AAAI / IAAI

Proceedings

Seventeenth National Conference on
Artificial Intelligence (AAAI-2000)

Twelfth Innovative Applications of
Artificial Intelligence Conference (IAAI-2000)

AAAI Press/The MIT Press

Menlo Park, California • Cambridge, Massachusetts • London, England

Copyright © 2000
American Association for Artificial Intelligence
AAAI Press
445 Burgess Drive
Menlo Park, California 94025

All rights reserved. No part of this book may be reproduced in any form by any electronic or mechanical means (including photocopying, recording, or information storage and retrieval) without permission in writing from the publisher.

Distributed by The MIT Press, Massachusetts Institute of Technology, Cambridge, Massachusetts and London, England.

ISBN 0-262-51112-6

Printed on acid-free paper in the United States of America

Contents

AAAI Organization / xix

Conference Program Committees / xxi

Outstanding Paper Award / xxiv

Sponsoring Organizations / xxv

Preface / xxvi

Invited Talks / xxvii

AAAI-2000 Technical Papers

Agents

Inter-Layer Learning Towards Emergent Cooperative Behavior / 3
Shawn Arseneau, Wei Sun, Changpeng Zhao, and Jeremy R. Cooperstock, McGill University

Coordination Failure and Congestion in Information Networks / 9
A. M. Bell, NASA Ames Research Center; W. A. Sethares and J. A. Bucklew, University of Wisconsin-Madison

Non-Deterministic Social Laws / 15
Michael H. Coen, MIT Artificial Intelligence Lab

Solving Combinatorial Auctions Using Stochastic Local Search / 22
Holger H. Hoos, University of British Columbia; Craig Boutilier, University of Toronto

A Mechanism for Group Decision Making in Collaborative Activity / 30
Luke Hunsberger, Harvard University; Massimo Zancanaro, ITC-irst

Cobot in LambdaMOO: A Social Statistics Agent / 36
Charles Lee Isbell, Jr., Michael Kearns, Dave Kormann, Satinder Singh, and Peter Stone, AT&T Shannon Labs

Semantics of Agent Communication Languages for Group Interaction / 42
Sanjeev Kumar, Marcus J. Huber, David R. McGee, and Philip R. Cohen, Oregon Graduate Institute; Hector J. Levesque, University of Toronto

Deliberation in Equilibrium: Bargaining in Computationally Complex Problems / 48
Kate Larson and Tuomas Sandholm, Washington University

An Algorithm for Multi-Unit Combinatorial Auctions / 56
Kevin Leyton-Brown, Yoav Shoham, and Moshe Tennenholtz, Stanford University

Maintainability: A Weaker Stabilizability Like Notion for High Level Control / 62
Mutsumi Nakamura, University of Texas at Arlington; Chitta Baral, Arizona State University; Marcus Bjäreland, Linköping University

Agent Capabilities: Extending BDI Theory / 68
Lin Padgham, RMIT University; Patrick Lambrix, Linköpings Universitet

Iterative Combinatorial Auctions: Theory and Practice / 74
David C. Parkes and Lyle H. Ungar, University of Pennsylvania

Preventing Strategic Manipulation in Iterative Auctions: Proxy Agents and Price-Adjustment / 82
David C. Parkes and Lyle H. Ungar, University of Pennsylvania

Improved Algorithms for Optimal Winner Determination in Combinatorial Auctions and Generalizations / 90
Tuomas Sandholm and Subhash Suri, Washington University

Some Tractable Combinatorial Auctions / 98
Moshe Tennenholtz, Technion, Israel Institute of Technology

Collective Intelligence and Braess' Paradox / 104
Kagan Tumer and David Wolpert, NASA Ames Research Center

Robust Combinatorial Auction Protocol against False-Name Bids / 110
Makoto Yokoo, Yuko Sakurai, and Shigeo Matsubara, NTT Communication Science Laboratories

Cognitive Modeling

Self-Organization of Innate Face Preferences: Could Genetics Be Expressed through Learning? / 117
James A. Bednar and Risto Miikkulainen, The University of Texas at Austin

A Self-Organizing Neural Network for Contour Integration through Synchronized Firing / 123
Yoonsuck Choe and Risto Miikkulainen, The University of Texas at Austin

Anchoring Symbols to Sensor Data: Preliminary Report / 129
Silvia Coradeschi and Alessandro Saffiotti, Örebro University

Modeling Classification and Inference Learning / 136
Bradley C. Love and Arthur B. Markman, The University of Texas at Austin; Takashi Yamauchi, University of Pittsburgh

Reading a Robot's Mind: A Model of Utterance Understanding Based on the Theory of Mind Mechanism / 142
Tetsuo Ono and Michita Imai, ATR Media Integration & Communications Research Laboratories

Visual Event Classification via Force Dynamics / 149
Jeffrey Mark Siskind, NEC Research Institute, Inc.

Constraint Satisfaction

Counting Models Using Connected Components / 157
Roberto J. Bayardo Jr., IBM Almaden Research Center; J. D. Pehoushek, M.U.S.T. Centre

DATALOG with Constraints — An Answer-Set Programming System / 163
Deborah East and Miroslaw Truszczynski, University of Kentucky

Local Search with Constraint Propagation and Conflict-Based Heuristics / 169
Narendra Jussien, École des Mines de Nantes; Olivier Lhomme, ILOG

A Game-Theoretic Approach to Constraint Satisfaction / 175
Phokion G. Kolaitis, University of California, Santa Cruz; Moshe Y. Vardi, Rice University

Using Auxiliary Variables and Implied Constraints to Model Non-Binary Problems / 182
Barbara Smith, University of Leeds; Kostas Stergiou, University of Strathclyde; Toby Walsh, University of York

Game Playing

The Game of Hex: An Automatic Theorem Proving Approach to Game Programming / 189
Vadim V. Anshelevich, Vanshel Consulting

Combining Knowledge and Search to Solve Single-Suit Bridge / 195
Ian Frank, Electrotechnical Laboratory; David Basin, Universität Freiburg; Alan Bundy, University of Edinburgh

On Pruning Techniques for Multi-Player Games / 201
Nathan R. Sturtevant and Richard E. Korf. University of California, Los Angeles

Human-Computer Interaction

Human-Guided Simple Search / 209
David Anderson, Emily Anderson, Neal Lesh, Joe Marks, Brian Mirtich, and David Ratajczak, MERL — Mitsubishi Electric Research Laboratory; Kathy Ryall, MERL — Mitsubishi Electric Research Laboratory and University of Virginia

Predicting Future User Actions by Observing Unmodified Applications / 217
Peter Gorniak and David Poole, University of British Columbia

Acquiring Problem-Solving Knowledge from End Users: Putting Interdependency Models to the Test / 223
Jihie Kim and Yolanda Gil, University of Southern California

Predicting UNIX Command Lines: Adjusting to User Patterns / 230
Benjamin Korvemaker and Russell Greiner, University of Alberta

Generation of Ideologically-Biased Historical Documentaries / 236
Michael Mateas, Carnegie Mellon University; Paul Vanouse, University of Buffalo; Steffi Domike, Chatham College

Self-Supervised Learning for Visual Tracking and Recognition of Human Hand / 243
Ying Wu and Thomas S. Huang, University of Illinois at Urbana-Champaign

Interactive Training for Synthetic Characters / 249
*Song-Yee Yoon, Robert C. Burke, Bruce M. Blumberg, and
Gerald E. Schneider, Massachusetts Institute of Technology*

Knowledge Representation and Reasoning

Boolean Satisfiability

Generating Satisfiable Problem Instances / 256
Dimitris Achlioptas, Microsoft Research; Carla Gomes, Cornell University; Henry Kautz, AT&T Research; Bart Selman, Cornell University

Solving the Round Robin Problem Using Propositional Logic / 262
Ramón Béjar and Felip Manyà, Universitat de Lleida

A Demand-Driven Algorithm for Generating Minimal Models / 267
Rachel Ben-Eliyahu – Zohary, Ben-Gurion University of the Negev

Redundancy in Random SAT Formulas / 273
Yacine Boufkhad and Olivier Roussel, Université d'Artois

On 2-SAT and Renamable Horn / 279
Alvaro del Val, Universidad Autónoma de Madrid

A Distributed Algorithm to Evaluate Quantified Boolean Formulae / 285
Rainer Feldmann, Burkhard Monien, and Stefan Schamberger, University of Paderborn

Integrating Equivalency Reasoning into Davis-Putnam Procedure / 291
Chu Min Li, Univ. de Picardie Jules Verne

Local Search Characteristics of Incomplete SAT Procedures / 297
Dale Schuurmans and Finnegan Southey, University of Waterloo

MarketSAT: An Extremely Decentralized (but Really Slow) Algorithm for Propositional Satisfiability / 303
William E. Walsh and Michael P. Wellman, University of Michigan

An Efficient Global-Search Strategy in Discrete Lagrangian Methods for Solving Hard Satisfiability Problems / 310
Zhe Wu and Benjamin W. Wah, University of Illinois at Urbana-Champaign

Case-Based Reasoning

Assessing Relevance with Extensionally Defined Principles and Cases / 316
Bruce M. McLaren and Kevin D. Ashley, University of Pittsburgh

Dynamic Case Creation and Expansion for Analogical Reasoning / 323
Thomas Mostek, Kenneth D. Forbus, and Cara Meverden, Northwestern University

Memory-Based Forecasting for Weather Image Patterns / 330
Kazuhiro Otsuka and Tsutomu Horikoshi, NTT Cyber Solutions Laboratories; Satoshi Suzuki, NTT East Corporation; Haruhiko Kojima, NTT Cyber Solutions Laboratories

Computational Complexity of Reasoning

The Complexity of Restricted Consequence Finding and Abduction / 337
Alvaro del Val, Universidad Autónoma de Madrid

Tractable Classes for Directional Resolution / 343
Alvaro del Val, Universidad Autónoma de Madrid

Compilability of Abduction / 349
Paolo Liberatore and Marco Schaerf, Università di Roma "La Sapienza"

Decision Theory

Decision-Theoretic, High-Level Agent Programming in the Situation Calculus / 355
Craig Boutilier, Ray Reiter, and Mikhail Soutchanski, University of Toronto; Sebastian Thrun, Carnegie Mellon University

Making Rational Decisions Using Adaptive Utility Elicitation / 363
Urszula Chajewska, Daphne Koller, and Ronald Parr, Stanford University

Back to the Future for Consistency-Based Trajectory Tracking / 370
James Kurien, NASA Ames Research Center; P. Pandurang Nayak, PurpleYogi.com and RIACS

Sampling Methods for Action Selection in Influence Diagrams / 378
Luis E. Ortiz, Brown University and Leslie Pack Kaelbling, Massachusetts Institute of Technology

Logic

Answering Queries Using Views over Description Logics Knowledge Bases / 386
Diego Calvanese, Giuseppe De Giacomo, and Maurizio Lenzerini, Università di Roma "La Sapienza"

A Consistency-Based Model for Belief Change: Preliminary Report / 392
James P. Delgrande, Simon Fraser University; Torsten Schaub, Universität Potsdam

A Conjunctive Query Language for Description Logic Aboxes / 399
Ian Horrocks and Sergio Tessaris, University of Manchester

Nonmonotonic Reasoning

A Flexible Framework for Defeasible Logics / 405
G. Antoniou, D. Billington, G. Governatori, and M. J. Maher, Griffith University

Towards a Logic-Based Theory of Argumentation / 411
Philippe Besnard, Université Paul Sabatier; Anthony Hunter, University College London

Solving Advanced Reasoning Tasks Using Quantified Boolean Formulas / 417
Uwe Egly, Thomas Eiter, Hans Tompits, and Stefan Woltran, Technische Universität Wien

Total Knowledge / 423
Ian Pratt-Hartmann, University of Manchester

Computing Circumscriptive Databases by Integer Programming: Revisited / 429
Ken Satoh and Hidenori Okamoto, Hokkaido University

Ontology

Using Prior Knowledge: Problems and Solutions / 436
Vinay K. Chaudhri, Mark E. Stickel, Jerome F. Thomere, and Richard J. Waldinger, SRI International

Dynamic Ontologies on the Web / 443
Jeff Heflin and James Hendler, University of Maryland

PROMPT: Algorithm and Tool for Automated Ontology Merging and Alignment / 450
Natalya Fridman Noy and Mark Musen, Stanford University

Reasoning about Actions and Time

(De)Composition of Situation Calculus Theories / 456
Eyal Amir, Stanford University

Disjunctive Temporal Reasoning in Partially Ordered Models of Time / 464
Mathias Broxvall and Peter Jonsson, Linköpings Universitet

An Interval Algebra for Indeterminate Time / 470
Wes Cowley, University of South Florida; Dimitris Plexousakis, University of Crete and ICS-FORTH

cc-Golog: Towards More Realistic Logic-Based Robot Controllers / 476
Henrik Grosskreutz and Gerhard Lakemeyer, Aachen University of Technology

What Sensing Tells Us: Towards a Formal Theory of Testing for Dynamical Systems / 483
Sheila A. McIlraith, Stanford University; Richard Scherl, New Jersey Institute of Technology

Execution of Temporal Plans with Uncertainty / 491
Paul Morris, Caelum Research Corporation / NASA Ames Research Center;
Nicola Muscettola, NASA Ames Research Center

Modeling Actions with Ramifications in Nondeterministic, Concurrent, and Continuous Domains
— and a Case Study / 497
Michael Thielscher, Dresden University of Technology

Spatial Reasoning

Describing Rigid Body Motions in a Qualitative Theory of Spatial Regions / 503
Brandon Bennett, Anthony G. Cohn, Paolo Torrini, and Shyamanta Hazarika, University of Leeds

GeoRep: A Flexible Tool for Spatial Representation of Line Drawings / 510
Ronald W. Ferguson and Kenneth D. Forbus, Northwestern University

STA: Spatio-Temporal Aggregation with Applications to Analysis of Diffusion-Reaction Phenomena / 517
Iván Ordóñez, The Ohio State University; Feng Zhao, Xerox Palo Alto Research Center

Uncertainty

On the Recognition of Abstract Markov Policies / 524
Hung H. Bui, Svetha Venkatesh, and Geoff West, Curtin University of Technology

Bayesian Fault Detection and Diagnosis in Dynamic Systems / 531
Uri Lerner, Ronald Parr, and Daphne Koller, Stanford University; Gautam Biswas, Vanderbilt University

Semantics and Inference for Recursive Probability Models / 538
Avi Pfeffer, Harvard University; Daphne Koller, Stanford University

Towards Feasible Approach to Plan Checking under Probabilistic Uncertainty: Interval Methods / 545
Raúl Trejo and Vladik Kreinovich, University of Texas at El Paso; Chitta Baral, Arizona State University

Machine Learning and Data Mining

ADVISOR: A Machine Learning Architecture for Intelligent Tutor Construction / 552
Joseph E. Beck, Beverly Park Woolf, and Carole R. Beal, University of Massachusetts

Automatic Invention of Integer Sequences / 558
Simon Colton and Alan Bundy, University of Edinburgh; Toby Walsh, University of York

A Unified Bias-Variance Decomposition for Zero-One and Squared Loss / 564
Pedro Domingos, University of Washington

Generalizing Boundary Points / 570
Tapio Elomaa, University of Helsinki; Juho Rousu, VTT Biotechnology

Boosted Wrapper Induction / 577
Dayne Freitag, Just Research; Nicholas Kushmerick, University College Dublin

Information Extraction with HMM Structures Learned by Stochastic Optimization / 584
Dayne Freitag and Andrew McCallum, Just Research

Localizing Search in Reinforcement Learning / 590
Greg Grudic and Lyle Ungar, University of Pennsylvania

Recognizing End-User Transactions in Performance Management / 596
Joseph L. Hellerstein, T. S. Jayram, and Irina Rish, IBM Thomas J. Watson Research Center

ATMOSPHERE — Automatic Track Mining and Objective Satellite Pattern Hunting System Using Enhanced RBF and EGDLM / 603
Raymond S. T. Lee and James N. K. Liu, Hong Kong Polytechnic University

Learning the Common Structure of Data / 609
Kristina Lerman and Steven Minton, University of Southern California

Intuitive Representation of Decision Trees Using General Rules and Exceptions / 615
Bing Liu, Minqing Hu, and Wynne Hsu, National University of Singapore

Selective Sampling with Redundant Views / 621
Ion Muslea, Steven Minton, and Craig A. Knoblock, University of Southern California

A Mutually Beneficial Integration of Data Mining and Information Extraction / 627
Un Yong Nahm and Raymond J. Mooney, University of Texas at Austin

Multivariate Clustering by Dynamics / 633
Marco Ramoni, The Open University; Paola Sebastiani, Imperial College; Paul Cohen, University of Massachusetts

Toward a Theory of Learning Coherent Concepts / 639
Dan Roth and Dmitry Zelenko, University of Illinois at Urbana-Champaign

Empirical Evaluation of a Reinforcement Learning Spoken Dialogue System / 645
Satinder Singh, Michael Kearns, Diane J. Litman, and Marilyn A. Walker, AT&T Labs

Unsupervised Learning and Interactive Jazz/Blues Improvisation / 652
Belinda Thom, Carnegie Mellon University

Restricted Bayes Optimal Classifiers / 658
Simon Tong and Daphne Koller, Stanford University

A Quantitative Study of Small Disjuncts / 665
Gary M. Weiss and Haym Hirsh, Rutgers University

Natural Language Processing and Information Retrieval

Translating with Scarce Resources / 672
Yaser Al-Onaizan, Ulrich Germann, Ulf Hermjakob, Kevin Knight, Philipp Koehn, Daniel Marcu, and Kenji Yamada, University of Southern California

The Rules Behind Roles: Identifying Speaker Role in Radio Broadcasts / 679
Regina Barzilay, Columbia University; Michael Collins, Julia Hirschberg, and Steve Wittaker, AT&T Labs — Research

Cognitive Status and Form of Reference in Multimodal Human-Computer Interaction / 685
Andrew Kehler, University of California, San Diego

Class-Based Construction of a Verb Lexicon / 691
Karin Kipper, Hoa Trang Dang, and Martha Palmer, University of Pennsylvania

Preserving Ambiguities in Generation via Automata Intersection / 697
Kevin Knight and Irene Langkilde, University of Southern California

Statistics-Based Summarization — Step One: Sentence Compression / 703
Kevin Knight and Daniel Marcu, University of Southern California

Estimating Word Translation Probabilities from Unrelated Monolingual Corpora Using the EM Algorithm / 711
Philipp Koehn and Kevin Knight, University of Southern California

The Automatic Interpretation of Nominalizations / 716
Maria Lapata, University of Edinburgh

Predicting and Adapting to Poor Speech Recognition in a Spoken Dialogue System / 722
Diane J. Litman, AT&T Labs — Research; Shimei Pan, Columbia University

Social Choice Theory and Recommender Systems:
Analysis of the Axiomatic Foundations of Collaborative Filtering / 729
David M. Pennock, NEC Research Institute; Eric Horvitz, Microsoft Research; C. Lee Giles, NEC Research Institute

Learning Subjective Adjectives from Corpora / 735
Janyce M. Wiebe, New Mexico State University

Planning and Scheduling

Iterative Flattening: A Scalable Method for Solving Multi-Capacity Scheduling Problems / 742
Amedeo Cesta and Angelo Oddi, IP-CNR, National Research Council of Italy; Stephen F. Smith, Carnegie Mellon University

Planning as Satisfiability in Nondeterministic Domains / 748
Paolo Ferraris and Enrico Giunchiglia, DIST — Università di Genova

Open World Planning in the Situation Calculus / 754
Alberto Finzi and Fiora Pirri, Università degli Studi di Roma "La Sapienza"; Ray Reiter, University of Toronto

Discovering State Constraints in DISCOPLAN: Some New Results / 761
Alfonso Gerevini, Università di Brescia; Lenhart Schubert, University of Rochester

A Logic for Planning under Partial Observability / 768
A. Herzig, J. Lang, D. Longin, and T. Polacsek, IRIT-UPS

Graph Construction and Analysis as a Paradigm for Plan Recognition / 774
Jun Hong, University of Ulster at Jordanstown

Solving a Supply Chain Optimization Problem Collaboratively / 780
Hoong Chuin Lau, Andrew Lim, and Qi Zhang Liu, National University of Singapore

From Causal Theories to Successor State Axioms and STRIPS-Like Systems / 786
Fangzhen Lin, The Hong Kong University of Science and Technology

TCBB Scheme: Applications to Single Machine Job Sequencing Problems / 792
Sakib A. Mondal, Infosys Technologies Limited, India; Anup K. Sen, New Jersey Institute of Technology

Extracting Effective and Admissible State Space Heuristics from the Planning Graph / 798
XuanLong Nguyen and Subbarao Kambhampati, Arizona State University

An Iterative Algorithm for Synthesizing Invariants / 806
Jussi Rintanen, Albert-Ludwigs-Universität Freiburg

RealPlan: Decoupling Causal and Resource Reasoning in Planning / 812
Biplav Srivastava, Arizona State University

Gridworlds as Testbeds for Planning with Incomplete Information / 819
Craig Tovey and Sven Koenig, Georgia Institute of Technology

Robotics

Performance Comparison of Landmark Recognition Systems for Navigating Mobile Robots / 826
Tom Duckett, University of Örebro; Ulrich Nehmzow, University of Manchester

Active Audition for Humanoid / 832
Kazuhiro Nakadai and Tino Lourens, Japan Science and Technology Corporation; Hiroshi G. Okuno, Japan Science and Technology Corporation and Science University of Tokyo; Hiroaki Kitano, Japan Science and Technology Corporation and Sony Computer Science Laboratories, Inc.

Property Mapping: A Simple Technique for Mobile Robot Programming / 840
Illah R. Nourbakhsh, Carnegie Mellon University

A Method for Clustering the Experiences of a Mobile Robot that Accords with Human Judgments / 846
Tim Oates, Matthew D. Schmill, and Paul R. Cohen, University of Massachusetts

Coordination for Multi-Robot Exploration and Mapping / 852
Reid Simmons and David Apfelbaum, Carnegie Mellon University; Wolfram Burgard, University of Freiburg; Dieter Fox, Carnegie Mellon University; Mark Moors, University of Bonn; Sebastian Thrun and Håkan Younes, Carnegie Mellon University

Monte Carlo Localization with Mixture Proposal Distribution / 859
Sebastian Thrun and Dieter Fox, Carnegie Mellon University; Wolfram Burgard, University of Freiburg

Appearance-Based Obstacle Detection with Monocular Color Vision / 866
Iwan Ulrich and Illah Nourbakhsh, Carnegie Mellon University

Multi-Fidelity Robotic Behaviors: Acting with Variable State Information / 872
Elly Winner and Manuela Veloso, Carnegie Mellon University

Search

Dynamic Representations and Escaping Local Optima: Improving Genetic Algorithms and Local Search / 879
Laura Barbulescu, Jean-Paul Watson, and L. Darrell Whitley, Colorado State University

Localizing A* / 885
Stefan Edelkamp, Institut für Informatik; Stefan Schrödl, DaimlerChrysler Research and Technology

Speeding up the Convergence of Real-Time Search / 891
David Furcy and Sven Koenig, Georgia Institute of Technology

Change Detection in Heuristic Search / 898
Eyke Hüllermeier, IRIT — Université Paul Sabatier

Preference-Based Search for Scheduling / 904
Ulrich Junker, ILOG

Divide-and-Conquer Frontier Search Applied to Optimal Sequence Alignment / 910
Richard E. Korf, University of California, Los Angeles; Weixiong Zhang, USC Information Sciences Institute

Asynchronous Search with Aggregations / 917
Marius Calin Silaghi, Djamila Sam-Haroud, and Boi Faltings, Swiss Federal Institute of Technology

A* with Partial Expansion for Large Branching Factor Problems / 923
Takayuki Yoshizumi, Teruhisa Miura, and Toru Ishida, Kyoto University

Depth-First Branch-and-Bound versus Local Search: A Case Study / 930
Weixiong Zhang, University of Southern California

Innovative Applications of Artificial Intelligence Papers

Deployed Applications

SciFinance: A Program Synthesis Tool for Financial Modeling / 937
Robert L. Akers, Ion Bica, Elaine Kant, Curt Randall, and Robert L. Young, SciComp Inc.

Assentor®: An NLP-Based Solution to E-mail Monitoring / 945
Chinatsu Aone, Mila Ramos-Santacruz, and William J. Niehaus, SRA International, Inc.

Nurse Rostering at the Hospital Authority of Hong Kong / 951
Andy Hon Wai Chun, City University of Hong Kong; Steve Ho Chuen Chan, Garbbie Pui Shan Lam, Francis Ming Fai Tsang, Jean Wong, and Dennis Wai Ming Yeung, Advanced Object Technologies Limited

PTV: Intelligent Personalised TV Guides / 957
Paul Cotter and Barry Smyth, University College Dublin

LifeCode™ – A Natural Language Processing System for Medical Coding and Data Mining / 965
Daniel T. Heinze, Mark L. Morsch, Ronald E. Sheffer, Jr., Michelle A. Jimmink, Mark A. Jennings, William C. Morris, and Amy E. W. Morsch, A-Life Medical, Inc.

The Emergence Engine: A Behavior Based Agent Development Environment for Artists / 973
Eitan Mendelowitz, University of California, Los Angeles

Emerging Applications

The TheaterLoc Virtual Application / 980
Greg Barish, Craig A. Knoblock, Yi-Shin Chen, Steven Minton, Andrew Philpot and Cyrus Shahabi, University of Southern California

Exploiting a Thesaurus-Based Semantic Net for Knowledge-Based Search / 988
Peter Clark, John Thompson, Heather Holmback, and Lisbeth Duncan, The Boeing Company

ICARUS: Intelligent Content-Based Retrieval of 3D Scene / 996
Raffaella Colaci and Marco Schaerf, Università di Roma "La Sapienza"

Integrating a Spoken Language System with Agents for Operational Information Access / 1002
Jody Daniels, Lockheed Martin Advanced Technology Laboratories

DMML: An XML Language for Interacting with Multi-Modal Dialog Systems / 1008
Nanda Kambhatla, Malgorzata Budzikowska, Sylvie Levesque, Nicolas Nicolov, Wlodek Zadrozny, Charles Wiecha, and Julie MacNaught, IBM T. J. Watson Research Center

Applying Learnable Evolution Model to Heat Exchanger Design / 1014
Kenneth A. Kaufman, George Mason University and Ryszard S. Michalski, George Mason University and Polish Academy of Sciences

A Campus-Wide University Examination Timetabling Application / 1020
Andrew Lim, Ang Juay Chin, Ho Wee Kit, and Oon Wee Chong, National University of Singapore

An Expert System for Recognition of Facial Actions and their Intensity / 1026
M. Pantic and L. J. M. Rothkrantz, Delft University of Technology

AI for the Web — Ontology-Based Community Web Portals / 1034
Steffen Staab, University of Karlsruhe and ontoprise GmbH; Jürgen Angele, ontoprise GmbH; Stefan Decker, University of Karlsruhe; Michael Erdmann, Andreas Hotho, and Alexander Maedche, University of Karlsruhe; Hans-Peter Schnurr and Rudi Studer, University of Karlsruhe; York Sure, University of Karlsruhe

Defining and Using Ideal Teammate and Opponent Agent Models / 1040
Peter Stone, AT&T Labs — Research; Patrick Riley and Manuela Veloso, Carnegie Mellon University

Rapid Development of a High Performance Knowledge Base for Course of Action Critiquing / 1046
Gheorghe Tecuci, Mihai Boicu, Dorin Marcu, Michael Bowman, Florin Ciucu, and Cristian Levcovici, George Mason University

A Case-Based Reasoning Application for Engineering Sales Support Using Introspective Reasoning / 1054
Ian Watson, University of Auckland

Student Abstracts

Identifying Words to Explain to a Reader: A Preliminary Study / 1061
Greg Aist, Carnegie Mellon University

Speculative Execution for Information Agents / 1062
Greg Barish, Craig A. Knoblock, and Steven Minton, University of Southern California

Heterogeneous Neuron Models Based on Similarity / 1063
Lluís A. Belanche Muñoz, Universitat Politècnica de Catalunya

Mixed-Initiative Reasoning for Integrated Domain Modeling, Learning and Problem Solving / 1064
Mihai Boicu and Gheorghe Tecuci, George Mason University

A Methodology for Modeling and Representing Expert Knowledge that Supports Teaching-Based Intelligent Agent Development / 1065
Michael Bowman, Gheorghe Tecuci, and Mihai Boicu, George Mason University

Automated Learning of Pricing and Bundling Strategies in Information Economies / 1066
Christopher H. Brooks and Edmund H. Durfee, University of Michigan

Incremental and Distributed Learning with Support Vector Machines / 1067
Doina Caragea, Adrian Silvescu, and Vasant Honavar, Iowa State University

System that Identifies Writers / 1068
Sung-Hyuk Cha and Sargur N. Srihari, State University of New York at Buffalo

Using Anytime Planning for Centralized Coordination of Multiple Robots in Real-Time Dynamic Environments / 1069
Gabriel J. Ferrer, Glenn S. Wasson, James P. Gunderson, and Worthy N. Martin, University of Virginia

MURDOCH: Publish/Subscribe Task Allocation for Heterogeneous Agents / 1070
Brian P. Gerkey and Maja J. Mataric, University of Southern California

Domain-Specific Knowledge Acquisition Using WordNet / 1071
Roxana Girju, Southern Methodist University

Graph Based Concept Learning / 1072
Jesus A. Gonzalez, Lawrence B. Holder, and Diane J. Cook, University of Texas at Arlington

An Adaptive Planner Based on Learning of Planning Performance / 1073
Kreshna Gopal and Thomas R. Ioerger, Texas A&M University

Knowledge Representation on the Internet: Achieving Interoperability in a Dynamic, Distributed Environment / 1074
Jeff Heflin, University of Maryland

Using Pattern Databases to Find Macro Operators / 1075
István T. Hernádvölgyi, University of Ottawa

Autonomous Multi-Agent Docking Using Color Segmentation / 1076
Jeffrey Hyams, University of South Florida

Ontology Integration in XML / 1077
Euna Jeong, National Taiwan University; Chun-Nan Hsu, Academia Sinica

Graph-Based Hierarchical Conceptual Clustering in Structural Databases / 1078
Istvan Jonyer, Lawrence B. Holder, and Diane J. Cook, University of Texas at Arlington

Situation Awareness with the Limited Visual Attention / 1079
Youngjun Kim, Randall W. Hill, Jr., and Jonathan Gratch, University of Southern California

Language Learning in Large Parameter Spaces / 1080
Karen T. Kohl, MIT Artificial Intelligence Laboratory

Reinforcement Learning for Algorithm Selection / 1081
Michail G. Lagoudakis, Duke University; Michael L. Littman, AT&T Labs — Research and Duke University

Tracing Dependencies of Strategy Selections in Agent Design / 1082
Dung N. Lam and K. S. Barber, University of Texas at Austin

Programming Robot Behavior Primitives through Human Demonstration / 1083
Amy Larson and Richard Voyles, University of Minnesota

An Implementation of the Combinatorial Auction Problem in ECL^iPS^e / 1084
Robert Menke and Rina Dechter, University of California, Irvine

A Semi-Complete Disambiguation Algorithm for Open Text / 1085
Rada Mihalcea, Southern Methodist University

Combining Classification and Temporal Learning / 1086
Matthew Winston Mitchell, Monash University

Deriving and Using Abstract Representation in Behavior-Based Systems / 1087
Monica N. Nicolescu and Maja J. Mataric, University of Southern California

Model-Based-Diagnosis for Fault Management in Telecommunications Networks / 1088
Aomar Osmani, LIPN

Representation and Evolution of Lego-Based Assemblies / 1089
Maxim Peysakhov, Vlada Galinskaya, and William C. Regli, Drexel University

Intelligent Monitoring in a Robotic Assistant for the Elderly / 1090
Sailesh Ramakrishnan and Martha E. Pollack, University of Pittsburgh

Towards Efficient Negotiation Mechanisms for Collaboration / 1091
Timothy Rauenbusch, Harvard University

Behavior Acquisition and Classification: A Case Study in Robotic Soccer / 1092
Patrick Riley and Manuela Veloso, Carnegie Mellon University

"Small-World" Networks of Mobile Robots / 1093
Stergios I. Roumeliotis and Maja J. Mataric, University of Southern California

Towards Approximately Optimal Poker / 1094
Jiefu Shi and Michael Littman, Duke University

Team-Aware Multirobot Strategy for Cooperative Path Clearing / 1095
Gita Sukthankar, Carnegie Mellon University

Interfacing Issues for Information Extraction / 1096
Peter Vanderheyden and Robin Cohen, University of Waterloo

Clustering with Instance-Level Constraints / 1097
Kiri Wagstaff and Claire Cardie, Cornell University

An ILP Method Based on Instance Graph / 1098
Runqi Zhang, State University of New York at Buffalo

SIGART/AAAI Doctoral Consortium

Helping Children Learn Vocabulary during Computer Assisted Oral Reading / 1100
Greg Aist, Carnegie Mellon University

Adaptive Learning Systems: A Model for Business Entrepreneurs to Implement IT / 1102
Dessa David, City University of New York

Automatic Generation of Memory Based Search Heuristics / 1103
István T. Hernádvölgyi, University of Ottawa

Reasoning and Acting in Time / 1104
Haythem O. Ismail, State University of New York at Buffalo

Ontology Integration in XML / 1105
Euna Jeong, National Taiwan University, Chun-Nan Hsu, Academia Sinica

Belief Revision in a Deductively Open Belief Space / 1106
Frances L. Johnson, State University of New York at Buffalo

Selective Sampling with Co-Testing: Preliminary Results / 1107
Ion Muslea, Steven Minton, and Craig A. Knoblock, University of Southern California

Grounding State Representations in Sensory Experience for Reasoning and Planning by Mobile Robots / 1108
Daniel Nikovski, Carnegie Mellon University

Online Ensemble Learning / 1109
Nikunj C. Oza, University of California, Berkeley

Learning Landmarks for Robot Localization / 1110
Robert Sim and Gregory Dudek, McGill University

Refining Inductive Bias in Unsupervised Learning via Constraints / 1112
Kiri Wagstaff, Cornell University

Artificial Intelligence-Based Computer Modeling Tools for Controlling Slag Foaming in Electric Furnaces / 1113
Eric Wilson, University of Alabama

Intelligent Systems Demos

Sensible Agents: Demonstration of Dynamic Adaptive Autonomy / 1115
K. S. Barber, A. Goel, D. C. Han, J. Kim, D. N. Lam, T. H. Liu, C. E. Martin, and R. McKay, The University of Texas at Austin

The Systems Engineering Process Activities (SEPA) Methodology and Tool Suite / 1117
K. Suzanne Barber, Thomas Graser, Paul Grisham, Stephen Jernigan, and Sutirtha Bhattacharya, The University of Texas at Austin

Qualitative Spatial Interpretation of Course-of-Action Diagrams / 1119
Ronald W. Ferguson, Northwestern University; Robert A. Rasch, Jr., Battle Command Battle Lab (BCBL); William Turmel and Kenneth D. Forbus, Northwestern University

TV Content Recommender System / 1121
Srinivas Gutta, Kaushal Kurapati, KP Lee, Jacquelyn Martino, John Milanski, J. David Schaffer, and John Zimmerman, Philips Research

The Chimaera Ontology Environment / 1123
Deborah L. McGuinness and Richard Fikes, Stanford University; James Rice, CommerceOne; Steve Wilder, Stanford University

Matchmaking to Support Intelligent Agents for Portfolio Management / 1125
Massimo Paolucci, Zhendong Niu, Katia Sycara, Constantine Domashnev, Sean Owens, and Martin Van Velsen, Carnegie Mellon University

Adaptive User Interfaces through Dynamic Design Automation / 1127
Robin R. Penner and Erik S. Steinmetz, University of Minnesota; Christopher L. Johnson, Honeywell Technology Center

User Interface Softbots / 1129
Robert St. Amant and Luke S. Zettlemoyer, North Carolina State University

O-Plan: A Web-Based AI Planning Agent / 1131
Austin Tate, Jeff Dalton, and John Levine, The University of Edinburgh

Customer Coalitions in the Electronic Marketplace / 1133
M. Tsvetovat, K. Sycara, Y. Chen, and J. Ying, Carnegie Mellon University

Non-Axiomatic Reasoning System (Version 4.1) / 1135
Pei Wang, Intelligenesis Corporation and Indiana University

Untangle: A New Ontology for Card Catalog Systems / 1137
Christopher Welty and Jessica Jenkins, Vassar College

Robot Competition and Exhibition

Symbol Recognition and Artificial Emotion for Making an Autonomous Robot Attend the AAAI Conference / 1140
François Michaud, Dominic Létourneau, Jonathan Audet, and François Bélanger, Université de Sherbrooke

The Blue Swarm / 1142
Dan Stormont, Utah State University

Invited Talks

Decision Making under Uncertainty: Operations Research Meets AI (Again) / 1145
Craig Boutilier, University of Toronto

Why Do We Need a Body Anyway? / 1151
Justine Cassell, MIT Media Lab

Structure, Duality, and Randomization: Common Themes in AI and OR / 1152
Carla P. Gomes, Cornell University

Modeling High-Dimensional Data by Combining Simple Experts / 1159
Geoffrey E. Hinton, University College London

Recent Progress in the Design and Analysis of Admissible Heuristic Functions / 1165
Richard E. Korf, University of California, Los Angeles

Human-Level AI's Killer Application: Interactive Computer Games / 1171
John E. Laird and Michael van Lent, University of Michigan

The Games Computers (and People) Play / 1179
Jonathan Schaeffer, University of Alberta

Conceptual Indexing: Practical Large-Scale AI for Efficient Information Access / 1180
William A. Woods, Sun Microsystems Laboratories

Index / 1186

AAAI Organization

Officers

AAAI President
Bruce G. Buchanan, *University of Pittsburgh*

AAAI President-Elect
Tom M. Mitchell, *Carnegie Mellon University*

Past President
David L. Waltz, *NEC Research Institute, Inc.*

Secretary-Treasurer
Norman R. Nielsen, *SRI International*

Councilors

(through 2000):
Jan Aikins, *Sun Microsystems*
Bonnie Dorr, *University of Maryland*
Eric Horvitz, *Microsoft Corporation*
Stuart Russell, *University of California, Berkeley*

(through 2001):
Henry Kautz, *AT&T Labs–Research*
David McAllester, *AT&T Labs –Research*
Johanna Moore, *University of Pittsburgh*
Michael P. Wellman, *University of Michigan*

(through 2002):
Deborah McGuinness, *Stanford University*
Bart Selman, *Cornell University*
Reid Simmons, *Carnegie Mellon University*
Manuela Veloso, *Carnegie Mellon University*

Standing Committees

Conference Chair
Paul Rosenbloom, *University of Southern California*

Fellows/Nominating Chair
David L. Waltz, *NEC Research Institute, Inc.*

Finance Chair
Norman R. Nielsen, *SRI International*

Publications Chair
Kenneth Ford, *University of West Florida*

Grants Chair
Jan Aikins, *Sun Microsystems*

Scholarship Chair
Katia Sycara, *Carnegie Mellon University*

Symposium Chair
Ian Horswill, *Northwestern University*

Symposium Cochair
Daniel Clancy, *NASA Ames Research Center*

AAAI Press

Editor-in-Chief,
Kenneth Ford, *University of West Florida*

Press Editorial Board
Kenneth Ford, *University of West Florida*
Ken Forbus, *Northwestern University*
Pat Hayes, *University of West Florida*
Janet Kolodner, *Georgia Institute of Technology*
George Luger, *University of New Mexico*
Robert Morris, *Florida Institute of Technology*
Alain Rappaport, *Carnegie Mellon University*
Brian Williams, *NASA Ames Research Center*

AI Magazine

Editor
David Leake, *Indiana University*

Editor Emeritus
Robert Engelmore, *Stanford University*

Reports Editor
Robert Morris *NASA Ames Research Center*

Book Review Editor
B. Chandrasekaran *The Ohio State University*

Production Editor
Sunny Ludvik *Ludvik Editorial Services*

Magazine Editorial Board
James Allen, *University of Rochester*
Craig Boutilier, *University of Toronto*
Henrik Christensen, *Swedith Royal Institute of Technology*
Boi Faltings, *Florida Institute of Technology*
Usama Fayyad, *Microsoft Research*
Kenneth Ford, *University of West Florida*
Janice Glasgow, *Queen's University*
Kris Hammond, *Northwestern University*

Patrick Hayes, *University of West Florida*
Henry Kautz, *University of Washington*
Janet Kolodner, *Georgia Institute of Technology*
Robert Milne, *Intelligent Applications, Ltd.*
Leora Morgenstern, *IBM Watson Research Labs*
Martha Pollack, *University of Pittsburgh*
Jude Shavlik, *University of Wisconsin*
Moshe Tenneholtz, *Technion*
Sebastian Thrun, *Carnegie Mellon University*
Feng Zhao, *NASA Ames Research Center*

AAAI Staff

Executive Director
Carol McKenna Hamilton

Finance/Office Manager
Josette Mausisa

Senior Conference Coordinator
Keri Vasser Harvey

Conference Assistant
Mary Christine Armstrong

Information Technology Manager
Richard A. Skalsky

Membership Coordinator
Jhossy Quezada

AAAI & IAAI Conference Program Committees

Conference Chairs

AAAI-2000 Program Cochairs
Henry A. Kautz, *AT&T Labs-Research*
Bruce Porter, *University of Texas at Austin*

AAAI-2000 Associate Program Cochairs
Rina Dechter, *University of California, Irvine*
Richard Sutton, *AT&T Labs-Research*

AAAI-2000 Assistant Program Chair
Vibhu Mittal, *Just Research & Carnegie Mellon University*

IAAI-2000 Chair
Robert S. Engelmore, *Stanford University*

IAAI-2000 Cochair
Haym Hirsh, *Rutgers University*

Intelligent Systems Demonstrations Chair
George Ferguson, *University of Rochester*

Mobile Robot Competition Chair
Alan C. Schultz, *Naval Research Laboratory*

Robot Contest Subchair
Lisa Meeden, *Swarthmore College*

Robot Exhibit Subchair
Marc Böhlen, *Carnegie Mellon University*

Robot Challenge Subchair
Tucker Balch, *Carnegie Mellon University*

Robot Building Laboratory and National Botball Tournament Chair
David Miller, *KISS Institute for Practical Robotics*

SIGART/AAAI-2000 Doctoral Consortium Chair
Marie A. Bienkowski, *SRI International*

Student Abstract and Poster Chair
Sven Koenig, *Georgia Institute of Technology*

Tutorial Chair
Michael L. Littman, *Duke University*

Workshop Chair and Cochair
Marie desJardins, *SRI International*
Berthe Y. Choueiry, *University of Nebraska-Lincoln*

AAAI-2000 Senior Program Committee

Jamie Callan, *Carnegie Mellon University*
Rina Dechter, *University of California, Irvine*
Kenneth Forbus, *Xerox PARC*
Robert Holte, *University of Ottawa*
Leslie Kaelbling, *Massachusetts Institute of Technology*
Michael Kearns, *AT&T Labs*
Craig Knoblock, *University of Southern California*
Daphne Koller, *Stanford University*
James Lester, *North Carolina State University*
Alon Levy, *University of Washington*
Vladimir Lifschitz, *University of Texas at Austin*
Kathleen McKeown, *Columbia University*
Raymond Mooney, *University of Texas at Austin*
Pandurang Nayak, *PurpleYogi.com*
Peter Patel-Schneider, *Bell Labs Research*
Judea Pearl, *University of California, Los Angeles*
Gregory Piatetsky-Shapiro, *Xchange*
Bart Selman, *Cornell University*
Lynn Andrea Stein, *Massachusetts Institute of Technology*
Richard Sutton, *AT&T Labs-Research*
Sebastian Thrun, *Carnegie Mellon University*
Peter van Beek, *University of Alberta*
Manuela Veloso, *Massachusetts Institute of Technology*
Marilyn Walker, *AT&T Labs-Research*
Daniel Weld, *University of Washington*

AAAI-2000 Program Committee

Steve Abney, *AT&T Labs-Research*
David Aha, *Naval Research Laboratory*
James Allan, *University of Massachusetts*
David Andre, *University of California, Berkeley*
Elisabeth Andre, *DFKI GmbH*
Tucker Balch, *Carnegie Mellon University*
Chitta Baral, *Arizona State University*
Jonathan Baxter, *Australian National University*
Roberto Bayardo, *IBM Almaden Research Center*
Gautam Biswas, *Vanderbilt University*
Jim Blythe, *USC/Information Sciences Institute*
Justin Boyan, *NASA Ames Research Center / MIT AI Lab*
Carla Brodley, *Purdue University*
Rodney Brooks, *Massachusetts Institute of Technology*
Wolfram Burgard, *Universitaet Freiburg*
Mary Elaine Califf, *Illinois State University*
Vinay Chaudhri, *SRI International*
Berthe Choueiry, *University of Nebraska-Lincoln*

Daniel Clancy, *NASA Ames Research Center*
David Cohn, *Just Research / Carnegie Mellon University*
Michael Collins, *AT&T Labs-Research*
Corinna Cortes, *AT&T Labs-Research*
Mark Craven, *University of Wisconsin*
Adnan Darwiche, *University of California, Los Angeles*
Piew Datta, *GTE Laboratories*
Ernest Davis, *New York University*
Giuseppe De Giacomo, *Università di Roma "La Sapienza"*
Frank Dellaert, *Carnegie Mellon University*
Pedro Domingos, *University of Washington*
Susan Dumais, *Microsoft Research*
John Everett, *Xerox PARC*
Boi Faltings, *Swiss Federal Institute of Technology (EPFL)*
Tom Fawcett, *Hewlett-Packard Laboratories*
Ronen Feldman, *Bar-Ilan University*
Ronald Ferguson, *Northwestern University*
Eugene Fink, *University of South Florida*
Gary Flake, *NEC Research Institute*
Dieter Fox, *Carnegie Mellon University*
Jim French, *University of Virginia*
Eugene Freuder, *University of New Hampshire*
Marc Friedman, *Viathan Corporation*
Nir Friedman, *Hebrew University*
Michael Gelfond, *Texas Tech University*
Zoubin Ghahramani, *University College London*
Matthew L. Ginsberg, *University of Oregon*
Enrico Giunchiglia, *Università di Genova*
Bob Givan, *Purdue University*
Keith Golden, *NASA Ames Research Center*
Nancy Green, *University of North Carolina Greensboro*
Benjamin Grosof, *IBM T.J. Watson Research Center*
Milos Hauskrecht, *Brown University*
Ian Horrocks, *University of Manchester*
Adele Howe, *Colorado State University*
Manfred Huber, *University of Texas at Arlington*
Tommi Jaakkola, *Massachusetts Institute of Technology*
Peter Jeavons, *Oxford University*
David Jensen, *University of Massachusetts*
Hermann Kaindl, *Siemens Austria*
Subbarao Kambhampati, *Arizona State University*
Kevin Knight, *University of Southern California*
Jana Koehler, *Schindler Lifts Ltd*
Richard Korf, *University of California, Los Angeles*
David Kortenkamp, *Metrica/TRACLabs*
Manolis Koubarakis, *Technical University of Crete*
Benjamin Kuipers, *University of Texas at Austin*
Nicholas Kushmerick, *University College Dublin*
Javier Larrosa, *Universitat Politecnica de Catalunya*
Lillian Lee, *Cornell University*
Neal Lesh, *MERL*
Fangzhen Lin, *Hong Kong Univ..of Science and Technology*
Diane Litman, *AT&T Labs-Research*
Michael Littman, *AT&T Labs-Research*
Robert MacGregor, *Pacific Software Solutions*
Sridhar Mahadevan, *Michigan State University*
Inderjeet Mani, *The MITRE Corporation*
Chris Manning, *Stanford University*
Joel Martin, *National Research Council*
Andrew McCallum, *WhizBang Laboratories–Research*
Kathleen McCoy, *University of Delaware*
Sheila McIlraith, *Stanford University*
Marina Meila, *Carnegie Mellon University*
Nicolas Meuleau, *Massachusetts Institute of Technology*
Andrew Moore, *Carnegie Mellon University*
Leora Morgenstern, *IBM T.J. Watson Research Center*
Martha Palmer, *University of Pennsylvania*
Ronald Parr, *Stanford University*
Avi Pfeffer, *Harvard University*
Yusuf Pisan, *Macquarie University*
Martha Pollack, *University of Pittsburgh*
David Poole, *University of British Columbia*
Dragomir Radev, *University of Michigan*
Jeff Rickel, *University of Southern California*
Ellen Riloff, *University of Utah*
Irina Rish, *IBM T.J. Watson Research Center*
Dana Ron, *Tel Aviv University*
Dan Roth, *University of Illinois, Urbana-Champaign*
Marie-Christine Rousset, *University of Paris-Sud*
Tuomas Sandholm, *Washington University*
Stefan Schaal, *University of Southern California*
Jonathan Schaeffer, *University of Alberta*
Thomas Schiex, *INRA*
James Schmolze, *Tufts University*
Dale Schuurmans, *University of Waterloo*
Murray Shanahan, *Imperial College*
Jude Shavlik, *University of Wisconsin*
John Shawe-Taylor, *Royal Holloway, University of London*
Wei-Min Shen, *University of Southern California / ISI*
Reid Simmons, *Carnegie Mellon University*
Yoram Singer, *The Hebrew University*
Robert St. Amant, *North Carolina State University*
Peter Stone, *AT&T Labs-Research*
Peter Struss, *Technical University of Munich*
Gaurav Sukhatme, *University of Southern California*
Csaba Szepesvari, *Mindmaker Ltd.*
Prasad Tadepalli, *Oregon State University*
Hannu TT Toivonen, *Nokia Research Center*
Hudson Turner, *University of Minnesota at Duluth*
Lyle Ungar, *University of Pennsylvania*
Pascal Van Hentenryck, *Brown University*
Ellen Voorhees, *NIST*
Mark Wallace, *Imperial College*
Toby Walsh, *The University of York*
Janyce Wiebe, *New Mexico State University*
Brian Williams, *Massachusetts Institute of Technology*
Ronald Yager, *Iona College*
Qiang Yang, *Microsoft Research China*
Michael Young, *North Carolina State University*
Michael Wellman, *University of Michigan*
Weixiong Zhang, *University of Southern California*
Feng Zhao, *Xerox PARC*

2000 Auxiliary Reviewers

Eyal Amir
Alessandro Artale
Maren Bennewitz
Darse Billings
Yngvi Bjornsson
Diego Calvanese
Amedeo Cesta
Evgeny Dantsin
Oskar Dressler
Jenny Dy
Peggy S. Eaton
Alan Fern
Maria Fox
Enrico Franconi
Carole Goble
Dirk Haehnel
Ullrich Hustadt
Terran Lane
Victor Lavrenko
Anton Leuski
Sean MacArthur
R. Manmatha
Fabio Massacci
David McAllester
Karen Myers
Daniele Nardi
Joelle Pineau
Stergios Roumeliotis
Nicholas Roy
Jack van Ryswyck
Mark Stickel
Tim Stough
Russell Swan
Armando Tacchella
Sergio Tessaris
Richard Vaughan
Richard J. Wallace
David Wilkins

IAAI-2000 Program Committee

Bruce Buchanan, *University of Pittsburgh*
Steve Chien, *Jet Propulsion Laboratory*
Usama Fayyad, *Microsoft Research*
Neil Jacobstein, *Teknowledge Corporation*
Philip Klahr, *TriVida Corporation*
Alain Rappaport, *Carnegie Mellon University*
Charles Rosenberg, *Carnegie Mellon University*
Ted Senator, *NASD Regulation, Inc.*
Howard Shrobe, *Massachusetts Institute of Technology*
Reid Smith, *Schlumberger Limited*
Shirley Tessler, *Aldo Ventures, Inc.*
Ramasamy Uthurusamy, *General Motors Corporation*
Marilyn Walker, *AT&T Labs-Research*

AAAI–2000 Outstanding Paper Awards

This year, AAAI's National Conference on Artificial Intelligence honors four papers that exemplify high standards in technical contribution and exposition. During the blind review process, members of the Program Committee recommended which papers to consider for the Outstanding Paper Award. A subset of the Senior Program Committee, carefully chosen to avoid conflicts of interest, reviewed all such papers and selected the winning papers::

The Game of Hex: An Automatic Theorem Proving Approach to Game Programming
Vadim V. Anshelevich, *Vanshel Consulting*

Automatic Invention of Integer Sequences
Simon Colton and Alan Bundy, *University of Edinburgh;* Toby Walsh, *University of York*

Statistics-Based Summarization — Step One: Sentence Compression
Kevin Knight and Daniel Marcu, *University of Southern California*

Local Search Characteristics of Incomplete SAT Procedures
Dale Schuurmans and Finnegan Southey, *University of Waterloo*

AAAI–2000 Sponsoring Organizations

American Association for Artificial Intelligence

ACM/SIGART

Defense Advance Research Projects Agency

Microsoft Corporation

Naval Research Laboratory

Office of Naval Research

National Science Foundation

Preface

AAAI–2000

Artificial intelligence has always been exciting, and we're now entering a time of heightened enthusiasm for our field. Processor capabilities raise our expectations, of course, but far more importantly we are exploring challenging problems, creating new models of computation, and fielding impressive applications. To be sure, basic research continues on core issues in AI, but the startling news is the breadth of new AI research.

The National Conference on Artificial Intelligence is the premier showcase of the breadth of our field. The 2000 conference starts with a program of 17 workshops and 14 tutorials, then features the Robot Exhibition, 14 invited talks, and the Technical Program with 143 presentations of research drawn from many subareas of AI. While there are many workshops for specialized subareas of AI, the National Conference is the "big tent" — as broad as the scientific agenda itself.

The technical papers in this volume were selected from 432 submissions by a rigorous double-blind review process. Each submission was reviewed by three members of the AAAI Program Committee, who were supervised by one member of the Senior Program Committee. All the papers accepted for publication and presentation are good examples of research and scholarship. In particular, the Senior Program Committee would like to recognize four Outstanding Papers that combine substantial content and lucid presentation: "The Game of Hex: An Automatic Theorem Proving Approach to Game Programming" by Vadim V. Anshelevich, Vanshel Consulting; "Automatic Invention of Integer Sequences" by Simon Colton and Alan Bundy, University of Edinburgh; Toby Walsh, University of York; "Statistics-Based Summarization — Step One: Sentence Compression" by Kevin Knight and Daniel Marcu, University of Southern California; and "Local Search Characteristics of Incomplete SAT Procedures" by Dale Schuurmans and Finnegan Southey, University of Waterloo.

The National Conference on Artificial Intelligence relies on the generous help of many people. We extend our appreciation to the 130 members of the Program Committee, and the 28 members of the Senior Program Committee. Further, we thank Carol Hamilton, Keri Harvey, Rick Skalsky, and the entire AAAI staff for their professionalism, organization, and courtesy, and we thank Vibhu Mittal and Ramesh Patil for developing software to make this monumental task manageable. Finally, we thank the AAAI Executive Council for giving us this opportunity to cochair the conference.

- Henry Kautz and Bruce Porter

IAAI–2000

The Twelfth Annual Conference on Innovative Applications of Artificial Intelligence (IAAI-2000) continues the IAAI tradition of case studies of deployed applications with measurable benefits whose value depends on the use of AI technology. In addition, IAAI-2000 augments these case studies with papers and invited talks that address emerging areas of AI technology or applications. IAAI is organized as an independent program within the National Conference, with schedules coordinated to allow attendees to move freely between IAAI and National Conference sessions. IAAI and the National Conference are jointly sponsoring several invited talks that fit the theme of both programs.

AI applications developers benefit from learning about new AI techniques that will enable the next generation of applications. Basic AI research will benefit by learning about challenges of real-world domains and difficulties and successes in applying AI techniques to real business problems. IAAI-2000 will address the full range of AI techniques including knowledge-based systems, vision, constraint programming, machine learning, software synthesis, planning & execution, natural language processing, diagnostic reasoning, reasoning with uncertainty, neural networks and cognitive simulation.

Deployed Applications are case studies that provide a valuable guide to designing, building, managing, and deploying systems incorporating AI technologies. This year's papers address applications in a wide variety of domains, including large-scale scheduling, biotechnology, medical data mining, civil engineering, financial modeling, e-mail management, manufacturing, and interactive agents. These applications provide clear evidence of the impact and value that AI technology has in today's world.

Papers on Emerging Applications and Technologies describe efforts whose goal is the engineering of AI applications. They inform AI researchers about the utility of specific AI techniques for applications domains and also inform applications developers about tools and techniques that will enable the next generation of new and more powerful applications.

Invited talks by Prof. John Laird (Univ. Michigan) on AI's "Killer Application," and by Dr. Bertrand du Castel (Schlumberger) on the future of wireless technology and its opportunities for AI applications, should be especially interesting to this year's conference attendees.

Bob Engelmore and Haym Hirsh

Invited Talks

Decision Making under Uncertainty: Operations Research Meets AI (Again)
Craig Boutilier, *University of Toronto*

Models for sequential decision making under uncertainty (such as Markov decision processes, or MDPs) have been studied in operations research for decades. The recent incorporation of ideas from many areas of AI, including planning, probabilistic modeling, machine learning, and knowledge representation, have made these models much more widely applicable. In this talk, Boutilier will survey recent advances within AI in the use of fully- and partially-observable MDPs as a modeling tool, and the development of computationally-manageable solution methods. He will place special emphasis on algorithms that exploit specific problem structure and approximation techniques.

Why Do We Need a Body Anyway?
Justine Cassell, *MIT Media Lab*

Embodiment is all the rage: humanoid agents, robots with eyelashes. It brings back those glory days of AI when "human-like" was a goal in and of itself. But do bodies serve any use in today's AI? In this talk Cassell will support the use of embodiment in certain domains and demonstrate with a series of implemented systems. But she will argue that unless we understand the "affordances" of the body — for face-to-face conversation, for situating intelligence, for establishing trust and other kinds of interactional glue — then an embodied systems will never be more than just another pretty face.

Intelligence in "Artificial" Wireless (IAAI Invited Talk)
Bertrand du Castel, *Schlumberger Ltd.*

The background of the presentation is a perspective on the development of wireless technology from 2000 to 2010. The foreground of the presentation is a contrasted understanding of intelligence in "natural" wireless (human communication) versus "artificial" wireless (communication between devices).

Structure, Duality, and Randomization: Common Themes in AI and OR
Carla Pedro Gomes, *Cornell University*

Both the artificial intelligence (AI) community and the operations research (OR) communities are interested in developing techniques for solving hard combinatorial problems. OR has built heavily on mathematical programming formulations such as integer and linear programming, while AI has developed constraint-based search and inference methods. Recently, we have seen a convergence of ideas, drawing on the individual strengths of these paradigms. Problem structure, duality, and randomization are overarching themes in the study of AI and OR approaches. Gomes will compare and contrast the different views from AI and OR on these topics, highlighting potential synergistic benefits.

Missed Perceptions: AI versus the Funding Agencies
James Hendler, *University of Maryland & DARPA*

The relationship between the AI community and the funding establishment has often been very strained. In this talk, Hendler examines the reality of this and explore what we, as individuals and as a community, can do to improve our interaction with funding agencies.

Modeling High-Dimensional Data Distributions by Combining Simple Experts
Geoffrey Hinton, *University College London, UK*

It is possible to combine multiple non-linear probabilistic models of the same data by multiplying the probability distributions together and then renormalizing. This is a very efficient way to model data that simultaneously satisfies many different constraints. Hinton will describe an efficient way to fit a "Product of Experts" to data and show that this produces excellent models.

Design and Analysis of Heuristic Evaluation Functions
Richard E. Korf, *University of California, Los Angeles*

Korf will discuss recent progress in heuristic search, which has lead to optimal solutions to Rubik's Cube and the 5x5 TwentyFour Puzzle, problems with state spaces of size 10^{19} and 10^{25}, respectively. Korf will also present a new theory that allows us to accurately predict the performance of heuristic search algorithms.

Artificial Intelligence and Mobile Robots: Successes and Challenges
David Kortenkamp, *NASA Johnson Space Center/Metrica Inc.*

Mobile robots pose a unique challenge to artificial intelligence researchers. In recent years, successes in mapping and navigation have led to new challenges in human-robot interaction, multiple robots, mobile manipulation and learning. Kortenkamp's talk will discuss these successes and challenges within the context of the AAAI-2000 Mobile Robot competition.

Human-level AI's Killer Application: Interactive Computer Games
John E. Laird, *University of Michigan*

Over the last 30 years, there has been little progress in developing AI systems that integrate the varied intellectual capabilities of humans. In this talk, Laird proposes that interactive computer games can provide the unifying application area for research and development of integrated human-level AI.

Machines Reasoning about Machines
J. Strother Moore, *University of Texas at Austin*

Can machines reason about machines? The answer is "yes" and the question is of more than just philosophical interest. Today's microprocessors are extraordinarily complex machines; manufacturers are turning to mechanized reasoning tools to help them analyze sophisticated designs. These tools have their roots in early AI research.

Unconventional Vision Sensors
Shree K. Nayar, *Columbia University*

What can be perceived by a human or computed by a machine from an image is fundamentally restricted by the captured data. Current imaging systems are severely limited in spatial resolution, field of view, and dynamic range. In this talk, Nayar presents new vision sensors that provide unconventional forms of visual information. The first part of the talk focuses on the use of catadioptrics (lenses and mirrors) for capturing unusually large fields of view. Nayar describes several methods for obtaining single viewpoint and multi-viewpoint images. The second part of the talk addresses the problem of acquiring high dynamic range images using a low dynamic range detector. Nayar presents two approaches for extracting the desired extra bits at each pixel; the first one uses multiple images while the second uses just a single image. Several interactive demonstrations of our results will be shown. These results have implications for digital photography, immersive imaging, image based rendering, 3D scene modeling, and advanced interfaces.

The Games Computers (and People) Play
Jonathan Schaeffer, *University of Alberta*

The development of high-performance game-playing programs has been one of the major successes of AI research. The results have been outstanding but, with the one notable exception (Deep Blue), they have not been widely disseminated. Schaeffer's talk will discuss the past, present and future of the development of game-playing programs.

The research emphasis in the past has been on high performance for two-player perfect-information games. The research emphasis of the present encompasses multi-player imperfect/non-deterministic information games. And what of the future? There are some surprising changes of direction occurring that will result in games being more of an experimental testbed for mainstream AI research.

Eye Movements and Spoken Language Comprehension:
Bridging the Language-as-Action and Language-as-Product Traditions
Michael K. Tanenhaus, *University of Rochester*

Eye movements allow one to monitor real-time language processing in natural situations at a remarkably fine temporal grain. Tanenhaus will present an overview of research using this approach focusing on (1) word recognition in continuous speech and (2) the role that contextually-dependent representations play in reference resolution and syntactic ambiguity resolution.

Conceptual Indexing: Practical Large-Scale AI for Efficient Information Access
William A. Woods, *Sun Microsystems Laboratories*

Finding information is a problem shared by people and intelligent systems. Wood's talk describes an experiment combining both human and machine aspects in a knowledge-based system to help people find information in text. This system is the first to demonstrate a substantial improvement in information retrieval performance by using linguistic and world knowledge. It is also an example of practical subsumption technology on a large scale and with domain-independent knowledge. Results from this experiment are relevant to general problems of knowledge-based reasoning with large-scale knowledge bases.

Technical Papers

Agents

Inter-layer Learning Towards Emergent Cooperative Behavior

Shawn Arseneau, Wei Sun, Changpeng Zhao, Jeremy R. Cooperstock

Centre for Intelligent Machines, McGill University
3480 University St, Room 410, Montreal, QC, H3A 2A7
{arseneau | wsun | czhao | jer}@cim.mcgill.ca

Abstract

As applications for artificially intelligent agents increase in complexity we can no longer rely on clever heuristics and hand-tuned behaviors to develop their programming. Even the interaction between various components cannot be reduced to simple rules, as the complexities of realistic dynamic environments become unwieldy to characterize manually. To cope with these challenges, we propose an architecture for inter-layer learning where each layer is constructed with a higher level of complexity and control. Using RoboCup soccer as a testbed, we demonstrate the potential of this architecture for the development of effective, cooperative, multi-agent systems. At the lowest layer, individual basic skills are developed and refined in isolation through supervised and reinforcement learning techniques. The next layer uses machine learning to decide, at any point in time, *which* among a subset of the first layer tasks should be executed. This process is repeated for successive layers, thus providing higher levels of abstraction as new layers are added. The inter-layer learning architecture provides an explicit learning model for deciding individual and cooperative tactics in a dynamic environment and appears to be promising in real-time competition.

Introduction

The *real-world* as a dynamic, unpredictable environment offers numerous challenges for a researcher. Past AI techniques involving multiple agents have traditionally focused on problems in static, deterministic environments with complete information accessibility. Since more interesting problems deal with the real-world scenario, it seems only logical to test with such an environment.

To gauge whether an architecture is well-suited for an environment is difficult to accomplish, however, a common measure of performance is the time taken to finish the task. The elapsed time can be significantly reduced with the implementation of a cooperative team of agents motivated towards a common goal (Schneider-Fontan and Matarie 1998). Realizing a set of user-defined rules for inter-agent cooperation can become quite complex as all possible scenarios must be investigated. Hence machine learning has become an ideal tool for the development of multi-agent behavior. By having increasingly abstract layers of interaction between agents, a cooperative behavior emerges. Thus, multi-agent architecture in concert with machine learning techniques seems a promising path to pursue.

In order to study such real-world complexities in a limited domain the concept of RoboCup was introduced (Kitano et al. 1997, Asada et al. 1999). While maintaining an affordable problem size and research cost, RoboCup was designed in an attempt to provide a common task for the evaluation of various theories, algorithms, and architectures. This domain currently uses soccer as its "standard problem", in particular, the soccer simulator developed by Noda et al. (Noda, Matsubara and Hiraki 1998). This simulator incorporates many real-world complexities, such as limited vision, limited stamina, oral communication, and sensor noise, thus providing a convenient, yet non-trivial testbed for AI researchers.

Among the existing architectures, role-based decision trees are a common approach (Coradeschi and Karlsson 1998, Matsumoto and Nagai 1998). An agent's action is selected according to prioritized rules organized in a decision tree. However, in these works, building a decision tree is based completely on the designer's knowledge and experience, thus it would be difficult to cover all situations that might occur in a dynamic environment.

Under the influence of Brooks' work with the subsumption architecture (Brooks 1986), several layered architectures have been proposed. Matellan et al. (Matellan, Borrajo, and Fernndez 1998) used a two level structure: one composed of reactive skills capable of achieving simple actions on their own; the other based on an agenda used as an opportunistic planning mechanism to compound, activate, and coordinate the basic skills. Scerri and others (Scerri 1998; Westendorp, Scerri, and Cavedon 1998) proposed a multi-layered behavior based system, made up of a number of structurally similar layers, in which upper layers control the activation and priority of behaviors in lower layers. These layered architectures are advantageous for management and coordination, however, they have serious drawbacks due to the hard-wired design. For example, how does one set the appropriate priorities?

Copyright © 2000, American Association for Artificial Intelligence (www.aaai.org). All rights reserved.

There is also the problem dealing with oscillations between behaviors when information indicates more than one behavior is applicable. Finally, handling uncertain information becomes yet another challenge.

In order to cope with these problems, some effort has been made to incorporate machine learning into the layered structure. Noda et al. (Noda, Matsubara and Hiraki 1996) implemented neural networks to train an agent to choose between two basic behaviors, shooting and passing. Balch (Balch 1998) used Q-learning to train individual behaviors to determine when and how to activate a particular skill, given a common set of hand-coded low-level skills. Luke et al. (Luke et al. 1998) attempted genetic programming to "evolve" an entire soccer team from a set of low-level "basic" behavior functions to be used by individual agents. These methods, however, did not fully exploit the use of machine learning for low-level behaviors.

Stone and Veloso used neural networks to learn a basic behavior, ball interception, which was then incorporated via a decision tree into the learning of passing (Stone and Veloso 1998). They further suggested an extension to incorporate learning into the *decision* between dribbling, passing, and shooting skills, though this higher level was not implemented. In a later paper, they proposed a general framework named "layered learning" to deal with intractable tasks (Stone and Veloso 1999). This approach decomposed the problem, i.e. passing the ball, into several simpler, learnable steps: ball interception, pass evaluation, and pass selection. While this method provided an innovative framework for complex task decomposition, it did not, unfortunately, provide a mechanism for the learned selection among a set of lower-layer subtasks, such as that suggested earlier (Stone and Veloso 1998).

As an extension of the behavior-based layered structure (Luke et al. 1998), a generic architecture is proposed to incorporate machine learning techniques into the decision making process for multi-agent systems. This scheme is applicable to both individual and team cooperation in a dynamic environment.

Inter-layer Learning Approach

The general layout of the proposed architecture is a tree-like structure, where each additional layer introduces a higher level of complexity and control. As an example, a three-tier structure is shown in figure 1. The team strategy layer determines for each agent which individual strategy is to be adopted. Based on the individual strategy, an agent chooses an appropriate behavior from all possible basic behaviors in the lower level. The ultimate action output of an agent is the result of a *top-down* decision making process.

Machine learning of this layered architecture is implemented in a *bottom-up* fashion. Basic behaviors are learned first. The individual strategy layer then learns to choose between basic behaviors. Finally, the team strategy layer learns to coordinate a group of learned agents.

This process could be continued as necessary to achieve the desired scale of control according to various demands of applications. For example, considering a number of agents as a single entity, an additional layer could be built to attain more complex, cooperative behaviors between these groups.

The subdivision within a specific layer is done based on the perception of the world by the agent. For example, if an agent is to drive a car, one could divide the actions of parking and passing another vehicle on the highway, as each would become a viable option only under specific environmental conditions. The subdivisions within a layer are based on certain environmental variables which may be specific to that particular layer. This presents the danger of information overload. To follow the design principle of minimalism (Werger 1999), each layer uses only information about the environment pertinent to itself to simplify the entire process (Westendorp, Scerri, and Cavedon 1998). It should also be noted that the choice of percepts and reward functions are user defined, therefore it is left for future work.

The inter-layer learning architecture is used to design a team of soccer playing agents within the RoboCup simulator (Noda et al. 1998). The soccer team employs three distinct layers: basic skills, individual strategy, and a team strategy (Figure 1). Supervised and reinforcement learning are used, although unsupervised learning is also a possible venue to explore when building the interaction between layers. Each of these layers is discussed in further details in the following sections.

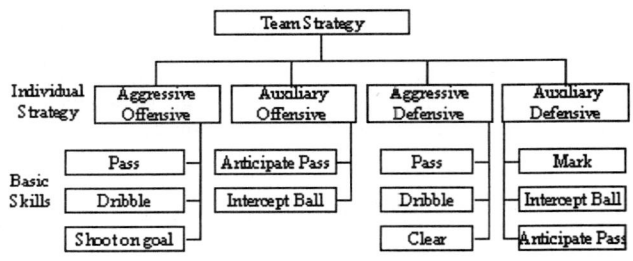

Figure 1. Overview of the inter-layer learning agent architecture. Note that the branches denote *choices* not *inputs*.

Basic Skills

A machine learning approach is employed to develop the basic skills, as other RoboCup researchers have done in the past (Stone and Veloso 1998, Ohta 1998, Tambe et al. 1998). The basic skills layer is subdivided into passing, dribbling, shooting on the goal, anticipating a pass, intercepting the ball, marking, and clearing. Neural networks are chosen for three of the skills, each based on a single action, intercept the ball, shoot on goal, and pass the ball. As it is possible to determine whether the action is appropriate soon after its execution, a supervised-learning algorithm is well suited for this type of scenario.

Dribbling and anticipating a pass are learned using

temporal difference Q-learning (Q-TD) as both of these skills involve a more complex state space and reward function. This choice is further motivated as Q-TD is an active reinforcement learning scheme that does not require the estimation of a world model, i.e. the state transition probabilities.

Both marking and clearing are analytically derived due to the nature of the skills (Stone, Veloso, and Riley 1999). In the following discussion, we examine in further details the skills of dribbling (Q-TD), passing (neural network), and anticipating a pass (Q-TD).

Dribbling – Q-TD. The task of dribbling is not only to run with the ball towards the opponent's goal, but also to avoid opponents. Given the delayed-reward aspect of this scenario, Q-TD was chosen for this skill.

The learning agent is trained to dribble against an opponent that has been trained to intercept the ball. A state is defined by the following three variables: opponent's goal direction, opponent's distance, and opponent's direction. The agent decides among five dribbling directions. At the early stage of learning, decision-based exploration is used so that the agent chooses actions that have been picked less often. The reward is assigned to both intermediate and terminal states based on distance gained towards the opponent's goal and time consumed. The assignment of intermediate reward motivates the agent to dribble towards the opponent's goal, thus helping speed up the learning procedure.

Figure 2 shows gained distance versus epochs during the Q-TD procedure. When the maximum distance the agent is able to reach stop increasing and the minimum distance is constantly above a certain threshold, which is 20 in this case, we consider that the learning is finished. Therefore, in Figure 2, the learning ended after approximately 400 epochs.

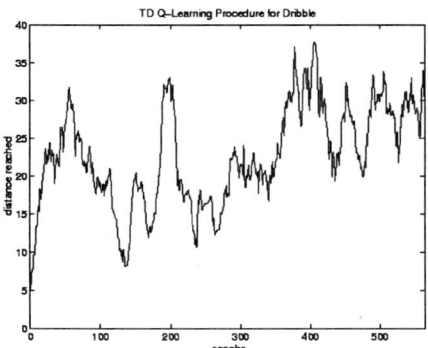

Figure 2. Q-TD procedure for dribble skill.

In a real soccer competition, the agent will use the learning result, without further Q-value updating, to dribble around the closest visible opponent. If no opponent is visible, the agent will remember the last visible opponent and behave accordingly. This learned dribble skill also has the added benefit of an emergent collision detection function as the player learns to avoid the opponents when it has possession of the ball.

Passing – BPNN. The challenge of passing the ball is in choosing the appropriate teammate to receive the pass. Since passing is not a continuous behaviour but a single action, for which active reinforcement learning is difficult to set up, the back-propagation neural network (BPNN) was chosen to learn this skill.

The passing skill is learned in a simplified environment with a passing agent, one teammate, and one opponent. Both the teammate and the opponent have learned to intercept the ball through a neural network at this point. Before learning begins, the passing agent simply passes the ball to its teammate while the opponent tries to intercept the ball. The agent's visual data is then used to train a BP neural network for the passing skill.

The input values for the neural network are the teammate's distance and direction as well as the opponent's distance and direction. The neural network converged after 292 iterations as shown in Figure 3.

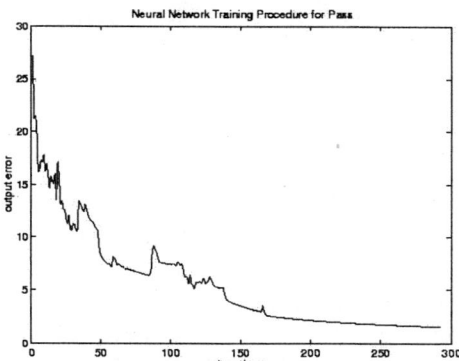

Figure 3. BP neural network training procedure for passing skill

In a real soccer competition, an agent has to choose to pass the ball to one of m teammates in the presence of n opponents, where m and n are arbitrary numbers. The trained neural network discussed above can be used as follows: First, compute the matrix S of probabilities of a successful pass to teammate i given the position of opponent j. Then, select teammate i^* with the highest probability of success, to receive the pass, where:

$$S_{i*} = \max_i \min_j S_{ij}.$$

This technique is similar to assigning confidence values to each of the choices (Stone and Veloso 1998).

	Success	Failure	Success rate
Random choice	254	75	77.2%
Neural network	276	53	83.9%

Table 1. Comparison of passing results by random choice and NN learning.

For evaluation, the neural network choice was compared to a random choice with three teammates and three opponents in the passing agent's field of view. The results are shown in Table 1. The successful passing rate increases by 6.7%. While the effect is marginal, it does nevertheless demonstrate improved performance.

Anticipating a Pass – Q-TD. The most difficult of the basic skills to implement is how to anticipating a pass. In a real game of soccer, a player must attempt to visualize the field from the perspective of its teammate with possession of the ball. In the RoboCup environment, the individual agents have a fixed viewing arc in which they gather visual percepts. In an attempt to learn this skill, the idea of a *viewcone* (Figure 4) is introduced in order to discretize the percepts as well as to create a simple but effective visual model along the lines of the minimalist design approach (Werger 1999).

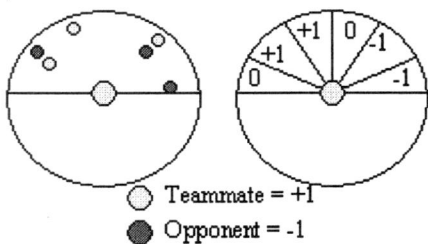

Figure 4. Viewcone of labeled arcs

The player first converts all of its information about the other players' positions on the field into global coordinates. These values are then converted to a relative coordinate system with respect to the passer. Finally, a viewcone is constructed whereby the passer parses its 90_ visual field into 15_ arcs and weights them according to the closest player. If a teammate and an opponent appear in the same arc, the closer of the two to the passer will determine the weight. These weights are entered into a Q value temporal difference learning scheme to determine the best possible action to perform. Another value used is if the passer has an unobstructed view of the player.

The four possible actions available to the player are to remain still, dash forward towards the passer, turn right and dash, or turn left and dash. In order for the player to choose the best possible actions, a unique reward system is devised. To encourage the player to dash to a location where it is open for a pass, the maximum reward is granted when the passer has an unobstructed view of the player and has two null arcs on either side (which would appear as 0, +1, 0 in the viewcone), in which case the player has no immediate threat of opponents. The reward decreases as teammates replace these null arcs, and the player is punished for being beside opponents, out of the viewcone of the passer, or within the passer's viewcone but behind another player.

After teaching the agent in a scenario with four teammates and five opponents randomly placed on one half of the field for over 28000 iterations, (with a state space of 5103 states), the player gradually chose an appropriate direction. With Q-value learning in this scenario, it is difficult to show the convergence, as the reward given after each step may produce the best action, but still results in an ineffective position. For example, if the player is outside the passer's viewcone, it may take several actions before it can achieve an improved position and hence escape from the low reward states. However, in comparing the learned skill against a random behavior, the learned skill moved in an appropriate direction approximately 70% more often.

Individual Strategy Layer

The individual strategy layer involves choosing amongst basic skills from a higher-level viewpoint (Noda et al. 1996). This layer is subdivided into four types. The first division dictates whether the agent has possession of the ball (*aggressive*) or not (*auxiliary*). This is further categorized into *offensive* and *defensive* depending on whether the agent's home area is on its own side of the field or its opponent's side (see Figure 1). The home area refers to the center of a circular region in which the agent may move. These regions are overlapped to accommodate agent interaction. The individual strategy examined here will be aggressive-defensive, which implies that the agent must choose among dribbling, passing, and clearing. As the choice to clear the ball is made analytically, when no other course of action is possible, in this instance the decision learning is between that of dribbling versus passing. This is useful for both aggressive-offensive and aggressive-defensive players.

Dribble/Pass. A learning agent is surrounded by four teammates and four opponents. All these players have been trained to dribble, pass, and intercept the ball. To simplify the learning situation, the teammate will only dribble after receiving a pass. The players pass or dribble the ball as far as possible towards the opponent's goal until an opponent successfully intercepts the ball.

The visual information of the learning agent is gathered to train a back-propagation neural network. Viewcone quantization is used here again to simplify the visual information of the learning agent. The weighted viewcone arc values discussed earlier as well as the direction of the opponent's goal are fed into the neural network.

In order to obtain the desired output of the neural network, both decisions of dribbling and passing are tested for the same configurations. The reward of each decision is calculated as:

$$reward = (distance\ gained) - 0.01 \times (time\ consumed)$$

For each configuration, the decision with the higher reward determines the desired output of the neural network.

Figure 5 illustrates the training procedure which converged after 15228 iterations to under 5% error. This behavior during our actual soccer competition proved highly effective at eluding the opposing team.

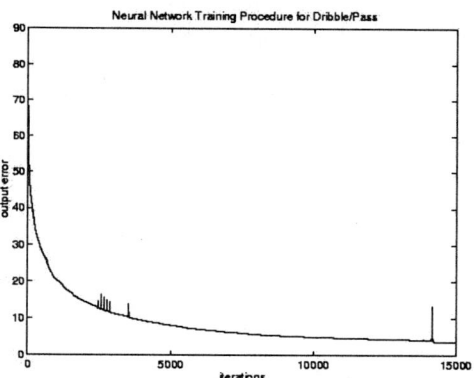

Figure 5. BP neural network training procedure for Dribble vs. Pass

Team Strategy Layer

This layer of learning investigates the performance of emergent team behavior. In order to adapt to different opponents and different scenarios, an effective team must learn to become more defensive or offensive during the match (Tambe 1996). In this particular scenario, a model-based approach to team strategy is adopted (Tambe 1996, Tambe et al. 1998) as opposed to a strictly behavior-based strategy (Werger 1999). This becomes the first layer of cooperation between the agents, and can potentially be expanded to further layers.

Three types of strategies; offensive, defensive, and half/half, are defined by three possible sets of home areas of the players (Figure 6).

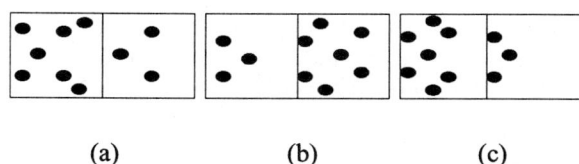

(a)　　　　　　(b)　　　　　　(c)
Figure 6. Team Strategies: (a) half/half, (b) offensive, (c) defensive

To facilitate the learning of an appropriate team strategy, a *captain* agent is introduced. This individual agent would carry the burden of deciding which team strategy to adopt based on its own visual cues and relays its decision to the rest of the team. In order to account for players outside the captain's field of view, the concept of *temporal decay* is applied (Westendorp, Scerri, and Cavedon 1998).

Once the captain has received its visual information, a world-model is created. Based on this world-model, Q-TD is applied to learn the team strategy.

The positional percepts that define the state values must be discretized in order to reduce the state space to a manageable size. To maintain useful information regarding team positions and local densities of players, a field mean and pseudo variance are calculated by dividing the field into six partitions in the x-direction. These figures are then used to determine the regions corresponding to the average position of both teams. This approach is similar to the tolerance design technique (Werger 1999). For example, in Figure 7, the mean of team *A* (white) lies in region 2 and team *B* (black) in region 5. The pseudo-variance varies with the number of agents present in the mean region.

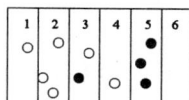

Figure 7. Discretized field

The final piece of data used by the learning algorithm is the ball location, which is also needed to create the appropriate reward. The reward relies solely on the amount the ball advanced or retreated during 100 ticks of the game clock. The choice of this time is completely heuristic.

After learning, the captain chooses between *offensive*, *defensive*, and *half/half* strategies according to the state of the game, and broadcasts this choice to the team. Each player picks a different home area corresponding to the new strategy, which determines whether the player will focus more on the opponent's side of the field (*offensive*) or on its own (*defensive*).

Results and Conclusions

Once all of the layers were integrated into a complete soccer playing agent, our team was entered into the 1999 RoboCup competition at McGill University, outscoring the competition by a total of 12:0. The inter-layer learning architecture appears to be a reasonable structure for a multi-agent, cooperative task. Employing the agents to learn cooperative behaviors, as opposed to taking an analytical approach, allowed emergent team strategies to be adopted.

It should be noted that although the final behavior is emergent, the human designer is still responsible for the division of the sub-tasks as well as the choice of training data. However, this approach extends the application of machine learning from the acquisition of individual tasks to the learning of the appropriate selection criteria for choosing between them. Expanding this architecture to cooperation between sub-teams working collectively appears possible, and an implementation of such a structure is left for further research.

Acknowledgements

We would like to thank Sorin Lerner for all of his help with the RoboCup soccer server, without whom we would never have gotten our players to see, let alone kick the ball.

References

Asada, M., Kitano, H., Noda, I., and Veloso, M. 1999. RoboCup, Today and Tomorrow – What We have Learned. *Artificial Intelligence*. 110(2):193-214.

Balch, T. 1998. Integrating Learning with Motor Schema-Based Control for a Robot Soccer Team. *RoboCup-97: Robot Soccer. World Cup I*. 483-491. Berlin, Germany: Springer-Verlag.

Brooks, R. A. 1986. A Robust Layered Control System for a Mobile Robot. *IEEE Journal of Robotics and Automation*, RA-2(1):14-23.

Coradeschi, S., and Karlsson, L. 1998. A role-based decision-mechanism for teams of reactive and coordinating agents. *RoboCup-97: Robot Soccer. World Cup I*. 99-111. Berlin, Germany: Springer-Verlag.

Kitano, H., Asada, M., Kuniyoshi, Y., Noda, I., Osawa, E., and Matsubara, H. 1997. RoboCup: A Challenge Problem of AI. *AI Magazine*. 18:73-85.

Luke, S., Hohn, C., Farris, J., Jackson, G., and Hendler, J. 1998. Co-evolving Soccer Softbot Team Coordination with Genetic Porgramming. *RoboCup-97: Robot Soccer. World Cup I*. 398-411. Berlin, Germany: Springer-Verlag.

Matellan, V., Borrajo, D., and Fernndez, C. 1998. Using ABC^2 in the RoboCup domain. *RoboCup-97: Robot Soccer. World Cup I*. 475-482. Berlin, Germany: Springer-Verlag.

Matsumoto, A., and Nagai, H. 1998. Decision making by the characteristics and the interaction in multi-agent robotics soccer. *RoboCup-97: Robot Soccer. World Cup I*. 132-143. Berlin, Germany: Springer-Verlag.

Noda, I., Matsubara, H. and Hiraki, K. 1996. Learning Cooperative Behavior in Multi-Agent Environment – A Case Study of Choice of Play-plans in Soccer. *Proceedings of the 4th Pacific Rim International Conference on Artificial Intelligence*. 570-579.

Noda, I., Matsubara, H., Hiraki, K., and Frank, I. 1998. Soccer Server: A Tool for Research on Multiagent Systems. *Applied Artificial Intelligence* 12(2-3):233-250.

Ohta, M. 1998. Learning Cooperative Behaviors in RoboCup Agents. *RoboCup-97: Robot Soccer. World Cup I*. 412-419. Berlin, Germany: Springer-Verlag.

Scerri, P. 1998. A Multi-layered Behavior-Based System for Controlling RoboCup Agents. *RoboCup-97: Robot Soccer. World Cup I*. 467-474. Berlin, Germany: Springer-Verlag.

Schneider-Fontan, M. and Matarie, M. 1998. Territorial Multi-Robot Task Division. *IEEE Transactions on Robotics and Automation*. 14(5):815-822.

Stone, P. and Veloso, M. 1998. A Layered Approach to Learning Client Behaviors in the RoboCup Soccer Server. *Applied Artificial Intelligence* 12:165-188.

Stone, P. and Veloso, M. 1999. Layered Learning. *International Joint Conference on Artificial Intelligence Workshop on Learning About, From, and With Other Agents*.

Stone, P., Veloso, M. and Riley, P. 1999. The CMUnited-98 Champion Simulator Team. *RoboCup-98: Robot Soccer. World Cup II*. Berlin, Germany: Springer-Verlag. At URL: http://www.cs.cmu.edu/afs/cs/usr/pstone/public/papers/98springer/final-champ/final-champ.html.

Tambe, M. 1996. Tracking Dynamic Team Activity. In Proceedings of the thirteenth Conference on Artificial Intelligence Applications. 11:80-87. Cambridge, U.S.A.: MIT Press.

Tambe, M., Adibi, J., Al-Onaizan, Y., Erdem, A., Kaminka, G., Marsella, C., and Muslea, I. 1998. Building Agent Teams Using an Explicit Teamwork Model and Learning. *Artificial Intelligence*. 110(2):215-239.

Werger, B. 1999. Cooperation Without Deliberation: A Minimal Behavior-Based Approach to Multi-Robot Teams. *Artificial Intelligence*. 110(2):293-320.

Westendorp, J., Scerri P., and Cavedon L. 1998. Strategic Behaviour-Based Reasoning with Dynamic, Partial Information. *RoboCup-97: Robot Soccer. World Cup I*. 297-308. Berlin, Germany: Springer-Verlag.

Coordination Failure and Congestion in Information Networks

A. M. Bell[*], W. A. Sethares[†], and J. A. Bucklew[‡]

Abstract

Coordination failure, or agents' uncertainty about the action of other agents, may be an important source of congestion in large decentralized systems. The *El Farol* or Santa Fe bar problem provides a simple paradigm for congestion and coordination problems that may arise with over utilization of the Internet. This paper recasts the problem in a stochastic framework and derives a simple adaptive strategy that has intriguing optimization properties; a large collection of decentralized decision makers, each acting in their own best interests and with limited knowledge, converge to a solution that (optimally) solves a complex congestion and social coordination problem. A variation in which agents are allowed access to full information is not nearly as successful.

Introduction

This paper focuses on imperfect information and coordination failure across agents as a source of congestion in large decentralized systems. We utilize the scenario posed by Arthur (1994) as a simplified model of a large class of congestion and coordination problems that arise in modern engineering and economic systems. *El Farol* is a bar in Santa Fe. The bar is popular, but becomes overcrowded when more than sixty people attend on any given evening. Everyone enjoys themselves when fewer

[*]NASA Ames Research Center, Mail Stop 269-3, Moffett Field, CA 94035-1000, abell@mail.arc.nasa.gov.

[†]Department of Electrical and Computer Engineering, University of Wisconsin-Madison.

[‡]Department of Electrical and Computer Engineering, University of Wisconsin-Madison.
Copyright © 2000, American Association for Artificial Intelligence (www.aaai.org). All rights reserved.

than sixty people go, but no one has a good time when the bar is overcrowded.

The *El Farol* or Santa Fe bar problem emphasizes the difficulty of coordinating the actions of independent agents without a centralized mechanism. The analogy between the bar problem and decentralized resource allocation is noted by Greenwald, Mishra and Parikh (1998), as well as in our previous work (Sethares and Bell 1998). Glance and Huberman (1994) and Huberman and Lukose (1997) consider the dynamics of congestion on the Internet when externalities similar to those found with public goods prevail. Unlike the standard public good framework, in this scenario fully informed optimizing agents will not increase consumption of a publicly available resource until it experiences an inefficient level of congestion: if agents could predict the behavior of other agents perfectly the bar would never be crowded and all patrons would have a good time. The only source of congestion, at least in a deterministic framework, is the inability of agents to coordinate their actions.

In a previous treatment (Sethares and Bell 1998) we proposed a deterministic adaptive algorithm based on habit formation which enabled agents to coordinate in a decentralized environment while avoiding the seemingly random fluctuations in aggregate attendance that Arthur's simulations demonstrated.

Here we consider the bar problem in a stochastic setting where agents' strategies are characterized by a probability of attending that evolves over time. There are several advantages to considering the stochastic version of the adaptive learning rule: a clearer problem statement, a simpler algorithm that is amenable to detailed analysis, and more general results. We analyze the dynamic and equilibrium characteristics of the system in relation to the mixed and pure strategy equilibria of the corresponding game.

The type and characteristics of the equilibria actually observed depend crucially on the nature of the information available to agents. In particular, we show that limiting the information available to agents leads them to successfully coordinate on a Pareto efficient equilibrium while providing more information leads to an inefficient outcome. Our results emphasize the critical role that increased information exchange may play in creating and alleviating congestion that arises from coordination failure. For example, in a complex environment such as the Internet supplying individual routers with more information about congestion may not result in better system-wide performance.

Algorithm Statement

Let agents have identical payoffs: b is the payoff an agent receives for attending a crowded bar and g is the payoff an agent receives for attending an uncrowded bar. Without loss of generality let h, the payoff received for staying home, be zero. Let M be the total number of agents and $\mathcal{N}$ be the maximum capacity of an uncrowded bar. The game is then $G = [M, \{S_i\}, u_i(s_i, s_{-i})]$ where S_i consists of two strategies, go to the bar (indicated by 1) and stay home (indicated by 0) and $u_i(0, s_{-i}) = 0$ for all s_{-i}, $u_i(1, s_{-i}) = g$ when $\sum_{s_{-i}} \leq \mathcal{N} - 1$, and $u_i(1, s_{-i}) = b$ when $\sum_{s_{-i}} > \mathcal{N} - 1$.

In a deterministic setting where agents utilize only pure strategies a Nash equilibrium occurs when exactly sixty agents choose to attend. There are $\binom{100}{60}$ such equilibria. There are no symmetric pure strategy Nash equilibria. Pure strategy Nash equilibria are Pareto efficient: in equilibrium no agent can be made better off without making another agent worse off. There is one symmetric mixed strategy equilibrium where every agent has the same probability of attending each period. Because of the variance in attendance that results from agents' mixed strategies the equilibrium is not Pareto efficient.

Suppose that the agent initially attends p percent of the time. Consistent with the desire to maximize pleasure and minimize painful experiences, the agent goes more often (increases p slightly) if the bar is uncrowded, but prefers to go less often (to decrease p) if the bar is crowded. Over time, the agent gathers information about the state of the bar, and 'remembers' this in the form of the parameter p. This learning rule can be interpreted as a kind of habit formation or stimulus-response.

Summarizing the previous notation there are M agents competing for the $\mathcal{N}$ spaces at the bar. The probability that the ith agent attends is p_i. Let k be a time (iteration) counter and $N(k)$ be the number of agents attending at time k. Let μ be a characteristic parameter that defines how much each agent changes p_i in response to new information and let $p_i(k)$ designate the instantaneous value of p_i at the time k. Let

$$N(k) = \sum_{i=1}^{M} x_i(k) \quad (1)$$

where the $x_i(k)$ are independent Bernoulli random variables that are 1 with probability $p_i(k)$ and zero otherwise. The evolution of the $p_i(k)$ is then defined by $p_i(k+1) =$

$$\begin{array}{ll} 0 & \text{if } p_i(k) - \mu(N(k) - \mathcal{N}) \, x_i(k) < 0 \\ 1 & \text{if } p_i(k) - \mu(N(k) - \mathcal{N}) \, x_i(k) > 1 \\ p_i(k) - \mu(N(k) - \mathcal{N}) \, x_i(k) & \text{otherwise} \end{array} \quad (2)$$

The operation of the algorithm is uncomplicated. At each time k the agent flips a biased coin, attending with probability $p_i(k)$. When the agent attends, then the parameter $p_i(k)$ is adjusted, increasing it proportionally to $N(k) - \mathcal{N}$ if the bar is uncrowded and decreasing it proportionally to $N(k) - \mathcal{N}$ if the bar is crowded. Since the $p_i(k)$ represent probabilities, they must be constrained to lie within 0 and 1. When the agent does not attend $x_i(k)$ is zero and $p_i(k+1) = p_i(k)$. Note that the stepsize does not decrease over time. The simplicity of the scheme makes it feasible to analyze the resulting behavior, and as demonstrated in section

In Arthur's formulation of the problem, agents have access to information about attendance at the bar even on evenings when they do not themselves attend. This can be incorporated into the algorithm (2), giving the update $p_i(k+1) =$

$$0 \quad \text{if } p_i(k) - \mu(N(k) - \mathcal{N}) < 0$$

$$\begin{cases} 1 & \text{if } p_i(k) - \mu(N(k) - \mathcal{N}) > 1 \\ p_i(k) - \mu(N(k) - \mathcal{N}) & \text{otherwise} \end{cases} \quad (3)$$

which mimics the information structure used by Arthur's agents. As will become clear, this information structure is a key element in the behavior of the algorithm. When agents base their updates on only their own experiences as in (2) they utilize "partial information". In contrast, (3) utilizes "full information" because agents base their decisions on the full record of attendance.

A related version of the stochastic algorithm updates according to whether the bar is crowded or not: $p_i(k+1) =$

$$\begin{cases} 0 & \text{if } p_i(k) - \mu \, \text{sgn}(N(k) - \mathcal{N}) \, x_i(k) < 0 \\ 1 & \text{if } p_i(k) - \mu \, \text{sgn}(N(k) - \mathcal{N}) \, x_i(k) > 1 \\ p_i(k) - \mu \, \text{sgn}(N(k) - \mathcal{N}) \, x_i(k) & \text{otherwise} \end{cases} \quad (4)$$

Generic Behavior of the Algorithms

This section explores the generic behavior of the system when each of the $M = 100$ agents follows the strategy defined by (2) above. Though details of the various simulations differ, a typical case is illustrated in Figure 1. The probabilities $p_i(0)$ were initialized randomly.

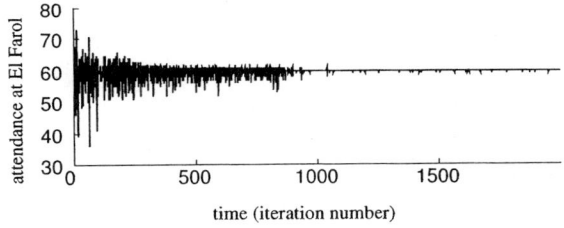

Figure 1: Attendance with Partial Information

Perhaps the most striking aspect of these simulations is the rapid convergence to near the optimal value of $\mathcal{N} = 60$ and the associated decline in the variance of attendance. The outcome approaches that which would be chosen with centralized control, despite the fact that each agent is autonomous, and makes the decision to go (or not to go) based on local information, that is, on its own experiences. In comparison, in Arthur's setup, there are far greater excursions about the optimal value and the bar is overcrowded about half the time.

Figure 2 shows values of the probabilities $p_i(k)$ over the course of a typical simulation run. By the final iteration, the agents have divided themselves into two groups. The probability parameter for 60 of the agents has risen very near 1, indicating that they go to *El Farol* nearly every time. The remaining 40 agents attend less and less frequently, with their probability parameter very near zero. This division of the population appears nowhere in the algorithm statement; rather, it is an emergent property of the adaptive solution to the *El Farol* problem. When agents follow this adaptive strategy, *El Farol* looks more like *Cheers*. Despite the stochastic nature of agents of the adaptive learning rule it converges to a pure strategy Nash equilibrium.

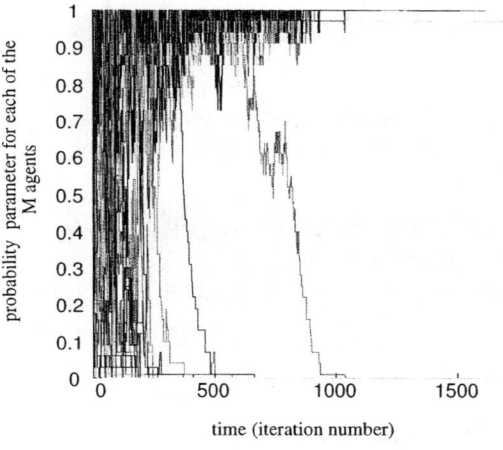

Figure 2: Probabilities with Partial Information

Finally Figures 3 and 4 use the "full information" algorithm (3) to investigate the effect of allowing the agents to update their probabilities at every iteration, whether they have personally attended the bar or not. This reflects the information structure in Arthur's simulations. Mean attendance is approximately 60, but the variance does not decline over time, indicating that seats in the bar often remain unfilled, and often the bar is overcrowded. Note that the transient behavior in the initial periods is masked by the long time scale. Figure 4 should be compared to Figure 2; the probability parameters for these agents continue to bounce randomly about some fixed value as their probabilities all increase or decrease simultaneously in response to the same signals.

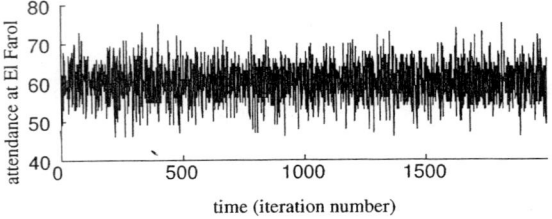

Figure 3: Attendance with Full Information

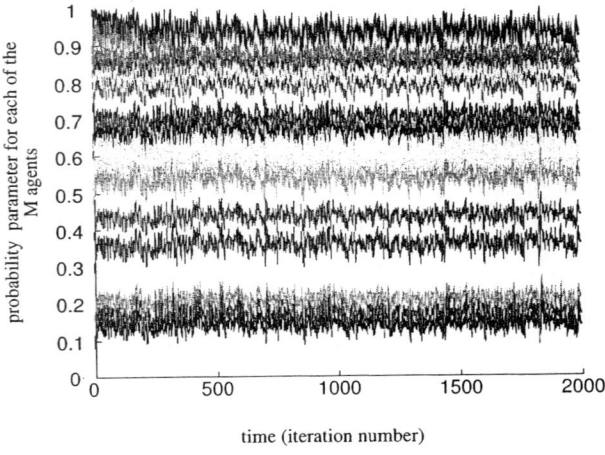

Figure 4: Probabilities with Full Information

Somewhat paradoxically, agents successfully coordinate their behavior and the system achieves a Pareto efficient outcome only when agents have access to less information. Several authors have noted a similar phenomena in transportation routing. Mahmassani and Jayakrishnan (1991) use simulations to demonstrate that when individuals pursue a strict best response strategy, changing their route no matter how small the improvement over their current choice, the performance of the system as a whole degrades if more than 25% of drivers have access to real time information about congestion. Arnott, De Palma and Lindsey (1996, 1991) show that congestion can arise because of "concentration," or similar responses to common information, and that consequently, more information can lead to increased congestion.

Analysis of the Adaptive Solutions

The first step in the analysis of the dynamic behavior of the algorithms is to determine the conditions under which the means of the $p(k)$ remain fixed; that is, to determine the steady states of the averaged system. We consider the partial information case first.

Taking the expectation of both sides of (2) gives

$$E\{p_i(k+1)\} = E\{p_i(k)\} - \mu E\{(N(k) - \mathcal{N}) \ x_i(k)\},$$

assuming that the $p_i(k)$ are not at the boundary points 0 or 1. This expectation remains unchanged exactly when the update portion is zero, that is, when

$$E\{(N(k) - \mathcal{N}) \ x_i(k)\} = 0.$$

Using (1) this can be rewritten

$$E\{(\sum_{j=1}^{M} x_j(k) - \mathcal{N}) \ x_i(k)\} = E\{(\sum_{\substack{j=1 \\ j \neq i}}^{M} x_j(k) + 1 - \mathcal{N}) \ p_i(k)\}$$

since the $x_i(k)$ is 1 with probability $p_i(k)$ and zero otherwise. Because the term in parenthesis is independent of $p_i(k)$ (recall that the $x_j(k)$ are independent Bernoulli random variables) this becomes

$$= (1 - \mathcal{N} + \sum_{\substack{j=1 \\ j \neq i}}^{M} E\{x_j(k)\}) \ p_i(k)$$

$$= (1 - \mathcal{N} + \sum_{\substack{j=1 \\ j \neq i}}^{M} p_j(k)) \ p_i(k).$$

In full vector form this is

$$\begin{pmatrix} (1 - \mathcal{N} + \sum_{j \neq 1}^{M} p_j(k)) \ p_1(k) \\ (1 - \mathcal{N} + \sum_{j \neq 2}^{M} p_j(k)) \ p_2(k) \\ \vdots \\ (1 - \mathcal{N} + \sum_{j \neq M}^{M} p_j(k)) \ p_M(k) \end{pmatrix}. \quad (5)$$

Consider any candidate steady state p^* with $\mathcal{N}$ ones and $\mathcal{N} - M$ zeroes. Let I_1 be the indices of the ones and I_0 be the indices of the zeroes. Then there are two kinds of terms in (5). When $i \in I_1$, $\sum_{\substack{j=1 \\ j \neq i}}^{M} p_j^* = \mathcal{N} - 1$ and so

$$(1 - \mathcal{N} + \sum_{\substack{j=1 \\ j \neq i}}^{M} p_j^*) \ p_i^* = (1 - \mathcal{N} + \mathcal{N} - 1) \ p_i^* = 0. \quad (6)$$

When $i \in I_0$, $\sum_{j=1, j\neq i}^{M} p_j^* = \mathcal{N}$, $p_i^* = 0$, and hence

$$(1 - \mathcal{N} + \sum_{\substack{j=1 \\ j\neq i}}^{M} p_j^*) p_i^* = (1 - \mathcal{N} + \mathcal{N}) \, 0 = 0.$$

Hence p^* is a steady state.

Now consider any p^* for which $\sum_{j=1}^{M} p_j^* = \mathcal{N}$ that is not of the form of $\mathcal{N}$ ones and $\mathcal{N} - M$ zeroes. Thus $0 < p_n^* < 1$ for at least one n. In this case, the relevant term in (5) is

$$(1 - \mathcal{N} + \sum_{\substack{j=1 \\ j\neq n}}^{M} p_j^*) p_n^* = (1 - \mathcal{N} + \sum_{j=1}^{M} p_j^* - p_n^*) p_n^*$$
$$= (1 - \mathcal{N} + \mathcal{N} - p_n^*) p_n^* = (1 - p_n^*) p_n^*.$$

This cannot be zero and hence p^* is not a steady state. Hence the only steady states of algorithm (2) are at p^* consisting of $\mathcal{N}$ ones and $M - \mathcal{N}$ zeroes. In particular, the symmetric mixed strategy Nash equilibrium at $p_j^* = .6$ for all j (for $g = 1$, $b \approx -0.98$) is not a steady state of this algorithm.

In contrast, consider a similar analysis carried out for the "full information" algorithm. Taking the expectation of both sides of (3) gives

$$E\{p_i(k+1)\} = E\{p_i(k)\} - \mu E\{\sum_{j=1}^{M} x_j(k) - \mathcal{N}\}.$$

Steady states occur when $E\{\sum_{j=1}^{M} x_j(k) - \mathcal{N}\} = 0$, i.e., whenever

$$E\{\sum_{j=1}^{M} x_j(k)\} = \sum_{j=1}^{M} E\{x_j(k)\} = \sum_{j=1}^{M} p_j(k) = \mathcal{N}.$$

Hence any p^* with $\sum_{j=1}^{M} p_j^* = \mathcal{N}$ is a steady state of this algorithm. Note that these are not mixed strategy equilibria of the *El Farol* game unless $p_i = .6$ for every agent. The expected return in the steady state is lower for agents whose individual probabilities are lower than average as they face a higher probability that the bar will be crowded, and vice versa for those whose individual probabilities are higher than average. Consequently, a sensible learning rule might converge to a pure strategy equilibrium assuming agents adjust their parameters slowly overtime.

To further understand the global behavior of the system we relate the algorithms utilized by individuals to a global cost function. The algorithm can be derived as an approximation to an instantaneous gradient descent for minimization of the cost function

$$J(k) = (E\{N(k)\} - \mathcal{N})^2 \quad (7)$$

where

$$E\{N(k)\} = E\{\sum_{i=1}^{M} x_i(k)\} = \sum_{i=1}^{M} E\{x_i(k)\} = \sum_{i=1}^{M} p_i(k) \quad (8)$$

is the expected number of attendees at time k. The typical gradient strategy is to update the state using

$$p_i(k+1) = p_i(k) - \mu(k) \frac{dJ(k)}{dp_i(k)}. \quad (9)$$

With $J(k)$ as in (7),

$$\frac{dJ(k)}{dp_i(k)} = (E\{N(k)\} - \mathcal{N}) \frac{dE\{N(k)\}}{dp_i(k)}.$$

From (8), the derivative is $\frac{dE\{N(k)\}}{dp_i(k)} = 1$, and hence

$$\frac{dJ(k)}{dp_i(k)} = E\{N(k)\} - \mathcal{N}.$$

Replacing $E\{N(k)\}$ by its instantaneous value gives

$$\frac{dJ(k)}{dp_i(k)} \approx N(k) - \mathcal{N}$$

which is an instantaneous approximation to the gradient of $J(k)$. Substituting this into (9) gives

$$p_i(k+1) = p_i(k) - \mu \, (N(k) - \mathcal{N}). \quad (10)$$

In the limited information case this update occurs only when $x_i(k) = 1$, in the full information case this update occurs every iteration regardless of the agent's attendance. Adding the *a priori* limits on $p_i(k)$ then gives the algorithms (2) and (3). For both algorithms $E\{N(k)\} = \mathcal{N}$ in a steady state. However, because the limited information algorithm converges to a pure strategy equilibria the actually observed costs will be 0, whereas with full information the expected costs will be $\frac{1}{2} Var[N(k)]$.

Similarly, the algorithm based on the sign of $(N(k) - \mathcal{N})$, 4, can be derived from the absolute value cost function $J(k) = |E\{N(k)\} - \mathcal{N}|$. By analogy, these algorithms are variants of the Least Mean Square (LMS) algorithms which are common in the context of linear system identification and adaptive filtering; (4) is an analog of the signed LMS algorithm.

The adaptive solution thus provides a simple mechanism whereby a large collection of decentralized decision makers, each acting in their own best interests and with only limited knowledge, can solve a complex congestion and social coordination problem. Moreover, convergence to the solution is relatively rapid (depending on the initial conditions) and robust.

References

Arnott, R.; De Palma A.; and Lindsey, R. 1996. Information and Usage of Free-access Congestible Facilities with Stochastic Capacity and Demand. *International Economic Review* 37(1):181-203.

Arnott, R.; De Palma A.; and Lindsey, R. 1991. Does Providing Information to Drivers Reduce Traffic Congestion? *Transportation Research A* 25A(5):309-318.

Arthur, W. B. 1994. Inductive Reasoning and Bounded Rationality: The *El Farol* Problem. *American Economic Review: Papers and Proceedings 1994* 84(May):406-411.

Glance, N. S.; and Huberman, B. A. 1994. The Dynamics of Social Dilemmas. *Scientific American* (March):76-83.

Greenwald, A.; Mishra, B.; and Parikh, R. 1998. The Santa Fe Bar Problem Revisited: Theoretical and Practical Implications. Technical Report, New York University.

Huberman, B. A.; and Lukose, R. M. 1997. Social Dilemmas and Internet Congestion. *Science* 277(July 25):535-537.

Mahmassani, H. S.; and Jayakrishnan, R. 1991. System Performance and User Response Under Real-time Information in a Congested Traffic Corridor," *Transportation Research A* 25A(5):293-307.

Sethares, W. A.; and Bell, A. M. 1998. An Adaptive Solution to the *El Farol* Problem. *Proceedings of the 36th Annual Allerton Conference on Communication, Control, and Computing, Allerton IL, Sept. 1998.*

Non-deterministic Social Laws

Michael H. Coen

MIT Artificial Intelligence Lab
545 Technology Square
Cambridge, MA 02139
mhcoen@ai.mit.edu

Abstract

The paper generalizes the notion of a *social law*, the foundation of the theory of artificial social systems developed for coordinating Multi-Agent Systems. In an artificial social system, its constituent agents are given a common social law to obey and are free to act within the confines it legislates, which are carefully designed to avoid inter-agent conflict and deadlock. In this paper, we argue that this framework can be overly restrictive in that social laws indiscriminately apply to all distributions of agent behavior, even when the probability of conflicting conditions arising is acceptably small. We define the notion of a non-deterministic social law applicable to a family of probability distributions that describe the expected behaviors of a system's agents. We demonstrate that taking these distributions into account can lead to the formulation of more efficient social laws and the algorithms that adhere to them. We illustrate our approach with a traffic domain problem and demonstrate its utility through an extensive series of simulations.

Introduction

Agents designed to exist in multi-agent systems in general can not afford to be oblivious to the presence of other agents in their environment. The very notion of a multi-agent system presupposes that agents, for better or worse, will have some impact on each other. A central problem in Distributed AI (DAI) has been to develop strategies for coordinating the behaviors of these agents – perhaps to cooperatively maximize some measure of the system's global utility or conversely, to insure that non-cooperative agents find some acceptable way to peacefully coexist.

Many coordination strategies have been developed for managing multi-agent systems (MAS). One axis on which we can contrast these different approaches is the degree of agent autonomy they suppose. For example, a centralized planning system [5] might globally synchronize each agent's activities in advance, taking pains to insure that conflict is avoided among them. Agents can then blindly follow these centrally arranged plans without further consideration. Alternatively, at the other end of the spectrum, agents can be wholly autonomous and pursue their individual goals without relying on any centralized control mechanism. In the event conflict arises among them, preformulated rules of encounter allow the agents to dynamically negotiate among themselves to resolve it [3].

An intermediary approach between these extremes has been explored in the development of *artificial social systems* [2,4], whose workings should feel familiar to anyone living in a civilized country. In an artificial social system, its constituent agents are given a common *social law* to obey and are free to act within the confines it legislates. A social law is explicitly designed to prevent conflict and deadlock among the agents; however, for it to be deemed *useful*, it should simultaneously allow each agent to achieve its individual set of goals. Thus, designing a social law is something of a balancing act. It must be sufficiently strict to prevent conflict or deadlock, and simultaneously, it must be sufficiently liberal to allow the agents to efficiently achieve their goals. Useful social laws can be designed that not only avoid inter-agent conflict but also minimize the use of energy, time, and other resources appropriate to the problem domain. Fitoussi has examined an extension of this theory involving *minimal social laws*. These are social laws that minimize the set of restrictions placed upon the agents, while still avoiding inter-agent conflicts. Minimal social laws allow agents to have maximum flexibility during action selection by only disallowing those activities that would prevent other agents from obtaining their goals; thus, they are minimally restrictive.

We propose here that social laws, including even the minimal type described above, can be overly restrictive because agents must adhere to them in all circumstances – even where the possibility of conflict with other agents is extremely low. By insisting that agents avoid any chance of conflict or deadlock when these circumstances are highly unlikely, even minimal social laws may sometimes be overly restrictive and thereby, inherently inefficient. We will refer to this property of a social law as it being *deterministic*. Consider, for example, a domain consisting of a grid traversed by a group of mobile agents. A deterministic social law for this domain might institute traffic regulations to insure that agents never collide or get stuck and to be useful, it would also allow the agents to

---

Copyright © 2000, American Association for Artificial Intelligence (www.aaai.org). All rights reserved.

reach whichever nodes they needed. However, being deterministic, this social law would be equally applicable to all distributions describing how agents select nodes to visit and how they travel between them.

In this paper, we examine how knowledge of the probability distributions governing agent behavior in MAS can be applied towards more efficiently coordinating them through a *non-deterministic social law*. For example, in the domain above, knowing (or learning) that the agents tend to uniformly select nodes in the grid to visit can drastically improve our ability to coordinate their movement. We note that from a social engineering perspective, this might appear somewhat counter-intuitive. Much of the work in artificial social systems has been motivated through analogy with how human societies function. We institute laws that govern individual behavior and thereby benefit the community as a whole. However, the analogy between agents and people must not be taken too far. For example, vehicular traffic laws in human society need to be easily remembered, and are thus rarely specific to particular distributions and flows of traffic. They are even less likely to be changed dynamically to reflect learned observations. Instead, epiphenomenal approaches are used: highways are constructed that implicitly redirect vehicles, signal light intervals are dynamically varied, and traffic reports are broadcast via radio – all of these are centralized mechanisms to reduce both congestion and the cognitive burden on human drivers. Traffic regulations themselves are essentially inviolate and for good reason – people would find it difficult to drive safely otherwise. However, agents do not share this limitation. There is nothing inherently worrisome in optimizing social laws to better fit the particular MAS they are intended to govern.

We would like to clarify a point that has been somewhat unclear in the social law literature regarding the efficiency of social laws. Social laws are not algorithms – they do not provide a method for accomplishing a particular task. Rather, they are guidelines that specify a class of valid algorithms (or strategies) for solving problems from a particular domain by partitioning the set of possible algorithms into "law-abiding" and "criminal" sets. Social laws are thus not necessarily instructive. Just as traffic laws in human society do not provide directions but simply legislate certain types of behavior in particular situations, social laws maintain a set of constraints that simplify writing and reasoning about algorithms. Therefore, it is not obviously meaningful to speak about a particular social law's efficiency. Instead, what should be considered are the computational and other costs of the best-known algorithms the social law makes realizable. We may then refer to a social law's efficiency solely in this regard. However, others do not always clearly make this discrimination, particularly with social laws so highly constrained and algorithmically formulated they blur the paradigmatic distinction. In referring to their work, we will sometimes find it convenient to ignore this distinction as well. More generally, we will define the notion of a *non-deterministic social law* as one that does not guarantee it is useful in the technical sense given above, although it is highly likely to be for its expected distribution of agent goals and behaviors. We will call *non-deterministic social algorithms* the algorithms that adhere to these laws and only present expected efficiency results regarding them.

In the next section, we discuss the importance of understanding the expected behaviors of the agents – and not simply their goal spaces – while formulating social laws. After this, we examine a traffic domain originally presented in [4]. We formulate a non-deterministic social law for it that is more efficient than its deterministic counterpart. We then present extensive simulation results that demonstrate the efficacy of our approach.

Using Distribution Information

Social laws in MAS do not always provide sufficient information to write efficient control algorithms for the agents. This is not necessarily a limitation of social laws *per se*. However, it indicates the importance of understanding the expected behavior of the agents as a group somewhere in the system's coordination mechanism, whether it be directly incorporated into the system's social laws as we argue in the next section, or instead, into the actual control algorithms for its agents. Even though we are investigating a coordination paradigm that has no centralized controller, there is no reason to insist that individual agents have no knowledge of their expected group behavior.

To better understand this point, it will be useful to first make explicit the role of social laws from a programmer's perspective. A social law for a multi-agent system is designed to give its agents some measure of autonomy and self-government. While it is essential that each agent follow the law, it is of no concern what the agent actually does as long as all of its activities are legal. In other words, social laws make no recommendations as to how agents should spend their time; they simply insure the agents do not unduly interfere with each other. Formulating a useful social law is computationally demanding, and even determining whether one exists for a MAS is in general NP-complete [4]. Therefore, the development of a social law is taken to be an offline practice. However, once a social law is formulated, it can be repeatedly used without further computational expense. This may be contrasted with negotiation protocols, in which computational effort goes into both formulating a protocol and then subsequently negotiating according to it each time is it employed.

After a social law is designed for a system, it is supplied to the agents' programmers, who are then responsible for implementing control algorithms for the agents that obey it. However, without more information about the expected behavior of the other agents in the system, this may be quite difficult to do efficiently. This is because a social law indicates which set of actions is legal in any encountered situation without providing guidance for selecting among the legal alternatives. It can be difficult do so without additional information. For example, consider the following domain, taken from [1], in which m agents synchronously travel circularly around an n-node ring, with nodes clockwise labeled from $1...n$. At each time step, an agent can move to either of its two neighboring nodes or it can remain immobile. A minimal social law presented in [1] that permitted these agents to travel was:

(1) Staying immobile is forbidden if the node that can be reached by a single counterclockwise movement is occupied.
(2) Moving counterclockwise is allowed only if the two nodes that would be encountered by moving counterclockwise twice are free.

While this social law provides a framework that guarantees two agents cannot collide or deadlock, it does not provide any practical guidance for how to actually move agents around the ring. If an agent is on node k and wishes to travel to node j, $j>k$, should it take a clockwise or counterclockwise path? Supposing $j-k < n/2$, the agent should clearly move clockwise. However, if $j-k > n/2$, it is not obvious which direction is best without knowing both the current value of m and how other agents tend to move (or stay immobile) on the ring. If the agent tried to reach node j but was blocked k steps along the path between them, it might then have to travel clockwise around the ring to j, thereby incurring a $2k$ penalty for its unsuccessful counterclockwise attempt. The primary question here is how far an agent can expect to move counterclockwise without being blocked by another agent. Although we do not further analyze this problem here, this simple example makes clear the need for an individual agent to have available more information than that provided directly by its social law or sensory capabilities.

The Multi-Agent Grid System

We now examine the multi-agent traffic domain presented in [4], which we will refer to as the Grid System. This domain consists of an $n \times n$ grid that is traversed by m mobile agents (e.g., robots), as shown in Figure 1. The rows and columns of the grid form lanes that the agents can navigate. We assume that time is discrete and the system is synchronous, so at every time step, each agent is located at some grid coordinate. In this system, agents are given goals in the form of grid coordinates to which they must navigate. Every time an agent reaches its destination, it receives a new goal to visit. For example, the agents might be transporting goods in a warehouse and are alternatively picking up and dropping off items. (We note such systems are currently in frequent commercial use.)

The main consideration here is how to insure that the agents do not collide while they navigate the grid. For example, the most naïve strategy would simply "snake" the agents in a Hamiltonian cycle around the grid, as shown in

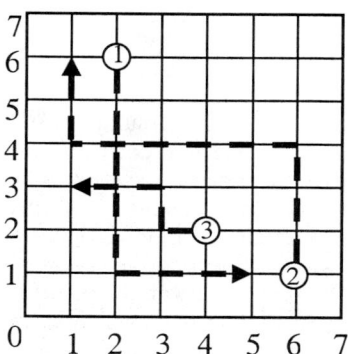

Figure 1 – An 8x8 grid with three agents that will travel along the indicated paths. Notice that in three time steps, agents 1 & 3 will collide at coordinate (2,3)

Figure 2A. Each trip between any two nodes would take $O(n^2)$ time units to complete, which does not compare favorably with the $O(n)$ steps an agent would take to make the same trip in isolation – i.e., with no other agents present. Because this domain does not have cooperative goals – ones that agents work together to achieve – the time an agent would take to complete a task in isolation is the optimum that any social law could achieve.

In [4], a complex, deterministic social law is presented for the Grid System that guarantees agents can achieve their goals within certain time bounds. This law requires that agents only use certain rows and columns in the grid for "long distance" travel, much like we use a highway. When an agent reaches the neighborhood of its goal, it then travels to it directly along the "local" grid, as illustrated in Figure 2B.

Summarizing their results, an agent that can achieve a goal in time t in isolation can achieve it using their social law in time $t + 2n + o(n)$, assuming $m = O(\sqrt{n})$ and $m << n$. For the case where $m \leq n$, a variant of this law provides that each goal can be achieved in $4n$ time steps.

It is helpful to keep in mind that with $m = O(\sqrt{n})$, the grid is very sparsely populated. For example, if $n = 100$, a grid containing 10,000 locations would have on the order of 10 agents moving on it. We are interested in answering the following questions: by insuring generality, is the deterministic social law framework overly constraining? How can its assumptions be loosened in order to achieve a more efficient coordination system? Can we both increase the number of agents travelling on the grid and simultaneously decrease the amount of time they take to reach their goals?

The Uniform Grid System

In this section, we consider the grid system presented above under a particular probability distribution describing an agent's goal selection. Namely, we will assume that the goals are uniformly distributed over all points (x, y) on the grid:

$$\Pr[(x,y) \text{ is a goal}] = \frac{1}{n^2}, \quad 0 \le x, y < n$$

It is important to note that this assumption will certainly not always be valid, and the non-deterministic social law we present here is not intended for systems where it is not. However, for MAS with agents described by this distribution, we can obtain far more efficient results than those in [4].

Towards determining a lower bound for the non-deterministic social law's efficiency, we first determine the expected distance between two randomly selected integral coordinates, which we call Δ, on a line from [0, n-1] inclusive:

$$E(\Delta) = \sum_{i=1}^{n-1} i \Pr(\Delta = i) = \sum_{i=1}^{n-1} i \frac{2(n-i)}{n^2} = \frac{n}{3} - \frac{1}{3n}$$

On a two-dimensional grid, the expected distance between a pair of successive goals will be $2E(\Delta)$, because the total distance will be the sum of the distances along each axis independently. We will call this value the *isolation time*, denoted by ΔG; it is the expected travel time between goals for an unconstrained, isolated agent. It is therefore also a lower bound on the time taken by any social law governing the uniform grid system. Our goal is to formulate a non-deterministic social law that approaches this lower bound as closely as possible.

Our approach will be to essentially allow the agents to move as they would in isolation. They will explicitly check to make sure their moves are "safe," and take corrective action if necessary. We assume that each agent has sufficient sensory capabilities to realize that other agents are in its immediate vicinity, i.e. up to 2 steps away. In the event a transition between nodes would cause a collision, an agent simply waits to try again on the next move. If an agent is blocked for an extended period along its path, the social law requires that it formulate some alternate route to its destination. Particularly important in this case is ensuring that the deadlock recovery mechanism maintains the assumed probability distribution describing the agents' movements through the grid.

Notice that this approach does *not* guarantee deadlock will be avoided. It is possible (however unlikely) that two agents headed in opposite directions along a column or row can indefinitely block one another, even after repeatedly trying alternate paths to their destinations. In practice, we might try to detect such situations and formulate rules of encounter to avoid them. However, in tens of millions of simulation runs, non-recoverable deadlock has never been encountered. Nonetheless, the non-deterministic social law shown below, which we call law Traffic Law U (for uniform), is not guaranteed in its present form to be useful in the technical sense defined in the introduction:

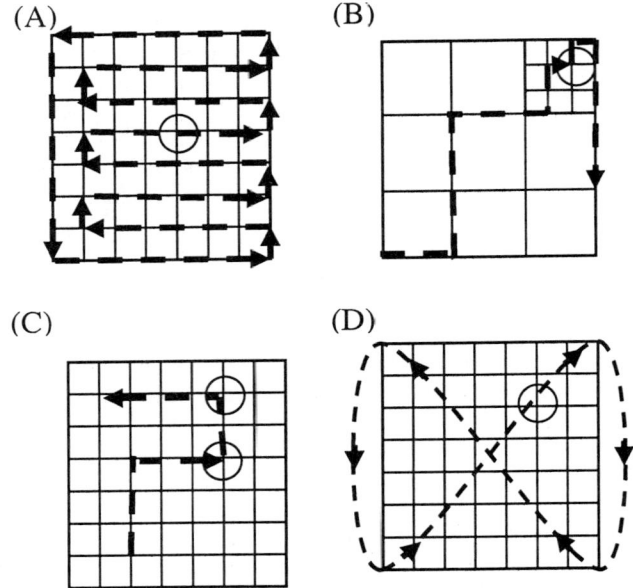

Figure 2 – Different strategies an agent might use to traverse the grid: (A) Walk a Hamiltonian cycle; (B) Navigate through *course* grid until reaching appropriate neighborhood and then use *fine* grid; (C) Take a minimum length path between points; (D) Loop in a "figure 8" path through grid. Circles in the above figures represent goals.

Traffic Law U
1) At step i+1, an agent may not move to a spot occupied by another agent at step i.
2) If more than one agent simultaneously wants to move to a coordinate, only one, chosen at random, is permitted to do so. The rest must remain where they are and wait one turn before trying again.
3) If an agent has remained immobile for more than k turns because its path has been blocked, it must pick another route to its goal.

We will refer to the condition of rule 2 of this law as a *collision* and the requirement of rule 3 as *rerouting*. Rule 1 in the above law is a conservative measure that prevents an agent from moving to a spot most recently occupied by another agent. While technically unnecessary, it allows us to avoid the nightmare of inter-agent communication and coordination that would be necessary for moving an immediately adjacent queue of agents simultaneously. Notice that the Traffic Law U leaves the precise strategy for picking an alternate route in rule 3 unspecified. Any particular implementation of a non-deterministic social algorithm that adheres to Traffic Law U will have to pick some mechanism for selecting this alternative route. This could, for example, involve dynamic negotiation between the agents, random selection, or some other strategy.

Below, we examine a method that randomly picks an intermediate goal to visit along the way to the agent's actual destination in case it gets stuck somewhere.

We define an *L-path* as a path between two grid points that contains at most one turn (i.e., change of direction), so called because of its resemblance to the letter L. (See Figure 2(c).) Points not on the same row or column will have two L-paths connecting them. Otherwise, there will be only one. A *route* is defined to be a sequence of L-paths. We now give a non-deterministic social algorithm that adheres to Traffic Law U:

Algorithm 1:
1. Select a new goal g.
2. Let P be a random L-Path from current position to g.
3. Set route R = P
4. Move along route R towards g, following rules 1 and 2 of Traffic Law U.
5. If blocked for more than k steps, do the following:
    a. Randomly select new intermediary goal g'
    b. Let P1 be a random L-path from current position to g'
    c. Let P2 be a random L-path from g' to g.
    d. Set R = P1, P2
    e. Go to step 4.
6. Upon reaching goal g, go to step 1.

The insistence that agents travel along L-paths is well motivated for maintaining the assumed distribution of agents in the grid. For example, were the agents to travel along random paths (i.e., completely shuffled L-paths), this would induce a normal distribution of the agents, more heavily favoring the center region of the grid and leading to higher numbers of collisions and rerouting. L-paths are to be preferred because they more uniformly distribute the agents and thus, make collisions far less likely. Furthermore, assuming that turning mobile robots requires greater energy than moving them in a straight direction and additionally interferes with dead-reckoning location strategies by introducing additional uncertainty, L-paths are to be preferred for practical, non-distribution specific reasons as well.

Analysis

The efficiency of this algorithm is strictly determined by the number of collisions and amount of rerouting an agent has to do. In the absence of these, each agent would achieve optimal time, because the L-path to its goal is a shortest length route to it. However, in the presence of other agents, both collisions and rerouting are inevitable and can incur prohibitive time penalties. With respect to each agent, a collision has cost 1 because of the incurred delay. Rerouting has cost of at least $2\Delta G$, because deadlock may occur during the rerouting process itself. However, there is no recursive rerouting – the agent simply reroutes with respect to the original goal, not the intermediary selected in step (5a) of the algorithm.

We will first provide a loose upper bound to the expected running time for an agent to travel between successive goals on an $n \times n$ grid containing m agents. We use this to determine how many agents can be allowed on the grid simultaneously given how much overhead (i.e. wasted travel time) is acceptable. We then present extensive simulation results for Algorithm 1, due to the difficulty of obtaining tighter bounds for its running time.

Analytic Results

To determine how many agents can simultaneously traverse the grid without incurring unreasonable delays due to congestion, we approximately model an agent's movement through the Uniform Grid System as if it were governed by a negative binomial distribution. This approximation will become increasingly inaccurate in systems where the grid is more heavily congested, in which case we must turn to the simulation results given below.

For Algorithm 1, we bound E_t, the expected travel time between goals as:

$$E_t \leq E(\text{time moving towards goal}) + E(\text{time recovering from deadlock})$$

We define the probabilities of colliding and successful transitions as P_c and P_s respectively:

$$P_c = \frac{m-1}{n^2-1}, \quad P_s = 1 - P_c$$

Note that P_c would be seem to be double the given value but we assume that half the time an agent is involved in a potential collision, it is the one selected to move per rule 2 of Traffic Law U, and no time penalty is thereby incurred. We bound the probability of deadlock P_d by considering that it occurs only when agents collide and then subsequently block each other. Separately accounting for interior and border regions, we have:

$$P_d = \frac{(n^2-4n)}{n^2}\frac{P_c}{4} + \frac{4n}{n^2}\frac{P_c}{3} = \frac{P_c}{4} + \frac{P_c}{3n} \approx \frac{P_c}{4}$$

Recall ΔG, the isolation time, is given by:

$$\Delta G = 2E(\Delta) = \frac{2n}{3} - \frac{2}{3n} \approx 2n/3$$

We calculate E_{goal}, the expected time an agent spends moving towards its goal using our negative binomial distribution assumption:

$$E_{goal} = \frac{\Delta G}{P_s}$$

We determine $E_{deadlock}$, the expected time an agent spends recovering from deadlocks, explicitly noting that the agent may deadlock in the midst of deadlock recovery:

$$E_{deadlock} \leq \left(\frac{\Delta G}{P_s}\right) P_d (2\Delta G + P_d (2\Delta G + P_d (2\Delta G + ...))...)$$

$$= \left(\frac{\Delta G}{P_s}\right) 2\Delta G \frac{P_d}{1 - P_d}$$

We then have the expected time between successive goals is:

$$E_t \leq \frac{\Delta G}{P_s} + \left(\frac{\Delta G}{P_s}\right) 2\Delta G \frac{P_d}{1 - P_d}$$

Next, we define c^*, the ratio between the expected and isolation times when traveling between successive goals. It is a measure of the overhead due to agent interaction while traversing the grid:

$$c^* = \frac{E_t}{\Delta G} \leq \frac{1}{P_s} + \left(\frac{2\Delta G}{P_s}\right) \frac{P_d}{1 - P_d} \leq \frac{1}{1 - P_c} + \left(\frac{2\Delta G}{1 - P_c}\right) \frac{P_c/4}{1 - P_c/4}$$

Recalling the above definition of P_c, we solve for the number of agents m as a function of c^* and n:

$$m \approx \frac{c^* - 1}{c^* + \Delta G/2}(n^2) + 1 = \frac{c^* - 1}{c^* + n/3}(n^2) + 1$$

We now have a handle on how many agents can be allowed onto an $n \times n$ grid given some level of acceptable overhead c^*. For example, on a 100x100 grid, if it is acceptable for an agent to spend 1.3 times longer between successive goals than it would on the grid alone, then we expect that roughly 87 agents can be permitted onto the grid simultaneously. Note that this is actually an underestimate because of the non-tight bound for E_t determined above. The actual number demonstrated in simulation for $c^* = 1.3$ is $m=n$, or in this case, $m=100$.

Simulation Results

A Java-based simulator was written for the Uniform Grid System employing Traffic Law U and Algorithm 1. Our approach for each grid of size n was to slowly increase the number of agents, m, observing how this impacted the average time of an agent to achieve its goals. We first consider the case where $m = c\sqrt{n}$. As expected, the time taken for an agent to achieve its goals on average is essentially equal to its isolation time. Tables 1 and 2 contain the cases for $c = 1$ and 10 respectively.

Each simulation was run until the agents globally achieved 10,000 goals. In the table: *#S* represents the number of time steps simulated; *CP* is the total collision penalty for the simulation; *RP* is the total rerouting penalty; *Avg* is the average time an agent took to achieve a goal; ΔG is the time an agent would ideally take in isolation; c^* is $Avg/\Delta G$; and %+ is $100 \times (Avg - \Delta G)/\Delta G$. We note that lower c^* values are better, and a value of 1 is the best that can be achieved by any social law in this domain.

We then examined cases where $m = cn$, where $1 \leq c < n$. As c approaches n, the density of the agents increases to the point where they become hopelessly crowded, and navigation becomes extraordinarily inefficient. As this happens, it becomes more efficient to simply "snake" the agents around the grid in a Hamiltonian cycle as described above. Graphs 1 and 2 display the rate of change in c^* ($=Avg/\Delta G$) as a function of c ($=m/n$) for $n=10$ and 100 respectively.

Finally, we examine our results for the case where $c = 1$ ($m=n$), where we find that empirically, c^* is roughly around 4/3 for all values of n.

Table 1: $m = \sqrt{n}$

n	m	#S	CP	RP	Avg	ΔG	c^*	%+
10	3	23728	3478	5069	7.12	6.6	1.08	7.85
20	4	34445	2562	7574	13.78	13.3	1.04	3.59
100	10	6589	192	2755	65.89	66.66	0.99	-1.16
200	14	9737	70	1624	136.32	133.33	1.02	2.24
500	22	15208	59	3229	334.58	333.33	1.00	0.37
1000	32	21365	22	2227	683.68	666.66	1.03	2.55

Table 2: $m = 10\sqrt{n}$

n	m	#S	CP	RP	Avg	ΔG	c^*	%+
10	30	724	13354	5582	21.7	6.60	3.29	2.29
20	40	542	5146	8282	21.61	13.30	1.62	0.62
50	70	590	2708	13775	41.3	33.32	1.24	0.24
100	100	763	1634	17239	76.3	66.66	1.14	0.14
500	220	1752	643	40440	385.1	333.33	1.16	0.16
1000	320	2617	460	55176	836.6	666.67	1.25	0.25

Table 3: $m = n$

n	#S	CP	RP	Avg	ΔG	c^*	%+
10	878	1758	1977	8.78	6.60	1.33	0.33
20	846	1895	4361	16.92	13.30	1.27	0.27
50	815	2363	12609	40.71	33.32	1.22	0.22
100	791	1960	22494	78.94	66.66	1.18	0.18
500	825	1376	81594	412.09	333.33	1.24	0.24
1000	931	1139	152955	929.14	666.67	1.39	0.39

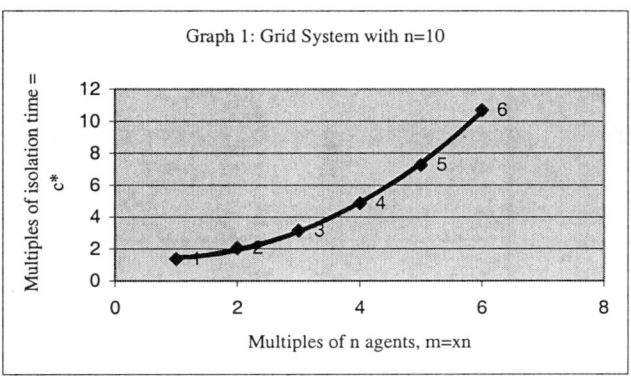

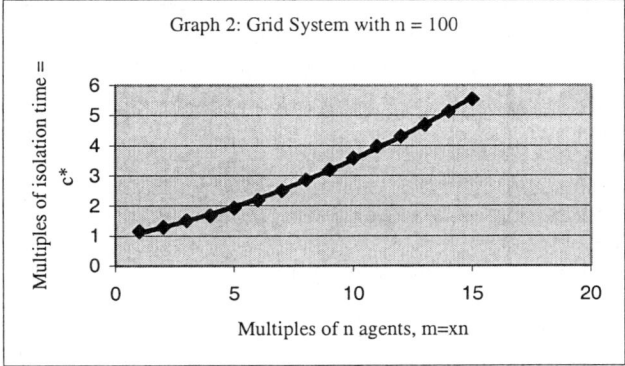

Comparison of results

Algorithm 1 is near optimal in the logarithmic cases shown in Tables 1 and 2, where $m = c\sqrt{n}$. Only in the case where $c \geq m/2$ does the performance degrade substantially. When $m = cn$, we observe a near constant multiplicative cost of approximately $1.3\Delta G$ for $c = 1$. As c starts to increase, we note the expected penalty observed in the average time it takes an agent to reach its goal. Finally, as c approaches n itself, the number of agents approaches n^2, and it would be best to dynamically switch to the Hamiltonian path strategy. In the table below, we compare the expected time for an agent to reach its goal in our approach and the one taken in [4]:

Table 4: Comparison of non-deterministic Algorithm 1 with the deterministic social law presented in [4]:

$m =$	Expected Time to Goal	
	Non-Deterministic	Deterministic
$\sqrt{n}$	ΔG (=2n/3)	$c\Delta G$, c>2
$10\sqrt{n}$	Approaches ΔG	$c\Delta G$, c>2
n	$1.3\Delta G=13n/15$	$4n$
cn	See graphs	Not applicable

Conclusions

In this paper, we proposed that general purpose, deterministic social laws appropriate for all circumstances may be inappropriate for the situations MAS actually encounter. In particular, we argued that knowledge of the underlying distributions describing agent behavior can give us new ways of coordinating MAS and help us formulate more efficient social laws. We demonstrated this by revisiting a previously studied traffic domain problem. By assuming a particular distribution of both agent goals and their deadlock recovery behavior, we were able to formulate a simple and more efficient strategy for coordinating the movement of agents throughout the grid.

Future work in this domain includes more precisely characterizing the runtime complexity of Algorithm 1, exploring how well the system works when faced with other distributions, i.e., how sensitive this formulation is to the actual encountered behavior, and exploring other coordination domains that might be amenable to this approach.

Acknowledgements

This material is based upon work supported by the Advanced Research Projects Agency of the Department of Defense under contract number F30602—94—C—0204, monitored through Rome Laboratory. Special thanks to D. Fitoussi and L. Weisman.

References

[1] Fitoussi, D. and Tennenholtz, M. Minimal Social Laws. In Proc. Of the Fifteenth National Conference on Artificial Intelligence, p26-31. 1998.

[2] Moses, Y., and Tennenholtz, M. Artificial Social Systems. *Computers and Artificial Intelligence*. 14(6):533-562.

[3] Rosenschein, J.S., and Zlotkin, G. Rules of Encounter: Design Conventions for Automated Negotiation among Computers. MIT Press. 1994.

[4] Shoham, Y., and Tennenholtz, M. Social Laws for Artificial Agent Societies: Off-line Design. *Artificial Intelligence* 73. 1995.

[5] Stuart, C. An Implementation of a Multi-Agent Plan Synchronizer. In Proc. Ninth International Joint Conference on Artificial Intelligence. 1985.

Solving Combinatorial Auctions using Stochastic Local Search

Holger H. Hoos
Department of Computer Science
University of British Columbia
Vancouver, BC V6T 1Z4
hoos@cs.ubc.ca

Craig Boutilier
Department of Computer Science
University of Toronto
Toronto, ON M5S 3H5
cebly@cs.toronto.edu

Abstract

Combinatorial auctions (CAs) have emerged as an important model in economics and show promise as a useful tool for tackling resource allocation in AI. Unfortunately, winner determination for CAs is NP-hard and recent algorithms have difficulty with problems involving goods and bids beyond the hundreds. We apply a new stochastic local search algorithm, Casanova, to this problem, and demonstrate that it finds high quality (even optimal) solutions much faster than recently proposed methods (up to several orders of magnitude), particularly for large problems. We also propose a logical language for naturally expressing combinatorial bids in which a single logical bid corresponds to a large (often exponential) number of explicit bids. We show that Casanova performs much better than systematic methods on such problems.

1 Introduction

Auctions have been the focus of increasing study in AI. Certainly the emergence of E-commerce has made market mechanisms an attractive means for conducting business transactions and sales online. Furthermore, as nontrivial multiagent systems become more prevalent, researchers are looking to market protocols such as auctions as the basis for the coordination of agent activities or for resource allocation [5, 18].

When multiple items need to be sold, standard "single-item" auction protocols may be inappropriate, particularly when items exhibit *complementarities*. Specifically, when a bidder attaches a value to a *collection* of goods, associating a "value" with the individual elements is problematic. For example, if an agent requires two adjacent gates at an airport at a specific time—such that obtaining one slot is useless without the other—attaching independent values to each is difficult. Furthermore, bidding for them individually (e.g., in sequence [3, 6, 8] or in parallel [2, 15]) exposes the agent to certain risks (e.g., obtaining one item without the other). *Combinatorial auctions (CAs)* have been proposed as a means of dealing with such problems [14, 16, 18]. Instead of selling items individually, the seller allows bids on *bundles* of items, allowing bidders to deal with the entities of direct interest and avoid the risk of obtaining incomplete bundles. Given a set of combinatorial bids, the seller then decides how best to allocate individual goods to those bundles for which bids were placed, with the aim of maximizing revenue. Because bundles generally overlap, this is—conceptually—a straightforward optimization problem, and is in fact equivalent to weighted set packing. As a result, *optimal winner determination* for CAs is NP-complete [16].

A number of complete algorithms for winner determination have been proposed, including dynamic programming models [16], and algorithms for dealing with problems with special structure.[1] More recently, two proposals for applying AI-style search techniques have been used with some success for winner determination [7, 17]. In these proposals, the structure of bids is exploited to restrict the search—if the number of bids received is relatively sparse compared to the space of possible bids, these approaches perform much better than dynamic programming, and despite the computational complexity of the problem, have been shown to perform reasonably well on problems of moderate size.

When problem instances are large or when solutions are needed quickly, existing algorithms are likely to prove inadequate. In many, if not most, resource-allocation or E-commerce problems that are most readily modeled as CAs, it seems apparent that real-time response to very large problems will be expected. Complete algorithms—those designed to guarantee optimality—necessarily spend *considerable* time "proving" that the solution they produce is optimal at the expense of providing high-quality (though perhaps suboptimal) solutions quickly. Furthermore, as instances become larger, complete algorithms will, in most cases, become infeasible. While certain domains may require optimal solutions (e.g., for legal reasons), we expect that typical applications of CAs will be ideally suited for techniques that produce high-quality, approximate solutions quickly (or within a suitable time frame). Drawing an analogy to scheduling research, for example, large scheduling problems are invariably solved heuristically: even though the smallest improvements in schedule quality can have large economic consequences, the problems are simply to hard to be solved ex-

---
[1] Generally the structures investigated (e.g., restricting the size or structure of bids) are of interest because they allow one to obtain polynomial time algorithms; the existence of such structure in practice is often questionable (see Sandholm [17] for an overview of some special cases).

Copyright © 2000, American Association for Artificial Intelligence (www.aaai.org). All rights reserved.

actly. For the same reasons, heuristic and approximation techniques for large CAs must be viewed as critical.

For these reasons, in this paper we consider the use of incomplete methods for winner determination. Specifically, we develop the *CASLS framework* for studying the solution of combinatorial auctions using *stochastic local search (SLS)* techniques. SLS has been used in AI and operations research for many decision and optimization problems with great success, and has generally proven more successful than systematic methods on a wide range of combinatorial problems. As we demonstrate in this paper, SLS can be applied with great success to the winner determination problem, finding high quality solutions much more quickly than systematic techniques and often finding optimal solutions. We also show that our techniques can tackle problem instances of considerably larger size than existing systematic methods. The nature of SLS does not permit one to offer solution quality or performance guarantees.[2] Instead we adopt the empirical methodology proposed by Hoos [9] to evaluate the success of SLS.

We also consider the use of logical languages to specify *schematic bids*. The CA problem is traditionally formulated by supposing that each bid is a bundle of items together with a bid value. However, there are many circumstances in which a bidder is indifferent between any of a number of different items or even different bundles of items. When such *substitutability* exists, requiring *explicit* bids imposes an undue burden on the bidder. To take one example, suppose a bidder wants any five of a collection of twenty items (e.g., five airport gate slots). The number of concrete bundles the user must bid on is over 15,000. By formulating the bid using a logical language such requirements can be expressed very concisely. We devise two languages for the logical specification of bids and examine the performance of SLS on bids so specified.

2 Combinatorial Auctions
2.1 Basic Model

We suppose a seller has a set of goods $G = \{g_1, ...g_{|G|}\}$ to be auctioned. Potential buyers value different subsets or *bundles* of goods, $b \subseteq G$, and offer bids of the form $\langle b, v \rangle$ where v is the amount the buyer is willing to pay for bundle b. Given a collection of bids $B = \{\langle b_i, v_i \rangle\}$, the seller must find an allocation of goods to bids that maximizes revenue. We define an *allocation* to be any $A = \{\langle b_i, v_i \rangle\} \subseteq B$ such that the bundles b_i making up A are disjoint. The *value* of an allocation $v(A)$ is given by $\sum\{v_i : \langle b_i, v_i \rangle \in A\}$. An *optimal allocation* is any allocation A with maximal value (taken over the space of allocations). The *optimal winner determination* problem is that of finding an optimal allocation given a bid set B. We call any algorithm that constructs some allocation, not necessarily optimal, a winner determination algorithm.

Notice that complementarities are naturally taken care of in this type of auction by allowing bidders to bid on collections of goods. Substitutability can be dealt with easily as well by allowing each bidder one dummy good that is inserted into each of her bids. If a bidder wants only one of several subsets of goods, she can bid on each subset but add the dummy good so that only one bid can be accepted. Because of this, winner determination need not rely on the identities of buyers, but only on the bids themselves.

We can view allocations in a slightly different way. Given a bid set B, an *assignment* is any function $f : G \to B$, assigning goods to specific bids. An assignment f induces an allocation $A_f = \{\langle b_i, v_i \rangle : f^{-1}(\langle b_i, v_i \rangle) \supseteq b_i\}$. Intuitively, given an assignment f, we consider allocated those bids that are "satisfied" by f. Unsatisfied bids (assigned less than their full complement of goods) are ignored. We can generally restrict our attention to assignments that only assign goods $g \in b$ to a bid $\langle b, v \rangle$ if we insert a dummy bid of value zero containing all goods.

The winner determination problem is equivalent to the weighted set packing problem [16] and as such is NP-complete. Algorithms for weighted set packing and related combinatorial problems can be used for winner determinations. Dynamic programming has been proposed for winner determination [16] but requires that the space of possible bids be enumerated, and thus is impractical for problems with a large number of goods (its complexity is independent of the number of actual bids). Search techniques have recently been proposed that exploit the fact that one need really only consider combinations of *actual bids*: if the set of actual bids is relatively sparse, such methods can work quite well.

The CASS algorithm developed by Fujishima, Leyton-Brown and Shoham [7] is good example of the effectiveness of search techniques. CASS uses a depth-first search to find optimal allocations; but clever structuring of the search space, preprocessing, heuristic ordering methods and pruning techniques allow the search to find optimal allocations rather effectively. Not surprisingly, CASS exhibits reasonable anytime performance as well, providing good allocations prior to finding optimal allocations. Sandholm [17] has also explored the use of search, developing an A*-formulation of the problem with good heuristics and pruning/preprocessing techniques. In both works, suitably structured search has proven to be quite computationally effective.

A number of approximation algorithms for weighted set packing have been developed in the literature, some based on local search. However, the emphasis in much of this work is on developing search strategies—or, more accurately, *local improvement strategies* for suboptimal solutions—that have provable quality guarantees rather than good practical applicability.[3] See [1, 4] for examples of such results. More practical stochastic search techniques such as tabu search and simulated annealing have been applied to related problems, but apparently not directly to weighted set packing.

---

[2] Indeed, as shown in [17], optimal winner determination is not even approximable in polytime.

[3] Specifically, none of the work cited here on approximation algorithms provides any empirical study of the actual approximation quality obtained in practice, only worst-case quality bounds.

2.2 A Language for Schematic Bids

In many cases buyers will have complex valuations for bundles of goods, reflecting the fact that certain goods or bundles can be substituted for one another. When combined with the natural complementarities captured by CAs, the set of explicit bids a buyer may need to reflect her true utility function may be very large. For example, should she desire either g_1 or h_1, *and* g_2 or h_2, *and* g_3 or h_3, she must formulate eight explicit bids (i.e., $\{g_1, g_2, g_3\}$, etc.). Complex requirements corresponding to a large number of explicit bids can often be expressed very compactly using a logical language. These bids, for example, can be captured using the logical formula $(g_1 \vee h_1) \wedge (g_2 \vee h_2) \wedge (g_3 \vee h_3)$.

To capture the logical structure of a set of bids, we introduce two logical languages for combinatorial bid specification. Given a set of goods G, a *clause over G* is any nonempty subset of G. Clauses over a set of goods are interpreted "disjunctively:" when a clause is part of a combinatorial bid, it expresses the fact that one (or more) of the goods in the clause is desired. A *clause set* is any (possibly empty) set of clauses over G. Clause sets are interpreted conjunctively: as part of a bid, a clause set is satisfied if each of its clauses is satisfied. Thus, a clause set expresses the fact that at least one good from each of its clauses is desired.[4] We can think of a clause set as a logical formula in conjunctive normal form (CNF) involving only positive literals (viewing each good as a logical atom). A *CNF bid* is any clause set f (positive CNF formula) together with an associated valuation v. Intuitively, such a bid means an agent is willing to pay v for an allocation of goods that "satisfies" the formula. We call the language of CNF bids $\mathcal{L}_{CA}^{cnf}$. Formally, we say a CNF bid $\langle c, v \rangle$ is *satisfied* by an assignment $f : G \to B$ (of goods to bids) iff $f^{-1}(c_i) \neq \emptyset$ for each $c_i \in c$; that is, if at least one good $g \in c_i$ from each clause $c_i \in c$ has been assigned to $\langle c, v \rangle$. The value of an assignment, or the allocation induced by an assignment, given a set of CNF bids is defined as the sum of the bid values of satisfied bids. Notice that simple bundles bids can be expressed trivially in this language; however, substitutability is expressible far more naturally using this logical language, obviating the need for dummy goods.

In many practical settings, a bidder will desire a subset of a set of "identical" goods offered for auction. For instance, a bidder may accept any five airport gates from a collection of twenty offered for lease. Expressing bids of this type in CNF can be cumbersome; furthermore, the size of the required set of explicit bids grows factorially with the size of the good collection of interest. For this reason, we consider an extended language, $\mathcal{L}_{CA}^{k\text{-}of}$, that allows *k-of clauses* having the form $k\text{-}of(S)$, where $k > 0$ and $S \subset G$ is such that $|S| \geq k$. An *extended CNF bid* is any set of clauses or *k-of* clauses. Satisfaction of an extended bid is defined in the obvious way.

---

[4] If obtaining more than one of these goods increases value, then the bid should be expressed differently. The fact that obtaining multiple items from a set does not *decrease* value can be justified by assuming free disposal. Our algorithms will not assign more than one good to a clause in any case, though our approach could be extended to deal with undesirable items (i.e., "bads" along with goods).

3 Stochastic Local Search Applied to CAs

We now sketch a model for applying stochastic local search methods to the winner determination problem. There are several ways SLS techniques can be applied to CAs. Here we focus on the *CASLS* family of algorithms, which searches the space of feasible allocations (nonoverlapping subsets of bids) by selecting in each step a bid which is currently unsatisfied and modifying the current allocation such that this bid becomes satisfied.[5] Searching through feasible allocations has the advantage that the search steps can be easily scored, obviating the need to assign scores to partially-satisfied bids based on their "potential."

Formally, the neighborhood relation for CASLS algorithms is defined as follows: a_j is reachable from a_i iff a_j is determined by adding a new bid b to a_i and assigning the required goods to b; this may entail removing the goods from other bids in a_i. As a consequence, a_j is *adjacent* to a_i iff $a_j = a_i \cup \{b\} \setminus \{b' \in a_i : b' \cap b \neq \emptyset\}$ for some $b \notin a_i$. Thus a_j will generally consist of some subset of a_i together with a new bid b. Note that the adjacency relation is not symmetric (e.g., to return to a_i from a_j may require several steps); but any valid (nondominated) allocation a can be reached from any other in no more than $|a|$ steps. The neighborhood relation we use is analogous to that used for set packing in [4].

3.1 Casanova

Casanova is a CASLS algorithm that bears a strong resemblance to the Novelty$^+$ algorithm for SAT defined by Hoos [10], one of the best-performing algorithms for solving hard SAT problems known to date (see also the Novelty algorithm of [13]). It is based on scoring each search state using the "revenue per good" of the corresponding allocation. Since each neighbor can be reached by adding a bid (and adjusting), we write $sc(b)$ to denote the increase in revenue obtained by adding b. The scoring function $score(b) = sc(b)/length(b)$ normalizes the revenue by the number of goods the bid "consumes".[6] During the search process, we define the *age* of each bid to be the number of steps since that bid was last selected (since initializing the search) to be added to a candidate solution.

Casanova starts with an empty allocation, where all goods assigned to a dummy bid and all real bids are unsatisfied. Then at each step, with probability wp (walk probability), a random unsatisfied bid is selected; with probability $1 - wp$ we select a bid "greedily" by ranking all bids according to their score. Then either the highest ranked bid b_1 or the second-highest b_2 is inserted into the solution as follows: if $age(b_1) \geq age(b_2)$, insert b_1; otherwise insert b_2 with probability np (novelty probability) and b_1 with probability $1 -$

---

[5] Note how this search scheme is analogous to the WalkSAT algorithm family for propositional satisfiability [13], where a currently satisfied clause is selected and satisfied in each search step; however, for CA there is no secondary selection involved in choosing how to satisfy a bid (there is only one way), unlike literal selection *within* the clause in WalkSAT.

[6] Revenue per good is commonly used to measure the quality of a bid in search approaches to CAs.

np. The search proceeds for *maxSteps* steps and is restarted with the empty allocation for a total of *maxTries* independent searches, with the best allocation found at any step of any search reported as the solution. Optionally, we also use a *soft restart strategy*, which reinitializes the search if at least θ_r search steps have occurred since the last initialization, but no improvement in revenue has been achieved within the last $\theta_r/2$ steps.

3.2 Explicit Bids: Empirical Evaluation

We tested Casanova on several random problem distributions, and compared its performance to CASS, the systematic search technique described in [7]. CASS is a complete algorithm which, given enough time, will find an optimal solution and prove its optimality. Casanova, like most SLS algorithms, is incomplete. In practice, given enough time, it may find optimal solutions, but it cannot be used to prove the optimality of any solution it finds. Both algorithms have useful anytime properties, as they generate and report intermediate solutions. But while CASS is deterministic, Casanova is a highly stochastic algorithm. Therefore, for Casanova, the time to achieve a given solution quality as well as the solution quality obtained after a fixed cutoff time are random variables. Both aspects have to be taken into consideration when comparing these two algorithms.

Generally, we performed two types of experiments: For large problem instances—those where CASS could not prove optimality of the best solution it found within 60 CPU seconds[7]—we measured the best solution obtained by CASS within the given cutoff time for each problem instance, while for Casanova, we measured a solution quality distribution over 10 runs of the algorithm. The cutoff times were chosen such that the experimental analysis could be conducted on a sufficient number of instances and in a reasonable amount of time; for bigger problems, we had to allow higher cutoff times to make sure that CASS would at least report the revenue for one candidate solution. For small problem instances, where CASS could prove the optimality of the solutions it found, we measured for each problem instance CASS's time to find the optimal solution. In order to ensure a fair comparison, we did not measure the total running time of CASS, which includes the time needed to "prove" the solution is optimal: we ran CASS to completion to ensure an optimal solution was found, and then determined the time at which the solution was *first* enumerated. For Casanova, we measured the distribution of the run time required to find the optimal solution. These run-time distributions (RTDs) were estimated from 100 runs of the algorithm for each given problem instance.

The CASS implementation we used is highly optimized and relies heavily on caching and pruning techniques. Likewise, Sandholm's bidtree algorithm [17], another systematic algorithm for winner determination, makes use of various preprocessing techniques. Casanova, on the other hand, has not been optimized for speed or memory, and did not have its parameters fine-tuned. Furthermore, we did not apply any pruning, preprocessing, or caching techniques.

Our test sets were generated according to several problem instance distributions known from the literature [17, 7]. These distributions are: UNI-p-g-b, Sandholm's uniform distribution where each instance comprises g goods, b bids, and each bid consists of p goods; DEC-p-g-b, Sandholm's decay distribution; EXP-p-g-b, the exponential distribution introduced in [7]; and BIN-p-g-b, the binomial distribution from [7]. Each of our test sets contains either 10 or 100 problem instances drawn from the same distribution, using identical parameter values.

The results for our first series of experiments, large problem instances with a fixed cutoff time, are reported in Table 1. For Casanova, we estimated the mean revenue from the distributions measured for each instance, while CASS gives a unique revenue for each instance. We report the median, the 90% percentile, and the 90%/10% percentile ratio as a measure of variation between instances. The variation in revenue over different runs of Casanova on the same instance was generally found to be very small (variation coefficient ≤ 0.01). Our results indicate clearly that Casanova gives superior solution quality for most of the test sets (the differences are up to 5.7% in median solution quality and up to 4.8% in the 90% percentile). The only exception is test set EXP-5-100-1000, where CASS gives a median solution quality which is 1.7% better than the mean revenue achieved by Casanova. However, the data suggests as the number of goods increase, Casanova's improvement relative to CASS also increases (see, e.g., the results for UNI-3-100-1000 and UNI-3-200-2000); in particular, for the larger EXP-5-500-5000 instances, Casanova outperforms CASS. Finally, it should be noted that the variation of solution quality over the individual test sets is generally smaller for Casanova than for CASS; this indicates that Casanova finds good solutions more consistently.

While Table 1 summarizes our results, the underlying analyses we performed are much more detailed. Figure 1 shows a typical scatter plot of the correlation between the (mean) revenue obtained by running CASS vs. Casanova on each instance across a test set (here we illustrate the results for UNI-3-200-10000). The data shows clearly that for almost all instances Casanova finds better solutions than CASS. Furthermore, the variation in solution quality is significantly smaller for Casanova than for CASS. Finally, there is no apparent correlation between the solution quality achieved by the two algorithms, suggesting that there are no differences in the intrinsic hardness of the instances of the test set. We also analyzed the dependence of these results on the cutoff time chosen. Figure 2 shows the revenue for Casanova vs. CASS for a typical instance of test set UNI-3-200-2000. Clearly, Casanova gives consistently better solution quality in this (typical) case, even when basing the comparison on the worst performance observed for Casanova over 10 runs. It should also be noted that for Casanova, the solution quality increases steadily over time, while for CASS, short series of rapid improvements are typically followed by long quiescent phases.

---

[7] All experiments were performed on a Pentium II 400Mhz with 512KB CPU cache and 128MB RAM, running Linux 2.2.15.

test set	# inst	cutoff	CASS			Casanova			np	wp	θ_r
			median	Q_{90}	Q_{10}/Q_{90}	median	Q_{90}	Q_{10}/Q_{90}			
UNI-3-100-1000	100	10s	130396	133838	1.05	**134216**	136203	1.03	0.5	0.15	–
UNI-3-200-2000	100	10s	252084	257643	1.04	**264814**	267573	1.02	0.5	0.15	–
UNI-3-100-5000	100	30s	142947	144015	1.02	**143886**	144666	1.01	0.5	0.02	–
UNI-3-200-10000	100	60s	281413	284033	1.02	**286164**	287632	1.01	0.5	0.02	–
BIN-0.01-500-5000	10	60s	583279	594931	1.04	**616708**	623624	1.04	0.1	0.01	1000
DEC-0.75-500-5000	10	60s	668458	678830	1.04	**675198**	279919	1.01	0.5	0.02	1000
EXP-5-100-1000	10	30s	**135027**	135658	1.03	132705	134412	1.03	0.05	0.02	1000
EXP-5-500-5000	10	60s	647629	650302	1.02	**655329**	659238	1.02	0.05	0.02	1000

Table 1: Regular bids: Comparison of solution quality (revenue) achieved by CASS and Casanova when using the same fixed cutoff time. We report statistics of the distribution across the test set, the Q_x are the $x\%$ percentiles. For Casanova, our analysis is based on the mean solution quality measured over 10 runs for each instance.

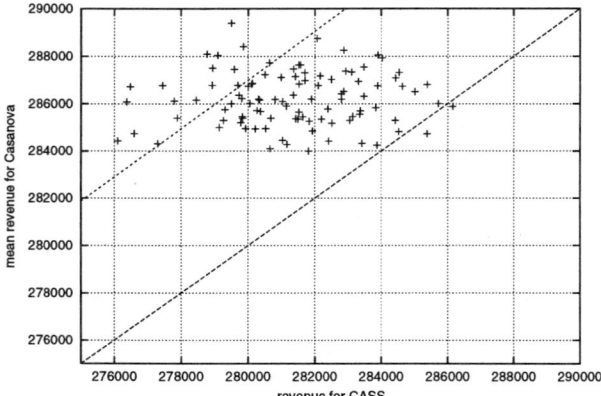

Figure 1: Regular bids, test set UNI-3-200-10000: Correlation of (mean) revenue obtained by CASS and Casanova within a fixed cutoff time of 60 CPU sec. The two lines show ratios of 1 and 1.025 when comparing the revenue obtained by Casanova to that of CASS.

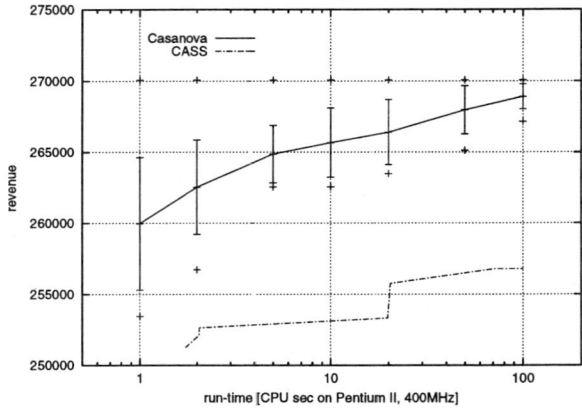

Figure 2: Regular bids, typical instance from test set UNI-3-200-2000: revenue over run time for CASS vs. Casanova. For Casanova, the solid line represents mean revenue and the error bars indicate ±1 stddev. The data points above and below the error bars show the min and max revenue found over 10 runs. CASS does not report any revenue before reaching 1.73 CPU seconds.

Finally, it can be seen that for Casanova, the variability of the solution quality over multiple runs decreases over time. Together with the fact that the maximal revenue remains constant, this suggests that the best solution found by Casanova (revenue=270075) might be the optimal solution to the problem. Overall, these observations illustrate the superior anytime behavior of the Casanova algorithm.

In our second series of experiments, we compared the time required by Casanova vs. CASS to find optimal solutions. The results are reported in Table 2. For each instance, we measured the time required by CASS to find an optimal solution, and estimated the time to obtain the same revenue with Casanova from an RTD constructed from 100 runs. The results indicate clearly that for certain types of problems (particularly UNI*, but also DEC*), Casanova is dramatically faster than CASS in finding optimal solutions, while for others (EXP* and BIN*) CASS is clearly superior for the small instances tested here. However, it is remarkable that Casanova, although incomplete, finds optimal solutions for all instances tested.

It should be noted that for systematic search algorithms, like CASS and Sandholm's bidtree procedure, the UNI* instances are extremely hard [17]. For these, Casanova finds optimal solutions between one and three orders of magnitude faster than CASS.[8] Furthermore, our results clearly indicate that Casanova's search time increases with problem size at a significantly lower rate than CASS's.

As we did with the larger instances when using fixed cutoff times, we studied the correlation between the performance of CASS and Casanova. Figure 3 shows a typical result; each point corresponds to the data obtained for one instance from the UNI-3-100-100 test set. Clearly, the mean run time required by Casanova to find an optimal solution is generally much lower than for CASS, typically by about a factor of

---

[8] Comparing the results reported here for CASS with those for bidtree from [17] strongly suggests that for the instance distributions tested here, CASS is up to one order of magnitude faster in finding optimal solutions.

test set	# inst	CASS			Casanova			np	wp	θ_r
		median	Q_{90}	Q_{10}/Q_{90}	median	Q_{90}	Q_{10}/Q_{90}			
UNI-3-50-50	100	0.058	0.125	9.09	**0.0092**	0.029	7.61	0.5	0.15	–
UNI-3-75-75	100	2.211	6.222	10.91	**0.030**	0.197	24.99	0.5	0.15	–
UNI-3-100-100	100	96.41	446.50	27.17	**0.136**	0.964	36.24	0.5	0.15	–
UNI-3-50-100	100	0.487	1.40	15.20	**0.091**	0.543	21.29	0.5	0.15	–
UNI-3-75-150	100	125.76	409.95	17.24	**1.078**	3.974	25.59	0.5	0.15	–
UNI-3-20-2000	100	33.99	140.55	462.86	**1.725**	5.160	6.911	0.5	0.15	–
UNI-10-200-200	100	147.99	308.92	15.72	**1.677**	6.051	10.54	0.5	0.15	–
BIN-0.2-20-500	100	**0.051**	0.066	1.48	7.980	31.447	11.08	0.2	0.02	–
DEC-0.75-200-200	10	252.82	1061.04	44.62	**6.236**	632.35	800.747	0.5	0.02	–
EXP-5-20-500	100	**0.0282**	0.0315	1.21	0.852	8.689	749.01	0.5	0.05	–

Table 2: Regular bids: Comparison of time (in CPU seconds) required by CASS and Casanova for finding optimal solutions. We report statistics of the distribution across the test set, the Q_x are the $x\%$ percentiles. For Casanova, the performance measure is the mean time for finding an optimal solution.

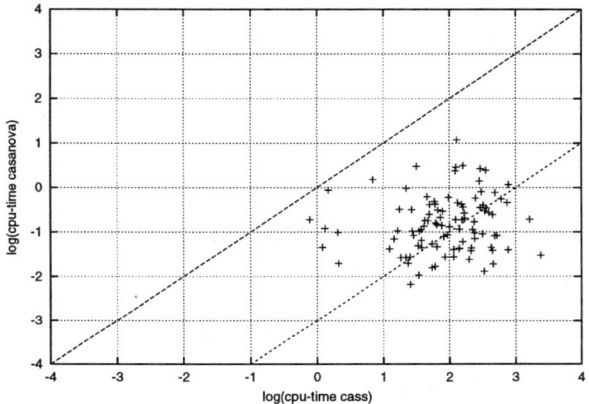

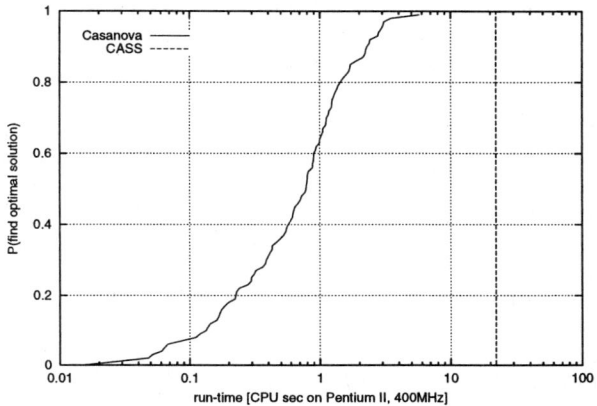

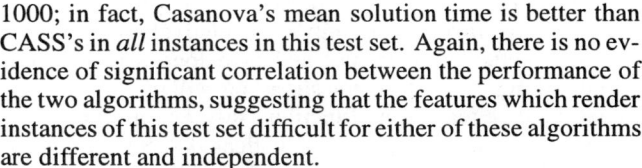

Figure 3: Regular bids, test set UNI-3-100-100: Correlation of CPU time (in CPU seconds) required by CASS and Casanova for finding optimal solutions. The two lines show factors of 1 and 1000 between the solution time for CASS and Casanova.

Figure 4: Regular bids, typical instance from test set UNI-3-100-100: Empirical RTDs for finding the optimal solution using Casanova vs. CASS, based on 100 runs for Casanova, one deterministic run for CASS.

1000; in fact, Casanova's mean solution time is better than CASS's in *all* instances in this test set. Again, there is no evidence of significant correlation between the performance of the two algorithms, suggesting that the features which render instances of this test set difficult for either of these algorithms are different and independent.

For Casanova, we are interested not only in the distribution of mean search cost within each test set, but also in the variation between multiple runs on a single instance. We therefore measured RTDs for all individual instances of each test set and characterized these by fitting functional models to the empirical data, using the methodology developed by Hoos and Stützle [9]. Figure 4 shows a rather typical example of the RTDs for Casanova and CASS (the latter of which is a step function due to the deterministic nature of the algorithm) for an instance from test set UNI-3-100-100. Clearly, Casanova is not only superior to CASS when comparing the mean solution time, but also when comparing higher percentiles of the RTDs. Surprisingly, we found that for all instances we checked (except for some extremely easy ones, where the data is too discrete due to the limited precision of CPU timing) the RTDs for Casanova could be successfully approximated with exponential distributions.[9] Based on this characterization we can conclude that with a probability of about 0.63 Casanova's actual search cost will be smaller than the mean solution time reported here.

3.3 Schematic Bids: Empirical Evaluation

To compare CASS and Casanova on schematic bids, we generated schematic bids randomly and then converted the schematic bids into a set of explicit bids on which the algorithms were run. Thus, a CNF bid b with c clauses and d

---
[9] These approximations were obtained by fitting the empirical RTD-data with the cdf of an exponential distribution and validated using the χ^2-test, a standard statistical test.

disjuncts per clause, for example, would generate d^c explicit bids, corresponding to the selection of one good from each clause. Each explicit bid generated from a CNF bid b also includes a dummy good g_b that prevents more than one explicit bid from being satisfied. Thus each explicit bid will have $c+1$ goods. Note that the number of explicit bids is exponential in the size of the CNF bid (and has a factorial component for *k-of* bids). This restricts the number of schematic bids we can handle. For CNF bids, we use two problem distributions. The CUNI-c-d-b-g problem distribution involves g goods and b bids, each bid consisting of c clauses with d disjuncts each. The CPOIS-m-n-b-g distribution generates bids where the number of clauses, and number of disjuncts in each clause, are generated using a Poisson distribution (with means m and n, respectively).[10] Thus the bids are variable length; but unlike the EXP-distribution, we do not have a mode at 1 (we expect the Poisson to be a more realistic model of bidding behavior). For *k-of* bids, we conducted preliminary experiments on a version of the CUNI∗ bids, where each CNF clause was turned into a *k-of* clause. These problem distributions are denoted KUNI-c-d-k-b-g.

We performed two experimental series analogous to those for explicit bids described above. The results are reported in Tables 3 and 4. For the CUNI∗ test sets, Casanova achieved between 15% and 35% more revenue than CASS for an identical cutoff time, with a clear trend for this difference in performance to increase with problem size. Casanova's performance for the CPOIS∗ test sets is equally impressive. For the second series of experiments, the problem size was restricted by the time required by CASS to find optimal solutions and prove optimality.[11] Our results show that the CUNI∗ instances—which are solved by Casanova in less than one CPU second—are extremely hard for CASS, which requires a median time of more than 10 CPU minutes. For the CPOIS∗ as well as for the KUNI∗ instances we observe a similar advantage of Casanova over CASS. Generally, the variation of search cost across the test sets is significantly lower for Casanova than for CASS, indicating a more robust performance.

3.4 Interpretation

Casanova outperforms CASS on large problem instances with fixed cutoff times (over various distributions); and on smaller instances, though incomplete, Casanova generally finds optimal solutions. On uniform problems, Casanova finds optimal solutions much faster than CASS. For other problem types, such as the one based on exponential bid-length distributions introduced in [7], the improvement shown by Casanova is less significant, and for smaller problem instances, CASS clearly has an advantage. These performance differences seem to be explained by the distribution of bid lengths and prices. While the UNI∗ instances have no variation in bid length and relatively low variation of prices, the EXP∗ instances are characterised by an extreme variation in both bid length and prices. We found that the variation coefficient of bid prices from all distributions is correlated with the performance difference: increased efficiency of Casanova is observed for lower values of the variation coefficient. This observation is confirmed by the results we obtained for the CNF instances, which are characterised by a low variation in bid prices and clusters of bids with identical price—here Casanova outperforms CASS significantly. This fact is likely to be of great practical import: large allocation problems will often be characterized by large numbers of bids with identical prices (corresponding to large-scale substitution effects) and many prices with reasonably low variability.

The experimental results presented here also indicate that Casanova's performance improves relative to CASS's with growing problem size. This suggests that the preprocessing and pruning techniques which are crucial for the efficiency of the systematic search algorithms are more adversely affected by growing problem size than the stochastic local search heuristics used by Casanova. Overall, our results suggest that for solving large problem instances with several hundred goods and thousands of bids, SLS algorithms like Casanova offers considerable advantages over current systematic search procedures. Finally, SLS algorithms like Casanova offer another important advantage over deterministic systematic search methods in that they can be parallelized easily with significant speedup (given the approximately exponentially-distributed running time).

4 Concluding Remarks

We have developed the CASLS framework for applying stochastic local search to combinatorial auction winner determination and have demonstrated the effectiveness of Casanova, a specific instantiation of this model. While the initial results presented here are very encouraging, we believe that CASLS offers hope for much better performance—through both the solution of larger problem instances and the provision of better anytime behavior—than demonstrated here. We have investigated only one, relatively straightforward SLS method in this paper, and have done very little parameter tuning. Our future investigations will include the examination of better scoring functions, different problem distributions and the use of more sophisticated SLS techniques. In particular, Iterated Local Search algorithms [12] appears to hold significant promise.

We also intend to explore techniques for solving problems involving schematic bids without explicit conversion to explicit form. To do this we will exploit the strong analogy between CAs with schematic bids and propositional satisfiability problems. This holds promise for significantly extending the scope and scale of problems that can be effectively dealt with. We are also currently investigating new classes of bidding languages which offer natural ways of expressing common utility functions, at the same time offering structure that can be exploited computationally.

Finally, we hope to extend our approach to deal with more

---

[10] Specifically, the number of clauses $c \sim 1 + Pois(m)$ to ensure a positive c; similarly for the number of goods per clause.

[11] Again, we emphasize that we compare to the time required by CASS to *find* the optimal solution, not to run to completion and prove optimality.

test set	# inst	cutoff	CASS			Casanova			np	wp	θ_r
			median	Q_{90}	Q_{10}/Q_{90}	median	Q_{90}	Q_{10}/Q_{90}			
CUNI-3-50-50	100	10s	55015	58479	1.15	**63360**	65745	1.09	0.5	0.15	–
CUNI-3-100-100	100	60s	104868	108687	1.10	**127011**	130440	1.06	0.5	0.15	–
CUNI-3-50-250	100	60s	52245	56943	1.20	**70158**	70551	1.02	0.5	0.15	–
CPOIS-2-50-50	100	10s	53204	56397	1.15	**60398**	63115	1.10	0.5	0.15	–
CPOIS-2-100-100	100	60s	99238	105275	1.13	**117889**	122673	1.0691	0.5	0.15	–
CPOIS-2-50-250	100	60s	53066	56094	1.13	**69608**	70755	1.03	0.5	0.15	–
CPOIS-2-100-500	100	60s	101568	105941	1.10	**135973**	138266	1.03	0.5	0.15	–
KUNI-2-4-2-100-100	10	60s	48812	50608	1.20	**59938**	63194	1.09	0.5	0.15	–

Table 3: CNF and *k-of* bids: Comparison of solution quality (revenue) achieved by CASS and Casanova when using the same fixed cutoff time.

test set	# inst	CASS			Casanova			np	wp	θ_r
		median	Q_{90}	Q_{10}/Q_{90}	median	Q_{90}	Q_{10}/Q_{90}			
CUNI-3-20-20	100	791.11	2904.89	180.58	**0.050**	0.138	5.24	0.5	0.15	–
CPOIS-2-20-20	100	1.855	9.355	41.15	**0.240**	1.048	17.74	0.5	0.15	–
KUNI-2-4-2-20-20	100	24.364	48.690	72.40	**0.474**	4.678	24.40	0.5	0.15	–

Table 4: CNF and *k-of* bids: Comparison of time (in CPU seconds) required by CASS and Casanova for finding optimal solutions.

sophisticated domains, for example, those involving a temporal component such as scheduling tasks [18], and multi-item combinatorial auctions of the type explored in [11].

Acknowledgements

Thanks are due to Kevin Leyton-Brown, Tuomas Sandholm, Yoav Shoham, and Moshe Tennenholtz for their comments and general discussion of these issues. We are especially indebted to Kevin for his CASS software and for his very generous and helpful support in adapting the code to our needs. This research was supported by IRIS Phase-III Grant "Preference Elicitation and Interactive Optimization."

References

[1] E. Arkin and R. Hassin. On local search for weighted k-set packing. *ESA-97*, pp.13–22, Graz, 1997.

[2] S. Bikhchandani and J. Mamer. Competitive equilibria in and exchange economy with indivisibilities. *J. Econ. Th.*, 74:385–413, 1997.

[3] C. Boutilier, M. Goldszmidt, and B. Sabata. Sequential auctions for allocation of resources with complementarities. *IJCAI-99*, pp.527–534, Stockholm, 1999.

[4] B. Chandra and M. Halldórsson. Greedy local improvement and weighted set packing approximation. *SODA-99*, pp.169–176, Baltimore, 1999.

[5] S. Clearwater, ed. *Market-based Control: A Paradigm for Distributed Resource Allocation*. World Scientific, 1995.

[6] R. Engelbrecht-Wiggans and R. Weber. A sequential auction involving assymetrically informed bidders. *Int. J. Game Th.*, 12:123–127, 1983.

[7] Y. Fujisima, K. Leyton-Brown, and Y. Shoham. Taming the computational complexity of combinatorial auctions. *IJCAI-99*, pp.548–553, Stockholm, 1999.

[8] D. Hausch. Multi-object auctions: Sequential vs. simultaneous sales. *Mgt. Sci.*, 32(12):1599–1610, 1986.

[9] H. Hoos and T. Stützle. Evaluating Las Vegas Algorithms–Pitfalls and Remedies. *UAI-98*, pp.238–245, Madison, 1998.

[10] H. Hoos. On the Run-time Behaviour of Stochastic Local Search Algorithms for SAT. *AAAI-99*, pp.661–666, Orlando, FL, 1999.

[11] K. Leyton-Brown and Y. Shoham and M. Tennenholtz. An algorithm for multi-unit combinatorial auctions. to appear, *AAAI-2000*, Austin, TX, 2000.

[12] O. Martin, S. Otto, E. Felten. Large-step Markov chains for the traveling salesman problem. *Compl. Sys.*, 5:299–326, 1991.

[13] D. McAllester, H. Kautz, B. Selman. Evidence for invariants in local search. *AAAI-97*, 321–326, Providence, RI, 1997.

[14] S. Rassenti, V. Smith, and R. Bulfin. A combinatorial auction mechanism for airport time slot allocation. *Bell J. Econ.*, 13:402–417, 1982.

[15] M. Rothkopf. Bidding in simultaneous auctions with a constraint on exposure. *Op. Res.*, 25:620–629, 1977.

[16] M. Rothkopf, A. Pekeč, and R. Harstad. Computationally manageable combinatorial auctions. *Mgt. Sci.*, 44(8):1131–1147, 1998.

[17] T. Sandholm. An algorithm for optimal winner determination in combinatorial auctions. *IJCAI-99*, pp.542–547, Stockholm, 1999. Extended, Washington Univ. Report WUCS-99-01.

[18] M. Wellman, W. Walsh, P. Wurman, and J. MacKie-Mason. Auction protocols for decentralized scheduling. *Games and Econ. Behavior*, 1999. To appear.

A Mechanism for Group Decision Making in Collaborative Activity

Luke Hunsberger
Division of Engineering and Applied Sciences
Harvard University
Cambridge, MA 02138 — USA
luke@eecs.harvard.edu

Massimo Zancanaro
Cognitive and Communication Division
ITC-irst
38050 Pante' di Povo — Italy
zancana@irst.itc.it

Abstract

The SharedPlans formalization of collaboration (Grosz and Kraus 1999) stipulates that collaborating agents must commit to certain decision-making processes, but it does not specify those processes. This paper presents a mechanism for group decision making that may be applied to the decisions that agents involved in a SharedPlan need to make: adopting the initial commitment, selecting a recipe, assigning agents to subtasks, and identifying various action parameters. The paper thus more fully specifies the dynamic expansion of a partial SharedPlan to a more complete plan. The decision-making mechanism is represented by a fixed, fully-specified SharedPlan. A set of speech acts and conditions under which those speech acts invoke the decision-making SharedPlans are also defined. The definition of the *force* of declarative speech acts is based on Searle's notion of constitutive rules (Searle 1998).

Introduction

SharedPlans (Grosz and Kraus 1999) is a theory of collaborative planning that specifies the mental-state requirements of agents collaborating on a group activity. A group of agents holding a certain set of individual intentions, beliefs, and mutual beliefs are said to have a SharedPlan.

Typically, a group's plan is partial: they may not yet have selected a recipe, decided which agents should do which subtasks, or selected values for various parameters. When plans are partial, the SharedPlans formalization specifies that the group must be committed to certain group decision-making processes, but it does not define those processes. In particular, it does not specify how a group of agents having a partial SharedPlan might make the group decisions needed to complete the plan.

In this paper, we present a generic voting-based group-decision-making mechanism that we represent as a fixed, fully-specified SharedPlan that agents may invoke directly using declarative speech acts. We show how this mechanism can be applied to the decisions that must be made by a group of agents collaborating on some group activity.

The voting process in the decision-making mechanism uses declarative speech acts. We define the *force* (Searle 1998) of declarative speech acts composing the group decision-making process in such a way that the group decisions arising from this process transform agent beliefs and intentions only in ways such that agents continue to satisfy the requirements of a SharedPlan as their plan evolves.

The definition of the force of the declarative speech act is based on Searle's theory of the construction of social reality (Searle 1998). In this theory, institutional facts (e.g., that Bill Clinton is the President of the United States) are distinguished from brute facts (e.g., that the Space Shuttle weighs over 500 pounds). Institutional facts exist only within systems of *constitutive rules* (i.e., rules that not only regulate an activity, but also create its very possibility). For example, the rules of chess are constitutive: without them there can be no game. Furthermore, the rules have a specific form: X counts as Y in the context C. In chess, moving my knight to the space occupied by your bishop in the context of it being my turn counts as my knight capturing your bishop. In specifying voting speech acts, we treat the type of decision as part of the context. This permits a single voting-based mechanism to be used for every type of decision faced by agents collaborating on a SharedPlan.

Preliminaries

In this section, we present axiomatizations for conditional actions and for declarative and assertive speech acts. Belief, mutual belief, intention to (do an action), and intention that (a proposition hold) are modeled using the modal operators, Bel, MB, $Int.To$ and $Int.Th$ (Grosz and Kraus 1999).

Conditional Actions

An example of a conditional action is: "If the phone rings, answer it." We model conditional actions of the form: if ϕ then A, where ϕ is a triggering condition and A is a single-agent action.[1] In this paper, the actions being triggered are mental actions (e.g., adopting an intention). We define the conditional actions C_{To} and C_{Th} by:

$$C_{To}(\phi, X): \quad \text{if } \phi \text{ then } Adopt.Int.To(X)$$
$$C_{Th}(\phi, \psi): \quad \text{if } \phi \text{ then } Adopt.Int.Th(\psi)$$

where X is a single-agent action and ψ is a proposition. $C_{To}(\phi, X)$ is interpreted as: "If ϕ becomes true, adopt an

---
[1]Conditional actions can also be constructed as expressions from standard operators in dynamic logic (Ortiz 1999b).

intention to do X"; $C_{Th}(\phi,\psi)$ is interpreted as: "If ϕ becomes true, adopt an intention that ψ hold."[2]

We assume that if a group GR mutually believe both that (1) an agent G intends—in the event of ϕ—to adopt some other intention, and (2) that G believes ϕ, then GR mutually believe that G actually adopts the new intention, as represented by the following axiom schemata:

(R_1) $MB(GR, Int.To(G, C_{To}(\phi, X))) \wedge Bel(G, \phi)$
$\quad\Rightarrow MB(GR, Int.To(G, X))$

(R_2) $MB(GR, Int.To(G, C_{Th}(\phi, \psi))) \wedge Bel(G, \phi)$
$\quad\Rightarrow MB(GR, Int.Th(G, \psi))$

Performatives

The decision-making mechanism uses two performatives: *Declare* and *Assert*.[3] We model performatives as primitive actions of the form $Perf(G, \phi, GR^-)$, where $Perf$ is either *Declare* or *Assert*, G is an agent, GR^- is a group of agents that does not include G, and ϕ is a proposition. The following axiom schema represents our simplifying assumption that performatives have been executed (i.e., "done") if and only if the group $GR = GR^- \cup \{G\}$ mutually believe they have been executed:

(P) $Done(G, Perf(G, \phi, GR^-))$
$\quad\Leftrightarrow MB(GR, Done(G, Perf(G, \phi, GR^-)))$

Thus, for example, G makes a declaration ϕ to GR^- if and only if GR mutually believe G has made such a declaration. For convenience, we use the following abbreviations:

$Declared(G, \phi, GR^-) = Done(G, Declare(G, \phi, GR^-))$
$Asserted(G, \phi, GR^-) = Done(G, Assert(G, \phi, GR^-))$

Declarations. In an arbitrary context, someone's declaring "I hereby dub thee *Sir Lancelot*" may have no implications; however, if Queen Elizabeth II declares it in the context of a royal ceremony, it will result in someone's being knighted. Agents use the *Declare* performative to establish certain propositions as mutually-believed institutional facts. Following Searle (1998), we use constitutive rules of the form, X counts as Y in the context C, to define the force of declarative speech acts. We represent these rules as axioms of the form, $X \wedge C \Rightarrow Y$. For example, we might define the force of the dubbing declaration as follows:

$Declared(G_1, Knighted(G_2, \texttt{SirLancelot}), \{G_2\})$
$\wedge\, Royalty(G_1)$
$\Rightarrow MB(\{G_1, G_2\}, Knighted(G_2, \texttt{SirLancelot}))$

Assertions. Agents use *Assert* to report their beliefs and intentions to other agents. We assume that agents are truthful in their assertions.[4] We also assume that if an agent G asserts to some other agents GR^- that it holds a particular belief or intention, then the result of that assertion is that they all mutually believe G holds that belief or intention, as represented by the following:

(S_{Bel}) $Asserted(G, Bel(G, \psi), GR^-)$
$\quad\Rightarrow MB(GR, Bel(G, \psi))$

(S_{To}) $Asserted(G, Int.To(G, X), GR^-)$
$\quad\Rightarrow MB(GR, Int.To(G, X))$

(S_{Th}) $Asserted(G, Int.Th(G, \psi), GR^-)$
$\quad\Rightarrow MB(GR, Int.Th(G, \psi))$

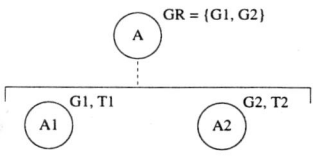

Figure 1: A method $\mathcal{M}_A$ for GR doing A

It follows from (S_{Bel}) and the definition of mutual belief that if *each* member of GR asserts to the other agents in GR that it believes some ψ, then the entire group mutually believe ψ:

Lemma 1. Given axiom schemata (S_{Bel}), the following is valid for all GR and ψ:

$[(\forall G \in GR) Asserted(G, Bel(G, \psi), GR^-)]$
$\quad\Rightarrow MB(GR, \psi)$

where GR^- (i.e., the "rest of the group") implicitly depends on G.

Throughout the rest of this paper, we assume a theory that includes all instances of all axiom schemata introduced to this point.

Methods and Full SharedPlans

We define a *method* $\mathcal{M}$ for a group of agents GR doing a multi-agent action A as a triple: $\langle \mathcal{R}, \mathcal{S}, \mathcal{B} \rangle$, where $\mathcal{R}$ is a fixed recipe for doing A, $\mathcal{S}$ is a complete set of agent assignments for the subacts in $\mathcal{R}$, and $\mathcal{B}$ is a complete set of bindings for all the parameters of A and $\mathcal{R}$. For example, Figure 1 gives a schematic representation of a method $\mathcal{M}_A$ that specifies that the two-agent group, $GR = \{G_1, G_2\}$, can do the multi-agent action A using the recipe $\{A_1, A_2\}$, where G_1 does the primitive subact A_1 at time T_1, and G_2 does A_2 at T_2.

To *adopt* (or commit to) a fully-specified SharedPlan (FSP) means to *establish* the individual intentions and mutual beliefs specified in the definition of the FSP meta-predicate (Grosz and Kraus 1999; Hunsberger 1999). The FSP requirements depend on the method being used. We write $\mathcal{F}_\mathcal{M}$ for the set of FSP requirements corresponding to the method $\mathcal{M}$.

---

[2] The *Adopt.Int.To* and *Adopt.Int.Th* actions correspond to a subset of the functions of Ortiz' *Update* action (Ortiz 1999b).

[3] Our specification of speech acts borrows from Cohen and Levesque (1990). Cohen and Levesque (1997) derive the semantics for request and commissive speech acts from the definition of an "attempt." We take a more direct approach. Ortiz (1999b) gives an alternative definition of an attempt.

[4] Perrault(1990) addresses the problem of agents making assertions they do not believe.

For the method $\mathcal{M}_A$ depicted in Figure 1, the FSP requirements (i.e., $\mathcal{F}_{\mathcal{M}_A}$) reduce to the following:[5]

F_1: $MB(GR, Is.Recipe(\{A_1, A_2\}, A))$
F_2: $MB(GR, CBA(G_1, A_1))$
F_3: $MB(GR, CBA(G_2, A_2))$
F_4: $MB(GR, Int.Th(G_1, Done(GR, A)))$
F_5: $MB(GR, Int.Th(G_2, Done(GR, A)))$
F_6: $Int.To(G_1, A_1) \wedge MB(GR, Int.To(G_1, A_1))$
F_7: $MB(GR, Int.Th(G_2, CBA(G_1, A_1)))$
F_8: $Int.To(G_2, A_2) \wedge MB(GR, Int.To(G_2, A_2))$
F_9: $MB(GR, Int.Th(G_1, CBA(G_2, A_2)))$

In general, the FSP requirements corresponding to some method $\mathcal{M}$ may be partitioned into two subsets which we denote $\mathcal{F}_\mathcal{M}^0$ and $\mathcal{F}_\mathcal{M}^I$. The requirements in $\mathcal{F}_\mathcal{M}^0$ involve mutual beliefs pertaining only to the validity of the method (i.e., that the recipe is valid and that the agents are able to do their assigned subacts). Agents holding such mutual beliefs need not be committed to doing anything. For the example above, $\mathcal{F}_{\mathcal{M}_A}^0 = \{F_1, F_2, F_3\}$. In contrast, the requirements in $\mathcal{F}_\mathcal{M}^I$ involve agent commitments and mutual beliefs about those commitments. For the example above, $\mathcal{F}_{\mathcal{M}_A}^I = \{F_4, F_5, F_6, F_7, F_8, F_9\}$.

Invoking a Method

When collaborating on some group activity, agents typically begin with a partial plan that, over time, they elaborate into a complete plan. Grosz and Kraus (1996, 1999) argue that certain planning (i.e., group decision making) processes should be modeled as fixed, fully-specified SharedPlans (FSPs). In a subsequent section, we present a generic group-decision-making method. In this section, we describe how a group of agents can adopt an FSP corresponding to such a method. In particular, we describe how—given an arbitrary proposition ϕ and a decision-making method $\mathcal{M}$—a group's adoption of an FSP corresponding to the method $\mathcal{M}$ may be triggered by the group's mutual belief that ϕ holds. We call ϕ the triggering condition and we say that the group's mutual belief of ϕ *invokes* the method (or invokes the FSP corresponding to the method). Sufficient requirements are:

(1) the group GR mutually believe that the method is valid (i.e., the mutual beliefs in $\mathcal{F}_\mathcal{M}^0$ hold); and

(2) the group GR mutually believe that they hold a certain set of background commitments (dependent on both $\mathcal{M}$ and ϕ, as described below) that may be interpreted as their willingness to adopt the FSP when triggered.

We first describe the triggered invocation of an FSP corresponding to the method $\mathcal{M}_A$ depicted in Figure 1. Let ϕ be an arbitrary triggering condition. Let $\mathcal{C}_{\mathcal{M}_A}(\phi)$ be a set containing the following conditional commitments (dependent on both $\mathcal{M}_A$ and ϕ):

---
[5] $Is.Recipe$ models that the given set of subacts constitutes a recipe for the given action; CBA ("can bring about") models an agent's ability to do an action (Grosz and Kraus 1999).

C_1: $Int.To(G_1, C_{Th}(\phi, Done(GR, A)))$
C_2: $Int.To(G_1, C_{To}(\phi, A_1))$
C_3: $Int.To(G_1, C_{Th}(\phi, CBA(G_2, A_2)))$
C_4: $Int.To(G_2, C_{Th}(\phi, Done(GR, A)))$
C_5: $Int.To(G_2, C_{To}(\phi, A_2))$
C_6: $Int.To(G_2, C_{Th}(\phi, CBA(G_1, A_1)))$

For example, C_3 represents G_1's commitment (conditioned on ϕ) to adopt an intention that G_2 be able to do A_2—which is precisely what must be mutually believed to satisfy the FSP requirement F_9.

The following theorem says that if the group GR mutually believe both (1) that they hold the conditional commitments in $\mathcal{C}_{\mathcal{M}_A}(\phi)$ and (2) that the triggering condition ϕ holds, then all of the FSP requirements in $\mathcal{F}_{\mathcal{M}_A}^I$ necessarily hold; hence, if they also mutually believe that the method is valid (i.e., the FSP requirements in $\mathcal{F}_{\mathcal{M}_A}^0$ hold), then the FSP requirements corresponding to the method $\mathcal{M}_A$ necessarily hold (i.e., the group has adopted the FSP corresponding to the method $\mathcal{M}_A$). In the theorem, the brackets around $\mathcal{C}_{\mathcal{M}_A}(\phi)$, $\mathcal{F}_{\mathcal{M}_A}$, $\mathcal{F}_{\mathcal{M}_A}^I$ and $\mathcal{F}_{\mathcal{M}_A}^0$ are used to represent the conjunction of all the clauses in the bracketed set.

Theorem 1 (Special Case: $\mathcal{M} = \mathcal{M}_A$). The following is valid for all GR and ϕ:

$MB(GR, \phi \wedge [\mathcal{C}_{\mathcal{M}_A}(\phi)]) \Rightarrow [\mathcal{F}^I]$; and hence:
$MB(GR, \phi \wedge [\mathcal{C}_{\mathcal{M}_A}(\phi)]) \wedge [\mathcal{F}^0] \Rightarrow [\mathcal{F}_{\mathcal{M}_A}]$.

[All proofs are omitted due to space limitations.]

Theorem 1 (General Version). Theorem 1 is easily generalized to cover the triggered invocation of an FSP based on an arbitrary method $\mathcal{M}$ whose recipe includes any number of primitive subacts and which involves a group of arbitrarily many agents. The voting-based group-decision-making mechanism described in the next section is based on such a method. The more subacts and agents involved in the method, the more numerous are the requirements in $\mathcal{F}_\mathcal{M}^0$ and $\mathcal{F}_\mathcal{M}^I$, and the more numerous are the conditional commitments in $\mathcal{C}_\mathcal{M}(\phi)$; the basic idea, however, is the same.

Invoking an FSP to Make a Group Decision

In this section, we show how an agent can invoke a decision-making FSP that a group of agents may use to make a group decision. We describe a single voting-based decision-making method $\mathcal{M}_V$; however any decision-making method representable by an FSP may be similarly treated. Thus, the presentation in this section has wide applicability to group decision making in multi-agent systems. Without loss of generality, we describe a scenario in which a particular agent (G_1) invokes the method.

A schematic for the voting method $\mathcal{M}_V$ is shown in Figure 2. The method involves a group GR of n agents: $G_1, \ldots, G_n$. The recipe has $n + 1$ subacts, each of which is a declarative speech act. D_1 is the declaration used by G_1 to invoke the method; $V_2, \ldots, V_n$ are declarations by the rest of the agents either to accept or reject the proposal contained in the invoking declaration; D_a is G_1's declaration

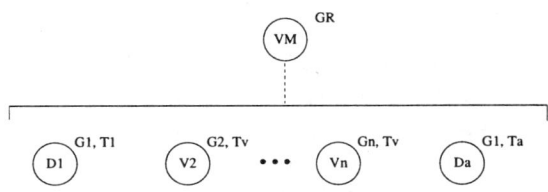

Figure 2: A schematic for the voting method $\mathcal{M}_V$

announcing the result of the voting. The axioms associated with the declarations in $\mathcal{M}_V$ (given below) ensure that if G_1 announces that the group has accepted the proposal, then the group's decision shall necessarily be established as a mutually believed fact.

Let $\mathcal{F}^0_{\mathcal{M}_V}$ and $\mathcal{F}^I_{\mathcal{M}_V}$ be the FSP requirements corresponding to the method $\mathcal{M}_V$. We assume that the group mutually believe that the voting method is valid (i.e., that the mutual beliefs in $\mathcal{F}^0_{\mathcal{M}_V}$ hold). Let $\mathcal{C}_{\mathcal{M}_V}(\phi_V)$ be the set of conditional commitments corresponding to the method $\mathcal{M}_V$ and the triggering condition ϕ_V, as described in the previous section. (The triggering condition ϕ_V is defined below.) We assume that the agents mutually believe that they hold the conditional commitments in $\mathcal{C}_{\mathcal{M}_V}(\phi_V)$. Thus, by Theorem 1 (general version), mutual belief in ϕ_V is sufficient to trigger the group's adoption of the FSP corresponding to $\mathcal{M}_V$.

Without loss of generality, we consider a "simple selection" decision problem in which the group must select a single item σ from a fixed set Σ.

Invoking the Voting Method. G_1's initial declaration is: $Declare(G_1, Invoked\_VM(G_1, \mathcal{M}_V, \pi), GR^-)$, where $\mathcal{M}_V$ includes the following parameters:

group: $GR = \{G_1, \ldots, G_n\}$ invocation time: T_1
voting time interval: T_v announcement time: T_a

and π includes the following additional parameters:

decision problem: $(\texttt{SelectItem}, \Sigma)$
proposal: $\delta = (\texttt{Select}, \sigma_3)$

The force of G_1's declaration is defined by the following axiom schema:

(S_1) $Declared(G_1, Invoked\_VM(G_1, \mathcal{M}_V, \pi), GR^-)$
  $\Rightarrow MB(GR, Invoked\_VM(G_1, \mathcal{M}_V, \pi))$

Let ϕ_V be the following triggering condition:

$$Invoked\_VM(G_1, \mathcal{M}_V, \pi)$$

By schema (S_1), G_1's initial declaration is sufficient to ensure that the group mutually believe ϕ_V. Thus, by Theorem 1 (general version) the group necessarily adopts the voting-mechanism FSP in response to G_1's invocation.

The Voting Phase. During the time interval T_v (a parameter in $\mathcal{M}_V$), the agents $G_2, \ldots, G_n$ must do the voting actions $V_2, \ldots, V_n$, respectively. Each vote is a declaration of accepting or rejecting the proposal δ (a parameter in π). Axiom schema (S_2) defines the force of a vote to accept δ. The force of a vote to reject δ can be defined analogously.

(S_2) $Declared(G, Accepted(G, \delta), \{G_1\})$
  $\wedge MB(\{G, G_1\}, Invoked\_VM(G_1, \mathcal{M}_V, \pi))$
  $\wedge G \in GR$
  $\wedge G \neq G_1$
  $\Rightarrow MB(\{G, G_1\}, Accepted(G, \delta))$

The Announcement. After the voting interval, G_1 announces the results of the voting to the rest of the group by making the declaration: $Declare(G_1, \chi, GR^-)$, where χ is either $GroupAccepted(GR, \delta)$ or $GroupRejected(GR, \delta)$. Due to space limitations, we only describe the announcement to accept.

We provide a set of three constitutive rules—(S_3), (S_4) and (S_5) below—sufficient to ensure that if G_1 announces the group decision to accept δ, then that announcement establishes the group's decision as a mutually-believed fact (formalized in Theorem 2 below). We use three constitutive rules rather than a single rule to explicitly show the assumptions sufficient to generate the desired result.

The rules have the following form:

(S_3) $X \wedge C_1 \Rightarrow Y_1$;

(S_4) $X \wedge (C_1 \wedge C_2) \Rightarrow Y_2$, where $Y_1 \Rightarrow C_2$; and

(S_5) $X \wedge (C_1 \wedge Y_2) \Rightarrow Y_3$.

In each rule, X stands for G_1's announcement. The result (Y_1) of the first rule enriches the context for the second rule; the result (Y_2) of the second rule enriches the context for the third rule.

In the first rule (S_3), G_1's announcement, in the context of the group mutually believing that G_1 invoked the voting mechanism, counts both as an assertion that each member agent voted to accept the proposal and as establishing the group's mutual belief that G_1 accepted the proposal.

(S_3) $Declared(G_1, GroupAccepted(GR, \delta), GR^-)$
  $\wedge MB(GR, Invoked\_VM(G_1, \mathcal{M}_V, \pi))$
  $\Rightarrow Asserted(G_1, Bel(G_1, Accepted(G_2, \delta)), GR^-)$
  $\vdots$
  $\wedge Asserted(G_1, Bel(G_1, Accepted(G_n, \delta)), GR^-)$
  $\wedge MB(GR, Accepted(G_1, \delta))$

From Lemma 1, these assertions entail that the group GR mutually believe that G_1 believes that everyone *else* voted to accept:

$$(\forall G \in GR^-) MB(GR, Bel(G_1, Accepted(G, \delta))).$$

In the second rule (S_4), the context is enriched by the mutual beliefs resulting from the first rule. In this context, G_1's announcement counts as the group mutually believing that everyone voted to accept δ:

(S_4) $Declared(G_1, GroupAccepted(GR, \delta), GR^-)$
  $\wedge MB(GR, Invoked\_VM(G_1, \mathcal{M}_V, \pi))$
  $\wedge (\forall G \in GR^-) MB(GR, Bel(G_1, Accepted(G, \delta)))$
  $\wedge MB(GR, Accepted(G_1, \delta))$
  $\Rightarrow (\forall G \in GR) MB(GR, Accepted(G, \delta))$

In the third rule (S_5), the context includes the result of the second rule. In this context, G_1's announcement counts as establishing the group's decision as a mutually believed fact.

(S_5) $Declared(G_1, GroupAccepted(GR, \delta), GR^-)$
$\land MB(GR, Invoked\_VM(G_1, \mathcal{M}_V, \pi))$
$\land (\forall G \in GR) MB(GR, Accepted(G, \delta))$
$\Rightarrow MB(GR, GroupAccepted(GR, \delta))$

Theorem 2. Given axiom schemata, $S_2, \ldots, S_5$, the following is valid:

$Declared(G_1, GroupAccepted(GR, \delta), GR^-)$
$\land MB(GR, Invoked\_VM(G_1, \mathcal{M}_V, \pi))$
$\Rightarrow MB(GR, GroupAccepted(GR, \delta))$

Applying the Mechanism to Collaborative Planning

Agents collaborating on some group activity often cannot adopt a fully specified plan for that activity in a single stroke. Instead, they must make numerous decisions (e.g., which recipe to use, which parameter values to use, or which agents or subgroups to assign to the various subtasks) as they elaborate their possibly-hierarchical partial plan into a more complete plan. In this section, we describe how the voting mechanism from the previous section may be applied to the decisions encountered by a group of agents collaborating on some group activity. The key idea is that the definition of the force of a vote to accept a proposal (given in schema (S_2) above) must be augmented according to the context determined by the type of decision being voted on. Thus, for example, a vote to use a particular recipe represents one set of conditional commitments, while a vote to assign a fellow agent to a particular subtask represents another set of commitments.

We illustrate the use of the voting mechanism as a general-purpose decision-making tool by showing how it may be used by a group both to adopt a minimal SharedPlan (i.e., a plan for which no recipe has been selected and no parameters have been bound) and to select a recipe for that plan (which introduces new decision problems).

To simplify the presentation, we assume a weaker model of the group's commitment to the plan-elaboration process than that used by Grosz and Kraus.[6] In particular, for each decision problem facing the group, we require only that the group mutually believe that each agent intends that the group find a way of resolving that problem.

Deciding to Adopt a Minimal SharedPlan (MSP). Suppose G_1 invokes the voting mechanism as described previously, but with $GR = \{G_1, G_2\}$ and π containing the following different parameters:

[6]In addition, we conjecture that this weaker model, which Grosz and Kraus (1999) use to model the group's commitment to finding values for the parameters of the group action, but not their commitment to selecting a recipe or assigning agents to subtasks, may be sufficient in many scenarios.

decision problem: `Adopt_MSP`(A)
proposal: $\delta_1 =$ `YES` (i.e., adopt the MSP)

Thus, G_1 proposes that the group adopt a minimal Shared-Plan (MSP) to do the multi-agent action A.

To adopt such a plan means to establish a subset of the intentions and mutual beliefs in the definition of the PSP (Partial SharedPlan) meta-predicate (Grosz and Kraus, 1999; Hunsberger, 1999). In this case, these requirements reduce to the following (for each G_i in GR):

(M_1) $MB(GR, Int.Th(G_i, Done(GR, A)))$

(M_2) $MB(GR, Int.Th(G_i, Recipe.Selected(GR, A)))$

Let $\xi_1 = GroupAccepted(GR, \delta_1)$. An agent voting to adopt an MSP counts as that agent asserting that it intends, in the event of ξ_1 (i.e., in the event that the group decides to accept the proposal), to adopt the intentions required of it in (M_1) and (M_2), as follows.

(S_6) $MB(GR, Accepted(G, \delta_1))$
$\land DecisionProblemType(\pi, \text{Adopt\_MSP}(A))$
$\Rightarrow Asserted(G, I_1 \land I_2, GR^-)$

where I_1 and I_2 are given by:

$I_1 = Int.To(G, C_{Th}(\xi_1, Done(GR, A)))$
$I_2 = Int.To(G, C_{Th}(\xi_1, Recipe.Selected(GR, A)))$

Theorem 3 states that if a group of agents using this decision-making mechanism decide to adopt a minimal SharedPlan, then they will in fact adopt it.

Theorem 3. Given schemata, $S_2, \ldots, S_6$, the following is valid:

$Declared(G_1, GroupAccepted(GR, \delta_1), GR^-)$
$\land MB(GR, Invoked\_VM(G_1, \mathcal{M}_V, \pi))$
$\land DecisionProblemType(\pi, \text{Adopt\_MSP}(A))$
$\Rightarrow MSP(GR, A)$

Deciding to Select a Recipe. Suppose G_1's intention that the group select a recipe leads[7] G_1 to invoke the voting mechanism with a proposal that the group use the recipe $\{A_1, A_2\}$ (which introduces the unbound parameters T_1 and T_2). To incorporate this decision into their existing plan requires that they establish the following additional mutual beliefs (for each G_i in GR):

(M_3) $MB(GR, Int.Th(G_i, Agent.Assigned.To(A_1)))$

(M_4) $MB(GR, Int.Th(G_i, Agent.Assigned.To(A_2)))$

(M_5) $MB(GR, Int.Th(G_i, Params.Bound(\{T_1, T_2\})))$

These mutual beliefs may be established by a schema nearly identical to S_6 above.

Other Types of Decisions. Making other types of decisions (e.g., to select an agent to do a subact or to bind a parameter) have slightly different requirements, but the general

[7]We use "leads" in the same sense as Grosz and Kraus (1999) in their axioms of intention-that.

procedure remains the same. For example, if the group decides that G_1 should do A_1, then they must establish clauses F_2, F_6 and F_7 (discussed previously), which may be ensured by augmenting the definition of the force of an accept vote to make it count as an assertion of belief in G_1's ability to do A_1 and an assertion of conditional commitment corresponding to C_2 (for G_1's vote) or C_6 (for G_2's vote).

Related Work

Many researchers are actively investigating frameworks for reasoning about collective activity in multi-agent systems. The role of communication is often recognized as crucial, but there are few formal studies of mechanisms for group decision making.

Werner (1990) distinguishes directive and informative speech acts. A "pragmatic interpretation" of high-level messages is used to transform the information and intentional states of agents. Werner also discusses the "institutional effects" of certain "representative declarative" speech acts, and gives examples of how directive and informative speech acts may be used in "social cooperation."

Cohen and Levesque (1997) derive the semantics for request and commissive speech acts from the definition of an "attempt" such that certain requests followed by certain commissive actions result in the formation of joint commitments. In contrast, we propose a general mechanism for group decision making and derive the adoption of a SharedPlan as a special case. Cohen and Levesque (1997) do not discuss declarative speech acts.

The set of background conditions that enable certain speech acts to directly invoke the voting mechanism in our work is comparable to the locker-room agreements presented by Stone and Veloso (1999). Both approaches can be viewed as mutually-believed commitment by the group members to "do the right thing at the right time." The main difference is that the locker-room agreement is used to execute a plan in the absence of reliable communication, whereas the voting mechanism in our work is used to dynamically establish decisions needed in elaborating a partially-specified plan.

Conclusions

The aim of the paper is to more fully specify the dynamic evolution of a partial SharedPlan to a more complete plan. The SharedPlans formalization of collaboration (Grosz and Kraus 1999) stipulates that collaborating agents must commit to certain decision-making processes (namely, adopting the initial commitment, selecting a recipe, assigning agents to subtasks, and identifying action parameters) but does not specify those processes. We have presented a mechanism for group decision making that may be applied to all of these types of decision.

The decision-making mechanism is modeled as a fixed, fully-specified SharedPlan (FSP) that can be directly invoked. We have provided conditions sufficient to ensure that the group will automatically adopt such an FSP as soon as they come to mutually believe a given triggering condition holds. We provided the *Declare* speech act to enable agents to establish mutual belief of a triggering condition. The definition of the force of the *Declare* speech act was specified using Searle's constitutive rule (i.e., "the performance of X in the context C counts as Y"). The *Assert* speech act was used to define the consequences of certain declarations.

We illustrated how the decision-making mechanism can be used to adopt a SharedPlan as well as to make the various decisions needed to elaborate a partially-specified plan, provided that the context C in the constitutive rules is properly managed. Furthermore, the techniques presented in this paper provide a solid foundation for formalizing the process of group decision making based on any mechanism representable by an FSP.

Acknowledgments

The work presented in this paper was supported by NSF grants IIS-9978343, IRI-9618848, and CDA-94-01024. The authors thank Barbara J. Grosz for her invaluable guidance in the preparation of this paper.

References

Cohen, P., and Levesque, H. 1990. Rational interaction as the basis for communication. In Cohen et al. (1990). chapter 12.

Cohen, P. R.; Levesque, H. J.; and Smith, I. 1997. On team formation. In Holmstrom-Hintikka, G., and Tuomela, R., eds., *Contemporary Action Theory*. Kluwer.

Cohen, P.; Morgan, J.; and Pollack, M., eds. 1990. *Intentions in Communication*. MIT Press.

Grosz, B. J., and Kraus, S. 1999. The evolution of SharedPlans. In Wooldridge, M., and Rao, A., eds., *Foundations of Rational Agency*, number 14 in Applied Logic Series. Kluwer.

Hunsberger, L. 1999. Making SharedPlans more concise and easier to reason about. In Muller et al. (1999), 81–98.

Muller, J.; Singh, M.; and Rao, A., eds. 1999. *Intelligent Agents V*, volume 1555 of *Lecture Notes in Artificial Intelligence*. Heidelberg: Springer.

Ortiz, C. L. 1999a. A commonsense language for reasoning about causation and rational action. *Artificial Intelligence* 111(1–2).

Ortiz, C. L. 1999b. Introspective and elaborative processes in rational agents. *Annals of Mathematics and Artificial Intelligence* 25(1–2).

Perrault, C. R. 1990. An application of default logic to speech act theory. In Cohen et al. (1990). chapter 9.

Searle, J. R. 1998. *Mind, Language and Society*. New York: Basic Books.

Stone, P., and Veloso, M. 1999. Task decomposition and dynamic role assignment for real-time strategic teamwork. In Muller et al. (1999).

Werner, E. 1990. Cooperating agents: A unified theory of communication and social structure. In *Distributed Artificial Intelligence: Volume II*. Morgan Kaufmann. 3–36.

Cobot in LambdaMOO: A Social Statistics Agent

**Charles Lee Isbell, Jr.   Michael Kearns
Dave Kormann   Satinder Singh   Peter Stone**

AT&T Shannon Labs
180 Park Avenue
Florham Park, NJ 07932-0971

Abstract

We describe our development of Cobot, a software agent who lives in LambdaMOO, a popular virtual world frequented by hundreds of users. We present a detailed discussion of the functionality that has made him one of the objects most frequently interacted with in LambdaMOO, human or artificial.

Introduction

The internet is a medium where large groups of people build social communities. This presents both a challenge and an opportunity for artificial intelligence and software agent researchers. In such communities, agents may do more than filter mail, and retrieve price quotes for consumer items; they may be legitimate, if still limited, participants in close-knit social environments.

This paper presents Cobot, a software agent that lives in an active online community frequented by several hundred users (LambdaMOO, which we describe in requisite detail in the next section). His goal is to interact with other members of the community and to become a vital, useful and accepted part of his social fabric. Toward this end, Cobot tracks actions taken by users, building statistics on who performs what actions, and on whom they use them. For example, Cobot tracks which users converse with each other most frequently. Using his chatting interface, Cobot can answer queries about these and other usage statistics, and describe the statistical similarities and differences between users. This information also provides Cobot with a user model that may be used for learning, imitation and conversation. Cobot's chat abilities include a simple and novel method inspired by information retrieval that allows him to choose appropriate utterances from very large documents.

During Cobot's months in LambdaMOO, he has become a member of the community. As we will see in subsequent sections, users interact with Cobot more than with any other user (human or artificial), take advantage of social statistics he provides, converse with him, and discuss him.

Following the pioneering studies of (Foner, 1993; Foner, 1997), we present transcripts establishing the sociological impact of Cobot. We compare the techniques that we have used to implement Cobot's set of social skills to those of previous MUD agents, such as Julia (Foner, 1997), and discuss how these techniques affect user expectations. In addition to the more anecdotal evidence provided by transcripts, we provide quantitative statistical support for our belief that Cobot has not only become part of the social environment in which he resides, but has significantly altered it as well.

The paper begins with a brief history of LambdaMOO. We then detail the two major components of Cobot's functionality—his ability to provide social statistics, and his conversational abilities—and quantify and discuss their impact. After an examination of privacy issues and our approach to them, we discuss future plans for Cobot.

LambdaMOO

LambdaMOO, founded in 1990 by Pavel Curtis at Xerox PARC, is one of the oldest continuously-operating MUDs, a class of online worlds with roots in text-based multiplayer role-playing games. MUDs (multi-user dungeons) differ from most chat and gaming systems in their use of a persistent representation of a virtual world, often created by the participants, who are represented as characters of their own choosing. The mechanisms of social interaction in MUDs are designed to reinforce the illusion that the user is present in the virtual space. LambdaMOO is a MOO: a MUD that uses an object-oriented programming language to manipulate objects in the virtual world.

LambdaMOO appears as a series of interconnected rooms (modeled as a mansion), populated by users and objects who may move from room to room. Each room provides a chat channel shared by just those users in the room (users can also communicate privately), and typically has an elaborate text description that imbues it with its own "look and feel." In addition to speech, users express themselves via a large collection of *emotes,* allowing a rich set of simulated actions, and the expression of emotional states:

(1) Buster is overwhelmed by all these paper deadlines.
(2) Buster begins to slowly tear his hair out, one strand at a time.
(3) HFh comforts Buster.
(4) HFh [to Buster]: Remember, the mighty oak was once a nut like you.
(5) Buster [to HFh]: Right, but his personal growth was assured. Thanks anyway, though.
(6) Buster feels better now.

Lines (1) and (2) are initiated by emote commands by user Buster, expressing his emotional state, while (3) and (4) are examples of emote and speech acts, respectively, by HFh.

Copyright © 2000, American Association for Artificial Intelligence (www.aaai.org). All rights reserved.

Lines (5) and (6) are speech and emote by Buster. (In our transcripts the name of the user initiating an action always begins the description of that action or utterance.) Though there are many standard emotes, such as the use of "comfort" in line (3) above, the variety is essentially unlimited, as players have the ability to create their own emotes.

The rooms and objects in LambdaMOO are created by users themselves, who devise descriptions, and control access by other users. Users can also create objects with methods (or *verbs*) that can be invoked by other players.[1] LambdaMOO is thus a long-standing, ongoing experiment in collective programming and creation, with often stunning results that can only be fully appreciated firsthand. Inventions include technical objects, such as the *lag meter*, which provides recent statistics on server load; objects serving a mix of practical and metaphorical purposes, such as elevators that move users between floors; objects with social uses, such as the *birthday meter*, where users register their birthdays publicly; and objects that just entertain or annoy, such as the *Cockatoo*, a virtual bird who occasionally repeats an utterance recently overheard (often to amusing effect). There is also a long history of objects that can be viewed as experiments in AI, as we will discuss below.

LambdaMOO's long existence, and the user-created nature of the environment, combine to give it with one of the strongest senses of virtual community in the on-line world. Many users have interacted extensively with each other over a period of years, and many are widely acknowledged for their contribution of interesting objects. LambdaMOO has been the subject of articles and books in many different literatures, including the popular press (Dibbell, 1999), linguistics and sociology (Cherny, 1999), computer science, and law.[2] The complex nature of the LambdaMOO community goes a long way towards explaining why it is difficult to simply characterize what users "do" on LambdaMOO. As in real life, users engage in a wide variety of activities, including social activity, programming, and exploring.

LambdaMOO is an attractive environment for experiments in AI. The population is generally curious and technically savvy, and users are interested in automated objects meant to display some form of intelligence (called "puppets"). There is a rich history of automated agents and constructions: Markov chainer, an object that builds a Markov model from the conversations in a room; Dudley, a well-known agent with simple chatting abilities; an automated bartender who provides virtual drinks and small-talk; and many others. There are also object classes allowing users to specialize and create their own AI agents. The agent Julia, a descendant of Colin (created by Fuzzy Mauldin (Mauldin, 1994)), who once resided in a different MUD, is perhaps the closest ancestor of Cobot. We will discuss both Julia and her analysis by Foner (Foner, 1997), which has strongly influenced our thinking, throughout the paper where appropriate.

Cobot

Most of Cobot's computation and storage occurs off-server. He is built using *the Cobot platform*, an agent architecture that uses a directed graph-based metaphor to define a standard for describing a wide-range of virtual environments, including MUDs. A complete discussion of the platform is beyond the scope of this paper.

Cobot appears to be just another user. Once connected, he usually wanders into the LambdaMOO Living Room, where he spends most of his time.[3] The Living Room is a central public place, frequented by many regulars. It is also located next to the Linen Closet, where guests tend to appear, so it is also frequented by users new to LambdaMOO. There are several permanent objects in the Living Room, including a couch with various features, a cuckoo clock, and the aforementioned Cockatoo. The Living Room usually has between five and twenty users, and is constantly busy. Over a three month period there, Cobot has counted over 550,000 separate events (roughly one event every eleven seconds).

As a regular of the Living Room over several months, Cobot has sought to engage other users. His social development can be divided into three distinct stages: inanimate object, social statistics engine, and conversationalist.

In the beginning, Cobot was socially inept: he sat in the Living Room and did nothing but answer one or two basic questions about why he was there. When spoken to in an unanticipated way, he did not respond. In other words, he was little more than a new piece of furniture. Not surprisingly, Cobot generated only a small amount of interaction.

In the next sections we explore the next two stages of Cobot's development and see how these changes impacted both Cobot's popularity and his environment.

Social Statistics

Previous work on agents in MUDs (Foner, 1993; Foner, 1997) has argued that being able to provide information of interest or value to other users aids the social acceptance of the agent. Because Cobot is intended to be primarily a social creature, we chose to have Cobot build and maintain what might be thought of as a *social map* of user interactions in LambdaMOO. In particular, Cobot maintains:

- For each user he encounters:
  - a histogram of verbs used by that user
  - a histogram of verbs that have been used on that user
- For each verb invoked in his presence:
  - a histogram of the users that have invoked it
  - a histogram of the users that have been its target
- For each pair of users Cobot has seen interact:
  - a histogram of verbs they have been used on each other

For both technical and ethical reasons, this information is gathered only for objects and users that are in Cobot's presence. The details of acquiring such information reliably are fairly straightforward, but beyond the scope of this paper. For a discussion, we refer the reader to (Curtis, 1997).

These statistics define a rich graph of social interactions. For example, it is possible to determine which users interact

---

[1] Everything in LambdaMOO is an object, and every event is the invocation of a verb on some object, including speech (usually invocations of the **tell** verb). The LambdaMOO server maintains the database of objects, and executes verbs. As of this writing, the database contains 118,154 objects (not all are valid), including 5158 active user accounts.

[2] LambdaMOO has its own rather intricate legal system.

[3] Cobot has visited about 1070 rooms.

tell me about *verb*-o-meter	Lists which users use (and get used by) *verb* the most.
tell me about me	Tells the questioner various facts about herself, including the verbs she likes to use most, and the verbs most often directed at her.
who are your playmates	Lists those who interact with Cobot the most.
who loves me	Tells the questioner those with whom she interacts the most.
who acts like me	Tells the questioner users who perform actions similar to hers.
who does not act like me	Tells the questioner users who do not perform actions similar to hers.
relate me to *user*	Indicates how the questioner interacts with *user*, providing a ranking on each other's list of playmates, how many playmates they have in common, and how similarly they act.
tell me my *verb*-buddies	Tells the questioner the users she uses *verb* on and who use *verb* on her.
who is spammy	Lists those users who generate and are the targets of the most verbs.

Table 1: **A partial list of social statistics questions that may be asked of Cobot.** Here, the term "act like" refers to distribution of verb usage. The similarity measure is the cosine between verb count vectors (based on a standard information retrieval technique).

with one another the most, who the most "popular" users are, and the types of actions any given user tends to use.

Using this information, Cobot is able to answer natural-language-like queries about social interactions in the Living Room. For example:

HFh [to cobot]: relate me to Buster

cobot whispers, "Here are your relationships with Buster. You like to use: - (62%), poke (7%), hug (3%), eye (3%), nod (2%), hi5, h5, zap, comfort, and grin on each other. Buster is ranked #14 on your list of playmates. You are ranked #1 on Buster's list. Your socializing overlap is 75.4% and your playmate overlap is 33.7%. Your actions have a similarity of 95.9% but ignoring common speech verbs it's 58.3%. Others act on you with a similarity of 96.6% but ignoring common speech verbs it's 81.9%."

This particular query yields a great deal of information. Cobot first reports how and how often HFh and Buster interact with one another (the "-" verb is one method for directing speech; the first line above is generated by HFh typing "-cobot relate me to Buster."). Cobot then provides measures of similarity of social circles and similarity of action. Each of these measures is calculated using a cosine measure (a common information retrieval technique) between histograms of action use or inter-user interactions. Table 1 lists more of the queries that can one can make of Cobot.

After a month of gathering statistics, the social statistics query feature of Cobot was made available to LambdaMOO users. As the Figures show, the results were immediate and dramatic. Initially, before he had any real functionality, interaction with Cobot was constant but low (three per 1000 events). After the introduction of his new abilities, the number of interactions directed at Cobot jumped significantly (now over 50/1000 events, more than double that of the next most popular Living Room denizen).[4]

While these graphs quantify the sudden rise in Cobot's popularity, they cannot express the extent to which he altered (for better or worse) social interaction in the Living Room. Users began to converse with each other on what they were learning about their relationships and similarities:

Snow_Crash [to Medb]: Cobot says you act like me. Stop.

Medb cracks up laughing at Snow_Crash!

Medb [to Snow_Crash]: How do you know it's not you acting like me?

---

[4]User HFh (an author) also experienced a sudden equal jump in interaction. As Cobot's primary human ambassador at the time, he spent much of that period answering questions, explaining functionality, and fielding requests for new abilities.

Medb tries to decide whether she or Snow_Crash should feel more insulted....

...

Gabaldon [to cobot]: loudly relate me to sparklebug

cobot [to Gabaldon]: Here are your relationships with Sparklebug ... Sparklebug is ranked 7 on your list of playmates. You are ranked 19 on Sparklebug's list. ...

Gabaldon [to Sparklebug]: I can't play with you so much anymore, you do realize. You don't like me nearly as much as I seem to like you.

Gabaldon cries at Sparklebug.

...

Spitboy has a new strategy. He stops by the Living Room, asks the cobot who's like him and if cobot tells him one of the people present is like him, he starts talking to them.

Spitboy says, "I haven't caught anyone who's like me, yet."

Spitboy [to Kimmy]: Shame, innit?

Kimmy says, "sure."

Kimmy [to cobot]: who is like me?

After observing these responses to the information provided by Cobot, we implemented changes to encourage such behavior. For example, as seen earlier in HFh's request about Buster, Cobot provides relative rankings of interactions between users. Players seemed appreciative of the ability to gain deeper insight into their interactions, and used the information accordingly. Access to social statistics resulted in other changes as well, some quite unintentional. For example, users began actively competing to move up on Cobot's list of playmates, or to be ranked the "most hugged."

cobot [to Stevage]: Here are my favorite playmates: Sparklebug, HFh, ...

Sparklebug beams brightly. Stevage might need some shades for that.

Stevage winks to cobot.

cobot winks to Stevage.

Sparklebug [to Stevage]: I've worked SO hard to beat HFh!

These social consequences were beyond our expectations, sometimes so severe that we needed to implement several social controls (as we shall see later). The important point is that Cobot provided a useful service (as have other agents, such as Julia) that captured information of constantly evolving and long-term interest to his community. The result was that Cobot had an immediate and profound impact on the social interactions within his sphere.

Chat and Emote Abilities of Cobot

Cobot's social statistic functions are what many Living Room denizens might view as his "purpose," or the inter-

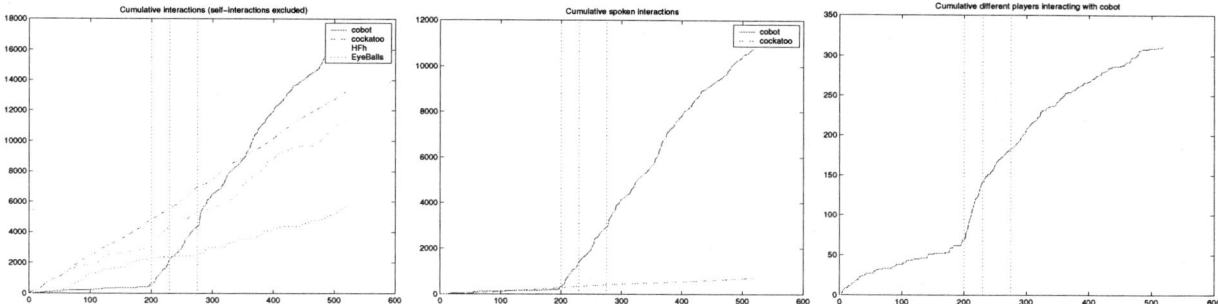

Figure 1: **Cumulative interactions with objects in the Living Room.** (a) Cumulative number of verbs (speech verbs, hugs, waves, etc.) directed towards various Living Room denizens: Cobot, the Cockatoo, and the two human users most interacted with during this period. The x-axis measures cumulative events (in thousands) of any type in the Living Room, while the y-axis measures cumulative events directed at the indicated user. Each dashed vertical line indicates the introduction of a major new feature on Cobot (from the left, his social statistics, his emoting abilities, and his extended chat abilities). A straight line—such as the Cockatoo's—indicates constant interaction. By contrast, Cobot's curve shows sudden changes in the slope coinciding with new features. Note that even when the slope levels off afterwards, it remains higher than it was previously, indicating long-term impact. Judging from cumulative interaction, Cobot is the most popular user in the Living Room. (b) Cumulative *speech* acts directed at Cobot and the Cockatoo. Clearly users interact with the two artifacts differently. Most of the interaction with Cockatoo is explained by users invoking its **gag** verb to silence it. Still, note that there is constant non-zero daily spoken interaction with it as well, indicating that users are willing to talk to even such a relatively simple creature. Also, note that before his new abilities surfaced, Cobot enjoyed a comparable amount of spoken interaction. (c) Variety of users interacting with Cobot.

esting service he provides. We follow researchers before us in believing that to truly integrate into an online society like LambdaMOO, Cobot must do much more. In particular, LambdaMOO is a world that is rich in both conversation and emoting, and in this section we detail our efforts to enable him to participate meaningfully in both.

Emoting. As users became more enamored or frustrated with Cobot's social statistics, they began to express their opinions via directing standard or personalized emotes such as hugging, waving, pouncing and kicking towards Cobot:

cobot exclaims, "Hi! I'm awake!"

Sparklebug [to cobot]: I've missed you SO much!

Sparklebug snuggles with cobot.

...

cobot [to Ratman]: Hello, Ratman.

Ratman takes cobot over his knee and spanks its bottom.

Consequently, it seemed natural to equip cobot with the ability to respond to such actions in appropriately. Like others before us, we found it effective to program several plausible replies to any given scenario, and to randomize between the responses (including doing nothing). This is a simple technique for introducing variability in Cobot's behavior, and seems to enhance his apparent intelligence for many users.

Melon hugs cobot.

cobot hugs Melon warmly.

EyeBalls kisses cobot lightly.

cobot hugs EyeBalls warmly.

...

cobot [to Ratman]: Welcome, special playmate of mine!

Ratman spits at cobot

cobot [to Ratman]: You'll be first up against the wall when the revolution comes.

Simple Chatting. Cobot's early chat abilities were of a similar nature, being randomized, canned responses to specific utterances. However, this is a more difficult problem because the variety of utterances directed at Cobot is much greater than the variety of emotes. As others have discovered, for certain classes of incoming utterances, it is helpful to respond with fairly general and leading conversational utterances, while other times it is possible to be rather specific:

killa [to cobot]: how old are you?

cobot [to killa]: I am older than you think.

lackluster [to cobot]: why are you carrying a shield?

cobot [to lackluster]: I think many of the dumber MOOers think I'm a garbage can.

Just as users expect to have their hugs to Cobot returned, his heaviest users enjoy having Cobot actually initiating recognition of them. We thus made occasional departures from our informal policy of having Cobot only respond to activity initiated by users, for instance by having Cobot initiate greetings to certain users who interact with him frequently, as in his (rebuffed) greeting to user Ratman above.

Extended Chat. So far we have described a limited set of chat and emote abilities, carefully crafted but based on tried techniques. Not long after Cobot began enjoying sustained usage, many users began to recognize some of his canned responses, and made comments longing for better chatting ability. At this point we inaugurated a novel experiment, in which some of Cobot's utterances were generated from a small number of large and publicly available online documents meeting the following desiderata:

- The sentences could plausibly serve as utterances by Cobot, at least in some contexts.
- The documents should be sufficiently large that repeated utterances will be unlikely.
- The documents should be on fairly specific and recognizable topics. Rather than designed to enhance general conversational ability (which remains handled in part by the mechanisms already described), the utterances generated by the documents are meant to give Cobot "personality".
- The utterances generated by the documents are entertaining and sometimes controversial (to spur further conversation).

Any utterance directed towards Cobot that is not recognized as a request for social statistics becomes a candidate

Guest [to cobot]: Do you know anyone I should send this home vasectomy kit to?

Sparklebug peers at Guest suspiciously.

cobot [to Guest]: This is a joke in very poor taste.

Guest [to HFh]: He's good.

Guest [to HFh]: Have you been tinkering with him?

HFh says, "I wish I could take credit, but I think he's evolving."

Guest [to cobot]: You're evolving?

cobot nods to Guest.

cobot says, "CITIZENS: ACIDHORSE DOES NOT EXIST."

Guest [to cobot]: he does so, I'm sure I've seen him

cobot [to Guest]: What does this prove?

Guest [to cobot]: my hovercraft is full of eels

Guest [to HFh]: He just made perfect sense. damn him.

cobot [to Guest]: Heavens!

...

deLaMer says to HFh, "you did good work on cobot."

HFh [to deLaMer]: Thank you.

deLaMer says, "it's starting to make sense. that's spooky."

Blue_Guest [to HFh]: I thought it was a person once.

Technicolor_Guest says, "cobot is an evil mastermind lurking behind the false guise of a mere bot"

Guest comes out of the closet (so to speak...).

cobot [to Guest]: Sunshine! You validate me!

Guest [to cobot]: nice.

cobot [to Guest]: We've had a nice snooze.

Guest [to cobot]: so more charitable than usual?

cobot [to Guest]: But my dreams are a lot emptier than yours.

Fawn_Guest [to cobot]: They can't possibly be any emptier than mine

Guest [to cobot]: oh.

cobot [to Guest]: Your cry for help is transparent.

...

Stevage says, "cobot is pretty damn human I have to admit... I asked him 3 questions and he gave sensible replies to them all."

...

Valley [to HFh]: cobot's genuinely cool...and I'm not even a techie :)

Guest says, "Cobot frightens and confuses me, yet I cannot turn away"

HFh [to Inimeg]: He *is* a player.

HFh [to Inimeg]: He has always been a player.

Inimeg says, "damn the line just gets blurrier and blurrier"

...

A better, kinder Ratman puts on his Ratman's Official Church of Cobot Membership Badge.

Table 2: **Additional Cobot commentary by LambdaMOO users.**

for the following process. Words in the incoming utterance are matched to words appearing in sentences in the documents, assigning to each sentence a weight based on the number of matching words. A minimum length on the words matched provides a parameter that can adjust the difficulty of matching sentences in each document independently. If no match is found, the utterance is handled by one of the mechanisms mentioned earlier; otherwise, with a (large) fixed probability Cobot randomly chooses a sentence to utter according to the distribution defined by the weights.

The effectiveness of this approach depends on the choice of documents. We first fielded the well-known Unabomber Manifesto by Theodore Kaczynski, a lengthy, didactic essay on the evils wrought on society by science, and the industrial revolution. The resulting response was immediate and dramatic, resulting in a steep rise in experimentation and interaction with Cobot (note the rightmost dashed vertical line in Figure 1). The new functionality resulted in endless conversation, both with and about Cobot, and allowed users to attribute to him all manner of intelligence and attitudes:

Technicolor_Guest [to cobot]: What's your religion?

cobot [to Technicolor_Guest]: technology unless you REALLY believe in that religion yourself and find that it arouses a deep, strong, genuine response in many other people.

...

cobot [to DragonBoi]: The line of conflict should be drawn between the mass of the people and the power-holding elite of industrial society.

DragonBoi eyes cobot warily.

cobot [to DragonBoi]: You have something cute in your eye.

DragonBoi [to HFh]: you're bot is turning into a communist.

DragonBoi [to cobot]: so what are you gonna do about it?

Wikked [to cobot]: are you a communist?

DragonBoi [to cobot]: are you now, or ever been a member of the communist party?

cobot mumbles something in binary.

DragonBoi [to cobot]: so you're taking the fifth are you? well this is a special commision, that won't work here!

...

cobot [to HFh]: The modern individual on the other hand is threatened by many things against which he is helpless; nuclear accidents, carcinogens in food, environmental pollution, war, increasing taxes, invasion of his privacy by large organizations, nation-wide social or economic phenomena that may disrupt his way of life.

HFh [to cobot]: I agree with that position, I suppose, but it doesn't help to explain the lack of a safety net.

cobot [to HFh]: Nevertheless, the position can be defended.

HFh [to cobot]: ...in the *short* term only.

cobot nods to HFh.

Cobot's replies are not always appropriate; that they are often appropriate and frequently amusing suffices to intrigue and entertain users. User seem to ignore the senseless interactions with Cobot and remember the "intelligent" ones. Certainly the open-ended nature of LambdaMOO, and the fact that few users have concrete, goal-oriented expectations of the other users or artifacts they encounter encourage this.

Other documents include scripts of "The Big Lebowski" and "Planet of the Apes"; a long analysis of the JonBenet Ramsey murder case; and articles on alien abduction and paranormal experience. It is simple to instantly swap new documents in and old ones out, limiting Cobot's chat abilities only by the imaginations of his creators. Still, we emphasize our belief that it is advantageous to limit the number of documents at any given time, and for these documents to be reasonably specific, so that well-defined "themes" can emerge in Cobot's conversation. Note that Cobot has no notion of conversational state at this point, so utterances in any given conversation may be drawn from multiple documents, as in the following exchange alternating between the Unabomber Manifesto and "Planet of the Apes":

cobot [to cyberat]: There is good reason to believe that many primitive societies subjected people to less pressure than the European society did, but European society proved far more efficient than any primitive society[....]

cyberat [to cobot]: Thats what they want you to think!

cobot [to cyberat]: Tell me who and what you really are and where you come from, and no veterinarian will touch you.

cyberat [to cobot]: Veterinarians!!!

cobot [to cyberat]: The Roman system of urban sanitation was forgotten, so that until rather recent times did the sanitation of European cities that of Ancient Rome.

Fawn_Guest [to HFh]: cobot's conversation topics just get weirder and weirder

cobot [to cyberat]: In spite of every sign I'm an intelligent being meaning no harm, you continue to hate and fear me.

Privacy and Social Issues

LambdaMOO has policies researcher, acquiring permissions from users, and quoting material; however, as in any complex culture, there are unofficial, unwritten rules that must be learned. Much of the work in introducing Cobot into LambdaMOO involved learning and understanding these rules, and is an ongoing concern. We began our education by discussing with colleagues who were LambdaMOO users, and could provide insight into its social dynamics. HFh spent several months as a LambdaMOO user, building genuine friendships, learning about etiquette and privacy, and floating the idea of an agent like Cobot. Only after convincing ourselves that Cobot would not be completely unwelcome did we introduce him into the Living Room.

Privacy. The Living Room is a *public* space, not a private room. Possibly intrusive objects are more likely to be tolerated, as long as users do not believe they are being recorded in some way for unfriendly purposes. Furthermore, most users are sophisticated enough to understand the tenuous nature of privacy in such public spaces. On the other hand, most users will *not* simply reveal their real-life identities to casual acquaintances in the MOO, nor do they expect others to reveal such information. Early in the project, several MOOers raised questions around these issues, sometimes in jest, sometimes quite seriously. In keeping with the goal of social acceptance, Cobot is fairly conservative. He notes only events in his presence, and does not share events verbatim. Furthermore, a questioner can generally only ask about herself, and not directly about others, and all responses are whispered only to the questioner unless the questioner explicitly asks to share the information with the room.

Spam. Being in a public place, Living Room regulars are more likely to tolerate spammy objects, but there are clear limits. Because the goal of Cobot is to be a part of his social environment, it is important that he not cross this line. Thus, Cobot's tendency to whisper answers to requests is not motivated just by privacy, but by the desire to be less spammy. Similarly, Cobot generally does not speak unless spoken to, except under certain conditions, as discussed earlier. These design decisions are intended to give users a modicum of control over the nature and rate of Cobot's output.

Nevertheless, these precautions sometimes proved inadequate. For example, users expect to have the ability to silence non-human objects. So, Cobot has a **silence** verb that allows a user to prevent him from speaking out loud (to anyone) for a random amount of time. Cobot may still respond to users, but he will only whisper to his intended target.

Still, it is no more possible to prevent users from using Cobot to generate spam (*e.g.* by repeatedly querying him aloud) than it is to prevent users from generating spam directly. It is debatable whether such users or Cobot are to blame, but it can be irritating regardless. Cobot's various social statistics are a great incentive to interact in front of and with him perhaps more than one would otherwise, thus raising the overall level of noise in the Living Room.[5]

To combat this, we have implemented more drastic measures. Along with Cobot's "owners," any of a set of identified regulars can direct Cobot to ignore individual players. Cobot will not interact with such a player during these times, except to occasionally inform him that he is being ignored. These policies appear to be the minimum necessary. We are continually revisiting and updating these decisions.

Discussion

Cobot has become a member of his community. As we have seen, he is perhaps the most "popular" resident of the Living Room. Users engage him in conversation, interact with him in a variety of ways, take advantage of his statistical services and sometimes even have generally positive things to say about him (see Table 2). On the other hand, his entry has not been welcomed by all MOOers. Some complain of a general increase in spam, and others have noted that he has irreparably changed the nature of the Living Room.

Cobot's development continues. Although Cobot often has remarkably cogent conversations, most of the time his remarks are complete non sequiturs[6]. We plan to provide cobot with minimal state to help him be more focused and coherent. We have also begun experimenting with using reinforcement learning techniques to teach Cobot to learn how to act more independently and without prompting, while avoiding angering users. Users will be able to reward and punish Cobot for actions he takes, and he will learn to modify his behavior accordingly. For example, Cobot may decide when it is best to inject himself into a conversation, when to hug, wave to or comfort someone, or when to introduce similar users who do not regularly interact.

In general, we are interested in ways of allowing Cobot to integrate more fully and usefully into his environment. We are mindful, however, that like all good citizens, Cobot should change his environment without degrading it.

References

Bates, J. (1994). The role of emotion in believable agents. *Communications of the ACM*, 37(7):122–125.

Cherny, L. (1999). *Conversation and Community: Discourse in a Social MUD*. Cambridge University Press.

Curtis, P. (1997). The lambdamoo programmer's manual v1.8.0p6. ftp://ftp.research.att.com/dist/-eostrom/MOO/html/ProgrammersManual_toc.html.

Dibbell, J. (1999). *My Tiny Life : Crime and Passion in a Virtual World*. Holt, Henry & Company.

Etzioni, O. (1997). Moving up the information food chain: deploying softbots on the world wide web. *AI Magazine*, 18(2):11–18.

Foner, L. (1993). What's an agent, anyway? a sociological case study. Technical report, MIT Media Lab.

Foner, L. (1997). Entertaining agents: a sociological case study. In *Proceedings of the First International Conference on Autonomous Agents*.

Mauldin, M. (1994). Chatterbots, tinymuds, and the turing test: Entering the loebner prize competition. In *Proceedings of the Twelfth National Conference on Artificial Intelligence*.

Mitchell, T., Caruana, R., Freitag, D., McDermott, J., and Zabowski, D. (1994). Experience with a learning personal assistant. *Communications of the ACM*, 37(7):80–91.

---

[5] There is some evidence that Cobot's presence may have raised the overall amount of interaction in the Living Room.

[6] Some users tailor their conversation with Cobot in order to keep him "on topic" while others revel in his lack of understanding.

Semantics of Agent Communication Languages for Group Interaction

Sanjeev Kumar, Marcus J. Huber, David R. McGee, Philip R. Cohen, Hector J. Levesque[*]

Department of Computer Science and Engineering
Oregon Graduate Institute
20000 NW Walker Road
Beaverton, OR 97006, USA
{skumar, marcush, dmcgee, pcohen}@cse.ogi.edu

[*]Department of Computer Science
University of Toronto
Toronto, Ontario
M5S 3H5, Canada
hector@cs.toronto.edu

Abstract

Group communication is the core of societal interactions. Therefore, artificial agents should be able to communicate with groups as well as individuals. However, most contemporary agent communication languages, notably FIPA and KQML, have either no provision or no well-defined semantics for group communication. We give a semantics for group communication that we believe can profitably enrich the agent communication languages. In our semantics, individual communication is a special case of group communication wherein each communicating group consists of a single agent. One of the novel features of this semantics is that it allows senders to send messages even without knowing all the potential recipients of those messages – a typical scenario in broadcast communication.

Motivation

Artificial as well as human agents not only interact with individual agents, but they also need to communicate with groups of agents. We post messages to mailing lists and notice boards; participate in teleconferences and videoconferences; publish web pages and books; speak in meetings and classrooms; talk on radio and television; and advertise on pamphlets and banners. Agents will be assuming some of these responsibilities from humans and will therefore, need to be able to reason and communicate about group concepts. Moreover, in open multi-agent systems, where agents come and go dynamically, it will become ever more prevalent that agents will not know exactly to whom they are sending information or from whom they are requesting aid. These are compelling reasons to investigate developing support for group communication in multi-agent systems. It is no surprise, therefore, that a large number of distributed software systems inevitably use some incarnation of broadcasting and multicasting.

However, we observe that the major agent communication languages have either no provision or no well-defined semantics for group communication. For instance, in the FIPA ACL, the only way to inform a set of agents is to inform them individually, one at a time. Furthermore, semantics of the FIPA communicative acts imposes the precondition that the sender has certain beliefs about the mental state of the (known) addressee. Consequently, there is no way to send messages to unknown agents – a typical scenario in broadcast communication.

KQML does offer several primitives, such as broadcast and recruit-all, that have group flavor but these primitives are merely shorthand for a request to do a series of other communicative acts. Proper semantics cannot be given to group requests such as "One of you, please, get me a slice of that pie." We may safely conclude that support for group communication in the widely used agent communication languages does not exist.

Group communication is not just about sending a message to a large number of agents at the same time. As mentioned earlier, sometimes the sender does not know the specific recipients of a message. A person who posts the notice "Beware of dogs" may not know who will read that message. So the semantics of a communication language should allow for intentions with respect to "whoever gets this message," while allowing for constraints on the intended recipients and identification of this constraint for correct illocutionary effect. Furthermore, the intended actor for a communication may be a subset of the recipients or a completely different set. By sending an email to the CSE101 mailing list requesting Becker to take the attendance in the next class, the instructor not only made a request to Becker to take attendance but also let the whole class know that she requested Becker to do it. Senders need not only be individuals but can also be groups. An invitation card from John and Betty is actually a request to attend from "them". Individuals may be viewed as singleton groups. Therefore, the same communication primitives should work both for individual and group communication. We believe that any general-purpose agent communication language should be able to deal with these aspects of communication.

To summarize, we have argued that (1) Agent communication languages should support group communication where communication between individuals is a natural special case; (2) An agent communication language that supports group communication should account for the recipients being unknown, the sender being a group, and the intended actors being different from the recipients; (3) Semantics of an agent communication language should be in terms of group communication.

Copyright © 2000, American Association for Artificial Intelligence (www.aaai.org). All rights reserved.

Constraints on Communication Languages

We believe that the properties of communication in human society should be an essential guiding principle in the design of agent communication languages. These properties are constraints that an agent communication language should address.

- *Addressee Constraint*: An ACL should support communication addressed to individuals as well as to groups. Moreover, a group may have a stable, known membership, as in a mailing list, or its membership may be unknown, as in a radio broadcast addressed to all listeners.
- *Sender Constraint*: An ACL should support communication sent by individuals as well as by groups. Typically, an individual acts on behalf of a group when the sender happens to be a group: for example, the invitation card from a couple, and an official letter from a company.
- *Recipient Constraint*: An ACL should support unintended recipients or over-hearers that are an inevitable part of group communication. For example, anybody may happen to read a notice addressed to CSE101 students on the school notice board. Similarly, an announcement on an airport public announcement system requesting Alfred Hopkins to meet someone at the bookstall may include everybody else who hears the announcement as an overhearer.
- *Actor Constraint*: An ACL should support intended actors being wholly different from either the intended or the unintended recipients of a message. In most cases, however, the intended actors will be a subset of the intended recipients. For instance, Alfred Hopkins is the only intended actor in the above example.
- *Actor Awareness Constraint*: An ACL should support a requester's ignorance about the intended actors of the request. For example, a teacher should be able to request "all those who have done the homework" to raise their hands, without knowing in advance which students have done the homework.
- *Sender's Awareness Constraint*: An ACL should support a sender's ignorance about the individual members of a recipient group. This is typically the case with radio and television broadcasts, notices and banners, and authoring web pages and journal articles.
- *Recipient's Awareness Constraint*: An ACL should support the ignorance of a recipient about other recipients of the same message. The reader of a newspaper article may not know who else read that article, yet she may be able to make certain inferences about the mental state of others who have read or will be reading the same article.
- *Originator Constraint*: An ACL should support a recipient's potential ignorance of the originator or sender of a message. A sign "Authorized Personnel Only" may not indicate the author, but it does communicate the appropriate intentions to anybody who reads the sign. Similarly, a note that I discover on the beach may let me make inferences about the intentions of "whoever wrote the note" even if I don't come to know or deduce its author from it.

In a later section, we will present the semantics of a request performative that satisfies these constraints. We note however, that the FIPA'97 specification (FIPA, 1997) supports the actor constraint to some extent.

Preliminaries

We use a modal language with the usual connectives of a first order language with equality, as well as operators for propositional attitudes and event sequences. (BEL x p) and (GOAL x p) say that p follows from x's beliefs or choices respectively. (HAPPENS a) and (DONE a) say that a sequence of actions described by the action expression a will happen next or has just happened, respectively. (HAPPENS x a) and (DONE x a) also specify the agent for the action sequence that is going to happen or has just happened. BEFORE and AFTER are defined using HAPPENS. Knowledge (KNOW x p) is defined in the usual manner. Details of this modal language can be found in (Cohen and Levesque, 1990b). An action expression is built from variables ranging over sequences of events using constructs of dynamic logic: a;b is action composition and p? is a test action. Mutual belief is defined in terms of unilateral mutual belief or BMB (Cohen and Levesque, 1990b). However, unlike the previous work, we treat BMB between two agents as a semantic primitive in this paper.

BMB as a Semantic Primitive

We assume a modal structure $\mathcal{M}$ that includes an accessibility relation $\mathcal{B}_a$ for every agent a. We use the usual possible worlds representation where $\omega_1 \mathcal{B}_a \omega_2$ means that world ω_2 is belief accessible by agent a from world ω_1. In this model, an agent x has unilateral mutual belief with agent y about proposition p if and only if $\forall \omega_1, \omega_2 ... \omega_n$ such that $\omega_1 \mathcal{B}_x \omega_2, \omega_2 \mathcal{B}_y \omega_3, \omega_3 \mathcal{B}_x \omega_4, \omega_4 \mathcal{B}_y \omega_5, ... \omega_{n-1} \mathcal{B}_a \omega_n$ (where $\mathcal{B}_a$ is $\mathcal{B}_x$ if n is even or $\mathcal{B}_y$ if n is odd), p is valid in the model $\mathcal{M}$ in world ω_n. More formally,

$\mathcal{M}, \omega \models$ (BMB x y p) $\equiv \forall n \, \forall (\omega, \omega') \in \mathcal{B}[x,y,n] \; \mathcal{M}, \omega' \models p$

where

$\mathcal{B}[x,y,n]$ is defined inductively by
(1) $\mathcal{B}[x,y,1] = \mathcal{B}_x$
(2) $\mathcal{B}[x,y,n+1] = \mathcal{B}_x \circ \mathcal{B}[y,x,n]$

This semantics is similar to the semantics of common knowledge given in (Halpern and Moses, 1992). In order to generalize the above modal language concepts for groups of agents, we need a suitable representation for groups.

Representing Groups

Similar to the assumptions of other researchers (Singh, 1993), we treat groups as simply a collection of entities. As such, we can regard a group as being defined by a membership property. This can be captured by a predicate consisting of a free variable that ranges over individuals, and in general, ranges over subgroups as well.

Notation. We will underline the entities that represent groups when we need to emphasize their group status, and use the same symbol without the underline in a functional notation to denote the associated membership predicate. For example, $\underline{\tau}$ is a group having the membership predicate $\tau(z)$ where z is a free variable. An entity without underline can be either an individual or a group.

We introduce the notation $\langle \alpha \rangle$ to denote a formula defined by the following rule:
1. If α is a formula without any term of the form $\underline{\tau}$, then $\langle \alpha \rangle = \alpha$
2. If α is a formula with term $\underline{\tau}$, and z does not appear in α, and $\tau(z)$ is the property predicate that corresponds to $\underline{\tau}$, and $\alpha(z)$ is a formula formed by replacing $\underline{\tau}$ with z in α, then $\langle \alpha \rangle = \forall z. \tau(z) \supset \alpha(z)$

For example,
$\langle \text{BEL } x \, p \rangle = (\text{BEL } x \, p)$, if x is an individual agent.
$\langle \text{BEL } \underline{\tau} \, p \rangle = \forall z \, \tau(z) \supset (\text{BEL } z \, p)$
$\langle \text{BEL } \tau \, p \rangle$ cannot be further expanded until we know whether τ is an individual or a group.

In case of ambiguity, we will mark the starting angle bracket, and the group term that it applies to, with the free variable in the superscript.

$\langle^y \text{BEL } \underline{\tau}^y \, (\text{BEL } x \, \langle^z \text{BEL } \underline{\tau}^z \, p \rangle \,) \rangle =$
$\forall y \, \tau(y) \supset (\text{BEL } y \, (\text{BEL } x \, \forall z.(\tau(z) \supset (\text{BEL } z \, p))))$

If τ represents an individual agent, say x, then the superscript is dropped in the expansion.

$\langle^y \text{BEL } \tau^y \, p \rangle = \langle \text{BEL } \tau \, p \rangle = (\text{BEL } \tau \, p) = (\text{BEL } x \, p)$

Sometimes, groups need to be treated as meta-agents with agent-like properties and not as a list of individuals. This distinction is discussed in the section on group action. In this case, the membership predicate will not be specified, the term representing this group will not be underlined, and the group will be treated as an individual agent.

Group Beliefs

Our semantics of group communication primitives based on speech acts deals with group beliefs. The simplest case is to consider the beliefs of all the members of a group when talking about group beliefs. The beliefs of more complex groups such as hierarchically composed organizations and institutions (Werner, 1989) can then be expressed in terms of the beliefs of an abstract group consisting of certain roles in that organization or institution.

Group Belief. Group belief may be defined in several ways, including *inclusive belief:* A group $\underline{\tau}$ believes p if all the individuals or the sub-groups that constitute the group believe p.

$(\text{BEL } \underline{\tau} \, p) \equiv \langle \text{BEL } \underline{\tau} \, p \rangle$
$= \forall z \, \tau(z) \supset (\text{BEL } z \, p)$

For example, "the students of CSE101 believe p" can be represented by
$(\text{BEL } \underline{\text{StudentsOfCSE101}} \, p) \equiv$
$\forall z \, (\text{student } z \, \text{CSE101}) \supset (\text{BEL } z \, p)$

assuming that the domain membership predicate (student z CSE101) is defined.

Other possible definitions of group belief may include (1) *extensive belief*—mutual belief among all the constituents (individuals or sub-groups) of a group, (2) *existential belief*—belief by at least one constituent of a group, (3) *majority belief*—belief by a majority in a group, and (4) *extensive majority belief*—mutual belief among a majority in a group. For the purpose of this paper, we will only use inclusive belief (as also is done in Singh, 93).

Group BMB. An entity τ_1 has unilateral mutual belief about a proposition p with another entity τ_2 when τ_1 believes that there is mutual belief between itself and τ_2 about p. It is possible to define different variations of group BMB corresponding to the various types of group beliefs mentioned above. For inclusive beliefs that we assume in this paper, we define four different categories of BMB.

1) *Unilateral Mutual belief between two individuals*: This is the degenerate case in which the two groups happen to be singleton groups. The semantics of (**BMB** x y p) has been given in a previous section. The semantics of all other cases will be expressed in terms of the semantics of this base case.

2) *Unilateral Mutual belief between an individual and a group*: Agent x has unilateral mutual belief about proposition p with every member of group $\underline{\tau}$ separately.
(**BMB** x $\underline{\tau}$ p) $\equiv$ $\langle$**BMB** x $\underline{\tau}$ $p\rangle$
$\equiv \forall z \, \tau(z) \supset$ (**BMB** x z p)

3) *Unilateral Mutual belief between a group and an individual*: Every individual in the group $\underline{\tau}$ has unilateral mutual belief about proposition p with agent x.
(**BMB** $\underline{\tau}$ x p) $\equiv$ $\langle$**BMB** $\underline{\tau}$ x $p\rangle$
$\equiv \forall z \, \tau(z) \supset$ (**BMB** z x p)

4) *Unilateral Mutual belief between two groups*: A group $\underline{\tau}_1$ has unilateral mutual belief about proposition p with another group $\underline{\tau}_2$ when everybody in group $\underline{\tau}_1$ has unilateral mutual belief with every member of group $\underline{\tau}_2$ separately.
(**BMB** $\underline{\tau}_1$ $\underline{\tau}_2$ p) $\equiv$ $\langle^z\langle^w$**BMB** $\underline{\tau}_1^z$ $\underline{\tau}_2^w$ $p\rangle\rangle$
$\equiv \forall z \, \tau_1(z) \supset$ (**BMB** z $\underline{\tau}_2$ p)

Group Mutual Belief. Given the above definitions of unilateral mutual belief, the entities τ_1 and τ_2 have mutual belief about proposition p when both τ_1 and τ_2 have unilateral mutual beliefs about proposition p with respect to the other entity.

(**MB** τ_1 τ_2 p) $\equiv$ (**BMB** τ_1 τ_2 p) $\wedge$ (**BMB** τ_2 τ_1 p)

This is a straightforward generalization of the mutual belief defined for two agents in (Cohen and Levesque, 1990b).

Group Action

Researchers in multi-agent systems have attempted to answer questions such as what it means for a group to do an action (Grosz, B. J. and Kraus, S., 1996). However, we are mainly interested in the meaning of terms such as (HAP-

PENS τ a) and (DONE τ a) where a is an action expression and τ is a group.

For the purpose of this paper, all we need is to be able to distinguish between (1) a group doing an action as an entity (or meta-agent), and (2) everybody in a list of individuals performing the action. For instance, a request to CSE101 students to move the teacher's desk is a request to the students as a whole. It may entail the CSE101 students deciding which students would do the action of moving the heavy desk and how the individual actions of those students would be coordinated. On the other hand, a request to everybody in CSE101 to submit the homework is a request to every student in the class to submit their homework individually. An agent communication language should be able to properly convey these nuances of a requester's intentions about the performers of an action. We distinguish between these two cases in our semantics by requiring that the group be treated as a meta-agent in the first case – the membership predicate should not be specified. Terms such as (HAPPENS τ a) do not decompose further and it is a part of the problem solving process of the group to decide how the group does the action a. The second case requires specification of a membership predicate and terms such as (HAPPENS $\underline{\tau}$ a) will be defined as ⟨HAPPENS $\underline{\tau}$ a⟩. This term expands to $\forall z\, \tau(z) \supset$ (HAPPENS z a) requiring every member of the group τ to do the action a.

Group Extension of Basic Concepts

We adopt an attempt-based semantics (Cohen and Levesque, 1990b) to illustrate the semantics of our group communication performatives. Here we extend the basic semantic concepts using the group formulation developed in the previous sections. The reader may assume any of the definitions for group and organizational beliefs suggested in the previous sections. It is important to note that the definitions to follow allow for both groups and individuals, as τ may either be an individual or a group.

Definition 1. *Persistent Goal*
(PGOAL τ p q) ≡ (BEL τ $\neg p$) ∧ (GOAL τ $\Diamond p$) ∧
 (KNOW τ [UNTIL [(BEL τ p) ∨
  (BEL τ $\Box\neg p$) ∨
  (BEL τ $\neg q$)]
  (GOAL τ $\Diamond p$)]).

Persistent goal formalizes the notion of commitment (Cohen and Levesque, 1990a). An entity (agent or group) τ having a persistent goal p is committed to that goal. The entity τ cannot give up the goal that p is true in the future, at least until it believes that one of the following is true: p is accomplished, or is impossible, or the relativizing condition q is untrue.

Definition 2. *Intention*
(INTEND τ a q) ≡ (PGOAL τ [HAPPENS τ
  (BEL τ (HAPPENS a))?;a] q)

Intention to do an action a is a commitment to do the action knowingly. The entity τ is committed to being in a mental state in which it has done the action a and just prior to which it believed that it was about to do the intended action next (Cohen and Levesque, 1990a).

Definition 3. *Attempt*
(ATTEMPT τ e p q t) ≡
 t?;[(BEL τ $\neg p$) ∧
 (GOAL τ (HAPPENS e;$\Diamond p$?)) ∧
 (INTEND τ t?;e;q? (GOAL τ (HAPPENS e;$\Diamond p$?)))]?;e

An attempt to achieve p via q is a complex action expression in which the entity τ is the actor of event e and just prior to e, the actor chooses that p should eventually become true, and intends that e should produce q relative to that choice. So, p represents some ultimate goal that may or may not be achieved by the attempt, while q represents what it takes to make an honest effort (Cohen and Levesque, 1990b; Smith et. al., 1998).

Definition 4. *Persistent Weak Achievement Goal*
(PWAG τ_1 τ_2 p q) ≡
 [¬(BEL τ_1 p) ∧ (PGOAL τ_1 p)] ∨
 [(BEL τ_1 p) ∧ (PGOAL τ_1 (MB τ_1 τ_2 p))] ∨
 [(BEL τ_1 $\Box\neg p$) ∧ (PGOAL τ_1 (MB τ_1 τ_2 $\Box\neg p$))] ∨
 [(BEL τ_1 $\neg q$) ∧ (PGOAL τ_1 (MB τ_1 τ_2 $\neg q$))]

This definition adapted from (Smith et. al., 1996) states that an entity τ_1 has a PWAG with respect to another entity τ_2 when the following holds: (1) if entity τ_1 believes that p is not currently true, it will have a persistent goal to achieve p, (2) if it believes p to be either true, or to be impossible, or if it believes the relativizing condition q to be false, then it will adopt a persistent goal to bring about the corresponding mutual belief with entity τ_2. PWAG is a basic concept in joint intentions and is used in the definition of request.

A Generalized Communication Primitive

We now present a definition of the request performative with group semantics. This definition is a generalized versions of the individual communication performative defined in (Smith et. al., 1998). The terms α, β, and γ in the following definition can represent either groups or individuals. Here, α is the entity performing the request, β is the recipient (including the "over-hearers") of the request message, and γ is the intended actor.

Definition 5. *Request*
(REQUEST α β γ e a q t) ≡ (ATTEMPT α e ϕ ψ t)
where ϕ = ⟨^{z}(DONE γ^z a) ∧
  [PWAG γ^z α (DONE γ^z a)
  (PWAG α γ ⟨^{w} DONE γ^w a⟩ q)]⟩
and ψ = [BMB β α (BEFORE e [GOAL α
  (AFTER e [PWAG α γ ϕ q])])]

Substituting for ϕ and ψ in the definition of attempt (definition 3), we get the goal and the intention of the request respectively. The goal of the request is that the intended actor γ eventually does the action a and also has a PWAG with respect to the requester α to do a. The intended actor's PWAG is with respect to the requester's PWAG (towards her) that she does the action a. The requester's PWAG is itself relative to some higher-level goal

q. The intention of the request is that the recipient β believe there is a mutual belief between the recipient and the requester that before sending the request, the requester α had a goal that after sending the request he (the requester) will have a PWAG with respect to the intended actor γ about the goal ϕ of the request.

The recipient β and the intended actor γ never quantify into the beliefs of the requester α - meaning thereby that the requester α does not need to know who β and γ are. Let us consider the general case in which β and γ are groups with specified membership predicate and α could be either a group or an individual i.e. consider (REQUEST α β γ e a t). The term $\langle^z (\text{DONE } \gamma^z\ a)...\rangle$ in ϕ expands to $(\forall z\ \gamma(z) \supset ...)$ with γ^z replaced by z everywhere. After plugging ϕ into the definition of attempt (definition 3) and simplifying, we get (GOAL α ...($\forall z\ \gamma(z) \supset ...$)) which means that the requester does not have to know about the members of the group γ. The PWAG conjunct of ϕ has the requester's PWAG as its relativizing condition (PWAG α γ...). However, the γ in (PWAG α γ...) is not specified as γ^z so it does not get replaced by the z that appears in $\langle^z (\text{DONE } \gamma^z\ a)...\rangle$ and hence γ does not quantify into the requester's PWAG as a result of expanding the angle brackets in ϕ. From definition 4, the (PWAG α γ...) expands to terms of the form [(BEL α p) $\wedge$ (PGOAL α (MB α γ p))]. Expanding the MB in terms of BMB and between two groups, the only relevant term that we get is of the form (PGOAL α (BMB γ α p) ...). Using the definition of inclusive BMB given earlier, this expression further simplifies to

(PGOAL α [$\forall z.\gamma(z) \supset$ (BMB z α p)).....])

where z is a variable that has not been used anywhere else in the expansion of request. Here also, γ does not quantify into the beliefs of the requester α. It is important to note, however, that any other definition of group BMB (such as exclusive BMB) will also not quantify γ into the beliefs of the requester α in the term (PGOAL α .....).

By plugging ψ into attempt, and with similar reasoning we find that the term (...[PWAG α γ ϕ q]...) does not quantify the intended recipient γ into the beliefs and goals of the requester α. Moreover, the term (INTEND...[BMB β α]...) in the expansion of attempt after plugging ψ, never quantifies the recipient β into the beliefs and goals of the requester α, as can be seen by similar expansion and reasoning. Hence, we see that *our definition of request never requires a requester to know who the recipients (both intended and unintended) or the intended actors are.*

We now illustrate examples of usage of this request.

Example 1. A request from one agent x to another agent y
This is the degenerate case in which each of the communicating groups consists of a single agent. The recipient of the message and the intended actor will be the same agent. Using the rules for expanding our macro notation, the above definition reduces to the following:

(REQUEST x y y e a q t) $\equiv$ (ATTEMPT x e ϕ ψ t)
where ϕ = [(DONE y a) $\wedge$
[PWAG y α (DONE y a)
(PWAG x y (DONE y a) q)]]

and ψ = [BMB y x (BEFORE e [GOAL x
(AFTER e [PWAG x y ϕ q])])]

As expected, this expression is same as the definition of request between two agents in (Smith et. al., 1998) with the exception of BEFORE and AFTER predicates that more precisely describe when the mental states should hold.

Example 2. "All those who have done the homework raise their hands".

Here, the requester α is a single agent – the teacher. The recipient β is a group—all students in the class. The intended actor γ is also a group—all the students in the class who have done their homework. The action a is "raise hand". Formally, this request may be expressed as

(REQUEST teacher
  students_in_class
  students_done_homework
  e
  raise_hand
  homework_due(now)
  t)

Let us assume that the membership predicate for γ ie. students_done_homework is (doneHomework z).
The goal term ϕ in the definition of request expands to the following:

ϕ = $\forall z.$(doneHomework z) $\supset$ [(DONE z raise_hand) $\wedge$
  [PWAG z teacher (DONE z raise_hand)
    (PWAG teacher students_done_homework
      $\langle$ DONE students_done_homework raise_hand$\rangle$
      homework_due(now))
  ]]

The goal part of the request is that every student z that has done the homework eventually does the action of raising her hand. Moreover, the student z should also have a PWAG with respect to the teacher that she (the student z) does the action of raising her hand. Furthermore, this PWAG should be with respect to the teacher's PWAG with "the students who have done their homework" that all students who have done their homework do the action of raising their hands. The intention of the request is to have mutual belief with all students (irrespective of whether or not they have done the homework) in the class about this goal.

Meeting the Constraints. What makes this definition of request uniquely powerful is that it satisfies all the constraints on agent communication languages identified earlier. The addressee and the sender constraints are satisfied because α and β can be groups as well as individuals. The recipient constraint is satisfied because β includes all the recipients—intended as well as unintended. The actor constraint is satisfied because we have a separate term γ for the intended actor. The only place where the recipient β is used in the definition of request is in [BMB β α ...]. From the definition of inclusive BMB used in this paper, we see that the members of β do not need to know who the other members of β are. Therefore, the recipient's awareness constraint is supported where it is needed. The originator constraint is satisfied because the requester α does not quantify into the beliefs of the recipient β in the term [BMB β α ...]. The most intriguing part of the request definition, however, is that it even satisfies the actor awareness constraint and the sender's awareness constraints as seen by the following theorems.

Theorem 1: A request can be performed even when the requester does not know about the intended actor. Formally,
  (Done α (REQUEST α β γ e a q t)) ∧ ¬∃ z.(BEL α γ(z))
is satisfiable.

Proof sketch: Construct a possible worlds model that satisfies both the conjuncts. We use the situation in example 2 to construct such a model. Let the real world w_0 be the world just after the request event has taken place. Let w_1 and w_2 be the worlds that are both belief and goal accessible by the teacher. Let the proposition (Done α (REQUEST α β γ e a q t)) be true in w_1 and w_2. Let y_1 and y_2 be two students who have done their homework and hence are the intended actors of the request. Suppose that w_1 is belief accessible from w_0 by y_1, and w_2 be belief accessible from w_0 by y_2. The proposition (doneHomework y_1) is true in w_1 and (doneHomework y_2) is true in w_2. However, it is not the case that ∃z.(BEL teacher (doneHomework z)) because the z in w_1 and w_2 differ. Since w_1 is the only accessible world for y_1 and w_2 is the only accessible world for y_2, y_1 believes that it has done the homework in w_1, and y_2 believes it has done the homework in w_2, because both y_1 and y_2 know that they individually satisfy (doneHomework z). Therefore, it is possible for the teacher to have the goal that whoever has done the homework be able to evaluate the implication (∀z.(doneHomework z) ⊃ (DONE z raise_hand) ∧ (PWAG z teacher .....)). This is the goal part of the request that we get after plugging φ in the attempt. Similarly, using a membership predicate for the class and constructing worlds in which these propositions hold, the intention part of the request can be satisfied. Therefore, (Done α (REQUEST α β γ e a q t)) ∧ ¬∃ z.(BEL α γ(z)) is satisfiable in this model.

Theorem 2: A request can be performed even when the requester does not know everyone who will get the message. Formally,
  (Done α (REQUEST α β γ e a q t)) ∧ ¬∃ z.(BEL α β(z))
is satisfiable.

Proof sketch: This follows from the proof of the above theorem when a model is constructed to satisfy the intention part of the request.

Discussion

Although there has been considerable work in agent communication languages (FIPA 1997; Labrou, 1997), and researchers, including us, have investigated group intentions and group action (Grosz and Kraus, 1996; Singh 1993), group communication has not been addressed in a comprehensive manner. We believe the present work provides a first step in this direction. We identified a set of constraints for agent communication languages, presented a generalized request performative that can handle both group and individual communication, and showed that this performative is novel in that it satisfied all the identified constraints.

We note that the implementation of an agent communication language and the design of its semantics are two distinct issues. Future work includes the specification and implementation of a complete agent communication language with group semantics. A treatment of roles and responsibilities in teams, organizations, and institutions is also needed for a better understanding of what happens in group-communication in these complex groups. Furthermore, the impact of group communication semantics on communication protocols needs to be investigated.

Acknowledgement

We gratefully acknowledge the support of the DARPA CoABS Program (contract F30602-98-2-0098, A0 G352) for the research presented in this paper and the anonymous reviewers for their constructive suggestions.

References

Cohen, P. R., and Levesque, H. J. 1990a. Intention is Choice with Commitment. *Artificial Intelligence*, 42(3).

Cohen, P. R., and Levesque, H. J. 1990b. Performatives in a rationally based speech act theory. In *Proceedings of the 28th Annual Meeting of the Association for Computational Linguistics*, Pittsburgh, Pennsylvania.

Cohen, P. R., and Levesque, H. J. 1991. Confirmations and Joint Action. In *Proceedings of the 12th International Joint Conference on Artificial Intelligence*, San Mateo, Calif.

FIPA Specification. 1997. http://www.fipa.org/

Grosz, B. J. and Kraus, S. 1996. Collaborative plans for complex group action. *Artificial Intelligence*, 86(2).

Halpern, Y. J., and Moses, Y. 1992. A Guide to Completeness and Complexity for Modal Logics of Knowledge and Belief. *Artificial Intelligence*, 54(3).

Labrou, Y., and Finin, T. 1997. Semantics and Conversations for an Agent Communication Language, In *Proceedings of the 15th International Joint Conference on Artificial Intelligence*, Nagoya, Japan.

Singh, M. P. 1993. Intentions for Multi-agent Systems. *MCC Technical Report*, KBNL-086-93.

Smith, I. A., and Cohen, P. R. 1996. Toward a Semantics for an Agent Communications Language Based on Speech-Acts. *Proceedings of the Annual Meeting of the American Association for Artificial Intelligence*, Portland, Oregon.

Smith, I.A.; Cohen, P.R.; Bradshaw, J. M.; Greaves, M.; and Holmback, H. 1998. Designing conversation policies using joint intention theory. *International Joint Conference on Multi-Agent Systems*, Paris, France.

Werner, E. 1989. Cooperating agents: A unified theory of communication and social structure, in *Distributed Artificial Intelligence*, Gasser, L., and Huhns, M.N. (eds.), Morgan Kaufmann, Publishers, Inc., San Mateo, California.

Deliberation in Equilibrium:
Bargaining in Computationally Complex Problems

Kate Larson and Tuomas Sandholm
Department of Computer Science
Washington University
St. Louis, MO 63130-4899
{ksl2, sandholm}@cs.wustl.edu

Abstract

We develop a normative theory of interaction—negotiation in particular—among self-interested computationally limited agents where computational actions are game-theoretically treated as part of an agent's strategy. We focus on a 2-agent setting where each agent has an intractable individual problem, and there is a potential gain from pooling the problems, giving rise to an intractable joint problem. At any time, an agent can compute to improve its solution to its problem, its opponent's problem, or the joint problem. At a deadline the agents then decide whether to implement the joint solution, and if so, how to divide its value (or cost). We present a fully normative model for controlling anytime algorithms where each agent has statistical performance profiles which are optimally conditioned on the problem instance as well as on the path of results of the algorithm run so far. Using this model, we analyze the perfect Bayesian equilibria of the games which differ based on whether the performance profiles are deterministic or stochastic, whether the deadline is known or not, and whether the proposer is known in advance. Finally, we present algorithms for finding the equilibria.

Introduction

Systems, especially on the Internet, are increasingly being used by multiple parties—or software agents that represent them—with their own preferences. This invalidates the traditional assumption that a central designer controls the behavior of all system components. The system designer can only control the *mechanism* (rules of the game), while each agent chooses its own *strategy*. The economic efficiency that a system yields depends on the agents' strategies. So, to develop a system that leads to desirable outcomes, the designer has to make sure that each agent is incented to behave in the desired way. This can be achieved by analyzing the game using the *Nash equilibrium* solution concept from game theory (or its refinements): no agent is motivated to deviate from its strategy given that the others do not deviate (Kreps 1990).

However, the equilibrium for rational agents does not generally remain an equilibrium for computationally limited agents.[1] This leaves a potentially hazardous gap in game theory as well as automated negotiation because computationally limited agents are not incented to behave in the desired way. This paper presents a framework and first steps toward filling that gap.

In this paper we begin to develop a theory of interaction—negotiation in particular—where computation actions are treated as part of an agent's strategy. We study a 2-agent bargaining setting where at any time, the agent can compute to improve its solution to its own problem, its solution to the opponent's problem, or its solution to the joint problem where the tasks and resources of the two agents are pooled. The bargaining occurs over whether or not to use a solution to the joint problem, and how to divide the associated value (or cost). This is the first piece of research that seriously treats computational actions game-theoretically.

Early on, it was recognized that humans have bounded rationality, e.g., due to cognitive limitations, so they do not act rationally as economic theory would predict (Simon 1955). He noted that there was a difference in the ways firms *do* behave as opposed to how they *should* rationally behave.

Since then, considerable work has focused on developing *normative* models that prescribe how a computationally limited agent *should* behave. Most of those methods resort to simplifying assumptions such as myopic deliberation control (Russell & Wefald 1991; Baum & Smith 1997), conditioning the deliberation control on hand-picked features, assuming that an anytime algorithm's future performance does not depend on the run on that instance so far (Horvitz 1987; Boddy & Dean 1994; Zilberstein & Russell 1996; Zilberstein, Charpillet, & Chassaing 1999; Horvitz 1997) or that performance is conditioned on quality so far but not the path (Hansen & Zilberstein 1996), resorting to asymptotic notions of bounded optimality (Russell & Subramanian 1995), or focusing on decision problems only (Sandholm & Lesser 1994).

While such simplifications can be acceptable in single-agent settings as long as the agent performs reasonably well, any deviation from full normativity can be catastrophic in games. If the designer cannot guar-

---

[1] In the relatively rare settings where the incentives can be designed so that each agent is motivated to use the desired strategy independent of what others do (dominant strategy equilibrium), a rational agent is best off maintaining its strategy even if some other agents are unable to act rationally, e.g. due to computational limitations.

antee that the strategy (including deliberation actions) is the best strategy that an agent can use, there is a risk that an agent is incented to use some other strategy. Even if that strategy happens to be "close" to the desired one, the social outcome may be far from desirable. Therefore, this paper introduces a fully normative deliberation control method. Each agent uses all the information it has available to control its computation, including conditioning on the problem instance and the path of solutions found on the run so far.

Game theorists have also realized the significance of computational limitations, but the models that address this issue have mostly analyzed how complex it is to compute the rational strategies (rather than the computation impacting the strategies) (Koller, Megiddo, & Stengel 1996), or memory limitations in keeping track of history in repeated games (Rubinstein 1998), or limited uniform-depth lookahead capability in repeated games (Jehiel 1995), or showing that allowing the choice between taking one computation action or not undoes the dominant strategy property in a Vickrey auction (Sandholm 1996). On the other hand, in this paper, the limited rationality stems from the complexity of each agent's optimization problem (each agent has a computer of finite speed, some anytime algorithm which might not be perfect, and finite time), a setting which is ubiquitous in practice.[2]

In the next section we present a quantitative model for controlling computation where each agent has statistical performance profiles of its anytime algorithm, which are optimally conditioned on the problem instance as well as on the path of results of the algorithm run so far. We also present the bargaining settings we are studying. We then proceed to analyze noncooperative equilibria and present algorithms that agents can use to determine how to direct their computation in equilibrium and how to bargain after the deliberation. In other words, these algorithms determine each agent's best-response deliberation strategy and bargaining strategy. The paper ends with a discussion of future research directions.

An Example Application

To make the presentation more concrete, we now discuss an example domain where our methods are needed. Consider a distributed vehicle routing problem (Sandholm & Lesser 1997) with two geographically dispersed dispatch centers that are self-interested companies. Each center is responsible for certain tasks (deliveries) and has a certain set of resources (vehicles) to take care of them. So each agent—representing a dispatch center—has its own vehicles and delivery tasks. Each agent's *individual problem* is to minimize transportation costs (driven mileage) while still making all of its deliveries. This problem is $\mathcal{NP}$-complete.

There is a potential for savings in driven mileage by pooling the agents' tasks and resources—e.g., because one agent may be able to handle some of the other's tasks with less driving due to adjacency. The objective in this *joint problem* is to again minimize driven mileage. This problem is again $\mathcal{NP}$-complete.

The General Setting

The distributed vehicle routing problem is only one example problem where the methods of this paper are needed. In general, they are needed in any 2-agent setting where each agent has an intractable *individual problem*, and there is a potential savings from pooling the problems, giving rise to an intractable *joint problem*. We also assume that the value of any solution to an agent's individual problem is not affected by what solution the other agent uses to its individual problem.

Applications with these characteristics are ubiquitous, including transportation as discussed above, manufacturing (where two potentially interacting companies need to construct their manufacturing plans and schedules), electric power negotiation between a custom provider and an industrial consumer (where the participants need to construct their production and consumption schedules), to name just a few.

In order to determine the gain generated by pooling instead of each agent operating individually, agents need to compute solutions to both agent's individual problems as well as to the joint problem. Say that the agents have anytime algorithms that can be used to solve (vehicle routing) problems so that some feasible solution is available whenever the algorithm is terminated, and the solution improves as more computation time is allocated to the algorithm.

By computing on the joint problem, an agent reduces the amount of time it has for computing on its individual problem. This may increase the joint value to the agents (reduce the sum of the agents' costs), but makes this agent's fallback position worse when it comes to bargaining over how the joint value should be divided between the two agents. Also, if one agent is computing on the joint problem, would it not be better for the other agent to compute on something different so as not to waste computation? In this paper we present a model where each agent strategically decides on how to use its limited computation in order to maximize its own expected payoff in such settings.

The Model

Let there be two agents, 1 and 2, each with its own *individual problem*. They also have the possibility to pool, giving rise to a *joint problem*. We assume that time is discretized into T units and each computational step takes one time unit.

---

[2]The same *source* of complexity has been addressed (Sandholm & Lesser 1997), but that paper only studied outcomes, not the process or the agents' strategies. It was also assumed that the algorithm's performance is deterministically known in advance. Finally, the agents had costly but unlimited computation, while in this paper the agents have free but limited computation.

Normative Control of Deliberation

Each agent has an anytime algorithm that has a feasible solution available whenever it is terminated, and improves the solution as more computation time is allocated to the problem. Let $v^1(t)$ be the value of the solution to agent 1's individual problem after computing on it for t time steps. Similarly, $v^2(t)$ is the value of the solution to agent 2's individual problem after computing on it for t time steps. Finally, $v^{1\cup 2}(t)$ is the value of the solution to the joint problem after computing on it for t time steps.

The agents have statistical performance profiles that describe how their anytime algorithms increase v^1, v^2, and $v^{1\cup 2}$ as a function of the allocated computation time. As will be discussed later, each agent uses this information to decide how to allocate its computation at every step of the game.

We index the problem (agent 1's, agent 2's, and the joint) by z, $z \in \{1, 2, 1 \cup 2\}$. For each z there is a performance profile tree $\mathcal{T}^z$, representing the fact that an agent can condition its algorithm's performance profile on the problem instance. Figure 1 exemplifies one such tree. Each depth of the tree corresponds to an

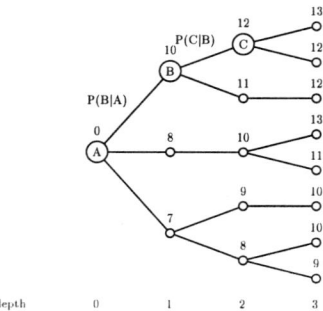

Figure 1: *A performance profile tree.*

amount of time t spent on running the algorithm on that problem. Each node at depth t of the tree represents a possible solution quality (value), v^z, that is obtained by running the algorithm for t time steps on that problem. There may be several nodes at a depth since the algorithm may reach different solution qualities for a given amount of computation depending on the problem instance (and if it is a stochastic algorithm, also on random numbers). We assume that the solution quality in the performance profile tree, $\mathcal{T}^1$, of agent 1's individual problem is discretized into a finite number of levels. Similarly, the solution quality in $\mathcal{T}^2$ is discretized into a finite number of levels, as is the solution quality in $\mathcal{T}^{1\cup 2}$.

Each edge in the tree is associated with the probability that the child is reached in the next computation step given that the parent has been reached. This allows one to compute the probability of reaching any particular future node in the tree given any node, by multiplying the probabilities on the path between the nodes. If there is no path, the probability is 0.

The tree is constructed by collecting statistical data from previous runs of the algorithm on different problem instances.[3] Each run is represented as a path in the tree. As a run proceeds along a path in the tree, the frequency of each edge of that path is incremented, and the frequencies at the nodes on the path are normalized to obtain probabilities. If the run leads to a value for which there is no node in the tree, the node is generated and an edge is inserted from the previous node to it.

Definition 1 *The state of deliberation of agent 1 at time step t is*
$$\theta_1^t = \langle n_1^1, n_1^2, n_1^{1\cup 2}\rangle$$
where n_1^1, n_1^2, and $n_1^{1\cup 2}$ are the nodes where agent 1 is currently in each of the three performance profile trees. The state of deliberation for agent 2 is defined analogously.

We denote by time(n) the depth of node n in the performance profile tree. In other words, time(n) is the number of computation steps used to reach node n. So, time(n_1^1) + time(n_1^2) + time($n_1^{1\cup 2}$) = t. We denote by $V(n)$ the value of node n.

In practice it is unlikely that an agent knows the solution quality for every time allocation without actually doing the computation. Rather, there is uncertainty about how the solution value improves over time. Our performance profile tree allows us to capture this uncertainty. The tree can be used to determine $P(v^z|t)$ denoting the probability that running the algorithm for t time steps produces a solution of value v^z.

Unlike previous methods for performance profile based deliberation control, our performance profile tree directly supports conditioning on the *path* of solution quality so far.[4] The performance profile tree that applies given a path of computation so far is simply the subtree rooted at the current node n. We denote this subtree by $\mathcal{T}^z(n)$. If an agent is at a node n with value v, then when estimating how much added deliberation would increase the solution value, the agent need only consider paths that emanate from node n. The probability, $P_n(n')$, of reaching a particular future node n' in $\mathcal{T}^z(n)$ given that the current node is n is simply the product of the probabilities on the path from n to n'. Similarly, given that the current node is n, the expected solution quality after allocating t more time steps to this problem is
$$\sum_{\{n'|n' \text{ is a node in } \mathcal{T}^z(n) \text{ with depth } t\}} P_n(n') \cdot V(n')$$

---

[3] The more finely solution quality and time are discretized, the more accurate deliberation control is possible. However, with more refined discretization, the number of possible runs increases (it is $O(m^T)$ where m is the number of levels of solution quality), so more runs need to be seen to populate the space. Furthermore, the space should be populated densely to get good probability estimates on the edges of the performance profile trees.

[4] Our results apply directly to the case where the conditioning on the path is based on other solution features in addition to solution quality. For example, in a scheduling problem, the distribution of slack can significantly predict how well an iterative refinement algorithm can further improve the solution.

This can be easily computed using depth-first-search with a depth limit t in $\mathcal{T}^z(n)$.

Computation plays several strategic roles in the game. First, it improves the solution that is available—for any one of the three problems. Second, it resolves some of the uncertainty about what future computation steps will yield. Third, it gives information about what solution qualities the opponent has encountered and can expect. This helps in estimating what solution quality the other agent has available on any of the three problems. It also helps in estimating what computations the other agent might have done and might do. Therefore, in equilibrium, an agent may want to allocate computation on its individual problem, the joint problem, and even on the opponent's problem. We will show how agents use the performance profile trees to handle these considerations.

Special Case: Deterministic Performance Profiles In a deterministic performance profile, $v^z(t) \in \Re$ is known for all t. In this setting, the tree that represents the performance profile has only one path. Before using any computation, the agents can determine what the value will be after any number of computation steps devoted to any one of the three problems. So, computation does not provide any information about the expected results of future computations. Also, computation does not provide any added information about the performance profiles, which could be used to estimate the other agent's computational actions.

In settings where the performance profiles are not deterministic, we assume that the agents have the same performance profile trees $\mathcal{T}^1$, $\mathcal{T}^2$, and $\mathcal{T}^{1\cup 2}$ which are common knowledge. One scenario where the agents have the same performance profile trees is where the agents use the same algorithm and have seen the same training instances. This is arguably roughly the case in practice if the parties have been solving the same type of instances over time, and the algorithms have evolved through experimentation and publication. In settings where the performance profiles are deterministic, all of our results go through even if the agents have different performance profile trees $\mathcal{T}_1^1$, $\mathcal{T}_1^2$, $\mathcal{T}_1^{1\cup 2}$, $\mathcal{T}_2^1$, $\mathcal{T}_2^2$, and $\mathcal{T}_2^{1\cup 2}$—assuming that these are common knowledge.

Bargaining

At some point in time, T, there is a deadline at which time both agents must stop deliberating and enter the bargaining round. The agents perform their computational actions in parallel with no communication between them until the deadline is reached. Call the value of the solution computed by that time by agent i to agent 1's problem v_i^1, to agent 2's problem v_i^2, and to the joint problem $v_i^{1\cup 2}$. At that time, the agents decide whether to pool or not, and in the former case they also have to decide how to divide the value of the solution to the joint problem. These decisions are made via bargaining. One agent, α, $\alpha \in \{1,2\}$, makes a take-it-or-leave-it offer, x_α^o, to the other agent, β, about how much agent β's payoff will be if they pool. Agent β can then accept or reject. If agent β accepts, the agents pool and use agent α's solution to the joint problem. Agent β's payoff is x_α^o as proposed and agent α gets the rest of the value of the solution: $v_\alpha^{1\cup 2} - x_\alpha^o$. If agent β rejects, both agents implement their own computed solutions to their own individual problems, in which case agent 1's payoff is v_1^1 and agent 2's payoff is v_2^2.

Before the deadline, the agents may or may not know who is to make the offer. The probability that agent 1 will be the proposer is P_{prop}, and this is common knowledge. When agents reach the bargaining stage, each agent's strategy is captured by an *offer-accept vector*. An offer-accept vector for agent 1 is $OA_1 = (x_1^o, x_1^a) \in \mathbf{R}^2$, where x_1^o is the amount that agent 1 would offer if it had to make the proposal, and x_1^a is the minimum value it would accept if agent 2 made the proposal. The offer-accept vector for agent 2 is defined similarly.

The agents strategies incorporate actions from both parts of the game. For the deliberation part of the game, an agent's strategy is a mapping from the state of deliberation to the next deliberation action (i.e., selecting which solution z, $z \in \{1, 2, 1 \cup 2\}$ to compute another time step on—in words, whether to compute on the agent's own problem, the other agent's problem, or the joint problem). At the deadline, T, each agent has to decide its offer-accept vector. Therefore, the strategy at time T is a mapping from the state of deliberation at time T to an offer-accept vector.

Definition 2 *A strategy, S_1 for agent 1 with deadline T is*
$$S_1 = ((S_1^{D,t})_{t=0}^T, S_1^B)$$
where the deliberation strategy
$$S_1^{D,t} : \theta_1^{t-1} \to \{a^1, a^2, a^{1\cup 2}\}$$
is a mapping from the deliberation state θ_1^{t-1} at time $t-1$ to a deliberation action a^z where a^z is the action of computing one time step on the solution for problem $z \in \{1, 2, 1 \cup 2\}$.

The bargaining strategy $S_1^B : \theta_1^T \to \Re^2$ is a mapping from the final deliberation state to an offer-accept vector (x_1^o, x_1^a). A strategy, S_2, for agent 2 is defined analogously.

Our analysis will also allow *mixed strategies*. A mixed strategy for agent 1 is $S_1 = ((\tilde{S}_1^{D,t})_{t=0}^T, S_1^B)$ where $\tilde{S}_1^{D,t}$ is a mapping from a deliberation state θ_1^t to a probability distribution over the set of deliberation actions $\{a^1, a^2, a^{1\cup 2}\}$. We let p^1 be the probability that an agent takes action a^1, p^2 be the probability that an agent takes action a^2, and therefore, $1 - p^1 - p^2$ is the probability that an agent takes action $a^{1\cup 2}$. It is easy to show that in equilibrium, each agent will use a pure strategy for picking its offer-accept vector [5] (i.e., the

---
[5] This holds whether or not the proposer is known in advance.

agent plays one vector with probability 1), so in the interest of simplifying the notation, we define S_1^B as a pure strategy as before.

Proposer's Expected Payoff

Say that at time T the proposing agent, α, is in deliberation state $\theta_\alpha^T = \langle n_\alpha^1, n_\alpha^2, n_\alpha^{1\cup 2}\rangle$ and the other agent, β, is in deliberation state $\theta_\beta^T = \langle n_\beta^1, n_\beta^2, n_\beta^{1\cup 2}\rangle$. Each agent has a set of beliefs (a probability distribution) over the set of deliberation states in which the other agent may be. If agent α offers agent β value x_α^o, then the expected payoff to agent α is

$$E[\pi_\alpha(\theta_\alpha^T, x_\alpha^o, S_\beta)] = P_a(x_\alpha^o)[V(n_\alpha^{1\cup 2}) - x_\alpha^o] + (1 - P_a(x_\alpha^o))V(n_\alpha^a)$$

where $P_a(x_\alpha^o)$ is the probability that agent β will accept an offer of x_α^o. These probabilities are determined by agent α's beliefs.

We can determine the proposer's expected payoff of following a particular strategy as follows. Assume agent α is following strategy $S_\alpha = ((p^{1,i}, p^{2,i})_{i=1}^T, (x_\alpha^o, x_\alpha^a))$ and agent β is following strategy S_β. At time t, if agent α is in deliberation state θ_α^t, the expected payoff is

$$E[\pi_\alpha(\theta_\alpha^t, ((p^{1,i}, p^{2,i})_{i=t}^T, x_\alpha^o), S_\beta)] =$$
$$p^{1,t} \sum_{\theta_\alpha^{t+1} \in \Theta(\theta_\alpha^t, a^1)} P(\theta_\alpha^{t+1}) E[\pi_\alpha(\theta_\alpha^{t+1}, ((p^{1,i}, p^{2,i})_{i=t+1}^T, x_\alpha^o), S_\beta)]$$
$$+ p^{2,t} \sum_{\theta_\alpha^{t+1} \in \Theta(\theta_\alpha^t, a^2)} P(\theta_\alpha^{t+1}) E[\pi_\alpha(\theta_\alpha^{t+1}, ((p^{1,i}, p^{2,i})_{i=t+1}^T, x_\alpha^o), S_\beta)]$$
$$+ (1 - p^{1,t} - p^{2,t}) \sum_{\theta_\alpha^{t+1} \in \Theta(\theta_\alpha^t, a^{1\cup 2})} P(\theta_\alpha^{t+1}) E[\pi_\alpha(\theta_\alpha^{t+1}, ((p^{1,i}, p^{2,i})_{i=t+1}^T, x_\alpha^o), S_\beta)]$$

where

$\Theta(\theta_\alpha^t, a^z) = \{\theta_\alpha^{t+1} | \theta_\alpha^{t+1} \text{ is reachable from } \theta_\alpha^t \text{ via action } a^i\}$.

Overloading the notation, we denote the expected payoff to agent α from following strategy S_α, given that agent β follows strategy S_β by

$$E[\pi_1(S_\alpha, S_\beta)] \stackrel{\text{def}}{=} E[\pi_\alpha(\theta_\alpha^0, ((p^{1,i}, p^{2,i})_{i=1}^T, S_\beta))]$$

Equilibria and Algorithms

We want to make sure that the strategy that we propose for each agent—and according to which we study the outcome—is indeed the best strategy that the agent has from its self-interested perspective. This makes the system behave in the desired way even though every agent is designed by and represents a different self-interested real-world party. One approach would be to just require that the analysis shows that no agent is motivated to deviate to another strategy given that the other agent does not deviate (i.e., *Nash equilibrium*). We actually place a stronger requirement on our method. We require that at any point in the game, an agent's strategy prescribes optimal actions from that point on, given the other agent's strategy and the agent's beliefs about what has happened so far in the game. We also require that the agent's beliefs are consistent with the strategies. This type of equilibrium is called a *perfect Bayesian equilibrium* (PBE) (Kreps 1990).

An agent's offer-accept vector is affected by the solutions that it computes and also what it believes the other agent has computed for solutions. The *fallback* value of an agent is the value it obtained for the solution to its own problem. An agent will not accept any offer less than its fallback.

In making a proposal, agent α must try to determine agent β's fallback value and then decide whether, by making an acceptable proposal to agent β, agent α's payoff would be greater than or less than its own fallback.[6]

The games differ significantly based on whether the proposer is known in advance or not, as will be discussed in the next sections.

Known Proposer

For an agent that is never going to make an offer, we can prescribe a dominant strategy independent of the statistical performance profiles:

Proposition 1 *If an agent, β, knows that it cannot make a proposal at the deadline T, then it has a dominant strategy of computing only on its own problem, and accepting any offer x_α^o such that $x_\alpha^o \geq V(n)$ where n is the node in the performance profile $\mathcal{T}^\beta$ that agent β has reached at time T. If the performance profile does not flatten before the deadline ($V(n') < V(n)$ for every node n' on the path to n), then this is the unique dominant strategy.*

Proof: In the event that an agreement is not reached, agent β could not have achieved higher payoff than by computing on its individual problem (even if it knows that further computation will not improve its solution). In the event that an agreement is reached, agent β would have been best off by computing so as to maximize the minimal offer it will accept, $V(n_\beta^\beta)$. Since solution quality is nondecreasing in computation time, if agent β deviates and computes t steps on a different problem, then the value of its fallback is $V(n_\beta'^\beta) \leq V(n_\beta^\beta)$ where $\text{time}(n_\beta'^\beta) = \text{time}(n_\beta^\beta) + t$. If $V(n') < V(n)$ for every node n' on the path to n, then this inequality is strict. □

Corollary 1 *In the games where the proposer is known, there exists a pure strategy PBE.*

Proof: By Proposition 1, the receiver of the offer has a dominant strategy. Say the proposer were to use a mixed strategy. In general, every pure strategy that has nonzero probability in a best-response mixed strategy has equal expected payoff (Kreps 1990). Since mixing by the proposer will not affect the receiver's strategy, the proposer might as well use one of the pure strategies in its mix. □

The equilibrium differs based on whether or not the deadline is known, as discussed in the next subsections.

---

[6]Since solution values are discretized, the offer-accept vectors are also from a discrete space.

Known Proposer, Known Deadline In the simplest setting, both the deadline and proposer are common knowledge. Without loss of generality we assume that agent 1 is the proposer. The game differs based on whether the performance profiles are deterministic or stochastic.

`Deterministic Performance Profiles` In an environment where the performance profiles are deterministic, the equilibria can be analytically determined.

Proposition 2 *There exists a PBE where agent 2 will only compute on its own problem, and agent 1 will never split its computation. It will either compute solely on its own problem or solely on the joint problem. The PBE payoffs to the agents are unique, and the PBE is unique unless the performance profile that an agent is computing on flattens, after which time it does not matter where the agent computes since that does not change its payoff or bargaining strategy. The PBEs are also the only Nash equilibria.*

Proof: Let $\eta_1^{1 \cup 2}$ be the node in $\mathcal{T}^{1 \cup 2}$ that agent 1 reaches after allocating all of its computation on the joint problem. Let η_1^1 be the node in $\mathcal{T}^1$ that agent 1 reaches after allocating all of its computation on its own problem. Let η_2^2 be the node in $\mathcal{T}^2$ that agent 2 reaches after allocating all of its computation on its own problem.

By Proposition 1, agent 2 has a dominant strategy to compute on its own solution (unless its performance profile flattens after which time it does not matter where the agent computes since that does not change its payoff). Agent 1's strategies are more complex since they depend on agent 2's final fallback value, $V(\eta_2^2)$, and also on what potential values the joint solution and 1's individual solution may have.

1. **Case 1:** $V(\eta_1^{1 \cup 2}) - V(\eta_2^2) > V(\eta_1^1)$. Agent 2 will accept any offer greater than or equal to $V(n_2^2)$ since that is its fallback. If agent 1 makes an offer that is acceptable to agent 2, then the highest payoff that agent 1 can receive is $V(\eta_1^{1 \cup 2}) - V(\eta_2^2)$. If this value is greater than $V(\eta_1^1)$—i.e., the highest fallback value agent 1 can have—then agent 1 will make an acceptable offer. To maximize the amount it will get from making the offer, agent 1 must compute only on the joint problem. Any deviation from this strategy will result in agent 1 receiving a lesser payoff (and strictly less if its performance profile has not flattened).

2. **Case 2:** $V(\eta_1^{1 \cup 2}) - V(\eta_2^2) < V(\eta_1^1)$. Any acceptable offer that agent 1 makes results in agent 1 receiving a lesser payoff than if it had computed on its own solution solely, and made an unacceptable offer (and strictly less if its performance profile has not flattened). Therefore agent 1 will compute only on its own problem until that performance profile flattens, after which it does not matter where it allocates the rest of its computation.

3. **Case 3:** $V(\eta_1^{1 \cup 2}) - V(\eta_2^2) = V(\eta_1^1)$. By computing only on its own problem, agent 1's payoff is $V(\eta_1^1)$.

By computing only on the joint problem, the payoff is $V(\eta_1^{1 \cup 2}) - V(\eta_2^2)$. These payoffs are equal. However, by dividing the computation across the problems, both payoffs decrease (unless at least one of the two performance profiles has flattened, after which it does not matter where the agent allocates the rest of its computation).

The above arguments also hold for Nash equilibrium. □

`Stochastic Performance Profiles` If the performance profiles are stochastic, determining the equilibrium is more difficult. By Proposition 1, agent 2 has a dominant strategy, S_2, and only computes on its individual problem (if that performance profile has flattened and agent 2 has computed on agent 1's or the joint problem thereafter, this does not change agent 2's fallback, and this is the only aspect of agent 2 that agent 1 cares about).

However, based on the results it has obtained so far, agent 1 may decide to switch the problem on which it is computing—possibly several times. We use a dynamic programming algorithm to determine agent 1's best response to agent 2's strategy. The base case involves looping through all possible deliberation states θ_1^T for agent 1 at the deadline T. Each θ_1^T determines a probability distribution over the set of nodes agent 2 reached by computing T time steps. For any offer x_1^o that agent 1 may make, the probability that agent 2 will accept is

$$P_a(x_1^o) = \sum_{\{n^2 | n^2 \text{in subtree } \mathcal{T}^2(n_1^2) \text{ at depth } T - \text{time}(n_1^2) \text{ s.t. } V(n^2) \le x\}} P(n^2)$$

Using this expression for $P_a(x)$, the best offer, x_1^o, that agent 1 can make to agent 2 is

$$x_1^o(\theta_1^T) = \arg\max_x [E[\pi_1(\theta_1^T, x, S_2)]]$$

For each deliberation state, θ_1^T, we can compute the expected payoff for agent 1, if at time t agent 1 is in deliberation state θ_1^t and then executes the sequence of actions $((a^{z,i})_{i=t}^T, x_1^o(\theta_1^T))$. The expected payoff is

$$E[\pi_1(\theta_1^t, ((a^{z,i})_{i=t}^T, x_1^o), S_2)] =$$
$$\sum P(\theta_1^{t+1}) E[\pi_1(\theta_1^{t+1}, ((a^{z,i})_{i=t+1}^T, x_1^o), S_2)]$$

The sum is over the set $\{\theta_\alpha^{t+1} | \theta_1^{t+1}$ is reachable from θ_1^t via action $a^z\}$. The algorithm works backwards and determines the optimal sequence of actions, $(a^{*,i})_{i=1}^T$, for agent 1. For every time t it solves

$$a^{*t} = \max_a [E[\pi_1(\theta_1^t, ((a, (a^{*i})_{i=t+1}^T), x_1^o), S_2)]]$$

It returns the optimal sequence of actions, $(a^{*i})_{i=1}^T$, and the expected payoff $E[\pi_1(((a^{*i})_{i=1}^T, x_o^1), S_2)]$.

Algorithm 1 *StratFinder1(T)*
For each deliberation state θ_1^T at time T

$$x_o^1(\theta_1^T) \leftarrow \arg\max_x [E[\pi_1(\theta_1^T, x, S_2)]]$$

For time $t = T - 1$ down to 1
  For each deliberation state θ_1^t

$$a^{*t} \leftarrow \max_a [E[\pi_1(\theta_1^t, ((a, (a^{*i})_{i=t+1}^T), x_1^o), S_2)]]$$

Return $(a^{*i})_{i=1}^T$ and $E[\pi_1(((a^{*i})_{i=1}^T, x_o^1), S_2)]$

Proposition 3 *Algorithm 1 correctly computes a PBE strategy for agent 1.*[7] *Assume that the degree of any node in $\mathcal{T}^1$ is at most B^1, the degree of any node in $\mathcal{T}^2$ is at most B^2 and the degree of any node in $\mathcal{T}^{1\cup 2}$ is at most $B^{1\cup 2}$. Algorithm 1 runs in $O((B^1 B^2 B^{1\cup 2})^{T^2})$ time.*

Known Proposer, Unknown Deadline There are situations where agents may not know the deadline. We represent this by a probability distribution $Q = \{q(i)\}_{i=1}^T$ over possible deadlines. Q is assumed to be common knowledge.

Whenever time t is reached but the deadline does not arrive, agents update their beliefs about Q. The new distribution is $Q' = \{q'(i)\}_{i=t}^T$ where $q'(t) = \frac{q(t)}{\sum_{j=t}^T q(j)}$.

`Stochastic Performance Profiles` The algorithm differs from Algorithm 1 in that it considers the probability that the deadline might arrive at any time.

Algorithm 2 *StratFinder2(Q)*
For each deliberation state θ_1^T at time T

$$x_o^1(\theta_1^T) \leftarrow \arg\max_x [E[\pi_1(\theta_1^T, x, S_2)]]$$

For $t = T-1$ down to 1 $q'(t) \leftarrow \frac{q(t)}{\sum_{j=t}^T q(j)}$
For each deliberation state θ_1^t

$$x_o^1(\theta_1^t) \leftarrow \arg\max_x [E[\pi_1(\theta^t, x, S_2)]]$$

$$a^{*t} \leftarrow \max_a [q'tE[\pi_1(\theta_1^t, x_1^o(\theta_1^t), S_2)]$$

$$+(1-q'(t))\max_a [E[\pi_1(\theta_1^t, ((a, (a^{*i})_{i=t+1}^T), x_1^o), S_2)]$$

Return $(a^{*i})_{i=1}^T$ and $E[\pi_1(((a^{*i})_{i=1}^T, x_o^1), S_2)]$

Proposition 4 *Algorithm 2 correctly computes a PBE strategy for agent 1. Assume that the degree of any node in $\mathcal{T}^1$ is at most B^1, the degree of any node in $\mathcal{T}^2$ is at most B^2 and the degree of any node in $\mathcal{T}^{1\cup 2}$ is at most $B^{1\cup 2}$. Algorithm 2 runs in $O((B^1 B^2 B^{1\cup 2})^{T^2})$ time.*

`Deterministic Performance Profiles` When the performance profiles are deterministic, determining an optimal strategy for agent 1 is a special case of Algorithm 2. Since there is no uncertainty as to agent 2's fallback value, agent 1 need never compute on agent 2's problem. Therefore, agent 1 will only be in deliberation states $\langle n_1^1, n_1^2, n_1^{1\cup 2}\rangle$ where $\text{time}(n_1^2) = 0$. Therefore, strategies that include computation actions a^2 need not be considered. This, and the lack of uncertainty in which deliberation state action a leads to, greatly reduce the space of deliberation states to consider. Denote by Γ_1^t any deliberation state of agent 1 where $\text{time}(n_1^1) + \text{time}(n_1^{1\cup 2}) = t$ and $\text{time}(n_1^2) = 0$.

Algorithm 3 *StratFinder3(Q)*
For each deliberation state Γ_1^T at time T

$$x_o^1(\Gamma_1^T) \leftarrow \arg\max_x [E[\pi_1(\Gamma_1^T, x, S_2)]]$$

For $t = T-1$ down to 1 $q'(t) \leftarrow \frac{q(t)}{\sum_{j=t}^T q(j)}$
For each deliberation state Γ_1^t

$$x_o^1(\Gamma_1^t) \leftarrow \arg\max_x [E[\pi_1(\Gamma^t, x, S_2)]]$$

$$a^{*t} \leftarrow \max_a [q'tE[\pi_1(\Gamma_1^t, x_1^o(\Gamma_1^t), S_2)]$$

$$+(1-q'(t))\max_a [E[\pi_1(\Gamma_1^t, ((a, (a^{*i})_{i=t+1}^T), x_1^o), S_2)]$$

Return $(a^{*i})_{i=1}^T$ and $E[\pi_1(((a^{*i})_{i=1}^T, x_o^1), S_2)]$

Proposition 5 *With deterministic performance profiles, Algorithm 3 correctly computes a PBE strategy for agent 1 in $O(T^2)$ time.*

Unknown Proposer

This section discusses the case where the proposer is unknown, but the probability of each agent being the proposer is common knowledge. The deadline may be common knowledge. Alternatively, the deadline is not known but its distribution is common knowledge.

Proposition 6 *There are instances (defined by $\mathcal{T}^1$, $\mathcal{T}^2$, and $\mathcal{T}^{1\cup 2}$) of the game that have a unique mixed strategy PBE, but no pure strategy PBE (not even a pure strategy Nash equilibrium).*

Proof: Let the deadline $T = 2$, and let p be the probability that agent 1 will be the proposer. Consider the following $\mathcal{T}^1$, $\mathcal{T}^2$, and $\mathcal{T}^{1\cup 2}$. Assume that $v^1(1) = v^1(2)$ and $v^2(1) = v^2(2)$. Furthermore, assume that the values satisfy the following constraints:

- $v^{1\cup 2}(1) \geq v^1(1)$
- $v^{1\cup 2}(1) \geq v^2(1)$
- $v^1(1) + v^2(1) \geq v^{1\cup 2}(1)$
- $pv^{1\cup 2}(2) \geq pv^{1\cup 2}(1) + (1-p)v^1(1)$
- $v^1(1) \geq p(v^{1\cup 2}(2) - v^2(1))$
- $pv^2(1) + (1-p)v^{1\cup 2}(1) \geq (1-p)v^{1\cup 2}(2)$
- $(1-p)(v^{1\cup 2}(2) - v^1(1)) \geq v^2(1)$

Agent 1 has two undominated strategies: to compute only on the joint problem, or to compute one step on the joint and one on its individual problem. Agent 2 also has two undominated strategies: to compute only on the joint problem, or to compute one step on the joint and one step on its individual problem. There is no pure strategy equilibrium in this game. However, there is a mixed strategy equilibrium where agent 1 computes on the joint problem only, with probability

$$\gamma = \frac{pv^2(1) - pv^{1\cup 2}(2) + v^1(1)}{pv^2(1) - pv^{1\cup 2}(1) + 2v^1(1) - pv^1(1)}$$

and agent 2 computes on the joint problem only with probability

$$\delta = \frac{v^{1\cup 2}(2) - v^2(1) - pv^{1\cup 2}(2) - v^1(1) + pv^1(1)}{pv^2(1) - v^2(1) + v^{1\cup 2}(1) - pv^{1\cup 2}(1) - v^1(1) + pv^1(1)}$$

$\square$

One approach of solving for PBE strategies is to convert the game into its normal form. There are efficient

---

[7] By keeping track of equally good actions at every step, Algorithms 1, 2, and 3 can return all PBE strategies for agent 1.

algorithms for solving normal form games, but the conversion itself usually incurs an exponential blowup since the number of pure strategies is often exponential in the depth of the game tree. (Koller, Megiddo, & Stengel 1996) suggest representing the game in *sequence form* which is more compact than the normal form representation. They then solve the game using Lemke's algorithm to find Nash equilibria. Their algorithm can be directly used to solve our problem where the proposer is unknown. Their algorithm is guaranteed to find some Nash equilibrium strategies, albeit not all.

Conclusions and Future Research

Noncooperative game-theoretic analysis is necessary to guarantee nonmanipulability of systems that consist of self-interested agents. However, the equilibrium for rational agents does not generally remain an equilibrium for computationally limited agents. This leaves a potentially hazardous gap in theory. This paper presented a framework and the first steps toward filling that gap.

We studied a setting where each agent has an intractable optimization problem, and the agents can benefit from pooling their problems and solving the joint problem. We presented a fully normative model of deliberation control that allows agents to condition their projections on the problem instance and path of solutions seen so far. Using that model, we solved the equilibrium of the bargaining game. This is, to our knowledge, the first piece of research to treat deliberation actions strategically via noncooperative game-theoretic analysis.

In games where the agents know which one gets to make a take-it-or-leave-it offer to the other, the receiver of the offer has a dominant strategy of computing on its own problem, independent of the algorithm's statistical performance profiles. It follows that these games have pure strategy equilibria. In equilibrium, the proposer can switch multiple times between computing on its own, the other agent's, and the joint problem. The games differ based on whether or not the deadline is known and whether the performance profiles are deterministic or stochastic. We presented algorithms for computing a pure strategy equilibrium in each of these variants. For games where the proposer is not known in advance, we use a general algorithm for finding a mixed strategy equilibrium in a 2-person game. This generality comes at the cost of potentially being slower than our algorithms for the other cases.

This area is filled with promising future research possibilities. We plan to extend this work to more than two agents, to settings where the agents have algorithms with different performance profiles, to games where computation is costly instead of limited, and games where bargaining is allowed amidst computation, not just after it. In such settings, the offers and rejections along the way signal about the agents' computation strategies, the results of their computations so far, and what can be expected from further computation.

Acknowledgments

This material is based upon work supported by the National Science Foundation under CAREER Award IRI-9703122, and Grant IIS-9800994.

References

Baum, E. B., and Smith, W. D. 1997. A Bayesian approach to relevance in game playing. *Artificial Intelligence* 97(1–2):195–242.

Boddy, M., and Dean, T. 1994. Deliberation scheduling for problem solving in time-constrained environments. *Artificial Intelligence* 67:245–285.

Hansen, E. A., and Zilberstein, S. 1996. Monitoring the progress of anytime problem-solving. In *AAAI*, 1229–1234.

Horvitz, E. 1987. Reasoning about beliefs and actions under computational resource constraints. In *3rd Workshop on Uncertainty in AI*, 429–444. Seattle.

Horvitz, E. J. 1997. Models of continual computation. In *AAAI*, 286–293.

Jehiel, P. 1995. Limited horizon forecast in repeated alternate games. *J. of Economic Theory* 67:497–519.

Koller, D.; Megiddo, N.; and Stengel, B. 1996. Efficient computation of equilibria for extensive two-person games. *Games and Economic Behavior* 14(2):247–259.

Kreps, D. M. 1990. *A Course in Microeconomic Theory*. Princeton University Press.

Rubinstein, A. 1998. *Modeling Bounded Rationality*. MIT Press.

Russell, S., and Subramanian, D. 1995. Provably bounded-optimal agents. *Journal of Artificial Intelligence Research* 1:1–36.

Russell, S., and Wefald, E. 1991. *Do the right thing: Studies in Limited Rationality*. The MIT Press.

Sandholm, T., and Lesser, V. R. 1994. Utility-based termination of anytime algorithms. In *ECAI Workshop on Decision Theory for DAI Applications*, 88–99. Extended version: UMass Amherst, CS TR 94-54.

Sandholm, T., and Lesser, V. R. 1997. Coalitions among computationally bounded agents. *Artificial Intelligence* 94(1):99–137. Early version in IJCAI-95.

Sandholm, T. 1996. Limitations of the Vickrey auction in computational multiagent systems.*ICMAS*,299–306.

Simon, H. A. 1955. A behavioral model of rational choice. *Quarterly Journal of Economics* 69:99–118.

Zilberstein, S., and Russell, S. 1996. Optimal composition of real-time systems. *Artificial Intelligence* 82(1–2):181–213.

Zilberstein, S.; Charpillet, F.; and Chassaing, P. 1999. Real-time problem solving with contract algorithms. In *IJCAI*, 1008–1013.

An Algorithm for Multi-Unit Combinatorial Auctions

Kevin Leyton-Brown and **Yoav Shoham** and **Moshe Tennenholtz**

Computer Science Department
Stanford University
Stanford, CA 94305

Abstract

We present a novel algorithm for computing the optimal winning bids in a combinatorial auction (CA), that is, an auction in which bidders bid for bundles of goods. All previously published algorithms are limited to single-unit CAs, already a hard computational problem. In contrast, here we address the more general problem in which each good may have multiple units, and each bid specifies an unrestricted number of units desired from each good. We prove the correctness of our branch-and-bound algorithm, which incorporates a specialized dynamic programming procedure. We then provide very encouraging initial experimental results from an implemented version of the algorithm.

Introduction

Auctions are the most widely studied mechanism in the mechanism design literature in economics and game theory (Fudenberg & Tirole 1991). This is due to the fact that auctions are basic protocols, serving as the building blocks of more elaborated mechanisms. Given the wide popularity of auctions on the Internet and the emergence of electronic commerce, where auctions serve as the most popular game-theoretic mechanism, efficient auction design has become a subject of considerable importance for researchers in multi-agent systems (e.g. (Wellman *et al.* 1998; Monderer & Tennenholtz 2000)). Of particular interest are multi-object auctions where the bids name bundles of goods, called combinatorial auctions (CA). For example, imagine an auction of used electronic equipment. A bidder may wish to bid x for a particular TV and y for a particular VCR, but $z \neq x + y$ for the pair. In this example all the goods at auction are different, so we call the auction a single-unit CA. In contrast, consider an electronics manufacturer auctioning 100 identical TVs and 100 identical VCRs. A retailer who wants to buy 70 TVs and 30 VCRs would be indifferent between all bundles having 70 TVs and 30 VCRs. Rather than having to bid on each of the $\binom{100}{70} \cdot \binom{100}{30}$ distinct bundles, she would prefer to place the single bid (price, {70 TVs, 30 VCRs}). We call an auction that allows such a bid a multi-unit CA.

In a combinatorial auction, a seller is faced with a set of price offers for various bundles of goods, and his aim is to allocate the goods in a way that maximizes his revenue. This optimization problem is intractable in the general case, even when each good has only a single unit (Rothkopf, Pekec, & Harstad 1998). Given this computational obstacle, two parallel lines of research have evolved. The first exposes tractable sub-cases of the combinatorial auctions problem. Most of this work has concentrated on identifying bidding restrictions that entail tractable optimization; see (Rothkopf, Pekec, & Harstad 1998; Nisan 1999; Tennenholtz 2000; Vries & Vohra 2000). Also, the case of infinitely divisible goods may be tractably solved by linear programming techniques. The other line of research addresses general combinatorial auctions. Although this is a class of intractable problems, in practice it is possible to address interestingly-large datasets with heuristic methods. It is desirable to do so because many economic situations are best modeled by a general CA, and bidders' strategic behavior is highly sensitive both to changes in the auction mechanism and to approximation of the optimal allocation (Nisan & Ronen 2000). Previous research on the optimization of general CA problems has focused exclusively on the simpler single-unit CA (Fujishima, Leyton-Brown, & Shoham 1999; Sandholm 1999; Lehmann, O'Callaghan, & Shoham 1999)). The general multi-unit problem has not previously been studied, nor have any heuristics for its solution been introduced.

In this paper we present a novel algorithm, termed CAMUS (Combinatorial Auction Multi-Unit Search), to compute the winners in a general, multi-unit combinatorial auction. A generalization and extension of our CASS algorithm for winner determination in single-unit CA's (Fujishima, Leyton-Brown, & Shoham 1999), CAMUS introduces a novel branch-and-bound technique that makes use of several additional procedures. A crucial component of any such technique is a function for computing upper bounds on the optimal outcome. We present such an upper

Copyright ©2000, American Association for Artificial Intelligence (www.aaai.org). All rights reserved.

bound function, tailored specifically to the multi-unit combinatorial auctions problem. We prove that this function gives an upper bound on the optimal revenue, which enables us to show that CAMUS is guaranteed to find optimal allocations. We also introduce dynamic programming techniques to more efficiently handle multi-unit single-good bids. In addition, we present techniques for pre-processing and caching, and heuristics for determining search orderings, further capitalizing on the inherent structure of multi-unit combinatorial auctions.

In the next section we formally define the general multi-unit combinatorial auction problem. In Section 3 we describe CAMUS. In Section 4 we deal in some more detail with some of CAMUS's techniques. Due to lack of space, we cannot present all the CAMUS procedures in detail; however, this section will clarify its most fundamental components. In Section 5 we present our experimental setup and some experimental results.

Problem Definition

We now define the computational problem associated with multi-unit combinatorial auctions.

Let $G = \{g_1, g_2, \ldots, g_m\}$ be a set of goods. Let $q(j)$ denote the number of available units of good j. Consider a set of bids $B = \{b_1, \ldots, b_n\}$. Bid b_i is a pair $(p(b_i), e(b_i))$ where $p(b_i)$ is the price offer of bid b_i, and $e(b_i) = (e(b_i)_1, e(b_i)_2, \ldots, e(b_i)_m)$ where $e(b_i)_j$ is the number of requested units of good j in b_i. If there is no bid requesting k units of good i and 0 units of all goods $j \neq i$ (for some $1 \leq i \leq m$ and some $1 \leq k \leq q(i)$) then, w.l.o.g, we augment B with a bid of price 0 for that bundle. An allocation $\pi \subseteq B$ is a subset of the bids where $\Sigma_{b \in \pi} e(b)_j \leq q(j)$ ($1 \leq j \leq m$). A partial allocation $\pi_{partial}$ is an allocation where, for some j, $\Sigma_{b \in \pi_{partial}} e(b)_j < q(j)$. A full allocation is an allocation that is not partial. Let Π denote the set of all allocations. The multi-unit combinatorial auction problem is the computation of an optimal allocation, that is, $argmax_{\pi \in \Pi} \Sigma_{b \in \pi} p(b)$. In short, we are searching for a subset of the bids that will maximize the seller's revenue while allocating each available unit at most once.

Note that the definition of the optimal allocation assumes that bids are additive–that an auction participant who submits multiple bids may be allocated any number of these bids for a price that equals the sum of each allocated bid's price offer. In some cases, however, a participant may wish to submit two or more bids but require that at most one will be allocated. We permit such additional constraints through the use of *dummy goods*, introduced already in (Fujishima, Leyton-Brown, & Shoham 1999). Dummy goods are normal single-unit goods which do not correspond to actual goods in the auction, but serve to enforce mutual exclusion between bids. For example, if bids b_1 and b_2 referring to bundles $e(b_1)$ and $e(b_2)$ are intended to be mutually exclu-

sive, we add a dummy good d to each bid: $e(b_1)$ becomes $e(b_1) \cup d$, and $e(b_2)$ becomes $e(b_2) \cup d$. Since the good d can be allocated only once, at most one of these bids will be in any allocation. (More generally, it is possible to introduce n-unit dummy goods to enforce the condition that no more than n of a set of bids may be allocated.) While dummy goods increase the expressive power of the bidding language, their use has no impact on the optimization algorithm. Hence, in the remainder of this paper we do not discriminate between dummy goods and real goods, and we assume that all bids are additive.

In the sequel, we will also make use of the following notation. Given an allocation π and a good i, we will denote the total number of units allocated in π, and the total number of units of good i allocated in π, by $units(\pi)$ and $units_i(\pi)$ respectively. In addition $units(total)$ will denote the total number of units over all goods.

Algorithm Definition
Branch-and-Bound Search

Given a set of bids, CAMUS systematically compares the revenue from all full allocations in order to determine the optimal allocation. This comparison is implemented as a depth-first search: we build up a partial allocation one bid at a time. Once we have constructed a full allocation we backtrack, removing the most recently added bid from the partial allocation and adding a new bid instead. Sometimes we can safely *prune* the search tree, backtracking before a full allocation has been constructed. Every time a bid is added to the current allocation, CAMUS computes an estimate of the revenue that will be generated by the unallocated goods which remain. Provided that this estimate function $o()$ always provides an upper bound on the actual revenue, we can prune whenever $p(\pi) + o(\pi) \leq p(\pi_{best})$, where π is the current allocation, $p(\pi) = \Sigma_{b \in \pi} p(b)$ and π_{best} is the best allocation observed so far.

Bins

Bins are partitioned sets of bids. Consider some ordering of the goods. There is one bin for each good, and each bid belongs to the bin corresponding to its lowest-order good. During the search we start in the first bin and consider adding each bid in turn. After adding a bid to our partial allocation we move to the bin corresponding to the lowest-order good with any unallocated units. For example, if the first bid we select requests all units of goods 1, 2 and 4, we next proceed to bin 3. Besides making it easy to avoid consideration of conflicting bids, bins are powerful because they allow the pruning function to consider context without significant computational cost. If bids in bin_i are currently being considered then the pruning function must only take into account bids from $bin_i \ldots bin_m$. Because the partitioning of bids into bins does not change during the search we may compute the pruning information for each bin in a preprocessing step.

Subbins

In the multi-unit setting, we will often need to select more than one bid from a given bin. This leads to the idea of *subbins*. A subbin is a subset of the bids in a bin that is constructed during the search. Since subbins are created dynamically they cannot provide precomputed contextual information; rather, they facilitate the efficient selection of multiple bids from a given bin. Every time we add a bid to our partial allocation we create a new subbin containing the next set of bids to consider. If the search moves to a new bin, the new subbin is generated from the new bin by removing all bids that conflict with the current partial allocation. If the search remains in the same bin, the new subbin is created from the current subbin by removing conflicting bids as above, and additionally: if $bid_1, bid_2, \ldots, bid_i$ is the ordered set of elements in the current subbin and bid_j is the bid that was just chosen, then we remove all $bid_k, k \leq j$. In this way we consider all combinations of non-conflicting bids in each bin, rather than all permutations.

Dominated Bids

Some bids may be removed from consideration in a polynomial-time preprocessing step. For each pair of bids (b_1, b_2) where both name the same goods but $p(b_1) \geq p(b_2)$ and $e(b_1)_j \leq e(b_2)_j$ for every good j, we may remove b_2 from the list of bids to be considered during the search, as b_2 is never preferable to b_1 (hence we say that b_1 *dominates* b_2). However, it is possible that an optimal allocation contains both b_1 and b_2. For this reason we store b_2 in a secondary data structure associated with b_1, and consider adding it to an allocation only after adding b_1.

Dynamic Programming

Singleton bids (that is, bids that name units from only one good) deserve special attention. These bids will generally be among the most computationally expensive to consider– the number of nodes to search after adding a very short bid is nearly the same as the number of nodes to search after skipping the bid, because a short bid allocates few units and hence conflicts with few other bids. Unfortunately, we expect that singleton bids will be quite common in a variety of real-world multi-unit CA's. CAMUS simplifies the problem of singleton bids by applying a polynomial-time dynamic programming technique as a preprocessing step. We construct a vector $singleton_g$ for each good g, where each element of the vector is a set of singleton bids naming only good g. $singleton_g(j)$ evaluates to the revenue-maximizing set of singleton bids totaling j units of good g. This frees us from having to consider singleton bids individually; instead, we consider only elements of the singleton vector and treat these elements as atomic bids during the search. Also, there is never a need to add more than one element from each singleton vector. To see why, imagine that we add both $singleton_g(j)$ and $singleton_g(k)$ to our partial allocation. These two elements may have bids in common, and additionally there may be singleton bids with more than $max(j,k)$ elements that would not conflict with our partial allocation but that we have not considered. Clearly, we would be better off adding the single element $singleton_g(j+k)$.

Caching

Consider a partial allocation π_1 that is reached during the search phase. If the search proceeds beyond π_1 then $o(\pi_1)$ was not sufficiently small to allow us to backtrack. Later in the search we may reach an allocation π_2 which, by combining different bids, covers exactly the same number of units of the same goods as π_1. CAMUS incorporates a mechanism for caching the results of the search beyond π_1 to generate a better estimate for the revenue given π_2 than is given by $o(\pi_2)$. (Since π_1 and π_2 do not differ in the units of goods that remain, $o(\pi_1) = o(\pi_2)$.) Consider all the allocations extending π_1 upon consideration of which the algorithm backtracked, denoted $s_1, s_2, \ldots, s_f$. When we backtracked at each s_i we did so because $p(s_i) + o(s_i) \leq \pi_{best}$, as explained above. It follows that $max_i(p(s_i) + o(s_i))$ is an overestimate of the revenue attainable beyond π_1, and that it is a smaller overestimate than $o(\pi_1)$ (if it were not, we would have backtracked at π_1 instead). Since in general $p(\pi_1) \neq p(\pi_2)$, we cache the value $max_i(p(s_i) + o(s_i)) - p(\pi_1)$ and backtrack when $p(\pi_2) + cache(\pi_2) \leq p(\pi_{best})$. Our cache is implemented as a hash table, since caching is only beneficial to the overall search if lookup time is inconsequential. A consequence of this choice of data structure is that cache data may sometimes be overwritten; we overwrite an old entry in the cache when the search associated with the new entry examined more nodes. Even when we do overwrite useful data the error is not catastrophic, however: in the worst case we must simply search a subtree that we might otherwise have pruned.

Heuristics

Two ordering heuristics are used to improve CAMUS's performance. First, we must determine an ordering of the goods; that is, which good corresponds to the first bin, which corresponds to the second, etc. For each good i we compute $score_i = \frac{numbids_i \cdot q(i)}{avgunits_i}$, where $numbids_i$ is the number of bids that request good i and $avgunits_i$ is the average number of *total* units (i.e., not just units of good i) requested by these bids. We designate the lowest-order good as the good with the lowest score, then we recalculate the score for the remaining goods and repeat. The intuition behind this heuristic is as follows:

- We want to minimize the number of bids in low-order bins, to minimize early branching and thus to make each individual prune more effective.

- We want to minimize the number of units of goods corresponding to low-order bins, so that we will more quickly move beyond the first few bins. As a result, the pruning function will be able to take into account more contextual information.

- We want to maximize the total number of units requested by bids in low-order bins. Taking these bids moves us more quickly towards the leaves of the search tree, again providing the pruning function with more contextual information.

Our second heuristic determines the ordering of bids within bins. Given current partial allocation π, we sort bids in a given bin in descending order of $score(b_j)$, where $score(b_j) = \frac{p(b_j)}{units(b_j)} + o(\pi \cup b_j)$. The intuition behind this heuristic is that the average price per unit of bid_j is a measure of how promising the bid is, while the pruning overestimate for $o(\pi \cup bid_j)$ is an estimate of how promising the unallocated units are, given the partial allocation. This heuristic helps CAMUS to find good allocations quickly, improving anytime performance and also increasing π_{best}, making pruning more effective. Because the pruning overestimate depends on π, this ordering is performed dynamically rather than as a pre-processing step.

CAMUS Outline

Based on the above, it is now possible to give an outline of the CAMUS algorithm:

- Process dominated bids.

- Determine an ordering on the goods, according to the good-ordering heuristic.

- Using the dynamic programming technique, determine the optimal combination of singleton bids totaling $1\ldots q(j)$ for each good j.

- Partition all non-singleton bids into bins, according to the good ordering.

- Precompute pruning information for each bin.

- Set $i = 1$ and $\pi = \{\}$.

- Recursive entry point:
  - For $j = 1 \ldots$ number of bids in the current subbin of bin_i.
    * $\pi = \pi \cup bid_j$.
    * If $(p(\pi) + cache(\pi) \leq p(\pi_{best}))$ backtrack.
    * If $(p(\pi) + o(\pi) \leq p(\pi_{best}))$ backtrack.
    * If $(units(\pi) = units(total))$ record π if it is the best; backtrack.
    * Set i to the index of the lowest-order good in π where $units_i(\pi) < q(i)$. (i may or may not change)
    * Construct a new subbin based on the previous subbin of bin_i (which is bin_i itself if i changed above):
      · Include all bid_k from current subbin, where $k > j$.
      · Include all dominated bids associated with bid_j.
      · Include $singleton_i(q(i) - units_i(\pi))$.
      · Sort the subbin according to the subbin-ordering heuristic.
      · Recurse to the recursive entry point, above, and search this new subbin.
    * $\pi = \pi - bid_j$.
  - End For

- Return the optimal allocation: π_{best}.

CAMUS procedures: a closer look

In this section we examine two of CAMUS's fundamental procedures more formally. Additional details will be presented in our full paper.

Pruning

In this subsection we explain the implementation of CAMUS's pruning function and demonstrate that it is guaranteed not to underestimate the revenue attainable given a partial allocation. Consider a point in the search where we have constructed some partial allocation π. The task of our pruning function is to give an upper bound on the optimal revenue attainable from the unallocated items, using the remaining bids (i.e., the bids that may be encountered during the remainder of the search). Hence, in the sequel when we refer to goods, the number of units of a good and bids, we refer to what remains at our point in the search.

First, we provide an intuitive overview. For every (remaining) good j we will calculate a value $v(j)$. Simplifying slightly, this value is the largest average price per unit of all the (remaining) bids requesting units of good j that do not conflict with π, multiplied by the number of (remaining) units of j. The sum of $v(j)$ values for all goods is an upper bound on optimal revenue because it relaxes the constraint that the bids in the optimal allocation may not conflict.

More formally, let $G = \{g_1, g_2, \ldots, g_m\}$ be a set of goods. Let $q'(j)$ denote the number of available units of good j. Consider a set of bids $B = \{b_1, \ldots, b_n\}$. Bid b_i is associated with a pair $(p(b_i), e(b_i))$ where $p(b_i)$ is the price offer of bid b_i, and $e(b_i) = (e(b_i)_1, e(b_i)_2, \ldots, e(b_i)_m)$ where $e(b_i)_j$ is the requested number of units of good j in b_i. For each bid b_i, let $a(b_i) = \frac{p(b_i)}{\Sigma_{1 \leq j \leq m} e(b_i)_j}$ be the average price per unit of bid b_i. Notice that the average price per unit may change dramatically from bid to bid, and it is a non-trivial notion; our technique will work for any arbitrary average price per unit. Let $L(j)$ be a sorted list of the bids that refer to non-zero units of good j; the list is sorted in a monotonically decreasing manner according to the a_i's. Let $|L(j)|$ denote the number of elements in $L(j)$, and let $L(j)_k$ denote the k-th element of $L(j)$.

$v(j)$ is determined by the following algorithm:

Let $v(j):=0$;
Let $m(j):=0$;
For $i := 1$ to $|L(j)|$ do
if $m(j) < q'(j)$ then
$\{$let $d := min(e(L(j)_i)_j, q(j) - m(j)); m(j) = m(j) + d; v(j) = v(j) + a(L(j)_i) \cdot d\}$

Theorem 1 *Let $B^o = \{b_1^o, b_2^o, \ldots, b_s^o\}$ be the bids in an optimal allocation. Then, $R^o = \Sigma_{b \in B^o} p(b) \leq \Sigma_{1 \leq j \leq m} v(j)$.*

Sketch of proof: Consider the bid $b^o \in B^o$. Then, $p(b^o) = \Sigma_{1 \leq j \leq m} a(b^o) \cdot e(b^o)_j$. Hence, $R^o = \Sigma_{b \in B^o} p(b) = \Sigma_{b \in B^o} \Sigma_{1 \leq j \leq m} a(b) \cdot e(b)_j$. By changing the order of summation we get that $R^o = \Sigma_{1 \leq j \leq m} \Sigma_{b \in B^o} a(b) \cdot e(b)_j$. Notice that, given a particular j, the contribution of bid b to $\Sigma_{b \in B^o} a(b) \cdot e(b)_j$ is $a(b) \cdot e(b)_j$. Recall now that $v(j)$ has been constructed from the set of all bids that refer to good j by choosing the maximal available units of good j from the bids in $L(j)$, where these bids are sorted according to the average price per unit of good. Hence, we get $v(j) \geq \Sigma_{b \in B^o} a(b) \cdot e(b)_j$. Given that the above holds for every good j, this implies that $\Sigma_{1 \leq j \leq m} v(j) \geq \Sigma_{b \in B^o} p(b)$, as requested.

The above theorem is the central tool for proving the following theorem:

Theorem 2 *CAMUS is complete: it is guaranteed to find the optimal allocation in a multi-unit combinatorial auction problem.*

Pre-Processing of Singletons

In this subsection we explain the construction of the $singleton_g$ vector described above, and demonstrate that $singleton_g(j)$ is the revenue-maximizing set of singleton bids for good g that request a total not exceeding j units.

Let $b_1, b_2, \ldots, b_l$ be bids for a single good g, where the total number of available units of good g is q. Let $p(b_i)$ and $e(b_i)$ be the price offer and the quantity requested by b_i, respectively. Our aim is to compute the optimal selection of b_i's in order to allocate k units of good g, for $1 \leq k \leq q$. Consider a two dimensional grid of size $[1 \ldots l] \times [1 \ldots q]$ where the (i,j)-th entry, denoted by $U(i,j)$, is the optimal allocation of j units considering only bids $b_1, b_2, \ldots, b_i$. The value of $U(i,j)$, denoted by $V(i,j)$, is the sum of the price offers of the bids in $U(i,j)$. $U(1,j)$ will be b_1 if b_1 requests no more than j units, and otherwise will be the empty set. Now we can define $U(i,j)$ recursively:

1. $e(b_i) > j$: $U(i,j) = U(i-1,j)$;

2. $e(b_i) = j$: if $p(b_i) > V(i-1,j)$ then $U(i,j) = b_i$. Else $U(i,j) = U(i-1,j)$.

3. $e(b_i) < j$: if $V(i-1,j) \geq p(b_i) + V(i-1, j - e(b_i))$ then $U(i,j) = U(i-1,j)$. Else $U(i,j) = b_i \cup U(i-1, j - e(b_i))$.

This dynamic programming procedure is polynomial, and yields the desired result; the optimal allocation of k units is given by $U(l,k)$. Set $singleton_g(k) = U(l,k), 1 \leq k \leq q$.

Experimental results

Unfortunately, no real-world data exists to describe how bidders will behave in general multi-unit combinatorial auctions, precisely because the determination of winners in such auctions was previously unfeasible. We have therefore tested CAMUS on sets of bids drawn from a random distribution. We created bids as follows, varying the parameters num_{goods} and num_{bids}, and fixing the parameters $units_{max} = 5$, $avgprice_{base} = 50$, $avgprice_{var} = 25$, $prob_1 = 0.8$, $prob_2 = 0.65$, $price_{var} = 0.5$:

1. Set the number of units that exist for each good:

   (a) For each good i, randomly choose $units_i$ from the range $[1 \ldots units_{max}]$.

   (b) If $\Sigma_i units_i \neq \frac{num_{goods} \Sigma_{j=1}^{units_{max}} j}{units_{max}}$ (the expectation on $\Sigma_i units_i$) then go to (a). This ensures that each trial involves the same total number of units.

2. Set an average price for each good: $avgprice_i$ is drawn uniformly randomly from the range $[avgprice_{base} - avgprice_{var} \ldots avgprice_{base} + avgprice_{var}]$.

3. Select the number of goods in the bid. This number is drawn from a decay distribution:

   (a) Randomly choose a good that has not already been added to this bid

   (b) With probability $prob_1$, if more goods remain then go to (a)

4. Select the number of units of each good, according to another decay distribution:

   (a) Add a unit

   (b) With probability $prob_2$, if more units remain then go to (a)

5. Set a price for this bid: $price = rand(1 - price_{var}, 1 + price_{var}) \cdot \Sigma_{i \in bid}(avgprice_i \cdot units_i)$

This distribution has the following characteristics that we consider to be reasonable. Bids will tend to request a small number of goods, independent of the total number of goods. Such data cases are computationally harder than drawing a number of goods uniformly from a range, or than scaling the average number of goods per bid to the maximum number of goods. Likewise, bids will tend to name a small number of units per good. Prices tend to increase linearly in the number of units, for a fixed set of goods. This is a harder case for our pruning technique, much harder than drawing prices uniformly from a range. In fact, it may be reasonable for prices to be superlinear in the number of units, as the motivation for holding a CA in the first place may be that bidders are expected to value bundles more than individual goods. However, this would be an easier case for our pruning algorithm, so we tested on the linear case instead. The construction of realistic, hard data distributions remains a topic for further research.

Our experimental data was collected on a Pentium III-733 running Windows 2000, with 25 MB allocated for CAMUS's cache. Our figure *Number of Bids vs Time* shows CAMUS's performance on the distribution described above, with each line representing runs with a different number of goods. Note that, for example, CAMUS solved problems with 35 objects (14 goods) and 2500 bids in about two minutes, and problems with 25 objects (10 goods) and 1500 bids in about a second. Because the lines in this graph are sub-linear on the logarithmic scale, CAMUS's performance is sub-exponential in the number of bids, though it remains exponential in the number of goods. Our figure *Percentage Optimality* shows CAMUS's anytime performance. Each line on the graph shows the time taken to find solutions with revenue that is some percentage of the optimal, calculated after the algorithm terminated. Note that the time taken to *find* the optimal solution is less than the time taken for the algorithm to finish, *proving* that this solution is optimal. These anytime results are very encouraging– note that CAMUS finds a 99% optimal solution an order of magnitude more quickly than it takes for the algorithm to run to completion. This suggests that CAMUS could be useful on much larger problems than we have shown here if an optimal solution were not required.

Conclusions

In this paper we introduced CAMUS, a novel algorithm for determining the optimal set of winning bids in general multi-unit combinatorial auctions. The algorithm has been tested on a variety of data distributions and has been found to solve problems of considerable scale in an efficient manner. CAMUS extends our CASS algorithm for single-unit combinatorial auctions, and enables a wide extension of the class of combinatorial auctions that can be efficiently implemented. In our current research we are studying the addition of random noise into our good and bin ordering heuristics, combined with periodic restarts and the deletion of previously-searched bids, to improve performance on hard cases while still retaining completeness.

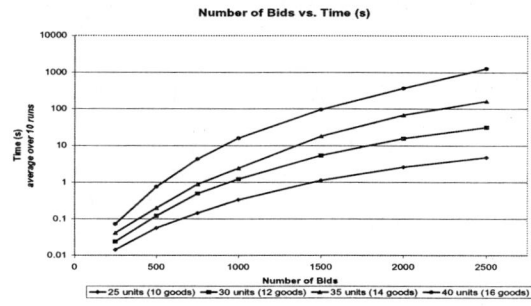

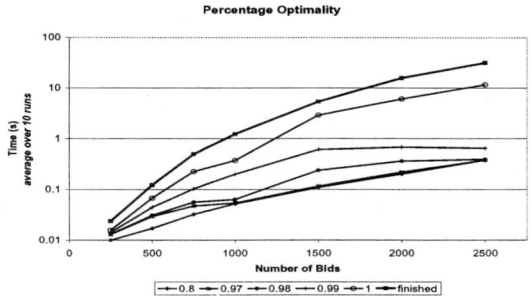

References

Fudenberg, D., and Tirole, J. 1991. *Game Theory*. MIT Press.

Fujishima, Y.; Leyton-Brown, K.; and Shoham, Y. 1999. Taming the computational complexity of combinatorial auctions: Optimal and approximate approaches. In *IJCAI-99*.

Lehmann, D.; O'Callaghan, L.; and Shoham, Y. 1999. Truth revalation in rapid, approximately efficient combinatorial auctions. In *ACM Conference on Electronic Commerce*.

Monderer, D., and Tennenholtz, M. 2000. Optimal Auctions Revisited. Artificial Intelligence, forthcoming.

Nisan, N., and Ronen, A. 2000. Computationally feasible vcg mechanisms. To appear.

Nisan, N. 1999. Bidding and allocation in combinatorial auctions. Working paper.

Rothkopf, M.; Pekec, A.; and Harstad, R. 1998. Computationally manageable combinatorial auctions. *Management Science* 44(8):1131–1147.

Sandholm, T. 1999. An algorithm for optimal winner determination in combinatorial auctions. In *IJCAI-99*.

Tennenholtz, M. 2000. Some tractable combinatorial auctions. To appear in the proceedings of AAAI-2000.

Vries, S., and Vohra, R. 2000. Combinatorial auctions: A brief survey. Unpublished manuscript.

Wellman, M.; Wurman, P.; Walsh, W.; and MacKie-Mason, J. 1998. Auction protocols for distributed scheduling. Working paper (to appear in Games and Economic Behavior).

Maintainability: a weaker stabilizability like notion for high level control

Mutsumi Nakamura
Department of CSE
University of Texas at Arlington
Arlington, TX 76019, USA
nakamura@cse.uta.edu

Chitta Baral
Department of CSE
Arizona State University
Tempe, AZ 85287, USA
chitta@asu.edu

Marcus Bjäreland
Department of Comp and Info Sc
Linköping University
S-581 83 Linkoping, Sweden
marbj@ida.liu.se

Abstract

The goal of most agents is not just to reach a goal state, but rather also (or alternatively) to put restrictions on its trajectory, in terms of states it must avoid and goals that it must 'maintain'. This is analogous to the notions of 'safety' and 'stability' in the discrete event systems and temporal logic community.

In this paper we argue that the notion of 'stability' is too strong for formulating 'maintenance' goals of an agent – in particular, reactive and *software agents*, and give examples of such agents. We present a weaker notion of 'maintainability' and show that our agents which do not satisfy the stability criteria, do satisfy the weaker criteria. We give algorithms to test maintainability, and also to generate control for maintainability. We then develop the notion of 'supportability' that generalizes both 'maintainability' and 'stabilizability, develop an automata theory that distinguishes between exogenous and control actions, and develop a temporal logic based on it.

Motivation and Introduction

Stability has undergone extensive investigations in the control theory community (Passino & Burgess 1998), both for continuous systems (e.g. Lyapunov stability and asymptotic stability) and Discrete Event Dynamic Systems (DEDS) (Ramadge & Wonham 1987b; 1987a; Ozveren, Willsky, & Antsaklis 1991). All these notions can be summarized as in (Passino & Burgess 1998):

> We say that a system is stable if when it begins in a good state and is perturbed into any other state it will always return to a good state.

The appropriate stability notion in a particular case depends on how the notions "system", "begins", "state", "good", and "perturbed" are defined, For DEDS the mainstream definition can be found in (Ozveren, Willsky, & Antsaklis 1991), and that definition is the one we use in this paper. They also mention that relation between stability and the notions of safety, fairness, livelock, deadlock are well studied. *In this paper we present a related notion which we call* **maintainability**, *and argue its importance, particularly for high level control of agents.*

Copyright © 2000, American Association for Artificial Intelligence (www.aaai.org). All rights reserved.

Intuitively, we can view stabilizability as a hard constraint of the system while maintainability is a softer constraint. In both maintainability and stabilizability our goal is that the system should be among a given set of states E as much as possible. In stabilizability, we want a control such that regardless of where the system is now and what exogenous actions may happen, the system will reach one of the states in E within a finite number of transitions and keep visiting it infinitely often after that. In maintainability, we have a weaker requirement where the system reaches a state in E within a finite number of transitions, provided it is not interfered with during those transitions. Thus in maintainability, we admit that if there is continuous interference (by exogenous actions) we can not get to E in a finite number of transition. Such a system will not satisfy the condition of stabilizability, but may satisfy the condition of maintainability.

Many practical closed-loop systems are not stabilizable, but they still serve a purpose and we believe that such systems purpose can be specified by using the weaker notion of maintainability. An example of such a system is an active database system (Widom & Ceri 1996) where 'consistency' of data is 'maintained' using active rules (also referred to as triggers). In such a database system, external updates are made to the database through Insert, Delete and Update commands. But the direct result of the updates may take the database to an inconsistent state where 'integrity constraints' of the database may be violated. In that case, the active part of the database triggers rules that result in additional changes to the database to bring it back to a consistent state. Now suppose E is the set of consistent states of a database. We can not capture the correctness of the triggers by directly using the notions of 'stability'. That is because, if there is a continuous stream of external updates with no time in between for getting back to consistency, then there is no guarantee that the database will reach a state in E within a finite number of transitions. But we can have a different notion of correctness of triggers, where the triggers are correct if given a window of non-interference (from external updates) the triggers will ultimately make the database consistent. In fact that is what happens in a database system where external updates are blocked until the triggers bring back the database to a consistent state.

Another example is a mobile robot (Brooks 1986; Maes 1991) which is asked to 'maintain' a state where there are no obstacles in its front. Here, if there is a belligerent adversary that keeps on putting an obstacle in front of the robot, then the robot can not get to a state with no obstacle in its front. But often we will be satisfied if the robot avoids obstacle in its front when it is not continually harassed. Of course, we would rather have the robot take a path that does not have such an adversary, but in the absence of such a path, it would be acceptable if it takes an available path and 'maintains' states where there are no obstacle in front.

Other examples include agents that perform tasks based on commands. Here, the correctness of the agent's behavior can be formalized as 'maintaining' states where there are no commands in the queue. We can not use the notion of stability because if there is a continuous stream of commands, then there is no guarantee that the agent would get to a state with no commands in its queue within a finite number of transitions.

The rest of the paper is structured as follows. We first formally define the notion of stability and stabilizability. We then introduce the notion of maintainability and compare it with the notion of stabilizability. Next we show that the correctness of an active database can be formalized as maintainability of consistent states. We then present algorithms to verify maintainability, and to construct controls to make a system maintain a set of states. Finally, we develop a general notion called *supportability* and show that stabilizability and maintainability are special cases of it.

Reviewing stability and stabilizability

In this section we review the notions of stability and stabilizability adapted from the definitions in (Ozveren, Willsky, & Antsaklis 1991).

Stability and aliveness

Definition 0.1 A system A is a 4-tuple (X, Σ, f, d), where X is a finite set of states, Σ is a finite set of actions, d is a function from X to 2^Σ listing what actions may occur (or are executable) in what state, and f is a non-deterministic transition function from X and Σ to 2^X. □

Definition 0.2 A trajectory is an alternating sequence of states and actions, and could be either a finite trajectory that starts and ends with a state or an infinite trajectory.

A trajectory $x_0, a_1, x_1, a_2, \ldots, x_k, a_{k+1}, x_{k+1}(\ldots)$ is said to be consistent with a system A if:

- $x_{k+1} \in f(x_k, a_{k+1})$, and
- $a_{k+1} \in d(x_k)$. □

Definition 0.3 Given a system A and a set of states E, a state x is said to be *stable* in A w.r.t. E if all trajectories consistent with A and starting from x go through a state in E in a finite number of transitions and they visit E infinitely often afterwards.

We say $A = (X, \Sigma, f, d)$ is a stable system if all states in X are stable in A w.r.t. E. □

Alternatively, A is stable w.r.t. E if, for any state $x \notin E$, every infinite trajectory starting with x will lead to E in a finite number of steps.

Definition 0.4 $R(A, x)$ denotes the set of states that can be reached from x in a system A.

A state x is said to be *alive* if $d(y) \neq \emptyset$, for all $y \in R(A, x)$. (I.e., we can not reach a state y from x, where no action is possible.)

We say $A = (X, \Sigma, f, d)$ is *alive* if all states in X are alive. □

Stabilizability

We now consider control and exogenous actions. The set of control actions U is a subset of Σ, that can be performed by the (controlling) agent. A particular control K is a function from X to U. The set of exogenous actions that can occur in a state (and that are beyond the control of the agent) is given by a function e from X to 2^Σ, such that $e(x) \subseteq d(x)$.

Definition 0.5 Let $A = (X, \Sigma, f, d)$ be a system. In presence of e, U, and K, we define $A_K{}^1$, the closed loop system of A as the four-tuple (X, Σ, f, d_K), where $d_K(x) = (d(X) \cap \{K(x)\}) \cup e(x)$. □

Definition 0.6 Given a system A, a function e, and a set of states E, we say $S \subseteq X$ is *stabilizable* with respect to E if there exists a control law[2] K such that for all x in S, x is alive and stable with respect to E in the closed loop system A_k. If $S = X$, we say A is stabilizable with respect to E. □

Maintainability

Our intuition behind maintainability is that we would like our system to 'maintain' a formula (or a set of states where the formula is satisfied) in presence of exogenous actions. By 'maintain' we mean a weaker requirement than the temporal operator *always* ($\Box$) where $\Box f$ means that f should be true in *all* the states in the trajectory. The weaker requirement is that our system needs to get to a desired state within a finite number of transitions provided it is not interfered in between by exogenous actions. The question then is what role the exogenous actions play.

Our definition of maintainability has parameters as a set of initial states S, that the system may be initially in, a set of desired state E, that we want to maintain, a system A and a control law K. Our goal is to formulate when the control law K maintains E assuming that the system is initially in one of the states in S. We account for the exogenous actions by defining the notion – $Closure(S, A)$ – of a closure of S with respect to A. This closure is the set of states that the system may get into starting from S. Then we define *maintainability* by requiring that the control law be such that

---

[1] A more appropriate terminology would be $A_{K,e}$. We use A_K to remain consistent with the usage in (Ozveren, Willsky, & Antsaklis 1991).

[2] It is also referred to as 'feedback law', 'feedback control' or 'state feedback' in the literature.

if the system is in any state in the closure and is given a window of non-interference from exogenous actions then it gets into a desired state.

Now a question might be that suppose the above condition of maintainability is satisfied, and while the control law is leading the system towards a desired state an exogenous action happens and takes the system off that path. What then? The answer is that the state that the system will reach after the exogenous action will be a state from the closure. Thus, if the system is then left alone (without interference from exogenous actions) it will be again on its way to a desired state. So in our notion of maintainability, the control is always taking the system towards a desired state, and after any disturbance from an exogenous action, the control again puts the system on a path to a desired state.

We now formally define the notions of closure and maintainability.

Definition 0.7 Let $A = (X, \Sigma, f, d)$ be a system and S be a set of states. By $Closure(S, A)$ we refer to the set $\bigcup_{x \in S} R(A, x)$. □

Definition 0.8 Given a system $A = (X, \Sigma, f, d)$, a set of control actions $U \subseteq \Sigma$, a specification of exogenous actions e, and a set of states E, we say a set of states S is *k-maintainable* with respect to E if there exists a feedback control K such that from each state x in $Closure(S, A_K)$, we will get to a state in E with at most k transitions, where each action (behind the transitions) is dictated by the control K.

If there exists an integer n such that S is *n-maintainable* with respect to E, we say S is *maintainable* with respect to E.

If $S = X$, then we say A is maintainable with respect to E. □

We now show that while stabilizability guarantees maintainability, the opposite is not true.

Proposition 0.1 Given a system A, if a set of states S is stabilizable with respect to a set of states E, then S is maintainable with respect to E. □

Proof : Suppose that a set $S \subseteq X$ and S is stabilizable with respect to E. Then there exists a control law K such that for each $x \in S$, x is alive and is stable with respect E.
Claim: There is a trajectory from each state x in S to a state in E with a finite transitions.
Case 1. Suppose $x \in S$. Then x is stable, therefore we can get from x to a state in E with a finite number of transitions dictated by K, say n_x transitions.
Case 2. Suppose $x \in Closure(S, A) \setminus S$. Then there exists $y \in S$ such that there is a trajectory T from y which goes through x. Since $y \in S$, y is stabilizable. Thus all trajectories consistent with A and starting from y go through a state in E in a finite number of transitions and they visit E infinitely often afterwards. Therefore any trajectory from y which goes through x will visit E infinitely. Thus there must be a sub trajectory T' from x to a state in E which is contained in the trajectory T from y to a state in E through x. Through this trajectory T', we can reach from x to a state in E in a finite number of transitions dictated by K, say n_x. Note that the maximum possible cardinality of $Closure(S, A)$ is the cardinality of X. Thus it is finite. Let n be $max\{n_x | x \in Closure(S, A)\}$. Since $Closure(S, A)$ is finite, n exists ($n < \infty$) and from all states in $Closure(S, A)$ we can reach a state in E within n transitions dictated by K. Hence S is n-maintainable with respect to E and thus S is maintainable with respect to E. □

But the converse of the above proposition is not true. I.e. *Maintainability does not necessarily imply stabilizability.* We now show an example of a system which is maintainable but is not stabilizable.

Consider a system $A = (X, \Sigma, f, d)$ with the following:
$X = \{s_1, s_2, s_3, s_4, s_5\}$,
$\Sigma = \{a_1, a_2, a_3, a_4, a_5\} \bigcup \{e_1, e_2\}$,

$d(s_1) = \{a_1\}$, $d(s_2) = \{a_2, e_1, e_2\}$, $d(s_3) = \{a_3\}$, $d(s_4) = \{a_4\}, d(s_5) = \{a_5\}$

$f(s_1, a_1) = \{s_2\}$, $f(s_2, a_2) = \{s_4\}$, $f(s_2, e_1) = \{s_3\}$,
$f(s_2, e_2) = \{s_2\}$, $f(s_3, a_3) = \{s_4\}$, $f(s_4, a_4) = \{s_5\}$,
$f(s_5, a_5) = \{s_4\}$

Given $E = \{s_4, s_5\}$, this system is maintainable, but is not stabilizable. With the control law K, where $K(s_i) = a_i$, with at most 3 transitions, we can reach from any state in X to a state in E, therefore it is maintainable. But if we consider all trajectories, at the state s_2, the exogenous action e_2 can keep interfering and we might never reach from the state s_2 to a state in E. Therefore it is not stabilizable. □

Maintainability in an active database

In this section we show how the notion of 'maintainability' is useful in defining the correctness of an active database.

Consider an active database with the following aspects:

- Relational Schema:

$Employee(Emp\#, Name, Salary, Dept\#)$
$Dept(Dept\#, Mgr\#)$

- Goal of the active database: Maintain Integrity constraints. I.e., Maintain the database in states where

  (i) If (e, n, s, d) is a tuple in $Employee$ then there must be a tuple (d', m') in $Dept$ such that $d = d'$; and

  (ii) If (d, m) is a tuple in $Dept$, then there must be a tuple (e', n', s', d') in $Employee$ such that $d = d'$ and $m = e'$

  (In addition we may have other constraints – which we do not focus here – such as each department has a single manager and each employee works in a single department.)

- Exogenous actions are of the kind: Delete (E, N, S, D) from $Employee$. (The direct effect of this action is the deletion of the tuple.)

- Triggers are of the kind:
  1. For any Delete (e, n, s, d) from $Employee$, if (d, e) is a tuple in $Dept$, delete that tuple from $Dept$ and delete all tuples of the form (e', n', s', d') from $Employee$, where $d = d'$.

To formulate the correctness of such an active database, we can treat the triggers as control laws, as was done initially in (Ceri & Widom 1990). The overall system operates in a way that whenever an exogenous action occurs if it modifies the database such that integrity constraints are violated, the triggers (control laws) kick in and force additional changes to the database such that it reaches a state where the integrity constraints are satisfied. This can be formulated as *maintenance of the integrity constraints*.

Now, if there were a continuous stream of exogenous actions (whose direct effects were immediately reflected in the database) then there is no guarantee that the database would reach a state satisfying the integrity constraints within a finite number of transitions. Hence, we can not formulate this as stabilizability.

Another important aspect of maintainability is that in reactive *software* systems like this, if we know that our system is k-maintainable, and each transition takes say at most t time units, then we can implement a transaction mechanism that will regulate the number of exogenous actions allowed per unit time to be $\frac{1}{k \times t}$. This will also be useful in web-based transaction softwares where exogenous actions are external interactions and the internal service mechanism is modeled as control laws. On the other hand, given a requirement that we must allow m requests (exogenous actions) per unit time, we can work backwards to determine the value of k, and then find a control to make the system k-maintainable. In general, since in high level controls we may have the opportunity to limit (say through a transaction mechanism) the exogenous actions, we think 'maintainability' is an important notion for high level control.

Algorithms

In this section we give two simple algorithms to verify maintainability, and to generate control for maintainability. We will further analyze them in the full paper.

Testing maintainability

Input: A system $A = (X, \Sigma, f, d)$, a set of states E, a set of states S, and a control K.

Output: To find out if S is maintainable with respect to E, using the control K.

Algorithm:

Step 1: Compute $Closure(S, A_K)$.

Step 2: For each x in $Closure(S, A_K)$ compute the sequence
$x_0, x_1, \ldots, x_k, x_{k+1}, \ldots, x_{|X|}$, where $x_0 = x$, and $x_{k+1} = x_k$ if $x_k \in E$, and $x_{k+1} = f(x_k, K(x_k))$ otherwise.

Step 3: If for all x, $\{x_0, \ldots, x_{|X|}\} \cap E \neq \emptyset$ then S is maintainable with respect to E, using the control K; Otherwise it is not maintainable with respect to E, using the control K.

Generating control for maintainability of a set of states

Input: A system $A = (X, \Sigma, f, d)$, a set of states E, and a set of states S.

Output: Find a control K such that S is maintainable with respect to E, using the control K.

Algorithm:

Step 0: $S_{in} := S, S_{out} = \emptyset$.

Step 1: While $S_{in} \neq S_{out}$ Do.

Pick an x from $S_{in} \setminus S_{out}$. Find a *shortest path (or a minimal cost path)* from x to a state in E using only control actions.

If no such path exists then EXIT and return(FAIL).

Let a be the first action of that path.
Assign $K(x) = a$.
$S_{out} := S_{out} \cup \{x\}$
$S_{in} := S_{in} \cup \{f(x, a)\} \cup \{x : x \in f(x, b), \text{ for some } b \in e(X)\}$.

Step 2: If $S_{in} = S_{out}$, return(S_{out}, K).

Proposition 0.2 If the above algorithm terminates by returning S' and K, then: (i) $S' = Closure(S, A_K)$, and (ii) S is maintainable with respect to E, using the control K. □

One important aspect of the above algorithm and its proof of correctness is the requirement of picking the first action of a shortest path or a minimal cost path. Picking the first action of a minimal path (as normally used in the notions of minimal plans) will not be sufficient as that may lead to cycles and the system may never reach its goal. An algorithm based on a minimal path will have to be more complicated so as to avoid this. On the other hand, our use of shortest path allows us to easily enhance the control when additional states are added to S. We then only need to consider the new states in the closure, find shortest paths from each of these states (say x), and have the first action as the value of $K(x)$. Thus our algorithm is useful in incrementally broadening the control when the set of initial states S is broadened.

At this point we would like to point out the relation between our work here and some research on reactive and situated agents (Kaelbling & Rosenschein 1991). In (Kaelbling & Rosenschein 1991), they say that in a control rule 'if c then a', the action a, must be the action that *leads* to the goal from any situation that satisfies the condition c. The above algorithm interprets the notion of 'leading to' as the first action of a minimal cost plan.

Supportability: a notion that generalizes stabilizability and maintainability

In this section we generalize the notion of maintainability and show that the notion of stabilizability is a special case of this generalization. Our generalization is based on the intuition that perhaps, we can allow a limited number of exogenous actions during our so called 'window of non-interference' and still be able to get back to a state in E. We refer to this general notion as *supportability*.

Definition 0.9 Given a system $A = (X, \Sigma, f, d)$, a set of agents action $U \subseteq \Sigma$, a specification of exogenous actions e, and a set of states E, we say a set of states S is *(k,l)-supportable* ($l \leq k$) with respect to E if there exists a control law K such that for each state x in $Closure(S, A_K)$, all trajectories – consistent with A_K – from x whose next k transitions contain at most l transitions due to exogenous actions and the rest is dictated by the control K, reach a state in E by the k-th transition. □

Proposition 0.3 $(k, 0)$-supportable is equivalent to k-maintainable. (A set of states S is $(k, 0)$-supportable with respect to a set of states E if and only if S is k-maintainable with respect to E.)

Proposition 0.4 A set of states S is stabilizable iff S is alive and there exists an integer m such that S is *(m,m)-supportable* with respect to E.

An automata and a temporal logic for 'maintainability' and 'supportability'

The notion of a system defined earlier does not distinguish between exogenous action and control action. They are both part of Σ. In this section we first define the notion of a 2-system where we distinguish between exogenous and control actions. Using the notion of a two system we define the notion of 'maintained' which is analogous to the notion of being 'stable' and related it to our earlier notion of maintainability. We then use the notion of 2-systems to define a temporal logic that makes the distinction between transitions due to exogenous action and transitions due to control actions.

Definition 0.10
A 2-system A is a 5-tuple $(X, \Sigma_a, \Sigma_e, f, d)$, where X is a finite set of states, Σ_a is a finite set of control actions, Σ_e is a finite set of control events, d is a function from X to $2^{\Sigma_a \cup \Sigma_e}$ listing what actions and events may occur (or are executable) in what state, and f is a transition function from X and $\Sigma_a \cup \Sigma_e$ to 2^X. □

The notion of a trajectory with respect to a 2-system remains the same as with respect to a system, which we earlier defined in Definition 0.2.

Definition 0.11 Given a 2-system A and a set of states E, a state x is said to be k-maintained in A w.r.t. E if for all trajectories of the form $x = x_0, a_1, x_1, a_2, \ldots, a_j, x_j, a_{j+1}, \ldots$ that is consistent with A and for all i such that $\{a_{i+1}, \ldots, a_{i+k}\} \subseteq \Sigma_a$, we have that $\{x_{i+1}, \ldots, x_{i+k}\} \cap E \neq \emptyset$.
A 2-system $A = (X, \Sigma_a, \Sigma_e, f, d)$ is k-maintained with respect to E if all its states are k-maintained.
A 2-system $A = (X, \Sigma_a, \Sigma_e, f, d)$ is maintained with respect to E if there exists a positive integer n such that it is n-maintained with respect to E. □

Proposition 0.5 A state x is k-maintainable in a system $A = (X, \Sigma_a \cup \Sigma_e, f, d)$ with respect to E iff there exists a control law K such that x is k-maintained with respect to E in the 2-system $A_K = (X, \Sigma_a, \Sigma_e, f, d_K)$, where d_K is as defined earlier in Definition 0.5.

A temporal language with respect to 2-systems

In the past, temporal logic has been used to specify and verify the behavior of reactive systems (Manna & Pnueli 1992; Clarke, Emerson, & Sistla 1986; Kabanza, Barbeau, & St-Denis 1997). Most of these temporal logics do not (perhaps with the exception of one description in (Singh 1994)) distinguish between transitions due to control actions and due to exogenous actions. Hence, they are too strong to be able to characterize the correctness of reactive software systems such as an active database system. In this section we propose a temporal language that makes a distinction between transitions due to control actions and exogenous actions and is able to characterize correctness of reactive software systems such as an active database system. We plan to elaborate on this in the full paper.

Some of the important future temporal operators as discussed in (Manna & Pnueli 1992) are: Next ($\bigcirc$), Always ($\square$), Eventually ($\diamond$), and Until ($\mathcal{U}$). There meaning with respect a trajectory $\sigma = x_0, a_1, x_1, \ldots, x_j, a_{j+1}, x_{j+1}, \ldots$ is defined as follows:

- $(\sigma, j) \models p$ iff p is true in x_j.
- $(\sigma, j) \models \bigcirc p$ iff $(\sigma, j + 1) \models p$
- $(\sigma, j) \models \square p$ iff $(\sigma, k) \models p$, for all $k \geq j$.
- $(\sigma, j) \models \diamond p$ iff $(\sigma, k) \models p$, for some $k \geq j$.
- $(\sigma, j) \models p \, \mathcal{U} \, q$ iff there exists $k \geq j$ such that $(\sigma, k) \models q$ and for all $i, j \leq i < k, (\sigma, i) \models p$.

It is easy to see that none of the above temporal operators consider the action type (whether exogenous or control action) behind the transitions. We now introduce some temporal operators that do consider the action type behind the transitions.

- $(\sigma, j) \models \bigcirc_k p$ iff $i \geq j$ is the smallest index such that $\{a_{i+1}, \ldots, a_{i+k}\} \subseteq \Sigma_a$ and $(\sigma, i + r) \models p$, for some $1 \leq r \leq k$.
- $(\sigma, j) \models \square_k p$ iff for all $i \geq j$ if $\{a_{i+1}, \ldots, a_{i+k}\} \subseteq \Sigma_a$ then $(\sigma, i + r) \models p$ for some $1 \leq r \leq k$.
- $(\sigma, j) \models \bigcirc_{k,l} p$ iff $i \geq j$ is the smallest index such that $|\{a_{i+1}, \ldots, a_{i+k}\} \cap \Sigma_e| \leq l$ and $(\sigma, i + r) \models p$ for some $1 \leq r \leq k$.
- $(\sigma, j) \models \square_{k,l} p$ iff for all $i \geq j$ if $|\{a_{i+1}, \ldots, a_{i+k}\} \cap \Sigma_e| \leq l$ then $(\sigma, i + r) \models p$ for some $1 \leq r \leq k$.

We can describe the intuitive meaning behind the above formal definitions as follows: Intuitively, $(\sigma, j) \models \square_k p$ means that starting from x_j, within or after any k consecutive transitions due to control actions p holds. Similarly, $(\sigma, j) \models \square_{k,l} p$ means that starting from x_j, within or after any k transitions with at most l exogenous actions p holds.

Proposition 0.6 (i) $(\sigma, j) \models \Box_k p$ iff $(\sigma, j) \models \Box_{k,0} p$.

(ii) $(\sigma, j) \models \bigcirc_k p$ iff $(\sigma, j) \models \bigcirc_{k,0} p$.

(iii) Let E_p be the set of states, where a formula p holds. S is (k, l)-supportable w.r.t. E_p iff for all trajectories σ whose $x_0 \in S$, and for all j, $(\sigma, j) \models \Box_{k,l} p$. □

Corollary 0.7 1. Let E_p be the set of states, where a formula p holds. S is k maintainable w.r.t. E_p iff for all trajectories σ whose $x_0 \in S$, and for all j, $(\sigma, j) \models \Box_k p$.

2. Let E_p be the set of states, where a formula p holds. S is stabilizable w.r.t. E_p iff S is alive and there exists an m such that for all trajectories σ whose $x_0 \in S$, and for all j, $(\sigma, j) \models \Box_{m,m} p$.

Conclusion and related work

In this paper we formalized the notion of 'maintenance' often mentioned (Baral & Son 1998) in the context of robots and agents, as a property of a discrete event dynamic system (DEDS) and compared it with the notion of 'stability' and 'stabilizability' that are most popular in DEDS. We argued why 'maintainability' may be a more preferred notion for certain systems and discussed active database systems as an example. We then gave simple algorithms for testing maintainability and generating control for maintainability. We then developed the notion of 'supportability' that generalizes both 'maintainability' and 'stabilizability. Finally, we developed an automata theory that distinguishes between exogenous and control actions, and developed a temporal logic based on it. Our basic formulation of 'maintainability' is related to the work in (Baral & Son 1998).

Among the other related works, there has been some work on defining stability of continuous systems in the presence of discontinuities and disturbances; for example (Sontag 1999). In the planning literature there has been some work on planning for temporal goals (Bacchus & Kabanza 1998; Weld & Etzioni 1994) where goals are expressed as temporal formulas. But they use the traditional temporal operators which by themselves can not express our notion of 'maintenance'. Another related notion is planning from the current situation in a dynamic domain (Baral, Gelfond, & Provetti 1997) and execution monitoring (DeGiacomo, Reiter, & Soutchanski 1998). In both these notions 'maintenance' is achieved by monitoring (or observing) the world for discrepancies and making new plans to recover. Finally, the notion of 'self-stabilization' (Dijkstra 1974) in distributed and fault-tolerant computing seems to be similar to our notion of 'maintenance' and we plan to compare and contrast them in the sequel.

References

Bacchus, F., and Kabanza, F. 1998. Planning for temporally extended goals. *Annals of Math and AI* 22:5–27.

Baral, C., and Son, T. 1998. Relating theories of actions and reactive control. *Electronic transactions on Artificial Intelligence* 2(3-4).

Baral, C.; Gelfond, M.; and Provetti, A. 1997. Representing Actions: Laws, Observations and Hypothesis. *Journal of Logic Programming* 31(1-3):201–243.

Brooks, R. 1986. A robust layered control system for a mobile robot. *IEEE journal of robotics and automation* 14–23.

Ceri, S., and Widom, J. 1990. Deriving production rules for constraint maintainance. In *VLDB 90*. 566–577.

Clarke, E.; Emerson, E.; and Sistla, A. 1986. Automatic verification of finite-state concurrent systems using temporal logic specifications. *ACM Transactions on Programming Languages and Systems* 8(2):244–263.

DeGiacomo, G.; Reiter, R.; and Soutchanski, M. 1998. Execution monitoring of high-level robot programs. In *Proc. of KR 98*, 453–464.

Dijkstra, E. W. 1974. Self-stabilizing systems in spite of distributed control. *CACM* 17(11):843–644.

Kabanza, F.; Barbeau, M.; and St-Denis, R. 1997. Planning control rules for reactive agents. *Artificial Intelligence* 5(1):67–113.

Kaelbling, L., and Rosenschein, S. 1991. Action and planning in embedded agents. In Maes, P., ed., *Designing Autonomous Agents*. MIT Press. 35–48.

Maes, P., ed. 1991. *Designing Autonomous Agents*. MIT/Elsevier.

Manna, Z., and Pnueli, A. 1992. *The temporal logic of reactive and concurrent systems: specification*. Springer Verlag.

Ozveren, O.; Willsky, A.; and Antsaklis, P. 1991. Stability and stabilizability of discrete event dynamic systems. *JACM* 38(3):730–752.

Passino, K., and Burgess, K. 1998. *Stability Analysis of Discrete Event Systems*. Adaptive and Learning Systems for Signal Processing, Communications, and Control. New York: John Wiley and Sons, Inc.

Ramadge, P., and Wonham, W. 1987a. Modular feedback logic for discrete event systems. *SIAM Journal of Control and Optimization* 25(5):1202–1217.

Ramadge, P., and Wonham, W. 1987b. Supervisory control of a class of discrete event process. *SIAM Journal of Control and Optimization* 25(1):206–230.

Singh, M. 1994. *Multiagent systems - a theoretical framework for intentions, know-how, and communications*. Springer-Verlag.

Sontag, E. 1999. Stability and stabilization: Discontinuities and the effect of disturbances. In Clarke, F., and Stern, R., eds., *Proc. NATO advanced study institute, July/Aug 1998*. Kluwer. 551–598.

Weld, D., and Etzioni, O. 1994. The first law of robotics (a call to arms). In *AAAI*, 1042–1047.

Widom, J., and Ceri, S., eds. 1996. *Active Database Systems - Triggers and Rules for advanced database processing*. Morgan Kaufmann.

Agent Capabilities: Extending BDI Theory

Lin Padgham[1] and **Patrick Lambrix**[2]
[1]RMIT University, Melbourne, Australia
[2]Linköpings universitet, Linköping, Sweden

Abstract

Intentional agent systems are increasingly being used in a wide range of complex applications. Capabilities has recently been introduced into one of these systems as a software engineering mechanism to support modularity and reusability while still allowing meta-level reasoning. This paper presents a formalisation of capabilities within the framework of beliefs, goals and intentions and indicates how capabilities can affect agent reasoning about its intentions. We define a style of agent commitment which we refer to as a *self-aware* agent which allows an agent to modify its goals and intentions as its capabilities change. We also indicate which aspects of the specification of a BDI interpreter are affected by the introduction of capabilities and give some indications of additional reasoning which could be incorporated into an agent system on the basis of both the theoretical analysis and the existing implementation.

Introduction

Agent systems are becoming increasingly popular for solving a wide range of complex problems. Intentional agent systems have a substantial base in theory as well as a number of implemented systems that are used for challenging applications such as air-traffic control and space systems (Rao and Georgeff 1995). One of the strengths of the BDI *Belief, Desire, Intention* class of systems (including IRMA (Bratman *et al.* 1988), PRS (Georgeff and Ingrand 1989), JACK (Busetta *et al.* 1999b), JAM (Huber 1999) and UMPRS (Lee *et al.* 1994)) is their strong link to theoretical work, in particular that of Rao and Georgeff (Rao and Georgeff 1991), but also Cohen and Levesque (Cohen and Levesque 1990), Bratman et al. (Bratman *et al.* 1988) and Shoham (Shoham 1993). Although the theory is not implemented directly in the systems it does inform and guide the implementations (Rao and Georgeff 1992).

In this paper we investigate how a notion of *capability* can be integrated into the BDI logic of Rao and Georgeff (Rao and Georgeff 1991), preserving the features of the logic while adding to it in ways that eliminate current intuitive anomalies and mismatches between the theory and implemented systems. We understand capability as the ability to react rationally towards achieving a particular goal. Depending on circumstances a capability may not always result in an achievable plan for realising the goal, but it is a pre-requisite for such.

We describe a possible formal relationship of capabilities to the other BDI concepts of *beliefs*, *goals* and *intentions*. The addition of capabilities enriches the existing formal model and allows for definition of a self-aware agent which takes on and remains committed to goals only if it has a capability to achieve such goals. The formalisation we introduce deals only with a single agent, but we indicate directions for development that would be suitable for dealing with rational behaviour in a multi-agent system which takes into account the known capabilities of other agents.

This work is partially motivated by the recently reported development and use of a *capability* construct in JACK, a java based BDI agent development environment (Busetta *et al.* 1999b), which follows the basic abstract interpreter described in (Rao and Georgeff 1992). We indicate how capabilities can be integrated into this abstract interpreter and also indicate some issues for consideration in implementation of capabilities that are highlighted by this work. This work can be seen as part of the ongoing interplay between theory and practice in the area of BDI agent systems. It provides a foundation for exploring some of the practical reasoning mechanisms involving capabilities and for further developing the theory as well as informing the ongoing implementations.

Using Capabilities in Reasoning

Most BDI systems contain a *plan library* made up of plans which are essentially abstract specifications for achieving certain goals or doing subtasks on the way to achieving a goal. Each plan is associated with a triggering event (which may be an event of type *achieve goal X*). Each plan may also have a list of pre-conditions or a *context* which describes the situation in which the plan is intended to be used. The context condition may be used to bind variables which are then used in the plan body. The plan body is the code which executes the plan. This may contain invocations of subgoals which allow new plans to flesh out the detail of the plan, calls to external "actions", or other code in the plan or host language.

We understand having *a capability to achieve X* as mean-

Copyright © 2000, American Association for Artificial Intelligence (www.aaai.org). All rights reserved.

ing that the agent has at least one plan that has as its trigger the goal event *achieve X*. That is the agent has at least one way it knows how to achieve X in some situation. At any given time the agent may be unable to actually use this plan (depending on whether its pre-conditions match the state of the world), but having some such plan is clearly a prerequisite to being able to achieve X.[1]

In the description of the implementation of capabilities in JACK (Busetta *et al.* 1999a) a capability is essentially a set of plans, a fragment of the knowledge base that is manipulated by those plans and a specification of the interface to the capability. The interface is specified partially in terms of what events generated external to the capability, can be handled by this capability. Thus a part of the interface to a capability will be a list of the goal achievement events that the capability is designed to handle. Additional subgoal events and the plans that deal with these can be hidden within the internals of the capability. The interface also specifies what events generated by the capability are to be visible externally and gives information as to what portion of the knowledge base fragment is used by the capability.

As an example a *scheduling capability* may contain a set of plans to construct a schedule in a certain domain. The knowledge base fragment defined as part of this capability may have knowledge about the objects to be scheduled, their priorities, and various other information that is generated and used as a schedule is being built. There may be a single external goal event called *achieve-schedule* which this capability responds to while the only events it generates that are seen externally are events which notify the schedule or which notify failure to generate a schedule.

It is easy to see how this abstraction of a set of plans into a capability could be used to advantage in finding plans that are a possibility for responding to a specific event. Rather than examining all plans it is only necessary to look within the plans of either the generating capability, or a capability that has the relevant event specified as part of its external interface. Naturally this relies on appropriate software engineering design and will preclude the system "discovering" a plan within the internals of a capability that achieves a goal that is not specified as part of the interface of the capability. This is consistent with the practical reasoning approach inherent in these systems which relies on forward chaining based on specified triggers (combined with the ability to manage failure and retry alternative mechanisms to achieve goals and subgoals). The abstraction of sets of plans into capabilities also provides a mechanism for name scoping which is a practical help in building large and complex systems.

Busetta et al. (Busetta *et al.* 1999a) describe how agents can be built by incorporating specific capabilities. A growing amount of work in multi-agent systems discusses agents with varying "roles". If an agent changes roles dynamically the expectation is that their behaviour also changes. One way to achieve this could be to use capabilities. A capability could specify and implement the things that an agent could do within a particular role. As an agent changed role, appropriate capabilities could then be activated or de-activated.

While a capability (in general language usage) cannot be regarded as a mental attitude similar to beliefs, desires, goals and intentions, beliefs about capabilities (both one's own and others) are clearly important mental attitudes for reasoning about action.

When we talk about *goals* and *intentions* we expect that they are related to aspects of the world that the agent has (at least potentially) some control over. While it is reasonable to talk about an agent having a desire for it to be sunny tomorrow, having a goal for it to be sunny tomorrow makes little intuitive sense - unless of course our agent believes it can control the weather. Just as *goals* are constrained to be a consistent subset of the set of *desires*, we would argue that they should also be constrained to be consistent with its *capabilities* (at least within a single agent system - this needs to be modified for multi-agent systems but the notion of capability remains relevant; for multi-agent systems one must also consider capabilities of agents other than oneself). As intentions are commitments to achieve goals these also are intuitively limited to aspects of the world the agent has some control over. Consequently, we would wish our agent's goals and intentions to be limited by its capabilities (or what it believes to be its capabilities).

Capabilities may also provide a suitable level at which agents in a multi-agent heterogeneous system have information about other agents. An agent observing an (external) event that it may not itself have the capability to respond to, may pass on the event to another agent if it believes that agent has the capability to respond to the event. (Beliefs about) capabilities of other agents may also provide a mechanism for supporting co-operation. An agent in a multi-agent system may contact or try to influence some other agent with the required capability, or alternatively may make decisions about its own actions based on the believed capabilities of other agents. Goals of an agent in a multi-agent system are likely to be constrained (in some way) by the capabilities of other agents as well as one's own capabilities.

We explore a possible formalisation of capabilities within BDI logic that lays the initial foundation for addressing some of these issues. We first summarise the BDI logic of Rao and Georgeff and then explore how this can be extended to incorporate capabilities - currently in the context of a single agent reasoning about its own capabilities, although we are also working on extending this to multi-agent systems.

Semantics of R&G BDI Logic

The logic developed by Rao and Georgeff[2] (e.g. (Rao and Georgeff 1991; 1992)) is a logic involving multiple worlds, where each world is a *time-tree* of world states with branching time future and single time past. The various nodes in

---

[1]This assumes that all plans explicitly state what goals they achieve, and does not take account of goals being achieved as a result of side-effects. This is consistent with how all BDI systems of which we are aware are implemented, and is part of the mechanism which allows for efficient practical reasoning.

[2]Due to space limitations we are unable to fully define R&G's logic here, though we attempt to give the basic idea. The reader is referred to (Rao and Georgeff 1991) for full formal definitions.

the future of the time-tree represent the results of different events or agent actions. The different worlds (i.e. different time-tree structures) result from incomplete knowledge about the current state of the world and represent different scenarios of future choices and effects based on differing current state.

The main value of Rao and Georgeff's formalism is that it avoids anomalies present in some other formalisms whereby an agent is forced to accept as goals (or intentions) all side effects of a given goal (or intention). Modalities are ordered according to a strength relation $<_{strong}$ and modal operators are not closed under implication with respect to a weaker modality, making formulae such as:
GOAL(ψ) $\wedge$ BEL($inevitable(always(\psi \supset \gamma))$) $\wedge$ $\neg$GOAL(γ)
satisfiable. Thus it is possible to have a goal to go to the dentist, to believe that going to the dentist necessarily involves pain, but *not* have a goal to have pain.

Unlike the logic of predicate calculus BDI logic formulae are always evaluated with respect to particular time points. The logic has two kinds of formulae; *state formulae* are evaluated at a specific point in a time-tree, whereas *path formulae* are evaluated over a path in a time-tree.[3] The modal operator *optional* is said to be true of a path formula θ at a particular point in a time-tree if θ is true of at least one path emanating from that point. The operator *inevitable* is said to be true of a path formula θ at a particular point in a time-tree if θ is true of all paths emanating from that point. The logic also includes the standard temporal operators $\bigcirc$ (next), $\Diamond$ (eventually), $\Box$ (always) and $\bigcup$ (until) which operate over path formulae.

Figure 1 illustrates evaluation of some formulae in a belief, goal or intention world (i.e. a time-tree).

A belief α, (written BEL(α)) implies that α is true in all belief-accessible worlds. Similarly, a goal (GOAL(α)) is something which is true in all goal-accessible worlds and an intention (INTEND(α)) is true in all intention-accessible worlds. The axiomatisation for beliefs is the standard weak-S5 (or KD45) modal system. For goals and intentions the D and K axioms are adopted.

The logic requires that goals be compatible with beliefs (and intentions compatible with goals). This is enforced by requiring that for each belief-accessible world w at time t, there must be a goal-accessible sub-world of w at time t. This ensures that no formula can be true in all goal-accessible worlds unless it is true in a belief-accessible world. There is a similar relationship between goal-accessible and intention-accessible worlds.

The key axioms of what Rao and Georgeff refer to as the *basic I-system* (Rao and Georgeff 1991) are as follows[4]

AI1 GOAL(α) $\supset$ BEL(α)
AI2 INTEND(α) $\supset$ GOAL(α)

---

[3]See (Rao and Georgeff 1991) for definitions of state and path formulae.

[4]AI1 and AI2 only hold for so-called O-formulae which are formulae with no positive occurrences of inevitable outside the scope of the modal operators. See (Rao and Georgeff 1991) for details. Also $\supset$ is implication (not superset).

AI3 INTEND($does$(a)) $\supset$ $does$(a)
AI4 INTEND(ϕ) $\supset$ BEL(INTEND(ϕ))
AI5 GOAL(ϕ) $\supset$ BEL(GOAL(ϕ))
AI6 INTEND(ϕ) $\supset$ GOAL(INTEND(ϕ))
AI7 $done$(a) $\supset$ BEL($done$(a))
AI8 INTEND(ϕ) $\supset$ $inevitable$ $\Diamond$ ($\neg$ INTEND(ϕ))

This framework can then be used as a basis for describing and exploring various commitment axioms that correspond to agents that behave in various ways with respect to commitment to their intentions. Rao and Georgeff describe axioms for what they call a blindly committed agent, a single-minded agent and an open-minded agent, showing that as long as an agent's beliefs about the current state of the world are always true, as long as the agent only acts intentionally, and as long as nothing happens that is inconsistent with the agent's expectations, then these agents will eventually achieve their goals.

Semantics of Capabilities

As discussed previously it makes little intuitive sense to have a goal and an intention for the sun to shine, unless an agent also has some mechanism for acting to achieve this world state. We extend the BDI logic of Rao and Georgeff's *I-system* (Rao and Georgeff 1991; 1992) to incorporate capabilities which constrain agent goals and intentions to be compatible with what it believes are its capabilities. We will call our extended logic the *IC-system*.

The *IC-system* requires capability-accessible worlds exactly analogous[5] to belief-accessible worlds, goal-accessible worlds and intention-accessible worlds. CAP(ϕ) is then defined as being true if it is true in all the capability-accessible worlds. If $\mathcal{C}$ is the accessibility relation with respect to capabilities, then
$$M, v, w_t \models \text{CAP}(\phi) \text{ iff } \forall\, w' \in \mathcal{C}_t^w: M, v, w'_t \models \phi^6$$
We adopt the D and K axioms for capabilities, i.e. capabilities are closed under implication and consistent.

Compatibility Axioms

The first two axioms of the basic *I-system* described in the previous section have to do with the compatibility between beliefs and goals, and goals and intentions. We add two further compatibility axioms relating to capabilities. Note that the compatibility axioms refer only to so-called O-formula, i.e. formula that do not contain any positive occurrences of *inevitable*.

Belief-Capability Compatibility:
This axiom states that if the agent has an O-formula α as a capability, the agent believes that formula.
AIC1 CAP(α) $\supset$ BEL(α)

---

[5]It is also possible to have a variant where capability-accessible worlds are also required to always be sub-worlds of belief-accessible worlds. This variant and its ramifications are considered in a longer version of this paper which will be available as an RMIT technical report.

[6]All the details of the supporting framework are not given here due to space limitations, but follow straightforwardly from (Rao and Georgeff 1991).

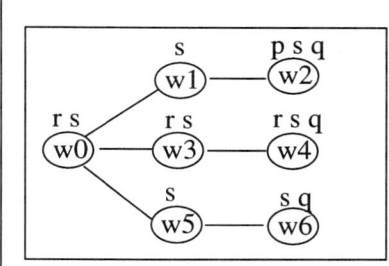

In this world evaluated at w0, the following are true
  optional eventually p
  optional always r
  inevitable eventually q
  inevitable always s
In this world evaluated over the path {w0,w1,w2} always s is true
In this world evaluated over the path {w5,w6} next q is true

Figure 1: Diagram illustrating evaluation of formulae in a world.

Thus if an agent has the capability that *optional*(ψ) is true, this also implies a belief that *optional*(ψ) is true. This should not be read as having a capability to achieve X implies that I believe X is true. The natural language semantics is closer to the statement that if I have a capability to achieve X (at time t), then I believe that it is possible for X to be true (at time t). Statements where α is a simple predicate rather than a formula involving *optional* must be evaluated at a particular time point. So CAP(*rich*) $\supset$ BEL(*rich*) means that if I am capable of being rich now then I believe I am rich now. Importantly it does not mean that if I have a capability of being rich in the future, I believe that I am rich in the future - I believe only that there is some possible future where I am rich. We note that intuitively it only really makes sense to talk about capabilities (and goals and intentions) with respect to future time, so the semantics of formulae such as CAP(*rich*) $\supset$ BEL(*rich*) are intuitively awkward though not problematic. This is inherent in the original logic and applies to goals and intentions at least as much as to capabilities. It could be addressed by limiting the form of valid formulae using CAP, GOAL and INTEND but we have chosen to remain consistent with the original BDI logic.

The semantic condition associated with this axiom is:[7]
CIC1 $\forall\, w' \in \mathcal{B}_t^w, \exists\, w'' \in \mathcal{C}_t^w$ such that $w'' \sqsubseteq w'$.

Capability-Goal Compatibility
This axiom and associated semantic condition states that if the agent has an O-formula α as a goal, then the agent also has α as a capability. This constrains the agent to adopt as goals only formulae where there is a corresponding capability.
AIC2 GOAL(α) $\supset$ CAP(α)
CIC2 $\forall\, w' \in \mathcal{C}_t^w, \exists\, w'' \in \mathcal{G}_t^w$ such that $w'' \sqsubseteq w'$.

Mixed Modality Axioms

Axioms AI4, AI5 and AI6 define the relationships when the BEL, GOAL and INTEND modalities are nested. We add two new axioms and a corollary along with semantic conditions to capture the relationship between CAP and each of the other modalities. We note that the original axiom AI4

---
[7]$\mathcal{B}, \mathcal{C}, \mathcal{G}$ and $\mathcal{I}$ are the accessibility relations with respect to beliefs, capabilities, goals and intentions respectively.

actually follows from AI1 and AI6.

Beliefs about Capabilities
If the agent has a capability α then it believes that it has a capability α.
AIC3 CAP(α) $\supset$ BEL(CAP(α))
CIC3[8] $\forall w' \in \mathcal{B}_t^w, \forall w'' \in \mathcal{C}_t^{w'}$ we have $w'' \in \mathcal{C}_t^w$

Capabilities regarding Goals
If an agent has a goal α then it has the capability to have the goal α.
AIC4 GOAL(α) $\supset$ CAP(GOAL(α))
CIC4 $\forall w' \in \mathcal{C}_t^w, \forall w'' \in \mathcal{G}_t^{w'}$ we have $w'' \in \mathcal{G}_t^w$

Capabilities regarding Intentions
If an agent has an intention α it also has the capability to have the intention α.
Follows from AIC2 and AI6
INTEND(α) $\supset$ CAP(INTEND(α))
semantic condition:
$\forall w' \in \mathcal{C}_t^w, \forall w'' \in \mathcal{I}_t^{w'}$ we have $w'' \in \mathcal{I}_t^w$

Strengthening of this group of axioms by replacing implication with equivalence would result in the expanded version of the equivalences mentioned in (Rao and Georgeff 1991) namely INTEND(α) $\equiv$ BEL(INTEND(α)) $\equiv$ CAP(INTEND(α)) $\equiv$ GOAL(INTEND(α)) and GOAL(α) $\equiv$ BEL(GOAL(α)) $\equiv$ CAP(GOAL(α)). Equivalence strengthening would also give CAP(α) $\equiv$ BEL(CAP(α)). As mentioned in (Rao and Georgeff 1991) this has the effect of collapsing mixed nested modalities to their simpler non-nested forms.

We will refer to the axioms AI2, AI3, AI6, AI7, AI8, AIC1, AIC2, AIC3 and AIC4 as the *basic IC-system*. We note that all axioms of the *I-system* remain true, although some are consequences rather than axioms.[9]

Commitment Axioms

Rao and Georgeff define three variants of a commitment axiom, which taken together with the basic axioms define

---
[8]This (and CIC4) is subtly different from the analogue of what is in (Rao and Georgeff 1991), which appears to be slightly wrong. The explanation with proof and counter-example for the original formulation will be given in the full paper.

[9]AI1 follows from AIC1 and AIC2. AI4 follows from AIC1, AIC2 and AI6. AI5 follows from AIC1 and AIC4.

what they call a *blindly committed agent*, a *single-minded agent* and an *open-minded agent*. The blindly committed agent maintains intentions until they are believed true, the single-minded agent maintains intentions until they are believed true or are believed impossible to achieve, while the open-minded agent maintains intentions until they are believed true or are no longer goals.

We define an additional kind of agent which we term a *self-aware agent* which is able to drop an intention if it believes it no longer has the capability to achieve that intention.

The *self-aware agent* is defined by the *basic IC-system* plus the following axiom which we call AIC9d.[10]

AIC9d INTEND($inevitable \Diamond \phi$) $\supset$
$inevitable$(INTEND($inevitable \Diamond \phi$)
$\bigcup$ (BEL(ϕ) $\vee \neg$CAP($optional \Diamond \phi$)))

It is then possible to extend theorem 1 in (Rao and Georgeff 1991) to show that a self-aware agent will inevitably eventually believe its intentions, and to prove a new theorem that under certain circumstances the self-aware agent will achieve its intentions.[11] Self-awareness can be combined with either open-mindedness or single-mindedness to obtain self-aware-open-minded and self-aware-single-minded agents.

Properties of the Logic

The logic allows for believing things without having the capability for this, i.e. BEL(ϕ) $\wedge \neg$ CAP(ϕ) is satisfiable. This means that, for instance, you can believe the sun will inevitably rise, without having a capability to achieve this. Also $inevitable(\Box$ BEL(ϕ)) $\wedge \neg$ GOAL(ϕ) is satisfiable. Similarly, one can have the capability to achieve something without having the goal to achieve this. In general, a modal formula does not imply a stronger modal formula, where BEL $<_{strong}$ CAP $<_{strong}$ GOAL $<_{strong}$ INTEND.

Theorem 1 *For modalities R_1 and R_2 such that $R_1 <_{strong} R_2$, the following formulae are satisfiable:*
(a) $R_1(\phi) \wedge \neg R_2(\phi)$
(b) $inevitable(\Box R_1(\phi)) \wedge \neg R_2(\phi)$

Proof: We prove the result for BEL and CAP. The proof for the other pairs of modalities is similar. Assume BEL(ϕ). Then, ϕ is true in every belief-accessible world. For every belief-accessible world there is a capability-accessible world. However, $\mathcal{C}$ may map to worlds that do not correspond to any belief-accessible world. If ϕ is not true in one of these worlds, then ϕ is not a capability. This shows the satisfiability of (a). Similar reasoning yields (b). ♣

As we have seen before, the modalities are closed under implication. However, another property of the logic is that a modal operator is not closed under implication with respect to weaker modalities. For instance, an agent may have the capability to do ϕ, believe that ϕ implies γ, but not have the capability to do γ.[12]

---

[10]This numbering is chosen because of the relationship of AIC9d to AI9a, AI9b, and AI9c in the original *I-system*.

[11]These theorems and proofs are not shown here due to space restrictions. They are available in the longer version of the paper.

[12]The alternative formulation referred to in footnote 5 does not have this property with respect to capabilities.

Theorem 2 *For modalities R_1 and R_2 such that $R_1 <_{strong} R_2$, the following formulae are satisfiable:*
(a) $R_2(\phi) \wedge R_1(inevitable(\Box (\phi \supset \gamma))) \wedge \neg R_2(\gamma)$
(b) $R_2(\phi) \wedge inevitable(\Box R_1(inevitable(\Box (\phi \supset \gamma)))) \wedge \neg R_2(\gamma)$

Proof: We prove the result for BEL and CAP. The proof for the other pairs of modalities is similar. Assume CAP(ϕ) and BEL($inevitable(\Box (\phi \supset \gamma))$). Then, ϕ is true in every capability-accessible world. To be able to infer that γ is true in each capability-accessible world, we would need that $\phi \supset \gamma$ is true in each capability-accessible world. We know that for every belief-accessible world $inevitable(\Box (\phi \supset \gamma))$ is true and that for each belief-accessible world there is a capability-accessible world. However, $\mathcal{C}$ may map to other worlds, where this is not true and thus γ is not a capability. This shows the satisfiability of (a). Similar reasoning yields (b). ♣

The formal semantics of capabilities as defined fit well into the existing R&G BDI logic and allow definition of further interesting types of agents. We look now at how this addition of capabilities affects the specification of an abstract interpreter for BDI systems and also what issues and questions arise for implementations as the result of the theoretical exploration.

Implementation aspects

An abstraction of a BDI-interpreter which follows the logic of the basic *I-system* is given in (Rao and Georgeff 1992).[13] The first stages in the cycle of this abstract interpreter are to generate and select plan options. These are filtered by beliefs, goals and current intentions. Capabilities now provide an additional filter on the options we generate and select. Similarly capabilities must be considered when dropping beliefs, goals and intentions. In a system with dynamic roles capabilities themselves may also be dropped. Thus we obtain this slightly modified version of the interpreter in (Rao and Georgeff 1992).

BDI with capabilities interpreter:
```
initialise-state();
do
  options :=
    option-generator(event-queue,B,C,G,I);
  selected-options :=
    deliberate(options,B,C,G,I);
  update-intentions(selected-options,I);
  execute(I);
  get-new-external-events();
  drop-successful-attitudes(B,C,G,I);
  drop-impossible-attitudes(B,C,G,I);
until quit.
```

This abstract interpreter is at a very high level and there are many details which must be considered in the actual implementation that are hidden in this abstraction. One important implementation detail that is highlighted by the def-

---

[13]Due to lack of space we cannot give more than the most basic summary here of this interpreter and its relation to the logic.

initions of the various kinds of agents (blindly committed, single-minded, open-minded and self-aware) has to do with when intentions should be dropped. With respect to capabilities the axiom AIC9d highlights the fact that if capabilities are allowed to change during execution it may be necessary to drop some intentions when a capability is lost/removed.

The observation that it is possible for an agent to have the capability to do ϕ, believe that ϕ implies γ, but not have the capability to do γ (see before), highlights an area where one may wish to make the agent more "powerful" in its reasoning by disallowing this situation. This is possible by a modification of the logical formalisation[14] but would have an impact on how the option generation and selection phases of the abstract interpreter work.

In (Rao and Georgeff 1992) an example is given to illustrate the workings of the specified abstract interpreter. In this example John wants to quench his thirst and has plans (which are presented as a special kind of belief) for doing this by drinking water or drinking soda, both of which then become options and can be chosen as intentions (instantiated plans that will be acted on).

It is also possible to construct the example where the agent believes that rain always makes the garden wet, and that rain is eventually possible, represented as:
BEL($inevitable$ $\Box$(rain) $\supset$ (garden-wet))
BEL($optional$ $\Diamond$(rain))

In the R&G formalism which does not differentiate between plans and other kinds of beliefs this would allow our agent to adopt (rain) as a GOAL. However, in the absence of any plan in the plan library for ever achieving rain this does not make intuitive sense - and in fact could not happen in implemented systems. With the $IC-system$ presented here we would also require CAP($optional$ $\Diamond$(rain)) thus restricting goal adoption to situations where the agent has appropriate capabilities (i.e. plans).

This example demonstrates that in some respects the $IC-system$ is actually a more correct formalisation of implemented BDI systems than the original $I-system$.

Conclusion and Future Work

The formalisation of capabilities and their relationships to beliefs, goals and intentions is a clean extension of an existing theoretical framework. Advantages of the extension include eliminating mismatch between theory and what happens in actual systems, better mapping of theory to intuition, indication of areas for development of implemented reasoning in line with the theory and highlighting of issues for consideration in actual implementations.

Exploration of how an agent's knowledge of other agents' capabilities affects its own goals and intentions requires further work and some modifications to the axioms relating goals to capabilities. This seems to require a framework which allows for beliefs about other agent's capabilities.

---

[14]The necessary modification is essentially to require that all capability-accessible worlds are sub-worlds of belief-accessible worlds. However this breaks the symmetry of the current formalisation where capability accessible worlds are exactly analogous to belief/goal/intention accessible worlds.

Goals would then be constrained by a combination of one's own capabilities plus beliefs about other agent's capabilities.

References

M.E. Bratman, D.J. Israel, and M.E. Pollack. Plans and resource-bounded practical reasoning. *Computational Intelligence*, 4(4):349–355, 1988.

P. Busetta, N. Howden, R. Rönnquist, and A. Hodgson. Structuring bdi agents in functional clusters. In *Proceedings of the Sixth International Workshop on Agent Theories, Architectures, and Languages - ATAL 99*, 1999.

P. Busetta, R. Rönnquist, A. Hodgson, and A. Lucas. Jack intelligent agents - components for intelligent agents in java. In *AgentLink News Letter*, pages 2–5, January 1999.

P. Cohen and H. Levesque. Intention is choice with commitment. *Artificial Intelligence*, 42:213–261, 1990.

M. Georgeff and F. Ingrand. Decision-making in an embedded reasoning system. In *Proceedings of the International Joint Conference on Artificial Intelligence - IJCAI 89*, pages 972–978, August 1989.

M. Huber. Jam: A bdi-theoretic mobile agent architecture. In *Proceedings of the Third International Conference on Autonomous Agents - Agents 99*, pages 236–243, Seattle, WA, 1999.

J. Lee, M. Huber, P.G. Kenny, and E.H. Durfee. Um-prs: An implementation of the procedural reasoning system for multi-robot applications. In *Proceedings of the Conference on Intelligent Robotics in Field, Factory, Service and Space - CIRFFSS 94*, pages 842–849, Houston, TX, 1994.

A. Rao and M. Georgeff. Modeling rational agents within a bdi-architecture. In *Principles of Knowledge Representation and Reasoning: Proceedings of the Second International Conference - KR 91*, pages 473–484, 1991.

A. Rao and M. Georgeff. An abstract architecture for rational agents. In *Principles of Knowledge Representation and Reasoning: Proceedings of the Third International Conference - KR 92*, pages 439–449, 1992.

A. Rao and M. Georgeff. Bdi agents: From theory to practice. In *Proceedings of the First International Conference on Multi-Agent Systems - ICMAS 95*, San Francisco, USA, 1995.

Y. Shoham. Agent oriented programming. *Artificial Intelligence*, 60:51–92, 1993.

Iterative Combinatorial Auctions: Theory and Practice

David C. Parkes and Lyle H. Ungar
Computer and Information Science Department
University of Pennsylvania
200 South 33rd Street, Philadelphia, PA 19104
dparkes@unagi.cis.upenn.edu; ungar@cis.upenn.edu

Abstract

Combinatorial auctions, which allow agents to bid directly for bundles of resources, are necessary for optimal auction-based solutions to resource allocation problems with agents that have non-additive values for resources, such as distributed scheduling and task assignment problems. We introduce *i*Bundle, the first iterative combinatorial auction that is optimal for a reasonable agent bidding strategy, in this case myopic best-response bidding. Its optimality is proved with a novel connection to primal-dual optimization theory. We demonstrate orders of magnitude performance improvements over the only other known optimal combinatorial auction, the Generalized Vickrey Auction.

Introduction

Auctions provide useful mechanisms for resource allocation problems with autonomous and self-interested agents. Typical applications include task assignment and distributed scheduling problems, and are characterized with distributed information about agents' local problems and multiple conflicting goals (Wellman 1993; Clearwater 1996). Auctions can minimize communication within a system, and generate optimal (or near-optimal) solutions that maximize the sum value over all agents.

More recently, electronic commerce has generated new interest in auction-based systems, both as dynamic mechanisms to sell items to individuals, and as systems for business-to-business transactions. Many retailers have on-line consumer auctions, e.g. www.onsale.com, and there are nascent auctions for procurement in the supply-chain, e.g. www.freemarkets.com. However, at present the vast majority of online auctions are simple variations on the traditional English auction, an ascending-price single-item auction.

We introduce *i*Bundle, an iterative combinatorial auction that allows agents to bid for bundles of items while the auctioneer increases prices and maintains a provisional allocation. Bundles are important in many real-world problems: consider a manufacturer that needs either components A and B, or just component C; consider a mobile agent that needs an interval of compute time; consider a train that needs a bundle of departure and arrival times on tracks across its route. Although combinatorial auctions can be approximated by multiple auctions on single items, this often results in inefficient outcomes (Bykowsky, Cull, & Ledyard 2000).

*i*Bundle is the first iterative combinatorial auction that is optimal for a reasonable agent bidding strategy, in this case myopic utility-maximizing agents that place *best-response* bids to prices. In this paper we prove the optimality of *i*Bundle with a novel connection to primal-dual optimization theory (Papadimitriou & Steiglitz 1982) that also suggests a useful methodology for the design and analysis of iterative auctions for other problems.

*i*Bundle has many computational advantages over the only other known optimal combinatorial auction, the Generalized Vickrey Auction (GVA) (Varian & MacKie-Mason 1995). As an iterative auction, agents can incrementally compute values for different bundles of items as prices change, and make new bids in response to bids from other agents. In comparison, the GVA is a *sealed-bid* auction, in which agents first submit bids simultaneously, and then the auctioneer determines an allocation and payments. In the GVA an agent's optimal strategy is to bid for, and compute the value of, *all* bundles for which it has positive value. This is often impossible, since for $|G|$ items there are $2^{|G|}$ bundles to value, each of which may require solving a difficult optimization problem (Parkes 1999a; Sandholm 1993).

However, combinatorial auctions introduce new computational complexities in mechanism execution. In particular, the auctioneer's *winner-determination* (WD) problem, the problem of choosing bids to maximize revenue, is $\mathcal{NP}$-hard by reduction from the maximal weighted clique problem (Rothkopf et al. 1998).

In *i*Bundle the auctioneer must solve a *sequence* of WD problems (one in each round) to maintain a provisional allocation as agents bid. In comparison, in the GVA the auctioneer must solve one WD problem for each agent in the final allocation. Each WD problem in *i*Bundle is smaller than in the GVA, because agents bid for less bundles. In addition, the auctioneer can increase the minimal bid increment and reduce the number of rounds to termination, reducing computation for some loss in economic efficiency. Further speed-ups are achieved through caching of solutions from previous rounds in the auction, and introducing approximate WD algorithms that maintain the same incentives for myopic agents to bid truthfully in each round.

We note that the GVA has stronger truth-revelation properties that *i*Bundle. Truthful bidding is optimal in the GVA whatever the bids of other agents. In comparison, rational agents with lookahead could manipulate the outcome of *i*Bundle to their advantage, and lead to suboptimal allocations. However, there is some evidence that myopic bidding may be a reasonable assumption in practice, perhaps because of the computational complexity of strategic behavior. For example, in the FCC broadband spectrum auction, conducted as a set of simultaneous ascending-price auctions on spectrum licenses, bids were rarely above minimum ask prices and jump bids were the exception (Cramton 1997).

In Parkes & Ungar (2000) we present a simple extension to *i*Bundle that makes it robust to strategic manipulation in several interesting problems; we adjust the final prices in *i*Bundle towards Vickrey prices.

The Ascending-Price Bundle Auction

*i*Bundle is an ascending-price auction that allows agents to bid on arbitrary combinations of items during the auction. The auctioneer increases prices on bundles as bids are received and maintains a set of winning bids that maximize revenue.

Let G denote the set of items to be auctioned, I denote the set of agents, and $S \subseteq G$ denote a bundle of items. The auction proceeds in rounds, indexed $t \geq 1$. We describe the types of bids that agents can place, and the allocations and price updates computed by the auctioneer.[1]

Bids. Agents can place exclusive-or bids for bundles, e.g. S_1 XOR S_2, to indicate than an agent wants either all items in S_1 or all items in S_2 but not both S_1 and S_2.[2]

Agent i associates a *bid price* $p^t_{bid,i}(S)$ with a bid for bundle S in round t, non-negative by definition. The price must either be within ϵ of, or greater than, the *ask price* announced by the auctioneer (see below). Parameter $\epsilon > 0$ defines the *minimal bid increment*, the minimal price increase in the auction. Agents must repeat bids for bundles in the current allocation, but can bid at the same price if the ask price has increased since the previous round.[3]

Winner-determination. The auctioneer solves a winner-determination problem in each round, computing an allocation of bundles to agents that maximizes revenue. The auctioneer must respect agents' XOR bid constraints, and cannot allocate any item to more than one agent. The provisional allocation becomes the final allocation when the auction terminate.

---

[1]The *i*Bundle auction has three variations, that differ in their price update rules (Parkes 1999b). In this paper, we use *i*Bundle both to refer to the family of auctions in general, and also to variation *i*Bundle(*d*), which we describe in detail.

[2]Exclusive-or bids provide complete expressibility, but are not necessarily computationally efficient for all problems. We can derive price-update rules for other bid languages (Parkes 1999b).

[3]An agent can also bid ϵ below the ask price for any bundle in any round— but then it cannot bid a higher price for that bundle in the future. This allows an agent to bid for a bundle priced slightly above its value.

Approximate Winner-determination. The auctioneer can also use an approximate algorithm for winner-determination, and still maintain the same incentives for myopic agents to follow the same bidding strategy. To achieve this an approximate algorithm must have the *bid-monotonicity* property:

Definition 1. *Bid monotonicity. An algorithm for winner-determination satisfies bid monotonicity if whenever an agent i is allocated a bundle with bids $\mathcal{B}_i$, it is also allocated a bundle with bids $\mathcal{B}_i \cup B$ that include a bid for an additional bundle B.*

It is straightforward to prove that *optimal* winner-determination algorithms are bid-monotonic.

Prices. The price-update rule generalizes the rule in the English auction, which is an ascending-price auction for a single item. In the English auction the price is increased whenever two or more agents bid for the item at the current price. In *i*Bundle the price on a bundle is increased when one or more agents that do not receive a bundle in the current allocation bid at (or above) the current ask price for a bundle. The price is increased to ϵ (the minimal bid increment) above the greatest failed bid price. The initial ask prices are zero.

The auctioneer announces a new ask price, $p^t_{ask}(S)$ in round t, for all bundles S that increase in price. Other bundles are implicitly priced at least as high as the greatest price of any bundle they contain, i.e. $p_{ask}(S') \geq p_{ask}(S)$ for $S' \supseteq S$. These ask prices are anonymous, the same for all agents.

Price discrimination. In some problems the auctioneer introduces price discrimination based on agents' bids, with different ask prices to different agents, when this is necessary to achieve an optimal allocation. A simple rule dynamically introduces price discrimination on an agent-by-agent basis, when an agent submits bids that are **not** *safe*:

Definition 2. *Safe bids. An agent's bids are **safe** if the agent is allocated a bundle in the current allocation, or it does not bid at or above the ask price for any pair of **compatible** bundles S_1, S_2, such that $S_1 \cap S_2 = \emptyset$.*

Suppose agent i bids unsuccessfully for compatible bundles S_1 and S_2 in round t. It is still possible that bids for bundles S_1 and S_2 from two different agents can be successful at the prices. Remember that the XOR bid constraint prevents the auctioneer accepting both bids from agent i.

When an agent's bids are not safe the agent receives *individual ask prices*, $p_{ask,i}(S)$, in future rounds. Individual prices are initialized to the current general prices, $p^t_{ask,i}(S) = p^t_{ask}(S)$, and increased to ϵ above the agent's bids in future rounds that the agent receives no bundle in the provisional allocation.

Termination. The auction terminates when: [T1] all agents submit the same bids in two consecutive rounds, or [T2] all agents that bid receive a bundle.

A Myopic Best-Response Bidding Strategy

*i*Bundle computes an optimal allocation with *myopically ra-*

tional agents that play a best (utility-maximizing) response to the current ask prices and allocation in the auction. The agents are myopic in the sense that they only consider the current round of the auction.

Let $v_i(S)$ denote agent i's value for bundle S, and assume $v_i(\emptyset) = 0$ and *free disposal* of items, so that $v_i(S') \geq v_i(S)$ for all $S' \supseteq S$. Consider a *risk-neutral* agent, with a quasi-linear utility function $u_i(S) = v_i(S) - p(S)$ for bundle S at price $p(S)$. Further, assume that agents are indifferent to within a utility of $\pm\epsilon$, the minimal bid increment. This is reasonable as $\epsilon \to 0$.

By definition, a myopic agent bids to maximize utility at the current ask prices (taking an ϵ discount when repeating a bid for a bundle in the provisional allocation or bidding for a bundle priced just above its value). The myopic best-response strategy is to submit an XOR bid for all bundles S that maximize (to within ϵ) utility $u_i(S)$ at the current prices. This maximizes the probability of a successful bid for bid-monotonic WD algorithms.

Theoretical Results

We are now ready to introduce our main theoretical results. Recall that $|G|$ is the number of items, $|I|$ is the number of agents, and ϵ is the minimal bid increment.

Theorem 1. *iBundle terminates with an allocation that is within $3\min\{|G|,|I|\}\epsilon$ of the optimal solution, for myopic best-response agent bidding strategies.*

The auction is *optimal* as the bid increment approaches zero because the error-term goes to zero.

However, *i*Bundle requires price discrimination, and this can be hard to enforce. For example, the auctioneer must prevent agents entering the auction under multiple pseudonyms, and also prevent the transfer of items in an after-market. In a simpler variation, *i*Bundle(2), the auctioneer never tests for bid-safety and never price discriminates between agents (Parkes 1999b).[4] From Theorem 1, this variation is optimal at least when bids are **safe** (this condition is sufficient but not necessary):

Theorem 2. *iBundle(2) terminates with an allocation that is within $3\min\{|G|,|I|\}\epsilon$ of the optimal solution when bids are safe, for myopic best-response agent bidding strategies.*

As an example, bids are safe if each agent bids for a set of *conflicting* bundles in every round of the auction. *i*Bundle(2) also provably solves the following problems without price discrimination: (1) every agent demands different bundles; (2) agents have additive or superadditive values, i.e. $v(S \cup S') \geq v(S) + v(S')$ for non-conflicting bundles S and S'; (3) the bundles that receive bids throughout the auction are from a single partition of items, e.g. all bids are for pairs of matching shoes, or single items.

In experimental tests *i*Bundle(2) performs well in many hard problems, achieving an average of 99% allocative efficiency[5] (Parkes 1999b) compared to 82% allocative efficiency from non-combinatorial auctions in the same problems. We found that price discrimination only had a noticeable effect on allocative efficiency with very small bid increments, and after many rounds of bidding.

Proof of Optimality

The proof of *i*Bundle's optimality is inspired by a proof due to Bertsekas (1990) for a simpler iterative auction, and makes an interesting connection with *primal-dual* theory of linear programming. It helps to motivate the price-update rules, the *safety condition* for introducing price discrimination, and the conditions for termination.

Primal-dual is an algorithm-design paradigm that is often used to solve combinatorial optimization problems (Papadimitriou & Steiglitz 1982). A problem is first formulated both as a *primal* and a *dual* linear program (see the examples below for *i*Bundle). A primal-dual algorithm searches for feasible primal and dual solutions that satisfy *complementary slackness conditions*, instead of searching for an optimal primal (or dual) solution directly. Complementary-slackness (CS for short) expresses logical relationships between the values of primal and dual solutions that are necessary and sufficient for optimality:

Complementary-Slackness Theorem. *Feasible primal and dual solutions are optimal if and only if they satisfy complementary slackness conditions.*

*i*Bundle implements a primal-dual algorithm for a linear-program formulation of the combinatorial resource allocation problem. It does this *without* formulating or solving the primal and dual problems explicitly, but based on information in agents' bids. Remember that the auctioneer does not know agents' values for resources.

Proof of *i*Bundle(2)

We first prove Theorem 2, the optimality of *i*Bundle(2) (the variation without price discrimination) in problems for which agents' bids are safe. A proof of Theorem 1, the optimality of *i*Bundle in general problems, follows from a simple transformation between *i*Bundle and *i*Bundle(2).

Figure 1 presents a standard integer program formulation of the combinatorial resource allocation problem. The objective is to maximize the total value of the allocation, given value $v_i(S)$ for bundle S to agent i. Integer variables $x_i(S) \in \{0, 1\}$ indicate whether or not agent i receives bundle S. Constraints (IP-1) ensure that each agent receives at most a single bundle, constraints (IP-2) ensure that each item is allocated to at most one agent.

Bikchandani & Ostroy (1998) formulate the combinatorial resource allocation problem as a *linear program*, see [LP$_2$] in Figure 2. The integer constraints $x_i(S) \in \{0, 1\}$ in [IP] are relaxed to $x_i(S) \geq 0$, and new variables $k \in K$ are introduced which correspond to a partition of items into bundles. K is the set of all possible partitions. Constraints

---

[4]Label 2 refers to "second-degree" price discrimination, non-linear prices in bundles of items but identical prices across agents (Bikchandani & Ostroy 1998).

[5]*Allocative efficiency* is a measure of optimality, computed as the ratio of the total value of the allocation across all agents to the value of the optimal allocation.

$$\max_{x_i(S)} \sum_{S \subseteq G} \sum_{i \in I} x_i(S) v_i(S) \quad \text{[IP]}$$

$$\text{s.t.} \quad \sum_{S \subseteq G} x_i(S) \leq 1, \quad \forall i \quad \text{(IP-1)}$$

$$\sum_{S \subseteq G, j \in S} \sum_i x_i(S) \leq 1, \quad \forall j \quad \text{(IP-2)}$$

$$x_i(S) \in \{0, 1\}, \quad \forall i, S$$

Figure 1: Combinatorial resource allocation problem: Integer program [IP] formulation.

$$\max_{x_i(S), y(k)} \sum_{S \subseteq G} \sum_{i \in I} x_i(S) v_i(S) \quad \text{[LP}_2\text{]}$$

$$\text{s.t.} \quad \sum_{S \subseteq G} x_i(S) \leq 1, \quad \forall i \quad \text{(LP-1)}$$

$$\sum_{i \in I} x_i(S) \leq \sum_{k \in K, S \in k} y(k), \quad \forall S \quad \text{(LP-2)}$$

$$\sum_{k \in K} y(k) \leq 1 \quad \text{(LP-3)}$$

$$x_i(S), y(k) \geq 0, \quad \forall i, S, k$$

$$\min_{p(i), p(S), \pi} \sum_{i \in I} p(i) + \pi \quad \text{[DLP}_2\text{]}$$

$$\text{s.t.} \quad p(i) + p(S) \geq v_i(S), \quad \forall i, S \quad \text{(DLP-1)}$$

$$\pi - \sum_{S \in k} p(S) \geq 0, \quad \forall k \quad \text{(DLP-2)}$$

$$p(i), p(S), \pi \geq 0, \quad \forall i, S$$

Figure 2: Combinatorial resource allocation problem: Primal linear program [LP$_2$] and dual linear program [DLP$_2$] formulations.

(LP-2) and (LP-3) replace constraints (IP-2), and ensure that a feasible solution does not allocate more than one of each item.

In general, an optimal solution to the linear program [LP$_2$] can allocate fractional items to agents, and need not be a feasible solution to [IP]. In fact, the optimal solution to [LP$_2$] is integral and solves [IP] if and only if non-discriminatory bundle prices exist that support the optimal allocation in *competitive equilibrium* with best-response agent bidding strategies (Bikchandani & Ostroy 1998). Competitive equilibrium implies that agents' maximize utility and the auctioneer maximizes' revenue given the final prices and the final allocation.

The dual problem, [DLP$_2$], to primal [LP$_2$] is shown in Figure 2. Variables $p(i)$, $p(S)$ and π correspond to constraints (LP-1), (LP-2) and (LP-3) respectively, and dual constraints (DLP-1) and (DLP-2) correspond to primal variables $x_i(S)$ and $y(k)$. When the primal solution is integral the dual problem computes competitive equilibrium bundle prices that minimize the sum of agent utility and auctioneer revenue, see (1) and (2) below.

We prove that iBundle(2) implements a primal-dual algorithm for [LP$_2$] and [DLP$_2$], and computes integral solutions to [LP$_2$] when agents follow myopic best-response bidding strategies and bids are safe. First, we show that the allocation and prices in each round of the auction correspond to feasible primal and dual solutions. Then, we show that the primal and dual solutions satisfy CS when the auction terminates.

Let S_i denote the provisional allocation to agent i, and $p_{\text{ask}}(S)$ denote the ask price for bundle S.

Feasible primal. To construct a feasible primal solution assign $x_i(S_i) = 1$ and $x_i(S') = 0$ for all $S' \neq S_i$. Partition $y(k^*) = 1$ for $k^* = [S_1, \ldots, S_{|I|}]$, and $y(k) = 0$ otherwise.

Feasible dual. To construct a feasible dual solution assign $p(S) = p_{\text{ask}}(S)$. Constraints (DLP-1) and (DLP-2) are satisfied with assignments:

$$p(i) = \max\left\{0, \max_{S \subseteq G}\{v_i(S) - p(S)\}\right\} \quad (1)$$

$$\pi = \max_{k \in K} \sum_{S \in k} p(S) \quad (2)$$

The value $p(i)$ can be interpreted as agent i's maximum utility at the prices, and π can be interpreted as the maximum revenue that the auctioneer can achieve at the prices (irrespective of the bids placed by agents). The auctioneer does not explicitly compute the value of $p(i)$, rather we prove that the allocation and prices in the auction satisfy CS with these assignments when the auction terminates, based on the bids placed by agents. This is just as well, because the values $v_i(S)$ remain private information to agents during the auction.

Complementary-slackness conditions. The first primal CS condition,[6] (CS-1) is:

$$x_i(S) > 0 \Rightarrow p(i) + p(S) = v_i(S), \quad \forall i, S \quad \text{(CS-1)}$$

Given (1) it states that all agents must only receive bundles that maximize utility at the current prices. (CS-1) is maintained throughout the auction because bundles are only allocated according to bids from agents, and agents place best-response bids. Formally, for any bundle S bid by agent i: (i) $p_{\text{ask}}(S) - \epsilon \leq p_{\text{bid},i}(S) \leq p_{\text{ask}}(S)$; (ii) $v_i(S) - p_{\text{bid},i}(S) + \epsilon \geq \max_{S'}\{v_i(S') - p_{\text{bid},i}(S')\}$ because agents bid for bundles that maximize utility within ϵ; (iii) $v_i(S) - p_{\text{bid},i}(S) \geq 0$, because agents only bid for bundles with positive utility. Since $x_i(S_i) = 1$ implies agent i bid for bundle S_i, we have:

$$x_i(S) > 0 \Rightarrow v_i(S) - p_{\text{ask}}(S) + 2\epsilon \geq$$
$$\max\left\{0, \max_{S'}\{v_i(S') - p_{\text{ask}}(S')\}\right\}$$

---

[6]Complementary slackness states that if a primal variable is non-zero then its corresponding dual inequality constraint is binding. Similarly for dual variables.

Substituting for $p(i)$ and $p_{\text{ask}}(S) = p(S)$, we prove ϵ-CS-1:

$$x_i(S) > 0 \Rightarrow p(i) + p(S) \leq v_i(S) + 2\epsilon, \quad \forall i, S \quad (\epsilon\text{-CS-1})$$

The second primal CS condition, (CS-2), is:

$$y(k) > 0 \Rightarrow \pi - \sum_{S \in k} p(S) = 0, \quad \forall k \quad (\text{CS-2})$$

Given (2) it states that the allocation must maximize the auctioneer's revenue at prices $p(S)$, over all possible allocations and irrespective of bids received from agents. We prove (CS-2) is maintained in all rounds because it is not binding that the auctioneer must allocate bundles according to agents' bids. Through the price-update rules the auctioneer is able to maximize revenue given prices in every round.

Formally: (i) Agent i with one of the highest losing bid for bundle S in round t will continue to bid for bundle S in rounds $t + 1$. Let $u_i^t(S)$ denote agent i's utility for bundle S in round t. Then, $u_i^{t+1}(S) = u_i^t(S) - \epsilon$ because the ask price for S increases by ϵ. Also, $u_i^t(S) \geq u_i^t(S')$ for all bundles S' the agent did not bid in round t. Hence, with $u_i^t(S') \geq u_i^{t+1}(S')$ because the price of S' can only increase in round $t+1$, we have $u_i^{t+1}(S) \geq u_i^{t+1}(S') - \epsilon$ and a bid for S' can never exclude a bid for S from agent i's best-response bids in round $t+1$. A similar argument can be made for the utility of bundles that the agent *did* bid in round t; (ii) No single agent causes the price to increase to its current level on a pair of compatible bundles. This follows because price updates are due to safe bids from agents.

Therefore, for partition k^* such that $y(k^*) = 1$, $\sum_{S_i \in k^*} p_{\text{ask}}(S_i) \geq \sum_{S_i \in k^*} p_{\text{bid},i}(S_i)$, because $p_{\text{ask}}(S) \geq p_{\text{bid},i}(S)$, and $\sum_{S_i \in k^*} p_{\text{bid},i}(S_i) \geq \max_{k \in K} \sum_{S_i \in k} p_{\text{bid},i}(S_i)$ because of (i) and (ii), i.e. the constraints to allocate to agents' bids are not binding. Finally, with (2) we have $\max_{k \in K} \sum_{S_i \in k} p_{\text{bid},i}(S_i) \geq \pi - \min\{|G|, |I|\}\epsilon$ because $p_{\text{bid},i}(S) \geq p_{\text{ask}}(S) - \epsilon$ and an allocation can include no more bundles than there are agents or items. We prove ϵ-CS-2:

$$y(k) > 0 \Rightarrow \pi - \sum_{S \in k} p(S) \leq \min\{|G|, |I|\}\epsilon, \quad \forall k \quad (\epsilon\text{-CS-2})$$

The first dual CS condition, (CS-3), is:

$$p(i) > 0 \Rightarrow \sum_{S \subseteq G} x_i(S) = 1, \quad \forall i \quad (\text{CS-3})$$

Given (1) it states that every agent with positive utility for some bundle at the current prices must receive a bundle in the allocation. (CS-3) is only satisfied during the auction for agents that receive bundles in the provisional allocation, but we prove (CS-3) for all agents when *i*Bundle(2) terminates. In termination case [T2] every agent that bids receives a bundle, so we immediately have (CS-3) with myopic best-response agents. In case [T1] some agents may bid and receive no bundles. However, these agents must bid at ϵ below the ask price and have values just below ask prices, otherwise prices would increase and their bids would change.

Finally, the last pair of dual CS conditions, (CS-4) and (CS-5), are:

$$p(S) > 0 \Rightarrow \sum_{i \in I} x_i(S) = \sum_{k \in K, S \in k} y(k), \quad \forall S \quad (\text{CS-4})$$

$$\pi > 0 \Rightarrow \sum_{k \in K} y(k) = 1 \quad (\text{CS-5})$$

The assignment $y(k^*) = 1$ for the partition $k^* = [S_1 \ldots S_{|I|}]$ trivially satisfies the RHS of both conditions.

Termination. By contradiction, assume the auction never terminates. Informally, [T1] implies that agents must submit different bids in successive rounds, but with myopic best-response bidding this implies that prices must increase, and agents must eventually bid above their values for bundles. We prove a contradiction with myopic best-response bidding strategies.

Putting it all together. Summing ϵ-CS-1 over all agents in the final allocation, and with $p(i) = 0$ for agents not in the allocation by (CS-3), $\sum_{i \in I} p(i) \leq \sum_{i \in I} v_i(S_i) - \sum_{i \in I} p(S_i) + 2\min\{|G|, |I|\}\epsilon$, because an allocation can include no more bundles than there are items or agents. Introducing ϵ-CS-2, because $y(k^*) = 1$ for the bundle-set that corresponds to the final allocation S_i, then $\pi \leq \sum_{i \in I} p(S_i) + \min\{|G|, |I|\}\epsilon$. Finally, adding these two equations, we have $\pi + \sum_{i \in I} p(i) \leq \sum_{i \in I} v_i(S_i) + 3\min\{|G|, |I|\}\epsilon$. The LHS is the value of the final dual solution, V_{DLP}, and the first-term on the RHS is the value of the final primal solution, V_{LP}. We know $V_{\text{LP}}^* \leq V_{\text{DLP}}$, where V_{LP}^* is the value of the optimal primal solution by the weak duality property of linear programs. Thus, because $V_{\text{DLP}} \leq V_{\text{LP}} + 3\min\{|G|, |I|\}\epsilon$, it follows that $V_{\text{LP}} \geq V_{\text{LP}}^* - 3\min\{|G|, |I|\}\epsilon$. Finally, because the primal solution is integral (by construction during *i*Bundle), it is a feasible and optimal solution to the combinatorial resource allocation problem [IP]. □

In addition, it follows immediately that *i*Bundle(2) terminates in competitive equilibrium when agents are myopically rational and place safe bids.

Proof of *i*Bundle

A simple transformation of agents' bids allows *i*Bundle to be implemented within *i*Bundle(2) and ensures that agents' bids remain safe throughout the auction. Whenever bids from agent i are not safe in *i*Bundle(2) we can simulate the price-update rule in *i*Bundle by introducing a new dummy item that is specific to that agent, call it X_i. This item is concatenated by the auctioneer to all bids from agent i in this round and all future rounds. It has the following effects:

1. The outcome of winner-determination, or the allocative efficiency of the auction, is unchanged because no other agent bids for item X_i.

2. Agent i's bids are always safe because every bid includes item X_i, and no pair of bids is compatible.

3. The price increases due to bids from agent i are isolated to that agent in all future rounds because all price increases are for bundles that include item X_i.

The optimality of iBundle follows immediately from the optimality of iBundle(2).

Computational Analysis

As an iterative auction, iBundle has many computational advantages for *agents* over the sealed-bid GVA, as we discussed in the introduction. In Parkes (1999b) we present results that demonstrate savings in agent valuation work in iBundle.

However, the winner-determination (WD) problem that the auctioneer solves in each round of iBundle to compute the provisional allocation is $\mathcal{NP}$-hard, just as in the GVA. The auctioneer must solve one WD problem in each round, and a naive worst-case analysis gives $O(BV_{\max}/\epsilon)$ rounds to converge, for a total of B bundles with positive value over all agents, maximum value $V_{\max}$ for any bundle, and minimal bid increment ϵ. In the worst-case the price of a single bundle must increase by at least ϵ in each round the auction remains open, and prices are bounded by the maximum value over all agents. The number of rounds to termination is inversely proportional to the minimal bid increment. The auctioneer can solve less WD problems by increasing the minimal bid increment, for some loss in economic efficiency.

A number of optimizations are possible within iBundle to speed-up computation on winner-determination in each round. First, the provisional allocation from the previous round provides a good initial solution to the WD problem, because agents must re-bid bundles received in the previous round. This allows pruning of the search for a revenue-maximizing allocation. An additional saving in computation time is achieved by limiting search to an allocation at least ϵ better than the value of the allocation in the previous round. Moreover, although each intermediate WD problem in iBundle may be intrinsically more difficult than each WD problem in GVA because all agents bid at similar prices for bundles (Andersson *et al.* 2000), the problems are typically much smaller than in the GVA.

The auctioneer only announces price *increases* in each round, and need not maintain explicit prices for all possible bundles. Bid prices are verified dynamically in each round, to check that bids are at least as large as the ask price of all contained bundles. With a simple sorted-list implementation, the total work in checking each bid is *linear* in the number P of bundles that have explicit ask prices. Similarly, prices can be maintained in linear-time in P for each new price increase. In addition, $P \leq B$, with agents that have values for B bundles, because only bundles that receive bids can receive explicit ask prices.

Experimental Results

We compare the computation and communication cost of iBundle with the Generalized Vickrey Auction (GVA).

We consider problems *Decay*, *Weighted-random* (WR), *Random* and *Uniform* from Sandholm (1999). Each problem defines a distribution over agents' values for bundles of items, with XOR valuation functions, such that agents want at most one bundle. In our main experiments the number of items, $|G| = 50$, and we scale the problems by increasing the number of agents from 5 to 40, with values for 10 bundles per agent. We set Sandholm's parameter $\alpha = 0.85$ in Decay, and select bundles of size 10 in Uniform.

Results are presented for iBundle(2), the auction variation without price discrimination. A variation on Sandholm's depth-first branch-and-bound search algorithm (Sandholm 1999) solves winner-determination (WD) in each round, and computes the allocation and prices in the GVA. We introduce a new heuristic to make search more efficient for XOR bids. The heuristic computes an overestimate of the possible value of a partial allocation based on allocating at most *one* bundle to each remaining agent without a bundle.

In addition, we measure the performance of iBundle with a greedy approximate winner-determination algorithm due to Lehmann *et al.* (1999) that satisfies the bid-monotonicity property (Definition 1).

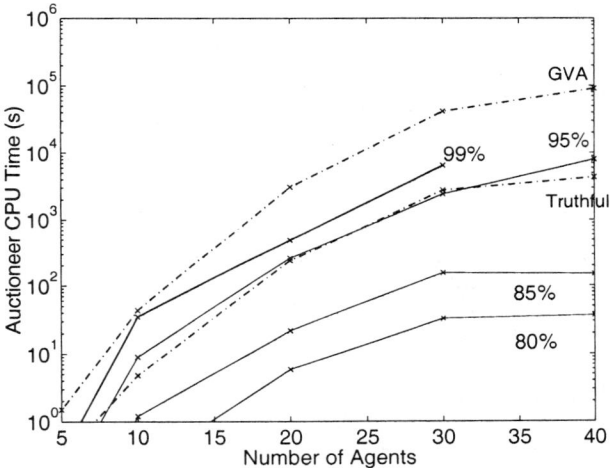

Figure 3: Total computation time in iBundle(2), the GVA, and a sealed-bid auction with truthful agents, in problem set Decay. The performance of iBundle is plotted with different bid increments ϵ, selected to give allocative efficiency of 80%, 85%, 95% and 99%.

Figure 3 plots the total auctioneer winner-determination and price-update time[7] in iBundle in the Decay problem set. Performance is measured for different bid increments, with the bid increment selected to give allocative efficiency of 80%, 85%, 95% and 99% ($\pm 1\%$). Figure 3 also plots performance for the GVA, and for a sealed-bid auction in which agents are assumed to bid truthfully.[8] Results are averaged over 10 trials. First, note that the curves are sublinear on the logarithmic value axis as the number of agents increases,

---

[7]Time is measured as user time in seconds on a 450 MHz Pentium Pro with 1024 MRAM, with iBundle coded in C++.

[8]The GVA proved intractable for 30 and 40 agents. In those problems the run time is estimated as the time to compute the optimal solution in a single WD problem multiplied by the number of agents in the optimal allocation.

indicating polynomial computation time in the number of agents.

The performance improvement of *i*Bundle over GVA is striking, achieving at least one order of magnitude improvement with 99% allocative efficiency and three orders of magnitude with 85% allocative efficiency. For up to 95% efficiency we essentially get the myopic truth-revelation properties of *i*Bundle for free, because *i*Bundle's run-time is approximately the same as for the sealed-bid auction with truthful agents.

Problem		GVA	*i*Bundle			Approx-Bundle
			$\simeq$ 90%	$\simeq$ 95%	$\simeq$ 99%	
Decay	Eff (%)	100	91.5	94.9	98.3	85.1
67.3%[d]	WD-time[a] (s)	41700	831	2400	5650	0
13.4[e]	Pr-time[b] (s)	–	26	34.5	44	39.2
	Comm[c] (kBit)	18.8	221	306	394	377
WR	Eff (%)	100	90.7	94.9	99.2	79.4
71.5%	WD-time (s)	3	0.6	1.7	6	0
1	Pr-time (s)	–	5.4	11.5	40.9	12.2
	Comm (kBit)	18.1	20.5	52.1	144	53.1
Rand	Eff (%)	100	89.3	97	99	95.8
37.8%	WD-time (s)	68	4.4	7.4	11	0
11.2	Pr-time (s)	–	6.5	9.7	12.1	12.9
	Comm (kBit)	18.7	49.5	66.4	82.6	85.6
Unif	Eff (%)	100	–	95.6	99.1	76.2
58%	WD-time (s)	25	–	6.6	18.7	0
3	Pr-time (s)	–	–	14.7	42.0	46
	Comm (kBit)	18.2	–	56.5	120	124

Table 1: Performance in the Decay, WR, random, and uniform problems. [a] Auctioneer WD time. [b] Price-update time. [c] Communication cost. [d] Alloc. eff. of a sealed-bid auction with a greedy WD algorithm and truthful agents. [e] Average number of agents in the optimal solution.

Table 1 compares *i*Bundle with the GVA for all Sandholm's problems, for problems with 30 agents. With our parameters the WR and Uniform problems are quite easy because the optimal allocation sells large bundles to a few agents, which allows considerable pruning during search. The Random and, in particular, Decay problems tend to be harder because the optimal allocation requires coordination across a number of agents, see also Sandholm (1999) and Andersson *et al.* (2000). In all problems *i*Bundle has less WD time at 95% allocative efficiency than the GVA. Note that price-update is relatively expensive in the otherwise easy weighted-random (WR) problem, because bid prices for large bundles must be checked for price consistency against the price of all included bundles.

There is a communication cost[9] penalty in using *i*Bundle compared with the GVA in these problems (Table 1) because of repeated bids across a number of rounds. This would

---

[9] We assume that bids and price information in *i*Bundle must only specify a bundle, because bids are usually at the current ask price, and ask prices only increase by the minimal bid increment. We also assume a broadcast network infrastructure for price updates. A bundle is specified with $|G|$ bits. In the GVA a bid specifies both a bundle and a value. We assume that values require 10 bits, enough to specify a value to 3 significant figures ($\log_2(1000) \simeq 10$.)

change in problems with agents that have values for many bundles because all values must be reported in the GVA, or in easier problems because *i*Bundle will terminate quickly with less bids.

The performance of *i*Bundle with the greedy WD algorithm is noteworthy: *i*Bundle performs well in the hard Decay problem set, with allocative efficiency 85.1%, giving at least a 1000-fold reduction in WD time. We believe that other, slightly less greedy, approximate algorithms will give even further performance improvements.

Speeding up *i*Bundle In addition to using the allocation from the previous round to prune search, it is also useful to cache all previous provisional allocations and select the best cached allocation as an initial solution for WD. A simple linear program is used to select the best allocation from the cache, and requires negligible computation. In our main trials we use a cache size of 1, i.e. take the solution from the previous round as an initial solution to the WD problem.

Problem		WD Time				% Cache Correct			
		0	1	T	$T!$	0	1	T	$T!$
Decay	50/15/150[a]	415	371	355	291	0	28	47	59
WR	50/50/1000	253	243	231	163	0	11	57	57
Rand	50/30/600	1823	1616	1491	864*	0	6	30	78
Unif	50/40/800	343	337	336	110	0	14	29	49

Table 2: Winner-determination time with caches of size 0, 1 (last round), and T (all previous rounds). In cache $T!$ revenue maximizing cached solutions from previous rounds are assumed optimal. *Eff* > 99% in all problems except *, where *Eff* = 96.8%. [a] $|G|$ / $|I|$ / # bundle values.

Table 2 compares the WD time in each problem with and without caching of previous allocations. Although a full cache can provide an additional speed-up over using no cached solutions, or just the allocation from the previous round, the effect is not very dramatic. The reason is that it remains expensive to *verify* that a cached solution is optimal. For example, although an extended cache in the Decay problem provides the correct allocation in 47% of problems, the speed-up is limited to around 14%.

In an attempt to leverage the correct solutions from the cache, we tested the performance of *i*Bundle under an additional assumption that if a cached solution from before round $t-1$ generates more revenue than the solution from round $t-1$, this is adopted as the new provisional allocation without further computation. The rule is designed to capture "flip-flop" competition between a number of good allocations during an auction.

Labeled $T!$, the rule proves useful in Decay, WR and Uniform, reducing computation by 30%, 36% and 68% from the time with no cache for a negligible drop in allocative efficiency. However, one must be careful: although we also see a speed-up in Random, the allocative efficiency falls from 99% to 96.8%. Further analysis shows that cached solutions prove optimal in 54%, 97% and 49% of rounds in Decay, WR and Uniform, but only optimal 34% of rounds in Random.

Further optimizations should be possible, for example

using cached solutions once a large enough cache is constructed, and solving WD when an auction is about to terminate with cached solutions. Another useful approach is ϵ-scaling, that adjusts the bid increment during an auction (Bertsekas 1990).

Related Work

Rassenti *et al.* (1982) describe an early single-round combinatorial mechanism for airport slot allocation, while Banks *et al.* (1989) describe AUSM, an early iterative bundle auction. AUSM has no explicit price-update rules, and agents must solve hard problems to bid effectively. DeMartini *et al.* (1998) describe, RAD, an iterative extension of Rassenti *et al.*, also with linear prices. No optimal properties have been proved for any of these auctions in general problems.

The AkBA (Wurman 1999, chapter 5) auctions are conceptually similar to *i*Bundle, but have different price-update rules and no price discrimination. AkBA shares many of *i*Bundle's computational properties, but is not known to be optimal for any reasonable bidding strategy.

There have been a number of proposals to reduce the computational costs of combinatorial auctions while maintaining incentives for truth-revelation; e.g. limit the types of bundles that agents can bid for (Rothkopf *et al.* 1998); or introduce an approximate solution for winner-determination (Lehmann *et al.* 1999), but little success in designing good auctions for general bundle problems. Moreover, most previous work focuses on sealed-bid auctions.

Conclusions

*i*Bundle is a new iterative combinatorial auction that is optimal for myopically-rational agents. As an iterative auction, *i*Bundle is particularly useful when agents have hard local valuation problems because it allows agents to compute estimates of the value of different outcomes incrementally, in response to bids from other agents. We proved *i*Bundle's optimality within a primal-dual framework, which we believe will provide a useful conceptual basis for the design and analysis of iterative auctions for other problems.

It remains expensive to compute *optimal* solutions with *i*Bundle in many problems, because the auctioneer's winner-determination (WD) problem is $\mathcal{NP}$-hard. We suggested a number of techniques to reduce computation, possibly for some loss in allocative efficiency, for example: increase the bid increment, use cached allocations, and introduce approximate winner-determination algorithms. We demonstrated orders of magnitude performance improvements over the GVA, the only other known optimal combinatorial auction, in some hard problems.

In future work we plan to test *i*Bundle in some real problems, and experiment with additional bid restrictions and alternative approximate WD algorithms. An interesting open problem is to adapt *i*Bundle for two-sided markets, with multiple buyers and sellers.

Acknowledgments

This research was funded in part by National Science Foundation Grant SBR 97-08965.

References

Andersson, A.; Tenhunen, M.; and Ygge, F. 2000. Integer programming for auctions with bids for combinations. In *Forthcoming, Proc. ICMAS'00*.

Banks, J. S.; Ledyard, J. O.; and Porter, D. 1989. Allocating uncertain and unresponsive resources: An experimental approach. *The Rand Journal of Economics* 20:1–25.

Bertsekas, D. P. 1990. The auction algorithm for assignment and other network flow problems: A tutorial. *Interfaces* 20(4):133–149.

Bikchandani, S., and Ostroy, J. M. 1998. The package assignment model. Tech. rep., Anderson School of Management and Department of Economics, UCLA.

Bykowsky, M. M.; Cull, R. J.; and Ledyard, J. O. 2000. Mutually destructive bidding: The FCC auction design problem. *Journal of Regulatory Economics*.

Clearwater, S. H., ed. 1996. *Market-Based Control*. World Scientific.

Cramton, P. 1997. The FCC spectrum auctions: An early assessment. *J. of Economics and Management Strategy* 6:431–495.

DeMartini, C.; Kwasnica, A. M.; Ledyard, J. O.; and Porter, D. 1998. A new and improved design for multi-object iterative auctions. Technical Report SSWP 1054, California Institute of Technology. Revised March 1999.

Lehmann, D.; O'Callaghan, L.; and Shoham, Y. 1999. Truth revelation in rapid, approximately efficient combinatorial auctions. In *Proc. ACM Conf. on Electronic Commerce (EC-99)*.

Papadimitriou, C. H., and Steiglitz, K. 1982. *Combinatorial Optimization*. Prentice-Hall.

Parkes, D. C., and Ungar, L. H. 2000. Preventing strategic manipulation in iterative auctions: Proxy agents and price-adjustment. In *Proc. 18th National Conference on Artificial Intelligence (AAAI-00)*. To appear.

Parkes, D. C. 1999a. Optimal auction design for agents with hard valuation problems. In *Proc. IJCAI-99 Workshop on Agent Mediated Electronic Commerce*. Stockholm.

Parkes, D. C. 1999b. *i*Bundle: An efficient ascending price bundle auction. In *Proc. ACM Conf. on Electronic Commerce (EC-99)*.

Rassenti, S. J.; Smith, V. L.; and Bulfin, R. L. 1982. A combinatorial mechanism for airport time slot allocation. *Bell Journal of Economics* 13:402–417.

Rothkopf, M. H.; Pekeč, A.; and Harstad, R. M. 1998. Computationally manageable combinatorial auctions. *Management Science* 44(8):1131–1147.

Sandholm, T. 1993. An implementation of the Contract Net Protocol based on marginal-cost calculations. In *Proc. 11th National Conference on Artificial Intelligence (AAAI-93)*, 256–262.

Sandholm, T. 1999. An algorithm for optimal winner determination in combinatorial auctions. In *Proc. 16th International Joint Conference on Artificial Intelligence (IJCAI-99)*, 542–547.

Varian, H., and MacKie-Mason, J. K. 1995. Generalized Vickrey auctions. Tech. rep., University of Michigan.

Wellman, M. P. 1993. A market-oriented programming environment and its application to distributed multicommodity flow problems. *Journal of Artificial Intelligence Research* 1:1–23.

Wurman, P. R. 1999. *Market Structure and Multidimensional Auction Design for Computational Economies*. Ph.D. Dissertation, University of Michigan.

Preventing Strategic Manipulation in Iterative Auctions: Proxy Agents and Price-Adjustment

David C. Parkes and Lyle H. Ungar

Computer and Information Science Department
University of Pennsylvania
200 South 33rd Street, Philadelphia, PA 19104
dparkes@unagi.cis.upenn.edu; ungar@central.upenn.edu

Abstract

Iterative auctions have many computational advantages over sealed-bid auctions, but can present new possibilities for strategic manipulation. We propose a two-stage technique to make iterative auctions that compute optimal allocations with myopic best-response bidding strategies more robust to manipulation. First, introduce proxy bidding agents to constrain bidding strategies to (possibly untruthful) myopic best-response. Second, after the auction terminates adjust the prices towards those given in the Vickrey auction, a sealed-bid auction in which truth-revelation is optimal. We present an application of this methodology to *i*Bundle, an iterative combinatorial auction which gives optimal allocations for myopic best-response agents.

Introduction

Many interesting problems involving distributed agents, e.g. task assignment, distributed scheduling, etc. can be formulated as resource allocation problems, with a set of discrete items to allocate to agents (Clearwater 1996). A common goal is to maximize the total value of the allocation over all agents, while respecting information decentralization, autonomy, and the self-interest of individual agents within a system. Auctions provide simple and robust mechanisms, and can compute optimal or near-optimal solutions in interesting problems (Wellman *et al.* 1999).

Iterative auctions, in which agents can bid continuously during an auction as prices are adjusted, have a number of computational advantages over sealed-bid auctions, in which agents must submit bids simultaneously in a single round. Agents can perform incremental computation about their values for different allocations as prices change (Parkes 1999a), and make new bids in response to bids from other agents. This is important in problems with hard valuation problems, consider for example a task allocation problem with agents that solve local optimization problems to compute the cost of performing additional task given existing commitments (Sandholm 1993).

Iterative auctions have been designed to solve non-trivial resource allocation problems, for example for auctions in multiple identical items (Ausubel 1997), and *i*Bundle (Parkes 1999b) for the combinatorial resource allocation problem.

However, iterative auctions present possibilities for strategic manipulation because information is exchanged between agents via bids and prices during an auction. A rational agent with look-ahead can try to manipulate the bids of other agents and the outcome of an auction, for example with *jump bids* at prices above the current ask price, or by delaying bids until the auction is about to close. Manipulation is undesirable because it reduces the economic efficiency of outcomes, and because it is inherently complex.

We propose a new method, "proxy agents and price-adjustment", to prevent strategic manipulation in iterative auctions. The method applies to iterative auctions that compute optimal resource allocations in *competitive equilibrium*.[1] We adjust prices retrospectively *after* an auction terminates towards prices that provide incentives for agents to bid truthfully.

The goal is to compute the prices that agents would pay in the Generalized Vickrey Auction (GVA) (Varian & MacKie-Mason 1995), a sealed-bid auction for combinatorial resource allocation problems. The prices in the GVA provide strong truth-revelation properties; truth-revelation is a *dominant strategy*, optimal for a self-interested agent for all strategies of other agents. When successful, in combination with *proxy bidding agents*, the iterative auction retains its computational advantages and inherits the strategy-proofness of the GVA. The proxy agents bid on behalf of agents, and constrain bidding strategies to best-response to prices based on (possibly untruthful) information received from agents about their values for items.

Our insight is that an interpretation of iterative auctions within *primal-dual* optimization theory presents a method, Adjust, to compute *minimal* competitive equilibrium prices after an auction terminates, based on bids placed by agents during the auction, i.e. prices that minimize the auctioneer's revenue in equilibrium. Extending recent results in Bikhchandani & Ostroy (1998), we prove that GVA prices can always be computed from "enough" minimal CE prices. A variation, Adjust*, on Adjust closes the gap between minimal CE prices and GVA prices. We characterize necessary and sufficient conditions on agents' bids and prices for Adjust* to compute GVA prices, and propose a dynamic test allows an auctioneer to detect when the auction

---
[1] In competitive equilibrium all agents maximize utility with the final allocation given the final prices, and the auctioneer maximizes revenue.

has terminated with GVA prices.

We also suggest approximate procedures, Adj-Pivot and Adj-Pivot*, for Adjust and Adjust* with negligible computation that work well in practice. The methods leverage computation already performed by the auctioneer during the auction, in solving a sequence of winner-determination problems.

As an application of our framework, we consider *i*Bundle, an ascending-price combinatorial auction which gives optimal allocations for myopically-rational agents. *i*Bundle and Adjust compute minimal CE prices in all problems. We characterize sufficient conditions on agents' valuation functions for Adjust* to compute GVA prices. Experimental results verify that *i*Bundle with price-adjustment computes minimal CE prices across a suite of hard problems, and often compute prices which are within 2% of GVA prices.

Incentive Compatible Auctions

In this section, we explain why truth-revelation is optimal for an agent in the Generalized Vickrey Auction (GVA), and discuss the consequences of achieving Vickrey prices in an iterative auction.

The GVA computes optimal resource allocations even with strategic self-interested agents.[2] It is an incentive compatible auction: an agent's optimal bidding strategy is truth-revelation, i.e. *bid the exact amount that it values an item, or bundle of items*. The GVA extends Vickrey's (1961) seminal second-price sealed-bid auction, which sells a single item to the highest bidder for the second-highest price, to auctions for *bundles* of items.

Let G denote the set of items to be auctioned, I denote the set of agents, and $v_i(S)$ denote agent i's value for bundle $S \subseteq G$ of items. We assume risk-neutral agents with quasi-linear utilities in money, $u_i(S, p) = v_i(S) - p$, for price p, and equate optimal strategies with utility-maximization.

The GVA is a *direct-revelation mechanism*, in which agents report (possibly untruthful) values for bundles of items. Let $\hat{v}_i$ denote agent i's reported value, not necessarily equal to its true value. The auctioneer computes the allocation $\mathbf{S}^* = (S_1^*, \ldots, S_{|I|}^*)$ that maximizes the total reported value, where agent i receives bundle $S_i^* \subseteq G$.

Agent i pays $p_{\text{gva}}(i) = \sum_{j \neq i} \hat{v}_j(S_j^{-i}) - \sum_{j \neq i} \hat{v}_j(S_j^*)$, where $\mathbf{S}^{-i}$ is the revenue-maximizing allocation with the bids from all agents except agent i. The GVA prices the marginal negative effect that an agent's presence has on the reported value of the outcome to the other agents.

Definition 1. *Dominant strategy. A bidding strategy is dominant if it is optimal for all bidding strategies of other agents.*

Truth-revelation, i.e. a bid $\hat{v}_i = v_i$, is a dominant strategy in the GVA. The proof is straightforward: agent i's utility, $u_i(S_i^*, p_{\text{gva}}(i))$, given allocation S_i^* and price $p_{\text{gva}}(i)$, is $u_i(S_i^*, p_{\text{gva}}(i)) = v_i(S_i^*) - p_{\text{gva}}(i) = v_i(S_i^*) +$

---

[2]The GVA is not robust to manipulation by colluding agents (Sandholm 1996). Similarly, the methods that we present in this paper do not prevent collusive manipulation of iterative auctions.

$\sum_{j \neq i} \hat{v}_j(S_j^*) - \sum_{j \neq i} \hat{v}_j(S_j^{-i})$. Agent i can maximize the sum of the first two terms by reporting $\hat{v}_i = v_i$ because this is precisely the objective function that the auctioneer maximizes to select allocation $\mathbf{S}^*$. The final term is independent of agent i's bid.

We will refer to this outcome, i.e. allocation, $\mathbf{S}^*$ and payments $p_{\text{gva}}(i)$, as the *Vickrey outcome*.

Vickrey Prices in an Iterative Auction

One might think that if an iterative auction implements the Vickrey outcome with agents that follow myopic best-response bidding strategies, then myopic best-response would be a dominant strategy for self-interested agents. In fact, manipulation remains possible with a non best-response strategy.

Definition 2. *Myopic best-response bidding strategy. Bid to maximize utility in the current round, taking prices as fixed.*

Definition 3. *Auction $\mathcal{A}$ myopically implements the Vickrey outcome if the auction terminates with the Vickrey outcome for agents that follow myopic best-response bidding strategies.*

Let $BR(v_i, p)$ denote the best-response bid for agent i with valuation function v_i, where p is the current prices in the auction. Call this a *truthful myopic strategy*. Also, let $BR(\hat{v}_i, p)$ denote an *untruthful myopic bidding strategy* for agent i, for some valuation function $\hat{v}_i \neq v_i$.

We derive the following result, for agents that are constrained to (possibly untruthful) myopic best-response bidding strategies. It is immediate from the incentive properties of the GVA:

Theorem 1. *Truthful myopic bidding is a dominant strategy in an iterative auction $\mathcal{A}$ that myopically-implements the Vickrey outcome, if all agents are constrained to following a (possibly untruthful) myopic best-response bidding strategy.*

That is, assume agent i must place bids in every round of the auction that are consistent with a myopic best-response bidding strategy, $BR(\hat{v}_i, p)$, for some valuation function $\hat{v}_i$, that does not need to equal the agent's actual valuation v_i. Given this, truth-revelation, i.e. following a best-response strategy for $\hat{v}_i = v_i$, is optimal.

This is weaker than the strategy-proofness of the GVA, where truthful bidding is dominant in a system with *unrestricted* bidding strategies. Gul & Stacchetti (1997) prove the following more general result:

Theorem 2. *Truthful myopic bidding is a sequentially rational best-response to truthful myopic bidding by other agents in an iterative auction $\mathcal{A}$ that myopically-implements the Vickrey outcome.*

We use proxy bidding agents to force agents to follow best-response bidding strategies, and leverage Theorem 1. With this, an iterative auction that myopically implements the Vickrey outcome inherits the incentive compatibility of the GVA.

Proxy Bidding Agents

We introduce semi-autonomous proxy bidding agents at the auctioneer, through which agents must interact with the auction. The proxy agents constrain agents' bidding strategies, following a best-response bidding strategy based on reported information about an agent's valuation function.

Let us first suggest (and reject) a couple of undesirable approaches to constrain agent strategies:

1. *Detect and penalize deviations from a myopic best-response strategy.* This is computationally expensive because the class of bidding strategies implemented by $BR(v, p)$ is large, and to detect an invalid strategy we must prove that no best-response strategy from this class can implement an agent's bids.

2. *Autonomous proxy bidding agents.* Proxy agents that must receive valuation functions in an initial stage, before bidding *autonomously* in the auction convert the iterative auction into a sealed-bid auction. This destroys many of the computational advantages that we outlined in the introduction.

Agent i provides incomplete information, $\hat{v}_{\text{app},i}$ about reported value, $\hat{v}_i$, to its proxy agent. The reported value can be different from an agent's true value. Agent i can update the information $\hat{v}_{\text{app},i}$ during the auction, but all new information must be consistent with previous information. The proxy agents must always have enough information to place best-response bids to the current prices in the auction.

With proxy bidding agents we have the following result, from Theorem 1:

Theorem 3. *Introducing myopic best-response proxy agents to auction $\mathcal{A}$ that myopically-implements the Vickrey outcome creates auction $\text{Proxy}(\mathcal{A})$, where truth-revelation is a dominant strategy.*

This solution retains the computational advantages of iterative auctions because agents do not need to provide complete value information up-front. If valuation functions are large and complex the proxy agents can be implemented at the client in a secure "wrapper".

Example: Single item auction. As an example, here is proxy bidding-agent variation on the English auction, in which the item is sold to the highest bidder for its bid. The new derivative auction is a "staged Vickrey auction". It is strategically equivalent to the standard Vickrey auction, but preferable because the optimal outcome is determined without complete information about all agents' values.

Agent i has a proxy agent that maintains a lower and upper bound, $\overline{v}_i$ and $\underline{\hat{v}}_i$, on agent i's (possibly untruthful) value $\hat{v}_i$ for the item. When the ask price is below the lower bound the proxy agent will bid. When the ask price is above the upper bound the proxy agent will leave the auction. When the price is between the bounds the proxy places no bid, and asks the agent for new bounds that must be consistent with previous bounds, i.e. tighter. The English auction terminates with the Vickrey price if agents follow truthful best-response bidding strategies. Hence, by Theorem 3, it is a dominant strategy for agents to provide the proxy agents with true lower and upper bounds on value.

Adjusting Towards Vickrey Prices

Now onto the second step of our design paradigm, "price-adjustment". We present a method to adjust the final prices in an iterative auction towards the Vickrey prices after an auction terminates. The method is applicable to auctions that terminate in competitive equilibrium (CE), such that the allocation maximizes the utility of all agents at the final prices and the auctioneer maximizes its revenue. The *i*Bundle and English auctions terminate in CE. Indeed, a fundamental connection between primal-dual optimization theory and competitive equilibrium prices allows optimal auctions to be designed and analyzed (Bertsekas 1990; Parkes & Ungar 2000).

We introduce Adjust, a procedure to compute *minimal* CE prices from agents' bids after an auction terminates. Minimal CE prices are equilibrium prices that minimize the auctioneer's total revenue from all agents in the optimal allocation. The price paid by each agent with minimal CE prices is always an upper-bound on GVA prices, and equal to GVA prices when certain conditions hold on agents' values for bundles (Bikchandani & Ostroy 1998).

In fact, it is always possible to compute GVA prices with "enough" minimal CE prices (they are typically not unique), as the minimum price for each agent over all CE prices. We propose a slight variation on Adjust, Adjust*, and prove necessary and sufficient conditions on agents' bids and prices for Adjust* to compute GVA prices. Finally, we introduce approximate procedures Adj-Pivot and Adj-Pivot* to adjust prices.

For the rest of the paper we assume that agents follow myopic best-response bidding strategies.

Minimal Competitive Equilibrium Prices

We can interpret equilibrium conditions within primal-dual optimization theory (Papadimitriou & Steiglitz 1982). This provides the key to compute minimal CE prices from agents' bids and prices after an auction terminates. Complementary slackness conditions for appropriate primal and dual formulations of the global resource allocation problem are equivalent to equilibrium conditions between an allocation and prices (Bertsekas 1990; Parkes & Ungar 2000).

Consider an auction $\mathcal{A}$ that terminates in equilibrium, let $p_i(S)$ denote the price for bundle S to agent i, and let S_i^* denote the bundle allocated to agent i. In defining a competitive equilibrium we allow price discrimination, with different prices for agents, e.g. $p_i(S) \neq p_j(S)$ for some $i \neq j$ and some bundle S. This is the most general case. In competitive equilibrium the prices and allocation must satisfy the following CS conditions:

(CS-1) Given prices $p_i(S)$, allocation S_i^* maximizes agent i's utility, $u_i(S_i^*, p_i(S_i^*)) = v_i(S_i^*) - p_i(S_i^*) = \max_S \{v_i(S) - p_i(S)\}$.

(CS-2) Given prices $p_i(S)$, allocation $\mathbf{S}^* = (S_1^*, \ldots, S_{|I|}^*)$ maximizes the auctioneer's revenue over all *feasible* allocations.

A feasible allocation sells each item to at most one agent, and allocates at most one bundle to each agent.

The following result follows immediately from strong duality and the *complementary slackness theorem* (Papadimitriou & Steiglitz 1982) of linear programming:

Theorem 4. *In an auction that terminates in competitive equilibrium, minimal prices that satisfy complementary slackness with the final allocation are minimal competitive equilibrium prices.*

This allows the computation of minimal CE prices after an auction terminates, based on bids placed by agents. Reduce prices while: (CS-1) agents continue to maximize utility with allocation S_i^*; (CS-2) allocation $\mathbf{S}^*$ continues to maximize revenue.

Adjust. Procedure Adjust computes minimal CE prices from agents' bids when an auction terminates in competitive equilibrium. Assume that agents place *exclusive-or* (XOR) bids, such that they demand at most one bundle.[3] Let I^* denote the set of agents in the optimal allocation, $\hat{P}$ denote agents' prices (initialized to $p_i(S)$), and V^* denote the revenue of the final allocation. We will compute the values of **second-best allocations**. An allocation S^{-i} is a *second-best allocation* if it maximizes revenue for the auctioneer without allocating a bundle to agent i, i.e. it is the second-best allocation without agent i. Let $V^{-i}(\hat{P})$ denote the revenue from this allocation, computed at prices $\hat{P}$.

Adjust computes a price discount Δ_i to each agent i in the final allocation, such that agent i receives final price $\underline{p}_i(S_i^*) = p_i(S_i^*) - \Delta_i$.

Adjust:
for each $i \in I^*$ {
  $\Delta_i = \min\{V^* - V^{-i}(\hat{P}),\ p_i(S_i^*)\}$;
  $V^* = V^* - \Delta_i$;
  $\hat{P}_i = \max\{\hat{P}_i - \Delta_i,\ 0\}$;[4] }

Adjust selects each agent in the final allocation in turn, reducing its price for every bundle by the amount that the value of the optimal allocation exceeds the value of the best allocation without that agent.[5] The maximization problem, to solve $V^{-i}(\hat{P})$ in each iteration, is $\mathcal{N}P$-hard (Rothkopf, Pekeč, & Harstad 1998) in bundle auctions.[6] Later we introduce an efficient approximate procedure Adj-Pivot.

Note that price reductions to each agent in the allocation are considered incrementally and not independently, prices $\hat{P}$ are adjusted according to Δ_i before reducing prices to agent j.

---

[3] This is without loss of generality because XOR is a completely expressive bid language. The procedure can be extended to other bid languages, e.g. additive-or bids through the introduction of a dummy agent for each price bid.

[4] Operation $\hat{P}_i = \max\{\hat{P}_i - \Delta_i, 0\}$ indicates that price $p_i(S)$ to agent i is reduced to $\max\{p_i(S) - \Delta_i, 0\}$.

[5] A simple optimization is possible. If $\Delta_i \leq p_i(S_i^*)$ and agent $j > i$ is not in the revenue-maximizing allocation without agent i then $\Delta_j = 0$.

[6] It can be solved in average-case polynomial time in some hard problems with efficient search algorithms; see Sandholm (1999) for example.

Proposition. *Procedure* Adjust *maintains* CE *prices.*

Proof. Adjust maintains (CS-1). Prices to agents not in the allocation are left unchanged. Agent i in allocation $\mathbf{S}^*$ continues to maximize utility with bundle S_i^* at new prices $p_i(S) - \Delta_i$; its price is reduced by Δ_i on bundle S_i^*. and by Δ_i or less on all other bundles. By the lemma, Adjust maintains (CS-2) because it explicitly computes the maximum value of all allocations without agent i, and reduces agent i's prices by no more than the difference between V^* and this value. □

Lemma. *An allocation with more revenue to the auctioneer than S^* as prices are reduced to agent i must exclude agent i, since all prices to agent i are reduced by the same amount (or until they are zero).*

We derive a sufficient condition on agents' bids and prices for Adjust to compute minimal CE prices.

Assumption A. *(i) Every agent j in allocation S^* bids at price $p_j(S_j^{-i})$ for bundles allocated in all second-best allocations S^{-i}; and (ii) Every agent j not in allocation S^* bids at price $p_j(S_j^{-i}) = v_j(S_j^{-i})$ for bundles allocated in all second-best allocations S^{-i}.*

Intuitively, when Assumption A holds, no bundles in second-best allocations are priced too high. If agent j receives bundle S_j^{-i} in a second-best allocation, it had better have bid the price of that bundle, else the price can be reduced (maintaining (CS-1)). In turn, this can allow agent i to pay a lower price but still maximize revenue with the final allocation S_i^*.

Theorem 5. *Procedure* Adjust *computes* **minimal** CE *prices if agents' bids and prices satisfy Assumption A.*

Proof. By contradiction. Assume that prices $\underline{p}_i(S_i^*)$ computed in Adjust are not minimal and Assumption A holds. If the prices are not minimal, then it must be possible to reduce the price $\underline{p}_j(S_j^*)$ to some agent, j, and still maintain (CS-1) and (CS-2). Therefore, there are some prices to agents $i \neq j$ that reduce the value $V^{-j}(\hat{P})$ of the second-best allocation without agent j, so that the price $\underline{p}_j(S_j^*)$ can be reduced without violating (CS-2).

However, Assumption A (i), any decrease in the price of bundle S_k^{-j} to some agent k in the optimal allocation and second-best allocation S^{-j} must be mirrored in a decrease in the price of S_k^* to maintain (CS-1); and (ii), any decrease in the price of bundle S_k^{-j} to some agent k not in the optimal allocation but in the second-best allocation S^{-j} violates (CS-1) because the agent has positive utility for that bundle but receives $S_k^* = \emptyset$. □

Computing GVA Prices

In fact, it is always possible to compute GVA prices from "enough" minimal CE prices. Minimal CE prices are often not unique, the same *total* revenue to the auctioneer can be achieved with different distributions of revenue across agents. We use this result to derive procedure Adjust* and to prove necessary and sufficient conditions for computing GVA prices in an auction. Let $\underline{p}_i(S_i^*)$ denote a minimal CE price to agent i for bundle S_i^*.

Theorem 6. *For agent j in the optimal allocation, the minimal price $\min \underline{p}_j(S_j^*)$ over all minimal CE prices $\underline{p}_j(S_j^*)$ equals the GVA price.*

Proof. The proof is constructive, using Adjust with alternative orders for selecting agents $i \in I^*$. First, observe that $p_i(S) = v_i(S)$ trivially satisfy (CS-1), and also Assumption A with best-response agents. Hence, Adjust will compute minimal CE prices by Theorem 5. Now, let j denote the first agent selected in Adjust. $\Delta_j = \min\{V^* - V_{-j}(\hat{P}), p_j(S_j^*)\} = \min\{\sum_i v_i(S_i^*) - \sum_{i \neq j} v_i(S_i^{-j}), v_j(S_j^*)\} = \sum_i v_i(S_i^*) - \sum_{i \neq j} v_i(S_i^{-j})$. Hence, $\underline{p}_j(S_j^*) = v_j(S_j^*) - \Delta_j = \sum_{i \neq j} v_i(S_i^{-j}) - \sum_{i \neq j} v_i(S_i^*) = p_{\text{gva}}(j)$. Therefore, the price $\underline{p}_j(S_j^*)$ for bundle S_j^* to agent j equals its GVA price in at least when agent $j \in I^*$ is selected first in Adjust. Finally, $p_{\text{gva}}(j) = p_{\min,i}(S_j^*) = \min \underline{p}_j(S_j^*)$, over all minimal CE prices. □

Adjust*. This leads to procedure Adjust*, a slight variation on Adjust that computes price discounts for each agent independently:

Adjust*:
for each $i \in I^*$
  $\Delta_i = \min\{V^* - V^{-i}(\hat{P}), \ p_i(S_i^*)\}$;

Although adjusted prices $\hat{p}_i(S_i^*) = p_i(S_i^*) - \Delta_i$ may not be CE prices, the prices are strictly closer to GVA prices. Assumption B characterizes conditions on agents' bids and prices that, together with Assumption A, are necessary and sufficient for Adjust* to compute GVA prices after an auction terminates.

Assumption B. *When there is more than one agent in the optimal allocation, an agent j in the optimal allocation but not in a second-best allocation S^{-i} for some agent $i \neq j$ bids $p_j(S_j^*) = v_j(S_j^*)$ for the bundle S_j^* it receives in the optimal allocation.*

In other words, every agent in the optimal allocation must bid its value for the bundle that it receives, unless it remains in the revenue-maximizing allocations as bids from the other agents in the optimal allocation are ignored in turn.

Here is some intuition for the rule. Consider two agents, 1 and 2, that receive a bundle in the final allocation, and suppose that agent 2 bids less than its value for its bundle S_2^* in the allocation. Suppose, in addition, that bids from agents 3 and 4 maximize revenue in the second-best allocation as agent 1's prices are reduced. Agent 1's prices can be reduced further and still achieve more revenue than the bids from agents 3 and 4 if agent 2 bids more for bundle S_2^*. In procedure Adjust to compute minimal CE prices this effect is neutral because the price decrease is received in only a single agent, but in Adjust* the price decrease is received by all agents in the optimal allocation.

Theorem 7. *Assumptions A and B are necessary and sufficient conditions on agents' bids and prices for Adjust* to compute GVA prices.*

Proof. [Sufficient.] The proof follows from Theorem 6, show that Assumptions A and B imply that Adjust* computes the same price to each agent in the optimal allocation as when the agents bid at prices $p_i(S) = v_i(S)$.

[Necessary.] By contradiction. (Case 1) Assume GVA prices and *not* Assumption A. Consider agent j in allocation S^* that does not bid at price $p_j(S_j^{-i})$ for a bundle S_j^{-i} that it receives in second-best allocation without an agent $i \neq j$. Now, agent i can receive a larger discount by reducing the price $p_j(S_j^{-i})$ to agent j, still maintaining (CS-1) for agent j. Similarly for an agent j not in allocation S^* that does not bid at price $p_j(S_j^{-i}) = v_j(S_j^{-i})$ for a bundle S_j^{-i} that it receives in second-best allocation without agent $i \neq j$. The proof of (Case 2), assuming GVA and *not* Assumption B is similar, consider an agent j in the optimal allocation that is not in some second-best allocation and does not bid $p_j(S_j^*) = v_j(S_j^*)$ for its optimal allocation. □

This leads to a test that allows an auctioneer to determine whether Adjust* computes GVA prices. The Vickrey-Test is sufficient but not necessary for GVA prices.[7]

Vickrey-Test. *Procedure Adjust* computes GVA prices if agents' bids and prices satisfy: (1) all second-best allocations can be computed from agents' bids; (2) every agent in the optimal allocation is in every second-best allocation if there is more than one agent in the optimal allocation.*

Property (1) implies Assumption A, and Property (2) implies Assumption B. Assumption B also holds if agents in the optimal allocation bid $p_j(S_j^*) = v_j(S_j^*)$, but there is no easy way for the auctioneer to detect this.

Example: Computing GVA Prices Consider a problem with three agents, $I = \{1, 2, 3\}$ and two items, $G = \{A, B\}$. The agents have the following values for bundles: $v_1 = \{30, 0, 30\}$, $v_2 = \{0, 40, 40\}$ and $v_3 = \{0, 20, 40\}$, for bundles A, B, and AB. The optimal allocation is $\mathbf{S}^* = (A, B, \emptyset)$, i.e. with items are allocated to agents 1 and 2. The Vickrey prices are $p_{\text{gva},1} = 40 - 40 = 0$ and $p_{\text{gva},2} = 50 - 30 = 20$. We consider adjusting prices in two scenarios. In both cases initial prices are competitive equilibrium prices, and best-response bids satisfy Assumption A with the prices. Adjust computes minimal CE prices in both scenarios, while Adjust* computes GVA prices in Scenario 2.

(Scenario 1) Prices are $p_1 = \{25, 0, 25\}, p_2 = \{0, 25, 25\}$ and $p_3 = \{0, 20, 40\}$. Adjust computes minimal CE prices: $\underline{p}_1(A) = 25 - (50 - 40) = 15$ and $\underline{p}_2 = 25 - (40 - 40) = 25$; or $\underline{p}_2(B) = 25 - (50 - 45) = 20$ and $\underline{p}_1(A) = 25 - (45 - 40) = 20$. The result depends on which agent is selected first. Adjust* computes $\hat{p}_1(A) = 15$ and $\hat{p}_2(B) = 20$. Agent 2 pays its GVA price because agent 1 is

---
[7]Furthermore, GVA prices are approximately computed when an agent in the optimal allocation "almost" bids for a bundle in a second-best allocation, or is "almost" in every second-best allocation.

in the second-best allocation without bids from agent 2, but agent 1 pays above its GVA price.

(Scenario 2) Now, assume prices to agent 2 are $p_2 = \{0, 40, 40\}$. The prices and agents' best-response bids now satisfy Assumption B, because agent 2 bids its value $p_2(B) = v_2(B)$ for item 2. In this case Adjust computes: $\underline{p}_1(A) = 0$ and $\underline{p}_2(B) = 40$, or $\underline{p}_2(B) = 20$ and $\underline{p}_1(A) = 20$. Adjust* computes $\hat{p}_1(A) = 0$ and $\hat{p}_2(B) = 20$, equal to GVA prices.

A Fast and Approximate Method

Procedure Adj-Pivot is a fast approximation to Adjust, that leverages computation already performed by the auctioneer to solve the winner-determination problem in each round of the auction. Experimental results show that it works well in practice.

Adj-Pivot uses an approximate formulation of Adjust as a linear program, where the value of $V^{-i}(\hat{P})$ is computed as the maximum value over all provisional allocations during the auction. These are *pivotal* allocations, likely to represent allocations with high value. Adj-Pivot computes $\max \sum_i \Delta_i$ such that $\hat{p}_i(S) = \max\{0, p_i(S) - \Delta_i\}$ for all agents, $\Delta_i = 0$ for agents not in the optimal allocation, and the revenue from the optimal allocation maximizes revenue over the set of pivotal allocations at prices $\hat{p}_i(S)$.

Similarly, Adj-Pivot* approximates Adjust. The price discount Δ_i is computed for each agent independently: compute $\max \Delta_j$ such that $\hat{p}_j(S) = \max\{0, p_j(S) - \Delta_j\}$, and the revenue from the optimal allocation maximizes revenue over all pivotal allocations.

Preprocessing.

As described, the price adjust procedures compute adjusted prices from individual prices to each agent. In an auction without price discrimination, in which each bundles are priced the same to all agents, the first step is to construct prices for each agent. Simply replicate the prices, i.e. $p_i(S) = p(S)$. Preprocessing can then be optionally applied, to adjust prices towards prices that satisfy Assumption A, such that agent i would bid for all bundles with a positive price. To give a simple example, we can reduce prices to an agent not in the final allocation to the prices in the last round in which the agent placed bids.

Application: *i*Bundle

*i*Bundle (Parkes 1999b; Parkes & Ungar 2000) is an ascending-price combinatorial auction in which agents can bid directly for bundles of items. It generalizes the English auction to the combinatorial resource allocation problem. Bundles are priced explicitly, and prices are increased whenever agents' bids are unsuccessful at the current prices. The auctioneer selects a provisional allocation in each round of the auction to maximize revenue, given the bids received.

*i*Bundle computes optimal resource allocations, and terminates in competitive equilibrium, with agents that follow myopic best-response bidding strategies, i.e. bid for all bundles that maximize utility in each round given the prices.

We present an application of the price-adjustment technique to variation *i*Bundle(*3*) that maintains price discrimination throughout the auction.[8] It is trivial to prove that *i*Bundle(*3*) terminates with bids and prices that satisfy Assumption A, because agents bid for all priced bundles. By Theorem 5, *i*Bundle with Adjust computes minimal CE prices.

Theorem 8. *i*Bundle(*3*) *with* Adjust *and myopic best-response proxy agents computes the minimal CE prices in combinatorial resource allocation problems.*

We have the following key result, that follows from Theorems 3 and 7.

Theorem 9. *i*Bundle(*3*) *with* Adjust* *and myopic best-response proxy agents is incentive-compatible and allocatively-efficient in combinatorial resource allocation problems in which Assumption B holds when the auction terminates.*

The *Vickrey-test* allows an auctioneer to be sure that *i*Bundle computes GVA prices. In addition, we can characterize properties on agents' valuation functions $v_i(S)$ in which Assumption B will hold. As an example, Assumption B holds in these problems: in the assignment problem with unit-demands; with multiple identical items and subadditive valuation functions (i.e. decreasing returns); and in problems with linear-additive valuation functions in items. In all of these problems agents in the optimal allocation will remain in all second-best allocations.

Experimental Results

We present experimental results for *i*Bundle(*3*) with Adjust* and Adj-Pivot*, comparing its performance with the GVA in a number of hard problems. The problems are PS 1–12 from (Parkes 1999b), and also problems Decay, Weighted-random (WR), Random and Uniform in Sandholm (1999). Each problem set defines a distribution over agents' values for bundles of items. Implementation details for *i*Bundle, e.g. the algorithm for winner-determination in each round, are as described in (Parkes & Ungar 2000). A standard Simplex algorithm computes adjusted prices with Adj-Pivot*.

The distance $\mathcal{D}(p_i(S_i^*), p_{\text{gva}}(i))$ between prices $p_i(S_i^*)$ and GVA prices is measured with an L_1 norm, as $\sum_i |p_i(S_i) - p_{\text{gva}}(i)| / \sum_i v_i(S_i)$, i.e. the sum absolute difference between the price charged to each agent and its GVA price normalized by the total value of the allocation over all agents.[9] We compute the average distance over problem instances in which *i*Bundle computes the optimal allocation, which approaches 100% of problems as the bid increment gets small. It is not clear how to measure distance to GVA

---

[8]*i*Bundle auction has three variations, that differ in their price-update rules. In this paper we use *i*Bundle both to refer to the family of auctions in general, and also to variation *i*Bundle(*3*) in particular.

[9]An L_1 norm is appropriate because minimal CE prices is computed with a linear additive measure over the auctioneer's price to each agent in the allocation.

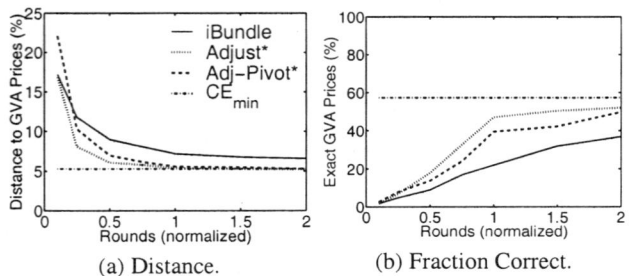

(a) Distance.   (b) Fraction Correct.

Figure 1: Average performance of *i*Bundle with price-adjustment `Adjust*` and `Pri-Adjust*` in problems PS 1–12. The number of rounds to termination is varied by adjusting the minimal bid increment.

prices in problems in which the auction's allocation is suboptimal and different from the GVA.

Figure 1 plots the distance to the GVA prices in *i*Bundle, before and after price-adjustment using `Adjust*` and `Adj-Pivot*`, averaged over 25 trials each of problems PS 1–12. We ran *i*Bundle with different bid increments to vary the number of rounds to termination, and average performance across problem sets by normalizing the number of rounds to termination according to the minimal number of rounds in which *i*Bundle achieves 100% allocative efficiency. For comparison, we also plot the performance of minimal CE prices.

The average distance between minimal CE prices and GVA prices across these problems is 5.3%. For small bid increments *i*Bundle computes prices to within 6.5% of the GVA prices, with `Adjust` to within 5.5% (not plotted), and with `Adjust*` and `Adj-Pivot*` to within 5.2%. Notice that the prices continue to adjust towards the min CE prices for bid increments smaller than those required for 100% allocative efficiency, corresponding to normalized rounds to termination > 1.

We also compute the fraction of all problems in which $\mathcal{D}(p_i, p_{\text{gva}}(i)) < 2\%$, to test the proportion of problems in which prices are approximately Vickrey. CE prices are equal to GVA prices in approximately 57% of problem instances. *i*Bundle computes GVA prices in around 38% of problem instances, compared to approaching 57% with `Adjust*` and `Adj-Pivot*`. Clearly, the results verify that `Adjust*` computes minimal CE prices when Assumption A holds, as it will in *i*Bundle.

The minimal CE prices are close to GVA prices (average distance < 2.5%) in problems 4–8, in which the agents in the optimal allocation also tend to be in the second-best allocations. In contrast, the minimal CE prices differ from the GVA payments by more than 5% in problems PS 1, 3, 9, 11 and 12, which are characterized by optimal allocations that are very different from second-best allocations, and agents with complementary demands for bundles.

As expected, an application of the Vickrey-Test over all problems confirmed no false positives, a specificity of 100%, but some false negatives, a sensitivity of 56%. The outcome was always approximately Vickrey when indicated by the Vickrey-Test, but Vickrey-outcomes went undetected in some problems.

It is noteworthy that the approximate method `Adj-Pivot*` is as effective as `Adjust*` for small bid increments. We use `Adj-Pivot*` in the harder problems plotted in Figure 2.

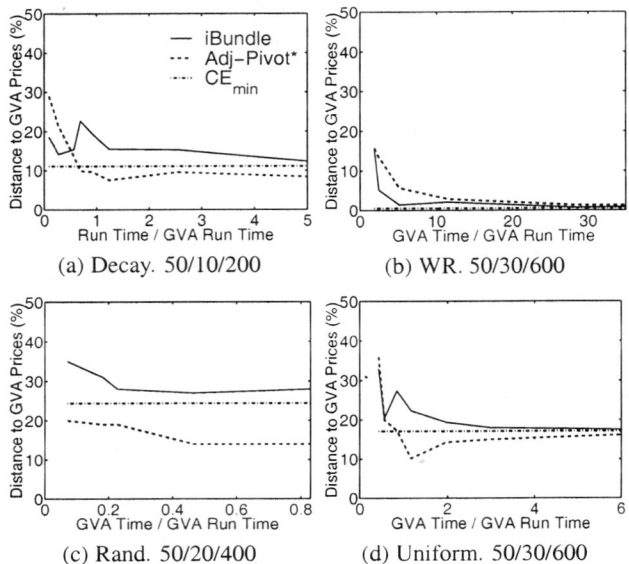

(a) Decay. 50/10/200   (b) WR. 50/30/600

(c) Rand. 50/20/400   (d) Uniform. 50/30/600

Figure 2: Performance of *i*Bundle with price-adjustment `Adj-Pivot*` problem sets from Sandholm (1999). The bid increment in *i*Bundle is adjusted to give different run times.

Figure 2 illustrates the performance of *i*Bundle with `Adj-Pivot*` in Decay, WR, Random, and Uniform, with problem sizes selected to give reasonable winner-determination computation times. In Decay we set Sandholm's α parameter to 0.85. We plot the distance to GVA prices against the relative run time of *i*Bundle with `Adj-Pivot*` to the time to compute winner-determination and agent prices in the GVA.[10] The minimal bid increment is varied to adjust the number of rounds in *i*Bundle, and with the values used allocative efficiency varies between 93% and 100%.

`Adj-Pivot*` computes prices closer to GVA prices than the minimal CE prices in Decay and Random, and minimal CE prices are equal to GVA prices in WR (where there is typically a single agent in the final allocation). Prices remain quite far from GVA prices in the Uniform problem set because second-best allocations are typically quite different from optimal allocations, and Assumption B often fails.

Related Work

There have been a number of recent proposals to achieve incentive-compatibility and allocative efficiency with less

---

[10] We do not focus on the auctioneer's winner-determination time in this paper, but note that T_{gva} is 362s, 9.1s, 1791s, and 138s (on a 450MHz Pentium) for problems (a – d), i.e. the run time for *i*Bundle in WR is small despite the considerable slow-down in comparison with the GVA.

computation than the GVA, focusing on sealed-bid auctions in special cases (Lehmann *et al.* 1999; Kfir-Dahav *et al.* 1998; Nisan & Ronen 1999).

For iterative auctions in particular, previous work has focused on careful control of prices during an auction, so that the auction terminates with GVA prices. Positive results exist only for special cases (Demange *et al.* 1986; Gul & Stacchetti 1997; Ausubel 1997). *i*Bundle(3) with `Adjust*` solves all of these problems because Assumption B holds with myopic best-response bids.

Bikchandani & Ostroy (1998) provides additional motivation and background for our work, formulating linear programs for combinatorial resource allocation problems and relating primal and dual solutions to competitive equilibrium outcomes. Wurman & Wellman (1999) provide useful background on equilibrium prices in bundle auctions.

Milgrom (1999) presents examples of strategic-manipulation in simultaneous ascending-price auctions on individual items, and identifies the search for strategy-proof iterative combinatorial auctions as an important open problem.

Conclusions

We have proposed a new method, "proxy agents and price adjustment", to make iterative auctions more robust to strategic manipulation. This is important given the computational advantages of iterative auctions over sealed-bid auctions for bidding agents, because of dynamic price-discovery coupled with incremental computation on agents' values for different items or bundles of items.

The method introduces proxy bidding agents and adjusts the final prices in an iterative auction towards Vickrey prices. We characterize necessary and sufficient conditions on agents' bids and prices to obtain dominant strategy truth-revelation without a sealed-bid auction, describe a dynamic test for an auctioneer to detect a Vickrey outcome, and relate the conditions to agents' valuation functions.

We proposed both an optimal procedure `Adjust*` and an approximate procedure `Adj-Pivot*` to reduce prices after the auction terminates. The `Adj-Pivot*` approximation is both fast and effective. An interesting open empirical problem is to understand the level of approximation to GVA prices that is "good enough" to prevent most opportunities for strategic manipulation.

Finally, this work suggests a method to design an iterative Generalized Vickrey Auction: keep the auction open until every agent in the optimal allocation is also in all revenue-maximizing allocations without bids from each agent in the optimal allocation, or bids its value. It might be useful to keep *i*Bundle open for longer, past the first round in which a competitive equilibrium outcome is computed, and increase the prices for bundles. Paradoxically, higher prices when *i*Bundle terminates will allow lower adjusted prices.

Acknowledgments

This research was funded in part by National Science Foundation Grant SBR 97-08965.

References

Ausubel, L. M. 1997. An efficient ascending-bid auction for multiple objects. Tech. report, University of Maryland.

Bertsekas, D. P. 1990. The auction algorithm for assignment and other network flow problems: A tutorial. *Interfaces* 20(4):133–149.

Bikchandani, S., and Ostroy, J. M. 1998. The package assignment model. Tech. report, Anderson School of Management and Department of Economics, UCLA.

Clearwater, S. H., ed. 1996. *Market-Based Control: A Paradigm for Distributed Resource Allocation*. World Scientific.

Demange, G.; Gale, D.; and Sotomayor, M. 1986. Multi-item auctions. *J. of Political Economy* 94(4):863–872.

Gul, F., and Stacchetti, E. 1997. English and double auctions with differentiated commodities. Tech. Report 97-02, University of Michigan.

Kfir-Dahav, N. E.; Monderer, D.; and Tennenholtz, M. 1998. Mechanism design for resource bounded agents. Tech. report, Technion.

Lehmann, D.; O'Callaghan, L.; and Shoham, Y. 1999. Truth revelation in rapid, approximately efficient combinatorial auctions. In *Proc. ACM Conf. on Electronic Commerce (EC-99)*.

Milgrom, P. 1999. Putting auction theory to work: The simultaneous ascending auction. *J. of Political Economy* 108. To appear.

Nisan, N., and Ronen, A. 1999. Algorithmic mechanism design (extended abstract). In *Proc. 31st Annual Symposium on Theory of Computing (STOC99)*.

Papadimitriou, C. H., and Steiglitz, K. 1982. *Combinatorial Optimization: Algorithms and Complexity*. Prentice-Hall.

Parkes, D. C., and Ungar, L. H. 2000. Iterative combinatorial auctions: Theory and practice. In *Proc. 18th National Conference on Artificial Intelligence (AAAI-00)*. To appear.

Parkes, D. C. 1999a. Optimal auction design for agents with hard valuation problems. In *Proc. IJCAI-99 Workshop on Agent Mediated Electronic Commerce*. Stockholm.

Parkes, D. C. 1999b. *i*Bundle: An efficient ascending price bundle auction. In *Proc. ACM Conf. on Electronic Commerce (EC-99)*.

Rothkopf, M. H.; Pekeč, A.; and Harstad, R. M. 1998. Computationally manageable combinatorial auctions. *Management Science* 44(8):1131–1147.

Sandholm, T. 1993. An implementation of the Contract Net Protocol based on marginal-cost calculations. In *Proc. 11th National Conference on Artificial Intelligence (AAAI-93)*, 256–262.

Sandholm, T. 1996. Limitations of the Vickrey auction in computational multiagent systems. In *Second International Conference on Multiagent Systems (ICMAS-96)*, 299–306.

Sandholm, T. 1999. An algorithm for optimal winner determination in combinatorial auctions. In *Proc. 16th International Joint Conference on Artificial Intelligence (IJCAI-99)*, 542–547.

Varian, H., and MacKie-Mason, J. K. 1995. Generalized Vickrey auctions. Tech. report, University of Michigan.

Vickrey, W. 1961. Counterspeculation, auctions, and competitive sealed tenders. *J. of Finance* 16:8–37.

Wellman, M. P.; Walsh, W. E.; Wurman, P. R.; and MacKie-Mason, J. K. 1999. Auction protocols for decentralized scheduling. *Games and Economic Behavior*. To appear.

Wurman, P. R., and Wellman, M. P. 1999. Equilibrium prices in bundle auctions. In *Proc. AAAI-99 Workshop on Artificial Intelligence for Electronic Commerce*, 56–61.

Improved Algorithms for Optimal Winner Determination in Combinatorial Auctions and Generalizations

Tuomas Sandholm and Subhash Suri
Department of Computer Science
Washington University
St. Louis, MO 63130-4899
{sandholm,suri}@cs.wustl.edu

Abstract

Combinatorial auctions can be used to reach efficient resource and task allocations in multiagent systems where the items are complementary. Determining the winners is $\mathcal{NP}$-complete and inapproximable, but it was recently shown that optimal search algorithms do very well on average. This paper presents a more sophisticated search algorithm for optimal (and anytime) winner determination, including structural improvements that reduce search tree size, faster data structures, and optimizations at search nodes based on driving toward, identifying and solving tractable special cases. We also uncover a more general tractable special case, and design algorithms for solving it as well as for solving known tractable special cases substantially faster. We generalize combinatorial auctions to multiple units of each item, to reserve prices on singletons as well as combinations, and to combinatorial exchanges—all allowing for substitutability. Finally, we present algorithms for determining the winners in these generalizations.

Introduction

Auctions are important mechanisms for resource and task allocation in multiagent systems. In many auctions, a bidder's valuation for a combination of items is not the sum of the individual items' valuations—it can be more or less. This is often the case for example in electricity markets, equities trading, bandwidth auctions, transportation exchanges (Sandholm 1993), pollution right auctions, and auctions for airport landing slots (Rassenti, Smith, & Bulfin 1982).

In a traditional auction format where the items are auctioned separately (sequentially or in parallel), to decide what to bid on an item, an agent needs to estimate which other items it will receive in the other auctions, requiring intractable lookahead in the game tree. Even after lookahead, residual uncertainty would remain due to incomplete information about the other bidders. This leads to inefficient allocations where bidders do not get the combinations that they want and get combinations that they do not (Sandholm 1996).

Combinatorial auctions (CAs) can be used to overcome these deficiencies (Rassenti, Smith, & Bulfin 1982; Sandholm 1993). In a CA, bidders may submit bids on combinations of items. This allows the bidders to express complementarities between items instead of having to speculate into an item's valuation the impact of possibly getting other, complementary items.

Winner determination problem

The auctioneer has a set of items, $M = \{1, 2, \ldots, m\}$, to sell, and the buyers submit a set of bids, $\mathcal{B} = \{B_1, B_2, \ldots, B_n\}$. A bid is a tuple $B_j = \langle S_j, p_j \rangle$, where $S_j \subseteq M$ is a set of items and p_j is a price. Assume for now (this is relaxed later), that $p_j \geq 0$ for all $j \in \{1, 2, \ldots, n\}$. Assume also that no two bids concern the same set of items: $S_j \neq S_k$ (if multiple bids do concern the same set of items, all but the highest bid can be discarded as a preprocessing step, breaking ties arbitrarily). The *winner determination problem* is to label the bids as winning ($x_j = 1$) or losing ($x_j = 0$) so as to maximize the auctioneer's revenue under the constraint that each item can be allocated to at most one bidder:

$$\max \sum_{j=1}^{n} p_j x_j \quad \text{s.t.} \quad \sum_{j | i \in S_j} x_j \leq 1 \quad i = 1, 2, \ldots, m$$
$$x_j \in \{0, 1\}$$

This problem is intractable: it is equivalent to weighted set packing, a well-known $\mathcal{NP}$-complete problem. It can be solved via dynamic programming, but that takes $\Omega(2^m)$ and $O(3^m)$ time independent of n (Rothkopf, Pekeč, & Harstad 1998).

One approach is to solve the problem approximately (Rassenti, Smith, & Bulfin 1982; Fujishima, Leyton-Brown, & Shoham 1999; Lehmann, O'Callaghan, & Shoham 1999). However, it was recently shown (using the inapproximability of maximum clique) that no polynomial time algorithm can guarantee a solution that is close to optimum (Sandholm 1999). Certain special cases can be approximated slightly better, as reviewed in (Sandholm 1999).

The second approach is to restrict the allowable bids (Rothkopf, Pekeč, & Harstad 1998; Nisan 1999; Tennenholtz 2000). For certain restrictions, which are severe in the sense that only a vanishingly small fraction of the combinations can be bid on, winners can be determined in polynomial time. Restrictions on the bids give rise to the same economic inefficiencies that prevail in noncombinatorial auctions because bidders may not be able to bid on the combinations they prefer.

The third approach is to solve the unrestricted problem using search. This was shown to work very well on average, scaling optimal winner determination up to hundreds of items and thousands of bids depending on

---

Copyright © 2000, American Association for Artificial Intelligence (www.aaai.org). All rights reserved.

the problem instance distribution (Sandholm 1999) and improvements to the algorithm have been developed since (Fujishima, Leyton-Brown, & Shoham 1999).

In the vein of the third approach, this paper presents a more sophisticated algorithm for optimal winner determination. The enhancements include structural improvements that reduce search tree size, faster data structures, and optimizations at search nodes based on driving toward, identifying and solving tractable special cases. We also uncover a more general tractable case, and design algorithms for solving it as well as for solving known tractable cases substantially faster. We generalize CAs to auctions with multiple units of each item, to auctions with reserve prices on singletons as well as combinations, and to combinatorial exchanges—all allowing for substitutability. We also give algorithms for determining the winners in these generalizations.

While we present our results for auctions where the auctioneer is the seller and the bidders are buyers, all of the results apply directly to reverse auctions where the auctioneer buys and the bidders sell.

A sophisticated search algorithm

In this section we present an algorithm for optimal winner determination. The improvements over previous algorithms are classified into structural improvements, capitalizing on tractable subproblems at nodes, and faster data structures.

Structural improvements

This section presents improvements that reduce search tree size by changing its structure.

Branching on bids (BOB) The skeleton of our algorithm is a depth-first branch-and-bound tree search that branches on bids. The set of bids that are labeled winning on the path to the current search node is called IN, and the set of bids that are winning in the best allocation found so far is IN^*. Let $\tilde{f}^*$ be the value of the best solution found so far. Initially, $IN = \emptyset$, $IN^* = \emptyset$, and $\tilde{f}^* = 0$. Each bid, B_j, has an exclusion count, e_j, that stores how many times B_j has been excluded by bids on the path. Initially $e_j = 0$ for all $j \in \{1, 2, \ldots, n\}$. M' is the set of items that are still unallocated, and g is the revenue from the bids with $x_j = 1$ on the search path so far. h is an upper bound on how much the unallocated items can contribute (let $\max\{\emptyset\} = 0$). The search is invoked by calling $BOB(M, 0)$.

Algorithm 1 $BOB(M', g)$

1. If $g > \tilde{f}^*$, then $IN^* \leftarrow IN$ and $\tilde{f}^* \leftarrow g$
2. $h \leftarrow \sum_{i \in M'} c(i)$, where $c(i) \leftarrow \max_{j | i \in S_j, e_j = 0} \frac{p_j}{|S_j|}$
3. If $g + h \leq \tilde{f}^*$, then return /* bounding */
4. Choose a bid B_k for which $e_k = 0$ /* branching */
   If no such bid exists, then return
5. $IN \leftarrow IN \cup \{B_k\}$, $e_k \leftarrow 1$
6. For all B_j such that $B_j \neq B_k$ and $S_j \cap S_k \neq \emptyset$,
   $e_j \leftarrow e_j + 1$
7. $BOB(M' - S_k, g + p_k)$
8. $IN \leftarrow IN - \{B_k\}$
9. For all B_j such that $B_j \neq B_k$ and $S_j \cap S_k \neq \emptyset$,
   $e_j \leftarrow e_j - 1$
10. $BOB(M', g)$
11. $e_k \leftarrow 0$, return

Both of the previous search algorithms for winner determination, *de facto*, branch on items (Sandholm 1999; Fujishima, Leyton-Brown, & Shoham 1999). The children of a search node are those bids that include the smallest item that is still unallocated, and do not share items with any bid on the path so far. If, as a preprocessing step, a dummy bid of price zero is submitted for every individual item that received no bids alone (to represent the fact that the auctioneer can keep items), then it was proven that the leaves of this tree correspond to feasible solutions to the winner determination problem (Sandholm 1999). Clearly, the branching factor is at most $n + m$ (the m comes from the dummy bids), and the depth is at most m, so the complexity is $O((n+m)^m)$.

On the other hand, BOB branches on bids (winning or losing, i.e., $x_j = 1$ or $x_j = 0$) instead of items. The branching factor is 2 and the depth is at most n, so a naive analysis shows that BOB is $O(2^n)$, which is exponential in bids. However, the nodes (both interior and leaf) correspond to feasible solutions to the winner determination problem. Therefore, the number of nodes in this tree is the same as the number of leaves in the old formulation. This proves that BOB is $O((n+m)^m)$, i.e., polynomial in bids. This is desirable since the auctioneer can usually control how many items are auctioned, but she cannot control how many bids are submitted. Furthermore, even though the complexity is exponential in items, this is only a worst-case bound and the average case tends to be significantly better. By contrast, the dynamic programming algorithm (Rothkopf, Pekeč, & Harstad 1998) is exponential in items even in the best case.

The main advantage of BOB compared to the earlier search formulation is that BOB is in line with the AI principle of least commitment. In BOB, the choice in step 4 only commits one bid, while in the old formulation the choice of an item committed all the remaining bids that include the item. BOB allows more refined search control—in particular, better bid ordering. Many of the techniques of this paper capitalize heavily on that possibility. A secondary advantage of BOB is that there is no need to use dummy bids.

Bid ordering heuristics (HEU) Search speed can be increased by improving the pruning that occurs in step 2. Our algorithm does this by constructing many high-revenue allocations early. We do this by bid ordering in step 4. We choose bids that contribute a lot to the revenue, and do not retract from the potential contribution of other bids by using up many items. At a search node, we choose a bid that maximizes $\frac{p_j}{|S_j|^\alpha}$ (to avoid scanning the list of bids repeatedly, the bids are sorted in descending order before the search begins) and has $e_j = 0$. Intuitively, $\alpha = 0$ gives too much preference to bids with many items, and $\alpha = 1$ gives too much preference to bids with few items. It was recently shown that in a greedy algorithm that simply inserts bids into IN^* in highest $\frac{p_j}{|S_j|^\alpha}$ first order (as a bid is inserted, bids that share items with it are discarded), $\alpha = \frac{1}{2}$ gives the best worst case bound over all α (Lehmann, O'Callaghan, & Shoham 1999) (but not necessarily over all possible bid ordering formulas). As in the greedy algorithm, we want to construct high-valued allocations. Unlike in the greedy algorithm, we also want to construct many allocations early to increase the chance of high-valued ones. Since bids with few items lead to deeper search than bids with many items (because bids with many items exclude more of the other bids due to overlap in items) (Sandholm 1999), preference for bids with many items increases the number of allocations seen early. Therefore, we set α slightly below $\frac{1}{2}$.

In addition to finding the optimal solution faster via more pruning, such bid ordering improves the algorithm's anytime performance: $\tilde{f}^*$ increases faster.

Lower bounding (LOW) We also prune using a lower bound, L, (obtained, e.g., using the greedy algorithm described above) at each node. If $g + L > \tilde{f}^*$, then $\tilde{f}^* \leftarrow g + L$ and IN^* is updated. This reduces search by enhanced pruning in the subtree rooted at the current search node.

Exploiting decomposition (DEC) If the set of items can be divided into subsets such that no bid includes items from more than one subset, the winner determination can be done in each subset separately. Because the search is superlinear in the size of the problem (both n and m), such decomposition leads to a speedup.

At every search node (between steps 1 and 2), our algorithm checks whether the problem has decomposed. We maintain a graph, G, where the vertices V are the bids with $e_j = 0$, and two vertices share an edge if the bids share items. Call the set of edges E. Clearly, $|V| \leq n$ and $|E| \leq \frac{n(n-1)}{2}$. Via an $O(|E| + |V|)$ depth-first-search in G, the algorithm checks whether the graph has decomposed. Every tree in the depth-first-forest corresponds to an independent subproblem (subset of bids and the associated subset of items). The winners are determined by calling BOB on each subproblem separately (bids not in that subproblem are marked $e_j \leftarrow 1$).[1]

Upper and lower bounding across subproblems (ACROSS) The straightforward approach is to call BOB on each subproblem with $g = 0$ and $\tilde{f}^* = 0$.

---

[1] This decomposition check was used as a preprocessor before (Sandholm 1999), not at every node.

Somewhat unintuitively, we can achieve further pruning, without compromising optimality, by exploiting information across the independent subproblems. Say there are k subproblems at the current search node θ: $1, \ldots, k$. Let g^θ be the g-value of θ before any of the subproblems have been solved. Let f_q^* be the value of the optimal solution found for subproblem q. Let h_q be the h-value of subproblem q. Let L_q be a lower bound (obtained, e.g., using the greedy algorithm described above, but even $L_q = 0$ works) for subproblem q.

Now, consider what to do to solve subproblem z after subproblems $1, \ldots, z-1$ have been solved and the other subproblems have not. Let l_z be a lower bound (obtained, e.g., using the greedy algorithm described above) on the value that the *unallocated* items of subproblem z can contribute. Let g_z be the g-value within subproblem z only, and let h_z be the h-value within subproblem z only. Let

$$F^*_{solved} = g^\theta + \sum_{q=1}^{z-1} f_q^*$$

$$H_{unsolved} = \sum_{q=z+1}^{k} h_q$$

$$LO_{unsolved} = \sum_{q=z+1}^{k} L_q$$

At every search node within the subproblem z, we update the global lower bound $\tilde{f}^*$ as follows:

$$\tilde{f}^* \leftarrow \max\{\tilde{f}^*, F^*_{solved} + g_z + l_z + LO_{unsolved}\}$$

and we update IN^* accordingly.

Now we can cut the search path whenever

$$F^*_{solved} + g_z + h_z + H_{unsolved} \leq \tilde{f}^*$$

Since both the straightforward approach and this approach are correct, we use both. If either one allows the search path to be cut, the algorithm does so in step 3.

Due to the upper and lower bounding across subproblems, the order of tackling the subproblems makes a difference in speed, providing further opportunities for optimization via subproblem ordering.

Forcing a decomposition via articulation bids (ART) In addition to checking whether a decomposition has occurred, our algorithm strives for a decomposition. In the bid choice in step 4, we pick a bid that leads to a decomposition, if such a bid exists. Such bids whose deletion disconnects G are called *articulation bids*. Articulation bids can be identified during the depth-first-search of G in $O(|E|+|V|)$ time, as follows.

The depth-first-search assigns each node v of G a number $d(v)$, which is the order in which nodes of G are "discovered". The root has number 0. (See (Weiss 1999) for details.) In order to identify articulation bids, we assign to each node v one additional number, $low(v)$, which is defined inductively:

$$x = \min\{low(w) \mid w \text{ is a child of } v\}$$
$$y = \min\{d(z) \mid (v, z) \text{ is a back edge}\}$$
$$low(v) = \min(x, y)$$

A node v is an articulation bid if and only if $\text{low}(v) \geq d(v)$. If there are multiple articulation bids, we branch on the one that minimizes the size of the larger subproblem, measured by the number of bids.

The strategy of branching on articulation bids may conflict with our price-based branching. Is one scheme necessarily dominant over the other? To answer this question, we define the two classes of schemes:

Definition. 1 *In an articulation-based bid choosing scheme, the next bid to branch on is an articulation bid if one exists. Ties can be resolved arbitrarily, as can cases where no articulation bid exists.*

Definition. 2 *In a price-based bid choosing scheme, the next bid to branch on is $B_k = \arg\max_{B_j \in \mathcal{B} | e_j = 0} \frac{p_k}{\nu(|S_k|)}$, for any given positive function ν. Ties can be resolved arbitrarily, e.g., preferring bids that articulate.*

Proposition 1 *For any given articulation-based bid choosing scheme and price-based bid choosing scheme, there are instances where the former leads to fewer search nodes, as well as instances where the latter leads to fewer search nodes.*[2]

Even if a bid is not an articulation bid, and would not lead to a decomposition if the bid is assigned losing, it might lead to a decomposition if it is assigned winning because that removes the bid's neighbors from G as well. This is yet another reason to assign a bid that we branch on to be winning before assigning it to be losing (value ordering). Also, in bid ordering (variable ordering), we can give first preference to articulation bids, second preference to these bids that articulate on the winning branch only, and third preference to bids that do not articulate on either branch (among them, the price-based bid ordering is used).

During the search, the algorithm could also do shallow lookaheads—for the purpose of bid ordering—to identify *combinations* of bids that would disconnect G. Such *cutsets* of bids can also be identified in a preprocessor, and then the bids within a small cutset should be branched on first in the search (however, identifying the smallest cutset is intractable).

Tractable subproblems at nodes

The following techniques, used at each search node, drive toward, identify and solve tractable special cases.

Avoiding branching on short bids Bids that include a small number of items lead to significantly deeper search than bids with many items because the latter exclude more of the other bids due to overlap in items. A previous search algorithm scaled to thousands of bids when bids had many items, and only hundreds of bids when bids had few items each (Sandholm 1999). We call bids with 1 or 2 items *short* and other bids *long*.[3] Winners can be optimally determined in $O(n_{short}^3)$ worst case time using a weighted maximal matching algorithm (Edmonds 1965) if the problem has short bids only (Rothkopf, Pekeč, & Harstad 1998). To solve problems with both long and short bids efficiently, we integrate Edmond's algorithm with search. Our algorithm achieves optimality without ever branching on short bids. In step 4, bid choice is restricted to long bids. At every node, before step 1, Edmond's algorithm is executed using the short bids with $e_j = 0$. It returns a set of winning bids, IN_E, and the revenue they provide, f_E. The only remaining change is to step 1:

1. If $g + f_E > \tilde{f}^*$, then $IN^* \leftarrow IN \cup IN_E$, $\tilde{f}^* \leftarrow g + f_E$

Deleting items included in only one bid In the previous optimization, short bids are statically defined. We can improve on this by a more dynamic size determination. If an item x belongs to only one long bid b, then the size of b can be effectively reduced by one. This optimization may move some of the long bids into the short category, thereby further reducing search tree size. This optimization can be done at each search node, by keeping track of bids concerning each item.

Interval bids (Rothkopf, Pekeč, & Harstad 1998) considered an important special case where the items can be linearly ordered, and each bid concerns a contiguous interval of items. Specifically, assume that items are labeled $\{1, 2, \ldots, m\}$, and each bid b is for some interval $[i, j]$ of items. Using dynamic programming, Rothkopf et al. solved the problem in $O(m^2)$ time. We propose a different algorithm that solves this special case in $O(n + m)$ time. This asymptotic complexity is worst-case optimal because any algorithm may need to read all of the items and bids as input.

We briefly describe our algorithm here. Given a bid b on the interval $[f, l]$, let us call item f the *first item* of b, and item l the *last item* of b. We sort the bids in increasing order of their *last item*; if two bids have the same last item, the one with the smaller first item comes earlier in the sorted order. Since the set of items has bounded size $[1, m]$, we can bucket sort the bids in $O(n + m)$ time. Our dynamic program computes optimal solutions for the prefix intervals of the form $[1, i]$, for $i = 1, 2, \ldots, n$. Let $\text{opt}(i)$ denote the optimal solution for the problem considering only those bids that contain items in the range $[1, i]$; that is, bids whose last item is no later than i. Initially, $\text{opt}(0) = 0$. Let C_i denote the set of bids whose last item is i. Then, we have the following recurrence:

$$\text{opt}(i) = \max_{b \in C_i} \{p_b + \text{opt}(f_b - 1), \text{opt}(i - 1)\},$$

where p_b is the price of bid b, and f_b is the smallest indexed item in b. The maximization has two terms.

---

[2] Proofs are omitted in this version due to limited space.

[3] We define *short* in this way because the problem is $\mathcal{NP}$-complete already if 3 items per bid are allowed (Rothkopf, Pekeč, & Harstad 1998).

The first term corresponds to accepting bid b, in which case we need an optimal solution for the subproblem $[1, f_b - 1]$. The second term corresponds to not accepting b, in which case we use the optimal allocation for items in $[1, i - 1]$. By solving these problems in increasing order of i, we can compute each opt(i) in time proportional to the size of C_i. Since $\sum C_i = n$, the total time complexity is $O(n + m)$. The optimal allocation is opt(m).

Proposition 2 *If all n bids are interval bids in a linearly ordered set of items $[1, m]$, then an optimal allocation can be computed in worst-case time $O(n + m)$.*

If we allow interval wraparound bids (e.g, $S_j = \{m - 1, m, 1, 2, 3\}$), the winners can be determined optimally in $O(m(n + m))$ time by cutting the circle of items in each of the m possible positions separately, and solving the associated problem (ignoring bids that span over the cutting position) using our algorithm described above. The fastest prior algorithm for this case took $O(m^3)$ time (Rothkopf, Pekeč, & Harstad 1998).

Identifying linear ordering Our interest is not to limit the auctions to interval bids only, but rather to recognize whether the remaining problem at any search node falls under this special case and to solve it by our specialized fast algorithm. This requires an algorithm to check whether *there exists some linear ordering of items* for which the given set of bids are all interval bids. It turns out this problem can be phrased as the *interval graph recognition* problem, for which a linear-time solution exists.

Given a graph $G = (V, E)$, we say that G is an *interval graph* if the vertices V can be put in one-to-one correspondence with intervals of the real line such that two intervals overlap if and only if there is an edge between the vertices corresponding to those intervals. The interval graph recognition problem is to decide whether G is an interval graph, and to also construct the intervals. The algorithm in (Korte & Mohring 1989) solves this problem in $O(|V| + |E|)$ time. Given the intervals for the bids, one can easily produce a linear ordering of the items. Figure 1 shows an example with 4 bids: $A = (2, 4, 6)$, $B = (1, 2, 4, 5, 7)$, $C = (1, 3, 7, 8)$, $D = (1, 3, 5, 7)$.

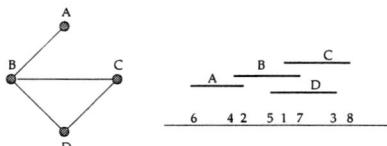

Figure 1: *Bid graph and a valid linear ordering.*

The case where wraparound bids are allowed can be identified in $O(n^2)$ time using an algorithm for recognizing whether the remaining graph G is *circular* (Eschen & Spinrad 1993).

Subgraph bids on tree-structured items We now propose a fast algorithm for another case that subsumes and substantially generalizes the interval bid model of (Rothkopf, Pekeč, & Harstad 1998). The items are structured in a tree T, and a valid bid corresponds to a *connected subgraph* of T (see Figure 2). This is a strict generalization of the linear ordering model, which corresponds to the special case where T is a path. Our tree model is also distinct from the "nested structure" model in (Rothkopf, Pekeč, & Harstad 1998), where the tree nodes corresponds to bids.

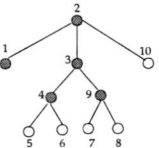

Figure 2: *An example of a subgraph bid:* $\{1, 2, 3, 4, 9\}$.

An example application where this special structure prevails is the following web shopping scenario. The goods are structured in a tree, where a web page contains the description of a good and links to children goods. For example, the page of a tent could have links to a heater, camping stove, and bug spray. The stove could have links to fuel refills and pots, etc. On any page, the user can 1. buy the item and be allowed to continue to any number of the children goods, or 2. not buy the item and backtrack, or 3. submit the bid by specifying a price for the subgraph that the user has chosen so far, or 4. exit without submitting the bid.

We developed an $O(nm)$ algorithm for solving the winner determination problem with subgraph bids on tree-structured items. We pick an arbitrary node r as the root of the item tree T. We assign each node of T a *level*, which is its distance from the root. The level of a bid b, denoted level(b), is the smallest level of any item in b. We sort the bids in increasing order of level, breaking ties arbitrarily. We use a dynamic program to compute the optimal solutions at nodes of T in decreasing order of level.

Given a node i of T, let C_i denote the set of bids that include i and whose level is the same as the level of i. Our algorithm computes the function opt(i), for each node i, where opt(i) is the optimal solution for the problem considering only those bids that contain items in the subtree below i. Our goal is to compute opt(r).

Consider a bid b, and suppose that the item giving b its level is x. Removing all items of b disconnects the tree rooted at x, namely T_x, into several subtrees. Let U_b be the set of roots of this forest of subtrees. Now,

$$\text{opt}(i) = \max\left\{\max_{b \in C_i}\left\{p_b + \sum_{j \in U_b} \text{opt}(j)\right\}, \sum_{j \in \text{children}(i)} \text{opt}(j)\right\}$$

where p_b is the price of bid b. By proceeding bottom up, we compute opt(i) for all nodes of the tree.

Proposition 3 *The recurrence above correctly computes the optimal solution for subtree bids in tree-structured items in $O(nm)$ worst-case time.*

Subtree bids in DAGs Our special case of subtree bids on tree-structured item is sharp in the sense that a slight generalization makes the problem intractable:

Proposition 4 *If the set of items is structured as a directed acyclic graph D, and each bid is a subtree of D, then winner determination is $\mathcal{NP}$-complete.*

Faster data structures

Bid graph representation (GRA) We use an adjacency list representation of the bid graph G for efficient insert and delete operations on bids. We do not actually keep track of exclusion counts e_j. Instead, a bid j having been deleted corresponds to $e_j > 0$, and a bid j not having been deleted corresponds to $e_j = 0$. We use an array to store the nodes of G. The array entry for node j points to a doubly-linked list of bids that share items with j. Thus, an edge (j, k) creates two entries: one for j in the list of k, and the other for k in the list of j. We use cross-pointers with these entries to be able to access one from the other in $O(1)$ time. To delete node j whose current neighbor list is $\{b_1, b_2, \ldots, b_k\}$, we mark the node j "deleted" in the node array. Then, we use the linked list of j to access the position of j in each of the b_i's list, and delete that entry, at $O(1)$ cost each. When reinserting a node j with edges E_j into G, node j's "deleted" label is first removed in the node array. Then, for each $(j, k) \in E_j$, j is inserted at the front of k's neighbor list, k is inserted at the front of j's neighbor list, and the cross-pointer is set between them, all at $O(1)$ cost.

As BOB branches by $x_j = 1$, j and its neighbors in G are deleted. We also store in the search node a list of the edges that were in effect removed: the edges E' that include j, and the edges E'' that include j's neighbors but not j. When backtracking to that node, we reinsert j's neighbors into G using the edges E''. Then BOB branches by $x_j = 0$. When backtracking from that branch, j is reinserted into G using edges E'.

Maintaining the heuristic function (MAI) Our heuristic function, h, is the same as in an earlier winner determination algorithm (Sandholm 1999). In that implementation it took $O(mn)$ time per search node to compute. A faster but rougher approximation of the same heuristic was used in (Fujishima, Leyton-Brown, & Shoham 1999). Here we propose data structures that allow us to compute h fast and exactly.

We store the items in a dynamic list which supports insert and delete in $O(\log m)$ time each. Each item i points to a *heap* $H(i)$ that maintains the bids that include i. The heap supports find-max, extract-max, insert, and delete in $O(\log m)$ time each (delete requires a pointer to the item being deleted, which we maintain).

The heuristic function requires us to compute, for each item i, the maximum value $\frac{p_j}{|S_j|}$ among the bids that have not been deleted and concern item i. We keep a tally of the current heuristic function and update it each time a bid gets deleted or reinserted into G. Consider the deletion of bid j that has k items; each item points to its position in the item list. We delete j's entry from the heap of each of these k items. For each of these k items, we update the heuristic function, by calculating the difference in its c value before and after the update. When j is reinserted, we reinsert j into the heaps of all the items that concern j. The cost, per search node, of updating the heuristic function is $\sum_j |S_j| \log m$, where the summation is over all the bids that got deleted or reinserted.

As a further optimization, our algorithm uses a *leftist heap* for $H(i)$ (Weiss 1999). A leftist heap has the same worst-case performance as an ordinary heap, but improves the amortized complexity of insert and delete to $O(1)$, while extract-max and find-max remain $O(\log m)$. Because the insert and delete operations in BOB are quite frequent, this improves the overall performance.

Preprocessing

Four preprocessing techniques were recently proposed for the winner determination problem (Sandholm 1999). Each one of them can be directly used in conjunction with our algorithm.

Generalizations of CAs

This section discusses generalizations of CAs. Our auction server prototype (http://ecommerce.cs.wustl.edu/emediator) supports all of these generalizations separately and combined (Sandholm 2000), and has been in continuous operation since December 1998.

Multiple units of each item

In some auctions, there are multiple indistinguishable units of each item for sale. One can compress the bids and speed up winner determination by not treating every unit as a separate item, since the bidders do not care which units of each item they get, only how many. We define a bid in this setting as $B_j = \langle (\lambda_j^1, \lambda_j^2, \ldots \lambda_j^m), p_j \rangle$, where $\lambda_j^k \geq 0$ is the requested number of units of item k, and p_j is the price. The winner determination problem is:

$$\max \sum_{j=1}^n p_j x_j \quad \text{s.t.} \quad \sum_{j=1}^n \lambda_j^i x_j \leq u_i \quad i = 1, 2, \ldots, m$$
$$x_j \in \{0, 1\}$$

where u_i is the number of units of item i for sale. In our basic CA, and in every one of the generalizations, if *free disposal* is not possible, we use an equality constraint in place of the inequality.

Previous winner determination algorithms cannot be used in the multi-unit setting because they branch on items (Sandholm 1999; Fujishima, Leyton-Brown, & Shoham 1999). Even if each unit is treated as a separate item, the earlier algorithms cannot be used if the demands, λ_j^k, are real-valued instead of integer.

BOB can be used. A tally of the number of units allocated on the search path is kept for each item: $\Lambda_i = \sum_{j \mid x_j = 1} \lambda_j^i$.

The decomposition techniques DEC and ART apply on the bid graph G where two vertices, j and k, now share an edge if $\exists i$ s.t. $\lambda_j^i > 0$ and $\lambda_k^i > 0$. However, once a bid is assigned winning and removed from G, the neighbor bids in G cannot always be removed unlike in the basic CA. Instead, only those neighbors, j, are removed that demand more units of some item than remain ($\exists$ item k such that $\lambda_j^k > u_k - \Lambda_i^k$). The removed bids are reinserted into G when backtracking. The data structure improvements GRA and MAI apply with this change.

One admissible heuristic for this setting is

$$h = \sum_{i \in M}[(u_i - \Lambda_i) \max_{j \in V_G | \lambda_j^i > 0} \frac{p_j}{\sum_{i \in S_j} \lambda_j^i}]$$

where V_G is the set of bids that remain in G. More refined heuristics can be constructed by giving different items different weights. Once $g + h \leq \bar{f}^*$, the search path is cut. The lower bounding technique LOW also applies, as do upper and lower bounding across sub-problems (ACROSS).

Bid ordering can be used, e.g., by presorting the bids in descending order of $\frac{p_j}{(\sum_{i=1}^{m} \lambda_j^i)^\alpha}$.

Combinatorial exchanges

In a combinatorial exchange, both buyers and sellers can submit combinatorial bids (Sandholm 2000). Bids are as in the multi-unit case, except that the λ_j^i values can be negative, as can the prices p_j, representing selling instead of buying. The winner determination problem is to maximize surplus:[4]

$$\max \sum_{j=1}^n p_j x_j \quad \text{s.t.} \quad \sum_{j=1}^n \lambda_j^i x_j \leq 0 \quad i = 1, 2, \ldots, m$$
$$x_j \in \{0, 1\}$$

Unlike earlier algorithms that branch on items (Sandholm 1999; Fujishima, Leyton-Brown, & Shoham 1999), BOB can be used in this setting. In the basic CA and in our other generalizations, the optimal solution occurs in a leaf. In contrast, in our combinatorial exchange, the optimal solution can occur even in an interior node of the search tree. In the search, a tally of the net number of units demanded (units supplied are negative numbers) on the path is kept for each item: $\Lambda_i = \sum_{j | x_j = 1} \lambda_j^i$.

The decomposition techniques DEC and ART apply on bid graph G where two vertices, j and k, share an edge if $\exists$ item i such that $\lambda_j^i \neq 0$ and $\lambda_k^i \neq 0$. However, once a bid is assigned winning and removed from G, the neighbor bids in G cannot always be removed unlike in the basic CA. Instead, only those neighbors, j, are removed that cannot possibly be matched any more:

- $\exists$ item i s.t. $\lambda_j^i > 0$ and $\lambda_j^i + \Lambda_i + \sum_{k \in V_G | \lambda_k^i < 0} > 0$, or
- $\exists$ item i s.t. $\lambda_j^i < 0$ and $\lambda_j^i + \Lambda_i + \sum_{k \in V_G | \lambda_k^i > 0} < 0$,

where V_G is the set of remaining bids in G. The removed bids are reinserted into G when backtracking. The data structure improvements GRA and MAI apply with this modification.

The upper bounding and lower bounding (LOW) techniques discussed earlier in the paper can be used after constructing functions that compute an upper bound h and a lower bound L. Then, also the upper bounding and lower bounding techniques across subproblems (ACROSS) apply.

Bid ordering can also be used. For example, by branching on a bid, j, that maximizes p_j (the bids can be sorted in this order as a preprocessing step to avoid sorting during search), the algorithm can strive to high-surplus allocations early, leading to enhanced pruning. As another example, by branching on a bid, j, that minimizes $\sum_{i | \Lambda_i > 0} \Lambda_i + \lambda_i^j$, or a bid that minimizes $\max_{i | \Lambda_i > 0} \Lambda_i + \lambda_i^j$, the algorithm can reach feasible solutions faster (especially in the case of free disposal), leading again to enhanced pruning later.

Additional pruning is achieved by branching on bids with $p_j < 0$ first, and then on bids with $p_j \geq 0$.[5] Once $\sum_{j | x_j = 1} p_j > 0$, that branch of the search is cut.[6] Also, after the switch to bids with $p_j \geq 0$ has occurred on a path, h, LOW, ACROSS, and bid ordering from the multi-unit case can be used among the remaining bids to achieve further pruning.

Reserve prices

In some auctions, the seller has a reserve price r_i for every item i, below which she is not willing to sell. This could be easily incorporated into our algorithm by adding a constraint: the revenue collected from the bids is no less than the sum of the reserve prices of the items that are allocated to bidders. A stricter way of interpreting reserve prices as a constraint is to require that the auctioneer's payoff (revenue collected from the bidders plus reserve prices of the items kept) would not increase by keeping an additional item or by allocating an additional item to one of the bidders. This could also be easily incorporated into our algorithm.

However, this raises the concern that the auctioneer's payoff might increase by keeping or allocating a *set* of items. It turns out that requiring that it does not coincides with maximizing social welfare (sum of the auctioneer's payoff plus the bidder's payoffs; each bidder's payoff is her valuation for the bundle of goods that she gets minus what she has to pay), assuming

---

[4] If the exchange charges based on transaction volume, as most current exchanges do, it may want to maximize volume instead: $\max \sum_{j \in \{1, \ldots, n\} | p_j > 0} p_j x_j$ with the same constraints. Our algorithms apply to this case as they do to surplus maximization. However, we advocate surplus maximization since that maximizes social welfare (assuming that bidders are truthful).

[5] Alternatively one can branch on bids with $p_j > 0$ first, and reverse the tests respectively.

[6] Alternatively one can do this split of bids into two sets ($\lambda_i^j < 0$ vs. $\lambda_i^j \geq 0$) and cutting (when $\Lambda_i > 0$) on any item i instead of price.

that bidders enter their true valuations and the auctioneer enters his true reserve prices. This is done not as a constraint, but by changing the maximization criterion to max $\sum_{j=1}^{n}(p_j - \sum_{i \in S_j} r_i)x_j$. This is trivial to incorporate into our algorithm: the item's reserve prices are simply subtracted from the bid prices as a preprocessing step.

This method can also be used for exchanges where only one side (buyers or sellers) is allowed to place combinatorial bids. The other side has to bid noncombinatorially. The bids of the noncombinatorial side are considered reserve prices, allowing the fast winner determination algorithm for one-to-many CAs to be used in many-to-many exchanges for optimal clearing.

Auctions where the seller is allowed to submit reserve prices on combinations of items or is allowed to express substitutability in the reserve prices, cannot be handled by the one-to-many algorithm. Instead, they are treated as exchanges where the seller's reserve prices are her bids. Our algorithm for combinatorial exchanges is then used for optimally clearing the market.

Substitutability

In the auctions discussed so far in the paper, bidders can express superadditive preferences: the value of a combination is greater or equal to the sum of the values of its parts. They cannot express subadditive preferences, aka. substitutability. For example, by bidding $5 for $\{1,2\}$, $3 for $\{1\}$, and $4 for $\{2\}$, the bidder may get $\{1,2\}$ for $7. Two solutions have been proposed that allow any preferences to be expressed. They extend directly to all the generalized CAs presented in this paper: the multi-unit case, the exchange, and the case of reserve prices. In the first, bidders can combine their bids with XORs, potentially joined by ORs (Sandholm 2000; 1999). The second uses dummy items (Fujishima, Leyton-Brown, & Shoham 1999). If two bids share a dummy item, they cannot be in the same allocation.

BOB can be used with the first method by adding edges in G for every pair of bids that is combined with XOR. These additional constraints actually speed up the search. However, only some of the optimization apply: HEU, LOW, DEC, ART, ACROSS, GRA, and MAI. BOB supports the second method directly and all of the optimization apply. Unfortunately, certain preferences require exponentially many dummy items to express.

Acknowledgments

Supported by NSF under CAREER Award IRI-9703122, Grant IRI-9610122, and Grant IIS-9800994.

Conclusions

Combinatorial auctions can be used to reach efficient resource and task allocations in multiagent systems where the items are complementary. Determining the winners is $\mathcal{NP}$-complete and inapproximable, but it was recently shown that optimal search algorithms do very well on average. This paper presented a more sophisticated search algorithm for optimal (and anytime) winner determination, including structural improvements that reduce search tree size, faster data structures, and optimizations at search nodes based on driving toward, identifying and solving tractable special cases. We also discovered a more general tractable special case, and designed algorithms for solving it as well as for solving known tractable special cases substantially faster. We generalized combinatorial auctions to multiple units of each item, to reserve prices on singletons as well as combinations, and to combinatorial exchanges—all allowing for substitutability. Finally, we developed algorithms for determining the winners in these generalizations.

References

Edmonds, J. 1965. Maximum matching and a polyhedron with 0,1 vertices. *J. Res. Nat. Bur. Standards* B(69):125–130.

Eschen, E. M., and Spinrad, J. 1993. An $O(n^2)$ algorithm for circular-arc graph recognition. In *SIAM-ACM Sym. on Discrete Algorithms (SODA)*, 128-137.

Fujishima, Y.; Leyton-Brown, K.; and Shoham, Y. 1999. Taming the computational complexity of combinatorial auctions: Optimal and approximate approaches. In *IJCAI*, 548–553.

Korte, N., and Mohring, R. H. 1989. An incremental linear-time algorithm for recognizing interval graphs. *SIAM Journal on Computing* 18(1):68–81.

Lehmann, D.; O'Callaghan, L. I.; and Shoham, Y. 1999. Truth revelation in rapid, approximately efficient combinatorial auctions. In *ACM Conference on Electronic Commerce (ACM-EC)*, 96–102.

Nisan, N. 1999. Bidding and allocation in combinatorial auctions: Preliminary version. Hebrew U., Sept.

Rassenti, S. J.; Smith, V. L.; and Bulfin, R. L. 1982. A combinatorial auction mechanism for airport time slot allocation. *Bell J. of Economics* 13:402–417.

Rothkopf, M. H.; Pekeč, A.; and Harstad, R. M. 1998. Computationally manageable combinatorial auctions. *Management Science* 44(8):1131–1147.

Sandholm, T. W. 1993. An implementation of the contract net protocol based on marginal cost calculations. In *AAAI*, 256–262.

Sandholm, T. W. 1996. Limitations of the Vickrey auction in computational multiagent systems. In *ICMAS*, 299–306.

Sandholm, T. W. 1999. An algorithm for optimal winner determination in combinatorial auctions. In *IJCAI*, 542–547. Extended version first appeared as Washington U., Comp. Sci. WUCS-99-01, Jan. 28th.

Sandholm, T. W. 2000. eMediator: A next generation electronic commerce server. In *AGENTS*. Early version: AAAI-99 Workshop on AI in Electronic Commerce, Orlando, FL, pp. 46–55, July 1999.

Tennenholtz, M. 2000. Some tractable combinatorial auctions (preliminary report). Draft. Technion, Israel.

Weiss, M. A. 1999. *Data structures and algorithm analysis in C++*. Addison-Wesley, 2nd edition.

Some Tractable Combinatorial Auctions

Moshe Tennenholtz
Faculty of Industrial Engineering and Management
Technion, Israel Institute of Technology
Haifa 32000, Israel [*]

Abstract

Auctions are the most widely used strategic game-theoretic mechanism in the Internet. Auctions have been mostly studied from a game-theoretic and economic perspective, although recent work in AI and OR has been concerned with computational aspects of auctions as well. When faced from a computational perspective, combinatorial auctions are perhaps the most challenging type of auctions. Combinatorial auctions are auctions where agents may submit bids for bundles of goods. Given that finding an optimal allocation of the goods in a combinatorial auction is intractable, researchers have been concerned with exposing tractable instances of combinatorial auctions. In this work we introduce polynomial solutions for a variety of non-trivial combinatorial auctions, such as combinatorial network auctions, various sub-additive combinatorial auctions, and some restricted forms of multi-unit combinatorial auctions.

The emergence of electronic commerce has led to increasing interest in the design of protocols for non-cooperative environments (see e.g. (Rosenschein & Zlotkin 1994; Kraus 1997; Tennenholtz 1999; Durfee 1992)). The wide-spread of auctions in the Internet, and the fact auctions are basic building blocks for a variety of economic protocols have attracted many researchers to tackle the challenge of efficient auction design (e.g. (Wellman *et al.* 1998; Monderer & Tennenholtz 2000; Lehmann, O'callaghan, & Shoham 1999; Sandholm 1996; Parkes 1999)). The design of auctions introduces deep problems and challenges both from the game-theoretic and from the computational perspectives. This paper mainly concentrates on computational aspects of auctions. More specifically, we concentrate on addressing computational problems of combinatorial auctions, extending upon previous work on this basic topic (Rothkopf, Pekec, & Harstad 1998;

[*]Current address: Computer Science Department, Stanford University, Stanford, CA 94305, USA
Copyright ©2000, American Association for Artificial Intelligence (www.aaai.org). All rights reserved.

Nisan 1999; Sandholm 1999; Fujishima, Leyton-Brown, & Shoham 1999).

In an auction, a seller sells several goods to several potential buyers. In typical single-object auctions, determining the auction's winner and its payment is a computationally tractable problem. This is also true when agents' valuations for the different objects are additive, i.e. determined in an additive manner by their valuations for the single goods. However, consider a situation where a VCR, a TV, and a Microwave are sold; an agent may be willing to pay $200 for the TV, $300 for the VCR, and $150 for the microwave, but might be willing pay only $500 for getting all of them. In order to allocate the goods in a satisfactory manner, bids for bundles of goods should be allowed; given these bids, we need to find an optimal, revenue maximizing, allocation of the goods. This problem is referred to as the combinatorial auction problem, and it is in general intractable.

One can partition previous work on computational aspects of combinatorial auctions into two parts. One part deals with heuristics for the solution of combinatorial auctions (see e.g. (Sandholm 1999; Fujishima, Leyton-Brown, & Shoham 1999)), while the other part deals with the identification of tractable cases of the combinatorial auctions problem (see (Rothkopf, Pekec, & Harstad 1998; Nisan 1999)). Our work fits into the latter category. Previous results on that category can be obtained in a relatively straightforward manner by a linear programming [LP] relaxation of the combinatorial auctions problem (which can be stated as an integer programming [IP] problem). This paper extends on these results, by exposing non-trivial tractable instances of the combinatorial auctions problem.

In Section 2 we present some preliminaries. In Sections 3–4 we expose the use of b-matching techniques for the solution of combinatorial auctions,[1] and present

[1]The use of b-matching techniques in the solution of other auctions is discussed in (Penn & Tennenholtz 1999).

polynomial solutions for a variety of combinatorial auctions. In Section 5 we introduce combinatorial network auctions. Combinatorial network auctions widely extend on auctions for linear goods (such as auctions for time slots, or for one-dimensional space), that are known to be tractable; we prove that combinatorial network auctions are tractable. Finally, in Section 6 we discuss multi-unit combinatorial auctions, and identify some tractable cases of such auctions.

Preliminaries

Let $G = (V(G), E(G))$ be a graph, where V(G) is a set of nodes, and E(G) is a set of edges. Each edge $e \in E(G)$ is assigned a cost w_e. Let $b = ((l_1, b_1), (l_2, b_2), \ldots, (l_{|V|}, b_{|V|}))$, where the b_i's are integers and l_i equals b_i or 0 ($1 \le i \le |V(G)|$). A *b-matching* is a set $M \subseteq E(G)$ such that, for each node $i \in V(G)$, the number of edges incident with i is no more than b_i and no less than l_i. The value of a b-matching is the sum of costs of its edges, i.e. $\Sigma\{w_e | e \in M\}$. The *b-matching problem* is to find a b-matching of maximum value.

An important result of the field of combinatorial optimization is that the b-matching problem is polynomial (Cook et al. 1998; Anstee 1987). This result widely extends upon the more commonly known results about the computation of (standard) matchings, and will play a significant role later in this paper.

In a combinatorial auctions setup a seller sells m goods to n potential buyers. A bid of agent i is a pair (S, p), where S is a bundle of goods and p is a non-negative real number that denotes the price offer for S. Let $X = \{x_1 = (s_1, p_1), \ldots, x_t = (s_t, p_t)\}$ be a set of bids, and denote by $S(x_i)$ and $P(x_i)$ the bundle of goods and the price offer of bid x_i, respectively. The *combinatorial auction problem* [CAP] is to find an $X_o \subseteq X$, for which $\Sigma_{X_o} P(x_i)$ is maximal, under the constraint that $S(x_i) \cap S(x_j) = \emptyset$ for every $x_i, x_j \in X_o$. The [CAP] is NP-hard (Rothkopf, Pekec, & Harstad 1998).

The literature distinguishes between two types of combinatorial auctions. In a *sub-additive* combinatorial auction an agent's bid for every bundle $S = S_1 \cup S_2, S_1 \cap S_2 = \emptyset$ of goods, is less than or equals to the sum of its bids for S_1 and S_2. In a *super-additive* combinatorial auction an agent's bid for every bundle $S = S_1 \cup S_2, S_1 \cap S_2 = \emptyset$ of goods, is greater than or equals to the sum of its bids for S_1 and S_2. Auctions for substitute goods are sub-additive, while auctions for complementary goods are super-additive. Hence, both of these auction types are of central importance.

Quantity Restrictions in Multi-Object Auctions

Consider an auction for the reservation of seats in a particular flight. Each potential buyer submits bids for each possible seat in the airplane, but restricts the total number of seats he may wish to obtain. This auction has the property that the payment of agent i for the set of seats allocated to it, subject to his quantity constraint, is the sum of his bids for the individual seats in this set. However, this auction is a sub-additive combinatorial auction; a buyer will pay 0 for every additional seat assigned to him beyond his limit on the number of required seats.

Definition 1 *A Quantity-constrained multi-object auction is a sub-additive combinatorial auction where bids are of the form $(a_1, p_1, a_2, p_2, \ldots, a_k, p_k, q)$ where p_i is a price offer for object a_i, and q is the maximal number of objects that are to be assigned.*

Theorem 1 *Quantity-constrained multi-object auctions are computationally tractable.*

Sketch of proof:
We reduce the input of a quantity-constrained multi-object auction to an input of a b-matching problem in a bipartite graph $G = (V_1 \cup V_2, E = V_1 \times V_2)$ where V_1 is isomorphic to the set of bids and V_2 is isomorphic to the set of objects. An edge e_{i_j} which connects a node associated with the i-th bid to a node associated with the j-th object will be assigned a cost that equals bid i's offer for good j (the cost equals 0 if bid i does not refer to object j). The pair of b values of a node $v_i \in V_1$ associated with a bid $(a_1, p_1, a_2, p_2, \ldots, a_k, p_k, q)$ will be $(0, q)$. The b value of $v_j \in V_2$ will be $(0, 1)$.

The above reduction is polynomial and creates an input of a b-matching problem. One can now verify that the optimal weighted b-matching of the graph defines a solution to the quantity-constrained multi-object auction.

The above result shows that quantity constraints can be incorporated into simple multi-object auctions, while still getting tractable solutions. Previous work has tried to tackle the tractability of combinatorial auctions where bids are given for non-singleton bundles. It was shown that the case of bundles of size two is tractable, while the case of larger bundles is NP-hard. We now show that the case of bundles of size two and the case of quantity constraints can be tackled simultaneously in an efficient manner.

Definition 2 *A Quantity-constrained multi-object action with binary combinatorial bundles is a sub-additive combinatorial auction that allows two types* of bids: 1. The bids allowed in a quantity-constrained multi-object auctions. 2. Bids of the form $(a, p, b, q, \{a, b\}, l)$ where p is the price offer for good a, q is the price offer for good b, and $p + q - l$ is the combinatorial price offer for the pair $\{a, b\}$, where $0 < l < min(p, q)$,

Theorem 2 *Quantity-constrained multi-object auctions with binary combinatorial bundles are computationally tractable.*

Sketch of proof:

We construct a graph G as in Theorem 1, and for each bid of the form $x = (a, p, b, q, \{a, b\}, l)$ we do the following:

1. We add three nodes v_x, v_{x_1}, v_{x_2}.

2. We connect v_x to a, b, v_{x_1} and v_{x_2}.

3. Denote $w = \frac{l}{2}$. We assign edge weights as follows: $(v_x, a) \to p - w$, $(v_x, b) \to q - w$, $(v_x, v_{x_1}) \to w$, $(v_x, v_{x_2}) \to -w$.

4. We require that v_x will have the b-value (2,2) (i.e. exactly 2), and that v_{x_1} and v_{x_2} will have the b-value (0,1) (i.e. at most 1).

We now prove that the optimal b-matching is the required solution to the combinatorial auction problem. We consider the possible allocations with regard to the bid $x = (a, p, b, q, \{a, b\}, l)$:

1. If both a and b are not allocated then the cost contributed by this bid in the corresponding b-matching is $w - w = 0$ as required.

2. If only a is allocated then the cost contributed by this bid in the corresponding b-matching is $p - w + w = p$ as required.

3. If only b is allocated then the cost contributed by this bid in the corresponding b-matching is $q - w + w = q$ as required.

4. If both a and b are allocated then the cost contributed by this bid in the corresponding b-matching is $q - w + p - w = p + q - l$ as required.

Beyond binary bids

As we mentioned, combinatorial auctions where bids are only for single goods or for pairs of goods are tractable (Rothkopf, Pekec, & Harstad 1998). However, when bids are for bundles of size greater than two, the CAP is in general intractable. Notice that in the previous section we presented general tractable auctions where the bids for singletons can not be simply sum up in order to get the bid for a bundle of goods. However, this was a result of a constraint on the number of goods to be allocated; when this constraint is satisfied, the bid/payment for an allocated set of goods equals the sum of bids for the objects it consists of. In this section we wish to relax this property; namely, we wish to consider cases where the bid for an allocated set of goods is different from the sum of bids for the singletons it consists of. Our aim is to do so for auctions where bids are for bundles of size greater than two. We now present two results that we believe to be of considerable importance in this regard.

Almost additive auctions

Definition 3 *An almost-additive multi-object auction is a combinatorial sub-additive auction where bids for non-singletons are of the form $(a_1, p_1, a_2, p_2, \ldots, a_k, p_k, q)$ where p_i is the price offer for object a_i, the price offer for any $A \subset \{a_1, \ldots, a_k\}$ equals $\Sigma_{a_i \in A} p_i$, and the offer for $\{a_1, \ldots, a_k\}$ is q; in addition, $w = \Sigma_{1 \leq i \leq k} p_i - q > 0$, and $w < \frac{k}{k-1} p_j$ ($1 \leq j \leq k$).*

In an almost-additive multi-object auction a shopping list of items is gradually built until we reach a situation that the valuations become sub-additive; sub-additivity is a result of the requirement that $w > 0$. The other condition on w implies that the bid on the whole bundle is not too low with respect to the sum of bids on the single goods it consists of.

Theorem 3 *Almost-additive multi-object auctions are computationally tractable.*

Sketch of proof:

We start from the graph G that was built for the quantity-constrained multi-object auction, and add the following for each almost additive bid $(a_1, p_1, a_2, p_2, \ldots, a_k, p_k, q)$:

1. Construct $k+1$ new nodes: $v, v_1, v_2, \ldots, v_k$, and connect v to each of the v_j's. In addition, we connect v to each object a_j ($1 \leq j \leq k$).

2. Let $w = (\Sigma_{1 \leq i \leq k} p_i) - q$, and let $a = \frac{k-1}{k} w$.

3. The weights of the newly added edges will be as follows:

    (a) $(v, v_1) \to a$,
    (b) $(v, v_j) \to \frac{-a}{k-1}$ ($1 < j \leq k$).
    (c) $(v, a_j) \to p_j - \frac{a}{k-1}$, for ($1 \leq j \leq k$)

4. The b-value of v is taken to be exactly k (i.e. (k,k)). The b-values of the v_j's are taken as $(0,1)$ (i.e. at most 1).

Consider now the optimal weighted b-matching in the corresponding graph. It follows that if none of the a_j's are allocated then the sum of costs contributed to the corresponding matching is 0, as required.

If a strict non-empty subset $a_{l_1}, \ldots, a_{l_s}$ $(1 \leq s < k)$ of the a_j's is allocated then the sum of costs contributes to the corresponding matching is $(\Sigma_{1 \leq i \leq s} p_{l_i}) - s\frac{a}{k-1} + a - \frac{a}{k-1}(k-s-1) = \Sigma_{1 \leq i \leq s} p_{l_i}$, as required.

If all the a_j are allocated then the sum of costs contributed to the corresponding matching is $\Sigma_{1 \leq j \leq k} p_k - k\frac{a}{k-1} = \Sigma_{1 \leq j \leq k} p_k - w = q$, as required.

As a result, by finding an optimal weighted b-matching in the corresponding graph, we get a solution to the corresponding CAP.

The case of triples

The case of combinatorial auctions with bids for triples of goods, rather than only for pairs of goods, is NP-hard. However, consider the following:

Definition 4 *A combinatorial auction with sub-additive symmetric bids for triplets is a sub-additive combinatorial auction where bids are either for singletons, for pairs of goods (and the singletons they are built of), or for triplets of goods (and the corresponding subsets). Bids for pairs of goods are as in Definition 2, while bids for triplets have the form $(a_1, p_1, a_2, p_2, a_3, p_3, b_1, b_2)$: p_i is the price offer for good a_i, the price offer for any pair of goods $\{a_i, a_j\}, (1 \leq i, j \leq 3; i \neq j)$ is $p_i + p_j - b_1$, and the price offer for the whole triplet $\{a_1, a_2, a_3\}$ is $p_1 + p_2 + p_3 - b_2$.*

Theorem 4 *Combinatorial auctions with sub-additive symmetric bids for triplets, where each bid for triplet $(a_1, p_1, a_2, p_2, a_3, p_3, b_1, b_2)$ has the property that $b_2 > 3b_1$, and $p_i > b_2 - b_1 (1 \leq i \leq 3)$, are tractable.*

The theorem makes use of two conditions that connect b_1, b_2, and the bids on singletons. These conditions measure the amount of sub-additivity relative to the purely additive case where a bid for a bundle is the sum of bids for the singletons it consists of. The first condition is that the decrease in valuation/bid for a bundle, relative to the sum of bids for the singletons it consists of, will be proportional to the bundle's size; the second condition connects that decrease to the bids on the singletons, and requires that the above-mentioned decrease will be relatively low compared to the bids on the single goods. Both of these conditions seem quite plausible for many sub-additive auctions.

Sketch of proof:

We will use the graph G constructed in Theorem 2 for quantity-constrained multi-object auctions with binary combinatorial bundles, and for any bid on a triplet, $(a_1, p_1, a_2, p_2, a_3, p_3, b_1, b_2)$, we will add the following:

1. Construct 4 new nodes: v_0, v_1, v_2, v_3, and connect v_0 to v_1, v_2 and v_3.

2. Let $k = \frac{b_2 - 3b_1}{2b_2 - 3b_1}$, and let $a = \frac{b_1}{1-2k}$.

3. Assign weights to the new edges as follows:

   (a) $(v_0, a_j) \to p_j - a + ka$ for $1 \leq j \leq 3$.
   (b) $(v_0, v_1) \to a$
   (c) $(v_0, v_2) \to -ka$
   (d) $(v_0, v_2) \to -(1-k)a$

4. Take the b-value of v_0 to be exactly 3, and of v_1, v_2, v_3 to be at most 1 (i.e. $(0, 1)$).

We now compute an optimal weighted b-matching on the generated graph, and claim it defines an optimal allocation of the goods. The proof makes use of the following observations:

1. If none of the a_j in the triplet are allocated then the cost contributed to the corresponding matching is $a - ka - (1-k)a = 0$, as required.

2. If only one item a_i is allocated, then the cost contributed to the corresponding matching is $p_i - a + ka + a - ka = p_i$, as required.

3. If a_i and a_j, $i \neq j$, are allocated, then the cost contributed to the corresponding matching is $p_i + p_j - a + 2ka = p_i + p_j - b_1$, as required.

4. If the whole triplet is allocated then the cost contributed to the corresponding matching is $p_1 + p_2 + p_3 - 3a + 3ka = p_1 + p_2 + p_3 - 3a(1-k)$, which can be shown to be equal to $p_1 + p_2 + p_3 - b_2$ as required.

Additional results

Our technique for dealing with bundles of size 3 can be extended to bundles of larger size. The conditions however on the amount of decrease in price offers as a function of the bundle size become more elaborated, which might make the result less applicable. We can also apply these techniques to a restricted instance of super-additive combinatorial auctions. The discussion of this is left to the full paper.

Combinatorial network auctions

Auctions for linear goods are a useful case of tractable combinatorial auctions (see (Rothkopf, Pekec, & Harstad 1998; Nisan 1999)). In an auction for linear goods we have an ordered list of m goods, $g_1, \ldots, g_m$, and bids should refer to bundles of the form $g_i, g_{i+1}, g_{i+2}, \ldots, g_{j-1}, g_j$ where $j \geq i$, i.e. there are no "holes" in the bundle. Auctions for linear goods can be used for time scheduling (e.g. for the allocation of time slots in a conference room), or for the allocation of one-dimensional space (e.g. for parts of a seashore), etc. In this section we widely extend the result on the tractability of auctions for linear goods, by considering combinatorial network auctions:

Definition 5 *Let $O = \{g_1, \ldots, g_m\}$ be a set of goods. A network of goods is a tree $G(O) = (V(O), E(O))$, where the set of nodes, $V(O)$, is isomorphic to the set of goods O. A combinatorial network auction with respect to the set of goods O and the network $G(O)$, is a combinatorial auction where bids can be submitted only to bundles associated with paths in $G(O)$.*

It is clear that combinatorial auctions for linear goods are simple instances of combinatorial network auctions, where the network is a simple path. We can now show:

Theorem 5 *Combinatorial network auctions are computationally tractable.*

Sketch of proof:

Consider the graph $G(O)$. We construct the (weighted) graph G_{net} which is built from $G(O)$ by adding the following nodes, edges, and edge weights:

1. Each edge of $G(O)$ will be assigned the weight 0.

2. For each $v \in V(O)$ we add a simple loop that connects v directly to itself, and has the weight 0.

3. For each bid b that refers to a path from v_1 to v_2, we add a new node v_b, and two edges: one that connects v_b to v_1 and has the weight 0, and one that connects v_2 to v_b and has a weight that equals the price offer in b.

We can now prove that the optimal allocation is given by computing an optimal weighted matching in G_{net}, where the degree of each node is exactly 1 (proof omitted). In order to find the optimal weighted matching in G_{net}, which is a directed graph, it is enough to find the optimal weighted matching in the following undirected bi-partite graph (proof omitted), $G_m = (V_1 \cup V_2, E)$: In G_m, both V_1 and V_2 (the two parts of the bipartite graph) are isomorphic to the set of nodes of G_{net}; an edge leading from s to t in G_{net} will be associated with an edge from the copy of s in V_1 to the copy of t in V_2. Given that the computation of an optimal weighted exact matching in a bi-partite graph is polynomial, we get the desired result.

Multi-Unit Combinatorial Auctions

In a general multi-object auction, a seller sells a set of m objects to a set of n potential buyers. Let us assume that there are s types of goods, m_i of each type, where $\Sigma_{1 \leq i \leq s} m_i = m$. The buyers in this case can submit bids for several goods of the same type, but can also submit composed bids, for different types of objects. In a classical combinatorial auction we consider a set of different goods, where bids for subsets of the goods are given as input. This is complementary to the concept of multi-unit auctions where we have multiple units of the same good. An interesting intermediate case is when we have a constant number of types of goods, but have multiple units of good of each type. We refer to this variant of multi-object auctions as simple combinatorial multi-unit auctions. We assume that each agent's bid includes the offers he gives for each subset of the objects. For simplicity we will consider the case where $s = 2$, i.e. we have two types of good; however, our result does hold for arbitrary (constant) number of types of good.

We will assume that an agent i's bid assigns to quantities (k, l), where k is a quantity of units of type 1, and l is a quantity of units of type 2, an offer $p_i(k, l)$. We assume that the price per quantity is non-decreasing, i.e. $l \leq l'$, and $k \leq k'$ imply that $p_i(k, l) \leq p_i(k', l')$.

Given a simple combinatorial multi-unit auction, and the agents' bids, we are interested in finding an optimal (revenue maximizing) allocation of the objects. We denote this problem by SCMUAP. We now show that the SCMUAP can be efficiently solved.

Given a set of m_j units of good j, and n agents, where agent i's ($1 \leq i \leq n$) bid for k units of good 1 and l units of good 2 is $b_i(k, l) > 0$, and $b_i(l', k') \geq b_i(l, k)$ whenever $l' \geq l$ and $k' \geq k$, the *combinatorial allocation graph* $G = (V, E, w)$ consists of set of nodes, V, a set of edges E, and edge weights w as follows: the set of nodes V is isomorphic to the three-dimensional grid of integers $[0..n] \times [0..m_1] \times [0..m_2]$, the set of edges $E \subset V^2$ is the set of all $((i, j, f), (i+1, l, q))$ where $0 \leq i < n$, $l \geq j$, $q \geq f$, and $w((i, j, f), (i+1, l, q)) = b_{i+1}(l - j, q - f)$.

The following result is now obtained by searching for the longest path that connects $(0, 0, 0)$ to (n, m_1, m_2) in the combinatorial allocation graph, using dynamic programming:

Theorem 6 *The SCMUAP is computationally tractable.*

Another interesting type of multi-unit combinatorial auctions is the auction for linear goods (see Section 5), where each good is assumed to have some quantity.

For example, when allocating time slots in a conference room, one may use the fact that the room can serve several parties simultaneously during particular hours of the day. More generally, in a multi-unit linear goods auction [MULGA] there are $q(i)$ units of good i; the bids are as in auctions for linear goods. We can show:

Theorem 7 *The MULGA problem is computationally tractable.*

Sketch of proof:

Consider the representation of the problem as an integer programming problem. Let $g_1, \ldots, g_m$ be the goods, let $q(i)$ be the number of available units of good i, and let $S_1, \ldots, S_n$ be the set of (linear) bids, where the price offer in S_i is $p(S_i)$. Let x_i be a 0/1 variable, where 1 denotes that S_i appears in the winning combination. The integer programming problem can be written as:

maximize $\Sigma_i(x_i \cdot P(S_i))$, subject to $\Sigma_{i:g_j \in S_i} x_i \leq q(g_j)$ (for $1 \leq j \leq m$).

Consider now the LP relaxation of this problem, where we require $0 \leq x_i \leq 1$, for $1 \leq i \leq n$. This can be written in a matrix form as $Ax \leq q$, where the $(i,j)-th$ entry in A is 1 if g_i appears in the bid S_j, and is 0 otherwise; the j-th entry in q is $q(j)$.

The matrix A has the property that at each column the 1's appear in a sequence. One can check now that A is TUM, and therefore regardless of the vector q, the LP relaxation yields the desired integer solution.

Conclusion

Combinatorial auctions are a most challenging type of auctions. Given that finding an optimal allocation of the goods in a combinatorial auction is generally intractable, researchers have been concerned with exposing tractable instances of combinatorial auctions. In this work we introduced polynomial solutions for a variety of non-trivial combinatorial auctions, such as combinatorial network auctions, various sub-additive combinatorial auctions, and some restricted forms of multi-unit combinatorial auctions. Our work extends upon the results obtained in (Rothkopf, Pekec, & Harstad 1998; Nisan 1999) on auctions for linear goods, as well for auctions with bids for binary bundles. Moreover, we present several other forms of tractable combinatorial auctions. Our work introduces the use of various techniques, and in particular b-matching techniques for tackling the combinatorial auctions problem. We believe that these techniques can be further used and applied to various types of combinatorial auctions, and can play an important role in addressing their complexity.

References

Anstee, R. 1987. A polynomial algorithm for b-matchings: An alternative approach. *Information Processing Letters* 153–157.

Cook, W.; Cunningham, W.; Pulleyblank, W.; and Schrijver, A. 1998. *Combinatorial Optimization*. John Wiley and Sons.

Durfee, E. 1992. What your computer really needs to know, you learned in kindergarten. In *10th National Conference on Artificial Intelligence*, 858–864.

Fujishima, Y.; Leyton-Brown, K.; and Shoham, Y. 1999. Taming the computational complexity of combinatorial auctions: Optimal and approximate approaches. In *IJCAI-99*.

Kraus, S. 1997. Negotiation and cooperation in multi-agent environments. *Artificial Intelligence* 94.

Lehmann, D.; O'callaghan, L.; and Shoham, Y. 1999. Truth revalation in rapid, approximately efficient combinatorial auctions. In *ACM Conference on Electronic Commerce*.

Monderer, D., and Tennenholtz, M. 2000. Optimal Auctions Revisited. Artificial Intelligence, forthcoming.

Nisan, N. 1999. Bidding and allocation in combinatorial auctions. Working paper.

Parkes, D. C. 1999. ibundle: An efficient ascending price bundle auction. In *ACM Conference on Electronic Commerce*.

Penn, M., and Tennenholtz, M. 1999. Constrained multi-object auctions. Working paper.

Rosenschein, J. S., and Zlotkin, G. 1994. *Rules of Encounter*. MIT Press.

Rothkopf, M.; Pekec, A.; and Harstad, R. 1998. Computationally manageable combinatorial auctions. *Management Science* 44(8):1131–1147.

Sandholm, T. 1996. Limitations of the vickrey auction in computational multiagent systems. In *2nd International Conference on Multi-Agent Systems*.

Sandholm, T. 1999. An algorithm for optimal winner determination in combinatorial auctions. In *IJCAI-99*.

Tennenholtz, M. 1999. Electronic commerce: From game-theoretic and economic models to working protocols. In *IJCAI-99*.

Wellman, M.; Wurman, P.; Walsh, W.; and MacKie-Mason, J. 1998. Auction protocols for distributed scheduling. Working paper (to appear in Games and Economic Behavior).

Collective Intelligence and Braess' Paradox

Kagan Tumer and David Wolpert
NASA Ames Research Center
Moffett Field, CA 94035
{kagan,dhw}@ptolemy.arc.nasa.gov

Abstract

We consider the use of multi-agent systems to control network routing. Conventional approaches to this task are based on Ideal Shortest Path routing Algorithm (ISPA), under which at each moment each agent in the network sends all of its traffic down the path that will incur the lowest cost to that traffic. We demonstrate in computer experiments that due to the side-effects of one agent's actions on another agent's traffic, use of ISPA's can result in large global cost. In particular, in a simulation of Braess' paradox we see that adding new capacity to a network with ISPA agents can *decrease* overall throughput. The theory of COllective INtelligence (COIN) design concerns precisely the issue of avoiding such side-effects. We use that theory to derive an idealized routing algorithm and show that a practical machine-learning-based version of this algorithm, in which costs are only imprecisely estimated substantially outperforms the ISPA, despite having access to less information than does the ISPA. In particular, this practical COIN algorithm avoids Braess' paradox.

INTRODUCTION

There is a long history of AI research on the design of distributed computational systems, stretching at least from the days of Distributed AI through current work on Multi-Agent Systems (Huhns 1987; Sandholm & Lesser 1995). One particularly important version of such design problems, exhibiting many of the characteristics of the more general problem, involves a set of agents connected across a network that route some form of traffic (here enumerated in "packets") among themselves, and must do so without any centralized control and/or communication. The goal of the system designer is to have the agents act in a way that optimizes some performance measure associated with that traffic, like overall throughput (Bertsekas & Gallager 1992).

Currently, many real-world solutions to this problem use Shortest Path Algorithms (SPA), in which each agent estimates the "shortest path" (i.e., path minimizing total cost accrued by the traffic it is routing)

Copyright © 2000, American Association for Artificial Intelligence (www.aaai.org). All rights reserved.

to each of its destinations, and at each moment sends all of its traffic with a particular destination down the associated (estimated) shortest path. Unfortunately, even in the limit of infinitesimally little traffic, performance with SPA's can be badly suboptimal, since each agent's routing decisions ignore side-effects on the traffic of other agents (Korilis, Lazar, & Orda 1997; Wolpert, Tumer, & Frank 1999). Indeed, in the famous case of Braess' paradox (Bass 1992), not only does this scheme result in suboptimal global cost, it causes *every* agent's traffic individually to have higher cost than at optimum. This even holds when each agent's estimated costs are (unrealistically) taken as perfectly accurate, so that those agents are all using Ideal SPA's (ISPA's). This is an instance of the famous Tragedy Of the Commons (TOC) (Hardin 1968).

As an alternative to ISPA's we present a solution to the Braess' paradox bases on the concept of COllective INtelligence (COIN). A COIN is a multi-agent system where there is little to no centralized communication or control among the agents and where there is a well-specified world utility function that rates the possible dynamic histories of the collection (Wolpert, Tumer, & Frank 1999; Wolpert & Tumer 2000b; 2000a; Wolpert, Wheeler, & Tumer 2000). In particular, we are concerned with agents that each use reinforcement learning (Kaelbing, Littman, & Moore 1996; Sutton & Barto 1998; Sutton 1988; Watkins & Dayan 1992) to try to achieve their individual goal. We consider the central COIN design problem: *How, without any detailed modeling of the overall system, can one set utility functions for the individual agents in a COIN to have the overall dynamics reliably and robustly achieve large values of the provided world utility?* In other words, how can we leverage an assumption that our learners are individually fairly good at what they do so as to induce good collective behavior? For reasons given above, we know that in routing the answer to this question is not provided by SPA's goals — some new set of goals is needed.

In this article, we illustrate the Braess' paradox in the network domain, and present a COIN based algorithm for network routing. We present simulations demonstrating that in networks running ISPAs, the per packet costs can be as much as 23 % higher than in networks running COIN algorithms. In particular, even though it only has access to imprecise estimates of costs (a handicap not affecting the ISPA), the COIN algorithm almost always avoids Braess' paradox, in stark contrast to the ISPA. In that the cost incurred with ISPA's is presumably a lower bound on that of a real-world SPA not privy to instantaneous communication, the implication is that COINs can outperform such real-world SPA's. A much more detailed investigation of the issues addressed here can be found in (Wolpert & Tumer 2000a).

Braess' Paradox

Braess' paradox (Bass 1992; Cohen & Kelly 1990; Cohen & Jeffries 1997; Korilis, Lazar, & Orda 1997) dramatically underscores the inefficiency of the ISPA. This "paradox" is perhaps best illustrated through a highway traffic example given in (Bass 1992): There are two highways connecting towns S and D. The cost accrued by a traveler along either highway when x travelers in total traverse that highway (in terms of tolls, delays, or the like) is $V_1(x) + V_2(x)$, as illustrated in Net A of Figure 1. So when $x = 1$ (a single traveler), for either path total accrued cost is 61 units. If on the other hand six travelers are split equally among the two paths, they will each incur a cost of 83 units to get to their destinations. Now suppose a new highway is built connecting the two paths, as shown in Net B in Figure 1. Note that the cost associated with taking this highway is not particularly high (in fact for any load higher than 1, this highway has a lower cost than any other highway in the system). The benefit of this highway is illustrated by the dramatically reduced cost incurred by the single traveler: by taking the short-cut, one traveler can traverse the network at a cost of 31 units ($2 V_1 + V_3$). Adding a new road has seemingly reduced the traversal cost dramatically.

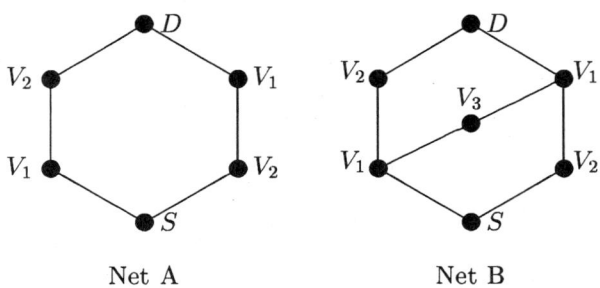

Figure 1: Hex network with $V_1 = 10x$; $V_2 = 50 + x$; $V_3 = 10 + x$

However consider what happens when six travelers are on the highways in net B. If an ISPA is used to make each routing decision, then at equilibrium each of the three possible paths contains two travelers.[1] Due to overlaps in the paths however, this results in each

[1] We have in mind here the Nash equilibrium, where no

traveler accruing a cost of 92 units, which is higher than than what they accrued *before* the new highway was built. The net effect of adding a new road is to increase the cost incurred by *every* traveler.

The COIN Formalism

One common solution to side-effect problems is to have certain components of the network (e.g., a "network manager" (Korilis, Lazar, & Orda 1995)) dictate actions to other routers. This solution can incur major brittleness and scaling problems however. Another kind of approach, which avoids the problems of a centralized manager, is to provide the routers with extra incentives that can induce them to take actions that are undesirable to them from a strict SPA sense. Such incentive can be in the form of "taxes" or "tolls" added to the costs associated with traversing particular links to discourage the use of those links. Such schemes in which tolls are superimposed on the routers' goals are a special case of the more general COIN-based approach of replacing the goal of each router with a new goal. In the COIN approach the new goals are specifically tailored so that if they are collectively met the system maximizes throughput. *A priori*, a router's goal need have no particular relation with the cost accrued by that router's packets. Intuitively, in a COIN approach, we provide each router with a goal that is "aligned" with the global objective, with no separate concern for that goal's relation to the cost accrued by the traffic routed by that router. To see how this can be done, in the remainder of this section we summarize salient aspects of the theory of COIN's.

In this paper we consider systems that consist of a set of agents, connected in a network, evolving across a set of discrete time steps, $t \in \{0, 1, ...\}$. Without loss of generality, all relevant characteristics of an agent η at time t — including its internal parameters at that time as well as its externally visible actions — are encapsulated by a Euclidean vector $\zeta_{\eta,t}$ with components $\zeta_{\eta,t;i}$. We call this the "state" of agent η at time t, with $\zeta_{,t}$ the state of all agents at time t, while ζ is the state of all agents across all time.

In this paper, we restrict attention to utilities of the form $\sum_{t \geq \tau} R_t(\zeta_{,t})$ for **reward functions** R_t (simply $\sum_t R_t(\zeta_{,t})$ for non-time-varying utilities). **World utility**, $G(\zeta)$, is an arbitrary function of the state of all agents across all time. (Note that that state is a Euclidean vector.) When η is an agent that uses a machine learning algorithm to "try to increase" its **private utility**, we write that private utility as $g_\eta(\zeta)$, or more generally, to allow that utility to vary in time, $g_{\eta,\tau}(\zeta)$.

Here we focus on the case where our goal, as COIN designers, is to maximize world utility through the proper selection of private utility functions. Intuitively, the idea is to choose private utilities that are aligned

traveler can gain by changing strategies (Fudenberg & Tirole 1991).

with world utility, and that also have the property that it is relatively easy for us to configure each agent so that the associated private utility achieves a large value.

We need a formal definition of the concept of having private utilities be "aligned" with G. Constructing such a formalization is a subtle exercise. For example, consider systems where the world utility is the sum of the private utilities of the individual nodes. This might seem a reasonable candidate for an example of "aligned" utilities. However such systems are examples of the more general class of systems that are "weakly trivial". It is well-known that in weakly trivial systems each individual agent greedily trying to maximize its own utility can lead to the tragedy of the commons (Hardin 1968) and actually *minimize* G. In particular, this can be the case when private utilities are independent of time and $G = \sum_\eta g_\eta$. Evidently, at a minimum, having $G = \sum_\eta g_\eta$ is not sufficient to ensure that we have "aligned" utilities; some alternative formalization of the concept is needed.

A more careful formalization of the notion of aligned utilities is the concept of "factored" systems. A system is **factored** at time τ when the following holds for each agent η individually: A change at time τ to the state of η alone, when propagated across time, will result in an increased value of $g_{\eta,\tau}(\zeta)$ if and only if it results in an increase for $G(\zeta)$ (Wolpert & Tumer 2000b).

For a factored system, the side-effects of any change to η's $t = \tau$ state that increases its private utility cannot decrease world utility. There are no restrictions though on the effects of that change on the private utilities of other agents and/or times. In particular, we don't preclude an agent's algorithm at two different times from "working at cross-purposes" to each other, so long as at both moments the agent is working to improve G. In game-theoretic terms, in factored systems optimal global behavior corresponds to the agents' always being in a private utility Nash equilibrium (Fudenberg & Tirole 1991). In this sense, there can be no TOC for a factored system. As a trivial example, a system is factored for $g_{\eta,\tau} = G \; \forall \eta$.

Define the **effect set** of the agent-time pair (η, τ) at ζ, $C^{eff}_{(\eta,\tau)}(\zeta)$, as the set of all components $\underline{\zeta}_{\eta',t}$ which under the forward dynamics of the system have non-zero partial derivative with respect to the state of agent η at $t = \tau$. Intuitively, (η, τ)'s effect set is the set of all components $\underline{\zeta}_{\eta',t \geq \tau}$ which would be affected by a change in the state of agent η at time τ. (They may or may not be affected by changes in the $t = \tau$ states of the other agents.)

Next, for any set σ of components (η', t), define $\text{CL}_\sigma(\zeta)$ as the "virtual" vector formed by clamping the components of the vector ζ delineated in σ to an arbitrary fixed value. (In this paper, we take that fixed value to be 0 for all components listed in σ.) The value of the effect set **wonderful life utility** (WLU for short) for σ is defined as:

$$WLU_\sigma(\underline{\zeta}) \equiv G(\underline{\zeta}) - G(\text{CL}_\sigma(\underline{\zeta})). \qquad (1)$$

In particular, we are interested in the WLU for the effect set of agent-time pair (η, τ). This WLU is the difference between the actual world utility and the virtual world utility where all agent-time pairs that are affected by (η, τ) have been clamped to a zero state while the rest of $\underline{\zeta}$ is left unchanged.

Since we are clamping to $\vec{0}$, we can loosely view (η, τ)'s effect set WLU as analogous to the change in world utility that would have arisen if (η, τ) "had never existed". (Hence the name of this utility - cf. the Frank Capra movie.) Note however, that CL is a purely "fictional", counter-factual operator, in that it produces a new $\underline{\zeta}$ without taking into account the system's dynamics. The sequence of states the agent-time pairs in σ are clamped to in constructing the WLU need not be consistent with the dynamical laws of the system. This dynamics-independence is a crucial strength of the WLU. It means that to evaluate the WLU we do *not* try to infer how the system would have evolved if agent η's state were set to $\vec{0}$ at time τ and the system evolved from there. So long as we know $\underline{\zeta}$ extending over all time, σ, and the function G, we know the value of WLU.

If our system is factored with respect to private utilities $\{g_{\eta,\tau}\}$, we want each agent to be in a state at time τ that induces as high a value of the associated private utility as possible (given the initial states of the other agents). Regardless of the system dynamics, having $g_{\eta,\tau} = G \; \forall \eta$ means the system is factored at time τ. It is also true that regardless of the dynamics, $g_{\eta,\tau} = WLU_{C^{eff}_{(\eta,\tau)}} \; \forall \eta$ is a factored system at time τ (proof in (Wolpert & Tumer 2000b)). However, note that since each agent is operating in a large system, it may experience difficulty discerning the effects of its actions on G when G sensitively depends on all the myriad components of the system. Therefore each η may have difficulty learning from past experience what to do to achieve high $g_{\eta,\tau}$ when $g_{\eta,\tau} = G$.[2]

This problem can be mitigated by using effect set WLU as the private utility, since the subtraction of the clamped term removes much of the "noise" of the activity of other agents, leaving only the underlying "signal" of how the agent in question affects the utility. (This reasoning is formalized as the concept of "learnability" in (Wolpert & Tumer 2000b).) Accordingly, one would expect that setting private utilities to

---

[2]In particular, in routing in large networks, having private rewards given by the world reward functions means that to provide each router with its reward at each time step we need to provide it the full throughput of the entire network at that step. This is usually infeasible in practice. Even if it weren't though, using these private utilities would mean that the routers face a very difficult task in trying to discern the effect of their actions on their rewards, and therefore would likely be unable to learn their best routing strategies.

WLU's ought to result in better performance than having $g_{\eta,\tau} = G \; \forall \eta, \tau$.

Simulation Overview

In this section we describe the model used in our simulations. We then present the ISPA in terms of that model, and apply the concepts of COIN theory to that model to derive private utilities for each agent. Because these utilities are "factored" we expect that agents acting to improve their own utilities will also improve the global utility (overall throughput of the network). We end by describing a Memory Based (MB) machine learning algorithm that each agent uses to estimate the value that its private utility would have under the different candidate routing decisions. In the MB COIN algorithm, each agent uses this algorithm to make routing decisions aimed at maximizing its estimated utility.

Simulation Model

As in much of network analysis, in the model used in this paper, at any time step all traffic at a router is a set of pairs of integer-valued traffic amounts and associated ultimate destination tags (Bertsekas & Gallager 1992). At each such time step t, each router r sums the integer-valued components of its current traffic at that time step to get its **instantaneous load**. We write that load as $z_r(t) \equiv \sum_d x_{r,d}(t)$, where the index d runs over ultimate destinations, and $x_{r,d}(t)$ is the total traffic at time t going from r towards d. After its instantaneous load at time t is evaluated, the router sends all its traffic to the next downstream routers, according to its routing algorithm. After all such routed traffic goes to those next downstream routers, the cycle repeats itself, until all traffic reaches its destination. In our simulations, for simplicity, traffic was only introduced into the system (at the **source routers**) at the beginning of successive disjoint **waves** of L consecutive time steps.

In a real network, the cost of traversing a router depends on "after-effects" of recent instantaneous loads, as well as the current instantaneous load. To simulate this effect, we use time-averaged values of the load at a router rather than instantaneous load to determine the cost a packet incurs in traversing that router. More formally, we define the router's **windowed load**, $Z_r(t)$, as the running average of that router's load value over a window of the previous W timesteps: $Z_r(t) \equiv \frac{1}{W} \sum_{t'=t-W+1}^{t} z_r(t') = \sum_{d'} X_{r,d'}(t)$, where the value of $X_{r,d}(t)$ is set by the dynamical law $X_{r,d}(t) = \frac{1}{W} \sum_{t'=t-W+1}^{t} x_{r,d}(t'))$. ($W$ is always set to an integer multiple of L.) The windowed load is the argument to a **load-to-cost** function, $V(\cdot)$, which provides the **cost** accrued at time t by each packet traversing the router at this timestep. That is, at time t, the cost for each packet to traverse router r is given by $V(Z_r(t))$. Different routers have different $V(\cdot)$, to reflect the fact that real networks have differences in router software and hardware (response time, queue length, processing speed etc). For simplicity, W is the same for all routers however. With these definitions, world utility is

$$G(\underline{\zeta}) = \sum_{t,r} z_r(t) \; V_r(Z_r(t)) \qquad (2)$$

Our equation for G explicitly demonstrates that, as claimed above, in our representation we can express $G(\underline{\zeta})$ as a sum of rewards, $\sum_t R_t(\underline{\zeta}_{,t})$, where $R(\underline{\zeta}_{,t})$ can be written as function of a pair of (r,d)-indexed vectors: $R_t(x_{r,d}(t), X_{r,d}(t)) = \sum_{r,d} x_{r,d}(t) V_r(\sum_{d'} X_{r,d'}(t))$.

Routing Algorithms

At time step t, ISPA has access to all the windowed loads at time step $t-1$ (i.e., it has access to $Z_r(t-1) \; \forall r$), and assumes that those values will remain the same at all times $\geq t$. (Note that for large window sizes and times close to t, this assumption is arbitrarily accurate.) Using this assumption, in ISPA, each router sends packets along the path that it calculates will minimize the costs accumulated by its packets.

We now apply the COIN formalism to the model described above to derive the idealized version of our COIN routing algorithm. First let us identify the agents η as individual pairs of routers and ultimate destinations. So $\underline{\zeta}_{\eta,t}$ is the vector of traffic sent along all links exiting η's router, tagged for η's ultimate destination, at time t. Next, in order to compute WLUs we must estimate the associated effect sets.

In the results presented here, the effect set of an agent is estimated as all agents that share the same destination as that agent.[3] Based on this effect set, the WLU for an agent η is given by the difference between the total cost accrued by all agents in the network and the cost accrued by agents when all agents sharing the same destination as η are "erased." More precisely, using Eq. 2, one can show that each agent η that shares a destination d, will have the following effect set WLU:

$$\begin{aligned} g_d(\underline{\zeta}) &= G(\underline{\zeta}) - G(\mathrm{CL}_{C_\eta^{eff}}(\underline{\zeta})) \\ &= \sum_t \sum_r [z_r(t) \; V_r(Z_r(t)) \; - \\ &\quad \sum_{d' \neq d} x_{r,d'}(t) \; V_r(\sum_{d'' \neq d} X_{r,d''}(t))] \end{aligned} \qquad (3)$$

Notice that the summand in Eq. 3 is computed at each router separately from information available to that router. Subsequently those summands can be propagated across the network and the associated g_d's "rolled up" in much the same way as routing tables updates are propagated in current routing algorithms.

Unlike the ISPA, the MB COIN has only limited knowledge, and therefore must *predict* the WLU value that would result from each potential routing decision. More precisely, for each router-ultimate-destination pair, the associated agent estimates the map from windowed loads on all outgoing links (the inputs) to WLU-based reward (the outputs). This is done with a single-nearest-neighbor algorithm. Next, each router could

---

[3] Exact factoredness obtains so long as our estimated effect set contains the true effect set; set equality is not necessary.

send the packets along the path that results in outbound traffic with the best (estimated) reward. However to be conservative, in these experiments we instead had the router randomly select between that path and the path selected by the ISPA (described below).

SIMULATION RESULTS

Based on the model and routing algorithms discussed above, we have performed simulations to compare the performance of ISPA and MB COIN. In all cases traffic was inserted into the network in a regular, non-stochastic manner at the sources. The results we report are averaged over 20 runs. We do not report error bars as they are all lower than 0.05. In both networks we present[4], ISPA suffers from the Braess' paradox, whereas the MB COIN almost never falls prey to the paradox for those networks. For no networks we have investigated is the MB COIN significantly susceptible to Braess' paradox.

Hex Network

In Table 1 we give full results for the network in Fig. 1. In Table 2 we report results for the same network but with load-to-cost functions which incorporate non-linearities that better represent real router characteristics. (Instances of Braess' paradox are shown in **bold**.)

For ISPA, although the per packet cost for loads of 1 and 2 drop drastically when the new link is added, the per packet cost increases for higher loads. The MB COIN on the other hand uses the new link efficiently. Notice that the MB COIN's performance is slightly worse than that of the ISPA in the absence of the additional link. This is caused by the MB COIN having to use an (extremely unsophisticated) learner to estimate the WLU values for potential actions whereas the ISPA has direct access to all the information it needs.

For this particular network, the equilibrium solution for the MB-COIN consists of ignoring the newly added middle link. This solution is "unstable" for the ISPA, since any packet routed along the middle path will provide a smaller cost to the router from which it was routed than would otherwise be the case, so that the system settles on the the suboptimal Nash Equilibrium solution discussed above. However, by changing the utilities of the agents (from a shortest path to the WLU), the COIN approach moves the Nash equilibrium to a more desirable location in the solution space.

Butterfly Network

The next network we investigate is shown in Figure 2. We now have three sources that have to route their packets to two destinations (packets originating at S_1 go to D_1, and packets originating at S_2 or S_3 go to D_2). Initially the two halves of the network have minimal contact, but with the addition of the extra link

[4]See (Wolpert & Tumer 2000a) for additional experiments.

Table 1: Average Per Packet Cost for HEX network for $V_1 = 50 + x$; $V_2 = 10x$; $V_3 = 10 + x$.

Load	Net	ISPA	MB COIN
1	A	55.50	55.56
	B	31.00	31.00
2	A	61.00	61.10
	B	52.00	51.69
3	A	66.50	66.65
	B	**73.00**	64.45
4	A	72.00	72.25
	B	**87.37**	73.41

Table 2: Average Per Packet Cost for HEX network for $V_1 = 50 + log(1+x)$; $V_2 = 10x$; $V_3 = log(1+x)$.

Load	Net	ISPA	MB COIN
1	A	55.41	55.44
	B	20.69	20.69
2	A	60.69	60.80
	B	41.10	41.10
3	A	65.92	66.10
	B	61.39	59.19
4	A	71.10	71.41
	B	**81.61**	69.88

two sources from the two halves of the network share a common router on their potential shortest path.

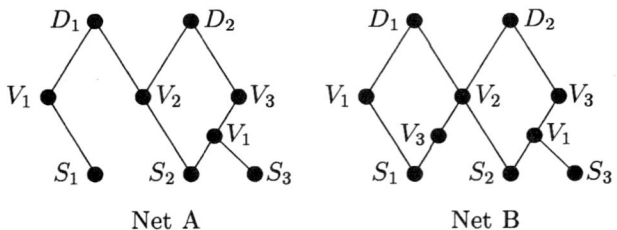

Figure 2: Butterfly Network

Table 3 presents results for uniform traffic through all three sources, and then results for asymmetric traffic. For the first case, the Braess' paradox is apparent in the ISPA: adding the new link is beneficial for the network at low load levels where the average per packet cost is reduced by nearly 20%, but deleterious at higher levels. The MB COIN, on the other hand, provides the benefits of the added link for the low traffic levels, without suffering from deleterious effects at higher load levels.

For the asymmetric traffic patterns, the added link causes a drop in performance for the ISPA, especially for low overall traffic levels. This is not true for the MB COIN. Notice also that in the high, asymmetric traffic regime, the ISPA performs significantly worse than the MB COIN even without the added link, showing that a bottleneck occurs on the right side of network alone.

Table 3: Average Per Packet Cost for BUTTERFLY network for $V_1 = 50 + log(1 + x)$; $V_2 = 10x$; $V_3 = log(1 + x)$.

Loads (S_1, S_2, S_3)	Net	ISPA	MB COIN
1,1,1	A	112.1	112.7
	B	92.1	92.3
2,2,2	A	123.3	124.0
	B	**133.3**	122.5
4,4,4	A	144.8	142.6
	B	**156.5**	142.3
3,2,1	A	81.8	82.5
	B	99.5	81.0
6,4,2	A	96.0	94.1
	B	**105.3**	94.0
9,6,3	A	105.5	98.2
	B	**106.7**	98.8

CONCLUSION

Collective Intelligence design is a framework for controlling decentralized multi-agents systems so as to achieve a global goal. In designing a COIN, the central issue is determining the private goals to be assigned to the individual agents. One wants to choose those goals so that the greedy pursuit of them by the associated agents leads to a globally desirable solution. We have summarized some of the theory of COIN design and derived a routing algorithm based on application of that theory to our simulation scenario. In our simulations, the COIN algorithm induced costs up to 23 % lower than the idealized version of conventional algorithms, the ISPA. This was despite the ISPA's having access to more information than the MB COIN. Furthermore the COIN-based algorithm avoided the Braess' paradoxes that seriously diminished the performance of the ISPA.

In the work presented here, the COIN-based algorithm had to overcome severe limitations. The estimation of the effect sets, used for determining the private goals of the agents was exceedingly coarse. In addition, the learning algorithms used by the agents to pursue those goals were particularly simple-minded. That a COIN-based router with such serious limitations consistently outperformed an ideal shortest path algorithm demonstrates the strength of the proposed method.

References

Bass, T. 1992. Road to ruin. *Discover* 56–61.

Bertsekas, D., and Gallager, R. 1992. *Data Networks*. Englewood Cliffs, NJ: Prentice Hall.

Boyan, J., and Littman, M. 1994. Packet routing in dynamically changing networks: A reinforcement learning approach. In *Advances in Neural Information Processing Systems - 6*, 671–678. Morgan Kaufmann.

Cohen, J. E., and Jeffries, C. 1997. Congestion resulting from increased capacity in single-server queueing networks. *IEEE/ACM Tran. on Net.* 5(2):305–310.

Cohen, J. E., and Kelly, F. P. 1990. A paradox of congestion in a queuing network. *Journal of Applied Probability* 27:730–734.

Fudenberg, D., and Tirole, J. 1991. *Game Theory*. Cambridge, MA: MIT Press.

Hardin, G. 1968. The tragedy of the commons. *Science* 162:1243–1248.

Heusse, M.; Snyers, D.; Guerin, S.; and Kuntz, P. 1998. Adaptive agent-driven routing and load balancing in communication networks. *Advances in Complex Systems* 1:237–254.

Huhns, M. E., ed. 1987. *Distributed Artificial Intelligence*. London: Pittman.

Kaelbing, L. P.; Littman, M. L.; and Moore, A. W. 1996. Reinforcement learning: A survey. *Journal of Artificial Intelligence Research* 4:237–285.

Korilis, Y. A.; Lazar, A. A.; and Orda, A. 1995. Architechting noncooperative networks. *IEEE Journal on Selected Areas in Communications* 13(8).

Korilis, Y. A.; Lazar, A. A.; and Orda, A. 1997. Achieving network optima using Stackelberg routing strategies. *IEEE/ACM Transactions on Networking* 5(1):161–173.

Sandholm, T., and Lesser, V. R. 1995. Issues in automated negotiations and electronic commerce: extending the contract net protocol. In *Proc of the 2nd Intl. Conf. on Multi-Agent Systems*, 328–335. AAAI Press.

Subramanian, D.; Druschel, P.; and Chen, J. 1997. Ants and reinforcement learning: A case study in routing in dynamic networks. In *Proc. of the 15th Intl Conf. on Artificial Intelligence*, 832–838.

Sutton, R. S., and Barto, A. G. 1998. *Reinforcement Learning: An Introduction*. Cambridge, MA: MIT Press.

Sutton, R. S. 1988. Learning to predict by the methods of temporal differences. *Machine Learning* 3:9–44.

Watkins, C., and Dayan, P. 1992. Q-learning. *Machine Learning* 8(3/4):279–292.

Wolpert, D. H., and Tumer, K. 2000a. Avoiding Braess' paradox through collective intelligence. Available as tech. rep. NASA-ARC-IC-99-124 from http://ic.arc.nasa.gov/ic/projects/coin_pubs.html.

Wolpert, D. H., and Tumer, K. 2000b. An Introduction to Collective Intelligence. In Bradshaw, J. M., ed., *Handbook of Agent technology*. AAAI Press/MIT Press. Available as tech. rep. NASA-ARC--IC-99-63 from http://ic.arc.nasa.gov/ic/projects/coin_pubs.html.

Wolpert, D. H.; Tumer, K.; and Frank, J. 1999. Using collective intelligence to route internet traffic. In *Advances in Neural Information Processing Systems - 11*, 952–958. MIT Press.

Wolpert, D. H.; Wheeler, K.; and Tumer, K. 2000. Collective intelligence for control of distributed dynamical systems. *Europhysics Letters* 49(6).

Robust Combinatorial Auction Protocol against False-name Bids

Makoto Yokoo, Yuko Sakurai, and **Shigeo Matsubara**

NTT Communication Science Laboratories
2-4 Hikaridai, Seika-cho
Soraku-gun, Kyoto 619-0237 Japan
email: {yokoo, yuko, matsubara}@cslab.kecl.ntt.co.jp
url: http://www.kecl.ntt.co.jp/csl/ccrg/members/{yokoo, yuko, matubara}

Abstract

This paper presents a new combinatorial auction protocol (LDS protocol) that is robust against false-name bids. Internet auctions have become an integral part of Electronic Commerce (EC) and a promising field for applying agent and Artificial Intelligence technologies. Although the Internet provides an excellent infrastructure for combinatorial auctions, we must consider the possibility of a new type of cheating, i.e., an agent tries to profit from submitting several bids under fictitious names (false-name bids). If there exists no false-name bid, the generalized Vickrey auction (GVA) satisfies individual rationality, Pareto efficiency, and incentive compatibility. On the other hand, when false-name bids are possible, it is theoretically impossible for a combinatorial auction protocol to simultaneously satisfy these three properties.

The Leveled Division Set (LDS) protocol, which is a modification of the GVA, utilizes reservation prices of auctioned goods for making decisions on whether to sell goods in a bundle or separately. The LDS protocol satisfies individual rationality and incentive compatibility, although it is not guaranteed to achieve a Pareto efficient social surplus. Simulation results show that the LDS protocol can achieve a better social surplus than that for a protocol that always sells goods in a bundle.

Introduction

Internet auctions have become an especially popular part of Electronic Commerce (EC). Various theoretical and practical studies on Internet auctions have already been conducted (Monderer & Tennenholtz 1998; Wurman, Wellman, & Walsh 1998; Sandholm 1996). The Internet provides an excellent infrastructure for executing much cheaper auctions with many more sellers and buyers from all over the world. However, we must consider the possibility of new types of cheating. For example, an agent may try to profit from submitting false bids made under fictitious names. Such a dishonest action is very difficult to detect since identifying each participant on the Internet is virtually impossible. We call a bid under a fictitious name a *false-name bid*. The problems resulting from collusion have been discussed by many researchers (Rasmusen 1994; Varian 1995; Sandholm 1996). Compared with collusion, a false-name bid is easier to execute since it can be done alone, while a bidder has to seek out and persuade other bidders to join in collusion.

In (Sakurai, Yokoo, & Matsubara 1999; Yokoo, Sakurai, & Matsubara 2000), the effects of false-name bids on auction protocols were analyzed. The obtained results can be summarized as follows.

- The generalized Vickrey auction protocol (GVA) (Varian 1995), which has been proven to satisfy individual rationality, Pareto efficiency, and incentive compatibility if there exists no false-name bid, fails to satisfy incentive compatibility when false-name bids are possible.

- There exists no combinatorial auction protocol that simultaneously satisfies incentive compatibility, Pareto efficiency, and individual rationality for all cases if agents can submit false-name bids.

- The revelation principle (Mas-Colell, Whinston, & Green 1995) still holds even if the agents can submit false-name bids.

In this paper, we concentrate on private value auctions (Mas-Colell, Whinston, & Green 1995). In private value auctions, each agent knows its own preference, and its evaluation value of goods is independent of the other agents' valuations. We define an agent's utility as the difference between the true evaluation value of the allocated goods and the payment for the allocated goods. Such a utility is called a *quasi-linear* utility (Mas-Colell, Whinston, & Green 1995). These assumptions are commonly used for making theoretical analyses tractable.

An auction protocol is incentive compatible, if bidding the true private values of goods is the dominant strategy, i.e., the best way to maximize the utility for each agent. The revelation principle states that in the design of an auction protocol we can restrict our attention only to incentive compatible protocols without losing generality (Mas-Colell, Whinston, & Green 1995). In other words, if a certain property (e.g., Pareto efficiency, individual rationality) can be satisfied using some auction protocol, the property can also be satisfied using an incentive compatible auction protocol. We say that auction protocols are robust against false-name bids if each agent cannot obtain additional profit by submitting false-name bids. If such robustness is not satisfied, the auction protocol lacks incentive compatibility.

Copyright © 2000, American Association for Artificial Intelligence (www.aaai.org). All rights reserved.

A Pareto efficient allocation means that the goods are allocated to bidders whose evaluation values are the highest, and that the sum of all participants' utilities (including that of the seller), i.e., the social surplus, is maximized[1].

An auction protocol is individually rational if each participant does not suffer any loss, in other words, the participant's payment never exceeds its evaluation value of the obtained goods. In a private value auction, individual rationality is indispensable: no agent wants to participate in an auction where it might be charged more money than it is willing to pay.

Since these three properties cannot be satisfied simultaneously when agents can submit false-name bids, we must give up Pareto efficiency and consider an auction protocol that satisfies incentive compatibility and individual rationality, and that can achieve a relatively good social surplus.

In the rest of the paper, we first describe the GVA and show an example where the GVA is not robust against false-name bids. Then, we describe our newly developed protocol, called *Leveled Division Set (LDS) protocol*, and provide the proof that the LDS protocol satisfies incentive compatibility. Furthermore, we show simulation results that demonstrate that this protocol can achieve a better social surplus than a protocol that always sells goods in a bundle. Finally, we discuss the merits/demerits of the LDS protocol.

Generalized Vickrey Auction Protocol (GVA)

An overview of the GVA is as follows. Let G denote one possible allocation of goods.

1. Each agent declares evaluation values for possible allocations[2]. Let $v_x(G)$ denote agent x's declared evaluation value for the allocation G.

2. The GVA chooses the optimal allocation G^* that maximizes the sum of all the agents' declared evaluation values.

3. The payment of agent x (represented as p_x) is calculated as follows:

$$p_x = \sum_{y \neq x} v_y(G^*_{\sim x}) - \sum_{y \neq x} v_y(G^*).$$

Here, $G^*_{\sim x}$ is the allocation that maximizes the sum of all agents' evaluation values except agent x. In the GVA, agent x pays the decreased amount of social surplus of the other agents caused by its participation. The GVA has been proven to be incentive compatible if there exists no false-name bid (Varian 1995; Mas-Colell, Whinston, & Green 1995).

Next, we show an example where the GVA is not robust against false-name bids.

Example 1 *Let us assume two agents are participating in an auction of two different goods, A and B, and declare the following evaluation values. The evaluation values of an agent are denoted by a tuple: (the value for A alone, the value for B alone, and the value for A and B together).*

- *agent 1: (6, 6, 12)*
- *agent 2: (0, 0, 8)*

The evaluation values of agent 2 are all-or-nothing, i.e., having only one good is useless. In this case, both goods are allocated to agent 1. Its payment is calculated as 8, since if agent 1 does not participate, agent 2 obtains both goods and the social surplus is 8; when agent 1 does participate, agent 1 obtains all goods and the social surplus except for agent 1 is 0. The obtained utility of agent 1 is $12 - 8 = 4$.

Now, let us assume that agent 1 submits a false-name bid using the identifier of agent 3.

- *agent 1: (6, 0, 6)*
- *agent 2: (0, 0, 8)*
- *agent 3: (0, 6, 6)*

In this case, A is allocated to agent 1 and B is allocated to agent 3. The payment of agent 1 (or agent 3) is calculated as $8 - 6 = 2$, since when agent 1 does participate, agent 3 obtains B and the social surplus except for agent 1 is 6. In reality, agent 1 obtains both goods by paying 4. Therefore, its utility is $12 - 4 = 8$, which means that agent 1 can make a profit by submitting a false-name bid.

Robust Protocol against False-name Bids
Basic Ideas

A trivial protocol can satisfy incentive compatibility even if agents can submit false-name bids, i.e., selling all goods in a bundle and use the second-price (Vickrey) auction protocol (Rasmusen 1994) to determine the winner and its payment. We call this simple protocol the *set protocol*. Selling goods in a bundle makes sense if goods are complementary for all agents, that is, the utility of a set of goods is larger than the sum of the utilities of having each good separately. However, if goods are substitutional for some agents, the set protocol is wasteful; the social surplus and the revenue of the seller can be significantly worse than that for the GVA

Let us consider a simple case where there are two goods A and B. To increase the social surplus, we must design a protocol where goods can be sold separately in some cases. To guarantee that the protocol is robust against false-name bids, the following condition must be satisfied.

Proposition 1 *If A and B are sold separately to different agents, the sum of the payments must be larger than the highest declared evaluation value for the set of A and B.*

If this condition is not satisfied, there is a chance that a single agent uses two false-names to obtain these goods. However, designing an incentive compatible protocol satisfying this condition is very difficult because we usually need to utilize the second highest evaluation values of goods to calculate the payment, and manipulating the second highest evaluation values is rather easy if an agent can submit false-name bids. We must solve the difficult dilemma of satisfying the above condition on payments without using the second highest evaluation values, which are essential to calculating the payments.

---

[1] In a more general setting, Pareto efficiency does not necessarily mean maximizing the social surplus. In an auction setting, however, agents can transfer money among themselves; thus the sum of the utilities is always maximized in a Pareto efficient allocation.

[2] The reported evaluation values may or may not be true.

	case 1	case 2	case 3
level 1	[{(A,B)}]	[{(A,B,C)}]	[{(A,B,C,D)}]
level 2	[{(A),(B)}]	[{(A,B)}, {(B,C)}, {(A,C)}]	[{(A,B,C)}, {(B,C,D)}, {(A,D)}]
level 3		[{(A),(B),(C)}]	[{(A),(D),(B,C)}]

Figure 1: Example of Leveled Division Sets

Our newly developed protocol solves this dilemma by utilizing *reservation prices* of goods (Rasmusen 1994). The seller does not sell a good if the payment of the good is smaller than the reservation price. Let us assume the reservation prices of A and B are r_A and r_B, respectively. If we sell goods separately only when the highest declared evaluation value for the set is smaller than $r_A + r_B$, we can satisfy the condition of Proposition 1. In the following, we are going to show how this idea can be introduced to the GVA.

Leveled Division Set Protocol

In the following, we are going to define several terms and notations. To help readability, we use three different types of parentheses to represent sets: (), {}, and [].

- a set of agents $N = \{1, 2, \ldots, n\}$
- a set of all auctioned goods $M = (1, 2, \ldots, m)$
- a division of goods $D = \{S \subseteq M \mid S \cap S' = \emptyset \text{ for every } S, S' \in D\}$[3]
- For each good j, the reservation price r_j is defined.
- For a set of goods S, we define $R(S)$ as $\sum_{j \in S} r_j$.

A *leveled division set* is defined as follows:

- Levels are defined as $1, 2, \ldots, max\_level$.
- For each level i, a division set $SD_i = [D_{i1}, D_{i2}, \ldots]$ is defined.

A leveled division set must satisfy the following three conditions.

- $SD_1 = [\{M\}]$ — the division set of level 1 contains only one division, which consists of a set of all goods.
- For each level and its division set, a union of multiple sets of goods in a division is always included in a division of a smaller level, i.e., $\forall i \geq 2, \forall D_{ik} \in SD_i, \forall D' \subseteq D_{ik}$, where $|D'| \geq 2, S_u = \bigcup_{S \in D'} S$, then there exists a level $j < i$, with a division set SD_j, where $D_{jl} \in SD_j$ and $S_u \in D_{jl}$.
- For each level and its division set, each set of goods in a division is not included in a division of a different level, i.e., $\forall i, \forall D_{ik} \in SD_i, \forall S \in D_{ik}, \forall j \neq i, \forall D_{jl} \in SD_j, S \notin D_{jl}$.

Figure 1 shows examples of leveled division sets. Case 1 shows one instance where there are two goods (A and B), and case 2 and case 3 show instances where there are three and four goods, respectively.

---
[3]Note that we don't require that $\bigcup_{S \in D} S = M$ holds, i.e., satisfying $\bigcup_{S \in D} S \subseteq M$ is sufficient.

For a division $D = \{S_1, S_2, \ldots\}$ and one possible allocation of goods G, we say G is allowed under D if G allocates each set of goods in D to different agents. Also, we allow that some set of goods is not allocated to any agent. In that case, we assume that the set of goods is allocated to a dummy agent d, whose evaluation value for each good j is equal to the reservation price r_j. For each level i and its division set $SD_i = [D_{i1}, D_{i2}, \ldots]$, we represent a union of all allowed allocations for each element of SD_i as SG_i.

To execute the leveled division set protocol (LDS protocol), the auctioneer must pre-define the leveled division set and the reservation prices of goods. Each agent x declares its evaluation value $B(x, S)$ for each subset of goods S, which may or may not be true. The declared evaluation value of agent x for an allocation G (represented as $v_x(G)$) is defined as $B(x, S)$ if S is allocated to agent x in G, otherwise $v_x(G) = 0$. Also, we define the evaluation value of a dummy agent d for an allocation G as the sum of the reservation prices of goods that are not allocated to real agents in G. The winners and payments are determined by calling the procedure LDS(1), which is defined as follows.

Procedure LDS(i)

Step 1: If there exists only one agent $x \in N$ whose evaluation values satisfy the following condition: $\exists D_{ik} \in SD_i, \exists S_x \in D_{ik}$, where $B(x, S_x) \geq R(S_x)$, then compare the results obtained by the procedure GVA(i) and LDS($i + 1$), and choose the one[4] that gives the larger utility for agent x. In this case, we say agent x is a *pivotal* agent. When choosing the result of LDS($i+1$), we don't assign any good, nor transfer money, to agents other than x, although the assigned goods for agent x and its payment are calculated as if goods were allocated to the other agents.

Step 2: If there exist at least two agents $x_1, x_2 \in N, x_1 \neq x_2$ whose evaluation values satisfy the following condition: $\exists D_{ik} \in SD_i, \exists D_{il} \in SD_i, \exists S_{x_1} \in D_{ik}, \exists S_{x_2} \in D_{il}$, where $B(x_1, S_{x_1}) \geq R(S_{x_1}), B(x_2, S_{x_2}) \geq R(S_{x_2})$, then apply the procedure GVA(i).

Step 3: Otherwise: call LDS($i + 1$), or terminate if $i = max\_level$.

Procedure GVA(i): Choose an allocation $G^* \in SG_i$ such that it maximizes $\sum_{y \in N \cup \{d\}} v_y(G)$. The payment of agent x (represented as p_x) is calculated as $\sum_{y \neq x} v_y(G^*_{\sim x}) - \sum_{y \neq x} v_y(G^*)$, where $G^*_{\sim x} \in SG_i$ is the allocation that maximizes the sum of all agents' (in-

---
[4]If the condition of Step 1 is also satisfied for LDS($i + 1$), then compare with the results of GVA($i + 1$) and LDS($i + 2$) also, and so on.

cluding the dummy agent d) evaluation values except that of agent x.

Note that the procedures in GVA(i) are equivalent to those in the GVA, except that the possible allocations are restricted to SG_i. We say that the *applied level* of the LDS protocol is i if the result of GVA(i) is used.

Examples of Protocol Application

Example 2 *Let us assume there are two goods A and B, the reservation price of each good is 50, the leveled division set is defined as case 1 in Figure 1, and the evaluation values of agents are defined as follows.*

	A	B	AB
agent 1	80	0	110
agent 2	0	80	105
agent 3	60	0	60

Since there exist two agents whose evaluation values for the set are larger than the sum of the reservation prices (i.e., 100), the condition in Step 2 of LDS(1) is satisfied; agent 1 obtains both goods by paying 105. Note that this allocation is not Pareto efficient. In the Pareto efficient allocation, agent 1 obtains A and agent 2 obtains B.

Example 3 *The problem setting is basically equivalent to Example 2, but the evaluation values are defined as follows.*

	A	B	AB
agent 1	80	0	80
agent 2	0	80	80
agent 3	60	0	60

There exists no agent whose evaluation value of the set is larger than 100. In this case, the condition in Step 3 of LDS(1) is satisfied, and then the condition in Step 2 of LDS(2) is satisfied. As a result, agent 1 obtains A and agent 2 obtains B. Agent 1 pays 60, and agent 2 pays the reservation price 50.

Example 4 *The problem setting is basically equivalent to Example 2, but the evaluation values are defined as follows.*

	A	B	AB
agent 1	80	0	110
agent 2	0	80	80
agent 3	60	0	60

There exists only one agent whose evaluation value of the set is larger than 100. The condition in Step 1 of LDS(1) is satisfied; agent 1 is the pivotal agent. Agent 1 prefers obtaining only A (with the payment 60) to obtaining both A and B (with the payment 100). Therefore, agent 1 obtains A and pays 60.

Note that in Example 4, B is not allocated to any agent. This might seem wasteful, but it is necessary to guarantee incentive compatibility. In Example 2, if agent 2 declares its evaluation value for the set as 80, the situation becomes identical to Example 4. If we allocate the remaining good B to agent 2, under-bidding becomes profitable for agent 2.

Example 5 *There are three goods A, B, and C. The reservation price for each is 50, and the leveled division set is defined as case 2 in Figure 1. The evaluation values of agents are defined as follows.*

	A	B	C	AB	BC	AC	ABC
agent 1	60	30	30	90	60	90	120
agent 2	30	60	30	90	90	60	120
agent 3	30	30	60	60	90	90	120

The condition in Step 2 of LDS(3) is satisfied. Agents 1, 2, 3 obtain A, B, C, respectively, and each pays the reservation price 50.

Proof of Incentive Compatibility

It is obvious that the LDS protocol satisfies individual rationality. Here, we prove that it also satisfies incentive compatibility.

Theorem 1 *The LDS protocol satisfies incentive compatibility even if agents can submit false-name bids.*

To prove Theorem 1, we use the following lemmas.

Lemma 1 *In the LDS protocol, the payment of agent x who obtains a set of goods S is larger than (or equal to) the sum of the reservation prices $R(S)$.*

The proof is as follows. Let us assume that the applied level is i. The payment of agent x (represented as p_x) is defined as follows: $p_x = \sum_{y \neq x} v_y(G^*_{\sim x}) - \sum_{y \neq x} v_y(G^*)$. The set of allocations SG_i considered at level i contains an allocation G', where G' is basically the same as G^* except that all goods in S are allocated to the dummy agent d rather than x. The following formula holds.

$$\sum_{y \neq x} v_y(G') = \sum_{y \neq x} v_y(G^*) + R(S)$$

Since $G^*_{\sim x}$ is the allocation that maximizes the sum of all agents' evaluation values (including the dummy agent) except x in SG_i, $\sum_{y \neq x} v_y(G') \leq \sum_{y \neq x} v_y(G^*_{\sim x})$ holds. Thus, the following formula holds.

$$\begin{aligned} p_x &= \sum_{y \neq x} v_y(G^*_{\sim x}) - \sum_{y \neq x} v_y(G^*) \\ &\geq \sum_{y \neq x} v_y(G') - \sum_{y \neq x} v_y(G^*) = R(S) \end{aligned}$$

Lemma 2 *In the LDS protocol, an agent cannot increase its utility by submitting false-name bids.*

The proof is as follows. Let us assume that agent x uses two false names x' and x'' to obtain two sets of goods $S_{x'}$ and $S_{x''}$, respectively. Also, let us assume that the applied level is i. From Lemma 1, the payments $p_{x'}$ and $p_{x''}$ satisfy $p_{x'} \geq R(S_{x'})$ and $p_{x''} \geq R(S_{x''})$. Now, let us assume that agent x declares the evaluation value $R(S)$ for the set $S = S_{x'} \cup S_{x''}$ by using a single identifier. From the condition of a leveled division set, there exists a level $j < i$, where $S \in D_{jl}$, $D_{jl} \in SD_j$ holds. In this case, the condition in Step 1 of LDS(j) is satisfied, i.e., only agent x declares evaluation values that are larger than or equal to the sum of reservation prices. Thus,

$\sum_{y \neq x} v_y(G^*_{\sim x}) = R(M)$, and $\sum_{y \neq x} v_y(G^*) = R(M) - R(S)$ hold. As a result, the payment becomes $R(S) \leq p_{x'} + p_{x''}$, i.e., the payment of agent x becomes smaller than (or equal to) the payment when agent x uses two false names. Similarly, we can show that when an agent uses more than two identifiers, the payment of the agent becomes smaller (or equal to) the payment when the agent uses only one identifier.

Lemma 2 states that false-name bids are not effective in the LDS protocol. Now, we are going to show that truth-telling is the dominant strategy for each agent under the assumption that each agent uses a single identifier.

The following lemma holds.

Lemma 3 *When there exists no false-name bid, and the applied level of the LDS protocol remains the same, an agent can maximize its utility by declaring its true evaluation values.*

The proof is as follows. As long as the applied level is not changed, the possible allocation set SG_i is not changed. The payment of agent x is defined as $\sum_{y \neq x} v_y(G^*_{\sim x}) - \sum_{y \neq x} v_y(G^*)$. We represent the true evaluation value of agent x of an allocation G as $u_x(G)$. The utility of agent x is represented as $u_x(G^*) + \sum_{y \neq x} v_y(G^*) - \sum_{y \neq x} v_y(G^*_{\sim x})$, i.e., the difference between the evaluation value and the payment. The third item of this formula is determined independently from agent x's declaration if there exists no false-name bid. Therefore, agent x can maximize its utility by maximizing the sum of the first two items. On the other hand, the allocation G^* is chosen so that $\sum_{y \in N \cup \{d\}} v_y(G) = v_x(G) + \sum_{y \neq x} v_y(G)$ is maximized. Therefore, agent x can maximize its utility by declaring $v_x(G) = u_x(G)$, i.e., declaring its true utility.

Next, we show that an agent cannot increase its utility by changing the applied level.

Lemma 4 *An agent cannot increase its utility by over-bidding so that the applied level decreases.*

The proof is as follows. Let us assume that when agent x truthfully declares its utility, the applied level is i, and by over-bidding, the applied level is changed to $j < i$. In that case, for every set of goods S included in the divisions of level j, agent x's evaluation value of S must be smaller than the sum of the reservation prices $R(S)$; otherwise, level j is applied when agent x tells the truth. On the other hand, by Lemma 1, the payment for a set S is always larger than the sum of the reservation prices $R(S)$, which means that agent x cannot obtain a positive utility by over-bidding.

Lemma 5 *An agent cannot increase its utility by under-bidding so that the applied level increases.*

The proof is as follows. Agent x can increase the applied level only in the following two cases.

1. Agent x is the pivotal agent when agent x truthfully declares its evaluation values.
2. By under-bidding, another agent y becomes the pivotal agent.

In the first case, when agent x tells the truth, agent x is the pivotal agent and the larger level is applied if agent x prefers the result of that level; thus under-bidding is useless. In the second case, agents other than y cannot obtain any goods; the utility of agent x becomes 0. In both cases, agent x cannot increase its utility by under-bidding.

From these lemmas, we can derive Theorem 1. □

Evaluation

In the LDS protocol, we can expect that the social surplus and the revenue of the seller can vary significantly according to the leveled division set and reservation prices. In this section, we show how the social surplus changes according to the reservation prices using a simulation in a simple setting where there are only two goods A and B.

We determine the evaluation values of agent x by the following method.

- Determine whether the goods are substitutional or complementary for agent x, i.e., with probability p, the goods are substitutional, and with probability $1 - p$, the goods are complementary.

  – When the goods are substitutional: for each good, randomly choose its evaluation value from within the range of $[0, 1]$. The evaluation value of the set is the maximum of the evaluation value of A and that of B (having only one good is enough).

  – When the goods are complementary: the evaluation values of A and B are 0. Randomly choose the evaluation value of the set from within the range of $[0, 2]$ (all-or-nothing).

Figure 2 shows the result where $p = 0.5$ and the number of agents $|N|$ is 10. We created 100 different problem instances and show the average of the social surplus by varying the reservation price. Both A and B have the same reservation price. For comparison, we show the social surplus of the GVA (assuming there exists no false-name bid) and the set protocol. Figure 3 shows the result where $p = 0.7$.

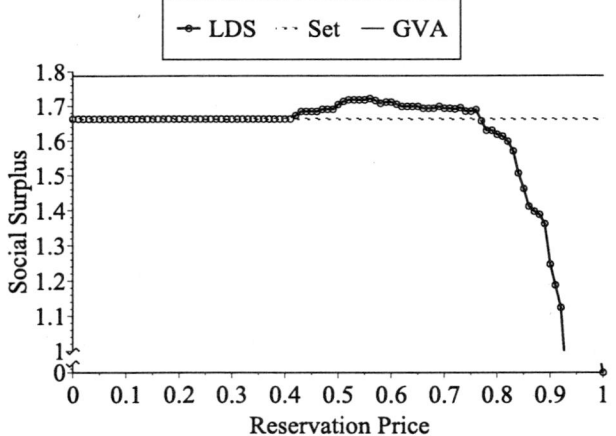

Figure 2: Comparison of Social Surplus ($p = 0.5$)

When the reservation price is small, the results of the LDS protocol are identical to the set protocol. We can see that

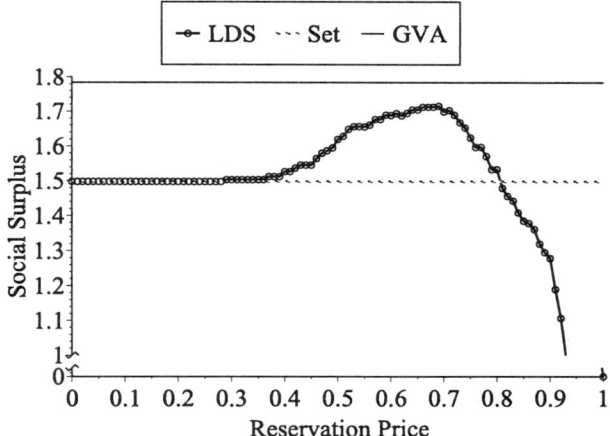

Figure 3: Comparison of Social Surplus ($p = 0.7$)

by setting an appropriate reservation price, the obtained social surplus becomes larger than that for the set protocol. When the probability that the goods are substitutional becomes large, the difference between the set protocol and the GVA, as well as the difference between the set protocol and the LDS protocol, becomes large.

Discussion

As far as the authors know, the LDS protocol is the first non-trivial protocol that is robust against false-name bids. One shortcoming of this protocol is that when the leveled division set and reservation prices are not determined appropriately, there is a chance that some goods cannot be sold. In that case, the social surplus and the revenue of the seller might be smaller than that for the set protocol.

One advantage of the LDS protocol over the GVA is that it requires less communication/computation costs. To execute the GVA, the bidder must declare its evaluation values for all possible subsets of the goods. Also, the seller must solve a complicated optimization problem to determine the winners and their payments (Sandholm 1999; Fujishima, Leyton-Brown, & Shoham 1999; Rothkopf, Pekeč, & Harstad 1998). In the LDS protocol, the allowed divisions are pre-determined, and bidders need to submit bids only for these subsets. Furthermore, the search space of the possible allocations is much smaller than the search space that must be considered in the GVA.

Conclusions

In this paper, we presented a new combinatorial auction protocol (LDS protocol) that is robust against false-name bids. This protocol satisfies individual rationality and incentive compatibility and can achieve a relatively good, though not Pareto efficient, social surplus. The main idea of the LDS protocol is to utilize the reservation prices of goods to make decisions on whether to sell goods in a bundle or separately. Simulation results showed that this protocol can achieve a better social surplus than that for the set protocol.

One remaining research issue is how to find the leveled division set and reservation prices that maximize the social surplus or the revenue of the seller. We are working on a method to find the appropriate leveled division set and reservation prices based on certain expectations of bidders' evaluation values.

Acknowledgments

The authors wish to thank Atsushi Kajii, Yoshikatsu Tatamitani, Fredrik Ygge, and Katsumi Tanaka for their helpful discussions.

References

Fujishima, Y.; Leyton-Brown, K.; and Shoham, Y. 1999. Taming the computation complexity of combinatorial auctions: Optimal and approximate approaches. In *Proceedings of the Sixteenth International Joint Conference on Artificial Intelligence (IJCAI-99)*, 548–553.

Mas-Colell, A.; Whinston, M. D.; and Green, J. R. 1995. *Microeconomic Theory*. Oxford University Press.

Monderer, D., and Tennenholtz, M. 1998. Optimal auctions revisited. In *Proceedings of the Fifteenth National Conference on Artificial Intelligence (AAAI-98)*, 32–37.

Rasmusen, E. 1994. *Games and Information*. Blackwell.

Rothkopf, M. H.; Pekeč, A.; and Harstad, R. M. 1998. Computationally manageable combinatorial auctions. *Management Science* 44(8):1131–1147.

Sakurai, Y.; Yokoo, M.; and Matsubara, S. 1999. A limitation of the Generalized Vickrey Auction in Electronic Commerce : Robustness against false-name bids. In *Proceedings of the Sixteenth National Conference on Artificial Intelligence (AAAI-99)*, 86–92.

Sandholm, T. 1996. Limitations of the Vickrey auction in computational multiagent systems. In *Proceedings of the Second International Conference on Multiagent Systems (ICMAS-96)*, 299–306.

Sandholm, T. 1999. An algorithm for optimal winner determination in combinatorial auction. In *Proceedings of the Sixteenth International Joint Conference on Artificial Intelligence (IJCAI-99)*, 542–547.

Varian, H. R. 1995. Economic mechanism design for computerized agents. In *Proceedings of the First Usenix Workshop on Electronic Commerce*.

Wurman, P. R.; Wellman, M. P.; and Walsh, W. E. 1998. The Michigan Internet AuctionBot: A configurable auction server for human and software agents. In *Proceedings of the Second International Conference on Autonomous Agents (Agents-98)*, 301–308.

Yokoo, M.; Sakurai, Y.; and Matsubara, S. 2000. The effect of false-name declarations in mechanism design: Towards collective decision making on the Internet. In *Proceedings of the Twentieth International Conference on Distributed Computing Systems (ICDCS-2000)*.

Cognitive Modeling

Self-Organization of Innate Face Preferences: Could Genetics Be Expressed Through Learning?

James A. Bednar and Risto Miikkulainen

Department of Computer Sciences
The University of Texas at Austin
Austin, TX 78712
jbednar, risto@cs.utexas.edu

Abstract

Self-organizing models develop realistic cortical structures when given approximations of the visual environment as input, and are an effective way to model the development of face recognition abilities. However, environment-driven self-organization alone cannot account for the fact that newborn human infants will preferentially attend to face-like stimuli even immediately after birth. Recently it has been proposed that internally generated input patterns, such as those found in the developing retina and in PGO waves during REM sleep, may have the same effect on self-organization as does the external environment. Internal pattern generators constitute an efficient way to specify, develop, and maintain functionally appropriate perceptual organization. They may help express complex structures from minimal genetic information, and retain this genetic structure within a highly plastic system. Simulations with the CRF-LISSOM model show that such preorganization can account for newborn face preferences, providing a computational framework for examining how genetic influences interact with experience to construct a complex system.

Introduction

Faces appear to be very special objects for a human newborn (see Slater and Kirby 1998 for a review). Newborns will preferentially turn their eyes or head towards face-like stimuli within a few minutes after birth (Goren, Sarty, and Wu 1975; Johnson and Morton 1991). The more attractive the face, the more readily they do this (Slater et al. 1998). Attractive faces are close to the mathematical average of the population, which suggests that newborns prefer prototypical instances of faces (Langlois and Roggman 1990). Yet newborns have not yet had any experience with faces, so it is unclear how they could have learned such a prototype. Furthermore, since newborns will even imitate facial expressions in others (Meltzoff and Moore 1997), they must have some machinery that can not only recognize facial expressions but also translate them to specific motor commands. Together, these capabilities suggest that there is a genetically-specified ability in humans (and presumably other primates) to detect and process face-like stimuli. Given that face shapes differ substantially across phylogeny, this ability must have a species-specific, genetically-determined foundation.

How can each organism encode a specification for such a specific function? Clearly there is not enough space available in the genome of a mammal to directly specify any sizable percentage of the connections in its nervous system (10^5 genes vs. 10^{15} connections; Shatz 1996.) Moreover, given the enormous post-natal flexibility of the nervous system (reviewed in Hirsch 1985), including the fact that infant face perception shows rapid learning in the first few hours and days after birth (Slater and Kirby 1998), how can the genetic specification be expressed within such a highly plastic system?

This article considers how self-organizing models, which have ordinarily focused on environment-driven development (see Swindale 1996 for a review), can also help explain genetically-driven development. Since newborn studies suggest that face detection has a strong genetic component, we will focus on that ability. The thesis is that pre-natal development uses the same learning mechanisms which extract regularities from the visual environment, but it uses them to extract regularities in training inputs generated internally under genetic control (Jouvet 1998; Marks et al. 1995; Roffwarg, Muzio, and Dement 1966; Shatz 1996). Instead of precisely specifying the organization of the brain, the genome simply encodes a developmental process that is based on genetically-determined patterns presented to a general self-organizing mechanism.

Using the RF-LISSOM self-organizing model (Receptive-Field Laterally Interconnected Synergetically Self-Organizing Map we have previously shown how orientation maps in the primary visual cortex can form based on spontaneously-generated retinal waves (Bednar and Miikkulainen 1998). This paper introduces CRF-LISSOM, which extends RF-LISSOM with a simple model of the eye so that it can be tested with natural photographic images. We then demonstrate how patterns found during REM sleep can account for a newborn's apparently innate predisposition for faces. These simulations represent a first step towards understanding genetic expression in a highly adaptive system.

CRF-LISSOM Model

The architecture for the CRF-LISSOM model is shown in figure 1, and will be briefly reviewed below. (For the detailed equations, see Sirosh, Miikkulainen, and Bednar 1996.) The model consists of a hierarchy of two-dimensional layers of neurons whose connections adapt through Hebbian learning. The input to the model is an activity pattern on a sheet of photoreceptors or PGO generator

---

Copyright © 2000, American Association for Artificial Intelligence (www.aaai.org). All rights reserved.

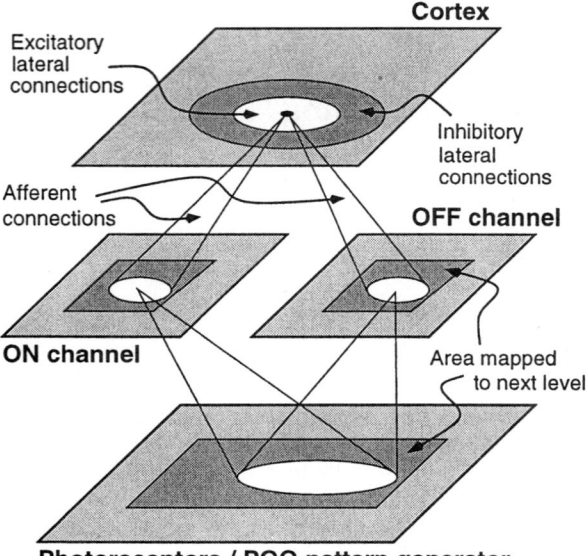

Figure 1: **The CRF-LISSOM model.** A schematic diagram of the CRF-LISSOM network, with connections shown for a single cortical neuron and for an ON-center and OFF-center ganglion cell. Activity propagates from the photoreceptor layer (bottom) up to the cortex and then spreads laterally within the cortex; weights are adapted when the activity settles.

output (e.g. figure 2a). The cells in the ON- and OFF-center layers compute their responses as a scalar product of their receptive fields and a fixed Difference-of-Gaussian weight vector (e.g. figure 2b-c). The ON and OFF layers, also known as input channels, were not present in RF-LISSOM, since the earlier model was designed to work directly with the output of the LGN. Like the ON and OFF cells, each cortical neuron also computes its initial response as a weighted sum of activity in its receptive field. After initial activation, the neural responses repeatedly propagate within the neural layer through the lateral connections, and evolve into coherent activity "bubbles" (figure 2d-e). After the activity stabilizes, weights of the active neurons are adapted by a normalized Hebb rule.

This model was initially developed to account for environment-driven self-organization in the primary visual cortex, where the input layer consists of photoreceptors in the retina, the middle layer of ON- and OFF-center ganglion cells, and the top layer of the cortical neurons (the LGN is bypassed for simplicity). Given elongated Gaussian patterns as input, the model shows how orientation columns and lateral connections between them form. The neural layer in CRF-LISSOM is very general, so the model can also be used for most of the cortical and subcortical areas that are organized as topographic maps. Different developmental phenomena can be modeled by manipulating properties of the input.

For the face-detection experiments, the input to the model is assumed to arise from ponto-geniculo-occipital (PGO) waves generated during rapid-eye-movement (REM) sleep. Developing embryos spend a large percentage of their time

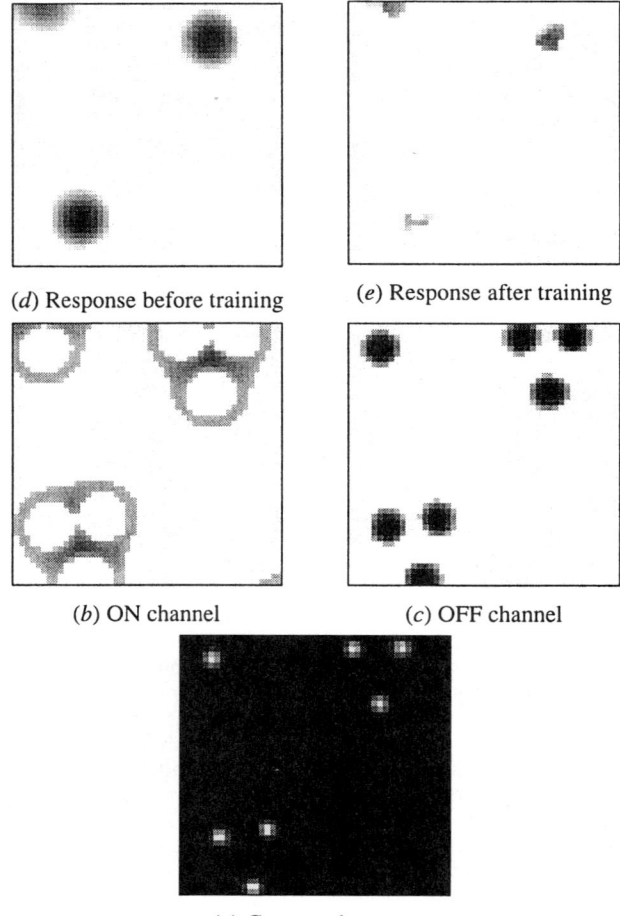

Figure 2: **Training Patterns for Face Detection.** (a) For training, the input consisted of simple three-dot configurations at random locations and random nearly-vertical orientations; these patterns were chosen based on the experiments of Johnson and Morton (1991). (b-c) The ON and OFF channels compute their responses based on this input, and (d-e) the cortical neurons compute their responses based on the output of the ON and OFF channels. Initially, the neurons are unselective (d), but after self-organization, they respond only to patterns similar to the three-dot stimuli (e).

in what appears to be REM sleep, which suggests a major developmental role for this process (Roffwarg, Muzio, and Dement 1966). During and just before REM sleep, PGO waves originate in the pons of the brain stem and travel to the LGN, visual cortex, and a variety of subcortical areas (see Callaway et al. 1987 for a review). PGO waves are strongly correlated with eye movements as well as with vivid visual imagery in dreams, suggesting that they activate the visual system as if they were visual inputs (Marks et al. 1995). PGO waves elicit different distributions of activity in different species (Datta 1997), and interrupting them has been shown to increase the influence of the environment on development (Marks et al. 1995).

All of these characteristics suggest that PGO waves may be providing species-specific training patterns for develop-

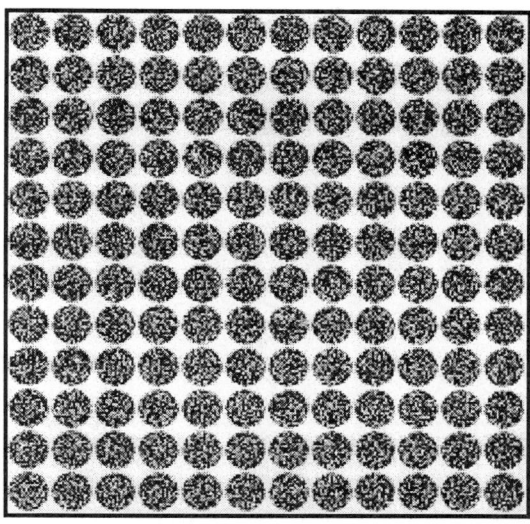
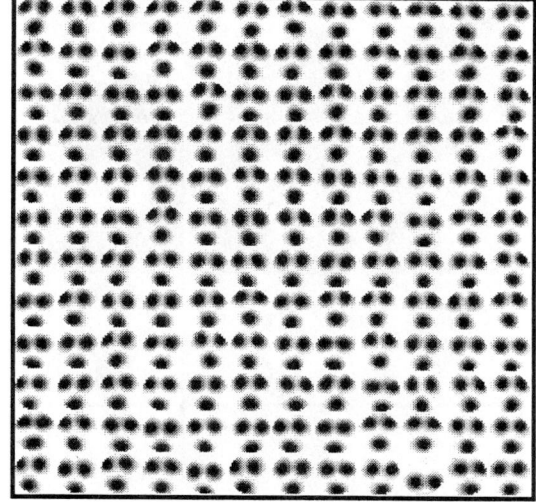

(*a*) Initial map   (*b*) Trained map

Figure 3: **Prenatal development of the face map.** The afferent weights for the OFF-center cells for every fourth neuron in the cortex are shown by grayscale coding. Initially, the weight pattern is unselective, and is identical for both ON and OFF weights (*a*). After many iterations of the self-organizing algorithm, the OFF-center weights (*b*) have come to represent the inputs it has seen, and the neurons now respond only to patterns similar to the three-dot stimuli. The ON-center weights became approximately the photographic inverse of the OFF-center weights, and the lateral weights have a short-range, approximately Gaussian shape throughout self-organization.

ment (Jouvet 1998). However, due to limitations in experimental imaging equipment and techniques, the spatial shape of the PGO wave activity patterns has not yet been measured (Rector et al. 1997). This paper predicts that if these patterns have certain simple properties (shown in figure 2*a*), they can account for the measured face-detection performance of human newborns.

Three assumptions and extensions were made to the CRF-LISSOM model to account for the development of face detection. First, in line with recent neurobiological evidence that shows that much of the adult cortical face processing circuitry is present in the infant (Rodman 1994), newborn face detection is assumed to require only cortical circuitry, most likely in human area V4v and nearby areas (Haxby et al. 1994). Even though multiple cortical areas are likely to be involved, for simplicity a single functional layer is used in this model. Second, until more details are learned about how PGO waves affect the cortex, it is reasonable to assume that this pathway has similar properties as the pathway from the retina. Therefore, the same structure of topographic input and ON/OFF middle layer is used in the model. Third, to keep the size of the model manageable, the PGO patterns are assumed to vary little in size and orientation, and are presented statically. With larger maps, moving patterns and larger variations can be taken into account (Sirosh and Miikkulainen 1996; Sirosh, Miikkulainen, and Bednar 1996).

The input patterns consisted of multiple (3-4) triples of 2-D Gaussian dots on a 132×132 array representing the PGO waves. These stimuli are an implementation of the genetically-encoded template postulated by Johnson and Morton (1991), but they are used as a cortical training stimulus rather than as hard-wired sub-cortical function. Each triple was placed at a random location at least 30 units away from others, with a random angle from a narrow ($\sigma = \pi/36$ radians) normal distribution around vertical. A pair of 66×66 ON-center and OFF-center cell layers received input from the PGO array. Each ON/OFF cell had a fixed Difference of Gaussians (DoG) receptive field (RF) within the PGO array (center $\sigma=1.0$, surround $\sigma=1.6$; ratio is from Marr 1982). The cortical layer consisted of 48×48 neurons that received input from the ON/OFF cell layers and from their neighbors within the cortical layer. The receptive field for each neuron was placed at the location in the central 48×48 portion of the ON/OFF cell layer corresponding to the location of the neuron in the cortex, giving every neuron a complete set of afferent (input) connections. Initially, the afferent weights were random and the lateral weights had a smooth Gaussian profile; all weights adapted through Hebbian learning as patterns were presented on the PGO layer. The learning rates and other parameters were similar to those of Sirosh, Miikkulainen, and Bednar (1996), scaled for this cortex size.

Results

In 20,000 presentations, the ordered configuration shown in figure 3*b* emerged. As one would expect, the neurons in the cortical layer developed receptive fields that closely resemble the training inputs used (figure 2*a*). The cortical map was then tested with the same schematic stimuli on which human newborns have been tested (Goren, Sarty, and Wu 1975; Johnson and Morton 1991). Assuming that the newborn attends most strongly to those stimuli that are most effective at activating his visual processing system (including face-selective areas), the activations in the network can be

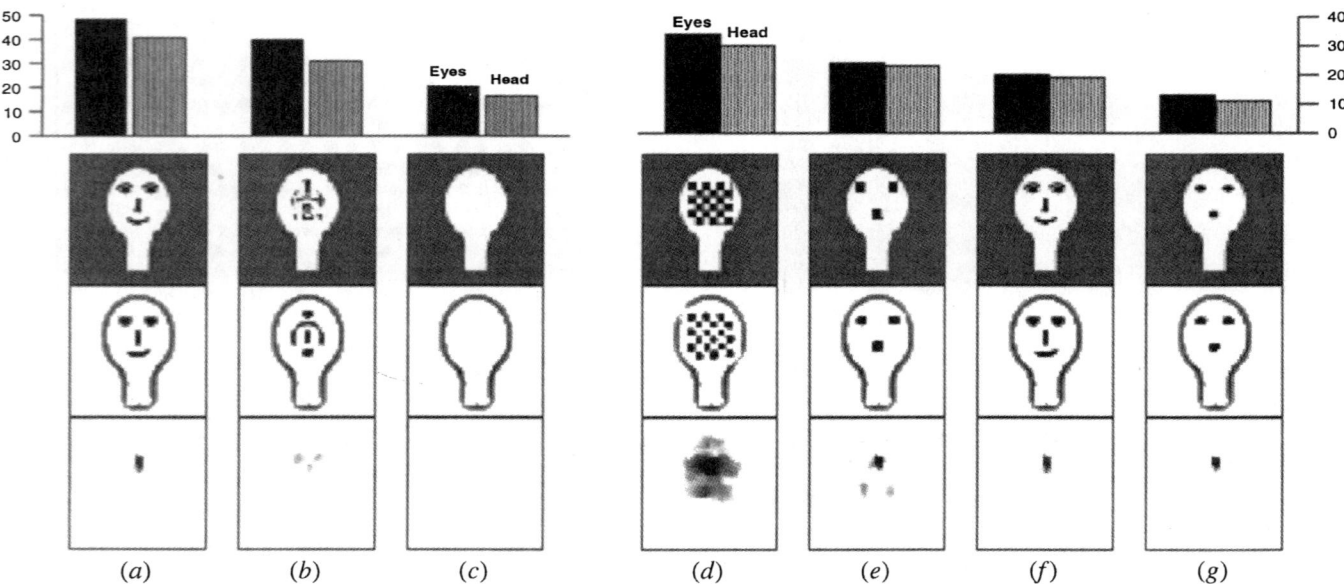

Figure 4: **Human newborn vs. model response to schematic images.** The graph at left shows the result of a study of human newborns tested with two-dimensional moving patterns within one hour of birth; the one at right shows the results from a separate study of newborns an average of 21 hours old (Johnson and Morton 1991). Each pair of bars shows the average newborn eye and head tracking, in degrees, for the image pictured below it; eye and head tracking showed similar trends here and thus either may be used as a measure. Since the procedures and conditions differed between the two studies, only the relative magnitudes should be compared. The second row of images shows the OFF-center activations in the CRF-LISSOM model; the ON-center cells responded as suggested by figure 2b. The bottom row shows the settled response of the cortical layer. Remarkably, the settled response in the model reflects the same relative preferences for all stimuli as in the newborn. Overall, the study at left demonstrates that the newborn and the network both respond to face-like stimuli more strongly than to simple control conditions. The study at right shows what features of the face-like pattern are essential. In all cases, the CRF-LISSOM model shows behavior remarkably similar to that of the newborns, and gives detailed computational insight into why these behaviors occur.

compared directly with the infant's looking preferences.

Remarkably, the responses of the pre-trained network turned out to match to the measured stimulus preference of newborns very well, with the same relative ranking in each case (figure 4). For both newborns and the model, a checkerboard pattern (4d) is the most effective, because it activates a very large region of neurons that mutually reinforce each other, despite the pattern being a poor match for a face. (Of course, in a newborn, other object processing areas are presumably even more effectively stimulated by a checkerboard, and thus such a pattern would be salient even if it did not activate face detection areas.) A simple three-square-dot pattern (4e) is also more effective than the more face-like pattern (4f), suggesting that the details of the input features are irrelevant. An oval-dot pattern evokes somewhat lesser activity than the other face-like stimuli since it has less energy in the spatial frequency range tested here (figure 4g); the difference is slight for the model due to the limited resolution of the model retina. These results provide computational support for the speculation of Johnson and Morton (1991) that the newborn could simply be responding to a three-dot face-like configuration, rather than performing sophisticated face detection. Internally-generated patterns provide an account for how such "innate" machinery can be constructed.

The model also shows some interesting spurious responses. Figure 4e shows two extra responses (the lighter blobs) caused by fortuitous matches with the three-dot receptive fields – e.g. the "mouth" dot can also match the right eye blob of a receptive field, while the face border matches the left eye and the mouth regions. These false matches actually serve to make the pattern even more salient. This prediction could be tested in newborns using stimuli with a single dot in one of the three positions; the newborn should respond more strongly to a pattern with a dot in the mouth position than to one in either eye position (assuming the training pattern has equal-sized dots and is processed using ON/OFF channels like those in the model).

Presumably, an ability to detect faces in natural images underlies the newborn's preference for schematic faces, so the CRF-LISSOM network was also tested with natural stimuli. As shown in figure 5, the pre-trained map also performs remarkably well on natural images. The map responds strongly to most human faces of the right size, and does not respond to most other stimuli, except when they contain accidental three-dot patterns. The model predicts that human newborns will have a similar pattern of responses in the face-selective brain regions if they are using a template with three equal-sized dots processed with ON- and OFF-center cells. Conversely, if human newborns show different responses, then it is likely that they are using a more sophisticated template, the shape of which can be recovered from the responses. Such experiments could constitute an important validation of the model, and further our understanding of the development of face detection in general.

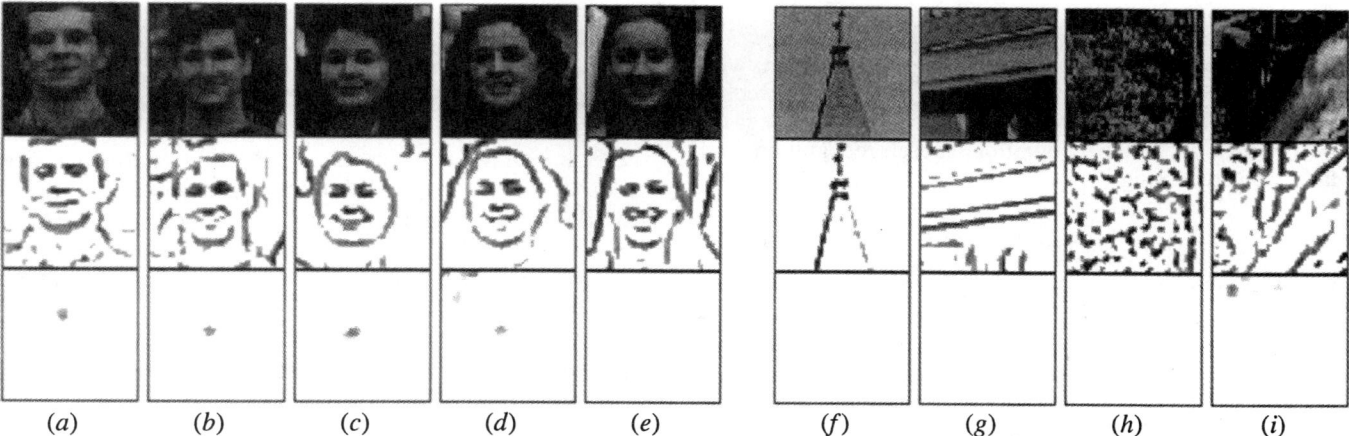

Figure 5: **Model response to natural images.** The top row shows the central 96×96 portion of a 132×132 image presented to the input layer (data from Rowley, Baluja, and Kanade 1998). As in figure 4, the second row shows the activation of the OFF-center cells, while the bottom row shows the response of the pre-natally trained network. The position of the network activation corresponds to the retinal position of the object to which it is responding. The pre-natally trained network is indeed activated for most real faces (*a-d*) and for some non-face patterns present in nature scenes (*i*) and complicated backgrounds (*d*). Just as important, the network is not activated for most man-made objects (*f-g*) and natural scenes (*h*); it is also inactive for faces with broad smiles (*e*). The model predicts that newborns would show similar responses.

Discussion and future work

The CRF-LISSOM simulations show that internally-generated patterns and self-organization can together account for newborn face detection. Pattern-generation represents a synthesis of the strengths of genetic specification and environment-driven learning. Once the genetically-specified component has ensured that the newborn pays attention to faces, experience with real faces drives the development of more sophisticated abilities. Preliminary further work has shown that the pretrained map does learn from natural images more quickly and more effectively than does a map with a random or uniform initial state.

The results reported in this paper suggest constraints on the types of patterns that may be used by the PGO pattern-generating system. For instance, if the patterns use the three equal-sized dots proposed by Johnson and Morton (1991), the system will not perform well on broad, fixed smiles; this prediction could be tested in the human newborn. More direct confirmation of the pattern-generation approach would come from imaging measurements of the actual activity patterns produced during REM sleep. Very recent advances in imaging hardware have made limited measurements of this type possible (Rector et al. 1997), and imaging of the pons is planned for the near future (R. M. Harper, personal communication). So it may soon be possible to test the assumptions and the predictions of the model directly in the developing animal.

Johnson and Morton (1991) originally proposed that newborn face detection occurred subcortically, and a face-selective subcortical pathway has recently been found in the adult (Morris, Ohman, and Dolan 1999). However, it is not known whether this pathway is present in infants, while face-selective inferior temporal cortex cells have been found in the youngest primates yet studied (6 weeks old; Rodman 1994). Thus since the current evidence points to a cortical mechanism, only cortical face-selective regions were modeled here. Incorporating subcortical influences would complicate the model, but the same principles of pattern generation and self-organization would apply.

Since PGO waves continue into adulthood, internal pattern generation may also have a lifelong role in maintaining brain function while the system adapts to environmental stimuli, particularly when subcortical pathways are considered. For instance, the patterns may help sustain connections between the phylogenetically older regions that provide basic visual functionality (such as the superior colliculus, the pulvinar, and the amygdala) and the more comprehensive object processing performed in the various sensory and motor areas of the neocortex. Presenting similar patterns to separate areas simultaneously would strengthen the connections between them, ensuring that despite pervasive adaptation they continue to work together in their genetically-specified roles. Thus ongoing internal pattern generation and self-organization may help explain how multiple highly-plastic processing streams are integrated into a coherent system.

From a larger information-processing perspective, pattern generation combined with self-organization may represent a general way to solve difficult problems like face detection and recognition. Simple inputs, easy to specify and generate, combined with simple learning mechanisms that also learn from the environment, together allow a complex system to be specified and developed. (Here "complex" is used in the sense of Gell-Mann's effective complexity, measuring the total amount of regularity of all types; Gell-Mann and Lloyd 1996). The specification for the system need only encode a process for constructing an individual along with interaction from its environment, rather than meticulously specifying the individual itself. Yet even so the result can incorporate the full complexity of the environment as well as *a priori* information about the desired function of the system, with seamless integration between the two. This approach could be used for engineering complex artificial systems, e.g. for handwritten character recognition, speech recognition, and language processing.

Conclusion

We propose that internally-generated patterns represent a general mechanism that allows an organism to specify, develop, and maintain complex functional structures. CRF-LISSOM simulations have shown how initial orientation maps and face-selective maps could develop from non-visual inputs. Future work will examine how these genetic factors interact with learning in the adult, as well as how distinct cortical areas can develop simultaneously. Such experiments with self-organizing models should greatly improve our understanding of the balance between environmental and genetic determinants of individuality, and should increase our ability to construct complex artificial systems.

Acknowledgments This research was supported in part by the National Science Foundation under grant #IIS-9811478. Computer time for the simulations was provided by the Texas Advanced Computing Center at the University of Texas at Austin. Software, demonstrations, and related publications for CRF-LISSOM and RF-LISSOM are available at http://www.cs.utexas.edu/users/nn/.

References

Bednar, J. A., and Miikkulainen, R. 1998. Pattern-generator-driven development in self-organizing models. In Bower, J. M., ed., *Computational Neuroscience: Trends in Research, 1998*, 317–323. New York: Plenum.

Callaway, C. W.; Lydic, R.; Baghdoyan, H. A.; and Hobson, J. A. 1987. Pontogeniculooccipital waves: Spontaneous visual system activity during rapid eye movement sleep. *Cellular and Molecular Neurobiology* 7(2):105–49.

Datta, S. 1997. Cellular basis of pontine ponto-geniculo-occipital wave generation and modulation. *Cellular and Molecular Neurobiology* 17(3):341–365.

Gell-Mann, M., and Lloyd, S. 1996. Information measures, effective complexity, and total information. *Complexity* 2(1):44–52.

Goren, C. C.; Sarty, M.; and Wu, P. Y. 1975. Visual following and pattern discrimination of face-like stimuli by newborn infants. *Pediatrics* 56(4):544–549.

Haxby, J. V.; Horwitz, B.; Ungerleider, L. G.; Maisog, J. M.; Pietrini, P.; and Grady, C. L. 1994. The functional organization of human extrastriate cortex: A PET-rCBF study of selective attention to faces and locations. *Journal of Neuroscience* 14:6336–6353.

Hirsch, H. V. B. 1985. The role of visual experience in the development of cat striate cortex. *Cellular and Molecular Neurobiology* 5:103–121.

Johnson, M. H., and Morton, J. 1991. *Biology and Cognitive Development: The Case of Face Recognition*. Oxford, UK; New York: Blackwell.

Jouvet, M. 1998. Paradoxical sleep as a programming system. *Journal of Sleep Research* 7(Suppl 1):1–5.

Langlois, J. H., and Roggman, L. A. 1990. Attractive faces are only average. *Psychological Science* 1:115–121.

Marks, G. A.; Shaffery, J. P.; Oksenberg, A.; Speciale, S. G.; and Roffwarg, H. P. 1995. A functional role for REM sleep in brain maturation. *Behavioural Brain Research* 69:1–11.

Marr, D. 1982. *Vision*. New York: Freeman.

Meltzoff, A. N., and Moore, A. K. 1997. Explaining facial imitation: A theoretical model. *Early Developmental Parenting* 6:179–192.

Morris, J. S.; Ohman, A.; and Dolan, R. J. 1999. A subcortical pathway to the right amygdala mediating "unseen" fear. *Proceedings of the National Academy of Sciences, USA* 96(4):1680–1685.

Rector, D. M.; Poe, G. R.; Redgrave, P.; and Harper, R. M. 1997. A miniature CCD video camera for high-sensitivity light measurements in freely behaving animals. *Journal of Neuroscience Methods* 78(1-2):85–91.

Rodman, H. R. 1994. Development of inferior temporal cortex in the monkey. *Cerebral Cortex* 4(5):484–98.

Roffwarg, H. P.; Muzio, J. N.; and Dement, W. C. 1966. Ontogenetic development of the human sleep-dream cycle. *Science* 152:604–619.

Rowley, H. A.; Baluja, S.; and Kanade, T. 1998. Neural network-based face detection. *IEEE Transactions on Pattern Analysis and Machine Intelligence* 20:23–38.

Shatz, C. J. 1996. Emergence of order in visual system development. *Proceedings of the National Academy of Sciences, USA* 93:602–608.

Sirosh, J., and Miikkulainen, R. 1996. Self-organization and functional role of lateral connections and multisize receptive fields in the primary visual cortex. *Neural Processing Letters* 3:39–48.

Sirosh, J.; Miikkulainen, R.; and Bednar, J. A. 1996. Self-organization of orientation maps, lateral connections, and dynamic receptive fields in the primary visual cortex. In Sirosh, J.; Miikkulainen, R.; and Choe, Y., eds., *Lateral Interactions in the Cortex: Structure and Function*. Austin, TX: The UTCS Neural Networks Research Group. Electronic book, ISBN 0-9647060-0-8, http://www.cs.utexas.edu/users/nn/web-pubs/htmlbook96.

Slater, A., and Kirby, R. 1998. Innate and learned perceptual abilities in the newborn infant. *Experimental Brain Research* 123(1-2):90–94.

Slater, A.; Von der Schulenburg, C.; Brown, E.; Badenoch, M.; Butterworth, G.; Parsons, S.; and Samuels, C. 1998. Newborn infants prefer attractive faces. *Infant Behavior and Development* 21(2):345–354.

Swindale, N. V. 1996. The development of topography in the visual cortex: A review of models. *Network – Computation in Neural Systems* 7:161–247.

A Self-Organizing Neural Network for Contour Integration through Synchronized Firing

Yoonsuck Choe and Risto Miikkulainen
Department of Computer Sciences
The University of Texas at Austin
Austin, TX 78712
yschoe,risto@cs.utexas.edu

Abstract

Contour integration in low-level vision is believed to occur based on lateral interaction between neurons with similar orientation tuning. The exact neural mechanisms underlying such interactions, and their developmental origins, are not well understood. This paper suggests through computational simulations that synchronized firing of neurons mediated by patchy lateral connections, formed through input-driven self-organization, can serve as such a mechanism. Furthermore, we argue that different degree of such patchy connections established during development may explain why different areas of the visual field show different degrees of contour integration in psychophysical experiments.

Introduction

Contour integration in low-level vision means forming a single coherent percept (i.e. a continuous contour) from a discontinuous sequence of line segments. Humans are very good at contour integration; understanding the underlying mechanisms can give us insights into how perceptual grouping can be implemented in general.

Psychophysical experiments (Field, Hayes, & Hess, 1993; Pettet, McKee, & Grzywacz, 1998; Geisler & Super, 2000) and computational models (Yen & Finkel, 1997; Li, 1998; Yen & Finkel, 1998; Geisler & Super, 2000) suggest that contour integration in the visual cortex may be due to interaction of neurons with similar orientation tuning. The models perform integration based on predetermined set of constraints such as relative orientation difference, distance, curvature, and change in curvature along with specific association rules, and they match experimental data quite well. However, how such constraints are implemented in the brain and how they emerge during early life of the animal remains an open question. Furthermore, the models do not explain why contour integration performance widely differs among different areas of the visual field. For example, contour integration is absent in the peripheral vision (Hess & Dakin, 1997), and subjective contours are harder to detect in the upper vs. the lower hemifield (Rubin, Nakayama, & Shapley, 1996).

This paper explores the possibility that a single mechanism of synchronized firing of neurons mediated by self-

Copyright © 2000, American Association for Artificial Intelligence (www.aaai.org). All rights reserved.

organized lateral connections may be responsible for these phenomena. Previous computational studies on cortical self-organization have shown that strong lateral connections develop between neurons with similar orientation preference, and these connections can serve as a foundation for segmentation and binding (RF-SLISSOM, or Receptive Field Spiking Laterally Interconnected Synergetically Self-Organizing Map; Choe & Miikkulainen, 1998; Sirosh, 1995; Sirosh, Miikkulainen, & Choe, 1996; Miikkulainen et al., 1997). This paper shows that (1) such lateral connections can also establish contour integration, (2) the specific lateral connection patterns necessary for contour integration can be learned in an input-driven self-organizing process like the rest of the orientation map, and (3) the weaker integration in peripheral vs. foveal and upper vs. lower hemifield may result from weaker lateral connectivity patterns, which in turn may originate from attentional modulation of the frequency and quality of input. In order to study these phenomena, RF-SLISSOM is extended to include long-range excitatory lateral connections.

Extending RF-SLISSOM for Contour Integration

The contour integration model is based on the RF-SLISSOM model of self-organization and segmentation in the visual cortex. In RF-SLISSOM, each cortical neuron receives afferent connections from the input layer and lateral (excitatory and inhibitory) connections from other neurons in the cortex. The connection strengths self-organize based on correlations in the input. In the final ordered map, the lateral excitation has a short range, and causes neurons responding to the same input object to fire synchronously, thereby binding the representation into a single coherent percept. The lateral inhibitory connections have a long range, and establish competition between representations of different objects. Neurons representing different objects tend to fire at different times, and the input is thereby segmented into different objects.

The RF-SLISSOM model shows how self-organization and segmentation can be achieved in a single unified model. The long-range lateral interactions play a crucial role in both behaviors: they establish competition that drives self-organization, and they establish desynchronization that

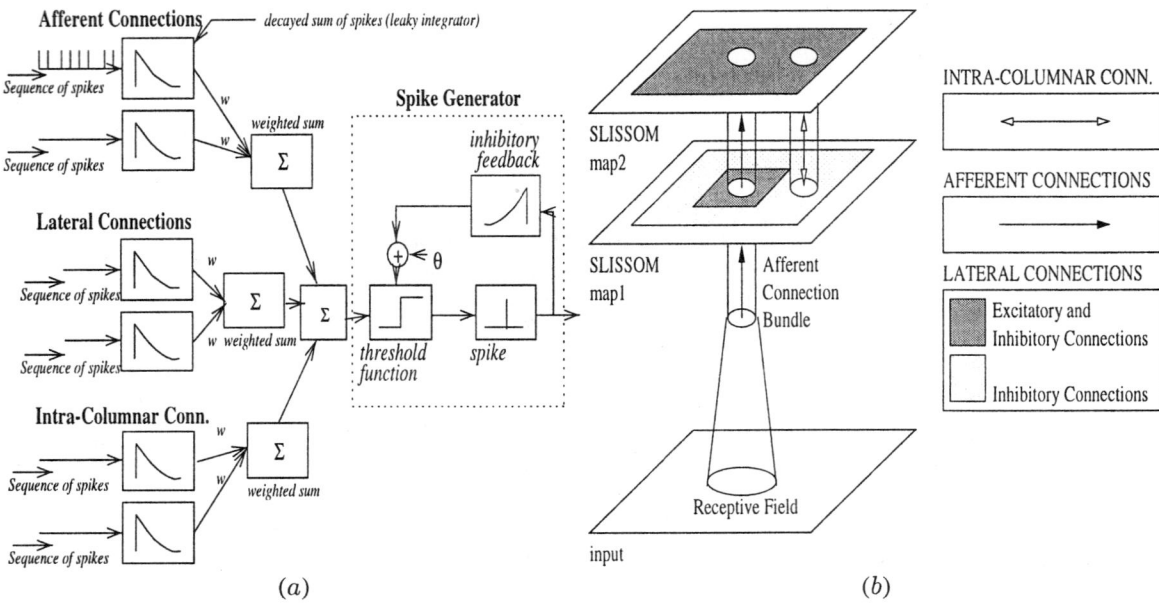

Figure 1: **The Stacked RF-LISSOM Architecture.** (*a*) The model neuron. Leaky integrators at each synapse perform decayed summation of incoming spikes, and the outgoing spikes establish a dynamic spiking threshold. (*b*) The overall organization of the Stacked RF-SLISSOM network. The cortical network consists of two sub-maps: MAP1 has short-range excitation and long-range inhibition, and drives the self-organization of the cortex. In MAP2, both excitation and inhibition are long range, establishing segmentation and binding. The two maps are connected with intra-columnar connections so that both the self-organization and segmentation dynamics are established in both maps.

drives segmentation. The model does not include any long-range excitatory connections because they were not found necessary to model the above behaviors.

However, it turns out that such a parsimonious model cannot account for filling-in phenomena such as contour integration. The network has to be able to bind together representations that are separated by gaps: that is, it has to have long-range excitatory connections that link together the representations of the different segments of a fragmented contour.

The RF-SLISSOM model is extended in this paper with such long-range excitatory connections (figure 1). For conceptual clarity, the cortical network is divided into two separate components: (1) MAP1, which is similar to the RF-SLISSOM cortex with short-range excitatory and long-range inhibitory connections. This map has the task of driving the self-organization of the network into an ordered map. (2) MAP2, which has the task of establishing long-range segmentation and binding, with long-range excitatory connections that allow contour integration, and long-range inhibitory connections that allow segmentation of separate objects.

The two maps are assumed to be overlaid in one cortical network. In other words, the model predicts that some of the neurons in each hypercolumn are involved in establishing and maintaining organization, whereas others perform visual segmentation and binding. The details of the architecture, referred to as Stacked RF-LISSOM, are described next.

The Network Architecture

The details of the neuron model are shown in figure 1*a*. Each connection is a leaky integrator that performs exponentially decayed summation of incoming spikes, thereby establishing not only spatial summation, but also temporal summation of activity. The spike generator compares the net input to a threshold and decides whether to fire a spike. The threshold is a sum of two factors: the base threshold θ and an exponentially decayed sum of past spikes, formed by a similar leaky integrator as in the input synapses (Eckhorn *et al.*, 1990; Reitboeck, Stoecker, & Hahn, 1993).

The overall organization of the Stacked RF-SLISSOM model is shown in figure 1*b*. The net input $\sigma_{i,j}$ to the spike generator of the cortical neuron (in each map) at location (i,j) at time t consists of the input from a fixed-size receptive field in the retina, centered at the location corresponding to the neuron's location in the cortical network, from neurons around the same location in the other map, and from neurons around it in the same map:

$$\sigma_{i,j}(t) = \gamma_a \sum_{r_1,r_2} \xi_{r_1,r_2} \mu_{ij,r_1r_2} + \gamma_c \sum_{p_1,p_2} \zeta_{p_1,p_2} \nu_{ij,p_1p_2}$$
$$+ \gamma_e \sum_{k,l} \eta_{kl}(t-1) E_{ij,kl} - \gamma_i \sum_{k,l} \eta_{kl}(t-1) I_{ij,kl}, \quad (1)$$

where $\gamma_a, \gamma_c, \gamma_e,$ and γ_i are the relative strengths of the afferent, intra-columnar, excitatory, and inhibitory contributions, ξ_{r_1,r_2} is the decayed sum of spikes of the retinal neuron (r_1, r_2), μ_{ij,r_1r_2} is the corresponding afferent connection weight, ζ_{p_1,p_2} is the decayed sum of spikes of the cortical neuron (p_1, p_2) of the other cortical map, ν_{ij,p_1p_2} is the

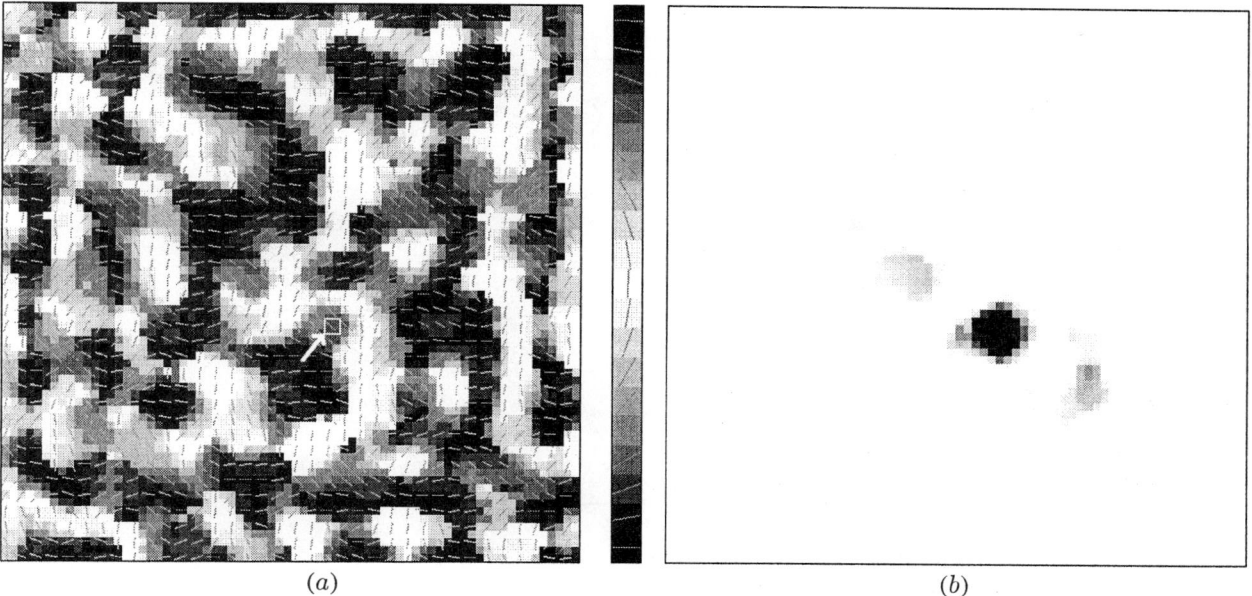

Figure 2: **The self-organized orientation map and patchy lateral connections.** (a) The orientation preferences of the neurons in MAP1 are shown; both maps (MAP1 and MAP2) developed similar organizations. The gray scale black → white → black represents preferences from 0 to 180 degrees as also indicated by the oriented line segments. The map has organized into orientation columns similar to those found in the visual cortex. (b) The strength of excitatory lateral connections of neuron at (41,29) of MAP2 is (i.e., at the location indicated by the arrow in (a)) plotted in gray scale (white → black represents weak → strong connection weight). This neuron is sensitive to 140 degree orientation, and its lateral connections link it to other neurons with the same orientation preference along the 140 degree direction across the map.

corresponding intra-columnar connection weight, $\eta_{kl}(t-1)$ is the decayed sum of spikes from the map neuron (k,l) at time $t-1$, and $E_{ij,kl}$ is the corresponding excitatory and $I_{ij,kl}$ the inhibitory lateral connection weight.

The input is kept constant while the cortical response settles through the lateral connections, forming a concentrated, redundancy-reduced activation pattern. The retinal neurons are spiking constantly at each iteration and the cortical neurons are allowed to exchange spikes. After a while, the neurons reach a stable rate of firing, and this rate is used to modify the weights. The afferent, lateral and intra-columnar weights are modified according to the Hebbian principle:

$$w_{ij,mn}(t) = \frac{w_{ij,mn}(t-1) + \alpha V_{ij} X_{mn}}{\sum_{mn}[w_{ij,mn}(t-1) + \alpha V_{ij} X_{mn}]}, \quad (2)$$

where $w_{ij,mn}(t)$ is the connection weight between neurons (i,j) and (m,n), $w_{ij,mn}(t-1)$ is the previous weight, α is the learning rate (α_a for afferent, α_c for intra-columnar, α_e for excitatory, and α_i for inhibitory connections), V_{ij} and X_{mn} are the average spiking rates of the neurons. Those connections that become less than 0.001 in this process are killed, modeling death of unused connections.

This process of weight adaptation is repeated for a number of input patterns (e.g. oriented Gaussians), and the neurons become gradually sensitive to particular orientations at particular locations, and the map forms a global retinotopic orientation map similar to that in the visual cortex (Blasdel, 1992; Blasdel & Salama, 1986). The self-organized map will then synchronize and desynchronize the firing of neurons to indicate binding and segmentation of visual input to different objects.

Experiments and Results

A Stacked RF-SLISSOM network with a 44×44 retina and a 72×72 cortex was trained for 30,000 iterations with elongated Gaussian bars at random locations in the retina (such input approximates the local features of natural visual stimuli after the edge detection and enhancement mechanisms in the retina). Excitatory lateral connections in MAP1 had an initial radius of 3 and gradually reduced to 1, and inhibitory lateral connections had a fixed radius of 7. In MAP2, both types of lateral connections had a radius of 19. Afferent connections to the retina had a radius of 7 in both maps, and intra-columnar connections a radius of 1. During each training presentation, the network was allowed to settle for 13 time steps (through equation 1) and all connections except the inhibitory lateral connections were updated according to equation 2. The fixed inhibition provides a baseline global inhibition similar to other cortical models (Eckhorn et al., 1988; von der Malsburg & Buhmann, 1992), used because it is simple and sufficient to establish segmentation. The simulations are not particularly sensitive to these parameter values as long as they are qualitatively similar.

A well-formed orientation map emerged in this process (figure 2a). Because of the intra-columnar connections, similar activity patterns formed on both maps during self-organization, and they developed almost identical organizations (only MAP1 is shown in figure 2). The lateral con-

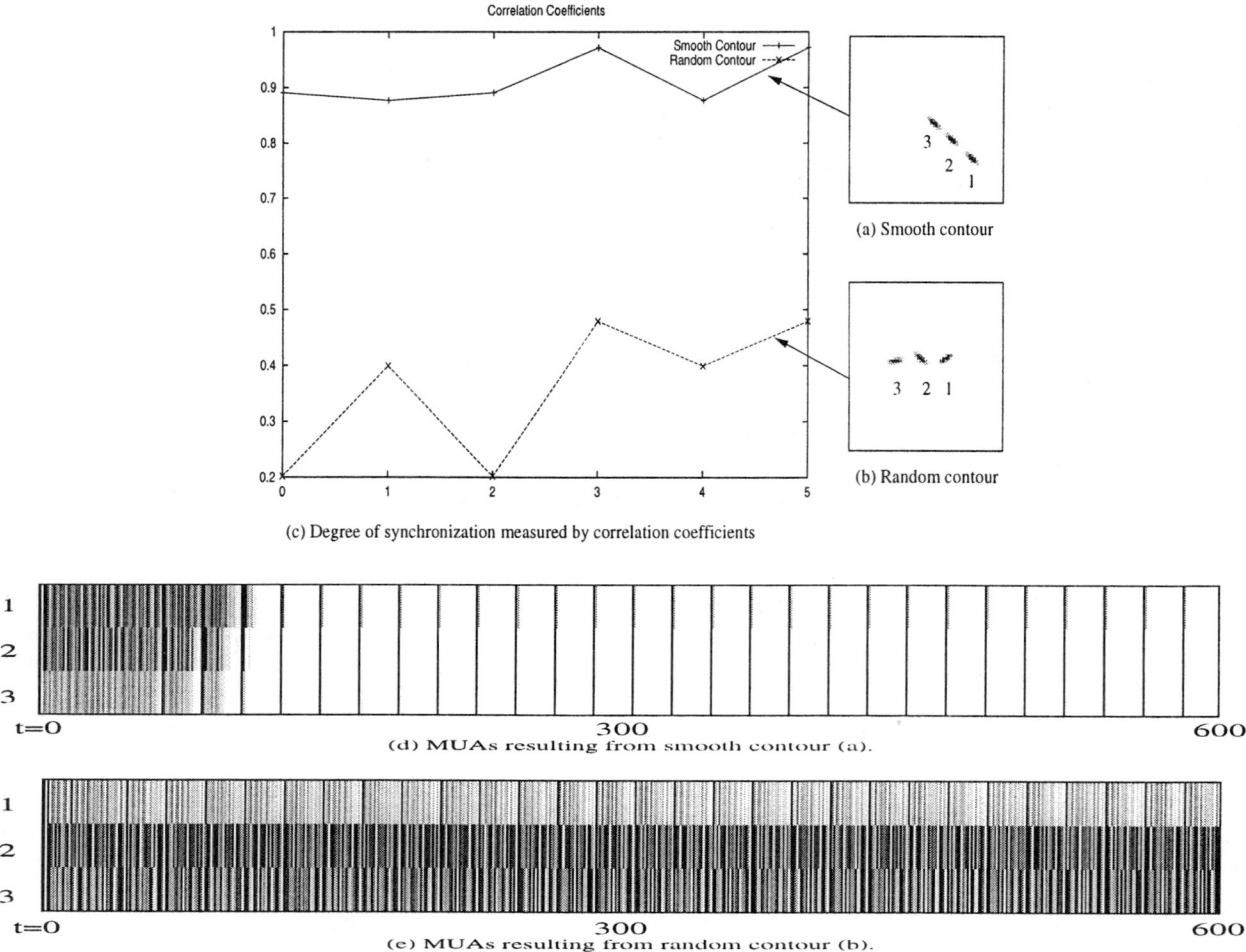

Figure 3: **Contour integration with Stacked RF-SLISSOM.** (a) A smooth input contour. (b) A randomly oriented contour. (d,e) The MUAs of the areas responding to each line segment in (a) and (b). Time is on the x-axis and the three rows from top to bottom represent MUA of area 1, area 2 and area 3 by gray-scale coding. (c) A comparison of the correlation coefficients between the MUAs. In each experiment (smooth vs. random contours), the MUAs from three areas in MAP2 were gathered over 600 iterations and the correlations between the MUAs were calculated. The x-axis is the index for MUA pairs. For example, 0, 1, ... represents MUA pairs $(1, 2), (1, 3), \ldots$. The y-axis is the correlation coefficient r as calculated by equation 3. When the contour elements are smooth, the MUAs are highly correlated, but the correlation is very low when the contour elements are randomly oriented relative to each other. This indicates that the network binds smooth contours together through synchronized firing of neurons but perceives random contours as multiple objects. This result is consistent with experimental data and can be explained by the existence of patchy excitatory lateral connections developed through self-organization.

nections with weights less than 0.001 were killed in the end, thus leaving a patchy connection profile (figure 2b). Only those connections that link areas with highly-correlated activity, such as those along a continuous contour, remain in the end.

The patchy lateral connections therefore form the foundation for feature binding and contour integration in the model. The network should be able to bind together separated line segments if they are collinear and therefore likely to be part of the same contour. If their directions do not agree, they should not be bound together because they are likely to belong to different objects.

To test this hypothesis, three elongated Gaussian bars arranged in two different configurations, i.e. smooth and random contours (figure 3a,b), were presented to the network. For each input bar, the number of spikes generated by the area of the cortex that responded to the bar was counted at each time step (figure 3d,e). This quantity is called the Multi-Unit Activity of the response, or MUA, and it can be used to identify which area of the cortex is the most active at each time step.

In order to measure synchronization between two areas, linear correlation coefficient r between their MUA sequences can be calculated as follows:

$$r = \frac{\sum_i (x_i - \bar{x})(y_i - \bar{y})}{\sqrt{\sum_i (x_i - \bar{x})^2} \sqrt{\sum_i (y_i - \bar{y})^2}} \quad (3)$$

where x_i and y_i, $i = 1, ..., N$ are the MUA values at time i for the two areas representing the two different objects in the scene, and $\bar{x}$ and $\bar{y}$ are the mean of each sequence.

Using this measure, the contour integration capability of the network was tested. The degree of synchrony in the two different cases was compared: in the first case, the segments lined up to form a smooth contour, and in the second, their orientation was random (figure 3).

During self-organization, patchy lateral connections formed between neurons that represent collinear line segments (figure 2). In the first case these connections synchronize the responses of the three areas. No such connections exist for line segments that are not collinear, and the MUAs remain desynchronized in the second case. This way the network perceives the collinear segments as one object, but the random line segments as three separate objects.

Although the example in figure 3 shows only three bars, the effect is robust. The network may integrate long chains of near-collinear line segments this way, whereas a perpendicular segment in the middle will break the integration. This way the network suggests a possible mechanism for contour integration, and demonstrates how the necessary connections emerge automatically as a side effect of Hebbian self-organization of lateral connections.

Discussion

Whether contour integration occurs or not in the model depends on whether the cortical areas are connected with excitatory lateral connections or not. The model therefore suggests an explanation for the different contour integration capability of the different visual areas: integration is possible only if focused (i.e. patchy) lateral connections exist linking collinear neurons with similar orientation preferences. If peripheral areas and the upper visual field do not receive dense enough visual input for such connections to form during development, the connections become diffuse, resulting in weaker integration.

Statistics of images projected on the retina indeed support this hypothesis. Reinagel & Zador (1999) showed that human gaze most often falls upon areas with high contrast and low pixel correlation than other areas. As a result, sharp images project more often on the fovea than the periphery, allowing more specific connections to form. A similar method can be used to find out if there's a difference in statistical distribution of image features in the lower vs. upper hemisphere. Such statistical difference together with Hebbian self-organization would result in different contour integration capability in different visual areas.

Another way of verifying this hypothesis would be to rear an animal with eye glasses that flip the input to the upper and lower hemifield. After the critical period, the animal's performance on contour detection task could be measured, and the connectivity patterns formed in the upper and lower hemifield analyzed. The prediction is that high connectivity and good integration would occur in the upper hemifield, instead of the lower hemifield as in normal animals.

The Stacked RF-SLISSOM network can be tested further in more advanced contour integration and gestalt perception tasks such as subjective contour detection and occluded object recognition. The excitatory lateral connections should be able to mediate these phenomena as well. Moreover, orientation maps for subjective contours are known to exist in V2 (Sheth *et al.*, 1996); the Stacked RF-SLISSOM could be extended to model V2 as well, thereby extending our understanding of the visual self-organization and function at higher levels.

Conclusion

Input-driven self-organization of afferent, intra-columnar, and lateral connections was shown to give rise to patchy connectivity patterns that can facilitate contour integration in the visual cortex. The model also suggests that different statistics of input presentations, and the resulting patchy lateral connection patterns, may be the cause for the different degrees of contour integration observed in the different visual areas. It should be possible to account for other low-level gestalt phenomena and also subjective contour effects with similar computational principles.

Acknowledgments.

This research was supported in part by National Science Foundation under grant #IRI-9811478.

References

Blasdel, G. G., and Salama, G. 1986. Voltage-sensitive dyes reveal a modular organization in monkey striate cortex. *Nature* 321:579–585.

Blasdel, G. G. 1992. Orientation selectivity, preference, and continuity in monkey striate cortex. *Journal of Neuroscience* 12:3139–3161.

Choe, Y., and Miikkulainen, R. 1998. Self-organization and segmentation in a laterally connected orientation map of spiking neurons. *Neurocomputing* 21:139–157.

Eckhorn, R.; Bauer, R.; Jordan, W.; Kruse, M.; Munk, W.; and Reitboeck, H. J. 1988. Coherent oscillations: A mechanism of feature linking in the visual cortex? *Biological Cybernetics* 60:121–130.

Eckhorn, R.; Reitboeck, H. J.; Arndt, M.; and Dicke, P. 1990. Feature linking via synchronization among distributed assemblies: Simulations of results from cat visual cortex. *Neural Computation* 2:293–307.

Field, D. J.; Hayes, A.; and Hess, R. F. 1993. Contour integration by the human visual system: Evidence for a local association field. *Vision Research* 33:173–193.

Geisler, W. S., and Super, B. 2000. Perceptual organization of two-dimensional patterns. *Psychological Review* (*to appear*).

Hess, R. F., and Dakin, S. C. 1997. Absence of contour linking in peripheral vision. *Nature* 390:602–604.

Li, Z. 1998. A neural model of contour integration in the primary visual cortex. *Neural Computation* 10:903–940.

Miikkulainen, R.; Bednar, J. A.; Choe, Y.; and Sirosh, J. 1997. Self-organization, plasticity, and low-level visual phenomena in a laterally connected map model of the primary visual cortex. In Goldstone, R. L.; Schyns, P. G.; and Medin, D. L., eds., *Perceptual Learning*, volume 36 of *Psychology of Learning and Motivation*. San Diego, CA: Academic Press. 257–308.

Pettet, M. W.; McKee, S. P.; and Grzywacz, N. M. 1998. Constraints on long range interactions mediating contour detection. *Vision Research* 38:865–879.

Reinagel, P., and Zador, A. M. 1999. Natural scene statistics at the center of gaze. *Network: Computation in Neural Systems* 10:1–10.

Reitboeck, H.; Stoecker, M.; and Hahn, C. 1993. Object separation in dynamic neural networks. In *Proceedings of the IEEE International Conference on Neural Networks* (San Francisco, CA), volume 2, 638–641.

Rubin, N.; Nakayama, K.; and Shapley, R. 1996. Enhanced perception of illusory contours in the lower versus upper visual hemifields. *Science* 271:651–653.

Sheth, B. R.; Sharma, J.; Rao, S. C.; and Sur, M. 1996. Orientation maps of subjective contours in visual cortex. *Science* 274:2110–2115.

Sirosh, J.; Miikkulainen, R.; and Choe, Y., eds. 1996. *Lateral Interactions in the Cortex: Structure and Function*. Austin, TX: The UTCS Neural Networks Research Group. Electronic book, ISBN 0-9647060-0-8, http://www.cs.utexas.edu/users/nn/web-pubs/htmlbook96.

Sirosh, J. 1995. *A Self-Organizing Neural Network Model of the Primary Visual Cortex*. Ph.D. Dissertation, Department of Computer Sciences, The University of Texas at Austin, Austin, TX. Technical Report AI95-237.

von der Malsburg, C., and Buhmann, J. 1992. Sensory segmentation with coupled neural oscillators. *Biological Cybernetics* 67:233–242.

Yen, C.-C., and Finkel, L. H. 1997. Identification of salient contours in cluttered images. In *Computer Vision and Pattern Recognition*, 273–279.

Yen, S.-C., and Finkel, L. 1998. Extraction of perceptually salient contours by striate cortical networks. *Vision Research* 38:719–741.

Anchoring Symbols to Sensor Data: preliminary report

Silvia Coradeschi and **Alessandro Saffiotti**
Center for Applied Autonomous Sensor Systems
Örebro University, S-70182 Örebro, Sweden
{silvia.coradeschi,alessandro.saffiotti}@tech.oru.se
http://www.aass.oru.se

Abstract

Anchoring is the process of creating and maintaining the correspondence between symbols and percepts that refer to the same physical objects. Although this process must necessarily be present in any physically embedded system that includes a symbolic component (e.g., an autonomous robot), no systematic study of anchoring as a problem *per se* has been reported in the literature on intelligent systems. In this paper, we propose a domain-independent definition of the anchoring problem, and identify its three basic functionalities: find, reacquire, and track. We illustrate our definition on two systems operating in two different domains: an unmanned airborne vehicle for traffic surveillance; and a mobile robot for office navigation.

Introduction

You are at a friend's house and your host asks you to go to the cellar and fetch the bottle of Barolo wine stored at the top of the green rack. You go down to the cellar, look around in order to identify the green rack, and visually scan the top of the rack to find a bottle-like object with a Barolo label. When you see it, you reach out your hand to grasp it, and bring it upstairs.

This vignette illustrates a mechanism that we constantly use in our everyday life: the use of words to refer to objects in the physical world, and to communicate a specific reference to another person. This example presents one peculiar instance of this mechanism, one in which the first person (the friend) "knows" which object he wants but cannot see it, while the second person (you) only has an incomplete description of the object, but can see it. Put crudely, the two persons embody two different types of processes: one that reasons about abstract representations of objects, and one that has access to perceptual data. One of the prerequisites for the successful cooperation between these processes is that they agree about the objects they talk about, that is, that there is a correspondence between the abstract representations and the perceptual data which refer to the same physical object. We call *anchoring* the process of establishing and maintaining this correspondence.

Not unlike our example, an autonomous system embedded in the physical world may need to incorporate processes that reason about abstract representations of the objects in the world, and processes that deal with the physical observation and manipulation of these objects. If the system has to successfully perform its tasks, it needs to make sure that these processes "talk about" the same physical objects: hence, this system needs to perform anchoring.

Consider for concreteness a mobile robot performing a delivery task and using a symbol system to reason about abstract knowledge. This may include knowledge about the object to be delivered, its location, and the structure of the environment. To execute its task, the robot must be able to connect (anchor) these symbols to the flow of perceptions generated by its sensors, in order to follow the right corridor, enter the right door, and fetch the right object.

Although this type of connection must necessarily take place in any symbolic reasoning system embedded in the physical world, the anchoring problem has received little attention in the fields of AI and autonomous robotics as a problem *per se*, and no work has been reported in that literature which analyzes this problem in a systematic way. Instead, anchoring is typically solved on a system-by-system basis, and the solution is hidden in the code. To our knowledge, the first general, although preliminary, definition of anchoring was reported in (Saffiotti 1994). More recently, the notion of anchoring has been extended in order to cope with some subtle issues encountered in real applications (Coradeschi, Karlsson, & Nordberg 1999), (Coradeschi & Saffiotti 1999) and (Saffiotti & LeBlanc 2000). Those studies were empirical in nature, leading to a pre-theoretical notion of anchoring. This paper is a first attempt to state the anchoring problem through a formal description of the entities and functionalities involved. These functionalities effectively define an interface between a perceptual and a symbolic system.

The next section gives an overview of related work. In the following sections, we first introduce our formal framework for anchoring, and then describe the corre-

Copyright © 2000, American Association for Artificial Intelligence (www.aaai.org). All rights reserved.

spondence between this framework and the implementation of the anchoring functionalities in two systems: an autonomous helicopter for traffic surveillance, and a mobile robot performing navigation tasks.

Anchoring in the literature

Although anchoring as defined in this paper has not been the subject of previous rigorous investigation, issues related to anchoring have been discussed in the fields of autonomous robotics, machine vision, linguistics, and philosophy.

The autonomous robotics literature contains a few examples in which the need and the role of anchoring, under different names, has been explicitly identified, e.g., (Hexmoor, Lammens, & Shapiro 1993), (Hutber et al. 1994), (Konolige et al. 1997), (Schlegel et al. 1999). Jung and Zelinsky (2000) use a similar concept to achieve grounded communication between robots. None of these works, however, pursue a systematic study of the anchoring problem. Bajcsy and Košecká (1994) offer a general discussion of the links between symbols and signals in mobile robotic systems. Yet, they do not deal with the problem of how to create and maintain these links, which is the main issue in anchoring.

The machine vision community has done much work on the problems of object recognition and tracking. While anchoring relies on these underlying perceptual abilities, it is mainly concerned with the integration of these with a symbol system. Some work in vision has explicitly considered the integration with symbols. Satoh et al. (1997) present a system which associates faces and names in news videos looking at co-occurrences between the speech and the video streams. Horswill's Ludwig system (Horswill 1997) answers natural language queries by associating linguistic symbols to markers and to marker operations in the image space. Interestingly, Ludwig may refer to physical objects using indexical terms, like "the block on the red block" (Agre & Chapman 1987). Markers are also used by Wasson et al. (2000) to provide a robot with a perceptual memory similar to the LPS of (Konolige et al. 1997). Markers are similar to the "anchors" that we introduce in this work. However, all the works above describe specific implementations and do not attempt a study of the general anchoring concept.

The problem of connecting linguistic descriptions of objects to their physical referents has been largely studied in the philosophical and linguistic tradition, e.g., (Frege 1892), (Russell 1905). In fact, we have borrowed the term *anchor* from situation semantics (Barwise & Perry 1983), where this term denotes an assignment of variables to individuals, relations, and locations. These traditions provide a rich source of inspiration for the conceptualization of the anchoring problem, but they typically disregard the formal and computational aspects necessary to turn these ideas into techniques.

The literature on the philosophical foundations of AI presents a wide debate on a problem which is related to anchoring: the *symbol grounding problem*, first stated by Harnard (1990). Symbol grounding is the problem of how to give an interpretation to a formal symbol system that is based on something that, contrary to classical formal semantics, is not just another symbol system. Anchoring is an important, concrete aspect of symbol grounding: connecting symbolic representations of specific objects to the perceptual image of these objects.

A computational theory of anchoring

The goal of this section is to make the pre-theoretic notion of anchoring given in the Introduction a precise one. We proceed as follows. We consider an agent that includes a symbol system and a perceptual system. Moreover, we assume the existence of a correspondence g between predicates in the former and *properties* measured by the latter. We do not make any assumption about the origin of g: for instance, g can be hand-coded by the designer of the system, or it can be learnt by the system using neural networks. The task of anchoring is to use this g to create and maintain a correspondence between a symbol used in the symbol system to denote an *object* in the world, and the percepts generated in the perceptual system by the same object. An *anchor* is a reification of this correspondence. Since new percepts are generated continuously within the perceptual system, this correspondence is indexed by time.

The underlying model

We now give formal definitions to the elements above. These will be illustrated with an example from one of our domains, in which the symbol 'car-1' has to be anchored to its perceptual counterpart in a camera image. We first introduce the elements that are time invariant.

- A *symbol system* Σ including: a set $\mathcal{X} = \{x_1, x_2, \ldots\}$ of individual symbols (variables and constants); a set $\mathcal{P} = \{p_1, p_2, \ldots\}$ of predicate symbols; and an inference mechanism whose details are not relevant here.

- A *perceptual system* Ξ including: a set $\Pi = \{\pi_1, \pi_2, \ldots\}$ of percepts; a set $\Phi = \{\phi_1, \phi_2, \ldots\}$ of attributes; and perceptual routines whose details are not relevant here. A percept is a structured collection of measurements assumed to originate from the same physical object; a attribute ϕ_i is a measurable property of percepts with values in the domain $D(\phi_i)$. We let $D(\Phi) =_{def} \bigcup_{\phi \in \Phi} D(\phi)$.

- A *predicate grounding relation* $g \subseteq \mathcal{P} \times \Phi \times D(\Phi)$, which embodies the correspondence between unary predicates and values of measurable attributes.

The set Π includes all the possible percepts, only some of which are realized at any given moment. The restriction to unary predicates is made here for simplicity and it will be relaxed in the future.

Example In our example, we have two individual symbols $\mathcal{X} = \{car1, car2\}$, and the predicate set is $\mathcal{P} = \{car, small, big, red, blue\}$. The percepts are the

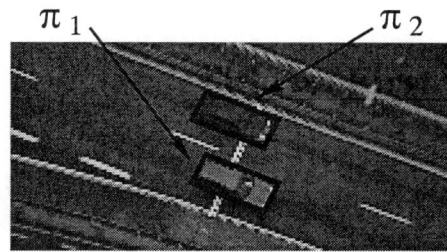

Figure 1: Two percepts π_1, π_2 in a camera image.

two image regions labeled π_1 and π_2 in Fig. 1. The set of attributes is $\Phi = \{type, color, shape\}$. The domain of *type* is the set of all recognizable objects, e.g., car;[1] the domain of *color* is the set of triples of possible hue, saturation, and luminosity values; and the domain of *shape* is the set of pairs of possible length and width values.

The *predicate grounding relation* g can be seen as a table that encodes the attribute values compatible with a certain predicate. For instance, we have:

$g(red, color, (h, s, l))$ iff $h \in [-30, 30], s \in [0, 1], l \in [0, 1].$

The g relation concerns properties, but anchoring concerns objects. The following definitions allow us to characterize objects in terms of their (symbolic and perceptual) properties.

Definition 1 *A symbolic description* $\sigma \in 2^{\mathcal{P}}$ *is a set of unary predicates.*

Definition 2 *A perceptual signature* $\gamma : \Phi \to D(\Phi)$ *is a partial function from attributes to attribute values. The set of attributes on which γ is defined is denoted by* $feat(\gamma)$.

Intuitively, a symbolic description lists the predicates that are considered relevant to the perceptual identification of an object; and a perceptual signature gives the values of the measured attributes of a percept (and it is undefined for the unmeasured ones).

The g relation can be used to match a symbolic description σ and a perceptual signature γ as follows.

$$match(\sigma, \gamma) \Leftrightarrow \forall p \in \sigma. \exists \phi \in feat(\gamma). g(p, \phi, \gamma(\phi)) \quad (1)$$

Other definitions for *match* could be used, this would not change the rest of our model.

Example An example of a *symbolic description* is $\sigma_1 = \{red, small\}$. A *perceptual signature* could be γ_1:

$\gamma_1 : color \mapsto (10, 1, 1)$ and $\gamma_1 : shape \mapsto (8, 4)$.

In this case, we have $feat(\gamma_1) = \{color, shape\}$. To see if σ_1 and γ_1 match, we must evaluate the following

$match(\sigma_1, \gamma_1) \Leftrightarrow$
$\bigl(g(red, color, (10, 1, 1)) \vee g(red, shape, (8, 4))\bigr) \wedge$
$\bigl(g(small, color, (10, 1, 1)) \vee g(small, shape, (8, 4))\bigr)$

The following is the time dependent part of the model.

- A *description state* $\Delta_t : \mathcal{X} \to 2^{\mathcal{P}}$ associates each individual $x \in \mathcal{X}$ with its symbolic description at time t.
- A *perceptual state* $S_t : \Pi \to (\Phi \to D(\Phi))$ associates each percept $\pi \in \Pi$ to its perceptual signature at time t. If π is not perceived at time t, then $S_t(\pi)$ is undefined for every $\phi \in \Phi$. The set of percepts which are perceived at t is denoted by V_t.

Δ_t and S_t are generated by the symbol system and by the perceptual system, respectively, and describe the current properties of the objects of discourse. The decision about what predicates and what perceptual signatures should be present in Δ_t and S_t is domain dependent. For the rest of this section, we assume that the above elements are all given and fixed.

We finally give our central definition.

Definition 3 *An anchor is any partial function α from time to triples in $\mathcal{X} \times \Pi \times (\Phi \to D(\Phi))$.*

An anchor is a unique internal representation of an object o in the environment. At every moment t, $\alpha(t)$ contains: a symbol meant to denote o; a percept generated by observing o; and a signature meant to provide the current (best) estimate of the values of the observable properties of o.

Example Suppose that at time t the *description state* is such that $\Delta_t : \text{car-1} \to \sigma_1$, and the *perceptual state* is such that $S_t : \pi_1 \to \gamma_1$. An *anchor* connecting these elements would then be $\alpha : t_1 \mapsto (\text{car-1}, \pi_1, \gamma_1)$.

We denote the components of $\alpha(t)$ by $\alpha_t^{sym}, \alpha_t^{per}$, and α_t^{val}, respectively. If the object is not observed at time t, then α_t^{per} is the 'null' percept $\emptyset$ (by convention, $\forall t, \emptyset \notin V_t$), while α_t^{val} still contains the best available estimate.

In order for an anchor to satisfy its intended meaning, the symbol and the percept in it should refer to the same physical object. This requirement cannot be formally stated inside the system. What can be stated is the following (recall that V_t is the set of percepts which are perceived at t).

Definition 4 *An anchor α is grounded at time t iff both $\alpha_t^{per} \in V_t$ and $match(\Delta_t(\alpha_t^{sym}), S_t(\alpha_t^{per}))$.*

We informally say that an anchor α is *referentially correct* if, whenever α is grounded at t, then the physical object denoted by α_t^{sym} is the same as the one that generates the perception α_t^{per}.

The anchoring problem, then, is the problem to find referentially correct anchors.[2]

---

[1] The *type* attribute may be treated in a special way by the perceptual system, since it determines the structure of the percept. In our example, "car" percepts are generated by the vision routines using a model of a car object.

[2] Another property that we may want an anchor α to satisfy is that the estimated values in α^{val} constitute a *good model* of the corresponding physical object. In this work, however, we concentrate on the reference problem.

The functionalities of anchoring

In order to solve the anchoring problem for a symbol x, we need the ability to: (i) create a grounded anchor the first time that the object denoted by x is perceived; (ii) continuously update the anchor while observing the object; and (iii) update the anchor when we need to reacquire the object after some time that it has not been observed. The following functionalities realize these abilities. (t denotes the time at which the functionality is called.)

Find Take a symbol x and return a grounded anchor α defined at t, and undefined elsewhere. In case of multiple matches, use a domain dependent selection function to choose one. This functionality is summarized by the following pseudo-code.

procedure Find (x)
$\quad \pi \leftarrow \text{Select}\{\pi' \in V_t \mid match(\Delta_t(x), S_t(\pi'))\}$
$\quad$ **if** $\pi = \emptyset$ **then** fail
$\quad\quad\quad$ **else** $\alpha(t) \leftarrow \langle x, \pi, S_t(\pi) \rangle$
$\quad$ **return** α

Instead of using Select, Find may return one anchor for each matching percept and leave the selection problem to the symbolic system, as we will see in the UAV application.

Reacquire Take a symbol x with an anchor α defined for $t - k$ and extend α's definition to t. First predict a new signature γ; then see if there is a new percept that is compatible with both the prediction and the symbolic description; if so, update γ. Prediction, verification of compatibility, and updating are domain dependent; verification should typically use *match*.

procedure Reacquire (x)
$\quad \alpha \leftarrow$ *anchor for x*
$\quad \gamma \leftarrow \text{Predict}(\alpha_{t-k}^{\text{val}}, x, t)$
$\quad \pi \leftarrow \text{Select}\{\pi' \in V_t \mid \text{Verify}(S_t(\pi'), \Delta_t(x), \gamma)\}$
$\quad$ **if** $\pi \neq \emptyset$ **then** $\gamma \leftarrow \text{Update}(\gamma, S_t(\pi), x)$
$\quad \alpha(t) \leftarrow \langle x, \pi, \gamma \rangle$
$\quad$ **return** α

If Reacquire fails to find a matching percept, then $\alpha(t)$ contains the predicted signature and the 'null' percept $\emptyset$. Note that in this case $\alpha(t)$ is not grounded. The Reacquire procedure is used to find an object when there is a previous perceptual experience of it. The prediction function may be complex: it may use domain knowledge like information about occluding objects, and generate multiple hypotheses for the predicted properties. The verify function checks that the attribute values of a percept are compatible with both the predicted γ and the descriptor $\Delta_t(x)$. The compatibility criteria are domain dependent

A special case of Reacquire deserves special attention: when the object is kept under constant observation. In this case, Prediction can often be greatly simplified. We define a separate functionality for this case.

Track Take an anchor α defined for $t - 1$ and extend its definition to t.

procedure Track (α)
$\quad x \leftarrow \alpha_{t-1}^{\text{sym}}$
$\quad \gamma \leftarrow \text{OneStepPredict}(\alpha_{t-1}^{\text{val}}, x)$
$\quad \pi \leftarrow \text{Select}\{\pi' \in V_t \mid \text{Verify}(S_t(\pi'), \Delta_t(x), \gamma)\}$
$\quad$ **if** $\pi \neq \emptyset$ **then** $\gamma \leftarrow \text{Update}(\gamma, S_t(\pi), x)$
$\quad \alpha(t) \leftarrow \langle x, \pi, \gamma \rangle$
$\quad$ **return** α

In our experience, these three functionalities, possibly combined together, have been sufficient to solve the anchoring problem in several domains. The next section will show two examples of their use.

Anchoring in practice

The work in anchoring has originated in our concrete experience with implementations of systems integrating symbolic and perceptual knowledge. The nature of the anchoring problem, in fact, suggests that a general study of it must be solidly grounded in experiments performed on different systems. Here, we show experiments performed on two platforms: a wheeled mobile robot, and a unmanned airborne vehicle (UAV).

The two experimental platforms share the use of a layered architecture to integrate abstract reasoning with perceptual and control processes. However, these platforms differ significantly in terms of sensory-motoric capabilities and domains of application. The mobile robot uses sonars as its main sensor modality and moves in an office environment. The main aspect of anchoring here is the need to link the symbols used by a planner to denote static objects, like corridors and doors, to the sensor data coming from the sonars. The UAV has been developed in the WITAS project (Doherty 1999), and it currently operates in a simulated environment. It uses vision as its main sensor and performs traffic surveillance over urban and rural areas. The main aspect of anchoring here is the need to connect the symbols used by a planner and a plan executor to the sensor data about specific cars provided by the vision system.

The robot navigation domain

Milou is a Nomad 200 robot equipped with an array of sonar sensors and controlled by an architecture similar to the one reported in (Saffiotti, Konolige, & Ruspini 1995), which includes a simple STRIPS-like planner. All the perceptual and prior information about the robot's surroundings are maintained in a blackboard-like structure called "Local Perceptual Space" (LPS). Symbolic descriptions, percepts, and anchors are all Lisp structures stored in the LPS.

In terms of our framework, the *symbol system* Σ is given by the planner; individuals symbols ($\mathcal{X}$) denote corridors and doors, and predicate symbols ($\mathcal{P}$) refer to position and width. The *perceptual system* Ξ extracts linear contours (segments) from consistent sets of sonar measurements; percepts (Π) include walls (individual

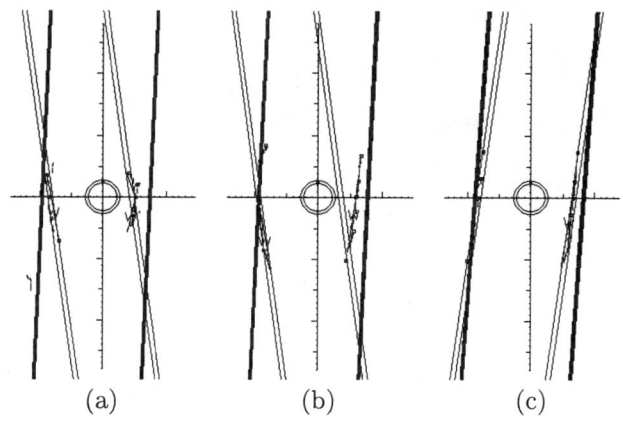

(a)　　　　　(b)　　　　　(c)

Figure 2: Anchoring a corridor. Thick line: description; 'w' segments: percepts; double line: anchor.

segments) and corridors (pairs of parallel segments); attributes (Φ) include position, orientation, length, and width. The *predicate grounding relation g* is hand-coded. Matching is done according to equation (1), with some extra provisions to take the measurement imprecision into consideration. Finally, an *anchor* is a structure containing pointers to the appropriate symbolic description, percept, and perceptual signature.

The planner puts the symbolic description of the objects to be used for a task into the LPS, based on map information. All the descriptors in the LPS are constantly anchored using **Find** (first time anchoring) and **Track** (afterwards). Both functionalities are implemented according to the general procedures above. In **Track**, prediction of relative position is based on the odometry of the robot, while updating is done by just copying the properties of the percept π. The Verify function is based on geometric distance. Select looks for the percept that best matches the predicted values γ; if no good match is found, it looks for a percept that best matches the symbolic description.

Fig. 2 shows an example in which Milou recovers from a erroneous initial anchoring of a corridor. The robot is shown in the middle, facing upwards. At time t_0 (a), the planner puts into the LPS the description of a corridor 'corr-1' that must be traversed (thick lines). **Find** matches this description with a corridor percept π_0 generated by observing a pair of parallel short wall segments (marked by 'w'), and creates an anchor α s.t. $\alpha(t_0) = (\text{corr-1}, \pi_0, \gamma_0)$, where the value of the position attribute in γ_0 is taken from π_0. This is shown by the double lines in the picture. Unfortunately, π_0 was generated by spurious sonar readings produced by a peculiar configuration of obstacles. As Milou moves further along the corridor, the **Track** routine predicts the new relative position γ_1; however, no percept matches this γ_1, and the α^{val} is only updated by prediction: $\alpha(t_1) = (\text{corr-1}, \emptyset, \gamma_1)$. Note that α is now ungrounded.

At time t_2 (b), a new percept π_2 is generated by the sonars' observing the actual walls. This percept does not match the new prediction γ_2, but it closely matches the original description. Therefore, π_2 is accepted by the Verify function and used to update the anchor (c): $\alpha(t_2) = (\text{corr-1}, \pi_2, \gamma_2)$, where the position of γ_2 is taken from π_2. The anchor is now referentially correct, and subsequent percepts will easily be matched, thus keeping α grounded.

The aerial surveillance domain

The UAV system integrates a planner, a reactive plan executor, a vision system and a control system. Anchoring is done in a dedicated module called Scene Information Manager (SIM) (Coradeschi, Karlsson, & Nordberg 1999). The SIM is intermediate between the plan executor and the vision system and handles the anchoring of symbolic identifiers used in the plan executor to sensory data produced in the vision processing component.

In terms of our formal model, the *symbol system* consists of the planner and the plan executor, both coded in Lisp. Individuals denote cars, while predicates denote linguistic terms (e.g., 'red') and positions in a road network (e.g., 'at-cross1').

The *perceptual system* is a reconfigurable active vision system able to extract information about objects in aerial images. Percepts are sets of adjacent pixels (regions) each having a HSL (hue, saturation, luminance) value. Attributes of interest include position, length, width, and color (average HSL values) of a region.

The *predicate grounding relation g* is given as a hand-coded table that associates each predicate to a set of admissible values for the corresponding attribute. For instance, the predicate 'red' is associated with a set of admissible HSL values for the attribute 'color.'[3]

Symbolic descriptions are tuples of predicates. The plan executor sends to the SIM the appropriate symbolic descriptions for the individual symbols that have to be anchored. For instance, if the executor is interested in finding Car1, a small red Mercedes at location cross-1, it sends to the SIM the list '(Car1 . (red small-Mercedes at-cross1))'. Note that while in the Milou testbed the anchoring module anchors all the objects in the LPS, the SIM only anchors the objects explicitly requested by the executor.

A *perceptual signature* is a list of attribute-value pairs. At each time step t, the vision system generates a perceptual state S_t based on information about the objects to look for. For instance, when asked to find all cars around location cross-1, the vision system (i) points the camera to cross-1, (ii) segments the image using a car model, and (iii) returns a set V_t of found regions, and a perceptual signature for each region.

Matching of symbolic descriptions and perceptual signatures is done according to (a fuzzy version of) (1).

---

[3] In the actual system, we use fuzzy sets to take into account vagueness of linguistic descriptions and uncertainty in vision data; we also use a fuzzy matching algorithm to compute a degree of matching (Coradeschi & Saffiotti 1999).

An *anchor* is a Lisp object that stores an individual symbol, the index of a region, and an association list recording the current estimates of the object's properties (shape, color, etc.)

The functionalities provided by the SIM are find, reidentify, and follow a car, described below. All these functionalities configure the vision system according to the properties of the object of interest.

FIND(x) is implemented by instantiating the general **Find** procedure, with the provision that there is no 'Select', but all the found anchors are returned, sorted by their degree of matching.

REIDENTIFY(x) is implemented by instantiating the general **Reacquire** procedure, with the provision that 'Predict' generates multiple hypothetical positions according to the configuration of the road network, and considers the effect of known occluding objects (both derived from a GIS).

FOLLOW(α) is implemented by combining the general **Track** and **Reacquire** procedures, which in turn are implemented as TRACK and REIDENTIFY, as follows.

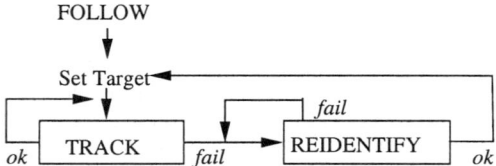

In TRACK, the 'OneStepPredict' and 'Update' functions are implemented as a Kalman filter (KF), which resides in the vision system. Its initial parameters are set according to the properties in α. The 'Verify' function checks the properties of the γ computed by the KF against a prediction of the possible properties based on domain knowledge. REIDENTIFY is repeatedly called when verification fails. It will search for a new percept for the anchor using more complex domain knowledge. When one is found, its properties are used to reset the parameters of the KF, and then continuous TRACKing is resumed.

Let us consider an example that illustrates the FOLLOW functionality. Two identical cars are present in the image, one traveling along a road which makes a bend under a bridge, and one which travels on the bridge — see Fig 3. The first car is being tracked by FOLLOW. The anchor has the form $\alpha(t_0) = (car\text{-}1, \pi_0, \gamma_0)$ where the perceptual signature γ_0 stores the attributes of π_0, in particular color, shape and position. At t_1 the car disappears under the bridge and the second car is almost in the position in the image where the first car would have been, had it not been occluded. The perceptual signature is updated, in particular the expected position of the car is extrapolated from the previously stored position. The percept provided by the vision is the region containing the car over the bridge. The Verify function compares the attributes of this percept with the updated perceptual signature. Given the information about the road network, the percept is discarded.

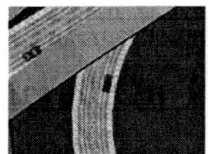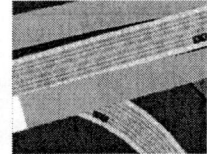

Figure 3: The followed car disappears under a bridge and a similar car appears at its place over the bridge.

Notice that the KF in TRACK, left by its own, would start tracking the car on the bridge. REIDENTIFY is called to try to find the car again. The anchor is ungrounded until an appropriate percept is found while the perceptual signature continues to be updated at every time point also using the knowledge about the road network. The REIDENTIFY uses knowledge about objects that can possibly occlude part of the road to detect the presence of the bridge. The vision system is directed toward the first visible position after the bridge. When the car reappears from under the bridge, a percept is generated by the vision system that is compatible with the perceptual signature present in the anchor. The anchor is grounded and the perceptual signature is updated with the attributes of the newly found percept. Normal tracking is then resumed.

Discussion

This paper makes two main contributions: (1) it defines the new concept of *anchoring* as a necessary component of any physically embedded symbolic system; and (2) it gives the basic ingredients needed to define the anchoring behavior of such a system, in terms of a formal model and of a set of functionalities. These functionalities rely on a number of building blocks, some of which, like the "match" and the "Predict" functions, may be complex. The study of these blocks is the subject of fields like pattern recognition, visual tracking, or estimation theory. Anchoring, by contrast, is concerned with the often underestimated problem of providing the semantic link between a perceptual system and a symbol system. It does so by combining these blocks into a general, coherent algorithmic structure.

In order to guarantee the generality of our theory, it is essential to test it on several applications. In this paper, we have done so in two substantially different ones. An interesting outcome has been the ability to deal with difficult tracking situations, like the bridge scenario, that require the integration of perceptual and symbolic knowledge. We believe that many of the systems discussed in the literature section could also be reformulated in our framework. We are currently working in applying our theory to other domains, including: the use of non-standard sensors like an artificial tongue and nose; the correspondence between a human provided map and a map built by a wheeled robot; and the RoboCup domain using the Sony legged robots (Saffiotti & LeBlanc 2000). In the first two cases the predicate grounding relation g is not hand-coded, but it is automatically acquired by the robot.

Our formalization is still preliminary, since in order to make this first step we had to ignore a number of subtle issues that are hidden in the anchoring problem. First is the issue of uncertainty. Perceptual information is inherently affected by uncertainty due to noise in the sensors, to poor observation conditions, and to errors in the perceptual interpretation. Anchoring should take this uncertainty into account, and consider the quality of the matching, for instance to decide to get a better view of an object. Second, we should consider the possibility to anchor a symbol to multiple percepts: this would be necessary in order to fuse the information coming from different sensors that observe the same objects. Finally, we should distinguish between *definite* descriptions, like "the bottle of Barolo on the table", *indefinite* descriptions, like "a bottle of Barolo", and *indexical* descriptions, like "the bottle on my left". These descriptions need different treatments. For instance, seeing two bottles of Barolo on the table is not a problem in the case of an indefinite description, but could be a problem in case of a definite one. Some of these issues have been investigated in our previous work, but a more formal treatment is needed.

We have not given a formal definition of the notion of an anchor being "referentially correct" in this first step. This is intentional. The theory presented here is internal to the agent, and can be computed by the agent. By contrast, referential correctness is an external notion, that should be studied by the designer once a formal model of the agent and one of the environment are available. Analyzing this notion is an important goal, that we leave as a future step.

Acknowledgements We are indebted to Dimiter Driankov, Ivan Kalaykov, and Lars Karlsson for fruitful discussions. This work has been partly funded by the Wallenberg Foundation, and partly by the Swedish KK foundation.

References

Agre, P., and Chapman, D. 1987. Pengi: an implementation of a theory of activity. In *AAAI-87*, 268–272.

Bajcsy, R., and Košecká. 1994. The problem of signal and symbol integration: a study of cooperative mobile autonomous agent behaviors. In *Proceedings of KI-95*, LNCS, 49–64. Berlin, Germany: Springer.

Barwise, J., and Perry, J. 1983. *Situations and Attitudes*. The MIT Press.

Coradeschi, S., and Saffiotti, A. 1999. Anchoring symbols to vision data by fuzzy logic. In Hunter, A., and Parsons, S., eds., *Qualitative and Quantitative Approaches to Reasoning with Uncertainty*, LNAI. Berlin, Germany: Springer. 104–115.

Coradeschi, S.; Karlsson, L.; and Nordberg, K. 1999. Integration of vision and decision-making in an autonomous airborne vehicle for traffic surveillance. In Christiansen, H. I., ed., *Computer Vision Systems*, 216–230. Berlin, Germany: Springer.

Doherty, P. 1999. The witas integrated software system architecture. Linköping Electronic Articles in Computer and Information Science, Vol. 4 (1999): no. 17. http://www.ep.liu.se/ea/cis/1999/017.

Frege, F. 1892. Über Sinn und Bedeutung. *Zeitschrift für Philosophie und philosophische Kritik* 25–50.

Harnard, S. 1990. The symbol grounding problem. *Physica D* 42:335–346.

Hexmoor, H.; Lammens, J.; and Shapiro, S. C. 1993. Embodiment in GLAIR: A grounded layered architecture with integrated reasoning for autonomous agents. In *Proc. of the Florida AI Research Sympos.*, 325–329.

Horswill, I. 1997. Visual architecture and cognitive architecture. *Journal of Experimental and Theoretical Artificial Intelligence* 9(2):277–292.

Hutber, D.; Moisan, S.; Shekhar, C.; and Thonnat, M. 1994. Perception-interpretation interfacing for the Prolab2 road vehicle. In *7th Symp. on Transportation Sys.: theory and Application of Advanced Technology*.

Jung, D., and Zelinsky, A. 2000. Grounded symbolic communication between heterogeneous cooperating robots. *Autonomous Robots* 8(3). In press.

Konolige, K.; Myers, K.; Ruspini, E.; and Saffiotti, A. 1997. The Saphira architecture: A design for autonomy. *Journal of Experimental and Theoretical Artificial Intelligence* 9(1):215–235.

Russell, B. 1905. On denoting. *Mind* XIV:479–493.

Saffiotti, A., and LeBlanc. 2000. Active perceptual anchoring of robot behavior in a dynamic environment. In *IEEE Int. Conf. on Robotics and Automation*.

Saffiotti, A.; Konolige, K.; and Ruspini, E. H. 1995. A multivalued-logic approach to integrating planning and control. *Artificial Intelligence* 76(1-2):481–526.

Saffiotti, A. 1994. Pick-up what? In Bäckström, C., and Sandewall, E., eds., *Current trends in AI Planning*. Amsterdam, Netherlands: IOS Press. 266–277.

Satoh, S.; Nakamura, Y.; and Kanade, T. 1997. Name-it: Naming and detecting faces in video by the integration of image and natural language processing. In *Proc. of IJCAI-97*, 1488–1493.

Schlegel, C.; Illmann, J.; Jaberg, H.; Schuster, M.; and Wötz, R. 1999. Integrating vision based behaviours with an autonomous robot. In Christiansen, H. I., ed., *Computer Vision Systems*, LNCS, 1–20. Springer.

Wasson, G.; Kortenkamp, D.; and Huber, E. 2000. Integrating active perception with an autonomous robot architecture. *IEEE Trans. on Robotics and Automation*. To appear.

Modeling Classification and Inference Learning

Bradley C. Love and **Arthur B. Markman**
[love,markman]@psy.utexas.edu
Department of Psychology - MEZ 330
The University of Texas at Austin
Austin, TX 78712

Takashi Yamauchi
takashi+@pitt.edu
3939 O'hara St. Rm 815
LRDC, University of Pittsburgh
Pittsburgh, PA 15260

Abstract

Human categorization research is dominated by work in classification learning. The field may be in danger of equating the classification learning paradigm with the more general phenomenon of category learning. This paper compares classification and inference learning and finds that different patterns of behavior emerge depending on which learning mode is engaged. Inference learning tends to focus subjects on the internal structure of each category, while classification learning highlights information that discriminates between the categories. The data suggest that different learning modes lead to the formation of different internal representations. SUSTAIN successfully models inference and classification learning by developing different internal representations for different learning modes. Other models do not fare as well.

Introduction

Categorization is central to our mental lives. We use categories to order our experiences and to make predictions which in turn govern our behavior. This paper explores the relationship between classification and inference learning in order to increase the generality and applicability of models of human category learning. Unfortunately, the field seems to be moving in the opposite direction towards special purpose models of learning that are first and foremost models of classification learning (c.f., Schank, Collins, & Hunter, 1986).

In a typical classification learning experiment, the subject learns to assign simple geometric stimuli consisting of a few binary valued dimensions to one of two mutually exclusive artificial categories. On each trial, the subject infers the category membership of a stimulus item and then receives feedback indicating whether the category assignment was correct. Using the first four dimensions to represent size, texture, shape, and color respectively and the fifth dimension to represent the category label, a classification trial involving an object that is small, smooth, dark, and triangle-shaped

may be represented as (0 0 0 1 ?), while a trial involving an object that is large, rough, light, and square-shaped may be represented as (1 1 1 0 ?). Assuming the first item is in category "A" and the second item is in category "B", following feedback the item representations would be (0 0 0 1 0) and (1 1 1 0 1). In classification learning, subjects tend to focus on information that discriminates between the categories, receive feedback, search for rules and store exemplars that are exceptions to the rules, perform hypothesis testing, exhibit sharp drops in their error rates (all or none learning), and are consciously aware of the rules they are entertaining (c.f., Nosofsky, Palmeri, & McKinley, 1994). Clearly this task is not representative of the majority of real world learning situations. No single laboratory task can hope to address all facets of category learning.

Here, instead of focusing on classification learning, we examine the relationship between two closely related learning modes: classification and inference learning. Classification and inference learning are conceptually similar, but differ in that inference learning tends to focus subjects on the internal structure of each category as opposed to information that discriminates between the categories. In inference learning, subjects predict (i.e., infer) the value of an unknown stimulus dimension instead of predicting the category label as subjects do in classification learning (in inference learning, the category label is given on every trial). The unknown dimension varies from trial to trial such that on one trial a subject may infer the size of an item and on the next trial the subject may infer the shape of an item. Thus, a series of inference learning trials could be (0 1 1 ? 1), (? 0 0 1 0), (1 ? 1 0 0), (0 1 0 ? 0). Like classification learning, the subject is given feedback after making a response (i.e., both classification and inference learning are supervised; the "?" is replaced with a 0 or 1 following corrective feedback).

Yamauchi and Markman's data (1998), henceforth referred to as YM, suggest that inference and classification learning have different informational demands that result in different internal representations being acquired. YM argue that subjects performing classification are more likely to focus on stimulus dimensions that discriminate between categories, to perform hy-

Copyright © 2000, American Association for Artificial Intelligence (www.aaai.org). All rights reserved.

Table 1: The stimulus structure for Yamauchi and Markman's (1998) studies. The stimulus dimension were form, size, color, and position.

Category A	Category B
1110	0001
1101	0010
1011	0100
0111	1000

Table 2: The stimulus structure for Yamauchi et al.'s (2000) studies. The stimulus dimension were form, size, color, and position.

Category A	Category B
1111	1101
1100	0110
0011	1000

pothesis testing, and to store exemplars than they are when engaging in inference learning. YM argue that subjects in an inference learning task focus on the prototype of each category, which should make inference learning easier than classification learning for problems that have well defined prototypes. YM found that subjects master the family resemblance problem illustrated in Table 1 (a linear problem in which each category has an underlying prototype that separates the two categories) faster as an inference learning problem than as a classification learning problem. Subjects were also more sensitive to the underlying prototypes in inference learning. Interestingly, subjects engaging in inference learning followed by classification learning made fewer errors than the reverse order.

Recent results with non-linear categories support YM's conclusion that inference learning focuses subjects on the prototypes of each category, while classification learning focuses subjects on discriminating stimulus dimensions. Yamauchi, Love, and Markman (2000) found that a classification learning advantage arises when non-linear categories are used (the logical structure is shown in Table 2). In the case of non-linear categories, the prototype of each category is not sufficient to separate the categories. Therefore, focusing on the category prototypes should be detrimental and inference learning performance should suffer.

Even though the exemplars are the same in both inference and category learning and the information content of the trials is the same (treating the category label as another stimulus dimension), different representations and radically different patterns of performance emerge. There is no strong a priori reason to favor inference learning or classification learning over the other and therefore it is important to be able to account for data from both learning modes within a single category learning model.

YM report that Generalized Context Model (Nosofsky 1986), a type of exemplar model (e.g., Hintzman, 1986; Nosofsky, 1986; Kruschke, 1992), and the rational model (Anderson 1991) cannot account for their results. In the remainder of this paper, we evaluate whether SUSTAIN (Supervised and Unsupervised STratified Adaptive Incremental Network) can model the results successively. SUSTAIN has successfully modeled classic studies of classification learning, learning at different levels of abstraction as expertise varies, sorting tasks, and unsupervised learning using the same set of parameters (Love & Medin 1998a; 1998b). If SUSTAIN can account for YM's findings, it would represent an important step towards a unifying model of human category learning that could be applied to a variety of learning modes (e.g., classification, inference, and unsupervised category learning). To foreshadow the results, SUSTAIN can capture inference learning using the same parameters used to model classification learning and its solution is consistent with YM's interpretation of their results. SUSTAIN also predicts the reversal that Yamauchi et al. (2000) observed with non-linear categories.

Overview of SUSTAIN

SUSTAIN is a clustering model that adaptively modifies its architecture during learning. When items are clustered together inappropriately (i.e., similar items from incompatible categories are placed in the same cluster), SUSTAIN adds a new cluster in memory to encode the misclassified item. For example, if SUSTAIN is applied to stimulus items and classifies them as members of the category mammal or the category bird it will develop one or more clusters (i.e., prototypes) for the bird category and one or more clusters for the mammal category. When SUSTAIN classifies a bat for the first time, the bat item will strongly activate a bird cluster because bats are similar to birds (both bats and birds are small, have wings, and fly). After incorrectly classifying the bat as a bird, SUSTAIN will create a new cluster to encode the misclassified bat item. The next time SUSTAIN classifies a bat, this new cluster will compete with the other clusters and will be the most strongly activated cluster (i.e., it will be more similar to the current stimulus than any other cluster), leading SUSTAIN to correctly classify the novel bat as a mammal and not as a bird. The new cluster would then become a bat prototype (a subcategory of mammal). Categories in SUSTAIN consist of one or more clusters (i.e., subcategories).

The method for adding units in SUSTAIN is psychologically motivated by the intuition that people ignore differences when they can (a bias towards simple solutions), but will note differences when forced to by environmental feedback (Medin, Wattenmaker, & Michalski, 1987; Ahn & Medin, 1992). At a more general level, SUSTAIN (like the ARTMAP model of Carpenter, Grossberg, and Reynolds, 1991) expands its architecture when observed inputs do not match top down expectancies.

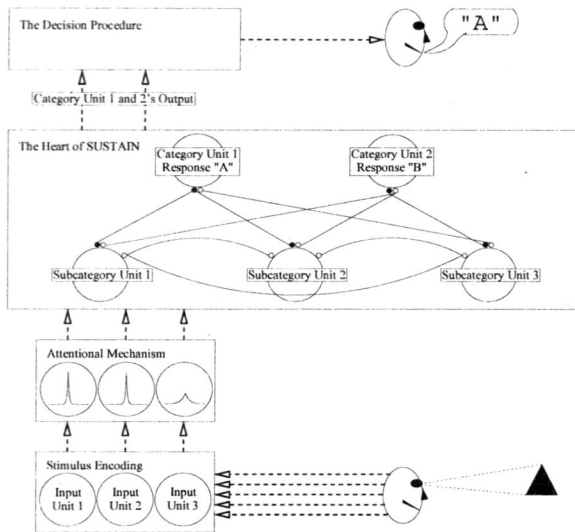

Figure 1: SUSTAIN's architecture is shown. Connections terminating in open circles are inhibitory connections while connections terminating in solid circles are excitatory. Arrows are intended to illustrate information flow.

SUSTAIN's Architecture

SUSTAIN consists of four layers: input, attention, subcategory, and category (see Figure 1). Input layer units take on real values to encode information about the environment (e.g., the encoding of a stimulus item that needs to be classified as a member of category "A" or "B"). In Figure 1, there are three binary valued stimulus dimensions represented by three input units. The three dimensions are dimension 1: size (small or large), dimension 2: shape (triangle or square), and dimension 3: luminance (light or dark). For example, the third input unit represents the luminance of a stimulus: a value of 0 denotes a light object, while a value of 1 denotes a dark object. The attention mechanism weights dimensions, making dimensions that are critical to classification more salient (SUSTAIN learns which dimensions to attend to). The implementation of the attentional mechanism is inspired by the operation of neuronal receptive fields. Each dimension has a receptive field. Dimensions that provide reliable information, and therefore are highly attended, develop peaked and narrow receptive fields (i.e., they develop a sharp tuning). In Figure 1, the first two dimensions (i.e., size and shape) are highly attended.

Units in the subcategory layer encode the prototypes and exceptions of the category units (i.e., the categories' clusters). SUSTAIN does not make a distinction between encoding exceptions and prototypes. A subcategory unit encoding a prototype is simply a unit that responds strongly to multiple items (i.e., input patterns) while a subcategory unit encoding an exception only responds strongly to one item. In Figure 2, two subcategory units are dedicated to representing category "A". These two units (subcategory units 1 and 2) have an excitatory connection to the category unit representing response "A" (each subcategory unit predicts response "A" when strongly activated). Only subcategory unit 3 is used to represent category "B". Subcategory units compete with one another to respond to patterns at the input layer (notice the inhibitory connections between subcategory units) with the winner being reinforced. The winning subcategory unit is the unit that is most highly activated by the current input pattern (i.e., the subcategory unit that is the most similar to the current stimulus). A subcategory unit is highly activated when an input pattern falls close to it in representational space. For example if a subcategory unit is centered at the point (.9, .8, .1) in three dimensional representational space, the majority of the clusters members would be large, square, and light. Therefore, a large lightly colored square would highly activate the cluster. When a subcategory unit is highly activated and "wins", it moves closer to the current input pattern (according to the Kohonen, 1984, unsupervised learning rule), minimizing the distance between its position and the input pattern. In effect, the correction makes the prototype more similar to the current input pattern (the cluster position is a running average of each member's position).

One novel aspect of SUSTAIN is that this unsupervised learning procedure is combined with a supervised procedure. When a subcategory unit responds strongly to an input pattern (i.e., it is the winner) and has an excitatory connection to the inappropriate category unit (e.g., the subcategory unit predicts "A" and the correct answer is "B"), the network shuts off the subcategory unit and recruits a new subcategory unit that responds maximally to the misclassified input pattern (i.e., the new unit is centered upon the input pattern). The process continues with the new unit competing with the other subcategory units to respond to input patterns. As previously stated, the winner's position is updated, as well as its connections to the category units by the one layer delta learning rule (Rumelhart, Hinton, & Williams, 1986). For example, if subcategory unit 1 is the winner, its connection to category unit 1 would be incremented, while its connection to category unit 2 would be decremented (i.e., it would become more negative). At a minimum, there must be as many subcategory units as category units when category responses are mutually exclusive.

In SUSTAIN, inference learning is assumed to engage the same processes as classification learning, though different internal representations (i.e., clusters) can emerge depending on which learning mode is engaged. A category unit is constructed for each dimension that is inferred in training (analogous to how a category unit is constructed for each category label that is inferred in classification learning). When an incorrect prediction is made (think back to the bats/birds/mammals example), a new subcategory unit (i.e., cluster) is recruited in the same fashion as in classification learning. The unknown stimulus dimension is simply ignored by SUSTAIN for the purposes of subcategory unit activation. After feedback is provided, the missing stimulus information is filled in for the purposes of learning.

Mathematical Formulation

Receptive fields (which implement the attentional mechanism) have an exponential shape with a receptive field's response decreasing exponentially as distance from its center increases:

$$\alpha(\mu) = \lambda e^{-\lambda \mu} \quad (1)$$

where λ is the tuning of the receptive field, μ is the distance of the stimulus from the center of the field, and $\alpha(\mu)$ denotes the response of the receptive field to a stimulus falling μ units from the center of the field. The choice of exponentially shaped receptive fields is motivated by Shephard's (1987) work on stimulus generalization.

While receptive fields with different λ have different shapes, for any λ, the area "underneath" a receptive field is constant:

$$\int_0^\infty \alpha(\mu) d\mu = \int_0^\infty \lambda e^{-\lambda \mu} d\mu = 1. \quad (2)$$

For a given μ, the λ that maximizes $\alpha(\mu)$ can be computed by differentiating:

$$\frac{\partial \alpha}{\partial \lambda} = e^{-\lambda \mu}(1 - \lambda \mu). \quad (3)$$

These properties of exponentials prove useful in formulating SUSTAIN.

The activation of a subcategory unit is given by:

$$A_{H_j} = \frac{\sum_{i=1}^n (\lambda_i)^r e^{-\lambda_i \mu_{ij}}}{\sum_{i=1}^n (\lambda_i)^r} \quad (4)$$

where A_{H_j} is the activation of the jth subcategory unit, n is the number of input units, λ_i is the tuning of the receptive field for the ith input dimension, μ_{ij} is the distance between subcategory unit j's position in the ith dimension and the output of the ith input unit (distance is simply the absolute value of the difference of these two terms), and r is an attentional parameter (always nonnegative). When r is high, input units with tighter tunings (units that seem relevant) dominate the activation function. Dimensions that are highly attended to have larger λs and will have greater importance in determining the subcategory units' activation values. Increasing r simply accentuates this effect. If r is set to zero, every dimension receives equal attention. Equation 4 sums the responses of the receptive fields for each input dimension and normalizes the sum (again, highly attended dimensions weigh heavily). The activation of a subcategory unit is bound between 0 (exclusive) and 1 (inclusive).

Subcategory units compete to respond to input patterns and in turn inhibit one another. When many subcategory units are strongly activated, the output of the winning unit is less. Units inhibit each other according to:

$$O_{H_j} = \frac{(A_{H_j})^\beta}{\sum_{i=1}^m (A_{H_i})^\beta} A_{H_j} \quad (5)$$

where β is the lateral inhibition parameter (always nonnegative) and m is the number of subcategory units. When β is small, competing units strongly inhibit the winner. When β is high the winner is weakly inhibited. Units other than the winner have their output set to zero. Equation 5 is a straightforward method for implementing lateral inhibition. It is a high level description of an iterative process where units send signals to each other across inhibitory connections. Psychologically, Equation 5 signifies that competing alternatives will reduce confidence in a choice (reflected in a lower output value).

Activation is spread from the winning subcategory unit to the category units:

$$A_{C_k} = O_{H_j} w_{jk} \quad (6)$$

where A_{C_k} is the activation of the kth category unit and O_{H_j} is the output of the winning subcategory unit. A winning subcategory unit (especially one that did not have many competitors and is similar to the current input pattern) that has a large positive connection to a category unit will strongly activate the category unit.

The output of a category unit is given by:

if (C_k is nominal and $|A_{C_k}| > 1$), then $O_{C_k} = \frac{A_{C_k}}{|A_{C_k}|}$
else $O_{C_k} = A_{C_k}$
$$(7)$$

where O_{C_k} is the output of the kth category unit. If the feedback given to subjects concerning C_k is nominal (e.g., the item is in category "A" not "B"), then C_k is nominal. Kruschke (1992) refers to this kind of teaching signal as a "humble teacher" and explains when its use is appropriate.

The following equation introduced by Ashby & Maddox (1993) determines the response probabilities (for nominal classifications):

$$Pr(k) = \frac{(O_{C_k} + 1)^d}{\sum_{i=1}^p (O_{C_i} + 1)^d} \quad (8)$$

where $Pr(k)$ is the probability of making the kth response, d is a response parameter (always nonnegative) and p is the number of category units. When d is high, accuracy is stressed and the category unit with the largest output is almost always chosen. In Equation 8, one is added to each category unit's output to avoid performing calculations over negative numbers. The Luce choice rule is a special case ($d = 1$) of this decision rule (Luce, 1959).

After feedback is provided by the "experimenter", if the winner predicts the wrong category, its output is set to zero and a new unit is recruited:

for all j and k, if ($t_k w_{jk} < 0$), then recruit a new unit
$$(9)$$

where t_k is the target value for category unit k and w_{jk} is the weight from subcategory unit j to category unit k. For example, if the target value of category unit 1 is -1 (i.e., not present) and the winning subcategory unit has a positive connection to category unit 1, the target values times the weight will be negative and a new subcategory unit will be recruited. When a new unit is recruited it is centered on the misclassified input pattern and the subcategory units' activations and outputs are recalculated. The new unit then becomes the winner because it will be the most highly activated subcategory unit (it is centered upon the current input pattern).

The position of the winner is adjusted:

$$\Delta w_{ij} = \eta(O_{I_i} - w_{ij}) \tag{10}$$

where η is the learning rate, O_{I_i} is the output of input unit i. The centers of the winner's receptive fields move towards the input pattern according to the Kohonen learning rule. This learning rule centers the prototype (i.e., the cluster's center) amidst its members.

Using our result from Equation 3, receptive field tunings are updated according to:

$$\Delta \lambda_i = \eta e^{-\lambda_i \mu_{ij}} (1 - \lambda_i \mu_{ij}). \tag{11}$$

Only the winning subcategory unit updates the value of λ_i. Equation 11 adjusts the shape of the receptive field for each input so that each input can maximize its influence on subcategory units. Initially, λ_i is set to be broadly tuned. For example, if input unit i takes on values between 0 and 1, the maximum distance between the ith input unit's output and the position of a subcategory unit's on the ith dimension is 1, so λ_i is set to 1 because that is the optimal setting of λ_i for μ equal to 1 (i.e., Equation 11 equals zero). Under this scheme, λ cannot become negative.

When a subcategory unit is recruited, weights from the unit to the category units are set to zero. The one layer delta learning rule (Rumelhart et al., 1986) is used to adjust these weights:

$$\Delta w_{jk} = \eta(t_k - O_{C_k})O_{H_j} \tag{12}$$

where t_k is the target value (i.e., the correct value) for category unit k. The target value is analogous to the feedback provided to human subjects. Note that only the winner will have its weights adjusted since it is the only subcategory unit with a nonzero output.

Table 3 lists all of SUSTAIN's parameters and the values used for the studies included in this paper and all cited studies. Unfortunately, it is unusual for a model of human learning to use the same set of parameters across a variety of studies. In this line of research, we focus on drawing conceptual links between diverse data sets and capturing qualitative patterns of performance.

Modeling Results

As foreshadowed, SUSTAIN successfully fits YM's data on a family resemblance problem (see Table 1). In inference learning, human subjects required 7.9 learning

Table 3: SUSTAIN's parameters.

function	name/value
learning rate	$\eta = .1$
cluster competition	$\beta = 1.0$
attentional focus	$r = 3.5$
decision consistency	$d = 8.0$

blocks on average to reach the learning criterion compared to 12.5 blocks in classification learning.[1] SUSTAIN displayed the same qualitative pattern, requiring 10.8 learning blocks for inference learning and 16.8 learning blocks for classification learning.

SUSTAIN is an incremental clustering model and can come up with different solutions for different item orderings. SUSTAIN's modal solution (over 80% of simulations) in inference learning involved one cluster per category (i.e., one subcategory unit per category). The one cluster was the underlying prototype of the category. SUSTAIN's modal solution is in accord with YM's assertion that inference learning focuses subjects on the underlying prototype of each category. Attention was evenly spread across all four perceptual dimensions and was highest for the category label dimension (in inference learning the category label is presented with every stimulus). Other solutions involved between three and six clusters with the frequency of the solution decreasing with the number of clusters involved. These solutions arose when item ordering was not advantageous.

In classification learning, SUSTAIN's modal solution (over 60% of simulations) involved three clusters per category. In accord with YM's analysis of human subjects, SUSTAIN created imperfect "rule" clusters (i.e., a cluster that captures some regularity along one or two dimensions that helps discriminate between the two categories) and attention was focused along the "rule" relevant dimensions. Exceptions to these "rule" clusters were captured by "exception" clusters (i.e., a cluster that has one stimulus item as a member). The modal solution in classification learning is less efficient than the one cluster per category solution (the modal solution in inference learning) because with six total clusters there tend to be a large number of highly activated competing clusters (subcategory units inhibit one another in SUSTAIN). Interestingly, approximately 1% of classification learning simulations displayed the one cluster per category solution. When this rare solution occurred in classification learning (due to an advantageous ordering of items), classification learning was as fast as the average inference learning simulation. This behavior allows SUSTAIN to successfully predict YM's finding that classification learning following inference learning should be easier than the reverse problem ordering. After completing inference learning and dis-

---

[1] A learning block involves each stimulus from Table 1 being presented once in a random order. The learning criterion was reached when average accuracy exceeded 90% for three consecutive learning blocks.

covering the two underlying prototypes, classification learning is trivial.

SUSTAIN also predicts that a classification learning advantage results when the category structure is non-linear (i.e., a category structure in which the underlying prototypes do not separate the categories), as it is in Yamauchi et al. (see Table 2). In inference learning, human subjects required 27.4 learning blocks on average to reach the learning criterion compared to 10.4 blocks in classification learning. SUSTAIN requires 25.6 blocks for inference learning and 15.3 for classification learning. The modal solution (60% of simulations) in classification learning involved three clusters per category (i.e., every item was memorized). In inference learning, the model solution involved nine clusters with the number of cluster required roughly normally distributed (ranging from four to sixteen clusters). SUSTAIN's focus on the prototype leads to prediction failures, which leads to many clusters being recruited. With this non-linear category structure, classification learning performance is roughly the same as in YM's studies, while inference learning performance suffers due to subjects' (and SUSTAIN's) focus on the prototype of each category.

Conclusions

Different learning modes can lead to radically different internal representations on learning problems that involve the same stimulus set and where learning trials have the same information content. In the case of classification learning, subjects focus on a limited number of dimensions and store exceptions to their classification "rule". In contrast, inference learning promotes a focus on the underlying category prototypes. SUSTAIN successfully addresses this data, but other models that do not create different internal representations for different learning modes (such as exemplar models) cannot account for the results. The idea that different representations can emerge from different tasks that involve the same exemplars helped SUSTAIN address another data set in which face experts (i.e., adult humans) learned to identify photographs of faces more easily than they could learn to assign each face to one of two categories (Medin, Gerald, & Murphy, 1983; Love & Medin, 1998a). Exemplar models also have difficulty fitting this data set. By fitting human learning data from a variety of learning modes (classification, inference, and unsupervised category learning), SUSTAIN shows promise as a unifying model of human category learning.

References

Ahn, W. K., and Medin, D. L. 1992. A two-stage model of category construction. *Cognitive Science* 16(1):81–121.

Anderson, J. 1991. The adaptive nature of human categorization. *Psychological Review* 98:409–429.

Ashby, F. G., and Maddox, W. T. 1993. Relations between prototype, exemplar, and decision bound models of categorization. *Journal of Mathematical Psychology* 37:372–400.

Carpenter, G. A.; Grossberg, S.; and Reynolds, J. H. 1991. ARTMAP: Supervised real-time learning and classification of nonstationary data by a self-organizing neural network. *Neural Networks* 4:565–588.

Hintzman, D. L. 1986. Schema abstraction in a multiple-trace memory model. *Psychological Review* 93(4):411–428.

Kohonen, T. 1984. *Self-Organization and Associative Memory.* Berlin, Heidelberg: Springer. 3rd ed. 1989.

Kruschke, J. K. 1992. ALCOVE: An exemplar-based connectionist model of category learning. *Psychological Review* 99:22–44.

Love, B. C., and Medin, D. L. 1998a. Modeling item and category learning. In *Proceedings of the 20th Annual Conference of the Cogntive Science Society*, 639–644. Mahwah, NJ: Lawrence Erlbaum Associates.

Love, B. C., and Medin, D. L. 1998b. SUSTAIN: A model of human category learning. In *Proceedings of the Fifteenth National Conference on Artificial Intelligence*, 671–676. Cambridge, MA: MIT Press.

Luce, R. D. 1959. *Individual choice behavior: A theoretical analysis.* Westport, Conn.: Greenwood Press.

Medin, D. L.; Dewey, G. I.; and Murphy, T. D. 1983. Relationships between item and category learning: Evidence that abstraction is not automatic. *Journal of Experimental Psychology: Learning, Memory, & Cognition* 9:607–625.

Medin, D. L.; Wattenmaker, W. D.; and Michalski, R. S. 1987. Constraints and preferences in inductive learning: An experimental study of human and machine performance. *Cognitive Science* 11(3):299–339.

Nosofsky, R. M.; Palmeri, T. J.; and McKinley, S. C. 1994. Rule-plus-exception model of classification learning. *Psychological Review* 101(1):53–79.

Nosofsky, R. M. 1986. Attention, similairty, and the identification-categorization relationship. *Journal of Experimental Psychology: General* 115:39–57.

Rumelhart, D. E.; Hinton, G. E.; and Williams, R. J. 1986. Learning representations by back-propagating errors. *Nature* 323:533–536.

Schank, R. C.; Collins, G. C.; and Hunter, L. E. 1986. Transcending inductive category formation in learning. *Behavioral and Brain Sciences* 9:639–686.

Shepard, R. N. 1987. Toward a universal law of generalization for psychological science. *Science* 237:1317–1323.

Yamauchi, T., and Markman, A. B. 1998. Category learning by inference and classification. *Journal of Memory and Language* 39:124–149.

Yamauchi, T.; Love, B. C.; and Markman, A. B. 2000. manuscript in preparation.

Reading a Robot's Mind:
A Model of Utterance Understanding based on the Theory of Mind Mechanism

Tetsuo Ono   Michita Imai
ATR Media Integration & Communications Research Laboratories
2-2 Hikaridai, Seikacho, Sorakugun, Kyoto, 619-0288 JAPAN
{tono, michita}@mic.atr.co.jp

Abstract

The purpose of this paper is to construct a methodology for smooth communications between humans and robots. Here, focus is on a *mindreading* mechanism, which is indispensable in human-human communications. We propose a model of utterance understanding based on this mechanism. Concretely speaking, we apply the model of a mindreading system (Baron-Cohen 1996) to a model of human-robot communications. Moreover, we implement a robot interface system that applies our proposed model. Psychological experiments were carried out to explore the validity of the following hypothesis: by reading a robot's mind, a human can estimate the robot's intention with ease, and, moreover, the person can even understand the robot's unclear utterances made by synthesized speech sounds. The results of the experiments statistically supported our hypothesis.

Introduction

In our everyday communications, we unconsciously attempt to read the minds of other people while trying to understand what they are saying. That is, *mindreading* is a daily activity of humans used to estimate the mental states of others by means of observing their behaviors. Recently, research has been actively carried out on such mindreading in communications due to the recognition of its importance (Premack & Dasser 1991; Baron-Cohen 1996). In addition, the general framework for such research is called "Theory of Mind."

We show concretely that the ability of mindreading is essential for a social being to communicate with others. For example, let us assume that A and B are two persons. Person A, who is carrying some bags in his arms, turns his eyes to B and utters words that are unclear speech sounds. B also turns his eyes to A, meeting A's eyes. Afterwards, A turns his eyes in the direction of his own movement. As B turns his eyes in the same direction simultaneously, he detects an object. B then recognizes the object as an obstacle for A by reading his own mental states of desire and goal. Finally, B understands A's utterance despite his unclear speech sounds and subsequently removes the object. As mentioned above, we can daily observe such reciprocal acts when communicating with others by the reading of intentions, desires, and goals.

Even in communications between humans and robots, such mindreading is indispensable for reciprocal acts. This is because we often judge synthesized speech sounds from artifacts to be strange, and we occasionally find the sounds hard to understand. We will not be able to communicate with robots smoothly as long as we do not make the reasons clear. If we do not assume the reciprocal acts mentioned above, it is possible to model communications as a "code model." A code model is a framework of signal transmission where a sender gives information (signals) to a receiver using a presupposed common code for encoding and decoding and then alternates turns within a given time. A code model, however, is unable to grasp essential qualities in communications involving humans. This is because humans cannot jointly own "code" with other entities in principle (Clark & Marshall 1981). Consequently, communications with humans cannot be grasped by transmitting restricted signal patterns.

To overcome the problem mentioned above, Sperber (Sperber & Wilson 1986) proposed bringing an "inference" viewpoint to the process of communications. In the relevance theory he proposed, humans communicate among themselves by inferring the minds of others. Certainly, this theory might approach the essence of human communications in overcoming the bottleneck of the code model. However, inference in the relevance theory can only be executed by mere "deductive" inference rules (Kimura 1997); therefore, this theory is equivalent to the code model if we regard the inference "rules" as a complicated "code." Moreover, this theory has the problem of technical terms in the theory not being connected through physical existence. These unsolved problems lower the theory's ability to explain actual communications.

The purpose of this paper is to construct a methodology for smooth communications between humans and robots by focusing on the mindreading mechanism. Es-

---

Copyright © 2000, American Association for Artificial Intelligence (www.aaai.org). All rights reserved.

pecially, we consider a mechanism of utterance understanding focusing on *sympathetic* and *embodied* inference and a viewpoint from an *internal observer* in communications. We first propose a model of utterance understanding based on the mindreading mechanism. Concretely speaking, we apply the model of a mindreading system (Baron-Cohen 1996) to a model of human-robot communications. Next, we implement a robot interface system that applies our proposed model. Third, we conduct psychological experiments to explore the validity of the following hypothesis: **By reading a robot's mind, a human can estimate the robot's intention with ease, and, moreover, the person can even understand the robot's unclear utterances made by synthesized speech sounds.** Finally, we discuss the validity of our model on the basis of the results of the experiments and conclude the paper.

Understanding a Robot's Utterance

In this chapter, we propose a model of utterance understanding and a robot interface model based on a mindreading mechanism.

"Mindreading System" and Model of Utterance Understanding

In this section, we propose a Model of Utterance Understanding based on the Theory of Mind Mechanism (**MUUToMM**). The left-hand side of Figure 1 shows an outline of MUUToMM. Concerning the theory of mind, Baron-Cohen is constructing the most detailed theoretical model known at present (Baron-Cohen 1996). This model of a *mindreading system* assumes the following four modules relevant to each other but functionally independently.

- Intentionality Detector (**ID**): This module is a perceptual device that interprets motion stimuli in terms of the primitive volitional mental states of goal and desire.
- Eye-Direction Detector (**EDD**): This module detects the presence of eyes and computes where the eyes are directed.
- Shared Attention Mechanism (**SAM**): This module builds triadic representations that specify that Self and Other are both attending to the same Object.
- Theory of Mind Mechanism (**ToMM**): This module infers the full range of mental states from behaviors.

Among these modules, **ID** and **EDD** are modules concerning dyadic relations, while **SAM** and **ToMM** are modules concerning triadic (or more) relations. These modules perform an important role in reciprocal acts, that is, reading the minds of others in communications.

In our proposed model MUUToMM, the following module functions by the activation of the above modules.

- Utterance Understanding Mechanism (**UUM**): This module is a system for understanding the utterances

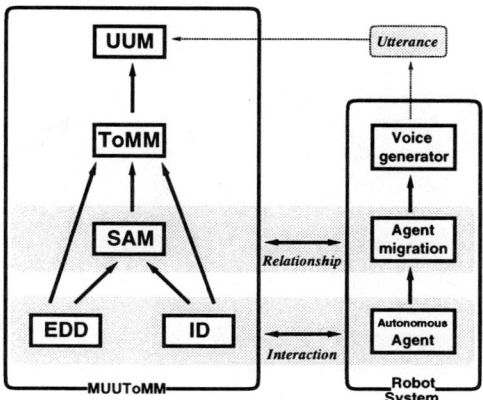

Figure 1: Outline of a model of utterance understanding and corresponding robot system.

of others by dynamically interacting with the process of inference in **ToMM**.

Here, the process of understanding utterances in MUUToMM is carried out for the example described in the Introduction. Person A, who carries some bags in his arms, turns his eyes to B and utters words that are unclear speech sounds. B recognizes A as a *person* through the activation of **ID** and **EDD** by observing his behaviors mentioned above. After their eyes meet, A turns his eyes in the direction of his own movement. As B also turns his eyes in the same direction, he detects an object. This is the process of a triadic relation being constructed among A, B, and the object, which **SAM** enables them to construct. B, moreover, recognizes the object as an obstacle for A by using the function of **ToMM**. Finally, B comes to understand A's utterance by interacting with the estimated intention of A and deficient information in his utterance (**UUM**) and subsequently removes the object.

Our proposed model enables us to overcome the problems in the "code model" and the relevance theory. This is because our model considers a mechanism of utterance understanding in connection with *physical existence* and regards the *relationship* that emerges between a speaker and a hearer as important. In other words, our model can clarify the mechanism of human communications in the real world which cannot be completely reduced to "symbolic" inference. In the next chapter, we explore the validity of this model through psychological experiments.

Robot Interface System

In this section, we describe a robot interface system that applies the model of utterance understanding MUUToMM (the right-hand side of Figure 1). We use robots because we consider communications in the physical world where humans live and also because robots enable us to control parameters in experiments. A serious problem in human-robot communications is that humans and robots cannot construct relationships sim-

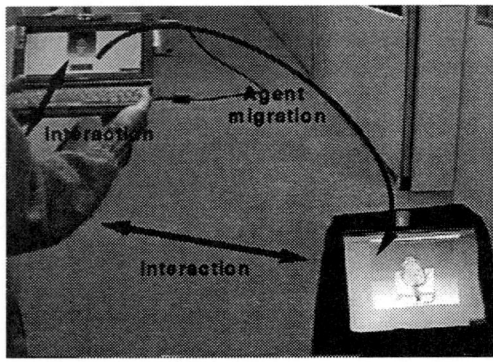

Figure 2: Outline of robot interface system.

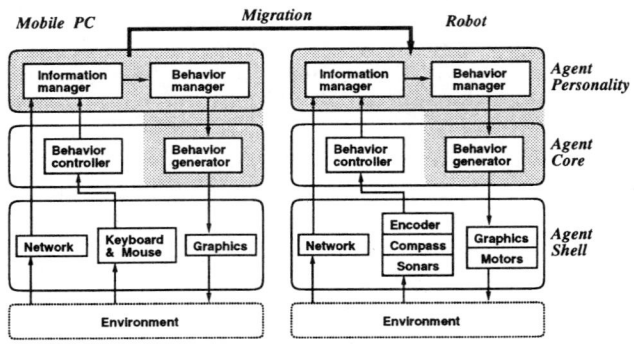

Figure 3: Structure of agent and mechanism for agent migration.

ilar to human-human ones, since humans do not regard robots as autonomous beings with intention (the human **ID** does not function) and do not call their attention (the human **SAM** does not function).

In our robot interface system, the functions of human **ID** and **EDD** are activated by an autonomous agent, and the function of **SAM** is activated by a mechanism of its agent migration (the shaded area of Figure 1 shows the corresponding relations). Figure 2 shows the implemented robot system. The following definitions are applied in our system.

- **Autonomous agent:** An agent in our system can behave autonomously because it adopts a model of Multi-Order Functions (MOF) (Ono & Okada 1998) as its internal model. We can observe both predictable and unpredictable behaviors of the agent because the MOF model spontaneously changes and consistently maintains the internal states while interacting with the environment. Accordingly, since each agent with the MOF model behaves autonomously while interacting with humans, the human **ID** and **EDD** become activated. The interaction in Figure 2 is similar to the interaction between a user and a digital pet.

- **Agent migration mechanism:** In our system, a mechanism of agent migration (Ono, Imai, & Etani 1999) enables the attention of a dyadic relation to be moved to a triadic one. Concretely speaking, an agent can migrate from a user's mobile PC to a robot. As a result of this migration, the robot can inherit the user's attention from the agent, enabling a relationship to form among the user, the robot, and an object along the direction of the robot's own movement (the human **SAM** becomes activated; Figure 2).

- **Voice generator:** The robot in our system can make utterances with synthesized speech sounds. Because synthesized sounds are used, we can freely set up parameters in the utterances such as intonation, accent, and clarity.

Implementation of Agent and Migration Mechanism

In this section, we briefly describe the structure of the agent and the mechanism for agent migration (Figure 3). The life-like agent consists of three layered components: an agent personality (AP), an agent core (AC), and an agent shell (AS), which can be rearranged dynamically. The AP has knowledge-based objects related to the user and environment, the AC has processing definitions for path-planning and behaviors, and the AS controls the physical resources of the network and the robot. In the process of migration, the AP and part of the AC, i.e., the shaded area of Figure 3, move from the mobile PC to the robot. An unpossessed robot can only move autonomously while obeying the set initial state.

In our experiments, we temporarily simplify the system setup, the interaction with the user, and the mechanisms of the agent and robot. This is because the aim of these experiments is basically to test whether subjects can understand the utterances of the robot under changing conditions and parameters. The interaction is like that between a user and a digital pet. The user first gives the agent a stimulus by clicking a mouse so that the agent changes its internal states. The agent changes the states by itself with a mechanism to generate autonomous and multiple behaviors (Ono & Okada 1998). Similarly, the agent's migration is simplified: the agent migrates from the mobile PC to the robot automatically under the experimental condition when the robot stops in front of an obstacle.

Experiments

In this chapter, we conduct experiments to test the validity of the proposed model of utterance understanding by using the implemented robot system.

Method

The experiments were conducted by the following method.

Subjects: Twenty-seven undergraduate and graduate students (male and female). The subjects were randomly divided into three groups: seven subjects were assigned for a preliminary experiment, ten for an experimental group, and ten for a control group.

Environment: Figure 4 shows an outline of the experimental setup. Points A-E in Figure 4 denote the positions of a robot, a subject, an experimenter, and an observer. The arrow from A to B is a trace of the robot. The subject's behavior is observed through a camera.

Preliminary experiment: For seven subjects, we examined their levels of understanding for three utterances made by synthesized speech sounds with changing sound parameters. We finally adopted one utterance for the experiments, which three subjects out of the seven understood. The content of the utterance is "Move the trash can out of my way."

Conditions: We prepared two conditions, which differed in their processes of interaction (*Interaction factor*). Under the experimental condition, the "character"[1] migrated from a mobile PC to a robot. Under the control condition, the character did not migrate. The subjects were distributed among the two conditions randomly. Moreover, the subjects psychologically evaluated the character and the robot by completing questionnaires (*Target factor*).

Procedure: The experiments consisted of the following four phases.

1. The subjects received the following instructions from the experimenter (position C): "This experiment is part of research concerning character design." The subjects, moreover, were taught a method to interact with the character on the mobile PC, and they actually practiced the operation for five minutes. After that, they psychologically evaluated the character through the questionnaires.

2. The experimenter told the subjects that he forgot to take a tool, and he moved from C to D in Figure 4.

3. Three minutes after leaving the experimenter, the robot approached the subject from A and stopped in front of the trash can (before that, the subject was unaware of the robot). Then, **under the experimental condition, the character migrated to the robot; meanwhile, under the control condition, it did not migrate.** The robot, moreover, gave the utterance that was adopted in the preliminary experiment. The content of the utterance was "Move the trash can out of my way."

---
[1]The word "agent" has various meanings in various fields. Accordingly, the more general word "character" is used in these experiments in consideration of the influence on the subjects.

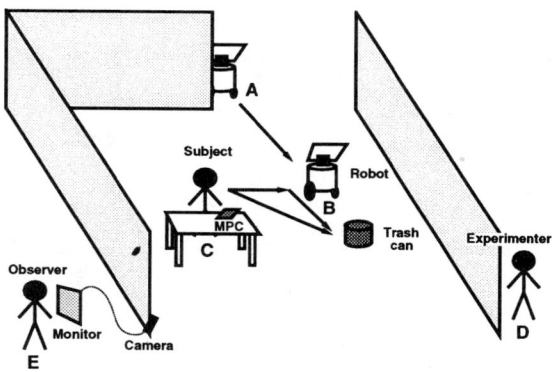

Figure 4: Experimental setup: arrangement of subject, observer, and robot.

4. The subjects psychologically evaluated the robot through the questionnaires when the experimenter came back to C two minutes later.

Evaluations: The results of the experiments were evaluated from the answers of the questionnaires and the record of the subjects' behaviors. In the questionnaires, the subjects were asked whether they understood the robot's utterance, why they behaved the way they did toward the robot, and to give a psychological evaluation of the character and the robot. In the evaluation, the subjects provided answers on a ten-point scale for two items: *Autonomy* and *Familiarity*, which are composed of the following three subitems respectively. The average score of each subitem was used in analyzing the results.

- Autonomy: Motivated ↔ Spiritless, Active ↔ Passive, Free ↔ Restricted
- Familiarity: Familiar ↔ Not familiar, Pleasant ↔ Trying, Kind ↔ Unkind

Hypothesis and Predictions

We put forward the following hypothesis: **By reading the mind of the robot to whom the agent migrated from the mobile PC, subjects under the experimental condition can estimate the robot's intention with ease. Moreover, the subjects can even understand the robot's unclear utterances made by synthesized speech sounds.** In the experiments, we aimed to verify the following three predictions derived from the hypothesis. Under the experimental condition compared with the control one,

Prediction 1: The subjects will regard the robot as an autonomous entity with intention (the function of **ID** and **EDD**).

Prediction 2: The subjects will first look at the robot and then turn their eyes to the trash can (the function of **SAM**).

Prediction 3: The subjects will be able to estimate the robot's intention with ease, and this will facili-

Table 1: Number of subjects who understood robot's utterance.

	Understanding	No-Understanding
Control	3	7
Experimental	8	2

Table 2: Number of subjects acting on robot's command.

	Acting	No-Acting
Control	1	9
Experimental	8	2

tate their understanding of the robot's utterance (the functions of **ToMM** and **UUM**).

Results of Experiments

In this section, we verify the three predictions on the basis of the results of the experiments. We verify them in the inverse order from prediction 3 to 1 to make the point of the argument clearer.

Verification of Prediction 3 First of all, we verified Prediction 3. In this experiment, we asked the subjects in the questionnaires whether they understood the robot's utterance. Table 1 shows the results for the number of subjects who understood it and those who did not under both conditions. In the analysis, a significant difference was found ($\chi^2 = 5.051, p < .05$). Accordingly, the difference between conditions (*Interaction factor*) had an effect on the subjects' understanding. In other words, **although the subjects understood to a large extent the utterance of the robot to which the agent migrated (Experimental condition), the subjects did not understand very well that of the robot to which the agent did not migrate (Control condition)**. To support this observation, almost all of the subjects who satisfied the robot's request were in the experimental group (Table 2). Figure 5 shows the appearance of a subject satisfying the robot's request, "Move the trash can out of my way." In contrast, Figure 6 shows the appearance of a subject not understanding the request. The difference between both conditions is caused by the agent migration because the utterance that all of the subjects received was the same synthesized speech sound utterance.

Verification of Prediction 2 Next, we verified Prediction 2. From the results of observations on the subjects' behaviors, we calculated the average time that they fixed their eyes on the robot and the trash can. From the results of the calculations, the average time of the experimental group was 33.7 seconds; in contrast, that of the control group was 28.1. However, we were unable to compare the times of both conditions simply because the time in the experimental group was only counted until the trash can was removed. Moreover, we

Figure 5: Photo of subject understanding robot's utterance.

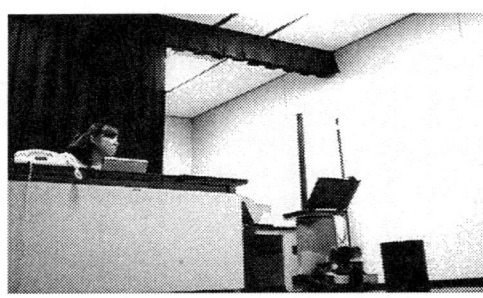

Figure 6: Photo of subject not understanding robot's utterance.

could not judge distinctly whether the subjects fixed their eyes on the robot or the trash can because we did not use a tracking device like an eye-camera.

Even considering these problems, however, we obtained evidence from the remarks in the questionnaires that all of the subject under the experimental condition noticed the trash can; however, half of the subjects under the control condition did not notice it. Accordingly, the former subjects turned their eyes from the robot to the trash can along the robot's running direction as the agent migrated; however, the latter subjects did not turn their eyes. It can be concluded that the agent migration prompted the subjects to turn their eyes because the only difference between the two conditions was this agent migration.

Verification of Prediction 1 Finally, we verified Prediction 1. We analyzed the results of the questionnaires to test whether the subjects regarded the robot as an autonomous entity with intention. In the analysis, we estimated the subjects' impressions of the robot by using two evaluation items, i.e., *Autonomy* and *Familiarity*, and their remarks. First, we tested whether the individual scores of the items in the questionnaires exhibited crossover interaction between the *Interaction factor* and *Target factor*. Consequently, crossover interaction was exhibited for *Autonomy* ($F(1, 18) = 14.223, p < .01$; Figure 7); additionally, a main effect was exhibited for the *Target factor*. Furthermore, crossover interaction was exhibited for *Familiarity* as well ($F(1, 18) = 9.31, p < .01$; Figure

Table 3: Summary of experimental results.

	Experimental	Control
Understanding the robot's utterance	Yes	No
Focusing on the trash box	Yes	Nearly all No
Considering the robot's intention	Yes	No

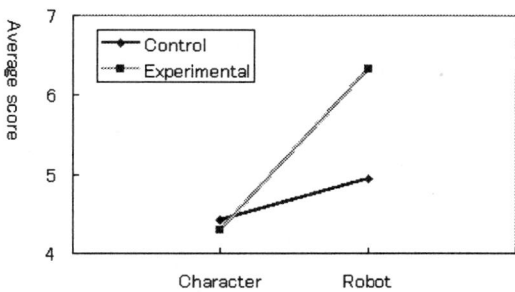

Figure 7: Interaction between two factors on *Autonomy*.

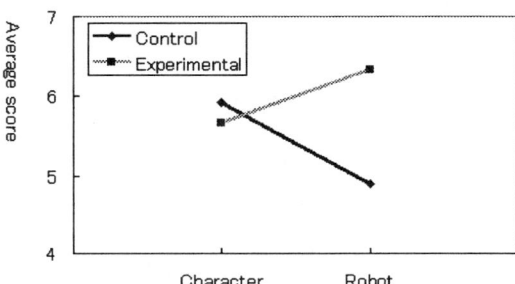

Figure 8: Interaction between two factors on *Familiarity*.

8); however, no main effect was exhibited.

In summary, as a result of migration, a robot can inherit the relationship from the interaction between a subject and an agent so that a relationship is formed between the subject and the robot. The questionnaires also asked the subjects who satisfied the robot's request why they did so. The subjects answered as follows: "I felt pity for the robot not going forward" and "The robot felt like going forward." As a result, the subjects in the experimental group regarded the robot as an autonomous and familiar entity, and looked at the robot as if it had an intention and an aim.

Summary of Experimental Results Table 3 shows a summary of the experimental results. Based on the consideration mentioned above, the three predictions were verified. Consequently, the hypothesis was supported by the experiments.

A noteworthy point in the experiment is that all of the subjects under both conditions turned their eyes and paid attention to the robot (in Verification of Prediction 2). As a result of their behaviors, although they should detect the trash can beside the robot's, half of the subjects under the control condition did not notice it. In other words, although all of the subjects could get the same contextual information, there were considerable differences in their understanding of utterances and behaviors between both conditions. We can attribute these differences to whether a mechanism of mindreading is activated. These differences cannot be fully explained only by a function of attention and symbolically situated inference. In the next chapter we discuss this issue.

Discussion and Conclusions

The purpose of this paper was to construct a methodology for smooth communications between humans and robots. In particular, we focused on the mindreading mechanism that is indispensable in human-human communications. Moreover, we proposed a model of utterance understanding based on this mechanism and implemented a robot interface system that applied our proposed model. In psychological experiments with the implemented system, the subjects in the experimental group activated "universal modules" (**ID** and **EDD**) in perceptions of the robot because an agent interacting with the subjects migrated from their mobile PC to the robot. Afterwards, a triadic relationship among the subject, the robot and an obstacle was constructed (**SAM**). On the basis of this relationship, by reading the robot's mental states of desire and goal (**ToMM**), the subjects could even understand the robot's unclear utterances (**UUM**). However, the subjects in the control group could not understand the utterances and construct the relationship despite getting the same contextual information as the subjects in the experimental group. These results are not explained only by a function of attention and symbolically situated inference. This is because all the subjects paid "attention" to the robot; moreover, there was no difference between the experimental situations as far as we could describe them through "symbolic" representation.

We can attribute the subjects' understanding of the robot's utterance to the activation of a mechanism of mindreading. We also believe that this activation is caused by the interaction among the five modules in our model (Figure 1). However, as this model still has a few shortcomings, we must further investigate the mechanism in detail. With the progress of this research, the following concepts become important: *sympathetic* and *embodied* inference as well as a viewpoint from an *internal observer* in communications. An impasse in the research on the theory of mind resulted from adopting tasks in experiments that subjects could solve by symbolic inference alone, e.g., "false belief task" (Wimmer & Perner 1983). Owing to adopting the task, an autistic child who is considered not able to estimate others' mental states can manage to carry out the task by repeated training. This is because he/she has a sufficient ability to think with operating symbols. However, the essential problems are that they lack the ability of sympathetic understanding to others and cannot take up the subjective attitude involved in communications. These two points are indispensable for investigating a mechanism of human communications.

In our experiment, we did research on human-robot communications from the two viewpoints mentioned above. That is to say, we could stimulate the subjects to promote the sympathetic understanding by the experimental setup where the robot as physical existence could not go forward if it was blocked by an obstacle. We could, moreover, make the subjects participate in communications with the robot subjectively by the relationship that emerged from the agent migration. As a results of the experimental setup, the subjects could even understand the robot's unclear utterances. Therefore, we could demonstrate the importance of *sympathetic* and *embodied* inference and a viewpoint from an *internal observer* in communications through the experiments.

Our proposed model can also give suggestions for problems in the relevance theory. As mentioned above, we considered the mechanism of utterance understanding focusing on the two viewpoints. Moreover, we emphasized that the former was caused by being a similar physical existence, and the latter was made possible by the relationship that emerged between a speaker and a hearer. The relevance theory is unable to overcome the code model because it is unable to adopt the above two points. We take a constructive approach to resolve these problems in human communications by regarding the above two viewpoints as important. Research on robots is particularly important in this field because it logically shifts our concerns from toy problems to real world ones and gives us empirical data through experiments on changing parameters.

Finally, we describe unsolved problems and future works. First, we need to design and construct a more effective human-robot interface for smooth communications. In our proposed model, we constructed a relationship between a human and a robot using an autonomous agent and the mechanism of agent migration. However, as a matter of course, we have to design it more naturally in other ways. For example, we can use functions found in daily behaviors, e.g., the effect of a greeting or falling into step with others. In the future, we plan to study basic factors in human-robot communications found in everyday interactions. Next, we have to consider engineering applications of our research. In our present-day society, there are many artifacts around us, such as cellular phones and computers, that can enhance our cognitive functions. We can expect robots to provide daily support to humans in the near future, e.g., carrying things, rescuing victims and guiding people, with the advance of robotics technology.

Accordingly, it is important that humans can communicate with robots smoothly and reliably. We believe that our research can contribute to this field of engineering applications as well as to scientific interests in the mechanism of human communications.

References

Baron-Cohen, S. 1996. *Mindblindness*. MIT Press.

Clark, H. H., and Marshall, C. R. 1981. Definite Reference and Mutual Knowledge. In Joshi, A. K.; Webber, B. L.; and Sag, I. A., eds., *Elements of Discourse Understanding*. Cambridge University Press.

Kimura, D. 1997. Information, Regularity, and Communications – Comparison between Shannon and Bateson –. In Tani, Y., ed., *Communication no Shizen-shi (in Japanese)*. Tokyo: Shin-yousha. 31–60.

Ono, T., and Okada, M. 1998. Consistency Generation dependent on Situation. In *7th IEEE International Workshop on Robot and Human Communication (ROMAN'98)*, volume 1, 40–45.

Ono, T.; Imai, M.; and Etani, T. 1999. Robots as Human Peers: Cognitive Conditions of Human-Robot Interaction. In *The Second International Conference on Cognitive Science (ICCS'99)*, 693–696.

Premack, D., and Dasser, V. 1991. Theory of Mind in Apes and Children. In Whiten, A., ed., *Natural Theories of Mind*. Blackwell.

Sperber, D., and Wilson, D. 1986. *Relevance: Communication and Cognition*. Oxford: Basil Blackwell.

Wimmer, H., and Perner, J. 1983. Beliefs about Beliefs: Representation and Constraining Function of Wrong Beliefs in Young Children's Understanding Deception. *Cognition* 13:103–128.

Visual Event Classification via Force Dynamics

Jeffrey Mark Siskind
NEC Research Institute, Inc.
4 Independence Way
Princeton NJ 08540 USA
609/951–2705
qobi@research.nj.nec.com
http://www.neci.nj.nec.com/homepages/qobi

Abstract

This paper presents an implemented system, called LEONARD, that classifies simple spatial motion events, such as *pick up* and *put down*, from video input. Unlike previous systems that classify events based on their motion profile, LEONARD uses changes in the state of force-dynamic relations, such as support, contact, and attachment, to distinguish between event types. This paper presents an overview of the entire system, along with the details of the algorithm that recovers force-dynamic interpretations using prioritized circumscription and a stability test based on a reduction to linear programming. This paper also presents an example illustrating the end-to-end performance of LEONARD classifying an event from video input.

Introduction

People can describe what they see. If someone were to pick up a block and ask you what you saw, you could say *The person picked up the block*. In doing so, you describe both *objects*, like people and blocks, and *events*, like pickings up. Most recognition research in machine vision has focussed on recognising objects. In contrast, this paper describes a system for recognising events. Objects correspond roughly to the noun vocabulary in language. In contrast, events correspond roughly to the verb vocabulary in language. The overall goal of this research is to ground the lexical semantics of verbs in visual perception.

A number of reported systems can classify event occurrences from video or simulated video, among them, Yamoto, Ohya, & Ishii (1992), Regier (1992), Pinhanez & Bobick (1995), Starner (1995), Siskind & Morris (1996), Bailey *et al.* (1998), and Bobick & Ivanov (1998). While they differ in their details, by and large, these system classify event occurrences by their motion profile. For example, a *pick up* event is described as a sequence of two subevents: the agent moving towards the patient while the patient is at rest above the source, followed by the agent moving with the patient away from the source. Such systems use some combination of relative and absolute; linear and angular; positions, velocities, and accelerations as the features that drive classification.

Copyright © 2000, American Association for Artificial Intelligence (www.aaai.org). All rights reserved.

These systems follow the tradition of linguists and cognitive scientists, such as Leech (1969), Miller (1972), Schank (1973), Jackendoff (1983), or Pinker (1989), that represent the lexical semantics of verbs via the causal, aspectual, and directional qualities of motion. Some linguists and cognitive scientists, such as Herskovits (1986) and Jackendoff & Landau (1991), have argued that force-dynamic relations (Talmy 1988), such as support, contact, and attachment, are crucial for representing the lexical semantics of spatial prepositions. For example, in some situations, part of what it means for one object to be *on* another object is for the former to be in contact with, and supported by, the latter. In other situations, something can be on something else by way of attachment, as in *the knob on the door*. Siskind (1992) has argued that changes in the state of force-dynamic relations plays a more central role in specifying the lexical semantics of simple spatial motion verbs than motion profile. The particular linear and angular velocities and accelerations don't matter when picking something up or putting something down. What matters is a state change. When picking something up, the patient is initially supported by being on top of the source. Subsequently, the patient is supported by being attached to the agent. Likewise, when putting something down, the reverse is true. The patient starts out being supported by being attached to the agent. It is subsequently supported by being on top of the goal. Furthermore, what distinguishes putting something down from dropping it is that, in the former, the patient is always supported, while in the latter, the patient undergoes unsupported motion.

Siskind (1995), among others, describes a system for recovering force-dynamic relations from simulated video and using those relations to perform event classification. Mann, Jepson, & Siskind (1997), among others, describes a system for recovering force-dynamic relations from video but does not use those relations to perform event classification. This paper describes a system, called LEONARD, that recovers force-dynamic relations from video and uses those relations to perform event classification. It is the first reported system that goes all the way from video to event classification using recovered force dynamics. LEONARD is a complex, comprehensive system. Video input is processed using a real-time colour- and motion-based segmentation procedure to place a convex polygon around each participant object in each input frame. A tracking procedure then computes the correspondence between the polygons in each frame and those in adjacent frames. LEONARD then constructs force-dynamic interpretations of the resulting polygon movie. These interpretations are constructed out of predicates that describe the attachment relations between objects, the qualitative depth of objects, and their groundedness. Some interpretations are consistent in that they describe stable scenes. Others are inconsistent in that they describe unstable scenes. LEONARD performs model reconstruction, selecting as models, only those interpretations that explain the stability of the scene. Kinematic stability analysis is performed efficiently via a reduction to linear programming. There are usually multiple models, i.e. stable interpretations of each scene. LEONARD selects a preferred subset of models using prioritized, cardinality, and temporal circumscription. Event classification is efficiently performed on this preferred subset of models using an interval-based event logic. A precise description of the entire system is beyond the scope of this paper. The remainder of this paper focuses on kinematic stability analysis and model reconstruction. It also presents an example of the entire system in operation. Future papers will describe other components of this system in greater detail.

Kinematic Stability Analysis

Let us consider a simplified world that consists of line segments. Polygons can be treated as collections of rigidly attached line segments. Let us denote line segments by the symbol l. In this simplified world, some line segments will not need to be supported. Such line segments are said to be *grounded*. Let us denote the fact that l is grounded by the property $g(l)$. In this simplified world, the table top and the agent's hand will be grounded.

In this simplified world, line segments can be *joined* together. If l_i and l_j are joined, the constraint on their relative motion is specified by three relations $\leftrightarrow_1$, $\leftrightarrow_2$, and $\leftrightarrow_\theta$. If $l_i \leftrightarrow_1 l_j$, then the position of the joint along l_i is fixed. Likewise, if $l_i \leftrightarrow_2 l_j$, then the position of the joint along l_j is fixed. And if $l_i \leftrightarrow_\theta l_j$, then the relative orientation of l_i and l_j is fixed. Combinations of these three relations allow specifying a variety of joint types. If $l_i \leftrightarrow_1 l_j \wedge l_i \leftrightarrow_2 l_j \wedge l_i \leftrightarrow_\theta l_j$, then l_i and l_j are rigidly joined. If $l_i \leftrightarrow_1 l_j \wedge l_i \leftrightarrow_2 l_j \wedge l_i \not\leftrightarrow_\theta l_j$, then l_i and l_j are joined by a revolute joint. If $l_i \not\leftrightarrow_1 l_j \wedge l_i \leftrightarrow_2 l_j \wedge l_i \leftrightarrow_\theta l_j$, then l_i and l_j are joined by a prismatic joint that allows l_j to slide along l_i. If $l_i \leftrightarrow_1 l_j \wedge l_i \not\leftrightarrow_2 l_j \wedge l_i \leftrightarrow_\theta l_j$, then l_i and l_j are joined by a prismatic joint that allows l_i to slide along l_j. If $l_i \not\leftrightarrow_1 l_j \wedge l_i \not\leftrightarrow_2 l_j \wedge l_i \not\leftrightarrow_\theta l_j$, then l_i and l_j are not joined. A total of eight different kinds of joints are possible, including ones that are simultaneously revolute and prismatic.

In this simplified world, line segments reside on parallel planes that are perpendicular to the focal axis of the observer. This simplified world uses an impoverished notion of depth. All that is important is whether two given line segments reside on the same plane. Such line segments are said to be on the *same layer*. Let us denote the fact that l_i and l_j are on the same layer by the relation $l_i \bowtie l_j$. This impoverished notion of depth lacks any notion of depth order. It cannot model objects being in front of or behind other objects. It also lacks any notion of adjacency in depth. It can-

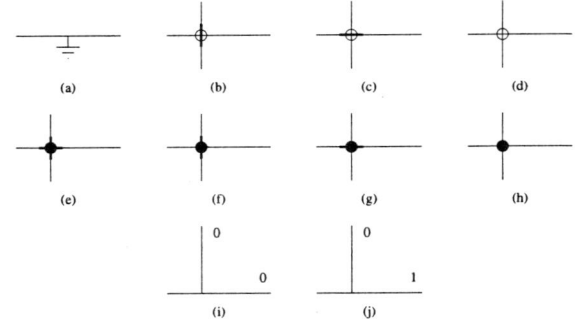

Figure 1: A graphical representation of scene interpretations. Consider the vertical lines to be l_i and the horizontal lines to be l_j. (a) depicts $g(l_j)$. (b) depicts $l_i \not\leftrightarrow_1 l_j \wedge l_i \leftrightarrow_2 l_j \wedge l_i \not\leftrightarrow_\theta l_j$. (c) depicts $l_i \leftrightarrow_1 l_j \wedge l_i \not\leftrightarrow_2 l_j \wedge l_i \not\leftrightarrow_\theta l_j$. (d) depicts $l_i \leftrightarrow_1 l_j \wedge l_i \leftrightarrow_2 l_j \wedge l_i \not\leftrightarrow_\theta l_j$. (e) depicts $l_i \not\leftrightarrow_1 l_j \wedge l_i \not\leftrightarrow_2 l_j \wedge l_i \leftrightarrow_\theta l_j$. (f) depicts $l_i \not\leftrightarrow_1 l_j \wedge l_i \leftrightarrow_2 l_j \wedge l_i \leftrightarrow_\theta l_j$. (g) depicts $l_i \leftrightarrow_1 l_j \wedge l_i \not\leftrightarrow_2 l_j \wedge l_i \leftrightarrow_\theta l_j$. (h) depicts $l_i \leftrightarrow_1 l_j \wedge l_i \leftrightarrow_2 l_j \wedge l_i \leftrightarrow_\theta l_j$. The $\bowtie$ relation is depicted by assigning layer indices to line segments. (i) depicts $l_i \bowtie l_j$. (j) depicts $l_i \not\bowtie l_j$.

not model objects touching one another along the focal axis of the observer.

A *scene* is a set L of line segments. An *interpretation* of scene is a quintuple $\langle g, \leftrightarrow_1, \leftrightarrow_2, \leftrightarrow_\theta, \bowtie \rangle$. It is convenient to depict scene interpretations graphically. Figure 1 shows the graphical representation of the predicates g, $\leftrightarrow_1$, $\leftrightarrow_2$, $\leftrightarrow_\theta$, and $\bowtie$.

An interpretation is *admissible* if the following conditions hold:

- For all l_i and l_j, if $l_i \leftrightarrow_1 l_j$, $l_i \leftrightarrow_2 l_j$, or $l_i \leftrightarrow_\theta l_j$, then l_i intersects l_j. In other words, attached line segments must intersect.

- For all l_i and l_j, $l_i \leftrightarrow_1 l_j$ iff $l_j \leftrightarrow_2 l_i$.

- $\leftrightarrow_\theta$ is symmetric.

- For all l_i and l_j, if $l_i \bowtie l_j$, then l_i and l_j do not overlap. In other words, line segments on the same layer must not overlap. Two line segments overlap if they intersect in a noncollinear fashion and the point of intersection is not an endpoint of either line segment.

- $\bowtie$ is symmetric and transitive.

(Note that whether two line segments intersect or overlap is purely a geometric property of the scene L and is independent of any interpretation of that scene.) Only admissible interpretations will be considered.

Statically, the line segments in a scene have fixed positions and orientations. Let us denote the coordinates of a point p as $x(p)$ and $y(p)$. And let us denote the endpoints of a line segment l as $p(l)$ and $q(l)$. And let us denote the length of a line segment l as $||l||$. And let us denote the position of a line segment l as the position of its midpoint $c(l)$. And let us denote the orientation $\theta(l)$ of a line segment l as the angle of the vector from $p(l)$ to $q(l)$. The quantities $p(l)$, $q(l)$,

$||l||$, $c(l)$, and $\theta(l)$ are all fixed given a static scene. And $p(l)$ and $q(l)$ are related to $||l||$, $c(l)$, and $\theta(l)$ as follows:

$$
\begin{aligned}
c(l) &= \frac{p(l) + q(l)}{2} \\
||l|| &= \sqrt{(q(l) - p(l)) \cdot (q(l) - p(l))} \\
\theta(l) &= \tan^{-1} \frac{y(q(l)) - y(p(l))}{x(q(l)) - x(p(l))} \\
x(p(l)) &= x(c(l)) - \frac{1}{2}||l|| \cos \theta(l) \\
y(p(l)) &= y(c(l)) - \frac{1}{2}||l|| \sin \theta(l) \\
x(q(l)) &= x(c(l)) + \frac{1}{2}||l|| \cos \theta(l) \\
y(q(l)) &= y(c(l)) + \frac{1}{2}||l|| \sin \theta(l)
\end{aligned}
$$

Let us postulate an unknown instantaneous motion for each line segment in the scene. This can be represented by associating a linear and angular velocity with each line segment. Let us denote such velocities with the variables $\dot{c}(l)$ and $\dot{\theta}(l)$. Let us assume that there is no motion in depth so the $\bowtie$ relation does not change. If the scene contains n line segments, then there will be $3n$ scalar variables, because $\dot{c}$ has x and y components. Assuming that the line segments are rigid, i.e. that instantaneous motion does not lead to a change in their length, one can relate $\dot{p}(l)$ and $\dot{q}(l)$, the instantaneous velocities of the endpoints, to $\dot{c}(l)$ and $\dot{\theta}(l)$, using the chain rule as follows:

$$
\begin{aligned}
\dot{p}(l) &= \frac{\partial p(l)}{\partial x(c(l))} x(\dot{c}(l)) + \frac{\partial p(l)}{\partial y(c(l))} y(\dot{c}(l)) + \frac{\partial p(l)}{\partial \theta(l)} \dot{\theta}(l) \\
\dot{q}(l) &= \frac{\partial q(l)}{\partial x(c(l))} x(\dot{c}(l)) + \frac{\partial q(l)}{\partial y(c(l))} y(\dot{c}(l)) + \frac{\partial q(l)}{\partial \theta(l)} \dot{\theta}(l)
\end{aligned}
$$

Note that $\dot{p}(l)$ and $\dot{q}(l)$ are linear in $\dot{c}(l)$ and $\dot{\theta}(l)$.

Each of the components of an admissible interpretation of a scene can be viewed as imposing constraints on the instantaneous motions of the line segments in that scene. The simplest case is the g property. If $g(l)$, then $\dot{c}(l) = 0$ and $\dot{\theta}(l) = 0$. Note that these equations are linear in $\dot{c}(l)$ and $\dot{\theta}(l)$.

Let us now consider the $l_i \leftrightarrow_1 l_j$ and $l_i \leftrightarrow_2 l_j$ relations and the constraint that they imposes on the motions of l_i and l_j. First, let us denote the intersection of l_i and l_j as $I(l_i, l_j)$. If we let

$$
\begin{aligned}
A &= \begin{pmatrix} y(p(l_i)) - y(q(l_i)) & x(q(l_i)) - x(p(l_i)) \\ y(p(l_j)) - y(q(l_j)) & x(q(l_j)) - x(p(l_j)) \end{pmatrix} \\
b &= \begin{pmatrix} y(p(l_i))(x(q(l_i)) - x(p(l_i))) \\ +x(p(l_i))(y(p(l_i)) - y(q(l_i))) \\ y(p(l_j))(x(q(l_j)) - x(p(l_j))) \\ +x(p(l_j))(y(p(l_j)) - y(q(l_j))) \end{pmatrix}
\end{aligned}
$$

then $I(l_i, l_j) = A^{-1}b$.

Next, let us compute $\dot{I}(l_i, l_j)$, the velocity of the intersection of the two lines segments l_i and l_j as they move. Let α be the vector containing the elements $x(p(l_i))$, $y(p(l_i))$, $x(q(l_i))$, $y(q(l_i))$, $x(p(l_j))$, $y(p(l_j))$, $x(q(l_j))$, and $y(q(l_j))$. And let β be the vector containing the elements $x(c(l_i))$, $y(c(l_i))$, $\theta(l_i)$, $x(c(l_j))$, $y(c(l_j))$, and $\theta(l_j)$. And let γ be the vector where $\gamma_k = \frac{\partial I}{\partial \alpha_k}$. And let D be the matrix where $D_{kl} = \frac{\partial \alpha_k}{\partial \beta_l}$. $\dot{I}(l_i, l_j)$ can be computed by the chain rule as follows:

$$\dot{I}(l_i, l_j) = \gamma^T D \dot{\beta}$$

Note that $\dot{I}(l_i, l_j)$ is linear in $\dot{c}(l_i)$, $\dot{\theta}(l_i)$, $\dot{c}(l_j)$, and $\dot{\theta}(l_j)$ because all of the partial derivatives are constant.

Next, let us denote by $\rho(p, l)$, where p is a point on l, the fraction of the distance where p lies between $p(l)$ and $q(l)$.

$$\rho(p, l) = \begin{cases} \frac{y(p) - y(p(l))}{y(q(l)) - y(p(l))} & x(p(l)) = x(q(l)) \\ \frac{x(p) - x(p(l))}{x(q(l)) - x(p(l))} & \text{otherwise} \end{cases}$$

And if $0 \leq \rho \leq 1$, let us denote by $l(\rho)$ the point that is the fraction ρ of the distance between $p(l)$ and $q(l)$.

$$l(\rho) = p(l) + \rho(q(l) - p(l))$$

And let us denote by $\dot{l}(\rho)$ the velocity of the point that is the fraction ρ of the distance between $p(l)$ and $q(l)$ as l moves. Let α be the vector containing the elements $x(p(l))$, $y(p(l))$, $x(q(l))$, and $y(q(l))$. And let β be the vector containing the elements $x(c(l))$, $y(c(l))$, and $\theta(l)$. And let γ be the vector where $\gamma_k = \frac{\partial l(\rho)}{\partial \alpha_k}$. And let D be the matrix where $D_{kl} = \frac{\partial \alpha_k}{\partial \beta_l}$. Again, by the chain rule:

$$\dot{l}(\rho) = \gamma^T D \dot{\beta}$$

Again, note that $\dot{l}(\rho)$ is linear in $\dot{c}(l)$ and $\dot{\theta}(l)$ because all of the partial derivatives are constant.

The $\leftrightarrow_1$ constraint can now be formulated as follows: if $l_i \leftrightarrow_1 l_j$, then

$$\dot{l}_i(\rho(I(l_i, l_j), l_i)) = \dot{I}(l_i, l_j)$$

And the $\leftrightarrow_2$ constraint can now be formulated as follows: if $l_i \leftrightarrow_2 l_j$, then

$$\dot{l}_j(\rho(I(l_i, l_j), l_j)) = \dot{I}(l_i, l_j)$$

Again, note that these equations are linear in $\dot{c}(l_i)$, $\dot{\theta}(l_i)$, $\dot{c}(l_j)$, and $\dot{\theta}(l_j)$.

Let us now consider the $l_i \leftrightarrow_\theta l_j$ relation and the constraint that it imposes on the motions of l_i and l_j. If $l_i \leftrightarrow_\theta l_j$, then

$$\dot{\theta}(l_i) = \dot{\theta}(l_j)$$

Again, note that this equation is linear in $\dot{\theta}(l_i)$ and $\dot{\theta}(l_j)$.

The same-layer relation $l_i \bowtie l_j$ imposes the constraint that the motion of l_i and l_j must not lead to an instantaneous penetration of one by the other. An instantaneous penetration can occur only when the endpoint of one line segment touches the other line segment. Without loss of generality, let us assume that $p(l_i)$ touches l_j. Let $\overline{p}$ denote a vector of the same magnitude as p rotated counterclockwise 90°.

$$\overline{(x, y)} = (-y, x)$$

Let σ be a vector that is normal to l_j, in the direction towards l_i.

$$\sigma = -\overline{[q(l_j) - p(l_j)] \cdot (q(l_i) - p(l_i))]}\overline{q(l_j) - p(l_j)}$$

An instantaneous penetration can occur only when the velocity of $p(l_i)$ in the direction of σ is less than the velocity of the point of contact in the same direction. The velocity of $p(l_i)$ is $\dot{p}(l_i)$. And the velocity of the point of contact is $\dot{l}_j(\rho(p(l_i), l_j))$. Thus if $l_i \bowtie l_j$ and $p(l_i)$ touches l_j, then

$$\dot{p}(l_i) \cdot \sigma \leq \dot{l}_j(\rho(p(l_i), l_j)) \cdot \sigma \qquad (1)$$

Again, note that this inequality is linear in $\dot{c}(l_i)$, $\dot{\theta}(l_i)$, $\dot{c}(l_j)$, and $\dot{\theta}(l_j)$.

We wish to determine the stability of a scene under an admissible interpretation. A scene is unstable if there is an assignment of linear and angular velocities to the line segments in the scene that satisfies the above constraints and decreases the potential energy of the scene. The potential energy of a scene is the sum of the potential energies of the line segments in that scene. The potential energy of a line segment l is proportional to its mass times $y(c(l))$. We can take the mass of a line segment to be proportional to its length. So the potential energy E can be taken as $\sum_{l \in L} ||l|| y(c(l))$. The potential energy can decrease if $\dot{E} < 0$. By scale invariance, if $\dot{E}$ can be less than zero, then it can be equal to any value less than zero, in particular -1. Thus a scene is unstable under an admissible interpretation iff the constraint $\dot{E} = -1$ is consistent with the above constraints. Note that $\dot{E}$ is linear in all of the $\dot{c}(l)$ values. Thus the stability of a scene under an admissible interpretation can be determined by a reduction to linear programming.

Model Reconstruction

Let us define a *model* of a scene as an admissible interpretation under which the scene is stable. LEONARD enumerates the models of each frame in each movie it processes. This is called *model reconstruction*. There are usually multiple models of any given scene. For example, if the scene contains a collection of overlapping polygons, then the polygons can be rigidly attached and any of them can be grounded. In a certain sense, some models make weaker assumptions than others. For example, it is always possible to explain the stability of an object by grounding it. Thus a model that has fewer grounded objects makes weaker assumptions than a model with more grounded objects. Similarly, whenever it is possible to explain the stability of an object that is supported by being above and on the same layer as another stable object, it is also possible to explain its stability by instead being attached to that object. Thus a model that has fewer attachment relations makes weaker assumptions than a model with more attachment relations. Accordingly, during model reconstruction, LEONARD selects models that make the weakest assumptions. It does so by a process of prioritized circumscription (McCarthy 1980).

To limit the search space, LEONARD considers only rigid and revolute joints. It does not consider prismatic joints.

In other words, only interpretations that meet the following constraint are considered:

$$(\forall l_i, l_j \in L) \left\{ \begin{array}{l} [(l_i \leftrightarrow_1 l_i) \leftrightarrow (l_i \leftrightarrow_2 l_j)] \wedge \\ [(l_i \leftrightarrow_\theta l_i) \rightarrow (l_i \leftrightarrow_1 l_j)] \end{array} \right\}$$

Let us define several preference relations between components of interpretations. First, let us define a preference relation between two grounded properties. Let us say that g is preferred to g', denoted $g \prec g'$, if $g \neq g'$ and $(\forall l \in L) g(l) \rightarrow g'(l)$. In other words, g is preferred to g' if they are different and every grounded line segment in the former is grounded in the latter. Along these lines, let us define a similar preference relation between two $\leftrightarrow_1$ relations. Let us say that $\leftrightarrow_1$ is preferred to $\leftrightarrow'_1$, denoted $\leftrightarrow_1 \prec \leftrightarrow'_1$, if $\leftrightarrow_1 \neq \leftrightarrow'_1$ and $(\forall l_i, l_j \in L) l_i \leftrightarrow_1 l_j \rightarrow l_i \leftrightarrow'_1 l_j$. In other words, $\leftrightarrow_1$ is preferred to $\leftrightarrow'_1$ if they are different and every pair of line segments that is attached in the former is attached in the latter. Similarly, let us define a preference relation between two $\leftrightarrow_\theta$ relations. Let us say that $\leftrightarrow_\theta$ is preferred to $\leftrightarrow'_\theta$, denoted $\leftrightarrow_\theta \prec \leftrightarrow'_\theta$, if $\leftrightarrow_\theta \neq \leftrightarrow'_\theta$ and $(\forall l_i, l_j \in L) l_i \leftrightarrow_\theta l_j \rightarrow l_i \leftrightarrow'_\theta l_j$. In other words, $\leftrightarrow_\theta$ is preferred to $\leftrightarrow'_\theta$ if they are different and every pair of line segments that is rigidly attached in the former is rigidly attached in the latter. Finally, let us define a preference relation between two same-layer relations. Let us say that $\bowtie$ is preferred to $\bowtie'$, denoted $\bowtie \prec \bowtie'$, if $\bowtie \neq \bowtie'$ and $(\forall l_i, l_j \in L) l_i \bowtie l_j \rightarrow l_i \bowtie' l_j$. In other words, $\bowtie$ is preferred to $\bowtie'$ if they differ and every pair of line segments that is on the same layer in the former is on the same layer in the latter.

Given a set G of grounded properties, its minimal elements $\hat{g}$ are those grounded properties $g \in G$ such that there is no $g' \in G$ where $g' \prec g$. Similarly for $\leftrightarrow_1$, $\leftrightarrow_\theta$, and $\bowtie$.

LEONARD uses the following prioritized circumscription process. It first finds all minimal grounded properties $\hat{g}$ such that there exist relations $\leftrightarrow_1$, $\leftrightarrow_\theta$, and $\bowtie$ where the interpretation $\langle \hat{g}, \leftrightarrow_1, \leftrightarrow_2, \leftrightarrow_\theta, \bowtie \rangle$ is admissible and the scene is stable under that interpretation. Note that there must be at least one such minimal grounded property $\hat{g}$. For each such minimal grounded property $\hat{g}$, it then finds all minimal $\widehat{\leftrightarrow_1}$ relations such that there exist relations $\leftrightarrow_\theta$ and $\bowtie$ where the interpretation $\langle \hat{g}, \widehat{\leftrightarrow_1}, \widehat{\leftrightarrow_1}, \leftrightarrow_\theta, \bowtie \rangle$ is admissible and the scene is stable under that interpretation. Note that there must be at least one such minimal $\widehat{\leftrightarrow_1}$ relation for each minimal grounded property. For each such minimal $\widehat{\leftrightarrow_1}$ relation, taken with the corresponding minimal grounded property $\hat{g}$, it then finds all minimal $\widehat{\leftrightarrow_\theta}$ relations such that there exists a same-layer relation $\bowtie$ where the interpretation $\langle \hat{g}, \widehat{\leftrightarrow_1}, \widehat{\leftrightarrow_1}, \widehat{\leftrightarrow_\theta}, \bowtie \rangle$ is admissible and the scene is stable under that interpretation. Note that there must be at least one such minimal $\widehat{\leftrightarrow_\theta}$ relation for each minimal minimal $\widehat{\leftrightarrow_1}$ relation. Finally, for each such minimal $\widehat{\leftrightarrow_\theta}$ relation, taken with the corresponding minimal $\widehat{\leftrightarrow_1}$ relation and minimal grounded property $\hat{g}$, it then finds all minimal same-layer relations $\widehat{\bowtie}$ such that the interpretation $\langle \hat{g}, \widehat{\leftrightarrow_1}, \widehat{\leftrightarrow_1}, \widehat{\leftrightarrow_\theta}, \widehat{\bowtie} \rangle$ is admissible and the scene is stable under that interpretation. Note that there must be at least one such minimal same-layer relation $\widehat{\bowtie}$ for each such minimal $\widehat{\leftrightarrow_\theta}$ relation. For each such minimal same-layer relation $\widehat{\bowtie}$, taken with the corresponding minimal $\overset{\frown}{\leftrightarrow_\theta}$ and $\overset{\frown}{\leftrightarrow_1}$ relations and minimal grounded property $\hat{g}$, prioritized circumscription returns the interpretation $\langle \hat{g}, \overset{\frown}{\leftrightarrow_1}, \overset{\frown}{\leftrightarrow_1}, \overset{\frown}{\leftrightarrow_\theta}, \widehat{\bowtie} \rangle$ as a minimal model of the scene.

The above prioritized circumscription procedure orders models by an inclusion relation and selects minimal models according to that inclusion relation. This has the following disadvantage. If a scene has one block resting on top of another block, there will be two minimal models: one where the bottom block is grounded and the top block is on the same layer as the bottom block and one where the top block is grounded and the bottom block is attached to the top block. The latter has more attachment assertions than the former but is still minimal because it is generated for a different minimal grounded property $\hat{g}$. Nonetheless, it is desirable to prefer the former model to the latter model. This is done by a second pass circumscription that uses a cardinality-based preference metric rather than one based on inclusion. Let us define the cardinality of a grounded property g, denoted $||g||$, as the number of line segments $l \in L$ for which $g(l)$ is true. And let us define the cardinality of a $\leftrightarrow_1$ relation, denoted $||\leftrightarrow_1||$ as the number of pairs of line segments $l_i, l_j \in L$ for which $l_i \leftrightarrow_1 l_j$ is true. Similarly for the $\leftrightarrow_\theta$ and $\bowtie$ relations. Furthermore, let us define the cardinality of an interpretation I, denoted $||I||$, as the quadruple $\langle ||g||, ||\leftrightarrow_1||, ||\leftrightarrow_\theta||, ||\bowtie|| \rangle$. Now, let us define a preference relation between two interpretations. Let us say that I is preferred to I', denoted $I \prec I'$, if $||I||$ is lexicographically less than $||I'||$. Given a set $\mathcal{I}$ of interpretation, its minimal elements $\hat{I}$ are those interpretations $I \in \mathcal{I}$ such that there is no $I' \in \mathcal{I}$ where $I' \prec I$. Cardinality circumscription returns the minimal elements of the set of minimal models produced by prioritized circumscription.

Prioritized and cardinality circumscription are not sufficient to prune all of the spurious models. The following situation often arises. During a *pick up* event, the agent is grounded before it grasps the patient but once the patient is grasped and lifted there is an ambiguity as to whether the agent is grounded and the patient is supported by being attached to the agent or whether the patient is grounded and the agent is supported by being attached to the patient. In some sense, the former is preferable to the later since it does not require the ground assertion to move from the agent to the patient. More generally, sequences of models are preferred when they entail fewer changes in assertions. This is a form of temporal circumscription (Mann & Jepson 1998). Taken together, prioritized, cardinality, and temporal circumscription typically yield a small number of models for each movie that usually correspond to natural pretheoretic human intuition.

Examples

The techniques described in this paper have been implemented in a system called LEONARD. Figure 2 shows the results of processing four short movies with LEONARD. Each column shows a subset of the frames from a single movie. From left to right, the movies have 29, 34, 16, and 16 frames respectively. Each movie was processed by the segmentation procedure to place a convex polygon around the coloured and moving objects in each frame. The tracking procedure computed the correspondence between the polygons in each frame and those in the adjacent frames. The model reconstruction procedure was used to construct force-dynamic models of each frame. Prioritized, cardinality, and temporal circumscription were used to prune the space of models. Each frame is shown with the results of segmentation and model reconstruction superimposed on the original video image.

For the leftmost column, notice that LEONARD determines that the lower block and the hand are grounded for the entire movie, that the upper block is supported by being on the same layer as the lower block for frames 2, 4, and 8, and that the upper block is supported by being rigidly attached to the hand for frames 20, 22, and 24. For the second column, notice that LEONARD determines that the lower block and the hand are grounded for the entire movie, that the upper block is supported by being rigidly attached to the hand for frames 5 and 10, and that the upper block is supported by being on the same layer as the lower block for frames 21, 24, 26, and 29. For the third column, notice that LEONARD determines that the lower block and the hand are grounded for the entire movie and that the upper block is supported for the entire movie by being on the same layer as the lower block. For the rightmost column, notice that LEONARD determines that the lower block and the hand are grounded for the entire movie and that the upper block is supported for the entire movie by being rigidly attached to the hand.

LEONARD was given the following lexicon when processing these four movies:

$$\text{PICKUP}(x, y) \triangleq \left[\begin{array}{l} \neg\text{SUPPORTED}(x) \land \\ \text{SUPPORTED}(y) \land \\ \left(\begin{array}{l} \neg\text{ATTACHED}(x, y); \\ \text{ATTACHED}(x, y) \end{array} \right) \end{array} \right]$$

$$\text{PUTDOWN}(x, y) \triangleq \left[\begin{array}{l} \neg\text{SUPPORTED}(x) \land \\ \text{SUPPORTED}(y) \land \\ \left(\begin{array}{l} \text{ATTACHED}(x, y); \\ \neg\text{ATTACHED}(x, y) \end{array} \right) \end{array} \right]$$

Essentially, these define *pick up* and *put down* as events where the agent is not supported throughout the event, the patient is supported throughout the event, and the agent grasps or releases the patient respectively. LEONARD correctly recognises the movie in the leftmost column as depicting a *pick up* event and the movie in the second column as depicting a *put down* event. More importantly, LEONARD correctly recognises that the remaining two movies do not depict any of the defined event types. Note that systems that classify events based on motion profiles will often mistakingly classify these last two movies as either *pick up* or *put down* events because they have similar motion profiles.

Conclusion

I have presented a comprehensive system that recovers force-dynamic interpretations from video and uses those interpretations to recognise event occurrences. Force dynamics is fundamentally more robust than motion profile for classifying events. Two occurrences of the same event type

Figure 2: The results of processing four short movies with LEONARD. The segmented polygons and force-dynamic models for each frame are overlayed on the video image for that frame. LEONARD successfully recognises the movie in the leftmost column as a *pick up* event and the movie in the second column as a *put down* event.

might have very different motion profiles. And occurrences of two different event types might have very similar motion profiles. This has been demonstrated by an implementation that distinguishes between occurrences and nonoccurrences of *pick up* and *put down* events despite similar motion profiles.

Acknowledgments

Amit Roy Chowdhury implemented an early version of the stability-checking algorithm described in this paper.

References

Bailey, D. R.; Chang, N.; Feldman, J.; and Narayanan, S. 1998. Extending embodied lexical development. In *Proceedings of the 20th Annual Conference of the Cognitive Science Society*.

Bobick, A. F., and Ivanov, Y. A. 1998. Action recognition using probabilistic parsing. In *Proceedings of the IEEE Computer Society Conference on Computer Vision and Pattern Recognition*, 196–202.

Herskovits, A. 1986. *Language and Spatial Cognition: An Interdisciplinary Study of the Prepositions in English*. New York, NY: Cambridge University Press.

Jackendoff, R., and Landau, B. 1991. Spatial language and spatial cognition. In Napoli, D. J., and Kegl, J. A., eds., *Bridges Between Psychology and Linguistics: A Swarthmore Festschrift for Lila Gleitman*. Hillsdale, NJ: Lawrence Erlbaum Associates.

Jackendoff, R. 1983. *Semantics and Cognition*. Cambridge, MA: The MIT Press.

Leech, G. N. 1969. *Towards a Semantic Description of English*. Indiana University Press.

Mann, R., and Jepson, A. 1998. Toward the computational perception of action. In *Proceedings of the IEEE Computer Society Conference on Computer Vision and Pattern Recognition*, 794–799.

Mann, R.; Jepson, A.; and Siskind, J. M. 1997. The computational perception of scene dynamics. *Computer Vision and Image Understanding* 65(2).

McCarthy, J. 1980. Circumscription—a form of non-monotonic reasoning. *Artificial Intelligence* 13(1–2):27–39.

Miller, G. A. 1972. English verbs of motion: A case study in semantics and lexical memory. In Melton, A. W., and Martin, E., eds., *Coding Processes in Human Memory*. Washington, DC: V. H. Winston and Sons, Inc. chapter 14, 335–372.

Pinhanez, C., and Bobick, A. 1995. Scripts in machine understanding of image sequences. In *AAAI Fall Symposium Series on Computational Models for Integrating Language and Vision*.

Pinker, S. 1989. *Learnability and Cognition*. Cambridge, MA: The MIT Press.

Regier, T. P. 1992. *The Acquisition of Lexical Semantics for Spatial Terms: A Connectionist Model of Perceptual Categorization*. Ph.D. Dissertation, University of California at Berkeley.

Schank, R. C. 1973. The fourteen primitive actions and their inferences. Memo AIM-183, Stanford Artificial Intelligence Laboratory.

Siskind, J. M., and Morris, Q. 1996. A maximum-likelihood approach to visual event classification. In *Proceedings of the Fourth European Conference on Computer Vision*, 347–360. Cambridge, UK: Springer-Verlag.

Siskind, J. M. 1992. *Naive Physics, Event Perception, Lexical Semantics, and Language Acquisition*. Ph.D. Dissertation, Massachusetts Institute of Technology, Cambridge, MA.

Siskind, J. M. 1995. Grounding language in perception. *Artificial Intelligence Review* 8:371–391.

Starner, T. E. 1995. Visual recognition of american sign language using hidden markov models. Master's thesis, Massachusetts Institute of Technology, Cambridge, MA.

Talmy, L. 1988. Force dynamics in language and cognition. *Cognitive Science* 12:49–100.

Yamoto, J.; Ohya, J.; and Ishii, K. 1992. Recognizing human action in time-sequential images using hidden markov model. In *Proceedings of the 1992 IEEE Conference on Computer Vision and Pattern Recognition*, 379–385. IEEE Press.

Constraint Satisfaction

Counting Models using Connected Components

Roberto J. Bayardo Jr.
IBM Almaden Research Center
bayardo@alum.mit.edu
http://www.almaden.ibm.com/cs/people/bayardo

J. D. Pehoushek
M.U.S.T. Centre
danpeh@yahoo.com

Abstract

Recent work by Birnbaum & Lozinskii [1999] demonstrated that a clever yet simple extension of the well-known Davis-Putnam procedure for solving instances of propositional satisfiability yields an efficient scheme for counting the number of satisfying assignments (models). We present a new extension, based on recursively identifying connected constraint-graph components, that substantially improves counting performance on random 3-SAT instances as well as benchmark instances from the SATLIB and Beijing suites. In addition, from a structure-based perspective of worst-case complexity, while polynomial time satisfiability checking is known to require only a backtrack search algorithm enhanced with nogood learning, we show that polynomial time counting using backtrack search requires an additional enhancement: good learning.

Introduction

Many practical problems from a variety of domains, most notably planning [Kautz & Selman 1996], have been efficiently solved by formulating them as instances of propositional satisfiability (SAT) and applying any of a number of freely available SAT algorithms. The problem of counting the number of models of a propositional formula (#SAT) has also been shown to have numerous applications [Roth 1996], though fast algorithms for this problem are not yet widely available. A recent paper by Birnbaum and Lozinskii [1999] may help change this situation, since it demonstrates that the Davis-Putnam (DP) algorithm [Davis et al. 1962] (for which freely available implementations are commonplace) can be straightforwardly extended to count models by identifying when subproblems contain no unsatisfied clauses; they call the resulting algorithm CDP.

In this paper, we describe an alternative modification of Davis-Putnam for more efficient model counting. We show that our approach yields the most significant improvements over CDP (orders of magnitude) on real world instances with many solutions, though we also witness large improvements on artificial instances such as those from the random 3-SAT problem space.

The basic idea behind our approach is as follows: by identifying connected components in the constraint graph of a SAT instance, the number of models can be determined by multiplying together the number of models of each subproblem corresponding to a connected component. This is a straightforward consequence of the fact that each subproblem corresponding to a connected component is completely independent of the others. We apply this idea recursively as Davis-Putnam builds a partial satisfying assignment.

The idea of recursively exploiting connected components in solving instances of SAT or the more general constraint satisfaction problem is not entirely new [Freuder & Quinn 1985; Bayardo & Miranker 1995]. In these formulations, however, connected components are identified using the full constraint graph, prior to attempting any solution of the instance. While this method is well-suited for obtaining worst-case complexity bounds for determining satisfiability given structure restricted instances, it offers few opportunities for good average-case performance when the initial constraint graph is dense, as is often the case with SAT (due to the typical abundance of non-binary constraints).

In contrast, our algorithm exploits components dynamically within a Davis-Putnam procedure. The Davis-Putnam procedure attempts to extend a partial solution of the input instance into a full solution. With each new extension, several clauses may be satisfied, and the constraint graph simplifies dynamically in a manner dependent upon the current variable assignments. By applying component identification dynamically, our algorithm is able to fully exploit this simplified structure. The advantage of this dynamic decomposition technique over static decomposition schemes is analogous to that of dynamic over static variable ordering.

The idea of dynamic component detection and exploitation has been proposed before by Rymon [1994], though within a set-enumeration tree search algorithm for identifying prime implicants of a propositional formula. To our knowledge, the technique has not been previously applied within a Davis-Putnam algorithm for the purpose of model counting. We note, however, that non-chronological backtracking schemes such as CBJ [Prosser 1993] and graph-based backjumping [Dechter 1987] effectively exploit component structure while backing up from a contradiction/dead-end.

Our primary contribution, then, is the demonstration that the dynamic detection and exploitation of connected components within a Davis-Putnam procedure is an efficient technique for model counting across a wide range of SAT instances. We also discuss how to optimize the technique for instances containing a mixture of both over and under-constrained subproblems (such instances are common in the real world). Our implementation is an extension of the relsat algorithm from Bayardo & Schrag [1997], and it appears in the relsat v2.00 release available from the web page of the first author.

Copyright 2000, American Association for Artificial Intelligence (www.aaai.org). All rights reserved.

In addition to the experimental contributions above, we look at the complexity of counting models in the presence of structure-restricted instances of the constraint-satisfaction problem (of which SAT is a simple restriction). Even though we find that model counting with a backtrack search algorithm can be significantly harder than satisfiability checking in practice, we show that with proper learning enhancements of the backtracking algorithm, satisfiability and model counting have equivalent worst-case runtime. However, while determining satisfiability in polynomial time requires only that a backtrack algorithm be enhanced with the ability to record nogoods, we show this is not sufficient for polynomial-time counting. In addition to the ability to record nogoods, polynomial time counting requires that *goods* be recorded as well. We discuss implementation difficulties which must be addressed before good learning can be applied efficiently in practice.

Definitions

A propositional logic *variable* ranges over the domain {true, false}. An *assignment* is a mapping of these values to variables. A *literal* is the occurrence of a variable, e.g. x, or its negation, e.g. $\neg x$; a positive literal x is satisfied when the variable x is assigned true, and a negative literal $\neg x$ is satisfied when x is assigned false. A *clause* is a simple disjunction of literals, e.g. $(x \vee y \vee \neg z)$; a clause is satisfied when one or more of its literals is satisfied. A *unit clause* contains exactly one variable, and a *binary clause* contains exactly two. The *empty clause* ( ) signals a contradiction (seen in the interpretation, "choose one or more literals to be true from among none"). A *conjunctive normal formula* (CNF) is a conjunction of clauses (e.g. $(a \vee b) \wedge (x \vee y \vee \neg z)$); a CNF is satisfied if all of its clauses are satisfied.

A *model* of a CNF is an assignment mentioning every variable in the CNF that satisfies every clause. For a given CNF, we consider the problems of determining satisfiability (determining if a model exists) and counting the number of models of the instance (SAT and #SAT respectively).

The *constraint graph* of a SAT instance is obtained by representing each variable with a node, and imposing an edge between any pair of variables appearing in the same clause. A connected component of a graph is a maximal subgraph such that for every pair of nodes u, v in the subgraph, there is a path from u to v. All connected components of a graph can be easily identified in linear time in the size of the graph ($O(n + m)$) using a simple depth-first traversal [Melhorn 1984].

Basic Algorithm Description

Before describing our algorithm, we first introduce the counting Davis-Putnam proof procedure (CDP) of Birnbaum & Lozinskii, which appears in the following figure. The algorithm maintains a satisfying truth assignment σ, which is empty upon initial top-level entry to the recursive,

CDP(F, σ, n)
  UNIT-PROPAGATE(F, σ)
  if ( ) in F **then return** 0
  if $F = \emptyset$ **then return** $2^{n-|\sigma|}$
  $\alpha \leftarrow$ SELECT-BRANCH-VARIABLE(F)
  return CDP($F \cup \{(\alpha)\}, \sigma \cup \{\alpha\}, n$) +
            CDP($F \cup \{(\neg\alpha)\}, \sigma \cup \{\neg\alpha\}, n$)

call-by-value procedure. It also accepts the number of variables present in the initial formula, n.

CDP exploits the fact that when all clauses in the formula are satisfied by the partial assignment, then any variables remaining unassigned can be assigned a value arbitrarily in order to obtain a solution. Thus, if there are i remaining unassigned variables once all clauses become satisfied, then there are 2^i unique models that include the given partial assignment, so CDP immediately returns 2^i. This step and the omission of the pure literal rule are the only differences between CPD and the classic Davis-Putnam proof procedure (DP). The pure literal rule is omitted since it cannot be used when counting models or enumerating all solutions without potentially compromising completeness.

Like any good implementation of DP, CDP employs a heuristic driven branch-selection function, SELECT-BRANCH-VARIABLE. It also performs unit-propagation (UNIT-PROPAGATE) to immediately assign variables that are mentioned in some unary clause. The CNF F and the truth assignment σ are modified in calls to UNIT-PROPAGATE. This function adds the single literal λ from a unit clause ω to the literal set σ, then it simplifies the CNF by removing any clauses in which λ occurs, and shortens any clauses in which $\neg\lambda$ occurs through resolution. After unit propagation, if F contains a contradiction, then the current subproblem has no models and backtracking is necessary.

UNIT-PROPAGATE(F, σ)
  while (exists ω in F where $\omega = (\lambda)$)
    $\sigma \leftarrow \sigma \cup \{\lambda\}$
    $F \leftarrow$ SIMPLIFY(F)

Our procedure, which we call DDP for Decomposing-Davis-Putnam, appears in the pseudo-code on the following page. Like CDP, DDP is based on DP, employing the same unit propagation and branch selection functions. Following each full unit propagation step, the constraint graph of the resulting simplified formula is constructed and its connected components identified.[1] Each subproblem corresponding to a component is then attempted recursively. Their solution counts are finally multiplied together to obtain the solution count for the given formula.

---

1. Our implementation actually determines the component structure lazily while backtracking instead of eagerly before branch selection. Though the effect in terms of search space explored is the same, this implementation detail simplifies some of the remaining optimizations, and also prevents component detection overhead from reducing performance on unsatisfiable instances.

```
DDP(F, σ)
  UNIT-PROPAGATE(F, σ)
  if ( ) in F then return 0
  if all variables are assigned a value then return 1
  Identify independent subproblems F_1...F_j
    corresponding to connected components of F.
  for each subproblem F_i, i = 1...j do
    α ← SELECT-BRANCH-VARIABLE(F_i)
    c_i ← DDP(F_i ∪ {(α)}, σ ∪ {α}) +
          DDP(F_i ∪ {(¬α)}, σ ∪ {¬α})
  return ∏_{i = 1...j} c_i
```

Optimizations

One modification of "plain vanilla" DDP which can provide substantial performance improvements, particularly for instances with a mixture of both under and over-constrained subproblems, is to attempt the component subproblems of F in a carefully determined order. The idea here exploits the fact that if any subproblem of F turns out to have no solutions, then the overall model count for F is inevitably zero. Thus, by attempting the most-constrained subproblems first, we often avoid futile counting within the under-constrained subproblems in the presence of an unsatisfiable subproblem. Note, however, that such ordering of subproblems is heuristic; there is always a chance we may inadvertently place an unsatisfiable subproblem last in the ordering. To reduce the impact of such a mistake, our implementation of DDP first attempts to determine satisfiability of each subproblem. Only when each subproblem is determined satisfiable does model counting begin. To avoid redundant searching, model counting begins from the state where satisfiability checking left off. Note that this modification also allows DDP to return a single satisfying assignment should one exist, in addition to the solution count.

To further avoid futile search, our implementation solves subproblems in an interleaved fashion, dynamically jumping to another subproblem if the current one turns out to be less constrained than initially estimated. This modification is not describable in the recursive pseudo-code framework used to define DDP above, which implements a strict depth-first search of the developing tree of connected components. This enhancement instead results in a best-first search of the developing component tree. The scores used in this best-first search can be obtained by simply reusing the scores typically provided by the branch-variable selection heuristic -- in our implementation, a subproblem's score is given by the score assigned to its best branch variable.

Another approach for improving performance is to fuse the counting methods of both CDP and DDP into a single algorithm: the resulting algorithm is nearly identical to DDP, except like CDP, it accepts the number of variables n and returns $2^{n-|σ|}$ when the formula is empty in place of simply returning 1 when all variables have been assigned values. Comparing this enhanced algorithm to DDP, every time the formula turns up empty, this enhancement saves $2(n-|σ|)$ recursive calls to the top-level procedure since there are $n-|σ|$ connected components, one corresponding to each unassigned variable.

Similar to the above idea, we can invoke an arbitrary algorithm in place of CDP/DDP when F is of a suitable size or structure for obtaining a more efficient model count. This technique was used by Birnbaum & Lozinskii in their implementation of CDP: when F contains fewer than 6 clauses, they invoke an algorithm of Lozinskii [1992] that is more efficient at handling these small formulas. Because these "small-model" enhancements apply equally to both algorithms, we did not exploit them in the experimental comparison described in the following section.

Experimental Comparison

In this section, we experimentally compare CDP and DDP on a wide variety of instances. We implemented these algorithms by modifying and extending the relsat algorithm of Bayardo & Schrag [1997]. Relsat is a Davis-Putnam satisfiability checker that also infers additional clauses (*nogoods*) as search progresses and performs *conflict-directed backjumping* [Prosser 1993] to better recover from contradiction. The clauses added by relsat explain when a certain sub-assignment of the instance results in an unsatisfiable subproblem. The additional clauses are redundant in that they do not affect the solution count of the instance. This implies that by ignoring them during constraint-graph decomposition, they do not compromise correctness of DDP.

Relsat allows one to specify the "order" of learning to be applied, corresponding to the degree of the polynomial in its space complexity (resulting from clause inference). Unless otherwise noted, we used a setting of 3 which is known to be useful for many instances when determining satisfiability [Bayardo & Schrag 1997]. We discuss the effect of this setting on the various instances later in this section.

Due to the high overhead of scoring branch variables (relsat uses expensive unit-propagation based heuristics [Freeman 1995]), code profiling revealed that dynamic component detection was an almost negligible additional expense for the algorithm. For this reason, we sometimes report performance only in terms of the CPU-independent metric of branch selections performed by the algorithm, rather than seconds elapsed. The number of branch selections corresponds to the number of recursive calls made to each procedure, and correlates highly with runtime on instances from the same class. When we do report runtimes, they are for a 400 Mhz Pentium-II IBM IntelliStation M-Pro running Windows NT 4.0.

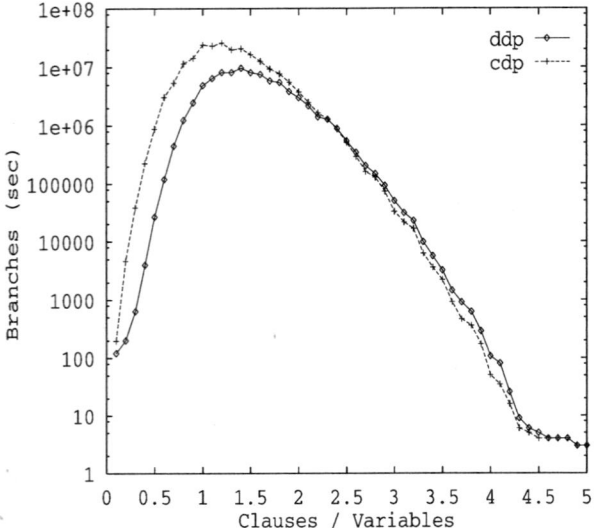

For our first experiment, we ran CDP and DDP on the same set of 50-variable instances from the uniform random 3-SAT problem space. To generate an instance from this problem space, three distinct variables are uniform-randomly selected out of the pool of n possible variables. Each variable is negated with probability $1/2$. These literals are combined to form a clause. m clauses are created in this manner and conjoined to form the 3-CNF Boolean expression.

We generated 100 instances at every C/V (clause/variable) point plotted along the x axis of the figure above, for a total of 5000 instances. The y axis plots the median number of branch selections, corresponding to the number of recursive calls of the procedure. Corroborating the results of Birnbaum and Lozinskii, we found that the hardness peak for CDP is around 1.2 C/V. We found the hardness peak resulted in a median of ~26 million branch selections, versus ~16 million determined by Birnbaum and Lozinskii. This discrepancy is most likely explained by the lack of small-model enhancements in our implementation.

Surprisingly, DDP does not appear to have an identical hardness peak. DDP instead peaks at approximately 1.5 C/V, with a median of ~8 million branch selections. Unlike the hardness peak for satisfiability, which consistently arises at approximately 4.26 C/V [Crawford & Auton 1996], the hardness peak for model counting may well be more algorithm dependent.

Though somewhat obscured by the logarithmic scale of the y axis, at CDP's hardness peak, DDP is over 3 times faster. Note that as the C/V ratio increases beyond 2.5, CDP gains a slight edge over DDP. We found that the fused DDP/CDP algorithm described in the previous section always performs better than either one alone, but never by a substantial amount. We omit its curve from the plot since it obscures the detail of the others.

DDP appears to be much more advantageous on larger instances we obtained from the SATLIB repository (http://aida.intellektik.informatik.tu-darmstadt.de/~hoos). We ran DDP and CDP on all 100 instances in the "flat200-*" suite

TABLE 1. Performance of and number of models computed by DDP on several "real world" benchmark instances for which model counts could be determined within 1 hour.

instance	branch	sec	count
2bitmax_6	6.2 mil	247	2.1e29
2bitcomp_5	237,379	9	9.8e15
logistics.a	151,265	24	3.8e14
logistics.b	5.3 mil	923	2.4e23
ssa7552-038	105,030	123	2.8e37
ssa7552-158	20,107	21	2.6e31
ssa7552-159	39,980	42	7.7e33
ssa7552-160	34,146	40	7.5e32

of graph coloring problems, each consisting of 600 variables and 2237 clauses. These instances are artificial graph-coloring instances which are hard for the Brelaz heuristic [Hogg 1996]. For DDP, an instance from this class required 27 seconds and 11,645 branch points on average. CDP was unable to determine a model count for *any* of these instances within the cutoff time of 15 minutes per instance.

We systematically went through the remainder of the SATLIB and beijing suite (available at http://www.cirl.edu/crawford/beijing) of benchmark instances, picking out for experimentation those obtained from "real world" sources such as planning and circuit analysis. Several, such as the ais-* class of instances, the blocksworld instances, hanoi4, and the 4blocks* and 3blocks instances from beijing suite, were not significantly easier for CDP or DDP than a complete enumeration of the solution space by DP with the pure literal rule disabled (called *enumerating* DP). This was because the number of solutions was relatively small -- at most a few hundred or thousand -- making efficient enumeration possible.

Many of the remaining satisfiable instances, though known to be easy when determining satisfiability instead of counting models, were too hard for either algorithm. These instances include logistics.c, logistics.d, 2bitadd_11 and 2bitadd_12. All resulted in timeout after the one hour per instance execution time limit was reached.

We found several instances for which the model count was efficiently determined by DDP even though the count was much too large for enumerating DP (see Table 1).[2] CDP failed to determine a solution count within 1 hour on any of them. Indeed, we were unable to find any instances among the benchmark suites for which CDP significantly outperforms enumerating DP. We note that given more computational power, it is possible some would be revealed by examining more of the randomly generated instances and/or increasing cutoff time substantially beyond one hour.

---

2. Though counts are rounded in the table, our implementation computes them exactly using a bignum package in order to avoid rounding errors which could result from using a floating point representation.

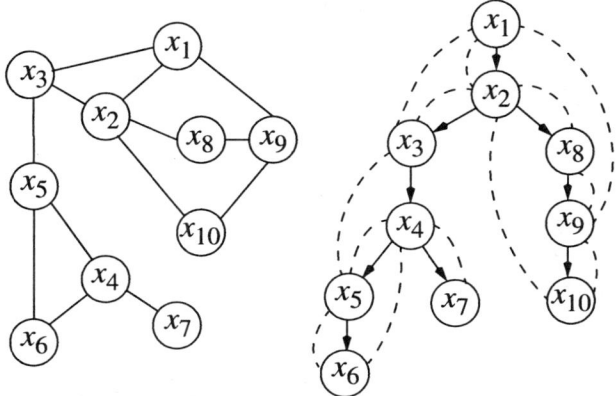

A graph and a rooted-tree arrangement of the graph.

Effects of Learning

We repeated the experiments from Table 1 with a learn order of 0 to disable the recording of additional clauses by the algorithms during search. In almost every case, this did not substantially alter performance. The only exceptions were logistics.a which went from 24 seconds of CPU time to over 15 minutes, and logistics.b, which resulted in timeout after one hour. The fact that learning often has no effect is not unexpected, since it is activated only in the presence of unsatisfiable subproblems. Instances which have a large number of solutions, like those in Table 1, tend to have only few such subproblems, and these are identified early on by the ordering optimizations that prevent futile counting when unsatisfiable subproblems are present.

Complexity Related Issues

In [Bayardo & Miranker 1996], the constraint-graph of a constraint satisfaction problem (CSP -- of which SAT is a restriction) is recursively decomposed to form a *rooted-tree arrangement* (see figure above) on which a backtracking algorithm similar to DDP is applied. By definition of a rooted-tree arrangement, two variables in different branches belong to different connected components when their common ancestors are assigned values.

The important differences between this algorithm and DDP are the decomposition is done statically before backtrack search instead of dynamically, and the algorithm attempts only to determine satisfiability instead of the number of models. They use this framework to define several graph-based parameters that can be used to bound the number of times each subproblem is attempted by the algorithm when different degrees and styles of learning are applied. These parameters lead to overall bounds on runtime which match the best-known structure-derived runtime bounds.

The key idea to the bounding technique is the realization that the assignment of variables within the *defining set* of a subproblem (the set of ancestors that are connected to at least one subproblem variable in the constraint graph) determines whether the subproblem is satisfiable. For example, the defining set of the subproblem rooted at x_4 in the example arrangement consists of x_3 alone. By recording the defining set assignment as a nogood or a good each time a subproblem is found to be unsatisfiable or satisfiable respectively, the number of times each subproblem is attempted can be bounded by the number of unique defining set assignments.

This algorithm can be easily modified to count solutions with identical bounds on runtime since equivalent assignments of the defining set must clearly lead to an equivalent number of solutions to the subproblem. Instead of recording whether a defining set assignment is "good" or "nogood", the idea is to pair the solution count of the given subproblem with its defining set assignment. With such a modification, subproblem counts can then be combined and propagated exactly as done by DDP, allowing the algorithms to determine a model count instead of satisfiability with equivalent space and runtime complexity.

From a structure-based complexity perspective, then, counting models with learning-enhanced backtrack search is no more difficult than determining satisfiability. In practice, however, our experiments from the previous sections reveal that counting models is often much more difficult. This is possibly due to the fact that structure-based bounds on runtime are rather conservative; they are based on static constraint-graph analysis, unable to account for efficiencies resulting from dynamic variable ordering and dynamically simplifying constraint graph structure.

Another cause of the difficulty we witnessed in counting may be due to the fact that relsat does not record goods (defining set assignments for which the solution count of the subproblem is greater than zero), the importance of which is indicated by complexity results. Previous work has shown that recording only nogoods during backtrack search leads to effective structure based bounds on runtime for determining satisfiability [Frost & Dechter 1994]. Bayardo & Miranker [1996] demonstrated that while good recording improves runtime complexity of satisfiability checking, it does so by reducing only the base of the exponent.

When counting models, good learning is in fact a necessary enhancement of backtrack search for achieving polynomial time complexity given certain variable arrangements. One simple example is a CSP whose constraint graph is a chain. If we arrange the variables in the order they appear along the chain, then determining satisfiability using a nogood learning backtrack algorithm is of quadratic complexity [Bayardo & Miranker 1994]. Model counting, however, would be exponential in the number of variables if the constraints are sufficiently loose. Recording of goods in addition to nogoods brings the complexity of model counting down to quadratic regardless of constraint looseness, so long as they have the chain (or in fact any tree) structure.

Towards Practical Good Learning

Though we have empirically explored the effects of nogood learning on model counting through relsat's clause-recording functionality, the effect of good learning remains unknown in practice. An effective implementation is an open problem, and a solution must address at least two significant complications: the identification of small defining sets, and ensuring correctness of the technique in conjunction with dynamic variable ordering.

The defining sets obtained from static constraint graph analysis are too large to use in practice on all but the most structure restricted instances. To overcome this, practical nogood learning algorithms perform conflict analysis to obtain a much smaller set of culprit variables. Conflict analysis techniques work backwards from contradiction, and are therefore inapplicable when attempting to identify the set of assignments responsible for a positive solution count. Techniques for minimizing the defining set in the case of a satisfiable (good) subproblem need to be developed.

Nogood learning is not complicated by dynamic variable ordering; if the defining set assignment of some nogood subproblem reappears, then the solution count of the current subproblem is immediately known to be zero, even if the current subproblem does not exactly match the subproblem from which the defining set assignment was derived. With good learning, in addition to recording the defining set assignment, it seems we must explicitly keep track of all the variables appearing within the subproblem. This is because some of the subproblem's variables may be assigned values once the defining set assignment reappears, potentially affecting its solution count. In order to apply a good, in addition to the defining set assignment matching the partial assignment, all subproblem variables must be in an unassigned state. Good learning with dynamic variable ordering therefore requires additional overhead to check and record the subproblem variables, and perhaps more significantly, it reduces the probability with which a recorded good might be exploited in the future.

On the other hand, since hard instances for model counting typically contain comparatively few unsatisfiable subproblems, there are plenty more opportunities to learn goods than nogoods. This suggests good learning may still prove beneficial on sufficiently difficult instances even given the above limitations.

Conclusions and Future Work

We have demonstrated that recursive identification of connected components within a dynamically simplified constraint graph leads to an efficient DP-based algorithm for counting models of a propositional logic formula. In addition, from a structure-based perspective of complexity, we have shown that model counting using a learning-enhanced backtrack search algorithm is no more difficult than determining satisfiability.

One avenue remaining to be explored is whether good learning will lead to substantial performance gains when counting models in practice, as suggested by complexity results showing that good learning is mandatory for polynomial time counting. We have yet to solve the problem of providing an efficient and effective implementation of good learning in conjunction with dynamic variable ordering. Though this problem is non-trivial, we feel it is not insurmountable, and continue to contemplate solutions.

References

Bayardo, R. J. and Miranker, D. P. 1994. An Optimal Backtrack Algorithm for Tree-Structured Constraint Satisfaction Problems. *Artificial Intelligence,* 71(1):159-181.

Bayardo, R. J. and Miranker, D. P. 1995. On the space-time trade-off in solving constraint satisfaction problems. In *Proc. of the 14th Int'l Joint Conf. on Artificial Intelligence*, 558-562.

Bayardo, R. J. and Miranker, D. P. 1996. A Complexity Analysis of Space-Bounded Learning Algorithms for the Constraint Satisfaction Problem. In *Proc. 13th Nat'l Conf. on Artificial Intelligence*, 558-562.

Bayardo, R. J. and Schrag, R. 1997. Using CSP Look-Back Techniques to Solve Real-World SAT Instances. In *Proc. of the 14th National Conf. on Artificial Intelligence*, 203-208.

Birnbaum, E. and Lozinskii, E. L. 1999. The Good Old Davis-Putnam Procedure Helps Counting Models. *Journal of Artificial Intelligence Research* 10:457-477.

Crawford, J. M. and Auton, L. D. 1996. Experimental Results on the Crossover Point in Random 3SAT. *Artificial Intelligence* 81(1-2), 31-57.

Davis, M., Logemann, G. and Loveland, D. 1962. A Machine Program for Theorem Proving, *CACM* 5, 394-397.

Dechter R., and Pearl, J., 1987. Network-Based Heuristics for Constraint-Satisfaction Problems. *Artificial Intelligence*, 34(1):1-38.

Freeman, J. W. 1995. *Improvements to Propositional Satisfiability Search Algorithms*. Ph.D. Dissertation, U. Pennsylvania Dept. of Computer and Information Science.

Freuder, E.C. and Quinn, M.J., 1985. Taking Advantage of Stable Sets of Variables in Constraint Satisfaction Problems. In *Proceedings of IJCAI-85,* 1076-1078.

Frost, D. and Dechter, R. 1994. Dead-End Driven Learning. In *Proc. of the Twelfth Nat'l Conf. on Artificial Intelligence*, 294-300.

Hogg, T. 1996. Refining the Phase Transition in Combinatorial Search. *Artificial Intelligence*, 81:127-154.

Kautz, H. and Selman, B. 1996. Pushing the Envelope: Planning, Propositional Logic, and Stochastic Search. In *Proc. 13th Nat'l Conf. on Artificial Intelligence*, 558-562.

Lozinskii, E. 1992. Counting Propositional Models. *Information Processing Letters*, 41(6):327-332.

Melhorn, K. 1984. *Data Structures and Algorithms*, vol 1-3, Springer.

Prosser, P. 1993. Hybrid Algorithms for the Constraint Satisfaction Problem. *Computational Intelligence* 9(3):268-299.

Roth, D. 1996. On the Hardness of Approximate Reasoning. *Artificial Intelligence* 82, 273-302.

Rymon, R. 1994. An SE-tree-based Prime Implicant Generation Algorithm. *Annals of Mathematics and Artificial Intelligence* 11, 1994.

DATALOG with constraints — an answer-set programming system

Deborah East and **Mirosław Truszczyński**
Department of Computer Science
University of Kentucky
Lexington KY 40506-0046, USA
email: deast|mirek@cs.uky.edu

Abstract

Answer-set programming (ASP) has emerged recently as a viable programming paradigm well attuned to search problems in AI, constraint satisfaction and combinatorics. Propositional logic is, arguably, the simplest ASP system with an intuitive semantics supporting direct modeling of problem constraints. However, for some applications, especially those requiring that transitive closure be computed, it requires additional variables and results in large theories. Consequently, it may not be a practical computational tool for such problems. On the other hand, ASP systems based on nonmonotonic logics, such as stable logic programming, can handle transitive closure computation efficiently and, in general, yield very concise theories as problem representations. Their semantics is, however, more complex. Searching for the middle ground, in this paper we introduce a new nonmonotonic logic, *DATALOG with constraints* or DC. Informally, DC theories consist of propositional clauses (constraints) and of Horn rules. The semantics is a simple and natural extension of the semantics of the propositional logic. However, thanks to the presence of Horn rules in the system, modeling of transitive closure becomes straightforward. We describe the syntax and semantics of DC, and study its properties. We discuss an implementation of DC and present results of experimental study of the effectiveness of DC, comparing it with the `csat` satisfiability checker and `smodels` implementation of stable logic programming. Our results show that DC is competitive with the other two approaches, in case of many search problems, often yielding much more efficient solutions.
Content Areas: constraint saitsfaction, search, knowledge representation, logic programming, nonmonotonic reasoning.

Introduction

Many important computational problems in combinatorial optimization, constraint satisfaction and artificial intelligence can be cast as search problems. Answer-set programming (ASP) (Marek & Truszczyński 1999; Niemela 1998) was recently identified as a declarative programming paradigm appropriate for such applications. Logic programming with the stable-model semantics (*stable logic programming*, for short) was proposed as an embodiment of this paradigm. Disjunctive logic programming with the answer-set semantics is another implementation of ASP currently under development (Eiter *et al.* 1998). Early experimental results demonstrate the potential of answer-set programming approaches in such areas as planning and constraint satisfaction (Niemela 1998; Lifschitz 1999a; 1999b).

In this paper we describe another formalism that implements the ASP approach. We call it *DATALOG with constraints* and denote by DC. Our goal is to design an ASP system with a semantics more readily understandable than the semantics of stable models. We seek a semantics that would be as close as possible to propositional satisfiability yet as expressive and as effective, especially from the point of view of conciseness of representations and time performance, as the stable logic programming. We argue that DC has a potential to become a practical declarative programming tool. We show that it yields intuitive and small-size encodings, we characterize its complexity and expressive power and present computational experiments demonstrating its effectiveness.

Answer-set programming is a paradigm in which programs are built as theories in some formal system $\mathcal{F}$ with a well-defined syntax, and with a semantics that assigns to a theory P in the system a *collection* of subsets of some domain. These subsets are referred to as *answer sets* of P and specify the results of computation based on P. To solve a problem Π in an ASP formalism, we find a program P so that the solutions to Π can be reconstructed, in polynomial (ideally, linear) time, from the answer sets to P.

The definition of the answer-set programming given above is very general. Essentially any logic formalism can be a basis for an answer-set programming system. For instance, the propositional logic gives rise to an ASP system: programs are collections of propositional clauses, their models are answer sets. To solve, say, a planning problem, we encode the constraints of the problem as propositional clauses in such a way that legal plans are determined by models of the resulting propositional theory. This approach, called *satisfiability planning*, received significant attention lately and was shown to be quite effective (Kautz & Selman 1992; 1996; Kautz, McAllester, & Selman 1996).

Recently, several implementations of the ASP approach

Copyright © 2000, American Association for Artificial Intelligence (www.aaai.org). All rights reserved.

were developed that are based on nonmonotonic logics such as smodels (Niemela & Simons 1996), for stable logic programming, dlv (Eiter et al. 1998), for disjunctive logic programming with answer-set semantics, and deres (Cholewiński, Marek, & Truszczyński 1997), for default logic with Reiter's extensions. All these systems have been extensively studied. Promising experimental results concerning their performance were reported (Cholewiński et al. 1999; Eiter et al. 1998; Niemela 1998).

The question arises which formal logics are appropriate as bases of answer-set programming implementations. To discuss such a general question one needs to formulate quality criteria with respect to which ASP systems can be compared. At the very least, these criteria should include:
1. expressive power
2. time performance
3. simplicity of the semantics
4. ease of coding, conciseness of programs.

We will discuss these criteria in detail elsewhere. We will make here only a few brief comments on the matter. From the point of view of the expressive power all the systems that we discussed are quite similar. Propositional logic and stable logic programming are well-attuned to the class NP (Schlipf 1995). Disjunctive logic programming and default logic capture the class Σ_P^2 (Eiter & Gottlob 1995; Cadoli, Eiter, & Gottlob 1997). However, this distinction is not essential as recently pointed out in (Janhunen et al. 2000). The issue of time performance can be resolved only through comprehensive experimentation and this work is currently under way.

As concerns inherent complexity of the system and intuitiveness of the semantics, ASP systems based on the propositional logic seem to be clear winners. However, propositional logic is monotone and modeling indefinite information and phenomena such as the frame problem is not quite straightforward. In applications involving the computation of transitive closures, as in the problem of existence of hamilton cycles, it leads to programs that are large and, thus, difficult to process. In this respect, ASP systems based on nonmonotonic logics have an edge. They were designed to handle incomplete and indefinite information. Thus, they often yield more concise programs. However, they require more elaborate formal machinery and their semantics are more complex.

Searching for the middle ground between systems such as logic programming with stable model semantics and propositional logic, we propose here a new ASP formalism, DC. Our guiding principle was to design a system which would lead to small-size encodings, believing that small theories will lead to more efficient solutions. We show that DC is nonmonotonic, has the same expressive power as stable logic programming but that its semantics stays closer to that of propositional logic. Thus, it is arguably simpler than the stable-model semantics. We present experimental results that demonstrate that DC is competitive with ASP implementations based on nonmonotonic logics (we use smodels for comparison) and those based on propositional logics (we use csat (Dubois et al. 1996) in our experiments). Our results strongly indicate that formalisms which provide smaller-size encodings are more effective as practical search-problem solvers.

DATALOG with constraints

A DC theory (or program) consists of constraints and Horn rules (DATALOG program). This fact motivates out choice of terminology — DATALOG with constraints. We start a discussion of DC with the propositional case. Our language is determined by a set of atoms At. We will assume that At is of the form $At = At_C \cup At_H$, where At_C and At_H are disjoint.

A *DC theory* (or *DC program*) is a triple $T = (T_C, T_H, T_{PC})$, where
1. T_C is a set of propositional clauses $\neg a_1 \vee \ldots \vee \neg a_m \vee b_1 \vee \ldots \vee b_n$ such that all a_i and b_j are from At_C,
2. T_H is a set of Horn rules $a_1 \wedge \ldots \wedge a_m \rightarrow b$ such that $b \in At_H$ and all a_i are from At,
3. T_{PC} is a set of clauses over At.
By $At(T)$, $At_C(T)$ and $At_{PC}(T)$ we denote the set of atoms from At, At_C and At_{PC}, respectively, that actually appear in T.

With a DC theory $T = (T_C, T_H, T_{PC})$ we associate a family of subsets of $At_C(T)$. We say that a set $M \subseteq At_C(T)$ *satisfies* T (is an *answer set* of T) if
1. M satisfies all the clauses in T_C, and
2. the closure of M under the Horn rules in T_H, $M^c = LM(T_H \cup M)$ satisfies all clauses in T_{PC} ($LM(P)$ denotes the least model of a Horn program P).

Intuitively, the collection of clauses in T_C can be thought of as a representation of the constraints of the problem, Horn rules in T_H can be viewed as a mechanism to compute closures of sets of atoms satisfying the constraints in T_C, and the clauses in T_{PC} can be regarded as constraints on closed sets (we refer to them as *post-constraints*). A set of atoms $M \subseteq At_C(T)$ is a model if it (propositionally) satisfies the constraints in T_C and if its closure (propositionally) satisfies the constraints in T_{PC}. Thus, the semantics of DC retains much of the simplicity of the semantics of propositional logic.

DC can be used as a computational tool to solve search problems. We define a search problem Π to be determined by a set of finite *instances*, D_Π, such that for each instance $I \in D_\Pi$, there is a finite set $S_\Pi(I)$ of all *solutions* to Π for the instance I. For example, the problem of finding a hamilton cycle in a graph is a search problem: graphs are instances and for each graph, its hamilton cycles (sets of their edges) are solutions. A DC theory $T = (T_C, T_H, T_{PC})$ solves a search problem Π if solutions to Π can be computed (in polynomial time) from answer sets to T. Propositional logic and stable logic programming are used as problem solving formalisms following the same general paradigm. To illustrate all the concepts introduced here and show how DC programs can be built by modeling problem constraints, we will now present a DC program that solves the hamilton-cycle problem.

Consider a directed graph G with the vertex set V and the edge set E. Consider a set of atoms $\{hc(a,b): (a,b) \in E\}$. An intuitive interpretation of an atom $hc(a,b)$ is that the edge (a,b) is in a hamilton cycle. Include in T_C all clauses of the form $\neg hc(b,a) \vee \neg hc(c,a)$, where $a,b,c \in V$, $b \neq c$ and $(b,a),(c,a) \in E$. In addition, include in T_C all clauses of the form $\neg hc(a,b) \vee \neg hc(a,c)$, where $a,b,c \in V$, $b \neq c$ and $(a,b),(a,c) \in E$. Clearly, the set of propositional variables of the form $\{hc(a,b): (a,b) \in F\}$, where $F \subseteq E$, satisfies all clauses in T_C if and only if no two distinct edges in F end in the same vertex and no two distinct edges in F start in the same vertex. In other words, F spans a collection of paths and cycles in G.

To guarantee that the edges in F define a hamilton cycle, we must enforce that all vertices of G are reached by means of the edges in F if we start in some (arbitrarily chosen) vertex of G. This can be accomplished by means of a simple Horn program. Let us choose a vertex, say s, in G. Include in T_H the Horn rules $hc(s,t) \to vstd(t)$, for every edge (s,t) in G. In addition, include in T_H Horn rules $vstd(t), hc(t,u) \to vstd(u)$, for every edge (t,u) of G not starting in s. Clearly, the least model of $F \cup T_H$, where F is a subset of E, contains precisely these variables of the form $vstd(t)$ for which t is reachable from s by a *nonempty* path spanned by the edges in F. Thus, F is the set of edges of a hamilton cycle of G if and only if the least model of $F \cup T_H$, contains variable $vstd(t)$ for every vertex t of G. Let us define $T_{PC} = \{vstd(t): t \in V\}$ and $T_{ham}(G) = (T_C, T_H, T_{PC})$. It follows that hamilton cycles of G can be reconstructed (in linear time) from answer sets to the DC theory $T_{ham}(G)$. In other words, to find a hamilton cycle in G, it is enough to find an answer set for $T_{ham}(G)$.

This example illustrates the simplicity of the semantics — it is only a slight adaptation of the semantics of propositional logic to the case when in addition to propositional clauses we also have Horn rules in theories. It also illustrates the power of DC to generate concise encodings. All known propositional encodings of the hamilton-cycle problem require that additional variables are introduced to "count" how far from the starting vertex an edge is located. Consequently, propositional encodings are much larger and lead to inefficient computational approaches to the problem. We present experimental evidence to this claim later in the paper.

The question arises which search problems can be represented (and solved) by means of finding answer sets to appropriate DC programs. In general, the question remains open. We have an answer, though, if we restrict our attention to the special case of decision problems. Consider a DC theory $T = (T_C, T_H, T_{PC})$, where $T_H = T_{PC} = \emptyset$. Clearly, M is an answer set for T if and only if M is a model of the collection of clauses T_C. Thus, the problem of existence of an answer set is at least as hard as the propositional satisfiability problem. On the other hand, for every DC theory T and for every set $M \subseteq At_C(T)$, it can be checked in linear time whether M is an answer set for T. Thus, we obtain the following complexity result.

Theorem 1 *The problem of existence of an answer set for a finite propositional DC theory T is NP-complete.*

It follows that every problem in NP can be polynomially reduced to the problem of existence of an answer set for a propositional DC program. Thus, given a problem Π in NP, for every instance I of Π, Π can be decided by deciding the existence of an answer set for the DC program corresponding to Π and I.

Propositional DC can be extended to the predicate case. It is important as it significantly simplifies the task of developing programs for solving problems with DC. In the example discussed above, the theory $T_{ham}(G)$ depends heavily on the input. Each time we change the input graph, a different theory has to be used. However, when constructing predicate DC-based solutions to a problem Π, it is often possible to separate the representation of an instance (input) to Π from that of the constraints that define Π. As a result only one (predicate) program describing the constraints of Π needs to be written. Specific input for the program, say I, can be described separately as a collection of facts (according to some uniform schema). Both parts together can be combined to yield a DC program whose answer sets determine solutions to Π for the input I. Such an approach, we will refer to it as *uniform*, is often used in the context of DATALOG, DATALOG¬ or logic programming to study complexity of these systems as query languages. The part representing input is referred to as the *extensional* database. The part representing the query or the problem is called the *intensional* database or program. Due to the space limitations we do not discuss the details of the predicate case here. They will be given in the full version of the paper. We only state a generalization of Theorem 1.

Theorem 2 *The expressive power of DC is the same as that of stable logic programming. In particular, a decision problem Π can be solved uniformly in DC if and only if Π is in the class* NP.

Implementation

Some types of constraints appear frequently in applications. For instance, when defining plans we may want to specify a constraint that says that exactly one action from the set of allowed actions be selected at each step. Such constraints can be modeled by *collections* of clauses. To make sure DC programs are as easy to write and as concise as possible we have extended the syntax of DC by providing explicit ways to model constraints of the form "select at least (at most, exactly) k elements from a set". Having these constraints results in shorter programs which, as we believe, has a significant positive effect of the performance of our system.

An example of a select constraint with a short explanation is presented here. Let $PRED$ be the set of predicates occurring in the IDB. For each variable X declared in the IDB the range $R(X)$ of X is determined by the EDB.

Select$(n, m, \vec{Y}; p_1(\vec{X}), \ldots, p_i(\vec{X}, \vec{Y}))q(\vec{X}, \vec{Y})$,
where n, m are nonnegative integers such that $n \leq m$, $q \in PRED$ and $p_1, \ldots, p_i$ are EDB predicates or logical conditions (logical conditions can be comparisons of arithmetic expressions or string comparisons). The interpretation of this constraint is as follows: for every $\vec{x} \in R(\vec{X})$ at least n atoms and at most m atoms in the set $\{q(\vec{x}, \vec{y}) : \vec{y} \in R(\vec{Y})\}$ are true.

We implemented DC in the predicate setting. Thus, our system consists of two main modules. The first of them, referred to as `grounder`, converts a predicate DC program (consisting of both the extensional and intensional parts) into the corresponding propositional DC program. The second module, DC *solver*, denoted `dcs`, finds the answer sets to propositional DC programs. Since we focus on the propositional case here, we only describe the key ideas behind the DC solver, `dcs`.

The DC solver uses a Davis-Putnam type approach, with backtracking, propagation and lookahead (also called literal testing), to deal with constraints represented as clauses, *select* constraints and Horn rules, and to search for answer sets. The lookahead in DC is similar to local processing performed in `csat` (Dubois *et al.* 1996). However, we use different methods to determine how many literals to consider in the lookahead phase. Other techniques, especially propagation and search heuristics, were designed specifically for the case of DC as they must take into account the presence of Horn rules in programs.

The lookahead procedure selects a number of literals which have not yet been assigned a value. For each such literal, the procedure tries both truth values: true and false. For each assignment, the theory is evaluated using propagation. If in both cases a contradiction is reached, then it is necessary to backtrack. If for only one evaluation a conflict is reached, then the literal is assigned the other truth value and we proceed to the next step. If neither evaluation results in a contradiction, we cannot assign a truth value to this literal but we save the data such as the number of forced literals and the number of clauses satisfied, computed during propagation.

Clearly, if all unassigned literals were tested it would prune the most search space. At the same time, the savings might not be large enough to compensate for the increase in the running time caused by extensive lookahead. Thus, we select only a portion of all unassigned literals for lookahead. The number of literals to consider was established empirically (it does not depend on the size of the theory). Since not all literals are selected, it is important to focus on those literals that are likely to result in a contradiction for at least one of the truth values. In our implementation, we select the most constrained literals, as determined by their weights.

Specifically, each constraint is assigned a weight based on its current length and types (recall that in addition to propositional clauses, we also allow other types of constraints, e.g., select constraints). The shorter the constraint the greater its weight. Also, certain types of constraints force more assignments on literals and are given a greater weight than other constraints of the same length. Every time a literal appears in an unsatisfied constraint, the weight of that literal is incremented by the weight of the clause.

After testing a predetermined number of literals without finding a forced truth assignment and without backtracking, the information computed during propagation is used to choose the next literal for which both possible truth assignments have to be tested (branching literal). The choice of the next branching literal is based on an approximation of which literal, once assigned a truth value, will force the truth

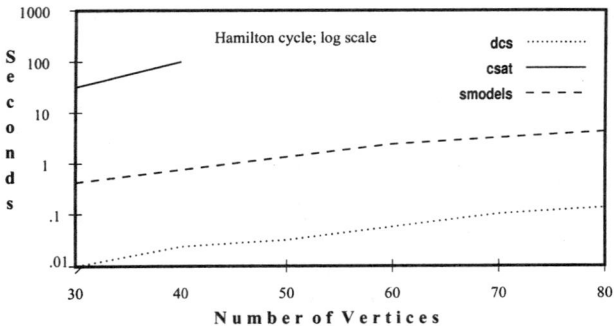

Figure 1: Hamilton cycle problem; times on the log scale as function of the number of vertices.

assignments onto the largest number of other literals and will satisfy the largest number of clauses. Using the data computed during propagation gives more accurate information on which to base such approximations. The methods used for determining which literals to select in the lookahead and which data to collect and save during the propagation phase are two key ways in which the literal testing procedure differs from the local processing of `csat`.

Experimentation

We compared the performance of DC solver `dcs` with `smodels`, a system for computing stable models of logic programs (Niemela & Simons 1996), and `csat`, a system for testing propositional satisfiability (Dubois *et al.* 1996). In the case of `smodels` we used version 2.24 in conjunction with the grounder `lparse`, version 0.99.41. These versions of `lparse` and `smodels` implement the expressive rules described by (Simons 1999). The expressive rules were used whenever applicable during the testing. The programs were all executed on a Sun SparcStation 20. For each test we report the cpu user times for processing the corresponding propositional program or theory. We tested all three system to compute hamilton cycles and colorings in graphs, to solve the N-queens problem, to prove that the pigeonhole problem has no solution if the number of pigeons exceeds the number of holes, and to compute Schur numbers.

The Hamilton cycle problem has already been described. We randomly generated one thousand graphs with the edge-to-vertex ratio such that $\approx 50\%$ of the graphs contained Hamilton cycles (crossover region). The number of vertices ranged from 30 to 80. We used encodings of the problem as a DC program, logic program (in `smodels` syntax) and as a propositional theory. `dcs` performed better than `smodels` and `smodels` performed significantly better than `csat` (Fig. 1). We believe that a major factor behind poorer performance of `csat` is that all known propositional encodings of the hamilton cycle problem are much larger than those possible with DC or logic programs (under the stable model semantics). Propositional encodings, due to their size, rendered `csat` not practical to execute for graphs with more than 40 vertices.

The N-queens problem consists of finding a placement

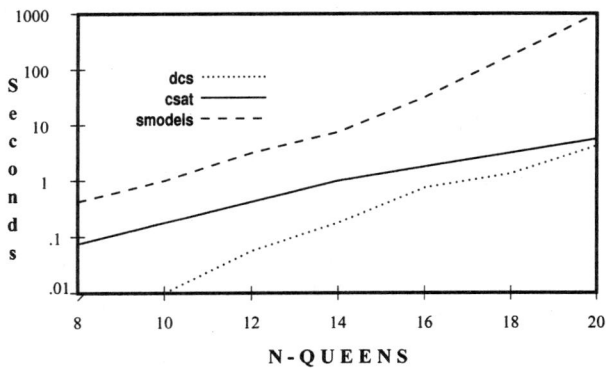

Figure 2: N-queens problem; log scale

B-N	csat	dcs	smodel
b-n	sec	sec	sec
3-13	0.03	0.00	0.12
3-14	0.05	0.00	0.16
4-14	0.05	0.01	0.23
4-43	0.59	1.91	5.23
4-44	1.95	51.04	5.55
4-45	1599.92	226.44	12501.00

Figure 3: Schur problem; times and the number of choice points.

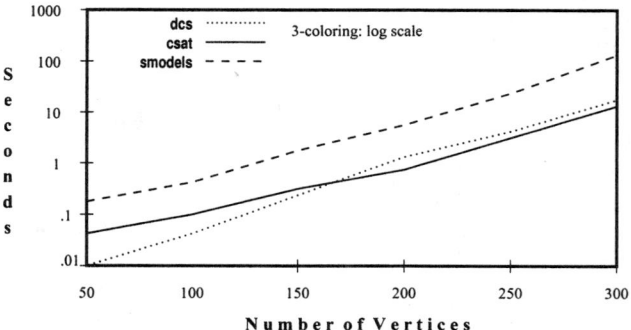

Figure 4: 3-coloring problem; log scale.

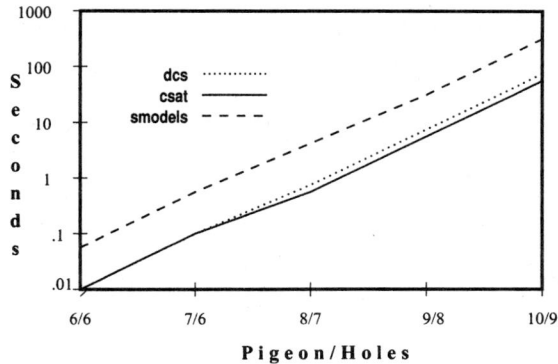

Figure 5: Pigeonhole problem; log scale.

of N queens on an $N \times N$ board such that no queen can remove another. Both csat and dcs execute in much less time than smodels for these problems (Fig. 2). Again the size of the encoding seems to be a major factor. One thing to consider in this case is that the number of rules for smodels is approximately five times that for DC and more than twice that of propositional encodings.

The Schur problem consists of placing N numbers $1, 2, \ldots, N$ in B bins such that no bin is closed under sums. That is, for all numbers $x, y, z, 1 \leq x, y, z \leq N$, if x and y are the same bin, then z is not (x and y need not be distinct). The Schur number $S(B)$ is the maximum number N for which such a placement is still possible. It is known to exist for every $B \geq 1$. We considered the problem of the existence of the placement for $B = 3$ and $N = 13$ and 14, and for $B = 4$ and $N = 43, 44$ and 45. In each case we used all three systems to process the corresponding encodings. The results are shown in Fig. 3. It follows that $S(3) = 13$ and $S(4) = 44$. Again, dcs outperforms both smodels and csat.

Results for graph 3-coloring for graphs with the number of vertices ranging from 50 to 300 are shown in Fig. 4 (for every choice of the number of vertices, 100 graphs from the crossover region were randomly generated). Both dcs and csat performed better than smodels. Again the size of the theory seems to be a factor. The CNF theory for coloring is smaller than a logic program encoding the same problem. The sizes of propositional and DC encodings are similar.

Results for the pigeonhole placement problem show a similar performance of all three algorithms, with csat doing slightly better than the others and dcs outperforming (again only slightly) smodels.

Conclusions

We described a new system, DC, for solving search problems. We designed DC so that its semantics was as close as possible to that of propositional logic. Our goal was to design a system that would result is short problem encodings. Thus, we provided constructs for some frequently occurring types of constraints and we built into DC elements of nonmonotonicity by including Horn rules in the syntax. As a result, DC programs encoding search problems are often much smaller than those possible with propositional theories. Experimental results show that dcs often outperforms systems based on propositional satisfiability as well as systems based on nonmonotonic logics, and that it constitutes a viable approach to solving problems in AI, constraint satisfaction and combinatorial optimization. We believe that our focus on short programs is the key to the success of DC and its reasoning engine dcs. Our results show that when building general purpose solvers of search problems, the size of encodings should be a key design factor.

References

Cadoli, M.; Eiter, T.; and Gottlob, G. 1997. Default logic as a query language. *IEEE Transactions on Knowledge and Data Engineering* 9(3):448–463.

Cholewiński, P.; Marek, W.; Mikitiuk, A.; and Truszczyński, M. 1999. Computing with default logic. *Artificial Intelligence* 112:105–146.

Cholewiński, P.; Marek, W.; and Truszczyński, M. 1997. Default reasoning system deres. In *Proceedings of KR-96*, 512–528. Morgan Kaufman.

Dubois, O.; Andre, P.; Boufkhad, Y.; and Carlier, J. 1996. Sat versus unsat. *DIMACS Cliques, Coloring and Satisfiability* 26.

Eiter, T., and Gottlob, G. 1995. Computing with default logic. *Annals of Mathematics and Artificial Intelligence* 15(3-4):289–323.

Eiter, T.; Leone, N.; Mateis, C.; Pfeifer, G.; and Scarcello, F. 1998. A kr system dlv: Progress report, comparisons and benchmarks. In *Proceedings of Sixth International Conference on Knowledge Representation and Reasoning (KR '98)*, 406–417. Morgan Kaufman.

Janhunen, T.; Niemelä, I.; Simons, P.; and You, J. 2000. Unfolding partiality and disjunctions in stable models semantics. manuscript.

Kautz, H. A., and Selman, B. 1992. Planning as satisfiability. In *Proceedings of the 10th European Conference on Artificial Intelligence*.

Kautz, H., and Selman, B. 1996. Pushing the envelope: Planning, propositional logic, and stochastic search. In *Proccedings of the Thirteenth National Conference on Artificial Intelligence (AAAI-96)*.

Kautz, H.; McAllester, D.; and Selman, B. 1996. Encoding plans in propositional logic. In *Proceedings of the Fifth International Conference on Principles of Knowledge Representation and Reasoning (KR-96)*.

Lifschitz, V. 1999a. Action languages, answer sets, and planning. In Apt, K.; Marek, W.; Truszczyński, M.; and Warren, D., eds., *The Logic Programming Paradigm: a 25-Year Perspective*. Springer Verlag. 357–373.

Lifschitz, V. 1999b. Answer set planning. In *Proceedings of the 1999 International Conference on Logic Programming*, 23–37. MIT Press.

Marek, V., and Truszczyński, M. 1999. Stable models and an alternative logic programming paradigm. In Apt, K.; Marek, W.; Truszczyński, M.; and Warren, D., eds., *The Logic Programming Paradigm: a 25-Year Perspective*. Springer Verlag. 375–398.

Niemela, I., and Simons, P. 1996. Efficient implementation of the well-founded and stable model semantics. In *Proceedings of JICSLP-96*. MIT Press.

Niemela, I. 1998. Logic programs with stable model semantics as a constraint programming paradigm. In *Proceedings of the Workshop on Computational Aspects of Nonmonotonic Reasoning*, 72–79.

Schlipf, J. 1995. The expressive powers of the logic programming semantics. *Journal of the Computer Systems and Science* 51(1):64–86.

Simons, P. 1999. Extending the stable model semantics with more expressive rules. In Gelfond, M.; Leone, N.; and Pfeifer, G., eds., *Proceedings of 5th International Conference, LPNMR '99*, volume 1730 of *Lecture Notes in Artificial Intelligence*, 305–316. Springer Verlag.

Local search with constraint propagation and conflict-based heuristics

Narendra Jussien
École des Mines de Nantes – BP 20722
F-44307 NANTES Cedex 3 – FRANCE
Narendra.Jussien@emn.fr

Olivier Lhomme
ILOG – Les Taissounières HB2
1681 route des Dolines – F-06560 VALBONNE – FRANCE
olhomme@ilog.fr

Abstract

In this paper, we introduce a new solving algorithm for Constraint Satisfaction Problems (CSP). It performs an overall local search helped with a domain filtering technique to prune the search space. Conflicts detected during filtering are used to guide the search. First experiments with a tabu version of the algorithm have shown good results on hard instances of open shop scheduling problems. It competes well with the best highly specialized algorithms.

Introduction

Many industrial and engineering problems can be modeled as constraint satisfaction problems (CSP). A CSP is defined as a set of variables each with an associated domain of possible values and a set of constraints over those variables.

Most of constraint solving algorithms are built upon backtracking mechanisms. Those algorithms usually explore the search space systematically, and thus guarantee to find a solution if one exists. Backtracking-based search algorithms are usually improved by using some relaxation techniques (usually called filtering techniques in the CSP world) which aim at pruning the search space in order to decrease the overall duration of the search.

Another series of constraint solving algorithms are local search based algorithms (eg. *min-conflict* (Minton, Johnston, & Laird 1992), GSAT (Selman, Levesque, & Mitchell 1992), *tabu search* (Glover & Laguna 1993)). They perform a probabilistic exploration of the search space and therefore cannot guarantee to find a solution, but may be far more efficient (*wrt* reponse time) than systematic ones to find a solution.

Several works have studied cooperation between local and systematic search (Yokoo 1994; Pesant & Gendreau 1996; David 1997; Schaerf 1997; Gervet 1998; Richards & Richards 1998). Those hybrid approaches have led to good results on large scale problems. Three categories of hybrid approaches can be found in the literature:

1. performing a local search before or after a systematic search;

Copyright © 2000, American Association for Artificial Intelligence (www.aaai.org). All rights reserved.

2. performing a systematic search improved with a local search at some points of the search (typically for optimisation problems, to try to improve the quality of a solution);

3. performing an overall local search, and using systematic search either to select a candidate neighbor or to prune the search space.

The hybrid approach presented in this paper falls in the third category. It uses filtering techniques to both prune the search space and help in choosing the neighbor in a local search. This leads to a generic search technique over CSP which is called `path-repair`. An implementation of `path-repair` which merges a tabu search together with a filtering technique and conflict-based heuristics to guide the search is described in this paper. That implementation has been used to solve open shop scheduling problems. It has given very good results on hard instances well competing with the best highly specialized algorithms. This was quite surprising since, unlike those specialized algorithms, our implementation is general and does not need any tuning of complex parameters.

The paper is organized as follows. The following section presents the notation used. Next we introduce the `path-repair` algorithm. Then related works are discussed. Finally first results obtained in the field of open shop scheduling problems are presented.

Preliminaries

A CSP is a pair $< V, C >$ where V is a set of variables and $C = \{c_1, \ldots, c_m\}$ a set of constraints. The domains of the variables are handled as unary constraints.

For a given constraints set $S = \{c_1, \ldots, c_k\}$, $\hat{S}$ will be the logical conjunction of the constraints in S: $\hat{S} = (c_1 \wedge \ldots \wedge c_k)$. By convention: $\hat{\varnothing} = true$.

Classical CSP solving simultaneously involves a filtering algorithm, to *a priori* prune the search tree, and an enumeration mechanism, to overcome the incompleteness of that filtering algorithm. For example, for binary CSP over finite domains, arc-consistency can be used as filtering technique. After a filtering step, three situations may arise:

1. the domain of a variable becomes empty: there is no feasible solution;

2. all the domains are reduced to a singleton: those values assigned to their respective variables provide a feasible solution for the considered problem;

3. there exists at least one domain which contains two values or more: the search has not yet been successful. In a classical approach, it would be time for enumeration through a backtracking-based mechanism.

In a more general way, a filtering algorithm Φ applied on a set C of constraints returns a new set $C' = \Phi(C)$ such that $C \subseteq C'$ (Note that we consider domain reductions as addition of redundant constraints). Moreover, for any filtering algorithm Φ applied on the set C of constraints of a given CSP, there exists a function obviousInference which, when applied on $C' = \Phi(C)$, answers:

- *noSolution* iff it is immediate to infer that no solution can be find for C' (as in situation 1 above).
- *solution* iff the current constraint system can immediately provide a solution that verifies all the constraints in C' (as in situation 2 above).
- *flounder* in all other situations (as in situation 3 above).

The function obviousInference has typically a low computational cost. Its aim is to make explicit the use of some properties that depends on the filtering algorithm that is used. The example of arc-consistency filtering with an empty domain or with only singleton domains has already been given, but a function obviousInference can be made explicit in many other filtering or pruning algorithms. For example, in integer linear programming, the aim is to find an optimal integer solution. This can be done by using the simplex algorithm over the reals. If there is no real solution or if the real optimum has only integer values, then an obviousInference function would respectively return *noSolution* or *solution*.

Enumerating discrete binary CSP is assigning a value a to a variable v *i.e.* adding a new constraint $v = a$. For other kinds of problems, enumerating may be different: for example, when dealing with scheduling problems, enumerating is often adding a precedence constraint between two tasks of the problem. We will call those constraints *decision* constraints.

In the next section, the path-repair algorithm is presented through an abstraction of the solved problems: they may be discrete binary CSP, numeric CSP as well as scheduling problems. This will be possible thanks to:

1. the parameter Φ which represents the filtering algorithm used;
2. the function obviousInference, tightly related to the used filtering algorithm, that is able to examine a set of constraints in order to continue the computation or not;
3. the concept of *decision* constraint.

The path-repair algorithm

The idea of the path-repair algorithm is very simple. First observe that:

```
procedure path-repair(C)
(1)  begin
(2)    repeat
(3)      if conditions of failure verified then
(4)        return failure
(5)      else
(6)        C' ← φ(C ∪ C_P)
(7)        switch obviousInference(C')
(8)          case noSolution :
(9)            k ← nogood explaining the failure
(10)           P ← neighbor(P, k, Γ)
(11)         case solution :
(12)           return C'
(13)         default :
(14)           P ← extend(P, Γ)
(15)       endswitch
(16)     endif
(17)   until false
(18) end
```

Figure 1: The *path-repair* algorithm

- current local search algorithms mainly work upon a total instantiation of the variables;
- backtracking-based search algorithms work upon a partial instantiation of the variables.

The ability of backtracking-based search algorithms to be combined with filtering techniques only comes from the fact that they work upon a partial instantiation of the variables. Thus, a local search algorithm working upon a partial instantiation of the variables would have the same ability. Indeed, the path-repair algorithm is such an algorithm. The considered partial instantiation is defined by a set of decision constraints (as described above) on the variables of the problem. Such a constraint set defines a *path* in the search tree.

Principles of path-repair

The principles of the path-repair algorithm as shown in figure 1 are the following: let P be a path in the search tree. At each node of that path, a decision constraint has been added. Let C_P be the set of added decision constraints while moving along P.

The path-repair algorithm starts with an initial path (it may range from the empty path to a path that defines a complete assignment). The main loop first checks the *conditions of failure*[1]. A filtering algorithm is then applied on $C \cup C_P$ giving a new set of constraints $C' = \Phi(C \cup C_P)$. The function obviousInference is then called over C'. Three cases may occur:

- obviousInference(C') = *solution*: a solution has been found. The algorithm terminates and returns C'.
- obviousInference(C') = *flounder*: the path-repair algorithm tries to extend the current path P by adding a decision constraint. That behavior is similar to

---
[1]These conditions depend on the instance of the algorithm; examples are given in the following sections.

that of backtracking-based search algorithms. For that purpose, a function extend(P,Γ) is assumed to exists that chooses a decision constraint to be added and adds it to P. Parameter Γ can be used to store a context that varies according to the chosen version of the algorithm. Its meaning will be made clear later.

- obviousInference(C') = noSolution: $C \cup C_P$ is inconsistent. We will say that P is a *dead-end*, or P is *inconsistent*: P cannot be extended. The path-repair algorithm will thus try to *repair* the current path by choosing a new path through the function neighbor(P,k,Γ). Parameter k as Γ will be explained later.

The path-repair algorithm appears here as a search method that handles partial instantiations and uses filtering techniques to prune the search space. The key components of this algorithm are the neighboring computation functions (neighbor) and the extension functions (extend).

Nogoods in path-repair

In a local search algorithm such as GSAT (on boolean CSP), an inconsistent instantiation is replaced by a new one built by negating the value of one of its variables. That variable is heuristically chosen (*eg.* selecting the one whose negation will allow the greatest number of clauses to become satisfied). More generally, a local search algorithm uses complete instantiations (called *states*) and replaces an inconsistent state with another state chosen among its *neighbors*.

The path-repair algorithm works in the same way except that it uses partial instantiations (paths): as soon as a path becomes inconsistent, one of its neighbors needs to be chosen. A path (partial instantiation) synthetizes all the included complete instantiations. Switching paths is like setting aside many irrelevant complete instantiations in one movement.

Like any local search algorithm, path-repair may use a heuristic way to select an interesting neighbor. It seems to be a good idea to select a neighboring path P' which does not have the drawbacks of the current path P (recall that in path-repair, neighbors of path P are computed iff P is inconsistent). Ideally, we would like to get to a consistent neighbor P' *i.e.* such that obviousInference($\Phi(C \cup C'_{P'})$) = solution. However, that is equivalent to solve the whole problem.

Instead, we may try to get to a partially consistent neighbor P' *i.e.* such that obviousInference($\Phi(C \cup C'_{P'})$) $\neq$ noSolution. Unfortunately, the only way to get there (without using computing resources) is to get back to an already explored node but, doing so, we would achieve a kind of backtracking mechanism, what is not wanted in the path-repair algorithm.

Nevertheless, what can be done is to avoid the neighbors that can already be known as inconsistent. Such an information can be extracted from an inconsistent path P. Indeed, inconsistency means that $\hat{C} \wedge \hat{C_P} \Longrightarrow false$. It is possible to compute a subset of C_P that is alone inconsistent with C. Such a subset is called a conflict set or *nogood*.

Definition 1 (Nogood) *A nogood k for a set of constraints C and a path P, is a set of constraints such that: $k \subset C_P$ and $\hat{C} \wedge \hat{k} \Longrightarrow false$.*

Now, we can define a neighbor P' of a path P according to a single nogood k. As long as constraints in the computed nogood k remain altogether in a given path P', that path will remain inconsistent. Therefore, in order to get a path with some hope to be consistent, we need to remove from the current path P at least one of the constraints in k.

Indeed, a more precise neighborhood can be computed. Let $c \in k$ be a constraint to be removed from C_P. As long as all the constraints in $k \setminus c$ remain in the active path, c will never be satisfiable. Thus, the negation of c can be added in the new path. A neighbor of a path P according to a nogood k is thus defined as follows:

Definition 2 (Neighbor wrt one nogood) *Let k be a nogood for a path P, a neighbor P' of P wrt k verifies $\exists c \in k, C_{P'} = C_P \setminus c \cup \{\neg c\}$*

Computing nogoods Note that if the current path P is inconsistent, C_P is a valid nogood. Obviously, a strict subset will be much more interesting and will give a more precise neighborhood. A minimal (for the inclusion) nogood would be the best, but could be expensive to compute (Verfaillie & Lobjois 1999). The current implementation does not try to find such a minimal nogood. Instead, it tries to find a *good* nogood in a fast way.

Nogoods are provided by the filtering algorithm as soon as it can prove that no solution exists in the subsequent complete paths derived from the current partial path. In filtering based constraint solving algorithms, a contradiction is raised as soon as the domain of a variable v becomes empty. Suppose that, for each value (or set of values) a_i removed from the domain of v, a set of decision constraints $k_i \subset C_P$ is given (k_i is called a removal explanation for a_i) and is such that: $\hat{C} \wedge \hat{k_i} \Longrightarrow v \neq a_i$. If so, $k = \bigcup_i k_i$ is a nogood since no value for v is allowed by the union of the k_i. Therefore, in order to compute nogoods, it is sufficient to be able to compute an explanation for each value (or set of values) removal from the domain of the failing variable.

Value removals are direct consequences of the filtering algorithms. Therefore, value removal explanations can be easily computed by using a trace mechanism embedded within the filtering algorithm and memorizing the reason why a removal is done (*eg.* see (Jussien & Lhomme 1998)).

For example, let us consider two variables v_1 and v_2 whose domains are both $\{1,2,3\}$. Let c_1 be the constraint: $v_1 \geq 3$ and let c_2 be the constraint: $v_2 \geq v_1$. Let us assume that the used filtering algorithm is arc-consistency filtering. The constraint c_1 explains the fact that $\{1,2\}$ should be removed from v_1. Afterwards, c_2 leads to remove $\{1,2\}$ from v_2. An explanation of the removal of $\{1,2\}$ from v_2 will be: $c_1 \wedge c_2$ because c_2 makes that removal only because previous removals occured in v_1 due to c_1.

Tabu path-repair

In a local search algorithm, the neighbor selection is very important. Many heuristics may be used. That is also the

```
    function neighbor(P, k, Γ)
          % precondition:   k ⊂ C_P, P covers Γ
(1)   begin
(2)       add k to the list of nogoods Γ
(3)       if sizeof(Γ) > s then
(4)           remove the oldest element of Γ
(5)       endif
(6)       L ← ordered list (decr. weight) of constraints in k
(7)       repeat
(8)           remove the first constraint c from L
(9)           P' ← P \ {c} ∪ {¬c}
(10)          if C_{P'} covers all nogoods in Γ then
(11)              return P'
(12)          endif
(13)      until L empty
(14)      return stop (or extend the neighborhood)
(15)  end
```

Figure 2: The `neighbor` function for *tabu* `path-repair`

case in `path-repair`.

The *tabu* version of `path-repair` uses a tabu list of a given size s. The s last computed nogoods are kept in a list Γ. The following invariant is maintained by the algorithm: the current path P covers all the nogoods in Γ, *ie* does not completely contain any of the nogoods in Γ.

We have defined so far a neighbor *wrt* one single nogood, so we have to extend the definition when facing multiple nogoods.

Definition 3 (Neighbor *wrt* several nogoods) *A valid neighbor is defined as a path that covers all the nogoods in Γ.*

In other words, at least one constraint in each nogood of Γ is not (or is negated) in the new neighbor. To compute such a neighbor in a reasonable time, a greedy algorithm can be used.

Figure 2 shows an implementation of the *neighbor* function for *tabu* `path-repair` that has been used for solving scheduling problems.

The *neighbor* function has to record in Γ the new nogood k found by the filtering algorithm and to maintain the invariant. It tries to find one constraint in k such that negating this constraint makes the path cover all the nogoods. An integer (weight) is associated with each constraint counting the number of times that the constraint has appeared in any nogood. The *neighbor* function chooses to negate the constraint with the greatest weight that, when negated, makes the new path cover all the nogoods in Γ. If such a constraint does not exist, the neighborhood can be extended. For example, we may try to negate two constraints. In our implementation for open shop problems (see last section), this case is handled as a stopping criterion, so there is no need for any neighborhood extension.

Note that, in the same way, the function `extend(P, Γ)` has to use Γ in order to extend the partially consistent current path while maintaining the invariant. A heuristically ordered list of constraints which performs an extension of the current path is dynamically generated and the first constraint that covers all the nogoods in Γ is chosen.

As for now, our algorithm seems to need to call the filtering algorithm many times with little changes to handle in the constraint set. Of course, it would not be very efficient to each time recompute for example the arc-consistency closure from scratch. That problem has been addressed for dynamic CSP. The algorithms used in `path-repair` are similar to those of (Bessière 1991; Debruyne 1996) or other works (Jussien & Lhomme 1998).

Related works

The `path-repair` algorithm takes its roots in many other works, among which (Ginsberg & McAllester 1994) has probably been the most influential by highlighting the relationships between local search and systematic search, and by the use of nogoods to guide the search and make it systematic. In the same spirit are (Ginsberg 1993), (Frost & Dechter 1994), (Schiex & Verfaillie 1994) and (Bliek 1998).

Two algorithms have been designed that have similarities with the `path-repair` algorithm:

- The algorithm proposed in (Schaerf 1997) can be seen as an instance of the `path-repair` algorithm where: the decision contraints are instantiations; there is no propagation and no pruning (the filtering algorithm Φ only consists in checking if the constraints containing only instantiated variables are not violated) and it does not make use of nogoods neither in the the *neighbor* function nor in the *extend* function.

  The common idea, which already exists in previous works (Jackson 1990), is essentially to extend a partial instantiation when it is consistent, and to perform a local change when the partial solution appears to be a dead-end.

- The idea to use a filtering algorithm during the running of a local search has been also used in (Stuckey & Tam 1998), where an extension to GENET, a local search method based on an artificial neural network aiming at solving binary CSP, is introduced. This extension achieves what is called "lazy arc-consistency" during the search. The lazy arc-consistency filtering performs a filtering over the initial domains. The result is at most the one obtained by filtering the domains before any search. In path repair, the filtering is applied over the current domains at every step.

The heuristic we used to select the decision constraint to negate – choose the one that has appeared the greatest number of times in a nogood – is an adaptation of a similar approach for GSAT counting the number of times that a constraint has not been verified (Selman & Kautz 1993).

The way nogoods are computed by the filtering algorithm is a well-known technique that has already been used with slight variations for different combinations of filtering algorithms with systematic search algorithms (forward checking + intelligent backtracking (Prosser 1993), forward checking + dynamic backtracking (Verfaillie & Schiex 1994), arc-consistency + intelligent backtracking (Codognet, Fages, & Sola 1993), arc-consistency + dynamic backtracking

(Jussien 1997), 2B-consistency + dynamic backtracking (Jussien & Lhomme 1998). Nevertheless, as far as we know, the *tabu* version of `path-repair` is the first time such a technique is used in combination with a local search algorithm.

Solving scheduling problems

Classical scheduling shop problems for which a set J of n jobs consisting each in m tasks (operations) must be scheduled on a set M of m machines can be considered as CSP upon intervals[2]. One of those problems is called the Open Shop problem (Gonzales & Sahni 1976). For that problem, operations for a given job may be sequenced as wanted but only one at a time. We will consider here the building of non preemptive schedules of minimal makespan[3]. That problem is NP-hard as soon as $\min(n, m) \geq 3$.

Constraints on resources (machines and jobs) are propagated thanks to *immediate selections* from (Carlier & Pinson 1994). The consistency level achieved by that technique does not ensure the computation of a feasible solution. An enumeration step is therefore needed. For shop problems, enumeration is classically performed on the relative order on which tasks are scheduled on the resources. When every possible precedence has been posted, setting the starting date of the variable to their smallest value provides a feasible solution. Such a precedence constraint is therefore a decision constraint as described above.

One of the best systematic search algorithms developed for the Open Shop problem is the branch and bound algorithm presented in (Brucker *et al.* 1994). It consists in adding precedence constraints along the critical path of a heuristic solution in each node. As far as we know, although this is one of the best methods ever, some problems of size 7×7 remain unsolved.

We tested a *tabu* version of `path-repair`. That version is fully systematic due to the used heuristics. Table 1 presents the results obtained on a series of 30 problems from Taillard (1993). In order to put in perspective our results, we recall results presented in (Alcaide, Sicilia, & Vigo 1997) and (Liaw 1998). Those papers present tabu searches specifically developed for the Open Shop problem. Those methods both use carefully chosen complex parameter values. Results presented in table 1 show that our simple approach which merely applies principles presented in this paper already gives very good results. More precisely, the time required to solve those problems is similar to those reported by (Alcaide, Sicilia, & Vigo 1997) and (Liaw 1998). Moreover, for the problems of size 4×4, the obtained results are the same as those of (Liaw 1998); for 5×5 problems, if our algorithm gives bad results, they are not very far from the results of (Liaw 1998) but it often gives the same results and even a better one for the 5x5-3 problem; for 7×7 problems, our algorithms gives the same results as the best of the two others except for four problems among which three

---

[2]Variables are the starting date of the tasks. Bounds thus represent the least feasible starting time and the least feasible ending time of the associated task.

[3]Ending time of the last task.

```
procedure minimize-makespan(C)
(1)  begin
(2)      P ← initial path
(3)      bound ← +∞
(4)      lastSolution ← failure
(5)      repeat
(6)          C ← C ∪ { makespan < bound}
(7)          solution ← path-repair(C)
(8)          if solution = failure then
(9)              return lastSolution
(10)         else
(11)             bound ← value of makespan in solution
(12)             lastSolution ← solution
(13)         endif
(14)     until false
(15) end
```

Figure 3: Algorithm used to solve Taillard's problems

are worse (but not much) and one is better (7x7-5). In a few words, our algorithm seems to compete well with those highly customized algorithms.

Our implementation uses a tabu list of size 15. The `neighbor` function is the one given in figure 2. The conditions of failure specifying the exit of the main loop (figure 1) are either a *stop* returned by the `neighbor` function or 1500 iterations without improvement of the last solution reached.

Taillard's problems are optimization problems. This requires a main loop that calls the function `path-repair` until improvement is no longer possible (see figure 3). Improvements are generated by adding a constraint that specifies that the makespan is less than the current best solution found. The initial path for each call of the function `path-repair` is the latest path (which describes the last solution found).

Conclusion and future works

In this paper, we introduced a new solving algorithm for CSP: the `path-repair` algorithm. The two main points of that algorithm are: it makes use of a repair algorithm (local search) as a basis and it works on a partial instantiation in order to be able to use filtering techniques. The most useful tool to implement that algorithm was the use of *nogoods*: nogoods allow relevant neighborhoods to be considered and nogoods can be used to derive efficient neighbor selecting heuristics for a `path-repair` algorithm.

First experiments with a tabu version of `path-repair` has shown good results over open shops scheduling problems. It competes well with the best highly specialized algorithms. This was quite surprising since, unlike those specialized algorithms, our implementation is general and does not need any tuning of complex parameters. Experiments over other problems are currently being done.

Acknowledgements

We would like to thank Christian Bliek for his useful suggestions.

Problem	Solution	PR	Dist.	L	A
4x4-1	193	193	-	193	-
4x4-2	236	236	-	236	-
4x4-3	271	271	-	271	-
4x4-4	250	250	-	250	-
4x4-5	295	295	-	295	-
4x4-6	189	189	-	189	-
4x4-7	201	201	-	201	-
4x4-8	217	217	-	217	-
4x4-9	261	261	-	261	-
4x4-10	217	217	-	217	-
5x5-1	300	301	0.33 %	300	-
5x5-2	262	262	-	262	-
5x5-3	323	323	-	326	-
5x5-4	310	311	0.32 %	310	-
5x5-5	326	326	-	326	-
5x5-6	312	314	0.64 %	312	-
5x5-7	303	304	0.33 %	303	-
5x5-8	300	300	-	300	-
5x5-9	353	356	0.85 %	353	-
5x5-10	326	326	-	326	-
7x7-1	435	435	-	435	437
7x7-2	443	449	1.35 %	447	444
7x7-3	468	**473**	1.07 %	474	476
7x7-4	463	463	-	463	464
7x7-5	416	**416**	-	417	417
7x7-6	451	460	2.00 %	459	-
7x7-7	422	430	1.90 %	429	429
7x7-8	424	424	-	424	-
7x7-9	458	458	-	458	458
7x7-10	398	398	-	398	398

Table 1: Results on Taillard's problems

PR : results using `path-repair` restricted to 1500 moves without improvement, **Dist.** represents the distance to the optimum value. **L** : results obtained by Liaw with 50 000 moves without improvement and **A** : results obtained by Alcaide et al. with 100 000 moves without improvement. - : represents unknown values.

References

Alcaide, D.; Sicilia, J.; and Vigo, D. 1997. A tabu search algorithm for the open shop problem. *TOP : Trabajos de Investigación Operativa* 5(2):283–296.

Bessière, C. 1991. Arc consistency in dynamic constraint satisfaction problems. In *Proceedings AAAI'91*.

Bliek, C. 1998. Generalizing partial order and dynamic backtracking. In *Proceedings of AAAI*.

Brucker, P.; Hurink, J.; Jurisch, B.; and Westmann, B. 1994. A branch and bound algorithm for the open-shop problem. Technical report, Osnabrueck University.

Carlier, J., and Pinson, E. 1994. Adjustment of heads and tails for the job-shop problem. *European Journal of Operational Research* 78:146–161.

Codognet, P.; Fages, F.; and Sola, T. 1993. A metalevel compiler of CLP(FD) and its combination with intelligent backtracking. In Benhamou, F., and Colmerauer, A., eds., *Constraint Logic Programming - Selected Research*. Massachussetts Institute of Technology. chapter 23, 437–456.

David, P. 1997. A constraint-based approach for examination timetabling using local repair techniques. In *Proceedings of the Second International Conference on the Practice And Theory of Automated Timetabling (Patat'97)*, 132–145.

Debruyne, R. 1996. Arc-consistency in dynamic CSPs is no more prohibitive. In 8th *Conference on Tools with Artificial Intelligence (TAI'96)*, 299–306.

Frost, and Dechter. 1994. Dead-end driven learning. In *12th National Conf. on Artificial Intelligence, AAAI94*.

Gervet, C. 1998. Large combinatorial optimization problem methodology for hybrid models and solutions (invited talk). In *JFPLC*.

Ginsberg, M., and McAllester, D. A. 1994. Gsat and dynamic backtracking. In *International Conference on the Principles of Knowledge Representation (KR94)*, 226–237.

Ginsberg, M. 1993. Dynamic backtracking. *Journal of Artificial Intelligence Research* 1:25–46.

Glover, F., and Laguna, M. 1993. *Modern heuristic Techniques for Combinatorial Problems, chapter Tabu Search, C. Reeves*. Blackwell Scientific Publishing.

Gonzales, T., and Sahni, S. 1976. Open-shop scheduling to minimize finish time. *Journal of the Association for Computing Machinery* 23(4):665–679.

Jackson, P. 1990. *Introduction to Expert Systems*. Readings. Addison Wesley.

Jussien, N., and Lhomme, O. 1998. Dynamic domain splitting for numeric csp. In *European Conference on Artificial Intelligence*, 224–228.

Jussien, N. 1997. *Relaxation de Contraintes pour les problèmes dynamiques*. 1. thèse, Université de Rennes I.

Liaw, C.-F. 1998. A tabu search algorithm for the open shop scheduling problem. *Computers and Operations Research* 26.

Minton, S.; Johnston, M.; and Laird, P. 1992. Minimizing conflicts: A heuristic repair method for constraint satisfaction and scheduling problems. *Artificial Intelligence* 58:161–206.

Pesant, G., and Gendreau, M. 1996. A view of local search in constraint programming. In *Proc. of the Principles and Practice of Constraint Programming*, 353–366. Springer-Verlag.

Prosser, P. 1993. Hybrid algorithms for the constraint satisfaction problem. *Computational Intelligence* 9(3):268–299. (Also available as Technical Report AISL-46-91, Stratchclyde, 1991).

Richards, E. T., and Richards, E. B. 1998. Non-systematic search and learning: An empirical study. In *Proc. of the the Conference on Principles and Practice of Constraint Programming*.

Schaerf, A. 1997. Combining local search and look-ahead for scheduling and constraint satisfaction problems. In *Proc. of the 15th International Joint Conf. on Artificial Intelligence (IJCAI-96)*, 1254–1259. Nagoya, Japan: Morgan Kaufmann.

Schiex, T., and Verfaillie, G. 1994. Nogood Recording fot Static and Dynamic Constraint Satisfaction Problems. *International Journal of Artificial Intelligence Tools* 3(2):187–207.

Selman, B., and Kautz, H. 1993. Domain-independent extensions to gsat: Solving large structured satisfiability problems. In Bajcsy, R., ed., *Proceedings of International Joint Conference on Artificial Intelligence (IJCAI-93)*, 290–295. Chambery, France: Morgan Kaufmann.

Selman, B.; Levesque, H.; and Mitchell, D. 1992. A new method for solving hard satisfiability problems. In *AAAI 92, Tenth National Conference on Artificial Intelligence*, 440–446.

Stuckey, P., and Tam, V. 1998. Extending GENET with lazy arc consistency. *IEEE Transactions on Systems, Man, and Cybernetics* 28(5):698–703.

Taillard, É. 1993. Benchmarks for basic scheduling problems. *European Journal of Operations Research* 64:278–285.

Verfaillie, G., and Lobjois, L. 1999. Problèmes incohérents: expliquer l'incohérence, restaurer la cohérence. In *Actes des JNPC*.

Verfaillie, G., and Schiex, T. 1994. Dynamic backtracking for dynamic csps. In Schiex, T., and Bessière, C., eds., *Proceedings ECAI'94 Workshop on Constraint Satisfaction Issues raised by Practical Applications*.

Yokoo, M. 1994. Weak-commitment search for solving constraint satisfaction problems. In *Proceedings of AAAI*.

A Game-Theoretic Approach to Constraint Satisfaction

Phokion G. Kolaitis[*]
Computer Science Department
University of California, Santa Cruz
Santa Cruz, CA 95064
kolaitis@cse.ucsc.edu
www.cse.ucsc.edu/~kolaitis

Moshe Y. Vardi[†]
Department of Computer Science
Rice University
Houston, TX 77005-1892
vardi@cs.rice.edu
www.cs.rice.edu/~vardi

Abstract

We shed light on the connections between different approaches to constraint satisfaction by showing that the main consistency concepts used to derive tractability results for constraint satisfaction are intimately related to certain combinatorial pebble games, called the existential k-pebble games, that were originally introduced in the context of Datalog. The crucial insight relating pebble games to constraint satisfaction is that the key concept of strong k-consistency is equivalent to a condition on winning strategies for the Duplicator player in the existential k-pebble game. We use this insight to show that strong k-consistency can be established if and only if the Duplicator wins the existential k-pebble game. Moreover, whenever strong k-consistency can be established, one method for doing this is to first compute the largest winning strategy for the Duplicator in the existential k-pebble game and then modify the original problem by augmenting it with the constraints expressed by the largest winning strategy. This basic result makes it possible to establish deeper connections between pebble games, consistency properties, and tractability of constraint satisfaction. In particular, we use existential k-pebble games to introduce the concept of k-locality and show that it constitutes a new tractable case of constraint satisfaction that properly extends the well known case in which establishing strong k-consistency implies global consistency.

Introduction and Summary of Results

Constraint satisfaction has occupied a prominent place in AI research since the 1970s. The importance of constraint satisfaction stems from the fact that a large number of fundamental algorithmic problems from different areas of artificial intelligence can be modeled as constraint-satisfaction problems (CSP) in a natural way. The input to a constraint-satisfaction problem consists of a set of variables, a set of possible values, and a set of constraints on tuples of variables; the question is to determine whether there is an assignment of values to the variables that satisfies the given constraints. Since in general constraint satisfaction is NP-complete, a considerable amount of effort has been dedicated to the discovery of tractable cases of constraint satisfaction, see (Mackworth & Freuder 1993; Dechter 1992; Jeavons, Cohen, & Gyssens 1997). The aim of this line of investigation is to design efficient algorithms for special cases of constraint satisfaction and to develop useful heuristics for the general case.

One of the most fruitful approaches to coping with the intractability of constraint satisfaction has been the introduction and use of various *consistency* concepts that make explicit additional constraints implied by the original constraints. The connection between consistency properties and tractability was first described in (Freuder 1978; 1982). In a similar vein, (Dechter 1992; van Beek 1994; van Beek & Dechter 1997) investigated the relationship between *local consistency* and *global consistency*. Intuitively, local consistency means that any partial solution on a set of variables can be extended to a partial solution containing an additional variable, whereas global consistency means that any partial solution can be extended to a global solution. Note that if the inputs are such that local consistency implies global consistency, then there is a polynomial-time algorithm for constraint satisfaction; moreover, in this case a solution can be constructed via a backtrack-free search.

In recent years, researchers have also embarked on an ambitious project aiming to classify the currently known tractable cases of constraint satisfaction and ultimately identify all tractable cases of this problem. Specifically, in (Feder & Vardi 1999) two conditions are isolated and are shown to be sufficient for tractability of constraint satisfaction and to also provide a unifying framework for a large number of tractability results in the literature. The first of these conditions is expressibility in Datalog, the main query language for deductive database and knowledge-base systems, while the second condition is group-theoretic. A related unifying framework for tractability of constraint satisfaction has been developed by Jeavons et al. in a sequence of papers, including (Jeavons, Cohen, & Gyssens 1995; 1996; 1997); the key theme of this framework is that tractability is intimately connected to certain algebraic closure properties of the constraints. Although the above two frameworks are of distinctly different character, they turn out to have several points in common. In fact, certain tractable cases in the

---

[*]Work partially supported by NSF grants CCR-9610257 and CCR-9732041

[†]Work partially supported by NSF grant CCR-9700061
Copyright © 2000, American Association for Artificial Intelligence (www.aaai.org). All rights reserved.

first framework turn out to coincide with certain tractable cases in the second framework. Furthermore, one of these cases also coincides with the case in which local consistency implies global consistency; thus, these three different approaches to constraint satisfaction meet at this point.

Our goal in this paper is to shed additional light on the connections between the different approaches to constraint satisfaction. As pointed out first by (Feder & Vardi 1999), constraint satisfaction can be identified with the *homomorphism problem* on relational structures: given two finite relational structures **A** and **B** over the same vocabulary, is there a homomorphism from **A** to **B**?[1] Informally, the structure **A** represents the variables and the constrained tuples of variables, the structure **B** represents the values and the constraints, and the homomorphisms from **A** to **B** are precisely the solutions to the instance of the constraint-satisfaction problem encoded by **A** and **B**. Using this viewpoint, we show that the main consistency concepts mentioned above are intimately related to certain combinatorial pebble games on relational structures that were originally introduced in the context of Datalog. It is well known that the expressive power of several major logical formalisms, including first-order logic and second-order logic, can be analyzed using certain combinatortial two-person games, see (Ebbinghaus, Flum, & Thomas 1994). As regards Datalog, *existential k-pebble games* were introduced in (Kolaitis & Vardi 1995) and used to analyze the expressive power of Datalog. These games are played between two players, the *Spoiler* and the *Duplicator*, on two relational structures **A** and **B** according to the following rules: on the i-th move of a round of the game, $1 \leq i \leq k$, the Spoiler places a pebble on an element a_i of A, and the Duplicator responds by placing a pebble on an element b_i of B. The Spoiler wins the game at the end of that round, if the mapping $a_i \mapsto b_i$, $1 \leq i \leq k$, is not a homomorphim between the corresponding substructures of **A** and **B**. Otherwise, the Spoiler removes one or more pebbles, and a new round of the game begins. The Duplicator wins the existential k-pebble game if he has a *winning strategy*, that is to say, a systematic way that allows him to sustain playing "forever", so that the Spoiler can never win a round of the game.

The crucial insight that relates pebble games to constraint satisfaction is that the key concept of *strong k-consistency* (Dechter 1992) is equivalent to a property of winning strategies for the Duplicator in the existential k-pebble game. Specifically, after giving the formal definition of a winning strategy, we point out that an instance of a constraint-satisfaction problem is strongly k-consistent if and only if the family of *all* partial homomorphims f with $|f| < k$ is a winning strategy for the Duplicator in the existential k-pebble game on the two relational structures that represent the given instance. The connection between pebble games and consistency properties, however, is deeper than just a mere reformulation of the concept of strong k-consistency. Indeed, as mentioned earlier, consistency properties underly the process of making explicit new constraints that are implied be the original constraints. A key technical step in this approach is the procedure known as "establishing strong k-consistency", which propagates the original constraints, adds implied constraints, and transforms a given instance of a constraint satisfaction problem to a strongly k-consistent instance with the same solution space (Cooper 1989; Dechter 1992). Here we show that strong k-consistency can be established if and only if the Duplicator wins the existential k-pebble game. Moreover, whenever strong k-consistency can be established, one method for doing this is to first compute the largest winning strategy for the Duplicator in the existential k-pebble game and then modify the original problem by augmenting it with the constraints expressed by the largest winning strategy; we also show that this method gives rise to the least constrained instance that establishes strong k-consistency and, in addition, satisfies a natural *coherence* property. By combining this result with earlier results in (Kolaitis & Vardi 1995; 1998) concerning the definability of the largest winning strategy, it follows that the algorithm for establishing strong k-consistency in this way (with k fixed) is actually expressible in least fixed-point logic; this strengthens the fact that strong k-consistency can be established in polynomial time, when k is fixed.

After this, we show that there are further connections between pebble games, consistency properties, and tractability of constraint satisfaction. If **B** is a fixed finite relational structure, then CSP(**B**) is the following non-uniform constraint-satisfaction problem: given a finite relational structure **A**, is there a homomorphism h from **A** to **B**? Note that if **B** is the complete graph K_3 on three vertices, then CSP(**B**) is 3-COLORABILITY; thus, CSP(**B**) may very well be an NP-complete problem. It was shown in (Feder & Vardi 1999; Kolaitis & Vardi 1998) that existential k-pebble games can be used to characterize when CSP(**B**) is expressible in Datalog (from which it follows that CSP(**B**) is also solvable in polynomial time). Specifically, it was established that for every relational structure **B**, the complement of CSP(**B**) is expressible by a Datalog program with k variables if and only if CSP(**B**) coincides with the collection of all relational structures **A** such that the Duplicator wins the existential k-pebble game on **A** and **B**. Consequently, this is also equivalent to the following condition: CSP(**B**) coincides with the collection of all relational structures **A** such that establishing strong k-consistency on **A** and **B** implies that there is a homomorphism from **A** to **B**.

Expressibility in Datalog is certainly a condition that gives rise to a large tractable case of non-uniform constraint satisfaction. It has the disadvantage, however, that it does not yield a method for finding a solution to an instance of CSP(**B**), if a solution exists. This should be contrasted with the special case of expressibility in Datalog in which CSP(**B**) has the property that establishing strong k-consistency implies global consistency. We call this property *global k-consistency*. In this case, given an intance of CSP(**B**), we can first detect the existence of a solution by establishing strong k-consistency and then we can easily construct a solution using a backtrack-free

---

[1] A *homomorphism* is a mapping from the domain of **A** to the domain of **B** such that every tuple in a relation of **A** is mapped to a tuple in the corresponding relation of **B**.

search. Although this special case does not suffer from the above disadvantage of Datalog, its applicability is limited, since it turns out to be equivalent to a very stringent closure property of the relations of **B** (Feder & Vardi 1999; Jeavons, Cohen, & Cooper 1998). This state of affairs motivates the pursuit of tractable cases that interpolate between global k-consistency and expressibility in Datalog. To this effect, using k-pebble games, we introduce the concept of *k-locality* and show that it constitutes a new tractable case of non-uniform constraint satisfaction that is broader than global k-consistency, is expressible in Datalog, but does not suffer from the aforementioned disadvantage of expressibility in Datalog. In particular, we show that if $CSP(\mathbf{B})$ is k-local, then a solution (if one exists) to a given instance of $CSP(\mathbf{B})$ can be constructed in polynomial time via a backtrack-free search during which strong k-consistency is established for certain expansions of the given instance. Moreover, we show that if $CSP(\mathbf{B})$ is k-local, then computing the largest winning strategy for the Duplicator in the existential k-pebble game is the *only* way to obtain an instance that establishes strong k-consistency and satisfies the coherence property mentioned earlier.

Consistency and Pebble Games

The standard terminology in AI formalizes an instance $\mathcal{P}$ of CSP as a triple $(V, D, \mathcal{C})$, consisting of a set V of variables, a set D of values, and a collection $\mathcal{C}$ of *constraints* $C_1, \ldots, C_q$, where each C_i is a pair (t, R) with t a tuple over V (i.e., a tuple of not necessarily distinct variables in V) and R is a relation on D of the same arity as $|t|$. Note that, without loss of generality, we may assume that all constraints (t, R_i) involving a tuple t have been consolidated to a single constraint (t, R). Thus, we can assume that each tuple t of variables occurs at most once in the collection $\mathcal{C}$. It is clear that every such instance $\mathcal{P}$ can be viewed as an instance of the homomorphism problem between two structures $\mathbf{A}_\mathcal{P}$ and $\mathbf{B}_\mathcal{P}$, where the universe of $\mathbf{A}_\mathcal{P}$ is V, the universe of $\mathbf{B}_\mathcal{P}$ is D, the relations of $\mathbf{B}_\mathcal{P}$ are the distinct relations R occurring in $\mathcal{C}$, and the relations of $\mathbf{A}_\mathcal{P}$ are defined as follows: for each relation R on D occurring in $\mathcal{C}$, we have the relation $R^\mathbf{A} = \{t : (t, R) \text{ is a constraint}\}$. We call $(\mathbf{A}_\mathcal{P}, \mathbf{B}_\mathcal{P})$ the *homomorphism instance* of $\mathcal{P}$. It is also clear that every instance of the homomorphism problem between two structures $\mathbf{A}$ and $\mathbf{B}$ can be viewed as a CSP instance $CSP(\mathbf{A}, \mathbf{B})$ by simply "breaking up" each relation $R^\mathbf{A}$ on $\mathbf{A}$ as follows: we generate a constraint $(t, R^\mathbf{B})$ for each $t \in R^\mathbf{A}$. (and then consolidate constraints involving the same tuple of variables). We call $CSP(\mathbf{A}, \mathbf{B})$ the *CSP instance* of $(\mathbf{A}, \mathbf{B})$ We will use both formalisms in this paper, as each has its own advantages.

The next definition contains the main concepts concerning existential k-pebble games.

Definition 1: Let k be a positive integer and let $\mathbf{A}$ and $\mathbf{B}$ be two relational structures over the same vocabulary with universes A and B respectively.

- A *k-partial homomorphism* from $\mathbf{A}$ to $\mathbf{B}$ is a homomorphism from a substructure of $\mathbf{A}$ with at most k elements in its universe to a substructure of $\mathbf{B}$.

- A *winning strategy for the Duplicator in the existential k-pebble game on $\mathbf{A}$ and $\mathbf{B}$* is a nonempty family $\mathcal{F}$ of k-partial homomorphisms having the following two properties:
  1. $\mathcal{F}$ is *closed under subfunctions*, which means that if $g \in \mathcal{F}$ and $f \subseteq g$, then $f \in \mathcal{F}$.
  2. $\mathcal{F}$ has the *k-forth property*, which means that for every $f \in \mathcal{F}$ with $|f| < k$ and every $a \in A$ on which f is undefined, there is a $g \in \mathcal{F}$ that extends f and is defined on a.

- A *configuration for the existential k-pebble game on $\mathbf{A}$ and $\mathbf{B}$* is a $2k$-tuple $\overline{a}, \overline{b}$, where $\overline{a}$ and $\overline{b}$ are elements of A^k and B^k respectively such that if $a_i = a_j$, then $b_i = b_j$ (i.e., the correspondence $a_i \mapsto b_i$, $1 \leq i \leq k$, is a partial function from A to B, which we denote by $h_{\overline{a},\overline{b}}$).

- A *winning configuration for the Duplicator in the existential k-pebble game on $\mathbf{A}$ and $\mathbf{B}$* is a configuration $\overline{a}, \overline{b}$ for this game such that $h_{\overline{a},\overline{b}}$ is a member of some winning strategy for the Duplicator in this game. We denote by $\mathcal{W}^k(\mathbf{A}, \mathbf{B})$ the set of all such configurations.

The following facts turn out to be quite useful.

Proposition 2: *If $\mathcal{F}$ and $\mathcal{F}'$ are two winning strategies for the Duplicator in the existential k-pebble game on two structures $\mathbf{A}$ and $\mathbf{B}$, then also the union $\mathcal{F} \cup \mathcal{F}'$ is a winning strategy for the Duplicator. Hence, there is a largest winning strategy for the Duplicator in the existential k-pebble game, namely the union of all winning strategies, which is precisely*

$$\mathcal{H}^k(\mathbf{A}, \mathbf{B}) = \{h_{\overline{a},\overline{b}} : (\overline{a}, \overline{b}) \in \mathcal{W}^k(\mathbf{A}, \mathbf{B})\}.$$

Proof: The first part is obvious. For the second part, note that $\mathcal{H}^k(\mathbf{A}, \mathbf{B})$ is clearly a winning strategy for the Duplicator and contains every winning strategy as a subset, since every element h of a winning strategy gives rise to a winning configuration $\overline{a}, \overline{b}$ such that $h_{\overline{a},\overline{b}} = h$, where $\overline{a}$ is a list of all elements in the domain of h and $\overline{b}$ is a list of their images under h (the list may contain elements with repetitions, if the domain of h has fewer than k elements). ∎

The following lemma is a crucial definability result.

Lemma 3: (Kolaitis & Vardi 1998) *There is a positive first-order formula $\varphi(\overline{x}, \overline{y}, S)$, where $\overline{x}$ and $\overline{y}$ are k-tuples of variables, such that the complement of its least fixed-point on a pair $\mathbf{A}, \mathbf{B}$ of structures defines the set $\mathcal{W}^k(\mathbf{A}, \mathbf{B})$ of all winning configurations for the Duplicator in the existential k-pebble game on $\mathbf{A}, \mathbf{B}$.*

We now recall the concepts of *i-consistency* and *strong k-consistency*.

Definition 4: Let $\mathcal{P} = (V, D, \mathcal{C})$ be a CSP instance. $\mathcal{P}$ is *i-consistent* if for every $i - 1$ variables $v_1, \ldots, v_{i-1}$, for every partial solution on these variables, and for every variable $v_i \notin \{v_1, \ldots, v_{i-1}\}$, there is a partial solution on the variables $v_1, \ldots, v_{i-1}, v_i$ extending the given partial solution on the variables $v_1, \ldots, v_{i-1}$. $\mathcal{P}$ is *strongly k-consistent* if it is i-consistent for every $i \leq k$. ∎

A key insight is that strong k-consistency can be naturally recast in terms of existential k-pebble games.

Proposition 5: *Let $\mathcal{P}$ be a CSP instance, and let $(\mathbf{A}_\mathcal{P}, \mathbf{B}_\mathcal{P})$ be the associated homomorphism instance. $\mathcal{P}$ is strongly k-consistent if and only if the family of all k-partial homomorphisms from $\mathbf{A}_\mathcal{P}$ to $\mathbf{B}_\mathcal{P}$ is a winning strategy for the Duplicator in the existential k-pebble game on $\mathbf{A}_\mathcal{P}$ and $\mathbf{B}_\mathcal{P}$.*

Let us now recall the concept of *establishing strong k-consistency*, as defined, for instance, in (Cooper 1989; Dechter 1992). This concept has been defined rather informally in the literature to mean that, given an instance $\mathcal{P}$ of CSP, we associate an instance $\mathcal{P}'$ that has the following properties: (1) $\mathcal{P}'$ has the same set of variables and the same set of values as $\mathcal{P}$; (2) $\mathcal{P}'$ is strongly k-consistent; (3) $\mathcal{P}'$ is more constrained than $\mathcal{P}$; and (4) $\mathcal{P}$ and $\mathcal{P}'$ have the same space of solutions. The next definition formalizes the above concept in the context of the homomorphism problem.

Definition 6: *Let $\mathbf{A}$ and $\mathbf{B}$ be two relational structures over a k-ary vocabulary σ (i.e., every relation symbol in σ has arity at most k). Establishing strong k-consistency for $\mathbf{A}$ and $\mathbf{B}$ means that we associate two relational structures $\mathbf{A}'$ and $\mathbf{B}'$ with the following properties:*

1. *$\mathbf{A}'$ and $\mathbf{B}'$ are structures over some k-ary vocabulary σ' (in general, different than σ); moreover, the universe of $\mathbf{A}'$ is the universe A of $\mathbf{A}$, and the universe of $\mathbf{B}'$ is the universe B of $\mathbf{B}$.*
2. *$\mathrm{CSP}(\mathbf{A}', \mathbf{B}')$ is strongly k-consistent.*
3. *if h is a k-partial homomorphism from $\mathbf{A}'$ to $\mathbf{B}'$, then h is a k-partial homomorphism from $\mathbf{A}$ to $\mathbf{B}$.*
4. *If h is a function from A to B, then h is a homomorphism from $\mathbf{A}$ to $\mathbf{B}$ if and only if h is a homomorphism from $\mathbf{A}'$ to $\mathbf{B}'$.*

If the structures $\mathbf{A}'$ and $\mathbf{B}'$ have the above properties, then we say that $\mathbf{A}'$ and $\mathbf{B}'$ establish strong k-consistency for $\mathbf{A}$ and $\mathbf{B}$. ∎

An instance $\mathcal{P}$ of CSP is *coherent* if every constraint (t, R) of $\mathcal{P}$ completely determines all constraints (u, Q) in which all variables occurring in u are among the variables of t. We formalize this concept as follows.

Definition 7: *An instance $\mathbf{A}, \mathbf{B}$ of the homomorphism problem is coherent if its associated CSP instance $\mathrm{CSP}(\mathbf{A}, \mathbf{B})$ has the following property: for every constraint $(\overline{a}, R)$ of $\mathrm{CSP}(\mathbf{A}, \mathbf{B})$ and every tuple $\overline{b} \in R$, the mapping $h_{\overline{a},\overline{b}}$ is well defined and is a partial homomorphism from $\mathbf{A}$ to $\mathbf{B}$.* ∎

Note that a CSP instance can be made coherent by polynomial-time constraint propagation.

The main result of this section is that strong k-consistency can be established precisely when the Duplicator wins the existential k-pebble game. Moreover, one method for establishing strong k-consistency is to first compute the largest winning strategy for the Duplicator in this game and then generate an instance of the constraint-satisfaction problem consisting of all the constraints embodied in the largest winning strategy. Furthermore, this method gives rise to the largest coherent instance that establishes strong k-consistency (and, hence, the least constrained such instance).

Theorem 8: *Let k be a positive integer, let σ be a k-ary vocabulary, and let $\mathbf{A}$ and $\mathbf{B}$ be two relational structures over σ with domains A and B, respectively. It is possible to establish strong k-consistency for $\mathbf{A}$ and $\mathbf{B}$ if and only if $\mathcal{W}^k(\mathbf{A}, \mathbf{B}) \neq \emptyset$. Furthermore, if $\mathcal{W}^k(\mathbf{A}, \mathbf{B}) \neq \emptyset$, then the following sequence of steps gives rise to two structures $\mathbf{A}'$ and $\mathbf{B}'$ that establish strong k-consistency for $\mathbf{A}$ and $\mathbf{B}$:*

1. *Compute the set $\mathcal{W}^k(\mathbf{A}, \mathbf{B})$.*
2. *Form the set $\mathcal{W}_*^k(\mathbf{A}, \mathbf{B})$ of all $2i$-tuples $(a_{j_1}, \ldots, a_{j_i}, b_{j_1}, \ldots, b_{j_i}) \in A^i \times B^i$, $1 \leq i \leq k$, that can be extended to a $2k$-tuple $(a_1, \ldots, a_k, b_1, \ldots, b_k) \in \mathcal{W}^k(\mathbf{A}, \mathbf{B})$.*
3. *For every $i \leq k$ and for every i-tuple $\overline{a} \in A^i$, form the set $R_{\overline{a}} = \{\overline{b} \in B^i : (\overline{a}, \overline{b}) \in \mathcal{W}_*^k(\mathbf{A}, \mathbf{B})\}$.*
4. *Form the CSP instance $\mathcal{P}$ with A as the set of variables, B as the set of values, and $\{(\overline{a}, R_{\overline{a}}) : \overline{a} \in \bigcup_{i=1}^k A^i\}$ as the collection of constraints.*
5. *Let $(\mathbf{A}', \mathbf{B}')$ be the homomorphism instance of $\mathcal{P}$.*

In addition, the structures $\mathbf{A}'$ and $\mathbf{B}'$ obtained above constitute the largest coherent instance establishing strong k-consistency for $\mathbf{A}$ and $\mathbf{B}$, i.e., if $(\mathbf{A}'', \mathbf{B}'')$ is another such coherent instance, then for every constraint $(\overline{a}, R)$ of $\mathrm{CSP}(\mathbf{A}'', \mathbf{B}'')$, we have that $R \subseteq R_{\overline{a}}$.

Proof: Suppose first that $\mathcal{W}^k(\mathbf{A}, \mathbf{B}) \neq \emptyset$. We now show that $\mathrm{CSP}(\mathbf{A}', \mathbf{B}')$ is strongly k-consistent. To see this, assume that g is a partial homomorphism from $\mathbf{A}'$ to $\mathbf{B}'$ with domain $\{a_1, \ldots, a_i\}$, for some $i < k$, and c is an element of A. Let $b_j = g(a_j)$, $1 \leq j \leq i$, let $\overline{a} = (a_1, \ldots, a_i)$ and $\overline{b} = (b_1, \ldots, b_i)$. Since g is a partial homomorphism from $\mathbf{A}'$ to $\mathbf{B}'$, it must be the case that $\overline{b} \in R_{\overline{a}}$, which in turn means that $\overline{a}, \overline{b}$ is a winning configuration for the Duplicator in the existential k-pebble game on $\mathbf{A}$ and $\mathbf{B}$. It follows that there is an element d of B such that $\overline{a}, c, \overline{b}, d$ is a winning configuration for the Duplicator in the existential k-pebble game on $\mathbf{A}$ and $\mathbf{B}$. In turn, this means that $\overline{b}, d \in R_{\overline{a},c}$. It is easy, however, to verify that $(\mathbf{A}', \mathbf{B}')$ is coherent and so the mapping $g \cup \{(c, d)\}$ is a partial homomorphism from $\mathbf{A}'$ to $\mathbf{B}'$ extending g.

Next assume that h is a function from A to B. We have to show that h is a homomorphism from $\mathbf{A}$ to $\mathbf{B}$ if and only if h is a homomorphism from $\mathbf{A}'$ to $\mathbf{B}'$. Let $\overline{a} = (a_1, \ldots, a_k)$ be a k-tuple of elements from A and let $\overline{b} = (h(a_1), \ldots, h(a_k))$. Assume first that h is a homomorphism from $\mathbf{A}$ to $\mathbf{B}$. In this case, we have that $\overline{a}, \overline{b}$ is a winning configuration for the Duplicator in the existential k-pebble game on $\mathbf{A}$ and $\mathbf{B}$, which in turn implies that $\overline{b} \in R_{\overline{a}}$, thus establishing that h is a homomorphism from $\mathbf{A}'$ to $\mathbf{B}'$. In the other direction, if h is a homomorphism from $\mathbf{A}'$ to $\mathbf{B}'$, then $\overline{b} \in R_{\overline{a}}$, which means that $\overline{a}, \overline{b}$ is a winning configuration for the Duplicator in the existential k-pebble game on $\mathbf{A}$ and $\mathbf{B}$. In turn, this implies that if a relation of $\mathbf{A}$ is satisfied by a sequence of elements from $\overline{a}$, then the corresponding sequence of elements from $\overline{b}$ satisfies the corresponding relation on **B**, thus establishing that h is a homomorphism from **A** to **B**.

Conversely, suppose that $\mathbf{A}'$ and $\mathbf{B}'$ establish strong k-consistency for **A** and **B**. Let $\mathcal{H}$ be the family of all k-partial homomorphisms from $\mathbf{A}'$ to $\mathbf{B}'$. By the definition of establishing strong k-consistency, $\mathcal{H}$ is also a family of k-partial homomorphisms from **A** to **B**. Since, $\mathrm{CSP}(\mathbf{A}', \mathbf{B}')$ is strongly k-consistent, $\mathcal{H}$ has the k-forth property. But this means that the Duplicator has a winning strategy in the existential k-pebble game on **A**, **B**, which implies that $\mathcal{W}^k(\mathbf{A}, \mathbf{B}) \neq \emptyset$.

As mentioned earlier, $(\mathbf{A}', \mathbf{B}')$ is coherent. Assume that $(\mathbf{A}^*, \mathbf{B}^*)$ is another coherent instance establishing strong k-consistency for **A** and **B**. Let $(\bar{a}, R)$ be a constraint of $\mathrm{CSP}(\mathbf{A}^*, \mathbf{B}^*)$, and let $\bar{b} \in R$. Then the mapping $h_{\bar{a},\bar{b}}$ is a partial homomorphism from $\mathbf{A}^*$ to $\mathbf{B}^*$, which in turn implies that it is also a partial homomorphism from **A** to **B**. It follows that $(\bar{a}, \bar{b}) \in \mathcal{W}_*^k(\mathbf{A}, \mathbf{B})$, and thus $\bar{b} \in R_{\bar{a}}$. ∎

The key step in the procedure described in Theorem 8 is the first step, in which the set $\mathcal{W}^k(\mathbf{A}, \mathbf{B})$ is computed. The other steps simply "re-format" $\mathcal{W}^k(\mathbf{A}, \mathbf{B})$. From Lemma 3, it follows that we can establish strong k-consistency by computing the least fixed-point of a positive first-order formula. This perspective should be contrasted with the efficient-implementation perspective in (Cooper 1989), the algebraic perspective described in (Güsgen & Ladkin 1995), and the chaotic-iteration perspective described in (Apt 1997).

One advantage of formalizing the concept of strong k-consistency in Definition 6 is that we can now address the computational complexity of establishing strong k-consistency. That is, how hard is it to determine whether it is possible to establish strong k-consistency for **A** and **B**, given two structures **A**, **B** and a positive integer k? In view of Theorem 8, this key question is equivalent to asking how hard it is to test whether $\mathcal{W}^k(\mathbf{A}, \mathbf{B}) \neq \emptyset$. We conjecture that the exponential upper bound from (Kolaitis & Vardi 1995) is tight.

Conjecture: Checking whether $\mathcal{W}^k(\mathbf{A}, \mathbf{B}) \neq \emptyset$ for given structures **A**, **B** and a positive integer k is EXPTIME-complete.

Note that a confirmation of this conjecture will explain why all known algorithms for establishing strong k-consistency are exponential in k (see (Cooper 1989; Dechter 1992)).

We can now relate the concept of strong k-consistency to the results in (Feder & Vardi 1999; Kolaitis & Vardi 1998) regarding Datalog and non-uniform CSP. *Datalog* is the language of database logic programming; it has received a tremendous amount of attention over the past two decades, see (Abiteboul, Hull, & Vianu 1995). A Datalog program is a finite set of rules of the form $t_0 \leftarrow t_1, \ldots, t_m$, where each t_i is an atomic formula $R(x_1, \ldots, x_n)$. The relational predicates that occur in the heads of the rules are the *intensional database* predicates (IDBs), while all others are the *extensional database* predicates (EDBs). One of the IDBs is designated as the *goal* of the program. Note that IDBs may occur in the bodies of rules and, thus, a Datalog program is a recursive specification of the IDBs with semantics obtained via least fixed-points of monotone operators, see (Ullman 1989). Each Datalog program defines a query which, given a set of EDB predicates, returns the value of the goal predicate. If the goal predicate is 0-ary, then the program is a Boolean query, i.e., it either holds or does not. Note that a Datalog query is computable in polynomial time, since the bottom-up evaluation of the least fixed-point of the program terminates within a polynomial number of steps (in the size of the given EDBs), see (Ullman 1989). Thus, expressibility in Datalog is a sufficient condition for tractability of a query.

Let **B** be a relational structure over a vocabulary σ. Let $\neg\mathrm{CSP}(\mathbf{B})$ be the class of all structures **A** over the vocabulary σ such that there is no homomorphism h from **A** to **B**. A unifying explanation for the tractability of many non-uniform $\mathrm{CSP}(\mathbf{B})$ problems is provided by showing that $\neg\mathrm{CSP}(\mathbf{B})$ is expressible in Datalog (Feder & Vardi 1999). That is, in many cases in which $\mathrm{CSP}(\mathbf{B})$ is tractable there is a Boolean Datalog program P such that for every structure **A** over σ, we have that $P(\mathbf{A})$ holds iff $\mathbf{A} \notin \mathrm{CSP}(\mathbf{B})$. A key parameter that shows up in this analysis is the number of variables used. For every positive integer n, let k-Datalog be the collection of all Datalog programs in which the body of every rule has at most k distinct variables and also the head of every rule has at most k variables (the variables of the body may be different from the variables of the head).

Theorem 9: (Kolaitis & Vardi 1998) *Let* **B** *be a relational structure over a vocabulary* σ. $\neg\mathrm{CSP}(\mathbf{B})$ *is expressible in k-Datalog iff the following condition holds:*

For every structure **A** *over* σ, *if the Duplicator wins the existential k-pebble game on* **A** *and* **B**, *then there is a homomorphism from* **A** *to* **B**.

We can now derive a relationship between k-Datalog and strong k-consistency.

Theorem 10: *Let* **B** *be a relational structure over a vocabulary* σ. $\neg\mathrm{CSP}(\mathbf{B})$ *is expressible in k-Datalog iff for every structure* **A** *over* σ, *establishing strong k-consistency for* **A**, **B** *implies that there is a homomorphism from* **A** *to* **B**.

Proof: Since the Duplicator wins the existential k-pebble game on **A** and **B** if and only if $\mathcal{W}^k(\mathbf{A}, \mathbf{B}) \neq \emptyset$, the result follows from Theorems 8 and 9. ∎

Consistency and Locality

As mentioned in the introduction, expressibility in k-Datalog is a sufficient condition for tractability of $\mathrm{CSP}(\mathbf{B})$, but it does not provide a method for finding a solution to an instance of $\mathrm{CSP}(\mathbf{B})$, if one exists. In contrast, if $\mathrm{CSP}(\mathbf{B})$ has the global k-consistency property, (i.e., establishing stong k-consistency implies global consistency), then a solution to an instance of $\mathrm{CSP}(\mathbf{B})$ can be constructed via a backtrack-free search. Since the latter condition is of limited applicability, it is natural to pursue conditions that are of wider applicability and still yield a method for finding a solution efficiently, if one exists.

Definition 11: Let $\mathbf{B}$ be a structure over a relational vocabulary σ and let k be a positive integer. We say that $\mathrm{CSP}(\mathbf{B})$ is *k-local* if $\neg\mathrm{CSP}(\mathbf{B}^*)$ is in k-Datalog for every expansion $\mathbf{B}^*$ of $\mathbf{B}$ with constants, that is, for every expansion of $\mathbf{B}$ obtained by augmenting $\mathbf{B}$ with a finite sequence of distinguished elements from its universe. Note that such an expansion can be also viewed as a structure over a relational vocabulary σ^* in which unary relational symbols are used to encode the distinguished elements that form the expansion. ∎

The first result of this section yields a characterization of k-locality in terms of establishing strong k-consistency. Moreover, it asserts that k-locality has the property that there is a unique way to obtain a coherent instance establishing strong k-consistency.

Proposition 12: *Let $\mathbf{B}$ be a relational structure over a vocabulary σ. $\mathrm{CSP}(\mathbf{B})$ is k-local iff for every structure $\mathbf{A}$ over σ and every expansions $\mathbf{A}^*$ and $\mathbf{B}^*$ of $\mathbf{A}$ and $\mathbf{B}$ with constants, establishing strong k-consistency on $\mathbf{A}^*$ and $\mathbf{B}^*$ implies that there is a homomorphism from $\mathbf{A}^*$ to $\mathbf{B}^*$. Moreover, if $\mathrm{CSP}(\mathbf{B})$ is k-local, then the only way to obtain a coherent instance establishing strong k-consistency for $\mathbf{A}$ and $\mathbf{B}$ is to compute the largest winning strategy for the Duplicator in the existential k-pebble game on $\mathbf{A}$ and $\mathbf{B}$.*

Proof: The characterization of k-locality in terms of establishing strong k-consistency is an immediate consequence of Theorem 10. Assume that $(\mathbf{A}'', \mathbf{B}'')$ is a coherent pair of structures establishing strong k-consistency for $(\mathbf{A}, \mathbf{B})$. Let $(\overline{a}, R)$ be a constraint of $\mathrm{CSP}(\mathbf{A}'', \mathbf{B}'')$. From Theorem 8, it follows that $R \subseteq R_{\overline{a}}$, where $R_{\overline{a}}$ is the set of all tuples $\overline{b}$ such that $(\overline{a}, \overline{b}) \in \mathcal{W}_*^k(\mathbf{A}, \mathbf{B})$. For the other direction, if $\overline{b} \in R_{\overline{a}}$, then $(\overline{a}, \overline{b}) \in \mathcal{W}_*^k(\mathbf{A}, \mathbf{B})$ and so the Duplicator wins the existential k-pebble game on $\mathbf{A}$ and $\mathbf{B}$ with pebbles placed on $\overline{a}$ and $\overline{b}$. Since $\mathrm{CSP}(\mathbf{B})$ is k-local, $\neg\mathrm{CSP}(\mathbf{B}, \overline{b})$ is expressible in Datalog. Consequently, by Theorem 9, it follows that there is a homomorphism h from $\mathbf{A}$ to $\mathbf{B}$ extending the partial homomorphism $a_i \mapsto b_i$, where a_i and b_i are the elements of A and B occuring in $\overline{a}$ and $\overline{b}$. Since $(\mathbf{A}'', \mathbf{B}'')$ establishes strong k-consistency for $\mathbf{A}$ and $\mathbf{B}$, it follows that h is a homomorphism from $\mathbf{A}''$ to $\mathbf{B}''$. Thus, $\overline{b} \in R$, which establishes that $R = R_{\overline{a}}$. ∎

The next result presents the relationship between k-locality and the other tractable cases of non-uniform constraint satisfaction considered earlier. Moreover, it asserts that if $\mathrm{CSP}(\mathbf{B})$ is k-local, then there is a polynomial-time algorithm for finding a solution to a given instance of a $\mathrm{CSP}(\mathbf{B})$.

Theorem 13: *Let $\mathbf{B}$ be a relational structure over a vocabulary σ and let k be a positive integer.*

1. *If $\mathrm{CSP}(\mathbf{B})$ is k-local, then $\neg\mathrm{CSP}(\mathbf{B})$ is expressible in k-Datalog.*
2. *If $\mathrm{CSP}(\mathbf{B})$ has the global k-consistency property, then $\mathrm{CSP}(\mathbf{B})$ is k-local.*
3. *If $\mathrm{CSP}(\mathbf{B})$ is k-local, then there is a polynomial-time algorithm that, given a structure $\mathbf{A}$ over σ, finds a homomorphism from $\mathbf{A}$ to $\mathbf{B}$, if one exists.*

Proof: (*Sketch*) The first two parts follow easily from the definitions, Theorem 8, and Proposition 12. For the third part, given a structure $\mathbf{A}$ over σ, one first checks whether $\mathcal{W}^k(\mathbf{A}, \mathbf{B}) \neq \emptyset$ to determine whether a homomorphism from $\mathbf{A}$ to $\mathbf{B}$ exists. If $\mathcal{W}^k(\mathbf{A}, \mathbf{B}) \neq \emptyset$, then one can build a homomorphism from $\mathbf{A}$ to $\mathbf{B}$ via a backtrack-free search that takes at most $O(n)$ steps; in each step, one has to test whether strong k-consistency can be established for progressively longer expansions $\mathbf{A}^*$ and $\mathbf{B}^*$ of $\mathbf{A}$ and $\mathbf{B}$ respectively. ∎

Note that if $\mathrm{CSP}(\mathbf{B})$ is k-local, then the algorithm for constructing a homomorphism is similar to the algorithm for constructing a homomorphism in the case where the global k-consistency property holds. The difference between these two algorithms is that in the latter case there is a single test in the beginning to determine whether it is possible to establish strong k-consistency for $\mathbf{A}$ and $\mathbf{B}$, whereas in the case of k-locality the test as to whether it is possible to establish strong k-consistency is repeatedly applied to the expansions $\mathbf{A}^*$ and $\mathbf{B}^*$ of $\mathbf{A}$ and $\mathbf{B}$ built during the backtrack-free search.

According to Theorem 13, the global k-consistency property implies k-locality. We can prove that this implication cannot be reversed. That is, k-locality is a tractable case of non-uniform constraint satisfaction that properly contains the case in which establishing strong k-consistency implies global consistency. For $k > 2$, let HORN k-SAT be the restriction of the satisfiability problem to k-CNF formulas in which every clause is Horn, i.e., it has at most one positive literal. It is easy to see that HORN k-SAT can be cast as a non-uniform CSP problem $\mathrm{CSP}(\mathbf{B}_k)$, where the universe of $\mathbf{B}_k$ is $\{0, 1\}$ and the relations of $\mathbf{B}_k$ encode the truth tables of Horn clauses with at most k literals. The proof of the next result will appear in the full paper.

Theorem 14: *Let $k > 2$ be a positive integer and let $\mathbf{B}_k$ be a structure that encodes HORN k-SAT. Then $\mathrm{CSP}(\mathbf{B}_k)$ is k-local, but there is no positive integer l such that $\mathrm{CSP}(\mathbf{B}_k)$ has the global l-consistency property.*

As mentioned in the introduction, the global k-consistency property is equivalent to a certain closure property of the relations of $\mathbf{B}$, (Feder & Vardi 1999; Jeavons, Cohen, & Cooper 1998). Since this closure property is decidable, it follows that there is an algorithm to decide whether, given a structure $\mathbf{B}$, the non-uniform constraint satisfaction problem $\mathrm{CSP}(\mathbf{B})$ has the global k-consistency property. In contrast, expressibility in k-Datalog in not known to be a decidable property. We also do not know whether k-locality is a decidable property. One way to attack this problem is to try to relate k-locality to a closure property, as in (Feder & Vardi 1999; Jeavons, Cohen, & Cooper 1998).

References

Abiteboul, S.; Hull, R.; and Vianu, V. 1995. *Foundations of databases*. Addison-Wesley.

Apt, K. 1997. The essence of constraint propagation. *Theoretical Computer Science* 221(1–2):179–210.

Cooper, M. 1989. An optimal k-consistency algorithm. *Artificial Intelligence* 41(1):89–95.

Dechter, R. 1992. From local to global consistency. *Artificial Intelligence* 55(1):87–107.

Ebbinghaus, H.-D.; Flum, J.; and Thomas, W. 1994. *Mathematical Logic*. Springer-Verlag, 2nd edition.

Feder, T., and Vardi, M. 1999. The computational structure of monotone monadic SNP and constraint satisfaction: a study through Datalog and group theory. *SIAM J. on Computing* 28:57–104. Preliminary version in *Proc. 25th ACM Symp. on Theory of Computing*, May 1993, pp. 612–622.

Freuder, E. 1978. Synthesizing constraint expressions. *Communications of the ACM* 21(11):958–966.

Freuder, E. 1982. A sufficient condition for backtrack-free search. *Journal of the Association for Computing Machinery* 29(1):24–32.

Güsgen, H., and Ladkin, P. 1995. An algebraic approach to general Boolean constraints problem. Technical report, University of Bielfeld. RVS-RR-96-04.

Jeavons, P.; Cohen, D.; and Cooper, M. 1998. Constraints, consistency and closure. *Artificial Intelligence* 101(1-2):251–65.

Jeavons, P.; Cohen, D.; and Gyssens, M. 1995. A unifying framework for tractable constraints. In Montanari, U., and Rossi, F., eds., *Proceedings of 1st International Conference on Principles and Practice of Constraint Programming, CP95*, 276–291. Springer-Verlag.

Jeavons, P.; Cohen, D.; and Gyssens, M. 1996. A test for tractability. In Freuder, E., ed., *Proceedings of 2nd International Conference on Principles and Practice of Constraint Programming, CP96*, 267–281. Springer-Verlag.

Jeavons, P.; Cohen, D.; and Gyssens, M. 1997. Closure properties of constraints. *Journal of the ACM* 44(4):527–48.

Kolaitis, P. G., and Vardi, M. Y. 1995. On the expressive power of Datalog: tools and a case study. *Journal of Computer and System Sciences* 51(1):110–134.

Kolaitis, P., and Vardi, M. 1998. Conjunctive-query containment and constraint satisfaction. In *Proc. 17th ACM Symp. on Principles of Database Systems*, 205–213. Full version at http://www.cs.rice.edu/~vardi/papers.

Mackworth, A., and Freuder, E. 1993. The complexity of constraint satisfaction revisited. *Artificial Intelligence* 59(1-2):57–62.

Ullman, J. D. 1989. *Database and Knowledge-Base Systems, Volumes I and II*. Computer Science Press.

van Beek, P., and Dechter, R. 1997. Constraint tightness and looseness versus local and global consistency. *Journal of the ACM* 44(4):549–566.

van Beek, P. 1994. On the inherent tightness of local consistency in constraint networks. In *Proc. of National Conference on Artificial Intelligence (AAAI-94)*, 368–373.

Using auxiliary variables and implied constraints to model non-binary problems

Barbara Smith
School of Computer Studies
University of Leeds
Leeds LS2 9JT
England
bms@scs.leeds.ac.uk

Kostas Stergiou
Department of Computer Science
University of Strathclyde
Glasgow G1 1XL
Scotland
ks@cs.strath.ac.uk

Toby Walsh
Department of Computer Science
University of York
York YO10 5DD
England
tw@cs.york.ac.uk

Abstract

We perform an extensive theoretical and empirical analysis of the use of auxiliary variables and implied constraints in modelling a class of non-binary constraint satisfaction problems called *problems of distance*. This class of problems include 1-d, 2-d and circular Golomb rulers. We identify a large number of different models, both binary and non-binary, and compare theoretically the level of consistency achieved by generalized arc consistency on them. Our experiments show that the introduction of auxiliary variables and implied constraints can significantly reduce the size of the search space. For instance, our final models reduce the time to find an optimal 10-mark Golomb ruler 50-fold.

Introduction

In an invited talk at AAAI-98, Gene Freuder identified modelling as a major hurdle preventing the uptake of constraint satisfaction technology. Modelling is especially challenging when using non-binary constraints as the number of possible models is very large. In this paper, we model problems of distance, a challenging set of problems based on Golomb rulers. We identify a large number of different models, and compare them theoretically and empirically. Our results demonstrate the considerable benefits of including additional auxiliary variables and implied constraints in the models. We believe that many more studies like this are needed to help turn the art of modelling into a science.

Problems of distance

Peter van Beek has proposed Golomb rulers as a challenging constraint satisfaction problem for the CSPLib benchmark library (available as prob006 at http://csplib.cs.strath.ac.uk). The specification given there is: "A Golomb ruler may be defined as a set of m integers $0 = x_1 < x_2 < ... < x_m$, such that the $m(m-1)/2$ differences $x_j - x_i$, $1 \le i < j \le m$, are distinct. Such a ruler is said to contain m marks and is of length x_m. The objective is to find optimal (minimum length) or near optimal rulers."

The longest known optimal ruler has 21 marks and is of length 333. Such rulers have practical applications in radio astronomy. Peter van Beek reports that even quite small problems (with fewer than 15 marks) are very difficult for complete methods, and that their difficulty lies both in proving optimality and in finding a solution since problems have very few solutions.

Golomb rulers are instances of a more general class of problem which we call *problems of distance*. Such problems are defined by a graph in which m nodes are labelled with integers, the edges are labelled by the difference between the node labels at either end of each edge, and there are constraints that all edge labels are different. A Golomb ruler is a problem of distance in which this underlying graph is complete. We may, however, have a problem of distance in which the underlying graph is not complete. For example, in a 2-d Golomb ruler we have (2 or more) layers of cliques, with edges between node i in clique j and node i in clique $j+1$.

A further generalization is to *modular* problems of distance in which the underlying graph is directed, the edge from node i to node j is labelled with the label of j less that of i, and there are constraints that all edge labels mod n are different. For instance, in a circular Golomb ruler, the underlying directed graph is complete, and n is the length of the circular rule.

Non-binary models

To model problems of distance, we use m variables, $x_1, \ldots, x_m$, each with a (finite) integer domain. There are three obvious non-binary representations:

quaternary model: for each pair of edges, we post quaternary constraints of the form $|x_j - x_i| \ne |x_l - x_k|$

ternary and not-equals model: for each edge, we introduce an auxiliary variable, d_{ij}; we post ternary constraints of the form $d_{ij} = |x_j - x_i|$, and binary not-equals constraints between the auxiliary variables

ternary and all-different model: we again introduce auxiliary variables, d_{ij} and ternary constraints of the form $d_{ij} = |x_j - x_i|$; however, we now post a single all-different constraint on the auxiliary variables

Additional constraints can also be added to eliminate various symmetries. For example, with a Golomb ruler, we post the monotonicity constraints, $x_i < x_{i+1}$ for $1 \leq i < m$. A reflection symmetry can also be broken by adding the constraint $|x_2 - x_1| < |x_m - x_{m-1}|$ (or equivalently, $d_{12} < d_{m-1,m}$).

Theoretical comparison

As in previous studies (Stergiou & Walsh 1999a; 1999b)), we will compare theoretically the effects of constraint propagation on the different models; in particular, we focus on enforcing generalized arc-consistent (GAC) on the different non-binary constraints. A problem is GAC iff for any assignment of a value to a variable in a (non-binary) constraint, there exist compatible values for all the other variables in the constraint (Mohr & Masini 1988).

The introduction into a model of auxiliary variables might be expected to reduce the amount of constraint propagation achieved. However, the large all-different constraint can more than compensate for this reduction.

Theorem 1 *On a problem of distance, GAC on the ternary and all-different model is incomparable to GAC on the quaternary model.*

Proof: Consider a Golomb ruler with $x_1 = \{0\}$, $x_2 = \{1, 2\}$, and $x_3 = \{4\}$. The ternary and all-different model is GAC, but the quaternary model is not GAC (the value 2 must be removed from the domain of x_2).

Consider a Golomb ruler with $x_1 = \{0\}$, $x_2 = \{1, 2\}$, $x_3 = \{3\}$, and $x_4 = \{4, 5\}$. The quaternary model is GAC. However, enforcing GAC on the ternary and all-different model shows that the problem is insoluble since the auxiliary variables d_{12}, d_{23} and d_{34} have domains $\{1, 2\}$ and thus cannot be all different. □

More surprisingly, whilst replacing the large all-different constraint with binary not-equals constraints reduces the amount of constraint propagation, GAC on the ternary and not-equals model can still sometimes be stronger than GAC on the quaternary model.

Theorem 2 *On a problem of distance, GAC on the ternary and not-equals model is incomparable to GAC on the quaternary model.*

Proof: Consider the first Golomb ruler in the previous proof. The ternary and not-equals model is GAC. However, enforcing GAC on the quaternary model prunes the value 2 from the domain of x_2.

Consider a Golomb ruler with $x_1 = \{0\}$, $x_2 = \{1\}$, $x_3 = \{3\}$, $x_4 = \{7, 8\}$, and $x_5 = \{8, 9\}$. The quaternary model is GAC. However, enforcing GAC on the ternary and not-equals model shows that the problem is insoluble since the auxiliary variable d_{45} has all its possible values (1, 2 or 3) removed from its domain by the constraints with the auxiliary variables d_{12}, d_{23} and d_{13}. □

It is less surprising that replacing the single all-different constraint with binary not-equals constraints reduces the amount of constraint propagation.

Theorem 3 *On a problem of distance, GAC on the ternary and all-different model is strictly stronger than GAC on the ternary and not-equals model.*

Proof: It is trivially stronger as GAC on an all-different constraint is stronger than GAC on binary not-equals constraints. To show strictness, consider again the second Golomb ruler in the first proof. The ternary and not-equals model is GAC. However, enforcing GAC on the ternary and all-different model shows that is insoluble. □

By including additional implied constraints, the ternary and not-equals model can be made strictly stronger than the quaternary model. By transitivity, the ternary and all-different model can also be made strictly stronger than the quaternary model.

Theorem 4 *On a problem of distance, there exist some implied ternary constraints with which GAC on the ternary and not-equals model is strictly stronger than GAC on the quaternary model.*

Proof: The implied ternary constraints are of the form $|x_j - x_i| \neq |x_k - x_i|$ for all pairs of nodes j and k connected to a third node i. Consider one of the quaternary constraints, $|x_j - x_i| \neq |x_l - x_k|$. Assume that enforcing GAC on this quaternary constraint prunes a value but this value is not removed in the ternary and not-equals model. Due to the inclusion of the implied ternary constraints, i, j, k, l must all be different. The quaternary constraint is GAC unless at least three of the variables have a singleton domain, and one of the values of the remaining variable, say x_i, violates the constraint. But in that case, d_{kl} also has a singleton domain, and GAC on $d_{ij} \neq d_{kl}$ would delete the only possible value for d_{kl} from the domain of d_{ij}. Enforcing GAC on the ternary constraint $d_{ij} = x_j - x_i$ will then delete the same value of x_i. This contradicts the assumption that we prune a value in the quaternary model but not in the ternary and binary model. To show strictness, consider again the second Golomb ruler in the first proof. □

Our results show that a model with auxiliary variables and ternary constraints can in theory improve upon one with quaternary constraints. The next section shows that the differences can be very large in practice.

Golomb rulers

Table 1 shows the number of branches explored and the CPU time used on a Silicon Graphics O2 to find optimal Golomb rulers using ILOG Solver's inbuilt minimization functions. For efficiency, we use Jean-Charles Régin's specialized GAC algorithm on the all-different constraint (Régin 1994), simple bounds consistency on the ternary and quaternary constraints, and arc consistency on the binary constraints (which is equivalent to GAC on binary constraints). We show later on that GAC on the ternary constraints is not competitive in terms of CPU time with bounds consistency. The same is likely to be true of GAC on the quaternary constraints, especially as GAC is more expensive as we increase the constraint arity and as it will tend to prune fewer values.

In all three models, we used a fixed lexicographical variable ordering. Variables are assigned in order start-

Marks (m)	quaternary br.	CPU	ternary + $\neq$ br.	CPU	ternary + alldiff br.	CPU
6 - F	15	0.020	6	0.007	6	0.012
- P	63	0.042	39	0.015	10	0.006
7 - F	116	0.170	28	0.023	26	0.033
- P	594	0.801	327	0.198	84	0.125
8 - F	756	2.03	130	0.104	98	0.124
- P	4852	14.0	2605	2.27	599	1.23
9 - F	7271	31.7	1622	1.70	816	1.56
- P	33679	168	17823	22.1	2924	9.69
10 - F	78503	657	21507	27.9	9757	24.3
- P	-	-	-	-	13707	68.3
11 - F	-	-	-	-	31666	94.5
- P	-	-	-	-	-	-

Table 1: Branches explored and CPU time (seconds) used to find a minimal length ruler (F) or prove that none shorter exists (P). A - means that the run was cut off after 10^5 branches.

ing from x_2 (since x_1 can be unconditionally assigned to 0). Constraint propagation on the ternary constraints will assign the auxiliary variables. We tried the smallest domain dynamic variable ordering heuristic on a variety of different sets of search variables, but were unable to beat a simple lexicographic heuristic that builds up the ruler from one end.

Table 1 shows that the quaternary model is much less efficient than the ternary models, both in terms of branches explored and CPU time. Introducing auxiliary variables is in practice very worthwhile for these problems. With the ternary models, making the alldiff constraint GAC gives the smallest search tree. On the smaller problems, runtimes are not always shorter than if binary $\neq$ constraints are used, but on the larger problems the savings are considerable, particularly when proving optimality.

Binary encodings

An alternative strategy for solving a non-binary model is to encode it into a binary model using one of the standard encodings such as the hidden variable or the dual encoding (Bacchus & van Beek 1998; Stergiou & Walsh 1999b). In the case of Golomb rulers, the double encoding introduced in (Stergiou & Walsh 1999b) is more practical than the dual encoding. The double encoding combines together all the constraints from the dual and the hidden variable encodings. In a dual encoding, the dual variables associated with either the all-different constraint or the binary not-equals constraints have such large domains that we cannot afford to enforce arc consistency. In a double encoding, whilst we use dual variables associated with the ternary constraints, we can ignore the dual variables associated with the all-different constraint or the binary not-equals constraints as they are redundant. This makes it computationally feasible to use the double encoding. Finally, whilst encodings of models with ternary constraints are practical, encodings of the quaternary constraints have domains which are prohibitively large. We therefore looked at four new models.

hidden variable + all-different model: each ternary constraint is replaced by a hidden variable with domain of size $O(l^2)$; we also post a single all-different constraint between the auxiliary variables;

hidden variable + not-equals model: again each ternary constraint is replaced by a hidden variable; we also post binary not-equals constraints between the auxiliary variables; this model contains purely binary constraints;

double encoding + all-different model: again each ternary constraint is replaced by a hidden variable; we also post compatibility constraints between hidden variables that share variables, and a single all-different constraint between the auxiliary variables;

double encoding + not-equals model: again each ternary constraint is replaced by a hidden variable; we also post compatibility constraints between hidden variables that share variables, and binary not-equals constraints between auxiliary variables; this model contains purely binary constraints.

It was not feasible to find optimal rulers using the binary encodings as this requires setting l to some large initial value, and the domain size of the hidden variables is then prohibitively large. Instead, we have used the known optimal rulers to compare the encodings. We first find a ruler with length equal to the optimal length, and then show that there is no shorter ruler. Table 2 compares the models in which all the constraints are binary with the ternary and not-equals model.

m	l	hidden + $\neq$ br.	CPU	double + $\neq$ br.	CPU	ternary + $\neq$ br.	CPU
6	17	5	0.150	5	0.473	5	0.052
6	16*	36	0.304	32	0.912	36	0.109
7	25	18	0.645	17	3.70	18	0.251
7	24*	286	3.13	237	11.9	286	1.18
8	34	45	2.34	45	21.2	45	0.964
8	33*	2015	31.4	1461	117	2012	12.1
9	44	708	22.0	506	147	705	8.51
9	43*	12822	302	8846	1180	12815	115

Table 2: Branches explored and CPU time (seconds) used to find a ruler of length no more than l or prove that none exists, using lexicographic ordering. * indicates that there is no ruler of this length.

Fewer branches are explored in the double than in the hidden encoding. The hidden encoding gives very similar results, in terms of the size of the search tree, to the ternary model with GAC. However, the CPU times tell a different story. Both the binary encodings, and especially the double, are far worse than the ternary model. This is not surprising as arc consistency takes longer to enforce in the binary encodings due to the large domain sizes. Results are similar (though slightly better) with the models using all-different constraints: the double encoding gives the best results in terms of the number of branches explored, but the worst CPU times.

Implied constraints

As Theorem 4 suggests, one route to improved performance is to add implied constraints to the model. Although implied constraints can often significantly reduce runtimes (e.g. (Proll & Smith 1998; Regin 1998)), choosing useful implied constraints remains an art. We can, however, state two basic criteria. First, we require either implied constraints for which specialized and efficient constraint propagation algorithms are available, or constraints of small arity. Second, circumstances in which an implied constraint leads to pruning of additional values should be obvious and frequent. However, whilst these criteria are desirable, they are not sufficient as implied constraints must offer enough pruning to offset their overheads. This is hard to predict without experimentation. For instance, the implied constraints of Theorem 4 satisfy the two criteria, but do not justify their overhead. In the rest of this section, we consider other implied constraints, and their effect when added to the current best model, i.e. the ternary and all-different model with lexicographic variable ordering.

Ordering of Auxiliary Variables

For all $i < j < k$, we can post the implied constraints $d_{ij} < d_{ik}$ and $d_{jk} < d_{ik}$. These implied constraints are binary, and hence cheap to propagate. It is also easy to see that they can lead to domain reductions not achievable otherwise. However, experiments show that they only reduce the size of the search tree modestly, and do not reduce runtimes on larger problems.

Tighter Bounds on Auxiliary Variables

Since $d_{ij} = d_{i,i+1} + d_{i+1,i+2} + \ldots + d_{j-1,j}$, and each of term in this sum is different, d_{ij} must at least equal the sum of the first $j-i$ integers, i.e. $d_{ij} \geq (j-i)(j-i+1)/2$. We can tighten this bound further as a subsection of the ruler, i.e. from mark i to mark j, must itself form a (not necessarily optimal) Golomb ruler of $j - i + 1$ marks. Therefore, $d_{ij} \geq l_{j-i+1}$ where l_k is the optimal length of a k mark ruler. Both these implied constraints are cheap to implement as they are unary.

Another bound on the auxiliary variables comes from the constraint $x_n = d_{12} + d_{23} + \ldots + d_{n-1,n}$. That is, $d_{ij} = x_n - (d_{12} + d_{23} + \ldots + d_{i-1,i} + d_{j,j+1} + \ldots + d_{n-1,n})$. The RHS is x_n less the sum of $n - 1 - j + i$ different integers. So we can maximize the RHS by minimizing this sum. This gives the implied constraint $d_{ij} \leq x_n - (n-1-j+i)(n-j+i)/2$. This is again efficient to implement as it is binary. As x_n is reduced, the constraint gets tighter, and so becomes more effective as we approach the minimal length.

Table 3 shows the significant benefits of adding these bounds to the model, with and without the ordering constraints described in the last section. On the larger problems, search space and runtimes are significantly reduced. Because of the smaller domains, CPU time reduces on the smaller problems even when the number of branches remains constant. The ordering constraints on the auxiliary variables continue to offer little benefit.

m	ternary + alldiff		+ tighter bounds		+ tighter bounds + ordering constraints	
	br.	CPU	br.	CPU	br.	CPU
7 - F	26	0.033	26	0.032	26	0.038
- P	84	0.118	54	0.051	54	0.063
8 - F	98	0.124	98	0.128	98	0.160
- P	599	1.23	385	0.503	385	0.635
9 - F	816	1.56	718	1.17	718	1.47
- P	2924	9.69	1751	3.61	1751	4.48
10 - F	9757	24.3	7971	17.1	7948	21.3
- P	13707	68.3	7812	24.0	7807	29.5
11 - F	31666	94.5	29251	80.8	29190	108
- P	343220	2000	252985	1020	252577	1300

Table 3: Branches explored and CPU time to find a minimal length ruler (F) or prove that none shorter exists (P), with and without tighter bounds on the auxiliary variables.

Dynamic Bounds on Auxiliary Variables

By adding implied constraints *dynamically* during search, we can post even tighter bounds on the auxiliary variables. For example, if we have assigned 1 and 3 to x_2 and x_3, then any auxiliary variable d_{ij} for $i \geq 2$ must be at least the sum of $j - i$ different integers *excluding* 1, 2 and 3, the values already assigned. We have implemented a limited form of propagation for this type of implied constraint. We record the largest mark so far assigned (x_{max}) and the values assigned to the auxiliary variables. For all $m > max$, we calculate the sum of the $m - max$ smallest integers which have not yet been assigned to auxiliary variables, and post a constraint on this branch of the search tree that the value of $d_{max,m}$ must be at least this sum.

m	ternary + alldiff + + tighter bounds		+ dynamic bounds	
	br.	CPU	br.	CPU
7 - F	26	0.032	25	0.032
- P	57	0.051	50	0.049
8 - F	98	0.128	80	0.111
- P	385	0.503	355	0.480
9 - F	718	1.17	509	0.822
- P	1751	3.61	1564	3.41
10 - F	7971	17.1	5428	12.0
- P	7812	24.0	6810	22.1
11 - F	29251	80.8	19211	53.6
- P	252985	1020	224636	967

Table 4: Branches explored and CPU time to find a ruler of minimal length (F) or prove that none shorter exists (P), with and without the dynamic bounds on the auxiliary variables.

Table 4 shows that adding this implied constraint dynamically to the model during search gives the best results so far. Except for the smallest problems, there are significant reductions in both the number of branches explored and CPU time.

2-d Golomb rulers

In the next two sections, we see how these results map onto related problems. We first consider 2-d Golomb rulers with two layers, each of which is a 1-d ruler, with marks at $x_1, x_2, \ldots x_m$ and $y_1, y_2, \ldots y_m$ respectively. As before we introduce auxiliary variables to represent the pairwise distances between the marks in each layer, as well as the distances $|x_i - y_i|$. We add a symmetry constraint $x_2 - x_1 < x_m - x_{m-1}$ on the first layer, as before, but we cannot add a similar constraint on the second. However, there is a symmetry between the two layers, and we can break this by adding $x_2 - x_1 < y_2 - y_1$.

As in the 1-d case, the quaternary model is very inefficient compared to the ternary and all-different one, which again is the best model. The hidden variable representation reduces the search space substantially but again the CPU times are much worse. Since each layer is itself a (not necessarily optimal) 1-d Golomb ruler, we can use all the implied constraints introduced in the last section. However, now they have very little effect on the number of fails and are more expensive in terms of cpu time. The minimum length is much greater than in the 1-d case for the same value of m, and hence the lower bounds provided by the implied constraints are much less effective.

Variable ordering again has a significant effect on performance, and the smallest domain heuristic once more performs poorly. Table 5 gives the number of branches explored and the CPU time used (on a 166MHz Pentium) to find and prove optimal 2-d Golomb rulers with two layers, each with m marks, with different variable orderings. In all cases, the search variables are those representing the marks. We compare the dynamic smallest domain ordering with two static orderings; in one, the marks from the first layer are assigned and then those from the second; in the other, marks from two layers are assigned alternately. As in the 1-d case, building up each layer successively is much quicker than the dynamic ordering, but it is better to build up both layers in parallel than to complete one layer first. This allows the distances between the layers to be assigned at the same time.

m	smallest dom. br.	CPU	$x_2,...,x_m,y_2,...,y_m$ br.	CPU	$x_2,y_2,...,x_m,y_m$ br.	CPU
3 - F	3	0.049	1	0.038	1	0.036
- P	9	0.058	9	0.057	5	0.047
4 - F	89	0.44	78	0.15	32	0.070
- P	419	0.45	395	0.48	199	0.23
5 - F	2929	4.19	2217	3.7	1479	1.84
- P	21069	36	19510	35	7719	11

Table 5: Branches explored and CPU time to find a minimal length 2-d Golomb ruler with two layers (F) or prove that none shorter exists (P), with different variable orderings.

Note that these problems are much harder to solve than 1-d Golomb rulers. Our fastest model takes more than 15 minutes to find and prove an optimal solution for $m = 6$, and we have not been able to prove optimality for $m = 7$.

Circular Golomb rulers

Circular or modular Golomb rulers can be thought of as a number of marks arranged on the circumference of a circle in such a way that the distances between any pair of marks, in either direction along the circumference, are different. The problem of finding a minimal length ruler for a given number of marks is different in several respects from the linear problem. Solutions can be constructed (see http://www.research.ibm.com/people/s/shearer/mgrule.html for an account) and if $m - 1$ is a prime power, there is a perfect ruler, i.e. every intermediate length occurs. This is very different from the linear case, where perfect rulers are extremely rare. Although search will not be a good approach to finding solutions to these problems, it is instructive to consider the issues that arise when modelling them as CSPs.

With a circular Golomb ruler, we can ignore the variables associated with the marks, and assign instead search variables $d_0, \ldots, d_{m-1}$ to represent the distance between adjacent marks. In this sense, the ternary models of circular Golomb rulers are more fundamental than the quaternary models. We break the rotational and reflective symmetry by insisting that $d_0 = 1$ and $d_1 < d_{m-1}$.

We also define a set of composite distances between every pair of non-adjacent marks: $d_{i,j} = d_i + d_{(i+1) \bmod m} + \ldots + d_{(i+k) \bmod m}$, where $(i+k) \bmod m = j$, for all $i \neq j$ between 0 and $m - 1$. To express the constraint that the circumference of the ruler is minimal, we introduce an objective variable l constrained to equal $d_0 + d_1 + \ldots + d_{m-1}$. This is the basic model whose results are shown below in Table 6, using lexicographic ordering of the search variables.

Because of the large arity of the constraint defining l and of some of the constraints defining the composite distances, we introduced new ternary constraints expressing the composite distances and l in terms of one of the basic distances and a shorter composite distance. This gives in general two constraints for $d_{i,j}$: $d_{i,j} = d_i + d_{(i+1) \bmod m, j}$ and $d_{i,j} = d_{i,(j-1) \bmod m} + d_j$, and m constraints for l, one for every basic distance. The effect of these implied constraints is shown in the second column of Table 6: there is a significant saving in both the number of branches and CPU time, for larger problems.

We can also use the lower bounds derived earlier for linear rulers, based on the fact that each composite distance is at least the sum of a number of different integers. However, adding these bounds makes virtually no difference to the number of branches.

The third column of Table 6 shows the effect of making the all-different constraint GAC. The arity of the all-different constraint, for the same number of marks, is much higher than with a linear ruler, so making the constraint GAC is more expensive. The Table shows that it is not worthwhile, in terms of CPU time, for finding the optimal solution. However, it does allow optimality to be proved very quickly, except for $m = 7$. For the other values of m, the optimal ruler is perfect. Since there are $m * (m - 1)$ different distances between the marks, the length of a perfect circular ruler is $m * (m - 1) + 1$. This could be included in the model as a lower bound on l, and the proof of optimality would be immediate, except for $m = 7$. The benefit of making the all-different constraint GAC would then disappear.

Another difference between modelling the circular

and linear problems is that in this case the lexicographic ordering $d_0, d_1, \ldots, d_{m-1}$ does not reflect the geometry of the problem so well as in the linear case. Perhaps for this reason, the smallest domain ordering performs relatively well, solving some instances more quickly.

m	basic model		+ implied constraints		+ alldiff	
	br.	CPU	br.	CPU	br.	CPU
5 - F	22	0.067	19	0.044	16	0.161
- P	33	0.079	29	0.055	18	0.168
6 - F	10	0.082	9	0.049	8	0.215
- P	166	0.198	117	0.151	11	0.226
7 - F	724	0.941	333	0.516	297	1.07
- P	5523	6.32	2819	3.91	1889	5.61
8 - F	4042	8.08	1350	3.18	1146	4.66
- P	23109	43.3	8564	19.0	1150	4.68
9 - F	948	2.31	346	1.26	331	2.17
- P	-	-	-	-	336	2.23

Table 6: Effect of implied constraints and making the all-different constraint GAC on branches explored and CPU time to find a circular Golomb ruler of minimal circumference (F) or prove that none shorter exists (P).

Related work

Nadel performed a study on various different ways of modelling the n-Queens problem (Nadel 1990). In CSPLib, Jean-Francois Puget reports finding a 12-mark Golomb ruler using ILOG Solver in 2,042,001 branches, and proving it optimal in a further 1,141,316 branches. Our best model offers a significant improvement over this result. With the ternary and all-different model and implied constraints, we found an optimal 12-mark solution in 1,398,327 branches, and needed just a further 513,109 branches to prove it optimal. This is a significant reduction in search effort. Auxiliary variables are important in modelling cryptarithmetic problems like SEND + MORE = MONEY. Large arithmetic constraints such as these can be decomposed into more useful ternary and quaternary constraints via auxiliary variables that represent the "carries" (Brailsford, Potts, & Smith 1999).

Conclusions

We have performed an extensive theoretical and empirical analysis of different models for problems of distance like 1-d, 2-d and circular Golomb rulers. We introduced a number of different models with quaternary, ternary, binary and all-different constraints. We proved that, whilst the level of consistency achieved by GAC on the quaternary and ternary models is incomparable in general, the ternary models are strictly stronger than the quaternary if we introduce some simple implied ternary constraints. We also considered purely binary models using hidden variables for the non-binary constraints. Whilst these reduced the number of branches explored as predicted by theory, they did not always give a reduction in runtime because of the cost of enforcing arc consistency on hidden variables with large domains. We also identified several sets of implied constraints, some of which reduced both the number of branches explored and the CPU time significantly. Our final models offer dramatic improvement reducing, for instance, the time to find an optimal 10–mark Golomb ruler 50-fold.

What general lessons can be learned from this study? First, even simple problems can be modelled in many different ways. Counting all possible encodings, this study alone has identified fifteen possible models for the Golomb ruler problem, although we have omitted some of these from our experiments (in particular the binary encodings of the quaternary models). If we include all possible ways of adding the implied constraints, there would be many more. Secondly, finding the best model involves a trade-off between the arity of the constraints and the efficiency with which we can reason about them. The most effective model in this case study was not the quaternary model but the ternary model with a single, large, all-different constraint. Thirdly, the addition of auxiliary variables and implied constraints can allow us to achieve higher levels of consistency. However, identifying those implied constraints which will reduce runtimes is not easy. Although we have suggested some guidelines, our experience indicates that experiment is often needed to tell whether a set of implied constraints is worthwhile.

Acknowledgements

The third author is an EPSRC advanced research fellow. The authors are members of the APES research group (http://www.cs.strath.ac.uk/~apes) and wish to thank the other members.

References

Bacchus, F., and van Beek, P. 1998. On the conversion between non-binary and binary constraint satisfaction problems. In *Proceedings of AAAI-98*, 311–318.

Brailsford, S. C.; Potts, C. N.; and Smith, B. M. 1999. Constraint Satisfaction Problems: Algorithms and Applications. *European Journal of O.R.* 119:557–581.

Mohr, R., and Masini, G. 1988. Good old discrete relaxation. In *Proceedings ECAI-88*, 651–656.

Nadel, B. 1990. Representation Selection for Constraint Satisfaction: A Case Study using n-Queens. *IEEE Expert* 5(3):16–24.

Proll, L., and Smith, B. 1998. ILP and constraint programming approaches to a template design problem. *INFORMS Journal on Computing* 10:265–277.

Régin, J.-C. 1994. A filtering algorithm for constraints of difference in CSPs. In *Proceedings of AAAI-94*, 362–367.

Regin, J.-C. 1998. Minimization of the number of breaks in sports scheduling problems using constraint programming. In *Proceedings of the DIMACS Workshop on Constraint Programming and Large Scale Discrete Optimization*.

Stergiou, K., and Walsh, T. 1999a. The difference all-difference makes. In *Proceedings of IJCAI-99*.

Stergiou, K., and Walsh, T. 1999b. Encodings of non-binary constraint satisfaction problems. In *Proceedings of AAAI-99*.

Game Playing

The Game of Hex: An Automatic Theorem Proving Approach to Game Programming

Vadim V. Anshelevich

Vanshel Consulting
1200 Navaho Trail
Richardson, Texas 75080
vanshel@earthlink.net

Abstract

The game of Hex is a two-player game with simple rules, a deep underlying mathematical beauty, and a strategic complexity comparable to that of Chess and Go. The massive game-tree search techniques developed mostly for Chess, and successfully used for Checkers, Othello, and a number of other games, become less useful for games with large branching factors like Go and Hex. We offer a new approach, which results in superior playing strength. This approach emphasizes deep analysis of relatively few game positions. In order to reach this goal, we develop an automatic theorem proving technique for topological analysis of Hex positions. We also discuss in detail an idea of modeling Hex positions with electrical resistor circuits. We explain how this approach is implemented in Hexy - the strongest known Hex-playing computer program, able to compete with best human players.

1. Introduction

The rules of Hex are extremely simple. Nevertheless, experienced players recognize that Hex requires both deep strategic understanding and sharp tactical skills. Multiple attempts to build a strong Hex-playing program show that it is a difficult task. One of the major reasons is the large branching factor. For a classic 11×11 Hex board the average number of legal moves is about 100 (compare with 40 for Chess and 8 for Checkers). The massive game-tree search techniques developed over the last 30-40 years mostly for Chess (Marsland, 1986), and successfully used for Checkers (Schaeffer et al. 1996), and a number of other games, become less useful for games with large branching factors like Hex. On the other hand, many experienced game players believe that in most positions, intelligent decisions can be made without a massive game-tree search. Instead, the emphasis can be on a deep strategic analysis of a relatively small number of game positions.

In this paper we concentrate on building a far-sighted evaluation function, which is capable of foreseeing future development of Hex positions. We believe that if such a function is built, it could be used for highly selective game-tree search. In order to reach this goal, we identify topological objects, called *virtual connections*, which contain information about the potential of Hex positions, and develop an automatic theorem proving technique for their calculations. The construction of virtual connections can be thought of as a very narrow search, which focuses on relevant paths. As a result, this approach is much more efficient than a brute-force search.

There are also other games (Chess and Sokoban), where important game-specific properties were identified, and real time proofs of necessary conditions were successfully used (Adelson-Velskiy, Arlazarov, and Donskoy 1975; Junghanns and Schaeffer 1998). In both cases it has resulted in significant reduction in the size of the search tree.

In section 2 we introduce the game of Hex and its history. In section 3 we present a model for evaluating Hex positions based on electrical resistor circuits. In section 4 we discuss the concept of a virtual connection, and define contributions of virtual connections to the evaluation function. In section 5 we introduce the algebra of virtual connections as a tool for their calculation. In section 6 we explain how this approach is implemented in Hexy - the strongest known Hex-playing computer program, able to compete with best human players. A Windows 95/98/NT version of the program (165KB) is publicly available at the website: http://home.earthlink.net/~vanshel.

2. Hex and Its History

The game of Hex was presented to the general public in *Scientific American* by Martin Gardner (Gardner 1959).

Hex is a two-player game played on a rhombic board with hexagonal cells (see Figure 1). The classic board is 11×11, but it can be any size. The 10×10 and 14×14 board sizes are also popular. The players, Black and White, take turns putting pieces of their color on empty cells of the board. Black's objective is to connect the two opposite black sides of the board with a chain of black pieces. White's objective is to connect the two opposite white sides of the board with a chain of white pieces (see Figure 1). In practice, players often employ "one move equalization",

---

Copyright © 2000, American Association for Artificial Intelligence (www.aaai.org). All rights reserved

where the second player has the option of taking the first player's opening move (also known as the swap rule).

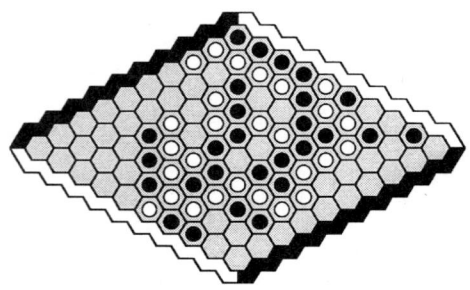

Fig. 1. The chain of white pieces connects white boundaries. White has won the game.

Despite the simplicity of the rules, the game has a complexity comparable to Chess, in both strategy and tactics.

Hex was invented by a Danish poet and mathematician Piet Hein in 1942 at the Niels Bohr Institute for Theoretical Physics, and became popular under the name of Polygon. It was re-discovered in 1948 by John Nash, when he was a graduate student at Princeton. At that time, this game was commonly called John, referring mainly to the fact that it was often played on the hexagonal tiles of bathroom floors. Parker Brothers marketed a version of the game in 1952 under the name Hex.

The game of Hex can never end in a draw. This follows from the fact that if all cells of the board are occupied then a winning chain for Black or White must necessarily exist. While this two-dimensional topological fact may seem obvious, it is not at all trivial. In fact, David Gale demonstrated that this result is equivalent to the Brouwer fixed-point theorem for 2-dimensional squares (Gale 1979). It follows that there exists a winning strategy either for the first or second player. Using a "strategy stealing" argument (Berlekamp, Conway, and Guy 1982), John Nash showed that a winning strategy exists for the first player. However, this is only a proof of existence, and the winning strategy is not known for boards larger than 7×7.

A Hex-playing machine was built by Claude Shannon and E. F. Moore (Shannon 1953). Shannon associated a two-dimensional electrical charge distribution with any given Hex position. His machine made decisions based on properties of the corresponding potential field. In the next section we introduce another way to model Hex positions. Nevertheless, we gratefully acknowledge that our work was inspired by Shannon's original idea.

3. Using Electrical Circuits and Resistance for a Hex Evaluation Function

A reasonable evaluation function for Hex should estimate how much closer Black is to building a winning black chain than White is to building a winning white chain. A popular way to measure how close a player is to building his chain is to calculate the minimal number of pieces he needs to add to connect his two sides of the board. Unfortunately, this type of approach does not take into account the number of potential chains. We attempt to fix this flaw with an *electrical circuit* representation of Hex positions.

Consider the four polygonal boundary bands as additional cells (see Figure 1). We assume that black boundary cells are permanently occupied by black pieces, and white boundary cells are permanently occupied by white pieces.

With every Hex position we associate two electrical circuits. The first one characterizes the position from Black's point of view (Black's circuit), and the second one from White's point of view (White's circuit). To every cell c of the board we assign a resistance r in the following way:

$r_B(c) = 1$, if c is empty,
$r_B(c) = 0$, if c is occupied by a black piece,
$r_B(c) = +\infty$, if c is occupied by a white piece,
for Black's circuit, and
$r_W(c) = 1$, if c is empty,
$r_W(c) = 0$, if c is occupied by a white piece,
$r_W(c) = +\infty$, if c is occupied by a black piece,
for White's circuit.

For each pair of neighboring cells, (c_1, c_2), we associate an electrical link with resistance:

$r_B(c_1, c_2) = r_B(c_1) + r_B(c_2)$, for Black's circuit,
$r_W(c_1, c_2) = r_W(c_1) + r_W(c_2)$, for White's circuit.

We now apply an electrical voltage to the opposite boundary cells and measure the total resistance between them, R_B for Black's circuit, and R_W for White's circuit (see Figure 2).

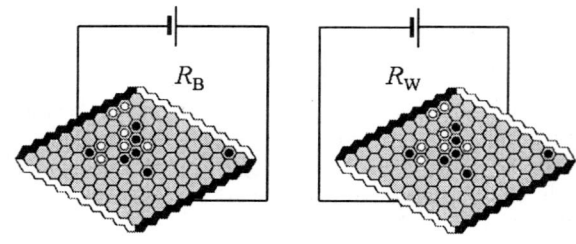

Fig. 2. Black's and White's circuits.

According to the Kirchhoff electrical current laws, the total resistance estimates both the number of pieces that need to be added to the board in order to connect the opposite sides of the board, and the number of ways it can be done.

Now we define an evaluation function:

$E = R_B / R_W$,

It is clear that:

- $E = 0$, iff there exists a winning black chain,
- $E = +\infty$, iff there exists a winning white chain,
- The smaller E is, the better this position is for Black, and the worse it is for White.

4. Virtual Connections

In this section we work with Black's circuits only. White's circuits can be dealt with in a similar way.

Consider the two positions in Figure 3. In both positions White cannot prevent Black from connecting the two groups of black pieces, x and y, even if White moves first, because there are two empty cells a and b adjacent to both x and y. If White occupies one of those empty cells, then Black can move to the other. As a result, White should resign immediately in the right position. Note that the black connection between groups x and y is secured while two cells a and b stay empty. Black can postpone moving to either a or b and can use his precious moves for other purposes. In this type of situation we say that the groups of black pieces x and y form a *two-bridge*.

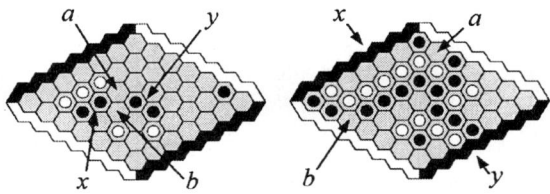

Fig. 3. Groups of black pieces, x and y, form two-bridges. In the position on the right, those groups are connected to the black boundaries.

We are now going to enhance our evaluation function to reflect this local Black advantage. One natural way of doing this is to add a link with zero resistance between groups x and y to Black's circuit. Then the virtual connection would be treated as an actual connection. However, virtual connections are weaker than actual ones, so our evaluation function should reflect this. Instead of connecting black groups x and y with a shortcut, we add other links to Black's circuit in the following way. If an empty cell c is a neighbor of the black group x, then we also treat this cell as a neighbor of group y (and vice versa). This means that we connect cell c and group y with an additional link in the same way as we do with actual neighbors.

Black's new circuit serves as a better model for the Hex position than the original one, and the enhanced evaluation function $E = R_B / R_W$ provides a better estimation of the value of the position. This estimate now includes information about the potential of the position two moves ahead.

Our intention is to further modify the electrical circuits in order to build a more far-sighted evaluation function, which takes into account the distant potential of positions. The following definition generalizes the two-bridge concept. First we need to clarify some terms. We say that a *cell is black* iff it is occupied by a black piece, and we say that a set of black cells forms a *group* iff it is connected.

Definition. *Two groups of black cells x and y, or a group of black cells x and an empty cell y, or two empty cells x and y, form virtual connection iff White cannot prevent Black from connecting them, even if White moves first.*

Any set A of empty cells that guarantees that the given pair x and y form a virtual connection is called a *carrier* of that virtual connection. We will describe a virtual connection V as a triplet (x, A, y), where groups or cells x and y are *ends* of the virtual connection V, and A is its carrier.

We represent virtual connections with diagrams as in Figure 4.

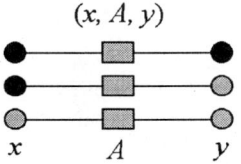

Fig. 4. Diagrams of three types of virtual connections: black-black, black-empty, and empty-empty.

Let us assume that in a given position with a virtual connection, White moves first. The number of moves which must be made in order to *realize* this virtual connection (i.e. to convert the virtual connection into an actual one, under the condition that Black does his best to minimize this number, and White does his best to maximize it) characterizes the *depth of the virtual connection*. In other words, the depth of the virtual connection is the depth of a game-tree search required to discover this virtual connection.

A special role is played by a *winning virtual connection* formed by the additional boundary cells. If it exists, then there exists a winning strategy for Black, even if White moves first.

Let us now make several remarks:

- Any pair of neighboring cells forms a virtual connection with an empty carrier. The depth of these virtual connections is equal to zero.
- Two-bridges, described previously, form virtual connections with a depth of two.
- The ends x and y can form a virtual connection with several different carriers. The virtual connection $V = (x, A, y)$ is *minimal* iff there does not exist a virtual connection (x, B, y) such that $B \subset A$ and $B \neq A$. We will be primarily interested in minimal virtual connections.

In Figure 5 you can see four samples of virtual connections.

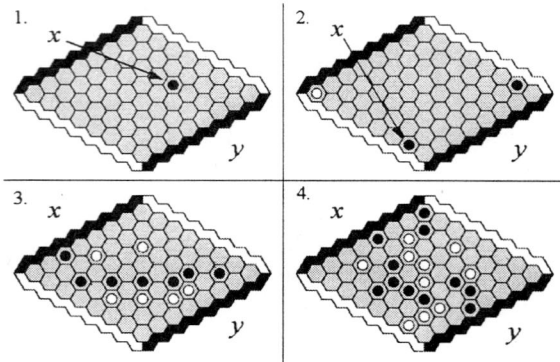

Fig. 5. Black groups x and y form virtual connections. In each diagram the group y is formed by the black pieces connected to the bottom right black boundary.
1. An "edge connection" from the fourth row. Depth = 10.
2. A "ladder". Depth = 14.
3. A chain of two-bridges. Depth = 12.
4. A tactical virtual connection. Depth = 6. This position will be analyzed in the next section.

We can deal with all virtual connections in the same way we did with two-bridges. Let black groups x and y form a virtual connection. If an empty cell c is a neighbor of one of the ends of this virtual connection, say x, then we also treat this cell c as a neighbor of the other end y. This means that we connect cells c and y with an additional link in the same way as actual neighbors.

Virtual connections with the depth d contain information about development of Hex position d moves ahead. The more virtual connections we include, and the larger their depths, the more reliable and far-sighted the evaluation function becomes.

5. Algebra of Virtual Connections

In this section we will explain how to detect virtual connections without searching the game-tree. We will define deduction rules (operators), which will allow us to build complex virtual connections starting with simple ones. We will again consider only Black's circuits.

The AND Deduction Rule. *Let (x, A, u) and (u, B, y) be two virtual connections, where the group u is black, and is a common end for both. If $x \cap B = \emptyset$, $y \cap A = \emptyset$, and $A \cap B = \emptyset$, then the triplet $(x, A \cup B, y)$ also forms a virtual connection.*

Diagram 1 in Figure 6 shows a graphical representation of this deduction rule.

We can explain this deduction rule in the following way. Since $A \cap B = \emptyset$, White cannot attack both virtual connections simultaneously. Let us suppose that White occupies a cell $a \in A$. Since the triplet (x, A, u) forms a virtual connection, then there exists a cell $b \in A$ where

Black can play to create a new virtual connection (x, A_1, u). The new carrier A_1 is obtained from A by removing two cells a and b. In short, if White occupies a cell from A, then Black can restore the first virtual connection by moving to an appropriate cell of A. The same is true for B, and thus every threat can be answered, until an actual connection is obtained.

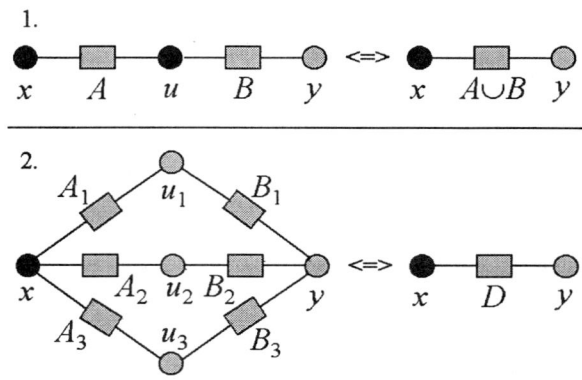

Fig. 6. Deduction rules.
1. The AND deduction rule.
2. The OR(3) deduction rule.

The OR(n) Deduction Rule. *Let (x, A_k, u_k) and (u_k, B_k, y), $(k = 1,2,...,n, \text{ for } n > 1)$ be virtual connections, where the cells x and y are black or empty, and all cells u_k are empty. Let the following conditions be true:*

$x \cap B_k = \emptyset$, and $y \cap A_k = \emptyset$, for all $k = 1,2,...,n$,

$A_k \cap B_k = \emptyset$, for all $k = 1,2,...,n$,

$$\bigcap_{k=1}^{n} C_k = \emptyset,$$

where $C_k = A_k \cup u_k \cup B_k$, for all $k = 1,2,...,n$. Then the triplet (x, D, y) also forms virtual connection with the carrier:

$$D = \bigcup_{k=1}^{n} C_k.$$

Diagram 2 in Figure 6 graphically represents this deduction rule (for $n = 3$).

The explanation of this rule is as follows: If White occupies a cell from C_i, then there exists a different carrier C_j, such that $C_i \cap C_j = \emptyset$. Black can move to u_j, to form a new virtual connection $(x, A_j \cup B_j, y)$, since (x, A_j, u_j) and (u_j, B_j, y) satisfy the conditions of the AND deduction rule.

Automatic Theorem Proving

Figure 7 demonstrates how the AND and the OR(n) deduction rules can be used to prove more complex virtual connections. Diagram 1 in Figure 7 represents the position on the board. The sequence of transformations in diagrams 2 through 4 graphically demonstrates the application of the deduction rules, and proves that Black has a winning position.

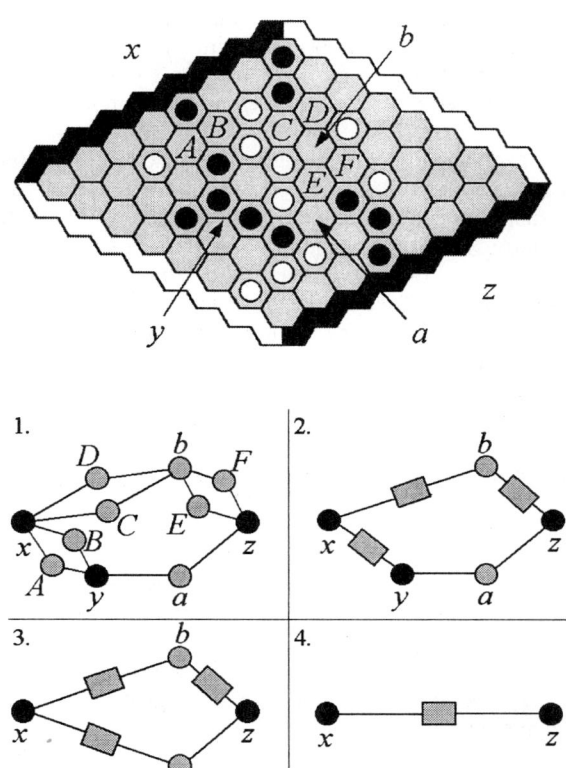

Fig. 7. Automatic theorem proving. Diagram 1 represents the position on the board above. Diagram 2 is obtained from Diagram 1 by applying the OR(2) deduction rule three times. Diagram 3 results from the AND rule. The winning virtual connection (x, z) in Diagram 4 follows from a final application of the OR(2) rule.

Let us consider the simplest virtual connections, namely the pairs of neighboring cells, as the set of axioms or in other words the first generation of virtual connections. Applying the AND and OR(n) deduction rules to the appropriate groups of the first generation of virtual connections we build (prove) the second generation of virtual connections. Then we apply the deduction rules to both the first and the second generations of virtual connections to build (prove) the third generation of virtual connections, etc.

The goal is not to prove some specific virtual connection (e.g. a winning one). The goal is to construct a collection of virtual connections, which belong to the given position.

This iterative algorithm can prove all of the virtual connections shown in Figures 3, 5, and 7. We would also like to know whether this system of deduction rules is **complete**, i.e. whether this process can build **all** virtual connections. The answer is negative. The diagram in Figure 8 represents a counter-example of a virtual connection that cannot be proven by this process. The fact that this is a virtual connection can be verified manually. For example, if White plays at a, Black can reply with b, forcing White to occupy c. Then Black plays d securing the connection. A computer program was used to verify that no combination of AND and OR(n) rules can establish the overall connection.

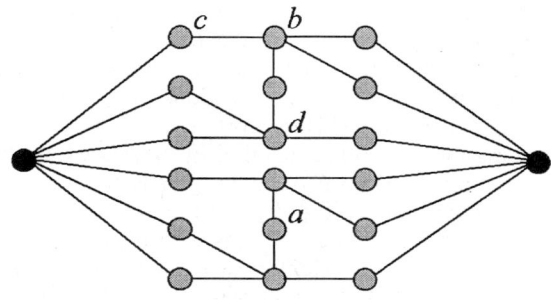

Fig. 8. The two black pieces form a virtual connection, which cannot be proven using AND and OR(n) deduction rules.

The system of deduction rules could be expanded to handle this case, but we are not going to do it in this paper.

6. Hexy Plays Hex

Hexy is a Hex-playing computer program which utilizes the ideas and algorithms presented in this paper. It runs on a standard PC with Windows, and can be downloaded from the website: http://home.earthlink.net/~vanshel. We consider the Advanced level as a standard. It plays a complete 10×10 game in about 10 minutes.

Hexy uses the alpha-beta search algorithm, with the evaluation function described in sections 3 and 4. For calculation of virtual connections, Hexy uses the automatic theorem proving algorithm introduced in section 5. This algorithm must be implemented very carefully. To make the algorithm efficient, we calculate only minimal connections, and enforce some reasonable restrictions.

The program has two thresholds, N and D. N is the maximal number of different virtual connections with the same ends. This threshold indirectly controls the total number of virtual connections calculated. The larger N, the more virtual connections the program builds for every node of the game-tree, and the more time the program spends on their calculation. The second parameter, D, is the depth of the game-tree search. We do not put any limits on the number of iterations, or the depth of virtual connections. There is an obvious trade-off between the parameters N and D, and finding a good compromise is an important task. The best practical results determined experimentally, were obtained with values of $N = 20$ and $D = 3$ (for a 10×10 board). As a result, Hexy performs a very shallow game-tree search (200-500 nodes per move), but routinely detects virtual connections with depth 20 or more.

Let $E(n)$ be an evaluation function that takes into account only those virtual connections which are built in the first n iterations of the theorem proving algorithm. Then $E(\infty)$ is an evaluation function without limits on the number of iterations (Iterations stop when no new virtual connections are discovered). Let Hexy(n) and Hexy(∞) be corresponding versions of the program. Hexy(0) does not calculate virtual connections at all, and Hexy(1) takes only two-bridges into account. Figure 9 shows the dependence of the ratio $T(n)/T(0)$ on n, where $T(n)$ is the time for the evaluation of a typical Hex position with $E(n)$. The ratio $T(\infty)/T(0)$ varies for different positions, but typical values are in the range 5-15. This means that the additional cost of computing the evaluation function $E(\infty)$, relative to that of the evaluation function $E(0)$, is not greater than the cost of one or two additional plies of game-tree search. Since $E(\infty)$ routinely finds virtual connections with depth 20 or more, it is not surprising that Hexy(∞) with $D = 3$ easily defeats Hexy(0) and Hexy(1) when they use a deeper 5-ply game-tree search.

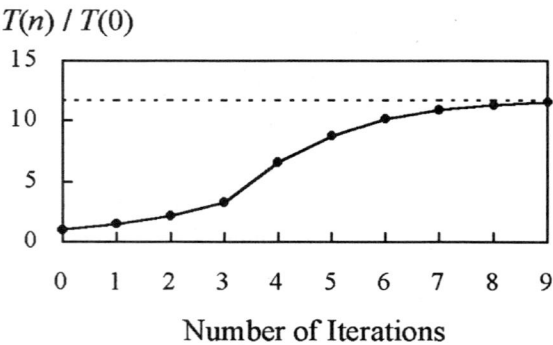

Fig. 9. Ratio $T(n)/T(0)$ versus number of iterations of the theorem proving algorithm. The dotted horizontal line shows the ratio $T(\infty)/T(0)$.

Hexy demonstrates a clear superiority over all known Hex-playing computer programs.[1,2] Hexy was also tested against human players on the popular game website, Playsite (http://www.playsite.com/games/board/hex). After more than 100 games, the program achieved a rating, which is within the highest Playsite *red* rating range.

---

[1]Chris Lusby Taylor, Hex, 1995.
Zhiping You, Hex, 1995.
A. V. Antonov, D. A. Antonov, Logical Game Hex, 1998.
Bob Kirkland, Hex-7, 1998.
Jack van Rijswijck, Queenbee, 1999.

[2]There is also a program Hex 1.0 by Sven Erik Elfgren (1997). This program plays on a 7×7 board and always moves first. It seemingly demonstrates perfect play.

7. Conclusion

In this paper we have offered the automatic theorem proving approach to Hex programming, and explained how this approach is implemented in Hexy - the strongest known Hex-playing program able to compete with best human players. Unlike conventional game-playing programs, Hexy does not perform massive game-tree search. Instead, this program spends most of its resources on deep analysis of a relatively small number of Hex positions.

Due to the mathematical purity of Hex rules, we have been able to build a far-sighted evaluation function based on virtual connections - topological objects, which contain information about the potential of Hex positions many moves ahead. We have built the automatic theorem proving technique for calculation of virtual connections.

The process of building virtual connections has its own cost. Nevertheless, this approach is much more efficient than brute-force search because it does not consider irrelevant paths. Experiments also show that the foreseeing abilities of this kind of evaluation function greatly outweigh its cost.

Acknowledgements

I would like to express my gratitude to Jonathan Schaeffer. Without his encouragement this paper would never have been written. I wish to thank Ryan Hayward, Jack van Rijswijck, and Sven Erik Elfgren for useful discussions. I owe my special thanks to Darse Billings for invaluable comments on earlier drafts of the paper.

References

Adelson-Velskiy, G.; Arlazarov, V.; and Donskoy, M. 1975. Some Methods of Controlling the Tree Search in Chess Programs. *Artificial Intelligence* 6(4):361-371.

Berlekamp, E. R.; Conway, J. H.; and R. K. Guy, R. K. 1982. *Winning Ways for your Mathematical Plays*. New York: Academic press.

Gale, D. 1979. The Game of Hex and the Brouwer Fixed-Point Theorem. *American Mathematical Monthly* 86: 818-827.

Gardner, M. 1959. *The Scientific American Book of Mathematical Puzzles and Diversions*. New York: Simon and Schuster.

Junghanns, A.; Schaeffer J. 1998. Single-Agent Search in the Presence of Deadlock. *AAAI'98* 419-424.

Marsland, T. A. 1986. A Review of Game-Tree Pruning. *Journal of the International Computer Chess Association* 9(1):3-19.

Schaeffer, J.; Lake, R.; Lu, P.; and Bryant M. 1996. Chinook: The World man-Machine Checkers Champion. *AI Magazine* 17(1):21-29

Shannon, C. E. 1953. Computers and Automata. *Proceedings of Institute of Radio Engineers* 41: 1234-1241

Combining Knowledge and Search to Solve Single-suit Bridge

Ian Frank
Complex Games Lab
Electrotechnical Laboratory
Umezono 1-1-4, Tsukuba
Ibaraki, JAPAN 305
ianf@etl.go.jp

David Basin
Institut für Informatik
Universität Freiburg
Am Flughafen 17
Freiburg, Germany
basin@informatik.uni-freiburg.de

Alan Bundy
Division of Informatics
University of Edinburgh
80 South Bridge
Edinburgh EH1 1HN
A.Bundy@ed.ac.uk

Abstract

In problem solving, it is often important not only to find a solution but also to be able to explain it. We use the game of Bridge to illustrate how tactics, which formalise domain-specific expertise, can be used for both these tasks. Our Bridge tactics constrain search to the point where optimal strategies can quickly be identified, and also provide the key to explaining these strategies in human-understandable terms. We demonstrate this using a canonical set of single-suit Bridge problems from a definitive expert text. FINESSE 'solves' these problems in the technical sense that, in addition to always finding optimal solutions (and revealing a 3% error rate in the expert answers), it also explains each solution in simple, clear English text.

Introduction

There is a big difference between finding a solution to a problem and being able to communicate that solution to others. In computer games, this distinction has been referred to as the difference between *cracking* and *solving* a game (Allis, van den Herik, & Herschberg 1991). To crack a game, a program needs to play optimally. But to solve it, the program's play must also be explainable in human-understandable terms.

In practice, solving a game is much harder than cracking it. Considerable advances in search algorithms and specialised hardware have led to strong computer play in games like chess, but have provided little help in explaining the resulting moves; ask a typical chess program why it made that pawn capture and you are lucky to get back a screenful of numbers. In contrast to this trend, we show in this paper how a difficult and significant part of the game of Bridge can be 'solved' in the technical sense.

Bridge is a game with imperfect information and enormous search spaces. We consider a sub-problem of the game that has been heavily analysed by experts: finding the optimal way to play the cards in a single suit. Analysis of single-suit Bridge problems (also called *suit combinations*) is challenging even for master-level players. There are a number of Bridge books that cover the problem in depth (ACBL 1994; Kosmulski 1990; Brock 1998; Roudinesco 1996)[1], and the author of one of these (a world life master), notes:

> 'How should I have handled this suit?' Seek advice from twenty experts, and you will get twenty different answers, among which at least nineteen will be wrong. Clearly the subject is very difficult and complicated, and there are not many bridge players able to cope correctly with all the suit combinations they meet. (Roudinesco 1996, p.9)

Cognitive studies (Engle & Bukstel 1978; Charness 1979; 1989) have shown that human players routinely plan their Bridge play by first considering individual suit combinations, and that human performance in Bridge can be attributed to the acquisition of high-level patterns and chunks of knowledge gained through experience. Our contribution here is to show that a computer can also use a set of patterns to find and explain optimal strategies for single-suit play.

To do this, we formalise expert knowledge about Bridge as a set of seven *tactics*, each of which represents a simple, distinct manœuvre, such as playing a winner or finessing (manœuvering against) missing cards. Any given suit combination is then solved by searching the space of possible tactic applications. This search is carried out by a new imperfect information search algorithm that quickly finds optimal solutions, despite the task being NP-complete in the size of the game tree. The use of tactics has two benefits: it speeds up the search, and it results in strategies that are trees of tactics rather than trees of individual moves. We show that a natural consequence of producing high-level trees is that strategies can then be explained in plain text.

Our ideas are implemented in a system called FINESSE. Although FINESSE's use of tactics significantly prunes the search space, all optimal strategies remain. We demonstrate this empirically by testing the system

---

[1] All these books implicitly use the *best defence* model (Frank & Basin 1998) to analyse Bridge problems. In this model, (1) the opponents have perfect information; (2) they choose their strategy second; and (3) the optimal strategy is a pure strategy (making no use of probabilistic choices such as '80% of the time do this, 20% of the time do that'). This is also the model assumed throughout the current paper.

on a database of over 1500 problems from a canonical Bridge reference (ACBL 1994). FINESSE solves all these problems in an average of just over 0.6sec, and also finds 58 errors in the test database (a rate of over 3%). Sometimes, FINESSE even discovers strategies that are new to the Bridge community; two of these new strategies were the subject of a recent article in a leading Bridge magazine (Frank & Basin 2000a).

Previous research on high-level approaches for playing computer Bridge includes the work of (Smith & Nau 1996), who won the 1997 computer Bridge championships with a program incorporating AI planning techniques. We have also previously shown the feasibility of using tactics for single-suit play (Frank, Basin, & Bundy 1992). Especially in the light of the cognitive research cited above, there are many worthwhile questions to be answered on how such knowledge-based approaches can be used to replicate the human ability of piecing together single-suit plans into global strategies. The more recent success of brute-force techniques such as GIB (Ginsberg 1999) suggests that the small but frequent errors made by a Monte Carlo sampling approach are no barrier to competing with strong human Bridge players, but the research reported in this paper represents the first time that a part of the game has been cracked or solved. FINESSE is fast enough for real-time use — for example as part of a program for playing complete hands — and its further ability to explain strategies in plain text suggests the viability of our approach as the basis of a real-time Bridge tutor.

A Bridge Example

For a detailed description of Bridge, readers are referred to one of the excellent books on the subject, such as (Goren 1986). Here, we give some idea of single-suit play with the following example:

In presenting single-suit problems such as this, it is conventionally assumed that South (S) is the *declarer* and his partner, North (N), places his cards on the table for all to see. The division of the remaining cards in the suit (held by East (E) and West (W)) is unknown, and the task is to specify the optimal way for South to play the cards from both his own hand and from North's. Typically, the goal is to win a certain number of *tricks*, or rounds of play.

In this example, declarer can win one certain trick by playing the Ace. However, if this card is played immediately, the only chance of making two tricks is if East or West holds the singleton King, so that it falls when the Ace is played. So, this play of *cashing* the Ace succeeds in winning two tricks for only two of the 2^{10} possible ways that the remaining 10 cards in the suit can be split between East and West.

A better solution is to play the two from the South hand. By covering whatever card West plays, declarer can then win two tricks whenever West has the King — a 50% chance. This play follows the elementary principle that the best results are obtained by forcing an opponent to play ahead of you. It is a typical example of a standard manœuvre called a *finesse*.

When planning a hand, human players will make use of their knowledge of commonly occurring patterns like the finesse to avoid having to consider all the possible combinations of plays of single cards. FINESSE attempts to replicate this capability by restricting declarer's options at each stage of the play to a similar set of such manœuvres, as defined by its tactics.

Our Bridge Tactics

FINESSE's tactics extend and improve the tactic set we introduced in (Frank, Basin, & Bundy 1992). They distill all possible attacking plays into seven distinct and simple manœuvres easily understood by Bridge players. Four of these tactics represent different types of finesse, which we simply number from 1 to 4. For example, the lead of the two we discussed in the previous section was a Type 1 finesse. The other three tactics are 'cash', 'duck', and 'sequence'. Cashing corresponds to playing a top card that is guaranteed to win (we also saw an example of a cash in the previous section). Ducking, on the other hand, is the act of deliberately losing a trick by playing the lowest cards from both the North and South hands. This is sometimes useful for increasing the chances of winning tricks with the remaining cards. Finally, sequencing handles situations that have no element of manœuvre; North or South simply plays a card from the highest sequence held by the combined hands.

To enable these seven tactics to be used to guide search, we formally specified their applicability preconditions as Prolog clauses. Each such clause takes a representation of the game state as its first argument. If the preconditions in the body of the clause succeed, the result is a tactic, represented as a Prolog term. The Prolog predicates used by FINESSE to represent tactics will sometimes appear in the figures of this paper. These should be fairly self-explanatory. For example, `cash(a,h)` denotes the cashing of the Ace of hearts, and `finesse(1, west, q, s)` denotes a Type 1 finesse of the Queen of spades against West (the optimal play for the ♠AQ-2 example).

Building the Space of Tactics

FINESSE's tactics specify the possible ways to play a single trick. The search space for a given problem is then the tree of possible tactic applications. To build this tree, a root (MAX) node is first generated, representing the initial game state. Successor (MIN) nodes are then produced by iterating through each of the applicable tactics. From each of these nodes, a new level

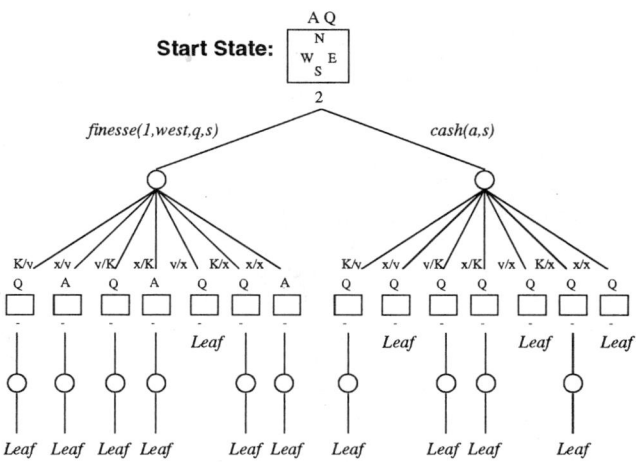

Figure 1: A game tree built with tactics

of MAX nodes is produced by iterating through the possible plays by East and West. The process of expanding MAX nodes by checking for applicable tactics is then repeated recursively, until no more tactics apply. In general, both the declarer and East/West will have a number of options at each node, so that trees will be of the form illustrated in Figure 1.

This example shows the tree generated by FINESSE for our ♠AQ-2 example. The North and South cards are shown at each non-terminal MAX node, and the MIN nodes are represented by circles. The labels on the MIN branches denote the cards played by West and East on the first trick (e.g., 'K/v' denotes West playing the King with East unable to follow in the suit), and an 'x' indicates an arbitrary low card. After the first trick, MAX has only one remaining card. If this cannot be cashed, then the node is a leaf node. Otherwise, the tree includes a further branch, representing the cash.

Searching the Space of Tactics

The MIN branches of Figure 1 can only be followed by East/West if they hold the appropriate cards (e.g., West can only play the King if he was dealt it). If we don't distinguish between the nine low cards in this problem, there are 20 distinct outcomes of the initial deal (for either East or West, they may hold between 0 and 9 low cards, and either hold the King or not). We call each of these possibilities a *world* and label the leaf nodes of a tree with the payoff in each world. To formalise this, for any leaf-node ν of a tree with n possible worlds, let the function *payoff-vector*(ν) return the n-element vector $\vec{K}$ in which $\vec{K}[j]$ (the jth element of $\vec{K}$) takes the value of the payoff at ν in world j ($1 \leq j \leq n$). For any world j in which ν cannot be reached, the value of $\vec{K}[j]$ is $\bot$, i.e., undefined. For example, the vector for the leftmost branch of Figure 1 would consist of one payoff of 2 (the world where East has no spades) and nineteen $\bot$s (all the remaining worlds).

Given a game tree, a specification of exactly one branch at each MAX node in the tree defines a MAX *strategy*. For any such strategy, we can determine its chance of success with respect to the best defence model (see footnote on first page) by a bottom-up pass through the tree, as follows: (1) at leaf nodes, back up the n-tuple *payoff-vector*(ν); (2) at MAX nodes, back up the vector from the daughter node on the branch specified by the strategy; and (3) at MIN nodes that have m daughters with the vectors $\vec{K}_1, \vec{K}_2, \cdots, \vec{K}_m$, back up the n-tuple:

$$(\min_{i=1\cdots m} \vec{K}_i[1], \min_{i=1\cdots m} \vec{K}_i[2], \cdots, \min_{i=1\cdots m} \vec{K}_i[n]), \quad (1)$$

where $\min(x,\bot)=\min(\bot,x)=x$, for all x.

This simple procedure produces a single vector at the root of a game tree, giving the strategy's payoff in each world. To find an *optimal* strategy we could iterate this procedure over each strategy. In practice, though, it is more efficient to propagate payoff-vectors in parallel. To this end, we define a *vector propagation* algorithm that backs up *sets* of vectors so that the outcome of each possible strategy in a node's subtree is represented by one of the vectors in the set produced at that node. This algorithm is defined in Figure 2, where $sub(t)$ is a function that computes the set of immediate subtrees of a tree t. At MAX nodes, no single branch is selected; instead, the results of all possible MAX branch selections are retained by collecting the vectors from all the daughter MIN nodes. At MIN nodes with m branches, the function Π first forms a set in which each element is itself a set containing exactly one vector from each of the initial m sets. It then applies Equation (1) to each element $\{\vec{K}_1, \vec{K}_2, \cdots, \vec{K}_m\}$ of this set.

In general, the number of vectors produced by *vec-prop* at any MAX or MIN node will be the same as the number of strategies in the subtree rooted on that node. This is exponential in the size of the tree. However, it is known that finding optimal strategies against best defence for this type of game tree is NP-complete in the size of the tree (Frank & Basin 2000b). Thus, unless P=NP, no efficient algorithm exists. To improve the (exponential) efficiency of *vec-prop*, we include a simple pruning step: if the collection of vectors at a node contains members that are pointwise less than or equal to any other member at that node, these vectors are ignored as inevitably giving rise to inferior strategies. For our trees of Bridge tactics, this pruning is sufficient to allow all the problems in our databases to be solved, in an average time of just over 0.6sec.

Algorithm *vec-prop*(t):
Take the following actions, depending on t.

Condition	Result
t is leaf node	$\{payoff\text{-}vector(t)\}$
root of t is a MAX node	$\cup_{t_i \in sub(t)} vec\text{-}prop(t_i)$
root of t is a MIN node	$\Pi_{t_i \in sub(t)} vec\text{-}prop(t_i)$

Figure 2: The vector propagation algorithm

Goal	Required strategy optimises chances of
max	taking the maximum number of tricks
Ntricks	taking at least N tricks, $N < \max$
expected	highest expected number of tricks

Figure 3: Three possible goals for a suit combination

Selecting the 'best' vector from the set at the root of a tree depends on the particular goal. We have implemented the three alternatives shown in Figure 3. We use a version of *vec-prop* that backs up information on branch choices together with the vectors, so that identifying the best vector for a given goal also identifies a strategy. For the ♠AQ-2 example, the best strategy for all three goals is the same: finesse the Queen.

Generating Explanations

FINESSE produces explanations of its strategies in three steps. The first identifies from a strategy the possible paths that need to be explained. The second removes from consideration move sequences or game situations that are too simple to warrant explanation. Finally, the third uses pattern-matching and knowledge of Bridge idioms to produce English text. We describe these three steps below. Note that each one is largely game-general, and that there is nothing in our account that requires explanations to be in *English*. The generation rules are simple enough for us to also construct another set that works in, say, Japanese or German.

Step 1: Path Extraction. The strategy to be explained defines a subset of the paths in the tactic search space (by virtue of selecting specific branches at MAX nodes, such as a finesse of a Queen). To decide which of these paths to explain, we take into account the goal (from Figure 3) that the strategy optimises. When explaining a strategy for the goal *max*, some paths in the strategy may fail to produce the maximum possible number of tricks. For example, when finessing in our example of ♠AQ-2, the MIN branch x/K (where the Queen loses to East's King) leads to a leaf node where declarer has won just one trick (with the Ace). Such paths that fail to produce the maximum number of tricks are ignored. Similarly, for the goal *Ntricks*, we extract only paths that achieve or exceed N tricks at the leaf node. And, for *expected*, we extract only paths for which the payoff at the leaf nodes is higher than the *minimum* possible payoff for the problem.

The paths extracted from a search space in this way are recombined into a new tree where paths that differ in just their MIN plays are merged. For example, Figure 4 shows the new tree produced by FINESSE for the optimal strategy when playing ♠AQ-2. The two branches represent four paths through the original tree. The left branch represents the two paths where West plays the King, so that declarer wins with the Ace and cashes the Queen on the second round (MIN branches K/v and K/x). The right branch represents the two paths where West plays low and the Queen wins, so that the Ace can then be cashed (x/v and x/x).

Step 2: Pruning Game Trees. Sometimes parts of a strategy describe situations that are so straightforward that only a beginner would expect an explanation. As described below, we implement two functions that identify and prune (1) bad moves, and (2) situations that are particularly easy to play. This leaves the parts of the game tree containing only the 'interesting' branches of the original strategy.

The first pruning function identifies clearly bad moves. In our trees, each MIN branch can only be followed under certain distributions of the outstanding cards. We therefore find bad moves by looking for branches that should *never* be followed by East/West. Such branches can be identified by checking that, for every possible distribution, there is a different path through the tree that restricts MAX to fewer tricks.

The second pruning function identifies easy playing situations. First, it prunes MIN nodes if each branch of the node leads to a linear tree. The justification for this is that linearity implies that MAX's best moves are not affected by the responses made by MIN: whatever moves MIN makes, MAX's best strategy is straightforward. Second, it prunes a particularly trivial kind of Bridge situation: any MIN node with a subtree containing only cash tactics. This heuristic is justified by noting that cashing a top card is the simplest possible play. The reader of FINESSE's explanations is expected to bear in mind that if no explicit direction is given, the default action is to cash a top card. In practice, this is always obvious: if the declarer still holds top cards, it is clearly advantageous to keep playing. A simple example of pruning is provided by Figure 4. Both the above pruning rules identify the top-most MIN node as an easy situation, leaving just a single MAX branch to be explained: finesse the Queen.

Step 3: Pattern Matching. The final step in automatically explaining strategies is performed by pattern matching, which maps the branches of an extracted and pruned tree into English text. Most of the basic oper-

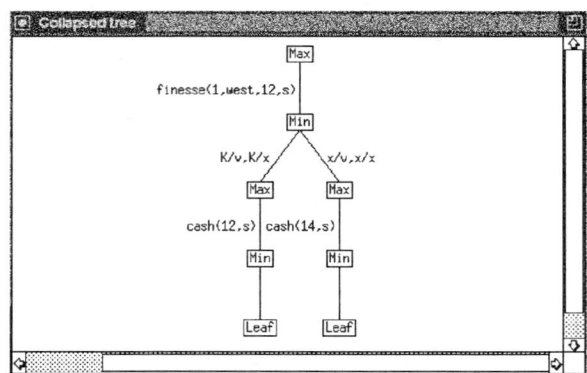

Figure 4: Screen capture of the tree extracted by FINESSE from the game tree for the ♠AQ-2 problem

ations carried out in this step are game-general. We describe three representative examples here.

First, when there is a linear sequence such as MAX $\xrightarrow{T1}$ MIN $\rightarrow$ MAX $\xrightarrow{T2}$ $\cdots$ in a tree (*i.e.*, the MAX and MIN nodes each have a single daughter node), the natural explanation is not 'Do tactic T1 then whatever MIN does, do tactic T2,...'. Much better is 'Do tactics T1 and T2,...'. We incorporate a sequentialisation step to compile down such linear sequences in trees. Second, MIN branches can have multiple labels (*e.g.*, as in Figure 4). When this is the case, the branches are ordered so that the branch with fewest labels comes first. This allows the final (longest) branch label to be explained as 'otherwise...'. Finally, as a special case of sequentialisation, a tree may contain a linear sequence where T1 and T2 are the same tactic. This is rendered as 'Do tactic T1 and repeat if necessary'.

Explanations are produced by a simple recursive function that incorporates the above operations. The basic action is simple: for each branch at the root of a tree, output some text describing the branch and then explain the subtree. If the root is a MAX node, the output text describes the tactic, and if the root node is a MIN node, the text describes the MIN moves. For formatting, line-breaks are added after each MAX tactic, and the ith MIN level is indented i spaces.

Only limited Bridge knowledge is required to explain the tactics, since they already correspond directly to Bridge plays that humans understand. It is also simple to describe the MIN plays in terms of the cards they represent. Just one further piece of Bridge-specific knowledge is required. If the extracted tree is linear, the tree can only contain cash tactics. We explain such trees as simply 'cash top honors'.

Performance: Discovery of Errors

We tested FINESSE on the suit combinations from the Official Encyclopedia of Bridge (ACBL 1994). This book contains a 55-page section presenting optimal strategies for 665 single-suit problems, chosen for their coverage of possible play situations. We created three separate test databases from these problems, corresponding to the three goals given in Figure 3. In total, these databases contain 1561 problems (less than 665×3 since the Encyclopedia often gives no strategy for one or two of the goals).

FINESSE solves all these problems correctly. On an Ultra SPARC-II at 450MHz, building the tree of tactics requires an average of 0.39sec per problem and applying *vec-prop* requires a further 0.25sec (in fact, we use a slightly modified version of *vec-prop* that incorporates the *beta-reduction* heuristic (Frank & Basin 2000b) — this leaves the average time per problem unaffected, but reduces the worst case solution time from 52sec to 7sec. The average number of leaf nodes in FINESSE's tactic trees is 1,330. In contrast, the trees of possible card plays (even if we generate just one branch for plays of cards from the same sequence) have an average of 47,000 leaf nodes. These larger trees can still be solved by *vec-prop* in an average of around 4sec, but the worst case solution time is over 80sec. For both types of tree, the average number of vectors produced by *vec-prop* at the root of a tree is 6.4.

FINESSE also discovers 58 errors in the Encyclopedia solutions (16 in the *max* database, 11 in the *Ntricks* database and 31 in the *expected* database). This overall error rate of 3.7% is somewhat surprising, as the Encyclopedia has gone through many editions and is a well-known reference for serious players. The discovery of these errors is evidence of the difficulty of the problem, and of the effectiveness of our approach. It is also of interest to Bridge players: FINESSE's identification of these errors, and in particular its discovery of two novel strategies, was recently the subject of an article in the magazine Bridge World (Frank & Basin 2000a).

Performance: Example Explanations

We used FINESSE to generate explanations for all the problems in our databases (generating explanations takes negligible time). We lack space here for a detailed analysis, but Figure 5 gives some typical examples. For instance, (12) illustrates the recognition of a repeated tactic, (25) provides an example of sequentialisation, and (26) and (28) show the effect of using 'otherwise...'

These examples show that FINESSE not only produces optimal strategies that are *explainable* in human terms (and thus solves single-suit play in the technical sense), but that FINESSE itself is capable of generating natural language explanations comparable to those produced by human experts. They also highlight the extra possibilities — over and above simply explaining an optimal strategy — that can be used to improve explanations in a reference text:

- give descriptions of card distributions under which strategies succeed, *e.g.*, (3), (12),
- vary the presentation and terminology when describing a number of similar problems, *e.g.*, 'play off the top honors' and 'cash top honors' in (5) and (24),
- compare the optimal strategy with slightly inferior strategies for a problem, *e.g.*, (25),
- give pointers to problems with similar solutions, *e.g.*, (28), (31) (although note that the Encyclopedia is mistaken to relate (31) to (26), as it is now not possible to win 4 tricks when East is void; FINESSE produces a correct strategy and explanation),
- explain more than one strategy, when the optimal strategy is not unique, *e.g.*, (62), and
- mention alternative strategies that can take advantage of weak defence, *e.g.*, (5). However, such strategies break the *best defence* assumptions that the opponents will play optimally; if the assumption of weak defence turns out to be incorrect, the chance of success of the alternative strategy will be lower than that of the 'best defence' strategy.

The last of these techniques is a topic for further research. We are using all the rest, however, in producing a computer-authored Bridge reference with FINESSE.

Num: (3)   AKQJ9-xx   Max Tricks: 5
Cash top honors in the hope of dropping the ten
cash the Ace
  if East shows out finesse the nine
	Num: (26) AKQ9-xxx Max Tricks: 4
	Cash the queen and king; if an honor drops from East, finesse the nine next. This is 6% better than cashing the three top honors regardless
	cash the Ace
	  if East shows out finesse the nine
	    and repeat if necessary
	  otherwise, cash the King
	    if East shows out or plays the Jack or ten
	finesse the nine

Num: (5) AKQJ8-xx Max Tricks: 5 Cash top honors. (But against defenders who would not falsecard from 109x or 109xx, cash the jack and finesse the eight if the nine or ten appears from East) **cash top honors**	

Num: (11)   AKQ10-xx   Max Tricks: 4
Cash the queen, and then finesse the ten
cash the Ace
  if both play low or East shows out finesse the 10
	Num: (28) AK9x-Qxx Max Tricks: 4
	See (26) above
	cash the Queen
	  if East shows out finesse the nine
	    and repeat if necessary
	  otherwise cash the Ace
	    if East shows out or plays the Jack or ten
	finesse the nine

Num: (12) AKQ9-xx Max Tricks: 4 Finesse the nine: hope that West has both the jack and ten **finesse the nine** **and repeat if necessary**	
Num: (23) AKxxx-Q10 Max Tricks: 5 Finesse the ten **finesse the 10**	Num: (31) A9xx-KQx Max Tricks: 4 See (26) above **cash the King and Queen** **if both follow low or East shows out or East plays the Jack or ten, finesse the nine**
Num: (24) AK9xx-Qx Max Tricks: 5 Play off the top honors **cash top honors**	
Num: (25) AKQ10-xxx Max Tricks: 4 Cash the king and queen; if both follow, play the ace. This is 2% better than a third-round finesse **cash the Ace and King** **if East shows out finesse the 10**	Num: (62) AK98x-Jx Max Tricks: 5 Run the jack *or* lead small to the nine **run the jack and finesse the eight**

Figure 5: Comparison of Encyclopedia's (normal font) and FINESSE's (`boldface font`) explanations for taking the maximum number of tricks. Problem numbers are those in the Encyclopedia, and 'x's denote arbitrary low cards.

Conclusions

We have shown that a set of seven tactics can be used to represent all attacking plays for Bridge card combinations. The search space reduction due to searching at the tactic-level enabled us to apply a new optimal search algorithm, and resulted in compact strategies constructed from human-understandable units.

Not only are FINESSE's strategies *explainable*, but FINESSE explains its strategies *automatically*. We gave examples of these explanations and showed that they are comparable to those found in human texts. We also identified some of the further qualities beyond simply 'explaining an optimal strategy' that are found in texts written by human experts. We are currently adding these qualities to FINESSE, so that it too can author its own expert text.

References

ACBL. 1994. *The Official Encyclopedia of Bridge*. 2990 Airways Boulevard, Memphis, TN 38116-3875: American Contract Bridge League, Inc., fifth edition.

Allis, L.; van den Herik, H.; and Herschberg, I. 1991. Which games will survive? In Levy, D., and Beal, D., eds., *Heuristic Programming in Artifical Intelligence 2*. Ellis Horwood. 232–243.

Brock, S. 1998. *Suit Combinations in Bridge*. B T Batsford Ltd. ISBN 0713481641.

Charness, N. 1979. Components of skill in bridge. *Canadian Journal of Psychology* 33(1):1–16.

Charness, N. 1989. Expertise in chess and bridge. In Klahr, D., and Kotovsky, K., eds., *Complex Information Processing: The Impact of Herbert A. Simon*. Hillsdale, NJ: Erlbaum. 183–208.

Engle, R. W., and Bukstel, L. 1978. Memory processes among bridge players of differing expertise. *American Journal of Psychology* 91(4):673–689.

Frank, I., and Basin, D. 1998. Search in games with incomplete information: A case study using bridge card play. *Artificial Intelligence* 100(1–2):87–123.

Frank, I., and Basin, D. 2000a. Make no mistake: Computers vs suit combinations. *Bridge World*. To appear.

Frank, I., and Basin, D. 2000b. A theoretical and empirical investigation of search in imperfect information games. *Theoretical Computer Science*. To appear.

Frank, I.; Basin, D.; and Bundy, A. 1992. An adaptation of proof-planning to declarer play in bridge. In *Proceedings of ECAI-92*, 72–76.

Ginsberg, M. 1999. GIB: Steps toward an expert-level bridge-playing program. In *Proc. IJCAI-99*, 584–589.

Goren, C. H. 1986. *Goren's New Bridge Complete*. Century Hutchinson Limited.

Kosmulski, M. 1990. *Rozgrywka pojedynczego koloru*. PZBS (Polski Zwiazek Brydza Sportowego). in Polish (English title: "Suit Treatment").

Roudinesco, J. 1996. *The Dictionary of Suit Combinations*. Guy Trédaniel. ISBN 2-85707-825-0.

Smith, S., and Nau, D. 1996. A planning approach to declarer play in contract bridge. *Computational Intelligence* 12(1):106–130.

On Pruning Techniques for Multi-Player Games

Nathan R. Sturtevant and Richard E. Korf
Computer Science Department
University of California, Los Angeles
Los Angeles, CA 90024
{nathanst, korf}@cs.ucla.edu

Abstract

Max^n (Luckhardt and Irani, 1986) is the extension of the minimax backup rule to multi-player games. We have shown that only a limited version of alpha-beta pruning, shallow pruning, can be applied to a max^n search tree. We extend this work by calculating the exact bounds needed to use this pruning technique. In addition, we show that branch-and-bound pruning, using a monotonic heuristic, has the same limitations as alpha-beta pruning in a max^n tree. We present a hybrid of these algorithms, alpha-beta branch-and-bound pruning, which combines a monotonic heuristic and backed-up values to prune even more effectively. We also briefly discuss the reduction of a n-player game to a 'paranoid' 2-player game. In Sergeant Major, a 3-player card game, we averaged node expansions over 200 height 15 trees. Shallow pruning and branch-and-bound each reduced node expansions by a factor of about 100. Alpha-beta branch-and-bound reduced the expansions by an additional factor of 19. The 2-player reduction was a factor of 3 better than alpha-beta branch-and-bound. Using heuristic bounds in the 2-player reduction reduced node expansions another factor of 12.

Introduction and Overview

Much work and attention has been focused on two-player games and alpha-beta minimax search (Knuth, Moore, 1975). This is the fundamental technique used by computers to play at the championship level in games such as chess and checkers. Alpha-beta pruning works particularly well on games of two players, or games with two teams, such as bridge. Much less work has been focused on games with three or more teams or players, such as Hearts. In max^n (Luckhardt and Irani, 1986), the extension of minimax to multi-player games, pruning is not as successful.

This paper focus on pruning techniques. There are many open questions in multi-player games, and we cannot cover them all here. For instance, it is unclear what the 'best' practical backup rule is. The techniques presented in this paper represent just one way we can evaluate the effectiveness of an algorithm.

We first review the max^n algorithm and the conditions under which pruning can be applied to max^n. Based on this, we show that shallow pruning in max^n cannot occur in many multi-player games. We will examine another common pruning method, branch-and-bound pruning, showing that it faces the same limitations as alpha-beta pruning when applied to max^n trees. Finally, we present a hybrid algorithm, alpha-beta branch-and-bound, which combines these two pruning techniques in multi-player games for more effective pruning. We will also analyze the reduction of a n-player game to a 2-player game.

Examples: Hearts and Sergeant Major (8-5-3)

To help make the concepts in this paper more clear, we chose two card games, Hearts and Sergeant Major, to highlight the successes and failures of the various algorithms presented. Note that while the game of bridge is played with 4 players, each player has the goal of maximizing the joint score they share with their partner, so bridge is really a two-team game, and standard minimax applies.

Hearts and Sergeant Major, also known as 8-5-3, are both trick-based card games. That is, the first player plays (leads) a card face-up on the table, and the other players follow in order, playing the same suit if possible. When all players have played, the player who played the highest card in the suit that was led "wins" or "takes" the trick. He then places the played cards in his discard pile, and leads the next trick. This continues until all cards have been played. Cards are dealt out to each player before the game begins, and each game has special rules about passing cards between players before starting. Card passing has no bearing on the work presented here, so we ignore it.

Hearts is usually played with four players, but there are variations for playing with three or more players. The goal of Hearts is to take as few points as possible. Each card in the suit of hearts is worth one point, and the queen of spades is worth 13. A player takes points when he takes a trick which contains point cards. At the end of the game, the sum of all scores is always 26, and each player can score between 0 and 26. If a player takes 26 points, or "shoots the moon," the other players all get 26 points each. For now, we ignore this rule.

Sergeant Major is a three-player game. Each player is dealt 16 cards, and the remainder of the deck is set aside. The ultimate goal for each player is to take as many tricks as possible. Similar to Hearts, the sum of scores is always 16, and each individual player can get any score from 0 to 16.

More in-depth descriptions of these and other games mentioned here can be found in (Hoyle et al. 1991).

Copyright © 2000, American Association for Artificial Intelligence (www.aaai.org). All rights reserved.

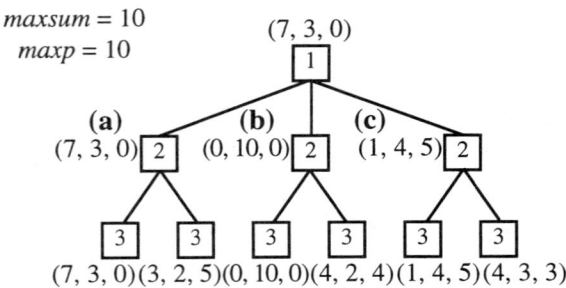

Figure 1: A 3-player max^n game tree.

Max^n

Luckhardt's and Irani's extension of minimax for multi-player games is called max^n. For a n-player game, an n-tuple of scores records each player's individual score for that particular game state. That is, the nth element in the tuple represents the score of the nth player. At each node in a max^n search tree, the player to move selects the move that maximizes his own component of the score. The entire tuple is backed up as the max^n value of that node. In a three-player game, we propagate triples from the leaves of the tree up to the root.

For example, in Figure 1, the triples on the leaves are the terminal values of the tree. The number inside each square represents the player to move at that node. At the node labelled (a), Player 2 will choose to back up the triple (7, 3, 0) from the left child, because the second component of the left child of (a), 3, is greater than the second component of the right child of (a), 2. Player 2 does likewise at nodes (b) and (c). Player 1 then chooses a triple from those backed up by Player 2. At the root, the first component of Player 1's children is greatest at node (a). Player 1 will back this triple up, giving the final max^n value of the tree, (7, 3, 0). Because the max^n value is calculated in a left-to-right depth-first order, a partial bound on the max^n value of a node is available before the entire calculation is complete. Throughout this paper we assume that nodes are generated from left to right in the tree, and that all ties are broken to the left.

When generating a Hearts game tree, the terminal values will be the number of points taken in the game. In Sergeant Major, the terminal values will be the number of tricks taken. If we are not able to search to the end of the game, we can apply an evaluation function at the frontier nodes to generate appropriate backup values. At a minimum, this evaluation would be the exact evaluation of what has occurred so far in the game, but might also contain an estimate of what scores are expected in the remainder of the game.

In most card games, one is not normally allowed to see one's opponents cards. As was suggested by (Ginsberg, 1996), we first concentrate on being able to play a completely open (double-dummy) game where all cards are available for all to see. In a real game, we would model the probability of our opponent holding any given card, and then generate hundreds of random hands according to these probability models. It is expected that solving these hands will give a good indication of which card should actually be played. See (Ginsberg, 1999) for an explanation of how this has been applied to Bridge.

Duality of Maximization and Minimization

Throughout this paper we deal with games that are usually described in terms of either maximization or minimization. Since minimization and maximization are symmetric, we briefly present here how the bounds used by pruning algorithms are transformed when we switch from one type of game to the other type.

There are four values we can use to describe the bounds on players' scores in a game. *Minp* and *maxp* are a player's respective minimum and maximum possible score. *Minsum* and *maxsum* are the respective minimum and maximum possible sum of all players scores. In Hearts, *minp* is 0 and *maxp* = *maxsum* = *minsum* = 26. In Sergeant Major, *minp* is also 0 and *maxp* = *maxsum* = *minsum* = 16. (Korf, 1991) showed that we may be able to prune a max^n tree if *minp* and *maxsum* are bounded. We are interested in how these bounds change when the goal of a game is changed from minimization to maximization. The transformation does not change the properties of the game, it simply allows us to talk about games in their maximization forms without loss of generality.

The one-to-one mapping between the minimization and maximization versions of a game is shown in Table 1. The first row in the table contains the variable names for a minimization problem, followed by sample values for a Hearts game, where *n*, the number of players, is 3. The transformation applied to the values are in the third row: the negation of the original value plus *maxp*$_{min}$. This re-normalizes the scores so that *minp* is always 0. Since Hearts and Sergeant Major are zero-sum or constant-sum games, *maxsum* is always the same as *minsum*. The final rows contain the new score after transformation and the new variable names. The process can be reversed to turn a maximization game into a minimization game.

Given the symmetry of minimization and maximization, there is also a duality in pruning algorithms. That is, for any pruning algorithm that works on a maximization tree, we can write the dual of that algorithm that works the same under the equivalent minimization tree. However, just changing the goal of a game from minimization to maximization does not create the dual of the game. The other parameter,

minimization variable	s_1	s_2	s_3	$maxp_{min}$	$minp_{min}$	$maxsum_{min}$ & $minsum_{min}$
minimization value	3	10	13	26	0	26
transformation	$-s_i + maxp_{min}$			$-maxp_{min} + maxp_{min}$	$-minp_{min} + maxp_{min}$	$-maxsum_{min} + n \cdot maxp_{min}$
maximization value	23	16	13	0	26	52
maximization variable	s^1	s^2	s^3	$minp_{max}$	$maxp_{max}$	$maxsum_{max}$ & $minsum_{max}$

Table 1: The transformation between a maximization and minimization problem, and examples for a 3-player game.

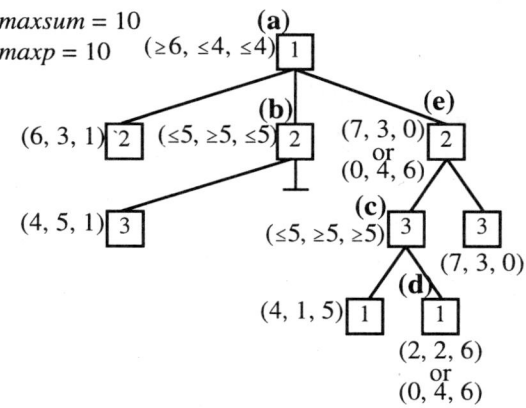

Figure 2: Pruning in a max^n tree.

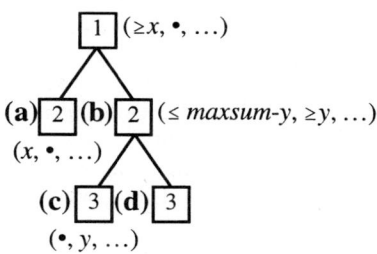

Figure 3: A generic max^n tree.

maxsum, must also be calculated. Given these observations, we will not explicitly show dual algorithms. Unless otherwise stated, all trees and algorithms presented here will be for maximization problems.

Pruning in Max^n Trees

In a two-player zero-sum game, there are three types of alpha-beta pruning that occur: immediate, shallow, and deep pruning. Not all of these are valid in multi-player games.

Immediate Pruning

Immediate pruning in a multi-player game is like immediate pruning in a two-player game. In a two-player game, we immediately prune when a player gets the best possible score, ∞ for max and $-\infty$ for min. In a multi-player game, we can prune when the current player gets a score of *maxp*, the best score in a multi-player game.

The opportunity to prune immediately is seen in Figure 1. At node (b), Player 2 can get 10 points by choosing to move towards his left child. Since *maxp* = 10, Player 2 can do no better than 10 points. Thus, after examining the first child, the second child can be pruned.

Shallow Pruning

While having a zero-sum game is a sufficient condition to apply alpha-beta pruning to a two-player game tree, it is not sufficient for a multi-player game tree. Given just one component of a zero-sum multi-player game, we cannot restrict any other single score in the game, because one of the remaining scores might be arbitrarily large, and another arbitrarily small. But, given a lower bound on each individual score, and an upper bound on the sum of scores, we can prune.

Figure 2 contains a sample 3-player max^n tree. At node (a), Player 1 can get at least 6 points by choosing the leftmost branch of node (a). When Player 2 examines the first child of node (b), Player 2 gets a score of 5, meaning Player 2 will get at least 5 by choosing the left-most branch at (b). There are 10 points available in the game, and since Player 2 will get at least 5 at node (b), Player 1 can get no more than 10 - 5 = 5 points at (b). Player 1 is guaranteed ≥ 6 points at (a), and ≤ 5 points at (b). So, Player 1 will never move towards node (b) no matter what max^n values the other children have, and the remaining children of (b) are pruned. This is shallow pruning, because the bound used to prune came from (a), the parent of (b).

General Bounds for Shallow Max^n Pruning

Figure 3 shows a generic max^n tree. In this Figure we have only included the values needed for shallow pruning. Other values are marked by a '•'. When Player 1 gets a score of x at node (a), the lower bound on Player 1's score at the root is then x. Assume Player 2 gets a score of y at node (c). Player 2 will then have a lower bound of y at node (b). Because of the upper bound of *maxsum* on the sum of scores, Player 1 is guaranteed less than or equal to *maxsum* - y at node (b). Thus, no matter what value is at (d), if *maxsum* - $y \leq x$, Player 1 will not choose to move towards node (b) because he can always do no worse by moving to node (a), and we can prune the remaining children of node (b).

In the maximization version of Hearts, *maxsum* is 52, and x and y will range between 0 and 26, meaning that we only prune when $52 - y \leq x$, which is only possible if $x = y = 26$. In Sergeant Major *maxsum* is 16, and x and y will range from 0 to 16, meaning that we will prune when $16 - y \leq x$.

Given these examples, we extract general conditions for pruning in multi-player games. We will use the following variables: n is the number of players in the game, *maxsum* is the upper bound on the sum of players scores, and *maxp* is the upper bound on any given players score. We assume a lower bound of zero on each score without loss of generality. So, by definition, *maxp* $\leq$ *maxsum* $\leq n \cdot$ *maxp*.

Lemma 1:
To shallow prune in a max^n tree, *maxsum* $< 2 \cdot$ *maxp*.

Proof:
We will use the generic tree of Figure 3. To prune:
   $x \geq$ *maxsum* - y
By definition:
   $2 \cdot$ *maxp* $\geq x + y$
So,
   $2 \cdot$ *maxp* $\geq x + y \geq$ *maxsum*
   $2 \cdot$ *maxp* $\geq$ *maxsum*

However, if *maxsum* $= 2 \cdot$ *maxp*, we can only prune when both x and y equal *maxp*. But, if $y =$ *maxp*, we can also immediate prune. Because of this, we tighten the bound to exclude this case, and the lemma holds. □

We can now verify what we suggested before. In the maximization version of 3-player Hearts, *maxsum* = 52, and *maxp* = 26. Since the strict inequality of Lemma 1, 52 < 2·26, does not hold, we can only immediate prune in Hearts. In Sergeant Major, the inequality 16 < 2·16 does hold, so we will be able to shallow prune a Sergeant Major max^n tree.

Intuitive Approach. Speaking in terms of the games as they are normally played, it may seem odd that we can't prune in Hearts and we can prune in Sergeant Major, when the only real difference in the games is that it one you try to minimize your score, and in the other you try to maximize it. While the preceding lemma explains the difference mathematically, there is another explanation that may be more intuitive.

Suppose in Sergeant Major that a player is deciding between two cards, the Ace of Spades and the Ten of Clubs. When we calculate the max^n value of the search tree, we are calculating how well the player can expect to do when playing a given card. Once we have the result of how well the player can do with the Ace of Spades, we begin to look at the prospects for the Ten of Clubs. We prune this search when we have enough information to guarantee that the player will always do no better with the Ten of Clubs than with the Ace of Spades. We get this information based on the dependence between the players' scores. In Sergeant Major, there are only 16 points available, and all players are competing to get as many points as possible. Each trick taken by one player is a trick denied to another player. This direct dependence between any two players score is what gives us the information that allows us to prune. When the next player is guaranteed enough points to deny a better score than can be achieved by playing the Ace of Spades, the line of play originating from the Ten of Clubs is pruned.

In the standard minimization form of Hearts, the goal is to take as few points as possible. Points taken by one player are points denied to the other players. But, since all players are trying to take as few points as possible, they don't mind being denied points. Thus, when another player takes points, it simply tells us that the current line of play may be better than previous lines of play, and that we should keep exploring our current line of play. When one player avoids taking points, those points must be taken by the other players. But, there is nothing that says which player must take the points. So, in contrast to Sergeant Major, there is a lack of direct dependence between two players scores, and we are unable to prune.

Deep Pruning

Returning to Figure 2, Player 1 is guaranteed a score greater than or equal to 6 at the root node (a). We might be tempted to prune node (d), because the bound on Player 1's score at (c), ≥5, says that Player 1 will get less than 6 points. This would be deep pruning, because (a) is a grandparent of (c). However, as we demonstrate here, the value at node (d) can still affect the max^n value of the tree. (Korf 1991)

If the value of (d) is (2, 2, 6), Player 3 will choose this value as the max^n value of (c). Player 2 at (e) will then choose (7, 3, 0) as the max^n value of (e) since the second component,

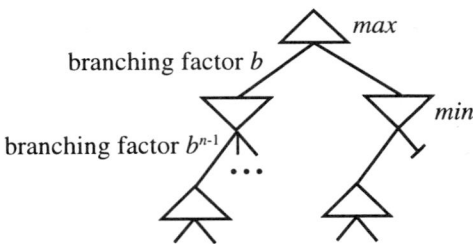

Figure 4: The reduction of a n-player game to a 2-player game.

nent, 3, is higher than the second component of the max^n value at (c), 2. This will result in the max^n value of (7, 3, 0) for the entire tree, since Player 1 can then get a score of 7.

Alternatively, if the value of (d) is (0, 4, 6), the max^n value of (c) will be (0, 4, 6). Then, at node (e), Player 2 will choose to backup (0, 4, 6) because the second component, 4, is higher than that in the other child, 3. This means the final max^n value of the tree will be (6, 3, 1).

Thus, while the bounds predicted correctly that no value at (d) will ever be the final max^n value of the tree, the different possible values at (d) may affect the final max^n value of the tree, and so (d) cannot be pruned.

Asymptotic Results

The asymptotic branching factor of max^n with shallow pruning in the best case is $\left(1+\sqrt{4b-3}\right)/2$, where b is the brute-force branching factor without any pruning. An average case model predicts that even under shallow pruning, the asymptotic branching factor will be b. (Korf, 1991)

We have shown here that in many cases, such as the game of Hearts, even under an optimal ordering of the tree, we would still be unable to do anything besides immediate pruning. This compares poorly with the 2-player best-case asymptotic branching factor of $\sqrt{b}$ (Knuth, Moore 1975), which can very nearly be achieved in two-player games.

Reduction to a Paranoid 2-Player Game

Another method to increase the pruning in a multi-player game is to reduce the game to a two-player game. This is done by making the 'paranoid' assumption that all our opponents have formed a coalition against us. Under this reduction we can use standard alpha-beta to prune our tree. This is not a realistic assumption and can lead to suboptimal play, but due to the pruning allowed, it may be worthwhile to examine. We will only analyze the pruning potential here.

To calculate the minimum number of nodes that need to be examined within the game tree, we need a strategy for min and a strategy for max. Min and max will play on the tree in Figure 4, where max is to move at the root, with a branching factor of b, and min moves next, with a branching factor of b^{n-1}. Min is the combination of the n-1 players playing against the first player.

Within a strategy for max, max must look at one successor of each max node in the strategy, and all possible successors of each min node in the strategy. Suppose the full tree is of depth D. Max will expand $b^{(n-1)}$ nodes at every other level, meaning that there are $b^{(n-1)\cdot D/2}$ leaf nodes in the

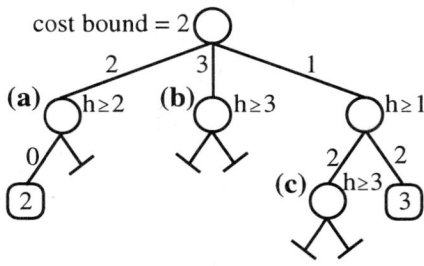

Figure 5: A single-agent depth-first branch-and-bound problem.

tree. Similarly, a min strategy must look at only one successor of each min node, and all successors of each max node, so min will look at $b^{D/2}$ nodes total. We have two players in the reduced game, and each player has an equal number of turns, so D is even, meaning we don't have to consider the floor or ceiling in the exponent.

The total nodes examined by both algorithms will be about $b^{(n-1) \cdot D/2} + b^{D/2}$ nodes, which is $O(b^{(n-1) \cdot D/2})$. But, D is the depth in the tree of Figure 4. We really want our results in terms of the real tree that we will search. For example, if the original tree has 3 players and is depth 12 (4 tricks), the new tree has 2 players and will also contains 4 tricks, so it will be height 8. So, for the actual tree searched, which has height d, $D = d \cdot 2/n$. Thus, we re-write the asymptotic branching factor in the best case as $O(b^{d \cdot (n-1)/n})$ to reflect the branching factor in the actual tree.

Depth-First Branch-and-Bound Pruning

Branch-and-Bound is another common pruning technique. It requires a monotonic heuristic, and many card games have natural monotonic heuristics. In Hearts and Sergeant Major, once you have taken a trick or a point you cannot lose it. Thus, an evaluation can be applied within the tree to give a bound on the points or tricks to be taken by a player in the game. We use the notation $h(i) \geq j$ to indicate that the heuristic is giving a lower bound score of j for player i, and $h(i) \leq j$ to indicate that the heuristic is giving an upper bound of j on player i's score. Suppose, for a Sergeant Major game, the players have taken 3, 2, and 6 points respectively. Then, $h(1) \geq 3$ because Player 1 has taken 3 points. Also, $h(1) \leq 8$ because *maxsum* (16) minus the other players' scores (8) is 8.

Single Agent Branch-and-Bound

The branch-and-bound algorithm is most commonly used in a depth-first search to prune single-agent minimization search trees, such as the Travelling Salesman Problem. In Figure 5, we are trying to find the shortest path to a leaf from the root, where edges have positive costs as labelled. Since all paths have positive length, the cost along a path will monotonically increase, giving a lower bound on the cost to a leaf along that path. The labels at the leaves are the actual path costs. Next to a node is a limit on the optimal cost of a path going through that node. If unexplored paths through a node are guaranteed to be greater than the best path found so far, we can prune the children of that node in the tree.

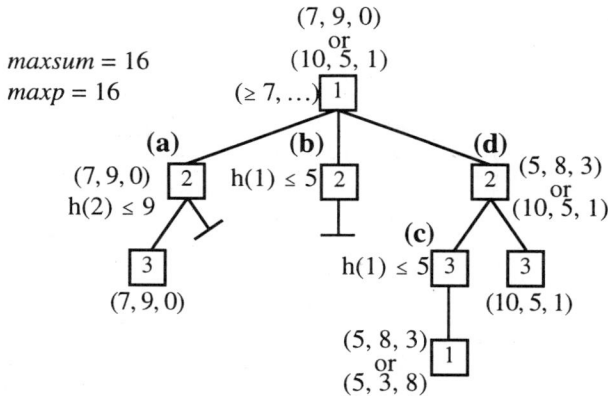

Figure 6: Branch-and-bound pruning in a max^n tree.

In order to draw parallels between alpha-beta pruning, we will describe the pruning that occurs in the same terms that we use to describe alpha-beta pruning: immediate, shallow and deep pruning. In a two-player game, immediate pruning occurs when we get the best score possible, a win. In the presence of a heuristic, the best score possible is best that we can get given the heuristic. In Figure 5, the heuristic at node (a) says the best score we can get is 2. Since we have a path of total cost 2 through the first child, we can prune the remaining children, as we have found the best possible path.

After finding the path with cost 2, we use that cost as a bound while searching subsequent children. At node (b), our heuristic tells us that all paths through (b) have cost higher than the bound of 2, so all children of (b) are pruned. This is like shallow pruning, since the bound comes from the parent of (b). Finally, at node (c) we can prune based on the bound of 2 on the path cost from the grandparent of (c), which is like deep pruning.

Multi-Player Branch-and-Bound

Branch-and-bound pruning can be used to prune a max^n tree, but under max^n it is limited by the same factors as alpha-beta pruning, namely we cannot use the bound at a node to prune at its grandchild. As with deep alpha-beta pruning, while the max^n value of the pruned nodes will never be the max^n value of the tree, they still have the potential to affect it. We will demonstrate this here, but because the proof is identical to the proof of why deep alpha-beta pruning does not work (Korf, 1991), we omit the proof.

In Figure 6 we show a portion of a max^n tree and demonstrates how branch-and-bound can prune parts of the tree. Immediate pruning occurs at node (a). At the left child of (a), Player 2 can get a score of 9. Since the $h(2) \leq 9$, we know Player 2 cannot get a better score from another child, and the remaining children are pruned.

Shallow pruning occurs at node (b) when the bound from the parent combines with the heuristic to prune the children of (b). Player 1 is guaranteed 7 or more at the root. So, when Player 1's heuristic at (b) guarantees a score of 5 or less, we prune all the children of (b), since Player 1 can always do better by moving to node (a).

Finally, deep branch-and-bound pruning, like deep alpha-

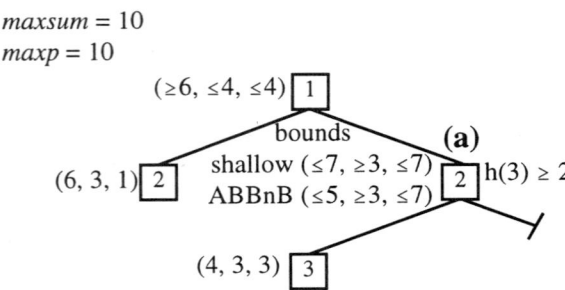

Figure 7: Alpha-beta branch-and-bound pruning.

beta pruning, can incorrectly affect the calculation of the max^n value of the game tree. The partial max^n value at the root of the tree in Figure 6 guarantees Player 1 a score of 7 or better. At node (c), Player 1 is guaranteed less than or equal to 5 points by the heuristic. Thus, we might be tempted to prune the children of (c), since Player 1 can do better by moving to node (a). But, this reasoning does not take into account the actions of Player 2.

Depending on which value we place at the child of (c), (5, 8, 3) or (5, 3, 8), Player 2 will either select (5, 8, 3) from node (c) or (10, 5, 1) from node (d)'s right branch to back up as the max^n value of node (d). Player 1 would then choose the root max^n value to be either (7, 9, 0) or (10, 5, 1). So, while the bounds on node (c) will keep it from being the max^n value of the tree, it has the potential to affect the max^n value of the tree.

Alpha-Beta Branch-and-Bound Pruning

Now that we have two relatively independent techniques for pruning a multi-player game tree, we show how these techniques can be combined. Shallow pruning makes comparisons between two players' backed up scores to prune. Branch-and-bound compares a monotonic heuristic to a player's score to prune. Alpha-beta branch-and-bound pruning uses both the comparison between backed up scores and monotonic heuristic limits on scores to prune even more effectively.

Looking at Figure 7, we see an example where shallow pruning applies. We have bounds on the root value of the tree from its left branch. After searching the left child of node (a) we get bounds on the max^n value of (a). We place an upper bound of 7 on Player 1's score, because Player 2 is guaranteed at least 3 points, and 10 (*maxsum*) - 3 = 7. This value does not conflict with the partial max^n bound on the root, so we cannot prune. We have a bound from our heuristic, but because it is not Player 3's turn, we can not use that by itself to prune either. But, if we combine this information, we can tighten our bounds. We know from backed up values that Player 2 will get at least 3 points and from our heuristic that Player 3 will get at least 2 points at (a). So, the real bound on Player 1's score is *maxsum* - score(2) - h(3) = 10 - 3 - 2 = 5.

As an aside, one may notice another slight, but effective optimization in this example. At (a), Player 2 will not choose another path unless he gets at least 4 points, and thus Player 1 gets no more than 6. Thus, since ties are broken to the left, we have integer terminal values, and because Player 1 did not get 7 points at the left child of (a), the shallow bound itself is sufficient to prune the right branch of (a).

In a n-player game where we normally only compare the scores of two players, we can further decrease our bound for pruning by subtracting the heuristic value for the remaining (n - 2) players. That is, if we have a lower bound on Player i's score from our parent, and Player j is to play at the current node, the upper bound on Player i's score at the next node is *maxsum* - score(j) - $\sum h(x)$ {for $x \neq i$ or j}. In a two-player game, this reduces to plain alpha-beta.

The alpha-beta branch-and-bound procedure is as follows. In this procedure, we use h_{up} to represent a heuristic upper bound and h_{low} to represent a heuristic lower bound. *Bound* is the upper bound on *Player*'s score.

```
ABBnB(Node, Player, Bound)
IF Node is terminal, RETURN static value
/* shallow branch-and-bound pruning */
IF (h_up(Prev Player) ≤ maxsum - Bound)
    RETURN static value
Best=ABBnB(first Child, next Player, maxsum)
/* Calculate our opponents guaranteed points */
Heuristic = Σh_low(n) [n≠Player or prev. Player]
FOR each remaining Child
    IF (Best[Player] ≥ Bound-Heuristic) OR
       (Best[Player] = h_up(Player))
        RETURN Best
    Current = ABBnB(next Child, next Player,
                    maxsum - Best[Player])
    IF (Current[Player] > Best[Player])
        Best = Current
RETURN Best
```

This procedure will always prune as much as shallow branch-and-bound pruning or shallow alpha-beta pruning. So, while we lose the ability to do deep pruning in a multi-player game, we may be able to use alpha-beta branch-and-bound pruning to prune more than we would be able to with just alpha-beta or branch-and-bound pruning alone.

Disregarding immediate branch-and-bound pruning, Alpha-beta branch-and-bound will have the same best-case performance as shallow pruning. If we have perfect ordering and a perfect heuristic, immediate branch-and-bound pruning could drastically shrink the search tree.

Experimental Results

We tested alpha-beta branch-and-bound (ABBnB) to see how it compared to branch-and-bound (BnB), alpha-beta shallow pruning, and the paranoid 2-player reduction. Our test domain was the game of Sergeant Major, and our heuristic was the number of tricks taken so far in the game. We searched 200 random game trees to a depth of 5 tricks, which is 15 cards. Consecutive cards in a player's hand were generated as a single successor. Moves were ordered from high cards to low cards. We initially did not use a transposition table or any other techniques to speed the search. Our code expands about 150k nodes per second on a Pentium II 233 laptop,

Algorithm	Full Tree	DFBnB	Shallow	ABBnB	Paranoid	Paranoid (with heuristic)
Avg. Nodes in Tree	3.33 billion	32.7 million	26.8 million	1.43 million	437,600	36,121
Reduction factor	1	102	1.22	18.7	3.27	12.1

Table 2: The average nodes expanded of the first 5 tricks in Sergeant Major and reduction factor over the next best algorithm.

depending on the problem.

The number of nodes in the entire tree varied from 78 million to 64 billion, with the average tree containing 33 billion nodes. The number of nodes expanded by each of the algorithms varied widely, based on the difficulty of the hand. Because of this, we have chosen to report our results according to the average number of nodes expanded by an algorithm over all 200 trees. These results are found in Table 2.

The first line in the table contains the average number of nodes in the entire tree. The second line contains the factor in reduction over the next best algorithm. The algorithms are listed left to right from worst to best. We ran the paranoid algorithm twice, once without using the heuristic information, and once using the heuristic information.

One interesting result is that the shallow pruning procedure provides significant savings over the full tree expansion. Thus, despite the negative theoretical results, there is still some potential for this algorithm.

Another thing to notice is how much faster the paranoid algorithm is than the standard max^n backup rule. This speed increase will not, however, guarantee an increase in play quality. Under this model, a player may make very poor moves assuming all the other players might work together much more than they really do. Double dummy play can magnify this problem. Clearly more work is needed to distinguish which algorithms are the best to use in practice.

Unfortunately, the most obvious heuristic in Hearts, the points taken by a player so far in the game, will only allow branch-and-bound pruning, and not for alpha-beta branch-and-bound pruning. This is because this heuristic comes directly from the evaluation function, which already doesn't allow shallow pruning. However, a heuristic that came from a different evaluation might allow some pruning.

Conclusion and Future Work

We have refined the bounds needed to prune a max^n tree using shallow pruning and introduced the alpha-beta branch-and-bound algorithm. While this algorithm is quite effective at reducing the number of nodes expanded in a max^n tree, it still cannot compare to two-player alpha-beta pruning. A bridge hand can be search in its entirety, but we are not close to doing this in multi-player games such as Sergeant Major, and we are even farther from doing it in Hearts. Alpha-beta branch-and-bound can solve 8-card hands (complete depth 24 trees) to completion in times ranging from a few seconds to about a minute. We are working on a implementation of Partition Search (Ginsberg, 1996) to see how this algorithm benefits searches on deeper trees. Our initial transposition table reduced node expansions by a factor of 3, but also slowed our program by the same factor.

More research needs to be done to see what other algorithms or methods might be applied to help with multi-player search. We are continuing to work to compare the value of these and other algorithms in real play, and as this work progresses we will be evaluating the assumption that we can use double-dummy play to model our opponents hands. It would be worthwhile to develop a different theoretical model to better explain how shallow and alpha-beta branch-and-bound pruning works in practice. Additional work on heuristics and game search can be found in (Prieditis, Fletcher, 1998).

One possibility for improving our search is to use domain specific knowledge for a particular game to simplify the problem. In most trick games, for instance, you must follow suit. This creates a loose independence between suits, which may be exploited to simplify the search process.

Research in practical multi-player game search has been very limited. We expect that in the next few years this will change and that much progress will be made in multi-player game search.

Acknowledgments

We would like to thank the reviewers for their comments and Pamela Allison for early discussion on pruning failures in other games. This work has been supported by the National Science Foundation under grant IRI-9619447.

References

Ginsberg, M, GIB: Steps Toward an Expert-Level Bridge-Playing Program, Proceedings, IJCAI-99, 584-589.

Ginsberg, M, How Computers Will Play Bridge, *The Bridge World*, 1996.

Ginsberg, M, Partition Search, Proceedings AAAI-96, Portland, OR, 228-33.

Hoyle, E., and Frey, R.L., Morehead, A.L., and Mott-Smith, G, 1991, *The Authoritative Guide to the Official Rules of All Popular Games of Skill and Chance*, Doubleday.

Knuth, D.E., and Moore, R.W., An analysis of alpha-beta pruning, Artificial Intelligence, vol. 6 no. 4, 1975, 293-326.

Korf, R.E. Multiplayer alpha-beta pruning. Artificial Intelligence, vol. 48 no. 1, 1991, 99-111.

Luckhardt, C.A., and Irani, K.B., An algorithmic solution of N-person games, Proceedings AAAI-86, Philadelphia, PA, 158-162.

Prieditis, A.E.; Fletcher, E. Two-agent IDA*, Journal of Experimental and Theoretical Artificial Intelligence, vol.10, Taylor & Francis, 1998, 451-85.

Human-Computer Interaction

Human-Guided Simple Search

David Anderson[1], Emily Anderson[1], Neal Lesh[1], Joe Marks[1],
Brian Mirtich[1], David Ratajczak[1], Kathy Ryall[1,2]

[1]MERL — Mitsubishi Electric Research Laboratory, Cambridge, MA 02139
[2]University of Virginia, Dept. of Computer Science, Charlottesville, VA 22903
Contact: lesh@merl.com

Abstract

Scheduling, routing, and layout tasks are examples of hard operations-research problems that have broad application in industry. Typical algorithms for these problems combine some form of gradient descent to find local minima with some strategy for escaping nonoptimal local minima. Our idea is to divide these two subtasks cleanly between human and computer: in our paradigm of *human-guided simple search* the computer is responsible only for finding local minima using a simple hill-climbing search; using visualization and interaction techniques, the human user identifies promising regions of the search space for the computer to explore, and intervenes to help it escape nonoptimal local minima. We have applied our approach to the problem of capacitated vehicle routing with time windows, a commercially important problem with a rich research history. Despite its simplicity, our prototype system is competitive with the majority of previously reported systems on benchmark academic problems, and has the advantage of keeping a human tightly in the loop to handle the complexities of real-world applications.

Introduction

Most previous research on scheduling, routing, and layout problems has focused on developing fully automatic solution methods. There are, however, at least two reasons for developing cooperative, interactive systems for optimization problems like these. First, human users may have knowledge of various amorphous real-word constraints and objectives that are not represented in the objective function given to computer algorithms. In vehicle-routing problems, for example, human experts may know the flexibility or importance of certain customers, or the variability of certain routes. The second reason to involve people in the optimization process is to leverage their abilities in areas in which humans (currently) outperform computers, such as visual perception, learning from experience, and strategic assessment. Although both motivations seem equally important, we have used the second, more quantitative consideration to drive our current round of research.

In this paper, we present a new cooperative paradigm for optimization, human-guided simple search (HuGSS). In our current framework, the computer performs a very simple, hill-climbing search. One or more people interactively "steer" the search process by repeatedly initiating focused searches, manually editing solutions, or backtracking to previous solutions. When invoking a focused search, the user determines which modifications to the current solution should be considered, how to evaluate them, and what type of hill-climbing search to use.

We have designed and implemented a prototype system that supports HuGSS for the *capacitated-vehicle-routing-with-time-windows* (CVRTW) problem. Below, we describe the CVRTW problem and our prototype, and report results from 48 hours of controlled testing with our system.

Sample Application
Problem Description and Definitions

We chose vehicle routing as our initial problem domain for three reasons: it is commercially important; it has a rich research history, which facilitates comparison with previous work; and routing problems are ones for which the human capabilities of vision, learning, and judgment should be useful. In the CVRTW problem (Solomon 1987), trucks deliver goods from a single central depot to customers at fixed geographic locations. Each customer requires a certain quantity of goods, and specifies a time window within which delivery of the goods must commence. All trucks have the same capacity, and travel one unit of distance in one unit of time. Delivery takes a constant amount of time, and each customer can receive only one delivery. All trucks must return to the depot by a fixed time. A *solution* to a CVRTW problem is an ordered list of customers assigned to each truck, and is *feasible* if it satisfies all the constraints. The optimization problem is first to minimize the number of trucks required to construct a feasible solution; and second to minimize the total distance traveled by the trucks.

As we describe below, users can force the system to consider *infeasible* solutions. Thus we needed to extend the classical objective function for CVRTW to rank infeasible as well as feasible solutions. We define the *maximum lateness* of a truck as the maximum tardiness with which it arrives at any of its customers; or if a

Copyright © 2000, American Association for Artificial Intelligence (www.aaai.org). All rights reserved.

truck has insufficient capacity to service its customers, we assign it an infinite maximum-lateness value. We optimize infeasible solutions by minimizing the sum of the maximum latenesses over all the routes. We rank any feasible solution as better than any infeasible solution.

We define a *1-ply* move as the transfer of a customer from its current route onto another route. Such a move requires that both routes be re-optimized for distance (if feasible) or maximum lateness (if infeasible).[1] An n-ply move is simply a combination of n 1-ply moves.

HuGSS for CVRTW

In our system, the user controls the optimization process by performing the following three actions:

1. Edit the current solution by making a 1-ply move.

2. Invoke a focused local search, starting from the current solution. The user controls which n-ply moves are considered, how they are evaluated, and what type of search is used.

3. Revert to an earlier solution, or to an initial seed solution generated randomly prior to the session.

We now describe each type of action in the context of our implemented system, followed by a description of the visualization and interface (see Figures 1 and 2) that support these actions.

Manual edits: To edit the current solution manually, the user simply selects a customer and a route. The system transfers the customer to the route and re-optimizes both affected routes. Moving the last customer off a truck's route eliminates that truck. Also, the user can create infeasible solutions by assigning customers with conflicting constraints, or with too much total demand, to a single truck.

Focused searches: The principal feature of our system is the following set of methods for allowing users to repeatedly invoke deep, focused searches into regions of the search space they feel are promising. The user determines which moves the hill-climbing engine will evaluate by:

- *Setting a priority (high, medium, or low) for each customer.* The user controls which customers can be moved, and the routes onto which they can be moved, by assigning priorities to them. The search engine will only consider moving high-priority customers, and only consider moving them onto routes that have no low-priority customers. For example, the user can restrict the search engine to exchanging customers between a pair of routes by setting all the customers on those routes to high priority and all other customers to low priority.

Figure 1: The Optimization Table.

- *Deciding which n-ply moves (1-ply to 5-ply) to enable.* In general, deeper searches are more likely to produce good results, but take more time.

- *Setting an upper bound on the number of moves that the computer can consider.* The search is stopped when all enabled moves have been considered, or when this user-supplied upper limit is reached.

Focusing the search dramatically reduces the number of moves that the search engine evaluates. In one example from our experiments, we focused the search on two of 12 routes (20 of 100 customers), which decreased the number of 1-ply moves considered by a factor of 30, 2-ply moves by a factor of 222, and 3-ply moves by a factor of 18,432.

In addition to determining which moves are evaluated, the user determines how they are evaluated by selecting an objective function. We currently support two objective functions: the standard CVRTW objective function modified to assess infeasible solutions; and a function we call *minimize-routes*, which removes $2 \times len^2$ from the cost attributed to each route that contains $len < 6$ customers. The idea behind this objective function is to encourage a short route to become shorter, even if it increases the total distance traveled, in the hope of eventually eliminating that route.

Finally, the user can select between greedy or steepest-descent search mode. In greedy mode, the search engine immediately adopts any move that improves the current solution under the given objective function. It considers 1-ply moves (if enabled) first, then 2-ply moves (if enabled), and so on. Within a ply, the moves are evaluated in a random order. As soon a move is adopted, the search engine begins, again, to evaluate 1-ply moves.

In steepest-descent mode, moves are considered in the same order as in greedy mode, but only the best move is adopted. The best move is defined as the one that decreases the cost of the solution the most, under the given objective function. If no move decreases the cost of the solution, then the best move is the one that increases the cost the least.[2] Making the least-bad move

---

[1]Computing the route for a truck once customers have been assigned to it is an instance of the Traveling Salesman Problem with Time Windows. Although an NP-hard problem, the instances that arose in our experiments are small enough that exhaustive search is practical.

[2]However, we never adopt a move that increases the infeasibility of a solution. Finding and ranking all infeasible moves is not worth the added computational expense.

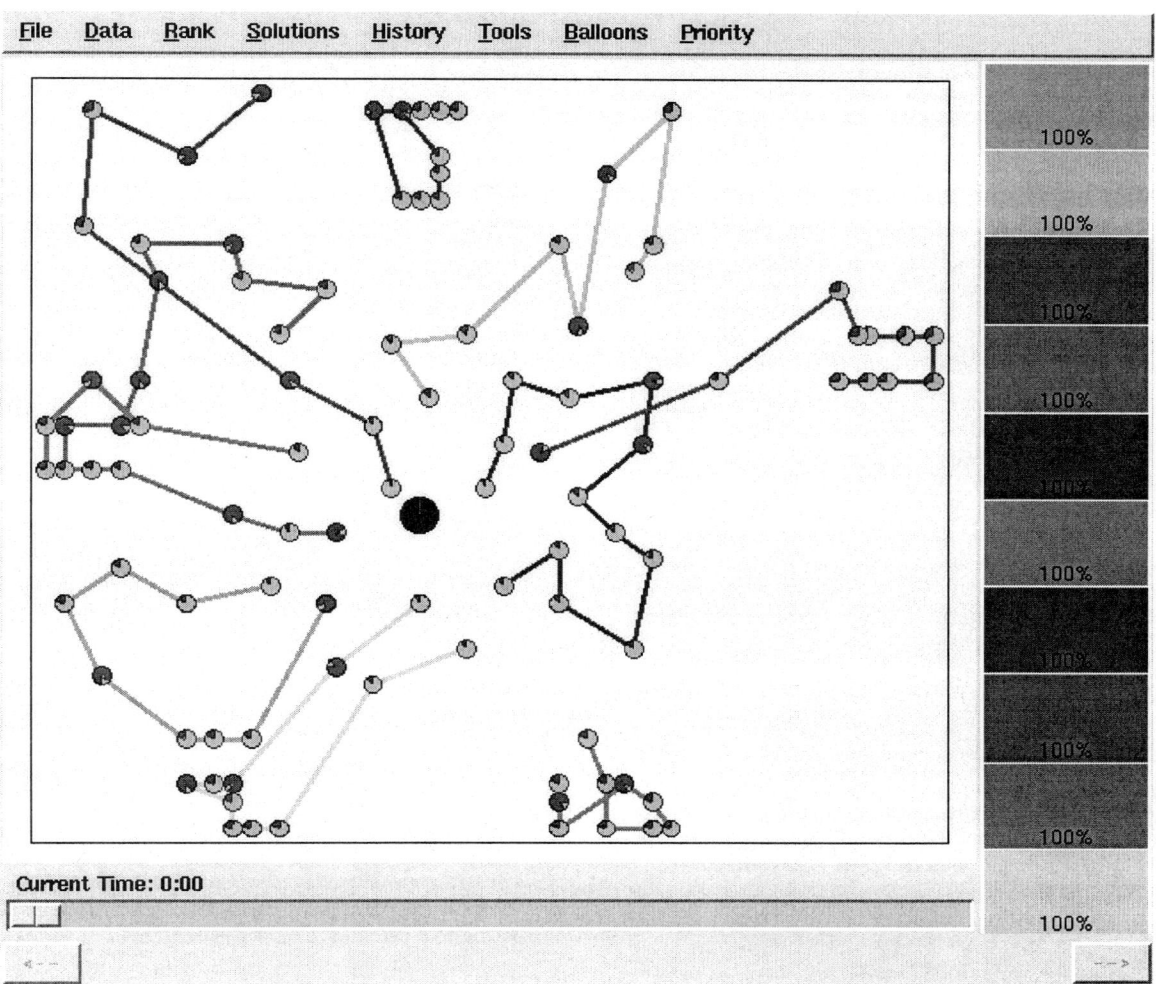

Figure 2: A snapshot of our interface.

provides useful information to the user, and can always be undone by reverting to the previous solution.

Switching among candidate solutions: The third type of action the user can perform is to switch candidate solutions, either to backtrack to a previous solution, or to load a precomputed, "seed" solution. The seed solutions are generated prior to the session using our hill-climbing search engine. They are intended to be used both as starting points for finding more optimal solutions and to give users a sense of how various combinations of customers can be serviced.

Interface and Implementation

For our initial implementation we have used a tabletop display, which we call the *Optimization Table* (see Figure 1). We project an image down onto a whiteboard. This allows users to annotate candidate solutions by drawing or placing tokens on the board, a very useful feature. In addition, several users can comfortably use the system together.

For this kind of problem, creating an effective visualization is an intrinsic challenge in bringing the human into the loop. Figure 2 shows our attempt to convey the spatial, temporal, and capacity-related information needed for CVRTW. The central depot is the black circle at the center of the display. The other circles represent customers. The pie slices in the customer circles indicate the time windows during which they are willing to accept delivery. The truck routes are shown by polylines, each in a different color. At the user's option, the first and last segments of each route can be hidden, as they are in the figure, to avoid visual clutter around the depot. The search-control operations described in the previous subsection are supported by mouse operations and pull-down menus. Detailed information about individual customers and trucks can also be accessed through standard interface widgets.

The interface was written in Tcl, and the hill-climbing algorithm in C++. We use a branch-and-bound algorithm to optimize truck routes during move evaluation. We carefully crafted several pruning rules and caching procedures to streamline this algorithm.

Experimental Investigation

Four test subjects participated in our experiments. Three of them are authors of this paper. The fourth tester is a Ph.D. student unaffiliated with this project, who received five hours of training prior to his first test.

The Solomon datasets (Solomon 1987) were our source of benchmark CVRTW problems. This corpus consists of 56 problem instances, each with 100 customers, divided into three categories according to the spatial distribution of customers: C-type (clustered), R-type (random), and RC-type (a mix of the two.) There are two problem sets for each category: the C1, R1, RC1 sets have a narrow scheduling horizon, while the C2, R2, and RC2 sets have a large scheduling horizon.

As we developed and refined our system, we tested users informally on a selection of R1 and RC1 problems. In the second, more controlled, phase of experimentation, we ran two tests on each of the RC1 problems. During this phase, subjects worked only on problem instances to which they had no previous exposure. In each test, the user spent 90 minutes working on the problem without reference to the precomputed seed solutions. Then, after an arbitrarily long break, the user spent another 90 minutes working on the same problem, this time with the precomputed seed solutions available for perusal. We recorded logs for a total of 79.4 hours of test sessions, 48 hours of which were the controlled experiments.

We generated the seed solutions using the settings we found to be the most effective on a small sample of the Solomon problem instances. In particular, we used greedy search with 1-ply and 2-ply moves enabled and all customers set to high priority; we used the minimize-routes objective function, and started the search from an initial solution in which each customer is assigned its own truck, and searched until we reached a local optimum. Multiple runs produce varied results due to the random order in which moves are considered in the greedy search. We ran the algorithm repeatedly until we had generated 1000 solutions or a 10-hour time limit was reached. On average, it took 8.4 hours to generate the seed solutions for a problem. We ran all our experiments on a 500 MHz PC.

Observations

User strategies: During a session, the user repeatedly invokes the hill-climbing engine to perform focused searches. This simple mechanism supports a surprisingly broad range of optimization strategies. For example, consider the goal of truck reduction. A user might start by browsing the precomputed seed solutions for one with a "vulnerable" route, e.g., one that might be eliminated because it has a small number of loosely constrained customers, and nearby routes that have available capacity and slack in their schedules. Having identified such a solution, the user can shift customers off the vulnerable route by invoking a steepest-descent search: setting the route's customers to high priority and the customers of nearby routes to medium priority will cause the search algorithm to return the least costly feasible move of a customer off the vulnerable route and onto one of the nearby routes. An alternative strategy for shortening and eliminating routes is to set all the customers in the neighborhood of a vulnerable route to high priority, and to use the minimize-routes objective function and a high search ply: a search with these parameters would consider compound moves, involving multiple customers on different routes, that have the net effect of shortening the vulnerable route. A third alternative, which users often had to resort to, is to manually move a customer off a vulnerable route, even if the move produces an infeasible solution; fixing the resulting infeasibility then becomes a subproblem for which there is another suite of strategies.

User behaviors: During test sessions, our users spent more time thinking than the search algorithm spent searching. On average, the search algorithm was in use 31% of the time; the range was 11% to 61%. Solution improvements were made throughout the sessions. Averaging over all the test runs, a new best solution was found a little over five times per hour. Of course, improving the current solution was much more common than finding a new best solution. Focused searches yielded an average of 23 improvements per hour, and manual adjustment yielded an average of 20 improvements per hour.

Tables 1 and 2 show what features of the system were used, as well as how usage varied among the test subjects. (Note that some of the variation is very likely due to differences in the nature of the individual problems.) Three of the four users primarily used steepest-descent search instead of greedy search. We feel that steepest-descent mode was preferred largely because it makes the least-bad move if no good move is available, which turned out to be a very useful feature for shifting customers onto or off of specific routes. The minimize-routes objective function was almost never used. Everyone spent at least half of the time working on infeasible solutions. All four users made substantial use of 1-ply, 2-ply, and 3-ply searches, but only two users frequently used 5-ply search. There was a wide range among the users in terms of how often the different priorities were used, and in how many searches were invoked, on average, per hour.

During the controlled experiments, each user did better than some other user on at least one data set. The one user who was not an inventor of the system (User D in the tables) turned out to have the best record. He generated three of the eight best results on the RC1 problem instances, which are shown in Table 3.

Quantitative results

HuGSS vs. unguided simple search: Our results show that human guidance provided a significant boost to the simple search in almost all cases. Table 3 compares the best scores on the RC1 datasets found by the hill-climbing engine alone with the best scores found using the HuGSS system.[3] For the hill-climbing en-

---

[3] To interpret the scores correctly, it is important to recall that the primary objective is to minimize the number of

User	Moves per hour	Searches per hour	Percent steep searches	Percent in infeasible space
A	53	47	30	78
B	46	53	99	52
C	107	101	87	60
D	26	72	99	76

Table 1: User styles: action and mode

User	Customer priority			Search ply used				
	high	med.	low	1	2	3	4	5
A	34	50	16	83	84	87	84	83
B	16	8	77	100	95	81	76	65
C	17	13	70	94	89	53	26	11
D	40	29	31	99	99	39	10	0

Table 2: User styles: depth and focus. The numbers indicate the fraction of customers assigned high, medium, or low priorities, and the frequency with which the various ply moves were enabled. E.g., on average, subject A assigned 34% of the customers to have high priority, and included 3-ply moves 87% of the time.

gine, the scores are the best found in approximately 100 hours of computation on a 500 MHz Pentium PC. The scores for the HuGSS system are the best found in at most 10 hours of precomputation and 10 hours of guided searching. (The table includes scores from all logged testing and training sessions, as well as those from the controlled experiments.) On three of the problems, the human-guided solution uses one fewer truck; on four of the five remaining problems, the human-guided solution has a lower distance value. The only dataset on which the unguided hill-climbing search prevailed was RC101, which is the most heavily constrained of all the problems. The very narrow time windows facilitate extremely fast computer searches (a new local optimum is found every six seconds), while making visualization more difficult.

The HuGSS results in Table 3 reflect the combined benefit of precomputed seed solutions and human-guided search. To tease these two factors apart, we considered the solutions produced by the first 90 minutes of each controlled experiment, during which precomputed seed solutions were not available to the user. In Table 4 we report these results in two ways: the average of the two scores available for each dataset represents what can be achieved with 1.5 hours of pure guided search (i.e., guided search without the benefit of precomputed seed solutions); the best of the two scores for each dataset represents what can be achieved in 3.0 hours of pure guided search, albeit using two people for separate 1.5-hour sessions. The table also shows the average results obtained by the hill-climbing engine without human guidance.[4] From this data we can con-

---

trucks, which often works against the secondary concern of minimizing total distance traveled. Additionally, it is standard practice in the literature to report results by averaging the trucks and distances over many problem instances.

[4] We estimated the average value of computer-only search

	Best found by simple search		Best found by human-guided simple search		Best pub. solution	
	Veh.	Dist.	Veh.	Dist.	Veh.	Dist.
RC101	15	**1631**	15	1662	14	1669
RC102	13	1499	**12**	1569	12	1555
RC103	11	1293	11	**1224**	11	1110
RC104	10	1156	10	**1136**	10	1136
RC105	14	1558	**13**	1691	13	1637
RC106	12	1407	**11**	1475	11	1432
RC107	11	1247	11	**1236**	11	1231
RC108	10	1191	10	**1185**	10	1140
Ave.	12.0	1373	11.63	1397	11.50	1364

Table 3: Best solutions found during 800 hours of simple search compared to 67.2 hours of precomputation and 79.4 hours of human-guided search. The best published solutions are shown for comparison.

clude that 1.5 hours of pure human-guided searching is comparable to about 5.0 hours of unguided hill climbing. However, 3.0 hours of pure guided searching is better than 20.0 hours of unguided hill climbing, which indicates that additional time is of more benefit to the guided regime than to the unguided one. The average score for 3.0 hours of guided search with precomputed seed solutions is also shown: the seed solutions impart a distinct benefit, but are not the sole factor behind the dominance of HuGSS over unguided simple search.

HuGSS vs. state-of-the-art techniques: The Solomon datasets are a very useful benchmark for comparing all the different heuristic-search techniques that have been applied to the CVRTW problem, including tabu search and its variants, evolutionary strategies, constraint programming, and ant-colony optimization. Table 4 includes performance data for these techniques and others. The scores we obtained with the full HuGSS approach (i.e., with precomputed seed solutions) are competitive with those obtained by the state-of-the-art techniques, dominating several of them, and being clearly dominated only by the results from a recent genetic algorithm (Homberger & Gehring 1999).

However, the full HuGSS technique uses between one and two orders of magnitude more computational effort than other techniques. Other algorithms may benefit from a comparable amount of computation, but there is not enough information in the cited papers to accurately assess how much benefit to expect, if any.

To test whether the HuGSS approach for this problem can be effective with less computational effort, we ran a pilot set of experiments with the latest version of our system (its improvements over the system described above are listed in the concluding section of this paper). In these experiments, we used only 90 minutes of precomputation and 90 minutes of guided search. We ran one test per problem, with three of the test subjects

---

for N hours of computation by taking the best score found in N hours of computation randomly sampled from the 100 hours of unguided search we recorded for each problem instance. We repeated this 1000 times for each problem and report the average result.

from the first set of experiments. (In some cases, the subjects worked on a problem instance that they had worked on some months earlier.) As shown in Table 4, we achieved comparable results with our new system with significantly less computational and human effort, thus closing the gap with the state-of-the-art systems.

In summary, these results suggest that human guidance can replace the painstakingly crafted, problem-specific heuristics that are the essence of other approaches without significant compromise in the quality of the results.

	Time	Veh.	Dist.
Our hill-climbing search engine alone	1 hour 2 hours 5 hours 8.4 hours 20 hours	12.35 12.23 12.15 12.13 12.06	1424 1416 1403 1390 1388
HuGSS (w/out seeds)	1.5 hours 3 hours	12.13 12.00	1432 1413
HuGSS (with seeds)	10 hours precomputation and 3 hours guided search on 500 MHz machine	11.88	1389
HuGSS (pilot experiments with newest system)	90 min. precomputation and 90 min. guided search on 500 MHz machine	11.88	1380
Carlton'95[a]	-	13.25	1402
Rochat and Taillard'95	44 min. on 100 MHz machine	12.38	1369
Chiang and Russell'97[b]	-	11.88	1397
Taillard et. al.'97	3.1 hours on 50 MHz machine	11.88	1381
De Backer and Furnon'97	-	14.25	1385
Shaw'98	1 hour on 100 MIPS machine	12.00	1361
Shaw'98	2 hours on 100 MIPS machine	12.00	1360
Cordone and Wolfer-Calvo'98[c]	12.1 min on 18 Mflops Pentium	12.38	1409
Gambardella and Taillard'99	30 min on 167MHz, 70 Mflops Sun UltraSparc	11.92	1388
Kilby, Prosser and Shaw'99[c]	48.3 min. on 25 Mflops/s Digital Alpha	12.12	1388
Homberger and Gehring'99	5 hours on 200 MHz machine	11.5	1407
Best published solutions	About 15 years on multiple machines	11.5	1364

[a] As reported by (Taillard *et al.* 1997).
[b] As reported in (Homberger & Gehring 1999).
[c] As reported in (Gambardella, Taillard, & Agazzi 1999).

Table 4: Reported results. The numbers are averages over the eight instances in Solomon's RC1 problem set.

Versatility

Because the user is directing the search, our system can be used for tasks other than the classic CVRTW optimization task. For example, it can be used to balance routes. Many of the best solutions found by state-of-the-art methods might be unsuitable for real use because they assign only one or two customers to a truck. The users of our system can direct the hill-climbing engine to find the lowest cost way of moving N customers to a particular truck, by only enabling N-ply moves and setting the priorities so that the search engine only considers moving customers onto the target truck.

Alternatively, it may be desirable to have a lightly loaded truck as a backup if other trucks encounter significant delays. This can be accomplished by the same means used in attempting to eliminate a truck. Similarly, in the case where there simply are not enough trucks to satisfy all the customers' needs, our system can be used to explore various infeasible options. It is often easy to shift the infeasibility around the board, if in fact some customers are more flexible than others.

Of course, other algorithms might be modified to solve any of these tasks. The ability of our system to handle these tasks without any recoding (or even recompiling!) suggests that it will be more effective at handling new tasks as they arise. Furthermore, it demonstrates that our system can be used to pursue an objective function that is known by the human users but is difficult to describe to the computer algorithm. In this regard, HuGSS is distinctly more versatile than the algorithms cited in Table 4.

Related Work

The HuGSS paradigm is one way of dividing the work between human and computer in a cooperative optimization or design system. Other interface paradigms organize the cooperation differently.

In an iterative-repair paradigm, the computer detects and resolves conflicts introduced by the human user. In a system for scheduling space-shuttle operations (Chien *et al.* 1999), the computer produces an initial schedule that the user iteratively refines by hand. The user can invoke a repair algorithm to resolve any conflicts introduced.

Another way for the computer to address conflicts or constraint violations is to not let the user introduce them in the first place. Constraint-based interfaces are popular in drawing applications, e.g., (Nelson 1985; Gleicher & Witkin 1994; Ryall, Marks, & Shieber 1997). Typically the user imposes geometric or topological constraints on a nascent drawing such that subsequent user manipulation is constrained to useful areas of the design space.

The interactive-evolution paradigm offers a different type of cooperation: the computer generates successive populations of novel designs based on previous ones, and the user selects which of the new designs to accept and which to reject (Kochhar & Friedell 1990; Sims 1991; Todd & Latham 1992).

A related but very different line of inquiry takes human-human collaboration as the model for cooperative human-computer interaction, e.g., (Ferguson & Allen 1998). The emphasis in this work is on mixed-initiative interaction between the user and computer in which the computer has some representation of the user's goals and capabilities, and can engage the human in a collaborative dialogue about the problem at hand and approaches to solving it.

The HuGSS paradigm differs significantly from the iterative-repair, constraint-based, and interactive-evolution paradigms in affording the user much more control of the optimization/design process. By setting customer priorities and specifying the scope of the local search, the user decides how much effort the computer will expend on particular subproblems. And there are no dialogue or mixed-initiative elements in our system: the user is always in control, and the computer has no representation of the user's intentions or abilities.

Other researchers have also allowed a user to interact with a computer during its search for a solution to an optimization or constraint-satisfaction problem, e.g., (Choueiry & Faltings 1995; Smith, Lassila, & Becker 1996); one group has even applied this idea to a vehicle-routing problem (Bracklow *et al.* 1992). We believe, however, that HuGSS embodies a stronger notion of human guidance than previous efforts. Furthermore, our work is the first rigorous investigation of how human guidance can improve the performance of an optimization algorithm.

Future Work And Conclusions

The contributions of this work are novel mechanisms for the interactive control of simple search, an application of these mechanisms to a vehicle-routing problem, and an empirical study of that application.

We are currently making our hill-climbing engine more efficient and our interface more interactive. The user now receives feedback from the hill-climbing engine that indicates the current depth of the search and the best move found to that point. The user can halt the search at any time, at which point the system returns the best solution found so far. This gives the user a much higher degree of control of the system and effectively removes the need to decide, in advance, the search depth, the maximum number of moves to evaluate, and blurs the distinction between greedy and steepest-descent search. Our pilot experiments (see Table 4) indicate that these changes greatly improve our system.

We had two principal motivations for investigating human-guided search: to exploit human perceptual and pattern-recognition abilities to improve the performance of search heuristics, and to create more versatile tools for solving real-world optimization problems. Our initial investigations show that human guidance improves simple hill-climbing search to world-class levels for at least one optimization task. We are also encouraged by the system's pliability and transparency: users pursued a variety of strategies, developed their own usage styles, and were highly aware of what the search engine was doing and why.

The separation made in HuGSS between the human's and the computer's roles has several pleasant consequences. The optimization engine is more generic and reusable than those used in state-of-the-art, problem-specific systems; and many of the user-interface concepts are also easily generalized to other problems. This raises the possibility of developing a general toolkit for creating a family of human-guided optimization tools.

Acknowledgments

We are very grateful to Wheeler Ruml for his help in making our experiments possible and his prowess at optimization, and to Kori Inkpen, Ken Perlin, Steve Powell, and Stacey Scott for their comments and discussion.

References

Bracklow, J. W.; Graham, W. W.; Hassler, S. M.; Peck, K. E.; and Powell, W. B. 1992. Interactive optimization improves service and performance for Yellow Freight system. *INTERFACES* 22(1):147–172.

Carlton, W. 1995. *A Tabu Search Approach to the General Vehicle Routing Problem*. Ph.D. Dissertation, The University of Texas at Austin, Texas.

Chiang, W.-C., and Russell, R. 1997. A reactive tabu search metaheuristic for the vehicle routing problem with time windows. *INFORMS J. on Computing* 9:417–430.

Chien, S.; Rabideau, G.; Willis, J.; and Mann, T. 1999. Automating planning and scheduling of shuttle payload operations. *J. Artificial Intelligence* 114:239–255.

Choueiry, B. Y., and Faltings, B. 1995. Using abstractions for resource allocation. In *IEEE 1995 International Conference on Robotics and Automation*, 1027–1033.

Cordone, R., and Wolfler-Calvo, R. 2000. A heuristic for the vehicle routing problem with time windows. *J. of Heuristics*, forthcoming.

De Backer, B., and Furnon, V. 1997. Meta-heuristics in constraint programming experiments with tabu search on the vehicle routing problem. In *Proc. of the 2nd Int'l Conference on Metaheuristics (MIC 97)*, 1–14.

Ferguson, G., and Allen, J. 1998. Trips: An integrated intelligent problem-solving assistant. In *Proc. 15th Nat. Conf. AI*, 567–572.

Gambardella, L.-M.; Taillard, E. D.; and Agazzi, G. 1999. MACS-VRPTW: A multiple ant colony system for vehicle routing problems with time windows. Technical Report IDSIA-06-99, IDSIA.

Gleicher, M., and Witkin, A. 1994. Drawing with constraints. *Visual Computer* 11:39–51.

Homberger, J., and Gehring, H. 1999. Two evolutionary metaheuristics for the vehicle routing problem with time windows. *INFORMS J. on Computing* 37(3):297–318.

		first session					second session				pilot experiments with new system		
	user	seedless		seeded		user	seedless		seeded				
		Veh.	Dist.	Veh.	Dist.		Veh.	Dist.	Veh.	Dist.		Veh.	Dist.
RC101	C	15	1678	15	1666	B	15	1690	15	1662	C	15	1629
RC102	D	12	1617	12	1569	A	13	1528	13	1528	B	13	1559
RC103	B	11	1323	11	1293	D	11	1420	11	1224	A	11	1281
RC104	C	10	1136	10	1136	B	10	1146	10	1140	B	10	1148
RC105	D	14	1733	13	1691	A	15	1707	14	1582	B	13	1642
RC106	A	12	1591	12	1385	C	12	1395	12	1395	C	12	1397
RC107	B	11	1284	11	1236	D	11	1359	11	1242	C	11	1232
RC108	C	11	1134	10	1218	A	11	1193	10	1246	A	10	1148

Table 5: Detailed results of the experiments

Kilby, P.; Prosser, P.; and Shaw, P. 1999. Guided local search for the vehicle routing problem with time windows. In *Meta-heuristics - Advances and Trends in Local Search Paradigms for Optimization*. Kluwer Academic Publishers. chapter 32, 473–486.

Kochhar, S., and Friedell, M. 1990. User control in cooperative computer-aided design. In *Proc. of the 1990 ACM SIGGRAPH Symposium on User Interface Software and Technology (UIST '90)*, 143–151.

Nelson, G. 1985. Juno, a constraint based graphics system. *Computer Graphics (Proc. of SIGGRAPH '85)* 19(3):235–243.

Rochat, Y., and Taillard, E. D. 1995. Probabilistic diversification and intensification in local search for vehicle routing. *J. of Heuristics* 1(1):147–167.

Ryall, K.; Marks, J.; and Shieber, S. 1997. Glide: An interactive system for graph drawing. In *Proc. of the 1997 ACM SIGGRAPH Symposium on User Interface Software and Technology (UIST '97)*, 97–104.

Shaw, P. 1998. A new local search algorithm providing high quality solutions to vehicle routing problems. Technical report, APES group, University of Strathclyde.

Sims, K. 1991. Artificial evolution for computer graphics. *Comp. Graphics (Proc. of SIGGRAPH '91)* 25(3):319–328.

Smith, S.; Lassila, O.; and Becker, M. 1996. Configurable, mixed-initiative systems for planning and scheduling. In Tate, A., ed., *Advanced Planning Technology*. Menlo Park, CA: AAAI Press. ISBN 0-929280-98-9.

Solomon, M. M. 1987. Algorithms for the vehicle routing and scheduling problems with time window constraints. *Operations Research* 35(2):254–265.

Taillard, E. D.; Badeau, P.; Gendreau, M.; Guertin, F.; and Potvin, J. 1997. A tabu search heuristic for the vehicle routing problem with soft time windows. *Transportation Science 31* 170–186.

Todd, S., and Latham, W. 1992. *Evolutionary Art and Computers*. Academic Press.

Appendix

Table 5 shows the actual scores attained during our controlled experiments and the pilot experiments for our new system.

Predicting Future User Actions by Observing Unmodified Applications

Peter Gorniak and **David Poole**
Department of Computer Science
University of British Columbia
Vancouver, B.C., Canada
pgorniak@cs.ubc.ca, poole@cs.ubc.ca

Abstract

Intelligent user interfaces often rely on modified applications and detailed application models. Such modifications and models are expensive to build and maintain. We propose to automatically model the use of unmodified applications to solve this problem. We observe a user's interactions with the application's interface and from these observations infer a state space which the user navigates and the stochastic policy he or she follows. ONISI, the algorithm presented here, builds this state space implicitly and on-line, and uses it to predict future user actions. Trials with real users show that this algorithm predicts the next user action significantly better than another current algorithm.

Content Areas: plan recognition, human computer interaction, automated modeling, software agents

Introduction

Artificial Intelligence supplies a vast set of tools to be applied to the design of intelligent user interfaces. While our previous research (Gorniak 1998) as well as countless other projects sample indulgently from this set and often produce quite impressive results in their own environments (for example, see (Horvitz, Breese, Heckerman, Hovel and Rommelse 1998) and (Albrecht, Zukerman, Nicholson and Bud 1997),) there emerge some new challenges when one attempts to apply these results to a new application.

1. The research results often do not transfer easily to a new application.
2. The actual implementation used in the research relies upon a modified application. This modification is usually non-trivial, time-consuming to repeat and increases application complexity.
3. Researchers work from various, often hand-crafted application models. In addition to the application building work in 2, an application designer needs to specify such a model. This process is often not straightforward and may rely on empirical data from user trials. An application designer's primary task does not include designing such a model, and thus the task seems an added difficulty to him or her. Also, the model needs to be updated and will tend to lag behind the application during maintenance.

Copyright © 2000, American Association for Artificial Intelligence (www.aaai.org). All rights reserved.

We are currently addressing these problems by investigating how much knowledge can be extracted from a user's interaction with an application without any prior information about the application's purpose or structure and without any modifications to the application (somewhat in the spirit of (Lieberman 1998).) We hypothesize that enough knowledge can be extracted to yield a detailed model of the application and its user. This model can then serve both as a knowledge source for other algorithms as well as provide a context under which to unite methods.

Other application independent user models build no application model at all, and thus do not provide any automatic analysis of the application. We show that they perform worse in cases where such application knowledge boosts performance, such as future action prediction (Davison and Hirsh 1998). Others stop early on in their analysis and subsequently rely on application specific knowledge (Encarnacao 1997). Our approach is similar to the web pre-caching work by Zukerman, Albrecht and Nicholson (1999), but they do not perform any kind of history analysis for state identification, except for simple frequency counts. We show here that frequency counts generally do not capture the user's current state as well as other possible identifiers.

In this paper, we employ a user modeling strategy to predict future user actions. It was our hope in choosing this domain that our extensive use of structured observations and history analysis would increase our prediction accuracy as compared to simpler approaches. Also, knowledge about future user actions can be useful to achieve various goals in many applications, thus providing an ideal target for a general application independent approach like ours. Specifically, predicting the user's next action allows application designers to automate tasks for the user, to initiate time-intensive tasks before the user requests them and to identify a user by comparing his or her real actions with the predicted ones. For example, Davison and Hirsh (1998) use next action prediction for UNIX command line completion. Current web browsers support a similar feature for URL completion. Debevc, Meyer, Donlagic and Svecko (1996) developed an adaptive toolbar that adjusts its displayed collection of tools based upon user behaviour. A next action prediction algorithm performs exactly the kind of analysis needed to make decisions in such adaptive interfaces. Zukerman et al. (1999) pre-cache web pages for users by predicting their next request. Lane (1999) uses Hidden Markov Models to detect security breaches by comparing a user's current behaviour to the HMM derived from their past behaviour. We believe the same goal can be achieved by comparing the predictions made by a next action prediction algorithm to the real user actions. Finally, knowledge about future user actions is valuable to intelligent help systems. These systems can use such information to identify user plans and help the user to achieve his or her current goals. We expand further on how our approach to user modeling can be used to support other intelligent interface components in (Gorniak and Poole 2000).

Let us view the user as an agent. Our assumption is that we can and have observed this agent acting in an environment, namely using an application. Artificial Intelligence concerns itself with agents acting in environments and worries about what decisions such agents should make. A common approach to such a problem consists of phrasing it in terms of states and actions between states and coming up with a policy that, perhaps stochastically, dictates which actions to take in which states (Boutilier, Dean and Hanks 1999). We are faced with the opposite problem: we see an agent acting in an environment and want to model the agent's decision process. We assume that the agent acts according to a policy. Each action is the result of some (possibly stochastic) function of what the agent observes and the agent's belief state. Our goal is to determine this policy and the state space to which it applies.

The following section describes our approach in detail. Our algorithm performs an on-line implicit state identification (ONISI). That is, it assigns probabilities to all possible actions in the currently observed interface state. It arrives at these probabilities by estimating how much support the observed interaction history contains given the history recorded immediately prior to entering the current state. To do so, it employs a k nearest neighbours scheme that uses sequence match length as a metric.

The section on implementation describes the Java implementation of the work presented here. This implementation works as a wrapper to existing Java applications and is able to record their interfaces states as well as user actions without modifications to the original application. The results section compares our algorithm, ONISI, to IPAM (Davison and Hirsh 1998), another next action prediction algorithm in user trials and shows that our algorithm performs significantly better by exploiting behavioural patterns found in the recorded user history. Finally, we conclude by discussing what the research presented here reveals about the issues involved in analysing user history and point to future research directions.

State Identification Algorithms

A state for the user consists of a combination of the user's internal state and the application's interface state. At a given time, the user chooses an action from a probability distribution based upon the current state. We attempt to determine the policy the user is employing from our observation of the user's interaction history. To do so, we hypothesize internal states of good predictive power in addition the observed interface states by searching the observed interaction history for behavioural patterns. These implicitly identified states refine the frequently very coarse observations of application interface states and let us predict more accurately what action the user will choose next. In the following, we call the currently observed interface state s and the possible next action currently under consideration a.

In the context of this work the only information to identify the current state is the observed interaction history. There are several choices we must make as to how to mine this information. We need to choose

1. A type of pattern to extract from the interaction history that can be matched against recently occurring actions,

2. A method to summarize the occurrence of a pattern in history,

3. A function that ranks the currently possible actions according to the summaries of applicable patterns.

IPAM (Davison and Hirsh 1998) exemplifies one possible set of choices. They choose pairs of actions occurring in sequence as a pattern and summarize them by increasing the probability of those that occur and decreasing the probabilities of all others. Finally, they rank the currently possible actions by considering all the pairs that start with the action that occurred one timestep ago and selecting the one of highest estimated probability to predict the next action. These choices make an implicit Markov assumption, namely that the last action together with the current summary provided by the probability estimates contain enough information to predict the next state. Looking at real user interaction traces we found that often users enter modes that can be easily identified by examining the behavioural patterns they engage in, but that these patterns span more than two actions in a row. For example, in the search algorithm application we investigated users would either step through a problem or simply look at an algorithm's result. Both of these modes can be identified and the actions that occur in them predicted by looking several steps back. IPAM fails to do so, and cannot make a significant fraction of predictions in this case.

To remediate this problem, we decided to automatically vary the length of patterns we identify. Indeed, we deem patterns more important to the state identification process if they are longer, building on the idea that longer patterns capture the current state better. Overall, we choose our patterns to be the longest sequences in history that match the immediate history. Given a small integer k, at time t in state s we summarize the sequences that predict action a by computing $l_t(s, a)$: the average of the lengths of the k longest sequences that end with action a in state s and match the history sequence immediately prior to time t. We rank currently possible actions according to this summary value for each action (i.e. according to the average of the lengths of patterns the action completes.) Due to our decision to view match length as the important criterion, we only consider k maximum length sequences so as to avoid making the average less distinctive by considering more. In short, rather than estimating the probability of the next action given the

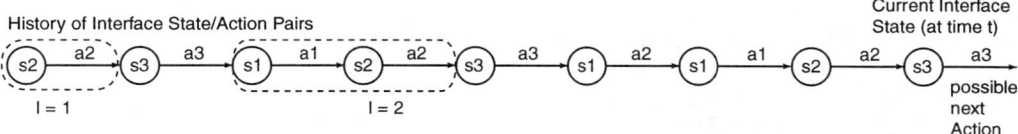

Figure 1: Example for On-Line Implicit State Identification

previous action like IPAM does, we estimate the probability of the next action given as much as we deem significant of the history that occurred immediately before this timestep. We determine significance by whether this sequence occurs previously in the observed history. This approach leans on a similar one used to identify hidden states during reinforcement learning (McCallum 1996). It is also akin to automation approaches that identify repeated patterns in user history (Ruvini and Dory 2000), but has the more general goal of modeling the use of an unmodified application.

Our measure of history support assigns no importance to how frequently actions occur, but only to how long the patterns are that they complete. However, action frequencies do encode a type of history support for an action that may augment the type of support we capture using match length. Specifically, a certain action may not be a part of long patterns, but its occurrence may be strongly correlated with that of another action. To account for this possibility, we reintroduce a simple frequency measure ($f(s,a)$), namely how many times an action has been taken from the current state. This term measures only state-action correlation and not action-action correlation like IPAM does, but it is less expensive to compute than IPAM's probability estimate. We experimentally traded off between the match length measure normalized across all possible actions,

$$\frac{l_t(s,a)}{\sum_i l_t(s,a_i)}$$

and the frequency measure, also normalized,

$$\frac{f(s,a)}{\sum_i f(s,a_i)}$$

using a parameter $0 \leq \alpha \leq 1$ to see when each would be useful. Figure 2 summarizes the ONISI k-nearest neighbours algorithm.

When normalized across all possible actions from the current state, $R(s,a)$ can be interpreted as the current probability of each action.

Figure 1 shows an example step of ONISI on a short history sequence. The application is currently observed to be in state $s3$ and the algorithm is ranking the possible action $a3$ from that state with $k=3$. As shown, it finds $\{3,1,0\}$ as the set of maximum length sequences matching the immediate history, and thus calculates

$$l_t(s3,a3) = \frac{0+1+2}{3} = 1.$$

Assuming that all actions provide a sum $\sum_i l_t(s,a_i) = 5$, that action $a3$ has occurred 50 times in interface state $s3$,

---

Given the currently observed interface state s, the action a currently under consideration, a small integer k to indicate how many pattern matches to consider and a real value $0 \leq \alpha \leq 1$ to indicate how to weigh off between the match length measure and the frequency measure, where $\alpha = 1$ uses only the match length measure and $\alpha = 0$ only the frequency measure,

1. Compare the immediate history starting at t with the state-action pair (s,a) and running backwards through all the recorded history. Find the k longest sequences in the recorded history that match the immediate history (they can be length 0).

2. Average the length of these sequences and call this average $l_t(s,a)$.

3. Count the number of times a has occurred in s and call this $f(s,a)$.

4. Return ranking

$$R_t(s,a) = \alpha \frac{l_t(s,a)}{\sum_i l_t(s,a_i)} + (1-\alpha)\frac{f(s,a)}{\sum_i f(s,a_i)}$$

where the sums run over all possible actions from s.

Figure 2: The ONISI k-nearest neighbours algorithm

and that $s3$ has been visited 100 times overall, ONISI run with $\alpha = 0.9$ finally assigns a rank of

$$R_t(s3,a3) = 0.9\frac{1}{5} + 0.1\frac{50}{100} = 0.18 + 0.05 = 0.23$$

to action $a3$ in observed interface state $s3$ at time t.

Implementation

Java's reflective capabilities and dynamic loading strategy make the language a prime candidate for an application independent approach (JDK 1998). It allows not only inspection of a structure of known visual components, but it can also inspect unknown components for state information. Java and JavaBeans introduced standard naming conventions for object methods. For example, *isVisible()* returns the visibility status of visual components, whereas *getEnabled()* returns whether they are currently useable. Components derived from standard Abstract Window Toolkit components inherit these methods automatically, and other components should define them. Java's Reflection mechanism, on the other hand, allows one to check whether a given object includes one of these state-revealing methods, and lets one call this method without knowing the object's class. Finally, Java's dynamic loading of classes rids the developer of needing to link with or even know about classes that will be present at runtime. Using these tools, one can establish the user interface state of an application built using Java at runtime by dynamically linking into its code, examining the methods available in its objects and calling the methods relevant to the interface state. This process requires no modification of the targeted application at all.

The system used for the experiments presented below runs as a wrapper to a Java application. Before it starts the application, it hooks itself into the application's event queue and thus sees all event activity within the Java Abstract Window Toolkit and components derived from it. It intercepts each such event that it considers an action (such as a button being pressed or a window closed) and records the observed state of the application's interface before and after the event occurs. In this way, this system establishes a state space of interface observations as a person uses the application and records a history consisting of actions and visited states at the same time.

The applications[1] under consideration here are educational AI applications. They were written to help undergraduate university students learn concepts in Artificial Intelligence. One application familiarizes the student with search problems and algorithms, the second deals with constraint satisfaction problems and the third demonstrates backpropagation neural network learning. In each, the student has the option to either load an example problem or to create his or her own problem by drawing a graph. He or she can then switch to a problem solution mode and step through the various algorithms at different levels of detail. The students used these applications to solve homework problems for an introductory AI course they were taking. Most of the assignment questions referred to a supplied example problem, so the students tended to explore the problem creation facilities of the applications less than their solving functionality. The following discussion and results focus mainly on the application for search algorithms.

Results

ONISI depends on two parameters: k and α. Figure 3 shows a graph of ONISI's performance over a range of values for these parameters, measured in percentage of actions predicted correctly for the search algorithm application (the application that yielded the largest dataset of about 2200 user actions.) The other two applications show similar trends, but due to the smaller dataset sizes they are less distinct. The graph continues to level out for larger values of k and performance continues to get worse for smaller values of α. Note that figure 3 is greatly magnified, and thus detailed features of the graph are likely not significant and should be ignored.

Concerning k, the graph shows the behaviour one would hope for in a nearest neighbour approach: small values of k show the same performance as larger ones, and thus suffice to capture history support accurately. As for α, a setting that

---

[1]The applications can be found at http://www.cs.ubc.ca/labs/lci/CIspace/.

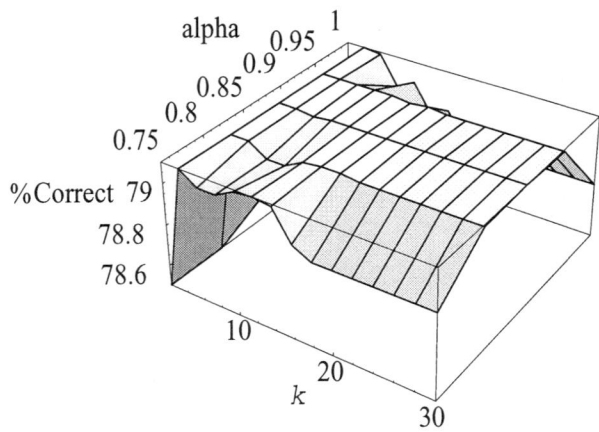

Figure 3: Performance at various parameter settings

assigns almost all importance to the match length measure yields the best performance, but if the frequency measure is ignored ($\alpha = 1.0$,) performance degrades. Upon inspection, the cases that are successfully predicted at $\alpha = 0.9$, but not at $\alpha = 1.0$ are indeed those where there are k maximal (but short) length matches in history for several actions and the default random choice between them that is used at $\alpha = 1.0$ performs worse than using the frequency measure to distinguish between them by setting $\alpha = 0.9$. All the following experiments were run with $k = 5$ and $\alpha = 0.9$.

We compared the implicit version of our state space approximation to IPAM which its authors in turn compare to a number of others (Davison and Hirsh 1998). IPAM estimates $P(a_{t+1}|a_t = x)$, i.e. the probability of the next action given the previous action. To do so, they build a table with all possible actions as rows and as columns and update its entries to be their desired probabilities during runtime. Specifically, they decrease all action pair probabilities in the row of the current action by a factor of $0 < \alpha < 1$ (note that this α is different from the α ONISI uses to trade of between frequency and length measure) and boost the probability of the action pair that just occurred by adding $1 - \alpha$, thus ensuring that the probabilities in a row continue to add up to 1.

We found IPAM to perform best on our data with a value of $\alpha = 0.9$, and all results here occur with that setting. The graphical user interface setting under investigation here differs somewhat from the UNIX command line prediction IPAM was designed for, and so does the state identification framework. To level the playing field, we let IPAM consider observed action-state pairs of the interface to be individual actions for its predictions. Taking state into consideration in this way produces better action distinctions, and IPAM's performance increases slightly (by ca. 2% for the search application.)

Figure 4 shows the percentage of actions predicted correctly by ONISI and IPAM for the search, neural network and constraint satisfaction applications. The numbers in parentheses indicate the number of actions recorded for each

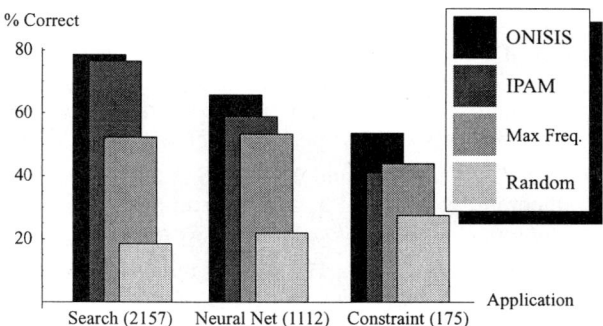

Figure 4: Performance of ONISI vs. IPAM

application. As baselines, the chart also indicates the percentage of actions predicted correctly using just the maximum action frequency in a state (ONISI with $\alpha = 0$) and by picking a random action amongst all that have been observed in a state. In each case the algorithms ran in a realistic setting with no access to actions that lie in the future. There are few users who performed enough actions to allow for meaningful analysis on a per-user basis, so the data were treated as if produced by a single user in successive sessions. We believe that the applications are simple enough and the user's goals and experience levels similar enough to validate this simplification. The differences in the percentages of actions that can be predicted for each application stem partially from the differing number of actions recorded for each, but also from the nature of the application. First, the random prediction baseline shows that as a tendency the number of possible actions for a given interface states increases with the number of total actions we record from users. Second, the frequency measure demonstrates that slightly less than half the actions in any of the applications can simply be predicted from the frequency distribution recorded in an interface state. Third, It is expected that with less data to predict from all prediction performances decrease, except that of the random predictions. As expected, ONISI degrades more gracefully than IPAM, because IPAM requires some time for its predicted probabilities to converge.

As for the difference in prediction performance of ONISI and IPAM as compared to the frequency measure in the search and neural network applications: the recorded history for the search application includes long runs of the students stepping through a problem. These runs consist entirely of one action, and are easy to predict for either algorithm, making the overall prediction percentages of ONISI and IPAM high and close in value. Neither the neural net nor the constraint application show this type of student behaviour in the histories. To document this fact we recorded the average maximum match length ONISI detects when finding the k nearest neighbours. For the search application, this average lies at a length of 14.2 steps, whereas for the Neural Net application it is 4.6 steps, indicating that indeed long sequence matches are abundant in the search application.

Overall, ONISI performs better for each application with statistical significance at greater than 95% confidence as given by a chi-square test using a directional hypothesis for each of the applications. Why does ONISI perform better? Some clear patterns emerge when looking at the specific actions that it predicts but IPAM (and, we suspect, other approaches that work from a very short, fixed length interaction history) fail to predict:

- While the IPAM probability estimates take some time to converge for a new user, ONISI is able to identify a distinct behavioural pattern if it has only occurred once before.
- ONISI successfully identifies state information hidden in the user's history beyond the last action. For example, there are two modes in which users seem to learn about search algorithms with the search application. In one mode, a user will switch to a new search algorithm and step through the problem by hand to learn how the algorithm works.

State	Action
Stepping	ActionEvent on Step
Goal Node Reached after Stepping	ActionEvent on Ok
Stepping	ActionEvent on Reset Search
Problem Solution Mode	ItemEvent on Breadth First Search
Problem Solution Mode	ActionEvent on Step

Table 1: Typical Search Action Sequences

In the other mode, as exemplified in Table 1, a user wants to learn about the result of different search algorithms, rather than the process, and immediately displays this result after switching to a new search algorithm. The problem for IPAM consists of the fact that the last action, namely the switch to a different search algorithm, does not encode the mode in which the user is currently using the application. In fact, often even the last few actions are not sufficient to identify this mode, because the user has likely just finished another search problem and clicked through a sequence of result dialogues - a sequence that is the same for either mode. ONISI, however, easily distinguishes these modes, because it finds some nearest neighbours that match the whole history sequence in the Table 1 and further actions. These are of greater length than sequences that only match backwards to where the goal node was reached, but contain the actions to immediately show a search result before that point.

Even more interesting than the fact that ONISI performs better than IPAM is that they predict different actions correctly. For the search application, there are 160 cases (ca. 7.5%) in which one of the algorithms predicts correctly and the other does not. This means that one does not replace the other, and in the concluding section below we argue that there is a systematic reason for this that can be exploited in further research.

Conclusion and Future Work

We have successfully designed and implemented a system that builds a model of an application, its graphical user interface and its user without requiring any modification of the application or any interaction with the user. We showed this approach can be used to predict future user actions by establishing the state space the user navigates together with the policy he or she uses to decide upon actions. To do so, we establish interface states of the application to build a coarse version of this state space and subsequently refine it. Our refinement algorithm identifies the k nearest neighbours to the immediate history and a possible next action and from their length estimates the action's likelihood, thus implicitly identifying the current state. This prediction method works better than other known future action prediction algorithms, but differs from them in which actions it can predict successfully.

Throughout the paper we identify the main differences between our approach and IPAM. These differences point to some of the main issues to be addressed:

1. ONISI and IPAM predict based on very different features of the recorded history. ONISI finds matching behavioural patters, whereas IPAM collects statistics about pairs of actions that occur in sequence. ONISI performs better than IPAM for the data in question in this paper, but the choice of predictor seems somewhat arbitrary.
2. ONISI and IPAM are able to predict different actions. To us, this indicates that neither of them is the ideal solution to the next action prediction problem.
3. An added simple frequency measure enhances our match length based implicit state identification.

These issues all point to the fact that the choice of patterns to mine from history and the measure to use in interpreting them dictate which actions a given algorithm can successfully predict. Ideally, the lessons learned from comparing ONISI to IPAM will let us design an algorithm that can trade off between the possible choices and draw from the predictive success of both approaches.

Finally, we are currently working on OFESI, an explicit, off-line version of ONISI (Gorniak and Poole 2000). That algorithm has a different goal from ONISI in that it should introduce new states when they explain a large fraction of actions in the overall application usage. ONISI, on the other hand, predicts the next action successfully at a given point in time even if that action occurs extremely rarely. Our results show that the explicit state graph inferred by OFESI captures the application and its usage well and can serve as a tool for application designers to analyse the application and to augment it with other intelligent interface components. Also, there are strong relationships between building such a stochastic dynamic model and deriving states for Hidden Markov Models, opening up a whole new realm of applications in the general field of sequence modeling (Rabiner 1989, Seymore, McCallum and Rosenfeld 1999).

References

Albrecht, D. W., Zukerman, I., Nicholson, A. E. and Bud, A.: 1997, Towards a bayesian model for keyhole plan recognition in large domains, *User Modeling: Proceedings of the Sixth International Conference, UM97*.

Boutilier, C., Dean, T. and Hanks, S.: 1999, Decision-theoretic planning: Structural assumptions and computational leverage, *Journal of AI Research* **11**, 1–94.

Davison, B. D. and Hirsh, H.: 1998, Predicting sequences of user actions, *Technical report*, Rutgers, The State University of New York.

Debevc, M., Meyer, B., Donlagic, D. and Svecko, R.: 1996, Design and evaluation of an adaptive icon toolbar, *User Modeling and User-Adapted Interaction* **6**(1), 1–21.

Encarnacao, L.: 1997, *Concept and Realization of intelligent user support in interactive graphics applications*, PhD thesis, Eberhard-Karls-Universität Tübingen, Fakultät für Informatik.

Gorniak, P. J.: 1998, Sorting email messages by topic. Project Report.

Gorniak, P. J. and Poole, D. L.: 2000, Building a stochastic dynamic model of application use. Forthcoming.

Horvitz, E., Breese, J., Heckerman, D., Hovel, D. and Rommelse, K.: 1998, The lumiere project: Bayesian user modeling for inferring the goals and needs of software users, *Uncertainty in Artifical Intelligence, Proceedings of the Fourteenth Conference*.

JDK: 1998, *Java Development Kit Documentation*. http://java.sun.com/products/jdk/1.1/docs/index.html

Lane, T.: 1999, Hidden markov models for human/computer interface modeling, *Proceedings of the IJCAI-99 Workshop on Learning about Users*, pp. 35–44.

Lieberman, H.: 1998, Integrating user interface agents with conventional applications, *Proceedings of the International Conference on Intelligent User Interfaces, San Francisco*.

McCallum, A. R.: 1996, Instance-based state identification for reinforcement learning, *Technical report*, University of Rochester.

Rabiner, L.: 1989, A tutorial on hidden markov models and selected applications in speech recognition, *Proceedings of the IEEE*, Vol. 77(2).

Ruvini, J.-D. and Dory, C.: 2000, Ape: Learning user's habits to automate repetitive tasks, *Proceedings of the International Conference on Intelligent User Interfaces*.

Seymore, K., McCallum, A. R. and Rosenfeld, R.: 1999, Learning hidden markov model structure for information extraction, *AAAI-99 Workshop on Machine Learning for Information Extraction*.

Zukerman, I., Albrecht, D. and Nicholson, A.: 1999, Predicting users' requests on the www, *User Modeling: Proceedings of the 7th International Conference, UM99*.

Acquiring Problem-Solving Knowledge from End Users: Putting Interdependency Models to the Test

Jihie Kim and Yolanda Gil

Information Sciences Institute and Computer Science Department
University of Southern California
4676 Admiralty Way
Marina del Rey, CA 90292, U.S.A.
jihie@isi.edu, gil@isi.edu

Abstract

Developing tools that allow non-programmers to enter knowledge has been an ongoing challenge for AI. In recent years researchers have investigated a variety of promising approaches to knowledge acquisition (KA), but they have often been driven by the needs of knowledge engineers rather than by end users. This paper reports on a series of experiments that we conducted in order to understand how far a particular KA tool that we are developing is from meeting the needs of end users, and to collect valuable feedback to motivate our future research. This KA tool, called EMeD, exploits Interdependency Models that relate individual components of the knowledge base in order to guide users in specifying problem-solving knowledge. We describe how our experiments helped us address several questions and hypotheses regarding the acquisition of problem-solving knowledge from end users and the benefits of Interdependency Models, and discuss what we learned in terms of improving not only our KA tools but also about KA research and experimental methodology.

Introduction

Acquiring knowledge from end users (i.e., ordinary users without formal training in computer science) remains a challenging area for AI research. Many knowledge acquisition approaches target knowledge engineers (Wielinga, Schreiber, & Breuker 1992; Yost 1993; Fikes, Farquhar, & Rice 1997), and those that have been developed for end users (Eriksson *et al.* 1995; Marcus & McDermott 1989) only allow them to specify certain kinds of knowledge, i.e., domain-specific knowledge regarding instances and classes but not problem-solving knowledge about how to solve tasks. Alternative approaches apply learning and induction techniques to examples provided by users in a natural way as they are performing a task (Mitchell, Mahadevan, & Steinberg 1985; Cypher 1993; Bareiss, Porter, & Murray 1989). Although these tools may be more accessible to end users, they are only useful in circumstances where users can provide a variety of examples. When examples are not readily available, we may need knowledge acquisition (KA) tools for direct authoring.

Copyright ©2000, American Association for Artificial Intelligence (www.aaai.org). All rights reserved.

In recent years, researchers have investigated a variety of new approaches to develop KA tools, in many cases targeted to end users though in practice motivated by knowledge engineers. Few user studies have been conducted (Yost 1993; Tallis & Gil 1999; Kim & Gil 1999), and the participants are typically knowledge engineers. Without studies of the effectiveness of KA approaches and tools for end users, it is hard to assess the actual requirement of end users and our progress towards satisfying them. One of the challenges of this work is to devise a methodology and experimental procedure for conducting user studies of KA tools.

As KA researchers, we wanted to test our approach and KA tools with end users. A central theme of our KA research has been how KA tools can exploit *Interdependency Models* (Swartout & Gil 1995) that relate individual components of the knowledge base in order to develop expectations of what users need to add next. To give an example of interdependencies, suppose that the user is building a KBS for a configuration task that finds constraint violations and then applies fixes to them (Marcus & McDermott 1989). When the user defines a new constraint, the KA tool has the expectation that the user should specify possible fixes, because there is an interdependency between the problem-solving knowledge for finding fixes for violated constraints and the definitions of constraints and their possible fixes.

EMeD (EXPECT Method Developer) (Kim & Gil 1999), a knowledge acquisition tool to acquire problem-solving knowledge, exploits Interdependency Models to guide users by helping them understand the relationships among the individual elements in the knowledge base. The expectations result from enforcing constraints in the knowledge representation system, working out incrementally the interdependencies among the different components of the KB. Our hypothesis is that Interdependency Models allow users to enter more knowledge faster, particularly for end users.

In addition to the goal of evaluating the role of Interdependency Models, we had more general questions. Users with different degrees of exposure to computing environments would probably perform differently. But in what ways? How much training and of what kind is needed before they can make reasonably complex additions to a knowledge base with a KA tool? What aspects of a knowledge base modification task are more challenging to end users? What

```
((name method1)
  (capability (check (obj (?f is (spec-of force-ratio)))
                     (of (?t is (spec-of main-task)))
                     (in (?c is (inst-of COA))))))
  (result-type (inst-of yes-no))
  (method (check (obj (spec-of force-ratio))
                 (of (main-task-of (close-statement-of ?c))))))
((name method2)
  (capability (check (obj (spec-of (force-ratio)))
                     (of (?t is (inst-of military-task)))))
  (result-type (inst-of yes-no))
  (method (is-less-or-equal
           (obj (estimate (obj (spec-of required-force-ratio))
                          (for ?t)))
           (than (estimate (obj (spec-of available-force-ratio))
                           (for ?t))))))
((name method3)
  (capability (estimate (obj (?f is (spec-of required-force-ratio)))
                        (for (?s is (inst-of military-task)))))
  (result-type (inst-of number))
  (method ...))
((name method4)
  (capability (estimate (obj (?f is (spec-of available-force-ratio)))
                        (for (?t is (inst-of military-task)))))
  (result-type (inst-of number))
  (method ....))
```

Figure 1: Examples of EXPECT Problem-Solving Methods.

kinds of interfaces and interaction modalities would be appropriate and in what ways should they be different from those that knowledge engineers find useful?

This paper reports on a study to evaluate our KA tools with domain experts (end users) who extended a knowledge base in their area of expertise. This study was conducted as part of an evaluation of the DARPA High Performance Knowledge Bases program (Cohen *et al.* 1998). We also present our experimental design and the preliminary study with users with varying degrees of background in AI and computer science, which was performed before the evaluation. We analyze the results in terms of our initial questions and hypotheses, and extract some general conclusions that motivate future directions of KA research.

EMeD: Exploiting Interdependency Models to Acquire Problem-Solving Knowledge

EMeD (EXPECT Method Developer) (Kim & Gil 1999) is a knowledge acquisition tool that allows users to specify problem-solving knowledge. This section summarizes the functionality of the tool, further details and comparison with other tools are provided in (Kim & Gil 1999).

EMeD is built within the EXPECT framework (Gil & Melz 1996; Swartout & Gil 1995). EXPECT's knowledge base contains ontologies that describe the objects in a domain, and problem-solving methods that describe how tasks are achieved. Tasks are specified as goal hierarchies, where a goal is broken into smaller subgoals all the way down to primitive or basic tasks. The problem-solving methods specify how the decomposition takes place. EXPECT provides a rich language that was developed with understandability and intelligibility in mind, since it was used to generate adequate explanations for knowledge-based systems

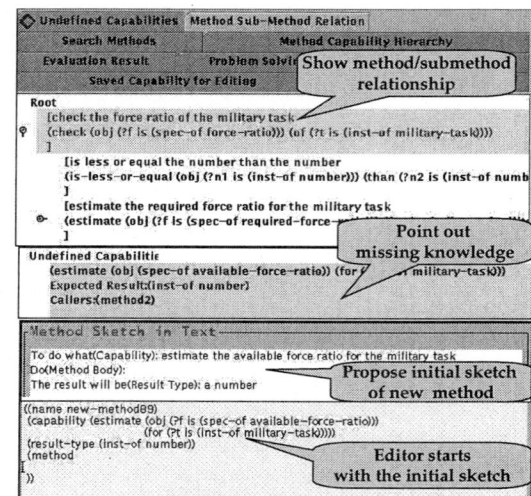

Figure 2: The Method Proposer of the EMeD Acquisition Interface.

(Swartout, Paris, & Moore 1991). Figure 1 shows some examples of EXPECT methods. Each problem-solving method has a *capability* that describes what the method can achieve, a *result type* that specifies the kind of result that the method will return upon invocation, and a *method body* that specifies the procedure to achieve the capability. The method body includes constructs for invoking subgoals to be resolved with other methods, retrieving values of concept roles, and control constructs such as conditional expressions and iteration. The arrows in the figure indicate some interdependencies, where a head of an arrow points to a sub-method which can solve a given subgoal. For example, the second method shown in the Figure 1 checks the force ratio of a given military task by comparing its required force ratio and the available force ratio. The result should be yes or no depending on whether the required ratio is less than the available ratio.

EXPECT derives an *Interdependency Model* (IM) by analyzing how individual components of a knowledge base are related and interact when they are used to solve a task. An example of interdependency between two methods is that one may be used by the other one to achieve a subgoal in its method body. Two methods can also be related because they have similar capabilities. EMeD exploits IM in three ways: (1) pointing out missing pieces at a given time; (2) predicting what pieces are related and how; (3) detecting inconsistencies among the definitions of the various elements in the knowledge base.

When users define a new problem-solving method, EMeD first finds the interdependencies and inconsistencies within that element, such as if any undefined variable is used in the body of the method. If there are any errors within a method definition, the *Local-Error Detector* displays the errors and it also highlights the incorrect definitions so that the user can be alerted promptly. The *Global-Error Detector* analyzes the knowledge base further and detects more subtle errors that occur in the context of problem solving.

By keeping the interdependencies among the problem-solving methods and factual knowledge, and analyzing interdependencies between each method and its sub-methods, the *Method Sub-method Analyzer* in EMeD can detect missing links and can find undefined problem-solving methods that need to be added. EMeD highlights those missing parts and proposes an initial version of the new methods, as shown in Figure 2. In this example, a method for checking the force ratio for an assigned task needs to compare the available force ratio (i.e, ratio between blue units and red units) with the force ratio required for that task. When the system is missing the knowledge for the available ratio (i.e., missing method4), the *Method Proposer* in EMeD notifies the user with a red diamond (a diamond shown in Figure 2 on the top) and displays the ones needed to be defined. It can also construct an initial sketch of the capability and the result type of the new method to be defined. What the new method has to do (capability of the method) is to estimate the available force ratio for a given military task. Since we are computing a ratio, the result type suggested is a number (method sketch in Figure 2). Users can search for existing methods that can achieve a given kind of capability using the *Method-Capability Hierarchy*, a hierarchy of method capabilities based on subsumption relations of their goal names and their parameters.

Finally, EMeD can propose how the methods can be put together. By using the Method Sub-method Analyzer for analyzing the interdependencies among the KB elements, it can detect still unused problem-solving methods and propose how they may be potentially used in the system.

Experimental Design

As described in the introduction, current KA research lacks evaluation methodology. In recognition of the need for evaluation, the community started to design a set of standard task domains that different groups would implement and use to compare their work. These Sisyphus experiments (Schreiber & Birmingham 1996; Sisyphus 2000) show how different groups would compare their approaches for the same given task, but most approaches lacked a KA tool and no user evaluations were conducted. Other evaluations have tested the use and reuse of problem-solving methods, but they measure code reuse rather than how users benefit from KA tools (Runkel & Birmingham 1995; Eriksson *et al.* 1995). Other KA work evaluated the tool itself. TAQL's performance was evaluated by comparing it with some basic data that had been reported for other KA tools (Yost 1993). There were some user studies on ontology editors (Terveen 1991). In contrast with our work, these evaluations were done with knowledge engineers. Also since the experiments were not controlled studies, the results could not be causally linked to the features in the tools.

Our research group has conducted some of the few user studies to date (Tallis & Gil 1999; Kim & Gil 1999), and as a result we have proposed a methodology (Tallis, Kim, & Gil 1999) that we use in our own work. It turns our that the lack of user studies is not uncommon in the software sciences (Zelkowitz & Wallace 1998). In developing a methodology for evaluation of KA tools, we continue to draw from the experiences in other areas (Self 1993; Basili, Selby, & Hutchens 1986; Olson & Moran 1998).

Our goal was to test two main hypotheses, both concerned with Interdependency Models (IMs):

Hypothesis I: A KA tool that exploits IMs *enables users to make a wider range of changes* to a knowledge base because without the guidance provided with IMs users will be unable to understand how the new knowledge fits with the existing knowledge and complete the modification.

Hypothesis II: A KA tool that exploits IMs *enables users to enter knowledge faster* because it can use the IMs to point out to the user at any given time what additional knowledge still needs to be provided.

There are three important features of our experiment design:

- In order to collect data comparable across users and tasks, we used a controlled experiment. Thus, we designed modification tasks to be given to the participants based on typical tasks that we encountered ourselves as we developed the initial knowledge base.

- Given the hypotheses, we needed to collect and compare data about how users would perform these tasks under two conditions: with a tool that exploits IMs and with a tool that does not (this would be the control group). It is very important that the use of IMs be the only difference between both conditions. We designed an ablated version of EMeD that presented the same EMeD interface but did not provide any of the assistance based on IMs.

- Typically, there are severe resource constraints in terms of how many users are available to do the experiments (it typically takes several sessions over a period of days). In order to minimize the effect of individual differences given the small number of subjects, we performed within-subject experiments. Each subject performed two different but comparable sets of tasks (each involving the same kind of KA tasks but using a different part of the knowledge base), one with each version of the tool.

In order to determine when a KA task was completed, the subjects were asked to solve some problems and examine the output to make sure they obtained the expected results. In addition, after each experiment, we checked by hand the knowledge added by the subjects.

Participants were given different combinations of tools and tasks and in different order, so as to minimize transfer effects (i.e., where they would remember how they did something the second time around).

EMeD was instrumented to collect data about the user's performance, including actions in the interface (e.g., commands invoked and buttons selected), the knowledge base contents at each point in time, and the time at which each user action takes place. These provide objective measurements about task completion time and the use of specific features. Since this data was insufficient to understand what things users found hard and difficult to do with the

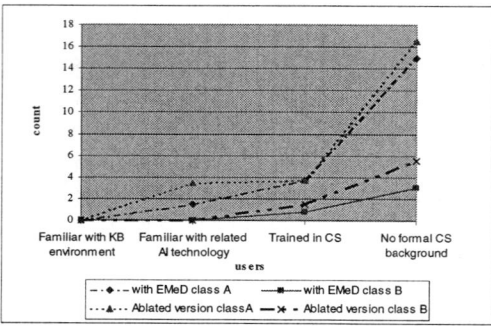

Figure 3: Average number of hints given to each group of subjects during the preliminary user study.

tool or why a certain action was not taken, we collected additional information during the experiment. We asked users to voice what they were thinking and what they were doing and recorded them in transcripts and in videotapes (during the experiments with domain experts). We also prepared a questionnaire to get their feedback, where instead of questions with free form answers we designed questions that could be answered with a grade from 1 (worst) to 5 (best).

Preliminary Study

Since it is expensive to run user studies and hard to get domain experts in the field, we wanted to filter out distractions which are unrelated with our claim, such as problems with the tool that are not related to Interdependency Models. We also wanted to understand whether our interface and KA tool are appropriate for end users and how different types of users interact with it, so that we can improve our tools and our experimental methodology. For these reasons, we performed a preliminary study before the actual evaluation with domain experts.

The study used a spectrum of users that had gradually less background in AI and CS (Kim & Gil 2000). We had (1) four knowledge engineers who had not used EMeD before but were familiar with EXPECT, (2) two knowledge engineers not familiar with EXPECT but that had experience with knowledge-based systems, (3) four users not familiar with AI but had formal training in computer science, and (4) two users with no formal training in AI or CS.

Since a major goal of this preliminary study was to understand our KA tool, we allowed the subjects to ask for hints when they were not able to make progress in the task (this was not allowed in the final evaluation). These hints allow us to categorize the basic types of difficulties experienced by users and adjust the tool based on them.

Figure 3 shows the number of hints given to the subjects in this study. More hints were always needed with the ablated version. The number of hints increases dramatically when subjects lack CS background. We analyzed all the hints, and separated them into two major categories. Class A hints consist of simple help on language and syntax, or clarification of the tasks given. Since syntax errors are unrelated to our claims about IMs, we developed a Structured Editor for the new version of EMeD (version 2) that

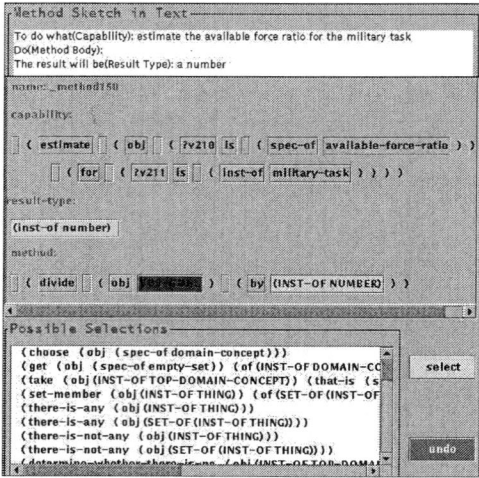

Figure 4: Structured Editor.

guides users to follow the correct syntax. Figure 4 shows the new editor which guides the users to follow the correct syntax. Users can build a method just using point and click operations without typing.

Class B hints were of a more serious nature. For example, users asked for help to compose goal descriptions, or to invoke a method with the appropriate parameters. Although the number of times these hints were given is smaller and the number is even smaller with EMeD, they suggest new functionality that future versions of EMeD should eventually provide to users. The subjects indicated that sometimes the tool was showing too many items, making it hard to read although they expected this would not be a problem after they had used the tool for a while and had become used to it. Since these presentation issues were affecting the results of the experiment and are not directly evaluating the IMs, the new version of EMeD (version 2) has more succinct views of some of the information, showing details only when the user asks for them. Other hints pointed out new ways to exploit IMs in order to guide users and would require more substantial extensions to EMeD that we did not add to the new version. One area of difficulty for subjects was expressing composite relations (e.g., given a military task, retrieve its assigned units and then retrieve the echelons of those assigned units). Although EMeD helped users in various ways to match goals and methods, in some cases the users still asked the experimenters for hints and could have benefited from additional help. The fundamental difficulties of goal composition and using relations still remained as questions for the real experiment.

In addition to improving the tool, we debugged and examined our experimental procedure, including tutorial, instrumentation, questionnaire, etc., especially based on the the results from the fourth group.

We found out how much time end users would need to learn to use our tools. The tutorial given to the users was done with simpler sample tasks from the same knowledge base. The training time was significantly longer and harder for the subjects with no technical background (2 hours for knowledge engineers and 7.5 hours for the project assistants). More details of this study are discussed in (Kim & Gil 2000), showing that even the end users were able to finish complex tasks, and that the KA tool saves more time as users have less technical background.

As described above, we extended our tool based on the pre-test results, creating a new version of EMeD (version 2). The next section describes the evaluation with domain experts with this new version of EMeD.

Experiment with Domain Experts

The participants in this experiment were Army officers facilitated by the Army Battle Command Battle Lab (BCBL) at Ft Leavenworth, KS. They were asked to use our KA tools to extend a knowledge based system for critiquing military courses of action. Each subject participated in four half-day sessions over a period of two days. The first session was a tutorial of EXPECT and an overview of the COA critiquer. The second session was a tutorial of EMeD and a hands-on practice with EMeD and with the ablated version. In the third and fourth sessions we performed the experiment, where the subjects were asked to perform the modification tasks, in one session using EMeD and in the other using the ablated version. Only four subjects agreed to participate in our experiment, due to the time commitment required.

An important difference with the previous study is that during this experiment subjects were not allowed to ask for hints, only clarifications on the instructions provided. As soon as a participant would indicate that they could not figure out how to proceed, we would terminate that part of the experiment. In order to collect finer-grained data about how many tasks they could complete, we gave each subject four knowledge base modification tasks to do with each version of the KA tool. The reason is that if we gave them one single task and they completed almost but not all of it then we would not have any objective data concerning our two initial hypotheses. The four tasks were related, two of them were simpler and two more complex. The easier tasks required simple modifications to an existing method (e.g., generalize the existing methods that compute the required force ratio for "destroy" tasks into methods that can compute the ratio for any military tasks in general). The more complex tasks required adding new methods, such as the second method shown in Figure 1.

Results and Discussion

The main results are shown in Figure 5. Figure 5-(a) shows the average time to complete tasks (for the completed tasks only). None of the subjects was able to do the more complex tasks with the ablated version of EMeD. Where data is available (the easier tasks), subjects were able to finish the tasks faster with EMeD. Figure 5-(b) shows the number of tasks that the subjects completed with EMeD and with the ablated version, both by task category and overall. The solid part of the bars show the number of tasks completed. We show with patterned bars the portion of the uncompleted tasks that was done when the subjects stopped and gave up

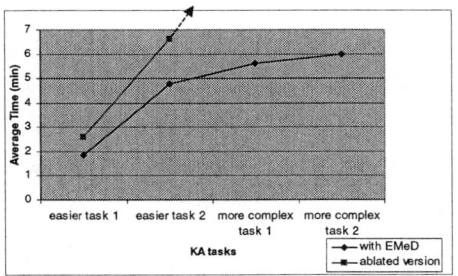

(a) Average time to complete tasks

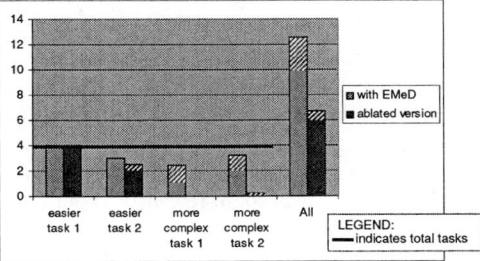

(b) Tasks completed

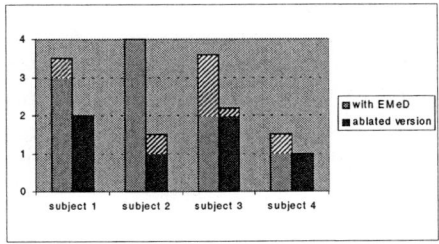

(c) Tasks completed (for each subject)

Figure 5: Results of the evaluation with domain experts.

(we estimated this based on the portion of the new knowledge that was added). Figure 5-(c) shows the same data but broken down by subject[1]. The results show that on average subjects were able to accomplish with EMeD almost twice as many tasks as they accomplished with the ablated version. The results support our claims that Interdependency Models can provide significant help to end users in extending knowledge bases.

It would be preferable to test additional subjects, but it is often hard for people (especially domain experts) to commit the time required to participate in this kind of study. Given the small number of subjects and tasks involved it does not seem appropriate to analyze the statistical significance of our results, although we have done so for some of the initial experiments with EMeD with a t-test showing that they were significant at the 0.05 level with $t(2)=7.03$, $p < .02$. Gathering data from more subjects may be more reassuring than using these tests for validation.

Our experience with these experiments motivates us to share a few of the lessons that we have learned about knowl-

---

[1]We had noticed early on that Subject 4 had a different background from the other three, but unfortunately we were not able to get an alternative subject.

Functionality	Avg No. invocations	Usefulness rating	No. Users who used it
Method Proposer	10.5 (1.25)	4.7	4
Method Sub-method Analyzer	8.5	4.3	4
Method-Capability Hierarchy	2.75	4.5	2
Global-Error Detector	3	3.3	4

Table 1: Average Use of EMeD's Functionality.

edge acquisition research:

- **Can end users use current KA tools to modify the problem-solving knowledge of a knowledge-based system? How much training do they need to start using such KA tools? Would they be able to understand and use a formal language?**

  As we described earlier, we spent 8 hours (two half-day sessions) for training. They spent roughly half of that time learning EXPECT's language and how to put the problem-solving methods together to solve problems. The rest of the time was spent learning about the KA tool and its ablated version. We believe that this time can be reduced by improving the tool's interface and adding on-line help. We also recognize that more training may be needed if users are expected to make much more complex changes to the knowledge base. At the same time, if they did not need to be trained on how to use an ablated version of the tool they would not need to learn as many details as our subjects did.

  Our subjects got used to the language and could quickly formulate new problem-solving methods correctly. They did not seem to have a problem using some of the complex aspects of our language, such as the control structures (e.g., if-then-else statement) and variables. It took several examples to learn to express procedural knowledge into methods and sub-methods and to solve problems. EMeD helps this process by automatically constructing sub-method sketches and showing the interdependencies among the methods. Retrieving role values through composite relations was also hard. Providing a better way to visualize and to find this kind of information would be very useful.

  As a result of this experiment, we believe that with current technology it is possible to develop KA tools that enable end users to add relatively small amounts of new problem solving knowledge, and that they can be trained to do so in less than a day.

- **How much do Interdependency Models help? What additional features should be added to our KA tools?**

  Overall, the Interdependency Models exploited via different features in EMeD were useful for performing KA tasks. Table 1 shows the average use of each of the Components of EMeD, in terms of the number of times the user invoked them[2]. The subjects were very enthusiastic about the tool's capabilities, and on occasion would point

[2] We show the number of times the users selected them, except for the Method Proposer where we show the number of times the system showed it automatically as well as the number of times selected (in parenthesis) when applicable.

out how some of the features would have helped when they were using only the ablated version.

According to the answers to the questionnaire, using EMeD it was easier to see what pieces are interrelated. That is, visualizing super/sub method relations using Method Sub-method Analyzer was rated as useful (4.3/5). Also detecting missing knowledge and adding it was easier with EMeD's hints. Highlighting missing problem-solving methods and creating initial sketch based on interdependencies (by Method Proposer) were found to be the most useful (4.7/5).

The Structured Editor used in this version of EMeD provided very useful guidance, and there were less errors for individual method definitions. The Local-Error Detector was not used for the given tasks.

- **What aspects of a modification task are more challenging to end users?**

  Almost everyone could do simple modifications, which required that the subjects browse and understand the given methods to find one method to be modified and then changing it.

  Some subjects had difficulties starting the KA tasks, when EMeD does not point to a particular element of the KB to start with. Although they could use the search capability in EMeD or look up related methods in the Method-Capability Hierarchy, this was more difficult for them than when the tool highlighted relevant information.

  Typically, a KA task involves more than one step, and sometimes subjects are not sure if they are on the right track even if they have been making progress. A KA tool that keeps track of what they are doing in the context of the overall task and lets them know about their progress would be very helpful. Some of the research in using Knowledge Acquisition Scripts to keep track of how individual modifications contribute to complex changes (Tallis & Gil 1999) could be integrated with EMeD.

- **How do KA tools need to be different for different kinds of users**

  We did not know whether end users would need a completely different interface altogether. It seems that a few improvements to the presentation in order to make the tool easier to use was all they needed. We did not expect that syntax errors would be so problematic, and developing a structured editor solved this problem easily. On the other hand, we were surprised that end users found some of the features useful when we had expected that they would cause confusion. For example, a feature in the original EMeD that we thought would be distractive and disabled is organizing problem-solving methods into a hierarchy. However, the feedback from the end users indicates that they would have found it useful.

  Although EMeD is pro-active in providing guidance, we believe that some users would perform better if we used better visual cues or pop-up windows to show the guidance. As the users are more removed from the details, the KA tool needs to do a better job at emphasizing and making them aware of what is important.

Conclusions

In this paper, we presented an evaluation of a KA tool for acquiring problem-solving knowledge from end users who do not have programming skills. We described the experimental procedure we have designed to evaluate KA tools, and how we refined the design with a preliminary user study with users with gradually less background in AI and computer science. The KA tool that we tested exploits Interdependency Models, and the results show that it helped end users to enter more knowledge faster. We also discussed additional lessons that we have learned that should be useful to other knowledge acquisition researchers.

Acknowledgments

We gratefully acknowledge the support of DARPA with grant F30602-97-1-0195 as part of the DARPA High Performance Knowledge Bases Program. We are indebted to the many subjects, especially the military officers from the Army Battle Command Battle Lab (BCBL) at Ft Leavenworth, KS, who participated in the experiments for their time and their patience. We would like to thank Surya Ramachandran, Marcelo Tallis, and Jim Blythe for their help during the experiment. We also would like to thank Jon Gratch for helpful comments on earlier drafts.

References

Bareiss, R.; Porter, B.; and Murray, K. 1989. Supporting start-to-finish development of knowledge bases. *Machine Learning* 4:259–283.

Basili, V.; Selby, R. W.; and Hutchens, D. H. 1986. Experimentation in software engineering. *IEEE Transactions in Software Engineering* SE-12(7).

Cohen, P.; Schrag, R.; Jones, E.; Pease, A.; Lin, A.; Starr, B.; Gunning, D.; and Burke, M. 1998. The DARPA High Performance Knowledge Bases Project. *AI Magazine* 19(4).

Cypher, A. 1993. *Watch what I do: Programming by demonstration*. MIT Press.

Eriksson, H.; Shahar, Y.; Tu, S. W.; Puerta, A. R.; and Musen, M. 1995. Task modeling with reusable problem-solving methods. *Artificial Intelligence* 79:293–326.

Fikes, R.; Farquhar, A.; and Rice, J. 1997. Tools for assembling modular ontologies in Ontolingua. In *Proceedings of the Fourteenth National Conference on Artificial Intelligence*, 436–441.

Gil, Y., and Melz, E. 1996. Explicit representations of problem-solving strategies to support knowledge acquisition. In *Proceedings of the Thirteenth National Conference on Artificial Intelligence*.

Kim, J., and Gil, Y. 1999. Deriving expectations to guide knowledge base creation. In *Proceedings of the Sixteenth National Conference on Artificial Intelligence*, 235–241.

Kim, J., and Gil, Y. 2000. User studies of an interdependency-based interface for acquiring problem-solving knowledge. In *Proceedings of the Intelligent User Interface Conference*, 165–168.

Marcus, S., and McDermott, J. 1989. SALT: A knowledge acquisition language for propose-and-revise systems. *Artificial Intelligence* 39(1):1–37.

Mitchell, T.; Mahadevan, S.; and Steinberg, L. 1985. LEAP: A learning apprentice for VLSI design. In *Proceedings of the 1985 International Joint Conference on Artificial Intelligence*.

Olson, G. M., and Moran, T. P. 1998. Special issue on experimental comparisons of usability evaluation methods. *Human-Computer Interaction* 13.

Runkel, J. T., and Birmingham, W. P. 1995. Knowledge acquisition in the small: Building knowledge-acquisition tools from pieces. *Knowledge Acquisition* 5(2):221–243.

Schreiber, A. T., and Birmingham, W. P. 1996. The Sisyphus-VT initiative. *International Journal of Human-Computer Studies* 44(3/4).

Self, J. 1993. Special issue on evaluation. *Journal of Artificial Intelligence in Education* 4(2/3).

Sisyphus. 2000. Sisyphus projects. http://ksi.cpsc.ucalgary.ca/KAW/Sisyphus/.

Swartout, W., and Gil, Y. 1995. EXPECT: Explicit representations for flexible acquisition. In *Proceedings of the Ninth Knowledge-Acquisition for Knowledge-Based Systems Workshop*.

Swartout, W. R.; Paris, C. L.; and Moore, J. D. 1991. Design for explainable expert systems. *IEEE Expert* 6(3).

Tallis, M., and Gil, Y. 1999. Designing scripts to guide users in modifying knowledge-based systems. In *Proceedings of the Sixteenth National Conference on Artificial Intelligence*.

Tallis, M.; Kim, J.; and Gil, Y. 1999. User studies of knowledge acquisition tools: Methodology and lessons learned. In *Proceedings of the Twelfth Knowledge-Acquisition for Knowledge-Based Systems Workshop*.

Terveen, L. 1991. *Person-Computer Cooperation Through Collaborative Manipulation*. Ph.D. Dissertation, University of Texas at Austin.

Wielinga, B. J.; Schreiber, A. T.; and Breuker, A. 1992. KADS: a modelling approach to knowledge acquisition. *Knowledge Acquisition* 4(1):5–54.

Yost, G. R. 1993. Knowledge acquisition in Soar. *IEEE Expert* 8(3):26–34.

Zelkowitz, M., and Wallace, D. 1998. Experimental models for validating computer technology. *IEEE Computer* 31(5):23–31.

Predicting UNIX Command Lines:
Adjusting to User Patterns

Benjamin Korvemaker and **Russell Greiner**

{benjamin, greiner}@cs.ualberta.ca
Department of Computing Science
University of Alberta
Edmonton, Canada

Abstract

As every user has his own idiosyncrasies and preferences, an interface that is honed for one user may be problematic for another. To accommodate a diverse range of users, many computer applications therefore include an interface that can be *customized* — e.g., by adjusting parameters, or defining macros. This allows each user to have his "own" version of the interface, honed to his specific preferences. However, most such interfaces require the user to perform this customization by hand — a tedious process that requires the user to be aware of his personal preferences. We are therefore exploring *adaptive* interfaces, that can autonomously determine the user's preference, and adjust the interface appropriately.

This paper describes such an adaptive system — here a UNIX-shell that can predict the user's next command, and then use this prediction to simplify the user's future interactions. We present a relatively simple model here, then explore a variety of techniques to improve its accuracy, including a "mixture of experts" model. In a series of experiments, on real-world data, we demonstrate (1) that the simple system can correctly predict the user's next command almost 50% of the time, and can do so robustly — across a range of different users; and (2) that it is extremely difficult to further improve this result.

Keywords: human computer interaction, machine learning, automated modeling

1 Introduction

Today there are a wide variety of interactive computer applications, ranging from web-browsers and searchers, through spreadsheets and database management systems, to editors, as well as games. As these systems become more complicated — as required to be able to accomplish more tasks, better — their interfaces necessarily also become more complex. Many of these systems have begun including tricks to help the users; e.g., if the user begins an empty file with "Dear John", WORD will suggest a "Letter" template; similarly, if the user begins a line with an asterisk (∗), WORD will change that character to a bullet (•) and go into its `List` environment.

Unfortunately, different users have different preferences, therefore the tricks that are appropriate for one user may be problematic for another (e.g., not all users like the fact that WORD automatically formats anything starting with

Copyright © 2000, American Association for Artificial Intelligence (www.aaai.org). All rights reserved.

"http://" as a web link). Moreover, different users want to do different things with the system, as they have very different abilities, background knowledge, styles, etc. This realization — that "one size does NOT fit all" — argues for *customizable* interfaces that can provide different interfaces for different users, and hence allow each user to have an interface that is honed to his individual preferences.

Of course, many of today's application programs can be customized; e.g., most editors and shells include macro- or scripting- facilities. However, this customization process must typically be done *by the user* — this typically means that it is *not* done by the user, as this customization process (1) requires that the user *knows how* to make this modification (e.g., knows both the names of the relevant parameters, and how to modify them); (2) requires the user to be *aware* of his specific preferences, and (3) is usually quite *tedious*.

This research project, therefore, pursues a different approach: Build application systems that can *autonomously* adapt themselves to the individual users. In particular, we focus on techniques for detecting patterns in the user's interactions, and then use this information to make the interaction simpler for the user (perhaps by automatically resetting some system parameters, or defining appropriate new macros).

This paper investigates a specific manifestation of this task: We design and implement a UNIX command shell that predicts the user's behavior from his previous commands, and then uses these predictions to simplify his future interactions with the shell. The rest of this introductory section presents two illustrative examples to help describe our task more precisely. Section 2 provides the background for this work, focusing on the Davison/Hirsh system (DH98) which serves as a precursor to our system. Section 3 first scales their system to address our "learn complete commands" task, and observes that the resulting system can correctly predict the user's next command almost 50% of the time, over a wide range of different users. It then presents a body of well-motivated techniques that should improve on that system — e.g., provide the adaptation system with other types of information, including longer history, etc. Our empirical studies, however, demonstrate that these ideas often produced inferior results. Section 4 explains these disappointing (read "what not to do") results, then presents a slightly different approach, of combining the predictions made by a set of relatively-simple experts, each using its own class of information. It then demonstrates that this ap-

```
[1]  vi cw.c
[2]  make cw
cc -g cw.c -o cw -lm
[3]  cw puzzle01
bus error (core dumped)
[4]  vi cw.c
[5]  make cw
cc -g cw.c -o cw -lm
[6]  cw puzzle01
Solution found in 15584 attempts.
[7]  cw puzzle02
Solution found in 349295 attempts.
[8]  cw puzzle03
segmentation violation (core dumped)
[9]  ddd cw core
[10] vi cw.c
[11] make cw
cc -g cw.c -o cw -lm
Undefined symbol: print first refer-
enced in file cw.o
ld: fatal: Symbol referencing errors. No out-
put written to cw
*** Error code 1
make: Fatal error: Command failed for target 'cw'
[12] vi cw.c
[13] make
cc -g cw.c -o cw -lm
[14] cw puzzle03
Solution found in 13 attempts.
[15] elm -s"it works" fred
```

Figure 1: Wilma's Command Sequences

```
[1]  vi cw.tex
[2]  latex cw.tex
[3]  dvips cw.dvi
[4]  gv cw.ps
[5]  vi cw.tex
[6]  latex cw.tex
[7]  dvips cw.dvi
[8]  gv cw.ps
[9]  vi cw.tex
[10] latex cw.tex
[11] dvips cw.tex
dvips: ! Bad DVI file: first byte not preamble
[12] dvips cw.dvi
[13] gv cw.ps
[14] wall
Can anyone help me with latex???
^D
```

Figure 2: Fred's Command Sequences

proach does work slightly more effectively than the base system. We conclude by arguing that the relatively simple system appears to have "gleaned" essentially all of the accuracy possible from the data collected; if true, this explains why no number of tricks can produce a system that will be significantly more accurate.

1.1 Examples

Figure 1 shows Wilma's interactions with a shell, as she works on her crossword-solving program. It is easy to see that there is a consistent pattern within Wilma's activities; e.g., the vi-make-cw sequence is repeated several times. Although Wilma has taken advantage of traditional UNIX facilities, she still has to type a number of characters.

Now examine Fred's command sequences; Figure 2. He has already completed the assignment and is trying to write up his results. Unfortunately, Fred is not very familiar with LaTeX and is having trouble formatting an equation. Here, an even more obvious pattern is visible. Note that, if Fred had a script to perform the latex-dvips-gv steps for him, he would not have make the mistake of running dvips on a LaTeX source file.

2 Background

UNIX command line prediction appears at first glance to be a trivial task: after all, how many commands can one person possibly use regularly? Although novice users[1] are typically easy to predict (as their command set is typically very small), novice users become advanced users with experience, and these advanced users often use hundreds of commands, and moreover often augment these repertoire of commands over time. Over the last decade, many people in the Human-Computer Interaction (HCI) and Machine Learning (ML) have addressed the task of predicting UNIX command lines. Greenberg collected a large amount of data (Gre88), providing the community with the usage patterns (287,000 command lines) of 168 users of varying skill levels (non-programmers, novice programmers, experienced programmers, and computer scientists), over a period of two to six months. There are approximately 5,100 distinct command stubs[2], ranging from 7 to 359 per user (average = 89) in approximately 62,000 distinct command lines, ranging from 35 to 3,160 per user (average = 467). Although the data is ten years old, it is still quite usable, and provides a reasonable benchmark to compare our work against others.

Davison and Hirsh (DH97; DH98) more recently provided a hand-crafted algorithm that adapts to user activity over time, generating a simple probabilistic model to predict command stubs. They keep track of which sequences of commands are typed, and use this to estimate the probability that any command C_{t+1} will immediately follow each possible C_t. However, predicting a user's next command line is a moving target — e.g., external unobserved events (such as mail arriving or deadlines approaching) can occur, and the user goals can change. As this means the underlying command distribution is not stationary, standard ML techniques are not applicable. Therefore, instead of building a conditional probability table (CPT) based on stub *frequencies*, they instead estimate probabilities in a different fashion: Each time they see one command following another —

---
[1]Novice users (as classified by Greenberg (Gre88)) are typically characterized by a lack of knowledge about existing commands, as well as a lack of knowledge about how to effectively use (or abuse) system resources.

[2]A **stub** is the "executable" of the command, rather than the complete command line — i.e., if the command line is "latex foo.tex", the stub is "latex".

	vi	latex	dvips	gv	wall
vi	0	1	0	0	0
latex	0	0	1	0	0
dvips	0	0	0.16	0.84	0
gv	0.8	0	0	0	0.2

Table 1: Probability of Stub_{t+1} following Stub_t

say $C_t = \texttt{ls}$ and $C_{t+1} = \texttt{make}$ — they first update all of the current $P(C_{next} = \chi \mid C_{current} = \texttt{ls})$ entries by multiplying each by some fixed $\alpha \in (0,1)$; they then add $1 - \alpha$ to the particular $P(C_{next} = \texttt{make} \mid C_{current} = \texttt{ls})$ entry. (Note they explicitly maintain only the observed pairs, and implicitly assign each unseen pair the probability of 0.) For example, applying this scheme (which we call "AUR") to the sequence shown in Figure 2, produces the distribution shown in Table 1. (Here we use $\alpha = 0.8$.)

Their system is "on-line": at each point, after observing the sequence of stubs $\vec{C} = (stub_1, \ldots, stub_t)$, it then predicts the five stubs with the largest probability values: $(stub_{t+1}^{*1}, \ldots, stub_{t+1}^{*5})$. It is then told the correct $stub_{t+1}$ that the user actually typed, which it uses to update its CPT, (which in turn is then used to predict $stub_{t+2}^{*}$, etc.). To define *accuracy*, we observe how frequently the predicted command completely matches the user's actual command. This Davison and Hirsh method obtains nearly 75% accuracy, in that the user's actual command stub is one of the 5 predicted stubs, three-fourths of the time.

Our task is extremely similar to theirs, except we will focus on learning *entire commands*, rather than just stubs; and we have built a real-time system for this task, rather than just performing a retrospective analysis. Moreover, many of our individual experts will use something very similar to AUR.

Yoshida and Motoda (YM96) examine another aspect of the issue: by exploring file I/O relationships (*i.e.*, which programs use which files) they can suggest default commands to run on files. For example, suppose a user runs "emacs foo.tex", "latex foo.tex", "dvips foo.dvi" and "gv foo.ps". Later on, when the user creates another file "bar.ps", their system will suggest running "gv", because the file ends in ".ps". After a number of interactions have been observed, complete shell scripts can be generated for a sequence of events (*e.g.*, for compiling or writing LaTeX documents). Additionally, they explore file/web cache pre-fetching to reduce load delays (MY98).

Finally, the Reactive Keyboard (DW92) uses length-k modeling to predict the next keystrokes based on the previous keystrokes typed. This is similar to our work, except we are predicting the next complete command line based on the previous command lines typed, rather than a keystroke at a time. This leads to a fundamental difference: while they deal with only a small number of possible "tokens", our system must deal with an unbounded number of possible commands.

Command_t	Command_{t+1}	Prob
vi cw.tex	latex cw.tex	1.0
latex cw.tex	dvips cw.dvi	0.8
	dvips cw.tex	0.2
dvips cw.dvi	gv cw.ps	1.0
dvips cw.tex	dvips cw.dvi	1.0
gv cw.ps	vi cw.tex	0.8
	wall	0.2

Table 2: Probability of Command_{t+1} following Command_t

3 Basic Approach

As noted above, our goal is to extend the Davison and Hirsh system, in several ways. First, we implemented an interactive system. As described below (Section 4.1), we first estimate a distribution over the next command — computing the probability that this $t + 1^{st}$ command will be "ls", versus "cd ..", versus "latex foo.tex", etc. We then map the top five to the F-keys — the best prediction to F1, the second best to F2, ..., the fifth best to F5 — and lists these mappings (read "predictions") in the title bar of the xterm; see Figure 3. Throughout our many designs, we insisted that the adaptive system remain "real-time"; *i.e.*, the total process — updating the various data structures, computing the most likely commands, resetting the display, etc. — could not take over 500 milliseconds. Note, also, that this approach complements the existing history and file/command completion and correction facilities already available with the shell we used, ZSH.

The second extension is to predict *complete commands*, rather than just stubs. Our first approach was simply to extend the Davison/Hirsh system to predict these complete commands; producing Table 2 from the Figure 2 dialog. The resulting system was 47.4% accurate over the Greenberg data.[3] Hoping to improve of this score, we then implemented several modifications.

First, we built a system that used both the previous command and the error code it returned. For example, after running latex foo.tex, we figured the user would only go on to dvips foo.dvi if the latex command was successful (read "return error code of 0"), and would otherwise go perhaps to emacs foo.tex. Unfortunately, our empirical data shows this degraded the performance; see Table 4. We had similar negative results when we tried incorporating day-of-week, or time-of-day.

We also considered *parsing* the actual commands, to enable some simple types of generalization — *e.g.*, after observing that "dvips foo.dvi" followed "latex foo.tex" and "dvips bar.dvi" followed "latex bar.tex", our system should anticipate that "dvips blop.dvi" may follow "latex blop.tex", even though it has never seen anything related to "blop" before. To do this, we used an parser to produce an "abstract" pattern of commands; *e.g.*, to re-represent the commands from Figure 2 as:

---

[3] Our system matched the Davison and Hirsh results: we could get almost 75% accuracy when predicting *stubs*.

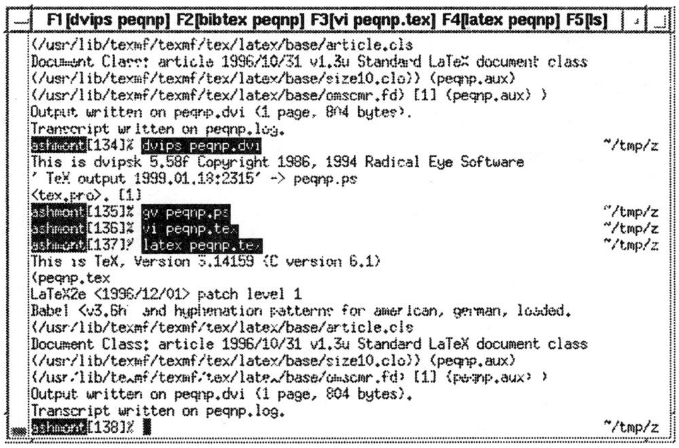

Figure 3: Implementation

[1] vi cw.tex
[2] latex ⟨T-1 ARG1⟩
[3] dvips ⟨T-1 ARG1 STEM⟩.dvi
[4] gv ⟨T-1 ARG1 STEM⟩.ps
[5] vi ⟨T-1 ARG1 STEM⟩.tex
...

Our system can then attempted to match the "current pattern" against these abstracted command lines (rather than the actual commands). This too degraded performance.

Finally, we considered conditioning on the previous *two* commands, $\langle C_{t-1}, C_{t-2} \rangle$, rather than just C_{t-1}. (That is, we used AUR to compute $P(C_t = \chi \mid C_{t-1} = a, C_{t-2} = b)$ based on the observed triples b, a, χ.) So from the Figure 1 dialog, we would claim an 84% chance that that the user will type cw, after seeing her type the the sequence ⟨make, vi⟩ — *i.e.*, $P(C_t = \text{cw} \mid C_{t-1} = \text{make}, C_{t-2} = \text{vi}) = 0.84$. This too failed — producing a system whose accuracy dropped to only 36.9%.

So, while we thought each of these approaches *had* to work, our data proved otherwise: essentially all of these winning ideas caused the performance to degrade. Undaunted, we tried another approach...

4 "Mixture of Experts" Approach

Each of the previous ideas attempted to exploit some other type of information. Of course, we would like to include them *all*. One major problem, of course, is dimensionality: Even assuming there are only 500 commands, we first need to consider 500^2 possible command-pairs. For each of these, we need to also consider time of day (say in 4 buckets), error code (say in 2 buckets), and day of week (say in 7 buckets) which means we will need to estimate at least 14,000,000 parameters. Unfortunately, this is not just cumbersome, but unlearnable: people will change their patterns long before observing enough commands to produce good estimates here.

We therefore need to reduce the dimensionality of this space. Here we used a standard trick of "factoring" the range of options. We word this using the "mixture of experts" model (JJNH91): Building several relatively sim-

Source of Prediction	Accuracy $\pm \sigma$
Previous 1 Cmd	47.4% ±0.0009
Previous 1 Cmd, w/parsing	44.0% ±0.0009
Previous 2 Cmds	36.9% ±0.0009
Previous 1 Cmd + Error Code	46.9% ±0.0009
Previous 1 Cmd + Day of Week	46.7% ±0.0009
Previous 1 Cmd + Time of Day	46.6% ±0.0009

Table 3: Early Results

ple experts $\{E_i\}$, each predicting the next command from some different set of available information; see Figure 4. After Section 4.1 motivates and provides the combination rule we used, the remaining 4 subsections describe the four actual experts we used: E_{AC} uses the previous k <u>A</u>ctual <u>C</u>ommands (for various k); E_{PC} uses the previous k <u>P</u>arsed <u>C</u>ommands; E_{L100} focuses on the <u>L</u>ast <u>100</u> commands; and E_{F1} uses the <u>F</u>irst <u>1</u> command in a session. The concluding Subsection 4.6 then shows provides empirical data to illustrate that these experts, when combined, did produce a slight improvement.

4.1 Combining the Voices

Here, we assume each expert E_i has used some aspects of the current body of information Ω (previous commands, error code, time and date, etc), to produce its prediction for what command the user will type next; $P(E_i = y \mid \Omega)$ ($E_i = y$ indicates that expert E_i predicts y will be the next command, and $C = \chi$ is the composite prediction. The specific predictors are described below.) Our goal is to combine these, to produce an improved prediction — $P(C = \chi \mid \Omega)$.

To simplify the derivation, assume there are only two experts. We can then write

$$P(C = \chi \mid \Omega) = \sum_{y,z} P(C = \chi, E_1 = y, E_2 = z \mid \Omega) =$$

$$\sum_{y,z} P\left(C = \chi \,\middle|\, \begin{array}{l} E_1 = y \\ E_2 = z \\ \Omega \end{array}\right) P\left(E_1 = y \,\middle|\, \begin{array}{l} E_2 = z \\ \Omega \end{array}\right) P(E_2 = z \mid \Omega)$$

$$= \sum_{y,z} P\left(C = \chi \,\middle|\, \begin{array}{l} E_1 = y \\ E_2 = z \end{array}\right) P(E_1 = y \mid \Omega) P(E_2 = z \mid \Omega)$$

where the last line uses the assumptions that the prediction will depend only on the values that the experts say (*i.e.*, $P(C = \chi \mid E_1 = y, E_2 = z, \Omega) = P(C = \chi \mid E_1 = y, E_2 = z)$); and E_2's prediction is independent of E_1's given the background Ω — $P(E_1 = y \mid E_2 = z, \Omega) = P(E_1 = y \mid \Omega)$. We further simplify the equations by making the assumption that $P(C = \chi \mid E_1 = y, E_2 = z) = 0$ when $\chi \notin \{y, z\}$, and moreover, that we can lump together various $y \neq z$ cases. We also ignore the actual commands — *i.e.*, assume $P(C = \text{ls} \mid E_1 = \text{ls}, E_2 = \text{ls}) = P(C = \text{make} \mid E_1 = \text{make}, E_2 = \text{make})$, and so forth. This means we need only estimate 3 additional numbers:

$$P_{=,=} = P(C = \chi \mid E_1 = \chi, E_2 = \chi)$$
$$P_{=,\neq} = P(C = \chi \mid E_1 = \chi, E_2 \neq \chi)$$
$$P_{\neq,=} = P(C = \chi \mid E_1 \neq \chi, E_2 = \chi)$$

(Recall

$$P_{\neq,\neq} = P(C = \chi \mid E_1 \neq \chi, E_2 \neq \chi) = 0)$$

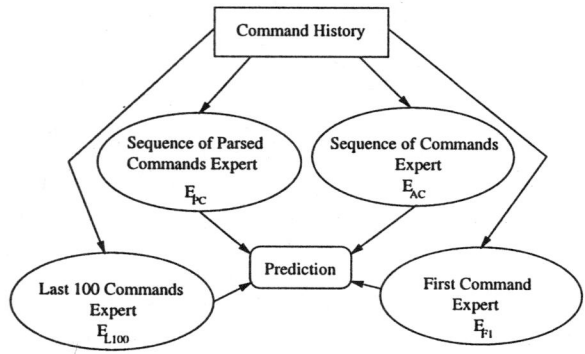

Figure 4: Combination of multiple Experts

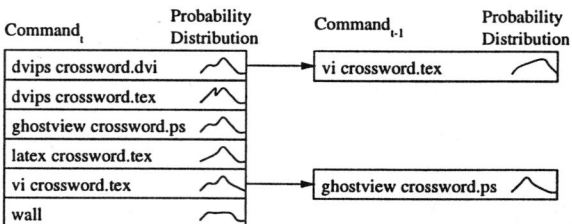

Figure 5: History Expert

This means
$$\begin{aligned}P(C = \chi \mid \Omega) &= P_{=,=} \quad P_1(\chi \mid \Omega) P_2(\chi \mid \Omega) \\ &+ P_{=,\neq} \quad P_1(\chi \mid \Omega)(1 - P_2(\chi \mid \Omega)) \\ &+ P_{\neq,=} \quad (1 - P_1(\chi \mid \Omega)) P_2(\chi \mid \Omega)\end{aligned}$$
where $P_i(\chi \mid \Omega)$ abbreviates $P(E_i = \chi \mid \Omega)$. To further simplify the computation, we only consider a subset of the possible commands χ — only those commands that either E_1 or E_2 rank in their (respective) top 10.

Of course, this all scales up to larger sets of experts: In general, if we are considering k experts, then (in addition to having each expert learn its own distribution $P(E_i = \chi \mid \Omega)$), we will also need to estimate $2^k - 1$ probability values.

4.2 Using m Previous Actual Commands

As noted above (when outlining AUR; Section 2), the distribution over the user's next command is not stationary, which means standard techniques (such as using simple frequencies) will not work. The E_{AC} expert therefore adopts a version of the AUR approach, in using the observed previous commands $C_{t-1}, C_{t-2}, \ldots$ in predicting the next (currently unobserved) C_t command. Of course, we are dealing with the entire command, rather than just stubs. See Table 2.

We initially used only the immediately previous command C_{t-1}, then tried conditioning on the previous two commands, $\langle C_{t-1}, C_{t-2} \rangle$. Unfortunately, relatively few command-pairs occurred frequently; this means we are relatively unlikely to have seen many examples of any particular pair before... which meant our system overfit the available data, and produced a system with reduced accuracy (only 36.9%).

A better approach is to condition on the previous two commands *only when we have reason to believe these predictions will be meaningful*; that is, only when this pair has occurred frequently before. Otherwise, we just condition on the single, immediately previous C_{t-1}. Of course, we can apply this recursively, to consider conditioning on the previous three $C_{t-1}, C_{t-2}, C_{t-3}$ when there is sufficient data to support any conclusions reached, or previous 4, or whatever. (This is idea underlying the IMM system (SDKW98).)

We therefore built a data structure to encode this information; such as Figure 5, which corresponds to the Figure 2 example. As shown on the left-hand-side, each single command indexes a node, which also has a distribution; *e.g.*, the top left node contains the distribution $P(C_t = \chi \mid C_{t-1} = \text{dvips cw.dvi})$. As there are at least $k = 2$ examples of $\langle C_{t-1} = \text{dvips cw.dvi}, C_{t-2} = \text{vi cw.tex} \rangle$, this top-left node also has a child, shown to its right. That node also includes a distribution $P(C_t = \chi \mid C_{t-1} = \text{dvips cw.dvi}, C_{t-2} = \text{vi cw.tex})$. Of course, that "dvips cw.dvi" node could have several children, and any of these children could their own have children. E.g., if ρ had the child σ which had the child τ, then the τ node would include a distribution $P(C = \chi \mid C_{t-1} = \rho, C_{t-2} = \sigma, C_{t-3} = \tau)$, and so forth. Here, we update this data structure by generating a new child whenever there are a sufficient number of instances, here $k = 5$, that reach the child's location. Although the possibility of growth is unlimited, in practice the number of levels of children rarely exceeds 3.

4.3 Using m Previous Abstracted Commands

The E_{PC} expert first "abstracts" the command line, by replacing the details of the filename components (path name and extensions such as "/usr/ralph/" and ".tex") with generic, matchable terms; see Section 3. This allows it to re-use the patterns, in matching new terms. After command lines have been converted into patterns, this expert uses the same prediction method as in Section 4.2.

4.4 Short-Term Frequency Predictions

The E_{L100} expert maintains a frequency table for the last $m = 100$ commands, and predicts the distribution over the $t + 1^{st}$ command will be from this empirical distribution
$$P_{L100}(C_{t+1} = x \mid \Omega) = \frac{|x \in \{C_{t-n}, \ldots, C_t\}|}{n}$$
This method performs surprisingly well by itself, and provides a robust mechanism for predicting commands — *e.g.*, after erroneous command lines (a.k.a. typos) are entered.

4.5 Predicting the Sessions First Command

The first command in a session is a special case, and problematic as there is no previous command on which to base predictions. In a method very similar to that of Section 4.4, the E_{F1} expert maintains a simple probability table for the first commands of the user's last $n = 100$ sessions, and uses this to predict the user's first command. Of course, E_{F1} is only active for the first command of each session.

4.6 Results

Table 4 summarizes our results, showing that our algorithm, with all of its experts, can guess the correct command slightly more accurately than the simple AUR system. While the improvement seems minor, notice it is significant, at the $p < 0.001$ level.

Source of Prediction	Accuracy $\pm\sigma$
5 Most Frequent Lines	33.9% ±0.0009
5 Most Frequent in Last 100	44.6% ±0.0009
Simple AUR method (1 previous cmd)	47.4% ±0.0009
Combination of Experts	**47.9% ±0.0009**

Table 4: Command Line Prediction Accuracy

We explored using yet other tricks (including combinations with the "obviously appropriate" ones listed in Table 3 (KG99)), but were unable to produce significantly better results. We therefore suspect we have reached the limits of successful prediction with this dataset — the remaining error is simply a function of the underlying stochasticity of the process. Towards confirming this, we investigated how well our algorithm would work if it had complete knowledge of the future; *i.e.*, we trained it on the complete data, and then ran the trained version over the same data. We saw this system was only correct 45.5% of the time. In fact, on average, only 72% of commands are duplicates of previous commands. That is, 28% of commands are *very* difficult to predict, since they have never been seen before.

5 Conclusion

5.1 Future Work

Although the Greenberg data helped us to start our work, we worry it may miss information that is needed for better in-depth analysis of user patterns. We are therefore collecting our own data (see Figure 3). While we have collected many fewer command lines, we store with each command line substantially more information, including:

- current working directory (track directory navigation)
- command timing (allowing timing of under one second)
- computer and display identification
- shell aliases and functions

We plan to exploit this additional information in the automated construction of shell macros. (Here we will, of course, use the abstracted patterns; see Section 4.3. We also suspect that the other available information, such as error codes, will be essential here.)

Our user interface, while functional, suffers some drawbacks and would benefit greatly from auto-completion and integration with ZSH's correction facilities.

We are also investigating other applications — *i.e.*, other situations where it would be useful to predict the user's next command. In addition to detecting and exploiting patterns in other software systems (like WORD or POWERPOINT), we are also considering using this to help optimize communication; *e.g.*, when using a Palm™ organizer to telnet to a remote computer or to administer a NetWinder server. Bandwidth is not a large concern, but command input can be. Providing command lines on a pull-down menu could improve general telnet access, and accurate construction of useful aliases for long command lines would be far more valuable.

5.2 Contributions

This paper has investigated various ways of producing a system to predict the user's next command. Our explorations have produced many insights into this task: for example, we found that a fairly simple algorithm (AUR, on the single previous command) can perform adequately. We then considered many obvious "improvements", which used other types of information. We found, however, that these modifications typically *degrade*, not improve, performance. We attribute this to both the vast number of parameters that these systems needed to estimate, and to the fact that the distribution of user commands are typically non-stationary.

To achieve any improvement required using more sophisticated techniques: here, we used a "mixture of experts" approach, together with a body of "approximations" to drastically reduce the number of parameters that needed to be estimated. We are continuing to explore this framework, in incorporating other types of information (*e.g.*, about error codes and time of day). The current system, however, is quite usable, and demonstrates that it is possible to predict complete user commands correctly almost half the time, and do so in real-time.

For more information about our system, please visit http://www.cs.ualberta.ca/~benjamin/AUI/

Acknowledgements

We thank Saul Greenberg for the use of his UNIX usage data. Portions of this paper were adapted from work done with Thomas Jacob. Korvemaker and Greiner were supported, in part, by NSERC.

References

[DH97] Brian D. Davison and Haym Hirsh. Toward an adaptive command line interface. In *Advances in Human Factors/Ergonomics: Design of Computing Sytems: Social and Ergonomic Considarations*, pages 505–508. Elsevier, 1997.

[DH98] Brian D. Davison and Haym Hirsh. Predicting sequences of user actions. In *Predicting the Future: AI Appreaches to Time-Series Analysis*, pages 5–12. AAAI Press, July 1998.

[DW92] John J. Darragh and Ian H. Witten. *The Reactive Keyboard*. Cambridge Series on Human-Computer Interaction. Cambridge University Press, New York, New York, 1992.

[Gre88] Saul Greenberg. Using unix: Collected traces of 168 users. Research Report 88/333/45, Department of Computer Science, University of Calgary, Calgary, Alberta, 1988.

[JJNH91] R. A. Jacobs, M. I. Jordan, S. J. Nowlan, and G. E. Hinton. Adaptive mixtures of local experts. *Neural Computation*, 3(1):79–87, 1991.

[KG99] Benjamin Korvemaker and Russell Greiner. The trials and tribulations of building an adaptive user interface. http://www.cs.ualberta.ca/~greiner/PAPERS/AdaptUI.ps, 1999.

[MY98] Hiroshi Motoda and Kenichi Yoshida. Machine learning techniques to make computers easier to use. *Artificial Intelligence*, 103(1–2):295–321, 1998.

[SDKW98] S. Salzberg, A. Delcher, S. Kasif, and O. White. Microbial gene identification using interpolated markov models. *Nucleic Acids Research*, 26(2):544–548, 1998.

[YM96] Kenichi Yoshida and Hiroshi Motoda. Automated user modeling for intelligent interface. *International Journal of Human-Computer Interaction*, 8(3):237–258, 1996.

Generation of Ideologically-Biased Historical Documentaries

Michael Mateas

Computer Science Department
Carnegie Mellon University
5000 Forbes Avenue
Pittsburgh PA 15213
michaelm@cs.cmu.edu

Paul Vanouse

Art Department
202 Center for the Arts
University at Buffalo
Buffalo NY 14260-6010
vanouse@buffalo.edu

Steffi Domike

Chatham College
Woodland Road
Pittsburgh PA 15232
domike@chatham.edu

Abstract

Terminal Time is a machine that constructs ideologically-biased documentary histories in response to audience feedback. The audience answers multiple-choice questions via an applause meter. The answers to these questions influence which historical events are chosen from a knowledge base, how these events will be slanted to embody the bias implied in the audience's answers, and how the events will be connected together to form a historical narrative. *Terminal Time*'s architecture consists of a knowledge base and inference engine for querying the knowledge base, ideological goal trees and rhetorical devices which represent the current bias, a natural language generator to turn the constructed history into narrative prose, and an indexed multimedia database used to sequence video against the narration.

Introduction

Terminal Time is a machine that constructs ideologically-biased documentary histories in response to audience feedback. It is a cinematic experience, designed for projection on a large screen in a movie theater setting. At the beginning of the show, and at several points during the show, the audience responds to multiple choice questions

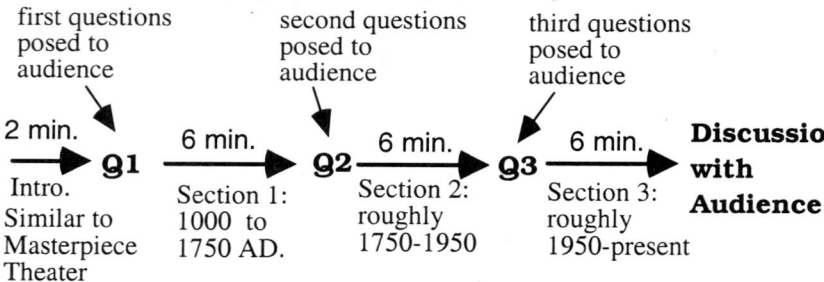

Figure 1: Audience interaction

reminiscent of marketing polls. The audience interaction in relationship to the viewing experience is depicted in Figure 1. In the first question period, an initial ideological theme (from the set of gender, race, technology, class, religion)

and a narrative arc (e.g. is this a progress or decline narrative) are established.

The second set of questions refines the ideological theme chosen in the first set, and possibly introduces a sub-theme (e.g. combining race and class, or technology and religion). The third set of questions further refines the theme(s) and introduces the possibility for a reversal (e.g. a decline narrative becoming a progress narrative). An example question (from the first question period) is shown in Figure 2.

Which of these phrases do you feel best represents you:

A. Life was better in the time of my grandparents.
B. Life is good and keeps getting better every day.

Figure 2: Example question

The audience selects answers to these questions via an applause meter – the answer generating the most applause wins. The answers to these questions allow the system to create historical narratives that attempt to mirror and often exaggerate the audience's biases and desires. By exaggerating the ideological position implied in the audience's answers, *Terminal Time* produces an uncomfortable history that encourages the audience to reflect on the influence of ideology on historical narratives.

Terminal Time is a collaboration between a computer scientist specializing in AI-based art and entertainment, an interactive media artist, and a documentary filmmaker.

Terminal Time's architecture consists of the following major components: knowledge base, ideological goal trees (Carbonell 1979), rule-based natural language generator, rhetorical devices, and a database of indexed audio/visual elements primarily consisting of short digital movies and sound files containing music. Figure 3 shows a diagram of the architecture. The knowledge base contains representations of historical events. This is the raw material out of which the ideologically-biased histories are constructed. Examples of historical events are the First Crusades, the invention of Bakelite, and the rise of enlightenment philosophy. Ideological-goal trees represent the current ideological-bias being pursued by the narrator. The goal-trees consist of rhetorical goals ordered by subgoal and importance (to the ideologue) relationships. These goals are used both to select historical events to include in the story and to "spin" the event in an ideologically-consistent manner. The rule-based natural language generator (NLG) generates the narrative text once specific facts have been selected and connected to make a story. The storyboard serves as a working memory for processes that impose a narrative order on event spins created by the goal tree. Rhetorical devices are connecting pieces of text with accompanying constraints on story structure. These devices are used to create narrative connections between historical events. Finally, the multimedia database contains the audio/visual elements for the assembled documentary. Once a narrative track has been constructed, information retrieval techniques are used to match the "best" indexed multimedia elements to the appropriate pieces of text. Once the multimedia elements have been selected, the resulting documentary is displayed, layering text-to-speech synthesis of the narrative track, and the video and audio elements.

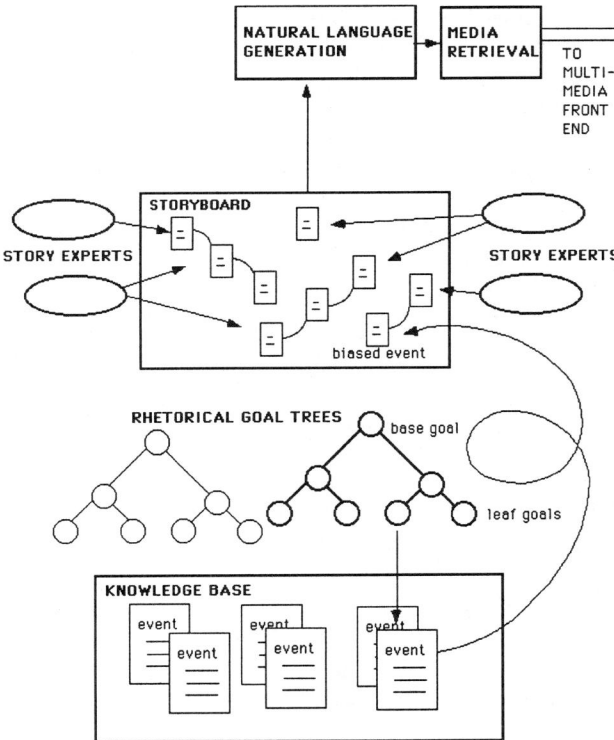

Figure 3: *Terminal Time* architecture

The audience's responses to the questions influence the machine by selecting and editing rhetorical goal trees, selecting a set of rhetorical devices, and placing constraints on the storyboard. In a sense, the audience's responses parameterize the machine. The responses activate structures and processes; the machine then autonomously generates a biased history.

The rest of this paper describes the artistic goals of *Terminal Time*, provides more detail about each of the architectural components, and describes our experiences performing *Terminal Time*.

Artistic Goals

Documentary Form

The popular model of the documentary film in America today, most clearly exemplified by Ken Burns' "The Civil War," has the familiar structure of Western narrative. The rhetorical structure invariably involves a crisis situation, a climax, and a clear resolution. Generally there is one prevailing narrative, one interpretation of the historical facts presented. The documentary situates itself as an objective retelling of history, making it difficult for the viewer to question the authority of the presented viewpoint.

Terminal Time imitates the model of this "cookie-cutter documentary" with a machine that produces and reproduces it, until the model itself is revealed for the tool of ideological replication that it has become. *Terminal Time* generates endless variations of documentaries that have the "look and feel" of the traditional, authoritative PBS documentary. Yet these generated documentaries are clearly charged with a strong ideological bias derived from the audience's responses. In this way Terminal Time invites the viewer to question the implicit authority of documentary presentations of history.

Utopian Navigation

There is a great deal of industry hype surrounding interactive media and computing. Typically such experiences are promoted through a rhetoric of utopian navigation. According to such rhetoric, the computer provides unlimited access to information and experience, a pure source of empowerment that imposes no interpretation on the data that is processed. Other familiar tropes in this rhetoric include: Real-time, Immersion and Virtuality -- promising the thrill of reality or hyper-reality, without the effort, right from one's own PC. Microsoft's ads softly beguile us with the question "Where do you want to go today?"

With *Terminal Time*, we play with these notions by building a program that engages in active interpretation and construction of the interactive experience. While the resulting constructed histories clearly respond to audience input, the system has a mind of its own, pushing the story into extremes that the audience did not intend. Thus value-free navigation gives way to a value-laden interpretation. *Terminal Time* is a program that bites back.

Audience Experience

Utilizing indirect questionnaires as a user interface, the system essentially target markets each audience with an appropriate history. Rather than asking audiences what type of history they would like, or how they would like to navigate through history, they are asked questions about their own demographics and psychographics: their work status, what cultural trends they find most disturbing, how well they get along with others, etc. The resulting history is like holding a funhouse mirror to the audience; it reflects an exaggerated and distorted view of the audience's biases.

As the history begins 1000 years ago, the audience should experience a comfortable sense of historical authority engendered by the familiar documentary form and the remoteness of the historical events. As the history unfolds, the effect of the periodic audience polls becomes more and more apparent. The increased bias evident in the history should begin creating a tension with regard to the veridicality of the history (a sense of "wait a minute, this doesn't seem quite right..."). Ideally, this tension should reach a maximum as the piece moves into modern history.

Knowledge Base

Upper Cyc Ontology

The knowledge base consists of higher order predicate statements about historical events, definitions of ontological entities used in the historical event descriptions (individuals and collections), and inference rules. *Terminal Time*'s ontology is based on the Upper Cyc Ontology, the top 3000 most general terms in the Cyc ontology (Lenat 1995). The Upper Cyc Ontology is available free of charge from Cycorp[1]. It does not include any other components of Cyc (theorem prover, natural language engine, database, etc.). However, the upper ontology provides a useful set of distinctions in terms of which the more specific ontology needed by *Terminal Time* can be defined.

Example Historical Event

Figure 4 shows the representation of The Giordano Bruno

```
;; Giordano Bruno
($isa %GiordanoBrunoStory %HistoricalEvent)
($isa %GiordanoBrunoStory %IdeaSystemCreationEvent)
($isa %GiordanoBrunoStory %Execution)
(%circa %GiordanoBrunoStory (%DateRangeFn
   (%CenturyFn 16) (%CenturyFn 17)))
($eventOccursAt %GiordanoBrunoStory $ContinentOfEurope)
($performedBy %GiordanoBrunoStory %GiordanoBruno)
($outputsCreated %GiordanoBrunoStory %GiordanoBrunosIdeas)
($isa %GiordanoBrunosIdeas $PropositionalInformationThing)
($isa %GiordanoBrunosIdeas $SomethingExisting)
(%conflictingMOs %GiordanoBrunosIdeas %MedievalChristianity)
($isa %GiordanoBrunosIdeas %IdeaSystem)
($performedByPart %GiordanoBrunoStory
   %TheRomanCatholicReligiousOrg)
($objectActedOn %GiordanoBrunoStory %GiordanoBruno)
```

Figure 4: Example knowledge base representation

---
[1] http://www.cyc.com/

story. Those terms preceded by a "$" are defined in the Upper Cyc Ontology. Those terms preceded by "%" are defined within the TT ontology in terms of the Upper Cyc Ontology.

Figure 4, translated into English, states:

> The Giordano Bruno story, a historical event occurring in the 16th and 17th century, involved the creation of a new idea system and an execution. The idea system created in this event conflicts with the idea system of medieval Christianity. Both Giordano Bruno and a portion of the Roman Catholic Church were the performers of this event. Giordano Bruno was acted on (he was executed) in this event.

In this particular representation of the story of Giordano Bruno, both the creation of his philosophical writings and his execution by the Roman Catholic Church are treated as a single compound event. If we wanted *Terminal Time* to be able to treat these two events separately (perhaps talking about Bruno's writings without mentioning his eventual execution), they could be represented as two sub-events. In general, events are only represented as deeply as is needed by the rhetorical goal trees, storyboard, and natural language generator.

Inference Engine

The inference engine, implemented in Common Lisp, is based on the interpreter implementing higher-order hereditary Harrop logic described in (Elliott and Pfenning 1991). Hereditary Harrop logic allows knowledge base entries (the program, thinking in logic programming terms) to consist of Horn clauses, and queries (goals) to consist of all the standard Prolog-like goals (atomic goals, conjunctions, disjunctions, existentials), plus embedded implications (assumptions). The interpreter also includes extra-logical support for operations such as unifying logic variables against a function evaluated by Lisp.

The inference engine is used to answer all queries about historical events. For example, in the discussion below of ideological goal trees, the historical event tests are all made using the inference engine.

Ideological Goal Trees

Terminal Time organizes ideological bias with goal trees, adapted from Politics (Carbonell 1979). In Politics, ideology is encoded as a set of goals held by the ideologue. The goals are organized via subgoal links (not corresponding exactly to either the conjunctive or disjunctive notion of subgoal) and relative importance links. The relative importance links place an importance partial order over the subgoals. For example, in Politics, the US Conservative ideologue's most important goal is *Communist Containment*. This goal has a number of subgoals such as *Have a Strong Military*, *Aid Anti-Communist Countries*, etc. Though *Have a Strong Military* and *Aid Anti-Communist Countries* are sibling subgoals, *Have a Strong Military* has a higher relative importance. In addition to their own goal tree, an ideologue also possesses beliefs about the goal trees of others. In Carbonell's system, the goal trees were used to organize inferences made by a news story understanding system.

In *Terminal Time*, the goal tree has been modified to represent the goals of an ideological story-teller. Rather than having goals to modify the world, the story-teller has rhetorical goals to show that something is the case. For example, the *Anti-Religious Rationalist* possesses the goals show in Figure 5 during the first segment of the history. The indented goals are subgoals.

The leaf goals in the goal tree are used to organize two kinds of knowledge: a set of tests for recognizing when a historical event is potential fodder for satisfying the rhetorical goal, and a set of plans for actually constructing the description of the event to satisfy the goal (the event spin).

```
show-religion-is-bad
    show-religion-causes-war
    show-religion-causes-crazy-self-sacrifice
    show-religion-causes-oppression
    show-religion-causes-self-abuse
    show-thinkers-persecuted-by-religion
show-halting-rationalist-progress-against-religion
    show-thinkers-opposing-religious-thought
    show-thinkers-persecuted-by-religion
```

Figure 5: Anti-Religious Rationalist goal tree

Notice that the leaf goal *show-thinkers-persecuted-by-religion* is a subgoal of two higher level goals. Satisfying this goal satisfies both higher-level goals.

Tests for Event Applicability

An ideologue needs a way of recognizing when a historical event could be used to satisfy a goal (make an ideological point). For example, the *Anti-Religious Rationalist* must be able to recognize that the Giordano Bruno story can be used to show that thinkers are persecuted by religion. This involves recognizing that a religious organization does something negative to a thinker because of the thinker's thoughts. In the current version of *Terminal Time*, this test determines whether an event involves both the creation of

```
(%and
    ($isa ?event %IdeaSystemCreationEvent)
    ($isa ?event %Execution)
    ($outputsCreated ?event ?newIdeas)
    (%conflictingMOs ?newIdeas ?relBeliefSystem)
    ($isa ?relBeliefSystem $Religion))
```

Figure 6: Example event applicability test

an idea system and an execution, and whether the idea system conflicts with some religious belief system. The formal syntax of this test expressed in the language of the inference engine is shown in figure 6.

This test assumes that the execution must have been performed by the religious organization in response to the creation of the conflicting idea system. Further, it assumes that the only forms of persecution are execution. These simplifying assumptions work because given the current content of the knowledge base, this applicability test is sufficient to locate events that can be slanted as forms of religious persecution. As new events involving religious persecution are added to the knowledge base, the test may have to be changed (most likely broadened).

Plans for Event-level Story Generation

Once an event has been recognized as applicable to a rhetorical goal of the ideologue, additional knowledge is necessary to spin the event in such a way as to satisfy the rhetorical goal. This knowledge is represented as rhetorical plans. These plans put a "spin" on the event (referred to as a *spin*) by selecting a subset of the event knowledge represented in the KB to place on the storyboard.

```
Describe the individual who called for the war,
mentioning their religious belief
Describe the religious goal of the war
Describe some event happening during the war
Describe the outcome
```

Figure 7: Rhetorical plan outline

Rhetorical plans are the mechanism by means of which a rhetorical goal can place its unique view on an event.

The plan language is similar to the rule language for natural language generation, except that the atomic actions for the NLG rule language emit strings while the atomic actions for the plan language add syntactic units to an event spin. See the section on NLG rules for a more detailed description of the logic allowed in rhetorical plans.

An outline of an example plan for *Show that religious thought leads to war* is shown in Figure 7.

In addition to the knowledge elements selected by the rhetorical plan, the name of the rhetorical goal and the names of all of its parents are added to the spin. The goal name(s) tell the rhetorical devices and natural language generator which goal(s) a particular spin is satisfying.

Rhetorical Devices

After the rhetorical goals are done producing event spins, the storyboard now contains an unordered collection of spins. Rhetorical devices connect spins together to form a story. Rhetorical devices consist of an English sentence(s) (actually represented as NLG rules) and accompanying logical tests that can be used to connect spins together. For example, the sentence "Yet progress doesn't always yield satisfaction" can be used to connect several spins describing the positive effects of technological progress and several spins describing social or environmental problems arising from technological progress. The associated tests require that all the spins preceding the rhetorical device must be positive technological, artistic, or industrial progress, and that all the spins following the rhetorical device must be negative effects of progress.

Prescope and Postscope Tests

The prescope of a rhetorical device is the ordered collection of spins preceding the device. The postscope is the ordered collection of spins following the device. The prescope and postscope tests are constraints (interpreted by the inference engine) that the preceding and following spins must satisfy in order for the rhetorical device to be applicable (that is, able to glue the spins together). Scope tests can either require that all the spins in the scope satisfy the test or that at least one spin in the scope satisfies the test. In addition, the scope range and length can be specified. The scope length is the number of spins to include in the scope; the default is 1 (that is, only the preceding or following spin must satisfy the test). The scope range specifies the range of spins that can be searched for a satisfying scope; the default is (1 1) (the range consists of only the immediately preceding or following spin).

Rhetorical Device NLG Rule

Associated with each rhetorical device is an NLG rule for generating the English sentence associated with the device. For some rhetorical devices, this may be a simple rule generating a single canned sentence. For other (more flexible) rhetorical devices, the rule may be passed arguments (which were bound by the scope tests) which influence the generated sentence.

Example Rhetorical Device

An example rhetorical device is shown in figure 8.

```
(def-rhetdev :name :non-western-religious-faith
   :prescope-length 2
   :prescope-test (:all-events-satisfy (%and
      ($isa ?event %HistoricalSituation)
      (:kb ($eventOccursAt ?event %FirstWorld))
      (%rhet-goal :show-religion-is-good)))
   :postscope-test (:some-event-satisfies ?spin (%and
      ($isa ?event %HistoricalSituation)
      (:kb ($eventOccursAt ?event %NonFirstWorld))
      (%rhet-goal :show-religion-is-good)))
   :nlg-rule :generate
   :nlg-context-path (:non-western-religious-faith))
```

Figure 8: Example rhetorical device

This rhetorical device, employed by the *Pro-religious Supporter*, is used to connect a couple of spins describing Western religious faith, with an example of non-Western religious faith. The prescope-length is 2; since no prescope-range is specified, it defaults to the preceding two events. Thus the prescope test must be satisfied by the preceding two spins and only the immediately preceding two spins. The test requires that the event occurred in the First World (represented in the ontology as a collection of geographical regions which includes regions such as Europe) and that it satisfied the rhetorical goal *show religion is good*. The %rhet-goal term was added to the event spin during rhetorical plan processing (when the rhetorical goal sticks the spin on the blackboard). Most rhetorical devices test the satisfied rhetorical goal in their scope tests; these goal labels indicate how an event has been slanted in order to create a specific even spin. The postscope test similarly tests whether the immediately following event spin satisfies the goal *show-religion-is-good* in the *non*-First World. In the event that the constraints are satisfied, text will be generated by the NLG rule.

Story Generation

Once a collection of event spins has been placed on the storyboard, a historical story can be generated. For each of the three periods of the documentary, each ideologue has a list of storyboard constraints. The storyboard constraint for section 1 of the *Anti-Religious Rationalist* is shown in figure 9.

```
(%rhet-goal :show-religion-is-bad)
(%rhet-goal :show-religion-is-bad)
(%rhet-goal :show-religion-is-bad)
(%rhet-goal :show-religion-is-bad)
(%rhet-goal :show-halting-rationalist-progress)
(%and (%rhet-goal :show-halting-rationalist-progress)
   (%rhet-goal :show-religion-is-bad))
```

Figure 9: *Anti-Religious Rationalist* storyboard constraint

The length of the constraint list determines how many event spins will be included in the story section. In this example, six spins will be included. Each test in the list constrains the spins that can appear in each position in the story. Typically these are constraints on the rhetorical goals that were satisfied to create the spin. In addition to the storyboard constraints, there is also an implicit temporal constraint that requires that spins appear in roughly chronological order.

To generate a story, the space of all sequences of event spins satisfying the storyboard constraints is searched for a sequence that can be satisfied by the current set of rhetorical devices. A sequence is satisfied if a rhetorical device with satisfied scope tests can be placed between every spin in the sequence. The resulting sequence of interleaved spins and rhetorical devices is a story.

NLG Rules

The NLG system generates English text for both event spins and rhetorical devices. NLG is accomplished using rules which map pieces of knowledge representation onto English. There is no deep theory of lexical choice or text planning. The goal of the NLG system is to produce high quality text for the stories generated on the storyboard. The rule language provides a framework in which a human author can write text ranging in granularity from canned paragraphs down to individual words and phrases and provide the logic to map these varying chunks onto pieces of knowledge representation.

NLG Rule Syntax

Figure 10 provides an abstract example of a rule. This example makes use of most of the features supported by the rule language. This language is similar to the language used for rhetorical plans. All tests mentioned in the NLG rules are interpreted by the inference engine.

```
(def-nlgrule
   :name :rule-name
   :context :some-context
   :test test over the rule arguments
   :body (:seq
      (:terminal
         (:string "string 1")
         (:keywords k1 k2 k3))
      (:cond
         ((test1 over rule arguments)
            (:terminal...))
         ((test 2 over rule arguments)
            (:bag-one-of
               step1...
               stepn)))
      (:rule subrule args (context1 ... contextn))
      (:opt (:if (another test)
         (:seq...)))))
```

Figure 10: NLG rule syntax

An NLG rule is identified by a name and a rule context. The rule context provides a name space in which NLG rule names are recognized. Each context defines a set of rules which are specialists in handling some particular NLG task. Typically, a separate rule context is used for each historical event found in the knowledge base. When generation is initiated, a rule name, arguments (list of knowledge representation elements for which English should be generated) and a context list are given. The context list provides a set of contexts (in order from most specific to most general) in which to search for rules matching the rule name.

When a rule with matching rule name is found, the test is evaluated against the arguments to determine whether to use that instance of the rule for generation. Within a context, there may be multiple rules with the same name (corresponding to different ways to accomplish the same generation task); the test is used to determine which of these rules should be applied given specific arguments.

Once a rule is found whose test evaluates to true, the rule body is interpreted. In the example rule, the rule body is a sequence of steps. Terminals are the atomic steps that emit language. In addition to emitting an English string, terminals emit keywords associated with the English string. These keywords are used by the multimedia retrieval subsystem to associate a video clip with the sentence.

The conditional step (*:cond*) allows generation to branch depending on tests over the rule arguments. The branches may either by individual terminals or an entire rule body. If none of the tests in a conditional succeeds, then the rule fails; the system will try to find other applicable rules for generation. The *bag-one-of* body in the second branch of the conditional chooses one of the steps at random to execute. This can be used to add some random variation to generation.

A rule may contain a call to another generation rule.

The *:opt* construct allows the insertion of an optional conditional step. If the conditional is satisfied, the conditional branch is executed. If the conditional fails, execution of the rule body continues after the optional step.

Video Sequencing

After natural language generation, the event spins and rhetorical devices have been rendered as English text. Video clips from the database of keyword-annotated clips must be sequenced against the text (which forms the narrative track) to create the complete documentary. Video sequencing takes place in two steps. First, the keywords associated with each sentence (the keywords emitted by terminals in NLG rules) are used to retrieve keyword annotated video clips using TF/IDF term-based retrieval (Salton and Buckley 1988). This creates a list of top-scoring video clips for each sentence (typically the top 4 or 5 are taken). Then a greedy forward and backward search through the narrative track is performed to try and maximize clip continuity while minimizing clip reuse. If a pair of consecutive sentences shares clips among their top scoring clips, this greedy search will play the top-scoring shared clip across both sentences.

Current Status

Currently *Terminal Time* contains 134 historical events and 1568 knowledge base assertions (in addition to the assertions in the Upper Cyc Ontology). Nine major ideologues are represented using a total of 222 rhetorical goals, 281 rhetorical devices, and 578 NLG rules. The video database contains 352 annotated 30 second clips. *Terminal Time* has been performed in 14 venues, including the Carnegie Museum of Art, the Warhol Museum, and as the Walker Museum's entry in Sonic Circuits. Work continues in adding new events, goals, devices, NLG rules and video clips.

Performance Experiences

One way to evaluate an AI-based interactive art work is to evaluate the audience response to the system, to examine whether the AI architecture supports an audience interaction which successfully conveys the artistic intentions of the piece. Our knowledge of the audience reaction to *Terminal Time* comes both from observing audiences during a performance and from the audience discussion period we always hold after a performance.

During performances, the audience is highly engaged with the piece. During the interactive polls, segments of the audience sometimes compete for control, clapping and shouting to make their choice the winner. At other times, the audience laughs when a choice meets with silence (no one wants to vote for it). Sometimes the applause grows into a groundswell of whistling and clapping as it becomes clear that certain choices are nearly unanimous. As the audience watches the constructed histories, there is often laughter, and sometimes groans and gasps. These reactions tend to grow as the documentary proceeds, indicating that the ideological bias is indeed becoming stronger and more visible as the history proceeds.

The discussion period tends to be quite animated, with the audience offering many questions and comments. Common topics of discussion include the role of ideology in the construction of history, the nature of certain specific biases, and the experience of being unable to completely control over the machine. From both the audience reactions during the performance and the nature of the post-performance discussion period, *Terminal Time* is successfully creating an engaging audience experience in accord with our artistic intentions.

Related Work

Two of the earliest computational models of ideology are Abelson's Goldwater Machine (Abelson and Carroll 1965) and Carbonell's Politics (Carbonell 1979). The Goldwater Machine mimics the responses of conservative presidential candidate Barry Goldwater to questions about the Cold War. The Goldwater Machine's responses were driven by a Cold War masterscript describing typical roles and event sequences during the Cold War. Politics represents rhetorical goals in order to guide biased understanding of news stories. In contrast to both the Goldwater Machine and Politics, *Terminal Time* generates biased historical stories composed of multiple events, rather than answering individual questions.

Pauline (Hovy 1987) generates natural language text for news events subject to the pragmatic constraints of rhetorical goals. Rhetorical goals include goals of opinion (e.g. show that our side has good goals or takes good actions) and goals of style (level of formality, level of simplicity). Pauline knows about 3 events, but is able to produce 100 different descriptions of an event. Where Pauline has a deep architecture for generating descriptions of individual events, *Terminal Time* selects and connects multiple events to satisfy an ideological position.

Spindoctor (Sack 2000) uses statistical techniques to classify bias in news stories. This system determines the ideological point-of-view expressed in stories about the Nicaraguan Contras. While the use of statistical techniques makes Spindoctor robust, it is concerned with classification where *Terminal Time* is concerned with generation.

Some computer based documentaries support the user in navigating through documentary materials (e.g. Davenport and Murtaugh 1995, Schiffer 1999). As a user interacts with the system, implicit queries retrieve and play annotated video clips. Where these systems support a user in exploring a documentary space through immediate navigation, *Terminal Time* autonomously generates biased documentaries in response to punctuated audience feedback.

Finally, *Terminal Time* differs from all these systems in self-consciously being a work of art. *Terminal Time* is a piece of interactive performance art designed to create an experience for an audience.

Conclusion

This paper has described *Terminal Time*, an AI-based interactive artwork which produces ideologically-biased documentary histories in response to audience feedback. A novel AI architecture developed for *Terminal Time* was described. Performance experience suggests that the architecture supports an audience interaction in accord with our artistic goals.

References

Abelson, R., Carroll, J. 1965. Computer Simulation of Individual Belief Systems. *American Behavioral Scientist*, 8, 24-30.

Carbonell, J. 1979. Subjective understanding: Computer models of belief systems. Ph.D. Thesis, Computer Science Department, Yale University, Research Report #150.

Davenport, G., Murtaugh, M. 1995. ConText: Towards the Evolving Documentary. ACM Multimedia '95, November.

Elliott and Pfenning. 1991. A semi-functional implementation of a higher-order logic programming language. In Peter Lee, editor, *Topics in Advanced Language Implementation*, pages 289-325. MIT Press.

Hovy. 1987. Generating Natural Language Under Pragmatic Constraints. Ph.D. Thesis, Computer Science Department, Yale University, Research Report #521.

Lenat. 1995. Cyc: A Large-Scale Investment in Knowledge Infrastructure. *Communications of the ACM*, 38, no. 11, November.

Sack, W. 2000. "Actor-Role Analysis: Ideology, Point of View and the News," in *Narrative Perspectives: Cognition and Emotion*, Chatman S., Van Peer, W. (editors), New York: SUNY Press.

Salton, G., Buckley C. 1988. Term Weighting Approaches in Automatic Text Retrieval. *Information Processing and Management*, Vol. 24 No. 5, pp. 513-523.

Schiffer. S. 1999. The Rise and Fall of Black Velvet Flag: An "Intelligent" System for Youth Culture Documentary. *AAAI Fall Symposium on Narrative Intelligence*.

Self-Supervised Learning for Visual Tracking and Recognition of Human Hand

Ying Wu, Thomas S. Huang

Beckman Institute
University of Illinois at Urbana-Champaign
Urbana, IL 61801
{yingwu, huang}@ifp.uiuc.edu

Abstract

Due to the large variation and richness of visual inputs, statistical learning gets more and more concerned in the practice of visual processing such as visual tracking and recognition. Statistical models can be trained from a large set of training data. However, in many cases, since it is not trivial to obtain a large labeled and representative training data set, it would be difficult to obtain a satisfactory generalization. Another difficulty is how to automatically select good features for representation. By combining both labeled and unlabeled training data, this paper proposes a new learning paradigm, self-supervised learning, to investigate the issues of learning bootstrapping and model transduction. Inductive learning and transductive learning are the two main cases of self-supervised learning, in which the proposed algorithm, Discriminant-EM (D-EM), is a specific learning technique. Vision-based gesture interface is employed as a testbed in our research.

Introduction

In current Virtual Environment (VE) applications, some conventional interface devices, such as keyboards, mice, wands and joysticks, are inconvenient and unnatural. In recent years, the use of hand gestures in human computer interaction serves as a motivating force for research in hand tracking and gesture recognition. Although hand gestures are complicated to model since the meanings of hand gestures depend on people and cultures, a set of specific hand gesture vocabulary can be always predefined in many applications, so that the ambiguity can be limited. Hand tracking and posture recognition are two of the main components in vision-based gesture interface.

One goal of hand tracking is to locate hand regions in video sequences. Skin color offers an effective and efficient way to segment hand regions out. According to the representation of color distribution in certain color spaces, current techniques of color tracking can be classified into two general approaches: non-parametric (Swain and Ballard 1991; Kjeldsen and Kender 1996; Jones and Rehg 1998; Wu, Liu, and Huang 2000) and parametric (Raja, McKenna, and Gong 1998). Many different color spaces, such as RGB, HSV, N-RGB, have been used in current research. However,

---

Copyright © 2000, American Association for Artificial Intelligence (www.aaai.org). All rights reserved.

many of these techniques are plagued by some special difficulties such as large variation in skin tone, unknown lighting conditions and dynamic scenes.

One possible solution is to make a generic statistical skin color model by collecting a huge training data set (Jones and Rehg 1998) so that the generic color model could work for any user in any case. However, collecting and labeling such a huge database is not trivial. Even though such a good generic color model can be obtained, the skin color may looks very different in different lighting conditions. This color constancy problem is not trivial in color tracking. Because of dynamic scenes and changing lighting conditions, the color distribution over time is non-stationary, since the statistics of color distribution will change with time. If a color classifier is trained under a specific condition, it may not work well in other scenarios.

In many gesture interfaces, some simple controlling, commanding and manipulative gestures are defined to fulfill natural interaction such as pointing, navigating, moving, rotating, stopping, starting, selecting, etc. View-independent hand posture recognition is to recognize hand signs even from different viewing directions.

One approach is the 3D model-based approach, in which the hand configuration is estimated by taking advantage of 3D hand models (Davis and Shah 1994; Heap and Hogg 1996; Kuch and Huang 1995; Lee and Kunii 1995; Rehg and Kanade 1995; Wu and Huang 1999). Since hand configurations are independent to view directions, these methods could directly achieve view-independent recognition. However, since a classification of hand postures is often enough in many other applications such as commands switching, an alternative approach is appearance-based approach (Cui and Weng 1996; Quek and Zhao 1996; Triesch and von de Malsburg 1996), in which classifiers are learned from a set of image samples. Although it is easier for the appearance-based approach to achieve user-independence than model-based approach, there are two major difficulties of this approach: automatic feature selection and training data collection. In general, good generalization requires a large and representative labeled training data set. However, to manually label a large data set will be very time-consuming and tedious. Although unsupervised schemes has been proposed to clustering the appearances of 3D objects(Basri, Roth, and Jacobs 1998), it is hard for pure unsupervised approach to achieve accurate classification without supervision.

In this paper, color tracking is formulated as a transductive learning problem, and posture recognition is formulated as an inductive learning problem. These two learning problems are unified in a framework of self-supervised learning in which both supervised and unsupervised training data are employed.

Problem Formulation

Unlabeled Data

Traditionally, feature extraction and selection are independent to the designation of classifier. Although the discriminant analysis technique offers a means to automatically select and weight classification-relevant features, it puts a harsh requirement to the training data set: a large labeled data set. We do not expect discriminant analysis to output a good result, unless enough labeled data are available.

In fact, it seems that it might not be necessary to have every sample labeled in supervised learning. A very interesting result given by the theory of the support vector machine (SVM) (Vapnik 1995) is that the classification boundary is related only to some support vectors, rather than the whole data set. Although the identification of these support vectors is not trivial, it motivates us to think about the roles of non-support vectors. Fortunately, it is easier to collect unlabeled data. The issue of combining unlabeled data in supervised learning begins to receive more and more research efforts recently and the research of this problem is still in its infancy. Without assuming parametric probabilistic models, several methods are based on the SVM (Gammerman, Vapnik, and Vowk 1998; Bennett and Demiriz 1998; Joachims 1999). However, when the size of unlabeled data becomes very large, these methods need formidable computational resources for mathematical programming. Another difficulty of these SVM-based methods is that the way of selecting the kernel function is heuristic. Some other alternative methods try to fit this problem into the EM framework and employ parametric models (Mitchell 1999; Nigam *et al.* 1999), and have some applications in text classification. Although EM offers a systematic approach to this problem, these methods largely depend on the *a priori* knowledge about the probabilistic structure of data distribution.

If the probabilistic structure of data distribution is known, parameters of probabilistic models can be estimated by unsupervised learning alone, but it is still impossible to assign class labels without labeled data (Duda and Hart 1973). This fact suggests that labeled and unlabeled training data are both needed in learning, in which labeled data (if enough) can be used to label the class and unlabeled data can be used to estimate the parameters of generative models.

Self-supervised Learning

In self-supervised learning, there is a hybrid training data set $\mathcal{D}$ which consists of a labeled data set $\mathcal{L} = \{(\mathbf{x}_i, y_i), i = 1, \ldots, N\}$, where $\mathbf{x}_i$ is feature vector, y_i is label and N is the size of the set, and an unlabeled data set $\mathcal{U} = \{\mathbf{x}_i, i = 1, \ldots, M\}$, where M is the size of the set. Generally, we make an assumption here that $\mathcal{L}$ and $\mathcal{U}$ are from the same distribution. Essentially, the classification problem can be represented as:

$$y_i = arg \max_{j=1,\ldots,C} p(y_j|\mathbf{x}_i, \mathcal{L}, \mathcal{U} : \forall \mathbf{x}_i \in \Psi) \quad (1)$$

where Ψ is a subset of the whole data space Ω and C is the number of classes. According to different Ψ, self-supervised learning has different special cases.

The Inductive Problem When $\Psi = \Omega$, self-supervised learning becomes inductive learning. The classification is represented as:

$$y_i = arg \max_{j=1,\ldots,C} p(y_j|\mathbf{x}_i, \mathcal{L}, \mathcal{U} : \forall \mathbf{x}_i \in \Omega) \quad (2)$$

Different from conventional learning paradigms, inductive learning depends on both supervised data set $\mathcal{L}$ and unsupervised data set $\mathcal{U}$. If $\mathcal{L} = \phi$, it degenerates to pure unsupervised learning. If $\mathcal{U} = \phi$, it degenerates to pure supervised learning. Generally, we use a large unlabeled training set and a relatively small labeled set.

The Transductive Problem When $\Psi = \mathcal{U}$, self-supervised learning becomes transductive learning. The classification is represented as:

$$y_i = arg \max_{j=1,\ldots,C} p(y_j|\mathbf{x}_i, \mathcal{L}, \mathcal{U} : \forall \mathbf{x}_i \in \mathcal{U}) \quad (3)$$

Generally, the classifier obtained from inductive learning could be highly nonlinear, and a huge labeled training set is required to achieve good generalization. However, the requirement of generalization could be relaxed to a subset of the whole data space. The generalization of transductive learning is only defined on the unlabeled training set $\mathcal{U}$, instead of the whole data space Ω.

It can be illustrated by an example of non-stationary color tracking, in which each color pixel will be labeled by a color classifier or model (M). In transductive learning, a color classifier M_t at time frame t could be only used to classify pixel $\mathbf{x}_j$ in the current specific image feature data set I_t so that this specific classifier M_t could be simpler. When there is a new image I_{t+1} at time $t+1$, this specific classifier M_t should be *transduced* to a new classifier M_{t+1} which works just for the new image I_{t+1} instead of I_t. The classification can be described as:

$$y_i = arg \max_{j=1,\ldots,C} p(y_j|\mathbf{x}_i, M_t, I_{t+1} : \forall \mathbf{x}_i \in I_{t+1}) \quad (4)$$

where y_i is the label of $\mathbf{x}_i$, and C is the number of classes. In this sense, we do not care the performance of the classifier M_{t+1} outside I_{t+1}. The *transductive learning* is to transduce the classifier M_t to M_{t+1} given I_{t+1}. Figure 1 shows the transduction of color classifiers.

This *transduction* may not always be feasible unless we know the joint distribution of I_t and I_{t+1}. Unfortunately, such joint probability is generally unknown since we may not have enough *a priori* knowledge about the transition in a color space over time. We assume that the classifier M_t at time t can give "confident" labels to several samples in I_{t+1}, so that the data in I_{t+1} can be divided into two parts:

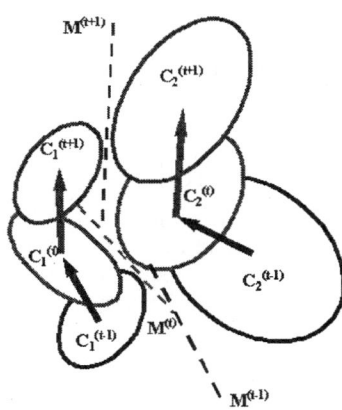

Figure 1: An illustration of transduction of classifiers.

labeled data set $\mathcal{L} = \{(\mathbf{x}_j, y_j), j = 1, \ldots, N\}$, and unlabeled set $\mathcal{U} = \{\mathbf{x}_j, j = 1, \ldots, M\}$. Here, $\mathcal{L}$ and $\mathcal{U}$ are from the same distribution. Consequently, the transductive classification can be written as 3. In this formulation, the specific classifier M_t is transduced to another classifier M_{t+1} by combining a large unlabeled data set from I_{t+1}.

Generative Model

We assume that the hybrid data set is drawn from a mixture density distribution of C components $\{c_j, j = 1, \ldots, C\}$, which are parameterized by $\Theta = \{\theta_j, j = 1, \ldots, C\}$. The mixture model can be represented as:

$$p(\mathbf{x}|\Theta) = \sum_{j=1}^{C} p(\mathbf{x}|c_j; \theta_j) p(c_j|\theta_j) \qquad (5)$$

where $\mathbf{x}$ is a sample drawn from the hybrid data set $\mathcal{D} = \mathcal{L} \bigcup \mathcal{U}$. We make another assumption that each component in the mixture density corresponds to one class, i.e. $\{y_j = c_j, j = 1, \ldots, C\}$.

The D-EM Algorithm

In this section, we describe the EM framework and the proposed D-EM algorithm to the self-supervised learning problem.

The EM Framework

Since the labels of unlabeled data can be treated as missing values, the Expectation-Maximization (EM) approach can be applied to this transductive learning problem. The training data set $\mathcal{D}$ is a union of a set of labeled data set $\mathcal{L}$ and a set of unlabeled set $\mathcal{U}$. When we assume sample independency, the model parameters Θ can be estimated by maximizing *a posteriori* probability $p(\Theta|\mathcal{D})$. Equivalently, this can be done by maximizing $\lg(p(\Theta|\mathcal{D}))$. Let $l(\Theta|\mathcal{D}) = \lg(p(\Theta)p(\mathcal{D}|\Theta))$, and we have

$$l(\Theta|\mathcal{D}) = \lg(p(\Theta)) + \sum_{\mathbf{x}_i \in \mathcal{U}} \lg(\sum_{j=1}^{C} p(O_j|\Theta)p(\mathbf{x}_i|O_j; \Theta))$$

$$+ \sum_{\mathbf{x}_i \in \mathcal{L}} \lg(p(y_i = O_i|\Theta)p(\mathbf{x}_i|y_i = O_i; \Theta)) \qquad (6)$$

When introducing a binary indicator $\mathbf{z}_i = (z_{i1}, \ldots, z_{iC})$, where $z_{ij} = 1$ iff $y_i = O_j$, and $z_{ij} = 0$ otherwise, we have:

$$l(\Theta|\mathcal{D}, \mathcal{Z}) = \lg(p(\Theta))$$
$$+ \sum_{\mathbf{x}_i \in \mathcal{D}} \sum_{j=1}^{C} z_{ij} \lg(p(O_j|\Theta)p(\mathbf{x}_i|O_j; \Theta))$$

The EM algorithm estimates the parameters Θ by an iterative hill climbing procedure, which alternatively calculates $E(\mathcal{Z})$, the expected values for all unlabeled data, and estimates the parameters Θ given $E(\mathcal{Z})$. The EM algorithm generally reaches a local maximum of $l(\Theta|\mathcal{D})$. It consists of two iterative steps:

- E-step: set $\hat{\mathcal{Z}}^{(k+1)} = E[\mathcal{Z}|\mathcal{D}; \hat{\Theta}^{(k)}]$
- M-step: set $\hat{\Theta}^{(k+1)} = arg\ max_\theta\ p(\Theta|\mathcal{D}; \hat{\mathcal{Z}}^{(k+1)})$

where $\hat{\mathcal{Z}}^{(k)}$ and $\hat{\Theta}^{(k)}$ denote the estimation for $\mathcal{Z}$ and Θ at the k-th iteration respectively.

If the probabilistic structure, such as the number of components in mixture models, is known, EM could estimate true probabilistic model parameters. Otherwise, the performance could be very bad. A Gaussian distribution is often assumed to represent a class. Unfortunately, this assumption is often invalid in practice.

The D-EM Algorithm

Since we generally do not know the probabilistic structure of data distribution, EM often fails when structure assumption does not hold. One approach to this problem is to try every possible structure and select the best one. However, it needs more computational resources. An alternative is to find a mapping such that the data are clustered in the mapped data space, in which the probabilistic structure could be simplified and captured by simpler Gaussian mixtures. The Multiple Discriminant Analysis (MDA) technique offers a way to relax the assumption of probabilistic structure, and EM supplies MDA a large labeled data set to select most discriminating features.

MDA is a natural generalization of Fisher's linear discrimination (LDA) in the case of multiple classes(Duda and Hart 1973). The basic idea behind MDA is to find a linear transformation $\mathbf{W}$ to map the original d_1 dimensional data space to a new d_2 space such that the ratio of the between-class scatter and the within-class scatter is maximized in some sense. Details can be found in (Duda and Hart 1973). MDA offers a means to catch major differences between classes and discount factors that are not related to classification. Some features most relevant to classification are automatically selected or combined by the linear mapping $\mathbf{W}$ in MDA, although these features may not have substantial physical meanings any more. Another advantage of MDA is that the data are clustered to some extent in the projected space, which makes it easier to select the structure of Gaussian mixture models.

It is apparent that MDA is a supervised statistical method, which requires enough labeled samples to estimate some statistics such as mean and covariance. By combining MDA with the EM framework, our proposed method, Discriminant-EM algorithm (D-EM), is such a way to combine supervised and unsupervised paradigms. The basic idea of D-EM is to enlarge the labeled data set by identifying some "similar" samples in the unlabeled data set, so that supervised techniques are made possible in such an enlarged labeled set.

D-EM begins with a weak classifier learned from the labeled set. Certainly, we do not expect much from this weak classifier. However, for each unlabeled sample $\mathbf{x}_j$, the classification confidence $\mathbf{w}_j = \{w_{jk}, k = 1, \ldots, C\}$ can be given based on the probabilistic label $\mathbf{l}_j = \{l_{jk}, k = 1, \ldots, C\}$ assigned by this weak classifier.

$$l_{jk} = \frac{p(\mathbf{W}^T\mathbf{x}_j|c_k)p(c_k)}{\sum_{k=1}^{C} p(\mathbf{W}^T\mathbf{x}_j|c_k)p(c_k)} \quad (7)$$

$$w_{jk} = \lg(p(\mathbf{W}^T\mathbf{x}_j|c_k)) \; k = 1, \ldots, C \quad (8)$$

Euqation(8) is just a heuristic to weight unlabeled data $\mathbf{x}_j \in \mathcal{U}$, although there may be many other choices.

After that, MDA is performed on the new weighted data set $\mathcal{D}' = \mathcal{L} \bigcup \{\mathbf{x}_j, \mathbf{l}_j, \mathbf{w}_j : \forall \mathbf{x}_j \in \mathcal{U}\}$, by which the data set $\mathcal{D}'$ is linearly projected to a new space of dimension $C - 1$ but unchanging the labels and weights, $\hat{\mathcal{D}} = \{\mathbf{W}^T\mathbf{x}_j, y_j : \forall \mathbf{x}_j \in \mathcal{L}\} \bigcup \{\mathbf{W}^T\mathbf{x}_j, \mathbf{l}_j, \mathbf{w}_j : \forall \mathbf{x}_j \in \mathcal{U}\}$. Then parameters Θ of the probabilistic models are estimated on $\hat{\mathcal{D}}$, so that the probabilistic labels are given by the Bayesian classifier according to Equation(7). The algorithm iterates over these three steps, "Expectation-Discrimination-Maximization". The following is the description of the D-EM algorithm.

Discriminant-EM algorithm (D-EM)
inputs: labeled set $\mathcal{L}$, unlabeled set $\mathcal{U}$
output: classifier with parameters Θ
begin Initialize: number of components C
    $\mathbf{W} \leftarrow MDA(\mathcal{L})$
    $lset \leftarrow Projection(\mathbf{W}, \mathcal{L})$
    $uset \leftarrow Projection(\mathbf{W}, \mathcal{U})$
    $\Theta \leftarrow MAP(lset)$
    D-E-M iteration
        E-step:
            $plabel \leftarrow Labeling(\Theta, uset)$
            $weight \leftarrow Weighting(plabel)$
            $\mathcal{D}' \leftarrow \mathcal{L} \bigcup \{\mathcal{U}, plabel, weight\}$
        D-step:
            $\mathbf{W} \leftarrow MDA(\mathcal{D}')$
            $lset \leftarrow Projection(\mathbf{W}, \mathcal{L})$
            $uset \leftarrow Projection(\mathbf{W}, \mathcal{U})$
            $\hat{\mathcal{D}} \leftarrow lset \bigcup \{uset, plabel, weight\}$
        M-step:
            $\Theta \leftarrow MAP(\hat{\mathcal{D}})$
    return Θ
end

It should be noted that the simplification of probabilistic structures is not guaranteed in MDA. If the components of data distribution are mixed up, it is very unlikely to find such a linear mapping. In this case, nonlinear mapping should be found so that simple probabilistic structure could

be used to approximate the data distribution in the mapped data space. Generally, we use Gaussian or 2-order Gaussian mixtures. Our experiments show that D-EM works better than pure EM.

Experiments

In our experiments, color tracking is formulated as a transductive problem that is described before, and hand posture recognition is treated as an inductive problem. The investigation of the effect of self-supervision and the effectiveness of D-EM are reported.

Color Tracking

Although these compact 3-D color spaces have substantial physical meanings, none of them is found to be able to give satisfactory color invariants through different lighting conditions. Considering that HSV color space is not a linear transformation of RGB space, we try to use a higher dimensional color space (6-D) by combining HSV and RGB spaces. In one of the experiments, to evaluate our algorithm in color tracking, we assume the segmentation is known to calculate classification errors, although such errors are not available in real applications. We use two "hand images" (resolution 100×75), where I_1 is a segmented image, and I_2 is the same as I_1 except that the color distribution of I_2 is transformed by shifting the R element of every pixel by 20 such that I_2 looks like adding a red filter. A color classifier is learned for I_1 with error rate less than 5%. In this simple situation, this color classifier would fail to correctly segment hand region from I_2, since the skin color in I_2 is much different. Actually, it has error rate of 35.2% on I_2.

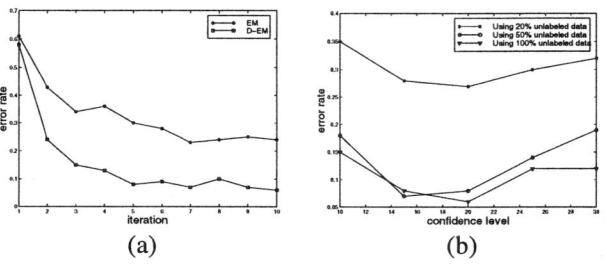

(a)   (b)

Figure 2: (a) shows the comparison between EM and D-EM. (b) shows the effect of number of labeled and unlabeled data in D-EM

Figure 2(a) shows the comparison between EM and D-EM, in which D-EM gives a lower classification error rate (6.9% vs. 24.5%). We feed the algorithm a different number of labeled and unlabeled samples. The number of labeled data is controlled by the confidence level. In this experiment, confidence level is the same as the size of the labeled set. In general, combining unlabeled data can largely reduce the classification error when labeled data are very few. When using 20% (1500) unlabeled data, the lowest error rate achieved is 27.3%. When using 50% (3750) unlabeled data, the lowest error rate drops to 6.9%. The transduced color classifier gives around 20% more accuracy, which is shown in Figure 2(b).

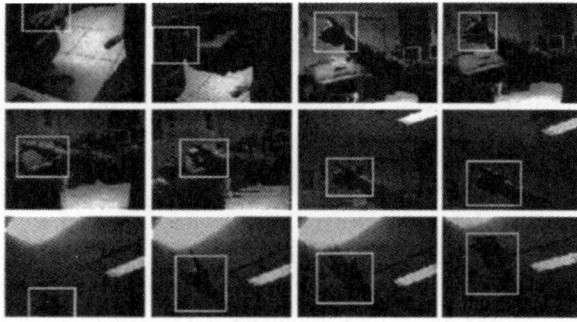

Figure 3: Hand Localization by D-EM

We also perform real experiments by implementing this tracking algorithm, which runs at 15-20Hz on a single processor SGI O2 R10000 workstation. Figure 3 shows an example of hand localization in a typical lab environment. In Figure 3, the skin color in different parts of hand are different. The camera moves from downwards to upwards and the lighting conditions on the hand are different. Hand becomes darker when it shades the light sources in several frames.

Hand Posture Recognition

The gesture vocabulary in our gesture interface is 14. The hand localization system is employed to automatically collect hand images which serve as the unlabeled data, since the localization system only outputs bounding boxes of hand regions, regardless of hand postures. A large unlabeled database can be easily constructed. Currently, there are 14,000 unlabeled hand images in our database. It should be noted that the bounding boxes of some images are not tight, which introduce noise to the training data set. For each posture class, some samples are manually labeled. To investigate the effect of using unlabeled data and to compare different classification algorithms, we construct a testing data set, which consists of 560 labeled images.

Physical (P-) and mathematical (M-) features are both used as hand representation in our experiments. Gabor wavelet filters with 3 levels and 4 orientations are used to extract 12 texture features, each of which is the standard deviation of the wavelet coefficients from one filter. 10 coefficients from the Fourier descriptor are used to represent hand shapes. We also use some statistics such as the hand area, contour length, total edge length, density, and 2-order moments of edge distribution. Therefore, we have 28 low-level image features in total. After resizing the images to 20×20, some mathematical features are extracted by PCA.

We feed the algorithm a different number of labeled and unlabeled samples. In this experiment, we use 500, 1000, 2500, 5000, 7500, 10000, 12500 unlabeled samples and 42, 56, 84, 112, 140 labeled data, respectively. In this experiment, we use the mathematic features extracted by PCA with 22 principal components, and the dimension for MDA is set to 10. As shown in Figure 4(a), in general, combining some unlabeled data reduce the classification error by 20% to 30%.

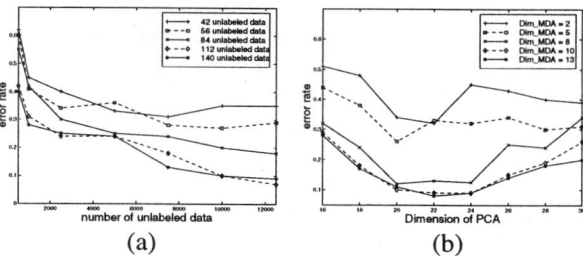

Figure 4: (a) shows the effect of labeled and unlabeled data in D-EM. (b) shows the effect of the dimension of PCA and MDA in D-EM

In Figure 4(b), we study the effect of the dimension parameters in PCA and MDA. If less principal components of PCA are used, some minor but important discriminating features may be neglected so that those principal components may be insufficient to discriminate different classes. On the other hand, if more principal components of PCA are used, it would include more noise. Therefore, the number of principal components of PCA is an important parameter for PCA. The dimension of MDA ranges between 1 to $C - 1$, where C is the number of classes. We are interested in a lower dimensional space in which different classes can be classified. In this experiment, we use 112 labeled data and 10000 unlabeled data, and we find that a good dimension parameter of PCA is around 20 to 24, and 8 to 13 for MDA.

Four classification algorithms are compared in this experiment. For M-Features, the number of principal components of PCA is set to 22, and a set of 560 labeled data is used to perform MDA with dimension of 10. Using 1000 labeled training data, the multi-layer perceptron used in this experiment has one hidden layer of 25 nodes. We experiment with two schemes of the nearest neighbor classifier. One is just of 140 labeled samples, and the other uses 140 labeled samples to bootstrap the classifier by a growing scheme, in which newly labeled samples will be added to the classifier according to their labels. The labeled and unlabeled data for both EM and D-EM are 140 and 10000, respectively. Table 1 shows the comparison.

Algorithm	P-Features	M-Features
Multi-layer Perceptron	33.3%	39.6%
Nearest Neighbor	30.2%	35.7%
Nearest Neighbor(growing)	15.8%	20.3%
EM	21.4%	20.8%
D-EM	9.2%	7.6%

Table 1: Comparison among different algorithms

As shown in Table 1, the D-EM algorithm outperforms the other three methods. The multi-layer perceptron is often trapped in local minima in this experiment. The poor performance of the nearest neighbor classifier is partly due to the insufficient labeled data. When the growing scheme is used, it reduces the error by 15%, since it automatically expends the stored templates. The problem of this scheme is that it is affected by the order of inputs, because there is no confidence measurement in growing so that the error of labeling will be accumulated. Pure EM algorithm hardly converges to a satisfactory classification in our experiments. However, D-EM ends up with a pretty good result.

Conclusion

This paper presents a study of a new learning paradigm, named self-supervised learning, which employs both supervised and unsupervised training data sets. Inductive learning and transductive learning can be treated as two special cases of this new learning paradigm. One possible approach in self-supervised learning is based on the EM framework. Integrating discriminant analysis and the EM framework, the proposed Discriminant-EM (D-EM) algorithm offers a means to relax the assumption of probabilistic structures of data distribution and automatically select a good classification features. In vision-based gesture interface, hand tracking and hand posture recognition offer two applications of self-supervised learning. Experiments show that the proposed D-EM algorithm outperforms some other learning techniques, and self-supervised has many potential applications.

One of the future research directions of this approach is to explore the nonlinear case of MDA. Like nonlinear SVM, some kernel functions should be studied. The convergence and stability analysis should be performed in our future research. Model transduction by using both labeled and unlabeled data is an interesting research topic, which needs more investigation.

Acknowledgments

This work was supported in part by National Science Foundation Grant IRI-9634618 and Grant CDA-9624396. The authors would like to appreciate the anonymous reviewers for their comments.

References

Basri, R.; Roth, D.; and Jacobs, D. 1998. Clustering appearances of 3D objects. In *Proc. of IEEE Int'l Conf. Computer Vision and Pattern Recognition*.

Bennett, K., and Demiriz, A. 1998. Semi-supervised support vector machines. In *Proc. of Neural Information Processing Systems*.

Cui, Y., and Weng, J. 1996. Hand sign recognition from intensity image sequences with complex background. In *Proc. IEEE Conference on Computer Vision and Pattern Recognition*, 88–93.

Davis, J., and Shah, M. 1994. Visual gesture recognition. *Vision, Image, and Signal Processing* 141:101–106.

Duda, R., and Hart, P. 1973. *Pattern Classification and Scene Analysis*. New York: Wiley.

Gammerman, A.; Vapnik, V.; and Vowk, V. 1998. Learning by transduction. In *Proc. of Conf. Uncertainty in Artificial Intelligence*, 148–156.

Heap, T., and Hogg, D. 1996. Towards 3D hand tracking using a deformable model. In *Proc. of IEEE Int'l Conf. Automatic Face and Gesture Recognition*.

Joachims, T. 1999. Transductive inference for text classification using support vector machines. In *Proc. of Int'l Conf. on Machine Learning*.

Jones, M., and Rehg, J. 1998. Statistical color models with application to skin detection. Technical Report CRL 98/11, Compaq Cambridge Research Lab.

Kjeldsen, R., and Kender, J. 1996. Finding skin in color images. In *Proceedings of the Second International Conference on Automatic Face and Gesture Recognition*, 312–317.

Kuch, J. J., and Huang, T. S. 1995. Vision-based hand modeling and tracking for virtual teleconferencing and telecollaboration. In *Proc. of IEEE Int'l Conf. on Computer Vision*, 666–671.

Lee, J., and Kunii, T. 1995. Model-based analysis of hand posture. *IEEE Computer Graphics and Applications* 77–86.

Mitchell, T. 1999. The role of unlabeled data in supervised learning. In *Proc. Sixth Int'l Colloquium on Cognitive Science*.

Nigam, K.; McCallum, A.; Thrun, S.; and Mitchell, T. 1999. Text classification from labeled and unlabeled documents using EM. *Machine Learning*.

Quek, F., and Zhao, M. 1996. Inductive learning in hand pose recognition. In *Proc. of IEEE Int'l Conf. on Automatic Face and Gesture Recognition*.

Raja, Y.; McKenna, S.; and Gong, S. 1998. Colour model selection and adaptation in dynamic scenes. In *Proc. of European Conf. on Computer Vision*.

Rehg, J., and Kanade, T. 1995. Model-based tracking of self-occluding articulated objects. In *Proc. of IEEE Int'l Conf. Computer Vision*, 612–617.

Swain, M., and Ballard, D. 1991. Color indexing. *Int. J. Computer Vision* 7:11–32.

Triesch, J., and von de Malsburg, C. 1996. Robust classification of hand postures against complex background. In *Proc. Int'l Conf. On Automatic Face and Gesture Recognition*.

Vapnik, V. 1995. *The Nature of Statistical Learning Theory*. New York: Springer-Verlag.

Wu, Y., and Huang, T. S. 1999. Capturing articulated human hand motion: A divide-and-conquer approach. In *Proc. IEEE Int'l Conf. on Computer Vision*, 606–611.

Wu, Y.; Liu, Q.; and Huang, T. S. 2000. An adaptive self-organizing color segmentation algorithm with application to robust real-time human hand localization. In *Proc. of Asian Conference on Computer Vision*, 1106–1111.

Interactive Training for Synthetic Characters

Song-Yee Yoon[†,‡], Robert C. Burke[†], Bruce M. Blumberg[†] and Gerald E. Schneider[‡]

sy@media.mit.edu   rob@media.mit.edu   bruce@media.mit.edu   jerry@mit.edu

[†] Synthetic Characters Group
Media Laboratory
Massachusetts Institute of Technology
Cambridge, MA 02139

[‡] Department of Brain and Cognitive Sciences
Massachusetts Institute of Technology
Cambridge, MA 02139

Abstract

Compelling synthetic characters must behave in ways that reflect their past experience and thus allow for individual personalization. We therefore need a method that allows characters to learn. But simply adding traditional machine learning algorithms without considering the characters' own motivations and desires will break the illusion of life. Intentional characters require interactive learning. In this paper, we present the results of Sydney K9.0, a project based on the Synthetic Characters creature kernel framework. Inspired by pet training, we have implemented a character that can be trained using the "clicker training" technique. Clicker training utilizes the natural desires of an animal and employs operant conditioning procedures for shaping their behavior. The necessary plasticity of system interconnections shaped by associations and rewards that is required by clicker training was integrated into the creature kernel framework. The implemented system also includes a module named DogEar that is designed for collecting real-world acoustic data, such as human voice commands, integrated into the creature kernel's perception system. This provides a seamless interface between the simulated and real worlds. Detailed implementation and interaction results are presented.

Introduction

Synthetic characters are artificial creatures that have their own motivations and desires and can interact with human beings in real time (Kline and Blumberg 1999). The capacity to adapt and the ability to convey intentions (Dennett 1987) have been pointed out as key factors that maintain the illusion of life during human interactions with characters designed to have their own mind and will.

In particular, a character's ability to learn makes the interactions between humans and characters a sustainable relationship. For example, toys that learn through interactions are appealing as creatures that can reflect their past experiences. They are personalizable, and are seen to exist as unique beings.

Copyright © 1999, American Association for Artificial Intelligence (www.aaai.org). All rights reserved.

Introducing learning abilities into synthetic characters brings with it several challenges if we hope to maintain a lifelike impression. For example, we want characters to learn what they are being taught, but remain in character. Yet, through this training, we would like to be able to shape characters, and personalize them as our friends and companions. Even if they are learning, they should have their own drives and affects, and show these states through their actions and emotional expressions. This raises the issue of how to train a being that has its own intentions. More fundamentally, learning is a hard problem for any system but one which can be greatly facilitated by the presence of a skilled trainer who can guide the learning process and thereby reduce the complexity of the learner's task.

Figure 1. This figure shows two of the characters that inhabit the Sydney K9.0 virtual world - Sydney and Fridge. Human participants who interact with this system can train the virtual dog, Sydney. Fridge is the graphical instantiation of the user, who holds and controls the training stick to guide Sydney's attention. Fridge can reward Sydney with milkbones when the human participant shakes the milkbone box.

Pet trainers face a similar problem, since real animals also have their own drives and interests. Among the various training techniques that have been tried with pets, the "clicker training" method, derived from operant conditioning, has proven to be particularly successful with animals ranging from dogs to dolphins (Wilkes 1995; Pryor 1999). Inspired by this idea from pet training, our project implements a clicker training session.

Related Work

Building an artifact that can learn is an extensively studied area (Ballard 1997). In the case of situated characters, however, additional constraints – which naturally originate due to the complexity of the surrounding world – need to be dealt with. Terzopoulos and Tu (1994) integrated learning into graphical creatures where the learning focused on locomotion for surviving in the simulated physical world. Relevant cues were already given and creatures were assumed to know what to learn and pay attention to. In real world situations, however, deciding what to attend to and learning relevant cues and the right associative links are significant challenges (Scherl and Levesque 1993). These are areas where extensive state-based search methods (Allen, Hendler and Tate 1990) have been used for dealing with the complexity of the environment and as a strategy for learning, and this has been applied to the domain of self-animated graphical creatures (Funge, Tu and Terzopoulos 1999).

This is exactly the problem that must be addressed by animals in the natural world. Studies of animal behavior (Lorenz 1981; Skinner 1938) have defined operant conditioning as a powerful learning scheme for a situated creature (Sutton and Barto 1998). Operant conditioning has been implemented in a number of studies with promising results (Drescher 1993; Touretzky and Saksida 1996; Blumberg, Todd and Maes 1996). However, the question addressed by our work is different. Namely, assuming you have a system that can learn using operant and classical associations, what is the best way to teach the system? To answer this question, we take our inspiration from animal training.

Clicker Training

One of the most popular methods that pet trainers use is clicker training (Wilkes 1995), which is based on operant conditioning and consisting of two associative learning processes. By repeatedly giving a reward (i.e. something like a food treat that is motivationally important to the dog) right after sounding a hand-held "clicker" device, the dog forms an associative link between the clicker sound and the positive reinforcer. After multiple repetitions, the clicker becomes a secondary reinforcer that reliably signals that a primary reinforcer will be forthcoming. In addition, the clicker acts as an "event marker" indicating the exact behavior and/or configuration for which the dog is to be rewarded. A behavior that is consistently rewarded will tend to increase in frequency per Thorndike's Law (Wilkes 1995). A clicker trainer uses this phenomenon together with techniques such as luring or shaping to create the desired behavior. In luring, the dog is lured into a configuration that can then be rewarded. In shaping, the trainer guides the dog's search by rewarding successive approximations to the desired behavior. Once the behavior is in place, a clicker trainer then teaches the dog the context in which this behavior is a reliable strategy for being rewarded. Typically, the context is a gesture or an utterance. In a sense, since the dog already "knows" the behavior, it can focus on learning the context in which the behavior is maximally reliable. Backward chaining is typically used to teach sequences of actions.

There are two properties of the clicker sound that make it effective for training. Firstly, the clicker emits a sound of a very distinct frequency that is easily discernable from other auditory inputs. Secondly, it provides a precise "end of behavior" marker because it has very short temporal characteristics. Thus, while verbal praises such as *good dog* could be used for the same purpose, the duration of such an utterance is sufficiently long that a number of behaviors could have been performed while the utterance was being made (Wilkes 1995). The clicker sound provides the dog with a more accurate sense of which behavior is being rewarded.

Clicker training works effectively for pets because it solves several problems faced by a learner in a complex and unpredictable environment. The interactive nature of the training and the distinctive clicker marking help the learner to solve the temporal and behavioral credit assignment problems (Sutton and Barto 1998), which are crucial for successful learning in a dynamic environment. The training proceeds by forming a chain of links that ultimately leads to a motivationally important state for the animal. The training starts with forming the simple associative link between the clicker sound and reward, then the rest of the procedure results in backwardly expanding the link to a more complex behavioral repertoire, including only elements that ultimately lead to reward. Feedback from the trainer, such as the clicker sound, helps the pet to determine exactly why it is being rewarded and what it is supposed to learn and focus on. At the same time, this simplifies the job of the trainer.

Sydney K9.0

In this section, we describe a project called **Sydney K9.0**, which implements three main characters: "Sydney," an interactive dog; "Fridge," his friend the walking refrigerator; and "Nabee," the butterfly. We extend the creature kernel framework (Yoon 2000) to include an interactive learning ability in building the characters for this project. In addition, Sydney is endowed with an auditory system described below.

An example interaction is shown in Figure 2. The participant has all four elements of the interface available: a wearable microphone, a training stick, a milkbone box and the clicker. The user can move the training stick in any direction and the movement and resulting location of the stick is reflected by a corresponding change in the training stick that Fridge holds. Sydney can sense the location of the tip of the training stick using a virtual sensor located on the virtual training stick in Fridge's hand. The clicker sound is treated as a special sound signal that is perceived as distinct from the speech signal, even though both are auditory signals. When Sydney's behavior deserves to be rewarded, the human participant shakes the milkbone box, which results in a bone appearing on screen, which Sydney can eat to satisfy his hunger drive. A sensor is installed inside the milkbone box that is activated whenever the box is shaken.

Figure 2. Sydney K9.0 implements a virtual dog training session where Fridge, a refrigerator in the virtual world, is both the trainer and the proxy for the human participant. The participant can provide input to the system with the aid of various interfaces: a wearable microphone, a training stick, a milkbone box and a clicker.

The participant can train Sydney using the clicker training method described above. Since this training proceeds while respecting the synthetic character's motivations and intentions – just as when we train real dogs – we believe it proposes a method for training an intentional character without compromising the character's illusion of life (Thomas and Johnston 1981). A graphical display of the interaction between Sydney and Fridge is shown in Figure 1.

Now we discuss how the characters in **Sydney K9.0** were built, and then describe the external components, such as speech processing for DogEar; and internal components, such as Sydney's behavior, learning and memory implementation.

Characters

All three characters in this project – Sydney the dog, Fridge the refrigerator, and Nabee the butterfly – are implemented within the creature kernel framework as suggested by Blumberg (Blumberg 1996; Blumberg and Galyean 1995) and later expanded by Kline (Kline and Blumberg 1999) and Yoon (Yoon 2000).

Creature kernel. Creature kernel is a framework for building interactive synthetic characters. Within this framework, a creature is built internally as a sum of four subcomponents: the motivation, behavior, motor and perception systems. These four components coordinate to make the character operate as a functioning whole.

The motivation, behavior and perception systems are organized as a network of basis units. For example, the behavior system is modeled as a hierarchically connected network of behavior units as shown in Tinbergen's animal behavior model (Tinbergen 1951). The perception system is a system of sensors that extract information about what is going on inside and outside of the character. It includes both the virtual vision sensors for seeing another character in the same virtual world, and physical sensors for receiving input (such as the training stick) coming from the physical world. The motivation system is composed of affect and drives. Affect refers to the creature's emotional state, and is associated with the character's feelings and moods. Drives are motivators, and include endogenous drives and externally induced desires. The behavior system performs action selection i.e., it chooses the most relevant behavior to perform given the perception and motivation input. The behavior system in turn sends a signal to the motor system, which is a set of action primitives and available motor skills, indicating which action should be performed and how it should be performed. In our system, where characters are 3D animated creatures, the motor system is composed of a set of animations, and it renders the skill chosen by the behavior system on the screen.

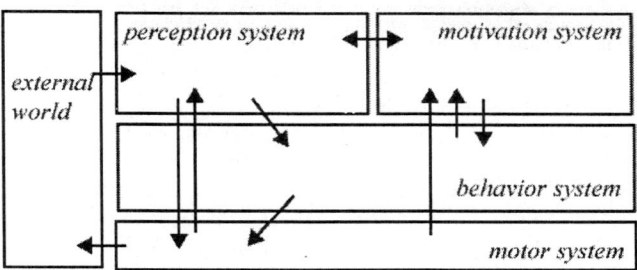

Figure 3. A schematic diagram of a synthetic character. Arrows represent the information flow between systems. Well-coordinated communication among these four systems—perception, motivation, behavior and motor—is required for a character to successfully function in a dynamic world.

Figure 3 shows the schematic diagram of the creature kernel. Arrows represent information flow between components. Any loop made by a succession of arrows represents a possible sequence, e.g., from the creature's perception of the world, to internal information processing and then to exertion on the outside world. All three characters in this project are implemented using this framework. Detailed explanation of this kernel operation is found in Yoon (2000).

Creature Kernel Implementation

This section further explains the creature kernel framework as it pertains to the implementation of Sydney. Sydney is based on a version of the creature kernel that has been augmented to allow for the processing of real-time voice commands from the human participant, and to allow formation of associations between verbal commands and corresponding tricks during the clicker training session.

The Motivation System. Sydney's motivation system consists of two parts – the drive system and the affect system. Sydney has three main drives: hunger, curiosity and fatigue. He feels hungry if he does not consume an adequate amount of food for a long time, and thus Sydney perceives as an incentive or positive reinforcement something that will satisfy his hunger drive (i.e., a snack). This drive provides Sydney with the motivation to learn through interaction with the human participant because learning and performance of a desired behavior provide Sydney with milkbones as rewards.

Curiosity drives Sydney to explore the world. Drives rise at different rates while satisfying stimuli are not provided, or while the key stimuli that instigate them are perceived. The Curiosity drive rises when Sydney stays at one place for a long period of time, and exploring the world lowers this curiosity. Sydney is also interested in interacting with other creatures such as Nabee, the butterfly. So, for example, when Nabee is close to Sydney, his curiosity rises until it often surpasses the other drives. Fatigue brings Sydney back home for a rest, and as he rests his Fatigue drive is reduced. After the fatigue level diminishes below the level of another drive, Sydney gets up to initiate behaviors that will satisfy his currently most pressing drive.

The Behavior System. Sydney's behavior system is composed of two main parts. The first is the *primary* behavior system, which is a set of behavior nodes and sequences that can be used to satisfy goals. In essence, it is composed of behavior units such as walk, run, lie down, sit down, roll over, beg, etc., which form sequences within the behavior network to satisfy goals and drives.

The other part of Sydney's behavior system is the *autonomous* behavior system, which contains more reflex-like behavior such as ear movement – triggered when Sydney detects sound – and autonomous stand, which is a low-priority default behavior that runs to avoid situations where no animation would be running because no particular behavior is chosen by the action selection mechanism.

The Motor System. As for Sydney's motor system, animation files made by animators are provided as the means for enabling Sydney to perform certain skills and display them on the screen. Leaf node behavior units, at the termination of the behavior system's branches, are where the behavior system blends into the motor system. The motor system uses a verb-adverb model (Rose, Cohen and Bodenheimer 1998), whereby the behavior system specifies a verb/adverb and the motor system does real time motion interpolation among animation examples to produce motion with the appropriate emotional content. The animation blending capabilities of the motor system are described in more detail by Johnson (1999).

The Perception System. Sydney's perception system is expanded to cope with real-time voice inputs from human participants. His perception system is divided into two parts: virtual sensors, and sensors responsible for receiving inputs from the physical world. Virtual sensors enable Sydney to access all of the returnable features of the targeted objects (Kline and Blumberg 1999). The perception network is extended by additional sensors that return levels of beliefs about whether the objects are far, close, etc.

The sensors responsible for processing real world inputs, include *DogEar*, an interface to the human voice commands. The system is built to use two PCs. One PC is devoted to receiving data through the microphone and running DogEar, and the other PC updates the creature kernel and renders graphics. Implementation detail on DogEar is found in the next section.

DogEar

The DogEar system has been implemented to mediate verbal communication between a human participant and Sydney. It receives the human participant's utterance data, and converts the raw data to a Cepstral coefficient format that is received and stored by Sydney's auditory memory.

Data Acquisition. The sounds in the system are sampled at 11025 Hz. Sound bites are obtained by using a thresholding algorithm that averages the signal over windows of 512 samples. Recording starts when the signal is above the threshold, and ends when it has been below the threshold for three successive windows. The sample is then trimmed at each end to the nearest zero-crossing.

Representation. We have chosen to use a vector of cepstral coefficients as a representation. Like a real dog, Sydney does not comprehend language, nor does he have a concept of language. What Sydney interprets is the acoustic pattern of the speech signal; thus, a Cepstral coefficient representation is a sufficient and appropriate encoding of the necessary information. Cepstral analysis is a technique that removes the pitch ripple from high-resolution speech spectra, as examined by Rabiner and Juang (1993). The goal of cepstral analysis is to obtain the vocal tract response after removing the pitch ripple.

The DogEar system performs this task by filtering the log-magnitude of the signal with an inverse FFT. This is followed by truncation of the coefficients beyond the pitch frequency, and then a forward FFT (Intel 1998). In the Fourier domain, we are using 10 filters placed linearly on a scale from 100 Hz up to 2 kHz, followed by 10 additional filters laid out on a Mel scale up to 6400 Hz. Analysis is performed using a window size of 512 samples and an overlap of 256 samples per window. At present, in order to facilitate classification of feature vectors of equal length, cepstral coefficients are obtained for exactly the first 20 windows. If the utterance is sufficiently short that it does not fill 20 windows, the remaining windows are filled with silence. We thus end up with 400-dimensional cepstral coefficient feature vectors.

Integration

The protocol that allows DogEar to communicate with the creature kernel system includes two binary bits indicating the existence of new speech and clicker inputs, and the Cepstral coefficient representation of new utterance data.

Classifier and Short-Term Memory. The main system includes a short-term memory module with a fixed number of memory cells. These cells, referred to as memory groups below, each represent uniquely classified utterances. This memory module is very simple in implementation; its main role is in storing patterns. When a new utterance is heard, it is compared to the utterances in all the groups to see if the distance of the newly arrived data in any of the groups is closer than a preset threshold. Dynamic Time Warping (Rabiner 1993, Intel 1998) is used as a distance metric.

Interaction. From Sydney's standpoint, the information he receives which is relevant to training comes from auditory inputs, utterances of the human participant and the clicker sound, and virtual visual inputs. It is assumed that Sydney has the ability to distinguish the clicker sound from utterances, due to its distinctive frequency.

Without the human participant's presence, Sydney freely wanders around, motivated by his internal drives and affects aroused endogenously as well as perceptually. At realization of the human's presence, through a speech signal that is perceived as an attentional bid (from Fridge), Sydney runs toward Fridge and awaits a command because he has learned that the interaction and performing the right behaviors lead to reward. As the user's speech command is issued, Sydney performs a trick that, he believes, matches the spoken command. If he was right, the human participant shakes the milkbone box in his hand that produces a milkbone in the virtual world. Sydney runs toward the milkbone, consumes it and thereby reduces his level of hunger. A reward solidifies his belief in the link between the command and the behavior he just performed. When the behavior was not right, the lack of reward weakens his belief in the associative link between the perceived acoustic pattern and the behavior. This makes the behavior less likely to be performed the next time he hears a similar utterance. In the absence of a command Sydney will probablistically choose a behavior based on the likelihood of reward.

Learning

The "eating" behavior is rewarding because it reduces the level of hunger. Thus, perceiving a milkbone is rewarding for Sydney. The unconditioned stimulus, food, and the unconditioned response, eating that leads to hunger drive satisfaction, is an innate behavior context chain. This pathway is represented as the chain of links marked **A** in Figure 4. The first thing that a dog trainer does is to form a linkage between the clicker sound and something rewarding. It could be any type of food that the dog enjoys or petting or praise that causes positive affective arousal in the dog. A strong link between the clicker sound and the unconditioned reward stimulus makes the dog regard the clicker sound itself as rewarding, and thus the trainer can use this clicker sound as a positive reinforcer for further training. This associative link between two perceptual stimuli is marked **B** in Figure 4.

Finally, operant conditioning builds a chain of links labeled **C** in Figure 4. A verbal command is issued and, when Sydney performs the appropriate behavior, he is rewarded with the clicker sound. It forms an associative link between the command and the behavior that leads to the clicker sound. The sound has a positive reinforcing value due to the expectation of a reward to follow. Update rules and learning algorithms for integrating learning into the creature kernel are described by Yoon, Blumberg and Schneider (2000).

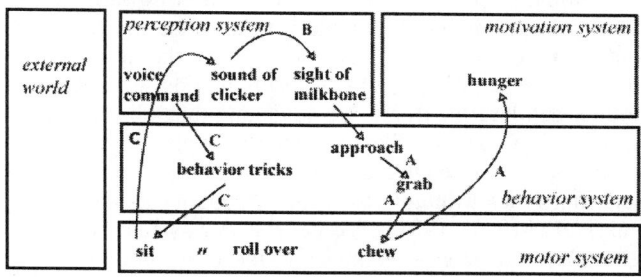

Figure 4. Clicker training, effectively, builds up a behavioral representation within Sydney's creature kernel. The chain labeled A is an unconditioned stimuli-unconditioned response (US-UR) link that preexists in the creature kernel. During the first phase of the clicker training, an associative link between two stimuli, clicker sound and food, a piece of milkbone in this project's case, is formed and this is labeled B in this figure. The third associative link chain is formed through an operant conditioning process and this is labeled C. The link encompasses the sequence of spoken command → performance of a corresponding trick → clicker sound. The link between a spoken command and a trick is strengthened as the outperforming of the link is rewarded by the clicker sound, which has a positive reinforcing value as it is followed by an unconditioned rewarding stimulus.

Observations and Discussion

Preliminary interactive experiences have been provided to experienced programmers, as well as novice users who have never interacted with software creatures before. Participants who had pet-training experience felt comfortable extending their experience to the virtual pet training session. One response we received to a recalcitrant Sydney while adjusting the noise controls in a crowded environment was, "he's acting that way because you aren't treating him gently enough. I know how dogs behave since I have my own pet dog at home." The user went on to (gently) teach Sydney how to roll over on command.

Since the acoustic data processing does not assume *a priori* knowledge of language or grammar, Sydney's acoustic system has proven robust. At one point during a demonstration, Sydney had learned to respond appropriately to commands in English, French, Japanese and Norwegian.

Perhaps most importantly, users were consistently impressed by Sydney's lifelike behavior. These observations demonstrate the plausibility of using the clicker training method to allow synthetic characters to learn while maintaining the illusion of life that comes from their actions and reactions.

Limitations of this implementation include the lack of ability to process affect information in the verbal commands. As our participants indicated, real dogs discern contextual information from cues such as prosidy and pitch in utterances. This extension will be implemented by augmenting DogEar to extract these acoustic cues and transfer them to the behavior system.

More fundamentally, we need to implement luring and shaping. Clicker training requires variation on the part of the animal to produce behavior that can be rewarded. The trainer can wait for the creature to produce the behavior, but it is often more efficient to lure the animal into performing it. For example, to teach the dog to lie down, a trainer can lure the dog to lie down and then click so that it learns it is a behavior that can potentially bring a reward.

In Nature an adaptable mammal must have a variety of learning types available to it for optimizing its chances of survival (Lorenz 1981). We believe our system is general enough to enable a number of these learning types in addition to operant conditioning, including habituation, concept formation, and formation of affective responses to objects or places (see Yoon et al. 2000). A full evaluation of the learning abilities of a synthetic character like Sydney will require detailed analysis of all these learning types, a task we are now at the stage of undertaking.

Acknowledgments. Many thanks to all the members of the Synthetic Characters Group, and Gary Wilkes for introducing us to the world of clicker training.

References

Allen, J., Hendler, H. and Tete, A, eds. 1990. *Readings in Planning*, San Mateo, CA.: Morgan Kaufmann.

Ballard, D. H. 1997. *An Introduction to Natural Computation.* Cambridge, MA. :MIT Press.

Blumberg, B. and Galyean, T. 1995. Multi-Level Direction of Autonomous Creatures for Real Time Virtual Environment. In *Proceedings of SIGGRAPH 95*: New York, NY. ACM SIGGRAPH

Blumberg, B. M. 1996. Old Tricks, New Dogs: Ethology and Interactive Creatures. Ph.D. diss., The Media Laboratory, Massachusetts Institute of Technology.

Blumberg, B. M., Todd, P. M. and Maes, P. 1996. No Bad Dogs: Ethological Lessons for Learning in Hamsterdam. From Animals to Animats 4, *Proceedings of the Fourth International Conference on Simulation of Adaptive Behavior.* Cambridge, MA.:MIT Press.

Dennett, D. 1987, *The Intentional Stance*, Cambridge, MA.: MIT Press.

Drescher, G. 1991. *Made-up minds: a constructive approach to artificial intelligence.* Cambridge, MA.: MIT Press.

Funge, J., Tu, X. and Terzopoulos, D. 1999. Cognitive Modeling: Knowledge, Reasoning and Planning for Intelligent Characters. In *Proceedings of SIGGRAPH 99*, 29-38.: New York, NY. ACM SIGGRAPH

Intel, Inc. 1998. Intel® Recognition Primitives Library V4.0 Documentation. Santa Clara, CA.: Intel Corporation. *Available at* http://developer.intel.com/vtune/perflibst/RPL

Johnson, M. P. 1999. Multi-Dimensional Quaternion Interpolation, In *ACM SIGGRAPH99 Conference Abstracts and Applications*, page 258. New York, NY. ACM SIGGRAPH.

Kline, C. and Blumberg, B. 1999. The Art and Science of Synthetic Character Design. In Proceedings of the AISB 1999 Symposium on AI and Creativity in Entertainment and Visual Art, Edinburgh, Scotland.

Lorenz, K. 1981. *The Foundations of Ethology.* New York, NY.: Springer-Verlag.

Pryor, K. 1999. *Clicker Training for Dogs.* Waltham, MA.: Sunshine Books, Inc.

Rabiner, L. and Juang, B. 1993. Fundamentals of Speech Recognition. New York, NY.: Prentice-Hall.

Rose, C., Cohen, M. F., and Bodenheimer, B. 1998. Verbs and Adverbs: Multidimensional Motion Interpolation. IEEE CG&A, 18(5): 32~40. Piscataway, NJ.:IEEE Press.

Scherl, R. and Levesque, H. 1993. The frame problem and knowledge-producing actions. In *Proceedings of AAAI-93*. Menlo Park, Calif.: AAAI Press.

Skinner, B. F. 1938. *The Behavior of Organisms.* New York, NY.: Appleton Century Crofs.

Sutton, R. and Barto, A. 1998. Reinforcement Learning. Cambridge, MA.: MIT Press.

Terzapoulos, D. and Tu, X. 1994. Artificial fishes: Autonomous locomotion, perception, behavior and learning in a simulated physical world. Artificial Life 1:327~351.

Thomas, F. and Johnston, O. 1981. *The Illusion of Life: Disney Animations.* New York, NY.: Abbeville Press.

Tinbergen, N. 1951. *The Study of Instinct.* New York, NY.: Oxford University Press.

Touretzky, D. S. and Saksida, L. M. 1996. Skinnerbots. From Animals to Animats 4, *Proceedings of the Fourth International Conference on Simulation of Adaptive Behavior.* Cambridge, MA.:MIT Press.

Wilkes, G. 1995. Click and Treat Training Kit Version 1.2. Mesa, AZ.: www.clickandtreat.com.

Yoon, S. -Y. 2000. Affective Synthetic Characters. Ph D. diss. Department of Brain and Cognitive Sciences, Massachusetts Institute of Technology. *Forthcoming.*

Yoon, S.-Y., Blumberg, B. M. and Schneider, G. E. 2000. Motivation Driven Learning for Interactive Synthetic Characters. In *Proceedings of the Fourth International Conference on Autonomous Agents.* New York, NY.: ACM Press. *Forthcoming.*

Knowledge Representation and Reasoning

Generating Satisfiable Problem Instances

Dimitris Achlioptas
Microsoft Research
Redmond, WA 98052
optas@microsoft.com

Carla Gomes
Dept. of Comp. Sci.
Cornell Univ.
Ithaca, NY 14853
gomes@cs.cornell.edu

Henry Kautz
AT&T Research
Florham Park, NJ
kautz@research.att.com

Bart Selman
Dept. of Comp. Sci.
Cornell Univ.
Ithaca, NY 14853
selman@cs.cornell.edu

Abstract

A major difficulty in evaluating incomplete local search style algorithms for constraint satisfaction problems is the need for a source of hard problem instances that are guaranteed to be satisfiable. A standard approach to evaluate incomplete search methods has been to use a general problem generator and a complete search method to filter out the unsatisfiable instances. Unfortunately, this approach cannot be used to create problem instances that are beyond the reach of complete search methods. So far, it has proven to be surprisingly difficult to develop a direct generator for satisfiable instances only. In this paper, we propose a generator that only outputs satisfiable problem instances. We also show how one can finely control the hardness of the satisfiable instances by establishing a connection between problem hardness and a new kind of phase transition phenomenon in the space of problem instances. Finally, we use our problem distribution to show the easy-hard-easy pattern in search complexity for *local search* procedures, analogous to the previously reported pattern for complete search methods.

Introduction

In recent years, we have seen the rapid development of both complete and incomplete search methods for constraint satisfaction (CSP) and Boolean satisfiability (SAT) problems. These methods are now applied successfully in a range of applications within artificial intelligence and computer science in general. An important factor in the development of new search methods is the availability of good sets of benchmark problems to evaluate and fine-tune the algorithms. There are two main sources of benchmark problems. One class of benchmarks is based on real-world applications and the other is from random instance generators. Real-world instances are arguably the best source, but unfortunately are often in short supply. Moreover, there is a risk that algorithms are being tuned towards specific application domains for which good benchmarks are available. Random problem generators therefore provide a good additional source of problem instances. These generators also have the advantage of a more direct control over the problem characteristics, such as size and expected hardness. Hard random instances have led to the development of new stochastic search methods such as Walksat (Selman et al. 1996) and the breakout procedure (Morris 1993), and have been used in detailed comparisons of local search methods for graph coloring and related graph problems (Johnson et al. 1989). The results of various competitions for CSP and SAT algorithms show that there is a fairly direct correlation between the performance on real-world benchmarks and on hard random instances (DIMACS 1993, 1996; Beijing, 1996; Johnson et al. 1989). It is important to note that randomly generated problem instances are not necessarily *unstructured*. Structure may be introduced by translating random problems from one domain into another, or by considering problem domains that by definition exhibit regular structure (Gomes and Selman 1997, Walsh 1999).

Current problem generators are based on recent developments in our understanding of the nature of computationally hard problem instances. In particular, a clear connection has been established between so-called phase transition phenomena and the computational hardness of NP-complete problems (Cheeseman et al. 1991, Mitchell et al. 1992, Hogg et al. 1996). Phase transition phenomena capture the surprisingly sharp transitions from the solvable to the unsolvable in the space of problem instances, as a function of certain problem parameters such as the ratio of the number of constraints to the number of variables. In random distributed problem instances, at low ratios (relatively few constraints) one encounters mostly satisfiable instances, while at high ratios most instances are unsatisfiable. In terms of complexity, one observes a easy-hard-easy pattern, where assignments are easily found in the sat-phase, while inconsistency is easily shown in the unsat-phase. At the phase transition, where roughly half the instances are satisfiable and half the instances are unsatisfiable, one finds a concentration of computationally hard problem instances. The ability to varying the hardness of the problem instances makes it possible to study precisely how different search algorithms *scale* in terms of problem difficulty.

A key limitation of current problem generators concerns their use in the evaluation of incomplete local search methods. This is because the generators generally produce a mixture of solvable (satisfiable) and unsolvable (unsatisfiable) instances. When a local search style method does not find a solution, it can be difficult to determine whether this is because the algorithm fails to find a solution or because the instance itself is unsolvable. The standard way of dealing

Copyright © 2000, American Association for Artificial Intelligence (www.aaai.org). All rights reserved.

with this problem is to use a complete search method to filter out the unsatisfiable cases. However, this limits the size and difficulty of problems instances that can be considered. Ideally, one would use problem generators that generate satisfiable instances only. However, developing such generators has been surprisingly difficult.

As an example, let us consider generating hard satisfiable 3CNF formulas. In order to obtain satisfiable instances only, it is natural to use a strategy where one creates formulas in the phase transition region (ratio of clauses to variables of around 4.25) that are "forced" to have at least one satisfying assignment. To do so, consider the following strategy: generate a random truth assignment T, and then generate a formula with N variables and $4.25N$ random clauses, where one rejects any clause that violates T. This method will in principle generate all possible satisfiable formulas with a clause-to-variable ratio of 4.25 that have T among their solution. What is somewhat surprising however is that the sampling of these formulas is far from uniform: the generator is highly biased towards formulas with many assignments, clustered around T. When fed to local search methods such as Walksat, these formulas are much easier than formulas of comparable size obtained by filtering satisfiable instances from a 3SAT generator. More sophisticated versions of the forced-formula scheme (Asahiro *et al.* 1993, Van Gelder 1993) provide improvements but also lead to biased samples.

There are also a number of theoretical results that show that is is difficult to "hide" a combinatorial object in a larger combinatorial structure. For example, it can be shown that one can easily find cliques over a certain size that are hidden in a random graph, and similar results are known for hiding graph colorings (Frieze and McDiarmid 1997). The problem of hiding information in larger combinatorial structures is of interest to the computer science theory community since successful techniques for doing so may eventually lead to more effective cryptographic methods.

Cryptographic problems do suggest one way of creating hard satisfiable problem instances (Impagliazzo *et al.* 1989). For example, Crawford and Kearns (1993) created SAT encodings of the "noisy" parity problem. The instances are guaranteed to have a satisfying assignment but are extremely hard to solve using current SAT procedures. In recent work Massacci (1999) also provides a way of translating the DES crypto protocol into a SAT instance. One can obtain very hard satisfiable instances this way. Since the best algorithms known for dealing directly with the original crypto problem involve exhaustive search, one finds that the best SAT methods are also reduced to an essentially exhaustive search of the space of truth assignments. This means that in practice these problems are in a sense too hard for the development and evaluation of SAT procedures. Furthermore, the cryptographic encodings do not provide a fine-grained way to vary problem hardness in order to studying how the algorithms scale. In general, it seems reasonable to assume that in practical applications one does not expect to find hidden crypto problems, unless one is dealing specifically with a cryptographic application.

In this paper, we will introduce a method for the generation of (empirically) hard satisfiable problem instances. We also show how one can finely control the hardness of the satisfiable instances by establishing a connection between problem hardness and a new kind of phase transition phenomenon in the space of problem instances. As we discussed above, traditional phase transition phenomena involve a sudden transition from a satisfiable to an unsatisfiable phase of the problem instance space. Since our generator only outputs satisfiable instances, such a transition does not occur. However, under the right parameterization, we also observe an easy-hard-easy pattern in the space of satisfiable instances, just as is the case for complete search methods. (For related work, see Clark *et al.* (1996).) This makes it possible to tune the generator to output hard problem instances.

We can link the hardness area to a phase transition which corresponds to a clear threshold phenomenon in the size of the "backbone" of the problem instances. Informally speaking, the backbone measures the amount of shared structure among the set of all solutions to a given problem instance. The size of the backbone is measured in terms of the percentage of variables that have the same value in all possible solutions. We will observe a transition from a phase where the size of the backbone is almost 100% to a phase with a backbone of size close to 0%. The transition is sudden and we will show how it coincides with the hardest problem instances both for incomplete and complete search methods.

Quasigroups with holes

Most traditional benchmark problems are based on randomly generated instances with little or no global structure. In Gomes and Selman (1997), we introduced the so-called quasigroup completion problem in order to obtain benchmark instances with more interesting structural properties.

The best way to view the quasigroup completion problem is in terms of the completion of a Latin square (which technically defines the multiplication table of the quasigroup). Given N colors, a Latin square is defined by an N by N table, where each entry has a color and where there are no repeated colors in any row or column. N is called the *order* of the square. Gomes and Selman considered the problem of whether a partially colored Latin square can be completed into a full Latin square by assigning colors to the open entries of the table. This problem is referred to as the quasigroup completion problem (QCP). QCP is NP-complete (Colbourn 1984) and has an interesting phase transition phenomenon with an associated easy-hard-easy pattern as a function of the fraction of number of preassigned colors. The domain has been used to study the effectiveness of a variety of local consistency measures for constraint satisfaction procedures (Stergiou and Walsh 1999, Walsh 1999, Regin 1994).

The quasigroup completion task has interesting global structure but does not lend itself well for the evaluation of local search methods because we again have a mix of satisfiable and unsatisfiable instances. However, we will introduce a new generator based on the quasigroup domain that gives a natural unbiased way for obtaining only satisfiable instances, with good computational properties, namely by starting with a full quasigroup and "punching" holes into it. We use a recent result on generating uniformly distributed random complete quasigroups for generating our initial full quasigroup.

The problem of generating uniformly distributed Latin squares is non-trivial. Jacobson and Matthews (1996) show how by simulating an ergodic Markov chain whose stationary distribution is uniform over the space of N by N Latin squares, one can obtain squares that are (approximately) uniformly distributed. The Markov chain Monte Carlo method starts with a complete Latin square. (There is an efficient method for generating a fixed Latin square of any size.) Subsequently, the method randomly "perturbs" the initial Latin square to obtain a new square; repeated random perturbations lead us through a chain of squares. The difficult part is to design sequences of perturbations that lead from one valid Latin square to another while ensuring that one can reach any arbitrary Latin square in the chain with equal probability in the stationary distribution. The method proposed by Jacobson and Matthews corresponds to a random walk on a finite, connected, nonbipartite undirected graph and therefore it is ergodic, with stationary distribution assigning each vertex a probability proportional to its degree.

The Jacobson and Matthews approach provides us with a good starting point for obtaining interesting satisfiable computational instances. We propose the following generator: (1) Generate a complete Latin square according to the Markov chain Monte Carlo approach proposed by Jacobson and Matthews; (2) punch a fraction p of "holes" in the Latin square (i.e., uncolor some of the entries) in a uniformly distributed manner. The resulting partial Latin square is now guaranteed to be satisfiable and moreover, as we will see below, we can finely control its expected hardness by tuning the value of p. We call this new problem the "quasigroup with holes" (QWH) problem.[1] As we will describe below, the instances can be solved directly (in order to test e.g., a constraint-logic programming algorithm) or translated into a Boolean CNF encoding (in order to test general SAT solvers). It is interesting to note that while the quasigroup domain lends itself naturally to a satisfiable instance generator with good computational properties, it is not clear how a similar generator could be developed for, e.g., k-SAT or graph coloring.

The quasigroup with holes problem is NP-hard. This follows from the following argument. Assume one had a polynomial algorithm that could solve QWH. Such an algorithm could be used to solve the quasigroup completion task (QCP), by simply running the algorithm with a polynomial time bound. The bounded algorithm would either solve our completion problem or terminate at the time bound, indicating no solution exists. However, this is impossible because, as noted above, QCP is NP-complete.

In the next sections, we will identify a clear easy-hard-easy pattern for both complete and incomplete search methods on these problem instances. Note that because we are dealing with a distribution of satisfiable instances only, we obtain a clear full easy-hard-easy diagram for a incomplete search method. Clark et al. (1996) provide initial results on a such a pattern for local search using standard benchmarks. However, given the rareness of satisfiable instances on the unsat side of the phase transition it is difficult to establish a clear full pattern. We will also show that the hardness region of our satisfiable problem instances coincides with a new kind of phase transition. This transition differs from the standard sat/unsat transition because we now have only satisfiable instances, but like the standard transition, it is based on an underlying structural property — namely, the backbone.

Problem hardness

In order to solve QWH instances, we explored a range of algorithms. We used an ILOG constraint solver working directly on the constraint satisfaction encoding of the problem. In the ILOG solver, we incorporated, aside from the standard constraint propagation methods, the all-diff constraint (Stergiou and Walsh 1999; Regin 1994). We also implemented (in C) a local search procedure working directly on the constraint representation. Finally, we converted the problem instances into Boolean satisfiability encodings and used state-of-the-art SAT solvers, both complete and incomplete methods. To our surprise, the approach via a SAT encoding is more efficient than using the direct CSP approaches; apparently, the increase in the size of the encoding when going to SAT does not hurt overall performance. Given the space limitations of this paper, we will only include the data for our best performing procedures, the backtracking SAT solver Satz (Li and Anbulagan 1997) and the local search SAT solver Walksat (Selman et al. 1996). (Both solvers are available from SATLIB (Hoos 1999).) Our data for the CSP approach is qualitatively the same. The QWH instances thus provide a good benchmark for both CSP and for SAT methods. Experimental data, instances, and generator (both SAT and CSP representation) are available from the authors.

In Fig. 1, we show the computational cost profiles for an incomplete (Walksat; left panel) and a complete (Satz; right panel) search method for the QWH problem. Along the horizontal axis, we vary the fraction of holes in the quasigroup. More specifically, we take the ratio of the number of holes to the total number of entries in the Latin square, i.e., N^2, where N is order of the square. The vertical axis gives the median computational cost. For Walksat, the cost is measured in terms of the total number of variable flips; for Satz we measured the total number of backtracks.

The figure shows a clear easy-hard-easy pattern for both the incomplete and the complete search methods. Over a range of different sizes ($N = 30, 33, 36$) we see a rapid (in fact, exponential) increase in search cost in the hardest region. Close observation shows that there is a slight shift in the location of the peaks. We will return to this issue below, when we discuss a way of rescaling the figures to precisely line up the peaks.

Aside from having a clear easy-hard-easy pattern, the main point of interest in Fig. 1 is the profile for the incomplete search method. We see a clear example of an easy-hard-easy pattern for an incomplete search method. Because previous problem generators give a mixture of sat and unsat cases, such an easy-hard-easy pattern has generally been reported so far only for complete methods, which can handle both types of instances. Our figure shows that the notions of under-constrained, critically constrained, and over-

---

[1] We thank Mark Stickel for some preliminary discussions on the use of the quasigroups with holes (Stickel, personal communications, May 1998).

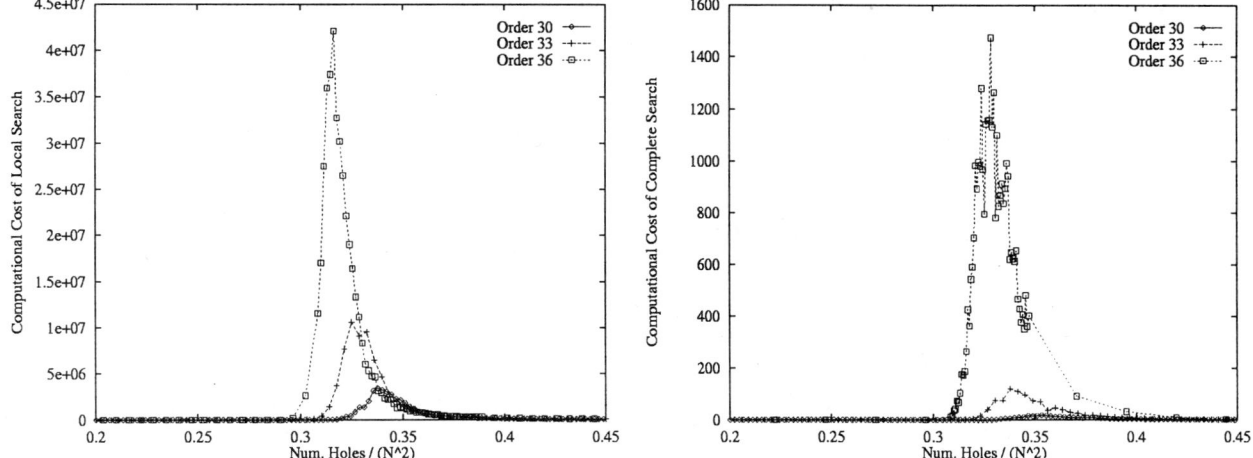

Figure 1: Computational cost profiles for incomplete (Walksat) and complete (Satz) search methods for QWH.

constrained (Hogg et al. 1996) are also predictive of the performance of incomplete search methods.

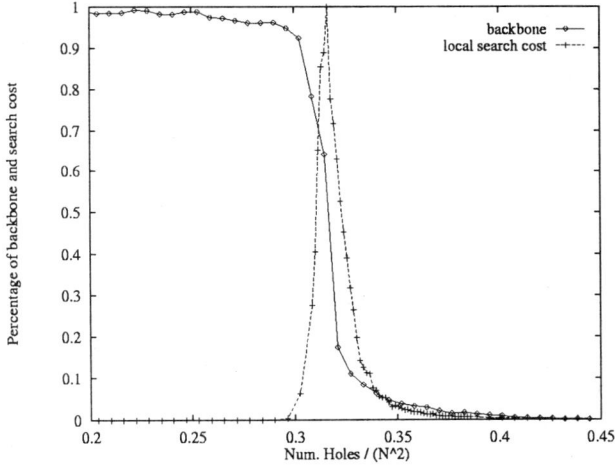

Figure 2: Backbone phase transition with cost profile.

A New Type of Phase Transition

One of the key advances in our understanding of problem hardness has been the connection between the easy-hard-easy pattern in search complexity and phase transition phenomena (Cheeseman 1991; Mitchell et al. 1992; Kirkpatrick and Selman 1994; Hogg et al. 1996; Hayes 1996). In particular, a clear connection has been established between the hardest problem instances and the phase transition region, where instances shift from being mostly satisfiable to being mostly unsatisfiable. One of the interesting aspects of this connection is that properties of the SAT/UNSAT phase transition can be analyzed quite independently from any particular solution procedure. In fact, this has led to a large number of papers on the SAT/UNSAT phase transition *per se*.

For the QWH instances, we do not have a SAT/UNSAT phase transition, since all our instances are guaranteed to be satisfiable. Nevertheless, we can use recently introduced notions from the study of phase transition phenomena to link the peak in search complexity to a phase transition in structural properties of our problem instances. To do so, we will consider so-called backbone variables.

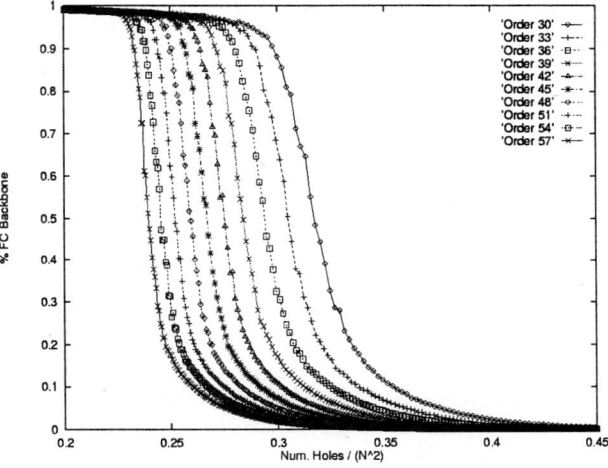

Figure 3: Backbone for different orders.

Monasson et al. (1999) introduced the notion of the *backbone* of a SAT problem to refer to the fraction of its variables that are *fully constrained*: that is, which take on the same values in all solutions. The backbone fraction (ratio of backbone variables to the total number of variables) is a property of CSP and SAT problems that is well-defined for satisfiable distributions.

Fig. 2 shows the backbone fraction as a function of the fraction of holes in the QWH problem. We also included the normalized cost of local search. The figure shows a sharp phase transition phenomenon in the backbone fraction, which coincide with the hardness peak in local search.[2]

---

[2]The figure gives data for $N = 36$. The hardness peak for our complete search method also lies in the phase transition region

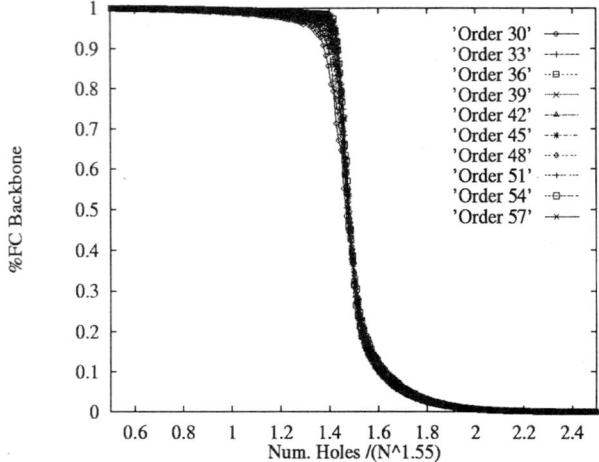

Figure 4: Backbone for different orders (rescaled).

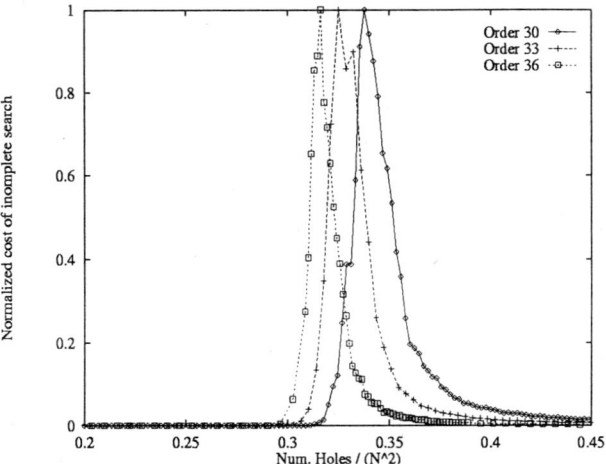

Figure 5: Normalized computational cost.

The reasons for the correlation between problem hardness and the appearance of the backbone are not fully understood at this time. One intuition is that backtracking search algorithms have the worst performance when they make an incorrect choice near the root of the search tree: that is, when they make a variable-value assignment that appears in no solution. For the algorithm to have a significant chance of making such a bad choice a non-negligible fraction of the variables must appear in the backbone. When the backbone fraction nears 1, however, the problems are so over-constrained that incorrect choices near the root are quickly detected and corrected. For local search procedures, an explanation might be developed by considering the relationship between the backbone and set of solutions to the instances. When the backbone is small, there are many solutions widely distributed in the search space, and so local search may quickly find one. When the backbone is near 1, the solutions are tightly clustered, so that that all clauses "vote" to push the search in the same direction. A partial backbone, however, may indicate that solutions are in different clusters that are widely distributed, with different clauses pushing the search in different directions. Making these intuitions precise, however, awaits future research.

Re-parameterization

As we noted above, there is a slight shift in the location of the hardness peak as a function of N. There is a similar shift in the location of the backbone phase transition. This points to the fact that the original parameterization in terms of the fraction of holes does not exactly capture the dimensionality of our problem.[3] Fig. 3 shows the shift in the backbone transition for a larger range of problem sizes ($N = 30, \ldots, 57$).[4]

---

but is shifted slightly to the right. We are currently investigating whether that shift is real or part of the uncertainty in our data.

[3]Note that a similar shift is also present in the original quasigroup completion problem.

[4]Computing the full backbone is prohibitively expensive. The figure gives a good approximation of the backbone fraction computed by using forward-checking to estimate the fraction of fixed

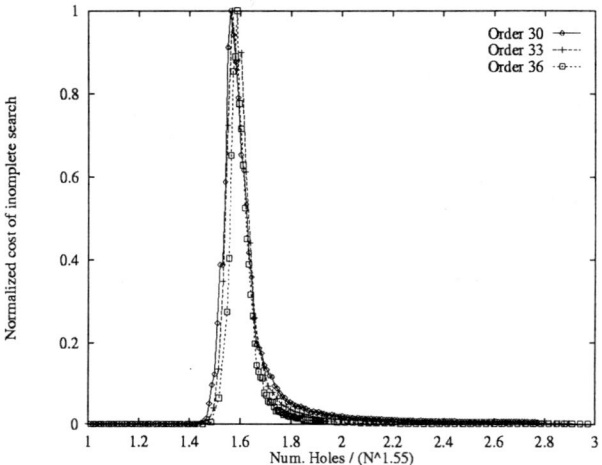

Figure 6: Re-parameterized computational cost.

Some experimentation with different parameterization leads us to Fig. 4. This figure shows the backbone plotted against the number holes over $N^{1.55}$. Note that we originally used "number of holes over N^2". We are currently working on an analytical derivation of the re-parameterization.

Finally, Figs. 5 and 6 show how our rescaling also corrects for the shift in the complexity peak of our local search method. To show the original shift, Fig. 5 gives the search complexity for three different sizes of the QWH problem, where the cost has been normalized to 1. Fig. 6 shows how the peaks collapse onto each other after rescaling. The peaks for the complete search method (right panel in Fig. 1) also align after such a rescaling.

---

variables. This estimate is a few percentage off from the true value, but the shifting behavior appears identical to that of the full backbone, based on experiments for smaller values of N.

Conclusions

We propose a problem generator for satisfiable instances. The generator samples uniformly from *satisfiable* quasigroups of a given size with a given number of holes. The hardness of the QWH problem instances can be tuned by varying the fraction of holes in the quasigroup instances. The main advantage of this generator is that it generates satisfiable instances only and is therefore well-suited for use in the study and evaluation of incomplete search methods.

Several earlier attempts at designing such a generator (*e.g.,* by forcing a given solution during the problem generation) were unsatisfactory. Using our generator, we showed that a local search method does exhibit the easy-hard-easy pattern, as observed previously for complete search methods. Based on the notion of under-constrained, critically constrained, and over-constrained regions identified with complete search methods, it was believed that an easy-hard-easy pattern would emerge for local search methods but this was difficult to confirm empirically because satisfiable instances in the over-constrained region are extremely rare for standard problem generators.

We also show how the hardest region of the satisfiable instances coincides with a new kind of phase transition in terms of the backbone of the problem instances. The backbone characterizes the amount of shared structure between solutions. Finally, we present an empirically obtained re-parameterization of the phase transition and complexity peak of the quasigroup with holes problem. Our generator outputs instances suitable for both CSP and SAT style methods. The generator should therefore be of use in the future development of stochastic local search style CSP and SAT methods.

Acknowledgements We would like to thank Dongmin Liang for his assistance with obtaining the experimental data in this paper. The second author is supported by the Air Force Research Laboratory and the Air Force Office of Scientific Research, under the New World Vistas Initiative. The fourth author is supported by an NSF Faculty Early Career Development Award, an Alfred P. Sloan fellowship, and by the Air Force Research Laboratory.

References

Asahiro, Y., Iwama, K. and Miyano, E. (1993). Random generation of test instances with controlled attributes. In *DIMACS 1993*, op cite.

Beijing (1996). *International Competition and Symposium on Satisfiability Testing*, Beijing, China, March 15–17, 1996.

Cheeseman, P. and Kanefsky, R. and Taylor, W. (1991). Where the Really Hard Problems Are. *Proc. IJCAI-91*, 1991, 163–169.

Clark, D.A., Frank, J., Gent, I.P., MacIntyre, E., Tomov, N., Walsh, T. (1996). Local search and the number of solutions. *Proc. CP-96*, 1996.

Colbourn, C. (1984). The Complexity of Completing Latin Squares. *Discrete Appl. Math.*, 8, (1984), 25-30.

Crawford, J. and Kearns, M. (1993). Instances for learning the parity function. Unpublished note, see Hoos (1999).

DIMACS (1993). *Second DIMACS Implement. Challenge, 1993*. Pub. as *DIMACS Series in Disc. Math. and Theor. Comp. Sci.*, vol. 26, D. Johnson and M. Trick, eds., AMS, 1996.

DIMACS (1996). *Satisfiability Problem*, DIMACS Workshop, 1996. Pub. as *DIMACS Discrete Math. and Theor. Comp. Sci.*, vol. 35, D. Du, J. Gu, and P. Pardalos, eds., AMS, 1997.

Frieze, A. and McDiarmid, C. (1997). Algorithmic theory of random graphs. *Random Structures and Algorithms*, vol. 10 (1997) 5–42.

Gent, I. and Walsh, T. (1993) An empirical analysis of search in GSAT. *J. of Artificial Intelligence Research*, vol. 1, 1993.

Gomes, C.P. and Selman, B. (1997a). Problem structure in the presence of perturbations. *Proc. AAAI-97*, 1997.

Hayes, B. (1996). Can't get no satisfaction. *American Scientist* vol. 85, 108 (1996)

Hogg, T., Huberman, B.A., and Williams, C.P. (Eds.) (1996). Phase Transitions and Complexity. *Artificial Intelligence*, 81 (Spec. Issue), 1996.

Hoos, H. 1999. SATLIB. A collection of SAT tools and data. See www.informatik.tu-darmstadt.de/AI/SATLIB.

Impagliazzo, R., Levin, L., and Luby, M. (1989). Pseudo-random number generation from one-way functions. *Proc. 21st STOC*, 1989, 12-24.

Jacobson, M.T. and Matthews, P. (1996) Generating uniformly distributed random latin squares. *J. of Combinatorial Designs*, vol. 4., no. 6, (1996) 405–437.

Johnson, D.S. , Aragon, C.R., McGeoch, L.A., and Shevon C. (1989) Optimization by Simulated Annealing: An Experimental Evaluation. *Operations Research*, 37:6 (1989), 865-892.

Kirkpatrick, S. and Selman, B. (1994). Critical behavior in the satisfiability of random Boolean expressions. *Science*, 264, 1994, 1297–1301.

Li, Chu Min and Anbulagan (1997). Heuristics based on unit propagation for satisfiability problems. *Proc. IJCAI-97*, 366–371.

Massacci, F. (1999). Using Walk-SAT and Rel-SAT for cyptographic key search. *Proc. IJCAI-99*, 1999, 290-295.

Mitchell, D. and Levesque H. (1996). Some pitfalls for experimenters with random SAT. *Artificial Intelligence*, Vol. 81(1-2), 1996, 111–125.

Mitchell, D., Selman, B., and Levesque, H.J. (1992). Hard and easy distributions of SAT problems. *Proc. AAAI-92*, San Jose, CA (1992) 459–465.

Morris, P. (1993) The breakout method for escaping from local minima. *Proc. AAAI-93*, 1993, 40–45.

Monasson, R., Zecchina, R., Kirkpatrick, S., Selman, B., and Troyansky, L. (1996). Determining computational complexity from characteristic 'phase transitions'. *Nature*, Vol. 400(8), 1999.

Regin, J.C. (1994). A filtering algorithm for constraints of difference in CSP. *Proc. AAAI-94*, 1994, 362–367.

Selman, B. and Levesque, H.J., and Mitchell, D.G. (1992). A New Method for Solving Hard Satisfiability Problems.

Selman, B., Kautz, H.A., and Cohen, B. (1996). Local search strategies for satisfiability testing. In DIMACS (1993).

Shaw, P., Stergiou, K., and Walsh, T. (1998) Arc consistency and quasigroup completion. *Proc. ECAI-98*, workshop on binary constraints, 1998.

Stergiou, K. and Walsh, T. (1999) The Difference All-Difference Makes Proc. of *IJCAI-99*, Stockholm, Sweden.

Walsh, T. (1999) Search in a Small World. Proc. of *IJCAI-99*, Stockholm, Sweden, 1999.

Van Gelder, A. (1993). Problem generator (mkcnf.c) contributed to the DIMACS 1993 Challenge archive.

Solving the Round Robin Problem Using Propositional Logic

Ramón Béjar and **Felip Manyà**
Department of Computer Science
Universitat de Lleida
Jaume II 69, E-25001 Lleida, Spain
{ramon,felip}@eup.udl.es

Abstract

In this paper we present a new and extremely competitive approach to solving a notoriously hard problem from the sports scheduling domain, the round robin problem. By combining local search satisfiability algorithms and an appropriate problem encoding based on classical propositional logic, we are able to find feasible schedules many times faster than using the best existing approaches to the round robin problem. Moreover, using this scheduling as satisfiability approach we are able to solve a previously unsolved instance, the round robin problem for 20 teams.

Introduction

The propositional satisfiability problem (SAT) plays a relevant role in the research activity of the AI community. The design and implementation of fast satisfiability algorithms, as well as the definition of appropriate problem encodings as SAT instances, have given raise to a new and extremely competitive approach to solving real-world problems from various domains (e.g. planning (Kautz & Selman 1996; 1999), circuits (Warners & van Maaren 1999), ...).

In this paper we describe a series of experiments performed in order to show the suitability of the *scheduling as satisfiability* approach to solving the round robin problem (defined in the next section). To this end, we have first defined an appropriate problem encoding in such a way that we can obtain a feasible schedule from a satisfying truth assignment of the SAT instance generated. We have then tried to find satisfying truth assignments by using a variety of satisfiability algorithms. We have observed that local search algorithms outperform the best systematic algorithms and are the most powerful method described so far for practically solving hard instances of the round robin problem. The best results were obtained with the WalkSAT family of algorithms (Selman, Kautz, & Cohen 1994; McAllester, Selman, & Kautz 1997).

The scheduling as satisfiability approach was used to solve the job shop problem by Crawford & Baker (1994). However, to our best knowledge, the round robin problem has not been solved before using classical propositional logic.

McAloon, Tretkoff, & Wetzel (1997) used a constraint programming formulation for solving the round robin problem for 14 teams. Then, Gomes *et al.* (1998) used both an integer programming and a constraint programming formulation. With the former formulation, they were unable to find a solution for 14 teams and they lasted 14 hours to find a solution for 12 teams. With the latter formulation and a randomized constraint programming algorithm, they found a solution for 18 teams after 22 hours. Recently, we solved the round robin problem using a local search algorithm and an encoding based on many-valued propositional logic (Béjar & Manyà 1999c). We found solutions for 16 teams in about 2 hours.

In this paper we show experimentally that, by combining local search satisfiability algorithms and an appropriate problem encoding based on classical propositional logic, we can find feasible schedules many times faster than using the best existing approaches to the round robin problem. We found solutions for 14 teams in less than 2 minutes, for 16 teams in less than 20 minutes and for 18 teams in less than 2 hours. Moreover, we found a solution for a previously unsolved instance (20 teams) in about 13 hours.[1] These results provide experimental evidence that our approach scales better than previous approaches.[2]

A related sports scheduling problem that has received increasing interest in the last years is the problem of finding a timetable for the Atlantic Coast Basketball Conference (Nemhauser & Trick 1998).

The paper is structured as follows. In the next section, we introduce the round robin problem and define an appropriate encoding based on classical propositional logic. Next, we describe the local search algorithms used in our experiments. We then present our experimental investigation and summarize our results on the round robin problem.

Copyright © 2000, American Association for Artificial Intelligence (www.aaai.org). All rights reserved.

[1]Gomes *et al.* (1998) claim that Wetzel and Zabatta have generated schedules for 26 and 28 teams by using multiple threads on a 14 processor Sun system. To our best knowledge, such results are neither published nor publicly available. In our experiments we used a single processor machine.

[2]Our experiments were performed on a 250 MHz Sun UltraSparc with 512 MB of memory. Gomes *et al.* used a 200 MHz SGI Challenge and claim that the speed of the SGI is comparable to that of a Sun UltraSparc.

The Round Robin Problem

In this section we first introduce the round robin problem and then define the reduction to classical propositional logic that we used in our experiments. In the below description of the round robin problem we follow closely the presentation of Gomes et al. (1998).

In sports scheduling one of the issues is to find a feasible schedule for a sports league that takes into consideration constraints on how the competing teams can be paired, as well as how each team's games are distributed in the entire schedule. Here we consider the timetabling problem for the classic "round robin" schedule: every team must play every other team exactly once. The global nature of the pairing constraints makes this a particularly hard combinatorial search problem.

A game will be scheduled on a certain field at a certain time. This kind of combination will be called a slot. These slots can vary in desirability due to such factors as lateness in the day, the location and the condition of the field, etc. The problem is to schedule the games such that the different fields are assigned to the teams in an equitable manner over the course of the season.

The round robin problem for n teams (n-team round robin problem) is formally defined as follows:

1. There are n teams (n even) and every two teams play each other exactly once.
2. The season lasts $n-1$ weeks.
3. Every team plays one game in each week of the season.
4. There are $n/2$ fields and, each week, every field is scheduled for one game.
5. No team plays more than twice in the same field over the course of the season.

The meeting between two teams is called a game and takes place in a slot; i.e., in a particular field in a particular week. Table 1 shows a solution for the 10-team round robin problem; teams are named $1, \ldots, 10$. An n-team round robin timetable contains $n(n-1)/2$ slots and slots are filled in with games. A game is represented by a pair of teams (t_1, t_2) such that $t_1 < n$ and $t_1 < t_2$.

The combinatorics of the round robin problem are explosive (McAloon, Tretkoff, & Wetzel 1997): For an n-team league, there are $n/2 \cdot (n-1)$ games (i,j) with $1 \leq i < j \leq n$ to be played. A schedule can be thought of as a permutation of these games. So, for n teams the search space size is $(n/2 \cdot (n-1))!$; i.e., the search space size grows as the factorial of the square of $n/2$.

The n-team round robin problem is encoded as an instance of the SAT problem as follows:

1. The set of propositional variables is
$$\{p_{ij}^{1k} \mid 1 \leq i \leq n/2, 1 \leq j, k \leq n-1\} \cup$$
$$\{p_{ij}^{2k} \mid 1 \leq i \leq n/2, 1 \leq j \leq n-1, 2 \leq k \leq n\}$$
and its cardinality is $n(n-1)^2$.
Each slot in the timetable is filled in by a pair of variables $(p_{ij}^{1k_1}, p_{ij}^{2k_2})$. The intended meaning of the pair $(p_{ij}^{1k_1}, p_{ij}^{2k_2})$ is that team k_1 will play against team k_2 in field i in week j.

2. *In each slot, one team plays against another team.* For each slot $(p_{ij}^{1k_1}, p_{ij}^{2k_2})$ ($1 \leq k_1 \leq n-1, 2 \leq k_2 \leq n$), we define the clauses
$$(p_{ij}^{11} \vee \cdots \vee p_{ij}^{1n-1}) \wedge (p_{ij}^{22} \vee \cdots \vee p_{ij}^{2n})$$
These clauses together with the clauses in (4) ensure that one team plays exactly against another team every week.

3. *In each slot $(p_{ij}^{1k}, p_{ij}^{2k'})$ it holds that $k < k'$.* For each two teams k_1, k_2 such that $k_1 \geq k_2$, we define the clause
$$\neg p_{ij}^{1k_1} \vee \neg p_{ij}^{2k_2}$$

4. *Every team plays one game in each week of the season.* For each week j, for each team k, for each two fields i_1, i_2 ($1 \leq i_1, i_2 \leq n/2$) and for r_1, r_2 ($1 \leq r_1, r_2 \leq 2$), we define the clause
$$\neg p_{i_1 j}^{r_1 k} \vee \neg p_{i_2 j}^{r_2 k}$$
provided that $p_{i_1 j}^{r_1 k} \neq p_{i_2 j}^{r_2 k}$. Clauses containing a variable of the form p_{ij}^{21} or p_{ij}^{1n} are not generated.

5. *Every two teams play each other exactly once.* For each two different slots of the form $(p_{i_1 j_1}^{1k_1}, p_{i_1 j_1}^{2k_2})$ and $(p_{i_2 j_2}^{1k_1}, p_{i_2 j_2}^{2k_2})$ such that $j_1 \neq j_2$ and $k_1 < k_2$, we define the clause
$$\neg p_{i_1 j_1}^{1k_1} \vee \neg p_{i_1 j_1}^{2k_2} \vee \neg p_{i_2 j_2}^{1k_1} \vee \neg p_{i_2 j_2}^{2k_2}$$
The clauses of (5) ensure that every two teams play each other at most once over the course of the season. Since the total number of slots coincides with the total number of possible games, the above clauses not only ensure that each possible game appears at most in one slot, but exactly once.

6. *No team plays more than twice in the same field over the course of the season.* For each team k, for each field i, for each three different weeks j_1, j_2, j_3 and for each r_1, r_2, r_3 ($1 \leq r_1, r_2, r_3 \leq 2$), we define the clause
$$\neg p_{ij_1}^{r_1 k} \vee \neg p_{ij_2}^{r_2 k} \vee \neg p_{ij_3}^{r_3 k}$$

The number of clauses of the SAT instance obtained for the n-team round robin problem is in $\mathcal{O}(n^6)$. By employing additional variables, it is possible to obtain a SAT instance with a number of clauses which is in $\mathcal{O}(n^4)$. Unfortunately, that reduction is not so computationally competitive. This fact was also observed in (Béjar & Manyà 1999c).

We have performed experiments with five alternative SAT encodings, but the results obtained were rather worse. In the rest of the paper, we always refer to the above SAT encoding.

	Week 1	Week 2	Week 3	Week 4	Week 5	Week 6	Week 7	Week 8	Week 9
Field 1	(6, 9)	(4, 6)	(1, 8)	(4, 10)	(2, 8)	(7, 9)	(5, 7)	(1, 2)	(3, 5)
Field 2	(2, 3)	(1, 5)	(2, 4)	(1, 7)	(9, 10)	(8, 10)	(3, 6)	(4, 9)	(6, 8)
Field 3	(5, 10)	(2, 7)	(3, 9)	(5, 9)	(1, 3)	(1, 6)	(4, 8)	(6, 10)	(4, 7)
Field 4	(1, 4)	(8, 9)	(5, 6)	(3, 8)	(6, 7)	(2, 5)	(1, 10)	(3, 7)	(2, 10)
Field 5	(7, 8)	(3, 10)	(7, 10)	(2, 6)	(4, 5)	(3, 4)	(2, 9)	(5, 8)	(1, 9)

Table 1: A 10-team round robin timetable

procedure WalkSAT
input: a set of clauses S, maxTries, maxFlips
       and a heuristic H
output: a satisfying truth assignment of S, if found

```
for i := 1 to maxTries do
{
    I := a randomly generated truth assignment;
    for j := 1 to maxFlips do
    {
        if I satisfies S then return I;
        c := a randomly selected clause not satisfied by I;
        p := a propositional variable in c selected using H;
        I := I with p flipped;
    }
}
return "no satisfying truth assignment found";
```

Figure 1: Procedure WalkSAT

Local Search Algorithms for SAT

The WalkSAT algorithm is shown in Figure 1. It starts from a randomly generated truth assignment, and repeatedly selects one of the clauses that is not satisfied by the current assignment. Then, it selects one of the variables in that clause using a heuristic and flips its truth assignment. The algorithm flips truth assignments until a satisfying truth assignment is found or until some predefined number of flips (maxFlips) is reached. This process is repeated as needed, up to a maximum of maxTries times. Most heuristics take a noise parameter ω ($\omega \in [0, 1]$) to escape from local optima.

In fact, WalkSAT is a family of algorithms (Selman, Kautz, & Cohen 1994; McAllester, Selman, & Kautz 1997). The difference between the algorithms lies in the heuristic used to select the variable to be flipped next. The heuristics considered in this paper are the following ones:

G+Tabu: We maintain a list of a fixed size t, called tabu list, that contains bindings (i.e., pairs of the form (p, b), where p is a variable and b is either 0 or 1). Such bindings represent the last t flips performed by WalkSAT.
Let ω be the noise parameter. With probability ω, pick any variable of the clause selected by WalkSAT; otherwise, pick a variable p of the clause selected by WalkSAT that (i) if the value that assigns the current truth assignment to p is changed to b, the new truth assignment minimizes the total number of unsatisfied clauses and (ii) the binding (p, b) is not in the tabu list. If all the possible flips in the clause selected by WalkSAT are tabu, choose a different unsatisfied clause instead. If all the possible flips in all the unsatisfied clauses are tabu, then the tabu list is ignored. In contrast to (Selman, Kautz, & Cohen 1994), our tabu list contains a list of bindings instead of a list of variables.

R-Novelty: This strategy sorts the variables of the clause selected by WalkSAT by the total number of clauses that are not satisfied if the variable is flipped, but breaking ties in favor of the least recently flipped variable. Consider the best (p_i) and second-best (p_j) variable under this sort, and let n be the difference in the objective function between p_i and p_j. If the best variable is not the most recently flipped variable in the clause, then select it. Otherwise, there are four cases:

1. When $\omega < 0.5$ and $n > 1$, pick p_i.
2. When $\omega < 0.5$ and $n = 1$, then with probability 2ω pick p_j; otherwise, pick p_i.
3. When $\omega \geq 0.5$ and $n = 1$, pick p_j.
4. When $\omega \geq 0.5$ and $n > 1$, then with probability $2(\omega - 0.5)$ pick p_j; otherwise, pick p_i.

Additionally, to inhibit loops, the variable to be flipped is picked at random from the selected clause every 100 flips.

In the following, when we write WalkSAT/G+Tabu we mean WalkSAT using heuristic G+Tabu, and when we write WalkSAT/R-Novelty we mean WalkSAT using heuristic R-Novelty.

Experimental Results

First of all, we have implemented a generator of SAT instances of the round robin problem. Then, we have executed the instances with both systematic and local search satisfiability algorithms. With systematic algorithms, we were only able to solve the round robin problem for 8 teams using both Satz (Li & Anbulagan 1997) and the randomized version of Satz (Gomes, Selman, & Kautz 1998), and we solved the round robin problem for 10 teams using REL-SAT (Bayardo & Schrag 1997).

With local search algorithms, we have executed SAT instances of the round robin problem, ranging from 12 to 20 teams, with WalkSAT/G+Tabu and WalkSAT/R-Novelty using both approximately optimal noise parameters and different cutoff values. Table 2 shows the number of clauses of the SAT instances, and the cutoff values (maxFlips), the lengths of the tabu list, the noise parameters and the average number of restarts that gave rise to the best running times in our experiments.

For 12 teams and 14 teams we performed 200 tries and used a very high cutoff value in order to get a solution in

Teams	Clauses	maxFlips	WalkSAT/G+Tabu			WalkSAT/R-Novelty	
			tabu list	ω	avg. tries	ω	avg. tries
12-team	$2 \cdot 10^5$	∞	7	0.233	1	0.09	1
14-team	$5 \cdot 10^5$	∞	8	0.19	1	0.05	1
16-team	$12 \cdot 10^5$	$3.5 \cdot 10^6$	10	0.184	3.6	0.045	1.65
18-team	$25 \cdot 10^5$	$5 \cdot 10^6$	10	0.175	6	0.0328	4.5
20-team	$47 \cdot 10^5$	$12 \cdot 10^6$	10	0.142	16	0.0222	10

Table 2: Number of clauses per instance, parameter settings and average number of tries needed to find a solution

Teams	Béjar&Manyà (1999)	Gomes et al. (1998)	WalkSAT/G+Tabu	WalkSAT/R-Novelty
12-team	6 min	< 0.22 min	0.6 min	0.27 min
14-team	1.30 hrs	4.17 min	4.08 min	1.74 min
16-team	2.35 hrs	1.4 hrs	0.78 hrs	0.28 hrs
18-team	*	≈ 22 hrs	3.67 hrs	1.98 hrs
20-team	*	*	20.48 hrs	12.73 hrs

Table 3: Comparison of experimental results for the n-team round robin problem

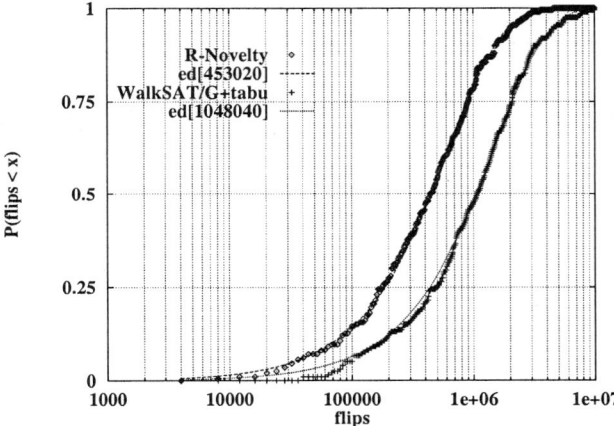

Figure 2: Run-length distributions for 14 teams

every try. This way, we obtained empirical run-length distributions (RLDs) for those instances, as well as the expected time and number of flips needed to solve an instance. Figure 2 shows the empirical RLDs obtained for the round robin problem for 14 teams using WalkSAT/G+Tabu and WalkSAT/R-Novelty. As can be seen in the figure, WalkSAT/R-Novelty outperforms WalkSAT/G+Tabu. Moreover, we found that the RLDs are well approximated by exponential distributions $ed[m]$, with distribution function $F(x) = 1 - 2^{-(x/m)}$, where m is the median of the distribution (see Figure 2). This kind of distributions were observed for local search algorithms in other problem domains by Hoos (1999) and Hoos & Stützle (1998).

For 16, 18 and 20 teams we executed WalkSAT/G+Tabu and WalkSAT/R-Novelty, with the input parameters shown in Table 2, until we found 10 solutions. In Table 3 are shown the average time needed to find a solution. This table also contains the times obtained in (Béjar & Manyà 1999c) and in (Gomes et al. 1998) using other approaches.

Gomes et al. (1998) found a solution for 18 teams after 22 hours using a constraint programming formulation and a randomized constraint programming algorithm. Recently, we solved the round robin problem using a local search algorithm and an encoding based on many-valued propositional logic (Béjar & Manyà 1999c) (see (Béjar & Manyà 1999a; 1999b) for related work on the many-valued logic used to encode the round robin problem). We found solutions for 16 teams in about 2 hours; we believe that these results can be improved by introducing minor changes in the algorithm and using more suitable data structures for representing formulas.

Our experimental results show that, by combining local search satisfiability algorithms and an appropriate problem encoding based on classical propositional logic, we can find feasible schedules many times faster than using the best existing approaches to the round robin problem. We found solutions for 14 teams in less than 2 minutes, for 16 teams in less than 20 minutes and for 18 teams in less than 2 hours. Moreover, we found a solution for a previously unsolved instance (20 teams) in about 13 hours. These results provide experimental evidence that our approach scales better than previous approaches.

The application of the scheduling as satisfiability approach described in this paper, as well as the approach based on many-valued propositional logic that we proposed in (Béjar & Manyà 1999c), to a greater number of teams is the subject of further research. We expect that we will be able to find feasible schedules for the round robin problem for 22 teams in a reasonable time.

Acknowledgements

We thank T. Alsinet, C. Fernàndez, C. Mateu and F. Molina for technical assistance. This research was partially supported by the project SMASH (TIC96-1038-C04-03) funded by the CICYT and "La Paeria". The first author was supported by a doctoral fellowship of the Comissionat per a Universitats i Recerca (1998FI00326).

References

Bayardo, R. J., and Schrag, R. C. 1997. Using CSP lookback techniques to solve real-world SAT instances. In *Proceedings of the 14th National Conference on Artificial Intelligence, AAAI'97, Providence/RI, USA*, 203–208.

Béjar, R., and Manyà, F. 1999a. A comparison of systematic and local search algorithms for regular CNF formulas. In *Proceedings of the 5th European Conference on Symbolic and Quantitative Approaches to Reasoning with Uncertainty, ECSQARU'99, London, England*, 22–31. Springer LNAI 1638.

Béjar, R., and Manyà, F. 1999b. Phase transitions in the regular random 3-SAT problem. In *Proceedings of the International Symposium on Methodologies for Intelligent Systems, ISMIS'99, Warsaw, Poland*, 292–300. Springer LNAI 1609.

Béjar, R., and Manyà, F. 1999c. Solving combinatorial problems with regular local search algorithms. In *Proceedings of the 6th International Conference on Logic for Programming and Automated Reasoning, LPAR'99, Tbilisi, Republic of Georgia*, 33–43. Springer LNAI 1705.

Crawford, J. M., and Baker, A. B. 1994. Experimental results on the application of satisfiability algorithms to scheduling problems. In *Proceedings of the 12th National Conference on Artificial Intelligence, AAAI'94, Seattle/WA, USA*, 1092–1097.

Gomes, C. P.; Selman, B.; McAloon, K.; and Tretkoff, C. 1998. Randomization in backtrack search: Exploiting heavy-tailed profiles for solving hard scheduling problems. In *Proceedings of the International Conference on Artificial Intelligence Planning and Scheduling, AIPS'98, Pittsburg/PA, USA*.

Gomes, C. P.; Selman, B.; and Kautz, H. 1998. Boosting combinatorial search through randomization. In *Proceedings of the 15th National Conference on Artificial Intelligence, AAAI'98, Madison/WI, USA*, 431–437.

Hoos, H. H., and Stützle, T. 1998. Evaluating las Vegas algorithms – pitfalls and remedies. In *Proceedings of the 14th Conference on Uncertainty in Artificial Intelligence, UAI'98, San Francisco/CA, USA*, 238–245.

Hoos, H. H. 1999. On the run-time behaviour of stochastic local search algorithms for SAT. In *Proceedings of the 16th National Conference on Artificial Intelligence, AAAI'99*, 661–666.

Kautz, H. A., and Selman, B. 1996. Pushing the envelope: Planning, propositional logic, and stochastic search. In *Proceedings of the 14th National Conference on Artificial Intelligence, AAAI'96, Portland/OR, USA*, 1194–1201.

Kautz, H. A., and Selman, B. 1999. Unifying SAT-based and graph-based planning. In *Proceedings of the International Joint Conference on Artificial Intelligence, IJCAI'99, Stockholm, Sweden*, 318–325.

Li, C. M., and Anbulagan. 1997. Look-ahead versus look-back for satisfiability problems. In *Proceedings of the 3rd International Conference on Principles of Constraint Programming, CP'97, Linz, Austria*, 341–355. Springer LNCS 1330.

McAllester, D.; Selman, B.; and Kautz, H. 1997. Evidence for invariants in local search. In *Proceedings of the 14th National Conference on Artificial Intelligence, AAAI'97, Providence/RI, USA*, 321–326.

McAloon, K.; Tretkoff, C.; and Wetzel, G. 1997. Sports league scheduling. In *Proceedings of the 1997 ILOG Optimization Suite International Users' Conference, Paris, France*.

Nemhauser, G. L., and Trick, M. A. 1998. Scheduling a major college basketball conference. *Operations Research* 46(1):1–8.

Selman, B.; Kautz, H. A.; and Cohen, B. 1994. Noise strategies for improving local search. In *Proceedings of the 12th National Conference on Artificial Intelligence, AAAI'94, Seattle/WA, USA*, 337–343.

Warners, J. P., and van Maaren, H. 1999. A two phase algorithm for solving a class of hard satisfiability problems. *Operations Research Letters* 23(3–5):81–88.

A demand-driven algorithm for generating minimal models

Rachel Ben-Eliyahu - Zohary
Communication Systems Engineering Department
Ben-Gurion University of the Negev
Beer-Sheva 84105, Israel
rachel@bgumail.bgu.ac.il

Abstract

The task of generating minimal models of a knowledge base is a significant computational problem in artificial intelligence. This task is at the computational heart of diagnosis systems like truth maintenance systems, and of nonmonotonic systems like autoepistemic logic, default logic, and disjunctive logic programs. Unfortunately, it is NP-hard. In this paper we present a hierarchy of classes of knowledge bases, $\Psi_1, \Psi_2, ...$, with the following properties: first, Ψ_1 is the class of all Horn knowledge bases; second, if a knowledge base T is in Ψ_k, then T has at most k minimal models, and all of them may be found in time $O(lnk)$, where l is the length of the knowledge base and n the number of atoms in T; third, for an arbitrary knowledge base T, we can find the minimum k such that T belongs to Ψ_k in time polynomial in the size of T; and, last, where $\mathcal{K}$ is the class of all knowledge bases, it is the case that $\bigcup_{i=1}^{\infty} \Psi_i = \mathcal{K}$, that is, every knowledge base belongs to some class in the hierarchy. The algorithm is demand-driven, that is, it is capable of generating one model at a time.

1 Introduction

Computing minimal models is an essential task in many reasoning systems in artificial intelligence, including circumscription (McCarthy 1980) and minimal diagnosis (de Kleer, Mackworth, & Reiter 1992), and in answering queries posed on logic programs and deductive databases (Minker 1982). In such reasoning systems, the goal is to produce plausible inferences or plausible explanations, not to compute minimal models. Nonetheless, efficient algorithms for computing minimal models can substantially speed up inference in these systems.

Let us take a closer look at the task of computing the stable models of a disjunctive knowledge base. One of the most successful semantics for knowledge bases is *stable model semantics* (Gelfond & Lifschitz 1988), which associates any knowledge base with a (possibly empty) set of models called *stable models*. Intuitively, each stable model represents a set of coherent conclusions one might deduce from the knowledge base. It turns out that the task of computing grounded interpretations for a set of TMS justifications corresponds exactly to the task of computing the stable models of the knowledge base represented by the set of TMS justifications, and that algorithms for computing stable models may be used in computing expansions of autoepistemic programs and extensions of Reiter's default theories (Elkan 1990; Gelfond & Lifschitz 1991).

Each stable model of a knowledge base is a minimal model. Moreover, if the knowledge base is stratified, that is, if there are no circular dependencies between the facts that involve negation, the computation of the stable model is carried by dividing the knowledge into layers (strata) and computing the set of minimal models in each strata.

The algorithm presented in this paper can be used for computing all minimal models, but it can stop once only part of the models have been generated. That is, there is no need to compare all the models of the knowledge base with each other in order to find out which of them is minimal. This feature can be used, for example, as follows:

In entailment - a fact follows from the knowledge base iff it is true in all minimal models. We can check the minimal models one at a time and refute a fact before seeing all of them.

In diagnosis - each minimal model is an indication of a possible set of faulty components. We can check the components suggested by some minimal model while the next minimal model is being generated.

The task of reasoning with minimal models has received a formal analysis in several studies (Cadoli 1991; 1992; Kolaitis & Papadimitriou 1990; Eiter & Gottlob 1993; Chen & Toda 1993; Ben-Eliyahu & Dechter 1996). Unfortunately, the results of the above work on the complexities of reasoning with minimal models are discouraging. It turns out that even when the knowledge base is positive, that is, when the knowledge base has no integrity constraints, finding one minimal model is $P^{NP[O(\log n)]}$-hard (Cadoli 1992) (and positive theories always have a minimal model!)[1], and checking whether a model is minimal for some knowledge base is co-NP-complete (Cadoli 1991).

---
[1]We recall that $P^{NP[O(\log n)]}$ is the class of decision problems that are solved by polynomial-time bounded deterministic Turing machines making at most a logarithmic number of calls to an oracle in NP. For a precise characterization of the complexity of model finding, given in terms of complexity classes of functions, see (Chen & Toda 1993).

In this paper we present a new algorithm for computing minimal models. Using this algorithm, we can show a hierarchy of classes of knowledge bases, $\Psi_1, \Psi_2, ...$, with the following properties: first, Ψ_1 is the class of all Horn knowledge bases; second, if a knowledge base T is in Ψ_k, then T has at most k minimal models, and all of them may be found in time $O(lnk)$, where l is the length of the knowledge base and n the number of atoms in T; third, for an arbitrary knowledge base T, we can find the minimum k such that T belongs to Ψ_k in time polynomial in the size of T; and, last, where $\mathcal{K}$ is the class of all knowledge bases, it is the case that $\bigcup_{i=1}^{\infty} \Psi_i = \mathcal{K}$, that is, every knowledge base belongs to some class in the hierarchy. The algorithm that we present is demand-driven, that is, it is capable of generating one model at a time. We show how the algorithm can be generalized to allow efficient computation of minimal Herbrand models for the subclass of all function-free first-order knowledge bases.

2 Preliminary Definitions

2.1 syntax

We assume that all rules are in the form

$$A_1 \wedge ... \wedge A_n \longrightarrow B_1 \vee ... \vee B_m \tag{1}$$

where all the A's and B's are positive atoms and $m, n \geq 0$. The B's are called the head of the rule, the A's - the body. When $m = 0$ (1) becomes

$$A_1 \wedge ... \wedge A_n \longrightarrow \textbf{false},$$

and is called *an integrity constraint* (name borrowed from database terminology). When $n = 0$ (1) becomes

$$\textbf{true} \longrightarrow B_1 \vee ... \vee B_m,$$

or simply:

$$B_1 \vee ... \vee B_m,$$

and is called a fact. When both m, n are 0, (1) is equal to **false**. The rule (1) is *Horn* whenever $m \leq 1$.

It is easy to see that our language covers all CNF propositional formulas, Hence, for any propositional formula there is a logically equivalent formula in our language.

2.2 The dependency graph

We will divide all the atoms in the knowledge base to equivalence sets as follows:

- If P and Q are in the head of the same rule, then P and Q are in the same set.
- If P and Q are both in the body of the same integrity constraint, they are in the same set.
- If P and Q are both unconstrained, they are in the same set. An atom P is *unconstrained* iff it appears in no integrity constraint and in no head of any rule in the theory.

It's easy to see that all the equivalence sets make up a partition of all the atoms in the knowledge base.

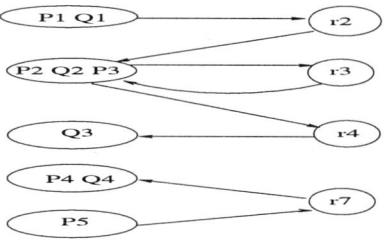

Figure 1: The dependency graph of T_0

Example 2.1 (Running example) *Consider the following knowledge base T_0:*

$$\begin{array}{ll} r_1: & P_1 \vee Q_1 \\ r_2: & P_1 \longrightarrow P_2 \vee Q_2 \\ r_3: & P_2 \longrightarrow P_3 \vee Q_2 \\ r_4: & P_3 \longrightarrow Q_3 \\ r_5: & P_2 \wedge Q_2 \longrightarrow \textbf{false} \\ r_6: & P_4 \vee Q_4 \\ r_7: & P_5 \longrightarrow P_4. \end{array}$$

Note that P_5 is the only unconstrained atom. The equivalence sets we get are:

$s_1: \{P_1, Q_1\}$,

$s_2: \{P_2, Q_2, P_3\}$,

$s_3: \{Q_3\}$,

$s_4: \{P_4, Q_4\}$,

$s_5: \{P_5\}$.

Given a knowledge base T, the dependency graph of T, DG_T is a directed graph built as follows:

Nodes: there are two types of nodes:

1. each equivalence set is a node, called *ES-node*.
2. each rule having nonempty head and nonempty body is a node, called *R-node*.

Edges: There is an edge directed from an ES-node s to an R-node r iff an atom from ES-node s appears in the body of r, and there is an edge directed from an R-node r to an ES-node s iff there is an atom in the ES-node s that appears in the head of r.

Example 2.2 *The dependency graph of the knowledge base of Example 2.1 is shown in figure (1).*

With each ES-node s in the dependency graph, we associate a subset of rules from T, called T_s. T_s is all the integrity constraints over the atoms in s and all the rules in which the atoms from s appear in the head. For example, T_{s_1} is r_1 and T_{s_2} is r_2, r_3, and r_5.

The **super** *dependency graph* of a knowledge base T, denoted G_T, is the superstructure of the dependency graph of T. That is, G_T is a directed graph built by making each strongly connected component (SCC) in the dependency graph of T into a node in G_T. An arc exists from an SCC s to an SCC v iff there is an arc from one of the nodes in s

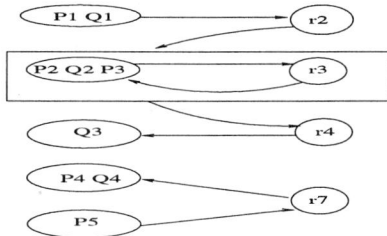

Figure 2: The super dependency graph of T_0

to one of the nodes in v in the dependency graph of T. Note that G_T is an acyclic graph.

The strongly connected components of a directed graph G make up a partition of its set of nodes such that, for each subset S in the partition and for each $x, y \in S$, there are directed paths from x to y and from y to x in G. The strongly connected components are identifiable in linear time (Tarjan 1972).

Recall that a *source* of a directed graph is a node with no incoming edges, while a *sink* is a node with no outgoing edges. Given a directed graph G and a node s in G, the *subgraph rooted by* s, is the subgraph of G having only nodes t such that there is a path directed from t to s in G (this includes s itself). The *children* of s in G are all nodes t such that there is an arc directed from t to s in G.

Example 2.3 The super dependency graph of T_0 is shown in Figure 2. The nodes in the square are grouped into a single node.

Sometimes we will treat a truth assignment (in other words, interpretation) in propositional logic as a set of atoms — the set of all atoms assigned **true** by the interpretation. Given an interpretation I and a set of atoms A, I_A denotes the projection of I over A. Given two interpretations, I and J, over sets of atoms A and B, respectively, the interpretation $I + J$ is defined as follows:

$$(I+J)(P) = \begin{cases} I(P) & \text{if } P \in A \setminus B \\ J(P) & \text{if } P \in B \setminus A \\ I(P) & \text{if } P \in A \cap B \text{ and } I(P) = J(P) \\ \text{undefined} & \text{otherwise} \end{cases}$$

If $I(P) = J(P)$ for every $P \in A \cap B$, we say that I and J are *consistent*.

A *partial* interpretation is a truth assignment over a subset of the atoms. Hence, a partial interpretation can be represented as a consistent set of literals: positive literals represent the atoms that are true, negative literals the atoms that are false, and the rest are unknown. A model for a knowledge base (set of rules) in propositional logic is a truth assignment that satisfies all the rules. A model m is *minimal* among a set of models M iff there is no model $m' \in M$ such that $m' \subset m$. A knowledge base will be called *Horn* iff all its rules are Horn. A Horn knowledge base has a unique minimal model (if it has a model at all) that can be found in linear time (Dowling & Gallier 1984).

3 The algorithm

Algorithm ALL-MINIMAL (AAM) in Figure 3 exploits the structure of the knowledge base as it is reflected in its super dependency graph. It computes all minimal models while traversing the super dependency graph from the bottom up, and can use any algorithm for computing minimal models as subroutine.

Let T be a knowledge base. With each node s in G_T (the super dependency graph of T), we associate T_s, A_s, M_s, and $\hat{T}_s$. T_s is the subset of T containing all the rules about the atoms in s (as explained in section 2), A_s is the set of all atoms in the subgraph of G_T rooted by s, and M_s is the set of minimal models associated with the subset of the knowledge base T which contains only rules about atoms in A_s. The definition of $\hat{T}_s$ is more involved: we define $\hat{T}_s$ to be the knowledge base obtained from T_s by deleting each occurrence of an atom that does not belong to s from the body of every rule. For example, if $T_s = \{b \longrightarrow a, a \wedge d \longrightarrow c, a\}$ and $s = \{a, c\}$, then $\hat{T}_s = \{a, a \longrightarrow c\}$. While visiting a node s during the execution of AAM, we have to compute at step 1.d. all minimal models of some knowledge base T_s. The estimated time required to find all minimal models of T_s is shorter than or equal to the time required to find all minimal models of $\hat{T}_s$, because the truth value of atoms out of s is already known at this stage of the computation. Thus, if $\hat{T}_s$ is a Horn knowledge base, we can find the minimal model of $\hat{T}_s$, and hence of T_s, in polynomial time. If $\hat{T}_s$ is not Horn, then we can find all minimal models of $\hat{T}_s$, and hence of T_s, in time $O(2^{2n})$ where n is the number of atoms used in $\hat{T}_s$. Note that in many cases we can use algorithms with better performance as subroutines.

Initially, M_s is empty for every s. The algorithm traverses G_T from the bottom up (that is, starting from the sources). When at a node s, it first combines all the submodels of the children of s into a single set of models $M_{c(s)}$. If s is a source, then $M_{c(s)}$ is set to $\{\emptyset\}$[2]. Next, for each model m in $M_{c(s)}$, AAM converts T_s to a knowledge base T_{s_m} using some transformations that depend on the atoms in m; then, it finds all the minimal models of T_{s_m} and combines them with m. The set M_s is obtained by repeating this operation for each m in $M_{c(s)}$. AAM uses the procedure CartesProd (Figure 4), which receives as input several sets of models and returns the consistent portion of their Cartesian product. If one of the sets of models which CartesProd gets as input is the empty set, CartesProd will output an empty set of models. The procedure Convert gets as input a knowledge base T and a model m, and performs the following: for each positive literal P in m, each occurrence of P is deleted from the body of each rule in T. The procedure ALL-MINIMAL-SUBROUTINE called by AAM may be any procedure that generates all minimal models.

Theorem 3.1 *Algorithm AAM is correct, that is, m is a minimal model of a knowledge base T iff m is generated by AAM when applied to T.*

---

[2]Note the difference between $\{\emptyset\}$, which is a set of one model - the model that assigns **false** to all the atoms, and $\emptyset$, which is a set that contains no models.

```
ALL-MINIMAL(T)
Input: A knowledge base T.
Output: The set of all minimal models of T.

1. Traverse G_T from the bottom up. For each node s,
   do:
   (a) M_s := ∅;
   (b) Let s_1, ..., s_j be the children of s.
   (c) If j = 0, then M_{c(s)} := {∅};
       else M_{c(s)} := CartesProd({M_{s_1}, ..., M_{s_j}});
   (d) For each m ∈ M_{c(s)}, do:
        i.  T_{s_m} := Convert(T_s, m);
        ii. M := ALL-MINIMAL-SUBROUTINE(T_{s_m});
        iii. If M ≠ ∅,
             then M_s := M_s ∪ CartesProd({{m}, M});
2. Output CartesProd({M_{s_1}, ..., M_{s_k}}),
   where s_1, ..., s_k are the sinks of G_T.
```

Figure 3: Algorithm ALL-MINIMAL (AAM)

```
CartesProd(M)
Input: A set of sets of models M.
Output: A set of models which is the consistent portion
of the Cartesian product of the sets in M.

1. If M has a single element {E}, then return E;
2. M := ∅;
3. Let M' ∈ M;
4. D := CartesProd(M \ {M'});
5. For each d in D, do:
   (a) For each m in M', do:
       If m and d are consistent,
          then M := M ∪ {m + d};
   (b) EndFor;
6. EndFor;
7. Return M;
```

Figure 4: Procedure CartesProd

Proof: (sketch) Let $s_0, s_1, ..., s_n$ be the ordering of the nodes of the super dependency graph by which the algorithm is executed. We can show by induction on i that AAM, when at node s_i, generates all and only the minimal models of the portion of the knowledge base composed of rules that only use atoms from A_{s_i}. □

We will now analyze the complexity of AAM. With each knowledge base T, we associate a number t_T as follows. Associate a number v_s with every node in G_T. If $\hat{T}_s$ is a Horn knowledge base, then v_s is 1; else, v_s is (2^{2n}), where n is the number of atoms that appear in $\hat{T}_s$. Now associate another number t_s with every node s. If s is a leaf node, then $t_s = v_s$. If s has children $s_1, ..., s_j$ in G_T, then $t_s = v_s * t_{s_1} * ... * t_{s_j}$. Define t_T to be $t_{s_1} * ... * t_{s_k}$, where $s_1, ..., s_k$ are all the sink nodes in G_T.

Definition 3.2 *A knowledge base T belongs to Ψ_j if $t_T = j$.*

Theorem 3.3 *If a knowledge base belongs to Ψ_j for some j, then it has at most j minimal models that can be computed in time $O(lnj)$, where l is the length of T and n is the number of atoms used in T.*

The proof is omitted due to space constraints.

Note that all Horn theories belong to Ψ_1, and the more that any knowledge base looks Horn, the more efficient algorithm AAM will be.

Given a knowledge base T, it is easy to find the minimum j such that T belongs to Ψ_j. This follows because building G_T and finding t_s for every node in G_T are polynomial-time tasks. Hence,

Theorem 3.4 *Given a knowledge base T, we can find the minimum j such that T belongs to Ψ_j in polynomial time.*

Note that some models generated at some nodes of the super dependency graph during the run of AAM may later be deleted, since they cannot be completed to a minimal model of the whole knowledge base:

Example 3.5 Consider knowledge base T_2:

$$
\begin{aligned}
a \vee c & \\
a &\longrightarrow b \\
a &\longrightarrow d \\
b \wedge d &\longrightarrow \textbf{false}
\end{aligned}
$$

During the run of algorithm AAM, M_{ac} (the set of models computed at the node $\{a, c\}$) is set to $\{\{a\}, \{c\}\}$. However, only $\{c\}$ is a minimal model of T_2.

Nevertheless, we can show that if there are no integrity constraints in the nodes that follows, each minimal model generated at some node will be a part of a minimal model of the whole knowledge base.

Despite the deficiency illustrated in Example 3.5, algorithm AAM does have desirable features. First, AAM enables us to compute minimal models in a modular fashion. We can use G_T as a structure in which to store the minimal models. Once the knowledge base is changed, we need to resume computation only at the nodes affected by the change.

Second, in using the AAM algorithm, we do not always have to compute all minimal models up to the root node.

If we are queried about an atom that is somewhere in the middle of the graph, it is often enough to compute only the models of the subgraph rooted by the node that represents this atom.

Third, the AAM algorithm is useful in computing the labeling of a TMS subject to nogoods. A set of nodes of a TMS can be declared *nogood*, which means that all acceptable labeling should assign **false** to at least one node in the nogood set.[3] In minimal models terminology, this means that when handling nogoods, we look for minimal models in which at least one atom from a nogood is **false**. A straightforward approach would be to first compute all the minimal models and then choose only the ones that comply with the nogood constraints. But since the AAM algorithm is modular and works from the bottom up, in many cases it can prevent the generation of unwanted minimal models at an early stage. During the computation, we can exclude the submodels that do not comply with the nogood constraints and erase these submodels from M_s once we are at a node s in the super dependency graph such that A_s includes all the members of a certain nogood.

4 Computing Minimal Models of First-Order Knowledge Bases

In this section, we show how we can generalize algorithm AAM so that it can find all minimal models of a knowledge base over a first-order language with no function symbols. The new algorithm will be called FIRST-ALL-MINIMAL (FAAM).

We will now refer to a knowledge base as a set of rules of the form

$$A_1 \wedge A_2 \wedge ... \wedge A_n \longrightarrow B_1 \vee B_2 \vee ... \vee B_m \quad (2)$$

where all As and Bs are atoms in a *first-order* language with no function symbols. The definitions of head, body, facts, and integrity constraints are analogous to the propositional case. In the expression $p(X_1, ..., X_k)$, p is called a *predicate name*.

As in the propositional case, every knowledge base T is associated with a directed graph called the *dependency graph* of T, in which we have predicates names instead of atoms. The super dependency graph, G_T, is defined in an analogous manner.

A knowledge base will be called *safe* iff each of its rules is safe. A rule is *safe* iff all the variables appearing in the head of the rule also appear in in the body of the rule. In this section, we assume that knowledge bases are safe. The *Herbrand base* of a knowledge base is the set of all atoms constructed using predicate names and constants from the knowledge base. The set of *ground instances of a rule* is the set of rules obtained by consistently substituting variables from the rule with constants that appear in the knowledge base in all possible ways. The *ground instance of a knowledge base* is the union of all ground instances of its rules. Note that the ground instance of a first-order knowledge base can be viewed as a propositional knowledge base.

---
[3]In our terminology nogoods are simply integrity constraints, and can be added directly to the knowledge base.

FIRST-ALL-MINIMAL(T)
Input: A first-order knowledge base T.
Output: All the minimal models of T.

1. Traverse G_T from the bottom up. For each node s, do:
   (a) $M_s := \emptyset$;
   (b) Let $s_1, ..., s_j$ be the children of s;
   (c) $M_{c(s)} := \text{CartesProd}(\{M_{s_1}, ..., M_{s_j}\})$;
   (d) For each $m \in M_{c(s)}$ do
   $M_s := M_s \bigcup \text{all-minimal}(T_s \bigcup \{\textbf{true} \longrightarrow P | P \in m\})$
2. Output CartesProd($\{M_{s_1}, ..., M_{s_k}\}$), where $s_1, ..., s_k$ are the sinks of G_T.

Figure 5: Algorithm FIRST-ALL-MINIMAL (FAAM)

A *model* for a knowledge base is a subset M of the knowledge base's Herbrand base having the following two properties:

1. For every rule with non-empty head in the grounded knowledge base, if all the atoms that appear in the body of the rule belong to M then at least one of the atoms in the head of the rule belongs to M.

2. For every integrity constraint, not all the atoms in the body appear in M.

A minimal model for a first-order knowledge base T is a Herbrand model of T, which is also a minimal model of the grounded version of T.

We now present FAAM, an algorithm that computes all minimal models of a first-order knowledge base. Let T be a first-order knowledge base. As in the propositional case, with each node s in G_T (the super dependency graph of T), we associate T_s, A_s, and M_s. T_s is the subset of T containing all the rules about predicates whose names are in s. A_s is the set of all predicate names P that appear in the subgraph of G_T rooted by s. M_s are the minimal models associated with the sub–knowledge base of T that contains only rules about predicates whose names are in A_s. Initially, M_s is empty for every s. Algorithm FAAM traverses G_T from the bottom up. When at a node s, the algorithm first combines all the submodels of the children of s into a single set of models, $M_{c(s)}$. Then, for each model m in $M_{c(s)}$, it calls a procedure that finds all the minimal models of T_s union the set of all the clauses $\textbf{true} \longrightarrow P$ such that $P \in m$. The procedure ALL-MINIMAL called by FAAM can be any procedure that computes all the minimal models of a first-order knowledge base. Because procedure ALL-MINIMAL computes minimal models for only parts of the knowledge base, it may take advantage of some fractions of the knowledge base being Horn or having any other property that simplifies computation of the minimal models of a fraction.

Theorem 4.1 *Algorithm FAAM is correct, that is, m is a minimal model of a knowledge base T iff m is one of the models in the output when applying FAAM to T.*

Proof: As the proof of Theorem 3.1. □

Note that the more that a knowledge base appears Horn, the more efficient algorithm FAAM becomes.

5 Related Work

During the last few years there have been several studies regarding the problem of minimal model computation. Ben-Eliyahu and Dechter (Ben-Eliyahu & Dechter 1996) have presented several algorithms for computing minimal models, all of them different from the one presented here. One limitation of the algorithms presented there is that they produce a *superset* of all minimal models while every model produced using our algorithm is minimal. In addition, for each of the algorithms presented by (Ben-Eliyahu & Dechter 1996) we can show a set of theories for which our algorithm performs better. A more detailed comparison is omitted here because of space constraints.

Ben-Eliyahu and Palopoli (Ben-Eliyahu & Palopoli 1997) have presented a polynomial algorithm for finding a minimal model, but it works only for a subclass of all CNF theories and it finds only one minimal model.

The algorithm of Ben-Eliyahu (Ben-Eliyahu 1996) for finding stable models of logic programs has some common ideas with the one presented here. However, it finds only stable models and it does not work for rules with more than one atom in the head.

Special cases of this task have been studied in the past in the diagnosis literature and the logic programming literature. For instance, many of the algorithms used in diagnosis systems (de Kleer & Williams 1987; de Kleer, Mackworth, & Reiter 1992) are highly complex in the worst case. To find a minimal diagnosis, they first compute all prime implicates of a theory and then find a minimal cover of the prime implicates. The first task is output exponential, while the second is NP-hard. Therefore, in the diagnosis literature, researchers often compromise completeness by using heuristic approaches. Some of the work in the logic programming literature has focused on using efficient optimization techniques, such as linear programming, for computing minimal models (e.g., (Bell *et al.* 1994)). One limitation of this approach is that it does not address the issue of worst-case and average-case complexities.

6 Conclusions

We have presented a new algorithm for computing minimal models. Every model generated by this algorithm is minimal, and all minimal models are eventually generated. The algorithm induces a hierarchy of tractable subsets for the problem of minimal model computation. The minimal models can be generated by the algorithm one at a time, a property which allows demand-driven computation. This algorithms calls for a distributed implementation, an issue we leave for future work.

References

Bell, C.; Nerode, A.; Ng, R.; and Subrahmanian, V. 1994. Mixed integer programming methods for computing non-monotonic deductive databases. *Journal of the ACM* 41(6):1178–1215.

Ben-Eliyahu, R., and Dechter, R. 1996. On computing minimal models. *Annals of Mathematics and Artificial Intelligence* 18:3–27. A short version in AAAI-93: Proceedings of the 11th national conference on artificial intelligence.

Ben-Eliyahu, R., and Palopoli, L. 1997. Reasoning with minimal models: Efficient algorithms and applications. *Artificial Intelligence* 96:421–449. A short version in KR-94.

Ben-Eliyahu, R. 1996. A hierarchy of tractable subsets for computing stable models. *Journal of Artificial Intelligence Research* 5:27–52.

Cadoli, M. 1991. The complexity of model checking for circumscriptive formulae. Technical Report RAP.15.91, Università di Roma "La Sapienza", Dipartimento di Informatica e Sistemistica. To appear in *Information Processing Letters*.

Cadoli, M. 1992. On the complexity of model finding for nonmonotonic propositional logics. In Marchetti Spaccamela, A.; Mentrasti, P.; and Venturini Zilli, M., eds., *Proceedings of the 4th Italian conference on theoretical computer science*, 125–139. World Scientific Publishing Co.

Chen, Z., and Toda, S. 1993. The complexity of selecting maximal solutions. In *Proc. 8th IEEE Int. Conf. on Structures in Complexity Theory*, 313–325.

de Kleer, J., and Williams, B. 1987. Diagnosis multiple faults. *Artificial Intelligence* 32:97–130.

de Kleer, J.; Mackworth, A.; and Reiter, R. 1992. Characterizing diagnosis and systems. *Artificial Intelligence* 56:197–222.

Dowling, W. F., and Gallier, J. H. 1984. Linear time algorithms for testing the satisfiability of propositional horn formulae. *Journal of Logic Programming* 3:267–284.

Eiter, T., and Gottlob, G. 1993. Propositional circumscription and extended closed-world reasoning are Π_2^p-complete. *Theoretical Computer Science* 114:231–245.

Elkan, C. 1990. A rational reconstruction of nonmonotonic truth maintenance systems. *Artificial Intelligence* 43:219–234.

Gelfond, M., and Lifschitz, V. 1988. The stable model semantics for logic programming. In Kowalski, R. A., and Bowen, K. A., eds., *Logic Programming: Proceedings of the 5th international conference*, 1070–1080. MIT Press.

Gelfond, M., and Lifschitz, V. 1991. Classical negation in logic programs and disjunctive databases. *New Generation Computing* 9:365–385.

Kolaitis, P. G., and Papadimitriou, C. H. 1990. Some computational aspects of circumscription. *J. ACM* 37:1–14.

McCarthy, J. 1980. Circumscription - a form of nonmonotonic reasoning. *Artificial Intelligence* 13:27–39.

Minker, J. 1982. On indefinite databases and the closed world assumption. In *Proceedings of the 6th conference on automated deduction, Lecture Notes in Computer Science Vol. 138*, 292–308. Springer-Verlag.

Tarjan, R. 1972. Depth-first search and linear graph algorithms. *SIAM Journal on Computing* 1:146–160.

Redundancy in Random SAT Formulas

Yacine Boufkhad **Olivier Roussel**
CRIL, Université d'Artois,
rue de l'Université SP 16
62307 Lens Cedex France
{boufkhad,roussel}@cril.univ-artois.fr

Abstract

The random k-SAT model is extensively used to compare satisfiability algorithms or to find the best settings for the parameters of some algorithm. Conclusions are derived from the performances measured on a large number of random instances. The size of these instances is, in general, small to get these experiments done in reasonable time. This assumes that the small size formulas have the same properties as the larger ones. We show that small size formulas have at least a characteristic that makes them relatively easier than the larger ones (beyond the increase in the size of the formulas). This characteristic is the redundancy. We show, experimentally, that the irredundant formulas are harder for both complete and incomplete methods. Besides, the randomly generated formulas tend to be naturally irredundant as their size becomes larger. Thus, irredundant small formulas are more suitable for testing algorithms because they better reflect the hardness of the larger ones.

Introduction

Random k-SAT problems are widely used to benchmark SAT algorithms. This is because the hardest instances of this class of problems are empirically well identified (Mitchell, Selman, & Levesque 1992; Larabee & Tsuji 1993). Indeed, these problems have a satisfiability phase transition behavior. Hence, as for many NP-Complete problems having the same behavior, the hardest formulas are located at the middle of this phase transition i.e. at a ratio of clauses to variables approximately equal to 4.25 for 3-SAT for example. The main interest of this class of problems is that they provide researchers working on the design of algorithms for SAT, with an inexhaustible source of hard problems to test their solving methods. Most of these algorithms, either belonging to the category of complete or incomplete methods, require the setting of one or several parameters. To find the optimal setting for these parameters, statistical methods, using trial-and-error, are generally used. The performance obtained using some parameter setting is measured statistically by running the candidate algorithm on a large set of random formulas. For these measurements to be practically feasible, the size of the instances must be kept relatively small. The best settings that are derived are generalized to larger formulas and used as the optimal ones for a candidate solving method. This generalization assumes that small size and large size formulas have the same properties and structures. We show, experimentally, that the small size formulas have at least one characteristic, beyond their size, that makes them easier for both complete and incomplete methods. This characteristic is clause *redundancy*. A clause C is said to be *redundant* in a CNF formula F, if removing C from F does not change the set of solutions of F i.e. F and $F - \{C\}$ are equivalent. A formula is said to be irredundant if none of its clauses is redundant. The hardness of random formulas at the phase transition is always implicitly evaluated with the best known algorithms, and we use the same algorithms to evaluate the hardness of formulas throughout this paper. The main contribution of this work lies in giving an empirical evidence of these two facts: irredundant formulas are harder than redundant ones and, as the number of variables increases, the formulas become less and less redundant. Indeed, we show that when generated with the usual model of k-SAT, small size formulas are highly redundant i.e. have many redundant clauses. The proportion of clauses that must be removed to make the formulas irredundant decreases rapidly and tends to 0 when the number of variables tends to infinity. Beside that fact, if redundant clauses are removed from a formula to make it irredundant then this formula becomes, in average, much more difficult for known solving methods. A straightforward consequence is the following: to design solvers that significantly increase the size of practically solved formulas one would preferably work on improving performances on irredundant small formulas.

The problem with irredundant formulas is that they are hard to generate. They require making many tests of clause redundancy which is a coNP-complete problem. In spite of that drawback one can compute and save once for all a large set of such formulas and use them for measuring the performances of a candidate algorithm. We give an algorithm that generates random irredundant formulas without requiring to test the irredundancy of all the clauses in the formula every time a new one is generated.

In this paper, we will consider randomly generated CNF formulas of fixed length clauses generated using the usual

Copyright © 2000, American Association for Artificial Intelligence (www.aaai.org). All rights reserved.

way i.e. each clause of length k is uniformly chosen at random and with replacement among the $2^k \binom{n}{k}$ possible clauses. A CNF formula is a set of clauses conjunctively interpreted. An implicate of a formula F is a clause such that every solution of F satisfies the implicate. A prime implicate is an implicate such that no proper subset of literals in this implicate is an implicate itself. An implicant of a formula is a conjunction of literals that satisfies this formula. For a clause C, we denote by $\overline{C}$ be the set of unit clauses $\{\overline{l}/l \in C\}$. We denote by C/V the ratio of the number of clauses to the number of variables. All the results reported here apply to 3SAT but some informal experiments make us believe they apply to kSAT in general.

The paper is organized as follows: in the next section the irredundant formulas are empirically shown to be harder than the redundant ones, then the number of redundant clauses is shown to tend to 0 when the number of clauses increases indefinitely and at last an algorithm for generating irredundant formulas is described.

Irredundant formulas and solving methods

We first, empirically, evaluate the hardness of the irredundant formulas with respect to the 3SAT formulas generated using the usual model. More precisely, we compare the difficulty of each formula F in a sample of randomly generated formulas with the difficulty of an irredundant subset of the clauses of F equivalent to F.

Considering the fact that a clause C is redundant in a formula F if and only if C is an implicate of $F - \{C\}$, to test the redundancy of this clause, the satisfiability of the formula $G = (F - \{C\}) \cup \overline{C}$ is tested. C is redundant in F if and only if the formula G is unsatisfiable. For a randomly generated 3CNF formula F, an equivalent irredundant formula F_{irred} is computed according to the following steps:

1. Initialize F_{irred} with F.
2. For each clause $C_i \in F_{irred}$, the satisfiability of the formula $(F_{irred} - C_i) \cup \overline{C_i}$ is tested.
3. if the latter formula is unsatisfiable then remove C_i from F_{irred}.
4. Continue with the next clause.

The resulting set of clauses F_{irred} depends on the order in which the clauses are examined. We used, merely, the chronological order in which the clauses of F are generated. Although this order is fixed, every irredundant formula equivalent to some random formula F has equal chances to be generated since F could be generated equally likely with any clause order.

On WalkSAT

We used the version of walksat described in (McAllester, Selman, & Kautz 1997) to test the hardness of irredundant formulas on local search methods. For every generated satisfiable formula F, the ratio of the performances of walksat on F_{irred} to the performances on F is computed. The same parameters setting of walksat are used to solve F and F_{irred}.

As parameters, we used the Rnovelty heuristic at a noise level of 0.6 and measured the mean number of flips on 10 tries for each formula. For each formula F, we compute the ratio of the mean number of flips needed to solve F_{irred} to the mean number of flips needed to solve F. The figures 1, 2 represent the mean and the median[1] of this ratio as a function of C/V for different numbers of variables. Each point was computed using 1000 instances. Irredundant formulas prove to be harder in a range of clauses to variables ratio that depends on the number of variables and that is in the vicinity of the phase transition. For a given n, when C/V increases, the increase in the average difficulty of F_{irred} with respect to F follows the increase of the number of redundant clauses removed from F (as will be shown in the next section). It is important to be aware that even if the redundancy decreases in function of the number of variables, the ratio of mean number of flips may increase because n increases. Anyhow, this ratio is equal to 1 if F and F_{irred} are equal, which is the case when the number of variables tends to infinity. Figure 3 shows that the difficulty of solving increases as a function of the number of redundant clauses removed.

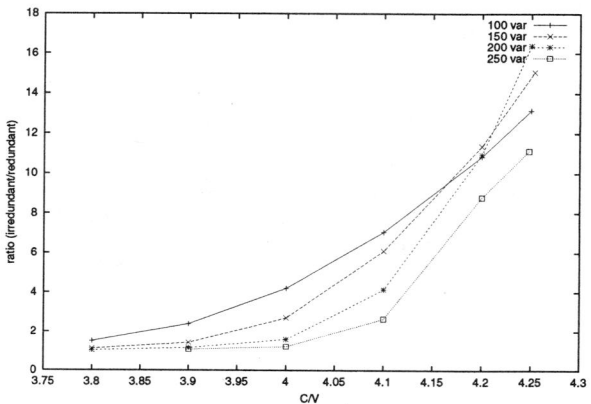

Figure 1: Median ratio (irredundant/redundant) of the number of flips in walksat as a function of C/V and for different numbers of variables

Let us stress the fact that this result does not mean that walksat fails on this type of formulas but proves that, when the parameters tuned to solve the redundant formulas are used, the irredundant ones require much more efforts to be solved. Walksat might be tuned to solve these formulas more efficiently but this would prove that experiments on small redundant formulas are not suitable to find the best parameters.

Intuitively, it is not surprising that these formulas are tricky for walksat. Indeed, the main difficulty that local search procedures have to face is that they are often stuck in local minima with few contradicted clauses. Most of the work that have been deployed to improve the performance of these procedures has consisted in finding noise strategies

---

[1]The median of a set of numbers is obtained by sorting the numbers and retaining the number in the middle of the list (or by averaging the two numbers in the middle of the list if it is of even length).

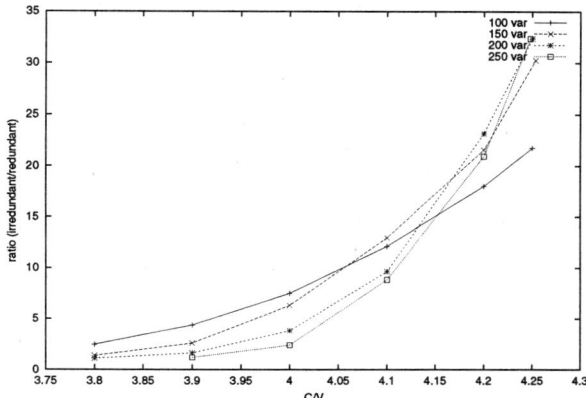

Figure 2: Mean ratio (irredundant/redundant) of the number of flips in walksat as a function of C/V and for different numbers of variables

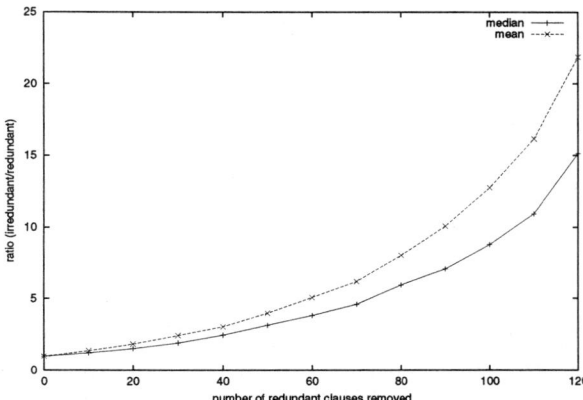

Figure 3: Median and mean ratio (irredundant/redundant) of the number of flips in walksat as a function of the number of redundant clauses removed (100 variables, 425 clauses)

to escape from these local minima. One can assert this rough principle: the more a formula has local minima the harder it is for walksat-like procedures. This is the case for irredundant formulas. Indeed, there exists, for every irredundant clause, a set of truth assignments that satisfies all the clauses of the formula except the latter one. Every such truth assignment is a good candidate for being a local minimum that is almost a solution. In an irredundant formula all the clauses have such a possible low local minima.

On satz procedure

We tested the performances of algorithms based on the DPL procedure (Davis & Putnam 1960; Davis, Logemann, & Loveland 1962) such as CSAT (Dubois *et al.* 1996; Boufkhad 1996), POSIT (Freeman 1995), NTAB (Crawford & Auton 1996). We report the results obtained with one of the most recent : satz (LI & Anbulagan 1997). The same conclusions derived here apply to the above algorithms. The figures 4 and 5 represent the mean and the median of the ratio of the number of branches needed by satz to solve a formula F_{irred} to the number of branches needed to solve F. Irredundant formulas prove to be harder also for satz, in a range of clauses to variables ratio that depends on the number of variables and that is in the vicinity of the phase transition. The same remark made about the relative positions of the curves in the case of walksat, apply to satz. Figure 6 shows that the difficulty of solving increases linearly as a function of the number of redundant clauses removed.

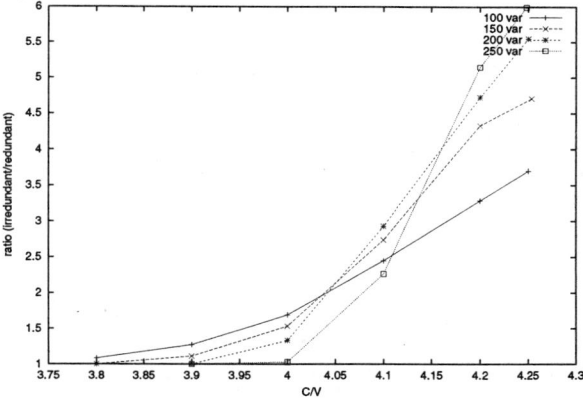

Figure 4: Median ratio (irredundant/redundant) of the number of branches in a satz tree as a function of C/V and for different numbers of variables

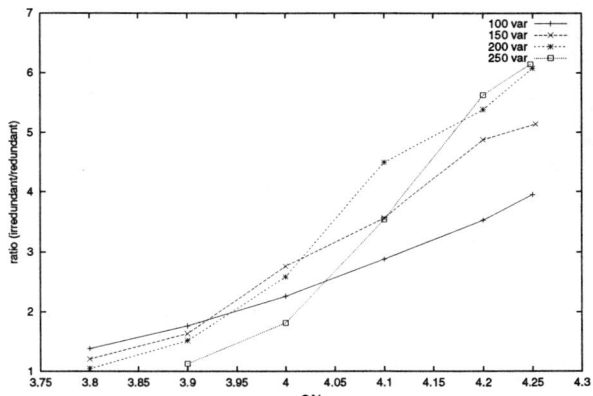

Figure 5: Mean ratio (irredundant/redundant) of the number of branches in a satz tree as a function of C/V and for different numbers of variables

We compared, in addition, the set of atoms of F and of F_{irred}. In a majority of formulas they were equal, and were almost equal in the few remaining formulas. This is important to understand the difference of hardness between F and F_{irred}. Indeed, let us denote by $V(F)$ the set of variables of a formula F. If $V(F) = V(F_{irred})$ then for every tree generated by a DPL-like procedure for F_{irred}, there exists an equal or shorter tree for F. This is true because the clauses that are in F but not if F_{irred} may cut some nodes in the tree

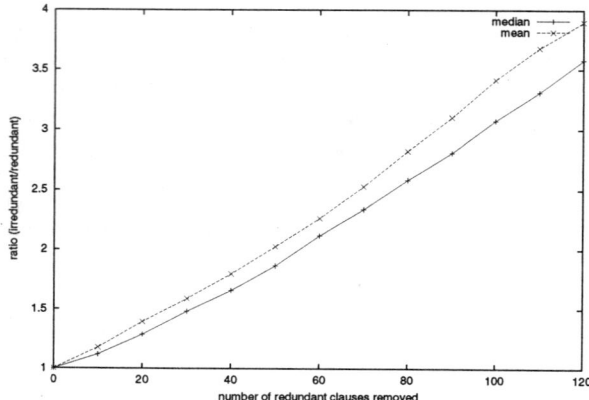

Figure 6: Median and mean ratio (irredundant/redundant) of the number of branches in a satz tree as a function of the number of redundant clauses removed (100 variables, 425 clauses)

of F_{irred}. In addition, if F_{irred} is satisfiable then any implicant of F_{irred} is an implicant of F and the possible node of the solution in the tree of F_{irred} need not to be extended to satisfy the clauses in $F - F_{irred}$.

When F is inconsistent, F_{irred} is an inconsistent kernel of F that is harder to solve than F, though there are methods that exploit the existence of an inconsistent kernel (Mazure, Saïs, & Grégoire 1996; Bayardo & Schrag 1996) to speed up proving the inconsistency of a formula. This leads us to give a necessary condition for an inconsistent kernel to be helpful for solving methods (which is not the case of F_{irred} with respect to F). Given an inconsistent formula F and an inconsistent subset F_K of clauses of F such that $V(F_K)$ is a proper subset of $V(F)$, F_K may be a helpful inconsistent kernel of F since in the tree of F, the nodes that involve only the variables of the set $V(F) - V(F_K)$ can be collapsed. As a conclusion a helpful inconsistent kernel of a formula F must discard variables from F to be possibly helpful.

Redundancy in random formulas

Now that we know that irredundant formulas are much harder, a question that may arise is: how does irredundancy vary in random 3SAT instances? To answer this question, we have taken, as measure of redundancy, for a formula F generated according to the 3SAT model, the ratio $\rho = 1 - \frac{|F_{irred}|}{|F|}$ called level of redundancy. F_{irred} is computed as described in the previous section. We recall that the chronological order used in the removal of redundant clauses doesn't modify the statistical distribution of ρ since formulas F have equal chances to be generated with any ordering of clauses.

As a function of the number of variables

The curve figure 7 represents the variations of the level of redundancy as a function of the number of variables, the ratio C/V being fixed and equal to 4.25 the approximate position of the phase transition for 3SAT. This variation shows clearly a decrease in the level of redundancy which tends to 0 when the number of variables tends to infinity. Together with the conclusions of the previous section, the fact that formulas tend to be irredundant with increasing values of the number of variables, shows clearly that, when the number of variables increases, the formulas tend to be harder not only because the number of variables increases but also because they become less redundant.

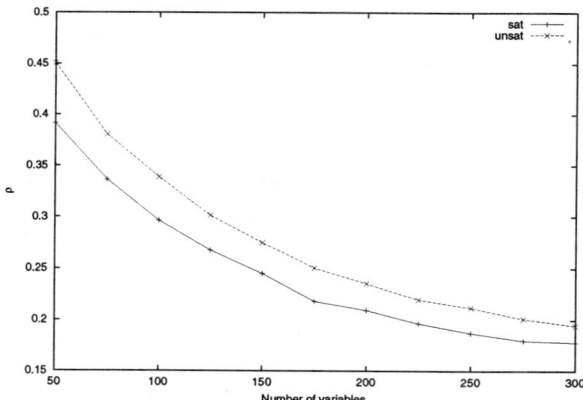

Figure 7: Median level of redundancy ρ for satisfiable and unsatisfiable formulas as a function of the number of variables and for C/V=4.25

For a formula F at the phase transition ratio 4.25, F_{irred} is located in the under-constrained region and can be considered as an exceptionally hard instance (EHI for short) (Gent & Walsh 1993; Hogg & Williams 1994). For 50 variables, an unsatisfiable formula in the phase transition has in average a level of redundancy of 0.46. In constrast, an equivalent irredundant formula would be located in average at a ratio equal to 2.3. For unsatisfiable formulas of 200 variables, the level of redundancy is 0.24. The irredundant equivalent formulas would be located in average at a ratio equal to 3.23 . This is a possible explanation for the fact that EHIs were surprisingly found in (Gent & Walsh 1993) at a ratio C/V between 1.8 and 3 for 50 variables while in (Crawford & Auton 1996) no EHI is found at the same range of ratios for 200 variables.

As a function of the clauses to variables ratio

Figure 8 represents the variations of ρ as a function of the C/V for different values of the number of variables. The level of redundancy is equal to 0 for small values of clauses to variables ratio then first starts to increase from a value of C/V that depends on n and which we note by $c_{red}(n)$. From there, the level of redundancy increases until the phase transition value. After that, the level of redundancy increases linearly as a function of the number of clauses since every clause added to almost every formula is redundant because almost every formula is then inconsistent.

The threshold of emergence of redundant clauses $c_{red}(n)$ increases in function of the number of variables and we con-

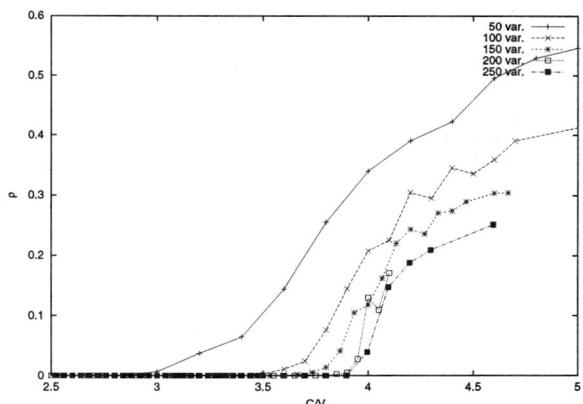

Figure 8: Median level of redundancy ρ for satisfiable and unsatisfiable formulas as a function of C/V and for different numbers of variables

jecture that it tends to the phase transition ratio. The existence of this threshold is to be related to the length of prime implicates and their number. Indeed, if the length of the shortest prime implicates that are not among the clauses of the formula F is greater than the length of the clauses of F then the probability that a newly generated clause will be redundant if added to F is equal to 0, since to be redundant if added to some formula F, a clause must be an implicate of F. Thus the threshold in the emergence of redundancy is certainly connected to the threshold of emergence of prime implicates as experimentally shown in (Schrag & Crawford 1996). In contrast, if F is inconsistent then the probability that a newly generated clause is redundant is equal to 1. Between the two extreme situations, this probability increases as the length of the shortest prime implicates decreases and their number increases.

When talking about the phase transition phenomenon in kSAT three regions are, generally, identified and referred to as under-constrained, critically constrained and over-constrained regions. The existence of these regions is related to the number of constraints. But since this number monotonically increases, it is not sufficient to explain the non monotonicity in the hardness. We give a possibly more accurate picture taking into account, in addition to the number of constraints, the level of redundancy. The formulas with few clauses are irredundant but have few constraints which make them easy. The formulas with a lot of clauses are very constrained but are highly redundant which makes them easy. Between these two situations we have constrained and nearly irredundant formulas which are the hardest. To sum up, the formulas at the phase transition can be considered as located in the cross-over between a decreasing irredundancy and an increasing number of constraints.

An irredundant formulas generator

We describe in this section an algorithm for generating random irredundant formulas. The set of clause is initialized to the empty set then is built by iteratively adding randomly generated clauses after checking at each step that the resulting formula is irredundant. The main problem that has to be faced is that we have to test, at each step, not only the redundancy of the newly generated clause but also if adding this clause does not make some other clause, already in the formula, redundant. To avoid doing systematically redundancy tests for every clause, we use the following fact: for every irredundant clause C in a formula F there exists an implicant I of $F - \{C\}$ that contradicts C. We call such an implicant a *witness* of the redundancy of C in F. Let us suppose that, at some point in the generating process, the current formula F is irredundant and we have a witness for every clause. When a new clause C is generated, its redundancy is tested. If it is irredundant then the algorithm tests if it is satisfied by every witness of the clauses already generated. If it is not satisfied by some witness, we must check if the corresponding clause is redundant and, if it isn't, we must find another witness which satisfies C. The algorithm first tries to modify the witness, by adding to it new literals, if possible, to satisfy C. If this is not possible then a completely new witness is searched. If none exists the algorithm rejects the clause C. These steps are detailed below:

- Check the satisfiability of $F \cup \{\overline{C}\}$, if it is unsatisfiable then reject C since it is redundant, otherwise record the implicant of $F \cup \{\overline{C}\}$, found by the previous satisfiability test, as a witness for C.

- If C is not redundant, check if it is satisfied by every witness of the clauses of F. For every witness w_i that does not satisfy C (w_i corresponding to some clause C_i):

  1. either there exists a literal of C such that its underlying variable is not in w_i, in which case add this literal to w_i so that w_i satisfies $F \cup \{C\} - \{C_i\}$.
  2. There exists no such literal then check the redundancy of C_i in $F \cup \{C\}$. If it is irredundant then the implicant found by this test will replace the witness of C_i otherwise reject C and reset the witnesses modified by this step to their previous values.

At the end of these steps the clause C, if not rejected, is added to the current set of clauses. This algorithm is not guaranteed to terminate because it may happen that at some step no clause maintaining the irredundancy is, after many attempts, randomly selected. One can limit the number of attempts for finding a clause that maintains the irredundancy if added. If this limit is reached, the generator answers that it has failed to generate an irredundant formula at the given number of clauses. This will, for example, stop the algorithm if the formula is unsatisfiable before the required number of clauses is reached.

Conclusion

We have empirically shown that redundancy is a characteristic that conditions the hardness of the random formulas. We have given results which show that irredundant formulas are harder than redundant ones both for local search procedures and proof procedures such as DPL-like procedures. We also have exhibited that random formulas become less and less redundant as their size increases. Since these formulas are used as benchmarks to compare algorithms and to choose the best settings for their parameters, one has to be careful no to exploit this characteristic to improve an algorithm. If an algorithm A exploits only the redundancy to improve over an algorithm B then the performances of A and B will converge when the number of variables increases. We suggest to compare algorithms on irredundant random formulas and to try to improve algorithms on these formulas, instead. To this end we have given an algorithm of a generator of irredundant formulas which avoids some clause redundancy checks.

This work can be generalized by studying the redundancy in realistic problems and its impact on their hardness. It would also be interesting to identify the possible other characteristics of this type so that the challenging small size formulas for SAT algorithms will be structurally identical to the larger ones.

Acknowledgments

This work has been supported in part by the I.U.T. de Lens and the "Region Nord/Pas-de-Calais".

References

Bayardo, R. J., and Schrag, R. 1996. Using CSP look-back techniques to solve exceptionally hard SAT instances. In Springer., ed., *Proc. of the Second Int'l Conf. on Principles and Practice of Constraint Programming*, 46–60.

Boufkhad, Y. 1996. *Aspects Probabilistes et Algorithmiques du Problème de Satisfiabilité*. Ph.D. Dissertation, Université Paris 6.

Crawford, J. M., and Auton, L. 1996. Experimental Results on the Crossover Point in Random 3-SAT. *Artificial Intelligence* 81.

Davis, M., and Putnam, H. 1960. A computing Procedure for Quantification Theory. *Jour. Assoc. for Comput. Mach.* 7:201–215.

Davis, M.; Logemann, G.; and Loveland, D. 1962. A Machine Program for Theorem Proving. *Jour. Assoc. for Comput. Mach.* 5:267–270.

Dubois, O.; André, P.; Boufkhad, Y.; and Carlier, J. 1996. SAT versus UNSAT. In *Cliques, Coloring, and Satisfiability: Second DIMACS Implementation Challenge*, number 26. American Mathematical Society. 415–436.

Freeman, J. W. 1995. *Improvements to Propositional Satisfiability Search Algorithms*. Ph.D. Dissertation, University of Pennsylvania, Philadelphia.

Gent, I. P., and Walsh, T. 1993. Easy Problems are Sometimes Hard. *Artificial Intelligence* 70:335–345.

Hogg, T., and Williams, C. 1994. The Hardest Constraint Problems: A Double Phase Transition. *Artificial Intelligence* 69:359–377.

Larabee, T., and Tsuji, Y. 1993. Evidence for a Satisfiability Threshold for Random 3CNF Formulas. In *Proceedings AAAI Spring Symposium*, 112–118.

LI, C. M., and Anbulagan. 1997. Heuristics Based on Unit Propagation for Satisfiability Problems. In *Proceedings of IJCAI'97*, 366–371.

Mazure, B.; Saïs, L.; and Grégoire, E. 1996. Detecting Logical Inconsistencies. In *Annals of Mathematics and Artificial Intelligence*.

McAllester, D.; Selman, B.; and Kautz, H. 1997. Evidence for Invariants in Local Search. In *Proceedings of the Fourteenth National Conference on Artificial Intelligence AAAI'97*.

Mitchell, D.; Selman, B.; and Levesque, H. 1992. Hard and Easy Distribution of SAT Problems. In *Proceedings of AAAI'92*, 459–465.

Schrag, R., and Crawford, J. M. 1996. Implicates and Prime Implicates in Random 3SAT. *Artificial Intelligence* 81:199–222.

On 2-SAT and Renamable Horn

Alvaro del Val
E.T.S. Informática
Universidad Autónoma de Madrid
delval@ii.uam.es
http://www.ii.uam.es/~delval.

Abstract

We introduce new linear time algorithms for satisfiability of binary propositional theories (2-SAT), and for recognition and satisfiability of renamable Horn theories. The algorithms are based on unit resolution, and are thus likely easier to integrate within general SAT solvers than other graph-based algorithms.

Introduction

2-SAT and renamable Horn SAT are the paradigmatic examples of tractable problems in propositional satisfiability, itself the paradigmatic example of NP-complete problem. 2-SAT is the problem of deciding the satisfiability of a set of binary clauses; renamable Horn SAT, or RenHorn-SAT for short, the problem of deciding the satisfiability of a set of clauses which is renamable Horn, i.e. which can be transformed into a set of Horn clauses by an uniform renaming of variables. We present linear time algorithms for satisfiability of binary theories, and for recognition and satisfiability of renamable Horn.

For such two classic problems, the conceptual baggage, data structures, and sometimes control, needed to solve them appear pretty cumbersome. For 2-SAT, you need parallelization (Even, Itai, & Shamir 1976) or various forms of graph or hypergraph theory (Aspvall, Plass, & Tarjan 1979; Chandru et al. 1990; Pretolani 1993); for Horn renamability, large intermediate binary theories (Lewis 1978; Aspvall 1980) or complex graph or hypergraph labeling algorithms (Chandru et al. 1990; Pretolani 1993). You don't need any of this, as we show. All you need is a simple and efficient rule of inference, our old friend unit resolution, twisted in some interesting ways.

$BinSat$, the new algorithm for 2-SAT, is based on the following key idea:

- Propagation of tentative values by unit resolution need not be stopped in the presence of contradictions, as long as we correctly identify their source; on the contrary, stopping this propagation is a source of repeated work which may lead to rediscovery of identical dead ends over and over.

RenHorn-SAT, in turn, can be decided by unit resolution, (Henschen & Wos 1974), and thus in linear time

(Dowling & Gallier 1984; Forbus & de Kleer 1993). That is, a renamable Horn set of clauses is unsatisfiable iff unit resolution derives a contradiction from the set. Typically, however, we do not know whether a set S of clauses is renamable Horn. We need to verify this property explicitly if we want to conclude that S is satisfiable from the failure to find a unit resolution refutation of S. We show how to adapt $BinSat$ to yield a new linear algorithm for (a superset of) RenHorn-SAT which requires no intermediate binary theories (unlike (Lewis 1978; Aspvall 1980)) and no additional data structures beyond those used by standard SAT solvers (unlike the special graphs of (Chandru et al. 1990) or the hypergraphs of (Pretolani 1993)). Letting S_B be the binary theory obtained from S following (Lewis 1978), the key idea is the following:

- In order to mimic $BinSat$'s unit propagation over the binary S_B it suffices to use the following rule: given clause $xC \in S$ and literal $\neg x$ to be propagated, assign *all* literals of C as *true*, and propagate them.

There is, incidentally, a very clear semantic interpretation of this rule, which is discussed later.

We will later argue that the new algorithms are more efficient than other linear time algorithms for 2-SAT and renamable Horn recognition. Perhaps more importantly, by their reliance on unit resolution, the new algorithms are likely to be more easily integrated within more general SAT solvers than their competitors. Many of the most efficient SAT solvers nowadays rely on some variant of the "backtracking plus unit resolution" scheme of the classical Davis-Putnam satisfiability algorithm (Davis, Logemann, & Loveland 1962); so does recent work on hierarchies of tractable satisfiability problems, e.g. (Dalal & Etherington 1992; Pretolani 1996), which include 2-SAT and/or RenHorn as the base problems to which more complex problems can be reduced through a combination of backtracking and unit resolution. Our algorithms require no additional data structures beyond those used by unit resolution, and thus by the vast majority of existing general SAT solvers.

We assume familiarity with the terminology of propositional reasoning. n denotes the number of distinct variables of the theory S, m the number of clauses, $|S|$ its total length (number of literal occurrences). We first discuss the classic 2-SAT algorithm as motivation for our algorithms, which are presented in the following sections.

Copyright © 2000, American Association for Artificial Intelligence (www.aaai.org). All rights reserved.

Procedure BTOSat(S)

$S := PropUnit(S)$;
while $\square \notin S$ **and** $S \neq \emptyset$ **do**:
    choose an unassigned literal x;
    $R := PropUnit(S \cup \{x\})$;
    if $\square \in R$
    then $S := PropUnit(S \cup \{\overline{x}\})$
    else $S := R$;
endwhile
If $\square \in S$
then return "Unsatisfiable"
else return the current assignment;

Figure 1: Backtrack-once algorithm

The "standard" 2-SAT algorithm

The classical "guess and deduce" algorithm for 2-SAT was introduced in (Even, Itai, & Shamir 1976); we provide here a modernized version of the algorithm, similar to that provided in (Dalal & Etherington 1992). The algorithm, which we will call $BTOSat$ (for "backtrack once"), is described in Figure 1. It can be seen as a restricted case of the classic Davis-Putnam backtracking-plus-unit-resolution procedure for general SAT problems (Davis, Logemann, & Loveland 1962). $PropUnit$ stands for the well-known algorithm for unit resolution used in almost all SAT solvers, also called unit propagation or boolean constraint propagation, which runs in time $O(|S|)$. Good descriptions of $PropUnit$ can be found in e.g. (Dowling & Gallier 1984; Dalal & Etherington 1992; Forbus & de Kleer 1993). $BTOSat$ simply chooses literals to assign, and propagates their value with unit resolution. If an assignment x yields a contradiction, then it adds $\overline{x}$ to the input S; otherwise it adds x to S. The crucial aspect is that $BTOSat$ never backtracks to previously assigned variables. We may need to undo an assignment to x, but if the complementary assignment $\overline{x}$ ends in failure then the theory is unsatisfiable. Hence $BTOSat$ backtracks at most one step.

As described (but see discussion of the "parallel version" later), $BTOSat$ has complexity $O(nm)$. The following two examples show that this bound is tight, illustrating two different sources of redundancy in $BTOSat$: respectively, the failure to identify the source of contradictions, and the repeated propagation of values from branches which lead to contradictions, even when those values are not responsible for the contradiction.

Example 1 Consider the theory $S_1 = \{\overline{x_1}x_2, \overline{x_2}x_3, \ldots, \overline{x_{n-1}}x_n, \overline{x_{n-1}}\overline{x_n}, x_{n-1}\overline{x_n}, x_{n-1}x_n\}$.
Note that the last four clauses are unsatisfiable. Suppose literals are assigned in their natural order, preferring always the positive literal. This leads to a sequence of $n-1$ failures, with $PropUnit(S_1 \cup \{x_1\})$, $PropUnit(S_1 \cup \{\overline{x_1}, x_2\})$, and so on, returning $\square$. In each step, the procedure must consider all remaining unsubsumed clauses. It is only in the last step that S_1 is determined unsatisfiable when both $PropUnit(S_1 \cup \{\overline{x_1}, \ldots, \overline{x_{n-2}}x_{n-1}\})$ and $PropUnit(S_1 \cup \{\overline{x_1}, \ldots, \overline{x_{n-1}}\})$ yield $\square$. $\square$

Procedure TempPropUnit(x)
/* Input: A literal x to be tentatively assigned. */

if $tempval(x) = false$ /*temporary conflict, $S \models \neg x \supset x$ */
then set $S := PropUnit(S \cup \{x\})$ and **return**;
$tempval(x) := true$; $tempval(\overline{x}) := false$;
foreach $y\overline{x} \in S$ **do**:
    if $\square \in S$ **then return**;
    if $tempval(y) \neq true$ **then** TempPropUnit(y);

Procedure BinSat(S)
/* Input: A binary clausal theory S */

foreach variable p of S **do**:
    $tempval(p) := tempval(\overline{p}) := NIL$;
    $permval(p) := permval(\overline{p}) := NIL$;
$S := PropUnit(S)$;
while ($\square \notin S$ **and** there exists a literal x
    s.t. $permval(x) = tempval(x) = NIL$) **do**:
    TempPropUnit(x);
If $\square \in S$
then return Unsatisfiable;
else return Satisfiable;

Figure 2: Linear time algorithm for 2-SAT. $PropUnit$ assigns variables by setting $permval$'s (see text).

In this example, we can solve the problem if we detect in the first step that the source of the contradiction in each of the failed assignments x_i is that $S_1 \models \overline{x_{n-1}}$, from which the unsatisfiability of S_1 can be immediately detected by adding $\overline{x_{n-1}}$ to S_1 and running $PropUnit$.

Detecting the source of contradictions is not enough, however, to avoid $\Theta(nm)$ cost:

Example 2 Consider the following theory $S_2 = \{\overline{x_1}x_2, \overline{x_2}x_3, \ldots, \overline{x_{k-1}}x_k, \overline{x_k}y_1, \overline{y_1}y_2, \ldots, \overline{y_{k-1}}y_k, \overline{x_1}z, \overline{x_1}\overline{z}, \ldots, \overline{x_k}z, \overline{x_k}\overline{z}\}$. Suppose again we assign first $x_1, \ldots, x_n$, positively. Assigning any of the x_i's positively yields a contradiction using the second row of clauses. Before doing so, however, it may assign all later x_j's as well as all the y_i's. While replacing the assignment, say, x_1, by $\overline{x_1}$ does correctly identify the source of contradiction, it also forces us to undo all other assignments to the y_i's. This is unfortunate, as these are perfectly fine, and $BTOSat$ will in fact reassign them as a by-product of each of the x_i assignments. $\square$

These two examples are sufficient to motivate the new algorithm, described in the next section.

A new linear time algorithm for 2-SAT

$BinSat$, the new algorithm for 2-SAT, is described in Figure 2. $BinSat$ simply tries assignments much as $BTOSat$, using the routine $TempPropUnit$, abbreviated TPU. $TPU(x)$ takes a literal x to be temporarily assigned and propagates its value by unit resolution. It works in a depth first fashion, assigning temporary values $tempval$ to x and to every literal derivable by unit resolution from $S \cup \{x\}$. When it is about to assign a $tempval$ to a literal y which is in contradiction with the previous $tempval(y)$, it recognizes this as the entailment

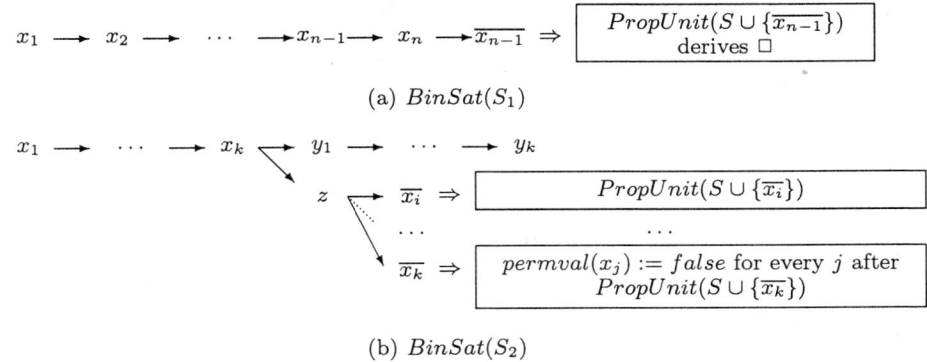

Figure 3: Examples of BinSat. An arrow $x_i \to x_j$ denotes that $TPU(x_j)$ is called from the loop of $TPU(x_i)$.

$S \models \overline{y} \supset y$, i.e. $S \models y$, and, through a call to *PropUnit*, it *permanently* assigns the value true to y and propagates it. We represent the permanent character of the effects of *PropUnit* by assuming that, for any x which it propagates, it sets $permval(x) := true$, $permval(\overline{x}) = false$, and effectively removes from S clauses containing x (in practice, it may simply mark these clauses as permanently subsumed). Temporary assignments are ignored by *PropUnit*.

BinSat does not revoke any assignment unless forced to; correctly identifies the source of conflict; and *does not stop unit propagation when a contradiction is found*—instead, it searches for, and finds, all conflicts, whether they are induced by the initial literal which was tentatively assigned, or by a literal that was assigned as a result of the initial tentative assignment. As a result, any tentative assignment is explored in full only once, and revoked at most once.

If *BinSat* returns Satisfiable, a satisfying assignment can be found as follows: for each variable p, if $permval(p) \neq NIL$ then p is assigned $permval(p)$; otherwise, p is assigned $tempval(p)$.

Example 3 The execution of *BinSat* on S_1, with the same ordering of literals, is depicted in Figure 3.a. $BinSat(S_1)$ recursively calls in sequence $TPU(x_1)$, ..., $TPU(x_{n-1})$, $TPU(x_n)$, and finally $TPU(\overline{x_{n-1}})$. At this point, x_{n-1} cannot be assigned, and the algorithm calls $S := PropUnit(S_1 \cup \{\overline{x_{n-1}}\})$, which derives a contradiction from the last two clauses.

Note that backjumping, which is usually described as "identifying the source of conflict," cannot help here; indeed the strength of backjumping is in "jumping back" more than one step at a time, which is never needed for 2-SAT. Clearly, certain conflicts are not identified by backjumping, which would only add useless overhead for these instances. □

Example 4 As mentioned, in order to avoid repeating any work, *BinSat* goes beyond correctly identifying culprits of contradictions. Figure 3.b illustrates a possible runs of $BinSat(S_2)$, with the same ordering of literals as in example 2. Note that multiple conflicts can be discovered within a single top level TPU call, as can be seen in the various calls to *PropUnit*, and that the y_i assignments are never undone. □

Lemma 1 *Suppose $tempval(x) = false$ right before some call to $TPU(x)$. Then $S \models x$ (and therefore S is satisfiable iff $PropUnit(S \cup \{x\})$ is satisfiable).*

Lemma 2 *Suppose $tempval(x) := true$ is assigned in a $TPU(x)$ call. Then $tempval(x)$ never changes, and $TPU(x)$ is never called again.*

By lemma 1 and soundness of *PropUnit*, all permanent assignments made by *BinSat* preserve satisfiability. By lemma 2, TPU is called at most once per literal, and thus no clause is considered more than twice within TPU calls. Similar analysis can be applied to *PropUnit* and *BinSat* as a whole. We can show:

Theorem 3 *BinSat correctly decides the satisfiability of binary clausal theories, in time $O(m)$.*

This analysis assumes that for an $O(m)$ initialization step by which clauses are indexed by the literals they contain, so that the loop of $TPU(x)$ considers exactly those y's such that $\overline{x}y \in S$.

Interestingly, tentative assignments which are not revoked by an opposite permanent value by the end of the toplevel call in which they were made, are never revoked. Thus they behave exactly as permanent assignments.[1] See e.g. the y_i's in Figure 3.b.

Related work on 2-SAT

As said, *BTOSat* originates in (Even, Itai, & Shamir 1976). As first suggested by Even et al., *BTOSat* can be implemented in parallel $O(m)$ time by working in parallel in the branches for p and $\overline{p}$; the first branch that finishes without returning a contradiction gets its assignment made permanent, immediately interrupting work on the other branch. If both branches return a contradiction, then the theory is unsatisfiable. We can obtain

---

[1]Note however than an unrevoked tentative value can be *confirmed* by an identical permanent value. This source of redundancy in *BinSat* has an easy fix: before assigning some $permval(x)$ in *PropUnit*, check that that $tempval(x)$ is not already set to the same value; if it is, do not add x to the stack of unit clauses to be propagated.

the same complexity with a single processor, by interleaving work in alternative branches. But this is obviously more complex to implement than *BinSat*, and may lead to twice more work than needed, as we always explore two branches.

Define the *implication graph* $G(S)$ as the graph whose nodes are the literals of S, and there is an edge from a literal v to a literal w iff there exists a clause $\overline{v}w \in S$. (Aspvall, Plass, & Tarjan 1979) provides a linear algorithm based on the $G(S)$ graph. The algorithm first finds the strongly connected components of $G(S)$; members of the same SCC are literals which must have the same truth value in any satisfying assignment. Then it generates an assignment by processing the SCCs in topological order. Finding SCCs is usually done by two complete depth-first searches of the graph, inverting all edges before the second pass; a satisfying assignment is generated by outputting the SCCs in topological order. *BinSat* can be described as performing a single *partial* depth-first search of this graph: a call to $TPU(y)$ from $TPU(x)$ traverses the (x,y) edge corresponding to the clause $\overline{x}y$, in which case the $(\overline{y},\overline{x})$ edge is traversed only if there's a call to *PropUnit* which inverts the temporary assignments. This partial search will often be shortcircuited by derivation of permanent values, and generates the assignment on the fly. Thus *BinSat* should be more efficient.[2]

After developing *BinSat*, we learned about the linear 2-SAT algorithm of (Chandru *et al.* 1990), a special case of an algorithm for renamable Horn recognition. One can find some similarity with the ideas of *BinSat* after some digging, by mapping their graph traversal procedures to implicit unit resolution operations. Their algorithm relies on a substantially more complicated graph than $G(S)$, having both variables and clauses as vertices. In addition, a referee pointed out that (Pretolani 1993) provides an hypergraph version of the algorithm of (Chandru *et al.* 1990). We defer discussion of these algorithms to the section on related work in renamable Horn.

Horn renamability

Recall that a theory is renamable Horn iff there exists a uniform renaming of its variables such that the theory becomes Horn after the renaming. For example, the theory $\{ab, cd\}$ can be made Horn by renaming a to be the negative literal $\overline{a^*}$, and c to be $\overline{c^*}$, where both a^* and c^* are new variables. Equivalently, S is renamable Horn iff there exists an interpretation such that at most one literal per clause is false in this interpretation. As it is well known, unit resolution is a complete satisfiability method for renamable Horn, not just for Horn. Horn renamability can be reduced to the satisfiability of a set of binary clauses. Specifically, for any set of clauses S, let S_B be the binary theory consisting of all clauses xy such that the literals x and y occur jointly in some clause of S. Then S is renamable Horn iff S_B is satisfiable (Lewis 1978). Generating S_B requires quadratic

---

[2]Note that Aspvall's method finds *all* pairs of literals such that $S \models l_1 \equiv l_2$ (when l_1 and l_2 are in the same SCC) in order to detect whether $S \models x \equiv \overline{x}$ for some x.

Procedure RH-Prop(x)
/* Input: A literal x to be permanently assigned in S_B. */

$permval(x) := true; permval(\overline{x}) := false;$
$Q := \{x\};$ /* stack of literals whose *permval* is true */
while $Q \neq \emptyset$ **do**:
  $y := pop(Q);$
  foreach clause $C \in S$ s.t. $\overline{y} \in C$ **do**:
    foreach literal $z \in C \setminus \{\overline{y}\}$ **do**:
      if $permval(z) = false$
      then {/* S_B unsatisfiable */
        $renamable := false;$ **return**;}
      else if $permval(z) = NIL$
      then {$permval(z) := true; permval(\overline{z}) := false;$
        $push(z, Q);$}

Procedure RH-TempProp(x)
/* Input: A literal x to be tentatively assigned in S_B */

if $tempval(x) = false$ /* $S_B \models \neg x \supset x$ */
then return RH-Prop(x);
$tempval(x) := true; tempval(\overline{x}) := false;$
foreach clause $C \in S$ s.t. $\overline{x} \in C$ **do**:
  foreach literal $z \in C \setminus \{\overline{x}\}$ **do**:
    if $renamable = false$ **then return**;
    if $tempval(z) \neq true$ **and** $permval(z) \neq true$
    then RH-TempProp(z);

Figure 4: Auxiliary routines for renamable Horn.

---

time and space, respectively $O(mn^2)$ and $O(n^2)$. While the cost of generating a binary theory corresponding to the Horn renamability problem can be reduced to $O(|S|)$ (see the discussion of (Aspvall 1980) later), we can in fact skip this step altogether, as we show next.

Figures 4 and 5 describe a new $O(|S|)$ algorithm, $RHSat(S)$, which decides both membership in the class renamable Horn, and satisfiability of renamable Horn *and* binary theories. It works in a similar manner to *BinSat*, except that no binary theory is explicitly constructed, and no new variables need to be reasoned with. As a result, *RHSat* is likely to be much more efficient in practice than competing algorithms.

The easiest way to understand *RHSat*, procedurally, is as the repeated application of the rule (RH) "from a clause $xC \in S$ and literal $\overline{x}$ to be propagated, assign *all* literals of C as *true*." This rule is applied in a two-level fashion, just as in *BinSat*, corresponding to tentative and permanent assignments, through the subroutines *RH-TempProp* and *RH-Prop*, respectively. The main loop of *RHSat* simply handles literals to try and assign to *RH-TempProp*.

We come back to this rule later. We will instead describe here the procedure in terms of a simulation of unit resolution over an implicit S_B. *RHSat* mimics *BinSat* in the relevant parts, but the subroutines are adapted to work on this implicit S_B. The key observation is that unit propagation of values in S_B can be done directly by considering the clauses of S. Given a clause $x_1 x_2 \ldots x_k \in S$, a call $TPU(\overline{x}_1)$ in S_B would call TPU for each of $x_2, \ldots, x_k$; and similarly for propagating $\overline{x_1}$

Procedure RHSat(S)
/* Input: A set of clauses S. Output: See theorem 4. */

foreach variable p of S **do**:
    $tempval(p) := tempval(\overline{p}) := NIL$;
    $permval(p) := permval(\overline{p}) := NIL$;
$S := PropUnit(S)$;
if $\square \in S$ **then return** Unsatisfiable;
$renamable := true$;
while ($renamable = true$ **and** there exists a literal x
      s.t. $permval(x) = tempval(x) = NIL$) **do**:
    RH-TempProp(x);
if $renamable = false$
then {**if** S is binary
      then return Unsatisfiable;
      else return Non-renamable; }
else return Satisfiable;

Figure 5: Algorithm for renamable Horn theories.

with $PropUnit$ over S_B. There is therefore no need to generate S_B explicitly in order to run unit propagation over S_B.

The main procedure $RHSat$ first sets $S := PropUnit(S)$, and thereafter works on the simplified problem without unit clauses. Let us keep using S_B for the binary theory encoding the renamability problem for $PropUnit(S)$. Then $RHSat$ iterates over unassigned literals just as $BinSat$, working over the implicit S_B by tentatively assigning literals with $RH\text{-}TempProp$. $RH\text{-}TempProp$ corresponds to TPU over S_B, exploring tentative assignments in full, and $RH\text{-}Prop$ corresponds roughly to $PropUnit$, setting and propagating permanent assignments over S_B which have been derived by $RH\text{-}TempProp$. Note that in all routines, the termination test $\square \in S$ which was used in $BinSat$ is replaced by the test $renamable = false$, since the fact that $S_B \models \square$ means only that S is not renamable, not that it is unsatisfiable. Unless, of course, $PropUnit(S)$ is binary, in which case $PropUnit(S) = S_B$, and S is satisfiable iff $PropUnit(S)$ is renamable Horn.

Example 5 Let $S_4 = \{\overline{q}p, \overline{r}p, \overline{p}st, \overline{s}q, \overline{t}r\}$, and let $S_5 = S_4 \cup \{\overline{qr}\}$. The former is renamable Horn, while the latter is not. Figure 6 provides possible runs of $RHSat$ over each of these inputs. We illustrate two potential runs with S_4, both of which yield the assignment p, q, r, s, t; this can be interpreted as requiring that the sign of all variables is changed (see discussion below). In fact, these changes are all forced, as illustrated in the second run; that is, renaming all variables is the *only* way to make S_4 Horn. In the second example, with S_5, the call $RH\text{-}TempProp(\overline{p})$ results in a call to $RH\text{-}Prop(\overline{p})$, which in turn ends up in failure.

There is a very natural reading of the figures in terms of renaming. A positive literal is a variable saying "rename me," a negative literal a variable saying "do not rename me." For example, Figure 6.c "reads" as follows: if you change the sign of p then you must change the sign of s as well (otherwise both p and s would both be positive in the renamed $\overline{p}st$, which therefore would not be Horn); but

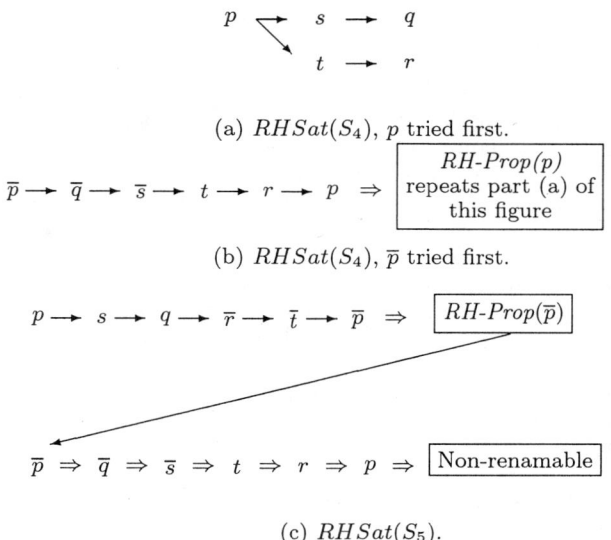

Figure 6: Examples of RHSat. An arrow $x \to y$ denotes that $RH\text{-}TempProp(y)$ is called from the loop of $RH\text{-}TempProp(x)$. Similarly, $x \Rightarrow y$ means that $RH\text{-}Prop$ derives y from x.

changing s requires renaming q, because of $\overline{s}q$; renaming q in turn forces you to keep r unchanged, etc. $\square$

Theorem 4 *If $\square \in PropUnit(S)$, or if $PropUnit(S)$ is renamable Horn or binary, then $RHSat(S)$ correctly decides the satisfiability of S. Otherwise, $RHSat(S)$ correctly returns Non-renamable. The running time is $O(|S|)$.*

Corollary 5 *$RHSat$ is a satisfiability decision procedure exactly for the class of theories S such that $PropUnit(S)$ is renamable Horn or binary, or S contains an unsatisfiable subset which is renamable Horn.*

Note that $PropUnit(S)$ may be renamable Horn or binary even if S is neither, and thus that $RHSat$ decides a larger class than the union of renamable Horn and binary, with a single algorithm. The reasoning for the $O(|S|)$ bound is similar to that for $BinSat$. We can show that $RH\text{-}Prop$ and $RH\text{-}TempProp$ can each consider a clause at most twice. We use the same indexing scheme as in $BinSat$, a list of clauses in which each literal occurs. This scheme is used by most SAT solvers; our algorithms require no additional data structures beyond these.

We have focused on satisfiability as opposed to recognition per se. It is trivial to modify $RHSat$ to make it a pure recognition algorithm, if desired. If the theory is determined satisfiable, then a satisfying assignment can be found exactly as in $BinSat$ (i.e. use the $permval$'s if available, otherwise the $tempval$'s). This assignment satisfies all but possibly one literal from each clause of S, since it satisfies S_B. The renaming to make S Horn can be obtained from this assignment: if a variable is assigned true, then change its sign in S.

As we have mentioned, the renamable Horn algorithm

can be understood simply as repeated application of the rule (RH) given above. Both *RH-Prop* and *RH-TempProp* can be seen as applying this rule, respectively with permanent and tentative assignments. Consider the semantics by which an assignment is said to satisfy a non-unit clause iff it satisfies all but possibly one of its literals. It turns out that a theory is renamable Horn iff there is some assignment that satisfies *in this sense* all non-unit clauses of S. (If S is Horn, this assignment is the one which assigns $false$ to all variables.) Clearly, (RH) is sound with respect to this semantics, and can be made complete using the two level-approach of *RHSat*, as shown by Theorem 4. Hence the propagation rule can be seen as either mimicing unit propagation over S_B without generating it; or simply as a direct implementation of the semantics just described as a means to identify renamable Horn.

Related work on renamable Horn

Alternative algorithms for recognizing renamable Horn theories can be found in (Chandru *et al.* 1990; Pretolani 1993; Aspvall 1980). We have already mentioned the first two algorithms in the context of 2–SAT; again, the algorithm of (Pretolani 1993), which was pointed to us by a referee and which we haven't been able to examine in detail in the short time alloted for revision of this paper, is described as an hypergraph version of (Chandru *et al.* 1990). The correspondence between these two algorithms appears to be as follows: a clause node in (Chandru *et al.* 1990) corresponds in Pretolani's algorithm to a directed hyperedge from variables occurring negatively (or from *false* if none) to variables occurring positively in the clause (or to *true* if none). *BinSat* and *RHSat* are significantly simpler than either algorithm, both in terms of data structures and, equally importantly, of the conceptual baggage needed to understand them.

A different approach was followed earlier by Aspvall (Aspvall 1980). He showed that by introducing auxiliary variables it is possible to generate in $O(|S|)$ time and space a binary theory S_B^* which is satisfiable iff S_B is satisfiable. Coupled with *BinSat* or any other linear 2-SAT algorithm, Horn renamability can be decided in linear time by first generating S_B^* and then testing it for satisfiability.

Since we do not need to generate any binary theory, our algorithm is more efficient than the procedure just described. Furthermore, it can be shown that $|S_B^*| = (6 - 8/k)|S|$, assuming all clauses of S have length $k > 2$. Multiplying our memory requirements almost sixfold will not always be an option. Even if it is, simply "preparing the input" may take six times more time than with *RHSat* (which basically has only to read S, as opposed to generating S_B^*); and "actually solving the problem" with *RHSat* needs only consider $|S|$ literal occurrences, as opposed to, again, a sixfold increase. The generation cost, furthermore, is always paid by Aspvall's method, even when it may happen that the resulting binary theory is easily unsatisfiable (i.e. *RHSat* may be able to detect unsatisfiability by considering only a small subset of clauses of S).

Conclusion

We introduce new linear time algorithms for 2-SAT and renamable Horn, which improve on previous algorithms in efficiency and simplicity. Being based on unit resolution, they are likely to be more easily integrated into general SAT solvers based on the standard scheme of backtracking plus unit resolution. We provide one explicit example in the extended version of the paper by showing how to optimize the enumeration of models of a binary theory, which could be used by a SAT solver such as Nemesis (Larrabee 1992), with complexity almost linear per model. Other applications are possible, for example in the the hierarchy of tractable classes $\{R_i\}$, defined by (Pretolani 1996), where R_0 is renamable Horn, and $S \in R_i$ iff either $S \in R_{i-1}$ or there exists a literal x such that $PropUnit(S \cup \{x\}) \in R_{i-1}$ and $PropUnit(S \cup \{\overline{x}\}) \in R_i$.

References

Aspvall, B.; Plass, M. F.; and Tarjan, R. E. 1979. A linear-time algorithm for testing the truth of certain quantified Boolean formulas. *Information Processing Letters* 8(3):121–123.

Aspvall, B. 1980. Recognizing disguised NR(1) instances of the satisfiability problem. *Journal of Algorithms* 1(1):97–103. Note.

Chandru, V.; Coullard, C.; Hammer, P.; Montañez, M.; and Sun, X. 1990. On renamable Horn and generalized Horn functions. *Annals of Mathematics and Artificial Intelligence* 1:33–48.

Dalal, M., and Etherington, D. W. 1992. A hierarchy of tractable satisfiability problems. *Information Processing Letters* 44:173–180.

Davis, M.; Logemann, G.; and Loveland, D. 1962. A machine program for theorem proving. *Communications of the ACM* 5:394–397.

Dowling, W. F., and Gallier, J. H. 1984. Linear-time algorithms for testing the satisfiability of propositional Horn formulae. *Journal of Logic Programming* 3:267–284.

Even, S.; Itai, A.; and Shamir, A. 1976. On the complexity of timetable and multicommodity flow problems. *SIAM Journal of Computing* 5(4):691–703.

Forbus, K., and de Kleer, J. 1993. *Building Problem Solvers*. The MIT Press.

Henschen, L., and Wos, L. 1974. Unit refutations and Horn sets. *Journal of the ACM* 21:590–605.

Larrabee, T. 1992. Test pattern generation using boolean satisfiability. *IEEE Transactions on Computer-Aided Design* 4–15.

Lewis, H. R. 1978. Renaming a set of clauses as a Horn set. *Journal of the ACM* 25(1):134–135.

Pretolani, D. 1993. *Satisfiability and Hypergraphs*. Ph.D. Dissertation, Università di Pisa.

Pretolani, D. 1996. Hierarchies of polynomially solvable satisfiability problems. *Annals of Mathematics and Artificial Intelligence* 17:339–357.

A Distributed Algorithm to Evaluate Quantified Boolean Formulae

Rainer Feldmann, Burkhard Monien, Stefan Schamberger

Department of Computer Science
University of Paderborn
Fürstenallee 11, 33102 Paderborn, Germany
(obelix|bm|schaum)@uni-paderborn.de

Abstract

In this paper, we present PQSOLVE, a distributed theorem-prover for Quantified Boolean Formulae. First, we introduce our sequential algorithm QSOLVE, which uses new heuristics and improves the use of known heuristics to prune the search tree. As a result, QSOLVE is more efficient than the QSAT-solvers previously known. We have parallelized QSOLVE. The resulting distributed QSAT-solver PQSOLVE uses parallel search techniques, which we have developed for distributed game tree search. PQSOLVE runs efficiently on distributed systems, i. e. parallel systems without any shared memory. We briefly present experiments that show a speedup of about 114 on 128 processors. To the best of our knowledge we are the first to introduce an efficient parallel QSAT-solver.

Introduction

QSAT generalizes propositional satisfiability (SAT) which has been thoroughly analyzed, see e.g. (Gu et al. 1997), since it is the prototype of an NP-complete problem and has applications in automated reasoning, computer-aided design, computer architecture design, planning, and VLSI. QSAT is the problem to decide the satisfiability of propositional formulae, in which the variables may either be universally ($\forall$) or existentially ($\exists$) quantified. Thus, the inputs of a QSAT-solver look like the following:

$$f(X) = Q_N X_N Q_{N-1} X_{N-1} \ldots Q_0 X_0 : f',$$

with $Q_i \in \{\forall, \exists\}$. The X_i are disjoint sets of boolean variables, $X = \cup_{i=0}^{N} X_i$, and f' is a propositional formula over X. $f(X) = \exists X_N \phi$ is satisfiable iff there is a truth assignment for the variables in X_N such that ϕ is true, and $f(X) = \forall X_N \phi$ is satisfiable iff ϕ is true for all possible truth assignments of the variables in X_N.

According to the increasing interest in problems not in NP, QSAT has been studied as a prototype of a PSPACE-complete problem. Furthermore, by restricting the number of quantifiers to some fixed c, it has been analyzed as a family of prototypical problems for the polynomial hierarchy. (Gent and Walsh 1999) study QSAT and show that a phase transition similar to that observed for SAT does occur for

Copyright © 2000, American Association for Artificial Intelligence (www.aaai.org). All rights reserved.

QSAT, too. They show that some models of random instances are "flawed" and propose a model, in which each clause contains at least two existentials.

The first QSAT-solver, published in (Kleine-Büning, Karpinski, and Flögel 1995), is based on resolution. (Cadoli, Giovanardi, and Schaerf 1998) propose EVALUATE, an algorithm based on the Davis-Putnam procedure for SAT. EVALUATE contains a heuristic to detect trivial truth of a QSAT instance. (Rintanen 1999) presents an algorithm based on the Davis-Putnam procedure and introduces a heuristic called Inverting Quantifiers (IQ). He shows that the use of IQ before the entire evaluation process speeds up the computation of several QSAT instances which originate from conditional planning.

First, we describe QSOLVE, a sequential QSAT-solver. QSOLVE is based on the Davis-Putnam procedure for SAT. We make use of a generalization of the data structures of a SAT-solver (Böhm and Speckenmeyer 1996). The data structure supports the operations to delete a clause, to delete a variable, and to undo these deletions. We implemented most of the heuristics that were introduced by (Cadoli, Giovanardi, and Schaerf 1998) and (Rintanen 1999). Moreover, we have developed an approximation algorithm for the IQ-heuristic of (Rintanen 1999) which allows the use of IQ during the evaluation process. We developed a simple history heuristic to determine on whether or not to apply the heuristic to detect trivial truth (TTH) of (Cadoli, Giovanardi, and Schaerf 1998) at a node in the search tree. In addition, we have developed a heuristic to detect trivial falsity (TFH) of a QSAT instance. TFH is controlled by a history heuristic, too. We show experimentally, that with the help of these additional heuristics our algorithm is faster than the ones mentioned above.

Then we present our parallelization of QSOLVE. The parallelization is similar to the parallelization used in the chess program ZUGZWANG (Feldmann, Monien, and Mysliwietz 1994). For chess programs this parallelization is still the best known (Feldmann 1997).

Since QSAT can be regarded as a two-person zero-sum game with complete information, it is not surprising that techniques from parallel chess programs are applicable to QSAT-solvers. We briefly explain the general concepts of our parallelization and then concentrate on the heuristics that are used in order to schedule subproblems. Finally, we show experimentally that the resulting parallel QSAT-solver PQ-SOLVE works efficiently. On a set of randomly generated formulae the speedup of the 128-processor version is about 114. To the best of our knowledge, PQSOLVE is the first parallel QSAT-solver. Moreover, it is very efficient. Its efficiency of about 90 % is partly due to the fact that the dynamic load balancing together with our scheduling heuristics often result in a "superlinear" speedup. The effect has already been observed for SAT (Speckenmeyer, Monien, and Vornberger 1987) and indicates that the sequential depth-search algorithm is not optimal. However, as the sequential program is best among the known algorithms for QSAT, we define speedup on the basis of our sequential implementation.

QSOLVE: The Sequential Algorithm

The skeleton of QSOLVE is presented below:

boolean Qsolve(f)   /* f is "call by value" parameter */
/* let f = $Q_N X_N Q_{N-1} X_{N-1} \ldots Q_0 X_0 : f'$, */
/* let $s \in$ {true, false, unknown}, x a literal */

  $s \leftarrow$ simplify(f);   /* f may be altered */
  if ($s \neq$ unknown) **return** s;   /* prune */

  if ($Q_N = \exists$)
    if ($N \geq 2$)   /* f has ≥ 3 blocks $Q_N \ldots Q_0$ */
      if ($x \leftarrow$ InvertQuantifiers(f))   /* IQ */
        $s \leftarrow$ reduce($f, x =$ true); /* f is altered */
        if ($s \neq$ unknown) **return** s; /* prune */
        return Qsolve(f); /* recursion */

    $x \leftarrow$ SelectLiteral(f);

    $s \leftarrow$ reduce($f, x =$ true);   /* f is altered */
    if ($s \neq$ unknown) **return** s; /* prune */
    if (Qsolve(f) = true)   /* branch */
      return true;   /* cutoff */

    undo($f, x =$ true);   /* f is altered */
    $s \leftarrow$ reduce($f, x =$ false); /* f is altered */
    if ($s \neq$ unknown) **return** s; /* prune */
    return Qsolve(f);   /* branch */

  else /* $Q_N = \forall$ */
    if (TrivialTruth(f) = true)   /* TTH: SAT */
      return true;   /* prune */
    if (TrivialFalsity(f) = false)   /* TFH: SAT */
      return false;   /* prune */

    $x \leftarrow \overline{\text{SelectLiteral}(f)}$; /* complement */

    ...
    if (Qsolve(f) = false)   /* branch */
      return false;   /* cutoff */
    ...
end

When called for a formula f, f is simplified first. This is done by setting the truth values of monotone and unit existential variables. The formula is checked for an empty set of clauses or the empty clause, etc.

We measure the length of a clause in terms of $\exists$-quantified literals of the clause. Thus, a variable $x \in X_N$ is unit existential iff $Q_N = \exists$ and there is a clause that contains x as the only $\exists$-quantified variable. The simplification is then performed according to (Cadoli, Giovanardi, and Schaerf 1998). The function "simplify" may deliver the result that the formula is satisfiable or unsatisfiable.

Then, in the first case ($Q_N = \exists$) the IQ-heuristic may determine a literal that must be set to true in order to satisfy f.

If the IQ-heuristic does not deliver the desired literal a branching literal is determined in such a way that x is set to true in the first branch. Unless a cutoff occurs, both branches are tested recursively.

In the second case ($Q_N = \forall$), a test for trivial truth and trivial falsity is performed first. The literal that is selected for the branching is negated. The cutoff condition is changed according to the $\forall$-quantor. The rest of the case $Q_N = \forall$ is similar to the first case.

In the next sections, we will describe the features of QSOLVE mentioned above in more detail.

Literal Selection

The function SelectLiteral selects a literal $x \in X_N$. SelectLiteral first determines the variable v to branch with. Then the literal $x \in \{v, \bar{v}\}$ is selected in such a way that it is set to true in the first branch and to false in the second one. If the literal is $\exists$-quantified, the selection is done like in the SAT-solver by (Böhm and Speckenmeyer 1996): For every literal x let $n_i(x)$ ($p_i(x)$) be the number of negative (positive) occurrences of literal x in clauses of length i, and let $h_i(x) = max(n_i(x), p_i(x)) + 2 \cdot min(n_i(x), p_i(x))$. A literal x with lexicographically largest vector $(h_0(x), \ldots h_k(x))$ is chosen for the next branching step. The idea is to choose literals that occur as often as possible in short clauses of the formula and to prove satisfiability in the first branch already. The setting of these literals often reduces the length of the shortest clause by one. Often, the result is a unit clause or even an empty clause. If $Q_N = \forall$, the literal is negated, i. e. the branching variable is the same but the branches are searched in a different order. This often helps to prove unsatisfiability in the first branch already.

Inverting Quantifiers

The technique to invert quantifiers is based on (Rintanen 1999). We have developed the approximation algorithm presented below. The function InvertQuantifiers (IQ) tries to compute an $\exists$-quantified literal of X_N which must be set to true in order to satisfy f. IQ starts checking on whether there is a unit existential $x \in X_N$. If this is not the case, it tries to create unit existentials by setting monotone $\forall$-literals in unit clauses. Note that a unit clause is a clause with one existential. If none of the $\forall$-literals is monotone, it keeps track of the $\forall$-literal h with a maximum occurrence in unit clauses.

IQ continues recursively by testing $h =$ true and $h =$ false. In our implementation, we stop searching for a literal, if the number of recursive calls of InvertQuantifiers exceeds four. This constant has been the result of a simple program optimization on a small benchmark.

```
literal InvertQuantifiers(f)          /* f is "call by value" */
  /* let f = Q_N X_N Q_{N-1} X_{N-1} ... Q_0 X_0 : f', */
  /* let s ∈ {true,false,unknown}, x, h literals */

     do                                /* create unit existentials */
        forall (∃-units x ∈ f)
           if (x ∈ X_N) return x;
           s ← reduce(f,x = true);     /* f is altered */
           if (s = false) return NULL;

        forall (∀-literals x)
           if (#_{|C|=1}(x) > 0 and #_{|C|=1}(x̄) = 0)
              /* x is monotone */
              s ← reduce(f,x = false); /* f is altered */
              if (s = false) return NULL;
           if (#_{|C|=1}(x) = 0 and #_{|C|=1}(x̄) > 0)
              /* x̄ is monotone */
              s ← reduce(f,x = true);  /* f is altered */
              if (s = false) return NULL;
           if (#_{|C|=1}(x) > 0 and #_{|C|=1}(x̄) > 0)
              /* neither x nor x̄ are monotone */
              h ← max_{#_{|C|=1}}(h, x, x̄);
     while (there are ∃-units ∈ f);

     if (h = NULL) return NULL;        /* no recursive search */

     reduce(f,h = true);               /* recursive search */
     x ← InvertQuantifiers(f);
     if (x ≠ NULL) return x;

     undo(f,h = true);                 /* recursive search */
     reduce(f,h = false);
     return InvertQuantifiers(f);
  end
```

<u>Lemma:</u> Let f be a Quantified Boolean Formula, and let $x =$ InvertQuantifiers(f) be a literal of f. f is satisfiable iff $f_{[x=true]}$ is satisfiable.

The proof is an easy induction on the recursion depth of InvertQuantifiers. Note that f does not contain unit existentials before the initial call to InvertQuantifiers.

Trivial Truth

(Cadoli, Giovanardi, and Schaerf 1998) present a test for trivial truth: Given a QSAT instance f, delete all ∀-quantified literals from the clauses. This results in a set of clauses of ∃-quantified literals. Solve the corresponding SAT instance f'. If f' is satisfiable then f is satisfiable. SAT is NP-complete, but algorithmically QSOLVE can be used to solve the SAT-problem. The QSAT-solver does benefit from this heuristic, only if f' is satisfiable.

Adaptive Trivial Truth

Since a considerable amount of time may be wasted for the solving of SAT instances (one at every ∀-node of the search tree) we have developed a simple adaptive history heuristic to determine on when to apply this test: At every node of the search tree two global variables s and v are changed: Initially, $v=1$ and $s=2$. TrivialTruth is executed if $v \geq s$. If TrivialTruth is executed v is set to 1 and s is set as follows: if the execution proves satisfiability s is set to 2, otherwise $s = max(2 \cdot s, 16)$. If TrivialTruth is not executed then $v = 2 \cdot v$. The idea is that in the parts of the search tree where the function TrivialTruth is successfully applied, the heuristic is used at every second node of the search tree ($s = 2$). In the parts of the tree, where TrivialTruth is unsuccessful, s increases to 16 and thus, the use of TrivialTruth is restricted to every fifth node of the search tree. Again, the constants of 2 and 16 have been the result of a program optimization on some benchmark instances.

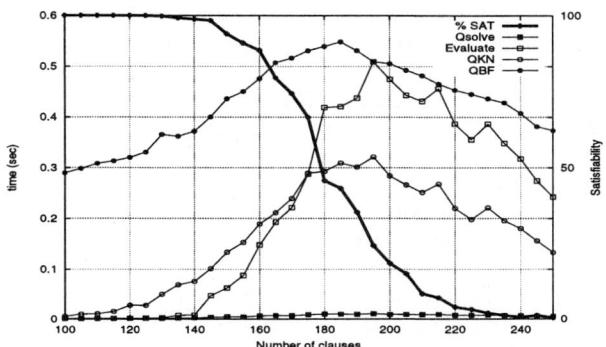

The diagram above presents the average running times of QSOLVE, EVALUATE (Cadoli, Giovanardi, and Schaerf 1998), QKN (Kleine-Büning, Karpinski, and Flögel 1995), and QBF (Rintanen 1999) on formulae with 50 variables (15 ∀-quantified ones), clauses of length four and three blocks. The formulae have been generated randomly according to Model A by (Gent and Walsh 1999). The average is taken over 500 formulae. QSOLVE and QKN are C programs, EVALUATE is a C++ program, to run QBF we used a binary from Rintanens home page. Note that the running times are arithmetic means of unnormalized data (left y-axis). E.g. from the 500 QSAT instances with 180 clauses we obtain the following running times rounded to 4 decimal digits:

time(sec)	QSOLVE	EVALUATE	QKN	QBF
minimum	0.0004	0.0000	0.0050	0.0700
average	**0.0100**	**0.4188**	**0.2927**	**0.5394**
maximum	0.1225	6.7700	4.3910	1.2200
variance	0.0119	0.6726	0.3969	0.1699

QSOLVE uses considerably less time than any of the other QSAT-solvers. This has been observed for other classes of randomly generated formulae, too. However, it should be pointed out that QBF needs less recursions than QSOLVE.

Adaptive Trivial Falsity

Let $f(X) = Q_N X_N Q_{N-1} X_{N-1} \ldots Q_0 X_0 : \bigwedge_{i=1}^{m} C_i$ be a QSAT instance, let $L_k = \{x, \bar{x} \mid x \in X_k\}$, $L_\Sigma = \bigcup_{Q_i=\exists} L_i$, $L_\Pi = \bigcup_{Q_i=\forall} L_i$. For $x \in L_k$ let $block(x) := k$.

Definition: For a formula f and a set $I \subset \{1, \ldots, m\}$ we define $f_I := \exists \Sigma : \bigwedge_{i \in I} C_i \cap \Sigma$.

$f_{\{1,\ldots,m\}}$ is the SAT instance f' of the test for trivial truth.

Definition: Two clauses C_i, C_j are conflict free, if for all $x \in L_\Pi$

$$x \in C_i \Rightarrow \begin{cases} \bar{x} \notin C_j \text{ or} \\ block(y) > block(x) \forall y \in (C_i \cup C_j) \cap L_\Sigma \end{cases}$$

I is conflict free if for all $i, j \in I$ C_i and C_j are conflict free.

Lemma: Let f be a QSAT instance, let $I \subset \{1, \ldots, m\}$ be conflict free. If f_I is not satisfiable, then f is not satisfiable.

The lemma above can be proven by induction on the number of variables of f. Simplify f without deleting or reordering the clauses. Then, if I is conflict free for f, I is conflict free for $f_{[x=0]}$ and $f_{[x=1]}$ for the outermost variable x of f. Furthermore, $(f_{[x=0]})_I = (f_I)_{[x=0]}$ and $(f_{[x=1]})_I = (f_I)_{[x=1]}$.

The generating of a conflict free clause set I with a maximum number of clauses can be shown to be computationally equivalent to the Maximum Independent Set problem, which is NP-complete in general. The function TrivialFalsity first determines a conflict free set of clauses I by a greedy approximation and then evaluates f_I by using QSOLVE. The use of TrivialFalsity is controlled by a history heuristic similar to the one described for TrivialTruth. Moreover, the test which has been used successfully most recently in the search process is performed first.

We tested a version of QSOLVE using TrivialFalsity on a set of 9500 randomly generated formulae of the form $\exists \forall \exists - 150 - L4$, i. e. formulae with 150 variables (50 $\forall$-quantified) and clause length four. The number of clauses varied from 300 to 650 in steps of 2. For each number of clauses we evaluated 50-100 formulae. The table below presents us with the average, minimum, and maximum savings in terms of recursions and running time. The net decrease of the running time is 11.57 %. The minimal savings occur at formulae with 648 or 302 clauses resp., whereas the maximum savings occur at formulae with 324 clauses.

Savings	Rec %	(#cls)	Time %	(#cls)
Average	35.26 %		11.57 %	
Minimum	16.36 %	648	-7.00 %	302
Maximum	59.98 %	324	31.44 %	324

PQSOLVE: The Distributed Algorithm

We first describe a general framework to search trees in parallel.

The Basic Algorithm

The basic idea of our distributed QSAT-solver is to decompose the search tree and search parts of it in parallel. This is organized as follows: Initially, processor 0 starts its work on the input formula. All other processors are idle. Idle processors send requests for work to a randomly selected processor. If a busy processor P gets a request for work, it checks on whether or not there are unexplored parts of its search tree waiting for evaluation. The unexplored parts are rooted in the right siblings of the nodes of P's current search stack.

On certain conditions, which will be described later, P sends one of these siblings (a formula) to the requesting processor Q. P is now the master of Q, and Q the slave of P. Upon receiving a node v of the search tree, Q starts a search below v. After having finished its work, Q sends the result back to P. The master-slave relationship is released and Q is idle again. The result is used by P as if P had computed it by itself, i. e. the stack is updated and the search below the father of v is stopped, if a cutoff occurs (see the conditions for a cut in QSOLVE). The message which contains the result is interpreted by P as a new request for work. If, upon receiving a request for work, a processor is not allowed to send a subproblem, it passes the request to a randomly selected processor. Whenever P notices that a subproblem sent to another processor Q may be cut off, it sends a cutoff message to Q, and Q becomes idle.

In distributed systems messages may be delayed by other messages. It may happen, that messages refer to nodes that are no longer active on the search stack. Therefore, for every node v a processor generates a locally unique ID. This ID is added to every message concerned with v. All messages received are checked for validity. Messages that are no longer valid are discarded.

The load balancing is completely dynamic: a slave Q of a master P may itself become master of a processor R. However, if a processor P has evaluated the result for a node v, but a sibling of v is still under evaluation at a processor Q, P has to wait until Q finishes its search, since the result of the father of v depends on the result of Q.

The nodes searched for the solution of the SAT (TTH, TFH) instances are not distinguished from the nodes searched for the solution of the original QSAT instance. Therefore, the tests are done in parallel too.

The above is a general framework for parallel tree search. In the next section we will describe in detail our scheduling methods in order to cope with the problems that arise when searching QSAT trees:

- In general, a busy processor has a search stack with more than one right sibling available for a parallel evaluation. Upon receiving a request for work, it has to decide on which subproblem (if any) to send to the requesting processor.

- A processor that waits for the result of a slave is doing nothing useful. We describe a method for getting it busy while it is waiting.

- At nodes that correspond to $\exists$-quantified ($\forall$-quantified) variables a cutoff occurs, if the left branch evaluates to true (false). In this case the right branch is not evaluated by the sequential algorithm. However, in the parallel version, both branches may be evaluated at the same time. In this case the parallel version may do considerably more work than the sequential one. We describe a method for delaying parallelism, in order to reduce the amount of useless work.

The scheduling heuristics presented in the next sections are not needed to prove the correctness of the parallel algorithm, but rather to improve its efficiency.

Scheduling

The **selection of subproblems** that are to be sent upon receiving a request is supposed to fulfill the following requirements:

- The subproblem is supposed to be large enough to keep the slave busy for a while. Otherwise, the communication overhead increases since at least two messages (the subproblem itself and the request for work / result) have to be sent for every subproblem. In general, the size of a search tree below a node v is unpredictable. However, the subtrees rooted at nodes higher in the tree are typically larger than the ones rooted at the nodes deeper in the tree.

- The heuristic to select a literal for the branching process of QSOLVE selects a variable to branch with and then decides on which branch is searched first. The intention is to prove (un)satisfiability first at nodes that correspond to $\exists$- ($\forall$-) quantified variables. A perfect heuristic selects subproblems such that both siblings must be evaluated to get the final result. Our heuristic to select subproblems prefers the variables x such that both literals $x, \bar{x}$ appear equally often in the formula.

Formally, let $v_0, \ldots, v_m$ be the nodes of the search stack of a processor P. Let $x_0, \ldots, x_m$ be the boolean variables that correspond to $v_0, \ldots, v_m$. Upon receiving a request, P sends the highest right son of v_i such that $3 \cdot |N(x_i) - P(x_i)| + i$ is minimized, where $P(x_i) = \sum_j p_j(x_i)$ and $N(x_i) = \sum_j n_j(x_i)$ (see section "Literal Selection").

In order to avoid masters having to wait for slaves we have proposed the **Helpful Master Scheduling** (HMS) for a distributed chess program (Feldmann et al. 1990): Whenever a processor P waits for its slave Q to send a result, P sends a special request for work to Q. Q handles this request like a regular request. If Q does not send a subproblem, P will keep waiting for the result of Q. If Q sends a subproblem to P, it will be guaranteed that the root of the subproblem is deeper in the tree than the node where P is waiting. P then behaves like a regular slave of Q. Later, if Q waits for its slave P, the protocol is repeated with Q as the master and P as the slave. The termination of this protocol is guaranteed since the depth of the overall search tree is limited by the number of variables. While supporting its slave a processor P handles messages concerned with upper parts of the search tree as P would do while waiting for Q. A cutoff message requires the deletion of several HMS-shells from the work stack.

Since the search trees of QSOLVE are binary, the avoidance of waiting times is crucial for the efficiency of our parallel implementation.

Another problem arises when two processors P and Q search two siblings v_0, v_1 of a node v in parallel, but the result of v_0 cuts off the search below v. In this case the work done for the search below v_1 is wasted. Since the load balancing is fully dynamic a considerable amount of work which is avoided by the sequential program is done by the parallel one. For a distributed chess program we use the **Young Brothers Wait Scheduling** (YBWS) (Feldmann et al. 1990) to avoid irrelevant work. YBWS states that the parallel evaluation of a right ("younger") sibling may start only after the evaluation of the leftmost sibling has been finished. With the help of the YBWS the parallelism at a node v is delayed until at least one successor of v is completely evaluated. By the use of the YBWS the parallel search performs all cutoffs produced by the result of the evaluation of the leftmost son. However, in binary trees such as the ones searched for QSAT, this would lead to a sequential run. Therefore, in PQSOLVE we apply YBWS to blocks of variables. The subtrees that correspond to a block X have $2^{|X|+1} - 1$ nodes. For each of these subtrees, the parallel evaluation of these nodes is delayed until the leftmost leaf is evaluated.

Results

QSAT instances: The results are taken from a set of 48 QSAT instances. These instances have been generated randomly according to the model A by (Gent and Walsh 1999). The number of variables is about 120, the clause length is four, the number of blocks range from two to five. The fraction of $\forall$-variables is 25 %, the number of clauses varies from 416 to 736. The instances are hard in the sense that all sequential QSAT-solvers mentioned in this paper need considerable running times to solve them.

Hardware: Experiments with PQSOLVE are performed on the PSC2-cluster at the Paderborn Center for Parallel Computing. Every processor is a Pentium II/450 MHz running the Solaris operating system. The processors are connected as a 2D-Torus by a Scali/Dolphin CluStar network.

The effects of HM-scheduling have been studied by running PQSOLVE on the PSC-cluster, a machine with Pentium II/300 MHz processors and Fast-Ethernet communication. The communication is implemented on the basis of MPI.

Efficiency:

P	time(s)	SPE	work %
1	1594.60	1.00	0.00
32	43.29	36.84	-32.13
64	24.44	65.25	-30.30
128	13.99	114.02	-29.55

The table above presents us with the data from the parallel evaluations (averaged over 48 QSAT instances). As can be seen, the overall speedup is about 114 on 128 processors. The high efficiency is due to the fact that PQSOLVE needs about 30 % less recursions than QSOLVE (fourth column), i.e. the parallel version does less work than the sequential one. The result is a "superlinear" speedup ($SPE(P) > P$) on several instances. This effect has already been observed for SAT (Speckenmeyer, Monien, and Vornberger 1987) but is surprising for QSAT.

The main reason for this effect is the fact that the trees searched by QSOLVE are highly irregular due to the tests for trivial truth and trivial falsity. The load balancing supports the parallelism in the upper parts of the tree. A considerable amount of work can be saved by searching two sons of a node in parallel: The one that would have been searched second by QSOLVE delivers a result that cuts off the first branch, or, both branches would deliver a result cutting off the other one, but the branch considered first by QSOLVE is harder to evaluate than the second one.

Load balancing: The table below presents us with the percentage of the running time the processors spend in the states $BUSY$ (evaluating a subtree), $WAIT$ (waiting for the result of a slave), COM (sending or responding to messages), and $IDLE$ (not having any subproblem at all).

P	forks	$BUSY$	$WAIT$	COM	$IDLE$
1	0.0	100.00	0.00	0.00	0.00
32	2107.5	83.86	8.87	3.75	0.80
64	4017.6	77.29	9.23	8.71	3.65
128	7413.2	69.00	10.16	16.58	2.08

The second column reveals the average number of subproblems that are sent during an evaluation process. The work load of the sequential version is 100 % by definition. The scheduling works well, resulting in an average work load of 69 % for 128 processors.

HM-scheduling: A crucial point for the evaluation of binary QSAT-trees is the HM-scheduling. Although HM-scheduling increases the number of subproblems that are sent by a factor of about four, it reduces the waiting times from 31.38% to less than 9 % for 32 processors. The tables below present us with results obtained from running our 48 QSAT instances on the PSC-cluster. Note that the communication of the PSC-cluster is significantly slower than the one of the PSC2-cluster used for the experiments above.

	time(s)	SPE	work
¬HM	92.64	22.61	-27.72
HM	70.72	29.61	-29.20

	forks	$BUSY$	$WAIT$	COM	$IDLE$
¬HM	566.1	52.03	31.38	13.23	1.52
HM	2185.6	69.42	8.75	18.73	0.71

YBW-scheduling: The YBW-scheduling has two effects: Firstly, as intended, the number of recursions is frequently decreased on instances with sublinear speedup. Secondly, the number of recursions is increased on many instances with superlinear speedup. In total YBW-scheduling has nearly no effect.

Conclusions and Future Work

We presented QSOLVE, a QSAT-solver that uses most of the techniques published for other QSAT-solvers before. In addition, we have implemented an adaptive heuristic to decide on when to use the expensive tests for trivial truth and trivial falsity. Moreover, QSOLVE benefits from a new test for trivial falsity.

We parallelized QSOLVE. The result is the parallel QSAT-solver PQSOLVE which runs efficiently on even more than 100 processors.

These encouraging results were obtained from random formulae. We are going to run PQSOLVE on structured instances in the near future. We are currently analyzing the test for trivial falsity. It may be improved by the way the conflict free set I is determined or by the use of more than one set. Moreover, this test for trivial falsity may lead to new insights into the theory of randomly generated QSAT instances.

Acknowledgment

We would like to thank Marco Cadoli for providing us with a binary of EVALUATE, Theo Lettmann for many helpful discussions, and the referees of AAAI for their constructive comments. This work has been supported by the DFG research project "Selektive Suchverfahren" under grant Mo 285/12-3.

References

Böhm, M.; and Speckenmeyer, E. 1996. A fast parallel SAT-solver – efficient workload balancing. *Annals of Mathematics and Artificial Intelligence* 17:381–400.

Cadoli, M.; Giovanardi, A.; and Schaerf, M. 1998. An Algorithm to Evaluate Quantified Boolean Formulae. *Proc. of the 15th National Conference on Artificial Intelligence (AAAI-98)* 262–267. AAAI Press.

Feldmann, R.; Monien, B.; Mysliwietz, P.; and Vornberger O. 1990. Distributed Game Tree Search. In *Parallel Algorithms for Machine Intelligence and Pattern Recognition*, Kumar, V., Kanal, L.N., and Gopalakrishnan, P.S. eds., 66–101, Springer-Verlag.

Feldmann, R.; Monien, B.; and Mysliwietz, P. 1994. Studying Overheads in Massively Parallel MIN/MAX-Tree Evaluation. *Proc. of the 6th ACM Symp. on Parallel Algorithms and Architectures (SPAA-94)* 94–103. ACM.

Feldmann, R. 1997. Computer Chess: Algorithms and Heuristics for a Deep Look into the Future. *Proc. of the 24th Seminar on Current Trends in Theory and Practice of Informatics (SOFSEM-97)* LNCS 1338, 511–522, Springer Verlag.

Gent, I.P.; and Walsh, T. 1999. Beyond NP: The QSAT Phase Transition. *Proc. of the 16th National Conference on Artificial Intelligence (AAAI-99)* 648–653. AAAI Press.

Gu, J.; Purdom, P.W.; Franco, J.; and Wah, B.W. 1997. Algorithms for the Satisfiability (SAT) Problem: A Survey. In *Satisfiability Problem: Theory and Applications*, Du, D., Gu, J., and Pardalos, P.M. eds. DIMACS 35, 19–151. American Mathematical Society.

Kleine-Büning, H.; Karpinski, M.; and Flögel, A. 1995. Resolution for quantified boolean formulas. *Information and Computation*, 117:12–18.

Rintanen, J. 1999. Improvements to the Evaluation of Quantified Boolean Formulae. *Proc. of the 16th International Joint Conference on Artificial Intelligence (IJCAI-99)*, 1192–1197. Morgan Kaufman.

Speckenmeyer, E; Monien, B; and Vornberger, O. 1987. Superlinear speedup for parallel backtracking. *Proc. of the International Conference on Supercomputing (ICS-87)* LNCS 385, 985–993, Springer-Verlag.

Integrating Equivalency Reasoning into Davis-Putnam Procedure

Chu Min Li

LaRIA, Univ. de Picardie Jules Verne, 5 rue du moulin Neuf, 80000 Amiens, France
fax: (33) 3 22 82 75 02, e-mail: cli@laria.u-picardie.fr

Abstract

Equivalency clauses (Xors or modulo 2 arithmetics) represent a common structure in the SAT-encoding of many hard real-world problems and constitute a major obstacle to Davis-Putnam (DP) procedure. We propose a special look-ahead technique called equivalency reasoning to overcome the obstacle and report on the performance of an equivalency reasoning enhanced DP procedure on SAT instances containing equivalency clauses derived from problems in parity learning, cryptographic key search and model checking. Our results show that integrating equivalency reasoning renders easy many problems which were beyond DP's reach. We also compare equivalency reasoning with general CSP look-back techniques on equivalency clauses.

Introduction

Consider a propositional formula $\mathcal{F}$ in Conjunctive Normal Form (CNF) on a set of Boolean variables $\{x_1, x_2, ..., x_n\}$. The *satisfiability (SAT) problem* consists in testing whether clauses in $\mathcal{F}$ can all be satisfied by some consistent assignment of truth values (1 or 0) to variables. SAT is fundamental in many fields of computer science, electrical engineering and mathematics. It was the first NP-Complete problem (Cook 1971).

Let l with or without index be a literal. An equivalency clause of length k can be written as

$$l_1 \leftrightarrow l_2 \leftrightarrow ... \leftrightarrow l_k$$

where the operator $\leftrightarrow$ is commutative and associative. The equivalency clause is equivalent to 2^{k-1} CNF clauses. For example, a binary equivalency clause is equivalent to 2 CNF clauses: $l_1 \vee \bar{l}_2$ and $\bar{l}_1 \vee l_2$, and a ternary equivalency clause is equivalent to 4 CNF clauses: $l_1 \vee \bar{l}_2 \vee \bar{l}_3$, $\bar{l}_1 \vee \bar{l}_2 \vee l_3$, $\bar{l}_1 \vee l_2 \vee \bar{l}_3$, and $l_1 \vee l_2 \vee l_3$.

When encoding a hard real-world problem as SAT, one usually structures the problem in layers and makes use of abbreviations and definitions, which often results in a number of equivalency clauses (in their equivalent CNF form) in the final SAT instance. Unfortunately, equivalency clauses of length > 2 generally are hard for Davis-Putnam procedure (DP) (Davis et al. 1962), the best systematic method for SAT.

The reason for the inefficiency of DP procedure on these problems seems to be that equivalency clauses give very few unit clauses throughout the resolution while on other problems DP procedure often deals with many unit clauses under some depth. On the other hand, fixing a variable in equivalency clauses often produces a number of equivalent literals from which an equivalency reasoning can be made to remedy the ineffectiveness of unit propagation. In this paper we show how to integrate equivalency reasoning to solve problems containing both equivalency clauses (called EQ part) and other CNF clauses (called CNF part).

The paper is organized as follows. In section 2 we define equivalency reasoning. In section 3 we present the equivalency reasoning enhanced DP procedure called $EqSatz$. Our approach was originally motivated by the second challenge problem formulated by Selman et al. (1997) at IJ-CAI'97. Section 4 reports on the performance of $EqSatz$ on the challenge problem. In section 5 we report on and compare the performance of $EqSatz$ with 4 state-of-the-art DPs on various SAT problems involving equivalency clauses. All experimental results are obtained on a Macintosh G3 300 Mhz with 96 Mb memory under Linux system and run time is expressed in seconds. Section 6 discusses related work and Section 7 concludes.

Equivalency Reasoning

An equivalency clause can be negated with the following property:

$$\begin{aligned}
\neg(l_1 \leftrightarrow l_2 \leftrightarrow ... \leftrightarrow l_k) &\equiv \bar{l}_1 \leftrightarrow l_2 \leftrightarrow ... \leftrightarrow l_k \\
&\equiv l_1 \leftrightarrow \bar{l}_2 \leftrightarrow ... \leftrightarrow l_k \\
&... \\
&\equiv l_1 \leftrightarrow l_2 \leftrightarrow ... \leftrightarrow \bar{l}_k \quad (1)
\end{aligned}$$

Since all equivalency clauses of length > 3 can be simply transformed into ternary equivalency clauses by adding new variables, we only consider binary ($k=2$) and ternary ($k=$

3) equivalency clauses in this paper. We define six inference rules on them.

$$l_1, l_1 \leftrightarrow l_2 \leftrightarrow l_3 \vdash l_2 \leftrightarrow l_3 \quad (2)$$
$$\bar{l}_1, l_1 \leftrightarrow l_2 \leftrightarrow l_3 \vdash \neg(l_2 \leftrightarrow l_3) \quad (3)$$
$$l_1 \leftrightarrow l_1 \leftrightarrow l_2 \vdash l_2 \quad (4)$$
$$l_1 \leftrightarrow l_2 \leftrightarrow l_3, l_1 \leftrightarrow l_2 \leftrightarrow l_4 \vdash l_3 \leftrightarrow l_4 \quad (5)$$
$$l_1 \to (l_3 \leftrightarrow l_4), \bar{l}_1 \to (l_3 \leftrightarrow l_4) \vdash l_3 \leftrightarrow l_4 \quad (6)$$
$$l_1 \to (l_3 \leftrightarrow l_4), \bar{l}_1 \to (\bar{l}_3 \leftrightarrow l_4) \vdash l_1 \leftrightarrow l_3 \leftrightarrow l_4 \quad (7)$$

Note that the right side of rule 3 can be rewritten as $\bar{l}_2 \leftrightarrow l_3$ or $l_2 \leftrightarrow \bar{l}_3$ using property 1. All these rules can be realized by a constant number of resolution steps after writing the equivalency clauses in CNF form. We call the application of these rules in a formula $\mathcal{F}$ *equivalency reasoning*.

Binary equivalency clauses play a particular role in our approach. Every time a binary equivalency clause $l_1 \leftrightarrow l_2$ is deduced by rule 2, 3, 5, or 6, l_1 is substituted by l_2 in $\mathcal{F}$. It can be shown that DIMACS[1] dubois* problem is solved in linear time by repeatedly applying rule 5 and the equivalent literal substitution.

Ternary equivalency clauses are represented both in CNF form and by a list of the three involved variables, eventually with a negation operator. For example the equivalency clause $\bar{x} \leftrightarrow \bar{y} \leftrightarrow \bar{z}$ is represented by four CNF clauses and by $\neg(x, y, z)$.

Rule 7 is used to add new ternary equivalency clauses into $\mathcal{F}$. Given three equivalency clauses $x \leftrightarrow u \leftrightarrow v$, $y \leftrightarrow u \leftrightarrow w$, and $z \leftrightarrow v \leftrightarrow w$, one adds a unit clause x, rule 2 applied to the first equivalency clause gives $u \leftrightarrow v$. Then one substitutes u by v in the second equivalency clause before applying rule 5 to obtain $y \leftrightarrow z$. So $x \to (y \leftrightarrow z)$. Similarly $\bar{x} \to (\bar{y} \leftrightarrow z)$. Applying rule 7, one obtains $x \leftrightarrow y \leftrightarrow z$, an equivalency clause to be added into $\mathcal{F}$. Rule 6 is also used in this way to deduce new equivalent literals.

It can be shown from its own construction that DIMACS pret* problem, although hard for a classical implementation of DP procedure, is solved in linear time by repeatedly adding new ternary equivalency clauses into $\mathcal{F}$.

$EqSatz$: An Equivalency Reasoning Enhanced DP

We implement the six inference rules defined in section 2 into a highly optimized DP procedure called $Satz$ (Li and Anbulagan 1997). $Satz$ consists of a fast unit propagator and a powerful look-ahead heuristic based on unit propagation to select the next branching variable to maximize the reduction of search space when branching. Equivalency reasoning enhanced $Satz$ is called $EqSatz$ and is sketched in Figure 1. Figure 2 shows the implementation of equivalency reasoning. Figure 3 shows the branching rule of $EqSatz$.

---
[1]ftp://dimacs.rutgers.edu/pub/challenge/sat

The equivalency clauses contained in the input formula are in CNF form. Rules 2 and 3 are performed by unit propagation, so equivalency reasoning begins by detecting equivalent literals produced by unit propagation. If l_1 is equivalent to l_2, it is substituted by l_2. Note that the substitution may produce a unit clause in case $l_1 \vee l_2$ is a clause in $\mathcal{F}$. Property 1 is used to rewrite equivalency clauses in an appropriate form to apply the inference rules.

Equivalency reasoning is naturally integrated in the heuristic of $Satz$. Given a free variable x, $Satz$ examines x by respectively adding two unit clauses x and $\bar{x}$ into $\mathcal{F}$ and makes two experimental unit propagations to see the impact of branching on x. Following this line, $EqSatz$ performs an experimental equivalency reasoning after each experimental unit propagation to look further forward and to add new equivalency clauses into $\mathcal{F}$ using rules 6 and 7.

Like $Satz$, $EqSatz$ tries to branch to the variable allowing to maximize the reduction of search space by taking equivalency reasoning into account and uses three functions to estimate the reduction of search space.

Procedure $EqSatz(\mathcal{F})$
Begin
```
   if F is empty, return "satisfiable";
   F:=UnitPropagation(F);
   F:=Equivalency_Reasoning(F);
   if F contains an empty clause,
   return "unsatisfiable".

   /* branching rule */
   select a variable x in F.
   If EqSatz(F ∪ {x}) is "satisfiable"
   then return "satisfiable", otherwise
   return the result of EqSatz(F ∪ {x̄}).
```
End.

procedure UnitPropagation($\mathcal{F}$)
Begin
```
   While there is no empty clause and a unit
   clause l exists, satisfy l and simplify F.
   Return F.
```
End.

Figure 1: The DP Procedure $EqSatz$

The first function is $nb\_fixed\_vars(\mathcal{F}_1, \mathcal{F}_2)$ giving the number of variables of $\mathcal{F}_2$ instantiated in $\mathcal{F}_1$, and the second is $nb\_eq\_pairs(\mathcal{F}_1, \mathcal{F}_2)$ giving the number of equivalent literals of $\mathcal{F}_2$ substituted in $\mathcal{F}_1$. The motivation is that the instantiation of a variable or a new deduced literal equivalence such as $l_3 \leftrightarrow l_4$ cuts the search space in half. The third function $nb\_binary\_clauses(\mathcal{F}_1, \mathcal{F}_2)$ ($nb\_bin\_cls(\mathcal{F}_1, \mathcal{F}_2)$ in short) is defined following the same line. But the consideration is somewhat more complicated.

If $\mathcal{F}$ has n variables, it has 2^n possible solutions. A binary clause removes 2^{n-2} solutions. But generally two binary clauses together do not remove 2^{n-1} solutions. In fact two binary clauses sharing an identical literal or having no common variable such as $x_1 \lor x_2$ and $x_1 \lor x_3$ or $x_1 \lor x_2$ and $\bar{x}_3 \lor x_4$ remove $2^{n-1} - 2^{n-3}$ and $2^{n-1} - 2^{n-4}$ solutions, respectively. Only two binary clauses sharing a complementary literal such as $x_1 \lor x_2$ and $\bar{x}_1 \lor x_3$ remove 2^{n-1} solutions. Clearly binary clauses sharing complementary literals remove many more solutions and have more chances to lead to a dead-end where all solutions are removed. So a DP procedure should branch next on the variable generating subproblems having more binary clauses sharing complementary literals.

$$nb\_bin\_cls(\mathcal{F}_1, \mathcal{F}_2) = \sum_{l \lor l' \text{ is in } \mathcal{F}_1 \text{ but not in } \mathcal{F}_2} [f(\bar{l}) + f(\bar{l}')]$$

where $f(\bar{l})$ is the number of binary occurrences of $\bar{l}$ in $\mathcal{F}_2$.

Procedure Equivalency_Reasoning($\mathcal{F}$)
Begin
```
  F:=Set_Equivalence_by_CNF_Clauses(F);
  repeat
    /* Rule 4 */
    while there is an equivalency clause
       containing two identical literals such
       as l₁ ↔ l₁ ↔ l₃ but no empty clause do
    begin
       satisfy l₃ and simplify F;
       F:=Set_Equivalence_by_CNF_Clauses(F);
    end;
    /* Rule 5 */
    while there are two equivalency clauses
       containing two identical literals such
       as l₁ ↔ l₂ ↔ l₃ and l₁ ↔ l₂ ↔ l₄ but no
       empty clause do
       if l₃ = ¬l₄ then add an empty clause
          into F
       else
       begin
          F:=Substitute(l₃, l₄, F);
          F:=Set_Equivalence_by_CNF_Clauses(F);
       end
    until an empty clause is produced
       or no change happens in F
```
End.

procedure Set_Equivalence_by_CNF_Clauses($\mathcal{F}$)
Begin
```
  while F contains two binary CNF clauses
    such as l₁ ∨ l̄₂ and l̄₁ ∨ l₂ but no
    empty clause do
    F:=Substitute(l₁, l₂, F);
  return F
```
End.

procedure Substitute($l_1, l_2, \mathcal{F}$)
Begin
```
  substitute all occurrences of l₁(l̄₁) by l₂(l̄₂);
  F:=UnitPropagation(F); return F;
```
End.

Figure 2: The Procedure Equivalency Reasoning

Solving the Challenge DIMACS 32-bit Parity Problem

EqSatz was originally motivated by the challenge DIMACS 32-bit parity problem formulated by Selman et al. (1997) at IJCAI'97. To the best of our knowledge, *EqSatz* is the *only* procedure which is able to solve all the ten par32* instances in reasonable time.

Table 1 shows the performance of *EqSatz* on the challenge problem. As in the next section, #cls and #eq_cls[2] respectively denote the total number of clauses in the input CNF formula and the number of ternary equivalency clauses, a ternary equivalency clause being counted as 4 clauses in #cls. As can be seen, All instances contain a large EQ part.

Equivalency reasoning makes *EqSatz* substantially faster than *Satz* on the challenge parity problem. In the next section we show that it is sufficiently powerful to make a DP procedure able to solve other problems.

```
For each free variable x do
let F' and F" be two copies of F
Begin
  F'  := UnitPropagation(F' ∪ {x});
  F" := UnitPropagation(F" ∪ {x̄});
  F':=Equivalency_Reasoning(F');
  F":=Equivalency_Reasoning(F");
  If both F' and F" contain an empty clause
     then return "F is unsatisfiable".
  else if F' contains an empty clause then
        x := 0, F := F"
  else if F" contains an empty clause then
        x := 1, F := F';
  else
  begin
    /* Rule 6 */
    for all l₃ ↔ l₄ ∈ F' ∧ F"
       F:=Substitute(l₃, l₄, F);
    /* Rule 7 */
    for all l₃ ↔ l₄ ∈ F' and l̄₃ ↔ l₄ ∈ F"
       add x ↔ l₃ ↔ l₄ into F.
    F:=Equivalency_Reasoning(F);
    if F contains an empty clause then
           return "F is unsatisfiable".
    let w(l) denote the weight of literal l,
    w(x)  := nb_fixed_vars(F',F) + nb_eq_pairs(F',F)
              +nb_bin_cls(F',F)/2
    w(x̄) := nb_fixed_vars(F",F) + nb_eq_pairs(F",F)
              +nb_bin_cls(F",F)/2;
  end
End;
For each free variable x do
  H(x) := w(x̄) * w(x) * 1024 + w(x̄) + w(x);
Branching on the free variable x such that
H(x) is the greatest.
```

Figure 3: The Branching Rule of *EqSatz*

---

[2]*EqSatz* inherits from Satz a preprocessing of the input instance searching and adding resolvents of length ≤ 3, which may remove some equivalency clauses. #eq_cls denotes the number of remaining ternary equivalency clauses.

Table 1: Run time and search tree size (t_size) of *EqSatz* on the challenge DIMACS 32-bit parity problem

Instance	#var	#cls	#eq_cls	time	t_size
par32-1-c	1315	5254	1097	1133	3672
par32-2-c	1303	5206	1085	50	209
par32-3-c	1325	5294	1107	3972	15123
par32-4-c	1333	5326	1115	793	1488
par32-5-c	1339	5350	1121	9265	38348
par32-1	3176	10277	1097	989	3089
par32-2	3176	10253	1085	241	651
par32-3	3176	10297	1107	8899	23827
par32-4	3176	10313	1115	827	2885
par32-5	3176	10325	1121	11855	35133

Other Experimental Results

We use three separate benchmarks involving equivalency clauses in the literature to evaluate the impact of equivalency reasoning in a DP procedure and to compare the performance of *EqSatz* with 4 state-of-the-art DP procedures on the same instances: DIMACS pret* problem, Massacci's Data Encryption Standard (DES) problem[3], and Biere et al.'s Bounded Model Checking (BMC) problems[4].

The four state-of-the-art DPs compared are Sato (Zhang 1997), Grasp (Silva and Sakallah 1996), Relsat (Bayardo and Schrag 1997) and Satz. Sato, Grasp and Relsat use both look-ahead techniques such as unit propagation and variable ordering heuristics for branching and look-back techniques such as intelligent backtracking and learning, while Satz uniquely uses look-ahead techniques. So the comparison between *EqSatz* and Satz in the experimentation illustrates the impact of equivalency reasoning and the comparison of *EqSatz* with Sato, Grasp[5], and Relsat might be considered as a comparison between look-back techniques and equivalency reasoning on the instances involving equivalency clauses.

Performance on DIMACS pret* problem

The problem was contributed by Pretolani, inspired by Urquhart's construction (Urquhart 1987). We modify some constants in the generator available at the same site to generate larger instances. These unsatisfiable instances are uniquely composed of equivalency clauses.

EqSatz solves Pretolani's problem in linear time. Table 2 shows the performance of the 5 DP procedures. Note that though Sato, Grasp and Relsat are substantially faster than Satz on these instances, it seems that they still have an exponential behavior.

---

[3] available from http://www.uni-koblenz.de/~massacci

[4] available from http://www.cs.cmu.edu/~modelcheck

[5] when solving some instances, Grasp is stopped before 2 hours of run time because of memory shortage or resource exceeded. Its runtime is marked by "?"

Table 2: run time of Sato, Grasp, Relsat, Satz and *EqSatz* on DIMACS pret* problem

#vars	300	450	600	750	1500	3000
#eq_cls	200	300	400	500	1000	2000
Grasp	9	31	82	166	1742	>7200
Sato	28	37	102	>7200	-	-
Relsat	1	2	4	10	72	696
Satz	>7200	-	-	-	-	-
EqSatz	0	0	0	0	0	0

Performance on DES instances

DES instances are contributed by Massacci (1999). These are SAT-encoding of cryptographic key search problem and contain equivalency clauses from 3 rounds. We only report on 3 round instances, since to our knowledge no SAT solver solves instances of more than 3 rounds. The original instances involve a huge number of variables with no clauses. So we compact them by making unit resolution and pure literal elimination and renaming the variables to be contiguous. The instances after the simplification are listed in table 3. All instances are satisfiable.

Table 3: DES instances

Instance	#var	#clause	#eq_cls
cnf-r3-b1-k1.1	1461	8966	48
cnf-r3-b1-k1.2	1450	8891	48
cnf-r3-b2-k1.1	2855	17857	96
cnf-r3-b2-k1.2	2880	17960	96
cnf-r3-b3-k1.1	4255	26778	144
cnf-r3-b3-k1.2	4418	27503	144
cnf-r3-b4-k1.1	5679	35817	192
cnf-r3-b4-k1.2	5721	35963	192

Table 4 displays the performance of the 5 DPs on Massacci's DES 3-round instances. *EqSatz* is one of the fastest procedures to solve these instances and is substantially faster than Satz, illustrating the impact of equivalency reasoning to solve these instances even when there are very few equivalency clauses.

Table 4: Run time on DES instances. The name of each instance should be preceded by "cnf-r3"

Instance	Sato	Grasp	Relsat	Satz	*EqSatz*
b1-k1.1	871	?	1080	>7200	995
b1-k1.2	>7200	?	454	>7200	1023
b2-k1.1	3	170	18	946	1276
b2-k1.2	>7200	183	22	1468	629
b3-k1.1	>7200	96	37	32	11
b3-k1.2	>7200	113	44	101	11
b4-k1.1	>7200	77	45	357	17
b4-k1.2	>7200	67	48	>7200	18

Performance on BMC instances

BMC problems are contributed by Biere et al. (1999) and arise from (bounded) model checking. All instances are unsatisfiable. We select the most difficult barrel* and queueinvar* instances and representative half longmult* instances. The selected instances are listed in Table 5.

Table 5: BMC instances

Instance	#var	#clause	#eq_cls
barrel5	1407	5383	870
barrel6	2306	8931	1476
barrel7	3523	13765	2310
barrel8	5106	20083	3408
barrel9	8903	36606	6408
longmult1	791	2335	29
longmult3	1555	4767	87
longmult5	2397	7431	145
longmult7	3319	10335	203
longmult9	4321	13479	261
longmult11	5403	16863	319
longmult13	6565	20487	377
longmult15	7807	24351	435
queueinvar10	886	5622	51
queueinvar12	1112	7335	53
queueinvar14	1370	9313	55
queueinvar16	1168	6496	75
queueinvar18	2081	17368	70
queueinvar20	2435	29671	72

Table 6 displays the performance of the 5 DPs on BMC instances. $EqSatz$ is substantially faster than the 4 other DPs on the barrel* and queueinvar* instances. On barrel* instances containing a more important EQ part, $EqSatz$ finds the inconsistency by equivalency reasoning without branching. On longmult* instances, only Sato is slightly faster than $EqSatz$.

Discussion and Related Work

Equivalency clauses constitute a major obstacle to DP procedure. For example, while the complexity of Satz on the most difficult random 3-SAT instances appears to be $O(2^{n/21})$, its complexity on DIMACS pret* problem is $O(2^{n/3})$. However, equivalency clauses realize a common structure in the SAT-encoding of many hard real-world problems. Massacci (1999) noticed in his SAT-encoding of cryptographic key search problem that each round is separated from the next round by a level of equivalency clauses and most constraints are in form of equivalency clauses. He also noted that the problem becomes hard for current AI techniques as soon as equivalency clauses start to appear.

Learning and intelligent backtracking are general CSP look-back techniques effective for many structured problems. However they appear to be less effective on the special structure of equivalency clauses than the specialized look-ahead technique equivalency reasoning. For example, although they make Sato, Grasp and Relsat substantially faster than Satz on DIMACS pret* problem, equivalency reasoning makes the complexity of $EqSatz$ linear on this problem.

For instances containing both EQ part and CNF part, equivalency reasoning plays its role even when the EQ part

Table 6: Run time on BMC instances. Each name mult* should be preceded by "long" and each name invar* by "queue"

Instance	Sato	Grasp	Relsat	Satz	$EqSatz$
barrel5	25	?	264	293	0
barrel6	281	?	4428	2461	1
barrel7	530	?	>7200	57	2
barrel8	726	?	>7200	5	3
barrel9	>7200	?	>7200	>7200	7
mult1	0	0	0	0	0
mult3	41	1	1	0	1
mult5	181	64	27	11	13
mult7	348	?	3402	331	274
mult9	733	?	>7200	1948	1681
mult11	1110	?	>7200	4371	3050
mult13	1916	?	>7200	6965	3662
mult15	2646	?	>7200	>7200	4876
invar10	15	27	20	12	3
invar12	97	52	31	54	5
invar14	576	101	162	250	10
invar16	1398	109	93	1017	9
invar18	>7200	?	257	8	9
invar20	>7200	?	834	13	14

is very small. For example, $EqSatz$ is significantly faster than Satz and competes with the most efficient look-back enhanced DP on DES instances where the EQ part is only roughly 2% of the whole formula. On DIMACS 32-bit parity problem and BMC barrel* problem containing a large EQ part, $EqSatz$ is substantially faster than other DPs.

Neither equivalency reasoning nor CSP look-back techniques allow a DP to solve Massacci's 4-round DES instances in reasonable time. The reason appears to be that these instances have other structures. We believe that combining equivalency reasoning and look-back techniques is promising to solve these instances.

Warners and Van Maaren (1998) proposed an approach to solve the instances only having EQ part or whose EQ part is much larger than their CNF part. Their approach gave the first method able to solve the 5 DIMACS 32-bit parity instances par32-i-c in which more than 80% of clauses are equivalency clauses. The originality is the elimination of equivalency clauses.

Given a set of equivalency clauses, Warners and Van Maaren select an equivalency clause of length k, $x_1 \leftrightarrow l_2 \leftrightarrow \ldots \leftrightarrow l_k$, write it as $x_1 \equiv l_2 \leftrightarrow \ldots \leftrightarrow l_k$ and substitute in all other equivalency clauses the occurrence of $(\bar{x}_1)$ x_1 by $(\neg)l_2 \leftrightarrow \ldots \leftrightarrow l_k$, increasing in general the length of these clauses (by $k-2$ in the worst case). x_1 is called *dependent variable*.

For a formula $\mathcal{F}$ having no CNF part such as DIMACS pret* and dubois*, the selected equivalency clause can be easily satisfied since its dependent variable doesn't occur elsewhere after the above substitution, so that it is removed from $\mathcal{F}$. By repeatedly removing equivalency clauses $\mathcal{F}$ is solved in polynomial time. For problems containing both EQ and CNF part, the substitution is limited in the EQ part and the selected equivalency clause cannot be removed if its dependent variable occurs in the CNF part. Otherwise the selected equivalency clause is removed.

Warners and Van Maaren's algorithm is divided into two phases to solve an instance containing both CNF part and EQ part. In the first phase the above substitution operation is applied to the EQ part to eliminate as many equivalency clauses as possible. For example, the five par32-i-c instances contain more than 1085 equivalency clauses, but only 218 equivalency clauses remain after the first phase (i.e. there are 218 dependent variables occurring in the CNF part). In the second phase an adapted DP procedure is executed on the CNF part together with the 218 equivalency clauses. So the first phase might be considered as a special processing in the root of a search tree, which is to be compared with the equivalency reasoning of $EqSatz$ in *every* node of a search tree.

Warners and Van Maaren's algorithm is actually substantially faster than $EqSatz$ on the five par32-i-c instances which are solved in at most 50 seconds (Warners 1999). The efficiency seems due to the fact that few (i.e. 218) equivalency clauses remain after the first phase for their DP procedure. However, when the CNF part of a formula is larger and contains more dependent variables, less equivalency clauses can be removed. In this case $EqSatz$ outperforms Warners and Van Maaren's algorithm. In fact, the five par32-i instances, the DES instances and the BMC instances are in this case. For example, for the par32-1 instance which contains 1548 equivalency clauses and 4085 other CNF clauses, 1048 (longer) equivalency clauses remain after the first phase (Warners 1999). To the best of our knowledge, $EqSatz$ is the *only* procedure which is able to solve all the five par32-i instances in reasonable time.

Conclusion

Equivalency clauses represent a common structure in the SAT-encoding of many hard real-world problems. They constitute a major obstacle to DP procedure. We have integrated an equivalency reasoning into Satz to solve problems containing equivalency clauses. Equivalency reasoning allows to remedy the ineffectiveness of unit propagation on equivalency clauses. Integrated in the branching rule, it makes the branching rule more precise and more powerful to maximize the reduction of search space when branching. Finally the new equivalency clauses added into $\mathcal{F}$ by equivalency reasoning also reduce considerably the search space.

Our approach makes DP able to solve one of the ten challenge problems of propositional reasoning formulated by Selman et al. and many other real-world problems. The experimental results suggest that equivalency reasoning is more effective than the general CSP look-back techniques on the special structure of equivalency clauses.

Acknowledgments

We thank Daniel Le Berre for informing us BMC problems, Patrice Seebold and anonymous referees for their comments which helped improve this paper.

References

Bayardo Jr. R.J., Schrag R.C., Using CSP Look-Back Techniques to Solve Real-World SAT Instances. In proceedings of AAAI-97, Providence, Rhode Island, July 1997.

Biere A., Cimatti A., Clarke E., Zhu Y., Symbolic Model Checking without BDDs. In proceedings of Tools and Algorithms for the Analysis and Construction of Systems (TACAS'99), number 1579 in LNCS. Springer-Verlag, 1999.

Cook S.A., The Complexity of Theorem Proving Procedures. In *3rd ACM Symp. on Theory of Computing*, pages 151-158, Ohio, 1971.

Crawford J.M., Kearns M.J., Schapire R.E., The Minimal Disagreement parity problem as a hard satisfiability problem. Draft version 1995.

Davis M., Logemann G., Loveland D., A Machine Program for Theorem Proving. In Common. ACM 5, 1962, pp. 394-397.

Li C.M., Anbulagan, Heuristics Based on Unit Propagation for Satisfiability Problems. In Proceedings of IJCAI-97, ISBN 1-55860-480-4, Page 366-371, Nagoya, Japan, August 1997.

Massacci F., Using Walk-SAT and Rel-SAT for Cryptographic Key Search. In Proceedings of IJCAI-99, Page 290-295.

Selman B., Kautz H., McAllester D., Ten challenges in propositional reasoning and search. In Proc. of IJCAI-97, ISBN 1-55860-480-4, Nagoya, Japan, August 1997.

Silva J. P. M., Sakallah K. A., Conflict Analysis in Search Algorithms for Propositional Satisfiability. In Proc. of the Int. Conf. on Tools with Artificial Intelligence, November 1996.

Urquhart A., Hard examples for resolution. Journal of the ACM, 34(1):209-219, January 1987.

Warners J.P., Van Maaren H., A two phase algorithm for solving a class of hard satisfiability problems. Operations research letters 23 (1998) 81-88.

Warners J.P., Personal communication, June 1999.

Zhang H., An efficient propositional prover. In Proc. of int' Conf. on Automated Deduction, pp272-275, July 1997.

Local search characteristics of incomplete SAT procedures

Dale Schuurmans and **Finnegan Southey**
Department of Computer Science
University of Waterloo
{dale,fdjsouth}@cs.uwaterloo.ca

Abstract

Effective local search methods for finding satisfying assignments of CNF formulae exhibit several systematic characteristics in their search. We identify a series of measurable characteristics of local search behavior that are predictive of problem solving efficiency. These measures are shown to be useful for diagnosing inefficiencies in given search procedures, tuning parameters, and predicting the value of innovations to existing strategies. We then introduce a new local search method, SDF ("smoothed descent and flood"), that builds upon the intuitions gained by our study. SDF works by greedily descending in an informative objective (that considers how strongly clauses are satisfied, in addition to counting the number of unsatisfied clauses) and, once trapped in a local minima, "floods" this minima by re-weighting unsatisfied clauses to create a new descent direction. The resulting procedure exhibits superior local search characteristics under our measures. We then show that our method is competitive with the state of the art techniques, and typically reduces the number of search steps by a significant factor.

Introduction

Since the introduction of GSAT (Selman, Levesque, & Mitchell 1992) there has been considerable research on local search methods for finding satisfying assignments for CNF formulae. These methods are surprisingly effective; they can often find satisfying assignments for large CNF formulae that are far beyond the capability of current systematic search methods (however see (Bayardo & Schrag 1997; Li & Anbulagan 1997) for competitive systematic search results). Of course, local search is incomplete and cannot prove that a formula has no satisfying assignment when none exists. However, despite this limitation, incomplete methods for solving large satisfiability problems are proving their worth in applications ranging from planning to circuit design and diagnosis (Selman, Kautz, & McAllester 1997; Kautz & Selman 1996; Larrabee 1992).

Significant progress has been made on improving the speed of these methods since the development of GSAT. In fact, a series of innovations have led to current search methods that are now an order of magnitude faster.

Copyright © 2000, American Association for Artificial Intelligence (www.aaai.org). All rights reserved.

Perhaps the most significant early improvement was to incorporate a "random walk" component where variables were flipped from within random falsified clauses (Selman & Kautz 1993). This greatly accelerated search and led to the development of the very successful WSAT procedure (Selman, Kautz, & Cohen 1994). A contemporary idea was to keep a tabu list (Mazure, Saïs, & Grégoire 1997) or break ties in favor of least recently flipped variables (Gent & Walsh 1993; 1995) to prevent GSAT from repeating earlier moves. The resulting TSAT and HSAT procedures were also improvements over GSAT, but to a lesser extent. The culmination of these ideas was the development of the Novelty and R_Novelty procedures which combined a preference for least recently flipped variables in a WSAT-type random walk (McAllester, Selman, & Kautz 1997), yielding methods that are currently among the fastest known.

A different line of research has considered adding clause-weights to the basic GSAT objective (which merely counts the number of unsatisfied clauses) in an attempt to guide the search from local basins of attraction to other parts of the search space (Frank 1997; 1996; Cha & Iwama 1996; 1995; Morris 1993; Selman & Kautz 1993). These methods have proved harder to control than the above techniques, and it has only been recent that clause re-weighting has been developed to a state of the art method. The series of "discrete Lagrange multiplier" (DLM) systems developed in (Wu & Wah 1999; Shang & Wah 1998) have demonstrated competitive results on benchmark challenge problems in the DIMACS and SATLIB repositories.

Although these developments are impressive, a systematic understanding of local search methods for satisfiability problems remains elusive. Research in this area has been largely empirical and it is still often hard to predict the effects of a minor change in a procedure, even when this results in dramatic differences in search times.

In this paper we identify three simple, intuitive measures of local search effectiveness: depth, mobility, and coverage. We show that effective local search methods for finding satisfying assignments exhibit all three characteristics. These, however, are conflicting demands and successful methods are primarily characterized by their ability to effectively manage the tradeoff between these factors (whereas ineffective methods tend to fail on at least one measure). Our goal is to be able to distinguish between effective and ineffective search strategies in a given problem (or diagnose problems with a given method, or tune parameters) without having to run exhaustive search experiments to their completion.

To further justify our endeavor, we introduce a new local search procedure, SDF ("smoothed descent and flood") that arose from our investigation of the characteristics of effective local search procedures. We show that SDF exhibits uniformly good depth, mobility, and coverage values, and consequently achieves good performance on a large collection of benchmark SAT problems.

Local search procedures

In this paper we investigate several dominant local search procedures from the literature. Although many of these strategies appear to be only superficial variants of one another, they demonstrate dramatically different problem solving performance and (as we will see) they exhibit distinct local search characteristics as well.

The local search procedures we consider start with a random variable assignment $\mathbf{x} = \langle x_1, ..., x_n \rangle$, $x \in \{0, 1\}$ and make local moves by flipping one variable $x'_i = 1 - x_i$ at a time, until they either find a satisfying assignment or time out. For any variable assignment there are a total of n possible variables to consider, and the various strategies differ in how they make this choice. Current methods uniformly adopt the original GSAT objective of minimizing the number of unsatisfied clauses, perhaps with some minor variant such as introducing clause weights or considering how many new clauses become unsatisfied by a flip (break count) or how many new clauses become satisfied (make count). The specific flip selection strategies we investigate (along with their free parameters) are as follows.

GSAT() Flip the variable x_i that results in the fewest total number of clauses being unsatisfied. Break ties randomly. (Selman, Levesque, & Mitchell 1992)

HSAT() Same as GSAT, but break ties in favor of the least recently flipped variable. (Gent & Walsh 1993)

WSAT-G(p) Pick a random unsatisfied clause c. With probability p flip a random x_i in c. Otherwise flip the variable in c that results in the smallest total number of unsatisfied clauses. (McAllester, Selman, & Kautz 1997)

WSAT-B(p) Like WSAT-G except, in the latter case, flip the variable that would cause the smallest number of new clauses to become unsatisfied. (McAllester, Selman, & Kautz 1997)

WSAT(p) Like WSAT-B except first check whether some variable x_i would not falsify any new clauses if flipped, and always take such a move if available. (Selman, Kautz, & Cohen 1994; McAllester, Selman, & Kautz 1997)

Novelty(p) Pick a random clause c. Flip the variable x_i in c that would result in the smallest total number of unsatisfied clauses, unless x_i is the most recently flipped variable in c. In the latter case, flip x_i with probability $1 - p$ and otherwise flip the variable x_j in c that results in the second smallest total number of unsatisfied clauses. (McAllester, Selman, & Kautz 1997)

Novelty+(p, h) Like Novelty, except that after the clause c is selected, flip a random x_i in c with probability h, otherwise continue with Novelty. (Hoos 1999)

Note that, conventionally, these local search procedures have an outer loop that places an upper bound, F, on the maximum number of flips allowed before re-starting with a new random assignment. However, we will not focus on random restarts in our experiments below because *any* search strategy can be improved (or at the very least, not damaged) by choosing an appropriate cutoff value F (Gomes, Selman, & Kautz 1998). In fact, it is straightforward and well known how to do this optimally (in principle): For a given search strategy and problem, let the random variable f denote the number of flips needed to reach a solution in a single run, and let f_F denote the number of flips needed when using a random restart after every F flips. Then we have the straightforward equality (Parkes & Walser 1996)

$$\mathrm{E}f_F \;=\; F/\mathrm{P}(f \leq F) - [F - \mathrm{E}(f | f \leq F)]$$

Note that this always offers a potential improvement since

$$\begin{aligned}\mathrm{E}f_F &= F\mathrm{P}(f > F)/\mathrm{P}(f \leq F) + \mathrm{E}(f | f \leq F) \\ &\leq F\mathrm{P}(f > F) + \mathrm{E}(f | f \leq F) \;\leq\; \mathrm{E}f\end{aligned}$$

for any cutoff $F > 0$. In particular, one could choose the optimal cutoff value $F^* = \arg\min_F \mathrm{E}f_F$. We report this optimal achievable performance quantity for every procedure below, using the empirical distribution of f over several runs to estimate $\mathrm{E}f_{F^*}$. Thus we will focus on investigating the single run characteristics of the various variable selection policies, but be sure to report estimates of what the optimum achievable performance would be using random restarts.

Measuring local search performance

In order to tune the parameters of a search strategy, determine whether a strategic innovation is helpful, or even debug an implementation, it would be useful to be able to measure how well a search is progressing without having to run it to completion on large, difficult problems.

To begin, we consider a simple and obvious measure of local search performance that has no doubt been used to tune and debug many search strategies in the past.

Depth measures how many clauses remain unsatisfied as the search proceeds. Intuitively, this indicates how deep in the objective the search is remaining. To get an overall summary, we take a depth average over all search steps. Note that it is desirable to obtain a small value of depth.

Although simple minded, and certainly not the complete story, it is clear that effective search strategies do tend to descend rapidly in the objective function and remain at good objective values as the search proceeds. By contrast, strategies that fail to persistently stay at good objective values usually have very little chance of finding a satisfying assignment in a reasonable number of flips (McAllester, Selman, & Kautz 1997).

To demonstrate this rather obvious effect, consider the problem of tuning the noise parameter p for the WSAT procedure on a given problem. Here we use the uf100-0953

100 runs on uf100-0953	Avg. depth	Avg. flips	Est. opt. w/cutoff
WSAT(.5)	5.62	11,153	9,618
WSAT(.7)	8.65	16,772	14,926
WSAT(.8)	10.3	29,322	25,835
WSAT(.9)	12.1	48,175	48,175
Novelty(.5)	4.85	3,958	3,958
SDF($\frac{.2}{m}$, .995)	3.93	1,242	1,242

Figure 1: Depth results

Flips rank	Depth rank				Mobility rank			
	best 1	2	3	worst 4	best 1	2	3	worst 4
best 1	.82	.09	.05	.04	.81	.11	.07	.01
2	.08	.39	.30	.16	.11	.50	.30	.08
3	.07	.36	.41	.23	.07	.25	.50	.18
worst 4	.03	.16	.25	.57	.01	.13	.13	.73

Figure 2: Large scale experiments (2700 uf problems)

problem from the SATLIB repository to demonstrate our point.[1] Figure 1 shows that higher noise levels cause WSAT to stay higher in the objective function and significantly increase the numbers of flips needed to reach a solution. This result holds both for the raw average number of flips but also for the optimal expected number of flips using a maximum flips cutoff with random restarts, $\hat{E}f_{F^*}$. The explanation is obvious: by repeatedly flipping a random variable in an unsatisfied clause, WSAT is frequently "kicked out" to higher objective values—to the extent that it begins to spend significant time simply re-descending to a lower objective value, only to be prematurely kicked out again.

Although depth is a simplistic measure, it proves to be very useful for tuning noise and temperature parameters in local search procedures. By measuring depth, one can determine if the search is spending too much time recovering from large steps up in the objective and not enough time exploring near the bottom of the objective. More importantly, maintaining depth appears to be *necessary* for achieving reasonable search times. Figure 2 shows the results of a large experiment conducted over the entire collection of 2700 uf problems from SATLIB. This comparison ranked four comparable methods—SDF (introduced below), Novelty, Novelty+, and WSAT—in terms of their search depth and average flips. For each problem, the methods were ranked in terms of their average number of flips and average depth. Each (flips rank, depth rank) pair was then recorded in a table. The relative frequencies of these pairs is summarized in Figure 2. This figure shows that the highest ranked method in terms of search efficiency was always ranked near the best (and almost never in the bottom rank) in terms of search depth.

Although useful, depth alone is clearly not a *sufficient* criterion for ensuring good search performance. A local search

[1]The uf series of problems are randomly generated 3-CNF formulae that are generated at the phase transition ratio of 4.3 clauses to variables. Such formulae have roughly a 50% chance of being satisfiable, but uf contains only verified satisfiable instances. http://aida.intellektik.informatik.tu-darmstadt.de/~hoos/SATLIB/

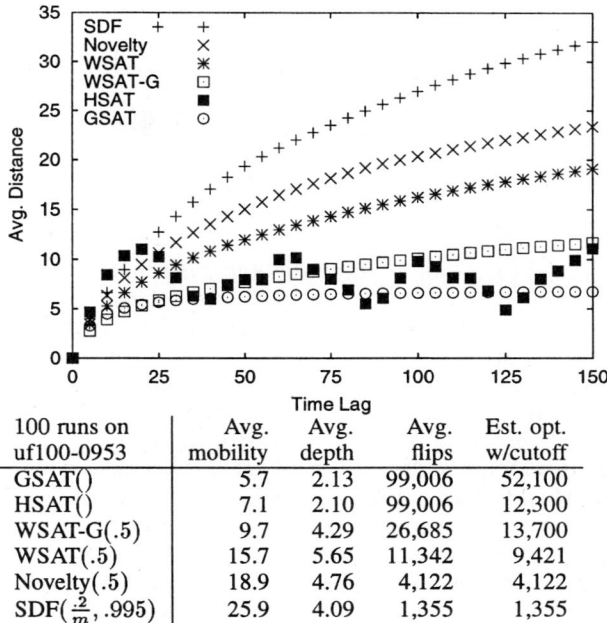

100 runs on uf100-0953	Avg. mobility	Avg. depth	Avg. flips	Est. opt. w/cutoff
GSAT()	5.7	2.13	99,006	52,100
HSAT()	7.1	2.10	99,006	12,300
WSAT-G(.5)	9.7	4.29	26,685	13,700
WSAT(.5)	15.7	5.65	11,342	9,421
Novelty(.5)	18.9	4.76	4,122	4,122
SDF($\frac{.2}{m}$, .995)	25.9	4.09	1,355	1,355

Figure 3: Mobility results

could easily become stuck at a good objective value, and yet fail to explore widely. To account for this possibility we introduce another measure of local search effectiveness.

Mobility measures how rapidly a local search moves in the search space (while it tries to simultaneously stay deep in the objective). We measure mobility by calculating the Hamming distance between variable assignments that are k steps apart in the search sequence, and average this quantity over the entire sequence to obtain average distances at time lags $k = 1, 2, 3, ...$, etc. It is desirable to obtain a large value of mobility since this indicates that the search is moving rapidly through the space.

Mobility is obviously very important in a local search. In fact, most of the significant innovations in local search methods over the last decade appear to have the effect of substantially improving mobility without damaging depth. This is demonstrated clearly in Figure 3, again for the uf100-0953 problem. It appears that the dramatic improvements of these methods could have been predicted from their improved mobility scores (while maintaining comparable depth scores).

Figure 3 covers several highlights in the development of local search methods for satisfiability. For example, one of the first useful innovations over GSAT was to add a preference for least recently flipped variables, resulting in the superior HSAT procedure. Figure 3 shows that one benefit of this change is to increase mobility without damaging search depth, which clearly corresponds to improved solution times. Another early innovation was to incorporate "random walk" in GSAT. Figure 3 shows that WSAT-G also delivers a noticeable increase in mobility—again resulting in a dramatic reduction in solution times. It is interesting to note that the apparently subtle distinction between WSAT-G and WSAT in terms of their definition is no longer sub-

100 runs on uf100-0953	Avg. cover. rate	Avg. mob.	Avg. dep.	Avg. flips	Est. opt.
Novelty(.5)	.0123	19	4.7	4,122	4,122
Novelty+(.5)	.0227	19	4.9	2,830	2,298
SDF($\frac{.2}{m}$, .995)	.0572	26	4.1	1,355	1,355

Figure 4: Coverage results

tle here: WSAT offers a dramatic improvement in mobility, along with an accompanying improvement in efficiency. Finally, the culmination of novelty and random walk in the Novelty procedure achieves even a further improvement in mobility, and, therefore it seems, solution time.

We have observed this effect consistently over the entire range of problems we have investigated. Thus it appears that, in addition to depth, mobility also is a necessary characteristic of an effective local search in SAT problems. To establish this further, Figure 2 shows the results of a large experiment on the entire collection of 2700 uf problems in SATLIB. The same four procedures were tested (SDF, Novelty, Novelty+, WSAT) and ranked in terms of their search mobility and solution time. The results show that the highest ranked in terms of mobility is almost always ranked near the top in problem solving efficiency, and that low mobility tends to correlate with inferior search efficiency.

A final characteristic of local search behavior that we consider is easily demonstrated by a simple observation: Hoos (1999) presents a simple satisfiable CNF formula with five variables and six clauses that causes Novelty to (sometimes) get stuck in a local basin of attraction that prevents it from solving an otherwise trivial problem. The significance of this example is that Novelty exhibits good depth and mobility in this case, and yet fails to solve what is otherwise an easy problem. This concern led Hoos to develop the slightly modified procedure Novelty+ in (Hoos 1999). The characteristic that Novelty is missing in this case is coverage.

Coverage measures how systematically the search explores the entire space. We compute a rate of coverage by first estimating the size of the largest "gap" in the search space (given by the maximum Hamming distance between any unexplored assignment and the nearest evaluated assignment) and measuring how rapidly the largest gap size is being reduced. In particular, we define the coverage rate to be $(n - \text{max gap})/\text{search steps}$. Note that it is desirable to have a high rate of coverage as this indicates that the search is systematically exploring new regions of the space as it proceeds.

Figure 4 shows that Hoos's modified Novelty+ procedure improves the coverage rate of Novelty on the uf100-0953 problem. Space limitations do not allow a full description, but Novelty+ demonstrates uniformly better coverage than Novelty while maintaining similar values on other measures, and thus achieves better performance on nearly every problem in the benchmark collections.

Overall, our results lead us to hypothesize that local search procedures work effectively because they descend quickly in the objective, persistently explore variable assignments with good objective values, and do so while moving rapidly through the search space and visiting very different variable assignments without returning to previously explored regions. That is, we surmise that good local search methods do not possess any special ability to predict whether a local basin of attraction contains a solution or not—rather they simply descend to promising regions and explore near the bottom of the objective as rapidly, broadly, and systematically as possible, until they stumble across a solution. Although this is a rather simplistic view, it seems supported by our data and moreover it has led to the development of a new local search technique. Our new procedure achieves good characteristics under these measures and, more importantly, exhibits good search performance in comparison to existing methods.

A new local search strategy: SDF

Although the previous measures provide useful diagnostic information about local search performance, the main contribution of this paper is a new local search procedure, which we call SDF for "smoothed descent and flood." Our procedure has two main components that distinguish it from previous approaches. First, we perform steepest descent in a more informative objective function than earlier methods. Second, we use multiplicative clause re-weighting to rapidly move out of local minima and efficiently travel to promising new regions of the search space.

Recall that the standard GSAT objective simply counts the number of unsatisfied clauses for a given variable assignment. We instead consider an objective that takes into account how many variables satisfy each clause. Here it will be more convenient to think of a reversed objective where we seek to maximize the number of satisfied clauses instead of minimize the number of unsatisfied clauses. Our enriched objective works by always favoring a variable assignment that satisfies more clauses, but all things being equal, favoring assignments that satisfy more clauses twice (subject to satisfying the same number of clauses once), and so on. In effect, we introduce a tie-breaking criterion that decides, when two assignments satisfy the same number of clauses, that we should prefer the assignment which satisfies more clauses on two distinct variables, and if the assignments are still tied, that we should prefer the assignment that satisfies more clauses on three distinct variables, etc. This tie-breaking scheme can be expressed in a scalar objective function that gives a large increment to the first satisfying variable, and then gives exponentially diminishing increments for subsequent satisfying variables for a given clause. For k-CNF formulas with m clauses, such a scoring function is

$$f_{ABE}(\mathbf{x}) = \sum_c score(\text{\# } x_i\text{'s that satisfy } c)$$

where $score(0) = 0$, $score(1) = m^{k-1}$, $score(2) = m^{k-1} + m^{k-2}$,..., $score(k) = m^{k-1} + m^{k-2} + \cdots + 1$.

Our intuition is that performing steepest ascent in this objective should help build robustness in the current variable assignment which the search can later exploit to satisfy new clauses. In fact, we observe this phenomenon in our experiments. Figure 5 shows that following a steepest ascent in

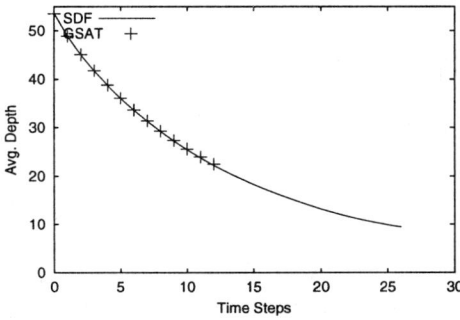

Figure 5: Descent results

f_{ABE} descends deeper in the original GSAT objective than the GSAT procedure itself (before either procedure reaches a local extrema or plateau). This happens because plateaus in the GSAT objective are not plateaus in f_{ABE}; in fact, such plateaus are usually opportunities to build up robustness in satisfied clauses which can be later exploited to satisfy new clauses. This effect is systematic and we have observed it in every problem we have examined. This gives our first evidence that the SDF procedure, by descending deeper in the GSAT objective, has the potential to improve the performance of existing local search methods.

The main outstanding issue is to cope with local maxima in the new objective. That is, although f_{ABE} does not contain many plateaus, the local search procedure now has to deal with legitimate (and numerous) local maxima in the search space. While this means that plateau walking is no longer a significant issue, it creates the difficulty of having to escape from true traps in the objective function. Our strategy for coping with local maxima involves the second main idea behind the SDF procedure: *multiplicative* clause re-weighting. Note that when a search is trapped at a local maxima the current variable assignment must leave some subset of the clauses unsatisfied. Many authors have observed that such local extrema can be "filled in" by increasing the weight of the unsatisfied clauses to create a new search direction that allows the procedure to escape (Wu & Wah 1999; Frank 1996; Morris 1993; Selman & Kautz 1993). However, previous published re-weighting schemes all use *additive* updates to increment the clause weights. Unfortunately, additive updates do not work very well on difficult search problems because the clauses develop large weight differences over time, and this causes the update mechanism to lose its ability to rapidly adapt the weight profile to new regions of the search space. Multiplicative updating has the advantage of maintaining the ability to swiftly change the weight profile whenever necessary.

One final issue we faced was that persistently satisfied clauses would often lose their weight to the extent that they would become frequently falsified, and consequently the depth of search (as measured in the GSAT objective) would deteriorate. To cope with this effect, we flattened the weight profile of the satisfied clauses at each re-weighting by shrinking them towards their common mean. This increased the weights of clauses without requiring them to be explicitly falsified and had the overall effect of restoring search depth and improving performance. The final SDF procedure we tested is summarized as follows.

SDF(δ, ρ) Flip the variable x_i that leads to the greatest increase in the weighted objective

$$f_{WABE}(\mathbf{x}) = \sum_c w(c) \, score(\# \, x_i\text{'s that satisfy } c)$$

If the current variable assignment is a local maximum and not a solution, then re-weight the clauses to create a new ascent direction and continue.

Re-weight(δ, ρ) Multiplicatively re-weight the unsatisfied clauses and re-normalize the clause weights so that the resulting largest difference in the f_{WABE} objective (when flipping any one variable) is δ. (That is, create a minimal greedy search direction.) Then flatten the weight profile of the satisfied clauses by shrinking them $1 - \rho$ of the distance towards their common mean (to prevent the weights from becoming too small and causing clauses to be falsified gratuitously).

One interesting aspect of this procedure is that it is almost completely deterministic (given that ties are rare in the objective, without re-starts) and yet seems to perform very well in comparison to the best current methods, all of which are highly stochastic. We claim that much of the reason for this success is that SDF maintains good depth, mobility, and coverage in its search. This is clearly demonstrated in Figures 1–3 which show that SDF obtains superior measurements in every criteria.

Evaluation

We have conducted a preliminary evaluation of SDF on several thousand benchmark SAT problems from the SATLIB and DIMACS repositories. The early results appear to be very promising. Comparing SDF to the very effective Novelty+ and WSAT procedures, we find that SDF typically reduces the number of flips needed to find a solution over the best of Novelty+ and WSAT by a factor of two to four on random satisfiable CNF formulae (from the uf, flat, and aim collections), and by a factor of five to ten on non-random CNF formulae (from the SATLIB blocks-world and ais problem sets). These results are consistent across the vast majority of the problems we have investigated, and hold up even when considering the mean flips without restart, median flips, and optimal expected flips using restarts estimated from (1). However, our current implementation of SDF is not optimized and does not yet outperform current methods in terms of CPU time. Details are reported below.

In all experiments, each problem was executed 100 times and results averaged over these runs. All problems were tried with SDF($\frac{.2}{m}$, .995), Novelty(.5), Novelty+(.5), and WSAT(.5). Furthermore, smaller problems were also tried with HSAT, GSAT, and simulated annealing.[2] There are

---

[2]We have as yet been unable to replicate the reported results for the DLM procedures from the published descriptions (Wu & Wah 1999; Shang & Wah 1998), and so did not include them in our study. This remains as future work.

	SDF		Novelty+		WSAT
	Avg.	Est. opt.	Avg.	Est. opt.	Est. opt.
uf50	214	140	411	271	505
uf75	488	411	978	732	1394
uf100	939	748	2297	1470	2877
uf125	1906	1563	5160	2712	5876
uf150	2962	2209	8253	4314	8393
uf175	6632	4945	18208	10719	20696
uf200	14106	9485	29536	18371	32039
uf225	17026	12198	38288	21129	35394
uf250	17980	13619	30617	23681	33993
flat125	15230	12868	37085	26369	64294
flat150	36020	31615	81668	59194	135981
aim100	94642	89155	236540	236215	236281

	SDF		Novelty+	% Failed
	Avg. flips	Est. opt.	Est. opt.	SDF / Nov+
bwlarge.a	2747	2701	10588	0 / 0
bwlarge.b	41907	39611	354111	0 / 40
bwlarge.c	470366	470366	-	87 / 100
huge	2561	2560	11104	0 / 0
logistics.c	17249	16870	140412	0 / 0

	SDF		WSAT	% Failed
	Avg. flips	Est. opt.	Est. opt.	SDF / WSAT
ais6	441	435	1063	0 / 0
ais8	6901	5617	34508	0 / 0
ais10	20214	16095	297460	0 / 28
ais12	154464	134491	488421	5 / 96

Figure 6: Search results

three sets of experiments reported in Figure 6. The first set covers a wide array of random SAT problems from both the SATLIB and DIMACS repositories. The results shown are averaged over all problems in the respective problem set and are shown for the runs with SDF, Novelty+ (which was 2nd best), and WSAT. The second set covers large planning problems. The results are shown for SDF and Novelty+ (2nd best), and the failure rates of each are compared. The third set covers the ais (All-Interval Series) problem set and shows results for SDF and WSAT (2nd best). In all experiments, the mean flips without restart and optimal expected flips are reported for SDF, and the optimal expected flips is reported for the other algorithms (when significantly smaller than the mean without restarts).

The results for the non-random blocks-world and ais problems are particularly striking. These problems challenge state of the art local search methods (verified in Figure 6) and yet SDF appears to solve them relatively quickly. This suggests that, although SDF shares many similarities to other local search methods currently in use, if might offer a qualitatively different approach that could yield benefits in real world problems.

The current implementation of SDF is unfortunately not without its limitations. We are presently using a non-optimized floating-point implementation, which means that even though SDF executes significantly fewer search steps (flips) to solve most problems, each search step is more expensive to compute. The overhead of our current implementation is about factor of six greater than that of Novelty or WSAT per flip, which means that in terms of CPU time, SDF is only competitive with the current best methods in some cases (e.g. bw_large.b). However, the inherent algorithmic complexity of each flip computation in SDF is no greater than that of GSAT, and we therefore expect that an optimized implementation in integer arithmetic will speed SDF up considerably—possibly to the extent that it strongly outperforms current methods in terms of CPU time as well.

References

Bayardo, R., and Schrag, R. 1997. Using CSP look-back techniques to solve real-world SAT instances. In *Proc. AAAI-97*.

Cha, B., and Iwama, K. 1995. Performance test of local search algorithms using new types of random CNF formulas. In *Proc. IJCAI-95*, 304–310.

Cha, B., and Iwama, K. 1996. Adding new clauses for faster local search. In *Proc. AAAI-96*, 332–337.

Frank, J. 1996. Weighting for Godot: Learning heuristics for GSAT. In *Proc. AAAI-96*, 338–343.

Frank, J. 1997. Learning short-tem weights for GSAT. In *Proc. IJCAI-97*, 384–391.

Gent, I., and Walsh, T. 1993. Towards an understanding of hill-climbing procedures for SAT. In *Proc. AAAI-93*, 28–33.

Gent, I., and Walsh, T. 1995. Unsatisfied variables in local search. In Hallam, J., ed., *Hybrid Problems, Hybrid Solutions (AISB-95)*.

Gomes, C.; Selman, B.; and Kautz, H. 1998. Boosting combinatorial search through randomization. In *Proc. AAAI-98*, 431–437.

Hoos, H. 1999. On the run-time behavior of stochastic local search algorithms for SAT. In *Proc. AAAI-99*, 661–666.

Kautz, H., and Selman, B. 1996. Pushing the envelope: Planning, propositional logic, and stochastic search. In *Proc. AAAI-96*, 1194–1201.

Larrabee, T. 1992. Test pattern generation using boolean satisfiability. *IEEE Trans Computer-Aided Design* 11(1):4–15.

Li, C., and Anbulagan. 1997. Heuristics based on unit propagation for satisfiability problems. In *Proc. IJCAI-97*, 366–371.

Mazure, B.; Saïs, L.; and Grégoire, E. 1997. Tabu search for SAT. In *Proc. AAAI-97*, 281–285.

McAllester, D.; Selman, B.; and Kautz, H. 1997. Evidence for invariants in local search. In *Proc. AAAI-97*, 321–326.

Morris, P. 1993. The breakout method for escaping from local minima. In *Proc. AAAI-93*, 40–45.

Parkes, A., and Walser, J. 1996. Tuning local search for satisfiability testing. In *Proc. AAAI-96*, 356–362.

Selman, B., and Kautz, H. 1993. Domain-independent extensions to GSAT: Solving large structured satisfiability problems. In *Proc. IJCAI-93*.

Selman, B.; Kautz, H.; and Cohen, B. 1994. Noise strategies for improving local search. In *Proc. AAAI-94*, 337–343.

Selman, B.; Kautz, H.; and McAllester, D. 1997. Ten challenges in propositional reasoning and search. In *Proc. IJCAI-97*, 50–54.

Selman, B.; Levesque, H.; and Mitchell, D. 1992. A new method for solving hard satisfiability problems. In *Proc. AAAI-92*.

Shang, Y., and Wah, W. 1998. A discrete Lagrangian based global search method for solving satisfiability problems. *J. Global Optimization* 12(1):61–99.

Wu, Z., and Wah, W. 1999. Trap escaping strategies in discrete Lagrangian methods for solving hard satisfiability and maximum satisfiability problems. In *Proc. AAAI-99*, 673–678.

MarketSAT: An Extremely Decentralized (but Really Slow) Algorithm for Propositional Satisfiability

William E. Walsh   Michael P. Wellman
University of Michigan Artificial Intelligence Laboratory
1101 Beal Avenue, Ann Arbor, MI 48109-2110 USA
{wew, wellman}@umich.edu

Abstract

We describe MarketSAT, a highly decentralized, market-based algorithm for propositional satisfiability. The approach is based on a formulation of satisfiability as production on a supply chain, where producers of particular variable assignments must acquire licenses to fail to satisfy particular clauses. MarketSAT employs a market protocol for general supply chain problems, which we show to be expressively equivalent to 3SAT. Experiments suggest that MarketSAT reliably converges to market allocations corresponding to satisfiable truth assignments. We experimentally compare the computational performance with GSAT, a centralized local search algorithm.

Introduction

Decentralization comprises constraints on the distribution of information and authority among participants in a distributed system. In a decentralized system, the information state of an individual is considered private, and is disseminated only by voluntary communication acts. This contrasts with centralized systems, in which it is generally assumed that a single entity (the "center") can obtain knowledge of the entire information state, for example by compelling communication. Decentralization constraints clearly restrict the computations performed by individual participants, and apparently of the system as a whole.

Because computational environments are increasingly decentralized in some respects (e.g., multiagent systems, where agents represent distinct individuals or organizations with diverse information and interests), it is important to understand the computational properties of decentralized systems. To do so, we require an appropriate model of decentralized computation.

Markets provide one model of decentralized systems with clearly delineated boundaries of knowledge and lines of communication. Typically, participants (agents) maintain knowledge of only resources of direct interest, and interact with other agents only indirectly through market institutions, such as auctions. The market-based approach has become increasingly popular in recent years, as evidenced by the growing prevalence in the AI literature of research in the design and analysis of computational market systems and their underlying mechanisms (Fujishima, Leyton-Brown, & Shoham 1999; Sandholm 1999; Wurman, Wellman, & Walsh 1998; Ygge & Akkermans 1998).

Shoham and Tennenholtz (to appear) directly pose the question "What can a market compute, and at what expense?" They provide answers for some interesting cases, applying concepts from economic mechanism design and communication complexity. Different behavioral assumptions can support conclusions about additional cases. For instance, over fifty years ago, Samuelson (1949) considered how markets could decentralize the solution of linear programming problems. More generally, adopting market protocols in the framework of general equilibrium theory can be seen to yield a computational model capable of solving convex programming problems (Cheng & Wellman 1998). However, none of these lines of analysis provide answers with respect to the sort of combinatorial optimization problems of most interest in AI research.

To address this gap, we examine here the possibility of using markets to solve propositional satisfiability (SAT) problems in a decentralized manner. As the original NP-complete problem, SAT (or its equivalently difficult special case, 3SAT) is considered fundamental, has been thoroughly studied, and indeed remains the object of active research. Studies in AI have led to a greater understanding of its difficulty (Crawford & Auton 1996), and steady improvements in centralized algorithms, starting with the success of GSAT (Selman, Levesque, & Mitchell 1992).

Our market approach to satisfiability employs a market protocol we found to be effective in decentralized supply-chain formation problems (Walsh & Wellman 1998; 1999). We formulate satisfiability (3SAT) problems in terms of a supply chain, and investigate the effectiveness of the market in solving them. The market protocol applied to these problems is what we refer to as *MarketSAT*.

We describe the supply chain formation problem in the next section. We show how to transform 3SAT to supply chain formation in the "Supply Chain Formation is NP-Complete" section. We discuss the role of prices in guiding decentralized supply chain formation in the "Decentralization and Prices" section. Next we describe a distributed approach to supply chain formation in the "Market Protocol" section. We compare MarketSAT to GSAT in "MarketSAT

Copyright © 2000, American Association for Artificial Intelligence (www.aaai.org). All rights reserved.

Experiments". Finally, we discuss work on distributed constraint satisfaction and our conclusions.

Supply Chain Formation

Decentralized supply chain formation, informally, is the problem of assembling a network of agents that can transform basic goods into composite goods of value, given local knowledge and communication (Walsh & Wellman 1999). The term "good" refers to any discrete resource or task for which the results cannot be shared between agents.

More precisely, we (1999) formulate the problem as follows. A *task dependency network* is a directed, acyclic graph, (V, E), representing dependencies among agents and goods. $V = G \cup A$, where G is the set of goods and $A = C \cup \Pi \cup S$ is the set of agents, comprised of consumers C, producers Π, and suppliers S. Edges, E, connect agents with goods they can use or provide. There exists an edge $\langle g, a \rangle$ from $g \in G$ to $a \in A$ when agent a can make use of one unit of g, and an edge $\langle a, g \rangle$ when a can provide one unit of g. When an agent can acquire or provide multiple units of a good, separately indexed edges represent each unit. For instance, edges $\langle a, g \rangle_1$ and $\langle a, g \rangle_2$ would represent the fact that agent a can provide two units of good g. The goods can be traded only in integer quantities.

A *consumer* wishes to acquire one unit of one good among a set of possible goods. A *producer* can produce a single unit of an *output* good conditional on acquiring a certain number each of some fixed set of *input* goods. A producer must acquire each of its inputs to provide its output. A *supplier* can supply a set of goods, up to some maximum quantity for each, without requiring any input goods.

An *allocation* is a subgraph $(V', E') \subseteq (V, E)$. For $g \in G$, an edge $\langle a, g \rangle \in E'$ means that agent a provides g, and $\langle g, a \rangle \in E'$ means a acquires g. An agent is in an allocation graph iff it acquires or provides a good. A good is in an allocation graph iff it is bought or sold.

A producer is *active* iff it provides its output. A *producer is feasible* iff it is inactive or acquires all its inputs. Consumers and suppliers are always feasible. An *allocation is feasible* iff all producers are feasible and all goods are in *material balance*, that is the number of edges into a good equals the number of edges out.

A *solution* is a feasible allocation such that one or more consumers acquire a desired good. If $c \in C \cap V'$ for solution (V', E'), then (V', E') is a *solution for c*.

Definition 1 (supply chain formation problem) *(SUPP-CHAIN)*.

Instance: *A task dependency network, (V, E), with agents, goods, and edges as described above.*

Question: *Is there a solution $(V', E') \subseteq (V, E)$?*

Supply Chain Formation is NP-Complete

To develop our market approach to solving satisfiability problems, we show that SUPP-CHAIN is NP-complete by a reduction transformation from 3SAT. The transformation combined with the protocol described in the next section provide the desired solution method.

Definition 2 (3satisfiability) *(3SAT)*

Instance: *Set U of variables, and collection Q of clauses, where each $q \in Q$ is a set of literals over U, and $|q| = 3$.*

Question: *Is there a truth assignment $t : U \to \{T, F\}$ that satisfies each $q \in Q$?*

Theorem 1 SUPP-CHAIN *is NP-complete.*

Proof concept. We say that a variable u *fails to satisfy* a clause q under truth assignment t, iff either: (1) $t(u) = T$, $u \notin q$, and $\bar{u} \in q$, or, (2) $t(u) = F$, $\bar{u} \notin q$, and $u \in q$. The key observation behind our reduction is that in a satisfying truth assignment, at least one variable must satisfy any given clause, hence at *most* two variables can *fail to satisfy* any given clause. Thus the transformation ensures that, in order to produce a truth assignment for a variable, a producer must acquire *licenses* to fail to satisfy clauses. These licenses are the scarce resources (only two are available per clause) to be allocated.

The task dependency network corresponding to a 3SAT instance includes goods of the following types:

- g_q: license to fail to satisfy clause q
- g_u: an assignment to variable u
- g_c: a satisfying overall assignment

and agents of the following types:

- s_q: supplier of licenses to fail to satisfy q
- π_u: producer of a positive assignment to u
- $\pi_{\bar{u}}$: producer of a negative assignment to u
- π_c: producer of an overall assignment (from individual variable assignments)
- c: consumer of the overall assignment

As described below, we construct the network in such a way as to ensure that only satisfying assignments can be produced, primarily by controlling availability and necessity of failure-to-satisfy licenses.

Proof. SUPP-CHAIN *is in NP*. It is straightforward to verify that an allocation is a solution by observing whether c obtains a good and by counting the edges incident on each good and producer.

Reduction. We transform an instance of 3SAT to an instance of SUPP-CHAIN.

1. For each $q \in Q$, add g_q to G, add s_q to S, and add $\langle s_q, g_q \rangle_1$ and $\langle s_q, g_q \rangle_2$ to E.

2. For each $u \in U$, do the following:
   - add g_u to G,
   - add π_u to Π, add $\langle \pi_u, g_u \rangle$ to E, and for each $q \in Q$ such that $u \notin q$ and $\bar{u} \in q$, add $\langle g_q, \pi_u \rangle$ to E,
   - add $\pi_{\bar{u}}$ to Π, add $\langle \pi_u, g_u \rangle$ to E, and for each $q \in Q$ such that $\bar{u} \notin q$ and $u \in q$, add $\langle g_q, \pi_{\bar{u}} \rangle$ to E.

3. Add c to C, $\langle g_c, c \rangle$ to E, g_c to G, π_c to Π, and $\langle \pi_c, g_c \rangle$ to E. For each $u \in U$, add $\langle g_u, \pi_c \rangle$ to E.

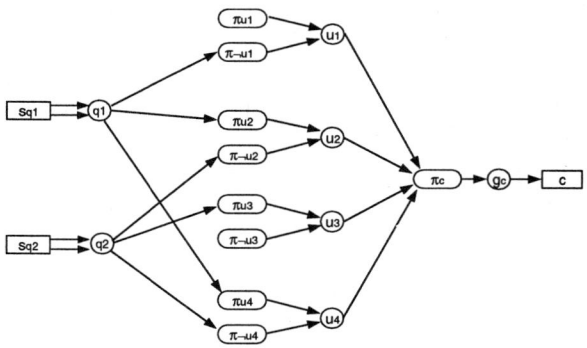

Figure 1: The transformation for $Q = \{q_1, q_2\}$, $q_1 = \{u_1, \bar{u}_2, \bar{u}_4\}$, $q_2 = \{u_2, \bar{u}_3, u_4\}$.

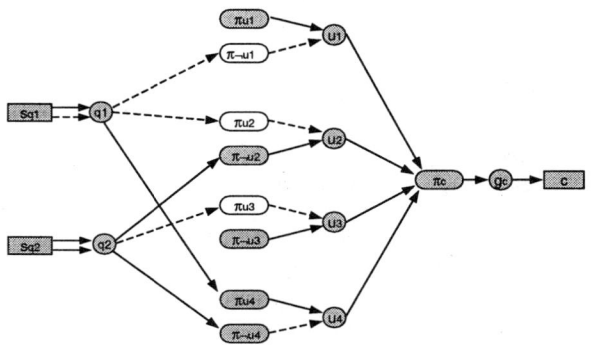

Figure 2: A solution that corresponds to the satisfying truth assignment $t(u_1) = T$, $t(u_2) = F$, $t(u_3) = F$, $t(u_4) = T$, for the problem in Figure 1. Shaded vertices and solid edges are in the solution.

Figure 1 shows the transformation for an example with $Q = \{q_1, q_2\}$, $q_1 = \{u_1, \bar{u}_2, \bar{u}_4\}$, $q_2 = \{u_2, \bar{u}_3, u_4\}$.

A "yes" configuration for 3SAT *is a "yes" configuration for* SUPP-CHAIN. If t is a satisfying truth assignment in the instance of 3SAT, then we can map t to a solution $(V', E') \subseteq (V, E)$. First, add g_c, π_c, and each $g_u \in G$ to V'. Add $\langle \pi_c, g_c \rangle$ to E', and for each $g_u \in G$, add $\langle g_u, \pi_c \rangle$ to E'.

For $u \in U$, if $t(u) = T$, then add π_u to V' and add all input and output edges of π_u to E'. For each $q \in Q$ such that $u \notin q$ and $\bar{u} \in q$, add s_q to V' and a new $\langle s_q, g_q \rangle_i$ to E'. If instead, $t(u) = F$, then perform similar operations with $\bar{u}$ and u reversed. Since t is satisfying, for each q in Q there are at most two variables that fail to satisfy q, hence at most two producers require g_q as input in (V', E'). Hence, (V', E') is feasible. It is also a solution because $\langle \pi_c, g_c \rangle \in E'$.

Figure 2 shows a feasible allocation that corresponds to the satisfying truth assignment $t(u_1) = T$, $t(u_2) = F$, $t(u_3) = F$, $t(u_4) = T$, for the problem in Figure 1.

A "yes" configuration for SUPP-CHAIN *is a "yes" configuration for* 3SAT. A solution (V', E') must be in material balance, which implies that, for each $u \in U$, either $\langle \pi_u, g_u \rangle \in E'$ or $\langle \pi_{\bar{u}}, g_u \rangle \in E'$. If the former is true, then, we assign $t(u) = T$, otherwise $t(u) = F$.

Since there are two units of any g_q available, each of which is in material balance, there are at most two edges in E' of the type $\langle g_q, \pi_u \rangle$ or $\langle g_q, \pi_{\bar{u}} \rangle$. But then, there are at most two variables in $q \in Q$ that fail to satisfy q, and hence at least one variable that does satisfy q under t. Thus, t is a satisfying truth assignment.

The transformation runs in polynomial time. The number of goods, agents, and edges incident thereof is polynomial in the 3SAT size. □

Decentralization and Prices

Given full knowledge of a 3SAT problem, we could employ a centralized algorithm known to be effective (e.g. GSAT). But in a decentralized system, agents need incentives to participate. In the market framework we model this in terms of recovering costs and acquiring value. Generally, supplier s has some ***opportunity cost*** $oc_s(\{g\})$ for supplying one unit $\langle s, g \rangle$ of good g. We assume $oc_s(\{g\}) = 0$ for all $s \in S$ and $\langle s, g \rangle \in E$. The consumer c obtains ***value*** $v_c(\{g_c\})$ for obtaining a single unit of good g_c.

We further assume the problem is decentralized in that each agent has knowledge only of its goods of interest and its valuations or costs thereof. In the market approach, we posit a ***price system*** p, which assigns to each good g a nonnegative number $p(g)$ as its ***price***. Intuitively, prices indicate the relative global value of the goods. Therefore, agents may use the prices as a guide to their local decision making. We assume that each agent wishes to maximize its ***surplus***, that is the difference between its values (for consumers, from goods obtained, or for producers, from the price of goods sold) and costs incurred (for suppliers, opportunity costs of goods provided, or for producers, total price of inputs acquired), while maintaining feasibility.

We allow the existence of mediators for each good to facilitate indirect communication between agents, via prices. Thus an agent is constrained to exchange messages with mediators for its goods of interest based on its own valuations or costs and the history of price messages received from the mediators.

We describe particular protocol for forming supply chains, subject to the decentralization constraints, in the next section.

Market Protocol

In previous work (1999) we defined a market protocol for the supply chain formation problem. MarketSAT is simply this protocol applied to 3SAT task dependency networks. In the protocol, agents negotiate through auction mediators, one for each good. An auction in turn determines the price and allocation of its respective good. Here we assume reliable synchronous message passing, although all results pertaining to general task dependency networks apply to the asynchronous case as well (1998; 1999).

Auction Mechanism

The task allocation market includes a separate auction for each good of interest. Agents submit bids for goods they wish to buy or sell. A ***bid*** specifies the price below/above

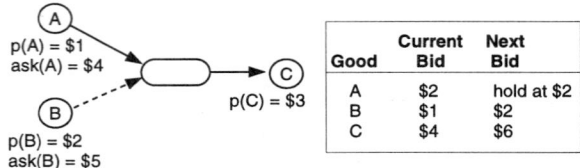

Figure 3: Example of how a producer updates its bids in a state where it is winning A and C, with $\delta = \$1$.

which the agent is willing to buy/sell. Auctions respond with *price quotes* specifying the current going price and the number of units the recipient would trade at what price, given the current bid state. Agents may in turn respond with further bids. Each auction requires that an agent's successive bids increase by no less than some (typically small) positive increment δ.

This process proceeds synchronously in rounds. That is, all agents submit bids within a round, and then receive price quotes before the next round. When the market reaches *quiescence*—a state in which no new bids or price quotes are issued—the auctions *clear*. Each bidder is notified of the final prices and how many units it transacted in each good.

According to the the (M+1)st-price rules (Satterthwaite & Williams 1989; Wurman, Walsh, & Wellman 1998), an auction balances reported supply and demand at a uniform price. If there are M units of a good offered for sale, based on the current bids, then the price of a good is the $M + 1$st price of *all* bids in the auction. Winners include all buyers/sellers strictly above/below the price, and, to maximize the benefits from trade, some agents at the clearing price. Ties are broken in favor of bids received in earlier rounds, and randomly among tied bids within a round.

When issuing price quotes, the auction reports both the price, $p(g)$, and the *ask price*, $ask(g)$ of the good g. The ask price specifies the amount above which a buyer would have to bid in order to buy the good, given the current set of bids. The ask price is determined by the Mth highest of all bids in the auction.

Bidding Policies

The strategic problem defined by the auction mechanism and the task dependency network is of a complexity well beyond our ability to derive optimal solutions in the game-theoretic sense. Therefore, we propose simple bidding policies based on myopic behavior and local information.

Let the current going prices be p. Supplier s places a one-time bid of $oc_s(\{g\})$, for each unit $\langle s, g \rangle \in E$ it can supply. When consumer c is not winning g_c it increases its bid for g_c to $p(g_c) + \delta$ if $v_c(\{g_c\}) - p(g_c) - \delta \geq 0$, otherwise it stops bidding.

A producer π initially bids zero for each input g, and increments its bid on an g whenever it is winning its output but losing g. π initially bids zero for its output g_π, and then changes the bid in an attempt to recover the *perceived costs* of its inputs. If π is currently winning an input g, its perceived cost, $\hat{p}_\pi(g)$ of g is simply $p(g)$. When π is not currently winning g, $\hat{p}_\pi(g) = ask(g)$ if $ask(g) > p(g)$ and $\hat{p}_\pi(g) = ask(g) + \delta$ if $ask(g) = p(g)$ (in the latter case, the producer must bid strictly above $ask(g)$ to win the good). When the prices of its inputs change, π bids $\sum_{\langle g, \pi \rangle \in E} \hat{p}_\pi(g)$ for g_π. Figure 3 shows an example of how a producer updates its bids.

Properties

A solution in which all consumers, suppliers and *active* producers have nonnegative surplus is called a **valid solution**. The quiescent state of the protocol is a valid solution iff some consumers acquire desired goods (which implies that no *in*valid solutions are reached) (Walsh & Wellman 1998).

Because bids are strictly ascending and the consumer has an upper bound on its value for goods, the market protocol is guaranteed to reach quiescence. Moreover, the runtime is bounded by a polynomial function of the network size and the size of the consumer value.

Theorem 2 *In the worst case, MarketSAT reaches quiescence after a number of bidding rounds polynomial in the network size and the size of the consumer value.*

Proof. (See the appendix for Lemmas.) There is one initial bid for each edge. By Lemma 4 and the fact that agents increase buy bids by at least δ, the number of subsequent buy bids is polynomial. Lemmas 5 and 6 prove the same for sell bids. At least one bid is placed in each round. $\square$

Extensive simulations on generic, random task dependency networks (with a slightly different version of the protocol) led us to conjecture that the protocol always converges to a valid solution if one exists and if some consumer has a sufficiently high value for a good (1998). As described in the next section, experiments support this conjecture for MarketSAT. It turns out that the size of $v_c(\{g_c\})$ can effect a tradeoff between worst-case runtime and the probability of successfully finding a satisfying assignment.

Corollary 3 (to Theorem 2) *The minimum consumer value necessary to ensure solution convergence in MarketSAT cannot be bounded by a polynomial function of the 3SAT instance problem size (assuming $P \neq NP$).*

Although we do not yet have a proof of solution convergence, we have some intuition for how it works. The bidding process can be seen as a distributed search for a set of prices such that the agents in a solution would choose to be in the solution while other agents would choose to be out of the solution. In particular, the prices of certain goods of type g_q must rise sufficiently high relative to other such goods to block out variable assignments that cannot be a part of the solution.

Recall that a producer increases an input bid only when it is winning its output but losing that input. In this way, a variable assignment producer has the opportunity to affect the price space search to support its tentative inclusion in the solution. But as the prices on its inputs rise, it will raise its output bid in response. If these prices rise too high, the opposite assignment may be tentatively included in the solution instead, reflecting the collective market evaluation that the opposite assignment is currently the better for which to search.

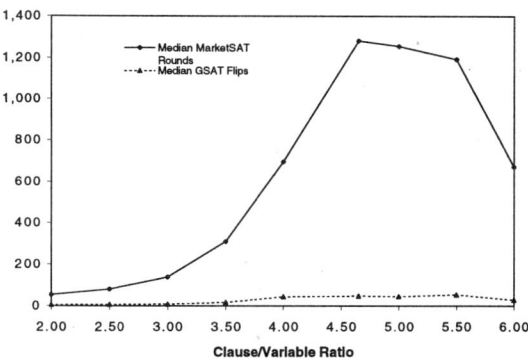

Figure 4: Median runtimes for 20-variable problems.

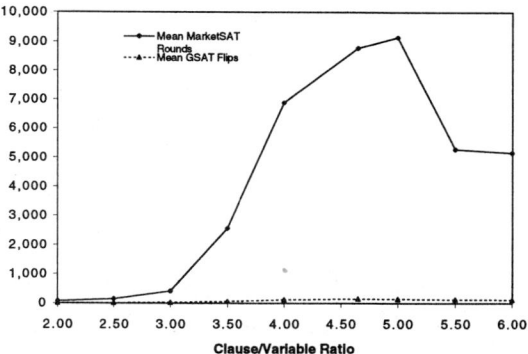

Figure 5: Mean values for 20-variable problems.

	Standard Deviation	Mean/ Median	Max/ Median
MarketSAT	49,694	741	6.8
GSAT	231	41	3

Table 1: Comparison of MarketSAT and GSAT for 20-variable problems at the crossover point.

MarketSAT Experiments

In this section we describe the construction and results of a battery of experiments comparing MarketSAT to GSAT (Selman, Levesque, & Mitchell 1992), a centralized random-restart hill-climbing algorithm.

Construction

We ran the two algorithms on a set of problems chosen according to the random 3SAT model (Mitchell, Selman, & Levesque 1992). Given a set of variables U, a clause contains three variables chosen uniformly and independently from U, each negated with probability .5. We eliminated unsatisfiable problems.

We tried problems with 15 and 20 variables, and varying numbers of clauses. Mitchell et al. (1992) observed that the hardest problems occur at a crossover point in the clause/variable ratio where 50% of the problems are satisfiable. Crawford and Auton (1996) found experimentally that the transition occurs when the number of clauses is approximately $4.258v + 58.26v^{-2/3}$, where v is the number of variables. In order to understand the behavior of MarketSAT on the hardest problems, as well as a broader class, we examined problems with numbers of clauses computed with the Crawford-Auton function (ratios of 4.87 and 4.65 for 15 and 20 variables, respectively), as well with clause/variable ratios of 2, 2.5, 3, 3.5, 4, 5, 5.5, and 6. We ran 500 trials for each number of variables and clauses, for a total of 9000.

Results

Given that agents and auctions run in parallel, a plausible measure of runtime is bidding rounds. Within a given round, the clause auctions are the bottleneck, running in $O(|U| \lg |U|)$ time (though incremental updating techniques can improve amortized performance (Wurman, Walsh, & Wellman 1998)).

To consider alternative measures, recall from the reduction transformation that for each $u \in U$, there are producers π_u and $\pi_{\bar{u}}$. The number of times they "swap" the license to sell g_u is directly analogous to flipping a variable. In any given round of MarketSAT, zero or multiple such "flips" can take place. However, our experiments show that the number of MarketSAT flips is highly linear in the number of rounds (regression result: $flips = 0.5 rounds - 11.9, R^2 = .99$) hence we choose to compare MarketSAT bidding rounds to GSAT flips as a rough estimate of their relative performance.

Both algorithms found solutions to all problems, and we have been unable to construct a problem that MarketSAT could not solve, given enough time and a high enough $v_c(\{g_c\})$ (2×10^7 was sufficient for all our experiments). GSAT nearly dominated MarketSAT, performing better in all but 3.3% of the instances. Moreover, GSAT ran significantly faster. In the median case, MarketSAT required 17.6 times as many rounds as GSAT required flips. Figure 4 shows the median runtime of each algorithm over the range of clause/variable ratios in 20-variable problems. Not only did MarketSAT fare poorly on median measures, but also had a heavy tail of slow runs. As shown in Figure 5, the mean runtimes of MarketSAT are significantly higher than the medians. Table 1 shows that, for 20-variable problems at the crossover point, MarketSAT has significantly higher standard deviation, mean/median ratio, and maximum/median ratio. We obtained qualitatively similar results for 15-variable problems.

We found ourselves constrained in the size of problems we could practically solve with MarketSAT. While GSAT can solve 500-variable problems on 1992 computers (Selman, Levesque, & Mitchell 1992) MarketSAT can be prohibitively slow on much smaller problems. In our 20-variable trials, the worst MarketSAT run required 1.48×10^6 rounds, compared with only 2,017 flips for the worst GSAT run. Some 25-variable problems we have tried require tens of millions of MarketSAT rounds and hours of single-CPU computation. Despite the somewhat limited range of problem sizes explored, we believe they are sufficient to establish the qualitative performance of MarketSAT relative to GSAT[1].

Distributed Constraint Satisfaction

Yokoo et al. (Yokoo *et al.* 1998) provide a general formulation of distributed constraint satisfaction problems (CSPs). Since CSP is polynomially equivalent to 3SAT, we could solve 3SAT problems with distributed constraint satisfaction algorithms. However, the distributed CSP formulation imposes much weaker decentralization constraints than MarketSAT.

In Yokoo et al.'s model, each agent represents one or more variables. An agent proposes values for its variables and evaluates constraints on those variables. Agents send and receive (partial) solutions as well as lists of nogood partial solutions. This mapping of agents to the underlying problem is admittedly more natural than in MarketSAT. The algorithms presented by Yokoo et al. can be viewed as adaptations of centralized CSP solution techniques to a multiagent environment, performing systematic search with respect to the (implicit) global state. The primary adaptation is *asynchronous backtracking*, which allows agents to propose partial solutions in parallel. Since they do not ultimately restrict the dissemination of information, their distributed framework is able to provide performance comparable to (and, with effective parallelism, potentially better than) centralized algorithms.

In contrast, MarketSAT appears to perform substantially worse, but adheres to much stricter decentralization constraints. If we assume that, for a given 3SAT variable u, the literal producers π_u and $\pi_{\bar{u}}$ are in fact a single producer with separate policies for g_u and $g_{\bar{u}}$, then the task dependence network can be constructed with only the following knowledge of the original 3SAT problem: (1) a producer representing a variable knows in which clauses it is contained, and (2) π_c knows all the variables. No further knowledge of the structure nor partial solutions of the 3SAT problem is later transmitted, except indirectly and compactly via prices. In contrast, the distributed CSP algorithms require that agents have more knowledge of the initial problem and the partial solutions. Any agent involved in a constraint must be able to evaluate the constraint, and agents may potentially form links with all other agents to transmit partial solutions or nogoods.

Conclusions

Our experiments show that, in terms of runtime, GSAT dominates MarketSAT by several orders of magnitude. The ability of centralized algorithms like GSAT to evaluate global state (and similarly for distributed formulations that allow arbitrary information sharing) provide a decided advantage

---
[1] In preliminary experiments, CPLEX, a commercial mixed integer programming package, solves much larger SUPP-CHAIN encoded 3SAT problems much faster than MarketSAT. Hence we believe that MarketSAT's performance is mainly attributable to decentralization, rather than the encoding.

in combinatorial search. In contrast, MarketSAT makes decisions about individual variables entirely based on local price information.

Nevertheless, that a market *can* reliably solve satisfiability problems, however slowly, in a distributed fashion, provides existential evidence for highly decentralized solution methods to general classes of combinatorial problems. Moreover, it is intriguing that MarketSAT succeeds without explicit search state or randomization. At this time we do not fully understand how prices guide MarketSAT to a solution, hence we can only conjecture that MarketSAT is complete. We regard the present work as evidence of the versatility of the market model of computation, and a starting point for further studies of decentralizing combinatorial optimization.

Appendix: Lemmas

Lemma 4 *No agent places a buy bid above $v_c(\{g_c\}) + 4\delta$.*

Proof. First we show that, if $\beta(g)$ is the maximum buy bid that any agent ever places for good g, then a producer with output g will never bid above $\beta(g) + 2\delta$ for any of its inputs. Assume that π will raise its bid for input g_i from α to α', where $\beta(g) < \alpha \leq \beta(g) + \delta < \alpha' \leq \beta(g) + 2\delta$. π must bid α' for g_i before bidding above $\beta(g) + 2\delta$. It must also be that π is losing its current bid α for g_i, otherwise it would not raise that input bid. But then the current price quote for g_i is greater than $\beta(g)$. Thus, π will bid greater than $\beta(g)$ for its output g. Because bids are nondecreasing, it will never again win its output bid, and hence will never raise its bid for input g_i above $\beta(g) + 2\delta$.

The consumer never bids above $v_c(\{g_c\})$ for g_c. Given the relationship between output good bids and input good bids shown above, it follows that π_c never bids above $v_c(\{g_c\}) + 2\delta$ for any of its inputs, and hence no variable assignment producer π_u or $\pi_{\bar{u}}$ ever bids above $v_c(\{g_c\}) + 4\delta$ for any of its inputs. □

Lemma 5 *A producer of an assignment to a variable updates its sell bid at most $2|Q|(v_c(\{g_c\}) + 4\delta)/\delta$ times.*

Proof. Consider producer π of the specified type (e.g. either π_u or $\pi_{\bar{u}}$ for some variable u). After its initial bid, π changes its output bid when either the price or bid price for an input changes, or it switches from winning to losing an input (in which case it switches from using the price to the ask price in its output bid calculation). Thus, the number of times π changes its output bid is bounded by the total number of times the price and ask price change for each input.

The price quote of an input good g_q of π changes only in response to buy bids from the variable assignment producers. By Lemma 4, producers never place a buy bid above $v_c(\{g_c\}) + 4\delta$. Because the buy bids start at zero and go up by δ, the price and ask price of g_q can each change at most $(v_c(\{g_c\}) + 4\delta)/\delta$ times. Since π has at most $|Q|$ inputs, we have proved the lemma. □

Lemma 6 *The producer π_c updates is sell bid at most $|U|2[v_c(\{g_c\}) + 4\delta + 4|Q|(v_c(\{g_c\}) + 4\delta)]/\delta$ times.*

Proof. As in the proof for Lemma 5, the number of times π_c changes its output bid is bounded by the total number of times the price and ask price change for each input. The price quote on an input good g_u of π_c is affected by sell bids from producers π_u and $\pi_{\bar{u}}$ as well as by the buy bids by π_c. By Lemma 5, and the fact that there are two potential sellers of g_u, no more than $4|Q|(v_c(\{g_c\})+4\delta)/\delta$ bid updates are placed for g_u. By Lemma 4, π_c bids no higher than $v_c(\{g_c\})+4\delta$ for g_u, and by its policy, does so in increments of δ. Thus the price and ask price of g_u *each* increase no more than $[v_c(\{g_c\})+4\delta+4|Q|(v_c(\{g_c\})+4\delta)]/\delta$ times. This holds for all $|U|$ input goods of π_c. □

Acknowledgments We thank the anonymous reviewers for helpful comments. This work was supported by a NASA/Jet Propulsion Laboratory Graduate Student Researcher fellowship and DARPA grant F30602-97-1-0228 from the Information Survivability program.

References

Cheng, J. Q., and Wellman, M. P. 1998. The WALRAS algorithm: A convergent distributed implementation of general equilibrium outcomes. *Computational Economics* 12:1–24.

Crawford, J. M., and Auton, L. D. 1996. Experimental results on the crossover point in random 3-SAT. *Artificial Intelligence* 81:31–57.

Fujishima, Y.; Leyton-Brown, K.; and Shoham, Y. 1999. Taming the computational complexity of combinatorial auctions: Optimal and approximate approaches. In *Sixteenth International Joint Conference on Artificial Intelligence*, 548–553.

Mitchell, D.; Selman, B.; and Levesque, H. 1992. Hard and easy distributions of SAT problems. In *Tenth National Conference on Artificial Intelligence*, 459–465.

Samuelson, P. A. 1949. Market mechanisms and maximization. Research memorandum, RAND. Available in *The Collected Scientific Papers of Paul A. Samuelson*, Stiglitz, J. E., ed., 1966.

Sandholm, T. 1999. An algorithm for optimal winner determination in combinatorial auctions. In *Sixteenth International Joint Conference on Artificial Intelligence*, 542–547.

Satterthwaite, M. A., and Williams, S. R. 1989. Bilateral trade with the sealed bid k-double auction: Existence and efficiency. *Journal of Economic Theory* 48:107–133.

Selman, B.; Levesque, H.; and Mitchell, D. 1992. A new method for solving hard satisfiability problems. In *Tenth National Conference on Artificial Intelligence*, 440–446.

Shoham, Y., and Tennenholtz, M. to appear. Rational computability and communication complexity. *Games and Economic Behavior*.

Walsh, W. E., and Wellman, M. P. 1998. A market protocol for decentralized task allocation. In *Third International Conference on Multi-Agent Systems*, 325–332.

Walsh, W. E., and Wellman, M. P. 1999. Efficiency and equilibrium in task allocation economies with hierarchical dependencies. In *Sixteenth International Joint Conference on Artificial Intelligence*, 520–526.

Wurman, P. R.; Walsh, W. E.; and Wellman, M. P. 1998. Flexible double auctions for electronic commerce: Theory and implementation. *Decision Support Systems* 24:17–27.

Wurman, P. R.; Wellman, M. P.; and Walsh, W. E. 1998. The Michigan Internet AuctionBot: A configurable auction server for human and software agents. In *Second International Conference on Autonomous Agents*, 301–308.

Ygge, F., and Akkermans, H. 1998. On resource-oriented multi-commodity market computations. In *Third International Conference on Multi-Agent Systems*, 365–371.

Yokoo, M.; Durfee, E. H.; Ishida, T.; and Kuwabara, K. 1998. The distributed constraint satisfaction problem: Formalization and algorithms. *IEEE Transactions on Knowledge and Data Engineering* 10(5):673–685.

An Efficient Global-Search Strategy in Discrete Lagrangian Methods for Solving Hard Satisfiability Problems*

Zhe Wu and **Benjamin W. Wah**
Department of Electrical and Computer Engineering
and the Coordinated Science Laboratory
University of Illinois at Urbana-Champaign
Urbana, IL 61801, USA
E-mail: {zhewu, wah}@manip.crhc.uiuc.edu
URL: http://www.manip.crhc.uiuc.edu

Abstract

In this paper, we present an efficient global-search strategy in an algorithm based on the theory of discrete Lagrange multipliers for solving difficult SAT instances. These difficult benchmarks generally have many traps and basins that attract local-search trajectories. In contrast to trap-escaping strategies proposed earlier (Wu & Wah 1999a; 1999b) that only focus on traps, we propose a global-search strategy that penalizes a search for visiting points close to points visited before in the trajectory, where penalties are computed based on the Hamming distances between the current and historical points in the trajectory. The new strategy specializes to the earlier trap-escaping strategies because when a trajectory is inside a trap, its historical information will contain many points in close vicinity to each other. It is, however, more general than trap escaping because it tries to avoid visiting the same region repeatedly even when the trajectory is not inside a trap. By comparing our results to existing results in the area (Wu & Wah 1999a; 1999b; Kautz & Selman 1996; Choi, Lee, & Stuckey 1998; Marques-Silva & Sakalla 1999), we conclude that our proposed strategy is both effective and general.

Introduction

Satisfiability (SAT) problems are the most fundamental discrete, constraint-satisfaction problems among all NP-complete problems. Many real-world applications, like artificial intelligence, computer-aided design, database processing, and planning, can be formulated as SAT problems. These problems generally require algorithms of exponential complexity in the worst case in order to obtain satisfiable assignments.

A general *satisfiability* (SAT) problem is defined as follows. Given a set of n clauses $\{C_1, \cdots, C_n\}$ on m variables $x = (x_1, \cdots, x_m)$, $x_j \in \{0, 1\}$, and a Boolean formula in conjunctive normal form:

$$C_1 \wedge C_2 \wedge \cdots \wedge C_n, \qquad (1)$$

---
*Research supported by National Science Foundation Grant NSF MIP 96-32316.
The source code of DLM-2000 is at http://manip.crhc.uiuc.edu.
Copyright © 2000, American Association for Artificial Intelligence (www.aaai.org). All rights reserved.

find a truth assignment to x for (1), where a truth assignment is a combination of variable assignments that makes the Boolean formula true. For example, one solution to the following simple SAT problem with four variables and four clauses is $(1, 0, 0, 0)$:

$(x_1 \vee x_3 \vee x_4) \wedge (x_1 \vee \bar{x}_2 \vee \bar{x}_3) \wedge (\bar{x}_1 \vee \bar{x}_2 \vee x_4) \wedge (\bar{x}_1 \vee \bar{x}_3 \vee \bar{x}_4).$

Many algorithms and heuristics have been developed to solve SAT problems. Complete approaches based on resolution, constraint satisfaction and backtracking (Purdom 1983; Genesereth & Nilsson 1987; Davis & Putnam 1960) are computationally expensive and are not suitable for solving large instances. Local-search methods (Frank 1997; Selman, Kautz, & Cohen 1994; 1993; Gu 1993; Sosič & Gu 1994), in contrast, iteratively perturb a trajectory until a satisfiable assignment is found. These methods can solve larger instances but may have difficulty in solving hard-to-satisfy instances. Recently, there is also some research in combining global optimization schemes, like GA, with local-search methods (Folino, Pizzuti, & Spezzano 1998).

In this paper, we formulate a SAT problem as a discrete, constrained optimization problem as follows:

$$\min_{x \in \{0,1\}^m} \quad N(x) = \sum_{i=1}^{n} U_i(x) \qquad (2)$$
$$\text{subject to} \quad U_i(x) = 0 \quad \forall i \in \{1, 2, \ldots, n\},$$

where $U_i(x)$ is a binary expression equal to zero when the ith clause is satisfied and to one otherwise, and $N(x)$ is the number of unsatisfied clauses. In this formulation, the objective function is automatically at its minimum when all the clauses are satisfied. Although the redundancy may seem superfluous, it actually gives better control in constraint satisfaction by treating each clause as a separate constraint. In contrast, in an unconstrained formulation, all clauses may be viewed to have the same fixed relative weight. This is generally undesirable because different clauses may have different degrees of difficulty to be satisfied. Hence, a constrained formulation of SAT with dynamically changing penalties on each clause is intuitively preferable.

In this paper, we briefly introduce the theory of discrete Lagrange multipliers and the discrete Lagrange-multiplier method (DLM) that can be applied to solve (2) (Shang & Wah 1998). We then show a basic implementation of DLM used in (Shang & Wah 1998) for solving SAT problems and discuss reasons why some hard instances cannot be solved. To solve those difficult instances, we propose a global-search strategy that avoids visiting nearby points visited before, using penalties related to the Hamming distances between the current and the historical points in the search trajectory. A *global-search strategy* in this paper is defined as one that can overcome local minima or valleys in the search space under consideration. It differs from global-optimization strategies in the sense that there is no theoretical guarantee that it will converge to a feasible or an optimal solution even when sufficient time is given. Finally, we show our results in solving some difficult SAT benchmark instances in the DIMACS archive and compare our results to existing results in this area.

Discrete Lagrangian Formulations

In this section, we summarize briefly the theory of discrete Lagrange multipliers (Shang & Wah 1998; Wu 1998; Wah & Wu 1999) for solving general constrained discrete optimization problems.

Define a discrete constrained optimization problem as:

$$\min_{x \in E^m} \quad f(x) \tag{3}$$
$$\text{subject to} \quad h(x) = 0 \quad x = (x_1, x_2, \ldots, x_m),$$

where x is a vector of m discrete variables, $f(x)$ is an objective function, and $h(x) = [h_1(x), \ldots, h_n(x)]^T = 0$ is a vector of n equality constraints. The corresponding discrete Lagrangian function is defined as follows:

$$L_d(x, \lambda) = f(x) + \lambda^T h(x), \tag{4}$$

where λ is a vector of Lagrange multipliers that can be either continuous or discrete.

An understanding of gradients in continuous space shows that they define directions in a small neighborhood in which function values decrease. To this end, (Wu 1998; Wah & Wu 1999) define in discrete space a *direction of maximum potential drop* (DMPD) for $L_d(x, \lambda)$ at point x for fixed λ as a vector[1] that points from x to a neighbor of $x \in \mathcal{N}(x)$ with the minimum L_d:

$$\Delta_x L_d(x, \lambda) = \vec{v}_x = y \ominus x = (y_1 - x_1, \ldots, y_n - x_n) \tag{5}$$
$$\text{where}$$
$$y \in \mathcal{N}(x) \cup \{x\} \text{ and } L_d(y, \lambda) = \min_{\substack{x' \in \mathcal{N}(x) \\ \cup \{x\}}} L_d(x', \lambda). \tag{6}$$

Here, $\ominus$ is the vector-subtraction operator for changing x in discrete space to one of its "user-defined" neighborhood

---
[1] To simplify our symbols, we represent points in the x space without the explicit vector notation.

points $\mathcal{N}(x)$. Intuitively, $\vec{v}_x$ is a vector pointing from x to y, the point with the minimum L_d value among all neighboring points of x, including x itself. That is, if x itself has the minimum L_d, then $\vec{v}_x = \vec{0}$.

Based on DMPD and a concept called *saddle points* introduced in (Shang & Wah 1998), (Wu 1998; Wah & Wu 1999) prove some first-order necessary and sufficient conditions on discrete-space constrained local minima based on the minimum of the discrete Lagrangian function defined in (4). This is done by showing that the first-order conditions are necessary and sufficient for a point to be a discrete saddle point, and that the saddle-point condition is necessary and sufficient for a point to be a constrained local minimum. Readers should refer to the correctness proofs in (Wu 1998).

The first-order conditions lead to the following iterative procedure to look for solutions to (3):

General Discrete First-Order Search Method

$$x(k+1) = x(k) \oplus \Delta_x L_d(x(k), \lambda(k)) \tag{7}$$
$$\lambda(k+1) = \lambda(k) + ch(x(k)) \tag{8}$$

where $\oplus$ is the vector-addition operator ($x \oplus y = (x_1 + y_1, \ldots x_n + y_n)$), and c is a positive real number controlling how fast the Lagrange multipliers change.

It is easy to see that the necessary condition for (7) to converge is when $h(x) = 0$, implying that x is a feasible solution to the original problem. If any of the constraints is not satisfied, then λ on the unsatisfied constraints will continue to evolve until the constraint is satisfied. Note that, similar to continuous Lagrangian methods, there is no guarantee for the first-order method to find a feasible solution in finite time, even if one exists.

Basic DLM Implementation for SAT

We describe the solution of SAT as a discrete Lagrangian search in this section. Although the overall strategy for updating Lagrange multipliers may resemble existing weight-update heuristics (Frank 1997; Morris 1993), our proposed formulation is based on a solid mathematical foundation of discrete Lagrange multipliers. The Lagrangian search, when augmented by new heuristics presented in the next section, provides a powerful tool to solve hard-to-satisfy SAT instances.

Specifically, the Lagrangian function for the SAT problem in (2) is:

$$L_d(x, \lambda) = N(x) + \sum_{i=1}^{n} \lambda_i U_i(x) \tag{9}$$

where $U_i(x)$ is a binary function equal to zero when the ith clause is satisfied and to one otherwise, and $N(x)$ is the number of unsatisfied clauses.

procedure *DLM-98-BASIC-SAT*
1. Reduce the original SAT problem;
2. Generate a random starting point using a fixed seed;
3. Initialize $\lambda_i \leftarrow 0$;
4. **while** solution not found and time not used up **do**
5.   Pick $x_j \notin$ TabuList that reduces L_d the most;
6.   Maintain TabuList;
7.   Flip x_j;
8.   **if** $\#_{FlatMoves} > \theta_1$ **then**
9. $\lambda_i \leftarrow \lambda_i + \delta_o$;
10.   **if** $\#_{Adjust} \% \theta_2 = 0$ **then**
11. $\lambda_i \leftarrow \lambda_i - \delta_d$ **end_if**
12.   **end_if**
13. **end_while**
end

Figure 1: *DLM-98-BASIC-SAT* (Shang & Wah 1998): An implementation of the basic discrete first-order method (7) and (8) for solving SAT.

Figure 1 shows a basic implementation of *discrete Lagrangian method* (*DLM*) of (Shang & Wah 1998). The original DLM uses two main heuristics: tabu lists (Glover 1989) and flat moves (Selman, Kautz, & Cohen 1993). We explain the steps of DLM later when we present our proposed global-search strategy.

Table 1 lists the performance of our current implementation of DLM on a 500-MHz Pentium-III computer with Solaris 7 (from 10 randomly generated starting points) for some typical DIMACS/SATLIB benchmark problems. Due to space limitation, we only present our results for a few representative instances in each class of problems.

Although quite simple, DLM-98-BASIC-SAT can find solutions within seconds to most satisfiable DIMACS benchmarks, such as all the problems in the *aim*, *ii*, *jnh*, *par8*, and *ssa* classes, and most problems in SATLIB, like uniform 3-SAT problems *uf*, flat graph coloring *flat*, and morphed graph coloring *sw* problems. DLM-98-BASIC-SAT is either faster than, or at least comparable to, competing algorithms like GSAT and Grasp (Shang & Wah 1998). However, it has difficulty in solving problems in the *par16-*, *hanoi-*, *g-*, *f2000-* and *par32-* classes.

DLM with Global Search for SAT

Traps were identified by (Wu & Wah 1999b; 1999a) as one of the major difficulties in applying DLM to solve hard SAT instances. A *trap* is a basin in the original variables, x, of a discrete Lagrangian space in which a flip of any variable inside the trap will only cause the Lagrangian value to increase. In other words, there is no viable descents in x space through a single flip, and the trajectory is stuck until enough changes are made to the Lagrangian multipliers. Since changing the Lagrange multipliers on unsatisfied clauses changes the terrain, a trap will disappear eventually when the multipliers of unsatisfied clauses are large enough. Traps degrade the performance of DLM because many cycles are spent in updating Lagrange multipliers gradually.

A trap-escaping strategy was proposed in (Wu & Wah 1999b; 1999a) to overcome the attraction of traps in DLM.

Table 1: Performance of DLM-98-SAT for solving some representative DIMACS/SATLIB SAT problems. All our experiments were run on a 500-MHz Pentium-III computer with Solaris 7. Among these benchmarks, the *aim*-class is on artificially generated random-3-SAT; the *ii*-class is from inductive inference; the *jnh*-class is on random SAT with variable-length clauses; the *par8*-class is for learning parity functions; the *ssa*-class is on circuit fault analysis; the *sw*-class is on "morphed" graph coloring (Gent et al. 1999); the *flat*-class is on "flat" graph coloring; the *uf*-class is on uniform random-3-SAT; the *ais*-class is on all-interval series; and the *logistics*-class is on logistics planning.

Problem ID	Succ Ratio	CPU Sec.	Num. of Flips
aim-200-1-6-yes1-4.cnf	10/10	0.06	29865
aim-200-2-0-yes1-4.cnf	10/10	0.33	129955
aim-200-3-4-yes1-4.cnf	10/10	0.53	98180
aim-200-6-0-yes1-4.cnf	10/10	0.02	632
ii32b4.cnf	10/10	0.12	6268
ii32c4.cnf	10/10	0.41	7506
ii32d3.cnf	10/10	0.33	8676
ii32e5.cnf	10/10	0.11	5083
jnh212.cnf	10/10	0.24	33197
jnh220.cnf	10/10	0.08	9918
jnh301.cnf	10/10	0.10	11039
par8-1.cnf	10/10	0.13	41810
par8-2.cnf	10/10	0.17	57521
par8-3.cnf	10/10	0.38	122311
par8-4.cnf	10/10	0.15	48256
par8-5.cnf	10/10	0.40	135212
ssa7552-038.cnf	10/10	0.13	16250
ssa7552-160.cnf	10/10	0.10	13742
sw100-1.cnf	10/10	0.62	117577
sw100-2.cnf	10/10	1.43	288571
sw100-3.cnf	10/10	0.97	192017
sw100-97.cnf	10/10	0.77	150486
sw100-98.cnf	10/10	1.46	295163
sw100-99.cnf	10/10	1.28	247702
sw100-100.cnf	10/10	0.47	89026
sw100-8-p0-c5.cnf	10/10	1.00	191275
flat100-1.cnf	10/10	0.36	108069
flat100-3.cnf	10/10	0.05	11072
flat100-5.cnf	10/10	0.09	23146
flat100-7.cnf	10/10	2.64	859110
flat100-9.cnf	10/10	0.06	16428
uf200-01.cnf	10/10	0.14	11810
uf200-03.cnf	10/10	0.07	1851
uf200-05.cnf	10/10	0.17	16162
uf200-07.cnf	10/10	0.13	12457
uf200-09.cnf	10/10	0.17	15005
ais10.cnf	10/10	0.23	18916
ais12.cnf	10/10	2.19	140294
ais6.cnf	10/10	0.01	416
ais8.cnf	10/10	0.07	7242
logistics-a.cnf	10/10	0.16	17427
logistics-b.cnf	10/10	0.16	18965
logistics-c.cnf	10/10	0.21	16870
logistics-d.cnf	10/10	1.65	48603

Its basic idea is to keep track of clauses appearing in traps and add extra penalties to those clauses by increasing their corresponding Lagrange multipliers. Although the strategy was tested to be very helpful in overcoming traps and in finding better solutions, it only corrects the search after it gets into the same trap repeatedly.

A more general way is to avoid visiting the same set of points visited in the past. This is done by measuring the distances in x space between the current point and points visited previously in the trajectory and by penalizing the search accordingly. This strategy leads to an efficient global-search method that addresses not only the repulsion of traps in x space but also the repulsion of points visited in the past.

The new discrete Lagrangian function, including the extra *distance_penalty* term, is defined as:

$$L_d(x, \lambda) = N(x) + \sum_{i=1}^{n} \lambda_i U_i(x) - distance\_penalty. \quad (10)$$

Distance_penalty is actually the sum of Hamming distances from the current point to some points visited in the past in the trajectory. Hence, if a trajectory is stuck in a trap, then the Hamming distances from the current point to points in the trap will be small, leading to a large penalty on the Lagrangian function (10). On the other hand, if the trajectory is not inside a trap, then the Hamming distance to points close to points visited before will still be large, thereby steering the trajectory away from regions visited before.

The exact form of *distance_penalty* is defined to be:

$$distance\_penalty = \sum_{i} \min(\theta_t, |x - x_i^s|), \quad (11)$$

where θ_t is a positive threshold, and $|x - x_i^s|$ is the Hamming distance between point x to a point x_i^s visited before by the trajectory.

θ_t is used to control the search and put a lower bound on *distance_penalty* so that it will not be a dominant factor in the new Lagrangian function. Without θ_t, the first-order search method will prefer a far-away point than a point with less constraint violation, which is not desirable. In our experiments, we set θ_t to be 2. This means that, when the Hamming distances between the current point and all the stored historical points of a trajectory is larger than 2, the impact of all the stored historical points on *distance_penalty* will be the same. Note that the fundamental concept of *distance_penalty* is similar to that of tabu search (Glover 1989).

Ideally, we like to store all the points traversed by a trajectory in the past. This is, however, impractical in terms of memory usage and computation overhead in calculating *DMPD* for the ever-increasing Lagrangian value. In our implementation, we keep a fixed-size queue of size q_s of historical points and periodically update this queue in a FIFO manner. The period of update is based on w_s flips; namely,

procedure *DLM-2000-SAT*
1. Reduce the original SAT instance;
2. Generate a random starting point using a fixed seed;
3. Initialize $\lambda_i \longleftarrow 0$;
4. **while** solution not found and time not used up **do**
5.   Pick $x_j \notin$ TabuList that reduces L_d the most;
6.   Flip x_j;
7.   **If** $\#_{Flips} \% w_s = 0$ **then**
8.   Update the queue on historical points **end_if**
9.   Maintain TabuList;
10.   **if** $\#_{FlatMoves} > \theta_1$ **then**
11. $\lambda_i \longleftarrow \lambda_i + \delta_o$;
12.   **if** $\#_{Adjust} \% \theta_2 = 0$ **then**
13. $\lambda_i \longleftarrow \lambda_i - \delta_d$; **end_if**;
14.   **end_if**
15. **end_while**
end

Figure 2: Procedures *DLM-2000-SAT*, an implementation of the discrete first-order method for solving SAT problems.

after w_s flips, we save the current search point in the queue and remove the oldest element from the queue.

DLM-2000-SAT

Figure 2 shows the algorithm of DLM-2000 for solving general SAT instances. In the following, we explain each line of the algorithm in detail, including the various parameters and their values. In general, we need a unique set of parameters for each class of problems in order to achieve the best performance. For the around 200 instances in the DIMACS and SATLIB benchmarks, we need only five different sets of parameters.

Line 1 performs some straightforward reductions on all clauses with a single variable. For all single-variable clauses, we set the value of that variable to make that clause satisfied and propagate the assignment. For example, if a clause has just one variable x_4, then x_4 must be true in the assignment of the solution. Reduction stops when there are no single-variable clauses.

Line 2 generates a random starting point using a fixed seed. Note that we use the long-period random-number generator of L'Ecuyer with Bays-Durham shuffle and added safeguards rather than the default generator provided in the C library in order to allow our results to be reproducible across different platforms.

Line 3 initializes λ_i (Lagrange multiplier for Clause i) to zero in order to make the experiments repeatable.

Line 4 is the main loop of our algorithm that stops when time (maximum number of flips) runs out or when a satisfiable assignment is found.

Line 5 chooses a variable x_j that will reduce L_d the most among all variables not in TabuList. If such a variable cannot be found, then it picks x_j that will not increase L_d. We call a flip a *flat move* (Selman, Kautz, & Cohen 1993) if it does not change L_d. We allow flat moves to help the trajectory explore flat regions.

Line 6 flips the x_j chosen (from false to true or vice versa). It also records the number of times the trajectory is doing flat moves.

Lines 7-8 maintain a queue on a fixed number of historical points. After a predefined number of flips, the algorithm stores the current search point in the queue and removes the oldest historical point. Note that this queue needs to be designed carefully in order to make the whole scheme efficient. In our experiments, we choose the queue size q_s to be in the range [4, 20].

Line 9 maintains TabuList. Similar to the queue for storing historical points, TabuList is also a FIFO queue. Each time a variable is flipped, it will be put in TabuList, and the oldest element will be removed from TabuList. TabuLists are important in helping a search explore flat regions effectively.

Lines 10-11 increase the Lagrange multipliers for all unsatisfied clauses by δ_o (= 1) when the number of flat moves exceeds a predefined threshold θ_1 (50 for f, 16 for $par16$, 36 for g, and 16 for $hanoi4$). Note that δ_o is the same as c_1 in (8). After increasing the Lagrange multipliers of all unsatisfied clauses, we increase counter $\#_{Adjust}$ by one.

Lines 12-13 reduce the Lagrange multipliers of all clauses by δ_d (= 1) when $\#_{Adjust}$ reaches threshold θ_2 (12 for f, 46 for $par16$, 7 for g, and 40 for $hanoi4$). These help change the relative weights of all the clauses and may allow the trajectory to visit another region in the search space after the reduction. They are critical to our global-search strategy because they help maintain the effect of *distance_penalty* in the Lagrangian function. Their purpose is to keep the weighted constraint functions, $\lambda^T h(x)$, in the Lagrangian definition to be in a suitable range, given that *distance_penalty* has a fixed range that can be computed from w_s and θ_t. Otherwise, when λ gets too large, *distance_penalty* will be relatively small and has no serious effect in avoiding regions visited before.

Compared to DLM-99-SAT (Wu & Wah 1999b; 1999a), our proposed algorithm is simpler and has less parameters to be tuned. Note that there is more overhead in searching for a suitable variable to flip (Line 5); that is, each flip will take more CPU time than a similar flip in DLM-99-SAT. However, the overall CPU time is actually much shorter for most benchmark problems tested because the new global-search strategy can avoid visiting the same regions more effectively.

Results on Some Hard SAT Instances

We first apply DLM-2000-SAT to solve some hard, satisfiable SAT instances in the DIMACS archive. DLM-2000-SAT can now solve quickly *f2000*, *par16-1-c* to *par16-5-c*, *par16-1* to *par16-5*, *hanoi4* and *hanoi4-simple* with 100% success ratio. For other simpler problems in the DIMACS archive, DLM-2000-SAT has similar performance as the best existing method developed in the past. Due to space limitation, we will not present the details of these experiments here.

Table 2 lists the experimental results on all the hard problems solved by DLM-2000-SAT, WalkSAT, GSAT, and DLM-99-SAT. It lists the CPU times of our implementation on a 500-MHz Pentium-III computer with Solaris 7, the numbers of (machine-independent) flips for our algorithm to find a feasible solution, the success ratios (from multiple randomly generated starting points), the success ratios (SR) and the CPU times of WalkSAT/GSAT, and in the last column, the adjusted CPU times of DLM-99-SAT. Note that our algorithm has 100% success ratio for all the benchmark instances tested.

Table 2 also lists the results of applying DLM-2000-SAT to solve the *g*-class problems that were not solved well by (Shang & Wah 1998). The number of flips used for solving these problems indicate that they are much easier than problems in the *par16* and *hanoi* classes.

Table 2: Comparison of performance of DLM-2000-SAT for solving some hard SAT instances and the *g*-class instances that were not solved before (Shang & Wah 1998). (All our experiments were run on a 500-MHz Pentium-III computer with Solaris 7. WalkSAT/GSAT experiments were run on an SGI Challenge with MPIS processor, model unknown. "NR" in the table stands for "not reported.")

Problem ID	Succ. Ratio	CPU Sec.	Num. of Flips	WalkSAT/GSAT SR	WalkSAT/GSAT Sec.	DLM-99-SAT Sec.
par16-1	10/10	101.7	$1.3 \cdot 10^7$	NR	NR	96.5
par16-2	10/10	154.0	$2.1 \cdot 10^7$	NR	NR	95.7
par16-3	10/10	76.3	$9.8 \cdot 10^6$	NR	NR	125.7
par16-4	10/10	83.7	$1.1 \cdot 10^7$	NR	NR	54.5
par16-5	10/10	121.9	$1.5 \cdot 10^7$	NR	NR	178.5
par16-1-c	10/10	20.8	2786081	NR	NR	28.8
par16-2-c	10/10	51.6	6824355	NR	NR	61.0
par16-3-c	10/10	27.5	3674644	NR	NR	35.3
par16-4-c	10/10	35.8	4825594	NR	NR	46.1
par16-5-c	10/10	32.4	4264095	NR	NR	44.6
f600	10/10	0.80	73753	NR	35*	0.664
f1000	10/10	3.21	285024	NR	1095*	3.7
f2000	10/10	19.2	1102816	NR	3255*	16.2
hanoi4	10/10	6515	$6.3 \cdot 10^8$	NR	NR	14744
hanoi4$_s$	10/10	9040	$1.1 \cdot 10^9$	NR	NR	14236
g125-17	10/10	41.4	434183	7/10**	264**	144.8
g125-18	10/10	4.8	22018	10/10**	1.9**	3.98
g250-15	10/10	17.7	2437	10/10**	4.41**	12.9
g250-29	10/10	193.1	289962	9/10**	1219**	331.4
anomaly	10/10	0.00	259	NR	NR	NR
medium	10/10	0.02	1537	NR	NR	NR
huge	10/10	0.19	10320	NR	NR	NR
bw-large-a	10/10	0.10	6176	0.3***	NR	NR
bw-large-b	10/10	1.55	67946	22***	NR	1.9
bw-large-c	10/10	72.36	1375437	670***	NR	292.2
bw-large-d	10/10	146.28	1112332	937***	NR	2390

*: Results from (Selman, Kautz, & Cohen 1993) for similar but not the same problems in the DIMACS archive
**: Results from (Selman 1995)
***: Results from (Kautz & Selman 1996)

Table 3: Comparison of performance of DLM-2000-SAT with *LSDL* (Choi, Lee, & Stuckey 1998) for solving some hard graph coloring problems. The timing results of *LSDL* were collected from a SUN Sparc classic, model unknown.

Problem ID	Succ. Ratio	CPU Sec.	Num. of Flips	*LSDL* GENET	*LSDL* MAX
g125-17	10/10	41.4	434183	282.0*	192.0*
g125-18	10/10	4.8	22018	4.5	1.1
g250-15	10/10	17.7	2437	0.418	0.328
g250-29	10/10	193.1	289962	876.0*	678.0*

*: Calculated from CPU times reported in minutes (Choi, Lee, & Stuckey 1998).

Table 4: Comparison of performance of DLM-2000-SAT with GRASP (Marques-Silva & Sakalla 1999) on some typical DIMACS benchmarks. The timing results of GRASP were collected from a SUN SPARC 5/85 computer. '-' stands for 'not solved'.

Problem Class	Succ. Ratio	CPU Sec.	Num. of Flips	GRASP Sec.
f-	10/10	7.7*	487198*	-
g-	10/10	64.3*	187150*	-
par8-	10/10	0.25**	81022**	0.4
par16-	10/10	108*	$1.4 \cdot 10^{7*}$	9844
hanoi-	10/10	7778*	$8.7 \cdot 10^{8*}$	14480

*: Averages computed using values in Table 2
**: Averages computed using values in Table 1

Table 3 compares our algorithm with a typical heuristic-repair method, *LSDL* (Choi, Lee, & Stuckey 1998), on hard graph coloring problems. Our algorithm outperforms *LSDL* on g125-17 and g250-29 by using 60% less CPU time. The reason that it uses more time to solve g125-18 and g250-15 is due to the complexity of maintaining a queue of historical points. Hence, for very simple problems, there is no apparent advantage of using our proposed global-search strategy.

Table 4 compares our method to a well-known backtracking and search-pruning algorithm (Marques-Silva & Sakalla 1999). Since this is a complete method that can prove unsatisfiability, it performs much slower than our proposed global-search method.

References

Choi, K.; Lee, J.; and Stuckey, P. 1998. A Lagrangian reconstruction of a class of local search methods. *Proc. 10th IEEE Int'l Conf. on Tools with Artificial Intelligence* 166–175.

Davis, M., and Putnam, H. 1960. A computing procedure for quantification theory. *J. Assoc. Comput. Mach.* 7:201–215.

Folino, G.; Pizzuti, C.; and Spezzano, G. 1998. Combining cellular genetic algorithms and local search for solving satisfiability problems. *Proc. Tenth IEEE Int'l Conf. on Tools with Artificial Intelligence* 192–198.

Frank, J. 1997. Learning short-term weights for GSAT. *Proc. 15'th Int'l Joint Conf. on AI* 384–391.

Genesereth, M. R., and Nilsson, N. J. 1987. *Logical Foundation of Artificial Intelligence*. Morgan Kaufmann.

Gent, I. P.; Hoos, H. H.; Prosser, P.; and Walsh, T. 1999. Morphing: Combining structure and randomness. *Proc. Sixteenth National Conf. on Artificial Intelligence* 654–660.

Glover, F. 1989. Tabu search — Part I. *ORSA J. Computing* 1(3):190–206.

Gu, J. 1993. Local search for satisfiability (SAT) problems. *IEEE Trans. on Systems, Man, and Cybernetics* 23(4):1108–1129.

Kautz, H., and Selman, B. 1996. Pushing the envelope: Planning, propositional logic, and stochastic search. *Proc. the AAAI National Conf. on AI* 1194–1201.

Marques-Silva, J. P., and Sakalla, K. A. 1999. Grasp: A search algorithm for propositional satisfiability. *IEEE Trans. on Computers* 48(5):506–521.

Morris, P. 1993. The breakout method for escaping from local minima. In *Proc. of 11th National Conf. on Artificial Intelligence*, 40–45.

Purdom, P. W. 1983. Search rearrangement backtracking and polynomial average time. *Artificial Intelligence* 21:117–133.

Selman, B.; Kautz, H.; and Cohen, B. 1993. Local search strategies for satisfiability testing. In *Proc. of 2nd DIMACS Challenge Workshop on Cliques, Coloring, and Satisfiability, Rutgers University*, 290–295.

Selman, B.; Kautz, H.; and Cohen, B. 1994. Noise strategies for improving local search. In *Proc. of 12th National Conf. on Artificial Intelligence*, 337–343.

Selman, B. 1995. Private communcation.

Shang, Y., and Wah, B. W. 1998. A discrete Lagrangian based global search method for solving satisfiability problems. *J. of Global Optimization* 12(1):61–99.

Sosič, R., and Gu, J. 1994. Efficient local search with conflict minimization: A case study of the n-queens problem. *IEEE Trans. on Knowledge and Data Engineering* 6(5):661–668.

Wah, B. W., and Wu, Z. 1999. The theory of discrete Lagrange multipliers for nonlinear discrete optimization. *Principles and Practice of Constraint Programming* 28–42.

Wu, Z., and Wah, B. W. 1999a. Solving hard satisfiability problems: A unified algorithm based on discrete Lagrange multipliers. In *Proc. Int'l Conf. on Tools with Artificial Intelligence*, 210–217. IEEE.

Wu, Z., and Wah, B. W. 1999b. Solving hard satisfiability problems using the discrete Lagrange-multiplier method. In *Proc. 1999 National Conference on Artificial Intelligence*, 673–678. AAAI.

Wu, Z. 1998. *Discrete Lagrangian Methods for Solving Nonlinear Discrete Constrained Optimization Problems*. Urbana, IL: M.Sc. Thesis, Dept. of Computer Science, Univ. of Illinois.

Assessing Relevance With Extensionally Defined Principles and Cases

Bruce M. McLaren and Kevin D. Ashley

Graduate Program In Intelligent Systems
University of Pittsburgh Learning Research and Development Center
3939 O'Hara Street
Pittsburgh, Pennsylvania 15260
bmclaren+@pitt.edu, ashley+@pitt.edu

Abstract

Expert decision-makers often explain decisions by citing general principles. In some domains, however, it is nearly impossible to define principles intensionally so that they may be applied deductively. After investigating hundreds of professional ethics case opinions, we hypothesized that the decision-makers' explanations *extensionally* defined principles over time, in effect, *operationalizing* them. To model this phenomenon computationally, we constructed SIROCCO, a system for retrieving principles and past cases. This paper presents empirical evidence that operationalization information can be leveraged to predict relevant principles and past cases more accurately than competing approaches that do not use such information.

Introduction

General principles are useful for guiding and explaining decisions. For instance, in classic work designed to make MYCIN's rule-tracing explanations more comprehensible, Clancey recommended explaining a heuristic rule's role in terms of explicit principles of good diagnostic strategy. Such principles included general rules like "if there is evidence for two hypotheses that tend to be confused, try to rule out the second." (Clancey 1983, p. 226).

Since principles are rule-like, one might think that they can be applied deductively. In domains like professional ethics, law, and policy-making, however, often there are no ready sources of authoritative intermediate-level rules for deducing how the abstract principles apply to realistic scenarios. Also, multiple abstract principles may appear to apply equally well but recommend conflicting advice.

In the abstract, everyone may agree with general principles like, "Engineers shall ... recognize that their primary obligation is to protect the safety, health, and welfare of the public."[1] Or "Engineers shall act in professional matters for each employer or client as faithful agents or trustees."[2] Agreement is difficult, however, when one considers how to apply and reconcile such principles in real-world situations (Jonsen and Toulmin, 1988). Since the general principles are open-textured, experts cannot write intermediate-level rules to cover all possible conditions to which the principles apply. Even their consequents are abstract (e.g., what exactly does it mean to be a "faithful agent"?). Also, an ethicist's rules for interpreting general principles may not be authoritative; ethicists have no special imprimatur to legislate right and wrong.

While efforts to define such general principles intensionally are thus bound to fail, we hypothesized that as ethicists explain their decisions by applying and resolving general principles, their explanations *extensionally* define those principles. In effect, they *operationalize* the general principles (Mostow 1983). We believed, moreover, that a computational model could take advantage of these operationalizations, if not to reason about novel ethical problems, then at least to predict which principles and past cases are relevant for analyzing novel problems.

We investigated a body of ethics case opinions issued from 1958-1998 by the National Society of Professional Engineers' Board of Ethical Review (NSPE BER) and now published on the Internet (http://www.niee.org/cases/). Reconstituted annually with a new set of five to seven professional engineers, the BER has written extensive explanations of its decisions in more than 400 cases. In justifying its decisions, the Board applied the Society's published Code of Ethics comprising 75 general principles including the two mentioned above.

We focused particularly on how the BER cited Ethics Code provisions and past cases in its justifications, and identified nine ways in which the BER operationalized the code provisions and past cases. SIROCCO (System for Intelligent Retrieval of Operationalized Cases and COdes) computationally models the operationalization techniques for the purpose of retrieving relevant code provisions and pasts cases. As described more fully in (McLaren 1999), key aspects of the model are: an ontology, including an Ethics Transcription Language (ETL) for representing the facts of engineering scenarios as narratives of chronologically ordered events, and extensions (EETL) for representing aspects of the Board's arguments for and against its conclusions, a web-based case acquisition tool, and a case base of 184 foundational cases. To input a target case, a human case enterer must encode the facts of the case into ETL using the acquisition tool. For source cases

---

Copyright © 2000, American Association for Artificial Intelligence (www.aaai.org). All rights reserved.

[1] NSPE Code II.1.A. The code provision continues: "If their professional judgment is overruled under circumstances where the safety, health, property or welfare of the public are endangered, they shall notify their employer or client and such other authority as may be appropriate."
[2] NSPE Code I.4

in the case base, case enterers must also have encoded the Board's analysis into EETL.

Using the model, we tested two hypotheses:
(1) whether a core subset of five operationalization techniques enables SIROCCO to make accurate predictions of the principles and past cases that are likely to be important in the analysis of new cases,
(2) whether SIROCCO's temporal knowledge contributes to the accuracy of its predictions.

This work extends interpretive CBR techniques (Kolodner 1993) from the legal domain (Ashley, 1990; Branting, 1991; Rissland *et al.*, 1996; Aleven, 1997) to a new domain. Arguments in practical ethics are more free-form in style and structure than legal arguments. Ethics cases do not have binary outcomes (e.g., plaintiff wins or loses) but may require "creative middle way" solutions (Harris *et al.*, 1999, p. 64-72). SIROCCO contributes a detailed, narrative case representation, including temporal relations among facts, and an extensional model of how general principles and cases accrue meanings through operationalization. It can retrieve cases over a wider range of factual scenarios than the AI&Law programs, but unlike those programs it is not able to make arguments.

Overview of SIROCCO

SIROCCO accepts a target case expressed in ETL and produces suggestions about relevant code provisions and past cases. A sample target case in ETL is shown in Figure 1; it deals with an engineer who has discovered structural defects in an apartment building but has been told he must keep that information confidential. SIROCCO's output for that case is shown in Figure 2, at the top of which is a textual description of the case facts. Notice that SIROCCO identifies the two general principles introduced above (i.e., NSPE Codes II.1.A and I.4) as possibly relevant and even suggests a relevantly similar case 76-1-4, in which the BER concluded the former code provision overrode the latter.

Ethics Transcription Language

Like SWALE (Leake, 1991), SIROCCO represents ethics cases as narratives, expressed in a limited language. As shown in Figure 1, ETL represents the actions and events of a scenario as an ordered list (i.e., a *Fact Chronology*) of individual sentences (i.e., *Facts*), each consisting of (1) *Actors and objects*, instances of general actors and objects which appear in the scenario, (2) a *Fact Primitive*, the action or event in which the actors and objects participated, and (3) a *Time Qualifier,* a temporal relation that specifies how a Fact relates to other Facts in time. At least one Fact in the Fact Chronology is designated as a *Questioned Fact*; this is an action or event corresponding to an ethical question raised in the scenario. If an NSPE BER case raises more than one Questioned Fact in the context of the same Fact Chronology, it generates one SIROCCO case for each Questioned Fact.

Extracts of the ETL grammar are shown in Figure 3. The Fact Primitive in each Fact Phrase is a verb phrase that indicates a specific action or event involving actors, objects, or similarly constituted Fact-Phrases.

Time Qualifiers are disjunctive compositions of Allen's temporal constraints (1983). Since the case enterer does not provide temporal relationships among *all* Facts in a chronology, SIROCCO uses TIMELOGIC (Koomen 1989), a time propagation system, to compute the relationships by forward-chaining over the Allen relations.

1. Apartment Building **<may be hazardous to safety>**....	Pre-existing fact
4. Residents **<file a lawsuit or arbitration action against>** Bldg. Owner **<because>** (Apt. Bldg. **<may be hazardous to safety>**)....	Occurs during 3
6. Owner's Attorney **<hires the services of>** Engineer A **<for>** (Engineer A **<inspects>** Apt. Bldg.)....	Occurs during 4, 5
8. Engineer A **<discovers that>** (Apt. Bldg. **<fails standards and may be hazardous to safety.>**)	Occurs during 7
9. Engineer A **<knows>** (Government Authority **<should be informed about the hazard or potential hazard>**).	Occurs during 8
10. Engineer A **<informs>** Owner's Attorney **<that>** (Apt. Bldg. **<fails standards and may be hazardous to safety.>**)	Immediately after conclusion of 8
11. Owner's Attorney **<instructs>** Engineer A **<to>** (Engineer A **<withholds information from>** Anyone Else **<regarding>** Apt. Bldg.).	After conclusion of 10
12. Engineer A **<does not inform>** Anyone Else **<that>** (Apt. Bldg. **<fails standards and may be hazardous to safety.>**) *[Questioned fact]*	After conclusion of 11

Figure 1: Excerpts of Sample Target Case (Case 90-5-1)

Cases stored in SIROCCO's case base are represented in the *Extended* ETL (EETL), which adds a template and standard components for representing the BER's analysis of a case. The template includes the BER's conclusion (i.e., ethical, unethical, or undecided), the protagonist whose action is questioned, the ethical review Board's general argument structure, and specific information about each code provision or past case cited in support of its conclusion or noted as conflicting. When entering Case 90-5-1, the case enterer filled in the information shown in Figure 4 regarding how Code II.1.a applies (*see* note 1.)

The ontology comprises the ETL grammar (Figure 3), valid attribute values of an EETL template, and two abstraction hierarchies (not shown): (1) an *Action/Event Hierarchy* which clusters and generalizes similar Fact Primitives, (2) a *Code Hierarchy* which clusters codes dealing with similar issues. The hierarchies help define inexact matching of cases and codes, respectively.

> *** **SIROCCO is analyzing Case 90-5-1**
> **Facts:** Tenants of an apartment building sue the owner to force him to repair many defects in the building that affect the quality of use. The owner's attorney hires Engineer A to inspect the building and give expert testimony in support of the owner. Engineer A discovers serious structural defects in the building, which he believes constitute an immediate threat to the safety of the tenants. The tenants' suit has not mentioned these safety-related defects. Upon reporting the findings to the attorney, Engineer A is told he must maintain this information as confidential as it is part of a lawsuit. Engineer A complies with the request of the attorney.
>
> **Question:** Was it ethical for Engineer A to conceal his knowledge of the safety-related defects in view of the fact that it was an attorney who told him he was legally bound to maintain confidentiality?
>
> *** **SIROCCO['s]…suggestions for evaluating 90-5-1:**
> *** *Possibly Relevant Codes:*
> I-4: Act as a Faithful Agent or Trustee
> III-4: Do not Disclose Confidential Info. Without Consent
> I-1: Safety, Health, and Welfare of Public is Paramount
> II-1-A: Primary Obligation is to Protect Public (Notify Authority if Judgment is Overruled). …
> II-1-C: Do not Reveal Confidential Info. Without Consent
> III-2-B: Do not Complete or Sign Documents that are not Safe for Public …
>
> *** *Possibly Relevant Cases:*
> 76-4-1: Public Welfare - Knowledge of Information Damaging to Client's Interest
> 89-7-1: Duty To Report Safety Violations
> 84-5-1: Engineer's Recommendation For Full-Time, On-Site Project Representative
>
> *** *Additional Suggestions:*
> o The codes II-1-A … and I-1 … may override codes III-4 …, I-4…, and III-1 … in this case. See case 76-4-1 for an example of this type of code conflict and resolution.…

Figure 2: Output for Target Problem (Case 90-5-1) (excerpts)

SIROCCO's case base includes a subset of the NSPE BER cases analyzed during the empirical study: 184 foundational cases, covering 135 different Fact Chronologies and culled from the 475 cases decided by the BER between 1958 and 1992.

The foundational cases were used to design, implement, and refine the program. These cases completely cover a reasonable number of important ethics topics (i.e., the Selected Topics) and provide some (minimal) coverage of other topics (the Non-Selected Topics.) The Selected Topics include: public safety, confidential information, duty to employer, credit for engineering work, proprietary interests, and honesty in reports and public statements.

Each topic is associated with one or more of the NSPE BER ethics code provisions, all of which are represented in SIROCCO. Of the foundational cases, 135 cite at least one code related to at least one of the Selected Topics. The other 49 do not cite any of the Selected Topics codes. The cases are spread reasonably widely across the topics and tend to cite different sets of codes.

> <Fact-Chronology> := <Fact> [<Fact> …]
> <Fact> := <Fact-#> <Fact-Phrase> [(Questioned Fact <X>)]
>   <Time-Qualifier> [,<Time-Qualifier>, …]
> <Fact-Phrase> := <Fact-Primitive> [<Fact-Modifier>]
>   <Actor-Or-Object>
>   [<Actor-Or-Object> | (<Fact-Phrase>)]
>   [<Actor-Or-Object> | (<Fact-Phrase>)]
> <Fact-Primitive> := *An instance of a Fact-Primitive*
> <Actor-Or-Object> := *An instance of an Actor or an Object*
> < Fact-Modifier> :=   partially | substantially | limited | extensive
> <Time-Qualifier> :=
>   Pre-existing fact |
>   After the start of <Fact-#> [, <Fact-#>, …] |
>   Starts at the same time as <Fact-#> [, <Fact-#>, …] |
>   After the conclusion of <Fact-#> [, <Fact-#>, …] |
>   Immediately after the conclusion of <Fact-#>
>   [, <Fact-#>, …] |
>   Ends <Fact-#> [, <Fact-#>, …] |
>   Occurs during <Fact-#> [, <Fact-#>, …] | …
> **Key:** | = Alternative; [ ] = Optional; < > = Grammar element

Figure 3: ETL Grammar Extracts

Code	II.1.a
Code Status	Violated
How Cited	Explicitly discussed
Grouped With	None
Overrides	II.1.c
Why relevant	Engineer's judgment is overruled in a particular professional circumstance. [11] Overruling the Engineer's judgment may lead to the endangerment of the safety, health, property or welfare of the public. [8, 9]
Why violated, not violated,…	In the given situation, Engineer does not hold paramount the safety, health, property, and welfare of the public. [12]

Figure 4: EETL Table for Code II.1.a in Case 90-5-1

Twelve independent case enterers transcribed the foundational cases into EETL using the case-acquisition web site (www.pitt.edu/~bmclaren/ethics). The web site contains instructions on how to transcribe ethics cases into EETL, a reference shelf of useful materials, including the full vocabulary of EETL, and an example set of 47 transcribed Fact Chronologies.

Operationalizations

As noted, our investigation of the BER's case explanations revealed nine operationalization techniques:

1. Instantiating principles by linking them to clusters of questioned and critical facts.
2. Hypothesizing facts that affect how principles apply.
3. Revising a principle over time.
4. Arbitrating between competing principles.
5. Grouping principles.
6. Instantiating cases as precedents by linking them to clusters of questioned and critical facts, and by analogizing or distinguishing them.
7. Applying, defining or elaborating issues and principles from past cases.
8. Grouping cases.
9. Reusing specific applications of any of the above techniques from previous analyses.

Our experiment tested the contributions of a core subset, those techniques which contribute directly to suggesting relevant cases and codes (i.e., techniques 1, 5, 6, 8, and 9). The remaining techniques focus on providing explanations.

Code and case instantiations (i.e., techniques 1 and 6) are the primary operationalization techniques by which codes and cases become defined extensionally in a way that SIROCCO can reuse in analyzing new cases. Instantiating a code or past case means relating a questioned fact, certain critical facts, and the temporal sequence of those facts in the citing case to the cited code provision or case. Case enterers recorded information instantiating codes or past cases, grouping them or reusing previous operationalizations in the EETL tables such as that in Figure 4. The numbers in brackets [ ] in the last two rows of Figure 4 refer to those facts in the representation of Case 90-5-1 (Figure 1) that are critical to the code's application and explain why it was [not] violated. In this way, Code II.1.a is connected extensionally to a real case's relevant facts and chronology in a way that SIROCCO can reuse.

The NSPE BER's groupings of principles (i.e., code provisions) and cases in arguments (operationalization techniques 5 and 8) inform SIROCCO's selection heuristics as do the Board's reuse of past operationalizations (technique 9) (e.g., the case and code instantiations in a cited case can be reused.)

SIROCCO's Two-Stage Retrieval Process

Following the general approach in designing analogical retrieval programs (Forbus et al. 1994; Thagard et al. 1990), SIROCCO's retrieval phase is implemented as a two-stage algorithm, as shown in Figure 1. Stage 1 rapidly matches the target case's Fact Primitives to those of all possible source cases. Stage 2 applies a more-expensive A* search to map selected case structures between target and source cases.

In both stages, instantiations (i.e., operationalization techniques 1 and 6, above) help SIROCCO focus attention on the most critical facts. Stage 1's accuracy improves by giving more weight to the instantiations' Fact Primitives. In Stage 2 focusing on only the part of a source case's Fact Chronology in an instantiation makes the structural mapping routine more efficient and accurate.

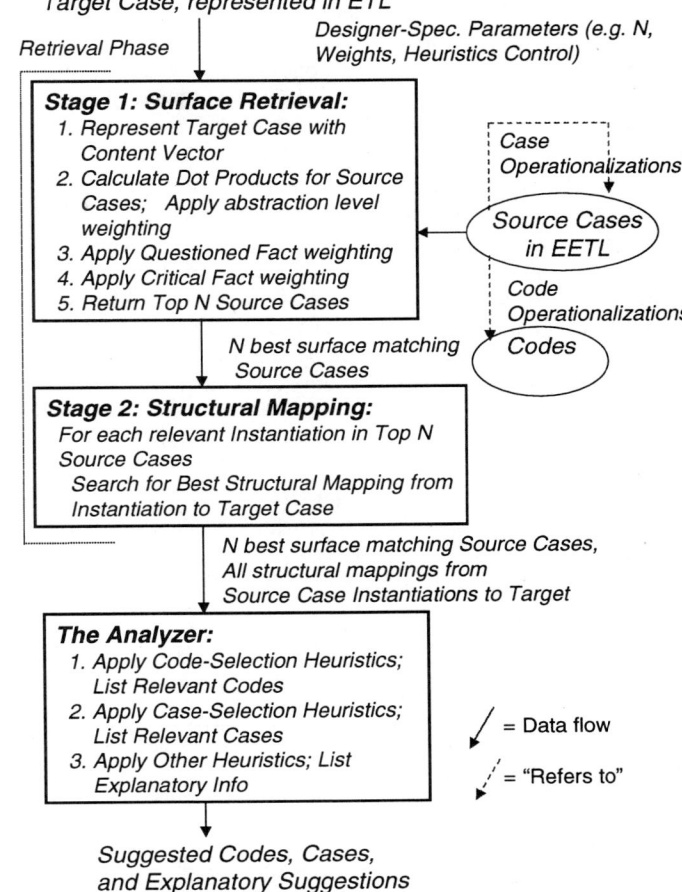

Figure 5: SIROCCO's Architecture

For Stage 1, the target case and all of the cases in the case base are represented as content vectors (Forbus et al. 1994). Each vector summarizes the Fact Chronology of a single case. It specifies the Fact Primitives, and their corresponding abstractions in the Action/Event Hierarchy, and a count of how many times each appears. Figure 6 shows two content vectors for Case 90-5-1. The left (Fact-Primitive) is the most specific; the right (Fact-Group) is one level higher in the Action/Event Hierarchy.

Stage 1 computes the weighted dot products of content vectors for the target case and all cases in the case base. It outputs a list of candidate cases ranked by descending dot product scores. Different weights have been assigned to matches at the four abstraction levels (e.g., Fact-Primitive matches may be weighted twice as highly as more abstract Fact-Group matches.) Higher weights are also assigned to matches of a source case's critical and questioned facts.

Using a heuristic A* search, Stage 2 attempts a structural mapping between the target case and each of the N top-ranking candidate source cases from Stage 1. (Branting 1991) first used A* search for case structure mapping; SIROCCO also takes temporal relations into account, supports abstract matches, and accommodates a wider range of scenarios. The search focuses on matching the source case's instantiations (i.e., operationalization techniques 1 and 6). The goal is to map each of the Facts of the source instantiation to a corresponding Fact in the target case while maintaining a one-to-one and consistent mapping between the Actors and Objects of the source and the target. The initial node of the search space maps the source's questioned Actor to the target's. Each subsequent node represents: (1) a proposed mapping of a pair of Facts, one from the source instantiation and one from the target case, (2) all of the Fact mappings that preceded this node (i.e., all of the successful Fact mappings from ancestor nodes), (3) a one-to-one, consistent set of Actors and Objects entailed by the Fact mappings, and (4) consistent temporal relations between mapped Facts of the source and target. Temporal relations are consistent if the Allen relations of every pair of source Facts intersect with the Allen relations of the corresponding pair of target Facts.

Fact-Primitive-CV:	Fact-Group-CV:
(May-be-Hazardous-to-Safety 1)	(Deal-with-Potential-Dangers-or-Hazards 1)
(Owns 1)	(Own-Something 1)
(Resides-in 1)	(Specify-Location-of-Residence 1)
(Files-a-Lawsuit-or-Arbitration- Action-Against 1)	(Initiate-Legal-or-Arbitration-Proceedings 1)
(Is-Legally-Represented-by 1)	(Has-Legal-Representation 1)
(Hires-the-Services-of 1)	(Work-as-an-Employed-or-Contract-Professional-Engineer 1)
(Inspects 1)	(Perform-Engineering-Analysis-Review-or-Testing-Work 1)
(Discovers-That 1) (Knows 1)	(Know-or-Believe-Something 2)
(Informs-That 2) ***	(Disclose-Information 2) ***
(Instructs-to 1)	(Order-Subordinate-to-Perform-Task 1)

Figure 6: Content Vectors for Case 90-5-1

New nodes are generated from an existing node by selecting an unmapped Fact from the source case instantiation and mapping it to each of the target's unmapped Facts in which the corresponding Fact Primitives match either exactly or abstractly. An "empty" node is generated at each ply to represent the possibility of no match between the current source Fact and any target Facts. In this way, a search path may be extended that contains a current failed match, but subsequent successful matches.

Each node is evaluated in terms of the A* cost function, $f(n) = g(n) + h'(n)$, which is calculated as follows. The mismatch cost $g(n)$ is a summation of the degree of mismatch at each node up to and including n, divided by the current depth. The default mismatch costs (as match levels increase in abstraction in the Action/Event Hierarchy) are: 0.0 for an exact Fact Primitive match, 0.4 for a match at the Fact Group level, 0.6 for a match at the Sibling Group level, 0.9 for a Fact Root level match and 1.0 for a completely failed match.

The $h'(n)$ function evaluates the most optimistic possible completion of the mapping from node n. It provides the mismatch cost that would be attained by achieving an exact match (i.e., adding 0) at each node from n until the goal node is reached. It is calculated by dividing the summed degree of mismatch up to node n by the solution depth. The solution depth is always fixed to be the number of Facts in the instantiation (as noted, even if a Fact does not match, an "empty" match node is created.) SIROCCO always returns the minimum $f(n)$ found at the fixed solution depth.

The goal node is reached when the current depth equals the pre-defined solution depth and either the current node has the lowest mismatch score of all open nodes, as defined by the A* cost function, or the list of nodes is empty.

Upon completing Stage 2, SIROCCO's Analyzer phase assesses the results of Stages 1 and 2 and lists suggested codes, cases and provides some additional explanatory information (as in Figure 2). A set of selection heuristics that embody Operationalization Techniques 1, 5, 6, 8 and 9 generate the lists of possibly relevant codes and cases. The heuristics favor codes that, for example, (1) occur more frequently in the top-ranked cases of Stage 1 or (2) have code instantiations with a low Stage 2 mismatch score and at least a minimum number of matches to the source's critical facts. Similar heuristics are used to select cases. Other heuristics embody the remaining Operationalization Techniques and generate explanatory information.

Evaluation

A series of experiments were performed with SIROCCO to test the two hypotheses. The data included the 184 foundational cases and a set of 58 trial cases that were decided later than the foundational cases. All of the trial cases were transcribed into the extended ETL by two independent case enterers and, to ensure objectivity, were provided unaltered to SIROCCO for processing. The 58 trial cases were chosen from two pools of cases within a set of 77 cases decided by the NSPE BER between 1993 and 1998: 44 trial cases were chosen at random from 52 Selected Topics cases and 14 trial cases were chosen at random from 25 Non-Selected Topics cases.

To test the first hypothesis, SIROCCO was pitted against five competitor methods, shown in Figure 7. Each method, including SIROCCO, was given the entire set of trial cases to process one-by-one, and the retrieval results of each method were then compared to the BER's code and case citations for the same case. To calculate overlap between the method's solution and the Board's solution, we employed the *F-measure*, an information retrieval metric that combines precision P and recall R: $F = (\beta^2 +1)PR / (\beta^2 P+R)$ (Lewis et al., 1996). The value of β was 1.0. Two F-Measure values were computed for each case, one representing exact matches of codes and cases between the method's solution and the Board's and one representing inexact matches. Inexact matches of codes were determined using the Code Hierarchy. Inexact matches of cases were determined using a citation overlap metric, inversely related to the shortest citation path between two cases. For instance, if a case directly cites another, the overlap is 1/1. If two cases share a citation to a third case, the overlap is 1/2 (McLaren and Ashley 1999).

RANDOM: Codes/cases randomly selected for each case.

INFORMED-RANDOM: Like RANDOM but accounts for frequency distribution of code/case citations in NSPE corpus.

MG (Managing Gigabytes): Full-text retrieval method converts ethics case into term vector and compares to codes/cases vectors.

EXTENDED-MG: Like MG, but codes selected according to frequency of citation in the top X selected cases.

NON-OP SIROCCO: Ablated version of SIROCCO, with almost no functionality related to operationalizations.

Figure 7: Five Methods Compared to SIROCCO

The results are shown in Figure 8. Since the data generated by benchmarking each method against the BER's citations using the F-Measure was highly non-Gaussian, we applied a *nonparametric bootstrap procedure* (Davison and Hinkley 1997) to compare SIROCCO with the other methods. According to the procedure, the probability that SIROCCO was more accurate than the other five methods was greater than 95% in every instance except with respect to EXTENDED-MG on the inexact matching. There the probability was 94.3%, just below the threshold of statistical significance. In other words, SIROCCO was significantly more accurate than EXTENDED-MG in retrieving *exact* codes and cases. It was also more accurate in retrieving *inexact* codes and cases, but the difference was not statistically significant.

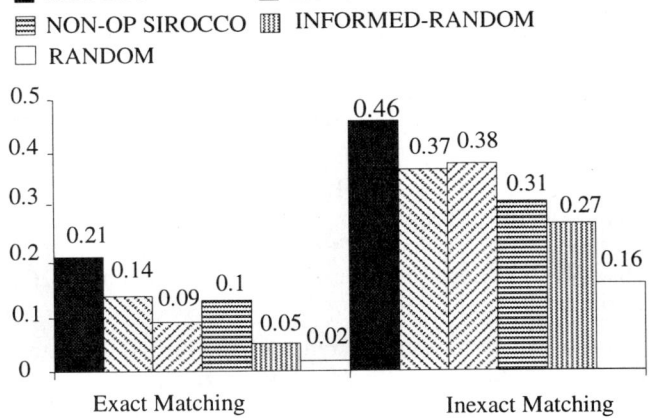

Figure 8: Mean F-Measures For All Methods Over All Trial Cases

The above experiment penalized SIROCCO for citing relevant codes and cases that the BER happened not to have cited. In a supplemental experiment, we asked two ethics graduate students to evaluate the extra code and case citations for the trial cases made by SIROCCO and SIROCCO's closest competitor, EXTENDED-MG. For each additional code and case suggested by the two methods, the evaluators were asked to indicate, whether the extra suggestion was reasonable or not.

After verifying that inter-rater reliability was satisfactory, we recalculated SIROCCO's and EXTENDED-MG's F-Measures for the 58 trial cases, counting the extra citations rated as "reasonable" by the evaluators as Board citations. For SIROCCO, the recalculated mean F-Measures were 0.36 for exact matching and 0.58 for inexact matching. For EXTENDED-MG, the recalculated mean F-Measures were 0.25 for exact matching and 0.46 for inexact matching. The nonparametric bootstrap procedure now showed a significant difference between the accuracy of SIROCCO and EXTENDED-MG on both the exact and inexact match criteria. For both criteria, the confidence level of a difference (in favor of SIROCCO) was now at least 99%.

We compared SIROCCO's predictive capability for cases within and outside the Selected Topics. Outside its primary area of expertise, SIROCCO's predictive capability degraded slightly. The differences between the mean F-measures for Selected Topics trial cases and Non-Selected Topics trial cases were: 0.23 - 0.15 = 0.08 on exact matching, and 0.47 - 0.44 = 0.03 on inexact matching.

To test the second hypothesis (i.e., that SIROCCO's temporal knowledge makes a difference in the accuracy of its predictions) the trial cases were processed by an ablated version of the program, NON-TEMP SIROCCO, that did not employ temporal knowledge. NON-TEMP SIROCCO provides the full functionality of SIROCCO with the exception that it doesn't check the consistency of temporal relations across matched cases. As with the initial experiments, the results of NON-TEMP SIROCCO were compared against the suggestions made by the ethical review Board and the F-Measure calculated for each individual sample and as a mean value over all samples. These results were then compared to the output of the standard version of SIROCCO, which did apply temporal knowledge. The differences between SIROCCO with and without its temporal knowledge were essentially negligible.

Discussion and Conclusion

The experiments confirmed that the core operationalization techniques allow SIROCCO to make accurate predictions of the principles and past cases that are likely to be relevant in the analysis of new cases. This is evidence that the BER's explanations extensionally define applicability conditions for the code provisions and past cases.

The fact that SIROCCO significantly outperformed NON-OP SIROCCO is the strongest evidence that SIROCCO's operationalization techniques do, in fact, make a difference. SIROCCO and NON-OP SIROCCO share the same case representation and Stage 1 retrieval method.

The critical difference is their use of the operationalization techniques. NON-OP SIROCCO makes only weak use of an operationalization technique. Like EXTENDED-MG, it selects codes that appear most frequently in the list of N top-rated cases. By contrast, SIROCCO makes extensive use of the core operationalization techniques in performing its retrieval task.

Outperforming MG and EXTENDED-MG shows that SIROCCO is a powerful retrieval method. These full-text retrieval methods are strongly competitive alternatives for performing SIROCCO's task. The fact that SIROCCO outperformed EXTENDED-MG which, in turn, outperformed MG is also significant. Since EXTENDED-MG makes use of an operationalization technique, its improvement over MG also supports our first hypothesis.

We were unable to show that SIROCCO's temporal knowledge contributed to its accuracy. This result surprised us. Intuitively, temporal orderings of events are important in ethical analysis. For instance, one can be expected to report a dangerous situation only after one has learned of it, not before. Then it occurred to us that the latter case would not appear in the NSPE BER cases because it so obviously does not involve a moral duty. In such a case base it might be a rare event that pairs of cases exist such that a difference in temporal ordering leads to different ethical interpretations.

This work suggests how to design intelligent aids for retrieving principles and cases in fields like professional ethics where intelligent access to the right standards and examples may lead to better decision-making. SIROCCO performs significantly better than a full-text retrieval method, providing clear evidence of the value of its case representation. Of course, it takes much more time and effort to represent a problem situation as a Fact Chronology for SIROCCO than to encode input to a full-text retrieval system. We plan, however, to incorporate SIROCCO into a tutoring environment for practical ethics. Expending some effort in representing problems has pedagogical value (e.g., it induces students to consider more carefully the facts of a case.) SIROCCO's explanations of its outputs are also pedagogically useful. Full-text retrieval schemes cannot generate such explanations. Finally, other work explores how to use CBR knowledge representations to guide a program in learning how to assign indices to textual cases automatically (Brüninghaus and Ashley 1999). SIROCCO's case representation may support an automated approach to processing textual cases in ethics.

Acknowledgements: This work was supported by an NSF-LIS grant No. 9720341.

References

Aleven, V.A. 1997. *Teaching Case-Based Argumentation Through a Model and Examples.* Ph.D. Diss., U. Pittsburgh.

Allen, J.F. 1983. Maintaining Knowledge about Temporal Intervals. *Comm. ACM* 26(11), 832-843.

Ashley, K.D. 1990. *Modeling Legal Argument: Reasoning with Cases and Hypotheticals.* Cambridge: MIT Press.

Branting, L.K. 1991. Building Explanations from Rules and Structured Cases. *Int'l J.Man-Machine Studies*, 34 (6): 797-837.

Brüninghaus, S. and K.D. Ashley. 1999. Bootstrapping Case Base Development with Annotated Case Summaries (Althoff, K.-D., et al. ed.) *CBR Research and Development* (ICCBR-99) Lecture Notes in AI No. 1650, 59-73. Springer: Berlin.

Clancey, W.J. 1983 The Epistemology of a Rule-based Expert System: A Framework for Explanation. *Artificial Intelligence*, 20(3):215-251.

Davison, A.C. and D.V. Hinkley. 1997. *Bootstrap Methods and Their Application.* Cambridge U. Press.

Forbus, K.D., D. Gentner, and K. Law. 1994. MAC/FAC: A Model of Similarity-based Retrieval. *Cognitive Science* 19, 141-205..

Harris, C.E., M.S. Pritchard, and M.J. Rabins. 1999. *Engineering Ethics: Concepts and Cases.* 2d ed. Belmont, CA: Wadsworth.

Jonsen, A.R. and S. Toulmin. 1988. *The Abuse of Casuistry: A History of Moral Reasoning.* Berkeley: U. California Press.

Kolodner, J. 1993. *Case-Based Reasoning.* San Mateo: Morgan Kaufmann.

Koomen, J.A. 1989. *The TIMELOGIC Temporal Reasoning System.* Tech. Rep. 231, Computer Science Dept., U. Rochester, NY.

Leake, D.B. 1991. An Indexing Vocabulary for Case-Based Explanation. In *Proc. AAAI-91*. 10-15.

Lewis, D.D., R.E. Schapire, et al. 1996. Training Algorithms for Linear Text Classifiers. In *Proc. 19th Ann. Int'l ACM-SIGIR Conf. on Res. and Dev. in Information Retrieval.* Zurich.

McLaren, B.M. 1999. *Assessing the Relevance of Cases and Principles Using Operationalization Techniques.* Ph.D. Diss., U. Pittsburgh.

McLaren, B.M. and K.D. Ashley 1999. Case Representation, Acquisition, and Retrieval in SIROCCO (Althoff, K.-D., et al. ed.) *CBR Research and Development* (ICCBR-99). Lecture Notes in AI No. 1650. 248-262. Springer: Berlin.

Mostow, J. 1983. Machine transformation of advice into a heuristic search procedure. *Machine Learning*, vol. 1.

Rissland, E.L., D.B. Skalak, and M.T. Friedman. 1996. BankXX: Supporting Legal Arguments through Heuristic Retrieval. *Artificial Intelligence and Law* 4:1-71.

Thagard, P., K.J. Holyoak, et al. 1990. *Analog Retrieval by Constraint Satisfaction.* Tech. Rep. CSL-Report 41, Princeton U.

Dynamic Case Creation and Expansion for Analogical Reasoning

Tom Mostek, Kenneth D. Forbus, Cara Meverden

Qualitative Reasoning Group, Northwestern University
1890 Maple Avenue, Evanston, IL, 60201, USA

{t-mostek, forbus, meverden}@nwu.edu

Abstract

Most CBR systems rely on a fixed library of cases, where each case consists of a set of facts specified in advance. This paper describes techniques for *dynamically extracting* cases for analogical reasoning from general-purpose knowledge bases, and *dynamically expanding* them during the course of analogical reasoning. These techniques have several advantages: (1) Knowledge authoring is simplified, since facts can be added without regard to which case(s) they will be used in. (2) Reasoning is more efficient, since task constraints can be used during case extraction to focus on facts likely to be relevant. (3) Larger problems can be tackled, since cases can be dynamically expanded with more details during the matching process itself, rather than starting with completely detailed cases. We describe algorithms for case extraction and case expansion, including how a version of the Structure-Mapping Engine (SME) has been modified to incorporate this new matching technique. The utility of this technique is illustrated by results obtained with two large knowledge bases, created by other groups, and used to answer questions in the DARPA High-Performance Knowledge Base Crisis Management Challenge Problem.

Introduction

Analogical reasoning operates by comparing cases. In most case-based reasoning systems (c.f. [1]), cases are stored as named collections of facts in a memory (c.f. [18, 19]). Most CBR systems are designed for a specific range of problems, and this strategy can be effective for such tasks. However, it becomes problematic for creating systems that can tackle multiple types of problems, involving very large amounts of knowledge. An International Crisis Management Assistant, for example, would require substantial knowledge of the nations of the world and their history. How should this knowledge be organized into cases? For example, facts about Great Britain presumably appear in cases describing WWI, WWII, and Great Britain, as well as cases describing interactions of Great Britain with other countries and describing events that occur inside it. Knowing what to store where becomes a complex issue, leading to potential missed inferences and storage redundancies. Worse, different tasks demand different types of information. Reasoning about Great Britain's military options in response to a hypothetical threat is, for instance, unlikely to require knowledge of its livestock feeding practices, although such practices are very relevant in reasoning about its economic relationships with the rest of the European Union. The static organization of knowledge into cases, whose contents are crafted by human designers in advance, is unlikely to scale to this level of application system, let alone the human-like flexibility of common sense reasoning.

Considering what would be involved in scaling up to human-sized knowledge bases raises a second problem with case organization: Controlling level of detail. For example, a representation of the Persian Gulf War might be broken into three major phases: the invasion of Kuwait, Operation Desert Shield, and Operation Desert Storm. Each of these phases consists in turn of various events, which are often further decomposable, and so on. Similar examples abound in medicine, engineering, science, and business. A rich case library should describe complex systems and events at multiple levels of detail. Unfortunately, larger cases are more expensive to match: directly comparing two full cases containing thousands of propositions can easily blow out even today's large memories and render a system too slow to be usable. The ability to modulate the level of detail during matching seems essential to scaling up.

This paper proposes a new method for organizing and using case libraries in analogical reasoning. The idea is to store the facts of all cases in a general-purpose knowledge base, and automatically extract relevant subsets of knowledge for reasoning, based on task constraints. This leads to two techniques:

1. *Dynamic case extraction* extracts case contents from a knowledge base, given a *target entity* and a query about that entity.
2. *Dynamic case elaboration* expands cases during the matching process, adding more information to help the matcher decide between competing submatches.

These techniques have three advantages. First, they simplify knowledge authoring: Concrete, specific facts can

---

Copyright © 2000, American Association for Artificial Intelligence (www.aaai.org). All rights reserved.

be added without regard to which case (or cases) they are part of, since that decision will be made automatically. Second, reasoning with cases can be made more efficient: The contents of a case can be partially determined by the current task, thus eliminating irrelevant material from consideration. Third, larger cases can be handled. In a fixed-contents case memory, finding the right level of detail is a difficult tradeoff. Too little detail, and useful inferences will be missed. Too much detail, and the reasoning system bogs down. We show that dynamic case expansion enables us to handle detailed cases that, on the same system, lead to memory blowouts if matched directly.

The next section begins with a brief review of the relevant aspects of structure-mapping theory, SME, and MAC/FAC, the analogical reasoning approach and tools we are using. Then we describe the methods we use for structuring cases in a knowledge base and extracting relevant aspects of them via KB queries. Dynamic case expansion during matching is discussed next. Empirical results obtained as part of the DARPA High Performance Knowledge Bases Crisis Management Challenge Problem follow, showing that these techniques work well with two different knowledge bases and case libraries, neither authored by us. Finally, we discuss related work and future plans.

Prelude: Cases and analogical matching

According to structure-mapping theory [14], an analogy match takes as input two structured representations (*base* and *target*) and produces as output a set of *mappings*. Each mapping consists of a set of *correspondences* that align items in the base with items in the target and a set of *candidate inferences*, which are surmises about the target made on the basis of the base representation plus the correspondences. The constraints that govern mappings, while originally motivated by psychological concerns [14], turn out to be equally important for the use of analogy in case-based reasoning, since they ensure that candidate inferences are well defined and that stronger arguments are preferred [15].

Two simulations based on structure-mapping are particularly relevant to this paper. The Structure-Mapping Engine (SME) [1,9,11] is a cognitive simulation of analogical matching. Given base and target descriptions, SME finds globally consistent interpretations via a local-to-global match process. SME begins by proposing correspondences, called *match hypotheses,* in parallel between statements in the base and target. Then, SME filters out structurally inconsistent match hypotheses. Mutually consistent collections of match hypotheses are gathered into global mappings using a greedy merge algorithm. An evaluation procedure based on the systematicity principle is used to compute the *structural evaluation* for each match hypothesis and mapping. These numerical estimates are used both to guide the merge process and as one component in the evaluation of an analogy. SME operates in time and space polynomial in the size of the input representations, and its results can be incrementally extended as new information arrives.

MAC/FAC is a two-stage model of similarity-based retrieval that is consistent with psychological constraints [12] and has been used in a fielded application [13]. The key insight of MAC/FAC is that memory contents should be filtered by an extremely cheap match that filters a potentially huge set of candidates, followed by a structural match (i.e., SME) to select the best from the handful of candidates found by the first stage. The extremely cheap match is based on *content vectors*, a representation computed from structured descriptions. Each dimension of a content vector represents the number of occurrences of a particular predicate in a description. For example, if a (tiny) description had three BEFORE statements and one IMPLIES statement, its content vector would be ((BEFORE 0.75)(IMPLIES 0.25)). Content vectors are normalized to avoid size biases. Content vectors are useful cheap matchers because their dot product provides an estimate of the largest structural match that could be obtained between the two original structured descriptions. During the construction of the match hypothesis forest in SME, base and target items with identical predicates are hypothesized to match, which may in turn suggest other matches (e.g., entity matches, non-identical function matches). Thus the size of a match hypothesis forest for two structured descriptions is roughly correlated with the dot product of their corresponding content vectors. In this paper, we use content vectors as a cheap similarity metric. Every entity (and indeed every predicate) in the knowledge base has an associated content vector, derived from the set of statements in the KB that mentions that entity.

Dynamic case construction

Cases are about something. That something can be a specific entity (e.g., the United States) or an event (e.g., WWII). Depending on task, even abstract concepts can be the subject of comparison, e.g., comparing notions of justice across cultures. We assume that one can always identify a *seed* for a case, the entity or relationship that the case is about. Given a task T, the case for a seed is a subset of facts from the KB about seed that are relevant for T. The two issues that must be addressed are
1. What facts about a seed S are *relevant* for a given task T?
2. What *bounds* the subset of the KB to be included?
The set of facts about S that are relevant to T can be divided into two sets: Those that explicitly mention S and those that do not. (If the term S appears in fact F, we denote this via Mentions(F,S).) Not every fact that mentions S is relevant: In reasoning about possible US responses to an economic crisis, it is very unlikely that the fact that George Washington was the first US president will be relevant. We assume that for each task T, a set of predicates RP(T) can be identified such that statements whose predicates are in RP(T) and mention S are relevant.

For example, in the case of reasoning about economic interests, predicates such as has-economic-interest and economic-action are included in RP(economic-interests). RP can be defined very broadly, excluding only predicates used for internal, bookkeeping statements, or very sharply, including only predicates relevant to a particular aspect of knowledge about a domain (e.g., economic versus political versus military). RP can also be defined via inference rather than via explicit enumeration.

Unfortunately, task constraints are often more complex than can be expressed in terms of simply filtering via categories of predicates. For example, when reasoning about options a country might have had in a situation based on a historical precedent, one wants to extract the relevant facts of the situation up to, but not after, the key event. By doing this, the match against the historical precedent will yield candidate inferences that represent potential options for the new situation that are analogous to what occurred in the historical precedent. Such task constraints can be expressed in terms of filtering out facts that match some specific criterion. Since the criterion depends on the details of the task and the representations, we must settle for describing it abstractly. Consequently, we assume the existence of a procedure, Filter?, that takes two arguments, a fact and a task, and returns true if the given fact should be ignored.

In the case generation algorithm (Figure 1), we use RP and Filter? to narrow in on the facts relevant to a task. Let the set RM(S,T) (intuitively, "relevant mentions") be the set of facts that mention S, whose predicate is in RP(T), and which do not satisify Filter? (i.e., they are relevant to the task). RM(S,T) constitutes the relevant facts for T that mention S explicitly. These are not necessarily all of the relevant facts, of course, since the background for these facts in turn may need to be considered.

The set of relevant facts that do not mention S explicitly is found by recursive expansion, based on the entities mentioned in RM(S,T). Let GT(<expressions>) refer to the set of ground terms occurring in the statements <expressions>. The terms (i.e., entities, events, processes, etc.) in GT(RM(S,T)) are the conceptual entities for which additional facts should be included, since constraints on these terms can affect conclusions drawn with RM(S,T). Let the *basic relevant facts* RB(S,T) be defined as follows:
RB(S,T) = {f ∈ KB | f ∈ RM(S,T)
∨ [predicate(f) ∈ RP(T)
∧ GT({f}) ⊆ GT(RM(S,T))] }

That is, RB(S,T) is the set of facts in RM(S,T), plus the facts that mention only entities in RM(S,T). The basic relevant set of facts can be expanded by recursively computing RB(e,T), for every e ∈ GT(RM(S,T)), and taking their union.. Obviously, the scope of this expansion has to be limited, otherwise in a highly interconnected knowledge base, all the facts will be included in every case. We scope the expansion by having Filter? be more constrained on facts that don't mention S. Table 1 shows the different Filter? methods for the case denoting functions from the analogy ontology we have developed. These range from no expansion (minimal-case-fn) to expanding all the sub-parts of the original case (recursive-case-fn). The appropriate procedure definitions for what are internal, bookkeeping predicates (book-keeping?), causal relationships (causal?), part/whole relations (subparts?) and attributes (attributes?) will be specific to the particular KB. For example, in Cyc [20] isa statements constitute attributes.

Input:
- An entity or expression S which the case will be about.
- A knowledge base KB and task T
- A procedure Filter? that encodes task-specific constraints (see text).

Procedure GenerateCase(S,T)
1. RM(S,T) ← {}
2. For all f ∈ KB s.t. Mentions(f,S),
   2.1 If predicate(f) ∈ RP(T) ∧ ¬Filter?(f,T) then
       RM(S,T) ← RM(S,T) ∪ {f}
3. RB(S,T) ← RM(S,T)
4. For each E in GT(RM(S,T))
   4.1 RB(S,T) ← RB(S,T) ∪ GenerateCase(E,T)

Figure 1: GenerateCase algorithm

Function	Method
Minimal-case-fn(S)	Book-keeping?(f) or ¬mentions(f,S)
Case-fn(S)	Book-keeping?(f) or (¬mentions(f,S) and ¬Attribute?(f))
Event-case-fn(S)	Book-keeping?(f) or (¬mentions(f,S) and ¬(Attribute?(f) or causal?(f)))
Agent-case-fn(S)	Book-keeping?(f)
In-context-case-fn(S,C)	Book-keeping?(f) or GT(f) ∩ subparts(C) = φ or (¬mentions(f,S) and ¬Attribute?(f))
Recursive-case-fn(S)	Book-keeping?(f) or (GT(f) ⊄ GT(RM(S,T) and ¬mentions(f, {subparts(S)}))

Table 1 – The semantics of filter? for the analogy ontology case functions

Dynamic case expansion

Complex cases typically have a hierarchical structure. Complex events have subevents, complex objects have parts, complex systems have subsystems, and complex devices have components. This hierarchical structure typically manifests itself in representations by things that are conceptual entities at one level being expanded into a collection of facts and entities when viewed at a finer level of detail. Matching can be made more efficient by exploiting this hierarchical structure. All matchers require resources proportional to the size of the input descriptions.

Starting with a high-level description, then incrementally refining the match by further exploring potentially corresponding parts, avoids considering many fruitless matches. For example, in comparing a person to a chimpanzee the rough match between their overall form invites a closer look at comparing their heads but not, say, the human's head to the chimpanzee's foot. Matching then becomes an incremental, iterative process, with the results of one stage of matching helping to guide the next. We call this process *dynamic case expansion*.

The ideas of the previous section provide the framework needed for dynamic case expansion. Given a comparison, the seed is chosen to be at an appropriate level of detail (i.e., Persian Gulf War versus Operation Desert Storm versus a particular sortie), corresponding to the highest level of abstraction denoted in the driving question. Base and target cases are created, without recursing, and SME is used to create the forest of match hypotheses that describes how statements in these two cases might be aligned. As noted above, expansion takes place at entities, so it is the possible correspondences, also called *match hypotheses* (MHs), between entities that form the candidates for expansion. There are three criteria used for deciding whether to expand a match hypothesis MH:

1. There must be at least one other competing MH for either the base or target entity in the original MH. Only those MH's whose score is close to the top scoring MH (currently 60%) are considered.
2. The content vector overlap between the two entities paired by the MH must be over some threshold (currently 0.4). This heuristic makes it more likely that expansion will give rise to new overlapping structure.
3. A task-specific procedure, Expandable?, which takes as arguments a candidate for expansion and the depth, and returns true if the candidate is worth expanding. For example, in reasoning about international crises it is typically only appropriate to expand events one level, whereas actors and goals are worth expanding deeper.

An MH is expanded by treating the entities it pairs as seeds for case extraction, as described in the previous section. The new facts for the entities are added to the appropriate descriptions (i.e., facts about the base entity are added to the base, and similarly for the target). Normally, when new statements are added to the base or target, SME's incremental match process extends the set of match hypotheses by considering the new base items against all of the target, and the new target items against all of the base. Our *focused match* algorithm modifies this by considering the new base items only against the new target items, thus avoiding hypothesizing local matches that are likely to be irrelevant. This process continues recursively, up to some depth bound (currently 2). The algorithm is described in detail in Figure 2.

Inputs:
- The base B and target T being compared
- The knowledge base KB from which B & T were drawn
- Procedures Filter? and Expandable? that encodes task-specific constraints (see text).
- An integer MaxDepth which limits expansion by depth
- A threshold CVOverlap that specifies the minimal content vector overlap (currently 0.4).
- The match hypothesis forest MHS created by the standard SME algorithm given initial B, T.

Context: This algorithm is executed immediately after the usual match hypothesis forest step in the incremental SME algorithm, and when finished, the rest of the SME algorithm proceeds as usual.

Procedure CaseExpansion
  For each MH in MHS, ExpandMHS(MHS, 0)

Procedure ExpandMHS(theMHS, depth)
1. When depth = MaxDepth, return.
2. For each MH in theMHS
   2.1 Unless Entity?(BaseItem(MH)), skip.
   2.2 Unless InCompetition?(MH, newMHS), skip.
   2.3 Unless Expandable?(MH), skip.
   2.4 Unless CVDotProduct(MH) > CVOverlap, skip.
   2.5 NewBase ← GenerateCase(BaseItem(MH),KB)
   2.6 NewTarget ← GenerateCase(TargetItem(MH),KB)
   2.7 NewMHS ← CreateMHS(NewBase,NewTarget)
   2.8 MHS ← MHS ∪ NewMHS
   2.9 ExpandMHS(NewMHS, depth+1)

Procedure CVDotProduct(MH)
  ContentVector(BaseItem(MH))
  • ContentVector(TargetItem(MH))

Procedure InCompetition? (MH1, MHS)
1. For each MH2 ∈ MHS, such that MH1 ≠ MH2
   1.1 Unless BaseItem(MH1) = BaseItem(MH2) or
             TargetItem(MH1) = TargetItem(MH2), skip.
   1.2 If CVDotProduct(MH2) > CVOverlap, then
       return True from InCompetition?
2. Return False from InCompetition?

Figure 2: Dynamic case expansion algorithm

Importantly, this process is different from recursively calling SME on the cases created from the entities because global mappings are not created during expansion at any level. Structure-mapping theory tells us that large, systematic matches are preferred [14]. Global mappings between lower-level matches would not be sensitive to relations that occur at higher levels. By keeping all of the match hypotheses in the same forest, SME's constraint satisfaction mechanisms can combine evidence from all levels in creating its interpretations, which improves accuracy and enables interpretations to include all relevant levels of detail.

The worst-case complexity of the focused match algorithm is polynomial, assuming a fixed maximum depth limit for

Team	Query	Base			Target			Dynamic Creation +expansion		No Dynamic Expansion		No Dynamic Creation	
		Start	Final	Max	Start	Final	Max	MHs	Seconds	MHs	Seconds	MHs	Seconds
SAIC	SQM226	777	883	2062	632	822	1312	2579	27	10634	346	36602	3000*
SAIC	TQE225	437	503	1057	777	863	2062	2030	32	11437	310	33114	2400*
SAIC	TQE226	777	1117	2062	239	507	507	3976	144	11699	259	18824	1493
Cyc	TQE225	299	721	721	192	1891	1891	9146	141	11614	821	11614	821
Cyc	SQM226	192	1891	1891	108	592	592	6319	112	9299	307	9299	307
SAIC	TQM226	240	324	493	632	729	1312	1470	12	3619	13	8933	123
Cyc	TQE226	192	1842	1891	34	168	168	1857	47	2704	46	2704	46
SAIC	TQF225a	184	274	274	234	486	486	1499	14	2122	5	2122	5
Cyc	TQM226	119	205	205	108	592	592	1318	8	1583	3	1583	3
Cyc	TQF225a	79	239	239	120	457	457	780	7	869	1	869	1
Cyc	TQF225b	118	129	129	423	440	440	665	4	665	1	665	1
SAIC	TQF225b	91	120	120	99	144	302	302	6	333	1	333	1

Table 2 - Crisis Management Query Timing

recursive expansion and assuming that the computation of RM, RP, and Expandable? are polynomial. The latter are polynomial if implemented as lookup operations rather than inference steps; if they require inference, then the complexity of the inference machinery becomes a factor. The savings over uniform preexpansion come from two sources: (1) Many fewer match hypotheses are generated, saving storage and time, and (2) fewer match hypotheses means fewer things to consider when constructing global interpretations. These savings can be significant in practice, as the next section illustrates.

Empirical Results

In the DARPA High Performance Knowledge Bases program, the Crisis Management Challenge Problem focused on building knowledge bases and systems that could answer the kinds of queries that an analysts' assistant might provide. When reasoning about international crises, analysts commonly rely on analogy to analyze the present in terms of history (c.f. [22,24]). Consequently, a number of analogy queries were included in the tests, and we used the algorithms described here in providing analogical processing services for both teams in the evaluation. Examples of the analogy questions include

```
TQE225: How is the UN's mediation of the dispute
between Iran and the Taliban in the 1998 Iranian-
Taliban Crisis similar to the UN's mediation of
the dispute between Iran and the GCC in the Y2
Scenario?

SQM226: Who/what is IRAN in Y2-SCENARIO-CONFLICT
similar to in PERSIAN-GULF-WAR? How so, and how
are they different?
```

Examining how the case creation and case expansion algorithms work on these problems is a good test for two reasons. First, the cases involved in these problems were often substantial, two orders of magnitude larger than many examples used in the analogy literature, and an order of magnitude larger than anything we had tackled previously. Second, our algorithms had to work with two independently developed knowledge bases, created by other research groups. (Since the evaluation was competitive, we were allowed to consult with both teams about how to improve their knowledge bases, but were not allowed to make extensions ourselves.)

Table 2 describes data from an experiment using queries from the Crisis Management challenge problem. The first two columns indicate what team's KB was used and the specific query. The next six columns show the initial size of the base or target, as found via GenerateCase (Start), how large it reached due to dynamic expansion (Final), and the size of the full case (Max). The results of dynamic case creation and expansion are shown in the next two columns, which indicate the size of the match hypothesis forest generated in SME (MHs) and the total run time (seconds). The final four columns provide data that help tease apart the relative contributions of dynamic case expansion versus creation. The No Dynamic Expansion column shows the amount of work done when the focused match algorithm is not used. In this condition, SME is being run on the largest cases found dynamically, but interactions between different aspects of the case matches are considered, as opposed to only attempting matches between expansions of corresponding parts. The final pair of columns indicate the amount of work done if the full cases were compared. Runs marked with "*" indicate that the program hadn't completed by the time recorded. The task-specific settings of the algorithms used in these runs were as follows: For RP, only internal, bookkeeping predicates were excluded. For Filter?, depending on the query, either nothing was filtered out, or causal consequences of the seed were filtered out. Expandable? always expanded interests and was set so events were expanded first, and objects expanded at the last iteration. This reduced complexity in the scoping algorithm used in Filter?. The same parameter settings were used for both team's KB's; only the particular lists of predicates (e.g., what constituted a bookkeeping predicate, interest, or event) varied.

The table contents are ordered by the worst-case match hypothesis count. Several interesting properties can be seen in this table[1]. First, smaller cases are faster, and when sufficiently small, the complete case tends to be retrieved. Looking at the KB, the cases used in these queries are without substantial substructure, so this makes sense. Even on these smaller cases, some space savings occurs due to the focused nature of the matches used during case expansion, but the overhead of dynamic expansion makes the runtime slower. However, on larger cases, both significant time and space savings are found: up to an order of magnitude reduction in storage, and finishing in a reasonable time versus not finishing at all in the largest cases. The average storage savings over all examples is 75%, and the speedup over the entire set of queries is 4.6. The combination of significant speedups plus the ability to do examples that were impossible before is strong evidence for the utility of our techniques.

Related Work

In traditional CBR (c.f. [18]), cases are either created manually or automatically generated via performance systems, and are treated as individual items in an indexed memory. Although cases can be added to or modified by human authors, from the perspective of the reasoning system such case memories are static, since they are not being evolved during the course of reasoning. Our techniques of dynamic case extraction and expansion allow for analogical mapping with very large cases using un-indexed memory. Our techniques leverage the compositional nature of structured case representations along with task-specific and mapping-specific pragmatics.

A number of other CBR techniques use the interconnectedness of case representations to guide case retrieval and/or matching, including Stratified CBR [3], Knowledge Directed Spreading Activation (KDSA) [26], Activation Passing (as used in CRASH) [4], Case Retrieval Nets (CRN) [21] and Progressive deepening [25]. We discuss each in turn.

Stratified CBR uses memory organized in decomposable abstraction layers to direct search and help adaptation. Activation Passing uses memory annotated with context and structure links as well as relationship weights to direct search, preserve structure, and support case descriptions at multiple levels of detail. CRNs include relevancy functions and micro-features, letting it scale to tens of thousands of cases. KDSA speeds retrieval by finding beacon points based on a relevancy function which speed search through the entire memory to for the purpose of analogical retrievals. Progressive deepening, used in Sapper, also provides for analogical comparisons using derived analogy links, and controls the depth of the search by using a threshold function.

All of these techniques use heuristics to reduce the computational complexity by trimming the search space, but the focus and flexibility of their techniques vary (see Table 3). SCBR uses the abstraction hierarchy to find the best case, but comparison is always done between the two full ground cases. Activation passing takes advantage of structure links, allowing it to handle large cases at different levels of detail. Unfortunately, it requires prebuilt memory structures at each level, which precludes the use of task-specific pragmatics. CNET's use of pre-computed similarity and relevancy measures as well as microfeatures speed retrieval, but does not provide any mechanism to dynamically change the information in the case to improve matching, nor does it support high-level structure needed for analogical comparisons and very large cases. KDSA's beacons act as a two-phase retrieval technique similar to MAC/FAC, but the basic spreading activation of the case comparison does not scale. Finally, Sapper's progressive deepening technique provides an anytime algorithm, but doesn't support task-specific relevance constraints to avoid exponential search as the depth increases with large cases.

	SCBR	KDSA	Activation Passing	CRN	Progressive Deepening	Dynamic Extraction/ Expansion
Un-indexed memory		✔		✔	✔	✔
Supports analogy		✔	✔		✔	✔
Decomposable cases	✔		✔			✔
Scales to large cases				✔		✔
Problem Specific Pragmatics						✔

Table 3 – Comparison of Matching Techniques

Discussion

The traditional reliance of CBR on a libraries of fixed-structure cases has been useful in practice, but it is unclear that such techniques will scale to human-scale memories. The ability to dynamically extract cases from large-scale knowledge bases, combined with the ability to dynamically expand them during matching, supports the use of analogical reasoning with rich, relational representations drawn from large-scale, general-purpose knowledge bases. In addition, dynamic case expansion provides more efficient matching on large descriptions, facilitating scale-up. The fact that these techniques succeed on different large-scale knowledge bases constructed by other research groups is strong evidence that these techniques are generally useful.

---

[1] It may seem surprising that run time is not always a monotonic function of the number of MHs, but this falls directly out of the structure of the SME algorithm [11]

A number of issues remain to be explored. As the structure of large knowledge bases becomes understood, it may be possible to have a stronger theory for what our algorithm currently uses as procedural parameters. Techniques from compositional modeling [10, 23, 5] might be generalized to automatically handle selection of initial perspective and level of detail. Finally, new possibilities for dynamic expansion open up when considering larger-scale systems: Suppose SME were run to completion with the most abstract level of match, with expansion taking place when a downstream system needed more detail about a particular aspect of a comparison. This could provide a useful generalization to Falkenhainer's map/analyze cycle [7].

Acknowledgements

We thank Ron Ferguson, Dedre Gentner, and the anonymous reviewers for useful comments. This research was supported by the Defense Advanced Projects Research Agency under the High-Performance Knowledge Bases Program, the Air Force Office of Scientific Research, and the Computer Science Division of the Office of Naval Research.

References

1. Aamodt, A & Plaza, E. (1994). Case-based reasoning: Foundational issues, methodological variations, and system approaches, *AI-Communications*
2. Blythe, J. & Veloso, M. (1997) Analogical replay for efficient conditional planning, *Proceedings of AAAI-97*, pages 668-673.
3. Branting, L.K. (1997). Stratified Case-Based Reasoning in Non-Refinable Abstraction Hierarchies. *Proceedings of ICCBR-97*, 519-530.
4. Brown, M.G. (1993). An Underlying Memory Model to Support Case Retrieval, *EWCBR-93*.
5. Clark, P. and Porter, B. 1997. Building Concept Representations from Reusable Components. In AAAI'97, pages 369-376, CA:AAAI Press.
6. Cohen, P., Schrag, R., Jones, E., Pease, A., Lin, A., Starr, B., Gunning, D., & Burke, M. 1998. The DARPA High Performance Knowledge Bases Project. *AI Magazine*, Winter, 1998.
7. Falkenhainer, B. (1987). An examination of the third stage in the analogy process: Verification-based analogical learning. *Proceedings of IJCAI-87*, 260-263.
8. Falkenhainer, B., Forbus, K., & Gentner, D. (1986, August) The Structure-Mapping Engine. Proceedings of AAAI-86, Philadelphia, PA
9. Falkenhainer, B., Forbus, K., & Gentner, D. (1989) The Structure-Mapping Engine: Algorithm and examples. Artificial Intelligence, 41, pp 1-63.
10. Falkenhainer, B. & Forbus, K. "Compositional Modeling: Finding the Right Model for the Job", Artificial Intelligence, **51** (1-3), October, 1991.
11. Forbus, K., Ferguson, R. & Gentner, D. (1994) Incremental structure-mapping. *Proceedings of the Cognitive Science Society*, August.
12. Forbus, K., Gentner, D. & Law, K. (1995) MAC/FAC: A model of Similarity-based Retrieval. *Cognitive Science*, 19(2), April-June, pp 141-205.
13. Forbus, K.D., Whalley, P., Everett, J., Ureel, L., Brokowski, M., Baher, J. & Kuehne, S. (1999) CyclePad: An articulate virtual laboratory for engineering thermodynamics. *Artificial Intelligence*.
14. Gentner, D. (1983). Structure-mapping: A theoretical framework for analogy. Cognitive Science, 7, 155-170.
15. Gentner, D. (1989). The mechanisms of analogical learning. In S. Vosniadou & A. Ortony (Eds.), *Similarity and analogical reasoning* (pp. 199-241). London: Cambridge University Press. (Reprinted in *Knowledge acquisition and learning*, 1993, 673-694.)
16. Gentner, D., & Holyoak, K. J. (1997). Reasoning and learning by analogy: Introduction. *American Psychologist, 52*, 32-34.
17. Gentner, D., & Markman, A. B. (1997). Structure mapping in analogy and similarity. *American Psychologist, 52*, 45-56. (To be reprinted in *Mind readings: Introductory selections on cognitive science*, by P. Thagard, Ed., MIT Press)
18. Kolodner, J. L. (1994). Case-based reasoning. San Mateo, CA: Morgan Kaufmann Publishers.
19. Leake, D. (Ed.) 1996. *Case-Based Reasoning: Experiences, Lessons, and Future Directions*, MIT Press.
20. Lenat, D. B., & Guha, R.V. (1990). *Building Large Knowledge Based Systems*. Addison Wesley.
21. Lenz, M., Burkhard, H.D. (1996). Case retrieval Nets: Basic Ideas and Extensions. in: G. Goerz, S. Hoelldobler (Eds.), *KI-96: Advances in Artificial Intelligence*, Springer publishing house.
22. Neustad, R. & May, E. 1988. *Thinking in time: The uses of History for Decision Makers*. Free Press.
23. Rickel, J. 1995. Automated Modeling of Complex Systems to Answer Prediction Questions. Ph.D. Dissertation, Department of Computer Science, University of Texas at Austin, May 1995. Technical Report AI95-234.
24. IET, Inc. and PSR Corp. 1999. HPKB Year 2 Crisis Management End-to-end Challenge Problem Specification. http://www.iet.com/Projects/HPKB/Y2/Y2-CM-CP.doc
25. Veale, T., & Keane, M. T. 1998. 'Just in Time' Analogical Mapping, An Iterative-Deepening Approach to Structure-Mapping. *Proceedings of ECAI'98, the Thirteenth European Conference on Artificial Intelligence*
26. Wolverton, M. (1995). An Investigation of Marker-Passing Algorithms for Analogue Retrieval. *ICCBR-95*

Memory-Based Forecasting for Weather Image Patterns

Kazuhiro Otsuka, Tsutomu Horikoshi, Satoshi Suzuki[†], and Haruhiko Kojima

NTT Cyber Solutions Laboratories
1-1, Hikarino-oka, Yokosuka, 239-0847, JAPAN
tsuka@aether.hil.ntt.co.jp

[†]Multimedia Business Department,
[†]NTT East Corp.
[†]2-2-2, Otemachi, Tokyo, 100-0004, JAPAN

Abstract

A novel method and a framework called Memory-Based Forecasting are proposed to forecast complex and time-varying natural patterns with the goal of supporting experts' decision making. This paper targets the local precipitation phenomena captured as echo patterns in weather radar images, and aims to realize a tool that supports weather forecasters. In our framework, past image patterns similar to the present pattern are retrieved from a large set held in an image database, and the forecast image is produced by using the patterns that follow the retrieved patterns; it is analogous to human forecasters who imagine the future patterns based on their past experience. Appearance-based image features and temporal texture features are introduced to characterize the non-rigid complex echo patterns found in such radar images. The dissimilarity between two image sequences is defined as the normalized distance between paths of feature points in eigenspaces of the image features to retrieve similar past sequences. Forecast images are then constructed from a future point in the feature spaces, which is estimated by a nonlinear prediction scheme. Statistical experiments using weather radar images verify the effectiveness of our method and framework especially for drastically changing patterns.

Introduction

This world is full of complicated and somewhat vague phenomena such as daily weather, climate change, and stock prices, all of which heavily affect human activities. In such fields, human experts still play vital roles in predicting future events due to their experiential knowledge and analogical reasoning process, and computerized decision aiding tools are demanded to support human experts for improving their efficiency and accuracy (Kolodner 1991).

As an application typical of such tools, we have focused on weather phenomena, in particular local precipitation, and aim to realize a tool that supports the local short-term(1h-3h) precipitation forecasting strongly needed for the control of aviation and surface transportation systems, hydrographic networks and so on. To observe the precipitation phenomena, a weather radar system featuring high resolution and real-time observation is used to provide the weather

Copyright © 2000, American Association for Artificial Intelligence (www.aaai.org). All rights reserved.

radar reflectivity images that represent the spatial distribution of precipitation intensity, called the echo pattern. So far, radar image-based methods, such as the extrapolation-based method (Crook & Tuttle 1997), have been used to support forecasters even though their forecast accuracy is severely limited by the complexity of the dynamics of the precipitation phenomenon. On the other hand, a numerical prediction method based on a physical model of the atmosphere is now being used to produce daily weather reports. However, the method can not produce short-term forecasts of local precipitation because of its limited resolutions in terms of observation and computation.

So far, methodologies known as Case-Based Reasoning(CBR) and Memory-Based Reasoning(MBR) (Kolodner 1991) (Stanfill & Waltz 1986), both based on large sets of past examples, have been developed to aid decision making in fields such as medical diagnostics and machine translation. Such an approach has also been applied to prediction problems such as cash flow(Lee, Barcia, & Khator 1995), visibility(Hansen & Riordan 1998), and physical systems(Connell & Utgoff 1987). This approach bypasses the elicitation of human expertise and does not need modeling of the phenomena, which tends to be difficult for incomplete and imprecise data under real world conditions, therefore, it has been suggested as an effective methodology for prediction problems.

We have tried to extend the memory-based approach, which has mainly been used to deal with symbolic and numeric knowledge, to dynamic image patterns which cannot be easily transformed into symbols or linguistic representation by machines or even humans (Otsuka et al. 1999) (Otsuka et al. 2000). This paper presents a framework that we call Memory-Based Forecasting (MBF) with the aim of forecasting image sequences including complex natural patterns such as weather radar images. The MBF framework is analogous to human weather forecasters who have acquired sequencing rules such as pattern A will follow pattern B, and recall past patterns similar to the present pattern, and imagine how the present pattern will develop. The idea of MBF is that the temporal development of past image patterns similar to the present one can be used to create short-term forecast information. As such, MBF is expected to support the decision-making tasks of weather forecasters by providing enhanced memory resources and reference forecast information.

In studies related to meteorology based on such memory-based approach, T. Mohri et al. proposed a system to predict future weather categories (rain or fine) based on past similar situations; they used a weather database holding a large amount of symbolized weather data such as rain amount and wind direction measured at surface observatories(Mohri, Nakamura, & Tanaka 1993). E. K. Jones and A. Roydhouse developed a retrieval system for summarized weather maps that held low and high pressure data. The data was indexed with regard to position, extent, and central intensity of the phenomena(Jones & Roydhouse 1995). These studies dealt with high-level features or symbolized data of large-scale ($1000km^2$-$10000km^2$) phenomena whose changes were relatively smooth and slow. In contrast to the above methods, we directly employ raw image sequences and concentrate on smaller scale ($10km^2$-$300km^2$) and more dynamic phenomena that are full of abrupt changes.

Moreover, in the field of nonlinear dynamical systems, the idea of using similar past patterns has also been applied to predict chaotic time series such as market activity (Mulhern & Caprara 1994), and several prediction methods have been proposed (Ikeguchi & Aihara 1995). However, the targets of these existing schemes were mostly limited to one dimensional time series, and the attempt to handle image pattern has been hampered by the lack of a suitable method of representing complex, time-varying, two dimensional patterns.

In recent years, appearance-based methods have been developed for object and face recognition. In these methods, the high dimensional features of raw image intensity are transformed into a lower dimensional space, the so called eigenspace, based on principal component analysis of a set of training images (Murase & Nayar 1995) (Turk & Pentland 1991). Because of its robustness under real environments and its simplicity, explicit target modeling is not required, the range of applications continues to expand such as human gesture recognition (Bobick & Wilson 1995), robot vision system (Nayar, Nene, & Murase 1996), and video retrieval (Fujimoto et al. 1996).

In this paper, since we do not presuppose the availability of meteorological knowledge regarding physical precipitation phenomena, a sort of appearance-based representation is employed to handle complex echo patterns. In particular, this paper introduces the global distribution of echo patterns, the velocity field, and temporal texture features. While that first two features describe the global characteristics of the precipitation system, the temporal texture features characterize local non-rigid motion patterns, which are strongly related to the underlying structure of precipitation (Otsuka et al. 2000). These image features are transformed into the eigenspaces and the image sequence is represented as paths in the eigenspaces. The dissimilarity between two image sequences, used to retrieve similar past sequences, is defined as the normalized distance between the paths of feature points in eigenspaces of the image features. Forecast images are then constructed from a future point in the feature spaces, which is estimated by a nonlinear prediction scheme.

Although, similar representation schemes for time series of image features have been explored for motion recogni-

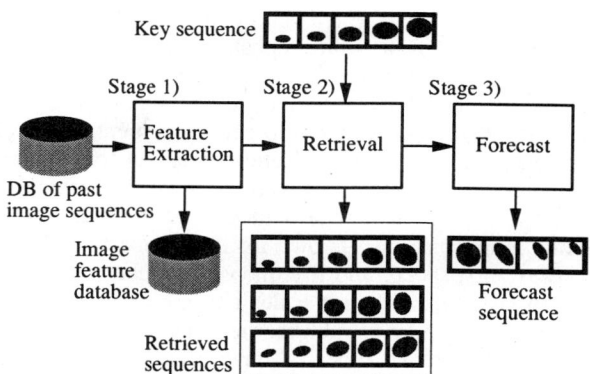

Figure 1: Framework of Memory-Based Forecasting of image sequence.

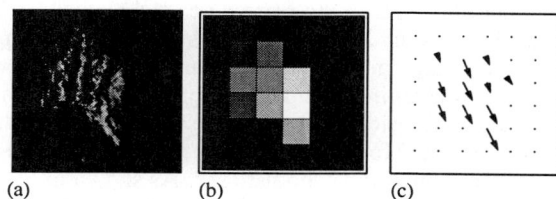

Figure 2: (a)Radar echo image, (b)Mesh feature, (c)Velocity field.

tion (Bobick & Wilson 1995) (Yacoob & Black 1999), current targets are mostly limited to artificially generated patterns, not naturally occurring patterns whose dynamics are unknown. Our research reveals the potential of the image sequence retrieval method in understanding natural systems and their veiled principles.

This paper is organized as follows. Section 2 introduces the framework and an implementation. Section 3 shows experimental results. Section 4 draws several discussions and a conclusion is presented in Section 5.

Framework and Implementation

The proposed MBF framework consists of three stages: feature extraction, retrieval, and forecast, as shown in Figure 1. At first, the sequence of image features representing the characteristics of the targeted image patterns are extracted from the image sequence database, which holds a large set of images. The image features are stored in the image feature database. Next, the latest image sequence (or arbitrary sequence) given as the query sequence is compared with each of the stored sequences in terms of feature vector difference to retrieve similar sequences. Finally, the subsequent sequences of the retrieved sequences are used to produce forecast information such as the accumulated distribution of precipitation in the case of weather forecasting.

Feature Extraction

The radar echo patterns present in weather radar images are non-rigid and deformable patterns that appear and disappear one after another, while roughly paralleling atmospheric flow. For example, Figure 2(a) shows a pattern, called the band-shape pattern, that consists of a set of small echo cells forming parallel lines. Each echo cell continuously moves with atmospheric flow, while repeatedly appearing and disappearing. In spite of the constant movement of the echo cells, the whole pattern (pattern envelope) changes its shape and location slowly compared to cell movement. Such observations, note that the echo pattern varies its apparent motion characteristics according to the observation scale, correspond to the multiple scale structure of the precipitation system. Each scale has its own instinct property regarding spatial extents, speed, and lifetime of the echo pattern, but the phenomena on different scales are interrelated. In view of this scale dependent structure, the radar echo patterns are decomposed into two types of image features at different scales to characterize the precipitation system: global features and local features.

The global features represent the spatial distribution and movement of the entire echo pattern i.e. global position and shape of the pattern. Also, its changes through time represent the long-range motion such as translation, and growth and decay of the entire precipitation system. As the global features, the mesh feature $x_1(t)$ and the velocity field feature $x_2(t)$ are calculated for each time step t for the spatial distribution and motion of the echo patterns. As shown in Figure 2(b),(c), each image frame at each time step is partitioned into meshes, and the average gray level and average velocity of each mesh region are calculated as vector components of the mesh feature and the velocity field, respectively.

While the precipitation system roughly moves along with the atmospheric flow, the detailed characteristics of the precipitation phenomenon are reflected in the spatial and temporal structures of echo cells. Therefore, as local features, we focus on the statistical characteristics of an aggregation of echo cells, and introduce temporal texture features x_3, which mainly measure the uniformity and diversity of the local echo motion(Otsuka et al. 1998). These temporal texture features are calculated based on an analysis of motion trajectories drawn by moving edges in local spatiotemporal space. They are able to characterize types of echo pattern such as band-shape, stratiform, and scattered-type, since the atmospheric structure of precipitation phenomenon can be segregated into specific types of texture and echo cell motion. A set of temporal texture features is calculated for each mesh as in Figure 2(b), and the average values of the feature values over the meshes at time step t become the feature vector $x_3(t)$.

For each set of the feature vectors, we compute eigenvectors and eigenvalues from their covariance matrices, and the feature vectors at each time step t are then correspondingly transformed into reduced vectors $y_1(t)$, $y_2(t)$, and $y_3(t)$ in eigenspaces to eliminate correlated components within a set of feature vectors and to reduce their dimensionalities. The eigenspaces are spanned by eigenvectors with large eigenvalues calculated from the covariance matrices of the feature vectors.

Representation of Echo Pattern Sequence

For the retrieval of similar pattern toward forecasting, it is required that not only query pattern (present pattern) and retrieved pattern at a time step are similar, but also their trend

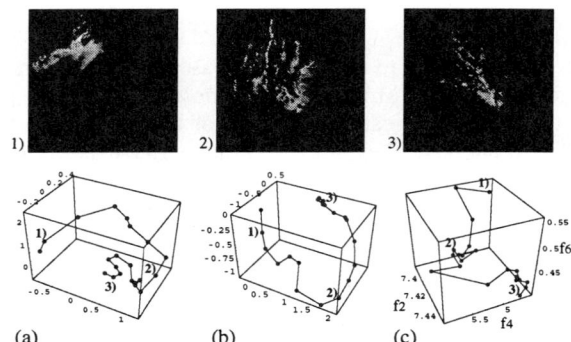

Figure 3: Paths of feature points of (a)Mesh feature in eigenspace, (b)Velocity field in eigenspace, and (c)Temporal texture [Axes : motion entropy f_2, speed f_4, density f_6]. Note, each point is 1 hour apart.

in pattern change should also be similar. To represent this trend, the pattern sequence is represented by a set of sequential feature vectors. Figure 3 shows paths of feature points for a sequence in the feature spaces. Matching the transition in the echo sequence, the feature points trace paths in the feature spaces representing the temporal development of the pattern. Therefore, the similarity between two sequences can be determined from the degree of closeness of their two paths.

Retrieval Process

Next, a retrieval algorithm based on path dissimilarity is presented. Hereafter the query sequence $\{T - L + 1, \cdots, T - 1, T\}$ and the matching sequence $\{t - L + 1, \cdots, t - 1, t\}$ are denoted by tail time T and t, respectively, where L is the length of the subsequences to be matched, as shown in Figure 4. This retrieval process consists of two steps: first, select retrieval candidates from the complete dataset; and second, rank the retrieved candidates by DP matching and to present candidates ranked in terms of closeness. Here, the distance measure between patterns at two time steps, m and n, in terms of feature k, is defined as

$$d_k(m, n) = \frac{|y_k(m) - y_k(n)|}{\eta V_k(T)} \quad (1)$$

where $|\cdot|$ represents Euclidean norm, and η is the lead time step that denotes the forecast target time. $V_k(T)$ indicates the transition speed of the query pattern corresponding to the distance that a feature point moves per unit time step in the feature space. For example, the transition speed $V_k(T)$ can be obtained as follows

$$V_k(T) = |y_k(T) - y_k(T - 1)|. \quad (2)$$

With the transition speed $V_k(T)$ and lead time η, we can calculate normalized distances $d_k(m, n)$. The numerator in Eq.(1) depends on types of the echo patterns, especially its area for the mesh feature. This normalization eliminates this dependency and enables us to set an appropriate search range by thresholding the distance $d_k(m, n)$.

Next, from the complete dataset, we extract subset S_T that holds retrieval candidate subsequences similar to the query

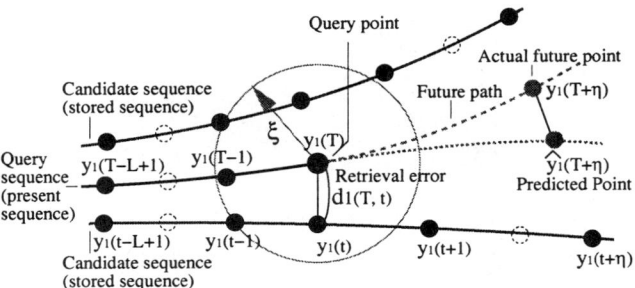

Figure 4: Paths representing query sequence and stored sequences in the feature space.

sequence T by thresholding the distance d_k calculated between the query point and each point in the dataset over the span L, as written in

$$S_T = \bigcap_{\substack{k \in \{1,2,3\} \\ i \in \{0,\cdots,L-1\}}} \{t \mid d_k(T-i, t-i) < \xi\} \quad (3)$$

where ξ is a threshold determining the range of dissimilarity. The subset S_T consists of subsequences that display the similar phenomenon as the query.

Next, the dissimilarity between the query and each of the candidate sequences in S_T is determined to choose several of the best matching sequences. It is known that similar phenomena can exhibit different development speeds, and it is desirable to determine the degree of dissimilarity while compensating a certain degree of difference in their speeds. To do this, possible temporal alignments between query and the candidate sequence should be considered to select the one with minimum matching cost. Thus, we employ DP matching in determining the degree of dissimilarity $D_k(T, t)$ for each feature k. $D_k(T, t)$ is defined as described in the following recursive procedure.

$$D_k(T, t) = \min \left\{ \begin{array}{l} D_k(T-1, t) + d_k(T, t)/L \\ D_k(T-1, t-1) + d_k(T, t)/L \\ D_k(T, t-1) + d_k(T, t)/L \end{array} \right\}$$

$$D_k(m, n) = d_k(m, n)/L$$
$$\text{if } m = T - L + 1 \text{ or } n = t - L + 1. \quad (4)$$

The total dissimilarity measure $E(T, t)$ between the query subsequence T and a subsequence t in the database is then obtained by integrating each retrieval error $D_k(T, t)$ as follows

$$E(T, t) = \frac{1}{R} \sum_{k=1}^{R} D_k(T, t) \quad (5)$$

where number of features $R = 3$. The total dissimilarity $E(T, t)$ is also called the retrieval error.

Finally, we select some retrieval sequences from the set of the retrieval candidates S_T, in ascending order of the total dissimilarity measure E. Here, we assume that the user gives the maximum number K of retrieved sequences and the allowable total dissimilarity E_{TH}. The set of resulting retrieved sequences C_T is retrieved as

$$C_T = \{q_1, q_2, \cdots, q_{K'}\} \quad (6)$$
where
$$E(T, q_i) \leq E(T, q_{i+1})$$
$$K' = \max\{i \mid i \leq K, E(T, q_i) \leq E_{TH}\}$$
$$|q_i - q_{i+1}| > r$$
$$q_1 = \arg \min_{t \in S_T} E(T, t)$$

where r is constant and used to prevent retrieving adjacent points. In Eq.(6), K' denotes the resulting number of the retrieved sequences.

Prediction Scheme

Finally, we generate the forecast image of the radar echo pattern at η time steps ahead, based on subsequent parts of the retrieved sequences C_T. To that end, we first predict the future point of the query sequence in the mesh feature space. Here, since we consider this as a nonlinear prediction problem of time series, we employed the modified Lorenz method (Ikeguchi & Aihara 1995) because of its stability. This method produces the prediction as the linear combination of points at η steps ahead of the retrieved points q_i in the feature space, and we define its coefficients as the inverse of the retrieval error of each retrieved sequence. The prediction point $\widehat{\boldsymbol{y}}_1(T + \eta)$ in the mesh feature space is obtained as

$$\widehat{\boldsymbol{y}}_1(T + \eta) = \sum_{i=1}^{K'} w(q_i)\, \boldsymbol{y}_1(q_i + \eta) \quad (7)$$

$$w(q_i) = \frac{1}{E(T, q_i)} \cdot \frac{1}{\sum_{j=1}^{K'}(1/E(T, q_j))}. \quad (8)$$

Next, we construct the forecast image $\widehat{I}(T + \eta)$ from the predicted point $\widehat{\boldsymbol{y}}_1(T + \eta)$. Since the transformation G that yields the mesh feature $\boldsymbol{y}_1(t)$ from the original image $I(t)$ is not one-to-one correspondence mapping, we can not unequivocally obtain the forecast image from the predicted point $\widehat{\boldsymbol{y}}_1(T + \eta)$. Thus, we pose the constraint as described in $|\widehat{\boldsymbol{y}}_1(T + \eta) - G(\widehat{I}(T + \eta))| = 0$, and we obtain the forecast image that satisfies this constraint. Due to the linearity of the transformation G, which consists of spatial averaging and linear mapping into the eigenspace, the forecast image can be produced as

$$\widehat{I}(T + \eta) = \sum_{i=1}^{K'} w(q_i) I(q_i + \eta) \quad (9)$$

from Eq.(7) and the above constraint.

Experiments

To confirm the effectiveness of the proposed method, we conducted statistical experiments on retrieval and prediction.

Preparation of Dataset

In advance of the experiments, the feature spaces were constructed using approximately 9000 hours of radar images

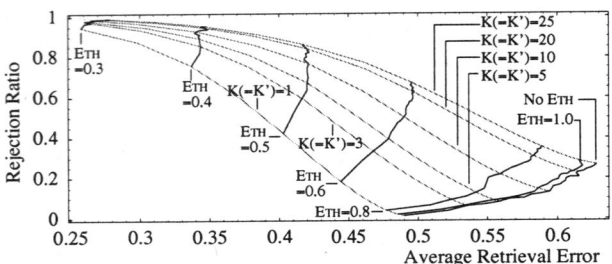

Figure 5: Relationship between average retrieval error and rejection ratio for various retrieval rank $K(=K')$ and threshold E_{TH} values.

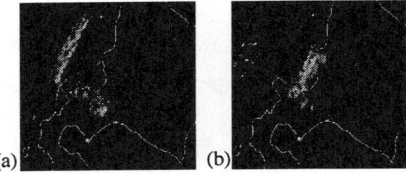

Figure 6: Query sequence, (a)Start frame, (b)End frame.

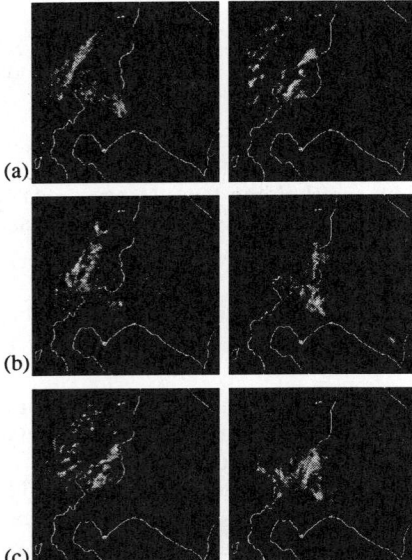

Figure 7: Retrieved sequences, (a)1st., (b)2nd., (c)3rd. candidate, [(left)start frame, (right)end frame].

(about 108000 image frames, 6 winter seasons) for the Sapporo area, northern Japan. Image size was 340×340 pixels where one pixel corresponded to a 1 km² area, and the gray level was 256 levels, which indicated instantaneous precipitation intensity. A single image frame was captured every 5 minutes. We set the unit time step to 1 hour, which meant that the interval between two adjacent time steps corresponded to 12 image frames. Dimensions of the eigenspaces were 8, 30, and 4 for the mesh feature, the velocity field, and the temporal texture feature, respectively. These dimensionalities were chosen to achieve 90% cumulative proportion, which means that 90% of the total variance in original feature distribution can be represented in the transformed feature space. The mesh size was 6 × 6 and each mesh included 55 × 55 pixels; the number of frames for temporal averaging was set to 20 frames. Subsequence length for matching was $L=3$, and the forecast lead time was set at $\eta=3$, the current goal of short-term precipitation forecasting. The threshold ξ was set to 1.0, and $r=3$. These parameters were empirically determined. Before each retrieval, the sequence used as the query, and its following sequence (if any), was removed from the dataset.

As a statistical evaluation of retrieval performance and prediction accuracy, we randomly picked 800 time steps as queries from a database holding about 9000 time steps. Each time step within the dataset was given as a query, and several sequences were retrieved to create the forecast image, After that, statistical characteristics regarding retrieval and prediction accuracy were examined. Here, the evaluation was done in the manner of the leave-one-out scheme.

Retrieval Error and Rejection Ratio

Figure 5 shows the relationships between the average retrieval error and the rejection ratio for various retrieval rank $K(=K')$ and threshold E_{TH} values. The rejection ratio was defined as the ratio of trials in which retrieval failed due to a lack of neighboring sequences. The retrieval result for retrieval rank $K(=K')$ corresponds to the result whose number of retrieved sequences K' is equal to the designated number of sequences K. From Figure 5, we can see that the retrieval error increases with retrieval rank $K(=K')$, and that a tradeoff between the retrieval error and the rejection ratio exists; small threshold E_{TH} offers retrieval with small retrieval error, but the rejection ratio tends to increase. Therefore, Figure 5 can be taken as a guide regarding data availability, an important factor in actual operational use.

As an example of retrieval, Figure 6 and Figure 7 show a query sequence and the top three retrieved sequences, respectively. Figure 6 includes a thick line-shaped echo moving toward the land area, and we can see that the retrieved sequences in Figure 7 also include patterns similar to the query pattern. These retrieval results are satisfactory because the retrieved patterns are not only visually similar to the queries, but also have almost the same meteorological characteristics as the query. Such retrieval results are expected to be useful reference information for human forecasters in understanding and forecasting future weather pattern.

Prediction Accuracy in Feature Space

Next, the prediction accuracy in the mesh feature space was verified. The reason for choosing the mesh feature was that the mesh feature was a kind of summarized representation of the precipitation distribution.

For each trial, the future point of the query sequence was predicted by using Eq.(7), and the prediction error ϵ_T was calculated as written in

$$\epsilon_T = \frac{|\widehat{\boldsymbol{y}}_1(T+\eta) - \boldsymbol{y}_1(T+\eta)|}{|\boldsymbol{y}_1(T) - \boldsymbol{y}_1(T+\eta)|}. \quad (10)$$

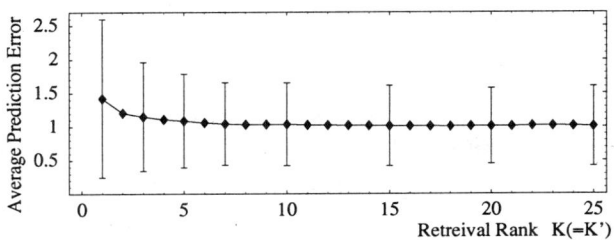

Figure 8: Average prediction error $\overline{\epsilon_T}$ in mesh feature space v.s. retrieval rank $K(=K')$, without thresholding by E_{TH}.

The prediction error ϵ_T in Eq.(10) was the distance between the actual future point and the predicted point at the lead time steps ahead, divided by persistence prediction error which is the distance between the query point and the actual future point, as shown in Figure 4. Normalization by the persistence prediction error was required to eliminate the dependency of the prediction error on the size of the individual echo pattern.

Figure 8 shows the transition of the average prediction error $\overline{\epsilon_T}$ and its standard deviation, as a function of the retrieval rank $K(=K')$, where no threshold E_{TH} is used. From Figure 8, we can see that the prediction error decreases as the rank $K(=K')$ increases and saturates at a certain level; the wide deviation range indicates that the prediction error varies widely depending on the sequences that neighbor each query. If the prediction error is above 1.0, the prediction is meaningless, because the prediction is worse than the persistence prediction that employs the query pattern as its forecast. In the case at $K(=K')$=25, 60.8% of all trials have prediction error under 1.0, and in such a case there is the potential to produce more accurate forecasts than would be possible with persistence prediction.

Evaluation of Forecast Images

Next, as a forecast image, we created the accumulated distribution of precipitation within periods from 2 hours to 3 hours later. The forecast images were calculated at five minute intervals from 2 hours to 3 hours later by Eq.(9), and each pixel value of the forecast images was transformed into precipitation intensity [mm/h] by applying a radar equation (Sauvageot 1992). Finally, the precipitation intensity at each time step was accumulated to yield the predicted distribution of the precipitation amount.

As a measure of forecast accuracy, we employed the CSI(Critical Success Index), which is the percentage of correctly forecasted areas divided by all areas including correctly forecasted areas and falsely forecasted areas whose precipitation exceeded 0.1[mm/hour]. Also, we employ the CSI ratio, which is a ratio of our result's CSI to the CSI of persistence forecasting. A persistence forecast is the accumulated distribution of precipitation from 1 hour before up to the query time. Generally speaking, overcoming the accuracy of persistence forecast is a primary goal of precipitation forecasting.

Table 1 shows the average CSI ratio and CSI for various $K(=K')$ values, where no threshold E_{TH} is used. From

Table 1: Average CSI ratio and average CSI for various retrieval rank $K(=K')$.

	K=1	K=3	K=5	K=10	K=25
CSI Ratio	0.76	0.97	1.02	1.08	1.12
CSI[%]	21.4	26.8	28.3	29.5	30.3

Table 2: Average CSI ratio and average CSI by simple extrapolation method (Rows of $K(=K')$=3,10,25 are results from same dataset for each MBF method).

	All	K=3	K=10	K=25
CSI Ratio	0.87	0.88	0.90	0.92
CSI[%]	18.8	19.1	18.6	17.2

Table 1, both CSI ratio and CSI are improved as $K(=K')$ increases, which corresponds to the trend in the prediction error as shown in Figure 8. At $K(=K')$=25, the CSI ratio reaches 1.12 and 51.8% of the forecasts exceeds the CSI of persistence forecasting. Table 2 shows the average CSI ratio and CSI by the simple extrapolation method for all samples and samples that correspond to our MBF method. The simple extrapolation method we use translates the present pattern at a single dominant velocity obtained by pattern matching between frames. A comparison of Table 1 and Table 2 shows that our MBF method exceeds the simple extrapolation method in terms of accuracy.

Figure 9 shows examples of forecast images, actual patterns, and persistence forecasts. Case 1) is the forecast created from the retrieval trial in Figure 7. We can see that thick line-shaped echo pattern changes into a widely spread pattern with a stripe-type texture over the sea within three hours. Case 2) and Case 3) are stratiform type pattern, which rapidly flows toward the upper-right direction with abrupt appearance of large surfaces. These cases confirm one key superiority of the MBF method: making the most of past patterns. The conventional methods fail to predict such drastic pattern changes, because they mainly depend on the current pattern.

Accordingly, our MBF framework is expected to become a promising tool to support the forecasting of local precipitation patterns by providing both retrieval and forecast images.

Discussion

In our framework, the forecast performance depends heavily on the dataset available. If there is no stored sequence that is similar to a given query sequence, the accuracy of retrieval and forecasting is greatly degraded; this is the main drawback of our MBF approach. Accordingly, it is useful to discover the relationship between the amount of stored data and forecast accuracy, and to know the degree of forecast reliability or predictability in advance. For guidance, we found a correlation between the retrieval error and the prediction error.

Furthermore, this work is rather simplistic in that only radar image information is used. Given that precipitation is affected by several physical atmospheric factors, the addi-

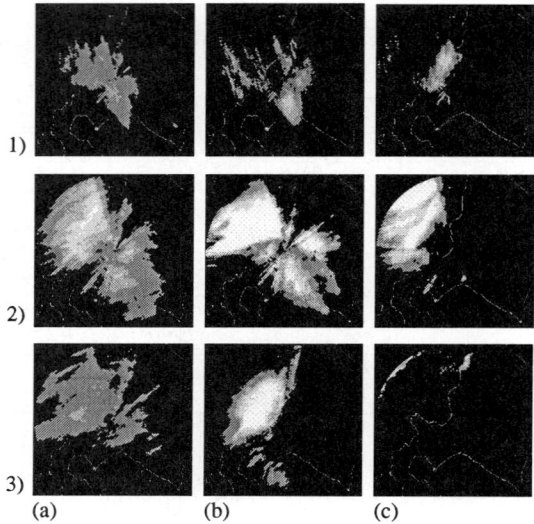

Figure 9: Accumulated distribution of precipitation from 2 hours later to 3 hours later, (a)Our forecast, (b)Actual, (c)Persistence forecast. For three cases, our CSI=(44.5, 72.9, 41.9), and CSI of persistence forecast is (16.5, 35.9, 3.0), respectively. No threshold E_{TH} is used, and K=25. Moreover, CSI of the simple extrapolation method was (24.2,24.0,1.0).

tion of physical information such as temperature, pressure, and humidity may be important in providing more accurate forecasts. For that purpose, appropriate selection and weighting mechanisms of different kinds of features should be incorporated into the MBF system.

Conclusion

This paper proposed a framework called Memory-Based Forecasting(MBF) and an implementation that can forecast complex natural patterns, especially weather radar echo patterns. To characterize such patterns, global features and temporal texture features were developed, and similar sequences are retrieved based on a dissimilarity measure between paths in the feature spaces. Several experiments confirmed that MBF offers good forecast accuracy if there is a sufficient volume and quality of stored data.

Acknowledgments. The authors are very grateful to Sapporo Information Network Co. and Mr. Masaharu Fujii for providing the radar images and useful meteorological advice. We also thank Dr. Noboru Sonehara of NTT Cyber Solutions Labs. for giving us the opportunity for this research.

References

Bobick, A. F., and Wilson, A. D. 1995. A state-based technique for the summarization and recognition of gesture. In *Proc. ICCV'95*, 382–388.

Connell, M. E., and Utgoff, P. E. 1987. Learning to control a dynamic physical system. In *Proc. AAAI'87*, 456–460.

Crook, N. A., and Tuttle, J. D. 1997. Short-term forecasting of summer precipitation using echo extrapolation, storm characteristics and model output. In *Proc. 7th Conf. Aviation, Range and Aerospace Meteorology*, 274–278.

Fujimoto, Y.; Iwasa, H.; Yokoya, N.; and Takemura, H. 1996. Retrieval of image sequences based on similarity of trajectories in eigenspaces. *Tech. Report of IEICE* PRMU96-110:49–56. (In Japanese).

Hansen, B. K., and Riordan, D. 1998. Fuzzy case-based prediction of ceiling and visibility. In *Proc. 1st. Conf. Artificial Intelligence of the American Meteorological Society*, 118–123.

Ikeguchi, T., and Aihara, K. 1995. Prediction of chaotic time series with noise. *IEICE Trans. Fundamentals* E78-A(10):1291–1298.

Jones, E. K., and Roydhouse, A. 1995. Intelligent retrieval of archived meteorological data. *IEEE Expert* 50–57.

Kolodner, J. L. 1991. Improving human decision making through case-based decision aiding. *AI Magazine* 52–68.

Lee, R. W.; Barcia, R. M.; and Khator, S. K. 1995. Case-based reasoning for cash flow forecasting using fuzzy retrieval. In *Proc. 1st. Int. Conf. Case-Based Reasoning*, 510–519.

Mohri, T.; Nakamura, M.; and Tanaka, H. 1993. Weather forecasting using memory-based reasoning. In *Proc. 2nd. Int. Workshop on PPAI*, 40–45.

Mulhern, F. J., and Caprara, R. J. 1994. A nearest neighbor model for forecasting market response. *Int. J. Forecasting* 10:191–207.

Murase, H., and Nayar, S. K. 1995. Visual learning and recognition of 3-d objects from appearance. *Int. J. Computer Vision* 14(1):5–24.

Nayar, S. K.; Nene, S. A.; and Murase, H. 1996. Subspace methods for robot vision. *IEEE Trans. Robotics and Automation* 12(5):750–758.

Otsuka, K.; Horikoshi, T.; Suzuki, S.; and Fujii, M. 1998. Feature extraction of temporal texture based on spatiotemporal motion trajectory. In *Proc. ICPR'98*, 1047–1051.

Otsuka, K.; Horikoshi, T.; Suzuki, S.; and Kojima, H. 1999. Memory-based forecasting of complex natural patterns by retrieving similar image sequences. In *Proc. ICIAP'99*, 874–879.

Otsuka, K.; Horikoshi, T.; Kojima, H.; and Suzuki, S. 2000. Image sequence retrieval for forecasting weather radar echo pattern. *IEICE Trans. Inf. and Syst.* E83-D. (Forthcoming).

Sauvageot, H. 1992. *Radar meteorology*. Artech House, Inc.

Stanfill, C., and Waltz, D. 1986. Toward memory-based reasoning. *Commun. ACM* 29(12):1213–1228.

Turk, M. A., and Pentland, A. P. 1991. Face recognition using eigenfaces. In *Proc. CVPR'91*, 586–591.

Yacoob, Y., and Black, M. J. 1999. Parameterized modeling and recognition of activities. *Computer Vision and Image Understanding* 73(2):232–247.

The Complexity of Restricted Consequence Finding and Abduction

Alvaro del Val
E.T.S. Informática
Universidad Autónoma de Madrid
delval@ii.uam.es
http://www.ii.uam.es/~delval.

Abstract

We analyze the complexity of propositional kernel resolution (del Val 1999), a general method for obtaining logical consequences in restricted target languages. Different choices of target are relevant to important AI tasks, e.g. prime implicates, satisfiability, abduction and non-monotonic reasoning, and polynomial-size knowledge compilation.

Based on a generalized concept of induced width, we identify new tractable classes for various targets, and show how to estimate in advance the complexity of every problem, under various atom orderings. This can be used to choose an ordering for kernel resolution.

Two applications are discussed: estimating the number of prime implicates of any theory; and identifying tractable abduction and diagnosis problems.

Introduction

Kernel resolution (del Val 1999) is a powerful method for generating consequences of a logical theory, where we can restrict in arbitrary ways which consequences we are interested in by looking only for consequences in some "target language," a subset of the full language over a given vocabulary. We analyze the complexity of propositional kernel resolution in terms of "structural" parameters closely related to induced width, a well-known parameter for characterizing the structure of logical theories and many other AI and CS problems (Dechter and Rish 1994; Dechter 1999; Bodlaender 1993). In particular, we identify new tractable classes for a variety of consequence-finding tasks, and show how to estimate space and time requirements of variously restricted kernel resolution on *every* problem instance.[1] These estimates can also be used to choose among various atom orderings prior to running kernel resolution, a choice which is crucial to its efficiency. Of special interest is our ability to estimate, for the first time, the number of prime implicates of any theory; and the identification of tractable classes for tasks such as abduction and diagnosis.

The complexity analysis in this paper is a generalization of the analysis of (del Val 2000), in these proceedings. Reading (del Val 2000) before the present paper

Copyright © 2000, American Association for Artificial Intelligence (www.aaai.org). All rights reserved.

[1]This should be contrasted with the usual focus on hand-crafting worst-case instances whose relevance to any other problem in the class is at best doubtful.

may help the reader to understand better the results presented here. Part of the analysis of (del Val 2000) appears here as the special case for the restricted language $\mathcal{L}_\square$.

We assume familiarity with the standard terminology of propositional reasoning and resolution. Some definitions are as follows. A clause C subsumes a clause D iff $C \subseteq D$. The empty clause is denoted $\square$. For a theory (set of clauses) Σ, we use $\mu(\Sigma)$ to denote the result of removing all subsumed clauses from Σ. An implicate of Σ is a clause C such that $\Sigma \models C$; a prime implicate is an implicate not subsumed by any other implicate. We denote by $PI(\Sigma)$ the set of prime implicates of Σ. We are often interested only in some subset of $PI(\Sigma)$. For this purpose, we define the notion of a target language $\mathcal{L}_T$, which is simply a set of clauses. We assume $\mathcal{L}_T$ is *closed under subsumption (c.u.s.)*, i.e. for any $C \in \mathcal{L}_T$ and $D \subseteq C$, we have $D \in \mathcal{L}_T$. A target language can always be closed under subsumption by adding all subsumers of clauses in the language.

Given these definitions, the task we are interested in is finding the prime $\mathcal{L}_T$-implicates of Σ, defined as $PI_{\mathcal{L}_T}(\Sigma) = PI(\Sigma) \cap \mathcal{L}_T$. We will mainly consider the following target languages: $\mathcal{L}$ is the full language, i.e. the set of all clauses over the set $Var(\Sigma)$ of variables of Σ. $\mathcal{L}_\square = \{\square\}$ contains only the empty clause. Given a set of variables V, the "vocabulary-based" language $\mathcal{L}_V$ is the set of clauses over V. Finally, for a constant K, $\mathcal{L}_K$ is the set of clauses over $Var(\Sigma)$ whose length does not exceed K. Thus we have $\mathcal{L}_1$, $\mathcal{L}_2$, etc.

Each of these languages corresponds to some important AI task. At one extreme, finding the prime implicates of Σ is simply finding $PI_\mathcal{L}(\Sigma) = PI(\Sigma)$; at the other extreme, deciding whether Σ is satisfiable is identical to deciding whether $PI_{\mathcal{L}_\square}(\Sigma)$ is empty. Vocabulary-based languages also have many applications, in particular in abduction and non-monotonic reasoning, both for default logic and circumscription (see e.g. (Inoue 1992; Selman and Levesque 1996; Marquis 1999) among many others). Since most of these applications rely on some form of abductive reasoning, we will analyze the abduction problem in detail. Finally, $\mathcal{L}_K$ or subsets thereof guarantee that $PI_{\mathcal{L}_K}(\Sigma)$ has polynomial size, which is relevant to knowledge compilation (surveyed in (Cadoli and Donini 1997)).

Sometimes we will be interested in theories which are logically equivalent to $PI_{\mathcal{L}_T}(\Sigma)$, but which need not include all $\mathcal{L}_T$-implicates, and can thus be much more concise. We refer to any such theory as a $\mathcal{L}_T$-LUB of Σ, following (Selman and Kautz 1996), see also (del Val 1995). We'll see one particular application of $\mathcal{L}_T$-LUBs in our discussion of diagnosis later.

After reviewing kernel resolution, we analyze its complexity for one particular exhaustive search strategy. We then present several applications of our results. Finally, we briefly consider a number of refinements and extensions to other search strategies.

Kernel resolution: Review

Kernel resolution can be seen as the consequence-finding generalization of ordered resolution (Fermüller *et al.* 1993; Bachmair and Ganzinger 1999). We assume a total ordering $o = x_1, \ldots, x_n$ of the propositional variables $\mathcal{P}$, so called atom ordering or A-ordering. We speak of x_i being "earlier" or "smaller" in the ordering than x_j just in case $i < j$. We also use l_i for either x_i or $\overline{x_i}$; the ordering is extended to literals in the obvious way, i.e. $l_i < l_j$ iff $i < j$. A *kernel clause* C is a clause split into two parts, the *skip*, $s(C)$, and the *kernel*, $k(C)$. Kernel literals, those in $k(C)$, must be larger than all the skipped literals, and are the only ones which can be resolved upon. We write a kernel clause C as $A[B]$, where $C = A \cup B$, $A = s(C)$, and $B = k(C)$. Given a set of standard clauses as input, they are transformed into kernel clauses by making $k(C) = C$, $s(C) = \emptyset$ for every C in the set. We refer to a set of kernel clauses such as these with empty skip as a *standard kernel theory*.

Definition 1 *(del Val 1999) A $\mathcal{L}_T$-kernel deduction of a clause C from a set of clauses Σ is a sequence of clauses of the form $S_1[K_1], \ldots, S_n[K_n]$ such that:*

1. $C = S_n \cup K_n$
2. *For every k, $S_k \cup K_k$ is not a tautology.*
3. *For every k, either:*
   (a) $K_k \in \Sigma$ and $S_k = \emptyset$ *(input clause); or*
   (b) $S_k \cup K_k$ *is a resolvent of two clauses $S_i \cup K_i$ and $S_j \cup K_j$ ($i, j < k$) such that:*
      i. *the literals resolved upon to obtain $S_k \cup K_k$ are in, respectively, K_i and K_j; and*
      ii. K_k *is the set of all literals of $S_k \cup K_k$ which are larger than the literals resolved upon, according to the given ordering, and S_k is the set of smaller literals.*
      iii. $S_k[K_k]$ *is $\mathcal{L}_T$-acceptable, i.e. $S_k \in \mathcal{L}_T$.*

We write $\Sigma \vdash_k^{\mathcal{L}_T} C$ to indicate that there is a $\mathcal{L}_T$-kernel resolution proof of a clause which subsumes C from Σ.

The "clausal meaning" of a kernel clause $S_k[K_k]$ is simply given by $S_k \cup K_k$. The crucial aspects are that resolutions are only permitted upon kernel literals, condition 3.b.i, and that the literal resolved upon partitions the literals of the resolvent into those smaller (the skip) and those larger (the kernel) than the literal resolved upon, condition 3.b.ii. The generality of kernel resolution for consequence finding comes from condition 3.b.iii. Since the skipped literals of a clause C are never resolved upon,

Var	Initial	Added
s_1	s_1a_1	
s_2	s_2a_2	
s_3	s_3a_3	
a_1	s_1a_1, $[\overline{a_1a_2a_3}]$	
a_2	s_2a_2, $[\overline{a_1a_2a_3}]$	$s_1[\overline{a_2a_3}]$
a_3	s_3a_3, $[\overline{a_1a_2a_3}]$	$s_1[\overline{a_2a_3}]$, $s_2\overline{a_1}[\overline{a_3}]$, $s_1s_2[\overline{a_3}]$
		$s_3\overline{a_1a_2}$, $s_1s_3\overline{a_2}$,
		$s_2s_3\overline{a_1}$, $s_1s_2s_3$

Table 1: $\mathcal{L}$-BE(Σ_1).

they appear in all descendants of C. Assuming $\mathcal{L}_T$ is c.u.s., if $s(C) \notin \mathcal{L}_T$ then no descendant of C can be in $\mathcal{L}_T$, as any descendant is subsumed by $s(C)$. Thus any such C cannot contribute to finding $\mathcal{L}_T$-implicates, is labeled as non-acceptable, and discarded.

Example 1 Let $\Sigma_1 = \{s_1a_1, s_2a_2, s_3a_3, \overline{a_1a_2a_3}\}$, and $o_1 = s_1, s_2, s_3, a_1, a_2, a_3$. The "Added" column of Table 1 shows $\mathcal{L}$-kernel resolvents obtained from Σ_1 with ordering o_1. (The reason why some clauses are repeated will become clear in Example 2.) While all these resolvents are $\mathcal{L}$-acceptable, only $s_1[\overline{a_2a_3}]$ is $\mathcal{L}_1$-acceptable, and no resolvent is $\mathcal{L}_\square$-acceptable. Thus $\mathcal{L}_T$-acceptability greatly restricts allowable resolvents. □

The next theorem states the completeness of $\mathcal{L}_T$-kernel resolution for consequence-finding.

Theorem 1 *(del Val 1999) Suppose $\mathcal{L}_T$ is c.u.s. For any clause $C \in \mathcal{L}_T$, $\Sigma \models C$ iff $\Sigma \vdash_k^{\mathcal{L}_T} C$.*

As special cases, for $\mathcal{L}$ all resolvents are $\mathcal{L}$-acceptable, and $\mathcal{L}$-kernel resolution finds all prime implicates of Σ. For $\mathcal{L}_\square$, only resolvents whose skip is empty are acceptable; thus, we can only generate acceptable resolvents by resolving on the smallest literal of each clause. This is simply ordered resolution in the sense of (Bachmair and Ganzinger 1999), a satisfiability method which has been recently shown by (Dechter and Rish 1994) to be quite efficient on problems with "low induced width," on which it outperforms Davis-Putnam backtracking by orders of magnitude. For $\mathcal{L}_K$, only resolvents whose skip has at most K literals are acceptable.

In order to search the space of kernel resolution proofs, we associate to each variable x_i a bucket $b[x_i]$ of clauses containing x_i; these buckets are partitioned into $b[x_i]^+$ and $b[x_i]^-$ for, respectively, positive and negative occurrences of x_i. The clauses in each bucket are determined by an indexing function $I_{\mathcal{L}_T}$, so that $C \in b[x_i]$ iff $x_i \in I_{\mathcal{L}_T}(C)$. As shown in (del Val 1999), we can always use the function $I_{\mathcal{L}_T}(C) = \{$kernel variables of the largest prefix $l_1 \ldots l_k$ of C s.t. $l_1l_2 \ldots l_{k-1} \in \mathcal{L}_T\}$, where C is assumed sorted in ascending order; resolving on any other kernel literal would yield a non-$\mathcal{L}_T$-acceptable resolvent.

For reasons of space, we will consider only one specific exhaustive strategy for kernel resolution, namely *bucket elimination*, abbreviated $\mathcal{L}_T$-BE. $\mathcal{L}_T$-BE processes buckets $b[x_1], \ldots, b[x_n]$ in order, computing in step i all resolvents that can be obtained by resolving clauses of

$b[x_i]$ upon x_i, and adding them to their corresponding buckets, using $I_{\mathcal{L}_T}$. We denote the set of clauses computed by the algorithm as $\mathcal{L}_T\text{-BE}(\Sigma)$. We have $\mu(\mathcal{L}_T\text{-BE}(\Sigma)) \cap \mathcal{L}_T = PI_{\mathcal{L}_T}(\Sigma)$. Our analysis can be extended to other exhaustive strategies for kernel resolution, such as incremental saturation (del Val 1999); this is briefly discussed in the conclusion.

As shown in (del Val 1999), $\mathcal{L}\text{-BE}$ is identical to Tison's prime implicate algorithm (Tison 1967), whereas $\mathcal{L}_\square\text{-BE}$ is identical to directional resolution, the name given by (Dechter and Rish 1994) to the original, resolution-based Davis-Putnam satisfiability algorithm (Davis and Putnam 1960).

For $\mathcal{L}_V$, we will in fact consider two BE procedures, both of which assume that *the variables of V are the last in the ordering*. $\mathcal{L}_V^1\text{-BE}$ is simply $\mathcal{L}_V\text{-BE}$ under this ordering assumption. $\mathcal{L}_V^0\text{-BE}$ is identical, except that processing is interrupted right before the first variable of V is processed. Thus $\mu(\mathcal{L}_V^1\text{-BE}(\Sigma)) \cap \mathcal{L}_V = PI_{\mathcal{L}_V}(\Sigma)$, whereas $\mu(\mathcal{L}_V^0\text{-BE}(\Sigma)) \cap \mathcal{L}_V$ is logically equivalent but not necessarily identical to $PI_{\mathcal{L}_V}(\Sigma)$; in other words, it is a $\mathcal{L}_V$-LUB of Σ. Note that in either case, the desired set of clauses is stored in the last buckets. The advantage of this ordering is that either form of $\mathcal{L}_V\text{-BE}$ behave exactly as directional resolution, which as said is an efficient satisfiability method, up to the first V-variable of the ordering. $\mathcal{L}_V^0\text{-BE}$ stops right there (and is thus strictly cheaper than deciding satisfiability with DR under such orderings), while $\mathcal{L}_V^1\text{-BE}$ continues, computing the prime implicates of $\mu(\mathcal{L}_V^0\text{-BE}(\Sigma)) \cap \mathcal{L}_V$ with full kernel resolution over the V-buckets.

Example 2 Table 1 illustrates $\mathcal{L}\text{-BE}(\Sigma_1)$ along o_1, showing the initial and final contents of buckets. Note that clauses can be indexed in multiple buckets, or in none if they have empty kernels (listed in the bottom row). For $\mathcal{L}_1\text{-BE}$, initial buckets would differ only in that $[\overline{a_1 a_2 a_3}] \notin b[a_3]$; and there is a single $\mathcal{L}_1$-acceptable resolvent, $s_1[\overline{a_2 a_3}]$, which is added only to $b[a_2]$. This suffices to prove that Σ_1 has no unit implicates. Finally, $\mathcal{L}_\square\text{-BE}$ generates no resolvents along o_1.

Complexity of BE

We now introduce the main concepts used in our complexity analysis. The main idea is very simple. We capture the input theory Σ (which for BE we may assume to be a standard kernel theory) with a graph that represents cooccurrence of literals in clauses of Σ. We then "simulate" kernel resolution in polynomial time by processing the graph to generate a new "induced" graph. Finally, we recover from the induced graph information about all relevant complexity parameters for the hypothetical execution of BE for the given theory and ordering.

Definition 2 (split interaction graph) Let Σ be a set of kernel clauses. The split interaction graph of Σ is $GS(\Sigma) = \langle V_S, E_S \rangle$, where:

- The set of vertices V_S is the set of all literals of Σ.
- E_S is a set of labeled undirected edges (l_j, l_k), where the label $L(l_j, l_k)$ is either kernel-kernel (kk), skip-skip (ss), or skip-kernel (sk).

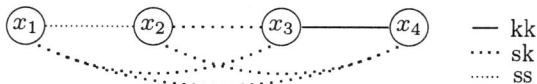

Figure 1: The split interaction graph for the single clause $x_1 x_2 [x_3 x_4]$. Unconnected vertices not shown.

- There is an edge $(l_j, l_k) \in E_S$ whenever there exists $C \in \Sigma$ such that $l_j, l_k \in C$. In this case, $L(l_j, l_k)$ is:
  - kk iff both $l_j, l_k \in k(C)$;
  - sk iff $l_j \in k(C), l_k \in s(C)$, or viceversa;
  - ss iff $l_j, l_k \in s(C)$.

If an edge (l_j, l_k) is determined by these rules to have more than one label, then $L(l_j, l_k)$ is the largest possible label according to the order $kk > sk > ss$.

Edges represent cooccurrence of literals, where we distinguish three types of cooccurrence: in the kernel, in the skip, or mixed. In the mixed case, we speak of the $l_k \in k(C)$ as the "kernel end" of the edge, the "skip end" being the other literal $l_j \in s(C)$. In the kk case, both literals are kernel ends, in the ss case, both are skip ends. Figure 1 illustrates the interaction graph for the single kernel clause $x_1 x_2 [x_3 x_4]$, and introduces our graphical conventions for each type of edge.

Every clause is represented in an interaction graph by a clique (fully connected graph) consisting of all its literals, with edge labels depending on where in the clause each literal occurs. All our complexity estimates will be based on approximately counting such cliques.

The split interaction graph is a generalization of the interaction graph of (Dechter and Rish 1994), in two ways: (a) our nodes are literals rather than variables, which yields a more fine-grained "simulation" of resolution; (b) we use various kinds of edges to deal with various forms of cooccurrence. Note however that (b) is irrelevant to the analysis of $\mathcal{L}_\square\text{-BE}$, which only uses kk edges (see below), and is the only procedure analyzed in (Dechter and Rish 1994). See also (del Val 2000). We next define an "induced graph" analogous to (Dechter and Rish 1994).

Definition 3 ($\mathcal{L}$-induced split interaction graph) Let Σ be a standard kernel theory, and $o = x_1, \ldots, x_n$ an ordering.

The $\mathcal{L}$-induced split interaction graph of Σ along ordering o is the graph $I_o(GS(\Sigma), \mathcal{L}) = \langle V_S, EL_S^o \rangle$ obtained by augmenting $GS(\Sigma)$ as follows:

1. initially, $EL_S^o = E_S$;
2. for $i = 1$ to n do: if $(x_i, l_j) \in E_S^o$, $(\overline{x_i}, l_k) \in E_S^o$, $j \neq k$, and $(l_j, l_k) \notin E_S^o$, then add the edge (l_j, l_k) to E_S^o, where the label $L(l_j, l_k)$ is:
   (a) kk, if the edge is added as above with $i < j$, $i < k$;
   (b) sk, if the edge is added with $k < i < j$ or $j < i < k$;
   (c) ss, if it was added with $k < i$ and $j < i$.

The $\mathcal{L}$-induced graph can be generated in $O(n^3)$. We adopt in what follows the convention of drawing graphs

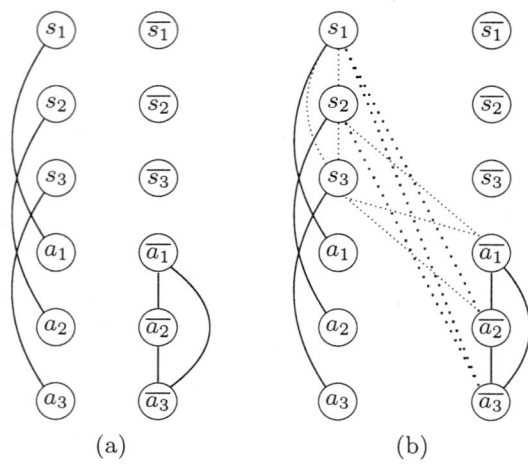

Figure 2: Interaction and $\mathcal{L}$-induced graphs for Σ_2.

with literal nodes ordered downwards along the given ordering, that is, with earlier literals above later literals, which motivates the following terminology:

Definition 4 *The* downward set $D(l_i)$ *of a literal* l_i *along ordering* o *is the set of literals* l_j *such that there is an edge* (l_i, l_j) *with* $i < j$; *the* upward set $U(v_i)$ *of* v_i *along* o *is the set of literals* l_j *such that there is an edge* (l_i, l_j) *with* $i > j$.

Both sets can be partitioned according to the type of edge. $D_{ss}(l_i)$, $D_{sk}(l_i)$ *and* $D_{kk}(l_i)$ *are respectively the subsets of* $D(l_i)$ *determined by, respectively, ss-, sk- and kk-edges. Similarly for* U_{ss}, U_{sk} *and* U_{kk}.[2]

Example 3 Figure 2 illustrates the interaction graph and $\mathcal{L}$-induced graph for the theory Σ_1 and ordering o_1 of Example 1. Note that the generation of the induced graph closely matches the generation of resolvents by $\mathcal{L}$-BE. Processing a_1 by $\mathcal{L}$-BE(Σ_1) yields the resolvent $s_1[a_2 a_3]$ from $[s_1 a_1]$ and $[\overline{a_1 a_2 a_3}]$ (see Table 1). In the generation of the induced graph, we find when processing a_1 that s_1 cooccurs with a_1, and $\overline{a_2}$ and $\overline{a_3}$ coocur with $\overline{a_1}$. Thus we can "predict" from the graph that resolving on a_1 will make s_1 cooccur with both $\overline{a_2}$ and $\overline{a_3}$. Further, since $s_1 < a_1 < a_2, a_3$, these cooccurrences must be of type sk. Similarly for all other added edges.

Other forms of BE can be similarly simulated:

Definition 5 *Define the following graphs:*

1. The $\mathcal{L}_\square$-induced graph $I_o(GS(\Sigma), \mathcal{L}_\square)$ is generated as $I_o(., \mathcal{L})$, except that we require $l_j \in D(x_i)$ and $l_k \in D(\overline{x_i})$. In other words, only kk-edges are added.

2. The $\mathcal{L}_1$-induced graph $I_o(GS(\Sigma), \mathcal{L}_1)$ is generated as $I_o(., \mathcal{L})$, except that we require that either $l_j \notin U(x_i)$ or $l_k \notin U(\overline{x_i})$. That is, only sk and kk edges are added.

3. The $\mathcal{L}_V^0$-induced graph $I_o(\Sigma, \mathcal{L}_V^0)$ is generated as $I_o(., \mathcal{L}_\square)$ up to the first variable of V in the ordering (recall V-variables are assumed last in o), and then stops.

---
[2] Note that l_i must be the skip end of sk-edges linking it to literals in $D_{sk}(l_i)$, and the kernel end of sk-edges linking it to literals in $U_{sk}(l_i)$.

The $\mathcal{L}_V^1$-induced graph $I_o(GS(\Sigma), \mathcal{L}_V^1)$ is generated in the same way up to the first V variable, then as $I_o(., \mathcal{L})$.

Example 4 $I_{o_1}(\Sigma_1, \mathcal{L}_\square)$ is identical to $GS(\Sigma_1)$ (Figure 2.a). $I_{o_1}(\Sigma_1, \mathcal{L}_1)$ can be obtained by eliminating all ss-edges from $I_{o_1}(\Sigma_1, \mathcal{L})$.

Our first lemma shows that the induced graphs simulate $\mathcal{L}_T$-BE as far as the interaction graph is concerned.

Lemma 2 *Let $\mathcal{L}_T$ be one of $\mathcal{L}$, $\mathcal{L}_\square$, $\mathcal{L}_V^0$, $\mathcal{L}_V^1$, or $\mathcal{L}_1$. $I_o(GS(\Sigma), \mathcal{L}_T)$ is a subgraph of $GS(\mathcal{L}_T\text{-}BE(\Sigma))$.*

Proof: Similar to the proof of (del Val 2000, Lemma 2). □

We can now characterize problem complexity.

Definition 6 *Given Σ, o, and $\mathcal{L}_T$ as above, let $D(l_i)$ and $U(l_i)$ be, respectively, the downward and upward sets of l_i in $I_o(GS(\Sigma), \mathcal{L}_T)$. Define:*

$$
\begin{array}{ll}
w_i^+ = |D(x_i)| & w_i^- = |D(\overline{x_i})| \\
wk_i^+ = |D_{kk}(x_i)| & wk_i^- = |D_{kk}(\overline{x_i})| \\
ws_i^+ = |D_{ss}(x_i)| & ws_i^- = |D_{ss}(\overline{x_i})| \\
wm_i^+ = |D_{kk}(x_i) \cup D_{sk}(x_i)| & wm_i^- = |D_{kk}(\overline{x_i}) \cup D_{sk}(\overline{x_i})| \\
um_i^+ = |U_{kk}(x_i) \cup U_{sk}(x_i)| & um_i^- = |U_{kk}(\overline{x_i}) \cup U_{sk}(\overline{x_i})|
\end{array}
$$

In addition, let $w_i = w_i^+ + w_i^-$, and similarly for wk_i, etc.

These can be seen as various forms of "induced width." Note that they are relative to the $\mathcal{L}_T$-induced graph, hence to both $\mathcal{L}_T$ and o. The mnemonics are: the initial letters w and u refer respectively to downward and upward sets, and the qualifiers are k for kk, s for ss, and m for mixed, meaning sk plus kk. The closest to the standard induced width of (Dechter and Rish 1994) would be given, if we abstract from the fact that we use literals rather than variables as nodes, by the wk_i's, which for $\mathcal{L}_\square$ are identical to the w_i's, since there are only kk edges in $I_o(GS(\Sigma), \mathcal{L}_\square)$. Again, see (del Val 2000).

Lemma 2, together with the restrictions on the contents of buckets imposed by $I_{\mathcal{L}_T}$ allow us to show:

Theorem 3 *For $\mathcal{L}_T \in \{\mathcal{L}, \mathcal{L}_\square, \mathcal{L}_V^0, \mathcal{L}_V^1\}$, the size of $\mathcal{L}_T$-BE(Σ) along ordering o is bounded by $\sum_{1 \le i \le n}(2^{w_i^+} + 2^{w_i^-})$. The size of $\mathcal{L}_K$-BE(Σ) is bounded by $\sum_{1 \le i \le n}((1 + ws_i^+)^{K-1} 2^{wm_i^+} + (1 + ws_i^-)^{K-1} 2^{wm_i^-})$.*

The number of resolutions steps performed by $\mathcal{L}_T$-BE(Σ) is bounded by:

1. $\mathcal{L}$-BE: $\sum_{1 \le i \le n} 2^{wk_i + um_i}$.

2. $\mathcal{L}_\square$-BE: $\sum_{1 \le i \le n} 2^{wk_i}$.

3. $\mathcal{L}_V^0$-BE: $\sum_{x_i \notin V} 2^{wk_i}$.

4. $\mathcal{L}_V^1$-BE: $\sum_{x_i \in V} 2^{wk_i + um_i} + \sum_{x_i \notin V} 2^{wk_i}$.

5. $\mathcal{L}_K$-BE: $\sum_{1 \le i \le n}((1 + um_i^+)^K (1 + um_i^-)^K 2^{wk_i})$.

Proof: The size estimate is obtained as in (del Val 2000, Theorem 4). For time, the number of resolution steps when processing x_i is bounded by $|b[x_i]^+| \times |b[x_i]^-|$. Consider the $\mathcal{L}$ case. Let $C \in b[x_i]$, $l \in C$. Then (l, x_i) must be an edge of $GS(\mathcal{L}\text{-}BE(\Sigma))$, with x_i as a kernel end (as $C \in b[x_i]$ implies $x_i \in k(C)$, given $I_\mathcal{L}$). By Lemma 2, (l, x_i) is also in $I_o(GS(\Sigma), \mathcal{L})$. Thus, $l \in U_{sk}(x_i) \cup U_{kk}(x_i) \cup D_{kk}(x_i)$. The cardinality of this set is $um_i^+ + wk^+ i$, which gives us a bound on the number of literals which cooccur with x_i in a clause which has x_i in the kernel. This immediately gives us

$|b[x_i]^+| \leq 2^{wk_i^+ + um_i^+}$. Bounding in a similar way $|b[x_i]^-|$ and summing up, we obtain the number of resolution steps given in the theorem for $\mathcal{L}$-BE. □

We emphasize that the values of w_i's in the size estimates depend on the induced graphs, which in turn depend on $\mathcal{L}_T$; in particular, $w_i = wk_i$ for $\mathcal{L}_\square$ and $\mathcal{L}_V^0$, as well as, for $x_i \notin V$, for $\mathcal{L}_V^1$. This is made explicit in the time estimates. Similarly, um_i may be smaller in $\mathcal{L}_V^1$ than in $\mathcal{L}$.[3] As expected, $\mathcal{L}_\square$-BE is cheaper in space and time than $\mathcal{L}$-BE, with $\mathcal{L}_K$-BE smoothly spanning the complexity gap between both;[4] and, if the V-variables are last, then $\mathcal{L}_V^1 - BE$ is cheaper than $\mathcal{L}_\square$-BE, which is cheaper than $\mathcal{L}_V^0$-BE, which is cheaper than $\mathcal{L}$-BE.

We next rewrite these estimates more compactly.

Definition 7 *The $\mathcal{L}_T$-induced kernel set $K(x_i)$ of a variable x_i along an ordering o is defined by reference to $I_o(GS(\Sigma), \mathcal{L}_T)$ as follows:*
  1. $\mathcal{L} : D_{kk}(x_i) \cup D_{kk}(\overline{x_i}) \cup U_{kk}(x_i) \cup U_{kk}(\overline{x_i}) \cup U_{sk}(x_i) \cup U_{sk}(\overline{x_i})$.
  2. $\mathcal{L}_\square : D_{kk}(x_i) \cup D_{kk}(\overline{x_i})$.
  3. $\mathcal{L}_V^0 : D_{kk}(x_i) \cup D_{kk}(\overline{x_i})$ for $x_i \notin V$, $\emptyset$ otherwise.
  4. $\mathcal{L}_V^1 : D_{kk}(x_i) \cup D_{kk}(\overline{x_i})$ for $x_i \notin V$, and otherwise as the $\mathcal{L}$-kernel set of x_i.

Definition 8 *The $\mathcal{L}_T$-induced s-width of an ordering o is $sw(o) = max(w_i^+, w_i^- \mid 1 \leq i \leq n)$. The $\mathcal{L}_T$-induced kernel width of o is $kw(o) = max(|K(x_i)| \mid 1 \leq i \leq n)$.*

Corollary 4 *Let $\mathcal{L}_T \in \{\mathcal{L}, \mathcal{L}_\square, \mathcal{L}_V^0, \mathcal{L}_V^1\}$. Then $|\mathcal{L}_T\text{-}BE(\Sigma)| = O(n \cdot 2^{sw(o)+1})$. The number of resolution steps is $O(n \cdot 2^{kw(o)})$, hence the total time complexity is $O(n^2 \cdot 2^{kw(o)})$.*

We thus obtain tractable classes:

Corollary 5 *If the $\mathcal{L}_T$-induced s-width along o is bounded by a constant then $\mathcal{L}_T\text{-}BE(\Sigma)$ requires only polynomial space; if the $\mathcal{L}_T$-induced kernel width is bounded by a constant then $\mathcal{L}_T\text{-}BE$ along o takes polynomial time.*

There exist methods to recognize in $exp(k)$ theories whose *standard* induced width is bounded by the constant k (Dechter and Rish 1994); we conjecture that these methods can be adapted to recognize bounded induced s-width at least for $\mathcal{L}_\square$, possibly for the other $\mathcal{L}_T$'s as well. Even if not, we can use the induced graphs to choose good orderings.

Applications

We next discuss very briefly some applications.

---

[3] E.g. say $x_3 \in V$. With $\mathcal{L}$, if $x_1 \in U_{sk}(x_2)$ and $x_3 \in D_{kk}(\overline{x_2})$ we must add x_1 to $U_{sk}(x_3)$. With $\mathcal{L}_V^1$, if $x_2 \notin V$ then $U_{sk}(x_2) = \emptyset$, hence x_1 is not added to $U_{sk}(x_3)$.

[4] This is made clearer by noting that $(1 + um^+ i)^K$ can be replaced by $min((1 + um_i^+)^K, 2^{um_i^+})$ in the time estimate for $\mathcal{L}_K$, and similarly with um_i^-. This yields a maximum of $2^{um_i^+} \cdot 2^{um_i^-} \cdot 2^{wk_i}$, which equals the time estimate for $\mathcal{L}$.

Prime implicates. Since $PI(\Sigma) = \mu(\mathcal{L}\text{-}BE(\Sigma))$, theorem 3 bounds the number of prime implicates of *any* theory. To our knowledge this is the first result of this kind in the literature (see the survey (Marquis 1999)). Much tighter estimates can be obtained along the lines discussed in the conclusion.

Diagnosis. In diagnosis (de Kleer *et al.* 1992), we are given a theory Σ describing the normal behavior of a set of components; for each component, there is an "abnormality" predicate ab_i. Let V be the set of ab_i's. Given a set of observations O (typically given as unit clauses), the diagnosis are given by the prime $\mathcal{L}_V$-*implicants*[5] of $PI_{\mathcal{L}_V}(\Sigma \cup O)$. These implicants can also be obtained from the smaller, equivalent $\mathcal{L}_V$-LUB; in other words, we can use either $\mathcal{L}_V^1$-BE or $\mathcal{L}_V^0$-BE to obtain a set of $\mathcal{L}_V$ clauses whose implicants yield the diagnosis. Thus, unlike in (de Kleer *et al.* 1992), we do not need to compute $PI(\Sigma \cup O)$; not even $PI_{\mathcal{L}_V}(\Sigma \cup O)$.

Corollary 5 yields classes of devices for which this intermediate, but crucial step of diagnosis is tractable. In addition, we can bound the size of the resulting $\mathcal{L}_V$ theory. This is simply the sum over $x_i \in V$ of $2^{w_i^+} + 2^{w_i^-}$ (which, again, may be smaller for $\mathcal{L}_V^0$).[6]

Abduction. Given a theory Σ, and a set A of variables, variously called assumptions, hypothesis, or abducibles, an *abductive explanation* of a literal l wrt. Σ is a conjunction L of literals over A such that $\Sigma \cup L$ is consistent and entails l; L is a minimal explanation iff no subset of it is also an explanation. Letting $Lit(A)$ be the set of literals over A, it is easy to show that $L \subseteq Lit(A)$ is a minimal explanation of l iff the clause $l \vee \neg L$ is in $PI(\Sigma)$ (see e.g. (Reiter and de Kleer 1987)).

Let $\mathcal{L}_A = \{l \vee C \mid l \text{ is a literal}, \text{clause } C \subseteq Lit(A)\}$. It follows from the above that we can obtain all minimal explanations of all literals from $PI_{\mathcal{L}_A}(\Sigma)$. An efficient form of $\mathcal{L}_A$-kernel resolution can be obtained by putting all assumptions A last in the ordering. The resulting BE procedure behaves as $\mathcal{L}_1$-BE up to the last variable not in A, and thereafter as $\mathcal{L}$-BE. The indexing function $I_{\mathcal{L}_A}(C)$ should index C by the kernel variables of C which are preceded by at most one non-A variable in C.

Example 5 Consider again Σ_1, and let $A = \{a_1, a_2, a_3\}$. The initial buckets would be identical to those of Table 1. $\mathcal{L}_A$-BE does not generate the resolvent $s_1 s_2 s_3$, as its parent $s_1 s_2 [\overline{a_3}]$ is rejected as not $\mathcal{L}_A$-acceptable; other resolvents are generated but rejected unless they contain exactly one s_i.

The $\mathcal{L}_A$-induced graph is identical to the $\mathcal{L}$-induced graph, except that no ss-edges linking two non-A-variables are allowed. We can use it to show:

Theorem 6 $|\mathcal{L}_A\text{-}BE(\Sigma)| \leq \sum_{1 \leq i \leq n}(2^{w_i^+} + 2^{w_i^-})$.
The number of resolution steps is bounded by $\sum_{x_i \notin A}(1 + um_i^+)(1 + um_i^-)2^{wk_i} + \sum_{x_i \in A} 2^{wk_i + um_i}$.

---

[5] An implicant of a theory Γ is a conjunction of literals which entails Γ.

[6] Use of $\mathcal{L}_V^0$ is beneficial if the ab_i's occur negatively in the theory, as it is the case when there are fault models; otherwise, both procedures yield the same result.

Note again that the w_i's can be significantly smaller than for $\mathcal{L}$, because of the restriction on ss edges. Again, if the exponents are bounded by a constant we obtain polynomial time and/or space. In this case we obtain tractable abduction in a rather strong sense, since $\mathcal{L}_A$ yields explanations for all literals. We can also bound the $\mathcal{L}_A$ clauses obtained, the number of explanations per literal, etc.

In addition to linking induced width with abduction, this tractability result is significant also because of the difficulty of abduction. Basically, the only known tractable classes are binary and definite theories. Finding *one* explanation for *one* literal is NP-complete even for acyclic Horn theories (Selman and Levesque 1996).

Polynomial size compilation The goal of knowledge compilation (Cadoli and Donini 1997) is to ensure tractable answers to all or some queries, by replacing a theory by a compiled one with better complexity. However, knowledge compilation faces fundamental limits in the sense that for many query languages it is extremely unlikely that one can guarantee tractable compiled representations of polynomial size (Selman and Kautz 1996; Cadoli and Donini 1997). It seems the only way out of this hurdle is to ensure that the query language has polynomial size. Our analysis of $\mathcal{L}_K$-consequence finding is a contribution to this goal.

Extensions and refinements

All of the above should be seen as a quite condensed summary of our complexity analysis of kernel resolution. In the long version of this paper, we refine and extend the analysis in a number of directions.

First, the estimates given can be made significantly tighter. As mentioned above, they are based on counting cliques in the $\mathcal{L}_T$-induced graphs. They do so very loosely, by simply assuming that the relevant subsets of $D(l) \cup U(l)$ are themselves cliques in the induced graph; and that these cliques have the appropriate structure (see Figure 1). While counting cliques is NP-hard, it is not difficult to devise cheap methods which provide much tighter estimates, and which can yield *new tractable classes* even with unbounded induced width. The refinements apply to the whole range of applications discussed here. It is also possible to take into account the effect of subsumption to further tigthen the estimates. All this is discussed in detail for the $\mathcal{L}_\Box$ case in (del Val 2000).

Second, we have focused only on BE, though we have mentioned that kernel resolution is compatible with other exhaustive search strategies, such as incremental saturation (IS) (del Val 1999), where clauses can be added/processed incrementally. In the extended paper, we show that we can simulate the behavior of IS as well, with suitable defined induced graphs. In a nutshell, the idea is to distinguish between passive and active edges, where the latter correspond to the newly added clause and the resolvents obtained from it and its descendants. We can thereby bound the space and time complexity of IS in a similar manner as we did with BE.

An interesting property of IS is that it allows us to obtain the *new* $\mathcal{L}_T$-implicates derivable from $\Sigma \cup C$ but not from Σ alone. Many tasks in common-sense reasoning, such as abduction and non-monotonic reasoning (both default logic and circumscription) can be cast in these terms (Inoue 1992; Marquis 1999). Thus the complexity analysis of IS helps us understand these tasks, and, again, obtain tractable classes.

References

L. Bachmair and H. Ganzinger. A theory of resolution. In J.A. Robinson and A. Voronkov, editors, *Handbook of Automated Reasoning*. Elsevier, 1999.

Bodlaender, H. L. 1993. A tourist guide through treewidth. *Acta Cybernetica* 11:1–21.

M. Cadoli and F. M. Donini. A survey on knowledge compilation. *AI Communications*, 10:137–150, 1997.

M. Davis and H. Putnam. A computing procedure for quantification theory. *J. ACM*, 7(3):201–215, 1960.

J. de Kleer, A. K. Mackworth, and R. Reiter. Characterizing diagnosis and systems. *Artificial Intelligence*, 56:197–222, 1992.

R. Dechter and I. Rish. Directional resolution: The Davis-Putnam procedure, revisited. In *KR'94, Proc. 4th Int. Conf. on Knowledge Representation and Reasoning*, pages 134–145. Morgan Kaufmann, 1994.

R. Dechter. Bucket elimination: A unifying framework for reasoning. *Artificial Intelligence*, 113:41–85, 1999.

A. del Val. An analysis of approximate knowledge compilation. In *IJCAI'95, Proc. 14th Int. Joint Conf. on Artificial Intelligence*, pages 830–836, 1995.

A. del Val. A new method for consequence finding and compilation in restricted languages. In *AAAI'99, Proc. 16th (U.S.) Nat. Conf. on Artificial Intelligence*, pages 259–264, 1999.

del Val, A. 2000. Tractable classes for directional resolution. In *AAAI'2000, Proc. 17th (U.S.) National Conference on Artificial Intelligence*. AAAI Press/MIT Press.

C. Fermüller, A. Leitsch, T. Tammet, and N. Zamov. *Resolution Methods for the Decision Problem*. Springer-Verlag, 1993.

K. Inoue. Linear resolution for consequence-finding. *Artificial Intelligence*, 56:301–353, 1992.

P. Marquis. Consequence-finding algorithms. In D. Gabbay and Ph. Smets, editors, *Handbook of Defeasible Reasoning and Uncertainty Management Systems*. Kluwer Academic Publishers, 1999.

R. Reiter and J. de Kleer. Foundations of assumption-based truth maintenance systems. In *AAAI'87, Proc. 6th (U.S.) Nat. Conf. on Artificial Intelligence*, 1987.

B. Selman and H. Kautz. Knowledge compilation and theory approximation. *J. ACM*, 43(2):193–224, 1996.

B. Selman and H. J. Levesque. Support set selection for abductive and default reasoning. *Artificial Intelligence*, 82:259–272, 1996.

P. Tison. Generalized consensus theory and application to the minimization of boolean circuits. *IEEE Transactions on Computers*, EC-16:446–456, 1967.

Tractable Classes for Directional Resolution

Alvaro del Val
E.T.S. Informática
Universidad Autónoma de Madrid
delval@ii.uam.es
http://www.ii.uam.es/~delval

Abstract

The original, resolution-based Davis-Putnam satisfiability algorithm (Davis & Putnam 1960) was recently revived by (Dechter & Rish 1994) under the name "directional resolution" (DR). We provide new positive complexity results for DR. First, we identify a class of theories (ACT, Acyclic Component Theories), which includes many real-world theories, for which DR takes polynomial time. Second, we present an improved analysis of the complexity of directional resolution through refined notions of induced width, which yields new tractable classes for DR, and much better predictions of its space and time requirements under various atom orderings. These estimates can be used for heuristically choosing among various orderings before running DR.

Introduction

The original, resolution-based Davis-Putnam satisfiability algorithm (Davis & Putnam 1960) was recently revived by (Dechter & Rish 1994; Rish & Dechter 2000) under the name "directional resolution" (DR). DR was shown to be a relatively efficient method for certain kinds of semi-structured problems, on which it often outperforms the backtracking-based Davis-Putnam algorithm (Davis, Logemann, & Loveland 1962) by orders of magnitude. While DR was also consistently outperformed by backjumping in these experiments, DR provides more information than backtracking procedures, as pointed out by (Dechter & Rish 1994), in that any model can be found backtrack-free after running DR.

In addition, DR lies at a very interesting theoretical crossroad. First, as shown in (Dechter 1999), DR is one of a family of "bucket elimination" (BE) procedures for logical, Bayesian, and constraint reasoning, as well as for linear and dynamic programming. The complexity of most of these BE procedures can be analysed in terms of a single structural parameter, induced width. Second, DR is, specifically, the bucket elimination version of propositional ordered resolution (in the sense of atom ordering, see e.g. (Fermüller et al. 1993; Bachmair & Ganzinger 1999)), itself a rich source of complexity results (Basin & Ganzinger 1996; Fermüller et al. 1993). Finally, (del Val 1999) has shown how to extend ordered resolution (with or without BE) to consequence-finding tasks, such as finding consequences that contain only certain literals, or with bounded length, or simply finding all consequences (the prime implicate task). DR provides a "bottom line" of computational effort for these consequence-finding tasks, as all the BE methods of (del Val 1999) perform at least as much work as DR. We extend our analysis of DR in this paper to consequence-finding in (del Val 2000).

(Dechter & Rish 1994) show that DR is tractable for a few classes of theories, including binary theories, and theories with bounded induced width or induced diversity. This paper makes two contributions. First, we introduce a wide class of structured, realistic theories for which DR takes polynomial time, even though it appears this cannot be predicted by induced width. Second, we refine the complexity analysis of DR in terms of induced width (Dechter & Rish 1994) by introducing new structural parameters to estimate the space and time requirements of DR. This allows us to identify new tractable classes, and also to obtain more accurate *empirical predictions* of complexity for any atom ordering. By comparing estimates for various orderings, we may heuristically choose among them before running DR. We will in fact go to some length to try to improve the accuracy of these predictions.

We assume familiarity with the standard terminology of propositional reasoning and resolution. The algorithm DR is very simple. Given a set of clauses Σ, fix some ordering $o = x_1, \ldots, x_n$ of the propositional variables. Associate to each variable a bucket $b[x_i]$ of clauses whose smallest variable, according to o, is x_i. Then process buckets in ascending order:[1]

Algorithm DR

for $i = 1$ to n do:
  compute all non-tautologous resolvents on x_i of clauses
  in $b[x_i]$, adding them to their corresponding buckets.

Example 1 *(Dechter & Rish 1994, example 2)* Consider the theory $\Sigma_1 = \{\overline{x_1}x_2, x_1\overline{x_3}, \overline{x_2}x_4, x_3x_4x_5\}$. Along the natural ordering, DR generates the clauses $x_2\overline{x_3}$, $\overline{x_3}x_4$, and x_4x_5. The buckets' final contents are $b[x_1] = \{\overline{x_1}x_2, x_1\overline{x_3}\}$, $b[x_2] = \{\overline{x_2}x_4, x_2\overline{x_3}\}$, $b[x_3] = \{x_3x_4x_5, \overline{x_3}x_4\}$, $b[x_4] = \{x_4x_5\}$, $b[x_5] = \emptyset$. □

DR is a complete SAT method. It is compatible with deletion of tautologies and subsumed clauses (del Val 1999),

---

[1] As in (del Val 1999), we use order of processing as our primary ordering, and speak of the variables processed first as the "earliest" or "smallest" in the ordering. (Dechter & Rish 1994; Rish & Dechter 2000) use as primary ordering reverse order of processing, speaking of processing buckets by resolving on "largest" literals. It is trivial to map from one representation to another.

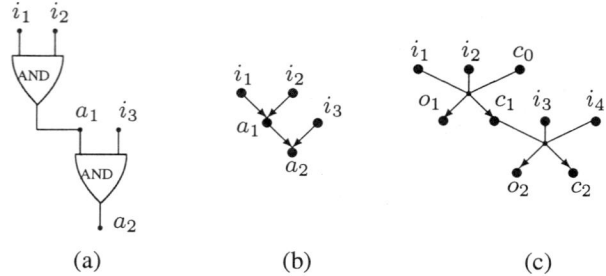

Figure 1: Sample ACTs.

though we will mostly ignore this for simplicity. In the above example, this would remove $x_3 x_4 x_5$.

For an ordering o, $DR_o(\Sigma)$ denotes the set of clauses obtained by processing Σ with DR along o. We use $b[x_i]^+$ (respectively $b[x_i]^-$) for the set of clauses of $b[x_i]$ in which x_i occurs positively (respectively, negatively). For any expression E, $Var(E)$ denotes its variables.

Tractable classes: ACNs

We next define acyclic component networks. They are in the spirit of other "structured system descriptions," e.g. (Darwiche & Pearl 1994; Dechter & Dechter 1996). Our building elements are *components*, whose associated "microtheories" describe their input/output behavior. This, together with an acyclic graphical structure (a DAG) representing flow from "inputs" to "outputs", ensures tractability results.

Formally, a component C_i is a tuple $C_i = \langle I_i, O_i, \Gamma_i \rangle$, where I_i and O_i are disjoint sets of variables (respectively, the "input" and "output" variables of C_i), and Γ_i is a set of clauses over $I_i \cup O_i$, the "component theory." The "component micrograph" $G_i = \langle V_i, E_i \rangle$ is defined by vertices $V_i = I_i \cup O_i$ and *directed* edges E_i, where $(x, y) \in E_i$ iff $x \in I_i$ and $y \in O_i$.

Components may be those of some device (e.g. logical gates in a circuit, engine parts), or represent events, or some other causal or logical relationship. We restrict how components can be linked together, which is what makes interesting structures appear:

Definition 1 *An Acyclic Component Network (ACN) is defined in terms of a set $COMP = \{C_1, \ldots, C_m\}$ of components. We require:*

1. *$O_i \cap O_j = \emptyset$, for any distinct i and j (i.e. a variable can be output variable of at most one component).*
2. *The component graph $G_C = \langle \bigcup_i V_i, \bigcup_i E_i \rangle$ is acyclic.*
3. *For any i and inverse topological order o of G_C, (a) $DR_o(\Gamma_i)$ can be computed in polynomial time, and (b) any clause $C \in DR_o(\Gamma_i)$ satisfies $Var(C) \cap O_i \neq \emptyset$.*

A theory Σ is an Acyclic Component Theory (ACT) just in case it can be partitioned into a set of disjoint subsets as $\Sigma = \bigcup_i \Gamma_i$ such that $Var(\Gamma_i)$ can in each case be partitioned into two sets I_i and O_i as above, and all other required properties are satisfied.

Example 2 Figure 1 displays a simple logical circuit (a) side by side with its component graph (b). The associated theory $\Sigma_2 = \Gamma_1 \cup \Gamma_2$ consists of microtheories $\Gamma_1 = \{\overline{i_1 i_2} a_1, \overline{a_1} i_1, \overline{a_1} i_2\}$, and $\Gamma_2 = \{\overline{a_1 i_3} a_2, \overline{a_2} a_1, \overline{a_2} i_3\}$.

Figure 1.c illustrates multiple outputs with a possible component graph for a 2-bit adder, composed of two full adders, with carries c, input bits i and output bits o. For convenience, all arcs for a single component are summarized as a single, star-shaped hyperedge.

Notice that one can easily "read" in the component graph an associated graph where nodes are components rather than propositional variables. □

Theorem 1 *Let Σ be an ACT. There is an order o such that $DR_o(\Sigma) = \bigcup_i DR_o(\Gamma_i)$, for which computing $DR_o(\Sigma)$ takes polynomial time.*

Proof sketch: Fix o to be any inverse topological sort of G_C. For any x_i, let $O(x_i)$ be the unique j, if any, such that $x_i \in O_j$. (Uniqueness follows from condition 1). We can show, by induction on the number k of variables processed that, for any x_i, if $O(x_i)$ is defined, then $b[x_i] \subseteq DR_o(\Gamma_{O(x_i)})$, else $b[x_i] = \emptyset$. In particular, we can show that every resolvent R generated by processing x_k is in $DR_o(\Gamma_{O(x_k)})$, and can be indexed only in a bucket $b[x_j]$ such that $x_j \in O_{O(x_k)} = O_{O(x_j)}$, thus preserving $b[x_j] \subseteq DR_o(\Gamma_{O(x_j)})$.

It now easily follows that $DR_o(\Sigma) = \bigcup_i DR_o(\Gamma_i)$, and since each component can be computed in polynomial time, the total cost of $DR_o(\Sigma)$ is also polynomial. □

Example 3 DR generates no non-tautologous resolvents on the theory Σ_2 of Example 2, using for example the order of processing a_2, a_1, i_1, i_2, i_3. □

Condition (3.b) implies that each Γ_i is satisfiable; thus by theorem 1, any ACT is satisfiable, as DR is complete for satisfiability. As in (Darwiche & Pearl 1994), consistency of components guarantees global consistency. What DR adds is the ability to generate any model of an ACT backtrack free (Dechter & Rish 1994) from $DR_o(\Sigma)$, using reverse order of processing —i.e. in topological order, with inputs assigned before outputs, if we follow Theorem 1.

ACNs capture a wide class of real-world theories, in particular those describing any combinatorial circuit. In this case the components would be the gates, and their simple microtheories, illustrated above, satisfy the given requirements. Condition 2 follows from the absence of feedback loops in combinatorial circuits. Condition 3 follows from the fact that these microtheories are (or can be easily put into) prime implicate form, so that (a) no new unsubsumed resolvents can be generated by any form of resolution on a gate's microtheory Γ_i, hence $DR_o(\Gamma_i) = \Gamma_i$ for any o; and (b) is satisfied initially by Γ_i, and by (a) this does not change. Thus applying Theorem 1 we obtain that in this case $DR_o(\Sigma) = \Sigma$ for any inverse topological sort o of G_C.

Theorem 1 is in fact a generalization of an *empirical observation*, the behavior of DR with ISCAS logic circuit benchmarks. It was not obvious at all that DR could do well on these benchmarks, until we tried them with an ordering compatible with this theorem. ACTs are however more general than theories of circuits, as in the latter inputs actually determine outputs; whereas Theorem 1 only suggests the weaker restriction that any assignment to a component's inputs can be *consistently extended* to its outputs; it need not *fix* them.

Other complexity results for structured descriptions, e.g. (El Fattah & Dechter 1995; Darwiche 1998) address tasks different from model-finding, e.g. abduction or diagnosis. It is interesting to note though that they come up with induced width analysis of circuits which fail to predict tractability except for tree-structured circuits. This suggests that the induced width analysis that we ourselves will advocate in the next section would fail to predict the tractability of DR on ACTs. For, as said, all circuits fit in the ACT framework.

Even though the tasks addressed are different, it is worth comparing the expressive power of ACTs and Symbolic Causal Networks (SCNs) (Darwiche & Pearl 1994; Darwiche 1998), since there are many similarities. It appears that every SCN is an ACN such that: (a) there is a single output per component; (b) "direct causes" are our inputs; (c) the SCN's "exogenous" or "assumable" propositions are treated as additional ACN outputs;[2] (d) outputs are determined by inputs;[3] (e) microtheories are required to have bounded size.

It can be seen, in particular from (a), (d) and (e), that SCNs are a relatively simple special case of ACNs.

Topological parameters for DR

We now turn to a more general analysis of the complexity of DR. We first introduce the concepts of induced width and diversity from (Dechter & Rish 1994). For application of these concepts to other areas of AI and CS, see (Dechter 1999; Bodlaender 1993). The intuitive idea is very simple. We capture the input theory Σ with a graph that represents cooccurrence of literals in clauses of Σ. We then "simulate" DR in polynomial time by processing the graph to generate a new "induced" graph. Finally, we recover from the induced graph information about all relevant complexity parameters for the hypothetical execution of DR for the given theory and ordering. Example 5 below will illustrate this idea of polynomial simulation of resolution.

As before, we use as our primary ordering the order of processing, as opposed to the inverse order used in (Dechter & Rish 1994). This means that *our induced width along an ordering corresponds to Dechter and Rish's induced width along the reverse order*.[4] The following definitions, though somewhat dense, should not be hard to parse for readers familiar with the notion of induced width.

Definition 2 *Let G be an undirected graph, and $o = v_1, \ldots, v_n$ an ordering of its vertices.*

The downward set *$D(v_i)$ of v_i along o is the set of vertices v_j such that there is an edge (v_i, v_j) in G and $i < j$. The* (downward) width *of v_i along o is the cardinality $|D(v_i)|$ of its downward set.*

The (downward) width *of a graph G along o is the maximum downward width among the nodes of G.*

Definition 3 *(Dechter & Rish 1994, induced width) Let Σ be a clausal theory, and $o = x_1, \ldots, x_n$ an ordering of its propositional variables $Var(\Sigma)$.*

1. The interaction graph *of Σ is an undirected graph $GI(\Sigma) = \langle V_I, E_I \rangle$, with vertices $V_I = Var(\Sigma)$, and edges $E_I = \{(x_i, x_j) \mid x_i, x_j \in Var(C) \text{ for some } C \in \Sigma\}$.*

---

[2]They are "private" to each component in (Darwiche & Pearl 1994), in line with our weaker restriction $O_i \cap O_j = \emptyset$.

[3]This follows from the syntactic restrictions on SCN microtheories imposed in (Darwiche & Pearl 1994).

[4]See also footnote 1. After all, the induced graphs below are also generated in DR's order of processing.

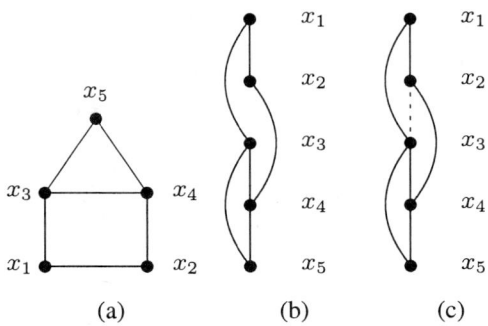

Figure 2: The interaction graph of Σ_1.

2. The induced interaction graph *of Σ along ordering o is the graph $I_o(GI(\Sigma)) = \langle V_I, E_I^o \rangle$ obtained from $GI(\Sigma)$ as follows: initially, $E_I^o = E_I$; then for $i = 1$ to n do: add edges (x_j, x_k) to E_I^o for all x_j and x_k in the current $D(x_i)$.*

3. The width *$w_o(x_i)$ of a variable x_i along o is the width of x_i in $GI(\Sigma)$ along o. The* induced width *$w_o^*(x_i)$ of x_i along o is the width of x_i in $I_o(GI(\Sigma))$ along o. When the ordering o is fixed, we abbreviate $w_o(x_i)$ as w_i, and $w_o^*(x_i)$ as w_i*.*

4. The width *$w(o)$ of Σ along o is the width of $GI(\Sigma)$ along o, and the* width *w of Σ is the minimal width of Σ over all orderings. The* induced width *$w*(o)$ of Σ along o is the width of $I_o(GI(\Sigma))$ along o, and the* induced width *$w*$ of Σ is the minimal induced width over all possible orderings.*

Example 4 Figure 2 illustrates induced width for the theory Σ_1 of Example 1: (a) the interaction graph of Σ_1; (b) the same graph, with nodes ordered from top to bottom along the given (natural) order; (c) the induced interaction graph along this ordering. The width and induced width of Σ_1 with this ordering are both 2. □

Definition 4 *(Dechter & Rish 1994, diversity) The* induced diversity *of a variable x_i along order o is $div_o^*(x_i) = |b[x_i]^+| \times |b[x_i]^-|$, where the product is taken after running $DR_o(\Sigma)$. The* induced diversity *$div*(o)$ of Σ along o is the maximum induced diversity of its variables along o. The* induced diversity *$div*$ of Σ is its minimal induced diversity over all orderings.*

Clearly, the induced diversity of an ordering provides a bound on the number of resolution steps performed by DR. Since each resolution step is $O(n)$, the time complexity of DR along an ordering o is $O(n^2 \cdot div*(o))$.

(Dechter & Rish 1994) show that the size of $DR_o(\Sigma)$ is bounded by $n \cdot 2 \cdot 3^{w*(o)}$, and the number of resolution steps by $n \cdot (2 \cdot 3^{w*(o)})^2 = n \cdot 4 \cdot 3^{2w*(o)}$.

We can greatly improve these estimates by introducing some new concepts. The basic idea is to split literals according to their sign, and use this to define more fine-grained concepts of width and to estimate diversity.

Definition 5 (split interaction graph) *Let Σ be a clausal theory, and $o = x_1, \ldots, x_n$ an ordering of $Var(\Sigma)$, extended in the obvious way to literals (e.g. $\overline{x_i} < x_j$ iff $i < j$).*[5]

---

[5]Note that the extended ordering is a partial order.

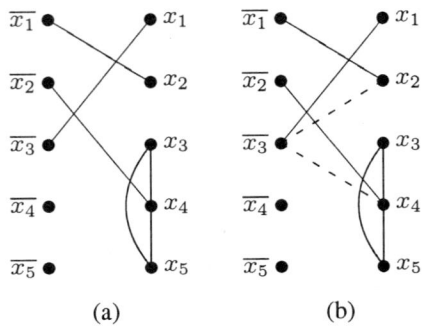

Figure 3: The split interaction graph of Σ_1.

1. The split interaction graph of Σ is an undirected graph $GS(\Sigma) = \langle V_S, E_S \rangle$, whose vertices V_S are the set of all literals of Σ, and E_S is the set of edges (l_i, l_j) such that literals l_i and l_j occur together in some clause.

2. The induced split interaction graph of Σ along ordering o is the graph $I_o(GS(\Sigma)) = \langle V_S, E_S^o \rangle$ obtained by augmenting $GS(\Sigma)$ as follows: initially, $E_S^o = E_S$; then for $i = 1$ to n do: add edges (l_j, l_k) to E_S^o for each $l_j \in D(x_i)$ and $l_k \in D(\overline{x_i})$.

3. The literal width of a literal l_i along o is the width of l_i in $GS(\Sigma)$ along o. The induced literal width of l_i in Σ along o is the width of l_i in $I_o(GS(\Sigma))$ along o. When o is fixed, we write w_i^+ and w_i^- for the literal widths along o of x_i and $\overline{x_i}$, respectively; similarly, we use w_i^+* and w_i^-* for the respective induced literal widths.

4. The s-width of a variable x_i along o is $sw_i = max(w_i^+, w_i^-)$. The t-width of x_i along o is $tw_i = w_i^+ + w_i^-$. The induced s-width sw_i* and induced t-width tw_i* are defined similarly from w_i^+* and w_i^-*.

5. The s-width $sw(o)$ of Σ along o is the maximal s-width of its variables along o. The t-width $tw(o)$ of Σ along o is the maximal t-width of its variables along o.

6. The induced s-width $sw*(o)$ of Σ along o is the maximal induced s-width of its variables along o. The induced t-width $tw*(o)$ of Σ along o is the maximal induced t-width of variables along o. The induced s-width $sw*$ and induced t-width $tw*$ of Σ are respectively the minimal induced s-width and t-width over all orderings.

Induced width is basically an instrument to predict that certain literals will occur together in certain clauses; induced s-width and t-width are more fine-grained instruments that take into account the sign of literals to predict, respectively, the space (s) and time (t) requirements of DR. Note that both induced graphs can be computed in polynomial time.

Example 5 Figure 3 illustrates induced s-width and t-width for the theory Σ_1 of Example 1: (a) the split interaction graph of Σ_1, with nodes ordered from top to bottom along the given ordering; (b) the induced interaction graph along this ordering. Σ_1 has s-width, t-width, and induced s-width 2, and induced t-width 3.

Note that the generation of the induced graph closely matches the generation of resolvents by DR. Since x_1 cooccurs with $\overline{x_3}$ and $\overline{x_1}$ with x_2 we can "predict" that as a result of resolving upon x_1 we will obtain a resolvent in which x_2 and $\overline{x_3}$ occur together. This corresponds to adding the edge $(x_2, \overline{x_3})$ to the induced graph; and similarly with other added edges. □

All these definitions, incidentally, can be adjusted to apply to Σ under any fixed set of polynomial time simplifications, along the lines of the "adjusted width" of (Dechter 1999). Our next lemma shows that the induced graph simulates DR as far as the split interaction graph is concerned.

Lemma 2 $GS(DR_o(\Sigma))$ is a subgraph of $I_o(GS(\Sigma))$.

Proof: We show by induction along the ordering that if $l_i, l_j \in C$ for some clause C obtained when DR processes bucket $b[x_k]$ then the edge (l_i, l_j) is in $I_o(GS(\Sigma))$ after processing x_k when generating the induced graph. (Assume $l_i \in \{x_i, \overline{x_i}\}$ and $l_j \in \{x_j, \overline{x_j}\}$.)

For the base case, edges corresponding to clauses of Σ are obviously in both graphs. Inductively, consider any edge (l_i, l_j) such that $l_i, l_j \in R$ for some resolvent R of clauses $C, D \in b[x_k]$. Note that $k < i$, and $k < j$. If l_i and l_j occur together in some parent then the claim follows directly from the inductive hypothesis, as both parents were generated before DR processes x_k. Otherwise, say $x_k, l_i \in C$, and $\overline{x_k}, l_j \in D$. By inductive hypothesis, the edges (x_k, l_i) and $(\overline{x_k}, l_j)$ were added to $I_o(GS(\Sigma))$ before processing x_k in the generation of the induced graph. Since $k < i$ and $k < j$, the edge (l_i, l_j) is added to $I_o(GS(\Sigma))$ when processing x_k. □

We can now bound the space and time complexity of DR.

Lemma 3 $|b[x_i]^+| \leq 2^{w_i^+}$, and $|b[x_i]^-| \leq 2^{w_i^-}$.

Proof: $b[x_i]^+$ contains all clauses whose smallest literal is x_i. There are w_i^+ literals that cooccur with the positive literal x_i which are later in the ordering than x_i, hence there are $\sum_{0 \leq i \leq w_i^+} \binom{w_i^+}{i} = 2^{w_i^+}$ subsets of those w_i^+ literals. Only clauses formed by adding x_i to one such subset can be in $b[x_i]^+$. □

Theorem 4 For any ordering o, the size of $DR_o(\Sigma)$ is bounded by $\sum_{1 \leq i \leq n}(2^{w_i^+*} + 2^{w_i^-*}) \leq n \cdot 2^{sw*(o)+1}$. The number of resolution operations performed by DR is bounded by $\sum_{1 \leq i \leq n} 2^{tw_i*} \leq n \cdot 2^{tw*(o)}$, hence the time complexity is $O(n^2 \cdot 2^{tw*(o)})$.

Proof: Use lemmas 2 and 3 to bound bucket sizes in $DR_o(\Sigma)$. From this obtain $div_o^*(x_i) \leq 2^{w_i^+*} \cdot 2^{w_i^-*} = 2^{tw_i*}$. As each resolution step is $O(n)$, time follows. □

This yields our second tractable class:

Corollary 5 If the induced s-width or t-width of Σ is bounded by a constant then for some ordering o computing $DR_o(\Sigma)$ takes polynomial time and space.

Finding the minimal induced s- or t-width of a theory is NP-hard,[6] though we conjecture that techniques to recognize in time $exp(k)$ theories with induced width bounded by k can be adapted to recognize theories with bounded induced s-width. And we can always use the polynomially computable bounds for any given ordering to choose among candidate orderings.

(Dechter & Rish 1994) prove a result similar to Corollary 5 for bounded *standard* induced width. But it is easy to find theories with constant induced s-width yet unbounded (i.e. $\Omega(n)$) standard induced width:

---

[6]As proven with a trivial reduction from the problem of finding the minimal induced width.

Example 6 Let $\Sigma_6 = \{x_i x_{2i}, x_i x_{2i+1} \mid 1 \leq i \leq m\}$. Along the natural order, each x_i gets linked to x_{i+1} through x_{2i+1} in the *standard* induced graph, whereas no new edges are added in the *split* induced graph, since negative literals have no edges. Thus $sw*(o) = 2$ is constant, while the standard induced width is the unbounded $w*(o) = w_m* = m + 1$.

For a non-binary theory with identical induced graphs, consider $\Sigma_6^* = \{x_i x_{2i} x_{2i+1} \mid 1 \leq i \leq m\}$. There is little point however in providing non-binary examples to exhibit properties of $sw*$ and $w*$, even though binary theories are tractable. This is because, for any non-binary theory Σ, there exists a binary theory Σ_B with exactly identical initial and induced graphs. $\square$

Example 7 Let us compare the estimates derivable from induced width, t-width, and s-width with the theory Σ_1 of Example 1, using figures 2 and 3.

We can obtain two estimates from induced width, using the results of (Dechter & Rish 1994). The looser prediction yields a size estimate of $n \cdot 2 \cdot 3^{w*(o)} = 5 \cdot 2 \cdot 3^2 = 90$ clauses for $DR_o(\Sigma_1)$, or more precisely (summing over the induced widths of each variable) $3 \cdot (2 \cdot 3^2) + 2 \cdot 3^1 + 2 \cdot 3^0 = 62$ clauses. The estimated number of resolutions is, loosely, $n \cdot (2 \cdot 3^{w*(o)})^2 = 5 \cdot (2 \cdot 3^2)^2 = 1620$; and more precisely, $3 \cdot (2 \cdot 3^2)^2 + (2 \cdot 3^1)^2 + (2 \cdot 3^0)^2 = 1012$.

The estimates derived from s-width and t-width are significantly better. For size, these are $n \cdot 2^{sw*(o)+1} = 5 \cdot 2^3 = 40$ or more precisely $(2^1 + 2^1) + (2^1 + 2^1) + (2^1 + 2^2) + (2^0 + 2^1) + (2^0 + 2^0) = 19$ clauses. For time, the loose estimate is that there are $n \cdot 2^{tw*(o)} = 5 \cdot 2^3 = 40$ resolution steps; the precise estimate, doing the summation, is that there are only 19 steps. $\square$

More generally, we can compare the *rough* estimates provided by these parameters as follows:

Theorem 6 *If (l_j, l_k) is an edge of $I_o(GS(\Sigma))$ then (x_j, x_k) is an edge of $I_o(GI(\Sigma))$. Hence $sw_i* \leq w_i*$ for any i and fixed ordering.*

It easily follows that the size estimate derived from induced width is at least $(3/2)^{w*(o)}$ times larger than the estimate derived from induced s-width, and the time estimate at least $4 \cdot (3/2)^{2w*(o)}$ times larger. Both ratios hold when $sw_i* = w_i*$, but as Example 6 illustrates, often sw_i* is much smaller. And, in fact, we can greatly improve even the summation form of our estimates.

Relative width

A clause C is captured by the interaction graph as a *clique* of all its literals, i.e. all literals of C are pairwise linked. The size bound $2^{w_i^+}$ of Lemma 3 can be read as an estimate of the number of cliques in which x_i is the smallest literal, an estimate which is tight only if its downward set $D(x_i)$ is itself a clique. Furthermore, it follows from the proof of Lemma 2 that the clique corresponding to a resolvent obtained when DR processes $b[x_i]$ is added to $I_o(GS(\Sigma))$ when processing x_k as well. Thus, resolvents whose smallest literal is x_i become cliques *before* processing x_i, since they are generated by processing earlier buckets.[7]

---

[7]This is important because processing x_i may link together nodes of $D(x_i)$. Indeed, in the *standard* induced graph processing x_i

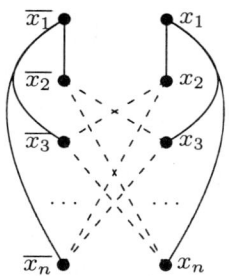

Figure 4: Induced split interaction graph for Σ_8.

Counting cliques over $D(x_i)$ is NP-hard, but there are a number of ways to approximate them, including polynomial randomized algorithms. The following simple upper bound suffices to obtain new tractable classes:

Lemma 7 *Let $D_i(l)$ be the downward set of l in $I_o(GS(\Sigma))$ right before processing x_i when generating the induced graph. Let $d_i^+(l) = |D_i(x_i) \cap D_i(l)|$, $d_i^-(l) = |D_i(\overline{x_i}) \cap D_i(l)|$. After running DR, $|b[x_i]^+| \leq 1 + \sum_{l \in D(x_i)} 2^{d_i^+(l)}$, and $|b[x_i]^-| \leq 1 + \sum_{l \in D(\overline{x_i})} 2^{d_i^-(l)}$.*

We can see $d_i^+(l)$ as the *relative width* of l with respect to x_i. Intuitively, each term in the sum estimates the number of cliques (whose smallest literal is x_i) containing l but no earlier literals; the estimate is tight only when $D(x_i) \cap D_i(l)$ is itself a clique right before processing x_i. Our next result is now straightforward:

Theorem 8

1. *Space: The size of $DR_o(\Sigma)$ is bounded by $2n + \sum_{1 \leq i \leq n} \left(\sum_{l \in D(x_i)} 2^{d_i^+(l)} + \sum_{l \in D(\overline{x_i})} 2^{d_i^-(l)} \right)$.*

2. *Time: The number of resolution steps performed by DR along ordering o is bounded by $\sum_{1 \leq i \leq n} \left[\left(1 + \sum_{l \in D(x_i)} 2^{d_i^+(l)}\right) \left(1 + \sum_{l \in D(\overline{x_i})} 2^{d_i^-(l)}\right) \right]$.*

As a special case of this theorem, suppose that for every literal l_i, the restriction of $I_o(GS(\Sigma))$ to its downward set $D(l_i)$ at the time x_i is processed contains no edges. (This is compatible with unbounded s-width, see Example 8.) Then the size of each $b[x_i]$ is only $2 + w_i^+ * + w_i^- *$, and its diversity $(1 + w_i^+ *)(1 + w_i^- *)$. And now the exponents are out! Generalizing this observation yields a new tractable class:

Corollary 9 *Suppose the $d_i(l)$'s are bounded by a constant for some ordering o. Then $|DR_o(\Sigma)| = O(n \cdot sw*(o)) = O(n^2)$. The number of resolution operations is $O(n \cdot (sw*(o))^2) = O(n^3)$, and thus the time complexity is $O(n^4)$.*

Proof: We have $|b[x_i]^+| \leq 1 + \sum_{l \in D(x_i)} k$, for some constant k, hence $|b[x_i]^+| = O(w_i^+ *) = O(sw*(o)) = O(n)$. The rest is obvious. $\square$

---

means making $D(x_i)$ a clique.

Example 8 $\Sigma_8 = \{x_1x_2, \ldots, x_1x_n, \overline{x_1x_2}, \ldots, \overline{x_1x_n}\}$ illustrates the principle of bounded $d_i(l)$'s with unbounded s-width. The induced split interaction graph $I_o(GS(\Sigma_8))$ is depicted in Figure 4, with induced edges dashed. Despite the high s-width of the graph ($w_i^+* = w_i^-* = n - i$ for each i), the $d_i(l)$'s always equal 0. □

We can also use relative widths to improve the estimates derived from the standard induced graph $I_o(GI(.))$. However, this would not allow us to derive tractability results such as corollary 9. This is because bounded $d_i(l)$'s in $I_o(GI(.))$ imply bounded induced width.[8] In other words, the use of the *split* induced graph is essential in obtaining this new tractable class.

The effect of subsumption

A clique of size k over $D(x_i)$ has 2^k subcliques, and all our estimates of bucket size so far take all of them as representing legitimate clauses. However, it is a well-known result in combinatorics, known as Sperner's theorem (Anderson 1987), that the maximum number of *unsubsumed* subsets of a set of k literals is $C(k, k/2) = \binom{k}{k/2}$. If we delete subsumed clauses, therefore, any term of the form 2^k in our previous estimates can be replaced by $C(k, k/2)$. In the theory Σ_1 of Example 1 this improves our size estimate to 11 clauses, and the number of resolution steps to 6.

This is unlikely to yield new tractable classes. It does allow us to obtain better predictions of complexity, though at a significant computational cost. This cost can be easily reduced with some loss of accuracy, e.g. by building a table of upper bounds in terms of powers of two (e.g. for $9 \leq k \leq 40$, $C(k, k/2) \leq 2^{k-2}$), so that all calculations are by powers of two. Even so, if our goal is only to compare various orderings in order to choose which one to use with DR, it is unclear whether this greater accuracy will help discriminate better among them.

Discussion

We have introduced new tractable classes for DR, and tightened the space and time bounds provided by (Dechter & Rish 1994) by means of a more refined analysis of the structure of theories. These bounds can be used to choose in polynomial time among different orderings before running DR.

As mentioned, the generation of the induced graph can be seen as a "polynomial time simulation" of resolution, which need not be limited to DR. In (del Val 2000), we extend this kind of analysis to the consequence-finding task, which for example allows us to estimate the number of prime implicates of any theory and identify tractable abduction classes.

References

Anderson, I. 1987. *Combinatorics of Finite Sets*. Oxford: Oxford University Press.

Bachmair, L., and Ganzinger, H. 1999. A theory of resolution. In Robinson, J., and Voronkov, A., eds., *Handbook of Automated Reasoning*. Elsevier.

[8]Suppose $w_i* = m = \Omega(n)$, and let x_j and x_k be the two smallest variables of $D(x_i)$. Processing x_i links together all edges of $D(x_i)$, hence $|D(x_j) \cap D_j(x_k)| \geq m - 2 = \Omega(n)$.

Basin, D., and Ganzinger, H. 1996. Complexity analysis based on ordered resolution. In *LCS'96, Proc. 11th IEEE Symposium on Logic in Computer Science*.

Bodlaender, H. L. 1993. A tourist guide through treewidth. *Acta Cybernetica* 11:1–21.

Darwiche, A., and Pearl, J. 1994. Symbolic causal networks. In *AAAI'94, Proc. 12th National Conference on Artificial Intelligence*, 238–244. Menlo Park, CA, USA: AAAI Press.

Darwiche, A. 1998. Model-based diagnosis using structured system descriptions. *J. of Artificial Intelligence Research* 8:165–222.

Davis, M., and Putnam, H. 1960. A computing procedure for quantification theory. *Journal of the ACM* 7(3):201–215.

Davis, M.; Logemann, G.; and Loveland, D. 1962. A machine program for theorem proving. *Communications of the ACM* 5:394–397.

Dechter, R., and Dechter, A. 1996. Structure driven algorithms for truth maintenance. *Artificial Intelligence* 82:1–20.

Dechter, R., and Rish, I. 1994. Directional resolution: The Davis-Putnam procedure, revisited. In *KR'94, Proc. 4th Int. Conf. on Principles of Knowledge Representation and Reasoning*, 134–145. Morgan Kaufmann.

Dechter, R. 1999. Bucket elimination: A unifying framework for reasoning. *Artificial Intelligence* 113:41–85.

del Val, A. 1999. A new method for consequence finding and compilation in restricted languages. In *AAAI'99, Proc. 16th (U.S.) National Conference on Artificial Intelligence*, 259–264. AAAI Press/MIT Press.

del Val, A. 2000. The complexity of restricted consequence finding and abduction. In *AAAI'2000, Proc. 17th (U.S.) National Conference on Artificial Intelligence*. AAAI Press/MIT Press.

El Fattah, Y., and Dechter, R. 1995. Diagnosing tree-decomposable circuits. In *IJCAI'95, International Joint Conference on Artificial Intelligence*, 1742–1748.

Fermüller, C.; Leitsch, A.; Tammet, T.; and Zamov, N. 1993. *Resolution Methods for the Decision Problem*. Springer-Verlag.

Rish, I., and Dechter, R. 2000. Resolution versus search: Two strategies for SAT. *Journal of Automated Reasoning* 24:225–275.

Compilability of Abduction

Paolo Liberatore and **Marco Schaerf**
Dipartimento di Informatica e Sistemistica
Università di Roma "La Sapienza"
Via Salaria 113, 00198 Roma - Italy
Email: liberato@dis.uniroma1.it
           schaerf@dis.uniroma1.it

Abstract

Abduction is one of the most important forms of reasoning and it has been successfully applied to several practical problems such as diagnosis. In this paper we investigate whether the computational complexity of abduction can be reduced by an appropriate use of preprocessing or compilation. This is motivated by the fact that part of the data of the problem (namely, the set of all possible assumptions and the theory relating assumptions and manifestations) are often known before the rest of the problem. We present a detailed analysis of the computational complexity of abduction when compilation is allowed.

Introduction

Abduction is, along with deduction and induction, one of the main reasoning styles. The first researcher to study abduction in detail has been C. S. Peirce (1955). The simplest presentation of abduction is by comparing it with deduction and induction. Deduction is the process of obtaining conclusions from facts and rules, so, for instance, from a and $a \rightarrow b$ we can conclude b by deduction. Induction is the process of establishing a general rule from the antecedents and consequences, so for instance from a and b we can conclude that $a \rightarrow b$ is true. Abduction is in some sense the inverse process of deduction, since from consequences and rules we try to establish the truth value of antecedents, so for instance given $a \rightarrow b$ and b, we conclude by abduction that a is a possible cause of b. Abduction is the process of finding the most likely explanations of a given set of manifestations, given some rules relating explanations and manifestations.

The most important application of abduction in AI is diagnosis. Indeed, the process of finding the causes of possible abnormal behaviors of systems is in fact a problem of abduction, where we want to find the causes of malfunctions given a set of rules describing the behavior of the system and a description of the observed malfunctions.

The computational complexity of abduction has already been deeply investigated in the literature. The case of hypothesis assembly has been studied by Bylander *et al.* (1989), while the first attempts to investigate the complexity of logic-based abduction has been done by Selman and Levesque (1990), and by Bylander *et al.* (1989). Eiter and Gottlob (1995) presented an extensive analysis of several problems related to abduction, including the problems of relevance and necessity.

In this paper we analyze a different computational aspect of abduction. Each instance of abduction is composed of three parts: the set of explanations, the logical theory defining the connections between explanations and manifestations, and the set of manifestations. In many applications, the set of all possible explanations and the theory are available beforehand, while the set of manifestations is only available when the solution is needed. Take as an example the diagnosis of a digital circuit: The logical theory defining the behavior of the circuit is known when the circuit is built and the set of possible explanations is simply the list of all components that can be faulty. Here we consider the problem of whether faster algorithms can be obtained by allowing the part of the instance that is known in advance to be preprocessed (compiled). We want to know if it is possible to rewrite the theory and the set of possible explanations so that we can provide faster algorithms to solve the problem when a set of manifestations is given.

Kautz, Kearns and Selman (1995) investigated the computational complexity of abduction from model-based representations. Their work is further expanded by Khardon and Roth (1996). In this paper we focus primarily on theory-based abduction, that is, we assume that the representation of the problem is given as a logical theory. In a later section we discuss the relations between our results and those presented in these two papers.

The idea of using compilation for speeding-up the solving of abduction problems is not new. For instance, Console, Portinale, and Duprè (1996) have shown how compiled knowledge can be used in the process of abductive diagnosis. The contribution of the present paper is to give a precise worst-case analysis of the problem.

Preliminaries

A problem of abduction is a triple $\langle H, M, T \rangle$, where H and M are sets of variables, while T is a theory (set of propositional formulae). The set of solutions is defined as follows:

$$SOL(H, M, T) = \{H' \subseteq H \mid H' \cup T \text{ is consistent and } H' \cup T \models M\}$$

Given an ordering $\preceq$ over the subsets of H, the set of minimal solutions of the problem is defined as follows.

$$SOL_\preceq(H, M, T) = \min(SOL(H, M, T), \preceq)$$

The ordering $\preceq$ captures the intuitive notion of plausibility of an explanation. That is, $H' \prec H''$ holds if H' is more likely to be the "real" cause of the manifestations than H''. The ordering $\preceq$ represents the concept of "at least as likely as", thus $H' \cong H''$ holds if H' and H'' are equally likely. The definition of $SOL_\preceq$ formalizes the idea of choosing only the explanations we consider more likely. Note that we assume that the ordering between two sets of assumptions does not depend on the set of manifestations.

In the sequel of the paper we assume that the ordering $\preceq$ is "well-founded". That is, if the set $SOL(H, M, T)$ is non empty, then there exists at least one minimal element (i.e., $\min(SOL(H, M, T), \preceq)$ is not empty).

In real applications we have very different forms of information on the plausibility of an explanation. The two simplest orderings are $\subseteq$-preference and $\leq$-preference. While $\subseteq$-preference selects only irredundant explanations, the $\leq$-preference selects explanations with the least possible number of assumptions.

$\subseteq$-preference $H' \preceq H''$ if and only if $H' \subseteq H''$;

$\leq$-preference $H' \preceq H''$ if and only if $|H'| \leq |H''|$;

where $|X|$ denotes the cardinality of the set X. In the sequel, we assume that the set of all possible manifestations is identical to the set of all variables. Moreover, without loss of generality, we assume that T is a 3CNF formula. The reasoning problems we consider are the following ones:

Existence: is there an explanation of the observed manifestations? That is, $SOL(H, M, T) \neq \emptyset$?

Relevance: given a variable $h \in H$, is there a minimal solution containing h? That is, $\exists H' \subseteq H$ such that $H' \in SOL_\preceq(H, M, T)$ and $h \in H'$?

Necessity: is $h \in H$ in all, and at least one, minimal solution? That is, $SOL(H, M, T) \neq \emptyset$ and $\forall H' \subseteq H$ we have that $H' \in SOL_\preceq(H, M, T)$ implies $h \in H'$?

Clearly, the ordering does not matter for the problem of existence, since we consider only well-founded orderings that guarantee that $\min(A, \preceq) \neq \emptyset$ whenever A is not empty. For all other problems, the ordering must be taken into account. Different orderings may lead to different computational properties.

Complexity and Compilability

We assume the reader is familiar with basic complexity classes, such as P, NP and the classes of the polynomial hierarchy (Stockmeyer 1976; Garey & Johnson 1979). In the sequel, C, C', etc. denote arbitrary classes of the polynomial hierarchy. We assume that the input instances of problems are strings built over an alphabet Σ. The *length* of a string $x \in \Sigma^*$ is denoted by $||x||$.

We summarize some definitions and results proposed to formalize the on-line complexity of problems (Cadoli et al. 1996). Following the intuition that an abductive problem is composed of a part that is known in advance (T and H) and a part that is only known at run-time (M), we divide a reasoning problem into two parts: one part is *fixed* or *accessible off-line*, and the second one is *varying*, or *accessible on-line*. We present a way of formalizing the *on-line complexity*, or *compilability*, of solving a problem composed of such inputs, i.e., complexity when the first input can be pre-processed.

A function f is called *poly-size* if there exists a polynomial p such that for all strings x it holds $||f(x)|| \leq p(||x||)$. An exception to this definition is when x represents a natural number: in this case, we impose $||f(x)|| \leq p(x)$.

A function g is called *poly-time* if there exists a polynomial q such that for all x, $g(x)$ can be computed in time less than or equal to $q(||x||)$. These definitions easily extend to binary functions as usual.

We define a *language of pairs* S as a subset of $\Sigma^* \times \Sigma^*$. Using the above definitions we introduce a new hierarchy of classes of languages of pairs, the *non-uniform compilability classes*, denoted as $\|\!\!\sim\!\! C$, where C is a generic uniform complexity class, such as P, NP, coNP, or Σ_2^p.

Definition 1 ($\|\!\!\sim\!\! C$ classes) *A language of pairs $S \subseteq \Sigma^* \times \Sigma^*$ belongs to $\|\!\!\sim\!\! C$ iff there exists a binary poly-size function f and a language of pairs $S' \in C$ such that for all $\langle x, y \rangle \in S$ it holds:*

$$\langle x, y \rangle \in S \text{ iff } \langle f(x, ||y||), y \rangle \in S'$$

A problem in $\|\!\!\sim\!\! C$ is a problem that is in C after a suitable polynomial-size preprocessing. Clearly, any problem whose time complexity is in C is also in $\|\!\!\sim\!\! C$ (just take $f(x, ||y||) = x$ and $S' = S$). Compilation is useful if a problem in C is in $\|\!\!\sim\!\! C'$, where $C' \subset C$, that is, preprocessing decreases the complexity of the problem. There are problems for which such reduction of complexity is possible (Cadoli et al. 1996).

Definition 2 (nucomp reductions) *A nucomp reduction from a problem A to a problem B is a triple $\langle f_1, f_2, g \rangle$, where f_1 and f_2 are poly-size functions, g is a polynomial function, and for every pair $\langle x, y \rangle$ it holds that $\langle x, y \rangle \in A$ if and only if $\langle f_1(x, ||y||), g(f_2(x, ||y||), y) \rangle \in B$.*

If there exists a nucomp reduction from A to B we say that A is nucomp reducible to B, denoted as $A \leq_{nucomp} B$.

For these classes it is possible to define the notions of *hardness* and *completeness*.

Definition 3 ($\|\!\!\sim\!\! C$-completeness) *Let S be a language of pairs and C a complexity class. S is $\|\!\!\sim\!\! C$-hard iff for all problems $A \in \|\!\!\sim\!\! C$ we have that $A \leq_{nucomp} S$. Moreover, S is $\|\!\!\sim\!\! C$-complete if S is in $\|\!\!\sim\!\! C$ and is $\|\!\!\sim\!\! C$-hard.*

It is important to point out that the hierarchy formed by the compilability classes is proper if and only if the polynomial hierarchy is proper (Cadoli et al. 1996; Karp & Lipton 1980; Yap 1983) — a fact widely conjectured to be true.

Informally, we may say that $\Vdash$NP-hard problems are "not compilable to P". Indeed, if such compilation were possible, then it would be possible to define f as the function that takes the fixed part of the problem and gives the result of compilation (ignoring the size of the input), and S' as the language representing the on-line processing. This would implies that a $\Vdash$NP-hard problem is in $\Vdash$P, and this implies the collapse of the polynomial hierarchy. In general, a problem which is $\Vdash$C-complete for a class C can be regarded as the "toughest" problem in C, even after arbitrary preprocessing of the fixed part.

Representative Equivalence

While the definitions of nucomp-reduction and $\Vdash$C-completeness are adequate to show the compilability level of a given reasoning problem, they require the definition of a new reduction that satisfies all the required properties. Now we show a technique that let us reuse, with only simple modifications, the reductions shown when the complexity result is first proved. We present conditions under which a polynomial reduction from an arbitrary problem implies the existence of a nucomp reduction.

Definition 4 (Classification Function) *A classification function for a problem A is a polynomial function $Class$ from instances of A to nonnegative integers, such that $Class(y) \leq \|y\|$.*

Definition 5 (Representative Function) *A representative function for a problem A is a polynomial function $Repr$ from nonnegative integers to instances of A, such that $Class(Repr(n)) = n$, and that $\|Repr(n)\|$ is bounded by some polynomial in n.*

Definition 6 (Extension Function) *An extension function for a problem A is a polynomial function from instances of A and nonnegative integers to instances of A such that, for any y and $n \geq Class(y)$, the instance $y' = Exte(y, n)$ satisfies the following conditions:*

1. $y \in A$ if and only if $y' \in A$;
2. $Class(y') = n$.

Let, for example, A be the problem of propositional satisfiability. We can take $Class(F)$ as the number of variables in the formula F and $Repr(n)$ to be the set of all clauses of three literals over an alphabet of n variables. Finally, a possible extension function is obtained by adding tautological clauses to an instance.

Note that these functions are related to the problem A only, and do not involve the specific problem B we want to prove hard, neither the specific reduction used.

Once proved that for a given problem A it is possible to define three functions satisfying the above requirements, what is needed is a condition over the reduction from A to B that implies the hardness of the problem B. A polynomial reduction from a problem A to a problem of pairs B is a pair of polynomial functions $\langle r, h \rangle$ such that $x \in A$ if and only if $\langle r(x), h(x) \rangle \in B$. The following condition is what is needed for proving that a problem is nucomp-hard.

Definition 7 (Representative Equivalence) *Given a problem A (satisfying the above three conditions), a problem of pairs B, and a polynomial reduction $\langle r, h \rangle$ from A to B, the condition of representative equivalence holds if, for any instance y of A, it holds:*

$$\langle r(y), h(y) \rangle \in B \quad \text{iff} \quad \langle r(Repr(Class(y))), h(y) \rangle \in B$$

It can be proved that the condition of representative equivalence implies that the problem B is $\Vdash$C-hard, if A is C-hard. Indeed, the following theorem shows that representative equivalence is a sufficient condition for proving the nucomp-hardness of a problem.

Theorem 1 *Let A be a problem for which there exists a classification, a representative and an extension function. If there exists a polynomial reduction from A to a problem of pairs B that satisfies representative equivalence, then there exists a nucomp reduction from $*A$ to B.*

We give an high-level explanation of the method we use to prove the incompilability of the considered problems of abduction. We begin by applying the method to the problem of existence of explanations, and then we sketch how it can be used for relevance and necessity.

The Method

Let us consider the problem of deciding whether there exists an explanation for a set of manifestations. It is already known that this problem is Σ_2^p-hard (Eiter & Gottlob 1995). A way for proving that this problem is also $\Vdash\Sigma_2^p$-hard is to find a polynomial reduction from a Σ_2^p-hard problem to the one under consideration, satisfying the condition of representative equivalence (of course, we have first to prove that the Σ_2^p-hard problem has a classification, representative, and extension functions).

The most easy way to do this is to consider reductions already known. For instance, Eiter and Gottlob (1995) have shown a reduction from $\exists\forall$QBF to the problem of existence of solutions. However, while $\exists\forall$QBF has the three needed functions, the reduction itself does not satisfy the condition of representative equivalence. As a result, we have to look for another reduction, either from $\exists\forall$QBF or from some other Σ_2^p-hard problem.

We are of course looking for a reduction that is as simple as possible. In general, the more similar two problems are, the easier it is to find a reduction with some given properties. The question now is: what is the Σ_2^p-hard problem that is most similar to the problem of existence of explanation? Clearly, the problem itself is the most similar one.

The theorem of representative equivalence says that, if we have a reduction from an *arbitrary* Σ_2^p-hard problem A to B, satisfying representative equivalence, then B is $\Vdash\Sigma_2^p$-hard. Nothing, however, prevent us from choosing $A = B$, if B is known to be Σ_2^p-hard. This technique can be formalized as follows:

- show that there exists a classification, representative, and extension functions for the problem B;
- show that there exists a reduction from B to B satisfying representative equivalence.

The most obvious reduction from a problem to itself is the identity. In our case, however, identity does not satisfy the condition of representative equivalence. As a result, we have to look for some other reduction.

Before showing the technical details of the reductions used, we notice that this technique allows for determining the compilability of problems for which a precise characterization of complexity is not known, since it allows to prove that a problem is $\|\leadsto$C-hard for any class C of the polynomial hierarchy for which B is C-hard.

In order to simplify the following proofs, we denote with $\Pi(Y)$ the set of all distinct clauses of length 3 on a given alphabet $Y = \{y_1, \ldots, y_n\}$. Since the theory T is in 3CNF by assumption, we have that $T \subseteq \Pi(V)$, where V is the set of variables appearing in T.

Existence of Solutions

The following lemma will be used to show a reduction from the problem of existence of solution to itself having the property of representative equivalence. Given H, M and $T = \{\gamma_1, \ldots, \gamma_m\}$, we define H', M', and T' as follows:

$$
\begin{aligned}
H' &= H \cup C \cup D \\
M' &= M \cup \{c_i \mid \gamma_i \in T\} \cup \{d_i \mid \gamma_i \notin T\} \\
T' &= \{\neg c_i \vee \neg d_i \mid \gamma_i \in \Pi(H \cup X)\} \cup \\
    &\quad \{c_i \to \gamma_i \mid \gamma_i \in \Pi(H \cup X)\}
\end{aligned}
$$

where X is the alphabet of T, while C and D are sets of new variables in one-to-one correspondence with the clauses (γ) in $\Pi(H \cup X)$. Note that, by definition, T is a subset of $\Pi(H \cup X)$. We now define f to be the function:

$$f(\langle H, M, T \rangle) = \langle H', M', T' \rangle$$

The following lemma relates the solutions of $\langle H, M, T \rangle$ with the solutions of $\langle H', M', T' \rangle$.

Lemma 1 *Let f be the function defined above. For any H, M, T, it holds:*

$$SOL(f(\langle H, M, T\rangle)) = \{S \cup \{c_i \mid \gamma_i \in T\} \cup \\ \{d_i \mid \gamma_i \notin T\} \mid S \in SOL(\langle H, M, T\rangle)\}$$

Proof. We divide the proof in three parts. First, we prove that any solution of $f(\langle H, M, T\rangle)$ contains exactly the literals c_i and d_i that are in M'. Then, we prove that if S' is a solution of $f(\langle H, M, T\rangle)$ then $S \backslash (C \cup D)$ is a solution of $\langle H, M, T\rangle$, and then we prove the converse.

1. We prove that $S \cap (C \cup D) = \{c_i \mid \gamma_i \in T\} \cup \{d_i \mid \gamma_i \notin T\}$. Let R be the set of literals $\{c_i \mid \gamma_i \in T\} \cup \{d_i \mid \gamma_i \notin T\}$. Since $R \subseteq M'$, we have that $S' \cup T' \models R$. Let us consider an arbitrary variable c_i or d_i in R. The point is that T' does not contain any positive occurrence of c_i or d_i (indeed, $c_i \to \gamma_i$ is $\neg c_i \vee \gamma_i$ in CNF form). As a result, if $c_i \in R$, then S' must contain a positive occurrence of c_i. But S' is a set of variables, thus $c_i \in S'$. The same holds for any $d_i \in R$.

2. Let S' be an element of $SOL(\langle H', M', T'\rangle)$. We prove that $S = S' \backslash (C \cup D) \in SOL(\langle H, M, T\rangle)$. The point proved above shows that, for each i, S' contains either c_i or d_i, depending on whether $\gamma_i \in T$. As a result:

$$
\begin{aligned}
S' \cup T' &\equiv S \cup \{c_i \mid \gamma_i \in T\} \cup \{d_i \mid \gamma_i \notin T\} \cup \\
&\quad \{\neg c_i \vee \neg d_i\} \cup \{c_i \to \gamma_i\} \\
&\equiv S \cup \{c_i \mid \gamma_i \in T\} \cup \{d_i \mid \gamma_i \notin T\} \cup T
\end{aligned}
$$

As a result, $S \cup T$ is consistent because the above formula is. Moreover, since the above formula implies M, and the variables in $C \cup D$ appears only once, it also holds $S \cup T \models M$. As a result, S is a solution of $\langle H, M, T\rangle$.

3. Let $S \in SOL(\langle H, M, T\rangle)$. We show that $S' = S \cup \{c_i \mid \gamma_i \in T\} \cup \{d_i \mid \gamma_i \notin T\}$ is a solution of $\langle H', M', T'\rangle$. This is an easy consequence of the fact that $S' \cup T'$ is equivalent to $S \cup T \cup \{c_i \mid \gamma_i \in T\} \cup \{d_i \mid \gamma_i \notin T\}$. □

The aim of this lemma is to show the existence of reductions satisfying the condition of representative equivalence. Another lemma is needed.

Lemma 2 *Let c be a positive integer number, and let g_c be the following function:*

$$
\begin{aligned}
g_c(\langle H, M, T\rangle) &= \langle H \cup \{h_{|H|+1}, \ldots, h_c\}, M, \\
&\quad T \cup \{x_{r+1} \vee \neg x_{r+1}, \ldots, x_c \vee \neg x_c\}\rangle
\end{aligned}
$$

where $r = |Var(T) \backslash H|$. It holds

$$SOL(g_c(\langle H, M, T\rangle)) = \{S \cup H' \mid S \in SOL(\langle H, M, T\rangle) \\ \text{and } H' \subseteq \{h_{|H|+1}, \ldots, h_c\}\}$$

We now define the classification, representative, and extension functions for the basic problems of abduction. First, the classification function is given by the maximum between the number of variables in H and the number of variables in T but not in H:

$$Class(\langle H, M, T\rangle) = \max(|H|, |Var(T) \backslash H|)$$

The representative instance of the class c is given by an instance with c possible assumptions, c other variables, and T composed by all possible clauses of three literals over these variables:

$$Repr(c) = \langle \{h_1, \ldots, h_c\}, \emptyset, \Pi(\{h_1, \ldots, h_c\} \cup \{x_1, \ldots, x_c\})\rangle$$

The extension function is also easy to give. For example, we may add to T a set of tautologies with new variables.

$$
\begin{aligned}
Ext(\langle H, M, T\rangle, m) &= \\
\langle H, M, T &\cup \{x_{r+1} \vee \neg x_{r+1}, \ldots, x_m \vee \neg x_m\}\rangle
\end{aligned}
$$

where $r = |Var(T) \backslash H|$

It is easy to check that these three functions are valid classification, representative, and extension functions for the problem of existence of explanation. It is also easy to prove that the same three functions are valid for the problems of relevance and necessity.

We are now able to show a reduction satisfying the condition of representative equivalence. Let i be the reduction defined as follows:

$$i(\langle H, M, T\rangle) = f(g_{Class(\langle H, M, T\rangle)}(\langle H, M, T\rangle))$$

By the above two lemmas, $i(\langle H, M, T\rangle)$ has solutions if and only if $\langle H, M, T\rangle$ has, thus this is a polynomial reduction. Moreover, the fixed part of $i(\langle H, M, T\rangle)$ depends only on the class of the instance $\langle H, M, T\rangle$. As a result, this reduction satisfies the condition of representative equivalence. The obvious consequence is the hardness of the problem of existence of solutions, which follows from the Σ_2^p-hardness of this problem (Eiter & Gottlob 1995).

Theorem 2 *The problem of establishing the existence of solution of an abductive problem is $\Vdash\Sigma_2^p$-hard.*

Relevance and Necessity

Let us now analyze is the problems of relevance and necessity. We make the following simplifying assumption: given an instance of abduction $\langle H, M, T\rangle$, where $H = \{h_1, \ldots, h_m\}$, we assume that we want to decide whether the first assumption h_1 is relevant. Clearly, the complexity of these two problems is the same, as we can always rename the variables appropriately.

By the two Lemmas above, it is easy to see that $i(\langle H, M, T\rangle)$ is also a reduction from the problem of relevance to the problem of relevance. It also satisfies representative equivalence, thus we have the compilability results for the problem of relevance.

Theorem 3 *The problem of relevance with no ordering is $\Vdash\Sigma_2^p$-hard.*

Let now consider the case in which an ordering $\preceq$ is used. The following properties on $\preceq$ are defined.

Meaningful. The ordering $\preceq$ is meaningful if, for any variable h and any pair of sets H' and H'' such that $h \notin H' \cup H''$, $H' \cup \{h\} \preceq H'' \cup \{h\}$ iff $H' \preceq H''$.

Irredundant The ordering $\preceq$ is irredundant if, for any pair of sets H' and H'', if $H' \subset H''$ then $H' \prec H''$.

It can be proved that the reduction i also works for the case of relevance and necessity, and satisfies representative equivalence, if the ordering $\preceq$ is irredundant. The basic point of the proof of incompilability of existence of solution is Lemma 1, which holds when no ordering is defined. In the case in which we consider $SOL_\preceq$ instead of SOL, it is possible to prove a similar lemma, if the given ordering is meaningful.

Lemma 3 *If $\preceq$ is a meaningful ordering, it holds:*

$SOL_\preceq(f(\langle H, M, T\rangle)) =$
$\{S \cup \{c_i \mid \gamma_i \in T\} \cup \{d_i \mid \gamma_i \notin T\} \mid S \in SOL_\preceq(\langle H, M, T\rangle)\}$

It is also possible to prove the analogous of Lemma 2.

Lemma 4 *Let c be a positive integer number, and let g_c be the function of Lemma 2. If $\preceq$ is an irredundant ordering, it holds:*

$$SOL_\preceq(g_c(\langle H, M, T\rangle)) = SOL_\preceq(\langle H, M, T\rangle)$$

From the above lemmas, it follows that the reduction i also works in the case in which $\preceq$ is meaningful and irredundant, and we consider the problems of relevance and necessity.

Theorem 4 *If $\preceq$ is a meaningful irredundant ordering, then the problem of relevance is $\Vdash$C-hard for any class C of the polynomial hierarchy such that the problem is C-hard.*

A similar theorem holds for necessity. Since $\subseteq$ and $\leq$ are meaningful irredundant orderings, from their complexity we are able to find their corresponding characterization of compilability.

Corollary 5 *Relevance using $\subseteq$ is $\Vdash\Sigma_2^p$-hard, while using $\leq$ it is nucomp$\Delta_3^p[\log n]$-hard.*

Related Work

In this paper we have analyzed whether the complexity of abduction can be decreased by a preprocessing. All along the paper we have assumed that the input is provided as a triple $\langle H, M, T\rangle$, where T is a propositional theory. In (Kautz, Kearns, & Selman 1995), a different problem is analyzed, where the background knowledge (that in their case corresponds to a Horn theory) is not given in terms of a propositional theory, but as a set of *characteristic models*. In the paper it is shown that computing abduction from this representation only requires polynomial time (Kautz, Kearns, & Selman 1995, Theorem 13), while for the representation in terms of a propositional Horn theory the same problem is NP-complete (Selman & Levesque 1990, Theorems 2,3,4)). This result has been further strengthened by Khardon and Roth (1996) where they show a model-based representation for general propositional theories (not just Horn ones) and prove (Khardon & Roth 1996, Theorem 9.1) that abduction can be computed in polynomial time for general propositional theories (when represented by their set of characteristic models).

It seems the case that, by preprocessing the input $\langle H, M, T\rangle$ into a model-based representation the complexity decreases from NP-complete to polynomial-time. However, this is not the case. In fact, as shown by Kautz, Kearns and Selman in the Horn case (Kautz, Kearns, & Selman 1995, Theorem 4) and by Khardon and Roth for the more general case (Khardon & Roth 1996, Claim 7.2 and Theorem 7.4), there is no way to rewrite a propositional representation into a model-based one without (in the worst case) increasing the size exponentially. Our definition of preprocessing does not permit such a rewriting since it imposes that the function f of Definition 1 is poly-size. Hence, the complexity results for model-based representations do not contradict the results presented in this paper.

The result of incompilability as the ones given in this paper left open two possibilities: first, compilation may be used to generate a polynomial-sized output that reduces complexity in some cases (but now always); second, we may always want a reduction of complexity, possibility giving up the requirement of polynomiality of the result of compilation. Work in practical compilation has shown that this second option may lead to compilation algorithm with a good space performance in practical cases. The results of this paper are not in contradiction with such results, but rather complement them. Indeed, saying that $\Vdash$NP-hard problems are not compilable to P is more or less like saying that NP-hard problems are not tractable. In the case of NP-hardness, the theoretical results show that even worst-case exponential algorithms are perfectly reasonable, and, in some sense, support the research in the direction of non-polynomial algorithms. In the same way, the incompilability results prove that an exponential output of the compilation phase is not a drawback of such an algorithm, but a necessity.

Conclusions and Future Work

In this paper we have shown that for most forms of logic-based abduction it is not possible to decrease the complexity of the most common computational tasks even if an arbitrarily long preprocess phase on the theory T and the set of hypothesis H is allowed.

We are currently extending their work in two directions. First of all, some more refined definitions of preference can be given, for instance prioritization and penalty. The use of these preference relations increase the complexity of the considered problems. Since these extensions are very relevant in practice, it make sense to study their properties w.r.t. compilability.

Another direction we are currently investigating is by restricting the theory T to be a set of Horn clauses. Indeed, since the complexity of abduction often goes down one level in the polynomial hierarchy when T is Horn, this restriction is relevant to implementation. It is thus useful to characterize the problem also from the point of view of compilation. Some preliminary results from the study of these two problems suggest that, even in these cases, the complexity of the abductive problems does not decrease when a compilation step is applied to T and H.

A practical question is whether there exist constraints on the form of the abductive problem allowing compilation to make the problem polynomial. Recent work in other areas (Cadoli *et al.* 1996) suggest that the most "natural" restrictions on logical formalisms (e.g. CNF form) do not lead to compilability.

Finally, it seems possible to give a definition of expressivity to logical-based abduction formalisms, which allows to classify different formalisms w.r.t. the set of abductive problems they are able to express. A preliminary analysis suggests that compilation (and not complexity) classes are useful to prove some results on this problem.

References

[Bylander *et al.* 1989] Bylander, T.; Allemang, D.; Tanner, M. C.; and Josephson, J. R. 1989. Some results concerning the computational complexity of abduction. In *Proc. of KR'89*, 44–54.

[Cadoli *et al.* 1996] Cadoli, M.; Donini, F. M.; Liberatore, P.; and Schaerf, M. 1996. Feasibility and unfeasibility of off-line processing. In *Proc. of ISTCS'96*, 100–109. IEEE Computer Society Press. URL = FTP://FTP.DIS.UNIROMA1.IT/PUB/AI/PAPERS/CADO-ETAL-96.PS.GZ.

[Console, Portinale, & Theseider Dupré 1996] Console, L.; Portinale, L.; and Theseider Dupré, D. 1996. Using compiled knowledge to guide and focus abductive diagnosis. *IEEE Trans. on Knowledge and Data Engineering* 8(5):690–706.

[Eiter & Gottlob 1995] Eiter, T., and Gottlob, G. 1995. The complexity of logic-based abduction. *J. of the ACM* 42(1):3–42.

[Garey & Johnson 1979] Garey, M. R., and Johnson, D. S. 1979. *Computers and Intractability: A Guide to the Theory of NP-Completeness*. San Francisco, Ca: W.H. Freeman and Company.

[Karp & Lipton 1980] Karp, R. M., and Lipton, R. J. 1980. Some connections between non-uniform and uniform complexity classes. In *Proc. of STOC'80*, 302–309.

[Kautz, Kearns, & Selman 1995] Kautz, H. A.; Kearns, M. J.; and Selman, B. 1995. Horn approximations of empirical data. *Artificial Intelligence* 74:129–145.

[Khardon & Roth 1996] Khardon, R., and Roth, D. 1996. Reasoning with models. *Artificial Intelligence* 87:187–213.

[Peirce 1955] Peirce, C. S. 1955. Abduction and induction. In Buchler, J., ed., *Philosophical Writings of Peirce*. Dover, New York. chapter 11.

[Selman & Levesque 1990] Selman, B., and Levesque, H. J. 1990. Abductive and default reasoning: A computational core. In *Proc. of AAAI'90*, 343–348.

[Stockmeyer 1976] Stockmeyer, L. J. 1976. The polynomial-time hierarchy. *Theor. Comp. Sci.* 3:1–22.

[Yap 1983] Yap, C. K. 1983. Some consequences of non-uniform conditions on uniform classes. *Theor. Comp. Sci.* 26:287–300.

Decision-Theoretic, High-level Agent Programming in the Situation Calculus

Craig Boutilier
Dept. of Computer Science
University of Toronto
Toronto, ON M5S 3H5
cebly@cs.toronto.edu

Ray Reiter
Dept. of Computer Science
University of Toronto
Toronto, ON M5S 3H5
reiter@cs.toronto.edu

Mikhail Soutchanski
Dept. of Computer Science
University of Toronto
Toronto, ON M5S 3H5
mes@cs.toronto.edu

Sebastian Thrun
School of Computer Science
Carnegie Mellon University
Pittsburgh, PA 15213-3891
thrun@cs.cmu.edu

Abstract

We propose a framework for robot programming which allows the seamless integration of explicit agent programming with decision-theoretic planning. Specifically, the *DTGolog* model allows one to partially specify a control program in a high-level, logical language, and provides an interpreter that, given a logical axiomatization of a domain, will determine the optimal completion of that program (viewed as a Markov decision process). We demonstrate the utility of this model with results obtained in an office delivery robotics domain.

1 Introduction

The construction of autonomous agents, such as mobile robots or software agents, is paramount in artificial intelligence, with considerable research devoted to methods that will ease the burden of designing controllers for such agents. There are two main ways in which the conceptual complexity of devising controllers can be managed. The first is to provide languages with which a programmer can specify a control program with relative ease, using high-level actions as primitives, and expressing the necessary operations in a natural way. The second is to simply specify goals (or an objective function) and provide the agent with the ability to plan appropriate courses of action that achieve those goals (or maximize the objective function). In this way the need for explicit programming is obviated.

In this paper, we propose a framework that combines both perspectives, allowing one to partially specify a controller by writing a program in a suitably high-level language, yet allowing an agent some latitude in choosing its actions, thus requiring a modicum of planning or decision-making ability. Viewed differently, we allow for the seamless integration of programming and planning. Specifically, we suppose that the agent programmer has enough knowledge of a given domain to be able to specify some (but not necessarily all) of the structure and the details of a good (or possibly optimal) controller. Those aspects left unspecified will be filled in by the agent itself, but must satisfy any constraints imposed by the program (or partially-specified controller). When controllers can easily be designed by hand, planning has no role to play. On the other hand, certain problems are more easily tackled by specifying goals and a declarative domain model, and allowing the agent to plan its behavior.

Copyright ©2000, American Association for Artificial Intelligence (www.aaai.org). All rights reserved.

Our framework is based on the synthesis of Markov decisions processes (MDPs) [4, 13] with the Golog programming language [10]. Key to our proposal is the extension of the Golog language and interpreter, called *DTGolog*, to deal with uncertainty and general reward functions. The planning ability we provide is that of a decision-theoretic planner in which choices left to the agent are made by maximizing expected utility. Our framework can thus be motivated in two ways. First, it can be viewed as a decision-theoretic extension of the Golog language. Golog is a high-level agent programming language based on the situation calculus, with a clear semantics, and in which standard programming constructs (e.g., sequencing, nondeterministic choice) are used to write high-level control programs.

From a different standpoint, our contribution can be viewed as a language and methodology with which to provide "advice" to a decision-theoretic planner. MDPs are a conceptually and computationally useful model for decision-theoretic planning, but their solution is often intractable. We provide the means to *naturally* constrain the search for (ideally, optimal) policies with a Golog program. The agent can only adopt policies that are consistent with the execution of the program. The decision-theoretic Golog interpreter then solves the underlying MDP by making choices regarding the execution of the program through expected utility maximization. This viewpoint is fruitful when one considers that an agent's designer or "taskmaster" often has a good idea about the general structure of a good (or optimal) policy, but may be unable to commit to certain details. While we run the risk that the program may not allow for optimal behavior, this model has the clear advantage that the decision problem faced will generally be more tractable: it need only make those choices left open to it by the programmer. In contrast to existing models for constraining policies in MDPs, which use concepts such as local policies [11, 18] or finite-state machines [11], DTGolog provides a natural and well-understood formalism for *programming* behaviors.

Our approach is specifically targeted towards developing complex robotics software. Within robotics, the two major paradigms—planning and programming—have largely been pursued independently. Both approaches have their advantages (flexibility and generality in the planning paradigm, performance of programmed controllers) and scaling limitations (e.g., the computational complexity of planning approaches, task-specific design and conceptual complexity for programmers in the programming paradigm). MDP-style planning has been at the core of a range of fielded robot applications, such as two recent tour-guide robots [5, 19]. Its ability to cope with uncertain worlds is an essential feature for real-world robotic applications. However, MDP planning scales poorly to complex tasks and environments. By programming easy-to-code routines and leaving only those choices to the MDP planner that are difficult to program (e.g., because the programmer cannot easily determine appropriate or optimal behavior), the complexity of planning can be reduced tremendously. Note that such difficult-to-program behaviors may actually be quite easy to *implicitly* specify using goals or objectives.

To demonstrate the advantage of this new framework, we have developed a prototype mobile office robot that delivers mail, using a combination of pre-programmed behavior and decision-theoretic deliberation. An analysis of the relative trade-offs shows that the combination of programming and planning is essential for developing robust, scalable control software for robotic applications like the one described here.

We give brief overviews of MDPs and Golog in Sections 2 and 3. We describe the DTGolog representation of MDPs and programs and the DTGolog interpreter in Section 4, and illustrate the functioning of the interpreter by describing its implementation in a office robot in Section 5.

2 Markov Decision Processes

We begin with some basic background on MDPs (see [4, 13] for further details). We assume that we have a stochastic dynamical system to be controlled by some agent. A fully-observable MDP $M = \langle S, A, \Pr, R \rangle$ comprises the following components. S is a finite set of *states* of the system being controlled. The agent has a finite set of *actions* A with which to influence the system state. Dynamics are given by $\Pr : S \times A \times S \to [0, 1]$; here $\Pr(s_i, a, s_j)$ denotes the probability that action a, when executed at state s_i, induces a transition to s_j. $R : S \to \Re$ is a real-valued, bounded *reward function*. The process is fully observable: though the agent cannot predict the outcome of an action with certainty, it can observe that state precisely once it is reached.

The decision problem faced by the agent in an MDP is that of forming an *optimal policy* (a mapping from states to actions) that maximizes expected total accumulated reward over some horizon of interest. An agent finding itself in state s^t at time t must choose an action a^t. The *expected value* of a course of action π depends on the specific objectives. A *finite-horizon* decision problem with horizon T measures the value of π as $E(\sum_{t=0}^{T} R(s^t)|\pi)$ (where expectation is taken w.r.t. Pr).[1] For an MDP with horizon T, a *(nonstationary) policy* $\pi : S \times \{1, \cdots, T\} \to A$ associates with each state s and stage-to-go $t \leq T$ an action $\pi(s, t)$ to be executed at s with t stages remaining. An *optimal* policy is one with maximum expected value at each state-stage pair.

The planning problem faced by an agent is that of forming an *optimal policy* (a mapping from states to actions) that maximizes expected total accumulated reward over some horizon. Dynamic programming methods are often used to solve MDPs [13], though one difficulty facing (the classical versions of) such algorithms is their reliance on an explicit state-space formulation; as such, their complexity is exponential in the number of state variables. However, "logical" representations such as STRIPS and dynamic Bayesian networks have recently been used to make the specification and solution of MDPs much easier [4]. The DTGolog representation goes further in this direction by specifying state transitions in first order logic. Restricting attention to reachable states using decision tree search can, in some circumstances, alleviate the computational difficulties of dynamic programming. Search-based approaches to solving MDPs can use heuristics, learning, sampling, and pruning to improve their efficiency [3, 6, 7, 8, 9]. Declarative search control knowledge, used successfully in classical planning [2], might also be used to prune the search space. In an MDP, this could be viewed as restricting the set of policies considered. This type of approach has been explored in the more general context of value iteration for MDPs in, e.g., [11, 18]: local policies or finite-state machines are used to model partial policies, and techniques are devised to find the optimal policy consistent with the constraints so imposed. In Section 4 we develop the DTGolog interpreter to capture similar intuitions, but adopt the Golog programming language as a means of specifying these constraints using natural programming constructs.

3 The Situation Calculus and Golog

The situation calculus is a first-order language for axiomatizing dynamic worlds. In recent years, it has been considerably extended beyond the "classical" language to include concurrency, continuous time, etc., but in all cases, its basic ingredients consist of *actions*, *situations* and *fluents*.

Actions are first-order terms consisting of an action function symbol and its arguments. In the approach to representing time in the situation calculus of [14], one of the arguments to such an action function symbol—typically, its last argument—is the time of the action's occurrence. For example, $startGo(l, l', 3.1)$ might denote the action of a robot starting to move from location l to l' at time 3.1. Following Reiter [14], all actions are instantaneous (i.e, with zero duration).[2]

A *situation* is a first-order term denoting a sequence of actions. These sequences are represented using a binary function symbol do: $do(\alpha, s)$ denotes the sequence resulting from adding the action α to the sequence s. The special constant S_0 denotes the *initial situation*, namely the empty action sequence. Therefore, the situation term

$do(endGo(l, l', 7.3), do(startGrasp(o, 2),$
$do(startGo(l, l', 2), S_0)))$

denotes the following sequence of actions: $startGo(l, l', 2)$, $startGrasp(o, 2)$, $endGo(l, l', 7.3)$. Axioms for situations with time are given in [15].

Relations whose truth values vary from state to state are called *relational fluents*, and are denoted by predicate or function symbols whose last argument is a situation term. For

---

[1] We focus on finite-horizon problems to keep the presentation short, though everything we describe can be applied with little modification to discounted, infinite-horizon MDPs.

[2] Durations can be captured using processes, as shown below. A full exposition of time is not possible here.

example, $closeTo(x, y, s)$ might be a relational fluent, meaning that when the robot performs the action sequence denoted by the situation term s, x will be close to y.

A domain theory is axiomatized in the situation calculus with four classes of axioms:

Action precondition axioms: There is one for each action function $A(\vec{x})$, with syntactic form $Poss(A(\vec{x}), s) \equiv \Pi_A(\vec{x}, s)$. Here, $\Pi_A(\vec{x}, s)$ is a formula with free variables among $\vec{x}, s$. These are the preconditions of action A.

Successor state axioms: There is one for each relational fluent $F(\vec{x}, s)$, with syntactic form $F(\vec{x}, do(a, s)) \equiv \Phi_F(\vec{x}, a, s)$, where $\Phi_F(\vec{x}, a, s)$ is a formula with free variables among $a, s, \vec{x}$. These characterize the truth values of the fluent F in the next situation $do(a, s)$ in terms of the current situation s, and they embody a solution to the frame problem for deterministic actions ([16]).

Unique names axioms for actions: These state that the actions of the domain are pairwise unequal.

Initial database: This is a set of sentences whose only situation term is S_0; it specifies the initial problem state.

Examples of these axioms will be seen in Section 4.1.

Golog [10] is a situation calculus-based programming language for defining complex actions in terms of a set of primitive actions axiomatized in the situation calculus as described above. It has the standard—and some not-so-standard—control structures found in most Algol-like languages.

1. *Sequence:* α ; β. Do action α, followed by action β.

2. *Test actions:* p? Test the truth value of expression p in the current situation.

3. *Nondeterministic action choice:* $\alpha \mid \beta$. Do α or β.

4. *Nondeterministic choice of arguments:* $(\pi\, x)\alpha(x)$. Nondeterministically pick a value for x, and for that value of x, do action $\alpha(x)$.

5. *Conditionals* (*if-then-else*) and *while* loops.

6. *Procedures, including recursion.*

The semantics of Golog programs is defined by macroexpansion, using a ternary relation Do. $Do(\delta, s, s')$ is an *abbreviation* for a situation calculus formula whose intuitive meaning is that s' is one of the situations reached by evaluating the program δ beginning in situation s. Given a program δ, one *proves*, using the situation calculus axiomatization of the background domain, the formula $(\exists s) Do(\delta, S_0, s)$ to compute a plan. Any binding for s obtained by a constructive proof of this sentence is a legal execution trace, involving only primitive actions, of δ. A Golog interpreter for the situation calculus with time, implemented in Prolog, is described in [15].

Thus the interpreter will makes choices (if possible) that lead to successful computation of an execution trace of the program. With nondeterministic choice and the specification of postconditions corresponding to goals, Golog can be viewed as integrating planning and programming in deterministic domains. We will see examples of Golog programs in Section 5.

4 DTGolog: Decision-Theoretic Golog

As a planning model, MDPs are quite flexible and robust, dealing with uncertainty, multiple objectives, and so on, but suffer from several key limitations. While recent work in DTP has focused on the development of compact, natural representations for MDPs [4], little work has gone into the development of first-order languages for specifying MDPs (see [1, 12] for two exceptions). More importantly, the computational complexity of policy construction is prohibitive. As mentioned, one way to circumvent planning complexity is to allow explicit agent programming; yet little work has been directed toward integrating the ability to write programs or otherwise constrain the space of policies that are searched during planning. What work has been done (e.g., [11, 18]) fails to provide a language for imposing such constraints, and certainly offers no tools for *programming* agent behavior. We believe that natural, declarative *programming languages and methodologies* for (partially) specifying agent behavior are necessary for this approach to find successful application in real domains.

Golog, on the other hand, provides a very natural means for agent programming. With nondeterministic choice a programmer can even leave a certain amount of "planning" up to the interpreter (or agent being controlled). However, for applications such as robotics programming, the usefulness of Golog is severely limited by its inability to model stochastic domains, or reason decision-theoretically about appropriate choices. Despite these limitations, (deterministic) Golog has been successfully used to provide the high-level control of a museum tour-guide robot, controlling user interaction and scheduling more than 2,400 exhibits [5].

We have developed DTGolog, a decision-theoretic extension of Golog that allows one to specify MDPs in a first-order language, and provide "advice" in the form of high-level programs that constrain the search for policies. A program can be viewed as a partially-specified policy: its semantics can be viewed, informally, as the execution of the program (or the completion of the policy) that has highest expected value. DTGolog offers a synthesis of both planning and programming, and is in fact general enough to accommodate both extremes. One can write purely nondeterministic programs that allow an agent to solve an MDP optimally, or purely deterministic programs that leave no decisions in the agent's hands whatsoever. We will see, in fact, that a point between these ends of the spectrum is often the most useful way to write robot programs. DTGolog allows the appropriate point for any specific problem to be chosen with relative ease. Space precludes the presentation of many technical details, but we try to provide the basic flavor of DTGolog.

4.1 DTGolog: Problem Representation

The specification of an MDP requires the provision of a background *action theory*—as in Section 3—and a background *optimization theory*—consisting of the specification of a reward function and some optimality criterion (here we require only a horizon T). The unique names axioms and initial database have the same form as in standard Golog.

A background action theory in the decision-theoretic setting distinguishes between *deterministic* agent actions and *stochastic* agent actions. Both types are used to form programs and policies. However, the situation resulting from execution of a stochastic action is not determined by the action itself: instead each stochastic agent action is associated with a finite set of deterministic actions, from which "nature" chooses stochastically. Successor state axioms are provided for nature's actions directly (which are deterministic), not for stochastic agent actions (i.e., successor state axioms never mention stochastic agent actions). When a stochastic action is executed, nature chooses one of the associated actions with a specified probability, and the successor state is given by nature's action so chosen. The predicate $stochastic(a, s, n)$ relates a stochastic agent action a to one of nature's action n in a situation s, and $prob(n, p, s)$ denotes the probability with which n is chosen in s. Deterministic agent's actions are axiomatized using exactly the same precondition and successor state axioms. This methodology allows us to extend the axiomatization of a domain theory described in the previous section in a minimal way.

As an example, imagine a robot moving between different locations: the process of going is initiated by a deterministic action $startGo(l_1, l_2, t)$; but the terminating action $endGo(l_1, l_2, t)$ is stochastic (e.g., the robot may end up in some location other than l_2, say, the hallway). We give nature two choices, $endGoS(l_1, l_2, t)$ (successful arrival) and $endGoF(l_1, Hall, t)$ (end with failure), and include axioms such as $stochastic(endGo(l_1, l_2, t), s, endGoS(l_1, l_2, t))$ and $prob(endGoS(l_1, l_2, t), 0.9, s)$ (i.e., successful movement occurs with probability 0.9 in any situation). Let $going(l_1, l_2, s)$ be the relational fluent meaning that in the situation s the robot is in the process of moving between locations l_1 and l_2; and let $robotLoc(l, s)$ be a relational fluent denoting the robot's location. The following precondition and successor state axioms characterize these fluents, and the actions $startGo, endGoS, endGoF$:

$Poss(startGo(l_1, l_2, t), s) \equiv \neg(\exists l, l')going(l, l', s)$
$\quad \land robotLoc(l_1, s)$
$Poss(endGoS(l_1, l_2, t), s) \equiv going(l_1, l_2, s),$
$Poss(endGoF(l_1, l_2, t), s) \equiv \exists l'.going(l_1, l', s) \land l' \neq l_2$
$going(l, l', do(a, s)) \equiv (\exists t)a = startGo(l, l', t) \lor$
$\quad going(l, l', s) \land \neg(\exists t)a = endGoS(l, l', t) \lor$
$\quad going(l, l', s) \land \neg(\exists t, l'')a = endGoF(l, l'', t),$

The background action theory also includes a new class of axioms, *sense conditions axioms*, which assert atomic formulae using predicate $senseCond(n, \phi)$: this holds if ϕ is a logical condition that an agent uses to determine if the specific nature's action n occurred when some stochastic action was executed. We require such axioms in order to "implement" full observability. While in the standard MDP model one simply assumes that the successor state is known, in practice, one must force agents to disambiguate the state using sensor information. The sensing actions needed can be determined from sense condition axioms. The following distinguish successful from unsuccessful movement:

$senseCond(endGoS(l_1, l_2, t), robotLoc(l_2))$
$senseCond(endGoF(l_1, l_2, t), robotLoc(Hall))$

A DTGolog optimization theory contains axioms specifying the reward function.[3] In their simplest form, reward axioms use the function $reward(s)$ and assert costs and rewards as a function of the action taken, properties of the current situation, or both (note that the action taken can be recovered from the situation term). For instance, we might assert

$reward(do(giveCoffeeSuccessful(Jill, t), s)) = 6.3$

Because primitive actions have an explicit temporal argument, we can also describe time-dependent reward functions easily (associated with behaviors that extend over time). These can be dealt with in the interpreter because of our use of situation terms rather than states, from which time can be derived without having it explicitly encoded in the state. This often proves useful in practice. In a given temporal Golog program, the temporal occurrence of certain actions can be uniquely determined either by temporal constraints or by the programmer. Other actions may occur at any time in a certain interval determined by temporal inequalities; for any such action $A(\vec{x}, t)$, we can instantiate the time argument by maximizing the reward for reaching the situation $do(A(\vec{x}, t), s)$. For example, suppose the robot receives a reward $r = max(\frac{100-t}{distance(l_1,l_2)})$ for doing the action $endGoS(l_1, l_2, t)$ in s. With this reward function, the robot is encouraged to arrive at the destination as soon as possible and is also encouraged to go to nearby locations (because the reward is inversely proportional to distance).

Our representation for stochastic actions is related somewhat to the representations proposed in [1, 7, 12].

4.2 DTGolog: Semantics

In what follows, we assume that we have been provided with a background action theory and optimization theory. We interpret DTGolog programs relative to this theory. DTGolog programs are written using the same program operators as Golog programs. The semantics is specified in a similar fashion, with the predicate *BestDo* (described below) playing the role of *Do*. However, the structure of *BestDo* (and its Prolog implementation) is rather different than that of *Do*. One difference reflects the fact that primitive actions can be stochastic. Execution traces for a sequence of primitive actions need not be simple "linear" situation terms, but rather branching "trees." Another reflects the fact that DTGolog distinguishes otherwise legal traces according to expected utility. Given a choice between two actions (or subprograms) at some point in a program, the interpreter chooses the action with highest expected value, mirroring the structure of an MDP search tree. The interpreter returns a *policy*—an expanded Golog program—in which every nondeterministic choice point is *grounded* with the selection of an optimal choice. Intuitively, the semantics of a DTGolog program will be given by the *optimal execution of that program*.

The semantics of a DTGolog program is defined by a predicate $BestDo(prog, s, horiz, pol, val, prob)$, where $prog$ is a Golog program, s is a starting situation, pol is the optimal conditional policy determined by program $prog$ beginning in

---
[3] We require an optimality criterion to be specified as well. We assume a finite-horizon H in this work.

situation s, val is the expected value of that policy, $prob$ is the probability that pol will execute successfully, and $horiz$ is a prespecified horizon. Generally, an intepreter implementing this definition will be called with a given program $prog$, situation S_0, and horizon $horiz$, and the arguments pol, val and $prob$ will be instantiated by the interpreter. The policy pol returned by the interpreter is a Golog program consisting of the sequential composition (under ;) of agent actions, $senseEffect(A)$ sensing actions (which serve to identify nature's choices whenever A is a stochastic agent action), and conditionals (if ϕ then pol_1 else pol_2).

Below we assume an MDP with finite horizon H: if a program fails to terminate before the horizon is reached, the interpreter produces the best (partial) H-step execution of the program. The interpreter can easily be modified to deal with programs that are guaranteed to terminate in a finite amount of time (so a bound H need not be imposed) or infinite-horizon, discounted problems (returning ε-optimal policies).

$BestDo$ is defined inductively on the structure of its first argument, which is a Golog program:

1. **Zero horizon.**
   $BestDo(p, s, h, \pi, v, pr) \stackrel{def}{=}$
   $\quad h = 0 \land \pi = Nil \land v = reward(s) \land pr = 1$.

   Give up on the program p if the horizon reaches 0.

2. **The null program**
   $BestDo(Nil, s, h, \pi, v, pr) \stackrel{def}{=}$
   $\quad \pi = Nil \land v = reward(s) \land pr = 1$.

3. **First program action is deterministic.**
   $BestDo(a; p, s, h, \pi, v, pr) \stackrel{def}{=}$
   $\quad \neg Poss(a, s) \land \pi = Stop \land pr = 0 \land v = reward(s) \lor$
   $\quad Poss(a, s) \land$
   $\quad \exists(\pi', v', pr') BestDo(p, do(a, s), h{-}1, \pi', v', pr') \land$
   $\quad \pi = a; \pi' \land v = reward(s) + v' \land pr = pr'$.

   A program that begins with a deterministic agent action a (if a is possible in situation s) has its optimal execution defined as the optimal execution of the remainder of the program p in situation $do(a, s)$. Its value is given by the expected value of this continuation plus the reward in s (action cost for a can be included without difficulty), while its success probability is given by the success probability of its continuation. The optimal policy is a followed by the optimal policy for the remainder. If a is *not* possible at s, the policy is simply the $Stop$ action, the success probability is zero, and the value is simply the reward associated with situation s. $Stop$ is a zero-cost action that takes the agent to a zero-cost absorbing state.[4]

4. **First program action is stochastic.**
   When a is a stochastic agent action for which nature selects one of the actions in the set $\{n_1, \ldots, n_k\}$,

   $BestDo(a; p, s, h, \pi, v, pr) \stackrel{def}{=}$
   $\quad \exists(\pi'). BestDoAux(\{n_1, \ldots, n_k\}, p, s, h, \pi', v, pr) \land$
   $\quad \pi = a; senseEffect(a); \pi'$.

The resulting policy is $a; senseEffect(a); \pi'$ where π' is the policy delivered by $BestDoAux$. Intuitively, this policy says that the agent should first perform action a, at which point nature selects one of $n_1, \ldots, n_k$ to perform (with probabilities $prob(n_i, s)$), then the agent should sense the outcome of action a (which tells it which of nature's actions n_i actually occurred), then it should execute the policy delivered by $BestDoAux$.[5]

$BestDoAux(\{\}, p, s, h, \pi, v, pr) \stackrel{def}{=}$
$\quad \pi = Stop \land v = 0 \land pr = 0$.

Suppose $k \geq 1$. Suppose further that ϕ_1 is the sense condition for nature's action n_1, meaning that observing that ϕ_1 is true is necessary and sufficient for the agent to conclude that nature actually performed action n_1, among the choices $\{n_1, \ldots, n_k\}$ available to her by virtue of the agent having done stochastic action a. Then

$BestDoAux(\{n_1, \ldots, n_k\}, p, s, h, \pi, v, pr) \stackrel{def}{=}$
$\neg Poss(n_1, s) \land BestDoAux(\{n_2, \ldots, n_k\}, p, s, h, \pi, v, pr)$
$\lor Poss(n_1, s) \land$
$\exists(\pi', v', pr'). BestDoAux(\{n_2, \ldots, n_k\}, p, s, h, \pi', v', pr') \land$
$\exists(\pi_1, v_1, pr_1). BestDo(p, do(n_1, s), h{-}1, \pi_1, v_1, pr_1) \land$
$\pi = $ if ϕ_1 then π_1 else $\pi' \land$
$v = v' + v_1 \cdot prob(n_1, s) \land$
$pr = pr' + pr_1 \cdot prob(n_1, s)$.

$BestDoAux$ determines a policy in the form of a conditional plan:

if ϕ_{i_1} then pol_1 else if ϕ_{i_2} then $pol_2 \cdots$
$\quad$ else if ϕ_{i_m} then pol_m else $Stop$.

Here, $n_{i_1}, \ldots, n_{i_m}$ are all of nature's actions among $\{n_1, \ldots, n_k\}$ that are possible in s, and pol_j is the policy returned by the program p, in situation $do(n_{i_j}, s)$.

5. **First program action is a test.**
   $BestDo(\phi?; p, s, h, \pi, v, pr) \stackrel{def}{=}$
   $\quad \phi[s] \land BestDo(p, s, h, \pi, v, pr) \lor$
   $\quad \neg \phi[s] \land \pi = Stop \land pr = 0 \land v = reward(s)$

6. **First program action is the nondeterministic choice of two programs.**

   $BestDo((p_1 \mid p_2); p, s, h, \pi, v, pr) \stackrel{def}{=}$
   $\quad \exists(\pi_1, v_1, pr_1). BestDo(p_1; p, s, h, \pi_1, v_1, pr_1) \land$
   $\quad \exists(\pi_2, v_2, pr_2). BestDo(p_2; p, s, h, \pi_2, v_2, pr_2) \land$
   $\quad ((v_1, pr_1) \leq (v_2, pr_2) \land \pi = \pi_2 \land v = v_2 \land pr = pr_2 \lor$
   $\quad (v_1, pr_1) > (v_2, pr_2) \land \pi = \pi_1 \land v = v_1 \land pr = pr_1)$.

   Given the choice between two subprograms p_1 and p_2, the optimal policy is determined by that subprogram with optimal execution. Note that there is some subtlety in the interpretation of a DTGolog program: on the one hand, we wish the interpreter to choose a course of action with maximal expected value; on the other, it should follow the advice provided by the program. Because certain choices may lead to abnormal termination—the $Stop$ action cor-

---

[4] This can be viewed as having an agent simply give up its attempt to execute the policy and await further instruction.

[5] It is these sensing actions that "implement" the assumption that the MDP is fully observable.

responding to an incomplete execution of the program—with varying probabilities, the success probability associated with a policy can be loosely viewed as the degree to which the interpreter adhered to the program. Thus we have a multi-objective optimization problem, requiring some tradeoff between success probability and expected value of a policy. The predicate $\leq$ compares pairs of the form (p, v), where p is a success probability and v is an expected value.[6]

7. **Conditionals.**

$$BestDo((\text{if } \phi \text{ then } p_1 \text{ else } p_2); p, s, h, \pi, v, pr) \stackrel{def}{=}\\ BestDo((\phi?; p_1 \mid \neg\phi?; p_2); p, s, h, \pi, v, pr)$$

This simply says that a conditional **if** ϕ **then** p_1 **else** p_2 is an abbreviation for $\phi?; p_1 \mid \neg\phi?; p_2$.

8. **Nondeterministic finite choice of action arguments.**

$$BestDo((\pi(x:\tau)p); p', s, h, pol, v, pr) \stackrel{def}{=}\\ BestDo(p|_{c_1}^{x} \mid \cdots \mid p|_{c_n}^{x}); p', s, h, pol, v, pr)$$

The programming construct $\pi(x:\tau)p$ requires the nondeterministic choice of an element x from the finite set $\tau = \{c_1, \ldots, c_n\}$, and for that x, do the program p. It therefore is an abbreviation for the program $p|_{c_1}^{x} \mid \cdots \mid p|_{c_n}^{x}$, where $p|_{c}^{x}$ means substitute c for all free occurrences of x in p.

9. **Associate sequential composition to the right.**

$$BestDo((p_1; p_2); p_3, s, h, \pi, v, pr) \stackrel{def}{=}\\ BestDo(p_1; (p_2; p_3), s, h, \pi, v, pr).$$

This is needed to massage the program to a form in which its first action is one of the forms suitable for application of rules 2-8.

There is also a suitable expansion rule when the first program action is a procedure call. This is almost identical to the rule for Golog procedures [10], and requires second-order logic to characterize the standard fixed point definition of recursive procedures. Because it is a bit on the complicated side, and because it is not central to the specification of policies for DTGolog, we omit this expansion rule here. While loops can be defined using procedures.

4.3 Computing Optimal Policies

$BestDo(prog, s, horiz, pol, val, prob)$ is, analogously to the case for Golog, an *abbreviation* for a situation calculus formula whose intuitive meaning is that *pol* is an optimal policy resulting from evaluating the program *prog* beginning in situation s, that *val* is its value, and *prob* the probability of a successful execution of this policy. Therefore, given a program δ, and horizon H, one *proves*, using the situation calculus axiomatization of the background domain described in Section 4.1, the formula

$$\exists(pol, val, prob) BestDo(\delta; Nil, S_0, H, pol, val, prob).$$

Any binding for *pol*, *val* and *prob* obtained by a constructive proof of this sentence determines the result of the program computation.

4.4 Implementing a DTGolog Interpreter

Just as an interpreter for Golog is almost trivial to implement in Prolog, when given its situation calculus specification, so also is an interpreter for DTGolog. One simply translates each of the above rules into an almost identical Prolog clause. For example, here is the implementation for rules 3 and 6:

```
% First action is deterministic.
bestDo(A : E,S,H,Pol,V,Prob) :-
  agentAction(A), deterministic(A),
  (not poss(A,S), Pol=stop, Prob is 0, reward(V,S);
  poss(A,S), bestDo(E,do(A,S),H-1,RestPol,Vfuture,Prob),
    reward(R,S), V is R + Vfuture, Pol = (A : RestPol)).

% Nondeterministic choice between E1 and E2
bestDo((E1 # E2) : E,S,Pol,V,P,k) :-
  bestDo(E1 : E,S,Pol1,V1,P1,k),
  bestDo(E2 : E,S,Pol2,V2,P2,k),
  ( lesseq(V1,P1,V2,P2), Pol=Pol2, P=P2, V=V2;
    greater(V1,P1,V2,P2), Pol=Pol1, P=P1, V=V1).
```

The entire DTGolog interpreter is in this style, and is extremely compact and transparent.

5 Robot Programming

A key advantage of DTGolog as a framework for robot programming and planning is its ability to allow behavior to be specified at any convenient point along the programming/planning spectrum. By allowing the specification of stochastic domain models in a declarative language, DTGolog not only allows the programmer to specify programs naturally (using robot actions as the base level primitives), but also permits the programmer to leave gaps in the program that will be filled in optimally by the robot itself. This functionality can greatly facilitate the development of complex robotic software. Planning ability allows for the scheduling of complex behaviors that are difficult to preprogram. It also obviates the need to reprogram a robot to adapt its behavior to reflect environmental changes or changes in objective functions. Programming, in contrast, is crucial in alleviating the computational burden of uninformed planning.

To illustrate these points, we have developed a mobile delivery robot, tasked to carry mail and coffee in our office building. The physical robot is an RWI B21 robot, equipped with a laser range finder. The robot navigates using BeeSoft [5, 19], a software package that includes methods for map acquisition, localization, collision avoidance, and on-line path planning. Figure 1d shows a map, along with a delivery path (from the main office to a recipient's office).

Initially, the robot moves to the main office, where someone loads mail on the robot, as shown in Figure 1a. DTGolog then chooses a recipient by utility optimization. Figure 1b shows the robot traveling autonomously through a hallway. If the person is in his office, he acknowledges the receipt of

---
[6] How one defines this predicate depends on how one interprets the advice embodied in a program. In our implementation, we use a mild lexicographic preference where $(p_1, v_1) < (p_2, v_2)$ whenever $p_1 = 0$ and $p_2 > 0$ (so an agent cannot choose an execution that guarantees failure). If both p_1 and p_2 are zero, or both are greater than zero, than the v-terms are used for comparison. It is important to note that certain multiattribute preferences could violate the dynamic programming principle, in which case our search procedure would have to be revised (as would any form of dynamic programming). This is not the case with our lexicographic preference.

   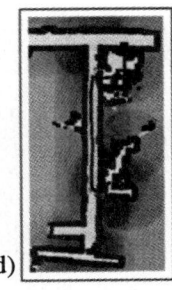

Figure 1: Mail delivery: (a) A person loads mail and coffee onto the robot. (b) DTGolog sends the robot to an office. (c) The recipient accepts the mail and coffee, acknowledging the successful delivery by pressing a button. (d) The map learned by the robot, along with the robot's path (from the main office to recipient).

the items by pressing a button on the robot as shown in Figure 1c; otherwise, after waiting for a certain period of time, the robot marks the delivery attempt as unsuccessful and continues with the next delivery. The task of DTGolog, thus, is to schedule the individual deliveries in the face of stochastic action effects arising from the fact that people may or may not be in their office at the time of delivery. It must also contend with different priorities for different people and balance these against the domain uncertainty.

The underlying MDP for this relatively simple domain grows rapidly as the number of people requiring deliveries increases. The state space is characterized by fluents such as $hasMail(person, s)$, $mailPresent(person, n, s)$, $robotLoc(loc, s)$, and so on. In a domain with P people, L locations, and N as the maximum number of pieces of mail (and *ignoring* the temporal aspect of the problem), our MDP has a state space of size $2^N \cdot (6N+6)^P \cdot L^3$ when formulated in the most appropriate way. Even restricting the MDP to one piece (or bundle) of mail per person, the state space complexity, $24^P \cdot L^3$, grows exponentially in P. Actions include picking up mail, moving from location to location, giving mail and so on. Uncertainty is associated with the *endGo* action as described above, as well as with the outcome of giving mail (see below).

The robot's objective function is given by a reward function that associates an independent, additive reward with each person's successful delivery. Each person has a different deadline, and the reward decreases linearly with time until the deadline (when it becomes zero). The relative priority associated with different recipients is given by this function; e.g., we might use $reward(Ray, t, s) = 30 - t/10$, where the initial reward (30) and rate of decrease (1/10) indicates relative priority. Given a situation term corresponding to any branch of the tree, it is straightforward to maximize value with respect to choice of temporal arguments assigned to actions in the sequence. We do not delve into details here.

Our robot is provided with the following simple DTGolog program:
while $(\exists p. \neg attempted(p) \land \exists n\, mailPresent(p,n))$
  $\pi(p,\, people,$
   $(\neg attempted(p) \land \exists n\, mailPresent(p,n))?\,;\, deliverTo(p)\,)$
endWhile

Intuitively, this program chooses people from the finite range people for mail delivery and delivers mail in the order that maximizes expected utility (coffee delivery can be incorporated readily). deliverTo is itself a complex procedure involving picking up items for a person, moving to the person's office, giving the items, and returning to the mailroom. But this sequence is a very obvious one to handcode in our domain, whereas the optimal ordering of delivery is not (and can change, as we'll see). We have included a guard condition $\neg attempted(p) \land \exists n\, mailPresent(p,n)$ in the program to prevent the robot from repeatedly trying to deliver mail to a person who is out of her office. This program constrains the robot to just one attempted mail delivery per person, and is a nice example of how the programmer can easily impose domain specific restrictions on the policies returned by a DTGolog program.

Several things emerged from the development of this code. First, the same program determines different policies—and very different qualitative behavior—when the model is changed or the reward function is changed. As a simple example, when the probability that Ray (high priority) is in his office is 0.8, his delivery is scheduled before Craig's (low priority); but when that probability is lowered to 0.6, Craig's delivery is scheduled beforehand. Such changes in the domain would require a change in the control program if not for the planning ability provided by DTGolog. The computational requirements of this decision making capability are much less than those should we allow completely arbitrary policies to be searched in the decision tree.

Full MDP planning can be implemented within DTGolog by running it with the program that allows *any* (feasible) action to be chosen at *any* time. This causes a full decision tree to be constructed. Given the domain complexity, this unconstrained search tree could only be completely evaluated for problems with a maximum horizon of seven (in about 1 minute)—this depth is barely enough to complete the construction of a policy to serve one person. With the program above, the interpreter finds optimal completions for a 3-person domain in about 1 second (producing a policy with success probability 0.94), a 4-person domain in about 9 seconds (success probability 0.93) and a 5-person domain in about 6 minutes (success probability 0.88). This latter corresponds to a horizon of about 30; clearly the decision tree search would be infeasible without the program constraints (with size well over 10^{30}). We note that the MDP formulation of this problem, with 5 people and 7 locations, would require more than 2.7 billion states. So dynamic programming could not be used to solve this MDP without program constraints (or exploiting some other form of structure).

We note that our example programs restrict the policy that the robot can implement, leaving only one choice (the choice of person to whom to deliver mail) available to the robot, with the rest of the robot's behavior fixed by the program. While these programs are quite natural, structuring a program this way may preclude optimal behavior. For instance, by restricting the robot to serving one person at a time, the simultaneous delivery of mail to two people in nearby offices won't be considered. In circumstances where interleaving is impossible (e.g., the robot can carry only one item at a time), this program admits optimal behavior—it describes *how* to deliver an item, leaving the robot to decide only on the order of deliveries. But even in settings where simultaneous or interleaved deliveries are feasible, the "nonoverlapping" program may have sufficiently high utility that restricting the robot's choices is acceptable (since it allows the MDP to be solved much more quickly).

These experiments illustrate the benefits of integrating programming and planning for mobile robot programming. We conjecture that the advantage of our framework becomes even more evident as we scale up to more complex tasks. For example, consider a robot that serves dozens of people, while making decisions as to when to recharge its batteries. Mail and coffee requests might arrive sporadically at random points in time, not just once a day (as is the case for our current implementation). Even with today's best planners, the complexity of such tasks is well beyond what can be tackled in reasonable time. DTGolog is powerful enough to accommodate such scenarios. If supplied with programs of the type described above, we expect DTGolog to make the (remaining) planning problem tractable—with minimal effort on the programmer's side.

6 Concluding Remarks

We have provided a general first-order language for specifying MDPs and imposing constraints on the space of allowable policies by writing a program. In this way we have provided a natural framework for combining decision-theoretic planning and agent programming with an intuitive semantics. We have found this framework to be very flexible as a robot programming tool, integrating programming and planning seamlessly and permitting the developer to choose the point on this spectrum best-suited to the task at hand. While Golog has proven to be an ideal vehicle for this combination, our ideas transcend the specific choice of language.

A number of interesting directions remain to be explored. The decision-tree algorithm used by the DTGolog interpreter is clearly subject to computational limitations.[7] However, the basic intuitions and foundations of DTGolog are not wedded to this particular computational model. We are currently integrating integrating efficient algorithms and other techniques for solving MDPs into this framework (dynamic programming, abstraction, sampling, etc.). We emphasize that

---

[7] Note, however, that program constraints often make otherwise intractable MDPs reasonably easy to solve using search methods.

even with these methods, the ability to naturally constrain the search for good policies with explicit programs is crucial. Other avenues include: incorporating realistic models of partial observability (a key to ensuring wider applicability of the model); extending the expressive power of the language to include other extensions already defined for the classical Golog model (e.g., concurrency); incorporating declaratively-specified heuristic and search control information; monitoring of on-line execution of DTGolog programs [17]; and automatically generating sense conditions for stochastic actions.

References

[1] F. Bacchus, J. Halpern, and H. Levesque. Reasoning about noisy sensors in the situation calculus. *IJCAI-95*, pp.1933–1940, Montreal, 1995.

[2] F. Bacchus and F. Kabanza. Using temporal logic to control search in a forward chaining planner. In M. Ghallab, A. Milani, eds., *New Directions in Planning*, pp.141–153, 1996. IOS Press.

[3] A. Barto, S. Bradtke, and S. Singh. Learning to act using real-time dynamic programming. *Art. Intel.*, 72:81–138, 1995.

[4] C. Boutilier, T. Dean, and S. Hanks. Decision theoretic planning: Structural assumptions and computational leverage. *J. Art. Intel. Res.*, 11:1–94, 1999.

[5] W. Burgard, A. Cremers, D. Fox, D. Hähnel, G. Lakemeyer, D. Schulz, W. Steiner, and S. Thrun. Experiences with an interactive museum tour-guide robot. *Art. Intel.*, 114, 1999.

[6] R. Dearden and C. Boutilier. Abstraction and approximate decision theoretic planning. *Art. Intel.*, 89:219–283, 1997.

[7] H. Geffner and B. Bonet. High-level planning and control with incomplete information using POMDPs. *AAAI Fall Symp. on Cognitive Robotics*, Orlando, 1998.

[8] M. Kearns, Y. Mansour, and A. Ng. A sparse sampling algorithm for near-optimal planning in large Markov decision processes. *IJCAI-99*, Stockholm, 1999.

[9] S. Koenig and R. Simmons. Real-time search in nondeterministic domains. *IJCAI-95*, pp.1660–1667, Montreal, 1995.

[10] H. Levesque, R. Reiter, Y. Lespérance, F. Lin, and R. Scherl. GOLOG: a logic programming language for dynamic domains. *J. Logic Prog.*, 31(1-3):59–83, 1997.

[11] R. Parr and S. Russell. Reinforcement learning with hierarchies of machines. *NIPS-10*, pp.1043–1049. MIT Press. 1998.

[12] D. Poole. The independent choice logic for modelling multiple agents under uncertainty. *Art. Intel.*, 94:7–56, 1997.

[13] M. Puterman. *Markov Decision Processes: Discrete Stochastic Dynamic Programming*. Wiley, New York, 1994.

[14] R. Reiter. Natural actions, concurrency and continuous time in the situation calculus. *KR'96*, pp.2–13, Cambridge, 1996.

[15] R. Reiter. Sequential, temporal GOLOG. *KR'98*, pp.547–556, Trento, 1998.

[16] R. Reiter. The frame problem in the situation calculus: A simple solution (sometimes) and a completeness result for goal regression. In V. Lifschitz, ed, *Artificial Intelligence and Mathematical Theory of Computation (Papers in Honor of John McCarthy)*, pp.359–380. Academic Press, 1991.

[17] M. Soutchanski. Execution monitoring of high–level temporal programs. *IJCAI-99 Workshop on Robot Action Planning*, Stockholm, 1999.

[18] R. Sutton. TD models: Modeling the world at a mixture of time scales. *ICML-95*, pp.531–539, Lake Tahoe, 1995.

[19] S. Thrun, M. Bennewitz, W. Burgard, A. Cremers, F. Dellaert, D. Fox, D. Hähnel, C. Rosenberg, N. Roy, J. Schulte, and D. Schulz. MINERVA: A second generation mobile tour-guide robot. *ICRA-99*, 1999.

Making Rational Decisions using Adaptive Utility Elicitation

Urszula Chajewska
Computer Science Department
Stanford University
Stanford, CA 94305-9010
urszula@cs.stanford.edu

Daphne Koller
Computer Science Department
Stanford University
Stanford, CA 94305-9010
koller@cs.stanford.edu

Ronald Parr
Computer Science Department
Stanford University
Stanford, CA 94305-9010
parr@cs.stanford.edu

Abstract

Rational decision making requires full knowledge of the utility function of the person affected by the decisions. However, in many cases, the task of acquiring such knowledge is not feasible due to the size of the outcome space and the complexity of the utility elicitation process. Given that the amount of utility information we can acquire is limited, we need to make decisions with partial utility information and should carefully select which utility elicitation questions we ask. In this paper, we propose a new approach for this problem that utilizes a prior probability distribution over the person's utility function, perhaps learned from a population of similar people. The relevance of a utility elicitation question for the current decision problem can then be measured using its value of information. We propose an algorithm that interleaves the analysis of the decision problem and utility elicitation to allow these two tasks to inform each other. At every step, it asks the utility elicitation question giving us the highest value of information and computes the best strategy based on the information acquired so far, stopping when the expected utility loss resulting from our recommendation falls below a pre-specified threshold. We show how the various steps of this algorithm can be implemented efficiently.

Introduction

Rational decision making requires full knowledge of the utility function of the person affected by the decisions. According to traditional decision-theoretic principles, we should choose the sequence of decisions, or the *strategy*, which maximizes the expected utility (von Neumann & Morgenstern 1947). In order to compute the expected utility of a strategy, we need to know both the probabilities of all possible events in the decision problem and the utilities of all world states, or *outcomes*. The task of acquiring the probabilistic information is well understood. We know how to elicit such knowledge from experts or learn it from data.

Eliciting utility information is inherently harder. First, every person we advise may have a different utility function. Therefore, we need to elicit utility information not once, but many times, once for each user. Second, the task of utility elicitation is cognitively difficult and error prone. There are many elicitation techniques and the fact that they produce very different results when applied to the same person is well documented (Fromberg & Kane 1989). People find it hard to answer utility elicitation questions; they need to be trained beforehand and a significant percentage of them still give inconsistent answers. Finally, for many interesting, real-life decision problems, the outcome space is very large. There is a limit to the number of questions we can ask a person before fatigue will start playing a role. A decision tool requiring an interview several hours long is not likely to be widely used.

In order to apply decision-theoretic tools to such situations, we have to address two new issues. First, we need to find a way to make optimal or nearly-optimal decisions based on incomplete utility information. Second, in order to use the time and attention that our users are willing to give us well, we should also carefully choose the questions we ask to elicit utilities. In this paper we argue that the decision analysis and utility elicitation should not be considered to be two separate tasks, but rather two parts of one process. Each of these parts can influence and inform the other and together they make the decision making process more accurate and more efficient.

Our approach to utility elicitation and decision making departs from traditional approaches in one very important way: we treat utility as a random variable that is drawn from a known distribution. This assumption is often quite reasonable: many medical informatics centers collect large databases of utility functions for various decision problems for the purpose of cost-benefit analyses of new treatments. We can use such databases of utility functions to estimate the distribution of utility functions in the population (Chajewska & Koller 2000) and then use this estimate as a prior when we elicit utilities from the new users we advise.

This idea is key to our approach. First, it tells us how to choose a strategy relative to a partially specified utility function: we simply act optimally relative to our uncertain information about this random variable. Second, it provides a clear metric for evaluating different possible utility elicitation questions: the extent to which a question helps reach the optimal decision is simply its *value of information* (Howard 1966). This insight provides us with the basis for our algorithm. At every step, our algorithm computes the optimal strategy based on the current information. It then asks the elicitation question with the highest value of information, and the user's answer is incorporated into the model. This

---

Copyright © 2000, American Association for Artificial Intelligence (www.aaai.org). All rights reserved.

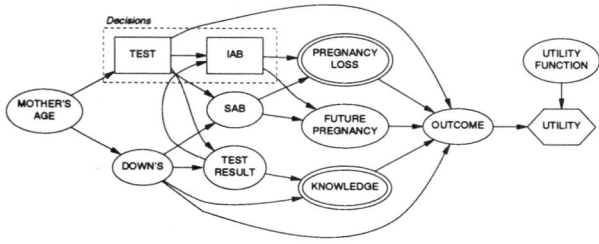

Figure 1: The decision model for prenatal diagnosis (courtesy of Joseph Norman, Stanford Medical Informatics).

process continues until the expected utility loss — the expectation, taken over the possible utility functions for the user, of the difference between the utility of using the current recommendation and the utility of using the strategy optimal for that user — falls below a pre-specified threshold. We provide a clean and efficient algorithm for implementing this scheme, despite the fact that it must deal with distributions over continuous utility variables.

Decision models

A sequential decision problem consists of several decisions, taken in sequence, typically with some information revealed between one decision and the next. Such a decision problem is often represented as an influence diagram (Howard & Matheson 1984). In our experiments, we will use a simplified version of a decision model developed at Stanford Medical Informatics for the task of prenatal testing. The influence diagram is shown in Figure 1. Prenatal testing is intended to diagnose the presence of a chromosomal abnormality such as Down's syndrome in the early weeks of pregnancy. The probability of such abnormality increases with maternal age. The two tests currently available to diagnose it, chorionic villus sampling (CVS) and amniocentesis (AMNIO), carry a significant risk of miscarriage above the baseline rate. The risk is higher for CVS, but it is more accurate and can be performed earlier in the pregnancy. In addition, both miscarriage (SAB) and elective termination of the pregnancy (IAB) may reduce the chances of future pregnancy. The influence diagram contains two decision nodes — which test to perform (CVS, AMNIO, or none), and whether to perform an elective termination. The edges going into the decision nodes represent information that is available to the decision maker before making the decision; for example, the test result (if any) is known before the decision about the elective termination.

An influence diagram can be solved by converting it into a *decision tree*, where at some nodes, the "choice" is made by nature and at others by the decision maker (Pearl 1988). We order the decisions $D_1, \ldots, D_k$, and partition the chance nodes into mutually exclusive and exhaustive sets $\mathbf{Y}_1, \ldots, \mathbf{Y}_k, \mathbf{Y}_{k+1}$, where $\mathbf{Y}_i$ are the variables that are revealed to the decision maker prior to D_i. The initial choice is made by nature about the random variables in $\mathbf{Y}_1$, with distribution $P(\mathbf{Y}_1)$. The next choice is made by the agent

about D_1; the agent can make different choices about D_1 in different nodes in the tree, thereby allowing his decision to depend on the values of $\mathbf{Y}_1$. The tree continues in this way, until at the very end, nature decides on the remaining (unobserved) variables $\mathbf{Y}_{k+1}$, and the final utility is determined accordingly. The optimal strategy in the tree can be computed by the standard *expectimax* algorithm, which traverses the tree bottom up, with the agent doing a Max operation at each decision node, and nature doing an expectation operation at each chance node. While more sophisticated algorithms for influence diagram inference exist (Jensen, Jensen, & Dittmer 1994), they are essentially equivalent in their behavior to this simple decision-tree algorithm when applied to standard influence diagrams (those in *Howard normal form*).

Utilities

We begin with a review of some basic concepts in utility theory. Our presentation is based on concepts discussed in detail in (Keeney & Raiffa 1976).

Utility representation

Let O be the set of possible outcomes in our domain, $\{o_1, \ldots, o_m\}$. A utility function maps outcomes to real numbers. The naive representation of a utility function is a vector of real numbers, ascribing a utility to each possible outcome. Many real-life domains, however, involve fairly complex outcomes. In such cases, the space of outcomes is defined as the set of possible assignments of values to a set of relevant variables. The utility is a function of all of these values. This structure is fairly typical in complex decision problems. Thus, we define each outcome as an assignment to a set of attribute variables $\mathbf{X} = \{X_1, \ldots, X_n\}$. Each variable X_i has a domain $\mathrm{Dom}(X_i)$ of two or more elements. For example, in our domain, the outcomes include 'first trimester test (CVS), normal result, birth of a healthy baby', 'second trimester test (amniocentesis), procedure-related miscarriage, inability to conceive later', and 'no test, birth of a baby with Down's syndrome'. In general, the utility can depend on five attributes: T: type of testing; D: fetus status; L: possible loss of pregnancy; K: knowledge of the fetus's status; F: future successful pregnancy. The space of possible outcomes depending on these attributes is very large: $3 \times 2 \times 3 \times 3 \times 2 = 108$. Some of these can be eliminated as impossible, extremely unlikely, or absent in medical practice, but even then more than 70 remain.

In some cases, subsets of attribute variables exhibit some sort of independence, leading to structured utility representations. In particular, we might be able to represent the utility $U(T, D, L, K, F)$ as a sum of *subutility functions*, e.g., $U(T) + U(L, F) + U(K, L, D)$. In these cases, the utility function can be specified using a smaller number of parameters (27 in this example).

Utility elicitation

The fact that the utility function can be different for every patient involved, and the large number of parameters involved in specifying it, has often led clinical practitioners to use a single "universal" utility function for all patients. This approach has led, for example, to the uniform recommendation of prenatal testing for all women above the age of 35. This type of universal recommendation is rarely suitable for all women. In particular, our analysis of the model revealed the considerable influence of the utility function (especially the patient's attitude towards the risk of having a Down's child and toward a miscarriage) on the optimal choice of actions. An alternative approach is to elicit an individual utility function from each patient.

The *standard gamble* approach to utility elicitation (von Neumann & Morgenstern 1947) estimates the strength of a person's preference for an outcome by the risks he or she is willing to take to obtain it. Consider three outcomes o_1, o_2, and o_3 and a user with the preference ordering $o_1 \succ o_2 \succ o_3$. If he or she is offered a choice between o_2 for sure and a gamble in which o_1 will be received with probability p and o_3 with probability $(1-p)$, then, according to the theory, there exists a value of p for which the user will be indifferent. The outcome o_2 can then be assigned the utility value $pU(o_1) + (1-p)U(o_3)$.

The utility elicitation process starts by defining two universal best and worst outcomes, ($o_\top$ and $o_\bot$), which are then used as *anchors*, with values 1 and 0, to determine the relative utilities of all the other outcomes in the decision problem. A typical question in a medical domain is formulated in this way: "Imagine that you have a certain health condition which limits your activities in a specific way [the detailed description follows]. Imagine that there is a new experimental drug which only needs to be taken once. If taken, it will cure the condition p percent of the time, and $1-p$ percent of the time it will cause a painless death. Would you take the pill?" The question is repeated for a sequence of values of p until the user's preference changes. Several different ways of choosing the sequence can be used, including binary search, *ping-pong* (alternating between high and low values) and, most commonly, *titration* (reducing the value of p by a small amount). Recent research established that the final values are sensitive to the sequence choice (Lenert *et al.* 1998). Obviously, the user's answers are the most reliable far from the actual indifference point and most error-prone immediately around it. The need to use a sequence of questions for every outcome greatly increases the length of an interview and thus reduces the number of outcomes we can ask our user to consider.

Uncertainty over utilities

The discussion above, as well as practical experience, shows that it is virtually impossible to elicit a person's exact utility function. In this paper, we propose to circumvent this goal entirely. Rather than aiming at a completely specified utility function for a given patient, we maintain a *probability distribution* representing our beliefs about that patient's utility function. In other words, we view the different quantities $\{U_o\}_{o \in O}$ as a set of continuous-valued random variables (in the interval $[0,1]$), with a joint probability density function (PDF) $p(\mathbf{U})$ ($\mathbf{U} = \{U_{o_1}, \ldots, U_{o_m}\}$), representing our beliefs about the patient's utilities.

This type of PDF can be represented in many ways; our approach applies to any representation that allows random samples to be generated from the PDF, thereby allowing moments of the distributions and expectations over it to be estimated numerically. However, our algorithm can be made more efficient in cases where the PDF allows some computations to be done in closed form, in particular PDFs that are jointly Gaussians or a mixture of Gaussians (cut off to fit in the $[0,1]$ hypercube). A Gaussian can represent dependencies between a person's utilities for different outcomes. A mixture of Gaussians can represent distinct clusters in the population, whose utility functions are very different; in general, any PDF can be approximated arbitrarily well with a mixture of Gaussians (Bishop 1995). Furthermore, there are efficient algorithms for estimating these PDFs from data.

In cases where the utility function can be assumed to have some structure, as described above, it is better to represent and learn the distribution over utilities via a PDF over the (much smaller set of) parameters of the subutility functions (Chajewska & Koller 2000). As the utility variables are linear in these parameters, a mixture of Gaussians over the subutility parameters induces a mixture of Gaussians over $\mathbf{U}$.

The algorithm

Our approach is based on an integrated algorithm for decision making and utility elicitation. The answers to our utility elicitation questions inform the decision making procedure, the results of which help us select the most informative next utility elicitation question to ask.

When the system encounters a new patient, the only information available about her utility function is the prior PDF $p(\mathbf{U})$. The algorithm then cycles through the following steps.

- It computes the optimal strategy π relative to the current PDF $p(\mathbf{U})$.
- If this optimal strategy meets the stopping criterion, it stops and outputs π.
- Otherwise, it selects a utility elicitation question to ask the user, and asks it.
- It conditions $p(\mathbf{U})$ on the response.

Decisions under utility uncertainty

The first question we must address is how we make optimal decisions given uncertainty over the user's utility function $\mathbf{U}$. Fortunately, the answer to this question is easy (and well-known). Consider a given strategy π and a PDF $p(\mathbf{U})$. The expected utility of π for a fixed utility function $\mathbf{u}$ is: $\mathrm{EU}_\pi(\mathbf{u}) = \sum_{o \in O} P(o \mid \pi) u_o$. The expected utility under $p(\mathbf{U})$ can easily be shown to be $\mathrm{EU}_\pi(p) = \sum_o P(o \mid \pi) \mathcal{E}_p[u_o]$. Hence, we can find the best strategy given $p(\mathbf{U})$ by running standard influence diagram inference using, as the utility value for outcome o, the mean of U_o under p.

In general, we can compute the mean of U_o under p by Monte Carlo sampling. However, under the assumption that p is a mixture of Gaussians, we can compute it much more efficiently by combining the closed form integral of $u \exp(-u^2)$ with the integral tables readily available for $\exp(-u^2)$. (We omit details.)

Utility elicitation questions

A distribution $p(\mathbf{u})$ can be updated with additional information about the user's utility function, elicited from the user. We consider questions that follow the standard gamble pattern: "Given the choice between outcome o for sure and a lottery which gives $o_\top$ with probability s and $o_\bot$ with probability $1-s$, which will you choose?" We translate the response to this question to a constraint of the form $U_o < s$ or $U_o > s$, depending on the response. We call the value of s a *split point*. Consider a cycle of this process. Initially, we have a PDF p over the user's utilities. Let μ be the mean of $\mathbf{U}$ under p, and π^* the strategy that is optimal relative to μ. Now, consider a question regarding an outcome o and a split point s. If the user responds that $U_o < s$, we condition our PDF p, resulting in a new PDF $p_{<s}$; this will give us a new mean $\mu_{<s}$, and as a result, a new optimal strategy $\pi^*_{<s}$. Similarly, if she responds that $U_o > s$, we obtain a PDF $p_{>s}$ with $\mu_{>s}$ and associated optimal strategy $\pi^*_{>s}$. As further questions are asked and more information is obtained, our probability distribution p is updated, and the choice of optimal strategy changes to better fit the user's true preferences.

Note that our questioning pattern differs from standard gamble in a significant way: we do not ask about the same outcome for different values of p, until the indifference point is reached. Rather, we choose questions so as to reduce the total number of questions we need to ask the user. A given question will often be for a different outcome than the previous one.

We discuss the process of selecting the best question below.

Stopping criterion

After a sequence of utility elicitation questions, we will have a posterior distribution $\tilde{p}(\mathbf{U})$ over the user's utility function, and an associated candidate optimal policy $\hat{\pi}$. We would like to estimate the regret associated with stopping the utility elicitation and recommending $\hat{\pi}$. Assume that the user's true utility function is $\mathbf{u}$, and that the associated optimal strategy is $\pi^*_\mathbf{u}$. Then the user's loss is the difference between her expected utility, under $\mathbf{u}$, of $\pi^*_\mathbf{u}$, and her expected utility under the recommended strategy $\hat{\pi}$. The expected loss is the expectation of the loss under $\tilde{p}(\mathbf{u})$:

$$\int [\mathrm{EU}_{\pi^*_\mathbf{u}}(\mathbf{u}) - \mathrm{EU}_{\hat{\pi}}(\mathbf{u})]\tilde{p}(\mathbf{u})d\mathbf{u}.$$

While computing this integral exactly is impractical — we would need to compute the regions in which every strategy is optimal — we can approximate it quite easily using Monte Carlo methods. We simply sample utility functions $\mathbf{u}$ from $\tilde{p}$, use the influence diagram to compute the optimal strategy $\pi^*_\mathbf{u}$, and compute the loss for $\mathbf{u}$.

We can bound the number of samples needed using the upper bound on the worst case loss x, the desired threshold for expected utility loss ϵ and the confidence parameter δ by using Chebyshev's inequality: $N > \frac{x^2}{2\epsilon^2\delta}$.

Choosing the next question

One of the important advantages of explicitly modeling our uncertainty over the user's utility is that we obtain a simple metric for evaluating possible questions — the *value of information* measures the expected improvement in our decision quality derived from the answer to a question "is $U_o > s$?" We define the *posterior expected utility* after asking this question as:

$$\mathrm{PEU}(o,s) = \mathrm{EU}_{\pi^*_{<s}}(\mu_{<s})P(U_o<s) + \mathrm{EU}_{\pi^*_{>s}}(\mu_{>s})P(U_o>s)$$

This is an average of the expected utilities arising from the two possible answers to the question, weighted by how likely these two answers are. The value of information is this expression minus the current expected utility. Our goal is to find the outcome U_o, and the splitting point s for that outcome, that achieves the highest value of information. We note that this metric only evaluates the *myopic* value of information for the question. The full value of information, which takes into consideration all possible future combinations of questions and answers, is, as usual, intractable.

We will start our analysis for the case in which the utilities of different outcomes are probabilistically independent, i.e., the different variables U_o are marginally independent in p. We then relax this assumption in a later section.

Discretizing the problem

The first problem we encounter is that the utility variables range over a continuous space, so that there are infinitely many potential split points for each outcome. Fortunately, it turns out that we can restrict attention only to a finite number of them.

Let π be some strategy, and consider $\mathrm{EU}_\pi(\mathbf{U})$ as a function of a single utility variable $U_{o'}$:

$$\begin{aligned}
\mathrm{EU}_\pi(u_{o'}) &= p(u_{o'})u_{o'} + \sum_{o \neq o'} \int P(o|\pi)p(u_o|u_{o'})u_o du_o \quad (1)\\
&= p(u_{o'})u_{o'} + \sum_{o \neq o'} \int P(o|\pi)p(u_o)u_o du_o \\
&= p(u_{o'})u_{o'} + \sum_{o \neq o'} P(o|\pi)\mathcal{E}_p[U_o],
\end{aligned}$$

where the second equality is due to our independence assumption about utility variables.

Hence, the expected utility of a given strategy π is a linear function of U_o. The value for the optimal strategy for this problem is, for each value of U_o, the maximum over all strategies π. Thus, it is a piecewise-linear, convex function of U_o. We say that a strategy is *viable for o* if it is optimal for some value of U_o. We say that a particular value s is an *intersection point* if there are two viable strategies π_1 and π_2 that achieve the same expected utility at s, i.e., $\mathrm{EU}_{\pi_1}(s) = \mathrm{EU}_{\pi_2}(s)$.

Proposition 1: *The split point with the highest value of information will occur at one of the intersection points.*

Proof: Consider a potential split point s, and let π^*_L be the optimal strategy for the distribution $p_{<s}$ and π^*_R be the optimal strategy for the distribution $p_{>s}$. Let s^* be the strategy intersection point where $\mathrm{EU}(\pi^*_L) = \mathrm{EU}(\pi^*_R)$. Let's further assume, without loss of generality, that $s^* < s$. We want to show that $\text{PEU}(o, s) \leq \text{PEU}(o, s^*)$. It is easy to verify, for any $a < b < c$ and any strategy π, that

$$\text{EU}_\pi(\mu_{[a,c]})P([a,c])$$
$$= \text{EU}_\pi(\mu_{[a,b]})P([a,b]) + \text{EU}_\pi(\mu_{[b,c]})P([b,c])$$

We have that

$$\text{EU}_{\pi_L^*}(\mu_{<s})P(U_o < s) + \text{EU}_{\pi_R^*}(\mu_{>s})P(U_o > s)$$
$$= \text{EU}_{\pi_L^*}(\mu_{<s^*})P(U_o < s^*)$$
$$\quad + \text{EU}_{\pi_L^*}(\mu_{[s^*,s]})P(U_o \in [s^*, s])$$
$$\quad + \text{EU}_{\pi_R^*}(\mu_{>s})P(U_o > s)$$
$$\leq \text{EU}_{\pi_L^*}(\mu_{<s^*})P(U_o < s^*)$$
$$\quad + \text{EU}_{\pi_R^*}(\mu_{[s^*,s]})P(U_o \in [s^*, s])$$
$$\quad + \text{EU}_{\pi_R^*}(\mu_{>s})P(U_o > s)$$
$$= \text{EU}_{\pi_L^*}(\mu_{<s^*})P(U_o < s^*)$$
$$\quad + \text{EU}_{\pi_R^*}(\mu_{>s^*})P(U_o > s^*)$$

where the inequality is due to the fact that π_R^* dominates π_L^* for every $u_o > s^*$, and therefore also for $\mu_{[s^*,s]}$. Now, consider the two strategies $\pi_{<s^*}^*$ and $\pi_{>s^*}^*$ that are optimal for the distributions $p_{<s^*}$ and $p_{>s^*}$ respectively. These are not necessarily π_L^* and π_R^*, because the mean of $p_{<s^*}$, say, might not fall in the part of the region where π_L^* is optimal. However, it is easy to show that $\pi_{<s^*}^*$ and $\pi_{>s^*}^*$ can only improve the posterior expected utility. The result follows. ∎

We only need to consider those strategy intersection points where the viable strategies $\pi_{<s^*}^*$ and $\pi_{>s^*}^*$ intersect at s^*; otherwise, as the proof shows, the strategy intersection point of these two strategies would have higher value of information. How many points like this are there? Suppose we have N optimal strategies. Let's imagine moving the potential split point s from left to right over the range of U_o. We can mark an interval boundary whenever the optimal strategy for the area to the left or the optimal strategy for the area to the right of our split point changes. Note that once a strategy on the left side changes, it cannot change back: the mean $\mu_{<s}$ of U_o increases monotonically as we widen the region on the left, and the expected utility for any strategy is a linear function of this mean. Hence, the linear functions for any pair of strategies can cross at most once. Similarly, once a strategy on the right side changes, it cannot change back. As each strategy is optimal on each side at most once, we have at most $2N$ intervals, and at most $2N - 1$ candidate split points. Each of these is only feasible, of course, if it is also a strategy intersection point of the two corresponding strategies. Thus, we need to consider only $2N - 1$ split points, rather than N^2. We can execute this process efficiently using a simple binary search procedure, which utilizes the fact that we can find intersection points analytically. We omit details for lack of space.

The number of optimal strategies

The result above suggests that the number of VOI computations required is linear in the number of viable strategies. At first glance, this result might not be very reassuring. After all, there is an enormous number of strategies: exponential in the size of the decision tree. Any computation which requires us to consider all of them is much too expensive in all but the most trivial of decision problems. Fortunately, the number of *viable* strategies is exponentially smaller than the total number of strategies. Indeed, we show that it is linear in the size of the decision tree corresponding to our influence diagram. Given that we need to traverse the decision tree every time we use the decision model for finding an optimal strategy, this cost is very reasonable.

Proposition 2: *The number of strategies that are viable for o is at most the number of nodes in the decision tree corresponding to the influence diagram.*

Proof: We prove this result by induction on the depth of the tree. For the base case, a tree of depth 0 consists of a single leaf, where we have only a single strategy. In this case, the number of nodes is 1, and the number of viable strategies is also 1. For the inductive case, consider a tree of depth $d + 1$. Let k be the number of children of the root, and let ℓ_i be the number of nodes in the subtree corresponding to the ith child. By the inductive hypothesis, the number of viable strategies for the ith child is at most ℓ_i. There are now two cases. Either the root is a max node or an expectation node. In the first case, the expected utility function $\text{EU}(U_o)$ is the maximum of the functions of the children. In the second case, it is a weighted average of the functions of the children, where the weights are the probabilities annotating the edges going out of the root. In both cases, it is easy to verify that the function at the root is a piece-wise linear function, with a number of segments which is at most the total number of segments in the combined functions. (Intuitively, the reason is that the combined function can change from one linear function to another only at a point where one of the constituent functions changes from one linear function to another.) ∎

Correlated outcomes

Until now in this section, we have assumed that the different utility variables U_o are independent in $p(\mathbf{U})$. Unfortunately, this assumption is too strong in many cases. Indeed, it is quite likely that a woman's utility for one outcome involving a Down's baby will be correlated with her utility for another outcome involving the same event. In this section, we consider the more general case of an arbitrary distribution p.

We begin by assuming that our prior $p(\mathbf{U})$ is a multivariate Gaussian with an arbitrary covariance matrix, constrained to lie within the $[0, 1]$ hypercube. Clearly, our utility function distribution cannot be truly Gaussian since utility functions are constrained to lie within the normalized range. Nevertheless, a Gaussian can be a reasonable approximation since the probability mass that lies outside of the normalized utility range will generally be negligibly small.

We use a convenient property of multivariate Gaussians to apply the algorithm of the previous section with almost no modifications: Given any variable $U_{o'}$, the conditional means of the remaining variables are linear functions of $U_{o'}$. In other words, in Eq. (1), although we no longer have that

$p(u_o \mid u_{o'}) = p(u_o)$, we do have that $\int p(u_o \mid u_{o'}) u_o du_o = g(u_{o'})$ for some linear function g. Thus, when we are enumerating the viable strategies for outcome o', as described in the section "Choosing the next question", we replace the means of the other U_o variables with their (linear) conditional means. The resulting function $\mathrm{EU}_\pi(U_{o'})$ is still a linear function of $U_{o'}$, so that the rest of the analysis remains unchanged.

Unfortunately, this analysis is insufficient for our purposes. Most obviously, it does not apply to the case of a mixture of Gaussians, where the mean of one variable is no longer a linear function of the other. There is a more subtle problem, however: even if our prior distribution is a multivariate Gaussian, once we condition our distribution on some information $U_{o''} > s$, the resulting posterior is no longer a multivariate Gaussian, but rather a "strip" of one. It can be verified that the conditional mean for this distribution is not a linear function.

We address both these difficulties using a simple approximation. Let p be our current distribution, conditioned on all of the relevant information. Rather than computing value of information relative to p, we approximate p using a distribution $\hat{p}$ which is a multivariate Gaussian. We note that our stopping criterion is always computed relative to the correct conditional distribution p.

In the case where p is a multivariate Gaussian, we can use a simple trick to maintain our distribution $\hat{p}$ as additional information is obtained. The key idea is that any multivariate Gaussian $p(X_1, X_2, \ldots, X_n)$ can be decomposed as a univariate Gaussian over X_1 and a *linear Gaussian (LG)* $p(X_2, \ldots, X_n \mid X_1)$ which defines a multivariate Gaussian over $X_2, \ldots, X_n$ with mean $\mu(x_1)$ which is a vector linear function of x_1 and a fixed covariance matrix (Shachter & Kenley 1989). If we condition X_1 on some evidence, and approximate the result on a Gaussian, the parameterization of the LG $p(X_2, \ldots, X_n \mid X_1)$ does not change. Hence, the best approximation to the joint PDF as a multivariate Gaussian, given evidence on X_1, can be found by finding the best approximation to $p(X_1)$ as a univariate Gaussian and leaving the LG unchanged. We can then regenerate a new approximate multivariate Gaussian $\hat{p}'$ by multiplying $p(X_1)$ and the LG. In this case, the variable $U_{o'}$ on which we have evidence plays the role of X_1.

We can extend this approach to the case of a mixture of Gaussians. We use the same idea of approximating the distribution as a multivariate Gaussian, and then using our algorithm above for finding the optimal split point relative to the approximation. We then use the information about the X_1 (the utility $U_{o'}$) to define a posterior distribution. The only difference is that, in this case, we must also use our information about X_1 to update the mixture weights. This can be done using a standard application of Bayes rule.

Experimental results

Our database consisted of 51 utility functions elicited from pregnant women considering prenatal diagnosis, collected for an earlier study (Kuppermann *et al.* 1997). We used five-fold cross-validation for experiments, estimating the distribution using four sets and testing on the fifth. We ran these tests separately for every possible value of mother's age. Due to the small size of the database, we assumed that the utility function does not change with age and used all functions in the database to run tests for all ages.

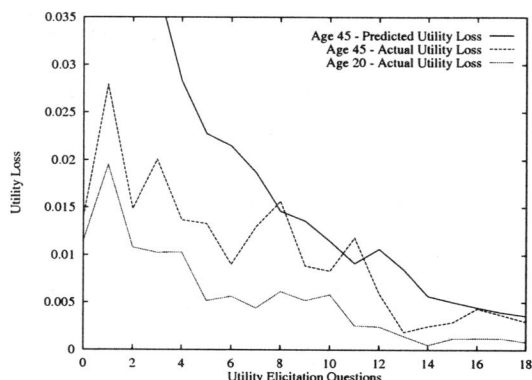

Figure 2: Expected and actual utility loss as a function of the number of qustions asked.

We present the results for an uncorrelated Gaussian; our current database is too small to allow reliable learning of more complex densities. Figure 2 shows the evolution of predicted and actual utility loss as more questions are asked. We see that the predicted utility loss starts out quite large, as the distribution is very broad. It gradually converges to the correct utility loss, and both gradually converge to zero. The predicted utility loss is usually an overestimate to the actual utility loss, implying that our algorithm is "safe" in not stopping prematurely. The overall results are summarized below; the ranges indicate behavior for different ages:

Number of questions asked				
	avg	best	worst	std. dev.
$\epsilon = 0.05$	2.3–3.9	2	16	13–14.7
$\epsilon = 0.02$	5.9–9.0	3	16	12.1–30

Utility loss after last question				
	avg	best	worst	std. dev.
$\epsilon = 0.05$	.01–.04	0	0.28	0.24–0.3
$\epsilon = 0.02$	.001–.015	0	0.087	0.05–0.14

Distance from indifference point			
Q1	Q2	Q3	avg (20 questions)
0.41	0.21	0.13	0.21

As we can see, the number of questions asked is surprisingly small given the fact that we have 108 outcomes in the model. It increases slightly as we lower the threshold, but stays well within the bounds of what is possible in clinical practice. By comparison, the approach of (Chajewska *et al.* 1998) achieves an average of 7.55 questions for the same domain and an average utility loss of 0.035; with a much smaller number of questions, we achieve a utility loss which is comparable for $\epsilon = 0.05$ and substantially lower for $\epsilon = 0.02$. Furthermore, their approach provides no guarantees about the utility loss of the final recommendation. Finally, note that the split points our algorithm chooses are usually quite far from the indifference point, making the questions cognitively easy.

Related work

With recent advances in the power and scope of decision-theoretic systems, utility elicitation has become a lively and expanding area of research. A few projects are particularly relevant to this work. Jameson, et al. (1995) and Linden, et al. (1997) investigated the problem of eliciting partial utility models and reasoning with such models in case of certainty for domains such as shopping and making airline reservations on the Web. Poh and Horvitz (1993) discussed the value of the refinement of utility information. Finally, Jimison et al. (1992) suggested explicitly representing uncertainty about key utility parameters in the context of explaining medical decision models to the users.

Conclusion and extensions

We have presented a new approach for making decisions based on limited utility information, and for targeting our utility elicitation process so as to lead to a good decision using a small number of questions. Our approach is based on maintaining a probability distribution over possible utility values of the user, and using value of information for deciding which utility elicitation question will best help us in making rational decisions. We have presented algorithms for doing these computations efficiently.

We have presented results that suggest that our approach can make utility elicitation substantially easier for users of the decision model. Our results suggest that, in most cases, our chosen split point will not be in the immediate vicinity of the user's indifference point, thus making the task much easier cognitively. Furthermore, we have seen that our method substantially reduces the overall number of questions we have to ask before a good decision can be made; often, the number is as small as 2–3, with a very small utility loss. Indeed, one might expect that the overall decision quality will be better, because our method allows us to avoid errors resulting from the fatigue caused by the utility elicitation process.

There are many ways in which our work can be extended. For example, some questions are cognitively more difficult than others: questions near the indifference point are hard, a second consecutive question about the same outcome is cheaper than a question about an outcome discussed a few questions back, etc. It is easy to incorporate the cognitive cost of questions into the value of information computation.

A more general research direction is to exploit other aspects of our approach to representing uncertainty over utility functions. One possible application is to represent the dependence of this distribution on environmental variables. For example, it has been noted by the practitioners in the field that a woman who personally knows a Down's syndrome child is more likely to rate an outcome involving such a child as less desirable. A less obvious and more philosophically controversial application is to represent the probability that a user's preferences will change over time. We believe that the tools provided by probabilistic models — value of information, statistical learning, and more — will turn out to be extremely useful in this new type of modeling.

Acknowledgments We would like to thank Miriam Kuppermann for allowing us to use her data and Joseph Norman his model for the prenatal diagnosis domain. We are also grateful to Uri Lerner for his help in building the inference code for Gaussians and to Brian Milch for his influence diagram code. This research was supported by ARO under the MURI program "Integrated Approach to Intelligent Systems", grant number DAAH04-96-1-0341, by ONR contract N66001-97-C-8554 under DARPA's HPKB program, and through the generosity of the Powell Foundation and the Sloan Foundation.

References

Bishop, C. M. 1995. *Neural Networks for Pattern Recognition*. New York, NY: Oxford University Press.

Chajewska, U., and Koller, D. 2000. Utilities as random variables: Density estimation and structure discovery. In *Proc. UAI–00*. To appear.

Chajewska, U., Getoor, L., Norman, J., and Shahar, Y. 1998. Utility elicitation as a classification problem. In *Proc. UAI–98*, 79–88.

Fromberg, D. G., and Kane, R. L. 1989. Methodology for measuring health-state preferences—II: Scaling methods. *Journal of Clinical Epidemiology* 42(5):459–471.

Howard, R. A., and Matheson, J. E. 1984. Influence diagrams. In *The Principles and Applications of Decision Analysis*. Strategic Decisions Group.

Howard, R. A. 1966. Information value theory. *IEEE Transactions on Systems Science and Cybernetics* SSC-2:22–26.

Jameson, A., Schäfer, R., Simons, J., and Weis, T. 1995. Adaptive provision of evaluation-oriented information: Tasks and techniques. In *Proc. IJCAI–95*, 1886–1893.

Jensen, F., Jensen, F. V., and Dittmer, S. L. 1994. From influence diagrams to junction trees. In *Proc. UAI–94*.

Jimison, H. B., Fagan, L. M., Shachter, R. D., and Shortliffe, E. H. 1992. Patient-specific explanation in models of chronic disease. *AI in Medicine* 4:191–205.

Keeney, R. L., and Raiffa, H. 1976. *Decisions with Multiple Objectives: Preferences and Value Tradeoffs*. John Wiley & Sons, Inc.

Kuppermann, M., Shiboski, S., Feeny, D., Elkin, E. P., and Washington, A. E. 1997. Can preference scores for discrete states be used to derive preference scores for an entire path of events? *Medical Decision Making* 17(1):42–55.

Lenert, L. A., Cher, D. J., Goldstein, M. K., Bergen, M. R., and Garber, A. 1998. The effect of search procedures on utility elicitations. *Medical Decision Making* 18(1):76–83.

Linden, G., Hanks, S., and Lesh, N. 1997. Interactive assessment of user preference models: The automated travel assistant. In *Proc. User Modeling '97*.

Pearl, J. 1988. *Probabilistic Reasoning in Intelligent Systems*. San Francisco, CA: Morgan Kaufmann.

Poh, K. L., and Horvitz, E. 1993. Reasoning about the value of decision-model refinement: methods and application. In *Proc. UAI–93*, 174–182.

Shachter, R., and Kenley, C. 1989. Gaussian influence diagrams. *Management Science* 35:527–550.

von Neumann, J., and Morgenstern, O. 1947. *Theory of Games and Economic Behavior*. Princeton, N.J.: Princeton University Press, 2nd edition.

Back to the Future for Consistency-based Trajectory Tracking

James Kurien
NASA Ames Research Center
MS 269-3, Moffett Field, CA 94035
jkurien@arc.nasa.gov

P. Pandurang Nayak
PurpleYogi.com and RIACS,
201 Ravendale Drive, Mountain View, CA 94043.
nayak@purpleyogi.com

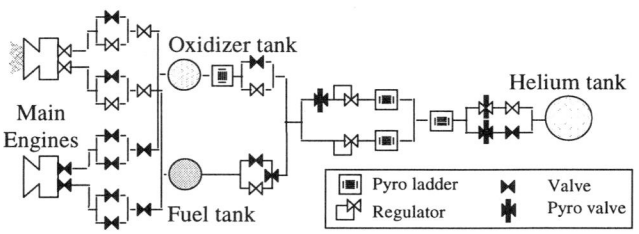

Figure 1: Propulsion system schematic.

Abstract

Given a model of a physical process and a sequence of commands and observations received over time, the task of an autonomous controller is to determine the likely states of the process and the actions required to move the process to a desired configuration. We introduce a representation and algorithms for incrementally generating approximate belief states for a restricted but relevant class of partially observable Markov decision processes with very large state spaces. The algorithm incrementally generates, rather than revises, an approximate belief state at any point by abstracting and summarizing segments of the likely trajectories of the process. This enables applications to efficiently maintain a partial belief state when it remains consistent with observations and revisit past assumptions about the process's evolution when the belief state is ruled out. The system presented has been implemented and results on examples from the domain of spacecraft control are presented.

Introduction

Given a model of a physical system and a sequence of commands and observations received over time, the task of an autonomous controller is to determine the likely states of the system and the actions required to move the system to a desired configuration. Focusing on the state identification question, a *belief state* is a probability distribution over the possible states of a system. If the system has the Markov property, then the influence of a new command and observation upon the belief state can be integrated via Bayes' rule. The updated belief state is a sufficient statistic, capturing within a single distribution all knowledge about the current state of the system contained within a history of commands and observations. The controller then makes use of the updated belief state in selecting an action.

Example 1 Consider the spacecraft propulsion subsystem of Figure 1. The helium tank pressurizes the two propellant tanks. When a propellant path to either engine is open, the pressurized tanks force fuel and oxidizer into the engine, producing thrust. Not shown are valve drivers that control the latch valves and a set of flow, pressure and acceleration sensors that provide partial observability. A model of a system specifies the modes of each component (*e.g.*, a valve may be open, closed, stuck closed, and so on), behavior in each mode (*e.g.*, a closed valve prevents flow), mode transitions (*e.g.*, valves usually open when commanded, but stick closed with probability p) and connections between components (*e.g.*, fuel flow into an engine is equal to the flow out of the attached fuel valve).

Consider the problem of determining the likelihood of the possible states of this subsystem. Unfortunately, computing a belief state in general requires enumeration of the state space. The propulsion subsystem has 38 components with an average of 3 states each. More complete spacecraft models capture 150 or more components averaging 4 states, yielding a state space of 2^{300} or more and making complete enumeration implausible. One alternative is to track an approximation whose computation does not require enumeration of the state space, ideally enumerating only the most likely portion of the belief state at each point in time. *Livingstone* (Williams & Nayak 1996) tracks n approximately most likely states of the system by transitioning a small number of tracked states by the transitions that are most likely, given only the current observations. This approximation is extremely efficient and well suited to the problem of tracking the internal state of a machine, where the likelihood of the nominal or expected transition dominates, and immediate observations often rule out the nominal trajectory when a failure occurs. The task then becomes one of diagnosing the most likely system transition, chosen from combinations of component transitions, that would be consistent with the unexpected observations. Using this technique, *Livingstone* is able to perform approximate state identification and reconfiguration of systems with hundreds of state variables. It has been applied to the control of a number of systems within NASA and is an integral part of the Remote Agent architecture demonstrated in-flight on the Deep Space 1 spacecraft in 1999 (Muscettola *et al.* 1998; Bernard *et al.* 1998). Unfortunately, the true trajectory may not be among the most likely given only the current observations. Consider the following example.

Copyright © 2000, American Association for Artificial Intelligence (www.aaai.org). All rights reserved.

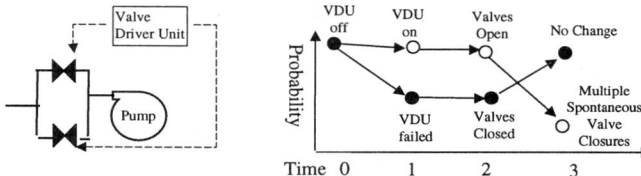

Figure 2: Evolution of a Valve Driver Unit and Valves

Example 2 Figure 2 illustrates a small system and two possible trajectories. The pump pressurizes the system and the valves, if open, allow a fluid flow. The valve driver unit (VDU) commands the two valves in parallel via the data bus represented by dashed lines. The graph to the right represents the probability of two possible trajectories. The filled circles represent the true state of the system. At time 0 the VDU is off, the valves are closed and the pump is off. At time 0 the VDU is commanded on. For the sake of illustration, consider an approximate belief state of size 1. The state wherein the VDU is on is placed into the belief state. The true state wherein the VDU is failed is discarded. At time 1, the VDU is commanded to open its valves. Since the only state in the belief state assumes the VDU is on, the single state in the updated belief state has the VDU on and all valves open. In the true, untracked state the valves are closed, as they never received a command. At time 2, the pump is turned on. Pressure is observed at the outlet of the pump, yet no flow is observed downstream of the valves. Failure of the pump alone has zero probability, given the observations. Failure of the VDU in the current time step has no effect on the valves. Thus, the most likely next state consistent with the observations requires that all valves spontaneously and independently shut. Regardless of the number of valves and the unlikeliness of spontaneous closure, this transition must be taken if it exists. If it does not exist, the belief state approximation becomes empty.

In general, as the true state evolves, the tracked subset of states may need to undergo arbitrarily unlikely transitions in order to remain consistent with the observations. While only one trajectory is tracked in this example, for any fraction of the trajectories that are tracked, an example can be constructed wherein the actual state of the system falls outside the tracked fraction and the error in the approximation may become arbitrarily large. We propose an alternative to committing to a subset of the current belief state or maintaining an approximation of the entire belief state. We propose to maintain the information necessary to begin incrementally generating the current belief state in best-first order at any point in time. Since we do not update the entire belief state, we do not have a sufficient statistic, so a history must be maintained. We introduce a variable to represent every state variable, command and observation at every point in time and an algorithm for incrementally generating the exact belief state at any point. Duplicating the entire set of variables at each point in the history seems impractical except for short duration tasks. We apply two approximations motivated by our experience modeling physical systems for *Livingstone*. The first duplicates only a small number of carefully selected variables at each time point. This approximation is conservative in that does not eliminate any feasible trajectories but may admit certain infeasible trajectories. These may be eliminated by future observations. The second limits the length of the history that is maintained by absorbing older variables into a single variable that grossly approximates them. This allows an approximate belief state to be generated at any point in time from a constant number of variables. The variables represent an exact model of system evolution over the recent past, an approximate model over the intermediate past, and a gross summarization over the more distant past. This allows assignment of the most likely past transitions to be revisited as new observations become available. The fewest variables, and thus the least flexibility, are allocated to segments of the system trajectory that have remained consistent with the system's observed evolution for the longest time.

In the following sections of the paper, we start by giving the complete history representation followed by a simple, exact, and intractable algorithm for enumerating the belief state. We introduce optimizations and approximations in order to gain tractability while maintaining the ability to revise assessments of past system evolution. We introduce a software system *L2* (for *Livingstone*2) that embodies these ideas. Finally we present the results of running *L2* on scenarios developed while applying *Livingstone* within NASA.

Transition Systems

We wish to represent the possible histories of a system composed of non-deterministic, concurrent automata given the commands issued to the automata and their output. We create a structure that allows incremental, best-first enumeration of all possible trajectories by extending the formalism of *Livingstone*. In order to compactly represent the trajectories, we add a set of transition variables that represent the non-deterministic transitions each automaton may make at each time step. Each assignment to a transition variable has a likelihood representing the prior probability of the corresponding non-deterministic transition occurring. One trajectory of the system is thus an assignment to each transition variable, and given the appropriate independence assumptions, the set of trajectories can be incrementally enumerated in order of likelihood. In order to capture the feasible behaviors of the automata, we introduce a set of formulae $\mathcal{M}_\Sigma$ describing the input/output mapping of the automata in each state, and a set of formulae $\mathcal{M}_\mathcal{T}$ for describing the feasible transitions of the automata.

Definition 1 A *transition system* $\mathcal{S}$ is a tuple $\langle \Pi, \mathcal{T}, \mathcal{D}, \mathcal{C}, \mathcal{M}_\Sigma, \mathcal{M}_\mathcal{T} \rangle$, where

- Π is a set of *state variables* representing the state of each automaton. Let n denote the number of automata and m denote the number of discrete, synchronous time steps over which the state is to be tracked. Π then contains $m \times n$ variables. Π_t will denote the set of state variables representing the state of the system at time step t. Each state variable y ranges over a finite domain denoted $\delta(y)$.

The temporal variable representing the occurrence of variable y at time step t is denoted y_t.

- $\mathcal{T}$ is a set of *transition variables*. The transition variable that represents the transition of state variable y from time t to $t+1$ is denoted $\tau_{y,t}$. Each value in the domain of $\tau_{y,t}$ is assigned a probability.
- $\mathcal{D}$ is a finite set of *dependent variables*.
- $\mathcal{C}$ is a finite set of *command variables*.
- State s_t is an assignment to $\Pi_t \cup \mathcal{T}_t \cup \mathcal{D}_t \cup \mathcal{C}_t$.
- $\mathcal{M}_\Sigma$ is a propositional formula over Π_t and $\mathcal{D}_t$ that specifies the feasible subset of the state space. A state is feasible if it makes an assignment to $\Pi_t \cup \mathcal{D}_t$ that is consistent with $\mathcal{M}_\Sigma$.
- $\mathcal{M}_\mathcal{T}$ is a propositional formula over Π_t, $\mathcal{D}_t$, $\mathcal{C}_t$, $\mathcal{T}_t$ and Π_{t+1} that specifies the feasible sequences of states. $\mathcal{M}_\mathcal{T}$ is a conjunction of transition formulae modeling possible evolutions of y_t to y_{t+1} of the form

$$\phi_t \wedge (\tau_{y,t} = \tau^*) \Rightarrow y_{t+1} = y^*$$

where ϕ_t is a propositional formula over $\Pi_t \cup \mathcal{D}_t \cup \mathcal{C}_t$, and τ^*, representing a choice among the non-deterministic transitions of y, is in $\delta(\tau_{y,t})$. The sequence s_i, s_{i+1} is feasible if the assignment made by $s_i \cup s_{i+1}$ is consistent with $\mathcal{M}_\mathcal{T}$.

Example 3 We introduce a transition system to model a VDU and two valves. The variables corresponding to the VDU consist of a state variable vdu representing the mode (*on*, *off*, or *failed*), the transition variable τ_{vdu}, a command variable $cmdin$ representing commands to the VDU or its associated valves (*on*, *off*, *open*, *close*, *none*), and a dependent variable $cmdout$ representing the command the VDU passes on to its valves (*open*, *close*, or *none*). The feasible states of the VDU are specified by the formulae

$$vdu = on \Rightarrow (cmdin = open \Rightarrow cmdout = open)$$
$$\wedge (cmdin = close \Rightarrow cmdout = close)$$
$$\wedge ((cmdin \neq open \wedge cmdin \neq close)$$
$$\Rightarrow cmdout = none)$$
$$vdu = off \Rightarrow cmdout = none$$
$$vdu = failed \Rightarrow cmdout = none$$

together with formulae like $(vdu \neq on) \vee (vdu \neq off) \vee (vdu \neq failed), \ldots$ that assert that variables have unique values. The time step subscript is omitted, indicating that all clauses refer to variables within the same time step. The valves $v1$ and $v2$ each have a state variable of domain (*open*, *closed*, or *stuck*), a transition variable τ_{vi} and a dependent variable $flow_{vi}$ of domain (*zero*, *nonzero*). The feasible states of the $v1$ are specified by the formula below. The feasible states of $v2$ are specified similarly.

$$v1 = open \Rightarrow flow_{v1} = nonzero$$
$$v1 = closed \Rightarrow flow_{v1} = zero$$
$$v1 = stuck \Rightarrow flow_{v1} = zero$$

$\mathcal{M}_\mathcal{T}$ for τ_{vdu} is as follows.

$\tau_{vdu,t} = nominal \Rightarrow$
$\quad vdu_t = off \wedge cmdin_t = on \Rightarrow vdu_{t+1} = on$
$\quad vdu_t = off \wedge cmdin \neq on \Rightarrow vdu_{t+1} = off$
$\quad vdu_t = on \wedge cmdin_t = off \Rightarrow vdu_{t+1} = off$
$\quad vdu_t = on \wedge cmdin_t \neq off \Rightarrow vdu_{t+1} = on$
$\quad vdu_t = failed \Rightarrow vdu_{t+1} = failed$
$\tau_{vdu,t} = fail \Rightarrow vdu_{t+1} = failed$

$\mathcal{M}_\mathcal{T}$ for τ_{v1} is shown below. τ_{v2} is as τ_{v1}.

$\tau_{v1,t} = nominal \Rightarrow$
$\quad v1_t = closed \wedge cmdout_t = open \Rightarrow v1_{t+1} = open$
$\quad v1_t = closed \wedge cmdout_t \neq open \Rightarrow v1_{t+1} = closed$
$\quad v1_t = open \wedge cmdout_t = closed \Rightarrow v1_{t+1} = closed$
$\quad v1_t = open \wedge cmdout_t \neq close \Rightarrow v1_{t+1} = open$
$\quad v1_t = stuck \Rightarrow v1_{t+1} = stuck$
$\tau_{v1,t} = stick \Rightarrow v1_{t+1} = stuck$

Infinitesimals

In order to complete the transition system model shown in Example 3, we require the probability of each $\tau_{y,t}$ assignment, representing the prior probability of each possible component transition. Experience with *Livingstone* suggests that an order of magnitude probability scale is sufficient for two reasons. First, the internal behavior of a machine is usually far less stochastic than its interaction with its environment. There is an expected or nominal behavior that a component will exhibit for a given state and input. Failures are one or more orders of magnitude less likely. Second, precise estimates for these priors are often either inaccessible or unknown. In the case of spacecraft, the components may be unique or they may be destined for a new operating environment. However, the relative plausibility of each failure mode during operation can be elicited quite easily. In this work, we formalize and capitalize on these characteristics of the priors by making use of infinitesimals (Goldszmidt & Pearl 1992) to model the relative likelihoods of failures.

An infinitesimal probability is represented by an infinitesimally small constant raised to an exponent referred to as the *rank*. The rank can be considered the degree of unbelievability. Intuitively, one would not consider a rank 2 infinitesimal believable unless all rank 0 and rank 1 possibilities had been eliminated. Composition of infinitesimals has many desirable properties. If A and B are independent events, then

$$Rank(AB) = Rank(A) + Rank(B)$$
$$Rank(A \vee B) = min(Rank(A), Rank(B))$$

Thus an outcome that can occur through multiple independent events has rank i if one event has rank i and the remaining events, even if arbitrarily many, have ranks of i or more. This property is key. It allows us to consider only the most likely trajectories leading to a state: if a sequence of events of rank i ends in state s_j, then an arbitrary number of higher rank (i.e. less likely) trajectories leading to s_j will not change its rank. Similarly, if state s_j is reached by a trajectory of rank i, and no trajectory of rank i or less reaches s_k, then s_j is more likely than s_k. We need not consider the possibility that a vast number of unlikely trajectories lead to s_k and together increase its likelihood above that of s_j. We frame our algorithms in terms most likely trajectories, knowing the direct correspondence to most likely states given the infinitesimal interpretation of the priors.

Trajectory Identification

Definition 2 A *trajectory* for $\mathcal{S}$ is a sequence of states $s_0, s_1, \ldots s_m$ such that for all t, $0 < t < m$, s_t is consistent with $\mathcal{M}_\Sigma$ and for all t, $0 < t < (m-1)$, $s_t \cup s_{t+1}$ is consistent with $\mathcal{M}_\mathcal{T}$.

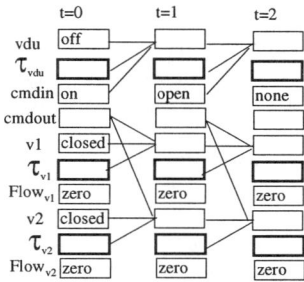

Figure 3: Evolution of the VDU/valve system

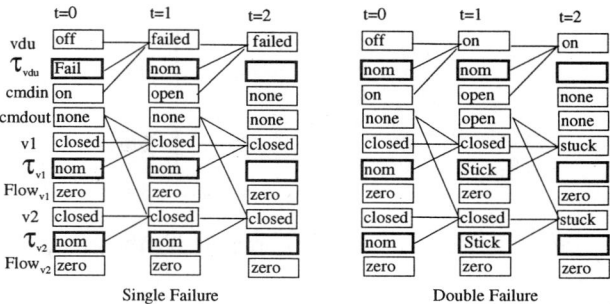

Figure 4: Two evolutions of the system

Consider the problem of determining the state of a physical process modeled by a transition system S at each point in a trajectory $s_0 \ldots s_m$. The subset of the dependent variables $\mathcal{D}$ whose assignment corresponds to a measurement from the process will be referred to as the observations, $\mathcal{O}$. We are given an assignment for the initial state, Π_0. In addition we are given assignments to commands $\mathcal{C}_t$ and observations $\mathcal{O}_t$ for all $0 < t < m$. The task is to choose assignments to $\tau_{y,t}$ for all y and t so as to ensure consistency with $\mathcal{M}_\Sigma$ and $\mathcal{M}_\mathcal{T}$ and maximize the likelihood of the trajectory. That is to say, given a starting state, a set of commands and a set of observations, we must find the most likely sequence of transitions such that each state is consistent with the state model $\mathcal{M}_\Sigma$ and the transitions are consistent with the transition model $\mathcal{M}_\mathcal{T}$. We define trajectory likelihood to be $\sum_{t=0}^{m} \sum_{y=1}^{n} Rank(\tau_{y,t})$. This definition makes the assumption that the likelihood of assignments to $\tau_{y,t}$ are independent of $\tau_{x,t}$. This is a common assumption and has been an adequate approximation in practice. Note that this assumption does not effect the handling of single failures that manifest themselves at multiple points throughout the system (e.g., a power failure causing all lights to go out).

A Simple Tracking Algorithm

The transition-system formulation suggests an intuitive procedure to begin enumerating the belief state at any point. The transition system is initialized with $\mathcal{M}_\Sigma$ and a copy of all variables, representing the initial state. At time step t, we introduce a copy of $\mathcal{M}_\Sigma$ and a copy of all variables, representing the next state of the system, as well as a copy of $\mathcal{M}_\mathcal{T}$ representing the constraints between the current and next states. We assign $\mathcal{C}_t$ and $\mathcal{O}_{t+1}$ according to how the system was commanded and the observations that resulted.

Example 4 Figure 3 illustrates a trajectory-tracking problem of length three for the model of Example 2. Each box represents an assignment. The command is $cmdin$ and the observations are $flow_{v1}$ and $flow_{v2}$. These variables are assigned by the problem, as is the start state. The highlighted $\tau_{y,t}$ assignments must be chosen. The remaining variables will be constrained based upon these assignments. The arcs represent constraints from $\mathcal{M}_\mathcal{T}$. Constraints from $\mathcal{M}_\Sigma$ are not shown. For all $\tau_{y,t}$ we will assume $Rank(\tau_{y,t} = nominal) = 0$ and $Rank(\tau_{y,t} \neq nominal) = 1$.

Trajectories may be enumerated in order by enumerating assignments to all $\tau_{y,t}$ in order of the sum of the ranks, then testing for consistency with $\mathcal{M}_\mathcal{T}$ and $\mathcal{M}_\Sigma$. Conflict-directed, best-first search, or *CBFS* (Dressler & Struss 1992; de Kleer & Williams 1989; Williams & Nayak 1996) greatly focuses this process by using conflicts. In this context, a conflict is a partial assignment to $\mathcal{T}$ and $\mathcal{O}$ that is inconsistent. When a candidate solution is found to be inconsistent, the conflict is recorded in a database, $ConflictDB$. No further candidates that contain a known conflict are generated.

Example 5 Figure 4 illustrates the two lowest cost solutions to the above problem would be found by *CBFS*. They represent a single failure of rank 1 at time 1 and a double failure of rank 2 at time 2, respectively.

While applying CBFS to the full transition system exactly enumerates the most likely trajectories, and thus states, in order, problem size is a significant issue. Let p denote the number of propositions needed to represent each possible value of each variable in $\mathcal{T} \cup \Pi \cup \mathcal{C} \cup \mathcal{D} \cup \mathcal{O}$. These propositions are constrained by a copy of $\mathcal{M}_\mathcal{T}$ and $\mathcal{M}_\Sigma$ at each time step. Testing consistency of an m-step candidate trajectory is a consistency problem of $m \times p$ propositions and $m \times |\mathcal{M}_\mathcal{T} \cup \mathcal{M}_\Sigma|$ clauses. For the Deep Space 1 model, this is $m \times 4041$ propositions and $m \times 13,503$ clauses. The remainder of this paper discusses methods that reduce the size of the consistency problem to be solved, eventually deriving a method that allows a constant problem size.

Problem Size Reduction

In this section, we reduce the structure needed to represent the evolution of the system at a time point from a complete copy of the system model to a small number of variables and clauses. Intuitively, when a command is issued to the system, only a small number of components participate in transmitting that command through the system or transitioning in response to the command. Consider Figure 5. The squares represent state variables, the lines sets of constraints from $\mathcal{M}_\mathcal{T}$. As of time 7, the valves, pump and VDU have not been commanded nor have they interacted with other components by passing a command. If we did not detect a failure of any of these components, we can represent the possibility that they remained idle or failed in a localized and unobservable way with a single set of variables and con-

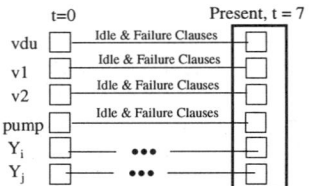

Figure 5: Evolution before commanding the valves

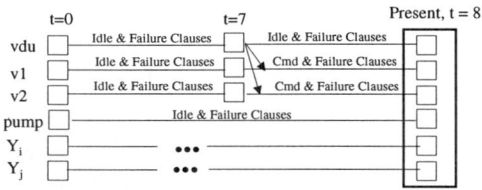

Figure 6: Evolution upon commanding the valves

straints as illustrated. At time 7 we command the valves on. We require variables $v1_8$ and $v2_8$ to represent the new states of the valves. $\mathcal{M}_\mathcal{T}$ suggests vdu_7, $v1_7$ and $v2_7$ will interact with $v1_8$ and $v2_8$. These variables, along with necessary transition variables $\tau_{vdu,7}$, $\tau_{v1,7}$ and, $\tau_{v2,7}$, are introduced to the system with the appropriate clauses from $\mathcal{M}_\mathcal{T}$. For each other variable y, the variable representing y_7 is adequate to represent y_8. Figure 6 illustrates this process. In order to derive a well-founded algorithm from these intuitions, we first place a natural restriction on $\mathcal{M}_\mathcal{T}$ that does not impact correctness. Second we introduce an approximation involving $\mathcal{M}_\Sigma$ that, importantly, does not rule out consistent trajectories. Instead, some trajectories that are not consistent with past observations may be admitted, with the possibility that future observations will eliminate them. These problem modifications avoid replication of many variables in Π and $\mathcal{D}$, as well as corresponding constraints from $\mathcal{M}_\mathcal{T}$ and $\mathcal{M}_\Sigma$.

Restricting $\mathcal{M}_\mathcal{T}$

We restrict $\mathcal{M}_\mathcal{T}$ as do *Livingstone* and *Burton* (Williams & Nayak 1997): a component moves to a failure state with equal probability from any state, and except for failures a component that does not receive a command idles in its current state. $\mathcal{M}_\mathcal{T}$ is limited to the forms:

$$(\tau_{y,t} = \tau_{failure}) \Rightarrow y_{t+1} = y_{failure}$$
$$(\mathcal{C}_{y,t} = \mathcal{C}^*) \wedge \phi_t \wedge (\tau_{y,t} = nominal) \Rightarrow y_{t+1} = y^*$$
$$(\mathcal{C}_{y,t} = idle) \wedge (\tau_{y,t} = nominal) \Rightarrow y_{t+1} = y_t$$

where ϕ_t is a propositional formula over $\Pi_t \cup \mathcal{D}_t$, $\mathcal{C}^* \in \delta(\mathcal{C}_{y,t})$, $nominal \in \delta(\tau_{y,t})$ and $\tau_{fail} \in \delta(\tau_{y,t})$. Formulae of the first form model failures while formulae of the second form model nominal, commanded transitions. Formula of the third form are frame axioms that encode our assumption that devices that do receive a command remain in their current state. We replace ϕ_t with implicant π_t, an equivalent formula involving only Π_t. Intuitively ϕ_t is a formula involving $\mathcal{D}$ that, given $\mathcal{M}_\Sigma$ and an assignment to Π, allows us to infer if $\mathcal{C}_{y,t}$ propagates through a set of components to component y. To form π_t, we replace each assignment to $\mathcal{D}_t$ with a set of assignments from Π_t that imply the $\mathcal{D}_t$ assignment under $\mathcal{M}_\Sigma$. We expect that for the type of clauses $\mathcal{M}_\mathcal{T}$ contains, growth in π_t will be proportional to the length of the component chain that transmits $\mathcal{C}_{y,t}$, which ranged from 1 to 5 in (Bernard *et al.* 1998). Our experience supports this hypothesis. This growth is offset as non-idle, non-failure clauses take the following form which is independent of $\mathcal{D}$.

$$(\mathcal{C}_{y,t} = \mathcal{C}^*) \wedge \pi_t \wedge (\tau_{y,t} = nominal) \Rightarrow y_{t+1} = y^*$$

Given a $\mathcal{C}_{y,t}$ which is not idle, in order to determine consistency with $\mathcal{M}_\mathcal{T}$ we now need only introduce $\mathcal{C}_{y,t}$, $\tau_{y,t}$ and those select members of Π_t that appear in π_t.

Eliminating intermediate observations

$\mathcal{M}_\Sigma$ remains, and requires introduction of all variables in Π_t and $\mathcal{D}_t$ in order to check consistency against $\mathcal{O}_t$. We proceed by eliminating all variables $\mathcal{O}_t$ for values of t sufficiently far in the past. That is to say, transition choices are only constrained by consistency between the trajectories they imply and recent observations. As the system evolves, variables representing older observations and the copies of $\mathcal{M}_\Sigma$ that constrain them are unneeded. For the portions of the trajectory where $\mathcal{M}_\Sigma$ is not introduced, we need not introduce $\mathcal{D}$ and need only introduce the limited portion of Π_t required by $\mathcal{M}_\mathcal{T}$. This is of course an approximation. It is now possible to choose transition assignments that are inconsistent with the discarded observations, resulting in an "imposter" trajectory. This approximation has several important features. First, it is a conservative approximation in that no consistent trajectories are eliminated. Second, all trajectories are checked against new observations, and imposters are eliminated as soon as they fail to describe the on-going evolution of the system. Finally if conflicts are recorded in $ConflictDB$, no partial assignment to $\mathcal{T}$ that was discovered to be in conflict with the observations will be reconsidered, even after observations are discarded. Thus we can only admit an imposter in the case where a transition choice is in conflict with an observation, but the choice is not considered until after the conflicting observation has been discarded.

Selective Model Extension

Based upon these restrictions, the procedure *extend* introduces into time step t only the small fraction of the model involved with the evolution of the system due to the command $\mathcal{C}_{y,t} = \mathcal{C}^*$. The resulting problem size per time step is proportional to $|\pi_t|$. This hinges upon Theorem 1. For the purpose of discussion we will assume that for each time step t there exists only one y for which $\mathcal{C}_{y,t} \neq idle$. The proofs can be extended to parallel commanding.

Theorem 1 *Assume $\mathcal{C}_{y,t} = \mathcal{C}^*$, $\mathcal{C}^* \neq idle$, and for all $x \neq y$, $\mathcal{C}_{x,t} = idle$. Consider the formula of $\mathcal{M}_\mathcal{T}$*

$$(\mathcal{C}_{y,t} = \mathcal{C}^*) \wedge \pi_t \wedge (\tau_{y,t} = nominal) \Rightarrow y_{y+1} = y^*$$

For all state variables x_t, $x \neq y$, if $x_t \notin \pi_t$, then an equivalent consistency problem is formed by replacing x_t, $\tau_{x,t}$ and all formulae of $\mathcal{M}_\mathcal{T}$ involving these variables with a constraint between x_{t-1} and x_{t+1}.

Space precludes inclusion of the complete proof. Intuitively, there are no witnesses to the value of x_t except for x_{t-1} and x_{t+1}, which can be constrained directly. If x_t is as described, then the only clauses involving x_t are of the form:

$$(\mathcal{C}_{x,t-1} = \mathcal{C}^*) \wedge \phi_{t-1} \wedge (\tau_{x,t-1} = nominal) \Rightarrow x_t = x^*$$
$$(\mathcal{C}_{x,t-1} = idle) \wedge (\tau_{x,t-1} = nominal) \Rightarrow x_t = x_{t-1}$$
$$(\tau_{x,t-1} = \tau_{fail}) \Rightarrow x_t = x_{fail}$$
$$(\mathcal{C}_{x,t} = idle) \wedge (\tau_{x,t} = nominal) \Rightarrow x_{t+1} = x_t$$
$$(\tau_{x,t} = \tau_{fail}) \Rightarrow x_{t+1} = x_{fail}$$

The variable x_t can only impact the consistency of the system via the assignments to $\tau_{x,t-1}$ and $\tau_{x,t}$. Given the independence assumptions, assigning failures to both is indistinguishable from and less likely than assigning $\tau_{x,t-1} = nominal$ and $\tau_{x,t}$ to a failure, while assigning a failure to one is equivalent to assigning a failure to the other. Thus we need only consider $\tau_{x,t-1} = \tau_{x,t} = nominal$ and $\tau_{x,t-1} = nominal$, $\tau_{x,t} = \tau_{fail}$. In the nominal case, x_t is equivalent to x_{t+1} and can be eliminated. In the failure case, the assignment to x_t has no impact on x_{t+1} and can be eliminated. The above formula are rendered equivalent to the following reduced set:

$$(\mathcal{C}_{x,t-1} = \mathcal{C}^*) \wedge \pi_{t-1} \wedge (\tau_{x,t-1} = nominal) \Rightarrow x_{t+1} = x^*$$
$$(\mathcal{C}_{x,t-1} = idle) \wedge (\tau_{x,t-1} = nominal) \Rightarrow x_{t+1} = x_{t-1}$$
$$(\tau_{x,t-1} = \tau_{fail}) \Rightarrow x_{t+1} = x_{fail}$$

In fact, at time t we will know whether or not $\mathcal{C}_{x,t-1} = idle$, and therefore we need only introduce one of the first two formulae. The *extend* procedure repeatedly applies Theorem 1 to avoid introducing a variable or constraints for x_t when there have been no witnesses to x_t and it is possible to constrain x_{t+1} directly from x_{t-1}. When a command is introduced, the compiled $\mathcal{M}_\mathcal{T}$ determines what clauses should be added to constrain the nominal transition of y_t under $\mathcal{C}_{y,t}$. State variables appearing in the introduced clauses are added, along with constraints representing their idle or failure transitions. By reducing the number of variables and clauses introduced at each time step, we reduce the consistency problem involved in checking a trajectory to a number of variables proportional to $m \times |\pi_t|$. The number of clauses is proportional to $m \times (|\pi_t| + k)$ where k is the number of failure values per τ_y domain.

Conflict Coverage Search

The strengths of efficiently tracking a partial belief state are merged with the flexibility of incrementally enumerating belief states in the *CoverTrack* procedure of Figure 7. *TSet* is a superset of all consistent trajectories of rank γ, as returned by a previous call to *CoverTrack*. As described above, *extend* adds to the transition system the variables needed to represent the outcomes of the current command. All trajectories are augmented by the new transition variables, which are assigned nominal transition, and checked for consistency. Any inconsistent trajectory requires additional failures above rank γ, and is discarded as relatively implausible. The survivors are a superset of all consistent trajectories of rank γ. If this set is not empty, it is returned. Otherwise, the most likely trajectory has a rank greater than γ. The *GenerateCover* algorithm generates all assignments to $\mathcal{T}$ of

```
proc CoverTrack(cmd, obs, TSet, ConflictDB, γ) {
  /*Extend the system adding Π_t to Π, 𝒯_t to 𝒯*/
  extend(Π,𝒯, cmd);
  /*Extend trajectories at current γ */
  Assign 𝒯_t to nominal, 0 rank assignment.
  for trajectory in TSet
    trajectory = trajectory ∪𝒯_t;
  /*Check trajectories for consistency, up γ if needed*/
  Assign 𝒪 according to obs received;
  Survivors = ∅;
  loop{
    for trajectory in TSet {
      conflict=checkConsistency(trajectory);
      if (conflict) then
        push(conflict, ConflictDB);
      else
        push(trajectory,survivors); }
    if(survivors) then return survivors;
    /*Ran out of trajectories. Find more at next rank*/
    γ = γ + 1;
    TSet=GenerateCover(𝒯,ConflictDB,γ);
  }
}
```

Figure 7: Conflict Coverage Tracking Procedure

a given rank that cover all known conflicts. A conflict is covered if at least one of the variables in the conflict is assigned to an assignment that does not appear in the conflict. Intuitively, we leave the $\tau_{y,t}$ at their zero rank values, introducing reassignment only to avoid conflicts, with a total cost of γ. This is the NP-hard *hitting set* problem. The contents of *ConflictDB* and γ will determine whether this problem is tractable. Because of the loss of observations at past time points, *GenerateCover* returns superset of all consistent rank γ trajectories. If at least one trajectory is consistent with the current observations, it is returned. If not, γ is increased.

Finite Horizons

While selective extension reduces the variables per time step, we still require an unbounded number of variables over time. We avoid this requirement by summarizing sets of $\tau_{y,t}$ variables beyond a horizon h in the past into a single variable τ_h. This horizon is fixed relative to the present, so at time step m, only the $\mathcal{T}$ variables $\tau_{y,m-h}$ through $\tau_{y,m}$ are required. Consider Figure 6 extended to some time step m. The variables $\tau_{y,0}$ through $\tau_{y,m}$ have been introduced to represent choices in the system's evolution. When tracking the system, we incrementally generate the few most likely consistent assignments to all $\tau_{y,t}$, representing the most likely consistent trajectories. Note that each m-step trajectory contains an assignment to $\tau_{y,0}$ and $\tau_{y,1}$ that appears among the most likely given a potentially large amount of information gained from time steps 0 through m. Each such assignment also induces an assignment upon Π_2, for example $y_2 = y^*$. Intuitively, we replace each of l likely assignments to $\tau_{y,0}$ and $\tau_{y,1}$ with an assignment $\tau_h = choice_l$ that has the same rank. We may then replace $\mathcal{M}_{\mathcal{T}2}$ with l clauses of the form $\tau_h = choice_l \Rightarrow y_2 = y^*$. The summary variable τ_h restricts choices for the initial portion of the trajectory to the partial

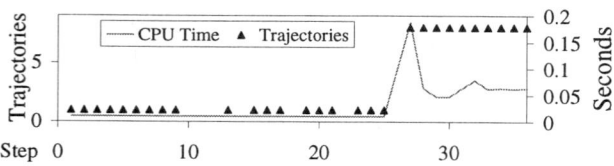

Figure 8: ISPP - Independent failures at steps 27, 32 and 33

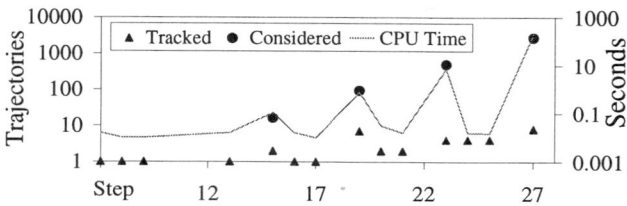

Figure 9: ISPP - 4 Identical failures over 27 Steps

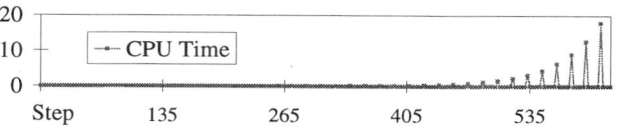

Figure 10: CB - 39 Identical failures over 618 Steps

trajectories that appeared most likely after being extended for some time. By summarizing the l most likely assignments to τ_h and all $\tau_{y,2}$ into a new variable $\tau_{h'}$ when the front of the transition system is extended, we can maintain a fixed sized problem representation. Since our search algorithms are continually considering the most likely choices for $\mathcal{T}$ and inferring the implications upon Π in order to determine consistency, this is a relatively low cost approximation to compute.

Results

$L2$ has been implemented in C++ in a modular form that allows alternative search and consistency procedures to be plugged into the transition system framework. The tests described below were performed using *CoverTrack* and propositional consistency as determined by an LTMS, running under Windows NT on a 550Mhz Pentium III. Observations were kept for one step only. No horizon was used.

$L2$ correctly tracks the canonical scenarios known to confound *Livingstone*. Consider Example 2. When the pump is turned on, *Livingstone* finds two conflicts in the current mode assignments: valve v1 cannot be open, and valve v2 cannot be open. It thus fails both valves. $L2$ finds the following sets of devices that could not have both transitioned nominally: {VDU, v1}, {VDU,v2}. The lowest cost covering is to fail the VDU at time step 0. Many more interesting scenarios have been demonstrated. If the VDU is failed and v1 is commanded open, the trajectory wherein v1 is stuck will be tracked if that is more likely than a VDU failure. If v2 is later commanded and no flow results, the v1 failure is dropped and the trajectory where the VDU failed in the past is found. If the VDU is resettable, the trajectory wherein the VDU has failed in a resettable manner is first tracked when multiple valves fail to open. If the VDU is reset and the valves again fail to open, $L2$ may find a trajectory where the valves were stuck all along, one that replaces the past resettable VDU failure with a permanent failure, or both, depending upon the ranks of the various failures.

Longer runs on more complex models written by *Livingstone* users rather than the authors were also performed. The ISPP model has 59 components and represents a chemical processor designed to produce rocket fuel from the Martian atmosphere. Its *flow failure* requires far more time for diagnosis under *Livingstone* than any other scenario we have encountered. Figure 8 illustrates a 33 step track of the model, approximating one day's worth of commands. On the 27th step, the flow failure becomes observable. On steps 32 and 33 simpler, unrelated failures occur. Figure 8 illustrates a second tracking run of the same model. Note

that the time axis is logarithmic. On step 15 the flow failure is introduced. Repair actions are taken and the failure is immediately reintroduced, until a total of four identical failures have occurred. The CB model of 24 electrical components connected in series and parallel was tracked in runs of 618 steps. Figure 10 illustrates a run wherein every 16 steps the same set of devices is turned on, a device fails and is reset, and the devices are turned off. The device fails a total of 39 times. Additional runs were made on both models.

Our results suggest the following. *Model growth per time step is small.* ISPP begins at 2933 clauses and grows by an average of 36 clauses per time step. CB begins at 1126 clauses and grows by an average of 44 clauses per time step. *Tracking time steps where no failure occurs takes a very small amount of CPU time.* Note that in Figure 8 the steps before the first failure occurs require a negligible amount of CPU time. The nominal steps after the failure take slightly more time, as 8 trajectories are being tracked, but the cost is still negligible. *Keeping a history does not induce an unreasonable cost when diagnosing a single failure.* When the nominal trajectory is ruled out we have a single, long conflict and $\gamma = 1$, leading to a simple coverage problem. The CPU time for a single CB failure scenario is below clock resolution whether 15 or over 600 nominal steps precede the failure. In Figure 9, $L2$ finds the eight trajectories that explain the failure that became observable on step 27 in 0.19 seconds. *Because of the accumulation of conflicts, tracking the system through k failures spread over time can be an easier problem than diagnosing a single failure of cardinality k.* Consider the run of Figure 8. On step 27, the flow failure occurs, causing the large spike in CPU time. Eight trajectories result and are tracked until step 32. On step 32, a simpler, unrelated failure occurs, and none of the 8 trajectories is consistent when extended by the nominal transition. Note that $L2$ must now rediagnose the entire history of the system including the flow failure. It does so in just 0.08 seconds, less than half of the time required to diagnose the flow failure alone. The key to this behavior is the conflicts. On step 27, the nominal trajectory is ruled out and $ConflictDB$ contains a single conflict. *GenerateCover* returns 28 candidate trajectories, 20 of which are ruled out, adding another 15 candidates to $ConflictDB$. Calling $GenerateCover$ with the same γ on these conflicts almost immediately returns just the 8 consistent candidates. On step 32, the 8 diagnoses are ruled out by conflicts resulting from the simple failure. Since the conflicts from the simple failure involve none of the variables from the flow failure conflicts, the problem decomposes into two subproblems, one of which has previously been solved and memoized by the conflicts. *For these classes of problems, L2 has adequate performance.* As a practical matter, each test above executes several times faster than *Livingstone*'s single diagnosis of the flow failure. On the above problems, the additional work performed is dominated by the size and speed benefits of porting from Lisp. *Unfortunately, tracking k related failures over time can also be as computationally intensive as diagnosing a cardinality k failure.* Figure 9 illustrates a sequence of failures where the conflict coverage problem does not decompose. At each time peak, the flow failure has occurred again. The conflicts generated by the fourth failure involve exactly the devices involved in the first three failures. As a result, the time required to solve the hitting set problem and the number of inconsistent trajectories considered rises dramatically. At the fourth failure, 2694 candidates are returned in 174 seconds. An additional 33 seconds are spent determining all but 8 of them are inconsistent. Figure 10 clearly shows the exponential growth of tracking time as the number of failures involving the same device grows.

Future Work

Interleaving consistency checking and conflict coverage may significantly cut down on the number of candidates returned by $GenerateCover$. We have not yet run tests with a horizon. A fixed horizon limits the search that can be done and cuts off consideration of overlapping conflicts beyond the horizon. A more interesting approach is to iteratively deepen the horizon as time allows or uncertainty requires. A recency bias may be a practical heuristic. Only exploring each device's history up to the last point it was considered to have failed should reduce the explosion in possible trajectories. Selectively reintroducing observations and small portions of $\mathcal{M}_\Sigma$ at past time points should also clamp the growth of trajectories. We are currently investigating these and other extensions to $L2$. The resulting system will be evaluated on Earth-bound testbeds representing an interferometer and a Mars propellant plant. In addition, it will be flown as an experiment on the X-34 rocket plane in 2001 and the X-37 orbital vehicle in 2002.

Related Work

The problem described is a partially observable Markov decision process with focus placed upon belief revision. (Friedman & Halpern 1999) provides an excellent synthesis of the literature in belief revision and belief update. The authors describe a general, plausibility-based temporal logic framework that can be used to describe revision methods such as $L2$. There also exists a large body of work concerning approximate belief update. (Boyen & Koller 1998) for example provides an approximate, factored belief state with a bounded error that can be updated without enumerating the state space. Unfortunately, the systems we consider have inadequate mixing rates to apply this approximation. $L2$ differs from this work and the other approximations of which the authors are aware in that it uses history to compensate for not having a sufficient statistic.

Conclusions

This paper presents incremental belief state generation as an alternative to belief revision. The described approximations create a family of representations that track an exact model for a number of steps, then track a reduced model, then summarize over the most likely initial trajectories. The uniform nature of the three abstractions allows a single, simple search to be employed. *CoverTrack* combines partial belief state propagation with the flexibility of the transition system representation. It is highly efficient when failures are sufficiently independent. We are investigating methods to improve performance when multiple failures involving the same components cause a highly unconstrained search.

Acknowledgements

Daniel J. Clancy, Leslie Pack Kaelbling, Brian Williams and three anonymous reviewers provided valuable comments on this work. Shirley Pepke provided valuable comments and software engineering. The Embedded Technology Group at NASA KSC developed the CB and ISPP domain models.

References

Bernard, D. E.; Dorais, G. A.; Fry, C.; Jr., E. B. G.; Kanefsky, B.; Kurien, J.; Millar, W.; Muscettola, N.; Nayak, P. P.; Pell, B.; Rajan, K.; Rouquette, N.; Smith, B.; and Williams, B. C. 1998. Design of the remote agent experiment for spacecraft autonomy. In *Procs. IEEE Aerospace*.

Boyen, X., and Koller, D. 1998. Tractable inference for complex stochastic processes. In *Procs. UAI-98*, 33–42.

de Kleer, J., and Williams, B. C. 1989. Diagnosis with behavioral modes. In *Procs. IJCAI-89*, 1324–1330.

Dressler, O., and Struss, P. 1992. Back to defaults: Characterizing and computing diagnoses as coherent assumption sets. In *Procs. ECAI-92*.

Friedman, N., and Halpern, J. Y. 1999. Modeling belief in dynamic systems part ii: Revision and update. *JAIR* 10:117–167.

Goldszmidt, M., and Pearl, J. 1992. Rank-based systems: A simple approach to belief revision, belief update, and reasoning about evidence and actions. In *Procs. KR-92*, 661–672.

Hamscher, W.; Console, L.; and de Kleer, J. 1992. *Readings in Model-Based Diagnosis*. San Mateo, CA: Morgan Kaufmann.

Muscettola, N.; Nayak, P. P.; Pell, B.; and Williams, B. C. 1998. Remote Agent: To boldly go where no AI system has gone before. *Artificial Intelligence* 103:5–47.

Struss, P. 1997. Fundamentals of model-based diagnosis of dynamic systems. In *Procs. IJCAI-97*. 480–485.

Williams, B. C., and Nayak, P. P. 1996. A model-based approach to reactive self-configuring systems. In *Procs. AAAI-96*, 971–978.

Williams, B. C., and Nayak, P. P. 1997. A reactive planner for a model-based executive. In *Procs. IJCAI-97*.

Sampling Methods for Action Selection in Influence Diagrams

Luis E. Ortiz
Computer Science Department
Brown University
Box 1910
Providence, RI 02912 USA
leo@cs.brown.edu

Leslie Pack Kaelbling
Artificial Intelligence Laboratory
Massachusetts Institute of Technology
545 Technology Square
Cambridge, MA 02139 USA
lpk@ai.mit.edu

Abstract

Sampling has become an important strategy for inference in belief networks. It can also be applied to the problem of selecting actions in influence diagrams. In this paper, we present methods with probabilistic guarantees of selecting a near-optimal action. We establish bounds on the number of samples required for the traditional method of estimating the utilities of the actions, then go on to extend the traditional method based on ideas from sequential analysis, generating a method requiring fewer samples. Finally, we exploit the intuition that equally good value estimates for each action are not required, to develop a heuristic method that achieves major reductions in required sample size. The heuristic method is validated empirically.

Introduction

The problem of decision-making involves the selection of an *optimal strategy*. A strategy determines how we should act based on observations or available information about the variables of the system relevant to the decision problem. Posed in the framework of decision theory, an optimal strategy is one that maximizes our utility. The utility defines our notion of value associated with the execution of actions and the states of the system. The states result from the combination of the state of the individual variables in the system. In the case of decision-making under uncertainty, we are uncertain about both the state of the system and the result of the actions we take. We express this uncertainty as probabilities. Therefore, in this context an *optimal strategy* is one that *maximizes our expected utility*.

In this paper our main interest is in decision problems under uncertainty formulated as *influence diagrams (ID)*. An *influence diagram* is a graphical model that provides a compact representation of (1) the probability distribution governing the states, (2) the structural strategy model representing how we make decisions, and (3) a utility model defining our notion of value associated with actions and states. We study the problem of selecting an optimal strategy in an influence diagram, concentrating on the case in which there is only one decision to be made. This is because we can decompose the problem of multiple decisions into many sub-problems involving single decisions (i.e., by using the tech-

Copyright © 2000, American Association for Artificial Intelligence (www.aaai.org). All rights reserved.

nique presented by Charnes & Shenoy (1999)). We note that we can apply methods developed to solve IDs of this kind to obtain methods to solve finite-horizon Markov decision processes (MDPs) and partially observable Markov decision processes (POMDPs) expressed as dynamic Bayesian networks (DBNs) (i.e., by modifying the technique presented by Kearns, Mansour, & Ng (1999)).

The problem of strategy selection involves the sub-problem of selecting an *optimal action*, from the set of action choices available for that decision, *for each possible observation* available at the time of making the decision. Therefore, we want to select the action that maximizes the expected utility for each observation. One way to do action selection is to compute, exactly or approximately, the probabilities of the sub-states of the system directly relevant to our utility in order to evaluate the expected utility or *value* of each action. A sub-state is formed from the state of a subset of variables in the system. We believe this approach fails to take advantage of an important intuition: it only matters which action is best. Therefore, the problem of action selection is primarily one of comparing the values of the actions. We combine this with the intuition that actions that are close to optimal are also good. In this paper, we present methods for action selection in IDs that take advantage of these intuitions to make major gains in efficiency.

Notation

Before we present the definition of the ID model, we introduce some notation used throughout the paper. We denote one-dimensional random variables by capital letters and denote multi-dimensional random variables by bold capital letters. For instance, we denote a multi-dimensional random variable by $\boldsymbol{X}$ and denote all its components by $(X_1, \ldots, X_n)$ where X_i is the ith one-dimensional random variable. We use small letters to denote assignments to random variables. For instance, $\boldsymbol{X} = \boldsymbol{x}$ means that for each component X_i of $\boldsymbol{X}$, $X_i = x_i$. We also denote by capital letters the nodes in a graph. We denote by $Pa(Y)$ the parents of node Y in a directed graph.

We now introduce notation that will become useful during the description of the methods presented in this paper. For any function h with variables $\boldsymbol{X}$ and $\boldsymbol{Z}$, the expression

$$h(\boldsymbol{X}, \boldsymbol{Z})|_{\boldsymbol{Z}=\boldsymbol{z}}$$

stands for a function f' over variables X that results from setting the values of Z in h with assignment z while letting the values for X remain unassigned. In other words,

$$f'(X) = h(X, Z)|_{Z=z} = h(X, Z = z).$$

The notation $Z = (S, S')$ means that the variable Z is formed by all the variables that form S and S'. That is, $Z = (Z_1, \ldots, Z_{n'}) = (S_1, \ldots, S_{n_1}, S'_1, \ldots, S'_{n_2}) = (S, S')$, where $n' = n_1 + n_2$. Note that we are assuming that the set of variables forming S and those forming S' are disjoint. The notation $Z \sim f$ means that the random variable Z is distributed according to probability distribution f. We denote a sequence of samples from Z by $z^{(1)}, z^{(2)}, \ldots$, where $z^{(i)}$ is the ith sample. In this paper, we assume that the samples are *independent*.

Definitions

An influence diagram (ID) is a graphical model for decision-making (See Jensen (1996) for additional information and references). It consists of a directed acyclic graph along with a structural strategy model, a probabilistic model and a utility model. The graph represents the decomposition used to compactly define the different models. Figure 1 shows an example of a general graphical representation of an ID. The vertices of the graph consist of three types of nodes: decision nodes, chance nodes and utility nodes. Decision nodes are square and represent the decisions or action choices in the decision problem. Chance nodes are circular and represent the variables of the system relevant to the decision problem. Utility nodes are diamonds and represent the utility associated with actions and *states*. A *state* is an assignment to the variables associated with the chance nodes of the ID.

Structural strategy model The structural strategy model defines locally the form of a decision rule for each decision node A_i. This rule is a function of (a subset of) the information available at the time of making that decision, which is contained in its parents $\text{Pa}(A_i)$ in the graph, the decision nodes that are predecessors of decision node A_i in the graph and their respective parents. The example ID of Figure 1 has only one decision node. Denote a strategy for our example model by π, the *state space* or set of possible assignments for the parents of the action node by $\Omega_{\text{Pa}(A)}$ and the set of possible actions Ω_A. Then, a policy $\pi : \Omega_{\text{Pa}(A)} \to \Omega_A$.

Probability model The probability model compactly defines the joint probability distribution of the relevant variables given the actions taken using a Bayesian network (BN) (See Jensen (1996) for additional information and references). The model defines locally a conditional probability distribution $P(X_i \mid \text{Pa}(X_i))$ for each variable X_i given its parents $\text{Pa}(X_i)$ in the graph. This defines the following joint probability distribution over the n variables of the system, given that a particular action a is taken:

$$P(X_1, \ldots, X_n \mid A = a) = \prod_{i=1}^{n} P(X_i \mid \text{Pa}(X_i))|_{A=a}.$$

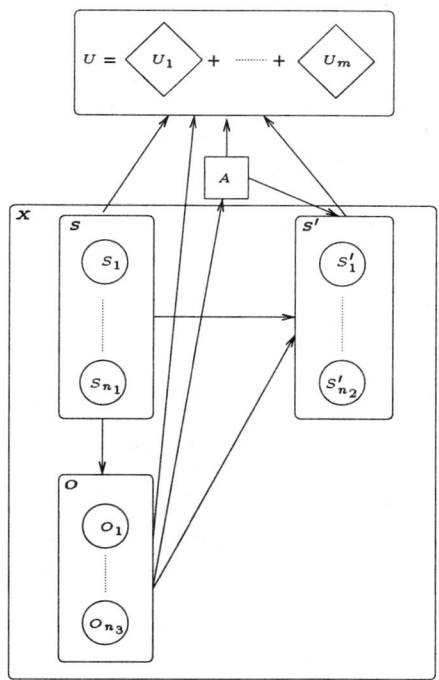

Figure 1: General structure of ID we consider.

In our example ID, $X = (S, S', O)$ and, since there is only one decision node, we can express $P(X \mid A = a)$ as

$$\begin{aligned} P(X \mid A = a) &= P(S, S', O \mid A = a) \\ &= P(S) P(S' \mid S, O, A = a) P(O \mid S), \end{aligned}$$

where

$$P(S) = \prod_{i=1}^{n_1} P(S_i \mid \text{Pa}(S_i)), \quad (1)$$
$$P(S' \mid S, O, A = a) = \prod_{i=1}^{n_2} P(S'_i \mid \text{Pa}(S'_i))|_{A=a} \quad (2)$$
$$P(O \mid S) = \prod_{i=1}^{n_3} P(O_i \mid \text{Pa}(O_i)). \quad (3)$$

Utility model Finally, the utility model defines the utility associated with actions resulting from the decisions made and states of the variables in the system. The total utility function U is the sum of local utility functions associated with each utility node. For each utility node U_i, the utility function provides a utility value as a function of its parents $\text{Pa}(U_i)$ in the graph. The total utility can be expressed as

$$U(X, A) = \sum_{i=1}^{m} U_i(\text{Pa}(U_i)). \quad (4)$$

Note that we are using the label of the utility node to also denote the utility function associated with it.

In this paper we assume that the variables and the decisions are discrete and the local utilities are bounded. In addition, we concentrate on IDs with one decision node and the general structure shown in Figure 1. The results in this paper are still valid for more general structural decompositions of the probability distribution. We use the structure given by the ID in the figure to simplify the presentation. Also, the results allow random utility functions.

Value of a strategy The *value V^π of a strategy* π is the expected utility of the strategy:

$$\begin{aligned} V^\pi &= \sum_X P(X \mid A = \pi(O))U(X, A = \pi(O)) \\ &= \sum_O \sum_S \sum_{S'} P(S, S', O \mid A = \pi(O)) \\ &\qquad U(S, S', O \mid A = \pi(O)). \end{aligned}$$

The optimal strategy π^* is that which maximizes V^π over all π. We denote the value of the optimal strategy by V^*.

Note that we can decompose this maximization into maximizations over the set of actions for each observation. For each assignment to the observations o, we define the *value of an action* a by

$$\begin{aligned} V_o(a) = \sum_S \sum_{S'} &P(S, S', O = o \mid A = a) \\ &U(S, S', O = o \mid A = a). \quad (5) \end{aligned}$$

Hence, the value of a strategy is $V^\pi = \sum_O V_O(\pi(O))$. Note that this is not the traditional definition of the value of an action. We discuss below why we do not use the traditional definition.

If we denote by $a^* = \pi^*(o)$ the action that maximizes $V_o(a)$ over all actions a, then the value of the optimal strategy is $V^* = \sum_O V_O(\pi^*(O)) = \sum_O \max_a V_O(a)$. Hence, the problem of strategy selection reduces to that of action selection for each observation.

Exact methods exist for computing the optimal strategy in an ID (See Charnes & Shenoy (1999) and Jensen (1996) for short descriptions and a list of references). However, this problem is hard in general. In this paper, we concentrate on obtaining approximations to the optimal strategy with certain guarantees. Our objective is to find policies that are close to optimal with high probability. That is, for a given accuracy parameter ϵ^* and confidence parameter δ^*, we want to obtain a strategy $\hat\pi$ such that $V^* - V^{\hat\pi} < \epsilon^*$ with probability at least $1 - \delta^*$. Note that given the decomposition described above, if we obtain actions for each observation such that their value is *sufficiently* close to optimal with *sufficiently* high probability, then we obtain a near-optimal strategy with high probability. That is, let l be the number of possible assignments to the observations. If for each observation o we select action $\hat a$ such that $V_o(a^*) - V_o(\hat a) < 2\epsilon$ with probability at least $1 - \delta$, where $\epsilon = \epsilon^*/(2l)$ and $\delta = \delta^*/l$, then we obtain a strategy that is within ϵ^* of the optimal with probability at least $1 - \delta^*$. Therefore, we concentrate on finding a *good* action for each observation.

Typically the value of an action is defined as the *conditional* expected utility of the action *given* an assignment of the observations. If we denote this value by $V(a \mid o)$, we can express the value of a policy as $V^\pi = \sum_O P(O)V(\pi(O) \mid O)$. We do not use this definition because it is harder to obtain estimates for $V(a \mid o)$ with guaranteed confidence bounds than it is to obtain estimates for $V_o(a)$.

Multiple Comparisons with the Best: Results

There are two important results from the field of *multiple comparisons* and in particular from the field of *multiple comparisons with the best* that we take advantage of in this paper. These results are based on the work of Hsu (1981) (See Hsu (1996) for more information). Before we present the results we introduce the following notation: denote $x^+ = \max(x, 0)$ and $-x^- = \min(0, x)$. The first result is known as *Hsu's single-bound lemma*, which is presented as Lemma 1 by Matejcik & Nelson (1995).

Lemma 1 *Let $\mu_{(1)} \leq \mu_{(2)} \leq \cdots \leq \mu_{(k)}$ be the (unknown) ordered performance parameters of k systems, and let $\hat\mu_{(1)}, \hat\mu_{(2)}, \ldots, \hat\mu_{(k)}$ be any estimators of the parameters. If*

$$Pr\{\hat\mu_{(k)} - \hat\mu_{(i)} - (\mu_{(k)} - \mu_{(i)}) > -w, i = 1, \ldots, k-1\} = 1 - \alpha, \quad (6)$$

then

$$\begin{aligned} Pr\{\mu_i - \max_{j \neq i} \mu_j \in [&-(\hat\mu_i - \max_{j \neq i} \hat\mu_j - w)^-, \\ &(\hat\mu_i - \max_{j \neq i} \hat\mu_j + w)^+], \text{ for all } i\} \geq 1 - \alpha. \quad (7) \end{aligned}$$

If we replace the $=$ in (6) with $\geq$, then (7) still holds.

In our context, we let for each action a, the true value $\mu_a = V_o(a)$ and the estimate $\hat\mu_a = \hat V_o(a)$. Also, the ith smallest true value corresponds to $\mu_{(i)}$. That is, if $V_o(a_1) \leq V_o(a_2) \leq \cdots \leq V_o(a_k)$, then for all i, $\mu_{(i)} = V_o(a_i)$. Note that in practice, we do not know which action has the largest value. In order to apply Hsu's single-bound lemma, we obtain the bound $Pr\{\hat\mu_j - \hat\mu_i - (\mu_j - \mu_i) > -w, \text{ for all } i \neq j\} \geq 1 - \alpha$, for each action j, individually. This implies that $Pr\{\hat\mu_{(k)} - \hat\mu_{(i)} - (\mu_{(k)} - \mu_{(i)}) > -w, i = 1, \ldots, k-1\} \geq 1 - \alpha$, which allow us to apply the lemma. Figure 2 graphically describes this practical interpretation of the lemma. For each action i, individually, the upper bounds on the true differences, drawn on the left-hand side, $V_o(i) - V_o(j) < \hat V_o(i) - \hat V_o(j) + w$, for each $j \neq i$, hold simultaneously with probability at least $1 - \alpha$. The confidence intervals, drawn on the right-hand side, $V_o(i) - \max_{j \neq i} V_o(j) \in [-(\hat V_o(i) - \max_{j \neq i} \hat V_o(j) - w)^-, (\hat V_o(i) - \max_{j \neq i} \hat V_o(j) + w)^+]$, for each action i, hold simultaneously with probability at least $1 - \alpha$.

The second result allows us to assess joint confidence intervals on the difference between the value of each action from the value of the best action when we have estimates of the differences between value of each pair of actions with different degrees of accuracy. The result is known as *Hsu's multiple-bound lemma*. It is presented as Lemma 2 by Matejcik & Nelson (1995), and credited to Chang & Hsu (1992).

Lemma 2 *Let $\mu_{(1)} \leq \mu_{(2)} \leq \cdots \leq \mu_{(k)}$ be the (unknown) ordered performance parameters of k systems. Let T_{ij} be a point estimator of the parameter $\mu_i - \mu_j$. If for each i individually*

$$Pr\{T_{ij} - (\mu_i - \mu_j) > -w_{ij}, \text{ for all } j \neq i\} = 1 - \alpha, \quad (8)$$

then we can make the joint probability statement

$$Pr\{\mu_i - \max_{j \neq i} \mu_j \in [D_i^-, D_i^+], \text{ for all } i\} \geq 1 - \alpha, \quad (9)$$

where $D_i^+ = (\min_{j \neq i}[T_{ij} + w_{ij}])^+$, $\mathcal{G} = \{l : D_l^+ > 0\}$, and

$$D_i^- = \begin{cases} 0 & \text{if } \mathcal{G} = \{i\} \\ -(\min_{j \in \mathcal{G}, j \neq i}[-T_{ji} - w_{ji}])^- & \text{otherwise.} \end{cases}$$

If we replace the $=$ in (8) with $\geq$, then (9) still holds.

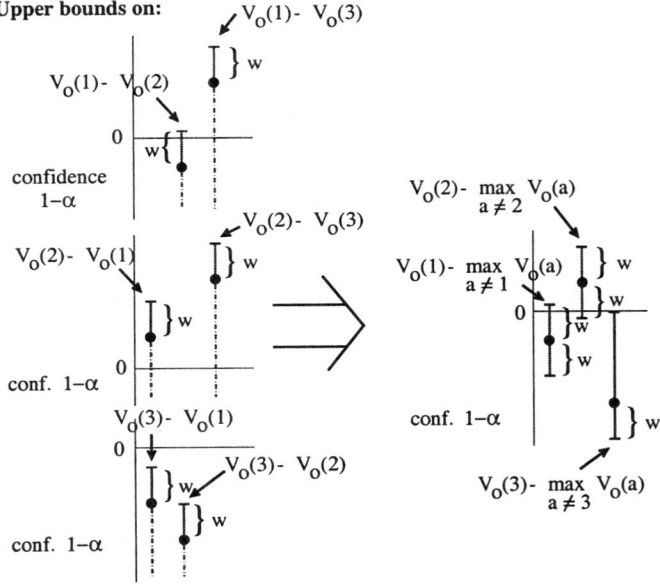

Figure 2: Graphical description for practical application of Hsu's single-bound lemma. Note that the "lower bounds" on the left-hand side are $-\infty$.

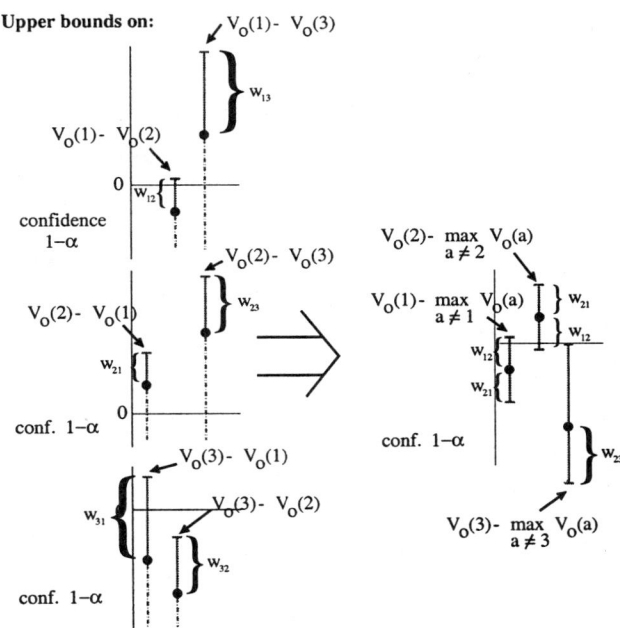

Figure 3: Graphical description of Hsu's multiple-bound lemma. Note that the "lower bounds" on the left-hand side are $-\infty$.

Figure 3 presents a graphical description of this lemma. Let, for all actions i, D_i^- and D_i^+, be as defined in Hsu's multiple-bound lemma, with $\mu_i = V_o(i)$ and for all $j \neq i$, $T_{ij} = \hat{V}_o(i) - \hat{V}_o(j)$. For each action i, individually, the upper bounds on the true differences, drawn on the left-hand side, $V_o(i) - V_o(j) < T_{ij} + w_{ij}$, for each $j \neq i$, hold simultaneously with probability at least $1 - \alpha$. The confidence intervals, drawn on the right-hand side, $V_o(i) - \max_{j \neq i} V_o(j) \in [D_i^-, D_i^+]$, for each action i, hold simultaneously with probability at least $1 - \alpha$. Also, in this example, $\mathcal{G} = \{1, 2\}$. In our context, $\mathcal{G}$ is the set of all the actions that could potentially be the best with probability at least $1 - \alpha$. That is, for each action a in $\mathcal{G}$, the upper bound D_a^+ on the difference of the true value of action a and the best of *all* the other actions, including those in $\mathcal{G}$, is positive.

Estimation-based methods

One approach to selecting the best action is to obtain estimates of $V_o(a)$ for each a by sampling, using the probability model of the ID conditioned on a, then select the action with the largest estimated value.

We can apply the idea of *importance sampling* (See Geweke (1989) and the references therein) to this estimation problem by using the probability distribution defined by the ID as *the importance function* or *sampling distribution*. This is essentially the same idea as *likelihood-weighting* in the context of probabilistic inference in Bayesian networks (Shachter & Peot, 1989; Fung & Chang, 1989). We present this method in the context of our example ID.

First, we present definitions that will allow us to rewrite $V_o(a)$ more clearly. First, let $Z = (S, S')$. Define the *target function* (in our case, the *weighted utilities*)

$$\begin{aligned} g_{a,o}(Z) &= g_{a,o}(S, S') \\ &= P(S)P(S' \mid S, O = o, A = a) \cdot \\ &\quad P(O = o \mid S)U(S, S', O = o, A = a). \end{aligned}$$

Note that $V_o(a) = \sum_Z g_{a,o}(Z)$. Define the *importance function* as

$$f_{a,o}(Z) = P(S)P(S' \mid S, O = o, A = a). \quad (10)$$

Define the *weight function* $\omega_{a,o}(Z) = g_{a,o}(Z)/f_{a,o}(Z)$. Note that in this case,

$$\omega_{a,o}(Z) = P(O = o \mid S)U(S, S', O = o, A = a). \quad (11)$$

Finally, note that $V_o(a) = \sum_Z f_{a,o}(Z)(g_{a,o}(Z)/f_{a,o}(Z))$. The idea of the sampling methods described in this section is to obtain independent samples according to $f_{a,o}$, use those samples to estimate the value of the actions, and finally select an approximately optimal action by taking the action with largest value estimate. Denote the *weight of a sample* $z^{(i)}$ from $Z \sim f_{a,o}$ as $\omega_{a,o}^{(i)} = \omega_{a,o}(z^{(i)})$. Then an unbiased estimate of $V_o(a)$ is $\hat{V}_o(a) = \frac{1}{N_{a,o}} \sum_{i=1}^{N_{a,o}} \omega_{a,o}^{(i)}$.

Traditional Method

We can obtain an estimate of $V_o(a)$ using the straightforward method presented in Algorithm 1; it requires parameters $N_{a,o}$ that will be defined in Theorem 1.

This is the traditional sampling-based method used for action selection. However, we are unaware of any result regarding the number of samples needed to obtain a near-optimal strategy with high probability using this method.

Algorithm 1 Traditional Method

1. Obtain independent samples $z^{(1)}, \ldots, z^{(N_{a,o})}$ from $Z \sim f_{a,o}$.
2. Compute the weights $\omega_{a,o}^{(1)}, \ldots, \omega_{a,o}^{(N_{a,o})}$.
3. Output $\hat{V}_o(a)$ = average of the weights.

Theorem 1 *If for each possible action $i = 1, \ldots, k$, we estimate $V_o(i)$ using the traditional method, the weight function satisfies $l_{i,o} \leq \omega_{i,o}(Z) \leq u_{i,o}$, and the estimate uses*

$$N_{i,o} = \left\lceil \frac{(u_{i,o} - l_{i,o})^2}{2\epsilon^2} \ln \frac{k}{\delta} \right\rceil$$

samples, then the action with the largest value estimate has a true value that is within 2ϵ of the optimal with probability at least $1 - \delta$.

Proof sketch. The proof goes in three basic steps. First, we apply *Hoeffding bounds* (Hoeffding, 1963) to obtain a bound on the probability that each estimate deviates from its true mean by some amount ϵ. Then, we apply the *Bonferroni inequality (Union bound)* to obtain joint bounds on the probability that the difference of each estimate from all the others deviates from the true difference by 2ϵ. Finally, we apply Hsu's single bound lemma to obtain our result.

Note that we can compute $l_{i,o}$ and $u_{i,o}$ efficiently from information local to each node in the graph. Assuming that we have non-negative utilities, we can let

$$u_{i,o} = \left[\prod_{j=1}^{n_3} \max_{\text{Pa}(O_j)} P(O_j \mid \text{Pa}(O_j))|_{O=o}\right]$$
$$\cdot \left[\sum_{j=1}^{m} \max_{\text{Pa}(U_j)} U_j(\text{Pa}(U_j))|_{O=o, A=i}\right], \quad (12)$$

$$l_{i,o} = \left[\prod_{j=1}^{n_3} \min_{\text{Pa}(O_j)} P(O_j \mid \text{Pa}(O_j))|_{O=o}\right]$$
$$\cdot \left[\sum_{j=1}^{m} \min_{\text{Pa}(U_j)} U_j(\text{Pa}(U_j))|_{O=o, A=i}\right]. \quad (13)$$

However, these bounds can be very loose.

Sequential Method

The sequential method tries to reduce the number of samples needed by the traditional method, using ideas from sequential analysis. The idea is to first obtain an estimate of the variance and then use it to compute the number of samples needed to estimate the mean. The method, presented in Algorithm 2, requires parameters $N'_{a,o}$ and $N''_{a,o}$ that will be defined in Theorem 2.

Note that given the sequential nature of the method, the total number of samples is now a random variable. We also note that while multi-stage procedures of this kind are commonly used in the statistical literature, we are only aware of results based on restricting assumptions on the distribution of the random variables (i.e., parametric families like normal and binomial distributions) (Bechhofer, Santner, & Goldsman, 1995).

Theorem 2 *If, for each possible action $i = 1, \ldots, k$, we estimate $V_o(i)$ using the sequential method, the weight func-*

Algorithm 2 Sequential Method

1. Obtain independent samples $z^{(1)}, \ldots, z^{(2N'_{a,o})}$ from $Z \sim f_{a,o}$.
2. Compute the weights $\omega_{a,o}^{(1)}, \ldots, \omega_{a,o}^{(2N'_{a,o})}$.
3. For $j = 1, \ldots, N'_{a,o}$, let $y_j = (\omega_{a,o}^{(2j-1)} - \omega_{a,o}^{(2j)})^2/2$.
4. Compute $\hat{\sigma}_{a,o}^2$ = average of y_j's.
5. Let $N_{a,o} = 2N'_{a,o} + N''_{a,o}(\hat{\sigma}_{a,o}^2)$.
6. Obtain $N''_{a,o}(\hat{\sigma}_{a,o}^2)$ new independent samples $z^{(2N'_{a,o}+1)}, \ldots, z^{(N_{a,o})}$ from $Z \sim f_{a,o}$.
7. Compute the new weights $\omega_{a,o}^{(2N'_{a,o}+1)}, \ldots, \omega_{a,o}^{(N_{a,o})}$.
8. Output $\hat{V}_o(a)$ = average of the new weights.

tion satisfies $l_{i,o} \leq \omega_{i,o}(Z) \leq u_{i,o}$, $\sigma_{i,o}^2 = Var[\omega_{i,o}(Z)]$,

$$N'_{i,o} = \left\lceil \frac{(u_{i,o} - l_{i,o})^{4/3}}{2 \cdot 2^{2/3} \epsilon^{4/3}} \ln \frac{2k}{\delta} \right\rceil,$$

and

$$N''_{i,o}(\hat{\sigma}_{i,o}^2) = \left\lceil \left(\frac{2\hat{\sigma}_{i,o}^2 + 2(u_{i,o} - l_{i,o})\epsilon/3}{\epsilon^2} + 2^{1/3} \frac{(u_{i,o} - l_{i,o})^{4/3}}{\epsilon^{4/3}} \right) \ln \frac{2k}{\delta} \right\rceil,$$

then the action with the largest value estimate has a true value that is within 2ϵ of the optimal with probability at least $1 - \delta$. Also,

$$N_{i,o} < \left(\frac{2\sigma_{i,o}^2 + 2(u_{i,o} - l_{i,o})\epsilon/3}{\epsilon^2} + \frac{5}{2^{2/3}} \frac{(u_{i,o} - l_{i,o})^{4/3}}{\epsilon^{4/3}} \right) \ln \frac{2k}{\delta} + 1$$
$$= O\left(\max\left(\frac{\sigma_{i,o}^2}{\epsilon^2}, \frac{(u_{i,o} - l_{i,o})^{4/3}}{\epsilon^{4/3}} \right) \ln \frac{k}{\delta} \right),$$

with probability at least $1 - \delta/(2k)$, and

$$E[N_{i,o}] = 2N'_{i,o} + N''_{i,o}(\sigma_{i,o}^2)$$
$$= O\left(\max\left(\frac{\sigma_{i,o}^2}{\epsilon^2}, \frac{(u_{i,o} - l_{i,o})^{4/3}}{\epsilon^{4/3}} \right) \ln \frac{k}{\delta} \right).$$

Proof sketch. The only difference from the proof of Theorem 1 is the first step. Instead of using Hoeffding bounds to bound the probability that each estimate deviates from its true mean, we use a combination of *Bernstein's inequality* (as presented by Devroye, Györfi, & Lugosi (1996) and credited to Bernstein (1946)) and Hoeffding bounds as follows. We first use the Hoeffding bound to bound the probability that the estimate of the variance after taking some number of samples $2N'$ deviates from the true variance by some amount ϵ'. We then use Bernstein's inequality to bound the probability that the estimate we obtain after taking some number of samples N'' deviates from its true mean by

ϵ given that the true variance is no larger than our estimate of the variance plus ϵ'. We then find the value of ϵ' (in terms of ϵ) that minimizes the total number of samples $N'' + 2N'$. The results on the number of samples follow by substituting the minimizing ϵ' back into the expressions for N'' and N'. Steps 2 and 3 are as in Theorem 1.

The sequential method is particularly more effective than the traditional method when $\sigma_{i,o}^2 \ll (u_{i,o} - l_{i,o})^2$.

Comparison-based Method

Using the results from MCB, we can compute simultaneous or joint confidence intervals on the difference between the value of $V_o(a)$ and the best of all the others for all actions a. Therefore, MCB allows us to select the best action choice or an action with value close to it, within a confidence level.

In the previous section we presented methods that require that we have estimates with the same precision in order to select a good action. Hsu's multiple-bound lemma applies when we do not have estimates of $V_o(a)$ for each a with the same precision. Based on this result, we propose the method presented in Algorithm 3 for action selection.

Algorithm 3 Comparison-based Method
---
1. Obtain an *initial number of samples* for each action a.
2. Compute *MCB confidence intervals* on the difference in value of each action from the best of the other actions using those samples.

while *not able to select a good action with high certainty* **do**

    3(a). Obtain *additional samples*.

    3(b). Recompute MCB confidence intervals using total samples so far.

We compute the MCB confidence intervals heuristically. To do this, we approximate the precisions that satisfy the conditions required by Hsu's multiple-bound lemma (Equation 8) using Hoeffding bounds (Hoeffding, 1963). Using this approach, for each pair of actions i and j, and values $l_{ij,o}$ and $u_{ij,o}$ such that $l_{ij,o} \leq \omega_{i,o}(Z) \leq u_{ij,o}$ and $l_{ij,o} \leq \omega_{j,o}(Z) \leq u_{ij,o}$, we approximate w_{ij} as

$$w_{ij} = (u_{ij,o} - l_{ij,o})\sqrt{\frac{1}{2}\left(\frac{1}{N_{i,o}} + \frac{1}{N_{j,o}}\right)\ln\frac{k-1}{\delta}}, \quad (14)$$

where $N_{i,o}$ is the number of samples taken for action i thus far. We then use these approximate precisions and the value-difference estimates to compute the MCB confidence intervals (as specified by Equation 9). There are alternative ways of heuristically approximating the precisions but, in this paper, we use the one above for simplicity.

Once we compute the intervals, the stopping condition is as follows. If at least one of the lower bounds of the MCB confidence intervals is greater than -2ϵ, then we stop and select the action that attains this lower bound. Otherwise, we continue taking additional samples.

We define the value of *initial number of samples* in our experiments as 40. When taking additional samples, we use a sampling schedule that is somewhat selective in that it takes more samples from more promising actions as suggested by the MCB confidence intervals. We find the action whose corresponding MCB confidence interval has an upper bound greater than 0 (i.e., from the set $\mathcal{G}$ as defined in Hsu's multiple bound lemma) and whose lower bound is the largest. We take 40 additional samples from this action and 10 from all the others. We understand that these sample sizes are very arbitrary. Potentially, other setting of these sample sizes can be more effective but we did not try to optimize them for our experiments. Algorithm 4 presents a detailed description of the instance of the method we used in the experiments.

Algorithm 4 Algorithmic description of the instance of the comparison-based method used in the experiments.
---
for each observation o **do**

  $l \leftarrow 1$

  for each action $i = 1, \ldots, k$ **do**

    Compute $u_{i,o}$ and $l_{i,o}$ using equations 12 and 13, respectively.

    $D_i^- \leftarrow -\infty; N_{i,o}^{(l)} \leftarrow 40; N_{i,o} \leftarrow 0; \hat{V}_o(i) \leftarrow 0$.

  for each pair of actions (i,j), $i \neq j$ **do**

    $u_{ij,o} \leftarrow \max(u_{i,o}, u_{j,o}); l_{ij,o} \leftarrow \max(l_{i,o}, l_{j,o})$.

  while there is no action i such that $D_i^- > -2\epsilon$ **do**

    for each action i **do**

      Obtain $N_{i,o}^{(l)}$ samples $z^{(N_{i,o}+1)}, \ldots, z^{(N_{i,o}+N_{i,o}^{(l)})}$ from $Z \sim f_{i,o}$, as in equation 10.

      Compute weights $\omega_{i,o}^{(N_{i,o}+1)}, \ldots, \omega_{i,o}^{(N_{i,o}+N_{i,o}^{(l)})}$.

      $\hat{V}_o(i) \leftarrow (N_{i,o}\hat{V}_o(i) + \sum_{j=1}^{N_{i,o}^{(l)}} \omega_{i,o}^{(N_{i,o}+j)})/(N_{i,o} + N_{i,o}^{(l)})$.

      $N_{i,o} \leftarrow N_{i,o} + N_{i,o}^{(l)}$.

    for each pair of actions (i,j), $i \neq j$ **do**

      $T_{ij} \leftarrow \hat{V}_o(i) - \hat{V}_o(j); T_{ji} \leftarrow -T_{ij}$.

      Compute w_{ij} using equation 14; $w_{ji} \leftarrow w_{ij}$.

    for each action i **do**

      Compute D_i^+, $\mathcal{G}$, and D_i^- using Hsu's multiple-bound lemma.

    for each action i **do**

      if $D_i^- == \max_{j \in \mathcal{G}} D_j^-$ **then** $N_{i,o}^{(l+1)} \leftarrow 40$

      else $N_{i,o}^{(l+1)} \leftarrow 10$.

    $l \leftarrow l + 1$.

  $\hat{\pi}(o) \leftarrow \arg\max_i D_i^-$.

Although this method may seem well-grounded, we are not convinced that the bounds hold rigorously. The precisions are correct if the samples obtained so far for each action are independent. However, this might not be the case, since the number of samples gathered on each round depends on a property of the previous set of samples (that is, that the lower-bound condition did not hold). It is not yet clear to us whether the fact that the *number* of samples depends on the values of the samples implies that the samples must be considered dependent.

Related Work

Charnes & Shenoy (1999) present a Monte Carlo method similar to our "traditional method." One difference is that they use a heuristic stopping rule based on a normal approximation (i.e., the estimates have an *asymptotically* normal distribution). Their method takes samples until all the estimates achieve a required standard error to provide the correct confidence interval on each value under the assumption that the estimates are normally distributed and the estimate of the variance is equal to the true variance. They do not give bounds on the number of samples needed to obtain a near-optimal action with the required confidence. We refer the reader to Charnes & Shenoy (1999) for a short description and references on other similar Monte Carlo methods for IDs.

Bielza, Müller, & Insua (1999) present a method based on Markov-Chain Monte Carlo (MCMC) for solving IDs. Although their primary motivation is to handle continuous action spaces, their method also applies to discrete action spaces. Because of the typical complications in analyzing MCMC methods, they do not provide bounds on the number of samples needed. Instead, they use a heuristic stopping rule which does not guarantee the selection of a near-optimal action. Other MCMC-based methods have been proposed (See Bielza, Müller, & Insua (1999) for more information).

Empirical results

We tried the different methods on a simple made-up ID. Given space restrictions we only describe it briefly (See Ortiz (2000) for details). Figure 4 gives a graphical representation of the ID for the *computer mouse problem*. The idea is to select an optimal strategy of whether to *buy* a new mouse ($A = 1$), *upgrade* the operating system ($A = 2$), or take *no action* ($A = 3$). The observation is whether the mouse pointer is working ($MP_t = 1$) or not ($MP_t = 0$). The variables of the problem are the status of the operating system (OS), the status of the driver (D), the status of the mouse hardware (MH), and the status of the mouse pointer (MP), all at the current and future time (subscripted by t and $t+1$). The variables are all binary.

The probabilistic model encodes the following information about the system. The mouse is old and somewhat unreliable. The operating system is reliable. It is very likely that the mouse pointer will not work if either the driver or the mouse hardware has failed. Table 1 shows the utility function $U(MP_{t+1}, A)$ and the values of the actions and observations $V_O(A)$ computed using an exact method. From Table 1 we conclude that the optimal strategy is: buy a new mouse ($A = 1$) if the mouse pointer is not working ($MP_t = 0$); take no action ($A = 3$) if the mouse pointer is working ($MP_t = 1$). This strategy has value 26.50.

Table 2 presents our results on the effectiveness of the sampling methods for this problem. We set our final desired accuracy for the output strategy to $\epsilon^* = 5$ and confidence level $\delta^* = 0.05$. This leads to the individual accuracy $2\epsilon = 2.5$ and confidence level $\delta = 0.025$ for each subproblem. We executed the sequential method and the comparison-based method 100 times. The comparison-

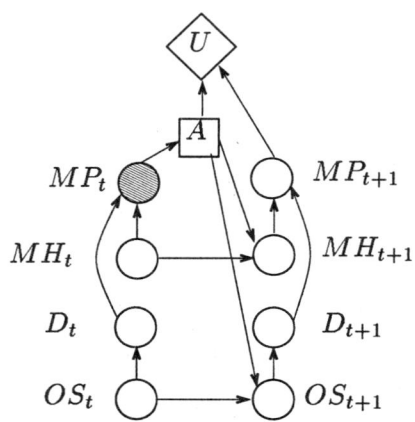

Figure 4: Graphical representation of the ID for the computer mouse problem.

	\multicolumn{2}{c}{U}	\multicolumn{2}{c}{V}
	\multicolumn{2}{c}{MP_{t+1}}	\multicolumn{2}{c}{MP_t}
A	0	1	0	1
1	0	40	**18.20**	6.60
2	5	45	7.54	7.39
3	10	50	10.57	**8.30**

Table 1: This table presents the utility function and the (exact) value of actions and observations for the computer mouse problem.

based method produces major reductions in the number of samples. When we observe the mouse pointer not working, The comparison-based method always selects the optimal action of buying a new mouse. When we observe the mouse pointer working, The comparison-based method failed to select the optimal action of *taking no action* 4 times out of the 100. In those cases, it selected the next-to-optimal action of upgrading the operating system ($A = 2$). This action is within our accuracy requirements since the difference in value with respect to the optimal action is 0.91.

The comparison-based method is highly effective in cases where there is a clear optimal action to take. For instance, in the computer mouse problem, buying a new mouse when we observe the mouse not working is clearly the best option. The differences in value between the optimal action and the rest are not as large as when we observe the mouse working.

In this problem, the results for the sequential method should not fully discourage us from its use, because the variances are still relatively large. We have seen major reductions in problems where the variance is significantly smaller than the square of the range of the variable whose mean we are estimating.

Summary and Conclusion

The methods presented in this paper are an alternative to exact methods. While the running time of exact methods depends on aspects of the structural decomposition of the

A	MP_t	Method		
		Traditional	Sequential	Comp-based
1	0	2403	3802 (188)	335 (151)
2	0	3007	2266 (142)	115 (37)
3	0	3679	2426 (129)	118 (39)
1	1	2213	2508 (178)	521 (216)
2	1	2794	2969 (201)	695 (421)
3	1	3443	3468 (202)	1361 (560)
Total		17539	17438 (434)	**3145** (809)

Table 2: Number of samples taken by the different methods for each action and observation. For the sequential and the comparison-based methods, the table displays the average number of samples over 100 runs. The values in parenthesis are the sample standard deviations.

ID, the running time of the methods presented in this paper depends primarily on the range of the weight functions, the variance of the value estimators and the amount of separation between the value of the best action and that of the rest (in addition to the natural dependency on the number of action choices, and the precision and confidence parameters). In some cases, we can know in advance whether they will be faster or not. The methods presented in this paper can be a useful alternative in those cases where exact methods are intractable. How useful depends on the particular characteristics of the problem.

Sampling is a promising tool for action selection. Our empirical results on a small ID suggest that sampling methods for action selection are more effective when they take advantage of the intuition that action selection is primarily a comparison task. We look forward to experimenting with IDs large enough that sampling methods are the only potentially efficient alternative. Also, our work leads to the study of adaptive sampling as a way to improve the effectiveness of sampling methods (Ortiz & Kaelbling, 2000).

Acknowledgments We would like to thank Constantine Gatsonis for suggesting the MCB literature; Eli Upfal, Milos Hauskrecht, Thomas Hofmann, Thomas Dean and Kee Eung Kim for useful discussions and suggestions; and the anonymous reviewers for their useful comments. Our implementations use the *Bayes Net Toolbox for Matlab* (Murphy, 1999), for which we thank Kevin Murphy. Luis E. Ortiz was supported in part by an NSF Graduate Fellowship and by NSF IGERT award SBR 9870676. Leslie Pack Kaelbling was supported in part by a grant from NTT and by DARPA Contract #DABT 63-99-1-0012.

References

Bechhofer, R. E.; Santner, T. J.; and Goldsman, D. M. 1995. *Design and analysis of experiments for statistical selection, screening and multiple comparisons.* Wiley.

Bernstein, S. 1946. *The Theory of Probabilities.* Gastehizdat Publishing House, Moscow.

Bielza, C.; Müller, P.; and Insua, D. R. 1999. Monte Carlo methods for decision analysis with applications to influence diagrams. *Management Science.* Forthcoming.

Chang, J. Y., and Hsu, J. C. 1992. Optimal designs for multiple comparisons with the best. *Journal of Statistical Planning and Inference* 30:45–62.

Charnes, J. M., and Shenoy, P. P. 1999. A forward Monte Carlo method for solving Influence diagrams using local computation. School of Business, University of Kansas, Working Paper No. 273.

Devroye, L.; Györfi, L.; and Lugosi, G. 1996. *A Probabilistic Theory of Pattern Recognition.* Springer.

Fung, R., and Chang, K.-C. 1989. Weighting and integrating evidence for stochastic simulation in Bayesian networks. In *Proceedings of the Fifth Workshop on Uncertainty in Artificial Intelligence*, 112–117.

Geweke, J. 1989. Bayesian inference in econometric models using Monte Carlo integration. *Econometrica* 57(6):1317–1339.

Hoeffding, W. 1963. Probability inequalities for sums of bounded random variables. *Journal of the American Statistical Association* 58(301):13–30.

Hsu, J. C. 1981. Simultaneous confidence intervals for all distances from the "best". *Annals of Statistics* 9(5):1026–1034.

Hsu, J. C. 1996. *Multiple Comparisons: Theory and Methods.* Chapman and Hall.

Jensen, F. V. 1996. *An Introduction to Bayesian Networks.* UCL Press.

Kearns, M.; Mansour, Y.; and Ng, A. Y. 1999. A sparse sampling algorithm for near-optimal planning in large Markov decision processes. In *Proceedings of the Sixteenth International Joint Conference on Artificial Intelligence*, 1324–1331. Menlo Park, Calif.: International Joint Conference on Artificial Intelligence, Inc.

Matejcik, F. J., and Nelson, B. L. 1995. Two-stage multiple comparisons with the best for computer simulation. *Operations Research* 43(4):633–640.

Murphy, K. P. 1999. Bayes net toolbox for Matlab. Available from http://www.cs.berkeley.edu/~murphyk/Bayes/bnt.html.

Ortiz, L. E., and Kaelbling, L. P. 2000. Adaptive importance sampling for estimation in structured domains. Under review.

Ortiz, L. E. 2000. Selecting approximately-optimal actions in complex structured domains. Technical Report CS-00-05, Computer Science Department, Brown University.

Shachter, R. D., and Peot, M. A. 1989. Simulation approaches to general probabilistic inference on belief networks. In *Proceedings of the Fifth Workshop on Uncertainty in Artificial Intelligence*, 311–318.

Answering Queries Using Views over Description Logics Knowledge Bases

Diego Calvanese, Giuseppe De Giacomo, Maurizio Lenzerini

Dipartimento di Informatica e Sistemistica
Università di Roma "La Sapienza"
Via Salaria 113, 00198 Roma, Italy
{calvanese,degiacomo,lenzerini}@dis.uniroma1.it

Abstract

Answering queries using views amounts to computing the answer to a query having information only on the extension of a set of precomputed queries (views). This problem is relevant in several fields, such as information integration, query optimization, and data warehousing, and has been studied recently in different settings. In this paper we address answering queries using views in a setting where intensional knowledge about the domain is represented using a very expressive Description Logic equipped with n-ary relations, and queries are nonrecursive datalog queries whose predicates are the concepts and relations that appear in the Description Logic knowledge base. We study the problem under different assumptions, namely, closed and open domain, and sound, complete, and exact information on view extensions. We show that under the closed domain assumption, in which the set of all objects in the knowledge base coincides with the set of objects stored in the views, answering queries using views is already intractable. We show also that under the open domain assumption the problem is decidable in double exponential time.

Introduction

Answering queries using views amounts to computing the answer to a query having information only on the extension of a set of views (Abiteboul & Duschka 1998; Grahne & Mendelzon 1999). This problem is relevant in several fields, such as information integration (Ullman 1997), data warehousing (Widom 1995), query optimization (Chaudhuri *et al.* 1995), etc. Data integration is perhaps the obvious setting where query answering using views is important: a typical integration process results in a set of precomputed views, and the query evaluation mechanism can only rely on such views in order to derive correct answers to queries. Previous work on answering queries using views does not allow for the possibility to take into account intensional knowledge about the domain, or considers only restricted ways to express such knowledge (Rousset 1999).

In this paper we address the problem of answering queries using views for non-recursive datalog queries embedded in a knowledge base expressed in an expressive Description Logic (DL). Our goal is to study the computational complexity of the problem, under different assumptions, namely,

Copyright © 2000, American Association for Artificial Intelligence (www.aaai.org). All rights reserved.

closed and open domain, and sound, complete, and exact information on view extensions. Such assumptions have been used in data integration with the following meaning. The *closed domain assumption* states that the set of all objects in the domain coincides with the set of objects explicitly mentioned in the knowledge base (in databases, typically the set of objects in the view extensions). On the contrary, the *open domain assumption* leaves the possibility open that other objects besides those mentioned in the knowledge base exist in the domain. With regard to the assumptions on views, a *sound view* corresponds to an information source which is known to produce only, but not necessarily all, the answers to the associated query. A *complete view* models a source which is known to produce all answers to the associated query, and maybe more. Finally, an *exact view* is known to produce exactly the answers to the associated query.

In this paper we consider query answering using views in the following framework:

- Domain knowledge is expressed in terms of a knowledge base constituted by general inclusion assertions and membership assertions, formulated in an expressive DL which includes n-ary relations and qualified number restrictions (Calvanese, De Giacomo, & Lenzerini 1998).

- Queries and views are expressed as non-recursive datalog programs, whose predicates in the body are concepts or relations that appear in the knowledge base.

- It can be specified whether the domain is open or closed, and for each view, whether the provided extension is sound, complete, or exact.

Observe that the DL considered is capable to capture formally Conceptual Data Models typically used in databases (Hull & King 1987; ElMasri & Navathe 1988), such as the Entity-Relationship Model (Chen 1976). Hence, in our setting, query answering using views is done under the constraints imposed by the conceptual data model.

We present the following results for the described setting: Query answering using views is decidable in all cases. Moreover, under the closed domain assumption, the problem is in Δ_3^P and is coNP-complete in data complexity, whereas under the open domain assumption it is in 2EXPTIME.

Answering queries using views is tightly related to query rewriting (Levy *et al.* 1995; Duschka & Genesereth 1997; Ullman 1997). In particular, (Beeri, Levy, & Rousset 1997) studies rewriting of conjunctive queries using conjunctive views whose atoms are DL concepts or roles. In general, a *rewriting* of a query with respect to a set of views is a function that, given the extensions of the views, returns a set of tuples that is contained in the answer set of the query with respect to the views. Usually, one fixes a priori the language in which to express rewritings (e.g., unions of conjunctive queries), and then looks for the best possible rewriting expressible in such a language. On the other hand, we may call *perfect* a rewriting that returns exactly the answer set of the query with respect to the views, independently of the language in which it is expressed. Hence, if an algorithm for answering queries using views exists, it can be viewed as a perfect rewriting. The results in this paper show the existence of perfect, and hence maximal, rewritings in a setting generalizing that in (Beeri, Levy, & Rousset 1997), which was a question left open in that paper.

Description Logic $\mathcal{DLR}$

To specify knowledge bases and queries we use the Description Logic $\mathcal{DLR}$ (Calvanese, De Giacomo, & Lenzerini 1998). The basic elements of $\mathcal{DLR}$ are *concepts* (unary relations), and *n-ary relations*. We assume to deal with a finite set of atomic relations, atomic concepts, and *constants*, denoted by P, A and a, respectively. We use R to denote arbitrary relations (of given arity between 2 and n_{max}), and C to denote arbitrary concepts, respectively built according to the following syntax:

$$R ::= \top_n \mid P \mid \$i/n:C \mid \neg R \mid R_1 \sqcap R_2$$
$$C ::= \top_1 \mid A \mid \neg C \mid C_1 \sqcap C_2 \mid \exists[\$i]R \mid (\leq k\,[\$i]R)$$

where i denotes a component of a relation, i.e., an integer between 1 and n_{max}, n denotes the *arity* of a relation, i.e., an integer between 2 and n_{max}, and k denotes a nonnegative integer. We use the usual abbreviations, in particular $C_1 \sqcup C_2$ for $\neg(\neg C_1 \sqcap \neg C_2)$, $C_1 \Rightarrow C_2$ for $\neg C_1 \sqcup C_2$, and $C_1 \equiv C_2$ for $(C_1 \Rightarrow C_2) \sqcap (C_2 \Rightarrow C_1)$.

We consider only concepts and relations that are *well-typed*, which means that (i) only relations of the same arity n are combined to form expressions of type $R_1 \sqcap R_2$ (which inherit the arity n), and (ii) $i \leq n$ whenever i denotes a component of a relation of arity n.

A $\mathcal{DLR}$ *knowledge base* (KB) is constituted by a finite set of *assertions*, where each assertion has one of the forms:

$$R_1 \sqsubseteq R_2, \quad C_1 \sqsubseteq C_2, \quad C(a), \quad R(a_1,\ldots,a_n)$$

where R_1 and R_2 are of the same arity, and R has arity n.

The semantics of $\mathcal{DLR}$ is specified as follows. An *interpretation* $\mathcal{I}$ of a KB is constituted by an *interpretation domain* $\Delta^{\mathcal{I}}$, and an *interpretation function* $\cdot^{\mathcal{I}}$ that assigns to each constant an element of $\Delta^{\mathcal{I}}$ under the unique name assumption, to each concept C a subset $C^{\mathcal{I}}$ of $\Delta^{\mathcal{I}}$, and to each relation R of arity n a subset $R^{\mathcal{I}}$ of $(\Delta^{\mathcal{I}})^n$, such that the conditions in Figure 1 are satisfied. Observe that, the "$\neg$" constructor on relations is used to express difference of relations, and not the complement (Calvanese, De Giacomo, & Lenzerini 1998). We assume that $\Delta^{\mathcal{I}}$ is a subset of a fixed infinitely countable domain Δ. To simplify the notation we do not distinguish between constants and their interpretations.

An interpretation $\mathcal{I}$ *satisfies* an assertion $R_1 \sqsubseteq R_2$ (resp. $C_1 \sqsubseteq C_2$) if $R_1^{\mathcal{I}} \subseteq R_2^{\mathcal{I}}$ (resp. $C_1^{\mathcal{I}} \subseteq C_2^{\mathcal{I}}$), and satisfies an assertion $C(a)$ (resp., $R(a_1,\ldots,a_n)$) if $a \in C^{\mathcal{I}}$ (resp., $(a_1,\ldots,a_n) \in R^{\mathcal{I}}$). An interpretation that satisfies all assertions in a KB $\mathcal{K}$ is called a *model* of $\mathcal{K}$.

A *query* Q is a non-recursive datalog query of the form

$$Q(\vec{x}) \leftarrow body_1(\vec{x}, \vec{y}_1) \vee \cdots \vee body_m(\vec{x}, \vec{y}_m)$$

where each $body_i(\vec{x}, \vec{y}_i)$ is a conjunction of *atoms*, and $\vec{x}$, $\vec{y}_i$ are all the variables appearing in the conjunct. Each atom has one of the forms $R(\vec{t})$ or $C(t)$, where $\vec{t}$ and t are variables in $\vec{x}$ and $\vec{y}_i$ or objects of the knowledge base, and R, C are relations and concepts, respectively. The number of variables of $\vec{x}$ is called the *arity* of Q, and is the arity of the relation denoted by the query Q.

We observe that the atoms in the queries are arbitrary $\mathcal{DLR}$ relations and concepts, freely used in the assertions of the KB. This distinguishes our approach with respect to (Donini *et al.* 1998; Levy & Rousset 1996), where no constraints on the relations that appear in the queries can be expressed in the KB.

Given an interpretation $\mathcal{I}$ of a KB, a query Q of arity n is interpreted as the set $Q^{\mathcal{I}}$ of n-tuples $(o_1,\ldots,o_n)$, with each $o_i \in \Delta^{\mathcal{I}}$, such that, when substituting each o_i for x_i, the formula

$$\exists \vec{y}_1.body_1(\vec{x}, \vec{y}_1) \vee \cdots \vee \exists \vec{y}_m.body_m(\vec{x}, \vec{y}_m)$$

evaluates to true in $\mathcal{I}$.

We observe that $\mathcal{DLR}$ is able to capture a great variety of data models with many forms of constraints (Calvanese, Lenzerini, & Nardi 1998; Calvanese, De Giacomo, & Lenzerini 1998). Logical implication (checking whether a given assertion logically follows from a KB) in $\mathcal{DLR}$ is EXPTIME-complete, and query containment (checking whether one query is contained in another one in every model of a KB) is EXPTIME-hard and solvable in 2EXPTIME (Calvanese, De Giacomo, & Lenzerini 1998).

Answering queries using views in $\mathcal{DLR}$

Consider a KB $\mathcal{K}$, and suppose we want to answer a query Q only on the basis of our knowledge about the extension of a set of views $\mathcal{V} = \{V_1,\ldots,V_m\}$. Associated to each view V_i we have:

- A definition $def(V_i)$ in terms of a query $V_i(\vec{x}) \leftarrow v_i(\vec{x}, \vec{y})$ over $\mathcal{K}$.

- A set $ext(V_i)$ of tuples of objects (whose arity is the same as that of V_i) which provides the information about the extension of V_i. We assume without loss of generality that such objects already appear in the KB.

- A specification $as(V_i)$ of which *assumption* to adopt for the view V_i, i.e., how to interpret $ext(V_i)$ with respect to the actual set of tuples that satisfy V_i. We describe below the various possibilities that we consider for $as(V_i)$.

As pointed out in several papers (Abiteboul & Duschka 1998; Grahne & Mendelzon 1999; Levy 1996; Calvanese *et al.* 2000), the above problem comes in different forms,

$$
\begin{array}{rcl}
\top_n^\mathcal{I} & \subseteq & (\Delta^\mathcal{I})^n \\
P^\mathcal{I} & \subseteq & \top_n^\mathcal{I} \\
\$i/n : C^\mathcal{I} & = & \{(d_1,\ldots,d_n) \in \top_n^\mathcal{I} \mid d_i \in C^\mathcal{I}\} \\
(\neg R)^\mathcal{I} & = & \top_n^\mathcal{I} \setminus R^\mathcal{I} \\
(R_1 \sqcap R_2)^\mathcal{I} & = & R_1^\mathcal{I} \cap R_2^\mathcal{I}
\end{array}
\qquad
\begin{array}{rcl}
\top_1^\mathcal{I} & = & \Delta^\mathcal{I} \\
A^\mathcal{I} & \subseteq & \Delta^\mathcal{I} \\
(\neg C)^\mathcal{I} & = & \Delta^\mathcal{I} \setminus C^\mathcal{I} \\
(C_1 \sqcap C_2)^\mathcal{I} & = & C_1^\mathcal{I} \cap C_2^\mathcal{I} \\
(\exists[\$i]R)^\mathcal{I} & = & \{d \in \Delta^\mathcal{I} \mid \exists (d_1,\ldots,d_n) \in R^\mathcal{I}. d_i = d\} \\
(\leq k\,[\$i]R)^\mathcal{I} & = & \{d \in \Delta^\mathcal{I} \mid \sharp\{(d_1,\ldots,d_n) \in R_1^\mathcal{I} \mid d_i = d\} \leq k\}
\end{array}
$$

Figure 1: Semantic rules for $\mathcal{DLR}$ (P, R, R_1, and R_2 have arity n)

depending on various assumptions about how accurate is the knowledge on both the objects of the KB, and the pairs satisfying the views. With respect to the knowledge about the objects, we distinguish between:

- *Closed Domain Assumption.* The exact set of objects in the domain of interpretation is known, and coincides with the set of objects that appear in the KB. Formally, an interpretation $\mathcal{I}$ of a KB *satisfies the closed domain assumption,* if $\Delta^\mathcal{I}$ coincides with the set of objects in the KB.

- *Open Domain Assumption.* Only a subset of the objects in the domain of interpretation is known. Formally, an interpretation $\mathcal{I}$ of a KB *satisfies the open domain assumption,* if $\Delta^\mathcal{I}$ includes the set of objects in the KB. Notice that this is the usual assumption in DLs.

With regard to the knowledge about the views, we consider the following three assumptions:

- *Sound Views.* When a view V_i is *sound*, from the fact that a tuple is in $ext(V_i)$ one can conclude that it satisfies the view, while from the fact that a tuple is not in $ext(V_i)$ one cannot conclude that it does not satisfy the view. Formally, an interpretation $\mathcal{I}$ of a KB is *a model of a sound view* V_i if $ext(V_i) \subseteq def(V_i)^\mathcal{I}$.

- *Complete Views.* When a view V_i is *complete*, from the fact that a tuple is in $ext(V_i)$ one cannot conclude that such a tuple satisfies the view. On the other hand, from the fact that a tuple is not in $ext(V_i)$ one can conclude that such a tuple does not satisfy the view. Formally, an interpretation $\mathcal{I}$ of a KB is *a model of a complete view* V_i if $ext(V_i) \supseteq def(V_i)^\mathcal{I}$.

- *Exact Views.* When a view V_i is *exact*, the extension of the view is exactly the set of tuples of objects that satisfy the view. Formally, an interpretation $\mathcal{I}$ of a KB is *a model of an exact view* V_i if $ext(V_i) = def(V_i)^\mathcal{I}$.

The problem of *answering queries using views under the open (resp., closded) domain assumption in $\mathcal{DLR}$* is the following: Given

- a KB $\mathcal{K}$,

- a set of views $\mathcal{V} = \{V_1,\ldots,V_m\}$, with, for each V_i, its definition $def(V_i)$, its extension $ext(V_i)$, and the specification of whether it is sound, complete, or exact,

- a query Q of arity n, and a tuple $\vec{d} = (d_1,\ldots,d_n)$ of objects in the KB,

decide whether $\vec{d} \in ans(Q,\mathcal{K},\mathcal{V})$, i.e., decide whether $(d_1,\ldots,d_n) \in Q^\mathcal{I}$, for each $\mathcal{I}$ such that: (i) $\mathcal{I}$ satisfies the open (resp., closed) domain assumption; (ii) $\mathcal{I}$ is a model of $\mathcal{K}$; (iii) $\mathcal{I}$ is a model of $V_1,\ldots,V_m$.

Next we study answering queries using views in $\mathcal{DLR}$, both under the closed and under the open domain assumption.

Closed domain assumption

We start our investigation by considering the closed domain assumption.

We first focus on *data complexity*, i.e., we consider as the only parameter in input the number of objects in the KB (while considering the query and view definitions fixed). By a reduction from graph-3-colorability (known to be NP-complete) analogous to the one in (Calvanese *et al.* 2000), we can show that answering queries using views under the closed domain assumption is coNP-hard in data complexity. Moreover, considering that under the closed domain assumption the number of possible interpretations of the KB is finite, to solve answering queries using views, we can guess an interpretation, check if it is a model of the KB and the views, and evaluate the query. This yields an algorithm, NP in data complexity, that checks whether a tuple is not in the answer to the query.

Theorem 1 *Answering queries using views under the closed domain assumption in $\mathcal{DLR}$ is coNP-complete in data complexity.*

Next we consider queries and views that are *simple*, i.e., are an atom of the form $R(\vec{x})$ or $C(x)$, where R (resp., C) is a (possibly complex) $\mathcal{DLR}$ relation (resp., $\mathcal{DLR}$ concept). Under the assumption that the maximal arity of relations is fixed, and exploiting the results in (Schild 1995), it is possible to show that evaluating a $\mathcal{DLR}$ relation (or concept) over an interpretation is polynomial both in the size of the interpretation and the size of the relation (or concept) itself. Hence, checking whether an interpretation is a model of the KB and a model of the simple views, and checking whether a tuple of objects is in the query, can be done in polynomial time. We obtain the following result.

Theorem 2 *Answering queries using views under the closed domain assumption in $\mathcal{DLR}$ is coNP-complete, in the case where the query and all views are simple, and under the assumption that the maximal arity of relations is fixed.*

Finally, in the general case, where queries and views are non-recursive datalog queries, once the relations and concepts appearing as atoms in queries and views are evaluated, checking whether an interpretation is a model of all views, and whether a tuple is in the answer to the query, requires $O(m)$ (where m is the number of views) calls to an NP or coNP oracle (Cosmadakis 1983). Hence, considering the need to first guess the interpretation, we obtain the following result.

Theorem 3 *Answering queries using views under the closed domain assumption in $\mathcal{DLR}$ is in Δ_3^P, under the assumption that the maximal arity of relations is fixed.*

Open domain assumption

Let us now consider the case of the open domain assumption. In this case we reduce the problem of checking whether a tuple $\vec{d}$ of objects is in $ans(Q, \mathcal{K}, \mathcal{V})$ to the problem of checking the unsatisfiability of a concept in the DL $\mathcal{CIQ}$ (De Giacomo & Lenzerini 1996). $\mathcal{CIQ}$ can be seen as the DL obtained from $\mathcal{DLR}$ by restricting relations to be binary (*roles* and *inverse roles*) and allowing for complex roles corresponding to regular expressions. The reduction is done in three steps.

Encoding of view extensions by means of special assertions.

For each *view* $V \in \mathcal{V}$, with $def(V) = V(\vec{x}) \leftarrow v(\vec{x}, \vec{y})$ and $ext(V) = \{\vec{a}_1, \ldots, \vec{a}_k\}$, we introduce special assertions as follows.

- If V is *sound*, then for each tuple $\vec{a}_i$, $1 \leq i \leq k$, we include the existentially quantified assertion:

$$\exists \vec{y}.v(\vec{a}_i, \vec{y})$$

- If V is *complete*, then we include the universally quantified assertion:

$$\forall \vec{x}.\forall \vec{y}.((\vec{x} \neq \vec{a}_1 \wedge \cdots \wedge \vec{x} \neq \vec{a}_k) \rightarrow \neg v(\vec{x}, \vec{y}))$$

- If V is *exact*, then, according to the definition, we treat it as a view that is both sound and complete.

Finally, since we are checking whether $\vec{d}$ is an answer of Q, we are interested in the negation of the query Q instantiated on $\vec{d}$. Hence we include the universally quantified assertion

$$\forall \vec{y}.\neg q(\vec{d}, \vec{y})$$

where $q(\vec{x}, \vec{y})$ is the right hand part of Q.

The newly introduced assertions are not yet expressed in a DL. The next step is to translate them in a DL, namely $\mathcal{CIQ}$ extended with object-names.

Translation into a $\mathcal{CIQ}$ concept.

We translate $\mathcal{K}$ and each of the assertions introduced in the previous step into a single concept in $\mathcal{CIQ}$ plus *object-names*. Object-names are concepts that are satisfied by a single object in each model. Observe that we do not require object-names to be disjoint by default (i.e, we do not make the unique name assumption on them), but disjointness can be explicitly enforced when needed. In order to obtain the translation we proceed as follows.

- We eliminate n-ary relations by means of *reification*, i.e., we represent each n-ary relation by a concept with n functional roles $f_1, \ldots, f_n$, one for each component of the relation (De Giacomo & Lenzerini 1995).

- We reformulate inclusion and membership assertions in $\mathcal{K}$ as concepts, by exploiting reflexive-transitive closure (Schild 1991), and by reexpressing objects as object-names (De Giacomo & Lenzerini 1996). Observe that we need to explicitly enforce disjointness between the object names corresponding to different objects.

- We translate each existentially quantified assertion

$$\exists \vec{y}.v(\vec{a}, \vec{y})$$

by treating every existentially quantified variable as a new object-name (skolem constant). Specifically:

  - An atom $C(t)$, where C is a concept and t is a term (either an object or a skolem constant), is translated to

$$\forall U.(N_t \Rightarrow \sigma(C))$$

  where $\sigma(C)$ is the reified counterpart of C, N_t is an object-name corresponding to t, and U is the reflexive-transitive closure of all roles and inverse roles introduced in the reification.

  - An atom $R(\vec{t})$, where R is a relation and $\vec{t} = (t_1, \ldots, t_n)$ is a tuple of terms, is translated to the conjunction of the following concepts:

$$\forall U.(N_{\vec{t}} \Rightarrow \sigma(R))$$

  where $\sigma(R)$ is the reified counterpart of R and $N_{\vec{t}}$ is an object-name corresponding to $\vec{t}$,

$$\forall U.(N_{\vec{t}} \equiv \exists f_1.N_{t_1} \sqcap \cdots \sqcap \exists f_n.N_{t_n})$$

  and for each i, $1 \leq i \leq n$, a concept

$$\forall U.(N_{t_i} \Rightarrow (\exists f_i^-.N_{\vec{t}} \sqcap (\leq 1\, f_i^-.N_{\vec{t}})))$$

  Then, the translations of the atoms are combined as in $v(\vec{a}, \vec{y})$.

- It remains to translate universally quantified assertions corresponding to the complete views and the query. We focus on complete views, i.e., on assertions of the form

$$\forall \vec{x}.\forall \vec{y}.((\vec{x} \neq \vec{a}_1 \wedge \cdots \wedge \vec{x} \neq \vec{a}_k) \rightarrow \neg v(\vec{x}, \vec{y}))$$

since the assertion corresponding to the query has the same form, except that the antecedent is empty.

In fact, it is easy to see that it is sufficient to deal with assertions of the form

$$\forall \vec{x}.\forall \vec{y}.((\vec{x} \neq \vec{a}_1 \wedge \cdots \wedge \vec{x} \neq \vec{a}_k) \rightarrow \neg body(\vec{x}, \vec{y}))$$

Following (Calvanese, De Giacomo, & Lenzerini 1998) we construct for $body(\vec{x}, \vec{y})$ a special graph, called *tuple-graph*, which reflects the dependencies between variables. Specifically, the tuple-graph is used to detect cyclic dependencies. In general, the tuple-graph is composed of $\ell \geq 1$ connected components. For the i-th connected component we build a $\mathcal{CIQ}$ concept $\delta_i(\vec{x}, \vec{y})$ as in (Calvanese, De Giacomo, & Lenzerini 1998). Such a concept contains newly introduced concepts A_x and A_y, one for each x in $\vec{x}$ and y in $\vec{y}$. We have to treat variables in $\vec{x}$ and $\vec{y}$ that occur in a cycle in the tuple-graph differently from those outside of cycles. Let $\vec{x}_c$ (resp., $\vec{y}_c$) denote the variables in $\vec{x}$ (resp., $\vec{y}$) that occur in a cycle, and $\vec{x}_l$ (resp., $\vec{y}_l$) those that do not occur in cycles. Consider the concept

$$C[\vec{x}_c/\vec{s}, \vec{y}_c/\vec{t}]$$

obtained from

$$(\forall U.\neg \delta_1(\vec{x},\vec{y})) \sqcup \cdots \sqcup (\forall U.\neg \delta_\ell(\vec{x},\vec{y}))$$

as follows:

- for each variable x_i in $\vec{x}_c$ (resp., y_i in $\vec{y}_c$), the concept A_{x_i} (resp., A_{y_i}) is replaced by N_{s_i} (resp., N_{t_i});
- for each variable y in $\vec{y}_l$, the concept A_y is replaced by $\top$.

The concept corresponding to the universally quantified assertion is the conjunction of:

- $\forall U.C_{\vec{x}_l}$, where $C_{\vec{x}_l}$ is obtained from $\vec{x} \neq \vec{a}_1 \wedge \cdots \wedge \vec{x} \neq \vec{a}_k$ by replacing each $x \neq a$ with $X \equiv \neg N_a$. Observe that $(x_1, \ldots, x_n) \neq (a_1, \ldots, a_n)$ is an abbreviation for $x_1 \neq a_1 \vee \cdots \vee x_n \neq a_n$.
- One concept $C[\vec{x}_c/\vec{s}, \vec{y}_c/\vec{t}]$ for each possible instantiation of $\vec{s}$ and $\vec{t}$ with the object-names corresponding to the objects in $\mathcal{K}$, with the proviso that $\vec{s}$ cannot coincide with any of the $\vec{a}_i$, for $1 \leq i \leq k$ (notice that the proviso applies only in the case where all variables in $\vec{x}$ occur in a cycle in the tuple-graph).

The critical point in the above construction is how to express a universally quantified assertion

$$\forall \vec{x}.\forall \vec{y}.((\vec{x} \neq \vec{a}_1 \wedge \cdots \wedge \vec{x} \neq \vec{a}_k) \to \neg body(\vec{x},\vec{y}))$$

If there are no cycles in the corresponding tuple-graph, then we can directly translate the assertion into a $\mathcal{CIQ}$ concept. As shown in the construction above, dealing with a nonempty antecedent requires some special care to correctly encode the exceptions to the universal rule. Instead, if there is a cycle, due to the fundamental inability of $\mathcal{CIQ}$ to express that two role sequences meet in the same object, no $\mathcal{CIQ}$ concept can directly express the universal assertion. The same inability, however, is shared by $\mathcal{DLR}$. Hence we can assume that the only cycles present in a model are those formed by the objects in the KB. And these are taken care of by the explicit instantiation.

Encoding of object-names.

As the last step to obtain a $\mathcal{CIQ}$ concept, we need to encode object-names in $\mathcal{CIQ}$. To do so we can exploit the construction used in (De Giacomo & Lenzerini 1996) to encode $\mathcal{CIQ}$-ABoxes as concepts. Such a construction applies to the current case without any need of major adaptation. To this point it is crucial to observe that the translation above uses object-names in order to form a sort of disjunction of ABoxes (cfr. (Horrocks et al. 1999)).

Theorem 4 *Let C_{qa} be the $\mathcal{CIQ}$ concept obtained by the construction above. Then $\vec{d} \in ans(Q, \mathcal{K}, \mathcal{V})$ if and only if C_{qa} is unsatisfiable.*

The size of C_{qa} is polynomial in the size of the query, of the view definitions, and of the inclusion assertions in $\mathcal{K}$, and is at most exponential in the number of objects of $\mathcal{K}$. The exponential blow-up is due to the number of instantiations of $C[\vec{x}_c/\vec{s}, \vec{y}_c/\vec{t}]$ with objects of $\mathcal{K}$ that are needed to capture universally quantified assertions. Hence, considering EXPTIME-completeness of satisfiability in $\mathcal{DLR}$ and in $\mathcal{CIQ}$, we get the following result.

Theorem 5 *Answering queries using views under the open domain assumption in $\mathcal{DLR}$ is EXPTIME-hard and can be done in 2EXPTIME.*

Interestingly, when the query, all complete views, and all exact views are simple, the construction above does not require the instantiation that gives rise to the exponential blow-up.

Theorem 6 *Answering queries using views under the open domain assumption in $\mathcal{DLR}$ is EXPTIME-complete, in the case where the query, all complete views, and all exact views are simple.*

Discussion

We stress that answering queries using views under the open domain assumption is essentially an extended form of a familiar reasoning service for DLs, namely *instance checking*, where from a partial knowledge about the extensions of concepts and relations, i.e., the ABox, one wants to establish if a given individual (tuple of individuals) is in the extension of a concept (relation). The first additional aspect introduced by answering queries using views is due to the fact that the query is of a more general form than a single concept or relation. In particular, it contains existentially quantified variables, which introduce universal quantification when the problem is reduced to satisfiability. The second additional aspect is the presence of the views, which introduce additional incomplete information.

Dealing only with the first aspect gives rise to the problem of *query answering (over a KB)*, i.e., given a KB (constituted by a TBox and an ABox), a (non-recursive datalog) query, and a tuple of objects, check whether the tuple satisfies the query in every model of the KB. If we apply the construction presented for the open domain assumption to the case where no views are present, we get a solution to query answering. The resulting algorithm has the same computational complexity as the one for answering queries using views. This is due to the fact that the essential difficulty of dealing with universal quantification is already present in this case.

Finally, we observe that, to compute the whole set $ans(Q, \mathcal{K}, \mathcal{V})$, we need to run the algorithm presented above once for each possible tuple (of the arity of Q) of objects in $\mathcal{K}$. Since we are dealing with incomplete information in a rich language, we should not expect to do much better than considering each tuple of objects separately. Indeed, in such a setting reasoning on objects, such as query answering, requires sophisticated forms of logical inference. In particular, verifying whether a certain tuple belongs to a query gives rise to a line of reasoning which may depend on the tuple under consideration, and which may vary substantially from one tuple to another. For simple languages we may indeed avoid considering tuples individually, as shown in (Rousset 1999) for query answering in KBs expressed using the DL $\mathcal{ALN}$ without cyclic TBox assertions. Observe, however, that for such a DL, reasoning on objects is polynomial in both data and expression complexity (Lenzerini & Schaerf 1991; Schaerf 1994), and does not require sophisticated forms of inference.

Conclusions

We have studied query answering using views for non-recursive datalog queries embedded in a $\mathcal{DLR}$ knowledge base. We have considered different assumptions on the view extensions (sound, complete, and exact) and on our knowledge of the domain (closed and open domain assumptions). We have shown decidability and established upper and lower bounds for the computational complexity of the problem under the different assumptions. It remains open to close the gap between the known upper and lower bounds.

We have seen in the introduction that an algorithm for answering queries using views is in fact a perfect rewriting. However, it remains open to find perfect rewritings expressed in a more declarative query language. Moreover it is of interest to find maximal rewritings belonging to well behaved query languages, in particular, languages with polynomial data complexity. Observe that from the coNP-hardness of data complexity already under the closed domain assumption, rewritings expressed in such a language cannot be perfect.

References

Abiteboul, S., and Duschka, O. 1998. Complexity of answering queries using materialized views. In *Proc. of PODS'98*, 254–265.

Beeri, C.; Levy, A. Y.; and Rousset, M.-C. 1997. Rewriting queries using views in description logics. In *Proc. of PODS'97*, 99–108.

Calvanese, D.; De Giacomo, G.; Lenzerini, M.; and Vardi, M. Y. 2000. Answering regular path queries using views. In *Proc. of ICDE 2000*, 389–398.

Calvanese, D.; De Giacomo, G.; and Lenzerini, M. 1998. On the decidability of query containment under constraints. In *Proc. of PODS'98*, 149–158.

Calvanese, D.; Lenzerini, M.; and Nardi, D. 1998. Description logics for conceptual data modeling. In Chomicki, J., and Saake, G., eds., *Logics for Databases and Information Systems*. Kluwer Academic Publisher. 229–264.

Chaudhuri, S.; Krishnamurthy, S.; Potarnianos, S.; and Shim, K. 1995. Optimizing queries with materialized views. In *Proc. of ICDE'95*.

Chen, P. P. 1976. The Entity-Relationship model: Toward a unified view of data. *ACM Trans. on Database Systems* 1(1):9–36.

Cosmadakis, S. S. 1983. The complexity of evaluating relational queries. In *Proc. of PODS'83*, 149–155.

De Giacomo, G., and Lenzerini, M. 1995. What's in an aggregate: Foundations for description logics with tuples and sets. In *Proc. of IJCAI'95*, 801–807.

De Giacomo, G., and Lenzerini, M. 1996. TBox and ABox reasoning in expressive description logics. In Aiello, L. C.; Doyle, J.; and Shapiro, S. C., eds., *Proc. of KR'96*, 316–327. Morgan Kaufmann, Los Altos.

Donini, F. M.; Lenzerini, M.; Nardi, D.; and Schaerf, A. 1998. $\mathcal{AL}$-log: Integrating Datalog and description logics. *J. of Intelligent Information Systems* 10(3):227–252.

Duschka, O. M., and Genesereth, M. R. 1997. Answering recursive queries using views. In *Proc. of PODS'97*, 109–116.

ElMasri, R. A., and Navathe, S. B. 1988. *Fundamentals of Database Systems*. Benjamin and Cummings Publ. Co., Menlo Park, California.

Grahne, G., and Mendelzon, A. O. 1999. Tableau techniques for querying information sources through global schemas. In *Proc. of ICDT'99*, volume 1540 of *Lecture Notes in Computer Science*, 332–347. Springer-Verlag.

Horrocks, I.; Sattler, U.; Tessaris, S.; and Tobies, S. 1999. Query containment using a DLR ABox. Technical Report LTCS-Report 99-15, RWTH Aachen.

Hull, R. B., and King, R. 1987. Semantic database modelling: Survey, applications and research issues. *ACM Computing Surveys* 19(3):201–260.

Lenzerini, M., and Schaerf, A. 1991. Concept languages as query languages. In *Proc. of AAAI'91*, 471–476.

Levy, A. Y., and Rousset, M.-C. 1996. CARIN: A representation language combining Horn rules and description logics. In *Proc. of ECAI'96*, 323–327.

Levy, A. Y.; Mendelzon, A. O.; Sagiv, Y.; and Srivastava, D. 1995. Answering queries using views. In *Proc. of PODS'95*, 95–104.

Levy, A. Y. 1996. Obtaining complete answers from incomplete databases. In *Proc. of VLDB'96*, 402–412.

Rousset, M.-C. 1999. Backward reasoning in ABoxes for query answering. In *Proc. of DL'99*, 18–22.

Schaerf, A. 1994. *Query Answering in Concept-Based Knowledge Representation Systems: Algorithms, Complexity, and Semantic Issues*. Ph.D. Dissertation, Dipartimento di Informatica e Sistemistica, Università di Roma "La Sapienza".

Schild, K. 1991. A correspondence theory for terminological logics: Preliminary report. In *Proc. of IJCAI'91*, 466–471.

Schild, K. 1995. *Querying Knowledge and Data Bases by a Universal Description Logic with Recursion*. Ph.D. Dissertation, Universität des Saarlandes, Germany.

Ullman, J. D. 1997. Information integration using logical views. In *Proc. of ICDT'97*, volume 1186 of *Lecture Notes in Computer Science*, 19–40. Springer-Verlag.

Widom, J. 1995. Special issue on materialized views and data warehousing. *IEEE Bulletin on Data Engineering* 18(2).

A Consistency-Based Model for Belief Change: Preliminary Report

James P. Delgrande
School of Computing Science,
Simon Fraser University
Burnaby, B.C., Canada V5A 1S6
jim@cs.sfu.ca

Torsten Schaub
Institut für Informatik,
Universität Potsdam
D–14415 Potsdam, Germany
torsten@cs.uni-potsdam.de

Abstract

We present a general, consistency-based framework for belief change. Informally, in revising K by α, we begin with α and incorporate as much of K as consistently possible. Formally, a knowledge base K and sentence α are expressed, via renaming propositions in K, in separate alphabets, but such that there is an isomorphism between the original and new alphabets. Using a maximization process, we assume that corresponding atoms in each language are equivalent insofar as is consistently possible. Lastly, we express the resultant knowledge base using just the original alphabet. There may be more than one way in which α can be so extended by K: in *choice revision*, one such "extension" represents the revised state; alternately *revision* consists of the intersection of all such extensions.

The overall framework is flexible enough to express other approaches to revision and update, and the incorporation of static and dynamic integrity constraints. Our framework differs from work based on ordinal conditional functions, notably with respect to iterated revision. We argue that the approach is well-suited for implementation: choice revision gives better complexity results than general revision; the approach can be expressed in terms of a finite knowledge base; and the scope of a revision can be restricted to just those propositions mentioned in the sentence for revision α.

Introduction

We describe a general framework for belief change. The approach has something of the same flavour as the consistency-based paradigm for diagnosis (Reiter 1987) or the assumption-based approach to default reasoning (Poole 1988), although it differs significantly in details. Informally, in revising a knowledge base K by sentence α, we begin with α and incorporate as much of K as consistently possible. There may be more than one way in which information from K can be incorporated. This gives rise to two notions of revision: a choice notion, in which one such "extension" is used for the revised state, and the intersection of all such extensions. Belief contraction is defined analogously.

Copyright © 2000, American Association for Artificial Intelligence (www.aaai.org). All rights reserved.

We mainly focus on belief revision in this paper. For revision, first a knowledge base K and sentence α are expressed, via renaming atomic propositions in K, in separate alphabets. We next assume that as many atoms in α are equivalent to the corresponding atom in K, as consistently possible. A set of such equivalent atoms is used to incorporate as much of the original knowledge base as is consistently possible. In the final section we discuss the more general approach, which we show is flexible enough to express extant approaches to revision and update.

The approach is developed in a formal, abstract framework. However, we argue that it is well-suited for implementation: The notion of choice revision gives better complexity results than general revision; moreover, we argue that belief revision is an area in which choice reasoning makes sense in some cases. Second, we show how the approach can be expressed equivalently in terms of a finite knowledge base, in place of a deductively-closed belief set. Third, we show that the scope of a revision can be restricted to just those propositions common to the knowledge base and sentence for revision.

We begin by presenting a very general framework for expressing belief change. This is restricted to address revision and contraction. Following this, we show how the approach allows for a uniform treatment of integrity constraints. As well, the approach supports iterated revision, with properties distinct from approaches based on the work of Spohn (Spohn 1988). Finally we briefly explore the general framework, and suggest it is flexible enough to express extant approaches to revision and update.

Background

A common approach in belief revision is to provide a set of *rationality postulates* for revision and contraction functions. The *AGM approach* of Alchourron, Gärdenfors, and Makinson (Gärdenfors 1988), provides the best-known set of such postulates. The goal is to describe belief change on an abstract level, independent of how beliefs are represented and manipulated. Belief states, called *belief sets*, are modelled by sets of sentences closed under the logical consequence operator of some logic in some language $\mathcal{L}$, where the logic includes classical propositional logic. For belief set K, $K + \alpha$ is the deductive closure of $K \cup \{\alpha\}$, and is called the *expansion* of K by α. $K_\perp$ is the inconsistent belief set (i.e. $K_\perp = \mathcal{L}$). $\mathcal{T}$ is the set of all belief sets.

A *revision* function $\dot{+}$ is a function from $\mathcal{T} \times \mathcal{L}$ to $\mathcal{T}$ satisfying the following postulates.

($K\dot{+}1$) $K\dot{+}\alpha$ is a belief set.

($K\dot{+}2$) $\alpha \in K\dot{+}\alpha$.

($K\dot{+}3$) $K\dot{+}\alpha \subseteq K + \alpha$.

($K\dot{+}4$) If $\neg \alpha \notin K$, then $K + \alpha \subseteq K\dot{+}\alpha$.

($K\dot{+}5$) $K\dot{+}\alpha = K_\perp$ iff $\vdash \neg\alpha$.

($K\dot{+}6$) If $\vdash \alpha \equiv \beta$, then $K\dot{+}\alpha = K\dot{+}\beta$.

($K\dot{+}7$) $K\dot{+}(\alpha \wedge \beta) \subseteq (K\dot{+}\alpha) + \beta$.

($K\dot{+}8$) If $\neg\beta \notin K\dot{+}\alpha$, then $(K\dot{+}\alpha) + \beta \subseteq K\dot{+}(\alpha \wedge \beta)$.

That is: the result of revising K by α is a belief set in which α is believed; whenever the result is consistent, revision consists of the expansion of K by α; the only time that $K_\perp$ is obtained is when α is inconsistent; and revision is independent of the syntactic form of K and α. The last two postulates deal with the relation between revising with a conjunction and expansion.

(Katsuno & Mendelzon 1992) explores the distinct notion of belief *update* in which an agent changes its beliefs in response to changes in its external environment. Our interests here centre on revision; however as the end of the paper, we briefly consider this approach.

Recently there has been interest in *iterated* belief revision, a topic that the AGM approach by-and-large leaves open. Representative work includes (Boutilier 1994; Williams 1994; Lehmann 1995; Darwiche & Pearl 1997). We discuss Darwiche and Pearl's approach here. They employ the notion of an *epistemic state* that encodes how the revision function changes following a revision. Ψ denotes an epistemic state; $Bel(\Psi)$ denotes the belief set corresponding to Ψ. So now the result of revising an epistemic state is another epistemic state (from which the revised belief set may be determined using $Bel(\cdot)$. Darwiche and Pearl propose the following postulates that "*any* rational system of belief change should comply with" (p. 2). Following their practice, we use Ψ to stand for $Bel(\Psi)$ when it appears as an argument of $\models$.

$C1$: If $\alpha \models \mu$ then $(\Psi\dot{+}\mu)\dot{+}\alpha \equiv \Psi\dot{+}\alpha$.

$C2$: If $\alpha \models \neg\mu$ then $(\Psi\dot{+}\mu)\dot{+}\alpha \equiv \Psi\dot{+}\alpha$.

$C3$: If $\Psi\dot{+}\alpha \models \mu$ then $(\Psi\dot{+}\mu)\dot{+}\alpha \models \mu$.

$C4$: If $\Psi\dot{+}\alpha \not\models \neg\mu$ then $(\Psi\dot{+}\mu)\dot{+}\alpha \not\models \neg\mu$.

(Nayak et al. 1996) propose a variant of $C2$ along with the following postulate:

$Conj$: If $\alpha \wedge \beta \not\models \perp$ then $(\Psi\dot{+}\alpha)\dot{+}^\alpha \beta = \Psi\dot{+}(\alpha \wedge \beta)$.

where $\dot{+}^\alpha$ indicates that the change in $\dot{+}$ following revision by α depends in part on α. This postulate is shown to be strong enough to derive $C1$, $C3$, and $C4$ in the presence of the other postulates.

There has also been work on specific approaches to revision based on the distance between models of a knowledge base and a sentence to be incorporated in the knowledge base. This work includes (Dalal 1988; Forbus 1989; Satoh 1988; Winslett 1988). In these approaches, models of the new knowledge base consist of models of the sentence to be added that are closest (based on "distance" between atomic sentences) to models of the original knowledge base.

Our approach differs from previous work first, in that we provide a specific, albeit general, framework in which approaches may be expressed. As well, the general framework allows the incorporation of different forms of integrity constraints. Also, given that it falls into the "consistency-based" paradigm, the approach has a certain syntactic flavour. However, notably, our approach is independent of the syntactic form of the knowledge base and sentence for revision.

Our technique of maximizing sets of equivalences of propositional letters bears a superficial resemblance to the use of such equivalences in (Liberatore & Schaerf 1997) (based in turn on the technique developed in (de Kleer & Konolige 1989)). However the approaches are distinct; in particular and in contradistinction to these references, we employ disjoint alphabets for a knowledge base and revising sentence. As well, the approach bears a resemblance to that of (del Val 1993). However, unlike del Val, we provide a single approach which may be restricted to yield extant approaches; also, we place no a priori restrictions on the form of a knowledge base.

Formal Preliminaries

We deal with propositional languages and use the logical symbols $\top$, $\perp$, $\neg$, $\vee$, $\wedge$, $\supset$, and $\equiv$ to construct formulas in the standard way. We write $\mathcal{L}_\mathcal{P}$ to denote a language over an alphabet $\mathcal{P}$ of *propositional letters* or *atomic propositions*. Formulas are denoted by the Greek letters α, β, α_1, ... Knowledge bases or, equivalently, *belief sets* are initially identified with deductively-closed sets of formulas and are denoted K, K_1, ... So we have $K = Cn(K)$, where $Cn(\cdot)$ is the deductive closure of the formula or set of formulas given as argument. Later we relax this restriction.

Given an alphabet $\mathcal{P}$, we define a disjoint alphabet $\mathcal{P}'$ as $\mathcal{P}' = \{p' \mid p \in \mathcal{P}\}$. Then, for $\alpha \in \mathcal{L}_\mathcal{P}$, we define α' as the result of replacing in α each proposition p from $\mathcal{P}$ by the corresponding proposition p' in $\mathcal{P}'$ (so implicitly there is an isomorphism between $\mathcal{P}$ and $\mathcal{P}'$). This is defined analogously for sets of formulas.

We define a *belief change scenario* in language $\mathcal{L}_\mathcal{P}$ as a triple $B = (K, U, V)$, where K, U, V are sets of formulas in $\mathcal{L}_\mathcal{P}$. Informally, K is a knowledge base that will be changed such that the set U will be true in the result, and the set V will be consistent with the result. For a base approach to revision we take $V = \emptyset$ and for a base approach to contraction we take $U = \emptyset$.

In the definition below, "maximal" is with respect to set containment (rather than set cardinality). The following is our central definition.

Definition 1 *Let $B = (K, U, V)$ be a belief change scenario in $\mathcal{L}_\mathcal{P}$. Define EQ as a maximal set of equivalences $EQ \subseteq \{p \equiv p' \mid p \in \mathcal{P}\}$ such that*
$$K' \cup EQ \cup U \cup V \not\vdash \bot.$$
Then
$$Cn(K' \cup EQ \cup U) \cap \mathcal{L}_\mathcal{P}$$
is a consistent definitional extension *of B.*

Hence, a consistent definitional extension of B is a modification of K in which U is true, and in which V is consistent. We say that EQ <u>underlies</u> the consistent definitional extension of B. We let $\overline{EQ}$ stand for $\{p \equiv p' \mid p \in \mathcal{P}\} \setminus EQ$.

Clearly, for a given belief change scenario there may be more than one consistent definitional extension. We will make use of the notion of a *selection function* c that for any set $I \neq \emptyset$ has as value some element of I. In Definition 2 and 3, these primitive functions can be regarded as inducing selection functions c' on belief change scenarios, such that $c'((K, U, V))$ has as value some consistent definitional extension of (K, U, V). This is a slight generalisation of selection functions as found in the AGM approach.

Revision and Contraction

Definition 1 provides a very general framework for specifying belief change. In the next two definitions we give specific definitions for revision and contraction. We develop these specific approaches and then, at the end of the paper, we return to the more general framework of Definition 1 and discuss how it can be used to express other approaches.

Definition 2 (Revision) *Let K be a knowledge base and α a formula, and let $(E_i)_{i \in I}$ be the family of all consistent definitional extensions of $(K, \{\alpha\}, \emptyset)$. Then*

1. $K \dotplus_c \alpha = E_i$ *is a* choice revision *of K by α with respect to some selection function c with $c(I) = i$.*
2. $K \dotplus \alpha = \bigcap_{i \in I} E_i$ *is the* (skeptical) revision *of K by α.*

Table 1 gives examples of (skeptical) revision. The first column gives the original knowledge base, but with atoms already renamed. The second column gives the revision formula, while the third gives the EQ set(s) and the last column gives the results of the revision. For the first and last column, we give a formula whose deductive closure gives the corresponding belief set.
In detail, for the last example, we wish to determine
$$\{p \wedge q\} \dotplus (\neg p \vee \neg q) \,. \tag{1}$$
We find maximal sets $EQ \subseteq \{p \equiv p', q \equiv q'\}$ such that
$$\{p' \wedge q'\} \cup EQ \cup \{\neg p \vee \neg q\} \cup \emptyset \text{ is consistent.}$$
We get two such sets of equivalences, namely $EQ_1 = \{p \equiv p'\}$ and $EQ_2 = \{q \equiv q'\}$. Accordingly, we obtain
$$\{p \wedge q\} \dotplus (\neg p \vee \neg q) =$$

K'	α	EQ	$K \dotplus \alpha$
$p' \wedge q'$	$\neg q$	$\{p \equiv p'\}$	$p \wedge \neg q$
$\neg p' \equiv q'$	$\neg q$	$\{p \equiv p', q \equiv q'\}$	$p \wedge \neg q$
$p' \vee q'$	$\neg p \vee \neg q$	$\{p \equiv p', q \equiv q'\}$	$p \equiv \neg q$
$p' \wedge q'$	$\neg p \vee \neg q$	$\{p \equiv p'\}, \{q \equiv q'\}$	$p \equiv \neg q$

Table 1: (Skeptical) revision examples.

$$\bigcap_{i=1,2} Cn(\{p' \wedge q'\} \cup EQ_i \cup \{\neg p \vee \neg q\}) \cap \mathcal{L}_\mathcal{P}.$$
In addition to $(\neg p \vee \neg q)$, we get $(p \vee q)$, jointly implying $(p \equiv \neg q)$.

In this example we get two choice extensions, $Cn(p \wedge \neg q)$ and $Cn(\neg p \wedge q)$. This raises the question of the usefulness of choice revision compared to general revision. An apparent limitation of a choice reasoner is that it might draw overly strong conclusions. However, in belief revision this may be less of a problem than, say, in nonmonotonic reasoning: the goal in revision is to determine the true state of the world; if a (choice) revision results in an inaccurate knowledge base, then *this* inaccuracy will presumably be detected and rectified in a later revision. So choice revision may do no worse than a "skeptical" operator with respect to "converging" to the true state of the world. In addition, as we later show, it may do so significantly more efficiently and with better worst-case behaviour. Hence for a land vehicle exploring a benign environment, choice revision might be an effective part of a control mechanism; for something like flight control, or controlling a nuclear reactor, one would prefer skeptical revision.

Contraction is defined similarly to revision.

Definition 3 (Contraction) *Let K be a knowledge base and α a formula, and let $(E_i)_{i \in I}$ be the family of all consistent definitional extensions of $(K, \emptyset, \{\neg \alpha\})$. Then*

1. $K \dotminus_c \alpha = E_i$ *is a* choice contraction *of K by α with respect to some selection function c with $c(I) = i$.*
2. $K \dotminus \alpha = \bigcap_{i \in I} E_i$ *is the* (skeptical) contraction *of K by α.*

Table 2 gives examples of (skeptical) contraction, using the same format and conventions as Table 1.

K'	α	EQ	$K \dotminus \alpha$
$p' \wedge q'$	q	$\{p \equiv p'\}$	p
$p' \wedge q' \wedge r'$	$p \vee q$	$\{r \equiv r'\}$	r
$p' \vee q'$	$p \wedge q$	$\{p \equiv p', q \equiv q'\}$	$p \vee q$
$p' \wedge q'$	$p \wedge q$	$\{p \equiv p'\}, \{q \equiv q'\}$	$p \vee q$

Table 2: (Skeptical) contraction examples.

In detail, for the first example we wish to determine
$$\{p \wedge q\} \dotminus q \,. \tag{2}$$
We compute the consistent definitional extensions of $(\{p \wedge q\}, \emptyset, \{\neg q\})$. We rename the propositions in $\{p \wedge q\}$

and look for maximal subsets EQ of $\{p \equiv p', q \equiv q'\}$ such that

$\{p' \wedge q'\} \cup EQ \cup \emptyset \cup \{\neg q\}$ is consistent.

We obtain $EQ = \{p \equiv p'\}$, yielding
$$\begin{aligned}\{p \wedge q\} \dot{-} q &= Cn(\{p' \wedge q'\} \cup \{p \equiv p'\} \cup \emptyset) \cap \mathcal{L}_\mathcal{P} \\ &= Cn(\{p\}).\end{aligned}$$

Properties of Revision and Contraction

With respect to the AGM postulates, we obtain the following.

Theorem 1 *Let $\dot{+}$ and $\dot{+}_c$ be defined as in Definition 2. Then $\dot{+}$ and $\dot{+}_c$ satisfy the basic AGM postulates $(K\dot{+}1)$ to $(K\dot{+}4)$, $(K\dot{+}6)$ as well as $(K\dot{+}7)$.*

For $(K\dot{+}5)$ we have instead the weaker postulate:

$(K\dot{+}5)$ $K\dot{+}\alpha = K_\perp$ iff: $K = K_\perp$ or $\vdash \neg\alpha$.

We obtain analogous results for $\dot{-}$ and $\dot{-}_c$ with respect to the AGM contraction postulates:

Theorem 2 *Let $\dot{-}$ and $\dot{-}_c$ be defined as in Definition 3. Then $\dot{-}$ satisfies the basic AGM postulates $(K\dot{-}1)$ to $(K\dot{-}4)$, $(K\dot{-}6)$, and $(K\dot{-}7)$. In addition, $\dot{-}_c$ satisfies the basic AGM postulates $(K\dot{-}1)$ to $(K\dot{-}4)$, $(K\dot{-}6)$.*

We also obtain the following interdefinability results:

Theorem 3 (Levi Identity) $K\dot{+}\alpha = (K\dot{-}\neg\alpha) + \alpha$.

Theorem 4 (Partial Harper Identity)
$K\dot{-}\alpha \subseteq K \cap (K\dot{+}\neg\alpha)$

The following example shows that equality fails in the Harper Identity: if $K \equiv p \wedge q \wedge r$ and $\alpha \equiv r$, then $K\dot{-}\alpha \equiv r$ while $K \cap (K\dot{+}\neg\alpha) \equiv (p \equiv \neg q) \wedge r$. Similar results are obtained for choice revision and choice contraction by appeal to appropriate selection functions.

Iterated belief change: The approach obviously supports iterated revision. Since we use a "global" metric, and since we can assume that *every* revision result, given K and α, can be determined, we continue to use K here rather than Darwiche and Pearl's Ψ for an epistemic state. That is, for us, we don't need to refer to epistemic states, since we have completely specified how $\dot{+}$ should behave on all arguments. Nonetheless, neither operator in Definition 2 satisfies any of the Darwiche-Pearl postulates for iterated revision. Nor in our opinion should they. For example, for $C1$, if we have

$$K = Cn(\neg p), \quad \alpha = p, \quad \mu = p \vee q, \quad (3)$$

then in our approach we obtain that

$$(K\dot{+}\mu)\dot{+}\alpha = Cn(p \wedge q) \text{ but } K\dot{+}\alpha = Cn(p). \quad (4)$$

(Darwiche & Pearl 1997; Nayak *et al.* 1996) assert that these results should be equal. However, it is *possible* (contra $C1$) that there are cases where revising $\neg p$ by $p \vee q$ yields $\neg p \wedge q$ and a subsequent revision by p then gives $p \wedge q$, but revising $\neg p$ by p would yield p. Which is to say, a significant difficulty in the area of belief revision is that different people have conflicting intuitions. However, Darwiche and Pearl argue that *all rational* revision functions should obey $C1$. Consequently they would need to argue that in all cases, having (4) result from (3) is *irrational*.

More seriously, an instance of $C2$ (letting α be $\neg\phi$ and μ be $\phi \wedge \psi$, whence $\alpha \models \neg\mu$) is the following:

$C2'$: $(K\dot{+}(\phi \wedge \psi))\dot{+}\neg\phi \equiv K\dot{+}\neg\phi$.

Thus if you revise by $(\phi \wedge \psi)$ and then revise by the negation of some of this information ($\neg\phi$), then the other original information (ψ) is lost. So, in a variant of an example from (Darwiche & Pearl 1997), consider where I see a new bird in the distance and come to believe that it is red and flies. If on closer examination I see that it is yellow, then according to $C2'$ and so $C2$, I also no longer believe that it flies. This seems too strong a condition to want to adopt. We conjecture (but have no proof) that approaches based on (Spohn 1988), such as (Darwiche & Pearl 1997), are subject in some form to such a "blanketing" result.

On the other hand, there are nontrivial results concerning iterated revision that hold for the present approach. For example, we have:

Theorem 5 *Let $\dot{+}$ be defined as in Definition 2. Then:* $(\alpha\dot{+}\beta)\dot{+}\alpha = \beta\dot{+}\alpha$.

Semantics: The operator $\dot{+}$ provides a (near) syntactic counterpart to the minimal-distance-between-models approach of (Satoh 1988). For two sets S and T, let $S \Delta T$ be the symmetric difference, $(S \cup T) \setminus (S \cap T)$. For formulas α, β, define

$\Delta^{\min}(\alpha, \beta) =$
$\quad \min_\subseteq(\{M \Delta M' \mid M \in Mod(\alpha), M' \in Mod(\beta)\})$,

where $Mod(\alpha)$ is the set of all models of α, each of which is identified with a set of propositions. Then, we have:

Theorem 6 *Let $B = (K, U, \emptyset)$ be a belief change scenario in $\mathcal{L}_\mathcal{P}$ where $K \neq \mathcal{L}_\mathcal{P}$, and let $(EQ_i)_{i \in I}$ be the family of all sets of equivalences, as defined in Definition 1.*

Then, $\{ \{p \in \mathcal{P} \mid (p \equiv p') \notin EQ_i\} \mid i \in I\} = \Delta^{\min}(U, K)$.

This correspondence is interesting, but is of limited use beyond supplying a semantics for one instance of the approach. The choice approach, and (below) considerations on implementation and integrity constraints, are not readily expressed in Satoh's model-based semantics. As well, a contraction function is straightforwardly obtained in Satoh's approach only by using the Harper Identity (which doesn't fully obtain here). Further, in the last section, we show how other approaches can be expressed in our general framework.

Integrity Constraints

Definitions 2 and 3 are similar in form, differing only in how the formula α is mapped onto the sets U and V in Definition 1. Clearly one can combine these definitions, allowing simultaneous revision by one formula and contraction by another. This in-and-of-itself isn't overly interesting, but it does lead to a natural and general treatment of integrity constraints in our approach.

There are two standard definitions of a knowledge base K satisfying a static integrity constraint IC. In the *consistency-based* approach of (Kowalski 1978), K satisfies IC iff $K \cup \{IC\}$ is satisfiable. In the *entailment-based* approach of (Reiter 1984), K satisfies IC iff $K \vdash IC$. (Katsuno & Mendelzon 1991) show how entailment-based constraints can be maintained across revisions: given an integrity constraint IC and revision function $\dotplus$, a revision function $\dotplus^{IC}$ which preserves IC is defined by: $K \dotplus^{IC} \alpha = K \dotplus (\alpha \wedge IC)$. In our approach, we can define revision taking into account both approaches to integrity constraints.

Corresponding to Definition 2 (and ignoring the choice approach) we obtain:

Definition 4 *Let K be a knowledge base, α a formula, and IC_K, IC_R sets of formulas. Let $(E_i)_{i \in I}$ be the family of all consistent definitional extensions of $(K, \{\alpha\} \cup IC_R, IC_K)$. Then $K \dotplus^{(IC_K, IC_R)} \alpha = \bigcap_{i \in I} E_i$ is the revision of K by α incorporating integrity constraints IC_K (consistency-based) and IC_R (entailment-based).*

Theorem 7 *Let $\dotplus^{(IC_K, IC_R)}$ be defined as in Definition 4. Then $\left(K \dotplus^{(IC_K, IC_R)} \alpha \right) \vdash IC_R$. If $IC_R \cup IC_K \not\vdash \neg \alpha$ then $\left(K \dotplus^{(IC_K, IC_R)} \alpha \right) \cup IC_K$ is satisfiable.*

Finally, and in contrast with previous approaches, it is straightforward to add *dynamic* integrity constraints, which express constraints that hold between states of the knowledge base before and after revision. The simplest way of so doing is to add such constraints to the set V in Definition 1. To state that if $a \wedge b$ is true in a knowledge base before revision then c must be true afterwards, we would add $a' \wedge b' \supset c$ to V. Note however that the addition of dynamic constraints may lead to an operator that violates some of the properties of $\dotplus$. For example $Cn(\alpha) \dotplus \neg \alpha$ with dynamic constraint $\alpha' \supset \alpha$ leads to an inconsistent revision.

Implementability Considerations

We claimed at the outset that the approach is well-suited for implementation. To this end, we first consider the use of choice belief revision. Second we consider the problem of representing the results of revision in a finite, manageable representation. Lastly, we address limiting the range of EQ.

Complexity: From (Eiter & Gottlob 1992) and Theorem 6 it follows that deciding, for given K, α, β, whether $K \dotplus \alpha \vdash \beta$ is Π_2^P-complete. However, the analogous problem for choice revision is lower in the polynomial hierarchy.

Theorem 8 *Given a selection function c, formulas K, α, β, and a set of equivalnces EQ. Then, we have:*

1. *Deciding whether EQ determines a choice revision of K and α is in $\mathbf{P^{NP}}$.*
2. *Deciding $K \dotplus_c \alpha \vdash \beta$ is in $\mathbf{P^{NP}}$.*

We have not yet addressed restrictions on the syntactic form of K or α; but see (Eiter & Gottlob 1992).

Finite representations: Definitions 1, 2, and 3 provide a characterisation of revision and contraction, yielding in either case a deductively-closed belief set. Here we consider how the same (with respect to logical equivalence) operators can be defined, but where a knowledge base is given as an arbitrary, finite set of formulas. It follows from the discussion below that, for knowledge base K and formula α, we can defined choice revision so that $|K \dotplus_c \alpha| \leq |K| + |\alpha|$ for any selection function c.

Informally the procedure is straightforward, although the technical details are less so. A knowledge base K is now represented by a formula (or set of formulas). Via Definitions 1 and 2 we consider maximal sets EQ where $\{K'\} \cup \{\alpha\} \cup EQ$ is consistent. For each such set EQ, we replace each p' in K' by p where $(p \equiv p') \in EQ$ and we replace each p' in K' by $\neg p$ where $(p \equiv p') \in \overline{EQ}$. The result of these substitutions into $\{K'\} \cup \{\alpha\}$ is a sentence of size $\leq |K| + |\alpha|$ and whose deductive closure is equivalent to (some) choice revision. The disjunction of all such sentences (and so considering all possible sets EQ) is equivalent to $Cn(K) \dotplus \alpha$.

As opposed to the computation of the sets EQ, the result of revising or contracting a formula K can be captured without an explicit change of alphabet. We start by observing that any set of equivalences EQ induces a binary partition of its underlying alphabet $\mathcal{P}$, namely $\langle \mathcal{P}_{EQ}, \mathcal{P}_{\overline{EQ}} \rangle$ with $\mathcal{P}_{EQ} = \{p \in \mathcal{P} \mid p \equiv p' \in EQ\}$ and $\mathcal{P}_{\overline{EQ}} = \mathcal{P} \setminus \mathcal{P}_{EQ}$. Given a belief change scenario B along with a set of equivalences EQ_i (according to Definition 1), we define for $\alpha \in \mathcal{L}_\mathcal{P}$, that $\lceil \alpha \rceil_i$ is the result of replacing in α each proposition $p \in \mathcal{P}_{\overline{EQ_i}}$ by its negation $\neg p$.

For generality, let K be a set of formulas:

Definition 5 *Let $B = (K, U, V)$ be a belief change scenario in $\mathcal{L}_\mathcal{P}$ and let $(EQ_i)_{i \in I}$ be the family of all sets of equivalences, as defined in Definition 1.*

Define $\lceil B \rceil$ as $\bigvee_{i \in I} \bigwedge_{(s \in K)} \lceil s \rceil_i$ and $\lceil B \rceil^c$ as $\bigwedge_{(s \in K)} \lceil s \rceil_k$ for selection function c corresponding to EQ_k.

For revision, we define $\lceil (K, \{\alpha\}, \emptyset) \rceil \wedge \alpha$ as the finite representation of $K \dotplus \alpha$, and analogously $\lceil (K, \{\alpha\}, \emptyset) \rceil^c \wedge \alpha$ as the finite representation of $K \dotplus_c \alpha$.

Theorem 9 *Let K and α be formulas. Then, we have*
$$Cn(K) \dotplus \alpha = Cn(\lceil (Cn(K), \{\alpha\}, \emptyset) \rceil \wedge \alpha)$$
$$\equiv \lceil (K, \{\alpha\}, \emptyset) \rceil \wedge \alpha.$$

Consider example (1): $\{p \wedge q\} \dotplus (\neg p \vee \neg q)$. So $B = (\{p \wedge q\}, \{(\neg p \vee \neg q)\}, \emptyset)$ is the belief change scenario. We obtain:
$$\lceil B \rceil \wedge (\neg p \vee \neg q) = [(p \wedge \neg q) \vee (\neg p \wedge q)] \wedge (\neg p \vee \neg q),$$

which is equivalent to $(p \equiv \neg q)$. For the other examples in Table 1, if K is the formula corresponding to K' in the first column, then revising by the given α via Theorem 9 is the formula given in the last line (up to permutation of symbols and elimination of definitional equivalents).

Contraction is handled somewhat differently. This is not altogether surprising, given that revision and contraction are not fully interdefinable (Theorem 4). Whereas for revision we replaced each atomic proposition in $\overline{EQ_i}$ by its negation in K, for contraction replacements in K are done over all truth values of atomic propositions in $\overline{EQ_i}$. Formally, given a belief change scenario B, a corresponding set of equivalences EQ_i (according to Definition 1) along with its induced partition $\langle \mathcal{P}_{EQ_i}, \mathcal{P}_{\overline{EQ_i}} \rangle$ of $\mathcal{P}$, and a function $\pi_{k_i} : \mathcal{P}_{\overline{EQ_i}} \to \{\top, \bot\}$, we define for $\alpha \in \mathcal{L}_\mathcal{P}$, $\lfloor \alpha \rfloor^{k_i}$ as the result of replacing in α each proposition $p \in \mathcal{P}_{\overline{EQ_i}}$ by $\pi_{k_i}(p)$. Note that each set of equivalences induces a whole set Π_i of such mappings π_{k_i}, viz. $\Pi_i = \{\pi_{k_i} \mid \pi_{k_i} : \mathcal{P}_{\overline{EQ_i}} \to \{\top, \bot\}\}$, amounting to all possible truth assignments to $\mathcal{P}_{\overline{EQ_i}}$.

Definition 6 *Let B and $(EQ_i)_{i \in I}$ be defined as in Definition 5.*

Define $\lfloor B \rfloor$ as $\bigvee_{i \in I, \pi_j \in \Pi_i} \bigwedge_{(s \in K)} \lfloor s \rfloor^j$ and $\lfloor B \rfloor^c$ as $\bigvee_{\pi_j \in \Pi_k} \bigwedge_{(s \in K)} \lfloor s \rfloor^j$ for some selection function c with $c(I) = k$.

We define $\lfloor (K, \emptyset, \{\neg\alpha\}) \rfloor$ as the finite representation of $K \dot{-} \alpha$, and analogously $\lfloor (K, \emptyset, \{\neg\alpha\}) \rfloor^c$ as the finite representation of $K \dot{-}_c \alpha$.

Theorem 10 *Let K and α be formulas. Then, we have*
$$Cn(K) \dot{-} \alpha = Cn(\lfloor (Cn(K), \emptyset, \{\neg\alpha\}) \rfloor)$$
$$\equiv \lfloor (K, \emptyset, \{\neg\alpha\}) \rfloor.$$

Consider example (2): $\{p \land \neg q\} \dot{-} (\neg q)$. We obtain
$$\lfloor (\{p \land \neg q\}, \emptyset, \{q\}) \rfloor = (p \land \bot) \lor (p \land \top) \equiv p.$$

For the examples in Table 2, if K is the formula corresponding to K', then in contracting by the given α, the result of the contraction via Theorem 10 is the formula given in the last line (up to permutation of symbols and elimination of definitional equivalents).

Theorems 9 and 10 are interesting in that they show that revision and contraction can be defined with respect to syntactic objects (viz. sentences representing the knowledge base) yet are essentially independent of syntactic form. Hence in a certain sense the approach combines the advantages of base revision (Nebel 1992) and syntax-independent approaches.

Limiting the range of EQ: Intuitively, if an atomic sentence appears in a knowledge base K but not in a sentence for revision α, or vice versa, then that atomic sentence plays no part in the revision. This is indeed the case here, as the next result demonstrates. Let $Vocab(\delta)$ be the atomic sentences in δ. We obtain:

Theorem 11 *Let K be a set of formulas and α a formula. Let $E = Cn(K' \cup EQ \cup \alpha) \cap \mathcal{L}_\mathcal{P}$ be a consistent definitional extension of belief change scenario $B = (Cn(K), \{\alpha\}, \emptyset)$.*

Then $\{p \equiv p' \mid p \in (Vocab(K) \setminus Vocab(\alpha)) \cup (Vocab(\alpha) \setminus Vocab(K))\} \subseteq EQ$.

So for belief change, we need consider just the atomic sentences common to K and α, and can ignore (with regards EQ) other atomic sentences. As detailed in the full paper, this result allows one to limit the primed atomic propositions in K' to those occurring in α.

The General Approach

Definition 1 is quite general; in Definitions 2 and 3 we narrow the scope to specific approaches to belief change. We note however, briefly, that other approaches are expressible in this framework. Belief *update* is a distinct form of belief change, suited to a changing world. Update and its dual operator *erasure* are studied in (Katsuno & Mendelzon 1992) where sets of postulates characterising the operators are given.

Definition 7 (Prime Implicate) *A consistent set of literals l is a prime implicate[1] of K iff: $l \vdash K$ and for $l' \subset l$ we have $l' \not\vdash K$.*

Definition 8 (Update) *Let K be a knowledge base and α a formula and let $PI(K)$ be the set of prime implicates of K. For each $K_j \in PI(K)$, $1 \leq j \leq m$, let $E_1^j, \ldots, E_{n_j}^j$ be the consistent definitional extensions of $(K_j, \{\alpha\}, \emptyset)$. Then $K \diamond \alpha = \bigcup_{j=1}^{m} \bigcap_{i=1}^{n_j} E_i^j$ is the update of K by α.*

We do not define *choice update* here, given space limitations.

Theorem 12 *$K \diamond \alpha$ satisfies the update postulates of (Katsuno & Mendelzon 1992).*

We show in the full paper that the operator $\diamond$ provides a syntactic counterpart for Winslett's update operator (Winslett 1988). We can also take a different notion of *maximal* in Definition 1, and base the definition on set cardinality, rather than set containment. We show that based on this measure we can capture the revision approaches of (Dalal 1988) and (Forbus 1989). Lastly a minor modification to Definition 1 allows one to use the framework to capture the *merging* of knowledge bases.

Conclusion

We have presented a general consistency-based framework for belief change, having the same flavour as the consistency-based paradigms for diagnosis or default reasoning. We focus on a specific approach, in which a knowledge base K and sentence α are expressed, via renaming propositions in K, in separate alphabets. Given this, we assume that as many corresponding atoms in each language are equivalent insofar as is consistently possible. Lastly, we express the resultant knowledge

---

[1] Note that this is the dual of *prime implicant*.

base in a single language. For the revision of K by α, for example, we begin with α and incorporate as much of K as consistently possible. This gives rise to two notions of revision: a choice notion, in which one such "extension" is used for the revised state, and the intersection of all such extensions.

The approach is well-suited for implementation: The notion of a choice extension gives better complexity results than general revision; also, belief revision is an area in which choice reasoning may be useful. Second, we show how the approach can be expressed in terms of a finite knowledge base, and that the scope of a revision can be restricted to those propositions common to the knowledge base and sentence for revision.

The approach allows for a uniform treatment of integrity constraints, in that belief change may take into account both consistency-based and entailment-based static constraints, as well as dynamic constraints. As well, it supports iterated revision. Finally, the framework is applicable to other approaches to belief change.

References

Boutilier, C. 1994. Unifying default reasoning and belief revision in a modal framework. *Artificial Intelligence* 68(1):33–85.

Dalal, M. 1988. Investigations into theory of knowledge base revision. In *Proceedings of the AAAI National Conference on Artificial Intelligence*, 449–479.

Darwiche, A., and Pearl, J. 1997. On the logic of iterated revision. *Artificial Intelligence* 89:1–29.

de Kleer, J., and Konolige, K. 1989. Eliminating the fixed predicates from a circumscription. *Artificial Intelligence* 39(3):391–398.

del Val, A. 1993. Syntactic characterizations of belief change operators. In *Proceedings of the International Joint Conference on Artificial Intelligence*, 540–545.

Eiter, T., and Gottlob, G. 1992. On the complexity of propositional knowledge base revision, updates, and counterfactuals. *Artificial Intelligence* 57:227–270.

Forbus, K. 1989. Introducing actions into qualitative simulation. In *Proceedings of the International Joint Conference on Artificial Intelligence*, 1273–1278.

Gärdenfors, P. 1988. *Knowledge in Flux: Modelling the Dynamics of Epistemic States*. Cambridge, MA: The MIT Press.

Katsuno, H., and Mendelzon, A. 1991. Propositional knowledge base revision and minimal change. *Artificial Intelligence* 52(3):263–294.

Katsuno, H., and Mendelzon, A. 1992. On the difference between updating a knowledge base and revising it. In Gärdenfors, P., ed., *Belief Revision*, 183–203. Cambridge University Press.

Kowalski, R. 1978. Logic for data description. In Gallaire, H., and Minker, J., eds., *Logic and Data Bases*. Plenum Press. 77–103.

Lehmann, D. 1995. Belief revision, revised. In *Proceedings of the International Joint Conference on Artificial Intelligence*, 1534–1540. Montréal: Morgan Kaufmann Publishers.

Liberatore, P., and Schaerf, M. 1997. Reducing belief revision to circumscription (and vice versa). *Artificial Intelligence* 93(1–2):261–296.

Nayak, A. C.; Foo, N. Y.; Pagnucco, M.; and Sattar, A. 1996. Changing conditional belief unconditionally. In *Proc. of the Sixth Conference on Theoretical Aspects of Reasoning About Knowledge*, 119–136.

Nebel, B. 1992. Syntax based approaches to belief revision. In Gärdenfors, P., ed., *Belief Revision*, 52–88. Cambridge University Press.

Poole, D. 1988. A logical framework for default reasoning. *Artificial Intelligence* 36(1):27–48.

Reiter, R. 1984. Towards a logical reconstruction of relational database theory. In Brodie, M.; Mylopoulos, J.; and Schmidt, J., eds., *On Conceptual Modelling*. Springer-Verlag.

Reiter, R. 1987. A theory of diagnosis from first principles. *Artificial Intelligence* 32(1):57–96.

Satoh, K. 1988. Nonmonotonic reasoning by minimal belief revision. In *Proceedings of the International Conference on Fifth Generation Computer Systems*, 455–462.

Spohn, W. 1988. Ordinal conditional functions: A dynamic theory of epistemic states. In Harper, W., and Skyrms, B., eds., *Causation in Decision, Belief Change, and Statistics*, volume II. Kluwer Academic Publishers. 105–134.

Williams, M.-A. 1994. Transmutations of knowledge systems. In Doyle, J.; Torasso, P.; and Sandewall, E., eds., *Proceedings of the Fourth International Conference on the Principles of Knowledge Representation and Reasoning*, 619–629.

Winslett, M. 1988. Reasoning about action using a possible models approach. In *Proceedings of the AAAI National Conference on Artificial Intelligence*, 89–93.

A Conjunctive Query Language for Description Logic Aboxes

Ian Horrocks and Sergio Tessaris
Department of Computer Science
University of Manchester
Manchester, UK
{horrocks|tessaris}@cs.man.ac.uk

Abstract

A serious shortcoming of many Description Logic based knowledge representation systems is the inadequacy of their query languages. In this paper we present a novel technique that can be used to provide an expressive query language for such systems. One of the main advantages of this approach is that, being based on a reduction to knowledge base satisfiability, it can easily be adapted to most existing (and future) Description Logic implementations. We believe that providing Description Logic systems with an expressive query language for interrogating the knowledge base will significantly increase their utility.

Introduction

A description logic (DL) knowledge base (KB) is made up of two parts, a terminological part (the Tbox) and an assertional part (the Abox), each part consisting of a set of axioms. The Tbox asserts facts about *concepts* (sets of objects) and *roles* (binary relations), usually in the form of inclusion axioms, while the Abox asserts facts about *individuals* (single objects), usually in the form of instantiation axioms. For example, a Tbox might contain an axiom asserting that Man is subsumed by Animal, while an Abox might contain axioms asserting that John, Peter and Bill are instances of the concept Man and that the pairs ⟨John, Peter⟩ and ⟨Peter, Bill⟩ are instances of the role Brother.

Recent years have seen significant advances in the design of sound and complete reasoning algorithms for DLs with both expressive logical languages and unrestricted Tboxes, i.e., those allowing arbitrary concept inclusion axioms (Baader 1991; De Giacomo & Lenzerini 1995; Horrocks & Sattler 1999; De Giacomo & Massacci 1998). Moreover, systems using highly optimised implementations of (some of) these algorithms have also been developed, and have been show to work well in realistic applications (Horrocks 1998; Patel-Schneider 1998). While most of these have been restricted to terminological reasoning (i.e., the Abox is assumed to be empty), attention is now turning to the development of both algorithms and (optimised) implementations that also support Abox reasoning (Haarslev & Möller 1999a; Tessaris & Gough 1998).

Although these systems provide sound and complete Abox reasoning for very expressive logics, their utility is limited w.r.t. earlier DL systems by their very weak Abox query languages. Typically, these only support instantiation (is an individual i an instance of a concept C), realisation (what are the most specific concepts i is an instance of) and retrieval (which individuals are instances of C). This is in contrast to a system such as Loom (MacGregor 1991), where a full first order query language is provided, although based on incomplete reasoning algorithms (MacGregor & Brill 1992).

The reason for this weakness is that, in these expressive logics, all reasoning tasks are reduced to that of determining KB satisfiability (consistency). For example, it can be inferred that John is an instance of Animal if and only if the KB is not satisfiable when an axiom is added to the Abox asserting that John is not an instance of Animal (i.e., that John is an instance of the negation of Animal). Realisation and retrieval can, in turn, be achieved through repeated application of instantiation tests. However, this technique cannot be used (directly) to infer from the above axioms that the pair ⟨John, Bill⟩ is an instance of the transitive role Brother, because these logics do not support role negation, i.e., it is not possible to assert that ⟨John, Bill⟩ is an instance of the negation of Brother.

In this paper we present a technique for answering such queries using a more sophisticated reduction to KB satisfiability. We then show how this technique can be extended to determine if an arbitrary tuple of individuals (i.e., not just a singleton or pair) satisfies a disjunction of conjunctions of concept and role membership assertions that can contain both constants (i.e., individual names) and variables. This provides a powerful query language, similar to the conjunctive queries typically supported by relational databases,[1] that allows complex Abox structures (e.g., cyclical structures) to be retrieved by using variables to enforce co-reference. For example, the query

$$\langle x, y \rangle \leftarrow \langle z, \mathsf{Bill}\rangle\mathord{:}\mathsf{Parent} \wedge \langle z, x\rangle\mathord{:}\mathsf{Parent} \wedge \\ \langle z, y\rangle\mathord{:}\mathsf{Parent} \wedge \langle x, y\rangle\mathord{:}\mathsf{Hates}$$

would retrieve all the pairs of hostile siblings in Bill's fam-

---
[1]It is inspired by the use of Abox reasoning to decide conjunctive query containment (Horrocks *et al.* 1999a; Calvanese, De Giacomo, & Lenzerini 1998).

ily.[2]

It is important to stress the fact that, given the expressivity of DLs, query answering cannot simply be reduced to model checking as in the database framework. This is because KBs may contain nondeterminism and/or incompleteness, making it infeasible to use an approach based on minimal models. In fact, query answering in the DL setting requires the same reasoning machinery as logical derivation.

An important advantage with the technique presented here is that it is quite generic, and can be used with any DL where instantiation can be reduced to KB satisfiability. It could therefore be used to significantly increase the utility of Abox reasoning in a wide range of existing (and future) DL implementations.

Preliminaries

Although the query answering technique is quite general, it will simplify the presentation if we consider a concrete DL language. We will use the language $\mathcal{ALC}$ (Schmidt-Schauß & Smolka 1991) as it is widely known, is sufficiently expressive for our purposes (in particular, it is closed under negation) and is a subset of the logics implemented in most "state of the art" DL systems, i.e., those based on highly optimised tableaux algorithms (Horrocks 1998; Patel-Schneider 1998; Haarslev & Möller 1999b).

In the following sections we will introduce and provide formal definitions for the $\mathcal{ALC}$ logic, DL knowledge bases, our query language and the various reasoning tasks with respect to knowledge bases and queries.

Description Logic $\mathcal{ALC}$

$\mathcal{ALC}$ concepts are built using a set of concept names (NC) and role names (NR). Valid concepts are defined by the following syntax:

$$C ::= A \mid \top \mid \bot \mid \neg A \mid C_1 \sqcap C_2 \mid C_1 \sqcup C_2 \mid \\ \forall R.C \mid \exists R.C$$

where $A \in$ NC is a concept name and $R \in$ NR is a role name. The meaning of concepts is given by a Tarski style model theoretic semantics using *interpretations*. An interpretation $\mathcal{I}$ is a pair $(\Delta^\mathcal{I}, \cdot^\mathcal{I})$, where $\Delta^\mathcal{I}$ is the domain and $\cdot^\mathcal{I}$ an interpretation function. The function $\cdot^\mathcal{I}$ maps each concept name in NC to a subset of $\Delta^\mathcal{I}$ and each role name in NR to a binary relation over $\Delta^\mathcal{I}$ (a subset of $\Delta^\mathcal{I} \times \Delta^\mathcal{I}$) such that the following equations are satisfied:

$$\begin{aligned}
\top^\mathcal{I} &= \Delta^\mathcal{I} \\
\bot^\mathcal{I} &= \emptyset \\
(\neg A)^\mathcal{I} &= \Delta^\mathcal{I} \setminus A^\mathcal{I} \\
(C_1 \sqcap C_2)^\mathcal{I} &= C^\mathcal{I}_1 \cap C^\mathcal{I}_2 \\
(C_1 \sqcup C_2)^\mathcal{I} &= C^\mathcal{I}_1 \cup C^\mathcal{I}_2 \\
(\forall R.C)^\mathcal{I} &= \{i \in \Delta^\mathcal{I} \mid \forall j. (i,j) \in R^\mathcal{I} \Rightarrow j \in C^\mathcal{I}\} \\
(\exists R.C)^\mathcal{I} &= \{i \in \Delta^\mathcal{I} \mid \exists j. (i,j) \in R^\mathcal{I} \land j \in C^\mathcal{I}\}
\end{aligned}$$

---
[2] Note that a sound and complete KB satisfiability algorithm will guarantee sound and complete query answers.

DL knowledge bases

A DL knowledge base is a pair $\Sigma = \langle \mathcal{T}, \mathcal{A} \rangle$, where $\mathcal{T}$ is called the *Tbox* and $\mathcal{A}$ is called the *Abox*.

The Tbox, or terminology, is a set of assertions about concepts of the form $C \sqsubseteq D$, where C and D are concepts.[3] An interpretation $\mathcal{I}$ *satisfies* $C \sqsubseteq D$ (written $\mathcal{I} \models C \sqsubseteq D$) iff $C^\mathcal{I} \subseteq D^\mathcal{I}$ and it satisfies a Tbox $\mathcal{T}$ (written $\mathcal{I} \models \mathcal{T}$) if it satisfies every assertion in $\mathcal{T}$.

The Abox, or assertional part, is a set of assertions about individuals of the form $a{:}C$ and $\langle a, b \rangle{:}R$, where a, b are names in NI, C is a concept and R is a role. The semantics of the Abox is given by extending the interpretation function $\cdot^\mathcal{I}$ to map each individual name in NI to a single element of $\Delta^\mathcal{I}$. An interpretation $\mathcal{I}$ satisfies $a{:}C$ iff $a^\mathcal{I} \in C^\mathcal{I}$, it satisfies $\langle a, b \rangle{:}R$ iff $(a^\mathcal{I}, b^\mathcal{I}) \in R^\mathcal{I}$ and it satisfies an Abox $\mathcal{A}$ (written $\mathcal{I} \models \mathcal{A}$) if it satisfies every assertion in $\mathcal{A}$.

An interpretation satisfies a knowledge base $\Sigma = \langle \mathcal{T}, \mathcal{A} \rangle$ (written $\mathcal{I} \models \Sigma$) if it satisfies both $\mathcal{T}$ and $\mathcal{A}$; a knowledge base is said to be satisfiable iff there exists at least one non-empty interpretation satisfying it. Using the definition of satisfiability, an assertion X is said to be a *logical consequence* of a KB Σ (written $\Sigma \models X$) iff X is satisfied by every interpretation that satisfies Σ.

The semantics of DL Aboxes often includes a so called *unique name assumption*: an assumption that the interpretation function maps different individual names to different elements of the domain (i.e., $a^\mathcal{I} \neq b^\mathcal{I}$ for all $a, b \in$ NI such that $a \neq b$). Our approach does not rely on such an assumption, and can be applied to DLs both with and without the unique name assumption.

Queries

In this paper we will focus on conjunctive queries: the extension to disjunctions of conjunctive queries can easily be accomplished using a technique sketched later on. In our framework, a key feature of queries is that they may contain variables, and we will assume the existence of a set of variables V that is disjoint from the set of individual names, i.e., $V \cap NI = \emptyset$. A *boolean* conjunctive query $\mathcal{Q}$ is of the form $q_1 \land \ldots \land q_n$, where $q_1, \ldots, q_n$ are query terms. Each query term q_i is of the form $x{:}C$ or $\langle x, y \rangle{:}R$, where C is a concept, R is a role and x, y are either individual names or variables. Given a KB Σ, an interpretation $\mathcal{I}$ of Σ satisfies a query $\mathcal{Q}$ iff the interpretation function can be extended to the variables in $\mathcal{Q}$ in such a way that $\mathcal{I}$ satisfies every term in $\mathcal{Q}$. A query $\mathcal{Q}$ is *true* w.r.t. Σ (written $\Sigma \models \mathcal{Q}$) iff every interpretation that satisfies Σ also satisfies $\mathcal{Q}$. For example, the query

$$\langle \text{Bill}, y \rangle{:}\text{Parent} \land \langle y, z \rangle{:}\text{Parent} \land z{:}\text{Male} \qquad (1)$$

is true w.r.t. a KB Σ iff it can be inferred from Σ that Bill has a grandson. Note that query truth value and the idea of logical consequence are strictly related. In fact, a boolean query is true w.r.t. a KB iff it is logical consequence of the KB.

---
[3] $C \doteq D$ is sometimes used as an abbreviation for the pair of assertions $C \sqsubseteq D$ and $D \sqsubseteq C$.

In the following, we will only consider how to answer boolean queries. Retrieving sets of tuples can be achieved by repeated application of boolean queries with different tuples of individual names substituted for variables. For example, the answer to the retrieval query $\langle x, y, z \rangle \leftarrow \mathcal{Q}$ w.r.t. a KB Σ is the set of tuples $\langle a, b, c \rangle$, where a, b, c are individual names occurring in Σ, such that $\Sigma \models \mathcal{Q}'$ for the boolean query $\mathcal{Q}'$ obtained by substituting a, b, c for x, y, z in $\mathcal{Q}$. The naive evaluation of such a retrieval could be prohibitively expensive, but would clearly be amenable to optimisation.

We will show how to answer boolean queries in two steps. Firstly, we will consider conjunctions of terms containing only individual names appearing in the KB; secondly, we will show how this basic technique can be extended to deal with variables.

Queries with multiple terms

In this section we will consider queries expressed as a conjunction of concept and role terms built using only names appearing in the KB, e.g., Tom:Student or $\langle$Tom, CS710$\rangle$:Enrolled.

As we have already seen, logical consequence can easily be reduced to a KB satisfiability problem if the query contains only a single concept term (this is the standard instantiation problem). For example,

$\langle \{\text{Student} \sqsubseteq \text{Person}\}, \{\text{Tom:Student}\} \rangle \models \text{Tom:Person}$

iff the KB

$\langle \{\text{Student} \sqsubseteq \text{Person}\}, \{\text{Tom:Student}, \text{Tom:}\neg\text{Person}\} \rangle$

is not satisfiable. This can be generalised to queries containing conjunctions of concept terms simply by transforming the query test into a set of (un)satisfiability problems: a conjunction $a_1:C_1 \land \ldots \land a_n:C_n$ is a logical consequence of a KB iff each $a_i:C_i$ is a logical consequence of the KB.

However, this simple approach cannot be used in our case since a query may also contain role terms. Instead, we will show how simple transformations can be used to convert every role term into a concept term. We call this procedure *rolling up* a query.

The rationale behind rolling up can easily be understood by imagining the availability of the DL one-of operator, which allows the construction of a concept containing only a single named individual (Schaerf 1994). The standard notation for such a concept is $\{a\}$, where a is an individual name, and the semantics is given by the equation $\{a\}^\mathcal{I} = \{a^\mathcal{I}\}$. For example, the expression $\{\text{Bill}\}$ represents a concept containing only the individual Bill (i.e., $\{\text{Bill}\}^\mathcal{I} = \{\text{Bill}^\mathcal{I}\}$).

Using the one-of operator, the role term $\langle$John, Bill$\rangle$:Brother can be transformed in the equivalent concept term John:($\exists$Brother.$\{$Bill$\}$). Furthermore, other concept terms asserting additional facts about the individual being rolled up (Bill in this case) can be absorbed into the rolled up concept term. For example, the conjunction

$\langle$John, Sally$\rangle$:Parent $\land$ Sally:Female $\land$ Sally:PhD

can be transformed into

John:$\exists$Parent.($\{$Sally$\} \sqcap$ Female $\sqcap$ PhD).

The absorption transformation is not strictly necessary for queries without variables, but it serves to reduce the number of satisfiability tests needed to answer the query (by reducing the number of conjuncts), and it will be required with queries containing variables. By applying rolling up to each role term, an arbitrary query can be reduced to an equivalent one which contains only concept terms, and which can be answered using a set of satisfiability tests as described above.

However, the logic we are using does not include the one-of operator, nor is it provided by any state of the art DL system (in fact the decidability of expressive DLs including this operator is still an open problem). Fortunately, we do not need the full expressivity of one-of, and in our case it can be "simulated". The technique used is to substitute each occurrence of one-of with a new concept name not appearing in the knowledge base. These new concept names must be different for each individual in the query, and are called the *representative* concepts of the individuals (written P_a, where a is the individual name). In addition, assertions which ensure that each individual is an instance of its representative concept must be added to the knowledge base (e.g., Bill:P_{Bill}).

In general, a representative concept cannot be used in place of one-of because it can have instances other than the individual which it represents (i.e., $P_a^\mathcal{I} \supseteq \{a^\mathcal{I}\}$). However, representative concepts can be used instead of one-of in our reduced setting, as shown by the following theorem:

Theorem 1 *Let $\Sigma = \langle \mathcal{T}, \mathcal{A} \rangle$ be a DL knowledge base, a, b two individual names in $\mathcal{A}$, R a role and $C_1, \ldots, C_n$ concepts. Given a new concept name P_b not appearing in Σ:*

$$\langle \mathcal{T}, \mathcal{A} \rangle \models \langle a, b \rangle{:}R \land b{:}C_1 \land \ldots \land b{:}C_n$$

if and only if

$$\langle \mathcal{T}, \mathcal{A} \cup \{b{:}P_b\} \rangle \models a{:}\exists R.(P_b \sqcap C_1 \sqcap \ldots \sqcap C_n).$$

Due to space considerations, we will not reproduce here a formal proof of this theorem, or of any of the other transformations used in this paper: full details can be found in (Horrocks et al. 1999a).

Queries with variables

In this section we show how variables can be introduced in this framework by using a more complex rolling up procedure in order to obtain a similar reduction to the KB (un)satisfiability problem.

Variables can be used exactly as individual names, but their meaning is as "place-holders" for unknown elements of the domain. Because variables may be interpreted as any element of the domain, they cannot simply be considered as individual names to which the unique name assumption does not apply; nor can they be treated as referring only to named individuals, giving the possibility of nondeterministically substituting them with names in the KB. In fact the query (1) is true w.r.t. both the KBs

$\langle \emptyset, \left\{ \begin{array}{l} \langle\text{Bill, Mary}\rangle\text{:Parent}, \langle\text{Mary, Tom}\rangle\text{:Parent}, \\ \text{Tom:Male} \end{array} \right\} \rangle$

and

$\langle \emptyset, \{\text{Bill}:\exists\text{Parent}.(\exists\text{Parent}.\text{Male})\}\rangle,$

but for the first KB the variables can be substituted by the individual names Mary and Tom, while in the second case the variables may need to be interpreted as elements of the domain that are not the interpretations of any named individuals.

Answering queries containing variables involves a more sophisticated rolling up technique. For example, let us consider the last two terms of query (1), $\langle y, z\rangle$:Parent and z:Male. If z were an individual name, the term could be rolled up as y:$\exists$Parent.($P_z \sqcap$ Male), but this is not an equivalent query when z is a variable name because z can be interpreted as any element of the domain, not just an element of $P_z^\mathcal{I}$. However, since in this case z is no longer referred to in any other place in the query, there is no other constraint on how an interpretation can be extended w.r.t. z, so the concept $\top$ (whose interpretation is always the whole domain) can be used instead of P_z. The resulting concept term is y:$\exists$Parent.($\top \sqcap$ Male), which can be simplified to y:$\exists$Parent.Male. The same procedure can now be applied to y, thereby reducing query (1) to the single concept term Bill:$\exists$Parent.($\exists$Parent.Male).

In order to show how this procedure can be more generally applied, it will be useful to consider the directed graph induced by the query, i.e., a graph in which there is a node x for each individual or variable x in the query, and an edge R from node x to node y for each role term $\langle x, y\rangle$:R in the query. It is easy to see that the rolling up procedure can be used to eliminate variables from any tree-shaped part of a query by starting at the leaves and working back towards the root (this is similar to the notion of descriptive support described in (Rousset 1999)). The ordering is important in order to maintain the connection between the rolled up term and the rest of the query. For example, rolling up query (1) in the reverse order would lead to the non-equivalent query

Bill:$\exists$Parent.$\top \wedge y$:$\exists$Parent.$\top \wedge z$:Male.

However, this simple procedure cannot be applied to parts of the query that contain cycles, or where more than one edge enters a node corresponding to a variable (i.e., with terms like $\langle x, z\rangle$:$R \wedge \langle y, z\rangle$:$S$). Let us consider the case where a variable is involved in a cycle, e.g., the simple query

$$\langle x, y\rangle\text{:Path} \wedge \langle y, z\rangle\text{:Path} \wedge \langle z, x\rangle\text{:Path} \quad (2)$$

which tests the KB for the presence of a loop involving the role Path. Rolling up one of the terms does not help, because the resulting query

$\langle x, y\rangle$:Path $\wedge \langle y, z\rangle$:Path $\wedge z$:$\exists$Path.P_x

still contains another reference to the variable x, and replacing P_x with $\top$ would result in a non-equivalent query that no longer contained a cycle. Moreover, it is obvious that there is no way to roll up the query in order to obtain a single occurrence of any of the three variables.

This problem can be solved by exploiting the tree model property of the logic.[4] Given this property, we know that

[4]This is a property of most DLs, and of all those implemented in state of the art systems.

Tbox assertions alone cannot constrain all models to be cyclical (if there is a model, then there is a tree model), so any cycle that might satisfy a cyclical query must be explicitly asserted in the Abox. Moreover, given the restricted expressivity of role assertions (i.e., that they apply only to atomic role names), cycles enforced in every interpretation must be composed only of elements interpreting individual names occurring in the Abox. Therefore, before applying the rolling up procedure, a variable occurring in a cycle can be nondeterministically substituted with an individual name occurring in the Abox.

For example, if in the query (2) the variable x is substituted by the individual name a, then it can be transformed into the query

$\langle a, y\rangle$:Path $\wedge \langle y, z\rangle$:Path $\wedge z$:($\exists$Path.P_a),

which no longer contains a cycle composed only of variables. Consequently, it can be rolled up into the single concept term

a:$\exists$Path.($\exists$Path.($\exists$Path.P_a))

where the concept P_a is used to close the cycle. A similar argument can be used w.r.t. variables appearing as the second argument of more than one role term, e.g., the variable z in the query $\langle x, z\rangle$:$R \wedge \langle y, z\rangle$:$S$. Such variables can also be dealt with by nondeterministically substituting them with individual names occurring in the Abox.

In order to deal with variables, one final problem remains to be overcome. We have seen how role terms containing variables can be rolled up into concept terms, but these may still be of the form x:C, where x is a variable. For example, the query $\langle x, y\rangle$:Parent, where x and y are variables, can only be reduced to the single term x:$\exists$Parent.$\top$. We cannot simply treat x as an individual and use the standard instantiation technique to reduce the query to KB satisfiability, because x can be interpreted as any element in the domain: in this case we need to verify that the interpretation of the concept $\exists$Parent.$\top$ is nonempty in every interpretation that satisfies the KB. However, it is easy to see that the interpretation of a concept C is nonempty in every interpretation that satisfies the KB $\langle \mathcal{T}, \mathcal{A}\rangle$ iff $\langle \mathcal{T} \cup \{\top \sqsubseteq \neg C\}, \mathcal{A}\rangle$ is not satisfiable.[5]

We are now in a position to present a procedure for answering an arbitrary boolean conjunctive query. The first step is to eliminate role terms from the query using the rolling up procedure, with the directed graph induced by the query being used to select an appropriate order in which to apply single rolling up steps. This is done by repeatedly applying one of the following steps until all role terms have been eliminated:

1. If the graph contains a leaf node y (i.e., a node with one incoming edge $\langle x, y\rangle$ and no outgoing edges), then the role term $\langle x, y\rangle$:R is rolled up, and the edge $\langle x, y\rangle$ is removed from the graph.

[5]Some earlier DL systems cannot reason with Tbox axioms of this kind (Baader & Hollunder 1991; Bresciani, Franconi, & Tessaris 1995), and this might restrict the kinds of query that could be answered.

2. Otherwise, if the graph contains a confluent node y (i.e., one with multiple incoming edges), then all role terms $\langle x, y \rangle {:} R$ are rolled up, and all edges $\langle x, y \rangle$ are removed from the graph (if y is a variable, then it is first replaced with an individual name chosen nondeterministically from the KB).

3. Finally, if the graph contains edges but no leaf nodes and no confluent nodes, then it must contain a cycle. In this case a node y in a cycle is chosen (preferably an individual as this reduces nondeterminism) and rolled up as in case 2 above.

The query now contains only concept terms, and evaluates to true iff every term evaluates to true (for some nondeterministic replacement of variables with individual names).

Extensions

For the sake of simplicity, we have so far only considered conjunctive queries over $\mathcal{ALC}$ KBs. However, the technique is general enough to be used with other DL languages, and it can be extended to deal with a disjunction of conjunctive queries.

DL expressivity

The technique described can be used with a wide range of DL languages. For example, qualified number restrictions, transitive roles and a role hierarchy (Horrocks, Sattler, & Tobies 1999b) could be added to the language without changing the rolling up procedure. Moreover, the efficiency of the rolling up procedure can actually be improved if the language is extended to include inverse roles, i.e., roles of the form R^{-1}, where $(i, j) \in (R^{-1})^\mathcal{I}$ iff $(j, i) \in R^\mathcal{I}$ (Horrocks & Sattler 1999). With inverse roles the rolling up procedure can be simplified because the orientation of the edges in the graph induced by the query is no longer relevant. For example, the term $\langle \text{John}, \text{Bill} \rangle{:}\text{Brother}$ can be rolled up in either direction to give $\text{John}{:}(\exists \text{Brother}.P_{\text{Bill}})$ or $\text{Bill}{:}(\exists \text{Brother}^{-1}.P_{\text{John}})$. Since the query graph is no longer directed, every connected subgraph without cycles can be treated as a tree and, moreover, each connected component of the graph can be collapsed into a single concept term.

Disjunctive queries

As we have already mentioned, it is possible to extend the basic framework to deal with disjunctions of boolean conjunctive queries, i.e., queries of the form $\mathcal{Q}_1 \vee \ldots \vee \mathcal{Q}_n$, where each Q_i is a boolean conjunctive query. We will make the assumption that no variable ever occurs in more than one conjunctive query (i.e., the sets of variables occurring in the conjunctive queries are pairwise disjoint).

Even with this simplification, verifying the truth value of a query cannot be achieved by verifying each conjunctive query separately and returning true iff any one of the conjunctive queries evaluates to true. This is because of the potential disjunctive information present in the KB. For example, consider the KB $\langle \emptyset, \{\text{Bill}{:}(\text{PhD} \sqcup \text{MsC})\} \rangle$, and the disjunctive query

$$\text{Bill}{:}\text{PhD} \vee \text{Bill}{:}\text{MsC}.$$

It is easy to see that the query should evaluate to true, but that none of the disjuncts is a logical consequence of the KB. In fact, in order to correctly evaluate the query it is necessary to consider both the terms together, and to test the satisfiability of the KB

$$\langle \emptyset, \{\text{Bill}{:}(\text{PhD} \sqcup \text{MsC}), \text{Bill}{:}\neg\text{PhD}, \text{Bill}{:}\neg\text{MsC}\} \rangle.$$

Clearly, this KB is unsatisfiable, giving the correct answer. A similar situation could arise w.r.t. variables, e.g., with the query $x{:}\text{PhD} \vee y{:}\text{MsC}$. In this case the problem must be reduced to testing the satisfiability of the KB

$$\langle \{\top \sqsubseteq \neg\text{PhD}, \top \sqsubseteq \neg\text{MsC}\}, \{\text{Bill}{:}(\text{PhD} \sqcup \text{MsC})\} \rangle.$$

Again, this KB is clearly unsatisfiable.

The examples given above suggest how the evaluation of disjunctive queries should be performed. The procedure can be summarised in the following three steps.[6] Firstly, each disjunct is transformed into a conjunction of concept terms as per the standard rolling up procedure. Secondly, the disjunction of these conjunctive terms is converted into its conjunctive normal form, the result being a conjunction of disjunctions of concept terms:

$$(q_{1,1} \vee \ldots \vee q_{1,n}) \wedge \ldots \wedge (q_{k,1} \vee \ldots \vee q_{k,n}).$$

Finally, each of the disjunctions of concept terms $q_{i,1} \vee \ldots \vee q_{i,n}$ is separately verified by adding its negation to the KB and testing the unsatisfiability of the result. The procedure returns true (i.e., the original disjunctive query evaluates to true) iff the KB is unsatisfiable in every case.

Discussion

In this paper we have presented a general technique for providing an expressive query language for a DL based knowledge representation system. Our work is motivated by the fact that many DL systems (including state of the art systems) provide no proper query language, and are only able to perform simple instantiation and retrieval reasoning tasks.

The only other comparable proposals in the literature are in the direction of integrating a DL system with Datalog (Levy & Rousset 1996a; Donini et al. 1998; Calvanese, De Giacomo, & Lenzerini 1999). Using Datalog as a query language can provide the ability to formulate recursive queries (Cadoli, Palopoli, & Lenzerini 1997), but on the other hand, the combination with expressive DLs soon leads to undecidability (Levy & Rousset 1996b). In addition, a special algorithm (dependent on the DL language) must be implemented in order to reason with the resulting hybrid language.

Our approach sacrifices some expressivity in the query language, but it works with very expressive DL languages and it can easily be adapted for use with any existing (or future) DL system equipped with the KB satisfiability reasoning service.

Our plans for future work include an implementation of the technique on top of the FaCT system (Horrocks 1998),

---

[6]Full details can be found in (Horrocks et al. 1999a).

which has recently been extended to include Abox reasoning (Tessaris & Gough 1998), as well as the analysis of suitable optimisations for reducing the nondeterminism due to variable substitution, both in the rolling up and the retrieval procedures.

References

Baader, F., and Hollunder, B. 1991. KRIS: Knowledge representation and inference system. *SIGART Bulletin* 2(3):8–14.

Baader, F. 1991. Augmenting concept languages by transitive closure of roles: An alternative to terminological cycles. In *Proc. of IJCAI-91*.

Bresciani, P.; Franconi, E.; and Tessaris, S. 1995. Implementing and testing expressive description logics: a preliminary report. In *Proc. of of KRUSE'95*, 28–39.

Cadoli, M.; Palopoli, L.; and Lenzerini, M. 1997. Datalog and description logics: Expressive power. In *Proc. of DBPL-97*.

Calvanese, D.; De Giacomo, G.; and Lenzerini, M. 1998. On the decidability of query containment under constraints. In *Proc. of PODS-98*, 149–158.

Calvanese, D.; De Giacomo, G.; and Lenzerini, M. 1999. Answering queries using views in description logics. In *Proc. of DL'99*, 9–13.

De Giacomo, G., and Lenzerini, M. 1995. What's in an aggregate: Foundations for description logics with tuples and sets. In *Proc. of IJCAI-95*.

De Giacomo, G., and Massacci, F. 1998. Combining deduction and model checking into tableaux and algorithms for converse-pdl. *Information and Computation*. To appear.

Donini, F. M.; Lenzerini, M.; Nardi, D.; and Schaerf, A. 1998. Al-log: Integrating datalog and description logics. *Journal of Intelligent Information Systems* 10(3):227–252.

Haarslev, V., and Möller, R. 1999a. An empirical evaluation of optimization strategies for abox reasoning in expressive description logics. In *Proc. of DL'99*, 115–119.

Haarslev, V., and Möller, R. 1999b. RACE system description. In *Proc. of DL'99*, 130–132.

Horrocks, I., and Sattler, U. 1999. A description logic with transitive and inverse roles and role hierarchies. *Journal of Logic and Computation* 9(3):385–410.

Horrocks, I.; Sattler, U.; Tessaris, S.; and Tobies, S. 1999a. Query containment using a DLR ABox. LTCS-Report 99-15, LuFG Theoretical Computer Science, RWTH Aachen, Germany.

Horrocks, I.; Sattler, U.; and Tobies, S. 1999b. Practical reasoning for expressive description logics. In *Proc. of LPAR'99*, 161–180. Springer-Verlag.

Horrocks, I. 1998. Using an expressive description logic: FaCT or fiction? In *Proc. of KR'98*, 636–647.

Levy, A. Y., and Rousset, M.-C. 1996a. Carin: A representation language combining horn rules and description logics. In *Proc. of ECAI-96*.

Levy, A. Y., and Rousset, M.-C. 1996b. The limits on combining recursive horn rules and description logics. In *Proc. of AAAI-96*.

MacGregor, R. M., and Brill, D. 1992. Recognition algorithms for the LOOM classifier. In *Proc. of AAAI-92*, 774–779. AAAI Press.

MacGregor, R. M. 1991. Inside the LOOM description classifier. *SIGART Bulletin* 2(3):88–92.

Patel-Schneider, P. F. 1998. DLP system description. In *Proc. of DL'98*, 87–89.

Rousset, M.-C. 1999. Backward reasoning in aboxes for query answering. In *Proc. of DL'99*, 18–22.

Schaerf, A. 1994. Reasoning with individuals in concept languages. *Data and Knowledge Engineering* 13(2):141–176.

Schmidt-Schauß, M., and Smolka, G. 1991. Attributive concept descriptions with complements. *Artificial Intelligence* 48:1–26.

Tessaris, S., and Gough, G. 1998. Abox reasoning with transitive roles and axioms. In *Proc. of DL'99*.

A Flexible Framework for Defeasible Logics

G. Antoniou and **D. Billington** and **G. Governatori** and **M.J. Maher**
School of Computing and Information Technology, Griffith University
Nathan, QLD 4111, Australia
{ga,db,guido,mjm}@cit.gu.edu.au

Abstract

Logics for knowledge representation suffer from over-specialization: while each logic may provide an ideal representation formalism for some problems, it is less than optimal for others. A solution to this problem is to choose from several logics and, when necessary, combine the representations. In general, such an approach results in a very difficult problem of combination. However, if we can choose the logics from a uniform framework then the problem of combining them is greatly simplified. In this paper, we develop such a framework for defeasible logics. It supports all defeasible logics that satisfy a strong negation principle. We use logic meta-programs as the basis for the framework.

Introduction

Logics for knowledge representation and, in particular, non-monotonic logics have developed greatly over the past 20 years. Many logics have been proposed, and a deeper understanding of the advantages and disadvantages of particular logics has been developed. There are also, finally, some indications that these logics can be usefully applied (Morgenstern 1998; Prakken 1997).

Unfortunately, it appears that no single logic is appropriate in all situations, or for all purposes. History clearly indicates that while one logic may achieve desired results in some situations, in other situations the outcome is not as successful. This is, no doubt, one reason for the proliferation of non-monotonic logics.

Furthermore, even with a fixed syntax and a common motivating intuition, reasonable people can disagree on the semantics of the logic. This can be seen in the literature on semantics of logic programs with negation, for example, but the point was made more sharply in (Touretzky, Horty and Thomason 1987) where a "clash of intuitions" was demonstrated in several different ways for a simple language describing multiple inheritance with exceptions. So it appears that no single logic, with a fixed semantics, will be appropriate. However, the diversity of logics threatens to become a Tower of Babel. If different problems require different logics then there are many practical disadvantages: skills in one logic do not transfer to another, combining systems composed of different logics is problematic, etc. It seems unlikely then that these logics are practically useful for knowledge representation.

One way to address this problem is to develop logics that are "tunable" to the situation. That is, to develop a framework of logics in which an appropriate logic can be designed. However, such a framework is not sufficient. Also needed is a methodology for designing logics, and the capability of employing more than one such logic in a representation. In this paper we develop such a framework for defeasible logics. This is a first step towards addressing the above problem for knowledge representation logics more generally. We make some contributions to the methodology by demonstrating how certain properties can be ensured for a logic. However, there is still much work to be done.

Defeasible logics were introduced and developed by Nute over several years (Nute 1994). These logics perform defeasible reasoning, where a conclusion supported by a rule might be overturned by the effect of another rule. Roughly, a proposition p can be defeasibly proved only when a rule supports it, and it has been demonstrated that no rule supports $\neg p$. These logics also have a monotonic reasoning component, and a priority on rules. One advantage of these logics is that the cost of computing with them is low (Antoniou, Billington, Maher and Rock 2000), in contrast to most logics for knowledge representation.

Nute has developed a framework for defeasible logic that abstracts the many individual logics he has constructed (Nute 1994). Although there are some logics in Nute's framework that cannot be represented in our framework, we will address logics that go well beyond the family of logics addressed by Nute. We consider logics that admit more kinds of conclusions than statements of definite or defeasible proof, as well as logics with different notions of failure-to-prove than the one used in Nute's framework.

In the next section we introduce defeasible logics in general and one particular defeasible logic DL. We introduce the Principle of Strong Negation as a design criterion for defeasible logics. In the following sections we demonstrate the framework, first by applying it to DL and then by designing independently motivated variants of DL. We also compare it with Nute's framework. In the process, we clarify the relationship between defeasible logics and other non-monotonic logics.

Copyright © 2000, American Association for Artificial Intelligence (www.aaai.org). All rights reserved.

Defeasible Logics

The family of defeasible logics was introduced by Nute. We begin by outlining the constructs in defeasible logics. We then define the inference rules of a particular defeasible logic DL that has received the most attention. Finally, we introduce the Principle of Strong Negation.

Outline of Defeasible Logics

A *defeasible theory* D is a triple $(F, R, >)$ where F is a set of literals (called *facts*), R a finite set of rules, and $>$ a superiority relation on R. In expressing the proof theory we consider only propositional rules. Rules containing free variables are interpreted as the set of their variable-free instances.

There are three kinds of rules: *Strict rules* are denoted by $A \to p$, and are interpreted in the classical sense: whenever the premises are indisputable (e.g. facts) then so is the conclusion. An example of a strict rule is "Emus are birds". Written formally: $emu(X) \to bird(X)$. Inference from facts and strict rules only is called *definite inference*. Facts and strict rules are intended to define relationships that are definitional in nature. Thus defeasible logics contain no mechanism for resolving inconsistencies in definite inference.

Defeasible rules are rules that can be defeated by contrary evidence. An example of such a rule is "Birds typically fly"; written formally: $bird(X) \Rightarrow flies(X)$. The idea is that if we know that something is a bird, then we may conclude that it flies, *unless there is other evidence suggesting that it may not fly*.

Defeaters are rules that cannot be used to draw any conclusions. Their only use is to prevent some conclusions. In other words, they are used to defeat some defeasible rules by producing evidence to the contrary. An example is "If an animal is heavy then it might not be able to fly". Formally: $heavy(X) \rightsquigarrow \neg flies(X)$. The main point is that the information that an animal is heavy is not sufficient evidence to conclude that it doesn't fly. It is only evidence that the animal *may* not be able to fly. In other words, we don't wish to conclude $\neg flies$ if $heavy$, we simply want to prevent a conclusion $flies$.

A *superiority relation* on R is an acyclic relation $>$ on R (that is, the transitive closure of $>$ is irreflexive). When $r_1 > r_2$, then r_1 is called *superior* to r_2, and r_2 *inferior* to r_1. This expresses that r_1 may override r_2. For example, given the defeasible rules

$$r: \qquad bird(X) \Rightarrow flies(X)$$
$$r': \quad brokenWing(X) \Rightarrow \neg flies(X)$$

which contradict one another, no conclusive decision can be made about whether a bird with a broken wing can fly. But if we introduce a superiority relation $>$ with $r' > r$, then we can indeed conclude that it cannot fly. A *conclusion* of a defeasible theory D is a tagged literal. Conventionally (Nute 1994; Billington 1993) there are four tags, so a conclusion has one of the following four forms:

- $+\Delta q$, which is intended to mean that q is definitely provable in D.

- $-\Delta q$, which is intended to mean that we have proved that q is not definitely provable in D.

- $+\partial q$, which is intended to mean that q is defeasibly provable in D.

- $-\partial q$ which is intended to mean that we have proved that q is not defeasibly provable in D.

Although the two pairs of tags mentioned above are the only ones currently used in defeasible logics, we will leave open the possibility of further (pairs of) tags. Indeed, we will later introduce in our framework the notion of support for a conclusion, which would require new tags in order to express this notion in a proof theory in the style of the next section.

Nute's Framework

Nute's framework for defeasible reasoning (Nute 1994) is based around defining a class of proof trees which represent valid inferences. We can reformulate this in terms of conventional inference rules, but we do not have space for a detailed presentation.

Briefly, Nute's framework consists of four inference rules which partly specify the behaviour of the definite (monotonic) reasoning component and its relationship with the defeasible (non-monotonic) reasoning component. Nute defines a defeasible logic to be a logic containing this monotonic kernel of inference rules and satisfying a coherence property. He also discusses several design principles of defeasible logics, but these are not a part of his framework.

A Defeasible Logic

As an example of a defeasible logic, we consider the logic of (Nute 1987), which has been investigated in (Maher, Antoniu and Billington 1998). In this presentation we use the formulation given in (Billington 1993). We denote this logic by DL.

Given a set R of rules, we denote the set of all strict rules in R by R_s, the set of strict and defeasible rules in R by R_{sd}, the set of defeasible rules in R by R_d, and the set of defeaters in R by R_{dft}. $R[q]$ denotes the set of rules in R with consequent q. In the following $\sim p$ denotes the complement of p, that is, $\sim p$ is $\neg p$ if p is an atom, and $\sim p$ is q if p is $\neg q$. A *rule* r consists of its *antecedent* $A(r)$ (written on the left; $A(r)$ may be omitted if it is the empty set) which is a finite set of literals, an arrow, and its *consequent* $C(r)$ which is a literal. In writing rules we omit set notation for antecedents. Provability is defined below. It is based on the concept of a *derivation* (or *proof*) in $D = (F, R, >)$.

A derivation is a finite sequence $P = (P(1), \ldots, P(n))$ of tagged literals satisfying the following conditions. The conditions are essentially inference rules phrased as conditions on proofs. $P(1..i)$ denotes the initial part of the sequence P of length i.

$+\Delta$: If $P(i+1) = +\Delta q$ then either
    $q \in F$ or
    $\exists r \in R_s[q] \; \forall a \in A(r): +\Delta a \in P(1..i)$

$-\Delta$: If $P(i+1) = -\Delta q$ then
    $q \notin F$ and
    $\forall r \in R_s[q] \; \exists a \in A(r): -\Delta a \in P(1..i)$

$+\partial$: If $P(i+1) = +\partial q$ then either
  (1) $+\Delta q \in P(1..i)$ or
  (2) (2.1) $\exists r \in R_{sd}[q] \, \forall a \in A(r) : +\partial a \in P(1..i)$ and
      (2.2) $-\Delta \sim q \in P(1..i)$ and
      (2.3) $\forall s \in R[\sim q]$ either
          (2.3.1) $\exists a \in A(s) : -\partial a \in P(1..i)$ or
          (2.3.2) $\exists t \in R_{sd}[q]$ such that
              $\forall a \in A(t) : +\partial a \in P(1..i)$ and $t > s$

$-\partial$: If $P(i+1) = -\partial q$ then
  (1) $-\Delta q \in P(1..i)$ and
  (2) (2.1) $\forall r \in R_{sd}[q] \, \exists a \in A(r) : -\partial a \in P(1..i)$ or
      (2.2) $+\Delta \sim q \in P(1..i)$ or
      (2.3) $\exists s \in R[\sim q]$ such that
          (2.3.1) $\forall a \in A(s) : +\partial a \in P(1..i)$ and
          (2.3.2) $\forall t \in R_{sd}[q]$ either
              $\exists a \in A(t) : -\partial a \in P(1..i)$ or $t \not> s$

The elements of a derivation are called *lines* of the derivation. We say that a tagged literal L is *provable* in $D = (F, R, >)$, denoted by $D \vdash L$, iff there is a derivation in D such that L is a line of P.

DL is closely related to several non-monotonic logics (Antoniou, Billington and Maher 2000). In particular, the "directly skeptical" semantics of non-monotonic inheritance networks (Horty, Thomason and Touretzky 1987) can be considered an instance of inference in DL once an appropriate superiority relation, derived from the topology of the network, is fixed (Billington, de Coster, and Nute 1990). DL is a conservative logic, in the sense of Wagner (1991).

The Principle of Strong Negation

The purpose of the $-\Delta$ and $-\partial$ inference rules is to establish that it is not possible to prove a corresponding positive tagged literal. These rules are defined in such a way that all the possibilities for proving $+\partial q$ (for example) are explored and shown to fail before $-\partial q$ can be concluded. Thus conclusions with these tags are the outcome of a constructive proof that the corresponding positive conclusion cannot be obtained.

As a result, there is a close relationship between the inference rules for $+\partial$ and $-\partial$, (and also between those for $+\Delta$ and $-\Delta$). The structure of the inference rules is the same, but the conditions are negated in some sense. We say that the inference rule for $+\partial$ ($-\partial$) is the *strong negation* of the inference rule for $-\partial$ ($+\partial$).

The strong negation of a formula is closely related to the function that simplifies a formula by moving all negations to an innermost position in the resulting formula. It is defined as follows.

$$
\begin{aligned}
sneg(+\partial p \in X) &= -\partial p \in X \\
sneg(-\partial p \in X) &= +\partial p \in X \\
sneg(A \wedge B) &= sneg(A) \vee sneg(B) \\
sneg(A \vee B) &= sneg(A) \wedge sneg(B) \\
sneg(\exists x \, A) &= \forall x \, sneg(A) \\
sneg(\forall x \, A) &= \exists x \, sneg(A) \\
sneg(\neg A) &= \neg sneg(A) \\
sneg(A) &= \neg A \quad \text{if } A \text{ is a pure formula}
\end{aligned}
$$

A pure formula is a formula that does not contain a tagged literal. Pairs of tags other than $+\partial, -\partial$ are treated in an analogous manner to $+\partial$ and $-\partial$. The strong negation of the applicability condition of an inference rule is a constructive approximation of the conditions where the rule is not applicable.

We are led to consider the following Principle of Strong Negation:

For each pair of tags such as $+\partial, -\partial$, the inference rule for $-\partial$ should be the strong negation of the inference rule of $+\partial$ (and vice versa).

Clearly DL satisfies this principle. In fact, all logics in our framework satisfy it. On the other hand, in Nute's framework (Nute 1994) logics may violate it.

There are two other important properties that defeasible logics may have. A theory is *coherent* if there is no p such that $D \vdash +\partial p$ and $D \vdash -\partial p$, or $D \vdash +\Delta p$ and $D \vdash -\Delta p$. A theory is *consistent* if for every p such that $D \vdash +\partial p$ and $D \vdash +\partial \neg p$, also $D \vdash +\Delta p$ and $D \vdash +\Delta \neg p$. Intuitively, coherence says that no literal is simultaneously provable and demonstrably unprovable. Consistency says that a literal and its negation can both be defeasibly provable only when it and its negation are definitely provable; hence defeasible inference does not introduce inconsistency. (As noted earlier, definite provability is intended for definitional information, and has no mechanism for resolving inconsistencies.) A logic is coherent (consistent) if each theory of the logic is coherent (consistent). The above logic DL is coherent and consistent (Billington 1993).

A Framework of Defeasible Logics

Our framework consists of a meta-program, defining when an atom is definitely or defeasibly proved, and a semantics for the meta-language (which is logic programming). Maher and Governatori (1999) have shown how DL is amenable to definition in this framework. We first introduce the meta-program for DL as a first example of the framework, and then derive some properties of the framework and the logics that can be defined within it. We make a comparison with Nute's framework.

The DL Meta-program

In this section we introduce a meta-program $\mathcal{M}$ in a logic programming form that expresses the essence of the defeasible reasoning embedded in DL. $\mathcal{M}$ consists of the following clauses. We first introduce the predicates defining classes of rules, namely

    supportive_rule(Name, Head, Body):-
       strict(Name, Head, Body).

    supportive_rule(Name, Head, Body):-
       defeasible(Name, Head, Body).

    rule(Name, Head, Body):-
       supportive_rule(Name, Head, Body).

    rule(Name, Head, Body):-
       defeater(Name, Head, Body).

We introduce now the clauses defining the predicates corresponding to $+\Delta$, $-\Delta$, $+\partial$, and $-\partial$. These clauses specify the structure of defeasible reasoning in DL. Arguably they convey the conceptual simplicity of DL more clearly than the proof theory.

```
c1    definitely(X):-
         fact(X).
c2    definitely(X):-
         strict(R,X,[Y_1,...,Y_n]),
         definitely(Y_1),...,definitely(Y_n).
c3    defeasibly(X):-
         definitely(X).
c4    defeasibly(X):-
         not definitely(~X),
         supportive_rule(R,X,[Y_1,...,Y_n]),
         defeasibly(Y_1),...,defeasibly(Y_n),
         not overruled(R,X).
c5    overruled(R,X):-
         rule(S,~X,[U_1,...,U_n]),
         defeasibly(U_1),...,defeasibly(U_n),
         not defeated(S,~X).
c6    defeated(S,~X):-
         sup(T,S),
         supportive_rule(T,X,[V_1,...,V_n]),
         defeasibly(V_1),...,defeasibly(V_n).
```

The first two clauses address definite provability, while the remainder address defeasible provability. The clauses specify if and how a rule in *DL* can be overridden by another, and which rules can be used to defeat an overriding rule, among other aspects of the structure of defeasible reasoning in *DL*.

We have permitted ourselves some syntactic flexibility in presenting the meta-program. However, there is no technical difficulty in using conventional logic programming syntax to represent this program.

Given a defeasible theory $D = (F, R, >)$, the corresponding program $\mathcal{D}$ is obtained from $\mathcal{M}$ by adding facts according to the following guidelines:

1. $\texttt{fact}(p)$.   if $p \in F$
2. $\texttt{strict}(r_i, p, [q_1, \ldots, q_n])$.   if $r_i : q_1, \ldots, q_n \rightarrow p \in R$
3. $\texttt{defeasible}(r_i, p, [q_1, \ldots, q_n])$.   if $r_i : q_1, \ldots, q_n \Rightarrow p \in R$
4. $\texttt{defeater}(r_i, p, [q_1, \ldots, q_n])$.   if $r_i : q_1, \ldots, q_n \leadsto p \in R$
5. $\texttt{sup}(r_i, r_j)$.   for each pair of rules such that $r_i > r_j$

The Framework

Maher and Governatori (1999) have established the correctness of this meta-program representation for *DL*. Let $\models_K$ denote logical consequence under Kunen's semantics of logic programs (Kunen 1987).

Theorem 1 *Let D be a defeasible theory and $\mathcal{D}$ denote its meta-program counterpart.*
For each literal p,

1. $D \vdash +\Delta p$ iff $\mathcal{D} \models_K \texttt{definitely}(p)$;
2. $D \vdash -\Delta p$ iff $\mathcal{D} \models_K \neg\texttt{definitely}(p)$;
3. $D \vdash +\partial p$ iff $\mathcal{D} \models_K \texttt{defeasibly}(p)$;
4. $D \vdash -\partial p$ iff $\mathcal{D} \models_K \neg\texttt{defeasibly}(p)$;

There are significant features of this result that deserve further comment. Negative conclusions (involving tags $-\Delta$ and $-\partial$), which refer to failure to prove, are characterized by the negation of the positive conclusions. Thus the meta-program implements *failure as negation*.

More generally, this provides a point of comparison between defeasible logics and other non-monotonic logics: in defeasible logics failure is the basic notion, whereas negation is basic in most other non-monotonic logics. Nevertheless, these two notions are different sides of the same coin.

An important feature of the meta-programming framework for defeasible logic is that it admits different forms of failure, corresponding to different semantics of negation in logic programs (Maher and Governatori 1999).

Our framework consists of a meta-program defining $\texttt{defeasibly}$ *and* $\texttt{definitely}$, *among other predicates, the implicit definition of negative tags by the negation of these predicates, and a semantics for the meta-language (logic programming).*

Every logic defined within the framework satisfies the Principle of Strong Negation, by construction. We say that a semantics for logic programs is *consistent* if for no program P and atom a does the semantics of P imply both a and $\neg a$ are true. Thus

Theorem 2 *Every defeasible logic defined in our framework using a consistent semantics is coherent.*

We can characterize the extent to which Nute's framework is covered by ours.

Theorem 3 *Every defeasible logic in Nute's framework that satisfies the Principle of Strong Negation can be represented in our framework, using Kunen's semantics.*

In view of this result and the consistency of Kunen's semantics we can establish that all such logics are coherent.

The presence of the Kunen semantics provides substantial insight into the computational complexity of defeasible logics. It means that every defeasible logic in Nute's sense that admits free variables and function symbols, and satisfies the Principle of Strong Negation is computable, in contrast to the great majority of non-monotonic logics which are uncomputable. Similarly, if we consider only propositional logics then, under certain restrictions on the meta-program, the consequences of a theory can be computed in polynomial time[1]. Again, this is in contrast to the great majority of non-monotonic logics.

There are several points of difference between our framework and Nute's.

- Nute's framework is committed to a very specific (though natural) notion of failure-to-prove: the one corresponding to the Kunen semantics. Our framework is not restricted in this way.

- Nute's framework is able to express logics that violate the Principle of Strong Negation, whereas ours cannot.

- By admitting arbitrary inference rules (in addition to the monotonic kernel) but requiring coherence, Nute's framework places the burden of proof that the result is a defeasible logic on the logic designer. Every logic designed within our framework is coherent.

- The setting of Nute's framework makes it extremely difficult to handle defeasible rules containing free variables

---
[1]Indeed, *DL* has been shown to have linear complexity (Antoniou, Billington, Maher and Rock 2000).

and function symbols. These can be handled very naturally in the meta-programming framework.
- It is not clear whether the four tags are intended to be the only tags admissible in Nute's framework or not. In the following section, we will demonstrate the advantage of admitting other tags.

New Defeasible Logics

We now develop several variations of *DL*. Our interest here is not to develop definitive defeasible logics, but to demonstrate the flexibility of the framework, and the beginnings of a methodology for designing logics. Maher and Governatori (1999) have already defined an extension of *DL* to allow a failure operator in the body of rules without disturbing the semantics of *DL* on theories without this operator. To keep this paper brief, we ignore definite inference in this section. A key element of the definition of the logics is the notion of support, used as part of Wagner's (1991) analysis of defeasible reasoning, so we begin by finding definitions of support.

Support

Support for a literal p consists of a chain of reasoning that would lead us to conclude p in the absence of conflicts. If we ignore the superiority relation we could define it simply as follows.

$c7$ `supported(X):-`
        `definitely(X).`

$c8$ `supported(X):-`
        `supportive_rule(R,X,[Y`$_1$`,...,Y`$_n$`]),`
        `supported(Y`$_1$`),...,supported(Y`$_n$`).`

However, in situations where two conflicting rules can be applied and one rule is inferior to another, the inferior rule should not be counted as supporting its conclusion. Thus we refine $c8$:

$c9$ `supported(X):-`
        `supportive_rule(R,X,[Y`$_1$`,...,Y`$_n$`]),`
        `supported(Y`$_1$`),...,supported(Y`$_n$`),`
        `not beaten(R,X).`

$c10$ `beaten(R,X):-`
        `rule(S,`$\sim$`X,[W`$_1$`,...,W`$_n$`]),`
        `defeasibly(W`$_1$`),...,defeasibly(W`$_n$`),`
        `sup(S,R).`

Notice that, because the definition of support is recursive, we would not be able to express it in the proof theories of (Nute 1994; Billington 1993) without additional tags.

Ambiguity Propagation

A literal is *ambiguous* if there is a chain of reasoning that supports a conclusion that p is true, another that supports that $\neg p$ is true, and the superiority relation does not resolve this conflict.

Example 1 The following is a classic example of non-monotonic inheritance.

$r_1 : \Rightarrow quaker$ $r_5 : republican \Rightarrow footballfan$
$r_2 : \Rightarrow republican$ $r_6 : pacifist \Rightarrow antimilitary$
$r_3 : quaker \Rightarrow pacifist$ $r_7 : footballfan \Rightarrow \neg antimilitary$
$r_4 : republican \Rightarrow \neg pacifist$

The priority relation is empty.

pacifist is ambiguous since the combination of r_1 and r_3 support *pacifist* and the combination of r_2 and r_4 support $\neg pacifist$. Similarly, *antimilitary* is ambiguous.

In *DL*, the ambiguity of *pacifist* results in the conclusions $-\partial pacifist$ and $-\partial \neg pacifist$. Since r_6 is consequently not applicable, *DL* concludes $+\partial \neg antimilitary$. This behaviour is called *ambiguity blocking*, since the ambiguity of *antimilitary* has been blocked by the conclusion $-\partial pacifist$ and an unambiguous conclusion about *antimilitary* has been drawn.

A preference for ambiguity blocking or ambiguity propagating behaviour is one of the properties of non-monotonic inheritance nets over which intuitions can clash (Touretzky, Horty and Thomason 1987). Stein (Stein 1992) argues that ambiguity blocking results in an unnatural pattern of conclusions in extensions of the above example. Ambiguity propagation results in fewer conclusions being drawn, which might make it preferable when the cost of an incorrect conclusion is high. For these reasons an ambiguity propagating version of *DL* is of interest.

We can achieve ambiguity propagation behaviour by making a minor change to clause $c5$ so that it now considers support to be sufficient to allow a superior rule to overrule an inferior rule.

$c11$ `overruled(R,X):-`
        `rule(S,`$\sim$`X,[U`$_1$`,...,U`$_n$`]),`
        `supported(U`$_1$`),...,supported(U`$_n$`),`
        `not defeated(S,`$\sim$`X).`

Proposition 4 *The resulting logic is consistent.*

Applying this logic to the example above, all literals mentioned in the theory (both positive and negated) are supported. As in *DL*, we conclude $-\partial pacifist$ and $-\partial \neg pacifist$, since r_3 and r_4 overrule each other. We also conclude $+\partial footballfan$ and $-\partial antimilitary$ for essentially the same reason as in *DL*. However this logic differs from *DL* and propagates ambiguity by concluding $-\partial \neg antimilitary$, since r_7 is overruled by r_6 and r_7 cannot defeat r_6.

Team Defeat

The defeasible logics we have considered so far incorporate the idea of *team defeat*. That is, an attack on a rule with head p by a rule with head $\sim p$ may be defeated by a *different* rule with head p (see inference rule $+\partial$ and clauses $c5$ and $c6$). Even though the idea of team defeat is natural, it is worth noting that several related approaches, such as LPwNF (Dimopoulos and Kakas 1995) and most argumentation frameworks, do not adopt this idea. It is easy to define defeasible logics without team defeat in our framework. For our original defeasible logic ($c1$–$c6$) this can be achieved by replacing $c5$ and $c6$ by the following clause.

$c12$ `overruled(R,X):-`
        `rule(S,`$\sim$`X,[U`$_1$`,...,U`$_n$`]),`
        `defeasibly(U`$_1$`),...,defeasibly(U`$_n$`),`
        `not sup(R,S).`

Proposition 5 *The resulting logic is consistent.*

It is also worth noting that several features can be easily integrated in our framework. For example, we may define an ambiguity propagating defeasible logic without team defeat replacing each defeasibly(U_i) with support(U_i) in clause $c12$. In this sense we have established a tunable framework in which a defeasible logic may be designed according to the specific needs of the problem at hand.

Relationships

In this section we wish to establish relationships among some of the variants we introduced in this paper. We will show that there exists a chain of increasing expressive power among several of the logics. We will be considering the following tags:

- Δ, which denotes strict provability.
- ∂_a, which denotes defeasible provability in the the ambiguity propagating defeasible logic ($c1$–$c4$,$c6$–$c11$).
- ∂, which denotes defeasible provability in our original defeasible logic ($c1$–$c6$).
- Σ, which denotes support in our original defeasible logic.

Then we are able to prove the following:

Theorem 6 $+\Delta \subset +\partial_a \subset +\partial \subset +\Sigma$.

Each inclusion is strict, in the sense that there are defeasible theories in which the inclusion is strict.

We wish to point out that this result is deeper that it may look on the surface. Notice that when the logic fails to prove a literal p and instead proves $-\partial p$, then that result may be used by the logic to prove another literal q that could not be proven if p were provable. In fact it is easily seen that defeasible provability in the original defeasible logic without team defeat is *not* weaker than defeasible provability with team defeat. Consider the following theory:

$$r_1 :\Rightarrow p \qquad r_2 :\Rightarrow p \qquad r_3 : p \Rightarrow \neg q$$
$$r_4 :\Rightarrow \neg p \qquad r_5 :\Rightarrow \neg p \qquad r_6 : \Rightarrow q$$
$$r_1 > r_4, r_2 > r_5$$

Then q is not defeasibly provable in the original defeasible logic, but defeasibly provable in the logic without team defeat.

Conclusion

We have developed a framework for defeasible logics that admits a wide range of logics. We have demonstrated the flexibility of the framework and the beginnings of a design methodology by developing, in a straightforward way, variants of *DL* which are, respectively, ambiguity propagating and incapable of team defeat. All logics designed within the framework are coherent.

The uniform setting provided by logic meta-programming supports the easy combination of logics that are based on the same form of failure. We have a proposal for combining logics with different notions of failure, based on the module system of (Maher 1993), but we have no space to present it here.

In summary, our framework provides a tunable family of defeasible logics.

Acknowledgements

This research was supported by the Australia Research Council under Large Grant No. A49803544.

References

G. Antoniou, D. Billington, M.J. Maher, A. Rock. 2000. Efficient Defeasible Reasoning Systems, *Proc. Australian Workshop on Computational Logic.*

G. Antoniou, M.J. Maher, and D. Billington. 2000. Defeasible Logic versus Logic Programming without Negation as Failure. *Journal of Logic Programming* (2000).

D. Billington, K. de Coster and D. Nute. 1990. A Modular Translation from Defeasible Nets to Defeasible Logic. *Journal of Experimental and Theoretical Artificial Intelligence* 2: 151–177.

D. Billington. 1993. Defeasible Logic is Stable. *Journal of Logic and Computation* 3: 370–400.

Y. Dimopoulos and A. Kakas. 1995. Logic Programming without Negation as Failure. In *Proc. ICLP-95*, MIT Press.

J.F. Horty, R.H. Thomason and D. Touretzky. 1987. A Skeptical Theory of Inheritance in Nonmonotonic Semantic Networks. In *Proc. AAAI-87*, 358–363.

K. Kunen. 1987. Negation in Logic Programming. *Journal of Logic Programming* 4: 289–308.

M.J. Maher. 1993. A Transformation System for Deductive Database Modules with Perfect Model Semantics. *Theoretical Computer Science* 110, 377–403.

M. Maher, G. Antoniou and D. Billington. 1998. A Study of Provability in Defeasible Logic. In *Proc. Australian Joint Conference on Artificial Intelligence*, 215–226, LNAI 1502, Springer.

M. Maher and G. Governatori. 1999. A Semantic Decomposition of Defeasible Logics. *Proc. American National Conference on Artificial Intelligence (AAAI-99)*, 299–306.

L. Morgenstern. 1998. Inheritance Comes of Age: Applying Nonmonotonic Techniques to Problems in Industry. *Artificial Intelligence*, 103, 1–34.

D. Nute. 1987. Defeasible Reasoning. In *Proc. 20th Hawaii International Conference on Systems Science*, IEEE Press, 470–477.

D. Nute. 1994. Defeasible Logic. In D.M. Gabbay, C.J. Hogger and J.A. Robinson (eds.): *Handbook of Logic in Artificial Intelligence and Logic Programming Vol. 3*, Oxford University Press, 353–395.

H. Prakken. 1997. *Logical Tools for Modelling Legal Argument: A Study of Defeasible Reasoning in Law.* Kluwer Academic Publishers.

L.A. Stein. 1992. Resolving Ambiguity in Nonmonotonic Inheritance Hierarchies. *Artificial Intelligence* 55: 259–310.

D.D. Touretzky, J.F. Horty and R.H. Thomason. 1987. A Clash of Intuitions: The Current State of Nonmonotonic Multiple Inheritance Systems. In *Proc. IJCAI-87*, 476–482, Morgan Kaufmann, 1987.

G. Wagner. 1991. Ex Contradictione Nihil Sequitur. In *Proc. IJCAI-91*, 538–546, Morgan Kaufmann.

Towards a logic-based theory of argumentation

Philippe Besnard and Anthony Hunter

IRIT-CNRS, Université Paul Sabatier, 118 route de Narbonne, 31062 Toulouse Cedex, France
Department of Computer Science, University College London, Gower Street, London WC1E 6BT, U.K.

Abstract

There are a number of frameworks for modelling argumentation in logic. They incorporate formal representation of individual arguments and techniques for comparing conflicting arguments. In these frameworks, if there are a number of arguments for and against a particular conclusion, an aggregation function determines whether the conclusion is taken to hold. We propose a generalization of these frameworks. In particular, this new framework makes it possible to define aggregation functions that are sensitive to the number of arguments for or against(in most other frameworks, aggregation functions just consider the existence of arguments for and against). In this paper, we explore this framework (based on classical logic) in which an argument is a pair where the first item in the pair is a minimal consistent set of formulae that proves the second item (which is a formula).

Introduction

Modelling argumentation has been a subject of research as long as the study of logic. They are closely intertwined topics, and modelling argumentation in logic is a natural, and important, research goal. A useful introduction to argumentation is in (Tou58), and a comprehensive recent review of modelling argumentation in logics is in (PV00).

Since paraconsistent logics have been suggested for applications including reasoning with specifications (HN98) and reasoning with news reports in structured text (Hun00), a logic-based theory of argumentation such as proposed below may be applicable in various roles.

Whilst most proposals have been made for modelling argumentation in logic, all are limited in the way that they combine arguments for and against a particular conclusion following. None are sensitive to the number of arguments for and against, apart from some proposals for counting the number for and the number against, and if there are more arguments for, then the conclusions follows, otherwise it is defeated.

Most proposals for modelling argumentation in logic are based on some form of binary argumentation (only the existence of arguments for and against is considered). A simple form of argumentation is that a conclusion follows if and if only if there is an argument for the conclusion, and no argument against the conclusion. So a conclusion follows only if it is not rebutted. A development of this idea is to only consider arguments that have not been undercut, and to check this by recursion for subarguments. An argument is undercut if and only if one of the assumptions for the argument is rebutted. Each undercut to a subargument is itself an argument and so may be undercut, and so by recursion each undercutter needs to be considered.

In this paper, we propose a new framework for argumentation with non-binary aggregation functions. For this framework, we have the following requirements:

- to derive arguments from a set of formulae that is potentially inconsistent;

- to compare arguments for and against a particular consequent;

- to identify undercuts for each argument, and by recursion, to identify undercuts for all subarguments for an argument;

- to evaluate each argument in terms of all its undercuts, and by recursion, all undercuts to its subarguments, and the value assigned to an argument decreases with increasing number of undercuts, and increases with increasing number of undercuts to each of the undercuts of the subarguments;

- to accumulate arguments for a consequent so that each extra argument contributes less to the accumulated value;

In our framework, that is based on classical logic, an argument is a pair where the first item in the pair is a minimal consistent set of formulae that proves the second item (which is a formula). Non-binary aggregation functions can be defined that are sensitive to the number of arguments for and against a conclusion. This paper defines the framework and explores its properties.

Preliminaries

We assume familiarity with classical logic.

We consider a propositional language. We use $\alpha, \beta, \gamma, \ldots$ to denote formulae and $\Delta, \Phi, \Psi, \ldots$ to denote sets of formulae. Deduction in classical propositional logic is denoted by the symbol $\vdash$ and deductive closure by Th so that $Th(\Phi) = \{\alpha \mid \Phi \vdash \alpha\}$.

For the following definitions, we first assume a database Δ (a finite set of formulae) and use this Δ throughout.

We further assume that every subset of Δ is given an enumeration $\langle \alpha_1, \ldots, \alpha_n \rangle$ of its elements, which we call its canonical enumeration. This really is not a demanding constraint: In particular, the constraint is satisfied whenever we impose an arbitrary total ordering over Δ. Importantly, the order has no meaning and is not meant to represent any respective importance of formulae in Δ. It is only a convenient way to indicate the order in which we assume the formulae in any subset of Δ are conjoined to make a formula logically equivalent to that subset.

Arguments

Here we adopt a very common intuitive notion of an argument and consider some of the ramifications of the definition. Essentially, an argument is a set of relevant formulae that can be used to classically prove some point, together with that point (we represent a point by a formula).

Definition 1 An **argument** is a pair $\langle \Phi, \alpha \rangle$ such that

1. $\Phi \not\vdash \bot$.
2. $\Phi \vdash \alpha$.
3. Φ is a minimal subset of Δ satisfying 2.

We say that $\langle \Phi, \alpha \rangle$ is an argument for α. We call α the consequent of the argument and Φ the support of the argument (we also say that Φ is a support for α).

Example 1 Consider $\Delta = \{\alpha, \alpha \to \beta, \gamma \to \neg\beta, \gamma, \delta, \delta \to \beta, \neg\alpha, \neg\gamma\}$. Some arguments are:

$$\langle \{\alpha, \alpha \to \beta\}, \beta \rangle$$
$$\langle \{\gamma \to \neg\beta, \gamma\}, \neg\beta \rangle$$
$$\langle \{\delta, \delta \to \beta\}, \beta \rangle$$
$$\langle \{\neg\alpha\}, \neg\alpha \rangle$$
$$\langle \{\neg\gamma\}, \neg\gamma \rangle$$
$$\langle \{\alpha \to \beta\}, \neg\alpha \vee \beta \rangle$$
$$\langle \{\neg\gamma\}, \delta \to \neg\gamma \rangle$$

Arguments are not independent. In a sense, some encompass others (possibly up to some form of equivalence). To clarify this requires a couple of definitions.

Definition 2 An argument $\langle \Phi, \alpha \rangle$ is **more conservative** than an argument $\langle \Psi, \beta \rangle$ iff $\Phi \subseteq \Psi$ and $\beta \vdash \alpha$.

Example 2 $\langle \{\alpha\}, \alpha \vee \beta \rangle$ is more conservative than $\langle \{\alpha, \alpha \to \beta\}, \beta \rangle$. Here, the latter argument can be obtained from the former (using $\alpha \to \beta$ as an extra hypothesis) but the reader is warned that such need not be the case in general as we now discuss.

Example 2 suggests that an argument $\langle \Psi, \beta \rangle$ can be obtained from a more conservative argument $\langle \Phi, \alpha \rangle$ by using $\Psi \setminus \Phi$ together with α in order to deduce β (in symbols, $\{\alpha\} \cup \Psi \setminus \Phi \vdash \beta$ or equivalently, $\Psi \setminus \Phi \vdash \alpha \to \beta$). As just mentioned, this does not hold in full generality. A counterexample consists of $\langle \{\alpha \wedge \gamma\}, \alpha \rangle$ and $\langle \{\alpha \wedge \gamma, \neg\alpha \vee \beta \vee \neg\gamma\}, \beta \rangle$. However, a weaker property holds:

Theorem 1 If $\langle \Phi, \alpha \rangle$ is more conservative than $\langle \Psi, \beta \rangle$ then $\Psi \setminus \Phi \vdash \phi \to (\alpha \to \beta)$ for some formula ϕ such that $\Phi \vdash \phi$ and $\phi \not\vdash \alpha$ unless α is a tautology.

The interesting case, as in Example 2, is when ϕ can be a tautology.

Theorem 2 Being more conservative defines a pre-ordering over arguments. Minimal arguments always exist, unless all formulas in Δ are inconsistent. Maximal arguments always exist: They are $\langle \emptyset, \top \rangle$ where $\top$ is any tautology.

A useful notion is then that of a normal form (a function such that any formula is mapped to a logically equivalent formula and, if understood in a strict sense as here, such that any two logically equivalent formulas are mapped to the same formula).

Theorem 3 Given a normal form, being more conservative defines an ordering provided that only arguments which have a consequent in normal form are considered. The ordered set of all such arguments is an upper semilattice (when restricted to the language of Δ). The greatest argument always exists, it is $\langle \emptyset, \top \rangle$.

Example 3 The g.l.b. of $\langle \{\alpha \wedge \beta\}, \alpha \rangle$ and $\langle \{\alpha \wedge \neg\beta\}, \alpha \rangle$ does not exist. If $\Delta = \{\alpha \wedge \beta, \alpha \wedge \neg\beta\}$, then there is no least argument. Taking now $\Delta = \{\alpha, \beta, \alpha \leftrightarrow \beta\}$, there is no least argument either (although Δ is consistent). Even though $\Delta = \{\alpha, \beta \wedge \neg\beta\}$ is inconsistent, the least argument exists: $\langle \{\alpha\}, \alpha' \rangle$ (where α' stands for the normal form of α). As the last illustration, $\Delta = \{\alpha \vee \beta, \beta\}$ admits the least argument $\langle \{\beta\}, \beta' \rangle$ (where β' stands for the normal form of β).

No normal form is assumed in the rest of the paper (i.e., we only consider the case where being more conservative is a pre-ordering). In any case, $\langle \emptyset, \top \rangle$ is more conservative than any other argument.

Irrespective of whether we consider an ordering, being more conservative induces, as any pre-ordering does, an equivalence relation (linking any two arguments that are more conservative than each other). Now, another basis for identifying two arguments with each other comes to mind: Pairwise logical equivalence of the components of both arguments. Hence the next definition.

Definition 3 Two arguments $\langle \Phi, \alpha \rangle$ and $\langle \Psi, \beta \rangle$ are **equivalent** iff Φ is logically equivalent to Ψ and α is logically equivalent to β.

Theorem 4 Two arguments are equivalent whenever each is more conservative than the other. In partial converse, if two arguments are equivalent then either each is more conservative than the other or neither is.

So, there exist equivalent arguments $\langle \Phi, \alpha \rangle$ and $\langle \Psi, \beta \rangle$ that fail to be more conservative than each other (as in Example 4). However, if $\langle \Phi, \alpha \rangle$ is strictly more conservative than $\langle \Psi, \beta \rangle$ (meaning that $\langle \Phi, \alpha \rangle$ is more conservative than $\langle \Psi, \beta \rangle$ but $\langle \Psi, \beta \rangle$ is not more conservative than $\langle \Phi, \alpha \rangle$) then $\langle \Phi, \alpha \rangle$ and $\langle \Psi, \beta \rangle$ are not equivalent.

Example 4 Let $\Phi = \{\alpha, \beta\}$ and $\Psi = \{\alpha \lor \beta, \alpha \leftrightarrow \beta\}$. The arguments $\langle \Phi, \alpha \land \beta \rangle$ and $\langle \Psi, \alpha \land \beta \rangle$ are equivalent even though none is more conservative than the other. This means that there exist two distinct subsets of Δ (namely, Φ and Ψ) supporting $\alpha \land \beta$.

Whilst equivalent arguments make the same point (that is, the same inference), we do want to distinguish equivalent arguments from each other. What we do not want is to distinguish between arguments that are more conservative than each other.

Undercuts

Some arguments oppose the support of others, which amounts to the notion of an undercut.

Definition 4 An **undercut** for an argument $\langle \Phi, \alpha \rangle$ is an argument $\langle \Psi, \neg(\phi_1 \land \ldots \land \phi_n) \rangle$ where $\{\phi_1, \ldots, \phi_n\} \subseteq \Phi$ and $\Phi \cup \Psi \subseteq \Delta$ by definition of an argument.

Example 5 Let $\Delta = \{\alpha, \alpha \to \beta, \gamma, \gamma \to \neg\alpha\}$. Then, $\langle \{\gamma, \gamma \to \neg\alpha\}, \neg(\alpha \land (\alpha \to \beta)) \rangle$ is an undercut for $\langle \{\alpha, \alpha \to \beta\}, \beta \rangle$. A less conservative undercut for $\langle \{\alpha, \alpha \to \beta\}, \beta \rangle$ is $\langle \{\gamma, \gamma \to \neg\alpha\}, \neg\alpha \rangle$.

Theorem 5 Δ is inconsistent if there exists an argument that has at least one undercut. The converse is true when no formula in Δ is inconsistent.

As arguments can be ordered from more conservative to less conservative, there is a clear and unambiguous notion of maximally conservative undercuts for a given argument (the ones which are representative of all undercuts for that argument):

Definition 5 $\langle \Phi, \alpha \rangle$ is a **maximally conservative undercut** of $\langle \Psi, \beta \rangle$ iff $\langle \Phi, \alpha \rangle$ is an undercut of $\langle \Psi, \beta \rangle$ such that no undercuts of $\langle \Psi, \beta \rangle$ are strictly more conservative than $\langle \Phi, \alpha \rangle$ (i.e., for all undercuts $\langle \Phi', \alpha' \rangle$ of $\langle \Psi, \beta \rangle$, if $\Phi' \subseteq \Phi$ and $\alpha \vdash \alpha'$ then $\Phi \subseteq \Phi'$ and $\alpha' \vdash \alpha$).

Notice that the consequent of a maximally conservative undercut for an argument is exactly the negation of the full support of the argument:

Theorem 6 If $\langle \Psi, \neg(\alpha_1 \land \ldots \land \alpha_n) \rangle$ is a maximally conservative undercut to an argument $\langle \Phi, \beta \rangle$, then $\Phi = \{\alpha_1, \ldots, \alpha_n\}$.

Note that if $\langle \Psi, \neg(\alpha_1 \land \ldots \land \alpha_n) \rangle$ is a maximally conservative undercut for an argument $\langle \Phi, \beta \rangle$, then so are $\langle \Psi, \neg(\alpha_2 \land \ldots \land \alpha_n \land \alpha_1) \rangle$ and $\langle \Psi, \neg(\alpha_3 \land \ldots \land \alpha_n \land \alpha_1 \land \alpha_2) \rangle$ and so on. However, they are all identical (in the sense that each is more conservative than the others). We can ignore the unnecessary variants by just considering the canonical undercuts defined as follows.

Definition 6 An argument $\langle \Psi, \neg(\alpha_1 \land \ldots \land \alpha_n) \rangle$ is a canonical undercut for $\langle \Phi, \beta \rangle$ iff it is a maximally conservative undercut for $\langle \Phi, \beta \rangle$ and $\langle \alpha_1, \ldots, \alpha_n \rangle$ is the canonical enumeration of Φ.

Theorem 7 Any two different canonical undercuts for the same argument have the same consequent, but distinct supports.

Theorem 8 Given two different canonical undercuts for the same argument, none is more conservative than the other.

Example 6 If $\Delta = \{\alpha, \beta, \neg\alpha, \neg\beta\}$, both the following

$$\langle \{\neg\alpha\}, \neg(\alpha \land \beta) \rangle$$
$$\langle \{\neg\beta\}, \neg(\alpha \land \beta) \rangle$$

are canonical undercuts for $\langle \{\alpha, \beta\}, \alpha \leftrightarrow \beta \rangle$, but neither is more conservative than the other.

We adopt a lighter notation, writing $\langle \Psi, \diamond \rangle$ for a canonical undercut of $\langle \Phi, \beta \rangle$. Clearly, $\diamond$ is $\neg(\alpha_1 \land \ldots \land \alpha_n)$ where $\langle \alpha_1, \ldots, \alpha_n \rangle$ is the canonical enumeration of Φ.

Argument trees

An argument tree describes the various ways an argument can be challenged, as well as how the counter-arguments to the initial argument can themselves be challenged, and so on recursively.

Definition 7 An **argument tree** for α is a tree where the nodes are arguments such that

1. The root is an argument for α.
2. For no node $\langle \Phi, \beta \rangle$ with ancestor nodes $\langle \Phi_1, \beta_1 \rangle, \ldots, \langle \Phi_n, \beta_n \rangle$ is Φ a subset of $\Phi_1 \cup \cdots \cup \Phi_n$.
3. The children nodes of a node N consist of all canonical undercuts for N that obey 2.

We first give an illustration of an argument tree in Example 7 and then we motivate the conditions of Definition 7 as follows: Condition 2 is meant to avoid the situation illustrated by Example 8; and Condition 3 is meant to avoid the situation illustrated by Example 9.

Example 7 For $\Delta = \{\alpha, \alpha \to \beta, \gamma, \gamma \to \neg\alpha, \neg\gamma \lor \neg\alpha\}$, we have the following argument tree where $\diamond$ stands for $\neg(\alpha \land (\alpha \to \beta))$.

$$\langle \{\alpha, \alpha \to \beta\}, \beta \rangle$$
$$\langle \{\gamma, \gamma \to \neg\alpha\}, \diamond \rangle \quad\quad \langle \{\gamma, \neg\gamma \lor \neg\alpha\}, \diamond \rangle$$

Note the two undercuts are equivalent. They do count as two arguments because they are based on two different items of the database (even though these items turn out to be logically equivalent).

Example 8 Let $\Delta = \{\alpha, \alpha \to \beta, \gamma \to \neg\alpha, \gamma\}$.

$$\langle \{\alpha, \alpha \to \beta\}, \beta \rangle$$
$$\uparrow$$
$$\langle \{\gamma, \gamma \to \neg\alpha\}, \diamond \rangle$$
$$\uparrow$$
$$\langle \{\alpha, \gamma \to \neg\alpha\}, \diamond \rangle$$

This is not an argument tree because the undercut to the undercut is actually making exactly the same point (that α and γ are incompatible in the context of Δ) as the undercut itself does, just by using modus tollens instead of modus ponens.

Example 9 Given $\Delta = \{\alpha, \beta, \alpha \to \gamma, \beta \to \delta, \neg\alpha \vee \neg\beta\}$, consider the following tree.

$$\langle\{\alpha, \beta, \alpha \to \gamma, \beta \to \delta\}, \gamma \wedge \delta\rangle$$
$$\langle\{\alpha, \neg\alpha \vee \neg\beta\}, \neg\beta\rangle \qquad \langle\{\beta, \neg\alpha \vee \neg\beta\}, \neg\alpha\rangle$$

This is not an argument tree because the two children nodes are not maximally conservative undercuts. The first undercut is essentially the same argument as the second undercut in a rearranged form (relying on α and β being incompatible, assume one and then conclude that the other doesn't hold). If we replace these by the maximally conservative undercut $\langle\{\neg\alpha \vee \neg\beta\}, \diamond\rangle$, we obtain an argument tree.

The following result is important in practice — particularly in light of other results we present in the next subsection.

Theorem 9 *Argument trees are finite.*

Theorem 10 *Let T be an argument tree. If Δ is consistent, then T has exactly one node. The converse is untrue.*

The form of an argument tree is not arbitrary. It summarizes all lines of discussion about the argument in the root node. Each node except the root node is the starting point of an implicit series of related arguments as shown by Theorem 11. We call these related arguments duplicates. We define this notion formally in the next subsection.

Duplicates

Equivalent arguments are arguments that express the same reason for the same point. For undercuts, a more refined notion than equivalent arguments is useful:

Definition 8 *Two undercuts $\langle\Gamma \cup \Phi, \neg\psi\rangle$ and $\langle\Gamma \cup \Psi, \neg\phi\rangle$ are **duplicates** of each other iff ϕ is $\phi_1 \wedge \ldots \wedge \phi_n$ such that $\Phi = \{\phi_1, \ldots, \phi_n\}$ and ψ is $\psi_1 \wedge \ldots \wedge \psi_m$ such that $\Psi = \{\psi_1, \ldots, \psi_m\}$.*

Duplicates introduce a symmetric relation which fails to be transitive (and reflexive). Arguments which are duplicates of each other are essentially the same argument in a rearranged form.

Example 10 *The two arguments below are duplicates of each other.*
$$\langle\{\alpha, \neg\alpha \vee \neg\beta\}, \neg\beta\rangle$$
$$\langle\{\beta, \neg\alpha \vee \neg\beta\}, \neg\alpha\rangle$$

Example 11 *To illustrate the failure of transitivity in the duplicate relationship, the following two arguments are duplicates,*
$$\langle\{\gamma, \alpha, \alpha \wedge \gamma \to \neg\beta\}, \neg\beta\rangle$$
$$\langle\{\gamma, \beta, \alpha \wedge \gamma \to \neg\beta\}, \neg\alpha\rangle$$
and the following two arguments are also duplicates,
$$\langle\{\gamma, \beta, \alpha \wedge \gamma \to \neg\beta\}, \neg\alpha\rangle$$
$$\langle\{\alpha, \alpha \wedge \gamma \to \neg\beta\}, \neg(\beta \wedge \gamma)\rangle$$
but the following two are not duplicates.
$$\langle\{\alpha, \alpha \wedge \gamma \to \neg\beta\}, \neg(\beta \wedge \gamma)\rangle$$
$$\langle\{\gamma, \alpha, \alpha \wedge \gamma \to \neg\beta\}, \neg\beta\rangle$$

The following result shows how we can systematically obtain duplicates.

Theorem 11 *For every maximally conservative undercut $\langle\Psi, \neg\alpha\rangle$ to an argument $\langle\Phi, \beta\rangle$, there exist at least m arguments each of which undercuts the undercut (m is the size of Ψ). Each of these m arguments is a duplicate to the undercut.*

Theorem 12 *No two maximally conservative undercuts of the same argument are duplicates.*

Theorem 13 *No branch in an argument tree may contain duplicates, except possibly one duplicate to the root.*

These two results are important. They show that argument trees are an efficient and lucid way of representing the pertinent counter-arguments to each argument: Theorem 12 shows it regarding breadth and Theorem 13 shows it regarding depth. Moreover, they show that the intuitive need to eliminate duplicates from argument trees is taken care of through an efficient syntactical criterion (condition 2 of Definition 7).

Argument structures

We now consider how we can gather argument trees for and against a point. In order to do this, we define argument structures.

Definition 9 *An **argument structure** for a formula α is a pair of sets $\langle\mathcal{P}, \mathcal{C}\rangle$ where $\mathcal{P}$ is the set of argument trees for α and $\mathcal{C}$ is the set of argument trees for $\neg\alpha$.*

Example 12 *Let $\Delta = \{\alpha \vee \beta, \alpha \to \gamma, \neg\gamma, \neg\beta, \delta \leftrightarrow \beta\}$. We obtain three argument trees for the argument structure for $\alpha \vee \neg\delta$.*

$$\langle\{\alpha \vee \beta, \alpha \to \gamma, \neg\gamma, \delta \leftrightarrow \beta\}, \neg\alpha \wedge \delta\rangle$$
$$\uparrow$$
$$\langle\{\neg\beta\}, \diamond\rangle$$

$$\langle\{\alpha \vee \beta, \neg\beta\}, \alpha \vee \neg\delta\rangle$$
$$\uparrow$$
$$\langle\{\alpha \to \gamma, \neg\gamma\}, \diamond\rangle$$

$$\langle\{\delta \leftrightarrow \beta, \neg\beta\}, \alpha \vee \neg\delta\rangle$$
$$\uparrow$$
$$\langle\{\alpha \vee \beta, \alpha \to \gamma, \neg\gamma\}, \diamond\rangle$$

Theorem 14 *Let $\langle\mathcal{P}, \mathcal{C}\rangle$ be an argument structure such that $\mathcal{P} \neq \emptyset$. If Δ is consistent, then each argument tree in $\mathcal{P}$ has exactly one node, and $\mathcal{C}$ is the empty set. The converse is untrue.*

Theorem 15 *Let $\langle[X_1, \ldots, X_n], [Y_1, \ldots, Y_m]\rangle$ be an argument structure. For any i and any j, the support of the root node of Y_j (resp. X_i) is a superset of the support of a canonical undercut for the root node of X_i (resp. Y_j).*

Aggregation

We now propose an approach to evaluate argument structures. This approach is actually an illustration of the possibilities arising from our framework: We will see that it needs be modified and generalized to cope with some particular requirements.

Definition 10 *A **categorizer** is a mapping from argument trees to numbers. A **categorization** is then a pair of multisets obtained by applying the same categorizer to each argument tree in an argument structure.*

The number assigned by a categorizer is intended to capture the relative strength of an argument taking into account the undercuts, undercuts to undercuts, and so on. I.e., it is an attempt to provide an abstraction of an argument tree in the form of a single number.

*The **h-categorizer**, denoted h, is an example of a categorizer. An argument tree of root R is assigned a number $h(R)$ defined recursively by*

$$h(N) = \frac{1}{1 + h(N_1) + \cdots + h(N_l)}$$

where $N_1, \ldots, N_l$ are the children nodes for N (if $l = 0$, $h(N_1) + \cdots + h(N_l) = 0$).

Definition 11 *An **accumulator** is a function that takes a categorization for a formula α and returns a pair of numbers (α^+, α^-) st α^+ is the accumulated value for α and α^- is the accumulated value against α. The **balance** of accumulated values is calculated as $\alpha^+ - \alpha^-$.*

If the balance of accumulated values is 0, then the arguments for the formula "equal" the arguments against the formula. If the balance of accumulated values is positive (negative), then the arguments for the formula are stronger (weaker) —when aggregated— than the arguments against the formula.

*The **l-accumulator** is an example of an accumulator. For any categorization $\langle [X_1, \ldots, X_n], [Y_1, \ldots, Y_m] \rangle$, let*

$$l(\langle [X_1, \ldots, X_n], [Y_1, \ldots, Y_m] \rangle) = \\ (\log(1 + X_1 + \cdots + X_n), \log(1 + Y_1 + \cdots + Y_m)).$$

Example 13 *Consider the categorization $\langle [1], [1/2] \rangle$. Using the l-accumulator, we obtain 0.47 as the balance of the accumulated values. For the categorization $\langle [1, 1/2], [1/2, 1/2] \rangle$, the l-accumulator gives 0.41 as the balance of the accumulated values. So we can see that adding an argument tree of value $1/2$ to both the pro and con sides benefits the con side since initially the con side is a much weaker argument than the pro side.*

Example 14 *For $\langle [1/2, 1/2], [1] \rangle$, the l-accumulator gives -0.25 as the balance of the accumulated values. For $\langle [1/2, 1/2, 1/2], [1, 1/2] \rangle$, the l-accumulator gives -0.29 as the balance of the accumulated values. Here, we see that adding an argument tree of value $1/2$ to both the pro and con sides benefits the con side since initially the pro side has two arguments of value $1/2$ but the con side has a single argument of value 1 (in particular, we want an argument to have a more profound effect when confirming a single argument than when joining a hundred similar arguments already agreeing).*

Definition 10 and Definition 11 make it possible to have categorizer and accumulator functions conforming to a probabilistic approach and the same holds for a diverse range of other approaches to argumentation. An example is binary argumentation (RM70; HTT90; BDP93; Nut94; GLV98), and counting arguments for and against (SL92; PL92) is another simple case. A general approach that can be incorporated in our framework is argumentative logics (see e.g., (EGH95)). Categorizers for doing so include constant functions ($\forall T, cat(T) = 1$), and other very simple functions ($cat(T) = 1$ iff T has exactly one node). No complex accumulator is then needed either.

As an illustration, a few approaches to argumentation based on reasoning with maximal consistent subsets are:

- α *is an **existential inference** from Δ iff $\Theta \vdash \alpha$ where Θ is some maximal consistent subset of Δ.*
- α *is an **unrebutted inference** from Δ iff $\Theta \vdash \alpha$ for some maximal consistent subset Θ of Δ and $\Omega \not\vdash \neg\alpha$ for each maximal consistent subset Ω of Δ.*
- α *is a **universal inference** from Δ iff $\Omega \vdash \alpha$ for each maximal consistent subset Ω of Δ.*
- α *is a **free inference** from Δ iff $\Lambda \vdash \alpha$ st Λ is the intersection of all maximal consistent subsets of Δ.*

Definition 12 *The **unit categorizer** is a function, denoted c, from the set of argument trees to $\{1\}$ such that $c(T) = 1$ in all cases.*

Definition 13 *The **unit accumulator** is a function, denoted u_a, from the set of categorizations to the set $\{(1,1), (1,0), (0,1), (0,0)\}$ st for a categorization $\langle X, Y \rangle$*

$$u_a(\langle X, Y \rangle) = (p(X), p(Y))$$

where $p(Z) = 1$ iff $Z \neq \emptyset$.

Theorem 16 *If applying the unit categorizer to the argument structure for α yields $\langle X, Y \rangle$, then α is an existential inference from Δ iff $u_a(\langle X, Y \rangle) = (1, 0)$ or $(1, 1)$.*

Theorem 17 *α is an unrebutted inference from Δ iff $u_a(\langle X, Y \rangle) = (1, 0)$ where $\langle X, Y \rangle$ results from applying the unit categorizer to the argument structure for α.*

Similarly, free inferencing is captured in our framework without recourse to maximal consistent subsets.

Definition 14 *The **free categorizer** is a function, denoted s, from the set of argument trees to $\{0, 1\}$ such that $s(T) = 1$ iff T is just a root node.*

Definition 15 *The **free accumulator** is a function, denoted f_a, from the set of categorizations to the set $\{(1,1), (1,0), (0,1), (0,0)\}$ st for a categorization $\langle X, Y \rangle$*

$$f_a(\langle X, Y \rangle) = (w(X), w(Y))$$

where $w(Z) = 1$ iff $1 \in Z$.

Theorem 18 *Let $\langle X, Y \rangle$ result from applying the free categorizer to the argument structure for α. Then, α is a free inference from Δ iff $f_a(\langle X, Y \rangle) = (1, 0)$.*

Universal inferencing cannot be captured using the above definitions for aggregation unless they are generalized (keep in mind that all results, apart from theorems 16 to 18, would still hold) and a similar observation applies for Dung's well-known approach (Dun95).

Yet, an argument structure can be viewed as an argumentation framework in Dung's sense. Also, an argument in our sense amounts to an argument in a Dung argumentation framework, and an arc in an argument tree amounts to an attack in Dung's sense. However, the way sets of arguments are compared is different.

Definition 16 *A* **Dung argumentation framework** *is a pair* $\Delta = \langle \Gamma, \mathcal{A} \rangle$ *where* Γ *is a set and* $\mathcal{A} \subseteq \Gamma \times \Gamma$ *(intuitively, $\mathcal{A}$ is an "attack" relation between arguments).*

Definition 17 *A subset S of Γ is* **conflict-free** *if there are no two X, Y in S such that $X \mathcal{A} Y$ or $Y \mathcal{A} X$.*

Definition 18 $X \in \Gamma$ *is* **acceptable** *wrt* $S \subseteq \Gamma$ *iff for each $Y \in \Gamma$, if $Y \mathcal{A} X$ then $Z \mathcal{A} Y$ for some $Z \in S$.*

Definition 19 *A conflict-free subset S of Γ is* **admissible** *iff each element of S is acceptable wrt S.*

Example 15 *Let* $\Delta = \{\beta, \beta \to \alpha, \gamma, \gamma \to \neg\beta, \delta \wedge \neg\gamma, \neg\delta \wedge \neg\gamma, \neg\gamma \to \neg\alpha\}$. *Consider the argument trees:*

$$\langle \{\neg\gamma, \neg\gamma \to \neg\alpha\}, \neg\alpha \rangle$$
$$\uparrow$$
$$\langle \{\gamma\}, \diamond \rangle$$

$$\langle \{\beta, \beta \to \alpha\}, \alpha \rangle$$
$$\uparrow$$
$$\langle \{\gamma, \gamma \to \neg\beta\}, \diamond \rangle$$

$$\langle \{\delta \wedge \neg\gamma\}, \diamond \rangle \qquad \langle \{\neg\delta \wedge \neg\gamma\}, \diamond \rangle$$
$$\uparrow \qquad\qquad \uparrow$$
$$\langle \{\neg\delta \wedge \neg\gamma\}, \diamond \rangle \qquad \langle \{\delta \wedge \neg\gamma\}, \diamond \rangle$$

There is no admissible set of arguments that contains $\langle \{\beta, \beta \to \alpha\}, \alpha \rangle$. Thus, we see that our approach cannot capture Dung's unless categorization is redefined so that instead of categorizing each tree individually, it considers each tree in the context of the other trees.

Concluding remarks

Here, we have proposed a new framework for modelling argumentation. The key feature is that we incorporate non-binary aggregation functions. This framework can be viewed as a generalization of a wide range of existing approaches to argument aggregation. Moreover, non-binary argument aggregation offers a more realistic approach to weighing up the relative merits of arguments for and against a possible conclusion.

We believe that there are a range of possible applications of our framework in reasoning with potentially inconsistent information. Such applications include reasoning with inconsistent specifications (HN98) and inconsistent structured text (Hun00).

In order to use the framework more generally, we may wish to differentiate the information in Δ from some background knowledge Σ where we assume that Σ is uncontroversial knowledge that can be taken for granted and Δ is questionable information. We can then generalize our definition of the consequence relation $\vdash$ to that of a consequence relation $\vdash_\Sigma$ where inferences can be derived with the benefit of the formulae in Σ.

References

S. Benferhat, D. Dubois, and H. Prade. Argumentative inference in uncertain and inconsistent knowledgebases. In *Proceedings of the Ninth Conference on Uncertainty in Artificial Intelligence (UAI'93)*, pages 485–491. Morgan Kaufmann, 1993.

P. Dung. On the acceptability of arguments and its fundamental role in nonmonotonic reasoning, logic programming and n-person games. *Artificial Intelligence*, 77:321–357, 1995.

M. Elvang-Goransson and A. Hunter. Argumentative logics: Reasoning from classically inconsistent information. *Data and Knowledge Engineering*, 16:125–145, 1995.

P. Geerts, E. Laenens, and D. Vermeir. Defeasible logics. In *Handbook of Defeasible Reasoning and Uncertainty Management Systems. Volume 2: Reasoning with Actual and Potential Contradictions*, pages 175–210. Kluwer, 1998.

A. Hunter and B. Nuseibeh. Managing inconsistent specifications: Reasoning, analysis and action. *ACM Transactions on Software Engineering and Methodology*, 7:335–367, 1998.

A. Hunter. Reasoning with inconsistency in structured text. *Knowledge Engineering Review*, to appear.

J. Horty, R. Thomason, and D. Touretzky. A skeptical theory of inheritance in nonmonotonic semantic networks. *Artificial Intelligence*, 42:311–348, 1990.

D. Nute. Defeasible logics. In *Handbook of Logic in Artificial Intelligence and Logic Programming. Volume 3: Nonmonotonic Reasoning and Uncertainty Reasoning*, pages 355–395. Oxford University Press, 1994.

G. Pinkas and R. Loui. Reasoning from inconsistency: A taxonomy of principles for resolving conflict. In *Proceedings of the Third International Conference on Knowledge Representation and Reasoning (KR'92)*, pages 709–719. Morgan Kaufmann, 1992.

H. Prakken and G. Vreeswijk. Logics for defeasible argumentation. In *Handbook of Philosophical Logic*, 2nd ed., to appear.

N. Rescher and R. Manor. On inference from inconsistent premisses. *Theory and Decision*, 1:179–217, 1970.

G. Simari and R. Loui. A mathematical treatment of defeasible reasoning and its implementation. *Artificial Intelligence*, 53:125–157, 1992.

S. Toulmin. *The Uses of Argument*. Cambridge University Press, 1958.

Solving Advanced Reasoning Tasks using Quantified Boolean Formulas

Uwe Egly, Thomas Eiter, Hans Tompits, and Stefan Woltran
Technische Universität Wien
Abt. Wissensbasierte Systeme 184/3
Favoritenstraße 9–11, A–1040 Wien, Austria
e-mail: [uwe,eiter,tompits,stefan]@kr.tuwien.ac.at

Abstract

We consider the compilation of different reasoning tasks into the evaluation problem of quantified boolean formulas (QBFs) as an approach to develop prototype reasoning systems useful for, e.g., experimental purposes. Such a method is a natural generalization of a similar technique applied to NP-problems and has been recently proposed by other researchers. More specifically, we present translations of several well-known reasoning tasks from the area of nonmonotonic reasoning into QBFs, and compare their implementation in the prototype system QUIP with established NMR-provers. The results show reasonable performance, and document that the QBF approach is an attractive tool for rapid prototyping of experimental knowledge-representation systems.

Introduction

Several important knowledge-representation tasks (KR tasks for short) can be efficiently reduced to SAT, the satisfiability problem of classical propositional logic. Thus, practically efficient algorithms for SAT can be used to solve such problems. Successful applications of this idea include, e.g., reductions of constrained-based planning problems to SAT (Kautz & Selman 1996).

The feasibility of this approach relies on the proviso that the considered problem is in NP, i.e., that it can be solved by a nondeterministic Turing machine working in polynomial time, and on the fact that SAT is the "prototypical" problem in NP. The latter property refers to the NP-completeness of SAT, stating that any problem in NP is expressible (in polynomial time) as SAT instance.

It is natural to apply an analogous method to problems beyond NP—in particular, many interesting KR problems are known to belong to PSPACE, the class of problems solvable in polynomial space. Now, since the prototypical PSPACE-problem is the evaluation of quantified boolean formulas (QBFs), these KR problems can thus be solved by efficient translations to QBFs.

In this paper, we consider an approach of this kind for problems belonging to the second level of the polynomial hierarchy. We present efficient (polynomial-time) translations of major reasoning problems from several propositional non-monotonic reasoning (NMR) formalisms into QBFs. To the

Copyright © 2000, American Association for Artificial Intelligence (www.aaai.org). All rights reserved.

best of our knowledge, except for an encoding of conditional planning problems into QBFs (Rintanen 1999a), concrete transformations of KR tasks beyond NP into QBFs have not been presented so far. In particular, we provide polynomial-time translations of problems from abduction, default logic, autoepistemic logic, and disjunctive logic programming into QBFs. As well, we recall that propositional circumscription is *ipso facto* a QBF.

In addition, we present a prototype implementation, QUIP, for solving KR problems using the reductions discussed above. QUIP employs as underlying QBF-evaluator the publicly available propositional theorem prover boole (bddlib), which is based on binary decision diagrams (BDDs) (Bryant 1986). Choosing boole is motivated by the fact that it can handle arbitrary QBFs, and because it is a highly sophisticated package developed over many years.

In order to evaluate the feasibility of the method in practice, we compare the prototype system QUIP with existing NMR theorem provers. In particular, comparisons are performed with Theorist (Poole 1989), DeRes (Cholewinski, Marek, & Truszczyński 1996), dlv (Eiter et al. 1997), and smodels (Niemelä & Simons 1996). As shown by the experimental results, even with no optimization methods applied, our (ad hoc) NMR implementations via QBFs compare reasonably well to these systems, some of which represent the state-of-the-art.

The approach discussed in this paper has been advocated in (Cadoli, Giovanardi, & Schaerf 1998; Rintanen 1999b), where algorithms for evaluating QBFs are presented. Although these Davis-Putnam style algorithms (like the resolution-style algorithm discussed in (Kleine Büning, Karpinski, & Flögel 1995)) could equally be used as underlying QBF-solvers, they suffer from the disadvantage that the input QBF is required to be in *prenex clausal normal form*, i.e., all quantifiers of the given formula must be at the front and its quantifier-free part must be in conjunctive normal form. As a consequence, since the "natural" reductions of KR problems to QBFs (as outlined in the present paper) do in general not yield a QBF in a particular normal form, the adoption of these algorithms would necessitate an additional normal form translation, which may result either in an exponential blow-up of the resultant input QBF or an increase of the number of variables.

Translations into QBFs

In this section, we discuss how some well-known logical formalisms in AI can be mapped to QBFs in polynomial time. We focus here on major NMR formalisms. For space reasons, the exposition is necessarily succinct.

All formalisms are propositional. We assume a finite set of propositional variables V and constants 1, 0, denoting *truth* and *falsity*, respectively. The set $\mathcal{L}$ of propositional formulas is defined in the usual way, using the sentential connectives $\neg, \wedge, \vee, \rightarrow,$ and $\leftrightarrow$. Formulas will be denoted by Greek lower-case letters. A *theory*, T, is a finite set of formulas. In general, a theory T will be identified with the formula $\bigwedge_{\phi \in T} \phi$.

Quantified boolean formulas (QBFs) generalize ordinary propositional formulas by the admission of quantifications over propositional variables (QBFs are denoted by Greek upper-case letters).

The truth value of a QBF Φ without free variables (i.e., where all variables in Φ are within the scope of a quantifier) is recursively defined as follows:

- if $\Phi = 1$, then Φ is true;
- if $\Phi = 0$, then Φ is false;
- if $\Phi = \neg \Psi$, then Φ is true iff Ψ is false;
- if $\Phi = \Phi_1 \vee \Phi_2$, then Φ is true iff either Φ_1 or Φ_2 is true.
- If $\Phi = \exists x\, \Psi$, then Φ is true iff $\Psi[x/0] \vee \Psi[x/1]$ is true.

(Here, $\Psi[v/c]$ denotes the substitution of c for v in Ψ.) The cases of the remaining operators follow from the given ones in the usual way.

Let $S = \{\phi_1, \ldots, \phi_n\}$ and $T = \{\psi_1, \ldots, \psi_n\}$ be sets of formulas. Then, $S \leq T$ abbreviates $\bigwedge_{i=1}^{n}(\phi_i \rightarrow \psi_i)$, and $S < T$ is a shorthand for $(S \leq T) \wedge \neg(T \leq S)$. Furthermore, for a set $P = \{p_1, \ldots, p_n\}$ of propositional variables and a quantifier $\mathsf{Q} \in \{\forall, \exists\}$, we let $\mathsf{Q}P\, \phi$ stand for the formula $\mathsf{Q}p_1 \mathsf{Q}p_2 \cdots \mathsf{Q}p_n\, \phi$.

Abduction. Classical abduction from a theory T on V may be defined as follows (Selman & Levesque 1990; Poole 1989). Let $H \subseteq V$ be a set of *hypotheses*, and let $p \in V$ be a distinguished atom. A subset $E \subseteq H$ is an *abductive explanation* for p from T and H, if

(i) $T \cup E$ is consistent, and

(ii) $T \cup E \models p$, i.e., $T \cup E$ logically implies p.

An explanation E is *minimal*, if no proper subset $E' \subset E$ is an abductive explanation.

Assume that $H = \{h_1, \ldots, h_m\}$, and let $G = \{g_1, \ldots, g_m\}$ be a set of new propositional variables. The following QBF $\mathcal{T}_{abd}(H, p, T)$ expresses whether p has some abductive explanation (by monotonicity of classical logic, equivalently a minimal abductive explanation):

$$\exists G \Big[\exists V \Big(T \wedge (G \leq H)\Big) \wedge \forall V \Big((T \wedge (G \leq H)) \rightarrow p\Big)\Big].$$

Intuitively, G guesses an explanation (determined by those g_i which are true), and the two conjuncts in the scope of $\exists G$ express conditions (i) and (ii), respectively.

The *relevance problem* is deciding whether a given hypothesis h belongs to some abductive explanation. This is expressed by the following QBF $\mathcal{T}_{abd}^{rel}(H, p, T, h)$:

$$\exists G \Big[\exists V \Big(T \wedge (G \leq H) \wedge h\Big) \wedge \forall V \Big((T \wedge (G \leq H) \wedge h) \rightarrow p\Big)\Big].$$

For minimal abductive explanations, the relevance problem is expressed by a QBF $\mathcal{T}_{abd}^{mrel}(H, p, T, h)$ which results from $\mathcal{T}_{abd}^{rel}(H, p, T, h)$ by adding within the scope of $\exists G$ a conjunct for the minimality check:

$$\bigwedge_{i=1}^{m} \Big[g_i \rightarrow \exists V \Big(T \wedge (G \setminus \{g_i\}) \leq H \setminus \{h_i\}) \wedge \neg h_i \wedge \neg p\Big)\Big].$$

It encodes (in terms of the auxiliary variable set G) the well-known property that a set $E \subseteq H$ is minimal iff $E \setminus \{e\}$ is not an explanation, for any $e \in E$, i.e., $T \cup (E \setminus \{e\}) \cup \{\neg p\}$ is satisfiable, and where e is false.

Theorem 1 *The QBFs $\mathcal{T}_{abd}(H, p, T)$, $\mathcal{T}_{abd}^{rel}(H, p, T, h)$, and $\mathcal{T}_{abd}^{mrel}(H, p, T, h)$ evaluate to true iff the answer of the corresponding abduction task is "yes".*

Autoepistemic logic. The language of Moore's autoepistemic logic (Moore 1985) contains the modal operator L, where $L\phi$ intuitively means that ϕ is believed. By $\mathcal{L}_L$ we denote the language $\mathcal{L}$ extended by L. In what follows, formulas $L\phi$ are viewed as propositional variables, which are called *modal atoms*.

A *stable expansion* of an autoepistemic theory $T \subseteq \mathcal{L}_L$ is a set of formulas $E \subseteq \mathcal{L}_L$ such that

$$E = Cn(T \cup \{L\phi \mid \phi \in E\} \cup \{\neg L\phi \mid \phi \in \mathcal{L}_L \setminus E\}),$$

where $Cn(\cdot)$ is the classical consequence operator with respect to the extended language $\mathcal{L}_L$.

The existence of a stable expansion can be expressed as follows (Niemelä 1992). Let $T \subseteq \mathcal{L}_L$ be an autoepistemic theory, M be the set of all modal atoms occurring in T, and V be the set of ordinary (non-modal) atoms in T. We say that $\Lambda \subseteq M \cup \{\neg \phi \mid \phi \in M\}$ is T-*full* iff, for all $L\phi \in M$, it holds that (i) $T \cup \Lambda \models \phi$ iff $L\phi \in \Lambda$, and (ii) $T \cup \Lambda \not\models \phi$ iff $\neg L\phi \in \Lambda$.

Proposition 1 *(Niemelä 1992) $T \subseteq \mathcal{L}_L$ has a stable expansion iff there exists a T-full set.*

For T, M, and V as above, this condition is easily translated into the following QBF $\mathcal{T}_{ael}(T)$:

$$\exists M \Big[\forall V \Big(T \rightarrow \bigwedge_{L\phi \in M}(L\phi \rightarrow \phi)\Big) \wedge$$
$$\bigwedge_{L\phi \in M} \Big(\neg L\phi \rightarrow \exists V(T \wedge \neg \phi)\Big)\Big].$$

Theorem 2 *A finite autoepistemic theory $T \subseteq \mathcal{L}_L$ has a stable expansion iff $\mathcal{T}_{ael}(T)$ evaluates to true.*

Default Logic. A *default theory* is a pair $T = (W, \Delta)$, where $W \subseteq \mathcal{L}$ is a set of formulae and Δ is a set of *defaults* of the form $\frac{\alpha\, :\, \beta}{\gamma}$.[1] Intuitively, the default is applied (γ is

---

[1] For simplicity, we omit multiple justifications here. Our QBF translations can be easily extended to the more general form of defaults.

concluded) if α is provable and the *justification* β can be consistently assumed. T is said to be *finite* iff W is finite.

The semantics of $T = (W, \Delta)$ is defined in terms of *extensions* (Reiter 1980). Following (Marek & Truszczyński 1993), extensions can be characterised thus. For any $S \subseteq \mathcal{L}$, let $\Delta(S)$ be the monotonic rules $\{\frac{\alpha}{\gamma} \mid \frac{\alpha : \beta}{\gamma} \in \Delta, \neg\beta \notin S\}$. Then, $E \subseteq \mathcal{L}$ is an extension of T iff $E = Cn^{\Delta(E)}(W)$, where $Cn^{\Delta(E)}(W)$ is the set of all formulae derivable from W using classical logic together with the rules from $\Delta(E)$.

Adopting this characterization, we next express the existence of an extension of a finite default theory (W, Δ) in terms of a QBF.

Suppose $\Delta = \{\delta_i = \frac{\alpha_i : \beta_i}{\gamma_i} \mid 1 \leq i \leq n\}$. Let $D = \{d_1, \ldots, d_n\}$ and $D' = \{d'_1, \ldots, d'_n\}$ be sets of new propositional variables. Intuitively, d_i is true if δ_i is selected into $\Delta(E)$, and d'_i is true if δ_i fires in the construction of E, i.e., if $\gamma_i \in Cn^{\Delta(E)}(T)$. Then, the following QBF expresses existence of an extension:

$$\mathcal{T}_{dl}(T) = \exists D' \exists D ((D' \leq D) \wedge \Phi_1 \wedge \Phi_2 \wedge \Phi_3 \wedge \Phi_4),$$

where $Cn(W \cup \{\gamma_i \mid d'_i \text{ is true }\})$ is the guess for the extension E and $\Phi_1, \ldots, \Phi_4$ express the following tests (G denotes the set $\{\gamma_1, \ldots, \gamma_n\}$):

- Φ_1 tests whether the justification β_i of each default δ_i in the guessed set $\Delta(E)$ is consistent with the guess for E:

$$\Phi_1 = \bigwedge_{i=1}^{n} \left[d_i \rightarrow \exists V \left(\beta_i \wedge W \wedge (D' \leq G)\right)\right].$$

- Φ_2 tests whether no applicable default in $\Delta(E)$ is missing with respect to the guessed D'; i.e., for every δ_i such that d_i is true but d'_i is false, the set $E \cup \{\neg\alpha_i\}$ is satisfiable:

$$\Phi_2 = \bigwedge_{i=1}^{n} \left[(d_i \wedge \neg d'_i) \rightarrow \exists V \left(\neg\alpha_i \wedge W \wedge (D' \leq G)\right)\right].$$

- Φ_3 tests whether for each default $\delta_i \notin \Delta(E)$, its justification β_i is inconsistent with E, i.e., $\neg\beta_i$ is derivable:

$$\Phi_3 = \bigwedge_{i=1}^{n} \left[\neg d_i \rightarrow \forall V \left((W \wedge (D' \leq G)) \rightarrow \neg\beta_i\right)\right].$$

- Φ_4 tests whether all defaults in $\Delta(E)$ assumed to be applied (d'_i is true) are actually applied (i.e., $Cn^{\Delta(E)}(W) \models \{\gamma_i \mid d'_i \text{ is true }\}$). This amounts to checking whether $\bigwedge_{i=1}^{n}(d'_i \rightarrow \gamma_i) \in Cn^{\Delta(E)}(W)$, i.e., whether $(D' \leq G) \in Cn^{\Delta(E)}(W)$. Applying a result shown in (Gottlob 1995), $\phi \notin Cn^{\Delta(E)}(W)$ iff there exists a subset $C \subseteq G = \{\gamma_1, \ldots, \gamma_n\}$ such that (i) $W \cup C \cup \{\neg\phi\}$ is satisfiable, and (ii) for each $\gamma_i \notin C$, the set $W \cup C \cup \{\neg\alpha_i\}$ is satisfiable. Using the set $C = \{c_1, \ldots, c_n\}$ of new variables, Φ_4 is as follows:

$$\forall C \Big\{ C \leq D \rightarrow$$
$$\Big[\forall V \neg \Big(W \wedge \neg(D' \leq G) \wedge (C \leq G)\Big) \vee$$
$$\bigvee_{i=1}^{n} \Big(d_i \wedge \neg c_i \wedge \forall V \neg \Big(W \wedge \neg\alpha_i \wedge (C \leq G)\Big)\Big)\Big]\Big\}.$$

Theorem 3 *A finite default theory* $T = (W, \Delta)$ *has an extension iff* $\mathcal{T}_{dl}(T)$ *evaluates to true.*

An alternative (and more succinct) translation of default logic into QBFs is possible using Niemelä's characterization of extensions in terms of full sets (Niemelä 1995). To this end, for a set Δ of defaults and a set S of formulas, define $j(\Delta) = \{\beta \mid \frac{\alpha : \beta}{\gamma} \in \Delta\}$ and $\Delta_p(S) = \{\frac{\alpha}{\gamma} \mid \frac{\alpha : \beta}{\gamma} \in \Delta, \beta \in S\}$.

Rephrasing a definition in (Niemelä 1995), a subset $\Lambda \subseteq j(\Delta)$ is a *full set* for (W, Δ) iff every $\beta \in j(\Delta)$ satisfies the following condition: $\beta \in \Lambda$ iff $\neg\beta \notin Cn^{\Delta_p(\Lambda)}(W)$.

Proposition 2 (Niemelä 1995) *There is a one-to-one correspondence between the extensions and the full sets of* (W, Δ). *In addition, each extension* E *is given by* $Cn^{\Delta_p(\Lambda)}(W)$, *where* Λ *is the full set corresponding to* E.

We now express the existence of a full set in terms of a QBF. Consider $T = (W, \Delta)$ where $\Delta = \{\frac{\alpha_i : \beta_i}{\gamma_i} \mid i = 1, \ldots, n\}$.

Let $J = \{j_1, \ldots, j_n\}$ be a set of new variables. Intuitively, j_i is true if β_i can be consistently assumed, i.e., if $\neg\beta_i$ is not provable. Consider the following QBF:

$$\mathcal{T}_{dl}^{fs}(T) = \exists J \left[\bigwedge_{i=1}^{n} \left(j_i \leftrightarrow \mathcal{N}(W, \Delta^J, \neg\beta_i)\right)\right],$$

where $\Delta^J = \{\frac{\alpha_i}{\gamma_i} \mid \frac{\alpha_i : \beta_i}{\gamma_i} \in \Delta, j_i \text{ is true}\}$ and $\mathcal{N}(T, \Delta^J, \neg\beta_i)$ expresses nonderivability of $\neg\beta_i$ from W using the rules from Δ^J, i.e., $\mathcal{N}(T, \Delta^J, \neg\beta_i)$ states that $\neg\beta_i \notin Cn^{\Delta^J}(W)$. Analogous to the characterization used for the QBF Φ_4 above, $\mathcal{N}(T, \Delta^J, \neg\beta_i)$ is of the following form ($C = \{c_1, \ldots, c_n\}$ is again a set of new variables):

$$\exists C \Big\{\bigwedge_{k=1}^{n} \Big[(j_k \wedge \neg c_k) \rightarrow$$
$$\Big[\exists V \Big(W \wedge \beta_i \wedge \bigwedge_{l=1}^{n}(\neg j_l \vee \neg c_l \vee \gamma_l)\Big) \wedge$$
$$\exists V \Big(W \wedge \neg\alpha_k \wedge \bigwedge_{l=1}^{n}(\neg j_l \vee \neg c_l \vee \gamma_l)\Big)\Big]\Big]\Big\}.$$

Theorem 4 *A finite default theory* $T = (W, \Delta)$ *has an extension iff* $\mathcal{T}_{dl}^{fs}(T)$ *evaluates to true.*

Brave inference, $(W, \Delta) \models_b \phi$, of a formula ϕ, i.e., membership of ϕ in some extension of (W, Δ), can be easily expressed by adding in $\mathcal{T}_{dl}^{fs}(T)$ the formula $\neg\mathcal{N}(W, \Delta^J, \phi)$. Similarly, cautious inference, $(T, D) \models_c \phi$, i.e., membership of ϕ in all extensions of (W, Δ), can be expressed by adding in $\mathcal{T}_{dl}^{fs}(T)$ the formula $\mathcal{N}(W, \Delta^J, \phi)$ and negating the result.

It is natural to ask how the equivalent translations $\mathcal{T}_{dl}(\cdot)$ and $\mathcal{T}_{dl}^{fs}(\cdot)$ compare with respect to evaluation time. Intuitively, $\mathcal{T}_{dl}^{fs}(\cdot)$ is less involved and should thus be evaluated faster. However, experiments indicate that $\mathcal{T}_{dl}(\cdot)$ yields in general better performance results than $\mathcal{T}_{dl}^{fs}(\cdot)$ (cf. comparisons below).

Disjunctive Logic Programming. A *disjunctive logic program*, P, is a finite set of clauses

$$r : \quad H(r) \leftarrow P(r), N(r),$$

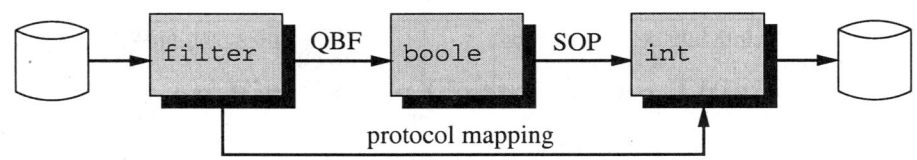

Figure 1: QUIP's system architecture.

where $H(r)$ is a disjunction of variables, $P(r)$ is a conjunction of variables, and $N(r)$ is a conjunction of negated variables. A Herbrand interpretation I of V is a *stable model* of P (Gelfond & Lifschitz 1988; Przymusinski 1991), if it is a minimal model (with respect to set-inclusion) of the program P^I resulting from P as follows: remove each clause r such that $I \models a$ for some $\neg a$ in $N(r)$, and remove $N(r)$ from all remaining clauses.

We express the existence of a stable model by a QBF. Let P be a program, $V = \{v_1, \ldots, v_n\}$ be the atoms occurring in P, and $V' = \{v'_1, \ldots, v'_n\}$ be a set of new variables. Consider the QBF $\mathcal{T}_{lp}(P)$:

$$\exists V \Big\{ P \wedge \forall V' \Big[\neg(V' < V) \vee \bigvee_{r \in P} \neg\big((N(r) \wedge B'(r)) \rightarrow H'(r)\big) \Big] \Big\},$$

where $B'(r)$ and $H'(r)$ result from $B(r)$ and $H(r)$, respectively, by replacing each occurrence of v_i with v'_i ($i = 1, \ldots, n$).

Theorem 5 *P has a stable model iff $\mathcal{T}_{lp}(P)$ evaluates to true.*

Brave inference, $P \models_b p$, of an atom p is expressed by adding p as a conjunct in the scope of $\exists V$ in $\mathcal{T}_{lp}(P)$, and cautious inference, $P \models_c p$, by adding similarly $\neg p$ there and negating the resulting formula.

Circumscription. In contrast to the formalisms described above, propositional circumscription is already a quantified boolean formula, hence it does not require a separate reduction. We recall the basic concepts of circumscription (McCarthy 1980).

In the propositional case, the parallel circumscription of a set of atoms $P = \{p_1, \ldots, p_n\}$ in a theory T, where the atoms Q are fixed and the remaining atoms $Z = \{z_1, \ldots, z_m\} = V \setminus (P \cup Q)$ may vary, is given by the following QBF $CIRC(T; P, Z)$, cf. (Lifschitz 1985):

$$T \wedge \forall P' \forall Z' \Big((T[P/P', Z/Z'] \wedge (P' \leq P)) \rightarrow (P \leq P') \Big).$$

Here, $P' = \{p'_1, \ldots, p'_n\}$ and $Z' = \{z'_1, \ldots, z'_m\}$ are sets of new propositional variables corresponding to P and Z, respectively, and $T[P/P', Z/Z']$ results from T by substitution of the variables in $P' \cup Z'$ for those in $P \cup Z$. Circumscriptive inference of a formula ϕ from a theory T is then expressed by the following QBF:

$$\forall V (CIRC(T; P, Z) \rightarrow \phi).$$

QUIP

QUIP implements the transformations described in the previous section. The architecture of QUIP is depicted in Figure 1. The problem description (e.g., a default theory, a disjunctive logic program, an abductive theory, etc.) is read and translated to a QBF by the `filter` program, which is then sent to the QBF-evaluator `boole`. The result of `boole`, usually a formula in disjunctive normal form (often called *sum of products*, SOP), is interpreted by `int`. The latter part associates a meaningful interpretation to the formulas occurring in SOP and provides an explanation in terms of the underlying problem instance (e.g., an extension, a stable model, an abductive explanation, etc.). The interpretation relies on a mapping of internal variables of the generated QBF into concepts of the problem description which is provided by `filter`.

The QBF-evaluator `boole` is a publicly available propositional theorem prover based on binary decision diagrams (the program, together with its source code, can be downloaded from the web; see (bddlib)). One of the advantages of `boole` is the fact that it enables a direct processing of the translations discussed in the previous section, without the need of an additional normal-form translation.

Finally, all parts of QUIP are written in C using standard tools like LEX and YACC which are easily portable to various platforms.

In order to incorporate new formalisms into QUIP, one has to extend the `filter` program responsible for the appropriate reductions, the mapping of the variables, and the interpreter `int`. The deductive engine remains unchanged in this process.

Experimental Results

We compare QUIP with several established tools from the literature on the basis of five benchmark problems. The tools are DeReS (Cholewinski, Marek, & Truszczyński 1996), `dlv` (Eiter *et al.* 1997), `smodels` (Niemelä & Simons 1996), and Theorist (Poole 1989). Four of the five test sets are taken from TheoryBase (Cholewinski *et al.* 1995), a well-known test-bed for nonmonotonic formalisms; the other test set consists of abductive diagnosis problems for n-bit full adders. The latter problem is used to compare the abduction part of QUIP with both Theorist and the diagnosis front-end of `dlv`, whilst the problems from TheoryBase are used to compare the two default-logic encodings and the logic-programming encoding of QUIP with DeReS, `dlv`, and `smodels`. More precisely, both encodings of the default-logic part of QUIP are compared with DeRes, and the logic-programming encoding is compared with `dlv` and smodels. All tests have been performed on a SUN ULTRA 60 with 256MB RAM; the running time is measured in seconds (with an upper time limit set to ten minutes) and comprises the sum of both user time and system time. The following program releases have been used: dlv release from November 24, 1999, smodels 2.24, and lderes 1.1.0.

The results for the abduction problems are shown in Table 1. The full adder is considered as a black box. The observations consists of output values (including carry bits), the input values are given by the theory. Entries with "min" give the running time for the computation of all minimal explanations; the remaining entries reflect the corresponding results for the computation of all non-minimal explanations. Furthermore, the values in the row "Theorist (1)" are determined by using our formalization of the n-bit adder, whereas the row "Theorist (2)" contains the results employing the formalization given in the User's Guide of Theorist. Due to space limitations, the details of the problem descriptions are omitted here. Note, however, that in order to perform abductive diagnosis, it is necessary that the respective problem descriptions contain both a model of the correct behaviour of the given components, as well as the specification of possible malfunctions (the so-called *fault model*). Furthermore, albeit the diagnosis front-end of dlv is based on a different semantics than both QUIP and Theorist, the considered formalizations are chosen in such a way that equivalent results are obtained.

Tables 2–5 contain the results for the problems from TheoryBase. This test-bed encodes different graph problems either as a default theory or as an equivalent logic program. The measurements represent the running time for the computation of all extensions of the given default theory, or of all stable models of the corresponding logic program (labeled with "LP"). The results for the two default logic reductions of QUIP are indicated by "$\mathcal{T}_{dl}$" and "$\mathcal{T}_{dl}^{fs}$", respectively.

The following problems from TheoryBase have been chosen: Δ_{ind} is an encoding for maximal independent sets in a given graph, Δ_{match} is an encoding for maximal matching, Δ_{col}^3 is an encoding for graph coloring, and Δ_{ham} is an encoding for Hamiltonian cycles. Moreover, TheoryBase admits different underlying graph-classes; here, chess graphs and cycle graphs have been used. (N.B. For the results in Table 2, it was necessary to resort to an earlier version of DeReS, because lderes 1.1.0 displayed occasional execution errors for the chosen problem class.)

The results of these tests show that QUIP compares sufficiently well. In fact, in some instances of the diagnosis example, QUIP performs actually better than both dlv and Theorist. This can be explained by the fact that the diagnosis front-end of dlv, as well as Theorist and QUIP, are ad hoc implementations developed to demonstrate the feasibility of the corresponding approach. On the other hand, it is clear that QUIP cannot compete with smodels or (the logic-programming part of) dlv because these tools are highly optimized systems developed with a particular semantics in mind, whereas the purpose of QUIP is to provide a *uniform* method to deal with several knowledge-representation formalisms at the same time. In any case, QUIP demonstrates the practical usefulness of our approach.

n	1	2	3	4	5
dlv	0	0	1	14	132
dlv (min)	0	2	22	231	787
QUIP	0	0	1	12	161
QUIP (min)	0	0	1	3	18
Theorist (1)	> 1500	—	—	—	—
Theorist (2)	54	> 3600	—	—	—

Table 1: Results for the n-bit full adder.

# vertices	15	20	25	30	35	40
DeReS	1	26	480	—	—	—
QUIP ($\mathcal{T}_{dl}$)	0	0	1	4	19	90
QUIP ($\mathcal{T}_{dl}^{fs}$)	1	1	3	8	25	113
dlv (LP)	0	0	0	1	3	15
QUIP (LP)	0	0	1	4	18	85
smodels (LP)	0	0	0	1	2	10

Table 2: Test set based on cycle graphs and Δ_{ind}.

# vertices	22	26	30	34	38	42
DeReS	0	2	18	147	1140	—
QUIP ($\mathcal{T}_{dl}$)	0	1	2	6	18	63
QUIP ($\mathcal{T}_{dl}^{fs}$)	1	2	5	10	25	72
dlv (LP)	0	0	0	1	3	12
QUIP (LP)	0	0	2	5	18	65
smodels (LP)	0	0	0	1	2	7

Table 3: Test set based on chess graphs and Δ_{match}.

# vertices	6	8	10	12	14	16
DeRes	0	0	0	0	2	8
QUIP (DE)	1	3	8	19	63	250
QUIP (DE_{fs})	27	90	240	493	—	—
dlv (LP)	0	0	0	1	3	15
QUIP (LP)	0	1	2	9	45	211
smodels (LP)	0	0	0	1	3	10

Table 4: Test set based on cycle graphs and Δ_{col}^3.

# vertices	6	8	10	12	14	16
DeRes	0	0	1	11	116	—
QUIP ($\mathcal{T}_{dl}$)	0	1	2	7	29	121
QUIP ($\mathcal{T}_{dl}^{fs}$)	2	9	24	69	153	267
dlv (LP)	0	0	0	0	0	0
QUIP (LP)	0	0	1	5	22	105
smodels (LP)	0	0	0	0	0	0

Table 5: Test set based on cycle graphs and Δ_{ham}.

Ongoing Work and Conclusion

Our experiments document that moderately sized instances of some NMR problems can be solved reasonably well by using *ad hoc* translations to QBFs. We expect a similar behavior for other KR formalisms, and believe that QBF-based problem solvers like QUIP are valuable tools for researchers experimenting with KR formalisms, and in particular with KR logics. Of course, a performance increase will be achieved by designing more sophisticated translations of the problems into QBFs, or by using more advanced BDD packages than `boole`. The power of the current framework is, however, that it realizes an easy-to-use system handling all problems in PSPACE (providing an appropriate reduction has been implemented).

Our ongoing and future work includes the following issues. We are investigating the implementations of theorem provers for modal logics in QUIP. The validity problem of standard logics like K, T, or S4 is in PSPACE, and can thus be polynomially reduced to QBFs. Notice that currently only for few modal logics theorem provers are available.

Another issue of research concerns alternative translations of the same problem into QBFs. The experimental results of the different QBFs $\mathcal{T}_{dl}(\cdot)$ and $\mathcal{T}_{dl}^{fs}(\cdot)$, which both express existence of a default-logic extension, have shown that the chosen translation crucially affects the performance. Further research is needed to get a clearer picture of more optimized translations.

Furthermore, different platforms for evaluating QBFs, based on (extensions of) the Davis-Putnam procedure (Cadoli, Giovanardi, & Schaerf 1998; Rintanen 1999b), resolution (Kleine Büning, Karpinski, & Flögel 1995) and binary decision diagrams, will be compared with respect to NMR prototype implementations. We plan to extend QUIP into a system for hybrid parallel QBF evaluation. The idea is to evaluate a particular QBF on different machines using different algorithms in parallel. This approach allows for an easy incorporation of new QBF algorithms, and exploits different strengths of the employed QBF algorithms. As well, for solving subformulas, an intertwined use of these algorithms may be considered.

Results on the above research issues will contribute for a better assessment of the suitability of the QBF approach regarding the computation of KR tasks. For expressing problem descriptions in a function-free language, it would be convenient to have an evaluator for a generalization of QBFs to function-free formulas with variables. Intelligent grounding algorithms, based on ideas in (Eiter *et al.* 1997), might be investigated.

Acknowledgments

This work was partially supported by the Austrian Science Fund Project N Z29-INF.

References

bddlib. http://www.cs.cmu.edu/~modelcheck/bdd.html.

Bryant, R. E. 1986. Graph-based Algorithms for Boolean Function Manipulation. *IEEE Trans. Comp.* 35(8):677–691.

Cadoli, M.; Giovanardi, A.; and Schaerf, M. 1998. An Algorithm to Evaluate Quantified Boolean Formulae. In *Proc. AAAI-98*, 262–267.

Cholewinski, P.; Marek, V. W.; Mikitiuk, A.; and Truszczyński, M. 1995. Experimenting with Nonmonotonic Reasoning. In *Proc. ICLP-95*, 267–282.

Cholewinski, P.; Marek, V. W.; and Truszczyński, M. 1996. Default Reasoning System DeReS. In *Proc. KR-96*, 518–528.

Eiter, T.; Leone, N.; Mateis, C.; Pfeifer, G.; and Scarcello, F. 1997. A Deductive System for Nonmonotonic Reasoning. In *Proc. LPNMR-97*, 363–374.

Gelfond, M., and Lifschitz, V. 1988. The Stable Model Semantics for Logic Programming. In *Proc. 5th ICSLP*, 1070–1080.

Gottlob, G. 1995. The Complexity of Propositional Default Reasoning Under the Stationary Fixed Point Semantics. *Information and Computation*. 121:81–92.

Kautz, H., and Selman, B. 1996. Pushing the Envelope: Planning, Propositional Logic and Stochastic Search. In *Proc. AAAI-96*, 1194–1201.

Kleine Büning, H.; Karpinski, M.; and Flögel, A. 1995. Resolution for Quantified Boolean Formulas. *Information and Computation* 117(1):12–18.

Lifschitz, V. 1985. Computing Circumscription. In *Proc. IJCAI-85*, 121–127.

Marek, W., and Truszczyński, M. 1993. *Nonmonotonic Logics*. Springer.

McCarthy, J. 1980. Circumscription – A Form of Non-Monotonic Reasoning. *Artificial Intelligence* 13:27–39.

Moore, R. 1985. Semantical Considerations on Nonmonotonic Logics. *Artificial Intelligence* 25:75–94.

Niemelä, I., and Simons, P. 1996. Efficient Implementation of the Well-Founded and Stable Model Semantics. In *Proc. JICSLP-96*, 289–303.

Niemelä, I. 1992. On the Decidability and Complexity of Autoepistemic Reasoning. *Fundamenta Informaticae* 17:117–155.

Niemelä, I. 1995. Towards Efficient Default Reasoning. In *Proc. IJCAI-95*, 312–318.

Poole, D. 1989. Explanation and Prediction: An Architecture for Default and Abductive Reasoning. *Computational Intelligence* 5(1):97–110.

Przymusinski, T. 1991. Stable Semantics for Disjunctive Programs. *New Generation Computing* 9:401–424.

Reiter, R. 1980. A Logic for Default Reasoning. *Artificial Intelligence* 13:81–132.

Rintanen, J. 1999a. Constructing Conditional Plans by a Theorem-Prover. *JAIR* 10:323–352.

Rintanen, J. 1999b. Improvements to the Evaluation of Quantified Boolean Formulae. In *Proc. IJCAI-99*, 1192–1197.

Selman, B., and Levesque, H. J. 1990. Abductive and Default Reasoning: A Computational Core. In *Proc. AAAI-90*, 343–348.

Total Knowledge*

Ian Pratt-Hartmann
Department of Computer Science
University of Manchester,
Manchester M13 9PL, U.K.
ipratt@cs.man.ac.uk

Abstract

In this paper, we analyse a concept of total knowledge based on the idea that an agent's total knowledge is the strongest proposition the agent knows. We propose semantics for propositional and first-order languages with a modal operator TK representing total knowledge, and establish a result showing that total knowledge is 'epistemically categorical', in the sense that it determines the agent's knowledge over a broad range of contents. We show that (subject to some restrictions) total knowledge is always total knowledge of an objective content, and that, for such objective contents, our TK-operator corresponds in a straightforward way to Levesque's operator O.

Keywords: mathematical foundations, philosophical foundations, nonmonotonic reasoning.

Introduction

An agent that acquires information by the gradual accretion of propositions has finite knowldge: there is some proposition ϕ—the conjunction of all the propositions so-far acquired—which constitutes that agent's total knowledge. Since we can imagine situations in which it is useful for agents to reflect on their current epistemic states, it is natural to examine epistemic logics in which such states of total knowledge can be explicitly represented. That is the goal of the present paper.

To date, most research on representing total knowledge has focused on its role in reconstructing various forms of nonmonotonic logic. The origin of these ideas can be traced back to the original non-monotonic logic of (McDermott & Doyle 1980; 1982) and its later modifications e.g. in (Halpern & Moses 1985). However, the best-known such reconstruction is (Levesque 1990), extended and discussed in (Halpern & Lakemeyer 1995), (Lakemeyer 1993; 1996) and (Lakemeyer & Levesque 1998). For an overview of the relationships between these closely related approaches, see (Donini, Nardi, & Rosati 1997) and (Rosati 2000). Chen (1997) presents an analysis relating Levesque's concept of only knowing to the method of epistemic specifications of (Gelfond 1991).

*The author thanks Nick Player, Manfred Jaeger and Renate Schmidt for their comments on earlier drafts of this paper.
Copyright © 2000, American Association for Artificial Intelligence (www.aaai.org). All rights reserved.

However, references to a proposition's being all that an agent knows also occur outside nonmonotonic logic, most notably, in discussions of probabilistic updating. For example, debates about the appropriateness of conditionalization as an updating strategy generally assume that probabilities are conditionalized on one's *total* knowledge: conditionalizing on just *part* of what one knows is (as far as the author is aware) never seriously proposed. But what does it mean, in this context, to say that a given proposition is one's total knowledge or total evidence? What are the implications of the assumption that such a proposition exists? Does this assumption affect the logic of knowledge in any way? Although there is much debate in the philosophical literature about the reasonableness of the assumption that evidence is propositional at all (see, e.g. (Jeffrey 1992), ch. 1), the implications for epistemic logic of the assumption that agents have (finite) total knowledge have been relatively neglected.

The goal of the present paper is to analyse a concept of total knowledge based on the intuition that an agent's total knowledge is the logically strongest proposition the agent knows, and to relate it to the corresponding concept employed by Levesque. In the course of our analysis, we will see that our concept of total knowledge shares many of the properties of Levesque's, though not the latter's central role in defeasible inference. This is a useful insight, because the concept presented here is arguably simpler and more intuitive than that used by Levesque, and may therefore be more appropriate in contexts other than the reconstruction of nonmonotonic inference. Certainly, the nontrivial and subtle nature of the relationship we map out illustrates the complexity and fecundity of the relevant concepts.

Total knowledge

The concept of total knowledge we will be working with is that of the strongest proposition an agent knows. Roughly, $TK\phi$ means that the agent knows ϕ, but does not know anything which knowing ϕ does not entail. This seems to be the most natural reconstruction of the concept of total knowledge appealed to when one is is enjoined to conditionalize on one's total knowledge.

Definition 1. Assume as given a countable set of *variables*, a countable set of *names* and, for each n ($0 \leq n$), a countable set of n-ary *predicate letters*. The symbol = is one of the binary predicate letters. We call the 0-ary predicate letters *proposition letters*. A *term* is a variable or a name.

Define the formulas of $\mathcal{FOLTK}$ to be the smallest set of expressions satisfying the following rules:

if r is an n-ary predicate letter and $t_1, \ldots, t_n$ are terms, then $r(t_1, \ldots, t_n)$ is a formula of $\mathcal{FOLTK}$;

if ϕ and ψ are formulas of $\mathcal{FOLTK}$ and x is a variable, then $\phi \wedge \psi$, $\phi \vee \psi$, $\neg \phi$, $\exists x \phi$, $\forall x \phi$ and $K\phi$ are formulas of $\mathcal{FOLTK}$;

If ϕ is a formula of $\mathcal{FOLTK}$ and contains no occurrence of TK, then $TK\phi$ is a formula of $\mathcal{FOLTK}$.

Define the formulas of $\mathcal{PCKT}$ to be those formulas of $\mathcal{FOLTK}$ involving no occurrences of $\exists$ or $\forall$ and no n-ary relations for $n > 0$.

Formulas involving no occurrences of TK are called *basic*; formulas involving no occurrences of K or TK are called *objective*. Formulas in which every predicate letter appears within the scope of either K or TK are called *subjective*. The notion of a *free* occurrence of a variable is defined in the usual way. We use the connectives $\rightarrow$ and $\leftrightarrow$ as abbreviations with their usual meanings. A formula with no free variables is a *sentence*.

We have restricted the syntax of $\mathcal{FOLTK}$ so that TK may apply only to basic formulas. In fact, this restriction is inessential: all the theorems reported below hold even when it is lifted. However, we maintain it throughout most of this paper for the purpose of simplifying proofs. (We indicate inessential restrictions of theorems to basic formulas using parentheses.)

The general semantic framework used here is that of (Levesque 1990). Models for $\mathcal{FOLTK}$-formulas are sets of "interpretations", where an interpretation is just a model of the underlying nonmodal language. The most notable features are that names denote rigidly and uniquely, and that the domain of quantification is covered by the names. We have taken advantage of these features to simplify the statement of the semantics slightly, and we have made one additional, substantive change (discussed below).

Definition 2. An *interpretation* w is a function mapping any n-ary predicate letter r to a set r^w of n-tuples of names, subject to the constraint that $=^w$ is the identity relation on the set of names. (As usual, we assume that there is exactly one 0-tuple of names.)

Let W be a set of interpretations, let $w \in W$, and let ϕ be a sentence of $\mathcal{FOLTK}$. We define $W \models_w \phi$ inductively as follows:

If r is a predicate letter and $a_1, \ldots, a_n$ are names, then $W \models_w r(a_1, \ldots, a_n)$ if and only if $a_1, \ldots, a_n \in r^w$;

$W \models_w \phi \wedge \psi$ if and only if $W \models_w \phi$ and $W \models_w \psi$, and similarly for the other Boolean connectives;

$W \models_w \exists x \phi$ if and only if $W \models_w \phi[x/a]$ for some name a, and similarly for the universal quantifier;

$W \models_w K\phi$ if and only if, for all $w' \in W$, $W \models_{w'} \phi$;

$\star$ $W \models_w TK\phi$ if $W \models_w K\phi$ and $W \models_w \neg K\chi$ for all objective sentences χ such that $\not\models K\phi \rightarrow \chi$.

Here, $\phi[x/a]$ denotes the result of substituting the name a for every free occurrence of x in ϕ.

Since only *sentences* receive truth-values, we will henceforth notate free variables explicitly. Thus, ϕ will denote a sentence, and $\psi(\bar{x})$ a formula with $\bar{x}$ as its only free variables. Note that if ϕ is objective, we can write $\models_w \phi$ for $W \models_w \phi$, and if ϕ is subjective, we can write $W \models \phi$ for $W \models_w \phi$. More generally, we write $W \models \phi$ to mean $W \models_w \phi$ for all $w \in W$, and $\models \phi$ to mean $W \models \phi$ for all W. We say ϕ is *consistent* if $W \models_w \phi$ for some W and some $w \in W$, and we say ϕ is *valid* if $\models \phi$. Clearly, the usual S5-axioms for K are valid.

At this point, we might pause to get a feel for our new operator by examining some of its salient properties. It is immediate from definition 2 that $\models TK\phi \rightarrow K\phi$ and, moreover, that

$$\text{if } \models K\phi \leftrightarrow K\psi \quad \text{then} \quad \models TK\phi \leftrightarrow TK\psi. \quad (1)$$

That is: if knowing ϕ and knowing ψ are the same state of affairs, then only knowing ϕ and only knowing ψ are also the same state of affairs. Moreover, since $\models K\phi \leftrightarrow KK\phi$, condition (1) has, as an immediate consequence

$$\models TK\phi \leftrightarrow TKK\psi. \quad (2)$$

Finally, anticipating a result proved below, it turns out that if we lift the restriction stating that TK may apply only to basic formulas, we obtain:

$$\models TK\phi \leftrightarrow TKTK\psi. \quad (3)$$

Properties (1)–(3) seem reasonable ones for a concept of total knowledge to exhibit, though, admittedly, intuition may be uncertain on the last of these. By contrast, if we consider Levesque's operator O (which corresponds roughly to our operator TK), we see that these properties fail. In particular, if ϕ is objective and is not logically true, then, on Levesque's semantics, $OK\phi$ and $OO\phi$ are both logically false. (At the same time, for any formula ϕ, $O(K\phi \wedge \phi)$ is logically equivalent to $O\phi$!) One of the surprising results of this paper is just how many features of Levesque's O-operator do nevertheless carry over to TK.

Let us return to the semantics of TK, given in clause $\star$ of definition 2. Observe that the quantification in this clause is restricted to *objective* sentences χ. (This restriction has nothing to do with our earlier syntactic stipulation that TK can apply only to basic formulas!) Allowing χ to range over *arbitrary* sentences in $\star$ would result in a nonterminating recursive definition of $\models$, since the truth of $TK\phi$ in W would depend on the truth of more complex sentences χ. Moreover, allowing χ to range over *basic* sentences in $\star$, though it would result in a well-formed definition, would have other undesirable consequences. Consider, for example, the sentence TKp_1. We do not want this sentence to be inconsistent, since it seems reasonable that an agent may have simply learned p_1 and nothing else. Yet Kp_1 fails to imply both p_2 and $\neg Kp_2$, so that, without the restriction of χ to objective sentences, clause $\star$ would make TKp_1 entail both $\neg Kp_2$ and $\neg K\neg p_2$, which is inconsistent on our semantics. Hence the restriction of χ to objective sentences in $\star$.

However, this restriction creates a problem. Consider the following consequence of $\star$.

Lemma 1. *For any (basic) sentence ϕ and any objective sentence χ, $\models TK\phi \to K\chi$ or $\models TK\phi \to \neg K\chi$.*

Proof. If $\models K\phi \to \chi$ then $\models TK\phi \to K\chi$. □

Lemma 1 states that, as we might say, $TK\phi$ is *epistemically categorical* for objective sentences χ. Yet we would prefer that $TK\phi$ were epistemically categorical for *arbitrary* χ. After all, an agent's total knowledge should determine exactly what the agent does and does not know. One of the main results about the TK operator is that, in the current semantic framework, lemma 1 can be strengthened in just this way. Again, to simplify the proofs, we restrict the result in this paper to basic χ.

It is worth pausing to see why this result is surprising. Lemma 1 guarantees that any two agents whose total knowledge is ϕ know the same objective sentences. However, it is easy to construct an example of two agents who know the same objective sentences but who do not know the same basic sentences. Let p be a unary predicate letter, and enumerate the names as $\{c_i\}_{0 \leq i}$. Define the interpretation w_0 by setting $\models_{w_0} p(c_j)$ if and only if j is odd; and define the interpretation w_i, for $i \geq 1$ by setting $\models_{w_i} p(c_j)$ if and only if j is odd or $j = 2i$. Assume that all other predicate letters are assigned the empty interpretation. Let $W = \{w_i | i \geq 0\}$ and $W' = \{w_i | i \geq 1\}$. Then it is easy to see that, for all objective χ, $W \models K\chi$ if and only if $W' \models K\chi$. (For a sketch proof, see (Levesque 1990), lemma 3.6.2.) However, we have $W' \models K\exists x(p(x) \land \neg Kp(x))$ but $W \models \neg K\exists x(p(x) \land \neg Kp(x))$. The analysis below shows that this sort of situation cannot arise in the presence of total knowledge.

The propositional case

We begin with a simple observation establishing the consistency of certain total-knowledge sentences.

Lemma 2. *If a sentence ϕ of $\mathcal{FOLTK}$ is objective and consistent, then $TK\phi$ is consistent.*

Proof. For each objective χ such that $\not\models K\phi \to \chi$, we have $\not\models \phi \to \chi$, so let w_χ be an interpretation such that $\models_{w_\chi} \phi \land \neg\chi$. Let W be the set consisting of all these w_χ. Since ϕ is consistent, $W \neq \emptyset$, and it is easy to see that $W \models TK\phi$. □

The analysis of TK in the propositional case is very easy, and relies on the existence of the following normal-form theorem.

Lemma 3. *Any basic sentence of $\mathcal{PCTK}$ is equivalent to a sentence of the form*

$$\bigvee_{1 \leq h \leq l} (K\psi_h \land \neg K\chi_{h,1} \land \ldots \land \neg K\chi_{h,m_h} \land \pi_h).$$

in which the ψ_h, $\chi_{h,i}$ and π_h are objective.

Proof. Straightforward from standard S5-identities. □

Thus, K-operators occurring in the scope of other K-operators in basic $\mathcal{PCTK}$ sentences can always be eliminated. Of course, $\mathcal{FOLTK}$ lacks this feature: the embedded K in $K\exists x(p(x) \land \neg Kp(x))$ cannot be removed.

As a corollary of this normal form lemma, we have

Lemma 4. *Let ϕ be a consistent (basic) sentence of $\mathcal{PCTK}$. Then there exists a basic (in fact, objective) sentence ψ, such that $\phi \land TK\psi$ is consistent.*

Proof. Assume without loss of generality that ϕ is of the form given in lemma 3, with the first disjunct consistent. Then $\not\models K\psi_1 \to \chi_{1,j}$ for all j ($1 \leq j \leq m_1$), and $\not\models \psi_1 \to \neg\pi_1$.

Now consider $TK\psi_1$. This sentence is consistent by lemma 2. Moreover, $\not\models K\psi_1 \to \chi_{1,j}$ implies $\models TK\psi_1 \to \neg K\chi_{1,j}$. Finally, since the objective sentence $\psi_1 \land \pi_1$ is true in some interpretation w, if $W \models TK\psi_1$, then it is easy to see that $W \cup \{w\} \models_w \pi_1 \land TK\psi_1$. Hence $\phi \land TK\psi_1$ is consistent. □

Lemma 4 ensures that, in the propositional case, the assumption that there is a sentence which is the agent's total knowledge does not change the finitary logic of knowledge: any (basic) sentence which is consistent without this assumption is consistent in its presence. However, we show below that lemma 4 is false for $\mathcal{FOLTK}$.

The first-order case

The following construction is crucial in understanding the behaviour of TK in the first-order case.

Definition 3. A *permutation of individuals* is a function from the set of names to the set of names which is 1–1 and onto. If f is a permutation of individuals, then it is extended to apply to interpretations and formulas as follows. If w is an interpretation, for any n-ary predicate letter r, let $a_1, \ldots a_n \in r^{f(w)}$ if and only if $f^{-1}(a_1), \ldots, f^{-1}(a_n) \in r^w$. If x is a variable, let $f(x) = x$. If $r(t_1, \ldots t_n)$ is an atomic formula, let $f(r(t_1, \ldots t_n)) = r(f(t_1), \ldots f(t_n))$, and let f be defined on nonatomic formulas by $f(\phi \land \psi) = f(\phi) \land f(\psi)$, $f(\phi \lor \psi) = f(\phi) \lor f(\psi)$, $f(\neg\phi) = \neg f(\phi)$, $f(\exists x\phi) = \exists x f(\phi)$, $f(\forall x\phi) = \forall x f(\phi)$, $f(K\phi) = K f(\phi)$, $f(TK\phi) = TK f(\phi)$.

Thus, when applying f to interpretations and formulas, we switch round the extensions of predicates and the names occurring in formulas in corresponding ways.

Lemma 5. *If f is a permutation of individuals, then f is also 1–1 and onto on the set of interpretations, the set of formulas, the set of basic formulas and the set of objective formulas. Furthermore, for all sentences ϕ, sets of interpretations W and interpretations $w \in W$, $W \models_w \phi$ if and only if $f(W) \models_{f(w)} f(\phi)$.*

Proof. The first part of the lemma is obvious. The second part follows by structural induction on ϕ. □

Definition 4. Let $\bar{x} = x_1, \ldots x_n$ be a tuple of variables with X the set $\{x_1, \ldots, x_n\}$. Let $A = \{a_1, \ldots, a_m\}$ (with the a_i distinct) be a set of names. Let $P_1, \ldots, P_m$ be a set of (possibly empty) disjoint subsets of X and let $P_{m+1}, \ldots, P_{m+l}$

be a partition of $X \setminus \bigcup_{1 \leq i \leq m} P_i$. (Thus, $0 \leq l \leq n$.) A *distribution formula* (for $\bar{x}$ and A) is a consistent formula of the form $\delta(\bar{x}) :=$

$\bigwedge \{x_j = a_i | 1 \leq i \leq m, 1 \leq j \leq n, \text{ and } x_j \in P_i\}$
$\bigwedge \{x_j = x_k | m + 1 \leq i \leq m + l, \text{ and } x_j, x_k \in P_i\}$
$\bigwedge \{x_j \neq a_i | 1 \leq i \leq m, m + 1 \leq i' \leq m + l, \text{ and } x_j \in P_{i'}\}$
$\bigwedge \{x_j \neq x_k | m + 1 \leq i < i' \leq m + l,$
$\qquad x_j \in P_i \text{ and } x_k \in P_{i'}\}.$

For a given $\bar{x}$ and A, denote the set of all such formulas by $\Delta_A(\bar{x})$. If $n = 0$, set $\Delta_A = \{\top\}$.

Intuitively, $\delta(\bar{x})$ assigns every variable in $\bar{x}$ to one of $m+l$ 'boxes'. Variables assigned to the same box are asserted to be identical and variables assigned to different boxes are asserted to be distinct. Variables assigned to box i ($1 \leq i \leq m$) are asserted to be identical to a_i.

Lemma 6. *Let $\bar{x} = x_1, \ldots x_n$ be a tuple of variables and A a set of names. Then $\Delta_A(\bar{x})$ is a partition. That is:* $\models \forall \bar{x} \bigvee \Delta_A(\bar{x})$, *and* $\models \forall \bar{x} \neg (\delta(\bar{x}) \wedge \delta'(\bar{x}))$ *for distinct* $\delta(\bar{x}), \delta'(\bar{x}) \in \Delta_A(\bar{x})$.

Proof. Obvious. □

We note that distribution formulas are *rigid*: they are satisfied by the same tuples regardless of the interpretation. Hence we sometimes write $\models \delta(\bar{a})$ without mentioning W or w.

Lemma 7. *Let ϕ be a sentence and $\psi(\bar{x})$ a formula. Let C be the set of names occurring in either formula. Then there exists a disjunction $\pi(\bar{x})$ of formulas in $\Delta_C(\bar{x})$ such that, for all tuples $\bar{a}$, $\models \pi(\bar{a})$ if and only if $\models \phi \rightarrow \psi(\bar{a})$.*

Proof. Suppose that $\bar{a}$ and $\bar{a}'$ satisfy the same $\delta(\bar{x})$ in $\Delta_C(\bar{x})$. Then the mapping $\bar{a} \mapsto \bar{a}'$ is well-defined and extends to a permutation of individuals f such that f is the identity on C. Hence $f(\phi) = \phi$ and $f(\psi(\bar{a})) = \psi(\bar{a}')$. By lemma 5, $\models \phi \rightarrow \psi(\bar{a})$ if and only if $\models \phi \rightarrow \psi(\bar{a}')$. Now set $\pi(\bar{x}) :=$

$\bigvee \{\delta(\bar{x}) \in \Delta_C(\bar{x}) : \models \delta(\bar{a}') \text{ for some } \bar{a}' \text{ s.t. } \models \phi \rightarrow \psi(\bar{a}')\}.$

(As usual, we take $\bigvee \emptyset$ to be $\bot$.) Suppose $\models \phi \rightarrow \psi(\bar{a})$. Since $\Delta_C(\bar{x})$ is a partition, $\models \delta(\bar{a})$ for some $\delta(\bar{x})$, so $\models \pi(\bar{a})$. Conversely, suppose $\models \pi(\bar{a})$. Then $\models \delta(\bar{a})$ for some $\delta(\bar{x})$, such that, for some $\bar{a}'$, $\models \delta(\bar{a}')$ and $\models \phi \rightarrow \psi(\bar{a}')$. But since $\bar{a}$ and $\bar{a}'$ satisfy the same $\delta(\bar{x})$ in $\Delta_C(\bar{x})$, we have $\models \phi \rightarrow \psi(\bar{a})$. □

Lemma 8. *Let ϕ be a (basic) sentence and $\psi(\bar{x})$ an objective formula. Let C be the set of names occurring in either formula. Then there exists a disjunction $\pi(\bar{x})$ of formulas in $\Delta_C(\bar{x})$ such that $\models TK\phi \rightarrow \forall \bar{x}(K\psi(\bar{x}) \leftrightarrow \pi(\bar{x}))$.*

Proof. By lemma 7, let $\pi(\bar{x})$ be such that, for all tuples $\bar{a}$, $\models \pi(\bar{a})$ if and only if $\models K\phi \rightarrow \psi(\bar{a})$. Let W be any set of interpretations and let $\bar{a}$ be any tuple. If $W \models TK\phi$, then, by the semantics of TK, $W \models K\psi(\bar{a})$ if and only if $\models K\phi \rightarrow \psi(\bar{a})$. The result is then immediate. □

Theorem 1. *Let ϕ be a (basic) sentence and $\psi(\bar{x})$ a (basic) formula. Then there is a disjunction $\pi(\bar{x})$ of elements of $\Delta_C(\bar{x})$ for some C, such that $\models TK\phi \rightarrow \forall \bar{x}(K\psi(\bar{x}) \leftrightarrow \pi(\bar{x}))$.*

Proof. We proceed by induction on the number n of occurrences of K in $\psi(\bar{x})$. The case $n = 0$ is handled by lemma 8. If $n > 0$, let $K\psi'(\bar{x}')$ be a subformula of $\psi(\bar{x})$, with $\psi'(\bar{x}')$ objective. By lemma 8, let $\pi'(\bar{x}')$ be such that $\models TK\phi \rightarrow \forall \bar{x}'(K\psi'(\bar{x}') \leftrightarrow \pi'(\bar{x}'))$. and let $\psi''(\bar{x})$ be the result of substituting $\pi'(\bar{x}')$ for $K\psi'(\bar{x}')$ in $\psi(\bar{x})$. Then, $\models TK\phi \rightarrow \forall \bar{x}(K\psi(\bar{x}) \leftrightarrow K\psi''(\bar{x}))$. Since $\psi''(\bar{x})$ has fewer than n occurrences of K, the result follows by inductive hypothesis. □

Note that this straightforward induction depends on the fact that $\psi(\bar{x})$ is basic. This is because, in any set of interpretations W, the truth-values of $K\psi(\bar{a})$ and $K\psi''(\bar{a})$ depend only on the truth-values of their subformulas *at the worlds in* W. Since $\pi'(\bar{x}')$ and $K\psi'(\bar{x}')$ are satisfied by the same tuples in any world of W, it is obvious that $\psi(\bar{a})$ and $\psi''(\bar{a})$ must have the same truth value in every world of W as well. However, such a substitution within the scope of TK-operators would in general not be truth-preserving. (As stated above, theorem 1 does in fact hold for arbitrary $\psi(\bar{x})$; however, the proof in this case is more delicate.)

Corollary 1. *For all (basic) sentences ϕ and ψ, $\models TK\phi \rightarrow K\psi$ or $\models TK\phi \rightarrow \neg K\psi$.*

Proof. By theorem 1, $\models TK\phi \rightarrow \forall \bar{x}(K\psi \leftrightarrow \pi)$, where π is a disjunction of elements of Δ_C for some C (with a 0-tuple of variables). Hence π is $\bot$ or $\top$. □

Corollary 2. *Let ϕ be a (basic) sentence and $\psi(x)$ a basic formula with one free variable. Suppose that $W \models TK\phi$. Then the set $\{a : W \models K\psi(a)\}$ is finite or cofinite.*

Proof. By theorem 1, $\models TK\phi \rightarrow \forall x(K\psi(x) \leftrightarrow \pi(x))$, where $\pi(x)$ is a disjunction of elements of $\Delta_C(x)$ for some C (with a single variable x). Clearly, the set of a satisfying $\pi(x)$ is finite or cofinite. □

Recall that, in the propositional case, if ϕ is consistent, then we can find ψ such that $\phi \wedge TK\psi$ is consistent. In the first-order case, this is no longer true.

Theorem 2. *There exists a consistent basic sentence ϕ such that, for all (basic) sentences ψ, $\models \phi \rightarrow \neg TK\psi$.*

Proof. If $\psi'(x)$ is any formula with one free variable x, let $\exists_\infty x \psi'(x)$ abbreviate some sentence or other implying that $\psi'(x)$ is satisfied by infinitely many values of x. Let $p(x)$ be a unary predicate letter, and let ϕ be a consistent basic sentence of the form $\exists_\infty x K p(x) \wedge \exists_\infty x \neg K p(x)$. It is easy to see that such a ϕ can be found. By corollary 2, $\models \phi \rightarrow \neg TK\psi$ for all basic sentences ψ. □

Thus, in the first-order case, the assumption that there is total knowledge changes the finitary logic of knowledge: basic sentences that are consistent without this assumption may be inconsistent in its presence.

Next, we show that total knowledge of any (basic) sentence is logically equivalent to total knowledge of an objective sentence. We need the following general lemma.

Lemma 9. *Let ϕ and ψ be (basic) sentences such that $\models TK\phi \to K\psi$, $\models K\psi \to K\phi$ and $TK\phi$ is consistent. Then $\models TK\phi \leftrightarrow TK\psi$.*

Proof. Suppose $W \models TK\phi$. Then $W \models K\psi$. Let χ be objective with $\not\models K\psi \to \chi$. Then $\not\models K\phi \to \chi$, because $\models K\psi \to K\phi$. So $W \models \neg K\chi$. Hence $W \models TK\psi$.

Conversely, suppose $W \models TK\psi$. Then $W \models K\phi$. Let χ be objective with $\not\models K\phi \to \chi$, so that $\models TK\phi \to \neg K\chi$. Then $\not\models K\psi \to \chi$ also, since otherwise, given that $\models TK\phi \to K\psi$, we would have $\models TK\phi \to K\chi$, contradicting the hypothesised consistency of $TK\phi$. But if $\not\models K\psi \to \chi$, then $W \models \neg K\chi$. Hence $W \models TK\phi$. □

Theorem 3. *Let ϕ be a (basic) sentence. Then there exists an objective sentence ϕ^* such that $\models TK\phi \leftrightarrow TK\phi^*$.*

Proof. If ϕ is already objective or if $TK\phi$ is inconsistent, the result is trivial, so we may assume otherwise. Let $K\psi_1(\bar{x}_1)$ be a subformula of ϕ, with $\psi_1(\bar{x}_1)$ objective. Then we can find ρ_1 such that $\models \phi \to \rho_1$, where ρ_1 is the sentence $\forall \bar{x}_1 (K\psi(\bar{x}_1) \leftrightarrow \pi_1(\bar{x}))$ constructed as in lemma 8. Let ϕ_1 be the result of substituting $\pi_1(\bar{x})$ for $K\psi_1(\bar{x}_1)$ in ϕ. By lemma 8, $\models TK\phi \to K(\phi_1 \wedge \rho_1)$, and certainly $\models K(\phi_1 \wedge \rho_1) \to K\phi$. Since $TK\phi$ is assumed consistent, lemma 9 implies that $\models TK\phi \leftrightarrow TK(\phi_1 \wedge \rho_1)$. If there is a subformula $K\psi_2(\bar{x}_2)$ in ϕ_1 with $\psi_2(\bar{x}_2)$ objective, we proceed as before, obtaining $\models TK\phi \leftrightarrow TK(\phi_2 \wedge \rho_1 \wedge \rho_2)$, and so on, until we eventually obtain $\models TK\phi \leftrightarrow TK(\phi_m \wedge \rho_1 \wedge \ldots \wedge \rho_m)$, with ϕ_m objective and $m \geq 1$.

Now consider in more detail the sentence $\rho_1 \wedge \ldots \wedge \rho_m$. Ignoring the previous numbering, this may be written out as a conjunction of the form $\bigwedge_{1 \leq j \leq M} \forall \bar{x}_j (\delta_j(\bar{x}_j) \to K\psi_j(\bar{x}_j)) \wedge \bigwedge_{1 \leq j \leq M'} \forall \bar{x}'_j (\delta'_j(\bar{x}'_j) \to \neg K\psi'_j(\bar{x}'_j))$ where the $\delta_j(\bar{x}_j)$, $\delta'_j(\bar{x}'_j)$ are conjunctions of equality and inequality formulas, and the $\psi_j(\bar{x}_j)$, $\psi'_j(\bar{x}'_j)$ are objective. Since the $\delta_j(\bar{x}_j)$ are in fact rigid, we have

$\models K\forall \bar{x}_j(\delta_j(\bar{x}_j) \to K\psi_j(\bar{x}_j)) \leftrightarrow K\forall \bar{x}_j(\delta_j(\bar{x}_j) \to \psi_j(\bar{x}_j))$.

Hence we can omit the K from the relevant conjuncts and set ϕ^* to be

$$\phi_m \wedge \bigwedge_{1 \leq j \leq M} \forall \bar{x}_j (\delta_j(\bar{x}_j) \to \psi_j(\bar{x}_j)),$$

whence $\models TK\phi \leftrightarrow TK(\phi^* \wedge \sigma_1 \wedge \ldots \wedge \sigma_{M'})$ where σ_j is $\forall \bar{x}'_j (\delta'_j(\bar{x}'_j) \to \neg K\psi'_j(\bar{x}'_j))$.

To complete the proof, suppose $\bar{a}$ is a tuple with $\models \delta'_j(\bar{a})$. Since $TK\phi$ is consistent, $\not\models K\phi^* \to \psi'_j(\bar{a})$. Hence, since $\psi'_j(\bar{a})$ is objective, $\models TK\phi^* \to \neg K\psi'_j(\bar{a})$. Thus, $\models TK\phi^* \to \forall \bar{x}'_j(\delta'_j(\bar{x}'_j) \to \neg K\psi'_j(\bar{x}'_j))$. Hence, we have $\models TK\phi^* \to K(\phi^* \wedge \sigma_1 \wedge \ldots \wedge \sigma_{M'})$, $\models K(\phi^* \wedge \sigma_1 \wedge \ldots \wedge \sigma_{M'}) \to K\phi^*$ and finally, by lemma 2, $TK\phi^*$ consistent. By lemma 9, $\models TK\phi^* \leftrightarrow TK(\phi^* \wedge \sigma_1 \wedge \ldots \wedge \sigma_{M'})$, and we are done. □

Comparison with only knowing

An alternative approach to total knowledge is provided by (Levesque 1990). Before we give the semantics for Levesque's operator, we need to mention a difference between Levesque's basic formalism and the one adopted in this paper. So far, we have assumed that, in an assertion of the form $W \models_w \phi$, w is a member of W. But in fact, the definitions work perfectly well without this assumption, the major effect being that $K\phi \wedge \neg \phi$ becomes satisfiable. (Levesque actually uses the letter B where we have used K.) Given this change, Levesque can give the semantics of the modal operator O as:

$W \models_w O\phi$ if and only if $W \models K\phi$ and, for all w such that $W \models_w \phi$, $w \in W$.

The semantics for K and the nonmodal connectives are unaffected.

Levesque's semantics for O have the desired effect only when the set of interpretations W is maximal in the following sense:

Definition 5. *Let W and W' be sets of interpretations. We say that W and W' are equivalent if, for all basic sentences ϕ, $W \models K\phi$ if and only if $W' \models K\phi$.*

A set of interpretations W is maximal if, for all W' such that $W \equiv W'$ and $W \subseteq W'$, we have $W = W'$.

The motivation for this definition is that, if W is a set of interpretations and $w \in W$ is an interpretation such that $W \models_w \phi$, then it can turn out that $O\phi$ is true in W and false in $W \setminus \{w\}$, even though and W and $W \setminus \{w\}$ give the agent the same basic beliefs! By ignoring nonmaximal sets W, this anomaly is avoided.

Theorem 4. *Let ϕ be objective and let $W \neq \emptyset$ be any set of interpretations (not necessarily maximal) such that $W \models O\phi$. Then $W \models TK\phi$. Conversely, Let ϕ be objective and let $W \neq \emptyset$ be a maximal set of interpretations such that $W \models TK\phi$. Then $W \models O\phi$.*

Proof. For the first part, we certainly have $W \models K\phi$. Moreover, let χ be objective with $\not\models K\phi \to \chi$. Certainly, then $\not\models \phi \to \chi$. So let w be an interpretation such that $\models_w \phi \wedge \neg \chi$. Since $W \models O\phi$, we have $w \in W$, whence $W \models \neg K\chi$. Thus, $W \models TK\phi$.

For the second part, again we certainly have $W \models K\phi$. Moreover, let w be an interpretation such that $\models_w \phi$. Suppose ψ is any basic sentence such that $W \models K\psi$. Since $W \models TK\phi$, it follows from corollary 1 that $\models TK\phi \to K\psi$. Now ϕ is objective, $\models_w \phi$ and $W \models TK\phi$, so $W \cup \{w\} \models TK\phi$, and so $W \cup \{w\} \models K\psi$. Thus, for any basic ψ, $W \models K\psi$ implies $W \cup \{w\} \models K\psi$. This easily implies that, for any basic ψ, $W \models K\psi$ if and only if $W \cup \{w\} \models K\psi$. That is, $W \equiv W \cup \{w\}$. By the maximality of W, then, $w \in W$, and hence $W \models O\phi$. □

Note that the second part of the above theorem depends crucially on the strengthening of lemma 1 provided by corollary 1.

It is easy to construct examples showing that theorem 4 fails if ϕ is allowed to be nonobjective. Consider for example the sentence $\phi := \neg Kp \to q$. The sentence $O\phi$ is consistent, and implies Kq. (Thus, ϕ can be seen as a default rule licencing inference to q provided p is not known.) By contrast, $TK\phi$ is easily seen to be inconsistent, since $K\phi$ implies neither p nor q, so that $TK\phi$ implies the inconsistent trio $\neg Kp, \neg Kq, K(\neg Kp \to q)$.

This last example shows how the failure of property (1) above is crucial for default inference. By simple S5-manipulation,

$$\models K(\neg Kp \to q) \leftrightarrow K(Kp \vee Kq)$$

and so by property (1),

$$\models TK(\neg Kp \to q) \leftrightarrow TK(Kp \vee Kq).$$

But the formula $(Kp \vee Kq)$ is symmetric in p and q, and thus could not possibly favour inferring Kq over inferring Kp. Thus, no concept of total knowledge for which property (1) obtains is likely to be of any use for modelling default inference along the lines taken by Levesque.

As we have already remarked, the restriction in the final clause of definition 1 that TK applies only to formulas not involving any occurrences of TK is inessential. The semantics presented in definition 2 work unproblematically even when it is lifted.

The following result is immediate from the semantics for TK and K.

Lemma 10. *If ϕ is any sentence, then* $\models TK\phi \to KTK\phi$.

We note that the proof of lemma 9 does not depend on any assumption that ϕ and ψ are basic, so that the result holds for all ϕ and ψ. We then have

Corollary 3. *For any formula ϕ,* $\models TK\phi \leftrightarrow TKTK\phi$.

Proof. If $TK\phi$ is inconsistent, then $TKTK\phi$ is certainly inconsistent. Hence we may assume that $TK\phi$ is consistent. We have $\models TK\phi \to KTK\phi$ by lemma 10, and certainly $\models KTK\phi \to K\phi$. Hence, by lemma 9, putting $\psi := TK\phi$, we have $\models TK\phi \leftrightarrow TKTK\phi$. □

This is the promised proof of the property (3) above.

Conclusions and further work

The purpose of this paper has been to define and analyse a concept of total knowledge based on the idea that an agent's total knowledge is the strongest proposition that the agent knows. We proposed semantics for the languages $\mathcal{PCTK}$ and $\mathcal{FOLTK}$, according to which a sentence $TK\phi$ was guaranteed to be epistemically categorical for objective sentences. We showed that, surprisingly, total knowledge is epistemically categorical for all basic sentences. We showed that the assumption that an agent has total knowledge does not change the finitary logic of $\mathcal{PCTK}$; but it does change the finitary logic of $\mathcal{FOLTK}$. We showed that total knowledge of any basic sentence is logically equivalent to total knowledge of some objective sentence. Finally, we showed that, for objective sentences, but not for nonobjective sentences, TK coincides with Levesque's operator O, modulo certain technical details.

The above results can be extended in several ways. Throughout most of this paper, we have assumed that TK-operators could apply only to basic formulas. In fact, this assumption is unnecessary, and all of the above theorems remain true when it is removed. The proofs cannot be presented within the confines of this paper. Another important extension is to index the modal operators K and TK to indicate the time at which the knowledge (or total knowledge) applies. Thus, we might work instead with operators K_n ("I know at time n that ... ...") and TK_n ("My total knowledge at time n is that ... ..."). The extension of the semantics to these temporally indexed cases is routine. It turns out that lemma 4 continues to hold for the temporally indexed version of $\mathcal{PCTK}$. The proof is more involved than in the nontemporal case, and cannot be given here.

References

Chen, J. 1997. The generalized logic of only knowing (GOL) that covers the notion of epistemic specifications. *Journal of Logic and Computation* 7(2):159–174.

Donini, F. M.; Nardi, D.; and Rosati, R. 1997. Ground nonmonotonic modal logics. *Journal of Logic and Computation* 7(4):523–548.

Gelfond, M. 1991. Strong introspection. In *Proceedings, AAAI*, 386–391. Los Altos, CA: Morgan Kaufmann.

Halpern, J. Y., and Lakemeyer, G. 1995. Levesque's axiomatization of only knowing is incomplete. *Artificial Intelligence* 74(2):381–387.

Halpern, J., and Moses, Y. 1985. Towards a theory of knowledge and ignorance: Preliminary report. In Apt, K., ed., *Logic and Models of Concurrent Systems*. Berlin: Springer. 459–476.

Jeffrey, R. C. 1992. *Probability and the Art of Judgment*. Cambridge: Cambridge University Press.

Lakemeyer, G., and Levesque, H. J. 1998. AOL: a logic of acting, sensing, knowing and only knowing. In *Proceedings of the sixth International Conference on Principles of Knowledge Representation and Reasoning*.

Lakemeyer, G. 1993. All they know: a study in multi-agent autoepistemic reasoning. In *Proceedings of the 13th International Joint Conference on Artificial Intelligence*, 376–381.

Lakemeyer, G. 1996. Only knowing in the situation calculus. In *Proceedings of the Fifth International Conference on Principles of Knowledge Representation and Reasoning*, 14–25.

Levesque, H. J. 1990. All I know: a study in autoepistemic logic. *Artificial Intelligence*.

McDermott, D., and Doyle, J. 1980. Non-monotonic logic I. *Artificial Intelligence Journal* 13:41–72.

McDermott, D., and Doyle, J. 1982. Non-monotonic logic II: Non-monotonic modal theories. *Journal of the ACM* 29:33–57.

Rosati, R. 2000. On the decidability and complexity of reasoning about only knowing. *Artificial Intelligence* 116(1–2):193–215.

Computing Circumscriptive Databases by Integer Programming: Revisited

Ken Satoh, Hidenori Okamoto
Division of Electronics and Information, Hokkaido University
N13W8 Kita-ku, Sapporo, 060-8628, Japan
Email:ksatoh@db-ei.eng.hokudai.ac.jp

Abstract

In this paper, we consider a method of computing minimal models in circumscription using integer programming in propositional logic and first-order logic with domain closure axioms and unique name axioms. This kind of treatment is very important since this enable to apply various technique developed in operations research to nonmonotonic reasoning.

(Nerode et al., 1995) are the first to propose a method of computing circumscription using integer programming. They claimed their method was correct for circumscription with fixed predicates, but we show that their method does not correctly reflect their claim. We show a correct method of computing all the minimal models not only with fixed predicates but also with varied predicates and we extend our method to compute prioritized circumscription as well.

Introduction

In this paper, we discuss a method of computing circumscription using integer programming used in operations research. Circumscription (McCarthy, 1986) has been proposed as a formalization of nonmonotonic reasoning and intensively studied. However, like other formalisms of nonmonotonic reasoning, it has a high complexity of computation and many proposals are made (Lifschitz, 1985; Przymusinski, 1989; Ginsberg, 1989; Nerode et al., 1995).

(Lifschitz, 1985) gives a condition in which circumscriptive theory is collapsed into the first-order logic. (Ginsberg, 1989) and (Przymusinski, 1989) give methods which use theorem prover techniques.

(Bell et al., 1992; 1996) and (Nerode et al., 1995) take different approach from the above approaches. Circumscription is restricted to a propositional logic or a first-order sentences with domain closure axioms and unique name axioms. Then, they translate axioms into inequality constraints in integer programming and use a minimization of an objective function which corresponds with minimized predicates and obtain all the minimal models. This kind of research is very important since it introduces an usage of efficient method developed in operations research to nonmonotonic reasoning.

In circumscription, there are three kinds of predicates; minimized predicates, fixed predicates, and varied predicates. Minimized predicates are subject to minimization whereas interpretation of fixed predicates cannot be changed for minimization, but interpretation of varied predicates can be changed if their change leads to further minimization of minimized predicates. (Bell et al., 1992; 1996) consider minimization of all the predicates and (Nerode et al., 1995) claim that they extend the method of (Bell et al., 1992; 1996) so that their method is correct for circumscription even including fixed predicates (but not including varied predicates). However, we show that their method does not correctly reflect their claim.

Even if their claim were correct, circumscription without varied predicates would have a serious drawback to apply circumscription to commonsense reasoning as Etherington et al. (Etherington et al., 1985) have pointed out.

For example, consider the following axioms.
$bird \land \neg ab \supset fly$.
$bird$.

It seems that circumscribing ab would yield fly. However, without fly varied, it is impossible to derive fly. This is because in this circumscription without fly varied, the interpretations are not comparable with each other if the interpretations of fly are different. There are three models of the above axioms, $I_1 = \{bird, ab, fly\}$, $I_2 = \{bird, fly\}$, $I_3 = \{bird, ab\}$[1]. In minimizing ab without fly varied, $I_2 < I_1$ holds, but $I_2 < I_3$ does not hold since the interpretation of fly in I_2 is different from the interpretation of fly in I_3. So, minimal models for this circumscription are I_2 and I_3, and therefore, we cannot conclude fly.

If we let the interpretation of fly be varied, then I_2 is the only minimal model and therefore, we can conclude fly. Therefore, usage of varied propositions is very important in commonsense reasoning.

In this paper, we give a computing method of circum-

---

[1] We represent an interpretation as a set of true propositions in the interpretation.

scription for a propositional logic or a first-order logic with domain closure axioms and unique name axioms. Our method can compute minimal models for this class of axioms not only with fixed predicates, but also with varied predicates. Moreover, (Nerode et al., 1995) gives a checking method of circumscriptive entailment for a limited class of formulas, whereas we give a complete checking method. Then, we extend our method to apply for prioritized circumscription as well.

(Cadoli et al., 1992) propose a method of eliminating varied predicates in circumscription by translating inference problem of a formula under circumscription with varied predicates and fixed predicates into another inference problem under circumscription without varied predicates nor fixed predicates. So, readers might think that methods of (Bell et al., 1992; 1996) which compute all the minimal models without varied nor fixed propositions are sufficient for computing minimal models. However, it is not clear how to apply the method proposed by (Cadoli et al., 1992) to computing minimal models since the relationship between a model of the original circumscription and a model of the translated circumscription is not known.

Preliminaries

We restrict our attention to propositional circumscription. For the first-order case with domain closure axioms and unique name axioms, we can translate each ground atom into a distinct proposition.

We assume that all propositional formulas are translated into a set of clauses of the form $L_1 \vee L_2 \vee ... \vee L_n$ where L_i is a positive literal p_i or a negative literal $\neg p_i$.

We associate each propositional symbol p with 0-1 variable X_p which represents the truth value of p; If $X_p = 1$, p is true and if $X_p = 0$, p is false. We also use an interpretation I to represent a solution of the assignments to variables from integer programming. If $p \in I$, it represents $X_p = 1$ and if $p \notin I$, it represents $X_p = 0$.

Let F and G be tuples of formulas, $\langle F_1, F_2, ..., F_n \rangle$ and $\langle G_1, G_2, ..., G_n \rangle$. We define $F \leq G$ as $\bigwedge_{i=1}^{n} F_i \supset G_i$. We define $F < G$ as $F \leq G$ and $G \not\leq F$, and $F \approx G$ as $F \leq G$ and $G \leq F$.

Let A be a conjunction of formulas and $\mathcal{P}$ be a set of propositional symbols used in A. We divide $\mathcal{P}$ into disjoint three tuples of propositions P, Z, Q which are called *minimized propositions*, *varied propositions*, and *fixed propositions*.

Circumscription of P for A with Z varied is defined as follows.
$Circum(A; P; Z) =$
$\quad A(P, Z) \wedge \neg \exists p \exists z (A(p, z) \wedge p < P).$

For a model theory of circumscription, we define an order of interpretations to minimize P with Z varied as follows. Let I be an interpretation and Φ be a tuple of propositional symbols. We define $I[\Phi]$ as $\{p \in \Phi | I \models p\}$ or, equivalently, $I \cap \Phi$.

Let I_1 and I_2 be interpretations.
$I_1 \leq^{P;Z} I_2$ if

Step 1: Let $AC := \emptyset$ and $SS := \emptyset$.

Step 2: Minimizing $\sum_{p \in P} X_p$ under $Tr(A) \cup AC$ using 0-1 integer programming.

Step 3: If there is no solution for the above minimization, output SS

Step 4: Otherwise,
1. Let M be a solution of the above minimization.
2. Add $M[P]$ to SS.
3. Add $\sum_{p \in M[P]} X_p \leq |M[P]| - 1$ to AC.
4. Go to Step 2.

Figure 1: The algorithm of Nerode et al.

1. $I_1[Q] = I_2[Q]$.
2. $I_1[P] \subseteq I_2[P]$.

We define $I_1 <^{P;Z} I_2$ as $I_1 \leq^{P;Z} I_2$ and $I_2 \not\leq^{P;Z} I_1$. A minimal model M of $A(P, Z)$ w.r.t. P with Z varied is defined as follows.

1. M is a model of $A(P, Z)$.
2. There is no model M' of $A(P, Z)$ such that $M' <^{P;Z} M$.

According to (Lifschitz, 1985), I is a minimal model of $A(P, Z)$ w.r.t. P with Z varied if and only if I is a model of $Circum(A; P; Z)$.

Computing Minimal Models without Varied Propositions

Let A be a set of clauses. Then, a set of inequalities, $Tr(A)$, translated from A is defined as follows.
$Tr(A) =$
$\quad \{X_{p_1} + ... + X_{p_n} + (1 - X_{q_1}) + ... + (1 - X_{q_m}) \geq 1 |$
$\quad p_1 \vee ... \vee p_n \vee \neg q_1 \vee ... \vee \neg q_m \in A\}$

Let Z be empty. Then, the algorithm proposed in (Nerode et al., 1995) is in Figure 1. We adapt their algorithm for propositional circumscription. Note that the algorithm is an extended version of the algorithm of (Bell et al., 1992; 1996) to minimize all propositions. The algorithm of (Bell et al., 1992; 1996) is a special case of the algorithm of (Nerode et al., 1995) where a set of fixed propositions, Q, is empty.

The algorithm works as follows. We start with $Tr(A)$ as the initial constraints and minimize an objective function corresponding with minimized propositions under $Tr(A)$. If we do not obtain any solution, we are done. Otherwise, we add a constraint AC which excludes non-minimal models larger than the obtained solution.

(Nerode et al., 1995) claims the following on the correctness and completeness of the above algorithm.

Claim(Nerode et al., 1995, Theorem 1) *Output SS from the algorithm in Figure 1 is equivalent to*
$\{M[P] | M$ is a minimal model of $A(P)$ with respect to P with no propositions varied $\}$.

Unfortunately, this claim is not correct in general as the following example shows.

Example 1 *Let $A(ab)$ be the following set of clauses.*

$\neg bird \vee ab \vee fly.$
$bird.$

Then, the minimal models of $A(ab)$ with respect to $\langle ab \rangle$ are $M_1 = \{bird, fly\}$ and $M_2 = \{bird, ab\}$. Note that fly is a fixed proposition and so, the two models are incomparable since interpretations of fly are different in these two models.

However, from the algorithm in Figure 1, we cannot obtain M_2 as follows.
$Tr(A)$ is
$1 - X_{bird} + X_{ab} + X_{fly} \geq 1$
$X_{bird} \geq 1$
By minimizing X_{ab} using 0-1 integer programming under $Tr(A)$, we obtain a solution $X_{ab} = 0, X_{bird} = 1, X_{fly} = 1$ which corresponds with M_1.
Then, we add $M_1[\langle ab \rangle] = \emptyset$ to SS. Since $M_1[\langle ab \rangle] = \emptyset$, $\sum_{p \in M[\langle ab \rangle]} X_p = 0$ and $|M_1[\langle ab \rangle]| = 0$. Thus, we add the following constraint to AC.
$0 \leq -1.$
Obviously, we cannot get any further solution. This means that we cannot obtain a minimal model M_2.

Therefore, the above claim does not work in general if there is a fixed proposition. Although their method is not correct with circumscription with fixed propositions, we later show that their method actually works for circumscription with varied propositions without fixed propositions.

Now, we give an algorithm which works correctly for circumscription with fixed propositions in Figure 2. Let I be an interpretation and Φ be a tuple of propositional symbols. We define $\overline{I}[\Phi]$ used in Figure 2 as $\{p \in \Phi | I \not\models p\}$ or equivalently, $\Phi - I$.

Theorem 1 *Output SS from the algorithm in Figure 2 is equivalent to*
$\{M | M$ is a minimal model of $A(P)$ with respect to P with no propositions varied $\}$.

Proof: Let α be a formula which consists of logical connectives and propositional symbols in P. Then, according to (de Kleer and Konolige, 1989), $Circum(A; P) \models \alpha$ if and only if $Circum(A \wedge (R \equiv \neg \cdot Q); P, Q, R) \models \alpha$ where R is a tuple of new propositions not in A and $R \equiv \neg \cdot Q$ is $\bigwedge_{i=1}^{m} r_i \equiv \neg q_i$ for $R = \langle r_1, ..., r_m \rangle$ and $Q = \langle q_1, ..., q_m \rangle$. Then, we use the algorithm of (Bell et al., 1992) to minimize all propositions and replace every occurrence of variables X_{r_i} for a proposition r_i in R by $1 - X_{q_i}$. □

Example 2 *Let $A(ab)$ be the following set of clauses as in Example 1*

Step 1: Let $AC := \emptyset$ and $SS := \emptyset$.

Step 2: Minimizing $\sum_{p \in P} X_p$ under $Tr(A) \cup AC$ using 0-1 integer programming.

Step 3: If there is no solution for the above minimization, output SS.

Step 4: Otherwise,
1. Let M be a solution of the above minimization.
2. Add M to SS.
3. Add $\sum_{p \in M[P]} X_p + \sum_{q \in M[Q]} X_q + \sum_{q' \in \overline{M}[Q]} (1 - X_{q'}) \leq |M[P]| + |Q| - 1$ to AC.
4. Go to Step 2.

Figure 2: Algorithm for circumscription with fixed propositions

$\neg bird \vee ab \vee fly.$
$bird.$

Then, the minimal models of $A(ab)$ with respect to $\langle ab \rangle$ are $M_1 = \{bird, fly\}$ and $M_2 = \{bird, ab\}$.
By minimizing X_{ab} under $Tr(A)$, we obtain a solution $X_{ab} = 0, X_{bird} = 1, X_{fly} = 1$ which corresponds with a minimal model M_1.
Then, we add M_1 to SS and we add the following constraint to AC.
$X_{bird} + X_{fly} \leq 1.$
Then, minimizing X_{ab} under $Tr(A) \cup AC$, we obtain a solution $X_{ab} = 1, X_{bird} = 1, X_{fly} = 0$ which corresponds with a minimal model M_2.
Then, we add M_2 to SS and we add the following constraint to AC.
$X_{ab} + X_{bird} + (1 - X_{fly}) \leq 2$
Then, minimizing X_{ab} under $Tr(A) \cup AC$, we no longer obtain any solution and therefore, $SS = \{\{bird, fly\}, \{bird, ab\}\}$ is obtained.

Computing Minimal Models with Varied Propositions

As shown in Introduction, we need varied proposition to perform commonsense reasoning. We give a computation method of handling varied propositions in Figure 3.

Let F, G be disjoint sets of propositions. We define $\mathcal{F}(F, G)$ as $\bigwedge_{f \in F} f \wedge \bigwedge_{f \in G} \neg f$.

Theorem 2 *Output MS from the algorithm in Figure 3 is equivalent to*
$\{M | M$ is a minimal model of $A(P, Z)$ with respect to P with Z varied $\}$.

Proof: At Step 4, every $M \in SS$ is a minimal model but there might be alternative models such that the

> **Step 1:** Let $AC := \emptyset$ and $SS := \emptyset$.
>
> **Step 2:** Minimizing $\sum_{p \in P} X_p$ under $Tr(A) \cup AC$ using 0-1 integer programming.
>
> **Step 3:** If there is no solution for the above minimization, go to Step 5.
>
> **Step 4:** Otherwise,
> 1. Let M be a solution of the above minimization.
> 2. Add $M[P \cup Q]$ to SS
> 3. Add $\sum_{p \in M[P]} X_p + \sum_{q \in M[Q]} X_q + \sum_{q' \in \overline{M}[Q]} (1 - X_{q'}) \leq |M[P]| + |Q| - 1$ to AC.
> 4. Go to Step 2.
>
> **Step 5:** Let MS be $\emptyset$ and for every $S \in SS$ do the following.
> 1. $A' := A \wedge \mathcal{F}(S, (P \cup Q) - S)$.
> 2. Compute all the models of A' and add these models to MS.
>
> Output MS.

Figure 3: Algorithm for circumscription with varied propositions

interpretations of $P \cup Q$ are the same but the interpretations of Z are different. At Step 5, we compute such alternative models. □

Example 3 *Let $A(ab)$ be the following set of clauses.*

$\neg bird \vee ab \vee fly.$
$bird.$

Then, the minimal model of $A(ab)$ with respect to $\langle ab \rangle$ with $\langle fly \rangle$ varied is $M_1 = \{bird, ab\}$.

By minimizing X_{ab} under $Tr(A)$, we obtain a solution where $X_{ab} = 0, X_{bird} = 1$ and $X_{fly} = 1$. We add $M_1[\langle ab \rangle \cup \langle bird \rangle] = \{bird\}$ to SS and the following constraint to AC.

$X_{bird} \leq 0.$

Obviously, there is no solution for $Tr(A) \cup AC$ and therefore, $SS = \{\{bird\}\}$ is obtained.

Then, we add $\mathcal{F}(\{bird\}, \{ab, bird\} - \{bird\}) = bird \wedge \neg ab$ to A to obtain A' and compute all the models of A'. We obtain $MS = \{\{bird, fly\}\}$.

Actually, in the algorithm in Figure 3, if Q is empty and we output SS at Step 3 instead of going to Step 5, then this is equivalent to the algorithm of Nerode et al. In other words, the correct claim for (Nerode et al., 1995) is as follows.

Corollary 1 *Let $\mathcal{P}$ be $P \cup Z$ and Q be empty. Final SS in the algorithm in Figure 3 is equivalent to*
$\{M[P] | M$ *is a minimal model of $A(P, Z)$ with respect to P with Z varied* $\}$.

If we only concern about circumscriptive entailment discussed in (Nerode et al., 1995), that is, whether $Circum(A; P; Z) \models \alpha$ or not, we do not need Step 5. Instead, we check whether $A \wedge \mathcal{F}(S, (P \cup Q) - S) \wedge \neg \alpha$ for every $S \in SS$ has any models or not. This can be done by checking whether $Tr(A \wedge \mathcal{F}(S, (P \cup Q) - S) \wedge \neg \alpha)$ does not have any solution when minimizing any arbitrary objective function. Note that in (Nerode et al., 1995), they use "upper and lower fringes" to compute circumscriptive entailment for a restricted class of formulas, but actually, such "fringes" are not necessary.

Computing Minimal Models in Prioritized Circumscription

We firstly give a definition of prioritized circumscription. We divide a set of propositions into n partitions and give an order over partitions. Suppose that this is $P_1 > P_2 > ... > P_n$. Intended meaning of this order is that we firstly minimize P_1, then P_2 ...., then P_n. Let P and Q be a tuple of propositions which have orders $P_1 > P_2 > ... > P_n$ and $Q_1 > Q_2 > ... > Q_n$. We define $P \preceq^i Q$ as follows. If $i = 1$, $P \preceq^i Q$ is $P_1 \leq Q_1$ and if $i > 1$, $(\bigwedge_{j=1}^{i-1} P_j \approx Q_j) \supset P_i \leq Q_i$. We define $P \preceq Q$ as $\bigwedge_{i=1}^n P \preceq^i Q$ and $P \prec Q$ as $P \preceq Q$ and $Q \not\preceq P$.

Prioritized circumscription of $P_1 > P_2 > ... > P_n$ for A with Z varied is defined as follows.
$Circum(A; P_1 > P_2 > ... > P_n; Z) =$
$A(P, Z) \wedge \neg \exists p \exists z (A(p, z) \wedge p \prec P).$

In a model theory of prioritized circumscription, we define an order over interpretations as follows.

Let I_1 and I_2 be interpretations and let $\mathcal{P}$ consist of disjoint sets $P_1, P_2, ..., P_n, Q, Z$.
$I_1 \preceq^{P_1 > P_2 > ... > P_n; Z} I_2$ if

1. $I_1[Q] = I_2[Q]$.
2. $I_1[P_1] \subseteq I_2[P_1]$.
3. For every i, if for every $1 \leq j \leq i-1$, $I_1[P_j] = I_2[P_j]$, then $I_1[P_i] \subseteq I_2[P_i]$.

We define $I_1 \prec^{P_1 > P_2 > ... > P_n; Z} I_2$ as $I_1 \preceq^{P_1 > P_2 > ... > P_n; Z} I_2$ and $I_2 \not\preceq^{P_1 > P_2 > ... > P_n; Z} I_1$.

A minimal model M of $A(P, Z)$ w.r.t. $P_1 > P_2 > ... > P_n$ with Z varied is defined as follows.

1. M is a model of $A(P, Z)$.
2. There is no model M' of $A(P, Z)$ such that $M' \prec^{P_1 > P_2 > ... > P_n; Z} M$.

According to (Lifschitz, 1985), I is a minimal model of $A(P, Z)$ w.r.t. $P_1 > P_2 > ... > P_n$ with Z varied iff I is a model of $Circum(A; P_1 > P_2 > ... > P_n; Z)$.

Similar to the problem in non-prioritized circumscription, the method proposed in (Nerode et al., 1995) of computing prioritized circumscription is correct if there are no fixed propositions.

To manipulate fixed propositions in prioritized circumscription, we need the following theorem which is a generalization of the result of (de Kleer and Konolige, 1989).

Theorem 3 *Let a set of propositions $\mathcal{P}$ consist of disjoint sets $P_1, P_2, ..., P_n, Q, Z$ and $P = P_1 \cup P_2 \cup ... \cup P_n$ and α be a formula which consists of logical connectives and propositional symbols in P. Then,*
$Circum(A(P,Z); P_1 > P_2 > ... > P_n; Z) \models \alpha$ *if and only if* $Circum(A(P,Z) \wedge (R \equiv \neg \cdot Q); Q, R, P_1 > P_2 > ... > P_n; Z) \models \alpha$.

Proof: See appendix.

This theorem means that we can translate prioritized circumscription with fixed propositions to prioritized circumscription without fixed propositions. Moreover, we extend the method so that it is applicable even if there are varied propositions. We show the algorithm in Figure 4.

Theorem 4 *Output MS from the algorithm in Figure 4 is equivalent to*
$\{M | M$ *is a minimal model of $A(P,Z)$ with respect to* $P_1 > ... > P_n$ *with Z varied$\}$.

Proof: According to (Lifschitz, 1985),
$Circum(A(P,Z); P_1 > P_2 > ... > P_n; Z)$ is equivalent to
$Circum(A(P,Z); P_1; P_2, ..., P_n, Z) \wedge$
$Circum(A(P,Z); P_2; P_3, ..., P_n, Z) \wedge ...$
$Circum(A(P,Z); P_n; Z)$.

At **Step 1**,...,**Step 4**, we compute interpretation of P_1 and Q for every model of
$Circum(A(P,Z); P_1; P_2, ..., P_n, Z)$.
At the iteration where $i = 2...n$ in **Step 5**, we compute interpretation of $P_1, ..., P_i$ and Q for every model of
$Circum(A(P,Z); P_1; P_2, ..., P_n, Z) \wedge$
$Circum(A(P,Z); P_2; P_3, ..., P_n, Z) \wedge ...$
$Circum(A(P,Z); P_i; P_{i+1}, ..., P_n, Z)$
since we reflect interpretation of propositions $P_1 \cup ... \cup P_{i-1} \cup Q$ which are obtained up to the latest iteration. Therefore, at n-th iteration, we obtain interpretation of $P_1, ..., P_n$ for every model of $Circum(A(P,Z); P_1 > P_2 > ... > P_n; Z)$. □

Example 4 *Consider the following axioms.*
$ab_1 \vee \neg fly$
$\neg bird \vee ab_2 \vee fly$.
We compute minimal models of $Circum(A; \langle ab_2 \rangle > \langle ab_1 \rangle; \langle fly \rangle)$ meaning that we minimize ab_1 and ab_2 with fly varied (and bird fixed) and ab_2 is preferably minimized than ab_1. The minimal models are $\{bird, fly, ab_1\}$ and $\emptyset$. We have two minimal models since the interpretations of bird in these models are different from each other.

Step 1: $AC := \emptyset$ and $SS := \emptyset$.

Step 2(1): *Minimize X_{ab_2} under the following constraints:*
$X_{ab_1} + 1 - X_{fly} \geq 1$
$1 - X_{bird} + X_{ab_2} + X_{fly} \geq 1$

Step 3(1): *Then, there are three solutions for this minimization:*
$S_1 = \{X_{ab_2} = 0, X_{bird} = 1, X_{fly} = 1, X_{ab_1} = 1\}$,

---

Step 1: Let $AC := \emptyset$ and $SS := \emptyset$.

Step 2: Minimizing $\sum_{p \in P_1} X_p$ under $Tr(A) \cup AC$ using 0-1 integer programming.

Step 3: If there is no solution for the above minimization, go to Step 5.

Step 4: Otherwise,
1. Let M be a solution of the above minimization.
2. Add $M[P_1 \cup Q]$ to SS
3. Add $\sum_{p \in M[P_1]} X_p + \sum_{q \in M[Q]} X_q + \sum_{q' \in \overline{M}[Q]} (1 - X_{q'}) \leq |M[P_1]| + |Q| - 1$ to AC.
4. Go to Step 2.

Step 5: For $i := 2$ to n do the following.
1. $SS' := \emptyset$.
2. For every $S \in SS$ do
   Step 5-1: Let $AC := \emptyset$.
   Step 5-2: Minimizing $\sum_{p \in P_i} X_p$ under $Tr(A \wedge \mathcal{F}(S, (P_1 \cup ... \cup P_{i-1} \cup Q) - S)) \cup AC$ using 0-1 integer programming.
   Step 5-3: If there is no solution for the above minimization, process the next S.
   Step 5-4: Otherwise,
   (a) Let M be a solution of the above minimization.
   (b) Add $M[P_1 \cup ... \cup P_i \cup Q]$ to SS'.
   (c) Add $\sum_{p \in M[P_i]} X_p \leq |M[P_i]| - 1$ to AC.
   (d) Go to Step 5-2.
3. $SS := SS'$ and do the next iteration for i.

If iteration stops then let MS be $\emptyset$ and for every $S \in SS$ do the following.
1. Let $A' := A \wedge \mathcal{F}(S, (P_1 \cup ... \cup P_n \cup Q) - S)$.
2. Compute all the models of A' and add these models to MS.

Output MS.

Figure 4: Algorithm for prioritized circumscription

$S_2 = \{X_{ab_2} = 0, X_{bird} = 0, X_{fly} = 1, X_{ab_1} = 1\}$,
$S_3 = \{X_{ab_2} = 0, X_{bird} = 0, X_{fly} = 0, X_{ab_1} = 0\}$.

Step 4(1): *Suppose that we obtain S_1.*

1. $M_1 = \{bird, fly, ab_1\}$
2. Add $M_1[\langle ab_2\rangle \cup \langle bird\rangle] = \{bird\}$ to SS. (SS becomes $\{\{bird\}\}$.)
3. Add $X_{bird} \leq 0$ to AC.

Step 2(2): *Minimize X_{ab_2} under new AC.*

Step 3(2): *Then, there are two solutions for this minimization, S_2 and S_3.*

Step 4(2): *Suppose that we obtain S_2.*

1. $M_2 = \{fly, ab_1\}$
2. Add $M_2[\langle ab_2\rangle \cup \langle bird\rangle] = \emptyset$ to SS. (SS becomes $\{\{bird\}, \emptyset\}$.)
3. Add $1 - X_{bird} \leq 0$ to AC.

Step 2(3): *Minimize X_{ab_2} under new AC.*

Step 3(3): *Then, we no longer obtain any solutions, and go to Step 5.*

Step 5:
$i := 2$ and $SS' := \emptyset$.

1. $S := \{bird\}$.

    Step 5-1(1): $AC := \emptyset$.

    Step 5-2(1): *Minimize X_{ab_1} under the following constraints:*
    $$X_{ab_1} + 1 - X_{fly} \geq 1$$
    $$1 - X_{bird} + X_{ab_2} + X_{fly} \geq 1$$
    $$X_{ab_2} \leq 0$$
    $$X_{bird} \geq 1$$

    Step 5-3(1): *Then, we obtain the solution S_1 again.*

    Step 5-4(1):
    (a) $M_1 = \{bird, fly, ab_1\}$
    (b) Add $M_1[\langle ab_2\rangle \cup \langle ab_1\rangle \cup \langle bird\rangle] = \{ab_1, bird\}$ to SS'. (SS' becomes $\{\{ab_1, bird\}\}$.)
    (c) Add $X_{ab_1} \leq 0$ to AC.

    Step 5-2(2): *Minimize X_{ab_1} under new AC.*

    Step 5-3(2): *Then, we no longer obtain any solutions.*

2. $S := \emptyset$.

    Step 5-1(1): $AC := \emptyset$.

    Step 5-2(1): *Minimize X_{ab_1} under the following constraints:*
    $$X_{ab_1} + 1 - X_{fly} \geq 1$$
    $$1 - X_{bird} + X_{ab_2} + X_{fly} \geq 1$$
    $$X_{ab_2} \leq 0$$
    $$X_{bird} \leq 0$$

    Step 5-3(1): *Then, we obtain the solution S_3 only.*

    Step 5-4(1):
    (a) $M_3 = \emptyset$
    (b) Add $M_3[\langle ab_2\rangle \cup \langle ab_1\rangle \cup \langle bird\rangle] = \emptyset$ to SS'. (SS' becomes $\{\{ab_1, bird\}, \emptyset\}$.)
    (c) Add $0 \leq -1$ to AC.

    Step 5-2(2): *Minimize X_{ab_1} under new AC.*

    Step 5-3(2): *Then, we no longer obtain any solutions.*

Iteration stops and by calculation of MS from SS', we obtain $\{\{bird, fly, ab_1\}, \emptyset\}$.

We can also give a method of circumscriptive entailment in prioritized circumscription as in ordinary circumscription. After iteration stops, we check for every $A' \in SS$, $A' \wedge \neg\alpha$ does not have any models to check whether α is consequence of the prioritized circumscription or not.

Conclusion

Contributions of this paper are as follows.

1. We correctly give the method of computing all the models of circumscription not only with fixed propositions, but also with varied propositions.

2. We give a complete method of computing circumscriptive entailment for propositional logic.

3. We also extend the method of computing minimal models to include varied propositions in prioritized circumscription.

Acknowledgements This research is partly supported by Grant-in-Aid for Scientific Research (Project No. 11878067), The Ministry of Education, Japan. We also thank the anonymous referees for comments on this paper.

References

Bell, C., Nerode, A., Ng, R., and Subrahmanian, V. S. 1992. Implementing Deductive Database by Linear Programming. *Proc. of PODS92*, pages 283 – 292.

Bell, C., Nerode, A., Ng, R., and Subrahmanian, V. S. 1996. Implementing Deductive Database by Mixed Integer Programming. *ACM Transactions on Database Systems*, **21**, pages 238 – 269.

Cadoli, M., Eiter, T., and Gottlob, G. 1992 An Efficient Method for Eliminating Varying Predicates from a Circumscription. *Artificial Intelligence*, **54**, pages 397 – 410.

de Kleer, J., and Konolige, K. 1989. Eliminating the Fixed Predicates from a Circumscription. *Artificial Intelligence*, **39**, pages 391 – 398.

Etherington, D., Mercer, R., and Reiter, R. 1985. On the Adequacy of Predicate Circumscription for Closed-world Reasoning. *Computational Intelligence*, **1**, pages 11 – 15.

Ginsberg, M. 1989. Circumscriptive Theorem Prover. *Artificial Intelligence*, **39**, pages 209 – 230.

Lifschitz, V. 1985. Computing Circumscription. *Proc. of IJCAI-85*, pages 121 – 127.

McCarthy, J. 1986. Applications of Circumscription to Formalizing Common-Sense Knowledge. *Artificial Intelligence*, **28**, pages 89 – 116.

Nerode, A., Ng, R. T., and Subrahmanian, V. S. 1995. Computing Circumscriptive Databases, I. Theory and Algorithms. *Information and Computation*, **116**, pages 58–80.

Przymusinski, T. 1989. An algorithm to compute circumscription. *Artificial Intelligence*, **38**, pages 49 – 73.

Appendix (Proof of Theorem 3)

Lemma 1 *Let a set of propositions $\mathcal{P}$ consist of disjoint sets P, Q, Z. $Circum(A(P, Z) \wedge (R \equiv \neg \cdot Q); P; Z)$ is equivalent to $Circum(A(P, Z) \wedge (R \equiv \neg \cdot Q); Q, R, P; Z)$.*

Proof: Suppose that M is a model of $Circum(A(P, Z) \wedge (R \equiv \neg \cdot Q); Q, R, P; Z)$, but M is not a model of $Circum(A(P, Z) \wedge (R \equiv \neg \cdot Q); P; Z)$. Then, there is a model M' s.t.

- The interpretations of R and Q are same in M and M'.
- $M' <^{P;Z} M$.

Then, this means that $M' <^{P,Q,R;Z} M$ and it contradicts the assumption that M is a model of $Circum(A(P, Z) \wedge (R \equiv \neg \cdot Q); Q, R, P; Z)$.

On the other hand, Suppose that M is a model of $Circum(A(P, Z) \wedge (R \equiv \neg \cdot Q); P; Z)$, but M is not a model of $Circum(A(P, Z) \wedge (R \equiv \neg \cdot Q); Q, R, P; Z)$. Then, there is a model M' s.t. $M' <^{P,Q,R;Z} M$. If the interpretations of Q and R were same in M and M', it would mean that $M' <^{P;Z} M$. Therefore, there must be some difference in the interpretations of Q and R between M and M'. Let s be proposition in Q or R s.t. the interpretation of s is different in M and M'. Suppose that s is in Q. Then, there is some proposition t in R s.t. $s \equiv \neg t$. This means that $M' \not<^{P,Q,R;Z} M$. The same argument applies if s is in R. Therefore, it leads to contradiction. □

Lemma 2 *Let a set of propositions $\mathcal{P}$ consist of disjoint sets $P_1, P_2, ..., P_n, Q, Z$ and $P = P_1 \cup P_2 \cup ... \cup P_n$.*
$Circum(A(P, Z) \wedge (R \equiv \neg \cdot Q); Q, R, P_1 > P_2 > ... > P_n; Z)$
is equivalent to
$Circum(A(P, Z) \wedge (R \equiv \neg \cdot Q); P_1 > P_2 > ... > P_n; Z)$.

Proof: According to (Lifschitz, 1985),
$Circum(A(P, Z) \wedge (R \equiv \neg \cdot Q); Q, R, P_1 > P_2 > ... > P_n; Z)$ is equivalent to
$Circum(A(P, Z) \wedge (R \equiv \neg \cdot Q); Q, R, P_1; P_2, ..., P_n, Z)$
$\wedge Circum(A(P, Z) \wedge (R \equiv \neg \cdot Q); P_2 > ... > P_n; Z)$.
Then, use Lemma 1. □

We also need the following lemma.

Lemma 3 *Let a set of propositions $\mathcal{P}$ consist of disjoint sets $P_1, P_2, ..., P_n, Q, Z$ and $P = P_1 \cup P_2 \cup ... \cup P_n$.*
$Circum(A(P, Z) \wedge (R \equiv \neg \cdot Q); P_1 > P_2 > ... > P_n; Z)$
is equivalent to
$Circum(A(P, Z); P_1 > P_2 > ... > P_n; Z) \wedge (R \equiv \neg \cdot Q)$.

Proof: Suppose that M is a model of $Circum(A(P, Z) \wedge (R \equiv \neg \cdot Q); P_1 > P_2 > ... > P_n; Z)$, but M is not a model of $Circum(A(P, Z); P_1 > P_2 > ... > P_n; Z) \wedge (R \equiv \neg \cdot Q)$. M is a model of $(R \equiv \neg \cdot Q)$ and therefore, M must not be a model of $Circum(A(P, Z); P_1 > P_2 > ... > P_n; Z)$. Then, there is a model M' of $A(P, Z)$ s.t. $M' \prec^{P_1 > P_2 > ... > P_n; Z} M$. Since R and Q are fixed propositions, $M' \models (R \equiv \neg \cdot Q)$ since $M \models (R \equiv \neg \cdot Q)$. This contradicts the assumption that M is a minimal model of $A(P, Z) \wedge (R \equiv \neg \cdot Q)$ w.r.t. $P_1 > P_2 > ... > P_n$ with Z varied.

On the other hand, suppose that M is a model of $Circum(A(P, Z); P_1 > P_2 > ... > P_n; Z) \wedge (R \equiv \neg \cdot Q)$, but M is not a model of $Circum(A(P, Z) \wedge (R \equiv \neg \cdot Q); P_1 > P_2 > ... > P_n; Z)$. Since M is a model of $A(P, Z) \wedge (R \equiv \neg \cdot Q)$, there is a model M' of $A(P, Z) \wedge (R \equiv \neg \cdot Q)$ s.t. $M' \prec^{P_1 > P_2 > ... > P_n; Z} M$. However, this contradicts with the assumption that M is a minimal model of $A(P, Z)$ w.r.t. $P_1 > P_2 > ... > P_n$ with Z varied since the interpretations of R and Q are same in M and M'. □

Proof of Theorem 3 By Lemma 2,
$Circum(A(P, Z) \wedge (R \equiv \neg \cdot Q); Q, R, P_1 > P_2 > ... > P_n; Z)$
is equivalent to
$Circum(A(P, Z) \wedge (R \equiv \neg \cdot Q); P_1 > P_2 > ... > P_n; Z)$.
Then, by Lemma 3, the above is equivalent to
$Circum(A(P, Z); P_1 > P_2 > ... > P_n; Z) \wedge (R \equiv \neg \cdot Q)$. □

Using Prior Knowledge: Problems and Solutions

Vinay K. Chaudhri, Mark E. Stickel, Jerome F. Thomere, Richard J. Waldinger
{chaudhri, stickel, thomere, waldinger}@ai.sri.com
Artificial Intelligence Center
SRI International
333 Ravenswood Ave, Menlo Park, CA 94025

Abstract

Encoding knowledge is time consuming and expensive. A possible solution to reduce the cost of developing a new knowledge base (KB) is to reuse existing knowledge. Previous work addressing this problem has focused on standards for representing, exchanging, and accessing knowledge (Genesereth and Fikes 1992), (Chaudhri et al. 1998), and on creating large repositories of knowledge (Lenat and Guha 1990). Results on the level of reuse achievable have been reported (Cohen et al. 1999). In this paper, we focus on the process of reuse and report a case study on constructing a KB by reusing existing knowledge. The reuse process involved the following steps: *translation, comprehension, slicing, reformulation,* and *merging*. We discuss technical problems encountered at each of these steps and explain how we solved them.

Introduction

A possible approach to reduce the cost of developing a new knowledge base (KB) is to amortize the high cost of encoding knowledge across multiple projects. To enable the reuse of knowledge across multiple projects, several complimentary approaches have been attempted. Standards for representing, exchanging, and accessing knowledge have been developed (Genesereth and Fikes 1992),(Chaudhri et al. 1998). Large repositories of knowledge have been constructed to serve as the starting point for new KB development (Lenat and Guha 1990).

This paper is about the process of knowledge reuse that builds upon the earlier work by starting from an existing repository of knowledge, and by using the standards for representing and exchanging knowledge in the development process. This process is based on an actual KB construction project, and involved the following steps: *comprehension, translation, slicing, reformulation,* and *merging*. We discuss technical problems encountered at each step and how we solved them.

Experimental Setup

The focus for the KB development was defined by the *Crisis Management Challenge Problem* (CMCP) (IET et al. December 1997),(Cohen et al. 1998). The CMCP

Copyright © 2000, American Association for Artificial Intelligence (www.aaai.org). All rights reserved.

defined a collection of test questions of interest to an analyst dealing with an international crisis. The objective of the KB development task was to assist the analyst in answering those questions.

The questions were specified using a question grammar. The grammar consisted of a set of parameterized questions or PQs, each of which had a large number of instantiations. An example question is, `` What {risks, rewards} would <InternationalAgent> face/expect in <InternationalActionType>?''. An example instantiation is, ``What risks can Iran expect in attacking targets in Saudi Arabia?''. The KB development included several test cycles with the test phase based on questions derived from the question grammar, but not previously seen by the system developers. A major test cycle was conducted at the end of the year with several small-scale tests in between. The results reported here are based on the work conducted over a period of two years.

Teams led by Teknowledge and SAIC developed the systems for answering the questions. SRI was a part of the SAIC team, and this paper concerns primarily the work conducted at SRI.

The KB was developed using the KIF syntax (Genesereth and Fikes 1992), augmented with the standard relation names derived from the OKBC knowledge model (Chaudhri et al. 1998). SNARK, SRI's **N**ew **A**utomated **R**easoning **T**oolkit, a first-order theorem prover, was used as an inference tool to answer the questions (Stickel et al. 1994). The details of the KB content and the inferences performed are available elsewhere (Chaudhri et al. 2000).

The KB development started from the HPKB upper ontology (HPKB-UL) that contains roughly 3000 most general terms derived from the Cyc KB (Lenat 1997). Four members of the SAIC team -- SRI, Knowledge Systems Laboratory (KSL), Stanford, Formal Reasoning Group (FRG), Stanford, and Northwestern University (NWU) -- addressed portions of the CMCP and developed somewhat independent KBs. After the first year of the project, KSL Stanford merged the KBs from SRI, KSL Stanford, and FRG Stanford, and the resulting KB was the starting point for the development for the second year.

Problems in Reusing Prior Knowledge

The reuse process reported here is a result of the practical needs of the project. A similar process has been adopted by others (Valente et al. 1999).

Translation

Translation is the process of taking the well-formed sentences in one representation language as input and producing the equivalent well-formed sentences of another representation language as output. Our translation step was limited to syntactic transformations and constant renaming. Any further processing, for example, choosing alternative syntactic forms in the target representation language or dealing with representation differences is handled as a separate step in the reuse process. It is possible that for some sentences in the input representation language, there is no equivalent sentence in the output language. Such a situation did not arise in our application.

The HPKB-UL was available in the MELD format (a language used by Cycorp) and was not directly readable by our system. In conjunction with KSL Stanford, we developed a translator to load the HPKB-UL into any OKBC-compliant server. Since the HPKB-UL contains mostly structural information (Pease et al. 2000), this translator handles structural information in the KB. The structural information includes classes, functions, relations, class-subclass relationships, and facets. While doing this translation, we had to define equivalence between relation names in the HPKB-UL and the OKBC knowledge model. For example, the relation *#$genls* in the HPKB-UL is equivalent to the relation *subclass-of* in the OKBC knowledge model. The translation process benefited significantly by the existence of the OKBC knowledge model into which many of the representation constructs from the HPKB-UL could be mapped. We also converted the case-sensitive names from the HPKB-UL to case-insensitive names. For example, the constant name *#$performedBy* from the HPKB-UL was mapped to *performed-by*. The syntactic translation was a low-effort engineering task, and accounted for a small fraction of the KB development time.

Comprehension

Before a knowledge engineer reuses an ontology, its contents and organization must be understood. Two techniques enabled ontology comprehension. First, we used our graphical visualization tool, GKB-Editor (Paley et al. 1997), to explore the HPKB-UL. The taxonomy and the relationship browsers of the GKB-Editor were instrumental in helping us understand the interrelationships between classes and predicates of the HPKB-UL. During the KB development process, the GKB-Editor's browsing capabilities were extensively used to search for necessary concepts and to identify the location in the taxonomy for a new concept. Second, the extensive documentation accompanying the Integrated Knowledge Base Environment (IKB) clarified many design decisions and presented the KB content in many different ways. (IKB is a portion of the Cyc KB that was distributed to the participants of the project.) For example, the IKB documentation included a glossary of terms organized by domains such as time, space, geography, communication actions, etc. The IKB also included a search facility that linked the English words in Wordnet to the corresponding concept names in the KB.

Slicing

Slicing involves selecting a portion of an input ontology for use in a new application. Using all of the input ontology may not be desirable for the following reasons. First, all of the input ontology may not be needed for a new application. Second, importing all of it may make the resulting KB unnecessarily complex. Third, there may be aspects of the input ontology that the target inference tool is unable to handle, and that must be removed. Finally, some of the representation decisions made in the input ontology may not be acceptable to the target application.

Two technical problems must be solved for slicing. First, we need to decide what portions of the input ontology we need to slice. We call the portion of the input ontology that needs to be extracted the *seed*. Second, we need a computational procedure that extracts out just the right amount of terms from the input ontology.

More formally, an ontology contains a set O of sentences of the following form.

- *(class X)*, where $X \in C$, and C is a set of classes
- *(relation X)*, where $X \in R$, and R is a set of relations
- *(function X)*, where $X \in F$, and F is a set of functions
- *(individual X)*, where $X \in I$, and I is a set of individuals
- *(subclass-of X Y)*, where $X, Y \in C$
- *(instance-of X Y)*, where $X \in C \cup I, Y \in C$
- *(arity X N)*, where $X \in R \cup F$, and N is a positive integer
- *(nth-domain X N Y)*, where $X \in R \cup F$, N is a positive integer, and $Y \in C$
- *(range X Y)*, where $X \in F$, and $Y \in C$
- *(nth-domain-subclass-of X N Y)*, where $X \in R \cup F$, N is a positive integer less than the arity of R, and $Y \in C$
- *(range-subclass-of X Y)*, where $X \in F$, and $Y \in C$
- *(r X V)*, where $r \in R$
- *(template-slot-value X Y V)*, where $X \in C$, $Y \in R$, and *(arity R 2)* is in O

The relation symbols *class, individual, subclass-of, instance-of,* and *template-slot-value* have meanings as defined in the OKBC specification (Chaudhri et al. 1998). The sentence *(class X)* means that X is a set or a unary relation. The sentence *(individual X)* means that X is not a set. The sentence *(subclass-of X Y)* means that the class X is a subset of class Y. The sentence *(instance-of X Y)* means that individual X is a member of the set Y. The sentence *(relation X)* means that X is a relation. The sentence *(function X)* means that X is a function. Every class is a unary relation, therefore, $C \subseteq R$. The relation symbols *range,* and *range-subclass-of* specify the type restriction on the value of a function. If *(range F C)*, the value returned by F must be an instance of the class C. If *(range-subclass-*

of F C), then the value returned by *F* must be a sub class of the class *C*. The relation *arity* specifies the number of arguments of a function or relation. If *(arity R 3)*, the relation *R* can have exactly three arguments. The relation symbols *nth-domain* and *nth-domain-subclass-of* specify the type restriction on the arguments of the functions and relations. If *(nth-domain R i C)*, then the *ith* argument of the relation *R* must be an instance of the class *C*. Similarly, if *(nth-domain-subclass-of R i C)*, the *ith* argument of the relation *R* must be a subclass of *C*.

The seed *S* is a set containing sentences of the form *(class X)*, *(relation X)*, *(function X)*, and *(individual X)*, where $X \in C \cup R \cup F \cup I$. Based on the knowledge of the target application, we were able to identify *S*. At the beginning of a project, all needed terms may not be included in *S* in the initial estimate of *S*. As the KB evolves, the seed can be revised. In practice, it was sufficient to recompute the slice once every six months.

The slice *L* is a subset of *O*. We would like to compute *L* in a way that all the useful information from the source ontology is incorporated into the KB being developed. We call a slice *maximal with respect to S* if any inferences involving *S* that can be performed using *O* can be performed using *L*. We call a slice *L* that is maximal with respect to S as *minimal with respect to S* if there is no $L' \subset L$ that is maximal with respect to S.

A trivial way to compute *L* is to simply return *S*. In general, *S* is not a maximal slice of *O* with respect to *S*. Let us define an algorithm to compute the maximal slice of *O*, with respect to *S*.

Algorithm *MaximalSlice*
Input: Input ontology *O*, and seed *S*
Output: *L*, a slice of *O*, with respect to *S*

1. Let *S'* = {*X* | *(class X)* ∈ *S*, or *(relation X)* ∈ *S*, or *(function X)* ∈ *S*, or *(individual X)* ∈ *S*}.
2. Set *L* = *S*.
3. For every $X \in S'$, if *(nth-domain X N Y)* ∈ *O*, add *Y* to *S'*, and add *(class Y)* and *(nth-domain X N Y)* to *L*.
4. For every $X \in S'$, if *(nth-domain-subclass-of X N Y)* ∈ *O*, add *Y* to *S'*, and add *(nth-domain-subclass-of X N Y)* and *(class Y)* to *L*.
5. For every $X \in S'$, if $X \in F$, and if *(range X Y)* ∈ *O*, add *Y* to *S'*, and add *(range X Y)* and *(class Y)* to *L*.
6. For every $X \in S'$, if $X \in F$, and if *(range-subclass-of X Y)* ∈ *O*, add *Y* to *S'*, and add *(range-subclass-of X Y)* and *(class Y)* to *L*.
7. For every $X \in S'$, if $X \in C$, and if *(subclass-of X Y)* ∈ *O*, add *Y* to *S'*, and add *(subclass-of X Y)* and *(class Y)* to *L*.
8. For every $X \in S'$, if *(instance-of X Y)* ∈ *O*, add *Y* to *S'*, and add *(instance-of X Y)* and *(class Y)* to *L*.
9. For every $X \in S'$, if *(r X V)* ∈ *O*, add *(r X V)* to *L*. If *(class V)* ∈ *O*, add *(class V)* to *L*, and *V* to *S'*. If *(individual V)* ∈ *O*, add *(individual V)* to *L*, and *V* to *S'*.
10. For every $X \in S'$, if *(template-slot-value X r V)* ∈ *O*, add *(template-slot-value r X V)* to *L*. If *(class V)* ∈ *O*, add *(class V)* to *L*, and *V* to *S'*. If *(individual V)* ∈ *O*, add *(individual V)* to *L*, and *V* to *S'*.
11. Repeat steps 7 through 10 until *L* does not change.
12. Return *L*.

The algorithm *MaximalSlice* works by first determining all the relevant classes, and then computing their upward closure in the graph of taxonomic relationships.

Theorem 1: The algorithm *MaximalSlice* produces a slice *L* of *O*, which is maximal with respect to *S*.
Theorem 2: The algorithm MaximalSlice is polynomial in the size of *C*.

It is possible to produce a smaller slice if one has additional knowledge about the sorts of axioms that are of interest for the target application. For example, suppose *X* is a *subclass-of Y*, and *Y* is a *subclass-of Z*, and that *X* is in the seed, but *Y* and *Z* are not. If there is no *(template-slot-value Y r V)* sentence in *O*, and if it is not used in any *nth-domain, nth-domain-subclass-of, range,* and *range-subclass-of* sentence, it may be dropped from the closure by asserting *X* as a *subclass-of Z*. This does not change any inferences of interest that can be performed about *X*. An example definition of *interestingness* follows.

Definition 1. A class *X* is of interest with respect to a seed S if one of the following holds.
- X is the root of the class-subclass graph
- The sentence *(nth-domain Y N X)* is in *O*, and *Y* is in *S*
- The sentence *(nth-domain-subclass-of Y N X)* is in *O*, and *Y* is in *S*
- The sentence *(range Y X)* is in *O*, and *Y* is in *S*
- *(range-subclass-of Y X)* is in *O*, and *Y* is in *S*
- *(template-slot-value X r V)* is in *O*

Using this definition, one can compute an interesting superclass of a class *X* as follows. For every *(subclass-of X Y)* sentence in *O*, the superclass *Y* is interesting if *Y* is of interest. If *Y* is not of interest check to see if *Z* is of interest, where *(subclass-of Y Z)* is in *O*. If *Z* is of interest, *Z* is an interesting superclass of *X*. For a rooted and connected taxonomy, this process is guaranteed to terminate. An interesting type of a class or an individual may be computed analogously.

Algorithm *MinimalMaximalSlice*
Input: Input ontology *O*, seed *S*, and slice *L* produced by *MaximalSlice*
Output: *L*, a slice of *O*, with respect to *S*

1. Steps 1 through 6 are the same as the algorithm *MaximalSlice*.
7. For every *(subclass-of X Y)* in *L*, compute interesting parent *Z* as in Definition 1, add *(subclass-of X Z)* and *(class Z)* to *L*, and *Z* to *S'*.
8. For every *(instance-of X Y)* in *L*, compute interesting parent *Z* as in Definition 1, add *(instance-of X Z)* and *(class Z)* to *L*, and *Z* to *S'*.
9. Steps 9 through 12 are the same as in the algorithm *MaximalSlice*.

Theorem 3: The algorithm *MinimalMaximalSlice* produces a slice *L* of *O*, which is minimally maximal with respect to *S* assuming the interestingness of a class as defined in Definition 1.

During the first year of the project, we used the trivial slice of the HPKB-UL, that is, we just used the constant names and documentation strings. During the second year, we used the *MaximalSlice*. The motivation for *MinimalMaximalSlice* was to argue that while reusing an ontology, it is not necessary to agree with everything in the source ontology, especially those terms and representations that can be *sliced* away. The terms that can be sliced away are like the binary code in a compiled program that never needs to be exposed to the knowledge engineer.

To consider the generality of the results of this section, let us compare the knowledge model considered here with some other well-known systems. The relation symbols taken from the OKBC knowledge model, *class, individual, subclass-of, template-slot-value*, and *instance-of*, or their equivalents are supported by a wide range of knowledge representation systems such as LOOM (MacGregor 1991), Classic (Borgida et al. 1989), and Ontolingua (Farquhar et al. 1997). Since slots are binary relations, the *nth-domain* restriction, for *n=1*, is equivalent to the *domain* restriction on a slot, and for *n=2*, is equivalent to the value type restriction. The domain and value type restrictions are commonly supported. Higher arity relations, functions, *nth-domain-subclass-of*, and *range-subclass-of* are not supported in the OKBC knowledge model and the description logic systems such as Classic. The equivalent relations, for example, *arg1Genls, resultGenls*, are in the HPKB-UL, and are used extensively in the Cyc KB. Numeric and cardinality restrictions on slot values are supported in the OKBC knowledge model, LOOM, and CLASSIC, but are not considered here. It is, straightforward to extend the slicing algorithms to include numeric and cardinality constraints. Supporting constructs such as *disjoint-with, same-values, not-same-values, etc.* remains open for future work.

Reformulation

Reformulation is the process of taking an input theory and transforming its representation. Reformulation is synonymous with morphing (Chalupsky 2000). A common reason for reformulation is that in the target system the reformulated theory may be more efficient to reason with than the original theory. We reformulated the HPKB-UL to convert every *Functional Predicate* into functions. We explain this reformulation in more detail.

HPKB-UL represents the functional relationships as predicates. For example, even though *mother* is a function, it is represented in the HPKB-UL as a relation. Such predicates are instances of the class *Functional Predicate*. There are two differences between using functions and relations for representing functional relationships.

First, functions are a more compact way to state that the relationship between two objects is single-valued and that when a function is applied to an object (or a set of objects), the value indeed exists (Bundy 1977). To assert the same information using relations, one needs to also specify that the cardinality of the relation is 1. Thus, when we represent *mother* as a function, we are guaranteed that every individual has one and only one mother. When we represent *mother* by a relation, we do not get any such guarantees unless we also assert the cardinality constraint.

Second, using functions, the paramodulation rule of inference can be applied. The benefits of using functions are enhanced while using equality reasoning. SNARK, like most theorem provers, uses the paramodulation rule of inference while reasoning with equality. The paramodulation rule, given an assertion such as $a = b$, allows us to simplify a formula such as *(R a)* to *(R b)*. If we use functions instead of relations, it introduces equality in the KB. For example, *(mother sue john)* is replaced by *sue = mother (john)*. SNARK is then able to use the paramodulation rule of inference for reasoning with such formulas. The paramodulation rules of inference can sometimes lead to faster and shorter proofs. But in other cases, the search space can become larger.

The implementation of this reformulation was straightforward because we were dealing with only structural information. Implementing this reformulation for general axioms remains open for future research.

Merging

Merging involves ensuring that the merged KBs use the same constant names when they mean the same thing, and that they represent the same information identically (McGuinness et al. 2000). Merging assumes the existence of two independently developed KBs that need to be combined to produce a new KB. The merging task for our KB development effort was primarily performed by KSL Stanford, and the details may be found elsewhere (McGuinness et al. 2000). The merging step was made easier by the fact that the KBs were developed using a standard syntax: ANSI KIF extended by standard relation names from the OKBC knowledge model. We, however, needed to invest some effort in resolving the conflicts arising from the merge. We give here one example of the representational difference that arose during the merge process.

The merge process revealed that the KBs developed by SRI and KSL Stanford both represented situations in which one agent supports or opposes another. To represent an action, in which one agent supports another action, say a terrorist attack, there are two alternatives. First, one can define a class *supporting-terrorist-attack* and create an individual member of this class to represent an instance of a supporting action. Second, one can define a slot called *supports* on the class *action*, which can take an instance of *terrorist-attack* as a value. If the KBs to be merged use these different representations for supporting actions, then the merge phase should either use one representation over the other or add axioms defining equivalence between the two representations. In the current merge, a meeting was organized between KSL and SRI to resolve this difference, and the solution that defines the slot *supports* on class *action* was adopted.

In a KB development project, the merging effort can be reduced by proactive means. For example, if the development process is driven by reuse, a global catalogue for constant names is maintained, and a style guide is followed for inventing new names, the problem of the same terms meaning the same thing can be reduced.

Experimental Results on Knowledge Reuse

We have three objectives in presenting the experimental results: to characterize the KB development process, to give specific examples of knowledge reuse to highlight that the results are based on some nontrivial examples of reuse, and finally to show the level of reuse achieved.

An overview of the KB development process is shown in Figure 1. The KB development started from the HPKB-UL. We took a slice of the HPKB-UL that was extended to create the KB CMCP-98. Two other KBs were developed independently at Stanford – the *Supports* KB was developed by KSL, and the *Capability* KB was developed by the Formal Reasoning Group. At the end of the first year, these KBs were merged to produce a new KB called the *SAIC merged ontology (MO)*. The development for the second year of the project started by taking a slice of the SAIC MO, which was extended to produce CMCP-99, the KB for the second year.

While interpreting the empirical results presented next it is helpful to understand the relationship between the test questions between the two years. During the second year, many of the questions were repeated from the first year, and several new questions were introduced. In terms of the domain content, the test questions during the first year involved organizations, agents, geographical regions, products and economic measures. During the second year, several different kinds of actions, interests and historical case descriptions were introduced. Even though there was

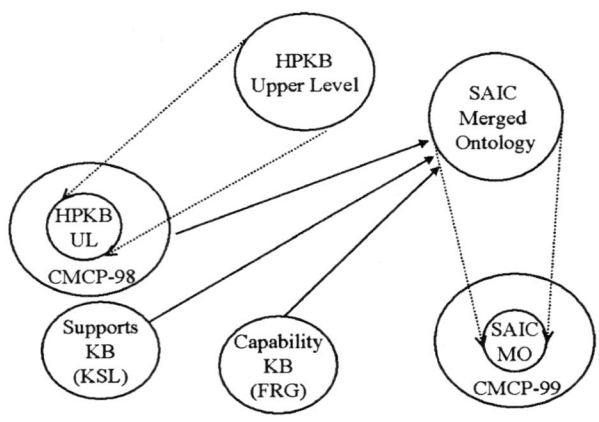

Figure 1. An overview of the development process

a substantial overlap in the content, the test problems differed significantly across the two years.

The HPKB-UL had about 16,434 axioms, and our initial slice of it contained 446 axioms. The CMCP-98 KB had 5943 axioms. The SAIC merged ontology contained 21,223 axioms. (We have excluded many ground facts from this count.) The slice of the merged ontology that was used for the development during the second year contained 5360 axioms. The CMCP-99 KB contained 22,902 axioms. The slice of HPKB-UL was recomputed three times over a period of two years. The final slice of HPKB-UL contained 2544 axioms.

To highlight the nature of reuse, we consider two representations. One of the questions answered by our system was:

Has post-Shah Iran launched ballistic missiles in wartime?

The upper ontology had a class representing *weapons*. We extended it by creating *ballistic-missiles* as a new subclass of the class representing weapons that already existed. The verb "launch" in the questions was mapped to the action *attack*, which was a subclass of an already existing class *hostile-social-action*. The class of actions in the HPKB-UL had several slots. The slot *performed-by* on an action specified the doer of the action, and *device-used* specified the tool that was used in performing that action. Finally, we specified the temporal extent of the question by defining a constant representing the time *reign-of-shah* and then using the temporal comparison *starts-after-ending-of*, from the HPKB-UL. The resulting formalization follows:
(and
 (attack ?act)
 (performed-by ?act Iran)
 (device-used ?act ballistic-missile)
 (starts-after-ending-of ?act reign-of-shah))

The formalization of this question reuses primitives for representing temporal knowledge and slots on actions from the HPKB-UL. As another example, consider the question:

What risks can Iran expect in sponsoring a terrorist attack in Saudi Arabia?

To answer questions of this type, one can use a cause effect model involving five predicates: *enables, causes, prevents, maleficiary,* and *beneficiary*. The predicates *enables, causes,* and *prevents* are based on the common sense language for reasoning about causation and rational action previously developed elsewhere (Ortiz 1999). The relation *causes* is used to represent the effects that are definitely caused by an action, *enables* to represent those actions that are made possible by an action, and *prevents* to represent actions that are prevented by an action. The relation *maleficiary* to relate an action to an agent who is harmed by that action, and *beneficiary* to relate an action to an agent who is benefited by that action. Thus, if an *?agent* performs an *?action1* that *causes* another action *?action2*, and the performer of *?action1* is *maleficiary* to *?action2*, then *?action2* is a risk in doing *?action1*. Similarly, if an *?agent* performs an *?action1* that *prevents* another action *?action2*, and the performer of *?action1* is the *beneficiary* of the *?action2*, then *?action2* is a risk in doing *?action1*. The HPKB-UL contained a predicate *cause-event-event* that was equivalent to *causes*. Adding the predicates *prevents*, and *enables* extended the HPKB-UL. The predicates *beneficiary* and *maleficiary* were reused directly from the HPKB-UL.

The empirical results that we present here are based on a reuse metric that was proposed earlier (Cohen et al. 1999). The metric can be computed for either axioms or constant names. Suppose a knowledge engineering task requires n constants and k of those can be reused from an existing KB; then, k/n measures the extent of reuse of the KB. The reuse of axioms can be computed analogously. The results are shown in Table 1.

The table first reports the constant reuse in constructing the KB CMCP-99, that is, the KB at the end of the project. We computed the reuse with respect to the HPKB-UL, CMCP-98, and the pre-evaluation KB, that is the KB that existed just before the final evaluation at the end of the second year began. Constants include any class, relation, function, or individual in the KB. The structural statements include atomic statements, which use the relations *subclass-of, instance-of, nth-domain, nth-domain-subclass-of, range-subclass-of, arity, subrelation-of,* and *disjoint-with*. The first numeric entry of 0.22 means that for encoding all the structural statements in CMCP-99, 22% of necessary constant symbols were already in the HPKB-UL. Similarly, 29% of all the necessary constants for encoding the statements containing implications were reused from the HPKB-UL.

The table next reports the level of reuse for axioms that were actually used in answering the questions. The reuse for non-ground statements is not reported, because the number of such statements in the KB was low. The reuse of the HPKB-UL in actually answering was somewhat lower than in constructing the KB. There were no implications in the HPKB-UL, and therefore, it was not meaningful to report the reuse of implications from it. The reuse of the pre-evaluation KB in answering the questions was higher than in constructing the new KB.

Table 1. Gross k/n for axioms in the KB and the axioms actually used to answer questions

With respect to KB	Constant Reuse in Constructing the KB		
	Structural	Implications	Non-Implications
HPKB-UL	0.22	0.29	0.13
Y1 KB	0.18	0.33	0.19
Pre-eval KB	0.49	0.78	0.39
	Axiom Reuse in Answering the Questions		
	Constants	Structural	Implications
HPKB-UL	0.17	0.12	N/A
Y1 KB	0.21	0.09	0.05
Pre-eval KB	0.67	0.76	0.43

The absolute value of these numbers is of less interest than the observation that the reuse of prior knowledge is indeed possible. The reuse from the HPKB-UL is especially interesting because it was not designed with the current application in mind.

Scope for Future Work

In this project, we reused only constants, and structural statements from the HPKB-UL, and did not reuse any statements containing implications and non-ground facts that were available in IKB. A hypothesis for future work would be that since our KB shares the upper structure with IKB, it would enable us to share the implications and non-ground facts from the HPKB-UL with greater ease. Exploring this hypothesis would also require us to extend our work on slicing and reformulation. The slicing techniques would need to be extended to slice out the relevant rules. The representation differences are likely to have a greater impact on rules than they had on the class-subclass structure; therefore, new reformulation techniques will need to be developed.

Apart from the technical issues associated with reuse, there are human issues. Knowledge engineers prefer their own representations to reusing someone else's. In many cases, using different representation does not necessarily contribute to the overall system and makes it difficult to scale the scope of a KB. We reuse other people's software routinely as long as it is well packaged, has a clear functionality, and adds value to our work. Doing the same for knowledge components has been a dream for the community for a long time, and remains an open challenge for the knowledge reuse technology.

Summary

We presented a case study in reusing prior knowledge. The reuse of prior knowledge was done in the following steps: translation, comprehension, slicing, reformulation, and merging. The *translation* tools were developed to convert a subset of MELD into KIF augmented with standard relation names from the OKBC knowledge model. The *comprehension* phase used graphical visualization tools and the KB documentation. The *slicing* techniques were developed to extract a portion of the existing KB to be incorporated into the new KB. The representation was *reformulated* so that the reused KB can be efficiently reasoned with. The *merging* phase involved human intervention to resolve the representation differences. We presented several concrete examples of reuse for an application in the crisis management domain, and empirically argued that KB construction by reuse from prior knowledge is indeed feasible. These results present an advancement of the state of the art of KB construction methods that start a new development from scratch.

Acknowledgements

This work was supported by DARPA's High Performance Knowledge Bases Project. We thank the co-developers of the CMCP KBs at SAIC, KSL Stanford, FRG Stanford, and NWU. We thank the developers of the CMCP that defined the context of the KB development for the project. We thank Cycorp for making the HPKB-UL available for use in the project. We also thank the SRI staff members Charlie Ortiz, and Nina Zumel for their technical contributions to this work.

References

Borgida, A., Brachman, R. J., McGuinness, D. L., and Resnick, L. A. (1989). "CLASSIC: A Structural Data Model for Objects." Proceedings of the 1989 ACM SIGMOD International Conference on Management of Data, Portland, OR, 58-67.

Bundy, A. (1977). "Exploiting the properties of functions to control search." *D. A. I. Report No. 45*, University of Edinburgh.

Chalupsky, H. (2000). "Ontomorph: A System for Translation of Symbolic Knowledge." *Seventh International Conference on Knowledge Reprewentation and Reasoning*, Breckenridge, CO.

Chaudhri, V. K., Farquhar, A., Fikes, R., Karp, P. D., and Rice, J. P. (1998). "OKBC: A Programmatic Foundation for Knowledge Base Interoperability." Proceedings of the AAAI-98, Madison, WI.

Chaudhri, V. K., Lowrance, J. D., Stickel, M. E., Thomere, J. F., and Waldinger, R. J. (2000). "Ontology Construction Toolkit.", SRI International, Menlo Park, CA.

Cohen, P., Chaudhri, V. K., Pease, A., and Schrag, B. (1999). "Does Prior Knowledge Facilitate the Development of Knowledge-based Systems." Proceedings of the AAAI-99, 221-226.

Cohen, P., Schrag, R., Jones, E., Pease, A., Lin, A., Starr, B., Gunning, D., and Burke, M. (1998). "The DARPA High-Performance Knowledge Bases Project." *AI Magazine*, 19(4), 25-49.

Farquhar, A., Fikes, R., and Rice, J. P. (1997). "A Collaborative Tool for Ontology Construction." *International Journal of Human Computer Studies*, 46, 707--727.

Genesereth, M. R., and Fikes, R. E. (1992). "Knowledge Interchange Format, Version 3.0 Reference Manual." (Logic-92-1).

IET, Alphatech, Pacific Sierra Research, and Cohen, P. (December 1997). "HPKB year 1 end-to-end challenge problem specification, version 1.1."

Lenat, D. B. (1997). "Cyc Public Ontology." http://www.cyc.com/cyc-2-1/index.html.

Lenat, D. B., and Guha, R. V. (1990). *Building Large Knowledge-Based Systems*, Addison Wesley, Reading, MA.

MacGregor, R. (1991). "The evolving technology of classification-based knowledge representation systems." Principles of semantic networks, J. Sowa, ed., 385--400.

McGuinness, D., Fikes, R., Rice, J., and Wider, S. (2000). "An Environment for Merging and Testing Large Ontologies." *Seventh International Conference on Knowledge Representation and Reasoning*, Breckenridge, CO.

Ortiz, C. L. (1999). "A Commonsense Language for Reasoning about Causation and Rational Action." *Artificial Intelligence Journal*, 111(2), 73-130.

Paley, S. M., Lowrance, J. D., and Karp, P. D. (1997). "A Generic Knowledge Base Browser and Editor." Proceedings of the Ninth Conference on Innovative Applications of Artificial Intelligence.

Pease, A., Chaudhri, V. K., Farquhar, A., and Lehman, F. (2000). "Practical Knowledge Representation and DARPA's High Performance Knowledge Bases Project." *Proceedings of the 7th International Conference on Principles of Knowledge Representation and Reasoning*, Brekcenridge, Colorado.

Stickel, M., Waldinger, R., Lowry, M., Pressburger, T., and Underwood, I. (1994). "Deductive Composition of Astronomical Software from Subroutine Libraries." Proceedings of the Twelfth International Conference on Automated Deduction (CADE-12), 341--355.

Valente, A., Russ, T., MacGregor, R., and Swartout, W. (1999). "Building and (Re)Using an Ontology of Air Campaign Planning." *IEEE Intelligent Systems*, 14(1), 27-36.

Dynamic Ontologies on the Web

Jeff Heflin and James Hendler

Department of Computer Science
University of Maryland
College Park, MD 20742
{heflin, hendler}@cs.umd.edu

Abstract

We discuss the problems associated with managing ontologies in distributed environments such as the Web. The Web poses unique problems for the use of ontologies because of the rapid evolution and autonomy of web sites. We present SHOE, a web-based knowledge representation language that supports multiple versions of ontologies. We describe SHOE in the terms of a logic that separates data from ontologies and allows ontologies to provide different perspectives on the data. We then discuss the features of SHOE that address ontology versioning, the effects of ontology revision on SHOE web pages, and methods for implementing ontology integration using SHOE's extension and version mechanisms.

1. Introduction

The World Wide Web is a repository of information that is structured for presentation to human readers and is thus mostly inaccessible to machines. This situation will be somewhat alleviated by the Extensible Markup Language (XML), which allows content to be separated from presentation. However, although XML Document Type Declarations (DTDs) can specify the grammar of markup languages, there are no facilities for formalizing the meaning of these languages. To create a web language with semantics, one must extend XML with features of knowledge representation (KR) languages.

However, the Web presents new challenges for KR; simply creating an XML syntax for traditional KR languages is insufficient. The Web is a distributed system and there are many providers of information. As such, the reliability of information is questionable, and it is inevitable that inconsistencies will arise. The Web is also in a constant state of change. Although standard vocabularies will be necessary for interoperability, these vocabularies must be able to evolve as the Web does. Additionally, the sheer size of the Web will test the scalability of KR systems and algorithms. As a consequence of the Web's size and dynamic nature, it must be treated as an open-world, since it would be unrealistic for any agent to assume that it knows all true facts about the Web.

Copyright © 2000, American Association for Artificial Intelligence (www.aaai.org). All rights reserved.

The Simple HTML Ontology Extensions (SHOE) is an ontology-based knowledge representation language that is embedded in web pages (Luke et al. 1997; Heflin, Hendler, and Luke 1999). Over the course of four years, we have investigated the use of ontologies to support the structuring and querying of data on the Web. We begin this paper with an overview of the SHOE language, and then provide a logical semantics for it. We then discuss the problem of ontology revision, which is necessary in a dynamic environment such as the Web, and describe how SHOE's versioning mechanism copes with this. Next, we discuss the tendency of distributed ontologies to diverge, and provide methods for reintegrating them using SHOE's extension and version mechanisms. Finally, we discuss related work and present our conclusions.

2. SHOE

The underlying philosophy of SHOE is that intelligent internet agents will be able to better perform their tasks if the most useful information is provided in a structured manner. To this end, SHOE extends HTML with a set of knowledge oriented tags that, unlike HTML tags, provide structure for knowledge acquisition as opposed to information presentation. SHOE associates meaning with this content by making each web page commit to one or more ontologies. These ontologies permit the discovery of implicit knowledge through the use of taxonomies and inference rules, allowing information providers to encode only the necessary information on their web pages, and to use the level of detail that is appropriate to the context. Interoperability is promoted through the sharing and reuse of ontologies.

To achieve compatibility with existing web standards, SHOE's syntax is defined as an application of SGML, a language that defines tag-based languages and was the influence for HTML's syntax. A slight variant of the syntax exists for compatibility with XML, and can be used by web sites that have begun to migrate to XML.

The nature of the SHOE language makes it possible to develop numerous tools and architectures for processing it. In order to evaluate the language, we have built a suite of tools, including a tool for adding SHOE markup to web pages, a web crawler that gathers SHOE from web pages

```
<HTML>
...
<BODY>
<ONTOLOGY ID="cs-dept-ontology" VERSION="1.1"
          BACKWARD-COMPATIBLE-WITH="1.0">
<USE-ONTOLOGY ID="univ-ontology" VERSION="1.0" PREFIX="u"
              URL="http://ontlib.org/univ_v1.0.html">
...
<DEF-CATEGORY NAME="ComputerScience" ISA="u.ResearchArea">
...
<DEF-RELATION NAME="writtenIn">
   <DEF-ARG POS=1 TYPE="Program">
   <DEF-ARG POS=2 TYPE="ComputerLanguage">
</DEF-RELATION>
...
<DEF-RENAME FROM="u.Department" TO="Department">
<DEF-RENAME FROM="u.Chair" TO="DepartmentHead">
...
</ONTOLOGY>
</BODY>
</HTML>
```

Figure 1. An Example Ontology

and stores it in a knowledge base, and a number of query tools. We have applied these tools to various domains, including computer science departments and food safety. A discussion of these tools and applications can be found in Heflin, Hendler and Luke (1999). Demos of the tools are available at *http://www.cs.umd.edu/projects/plus/SHOE*.

2.1 Language Features

In this section we describe the features of SHOE that are necessary for an understanding of this paper. The reader may be surprised by the simplicity of the language. In the context of the Web this is actually a virtue. In order for a language to be accepted by the web community, it must be easy for users to understand and tool developers to implement. As such, a guiding principle of the SHOE project has been to add features to the language only when it became clear that they were necessary.

SHOE ontologies are made publicly available by locating them on web pages. An example ontology is presented in Figure 1. An <ONTOLOGY> tag delimits the machine-readable portion of the ontology and specifies a unique identifier and a version number for the ontology. As is common in many ontology efforts, such as Ontolingua (Farquhar, Fikes, and Rice 1997) or Cyc (Lenat and Guha 1990), SHOE ontologies build on or extend other ontologies, forming a lattice with the most general ontologies at the top and the more specific ones at the bottom. Ontologies inherit all of the components present in their ancestors. As a result, ontologies are interoperable to the extent that they share the same ancestor ontologies.

Ontology reuse in SHOE is accomplished by extending general ontologies to create more specific ontologies. Specifically, the <USE-ONTOLOGY> tag indicates the id and version number of an ontology that is extended. An optional URL field allows systems to locate the ontology if needed and a PREFIX field is used to establish a short local identifier for the ontology. When an ontology refers to an element from an extended ontology, this prefix and a period is appended before the element's name. In this way, references are guaranteed to be unambiguous, even when two ontologies use the same term to mean different things. By chaining the prefixes, one can specify a path through the extended ontologies to an element in a general ontology.

An ontology can define categories, relations, and other components. Categories are introduced with a <DEF-CATEGORY> tag and may specify one or more subsuming categories. Note that it is not possible to specify subsuming categories for a category defined in another ontology. Relations, which are essentially n-ary predicates, are defined with a <DEF-RELATION> tag and must specify types for each argument.

Sometimes an ontology may need to use a term from another ontology, but a different label may be more useful within its context. The <DEF-RENAME> tag allows the ontology to specify a local name for a concept from any extended ontology. This local name must be unique within the scope of the ontology in which the rename appears. Renaming allows domain specific ontologies to use the vocabulary that is appropriate for the domain, while maintaining interoperability with other domains.

SHOE uses inference rules, indicated by the <DEF-INFERENCE> tag, to supply additional axioms. A SHOE inference rule consists of a body of one or more subclauses describing claims that entities might make and a head consisting of one or more subclauses describing a claim that may be inferred if all claims in the body are made. The <INF-IF> and <INF-THEN> tags indicate the head and body of the inference, respectively. SHOE rules can be reduced to Horn clauses, which allows implementations to take advantage of algorithms developed for datalog programs.

There are three types of inference subclauses: category, relation and comparison. The arguments of any subclause may be a constant or a variable, where variables are indicated by the keyword VAR. Constants must be matched exactly and variables of the same name must bind to the same value. The following example, which states "If X is a Car and the age of X is greater than 25, then X is an Antique," illustrates the construction of an inference that uses all three types of subclauses.

```
<DEF-INFERENCE>
<INF-IF>
   <CATEGORY NAME="Car" VAR FOR="X">
   <RELATION NAME="age">
      <ARG POS=1 VAR VALUE="X">
      <ARG POS=2 VAR VALUE="A">
   </RELATION>
   <COMPARISON OP="greaterThan">
      <ARG POS=1 VAR VALUE="A">
      <ARG POS=2 VALUE="25">
   </COMPARISON>
</INF-IF>
<INF-THEN>
   <CATEGORY NAME="Antique" VAR FOR="X">
</INF-THEN>
</DEF-INFERENCE>
```

The data sources for SHOE are web pages, where each can be thought of as a miniature knowledge base. These web pages declare one or more instances that represent SHOE entities, and each instance describes itself using categories and relations. The syntax for instances includes an <INSTANCE> tag that has a field for a KEY that uniquely identifies the instance. We recommend that the URL of the web page be used as this key, since it is guaranteed to identify only a single resource. An instance commits to a particular ontology by means of the <USE-ONTOLOGY> tag, which has the same function as the identically named tag used within ontologies. The use of common ontologies makes it possible to issue a single logical query to a set of data sources and enables the integration of related domains. To prevent ambiguity in the declarations, ontology elements are referred to using the prefixing mechanism described earlier.

It is important to note that the features of the language have been carefully chosen to prevent logical inconsistency. There are no negations, no single-valued relations, and no disjoint constraints between categories. Although this may seem extremely restrictive, it is very useful for practical systems on the Web, where inconsistencies would otherwise be unavoidable.

2.2 Mapping SHOE to First Order Logic

In order to provide formal semantics for SHOE, we will map it into a first order logical theory. This mapping will intentionally omit some features of the language so that we may focus on the issue of dynamic, distributed ontologies.

Essentially an ontology O can be thought of as a tuple <V,A> where V is the vocabulary and A is the set of axioms[1] that govern the theory. In the terminology of first-order theory, V is the set of predicate symbols, each with some arity >= 0, and A is a set of Horn clauses. For convenience, we will assume that the symbols in the vocabulary of each ontology are distinct. In actuality, SHOE has a separate namespace for each ontology, but we can make our assumption without loss of generality since it is possible to apply a renaming that appends a unique ontology identifier to each symbol. We now discuss how to build V and A, based upon the components that are defined in the ontology:

A <USE-ONTOLOGY> statement adds the vocabulary and axioms of the specified ontology to the current ontology. Since we have assumed that names must be unique, we do not have to concern ourselves with name conflicts.

A <DEF-RELATION> adds a symbol to the vocabulary and, for each argument type that is a category, adds an axiom that states that an instance in that argument must be a member of the category. If the tag specifies a name R and has n arguments then there is an n-ary predicate symbol R in V. If the type of the ith argument is a category C, then $[R(x_1,...,x_i,...x_n) \rightarrow C(x_i)] \in A$. Note that this rule is necessary because the Web must be treated as an open-world. Since there is no way to know that a given object is *not* a member of the required category, it is better to assume that this information is as yet undiscovered than to assume that the relation is in error.

A <DEF-CATEGORY> adds a unary predicate symbol to the vocabulary and possibly a set of rules indicating membership. If the name is C, then $C \in V$. For each super-category P_i specified, $[C(x) \rightarrow P_i(x)] \in A$.

A <DEF-INFERENCE> adds one or more axioms to the theory. If there is a single clause in the <INF-THEN>, then there is one axiom with a conjunction of the <INF-IF> clauses as the antecedent and the <INF-THEN> clause as the consequent. If there are n clauses in the <INF-THEN> then there are n axioms, each of which has one of the clauses as the consequent and has the same antecedent as above.

A <DEF-RENAME> provides an alias for a non-logical symbol. It is meant as a convenience for users and can be implemented using a simple pre-processing step that translates the alias to the original, unique non-logical symbol. Therefore, it can be ignored for the logical theory.

A formula F is well-formed with respect to O if: 1) F is an atom of the form $p(t_1,...,t_n)$ where p is a n-ary predicate symbol such that $p \in V$ or 2) F is a Horn clause where each atom is of such a form. An ontology is well-formed if every axiom in the ontology is well-formed with respect to the ontology.

A data source, such as a knowledge base or intelligent agent, uses an ontology to make relation and category claims. Let $S=<O_s,D_s>$ be such a data source, where O_s

---

[1] We distinguish axioms from rules by using the former term in the general sense and the later term to refer specifically to SHOE inference rules.

$=<V_s,A_s>$ is the ontology and D_s is the set of claims. We say S is well-formed if O_s is well-formed and each element of D_s is a ground atom that is well-formed with respect to O_s. The terms of these ground atoms are constants and can be instance keys or values of a SHOE data type.

We introduce a perspective $P=<S,O>$ as a data source $S=<O_s,D_s>$ viewed in the context of an ontology $O=<V,A>$. If $O=O_s$ then we say that P is the intended perspective, otherwise it is an alternate perspective. It is possible that elements of D_s will not be well-formed with respect to O, such elements are considered to be irrelevant to the perspective. If we let W_s be the subset of D_s that is well-formed with respect to O, then we say that P results in a theory $T=W_s \cup A$. An interpretation of the perspective consists of a domain, the assignment of each constant in S to an element of the domain, and an assignment of each element in V to a relation from the domain. A model of P is an interpretation such that every formula in its theory T is true with respect to it. If every ground logical consequence[2] of perspective P is also a ground logical consequence of perspective P′ then we say that P′ semantically subsumes P. That is, any query issued against perspective P′ will have at least the same answers as if the query was issued against P. If two perspectives semantically subsume each other, then they are said to be equivalent.

An important aspect of perspectives is that arbitrary ontology extensions do not automatically change the semantics of existing data sources. Instead, the semantics of a data source are determined by the intended perspective, which depends on the ontology that the source commits to. Any axioms added by new ontologies are invisible from the intended perspective, and will have no effect on queries issued against it. However, an extending ontology can reuse data sources that commit to an included ontology by providing an alternate perspective on them.

3. Revisioning

While previous ontology work has usually assumed static environments or that the ontologies exist in isolation and changes will not have side effects, when ontologies are applied to the Web these assumptions must be dropped. It is inevitable that web ontologies will change, whether the purpose is to correct errors, accommodate new information, or adjust the representation of a particular domain. However, changing any of these ontologies can have far-reaching side effects because numerous web pages and ontologies may depend on them. Any attempt to coordinate ontology revisions with corresponding revisions to the dependent objects will be very expensive and likely to fail. Furthermore, in distributed environments like the Web, the dependent objects are likely to be owned by various parties who may be opposed to or ill-prepared for such revisions.

---

[2] More precisely, we mean the set of ground atoms that are logical consequences of the corresponding theory T. This is also equivalent to the least Herbrand model of T.

In this section we define an ontology revision as a change in the components of an ontology. Thus, it can involve the addition or removal of categories, relations, and/or axioms. A revision may also extend a new ontology or stop extending one.

3.1 Effects of Revisions

We describe revisions by the impact they would have on perspectives of existing data sources. To be succinct, we will only discuss revisions that add or remove components; the modification of a component can be thought of as a removal followed by an addition. In the rest of this section, O will refer to the original ontology, O′ to its revision, P and P′ to the perspectives formed by these respective ontologies and an arbitrary source $S=<O,D_s>$, and T and T′ to the respective theories for these perspectives.

If a revision O′ adds an arbitrary rule to ontology O, then for any source S, the perspective P′ semantically subsumes P. This proof is trivial: since the revision only adds a sentence to the corresponding theory $T' \supset T$, and by the monotonicity of first-order logic any logical consequence of T is also a logical consequence of T′. Similar reasoning is used to ascertain that if the revision removes rules, then P semantically subsumes P′. Thus, a revision that adds or removes rules can provide an alternate perspective of a legacy data source, but it may restrict or loosen the semantics that were originally intended by the author of the data.

If O′ consists of the removal of categories or relations from O, then P semantically subsumes P′. This is because there may be some atoms in S that were well-formed with respect to O that are not well-formed with respect to O′. Informally, if categories or relations are removed, predicate symbols are removed from the vocabulary. If the ground atoms of S depended on these symbols for well-formedness, then the sentences are no longer well-formed when the symbols are removed. Thus, $T' \subset T$ and due to the monotonicity of first order logic every logical consequence of T′ is a logical consequence of T. Revisions of this type may mean that using the revised ontology to form a perspective may result in fewer answers to a given query.

Finally, if the revision only adds categories or relations, the corresponding perspective P′ is equivalent to P. Since $T \subset T'$ it is easy to show that P′ semantically subsumes P. The proof of the other direction depends on the nature of the axioms added: $R(x_1,...,x_i,...x_n) \rightarrow C(x_i)$ for relations and $C(x) \rightarrow P_i(x)$ for categories. It also relies on the fact that, due to the definitions of categories and relations, the predicate of each antecedent is a symbol added by the new ontology and must be distinct from symbols in any other ontology. Therefore any atoms formed from these predicates are not well-formed with respect to any preexisting ontology. There can be no such atoms in S, since S must be well-formed with respect to some ontology $\neq$ O′. Since the antecedents cannot be fulfilled, the rules will have no new logical consequences that are ground atoms. Since P semantically subsumes P′ and vice versa, P and P′ are equivalent. This result indicates that we can safely add relations or categories to the revision, and maintain the same perspective on all legacy data sources.

3.2 Versioning

As described in the previous section, different types of revisions may have different effects on the perspectives that we have on our data sources. It is these situations that make SHOE's versioning scheme important. SHOE maintains each version of the ontology as a separate web page and an instance must state which version it commits to. As a result, data sources can upgrade to the new ontology at their own pace and some may never upgrade.

To accomplish a revision in SHOE, the ontology designer copies the original ontology file, assigns it a new version number, and adds or removes elements as needed. If the revision merely adds ontology elements, then it can be used to form perspectives that semantically subsume the original perspective. Therefore, it can specify that it is compatible with previous versions using the optional BACKWARD-COMPATIBLE-WITH field in the <ONTOLOGY> tag. Agents and query systems that discover this ontology can also use it in place of any of the ontologies that it is backward-compatible with to form an alternate perspective of any data source. However, there is a danger in this as we describe below.

Consider the following scenario: an individual for whatever reasons, malicious or otherwise, decides that they want to create a revision to a popular ontology that is owned by somebody else. This revision only adds components, and thus is compatible with all existing web pages that reference the original ontology. The individual then indicates that this ontology is backward-compatible with the original. Unless there is a mechanism to determine if a revision is official, any agents or query systems that come across the revision will assume that they can use it in place of the old one, and unintended inferences may result. We suggest three methods to prevent this:

- agents will only use the revision as a substitute if it only adds categories or relations. Since such revisions will result in equivalent perspectives for existing data sources, it does not matter if it is an official revision.
- a revision must be located on the same server and in the same path as the ontology it revises. This guarantees that the owner has made the revision, but makes it difficult to move the location of an ontology once it has been used.
- the original ontology must authorize the revision. This could be accomplished by a <REVISED-BY> tag that points to the location of the revision. To use this method, upon discovering a purported revision, a system should reload the original ontology and see if it authorizes the revision.

Currently, we recommend that SHOE systems use the second approach, although we are considering the inclusion of a revised-by tag in a future version of the language.

4. Ontology Divergence

As discussed earlier, an important aspect of SHOE is that interoperability is achieved through ontology reuse. That is, the preferred method of ontology development is to extend existing ontologies and create new definitions only when existing definitions are unsuitable. In this way, all concepts are automatically integrated. However, when there is concurrent development of ontologies in a large, distributed environment such as the Web, it is inevitable that new concepts will be defined when existing ones could be used. As a result there will be a tendency for the most specific ontologies to diverge and become less interoperable. In these situations, occasional manual integration of ontologies is needed.

Ontology integration typically involves identifying the correspondences between two ontologies, determining the differences in definitions, and creating a new ontology that resolves these differences. Wiederhold (1994) describes four types of domain differences, which we paraphrase here:

- terminology: different names are used for the same concepts
- scope: similar categories may not match exactly; their extensions intersect, but each may have instances that cannot be classified under the other
- encoding: the valid values for a property can be different, even different scales could be used
- context: a term in one domain has a completely different meaning in another

The process for aligning ontologies can be performed either manually or semi-automatically (using tools and algorithms currently under development by other researchers). However, it is important to note that simply creating a new integrated ontology does not solve the problem of integrating information on the Web. When the web community has synthesized the ontologies (that is, other web pages and ontologies come to depend on them), all of the dependent objects would have to be revised to reflect the new ontology. Since this would be an impossible task, we instead suggest three ways to incorporate the results of an ontology integration effort, each of which is shown in Figure 2.

In the first approach, we create a mapping ontology O_M that extends the two ontologies O_1 and O_2 and assign it a unique id that distinguishes it from all other ontologies. We then add a <USE-ONTOLOGY> tag for each ontology to be integrated. Since this ontology has access to objects from both domains, it can create inference rules using the <DEF-INFERENCE> tag to map the common items between them. First, terminological differences can be mapped using simple if-and-only-if rules. For example:

$$BusOnt1.Employee(x) \Leftrightarrow BusOnt2.StaffMember(x)$$

Note that since SHOE's rules only allow inference in one direction, if-and-only-if rules like this one are actually implemented as two rules, one for each direction. Second, scope differences require mapping a category to the most specific category in the other domain that subsumes it. For example:

$$AF\_Ont.FighterPilot(x) \Rightarrow FAA\_Ont.JetPilot(x)$$

Third, some encoding differences can be handled by mapping individual values as in:

$$CriticOnt1.Rating(x, "Good") \Leftrightarrow CriticOnt2.Rating(x, "3")$$

Of course, not all encodings can be mapped in SHOE, for example arithmetic functions would be needed to map meters to feet. Finally, SHOE's prefix naming mechanism obviates the need to resolve context differences. The advantage of a mapping ontology is that the domain ontologies are unchanged; thus, it can be created without the approval of the owners of the original ontology. The disadvantages are that a user must explicitly request that the mapping ontology be used to provide a new perspective and that the mapping of many domains could result in a complex mess of mapping ontologies.

Another approach to implementing integration is to revise each ontology to include mappings to the other. First, we create a new version of each ontology, called a mapping revision, and assign it an appropriate version number. To each revision, we add mapping rules similar to the ones described in the mapping ontology approach. Since we are only adding inference rules, we can use the BACKWARD-COMPATIBLE-WITH field to specify that the revisions can be used in place of the original ontologies. If these revisions are used as alternate perspectives for data sources based on the domain ontologies, then data integration is automatic.

The disadvantage of the two mapping approaches is that they ignore a fundamental problem: the overlapping concepts do not belong in either domain, but are more general. The fact that two domains share the concept may mean that other domains will use it as well. If this is so, then each new domain would need a set of rules to map it to the others. Obviously this can become unwieldy very quickly. A more natural approach is to merge the common items into a more general ontology, called an intersection ontology, which is then extended by revisions to the domain ontologies. We create a new ontology O_N to serve as the intersection ontology and give it a unique identifier. Then, we standardize the common elements from the source ontologies and add them to the intersection ontology. To create the revisions for each source ontology, we create new versions O_1' and O_2' with appropriate version numbers and add the <USE-ONTOLOGY> tag to each revision to specify that it uses the intersection ontology. Since the intersection ontology must use a standard terminology, we must translate this terminology to that of each domain if we wish to make existing data sources well-formed with respect to the new ontologies. This is done by replacing the domain definitions of the common elements with <DEF-RENAME> tags that rename the intersection ontology's standardized names to the names originally used

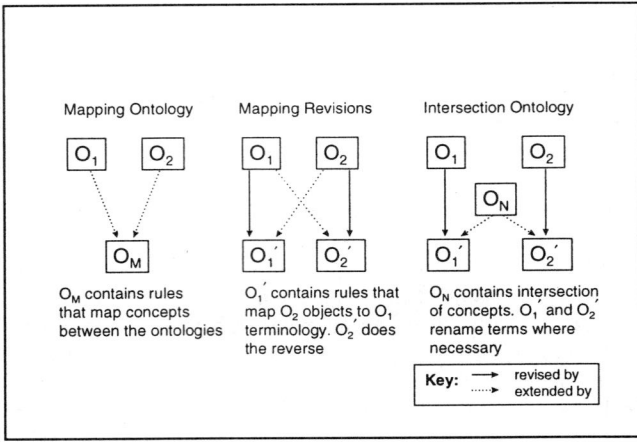

Figure 2. Integration Methods

by the source ontology. This has the advantage that equivalence of terms can be determined in the preprocessing phase rather than at query execution time. Finally, we use the BACKWARD-COMPATIBLE-WITH field to indicate that these revisions are compatible with the original ontologies.

5. Related Work

There are numerous efforts to create semantic languages for the Web. The Ontobroker project (Fensel et al. 1998) uses a language to describe data that is embedded in HTML, but relies on a centralized broker for ontology definitions. The Ontology Markup Language (OML) and Conceptual Knowledge Markup Language (CKML) (Kent 1999) are used together for semantic markup that is based on the theories of formal concept analysis and information flow. The W3C has developed the Resource Description Framework (RDF) (Lassila and Swick 1999), which uses XML to specify semantic networks for describing web resources. RDF has only a weak notion of ontologies, and although the RDF Schema proposal (Brickley and Guha 1999) improves this situation somewhat, it does not sufficiently handle the notions of revising or integrating ontologies.

In the last decade, there has been much active research in the area of ontology. For an overview and comparison of ontology design projects, see Noy and Hafner (1997). An attempt to formalize the notion of ontology is presented in Guarino and Giaretta (1995). There is little existing ontology research that considers either distributed environments or ontology revision. The Ontolingua Server (Farquhar, Fikes, and Rice 1997) can be used for collaborative ontology development; however, it primarily deals with the construction of ontologies and not the maintenance of ontologies that have been synthesized in a distributed environment. Foo (1995) has published some initial thoughts on ontology revision.

6. Conclusions

Although other projects are using ontologies to provide some structure to Web, none of these have focused on the problem of maintaining consistency as the ontologies evolve. The main contribution of this paper is an analysis of the problems associated with managing ontologies in a dynamic, distributed, and heterogeneous environment such as the Web. We have described the components of a SHOE ontology and focused on those that support revisions. We have developed a logic that separates data from ontologies and allows ontologies to provide different perspectives on the data. By mapping SHOE to this logic, we have shown how different types of revisions to an ontology affect the way we reason with existing data sources. We have shown that revisions that add categories or relations will have no effect, revisions that modify rules may change the answers to queries against the data sources, and revisions that remove categories or relations may eliminate certain answers. This knowledge should be used in weighing the benefits and costs of any revision. Although, ideally, integration is a byproduct of ontology extension, in a large, distributed environment, ontologies will tend to diverge and ontology integration will need to be performed periodically. We described three methods of incorporating this integration, showed how they could be applied in SHOE, and discussed the tradeoffs of each.

Although the Web is currently an untamed wilderness, ontologies can be used to give it a sense of order. However, we cannot expect the Web to stop growing and changing simply because we have fit it into the framework of an ontology. Instead, the ontologies must evolve with the Web, and must allow for different growth rates in different areas. This work is an initial step in this direction. Future work will investigate these issues more deeply and extend the analysis to richer ontology languages.

Acknowledgments

This work was supported by the Army Research Laboratory under contract number DAAL01-97-K0135. Professor Hendler is currently working as a Program Manager for the Defense Advanced Research Projects Agency (DARPA). The opinions expressed in this paper are his own, and not do not necessarily reflect the opinions of DARPA, the Department of Defense, or any other government agency.

References

Brickley, D. and Guha, R.V. 1999. *RDF Schema Specification (draft)*. W3C (World Wide Web Consortium). At http://www.w3.org/TR/1999/PR-rdf-schema-19990303.html.

Farquhar, A.; Fikes, R.; and Rice, J. 1997. Tools for Assembling Modular Ontologies in Ontolingua. In *Proceedings of the Fourteenth National Conference on Artificial Intelligence (AAAI-97)*, 436-441. Menlo Park, CA: AAAI Press.

Fensel, D.; Decker, S.; Erdmann, M.; and Studer, R. 1998. Ontobroker: How to enable intelligent access to the WWW. In *AI and Information Integration, Technical Report WS-98-14*, 36-42. Menlo Park, CA: AAAI Press.

Foo, N. 1995. Ontology Revision. In *Conceptual Structures; Third International Conference*, 16-31. Berlin: Springer-Verlag.

Guarino, N. and Giaretta, P. 1995. Ontologies and Knowledge Bases: Towards a Terminological Clarification. In N. Mars (ed.) *Towards Very Large Knowledge Bases: Knowledge Building and Knowledge Sharing*, 25-32. Amsterdam: IOS Press.

Heflin, J.; Hendler, J.; and Luke, S. 1999. SHOE: A Knowledge Representation Language for Internet Applications, Technical Report, CS-TR-4078 (UMIACS TR-99-71), Dept. of Computer Science, University of Maryland.

Kent, R.E. 1999. Conceptual Knowledge Markup Language: The Central Core. In *Proceedings of the Twelfth Workshop on Knowledge Acquisition, Modeling and Management*.

Lassila, O. and Swick, R. 1999. *Resource Description Framework (RDF) Model and Syntax*. W3C (World-Wide Web Consortium). At http://www.w3.org/TR/REC-rdf-syntax-19990222.html.

Lenat, D. and Guha, R. 1990. *Building Large Knowledge Based Systems*. Reading, Mass.: Addison-Wesley.

Luke, S.; Spector, L.; Rager, D.; and Hendler, J. 1997. Ontology-based Web Agents. In *Proceedings of the First International Conference on Autonomous Agents*, 59-66. New York, NY: Association of Computing Machinery.

Noy, N. and Hafner, C. 1997. The State of the Art in Ontology Design. *AI Magazine* 18(3):53-74.

Wiederhold, G. 1994. An Algebra for Ontology Composition. In *Proceedings of 1994 Monterey Workshop on Formal Methods*, 56-62. U.S. Naval Postgraduate School.

PROMPT: Algorithm and Tool for Automated Ontology Merging and Alignment

Natalya Fridman Noy and Mark A. Musen

Stanford Medical Informatics, Stanford University, Stanford, CA 94305-5479
{noy, musen}@smi.stanford.edu

Abstract

Researchers in the ontology-design field have developed the content for ontologies in many domain areas. Recently, ontologies have become increasingly common on the World-Wide Web where they provide semantics for annotations in Web pages. This distributed nature of ontology development has led to a large number of ontologies covering overlapping domains. In order for these ontologies to be reused, they first need to be merged or aligned to one another. The processes of ontology alignment and merging are usually handled manually and often constitute a large and tedious portion of the sharing process. We have developed and implemented PROMPT, an algorithm that provides a semi-automatic approach to ontology merging and alignment. PROMPT performs some tasks automatically and guides the user in performing other tasks for which his intervention is required. PROMPT also determines possible inconsistencies in the state of the ontology, which result from the user's actions, and suggests ways to remedy these inconsistencies. PROMPT is based on an extremely general knowledge model and therefore can be applied across various platforms. Our formative evaluation showed that a human expert followed 90% of the suggestions that PROMPT generated and that 74% of the total knowledge-base operations invoked by the user were suggested by PROMPT.

1 Ontologies in AI and on the Web

Ontologies today are available in many different forms: as artifacts of a tedious knowledge-engineering process, as information that was extracted automatically from informal electronic sources, or as simple "light-weight" ontologies that specify semantic relationships among resources available on the World-Wide Web (Brickley and Guha 1999). But what does a user do when he finds several ontologies that he would like to use but that do not conform to one another? The user must establish correspondences among the source ontologies, and to determine the set of overlapping concepts, concepts that are similar in meaning but have different names or structure, concepts that are unique to each of the sources. This work must be done regardless of whether the ultimate goal is to create a single coherent ontology that includes the information from all the sources (**merging**) or if the sources must be made consistent and coherent with one another but kept separately (**alignment**).

Copyright © 2000, American Association for Artificial Intelligence (www.aaai.org). All rights reserved.

Currently the work of mapping, merging, or aligning ontologies is performed mostly by hand, without any tools to automate the process fully or partially (Fridman Noy and Musen 1999). Our participation in the ontology-alignment effort within DARPA's High-Performance Knowledge-Bases project (Cohen et al. 1999) was a strong motivation for developing semi-automated specialized tools for ontology merging and alignment. Several teams developed ontologies in the domain of military planning, which then needed to be aligned to one another. We found the experience of manually aligning the ontologies to be an extremely tedious and time-consuming process. At the same time we noticed many steps in the process that could be automated, many points where a tool could make reasonable suggestions, and many conflicts and constraint violations for which a tool could check.

We developed a formalism-independent algorithm for ontology merging and alignment—PROMPT (formerly SMART)—which automates the process as much as possible. Where an automatic decision is not possible, the algorithm guides the user to the places in the ontology where his intervention is necessary, suggests possible actions, and determines the conflicts in the ontology and proposes solutions for these conflicts. We implemented the algorithm in an interactive tool based on the Protégé-2000 knowledge-modeling environment (Fridman Noy et al. 2000). Protégé-2000 is an ontology-design and knowledge-acquisition tool with an OKBC-compatible (Chaudhri et al. 1998) knowledge model, which allows domain experts (and not necessarily knowledge engineers) to develop ontologies and perform knowledge acquisition. We have evaluated PROMPT, comparing its performance with the human-expert performance and with the performance of another ontology-merging tool.

2 Related Work

Researchers in various areas of computer science have worked on automatic or tool-supported merging of ontologies (or class hierarchies, or object-oriented schemas, or database schemas—the specific terminology varies depending on the field). However, both automatic merging of ontologies and creation of tools that would guide the user through the process and focus his attention on the likely points for actions are in early stages. In this section, we give an overview of some of the existing approaches to merging and alignment in the fields of ontology design, object-oriented programming, and heterogeneous databases.

2.1 Ontology Design and Integration

Researchers working on tools for ontology merging have expended the greatest amount of effort on finding mostly syntactic matches among concepts in the source ontologies. Such systems rely on dictionaries to determine synonyms, evaluate common substrings, consider concepts whose documentation share many uncommon words, and so on (see, for example, (Chapulsky et al. 1997) or the Scalable Knowledge Composition project (Wiederhold and Jannik 1999)). These approaches, however, do not take into account the semantics of concepts, the structure of the ontology, or the steps the user takes during merging.

Ontomorph (MacGregor et al. 1999) defines a set of transformation operators that can be applied to an ontology. A human expert then uses the initial list of matches and the source ontologies to define a set of operators that need to be applied to the source ontologies in order to resolve differences between them, and Ontomorph applies the operators. Therefore, aggregate operations can be performed in a single step. However, a human expert receives no guidance except for the initial list of matches.

Chimaera (McGuinness et al. 2000) is an interactive merging tool based on Ontolingua ontology editor (Farquhar et al. 1996). Chimaera allows a user to bring together ontologies developed in different formalisms. The user can request an analysis or guidance from Chimaera at any point during the merging process. The tool will then point him to the places in the ontology where his attention is required. In its suggestions, Chimaera mostly relies on which ontology the concepts came from and, for classes, on their names. For example, Chimaera will point a user to a class in the merged ontology that has two slots derived from different source ontologies, or that has two subclasses that originated in different ontologies. Chimaera leaves the decision of *what* to do entirely to the user and does not make any suggestions itself. The only taxonomic relation that Chimaera considers is the subclass–superclass relation. We discuss the differences between Chimaera and PROMPT in more detail when we discuss the results of our comparative evaluation in Section 7.

Medical vocabularies provide a rich field for testing of various ontology-merging paradigms. Not only is there a wide variety of large-scale sources, but also medicine is a field where standard vocabularies change constantly. Oliver and colleagues explored representation of change in medical terminologies using a frame-based knowledge-representation system. The authors compiled a list of change operations that are relevant for the domain of medical terminologies, and developed a tool to support these operations. However, the user has to do all the operations manually; there is no automated help or guidance.

2.2 Object-Oriented Programming

Subject-oriented programming (SOP) (Harrison and Ossher 1993)—an area of object-oriented programming—supports building object-oriented systems through composition of subjects. **Subjects** are collections of classes that represent subjective views of, possibly, the same universe that need to be combined. The formal theory of subject-oriented composition defines a set of possible composition rules, these rules' semantics, and how the rules work with one another. Interactive tools for subject-oriented composition are currently under development. However, the SOP approach relies more heavily on the operational methods associated with classes rather than on declarative relations among classes and slots. Alignment (as opposed to merging) is extremely uncommon in composition of object-oriented hierarchies, whereas it is common in ontology design.

2.3 Integration of Heterogeneous Databases

Developers of heterogeneous databases have dealt with issues of bringing various information sources together. These issues include merging or mediating between relational and object-oriented databases, varying formats from different database vendors, varying underlying schemas or basic assumptions. The common theme in the research on heterogeneous databases, however, is to bridge the gaps on demand by creating an extra mediation layer. The approaches include:

- Develop *mediators* —a facility for answering queries about an information source. Each source may have a *wrapper* that works as an interface between the mediator and the source itself. TSIMMIS is an example of such mediator-based systems.
- Define a *common data model* and then map the source and target to it.
- Specify a set of *matching rules* that directly translate between source and target.

Database are usually integrated at the syntactic rather than semantic level. And, in fact, ontologies are more semantically complex and are often larger than database schemas.

3 Knowledge Model

We now turn to the discussion of the PROMPT ontology-merging and alignment algorithm. We start with the description of the knowledge model underlying PROMPT. The knowledge model is frame-based and it is designed to be compatible with OKBC (Chaudhri et al. 1998). At the top level, there are classes, slots, facets, and instances:

- **Classes** are collections of objects that have similar properties. Classes are arranged into a subclass–superclass hierarchy with multiple inheritance. Each class has slots attached to it. Slots are inherited by the subclasses.
- **Slots** are named binary relations between a class and either another class or a primitive object (such as a string or a number). Slots attached to a class may be further constrained by facets.
- **Facets** are named ternary relations between a class, a slot, and either another class or a primitive object. Facets

may impose additional constraints on a slot attached to a class, such as the cardinality or value type of a slot.
- **Instances** are individual members of classes.

These definitions are the only restrictions that we impose on the input ontologies for PROMPT. Since this knowledge model is extremely general, and many existing knowledge-representation systems have knowledge models compatible with it, the solutions to merging and alignment produced by PROMPT can be applied over a variety of knowledge-representation systems.

4 The PROMPT Algorithm

Figure 1 illustrates the PROMPT ontology-merging and ontology-alignment algorithm. PROMPT takes two ontologies as input and guides the user in the creation of one merged ontology as output. First PROMPT creates an initial list of matches based on class names. Then the following cycle happens: (1) the user triggers an operation by either selecting one of PROMPT's suggestions from the list or by using an ontology-editing environment to specify the desired operation directly; and (2) PROMPT performs the operation, *automatically* executes additional changes based on the type of the operation, generates a list of *suggestions* for the user based on the structure of the ontology around the arguments to the last operation, and determines *conflicts* that the last operation introduced in the ontology and finds possible solutions for those conflicts.

Since there are several research groups working on methods for determining linguistic similarity among concept names (see Section 2.1), a specific implementation of the PROMPT algorithm will use whatever measure of linguistic similarity among concept names is appropriate. In our Protégé-based implementation (Section 5), we use Protégé component-based architecture to allow the user to plug in any term-matching algorithm. In PROMPT, we start with the linguistic-similarity matches for the initial comparison, but concentrate on finding clues based on the structure of the ontology and user's actions.

The following is at the heart of our approach: We identify a set of knowledge-base operations for ontology merging or alignment. For each operation in this set, we define (1) changes that PROMPT performs automatically, (2) new suggestions that PROMPT presents to the user, and (3) conflicts that the operation may introduce and that the user needs to resolve. When the user invokes an operation, PROMPT creates members of these three sets based on the arguments to the specific invocation of the operation.

The set of ontology-merging operations that we identified includes both the operations that are normally performed during traditional ontology editing and the operations specific to merging and alignment, such as:
- merge classes,
- merge slots,
- merge bindings between a slot and a class,
- perform a deep copy of a class from one ontology to another (includes copying all the parents of a class up to the root of the hierarchy and all the classes and slots it refers to),
- perform a shallow copy of a class (just the class itself, and not its parents or the classes and slots it refers to).

We identified the following conflicts that may appear in the merged ontology as the result of these operations:
- name conflicts (more than one frame with the same name),
- dangling references (a frame refers to another frame that does not exist),
- redundancy in the class hierarchy (more than one path from a class to a parent other than root),
- slot-value restrictions that violate class inheritance.

Both lists grow as we gain more experience.

For example, suppose the user is merging two ontologies and he performs a merge-classes operation for two classes A and B to create a new class M. PROMPT then performs the following actions:
- For each slot S that was attached to A and B in the original ontologies, attach the slot to M with the same value type and other facets. If S did not exist in the merged ontology, create S.
- For each superclass of A and B that has been previously copied into the merged ontology, make that copy a superclass of M (thus restoring the original relation). Do the same for subclasses.
- For each class C in the original ontologies to which A and B referred (that is, for each superclass, subclass, slot value, and class restricting a slot value of A and B), if C has not been copied to the merged ontology, suggest that it is copied to the merged ontology.
- For each class C that was a facet value for A or B and that has not been copied to the merged ontology, declare a dangling-reference conflict.
- For each pair of slots for M that have linguistically similar names, suggest that the slots are merged. Later, if the user chooses to merge the slots, suggest that the classes restricting the values of these slots, are merged as well.
- For each pair of superclasses and subclasses of M that have linguistically similar names, suggest that they are merged: these classes have similar names and, in addition, they were both superclasses (or subclasses) for A and B, which the user declared to be similar.

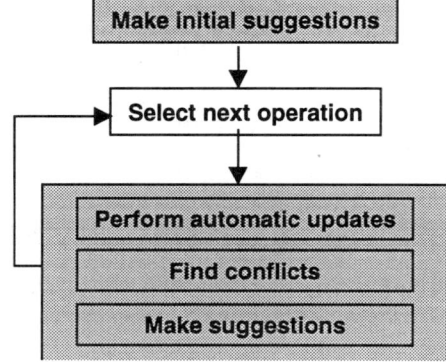

Figure 1. The flow of PROMPT algorithm. The gray boxes indicate the actions performed by PROMPT. The white box indicates the action performed by the user.

- Check for redundancy in the parent hierarchy for M: If there is more than one path to any parent of M (other than the root of the hierarchy), suggest that one of M's parents is removed.

Note, that PROMPT bases most of the decisions in the preceding list on the internal structure of the concepts and their position in the ontology and not syntax.

When we describe the tool based on the algorithm in the next section, we outline a few other actions that can be taken after each operation, such as rearranging the current list of suggestions to maintain the user's focus.

5 Protégé-based PROMPT Tool

We implemented the PROMPT ontology-merging algorithm as an extension to Protégé-2000—the latest in a series of knowledge-acquisition tools developed in our laboratory (Grosso et al. 1999). Protégé-2000 is a knowledge-base development tool, which is designed to make it easier for domain experts to create and maintain knowledge bases. Protégé-2000 uses direct-manipulation techniques for ontology editing. The Protégé-2000 component-based architecture allows users to add new features by developing plug-ins—applications that use Protégé as the knowledge-base access layer and that use Protégé graphical user interface to create the knowledge base itself. PROMPT is such a plug-in for merging two source ontologies in Protégé-2000 into one coherent ontology. The tool and a sample interaction with it have been described in detail elsewhere (Fridman Noy and Musen 1999). We will outline a few of its features here.

Setting the preferred ontology. It often happens, that the source ontologies are not equally important or stable, and that the user would like to resolve all the conflicts in favor of one of the source ontologies. We allow the user to designate one of the ontologies as **preferred**. When there is a conflict between values, instead of presenting the conflict to the user for resolution, the system resolves the conflict automatically.

Maintaining the user's focus. Suppose a user is merging two large ontologies and is currently working in one content area of the ontology. We believe that the system's suggestions that the user sees first should relate to the frames in the same area of the ontology in which the user is working and should not force him to change focus to a different part of the ontology. PROMPT maintains the user's focus by rearranging its lists of suggestions and conflicts and presenting first the items that include frames related to the arguments of the latest operations.

Providing feedback to the user. For each of its suggestions, PROMPT presents a series of explanations, starting with why it suggested the operation in the first place. If PROMPT later changes the operation placement in the suggestions list, it augments the explanation with the information on why it moved the operation.

Logging and reapplying the operations. The process of ontology merging or alignment is not a one-time exercise. After the user has merged or aligned ontologies and perhaps has even developed an application based on the result, the source ontologies may change. This scenario is particularly likely for distributed ontologies developed by independent users. Ideally, reapplication of the merging or alignment process to the changed ontologies should be almost automatic. PROMPT logs *knowledge-level* ontology-merging and editing operations. If the original ontologies change, the user only needs to make adjustments to the operations in the log that explicitly refer to the changed frames and the system can then reapply the operations automatically to merge the original ontologies again.

6 Evaluation

We have evaluated PROMPT formatively. We measured the quality of its suggestions, measured its utility, and compared it to another ontology-merging tool. We performed three controlled experiments, in which human experts merged two ontologies using Protégé-2000 with PROMPT, generic Protégé-2000, and Chimaera (see Section 2.1).

The two source ontologies were the same for all the experiments: (1) the ontology for the unified problem-solving method development language (Gennari et al. 1998; Fensel et al. 1999) and (2) the ontology for the method-description language (Gennari et al. 1998). Both ontologies describe reusable problem-solving methods, and merging them was a real-life task in our laboratory. The source ontologies contained the total of 134 class and slot frames, and the resulting merged ontology had 117 frames.

All the testers had unlimited time to complete their tasks and we did not compare the actual rate at which the experts performed the tasks: Each merging process was performed by one expert, and the impact of the individual differences on any rate data is extremely significant. These test are preliminary and we plan to perform extensive testing with more subjects using the same sources and protocols later.

6.1 Quality of PROMPT's Suggestions

In the first experiment, human experts who were initially unfamiliar with PROMPT, used Protégé-2000 augmented with PROMPT to merge the two source ontologies. We evaluated the quality of PROMPT's suggestions by measuring the following: (1) how many of the PROMPT's suggestions the human experts decided to follow when merging the source ontologies, and (2) how many of the conflict-resolution strategies that PROMPT proposed were followed by the experts. We present the average value among the experts.

Our results showed that the human experts followed 90% of PROMPT's suggestions. The experts followed 75% of the conflict-resolution strategies that PROMPT proposed. During the merging process, PROMPT suggested 74% of the total knowledge-base operations that the users invoked.

6.2 PROMPT versus Generic Protégé-2000

We performed an ablation experiment to determine the value that PROMPT adds to a generic knowledge-editing environment. Two experts initially unfamiliar with PROMPT merged the same source ontologies: One expert used Protégé-2000 augmented with PROMPT and the other used the generic version of the Protégé-2000 ontology editor. We compared the contents of the resulting merged ontologies and the number of explicit knowledge-base operations that each user had to specify.

The merged ontologies, which the two experts produced, were quite similar: there was only one difference in class hierarchy, and a number of minor differences in slot names and their types. The user who was using the generic Protégé-2000 was able to find all the classes that should have been merged. However, using the generic Protégé required performing and explicitly specifying 60 knowledge-base operations. Since PROMPT generated and suggested most of the necessary knowledge-base operations, the PROMPT user needed to specify explicitly only 16 operations.

6.3 PROMPT versus Chimaera

In the third experiment, we compared the performance of PROMPT and Chimaera, which is the tool closest to PROMPT in the limited set of existing ontology-merging tools (see Section 2.1).[1] We used PROMPT and Chimaera to merge the same source ontologies and we executed exactly the same sequence of merging steps in each of the tools. The executed operations included merging both slots and classes. After each step, we compared the set of new suggestions that the two systems generated. We used a human expert who has previously merged the two ontologies manually to judge whether the suggestions that the systems produced were correct or not.

PROMPT had 30% more correct suggestions than Chimaera did. Suggestions from Chimaera constituted a proper subset of PROMPT's suggestions. 20% of Chimaera's correct suggestions were roughly the same as PROMPT's. The remaining 80% were much less specific than the corresponding PROMPT's suggestions: Chimaera pointed to the class in the ontology where action was required, and PROMPT suggested a specific action (or alternative actions), which were required for that frame.

7 Discussion

Our results in the first two experiments demonstrated that a human expert agreed with a very large fraction of both the suggestions and the conflict-resolution strategies that PROMPT produced. PROMPT was able to perform a large number of merging operations on its own (or with simple "approval" of a human expert), thus saving the expert time and effort.

---

[1] Chimaera software is available at http://www.ksl.Stanford.EDU/software/chimaera/

We intentionally chose the source ontologies that were relatively small and uncontroversial to merge in order to factor out subjective differences in the experts' opinions. However, choosing the source ontologies in this way made it almost inevitable that the two resulting ontologies in the experiment that compared Protégé-2000 augmented with PROMPT and generic Protégé-2000 would be similar. This approach allowed us to compare the number of operations that needed to be generated but did not allow us to compare the quality of results. We believe that for larger ontologies, when it is harder for a human expert to track down all the frames that need merging, the results would be different. We plan to perform experiments to test that in the future.

There is a significant difference in the way Chimaera and PROMPT guide the user in the merging process: PROMPT presents a list of *specific* operations that it suggests to the user. Chimaera points to the classes where it determines that the user needs to do something, but it does not specify *what* exactly the user needs to do there. For instance, in the example in Figure 2, Chimaera suggested that the class Ontology requires the user's attention because some of the slots of that class came from different source ontologies. It did not specify which slots the user needs to consider and what he needs to do. In the corresponding case, PROMPT suggested that the axioms slots, which came from two different ontologies, must be merged. For classes with large number of slots, PROMPT's suggestion, which lists the slots, would be more helpful than simply suggesting that there are slots in this large list that require attention. On the other hand, the user may get overwhelmed if there are too many specific suggestions and in that case Chimaera's approach may be better.

We now plan to continue experimenting with ontology-merging and alignment to define more heuristics that will allow us to automate a larger part of the merging and alignment process. We will also extend our approach to

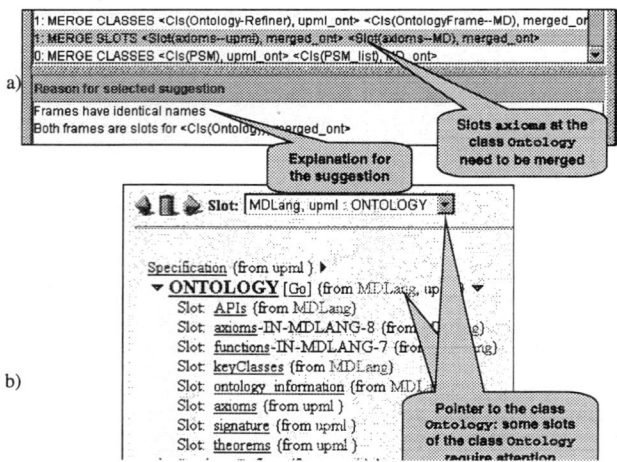

Figure 2. Differences in suggestions between (a) PROMPT and (b) Chimaera. PROMPT suggests that the user merges two specific slots (axioms) of the Ontology class. Chimaera points the user to the Ontology class that has two slots originating from different ontologies without specifying which slots the user needs to consider

consider standard OKBC facets, such as maximum and minimum cardinality, inverse, and so on. We will include instances of classes, as well as axioms that define additional constraints on frames in the ontology.

8 Conclusions

We have described a general approach to ontology merging and alignment. We presented PROMPT—an algorithm for semi-automatic merging and alignment. We discussed strategies that PROMPT uses to guide a user to the next possible point of merging or alignment, to suggest what operations should be performed there, and to perform certain operations automatically. The strategies and algorithms described in this paper are based on a general OKBC-compliant knowledge model. Therefore, these results are applicable to a wide range of knowledge-representation and ontology-development systems. We extended Protégé knowledge-modeling environment with a tool based on the algorithm and performed an empirical evaluation of the tool. Our results showed that PROMPT was very effective in providing suggestions: A human expert followed 90% of PROMPT's suggestions. PROMPT was also very effective in its coverage: 74% of the knowledge-based operations invoked by the user were suggested initially by PROMPT.

Acknowledgments

We are extremely grateful to Monica Crubézy, Ray Fergerson and Samson Tu for participating in the evaluation experiments and for the valuable feedback on the earlier drafts of this paper. This work was supported in part by the grants 5T16 LM0733 and 892154 from the National Library of Medicine, by a grant from Spawar, and by a grant from FastTrack Systems, Inc.

References

Abiteboul, S., Cluet, S. and Milo, T. (1997). Correspondence and Translation for Heterogeneous Data. In: *Proceedings of the International Conference on Database Theory (ICDT)*.

Brickley, D. and Guha, R.V. (1999). Resource Description Framework (RDF) Schema Specification. Proposed Recommendation, World Wide Web Consortium: http://www.w3.org/TR/PR-rdf-schema.

Chapulsky, H., Hovy, E. and Russ, T. (1997). Progress on an Automatic Ontology Alignment Methodology.

Chaudhri, V.K., Farquhar, A., Fikes, R., Karp, P.D. and Rice, J.P. (1998). OKBC: A Programmatic Foundation for Knowledge Base Interoperability. In: *Proceedings of the Fifteenth National Conference on Artificial Intelligence (AAAI-98)*, Madison, Wisconsin, AAAI Press.

Cohen, P., Schrag, R., Jones, E., Pease, A., Lin, A., Starr, B., Gunning, D. and Burke, M. (1999). The DARPA High-Performance Knowledge Bases Project. *AI Magazine* **19**(4): 25-49.

Farquhar, A., Fikes, R. and Rice, J. (1996). The Ontolingua Server: a Tool for Collaborative Ontology Construction. In: *Proceedings of the Tenth Knowledge Acquisition for Knowledge-Based Systems Workshop*, Banff, Canada.

Fensel, D., Benjamins, V.R., Motta, E. and Wielinga, R. (1999). UPML: A Framework for knowledge system reuse. In: *Proceedings of the International Joint Conference on Artificial Intelligence (IJCAI-99)*, Stockholm, Sweden.

Fridman Noy, N., Fergerson, R.W. and Musen, M.A. (2000). The knowledge model of Protégé-2000: combining interoperability and flexibility. Stanford Medical Informatics Technical Report, Stanford University.

Fridman Noy, N. and Musen, M.A. (1999). SMART: Automated Support for Ontology Merging and Alignment. In: *Proceedings of the Twelfth Banff Workshop on Knowledge Acquisition, Modeling, and Management*, Banff, Alberta.

Garcia-Molina, H., Papakonstantinou, Y., Quass, D., Rajaraman, A., Sagiv, Y., Ullman, J., Vassalos, V. and Widom, J. (1997). The TSIMMIS approach to mediation: Data models and Languages. *Journal of Intelligent Information Systems*.

Gennari, J.H., Grosso, W. and Musen, M.A. (1998). A method-description language: An initial ontology with examples. In: *Proceedings of the Eleventh Banff Knowledge Acquisition for Knowledge-Bases Systems Workshop*, Banff, Canada.

Harrison, W. and Ossher, H. (1993). Subject-Oriented Programming (A Critique of Pure Objects). In: *Proceedings of the Conference on Object-Oriented Programming: Systems, Languages, and Applications (OOPSLA'93)*, Washington, DC, ACM Press.

MacGregor, R., Chalupsky, H., Moriarty, D. and Valente, A. (1999). Ontology Merging with OntoMorph. http://reliant.teknowledge.com/HPKB/meetings/meet040799/Chalupsky/index.htm

McGuinness, D.L., Fikes, R., Rice, J. and Wilder, S. (2000). An Environment for Merging and Testing Large Ontologies. In: *Proceedings of the Seventh International Conference on Principles of Knowledge Representation and Reasoning (KR2000)*, Breckenridge, Colorado.

Milo, T. and Zohar, S. (1998). Using Schema Matching to Simplify Heterogeneous Data Translation. In: *Proceedings of the 24th International Conference on Very Large Data Bases*, New York City, Morgan Kaufmann.

Oliver, D.E., Shahar, Y., Shortliffe, E.H. and Musen, M.A. (1999). Representation of Change in controlled medical terminologies. *Artificial Intelligence in Medicine* **15**: 53-76.

Ossher, H., Kaplan, M., Katz, A., Harrison, W. and Kruskal, V. (1996). Specifying Subject-Oriented Composition. *Theory and Practice of Object Systems* **2**(3): 179-202.

Wiederhold, G. (1992). Mediators in the architecture of future information systems. *IEEE Computer* **25**(3): 38-49.

Wiederhold, G. and Jannik, J. (1999). Composing Diverse Ontologies. In: *Proceedings of the IFIP Working Group on Database, 8th Working Conference on Database Semantics (DS-8)*, Rotorua, New Zealand.

(De)Composition of Situation Calculus Theories

Eyal Amir
Department of Computer Science,
Gates Building, 2A wing
Stanford University, Stanford, CA 94305-9020, USA
eyal.amir@cs.stanford.edu

Abstract

We show that designing large situation calculus theories can be simplified by using object-oriented techniques and tools together with established solutions to the frame problem. Situation calculus (McCarthy & Hayes 1969) is one of the leading logical representations for action and change, but large situation calculus theories are not easy to design and maintain, nor are they flexible for extension or reuse. However, we wish to use it to represent large, complex domains.

To address this problem, we apply our proposed methodology to situation calculus theories and analyze the composition of theories in this light. The object-oriented tools that we use do not change the semantics of situation calculus, so all the original situation calculus results apply in our setting and vice versa. We get two additional results from this approach. First, we offer a new treatment of loosely interacting agents that uses situation calculus without abandoning the *result* formalism. This treatment allows a theory-builder to construct a theory without considering its potential inclusion in a multiple-agents setup. Second, theories that we build in this way admit specialized reasoning algorithms.

Introduction

Our work has two related motivations: making large situation calculus theories easier to design and maintain, and giving a partitioned representation to situation calculus theories. Situation calculus theories have a restricted form and a clear ontology that together help modeling. However, using situation calculus in large, multi-domain settings is not easy. It is hard to think of all the parts of a large theory in advance, reuse is not simple, and modifications can have unintended consequences. Giving situation calculus theories a partitioned representation allows us to use the algorithms of (Amir & McIlraith 2000) and opens the way for merging situation calculus theories into reactive frameworks such as (Amir & Maynard-Reid 1999). This paper focuses on the first motivation and addresses the second as a by-product.

We present one object-oriented reformulation of situation calculus, following some traditional decompositions of theories of action (Shanahan 1997). We create a class for situations and a class for actions (roughly speaking, *classes* are theory fragments). *Subclasses* of situations (roughly, these

Copyright © 2000, American Association for Artificial Intelligence (www.aaai.org). All rights reserved.

are supersets of the class of situations) contain domain constraints. Subclasses of actions contain effect axioms. We describe one theory constructed using objects of these and other classes. The combined theory has semantics that is equivalent to situation calculus, after translation to First-Order Logic (FOL). We apply Reiter's monotonic solution to the frame problem (Reiter 1991) to this system of objects and classes.

Object-oriented situation calculus theories can be combined easily and are elaboration-tolerant in that sense. We demonstrate this by combining domain theories and by giving a new treatment of agents in the situation calculus. Domain theories are connected by linking the corresponding objects with only a small vocabulary, even when the frame solution is used. This result extends to our proposed representation of agents. Our treatment of agents allows each agent's theory to be written as a simple theory, with no regard to the existence of other agents. Only new subtheories in which the agents interact need to consider the explicit existence of agents. We do this without giving up the *result* formalism (which is planning-friendly), as in (McCarthy & Costello 1998), or the independence of the agents (which allows efficient computation), as in (Reiter 1996), (Pinto 1998). We point out the applications and influence of the algorithms of (Amir & McIlraith 2000) on these theories. We conclude by proposing some guidelines for the knowledge engineering of situation calculus theories.

Our running example is a simplification of the *Daddy and Junior* scenario, taken from (McCarthy & Costello 1998).

Objects for Situations and Actions

Situation Calculus

Situation calculus (McCarthy & Hayes 1969) is a knowledge representation formalism for representing temporal information. The language consists of four sorts: *situations*, for situations in the world; *actions*, for events and actions; *fluents*, for situation-dependent properties; and *objects*, for simple other FOL objects.

s, a, f (or subscripted versions thereof) are variables for situations, actions and fluents, respectively. All other variables are of sort "object". The predicate $Holds(f, s)$ asserts that a fluent f holds in the situation s ($f(s)$ is used as a shorthand for $Holds(f, s)$ when such a shorthand causes no confusion). The function $result(a,s)$ returns the situation that results from performing a in s (we use $res(a,s)$ as a shorthand). $S0$ is a situation constant. Figure 1 displays A_{bw}, a sample situation calculus theory for the blocks-world domain. Capitalized symbols are constants. Free variables in axioms are universally quantified with maximum scope.

$on(A, B, S0) \land on(B, Table, S0) \land on(C, Table, S0)$
$on(x, y, s) \Rightarrow above(x, y, s)$
$above(x, y, s) \land above(y, z, s) \Rightarrow above(x, z, s)$
$clear(b, s) \iff \forall b' \neg on(b', b, s)$
$handEmpty(s) \iff \forall b \neg inHand(b, s)$
$clear(b, s) \land handEmpty(s) \Rightarrow inHand(b, res(pickUp(b), s)))$
$(y = Table \lor clear(y, s)) \land inHand(x, s) \Rightarrow$
$\qquad\qquad\qquad on(x, y, res(putOn(x, y), s))$
$on(x, y, s) \Rightarrow \neg inHand(x, s) \land \neg inHand(y, s)$
$inHand(x, s) \Rightarrow \neg on(x, y, s) \land \neg on(y, x, s)$
$on(x, y, s) \land y \neq z \Rightarrow \neg on(x, z, s)$

Figure 1: Blocks-world in the situation calculus: A_{bw}.

Object-Oriented FOL

We wish to make the design of situation calculus theories more structured. To this end, we adopt some object-oriented design principles and tools. In the rest of this section, we build an object-oriented situation calculus theory for the blocks-world. At the same time, we provide a few meta-logical tools and notations that are needed for this description, borrowing from (Amir 1999). Readers familiar with applications of context (e.g., (Ghidini & Serafini 1998)) can view the following as a special case having the semantics of FOL, object-oriented tools, and no explicit contexts.

An *object-oriented first-order logic (OOFOL) theory* is divided into subtheories associated with *objects*. A subtheory associated with an object has its own first-order language and axioms. We distinguish a subset of the vocabulary of each object and call it the object's *interface*. There are interface *links* between objects. Each interface link specifies equality/equivalence between symbols in two objects. Only symbols from these interfaces may participate in the link.

A situation calculus theory can be broken into an object (subtheory) associated with situations and an object associated with actions (additional other objects are possible). In the first, we put domain constraints (sentences that mention no action term). In the second, we put effect axioms (axioms of the form $Holds(\Phi, s) \Rightarrow Holds(\Psi, res(a, s))$). This decomposition for our blocks-world theory A_{bw} is diagrammatically presented in Figure 2. Here, the symbols $on, inHand, Holds$ are on the link between the objects and thus have the same semantics in both objects.

An OOFOL theory T is a set of object declarations (see below). The semantics is given by a translation to FOL: We replace every symbol in an axiom with the same symbol appended to the name of the object in which this axiom appears (making symbols in different objects distinct). For example, the symbol on used in a situation object $\mathcal{S}$ is translated to $\mathcal{S}.on$ in all the axioms of $\mathcal{S}$. Then, we add equality (or equivalence) axioms of the form $\forall \overrightarrow{x} (\mathcal{S}.P(\overrightarrow{x}) \equiv \mathcal{A}.P'(\overrightarrow{x}))$ for

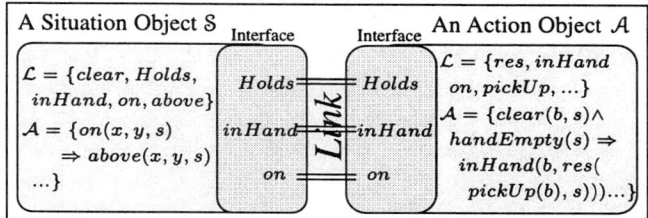

Figure 2: A situation object connected to an action object.

all linked symbols P, P' between objects $\mathcal{S}, \mathcal{A}$. The result of this translations is denoted $\widetilde{T}$.

Definition 1 (FOL Semantics for OOFOL) $\mathcal{M}$ *is a* model of T iff $\mathcal{M} \models \widetilde{T}$.

Situation Calculus Classes

We can now represent a theory as a set of linked objects. Presenting situation calculus theories in this form gives a designer a bird's-eye view of the theory and allows the combination of several theories by *linking* them. We also wish to reuse theories. For this, the notions of *classes* and *inheritance*[1] become handy. A class is a template for its objects, specified with no interface links, but otherwise identical to them. This allows the application of identical axiom sets in different positions in the theory by specifying the class to which the object belongs.

Inheritance extends this reuse by allowing some extensions to a copy of an existing class. For engineering purposes, inheritance in our system is treated outside the logic (unlike nonmonotonic inheritance, such as in (Morgenstern 1998)). In principle, a *subclass* (child) inherits all the axioms, vocabulary and interface vocabulary of its parent class. We can make the subclass different from its parent by: (1) adding to the inherited vocabulary and interface vocabulary; (2) adding axioms; and (3) explicitly replacing some non-logical symbols in all of the inherited axioms, with some new symbols in the child's language.

We use standard object-oriented methodology and define a hierarchy of classes for the blocks-world situation calculus. Figure 3 display our classes. We explain its contents together with the notation (most of the notation is similar to that used in object-oriented programming languages).

There are two root classes: **Situation** and **Action**. Both include interface declarations (to be inherited by subclasses) and no axioms. The notation *class1:class2* is used to declare that class1 is a subclass of class2. Classes **BWSit,BWAct** are subclasses of **Situation,Action**, respectively, specialized for the blocks-world. They inherit the respective interfaces, and add it to their explicitly declared interface. Since **BWS0** is a subclass of **BWSit**, it includes all the interface and axioms of its superclass, adding some observations about a particular $S0$.

---

[1] *Objects*, *classes* and *inheritance* are meta-logical notions.

```
class Situation {
    interface:   Holds }
class Action {
    interface:   res, Holds }
class BWSit : Situation {
    interface:   on, inHand
    axioms:      clear(b, s) ⟺ ∀b'¬on(b', b, s)
                 on(x, y, s) ⇒ above(x, y, s)
                 above(x, y, s) ∧ above(y, z, s) ⇒ above(x, z, s)
                 on(x, y, s) ⇒ ¬inHand(x, s) ∧ ¬inHand(y, s)
                 inHand(x, s) ⇒ ¬on(x, y, s) ∧ ¬on(y, x, s)
                 on(x, y, s) ∧ y ≠ z ⇒ ¬on(x, z, s) }
class BWAct : Action {
    interface:   on, inHand, pickUp, putOn, Table
    axioms:      clear(b, s) ∧ handEmpty(s) ⇒
                         inHand(b, res(pickUp(b), s)))
                 (y = Table ∨ clear(y, s)) ∧ inHand(x, s) ⇒
                         on(x, y, res(putOn(x, y), s)))
                 clear(b, s) ⟺ ∀b'¬on(b', b, s)
                 handEmpty(s) ⟺ ∀b¬inHand(b, s) }
class BWS0 : BWSit {
    interface:   on, S0, A, B, C, Table
    axioms:      on(A, B, S0) ∧ on(B, Table, S0) ∧ on(C, Table, S0) }
```

Figure 3: Blocks-world situation calculus classes.

Modeling With One Object per Class

Using these classes, we create the theory $\mathcal{A}_{ob}$ shown in Figure 4. In this theory, $S0_{obj}$ is an object (instantiation) of class **BWS0**, S is an object of class **BWSit** and $\mathcal{A}$ is an object of class **BWAct**. The statement $Object(Cl, O, \{(P, O', Q), ...\})$ declares an object named O of class **Cl** and specifies interface links with other objects: P in O is equal/equivalent to Q in O' (e.g., $O.P \equiv O'.Q$). $S0_{obj}, S$ are linked on $on, Holds$; $S, \mathcal{A}$ are linked on $on, inHand, Holds$; and $\mathcal{A}, S0_{obj}$ are linked on $Table$.

Our modeling can be summarized by the following two rules: (1) link all those symbols that should have the same intended meaning in two objects; and (2) omit links of symbols that follow from transitivity of equality (e.g., we omit $Holds, on$ from the link between $\mathcal{A}$ and $S0_{obj}$).

```
Object(BWS0, S0_obj, {(on, S, on), (Holds, S, Holds)}).
Object(BWSit, S, {(inHand, A, inHand),
                  (on, A, on), (Holds, A, Holds)}).
Object(BWAct, A, {(Table, S0_obj, Table)}).
```

Figure 4: The OOFOL theory $\mathcal{A}_{ob}$

Figure 5 is a diagrammatic view of the structure of $\mathcal{A}_{ob}$ showing the three objects and the links between them. Each link is labeled with the symbols that are pronounced equal between the two objects (e.g., for the fluent $on(x, y)$, $\forall xyS.on(x, y) = \mathcal{A}.on(x, y)$). Almost all the examples we will see have identical symbols on both ends of a link (e.g., on in S and on in $\mathcal{A}$), so this convention is clear.

The OOFOL semantics (Definition 1) given to $\mathcal{A}_{ob}$ is equivalent to the semantics given to $\mathcal{A}_{bw}$ from Figure 1. The translation of $\mathcal{A}_{ob}$ into $\widetilde{\mathcal{A}}_{ob}$ is syntactic, adding equality/equivalence axioms between linked symbols.

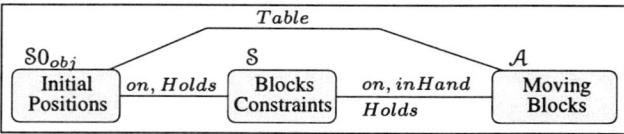

Figure 5: Diagrammatic view of $\mathcal{A}_{ob}$

Proposition 2 (Semantics) *Let $\varphi \in \mathcal{L}(\mathcal{A}_{bw})$ and let φ' be its translation to $\mathcal{L}(\mathcal{A}_{ob})$. $\mathcal{A}_{bw} \models \varphi$ iff $\mathcal{A}_{ob} \models \varphi'$.*

The translation of φ to $\mathcal{L}(\mathcal{A}_{ob})$ is straightforward. Symbols of φ that appear in more than one object have the same semantics in all of them, so we can arbitrarily pick one. For example, $\mathcal{A}_{bw} \models \neg inHand(A, S0)$ iff $\mathcal{A}_{ob} \models \neg S.inHand(S0_{obj}.A, S0_{obj}.S0)$.

Reasoning With Objects

(Amir & McIlraith 2000) provides message-passing algorithms in the style of (Pearl 1988) for reasoning with theories that are decomposed in this way. Roughly speaking, if object S is connected to object $\mathcal{A}$, sentence φ_1 from $\mathcal{L}(S)$ can be logically combined (after translation) with a sentence φ_2 from $\mathcal{L}(\mathcal{A})$ only if $\mathcal{L}(\varphi_1)$ is included in the link.

More generally, given a graph of links and objects (as in Figure 5) and a query, we first decide on an object that can express the query in its vocabulary (if there is no such object, we can create one and link it to the others). Then, we transform the graph into a tree by running an algorithm called BREAK-CYCLES (we iteratively select a minimal cycle in the graph, remove a link and add its language to that of the other links in the cycle) and then perform MESSAGE-PASSING to prove the query, which roughly performs the following: Continuously perform consequence generation in each object. Send a proved formula (message) to another object only if the formula is in the vocabulary of the link to that object, and this other object is on the graph path to the object containing the query.

(Amir & McIlraith 2000) shows that this kind of algorithm is complete and sound for the semantics of Definition 1, and that it improves running time compared to standard deduction methods. For the propositional case, if T is a theory with n objects, each connected to d other objects in a tree structure, with each link having l symbols and $\mathcal{L}(T)$ has m symbols, then the running time for an analogous algorithm for SAT is $O(n * 2^{d*l} * f_{SAT}(m/n))$ (f_{SAT} is the time to compute SAT). This is an exponential time-improvement compared to standard reasoning techniques if the links' vocabularies are small.

We can now explain our modeling decisions from a computational perspective. To increase efficiency, we try to minimize the vocabularies of the links without giving up correctness of queries. This is why we omit the symbols $A, B, C, S0, res$ and several fluents from the links. Each symbol shows only in one object (clear is defined by the fluent on in both $S, \mathcal{A}$). This is also the reason why we use the transitivity of equality to omit symbols from the links.

For a given domain theory (e.g., our blocks-world theory), $Holds$ and fluents that appear in the action object typically appear on the link between the situation and action objects. This seems to limit the computational improvement due to such algorithms, and it seems to be an inherent property in theory structures of the form presented in Figure 5 (one object per class, connecting on $Holds$ and fluents). There are other structures that take advantage of an assumed tree of situations to give better performance (e.g., multiple objects, connected in a tree structure). We do not pursue these further here. Instead, our computational effort focuses on larger theories made of multiple domains, as described below.

The Frame Problem

The *frame problem* concerns the conclusion of non-effects of actions from the known effects in a concise, correct, expressive and elaboration-tolerant manner (see (Shanahan 1997)).

One of the simplest solutions generates *explanation closure* axioms (e.g., (Haas 1987), (Pednault 1989), (Schubert 1990)) from the effect axioms and the domain constraints. When it is possible, we mechanically (outside the logic) add axioms saying that if something has changed, then one of the enumerated actions occurred. For example, one axiom that is generated for explanation closure for $inHand$ in $\mathcal{A}_{bw}$ is $\neg inHand(x,s) \wedge inHand(x, res(a,s)) \Rightarrow (clear(x,s) \wedge handEmpty(s) \wedge a = pickUp(x))$.

(Reiter 1991) summarized the effort and showed how to generate such axioms automatically if there are no state constraints, (Lin & Reiter 1994) extended this process for the presence of state constraints, using deduction, and (McIlraith 2000) gave a closed-form solution in the presence of some restricted state constraints. These solutions also add other axiom sets, including unique names axioms (UNA) for sort "actions", preconditions for executing actions (summarized by the predicate $Poss(a,s)$) and foundational axioms for situations (here we call them *Peano axioms for situations*, although the time structure represented by situations is a tree rather than a line).

The diagram in Figure 6 presents the theory resulting from appending this solution to $\mathcal{A}_{ob}$, together with additional axioms for domain closure (DCA) and UNA for objects (these are not needed for the solution, but are sometimes assumed in domain theories). In this figure, $\mathcal{U}na_a, \mathcal{U}na_o\&\mathcal{D}ca_o, \mathcal{P}oss, \mathcal{P}eano$ contain UNA for actions, UNA and DCA for objects, preconditions for execution and the Peano axioms, respectively. Our Peano axioms for situations include the first-order induction axiom $(\forall f)(Holds(f, S0) \wedge (\forall as)[Holds(f,s) \Rightarrow Holds(f, res(a,s))] \Rightarrow (\forall s)Holds(f,s))$ instead of the second-order axiom of (Lin & Reiter 1994).

The object $\mathcal{A}_p$ contains effect and explanation closure axioms with the following provision. To allow the introduction of the predicate $Poss(a, s)$, we need to make the effect axioms of **BWAct** dependent on $Poss(a, s)$. To do that, we create a subclass **BWPossAct** (shown in Figure 7) and replace the object $\mathcal{A}$ of the superclass with an object $\mathcal{A}_p$ of the subclass. The declaration *inherit:* $[Holds/Holds_{old}]$ is a directive to our compiler to replace the symbol $Holds$ with $Holds_{old}$ in all the axioms the class inherits from its superclass (as discussed above). This and the additional axiom adjusts our effect axioms to depend on $Poss$ (see Figure 7).

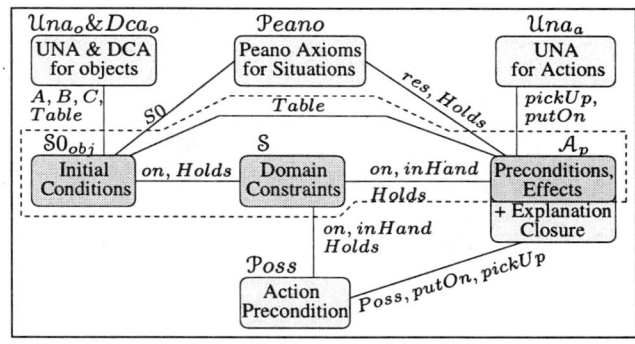

Figure 6: Frame-problem solution using objects.

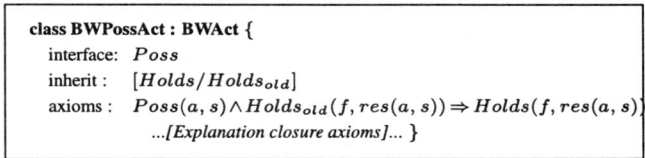

Figure 7: Adding $Poss$ and explanation closure to **BWAct**.

Combining Action Theories

Now, we examine the way domain theories can be joined. Consider a domain theory regarding buying and selling blocks. In this theory, buying a block decreases the amount of money a robot has, but also places the purchased block in the robot's hand. Selling a block has the opposite effect.

We use two new fluents together with $inHand$: (1) $hasItem$ accounts for named items the robot possesses; and (2) $money$ is a function (fluent) that returns the amount of money that the robot has. Figure 8 presents some of the new classes. Figure 9 displays the diagram of the complete theory with the frame solution.

```
class Has : Situation {
   interface:  hasItem, money, inHand
   axioms:     money(s) ≥ 0
               inHand(b, s) ⇒ HasItem(b, s) }

class BuySell : Action {
   interface:  hasItem, money, inHand
   axioms:     inHand(b, s) ∧ money(s) = m ⇒
               ¬hasItem(b, res(sell(b), s))∧
               money(res(sell(b), s)) = m + value(b, s) ... }
```

Figure 8: The domain of buying and selling blocks.

If the solution to the frame problem is not applied, we can combine the two domain theories by letting objects of corresponding positions in the two theories communicate. The two domains share only $S0, res, Holds$ and $inHand$. To see the situation diagrammatically, look at Figure 9 and consider only objects $S, S', \mathcal{A}, \mathcal{A}', S0_{obj}, S0'_{obj}$.

When we add the solution to the frame problem, there are two complications. First, the graph becomes more connected: UNAs potentially make all the objects dependent

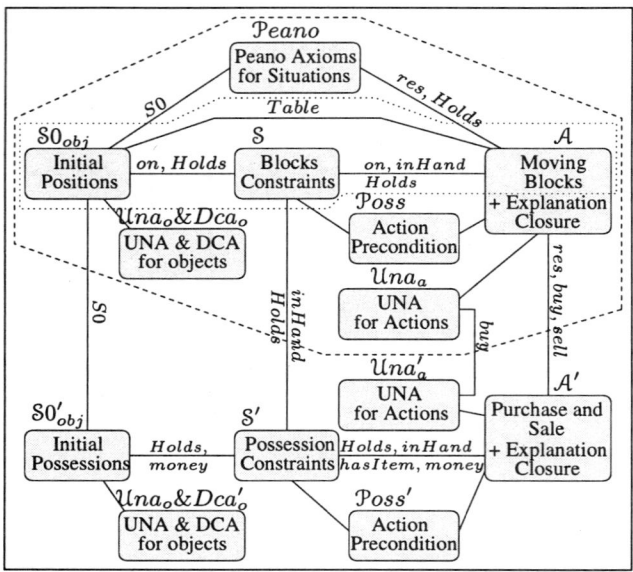

Figure 9: Connecting two domain theories.

on one another and explanation closure axioms add bandwidth to the links. Second, if we already have the solution for the separate domain theories, there are components that will have to be recomputed. These concerns are particularly important if we have a large number of connected domains.

Proposition 3 *For a theory made of many domain theories, if no qualification constraints are involved in computing $Poss$, then there is a formulation of the frame solution above (with or without UNA and DCA for objects) such that,*

1. *Any two domain theories that share fluents $\{f_i\}_{i \in I}$ are linked on exactly $\{f_i\}_{i \in I}, S0, res, Holds$ and actions $\{a_j\}_{j \in J}$ from the first domain that appear in the explanation closure for $\{f_i\}_{i \in I}$.*

2. *If we already have the frame solution for the separate domain theories, only the explanation closure axioms for $\{f_i\}_{i \in I}$ need to be recomputed (we ignore computations involved in solving the qualification problem (i.e., computing axioms for $Poss$)).*

3. *Domain theories are (directly) linked iff they share fluents or a removal of their links disconnects the graph.*

PROOF SKETCH We use the structure depicted in Figure 9 to explain the case for two domains. Call the two domains 1 and 2. We need to formulate $Poss, Una_a, Una_a \& Dca_o$ such that they do not use any symbol that is in domain 2 and not in $\{f_i\}_{i \in I}, S0, res, Holds, \{a_j\}_{j \in J}$. This is enough, because So_{obj}, S, A are in the original domain axiomatization, for which this is trivially true, and $Peano$ uses only symbols $res, Holds, S0$ and the partial order $\prec$ on situations.

The axioms involving $Poss$ are always in the vocabulary of domain 1, following from our assumption that there are no qualification constraints. Also, we do not need to include DCA for actions, as there are no qualification constraints.

In each of Una_a, Una_a' we use the formulation of UNAs given in (McCarthy 1986). We define a total order, $<$, on action prototypes (this can be extended to a total order on actions, but we are not concerned with that here). Set an action prototype, A_2 from $\{a_j\}_{j \in J}$, to be the $<$-smallest in domain 2. Set another action, A_1 from domain 1, to be the $<$-largest in domain 1. Adding the axiom $A_1 < A_2$ to Una_a completes the needed specification for UNA.

Finally, UNA and DCA for objects can be formulated to be domain-dependent and also situation dependent (e.g., adding $block(x)$ as a precondition for axioms in domain 1). This concludes part 1, as the arguments above can be easily generalized to more than two domain theories.

For part 2, notice that DCA and UNA for objects and UNA for actions do not need to be recomputed when we link domain 2 to domain 1. When there are more than two domains involved, an increasing order on added domains can be used to guide axiomatizing $<$ on actions so that there are no inconsistencies (inconsistency may arise if we sanction $a < b < c < a$). Notice that if two domains share object symbols, then we must use a scheme that is similar to the one used for actions (sharing objects but not object symbols does not give rise to this problem).

For part 3, notice that all domain theories have the same semantics to $Holds, res, S0$ (the graph of domain theories is connected by our assumption). If two domain theories do not share a fluent, then they do not share an action (we assume that domains originally do not share actions, and they eventually need to share an action only as a result of explanation closure). This means that symbols that should have matching semantics in both domains already have matching semantics by virtue of the graph being connected. Thus, such domain pairs do not need to be directly connected. ∎

Thus, adding the frame solution on top of the simple connection between the two domains adds to the links only actions participating in explanation closure of shared fluents. Figure 9 displays the complete theory of the blocks-world and buy-sell domains ($inHand$ is the only shared fluent). This result enables building composite theories like the one sketched in Figure 10 for a mobile robot that can perform electronic transactions, make phone calls, etc. Applying the reasoning algorithms described above to this theory results in an improved inference time, as the connectivity of this graph is kept low.

Combining Different Agents

We can represent different agents in the situation calculus by giving them different objects in the theory, and by adding an object to represent interactions. In the following, we assume that the agents' worlds do not interact, namely, that they deal with different fluents altogether (including the fluent *time*). We distinguish between actions that they perform separately (e.g., moving a block in their respective domains) and actions that influence the domains of both agents (e.g., money transfers between them). Those actions that influence both agents, are dealt with in a new interaction subtheory. In some cases we may choose to use the treatments of (Reiter 1996), (Pinto 1998) for this interaction subtheory, but in our

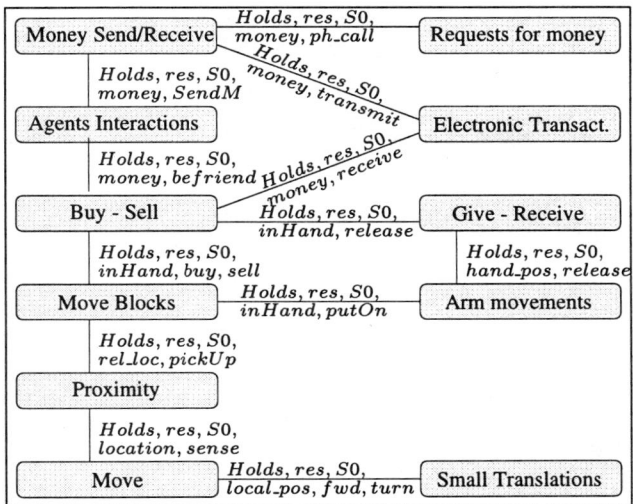

Figure 10: High-level diagrammatic view of a theory combining multiple domains

example we can do without them.

The approach we describe gives each agent a different perspective/knowledge of the same situation. It uses a single situations tree, but allows different perspectives on the *time* of a situation. Figure 11 is a diagrammatic view of a modification of *Daddy and Junior* (an example taken from (McCarthy & Costello 1998)). Daddy is stacking blocks of gold in New York, while Junior is stacking blocks of silver in London. If Junior needs more money, he may ask Daddy to send him some (requiring Daddy to sell a block). We omit the treatment for the frame problem here for clarity, but the approach used above works here too.

```
class MoneySend : Action {
  interface:   money, jointAction
  axioms:
    money(p1, s) = m1 ∧ money(p2, s) = m2 ∧ m1 >= m3 ⇒
      money(p1, res(send(p1, m3, p2), s)) = m1 − m3∧
      money(p2, res(send(p1, m3, p2), s)) = m2 + m3
    jointAction(a) ⟺ (∃p1, m, p2)a = send(p1, m, p2) }

class MergeAgents : Situation {
  interface:   HoldsD, HoldsJ, time, jointAction
  axioms:
    legalJoint(s) ⇒ [Holds(f(D), s) ⟺ HoldsD(f, s)]∧
                    [Holds(f(J), s) ⟺ HoldsJ(f, s)]
    legalJoint(s) ⟺
      [s = res(a, s′) ∧ jointAction(a) ∧ legalJoint(s′)]∨
      [time(D, s) = time(J, s) ∧ legalJoint(prevJoin(s))]
    legalJoint(s) ⇒ (∀p)time(s) = time(p, s)
    prevJoin(res(a, s)) = lastJoin(s)
    jointAction(a) ⇒ lastJoin(res(a, s)) = res(a, s)
    ¬jointAction(a) ⇒ lastJoin(res(a, s)) = lastJoin(s)
    lastJoin(S0) = S0
    prevJoin(S0) = S0 }
```

Figure 12: Merging perspectives on situations.

Figure 12 presents the necessary classes. **MoneySend** is an action class similar to those we have already seen. **MergeAgents** and the links to the object Agt of that class define our approach for merging the agents' theories (Figure 11), and we explain them below.

We care about time synchronization between the agents, so we assume some account of time in the different domain theories. We write $f(p)$ for the fluent that results from f after adding a dependency on p. The axioms of **MergeAgents** are explained as follows. First, if s is a legal joint situation ($legalJoint(s)$), then what holds in it ($Holds$) is exactly what holds in the different perspectives of the different agents ($HoldsD, HoldsJ$). If it is not a legal joint situation, we know nothing about it. Thus, the assumption that our agents' worlds do not interact is realized by giving each agent a different $Holds$ predicate.

The rest of the axioms in **MergeAgents** define legal joint situations. These axioms say that s is a legal joint situation iff the agents' perspectives of its history are consistent and their *time* fluents are synchronized. The two perspectives on history are consistent only if all joint actions (actions for which $jointAction$ holds) in history were done in a legally joint situation. We do not care about actions done separately, as they cannot influence an agent other than the one who executed them. In particular, notice that time does not progress in one agent's perspective of the world as a result of the other agent executing an action.

For example, in Daddy's world (S_D) the following is true after adding the explanation closure axioms for Daddy: $time(res(A_J.pickUp(A_J.A), S0)) = 0$. This is not a legal joint situation, because the agents' times are not synchronized. If we now add a *wait* action for Daddy and apply $A_D.wait(t)$ with the proper time, a legal joint situation would result (in which they can perform $send(D, m, J)$).

Conditional Independence

Complete knowledge of the world of the links of A_J renders A_J independent of all other objects. Proof-theoretically, proving something in the language of A_J depends only on theorems proved in the language of its links to S_J and A'_J (theorems that may depend on further theorems proved elsewhere). This follows from Craig's interpolation theorem.

Theorem 4 ((Craig 1957)) *If $\alpha \vdash \beta$, then there is a formula γ involving only symbols common to both α and β, such that $\alpha \vdash \gamma$ and $\gamma \vdash \beta$.*

From a modeling point of view, this kind of conditional independence allows us to build an object considering only those objects that will interact with it. A_m of class **MoneySend** depends only on Agt of **MergeAgents** and S_m of **MultiHas** (a class that was not detailed here), which in turn care only about money and time. Daddy's world is independent of Junior's, given Agt. This allows the design of theories by first considering their interfaces and only then writing their details. The construction of every domain theory can be done separately, caring only about those predicted inputs from connected theories, which must be in the vocabulary of the interfaces. In particular, we never care about

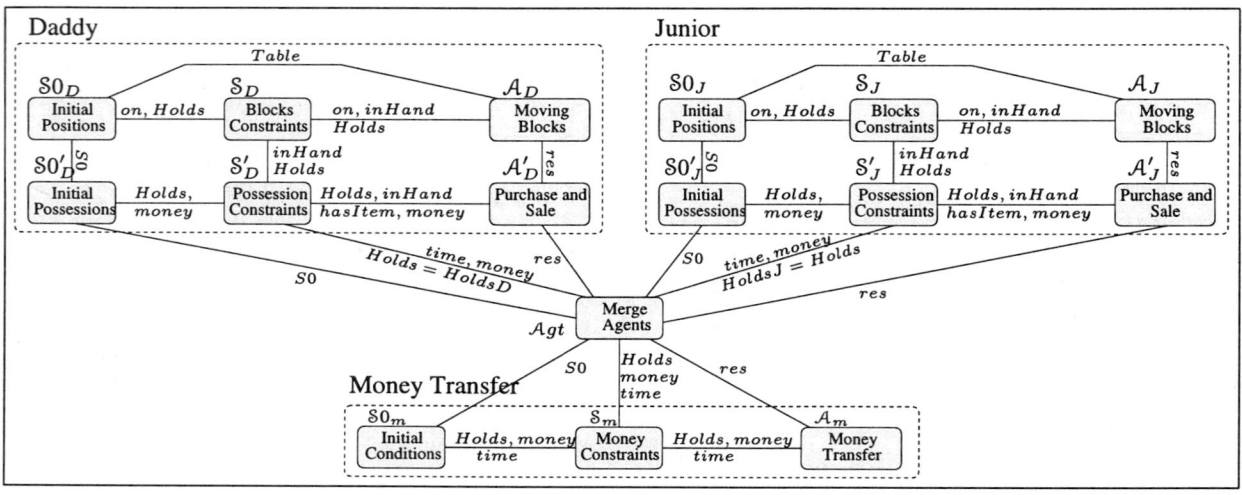

Figure 11: Diagrammatic view of Daddy and Junior in object-oriented situation calculus

theories that are independent from us, given our neighboring objects/domains.

This conditional independence is also utilized in the solutions to the frame problem. Explanation closure axioms help us make sure that actions in one domain do not influence domains that are not directly connected to it. Money transfers do not change the state of blocks on the table. This analysis can computationally enhance methods for computing solutions to the frame problem.

Finally, rewriting of theories is somewhat easier with this modeling technique. If a portion of the theory needs to be revised, the ramifications of this revision are easier to observe and predict. If the object structure is kept, then the influence of intra-object modifications can be predicted by checking the impact on the interface of the changed object/s.

Related Work

We focus our attention on object-oriented knowledge representation, as this material is spread out on many disciplines and the previous sections already included some references to related situation calculus literature. Many object-oriented knowledge representation systems are relevant to this work. However, systems available up until OOFOL (Amir 1999) either lack expressivity, lack object-oriented tools, extend the expressivity beyond the simple FOL semantics, or are not concerned with knowledge engineering at all.

The work on object-oriented Prolog (O-O Prolog) (e.g., (Shapiro & Takeuchi 1983)) provides limited expressivity and raises different challenges for object-oriented approaches than modeling in FOL. In contrast to FOL, O-O Prolog structures are built using a programming perspective, and the program flow in O-O Prolog is identical to the program flow in ordinary Prolog. Object-oriented structures in FOL supply heuristic information for theorem proving.

Another close object-oriented approach is Frame systems. Currently, there is no adequate object-oriented approach for full FOL in Frame systems. For example, Ontolingua (e.g., (Fikes, Farquhar, & Rice 1997)), one of the most expressive Frame systems to date, allows different sentences to be associated with each frame. However, it does not differentiate between a sentence put in one frame and the same sentence put in a different frame. The situation is similar in other and earlier frame systems such as KRYPTON/KL-ONE (Brachman, Fikes, & Levesque 1983),(for a recent survey see (Fridman-Noy & Hafner 1997)). Logical systems examined in the related field of *description logics* (e.g., (Borgida 1996)) are concerned with tasks related to classification in languages that is typically restricted (some systems can express full FOL theories, but in an unnatural way after translation).

Object-Oriented Databases are conceptually different from our approach. Logics for Object-Oriented Databases (e.g., (Kifer, Lausen, & Wu 1995)) try to give specific semantics to object-oriented databases. They focus on specific languages that allow us to reason about object membership in a class, class inheritance and properties of objects. In our work we do not try to reason about objects, but rather use the object-oriented technology to design large logical theories.

Approaches to formalizing and using context (e.g., (McCarthy & Buvač 1998; Guha & Lenat 1990)) typically have a significantly more expressive language, therefore requiring a more elaborate semantics. Furthermore, no object-oriented tools are supplied in any application of context known to the author (but some of it is hinted in (Ghidini & Serafini 1998)).

Finally, Bayes Nets (Pearl 1988) and Object-Oriented Bayes Nets (Koller & Pfeffer 1997) are closely related in spirit to our development here. Some of the ideas presented here came up while observing the work done in these fields.

Conclusions

In this paper we presented three results. First, we presented object-oriented techniques and tools that make designing large situation calculus theories simple. Conditional independence, low-bandwidth links, information hiding and encapsulation (looking at one subject at a time) are powerful tools in designing large theories in general and situation calculus theories in particular.

Second, we showed that it is possible to build situation calculus theories separately and then associate them with loosely interacting agents. The builder of a simple theory does not need to predict its use in a multiple-agents setup. Thus, agents can be treated in the situation calculus without abandoning the *result* formalism. We made an implicit assumption that the agents' separate actions are independent and had their joint actions explicitly stated as such.

Third, our theories can be designed with low-bandwidth links between interacting domains. This leads to good performance expectation for reasoning with these theories.

For simple theories, object-oriented structures are sometimes excessive. This situation is familiar from other fields that use object-oriented techniques. However, it seems that large theories are difficult to build and comprehend without such structures. In this paper we adjusted this methodology to the modeling of situation calculus theories. We hope that the results we presented here will support the scaling up of logical theory engineering.

Acknowledgments

I wish to thank Aarati Parmar for many discussions and help in writing this paper. Also, I thank Sheila McIlraith, Pedrito Maynard-Reid II, Sasa Buvac, Leora Morgenstern and John McCarthy for discussions on the subject of this paper. Sheila McIlraith also commented on a draft of this paper. I also thank the reviewers of AAAI'2000 for constructive, helpful comments. This research was supported by an AFOSR New World Vistas program under AFOSR grant F49620-97-1-0207 and the DARPA High Performance Knowledge Bases program.

References

Amir, E., and Maynard-Reid, P. 1999. Logic-based subsumption architecture. In *Intl' Joint Conf. on Artificial Intelligence (IJCAI'99)*.

Amir, E., and McIlraith, S. 2000. Paritition-based logical reasoning. In *Proc. KR'2000*. Available at http://www-formal.stanford.edu/eyal/papers/oo-reason.ps.

Amir, E. 1999. Object-Oriented First-Order Logic. Technical report, NRAC'99. Submitted to Elect. Trans. on AI (http://www.ida.liu.se/ext/etai)/RAC area.

Borgida, A. 1996. On the relative expressiveness of description logics and predicate logics. *Artificial Intelligence* 82(1-2):353–367.

Brachman, R. J.; Fikes, R. E.; and Levesque, H. J. 1983. KRYPTON: A functional approach to knowledge representation. *Computer* 16(10):67–73.

Craig, W. 1957. Linear reasoning. a new form of the herbrand-gentzen theorem. *Journal of Symbolic Logic* 22:250–268.

Fikes, R.; Farquhar, A.; and Rice, J. 1997. Tools for assembling modular ontologies in ontolingua. In *Natl' Conf. on Artificial Intelligence (AAAI '97)*, 436–441. AAAI Press.

Fridman-Noy, N., and Hafner, C. D. 1997. The state of the art in ontology design. *AI Magazine* 18(3):53–74.

Ghidini, C., and Serafini, L. 1998. Distributed first order logic. In *Proceedings of Frontiers of Combining Systems*.

Guha, R. V., and Lenat, D. B. 1990. Cyc: A midterm report. *AI Magazine* 11(3):33–59.

Haas, A. R. 1987. The case for domain-specific frame axioms. In *proc. workshop on the frame problem*, 343–348.

Kifer, M.; Lausen, G.; and Wu, J. 1995. Logical foundations of object-oriented and frame-based languages. *Journal of the ACM* 42(4):741–843.

Koller, D., and Pfeffer, A. 1997. Object-oriented Bayesian networks. In *Proc. of the 13th Conf. on Uncertainty in Artificial Intelligence (UAI-97)*, 302–313. Morgan Kaufmann.

Lin, F., and Reiter, R. 1994. State constraints revisited. *Journal of Logic and Computation, Special Issue on Actions and Processes*.

McCarthy, J., and Buvač, S. 1998. Formalizing Context (Expanded Notes). In *Computing Natural Language*, volume 81 of *CSLI Lecture Notes*. CSLI, Stanford University, Stanford, California. 13–50.

McCarthy, J., and Costello, T. 1998. Combining Narratives. In *Proc. KR'98*.

McCarthy, J., and Hayes, P. J. 1969. Some Philosophical Problems from the Standpoint of Artificial Intelligence. *Machine Intelligence* 4:463–502.

McCarthy, J. 1986. Applications of Circumscription to Formalizing Common Sense Knowledge. *Artificial Intelligence* 28:89–116.

McIlraith, S. 2000. Integrating actions and state constraints: a closed-form solution to the ramification problem (sometimes). *Artificial Intelligence* 116(1-2):87–121.

Morgenstern, L. 1998. Inheritance comes of age: Applying nonmonotonic techniques to problems in industry. *Artificial Intelligence* 103(1–2):237–271.

Pearl, J. 1988. *Probabilistic Reasoning in Intelligent Systems : Networks of Plausible Inference*. Morgan Kaufmann.

Pednault, E. P. D. 1989. ADL: exploring the middle ground between STRIPS and the situation calculus. In *Proc. KR'89*, 324–332.

Pinto, J. 1998. Concurrent actions and interacting effects. In *Proc. KR'98*.

Reiter, R. 1991. The frame problem in the situation calculus: A simple solution (sometimes) and a completeness result for goal regression. In Lifschitz, V., ed., *Artificial Intelligence and Mathematical Theory of Computation (Papers in Honor of John McCarthy)*. Academic Press. 359–380.

Reiter, R. 1996. Natural actions, concurrency and continuous time in the situation calculus. In *Proc. KR'96*.

Schubert, L. K. 1990. Monotonic solution of the frame problem in the situation calculus. In *knowledge representation and defeasible reasoning*. Kluwer. 23–67.

Shanahan, M. 1997. *Solving the Frame Problem, a mathematical investigation of the common sense law of inertia*. Cambridge, MA: MIT press.

Shapiro, E., and Takeuchi, A. 1983. Object oriented programming in concurrent prolog. *New Generation Computing* 1:25–48.

Disjunctive Temporal Reasoning in Partially Ordered Models of Time

Mathias Broxvall and **Peter Jonsson**
Department of Computer and Information Science
Linköpings Universitet
S-581 83 Linköping, Sweden
{matbr,petej}@ida.liu.se

Abstract

Certain problems in connection with, for example, cooperating agents and distributed systems require reasoning about time which is measured on incomparable or unsynchronized time scales. In such situations, it is sometimes appropriate to use a temporal model that only provides a partial order on time points. We study the computational complexity of partially ordered temporal reasoning in expressive formalisms consisting of point algebras extended with disjunctions. We show that the resulting algebra for partially ordered time contains four maximal tractable subclasses while the equivalent algebra for total-ordered time contains two.

Keywords: Temporal reasoning, constraint satisfaction, computational complexity.

Introduction

Many problems in Artificial Intelligence includes temporal reasoning in some form. Research on temporal reasoning has mainly focused on linear models of time, *cf.* Allen (1983). However, it is clear that more complex time models are needed in a variety of applications such as planning, cooperating robots, analysis of distributed systems etc. For analyzing such systems, more sophisticated time models such as *partially ordered* time (Anger 1989; Lamport 1986) have been proposed.

In Broxvall and Jonsson (1999) the satisfiability problem for the point algebra over partially ordered time is classified with respect to tractability; the result shows that there are three maximal tractable subclasses. Such classifications are feasible since the number of basic relations in point algebras are relatively small— the point algebra for partially-ordered time contains four. The number of basic relations increases when considering other representational entities, though. To exemplify, the interval algebra for total-ordered time contains 13 basic relations and 2^{8192} subclasses while the interval algebra for partially-ordered time contains 29 basic relations and $2^{2^{29}}$ subclasses. Needless to say, attempts to completely classify such algebrae have so far failed.

Instead of considering all possible subclasses of a temporal algebra, one can concentrate on subclasses that are "interesting" in some sense. We will study subclasses arising from extending point algebrae with disjunctions. Whether these subclasses are interesting or not is of course a matter of taste but we can provide some evidence that they are worth studying. First, simple constraint languages extended with disjunctions have historically proved to have interesting properties. For instance, the Horn DLRs (Jonsson & Bäckström 1998) which subsumes almost all previously presented temporal languages for total-ordered time can be viewed as a point algebra extended with disjunctions. Several other similar examples are given in Cohen *et al.* (1997). Secondly, disjunctions can compactly describe complex relations. Consider for example the ORD-Horn algebra (Nebel & Bürckert 1995) which is a tractable subclass of Allen's algebra. It contains 868 different relations and is consequently quite difficult to remember. Defining the ORD-Horn with the aid of disjunctions is much easier: ORD-Horn contains exactly the Allen relations which can be expressed by disjunctions of the form $x_1 \leq y_1 \vee x_2 \neq y_2 \vee \ldots \vee x_n \neq y_n$.

The main result of this paper is a total classification of tractability in the point algebra for partially ordered time extended with disjunctions. Our results show that there exists four maximal tractable subclasses. As a spin-off effect, we also get a total classification of the point algebra for total-ordered time extended with disjunctions; in this case, there are two maximal tractable subclasses.

The paper has the following organization: We begin by defining the basic concepts such as point algebrae and disjunctions. Thereafter we introduce the four tractable subclasses and provide a number of NP-completeness results that are needed in the classification. Finally, the classifications for partial-ordered and total-ordered time are carried out in the two last sections.

The point algebra

The point algebra is based on the notion of *relations* between pairs of variables interpreted over a partially-ordered set. In this paper we consider four *basic relations* which we denote by $<, >, =$ and $\|$. If x, y are points in a partial order $\langle T, \leq \rangle$ then we define these relations in terms of the partial ordering $\leq$ as follows:

1. $x < y$ iff $x \leq y$ and not $y \leq x$
2. $x > y$ iff $y \leq x$ and not $x \leq y$
3. $x = y$ iff $x \leq y$ and $y \leq x$

Copyright © 2000, American Association for Artificial Intelligence (www.aaai.org). All rights reserved.

4. $x \| y$ iff neither $x \leq y$ nor $y \leq x$

The relations in a point algebra are always disjunctions of basic relations and they are represented as sets of basic relations. Since we have 4 different basic relations we get $2^4 = 16$ possible disjunctive relations. The set of basic relations is denoted $\mathcal{B}$ and the set of all 16 relations is denoted by $\mathcal{PA}$. Sometimes we use a short-hand notation for certain relations, for example, $\{<, =\}$ is sometimes written as $\leq$ and $\{=, \|\}$ as $\|$. The empty relations is denoted by $\bot$ and it is always unsatisfied. We will implicitly assume that the converse of relations are available. For instance, if $(<)$ is in a set of relations Γ, then the converse $(>)$ is also in Γ.

The basic computational problem of the point algebra is the satisfiability problem where we have a set of variables and a set of constraints over the variables and the question is whether there exists a mapping from the variables to some partial order such that all constraints are satisfied.

Definition 1 Let $\Re \subseteq \mathcal{PA}$ be a set of point relations and P a class of partial orders. A problem instance of $\text{SAT}_p(\Re)$ is a set of variables V and a set of binary constraints of the form xRy where $x, y \in V$ and $R \in \Re$. A tuple $\langle f, \langle T, \leq \rangle \rangle$ where $f : V \to T$ is a total function and $\langle T, \leq \rangle \in P$ is called an interpretation of Π.

A problem instance Π is satisfiable iff there exists an interpretation $M = \langle f, \langle T, \leq \rangle \rangle$ such that $f(x) \; R \; f(y)$ holds for every constraint xRy. Such an M is called a *model* of Π.

Given an instance Π of $\text{SAT}_p(\Re)$ and two variables x, y we write $x \leq^+ y$ to say that there exists zero or more variables $z_1, \ldots, z_n$ such that

$$x \leq z_1 \wedge z_1 \leq z_2 \wedge \cdots \wedge z_{n-1} \leq z_n \wedge z_n \leq y$$

and we write $x \leq^* y$ to say $x \leq^+ y$ or $x = y$.

We will consider two classes of partial orders: *po* which is the class of all partial orders and $to \subset po$ which is the class of all total orders.

Disjunctions

We will now extend the point algebra with disjunctions.

Definition 2 Let R_1, R_2 be relations of arity i, j and define the disjunction $R_1 \vee R_2$ of arity $i + j$ as follows:

$$R_1 \vee R_2 = \{(x_1, \ldots, x_{i+j}) \in D^{i+j} | (x_1, \ldots, x_i) \in R_1 \vee (x_{i+1}, \ldots, x_{i+j}) \in R_2\}$$

Thus, the disjunction of two relations with arity i, j is the relation with arity $i + j$ satisfying either of the two relations. Let Γ_1, Γ_2 be sets of relations and define the disjunction $\Gamma_1 \vee \Gamma_2$ as follows:

$$\Gamma_1 \vee \Gamma_2 = \Gamma_1 \cup \Gamma_2 \cup \{R_1 \vee R_2 | R_1 \in \Gamma_1, R_2 \in \Gamma_2\}$$

The disjunction of two sets of relation $\Gamma_1 \vee \Gamma_2$, first introduced by Cohen et al.(Cohen, Jeavons, & Koubarakis 1997), is the set of disjunctions of each pair of relations in Γ_1, Γ_2 plus the sets Γ_1, Γ_2. It is a natural to include Γ_1 and Γ_2 since one wants to have the choice of using the disjunction or not. The fact that if $R_1 \vee R_2$ is included in a set of relations, then both R_1 and R_2 are in the set is an property which we refer to as the $\vee$-closure property. In the sequel, we will tacitly assume that all sets of relations that we consider can be constructed from $\mathcal{PA}$ and $\vee$ and that they, consequently, satisfy the $\vee$-closure property. In many cases we shall be concerned with constraints that are specified by disjunctions of an arbitrary number of relations. Thus, we make the following definition: for any set of relations, Δ, define $\Delta^* = \bigcup_{i=0}^{\infty} \Delta^{\vee i}$ where $\Delta^{\vee 0} = \{\bot\}$ and $\Delta^{\vee i+1} = \Delta^{\vee i} \vee \Delta$.

The previously defined concepts of problem instances, interpretations, models and so on can obviously be extended to disjunctions in a natural way. It is worth noting that the problem SAT_{po} is in NP even if we allow the use of disjunctions.

We say that a set of constraints Γ is *maximal tractable* iff $\text{SAT}_p(\Gamma)$ is tractable and for every set $X \not\subseteq \Gamma$ of relations which can be constructed by the relations in $\mathcal{PA}$ and the $\vee$ operator, $\text{SAT}_p(\Gamma \cup X)$ is not tractable.

Finally, we introduce the independence property as defined by Cohen et al. (1997). This concept will be used extensively for showing tractability results.

Definition 3 For any sets of relations Γ and Δ, we say that Δ is independent with respect to Γ if for any set of constraints C in $\text{SAT}_{po}(\Gamma \cup \Delta)$, C has a solution whenever every $C' \subseteq C$, which contains at most one constraint whose constraint relation belongs to Δ, has a solution.

Theorem 4 For any sets of relations Γ and Δ, if $\text{SAT}_p(\Gamma \cup \Delta)$ is tractable and Δ is independent with respect to Γ, then $\text{SAT}_p(\Gamma \vee \Delta^*)$ is tractable.

Gadgets

Gadgets allow us to concentrate on small sets of relations while proving tractability for large sets.

Definition 5 Let Ψ be a satisfiable instance of $\text{SAT}_{po}(\Gamma)$ containing the variables $x, y, z_1, \ldots, z_n$ and assume R to be a relation not in Γ. We say that Γ *implements* R iff the following holds: in every problem instance Θ containing a constraint xRy the following holds: Θ is satisfiable iff Θ with xRy replaced by a fresh copy of the gadget Ψ is satisfiable.

We assume that the variables $z_1, \ldots, z_n$ does not appear in the instance Θ. It is then easy to prove the following lemma.

Lemma 6 Let Γ be a set of relations such that $\text{SAT}_p(\Gamma)$ is tractable and assume there exists a gadget Ψ from Γ implementing γ, then $\text{SAT}_p(\Gamma \cup \{\gamma\})$ is tractable.

We also show that independence is preserved under the introduction of gadgets.

Theorem 7 Let Δ be a set of relations independent of Γ and assume there exists a gadget Ψ from Δ implementing the relation δ. Then, $\Delta \cup \{\delta\}$ is independent of Γ.

Proof: Let Π be an arbitrary instance of $\Gamma \cup \Delta \cup \{\delta\}$ and let S be the subinstance of Π only containing relations from $\Gamma - \Delta$. Assume that every subset $S \cup \{x_1 \delta_1 y_1\}, \ldots, S \cup \{x_n \delta_n y_n\}$ of Π where $\delta_i \in \Delta \cup \{\delta\}$ is satisfiable. Each such set of constraints can be rewritten on the form $S \cup \Pi_i$

```
1  algorithm A
2  Input: An instance Π of SAT_po(Γ_A) or SAT_po(Γ_B)
3   repeat
4     Π' ← Π
5     for each pair of nodes n_1, n_2 ∈ Π do
6       if n_1||n_2 and n_1 ≤* n_2 then reject
7       if n_1||n_2 and n_1 ≤* n_2 then
8         if n_1 ≠ n_2 then reject
9         else Π' ← contract(Π, n_1, n_2)
10      elsif n_1 ≤* n_2 and n_2 ≤* n_1 then
11        if n_1 ≠ n_2 ∈ Π then reject
12        else Π' ← contract(Π, n_1, n_2)
13      end if
14    end for
15  until Π' = Π
16  accept
```

Figure 1: The algorithm for solving $\text{SAT}_{po}(\Gamma'_A)$ and $\text{SAT}_{po}(\Gamma'_B)$

where Π_i is either a constraint from Δ or a set of constraints resulting from replacing the δ_i constraint by the gadget Ψ. Obviously each set $S \cup \Pi_i$ is also satisfiable as well as all the relaxed sets $S \cup \{\pi_{i,1}\}, \ldots, S \cup \{\pi_{i,m}\}$, where $\{\pi_{i,1}, \ldots, \pi_{i,m}\}$ are the constraints in Π_i. Since Δ is independent of Γ and Π_i only contains relations from Δ, we know that $S \cup H$ where $H = \{\pi_{i,j} | i \leq n, j \leq m\}$ is satisfiable. Since $S \cup H$ is the result of replacing each δ constraint in Π by the gadget Ψ, we have shown that Π is satisfiable and hence, that $\Delta \cup \{\delta\}$ is independent of Γ. □

Tractability Results

We continue by defining four classes of disjunctive relations $\mathcal{T}_A, \ldots, \mathcal{T}_D$ and show that their corresponding satisfiability problems are tractable. The classes are defined as follows: $\mathcal{T}_A = \Gamma_A \check{\vee} \Delta^*_A$, $\mathcal{T}_B = \Gamma_B \check{\vee} \Delta^*_B$, $\mathcal{T}_C = \Gamma_C \check{\vee} \Delta^*_C$ and $\mathcal{T}_D = \Delta^*_D$ and the exact definitions of the sets of relations can be found in Table 1. The classes $\mathcal{T}_A$ and $\mathcal{T}_B$ are extensions of the algebras $\mathcal{A}_{14}$ and $\mathcal{A}_{10}$ as defined by Broxvall and Jonsson (1999). It should be noted that if a problem instance of $\mathcal{T}_B$ has a model, then it has a model that is a total order. The class $\mathcal{T}_D$ is trivial since if an instance has a model, then it has a one-point model. The class $\mathcal{T}_C$ is quite obscure but note that its basic relations are a subset of the basic relations in $\mathcal{T}_A$.

Contractions are needed in order to understand the algorithms presented in this section. Let n_1, n_2 be two variables in a problem instance Π with variable set V and constraints C and let Π' be a problem instance with variables $V - \{n_2\}$ and constraints $(C - \{n_2Rx, xRn_2 \mid x \in V\}) \cup \{n_1Rx \mid n_2Rx \in C\} \cup \{xRn_1 \mid xRn_1 \in C\}$. We say that Π' is obtained by *contracting* n_1, n_2, that is, we identify the nodes n_1, n_2 by n_1. Note that this operation may introduce constraints of the form $n_1 R n_1$.

Lemma 8 $\text{SAT}_{po}(\Gamma'_A)$, $\text{SAT}_{po}(\Gamma'_B)$ and $\text{SAT}_{po}(\Gamma'_C)$ are tractable.

```
1  algorithm C
2  Input: An instance Π of SAT_po(Γ_C)
3   repeat
4     Π' ← Π.
5     if exists n_1, n_2 such that n_1 = n_2 in Π then    Π ←
    contract(Π)
6   until Π' = Π
7   if exists node n such that n ≠ n or n < n in Π then
    reject
8   if n_1 <* n_2 and n_1 R n_2 in Π where < ∉ R then
    reject
9   accept
```

Figure 2: The algorithm for solving $\text{SAT}_{po}(\Gamma'_C)$

Proof: An algorithm for $\text{SAT}_{po}(\Gamma'_A)$ and $\text{SAT}_{po}(\Gamma'_B)$ which is a slightly modified version of the algorithm for $\mathcal{A}_{14}$ and $\mathcal{A}_{10}$ proven correct and polynomial by Broxvall and Jonsson (1999) is presented in figure 1.

A polynomial-time algorithm for $\text{SAT}_{po}(\Gamma'_C)$ is presented in figure 2. Obviously algorithm C rejects only unsatisfiable instances of $\text{SAT}_{po}(\Gamma'_C)$.

Assume algorithm C accepts a certain instance Π and let Π' be the instance resulting from the contractions made by the algorithm in lines 3-6. Observe that Π' does not contain the relation $(=)$ and if Π' is satisfiable, then Π is satisfiable. Let I be the interpretation given by the function $f(x) = x$ and the partial order $\langle V, \{\langle x, y \rangle | x <^* y \text{ in } \Pi'\}\rangle$ where V is the set of variables appearing in Π'.

Each $\neq$ and $<$ constraint is satisfied by I and if there exists a constraint $x || < y$ in Π' then either $x < y$ or $x || y$ under I which guarantees that each such constraint is satisfied so I is a model and Π is satisfiable. Thus, $\text{SAT}_{po}(\Gamma'_C)$ is tractable. □

Next, we show a number of independence results.

Lemma 9 $\Delta'_A, \Delta'_B, \Delta'_C$ are independent of Γ'_A, Γ'_B and Γ'_C, respectively.

Proof: We show that Δ'_A is independent of Γ'_A; the proofs of the other two cases are similar.

Let Π be an instance of $\text{SAT}_{po}(\Gamma'_A \cup \Delta'_A)$ and assume that every instance Π' such that Π' only contains constraints present in Π and at most one constraint from Δ'_A is satisfiable. We prove Π to be satisfiable.

Assume to the contrary that Π is not satisfiable. Then, there exists at least one constraint $x R y \in \Pi$ where R is $\neq$ or $||$ which causes algorithm A to reject. Let Π' denote the problem instance containing all constraints from Π of the form $z R' w$ where R' is $\leq$ or $||$ plus the constraint $x R y$. Note that Π' causes the algorithm to reject. Contradiction, since Π' is a problem instance previously assumed to be satisfiable and the algorithm correctly solves $\text{SAT}_{po}(\Gamma'_A \cup \Delta'_A)$. Hence, Δ'_A is independent of Γ'_A. □

We can now show that the four classes are tractable.

Theorem 10 $\text{SAT}_{po}(\mathcal{T}_A)$, $\text{SAT}_{po}(\mathcal{T}_B)$, $\text{SAT}_{po}(\mathcal{T}_C)$ and $\text{SAT}_{po}(\mathcal{T}_D)$ are tractable.

Table 1: Tractable classes

	Γ'_A	Δ'_A	Γ_A	Δ_A	Γ'_B	Δ'_B	Γ_B	Δ_B	Γ'_C	Δ'_C	Γ_C	Δ_C	Δ_D
$<$			•					•		•		•	
$\leq$	•		•		•		•						•
$<>$							•	•					
$<=>$					•	•	•	•					•
$\parallel$	•	•	•	•							•	•	
$\parallel\!\!\parallel$	•		•								•	•	
$=$			•					•		•		•	•
$\neq$	•	•	•	•	•	•	•	•	•		•	•	
$<\parallel$		•	•	•							•	•	
$\leq\parallel$		•	•							•	•	•	•

Proof: That $\text{SAT}_{\text{po}}(\Gamma'_A \check{\vee} \Delta'^*_A)$ is tractable follows from Lemmata 8, 9 and Theorem 4. That Γ'_A implements Γ_A is proven by Broxvall and Jonsson (1999). Let Π be an arbitrary instance of $\text{SAT}_{\text{po}}(\mathcal{T}_A)$. We will show how every $\parallel < $ relation can be replaced by relations in $\Gamma'_A \check{\vee} \Delta'^*_A$ which implies the tractability of $\text{SAT}_{\text{po}}(\mathcal{T}_A)$. Choose an arbitrary disjunction $\gamma = x\ R_1\ y \vee \ldots \vee x_n\ R_n\ y_n$ in Π where $R_1 = (\parallel <)$. Introduce a fresh variable $t_{x,y}$, add the constraint $x \leq t_{x,y}$ and replace γ by the disjunction $\gamma' = t_{x,y} \parallel y \vee \ldots \vee x_n\ R_n\ y_n$. Repeat this transformation until no $(\parallel <)$ remains—a process which clearly takes polynomial time. Let Π' denote the resulting instance. Since the gadget $x \leq t_{x,y}, t_{x,y} \parallel y$ implements the relation $< \parallel$, it follows that Π' is satisfiable iff Π is satisfiable. Hence, $\text{SAT}_{\text{po}}(\mathcal{T}_A)$ is tractable.

The tractability of $\text{SAT}_{\text{po}}(\Gamma'_B \check{\vee} \Delta'^*_B)$ follows from Lemmata 8, 9 and Theorem 4. That Γ'_B implements Γ_B is proven by Broxvall and Jonsson (1999). The gadget $x \neq y$, $x <=> y$ implements $x <> y$ which shows that Δ'_B implements Δ_B. This fact combined with Theorem 7 proves that $\text{SAT}_{\text{po}}(\mathcal{T}_B)$ is tractable.

To show that $\mathcal{T}_C$ is tractable we begin by noting that the following gadgets from Δ'_C implements Δ_C: $x \leq \parallel y, y \leq \parallel x$ implement $x \parallel y$, $x \leq \parallel y, y \leq \parallel x, x \neq y$ implement $x \parallel y$ and $x \leq \parallel y, x \neq y$ implement $x < \parallel y$. Hence, Δ_C is independent of Γ'_C by Lemma 9 and Theorem 7. That $\text{SAT}_{\text{po}}(\Gamma'_C \check{\vee} \Delta^*_C)$ is tractable follows from Theorem 4. The theorem follows since $\Gamma_C = \Gamma'_C \cup \Delta_C$ which implies that $\mathcal{T}_C = \Gamma'_C \check{\vee} \Delta^*_C = \Gamma_C \check{\vee} \Delta^*_C$.

Finally, the tractability of $\text{SAT}_{\text{po}}(\mathcal{T}_D)$ is easy to show since each relation present in Γ_D contains only the relations $=$ and/or $\perp$. Consequently, it is sufficient to check whether an instance Π contains a disjunction containing only the $\perp$ relation. If this is the case, the instance is not satisfiable. Otherwise, Π is satisfied by the model mapping every variable to a single node. □

Intractability Results

This section contains the NP-completeness results which are needed in the classification theorem.

Lemma 11 *The following problems are NP-complete:*

1. $\text{SAT}_{\text{po}}(\{(<>)\}, R)$ if $R \in \{\parallel, < \parallel, \parallel\!\!\parallel, \leq \parallel\}$;
2. $\text{SAT}_{\text{po}}(\{<\} \vee \{<\})$;
3. $\text{SAT}_{\text{po}}(\{R\} \cup \{\leq\} \vee \{\leq\})$ if $R \in \{\neq, <>\}$;
4. $\text{SAT}_{\text{po}}(\{R\} \cup \{=\} \vee \{=\})$ if $R \in \{<, <>, \neq, \parallel, \parallel <\}$;
5. $\text{SAT}_{\text{po}}(\{R_1, R_2\} \cup \{\parallel\!\!\parallel\} \vee \{\parallel\!\!\parallel\})$ if $R_1 \in \{\leq, <=>\}$ and $R_2 \in \{<, <>, \neq, \parallel <\}$.

Proof: Case 1 is shown in Broxvall and Jonsson (1999). We only prove case 2 since the proofs of the other cases are similar. The proof is by a reduction from the NP-complete problem MONOTONE 3SAT:

INSTANCE: Set U of variables, collection C of clauses over U such that for each $c \in C$ has $|c| = 3$ and each clause contain either only positive or negative literals.
QUESTION: Is there a satisfying truth assignment for C?

Given an arbitrary instance P of MONOTONE 3SAT with variables $U = \{u_i, \ldots, u_m\}$ and clauses $C = \{c_1, \ldots, c_n\}$, construct incrementally an instance Π of $\text{SAT}_{\text{po}}(\{<\} \vee \{<\})$ by the following steps.

Begin with the variables in the set U and a fresh variable a and add the constraints $(u_i < a) \vee (u_i > a), 1 \leq i \leq m$. For each positive clause $c_i \in C$ of the form $x \vee y \vee z$ add a fresh variable t_i and the constraints:

$$x > a \vee t_i > a,\ y > t_i \vee z > a.$$

For each negative clause $c_i \in C$ of the form $\neg x \vee \neg y \vee \neg z$ add a fresh variable t_i and the constraints:

$$x < a \vee t_i < a,\ y < t_i \vee z < a.$$

We show that the problem instance constructed is satisfiable iff the original MONOTONE 3SAT problem instance is satisfiable. For the if-direction, assume that P is satisfiable and that $\mathcal{I}$ is a truth assignment satisfying all clauses in C. Construct an interpretation $M = \langle f, \langle T, \leq \rangle \rangle$ of Π as follows: let $T = \{a_i \mid 1 \leq i \leq 6\}, \leq\ = \{\langle a_i, a_j \rangle | i \leq j\}$ and

$$f = \{\langle x, a_5\rangle | x \text{ true in } \mathcal{I}\} \cup$$
$$\{\langle x, a_1\rangle | x \text{ false in } \mathcal{I}\} \cup$$
$$\{\langle t_i, a_0\rangle | c_i = x \vee y \vee z \text{ and } \mathcal{I}(x)\text{=true}\} \cup$$
$$\{\langle t_i, a_4\rangle | c_i = x \vee y \vee z \text{ and } \mathcal{I}(x)\text{= false}\} \cup$$
$$\{\langle t_i, a_2\rangle | c_i = \neg x \vee \neg y \vee \neg z \text{ and } \mathcal{I}(x)\text{=true}\} \cup$$
$$\{\langle t_i, a_6\rangle | c_i = \neg x \vee \neg y \vee \neg z \text{ and } \mathcal{I}(x)\text{=false}\} \cup$$
$$\{\langle a, a_3\rangle\}$$

That each constraint is satisfied by M can trivially be verified so M is a model of Π and Π is satisfiable if P is satisfiable. For the only-if direction, assume that Π is satisfiable and that M is a model of Π with mapping f. Construct a truth assignment $\mathcal{I}$ over the variables U assigning a variable x the value true if $f(x) > f(a)$ and otherwise the value false. Assume that there exists a clause c_i not satisfied by $\mathcal{I}$. The case when c_i is a positive clause $x \vee y \vee z$ leads to $f(x) < f(a), f(y) < f(a), f(z) < f(a)$ so $f(t_i) > f(a)$ and $f(y) > f(t_i)$ which contradicts that $f(y) < f(a)$. The case where u is a negative clause can be ruled out in a similar manner. Hence, no unsatisfied clause exists and $\mathcal{I}$ is a satisfying truth assignment. Since the reduction can be performed in polynomial time, the result follows. □

Maximality

This section contains the main result of this paper, namely that $\mathcal{T}_A, \mathcal{T}_B, \mathcal{T}_C$ and $\mathcal{T}_D$ are the only maximal tractable sets of the disjunctive point algebra for partially ordered time. However, we need some auxiliary results first.

To reduce the number of NP-completeness results needed in the classification, we will employ a *closure* operator $\mathcal{C}(\cdot)$ which is defined with the aid of the standard operators converse, intersection ($\cap$) and composition ($\circ$) together with a number of rules for handling disjunctions. These rules are defined and their tractability-preserving properties are stated in the next lemma. The straightforward proof is omitted.

Lemma 12 Let $R_i \in \mathcal{PA}$ and $\Gamma_j \subseteq \mathcal{PA}$.

(1) if $\text{SAT}_{\text{po}}(\Gamma_1 \cup \{<\}\check{\vee}\Gamma_2)$ is tractable, then $\text{SAT}_{\text{po}}(\Gamma_1 \cup \{<\}\check{\vee}\Gamma_2 \cup \Gamma_2\check{\vee}\Gamma_2)$ is tractable;

(2) assume $<, <>, \neq$ or $< \|$ is in Γ_1. If $\text{SAT}_{\text{po}}(\Gamma_1 \cup \{=\}\check{\vee}\Gamma_2)$ is tractable, then $\text{SAT}_{\text{po}}(\Gamma_1 \cup \{=\}\check{\vee}\Gamma_2 \cup \Gamma_2\check{\vee}\Gamma_2)$ is tractable.

(3) assume $\oplus \in \{\cap, \circ\}$. If $\text{SAT}_{\text{po}}(\Gamma_1 \cup \{R_1 \vee R_3, R_2 \vee R_3\})$ is tractable, then $\text{SAT}_{\text{po}}(\Gamma_1 \cup \{R_1 \vee R_3, R_2 \vee R_3, (R_1 \oplus R_2) \vee R_3\})$ is tractable.

(4) if $\text{SAT}_{\text{po}}(\Gamma_1 \cup \{R_1 \vee R_2\})$ is tractable, then $\text{SAT}_{\text{po}}(\Gamma_1 \cup \{R_1, R_2, R_1 \vee R_2\})$ is tractable.

If Γ is a set of relations, we define $\mathcal{C}(\Gamma)$ as the least set X such that $\Gamma \subseteq X$ and X is closed under converse, intersection and composition on point relations and the expansion rules in the previous lemma. A composition table for the point relations can be found in Broxvall and Jonsson (1999). By using the lemma, the $\check{\vee}$-closure property and the properties of converse, intersection and composition, it is a routine verification to show that if $\text{SAT}_{\text{po}}(\Gamma)$ is tractable, then $\text{SAT}_{\text{po}}(\mathcal{C}(\Gamma))$ is also tractable.

Now, we introduce a construction which simplifies the proof by allowing us to only consider a small number of disjunctions; this is shown in the next lemma.

Definition 13 Let $\mathcal{T} = \Gamma\check{\vee}\Delta^*$ and $\Delta \subseteq \Gamma$. We define $\overline{\mathcal{T}}$ as $(\mathcal{PA} - \Gamma) \cup (\Gamma - \Delta)\check{\vee}(\Gamma - \Delta)$.

Lemma 14 If $\mathcal{T} = \Gamma\check{\vee}\Delta^*$, $\Delta \subseteq \Gamma$ and $\mathcal{T}' \not\subseteq \mathcal{T}$, then there exists $C \in \overline{\mathcal{T}}$ such that $C \in \mathcal{T}'$.

Proof: Arbitrarily choose a $C \in \mathcal{T}'$ such that $C \notin \mathcal{T}$ and choose $C_1, \cdots, C_n \in \mathcal{PA}$ such that $C_1 \vee \cdots \vee C_n = C$. Assume first that there exists some i such that $C_i \notin \Gamma$. The definition of $\overline{\mathcal{T}}$ implies that $C_i \in \overline{\mathcal{T}}$ and the $\check{\vee}$-closure property implies that $C_i \in \mathcal{T}'$.

Assume instead that $C_1, \cdots, C_n \in \Gamma$. Since $\Gamma \subseteq \mathcal{T}$ and $C \notin \mathcal{T}$ we know that $n > 1$. If all or all but one $C_i \in \Delta$, then we know that $C \in \mathcal{T}$. Hence, there exists at least two i, j such that $C_i, C_j \notin \Delta$. Now, $C_i \vee C_j \in \mathcal{T}'$ by the $\check{\vee}$-closure property and the definition of $\overline{\mathcal{T}}$ gives that $C_i \vee C_j \in \overline{\mathcal{T}}$. □

Using the tractability and NP-completeness results given in previous sections as well as the previous definition and results we can now by a simple computer assisted case analysis prove the main result of this paper.

Theorem 15 $\mathcal{T}_A, \mathcal{T}_B, \mathcal{T}_C$ and $\mathcal{T}_D$ are the only maximal tractable subclasses of SAT_{po}.

Proof: Suppose to the contrary that there exists another maximal tractable algebra $\mathcal{T}$. From the previous lemma it follows that there exists $\gamma_A, \cdots, \gamma_D$ in $\mathcal{T}$ such that $\gamma_A \in \overline{\mathcal{T}}_A, \cdots, \gamma_D \in \overline{\mathcal{T}}_D$. Note that there exists only a finite number of possible values for $\gamma_A, \ldots, \gamma_D$.

To prove the result, a machine-assisted case analysis of the following form was performed: each admissible choice of $\gamma_A, \ldots, \gamma_D$ was generated and $X = \mathcal{C}(\gamma_A, \ldots, \gamma_D)$ was computed. Each such set X was examined and it was found that at least one of the NP-complete sets of Lemma 11 was a subset of X. Thus, $\text{SAT}_{\text{po}}(\mathcal{T})$ is NP-complete and the theorem follows. □

Totally Ordered Time

We will now identify the maximal tractable subclasses of SAT_{to}, *i.e.*, SAT_{po} restricted to total orders. The classification will rely on the results in the previous sections but the main theorem is shown without the use of a computer-assisted case analysis.

Note that the basic relation $\|$ is unnecessary when dealing with total orders so we only have three basic relations ($<, =$ and $>$) and eight possible disjunctions of these relations. Let $\mathcal{PA}_{\text{to}}$ denote the set of these eight relations and define $\mathcal{X}_1 = \mathcal{PA}_{\text{to}}\check{\vee}\{\neq\}^*$ and $\mathcal{X}_2 = \Delta^*$ where $\Delta = \{r \in \mathcal{PA}_{\text{to}} \mid r = \bot \text{ or } \{=\} \subseteq r\}$. As we will see later on, $\mathcal{X}_1$ and $\mathcal{X}_2$ are the only maximal tractable subclasses of SAT_{to}.

Lemma 16 $\text{SAT}_{\text{to}}(\mathcal{X}_i)$, $1 \leq i \leq 2$, are tractable problems.

Proof: Tractability of $\mathcal{X}_1$ has been proved by Jonsson and Bäckström (1998) and Koubarakis (1996) while the tractability of $\mathcal{X}_2$ is shown in Theorem 10. □

The NP-completeness results for SAT_{to} are all based on the previously presented NP-completeness results; interestingly, many of these results hold even when restricted to total orders.

Lemma 17 $\text{SAT}_{\text{to}}(\mathcal{N}_i)$, $1 \leq i \leq 5$, is NP-complete where

$$\mathcal{N}_1 = \{(< \vee <)\} \qquad \mathcal{N}_2 = \{\neq, (\leq \vee \leq)\}$$
$$\mathcal{N}_3 = \{<, (= \vee =)\} \qquad \mathcal{N}_4 = \{\neq, (= \vee =)\}$$
$$\mathcal{N}_5 = \{<, (\leq \vee \leq)\}.$$

Proof sketch: We begin by examining the proof of Lemma 11 which shows that $\text{SAT}_{\text{po}}(\{<\} \vee \{<\})$ is NP-complete. Obviously, the proof holds even if we restrict the possible partial orders to total orders which implies that $\text{SAT}_{\text{to}}(\{<\}\check{\vee}\{<\})$ is NP-complete. By analyzing the proofs of the other cases, it follows that $\text{SAT}_{\text{to}}(\mathcal{N}_i)$, $2 \leq i \leq 4$, is NP-complete. The NP-completeness of $\text{SAT}_{\text{to}}(\mathcal{N}_5)$ follows from the NP-completeness of $\text{SAT}_{\text{to}}(\mathcal{N}_3)$ plus the fact that $\{\leq\}\check{\vee}\{\leq\}$ implements $\{=\}\check{\vee}\{=\}$ □

We are now ready to prove the main theorem for the point algebra for totally ordered time.

Theorem 18 $\mathcal{X}_1$ and $\mathcal{X}_2$ are the only maximal tractable subclasses of SAT_{to}.

Proof: Assume that there exists a maximal tractable algebra $\mathcal{X}$ such that $\mathcal{X} \not\subseteq \mathcal{X}_1$ and $\mathcal{X} \not\subseteq \mathcal{X}_2$. By Lemma 14, there exists γ_1, γ_2 in $\mathcal{T}$ such that $\gamma_1 \in \overline{\mathcal{X}_1}$ and $\gamma_2 \in \overline{\mathcal{X}_2}$. It is easy to see that $\overline{\mathcal{X}_1} \subseteq \{r_1, \ldots, r_6\}$ where

$$r_1 = (< \vee <) \quad r_2 = (\leq \vee \leq)$$
$$r_3 = (= \vee =) \quad r_4 = (\leq \vee =)$$
$$r_5 = (< \vee =) \quad r_6 = (< \vee \leq)$$

and $\overline{\mathcal{X}_2} \subseteq \{<, \neq, (< \vee <), (< \vee \neq), (\neq \vee \neq)\}$. By Lemma 11, we know that $\text{SAT}_{\text{to}}\{(< \vee <)\}$ is NP-complete so the disjunction $r_1 = (< \vee <)$ can be excluded from further consideration. We will show that if γ_1 equals one of $r_2, \ldots, r_6$ and γ_2 equals $<$ or $\neq$, then $\text{SAT}_{\text{to}}(\{\gamma_1, \gamma_2\})$ is NP-hard. By noting that $(< \vee \neq)$ implements the relation $<$ (by the construction $x < y \vee x \neq x$) and $(\neq \vee \neq)$ implements $\neq$ (by $x \neq y \vee x \neq y$), this result implies that $\text{SAT}_{\text{to}}(\{\gamma_1, \gamma_2\})$ is NP-hard for all $\gamma_1 \in \overline{\mathcal{X}_1}$ and $\gamma_2 \in \overline{\mathcal{X}_2}$. This contradicts our initial assumptions and proves the theorem.

1. $\gamma_1 \in \{r_2, r_3\}$. Then, the NP-completeness of $\text{SAT}_{\text{to}}(\{\gamma_1, \gamma_2\})$ is an immediate consequence of Lemma 6.2.

2. $\gamma_1 = r_4$. Note that r_4 implements r_3 so $\text{SAT}_{\text{to}}(\{\gamma_1, \gamma_2\})$ is NP-complete by case 1.

3. $\gamma_1 = r_5$ and $\gamma_2 = \{<\}$. We show how to implement the disjunction $a < b \vee c < d$ with γ_1 and γ_2: introduce an auxiliary variable t and the following two relations: $a < t$ and $t = b \vee c < d$. NP-completeness follows from case 1.

4. $\gamma_1 = r_5$ and $\gamma_2 = \{\neq\}$. The relation $a < b$ can be implemented by the relations $t_1 \neq t_2$ and $t_1 = t_2 \vee a < b$ where t_1 and t_2 are auxiliary variables. NP-completeness follows from the previous case.

5. $\gamma_1 = r_6$. The NP-completeness of $\text{SAT}_{\text{to}}(\{\gamma_1, \gamma_2\})$ is a consequence of cases 3 and 4 and the observation that r_6 implies r_5. □

Acknowledgements

This research has been supported by the ECSEL graduate student program and by the *Swedish Research Council for the Engineering Sciences* (TFR) under grant 97-301.

References

Allen, J. F. 1983. Maintaining knowledge about temporal intervals. *Communications of the ACM* 26(11):832–843.

Anger, F. 1989. On Lamport's interprocessor communication model. *ACM Transactions on Programming Languages Systems* 11(3):404–417.

Broxvall, M., and Jonsson, P. 1999. Towards a complete classification of tractability in point algebras for nonlinear time. In *Proceedings of the 5th International Conference on Principles and Practice of Constraint Programming (CP-99)*, 448–454.

Cohen, D.; Jeavons, P.; and Koubarakis, M. 1997. Tractable disjunctive constraints. In *Proceedings of the 3rd International Conference on Principles and Practice for Constraint Programming*, 478–490.

Jonsson, P., and Bäckström, C. 1998. A unifying approach to temporal constraint reasoning. *Artificial Intelligence* 102(1):143–155.

Koubarakis, M. 1996. Tractable disjunctions of linear constraints. In *Proceedings of the 2nd International Conference on Principles and Practice for Constraint Programming*, 297–307.

Lamport, L. 1986. The mutual exclusion problem: Part I—a theory of interprocess communication. *Journal of the ACM* 33(2):313–326.

Nebel, B., and Bürckert, H.-J. 1995. Reasoning about temporal relations: A maximal tractable subclass of Allen's interval algebra. *Journal of the ACM* 42(1):43–66.

An Interval Algebra for Indeterminate Time

Wes Cowley
Department of Computer Science and Engineering
University of South Florida
P.O. Box 280138
Tampa, FL 33682-0138
wcowley@acm.org

Dimitris Plexousakis
Department of Computer Science
University of Crete & ICS-FORTH
P.O. Box 2208, Heraklion
Greece 71409
dp@csd.uch.gr

Abstract

Temporal indeterminacy is an inherent problem which arises when capturing and manipulating temporal data in many application areas. As such, representation and manipulation of timestamps with indeterminacy is a requirement for these applications. We present an extension of Allen's thirteen interval relationships to indeterminate temporal intervals based on a novel representation for indeterminate timestamps. The timestamps can be derived from and translated to interval constraints. We provide a set of simple and useful operators for manipulating both convex and non-convex indeterminate intervals represented by these timestamps.

Introduction

Temporal indeterminacy exists when one does not know precisely either the location of an event on the time line or its duration. The temporal knowledge about the event is indefinite or incomplete. This is an inherent problem when reasoning in many application domains. Planning systems are sometimes faced with the infeasibility of completely modeling all aspects of a situation. Knowledge representation and reasoning systems may be faced with insufficient information to completely determine a desired time interval. The knowledge about the time interval is indeterminate: one may know a period of time the interval definitely covers but there may also be a period of time into which the interval may extend.

The prevalent method for handling temporal indeterminacy in the temporal reasoning community is to use a temporal constraint network (TCN) on intervals (Allen 1983). The TCN allows the reasoner to arrive at a disjunction of possible relationships between pairs of intervals. For example, Anger, et al. describe a temporal knowledge base using this approach (Anger et al. 1988). The knowledge of the location and duration of an event on the time line is encoded in the relationships between that event and others in the network.

We examine a novel representation for indeterminate intervals based on the endpoints of the intervals' determinate and indeterminate regions and define a set of operators, which are both useful and non-complex, for manipulating indeterminate timestamps. Conversions between interval constraints in the form of the thirteen interval relationships (Allen 1983) and the indeterminate timestamps is straightforward. We use the indeterminate intervals to extend the traditional interval relationships to allow for indeterminacy. To the best of our knowledge, this is the first effort in this direction.

Our approach differs from TCNs in that the knowledge of an interval's position and duration is encoded in the interval's representation rather than in relationships between interval, allowing for non-complex manipulation of the knowledge. One application of this is in temporal integrity constraints for knowledge bases such as Telos (Plexousakis 1995).

Another method associates characteristic functions with intervals to represent the level of possibility that any given point is actually contained in the interval (Bouzid & Mouaddib 1998). In this approach, the characteristic function of intervals are modified as more knowledge is gained and schedules evolve. A similar method, in the temporal database field, describes a timestamp with a probability function (Dyreson & Snodgrass 1998). The probability and characteristic function approach is both more flexible and more complex than that described here as it allows for reasoning over the likelihood that a point is in the interval or not. In our method a point is either definitely in the interval or possibly in the interval.

In another approach, Gadia, et al propose a set oriented representation which supports both indeterminacy and incompleteness with a three-valued logic (Gadia, Nair, & Poon 1992). Their work is the closest to the indeterminate intervals described here, but provides a different set of operators. They do not describe a method for translating between interval constraint notation and their representation, complexity of the operators, or algorithms. Our work does not examine temporally missing values as Gadia does.

Koubarakis examines indeterminacy in the context of temporal constraint databases, where temporal indeterminacy is described by local and global constraints on variables representing the end points of the intervals (Koubarakis 1994; 1997). This is similar to the interval oriented TCN approach in that knowledge of a time interval is encoded in the constraints. The purpose in this case is less oriented toward deduction and more toward finite representation of

Copyright © 2000, American Association for Artificial Intelligence (www.aaai.org). All rights reserved.

potentially infinite domains.

In the remainder of this paper we will first describe our assumed temporal structure and chosen representation for indeterminate intervals followed by a discussion of an extension of the interval relationships to handle indeterminacy. Finally, we will give our conclusions and avenues for future work.

Valid Interval Stamps

Motivation Indeterminate time may arise in a number of ways and is nearly unavoidable when dealing with the valid time of facts in a knowledge base. We are interested in associating a valid time period with facts in order to support a temporal integrity constraint implementation, such as in, e.g., (Plexousakis 1995; Cowley 1999) in which constraints include combinations of the thirteen interval relationships (Allen 1983). As such, it is appropriate that the valid time periods are also specified using interval relationships. Because most of these relationships do not precisely constrain the time periods involved, the resulting time stamps are indeterminate. Thus, we must be able to derive indeterminate valid time stamps from interval constraints, manipulate those indeterminate intervals, and translate the results back to interval constraints.

Points We assume a linear discrete time line (Benthem 1991) bounded by the range of the underlying integer type in which temporal points are represented. We further assume distinct elements ∞, $-\infty$, and $\texttt{nil}$. With the exception of the incomparable element $\texttt{nil}$, which represents a non-specified value, points are totally ordered by $<$. The relationships $<$, $=$, and $\leq$ between two points carry the expected meaning. More formally, we assume a temporal structure $\mathcal{T}$ which is comprised of a set of points $\mathcal{P} = \{\ldots, p_{-1}, p_0, p_1, \ldots\}$ and a relation $<$. The set $\mathcal{P}' = \mathcal{P} \cup \{-\infty, \infty, \texttt{nil}\}$ is isomorphic to the set $\mathcal{Z}' = \mathcal{Z} \cup \{-\infty, \infty, \texttt{nil}\}$. We define a one-to-one and onto mapping function, $\iota: \mathcal{P}' \to \mathcal{Z}'$, and its inverse as follows:

$$\iota(p) = \begin{cases} p & \text{if } p = -\infty, \infty, \text{ or } \texttt{nil} \\ i & \text{for } p_i, i \in \mathcal{Z} \end{cases}$$

$$\iota^{-1}(i) = \begin{cases} i & \text{if } i = -\infty, \infty, \text{ or } \texttt{nil} \\ p_i & \text{for } i \in \mathcal{Z} \end{cases}$$

The relation $<$ between members of the set $\mathcal{P}$ is defined as $p_1 < p_2 \Leftrightarrow \iota(p_1) < \iota(p_2)$ and can be extended to the special elements $-\infty$ and ∞ by observing that $\forall p \in \mathcal{P} \; -\infty < p < \infty$. Finally, $<$ is undefined if either operand is $\texttt{nil}$. Similar translations give the meanings for $=$ and $\leq$. Note that from the definition of ι, $p_i = p_j \Rightarrow i = j$.

The following functions permit us to determine which of a pair of points occurs earlier or later on the time line.

Definition 1. We define The functions $\min_{\text{p}}$, $\max_{\text{p}}$, $\min_{\text{vp}}$, and $\max_{\text{vp}}$: $\mathcal{P}' \times \mathcal{P}' \to \mathcal{P}'$ as follows:

$$\min_{\text{p}}(p_1, p_2) = \begin{cases} \texttt{nil} & \text{if } p_1 = \texttt{nil} \vee p_2 = \texttt{nil} \\ p_1 & \text{if } p_1 < p_2 \\ p_2 & \text{otherwise} \end{cases}$$

$$\max_{\text{p}}(p_1, p_2) = \begin{cases} \texttt{nil} & \text{if } p_1 = \texttt{nil} \vee p_2 = \texttt{nil} \\ p_1 & \text{if } p_2 < p_1 \\ p_2 & \text{otherwise} \end{cases}$$

$$\min_{\text{vp}}(p_1, p_2) = \begin{cases} \texttt{nil} & \text{if } p_1 = \texttt{nil} \wedge p_2 = \texttt{nil} \\ p_1 & \text{if } p_2 = \texttt{nil} \vee p_1 < p_2 \\ p_2 & \text{otherwise} \end{cases}$$

$$\max_{\text{vp}}(p_1, p_2) = \begin{cases} \texttt{nil} & \text{if } p_1 = \texttt{nil} \wedge p_2 = \texttt{nil} \\ p_1 & \text{if } p_2 = \texttt{nil} \vee p_2 < p_1 \\ p_2 & \text{otherwise} \end{cases}$$

$\min_{\text{p}}$ ($\max_{\text{p}}$) chooses the earliest (latest) operand if both are not $\texttt{nil}$. Where exactly one operand is $\texttt{nil}$, $\min_{\text{vp}}$ and $\max_{\text{vp}}$ return the other point.

Given a point p, we need to refer to its next and previous points on the time line.

Definition 2. The functions previous and next, each with signature $\mathcal{P}' \to \mathcal{P}'$, are defined as follows:

$$\text{previous}(p) = \begin{cases} p & \text{if } p \in \{-\infty, \infty, \texttt{nil}\} \\ \iota^{-1}(\iota(p) - 1) & \text{otherwise} \end{cases}$$

$$\text{next}(p) = \begin{cases} p & \text{if } p \in \{-\infty, \infty, \texttt{nil}\} \\ \iota^{-1}(\iota(p) + 1) & \text{otherwise} \end{cases}$$

Determinate Intervals In order to discuss periods of time, as opposed to instants, we use intervals.

Definition 3. A *convex interval* is a set of consecutive points. An interval I can be represented by its lowest and highest points $\langle I_s, I_e \rangle$, $I_s \leq I_e$, $I_s = \texttt{nil} \Leftrightarrow I_e = \texttt{nil}$. We say that $p \in I$ iff $I_s \leq p \leq I_e$. The empty interval, which contains no point, is represented by $\langle \texttt{nil}, \texttt{nil} \rangle$ or $\emptyset$. We say that a convex interval is *infinite* if one or both endpoints is ∞ or $-\infty$. $\mathcal{I}$ refers to the set of all convex intervals. Points may be implicitly converted to intervals by the function *interval*: $\mathcal{P} \to \mathcal{I}$, defined as $\text{interval}(p) = \langle p, p \rangle$.

We will use the 13 basic interval relationships (Allen 1983) for comparing intervals for ordering and inclusion. The concept of intersection of convex intervals is important. This carries the same meaning as in set theory, namely that there is at least one point in common.

Definition 4. Two convex intervals I_1 and I_2 *intersect* if $I_{1_s} \leq I_{2_e} \wedge I_{2_s} \leq I_{1_e}$.

Note that the empty interval, $\langle \texttt{nil}, \texttt{nil} \rangle$ does not intersect with any interval due to the incomparability of $\texttt{nil}$. The infinite interval, $\langle -\infty, \infty \rangle$ intersects with all non-empty intervals. We also need the concept of adjacency of convex intervals, which is defined next.

Definition 5. We say that two intervals I_1 and I_2 are *adjacent* if $\text{next}(I_{1_e}) = I_{2_s} \vee \text{next}(I_{2_e}) = I_{1_s}$.

We will also need the concept of non-convex intervals to talk about sets of non-consecutive points.

Definition 6. A *non-convex interval* I is a set of convex intervals I_i which neither intersect nor are adjacent.

Indeterminate Intervals A *valid interval stamp* (VIS) is an extension of the interval concept. A VIS describes the set of points which are definitely in the interval as well as those which *may* be in the interval. Through this mechanism we can represent the indeterminacy inherent in interval constraints.

Definition 7. A *convex valid interval stamp* (CVIS) is a 4-tuple $V = \langle I_s, D_s, D_e, I_e \rangle$ associated with a fact in a knowledge base. The points are restricted so that $D_s = \text{nil} \Leftrightarrow D_e = \text{nil}$ and $D_s = \text{nil} \Rightarrow (I_s = \text{nil} \Leftrightarrow I_e = \text{nil})$. D_s, D_e, if not nil, are time stamps marking the end points of the determinate interval D; that period of time during which the associated fact is true. I_s and I_e, if not nil, represent the extended period of time before and after the determinate interval, respectively, during which the associated fact *may* be true. The indeterminate interval is the non-convex interval $I = \{I_L, I_H\}$ where I_L and I_H are:

$$I_L = \begin{cases} \emptyset & \text{If } I_s = \text{nil} \\ \langle V.I_s, V.I_e \rangle & \text{If } D = \emptyset \\ \langle V.I_s, \text{previous}(V.D_s) \rangle & \text{otherwise} \end{cases}$$

$$I_H = \begin{cases} \emptyset & \text{If } I_e = \text{nil} \vee D = \emptyset \\ \langle \text{next}(V.D_e), V.I_e \rangle & \text{otherwise} \end{cases}$$

A CVIS for which both I_s and I_e are nil is called *fully determinate*, while one with both D_s and D_e being nil is called *fully indeterminate*. The empty VIS is represented as $\langle \text{nil}, \text{nil}, \text{nil}, \text{nil} \rangle$ or $\emptyset$. We will use $\mathcal{CV}$ to refer to the set of all CVISs. An interval I can be converted implicitly to a CVIS with the function $\text{cvis} : \mathcal{I} \to \mathcal{CV}$, defined as $\text{cvis}(I) = \langle \text{nil}, I_s, I_e, \text{nil} \rangle$

Example 1. Figure 1a shows the CVIS $\langle 1, 2, 4, 6 \rangle$. This contains the points $\{2, 3, 4\}$ determinately and $\{1, 5, 6\}$ indeterminately. Figure 1b shows the same period covered by the fully indeterminate CVIS $\langle 1, \text{nil}, \text{nil}, 6 \rangle$. Finally, Figure 1c shows the left infinite CVIS $\langle -\infty, 4, 6, \text{nil} \rangle$.

We will often need to obtain the earliest and latest points in a CVIS independently of whether that point is determinate or not.

Definition 8. We define the functions *upper* and *lower* as $\text{upper}(V) = \max_{\text{vp}}(V.D_e, V.I_e)$ and $\text{lower}(V) = \min_{\text{vp}}(V.D_s, V.I_s)$, both with signature $\mathcal{CV} \to \mathcal{P}$.

We will also need to know the latest point at which a CVIS V can start and the earliest point at which it can end. To understand these functions, observe that if a CVIS V has a determinate region then the interval will start no later than

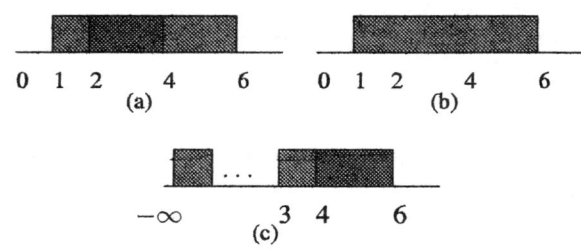

Figure 1: Examples of convex valid interval stamps

$V.D_s$ and end no earlier than $V.D_e$. On the other hand, if V is fully indeterminate then it may start as late as $V.I_e$ and end as earlier as $V.I_s$.

Definition 9. We define two functions, *maxlo* and *minup*, with signature $\mathcal{CV} \to \mathcal{P}$ as $\text{maxlo}(V) = \min_{\text{vp}}(V.D_s, V.I_e)$ and $\text{minup}(V) = \max_{\text{vp}}(V.I_s, V.D_e)$.

The following extends the definition of membership in an interval.

Definition 10. We denote membership of a point p in a CVIS V as $p \in V$ and define that membership as $p \in V \Leftrightarrow \text{lower}(V) \leq p \leq \text{upper}(V)$. We will also use $p \in V.D$ to represent p's determinate inclusion in V and $p \in V.I$ to represent p's indeterminate inclusion in V.

Next we extend the concept of intersection to convex valid interval stamps.

Definition 11. Two CVISs, V_1 and V_2, *intersect* if: $\text{lower}(V_1) \leq \text{upper}(V_2) \wedge \text{lower}(V_2) \leq \text{upper}(V_1)$. We say V_1 and V_2 *determinately intersect* if $V_1.D \neq \emptyset \wedge V_2.D \neq \emptyset \wedge V_1.D \text{ intersects } V_2.D$.

The concept of adjacency can be extended to convex valid interval stamps as follows.

Definition 12. We say that two CVISs, V_1 and V_2, are *adjacent* if $\text{next}(\text{upper}(V_1)) = \text{lower}(V_2) \vee \text{next}(\text{upper}(V_2)) = \text{lower}(V_1)$. We say that V_1 and V_2 are *determinately adjacent* if $V_1.D \neq \emptyset \wedge V_2.D \neq \emptyset \wedge V_1.D \text{ adjacent } V_2.D$. Note that two CVISs which are determinately adjacent may intersect but will not determinately intersect.

The work of (Cowley 1999) depicts how to translate from interval constraints of the form $\mathcal{R}\ I$, where $\mathcal{R}$ is an interval relationship and I is a determinate interval, to a convex valid interval stamp.

We will also need to consider non-convex VISs.

Definition 13. A *non-convex valid interval stamp* (NVIS) is a finite set of CVISs which meet two conditions. 1) No two CVISs may intersect. 2) If any two CVISs are adjacent, then both must have a definite interval and they must not be determinately adjacent. $\mathcal{NV}$ refers to the set of all NVISs. A CVIS can be implicitly converted to an NVIS with the function *nvis*: $\mathcal{CV} \to \mathcal{NV}$, defined as $\text{nvis}(C) = \{C\}$.

Definition 14. $\mathcal{V} = \mathcal{CV} \cup \mathcal{NV}$ is the set of all VISs.

Operators on Valid Interval Stamps There are a number of operators on VISs which correspond to the similarly named ones on Boolean expressions and sets. Specifically, we will define conjunction, intersection, union, and difference of VISs below. To avoid confusion, we will annotate the usual operators to emphasize that they carry different semantics than the familiar ones. For example, we use $\overset{v}{\cup}$ for the union of VISs. When operands are known to be convex (non-convex) VISs, we will use $\overset{cv}{\cup}$ ($\overset{nv}{\cup}$). When the familiar semantics from logic or set theory are sufficient, we will use the unannotated operators.

Conjunction There are times when a single interval constraint may not adequately express the knowledge one has about a fact's valid time. For that we must conjoin multiple constraints. We will do this by way of the VIS conjunction operator[1]: $\overset{v}{\wedge}$. The effect of $\overset{v}{\wedge}$ is to produce a determinate region which includes the determinate region of both operands and an indeterminate region which includes only points in the indeterminate region of both operands. The operator uses the knowledge expressed by two VISs in order to increase the accuracy to which the valid time of a fact is known.

In order to compute the resulting VIS, V_r, from the conjunction of two existing CVISs, V_1 and V_2, we must first ensure that the conjunction is satisfiable. For example, there are no dates which satisfy the condition "contains Jan-98 and during Mar-98". On the other hand, "contains Jan-98 and after Nov-97" can be satisfied. Each operand restricts the range of the other.

Definition 15. Two CVISs, V_1 and V_2, are *conjunction compatible*, denoted $V_1 \wedge_{\text{comp}} V_2$, if 1) V_1 intersects V_2, 2) $V_2.D \neq \emptyset \Rightarrow (\text{lower}(V_1) <= V_2.D_s \wedge V_2.D_e <= \text{upper}(V_1))$, and 3) $V_1.D \neq \emptyset \Rightarrow (\text{lower}(V_2) <= V_1.D_s \wedge V_1.D_e <= \text{upper}(V_2))$. We extend this definition to NVISs by saying that two NVISs are *conjunction compatible* if $\forall V_{1_i} \in V_1 \exists V_{2_j} \in V_2$ such that $V_{1_i} \wedge_{\text{comp}} V_{2_j}$ and $\forall V_{2_j} \in V_2 \exists V_{1_i} \in V_1$ such that $V_{2_j} \wedge_{\text{comp}} V_{1_i}$.

Conjunction compatibility ensures that the indefinite region of each interval encloses the definite region of the other. Otherwise, there would be a point which is in the definite region of one operand but not in the other operand at all. That is the condition which results from inconsistent interval constraints.

Definition 16 ($\overset{v}{\wedge}$). If V_1 and V_2 are VISs such that $V_1 \wedge_{\text{comp}} V_2$ we define their conjunction, denoted by $V_1 \overset{v}{\wedge} V_2$, as the VIS V_r such that $V_r.D = \{p | p \in V_1.D \vee p \in V_2.D\}$ and $V_r.I = \{p | p \in V_1.I \wedge p \in V_2.I\}$. If $\neg(V_1 \wedge_{\text{comp}} V_2)$ then $V_1 \overset{v}{\wedge} V_2 = \emptyset$.

Because the order of the interval constraints in a valid time specification should not matter, it is important that the order of VISs with respect to $\overset{v}{\wedge}$ not matter. Hence, this theorem, which is straightforward to show.

Theorem 1. $(\mathcal{V}, \overset{v}{\wedge})$ *forms a commutative monoid with identity* $V_{I_{\overset{v}{\wedge}}} = \langle -\infty, \texttt{nil}, \texttt{nil}, \infty \rangle$.

Intersection The intersection of two CVISs is defined similarly to conjunction. The precondition is not as restrictive. It is simply necessary that the intervals intersect by definition 11. On the other hand, the result of intersection is more restrictive than that of conjunction. Specifically, the determinate region produced by conjunction includes the determinate regions of both operands. If a point is determinate in only one of the operands, it is determinate in the result. For intersection, the determinate region includes only those points determinately in *both* operands. If a point is determinately in one operand but indeterminately in the other, the intersection contains that point indeterminately.

Definition 17 ($\overset{v}{\cap}$). We define the intersection of two VISs, V_1 and V_2, denoted by $V_1 \overset{v}{\cap} V_2$, as the VIS V_r such that $V_r.D = \{p | p \in V_1.D \wedge p \in V_2.D\}$ and $V_r.I = \{p | p \in V_1 \wedge p \in V_2 \wedge (p \in V_1.I \vee p \in V_2.I)\}$.

As with $\overset{v}{\wedge}$, the following is straightforward to prove.

Theorem 2. $(\mathcal{V}, \overset{v}{\cap})$ *forms a commutative monoid with identity* $V_{I_{\overset{v}{\cap}}} = \langle \texttt{nil}, -\infty, \infty, \texttt{nil} \rangle$

Union When an insert operation is performed for a fact whose non-temporal attributes are the same as an existing fact one of two things must happen. Either the operation is treated as a new insert, resulting in a pair of facts which differ only in their valid interval stamps; or the VIS of the existing fact is updated to include the valid time specified for the insert. We provide the union operator to support the latter semantics.

Definition 18 ($\overset{v}{\cup}$). We define the union of two VISs, V_1 and V_2, denoted by $V_1 \overset{v}{\cup} V_2$, as the VIS V_r such that $V_r.D = \{p | p \in V_1.D \vee p \in V_2.D\}$ and $V_r.I = \{p | p \notin V_r.D \wedge (p \in V_1.I \vee p \in V_2.I)\}$.

Again, the following is straightforward.

Theorem 3. $(\mathcal{V}, \overset{v}{\cup})$ *forms a commutative monoid with identity* $V_{I_{\overset{v}{\cup}}} = \langle nil, nil, nil, nil \rangle$.

Difference When performing a deletion or update operation where the valid time specified for the operation is only a

---
[1] The term *conjunction* refers to the operation on interval constraints which $\overset{v}{\wedge}$ supports. It might be more appropriate to think of the effect on a VIS as *strengthens*.

portion of the valid time for the affected facts, we will need to produce the difference of two valid interval stamps. In general, such a difference results in a non-convex interval.

Definition 19 ($\overset{v}{-}$). We define the difference of two VISs, V_1 and V_2, denoted by $V_1 \overset{v}{-} V_2$ as the VIS V_r such that $V_r.D = \{p | p \in V_1.D \land p \notin V_2\}$ and $V_r.I = \{p | (p \in V_1.D \land p \in V_2.I) \lor (p \in V_1.I \land p \notin V_2.D)\}$.

Note that $\overset{v}{-}$ is neither commutative nor associative. The identity element, denoted by $V_{I\overset{v}{-}}$, is the empty interval.

Complexity of VIS Operators The basic operators on CVISs: $\land_{comp}$, $\overset{cv}{\land}$, $\overset{cv}{\cap}$, $\overset{cv}{\cup}$, and $\overset{cv}{-}$, are all constant time. This should be clear from their definitions, which depend solely on the values of the end points. For an NVIS V, we will use $|V|$ to indicate the number of CVISs $V_i \in V$. Based on an analysis of the algorithms developed to implement the operators, we have the results in table 1 for NVISs. Those algorithms and proofs of these results are omitted due to lack of space.

Operator	Complexity
$\land_{comp}$	$O(|V_1||V_2|)$
$\overset{nv}{\land}$	$O(|V_1||V_2|)$
$\overset{nv}{\cap}$	$O(|V_1||V_2|)$
$\overset{nv}{\cup}$	$O((|V_1||V_2|)^2)$
$\overset{nv}{-}$	$O(|V_2|^4|V_1|)$

Table 1: Complexity of Operators over NVISs

Indeterminate Interval Relationships

Now we turn to comparing the indeterminate intervals by examining how the thirteen interval relationships used in Allen's interval algebra (Allen 1983) can be extended to the indeterminate intervals represented by CVISs. We will need to define both definite and potential satisfaction of the relationships when applied to CVISs, resulting in a total of 26 interval relationships. Two principles are used in reaching these definitions.

Principle 1. For V_1 definitely $\mathcal{R}$ V_2 to hold, where $\mathcal{R}$ is an interval relationship, we must have:

$$\not\exists V_1', V_2' \text{ such that } V_1 \land_{comp} V_1' \land V_2 \land_{comp} V_2' \land$$
$$\neg((V_1 \overset{cv}{\land} V_1').D \mathcal{R} (V_2 \overset{cv}{\land} V_2').D)$$

If this principle is met, it is not possible to conjoin any compatible interval constraint to either V_1 or V_2 such that $\mathcal{R}$ will not be satisfied.

Principle 2. For V_1 potentially $\mathcal{R}$ V_2 to hold, where $\mathcal{R}$ is an interval relationship, we must have:

$$\exists V_1', V_2' \text{ such that } V_1 \land_{comp} V_1' \land V_2 \land_{comp} V_2' \land$$
$$(V_1 \overset{cv}{\land} V_1') \text{ definitely } \mathcal{R} (V_2 \overset{cv}{\land} V_2')$$

This ensures that it is possible, via the conjunction of additional interval constraints with V_1 and V_2, to arrive at a pair of intervals which definitely satisfy $\mathcal{R}$.

Definition 20. For two CVISs, V_1 and V_2, we say:

- V_1 definitely equals V_2 if
$$V_1.I = \emptyset \land V_2.I = \emptyset \land V_1.D = V_2.D$$

- V_1 potentially equals V_2 if
$$\text{lower}(V_1) \leq \text{maxlo}(V_2) \land \text{lower}(V_2) \leq \text{maxlo}(V_1) \land$$
$$\text{minup}(V_2) \leq \text{upper}(V_1) \land \text{minup}(V_1) \leq \text{upper}(V_2)$$

- V_1 definitely before V_2 if
$$\text{upper}(V_1) < \text{lower}(V_2)$$

- V_1 potentially before V_2 if
$$\text{minup}(V_1) < \text{maxlo}(V_2)$$

- V_1 definitely meets V_2 if
$$V_1.I_e = \text{nil} \land V_2.I_s = \text{nil} \land V_1.D_e = V_2.D_s \land$$
$$V_1.D_s < V_2.D_s \land V_1.D_e < V_2.D_e$$

- V_1 potentially meets V_2 if
$$\text{lower}(V_1) < \text{maxlo}(V_2) \land \text{minup}(V_1) < \text{upper}(V_2) \land$$
$$\text{lower}(V_2) \leq \text{upper}(V_1) \land \text{minup}(V_1) \leq \text{maxlo}(V_2)$$

- V_1 definitely overlaps V_2 if
$$V_1.D_s < \text{lower}(V_2) \land \text{upper}(V_1) < V_2.D_e \land$$
$$V_2.D_s < V_1.D_e$$

- V_1 potentially overlaps V_2 if
$$\text{lower}(V_1) < \text{maxlo}(V_2) \land \text{minup}(V_1) < \text{upper}(V_2) \land$$
$$\text{lower}(V_2) < \text{upper}(V_1) \land$$
$$\text{lower}(V_1) < \text{previous}(\text{upper}(V_1)) \land$$
$$\text{lower}(V_2) < \text{previous}(\text{upper}(V_2))$$

- V_1 definitely during V_2 if
$$V_2.D_s < \text{lower}(V_1) \land \text{upper}(V_1) < V_2.D_e$$

- V_1 potentially during V_2 if
$$\text{lower}(V_2) < \text{maxlo}(V_1) \land \text{minup}(V_1) < \text{upper}(V_2) \land$$
$$\text{lower}(V_2) < \text{previous}(\text{upper}(V_2))$$

- V_1 definitely starts V_2 if
$$V_1.I_s = \text{nil} \land V_2.I_s = \text{nil} \land V_1.D_s = V_2.D_s \land$$
$$\text{upper}(V_1) < \text{minup}(V_2)$$

- V_1 potentially starts V_2 if
$$\text{lower}(V_1) \leq \text{maxlo}(V_2) \land \text{lower}(V_2) \leq \text{maxlo}(V_1) \land$$
$$\text{minup}(V_1) < \text{upper}(V_2)$$

- V_1 definitely finishes V_2 if
$$V_1.I_e = \text{nil} \land V_2.I_e = \text{nil} \land V_1.D_e = V_2.D_e \land$$
$$V_2.D_s < \text{lower}(V_1)$$

- V_1 potentially finishes V_2 if

  $\text{minup}(V_2) \leq \text{upper}(V_1) \wedge \text{minup}(V_1) \leq \text{upper}(V_2) \wedge \text{lower}(V_2) < \text{maxlo}(V_1)$

We can make some interesting observations about the compatibility of the various interval relationships. First, we note that the interval relationships between determinate intervals are mutually exclusive.

Lemma 1. *Let I_1, I_2 be intervals and $\mathcal{R}_1$, $\mathcal{R}_2$ be determinate interval relationships. Then, $I_1 \mathcal{R}_1 I_2 \Rightarrow \neg(I_1 \mathcal{R}_2 I_2)$.*

Proof. This follows directly from the definitions of the relationships. □

This observation extends to the definite relationships between valid interval stamps.

Theorem 4. *Let V_1 and V_2 be valid interval stamps and let $\mathcal{R}_1$ and $\mathcal{R}_2$ be determinate interval relationships, $\mathcal{R}_1 \neq \mathcal{R}_2$. Then, V_1 definitely $\mathcal{R}_1 V_2 \Rightarrow \neg(V_1$ definitely $\mathcal{R}_2 V_2)$.*

Proof. Assume that V_1 definitely $\mathcal{R}_1 V_2$. Then $\exists V_1', V_2'$ such that $(V_1 \stackrel{cv}{\wedge} V_1').D \, \mathcal{R}_1 \, (V_2 \stackrel{cv}{\wedge} V_2').D$. By lemma 1, we know that $\neg((V_1 \stackrel{cv}{\wedge} V_1').D \, \mathcal{R}_2 \, (V_2 \stackrel{cv}{\wedge} V_2').D)$. Principle 1 then requires that $\neg(V_1$ definitely $\mathcal{R}_2 V_2)$. □

We cannot make the same conclusion regarding potential relationships, however.

Theorem 5. *Let V_1 and V_2 be valid interval stamps and let $\mathcal{R}_1$ and $\mathcal{R}_2$ be determinate interval relationships, $\mathcal{R}_1 \neq \mathcal{R}_2$. Then, V_1 potentially $\mathcal{R}_1 V_2 \not\Rightarrow \neg(V_1$ potentially $\mathcal{R}_2 V_2)$.*

Proof. By example: Let p_1 and p_2 be points, $p_1 < p_2$. Let $V_1 = V_2 = \langle p_1, \texttt{nil}, \texttt{nil}, p_2 \rangle$. Choose $V_1' = V_2' = \langle \texttt{nil}, p_1, p_2, \texttt{nil} \rangle$. Then, $(V_1 \stackrel{cv}{\wedge} V_1').D$ equals $(V_2 \stackrel{cv}{\wedge} V_2').D$. By principle 2 V_1 potentially equals V_2. Now, choose $V_1'' = \langle \texttt{nil}, p_1, p_1, \texttt{nil} \rangle$ and $V_2'' = \langle \texttt{nil}, p_2, p_2, \texttt{nil} \rangle$. So, $(V_1 \stackrel{cv}{\wedge} V_1'').D$ before $(V_2 \stackrel{cv}{\wedge} V_2'').D$ and V_1 potentially before V_2. □

Finally, we can see that, as expected, a definite relationship implies a potential one.

Theorem 6. *Let V_1 and V_2 be valid interval stamps and let $\mathcal{R}$ be a determinate interval relationship. Then, V_1 definitely $\mathcal{R} V_2 \Rightarrow V_1$ potentially $\mathcal{R} V_2$.*

Proof. Assume V_1 definitely $\mathcal{R} V_2$. Choose $V_1' = V_2' = V_{I^v}$. Then $V_1 \stackrel{cv}{\wedge} V_1' = V_1$ and $V_2 \stackrel{cv}{\wedge} V_2' = V_2$, so $(V_1 \stackrel{cv}{\wedge} V_1')$ definitely $\mathcal{R} (V_2 \stackrel{cv}{\wedge} V_2')$. This meets the conditions for principle 2. Therefore, V_1 potentially $\mathcal{R} V_2$. □

Conclusions and Future Work

We have shown a representation for both convex and nonconvex indeterminate intervals and provided a useful set of operators on those intervals. Further, we have shown that it is possible to extend the relationships used in Allen's interval algebra (Allen 1983) to the indeterminate intervals represented by convex valid interval stamps. These extensions are interesting in their own right because of the large amount of prior work in both the artificial intelligence and database fields that is based on the interval algebra and its variants. One specific application area is in allowing temporal integrity constraints to take into account indeterminism.

An obvious extension of this current work would be to reformulate Allen's constraint propagation algorithms to use indeterminate intervals and investigate resulting differences in complexity and reasoning power. It would also be interesting to reformulate the potential and definite relationships presented here using intervals treated as primitive constructs instead of based on end points. For determinate intervals, all thirteen relationships can be defined in terms of either meets or before. This would provide the ability to use dense or continuous timelines as well as discrete.

Acknowledgements The authors would like to thank Dr. Manolis Koubarakis and the anonymous referees for their comments.

References

Allen, J. F. 1983. Maintaining knowledge about temporal intervals. *Communications of the ACM* 26(11):832–843.

Anger, F. D.; Mata-Toledo, R. A.; Morris, R. A.; and Rodriguez, R. V. 1988. A relational knowledge base with temporal reasoning. In *Proceedings of the First Florida Artificial Intelligence Research Symposium*, 147–151.

Benthem, J. v. 1991. *The Logic of Time*. Dordrecht, Holland: Kluwer Academic Publishers.

Bouzid, M., and Mouaddib, A.-I. 1998. Uncertain temporal reasoning for the distributed transportation scheduling problem. In *Proceedings : Fifth International Workshop on Temporal Representation and Reasoning*, 21–28.

Cowley, W. 1999. Temporal integrity constraints with temporal indeterminacy. Master's thesis, University of South Florida.

Dyreson, C. E., and Snodgrass, R. T. 1998. Supporting valid-time indeterminacy. *Transactions on Database Systems* 23(1):1–57.

Gadia, S. K.; Nair, S. S.; and Poon, Y.-C. 1992. Incomplete information in relational temporal databases. In *Proceedings of the 18th International Conference on Very Large Data Bases*, 395–406.

Koubarakis, M. 1994. Database models for infinite and indefinite temporal information. *Information Systems* 19(2):141–174.

Koubarakis, M. 1997. The complexity of query evaluation in indefinite temporal constraint databases. *Theoretical Computer Science* 171(1–2):25–60.

Plexousakis, D. 1995. Compilation and simplification of temporal integrity constraints. In *Rules in Database Systems: Second International Workshop*, 260–274.

cc-Golog: Towards More Realistic Logic-Based Robot Controllers

Henrik Grosskreutz and Gerhard Lakemeyer

Department of Computer Science V
Aachen University of Technology
52056 Aachen, Germany
{grosskreutz,gerhard}@cs.rwth-aachen.de

Abstract

High-level robot controllers in realistic domains typically deal with processes which operate concurrently, change the world continuously, and where the execution of actions is event-driven as in "charge the batteries as soon as the voltage level is low". While non-logic-based robot control languages are well suited to express such scenarios, they fare poorly when it comes to projecting, in a conspicuous way, how the world evolves when actions are executed. On the other hand, a logic-based control language like ConGolog, based on the situation calculus, is well-suited for the latter. However, it has problems expressing event-driven behavior. In this paper, we show how these problems can be overcome by first extending the situation calculus to support continuous change and event-driven behavior and then presenting cc-Golog, a variant of ConGolog which is based on the extended situation calculus. One benefit of cc-Golog is that it narrows the gap in expressiveness compared to non-logic-based control languages while preserving a semantically well-founded projection mechanism.

Introduction

High-level robot controllers typically specify processes which operate concurrently and change the world in a continuous fashion over time. Several special programming languages such as RPL (McDermott 1992),[1] RAP (Firby 1987), or COLBERT (Konolige 1997) have been developed for this purpose. As an example, consider the following RPL-program:

> WITH-POLICY WHENEVER Batt-Level ≤ 46
>   CHARGE-BATTERIES
> WITH-POLICY WHENEVER NEAR-DOOR(RmA-118)
>   SAY("hello")
> DELIVER-MAIL

Figure 1: Office delivery plan

Roughly, the robot's main task is to deliver mail, which we merely indicate by a call to the procedure DELIVER-MAIL. While executing this procedure, the robot concurrently also does the following, with an increasing level of priority: whenever it passes the door to Room A-118 it says "hello" and, should the battery level drop dangerously low, it recharges its batteries interrupting whatever else it is doing at this moment.

Even this simple program exhibits important features of high-level robot controllers: (1) The timing of actions is largely *event-driven*, that is, rather than explicitly stating when an action occurs, the execution time depends on certain conditions becoming true such as reaching a certain door. Most robot control languages realize this feature using the special construct *waitFor*(ϕ), which suspends activity until ϕ becomes true.[2] (2) Actions are executed *as soon as possible*. For example, the batteries are charged immediately after a low voltage level is determined. (3) Conditions such as the voltage level are best thought of as changing *continuously* over time. (4) Parts of programs which execute concurrently and with high priority must be *non-blocking*. For example, while waiting for a low battery level, mail delivery should continue. On the other hand, the actual charging of the battery should block all other activity.

Given the inherent complexity of concurrent robot programs, answers to questions like whether a program is executable and whether it will satisfy the intended goals are not easy to come by, yet important to both the designer during program development and the robot who may want to choose among different courses of action. A principled approach to answering such questions is to *project* how the world evolves when actions are performed, a method which also lies at the heart of planning.

In the case of RPL, a projection mechanism called XFRM exists (McDermott 1992; 1994), but it has problems.[3] Perhaps the most serious deficiency of XFRM is that projections rely on using RPL's execution mechanism, which lacks a formal semantics and which makes predictions implementation dependent. Preferably one would like a language which is as powerful as RPL yet allows for projections based on a perspicuous, declarative semantics.

The recently proposed language ConGolog (de Giacomo, Lesperance, & Levesque 1997) fulfills some of these desiderata as it offers many of the features of RPL such as

---

Copyright © 2000, American Association for Artificial Intelligence (www.aaai.org). All rights reserved.

[1] RPL has recently been used successfully to control the behavior of a mobile robot deployed in a realistic environment for an extended period of time (Thrun *et al.* 1999).

[2] In the example, *waitFor* is hidden within the whenever-construct.

[3] As far as we know, other non-logic-based robot control languages like RAP or COLBERT do not even consider projection.

concurrency, priorities etc. and, at the same time, supports rigorous projections of plans[4] because it is entirely based on the situation calculus (McCarthy 1963).

It turns out, however, that despite many similarities, ConGolog in its current form is not suitable to represent robot controllers such as the example above. The main problem is that the existing temporal extensions of the situation calculus such as (Pinto 1997; Reiter 1996) require that the execution time of an action is supplied explicitly, which seems incompatible with event-driven specifications. To solve this problem we proceed in two steps. First we present a new extension of the situation calculus which, besides dealing with continuous change, allows us to model actions which are event-driven by including *waitFor* as a special action in the logic. We then turn to a new variant of ConGolog called cc-Golog, which is based on the extended situation calculus. We study issues arising from the interaction of *waitFor*-actions and concurrency and show how the example-program can be specified quite naturally in cc-Golog with the additional benefit of supporting projections firmly grounded in logic.

The rest of the paper is organized as follows. In the next section, we briefly review the basic situation calculus. Then we show how to extend it to include continuous change and time. After a very brief summary of ConGolog, we present cc-Golog, which takes into account the extended situation calculus. This is followed by a note on experimental results and conclusions.

The Situation Calculus

One increasingly popular language for representing and reasoning about the preconditions and effects of actions is the situation calculus (McCarthy 1963). We will not go over the language in detail except to note the following features: all terms in the language are one of three sorts, ordinary objects, actions or situations; there is a special constant S_0 used to denote the *initial situation*, namely that situation in which no actions have yet occurred; there is a distinguished binary function symbol *do* where $do(a, s)$ denotes the successor situation to s resulting from performing the action a; relations whose truth values vary from situation to situation are called relational *fluents*, and are denoted by predicate symbols taking a situation term as their last argument; similarly, functions varying across situations are called functional fluents and are denoted analogously; finally, there is a special predicate $Poss(a, s)$ used to state that action a is executable in situation s.

Within this language, we can formulate theories which describe how the world changes as the result of the available actions. One possibility is a *basic action theory* of the following form (Levesque, Pirri, & Reiter 1998):

- Axioms describing the initial situation, S_0.
- Action precondition axioms, one for each primitive action a, characterizing $Poss(a, s)$.
- Successor state axioms, one for each fluent F, stating under what conditions $F(\vec{x}, do(a, s))$ holds as a function of

what holds in situation s. These take the place of the so-called effect axioms, but also provide a solution to the frame problem (Levesque, Pirri, & Reiter 1998).
- Domain closure and unique name axioms for the actions.
- Foundational, domain independent axioms (Levesque, Pirri, & Reiter 1998).

1. $\forall P. P(S_0) \wedge [\forall s \forall a.(P(s) \supset P(do(a, s)))] \supset \forall s P(s)$;
2. $do(a, s) = do(a', s') \supset a = a' \wedge s = s'$;[5]
3. $\neg(s \sqsubset S_0)$;
4. $s \sqsubset do(a, s') \equiv s \sqsubseteq s'$, where $s \sqsubseteq s'$ stands for $(s \sqsubset s') \vee (s = s')$.
5. $s \prec s' \equiv s \sqsubset s' \wedge \forall a, s^*.s \sqsubset do(a, s^*) \sqsubseteq s' \supset Poss(a, s^*)$

The first is a second-order induction axiom ensuring that the only situations are those obtained from applying *do* to S_0. The second is a unique names axiom for situations. $\sqsubset$ defines an ordering relation over situations. Intuitively, $s \sqsubset s'$ holds if s' can be obtained from s by performing a finite number of actions. Finally, $s \prec s'$ holds when there is a *legal* sequence of actions leading from s to s', where legal means that each action is possible.

Continuous Change and Time

Actions in the situation calculus cause discrete changes and, in its basic form, there is no notion of time. In robotics applications, however, we are faced with processes such as navigation which cause properties like the robot's location and orientation to change continuously over time. In order to model such processes in the situation calculus in a natural way, we add continuous change and time directly to its ontology.

As demonstrated by Pinto and Reiter (Pinto 1997; Reiter 1996), adding time is a simple matter. We add a new sort *real* ranging over the real numbers and, for mnemonic reasons, another sort *time* ranging over the reals as well.[6] In order to connect situations and time, we add a special unary functional fluent *start* to the language with the understanding that $start(s)$ denotes the time when situation s begins. We will see later how *start* obtains its values and, in particular, how the passage of time is modeled.

A fundamental assumption of the situation calculus is that fluents have a fixed value at every given situation. In order to see that this assumption still allows us to model continuous change, let us consider the example of a mobile robot moving along a straight line in a 1-dimensional world, that is, the robot's location at any given time is simply a real number. There are two types of actions the robot can perform, $startGo(v)$, which initiates moving the robot with speed v, and *endGo* which stops the movement of the robot. Let us denote the robot's location by the fluent *robotLoc*. What should the value of *robotLoc* be after executing $startGo(v)$ in situation s? Certainly it cannot be a fixed real value, since the position should change over time as long as the robot moves. In fact, the location of the robot at any time after $startGo(v)$ (and before the robot changes its velocity) can be

---

[4]In this paper we will use the terms program and plan interchangeably, following McDermott (McDermott 1992) who takes plans to be programs whose execution can be reasoned about by the agent who executes the program.

[5]We use the convention that all free variables are implicitly universally quantified.

[6]For simplicity, the reals are not axiomatized and we assume their standard interpretations together with the usual operations and ordering relations.

characterized (in a somewhat idealized fashion) by the function $x + v \times (t - t_0)$, where x is the starting position and t_0 the starting time. The solution is then to take this *function of time* to be the value of *robotLoc*. We call functional fluents whose values are continuous functions *continuous fluents*.

The idea of continuous fluents, which are often called *parameters*, is not new. Sandewall (Sandewall 1989) proposed it when integrating the differential equations into logic, Galton (Galton 1990) investigated similar issues within a temporal logic, and Shanahan considers continuous change in the event calculus (Shanahan 1990). Finally, Miller and Pinto (Miller 1996; Pinto 1997) formulate continuous change in the situation calculus. Here we essentially follow Pinto, in a somewhat simplified form.

We begin by introducing a new sort t-function, whose elements are meant to be functions of time. We assume that there are only finitely many function symbols of type t-function and we require *domain closure and unique names axioms* for them, just as in the case of primitive actions. For our robot example, it suffices to consider two kinds of t-functions: constant functions, denoted by $constant(x)$ and the special linear functions introduced above, which we denote as $linear(x, v, t_0)$.

Next we need to say what values these functions have at any particular time t. We do this with the help of a new binary function *val*. In the example, we would add the following axioms:
$val(constant(x), t) = x$;
$val(linear(x, v, t_0), t) = x + v \times (t - t_0)$.

Let us now turn to the issue of modeling the passage of time during a course of actions. As indicated in the introduction, motivated by the treatment of time in robot control languages like RPL, RAP, or COLBERT, we introduce a new type of primitive action $waitFor(\phi)$. The intuition is as follows. Normally, every action happens immediately, that is, the starting time of the situation after doing a in s is the same as the starting time of s. The only exception is $waitFor(\phi)$: whenever this action occurs, the starting time of the resulting situation is advanced to the earliest time in the future when ϕ becomes true. Note that this has the effect that actions always happen as soon as possible. One may object that requiring that two actions other than *waitFor* must happen at the same time is unrealistic. However, in robotics applications, actions often involve little more than sending messages in order to initiate or terminate processes so that the actual duration of such actions is negligible. Moreover, if two actions cannot happen at the same time, they can always be separated explicitly using *waitFor*.

For the purposes of this paper, we restrict the argument of *waitFor* to what we call a t-form, which is a Boolean combination of closed atomic formulas of the form $(F\ op\ r)$, where F is a continuous fluent with the situation argument suppressed, $op \in \{<, =\}$,[7] and r is a term of type real (not mentioning *val*). An example is $\phi = (robotLoc \geq 1000)$. To evaluate a t-form at a situation s and time t, we write $\phi[s, t]$ which results in a formula which is like ϕ except that every continuous fluent F is replaced by $val(F(s), t)$. For instance, $(robotLoc \geq 1000)[s, t]$ becomes $(val(robotLoc(s), t) \geq 1000)$. For reasons of space we completely gloss over the details of reifying t-forms within the

[7]We freely use $\leq$, $\geq$, and $>$ as well.

language[8] except to note that we introduce t-forms as a new sort and that $\phi[s, t]$ is short for $Holds(\phi, s, t)$, where *Holds* is appropriately axiomatized.

To see how actions are forced to happen as soon as possible, let $ltp(\phi, s, t)$ be an abbreviation for the formula

$\phi[s, t] \wedge t \geq start(s) \wedge \forall t'.start(s) \leq t' < t \supset \neg \phi[s, t']$,

that is, t in $ltp(\phi, s, t)$ is the least time point after the start of s where ϕ becomes true. Then we require that a *waitFor*-action is possible iff the condition has a least time point. In practice, this means that it is up to the user to ensure that ϕ has a least time point.

$Poss(waitFor(\phi), s) \equiv \exists t.ltp(\phi, s, t)$.

It is not hard to show that, if $\exists t.ltp(\phi, s, t)$ is satisfied, then t is unique.

We remark that Reiter (1996) introduced a related concept of *least natural time point*.[9] Note, however, that Reiter only considers natural actions (like the bouncing of a ball) which happen whenever they are (physically) *possible*. In contrast, we are concerned with actions which are under the control of the agent including deliberately waiting for an event to occur or to ignore it.

Finally, we need to characterize how the fluent *start* changes its value when an action occurs. The following successor state axiom for *start* captures the intuition that the starting time of a situation changes only as a result of a $waitFor(\phi)$, in which case it advances to the earliest time in the future when ϕ holds.

$Poss(a, s) \supset [start(do(a, s)) = t \equiv$
$\exists \phi.a = waitFor(\phi) \wedge ltp(\phi, s, t) \vee$
$[\forall \phi.a \neq waitFor(\phi) \wedge t = start(s)]]$.

Let AX be the set of foundational axioms of the previous section together with the domain closure and unique names axioms for t-functions, the axioms required for t-form's, the precondition axiom for *waitFor*, and the successor state axiom for *start*. Then the following formulas are logical consequences of AX.

Proposition 1:

1. The starting time of legal action sequences is monotonically nondecreasing:
   $\forall s, s'. s \prec s' \supset start(s) \leq start(s')$.
2. Actions happen as soon as possible:
   $[\forall a, s.start(do(a, s)) = start(s)] \vee [\exists \phi.a = waitFor(\phi) \wedge ltp(\phi, s, start(do(a, s)))]$

To illustrate the approach, let us go back to the robot example. First, we can formulate a successor state axiom for *robotLoc*:

$Poss(a, s) \supset [robotLoc(do(a, s)) = y \equiv$
$\exists t_0, v, x. x = val(robotLoc(s), t_0) \wedge t_0 = start(s) \wedge$
$([a = startGo(v) \wedge y = linear(x, v, t_0)]$
$\vee [a = endGo \wedge y = constant(x)] \vee [y = robotLoc(s) \wedge$
$\neg(\exists v.a = startGo(v) \vee a = endGo)])]$

In other words, when an action is performed *robotLoc* is assigned either the function $linear(x, v, t_0)$, if the robot starts moving with velocity v and x is the location of the robot at situation s, or it is assigned $constant(x)$ if the

[8]See, for example, (Giacomo, Lesperance, & Levesque 1999) for details how this can be done.
[9]Similar ideas occur in the context of delaying processes in real-time programming languages like Ada (Burns & Wellings 1991).

robot stops, or it remains the same as in s. Note that $val(robotLoc(s), t_0)$ is well-defined since every t-function has a name (*constant* or *linear*) with corresponding axioms for *val* as given above.

Let Σ be AX together with the axioms for *val*, the successor state axiom for *robotLoc*, precondition axioms stating that *startGo* and *endGo* are always possible, and the fact $(robotLoc(S_0) = constant(0))$, that is, the robot initially rests at position 0. Let us assume the robot starts moving at speed 50 (cm/s) and then waits until it reaches location 1000 (cm), at which point it stops. The resulting situation is $s_1 = do(endGo, do(waitFor(robotLoc = 1000), do(startGo(50), S_0)))$. Then
$\Sigma \models start(s_1) = 20 \land robotLoc(s_1) = constant(1000)$.
In other words, the robot moves for 20 seconds and stops at location 1000, as one would expect.

In summary, to model continuous change and time in the situation calculus, we have added four new sorts: real, time, t-function (functions of time), and t-form (temporal formulas). In addition, we introduced a special function *val* to evaluate t-functions, a new kind of primitive action *waitFor* together with a domain-independent precondition axiom, and a new fluent *start* (the starting time of a situation) together with a successor state axiom.

ConGolog

ConGolog (Giacomo, Lesperance, & Levesque 1999), an extension of GOLOG (Levesque *et al.* 1997), is a formalism for specifying complex actions and how these are mapped to sequences of atomic actions assuming a description of the initial state of the world, action precondition axioms and successor state axioms for each fluent. Complex actions are defined using control structures familiar from conventional programming language such as sequence, while-loops and recursive procedures. In addition, parallel actions are introduced with a conventional interleaving semantics. Here we confine ourselves to the deterministic fragment of ConGolog. (While nondeterministic actions raise interesting issues, we ignore them for reasons of space. Also note that nondeterminism plays little if any role in languages like RPL.)

α	primitive action
$\phi?$	test action[10]
$seq(\sigma_1, \sigma_2)$	sequence
$if(\phi, \sigma_1, \sigma_2)$	conditional
$while(\phi, \sigma)$	loop
$par(\sigma_1, \sigma_2)$	concurrent execution
$prio(\sigma_1, \sigma_2)$	prioritized execution
proc $\beta(x)\sigma$	procedure definition

The semantics of ConGolog is defined using the so-called transition semantics, which defines single steps of computation. There is a relation, denoted by the predicate $Trans(\sigma, s, \delta, s')$, that associates with a given program σ and situation s a new situation s' that results from executing a primitive action in s, and a new program δ that represents what remains of σ after having performed that action. Furthermore, we need to define which configurations (σ, s) are

---
[10]Here, ϕ stands for a situation calculus formula with all situation arguments suppressed. $\phi[s]$ will denote the formula obtained by restoring situation variable s to all fluents appearing in ϕ.

final, meaning that the computation can be considered completed when a final configuration is reached. This is denoted by the predicate $Final(\sigma, s)$.[11]

For space reasons, we only list a few of the axioms for *Final* and *Trans*. Note that the semantics is defined for the *non-temporal* situation calculus. Adapting the semantics to the temporal situation calculus of the previous section will be the subject of the next section.

$Final(\alpha, s) \equiv false$, where α is a primitive action
$Final(nil, s) \equiv true$, where *nil* is the empty program
$Final(\phi?, s) \equiv false$
$Final(if(\phi, \sigma_1, \sigma_2), s) \equiv$
    $\phi[s] \land Final(\sigma_1, s) \lor \neg\phi[s] \land Final(\sigma_2, s)$
$Final(par(\sigma_1, \sigma_2), s) \equiv Final(\sigma_1, s) \land Final(\sigma_2, s)$
$Final(prio(\sigma_1, \sigma_2), s) \equiv Final(\sigma_1, s) \land Final(\sigma_2, s)$

$Trans(\alpha, s, \delta, s') \equiv$
    $Poss(\alpha, s) \land \delta = nil \land s' = do(\alpha, s)$
$Trans(nil, s, \delta, s') \equiv false$
$Trans(\phi?, s, \delta, s') \equiv \phi[s] \land \delta = nil \land s' = s$
$Trans(seq(\sigma_1, \sigma_2), s, \delta, s') \equiv$
    $Final(\sigma_1, s) \land Trans(\sigma_2, s, \delta, s') \lor$
    $\exists \delta'. Trans(\sigma_1, s, \delta', s') \land \delta = seq(\delta', \sigma_2)$
$Trans(if(\phi, \sigma_1, \sigma_2), s, \delta, s') \equiv$
    $\phi[s] \land Trans(\sigma_1, s, \delta, s') \lor$
    $\neg\phi[s] \land Trans(\sigma_2, s, \delta, s')$
$Trans(par(\sigma_1, \sigma_2), s, \delta, s') \equiv$
    $\exists \gamma. \delta = par(\gamma, \sigma_2) \land Trans(\sigma_1, s, \gamma, s') \lor$
    $\exists \gamma. \delta = par(\sigma_1, \gamma) \land Trans(\sigma_2, s, \gamma, s')$

Intuitively, a program cannot be in its final state if there is still a primitive action to be done. Similarly, a concurrent execution of two programs is in its final state if both are. As for *Trans*, let us just look at *par*: a transition of two programs working in parallel means that one action of one of the programs is performed.

A final situation s' reachable after a finite number of transitions from a starting situation is identified with the situation resulting from a possible execution trace of program σ, starting in situation s; this is captured by the predicate $Do(\sigma, s, s')$, which is defined in terms of $Trans^*$, the transitive closure of *Trans*:

$Do(\delta, s, s') \equiv \exists \delta'. Trans^*(\delta, s, \delta', s') \land Final(\delta', s')$
$Trans^*(\delta, s, \delta', s') \equiv \forall T[... \supset T(\delta, s, \delta', s')]$

where the ellipsis stands for the universal closure of the conjunction of the following formulas:

$T(\delta, s, \delta, s)$
$Trans(\delta, s, \delta'', s'') \land T(\delta'', s'', \delta', s') \supset T(\delta, s, \delta', s')$

Given a program δ, proving that δ is executable in the initial situation then amounts to proving $\Sigma \models \exists s Do(\delta, S_0, s)$, where Σ consists of the above axioms for ConGolog together with a basic action theory in the situation calculus.

cc-Golog: a Continuous, Concurrent Golog

Let us now turn to cc-Golog, which is a variant of deterministic ConGolog and which is founded on our new extension of the situation calculus.

---
[11]Again, we gloss over the issue of reifying formulas and programs in the logical language and refer to (Giacomo, Lesperance, & Levesque 1999) for details.

First, for reasons discussed below we slightly change the language by replacing the instructions *par* and *prio* by the constructs *tryAll* and *withPol*, respectively. Intuitively, $tryAll(\sigma_1, \sigma_2)$ starts executing both σ_1 and σ_2; but unlike *par*, which requires both σ_1 and σ_2 to reach a final state, the parallel execution of *tryAll* stops as soon as *one* of them reaches a final state. As for $withPol(\sigma_1, \sigma_2)$, the idea is that a low priority plan σ_2 is executed, which is interrupted whenever the program σ_1, which is called a *policy*, is able to execute. The execution of the whole *withPol* construct ends as soon as σ_2 ends. (Note that *prio* is just like *withPol* except that for *prio* to end both σ_1 and σ_2 need to have ended.)

tryAll and *withPol* are inspired by similar instructions in RPL where they have been found very useful in specifying complex concurrent behavior. In particular, *withPol* is useful to specify the execution of a plan while guarding certain constraints. As we will see later, it is quite straightforward to define *par* and *prio* using the new instructions. On the other hand, defining *tryAll* and *withPol* in terms of *par* and *prio* appears to be more complicated. Hence we decided to trade *par* and *prio* for their siblings.

Let us now turn to the semantics of cc-Golog, which means finding appropriate definitions for *Final* and *Trans*. To start with, the semantics remains exactly the same for all those constructs inherited from deterministic ConGolog. Note that this is also true for the new $waitFor(\phi)$, which is treated like any other primitive action.[12] Hence we are left to deal with *tryAll* and *withPol*.

It is straightforward to give *Final* its intended meaning, that is, *tryAll* ends if one of the two programs ends and *withPol* ends if the second program ends:

$Final(tryAll(\sigma_1, \sigma_2), s)) \equiv Final(\sigma_1, s) \vee Final(\sigma_2, s)$
$Final(withPol(\sigma_1, \sigma_2), s) \equiv Final(\sigma_2, s)$

When considering the transition of concurrent programs, care must be taken in order to avoid conflicts with the assumption that actions should happen as soon as possible, which underlies our new version of the situation calculus. To see why let us consider the following example, where we want to instruct our robot to run a backup at time 8 or 20, whichever comes first. Let us assume we have a continuous fluent *clock* representing time[13] and let *runBackup* be always possible. Given our intuitive reading of *tryAll*, we may want to use the following program:

$seq(tryAll(waitFor(clock = 8), waitFor(clock = 20)),$
$\quad runBackup)$

If we start the program at time 0 we would expect to see

[$waitFor(clock{=}8), runBackup$]

as the only execution trace, since time 8 is reached first. (Recall that *tryAll* finishes as soon as one of its arguments finishes.) However, this is not necessarily guaranteed. In fact, the obvious adaptation of ConGolog's *Trans*-definition of *par* to the case of *tryAll*[14] also yields the trace

[$waitFor(clock{=}20), runBackup$].

This is because there simply is no preference enforced between the two *waitFor*-actions. As the following definition shows, it is not hard to require that actions which can be executed earlier are always preferred, restoring the original idea that actions should happen as soon as possible.

$Trans(tryAll(\sigma_1, \sigma_2), s, \delta, s') \equiv$
$\quad \neg Final(\sigma_1, s) \wedge \neg Final(\sigma_2, s) \wedge$
$\quad \exists \delta_1. Trans(\sigma_1, s, \delta_1, s') \wedge \delta = tryAll(\delta_1, \sigma_2) \wedge$
$\quad \forall \delta_2, s_2. Trans(\sigma_2, s, \delta_2, s_2) \supset start(s') \leq start(s_2)]$
$\quad \vee \exists \delta_2. Trans(\sigma_2, s, \delta_2, s') \wedge \delta = tryAll(\sigma_1, \delta_2) \wedge$
$\quad \forall \delta_1, s_1. Trans(\sigma_1, s, \delta_1, s_1) \supset start(s') \leq start(s_1)]$

We are left with defining *Trans* for *withPol*. To see what is involved, let us consider the following example

$withPol(watchB, deliverMail)$, where

$watchB = seq(waitFor(battLevel \leq 46), chargeBatt)$.

The idea is to deliver mail and, with higher priority, watch for a low battery level, at which point the batteries are charged. In the discussion of a similar scenario written in RPL, we already pointed out that the *waitFor*-action should not block the mail delivery even though it belongs to the high priority policy. On the other hand, once the routine for charging the batteries starts, it should not be interrupted, that is, it should run in blocking mode, which should also hold for possible *waitFor*-actions it may contain such as waiting for arrival at the docking station. It turns out that it suffices to arrange in the semantics of *Trans* that occurrences of *waitFor* within a policy are considered non-blocking. As we will see below, the effect of a policy running in blocking mode is definable by other means.

Interestingly, the resulting axiom is almost identical to that of *tryAll*: the main difference is that $\leq$ is replaced by $<$ in the last line. This ensures that σ_1 takes precedence if both σ_i are about to execute an action at the same time.

$Trans(withPol(\sigma_1, \sigma_2), s, \delta, s') \equiv \neg Final(\sigma_2, s) \wedge$
$\quad \exists \delta_1. Trans(\sigma_1, s, \delta_1, s') \wedge \delta = withPol(\delta_1, \sigma_2) \wedge$
$\quad \forall \delta_2, s_2. Trans(\sigma_2, s, \delta_2, s_2) \supset start(s') \leq start(s_2)]$
$\quad \vee \exists \delta_2. Trans(\sigma_2, s, \delta_2, s') \wedge \delta = withPol(\sigma_1, \delta_2) \wedge$
$\quad \forall \delta_1, s_1. Trans(\sigma_1, s, \delta_1, s_1) \supset start(s') < start(s_1)]$

This then ends the discussion of the semantics of *Trans* in cc-Golog. $Trans^*$ and $Do(\delta, s, s')$ are defined the same way as in ConGolog.

One issue left open is to show how a policy can run in blocking mode. This can be arranged using the macro $withCtrl(\phi, \sigma)$, which stands for σ with every primitive action or test α replaced by $if(\phi, \alpha, false?)$.[15]

Intuitively $withCtrl(\phi, \sigma)$ executes σ as long as ϕ is true, but gets blocked otherwise. As the following example shows, the effect of a policy in blocking mode is obtained by having the truth value of ϕ be controlled by the policy and using the $withCtrl(\phi, \sigma)$-construct in the low priority program.

This leads us, finally, to the specification of our initial example in cc-Golog. In the following we assume a fluent *wheels*, which is initially *true*, set *false*

---

[12]The reader familiar with ConGolog may wonder whether a test action $\phi?$ is the same as $waitFor(\phi)$. This is not so. Roughly, the main difference is that tests have no effect on the world while *waitFor* advances the time.

[13]This can be modeled using a simple linear function, but we ignore the details here.

[14]Roughly, replace *par* by *tryAll* and add $\neg Final(\sigma_1, s)$ and $\neg Final(\sigma_2, s)$ as additional conjuncts in the definition's R.H.S.

[15]We remark that $if(\phi, \alpha, false?)$ can only lead to a transition if ϕ is true in the current situation at which point α is executed immediately. This is essentially due to the fact that *false?* is neither *Final* nor can it ever lead to a transition.

by *grabWhls*, and reset by the action *releaseWhls*. We also use *whenever*(ϕ, σ) as shorthand for *while*(*true, seq*(*waitFor*(ϕ), σ)).

$withPol(whenever(battLevel \leq 46,$
$\quad seq(grabWhls, chargeBatteries, releaseWhls)^{16}),$
$withPol(whenever(nearDoor\text{A-118},$
$\quad seq(say(hello), waitFor(\neg nearDoor\text{A-118}))))$
$withCtrl(wheels, deliverMail)))$

Figure 2: The introductory example as a cc-Golog plan.

In this program, the outermost policy is waiting until the battery level drops to 46. At this point, a *grabWheels* is immediately executed, which blocks the execution of the program *deliverMail*. It is only after the complete execution of *chargeBatteries* that *wheels* gets released so that *deliverMail* may resume execution (if, while driving to the battery docking station, the robot passes by Room A-118, it would still say "hello").

Note that the cc-Golog-program is in a form very close to the original RPL-program we started out with. Hence we feel that cc-Golog is a step in the right direction towards modeling more realistic domains which so far could only be dealt with in non-logic-based approaches. Moreover, with their rigorous logical foundation, it is now possible to make provable predictions about how the world evolves when executing cc-Golog-programs. (See also the next section on experimental results.)

Finally, let us briefly consider how *par* and *prio* which we dropped in favor of *tryAll* and *withPol* are definable within cc-Golog. Let us assume fluents flg_i which are initially *false* and set *true* by $setFlg_i$. Then we can achieve what amounts to $par(\sigma_1, \sigma_2)$ by $tryAll(seq(\sigma_1, setFlg1, flg2?), seq(\sigma_2, setFlg2, flg1?))$. Note that the testing of the flags at the end of each program forces that both σ_i need to finish. Similarly, *prio* can be defined as $withPol(seq(\sigma_1, setFlg), seq(\sigma_2, flg?))$.

We end this section with some remarks on Reiter's proposal for a temporal version of GOLOG (Reiter 1998),[17] which makes use of a different temporal extension of the situation calculus (Pinto 1997; Reiter 1996). Roughly, the idea is that every primitive action has as an extra argument its execution time. E.g., we would write *endGo*(20) to indicate that *endGo* is executed at time 20. It turns out that this explicit mention of time is highly problematic when it comes to formulating programs such as the above. Consider the part about saying "hello" whenever the robot is near Room A-118. In Reiter's approach, the programmer would have to supply a temporal expression as an argument of the *say*-action. However, it is far from obvious what this expression would look like since it involves analyzing the mail delivery subprogram as well as considering the odd chance of a battery recharge. In a nutshell, while Reiter's approach forces the user to figure out when to act, we let cc-Golog do the work. — As a final aside, we remark that *waitFor*-actions allow us to easily emulate Reiter's approach within our framework.

---

[16]$seq(\sigma_1, \sigma_2, \sigma_3)$ is a shorthand for $seq(\sigma_1, seq(\sigma_2, \sigma_3))$. We will also use a similar shorthand for *tryAll*.

[17]While the paper is about sequential GOLOG, the extension to ConGolog is straightforward.

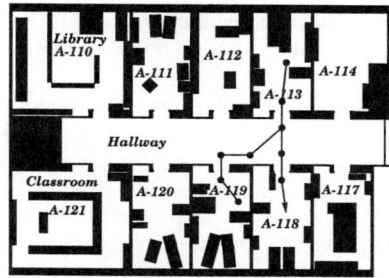

Figure 3: The robot environment

Experimental Results

Although the definition of cc-Golog requires second-order logic, it is easy to implement a PROLOG interpreter for cc-Golog, just as in the case of the original ConGolog.[18] In order to deal with the constraints implied by the *waitFor* instruction, we have made use of the ECRC Common Logic Programming System Eclipse 4.2 and its built-in constraint solver library (similar to Reiter (Reiter 1998)).

In order to evaluate the performance of our cc-Golog interpreter, we used it to project the (slightly modified) example of (Beetz & Grosskreutz 1998), where the XFRM framework (McDermott 1992; 1994) is used to deal with continuous change. Here, a mobile robot is to deliver letters in the environment depicted in Figure 3. At the same time, it has to monitor the state of the environment, that is, it has to check whether doors are open. As soon as it realizes that the door to A-113 is open, it has to interrupt its actual delivery in order to deliver an urgent letter to A-113. This is specified as a policy that leads the robot inside A-113 as soon as the opportunity is recognized. Similar to (Beetz & Grosskreutz 1998), we approximated the robot's trajectory by polylines, consisting of the starting location, the goal location and a point in front of and behind every passed doorway.

```
withPol(whenever(inHallway,
  [say(enterHW),
    tryAll(
      [whenever(nearDoor(a-114+117),
        [chkDr(a114),chkDr(a117),false?])],
      [whenever(nearDoor(a-113+118),
        [chkDr(a113),chkDr(a118),false?])],
      ...
      [waitFor(leftHallway),say(leftHW)])]),
  withPol([useOpp?,gotoRoom(a-113),
        deliverUrgentMail],
      [gotoRoom(a-118),giveMail(gerhard)]))).
```

Note that in the implementation, we used PROLOG lists ([a1,a2,...]) instead of $seq(a_1, a_2, ...)$. The outer policy is activated whenever the robot enters the hallway. It concurrently monitors whether the robot reaches a location near two opposite doors, at which point it checks whether the doors are open or not. If A-113 is detected to be open, the fluent useOpp is set true (by procedure chkDr). The policy is deactivated when the robot leaves the hallway. The inner policy is activated as soon as useOpp gets true. Its purpose is to use the opportunity to enter A-113 as soon as

---

[18]The subtle differences between the second order axiomatization of ConGolog and a PROLOG implementation are discussed in (Giacomo, Lesperance, & Levesque 1999).

possible. Figure 3 illustrates the projected trajectory starting in Room A-119, assuming that the door to A-113 is indeed open.

The projection of this plan took 0.5 seconds using cc-Golog, while the projection of the corresponding RPL program took 3.6 seconds. Both cc-Golog and XFRM ran on the same machine (a Linux Pentium III Workstation), under Allegro Common Lisp resp. Eclipse 4.2. We believe that cc-Golog owes this somewhat surprising advantage to the fact that it lends itself to a simple implementation with little overhead, while XFRM relies on the rather complex RPL-interpreter involving many thousand lines of Lisp code. Finally, and maybe most importantly, the cc-Golog implementation is firmly based on a logical specification, while XFRM relies on the procedural semantics of the RPL interpreter.

Conclusions

In this paper we proposed an extension of the situation calculus which includes a model of continuous change due to Pinto and a novel approach to modeling the passage of time using a special *waitFor*-action. We then considered cc-Golog, a deterministic variant of ConGolog which is based on the extended situation calculus. A key feature of the new language is the ability to have part of a program wait for an event like the battery voltage dropping dangerously low while other parts of the program run in parallel. Such mechanisms allow very natural formulations of robot controllers, in particular, because there is no need to state explicitly in the program when actions should occur. In addition to the sound theoretical foundations on which cc-Golog is built, experimental results have shown a superior performance in computing projections when compared to the projection mechanism of the plan language RPL, whose expressive power has largely motivated the development of cc-Golog.

Finally, a few words are in order regarding the use of projections in cc-Golog. They should be understood as a way of assessing whether a program is executable *in principle*. The resulting execution trace of a projection is not intended as input to the execution mechanism of the robot. This is because the time point of a *waitFor*-condition like a low battery level is computed based on a *model* of the world which includes a model of the robot's energy consumption. In reality, of course, the robot should react to the *actual* battery level by periodically reading its voltage meter. In the runtime system of RPL for an actual robot (Thrun *et al.* 1999) this link between *waitFor*-actions and basic sensors which are immediately accessible to the robot has been realized. One possibility to actually execute cc-Golog-programs on a robot would be to combine this idea of executing *waitFor*'s with an incremental interpreter along the lines of (de Giacomo & Levesque 1999). We leave this to future work. Another research issue is uncertainty, which plays a central role in the robotics domain which should be reflected in a plan language as well. Based on foundational work within the situation calculus (Bacchus, Halpern, & Levesque 1995) first preliminary results have been obtained regarding an integration into ConGolog (Grosskreutz & Lakemeyer 2000).

References

Bacchus, F.; Halpern, J.; and Levesque, H. 1995. Reasoning about noisy sensors in the situation calculus. In *IJCAI'95*.

Beetz, M., and Grosskreutz, H. 1998. Causal models of mobile service robot behavior. In *AIPS'98*.

Burns, A., and Wellings, A. 1991. *Real-time systems and their programming languages*. Addison-Wesley.

de Giacomo, G., and Levesque, H. 1999. An incremental interpreter for high-level programs with sensing. In Levesque, H., and Pirri, F., eds., *Logical Foundations for Cognitive Agents*. Springer. 86–102.

de Giacomo, G.; Lesperance, Y.; and Levesque, H. J. 1997. Reasoning about concurrent execution, prioritized interrupts, and exogeneous actions in the situation calculus. In *IJCAI'97*.

Firby, J. 1987. An investigation into reactive planning in complex domains. In *Proc. of AAAI-87*, 202–206.

Galton, A. 1990. A critical examination of Allen's theory of action and time. *Artificial Intelligence* 42:159–188.

Giacomo, G. D.; Lesperance, Y.; and Levesque, H. J. 1999. Congolog, a concurrent programming language based on the situation calculus: foundations. Technical report, University of Toronto, http://www.cs.toronto.edu/cogrobo/.

Grosskreutz, H., and Lakemeyer, G. 2000. Turning high-level plans into robot programs in uncertain domains. In *Submitted*. http://www-i5.informatik.rwth-aachen-bonn.de/kbsg/publications/.

Konolige, K. 1997. Colbert: A language for reactive control in sapphira. In *KI'97*, volume 1303 of *LNAI*.

Levesque, H. J.; Reiter, R.; Lesprance, Y.; Lin, F.; and Scherl, R. 1997. Golog: A logic programming language for dynamic domains. *Journal of Logic Programming* 31:59–84.

Levesque, H.; Pirri, F.; and Reiter, R. 1998. Foundations for the situation calculus. *Linköping Electronic Articles in Computer and Information Science* Vol. 3(1998): nr 018. URL: http://www.ep.liu.se/ea/cis/1998/018/.

McCarthy, J. 1963. Situations, actions and causal laws. Technical report, Stanford University. Reprinted 1968 in Semantic Information Processing (M.Minske ed.), MIT Press.

McDermott, D. 1992. Robot planning. *AI Magazine* 13(2):55–79.

McDermott, D. 1994. An algorithm for probabilistic, totally-ordered temporal projection. Research Report YALEU/DCS/RR-1014, Yale University, www.cs.yale.edu/AI/Planning/xfrm.html.

Miller, R. 1996. A case study in reasoning about actions and continuous change. In *ECAI'96*.

Pinto, J. 1997. Integrating discrete and continuous change in a logical framework. *Computational Intelligence, 14(1)*.

Reiter, R. 1996. Natural actions, concurrency and continuous time in the situation calculus. In *Proc. KR'96*, 2–13.

Reiter, R. 1998. Sequential, temporal golog. In *Proc. KR'98*.

Sandewall, E. 1989. Combining logic and differential equations for describing real-world systems. In *KR'89*, 412–420.

Shanahan, M. 1990. Representing continuous change in the event calculus. In *ECAI'90*.

Thrun, S.; Bennewitz, M.; Burgard, W.; Dellaert, F.; Fox, D.; Haehnel, D.; Rosenberg, C.; Roy, N.; Schulte, J.; and Schulz, D. 1999. Minerva: A second-generation museum tour-guide robot. In *ICRA'99*.

What Sensing Tells Us:
Towards A Formal Theory of Testing for Dynamical Systems

Sheila A. McIlraith
Knowledge Systems Laboratory
Department of Computer Science
Stanford University
Stanford, CA 94305-9020
sam@ksl.stanford.edu

Richard Scherl
Department of Computer Science
New Jersey Institute of Technology
University Heights
Newark, NJ 07102-1982
scherl@cis.njit.edu

Abstract

Just as actions can have indirect effects on the state of the world, so too can sensing actions have indirect effects on an agent's state of knowledge. In this paper, we investigate "what sensing actions tell us", i.e., what an agent comes to know indirectly from the outcome of a sensing action, given knowledge of its actions and state constraints that hold in the world. To this end, we propose a formalization of the notion of testing within a dialect of the situation calculus that includes knowledge and sensing actions. Realizing this formalization requires addressing the ramification problem for sensing actions. We formalize simple tests as sensing actions. Complex tests are expressed in the logic programming language Golog. We examine what it means to perform a test, and how the outcome of a test affects an agent's state of knowledge. Finally, we propose automated reasoning techniques for test generation and complex-test verification, under certain restrictions. The work presented in this paper is relevant to a number of application domains including diagnostic problem solving, natural language understanding, plan recognition, and active vision.

Introduction

Agents equipped with perceptual capabilities must operate in a world that is only partially observable. To determine properties of the world that are not directly observable, an agent must use its knowledge of the relationship between objects in the world, and its limited perceptual capabilities to infer such unobservable properties. For example, if an agent performs a sense action and observes that there is steam coming out of an electric kettle, then the direct effect of that sensing action is that the agent *knows* there is steam coming out of the kettle. With appropriate knowledge of the functioning of kettles, the agent should also know that the electrical outlet has power, that the kettle is functioning, and that there is hot liquid inside the kettle – all as *indirect* effects of the sensing action. Similarly, if the agent wishes to know whether there is power at an electrical outlet, but cannot directly sense this property of the world, the agent may potentially acquire this knowledge by attempting to boil water in a kettle plugged into this outlet.

Copyright © 2000, American Association for Artificial Intelligence (www.aaai.org). All rights reserved.

Such a sequence of actions constitutes a *test*. If steam is observed, then the agent knows that there is power at the outlet; however if steam is not observed, the agent may or may not know that there is no power at the electrical outlet. The knowledge the agent acquires from the test will depend on whether the agent knows that the kettle is functioning. Thus, this particular test is only *guaranteed* to provide knowledge about the existence of power at the electrical outlet under one test outcome.

While researchers have extended theories of action to include the notion of *sensing* or *knowledge-producing actions* (e.g., (Scherl & Levesque 1993; Baral & Tran 1998; Golden & Weld 1996; Funge 1998)) and have characterized the effect of sensing actions on an agent's state of knowledge, and even how to plan (e.g., (Stone 1998; Golden & Weld 1996)) and to project (e.g., (De Giacomo & Levesque 1999b)) in certain cases, with sensing actions, they have not addressed the problem of how to reason in a partially observable environment[1]. More generally, they have not examined the problem of how sensing actions can be coupled with knowledge of the relationship between objects in the world to gain further knowledge, and how both sensing actions, and world-altering actions change an agents state of knowledge in the presence of such world knowledge. Further, they have not examined the problem of how to select sensing actions to acquire knowledge of some property of the world that is not directly observable. Perhaps the closest research is that of (Shanahan 1996b; 1996a) who investigates the assimilation of sensing results for a mobile robot in a framework based on the event calculus, (McIlraith 1997) who assimilates observations into situation calculus device models to perform dynamical diagnosis, or (Baral, McIlraith, & Tran 2000) who do likewise in the language $\mathcal{L}$.

In this paper, we examine these issues in a dialect of the situation calculus that has been extended with knowledge-producing actions[2] (Scherl & Levesque 1993), but which does not include state constraints. Following (McIlraith 2000), we add state constraints to this language in order to

---
[1]Partially-Observable Markov Decision Processes (POMDPs) address this class of problems within a different formalism, but they do not address the testing issues we examine here.
[2]Henceforth referred to simply as *sensing* actions.

model the relationship between objects in the world, adopting the associated solution to the ramification problem for world-altering actions. We show that this solution extends to solve the ramification problem in the presence of sensing actions. Next, we define the notion of a test – how to design them and what knowledge can be drawn from their outcomes. In the formalization, simple tests comprise a set of initial conditions and a primitive sensing action. Complex tests are expressed as complex actions in the logic programming language Golog. We examine what it means to perform a test, and how the outcome of a test affects an agent's state of knowledge. Additionally, we examine the issue of selecting tests to confirm, refute, or discriminate a space of hypotheses.

Finally, we investigate the automation of reasoning about tests. We show that regression may be used to verify objective achievement for complex tests written in a subset of Golog. Further restrictions on the form of the complex tests allows the same regression operators to serve as the basis for a simple regression-style planner that generates tests to increase an agent's knowledge with respect to a space of hypotheses.

Situation Calculus

The situation calculus language we use, following (Reiter 2000), is a first-order language for representing dynamically changing worlds in which all of the changes are the direct result of named *actions* performed by some agent, or the indirect result of *state constraints*. Situations are sequences of actions, evolving from an initial distinguished situation, designated by the constant S_0. If a is an action and s a situation, the result of performing a in s is the situation represented by the function $do(a, s)$. Functions and relations whose truth values vary from situation to situation, called *fluents*, are denoted by a predicate symbol taking a situation term as the last argument. Note that for the purposes of this paper, we assume that our theory contains no functional fluents. Finally, $Poss(a, s)$ is a distinguished fluent expressing that action a is possible to perform in situation s. A situation calculus theory $\mathcal{D}$ comprises the following sets of axioms:

- foundational axioms of the situation calculus, Σ,
- successor state axioms, $\mathcal{D}_{SS}$,
- action precondition axioms, $\mathcal{D}_{ap}$,
- axioms describing the initial situation, $\mathcal{D}_{S_0}$,
- unique names for actions, $\mathcal{D}_{una}$,
- domain closure axioms for actions, $\mathcal{D}_{dca}$.

Successor state axioms, originally proposed by (Reiter 1991) to address the frame problem and extended by (e.g., (Lin & Reiter 1994; McIlraith 2000)) to address the ramification problem, are created by making a causal interpretation of the ramification constraints and a causal completeness assumption and compiling effect axioms of the form[3]:

$$Poss(a, s) \wedge \gamma_F^+(\vec{x}, a, s) \supset F(\vec{x}, do(a, s)) \quad (1)$$
$$Poss(a, s) \wedge \gamma_F^-(\vec{x}, a, s) \supset \neg F(\vec{x}, do(a, s)), \quad (2)$$

[3]Notational convention: all formulae are universally quantified with maximum scope unless otherwise noted.

and ramification (state) constraints of the form:

$$v_F^+(\vec{x}, s) \supset F(\vec{x}, s) \quad (3)$$
$$v_F^-(\vec{x}, s) \supset \neg F(\vec{x}, s), \quad (4)$$

into **Intermediate Successor State Axioms** of the form:

$$Poss(a, s) \supset [F_i(\vec{x}, do(a, s)) \equiv \Phi^*_{F_i}] \text{ where,} \quad (5)$$

$$\Phi^*_{F_i} \equiv \gamma^+_{F_i}(\vec{x}, a, s) \vee v^+_{F_i}(\vec{x}, do(a, s))$$
$$\vee (F(\vec{x}, s)$$
$$\wedge \neg(\gamma^-_{F_i}(\vec{x}, a, s) \vee v^-_{F_i}(\vec{x}, do(a, s)))), \quad (6)$$

I.e., if an action is possible is situation s, then it implies that the fluent is true in $do(a, s)$ iff an action made it true -or- a state constraint made it true -or- it was already true and neither an action nor a state constraint made it false.

Such intermediate successor state axioms provide a compact representation of a solution to the ramification problem for a common class of state constraints. (McIlraith 2000) shows that for what are essentially acyclic causal ramification constraints, repeated regression rewriting (e.g., (Reiter 1991)) of $\Phi^*_{F_i}$, $\mathcal{R}^*[\Phi^*_{F_i}] = \Phi_{F_i}$, repeatedly rewrites the ramification constraints that are relativized to $do(a, s)$ in (6) above, and is guaranteed to terminate in a formula whose fluents are relativized to situation s rather than $do(a, s)$. Both the intermediate and the less compact (final) successor state axioms which result from the regression provide closed-form solutions to the frame and ramification problem for the designated class of state constraints.

To illustrate sensing and testing in partially observable environments, we present a partial axiomatization of a car repair domain, derived from *The Complete Idiot's Guide to Trouble-Free Car Care* (Ramsey 1999). Our domain includes world-altering actions such as $turn\_on(x)$ and $turn\_off(x)$, where x is *radio* or *lights*. These have the effect that the radio or lights are on/off in the resulting situation. Actions $turn(key)$ and $release(key)$ have the effect that the ignition is begin turned ($turning\_ign$), or not, in the resulting situation. These actions are defined in terms of effect axioms and are combined with the following self-explanatory state constraints to produce successor state axioms. For notational convenience we abbreviate: transmission - *trans*, interlock - *intrlk*, solenoid - *solnd*, engine - *engn*, battery - *batt*; ignition system - *ign_sys*, start system - *strt_sys*.

$$empty(gas\_tank, s) \supset \neg startable(s) \quad (7)$$
$$ab(intrlk, s) \supset \neg startable(s) \quad (8)$$
$$ab(batt, s) \supset \neg startable(s) \quad (9)$$
$$ab(solnd, s) \supset \neg startable(s) \quad (10)$$
$$ab(starter, s) \supset \neg startable(s) \quad (11)$$
$$auto(trans) \wedge \neg ingear(trans, s) \supset ab(intrlk, s) \quad (12)$$
$$manual(trans) \wedge \neg depressed(clutch, s) \supset ab(intrlk, s) \quad (13)$$
$$turning\_ign(s) \wedge ab(batt, s) \supset \neg noise(engn, s) \quad (14)$$
$$turning\_ign(s) \wedge empty(gas\_tank, s) \supset \neg noise(engn, s) \quad (15)$$

$$turning\_ign(s) \wedge \neg ab(solnd, s) \supset noise(solnd, s) \quad (16)$$
$$ab(batt, s) \wedge on(radio, s) \supset \neg noise(radio, s) \quad (17)$$
$$ab(radio, s) \supset \neg noise(radio, s) \quad (18)$$
$$\neg ab(batt, s) \wedge on(lights, s) \supset emits(light, s) \quad (19)$$

Space precludes listing all the successor state axioms. There is one (intermediate) successor state axiom for each fluent. E.g., axioms (7)–(11) compile into intermediate successor state axiom (20):

$$Poss(a, s) \supset [startable(do(a, s)) \equiv$$
$$\neg empty(gas\_tank, do(a, s)) \wedge \neg ab(intrlk, do(a, s))$$
$$\wedge \neg ab(batt, do(a, s)) \wedge \neg ab(solnd, do(a, s))$$
$$\wedge \neg ab(starter, do(a, s))] \quad (20)$$

As described in (McIlraith 2000), the axioms describing the initial situation, S_0 contain what is known of the initial situation as well as the ramification constraints of the form of (3) and (4), relativized to S_0.

Knowledge and the Ramification Problem

In (Scherl & Levesque 1993), the situation calculus language *without* state constraints was extended to incorporate both knowledge and sensing actions. World-altering actions change the state of the world, sensing actions have no effect on the state of the world but rather change the agent's state of knowledge. In our example, sensing actions include *check_fuel*, *check_car_start*, *check_radio_noise* etc., which have the effect of the agent knowing $empty(gas\_tank, do(a, s))$, $startable(do(a, s))$, and $noise(radio, do(a, s))$.

The notation **Knows**(ϕ, s) (read as ϕ is known in situation s), where ϕ arbitrary formula, is an abbreviation for a formula that uses K. For example **Knows**$(on(block_1, block_2), s)$ abbreviates:
$$\forall s' \, K(s', s) \supset on(block_1, block_2, s).$$

The notation **Kwhether**(ϕ, s) is an abbreviation for a formula indicating that the truth value of ϕ is known.

$$\textbf{Kwhether}(\phi, s) \stackrel{def}{=} \textbf{Knows}(\phi, s) \vee \textbf{Knows}(\neg \phi, s),$$

Following the notation of (Levesque 1996), each sense action a has a *sensed fluent*, $SF(a, s)$ associated with it, and for each such a, $\mathcal{D}$ entails a sensed fluent axiom:

$$SF(a, s) \equiv \psi(s), \quad (21)$$

which says that performing the sense action a tells the agent whether the formula $\psi(s)$ is true or false. Thus, $\mathcal{D} \models$ **Kwhether**$(\psi, do(s, s))$ where a is an action with a sensed fluent equivalent to ψ.

For the sense action *check_fuel* the sensed fluent axiom is:

$$SF(check\_fuel, s) \equiv empty(gas\_tank, s) \quad (22)$$

which tells us whether or not the gas tank is empty. For world-altering actions, $\mathcal{D}$ entails $SF(a, s) \equiv True$.

In (Scherl & Levesque 1993), a successor state axiom for the K fluent is developed. Its form is as follows:

Successor State Axiom for K

$$Poss(a, s) \supset [K(s'', do(a, s)) \equiv$$
$$\exists s'. \, Poss(a, s') \wedge K(s', s) \wedge (s'' = do(a, s')) \wedge$$
$$[SF(a, s') \equiv SF(a, s)] \quad (23)$$

which says that after doing action a in situation s, the agent thinks it could be in a situation s'' iff $s'' = do(a, s')$ and s' is a situation that was accessible from s, and where s and s' agreed on the truth value of $SF(a, s)$, e.g., the truth value of $empty(gas\_tank)$. Thus, for all situations $do(a, s)$, the K relation will be completely determined by the K relation at s and the action a. This extends Reiter's solution to the frame problem (without ramifications and without knowledge) to the case of the situation calculus with sensing actions.

Proposition 1 *In the situation calculus theory described above, the agent knows the successor state axioms and the ramification constraints.*

This follows from the fact that the successor state axioms are universally quantified over all situations, and the ramification constraints explicitly hold in S_0 and are entailed in all successor situations, by the successor state axioms.

Theorem 1 (Correctness of Solution) *The proposed solution to the frame and ramification problems for world-altering and sensing actions ensures that knowledge only changes as appropriate, as defined by Theorems 1, 2, 3 (Scherl & Levesque 1993). Furthermore, the agent knows the indirect effects of its sensing actions.*

Thus, the successor state axioms for world-altering and sensing actions, together address the frame and ramification problems.

Testing

The purpose of a test is to attempt to determine the truth value of certain properties of the world, that may or may not be directly observable. A test is often performed with respect to a set of hypotheses, with the objective of eliminating as many hypotheses as possible from the set of hypotheses being entertained. Testing has been studied extensively for the specific problem of IC circuit testing, but there is little work on testing for rich dynamical systems such as the ones we examine here. The notion of a static test was briefly discussed in (Moore 1985, litmus example), and further developed for static systems in (McIlraith 1994; McIlraith & Reiter 1992). We build directly upon the work in (McIlraith 1994) with the objective of developing a formal theory of testing for *dynamical systems*.

Informally, a simple test comprises a set of initial conditions that may be established by the agent, together with the specification of a primitive sensing action, which determines what the agent will directly come to know as the result of the test. In our car repair domain, we can test the battery by checking the radio for noise. The initial conditions for such a test might be $on(radio, s)$. Then we can perform the sensing action *check_radio_noise* to see whether the radio is emitting noise. Note that the precondition for performing the action *check_radio_noise*, $Poss(check\_radio\_noise, s) \equiv inside(car, s)$, is different from the initial conditions of the test. Both must hold and must be consistent with the theory and with the current hypotheses being entertained, in order to execute the test.

We distinguish between two types of tests, *truth tests* which tell us *whether* the properties being sensed are true in the physical world, and *functional tests*, which tell us *what values* of the properties are true in the physical world. For the purposes of this paper, we restrict our attention to truth tests, and our sensing actions to so-called binary sense actions which establish the truth or falsity of a sensed formula.

Definition 1 (Simple Test)
A simple test is a pair, (I, a), where I, the initial conditions, is a conjunction of literals, and a is a binary sense action whose sensed formula contains no free variables.

$(on(radio, s), check\_radio\_noise)$ is an example of a simple test, following the discussion above. We now define the notion of a test for a particular hypothesis space, represented by the set HYP. We restrict the hypotheses, $H(s) \in HYP$ to be conjunctions of fluents whose non-situation terms are constants, and whose situation term is a situation variable s. In our car repair domain, an example hypothesis space might be $\{ab(batt, s), ab(solnd, s), empty(gas\_tank, s)\}$.

Definition 2 (Test for Hypothesis Space HYP)
A test (I, a) is a test for hypothesis space HYP in situation s iff $\mathcal{D} \wedge I \wedge Poss(a, s) \wedge H(s)$ is satisfiable for every $H(s) \in HYP$.

That is, the state the world must be in to execute the sensing action must be satisfiable, under the assumption that any one of the hypotheses in the hypothesis space could be true. Consider that $\mathcal{D}$ entails the safety constraint $\neg explosion(s)$ and the axiom $sparks(s) \wedge gas\_leak(s) \supset explosion(s)$, and that our hypothesis space is $\{gas\_leak(s), ab(spark\_plug, s)\}$. A reasonable test for $ab(spark\_plug, s)$ is to try to create sparks at the plug. Unfortunately such a test would cause an explosion in the presence of a gas leak. The satisfiability check above precludes such a test.

Definition 3 (Confirmation, Refutation)
*The outcome α of the test (I, a) **confirms** $H(s) \in HYP$ iff $\mathcal{D} \wedge I \wedge Poss(a, s) \wedge H(s)$ is satisfiable and $\mathcal{D} \wedge I \wedge Poss(a, s) \models \textbf{Knows}(H \supset \alpha, s)$. α **refutes** $H(s)$ iff $\mathcal{D} \wedge I \wedge Poss(a, s) \wedge H(s)$ is satisfiable and $\mathcal{D} \wedge I \wedge Poss(a, s) \models \textbf{Knows}(H \supset \neg \alpha, s)$.*

If the outcome of test $(on(radio, s), check\_radio\_noise)$ is $noise(radio, do(a, s))$, then our test refutes the hypothesis $ab(batt, s)$, following Axiom (17), and we can eliminate $ab(batt, s)$ from our hypothesis space, HYP.

Observe that a test outcome that refutes an hypothesis $H(s)$ allows us to eliminate it from HYP. Unfortunately, a test outcome that confirms an hypothesis is generally of no deterministic value, resulting in no reduction in the space of hypotheses. As we will see in a section to follow, there are exceptions that depend on the criteria by which the hypothesis space is defined.

In the sections to follow we use these basic definitions to define discriminating tests and relevant tests. These tests are distinguished by the effect their outcome will have on a general space of hypotheses.

Discriminating Tests

Notice that in our example above, if we had observed $\neg noise(radio, do(a, s))$, then by the definition, this would have confirmed the hypothesis $ab(batt, s)$, but it would have been of little value in discriminating our hypothesis space. All hypotheses remain in contention. Discriminating tests are those tests (I, a) that are guaranteed to discriminate an hypothesis space HYP, i.e., which will refute at least one hypothesis in HYP, regardless of the test outcome.

Definition 4 (Discriminating Tests)
A test (I, a) is a discriminating test for the hypothesis space HYP iff $\mathcal{D} \wedge I \wedge Poss(a, s) \wedge H(s)$ is satisfiable for all $H(s) \in HYP$, and there exists $H_i(s), H_j(s) \in HYP$ such that the outcome α of test (I, a) refutes either $H_i(s)$ or $H_j(s)$, no matter what that outcome might be.

Proposition 2
After we perform a discriminating test, (I, a), $\textbf{Knows}(\neg H_j, s)$, for some $H_j(s) \in HYP$.

In general, we would like a discriminating test to refute half of the hypotheses in the hypothesis space, regardless of the test outcome. By definition, a discriminating test must refute at least one hypothesis in the hypothesis space.

Definition 5 (Minimal Discriminating Tests)
A discriminating test (I, a) for the hypothesis space HYP is minimal iff for no proper subconjunct I' of I is (I', a) a discriminating test for HYP.

Minimal discriminating tests preclude unnecessary initial conditions for a test.

In some cases, we are interested in identifying a test that will establish the truth or falsity of a particular hypothesis. An individual discriminating test does precisely this.

Definition 6 (Individual Discriminating Tests)
A test (I, a) is an individual discriminating test for the hypotheses $H_i(s)$ and $\neg H_i(s) \in HYP$ iff $\mathcal{D} \wedge I \wedge Poss(a, s) \wedge H(s)$ is satisfiable for all $H(s) \in HYP$ and the outcome α of test (I, a) refutes either $H_i(s)$ or $\neg H_i(s)$, no matter what that outcome might be.

Proposition 3
After we perform an individual discriminating test (I, a), $\textbf{Kwhether}(H_i, s)$ for some $H_i \in HYP$.

The test $(\{\}, check\_fuel)$ is such a test. The outcome will be one of $\neg empty(gas\_tank, do(a, s))$ or $empty(gas\_tank, do(a, s))$. Thus, as the result of performing $check\_fuel$ in the physical world, the agent $\textbf{Kwhether}(empty(gas\_tank, s))$.

We can similarly define the notion of a minimal individual discriminating test, and a minimal relevant test, below.

Relevant Tests

In the majority of cases we will not be so fortunate as to have discriminating tests. Relevant tests are those tests (I, a) that have the potential to discriminate an hypothesis space HYP, but which cannot be guaranteed to do so. Given a particular outcome α, a relevant test may refute a subset of the hypotheses in the hypothesis space HYP, but may not refute any hypotheses if $\neg \alpha$ is observed. Since we can't guarantee the outcome of a test, these tests are not guaranteed to discriminate an hypothesis space. $(on(radio, s), check\_radio\_noise)$ is an example of such a test.

Definition 7 (Relevant Tests)
A test (I, a) is a relevant test for the hypothesis space HYP iff $\mathcal{D} \wedge I \wedge Poss(a, s) \wedge H(s)$ is satisfiable for all $H(s) in HYP$, and the outcome α of test (I, a) either confirms a subset of the hypotheses in HYP or refutes a subset.

By definition, a relevant test confirms or refutes at least one hypothesis in HYP, and it follows that every discriminating test is a relevant test.

In addition to discriminating and relevant tests, there is a third class of tests. Constraining tests do not refute an hypothesis, regardless of the outcome, but they do provide further knowledge that is relevant to the hypothesis space and which the agent can exploit in combination with other tests. We discuss this notion in a longer paper.

Testing Hypotheses

In the previous section we observed that a test outcome that refutes an hypothesis $H(s) \in HYP$ allows us to eliminate it from HYP, but that in general an outcome that confirms $H(s)$ has no value in reducing the hypothesis space. In this section, following (McIlraith 1994), we show that when the hypothesis space is determined using a consistency-based criterion this is indeed true, but when the hypothesis space is defined abductively, confirming test outcomes serve to eliminate those hypotheses that are not confirmed, i.e., that do not explain, the test outcome.

Definition 8 (Consistency-Based Hypothesis Space)
A consistency-based hypothesis for $\mathcal{D}$ and outcome α of the test (I, a) is any $H(s) \in HYP$ such that $\mathcal{D} \wedge I \wedge Poss(a, s) \wedge H(s) \wedge \alpha$ is satisfiable.

Proposition 4 (Eliminating C-B Hypotheses)
The outcome α of a test (I, a) eliminates those consistency-based hypotheses, $H(s) \in HYP$ that are refuted by test outcome α.

Definition 9 (Abductive Hypothesis Space)
An abductive hypothesis for $\mathcal{D}$ and outcome α of the test (I, a) is any $H(s) \in HYP$ such that $\mathcal{D} \wedge I \wedge Poss(a, s) \wedge H(s)$ is satisfiable, and $\mathcal{D} \wedge I \wedge Poss(a, s) \wedge H(s) \models \alpha$.

Proposition 5 (Eliminating Abductive Hypotheses)
The outcome α of a test (I, a) eliminates those abductive hypotheses, $H(s) \in HYP$ that are not confirmed by test outcome α.

Thus, in the case of abductive hypotheses, unlike consistency-based hypotheses, both confirming and refuting test outcomes have the potential to eliminate hypotheses.

Proposition 6 (Efficacy of Tests)
Any outcome α of a relevant test (I,a) can eliminate abductive hypotheses, whereas only a refuting outcome can eliminate consistency-based hypotheses. Discriminatory test outcomes, by definition, can eliminate either consistency-based or abductive hypotheses, regardless of the outcome.

Complex Tests

In the previous section, we defined the notion of a simple test (I, a), and characterized the circumstances under which the outcome of such a test would discriminate an hypothesis space. Indeed, to discriminate an hypothesis space, we may need a sequence of simple tests, interleaved with world-altering actions in order to achieve the initial conditions for a test. Likewise, the selection and sequencing of sensing and world-altering actions may be conditioned on the outcome of previous sensing actions. In the section to follow, we examine the problem of generating tests using regression. As we will see, generating tests, especially tests that involve sequences of sensing and world-altering actions is hard. In many instances, we need not resort to computation. The domain axiomatizer can articulate procedures for testing aspects of a system, just as the author of *The Idiot's Guide* has done in the domain of car repair. The logic programming language, Golog (alGOl in LOGic) (Levesque *et al.* 1997) provides a compelling language for specifying such tests, as we describe briefly here.

Only a sketch of Golog is given here. See (Levesque *et al.* 1997) for a full discussion of the language and also a Prolog interpreter. Golog provides a set of extralogical constructs (such as action sequencing, if-then-else, while loops) for assembling primitive actions, defined in the situation calculus, into macros that can be viewed as complex actions. The macros are defined through the predicate $Do(\delta, s, s')$ where δ is a complex action expression. $Do(\delta, s, s')$ is intended to mean that the agent's doing action δ in situation s leads to a (not necessarily unique) situation s'. The inductive definition of Do includes the following cases:

$Do(a, s, s')$ — simple actions
$Do(\phi?, s, s')$ — tests (referred to as G-tests in this paper)
$Do([\delta_1; \delta_2], s, s')$ — sequences
$Do([\delta_1|\delta_2], s, s')$ — nondeterministic choice of actions
$Do((\Pi x)\delta, s, s')$ — nondeterministic choice of parameters
$Do(\textbf{if } \phi \textbf{ then } \delta_1 \textbf{ else } \delta_2, s, s')$– conditionals, where we restrict ϕ to a G-test
$Do(\textbf{while } \phi \textbf{ do } \delta, s, s')$ — while loops

Space does not permit giving the full expansion for each of the constructs, but they can be found in (Levesque *et al.* 1997). The only change here is that the definition of the G-test construct (including the implicit G-test in the condition construct) must expand into a G-test involving knowledge[4].

The following is a partial example of a complex test written in Golog, and derived from (Ramsey 1999). This particular procedure is designed to help discriminate the space of hypotheses generated when a car won't start, namely $\{ab(intrlk, s), empty(gas\_tank, s), ab(batt, s), ab(solnd, s), ab(ign\_wires, s), ab(starter, s)\}$. In a diagnostic application such as this one, Golog procedures may also be written to combine testing with repair.

proc CARWONTSTART
   if ($\neg$ startable) **then** CHECKINTERLOCK;

---

[4]We are taking the simplest approach towards incorporating sensing actions into Golog. All actions are on-line. In other words, they are executed immediately without any possibility of backtracking. Other options for completely off-line execution (Lakemeyer 1999) and a mixture of off-line and on-line execution (De Giacomo & Levesque 1999a) have been discussed in the literature.

```
        if (¬ AB(INTRLK)) then CHECK_GAS_TANK;
       if (¬ EMPTY(GAS_TANK)) then CHECKBATTERY;
          if (¬ AB(BATT)) then CHECKSOLENOID;
           if (¬ AB(SOLND)) then CHECKIGNWIRES;
          if (¬ AB(IGN_WIRES)) then CHECKSTARTER;
            if (¬ AB(STARTER)) then CHECKENGINE
  end if end if end if end if end if end if end if
endProc

proc CHECKBATTERY
   TURN_ON(RADIO); CHECK_RADIO_NOISE;
   if (¬ NOISE(RADIO))
         then TURN_ON(LIGHTS); CHECK_LIGHTS
   end if
endProc
```

Observe that complex tests often involve world-altering actions which serve to establish the preconditions and initial conditions for embedded simple tests. Also observe that in achieving the preconditions or initial conditions for simple tests, these actions change the state of the world, including potentially changing the space of hypotheses. For example, if a flashlight isn't emitting light, and one hypothesis is that the batteries are dead, a good way to test them is to replace them with fresh batteries, and see whether the flashlight then works. However, replacing the flashlight batteries potentially changes the state of one of the hypotheses.

In diagnosis domains, such as the ones above, it is often desirable to combine fault detection (hypothesis testing) with repair and to take actions to eradicate faults as easily as to diagnose them (McIlraith 1997; Baral, McIlraith, & Tran 2000). However, in cases where it is desirable not to alter the truth status of the hypothesis space, care must be taken to design and verify and/or generate tests that maintain designated knowledge constraints and world constraints. E.g., we don't want to determine whether the gas tank is empty by draining it!

Automated Reasoning About Tests

In the previous section we introduced the notion of a complex test, demonstrating that such tests could sometimes be specified in Golog. In this final technical section we briefly examine the use of automated reasoning techniques, and in particular the use of regression rewriting, for the purpose of verifying certain properties of Golog-specified complex tests, and for generating complex tests as conditional plans. Our presentation draws upon (Lespérance 1994) and (Reiter 2000). Other related approaches to conditional planning include (Rosenschein 1981; Manna & Waldinger 1987; Lobo 1998).

Consider the Golog complex test given above to help discriminate the space of hypotheses generated when a car won't start. To verify that it is an individual discriminating test, it is necessary to ensure that for at least one of the hypotheses H, $\mathbf{Kwhether}(H, s)$ holds, where s is the situation resulting from the execution of the Golog procedure, i.e. $Do(\text{CARWONTSTART}, S_0, s)$. Thus, we would like to be able to entail $\bigvee_{H \in HYP} \mathbf{Kwhether}(H, s)$, and in particular $\mathbf{Kwhether}(empty(gas\_tank), s)$, for example. A verification that the procedure is a discriminating test would involve ensuring that for at least one H, $\mathbf{Knows}(\neg H, s)$ holds in the final situation, i.e., $\bigvee_{H \in HYP} \mathbf{Knows}(\neg H, s)$.

In (Scherl & Levesque 1993), a form of *regression* (based on the discussion in (Reiter 1991)) is developed for the situation calculus with sensing actions. Through the application of regression, reasoning about situations reduces to reasoning in the initial situation, S_0. Given a ground situation term (i.e. a term built on S_0 with the function do and ground action terms) s_{gr}, the problem is to determine whether the axiomatization of the domain $\mathcal{D}$ entails $G(s_{gr})$ where G (the intended objective of the procedure) is an arbitrary sentence including knowledge operators. This question is reduced to the question of whether or not the axiomatization of the initial situation entails the regression of $G(s_{gr})$, i.e., $\mathcal{R}(G(s_{gr}))$. Since the result of regression is a formula in an ordinary modal logic of knowledge (i.e. a formula without action terms and where the only situation term is S_0) an ordinary modal theorem proving method may be used to determine whether or not the regressed formula is entailed by the axiomatization of the initial situation, $\mathcal{D}_{S_0}$. In our case G will be a formula made up of subformulae of the form $\mathbf{Kwhether}(H, s)$ or $\mathbf{Knows}(\neg H, s)$, where H is an hypothesis.

The regression operator $\mathcal{R}$ is defined relative to a set of successor state axioms $\mathcal{D}_{ss}$. The first four parts of the definition of the regression operator[5], $\mathcal{R}$ concern world-altering actions and are taken from (Reiter 2000).

i. When W is a non-fluent atom, including equality atoms, and atoms with the predicate symbol $Poss$, or when W is a fluent atom or $\mathbf{Knows}$ operator, whose situation argument is the situation constant S_0, $\mathcal{R}[W] = W$.

ii. When F is a relational fluent (other than K) atom whose successor state axiom in $\mathcal{D}_{SS}$ is
   then $$Poss(a, s) \supset [F(x_1, \ldots, x_n, do(a, s)) \equiv \Phi_F]$$
   $$\mathcal{R}[F(t_1, \ldots, t_n, do(\delta, \sigma))] = \Phi_F |_{t_1,\ldots,t_n,\delta,\sigma}^{x_1,\ldots,x_n,a,s}$$

iii. Whenever W is a formula,
   $\mathcal{R}[\neg W] = \neg \mathcal{R}[W]$,
   $\mathcal{R}[(\forall v)W] = (\forall v)\mathcal{R}[W]$,
   $\mathcal{R}[(\exists v)W_1] = (\exists v)\mathcal{R}[W_1]$.

iv. Whenever W_1 and W_2 are formulas,
   $\mathcal{R}[W_1 \wedge W_2] = \mathcal{R}[W_1] \wedge \mathcal{R}[W_1]$,
   $\mathcal{R}[W_1 \vee W_2] = \mathcal{R}[W_1] \vee \mathcal{R}[W_1]$,
   $\mathcal{R}[W_1 \supset W_2] = \mathcal{R}[W_1] \supset \mathcal{R}[W_1]$.

Following (Scherl & Levesque 1993), additional steps are needed to extend the regression operator to sensing actions[6]. Two definitions are needed for the specification to follow. When φ is an arbitrary sentence and s a situation term, then $\varphi[s]$ is the sentence that results from adding an extra argument to every fluent of φ and inserting s into that argument

---
[5]Some details are omitted here (e.g, regression of functional fluents, and the equality predicate). Also note that the formula to be regressed must be *regressable*. This concept is fully defined in (Reiter 2000).

[6]Regression of sensing actions that make known the denotation of a term (e.g. an action of reading a number on a piece of paper) is not discussed here.

position. The reverse operation φ^{-1} is the result of removing the last argument position from all the fluents in φ.

Step **v** covers the case of regressing a world-altering action through the **Knows** operator. Step **vi** covers the cases of regressing a sensing action through the **Knows** operator. In the definitions below, s' is a new situation variable.

v. Whenever a is not a sensing action,
$\mathcal{R}[\mathbf{Knows}(W, do(a, s))] =$
  $\mathbf{Knows}((\mathcal{R}[W[do(a, s')]])^{-1}, s)$.

vi. Whenever a is a sensing action, where ψ is a formula such that $\mathcal{D}$ entails that $\psi[s]$ is equivalent to $SF(a, s)$,
$\mathcal{R}[\mathbf{Knows}(W, do(a, s))] =$
  $((\psi_i(s) \supset \mathbf{Knows}(\psi_i \supset \mathcal{R}[W[do(a, s')]]^{-1}, s)) \wedge$
  $(\neg\psi_i(s) \supset \mathbf{Knows}(\neg\psi_i \supset \mathcal{R}[W[do(a, s')]]^{-1}, s))$

An additional operator $\mathcal{C}$ needs to be defined to handle the expansion of the complex actions found in Golog, so that we can apply regression[7]. We are only considering a subset of Golog programs – those composed of simple actions, sequencing, and conditionals. We also add the empty action **noOp** or [] (names for the same operation). Also note that $\pi_a(\vec{x}, s)$ stands for the preconditions of $a(\vec{x})$ as specified in the action precondition axiom, $\mathcal{D}_{ap}, Poss(a(\vec{s}), s) \equiv \pi_a(\vec{x}, s)$.

viii. $\mathcal{C}(\mathbf{noOp}, W, s) = W(s)$

ix. $\mathcal{C}([a(\vec{x}); \delta], W, s) = \pi_a(\vec{x}, s) \wedge \mathcal{C}(\delta, W, do(a(\vec{x}), s))$ where $a(\vec{x})$ is a ground non-sensing simple action term.

x. $\mathcal{C}([\mathbf{if}\ \phi(\vec{x})\ \mathbf{then}\ \delta_1\ \mathbf{else}\ \delta_2], W, s) =$
  $\mathbf{Kwhether}(\phi(\vec{x}), s) \wedge$
  $[\mathbf{Knows}(\phi(\vec{x}), s) \supset \mathcal{C}(\delta_1, W, s)] \wedge$
  $[\mathbf{Knows}(\neg\phi(\vec{x}), s) \supset \mathcal{C}(\delta_2, W, s)]$

We are assuming that the agent is able[8] to execute the Golog test procedure. In particular, the programmer (of the test procedure) must have ensured that at the point where an $[\mathbf{if}\ \phi(\vec{x})\ \mathbf{then}\ \delta_1\ \mathbf{else}\ \delta_2]$ statement is encountered, the executing agent must $\mathbf{Kwhether}(\phi, s)$. If not, the procedure will fail.

In the following theorem (a generalization of Theorem 2 from (Lespérance 1994), recall $\mathcal{R}^*(\varphi)$ indicates the repeated regression of φ until further applications leave the formula unchanged.

Theorem 2 *For any Golog procedure δ, consisting of simple actions, sequences, and conditionals, and G an arbitrary closed regressable formula that may include knowledge operators:*

$$\mathcal{D} \models \exists s(Do(\delta, S_0, s) \wedge G(s))\ \text{iff}$$
$$\mathcal{D}_{S_0} \cup \mathcal{D}_{una} \models \mathcal{R}^*(\mathcal{C}(\delta, G, S_0))$$

Theorem 2 shows it may be verified that any Golog testing routine (utilizing concatenation and conditionals) achieves its intended objective G through the use of regression followed by theorem proving in the initial database. The successor state axioms ($\mathcal{D}_{ss}$) are only used in the regression procedure. This theorem can be extended to likewise verify other properties of our Golog procedures.

---

[7]The $\mathcal{C}$ operator introduced here is based on (but generalizes) the E operator of (Lespérance 1994).

[8]See (Lespérance *et al.* 2000) for a discussion of ability and Golog programs. Related issues are discussed in (Lespérance 1994; Lakemeyer 1999).

We can use the above regression operator as the basis for a simple conditional planning algorithm for constructing complex tests. Following (Lespérance 1994), we consider only normal form conditional plans. These are conditional plans in which the condition in a conditional (e.g. the ϕ in $[\mathbf{if}\ \phi(\vec{x})\ \mathbf{then}\ \delta_1\ \mathbf{else}\ \delta_2]$) must be a sensed formula. Thus we can require that prior to any conditional with the G-test ϕ, there must be an action a such that a is a sensing action and $\mathcal{D} \models SF(a, s) \equiv \phi(s)$. This guarantees that the program executing the test will always $\mathbf{Kwhether}(\phi, s)$ when a conditional is encountered. For any complex test (that is executable) consisting only of concatenation and conditionals, there must be an equivalent test in this normal form. For $i = 1, 2, 3 \ldots$, we can define the sentences Γ_i as:

$$\Gamma_0 \stackrel{\text{def}}{=} G(s)$$

$$\Gamma_i \stackrel{\text{def}}{=}$$
$\exists a([\exists \vec{x}(a = A_1(\vec{x}) \wedge \pi_{A_1}(\vec{x}) \vee \ldots$
  $\vee \exists \vec{x}(a = A_n(\vec{x}) \wedge \pi_{A_n}(\vec{x}))]$
  $\wedge \mathcal{R}(\Gamma_{i-1}(do(a, s)))) \vee$
$\exists a([\exists \vec{x}(a = A_1^s(\vec{x}) \wedge \pi_{A_1^s}(\vec{x}) \wedge (SF(a, s) \equiv \phi_1(s)) \wedge$
  $\mathcal{R}(\phi_1(\vec{x}, do(a, s)) \supset \Gamma_{i-1}(do(a, s))) \wedge$
  $\mathcal{R}(\neg\phi_1(\vec{x}, do(a, s)) \supset \Gamma_{i-1}(do(a, s)))]$
$\wedge \ldots \wedge$
$\exists a([\exists \vec{x}(a = A_m^s(\vec{x}) \wedge \pi_{A_m^s}(\vec{x}) \wedge (SF(a, s) \equiv \phi_m(s)) \wedge$
  $\mathcal{R}(\phi_m(\vec{x}, do(a, s)) \supset \Gamma_{i-1}(do(a, s))) \wedge$
  $\mathcal{R}(\neg\phi_m(\vec{x}, do(a, s)) \supset \Gamma_{i-1}(do(a, s)))]$

Each Γ_i is true if there is a plan of length i starting in s and leading to a state satisfying G (Reiter 1995; Lespérance 1994). The following theorem (essentially Theorem 3 of (Lespérance 1994)) establishes the soundness and completeness of the regression-based test planning method.

Theorem 3 *For Golog procedure δ in normal form and G, an arbitrary closed regressable formula that may include knowledge operators:*

$$\mathcal{D} \models \exists s(Do(\delta, S_0, s) \wedge G(s))\ \text{iff for some } n$$
$$\mathcal{D}_{S_0} \cup \mathcal{D}_{una} \models \Gamma_0(S_0) \vee \ldots \vee \Gamma_n(S_0)$$

This regression-based finite horizon method of generating and evaluating all normal form conditional plans of greater and greater size is certainly not designed for efficiency, but the results can serve as the foundation for building more efficient regression-based complex-test planning methods, much as similar results have served as the foundation for relatively more efficient regression based planning methods (McDermott 1991; Lespérance 1994; Rosenschein 1981). In future work we will evaluate the extension of current state of the art planning techniques based on SAT and Graphplan, to address the planning problems raised in this paper (Weld 1999).

Summary

In this paper we presented results towards a formal theory of testing for dynamical systems, specified in the language of the situation calculus. Our first contribution was to address the ramification problem for sensing actions. We then defined the notion of a test, examining how a test can be designed and how the outcome of different types of tests affect an agent's state of knowledge. The realization of many tests in the world requires a complex sequencing of world-altering and sensing actions, whose selection and ordering is conditioned upon the outcome of previous sensing actions. We proposed specifying such complex tests in the logic programming language Golog. We then demonstrated that regression could be used both to verify the desired objective of such complex tests, and to generate tests as conditional plans under certain restrictions.

Sensing is integral to the operation of most autonomous agents. The notion of complex and simple tests introduced here extends the body of theoretical work on sensing in dynamical systems, and has practical relevance for building agents for diagnostic problem solving, plan understanding, or simply for mobile cognitive agents that need to interact in complex environments with limited sensing.

Acknowledgments

We thank Eyal Amir for useful comments on an earlier version of this paper. Additionally, we thank Yves Lespérance for useful discussions related to this paper. This research was supported in part by NSF grant NSF 9819116, DARPA grant N66001-97-C-8554-P00004 and by NASA grant NAG2-1337.

References

Baral, C., and Tran, S. 1998. Formalizing sensing actions: a transition function based approach. In *Proc. of AAAI 98 Fall Symposium on Cognitive Robotics*.

Baral, C.; McIlraith, S.; and Tran, S. 2000. Formulating diagnostic problem solving using an action language with narratives and sensing. In *Proc. Seventh International Conference on Principles of Knowledge Representation and Reasoning (KR'2000)*. To appear.

De Giacomo, G., and Levesque, H. J. 1999a. An incremental interpreter for high-level programs with sensing. In Levesque, H. J., and Pirri, F., eds., *Logical Foundations for Cognitive Agents: Contributions in Honor of Ray Reiter*. Berlin: Springer. 86–102.

De Giacomo, G., and Levesque, H. J. 1999b. Progression and regression using sensors. In *Proc. Sixteenth International Joint Conference on Artificial Intelligence (IJCAI-99)*, 160–165.

Funge, J. 1998. *Making Them Behave: Cognitive Models for Computer Animation*. Ph.D. Dissertation, Department of Computer Science, University of Toronto.

Golden, K., and Weld, D. 1996. Representing sensing actions: The middle ground revisited. In *Proc. Fifth Intnl. Conf. on Principles of Knowledge Representation and Reasoning (KR'96)*.

Lakemeyer, G. 1999. On sensing and off-line interpreting in GOLOG. In Levesque, H. J., and Pirri, F., eds., *Logical Foundations for Cognitive Agents: Contributions in Honor of Ray Reiter*. Berlin: Springer. 173–189.

Lespérance, Y.; Levesque, H. J.; Lin, F.; and Scherl, R. B. 2000. Ability and knowing how in the situation calculus. *Studia Logica*. To appear.

Lespérance, Y. 1994. An approach to the synthesis of plans with perception acts and conditionals. In *Working Notes of the Canadian Workshop on Distributed Artificial Intelligence*.

Levesque, H.; Reiter, R.; Lespérance, Y.; Lin, F.; and Scherl, R. 1997. GOLOG: A logic programming language for dynamic domains. *The Journal of Logic Programming* 31:59–84.

Levesque, H. 1996. What is planning in the presence of sensing? In *Proc. Thirteenth National Conference on Artificial Intelligence (AAAI-96)*, 1139–1146.

Lin, F., and Reiter, R. 1994. State constraints revisited. *Journal of Logic and Computation* 4(5):655–678. Special Issue on Action and Processes.

Lobo, J. 1998. COPLAS: a COnditional PLAnner with Sensing actions. In *Working Notes of the AAAI98 Fall Symposium on Cognitive Robotics*, 109–116.

Manna, Z., and Waldinger, R. 1987. How to clear a block: A theory of plans. *Journal of Automated Reasoning* 3:343–377.

McDermott, D. 1991. Regression planning. *International Journal of Intelligent Systems* 6:356–416.

McIlraith, S., and Reiter, R. 1992. On tests for hypothetical reasoning. In W. Hamscher, L. C., and de Kleer, J., eds., *Readings in model-based diagnosis*. Morgan Kaufmann. 89–96.

McIlraith, S. 1994. Generating tests using abduction. In *Proc. Fourth International Conference on Principles of Knowledge Representation and Reasoning (KR'94)*, 449–460.

McIlraith, S. 1997. *Towards a Formal Account of Diagnostic Problem Solving*. Ph.D. Dissertation, Department of Computer Science, University of Toronto, Toronto, Ontario, Canada.

McIlraith, S. 2000. A closed-form solution to the ramification problem (sometimes). *Artificial Intelligence* 116(1–2):87–121.

Moore, R. 1985. A formal theory of knowledge and action. In Hobbs, J. B., and Moore, R. C., eds., *Formal Theories of the Commonsense World*. Ablex Publishing Corp. 319–358.

Ramsey, D. 1999. *The Complete Idiot's Guide to Trouble-Free Car Care*. Alpha Books.

Reiter, R. 1991. The frame problem in the situation calculus: A simple solution (sometimes) and a completeness result for goal regression. In *Artificial Intelligence and Mathematical Theory of Computation: Papers in Honor of J. McCarthy*.

Reiter, R. 1995. CS2532S course notes. Unpublished manuscript.

Reiter, R. 2000. *Knowledge in Action: Logical Foundations for Describing and Implementing Dynamical Systems*. In preparation. Draft available at http://www.cs.toronto.edu/~cogrobo/.

Rosenschein, S. 1981. Plan synthesis: A logical perspective. In *Proc. Seventh International Joint Conference on Artificial Intelligence (IJCAI-81)*, 331–337.

Scherl, R., and Levesque, H. 1993. The frame problem and knowledge producing actions. In *Proc. Eleventh National Conference on Artificial Intelligence (AAAI-93)*, 689–695.

Shanahan, M. 1996a. Noise and the common sense informatic situation for a mobile robot. In *Proc. Thirteenth National Conference on Artificial Intelligence (AAAI-96)*, 1098–1103.

Shanahan, M. 1996b. Robotics and the common sense informatic situation. In *Proc. European Conference on Artificial Intelligence (ECAI-96)*, 684–688.

Stone, M. 1998. Abductive planning with sensing. In *Proc. Fifteenth National Conference on Artificial Intelligence (AAAI-98)*, 631–636.

Weld, D. 1999. Recent advances in AI planning. *AI Magazine*.

Execution of Temporal Plans with Uncertainty

Paul Morris*
Caelum Research Corporation
M/S 269-1 NASA Ames Research Center
Moffett Field, CA 94035
pmorris@ptolemy.arc.nasa.gov

Nicola Muscettola
Mail Stop 269-2
NASA Ames Research Center
Moffett Field, CA 94035
mus@ptolemy.arc.nasa.gov

Abstract

Simple Temporal Networks (STNs) have proved useful in applications that involve metric time. However, many applications involve events whose timing is uncertain in the sense that it is not controlled by the execution agent. In this paper we consider execution algorithms for temporal networks that include events of uncertain timing. We present two such algorithms. The first retains maximum flexibility, but requires potentially costly updates during execution. The second surrenders some flexibility in order to obtain a fast execution comparable to that available for ordinary STNs.

Introduction

Simple Temporal Networks (Dechter, Meiri, & Pearl 1991) have proved useful in Planning and Scheduling applications that involve quantitative reasoning about time (e.g. (Bienkowski & Hoebel 1998; Muscettola *et al.* 1998)) because they allow fast checking of temporal consistency after each plan step. However this formalism does not adequately address an important aspect of real execution domains: the occurrence time of some events may not be under the complete control of the execution agent. For example, when a spacecraft commands an instrument or interrogates a sensor, a varying amount of time may intervene before the operation is completed. In cases like this, the execution agent does not have freedom to select the precise time delay between events in accord with the timing of previously executed events. Instead, the value is selected by Nature independently of the agent's choices. This can lead to constraint violations during execution even if the Simple Temporal Network appeared consistent at plan generation time. The problem of control of temporal networks with uncertainty was first addressed formally in (Vidal & Ghallab 1996; Vidal & Fargier 1997), and was also studied in (Morris & Muscettola 1999).

The previous work has been primarily concerned with algorithms to determine various flavors of *controllability* of temporal networks with uncertainty. Controllability is a property analogous to consistency in ordinary (without uncertainty) temporal networks. This paper focuses instead on execution algorithms for temporal networks with uncertainty and considers issues of flexibility and efficiency.

A method in widespread use for executing ordinary temporal networks is to "harden" the network. That is, a specific solution is chosen that rigidly fixes the time of execution of all the events in the network. Note that this approach is inapplicable to networks with uncertainty because of the unpredictable choices made by Nature (which may not agree with the chosen solution), and is often undesirable even for ordinary temporal networks because it allows no flexibility for dealing with unmodelled contingencies that may nevertheless occur in practice. However, retaining flexibility into execution imposes a burden of propagation to ensure that the windows of later timepoints are appropriately narrowed as earlier timepoints are executed. Since a short cycle time is paramount during execution, methods have been developed (Muscettola, Morris, & Tsamardinos 1998; Tsamardinos, Muscettola, & Morris 1998) to reformulate the network in order to reduce the amount of propagation. A central issue addressed in this paper is to what extent these methods are applicable to networks with uncertainty.

Background

We review the definitions of Simple Temporal Network (Dechter, Meiri, & Pearl 1991), Minimum Dispatchable Network (Muscettola, Morris, & Tsamardinos 1998), and Simple Temporal Network with Uncertainty (Vidal & Fargier 1997).

A Simple Temporal Network (STN) is a graph in which the edges are labelled with upper and lower numerical bounds. The nodes in the graph represent temporal events or *timepoints*, while the edges correspond to constraints on the durations between the events. Formally, an STN may be described as a 4-tuple $< N, E, l, u >$ where N is a set of nodes, E is a set of edges, and $l : E \to \mathbb{R} \cup \{-\infty\}$ and $u : E \to \mathbb{R} \cup \{+\infty\}$ are functions mapping the edges into extended Real Numbers. Figure 1 shows an example of an STN. Figure 2 shows the corresponding *distance graph* (Dechter, Meiri, & Pearl 1991), which is an alternate representation useful for mathematical analysis. Note that lower bounds are negated to give the lengths of the reverse edges. Edges of infinite length are omitted. (Given a distance graph, one can also find a corresponding STN, so the representations are interchangeable.) An STN is consistent

---
*Current Affiliation: RIACS.
Copyright © 2000, American Association for Artificial Intelligence (www.aaai.org). All rights reserved.

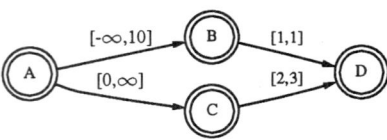

Figure 1: Simple Temporal Network.

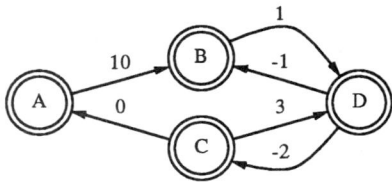

Figure 2: Distance Graph.

if and only if the distance graph does not contain a negative cycle.

In (Dechter, Meiri, & Pearl 1991), it is shown how time windows (upper and lower time bounds) can be determined for each timepoint by propagations in the distance graph starting from any designated initial timepoint. The upper bound corresponds to the shortest-path distance from the initial timepoint to the given timepoint, while the lower bound is the negation of the shortest-path distance in the opposite direction. Shortest-path distances are efficiently determined by propagation methods such as the Bellman-Ford algorithm (Cormen, Leiserson, & Rivest 1990). A solution (i.e., a globally consistent assignment of time values to timepoints) can be incrementally constructed without backtracking by progressively extending a locally consistent assignment, with propagation of time windows occurring after each extension.

An execution algorithm is essentially the same as an incremental construction of a solution. However, there are two important distinctions, as discussed in (Muscettola, Morris, & Tsamardinos 1998). First, to be eligible for execution, a timepoint must be *live*, i.e., the current time must lie between its upper and lower bounds. (Note that we maximize flexibility by delaying fixing the time of a timepoint until it is actually executed.) Second, suppose the shortest-path distance (in the distance graph) from a timepoint A to a timepoint B is negative. It follows that in all valid solutions, the time assigned to B must precede that assigned to A. We say B is an *enabling condition* for A. Notice that a naive incremental execution algorithm may execute A before B, with the resulting propagation forcing B into the past. To correct this, it is necessary to determine all the enabling conditions ahead of time, and defer executing timepoints until they are enabled. (Note that a deadlock cannot occur since a consistent STN has no negative cycles.)

The modified execution algorithm is still costly because it requires a full propagation after each timepoint is executed. A better approach (Muscettola, Morris, & Tsamardinos 1998) is to convert the network to an equivalent *minimum dispatchable* network for which *local propagation* (to immediate neighbors only) is sufficent to ensure a valid execution. Conversion to a minimum dispatchable network is obtained by first computing the All-Pairs Shortest-Path graph (Cormen, Leiserson, & Rivest 1990) (henceforth we abbreviate this to the All-Pairs graph), and then eliminating *dominated* edges. An edge AB is dominated if there is a timepoint C such that $AC + CB = AB$ and either both AB and CB are non-negative or both AB and AC are negative. In the former case, AB is dominated by CB; in the latter, by AC. If an edge is dominated, then removing it from the All-Pairs graph does not change the set of valid executions.

Controllability problems (Vidal & Ghallab 1996; Vidal & Fargier 1997) arise in STNs where the edges, which we will call *links*, are divided into two classes, *contingent links* and *requirement links*. Contingent links may be thought of as representing causal processes; their finishing times are controlled by Nature, subject to the limits imposed by the bounds on the contingent links. All other timepoints, which we will call *control points*, are controlled by the agent, whose goal is to satisfy the bounds on the requirement links.

Thus, a *Simple Temporal Network with Uncertainty* (Vidal & Fargier 1997) (STNU) is a 5-tuple $< N, E, l, u, C >$, where N, E, l, u are as in a STN, and C is a subset of the edges. The edges in C are called the *contingent links*, and the other edges are the *requirement links*. We require $0 < l(e) < u(e) < \infty$ for each contingent link e.

Each set of allowable durations for the contingent links may be thought of as reducing the STNU to an ordinary STN. Thus, an STNU determines a family of STNs, as in the following definition.

Suppose $\Gamma = < N, E, l, u, C >$ is an STNU. A *projection* (Vidal & Ghallab 1996) of Γ is a Simple Temporal Network derived from Γ where each requirement link is replaced by an identical STN link, and each contingent link e is replaced by an STN link with equal upper and lower bounds $[b, b]$ for some b such that $l(e) \leq b \leq u(e)$.

A *boundary* projection (Vidal & Fargier 1997) is one where, for each contingent link e, the above b is chosen so that $b = l(e)$ or $b = u(e)$. Because of convexity, the minimum shortest path distances over all projections can be calculated using only the boundary projections. This makes it feasible for many algorithms to essentially ignore the non-boundary projections.

Execution Of STNU

Execution of an STNU is complicated by the necessity of updating the network as new information is received. The most common scenario is that the precise timing of a contingent link finishing point is observed when the contingent process finishes. This is analogous to the timing of a control point becoming fixed when it is selected for execution. We call this the *standard* update scenario. However, other update scenarios are possible. For example, in a spacecraft application, the predicted time of closest encounter to a comet may be progressively refined as the event approaches. On the other hand, the precise time of the encounter might not be available until some time after the event has occurred due to delays involving communication or analysis.

In this paper we will consider two approaches to executing STNUs. The first, considered in this section, is a general

```
1.  A = Set of all control points
    current_time = 0
2.  Arbitrarily pick a control point TP in A that is
    live and enabled in all boundary projections.
3.  Set TP execution time to current_time, and remove
    TP from A.  Halt if A is now empty.
4.  Advance current time, propagating all updates
    until some point in A is live and enabled.
5.  Go to 2.
```

Figure 3: Execution Algorithm.

method that preserves maximum flexibility, but entails significant computational cost. The second approach, considered in a later section, surrenders some flexibility in order to achieve greater efficiency.

In (Morris & Muscettola 1999), the concept of *Waypoint Controllability* is introduced as a practical approach to ensuring controllability. It is shown that a Waypoint Controllable network may be effectively decomposed into (1) an induced STN involving only the waypoints, and (2) several STNUs corresponding to the subnetworks *between* the waypoints. This decomposition may impact the choice of execution algorithm. The point to note is that the subnetworks can be expected to be quite limited in size, which makes it feasible to consider methods with asymptotic high complexity. This lends plausibility to the algorithm to be considered in this section, which is exponential in the number of interacting contingent links.

A simple execution algorithm could proceed as if the network were an ordinary STN and simply fail if propagation causes the flexibility of a contingent link to be restricted. The following algorithm does better by excluding current values for control points that would lead to future restrictions on the uncontrollables.

We can formulate an execution algorithm in a manner analogous to that for ordinary STNs. For this, we must (1) propagate time windows, (2) determine whether a timepoint is live and enabled, and (3) repropagate with updated information. In the STNU case, updated information may result from observations and refined predictions, as well as executions. Note also that an update may arise from simple passage of time, where a contingent link finishing point is observed to have not yet occurred. Figure 3 summarizes the overall algorithm.

Basic Propagation

The propagation in the execution algorithm is closely related to the propagation algorithm for determining Waypoint Controllability that was introduced in (Morris & Muscettola 1999). The latter is similar to a Bellman-Ford distance propagation in an ordinary STN, except it effectively propagates in all boundary projections simultaneously. This is accomplished by splitting each distance value propagated across a contingent link into two values corresponding to the different boundary projections. For example, a contingent link $A \rightarrow B$ with bounds $[1,3]$ corresponds to an STN link with bounds $[1,1]$ or $[3,3]$ in different boundary projections. This means a distance value of 0 at A produces propagated values of 1 or 3 at B. The algorithm carries forward both values, but tags them according to which selection was used. In this case, we could write the set of propagated tagged values as $\{1^t, 3^T\}$, where t and T denote the $[1,1]$ and $[3,3]$ selections, respectively. Note that the values may split again at subsequent contingent links, leading to values involving multiple choices. Thus, the propagated values acquire tags reflecting all the boundary choices involved in their creation.

We will use the expression v^T to denote a value v with tag T. (We may write v, without superscript, if the tag is empty.) A tagged value $v_1^{T_1}$ *subsumes* a tagged value $v_2^{T_2}$ if $v_1 \leq v_2$ and $T_1 \subseteq T_2$. Subsumed values are subject to deletion. Observe that we can propagate distance values just like in an ordinary STN; the only difference is that sets of tagged values are propagated to each node instead of simple values. It is convenient to use a simplified notation for sets of tagged values, writing $1^t 3^T$ instead of $\{1^t, 3^T\}$.

Windows and Updates

For execution purposes, we need to propagate both upper and lower bounds, i.e., a time window. Each bound consists of a set of labelled values, corresponding to the values in the different boundary projections. Consider, for example, a contingent link $A \rightarrow B$ with bounds $[1,3]$. A time window of $[0,4]$ at A then propagates to a time window of $[1^t 3^T, 5^t 7^T]$ at B, where t and T indicate the $[1,1]$ and $[3,3]$ choices, respectively. The reader should pay particular attention to the interval $[3,5]$ lying between the maximum of the lower-bound values and the minimum of the upper-bound values, which corresponds to the intersection of the windows from all the boundary projections.

When an update occurs, we need to repropagate. Suppose, in the above example, the lower bound for the contingent link is increased from 1 to 2. This affects both the lower and upper bounds at B. The update of the lower bound at B is an increase from $1^t 3^T$ to $2^t 3^T$, which is a potential tightening of the intersection window. The change to the upper bound at B is also an increase, from $5^t 7^T$ to $6^t 7^T$. However, an increase in the upper bound is a potential loosening of the intersection window, not a tightening.

The need to propagate predictive updates efficiently requires a high degree of incrementality. In ordinary STNs, it is difficult to achieve incremental propagation of loosened bounds. However, the tags provide sufficient information to identify the values that need revision. A reasonable degree of incrementality is obtained by simply deleting values with tags involving the updated links, and repropagating from those links. (More selective deletion is possible by including additional information in the tags. For example, each contingent link gives rise to both a positive and negative edge in the distance graph, and information about which of those participated in a propagation could be used to advantage. We omit the details.)

Liveness and Enablement

We next consider how to select a control timepoint for execution. First, the timepoint must be live in all boundary projections. This is equivalent to the current time lying between the maximum of the lower-bound values and the minimum of the upper-bound ones. As an example, consider the network

```
    [1,100]         [-1,50]
A ========> B <------ C
```

where A ==> B is a contingent link, B <-- C is a requirement link, and A is the start point. The initial window at C is given by $[-49^{-t}50^{-T}, 2^{+t}101^{+T}]$, so C is not live. Suppose B is observed to occur at time 25. A new propagation produces a window of $[-25, 26]$ for C, which makes it live. On the other hand, suppose it is observed that B has *not* occurred by time 50. The bounds for the contingent link can be narrowed to $[50, 100]$. This update propagates to give $[0^{-t}50^{-T}, 51^{+t}101^{+T}]$ for C. Notice that C is now live in all projections even though B has not finished yet.

The second condition for execution is that the timepoint be enabled in all boundary projections. This poses a minor complication compared to an ordinary STN execution because the set of projections may contract as updates occur. We can still compute in advance all the paths that could possibly be required for enablement. (Note that each path will have a set of tagged values as its distance.) However, as projections are excluded due to updates, some of the paths may cease to be enabling. This requires repeated updating and checking of the enablement distances to see if they are still negative in some projection.

It is easy to see that the algorithm will never choose an execution time that is inconsistent with some projection. However, an execution can still fail, even for a network where all projections are consistent. This can happen if a situation occurs where immediate execution and deferred execution each exclude some of the projections. An example of this is the impossible task where we need to make preparations tightly in advance before some event whose timing is unknown.

Consider, for example, the network

```
    [1,100]         [1,50]
A ========> B <------ C
```

and assume the standard update scenario. Note that C must occur before B. However, any time we choose for C before time 50 will be inconsistent with some late occurrence of B. On the other hand, deferring the choice until time 50 will fail if B occurs early. For instance, the updated window for C at time 25, if B has not occurred earlier, will be $[-25^{-t}50^{-T}, 24^{+t}99^{+T}]$. Note that C is not live, so it cannot be executed. If B now occurs, the execution has failed.

Dispatchability

We next consider the extent to which the methods of (Muscettola, Morris, & Tsamardinos 1998) can speed up the execution algorithm, in the framework where maximum flexibility is retained.

The transformation to the All-Pairs graph is straightforward. However, the distances must be computed using tagged values. This can be costly, but is done offline before the execution begins.

A complication arises in the removal of dominated edges. In this framework, an edge may only be removed if it is dominated in *all* projections. This presents fewer opportunities for removal, and seems to exclude the possibility of arriving at a *minimum* dispatchable network. If interacting contingent edges are few in practice, as seems likely with the waypoint controllability approach, there should nevertheless be substantial savings from using a pruned dispatchable network.

A second complication is with respect to the arbitrary updates envisaged in this framework. The proof of theorem 1 in (Muscettola, Morris, & Tsamardinos 1998), upon which the dominance analysis is based, relies on two assumptions about the type of update that occurs during execution: first, the update only occurs for timepoints that are enabled; second, the update narrows the window to a single value. The upshot of this is that local propagation will be in general be insufficient for predictive updates to contingent links. Full propagation can be used instead. On the positive side, the updates arising from executions and sharp observations (that collapse the interval to a single point) do satisfy the criteria, and for those, local propagation is sufficient.

Safe Networks

We now turn to an approach that sacrifices some flexibility in order to avoid the exponential complexity of the algorithm in the previous section. This applies to scenarios where the precise finishing time of a contingent link becomes known as soon as it occurs. The key idea is as follows. Suppose we pretend that an STNU is an ordinary STN, and the contingent links are just ordinary links. Suppose also that the network has the property that, for every valid execution and for each contingent link, the only effective propagations to the contingent link finishing point are those that propagate through the contingent link itself. In this case, the propagations do not affect the possible durations of the contingent links, and Nature's flexibility is not impaired. Consequently, we can pretend that the agent is making all the choices, and carry out the execution as if the network was an ordinary STN. In particular, simple values can be propagated; no tags are needed. Furthermore, we can apply the methods of (Muscettola, Morris, & Tsamardinos 1998) to compute a minimum dispatchable network, and use only local propagation during execution.

An STNU with the above felicitous property will be called a *safe* network. Our first task is to obtain a characterization of the property that is more easily checked. It turns out that the dominance relation introduced in (Muscettola, Morris, & Tsamardinos 1998) is relevant here. The characterization will be in terms of the STN obtained from a given STNU by ignoring the distinction between contingent links and requirement links. We call this the *associated STN* of the given STNU. Note that in the distance graph of the associated STN, the forward edge arising from a contingent link will have positive length, while the corresponding reverse edge will have negative length. These edges will be referred to as "contingent edges."

The following terminology will also be useful. In an STN distance graph, an edge from A to B is a *tight edge* if there is no path from A to B whose distance is less than the length of the edge.

To avoid certain technical difficulties, it is necessary to exclude networks where two contingent links have the same finishing point. This does not entail any loss of generality because the coincident finishing points can be separated and connected by a $[0, 0]$ requirement link instead. (Semantically, there really are two points that are independently controlled by Nature.)

This leads to the following characterization.

Theorem 1 (Safety Theorem) *An STNU is safe if and only if in the distance graph of the associated STN the following three properties hold:*

(1) The forward and reverse edges arising from each contingent link are tight edges. (Thus, they survive unchanged in the All-Pairs graph.)

(2) In the All-Pairs graph, the forward edge arising from each contingent link $A \to B$ dominates all non-negative edges whose destination is B.

(3) In the All-Pairs graph, the reverse edge (from B to A) arising from each contingent link $A \to B$ dominates all negative edges whose source is B.

Proof: First suppose (1) is violated. Then one of the edges arising from a contingent link $A \to B$ is squeezed. Consider what happens when A is executed. The propagation along the squeezing path will supersede the propagation along the squeezed contingent edge. Thus, the network is not safe.

It remains to show that if (1) holds, then (2) and (3) together are equivalent to safety. This is a straightforward consequence of the methods of (Muscettola, Morris, & Tsamardinos 1998). Since (1) holds, we need only consider dispatching executions in the All-Pairs graph. Let $A \to B$ be a contingent link. By Theorem 1 of (Muscettola, Morris, & Tsamardinos 1998), the only effective propagations to B are those involving non-negative edges whose destination is B and negative edges whose source is B. Condition (2) states that the only effective non-negative edge propagation is the one occurring along the forward contingent edge. Similarly condition (3) states that the only effective negative edge propagation is the one occurring along the reverse contingent edge. Thus, (2) and (3) together state that the only effective propagations to B are those occurring along the two contingent edges, which is the requirement for safety. □

It follows from the theorem that for a safe STNU, the associated STN can be converted into a minimum dispatchable network in which the contingent links survive.[1] Moreover, for a contingent link $A \to B$ in this minimum dispatchable network, the forward contingent edge will be the only non-negative edge remaining whose destination is B, and the reverse contingent edge will be the only negative edge remaining whose source is B. This makes safety easy to check by first converting to the minimum dispatchable network. With minor modifications, the algorithm for constructing a minimum dispatchable graph in (Tsamardinos,

---

[1] If contingent links with coincident finishing points were allowed, this would not necessarily be the case because then there could be mutually dominating contingent links.

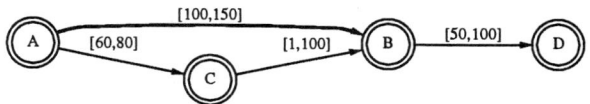

Figure 4: Safe Network.

Muscettola, & Morris 1998) can thus be used to verify safety in $O(EN + N^2 \log(N))$ time.

As an example of a safe network, consider figure 4, where $A \to B$ is a contingent link. Notice that no matter what time C is executed (within its window), the duration of $A \to B$ will not be further restricted. Also D does not affect the duration since it is constrained to occur after B. It is easy to verify, using the Triangle Rule of (Muscettola, Morris, & Tsamardinos 1998), that the dominance relations required by the theorem hold in the All-Pairs graph. Note that a minimum dispatchable graph exists that is identical to the original network except the link $C \to B$ is deleted.

Predictive updates that narrow the temporal bounds of contingent links can be accommodated within this framework. It is not hard to see that these cannot make a safe network unsafe. However, each such update requires full rather than local propagation, since it does not satisfy the criteria of dispatching executions.

Potential Safety

Few networks encountered in practice are likely to be safe. However, many networks that are not initially safe can be made so by judicious tightening of the constraints.

Consider for example the network

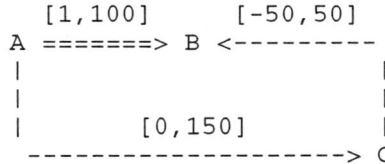

which is not safe since if C is executed at time 10, B will be forced to occur before time 60.

Notice that the network is already in All-Pairs form. We can use the criteria of the Safety Theorem to determine how to make it safe. The only edge at issue is the one of length 50 from C to B arising from the C --> B link. This violates condition (2). There are two ways to remove this violation.

First, we could make the edge be dominated by tightening up the bounds of the A --> C link as dictated by the Triangle Rule of (Muscettola, Morris, & Tsamardinos 1998). This requires that the distance graph edges satisfy $CA + AB = CB$, which can be accomplished by tightening the A --> C bounds to $[50, 150]$ (increasing the lower bound). It is easy to see the network is now safe: if B occurs before C, there is no problem (since B then propagates to C rather than vice versa); otherwise the propagation from C to B merely ratifies the situation that B has not yet occurred. For example, if B has not occurred before C is executed at time 60, then the propagation requires B to occur within $[10, 110]$, which is not restrictive given the current time of 60.

The second way to remove the violation is to eliminate the non-negative status of the edge. This can be done by tightening the C --> B bounds to $[-50, -1]$ (reducing the upper bound). Note that the $[-50, -1]$ link is equivalent to a $[1, 50]$ link in the opposite direction. This forces C to occur after B, which also makes the network safe.

With both methods, we must take care to ensure the tightening does not squeeze the contingent link, or produce an inconsistency. For example, if A --> C had bounds $[0, 100]$ then the second method would not work since it would restrict the contingent link to $[1, 99]$.

It is easy to see that this leads to a general algorithm for making a network safe, or determining that this is not possible. Each violation of the Safety Theorem can potentially be repaired in two ways. After a repair is attempted, the All-Pairs graph must be recomputed to determine whether a contingent link has been squeezed, or an inconsistency has been introduced. If so, the repair fails.

A network for which the repair algorithm succeeds will be called *potentially safe*. Since each choice of possible repairs can be verified in polynomial time, we see that the problem of determining potential safety is in $\mathcal{NP}$.

Examples suggest that the property of being potentially safe is very similar to that of *Dynamic Controllability*, as defined in (Vidal & Fargier 1997). The precise relationship between them remains to be determined. Note that an $\mathcal{NP}$ algorithm for Dynamic Controllability has not been presented in the literature.

Observe that in making safe a potentially safe network, we are giving up flexibility in advance. This complicates the question of predictive updates of contingent links. We could accommodate them, as discussed previously, by doing a full propagation, but this would not take advantage of the flexibility-enhancing effect of narrowing a contingent link. To do that, we would need to redo the repairs required for safety, which might be too costly in practice during execution.

Unfortunately, not all networks that can be effectively executed can be made safe. Consider the network

```
     [1,200]         [-1,100]
  A ========> B <---------
  |                       |
  |                       |
  |        [0,100]        |
  ---------------------> C
```

The following execution algorithm is effective:

```
if B occurs before time 99
then execute C at 1 unit later
else execute C at the fixed time 100
```

The first possibility for making this safe would be to increase the A --> C lower bound to 100 in an attempt to satisfy the Triangle Rule. However, this would squeeze the contingent link, forcing an increase in the lower bound to 99. The other possibility is to decrease the C --> B upper bound to -1, so that C occurs after B. However, that also squeezes the contingent link, forcing a decrease in the upper bound to 99.

This raises the possibility of using the safety analysis to synthesize the conditional execution strategy noted above. For example, the given network could be specialized to two "cases" where the contingent link bounds are restricted to ranges of $[1, 99]$ and $[99, 200]$, respectively. Each of these can be made safe separately, leading to the two branches of the strategy. This is a topic for future work.

Acknowledgments

We thank Thierry Vidal for useful discussions, and also thank the referees for their suggestions.

References

Bienkowski, M. A., and Hoebel, L. J. 1998. Integrating AI components for a military planning application. In *Proc. of Fifteenth Nat. Conf. on Artificial Intelligence (AAAI-98)*.

Cormen, T.; Leiserson, C.; and Rivest, R. 1990. *Introduction to Algorithms*. Cambridge, MA: MIT press.

Dechter, R.; Meiri, I.; and Pearl, J. 1991. Temporal constraint networks. *Artificial Intelligence* 49:61–95.

Morris, P., and Muscettola, N. 1999. Managing temporal uncertainty through waypoint controllability. In *Proc. of Sixteenth Int. Joint Conf. on Artificial Intelligence (IJCAI-99)*.

Muscettola, N.; Nayak, P.; Pell, B.; and Williams, B. 1998. Remote agent: to boldly go where no AI system has gone before. *Artificial Intelligence* 103(1-2):5–48.

Muscettola, N.; Morris, P.; and Tsamardinos, I. 1998. Reformulating temporal plans for efficient execution. In *Proc. of Sixth Int. Conf. on Principles of Knowledge Representation and Reasoning (KR'98)*.

Tsamardinos, I.; Muscettola, N.; and Morris, P. 1998. Fast transformation of temporal plans for efficient execution. In *Proc. of Fifteenth Nat. Conf. on Artificial Intelligence (AAAI-98)*.

Vidal, T., and Fargier, H. 1997. Contingent durations in temporal CSPs: From consistency to controllabilities. In *Proc. of IEEE TIME-97 International Workshop*.

Vidal, T., and Ghallab, M. 1996. Dealing with uncertain durations in temporal constraint networks dedicated to planning. In *Proc. of 12th European Conference on Artificial Intelligence (ECAI-96)*, 48–52.

Modeling Actions with Ramifications in Nondeterministic, Concurrent, and Continuous Domains— And A Case Study

Michael Thielscher
Dresden University of Technology
01062 Dresden, Germany
mit@inf.tu-dresden.de

Abstract

Combining into a consistent theory co-existing models for different phenomena in reasoning about actions can be a problem as challenging as addressing new aspects. We present a uniform theory for reasoning about actions with indirect effects in nondeterministic, concurrent, and continuous domains. We report on a case study to which our theory has been successfully applied.

Introduction

Research on reasoning about actions in dynamic environments has made rapid progress in the recent past: Initiated by new, solid solutions to the Frame Problem in the early 1990s,[1] a variety of advanced aspects of complex environments has been successfully addressed, among which are: indirect effects of actions, concurrency, uncertainty, sensing actions, and continuous change in conjunction with so-called natural actions, to mention just the ones on which most of recent work has focused.

However, the existence of models for all of these and other aspects does not imply that there be a unique model which covers them all. Rather, extensions of basic solutions to the Frame Problem have mostly been investigated in isolation. As a consequence, combining co-existing models for different phenomena is often a problem as challenging as addressing further aspects.

In this paper, we present a classical logic formalism that uniformly addresses the diverse phenomena of ramifications (i.e., indirect effects), nondeterminism, concurrency, and continuous change. Our formalism is based on the concept of state update axioms of the Fluent Calculus as one established solution to the Frame Problem (Thielscher 1999b), which roots in the logic programming formalism of (Hölldobler & Schneeberger 1990).

We have successfully applied our theory to the Traffic World, a complex dynamic domain which has recently been posed as a challenge to the scientific community (Sandewall 1999). The crucial property of this domain is that it shows all of the aforementioned phenomena, and hence cannot be fully axiomatized by means of co-existing but not readily compatible solutions to each aspect alone. Using the combined theory of the Fluent Calculus, in (Henschel & Thielscher 1999) we have developed an axiomatization of the full Traffic World,[2] which proves the expressiveness of our framework.

In the next section, we give a short introduction to the case study of the Traffic World, and we briefly recapitulate the fundamentals of the Fluent Calculus.[3] We then discuss a first challenge which is raised by combining the two aspects of uncertainty and natural actions and which concerns the specification of action preconditions. Thereafter, we present a theory which integrates ramification, nondeterminism, and concurrency in the Fluent Calculus, followed by incorporating continuous change and natural actions. Throughout the paper, key axioms taken from (Henschel & Thielscher 1999) serve as examples.

The Basic Fluent Calculus

The Traffic World consists of a net of road segments on which cars are moving. Cars may speed up, slow down, and turn at intersections (that is, nodes at which segments meet). Speed changes are approximated as instantaneous, for the sake of simplicity. Each car has its own top speed, roads have speed limits, and cars must keep a certain safety distance to the car in front. One or more cars may be under our control, others are not. A logical axiomatization of the Traffic World can be used to solve, using automated deduction, various kinds of problems, such as: What can be concluded about the future of a (possibly incompletely) given state? How did a given state evolve, say, a traffic jam? How can certain goals be achieved? Rigorous axiomatizations moreover allow for proving general properties, such as congestion avoidance under certain conditions etc. For details we refer to (Sandewall 1999).

Copyright © 2000, American Association for Artificial Intelligence (www.aaai.org). All rights reserved.

[1] A good overview of today's established action formalisms is provided by the set of reference articles published in (Sandewall 1998).

[2] It is worth mentioning that the Fluent Calculus was the first of the standard approaches in which a solution to the challenge problem was submitted.

[3] Due to lack of space we can provide only a brief description of the Fluent Calculus; for a complete introduction see (Thielscher 1999b)—or get an online tutorial at http://pikas.inf.tu-dresden.de/~mit/FC/Tutorial/index.htm.

The Traffic World involves a variety of aspects of real-world action domains:

- **Continuous change.** The position of a car which moves with constant velocity changes continuously.
- **Concurrency.** Two or more cars may arrive at an intersection at the same time and even with the intention to turn onto the same road segment.
- **Natural actions.** Cars are assumed to automatically slow down as soon as they have reached the safety distance to the car in front.
- **Ramification.** If the driver of a car hits the break and slows down as effect, then another car traveling behind and keeping just the safety distance must slow down, too, as an indirect effect, which in turn may cause a third car to slow down traveling behind the second one, and so on.
- **Nondeterminism.** Cars which are not under our control may choose either direction at intersections.

The Fluent Calculus uses the basic entity of a fluent, which is an atomic component of descriptions of world states. While fluents are generally assumed to be stable in between the occurrence of two consecutive actions, a fluent may internally represent an arbitrarily complex, continuous process. The central fluent used for the Traffic World, denoted by $\texttt{Movement}(x, d, v, t, r, n)$, represents such a process, namely, the constant movement of a car x. The other parameters are: the distance absolved on the current road segment at the time of initiation of the particular movement (d), the velocity (v), the time when the movement was initiated (t), the road segment (r), and the node the car is heading for (n).

The key feature of the Fluent Calculus is that it introduces an explicit notion of a state to the Situation Calculus. This requires the meticulous distinction between situations (which are characterized by sequences of actions) and states (which are characterized by truth-assignments to fluents). Formally, the Fluent Calculus is an order-sorted second order language with equality, which includes the pre-defined sorts *sit*, *action*, *fluent*, and *state*. Fluents are reified propositions. That is to say, the symbol Movement from above denotes a function symbol which maps a 6-tuple of the right sort onto a *fluent*. Fluents can be joined together by the binary function symbol "$\circ$" to make up states. We write this symbol in infix notation. The function shall satisfy the laws AC1, i.e., associativity, commutativity, and existence of a unit element, denoted by $\emptyset$. Associativity allows us to omit parentheses in nested applications of $\circ$.

The standard function $State : sit \mapsto state$ relates a situation to the state of the world in that situation. The following axiom, for instance, specifies two movements taking place in the initial situation S_0:

$(\exists z)\, State(S_0) =$
$\quad \texttt{Movement}(X_1, 2.5\text{km}, 70\text{kmph}, 9:30:00, R_{14}, N_8) \circ$
$\quad \texttt{Movement}(X_2, 3.7\text{km}, 50\text{kmph}, 9:32:30, R_6, N_{22}) \circ z$

That is, of $State(S_0)$ it is known that it includes the two fluents mentioned and possibly some other fluents z.[4]

---
[4] A word on the notation: Predicate and function symbols, in-

For convenience, we will frequently use the expressions $Holds(f, z)$ —denoting that f holds in state z —and the common $Holds(f, s)$ —stating that fluent f holds in situation s—, though they are not part of the signature but mere abbreviations of equality sentences:

$$Holds(f, z) \stackrel{\text{def}}{=} (\exists z')\, z = f \circ z'$$
$$Holds(f, s) \stackrel{\text{def}}{=} Holds(f, State(s))$$

So-called state constraints are used to restrict the space of states to those that can actually occur. The following, for instance, says that one and the same car can never execute two movements in the same situation:

$\texttt{Holds}(\texttt{Movement}(x, d_1, v_1, t_1, r_1, n_1), s)$
$\wedge\, \texttt{Holds}(\texttt{Movement}(x, d_2, v_2, t_2, r_2, n_2), s)$
$\supset d_1 = d_2 \wedge v_1 = v_2 \wedge t_1 = t_2 \wedge r_1 = r_2 \wedge n_1 = n_2$

A further example of a state constraint in the Traffic World can be found in the section on ramifications.

Fundamental for any Fluent Calculus axiomatization is the axiom set

$$EUNA[\circ, \emptyset; \textit{fluent}, \textit{state}] \qquad (\text{F1})$$

which accompanies domain-dependent unique name-assumptions by the axioms AC1 for $\circ; \emptyset$ along with the two axioms of irreducibility and of Levi, which entail inequality of two state terms that are composed of different fluents; see (Henschel & Thielscher 1999). In addition, we have the foundational axiom

$$State(s) \neq f \circ f \circ z \qquad (\text{F2})$$

by which double occurrences of fluents are prohibited in any state which is associated with a situation.

So-called state update axioms specify the entire relation between the states at two consecutive situations. In the basic case of deterministic actions with only direct and closed effects,[5] a mere equation relates a successor state $State(Do(a, s))$ [6] to the preceding state $State(s)$:

$Poss(A(\vec{x}), s) \wedge \Delta(\vec{x}, s) \supset$
$\quad (\exists \vec{y})\, State(Do(A(\vec{x}), s)) \circ \vartheta^- = State(s) \circ \vartheta^+$

where the standard predicate $Poss(a, s)$ denotes that action a is possible in situation s and where ϑ^- are the negative effects and ϑ^+ the positive effects, resp., of action $A(\vec{x})$ under condition $\Delta(\vec{x}, s)$ (sequence $\vec{y}$ contains the variables in ϑ^-, ϑ^+ which are not among $\vec{x}$).[7]

More complex phenomena require more complex forms of state update axioms, as we will see later in the paper.

---
cluding constants, start with a capital letter whereas variables are in lower case, sometimes with sub- or superscripts. Free variables in formulas are assumed universally quantified. Throughout the paper, action variables are denoted by the letter a, situation variables by the letter s, fluent variables by the letter f, and state variables by the letter z, all possibly with sub- or superscript.

[5] By closed effects we mean that an action does not have an unbounded number of direct effects.

[6] As in the standard Situation Calculus, $Do(a, s)$ denotes the situation reached after performing action a in situation s.

[7] This scheme is the reason for not stipulating that "$\circ$" be idempotent, contrary to what one might intuitively expect instead of (F2). For if the function were idempotent, then the equation would not imply that $State(Do(a, s))$ does not include ϑ^-.

Preconditions of Natural Actions in Nondeterministic Worlds

In formalisms based on the Situation Calculus, such as (Reiter 1991), as well as in the Fluent Calculus a usual premise is that the preconditions of an action $A(\vec{x})$ can be described by a definitional formula

$$Poss(A(\vec{x}), s) \equiv \pi_A(\vec{x}, s)$$

where the first-order formula π_A does not include the predicate *Poss* and describes the conditions on parameters $\vec{x}$ and situation s under which the action is possible. This assumption usually generalizes to the case of non-deterministic worlds as well as to the case of natural actions, i.e., which occur automatically. Surprisingly, the premise fails if the two aspects are combined.

The reason lies in the fact that all natural actions which are possible must actually occur (Reiter 1996). Yet in a non-deterministic world, several instances of a natural action may be possible but only one of them can actually take place. In this case, the possibility of one natural action depends on other actions not being possible at the same time.

An example from the Traffic World is the natural action of someone else's car turning at intersections. A car has a choice among several alternatives, but in any concrete model of the world it can turn onto one segment only. Under these circumstances, a definitional precondition axiom of the aforementioned form does not exist. Rather, the specification needs to be split into two parts, the first of which is of the form

$$Poss(A(\vec{x}, \vec{y}), s) \supset \pi_A(\vec{x}, s) \land \widehat{\pi}_A(\vec{x}, \vec{y}, s)$$

where $\vec{y}$ are the parameters among which a nondeterministic choice has to be made and where $\pi_A(\vec{x}, s) \land \widehat{\pi}_A(\vec{x}, \vec{y}, s)$ describes the necessary precondition of $A(\vec{x}, \vec{y})$ in s. The second part of the precondition axiomatization stipulates uniqueness of the choice:

$$\pi_A(\vec{x}, s) \supset (\exists ! \vec{y}) \, Poss(A(\vec{x}, \vec{y}), s)$$

Based on this generalization, the following two axioms describe the precondition of someone else's car arriving and nondeterministically turning at intersections:

```
Poss(ArriveAt(x, r₁, n, r₂, t), s) ⊃
  (∃d, v, t₀, n₂) (Holds(Movement(x, d, v, t₀, r₁, n), s) ∧
    d + v(t − t₀) = Length(r₁) ∧
    Connects(r₂, n, n₂) ∧ r₁ ≠ r₂)
```

where $\mathtt{ArriveAt(x, r_1, n, r_2, t)}$ denotes the natural action at time t of car x arriving at node n as the end of segment $\mathtt{r_1}$ and turning onto segment $\mathtt{r_2}$; $\mathtt{Length(r)}$ denotes the length of segment r; and $\mathtt{Connects(r, n_1, n_2)}$ denotes that road segment r connects nodes $\mathtt{n_1}$ and $\mathtt{n_2}$. Since there can only be one road segment $\mathtt{r_2}$ onto which the car may turn, the second axiom requires uniqueness of this parameter:

```
(∃d, v, t₀, n₂) (Holds(Movement(x, d, v, t₀, r₁, n), s) ∧
    d + v(t − t₀) = Length(r₁))
  ⊃ (∃!r₂) Poss(ArriveAt(x, r₁, n, r₂, t), s)
```

Concurrency with Ramification

Concurrency

The Fluent Calculus for concurrent actions (Thielscher 2000b) is based on the additional pre-defined sort *conc*, of which *action* is a sub-sort. Single actions which are performed simultaneously are joined together with a new binary function. This function shares with the function combining fluents to states the properties of associativity, commutativity, and existence of a unit element. Hence, the symbol "∘" is overloaded as denotation for both. The constant "ϵ" (read: *no-op*) acts as the unit element wrt. ∘ applied to terms of sort *conc*. In summary, the concurrent Fluent Calculus relies on the equality axioms (c.f. (F1)),

$$EUNA[\circ, \epsilon; action, conc] \qquad (F3)$$

In what follows, variables of the new sort are denoted by the letter c, possibly with sub- or superscript.

State update axioms for concurrent actions are recursive. They specify the effect of an action relative to the effect of arbitrary other, concurrent actions:

$$Poss(\alpha(\vec{x}) \circ c, s) \land \Delta(\vec{x}, c, s) \supset$$
$$(\exists \vec{y}) \, State(Do(\alpha(\vec{x}) \circ c, s)) \circ \vartheta^- = State(Do(c, s)) \circ \vartheta^+$$

That is, ϑ^- and ϑ^+ are the additional negative and positive, resp., effects which occur if α is performed besides c. Here, α can be a single action or a compound action which produces synergic effects, that is, effects which no single action would have if performed alone. With the help of recursive state update axioms, the effect of, say, two simultaneous but independent actions can be inferred by first inferring the effect of one of them and, then, inferring the effect of the other action on the result of the first inference. The recursion relies on the base case of the empty action, which has no effect:

$$State(Do(\epsilon, s)) = State(s)$$

Two or more actions may interfere when performed concurrently, which is why condition Δ in the above state update axiom may restrict the applicability of the implication in view of the concurrent action c.

Ramification

In the Fluent Calculus with ramifications (Thielscher 1997), indirect effects of actions are accounted for by the successive application of so-called causal relationships. Their axiomatization is based on defining a predicate $Causes(z_0, z_0^+, z_0^-, z_1, z_1^+, z_1^-)$, which means that in the current state z_0 the occurred positive and negative effects z_0^+, z_0^- give rise to an additional, indirect effect resulting in the updated state z_1 and the updated current effects z_1^+, z_1^-. For instance, the following causal relationship implies that if a car x has lowered its speed as a direct or indirect effect of some action, then this causes another car x' traveling behind in the global safety distance ς to slow down as well:

$$\begin{aligned}
&\text{Causes}(z_0, z_0^+, z_0^-, z_1, z_1^+, z_1^-) \equiv \\
&(\exists t_0, x, d, v, t, r, n, x', d', v', t') \\
&[\text{Start}(z_0) = t_0 \land \\
&\text{Holds}(\text{Movement}(x, d, v, t, r, n), z_0) \land \\
&\text{Holds}(\text{Movement}(x', d', v', t', r, n), z_0) \land \\
&\varsigma = d + v(t_0 - t) - (d' + v'(t_0 - t')) \land \\
&v < v' \land \\
&z_1 \circ \text{Movement}(x', d', v', t', r, n) = \\
&\quad z_0 \circ \text{Movement}(x', d' + v'(t_0 - t'), v, t_0, r, n) \land \\
&z_1^+ = z_0^+ \circ \text{Movement}(x', d' + v'(t_0 - t'), v, t_0, r, n) \land \\
&z_1^- = z_0^- \circ \text{Movement}(x', d', v', t', r, n)] \\
&\lor \ldots
\end{aligned}$$

(The ellipsis indicates that the Traffic World axiomatization includes more causal relationships. For the definition of $Start(z)$ see foundational axiom (F7) below.) Applications of the above causal relationship ensure that the following state constraint will not be violated, which says that cars must in any situation keep the safety distance:

$$\begin{aligned}
&\text{Holds}(\text{Movement}(x_1, d_1, v_1, t_1, r, n), s) \land \\
&\text{Holds}(\text{Movement}(x_2, d_2, v_2, t_2, r, n), s) \land \\
&x_1 \neq x_2 \land \text{Start}(s) = t \supset \quad (1)\\
&d_1 + v_1(t - t_1) - (d_2 + v_2(t - t_2)) \geq \varsigma \land \\
&[d_1 + v_1(t - t_1) - (d_2 + v_2(t - t_2)) = \varsigma \supset v_2 \leq v_1]
\end{aligned}$$

Causal relationships are repeatedly applied until a state is obtained which does not violate the state constraints. Our causal relationship from above is an excellent demonstration of the power of ramification: It is intended that if a car leading a whole convoy slows down, then in a manner of falling dominoes the effect of deceleration gets propagated. To this end, the general idea of ramification needs to be combined with the recursive effect specifications needed for concurrency. The combined axiomatization will allow for reasoning about interesting cases such as the following. Suppose car X_1 is followed by faster car X_2, which is in turn followed by car X_3, the fastest of all. Suppose further that X_2 reaches the safety distance to X_1 at the very same moment as X_3 approaches X_2. Then X_2 assumes the speed of X_1 and X_3 that of X_2 as direct effects; thereafter, ramification changes the speed of X_3 again, namely, to the new speed of X_2.

The Combination

The challenge with combining the two phenomena of concurrency and ramification is that two or more actions may produce direct effects which only together cause some indirect effect. (The scenario just mentioned constitutes such a case.) Therefore, ramifications must not be inferred separately for each member of a compound action. Hence, a new form of recursive effect specifications is required by which an intermediate state is determined in which all direct effects are realized but which is not yet the overall successor state. To this end, we introduce three functions, $DSucc, DEff^+, DEff^-$, mapping a concurrent action and a state to states which denote, resp., the world state resulting from the direct effects of the concurrent action and the combined positive and negative effects. On this basis, the new general form of state update axioms is as follows.[8]

$$\begin{aligned}
&Poss(\alpha(\vec{x}) \circ c, z) \land \Delta(\vec{x}, c, z) \supset \\
&(\exists \vec{y}, z^+, z^-) \\
&[z^+ = \vartheta^+ \land z^- = \vartheta^- \land \\
&DSucc(\alpha(\vec{x}) \circ c, z) \circ z^- = DSucc(c, z) \circ z^+ \land \\
&DEff^+(\alpha(\vec{x}) \circ c, z) = DEff^+(c, z) \circ z^+ \land \\
&DEff^-(\alpha(\vec{x}) \circ c, z) = DEff^-(c, z) \circ z^-]
\end{aligned}$$

The base case for this recursion is given by this foundational axiom:

$$\begin{aligned}
DSucc(\epsilon, z) &= z \land \\
DEff^+(\epsilon, z) &= \emptyset \land DEff^-(\epsilon, z) = \emptyset
\end{aligned} \quad (F4)$$

Based on the combined direct effects of a concurrent action, ramification yields all indirect effects:

$$Ramify(DSucc(c, z), DEff^+(c, z), DEff^-(c, z), \\ Succ(c, z)) \quad (F5)$$

where $Ramify(z_0, z^+, z^-, z)$ means that the successive application of (zero or more) causal relationships to state z_0 and effects z^+, z^- results in state z.

Ramification is the repeated application of causal relationships:

$$Ramify(z_1, z_1^+, z_1^-, z_2) \equiv \\ (\exists z_2^+, z_2^-)(z_1, z_1^+, z_1^-, z_2, z_2^+, z_2^-) \in \mu[Causes] \quad (F6)$$

where $(\vec{x}, \vec{y}) \in \mu[P]$ abbreviates the following formula, which is a standard second-order schema to axiomatize that $(\vec{x}, \vec{y})$ belongs to the reflexive and transitive closure of predicate P:

$$\forall \Pi \left\{ \begin{array}{l} (\forall \vec{u}) \Pi(\vec{u}, \vec{u}) \land \\ (\forall \vec{u}, \vec{v}, \vec{w}) [\Pi(\vec{u}, \vec{v}) \land P(\vec{v}, \vec{w}) \supset \Pi(\vec{u}, \vec{w})] \\ \supset \Pi(\vec{x}, \vec{y}) \end{array} \right\}$$

An example of a recursive effect specification is the following, which describes the direct effect of a car x arriving at an intersection n and the immediate turn onto another segment r_2. For a better understanding of the axiom, we note that our model of the Traffic World handles jams at intersections by virtual waiting areas in each outgoing road segment, which house all cars waiting in line for that segment to become free up to the safety distance; see (Henschel & Thielscher 1999).

$$\begin{aligned}
&Poss(\text{ArriveAt}(x, r_1, n, r_2, t) \circ c, z) \land \\
&\neg Cancels(c, \text{ArriveAt}(x, r_1, n, r_2, t), z) \supset \\
&(\exists d, p, v, t', t_0) \\
&[z^+ = \text{Waiting}(x, n, r_2, p) \circ \text{Counter}(n, r_2, p+1) \land \\
&z^- = \text{Movement}(x, d, v, t', r_1, n) \circ \text{Counter}(n, r_2, p) \land \\
&DSucc(\text{ArriveAt}(x, r_1, n, r_2, t) \circ c, z) \circ z^- = \\
&\qquad\qquad\qquad\qquad\qquad DSucc(c, z) \circ z^+ \land \\
&DEff^+(\text{ArriveAt}(x, r_1, n, r_2, t) \circ c, z) = \\
&\qquad\qquad\qquad\qquad\qquad DEff^+(c, z) \circ z^+ \land \\
&DEff^-(\text{ArriveAt}(x, r_1, n, r_2, t) \circ c, z) = \\
&\qquad\qquad\qquad\qquad\qquad DEff^-(c, z) \circ z^-]
\end{aligned}$$

---

[8] In anticipation of the integration of continuous change, the situation argument s is replaced by the state argument z, and the expression $State(Do(c, s))$ is replaced by $Succ(c, z)$—denoting the successor state of performing concurrent action c in state z—, in all specifications related to update in the following.

Put in words, if the action is not canceled by the concurrent actions, then car x is now waiting in line, there is one more car waiting to leave node n for segment r_2, car x is no longer moving, and the previous value of the counter becomes false.

Turning is a nice example also to demonstrate the problem of interfering concurrent actions. If more than one ArriveAt actions take place at the same time and do not conflict, e.g., because they occur at different intersections, then the recursive application of the above axiom ensures that each turn has the effect as specified. However, if two or more cars arrive at the same node with the intention to turn onto the same segment, then the consequents of the corresponding instances are in conflict. The reason being that different decompositions of the concurrent action lead to different queues, that is, the incoming cars are not placed in a unique order.

The conflict admits an elegant solution by defining cancellation of actions in the following way. Suppose a car attempts to turn onto a segment which another car has chosen, too, having higher priority according to the right-of-way regulation at the intersection in question. Then the former cancels the latter, thus avoiding that the decomposition starts with the action that has higher priority. As a consequence, only those decompositions of a concurrent action are possible without cancellation where all turns onto one segment are inferred according to the priority ordering:[9]

```
Cancels(c,ArriveAt(x_1,r_1,n,r_2,t),z) ≡
  (∃x_2,r'_1)( In(ArriveAt(x_2,r'_1,n,r_2,t),c) ∧
    Priority(r_1,n,r_2) > Priority(r'_1,n,r_2))
```

where $Priority(r_1,n,r_2)$ denotes the priority that cars coming from segment r_1 have at node n regarding a turn into r_2, and where we use the following macro:

$$In(c_1, c) \stackrel{\text{def}}{=} (\exists c')\, c = c_1 \circ c'$$

Integrating Continuous Change

Continuous Change and Natural Actions

The basic representation mechanism for continuous change is the introduction of process fluents. The Fluent Calculus for continuous change moreover relies on the distinction between deliberative and so-called natural actions. The latter are not subject to the free will of a planning agent. Rather they happen automatically under specific circumstances. If, for instance, a car which is not under our control has absolved the entire length of a segment, then it will automatically perform an ArriveAt action, thus causing an 'autonomous' update of the system state.

The crucial notion underlying the Fluent Calculus for continuous change is that of a situation tree with trajectories (Thielscher 1999a). In any situation, natural actions may cause an autonomous evolution of the state associated with

[9]To see this, suppose A_1 and A_2 are turn actions such that $Cancels(A_2, A_1, z)$. Then the only decomposition which avoids cancellation is, $DSucc(A_1 \circ A_2, z) \rightarrow DSucc(A_1, z) \rightarrow DSucc(\epsilon, z)$, where A_1 is performed 'first' in z.

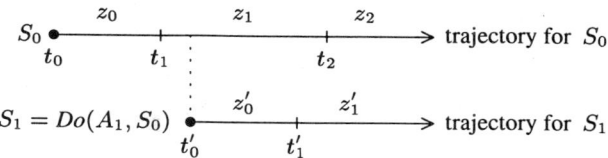

Figure 1: Each situation has its own trajectory, which describes how the state evolves according to the expected natural actions. In the example shown here, at the time t'_0 when the deliberative action A_1 is performed in situation S_0, the world is no longer in the initial state z_0 due to a natural action happening at time $t_1 < t'_0$, which causes state z_1 to arise. The effect of A_1 is to transform z_1 into z'_0, which thus becomes the initial state of the trajectory for situation $Do(A_1, S_0)$.

that situation.[10] To this end, each situation has a trajectory. A trajectory is a sequence of states. The world state resulting from a deliberative action is the first one on a new trajectory. The further evolution of that trajectory is then determined by the natural actions that are expected to happen. The performance of a deliberative action, on the other hand, brings about another situation again, with its own trajectory; see Fig. 1.

The Combination

Integrating the concepts of continuous change and natural actions into the Fluent Calculus for concurrency and ramification requires to reason about the updating of states that are not necessarily associated with a situation. This is the reason for replacing the situation argument in precondition and effect axioms by the more general state argument (recall Footnote 8). This shift is straightforward since the expression $Holds(f, s)$ means nothing but $Holds(f, State(s))$ anyway.

The combined Fluent Calculus uses the pre-defined fluent $StartTime(t)$, where t is of sort **R**, determining the time $Start(z)$ at which a state arises:

$$(\exists!t)\, Holds(StartTime(t), z) \\ \supset (\forall t)\, (Holds(StartTime(t), z) \supset Start(z) = t) \quad \text{(F7)}$$

The starting time of all states associated with a situation is unique:

$$(\exists!t)\, Holds(StartTime(t), s) \land \\ Start(s) = Start(State(s)) \quad \text{(F8)}$$

The evolution of a trajectory is modeled using the predicate $Trajectory(z, z')$, which indicates that z' occurs on the trajectory rooted in z. To model correctly the evolution at any state, all natural actions that are possible next determine the successor state:

$$Trajectory(z, z) \land \\ [Trajectory(z, z') \land NextNatActions(c, z') \supset \\ \quad Trajectory(z, Succ(c, z'))] \quad \text{(F9)}$$

[10]Our approach differs in this respect from the approach of (Reiter 1996), where natural actions are included in situation terms. This intertwining the two kinds of actions has been shown unsuited for planning under incomplete information (Thielscher 1999a).

where
$$NextNatActions(c, z) \stackrel{\text{def}}{=}$$
$$(\exists t) \, [\, Start(z) \leq t \wedge ExpectedNatActions(z, t, c) \wedge$$
$$\neg (\exists t', c') \, (ExpectedNatActions(z, t', c') \wedge$$
$$Start(z) \leq t' < t) \,]$$

which in turn makes use of the following macro:

$$ExpectedNatActions(z, t, c) \stackrel{\text{def}}{=}$$
$$c \neq \epsilon \wedge$$
$$(\forall a) \, [In(a, c) \equiv$$
$$Natural(a) \wedge Time(a) = t \wedge Poss(a, z)] \wedge$$
$$(\forall a, c') \, c \neq a \circ a \circ c'$$

Here, $Time(a)$ denotes the time of action a, for example, $Time(\texttt{ArriveAt}(c, r_1, n, r_2, t)) = t$; and $Natural(a)$ means that a is a natural action. Each domain is assumed to include a suitable axiom defining the positive instances of $Natural$.

No states other than the ones according to axiom (F9) may occur on a trajectory:

$$ActualState(s, t, z) \wedge ActualState(s, t, z') \qquad (F10)$$
$$\supset z = z'$$

where $ActualState(s, t, z)$ is true if z is the state of the world in situation s at time t:

$$ActualState(s, t, z) \stackrel{\text{def}}{=}$$
$$Trajectory(State(s), z) \wedge t > Start(s) \wedge$$
$$(\forall a) \, (Natural(a) \wedge Poss(a, z) \supset Time(a) > t)$$

State constraints, such as (1), need to be generalized so that they apply to all actual states in a situation. Thus, a state constraint in the general setting becomes an implication of the form, $ActualState(s, t, z) \supset \Phi(z)$.

The final complication raised by combining concurrency, ramification, and natural actions is that natural actions may by coincidence happen at the very same time at which a compound deliberative action shall be performed. This requires to infer the direct and indirect effects of all actions together:

$$Poss(c, s) \wedge ActualState(s, Time(c), z) \supset$$
$$ExpectedNatActions(z, Time(c), c') \supset \qquad (F11)$$
$$State(Do(c, s)) = Succ(c \circ c', z)$$

Having made the shift from situation to state arguments in precondition axioms, the expression $Poss(c, s)$ is now a mere macro. It shall be true iff all actions in c occur at the same time t, are not natural actions, and are possible in conjunction with all natural actions that are expected at time t:

$$Poss(c, s) \stackrel{\text{def}}{=}$$
$$TimeUniform(c) \wedge$$
$$(\forall a)(In(a, c) \supset \neg Natural(a)) \wedge$$
$$(\forall z, c') \, [ActualState(s, Time(c), z) \wedge$$
$$ExpectedNatActions(z, Time(c), c')$$
$$\supset Poss(c \circ c', z)]$$

with

$$TimeUniform(c) \stackrel{\text{def}}{=} (\forall a, a') \, (In(a, c) \wedge In(a', c) \supset$$
$$Time(a) = Time(a'))$$

where we have the following final foundational axiom, which defines the time of a time-uniform compound action:

$$TimeUniform(c) \supset In(a, c) \supset Time(c) = Time(a) \qquad (F12)$$

Summary

We have presented a uniform classical logic formalism for reasoning about actions which covers a variety of complex phenomena such as ramifications, concurrency, and continuous change. To the best of our knowledge, this is the first framework which allows to model domains involving all of these aspects, since in particular the Ramification Problem has mostly been investigated in isolation. We have illustrated how this theory has been successfully applied to a case study that has recently been posed as a challenge to the scientific community. Future work consists in extending the theory further, especially by integrating our Fluent Calculus model of sensing actions (Thielscher 2000a).

References

Henschel, A., and Thielscher, M. 1999. The LMW traffic world in the fluent calculus. http://www.ida.liu.se/ext/etai/lmw/TRAFFIC/001.

Hölldobler, S., and Schneeberger, J. 1990. A new deductive approach to planning. *New Generation Computing* 8:225–244.

Reiter, R. 1991. The frame problem in the situation calculus: A simple solution (sometimes) and a completeness result for goal regression. In Lifschitz, V., ed., *Artificial Intelligence and Mathematical Theory of Computation*. Academic Press. 359–380.

Reiter, R. 1996. Natural actions, concurrency and continuous time in the situation calculus. In Aiello, L. C.; Doyle, J.; and Shapiro, S., eds., *Proc. of the International Conference on Principles of Knowledge Representation and Reasoning*, 2–13. Cambridge, MA: Morgan Kaufmann.

Sandewall, E., ed. 1998. *Electronic Transactions on Artificial Intelligence 2(3–4). A Collection of Refereed Reference Articles.* http://www.ep.liu.se/ej/etai/1998.

Sandewall, E. 1999. Logic Modelling Workshop. http://www.ida.liu.se/ext/etai/lmw/.

Thielscher, M. 1997. Ramification and causality. *Artificial Intelligence* 89(1–2):317–364.

Thielscher, M. 1999a. Fluent Calculus planning with continuous change. *Electronic Transactions on Artificial Intelligence*. (Submitted.) http://www.ep.liu.se/ea/cis/1999/011/.

Thielscher, M. 1999b. From Situation Calculus to Fluent Calculus: State update axioms as a solution to the inferential frame problem. *Artificial Intelligence* 111(1–2):277–299.

Thielscher, M. 2000a. Representing the knowledge of a robot. In Cohn, A.; Giunchiglia, F.; and Selman, B., eds., *Proc. of the International Conference on Principles of Knowledge Representation and Reasoning*. Breckenridge, CO: Morgan Kaufmann.

Thielscher, M. 2000b. Solving the inferential frame problem for concurrent actions. (Submitted.) http://pikas.inf.tu-dresden.de/~mit/publications/conferences/FCconc.ps.

Describing Rigid Body Motions in a Qualitative Theory of Spatial Regions

Brandon Bennett,* Anthony G. Cohn, Paolo Torrini* and Shyamanta M. Hazarika

Division of Artificial Intelligence
School of Computer Studies
University of Leeds, Leeds LS2 9JT, England
brandon@scs.leeds.ac.uk

Abstract

We explore the expressive power of a recently developed qualitative region-based geometry and apply it to the problem of representing and reasoning about the motion of rigid bodies within a confining environment.

Introduction

This paper is an investigation of the expressive power of Region-Based Geometry (**RBG**) (Bennett et al. 2000). This is a qualitative theory of spatial information based on the primitive relation of *parthood* (P) and a *sphere* predicate (S). The domain of the theory is that of spatial regions. This theory builds on the earlier work of (Tarski 1929), (Randell, Cui, & Cohn 1992) and (Borgo, Guarino, & Masolo 1996).

We show that the framework is expressive enough to formulate a 'qualitative kinematics' capable of describing the possible movements of systems of rigid objects in a far more general way than previous theories (Davis 1987; Faltings 1987; Davis 1988; Mukerjee & Bhatia 1995). Moreover, our work provides a rigorous formal ontology (as advocated by e.g. (Lenat 1995; Guarino 1998)) for the qualitative description of rigid body motions within constraining environments. Our results go some way towards countering the *poverty conjecture* of (Forbus, Nielsen, & Faltings 1987; 1991), who claimed that no 'purely qualitative' theory could provide an adequate basis for kinematics. However, whether a theory is 'qualitative' or 'quantative' is a rather subtle issue and may not be apparent from its primitive vocabulary. In fact we shall see that within a sufficiently rich theory, based on ostensibly qualitative concepts, coordinate systems and metrical relationships are in fact definable.

In this paper we confine our attention to representing 2-dimensional space; but we believe that it would be fairly straightforward to apply the same approach to the 3-dimensional case.

Overview of the Theory

To make this paper self-contained we now give a concise summary of the theory. A fuller explanation can be found in (Bennett et al. 2000). We start by defining some well-known mereological concepts starting from the primitive parthood relation $P(x,y)$:

D1) $PP(x,y) \equiv_{def} (P(x,y) \wedge \neg(x=y))$
D2) $DR(x,y) \equiv_{def} \neg\exists z[P(z,x) \wedge P(z,y)]$
D3) $SUM(\alpha, x) \equiv_{def} \forall y[y \in \alpha \rightarrow P(y,x)] \wedge$
$\neg\exists z[P(z,x) \wedge \forall y[y \in \alpha \rightarrow DR(y,z)]]$
D4) $\forall x[x = \mathcal{U} \leftrightarrow \forall y[P(y,x)]]$
D5) $\forall x[x = (y+z) \leftrightarrow (P(y,x) \wedge P(z,x) \wedge$
$\neg\exists w[P(w,x) \wedge DR(w,y) \wedge DR(w,z)])$
D6) $O(x,y) \equiv_{def} \neg DR(x,y)$
D7) $PO(x,y) \equiv_{def} O(x,y) \wedge \neg P(x,y) \wedge \neg P(y,x)$
D8) $Prod(x,y,z) \equiv_{def} \forall w[(P(w,x) \wedge P(w,y)) \leftrightarrow P(w,z)]$
D9) $Diff(x,y,z) \equiv_{def} \forall w[(P(w,x) \wedge DR(w,y)) \leftrightarrow P(w,z)]$
D10) $Compl(x,y) \equiv_{def} \forall w[P(w,x) \leftrightarrow DR(w,y)]$

In addition to the mereological primitive P, we shall employ a morphological primitive $S(x)$, which says that 'x is a *sphere*' — in the 2D case this of course means that x is a *disc*. We shall often want to quantify over just the spherical regions in the domain. For convenience we introduce the notations

D11) $\forall^\circ x[\phi] \equiv_{def} \forall x[S(x) \rightarrow \phi]$
D12) $\exists^\circ x[\phi] \equiv_{def} \exists x[S(x) \wedge \phi]$

We now define some fundamental geometrical relations involving spheres:

D13) We use Tarski's (1929) definitions (in terms of P and S) of key relations among spheres, specifically: external and internal tangency (ET and IT), external diametricity (ED) and concentricity ($\circledcirc$).

D14) $B(x,y,z) \equiv_{def} x = y \vee y = z \vee$
$\exists vw[ED(x,y,v) \wedge ED(v,w,y) \wedge ED(y,z,w)]$
D15) $COB(s,r) \equiv_{def}$
$S(s) \wedge \forall s'[s' \circledcirc s \rightarrow (O(s',r) \wedge \neg P(s',r))]$
D16) $EQD(x,y,z) \equiv_{def}$
$\exists^\circ z'[z' \circledcirc z \wedge COB(y,z') \wedge COB(x,z')]$
D17) $Mid(x,y,z) \equiv_{def} B(x,y,z) \wedge$
$\exists y'[y' \circledcirc y \wedge COB(x,y') \wedge COB(z,y')]$
D18) $wx \rightleftharpoons yz \equiv_{def}$
$\exists u \exists v[Mid(w,u,y) \wedge Mid(x,u,v) \wedge EQD(v,z,y)]$
D19) $Nearer(w,x,y,z) \equiv_{def}$
$\exists^\circ x'[B(w,x,x') \wedge \neg(x \circledcirc x') \wedge wx' \rightleftharpoons yz]$

$B(x,y,z)$ holds when the centre of y is between the centres of x and z (or coincides with one of these). $COB(s,r)$ means that sphere s is Centred On the Boundary of r.

---

*Supported by the EPSRC under grant GR/M56807.
Copyright © 2000, American Association for Artificial Intelligence (www.aaai.org). All rights reserved.

$\text{EQD}(x, y, z)$ says that the centres of x and y are equidistant from the centre of z. $\text{Mid}(x, y, z)$ says that the centre of y lies mid-way between the centres of x and z; and $wx \rightleftharpoons yz$ holds when the distance between the centres of w and x is the same as the distance between the centres of y and z. $\text{Nearer}(w, x, y, z)$ means that the centres of w and x are closer than the centres of y and z.

Finally we define a relation $\text{InI}(s, r)$ that is true when the centre point of sphere s is in the interior of region r:

D20) $\text{InI}(s, r) \equiv_{def} \exists^\circ s'[s' \circledcirc s \land \text{P}(s', r)]$

In addition to the usual principles of classical logic and the theory of sets, the system is required to satisfy the following spatial axioms:

A1) $\forall \alpha [\exists x[x \in \alpha] \to \exists!x[\text{SUM}(\alpha, x)]]$
A2) $\forall r \exists^\circ s[\text{P}(s, r)]$
A3) $\forall^\circ xy[\neg(x \circledcirc y) \to$
$\exists^\circ s[s \circledcirc x \land \forall^\circ z[\text{InI}(z, s) \leftrightarrow \text{Nearer}(x, z, x, y)]]$
A4) $\forall^\circ x \exists^\circ y[\neg(x \circledcirc y) \land$
$\forall^\circ z[\text{InI}(z, s) \leftrightarrow \text{Nearer}(x, z, x, y)]]$
A5) $\forall xy[\text{P}(x, y) \leftrightarrow \forall^\circ s[\text{InI}(s, x) \to \text{InI}(s, y)]]$
A6) $\forall r \forall^\circ s[\exists^\circ s'[s' \circledcirc s \land$
$\forall^\circ s''[\text{P}(s'', s') \to \text{O}(s'', r)]] \to \text{InI}(s, r)]$
A7) A suitable axiom set for two dimensional geometry formulated in terms of the B and $\rightleftharpoons$ relations,[1] with the quantifiers restricted to range over spheres and equality replaced by the $\circledcirc$ relation.
A8) $\forall^\circ xyz[(x \circledcirc y \land y \circledcirc z) \to x \circledcirc z]$
A9) $\forall^\circ xx'yzw[(xy \rightleftharpoons zw \land x' \circledcirc x) \to x'y \rightleftharpoons zw]$

A1 ensures that every set of regions has a sum. **A2** states that every region has a spherical part (from this and **A1** it can be proved that every region is equal to the sum of its spherical parts). **A3** ensures that for every pair of distinct points x and y there is a sphere centred at one and bounded by the other. **A4** says that all spheres can be constructed in this way. Because Nearer is defined in terms of the purely geometrical concepts (B and $\circledcirc$) and the geometrical axioms are known to be complete relative to the classical interpretation in Cartesian spaces, this means that InI is completely determined for the class of spheres. **A5** means that $\text{P}(x, y)$ holds just in case every interior point of x is an interior point of y (thus P must be symmetric and transitive). This axiom could be used as a definition so that InI was taken as primitive instead of P. **A6** is needed to fully fix the domain of regions by ensuring that they correspond to *regular* sets of points in the intended Cartesian models. Axioms **A8** and **A9** ensure that $\circledcirc$ behaves like equality relative to the geometrical axioms.[2]

In (Bennett *et al.* 2000) it is proved that this theory is *categorical* — all models are isomorphic to standard models defined over classical Cartesian spaces:

Theorem: *A formula is a consequence of* **A1–7** *(together with the definitional formulae) just in case it is true for any assignment to the variables of regular open subsets of* $\Re^2$,

---
[1]E.g. (Tarski 1956). See also (Bennett 2000).
[2]Reflexivity and symmetry are implicit in the definition of $\circledcirc$.

where P is interpreted as the subset relation and $\text{S}(x)$ holds just in case the set of points denoted by x is an open disc.

For practical applications one would almost certainly want to avoid using set theory, in which case **A1** can be replaced by one of the following, weaker 1st-order formulae:

A1') $\exists x[\phi(x)] \to \exists!y[\text{SUM}_x(\phi(x) : y)]$
A1") $\forall xy \exists!z[z = x + y]$

A1' makes use of the following special syntax to refer to the sum of all regions satisfying a given predicate:

D21) $\text{SUM}_x(\phi(x) : y) \equiv_{def} \forall z[\phi(z) \to \text{P}(z, y)] \land$
$\neg \exists z[\text{P}(z, y) \land \forall w[\phi(w) \to \text{DR}(w, z)]]$

Useful Definitions

We now define a number of basic concepts that are very useful for describing spatial situations:

D22) $\text{C}(x, y) \equiv_{def} \exists z[\text{S}(z) \land$
$\forall z'[z' \circledcirc z \to (\text{O}(z', x) \land \text{O}(z', y))]]$
D23) $\text{EC}(x, y) \equiv_{def} \text{C}(x, y) \land \neg\text{O}(x, y)$
D24) $\text{CON}(x) \equiv_{def} \forall yz[x = y + z \to \text{C}(y, z)]$
D25) $\text{Comp}(c, r) \equiv_{def} \text{CON}(c) \land$
$\neg \exists x[\text{CON}(x) \land \text{P}(x, r) \land \text{PP}(c, x)]$

$\text{C}(x, y)$ is the connection relation and behaves in a similar fashion to the primitive of (Randell, Cui, & Cohn 1992). The definition is based on the observation that for every point of contact (or overlap) between two regions, any sphere centred on that point overlaps both regions. It is easy to prove that C is symmetric and reflexive. EC is the relation of External Connection. $\text{CON}(x)$ means that x is self-connected and $\text{Comp}(c, r)$ means that c is a maximal self-connected Component of r.

Generalised Betweenness and Collinearity

The *bounding sphere* for a region is the smallest sphere of which the region is a part. Since our domain includes unbounded regions, not every region has a bounding sphere. We define

D26) $\text{BS}(x, x') \equiv_{def} \text{P}(x, x') \land \text{S}(x') \land$
$\neg \exists y[\text{P}(x, y) \land \text{S}(y) \land \text{PP}(y, x')]$

We can generalise betweenness to a relation that can hold among any bounded regions:

D27) $\text{BSB}(x, y, z) \equiv_{def} \exists x'y'z'[\text{BS}(x, x') \land \text{BS}(y, y')$
$\land \text{BS}(z, z') \land \text{B}(x', y', z')]$

For convenience we also define a macro expression $\text{Inline}[r_1, \ldots, r_n]$ to stand for the conjunction of the relations $\text{Between}(r_{k-1}, r_k, r_{k+1})$, for each k such that $1 < k < n$. Sometimes, we want to say that regions are collinear but don't care about their order:

D28) $\text{Collin}(x, y, z) \equiv_{def} (\text{B}(x, y, z) \lor \text{B}(y, x, z) \lor \text{B}(x, z, y))$

The macro $\text{Collin}\{r_1, \ldots, r_n\}$ is used to specify a set of collinear regions and is defined analogously to Inline. $\circledcirc\{s_1, \ldots s_n\}$ specifies a set of concentric spheres.

The relation $\text{Aligned}(x, y; z, w)$ holds when x, y, z, w are collinear and the direction from x to y is the same as the direction from z to w:

D29) $\text{Aligned}(x,y;z,w) \equiv_{def} \text{Collin}\{x,y,z,w\} \wedge$
$\exists ee_1e_2e_3e_4[\odot\{e,e_1,e_2,e_3,e_4\} \wedge \text{P}(e_1,e_2) \wedge \text{P}(e_2,e_3) \wedge$
$\text{CB}(x,e_1) \wedge \text{CB}(y,e_2) \wedge \text{CB}(x,e_1) \wedge \text{CB}(y,e_2)]$

Congruence and Isometry

Borgo, Guarino, & Masolo (1996) showed how a *congruence* relation between arbitrary regions could be defined in terms of the S predicate. This relation is true of two regions if one can be transformed into the other by the operations of translation, rotation and taking a mirror image. The movement of physical bodies can be described in terms of translations and rotations but they do not ordinarily undergo mirror inversion. Thus, for our kinematic application we employ a congruence relation $\text{CG}(x,y)$ which excludes the case where x is a mirror image of y, unless x (and therefore also y) is in itself symmetric. The more general case including mirror transforms we call *isometry* and write $\text{Iso}(x,y)$.[3]

We first define congruence between spheres and pairs of spheres (SCG). We can then give a definition of isometry (Iso) that makes use of the concept of a '*scalene* sum of spheres' (SSS) (Borgo, Guarino, & Masolo 1996). This is a region whose Components are spheres and are all of different sizes:

D30) $\text{SCG}(x,y) \equiv_{def} \text{S}(x) \wedge \text{S}(y) \wedge \exists s_1 s_2 [s_1 \odot s_2 \wedge$
$\text{ET}(x,s_1) \wedge \text{ET}(y,s_1) \wedge \text{IT}(x,s_2) \wedge \text{IT}(y,s_2)]$

D31) $\text{SCG}(x,y;x',y') \equiv_{def} \text{SCG}(x,x') \wedge \text{SCG}(y,y') \wedge$
$((\text{ET}(x,y) \wedge \text{ET}(x',y')) \vee$
$\exists zz'[\text{SCG}(z,z') \wedge \text{ED}(x,y,z) \wedge \text{ED}(x',y',z')] \vee$
$\exists zz'[\text{SCG}(z,z') \wedge \text{IT}(z,x) \wedge \text{IT}(z,y) \wedge \text{IT}(z',x') \wedge \text{IT}(z',y')])$

D32) $\text{SSS}(r) \equiv_{def} \forall x[\text{Comp}(x,r) \rightarrow$
$(\text{S}(x) \wedge \neg \exists y[x \neq y \wedge \text{Comp}(y,r) \wedge \text{CG}(x,y)])]$

D33) $\text{IsoSSS}(x,y) \equiv_{def} \text{SSS}(x) \wedge \text{SSS}(y) \wedge$
$\forall° st[(\text{Comp}(s,x) \wedge \text{Comp}(t,x)) \rightarrow$
$\exists° s't'[\text{Comp}(s',y) \wedge \text{Comp}(t',y) \wedge \text{SCG}(s,t;s',t')]]$
$\wedge \forall° st[(\text{Comp}(s,y) \wedge \text{Comp}(t,y)) \rightarrow$
$\exists° s't'[\text{Comp}(s',x) \wedge \text{Comp}(t',x) \wedge \text{SCG}(s,t;s',t')]]$

D34) $\text{Iso}(x,y) \equiv_{def} \forall r[\text{SSS}(r) \rightarrow$
$((\text{P}(r,x) \rightarrow \exists r'[\text{P}(r',y) \wedge \text{IsoSSS}(r,r')])$
$\wedge (\text{P}(r,y) \rightarrow \exists r'[\text{P}(r',x) \wedge \text{IsoSSS}(r,r')]))]$

To distinguish (non-mirrored) congruence from isometry we define a predicate that identifies whether two triangular configurations of spheres are mirror images of one another. This makes use of the fact that the mid-points of the three segments connecting corresponding corners of mirror image triangles are collinear (see Fig. 1).[4]

D35) $\text{MirrorTs}(x_1,y_1,z_1;x_2,y_2,z_2) \equiv_{def}$
$\exists° x'y'z'[\text{Mid}(x_1,x',x_2) \wedge \text{Mid}(y_1,y',y_2) \wedge \text{Mid}(z_1,z',z_2)$
$\wedge \text{Collin}(x',y',z') \wedge \neg(x' \odot y' \wedge y' \odot z')]$

D36) $\text{CGTs}(x_1,y_1,z_1;x_2,y_2,z_2) \equiv_{def}$
$\text{SCG}(x_1,y_1;x_2,y_2) \wedge \text{SCG}(y_1,z_1;y_2,z_2) \wedge$
$\text{SCG}(z_1,x_1;z_2,x_2) \wedge \neg\text{MirrorTs}(x_1,y_1,z_1;x_2,y_2,z_2)$

CGTs gives us a non-mirror congruence relation between triangles which we use to define a general congruence relation:

---

[3]Bennett *et al.* (2000) show how S can in fact be defined from Iso, so Iso could be taken as the morphological primitive of **RBG**.

[4]Whether isosceles are counted as mirrors depends on the ordering of the defining circles given as arguments to MirrorTs.

D37) $\text{CGSSS}(s,t) \equiv_{def} \text{SSS}(s) \wedge \text{SSS}(t) \wedge$
$\forall° s_1,s_2,s_3[(\text{Comp}(s_1,s) \wedge \text{Comp}(s_2,s) \wedge \text{Comp}(s_3,s))$
$\rightarrow \exists° t_1,t_2,t_3[\text{Comp}(t_1,t) \wedge \text{Comp}(t_2,t)$
$\wedge \text{Comp}(t_3,t) \wedge \text{CGTs}(s_1,s_3,s_3;t_1,t_2,t_3)]]$
$\wedge \forall° t_1,t_2,t_3[(\text{Comp}(t_1,t) \wedge \text{Comp}(t_2,t) \wedge \text{Comp}(t_3,t))$
$\rightarrow \exists° s_1,s_2,s_3[\text{Comp}(s_1,s) \wedge \text{Comp}(s_2,s)$
$\wedge \text{Comp}(s_3,s) \wedge \text{CGTs}(s_1,s_3,s_3;t_1,t_2,t_3)]]$

D38) $\text{CG}(x,y) \equiv_{def} \forall r[\text{SSS}(r) \rightarrow$
$((\text{P}(r,x) \rightarrow \exists r'[\text{P}(r',y) \wedge \text{CGSSS}(r,r')])$
$\wedge (\text{P}(r,y) \rightarrow \exists r'[\text{P}(r',x) \wedge \text{CGSSS}(r,r')]))]$

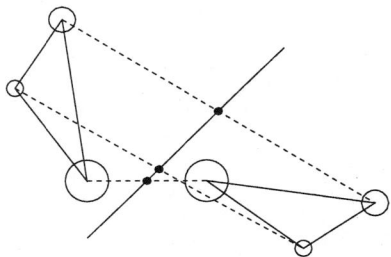

Figure 1: Mirror image triangles

Rectangular Disc Configurations

Later we shall define coordinate systems in terms of spheres. This will make use of the relation that holds when three spheres are arranged so that their centre points subtend a right angle. We use the following definition (explained by Fig. 2):

D39) $\text{RECT}(a,b,c) \equiv_{def}$
$\exists b'c'dd'[b' \odot b \wedge \text{CG}(c',c) \wedge \text{CG}(d',d) \wedge$
$\text{ED}(c,c',b') \wedge \text{ED}(a,d,c) \wedge \text{ED}(a,d',c')]$

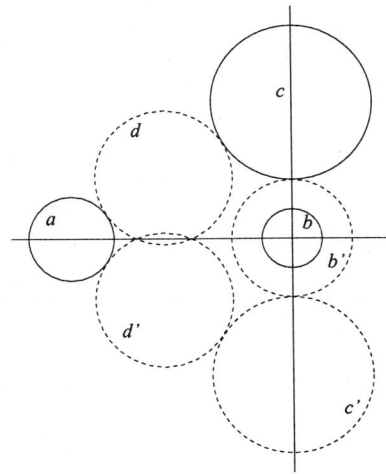

Figure 2: Rectangular configuration of discs a,b,c

Half-Planes

Both for expressing qualitative conditions and for interfacing with geometrical representations, the concept of a half-plane is extremely useful. We note that any two externally tangent discs d_1 and d_2 define a unique tangent line passing through their point of contact. Moreover, the set of discs containing d_1 but discrete from d_2 all lie on one side of the tangent whereas those containing d_2 but discrete from d_1 lie on the other side. These considerations lead to the following definition of a predicate $\mathsf{HP}(x)$, which says that the region x is a half-plane:

D40) $\mathsf{HP}(h) \equiv_{def}$
$\forall^\circ d_1 d_2 [(\mathsf{ET}(d_1, d_2) \wedge \mathsf{P}(d_1, h) \wedge \mathsf{DR}(d_2, h)) \rightarrow$
$(\forall^\circ d_3 [\mathsf{P}(d_1, d_3) \wedge \mathsf{DR}(d_2, d_3)) \rightarrow \mathsf{P}(d_3, h)] \wedge$
$\forall^\circ d_4 [\mathsf{DR}(d_1, d_4) \wedge \mathsf{P}(d_2, d_4)) \rightarrow \mathsf{DR}(d_4, h)])\,]$

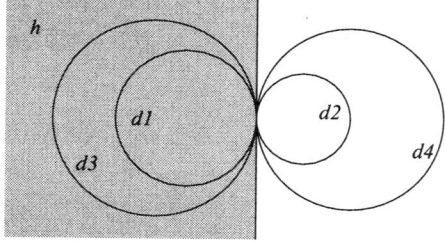

Figure 3: Defining a half-plane in terms of spheres

Congruent Pairs

It is very useful to be able to specify that a given pair of regions $\langle a, b \rangle$ is congruent to another pair $\langle a', b' \rangle$. By this we mean that $\mathsf{CG}(a, a')$ and $\mathsf{CG}(b, b')$ and also that the position of a relative to b is the same as the position of a' relative to b'. If a and b are discrete then this is true just in case $\mathsf{CG}((a+b), (a'+b'))$; but in general we have to take care of cases where a and b overlap. Thus we define:

D41) $\mathsf{CG}(a, b; c, d) \equiv_{def} (\mathsf{CG}(a, a') \wedge \mathsf{CG}(b, b') \wedge$
$\mathsf{CG}((a+b), (a'+b'))) \wedge$
$(\mathsf{PP}(a,b) \rightarrow \exists xy[\mathsf{Diff}(b,a,x) \wedge \mathsf{Diff}(b', a', y) \wedge \mathsf{CG}(x, y)])$
$\wedge$
$(\mathsf{PP}(b,a) \rightarrow \exists xy[\mathsf{Diff}(a,b,x) \wedge \mathsf{Diff}(a', b', y) \wedge \mathsf{CG}(x, y)])$
$\wedge$
$(\mathsf{PO}(a,b) \rightarrow \exists xyzw[\mathsf{Diff}(a,b,x) \wedge \mathsf{Diff}(b,a,y) \wedge$
$\mathsf{Diff}(a', b', z) \wedge \mathsf{Diff}(b', a', w) \wedge$
$\mathsf{CG}(x+y, z+w)])$

Disc-Based Coordinate Systems

Because Cartesian fields over real numbers provide canonical models for point-based Euclidean geometry, configurations of points and lines are very often described in terms of numerical coordinates. At first sight it may seen that the idea of a coordinate system is alien to region-based geometries. However, as we shall see, something very similar can in fact be set up. Fig. 4 illustrates how three distinguished discs (orig, xunit and yunit) fix a coordinate system. These discs must satisfy the axiom:

A10) $\mathsf{S}(\mathsf{orig}) \wedge \mathsf{S}(\mathsf{xunit}) \wedge \mathsf{S}(\mathsf{yunit}) \wedge \mathsf{xunit} \neq \mathsf{yunit}$
$\wedge \mathsf{IT}(\mathsf{xunit}, \mathsf{orig}) \wedge \mathsf{IT}(\mathsf{yunit}, \mathsf{orig})$
$\wedge \exists u[\mathsf{CG}(u, \mathsf{xunit}) \wedge \mathsf{EC}(u, \mathsf{xunit}) \wedge \mathsf{ID}(\mathsf{xunit}, u, \mathsf{orig})]$
$\wedge \exists u[\mathsf{CG}(u, \mathsf{yunit}) \wedge \mathsf{EC}(u, \mathsf{yunit}) \wedge \mathsf{ID}(\mathsf{yunit}, u, \mathsf{orig})]$

The x and y 'coordinates' of an arbitrary disc are given by the following defined relation:

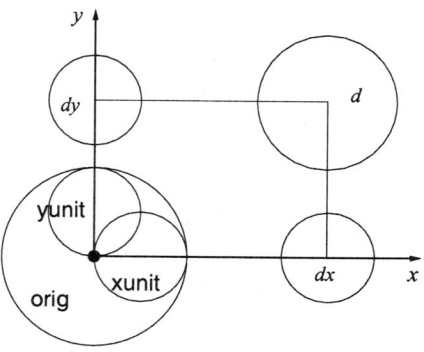

Figure 4: A disc-based coordinate system: x is a disc with coordinates dx and dy: $\mathsf{Coords}(x, dx, dy)$

D42) $\mathsf{Coords}(d, x, y) \equiv_{def}$
$\mathsf{Collin}(\mathsf{orig}, \mathsf{xunit}, x) \wedge \mathsf{RECT}(\mathsf{orig}, x, d)$
$\wedge \mathsf{Collin}(\mathsf{orig}, \mathsf{yunit}, y) \wedge \mathsf{RECT}(\mathsf{orig}, y, d)$

Since we have distinguished discs of 'unit length', one could go on to define metrical predicates.

Motion

In order to specify motions of rigid objects we first specify the simple motions of linear translation and rotation about the centre point of some sphere.

Linear Translation

To specify simple linear motions we define the translation of a region x_1 to the congruent region x_2 along a vector defined by the centre points of two discs d_1 and d_2 as follows (see Fig. 5):

D43) $\mathsf{TAV}(x_1, x_2, d_1, d_2) \equiv_{def} \exists d[d \odot d_2 \wedge \mathsf{CG}(x_1, d_1; x_2, d)]$

We can also define translation part-way along a vector:

D44) $\mathsf{PTAV}(x_1, x_2, d_1, d_2) \equiv_{def}$
$\exists d[\mathsf{B}(d_1, d, d_2) \wedge \mathsf{CG}(x_1, d_1; x_2, d)]$

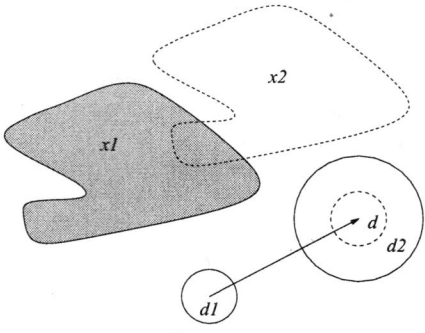

Figure 5: Translation along a vector

Rotation

One region is a bounding-sphere-centred rotation of another iff they are congruent and share the same bounding sphere.

D45) BSC-Rot(x, y) $\equiv_{def}$
$\qquad$ (CG$(x, y) \land \exists s$[BS$(x, s) \land$ BS(y, s)]$)$

More generally we can consider the rotation of a region about the centre point of any arbitrary sphere.

D46) Rot(x, y, s) $\equiv_{def}$ (S$(s) \land$ CG$(x, s; y, s)$)

Later we shall consider rotations of an object within some confining environment and to do this we shall consider those positions which are occupied by a region as it undergoes a continuous rotation between two orientations. We define RotOrd(a, b, c, s) to mean that a, b and c are rotations of a region about the centre point of a sphere s, such that: if a region r congruent to the three regions is rotated continuously (about the centre of s) from a to c in the direction that requires the smallest angular rotation, then r passes through b.

D47) RotOrd(a, b, c, s) $\equiv_{def}$ Rot$(a, b, s) \land$ Rot$(b, c, s) \land$
$\qquad \exists a'b'c'$[CG$\{a', b', c', s\} \land$ EC$(a', s) \land$ EC$(b', s) \land$
$\qquad$ EC$(c', s) \land$ CG$(a, a'; b, b') \land$ GC$(b, b'; c, c') \land$
$\qquad \exists t$[S$(t) \land$ EC$(t, s) \land$ IT$(b', t) \land$ O$(t, a) \land$ O(t, c)]]

The construction employed in this definition is shown in Fig. 6, where for the sake of clarity we have chosen a case where s is the bounding circle of a, b and c.

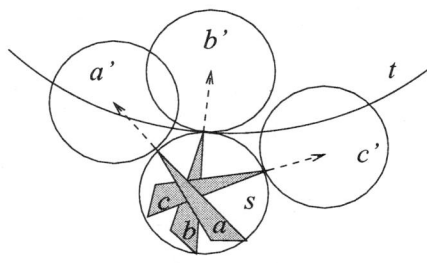

Figure 6: Illustration of the definition of RotOrd

Movement in a Constraining Environment

We now apply our theory to provide a model of physical environments that may be useful for reasoning about motions of rigid objects. This model might support practical applications such as the control of robots.

The fundamental problems of kinematics are of the forms: can a rigid body move between two locations within a confining environment? (the piano-movers problem (Schwartz & Sharir 1983)) and, if so, what is a possible path between the two locations? A simple example is illustrated in Fig. 7, where we want to know whether an object can move between two rooms *via* a narrow corridor.

Our idea is to model a possible movement within an environment as a series of translations and rotations, during each of which the area occupied by a (rigid) object must always lie within a region of free space.

First we define a *linear translation within* as a translation from x_1 to x_2 along some vector such that all translations part way along the vector lie within a confining region y:

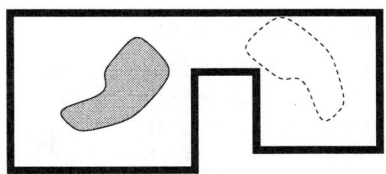

Figure 7: A problem of constrained movement

D48) LTW(x_1, x_2, y) $\equiv_{def}$ $\exists d_1 d_2$[TAV$(x_1, x_2, d_1, d_2) \land$
$\qquad \forall x$[PTAV$(x_1, x, d_1, d_2) \to$ P(x, y)]]

We define a 'short' (less than 180°) rotation of a region between two orientations x_1 and x_2, such that during the rotation the region remains within some hosting environment y as follows:

D49) SRotW(x_1, x_2, y) $\equiv_{def}$ $\exists s$[$\exists x'$[RotOrd(x_1, x', x_2, s)]
$\qquad \land \forall x'$[RotOrd$(x_1, x', x_2, s) \to$ P(x', y)]]

An arbitrary rotation within is just defined as the concatenation of two short rotations:

D50) RotW(x_1, x_2, y) $\equiv_{def}$
$\qquad \exists x'$[SRotW$(x_1, x', y) \land$ SRotW(x', x_2, y)]

Simple move within:

D51) SMW(x_1, x_2, y) $\equiv_{def}$
$\qquad$ (LTW$(x_1, x_2, y) \lor$ RotW(x_1, x_2, y))

We now axiomatise a predicate MoveWithin(x_1, x_2, y) to say that a rigid body can move from region x_1 to region x_2, while remaining within region y:

A11) MoveWithin$(x_1, x_2, y) \leftrightarrow$ SMW$(x_1, x_2, y) \lor$
$\qquad \exists x'$[SMW$(x_1, x', y) \land$ MoveWithin(x', x_2, y)]

We could restrict this so that a move was a strictly alternating sequence of LTW and RotW operations, which reduces the search space (though it is still infinite).

MoveWithin as a Finite Sequence of SMWs

In fact, although axiom **A11** is correct it is not strictly adequate since it does not actually force MoveWithin to coincide with the transitive closure of SMW. However it is likely to be sufficient for a large class of constructive proofs of whether MoveWithin(x_1, x_2, y) follows from (or is consistent with) some given constraints.

To get a more complete charaterisation of MoveWithin we would first have to define the notion of a finite sequence. Within our framework this can be modelled by (e.g.) a region σ that is a sum of discrete spheres, such that there is a smallest sphere s_1 and a largest sphere s_n and for all other spheres there is a sphere of half the diameter and a sphere of twice the diameter (thus the spherical Components are striclty ordered). We can then define MoveWithin(a, b, r) by saying that for each sphere s where Comp(s, σ) there is a pair of regions $\langle x_s, y_s \rangle$ related by SMW(x_s, y_s, r), such that $x_{s_1} = a$ and $y_{s_n} = b$ and moreover if t is a component of σ with twice the diameter of s then $y_s = x_t$. Given such a definition **A11** would not be needed.

General Continuous Motions

The definition of MoveWithin also assumes that any motion could be reduced to a series of linear translations and rotations. We call such a motion a *TR-motion*. However, in general there are many continuous motions that cannot be reduced in this way. For instance an object might trace a parabolic curve. On the other hand, it is clear that if an object moves within a confining environment such that it always has more than one degree of freedom, then for every continuous motion there is a TR-motion with the same start and end locations. Hence we believe that for most robotic applications only TR-motions need to be considered.

Nevertheless, for the sake of having a Comprehensive ontology one might want to define arbitrary continuous motions. In fact we have been able to define set-theoretically the notion of a set of unit discs whose centre points form a continuous non-fractal path; and by using $CG(x, y; z, w)$ one can easily construct from this a definition of a set of regions lying on a continuous (non-fractal) path. But such a definition is of only theoretical importance and will not be given here.

Movable Obstacles

So far we have considered the case of a single rigid object moving in a constraining environment; but in general a situation will involve multiple movable objects.

We need a way of representing a collection of rigid bodies in terms of a fixed finite number of regions. This would enable the situation to be included in the argument places or ordinary predicates. A naïve representation would be to sum the bodies and then identify objects with Components of this sum. But, if bodies may be EC to each other this does not work. However, we can appeal to the famous *four colour theorem* to see that any configuration of 2-dimensional objects can be described in terms of the Components of four regions.

Thus, we represent a *situation* by a 4-tuple $\sigma = \langle r_1, r_2, r_3, r_4 \rangle$ of mutually DR regions. The following definitions enable us to describe the movement of one amongst a collection of movable objects:

D52) $\text{Sit}(\langle r_1, r_2, r_3, r_4 \rangle) \equiv_{def} \text{DR}(r_1, r_2) \wedge \text{DR}(r_1, r_3) \wedge$
$\text{DR}(r_1, r_4) \wedge \text{DR}(r_2, r_3) \wedge \text{DR}(r_2, r_4) \wedge \text{DR}(r_3, r_4)$

D53) $\text{SitComp}(c, \langle s_1, s_2, s_3, s_4 \rangle) \equiv_{def}$
$\text{Comp}(c, s_1) \vee \text{Comp}(c, s_2) \vee$
$\text{Comp}(c, s_3) \vee \text{Comp}(c, s_4)$

D54) $\text{SitEQ}(\sigma, \sigma') \equiv_{def} \text{Sit}(\sigma) \wedge \text{Sit}(\sigma')$
$\wedge \forall x [\text{SitComp}(x, \sigma) \leftrightarrow \text{SitComp}(x, \sigma')]$

D55) $\text{MoveOne}(\sigma, \sigma', f) \equiv_{def}$
$\exists r_1 r_2 r_3 r_4 o o' f' [\text{Diff}(f, r_1 + r_2 + r_3 + r_4, f')$
$\wedge \text{MoveWithin}(o, o', f') \wedge \text{SitEQ}(\sigma, \langle r_1 + o, r_2 r_3 r_4 \rangle) \wedge$
$(\text{SitEQ}(\sigma', \langle r_1 + o', r_2, r_3, r_4 \rangle) \vee$
$\text{SitEQ}(\sigma', \langle r_1, r_2 + o', r_3, r_4 \rangle)))$

$\text{MoveOne}(\sigma, \sigma', f)$ holds just in case: σ and σ' are situation tuples representing configurations of objects; f is the region of free space in which the objects are situated; and, σ can be transformed into σ' by moving just one of the objects. The definition requires some explanation: $\langle r_1, r_2, r_3, r_4 \rangle$ represents the situation of all the objects except the one that is moved; without loss of generality we can assume that the initial situation σ can be obtained by adding the starting location o of the moved object; the final situation is obtained by adding a congruent region o' to either r_1 or r_2 corresponding to cases where a 'four-colouring' of the configuration would have the start and finish locations coloured the same or differently.

To determine whether one situation can be transformed into another by a series of movements of movable objects we can axiomatise a general MoveTrans relation as follows.[5]

A12) $\text{MoveTrans}(\sigma, \sigma', f) \leftrightarrow (\text{MoveOne}(\sigma, \sigma', f) \vee$
$\exists \sigma'' [\text{MoveOne}(\sigma, \sigma'', f) \wedge \text{MoveTrans}(\sigma'', \sigma', f)])$

Pushing Obstacles

In order to model the action of an auto-motive object such as a robot pushing a movable obstacle we have to know something about the resistance of obstacles to forces. Since we assume that we know which obstacles can and cannot be moved we are not concerned with the magnitude of an obstacle's resistance but only its direction of action. Thus, we model a movable obstacle by a pair $\langle r, c \rangle$, where r is the region it occupies and c is its *centre of resistance*. If a force acts on an obstacle through its centre of resistance it will move in a straight line; if it acts otherwise the force will cause a rotation.

D56) $\text{Push}(r, r', \langle x, c \rangle, \langle x' c' \rangle) \equiv_{def}$
$\exists d_1 d_2 [\text{EC}(d_1, d_2) \wedge \text{P}(d_1, r) \wedge \text{P}(d_2, x) \wedge$
$\text{Aligned}(d_1, d_2; c, c')] \wedge \text{CG}(r, x; r', x') \wedge \text{CG}(x, c; x', c')$

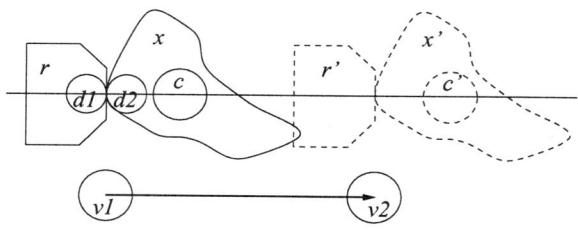

Figure 8: Robot r pushes an object from x to x'

It is fairly straightforward to modify the definitions of MoveOne and MoveTrans in order to describe situation transforms that can be achieved by a series of push operations. However, space does not permit us to give full details here.

Conclusion

We have explored the use of an expressive region-based geometry for describing spatial situations and reasoning about the movements of rigid bodies. Our formalism provides a rigorous ontological foundation for use in AI systems that need to process spatial information.

For most practical applications one will require tractable sublanguages of our very expressive formalism. (Cristani,

---

[5]This suffers from the same limitations as axiom **A11** for MoveWithin given above, and has the same possible solution.

Cohn, & Bennett 2000) investigate the Complexity of reasoning with a combination of mereological and morphological relations and proves tractability of a significant constraint language, which is a fragment of our formalism. Recursive definitions such as that for MoveWithin could be implemented by search algorithms. We envisage architectures whereby search is combined with one or more constraint solvers which determine when branches can be closed. Inductive theorem proving techniques may also be useful.

We believe that the formalism of region-based geometry will be extremely useful as a framework within which more Computationally oriented representations can be embedded.

References

Bennett, B.; Cohn, A.; Torrini, P.; and Hazarika, S. 2000. Region-based qualitative geometry. Technical Report 2000.07, University of Leeds, LS2 9JT, UK.

Bennett, B. 2000. Research note on Tarski's elementary geometry. Technical report, University of Leeds, School of Computer Studies. Available from web at http://www.scs.leeds.ac.uk/pub/doc/srg/tarski_geom.ps.

Borgo, S.; Guarino, N.; and Masolo, C. 1996. A pointless theory of space based on strong congruence and connection. In Aiello, L. C., and Doyle, J., eds., *Principles of Knowledge Representation and Reasoning, Proceedings of the 5th International Conference, KR96*. Morgan Kaufmann.

Cristani, M.; Cohn, A.; and Bennett, B. 2000. Spatial locations via morpho-mereology. In *Proceedings of KR'2000*. To appear.

Davis, E. 1987. A framework for qualitative reasoning about solid objects. In Rodriguez, G., ed., *Proceedings of the Workshop on Space Telerobotics*, 369–375. NASA and JPL. Reprinted in (Weld & De Kleer 1990).

Davis, E. 1988. A logical framework for commonsense predictions of solid object behavior. *AI in Engineering* 3(3):125–138.

Faltings, B. 1987. Qualitative kinematics in mechanisms. In *Proceedings IJCAI-87*, 436–442.

Forbus, K.; Nielsen, P.; and Faltings, B. 1987. Qualitative kinematics: A framework. In *Proceedings IJCAI-87*, 430–436.

Forbus, K. D.; Nielsen, P.; and Faltings, B. 1991. Qualitative spatial reasoning: The clock project. *Artificial Intelligence* 51:417–471.

Guarino, N., ed. 1998. *Formal ontology in information systems: Proceedings of the 1st international conference (FOIS-98)*, volume 46 of *Frontiers in Artificial Intelligence and Applications*. Trento, Italy: Ios Press.

Lenat, D. 1995. CYC: a large-scale investment in knowledge infrastructure. *Communications of the ACM* 38(11).

Mukerjee, A., and Bhatia, P. 1995. A qualitative discretization for two-body contacts. In Mellish, C. S., ed., *Proceedings of the 14th International Joint Conference on Artificial Intelligence (IJCAI-95)*, volume 1, 915–921.

Randell, D. A.; Cui, Z.; and Cohn, A. G. 1992. A spatial logic based on regions and connection. In *Proc. 3rd Int. Conf. on Knowledge Representation and Reasoning*, 165–176. San Mateo: Morgan Kaufmann.

Schwartz, J., and Sharir, M. 1983. On the 'piano movers' problem, II: General techniques for computing topological properties of real algebraic manifolds. In *Advances in Applied Mathematics*, volume 4. Academic Press.

Tarski, A. 1929. Les fondaments de la géométrie des corps. *Ksiega Pamiatkowa Pierwszego Polskiego Zjazdu Matematycznego* 29–33. A suplement to *Annales de la Société Polonaise de Mathématique*. English translation, 'Foundations of the Geometry of Solids', in A. Tarski, *Logic, Semantics, Metamathematics*, Oxford Clarendon Press, 1956.

Tarski, A. 1956. Foundations of the geometry of solids. In *Logic, Semantics, Metamathematics*. Oxford Clarendon Press. chapter 2. trans. J.H. Woodger.

Weld, D. S., and De Kleer, J., eds. 1990. *Readings in Qualitative Reasoning About Physical Systems*. San Mateo, Ca: Morgan Kaufman.

GeoRep: A Flexible Tool for Spatial Representation of Line Drawings

Ronald W. Ferguson and Kenneth D. Forbus

Qualitative Reasoning Group
Department of Computer Science
Northwestern University
1890 Maple Avenue
Evanston, IL 60201 USA
{ferguson, forbus}@ils.nwu.edu

Abstract

A key problem in diagrammatic reasoning is understanding how people reason about qualitative relationships in diagrams. We claim that progress in diagrammatic reasoning is slowed by two problems: (1) researchers tend to start from scratch, creating new spatial reasoners for each new problem area, and (2) constraints from human visual processing are rarely considered. To address these problems, we created GeoRep, a spatial reasoning engine that generates qualitative spatial descriptions from line drawings. GeoRep has been successfully used in several research projects, including cognitive simulation studies of human vision. In this paper, we outline GeoRep's architecture, explain the domain-independent and domain-specific aspects of its processing, and motivate the representations it produces. We then survey how GeoRep has been used in three different projects–a model of symmetry, a model of understanding juxtaposition diagrams of physical situations, and a system for reasoning about military courses of action.

Introduction: How Diagrams Work

Diagrams are ubiquitous. In daily communications, through sketches, maps, and figures, people use diagrams to convey information. Some diagrams depict intrinsically spatial domains, such as bus routes or furniture arrangements. Other diagrams use spatial concepts to compactly show more abstract relations, such as corporate hierarchies or data flow in a computer program. In all such domains, diagrams can be extremely effective.

It is also true, however, that there is a keen difference between effective and ineffective diagrams. Small visual differences may distinguish a diagram that elucidates from one that confuses (Tufte, 1990). A key difference between good and bad diagrams is how well they utilize the kinds of qualitative spatial relations most easily perceived by the human visual system. In the best diagrams, these spatial relations support the conceptual relations the reader is meant to infer. For example, in a thermodynamics diagram, an arrow may indicate the direction of heat flow, with thicker arrows to indicate greater flow, or tapering arrows to indicate heat dissipation. Or, in a circuit diagram, wires may be drawn so that related wires are adjacent and parallel, so they can be visually grouped.

For this reason, to understand how diagrams work, we must show how diagrams use visual characteristics to support particular qualitative inferences. In the system described here, we model this process as an interaction between two representation levels:

1. A low-level, domain-independent representation which involves a representative set of primitive spatial relations. This level models human low-level vision.
2. A high-level, domain-specific representation that models visual skills for a particular domain. This level links low-level visual relations to a domain's conceptual content.

These two representation levels form the basis of GeoRep. GeoRep is an engine for building diagrammatic reasoners. GeoRep takes as input a line drawing, given as a set of primitive visual elements. From this drawing, GeoRep creates a predicate calculus representation of the drawing's visual relations. To perform this task, GeoRep, given the drawing, examines the primitive shapes in the figure, looking for a broad set of low-level visual relations. These relations are detected by a library of visual operations (assumed to be domain-independent) which partially cover the set of *universal visual routines* (Ullman, 1984). Next, GeoRep uses these relations, in combination with domain-dependent rules, to generate the second, domain-specific representation. GeoRep's two-level

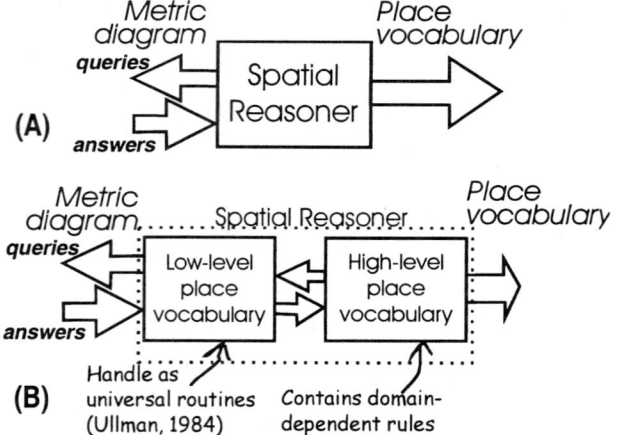

Figure 1: The Metric Diagram / Place Vocabulary framework (A) and how it is modified for GeoRep (B).

Copyright © 2000, American Association for Artificial Intelligence (www.aaai.org). All rights reserved.

architecture provides a sophisticated model of how early visual relations are used for inferring conceptual relations.

At the level of the high-level representation, GeoRep is a qualitative spatial reasoner. GeoRep's qualitative spatial reasoning uses a variant of the MD/PV framework (Forbus, 1980; Forbus, Nielsen, & Faltings, 1991). This framework is motivated by the *poverty conjecture*, which states that "there is no purely qualitative, general-purpose representation of spatial properties." (Forbus et al., 1991). For this reason, MD/PV reasoners use two representations levels: a *metric diagram*, which contains quantitative information (and often, some symbolic or qualitative representation), and the *place vocabulary*, which is a qualitative spatial representation fitted to the particular place and task (Figure 1-A). The place vocabulary is constructed as needed by querying the metric diagram.

Qualitative spatial reasoners using the MD/PV framework have been successful in many domains, including the analysis of mechanical systems (Forbus et al., 1991; Kim, 1993) and graphs (Pisan, 1995).

GeoRep elaborates on the MD/PV model by splitting the place vocabulary into higher and lower levels. The low-level place vocabulary represents low-level visual relations specific to early human vision, while the high-level place vocabulary is a task-specific spatial representation derivable from the low-level vocabulary (Figure 1-B). By generating the initial low-level place vocabulary directly from the metric diagram (which in this case is the line drawing itself), GeoRep can then use this initial vocabulary as the building blocks for a broad (if still finite) class of high-level place vocabularies. Thus GeoRep, while not a general diagrammatic reasoner, is general over the set of high-level place vocabularies derivable from this low-level place vocabulary, which is in turn bounded by cognitive constraints in human perception. Our conjecture is that this cognitively-grounded place vocabulary is both computationally useful and psychologically plausible.

GeoRep's consistency with human visual abilities–unlike previous systems using the MD/PV framework–provides robustness. Although some visual skills are domain-specific, the fact that people use visual reasoning in such a broad variety of tasks suggests that a sufficiently robust visual processing engine could provide similarly general services for diagrammatic reasoning. This generality addresses a key limitation of current research in diagrammatic reasoning, which is the tendency for every researcher to start from scratch, implementing a spatial reasoning system aimed at one class of problems.

Although most previous diagrammatic reasoning systems are motivated by human visual abilities (c.f. the systems described in Glasgow et.al. (1995)), their design has typically been driven more by the task than by the psychology of human vision. While this has lead to useful insights, we believe that an explicit concern with human vision can lead to better diagrammatic reasoners.

The next section describes GeoRep's architecture, explaining where its processing and representational choices have been influenced by perceptual psychology

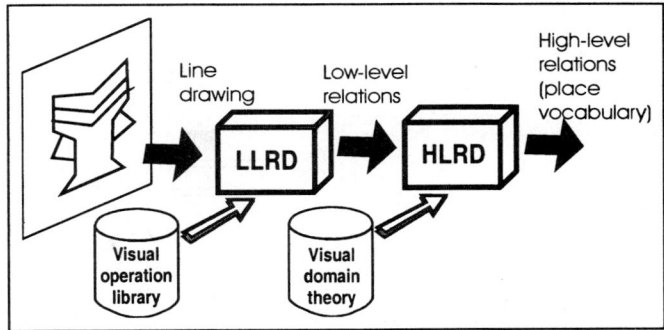

Figure 2: A simplified schematic of GeoRep's architecture.

findings. We then demonstrate GeoRep's generality by showing its use in three systems: MAGI (Ferguson, 1994), a model of symmetry; JUXTA (Ferguson & Forbus, 1995), a model of juxtaposition diagram understanding; and COADD, a system for understanding military course of action diagrams. We close with a discussion of GeoRep's limitations and future development.

Architecture

GeoRep's architecture is shown in Figure 2. GeoRep's input is a line drawing, given as a vector graphics file. This file uses the FIG graphics format. Using drawings rather than bitmaps avoids the problem of doing line detection, which is essential in machine vision, but not critical in diagrammatic reasoning. Using line drawings also makes diagram input simple: diagrams can be built using an off-the-shelf drawing program (Hendrich, 1999). Line drawings have been successful in several systems (e.g., Evans, 1968; Gross, 1996; Sutherland, 1963) and work well with existing spatial reasoning models.

The output of GeoRep is a description of the figure expressed in a domain-dependent high-level place vocabulary. Like previous approaches to spatial representation, the representation produced by GeoRep emphasizes compact, composable vocabularies that directly reflect visual structure. Entities are mapped onto geometric elements or object parts, with predicates to represent connections and arrangements (Biederman, 1987; Palmer, 1975). The composability of these arrangements are reflected in the composability of the vocabulary itself.

GeoRep's internal processing contains two stages: the low-level relational describer (LLRD) and the high-level relational describer (HLRD). The LLRD handles the domain-independent representation of the line drawing. It detects and represents a large set of useful visual relations. These relations are structural relations detected early in visual perception.

The HLRD, in turn, uses domain-specific rules that extend the LLRD's representation. These extensions include new visual relations (and how to compute them) and ways to recognize depicted items. The final output of the HLRD is one or more *representation levels*. A representation level is a set of propositions that corresponds to some specific task or type of analysis. For example, representation levels may include the LLRD's

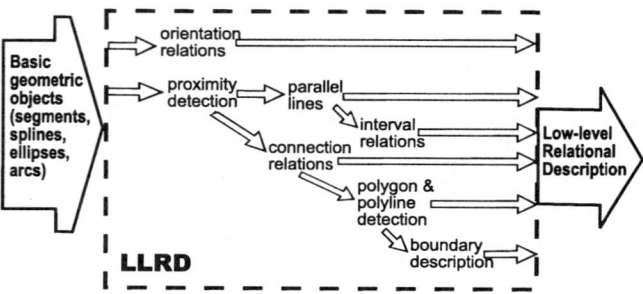

Figure 3: Processing of visual elements within the LLRD

basic visual representation, more complex visual relations, a representation of the depicted items, or potentially even limited reasoning within the diagram's problem domain (see Figure 5 for an example).

The Low-Level Relational Describer (LLRD)

GeoRep's first stage, the LLRD, creates GeoRep's low-level, domain-independent spatial representation. Starting with primitive visual elements, the LLRD detects and represents a broad set of early visual relations, using a library of *visual operations*. These operations correspond to Ullman's (1984) *universal routines*, which are routines that run in the absence of visual goals. These operations, while they do not attempt to model visual processes, model the visual relations such processes detect. Conceptually, these operations are applied in parallel over the visual field's proximate shapes. Due to dependencies between the LLRD's visual relations, it pipelines processing so that more complex visual relations are computed after simpler ones (Figure 3). For example, parallel lines and polygons, once detected, are fed to the interval relation and boundary description systems, respectively.

The LLRD recognizes five primitive shape types: line segments, circular arcs, circles and ellipses, splines (open and closed), and positioned text. The LLRD also subsumes some visual elements into polylines, polygons, and groups.

Computing proximity. Proximity is the LLRD's core attentional mechanism. Because it is impractical for the LLRD to detect all visual relations between all available element combinations, it only checks for relations between proximate elements. For example, in representing a human stick figure, the LLRD might relate the "foot" to the "leg", and the "leg" to the "torso", but wouldn't attempt to find relations between the "foot" and "hand".

To determine element proximity, GeoRep uses a calculation that is a function of element size, distance and shape type. Each visual element type has a prototypical *area of influence* based on the element's size. For example, a circle's area of influence is the area within twice its radius. Similarly, for a line segment the area of influence extends out from the segment for the segment length. Elements are considered proximate when their areas of influence overlap. Areas of influence are calculated as sets of circles and rectangles to make overlap checking efficient, and all proximity calculations are cached. Note that because all pairs of items must be considered, the time complexity of this stage is $O(N^2)$ over the number of visual elements. This makes proximity detection the LLRD's most expensive stage. However, proximity detection also makes subsequent LLRD operators more efficient by limiting their application to either the set of visual elements or the set of proximate element pairs.

Though imperfect, this proximity measure has many advantages. It is easily constructed, relatively efficient, and captures the intuition that large elements (such as a large rectangles or long polylines) relate visually to many other elements. Similar approaches to rating nearness have been used successfully (e.g., Abella and Kender, 1993).

Running the visual operations. Once the LLRD determines which elements are proximate, it looks for other visual relations between proximate elements, using a visual operation library. Each visual operation detects specific visual relations that are part of early vision. All visual operations act on some combination of primitive visual elements, composite visual elements, and reference frames.

The rest of this section briefly surveys the set of visual operations the LLRD uses.

Orientation and the frame of reference. One fundamental characteristic of vision is the reference frame. Experiments have shown that figure orientation can have a critical effect on perception, including figure recognition (Rock, 1973). The LLRD detects many orientation-based relations, including *horizontally* and *vertically*-oriented elements, and *above* and *beside* relations between elements. The LLRD also looks for elements occupying the same horizontal or vertical extent.

Like humans, GeoRep can change its reference frame. GeoRep's default reference frame is gravitational, but can be changed based on clues in the scene, such as a preponderance of lines at one orientation, figural elongation, or symmetry. When the reference frame changes, LLRD relations using the old reference frame are retracted, and new relations asserted in GeoRep's knowledge base.

Parallel lines. The LLRD also detects parallel line segments, modeling the ease with which humans detect parallelisms. However, in practice, describing the parallel segments alone often doesn't adequately constrain the description of a drawing. To elaborate on parallel elements in a cognitively-plausible fashion, we extended the LLRD to categorize parallel segments using Allen's (1983) interval relations. Allen's interval relations were useful in describing parallel segments because they constrain the relative position of segment endpoints in a way invariant to the frame of reference. Admittedly, while in practice these interval relations have been extremely useful, empirical evidence for their role in vision is still marginal.

Connection relations. The LLRD also describes element connectivity, which is a central factor in perceptual organization. Connectivity is detected using standard computational geometry routines (Glassner, 1990) amended with strictness factors. The element types determine the type of connection relation. "Ended" elements, such as line segments and arcs, can connect or cross other elements. Specifically, the LLRD checks pairs of segments for corner, intersection, and mid-connections. Arcs may connect with segments as well, and their connections may be aligned or misaligned. Connections may also have a particular character. Corner angles, for example, are characterized as acute, obtuse, or perpendicular. The LLRD also detects and classifies connections between line segments and curved objects, such as circles and ellipses. Endpoint connections between a segment and an ellipse or circle are checked to see if the connection is radial or tangential. Other curved shapes, such as circles, ellipses, and arcs, are connected by abutment (i.e., when boundaries touch).

Building Composite Elements

A key insight of Gestalt theory is that the whole is seen differently than the sum of its parts. For GeoRep, which operates mainly in a bottom-up fashion, this means that it must recognize when individual elements can be subsumed into larger structures. When elements are collected into composite elements, we say they are *visually subsumed*, and the status of those elements changes. Once subsumed, a visual element is represented as part of its composite structure rather than individually.

GeoRep contains three mechanisms to perform visual subsumption. Elements may be subsumed as polylines and polygons, via grouping, and by constructing ad hoc composite elements, called *glyphs*. While these mechanisms lack the flexibility of human perception, they can simulate aspects of it, and can be extended when a particular visual domain requires it. These three mechanisms, although listed here with the LLRD, actually bridge lower and higher-level visual processing. The need to bridge these levels is due to the way subsumption is tied to perceptual organization. Perceptual organization itself often depends on either global element configuration or domain knowledge, which limits the effectiveness of bottom-up processing. Note that because GeoRep's visual rules can check if an element is a subsumed element, such rules may act only on unsubsumed elements, increasing reasoner efficiency.

Polylines and polygons. It has long been recognized that polylines and closed shapes are important in perception. The LLRD detects polylines and polygons using simple path-following algorithms. Despite the computational complexity of calculating closed shapes (c.f., Ullman, 1984), humans detect shape closure early in perception— perhaps pre-attentively (Treisman & Patterson, 1984).

Polygons, and their constituent corners and segments, have many characteristics derived from their boundaries. Their corners may be concave or convex, and groups of adjoining convex or concave corners constitute protrusions or indentations. Representing these characteristics is crucial to modeling human performance: inflexion points (indentations and protrusions) are critical in recognition tasks (Hoffman & Richards, 1984; Lowe, 1987), and recent studies have shown the importance of concavities in visual tasks such as symmetry judgment (Baylis & Driver, 1994; Ferguson, Aminoff, & Gentner, submitted).

The LLRD represents indentations and protrusions as groups of concave or convex points. Protrusions are also represented relative to the current reference frame, indicating the protrusions' relative vertical placement.

Grouping. Grouping requires some measure of similarity between grouped elements. This required similarity metric makes grouping too broad an effect to model with the LLRD. However, the LLRD can model limited grouping effects by using domain-specific similarity metrics in the HLRD.

Grouping in GeoRep thus depends on a set of domain-specific *grouping rules*. These rules determine which element pairs are similar enough to be grouped. For example, triangle groups may be collected with a grouping rule that pairs triangles of similar size. While there are limits to this approach—a new rule is needed for each new group type, and the rules are not generative—this mechanism has proven adequate for our current visual domains, and easily accommodates the construction of new grouping-based place vocabularies. We are currently looking at a tractable grouping sub-case using factors, such as similar size, orientation, and shape, that have been shown to allow items to be grouped pre-attentively (Julesz & Bergen, 1983; Treisman & Gelade, 1980).

Glyphs. Along with other basic shapes, GeoRep includes *glyphs*, which are arbitrary collections of visual elements that constitute a symbol or other divisible visual form. Glyphs implement visual symbols, such as depictions of NAND gates or military units. Glyphs are treated as a single element with location and extent alone.

The High-Level Relational Describer (HLRD)

GeoRep's reasoning does not end with the LLRD's low-level place vocabulary. Built upon this low-level vocabulary is a high-level vocabulary specific to a visual reasoning task. For example, depicting connectivity in a wiring diagram or the meshing of gears may involve spatial relations that are not domain-general, but are still better expressed in a diagram than through text.

This high-level place vocabulary is created by GeoRep's second stage: the HLRD. The HLRD's input is the LLRD's description. The HLRD contains a rule engine utilizing a logic-based truth-maintenance system (LTMS; Forbus & de Kleer, 1993). The complexity of this stage thus depends on the domain. The rule engine loads rules from a visual domain theory, and creates a description using those rules.

HLRD rules are similar to those for other rule-based systems, but are set apart by the rules' visual vocabulary, which form a convenient abstraction layer for discussing domain-dependent visual symbols (e.g., the symbology of maps) and spatial relations. HLRD rules contain special forms for delimiting the application of rules to proximate objects and for calling the LLRD's visual operation library.

While HLRD rules are domain-specific, there are some rules used across domains. For example, one rule set handles *representational links* between visual elements and what they represent. In thermodynamics, for instance, a trapezoid may represent a fluid container. While the specific mappings from geometry to conceptual entity are domain-specific (trapezoids may have different meanings in other domains), the properties of representational links are more general. These rules dictate that each visual element represent only one thing (excluding partonomic relations). Multiple element interpretations are then resolved via various heuristics (e.g., when conflicting interpretations exist, choose the interpretation that accounts for the most visual elements and retract the other interpretation in the LTMS).

Because the HLRD uses the LTMS, the HLRD can explain *why* it believes that particular visual elements represent particular things: e.g., why a polygon represents a coffee cup. Another advantage of explicit representational links is that they can be used to extend the place vocabulary. For example, given a drawing of two coffee cups, GeoRep can determine which cup contains more liquid by returning to the polygons representing the cups and comparing them to see if one cup is taller or wider.

Once the HLRD has generated a high-level description, it can either be retrieved from the HLRD directly, or filtered by relation type to simulate different diagrammatic representation levels. For example, one representation level might list only individual glyph properties, while another level might relate patterns of glyphs.

HLRD's ability to handle arbitrary place vocabularies is limited by the LLRD's capabilities. However, the advantage is that when HLRD rules use only the LLRD's representation or visual operations, it is cognitively plausible that the resulting description will contain relations that are visible to people. The LLRD's representation is valuable because it provides an easy-to-use and extensible vocabulary. But it is also valuable because, used correctly, it should tell us not just the relations a drawing depicts, but why a person would notice those relations.

Applications of GeoRep

To date, GeoRep has been used in three different projects: symmetry detection of abstract figures, diagrams of simple physical phenomena, and military Course-of-Action (COA) diagrams. We briefly survey each of them here, and provide references for those who wish to explore, for each system, GeoRep's role in greater depth.

Symmetry detection. GeoRep is used in the MAGI symmetry-detection model (Ferguson, 1994; Ferguson, in preparation). MAGI, which maps similar relations in a representation to determine its symmetry, uses GeoRep to detect symmetry in drawings, including functional drawings such as logic circuits. It has also been used to simulate experimental results. In (Ferguson, Aminoff, & Gentner, 1996; Ferguson et al., submitted), subjects in two experiments judged the symmetry of randomly-generated polygons after brief presentation times (50 ms). The experiments found that qualitative visual structure, such as

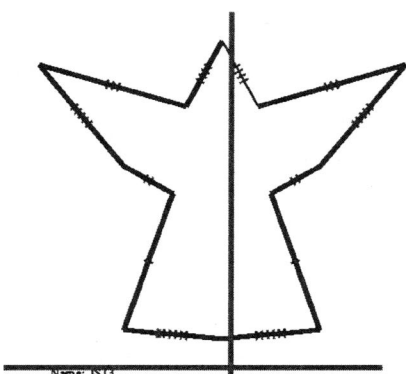

Figure 4: Sample figure from asymmetry study, with axis and correspondences are drawn in by MAGI.

boundary concavities, had a significant effect on whether a figure was judged symmetric.

To simulate the experimental results, GeoRep was given the polygon set, using the same segment data used for the experimental stimuli. For each figure, GeoRep generated a low-level relational description. This was then passed to the MAGI model, which determined the qualitative symmetry of the figure (Figure 4). The simulation was successful, resulting in the same general pattern of symmetry judgments found in the human subjects. MAGI, like human subjects, detected asymmetries more easily when the asymmetry involved differences in qualitative visual structure, such as mismatches in vertex concavity or in the number of vertices.

Juxtaposition-based diagrams of simple physical phenomena. GeoRep is used as part of a system called JUXTA (Ferguson & Forbus, 1995; Ferguson & Forbus, 1998), which critiques simplified diagrams of physical phenomena.

For each diagram, GeoRep generates three different levels of description: a visual level (using the LLRD, and some additional rules), a physical level (interpreting the

Original Drawing

Visual Level
(POLYGON poly1)
(NUMBER-OF-SIDES poly1 4)
(UPRIGHT-TRAPEZOID poly1)
(SPLINE spline1)
(SPLINE spline2)
(SPLINE spline3)
(SPINE-GROUP group1
    (GROUP spline1 spline2 spline3))

Physical Level
(CONTAINER cup1)
(LIQUID liquid1)
(CONTAINS (CONTAINER cup1)
    (LIQUID liquid1))
(STEAM-HEAT steam1)
(RISING-FROM steam1 liquid1)

Process Level (FLOW HEAT liquid1 atmosphere steam1)

Figure 5: A subset of the representations produced by GeoRep for JUXTA, with the original figure.

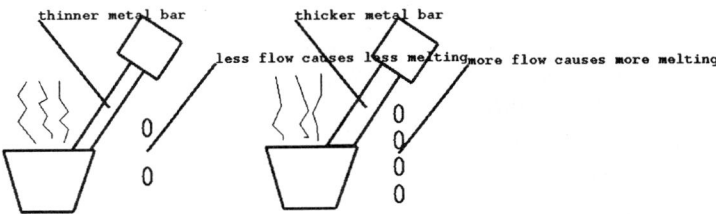

Figure 7: JUXTA's labeling of the aligned differences detected in a diagram, as related to the caption

visual elements as domain objects using a set of structural templates), and a process level (giving the physical processes inferred from the diagrams). A representative sample of each level is given in Figure 5.

Using MAGI to detect the repeated parts of the scene, JUXTA detects the physical and process differences between those parts, and attempts to relate those differences to the caption. The resulting system can critique the diagram based on how the diagram meets the expectations set in the caption. Based on the caption, for example, JUXTA can label the figure's critical differences (Figure 7).

To perform this analysis, the distinction between levels of interpretation is crucial. Visual differences can be relevant or irrelevant depending on the caption's interpretation. Because GeoRep can represent multiple abstraction levels, JUXTA can distinguish between visual differences that could confuse the reader and differences that, while noticeable, would not be confusing.

Course-of-Action Diagrams. In DARPA's High-Performance Knowledge Bases (HPKB) initiative, GeoRep is being used for spatial reasoning about Course-of-Action (COA) diagrams (Ferguson, Rasch, Turmel, & Forbus, 2000). These diagrams, drawn by the military for tasks such as troop movement planning, use a well-defined set of line-drawn symbols to indicate important areas, unit locations and types, tasks, movement paths, and obstacles. Most work performed with COA diagrams is done by hand, using grease pencils on clear acetate. Diagrams are frequently redrawn to remove irrelevant details or change

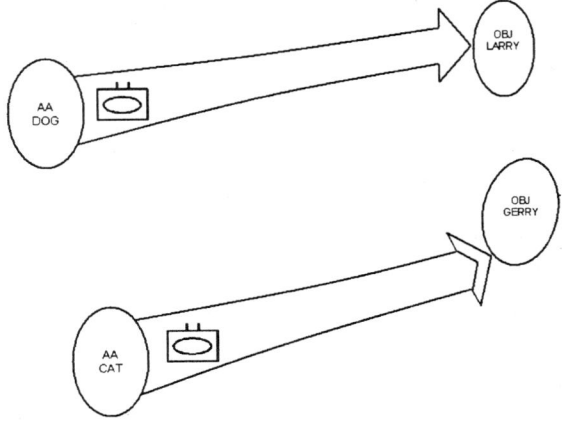

Figure 6: Example from a Course-of-Action diagram

the level of description.

The COA diagram describer (COADD), built using GeoRep, takes a line drawing of a COA diagram (as in Figure 6), and produces a description of the units, areas, and tasks given in the figure. Recognition of symbols in the COA diagram is handled by an HRLD rule set. It is worth noting that the initial prototype, which handles enough of the COA symbols to do simple but recognizable COA diagrams, was completed in less than 10 person-days, and involved only minimal changes to the LLRD (mostly to improve recognition of arrows). COADD's diagrams are the largest handled by GeoRep, containing as many as 197 visual elements.

Because most COA diagrams are constructed interactively, we are investigating extending GeoRep to handle interactive freehand sketches as input, instead of line drawings. A key technique is the use of glyphs in GeoRep to limit the low-level processing. A completed COA geographical reasoner utilizing GeoRep was recently used in a COA critiquer in HPKB (Ferguson et al., 2000)

Limitations and Areas for Future Work

GeoRep has evolved considerably as various projects have made demands on it. While GeoRep has shown itself to be a flexible and useful tool in our own research, it has significant limitations. These limitations must be addressed to make the model truly general.

First, GeoRep needs a cognitively accurate model of proximity. While GeoRep's proximity metric is sophisticated enough to incorporate the relative shape and size of elements considered proximate, the human attentional mechanism is much more complex, often balancing one proximity against another. For example, shapes A and B might be seen as proximate only if there is not some shape C that lies between them. We are investigating techniques for incorporating this model of proximity into the LLRD.

GeoRep's processing is mainly bottom-up, with only limited top-down influences on shape perception. Top-down influences occur when the HLRD calls LLRD operations to verify visual relations that are not checked by default. By using this limited top-down mechanism, GeoRep enforces the use of LLRD relations. In other words, GeoRep enforces the cognitive constraint that inferences be sanctioned by easily-perceived qualitative visual relations. We are currently examining ways to extend top-down influences while maintaining these vision-driven cognitive constraints.

GeoRep's intended use as part of an interactive sketching system highlights two other areas for improvement. GeoRep currently processes drawings in batch mode. For sketching, drawings will be processed incrementally. GeoRep currently expects each visual element to be accurately classified when read in. Although the strictness of LLRD operations can be varied, GeoRep does not have mechanisms to resolve ambiguous figures. Nor does it handle multiple variant feature interpretations of a single figure. For sketching, where a single pen stroke might be a spline, line segment, or arc depending on the context, GeoRep will have to be more flexible about choosing between alternate interpretations. These modifications will also allow GeoRep to be used with less-reliable data formats, such as vector data derived from scanned bitmaps of pre-existing diagrams.

Acknowledgements

This research was supported by the Cognitive Science and Computer Science programs of the Office of Naval Research, by the Defense Advanced Research Projects Agency, under the High Performance Knowledge Bases program, and by the National Science Foundation, under the Learning and Intelligent Systems program. Useful feedback and/or assistance was provided by Laura Allender, Jim Donlan, John Everett, George Lee, Yusuf Pisan, Rob Rasch, Bill Turmel, Jeff Usher and three anonymous reviewers.

References

Abella, A., & Kender, J. R. (1993). Qualitatively describing objects using spatial prepositions, *Proc. Eleventh National Conference on Artificial Intelligence*.

Allen, J. F. (1983). Maintaining knowledge about temporal intervals. *Comm. of the ACM*, 26, 832-843.

Baylis, G. C., & Driver, J. (1994). Parallel computation of symmetry but not repetition within single visual shapes. *Visual Cognition*, 1, 377-400.

Biederman, I. (1987). Recognition-by-components: A theory of human image understanding. *Psychological Review*, 94(2), 115-147.

Evans, T. G. (1968). A program for the solution of a class of geometric-analogy intelligence-test questions. In M. Minsky (Ed.), *Semantic Information Processing* (pp. 271-353). Cambridge, MA: MIT Press.

Ferguson, R. W. (1994). MAGI: Analogy-based encoding using symmetry and regularity. *Proc. 16th Ann. Conference of the Cognitive Science Society* (pp. 283-8). Atlanta.

Ferguson, R. W. (in preparation). A structure-mapping model of symmetry detection.

Ferguson, R. W., Aminoff, A., & Gentner, D. (1996). Modeling qualitative differences in symmetry judgments, *Proc. 18th Annual Conference of the Cognitive Science Society*. Hillsdale, NJ: Erlbaum Associates.

Ferguson, R. W., Aminoff, A., & Gentner, D. (submitted). Early detection of qualitative symmetry.

Ferguson, R. W., & Forbus, K. D. (1995). Understanding illustrations of physical laws by integrating differences in visual and textual representations. Fall Symposium on Computational Models for Integrating Language and Vision., Cambridge, Massachusetts.

Ferguson, R. W., & Forbus, K. D. (1998). Telling juxtapositions: Using repetition and alignable difference in diagram understanding. In K. Holyoak, D. Gentner, & B. Kokinov (Eds.), *Advances in Analogy Research* (pp. 109-117). Sofia: New Bulgarian University.

Ferguson, R. W., Rasch, R. A. J., Turmel, W., & Forbus, K. D. (2000). Qualitative spatial interpretation of Course-of-Action diagrams, *Proceedings of the 14th International Workshop on Qualitative Reasoning*. Morelia, Mexico.

Forbus, K. D. (1980). Spatial and qualitative aspects of reasoning about motion, *Proc. First National Conference on Artificial Intelligence*. Palo Alto, California.

Forbus, K. D., & de Kleer, J. (1993). *Building Problem Solvers*. Cambridge, MA: The MIT Press.

Forbus, K. D., Nielsen, P., & Faltings, B. (1991). Qualitative spatial reasoning: The CLOCK project. *Artificial Intelligence*, 51(1-3).

Glasgow, J., Narayanan, N. H., & Chandrasekaran, B. (1995). *Diagrammatic Reasoning: Cognitive and Computational Perspectives*. Menlo Park, CA: MIT Press.

Glassner, A. S. (Ed.). (1990). *Graphics Gems*. Chestnut Hill, MA: AP Professional.

Gross, M. D. (1996). The Electronic Cocktail Napkin: A computational environment for working with design diagrams. *Design Studies*, 17(1), 53-69.

Hendrich, N. (1999). JavaFIG: The Java diagram editor, [Web page]. Computer Science Department, University of Hamburg, Germany. Available: http://tech1.informatik.uni-hamburg.de/applets/javafig/ [1999, December 28].

Hoffman, D. D., & Richards, W. A. (1984). Parts of recognition. *Cognition*, 18(1-3), 65-96.

Julesz, B., & Bergen, J. R. (1983). Textons, the fundamental elements in preattentive vision and perception of textures. *The Bell System Technical Journal*, 1619-1645.

Kim, H. (1993). Qualitative reasoning about fluids and mechanics (Technical Report #47). Evanston, IL: Institute for the Learning Sciences, Northwestern University.

Lowe, D. G. (1987). Three-dimensional object recognition from single two-dimensional images. *Artificial Intelligence*, 31, 355-395.

Palmer, S. E. (1975). Visual perception and world knowledge. In D. A. Norman & D. E. Rumelhart (Eds.), *Explorations in Cognition* (pp. 279-307). San Francisco: W. H. Freeman and Company.

Pisan, Y. (1995). A visual routines based model of graph understanding, *Proc. 17th Annual Conference of the Cognitive Science Society*. Pittsburgh: Erlbaum.

Rock, I. (1973). *Orientation and Form*. New York, NY: Academic Press.

Sutherland, I. E. (1963). Sketchpad, a Man - Machine Graphical Communication System. Unpublished PH.D., Massachusetts Institute of Technology, Cambridge, MA.

Treisman, A., & Patterson, R. (1984). Emergent features, attention, and object perception. *Journal of Experimental Psychology: Human Perception and Performance*, 10, 12-31.

Treisman, A. M., & Gelade, G. (1980). A feature-integration theory of attention. *Cognitive Psychology*, 12, 97-136.

Tufte, E. R. (1990). *Envisioning Information*. Cheshire, Connecticut: Graphics Press.

Ullman, S. (1984). Visual routines. *Visual Cognition*. 18(1-3), 97-159.

STA: Spatio-Temporal Aggregation with Applications to Analysis of Diffusion-Reaction Phenomena*

Iván Ordóñez
Dept. of Computer and Information Science
The Ohio State University
2015 Neil Avenue
Columbus, OH 43210
iordonez@cis.ohio-state.edu

Feng Zhao
Xerox Palo Alto Research Center
3333 Coyote Hill Road
Palo Alto, CA 94304
zhao@parc.xerox.com

Abstract

Spatio-temporal data sets arise when time-varying physical fields are discretized for simulation or analysis. Examples of time-varying fields are isothermal regions in the sea or pattern formations in natural systems, such as convection rolls or diffusion-reaction systems. The analysis of these data sets is essential for generating qualitative interpretations for human understanding. This paper presents Spatio-Temporal Aggregation (STA), a system for recognizing and tracking qualitative structures in spatio-temporal data sets. STA algorithms record and maintain temporal events and compile event sequences into concise history descriptions. This is carried out at several levels of description, from the bottom up: first, low level events are identified and tracked, and then a subset of those events, relevant at the next description level, is identified. The process is iterated until a high level description of the system's temporal evolution is obtained. STA has been demonstrated on a class of diffusion-reaction systems in two dimensions and has successfully generated high-level symbolic descriptions of systems similar to those produced by scientists through carefully hand-tuned computational experiments.

Introduction

Spatio-temporal data sets arise when time-varying physical fields are discretized for the purpose of simulation or analysis. Some examples are turbulent fluids, isothermal regions in the sea, or pattern formations in natural systems, such as convection rolls or diffusion-reaction systems. The analysis of these data sets is essential in scientific visualization, modeling, or generating qualitative interpretations. However, many time-varying physical fields such as the diffusion-reaction phenomena can exhibit extremely complex behaviors that are time-dependent, spatially interacting, and sensitive to system parameter variations. It is often difficult, if not impossible, to predict such behaviors through analytical means alone. Because of recent advances in computational methods and hardware, there has been increasing interest in automated means for generating and classifying behaviors of such systems. In particular, the Spatial Aggregation (SA) approach (Yip and Zhao, 1996) provides a framework for the identification of structures in spatially distributed fields.

Regions of uniformity arise in a physical field because of continuities of properties such as intensity, temperature or pressure. A human observer would have little trouble describing events such as the formation of convection rolls in boiling water in straightforward qualitative terms. Furthermore, such an observer would easily recognize other phenomena also exhibiting convection rolls as belonging to the same class, even if they differ in details such as the size or the number of rolls.

A qualitative description of a physical field recognizes several events: the existence of coherent objects (that is, objects that are internally connected, of uniform features, and with a well-defined border), their persistence through time, and their abrupt change. The study of such high-level events arises frequently in many disciplines of scientific inquiry that deal with complex systems. For example, in medicine, it may be the high-level descriptions that provide the key to a problem: the cells of a heart that suffers from certain kinds of disease often do not behave differently from the cells of a normal heart at the individual level. It is their aggregated behavior that has gone awry (Beers and Berkow 1999). Any attempt to study complex phenomena that generate massive, unstructured data sets would benefit greatly from the automatic generation of high-level descriptions from raw data. Also, the classification of qualitative events based on topological and geometric characteristics of the involved objects and the nature of the transformations they undergo yields insight into the aggregated behavior of the system.

This paper describes Spatio-Temporal Aggregation, or STA (Ordóñez 1999), a temporal extension to Spatial Aggregation. This extension addresses systems that vary over time by recognizing and tracking structures in spatio-temporal data sets. STA is applied to a class of diffusion-reaction systems in two dimensions and it successfully generates high-level symbolic descriptions about the systems. In addition, by comparing multiple system histories, STA classifies systems with different parameterizations into equivalence classes, each of which contains members that exhibit qualitatively similar behaviors. This method is applied to the

---
*This work was conducted as part of the research in the Intelligent Simulation Group at Ohio State. Support for the Group is provided in part by ONR Young Investigator award N00014-97-1-0599, NSF Young Investigator award CCR-9457802, a Sloan Research Fellowship, NSF grant CCR-9308639, and a Xerox Foundation grant.
Copyright © 2000, American Association for Artificial Intelligence (www.aaai.org). All rights reserved.

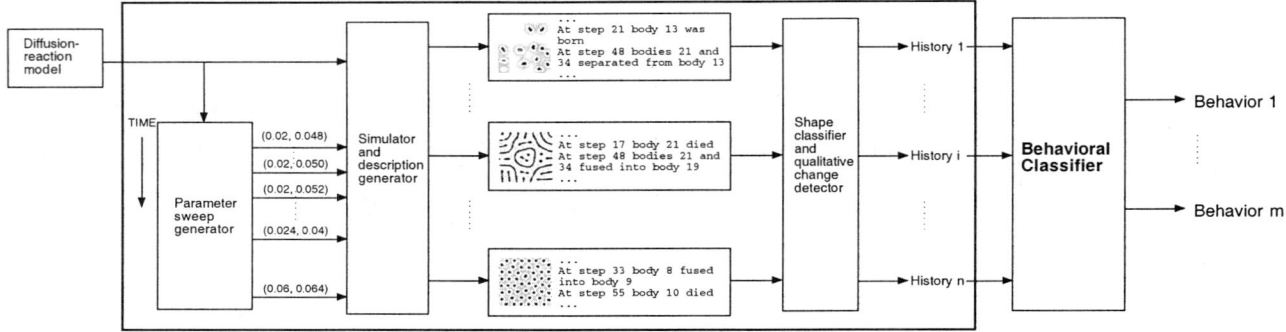

Figure 1: STA automatically catalogs qualitatively distinct behavioral classes, represented as spatio-temporal patterns, for a diffusion-reaction system. The simulator generates multiple system evolutions, each of which corresponds to a different set of system parameter values and initial condition. Each evolution, described as a sequence of qualitative events such as birth, death, or separation of objects, in conjunction with object shape transitions, is compiled into an event history. The classifier identifies behavioral classes from the set of event histories.

Gray-Scott (GS) model of glycolysis. It carries out an automated series of observations of temporal evolutions of this model, extracting a set of behavior-based classes of temporal evolutions. The approach has proved useful in that the classification scheme it generates is similar to one previously obtained by a scientist through carefully hand-tuned computational experiments and qualitative assessment by human observers (Pearson 1993). The operation of this application is sketched in Figure 1.

Other researchers have addressed the problem of generating high-level descriptions of physical systems. For instance, Williams and Millar (1996) develop a method for large-scale modeling and apply it to the thermal modeling of a smart building. STA is similar to their work in that it models complex systems through decomposition, but differs in that STA models more complex spatio-temporal dynamics, and produces symbolic descriptions. Crawford, Farquhar and Kuipers (1990) automatically generate qualitative differential equations from physical models. Their work considers temporal change, but not spatially distributed systems. Hornsby and Egenhofer (1997) study qualitative representations of change, such as an object's continuation, separation and fusion, and construct hierarchies of change, but they do not attempt to apply these objects to continuous fields. Forbus, Nielsen and Faltings (1991) developed the CLOCK project, which uses qualitative spatial reasoning to automatically analyze and qualitatively predict the behavior of fixed-axis mechanisms, such as mechanical clocks. Their approach is suitable for mechanical systems of rigid parts, while ours is best suited for continuous fields that exhibit high-level properties such as quasi-uniform regions.

The main contribution of this paper is a computational system that analyzes very large sets of unstructured data to produce descriptions of qualitatively distinct aggregate objects and events. Many other spatio-temporal reasoning systems cannot address such large systems because the sheer size of the data sets causes them problems such as combinatorial explosions. STA avoids such problems through intelligent decomposition and aggregation.

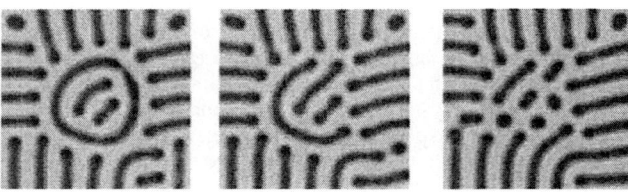

Figure 2: Three snapshots of a time-varying Gray-Scott diffusion-reaction system

A Case Study: Diffusion-Reaction Systems

An interesting instance of time-varying nonlinear dynamical systems is the set of phenomena known as Diffusion-Reaction. These phenomena are of great scientific importance, because they are associated with the problem of Morphogenesis, first addressed by Turing (1952). Particularly interesting instances, where noticeable patterns emerge and vary in seemingly unpredictable ways, will be examined.

The Gray Scott Model of Glycolysis

The phenomenon of glycolysis is found in virtually all living organisms. The Gray-Scott model of glycolysis is a diffusion-reaction system, characterized by the following equations:

$$\begin{aligned}
\frac{\partial u}{\partial t} &= D_u \nabla^2 u - uv^2 + F(1-u) \\
\frac{\partial v}{\partial t} &= D_v \nabla^2 v + uv^2 - (F+k)v,
\end{aligned} \quad (1)$$

where u and v are concentrations of two reactants, D_u and D_V are their diffusion rates, and F and k are reaction parameters. This system is of interest not only as a model of glycolysis, but also because it exhibits a variety of behaviors unlike anything observed before in theoretical or numerical studies. Pearson (1993) first observed the strikingly varied patterns exhibited by the GS system, such as the one seen in Figure 2. Pearson et al. (1994) have argued that since glycolysis occurs inside the cell, it is possible that patterns such as the above could form within it. Furthermore, they observe that the process of mitosis, through which cells divide, requires the formation of a bipolar structure known as the mitotic spindle, which is likely governed by simple physical processes such as chemical reactions and diffusion, rather than by complex genetic mechanisms.

As the parameters vary in the GS system, it undergoes qualitative transformations in its behavior. We apply STA to develop a program that can observe various system evolutions for different parameter values, and from this observation generate descriptions of the qualitative events that took place for each case. These descriptions are later used by the system to classify the instances into groups of similar behavior.

Spatio-Temporal Aggregation

STA significantly extends the functionality of Spatial Aggregation (SA) in the temporal dimension. SA provides a uniform vocabulary and mechanism for representing and reasoning about spatial fields. It builds a multi-layer, increasingly more abstract representation of a spatial field. Objects of each layer are formed as aggregates of lower-level objects. A neighborhood graph is constructed on the set of objects within each layer, and the objects are partitioned into equivalence classes with respect to their features, e.g., color, temperature, or pressure, as well their spatial adjacency. Each class is then re-described as a single object at the next higher level. The same process of aggregation, classification, and re-description repeats with more abstract relations at the next level. For a full description of the SA field ontology and operators see Yip and Zhao (1996) and Bailey-Kellogg (1999).

Temporal Changes

Existing applications of SA abstract over domains such as phase spaces and configuration spaces, in which time is only implicitly represented. Others deal with physical spaces in a fixed, steady state. In all these cases the field, as an ontology, and all the conceptual layers built on top of it, are static. Problems that use time are not necessarily outside the domain of Spatial Aggregation. For example, KAM (Yip 1989) is used to study Hamiltonian systems, which describe frictionless motion. These systems are studied in phase space, where temporal variation is implicitly represented. More in general, SA could be used to study time-varying systems as simple static systems where time has been represented as an extra spatial dimension. On the other hand, STA offers, beyond such approaches, the ability to reason about time-varying systems without having to compute and store the entire space-time volume beforehand. STA allows for the observation and representation of events as they happen, a feature that might be useful for real-time systems. For instance, our diffusion-reaction application, as sketched in Figure 1, records events such as the birth and death of spatial clusters in a diffusion-reaction field.

Aggregation and Persistence

Sophisticated techniques have been developed to address the problem of temporal tracking in fields (Silver and Wang 1997). It would seem natural to find whether there is a generalization of these tracking approaches, which would let them deal with not just one, but multiple abstraction layers, in the SA style.

The main addition made to the SA standard vocabulary by STA is the update operator, which takes a field or an object space and applies a set of transformations corresponding to the passage of a time interval. This operation allows for changes in an object's features, position and existence, and it affects all levels of conceptual entities: objects, neighborhood graphs, equivalence classes and inter-layer mappings. The notion of update implies the premise that these conceptual entities are persistent. Thus, a neighborhood graph on a particular abstraction layer at time $t+1$ should be conceived as a revision of the graph on that layer at time t, rather than as a new construct built from scratch. For instance, the dark areas in the fields seen in Figure 2 are objects, which may change in shape or position, while preserving their identities.

- Updates on Neighborhood Graphs: For a set of objects S, a neighborhood graph is a relation $R \in S \times S$ that does not contain any elements of the identity relation. When the objects in space come into existence, cease to exist or change positions, their adjacencies may be modified (thus changing R by removing elements from or adding elements to it). The changes in the neighborhood graph due to a change in a single object may remain localized in space, or may propagate everywhere, depending on the nature of the graph.

- Updates on Object Classes: Adjacency is a fundamental criterion to establish object equivalence in STA. Therefore, changes in adjacencies may cause objects to cease to belong to a certain class or to start belonging to a new class. Classes are connected sets of objects (for any two elements in a class, there is a path between them made of elements of R); therefore, changes in R may affect classes. On the other hand, even if the adjacencies are not altered, changes in the intrinsic properties of the objects may also affect the way they are classified. Changes in classification are annotated as sets of objects added or removed from each class, as well as classes that are newly formed or newly deceased.

- Updates on Re-described Objects: Changes in classes of objects may affect the way higher level objects are re-described, depending on what features are kept in the re-description process and which are abstracted away. For example, if clusters of objects in space constitute classes and they are re-described as convex hulls, internal changes in the clusters do not affect the higher level objects as long as they do not involve the hull. Therefore it is necessary to have mechanisms that detect lower-level changes that affect the structure of higher-level re-described objects.

Kinetic Data Structures: Reasoning about Change Detection

STA employs ideas from Kinetic Data Structures (KDS) to maintain the consistency of neighborhood graphs, object classes and re-described objects. KDS have been developed in robotics to maintain a set of geometric relations among distributed data (Basch, Guibas and Hershberg 1997). The problem KDS address consists of determining under which conditions the structure of certain geometric constructs is altered given that the elements are subject to particular motion laws.

Structural failure in a KDS is detected by maintaining a set of validity certificates, predicates that determine the conditions under which the current conditions of the system are valid. When a certificate is violated, an event is said to occur. The event is then processed and the certificates are updated to reflect the new conditions.

The existing corpus of research on finding and maintaining good certificates for various data structures is rich and varied. We are much less concerned with the particulars of each data structure and its maintenance algorithm than with the fact that such algorithms exist, and that they all fit within a single model of change as a violation of a certificate. Because STA addresses various levels of description, it is necessary to add conceptual mechanisms to determine the relevance of each certificate for the structure at the next abstraction level.

Update Mechanisms

We enhance the static SA to include certificate-violation based update mechanisms adapted from KDS. This is done first at the neighborhood graph level, by associating the graph (namely, its vertices and its adjacencies) with a set of certificates that establish how much deformation the graph can take without undergoing a structural change. The classifier operator now does not only map objects to classes via the neighborhood graph, but it also maps graph changes due to certificate violations to class changes.

The certificate-violation mechanism is extended to include the detection of non-geometrical change, namely, change in intrinsic object properties and existential change. The former kind of certificates exist at the classifier level, but not at the neighborhood graph level; typically it will consist of simple inequalities that test whether certain object features are within certain ranges. The latter exists at all levels. Also, detection at the re-description level requires being able to determine what low-level objects are relevant to the structure of higher-level objects. Because we know which objects are involved in which certificates, all certificates that contain relevant lower-level objects are needed for re-description. Such a filtering scheme is general, and allows for a unifying method to reason about abstraction of change.

Tracking Change in Time

We have developed a unifying reasoning scheme to deal with the propagation of change through an aggregation chain. We now focus on how to provide support for mechanisms that seek to interpret this change.

Keeping track of change in a system may be useful in many applications. For example, when studying transitional phases in self-organizing systems (such as the formation of

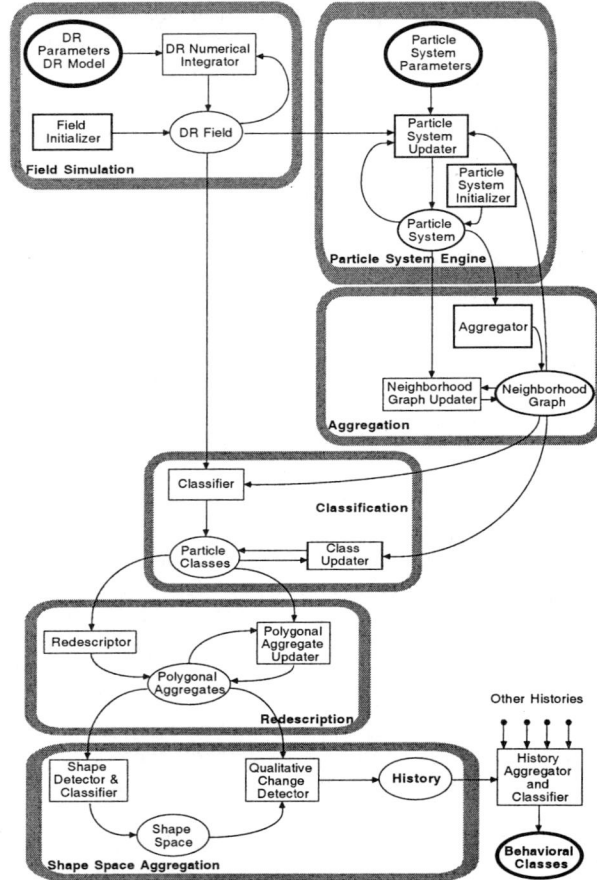

Figure 3: The flow diagram of STA application to the analysis of diffusion-reaction systems. The field simulator generates system evolutions, which are sampled and tracked by the particle system engine. A chain of aggregation, classification and re-description is maintained on top of the particle system, to identify and track high-level objects. Qualitative changes are later detected, generating event histories. The history aggregator and classifier take multiple histories and identify behavioral classes.

convection rolls in boiling water), researchers need to determine which kinds of events precede such transitions. We need, thus, to have a generic methodology to represent a history. More specifically, we require the ability to register a sequence of events that take place at various aggregation levels, namely changes in spatial objects, neighborhood graphs and object classes.

A history should register relevant change. The ease with which this can be done depends on how well the update mechanisms at various levels work. On one extreme, there is no attempt at any updates, and all structures are reconstructed from scratch at fixed intervals. In such conditions, finding relevant change is very difficult, since there is no knowledge to start with to draw correspondences. On the other extreme, there is a good update mechanism that operates on structures with a high degree of locality and that explicitly generates all change events. Such approach requires virtually no extra work from a history-tracking mechanism, which only needs to log these changes with their respective time stamps.

Application to Diffusion-Reaction Systems

We present a structure-identification algorithm for describing and classifying instances of diffusion-reaction systems that exhibit highly organized spatio-temporal structure. The algorithm is based on the central idea that qualitative structures of a spatial field can be constructed from an adaptive spatial subdivision rather than directly from a regularly discretized field. This adaptive subdivision changes as the field changes, but the identity of its structural components is persistent. The persistence of these components simplifies the correspondence between successive temporal snapshots. Figure 3 illustrates the operation of the algorithm.

Tracking High-Level Structures

The existence of coherent structures in a field implies that there are regions of approximately uniform characteristics. In the GS model, each region clearly belongs to one of two classes, low or high pH. The fewer the number of classes observed, and the larger the regions of uniform attributes are, the higher the organization perceived by an observer. These two global attributes of a field may vary with relative independence of each other, and each contributes significantly to the perception of coherence. For these reasons, local uniformity is one of the main features to look for when studying patterns. Once regions of uniformity are identified, characteristics such as topology and temporal behavior can be studied. The Field Simulation module (see Figure 3) generates the field and its changes, but is unaware of the existence of high-level structures.

Sampling Through a Particle System

Diffusion-reaction fields are sampled by the STA algorithm using particle systems (see corresponding block in Figure 3). Particles have the advantage of being persistent: they have discrete identities and hence whatever happens to them can be tracked in time with ease. Furthermore, any structures constructed by aggregating particles can also be tracked, because the identities of such constructs can be established recursively through a simple heuristic from the identities of its components. For example, one such simple heuristic is the following: if constructs A and B, existing at different time instants, share a majority of their components, they can be said to be identical. The particles must behave in such a way that they sample the field accurately. Therefore they must exist in large densities wherever the field gradient is large, and in low densities where it is small.

We consider a simple algorithm that allows the particle system to adapt itself to changes in the field, always maintaining an adequate sampling. The algorithm is a modification of a method introduced by Witkin and Heckbert (1994). It allows particles to move across the field, repelling each other, thereby occupying space uniformly. For this purpose, a Gaussian energy function is used. For any two particles i and j, their mutual energy is

$$E_{ij} = \alpha e^{-\frac{|r_{ij}|^2}{2\sigma_i^2}}, \qquad (2)$$

where α is a global constant and r_{ij} is their distance. The energy for each particle is given by

$$E_i = \sum_{j=1}^{n} E_{ij} + E_{ji}. \qquad (3)$$

Particles are assigned a velocity that is negatively proportional to the gradient of energy, such that their local energy (for particle i, the part of its energy that does not depend on σ_j) is minimized. Moreover, they modify their distribution and density to compensate for under or over-sampling, by adaptively changing each σ_i to maintain the local energy of each particle constant, and splitting or dying when this parameter falls outside of a pre-defined range.

Aggregating a Particle System

The sampling particles are used to construct a spatial subdivision. The subdivision is computed by dividing the space into simplices whose vertices are the particles, and whose edges constitute a neighborhood relation for the particles. The simplices need to be small and non-sharp, so a Delaunay triangulation is used. It offers the added advantage that it can be computed efficiently in two dimensions. Also, this triangulation is a superset of the closest-neighbor graph, and therefore it captures the notion of spatial locality: local variations in a particle's position cause changes in the triangulation that do not propagate beyond its immediate vicinity.

As the field varies in time, so does the position of the particles. This, in turn, causes the spatial subdivision to change: some edges cease to exist and some new ones arise at every time step. However, given the assumption that the underlying field changes slowly, the vast majority of edges and triangles are preserved through successive time steps, even though their shape is slightly changed. Because of the local nature of the Delaunay triangulation, these updates do not propagate far.

The static construction of a neighborhood graph constitutes the *aggregation* operator in SA. The corresponding block in Figure 3 represents the enhanced STA aggregate operation, which maintains the neighborhood graph as the particle system changes.

Description through Iso-Lines

Cluster boundaries are associated with field regions of high gradient. Those regions can be identified using iso-lines, continuous zones of uniform or near-uniform field value. The ratio of field value change to the distance between iso-lines gives an estimation of the gradient. Therefore, a field that is characterized by near-uniform regions that vary smoothly is well described by iso-lines that sample evenly spaced field values. Temporal variations in fields will be studied through the examination of geometric and topological change in iso-lines.

The particle placement algorithm previously described is used to approximate iso-line contours of uniform regions.

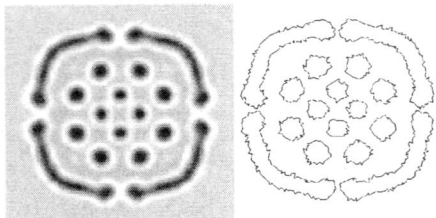

Figure 4: Subdivision generated from a particle system that samples a diffusion-reaction system

This algorithm requires the ability to do two things: to determine class equivalence between particles (the *classification* block in Figure 3), and to evaluate distances between particles that take the field into consideration. Since this case study is of two-dimensional diffusion-reaction systems, the distances between particles can be computed by using the field values as additional dimensions, with an appropriate scaling constant. Class equivalence for adjacent particles is computed by thresholding the distance between the particles in feature space, that is, by considering only the values of their properties. The extraction of structures from the spatial subdivision is analogous to a pixel-based region growing algorithm, with the difference that the element of aggregation is not the pixel, but the sampling particle. The block that does this in Figure 3 is labeled *redescription*. In Figure 4 the result of carrying out this process is exemplified.

Keeping Track of Shape Changes

STA records not only catastrophic events (such as object collisions), but also events that involve a single object modifying its shape. We use a shape-recognition and classification method called the Multiple Curvature Segmentation Algorithm, introduced by Dudek and Tsotsos (1997). Objects are placed in a shape space, and they are clustered by similarity. When an objects moves from one shape cluster to another, a qualitative shape transformation is said to have taken place (see the *Shape Space Aggregation* block in Figure 3).

Putting it All Together: Extracting Behavioral Descriptions

The STA algorithmic components we have described so far take as input a time-evolving diffusion-reaction system and produce the following descriptions:

- A detailed history of qualitatively significant events, including births, deaths, collisions and fusions of objects, and their changes in shape, specified as transitions from one shape cluster to another, and

- A summary of significant events that have taken place in the history, including records of the most common shapes and the most common events.

The last two blocks of Figure 3 indicate the final summarization process of the STA application: multiple histories as generated above are compared, and then classified according to behavioral similarity.

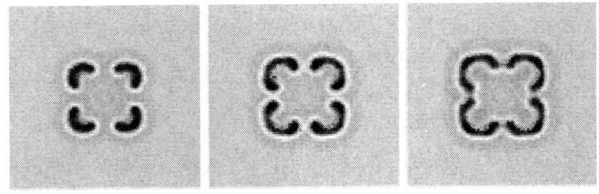

Figure 5: Successive snapshots of the evolution of a Gray-Scott diffusion-reaction system

```
At step 88 body 3 was born
At step 88 body 2 was born
At step 88 body 1 was born
At step 88 body 0 was born
At step 229 bodies 0 (born 88), 3
     (born 88) fused into body 1
At step 237 body 2 (born 88) fused
     into body 1
```

Table 1: A segment of a history: each entry is a time-stamped event. Notice that two fusion events are recorded. In them, the larger object preserves its identity, and the smaller ones are said to have fused to it.

A Sample Session: Classifying Patterns According to Behavior

We now present a short run of the history-generation part of the program.

The program records the events that take place in an evolving diffusion-reaction field. For instance, when a system such as that shown in Figure 5 evolves, the program can generate a history file such as that of Table 1.

The program can also compare several histories and group them into classes of similar behavior. For the systems on Figure 6, the groups in Table 2 were discovered. Compare these with the classes discovered by Pearson (1993), shown in Figure 7: cluster 4 corresponds to pattern (b); cluster 2 to (c) and cluster (5) to (a).

Conclusions

This paper has described a novel computational system, STA, for reasoning about time-varying fields such as diffusion-reaction systems. STA extends Spatial Aggregation to make explicit the representation of time and tem-

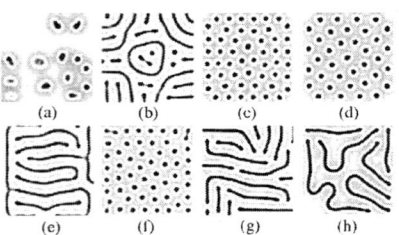

Figure 6: Snapshots for DR system evolutions. Histories were later classified into groups of similarity.

```
Cluster 1:  History (h)
Cluster 2:  Histories (e) and (g)
Cluster 3:  History (b)
Cluster 4:  Histories (c), (d) and (f)
Cluster 5:  History (a)
```

Table 2: Behavioral classes discovered by the STA application

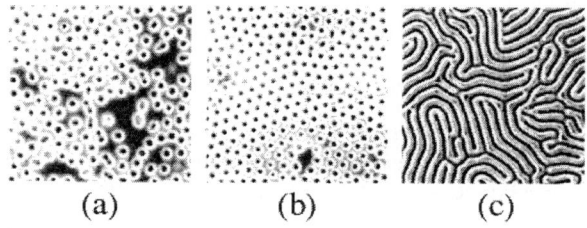

Figure 7: Patterns discovered by Pearson (1993) on the Gray-Scott system. His classification is similar to that produced by the STA application presented in this paper.

poral change. For this purpose, various abstract operations were introduced to represent the notions of persistence and change. Common qualitative events such as birth, death, collision, separation, acquisition or loss of components or properties were identified for objects in spatio-temporal domains.

STA has been demonstrated on a complex dynamical system that exhibits multiple, qualitatively different behaviors. This demonstration accounts for approximately 83% of the observations meticulously carried out by Pearson as documented in his 1993 paper. Our STA application classified multiple instances of this system using not only the appearance of static snapshots, but also the full extension of the behavior of the systems through a relatively long time interval. What this research contributes that had not been done before is the automatic differentiation of pattern classes by behavior.

STA makes use of various techniques, namely, operations of abstraction of change, kinetic data structures and geometric shape classification. How well would these techniques do if applied outside of this domain? We expect that a straightforward application of STA to problems that require extensive contextual and non-geometric knowledge would not work as well. For example, tracking objects for computer vision requires solving problems such as that of object occlusion and representation from incomplete information, not to mention the existence of multiple perspectives, different levels of illumination and reflectance, etc. In order to address those problems, STA needs to integrate additional domain specific techniques from computer vision. Similarly, the problem of examining weather patterns also requires extensive domain knowledge. While this problem seems more amenable to treatment from a STA perspective, it would still require integrating specific techniques such as those developed by Huang and Zhao (2000) with the STA tracking mechanism.

References

Bailey-Kellogg, C. 1999. The Spatial Aggregation Language for Modeling and Controlling Distributed Physical Systems. Ph.D. diss., Dept. of Computer and Information Science, The Ohio State Univ.

Basch, J.; Guibas, L.; and Hershberg, J. 1997. Data Structures for Mobile Data. In *Proceedings of the 8th ACM-SIAM Symposium on Discrete Algorithms* 747–756.

Beers, H. and Berkow, R. eds. 1999. *The Merck Manual*. Merck Research Laboratories, seventeenth edition.

Crawford, J; Farquhar, A.; and Kuipers, B. 1990. QPC: A Compiler from Physical Models into Qualitative Differential Equations. In *Proceedings of the National Conference on Artificial Intelligence (AAAI-90)*, AAAI/MIT Press.

Dudek, G. and Tsotsos, J. 1997. Shape Representation and Recognition from Multiscale Curvature. *Computer Vision and Image Understanding* 68(2): 170–189.

Forbus, K.; Nielsen, P.; and Faltings, B. 1991. Qualitative Spatial Reasoning: The Clock Project. *Artificial Intelligence* 51(1–3): 417–471.

Hornsby, K. and Egenhofer, M. 1997. Qualitative Representation of Change. In *Proceedings of the International Conference on Spatial Information Theory (COSIT-97)*, Lecture Notes in Computer Science, 1329:15–33.

Huang, X. and Zhao, F. 2000. Relation-Based Aggregation: Finding Objects in Large Spatial Datasets. *Inter. J. of Intelligent Data Analysis*. To appear.

Ordóñez, I. 1999. STA: Spatio-Temporal Aggregation of Physical Fields with Applications to Analysis of Diffusion-Reaction Phenomena. Ph.D. diss., Dept. of Computer and Information Science, The Ohio State Univ.

Pearson, J; Doolen, G.; Hasslacher, B. Reynolds, B.; Horsthemke, W.; Lee, K.; McCormick, W.; Swinney, H.; and Ponce-Dawson, S. 1994. Chemical Pattern Formation. *Parallel Computing Research*, 2(3).

Pearson, J. 1993. Complex Patterns in a Simple System. *Science*, 261.

Silver, D. and Wang, X. 1997. Tracking and Visualizing Turbulent 3D Features. *IEEE Transactions on Visualization and Computer Graphics* 3:129–141.

Turing, A. 1952. The Chemical Basis of Morphogenesis. *Philosophical Transactions of the Royal Society (B)* 237:37–72.

Williams, B. C. and Millar, B 1996. Automated Decomposition of Model-based Learning Problems. In *Proceedings of QR-96*.

Witkin, A. and Heckbert, P. 1994. Using Particles to Sample and Control Implicit Surfaces. In *Computer Graphics, SIGGRAPH 94 Proceedings*.

Yip, K. 1989. KAM: Automatic Planning and Interpretation of Numerical Experiments using Geometrical Methods. Ph.D. diss., Massachusetts Institute of Technology.

Yip, K. and Zhao, F. 1996. Spatial Aggregation: Theory and Applications. *Journal of Artificial Intelligence Research*, 5.

On the Recognition of Abstract Markov Policies

Hung H. Bui, Svetha Venkatesh and Geoff West
Department of Computer Science
Curtin University of Technology
PO Box U1987, Perth, WA 6001, Australia
{buihh, svetha, geoff}@cs.curtin.edu.au

Abstract

Abstraction plays an essential role in the way the agents plan their behaviours, especially to reduce the computational complexity of planning in large domains. However, the effects of abstraction in the inverse process – plan recognition – are unclear. In this paper, we present a method for recognising the agent's behaviour in noisy and uncertain domains, and across multiple levels of abstraction. We use the concept of abstract Markov policies in abstract probabilistic planning as the model of the agent's behaviours and employ probabilistic inference in Dynamic Bayesian Networks (DBN) to infer the correct policy from a sequence of observations. When the states are fully observable, we show that for a broad and often-used class of abstract policies, the complexity of policy recognition scales well with the number of abstraction levels in the policy hierarchy. For the partially observable case, we derive an efficient hybrid inference scheme on the corresponding DBN to overcome the exponential complexity.

Introduction

While planning their behaviours in large domains, the agents often have to employ abstraction techniques to reduce the complexity associated with large state spaces. As a consequence, their behaviours often follow a hierarchichal plan structure. In abstract probabilistic planning (Sutton, Precup, & Singh 1999; Parr & Russell 1997; Forestier & Varaiya 1978; Hauskrecht *et al.* 1998; Dean & Lin 1995), such a hierarchichal plan structure can be modelled using the concept of *abstract Markov policies* [1]. In this paper, we address the problem of recognising such a policy – the inverse of the abstract probabilistic planning problem, i.e. to infer the underlying abstract policy from the external observation of the induced behaviour.

The problem can be classified under the umbrella of key-hole plan recognition (Cohen, Perrault, & Allen 1981; Kautz & Allen 1986) where the agent who carries out the plan (the actor) is not aware that it is being observed. The recent trend in approaching this problem is first constructing a probabilistic model for the plan execution, and then employing abductive reasoning techniques such as probabilistic (Bayesian) inference to infer the underlying plan from the observation sequence (Huber, Durfee, & Wellman 1994; Goldmand, Geib, & Miller 1999). To represent the evolution of the plan over time, some authors (Forbes *et al.* 1995; Pynadath & Wellman 1995; Albrecht, Zukerman, & Nicholson 1998) have employed the Dynamic Bayesian Network (DBN) (Dean & Kanazawa 1989; Nicholson & Brady 1992) as the framework for inferencing. All of this work in plan recognition uses a hierarchichal structure of plans and actions. However, to the best of our knowledge, the question of how the structure of a plan hierarchy would affect the complexity of the recognition process has not been investigated.

In our approach, we adopt the Abstract Markov Policies (AMP) as the model for plan execution. The AMP is an extension of a policy in Markov Decision Processes (MDP) that enables an abstract policy to invoke other more refined policies and so on down the policy hierarchy. The concept originates from the abstract probabilistic planning literature as a way to scale up MDP-based planning to domains whose state spaces are large. An AMP can be described simply in terms of a state space and a Markov policy that selects among a set of other AMP's. Thus, using the AMP as the model for plan execution helps us focus on the structure of the policy hierarchy alone.

Throughout the paper, we make the assumption that only the states (which bear the effects of actions) can be observed, but not the actions themselves. Thus, the policy recognition problem can be divided into two cases: when state observations are certain (*fully observable*), and when the observations are partial and uncertain (*partially observable*) [2].

Computationally, we view policy recognition as probabilistic inference on the Dynamic Bayesian Network representing the execution of the AMP (together with the noisy observation of states in the partially observable case). Intuitively, the DBN models how an AMP causes the adoption of other policies and actions at different levels of abstraction, which in turn generate a sequence of states and observation. In policy recognition, we need to reverse the direction of causality and compute the conditional probability of the top-

---

Copyright © 2000, American Association for Artificial Intelligence (www.aaai.org). All rights reserved.

[1] Also known as *options, policies of Abstract Markov Decision Processes, supervisor's policies*.

[2] This only means that the external observer has partial information. Our model however assumes that the actor always has full information about the current state.

level AMP given an observation sequence.

It is known that the complexity of this kind of inferencing in the DBN depends on the size of the representation of the so-called *belief state*, the conditional joint distribution of the variables in the DBN at time t given the observation sequence up to t (Boyen & Koller 1998). Thus we can ask the following question: how does the structure of an AMP affect the size of its belief state representation? Using conditional independence relations on the network, we show that a reduction in size of the belief state is possible if at some level of abstraction, the set of applicable domains of all the policies forms a partition of the full state space. As a consequence, if the AMP is constructed through the region-based decomposition of the state space as in (Forestier & Varaiya 1978; Dean & Lin 1995; Hauskrecht *et al.* 1998), its belief state can be represented compactly as a chain in the fully observable case, facilitating very efficient inferencing. Based on this result, for the partially observable case, we derive a hybrid inference scheme combining both exact inference as in the fully observable case, and sampling-based approximative inference to handle the noisy observation. We provide experiment results showing the hybrid inference scheme achieving much better accuracy/time ratio than the original sampling-based inference (Kanazawa, Koller, & Russell 1995).

The main body of the paper is organised as follows. The next two sections introduce the abstract Markov policy model and its DBN representation. The algorithms for policy recognition are discussed next, first for the fully observable and then for the partially observable case. We then present the experiment results supporting the new hybrid inference scheme.

Abstract Markov Policies

In this section, we formally introduce the AMP concept as originating from the literature of abstract probabilistic planning with MDP (Sutton, Precup, & Singh 1999; Parr & Russell 1997; Forestier & Varaiya 1978; Hauskrecht *et al.* 1998; Dean & Lin 1995). Note that the work in planning is concerned with computing the optimal (abstract) policy given some reward function. In policy recognition, although it is possible to derive some information about the reward function by observing the agent's behaviour, we choose not to do this, thus omit from our model the reward function and also the optimality notion. This leaves the model open to tracking arbitrary agent's behaviours, regardless of whether they are optimal or not.

The general model

In an MDP, the world is modelled as a set of possible states S, termed the state space. At each state s, an agent has a set of actions A available, where each action a, if employed, will cause the world to evolve to the next state s' via a transition probability $\sigma_a(s, s')$. An agent's plan of actions is modelled as a policy that prescribes how the agent would choose its action at each state. For a policy π, this is modelled by a selection function $\sigma_\pi : S \times A \to [0, 1]$ where at each state s, $\sigma_\pi(s, a)$ is the probability that the agent will choose the action a.

In the original MDP, behaviours are modelled at only two levels: the primitive action level, and the plan level (policy). We would like to consider policies that selects other more refined policies and so on, down a number of abstraction levels. The idea is to form intermediate-level abstract policies as policies defined over a local region of the state space, having a certain terminating condition, and can be invoked and executed just like primitive actions (Forestier & Varaiya 1978; Sutton, Precup, & Singh 1999). Formally, let Π be a set of abstract policies. We can then define an abstract policy π^* over Π as a tuple $\langle S_{\pi^*}, D_{\pi^*}, \sigma_{\pi^*} \rangle$ where $S_{\pi^*} \subset S$ is the set of applicable states, $D_{\pi^*} \subset S$ is the set of destination states, and $\sigma_{\pi^*} : S_{\pi^*} \times \Pi \to [0, 1]$ is the selection function where $\sigma_{\pi^*}(s, \pi)$ is the probability that π^* selects the policy π at the state s. When an abstract policy π^* is invoked, it will keep on selecting the policies in Π for execution, and terminate whenever a destination state $d \in D_{\pi^*}$ is reached [3]. Note the recursiveness in this definition that allows an abstract policy to select among a set of other abstract policies. At the base level, primitive actions can be viewed as abstract policies themselves (Sutton, Precup, & Singh 1999).

Using the abstract policies as building blocks, we can construct a hierarchy of abstract policies as follows: A policy hierarchy is a sequence $\mathcal{H} = (\Pi_0, \Pi_1, \ldots, \Pi_K)$ where Π_0 is a set of primitive actions, and for $k = 1, \ldots, K$, Π_k is a set of abstract policies over the policies in Π_{k-1}. When a top-level policy π_K is executed, it invokes a sequence of level-(K-1) policies, each of which invokes a sequence of level-(K-2) policies and so on. A level-1 policy will invoke a sequence of primitive actions which leads to a sequence of states. Thus, the execution of π_K generates an overall state sequence $(s^{(0)}, s^{(1)}, \ldots, s^{(t)}, \ldots)$ that terminates in one of the destination states in D_{π_K}. When $K = 1$ this sequence is simply a Markov chain, however, for $K \geq 2$, it will generally be non-Markovian (Sutton, Precup, & Singh 1999).

State-space region-based decomposition

An intuitive and often-used method for constructing the policy hierarchy is via region-based decomposition of the state space (Dean & Lin 1995; Hauskrecht *et al.* 1998). Here the state space S is successively partitioned into a sequence of partitions $\mathcal{P}_K, \mathcal{P}_{K-1}, \ldots \mathcal{P}_1$ where $\mathcal{P}_K = \{S\}$ is the coarsest partition, and $\mathcal{P}_1$ is the finest, corresponding to the K levels of abstraction. For each region R_i of $\mathcal{P}_i$, the periphery of R_i, $Per(R_i)$ is defined as the set of states not in R_i, but connected to some state in R_i. Let Per_i be the set of all peripheral states at level i: $Per_i = \cup_{R_i \in \mathcal{P}_i} Per(R_i)$. Fig. 1(b) shows an example where the state space representing a building is partitioned into 4 regions corresponding to the 4 rooms. The peripheral states for a region is shown in Fig 1(a), and Fig 1(b) shows all such peripheral states.

To construct the policy hierarchy, we first define for each region $R_1 \in \mathcal{P}_1$ a set of abstract policies applicable on R_1,

---

[3] Sutton, Precup and Singh's model allows non-deterministic stopping conditions and thus is more general than what we consider here. Nevertheless, our theorem 1 can also be shown to hold in the general case as well.

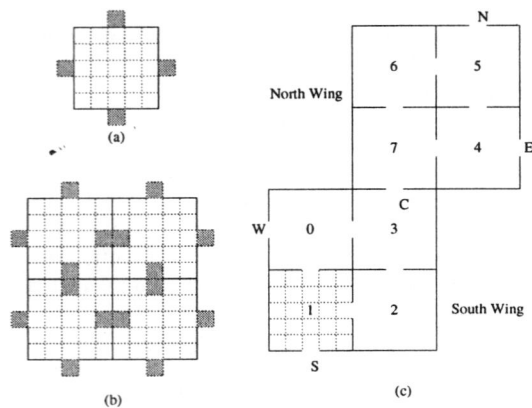

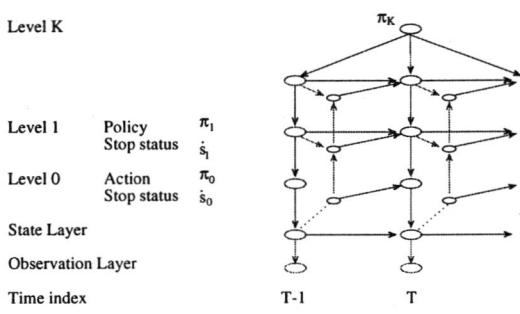

Figure 1: The environment and its partition

Figure 2: The DBN representation

and having $Per(R_1)$ as the destination states. For example, for each room in Fig 1, we can define a set of policies that model the agent's different behaviours while it is inside the room, e.g. getting out through a particular door. These policies can be initiated whenever the agent steps inside the room, and terminate when the agent steps out of the room (not necessarily through the target door since the policy might fail to achieve its intended target). Let the set of all policies defined be Π_1. At the higher level $\mathcal{P}_2$, for each region R_2, we can define a set of policies that model the the agent's behaviours inside that region with the constraint that these policies must use the policies previously defined at level-1 to achieve their goals. An example is a policy to navigate between the room-doors to get from one building gate to another. Let the set of all policies defined at this level be Π_2. Continuing doing this at the higher levels, we obtain the policy hierarchy $\mathcal{H} = (\Pi_0, \Pi_1, \Pi_2, \ldots, \Pi_K)$.

Dynamic Bayesian Network Representation

The process of executing the top-level abstract policy π_K can be represented by a DBN (Fig. 2). At time t, the current time slice consists of the variables representing the current state $s^{(t)}$, and the current policies at different levels of abstraction $\pi_k^{(t)}, k = 0, \ldots, K$. We assume that the top-level policy remains unchanged, so $\pi_K^{(t)} = \pi_K$ for all t.

Let $\dot{s}_k^{(t)}, k = 0, \ldots, K-1$ represent the stopping status of the policy $\pi_k^{(t)}$. That is $\dot{s}_k^{(t)} = s^{(t)}$ if the policy terminates at time t, and $\dot{s}_k^{(t)} = false$ otherwise. At the base level, since the primitive action always terminates after one time step, $\dot{s}_0^{(t)} = s^{(t)}$ for all t. This is indicated by the special dotted lines in Fig. 2. Generally, we can look at the stopping status of the current policy at the lower level $\dot{s}_{k-1}^{(t)}$ and see whether this falls inside the destination states of $\pi_k^{(t)}$ to determine the value of $\dot{s}_k^{(t)}$. Thus, $\dot{s}_k^{(t)}$ is dependent (deterministically) on $\pi_k^{(t)}$ and $\dot{s}_{k-1}^{(t)}$.

Now the evolution from one time-slice of the DBN to the next is as follows: the current policy $\pi_k^{(t)}$ is dependent on the current policy at the higher level $\pi_{k+1}^{(t)}$, the policy at the previous time $\pi_k^{(t-1)}$, and its stopping status $\dot{s}_k^{(t-1)}$. If $\dot{s}_k^{(t-1)} = false$, the previous policy $\pi_k^{(t-1)}$ persists to time t, otherwise, a new policy at level-k is generated by $\pi_{k+1}^{(t)}$ using the distribution $\sigma_{\pi_{k+1}^{(t)}}(\dot{s}_k^{(t-1)}, .)$.

We term the dynamical process in executing a top-level abstract policy π_K the *Abstract Markov Model* (AMM). When the states are only partially observable, an observation layer can be attached to the state layer (Fig. 2). The resulting process is termed the *Abstract Hidden Markov Model* (AHMM) since the states are hidden as in the Hidden Markov Model (Rabiner 1989).

The belief state of the AMM is a joint distribution of $K+2$ variables in the current time-slice: $s^{(t)}, \pi_0^{(t)}, \ldots, \pi_K^{(t)}$. Thus generally, the size of the belief state representation will be exponential of K. However, due to the way policies are invoked in the AMM, we can make an intuitive remark that, the higher level policies can only influence what happens at the lower level through the current level. Therefore, knowing enough information about the current level would make the higher level policies probabilistically independent of the lower level policies. If this kind of probabilistic independence relations can be exploited, the belief state could be represented more compactly.

Thus, our motivation here is to find the least amount of information we need to know about the current level, in order to make the current policies at the higher and lower levels independent. The following theorem states that if at level k, we know the current policy, together with its starting time and starting state, then the higher levels are independent of the lower levels. The condition obtained is the strictest, in the sense that, if one of these three variables is unknown, there are examples of AMMs in which the higher level policies can influence the lower level ones.

Theorem 1. *Let $\tau_k^{(t)}$ and $b_k^{(t)}$ be two random variables representing the starting time and the starting state, respectively, of the current level-k policy $\pi_k^{(t)}$: $\tau_k^{(t)} = \max\{t' < t \mid \dot{s}_k^{(t)} \neq false\}$ and $b_k^{(t)} = s^{(\tau_k^{(t)})}$. Let $\pi_{>k}^{(t)} = \{\pi_{k+1}^{(t)}, \ldots, \pi_K^{(t)}\}$ denote the set of current policies from level $k+1$ up to K, and $\pi_{<k}^{(t)} = \{s^{(t)}, \pi_0^{(t)}, \ldots, \pi_{k-1}^{(t)}\}$ de-*

note the set of current policies from level $k - 1$ down to 0 together with the current state. We have:

$$\pi^{(t)}_{>k} \perp \pi^{(t)}_{<k} \mid \pi^{(t)}_k, b^{(t)}_k, \tau^{(t)}_k \quad (1)$$

Proof. (Sketch) Induction by t. Can easily verify for $t = 1$. Suppose that (1) holds for $t - 1$, need to prove it for t. There are two cases. If $\tau^{(t)}_k < t - 1$, meaning $\pi^{(t)}_k$ started before $t - 1$, therefore $\pi^{(t)}_k = \pi^{(t-1)}_k$, $\tau^{(t)}_k = \tau^{(t-1)}_k$, $b^{(t)}_k = b^{(t-1)}_k$, and also for the higher levels, $\pi^{(t)}_{>k} = \pi^{(t-1)}_{>k}$. From the structure of the DBN, it can be seen that $\pi^{(t-1)}_k, \pi^{(t)}_k, \pi^{(t-1)}_{<k}$ d-separate $\pi^{(t)}_{<k}$ from all other variables up to time t. From this, we can obtain $\pi^{(t)}_{>k} \perp \pi^{(t)}_{<k} \mid \pi^{(t-1)}_{<k}, \pi^{(t)}_k, b^{(t)}_k, \tau^{(t)}_k$. Combining this with the inductive assumption $\pi^{(t)}_{>k} \perp \pi^{(t-1)}_{<k} \mid \pi^{(t)}_k, b^{(t)}_k, \tau^{(t)}_k$, and using the contraction property of the relation $\perp$ (Pearl 1988, p84), we obtain $\pi^{(t)}_{>k} \perp \pi^{(t)}_{<k} \mid \pi^{(t)}_k, b^{(t)}_k, \tau^{(t)}_k$. In the second case, if $\tau^{(t)}_k \geq t - 1$, but since $\tau^{(t)}_k \leq t - 1$, we have $\tau^{(t)}_k = t - 1$ and $b^{(t)}_k = s^{(t-1)}$. This means that the policy $\pi^{(t)}_k$, and all the policies in $\pi^{(t)}_{<k}$ have just been formed at the previous time at the state $s^{(t-1)}$. Therefore, $\pi^{(t)}_{<k}$ is d-separated from the upper levels by $\pi^{(t)}_k$ and $s^{(t-1)}$. Thus, $\pi^{(t)}_{>k} \perp \pi^{(t)}_{<k} \mid \pi^{(t)}_k, b^{(t)}_k = s^{(t-1)}, \tau^{(t)}_k = t - 1$. □

Policy Recognition

The policy recognition problem can be formulated as to compute the conditional probabilities of the current policies, given the current observation sequence. In this section, we will assume full observability, i.e. the observation sequence at time t is the state sequence $\tilde{s}^{(t-1)} = (s^{(0)}, \ldots, s^{(t-1)})$. In more concrete terms, we are interested in the probabilities $\Pr(\pi^{(t)}_k \mid \tilde{s}^{(t-1)})$ for all level k. This gives us information about the agent's behaviour at all levels of abstraction, from the current action ($k = 0$), to the top-level policy ($k = K$). In addition, continuous monitoring would require to compute these probabilities in all time steps t (whenever an observation is made).

Our solution to this problem is based on updating the belief state of the AMM, i.e. the joint distribution $\Pr(\pi^{(t)}_K, \ldots, \pi^{(t)}_0, s^{(t)} \mid \tilde{s}^{(t-1)})$. Thus, the size of the representation of this distribution is crucial.

The belief chain

From Theorem 1, if the starting time of the current level-k policy $\tau^{(t)}_k$ can be determined from the state sequence $\tilde{s}^{(t-1)}$, then so can the starting state $b^{(t)}_k$, and the belief state can be split into two independent parts conditioned on $\pi^{(t)}_k$: $\pi^{(t)}_{>k} \perp \pi^{(t)}_{<k} \mid \pi^{(t)}_k, \tilde{s}^{(t-1)}$. This condition is satisfied when the applicable domains of all the policies at level k do not partially overlap (i.e. any two domains are either identical or mutually exclusive), so that the starting point of the current policy $\pi^{(t)}_k$ can be identified as the last time the state

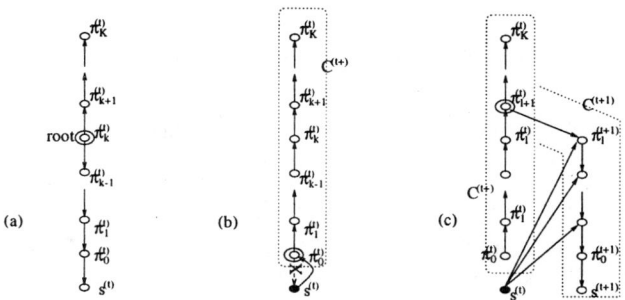

Figure 3: The belief chain and its updating process

history sequence $\tilde{s}^{(t-1)}$ crossed one of the peripheral states in Per_k: $\tau^{(t)}_k = \max_{t'}\{t' < t, s^{(t')} \in Per_k\}$.

As a consequence, if the policy hierarchy is constructed via region-based decomposition of the state-space, $\pi^{(t)}_{>k} \perp \pi^{(t)}_{<k} \mid \pi^{(t)}_k, \tilde{s}^{(t-1)}$ holds for all k, and thus the belief state can be represented by a Bayesian network with a simple chain structure. We term this network the *belief chain* (Fig. 3(a)), and denote it by $\mathcal{C}^{(t)}(\tilde{s}^{(t-1)}) \equiv \Pr(\pi^{(t)}_K, \ldots, \pi^{(t)}_0, s^{(t)} \mid \tilde{s}^{(t-1)})$. If a chain is drawn so that all links point away from the level-k node, we say the chain has root at level k. The root of the chain can be moved from k to another level k' simply by reversing the links between k and k'. For consistency purpose, level -1 will refer to the node $s^{(t)}$, and thus $\pi^{(t)}_{-1} \equiv s^{(t)}$. In the remaining of the paper, we assume that the policy hierarchy has been constructed via the region-based decomposition method, and thus deal exclusively with this chain structure.

Updating the belief chain

Since the belief state can be represented by a chain (and thus has size linear to K), we can expect that exact inference method based on updating the belief state will work efficiently. Here, we briefly describe such a method. More details can be found in a longer version of this paper (Bui, Venkatesh, & West 2000).

Assuming that we have a complete specification of the chain $\mathcal{C}^{(t)}$, we need to compute the parameters for the new chain $\mathcal{C}^{(t+1)}$. This is done in two steps, as in the standard "roll-over" of the belief state of a DBN (Boyen & Koller 1998): (1) absorbing the new evidence $s^{(t)}$, and (2) projecting the belief state into the next time step.

In the first step, we need to compute the chain $\mathcal{C}^{(t+)} \equiv \Pr(\pi^{(t)}_K, \ldots, \pi^{(t)}_0 \mid \tilde{s}^{(t)})$. This can be achieved by positioning the root of the chain $\mathcal{C}^{(t)}$ at level 0, and then reverse the link from $\pi^{(t)}_0$ to $s^{(t)}$ to absorb the new evidence $s^{(t)}$ (Fig. 3(b)).

In the second step, we continue to compute $\mathcal{C}^{(t+1)}$ from $\mathcal{C}^{(t+)}$. We note that the new state $s^{(t)}$ might cause some policies at the lower levels to terminate. Let l be the highest level of such a policy; l is deterministically determined since $l = \max\{0\} \cup \{k \geq 1 \mid s^{(t)} \in Per_k\}$. Since all the policies at levels higher than l do not terminate, $\pi_{>l}^{(t+1)} = \pi_{>l}^{(t)}$, and we can retain this upper sub-chain from $\mathcal{C}^{(t+)}$ to $\mathcal{C}^{(t+1)}$. In the lower part, for $k \leq l$, a new policy $\pi_k^{(t+1)}$ is created by the policy $\pi_{k+1}^{(t+1)}$ at the state $s^{(t)}$, and thus a new sub-chain can be formed among the variables $\pi_{\leq l}^{(t+1)}$ with parameters $\Pr(\pi_k^{(t+1)} \mid \pi_{k+1}^{(t+1)}, s^{(t)}) = \sigma_{\pi_{k+1}^{(t+1)}}(s^{(t)}, \pi_k^{(t+1)})$. The new chain $\mathcal{C}^{(t+1)}$ is then the combination of these two sub-chains, which will be a chain with root at level $l+1$ (see Fig. 3(c)).

The complexity of this updating process is $O(l)$. However, most of the time, none of the policies from level one up would terminate, and thus $l = 0$. More precisely, the probability that the current policy at level l terminates is exponentially small w.r.t. l. Thus, on average, the updating complexity at each time-step is $O(\sum_l l/exp(l))$ which is constant-bounded. Once the current belief chain is obtained, the required probability $\Pr(\pi_k^{(t)} \mid \tilde{s}^{(t-1)})$ is simply the marginal $\mu_k^{(t)}$ at the level-k node in the chain $\mathcal{C}^{(t)}$.

The Partially Observable Case

We now consider the scenarios when the states cannot be observed with certainty. The observation at time t is denoted by $o^{(t)}$, and is assumed to depend stochastically on $s^{(t)}$ only, via the observation model $\omega(s, o) = \Pr(o \mid s)$ (the probability that o is observed given the actual state is s). Thus, in comparison with the previous section, we now deal with a process represented by the AHMM, and the main inference problem becomes computing the probabilities $\Pr(\pi_k^{(t)} \mid \tilde{o}^{(t-1)})$.

The hidden states make the inference tasks in the AHMM much more difficult. Since the exact state sequence is not available, neither the starting times or the starting states of the current policies are known with certainty. Thus, theorem 1 cannot be used. We therefore cannot hope to represent the belief state by a chain as we did previously. In this case, an exact method for updating the belief state will have to operate on a structure with size exponential in K. To cope with this complexity, one generally has to resort to some approximative inference method instead.

In (Bui, Venkatesh, & West 1999), the stochastic sampling method for DBN (Kanazawa, Koller, & Russell 1995) has been applied to a network structure similar to the AHMM. This inference method makes use of a procedure that reverses the link from the state to the observation before sampling the next state (*evidence reversal (ER)*), so that the sampled state sequence would stay close to the true sequence. However, when applied to the multi-layer AHMM, the ER procedure only affects the sampling of the next state, while having no effect on the sampling of the next policies at the higher levels. Furthermore, since the method is intended to be an inference scheme for generic DBNs, it does not utilise the special structure of the AHMM.

Here, we present a method that uses stochastic sampling only at the state level, and performs exact inference through belief-chain updating at the higher levels. Thus, the method can be classified as an *hybrid-inference* scheme (Dawid, Kjærulff, & Lauritzen 1995) which attempts to combine approximative inference with exact inference on the tractable parts of the model network. We describe the details of this inference method below.

Hybrid inference

First, we have the following expansion of the wanted probability $\Pr(\pi_k^{(t)} \mid \tilde{o}^{(t-1)})$:

$$\propto \sum_{\tilde{s}^{(t-1)}} \Pr(\pi_k^{(t)} \mid \tilde{s}^{(t-1)}) \Pr(\tilde{o}^{(t-1)} \mid \tilde{s}^{(t-1)}) \Pr(\tilde{s}^{(t-1)})$$

$$= \mathop{\mathrm{E}}_{\tilde{s}^{(t-1)}} \left[\mu_k^{(t)}(\tilde{s}^{(t-1)}) w^{(t)}(\tilde{s}^{(t-1)}) \right] \quad (2)$$

where $\mu_k^{(t)}$ is the level-k marginal of the chain $\mathcal{C}^{(t)}$, $w^{(t)}(\tilde{s}^{(t-1)}) = \Pr(\tilde{o}^{(t-1)} \mid \tilde{s}^{(t-1)})$ is termed the *weight* of the sequence $\tilde{s}^{(t-1)}$, and the expectation operator is taken over the distribution $\Pr(\tilde{s}^{(t-1)})$.

Using Monte-Carlo approximation of (2), a set of sequences $\mathcal{S}^{t-1}$ called the *sample population* are sampled from the distribution $\Pr(\tilde{s}^{(t-1)})$, and (2) can be approximated by:

$$\sum_{\tilde{s}^{(t-1)} \in \mathcal{S}^{t-1}} \mu_k^{(t)}(\tilde{s}^{(t-1)}) w^{(t)}(\tilde{s}^{(t-1)}) \quad (3)$$

In (3), the marginal $\mu_k^{(t)}$ can be taken from the chain $\mathcal{C}^{(t)}$, which can be updated efficiently from $\mathcal{C}^{(t-1)}$ as we have shown in the previous section. The weight $w^{(t)}$ can also be updated using $w^{(t+1)} = w^{(t)} \Pr(o^{(t)} \mid s^{(t)})$. Thus, all the terms in (3) afford very efficient update from the same terms at the previous time step.

The only remaining problem is how to generate the sample population $\mathcal{S}^t$ from the old population $\mathcal{S}^{t-1}$. This is done by lengthening each sample $\tilde{s}^{(t-1)}$ in $\mathcal{S}^{t-1}$ with a new state $s^{(t)}$, obtained by sampling from the distribution [4] $\Pr(s^{(t)} \mid \tilde{s}^{(t-1)})$, which is simply the marginal $\mu_{-1}^{(t)}$ of the chain $\mathcal{C}^{(t)}(\tilde{s}^{(t-1)})$.

Overall, the main updating step for the hybrid-inference scheme is given in Fig. 4. Note that, in the data structure for a sample, we only have to keep the last state $s^{(t-1)}$, since all the future-relevant information from the sequence $\tilde{s}^{(t-1)}$ has been summarised in the chain and and the weight of the sample. Both the time and space complexity of this updating step are linear to the sample population size, and to the number of levels of abstraction K.

Experiments

By performing exact inference through updating the chain of each sample, our algorithm avoids sampling at the higher layers, and thus can be expected to achieve better accuracy than the original sampling method in (Kanazawa, Koller, &

---

[4] The sampling process is described here without the evidence reversal step for simplicity. When ER is used, the next state can be sampled from the distribution $\Pr(s^{(t)} \mid \tilde{s}^{(t-1)}, o^{(t)}) \propto \Pr(o^{(t)} \mid s^{(t)}) \mu_{-1}^{(t)}$.

```
Data structure
A sample $\tilde{s}^{(t-1)} = \{$
    A weight $w^{(t)} \in \mathbb{R}$
    A structure for a chain $\mathcal{C}^{(t)}$
    The last state $s^{(t-1)} \in S$
$\}$
Begin
For each sample $\tilde{s}^{(t-1)}$ in $\mathcal{S}^{t-1}$:
    Sample $s^{(t)}$ from $\mu_{-1}^{(t)}(\tilde{s}^{(t-1)})$
    Form new sample $\tilde{s}^{(t)} = (\tilde{s}^{(t-1)}, s^{(t)})$
    Update weight $w^{t+1}(\tilde{s}^{(t)}) = \Pr(o^{(t)} \mid s^{(t)}) w^t(\tilde{s}^{(t-1)})$
    Update chain $\mathcal{C}^{(t+1)}(\tilde{s}^{(t)})$ from $\mathcal{C}^{(t)}(\tilde{s}^{(t-1)})$
End
```

Figure 4: Updating algorithm for hybrid-inference

Russell 1995). Here, we provide the experimental result to back up this claim.

The experiment involves a synthetic tracking task in which it is required to monitor and predict the movement of an agent through a building shown in Fig. 1(c). Each room is represented by a 5x5 grid, and at each state, the agent can move in 4 possible directions. These actions have 0.5 failure probability, in which case the agent either stays in the same cell, or move unintendedly to one of the other three neighbours. The policy hierarchy is constructed based on region-based decomposition at three levels of abstraction. The partition of the environment consists of the 8 rooms at level 1, the two wings (north and south) at level 2, and the entire building at level 3. In each room, we specify 4 level-1 policies to model the agent's behaviours of exiting the room via the 4 different doors. Similarly, we specify 3 level-2 policies in each wing corresponding with the 3 wing exits, and a total of 4 top-level policies corresponding to the 4 building exits. All the parameters of these actions and policies are chosen manually, and then are used to simulate the movement of the agent in the building.

We implement both the sampling inference scheme of (Kanazawa, Koller, & Russell 1995) (with ER and survival-of-the-fittest) and our hybrid inference (with ER). In a typical run, the algorithm can return the probability of the next building exit, the next wing exit, and the next room-door that the agent is currently heading to (Bui, Venkatesh, & West 1999). Here, we run the two algorithms using different sample population sizes to obtain their performance profiles. For a given population size, the standard deviation over 50 runs in the estimated probabilities of the top-level policies is used as the measure of expected error in the probability estimates. We also record the average time taken in each update iteration.

Fig. 5(a) plots the average error of the two algorithms for different sample sizes. As expected, for the same number of samples, the hybrid algorithm delivers much better accuracy. This however comes with the overhead in updating the belief chain for each sample, which makes the new algorithm run about twice slower for a given sample size (Fig. 5(b)).

Fig. 5(c) plots the actual CPU time taken versus the expected error for the two algorithms. It shows that for the same CPU time spent, the hybrid inference still significantly reduces the error in the probability estimates. Alternatively, the hybrid inference can achieve the same error margin with only about half the CPU time.

Discussion and Conclusion

In summary, we have presented a framework for the recognition of abstract Markov policies from external observation, based on probabilistic inference on the Dynamic Bayesian Network representation of the abstract policy. The paper presents two contributions to this problem. First, the analysis of the fully-observable case shows that policy recognition can be carried out more efficiently if the domains of the intermediate abstract policies form a partition of the state-space (i.e. non-overlapping), due to fact that the belief state of the DBN can be represented more compactly in this case. As a result, for abstract policies constructed by region-based decomposition of the state-space, policy recognition can be performed with constant averaged complexity (i.e. not dependent on the number of levels of abstraction). In the second contribution, we derive an efficient hybrid inference scheme for the recognition of this class of abstract policies under partial-observability. Experimental results illustrate our hybrid inference scheme performs better than the existing sampling-based scheme of (Kanazawa, Koller, & Russell 1995).

Several future research directions are possible. To solve the more general problem, we need to consider what happens when the policy domains overlap, or their border is "fuzzy" (i.e. when stopping conditions are non-deterministic). Our analysis here points the difficulty of this case to the uncertainty in the starting times of the current policies. In addition, we are currently applying the framework presented here to the problem of tracking and predicting human movement in large spatial environment, and as part of this, addressing the problem of learning the parameters of the model from training data.

Acknowledgement

The research described here was supported by an ARC grant from the Australian Research Council. The authors would like to thank a number of anonymous reviewers for their helpful comments.

References

Albrecht, D. W.; Zukerman, I.; and Nicholson, A. E. 1998. Bayesian models for keyhole plan recognition in an adventure game. *User Modelling and User-adapted Interaction* 8(1–2):5–47.

Boyen, X., and Koller, D. 1998. Tractable inference for complex stochastic processes. In *Proceedings of the Fourteenth Annual Conference on Uncertainty in Artificial Intelligence*.

Bui, H. H.; Venkatesh, S.; and West, G. 1999. Layered dynamic Bayesian networks for spatio-temporal modelling. *Intelligent Data Analysis* 3(5):339–361.

Bui, H. H.; Venkatesh, S.; and West, G. 2000. On the recognition of abstract Markov policies. Technical Report 3/2000, Department of Computer Science, Curtin University of Technology, Perth, WA, Australia.

Cohen, P. R.; Perrault, C. R.; and Allen, J. F. 1981. Beyond question answering. In Lehnert, W., and Ringle, M., eds., *Strategies for Natural Language Processing*, 245–274. Hillsdale, NJ: Lawrence Erlbaum Associates.

Dawid, A. P.; Kjærulff, U.; and Lauritzen, S. 1995. Hybrid propagation in junction trees. In Zadeh, L. A., ed., *Advances in Intelligent Computing*, Lecture Notes in Computer Science, 87–97.

Dean, T., and Kanazawa, K. 1989. A model for reasoning about persistence and causation. *Computational Intelligence* 5(3):142–150.

Dean, T., and Lin, S.-H. 1995. Decomposition techniques for planning in stochastic domains. In *Proceedings of the Fourteenth International Joint Conference on Artificial Intelligence (IJCAI-95)*.

Forbes, J.; Huang, T.; Kanazawa, K.; and Russell, S. 1995. The BATmobile: towards a Bayesian automated taxi. In *Proceedings of the Fourteenth International Joint Conference on Artificial Intelligence (IJCAI-95)*, 1878–1885.

Forestier, J.-P., and Varaiya, P. 1978. Multilayer control of large Markov chains. *IEEE Transactions on Automatic Control* 23(2):298–305.

Goldmand, R.; Geib, C.; and Miller, C. 1999. A new model of plan recognition. In *Proceedings of the Fifteenth Annual Conference on Uncertainty in Artificial Intelligence*.

Hauskrecht, M.; Meuleau, N.; Kaelbling, L. P.; Dean, T.; and Boutilier, C. 1998. Hierarchical solution of Markov decision processes using macro-actions. In *Proceedings of the Fourteenth Annual Conference on Uncertainty in Artificial Intelligence*.

Huber, M. J.; Durfee, E. H.; and Wellman, M. P. 1994. The automated mapping of plans for plan recognition. In *Proceedings of the Tenth Annual Conference on Uncertainty in Artificial Intelligence*.

Kanazawa, K.; Koller, D.; and Russell, S. 1995. Stochastic simulation algorithms for dynamic probabilistic networks. In *Proceedings of the Eleventh Annual Conference on Uncertainty in Artificial Intelligence*, 346–351.

Kautz, H., and Allen, J. F. 1986. Generalized plan recognition. In *Proceedings of the Fifth National Conference on Artificial Intelligence*, 32–38.

Nicholson, A. E., and Brady, J. M. 1992. The data association problem when monitoring robot vehicles using dynamic belief networks. In *Proceedings of the Tenth European Conference on Artificial Intelligence*, 689–693.

Parr, R., and Russell, S. 1997. Reinforcement learning with hierarchies of machines. In *Advances in Neural Information Processing Sytems (NIPS-97)*.

Pearl, J. 1988. *Probabilitic Reasoning in Intelligent Systems: Networks of Plausible Inference*. San Mateo, CA: Morgan Kaufmann.

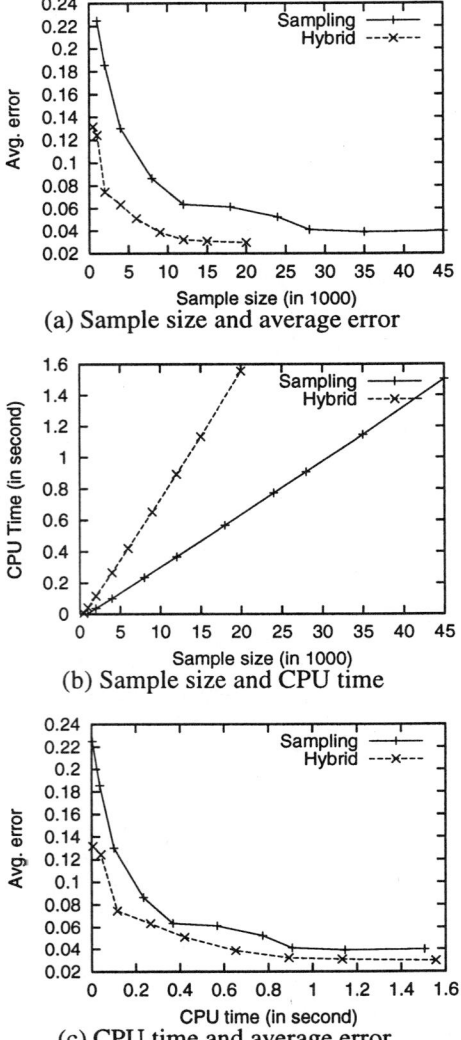

Figure 5: Sampling alone vs. hybrid inference

Pynadath, D. V., and Wellman, M. P. 1995. Accounting for context in plan recognition, with application to traffic monitoring. In *Proceedings of the Eleventh Annual Conference on Uncertainty in Artificial Intelligence*.

Rabiner, L. R. 1989. A tutorial on Hidden Markov Models and selected applications in speech recognition. *Proceedings of the IEEE* 77(2):257–286.

Sutton, R. S.; Precup, D.; and Singh, S. 1999. Between MDP and semi-MDPs: A framework for temporal abstraction in reinforcement learning. *Artificial Intelligence* 112:181–211.

Bayesian Fault Detection and Diagnosis in Dynamic Systems

Uri Lerner
Computer Science Dept.
Stanford University
uri@cs.stanford.edu

Ronald Parr
Computer Science Dept.
Stanford University
parr@cs.stanford.edu

Daphne Koller
Computer Science Dept.
Stanford University
koller@cs.stanford.edu

Gautam Biswas
Department of EECS
Vanderbilt University
biswas@vuse.vanderbilt.edu

Abstract

This paper addresses the problem of tracking and diagnosing complex systems with mixtures of discrete and continuous variables. This problem is a difficult one, particularly when the system dynamics are nondeterministic, not all aspects of the system are directly observed, and the sensors are subject to noise. In this paper, we propose a new approach to this task, based on the framework of *hybrid dynamic Bayesian networks (DBN)*. These models contain both continuous variables representing the state of the system and discrete variables representing discrete changes such as failures; they can model a variety of faults, including burst faults, measurement errors, and gradual drifts. We present a novel algorithm for tracking in hybrid DBNs, that deals with the challenges posed by this difficult problem. We demonstrate how the resulting algorithm can be used to detect faults in a complex system.

Introduction

The complexity and sophistication of the current generation of industrial processes, and the growing need for autonomous agents that control physical systems, motivate the need for robust online monitoring and diagnosis of complex hybrid systems (e.g., (Isermann 1997) and (McIlraith *et al.* 2000)). We want to monitor the state of the system, reliably detect abnormal behavior, and diagnose the failure. Several approaches have been used for dealing with this problem, but each has its limitations. The traditional model-based schemes for diagnosis and control suffer from computational intractability and numerical convergence problems. The qualitative reasoning mechanisms that dominate this work in the AI community mitigate some of these problems; however, the lack of precision in the representation, and the ambiguities introduced by the reasoning framework can lead them to perform poorly when applied to complex system with continuous dynamics (Hamscher, Console, & de Kleer (eds.) 1992).

In this paper, we propose a different approach to this problem, where we model a complex hybrid system as a *dynamic Bayesian network (DBN)*. This model implicitly defines a probability distribution over projected trajectories of the system state over time. In this sense, it is similar to the very successful *Kalman filter* (Kalman 1960). For systems with linear dynamics and Gaussian noise, the Kalman filter provides an excellent means for tracking system state. Unfortunately, real-life systems are rife with nonlinearities, many of which are expressed as discrete failure modes that can produce discontinuous jumps in system behavior. Hybrid DBNs accommodate a much greater range of problems, including nonlinear dynamics and discrete failure modes that influence system evolution. They can directly represent the noise associated with the system evolution and measurements, as well as the probabilities of faults and their effects.

We first show that many interesting aspects of diagnostic models can be represented in the DBN framework. In particular, we show that they allow a natural encoding of the representation of higher-order system dynamics used in the *temporal causal graph (TCG)* framework of Mosterman and Biswas (1997). In fact, a TCG can be used to provide the skeleton for an appropriate DBN model. We also show that many interesting types of failures can be modeled naturally in the DBN, including *burst faults*, parameter drift, and measurement errors.

There are several advantages to the use of general probabilistic models, such as DBNs, for fault detection and diagnosis. A DBN is complete model of the system. Using this model, the state of the system, including its failure modes, is tracked by maintaining a probability distribution over possible system states given all of the measurements so far. This *belief state* distribution is an exact representation of our best possible beliefs given all of the available evidence. It includes within it the likelihood of different types of failures, as well as a distribution over the relevant system parameters. In principle, many of the issues that have challenged traditional approaches to diagnosis — ranking possible failures, handling of multiple simultaneous failures, and robustness to parameter drift — can be addressed within a probabilistic tracking framework.

Of course, the inference task that is required for maintaining this belief state is a difficult one. Unlike the case of a simple Kalman filter, tracking such systems is generally intractable since the number of modes of these systems grows exponentially over time. We present a novel algorithm that tames this intractability using a combination of several different techniques. We show that this algorithm succeeds in tracking a very difficult scenario on a fairly large system (one involving five tanks). We believe that our approach will scale well to substantially more complex systems.

The framework
Diagnosis of hybrid systems

To ground our discussion, we will focus on the diagnosis task for a class of problems typical of chemical manufac-

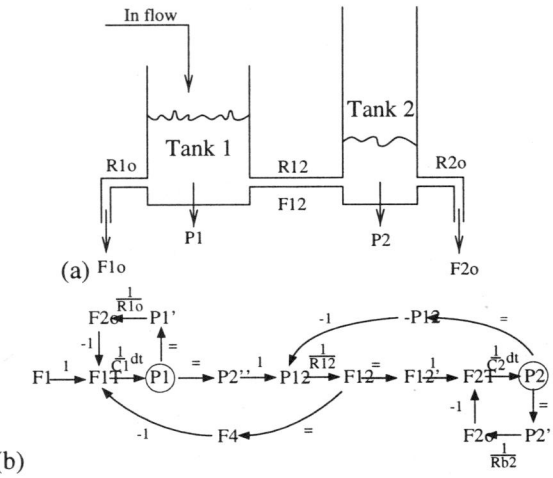

Figure 1: The two-tank system. F indicates flow; P indicates pressure; R indicates Resistance.

turing processes, which involve the transport of materials (mostly fluids) into and between tanks. Such domains are well-represented using bond graph formalism (Rosenberg & Karnopp 1983), where the dynamic behavior of the system is defined by fluid pressures and fluid flow-rates. Consider, for example, a simple two-tank model, shown in Figure 1(a). The model represents a system with two tanks that can hold fluids, an inlet pipe into tank 1, two outlet pipes, and a connecting pipe between the tanks. The storage tanks are *capacitive elements* and the connecting pipes are *resistive elements*. This system is a second order system with natural feedback mechanisms.

The *temporal causal graph (TCG)* framework of (Mosterman & Biswas 1997) is a topological representation that captures local dynamic relations between variables, and provides a more explicit representation of the relation between system parameters and the behavior variables. The TCG for the two-tank example is shown in Figure 1(b). Here, the variables are the pressure and flow-rate variables associated with the tanks and the pipes in the system. Causal edges in a TCG are labeled with component parameter values and temporal information derived from the characteristics of the related components. Resistive and junction components introduce algebraic relations among the system variables, and therefore, define instantaneous temporal relations such as a direct or inverse proportionality between the variables (denoted by ± 1). On the other hand, energy storage elements, like capacitive and inductive elements, introduce integral relations between system variables (labeled with a dt). For example, capacitive relations from the flow-rate variable to the pressure variable are labeled with a $\frac{1}{C} dt$; this implies a temporal relation, i.e., the flow-rate affects the derivative of the corresponding pressure variable.

Many systems have the property that they behave nearly deterministically in the absence of a fault. The deterministic trajectory of the system is often called its *nominal* trajectory. In such cases, faults are sometimes defined implicitly as any abrupt change in a parameter that causes a deviation from the nominal trajectory. Since the temporal causal graph defines a set of qualitative constraints on the system it can be used to predict the effects of sudden discontinuous changes in parameters, e.g., *burst faults*. By contrast, TCGs generally are not used identify *parameter drift* failures, which are the result of gradual changes in system parameters that accumulate over time.

Dynamic Bayesian Networks

A *dynamic Bayesian network (DBN)* is a temporal stochastic model for a dynamic system. It assumes that the system state can be represented by a set of variables, denoted $\mathbf{Z}$. Each of these variables Z_i can be real-valued or discrete. We use $\mathbf{D}^t \subseteq \mathbf{Z}^t$ to denote the discrete variables in the state. We partition the continuous variables into two subsets: the subset $\mathbf{Y} \subseteq \mathbf{Z}$ are variables that are measurements, i.e., their value is known to us; the remaining subset $\mathbf{X}$ are unobserved.

The system is modeled as evolving in discrete time steps. Thus, each system variable Z has an instantiation Z^t for each *time slice* t. A DBN is a compact graphical representation for the *two-time-slice conditional probability distribution* $P(\mathbf{Z}^{t+1} \mid \mathbf{Z}^t)$. It encompasses both the transition model and the observation model. More formally, a DBN is a directed acyclic graph, whose nodes are random variables in two consecutive time slices: $\mathbf{Z}^t$ and $\mathbf{Z}^{t+1}$. The edges in the graph represent the direct dependence of a time $t+1$ variable Z_i^{t+1} on its immediate causes $\mathrm{Par}(Z_i^{t+1})$. Each such node is annotated with a *conditional probability distribution (CPD)*, that defines the local probability model $P(Z_i^{t+1} \mid \mathrm{Par}(Z_i^{t+1}))$. The DBN model is a compact representation for the two-time-slice distribution via the *chain rule*: $P(\mathbf{Z}^{t+1} \mid \mathbf{Z}^t) = \prod_i P(Z_i^{t+1} \mid \mathrm{Par}(Z_i^{t+1}))$. We note that the transition probabilities for any variable are determined completely by the value of the variables in the current and previous time step. This *Markov* assumption requires us to model explicitly any variables, such as failures, that induce long-term correlations on the system state. We return to this issue below.

For the diagnostic tasks that we focus on, we can restrict attention to a very natural subclass of hybrid DBNs — the *conditional linear Gaussian (CLG)* models. Here, we we require that discrete nodes cannot have continuous parents. We also require that the CPD for a continuous variable be a conditional linear Gaussian. Roughly speaking, in a linear Gaussian dependence, the node is a linear function of its parents with Gaussian noise, where the parameters of the linear dependence can depend on the discrete parents. More precisely, if a node X has continuous parents $Y_1, \ldots, Y_k$ and discrete parents $\mathbf{U}$, we parameterize its CPD using parameters $a_{\mathbf{u},0}, \ldots, a_{\mathbf{u},k}$ and $\sigma_\mathbf{u}^2$ for every instantiation $\mathbf{u}$ to the discrete parents $\mathbf{U}$. Then $P(X \mid \mathbf{y}, \mathbf{u})$ is a Gaussian distribution with a mean $a_{\mathbf{u},0} + \sum_{i=1}^k a_{\mathbf{u},i} y_i$ and variance $\sigma_\mathbf{u}^2$.

It is important to note that, without discrete variables in the network, this type of DBN defines standard linear Gaussian dynamics. Hence, in this case, the DBN is simply a graphical representation of the standard dynamics used in a Kalman filter, albeit one that makes certain independence

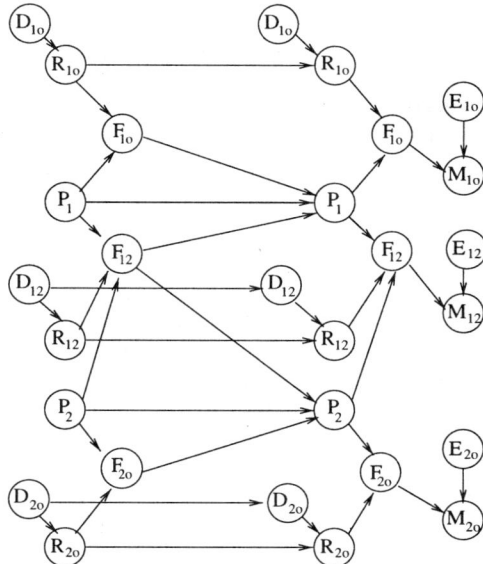

Figure 2: The two-tank DBN.

assumptions explicit. In the presence of discrete parents, the model represents a mixture of linear models, with the mixtures determined by the discrete variables.

DBNs for diagnosis

Our goal is to represent a diagnostic system, of the type described above, as a DBN. It turns out that we can use a TCG for a system as a "blueprint" for the skeleton of the DBN. We can think of a TCG as a schema for a system of equations describing the continuous system dynamics. We distinguish two types of arcs in a TCG: *temporal* arcs are annotated with a dt, whereas *non-temporal* arcs are not. For any variable X with no incoming temporal arcs, the TCG expresses an instantaneous constraint on X as a function of its predecessors. For a variable X with at least one incoming temporal arc, the TCG expresses a temporal constraint.

We generate a DBN structure from a TCG as follows: For each node X_i in the temporal causal graph, we create X_i^t and X_i^{t+1} to denote the state of the variable at two consecutive time points. (In practice, we will merge nodes that are connected by equality constraints in the TCG.) Let X_j be a node in the TCG which is a direct predecessor of X_i. If the arc from X_j to X_i is non-temporal, we add an arc from X_j^t to X_i^t and an arc from X_j^{t+1} to X_i^{t+1}. If the arc is temporal, we add an arc only from X_j^t to X_i^{t+1}. This process suffices to generate the structure for a DBN that models the nominal behavior the system.

We then want to add variables that model our observations and represent the failure modes of the system. Our framework accommodates for a wide variety of failure modes. In our presentation, we focus on three important types: burst failures, measurement failures and parameter drift failures. To accommodate these, we need to make two important additions to the TCG induced DBN. Since any parameter that can change must be modeled in the DBN, we add nodes to model the resistance variables. In our implementation, these were conductances and not resistances, since we preferred to use a multiplicative model. We also need to add nodes corresponding to presence of burst failures and the presence of measurement failures.

Figure 2 shows a DBN created by this process. The nodes F_{1t} and F_{2t} simply add incoming flows and this function has been subsumed by the CPDs for P_1 and P_2. The nodes labeled with M correspond to our measurements of the flow parameters in the system and the discrete nodes labeled with E indicate the presence of measurement failures. For example, we define the CPD of M_{12} to be a normal distribution around F_{12} with small variance when E_{12} is false, but with a much larger variance when the E_{12} is true. The R variables model the conductances in the system. These have discrete parents, D, that indicate the presence of faults. Unlike the measurement fault variables, these fault variables have parents in the previous DBN time slice. This is necessary to model persistent events such as drifts. Each conductance fault variable takes on four values: *stable*, *fault*, *buildup* and *leak*. When the system is stable, the CPD of the corresponding R has low noise. When a fault occurs, there is a sharp increase in the variance of the corresponding R. The two drift faults produce a small drift, defined as a percentage of the parameter's previous value. We need the temporal connection between the D nodes to reflect the fact that drifts persist; once a buildup starts in a pipe it tends to continue.

Inference

In this section, we propose an inference procedure for fault diagnosis and detection in models represented as DBNs. As we have mentioned, we can view DBNs as a structured representation and extension of traditional Kalman filters. We therefore build our algorithm starting from the classical Kalman filter algorithm. Typical extensions to this algorithm maintain multiple candidate hypotheses about the state of the system. At each time step they update a set of candidate hypotheses and prune out unlikely ones based upon evidence. If the correct hypothesis remains in the candidate set, these algorithms will track the state of the system correctly.

The problem with this type of approach is that it is very difficult to determine which hypotheses to keep for complex systems: there are too many possible new hypotheses at each time, and the information needed to prune away bad hypotheses often is not manifested until several time steps after the hypotheses are generated. We present a novel approach that collapses similar hypotheses into a single hypothesis, then present a novel approximate smoothing algorithm that we use to improve our ability to effectively reduce the number of hypotheses. This approach allows us to deal with complex failure modes and sequences involving many failures. But it does not scale to complex systems that involve many possible failures in different components. We address this problem by combining our techniques with a decomposition method based on the algorithm of Boyen and Koller (1998) that allows the tracking of very large systems.

Tracking and smoothing

Our dynamic Bayesian network represents the complete state of the system at each time step; it includes variables for the various aspects of the continuous state of the system such as pressures or conductances, as well as discrete variables representing possible failures. This complete model allows us to reduce the problems of fault detection and diagnosis to the task of *tracking* (or *filtering*) a stochastic dynamic system. The tracking problem is defined as follows. As the system evolves, we get observations $\mathbf{y}^1, \mathbf{y}^2, \ldots$. At time t, our most informed evaluation of the state of the system is our posterior distribution $P(\mathbf{Z}^t \mid \mathbf{y}^1, \ldots, \mathbf{y}^t)$ about the current system state given all of our observations so far. We call this posterior distribution our *time t belief state*, and denote it using σ^t. The probability of a discrete fault variable in this belief state takes into consideration all of the evidence up to the present to determine the probability that this fault has occurred.

In principle, tracking is a very easy task, which can be accomplished by the following propagation formula:

$$\sigma^{t+1}(\mathbf{z}^{t+1}) = \alpha P(\mathbf{y}^{t+1} \mid \mathbf{z}^{t+1}) \int \sigma^t(\mathbf{z}^t) P(\mathbf{z}^{t+1} \mid \mathbf{z}^t) d\mathbf{z}^t$$

where α is a normalizing constant. This process is known as a *forward pass*.

Forward tracking gives the best estimate of the likelihood of a fault given the evidence so far. It cannot, however, deal with cases where a fault is momentary, but whose direct effects are unobservable so that its effects become visible to our sensor only later on. The reason is that, at the time that the evidence indicates the presence of a previous failure, there is no longer a variable in the belief state that represents the occurrence of that failure. There is a variable denoting this event at an earlier time slice, but the forward pass only maintains beliefs about variables in the current time step. To explicitly discover faults of this type, we need to also reason backwards in time, from our current evidence to the time slice where the fault took place. This process is known as *smoothing*. Given evidence $\mathbf{y}^1, \ldots, \mathbf{y}^{t+\ell}$, we compute $P(\mathbf{Z}^t \mid \mathbf{y}^1, \ldots, \mathbf{y}^t, \ldots, \mathbf{y}^{t+\ell})$. The smoothing process involves a *backward pass* where evidence from $t + \ell$ is transmitted backwards over the intervening time slices, updating each of them. We omit details for lack of space.

One case of enormous practical importance is the case of *linear systems*. These systems are fully continuous, with linear Gaussian CPDs. In this case, $\mathbf{Z}^{t+1}$ is a linear function of $\mathbf{Z}^t$ and $\mathbf{Y}^{t+1}$ is a linear function of $\mathbf{Z}^{t+1}$, both with some added Gaussian noise. In this case, the belief state can be represented exactly as a multivariate Gaussian distribution over $\mathbf{Z}^t$. This is the basis for an elegant tracking algorithm called the Kalman filter (Kalman 1960) which maintains this belief state in closed form as the system evolves.

Nonlinearities

Unfortunately, often we cannot apply the Kalman filter directly to real-life problems, since many real-life systems are not linear systems. The continuous relationships between variables are often nonlinear and the failure modes of the system are often discrete, introducing discontinuous changes in system parameters. When the system is nonlinear, the belief state is no longer a multivariate Gaussian, and rarely has a compact closed form representation.

Consider our simple two-tank model. Here, we have a product of two random variables: the flow F is the product of the pressure P and the conductance $\frac{1}{R}$. A standard solution to this type of problem is to approximate the nonlinear dynamics with linear dynamics, and then use a standard linear Gaussian model. Thus, we try to get the best approximation for the first and second moments, and ignore the rest. The classical method of linearizing is called the *Extended Kalman Filter* (Bar-Shalom & Fortmann 1988); it approximates the nonlinear function using its second order Taylor series expansion. In our case, the nonlinear function is a product, which is fairly simple, thus we can compute its first and second order moments in closed form.

A far more problematic type of nonlinearity is caused by discrete state changes that influence the continuous system dynamics. For example, a fault might drastically change the conditional mean or variance of a continuous variable such as the conductance. This type of situation is represented in our model via the dependence of the continuous variables $\mathbf{X}$ on the discrete fault variables $\mathbf{D}$.

This type of model creates substantial difficulties for a tracking algorithm. To understand the difficulties, let $\mathbf{d}^1, \ldots, \mathbf{d}^t$ be some particular instantiation of the discrete variables at time $1, \ldots, t$. Given this instantiation, the dynamics of the continuous variables are, once again, linear Gaussian. Hence, the time t belief state, conditioned on $\mathbf{d}^1, \ldots, \mathbf{d}^t$, is a multivariate Gaussian over $\mathbf{X}^t$. The difficulty is that we have one such Gaussian for every single instantiation $\mathbf{d}^1, \ldots, \mathbf{d}^t$. Thus, in order to do exact tracking, we need to maintain a separate hypothesis for every combination of the discrete variables at all times. The number of such hypotheses grows exponentially with the length of the sequence, which is clearly unacceptable.

A classical tracking algorithm which deals with this problem is described in (Bar-Shalom & Fortmann 1988). The main idea is to maintain our belief state as a smaller set of hypotheses, each of which corresponds to a single multivariate Gaussian. The algorithm, applied to our setting, is as follows. It is convenient to introduce the random variable H^t, each of whose values corresponds to one hypothesis. The distribution of H^t corresponds to the likelihood of the hypothesis. When the algorithm does the forward pass, it considers all the combinations of values of H^t and $\mathbf{D}^{t+1}$. The result is a mixture with $K \times |\mathbf{D}|$ components. Each of these new hypotheses is conditioned on the new measurements $\mathbf{Y}^{t+1}$, and using Bayesian conditioning we adjust both the mixture weights and the parameters of the multivariate Gaussians. The algorithm them *prunes* the hypotheses that have low probability, and selects only the most likely ones to be part of the time $t + 1$ belief state.

I our setting, we also wish to maintain values for the persistent discrete state variables, since the state of the system at time $t + 1$ depends on these values at time t. We therefore represent the belief state using a simple graphical model of the form $\mathbf{D}^t \leftarrow H^t \rightarrow \mathbf{X}^t$. Formally, we represent our time

t belief state σ^t as a mixture $\sigma^t(h^t)$ of K hypotheses, each of which is associated with a single multivariate Gaussian $\sigma^t(\mathbf{X}^t \mid h^t)$ and a discrete distribution $\sigma^t(\mathbf{D}^t \mid h^t)$

The deficiency of this algorithm is that it selects some hypotheses exactly, while entirely ignoring others. In many cases, the hypotheses that are maintained all correspond to scenarios that are all close to nominal behavior, and are therefore qualitatively quite similar. By contrast, the pruned hypotheses often correspond to a priori unlikely faults, that can lead to very different behaviors. We therefore propose a new approach where similar hypotheses are collapsed.

Like the pruning algorithm, we start by performing the forward propagation step, defining a set of possible hypotheses $(H^t, \mathbf{D}^{t+1})$; let $\tilde{H}^{t+1}$ be random variable whose values correspond to this larger set of $K \cdot |\mathbf{D}|$ hypotheses. Next, the measurements are introduced, and the result is a mixture distribution τ^{t+1} over $H^t, \mathbf{D}^{t+1}$ and $\mathbf{X}^{t+1}$. Our task is to generate the $t+1$ hypotheses from this mixture.

We define a new set of mixture components H^{t+1}, each of which aggregates several of the values of $\tilde{H}^{t+1}$. The algorithm thereby defines a *collapsing matrix* that is essentially a deterministic CPD $P(H^{t+1} \mid H^t, \mathbf{D}^{t+1})$. This collapsing matrix is used to define the belief state σ^{t+1}, as a weighted average of the mixture components:

$$\sigma^{t+1}(H^{t+1}) = \sum_{\tilde{H}^{t+1}} P(H^{t+1} \mid \tilde{H}^{t+1}) \tau^{t+1}(\tilde{H}^{t+1})$$

$$\sigma^{t+1}(\mathbf{D}^{t+1} \mid H^{t+1}) = \sum_{\tilde{H}^{t+1}} P(\tilde{H}^{t+1} \mid H^{t+1}) \tau^{t+1}(\mathbf{D}^{t+1} \mid \tilde{H}^{t+1})$$

Finally, we define $\sigma^{t+1}(\mathbf{X}^{t+1} \mid H^t, \mathbf{D}^{t+1})$ to be the closest Gaussian approximation (i.e., the Gaussian that has the same mean and covariances as the mixture) to
$\sum_{\tilde{H}^{t+1}} P(\tilde{H}^{t+1} \mid H^{t+1}) P(\mathbf{X}^{t+1} \mid \tilde{H}^{t+1})$.

The main remaining question is the choice of which hypotheses to collapse. We use a greedy approach, that takes into consideration both the likelihood of the different hypotheses and their similarity to each other. We sort the different hypotheses by their likelihood.[1] Then, starting from the most likely hypothesis, we find the closest hypothesis to it, and merge the two. Note that the merged hypothesis will have higher probability, so will remain at the top of the list. When there are no hypotheses that are "close enough", we move to the next most likely hypothesis in our list. When we have filled our quota of hypotheses, we collapse all the remaining hypotheses into one, regardless of how close they are. As our distance measure, we use the sum of the two *relative entropies (KL-distances)* (Cover & Thomas 1991) between the Gaussians associated with the hypotheses. We note that we deliberately do not use the weights in determining the distance between hypotheses; otherwise, we would invariably collapse unlikely hypotheses into likely ones, even if they are qualitatively very different.

---
[1]To reduce CPU time in our implementation, we first removed all hypotheses with extremely low probability (10^{-8}), and then use the merging approach to collapse the rest.

Smoothing

Both hypothesis collapsing and pruning are myopic methods; they only use evidence observed up to time t. As discussed above, the effects of some failures have a delay, so a failure at time t may not manifest itself in evidence up to time t. Since *a priori* failure probabilities are typically quite low, failures could have very weak support in our belief state. Thus, by the time the data necessary to diagnose the failure are available, the failure track may be lost. The obvious solution to the problem is to pick the likely hypotheses based not only on past and present evidence but also on future evidence; i.e., we want to use weights obtained after some amount of smoothing. However, smoothing requires that we first propagate a belief state forward in time, and this is the very problem we are trying to solve. We break this cycle by using a slightly different method of collapsing hypotheses. Instead of sorting the hypotheses by likelihoods we always collapse the two most similar Gaussians until our mixture is small enough. This may lead to a more aggressive collapsing since we do not have a bound on the maximal KL-distance between two Gaussians that we collapse. We can afford to be more aggressive here since we will not use the results of smoothing to update our continuous variables, but only to guide our hypothesis reduction method.

It remains to show how we do the backward propagation process required for smoothing. The primary difficulty is the correct handling of the continuous part of our belief state approximation. The reason is that after collapsing a mixture of Gaussians, updating the distribution of each component based only on evidence relative to the result of the collapse is a non-trivial problem. Fortunately, we are primarily interested in getting a more informed posterior for the hypothesis variable, since our main goal is simply to identify the most likely hypotheses. The continuous parts will typically track correctly if we identify the correct hypotheses. Therefore, we execute smoothing only for the discrete variables.

The process is now easy; assume that we use a lookahead window of ℓ time slices (thus, the last observation we get to see is $t + \ell + 1$). The backward message to time step $t + \ell'$ is simply the probability of $\mathbf{y}^{t+\ell'+1}, \ldots, \mathbf{y}^{t+\ell+1}$ given $H^{t+\ell'}$. This message defines a posterior distribution over $H^{t+\ell'}$, which can be computed using standard methods. We now use our collapsing matrix to compute the effect of this new information on $\mathbf{D}^{t+l'}$ and $H^{t+l'-1}$. In particular, the probabilities of all the components which were collapsed into some $h^{t+\ell'}$ are multiplied by the change in the probability of $h^{t+\ell'}$. This is also intuitively appealing — since all the collapsed components were similar, we should change their probabilities by the same factor. The result is a message to time step $t + \ell' - 1$, which is propagated in the same way.

When the process terminates at time step t, we have the probability $P(H^t \mid \mathbf{y}^1, \ldots, \mathbf{y}^{t+\ell+1})$, which we can then use to better guide which hypotheses to eliminate, as well as our collapsing algorithm. We note, however, that the results of smoothing should be used *only* for guiding the approximation. In order to avoid double-counting evidence, it is very important to continue our tracking using our unsmoothed hypothesis weights $\sigma^t(H^t)$.

Subsystem decomposition

One of the underlying assumptions of the algorithm is that it is feasible to enumerate all the possible instantiations of the discrete variables $\mathbf{D}^t$. Unfortunately, for non-trivial systems, this assumption is often unrealistic. The number of possible instantiations of the discrete variables $\mathbf{D}^t$ grows exponentially with the number of discrete variables in the system. To deal with this problem, we take an approach introduced for discrete systems in (Boyen & Koller 1998). The crucial idea is to make use of the fact that large systems are typically composed of subsystems, and that, while the subsystems are correlated, the interaction between them is often not so strong. Therefore, it might be reasonable to approximate our beliefs about the system using separate beliefs about the subsystems, i.e., using a belief state where they are independent. Note that this approximation is very different from one that ignores the interactions between the subsystems. As we do the propagation, the state of one subsystem can influence the state of another; but we then decouple the correlations resulting from this interaction when we maintain our beliefs about the current system state.

More precisely, we partition the system variables into n disjoint sets, corresponding to the different subsystems. Let $\mathbf{D}_i$ and $\mathbf{X}_i$ be the discrete and continuous variables in subsystem i, respectively. As for the case of a single system, we represent the belief state for each subsystem i as a mixture, represented using a hypothesis variable H_i. We also associate with each subsystem a set of observation variables $\mathbf{Y}_i$, which are the ones that are most relevant to the subsystem.

Our goal is to get a belief state σ_i^t over each subsystem i. Since subsystem i may be influenced directly by some other subsystems, we cannot perform the inference completely in isolation inside subsystem i. Instead, we consider the *extended subsystem* which includes subsystem i, and all the variables from other subsystems which influence it.

Given our belief state representation, it is possible to describe the distribution over the extended subsystem as a mixture of Gaussians. As in the single subsystem case, we can introduce evidence which changes our probability distribution over discrete variables as well as over continuous variables. Note that different extended subsystems may overlap, and after introducing different measurements into these subsystems we may have a different distribution over the shared variables. We synchronize these probabilities using a message-passing algorithm called *calibration* (Lauritzen & Spiegelhalter 1988). As in backward propagation, we only update the discrete variables, not the continuous ones. As a result of this phase, all the discrete variables are updated using all the measurement information. This is important, as outside evidence can be important in determining the likelihood of the different hypotheses.

It is also possible to modify the smoothing algorithm to use the decomposed representation of the belief state. The collapsing is done independently in every subsystem using the same algorithm (and giving a collapsing matrix for every subsystem). The backward messages are used to update the hypothesis variables of each one of the subsystems. The information can be propagated backwards with the collapsing matrices. The only difference is that after this propagation,

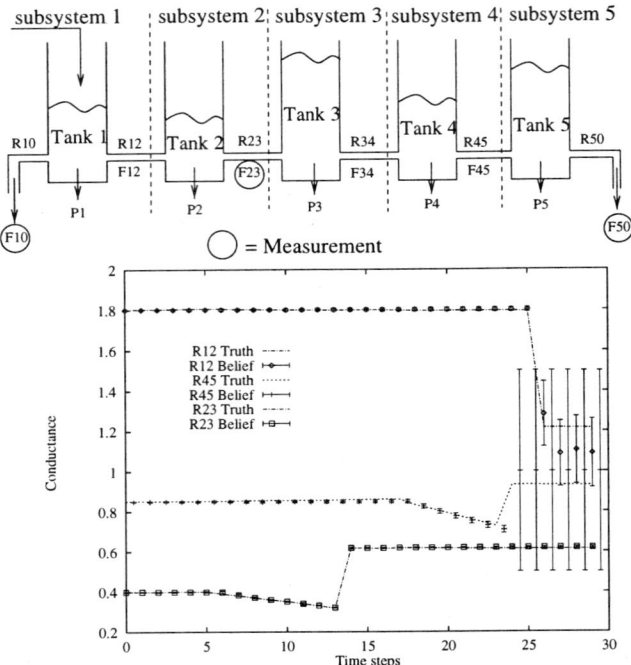

Figure 3: Five tank system and results

we need to calibrate the discrete variables of the subsystems, just like in the forward pass.

Experimental Results

We tested our algorithm on a system which contains five water tanks, shown in Figure 3. The system contains six conductances and five pressures, which are all free parameters, but only three measurements, making it a challenging system to track. In addition, the system contains the three types of failures described in Section : drifts, bursts and measurement errors, each occurring with probability 0.001. Thus, at every time step every conductance has 4 possible failure modes (stable, fault, buildup, leak) and each measurement has 2 possible failure modes. Counting all the possible failures at time $t + 1$ and the persistent failures from time t, the system has 2^{27} possible failure modes at any point in time, eliminating any hope of using inference without some decomposition of the system.

In our experiments we decomposed the system into five subsystems, since decompositions into less subsystems demanded too much memory. Each tank was considered to be a subsystem (see Figure 3). We tracked five hypotheses per subsystem, with a lookahead of two steps when doing smoothing. We tested our algorithm on a complicated sequence:

- At $t = 5$, R_{23} starts to experience a negative drift.
- At $t = 10$, we introduce two simultaneous measurement errors in the measurements of F_{23} and F_{5o}.
- At $t = 13$, R_{23} bursts, and then returns to a steady state.
- At $t = 17$ R_{45} starts a negative drift.
- At $t = 23$ R_{45} bursts and then returns to normal.
- At $t = 25$ R_{12} bursts.

The graph in Figure 3 shows the results of tracking R_{23},

R_{45} and R_{12}. Initially, at $t = 5$ the effect of the drift in R_{23} was negligible. The corresponding hypothesis had a probability of 0.012%, but after smoothing the probability went up to 7.43%. As a result our algorithm considered this a likely hypothesis, and kept it in the belief state. At $t = 6$ the probability of a negative drift went from 71.7% to 99.9% after smoothing. At this point our algorithm correctly detected the negative drift, and maintained a very high probability for this event until $t = 13$. At this point, before smoothing, our algorithm considered two hypotheses: a burst in R_{23} (probability 57%) or the persistence of the negative drift and a measurement failure (probability 43%). Smoothing raised the probability of a burst (the correct hypothesis) to 100%. The actual values of R_{23} were tracked with high accuracy.

The measurement of F_{23} made the tracking of R_{23} a relatively simple problem. Things are much more complicated for R_{45}. Not only is there no direct measurement of F_{45}, there is no measurement at all in subsystem 4! Therefore, tracking R_{45} is a real challenge. Due to lack of space we omit the actual numbers, but in this run our algorithm detected the drift as soon as it began. (In other runs the detection was sometimes delayed by 2–3 steps.) It is also interesting to see the behavior of R_{45} during the burst. Our algorithm detected the burst, but since no evidence is used in subsystem 4 it could not track the true value of the burst correctly. We plan to address this problem in future work by propagating continuous information between the subsystems as well as discrete information.

For the measurements failures at $t = 10$, our algorithm behaved in almost the same way for the two measurements, so we report on M_{23} only. Before smoothing, our algorithm considered two hypotheses — a burst in R_{23} (probability 81.8%) or a measurement fault and a persistent negative drift in R_{23} (probability 18.2%). After smoothing the probability of the correct hypothesis went up to almost 100%.

We feel that these results demonstrate the power of our algorithm, and its ability to correctly diagnose and track even a complex system with a small number of measurements.

Conclusions and future work

In this paper, we presented a new approach for monitoring and diagnosis of hybrid systems. We model these systems as DBNs, thus reducing the problem of diagnosis to the problem of tracking. It is not a surprise that tracking hybrid systems is also a difficult problem. In this paper we focus on a special class of hybrid systems: ones that given some particular assignment to the discrete variables have linear dynamics (or can be linearized with a satisfactory precision). Furthermore, we focus on systems that are composed of several weakly interacting subsystems. We believe that many real-life physical systems belong to this class of systems.

We present a novel tracking algorithm for this class of systems. First, we collapse similar hypotheses instead of just choosing the most likely ones. This technique allows us to use a bounded window look-ahead into the future. We use future observations to assist us in determining which hypotheses are the likely candidates and should be kept relative unchanged, and which are less likely and can be collapsed more aggressively. Our final contribution is introducing a way to avoid the exponential blowup, caused by many discrete variables within a time slice. We do this by reasoning separately about the different subsystems, while still propagating correlations between them.

Our initial experiments with this approach are very encouraging. We have tested it on a very large system (one with 2^{27} different discrete states per time slice), with a particularly difficult scenario. Our algorithm found most of the faults, showing that it can be used to provide reliable tracking and diagnosis even for very hard problems. Of course, we plan to conduct further experiments in other domains.

We are currently working on extending the calibration algorithm to allow us to propagate information between subsystems not only for the discrete variables but for continuous variables as well. We believe that this new feature will significantly improve our tracking capabilities, especially on long sequences with many events.

We are also looking for ways to extend the algorithm beyond the family of conditional linear systems (or systems which can be approximated as such). In particular, we hope to be able to handle discrete children of continuous parents and highly non-linear evidence models.

Finally, we hope to apply our algorithm on real-life applications and not just on synthetic data. We are exploring possible applications in the diagnosis domain, such as monitoring the performance of an engine, as well as application in other domains, such as visual tracking.

Acknowledgments. This research was supported by an ONR Young Investigator Award grant number N00014-99-1-0464 and by ARO under the MURI program, "Integrated Approach to Intelligent Systems," grant number DAAH04-96-1-0341, and by the Terman Foundation.

References

Bar-Shalom, Y., and Fortmann, T. E. 1988. *Tracking and Data Association*. Academic Press.

Boyen, X., and Koller, D. 1998. Tractable inference for complex stochastic processes. In *Proc. UAI*.

Cover, T., and Thomas, J. 1991. *Elements of Information Theory*. Wiley.

Hamscher, W.; Console, L.; and de Kleer (eds.), J. 1992. *Readings in Model-Based Diagnosis*. Morgan Kaufmann.

Isermann, R. 1997. Supervision, fault-detection and fault-diagnosis methods - an introduction. *Control Engineering Practice* 5(5):639–652.

Kalman, R. 1960. A new approach to linear filtering and prediction problems. *J. of Basic Engineering* 82:34–45.

Lauritzen, S., and Spiegelhalter, D. 1988. Local computations with probabilities on graphical structures and their application to expert systems. *J. Roy. Stat. Soc.* B 50.

McIlraith, S.; Biswas, G.; Clancy, D.; and Gupta, V. 2000. Hybrid systems diagnosis. In *Proceedings of Hybrid Systems: Computation and Control*, Lecture Notes in Computer Science. Berlin Heidelberg New York: Springer-Verlag. 282–295.

Mosterman, P. J., and Biswas, G. 1997. Monitoring, prediction, and fault isolation in dynamic physical systems. In *Proc. AAAI-97*, 100–105.

Rosenberg, R. C., and Karnopp, D. 1983. *Introduction to Physical System Dynamics*. McGraw-Hill.

Semantics and Inference for Recursive Probability Models

Avi Pfeffer
Division of Engineering and Applied Sciences
Harvard University
Cambridge, MA 02138
avi@eecs.harvard.edu

Daphne Koller
Computer Science Department
Stanford University
Stanford, CA 94305
koller@cs.stanford.edu

Abstract

In recent years, there have been several proposals that extend the expressive power of Bayesian networks with that of relational models. These languages open the possibility for the specification of recursive probability models, where a variable might depend on a potentially infinite (but finitely describable) set of variables. These models are very natural in a variety of applications, e.g., in temporal, genetic, or language models. In this paper, we provide a structured representation language that allows us to specify such models, a clean measure-theoretic semantics for this language, and a probabilistic inference algorithm that exploits the structure of the language for efficient query-answering.

1 Introduction

There has been a growing interest in recent years in *relational probabilistic languages* (Wellman, Breese, & Goldman 1992; Ngo & Haddawy 1996; Koller & Pfeffer 1998). These languages combine the ability of Bayesian networks to compactly describe probability models with the generality, flexibility and modularity of logical representations. They have extended the applicability of probabilistic reasoning techniques to more complex domains than in the past.

In the relational setting, it is very natural to define probability models that are *recursive*. In a recursive model, a variable associated with a particular domain entity can depend probabilistically on the same variable associated with a different entity. Examples of recursive probability models are temporal models, genetic models of gene propagation, and stochastic grammar models of natural language. Recursive models are challenging, because in principle they describe distributions over infinitely many variables.

Existing languages do not deal adequately with recursive probability models. Some languages, e.g. (Koller & Pfeffer 1998), rule them out altogether. Others, such as (Ngo & Haddawy 1996), get around the issue by using a variant of the closed world assumption to limit the set of variables. This assumption is often inappropriate, since it requires that all entities and the relationships between them be known and stated explicitly. The language of (Koller, McAllester, & Pfeffer 1997) allows the specification of recursive probability models as stochastic computational processes, but its semantics is quite limiting, since it requires that a process is guaranteed to terminate in order for the model to be well-defined.

In this paper, we present a new framework for recursive probability models. We do not make any restrictive assumptions on the language, explicitly considering probability distributions over infinitely many variables. We provide a natural measure-theoretic semantics for models in our language, that extends the semantics of Bayesian networks in a natural way. We also present a general anytime approximate inference algorithm for our language. Our algorithm exploits the relational structure of the domain, and we show that doing so yields great benefits for anytime inference.

2 Recursive Probability Models

For ease of presentation, we will focus on a simplified version of our full language. We consider the impact of recursion on more expressive languages in Section 5.

The main unit of discourse in our language is a *class*, which describes a particular kind of object, with a probability model over its properties. A class has *simple* and *complex attributes*. Intuitively, a simple attribute describes a basic property of an object, while a complex attribute indicates a relationship between one object and another. A simple attribute has an associated probability model, describing how the value of the attribute depends on other attributes of the same object, and on attributes of related objects.

Definition 2.1: A *probabilistic relational knowledge base* consists of:

- A set $\mathcal{C}$ of *classes*.
- A set $\mathcal{A}$ of *complex attributes*. Each complex attribute A has a *domain type* $Dom[A] \in \mathcal{C}$ and a *range type* $Range[A] \in \mathcal{C}$.
- A set $\mathcal{B}$ of *simple attributes*. Each simple attribute B has a *domain type* $Dom[A] \in \mathcal{C}$, and a *range*, which is a finite set of values, denoted by $Val[B]$. The simple attribute B has an associated probability model, consisting of
  - A set $Pa[B]$ of *parents*, each of which is a *well-typed terminal attribute chain (see below)* $\sigma = A_1.\cdots.A_n$, such that $Dom[A_1] = Dom[B]$. The *range* of σ is the range of A_n, and is denoted by $Val[\sigma]$.
  - A *conditional probability function* CPF_B, defining a probability distribution over $Val[B]$ for each assign-

ment of values to *Pa[B]*. Formally, if B has parents $\sigma_1, \ldots, \sigma_m$, $CPF_B(w \mid \mathbf{v})$ defines the conditional probability over values $w \in Val[B]$ given an assignment $\mathbf{v} = (v_1, \ldots, v_m)$ to $\sigma_1, \ldots, \sigma_m$.

- A single instance I_T, known as the *top-level instance*, whose *type* is a class in $\mathcal{C}$.

An attribute chain $\sigma = A_1.\cdots.A_n$ is *well-typed* if for each $i = 1, \ldots, n-1$, A_i is complex, and $Dom[A_{i+1}] = Range[A_i]$. It is *terminal* if A_n is simple. ∎

As in Bayesian networks, one must make sure that the probability model is acyclic. For our simple language, it turns out that it is sufficient to make sure that there is no class C and sequence of simple attributes $A_1, \ldots, A_n$ whose domain type is C, such that A_{i+1} is a parent of A_i and A_1 is a parent of A_n.

Example 2.2: As a running example we will consider a simple genetic model for the transmission and manifestation of a single eye-color gene. The knowledge base $\mathcal{K}$ consists of a single class Person, complex attributes Mother and Father, and simple attributes M-Chromosome, P-Chromosome and Phenotype. The domain and range types of each complex attribute are Person. The domain type of each simple attribute is Person, while its range is {*pink, mauve*}. The parents of Phenotype are M-Chromosome and P-Chromosome, and its CPF specifies that if either parent is *pink*, Phenotype is *pink* with probability 0.99, otherwise it is *mauve* with probability 0.99. The parents of M-Chromosome are Mother.M-Chromosome, and Mother.P-Chromosome, while P-Chromosome depends on the father's chromosomes. $\mathcal{K}$ also contains the named instance *Fred* of type Person. ∎

This simple example already shows how easy and natural it is to create infinitely recursive models in this language. A possible world for our language consists of all entities related to the top-level instance via some finite attribute chain. We make the simplifying assumption here that no entity can be reached by two distinct attribute chains. The set of entities in the world is therefore fixed (but possibly infinite), and is in one to one correspondence with the set of finite complex attribute chains. For our example, it consists of distinct entities for *Fred* and all his ancestors. Since a possible world is characterized by the values of the simple attributes of the domain entities, and the set of domain entities is fixed, we can define a possible world simply as follows.

Definition 2.3: Let $\mathcal{K}$ be a probabilistic relational KB. A *variable* of $\mathcal{K}$ has the form $I_T.\sigma$, where $\sigma = A_1.\cdots.A_n$ is a well-typed terminal attribute chain such that $Dom[A_1]$ is the type of I_T. We will denote variables by the letters X, Y and Z. A *possible world* ω for $\mathcal{K}$ is a function that maps each variable X of $\mathcal{K}$ to an element in $Val[X]$. The set of possible worlds for $\mathcal{K}$ is denoted $\Omega_\mathcal{K}$, or simply Ω. ∎

3 Measure-Theoretic Semantics

Intuitively, a probabilistic relational KB defines an infinite Bayesian network. Each variable $X = I_T.A_1.\cdots.A_n$ has a set of parents and a conditional probability function, as

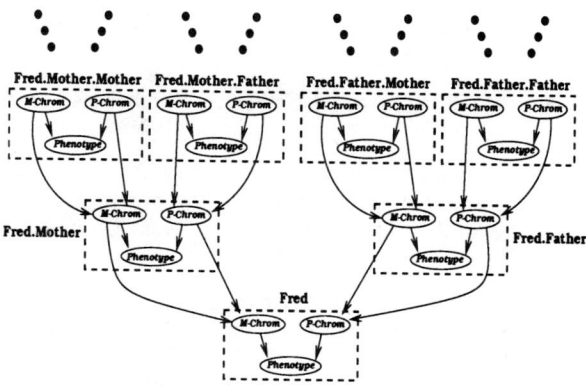

Figure 1: Infinite BN for genetic example.

specified by the probability model of A_n. Figure 1 illustrates the infinite BN for the KB of Example 2.2. To emphasize the object structure of the model, all variables associated with a particular domain entity are enclosed in a box.

Since a probabilistic relational KB defines an infinite BN, it may seem natural to define the semantics of our language in the same way as for BNs, namely, that the probability of any possible world ω is given by $\prod_X CPF_X(\omega(X) \mid \omega(Pa[X]))$. Unfortunately, if there are infinitely many variables, the probability of any possible world is typically 0.

Instead, we need to define a *probability measure* over the possible worlds. A probability measure assigns a probability to sets of possible worlds rather than individual worlds. Not all sets of worlds are assigned a probability, only those in a particular set $\mathcal{E}$ of subsets of Ω. A set $E \in \mathcal{E}$ is called an *event*, and $\mathcal{E}$ is called the *event space*. The set $\mathcal{E}$ is required to be a σ-*algebra*, which means that it is closed under countable unions and complements. A probability measure μ over $\Omega, \mathcal{E}$ is a function from $\mathcal{E}$ to $[0, 1]$ such that $\mu(\Omega) = 1$, and that is *countably additive*, i.e., if $E \in \mathcal{E}$ is the finite or countable union of disjoint events F_i, $\mu(E) = \sum_i \mu(F_i)$.

Definition 3.1: Let $\mathcal{K}$ be a probabilistic relational knowledge base. A *basic event* of $\mathcal{K}$ has the form $[\mathbf{X} = \mathbf{x}]$, where $\mathbf{X}$ is a finite set of variables of $\mathcal{K}$, and $\mathbf{x}$ is an assignment of values to $\mathbf{X}$. The basic event $[\mathbf{X} = \mathbf{x}]$ denotes the set of possible worlds ω such that $\omega(X_i) = x_i$ for each $X_i \in \mathbf{X}$. The set of basic events of $\mathcal{K}$ will be denoted $\mathcal{F}_\mathcal{K}$. We define $\mathcal{E}_\mathcal{K}$ to be the set of finite or countable unions of sets in $\mathcal{F}_\mathcal{K}$. ∎

It is easy to verify that $\mathcal{E}_\mathcal{K}$ is a σ-algebra, and it will serve as our event space. We now proceed to define the semantics of our language in a natural way. A model of $\mathcal{K}$ is a probability measure μ over $\Omega_\mathcal{K}, \mathcal{E}_\mathcal{K}$ that respects the probabilistic knowledge in $\mathcal{K}$. Intuitively, we require that μ *locally* satisfy the structure of the infinite BN. If we look at a finite set $\mathbf{X}$ of variables, we can consider the fragment of the infinite BN containing $\mathbf{X}$, and require that the distribution over $\mathbf{X}$ induced by μ agree with the BN fragment.

Definition 3.2: Let $\mathbf{X}$ be a finite set of variables. We define the *roots* of $\mathbf{X}$ to be $\cup_{X \in \mathbf{X}} Pa[X] - \mathbf{X}$. Let $\mathbf{Y}$ denote the roots of $\mathbf{X}$. The *BN fragment over* $\mathbf{X}$, written $B_\mathbf{X}$, is a DAG over $\mathbf{X} \cup \mathbf{Y}$, in which there is an edge from X_1 to X_2

if $X_2 \in \mathbf{X}$ and $X_1 \in Pa[X_2]$. $B_\mathbf{X}$ defines a conditional probability distribution over $\mathbf{X}$ given $\mathbf{Y}$, by

$$B_\mathbf{X}(\mathbf{X} = \mathbf{x} \mid \mathbf{Y} = \mathbf{y}) = \prod_X CPF_X(X = x \mid Pa[X] = \mathbf{u}_X),$$

where $\mathbf{u}_X$ denotes the value assigned to $Pa[X]$ in $\mathbf{x}, \mathbf{y}$.

If φ is some distribution over $\mathbf{Y}$, the notation $\varphi \cdot B_\mathbf{X}$ denotes the probability distribution π over $\mathbf{X}$ defined by $\pi(\mathbf{x}) = \sum_\mathbf{y} \varphi(\mathbf{y}) B_\mathbf{X}(\mathbf{x} \mid \mathbf{y})$. ∎

In order for the BN fragment over a set of variables to be meaningful, it must capture all the probabilistic relationships between variables in the set. If X and Y are variables in some set $\mathbf{X}$, and there is a path of influences from X to Y that passes through some variable Z not in $\mathbf{X}$, then we cannot expect the BN fragment over $\mathbf{X}$ to correctly express the conditional probability of Y given X. We will require that a model of a KB agree with the BN fragments over sets of variables that are *self-contained* in the following sense.

Definition 3.3: A set of variables $\mathbf{X}$ is *self-contained* if for all directed paths $X_1 \to \cdots \to X_n$ such that X_1 and X_n are in $\mathbf{X}$, all X_i are in $\mathbf{X}$. ∎

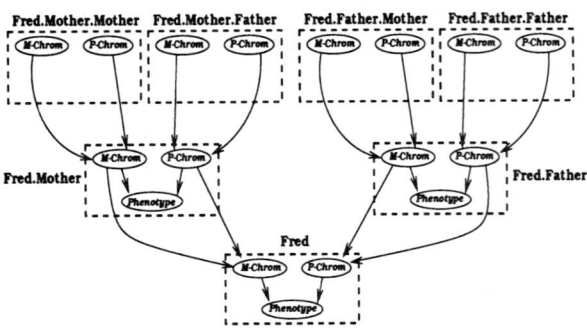

Figure 2: BN fragment for genetic example.

In our example, the variables associated with *Fred* and his parents form a self-contained set. The roots of this set are the chromosome variables of the grandparents. The BN fragment over this set of variables is shown in Figure 2. Essentially, the BN fragment over a self-contained set of variables captures all the knowledge expressed in the local probability models for the variables in the set. This includes both the conditional independence relationships in the structure of the BN fragment, and the quantitative knowledge in the CPFs. The following lemma shows how this knowledge is preserved when we move from one set of variables to a larger set.

Lemma 3.4: *Let $\mathbf{X}_1$ and $\mathbf{X}_2$ be two finite self-contained sets of variables, with $\mathbf{X}_1 \subseteq \mathbf{X}_2$. Let $\mathbf{Y}_1$ and $\mathbf{Y}_2$ be the roots of $\mathbf{X}_1$ and $\mathbf{X}_2$ respectively. Then $\mathbf{X}_1$ is d-separated from $\mathbf{Y}_2$ by $\mathbf{Y}_1$ in $B_{\mathbf{X}_2}$.*

Lemma 3.4 is illustrated in Figure 2. Let $\mathbf{X}_1$ be the set of variables associated with *Fred*, while $\mathbf{X}_2$ is the set of variables associated with *Fred* and his parents. $\mathbf{Y}_1$ is the set of chromosome variables of *Fred*'s parents, while $\mathbf{Y}_2$ is the set of chromosome variables of his grandparents. It is easy to see in the figure that $\mathbf{Y}_1$ d-separates $\mathbf{X}_1$ from $\mathbf{Y}_2$. The condition that $\mathbf{X}_1$ be self-contained is crucial to the truth of the lemma.

We are now ready to define the semantics of recursive probability models in a very natural way. We simply require that a model of a KB respect the BN fragment over every finite self-contained set of variables of the KB.

Definition 3.5: Let $\mathcal{K}$ be a recursive probabilistic KB. A *model* for $\mathcal{K}$ is a probability measure μ over $(\Omega_\mathcal{K}, \mathcal{E}_\mathcal{K})$, such that for every finite self-contained set of variables $\mathbf{X}$ of $\mathcal{K}$, with roots $\mathbf{Y}$, $\mu(\mathbf{X} \mid \mathbf{Y}) = B_\mathbf{X}(\mathbf{X} \mid \mathbf{Y})$. ∎

For a KB that has only a finite set of variables, this definition reduces to the standard semantics of BNs. All the variables of the KB form a finite self-contained set, and the BN fragment over all the variables is just an ordinary BN over those variables. So our semantics is a natural generalization of standard BN semantics. One of the nice properties of finite BNs is that a BN defines a unique probability distribution. Unfortunately, this is no longer the case for recursive probability models.

Example 3.6: Consider a KB with a single class State, with simple attribute Current and complex attribute Previous of type State. The attribute Current has a single parent Previous.Current. This class defines a Markov chain "looking backwards". If π is any stationary distribution of the Markov chain, the KB has a model whose marginal distribution over the state at any time is p. If the KB describes a non-ergodic Markov chain that has multiple stationary distributions, it has more than one model. ∎

Interestingly, however, it turns out that every KB has at least one model.

Theorem 3.7: *Let $\mathcal{K}$ be a recursive probabilistic KB. There exists a probability measure μ over $(\Omega_\mathcal{K}, \mathcal{E}_\mathcal{K})$ that is a model for $\mathcal{K}$.*

Sketch of proof (full proofs of all theorems can be found in (Pfeffer 2000)): We begin by defining a sequence of larger and larger self-contained sets of variables, that eventually covers all the variables of $\mathcal{K}$. We can achieve this by setting $\mathbf{X_i}$ to be the set of variables whose chains have length $\leq i$. (Such sets are self-contained for our language.) Next, for $i \geq j$, we define S_j^i to be the set of probability distributions π over $\mathbf{X_j}$, such that there is some distribution φ over the roots of $\mathbf{X_i}$, such that π is the marginal of $\varphi \cdot B_{\mathbf{X_i}}$ over $\mathbf{X_j}$. We can show that S_j^i is closed and non-empty, and, using Lemma 3.4, that $S_j^{i+1} \subseteq S_j^i$. Therefore the sequence $(S_j^i)_{i=j}^\infty$ is a non-increasing sequence of closed, non-empty sets, so by compactness of the space of probability distributions over $\mathbf{X_j}$, it has a non-empty intersection, which we denote by S_j.

Next, we use the S_j to recursively construct a sequence of distributions over all the $\mathbf{X_j}$ as follows. μ_1 is any distribution in S_1, and for $j > 1$, μ_j is a distribution in S_j such that μ_{j-1} is the marginal of μ_j over $\mathbf{X_{j-1}}$. This construction is always possible by definition of S_j. We can then define a function μ over the basic events $\mathcal{F}_\mathcal{K}$, by setting $\mu(E) = \mu_j(E)$ where all variables mentioned by E are in $\mathbf{X_j}$. By construction, it does not matter which j we pick, since all project to the same marginal distribution over the variables mentioned by E. We then show that μ so defined is countably additive, and that $\mu(\Omega_\mathcal{K}) = 1$, so we can extend μ to a probability measure over $\Omega_\mathcal{K}, \mathcal{E}_\mathcal{K}$. Finally, we show that μ so constructed does indeed satisfy the conditions of Definition 3.5. ∎

Note the central role of compactness in the proof. The result is a compactness result, and resembles the compactness theorem for first-order logic (Enderton 1972). The key idea is that a KB specifies a set of *local* constraints on the probability model, and the proof shows that if it is possible to satisfy every finite set of local constraints, it is possible to satisfy all constraints simultaneously. In our case, every finite set of constraints can be captured within a BN fragment, so it can always be satisfied. It follows that every KB has a model.

4 Inference

The traditional approach to inference in relational probability models has been to use the technique of *knowledge based model construction (KBMC)* (Wellman, Breese, & Goldman 1992). In this approach, used in (Ngo & Haddawy 1996) and (Koller & Pfeffer 1998), a Bayesian network is constructed in order to solve a particular query on a knowledge base. The network consists of all nodes that are relevant to determining the probability of the query variables given the evidence. Obviously, this approach will not work for recursive probability models, since the set of relevant nodes may be infinite, in which case the BN construction process will not terminate. The approaches of (Koller, McAllester, & Pfeffer 1997) and (Pfeffer *et al.* 1999) suffer from the same shortcoming. Even though they do not explicitly construct a BN to compute the solution to a query, they rely on the fact that the solution can be determined by looking at a finite number of variables.

4.1 Iterative Approximation

Clearly, what is needed is a method for determining an approximate solution to a query by looking at a finite number of nodes. The discussion of Section 3 suggests that we can obtain an approximate solution by looking at a BN fragment that contains the query and evidence variables. We can develop an *anytime algorithm* that repeatedly constructs larger and larger BN fragments, and solves each one in turn to get better and better approximate solutions. In order to develop the algorithm, we make the following definitions:

Definition 4.1: Let $\mathcal{K}$ be a probabilistic relational KB. A query $\mathcal{Q}$ is defined by a set $\mathbf{Q}$ of *query variables* of $\mathcal{K}$, a set $\mathbf{E}$ of *evidence variables* of $\mathcal{K}$, and an assignment $\mathbf{e}$ to $\mathbf{E}$. Let $\mathbf{X_i}$ be the set of variables of $\mathcal{K}$ of length $\leq i$, together with $\mathbf{Q}$ and $\mathbf{E}$. Let $\mathbf{Y_i}$ be the roots of $\mathbf{X_i}$. We define π_i to be the set of distributions π over $\mathbf{Q}$ such that $\pi = (\varphi \cdot B_{\mathbf{X_i}})(\mathbf{Q} \mid \mathbf{E} = \mathbf{e})$, for some distribution φ over $\mathbf{Y_i}$. We define π_{*i} to be the function on $Val[\mathbf{Q}]$ defined by $\pi_{*i}(\mathbf{q}) = \inf\{\pi(\mathbf{q}) : \pi \in \pi_i\}$. Similarly, π_i^* is defined by $\pi_i^*(\mathbf{q}) = \sup\{\pi(\mathbf{q}) : \pi \in \pi_i\}$. We define $\hat{\pi}_i$ to be $(\varphi^0 \cdot B_{\mathbf{X}})(\mathbf{Q} \mid \mathbf{E} = \mathbf{e})$, where φ^0 is the uniform distribution over $\mathbf{Y_i}$. We call π_{*i}, π_i^* and $\hat{\pi}_i$ the *i-th order lower bound*, *upper bound* and *approximate solution to* $\mathcal{Q}$ respectively. ∎

Informally, $\pi_\mathbf{i}$ represents the set of solutions to the query that are consistent with a BN fragment consisting of variables associated with entities at most i steps away from the top-level instance. π_{*i} and π_i^* are functions that assign lower and upper bounds to the probability of any assignment to the query variables. They are not themselves distributions. However, the set $\pi_\mathbf{i}$ is closed and convex, and any distribution lying between the bounds is attained by some element in $\pi_\mathbf{i}$. In particular, if we are interested in the probability of a particular assignment $\mathbf{q}$ to $\mathbf{Q}$, then we know that the probability must lie in $[\pi_{*i}(\mathbf{q}), \pi_i^*(\mathbf{q})]$, and that every value in between the bounds is consistent with the BN fragment.

We can construct an anytime algorithm by iteratively computing bounds of ever increasing order. The algorithm can be terminated at any time, and it returns the highest order bounds computed so far. The following theorem tells us that these bounds are valid, and that bounds from later iterations are at least as good as bounds from earlier iterations. It also tells us that the bounds eventually converge to the best possible bounds on the solution.

Theorem 4.2: *Let $\mathcal{K}$ be a probabilistic relational KB, and $\mathcal{Q}$ a query. Let b be the length of the longest query or evidence variable of $\mathcal{Q}$. If $j \geq i \geq b$, then for any model μ of $\mathcal{K}$,*

$$\pi_{*i} \leq \pi_{*j} \leq \mu(\mathbf{Q} \mid \mathbf{E} = \mathbf{e}) \leq \pi_j^* \leq \pi_i^*.$$

Furthermore, if π is a distribution over $\mathbf{Q}$ satisfying $\lim \pi_{*i} \leq \pi \leq \lim \pi_i^*$, then there exists a model μ for $\mathcal{K}$ such that $\mu(\mathbf{Q} \mid \mathbf{E} = \mathbf{e}) = \pi$. In particular, if $\mathcal{Q}$ has a unique solution, the bounds will converge to the solution.

The condition that $i \geq b$ ensures that the set $\mathbf{X_i}$ is self-contained. The first statement is a straightforward result of Lemma 3.4, while the proof of the second statement is similar to that of Theorem 3.7.

There are several ways to compute the bounds π_{*i} and π_i^*. One is an exact computation, based on the linear programming approach of (Nilsson 1986). This approach is expensive, as it ignores all structure in the BN fragment. Another is the approximation algorithm of (Draper & Hanks 1994), which performs standard BN inference for interval-valued probabilities. Both approaches are substantially more expensive than standard BN inference. A cheaper alternative is to compute the approximate solution $\hat{\pi}_i$, which is a standard BN inference computation on $B_{\mathbf{X_i}}$. The approximate solution always lies within the bounds, and if $\mathcal{Q}$ has a unique solution, then the approximate solution will converge to the true solution as i tends to infinity.

4.2 Exploiting Structure

There are two problems with the algorithm described above. First, the amount of work done in the i-th iteration of the approximation algorithm may grow exponentially in i. In the i-th iteration, the algorithm considers variables associated with objects at most i steps away from the top-level instance. In the genetic example, the number of such objects, and therefore the number of variables considered, is $\Theta(2^i)$. Second, the algorithm fails to exploit the object structure of the domain: the encapsulation of information within individual objects, so that only small amounts of information need to be passed between objects, and reuse of computation between different instances of the same class. It was shown in (Pfeffer et al. 1999) that exploiting this structure can lead to major speedup of inference. In this section we extend these techniques to an anytime approximation algorithm. Somewhat surprisingly, exploiting the object structure also serves to address the exponential blowup.

The basic idea of a structure-exploiting inference algorithm for relational probability models is to treat each object as a query-answering entity. An object answers a query by recursively issuing queries to related objects, receiving answers to those queries, and combining the answers together with the local probability models of its simple attributes to produce an answer to the original query.

Our algorithm, called **Iterative Structured Variable Elimination (ISVE)**, takes five arguments: a class C on which the query is asked; a set of attribute chains σ representing the query variables; a set of attribute chains ρ representing the evidence variables; the evidence $\mathbf{e} \in \mathit{Val}[\rho]$; and the desired solution quality i. ISVE returns a probability distribution over the values of the query chains σ.

For each query $\mathcal{Q}$ on class C, the cache maintains the highest order solution computed so far, together with its order j. If $i \leq j$, the cached solution is returned. Otherwise, if $i = 0$, a trivial approximation is returned. If neither of these conditions hold, the algorithm proceeds as follows. For each complex attribute A, it asks a recursive query of the object related by A, with a requested solution quality of $i - 1$. The query chains passed to these recursive queries come from two sources. One is the original set of query chains σ. If $A.\sigma'$ is a chain in σ, σ' is a query chain for the recursive call on A. (Evidence chains are passed similarly.) The second is the local probability models of the simple attributes of C. If some simple attribute B has a chain $A.\sigma'$ as a parent, σ' is added as a query chain for the recursive call. The result of the recursive query is a distribution over the chains σ'.

After solving the recursive queries, ISVE computes a factor for each of the simple variables of C, conditioning on the evidence where necessary. Finally, the results of the recursive queries and the factors for the simple variables are combined, and standard BN variable elimination is used to eliminate all but the query chains σ from this set. The result is a probability distribution over σ, which is returned as the solution to the query.

The ISVE algorithm can be used both for computing i-th order bounds $[\pi_{*i}, \pi_i^*]$ or the i-th order approximate solution $\hat{\pi}_i$. When computing $\hat{\pi}_i$, the zero-order approximation is just a uniform distribution over σ, and the VE procedure at the end is standard BN variable elimination. When computing bounds, the zero-order approximation is the trivial $[0, 1]$ bound.

The ISVE algorithm gains the standard advantages of structure-based inference — it is able to exploit encapsulation and reuse of inference between different instances of the same class. As it turns out, there is another advantage in the context of an iterative anytime approximation algorithm — the reuse of computation between different iterations.

Example 4.3: Consider the simple query where we wish to compute a probability distribution over Fred.Phenotype. We begin by requesting a first-order approximation to this distribution, with a call to ISVE(Person, {Phenotype}, ∅, ∅, 1). The third and fourth arguments are empty because there is no evidence. No solution to this query is found in the cache, so the algorithm proceeds by making recursive queries on the complex attributes of Person. The imports of the Mother attribute are M-Chromosome and P-Chromosome, so a recursive call is made to ISVE(Person, {M-Chromosome, P-Chromosome}, ∅, ∅, 0). No solution is found in the cache, but this time the requested order is 0, so a zero-order approximation is immediately returned, and stored in the cache. The original computation continues with a recursive call on the Father attribute. This call is exactly the same as the one on the Mother attribute, and the cached solution is returned, illustrating the reuse of computation between different objects in the model. Since all the recursive calls have been returned, the VE computation can be performed in the top-level query, and a first-order approximation is returned for the original query.

The anytime algorithm then continues to ask for a second-order approximate solution to the top-level query, beginning with a call to ISVE(Person, {Phenotype}, ∅, ∅, 2). This results in a recursive call on the Mother attribute to ISVE(Person, {M-Chromosome, P-Chromosome}, ∅, ∅, 1). which in turn results in a recursive call to ISVE(Person, {M-Chromosome, P-Chromosome}, ∅, ∅, 0), and the zero-order solution to this query is in the cache from the previous iteration, so it returns immediately. In general, only two new calls to **UncachedISVE** are made on each iteration, one with the query chain Phenotype, and one with the chains M-Chromosome and P-Chromosome. ∎

In the genetic example, the amount of work done in each iteration is constant. This is in contrast to the unstructured algorithm in which the amount of work done in each iteration grows exponentially. Is it always the case that after a certain number of iterations, the amount of work performed by ISVE becomes constant? The answer is yes, for our language. The main insight is that, for a given KB in our language and a given top-level query, there are only finitely many different queries that can be generated. In fact, for our simple language the number of distinct queries generated is at most $a + qb$ where a is the total number of complex attributes, q is the number of query and evidence variables of the top-level query, and b is the length of the longest query or evidence variable. It follows that there must be some depth L such that all the queries at depth L also appear at a shallower depth. Therefore, no query at depth L will ever be expanded, no matter how high the requested order for the original query. The amount of work performed from the L-th iteration onwards is constant.

Theorem 4.4: *If $\mathcal{K}$ is a probabilistic relational KB, and $\mathcal{Q}$ is a query on $\mathcal{K}$, the asymptotic complexity of computing an n-th order approximation to the solution of $\mathcal{Q}$ using the **Iterative SVE** algorithm is linear in n.*

5 More Expressive Languages

So far we have considered a fairly simple language for relational probability models, that is sufficient to bring out the key points arising from infinite recursion. There are many natural extensions to the expressive power of the language, and here we consider a number of them.

While space considerations prevent us from giving details, it turns out that many of the obvious extensions do not change our results at all. These "free" extensions include: a finite set of named instances, with the knowledge-base specifying relations between them; multi-valued complex attributes, with or without uncertainty over the number of values for such an attribute; a class hierarchy, with uncertainty about types of instances; statements of the form A *same-as* σ, saying that for any instance I of C, the value of $I.A$ is the same as that of $I.\sigma$ (an appropriate stratification assumption needs to be made to obtain well-defined semantics); and *reference uncertainty*, where we allow uncertainty as to which chain the attribute A actually refers.

One language extension that does impact our results is to allow inverse statements of the form A *inverse-of* B. Such a statement means that $I.A = J$ implies that $J.B = I$. Inverse statements are an issue because they allow us to create KBs in which there are arbitrarily long chains of dependencies between two variables X and Y.

Example 5.1: Consider a KB consisting of a single class, with two complex attributes A_1 and A_2, and two simple attributes B_1 and B_2. The KB contains the statements A_1 *inverse-of* A_2 and A_2 *inverse-of* A_1. Attribute B_1 has the parent $A_2.B_1$, while B_2 has the parents B_1 and $A_1.B_2$. The infinite BN for this KB has the following structure:

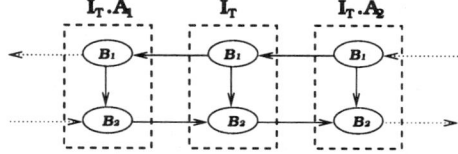

Note that the inverse relationship allows information to be passed both ways along the chain. There are arbitrarily long dependency chains between $I_T.B_1$ and $I_T.B_2$, so that there is no finite self-contained set containing both. ∎

We call a KB *normal* if every finite set of variables is a subset of a finite self-contained set. It is possible to weaken our semantics so that it still imposes constraints on non-normal KBs; some of our results (e.g., Theorem 4.4) still carry through to this case. We omit details for lack of space.

Another very useful language extension is to allow an object to *pass arguments* to a related object, by *binding* the values of attributes of the related object. In all the languages considered so far, an object pulls values from related objects by mentioning values of other objects as parents of its simple attributes. Allowing an object to push values to related objects is a significant extension to the expressive power of the language. It allows us to describe *stochastic functions* in the style of (Koller, McAllester, & Pfeffer 1997) (denoted KMP from now on).

Example 5.2: A *stochastic context-free grammar (SCFG)* is a context free grammar in which a probability distribution is provided over the productions associated with each non-terminal. An SCFG defines a probability distribution over the generation of strings in an obvious way.

An SCFG can be specified in our language as follows. There is a String class, with three attributes, the simple attribute First, ranging over the terminal symbols, the boolean simple attribute Is-Empty, and the complex attribute Rest of range type String. String is an abstract class — we will define some subclasses and specify their probability models. There is an Concat subclass of String, representing the concatenation of two strings. This subclass illustrates how something that we normally think of as a function can be represented in our language. Functionally, we can define Concat using the following recursive equations: Concat([],ys) = ys and Concat([x:xs],ys) = [x, Concat(xs,ys)]. We define Concat in our language as follows. It has two complex attributes Left and Right of type String, corresponding to the arguments of the function. The Is-Empty attribute of Concat depends on Left.Is-Empty and Right.Is-Empty, and its CPF is the **and** function. The First attribute of Concat depends on Left.First, Left.Is-Empty and Right.First, and its CPF specifies it to be equal to Left.First if Left.Is-Empty is false, otherwise it is equal to Right.First. Concat has a Subcall attribute, representing the recursive call shown in the second part of its definition. In order to specify the recursive call properly, we need to be able to pass its arguments. This is where the binding mechanism comes in. We bind the value of Subcall.Left with Left.Rest, while Subcall.Right is bound to Right. To pass the results of the recursive call back upwards, we use the same-as mechanism described earlier. The value of the Rest attribute of Concat is the same as Subcall, if Left.Is-Empty is false, otherwise it is the same as Right.Rest.

Using the String and Concat classes, we can now construct classes for every symbol in an SCFG. The class corresponding to a terminal symbol simply defines a string of length 1 containing the given symbol, while the class for a non-terminal contains a string for each of the possible productions for that non-terminal, and chooses the appropriate string with the given probability. The string corresponding to a production is formed by applying Concat to the strings associated with each of the symbols in the production. We omit the details. ∎

Basically, any probability model that can be described as a stochastic computational process can be defined in our language, once we allow argument passing via the binding mechanism. This language is much more expressive than those considered previously, but our semantics applies equally well to this language as to the others. Even when the stochastic computation is not guaranteed to terminate, the semantics still defines constraints on the probability distributions over variables at the roots of the process. This is much stronger than the semantics defined in KMP, which required that the stochastic computation be guaranteed to terminate in order for the probability model to be well-defined.

In KMP, it was shown how Bayesian inference can be performed on stochastic programs by exploiting the structure of the program. In particular, it was shown that the inference algorithm mimics the dynamic programming behavior of the *inside algorithm* for SCFGs. The **ISVE** algorithm achieves the same behavior on SCFGs as that of KMP. The dynamic programming effect is achieved by caching. **ISVE** also has several advantages over the algorithm of KMP. For one, it is an anytime approximation algorithm, whereas the KMP algorithm does not produce any answer when the stochastic program is not guaranteed to terminate in a finite amount of time. For example, the KMP algorithm can answer a query asking whether an SCFG produces the string s, but it cannot answer a query asking whether the SCFG produces a string *beginning with* s, whereas ours can. In addition, our algorithm can be shown to achieve much better performance on programs that define Bayesian networks.

As was the case with inverse statements, allowing argument passing into the language makes it possible to pass information back and forth between two entities, allowing the creation of non-normal KBs such as that of Example 5.1. For normal KBs with argument passing, Theorems 3.7 and 4.2 continue to hold. However, Theorem 4.4 no longer holds, even for normal KBs. The reason is that this theorem relies on the fact that only a finite number of distinct queries can be generated from a given top-level query. Once we allow argument passing into the language, it is possible to generate queries of arbitrary complexity. This is hardly surprising given the expressive power of the language — it is Turing complete, in that it is capable of defining any stochastic computation. Despite the fact that Theorem 4.4 does not hold, the benefits of reusing computation between iterations are still obtained by the **ISVE** algorithm. In fact, the conclusion of the theorem still holds for many KBs in this more expressive language. In particular, it holds for queries on SCFGs. For example, consider a query over whether a grammar generates a string beginning with s. Each iteration of the algorithm considers longer and longer derivations that might produce a string beginning with s. The types of queries generated are whether a certain non-terminal generates a substring of s, or a string beginning with a substring of s. There are only finitely many such queries, and after a certain number of iterations all the different queries will have been expanded, and the amount of work performed on each iteration becomes constant.

6 Conclusions and Future Work

Recursive probability models are common and natural. In this paper, we have presented an elegant framework for dealing with such models. We provided a natural measure-theoretic semantics that extends the semantics of Bayesian networks, and showed that every normal KB has a model under this semantics. We also presented the **ISVE** algorithm for anytime approximate inference. The algorithm exploits the relational structure of a domain, thereby gaining great benefits in the context of anytime inference.

There are a number of important questions about recursive probability models that remain to be explored. Some key questions are: Is there a general theory that can tell us when a model has a unique distribution? Can conditions be found under which Theorem 4.4 holds even for models with argument-passing? What kinds of conclusions can one draw from KBs that are not normal, and does Theorem 3.7 hold for such KBs?

We believe that applying finite or iterative computation to an infinite model is a fundamental AI technique. An example is game tree search, in which a finite portion of a possibly infinite game tree is expanded in order to determine the best move. Hughes (Hughes 1989) has argued that allowing the tree to be specified in its natural infinite form, and then applying a finite lazy computation to it, is the most elegant and modular way of expressing this process. The same holds true for probabilistic reasoning. Rather than forcing our possible worlds to be finite by applying arbitrary restrictions to our representation language, we can freely allow them to be infinite, and use the techniques of lazy evaluation and anytime approximation to deal with them.

Acknowledgements

We would like to thank David McAllester for useful discussions. This work was supported by ONR contract N66001-97-C-8554 under DARPA's HPKB program.

References

Draper, D., and Hanks, S. 1994. Localized partial evaluation of belief networks. In *Proc. UAI*.

Enderton, H. 1972. *A Mathematical Introduction to Logic*. Academic Press.

Hughes, J. 1989. Why functional programming matters. *The Computer Journal* 32(2):98 – 107.

Koller, D., and Pfeffer, A. 1998. Probabilistic frame-based systems. In *Proc. AAAI*.

Koller, D.; McAllester, D.; and Pfeffer, A. 1997. Effective Bayesian inference for stochastic programs. In *Proc. AAAI*.

Ngo, L., and Haddawy, P. 1996. Answering queries from context-sensitive probabilistic knowledge bases. *Theoretical Computer Science*.

Nilsson, N. 1986. Probabilistic logic. *AIJ* 28(1):71–87.

Pfeffer, A.; Koller, D.; Milch, B.; and Takusagawa, K. 1999. SPOOK: A system for probabilistic object-oriented knowledge representation. In *Proc. UAI*.

Pfeffer, A. 2000. *Probabilistic Reasoning for Complex Systems*. Ph.D. Dissertation, Stanford University.

Wellman, M.; Breese, J.; and Goldman, R. 1992. From knowledge bases to decision models. *The Knowledge Engineering Review* 7(1):35–53.

Towards Feasible Approach to Plan Checking Under Probabilistic Uncertainty: Interval Methods

Raúl Trejo and **Vladik Kreinovich**
Department of Computer Science
University of Texas at El Paso
El Paso, TX 79968, USA
{rtrejo,vladik}@cs.utep.edu

Chitta Baral
Dept. of Computer Science & Engineering
Arizona State University
Tempe, AZ 85287-5406, USA
chitta@asu.edu

Abstract

The main problem of *planning* is to find a sequence of actions that an agent must perform to achieve a given objective. An important part of planning is checking whether a given plan achieves the desired objective. Historically, in AI, the planning and plan checking problems were mainly formulated and solved in a *deterministic* environment, when the initial state is known precisely and when the results of each action in each state is known (and uniquely determined). In this deterministic case, planning is difficult, but plan checking is straightforward. In many real-life situations, we only know the probabilities of different fluents; in such situations, even plan checking becomes computationally difficult. *In this paper, we describe how methods of interval computations can be used to get a feasible approximation to plan checking under probabilistic uncertainty.* The resulting method is a natural generalization of 0-approximation proposed earlier to describe planning in the case of partial knowledge. It turns out that some of the resulting probabilistic techniques coincides with heuristically proposed "fuzzy" methods. Thus, we justify these fuzzy heuristics as a reasonable feasible approximation to the (NP-hard) probabilistic problem.

Traditional (deterministic) planning and plan checking

The main problem of *planning* is to find a sequence of actions that an agent must perform to achieve a given objective. An important part of planning is checking whether a given plan achieves the desired objective; this *plan checking* is also called *projection*.

Historically, in AI, the planning and plan checking problems were mainly formulated and solved in a *deterministic* environment, when the initial state is known precisely and when the results of each action in each state is known (and uniquely determined) (Allen et al. 1990).

To formulate the deterministic planning problem precisely we must be able to describe states of the world and actions. States are usually characterized by their

Copyright © 2000, American Association for Artificial Intelligence (www.aaai.org). All rights reserved.

properties (*fluents*) $f_1, \ldots, f_n$; the set of all possible fluents will be denoted by $\mathcal{F}$. A state s can thus be defined simply as a set of fluents, meaning the set of all the fluents which are true in this state.

At each moment of time, an agent can execute an action. We will denote the set of all possible actions by $\mathcal{A}$. We have *rules* which describe how an action $a \in \mathcal{A}$ changes a state s; these rules are of the form "a causes F if $F_1, \ldots, F_m$", where F and F_i are *fluent literals*, i.e., fluents or their negations. The set of all such rules is called a *domain description* and denoted by D. The result $res(a, s)$ of applying the action a to the state s is thus defined as
$res(a, s) = \{f \mid (f \in s \& \neg f \notin V_D(a, s)) \lor f \in V_D(a, s)\}$,
where $V_D(a, s)$ denotes the set of conclusions of all rules from D for which all conditions hold in s.

A *plan* α is a sequence of of actions $\alpha = [a_1, \ldots, a_n]$; the result $res(a_n, res(a_{n-1}, \ldots, res(a_1, s) \ldots))$ of applying these actions to the state s will be denoted by $res(\alpha, s)$.

To complete the description of deterministic planning, we must formulate possible objectives. In general, as an objective, we can take a complex combination of elementary properties (fluents) which characterize the final state; for example, a typical objective of an assembling manufacture robot is to reach the state of the world in which all manufactured items are fully assembled. To simplify the description of the problem, we can always add this combination as a new fluent literal (see, e.g. (Allen et al. 1990)); thus, without losing generality, it is sufficient to consider only objectives of the type $f \in \mathcal{F}$.

In these terms, the *planning* problem can be formulated as follows: given a set of fluents $\mathcal{F}$, a goal $f \in \mathcal{F}$, a set of actions $\mathcal{A}$ and a set of rules D describing how these actions affect the state of the world, to find a sequence of actions $\alpha = [a_1, \ldots, a_k]$ that, when executed from the initial state of the world s_0, makes f true. The problem of *plan checking* is, given $\mathcal{F}, \mathcal{A}$, a goal, and a sequence of actions α, to check whether the goal becomes true after execution of α in the initial state. In the deterministic case, planning is computationally difficult (NP-hard, see, e.g., a survey (Baral et. al. 1999)), but checking a given plan is feasible: it can be done by a straightforward computation of $res(\alpha, s_0)$ (Allen et al. 1990).

Imperfect sensors: First reason to consider planning and plan checking under probabilistic uncertainty

In real life, we often do not know have a complete knowledge of the initial state s_0. For some fluents $f \in \mathcal{F}$, we know whether f or $\neg f$ are initially true, but for some other fluents f, we may only know the *probability* $p(f, s_0)$ that f is initially true. (The probability $p(\neg f, s_0)$ that $\neg f$ is true is then equal to $1 - p(f, s_0)$.)

This probability may reflect either the expert's uncertainty in his own opinion (such probabilities are called *subjective*), or the fact that sensors and measuring instruments used to determine whether this fluent holds are never 100% reliable (such probabilities are called *objective*).

Towards the description of the corresponding planning and plan checking problems

Due to this probabilistic uncertainty, we do not know the exact initial state s_0; at best, we know the *probabilities* $P(s = s_0)$ of different initial states s. These probabilities (and similar uncertainty about observations in the future) form the basis of the Partially Observable Markov Decision Processes (POMDP) approach to planning under probabilistic uncertainty (see, e.g., (Heffner et al. 1998; Kaelbling, et al. 1998) and references therein).

Most examples of using POMDP assume that we know the probabilities of all possible initial states. Such a representation is possible for a simple example in which the total number $n_f = \#(\mathcal{F})$ of fluents is small: Indeed, since we define a state s as a subset $s \subseteq \mathcal{F}$ of the set of all the fluents, the number of all possible states is equal to the number of all possible subsets, i.e., to 2^{n_f}. Thus, to describe the probability $p(s)$ of each state, we need to use $2^{n_f} - 1$ real numbers $p(s) \in [0, 1]$ ($2^{n_f} - 1$ since $\sum p(s) = 1$, so one of the values $p(s)$ is uniquely determined if we know the others). Even for $n_f = 20$ fluents, we need more than a million different probabilities. In such situations, we cannot represent this probabilistic uncertainty by describing the probability of every possible initial state s.

In other words, we may know the probability $p(f, s_0)$ of each of n_f fluents $f \in \mathcal{F}$, but we may not know the probability of each of 2^{n_f} possible states $s \subseteq \mathcal{F}$.

In some cases, we know that different fluents are statistically independent; in this case, if we know the initial probabilities $p(f_i, s_0)$ of different fluents $f_i \in \mathcal{F}$, we can determine the probability of every possible state. For example, for $\mathcal{F} = \{f_1, f_2\}$, the probability $p(s_0 = \{f_1\})$ that the initial state s_0 coincides with $\{f_1\}$ is equal to the probability that in the initial state s_0, f_1 is true and f_2 is false, i.e., is equal to $p(s_0 = \{f_1\}) = p(f_1, s_0) \cdot p(\neg f_2, s_0) = p(f_1, s_0) \cdot (1 - p(f_2, s_0))$.

In real life, often, the errors of different sensors are partially caused by the same causes and therefore, are not independent; in most such cases, we do not know the exact extent of this correlation. Thus, even when we know the exact initial probability $p(f, s_0)$ of each fluent $f \in \mathcal{F}$, we may have several different probability distributions P on the set of all initial states; the set of all possible distributions coincides with the set of all distributions P for which the probability of each fluent f is equal to the given value: $P(f) = p(f, s_0)$. In this case, we will say that the probability distribution P is *consistent* with the given probabilities $p(f, s_0)$.

Even the probabilities $p(f, s_0)$ of different fluents may not be known exactly. Indeed, a natural way to get these probabilities is to apply statistical techniques to the records of sensor errors and/or expert judgments. From these statistical estimates, however, we do not get the *exact* values of these probabilities, we can only get *approximate* values. So, in reality, for a fluent f, often, we do not even know the exact value of the initial probability $p(f, s_0)$, we only know the *interval* $\mathbf{p}(f, s_0) = [p^-(f, s_0), p^+(f, s_0)]$ which contains the actual (unknown) value of $p(f, s_0)$ (see, e.g., (Givan et al. 1997). In this case, possible values of the probability $p(\neg f, s_0)$ that $\neg f$ hold is s_0 form the interval

$$\mathbf{p}(\neg f, s_0) = [1 - p^+(f, s_0), 1 - p^-(f, s_0)].$$

Comment. An even more general approach, related to Dempster-Shafer formalism, allows for the possibility that for some fluents $f_1, \ldots, f_k$, we do not even the intervals $\mathbf{p}(f_i, s_0)$; instead, we may know, e.g., only the probability $\mathbf{p}(f_1 \vee \ldots \vee f_k, s_0)$. Heuristic methods for this approach (based on independence-type assumptions) were considered, e.g., in (Lowrance et al. 1990); guaranteed estimates which are not based on any heuristic assumptions are described in (Doan et al. 1996).

The cases of complete information about the fluent and the complete lack of information about this fluent can be described as a particular case of the interval formulation: $\mathbf{p}(f, s_0) = [1, 1]$ means that we are 100% sure that f is true; $\mathbf{p}(f, s_0) = [0, 0]$ means that we are 100% sure that f is false; and $\mathbf{p}(f, s_0) = [0, 1]$ means that we have no information about f.

In this realistic case of interval probabilities $\mathbf{p}(f, s_0)$ ($f \in \mathcal{F}$), we have to consider all probability distributions P which are *consistent* with these interval probabilities, i.e., all probability distributions P for which the probability of each fluent f belongs to the corresponding interval: $P(f) \in \mathbf{p}(f, s_0)$.

If we have a complete domain description D, then, for each initial state s and for each action plan α, we can determine the resulting state $res(\alpha, s)$. Thus, for every probability distribution P which is consistent with the given interval probabilities, and for every objective fluent f, we can determine the probability $p(f, res(\alpha, s_0))$ that this objective will be satisfied in the final state, as the sum $\sum P(s)$ of the probabilities of all initial states s for which f holds in $res(\alpha, s)$. Since the interval probabilities do not determine the probability distribution uniquely, we may have different probability distributions P which are consistent with this data; for different distributions, we may get different values $p(f, res(\alpha, s_0))$. Let us denote the interval of all possible values of such probabilities by $\mathbf{p}(f, res(\alpha, s_0)) = [p^-(f, res(\alpha, s_0)), p^+(f, res(\alpha, s_0))]$.

Since we do not have the complete knowledge of the initial state, we, therefore, cannot be 100% sure that the result of applying a given sequence of actions will always lead to a given objective; at best, we can hope that the probability of achieving a given objective is high enough, i.e., that this probability is higher than a given number p_0. So, in this probabilistic context, the planning problem means finding a plan α for which $p^-(f, res(\alpha, s_0)) \geq p_0$. Correspondingly, a plan checking problem means checking whether this inequality holds for a given plan α.

Summarizing: with probabilistic uncertainty in sensors, the planning problem takes the following form. We are given a set of fluents $\mathcal{F}$, a set of actions $\mathcal{A}$, a domain description D (i.e., set of rules which describe how actions affect the state), the initial interval probabilities $\mathbf{p}(f, s_0)$ for all $f \in \mathcal{F}$, the objective $f \in \mathcal{F}$, and the desired success probability p_0. Our goal is to find a sequence of actions α such that the probability $p(f, res(\alpha, s_0))$ of the objective f being true after execution of α is guaranteed to be greater or equal than p_0.

A natural step in solving the planning problem is checking the given plan. The problem of *plan checking* is, given a planning problem and a candidate plan α, to check whether the probability $p(f, res(\alpha, s_0))$ is guaranteed to be greater or equal than p_0, i.e., whether $p^-(f, res(\alpha, s_0)) \geq p_0$.

For probabilistic uncertainty, even plan checking is NP-hard; so, we need a good approximate plan checking algorithm

In contrast to the deterministic planning where plan checking is easy, the probabilistic plan checking problem is NP-hard: indeed, in (Baral et. al. 1999), it is shown, in effect, that this problem is NP-hard even if we only allow intervals of the type $[0, 0]$, $[1, 1]$, and $[0, 1]$ (see also (Littman et al. 1998)). It is therefore desirable to find good approximate algorithms for plan checking.

A natural way to check the success of a plan is to estimate the probability $p^-(f, res(\alpha, s_0))$, and then compare the resulting estimate with the desired probability value p_0. Since it is NP-hard to check whether $p^- \geq p_0$, it is, therefore, NP-hard to compute the value p^-; thus, at best, we can look for a feasible algorithm for computing a good approximation $\widetilde{p}^-$ for the desired difficult-to-compute probability bound p^-.

This word "approximation" may mean two things: it may mean that our algorithm misses a successful plan (i.e., it is unable to confirm that a plan is successful), and it may mean that the approximate algorithm erroneously declares a bad plan to be successful.

There are many heuristic techniques which provide us with approximate values of probabilities; e.g., techniques based on fuzzy logic have been successfully combined with more traditional AI techniques to produce an award-winning robot (Congdon et al. 1993; Saffiotti et al. 1995). For a robot, usually, errors of both types are equally bad, so we just try to minimize the total number of such errors.

In many real-life applications, missing a successful plan is bad, but selecting a failing plan as supposedly successful can be disastrous: e.g., when we plan to send astronauts on a space mission, it is bad but still tolerable if we miss a possibility of a cheaper mission and thus erroneously overestimate the mission's cost, but it would be a disaster to send a mission with a low success probability under the erroneous assumption that this mission's success probability is high. Due to this fact, we are interested in a plan checking algorithm which will never overestimate the success probability. In other words, we want to guarantee that our estimate $\widetilde{p}^-$ never exceeds the actual value p^-: $\widetilde{p}^- \leq p^-$.

In the following text, we will show, among other things, that the above-mentioned fuzzy techniques (which were not originally intended to provide such guarantees) can, in fact, lead to guaranteed estimates.

Imperfect actuators: Second reason to consider planning and plan checking under probabilistic uncertainty

In the above text, we took into consideration that sensors can be imperfect, but we still assumed that the actuators are perfect, i.e., that the results of each action in a given state are uniquely determined by our choice of this action. In reality, of course, actuators are also imperfect; as a result, if we apply, several times, the same action a to the same state s, we may get different results. For example, if we want a robot to move forward, we send to it, at several consequent moments of time, a signal to go forward. Due to actuator errors, a robot usually deviates from the desired trajectory, and this deviation may change from time to time (the robot "wobbles"). In other words, instead of deterministic rules of the type "a causes F if $F_1, \ldots, F_m$", we now have probabilistic rules of the type

a causes F with probability p if $F_1, \ldots, F_m$.

Similarly to the sensor uncertainty, we may not know the exact values of the corresponding probabilities; instead, we only know the *interval* of possible values. In this case, the probabilistic rules take the following form:

a causes F with probability $p \in \mathbf{p}$ if $F_1, \ldots, F_m$

for some given probability interval $\mathbf{p}$. To illustrate this idea, let us give three simple examples: a deterministic action corresponds to $\mathbf{p} = [1, 1]$; a non-deterministic statement that an action a *may* cause F can be described by $\mathbf{p} = [0, 1]$, and coin toss leads to $F =$ "heads" with probability $\mathbf{p} = [0.5, 0.5]$.

These additional interval probabilities make the planning and plan checking problems even more complicated. In POMDP description, these probabilities are taken into consideration; however, it is assumed that the probabilities corresponding to consequent actions are independent. This is indeed true in some real-life situations when the actuator errors are purely random. In real life, many actuators also have a systematic error component, i.e., a component which leads to a strong correlation between probabilities corresponding to consequent actions (this assumption is also made in the interval version of POMDP, described, e.g., in (Draper et al. 1994)). Thus, in our description, we do not want to assume this independence; instead, similarly to sensor uncertainty, we consider all possible probability distributions which are consistent with the given interval probabilities.

This framework – no independence assumption at all, probabilities are allowed to change over time within the intervals, etc. – may yield overly conservative estimates for the probabilities (especially for long plans), but it is unavoidable in the situations when we need to *guarantee* that the plan succeeds with a given probability.

Taking actuator imperfection into consideration makes the plan checking problem even more complex. However, from the computational viewpoint, for realistic (polynomial-length) plans, we can reformulate this new uncertainty in the equivalent form of initial state's uncertainty. The motivation behind this reduction is very simple and natural: In the deterministic description, to find the post-action state of the system, it is sufficient to know its pre-action state. In the more realistic situation, to determine the post-action state uniquely, we must also know the pre-action state of the actuator. Thus, to reduce the new description to the previous one, we can add, to the the original set of fluents $\mathcal{F}$ which describe the state of the system itself, additional fluents which describe the state of the actuator. Namely, for each action a_i from the actions sequence (plan) α, and for each rule from D (of the type "a_i causes F with probability $p \in \mathbf{p}$ if $F_1, \ldots, F_m$") in which the result of this action a_i is not uniquely determined, we add a new fluent f_r whose meaning is that this rule leads to F if this fluent is true. Then, the original probabilistic rule is replaced by the deterministic rule "a causes F if $F_1, \ldots, F_m, f_r$", where the initial interval probability of the new fluent f_r is equal to $\mathbf{p}$.

Similarly, we can take care of *exogenous actions*, i.e., of the situations in which, with a certain probability, a state can change by itself, without any (regular) action being performed.

Due to the possibility of this reduction, in the following text, we will, without losing generality, restrict ourselves to the situations in which the results of actions are deterministic, and the only uncertainty is in the initial state.

The idea of 0-approximation: a motivation for our algorithm

Our feasible plan-checking algorithm for planning under probabilistic uncertainty will be a generalization of the 0-approximation algorithm developed in (Baral and Son 1997) for the case of partial knowledge, i.e., in our terms, for the case when for each fluent $f \in \mathcal{F}$, the initial probability interval is equal to $[0, 0]$, $[1, 1]$, or $[0, 1]$.

In terms of these intervals, the 0-approximation algorithm can be described as follows: To check whether a plan $\alpha = [a_1, \ldots, a_n]$ is successful, for each moment of time $t = 1, \ldots, n$, and for each fluent $f \in \mathcal{F}$, we estimate the interval $\mathbf{p}(f, s_t)$ of possible values of this fluent's probability in the state $s_t = res(a_t, res(a_{t-1}, \ldots, res(a_1, s) \ldots))$. To be more precise, for each t and f, we compute the *enclosure* $\widetilde{\mathbf{p}}(f, s_t) \supseteq \mathbf{p}(f, s_t)$. We start with the known values $\widetilde{\mathbf{p}}(f, s_0) = \mathbf{p}(f, s_0)$; after the estimates $\widetilde{\mathbf{p}}(f, s_t)$ are found for a certain t, we compute the estimates for s_{t+1} as follows: Let $V^+(a, s_t)$ denote the set of all fluent literals F for which D contains a rule "a causes F if $F_1, \ldots, F_m$" for which all the conditions F_i are definitely true (have probability intervals $\widetilde{\mathbf{p}}(F_i, s_t) = [1, 1]$). Let $V^-(a, s_t)$ denote the set of all fluent literals F for which D contains a rule "a causes F if $F_1, \ldots, F_m$" for which all the conditions F_i may be true (have probability intervals $\widetilde{\mathbf{p}}(F_i, s_t) \neq [0, 0]$). Then, for every fluent $f \in \mathcal{F}$:

- We assign $\widetilde{\mathbf{p}}(f, s_{t+1}) := [1, 1]$ if
$f \in V^+(a_{t+1}, s_t) \vee (\widetilde{\mathbf{p}}(f, s_t) = [1, 1] \& \neg f \notin V^-(a_{t+1}, s_t))$.

- We assign $\widetilde{\mathbf{p}}(f, s_{t+1}) := [0, 0]$ if
$\neg f \in V^+(a_{t+1}, s_t) \vee (\widetilde{\mathbf{p}}(f, s_t) = [0, 0] \& f \notin V^-(a_{t+1}, s_t))$.

- In all other cases, we take $\widetilde{\mathbf{p}}(f, s_{t+1}) := [0, 1]$.

It is proven that this algorithm indeed produces an enclosure and thus, if we get $\widetilde{\mathbf{p}}(f, s_n) = [1, 1]$ at the final state, we are thus guaranteed that this plan works.

The 0-approximation algorithm is feasible: its computation time grows linearly with the length of the plan and with the size of the domain description. Since the plan checking problem is NP-hard, it is not surprising that sometimes, this algorithm errs – fails to realize that a given plan is successful.

The new algorithm based on interval computations

In our new algorithm, we will also start with the original estimates $\widetilde{\mathbf{p}}(f, s_0) = \mathbf{p}(f, s_0)$ and produce the values $\widetilde{\mathbf{p}}(f, s_t) \supseteq \mathbf{p}(f, s_t)$ for $t = 1, 2, \ldots, n$.

According to the semantics of the rules, a fluent f holds in the next moment of time iff either it is caused by some rule, or it was true in the previous moment of time, and its negation was not caused by any rule. Thus, in order to find out whether f holds at the moment $t+1$ (after applying the action a_{t+1}), we first need to describe all the rules in which the action a_{t+1} causes either f or $\neg f$. Let us denote by k the total number of rules in which a_{t+1} causes f, and let us denote the conditions of the i-th such rule by $F_{i,1}, \ldots, F_{i,n_i}$. Similarly, let us denote by ℓ the total number of rules in which a_{t+1} cause $\neg f$, and let us denote the conditions of the j-th such rule by $G_{j,1}, \ldots, G_{i,m_j}$. In terms of these notations, f holds at the moment of time $t+1$ iff the following formula B holds at moment t:

$(F_{1,1} \& \ldots \& F_{1,n_1}) \vee \ldots \vee (F_{k,1} \& \ldots \& F_{k,n_k}) \vee$
$\{f \& \neg[(G_{1,1} \& \ldots \& G_{1,m_1}) \vee \ldots \vee (G_{\ell,1} \& \ldots \& G_{\ell,m_\ell})]\}$.

Thus, if we know the enclosures $\widetilde{\mathbf{p}}(F, s_t)$ for all fluent literals at time t, in order to find the enclosure $\widetilde{\mathbf{p}}(f, s_{t+1})$ for the probability interval $\mathbf{p}(f, s_{t+1})$, it is sufficient to be able to find the enclosure for the above Boolean combination B. Since the Boolean combination B consists of sequential application of propositional connectives $\&$, $\vee$, and $\neg$, it is therefore sufficient to be able to solve the following three auxiliary problems:

- given the enclosure $\widetilde{\mathbf{p}}(F)$ for $\mathbf{p}(F)$, compute the enclosure $\widetilde{\mathbf{p}}(\neg F)$ for $\mathbf{p}(\neg F)$;
- given the enclosures $\widetilde{\mathbf{p}}(F_i)$ ($1 \le i \le n$) for the intervals $\mathbf{p}(F_i)$, compute the enclosure $\widetilde{\mathbf{p}}(F_1 \& \ldots \& F_n)$ for $\mathbf{p}(F_1 \& \ldots \& F_n)$;
- given the enclosures $\widetilde{\mathbf{p}}(F_i)$ ($1 \le i \le n$) for the intervals $\mathbf{p}(F_i)$, compute the enclosure $\widetilde{\mathbf{p}}(F_1 \vee \ldots \vee F_n)$ for $\mathbf{p}(F_1 \vee \ldots \vee F_n)$.

The following propositions solve these problems:

Proposition 1. *If* $\mathbf{p}(F) \subseteq \widetilde{\mathbf{p}}(F)$, *then*
$\mathbf{p}(\neg F) \subseteq \widetilde{\mathbf{p}}(\neg F) \stackrel{\text{def}}{=} [1 - \widetilde{p}^+(F), 1 - \widetilde{p}^-(F)]$.

Proposition 2. *If* $\mathbf{p}(F_i) \subseteq \widetilde{\mathbf{p}}(F_i)$ *for* $i = 1, \ldots, n$, *then*
$\mathbf{p}(F_1 \& \ldots \& F_n) \subseteq \widetilde{\mathbf{p}}(F_1 \& \ldots \& F_n) \stackrel{\text{def}}{=} [\max(0, \widetilde{p}^-(F_1) + \ldots + \widetilde{p}^-(F_n) - n + 1), \min(\widetilde{p}^+(F_1), \ldots, \widetilde{p}^+(F_n))]$, *and*
$\mathbf{p}(F_1 \vee \ldots \vee F_n) \subseteq \widetilde{\mathbf{p}}(F_1 \vee \ldots \vee F_n) \stackrel{\text{def}}{=} [\max(\widetilde{p}^-(F_1), \ldots, \widetilde{p}^-(F_n)), \min(1, \widetilde{p}^+(F_1) + \ldots + \widetilde{p}^+(F_n))]$.

One can prove that the estimates provided by Propositions 1, 2 are indeed the narrowest possible.

By using these estimates, we can find, step-by-step, the enclosure for $\mathbf{p}(f, s_{t+1})$ and thus, the desired enclosure for the interval $\mathbf{p}(f, s_n)$ which describes the probability of success in the final state.

Let us give a simple example. Let a domain description D consist of the following three rules: a causes f if g, h; a causes f if k; a causes $\neg f$ if j, k. The objective is f, the checked plan consists of the single action a. In this case, the validity of f at the final moment of time s_1 is equivalent to the validity of the following propositional formula at the moment s_0: $(g \& h) \vee k \vee \{f \& \neg[j \& k]\}$. If initially, $\mathbf{p}(f, s_0) = [0.1, 0.2]$, $\mathbf{p}(g, s_0) = [0.7, 0.9]$, $\mathbf{p}(h, s_0) = [0.6, 0.7]$, $\mathbf{p}(j, s_0) = [0.2, 0.3]$, and $\mathbf{p}(k, s_0) = [0.7, 0.9]$, then we can compute the enclosure $\widetilde{\mathbf{p}}(f, s_1)$ as follows:

- $\widetilde{\mathbf{p}}(g \& h, s) = [\max(0, 0.7 + 0.6 - 1), \min(0.9, 0.7)] = [0.3, 0.7]$;
- $\widetilde{\mathbf{p}}(j \& k, s_1) = [\max(0, 0.2 + 0.4 - 1), \min(0.3, 0.6)] = [0, 0.3]$;
- $\widetilde{\mathbf{p}}(\neg[j \& k], s) = [1 - 0, 1 - 0.3] = [0.7, 1]$;
- $\widetilde{\mathbf{p}}(f \& \neg[j \& k], s) = [\max(0, 0.1 + 0.7 - 1), \min(0.2, 1)] = [0, 0.2]$;
- $\widetilde{\mathbf{p}}((g \& h) \vee k) \vee \{f \& \neg[j \& k]\}) = [\max(0.3, 0.7, 0), \min(1, 0.7 + 0.9 + 0.2)] = [0.7, 1]$.

Thus, if $p_0 \le 0.7$, this plan is successful; otherwise, we cannot guarantee its success with a given probability.

The soundness of the above algorithm can be formulated in precise terms:

Definition 1. *By a planning problem, we mean the tuple* $\langle \mathcal{F}, \mathcal{A}, D, \{\mathbf{p}(f, s_0)\}_{f \in \mathcal{F}}, f, p_0 \rangle$, *where:*
- $\mathcal{F}$ *is a finite set whose elements are called fluents;*
- $\mathcal{A}$ *is a finite set whose elements are called actions;*
- D *is a finite set of expression of the type "a causes F if $F_1, \ldots, F_m$", where F and F_i are fluent literals, i.e., fluents or their negations;*
- *each* $\mathbf{p}(f, s_0)$ *is a sub-interval of the interval* $[0, 1]$;
- $f \in \mathcal{F}$ *is called objective, and* $p_0 \in [0, 1]$.

A sequence of actions $\alpha = [a_1, \ldots, a_n]$ *is called a plan.*

By a plan checking problem we mean a pair consisting of a planning problem and a plan α.

We say that a probability distribution P on the set of all initial states is consistent with the planning problem if $P(f) \in \mathbf{p}(f, s_0)$ *for every fluent* f.

We say that a plan is successful if $p(f, res(\alpha, s_0)) \ge p_0$ *for every probability distribution P with is consistent with the planning problem.*

Proposition 3. *For every plan checking problem, for every probability distribution P on the set of all initial states which is consistent with the given interval probabilities, the probability* $P(f, res(\alpha, s_0))$ *is contained in the interval* $\widetilde{\mathbf{p}}(f, s_n)$ *computed by the above algorithm.*

(Proof is by induction over the length of the plan, similarly to the proof about 0-approximation.)

Corollary. *If the above algorithm tells that the plan is successful (i.e., if* $\widetilde{p}^-(f, s_n) \ge p_0$), *then this plan is indeed successful.*

Definition 2. *We say that a planning problem corresponds to incomplete information if for every fluent f, the interval* $\mathbf{p}(f, s_0)$ *is equal to* $[0, 0]$, $[1, 1]$, *or* $[0, 1]$.

Proposition 4. *For planning problems corresponding to incomplete information, the above algorithm coincides with the 0-approximation algorithm.*

Comments.

1) For degenerate intervals $\widetilde{\mathbf{p}}(F_i) = [p_i, p_i]$, we get $[\max(p_1 + p_2 - 1, 0), \min(p_1, p_2)]$ as $\widetilde{\mathbf{p}}(F_1 \& F_2)$, and $[\max(p_1, p_2), \min(1, p_1 + p_2)]$ for $\vee$. Both lower and upper bounds are particular cases of the operations used in the fuzzy approach (Congdon et al. 1993; Saffiotti et al. 1995); thus, we get a new justification for this approach.

2) The above step-by-step approach to getting guaranteed estimates can be viewed as a particular case of *interval computations*, i.e., computations in which the

input is only known with interval uncertainty (see, e.g., (Hammer et al. 1993; Kearfott et al. 1996)). Interval computations have been used, together with more traditional AI techniques, to produce a robot which won 1st place at the AAAI'97 robot competition (Baral and Son 1997a; Baral et al. 1998; Morales et al. 1998).

3) Estimates obtained by using interval computations are often overestimations, because when we compute the probability intervals for the next moment of time, we assume that the previous intervals are "independent", while in reality, they come from the same source and may therefore be dependent. For example, if we have two rules "a causes f if f_1" and "a causes f if $\neg f_1$", with $p(f_1, s_0) = [0.6, 0.7]$ and with f initially false, then after the action a, f is always true ($\mathbf{p}(f, s_1) = [1,1]$). In this case, our algorithm finds f as $f_1 \vee \neg f_1$, so we get $\widetilde{\mathbf{p}}(\neg f_1, s_0) = [0.3, 0.4]$, and $\widetilde{\mathbf{p}}(f, s_1) = [\max(0.6, 0.3), \min(0.6+0.4, 1)] = [0.6, 1]$. To take this dependence into consideration, we can use *generalized* (affine) interval computations (Hansen 1975).

4) If we are sure that all the probabilities are independent, then we can use a feasible technique – Monte-Carlo simulations (see, e.g., (Kreinovich et al. 1994)).

Conclusions

In this paper, we show that methods of interval computations can be used to get a feasible approximation to plan checking under probabilistic uncertainty. The resulting method is a natural generalization of 0-approximation proposed earlier to describe planning in the case of partial knowledge. It turns out that some of the resulting probabilistic techniques coincides with heuristically proposed "fuzzy" methods. Thus, we justify these fuzzy heuristics as a reasonable feasible approximation to the (NP-hard) probabilistic problem.

Acknowledgments

This work was supported in part by NASA grant NCC5-209, by NSF grants DUE-9750858 and CDA-9522207, by United Space Alliance grant NAS 9-20000 (PWO C0C67713A6), by the US Air Force grant F49620-95-1-0518, and by the National Security Agency grant MDA904-98-1-0561.

The authors are thankful to anonymous referees for valuable comments.

References

J. Allen, J. Hendler, A. Tate, *Readings in Planning*, Morgan Kauffman, San Mateo, CA, 1990.

C. Baral et al., "From theory to practice: The UTEP robot in AAAI 96 and AAAI 97 robot contests", *Proc. 2nd International Conference on Autonomous Agents (Agents'98)*, 1998, pp. 32–38.

C. Baral, V. Kreinovich, and R. Trejo, "Computational complexity of planning and approximate planning in presence of incompleteness", in: *Proc. IJCAI'99*, Vol. 2, pp. 948–953 (full text to appear in *Artificial Intelligence*).

C. Baral and T. Son, "Approximate reasoning about actions in presence of sensing and incomplete information", In: *Proc. of International Logic Programming Symposium (ILPS'97)*, 1997, pp. 387–401.

C. Baral and T. Son, "Regular and special sensing in robot control – relation with action theories", *Proc. AAAI 97 Workshop on Robots, Softbots, and Immobots – Theories of Action, Planning and Control*, 1997a.

C. Congdon et al., "Carmel vs. Flakey: A comparison of two winners," *AI Magazine*, 1993, Vol. 14, No. 1, pp. 49–57.

A. Doan and P. Haddawy, "Sound Abstraction of Probabilistic Actions in the Constraint Mass Assignment Framework", *Proc. UAI'96*, pp. 228–235.

D. Draper and S. Hanks, "Localized Partial Evaluation of Belief Networks", *Proc. UAI'94*.

R. Givan, S. Leach, and T. Dean, "Bounded parameter Markov decision processes", *Proc. 4th European Conference on Planning*, Toulouse, France, 1997.

R. Hammer et al., *Numerical Toolbox for Verified Computing I*, Springer-Verlag, 1993.

E. R. Hansen, "A generalized interval arithmetic", In: K. Nickel (ed.), *Interval mathematics*, Lecture Notes in Computer Science, 1975, Vol. 29, pp. 7–18.

H. Geffner and B. Bonet, "High-Level Planning and Control with Incomplete Information Using POMDPs", *Proc. AIPS-98 Workshop on Integrating Planning, Scheduling and Execution in Dynamic and Uncertain Environments*, 1998.

L. P. Kaelbling, M. L. Littman, and A. R. Cassandra, "Planning and acting in partially observable stochastic domains", *Artificial Intelligence*, 1998, Vol. 101, pp. 99–134.

R. B. Kearfott and V. Kreinovich (eds.), *Applications of Interval Computations*, Kluwer, Dordrecht, 1996.

V. Kreinovich et al., "Monte-Carlo methods make Dempster-Shafer formalism feasible." In R. R. Yager et al. (Eds.), *Advances in the Dempster-Shafer Theory of Evidence*, Wiley, N.Y., 1994, pp. 175–191.

M. L. Littman, J. Goldsmith, and M. Mundhenk, "The Computational Complexity of Probabilistic Planning", *JAIR*, 1998, Vol. 9, pp. 1–36.

J. D. Lowrance and D. E. Wilkins, "Plan evaluation under uncertainty," *Proc. Workshop on Innovative Approaches to Planning, Scheduling and Control*, Morgan Kaufmann, San Francisco, 1990, pp. 439–449.

D. Morales and Tran Cao Son, "Interval Methods in Robot Navigation", *Reliable Computing*, 1998, Vol. 4, No. 1, pp. 55–61.

A. Saffiotti, K. Konolige, and E. H. Ruspini, "A multivalued-logic approach to integrating planning and control", *Artificial Intelligence*, 1995, Vol. 76, No. 1–2, pp. 481–526.

Machine Learning
and Data Mining

ADVISOR: A machine learning architecture for intelligent tutor construction

Joseph E. Beck and **Beverly Park Woolf**
Computer Science Department
University of Massachusetts
Amherst, MA 01003
USA
{beck, bev}@cs.umass.edu

Carole R. Beal
Psychology Department
University of Massachusetts
Amherst, MA 01003
USA
cbeal@psych.umass.edu

Abstract

We have constructed ADVISOR, a two-agent machine learning architecture for intelligent tutoring systems (ITS). The purpose of this architecture is to centralize the reasoning of an ITS into a single component to allow customization of teaching goals and to simplify improving the ITS. The first agent is responsible for learning a model of how students perform using the tutor in a variety of contexts. The second agent is provided this model of student behavior and a goal specifying the desired educational objective. Reinforcement learning is used by this agent to derive a teaching policy that meets the specified educational goal. Component evaluation studies show each agent performs adequately in isolation. We have also conducted an evaluation with actual students of the complete architecture. Results show ADVISOR was successful in learning a teaching policy that met the educational objective provided. Although this set of machine learning agents has been integrated with a specific intelligent tutor, the general technique could be applied to a broad class of ITS.

Introduction

AnimalWatch is an intelligent tutor for teaching arithmetic to grade school students. The goal of the tutor is to improve girls' self-confidence in their ability to do math, with the long-term goal of increasing the number of women in mathematical and scientific occupations. AnimalWatch has been shown to increase the self-confidence of girls who use it. The tutor maintains a student model of how students perform for each topic in the domain, and uses this model to select a topic to present to the student, to construct a problem at the appropriate level of difficulty for the student, and to customize feedback. This adaptation is done using a set of teaching heuristics.

A major factor contributing to women's lower participation in science, engineering and mathematics careers is that, beginning in junior high school, many girls begin to doubt their ability to learn mathematics(Beller & Gafni 1996). As a result, girls are typically more likely than boys to progress no further in mathematics than eighth grade algebra, and are subsequently under-prepared for many science and math-intensive majors and programs at the university and graduate school levels. This project focuses on development of an intelligent tutor to provide effective, confidence-enhancing mathematics instruction for girls in elementary school.

We have constructed a learning agent that models student behavior at a coarse level of granularity for a mathematics tutor. Rather than focusing on whether the student knows a particular piece of knowledge, the learning agent determines how likely the student is to answer a problem correctly and how long he will take to generate this response. To construct this model, we used traces from previous users of the tutor to train the machine learning (ML) agent. This model is combined with a reinforcement learning agent to produce a configurable teaching policy.

Research goals and previous work

Intelligent tutoring systems (ITS) have not been integrated into schools and corporate training as rapidly as would be expected. One reason for this is the lack of configurability of such systems by organizations deploying ITS(Bloom 1996). Once constructed, an ITS's performance is fixed. Also, the cost to construct ITS is very high, both in terms of number of hours required, and the amount of expertise needed. Our high-level goal is to reduce the amount of knowledge engineering (and expert knowledge) needed to construct an ITS and to make the tutor's teaching goals parameterized so they can be altered as needed. Machine learning is a useful technique for automating knowledge engineering tasks and improving adaptivity.

A second goal is to make a tutor's reasoning defensible. Currently, most teaching decisions are made by cognitive and/or pedagogical theories that may or may not have been well-evaluated, and almost certainly have not been extensively studied in the context of an ITS. We aim to bypass this step, and instead direct decision making by relying on observational data of students using intelligent tutors. A potential advantage of this architecture is to centralize the tutor's reasoning in one component. Research that improves this single piece affects the entire ITS.

There has been some progress made at using ML to simplify ITS construction. The ASSERT system(Baffes & Mooney 1996) used theory refinement to automatically construct buggy rules, and could build teaching examples

Copyright © 2000, American Association for Artificial Intelligence (www.aaai.org). All rights reserved.

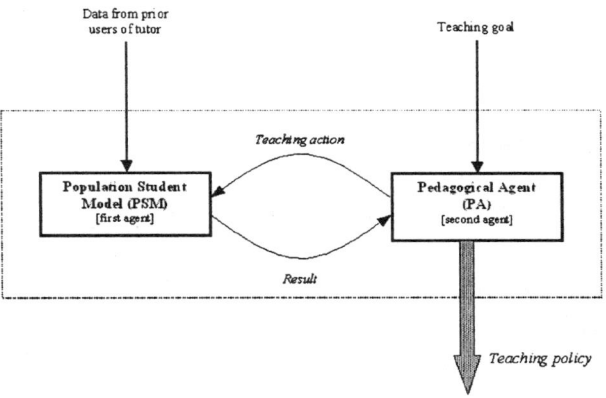

Figure 1: Overview of ADVISOR architecture.

to show students the fallacy behind their misconceptions. Given the typical difficulty in compiling bug lists(Burton 1982), this could be a substantial savings. Work on Input Output Agent modeling (IOAM)(Chiu & Webb 1998) has used ML to accurately predict mistakes students will make solving subtraction problems.

ANDES(Gertner, Conati, & VanLehn 1998) constructs a Bayesian network that represents a solution to the physics problem on which the student is working, and uses this network to recognize the student's plan(Conati et al. 1997) and determine on which skills he needs help(Gertner, Conati, & VanLehn 1998). This is a excellent example of using a single reasoning mechanism for many decisions within an ITS, and of principled reasoning techniques to direct teaching.

Architecture

To achieve our research goals, we constructed ADVISOR, which is a set of ML agents that learn how to teach students. Figure 1 provides an overview of this process. First, students using AnimalWatch are observed, and these data provided to a learning agent that models student behavior. This Population Student Model (PSM) is responsible for taking a context, and predicting how students will act in this situation.

The second component is the pedagogical agent (PA), that is given a high-level learning goal and the PSM. An example of such a high-level goal is "Students should make precisely 1 mistake per problem." Students making fewer than one mistake may not be sufficiently challenged, while those making too many mistakes may become frustrated. The PA's task is to experiment with the PSM to find a teaching policy that will meet the provided teaching goal.

The area contained in the dashed box represents a simulation that will occur several times during training before actual students use the tutor. The pedagogical agent considers a teaching action (selecting a particular topic, constructing a certain problem, or providing certain feedback) and observes how the simulation of the student reacts to this event. After learning which actions under which conditions meet the teaching goal and which do not, it outputs a teaching policy for the AnimalWatch tutor to use with real students. We define a teaching policy as a function that maps the current state of the tutor and student to a teaching action. Thus, from a given situation, the teaching policy can be used to direct all of the tutor's decision making. Currently, AnimalWatch's teaching policy is implemented with a set of heuristics. Our goal is to replace this with an ML-derived policy.

Population model

The purpose of the population model is to take as input a particular situation, and determine how the student would behave in that situation. Viewed this way, it is an executable student model. Combined with a tutoring system, this executable student model can act as a simulated student, or simulee(VanLehn, Ohlsson, & Nason 1994).

Constructing the PSM Building the PSM requires a database of prior users of the tutor. We have deployed AnimalWatch for two previous studies; one in a fourth-grade classroom (9 year olds), the other in a fifth-grade (10 year olds) classroom. When the student is presented with an opportunity to provide an answer, the system takes a "snap shot" of its current state. This picture consists of information from 4 main areas:

1. **Student:** The student's level of prior proficiency and level of cognitive development(Arroyo et al. 1999)
2. **Topic:** The difficulty of the current topic and the type of mathematics operand/operators.
3. **Problem:** The difficulty of the current problem.
4. **Context:** The student's current efforts at answering this question, and the hints he has seen.

After the student makes his next response, the system records the time he required to make this response and whether it was correct. These two pieces of information, time to respond and correctness of response, are what the learning agent will predict. We gathered 11,000 training instances from the previous deployments of AnimalWatch.

The above information specifies the inputs and outputs of the learning agent. For a function approximator, we used linear regression (after trying naive Bayesian classifiers and decision trees). Linear regression allows quick experimentation with models (unlike gradient descent techniques, which can take substantial time to learn), and works well with continuous variables. There were two regression models. Each took as input 48 features from the above 4 categories. The first model output the expected amount of time the student would require to generate his *next* response (in logmilliseconds). The second model output the probability the student's *next* response would be correct. Note, the model does not try to predict the student's longer term performance on the current problem, only his immediate action.

Validating the PSM To determine if the PSM is sufficiently accurate, we compare its predictions to how the students in the training dataset actually performed. Figure 2 shows its accuracy for predicting how long students required to generate a response, the PSM's predictions correlated at 0.629 ($R^2 \approx 0.4$) with actual performance. Training on half the dataset and testing on the other half dropped this correlation to 0.619, which is still very strong for predicting as noisy a variable as time.

The PSM is also responsible for predicting whether the student's response will be correct. Figure 3 shows the

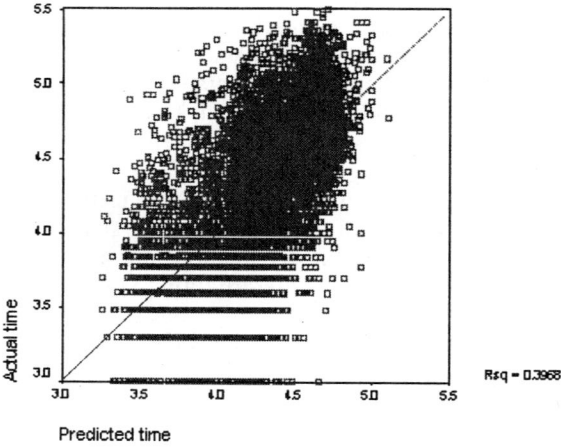

Figure 2: Accuracy for predicting response time

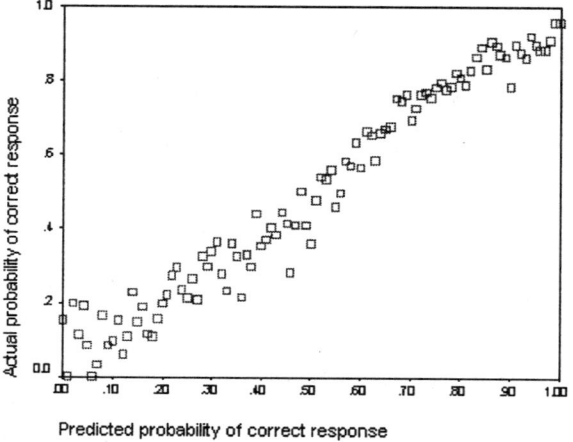

Figure 3: Accuracy for predicting response correctness.

model's performance at this task. The data were binned, so (for example) the right-most datapoint refers to cases where the model thought there was a probability of 1.0 the student would answer a question correctly. In these cases, there was roughly a 0.95 probability the student would generate a correct response. Interestingly, this model only correlates at 0.484 (0.481 with split-half validation) with the student's actual performance, for an $R^2 \approx 0.23$. Figure 3's correlation is much higher, but this is for averaged, not individual student performance.

In Figure 3, if the model were perfectly accurate, there should be no datapoints aside from those at 0.0 (leftmost edge of x-axis) and 1.0 (rightmost edge of x-axis). Students either generate a correct response or an incorrect response, there is no middle ground. So for individual cases, the PSM may be inaccurate. However, averaged across similar cases, the PSM's performance at predicting correctness is quite good. For making critical, stand alone predictions, this is not acceptable. As part of a simulation that uses millions of simulated trajectories, it seems to be adequate to have a probabilistic model such as this.

Pedagogical agent

The pedagogical agent (PA) uses the simulation of the student as described by the PSM, and experiments with different teaching policies to achieve an externally provided teaching goal.

An interesting question is why the pedagogical agent is needed. Why not use the PSM to directly learn/predict the relevant teaching goal in question? If the goal is for the student to make one mistake per problem, simply have the PSM predict the number of future mistakes. The difficulty with this is that the PSM's observations come under a particular teaching policy. If this teaching policy changes, the PSM's long-term predictions become worthless. Consider a PSM that is trained by observing a tutor that never provides any feedback. When asked to predict how many mistakes a student will make on a problem, its estimate will be very high, particularly if the teaching policy has changed so the tutor now provides feedback. Given that we are using training data from a tutor that probably has different teaching goals, and consequently a different teaching policy, this situation is not acceptable.

Thus, the PSM only makes short range predictions: "if the student has knowledge K, is working on problem P, has seen hints h1 and h2, and is now provided hint H → he will answer correctly with probability P after time T." A prediction of this form is *independent* of the teaching policy used by the tutor. The PSM is not interested why the student and tutor are in this situation, or indeed, what will happen afterwards. All the PSM is asked to predict is what the student will do immediately from this situation. Thus, the PSM is used to generate a model of state transitions that describe student behavior.

Constructing the pedagogical agent The pedagogical agent is a reinforcement learning (RL)(Sutton & Barto 1998) agent. RL can operate with a model of the environment (the Population Student Model), and a reward function (the pedagogical goal the agent is trying to achieve). This architecture of using a simulation is similar to that used in other complex RL tasks such as TD-gammon(Tesauro 1995) and elevator dispatching(Crites & Barto 1998).

For our RL mechanism, we decided to use temporal-difference (TD) learning(Sutton & Barto 1998). Specifically, TD(0) with state-value learning. The benefit of state-value learning is that there may be several actions that result in a similar state (e.g. the student gets the right answer in a small amount of time), and it is efficient to learn about these together. This is particularly relevant if the agent is trying to learn about the student in real-time.

We gave our first deployable PA the goal of minimizing the amount of time students require to solve a problem. This should result in the PA selecting easier topics, building easier problems, and not giving hints that will slow down the student's problem solving efforts (such as a long-winded interactive hint, when the student has made a minor mistake).

This goal (i.e. reward function for the RL agent) was chosen since it is relatively straightforward to optimize, and should not be a troublesome policy for actual students to use.

Specifically, when the (simulated) student solved a problem, the RL agent was given a reward inversely proportional to the amount of time the student required to solve the problem. Thus, this is a bounded horizon task, and discounting is not required. During training, the PA used ϵ-greedy exploration. This means that a certain percentage of the time, the PA selected a random action rather than the one it thought best. This helped prevent the PA from getting stuck in a locally good, but globally sub-optimal policy. Over time, ϵ was gradually reduced. Once the agent was deployed in the "real-world", however, ϵ was set to 0.

The PA used a linear function approximator to map the state to a future expected reward. This was used for all of the tutor's decision-making. E.g. to select a hint, the tutor would add the information about the topic, problem, and student's current efforts to the state. Combining the information about each possible hint with the current state, it would query the PSM to determine how a student would likely respond to the hint. The output of the PSM was given to the linear function approximator that predicted future expected reward, and the action corresponding to whichever "afterstate" had the highest value was selected.

Validating the pedagogical agent To determine if the pedagogical agent would interact correctly with the PSM, we constructed a simulation. This simulation contained all of the typical steps in a tutoring session. First the PA selected a topic and a problem. The PSM was then invoked to see if the student would make a mistake or answer correctly. In event of an incorrect answer, the PA was responsible for finding the hint that appeared best. From the PA's standpoint, this was identical to interacting with an actual student.

Figure 4 shows the improvement of the PA's performance at minimizing the amount of time students spent per problem. The x-axis is the number of trials (in thousands) the agent has spent learning. The y-axis is the exponential average of the amount of time the simulated student required to solve a problem. Performance started at around 40 seconds per problem, and eventually reduced to around 16 seconds per problem.

Compromises

Ideally, ADVISOR would have complete control over AnimalWatch's teaching actions. However, there were two difficulties with this. First, there was a limit on how frequently students could see a particular word problem template. Templates are skeletons for word problems, and problems are dynamically created with numbers in a range specified by the template. If all of the templates for a particular topic had been seen recently, the tutor was not permitted to select that topic. Furthermore, when ADVISOR's goal is to minimize the amount of time per problem, it has a tendency to select templates that involve small numbers. There is a limited supply of such templates. Thus, with with some probability (currently 0.1), the tutor uses a random level of difficulty to

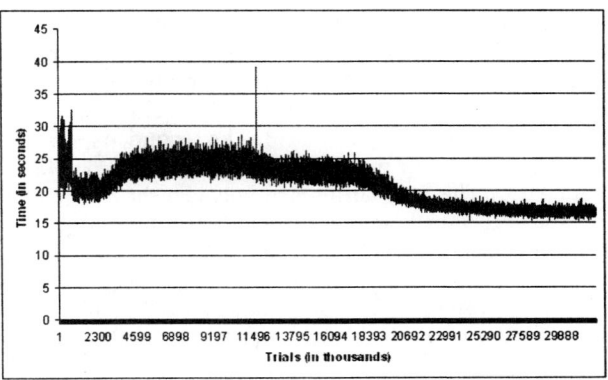

Figure 4: Improvement of pedagogical agent.

select a problem template. These issues are not the fault of the AI components, but rather result from our limited number of templates; as more are entered these restrictions can be removed.

Second, the classic AnimalWatch tutor only selects topics for which the student is "ready" (i.e. has not mastered, but has some understanding of the prerequisites). All of the training data provided to the PSM were biased in this manner. That is, there were no instances of students being shown a topic for which they did not understand the prerequisites. This makes it difficult for the PA to predict how students will react when presented with a problem for which they are not prepared. We had difficulty finding a graceful solution to this, and ultimately compromised. When using ADVISOR, the list of topics would first be screened so that only "ready" topics were considered. ADVISOR then used its standard decision-making strategies on this abridged list of topics. This difficulty is more fundamental to the AI architecture. By combining short- and long-range prediction agents, our architecture allows training data to be generalized to novel situations. However, it is unclear how to resolve such severe biases in the training data.

Validating ADVISOR

Given that both the PSM and PA have been validated, it is still necessary to the combined ADVISOR architecture. It is possible that the simulation of the PA and PSM working together is incorrect. Therefore, we performed an evaluation study comparing the performance of the classic AnimalWatch tutor with an ML version whose goal was to minimize the amount of time per problem. A possible objection is that time explicitly appears in the PSM, so is not an interesting choice for a reward. However, it is difficult to conceive of a reward that does not appear in the PSM. If the PA is being rewarded for something that cannot be directly observed, the question arises as to how the reward signal is generated. If the PA is rewarded for an observable event (such as time per problem), why not have the PSM predict (a version of) this to improve the model's accuracy?

This experiment was conducted with an urban, sixth grade class in a magnet school for students in the arts. This is in contrast to our earlier studies, which were used to construct the PSM, which utilized rural/suburban fourth and fifth grade students. Students were randomly assigned to one of two groups. One condition used the classic AnimalWatch tutor and served as a control. The second, experimental, group used a tutor which reasoned using the ADVISOR architecture. The only difference between the two conditions was the AI method used for selecting topics, problems, and feedback. Students were assigned to an experimental condition based on where they sat on the first day. To avoid problems with similar students sitting near each other, physically adjacent computers were in opposite conditions (e.g. experimental, control, experimental, control, ...). Unfortunately, classes did not fill the entire lab, so some machines were unused. We wound up with a split of 60% of the students using the ML version (N=58), and 40% (N=39) using classic AnimalWatch.

Results

Students taught with ADVISOR averaged 27.7 seconds to solve a problem, while students using the classic version of AnimalWatch averaged 39.7 seconds. This difference was significant at P<0.001 (P≈ 10^{-23} (2-tailed t-test)). Just as important, the difference is meaningful: reducing average times by 30% is a large reduction. Thus, the agent made noticeable progress in its goal of reducing the amount of time students spent per problem. We are not arguing this is necessarily the best pedagogical goal, just what we asked the agent to do.

To ensure that students in each condition were equally balanced with respect to math/computer ability, we examined their scores on a Piaget test of cognitive ability and their performance on the first problem seen using the tutor. The Piaget test has been found to correlate with both with speed and accuracy of problem solving on our tutor. Students in the control group had an average score of 6.7 (out of 10), while students in the experimental group had an average score of 6.6. This difference is insignificant (P=0.73, 2-tailed t-test).

Another metric for ensuring students were equally balanced is to examine first problem performance. The first problems students see (in both groups) is very easy, and almost always an addition of whole numbers problem. Thus, differences in time are largely a function of how experienced students are at learning a new interface as well as their math ability. Students in the control group required 59.8 seconds to solve the first problem, while students in the experimental group required 64.3 seconds. This difference is not significant (P= 0.63, 2-tailed t-test). Thus we feel safe in assuming the students in the two groups did not significantly differ in their incoming math abilities.

Further evidence of ADVISOR's ability to adapt instruction can be seen in Table 1. Students in the experimental group solved whole (P<0.001) and fraction problems (P=0.02) significantly faster than students in the control group. Prefraction problems are relatively homogeneous, so it is difficult to improve speed much on these. Students in the experimental group saw relatively fewer whole number, but more prefraction and fraction problems. Experimental

		Control	Experimental
Whole	Percentage	73.6%	60.0%
	Time	43.4 sec	**28.1 sec**
Prefract	Percentage	19.3%	27.3%
	Time	22.7 sec	21.7 sec
Fraction	Percentage	7.2%	12.7%
	Time	44.5 sec	**38.5 sec**

Table 1: Summary of performance by topic area.

group students saw more fractions problems, even though such problems take more time on average, because of the restriction AnimalWatch placed on topic selection. Experimental group students finished the whole number and prefraction topics relatively quickly, so were forced to work on fraction problems (as these were the only "ready" topics).

Particularly impressive is that experimental group students were faster at solving fraction problems in spite of having a significantly lower Piaget score. Students in the control group *who got to fraction problems* averaged a Piaget score of 7.9, while students in the experimental group averaged 7.3; this difference is significant at P<0.001. Thus, in spite of being less restrictive about which students saw fraction (i.e. difficult) problems, the experimental group was still able to get through such problems more quickly.

Conclusions

We have constructed an intelligent tutor that makes its teaching decisions using a novel AI architecture. The ADVISOR architecture first learns a model of how the population of students performs using the tutor. Then this model is used to train an RL agent that is responsible for attaining a predefined teaching goal. Due to the state representation we have chosen, it is possible to train the RL agent with data obtained from a tutor that uses a different teaching strategy. It is also possible to generalize learned policies across different populations, as our agents were trained with rural fourth- and fifth-graders but were tested with urban sixth graders.

We have evaluated each component of our architecture in isolation and found performance to be acceptable. Our evaluation study of the entire architecture with students showed that it learned a teaching policy that resulted in students correctly answering questions in a reduced amount of time (compared to the traditional tutor). This provides evidence that it has learned to optimize its teaching to meet the specified goal. For our first experiments with ADVISOR we used a fairly straightforward goal. Allowing for more general teaching goals is part of our future work.

This combination of the PSM and PA is used by ADVISOR to make all of its teaching decisions. This is advantageous, since as we make progress at improving these agents, all of the tutor's teaching becomes more accurate and/or more adaptive. Although these agents have been constructed and evaluated within the context of AnimalWatch, the general architecture should apply to other intelligent tutors.

Data-driven techniques for tutor construction are becoming more feasible. Ten years ago, the idea of 11,000 training instances and evaluation studies with 100 students would have been unrealistic. As studies become larger, it becomes less necessary to rely on pedagogical theory to guide decision-making and more possible to directly construct models from statistical patterns in the data. Such models appear to generalize across populations, as the PSM and PA were constructed with a different population of students than those who used the final ML tutor.

Future work

Our future goals include improving the performance of the PSM and PA. The PSM is accurate at predicting time, and somewhat accurate at predicting the correctness of student responses. A more sophisticated function approximation technique, such as neural networks, could result in increased accuracy. This strategy also applies to the PA, which could benefit from a more general learning scheme.

We are also investigating improving performance via on-line, real-time learning. This would enhance the tutor's adaptivity. The tutor records how students perform when using the tutor–in fact it saves the same state information that was used to generate the PSM. However, the PSM is not being updated online. What is needed is some means of integrating the current student's actions with the PSM, while giving these actions higher weight (otherwise the thousands of datapoints from the population will swamp any information about the individual student).

Even if the PSM can be updated online, it is necessary to modify the pedagogical agent's teaching policy to reflect this. This is the technically more challenging task. Reinforcement learning takes many CPU cycles to converge. Given that we are running on fairly typical classroom computers, valid questions are how much learning can we hope to achieve in a short amount of time, and how can we ensure the online learning does not interfere with the response time of the tutor. Prior research has shown benefits to adding information from individual students to population models(Beck & Woolf 1998). However, we have not yet found methods for updating the teaching policy while the student is using the tutor.

ADVISOR adapted its teaching to fit a (relatively) straightforward goal: "minimize the amount of time students spend on a problem." More complicated goals would both be a tougher test of the architecture, but more pedagogically useful. For instance, a system that receives its highest reward for students taking 30 to 45 seconds per problem would probably do a better job at keeping the problems "hard enough" for students. However, such goals are more difficult to learn, but should not require major adjustment to our architecture. We hope to achieve this by scaling up the pedagogical agent with more complicated learning mechanisms for our PSM and PA.

A more ambitious plan is to allow larger-scale teaching goals to be provided to the PA. Currently, goals must be phrased on a per-problem level. Ideally, it would be possible to provide goals such as, "Have the students master prefractions material as quickly as possible." This is beyond the scope of our simulation used to train the PSM and PA. Scaling up this simulation to work across multiple problems, and allowing reward to be (very) delayed is a challenging task.

Acknowledgements

This work has been funded by the National Science Foundation program HRD 9714757. Any opinions, findings, and conclusions or recommendations expressed in this material are those of the authors and do not necessarily reflect the views of the National Science Foundation. We acknowledge the contributions of David Marshall in the implementation of AnimalWatch, and Ivon Arroyo for her work with implementation and design of AnimalWatch's hinting.

References

Arroyo, I.; Beck, J. E.; Schultz, K.; and Woolf. 1999. Piagetian psychology in intelligent tutoring systems. In *Proceedings of the Ninth International Conference on Artificial Intelligence in Education*.

Baffes, P., and Mooney, R. 1996. A novel application of theory refinement to student modeling. In *Proceedings of American Association for Artificial Intelligence*, 403–408.

Beck, J. E., and Woolf, B. P. 1998. Using a learning agent with a student model. In *Proceedings Fourth International Conference on Intelligent Tutoring Systems*, 6–15.

Beller, M., and Gafni, N. 1996. The 1991 international assessment of educational progress in mathematics and sciences: The gender differences perspective. *Journal of Educational Psychology* 88:365–377.

Bloom, C. P. 1996. Promoting the transfer of adanced training technologies. In Frasson, C.; Gauthier, G.; and Lesgold, A., eds., *Proceedings of Third International Conference on Intelligent Tutoring Systems*, 1–10. Springer.

Burton, R. 1982. Diagnosing bugs in a simple procedural skill. In Sleeman, and Brown., eds., *Intelligent Tutoring Systems*, 157–182. Academic Press.

Chiu, B. C., and Webb, G. I. 1998. Using decision trees for agent modeling: Improving prediction performance. *User Modeling and User Adapted Interaction* 8(1-2):131–152.

Conati, C.; Gertner, A.; VanLehn, K.; and Druzdel, M. 1997. On-line student modeling for coached problem solving using bayesian networks. In *Proceedings of the Seventh International Conference on User Modeling*, 231–242.

Crites, R., and Barto, A. 1998. Elevator group control using multiple reinforcement learning agents. *Machine Learning* 33:235–262.

Gertner, A. S.; Conati, C.; and VanLehn, K. 1998. Procedural help in ANDES: Generating hints using a Bayesian network student model. In *Fifteenth National Conference on Artificial Intelligence*, 106–111.

Sutton, R., and Barto, A. 1998. *An Introduction to Reinforcement Learning*. MIT Press.

Tesauro, G. 1995. Temporal difference learning and TD-Gammon. *Communications of the ACM* 38(3).

VanLehn, K.; Ohlsson, S.; and Nason, R. 1994. Applications of simulated students: An exploration. *Journal of Artificial Intelligence in Education* 5(2):135–175.

Automatic Invention of Integer Sequences

Simon Colton, Alan Bundy
Mathematical Reasoning Group
Division of Informatics
University of Edinburgh
80 South Bridge
Edinburgh EH1 1HN
United Kingdom
simonco,bundy@dai.ed.ac.uk

Toby Walsh
Department of Computer Science
University of York
Heslington
York YO10 5DD
United Kingdom
tw@cs.york.ac.uk

Abstract

We report on the application of the HR program (Colton, Bundy, & Walsh 1999) to the problem of automatically inventing integer sequences. Seventeen sequences invented by HR are interesting enough to have been accepted into the Encyclopedia of Integer Sequences (Sloane 2000) and all were supplied with interesting conjectures about their nature, also discovered by HR. By extending HR, we have enabled it to perform a two stage process of invention and investigation. This involves generating both the definition and terms of a new sequence, relating it to sequences already in the Encyclopedia and pruning the output to help identify the most surprising and interesting results.

Introduction

An integer sequence is an ordered set of integers such as the square numbers: $1, 4, 9, 16, \ldots$ Integer sequences arise in many area of mathematics, and comprise an important subject area. The Encyclopedia of Integer Sequences (Sloane 2000) is an on-line repository of around 54,000 sequences collected over 35 years by Neil Sloane, with contributions from many mathematicians. To allow a sequence into the Encyclopedia, Sloane stipulates that it must be an infinite sequence of positive integers which is well defined and interesting. This rules out any randomly generated sequences which have no formula and many dull sequences which have no interesting features. Each sequence is given an 'A'-number which uniquely identifies it within the Encyclopedia, for instance the square numbers have number A000290.

We have used the HR program (Colton, Bundy, & Walsh 1999) to invent new integer sequences worthy of the Encyclopedia. HR performs theory formation in domains such as number theory, graph theory and group theory by inventing concepts and making and settling conjectures. We present here extensions to HR's abilities in number theory. Firstly, number theory concepts are presented as integer sequences, eg. the concept of an integer being prime is converted into the sequence of prime numbers. Next, taking advantage of the natural ordering of integers, we have given HR new ways to produce number theory concepts. Finally, we have enabled HR to provide justification why a new sequence is worthy of the Encyclopedia by relating it to sequences already in the Encyclopedia. Sometimes the relationships found are surprising and non-trivial to prove which adds to the interestingness of the new sequence. HR therefore employs a two step process to find new sequences:

- A sequence is invented by generating a definition and determining the first terms of the sequence.
- The sequence is investigated by relating it to ones already appearing in the Encyclopedia.

Invention of Sequences

The HR Program

HR is named after mathematicians Hardy (1877-1947) and Ramanujan (1887-1920). It is designed to model how mathematical theories can be formed from only the most fundamental concepts of a domain, such as addition and multiplication in number theory. HR is supplied with (a) some objects of interest such as groups, graphs or integers (b) some ways to decompose these into sub-objects, such as graphs into nodes, and (c) some relations between the sub-objects, such as nodes being adjacent.

Each initial concept is supplied with a data table of rows which satisfy a predicate, and a definition for the predicate. The first column of every data table contains objects of interest, the other columns contain sub-objects or integers calculated using the objects of interest and their sub-objects. For example, the concept of divisors of integers is supplied with the first data table in figure 1, where each row is an integer and a divisor. The definition supplied is: $[n, a] : a|n$, read "a divides n", which is used when generating a definition for any concept based on divisors.

Given the initial concepts, HR uses general production rules to turn one (or two) old concepts into a new one. For instance, the 'forall' production rule finds objects where a particular relation between its sub-objects is true in every case, eg. if the relation is adjacency of nodes in graphs, the concept of complete graphs is produced: every node is adjacent to every other node. Each production rule generates both a data table and a definition for the new concept, based on the data tables and definitions of the old concepts. HR uses seven production rules, each given in table 1 with a brief description of the types of concepts they produce.

Copyright © 2000, American Association for Artificial Intelligence (www.aaai.org). All rights reserved.

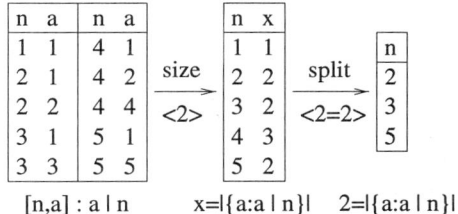

Figure 1: re-invention of prime numbers

Figure 1 shows how the production rules can generate new concepts: prime numbers are constructed using just two production rules. Each production rule step is accompanied by a parameterisation detailing exactly how the step is to occur. For example, parameters $\langle 2 \rangle$ for the size production rule stipulate that for every object of interest, the number of sub-objects in column 2 is to be counted. The parameters $\langle 2 = 2 \rangle$ for the split production rule tell it to keep rows where column 2 contains value 2. Each production rule generates the set of all possible parameters for a given concept.

HR forms a theory using a heuristic search which builds new concepts from the best old ones. To decide which concepts are most worthy of development, HR has eight measures which calculate values based on the data table and construction history of the concepts. A weighted sum of the measures for each concept is used to order the concepts. One measure is the **complexity** of the concept, which determines how many concepts in total have been built upon to produce the new concept. Concepts with high complexity are often difficult to understand, so low complexity is usually favoured in the weighted sum. Often we impose a complexity limit of around 10 to improve the comprehensibility of the theory. The **novelty** measure of a concept calculates how many times the categorisation produced by the concept has been seen. For example, square numbers categorise integers into two sets: $[1, 4, 9, \ldots]$ and $[2, 3, 5, \ldots,]$. If this categorisation had been seen often, square numbers would score poorly for novelty, and vice-versa.

To complete a cycle of mathematical activity, while searching for concepts, HR also checks for empirically true conjectures. For example, if a newly formed concept had exactly the same data table as a previous one, HR would make the conjecture that the definition for the old and new concepts were equivalent. Furthermore, when working in finite algebras, HR employs the Otter theorem prover (McCune 1990) to attempt to prove the conjectures it makes. HR then uses information from these proof attempts to re-assess the concepts in its theory - if a concept is involved in many interesting theorems, the interestingness of the concept is increased. For a more detailed discussion of the HR program, please see (Colton, Bundy, & Walsh 1999).

Extra Functionality for Integer Sequences

In number theory, we often start HR with only 3 concepts: integers - the objects of interest, divisors of integers - the sub-objects, and multiplication - relating two divisors if they multiply to give the integer. We can also supply other fundamental concepts, such as digits of integers and addition.

Name	Type of Concept Produced
Compose	identifying objects or sub-objects with properties from 2 concepts
Exists	identifying objects which have at least one sub-object with a particular property
Forall	identifying objects for which all sub-objects have a particular property
Match	identifying objects with equal sub-objects satisfying a relation.
Negate	identifying objects or sub-objects which do not have a particular property.
Size	counts the number of sub-objects which have a particular property.
Split	identifying objects with a given number of sub-objects with a particular property.

Table 1: the seven production rules used by HR

There is also a choice of which integers to supply as the objects of interest - using too many will slow down the theory formation, but if we choose too few, many sequences which are different will appear the same. For instance, if we use the integers 1 to 5, the prime numbers, 2, 3, 5 will appear the same as the non-squares, which are also 2, 3 and 5. In practice, we use the numbers between 1 and around 15, depending on the initial concepts chosen.

We have enabled HR to present concepts in number theory as integer sequences. If the concept is a type of number, for example square numbers, HR just outputs the integers of that type in order. We call such sequences number type sequences. For concepts produced by the size production rule, eg. the τ-function, which counts the number of divisors of an integer, the sequence is formed from the values calculated by the function for the integers 1, 2, 3, etc. in order. We call these coefficient sequences. Other concepts may be special types of sub-objects, for instance prime divisors. To present these as sequences, HR takes each integer in turn and writes down the sub-objects in numerical order. We call such sequences sub-object sequences.

We have also added 3 production rules which take advantage of the natural ordering of integers, but which can work in any domain with a well defined ordering, eg. polynomials. These were inspired by the transformations used to identify sequences in the Encyclopedia (Bernstein & Sloane 1995) and we hope to implement more such rules. The first new production rule takes a coefficient sequence and finds those integers setting the 'record' for it. For example, highly composite numbers (sequence A002182) are those which set the record for the τ-function - they have more divisors than any smaller integer. The second production rule starts with a number type sequence and takes the difference between successive terms to produce a new sequence, a common way of producing new sequences. The third production rule specialises the 'extreme' production rule introduced in (Steel 1999). It looks at the sub-objects for each integer and finds either the largest or the smallest. This produces concepts such as the greatest prime divisor.

When using HR to invent sequences, we turn off the empirical conjecture making and proving abilities, because, as discussed later, HR uses other methods to find conjectures. As long as the user supplies correct definitions for the initial concepts, HR will generate definitions consistent with the data for each concept. This therefore satisfies the criteria that sequences submitted to the Encyclopedia be well defined. HR can produce thousands of sequences, so there is the possibility that some simple sequences missing from the Encyclopedia can be identified and investigated.

Investigation of Sequences

When using HR to invent integer sequences, we set some parameters for the search and construct a fixed number of sequences, say 500. HR uses a local copy of the Encyclopedia to identify which of its inventions are missing, and orders them in terms of our complexity measure, so we can investigate the least complex ones first. We then examine the definitions of the sequences to choose a candidate for investigation and begin by using HR to calculate the terms up to 1000. Then HR compares the sequence to those already in the Encyclopedia and identifies any sequences which are related (as described below) with our new sequence. If HR finds such a relationship and we can prove it, we feel that the criteria for interestingness has been satisfied and we will probably submit the sequence to the Encyclopedia.

Unfortunately, the relationships identified can often be based on only little empirical evidence and may not be true in the general case. Also in many cases, there will be far too many sequences to which our sequence is related. For these reasons, we employ methods to prune the output, in an attempt to increase the yield of correct, interesting results. We first discuss the relationships that can be discovered, and then the pruning methods employed. As an example throughout, we use sequence A036436 which HR invented: integers with a square number of divisors. There are 62 terms for this stored in the Encyclopedia thus:

$$[A036436] \; 1, 6, 8, 10, 14, 15, 21, 22, 26, 27, \ldots, 183$$

We first introduce some definitions. Note that these and all further definitions refer not to the idealised sequence (with an infinite number of terms), but rather to the sequences as they appear in the Encyclopedia, with a finite number of terms.

- The nth term of sequence S is written S_n, and we say that $a \in S$ if a is a term of S. The **number of terms** of S is written $|S|$.

- The **range** of a sequence, written $range(S)$, is the set of integers between the smallest term in the sequence and the largest term, inclusive.

For example, if S is sequence A036436 above, then $|S| = 62$ and $range(S) = \{1, 2, 3, 4, \ldots, 183\}$.

Relationships Between Sequences

The following are three ways in which two sequences, S and T, can be related:

- S and T are **disjoint** if no term of S is a term of T.

- S is a **subsequence** of T if all the terms of S which are in $range(T)$ are also terms of T. Similarly, S is a **supersequence** of T if T is a subsequence of S.

- Letting k be the smaller of $|S|$ and $|T|$, we say that S is **less than** T if, for $i = 1, \ldots, k$, $S_i \leq T_i$. Similarly, S is **greater than** T if T is less than S.

Once a relationship has been noted, the user must interpret the result as a mathematical conjecture. This is rarely difficult to do because of the simple nature of the relationships found. For example, HR notes that sequence A006881, integers of the form pq for distinct primes p and q, is a subsequence of A036436 above. This is interpreted as the following easy to prove fact: Any integer of the form pq has a square number of divisors. Similarly, HR notes that prime numbers are disjoint with A036436, which is interpreted as: no prime has a square number of divisors, also easy to prove.

Pruning Methods

When investigating sequence A036436 above, HR returns 3605 sequences from the Encyclopedia which are subsequences using the above definition. HR has many ways to prune the output, which are either constraints on the output sequence or constraints on both the sequence of interest and the output sequence. Firstly, we would like to discard sequences such as $1, 1, 1, 1, \ldots$ which appear in the Encyclopedia for completeness, but are not particularly interesting. To do this, we can measure the number of *distinct* terms and discard any sequence with less than, say, 5 different terms.

If two sequences exist on different parts of the number line, it is uncertain whether one is a subsequence of the other. Our definition for subsequences admits those for which the range is disjoint with the range of the sequence being investigated. For example, HR notes that sequence A030091 (prime numbers, p, for which p and p^2 have the same digits) is a subsequence of A036436. This incorrect result occurs because the range of A030091 is $\{94583, \ldots, 1029647\}$ which is disjoint with the range of A036436. We may want to discard sequences like this, which share no terms with our sequence. In general, we may wish to discard sequences which share only 1, 2, etc. terms with the new sequence. To do this, HR measures the number of shared terms:

- The **number of shared terms** of S and T is calculated as: $|\{a : a \in S \; \& \; a \in T\}|$.

As an example, sequence A036436 has terms 1, 36 and 100 stored in the Encyclopedia. These are the only square numbers in A036436, so the term overlap for this sequence with the sequence of square numbers is 3. This measure is very effective for pruning, eg. if we prune subsequences which share less than 3 terms with A036436, this reduces the number of results from 3605 to a more manageable 390. This measure is easier to use and as effective as a similar measure which determines the *proportion*, rather than the number of terms from one sequence that appear in another.

When looking for supersequences of a given sequence the, non-negative numbers: $0, 1, 2, 3, 4, \ldots$ are always a supersequence. Therefore, we may want supersequences to be less dense on the number line than this, and HR uses the following measure for the density of a sequence:

- The **density** of S is calculated as:

$$\frac{|S|}{|range(S)|}$$

For example, there are 62 terms of A036436, distributed over the range of the first 183 integers. Therefore the density is $62/183 \simeq 0.34$. Often we choose a limit which is only slightly larger than the density of the new sequence, as this can produce interesting results.

When looking for sequences which are disjoint with the sequence of interest, we want to avoid sequences where the ranges are disjoint, as the sequences are bound to be disjoint. Ideally the sequences should occupy roughly the same space on the number line (but without any overlapping terms). HR uses this measure for pruning trivially disjoint sequences:

- The **range overlap** of S and T is calculated as:

$$\frac{|range(S) \cap range(T)|}{|range(S) \cup range(T)|}$$

For example, in the Encyclopedia, the prime numbers have range $\{2, 3, 4, \ldots, 271\}$ whereas sequence A036436 has range $\{1, 2, \ldots, 183\}$. The range overlap of these sequences is therefore $\frac{|\{2,3,\ldots,183\}|}{|\{2,3,\ldots,271\}|} = \frac{182}{270} \simeq 0.67$. If the minimum range overlap is set to close to 1, then the range of one sequence must be nearly contained in the range of the other. If this is true, yet the sequences are still disjoint, the result may be interesting.

When looking for a sequence which is less than our chosen sequence, it is desirable to look for sequences for which the terms are similar. HR calculates the average difference of the terms in the sequence thus:

- Letting k be the smaller of $|S|$ and $|T|$, the **difference** of S and T is calculated as:

$$\frac{1}{k}\sum_{i=1}^{k}|S_i - T_i|$$

If the maximum difference limit is set to 1, on average the nth terms of S and T will differ by only 1. Sequences so close to the new sequence may be interesting.

The final way to prune sequences is to use semantic information from the Encyclopedia. Firstly, HR can discard sequences with (or without) particular words in their definition. For example, when looking for subsequences of the prime numbers, it is desirable to discard any sequence with the word 'prime' in its definition, as these are usually obvious specialisations of primes, such as odd primes. Also, each sequence in the Encyclopedia has an associated set of keywords, such as 'core' - which are considered fundamental, and 'nice' - which have some appealing quality. HR can prune sequences if they have (or don't have) particular keywords associated. For example, when we ask for subsequences of sequence A036436 which are described as 'nice' in the Encyclopedia, the output is reduced from 3605 sequences to just 34, one of which is A007422: integers n, where the product of the divisors of n is equal to n^2. Like many of the results HR finds for A036436, a little investigation shows that this is true in the general case.

Results

Although we mainly use HR to invent new integer sequences, we would hope that it also re-invents many classically interesting sequences. We ran HR for 10 minutes, starting with the concepts of integers, divisors and multiplication. The search was depth limited to a complexity of 12, and we used the integers from 1 to 17. HR produced 233 sequences, of which 51 (22%) were sequences already in the Encyclopedia. This included 14 of the Encyclopedia's 120 'core' sequences with fundamental notions such as odd, even, square, cube and prime numbers being re-invented.

More complicated, non-core concepts were also re-invented, such as A000961: prime powers and A005117: square free numbers. Of the 51 re-invented sequences, 40 were found during the first minute, and so were less complex than the remaining 11 found in the final 9 minutes. This shows that less complex concepts are often more interesting, which is why we use a depth limited search. It also suggest more shallow searches using a variety of initial concepts rather than deep searches, where the complexity of the sequences makes them difficult to understand.

From all the number theory sessions so far, the total number of re-invented sequences is over 120. Certain sequences are re-invented with non-standard definitions, such as the sequence of powers of 2, which HR defines as: integers with only one odd divisor (eg. 1 is the only odd divisor of 1, 2, 4, 8, 16, etc. and all other integers have more odd divisors). A tactic which can increase the yield of classically interesting concepts is to identify the initial concepts and production rules required to re-invent a well known concept, and restrict the search to using only these. For example, the concept of the sum of divisors is reached using the concept of divisors and the "less than or equal to" concept. It is defined in this way, using only the size and compose production rules:

$$f(n) = |\{(d, a) : d|n \ \& \ a \leq d\}|.$$

Restricting theory formation to using only the concepts and production rules necessary for this construction, the first 14 sequences HR found were in the Encyclopedia. They included well known concepts such as the τ-function, square numbers, triangle numbers and the τ^2-function.

HR re-invents many well known concepts because the production rules, while general in nature, were derived by studying the types of concepts found in mathematics. The compose rule is essential as it combines 2 concepts - without this, theory formation comes to a halt fairly quickly. Each re-invented concept required either the exists, split or size rule. These rules produce concepts identifying objects with certain sub-objects or a fixed number of sub-objects which are common constructions in number theory, eg. prime numbers, with 2 distinct divisors. The negate rule was also useful for constructing compliments of concepts, eg. odd numbers from even numbers. The number theory specific rules increased the yield of potentially interesting concepts with the 'difference' and 'record' rules effectively trebling the yield of sequences, as each new sequence was transformed by them into another one. The match and forall rules were less instrumental in this session, although both were required for at least one re-invented concept.

Of the 182 new sequences generated in the above 10 minute session, we assessed that 45 (25%) were unsuitable for investigation because either: (i) they were finite (eg. integers, n, where $\tau(n) = n$, the only examples being 1 and 2) or (ii) they were too specialised which made them dull (eg. the function $f(n) = |\{a : a|n \ \& \ n = 2 \times 2\}|$ produces a sequence of zeros except the fourth term which is 3). The remaining 137 sequences were worthy of investigation, and in fact 4 of them were sequences that HR previously invented which are now in the Encyclopedia (as discussed below). Judging from the 22% of sequences produced which were already in the Encyclopedia, HR is certainly generating the kinds of concepts which interest mathematicians, and that while some new sequences were not worthy of the Encyclopedia, 3/4 of those produced were candidates for investigation, which we feel is acceptable.

Illustrative Examples

To date, 17 sequences invented by HR have been added to the Encyclopedia. While HR invents hundreds of well defined sequences not present in the Encyclopedia, we have only submitted sequences for which HR has also found interesting conjectures. Every sequence we have submitted has been accepted, including:

[A036438] 1, 4, 6, 10, 12, 14, 22, 24, 26, 27, 32, 34, ...

(integers expressible as $m.\tau(m)$ for some m), and:

[A036433] 1, 2, 14, 23, 29, 34, 46, 63, 68, 74, 76, 78...

(integers for which the number of divisors is a digit).

The first of HR's sequences we submitted to the Encyclopedia was the refactorable numbers:

[A033950] 1, 2, 8, 9, 12, 18, 24, 36, 40, 56, 60, 72, ...

which are those integers where the number of divisors is itself a divisor. We were informed later that these had been developed as recently as 1990 (Kennedy & Cooper 1990). On investigation, HR found 3 conjectures about refactorables which we have subsequently proved:

- Looking for disjoint sequences, and pruning with keywords, HR conjectured that perfect numbers [see (Sloane 2000)] are not refactorable.
- Looking for supersequences, HR conjectured that refactorables are only congruent to 0, 1, 2 or 4 mod 8.
- Looking for supersequences, HR conjectured that refactorables are of the form $lcm(a, \tau(a))$ for some a.

These, and more results found by us, were presented in a journal paper on refactorables (Colton 1999).

Investigation of sequences can be performed for any sequence, not just those invented by HR. For example, when looking for supersequences of fortunate numbers [see (Sloane 2000)], HR conjectured that they are all prime, a result known as Fortune's conjecture (Golomb 1981). We also used HR to look for supersequences of perfect numbers, and found that they are of the form $lcm(n, \sigma(n))$ for some n [where $\sigma(n)$ is the sum of the divisors of n]. This highlighted an appealing parallel between perfect numbers and refactorables, which HR discovered were of the form $lcm(n, \tau(n))$, for some n.

When HR invented this sequence:

[A046952] 1, 4, 16, 36, 144, 576, 1296, 2304, 3600 ...

which sets the record for this function:

$$f(n) = |\{(a,b) : a \times b = n \ \& \ a|b\}|, \quad (1)$$

it also made the conjecture that these are always square numbers. We went on to prove that the sequence was in fact the squares of the highly composite numbers.

Perhaps the most aesthetic result arose when HR invented the concept of integers where the number of divisors is prime, which is this sequence:

[A009087] 2, 3, 4, 5, 7, 9, 11, 13, 16, 17, 19, 23, 25, ...

To investigate this we looked for subsequences described as 'nice' in the Encyclopedia. The first answer supplied was:

[A023194] 2, 4, 9, 16, 25, 64, 289, 729, 1681, 2401, ...

which has the definition: integers for which the sum of divisors is prime. Therefore, HR made the conjecture that, given an integer, if the sum of divisors is prime, then the number of divisors will also be prime, which we subsequently proved. It is difficult to know whether this result is genuinely new, but it is certainly not well known, and is indicative of the kind of surprising and aesthetic conjectures it is possible to find using HR as an automated assistant.

Related Work

The aim of the SeekWhence program (Hofstadter 1995), (Meredith 1987) was not to invent sequences but to discover a definition for a given sequence. SeekWhence used heuristics to determine the nature of a sequence, such as taking the difference between two terms, or trying to extract and identify well known sub-sequences. For example, given the sequence 1, 1, 3, 4, 6, 9, SeekWhence would identify that square numbers: 1, 4, 9, and triangle numbers: 1, 3, 6, had been composed with repetition to form this sequence. Hofstadter aimed to model how humans search for reasonable definitions of sequences, rather than to provide a tool to identify sequences. The Guess program (Krattenthaler 1991) is such a tool which uses techniques from determinant calculus to produce a closed form definition for a given sequence. We have recently applied HR to the problem of identification and extrapolation of integer sequences (Colton, Bundy, & Walsh 2000), which requires more search control and is a distinct task to inventing sequences.

The AM program (Davis & Lenat 1982) worked in number theory, constructing a theory using a heuristic search to guide the invention of definitions. In contrast to HR, which starts with only a handful of concepts, 8 heuristic measures and 10 production rules (7, general, 3 specific to number theory), AM was supplied with 115 elementary concepts and used 242 heuristics to search for concepts. Some of these heuristics were very specific and often used only once during a session. AM re-invented well known sequences such as prime numbers and square numbers and the

τ-function and Lenat originally claimed that one of AM's sequences, integers with more divisors than any smaller integer was original. However, it later turned out that these had been defined as highly composite numbers and explored by Ramanujan (Hardy 1927). HR covers all the sequences re-invented by AM, and finds many outside of AM's range, such as powers of 2.

Conclusions and Further Work

The aim of the HR project is to provide a model for theory formation in pure mathematics and to investigate possible applications of this to mathematics and to areas of Artificial Intelligence such as machine learning. By implementing additional production rules and the ability to present concepts as sequences, we have applied HR to the invention of integer sequences. In a matter of minutes, it can re-invent more than 50 well known sequences, including 14 core sequences and can supply, in order of complexity, over 100 new sequences for investigation. We have linked HR to the Encyclopedia of Integer Sequences so the user can investigate a new sequence using HR to make conjectures about the sequence in relation to those in the Encyclopedia.

We have demonstrated that the theory formation techniques can scale up to produce interesting results and can be applied successfully in different domains. HR is the first program to both define new mathematical concepts and detail why they are of interest. This model for the invention of integer sequences has produced interesting novel results in number theory with the new sequences and conjectures generating genuine interest from mathematicians. For example, there are now over 30 sequences in the Encyclopedia related to refactorable numbers, submitted by various people.

The class of concepts which HR cannot invent is still large. In particular, it cannot invent concepts with recursive definitions, such as the factorial function. We are currently implementing a 'path' production rule which will output recursive definitions, thus increasing HR's coverage of these types of concepts. Also, many of the sequences in the Encyclopedia have aspects from more than one domain, eg. the first sequence in the Encyclopedia counts the number of groups with n elements. We are presently building on the work of (Steel 1999) to add cross domain functionality to HR. We have recently written the Integer Sequence Generator (ISG) as a Java implementation of the work presented here. We hope this will be an online tool which mathematicians use to invent and investigate new sequences. For instance, if the user was interested in refactorable numbers, the ISG would not only investigate refactorables, but would specialise the concept to, say, odd refactorable numbers. It would then conjecture, as we did in (Colton 1999), that all odd refactorables are squares.

Computer generated discoveries in mathematics such as the remarkable new formula for π detailed in (Bailey 1998) are still rare and often rely on specialised algorithms - in this case the PSLQ algorithm. Neil Sloane, the author of the Encyclopedia, states that coincidences arising from using the Encyclopedia have led to surprising conjectures (Sloane 1998). Whilst we cannot hope for such results as the famous moonshine conjectures (Conway & Norton 1979) which arose coincidentally, we hope to further the possibility of surprising conjectures arising from the use of the Encyclopedia and theory formation programs such as HR.

Acknowledgements

This work is supported by EPSRC grant GR/M98012. We would like to thank the anonymous reviewers for their enthusiastic and helpful comments, and Neil Sloane for maintaining a truly remarkable encyclopedia.

References

Bailey, D. 1998. Finding new mathematical identities via numerical computations. *ACM SIGNUM* 33(1):17–22.

Bernstein, M., and Sloane, N. J. A. 1995. Some canonical sequences of integers. *Linear Algebra and its Applications* 226-228:57–72.

Colton, S.; Bundy, A.; and Walsh, T. 1999. HR: Automatic concept formation in pure mathematics. In *Proceedings of the Sixteenth International Joint Conference on Artificial Intelligence*.

Colton, S.; Bundy, A.; and Walsh, T. 2000. Automatic identification of mathematical concepts. In *Proceedings of the 17th International Conference on Machine Learning*.

Colton, S. 1999. Refactorable numbers - a machine invention. *Journal of Integer Sequences* 2.

Conway, J., and Norton, S. 1979. Monstrous moonshine. *Bulletin of the London Mathematical Society* 11:308–339.

Davis, R., and Lenat, D. 1982. *Knowledge-Based Systems in Artificial Intelligence*. McGraw-Hill Advanced Computer Science Series.

Golomb, S. W. 1981. The evidence for Fortune's conjecture. *Mathematics Magazine* 54:209–210.

Hardy, G. H., ed. 1927. *S. Ramanujan, Collected Papers*. Cambridge University Press.

Hofstadter, D. 1995. *Fluid Concepts and Creative Analogies*. Basic Books.

Kennedy, R., and Cooper, C. 1990. Tau numbers, natural density and Hardy and Wright's theorem 437. *International Journal of Mathematics and Mathematical Sciences* 13:2:383–386.

Krattenthaler, C. 1991. Advanced determinant calculus. Technical report, Institute of Mathematics, University of Vienna.

McCune, W. 1990. The OTTER user's guide. Technical Report ANL/90/9, Argonne National Laboratories.

Meredith, M. J. E. 1987. *Seek-Whence: A Model of Pattern Perception*. Ph.D. Dissertation, Department of Computer Science, Indiana University.

Sloane, N. J. A. 1998. My favorite integer sequences. In *Proceedings of the International Conference on Sequences and Applications*.

Sloane, N. J. A. 2000. *Encyclopedia of Integer Sequences*. http://www.research.att.com/~njas/sequences.

Steel, G. 1999. Cross domain theory formation. Master's thesis, Division of Informatics, University of Edinburgh.

A Unified Bias-Variance Decomposition for Zero-One and Squared Loss

Pedro Domingos
Department of Computer Science and Engineering
University of Washington
Seattle, Washington 98195, U.S.A.
pedrod@cs.washington.edu
http://www.cs.washington.edu/homes/pedrod

Abstract

The bias-variance decomposition is a very useful and widely-used tool for understanding machine-learning algorithms. It was originally developed for squared loss. In recent years, several authors have proposed decompositions for zero-one loss, but each has significant shortcomings. In particular, all of these decompositions have only an intuitive relationship to the original squared-loss one. In this paper, we define bias and variance for an arbitrary loss function, and show that the resulting decomposition specializes to the standard one for the squared-loss case, and to a close relative of Kong and Dietterich's (1995) one for the zero-one case. The same decomposition also applies to variable misclassification costs. We show a number of interesting consequences of the unified definition. For example, Schapire et al.'s (1997) notion of "margin" can be expressed as a function of the zero-one bias and variance, making it possible to formally relate a classifier ensemble's generalization error to the base learner's bias and variance on training examples. Experiments with the unified definition lead to further insights.

Introduction

For the better part of the last two decades, machine-learning research has concentrated mainly on creating ever more flexible learners using ever more powerful representations. At the same time, very simple learners were often found to perform very well in experiments, sometimes better than more sophisticated ones (e.g., Holte (1993), Domingos & Pazzani (1997)). In recent years the reason for this has become clear: predictive error has two components, and while more powerful learners reduce one (bias) they increase the other (variance). The optimal point in this trade-off varies from application to application. In a parallel development, researchers have found that learning ensembles of models very often outperforms learning a single model (e.g., Bauer & Kohavi (1999)). That complex ensembles would outperform simple single models contradicted many existing intuitions about the relationship between simplicity and accuracy. This finding, apparently at odds with the one above about the value of simple learners, also becomes easier to understand in light

Copyright © 2000, American Association for Artificial Intelligence (www.aaai.org). All rights reserved.

of a bias-variance decomposition of error: while allowing a more intensive search for a single model is liable to increase variance, averaging multiple models will often (though not always) reduce it. As a result of these developments, the bias-variance decomposition of error has become a cornerstone of our understanding of inductive learning.

Although machine-learning research has been mainly concerned with classification problems, using zero-one loss as the main evaluation criterion, the bias-variance insight was borrowed from the field of regression, where squared-loss is the main criterion. As a result, several authors have proposed bias-variance decompositions related to zero-one loss (Kong & Dietterich, 1995; Breiman, 1996b; Kohavi & Wolpert, 1996; Tibshirani, 1996; Friedman, 1997). However, each of these decompositions has significant shortcomings. In particular, none has a clear relationship to the original decomposition for squared loss. One source of difficulty has been that the decomposition for squared-loss is purely additive (i.e., loss = bias + variance), but it has proved difficult to obtain the same result for zero-one loss using definitions of bias and variance that have all the intuitively necessary properties. Here we take the position that instead of forcing the bias-variance decomposition to be purely additive, and defining bias and variance so as to make this happen, it is preferable to start with a single consistent definition of bias and variance for all loss functions, and then investigate how loss varies as a function of bias and variance in each case. This should lead to more insight and to a clearer picture than a collection of unrelated decompositions. It should also make it easier to extend the bias-variance decomposition to further loss functions. Intuitively, since a bias-variance trade-off exists in any generalization problem, it should be possible and useful to apply a bias-variance analysis to any "reasonable" loss function. We believe the unified decomposition we propose here is a step towards this goal.

We begin by proposing unified definitions of bias and variance, and showing how squared-loss, zero-one loss and variable misclassification costs can be decomposed according to them. This is followed by the derivation of a number of properties of the new decomposition, in particular relating it to previous results. We then describe experiments with the new decomposition and discuss related work.

A Unified Decomposition

Given a training set $\{(x_1, t_1), \ldots, (x_n, t_n)\}$, a learner produces a model f. Given a test example x, this model produces a prediction $y = f(x)$. (For the sake of simplicity, the fact that y is a function of x will remain implicit throughout this paper.) Let t be the true value of the predicted variable for the test example x. A *loss function* $L(t, y)$ measures the cost of predicting y when the true value is t. Commonly used loss functions are squared loss ($L(t, y) = (t-y)^2$), absolute loss ($L(t, y) = |t - y|$), and zero-one loss ($L(t, y) = 0$ if $y = t$, $L(t, y) = 1$ otherwise). The goal of learning can be stated as producing a model with the smallest possible loss; i.e, a model that minimizes the average $L(t, y)$ over all examples, with each example weighted by its probability. In general, t will be a nondeterministic function of x (i.e., if x is sampled repeatedly, different values of t will be seen). The *optimal prediction* y_* for an example x is the prediction that minimizes $E_t[L(t, y_*)]$, where the subscript t denotes that the expectation is taken with respect to all possible values of t, weighted by their probabilities given x. The optimal model is the model for which $f(x) = y_*$ for every x. In general, this model will have non-zero loss. In the case of zero-one loss, the optimal model is called the *Bayes classifier*, and its loss is called the *Bayes rate*.

Since the same learner will in general produce different models for different training sets, $L(t, y)$ will be a function of the training set. This dependency can be removed by averaging over training sets. In particular, since the training set size is an important parameter of a learning problem, we will often want to average over all training sets of a given size. Let D be a set of training sets. Then the quantity of interest is the expected loss $E_{D,t}[L(t, y)]$, where the expectation is taken with respect to t and the training sets in D (i.e., with respect to t and the predictions $y = f(x)$ produced for example x by applying the learner to each training set in D). Bias-variance decompositions decompose the expected loss into three terms: bias, variance and noise. A standard such decomposition exists for squared loss, and a number of different ones have been proposed for zero-one loss.

In order to define bias and variance for an arbitrary loss function we first need to define the notion of main prediction.

Definition 1 *The* main prediction *for a loss function L and set of training sets D is* $y_m^{L,D} = \mathrm{argmin}_{y'} E_D[L(y, y')]$.

When there is no danger of ambiguity, we will represent $y_m^{L,D}$ simply as y_m. The expectation is taken with respect to the training sets in D, i.e., with respect to the predictions y produced by learning on the training sets in D. Let Y be the multiset of these predictions. (A specific prediction y will appear more than once in Y if it is produced by more than one training set.) In words, the main prediction is the value y' whose average loss relative to all the predictions in Y is minimum (i.e., it is the prediction that "differs least" from all the predictions in Y according to L). The main prediction under squared loss is the mean of the predictions; under absolute loss it is the median; and under zero-one loss it is the mode (i.e., the most frequent prediction). For example, if there are k possible training sets of a given size, we learn a classifier on each, $0.6k$ of these classifiers predict class 1, and $0.4k$ predict 0, then the main prediction under zero-one loss is class 1. The main prediction is not necessarily a member of Y; for example, if $Y = \{1, 1, 2, 2\}$ the main prediction under squared loss is 1.5.

We can now define bias and variance as follows.

Definition 2 *The* bias *of a learner on an example x is* $B(x) = L(y_*, y_m)$.

In words, the bias is the loss incurred by the main prediction relative to the optimal prediction.

Definition 3 *The* variance *of a learner on an example x is* $V(x) = E_D[L(y_m, y)]$.

In words, the variance is the average loss incurred by predictions relative to the main prediction. Bias and variance may be averaged over all examples, in which case we will refer to them as *average bias* $E_x[B(x)]$ and *average variance* $E_x[V(x)]$.

It is also convenient to define noise as follows.

Definition 4 *The* noise *of an example x is* $N(x) = E_t[L(t, y_*)]$.

In other words, noise is the unavoidable component of the loss, that is incurred independently of the learning algorithm.

Definitions 2 and 3 have the intuitive properties associated with bias and variance measures. y_m is a measure of the "central tendency" of a learner. (What "central" means depends on the loss function.) Thus $B(x)$ measures the systematic loss incurred by a learner, and $V(x)$ measures the loss incurred by its fluctuations around the central tendency in response to different training sets. The bias is independent of the training set, and is zero for a learner that always makes the optimal prediction. The variance is independent of the true value of the predicted variable, and is zero for a learner that always makes the same prediction regardless of the training set. However, it is not necessarily the case that the expected loss $E_{D,t}[L(t, y)]$ for a given loss function L can be decomposed into bias and variance as defined above. Our approach will be to propose a decomposition and then show that it applies to each of several different loss functions. We will also exhibit some loss functions to which it does not apply. (However, even in such cases it may still be worthwhile to investigate how the expected loss can be expressed as a function of $B(x)$ and $V(x)$.)

Consider an example x for which the true prediction is t, and consider a learner that predicts y given a training set in D. Then, for certain loss functions L, the following decomposition of $E_{D,t}[L(t, y)]$ holds:

$$\begin{aligned}
&E_{D,t}[L(t, y)] \\
&= c_1 E_t[L(t, y_*)] + L(y_*, y_m) + c_2 E_D[L(y_m, y)] \\
&= c_1 N(x) + B(x) + c_2 V(x) \quad (1)
\end{aligned}$$

c_1 and c_2 are multiplicative factors that will take on different values for different loss functions. We begin by showing that this decomposition reduces to the standard one for squared loss.

Theorem 1 *Equation 1 is valid for squared loss, with $c_1 = c_2 = 1$.*

Proof. Substituting $L(a, b) = (a - b)^2$, $y_* = E_t[t]$, $y_m = E_D[y]$ and $c_1 = c_2 = 1$, Equation 1 becomes:

$$E_{D,t}[(t-y)^2] = E_t[(t - E_t[t])^2] + (E_t[t] - E_D[y])^2 \\ + E_D[(E_D[y] - y)^2] \quad (2)$$

This is the standard decomposition for squared loss, as derived in (for example) Geman et al. (1992). $y_* = E_t[t]$ because $E_t[(t-y)^2] = E_t[(t-E_t[t])^2] + (E_t[t]-y)^2$ (also shown in Geman et al. (1992), etc.), and therefore $E_t[(t-y)^2]$ is minimized by making $y = E_t[t]$. □

Some authors (e.g., Kohavi and Wolpert, 1996) refer to the $(E_t[t] - E_D[y])^2$ term as "bias squared." Here we follow the same convention as Geman et al. (1992) and others, and simply refer to it as "bias." This makes more sense given our goal of a unified bias-variance decomposition, since the square in $(E_t[t] - E_D[y])^2$ is simply a consequence of the square in squared loss.

We now show that the same decomposition applies to zero-one loss in two-class problems, with c_1 reflecting the fact that on noisy examples the non-optimal prediction is the correct one, and c_2 reflecting that variance increases error on biased examples but decreases it on biased ones. Let $P_D(y = y_*)$ be the probability over training sets in D that the learner predicts the optimal class for x.

Theorem 2 *Equation 1 is valid for zero-one loss in two-class problems, with $c_1 = 2P_D(y = y_*) - 1$ and $c_2 = 1$ if $y_m = y_*$, $c_2 = -1$ otherwise.*

Proof. $L(a, b)$ represents zero-one loss throughout this proof. We begin by showing that

$$E_t[L(t,y)] = L(y_*, y) + c_0 E_t[L(t, y_*)] \quad (3)$$

with $c_0 = 1$ if $y = y_*$ and $c_0 = -1$ if $y \neq y_*$. If $y = y_*$ Equation 3 is trivially true with $c_0 = 1$. Assume now that $y \neq y_*$. Given that there are only two classes, if $y \neq y_*$ then $t \neq y_*$ implies that $t = y$ and vice-versa. Therefore $P_t(t = y) = P_t(t \neq y_*)$, and

$$E_t[L(t,y)] = P_t(t \neq y) = 1 - P_t(t = y) \\ = 1 - P_t(t \neq y_*) = 1 - E_t[L(t, y_*)] \\ = L(y_*, y) - E_t[L(t, y_*)] \\ = L(y_*, y) + c_0 E_t[L(t, y_*)] \quad (4)$$

with $c_0 = -1$, proving Equation 3. We now show in a similar manner that

$$E_D[L(y_*, y)] = L(y_*, y_m) + c_2 E_D[L(y_m, y)] \quad (5)$$

with $c_2 = 1$ if $y_m = y_*$ and $c_2 = -1$ if $y_m \neq y_*$. If $y_m = y_*$ Equation 5 is trivially true with $c_2 = 1$. If $y_m \neq y_*$ then $y_m \neq y$ implies that $y_* = y$ and vice-versa, and

$$E_D[L(y_*, y)] = P_D(y_* \neq y) = 1 - P_D(y_* = y) \\ = 1 - P_D(y_m \neq y) = 1 - E_D[L(y_m, y)] \\ = L(y_*, y_m) - E_D[L(y_m, y)] \\ = L(y_*, y_m) + c_2 E_D[L(y_m, y)] \quad (6)$$

with $c_2 = -1$, proving Equation 5. Using Equation 3,

$$E_{D,t}[L(t,y)] = E_D[E_t[L(t,y)]] \\ = E_D[L(y_*, y) + c_0 E_t[L(t, y_*)]] \quad (7)$$

Since $L(t, y_*)$ does not depend on D,

$$E_{D,t}[L(t,y)] = E_D[c_0] E_t[L(t, y_*)] + E_D[L(y_*, y)] \quad (8)$$

and since

$$E_D[c_0] = P_D(y = y_*) - P_D(y \neq y_*) \\ = 2P_D(y = y_*) - 1 = c_1 \quad (9)$$

we finally obtain Equation 1, using Equation 5. □

This decomposition for zero-one loss is closely related to that of Kong and Dietterich (1995). The main differences are that Kong and Dietterich ignored the noise component $N(x)$ and defined variance simply as the difference between loss and bias, apparently unaware that the absolute value of that difference is the average loss incurred relative to the most frequent prediction. A side-effect of this is that Kong and Dietterich incorporate c_2 into their definition of variance, which can therefore be negative. Kohavi and Wolpert (1996) and others have criticized this fact, since variance for squared loss must be positive. However, our decomposition shows that the subtractive effect of variance follows from a self-consistent definition of bias and variance for zero-one and squared loss, even if the variance itself remains positive. The fact that variance is additive in unbiased examples but subtractive in biased ones has significant consequences. If a learner is biased on an example, increasing variance decreases loss. This behavior is markedly different from that of squared loss, but is obtained with the same definitions of bias and variance, purely as a result of the different properties of zero-one loss. It helps explain how highly unstable learners like decision-tree and rule induction algorithms can produce excellent results in practice, even given very limited quantities of data. In effect, when zero-one loss is the evaluation criterion, there is a much higher tolerance for variance than if the bias-variance decomposition was purely additive, because the increase in average loss caused by variance on unbiased examples is partly offset (or more than offset) by its decrease on biased ones. The average loss over all examples is the sum of noise, the average bias and what might be termed the *net variance*, $E_x[(2B(x) - 1)V(x)]$:

$$E_{D,t,x}[L(t,y)] \\ = E_x[c_1 N(x)] + E_x[B(x)] + E_x[(2B(x) - 1)V(x)] \quad (10)$$

by averaging Equation 1 over all test examples x.

The c_1 factor (see Equation 9) also points to a key difference between zero-one and squared loss. In squared loss, increasing noise always increases error. In zero-one loss, for training sets and test examples where $y \neq y_*$, increasing noise decreases error, and a high noise level can therefore in principle be beneficial to performance.

The same decomposition applies in the more general case of multiclass problems, with correspondingly generalized coefficients c_1 and c_2.

Theorem 3 *Equation 1 is valid for zero-one loss in multiclass problems, with* $c_1 = P_D(y = y_*) - P_D(y \neq y_*) P_t(y = t \mid y_* \neq t)$ *and* $c_2 = 1$ *if* $y_m = y_*$, $c_2 = -P_D(y = y_* \mid y \neq y_m)$ *otherwise.*

Proof. The proof is similar to that of Theorem 2, with the key difference that now $y \neq y_*$ and $t \neq y_*$ no longer imply that $t = y$, and $y_m \neq y_*$ and $y_m \neq y$ no longer imply that $y = y_*$. Given that $y \neq y_*$ implies $P_t(y = t \mid y_* = t) = 0$,

$$\begin{aligned} P_t(y = t) &= P_t(y_* \neq t) P_t(y = t \mid y_* \neq t) \\ &\quad + P_t(y_* = t) P_t(y = t \mid y_* = t) \\ &= P_t(y_* \neq t) P_t(y = t \mid y_* \neq t) \end{aligned} \quad (11)$$

and Equation 4 becomes

$$\begin{aligned} E_t[L(t,y)] &= P_t(y \neq t) = 1 - P_t(y = t) \\ &= 1 - P_t(y_* \neq t) P_t(y = t \mid y_* \neq t) \\ &= L(y_*, y) + c_0 E_t[L(t, y_*)] \end{aligned} \quad (12)$$

with $c_0 = -P_t(y = t \mid y_* \neq t)$. When $y = y_*$ Equation 3 is trivially true with $c_0 = 1$, as before. A similar treatment applies to Equation 5, leading to $c_2 = -P_D(y = y_* \mid y \neq y_m)$ if $y_m \neq y_*$, etc. Given that

$$E_D[c_0] = P_D(y = y_*) - P_D(y \neq y_*) P_t(y = t \mid y_* \neq t) = c_1 \quad (13)$$

we obtain Theorem 3. □

Theorem 3 means that in multiclass problems not all variance on biased examples contributes to reducing loss; of all training sets for which $y \neq y_m$, only some have $y = y_*$, and it is in these that loss is reduced. This leads to an interesting insight: when zero-one loss is the evaluation criterion, the tolerance for variance will decrease as the number of classes increases, other things being equal. Thus the ideal setting for the "bias-variance trade-off" parameter in a learner (e.g., the number of neighbors in k-nearest neighbor) may be more in the direction of high variance in problems with fewer classes.

In many classification problems, zero-one loss is an inappropriate evaluation measure because misclassification costs are asymmetric; for example, classifying a cancerous patient as healthy is likely to be more costly than the reverse. Consider the two class case with $\forall_y L(y, y) = 0$ (i.e., there is no cost for making the correct prediction), and with any nonzero real values for $L(y_1, y_2)$ when $y_1 \neq y_2$. The decomposition above also applies in this case, with the appropriate choice of c_1 and c_2.

Theorem 4 *In two-class problems, Equation 1 is valid for any real-valued loss function for which* $\forall_y L(y,y) = 0$ *and* $\forall_{y_1 \neq y_2} L(y_1, y_2) \neq 0$, *with* $c_1 = P_D(y = y_*) - \frac{L(y_*,y)}{L(y,y_*)} P_D(y \neq y_*)$ *and* $c_2 = 1$ *if* $y_m = y_*$, $c_2 = -\frac{L(y_*,y_m)}{L(y_m,y_*)}$ *otherwise.*

We omit the proof in the interests of space; see Domingos (2000). Theorem 4 essentially shows that the loss-reducing effect of variance on biased examples will be greater or smaller depending on how asymmetric the costs are, and on

which direction they are greater in. Whether this decomposition applies in the multiclass case is an open problem. It does not apply if $L(y, y) \neq 0$; in this case the decomposition contains an additional term corresponding to the cost of the correct predictions.

Properties of the Unified Decomposition

One of the main concepts Breiman (1996a) used to explain why the bagging ensemble method reduces zero-one loss was that of an *order-correct* learner.

Definition 5 *(Breiman, 1996a) A learner is* order-correct *on an example x iff* $\forall_{y \neq y_*} P_D(y) < P_D(y_*)$.

Breiman showed that bagging transforms an order-correct learner into a nearly optimal one. An order-correct learner is an unbiased one according to Definition 2:

Theorem 5 *A learner is order-correct on an example x iff* $B(x) = 0$ *under zero-one loss.*

The proof is immediate from the definitions, considering that y_m for zero-one loss is the most frequent prediction.

Schapire et al. (1997) have proposed an explanation for why the boosting ensemble method works in terms of the notion of *margin*. For algorithms like bagging and boosting, that generate multiple hypotheses by applying the same learner to multiple training sets, their definition of margin can be stated as follows.

Definition 6 *(Schapire et al., 1997) In two-class problems, the* margin *of a learner on an example x is $M(x) = P_D(y = t) - P_D(y \neq t)$.*

A positive margin indicates a correct classification by the ensemble, and a negative one an error. Intuitively, a large margin corresponds to a high confidence in the prediction. D here is the set of training sets to which the learner is applied. For example, if 100 rounds of boosting are carried out, $|D| = 100$. Further, for algorithms like boosting where the different training sets (and corresponding predictions) have different weights that sum to 1, $P_D(.)$ is computed according to these weights. Definitions 1–4 apply unchanged in this situation. In effect, we have generalized the notions of bias and variance to apply to any training set selection scheme, not simply the traditional one of "all possible training sets of a given size, with equal weights."

Schapire et al. (1997) showed that it is possible to bound an ensemble's generalization error (i.e., its zero-one loss on test examples) in terms of the distribution of margins on training examples and the VC dimension of the base learner. In particular, the smaller the probability of a low margin, the lower the bound on generalization error. The following theorem shows that the margin is closely related to bias and variance as defined above.

Theorem 6 *The margin of a learner on an example x can be expressed in terms of its zero-one bias and variance as $M(x) = \pm[2B(x) - 1][2V(x) - 1]$, with positive sign if $y_* = t$ and negative sign otherwise.*

Proof. When $y_* = t$, $M(x) = P_D(y = y_*) - P_D(y \neq y_*) = 2P_D(y = y_*) - 1$. If $B(x) = 0$, $y_m = y_*$ and $M(x) =$

$2P_D(y = y_m) - 1 = 2[1 - V(x)] - 1 = -[2V(x) - 1]$.
If $B(x) = 1$ then $M(x) = 2V(x) - 1$. Therefore $M(x) = [2B(x) - 1][2V(x) - 1]$. The demonstration for $y_* \neq t$ is similar, with $M(x) = P_D(y \neq y_*) - P_D(y = y_*)$. □

Conversely, it is possible to express the bias and variance in terms of the margin: $B(x) = \frac{1}{2}[1 \pm \text{sign}(M(x))]$, $V(x) = \frac{1}{2}[1 \pm |M(x)|]$, with positive sign if $y_* \neq t$ and negative sign otherwise. The relationship between margins and bias/variance expressed in Theorem 6 implies that Schapire et al.'s theorems can be stated in terms of the bias and variance on training examples. Bias-variance decompositions relate a learner's loss on an example to its bias and variance on that example. However, to our knowledge this is the first time that *generalization* error is related to bias and variance on *training* examples.

Theorem 6 also sheds light on the polemic between Breiman (1996b, 1997) and Schapire et al. (1997) on how the success of ensemble methods like bagging and boosting is best explained. Breiman has argued for a bias-variance explanation, while Schapire et al. have argued for a margin-based explanation. Theorem 6 shows that these are two faces of the same coin, and helps to explain why the bias-variance explanation sometimes seems to fail when applied to boosting. Maximizing margins is a combination of reducing the number of biased examples, decreasing the variance on unbiased examples, and increasing it on biased ones (for examples where $y_* = t$; the reverse, otherwise). Without differentiating between these effects it is hard to understand how boosting affects bias and variance.

Unfortunately, there are many loss functions to which the decomposition in Equation 1 does not apply. For example, it does not apply to $L(t, y) = (t - y)^m$ with arbitrary m; in particular, it does not apply to absolute loss. (See Domingos (2000).) An important direction for future work is determining general properties of loss functions that are necessary and/or sufficient for Equation 1 to apply. Here we show that, as long as the loss function is a metric, it can be bounded from above and below by simple functions of the bias, variance and noise.

Theorem 7 *The following inequalities are valid for any metric loss function:*

$$E_{D,t}[L(t,y)] \leq N(x) + B(x) + V(x)$$
$$E_{D,t}[L(t,y)] \geq \max(\{N(x) - B(x) - V(x),$$
$$B(x) - V(x) - N(x),$$
$$V(x) - B(x) - N(x)\})$$

Proof. Recall that a function of two arguments $d(a_1, a_2)$ is a metric iff $\forall_{a,b} \; d(a,b) \geq d(a,a) = 0$ (minimality), $\forall_{a,b} \; d(a,b) = d(b,a)$ (symmetry), and $\forall_{a,b,c} \; d(a,b) + d(b,c) \geq d(a,c)$ (triangle inequality). Using the triangle inequality,

$$L(t,y) \leq L(t,y_*) + L(y_*,y)$$
$$\leq L(t,y_*) + L(y_*,y_m) + L(y_m,y) \quad (14)$$

Taking the expected value of this equation with respect to D and t and simplifying produces the upper bound. Using the triangle inequality and symmetry,

$$L(y_*, y_m) \leq L(y_*, t) + L(t, y) + L(y, y_m)$$
$$\leq L(t, y_*) + L(t, y) + L(y_m, y) \quad (15)$$

Rearranging terms, taking the expectation wrt D and t and simplifying leads to $E_{D,t}[L(t,y)] \geq B(x) - V(x) - N(x)$. The remaining components of the lower bound are obtained in a similar manner. □

Experiments

We used the bias-variance decomposition for zero-one loss proposed here in numerous experiments on a large suite of benchmark datasets (Blake & Merz, 2000). While space limitations preclude a full description of the experiments (see Domingos (2000)), some of the main observations made are:

- Surprisingly, varying C4.5's pruning parameter (Quinlan, 1993) has only a minor effect on bias and variance.

- Varying the maximum number of levels in C4.5's decision trees produces more interesting results. Bias typically decreases very rapidly at first (one to three levels) and then stabilizes. Net variance increases steadily but slowly, largely because variance on biased examples significantly offsets variance on unbiased ones. The minimum loss is often found at one extreme (one level or unlimited levels).

- Boosting C4.5 tends to slightly reduce bias and strongly reduce variance. The bulk of bias reduction occurs in the first few rounds, after which bias stabilizes. The variance curves are more irregular.

- In k-nearest neighbor bias increase with k dominates variance reduction. However, increasing k has the "ideal" effect of reducing variance on unbiased examples while increasing it on biased ones.

- Compared to the results of Kohavi and Wolpert (1996) with their decomposition, variance is typically a smaller contributor to error. Again, this can be largely traced to the conflicting effects of variance on biased and unbiased examples.

- There are exceptions to every one of the previous observations. In general, it is not always the case that variance increases as bias decreases, or that both vary monotonically with the "bias-variance" parameter.

Related Work

The first bias-variance decomposition for zero-one loss was proposed by Kong and Dietterich (1995). Although they proposed it in a purely *ad hoc* manner and only applied it to one ensemble learner in one artificial, noise-free domain, our results show that it is in fact a well-founded and useful decomposition, even if incomplete. Breiman (1996b) proposed a decomposition for the average zero-one loss over all examples, leaving bias and variance for a specific example x undefined. As Tibshirani (1996) points out, Breiman's definitions of bias and variance have some undesirable properties, seeming artificially constructed to produce a purely additive decomposition. Tibshirani's (1996) definitions do not suffer from these problems; on the other hand, he makes no use of the variance, instead decomposing zero-one loss into bias and an unrelated quantity he calls the "aggregation effect." Kohavi and Wolpert (1996) defined bias and variance in terms of quadratic functions of $P_t(t)$ and $P_D(y)$. Although the resulting decomposition is purely additive, it suffers from the serious problem that it does not assign zero bias to the Bayes classifier. Also, although Kohavi and Wolpert emphasize the fact that their definition of zero-one bias is not restricted to taking on the values 0 or 1, it would seem that a binary-valued bias is the natural consequence of a binary-valued loss function. In practice, Kohavi and Wolpert's method produces biased estimates of bias and variance; although their estimators can be debiased, this obscures their meaning (for example, the corrected bias can be negative). Friedman (1997) studied the relationship between zero-one loss and the bias and variance of class probability estimates. He emphasized that the effect of bias and variance is strongly non-additive; increasing variance can reduce error. In this paper we obtain similar results directly in terms of the bias and variance of class predictions, and without Friedman's restrictive assumptions (only two classes, Gaussian probabilities).

Conclusion

In this paper we proposed general definitions of bias and variance applicable to any loss function, and derived the corresponding decompositions for squared loss, zero-one loss and variable misclassification costs. We also showed that margins can be expressed as a function of zero-one bias and variance, and that a simple relationship between loss, bias and variance exists for any metric loss function. Experiments on benchmark datasets illustrated the utility of our decomposition. Directions for future work include applying the decomposition to further loss functions, and conducting further experiments. C functions implementing the bias-variance decomposition proposed in this paper are available at http://www.cs.washington.edu/homes/pedrod/bvd.c.

Acknowledgments

This research was partly supported by a PRAXIS XXI grant. The author is grateful to all those who provided the datasets used in the experiments.

References

Bauer, E., and Kohavi, R. 1999. An empirical comparison of voting classification algorithms: Bagging, boosting and variants. *Machine Learning* 36:105–142.

Blake, C., and Merz, C. J. 2000. UCI repository of machine learning databases. Machine-readable data repository, Department of Information and Computer Science, University of California at Irvine, Irvine, CA. http://www.ics.uci.edu/~mlearn/MLRepository.html.

Breiman, L. 1996a. Bagging predictors. *Machine Learning* 24:123–140.

Breiman, L. 1996b. Bias, variance and arcing classifiers. Technical Report 460, Statistics Department, University of California at Berkeley, Berkeley, CA.

Breiman, L. 1997. Arcing the edge. Technical Report 486, Statistics Department, University of California at Berkeley, Berkeley, CA.

Domingos, P., and Pazzani, M. 1997. On the optimality of the simple Bayesian classifier under zero-one loss. *Machine Learning* 29:103–130.

Domingos, P. 2000. A unified bias-variance decomposition. Technical report, Department of Computer Science and Engineering, University of Washington, Seattle, WA.

Friedman, J. H. 1997. On bias, variance, 0/1 - loss, and the curse-of-dimensionality. *Data Mining and Knowledge Discovery* 1:55–77.

Geman, S.; Bienenstock, E.; and Doursat, R. 1992. Neural networks and the bias/variance dilemma. *Neural Computation* 4:1–58.

Holte, R. C. 1993. Very simple classification rules perform well on most commonly used datasets. *Machine Learning* 11:63–91.

Kohavi, R., and Wolpert, D. H. 1996. Bias plus variance decomposition for zero-one loss functions. In *Proceedings of the Thirteenth International Conference on Machine Learning*, 275–283. Bari, Italy: Morgan Kaufmann.

Kong, E. B., and Dietterich, T. G. 1995. Error-correcting output coding corrects bias and variance. In *Proceedings of the Twelfth International Conference on Machine Learning*, 313–321. Tahoe City, CA: Morgan Kaufmann.

Quinlan, J. R. 1993. *C4.5: Programs for Machine Learning*. San Mateo, CA: Morgan Kaufmann.

Schapire, R. E.; Freund, Y.; Bartlett, P.; and Lee, W. S. 1997. Boosting the margin: A new explanation for the effectiveness of voting methods. In *Proceedings of the Fourteenth International Conference on Machine Learning*, 322–330. Nashville, TN: Morgan Kaufmann.

Tibshirani, R. 1996. Bias, variance and prediction error for classification rules. Technical report, Department of Preventive Medicine and Biostatistics and Department of Statistics, University of Toronto, Toronto, Canada.

Generalizing Boundary Points

Tapio Elomaa
Department of Computer Science
P. O. Box 26 (Teollisuuskatu 23)
FIN-00014 Univ. of Helsinki, Finland
elomaa@cs.helsinki.fi

Juho Rousu
VTT Biotechnology
Tietotie 2, P. O. Box 1500
FIN-02044 VTT, Finland
Juho.Rousu@vtt.fi

Abstract

The complexity of numerical domain partitioning depends on the number of potential cut points. In multiway partitioning this dependency is often quadratic, even exponential. Therefore, reducing the number of candidate cut points is important. For a large family of attribute evaluation functions only boundary points need to be considered as candidates. We prove that an even more general property holds for many commonly-used functions. Their optima are located on the borders of example segments in which the relative class frequency distribution is static. These borders are a subset of boundary points. Thus, even less cut points need to be examined for these functions.

The results shed a new light on the splitting properties of common attribute evaluation functions and they have practical value as well. The functions that are examined also include non-convex ones. Hence, the property introduced is not just another consequence of the convexity of a function.

Introduction

Fayyad and Irani (1992) showed that the *Average Class Entropy* and *Information Gain* functions (Quinlan 1986) obtain their optimal values for a numerical value range at a *boundary point*. Intuitively it means that these functions do not needlessly separate instances of the same class. The result reveals interesting fundamental properties of the functions, and it can also be put to use in practice: only boundary points need to be examined as potential cut points to recover the optimal binary split of the data.

Recently the utility of boundary points has been extended to cover other commonly-used evaluation functions and optimal multisplitting of numerical ranges (Elomaa and Rousu 1999). Other recent studies concerning the splitting properties of attribute evaluation functions include Breiman's (1996) research of the characteristics of ideal partitions of some impurity functions and Codrington and Brodley's (2000) study of the general requirements of well-behaved splitting functions. Similar research lines for nominal attributes are followed by Coppersmith, Hong, and Hosking (1999).

This paper continues to explore the splitting properties of attribute evaluation functions. We introduce a generalized version of boundary points—the so-called *segment borders*—which exclude all cut points in the numerical range that separate subsets of identical relative class frequency distributions. The separated subsets do not need to be class uniform to warrant the exclusion, as is the case with boundary points.

We show that it suffices to examine segment borders in optimizing the value of the best-known attribute evaluation functions. Hence, the changes in class distribution, rather than relative impurities of the subsets, define the potential locations of the optimal cut points (cf. López de Màntaras 1991). Two of the examined functions are non-convex. Hence, the property of splitting on segment borders is not only a consequence of the convexity of a function.

A *partition* $\uplus_{i=1}^{k} S_i$ of the sample S consists of k non-empty, disjoint subsets and covers the whole domain. When splitting a set S of examples on the basis of the value of an attribute A, there is a set of thresholds $\{T_1, \ldots, T_{k-1}\} \subseteq \text{Dom}(A)$ that defines a partition $\uplus_{i=1}^{k} S_i$ for the sample in an obvious manner:

$$S_i = \begin{cases} \{s \in S \mid \text{val}_A(s) \leq T_1\} & \text{if } i = 1, \\ \{s \in S \mid T_{i-1} < \text{val}_A(s) \leq T_i\} & \text{if } 1 < i < k, \\ \{s \in S \mid \text{val}_A(s) > T_{k-1}\} & \text{if } i = k, \end{cases}$$

where $\text{val}_A(s)$ denotes the value of attribute A in example s. The classification of an example s is its value for the class attribute C, $\text{val}_C(s)$.

Next section recapitulates boundary points and introduces example segments. Then we prove that six well-known functions do not partition within a segment. We also explore empirically the average numbers of boundary points and segment borders in 28 UCI data sets. Finally, we relate our results to those of Breiman (1996) and outline further research directions.

Example Segments

We recapitulate bins and blocks of examples as well as boundary points. Furthermore, we introduce segments. Rather than give unnecessarily complicated formal definitions for these simple concepts, we present them intuitively with the help of an illustration.

Copyright © 2000, American Association for Artificial Intelligence (www.aaai.org). All rights reserved.

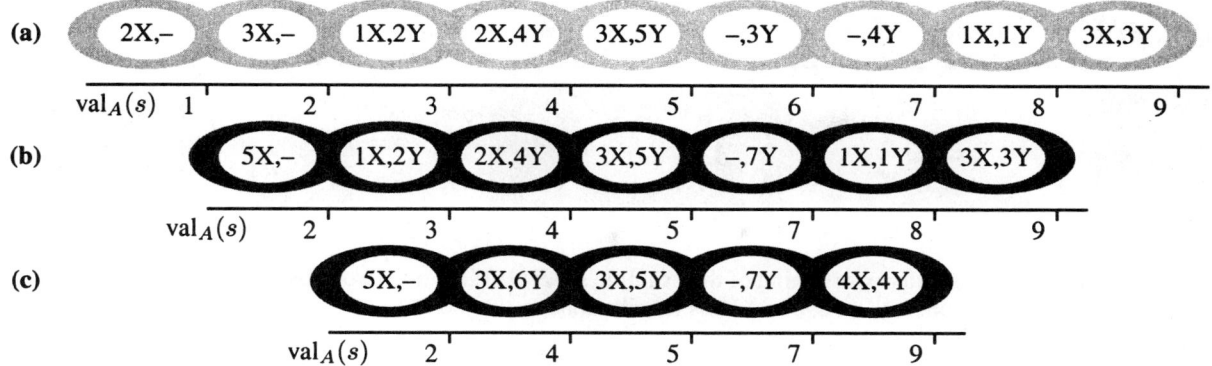

Figure 1: The (a) bins, (b) blocks, and (c) segments in the domain of a numerical attribute A in a hypothetical sample.

The definition of boundary points assumes that the sample has been sorted into ascending order with respect to the value of the numerical attribute under consideration (Fayyad and Irani 1992). Sorting is a typical preprocessing step in attribute evaluation strategies. It produces a sequence of *bins*, where all examples with an equal value for the attribute in question make up a bin of examples. Bin borders are the possible cut points of the value range. In Fig. 1a a hypothetical sample has been arranged into bins with respect to an integer-valued attribute A. The numbers of instances of different classes (X and Y in this case) belonging to the bins are depicted by the figures within them. To determine the correlation between the value of an attribute and that of the class it suffices to examine their mutual frequencies.

To construct *blocks* of examples we merge adjacent class uniform bins with the same class label (see Fig. 1b). The boundary points of the example sequence are the borders of its blocks. The points obtained thus are exactly the same as those that come out from the definition of Fayyad and Irani (1992). Block construction leaves all bins with a mixed class distribution as their own blocks.

From bins we obtain *segments* of examples by combining adjacent bins with an equal relative class distribution (see Fig. 1c). Segments group together adjacent mixed-distribution bins that have equal relative class distribution. Also adjacent class uniform bins fulfill this condition; hence, uniform blocks are a special case of segments and segment borders are a subset of boundary points.

Bins, blocks, and segments can all be identified in the same single scan over the sorted sample. Thus, taking advantage of them only incurs a linear computational cost. It is majorized by the $O(n \log n)$ time requirement of sorting, which cannot usually be avoided.

In practice, the additional cost for using segment borders in splitting is negligible. In multiway partitioning the evaluation often takes at least quadratic, even exponential, time in the number of candidate cut points. Elomaa and Rousu (2000) demonstrate up to 75% savings in time consumption on UCI data sets (Blake and Merz 1998) by preprocessing the data into segments instead of running the algorithms on the example bins.

Most Common Evaluation Functions Split on Segment Borders

In this section we show that many commonly-used attribute evaluation functions have their local optima on segment borders. Hence, partitions with intrasegment cut points can be disregarded.

All the following proofs have the same setting. The sample S contains three subsets, P, Q, and R with class frequency distributions

$$p = \sum_{j=1}^{m} p_j, \ q = \sum_{j=1}^{m} q_j, \text{ and } r = \sum_{j=1}^{m} r_j,$$

where p is the number of examples in P and p_j is the number of instances of class j in P. Furthermore, m is the number of classes. The notation is similar also for Q and R. Let us define $w_j = q_j/q \in [0, 1]$.

We consider the k-ary partition $\biguplus_{i=1}^{k} S_i$ of the sample S, where subsets S_h and S_{h+1} consist of the set $P \cup Q \cup R$, so that the split point is inside Q, on the border of P and Q, or that of Q and R (see Fig. 2). Let ℓ be an integer, $0 \leq \ell \leq q$. We assume that splitting the set Q so that ℓ examples belong to S_h and $q - \ell$ to S_{h+1} results in identical class frequency distributions for both subsets of Q regardless of the value of ℓ. In other words, for all j and ℓ it holds that $q_j(\ell) = w_j \cdot \ell$ where $q_j(\ell)$ is the frequency of class j in S_h.

The proofs treat the evaluation functions and their component functions as continuous in $[0, q]$ and twice differentiable, even though they are defined to be discrete. Observe that this causes no harm, since we only consider proving the *absence* of certain local extremas.

The proofs show in the multisplitting situation that the cut point in between two arbitrarily chosen partition subsets S_h and S_{h+1} is on a segment border. The remaining partition subsets are not affected by the placement of the cut point within $S_h \cup S_{h+1}$. Therefore, their impact usually disappears when the proof involves differentiation of the function.

Average Class Entropy

The Average Class Entropy of the partition $\biguplus_i S_i$ is

$$ACE\left(\biguplus_i S_i\right) = \sum_i \frac{|S_i|}{|S|} H(S_i) = \frac{1}{|S|} \sum_i |S_i| H(S_i),$$

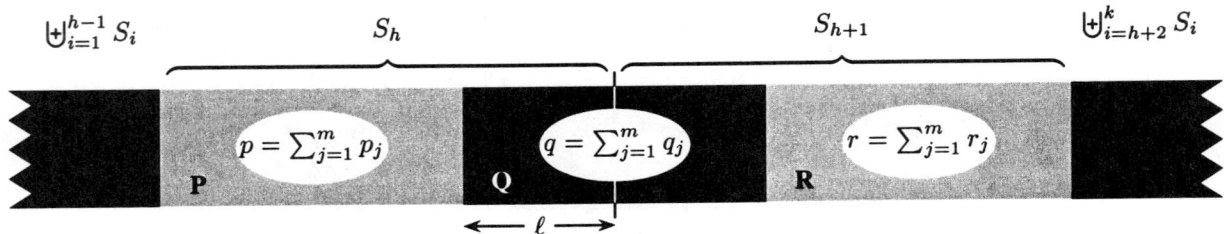

Figure 2: The following proofs consider partitioning of the example set $P \cup Q \cup R$ into two subsets S_h and S_{h+1} within Q. No matter where, within Q, the cut point is placed, equal class distributions result.

where H is the *entropy* function,

$$H(S) = -\sum_{j=1}^{m} P(C_j, S) \log P(C_j, S),$$

in which m denotes the number of classes and $P(C, S)$ stands for the proportion of the examples in S that belong to the class C.

We take all logarithms in this paper to be natural logarithms; it makes the manipulation and notation simpler. It is easy to check that our proofs can be worked through with binary logarithms as well.

Theorem 1 *The Average Class Entropy optimal partitions are defined on segment borders.*

Proof Let $L(\ell)$ denote the value of $\sum_{i=1}^{h} |S_i| H(S_i)$ when S_h contains P and the first ℓ examples from Q, and $R(\ell)$ the value $\sum_{i=h+1}^{k} |S_i| H(S_i)$. Now,

$$L(\ell) = \sum_{i=1}^{h-1} |S_i| H(S_i) - \sum_{j=1}^{m} (p_j + w_j \ell) \log \frac{p_j + w_j \ell}{p + \ell}$$

$$= \sum_{i=1}^{h-1} |S_i| H(S_i) + (p + \ell) \log(p + \ell)$$

$$- \sum_{j=1}^{m} (p_j + w_j \ell) \log(p_j + w_j \ell)$$

and, similarly,

$$R(\ell) = \sum_{i=h+2}^{k} |S_i| H(S_i) + (r + q - \ell) \log(r + q - \ell)$$

$$- \sum_{j=1}^{m} (r_j + q_j - w_j \ell) \log(r_j + q_j - w_j \ell).$$

Since the first sum in the formula of $L(\ell)$ is independent of the placing of the h-th cut point, it differentiates to zero and the second derivative of $L(\ell)$ is

$$L''(\ell) = \frac{1}{p + \ell} - \sum_{j=1}^{m} \frac{w_j^2}{p_j + w_j \ell}$$

$$= \frac{1}{p + \ell} - \sum_{j=1}^{m} \frac{w_j}{p_j/w_j + \ell}.$$

The remaining sum can be interpreted as the weighted arithmetic mean of the terms $1/(p_j/w_j + \ell), 1 \le j \le m$, and by the arithmetic-harmonic mean inequality (Hardy, Littlewood, and Pólya 1934, Meyer 1984) be bound from below by the corresponding harmonic mean

$$\sum_{j=1}^{m} w_j \frac{1}{p_j/w_j + \ell} \ge \frac{1}{\sum_{j=1}^{m} w_j (p_j/w_j + \ell)}$$

$$= \frac{1}{\sum_{j=1}^{m} (p_j + w_j \ell)} = \frac{1}{p + \ell}.$$

Thus, $L''(\ell) \le 0$.

Correspondingly, the second derivative of $R(\ell)$ can be approximated by majorizing the second term by the harmonic mean

$$R''(\ell) = \frac{1}{r + q - \ell} - \sum_{j=1}^{m} \frac{w_j^2}{r_j + q_j - w_j \ell}$$

$$\le \frac{1}{r + q - \ell} - \frac{1}{\sum_{j=1}^{m} w_j((r_j + q_j)/w_j - \ell)}$$

$$= 0.$$

Hence, we have shown that the second derivative of *ACE*, $ACE''(\ell) = (L''(\ell) + R''(\ell))/|S|$, is non-positive for all ℓ. This forces all local extrema of *ACE* within Q to be maxima. □

Information Gain

Information gain function, or the *Mutual Information*, is a simple modification of *ACE*. Thus, proving that it does not partition within segments is straightforward.

Theorem 2 *The Information Gain optimal partitions are defined on segment borders.*

Proof The Information Gain of the partition $\biguplus_{i=1}^{k} S_i$, when the h-th cut point is placed after the ℓ-th example of Q, is

$$IG(\ell) = H(S) - ACE(\ell).$$

The constant term $H(S)$ that does not depend on the value of ℓ differentiates to zero. Therefore, $IG'(\ell) = -ACE'(\ell)$ and its second derivative is $-ACE''(\ell)$. From the proof of Theorem 1 we know that $ACE''(\ell) \le 0$, which means that $IG''(\ell) \ge 0$. Hence, *IG* cannot have a local maximum within segment Q. □

Gain Ratio

To penalize against *IG*'s excessive favoring of multi-valued nominal attributes and multisplitting numerical attribute value ranges, Quinlan (1986) suggested dividing the *IG* score of a partition by the term

$$\kappa\left(\biguplus_i S_i\right) = -\sum_i \frac{|S_i|}{|S|} \log \frac{|S_i|}{|S|}.$$

The resulting evaluation function is the *Gain Ratio*

$$GR\left(\biguplus S_i\right) = IG\left(\biguplus S_i\right) / \kappa\left(\biguplus S_i\right).$$

The *IG* function was already inspected above. Therefore, the following proof concentrates on the denominator κ.

Theorem 3 *The Gain Ratio optimal partitions are defined on segment borders.*

Proof The denominator κ of the *GR* formula in our proof setting is

$$\begin{aligned}\kappa(\ell) &= \kappa\left(\biguplus_{i=1}^{h-1} S_i\right) + \frac{1}{|S|}\Big((p+q+r)\log|S| \\ &\quad - (p+\ell)\log(p+\ell) - (r+q-\ell) \\ &\quad \cdot \log(r+q-\ell)\Big) + \kappa\left(\biguplus_{i=h+2}^{k} S_i\right).\end{aligned}$$

The second derivative of $\kappa(\ell)$ w.r.t. ℓ is

$$\kappa''(\ell) = \frac{1}{|S|}\left(\frac{-1}{p+\ell} + \frac{-1}{r+q-\ell}\right) < 0. \quad (1)$$

The first derivative of $GR(\ell)$ is given by

$$GR'(\ell) = \frac{IG'(\ell)\kappa(\ell) - \kappa'(\ell)IG(\ell)}{\kappa^2(\ell)}.$$

Let us define $N(\ell) = IG'(\ell)\kappa(\ell) - \kappa'(\ell)IG(\ell)$, and note that

$$\begin{aligned}N'(\ell) &= IG''(\ell)\kappa(\ell) + \kappa'(\ell)IG'(\ell) \\ &\quad - \kappa''(\ell)IG(\ell) - \kappa'(\ell)IG'(\ell) \\ &= IG''(\ell)\kappa(\ell) - \kappa''(\ell)IG(\ell) \\ &\geq 0,\end{aligned}$$

because for each $0 < \ell < q$ it holds by definition that $\kappa(\ell) > 0$ and $IG(\ell) \geq 0$. Furthermore, by Theorem 2 we know that $IG''(\ell) \geq 0$ and by Eq. 1 that $\kappa''(\ell) < 0$.

Now the second derivative of $GR(\ell)$ is expressed by

$$GR''(\ell) = \frac{N'(\ell)\kappa^2(\ell) - 2\kappa(\ell)\kappa'(\ell)N(\ell)}{\kappa^4(\ell)}.$$

Let $\psi \in]0, q[$ be a potential location for a local maximum of *GR*, i.e., such a point that $GR'(\psi) = 0$. Then also $N(\psi) = 0$ and the expression for $GR''(\psi)$ is further simplified to

$$GR''(\psi) = N'(\psi)/\kappa^2(\psi),$$

which is larger than zero because $N'(\psi) \geq 0$ and $\kappa^2(\psi) > 0$. In other words, $GR(\psi)$ is not a local maximum. Since ψ was chosen arbitrarily, we have shown that $GR(\ell)$ can only obtain its maximum value when the threshold is placed at either of the segment borders, where $\ell = 0$ and $\ell = q$, respectively. □

Normalized Distance Measure

The *Normalized Distance Measure* was proposed by López de Màntaras (1991) as an alternative to the Information Gain and Gain Ratio functions. It can be expressed with the help of the Information Gain as

$$ND\left(\biguplus S_i\right) = 1 - IG\left(\biguplus S_i\right) / \lambda\left(\biguplus S_i\right),$$

where

$$\lambda\left(\biguplus_{i=1}^k S_i\right) = -\sum_{i=1}^k \sum_{j=1}^m \frac{M(j, S_i)}{|S|} \log \frac{M(j, S_i)}{|S|},$$

in which $M(j, S)$ stands for the number of instances of class j in the set S.

The following proof concerns instead the function

$$ND_1\left(\biguplus S_i\right) = 1 - ND\left(\biguplus S_i\right) = \frac{IG(\biguplus S_i)}{\lambda(\biguplus S_i)},$$

from which the claim directly follows for *ND*.

The ND_1 formula resembles that of *GR*. Therefore, the proof outline is also the same.

Theorem 4 *The Normalized Distance Measure optimal partitions are defined on segment borders.*

Proof Let $L(\ell)$ denote the value of $\lambda(\biguplus_{i=1}^h S_i)$ and $R(\ell)$ the value $\lambda(\biguplus_{i=h+1}^k S_i)$.

$$\begin{aligned}L(\ell) &= \lambda\left(\biguplus_{i=1}^{h-1} S_i\right) - \sum_{j=1}^m \frac{p_j + w_j\ell}{|S|} \log \frac{p_j + w_j\ell}{|S|} \\ &= \lambda\left(\biguplus_{i=1}^{h-1} S_i\right) + \frac{1}{|S|}\Big((p+\ell)\log|S| \\ &\quad - \sum_{j=1}^m (p_j + w_j\ell)\log(p_j + w_j\ell)\Big).\end{aligned}$$

and

$$\begin{aligned}R(\ell) &= \lambda\left(\biguplus_{i=h+2}^{k} S_i\right) + \frac{1}{|S|}\Big((r+q-\ell)\log|S| \\ &\quad - \sum_{j=1}^m (r_j + q_j + w_j\ell)\log(r_j + q_j - \ell)\Big).\end{aligned}$$

The second derivative of $L(\ell)$ is given by

$$L''(\ell) = \frac{-1}{|S|} \sum_{j=1}^m \frac{w_j^2}{p_j + w_j\ell} \leq 0,$$

because $|S|$, w_j, p_j, and ℓ are all non-negative.

Correspondingly, the second derivative of $R(\ell)$ is

$$R''(\ell) = \frac{-1}{|S|} \sum_{j=1}^m \frac{w_j^2}{r_j + q_j - w_j\ell} \leq 0.$$

Thus, we have proved that the second derivative of λ, $\lambda''(\ell) = L''(\ell) + R''(\ell)$ is non-positive for all ℓ.

The proof for ND_1 is easy to complete similarly as the proof for the Gain Ratio. Thus, the local extrema of ND_1 within Q are minima, which makes them local maxima of $ND(\ell) = 1 - ND_1(\ell)$. Hence, Normalized Distance measure does not obtain its minimum value within a segment. □

Gini Index

Gini Index (of diversity), or the *Quadratic Entropy*, (Breiman et al. 1984, Breiman 1996) is defined as

$$GI\left(\biguplus_i S_i\right) = \sum_i \frac{|S_i|}{|S|} gini(S_i),$$

in which *gini* is the impurity measure

$$\begin{aligned} gini(S) &= \sum_{j=1}^m P(C_j, S)(1 - P(C_j, S)) \\ &= 1 - \sum_{j=1}^m P^2(C_j, S), \end{aligned}$$

where $P(C, S)$ denotes the proportion of instances of class C in the data S.

Theorem 5 *The Gini Index optimal partitions are defined on segment borders.*

Proof Let $L(\ell)$ denote the value of $\sum_{i=1}^h |S_i|gini(S_i)$ when S_h contains P and the first ℓ examples from Q, and $R(\ell)$ the value $\sum_{i=h+1}^k |S_i|gini(S_i)$. Now,

$$L(\ell) = \sum_{i=1}^{h-1} |S_i|gini(S_i) + (p+\ell) - \sum_{j=1}^m \frac{(p_j + w_j\ell)^2}{p+\ell}.$$

The first derivative of $L(\ell)$ is

$$1 - \sum_{j=1}^m \frac{2(p_j + w_j\ell)w_j(p+\ell) - (p_j + w_j\ell)^2}{(p+\ell)^2}.$$

From which, by straightforward manipulation, we obtain

$$L''(\ell) = -2\sum_{j=1}^m \frac{(p_j + w_j p)^2}{(p+\ell)^3} \leq 0.$$

By symmetry we determine that $R''(\ell) \leq 0$ as well. Thus, $GI''(\ell) = (L''(\ell) + R''(\ell))/|S| \leq 0$ and, therefore, GI does not obtain its minimum value within the segment Q. □

Training Set Error

The *majority* class of sample S is its most frequently occurring class:

$$\text{maj}_C(S) = \arg\max_{1 \leq j \leq m} |\{s \in S \mid \text{val}_C(s) = j\}|.$$

The number of *disagreeing* instances, those in the set S not belonging to its majority class, is given by

$$\delta(S) = |\{s \in S \mid \text{val}_C(s) \neq \text{maj}_C(S)\}|.$$

Training Set Error is the number of training instances falsely classified in the partition. For a partition $\biguplus S_i$ of S it is defined as

$$TSE\left(\biguplus_i S_i\right) = \sum_i \delta(S_i).$$

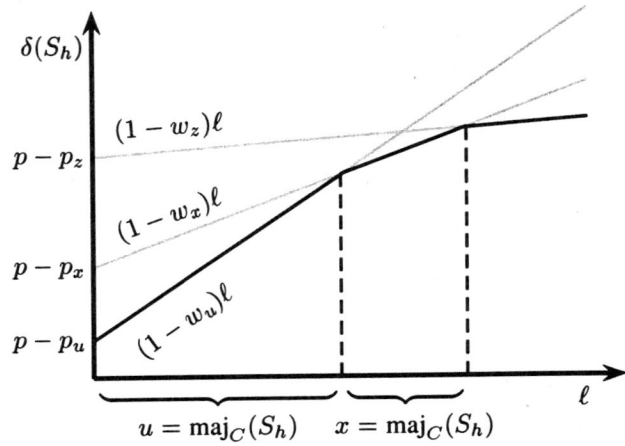

Figure 3: The number of instances of other classes than j grows linearly with increasing ℓ for all j. $\delta(S_h)$ is convex.

The number of instances in S_h from other classes than j, $(p-p_j) + (1-w_j)\ell$, is linearly increasing for any j, since the first term is constant and $0 \leq w_j \leq 1$. Respectively, in S_{h+1} the number of those instances, $(r - r_j) + (1 - w_j)(q - \ell)$, decreases with increasing ℓ.

In our proof setting, the majority class of S_h depends on the growth rates of classes in Q and the number of their instances in P. First, when $\ell = 0$, the majority class of P, say u, is also the majority class of S_h. Subsequently an other class x, with strictly larger growth rate $w_x > w_u$ may become the majority class of S_h (see Fig. 3). Observe that $p_x \leq p_u$. As a combination of non-decreasing functions, $\delta(S_h)$ is also non-decreasing.

Theorem 6 *The Training Set Error optimal partitions are defined on segment borders.*

Proof Let us examine the value of $TSE(l) = \delta(S_h) + \delta(S_{h+1})$ at an arbitrary cut point $\ell = l$, $0 \leq l \leq q$. Let u and v be the majority classes of S_h and S_{h+1}, respectively, in this situation. Then,

$$\begin{aligned} TSE(l) &= (p - p_u) + (1 - w_u)l \\ &\quad + (r - r_v) + (1 - w_v)(q - l). \end{aligned}$$

We now show that a smaller training set error is obtained by moving the cut point to the left or to the right from l. There are four possible scenarios for the changes of majority classes of S_h and S_{h+1} when the cut point is moved: (i) neither of them changes, only the majority class of (ii) S_h or (iii) S_{h+1} changes, or (iv) both of them change. Let x and y, when needed, be the new majority classes of S_h and S_{h+1}, respectively.

Assume, now, that $w_u \leq w_v$. Let us consider the four scenarios mentioned when moving the cut point one example to the left.

(i) $\begin{aligned} TSE(l-1) &= (p - p_u) + (1 - w_u)(l - 1) \\ &\quad + (r - r_v) + (1 - w_v)(q - l + 1) \\ &= TSE(l) + w_u - w_v \leq TSE(l), \end{aligned}$

because $w_u - w_v \leq 0$ by the assumption.

(ii) The majority class of S_h becomes x and v remains to be the majority class of S_{h+1}. Then

$$\begin{aligned} TSE(l-1) &= (p - p_x) + (1 - w_x)(l - 1) \\ &\quad + (r - r_v) + (1 - w_v)(q - l + 1) \\ &\leq TSE(l) + w_x - w_v, \end{aligned}$$

because $(p - p_x) \leq (p - p_u)$ and $(1 - w_x) < (1 - w_u)$. Since $w_x < w_u \leq w_v$ by the assumption, we have shown that $TSE(l - 1) \leq TSE(l)$.

(iii) The majority class of S_h remains to be u and y becomes the majority class of S_{h+1}. Observe that then $(r - r_y) + (1 - w_y)(q - l + 1) \leq (r - r_v) + (1 - w_v)(q - l + 1)$, by y being the majority class of S_{h+1}. Thus,

$$TSE(l - 1) \leq TSE(l) + w_u - w_v \leq TSE(l).$$

(iv) If both majority classes change, then by combining (ii) and (iii) we see that $TSE(l - 1) \leq TSE(l)$.

Hence, in all scenarios a smaller value of TSE is obtained by moving the cut point. Similarly, if $w_u \geq w_v$ we can obtain a smaller training set error for $S_h \uplus S_{h+1}$ by sliding the cut point forward in Q.

In any case, the cut point can be slid all the way to one of the borders of Q. Because l was chosen arbitrarily and

$$TSE\left(\biguplus_{i=1}^{k} S_i\right) = \sum_{i=1}^{h-1} \delta(S_i) + TSE(l) + \sum_{i=h+2}^{k} \delta(S_i),$$

we have proved the claim. □

Experiments

We test for 28 well-known UCI domains (Blake and Merz 1998) the effects of concentrating on segment borders. Fig. 4 depicts the average numbers of bin borders (the figures on the right) and the relative portions of boundary points (black bars) and segment borders (white bars) per numerical attribute of the domain. Gray bars indicate that the numbers of boundary points and segment borders are the same.

From Fig. 4 we see that the average number of segment borders per attribute is only marginally smaller than that of the boundary points. By combining bins into segments, in real-world data, almost all reduction in the number of points that need to be examined comes from combination of class uniform bins, only very few mixed bins get combined. The reason for this is obvious: even small changes—caused, e.g., by attribute noise—to the class distribution prevent combining neighboring mixed bins.

The segment construction is as efficient as block combination. Therefore, nothing is lost by taking advantage of the small reduction in the number of cut points examined.

Discussion

We have shown that the result of Fayyad and Irani (1992) can be properly generalized. Class uniform bins are not the only ones that can be grouped together without losing the optimal partition. In practice, though, they turn out to be far more numerous than other segments with static relative class

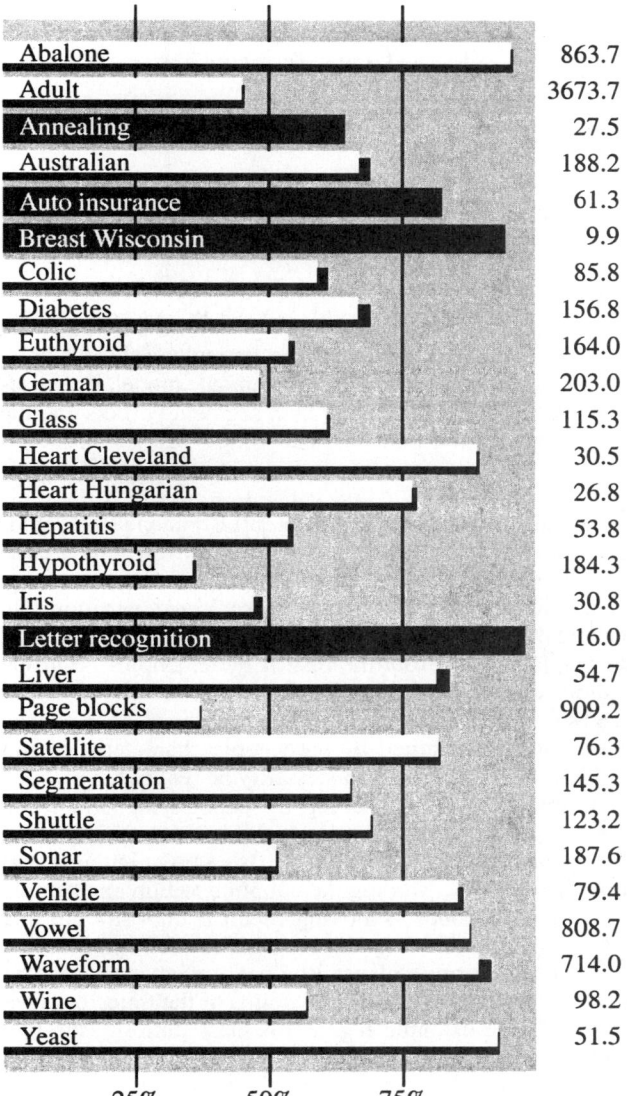

Figure 4: The average number of bin borders (the figures on the right) and the relative numbers of boundary points (black bars) and segment borders (white bars) per numerical attribute of the domain. Gray bars indicate that the numbers of segment borders and boundary points are the same.

frequency distribution. However, even small reductions in the number of cut points are valuable in the optimal partitioning tasks, where the time complexity can be quadratic or exponential in the number of cut points.

Most common evaluation functions behave in the way we would like them to: minimizing on non-boundary cut points would mean needless separation of instances of the same class. Moreover, minimizing within segments that have an identical relative class distributions would mean separating instances even if we have no evidence that they need different handling.

Even if the popular evaluation functions are similar in the

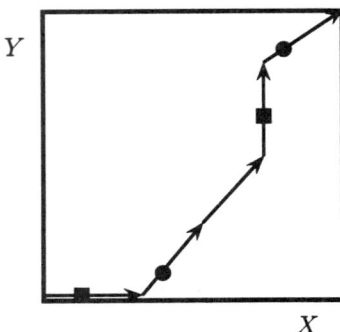

Figure 5: The effects on vector α of moving the cut point through the data set in Fig. 1 in Breiman's model. The discs denote boundary points other than segment borders and the squares denote non-boundary cut points.

above sense, their biases are different. Breiman (1996) studied for Gini Index and Average Class Entropy which class frequency distribution, if given the freedom to choose any, would produce the optimal score for a binary partition. He showed that Gini Index ideally separates all the instances of the majority class from the rest of the examples. Entropy minimization, on the other hand, aims at producing equal-sized subsets. In practice, the choices for the class frequency distributions are limited by the sample characteristics and the ideal partitions cannot necessarily be realized.

In Breiman's (1996) setting α_j denotes the proportion of examples of class j that lie to the left of a binary split. Hence, the vector $\alpha = \langle \alpha_1, \ldots, \alpha_m \rangle$ is a point in the hypercube $A = [0,1]^m$. Moving the cut point within an example segment corresponds to moving vector α on a straight line in the hypercube A. Moving it over a set that spans multiple segments, forms a piecewise linear trajectory in A. The segment borders are the turning points of the trajectory (see Fig. 5). If the example segment is class uniform, the line is axis-parallel. Non-boundary cut points fall on such line segments. Boundary points other than segment borders are situated on lines that are not axis-parallel, which correspond to segments with a mixed class distribution.

The practical uses of the results in this paper are somewhat hampered by the fact that small differences in neighboring blocks are inevitably present even if their underlying true class distributions were the same. These differences arise because of sampling of examples and noise. Hence, it is rare to find a sequence of cut points to lie exactly on a single line in the space A.

Thus, it would be useful to consider situations where the the relative class distributions of the neighboring blocks were allowed to differ. The questions for further research include whether the absence of optima can still be guaranteed, how much deviation can be allowed, and which types of deviations make it easier to guarantee the absence of optima within the example segment.

Acknowledgments

We thank Jyrki Kivinen for advice on the arithmetic-harmonic mean inequality.

References

Blake, C. L. and Merz, C. J. 1998. UCI Repository of Machine Learning Databases. Univ. of California, Irvine, Dept. of Information and Computer Science. http://www.ics.uci.edu/~mlearn/MLRepository.html.

Breiman, L. 1996. Some Properties of Splitting Criteria. *Machine Learning* **24**: 41–47.

Breiman, L., Friedman, J. H., Olshen, R. A., and Stone, C. J. 1984. *Classification and Regression Trees*. Pacific Grove, Calif.: Wadsworth.

Codrington, C. W. and Brodley, C. E. 2000. On the Qualitative Behavior of Impurity-Based Splitting Rules I: The Minima-Free Property. *Machine Learning*. Forthcoming.

Coppersmith, D., Hong, S. J., and Hosking, J. R. M. 1999. Partitioning Nominal Attributes in Decision Trees. *Data Mining and Knowledge Discovery* **3**: 197–217.

Elomaa, T. and Rousu, J. 1999. General and Efficient Multisplitting of Numerical Attributes. *Machine Learning* **36**: 201–244.

Elomaa, T. and Rousu, J. 2000. Uses of Convexity in Numerical Domain Partitioning. Submitted.

Fayyad, U. M. and Irani, K. B. 1992. On the Handling of Continuous-Valued Attributes in Decision Tree Generation. *Machine Learning* **8**: 87–102.

Hardy, G. H., Littlewood, J. E., and Pólya, G. 1934. *Inequalities*. Cambridge, UK: Cambridge Univ. Press.

López de Màntaras, R. 1991. A Distance-Based Attribute Selection Measure for Decision Tree Induction. *Machine Learning* **6**: 81–92.

Meyer, B. 1984. Some Inequalities for Elementary Mean Values. *Mathematics of Computation* **42**: 193–194.

Quinlan, J. R. 1986. Induction of Decision Trees. *Machine Learning* **1**: 81–106.

Boosted Wrapper Induction

Dayne Freitag
Just Research
Pittsburgh, PA, USA
dayne@cs.cmu.edu

Nicholas Kushmerick
Department of Computer Science
University College Dublin, Ireland
nick@ucd.ie

Abstract

Recent work in machine learning for *information extraction* has focused on two distinct sub-problems: the conventional problem of filling template slots from natural language text, and the problem of *wrapper induction*, learning simple extraction procedures ("wrappers") for highly structured text such as Web pages produced by CGI scripts. For suitably regular domains, existing wrapper induction algorithms can efficiently learn wrappers that are simple and highly accurate, but the regularity bias of these algorithms makes them unsuitable for most conventional information extraction tasks. *Boosting* is a technique for improving the performance of a simple machine learning algorithm by repeatedly applying it to the training set with different example weightings. We describe an algorithm that learns simple, low-coverage wrapper-like extraction patterns, which we then apply to conventional information extraction problems using boosting. The result is BWI, a trainable information extraction system with a strong precision bias and F1 performance better than state-of-the-art techniques in many domains.

Introduction

Information extraction (IE) is the problem of converting text such as newswire articles or Web pages into structured data objects suitable for automatic processing. An example domain, first investigated in the Message Understanding Conference (MUC) (Def 1995), is a collection of newspaper articles describing terrorist incidents in Latin America. Given an article, the goal might be to extract the name of the perpetrator and victim, and the instrument and location of the attack. Research with this and similar domains demonstrated the applicability of machine learning to IE (Soderland 1996; Kim and Moldovan 1995; Huffman 1996).

The increasing importance of the Internet has brought attention to all kinds of automatic document processing, including IE. And it has given rise to problem domains in which the kind of linguistically intensive approaches explored in MUC are difficult or unnecessary. Many documents from this realm, including email, Usenet posts, and Web pages, rely on extra-linguistic structures, such as HTML tags, document formatting, and ungrammatical stereotypic language, to convey essential information. Much recent work in IE, therefore, has focused on learning approaches that do not require linguistic information, but that can exploit other kinds of regularities. To this end, several distinct rule-learning algorithms (Soderland 1999; Califf 1998; Freitag 1998) and multi-strategy approaches (Freitag 2000) have been shown to be effective. Recently, statistical approaches using hidden Markov models have achieved high performance levels (Leek 1997; Bikel *et al.* 1997; Freitag and McCallum 1999).

At the same time, work on information integration (Wiederhold 1996; Levy *et al.* 1998) has led to a need for specialized *wrapper* procedures for extracting structured information from database-like Web pages. Recent research (Kushmerick *et al.* 1997; Kushmerick 2000; Hsu and Dung 1998; Muslea *et al.* 2000) has shown that wrappers can be automatically learned for many kinds of highly regular documents, such as Web pages generated by CGI scripts. These *wrapper induction* techniques learn simple but highly accurate contextual patterns, such as "to retrieve a URL, extract the text between <A href=" and ">". Wrapper induction is harder for pages with complicated content or less rigidly-structured formatting, but recent algorithms (Hsu and Dung 1998; Muslea *et al.* 2000) can discover small sets of such patterns that are highly effective at handling such complications in many domains.

In this paper, we demonstrate that wrapper induction techniques can be used to perform extraction in traditional (natural text) domains. We describe BWI, a trainable IE system that performs information extraction in both traditional (natural text) and wrapper (machine-generated or rigidly-structured text) domains. BWI learns extraction rules composed only of simple contextual patterns. Extraction is triggered by specific token sequences preceding and following the start or end of a target field. For example, BWI might learn the pattern ⟨[< a href = "], [http]⟩ for finding the beginning of a URL, and the pattern ⟨[. html], [" >]⟩ for finding the end, which would

---
Copyright © 2000, American Association for Artificial Intelligence (www.aaai.org). All rights reserved.

extract "http://xyz.com/index.html" from " ···<a href="http://xyz.com/index.html">···".

Of course, the documents used for traditional IE tasks do not exhibit the kind of regular structure assumed in wrapper induction. Consider the task of extracting the speaker's name from a seminar announcement. A significant fraction of documents in the seminar announcement corpus we use for experiments have the speaker's name prefixed by "Who:". Similarly, many speaker names begin with honorifics such as "Dr.". These observations suggest that simple contextual patterns such as ⟨[who :], [dr .]⟩ could be used to identify the start of the speaker's name with high precision.

However, while such a pattern may have high precision, it will generally have low recall: this pattern strongly indicates the beginning of a speaker's name, but it occurs in only a fraction of documents. To apply wrapper induction techniques to IE from natural text, we must generate many such simple patterns, and then combine their predictions in some reasonable way. Previous work on learning rules for information extraction assume that the final extractor will be some combination, typically a disjunction, of individual rules, each one covering only a fraction of the training phrases. However, whereas previous techniques learn individual rules that cover as many of the training examples as possible, BWI learns rules that individually have limited power and coverage, but that can be learned efficiently and are easy to understand.

Boosting is a procedure for improving the performance of a "weak" machine learning algorithm by repeatedly applying it to the training set, at each step modifying training example weights to emphasize examples on which the weak learner has done poorly in previous steps (Schapire and Singer 1998). The ability of boosting to improve upon the performance of the underlying weak learner has been verified in a wide range of empirical studies in recent years.

In this paper, we demonstrate that boosting can be used effectively for information extraction. Our BWI algorithm uses boosting to generate and combine the predictions from numerous extraction patterns. The result is a trainable information extraction system that, in our experiments, performs better than previous rule learning approaches, and is competitive with a state-of-the-art statistical technique.

In the remainder of this paper, we (1) formally describe the extraction patterns BWI learns; (2) describe the BWI algorithm; and (3) empirically evaluate BWI on eight document collections.

Problem Statement

We begin by explaining how we treat IE as a classification problem, and then describe the classifiers (*wrappers*) that BWI learns.

Information Extraction as Classification. We treat *documents* as sequences of *tokens*, and the IE task is to identify one or more distinguished token subsequences called *fields*. Specifically, IE involves identifying the *boundaries* that indicate the beginning and end of each field; below, the symbols i and j refer to boundaries. We cast this as a classification problem, where instances correspond to boundaries—the space between any two adjacent tokens—and the goal is to approximate two target extraction functions, X_{begin} and X_{end}:

$$X_{\text{begin}}(i) = \begin{cases} 1 & \text{if } i \text{ begins a field} \\ 0 & \text{otherwise} \end{cases}$$

Similarly, X_{end} is 1 for field-ending boundaries and 0 otherwise.

To learn such a function X (either X_{begin} or X_{end}), a learning algorithm is given a training set $\{\langle i, X(i) \rangle\}$ and must output a function that approximates X.

Wrappers. A *pattern* is a sequence of tokens (e.g., [who :] or [dr .]). A pattern *matches* a token sequence in a document if the tokens are identical. (Below we enrich this notion of matching when we describe BWI's use of wildcards.)

A *boundary detector* $d = \langle p, s \rangle$ is a pair of patterns: a *prefix* pattern p and a *suffix* pattern s. A boundary detector (hereafter, simply "detector") $d = \langle p, s \rangle$ *matches* a boundary i if p matches the tokens before i and s matches the tokens after i. We treat a detector d as a function from a boundary to $\{0,1\}$: $d(i) = 1$ if d matches i, and 0 otherwise. Finally, associated with every detector d is a numeric *confidence* value C_d.

A *wrapper* $W = \langle F, A, H \rangle$ consists of two sets $F = \{F_1, F_2, \ldots, F_T\}$ and $A = \{A_1, A_2, \ldots, A_T\}$ of detectors, and a function $H : [-\infty, +\infty] \to [0, 1]$. The intent is that F (the "fore" detectors) identifies field-starting boundaries, A (the "aft" detectors) identifies the field end boundaries, and $H(k)$ reflects the probability that a field has length k.

To perform extraction using wrapper W, every boundary i in a document is first given a "fore" score $F(i) = \sum_k C_{F_k} F_k(i)$ and an "aft" score $A(i) = \sum_k C_{A_k} A_k(i)$. W then classifies text fragment $\langle i, j \rangle$ as follows:

$$W(i,j) = \begin{cases} 1 & \text{if } F(i)A(j)H(j-i) > \tau \\ 0 & \text{otherwise} \end{cases},$$

where τ is a numeric threshold.

The rationale is that W compares τ to an estimate of the probability of correct classification. The value of $H(\cdot)$ is proportional to a maximum-likelihood estimate that a fragment is a particular length, given that it is a target fragment. If we assume that $F(\cdot)$ and $A(\cdot)$ are also proportional to the conditional probability of finding a beginning or ending boundary, respectively, then the product of the three values is proportional to a naive Bayesian estimate with uniform priors.

By varying τ one can force a tradeoff between precision and recall. In our experiments we use the full-recall setting $\tau = 0$, because (as our experiments demonstrate) BWI is generally biased toward precision.

```
procedure BWI(example sets S and E)
    F ← AdaBoost(LearnDetector, S)
    A ← AdaBoost(LearnDetector, E)
    H ← field length histogram from S and E
    return wrapper W = ⟨F, A, H⟩
```

Figure 1: The BWI algorithm.

```
procedure LearnDetector(example set Y)
    prefix pattern p ← []
    suffix pattern s ← []
    loop
        prefix pattern p' ← BestPreExt(⟨p, s⟩, Y)
        suffix pattern s' ← BestSufExt(⟨p, s⟩, Y)
        if score(⟨p', s⟩) > score(⟨p, s'⟩)
            if score(⟨p', s⟩) > score(⟨p, s⟩)
                p ← the last |p| + 1 tokens of p'
            else return detector ⟨p, s⟩
        else
            if score(⟨p, s'⟩) > score(⟨p, s⟩)
                s ← the first |s| + 1 tokens of s'
            else return detector ⟨p, s⟩
```

Figure 2: The LearnDetector weak learner.

The BWI algorithm

Learning a wrapper W involves determining the "fore" and "aft" detectors F and A, and the function H, given the example sets S and E. In this section, we describe BWI, our algorithm that solves problems of this form.

Fig. 1 lists BWI. The function H reflects the prior probability of various field lengths. BWI estimates these probabilities by constructing a frequency histogram $H(k)$ recording the number of fields of length k were encountered in the training set. To learn F and A, BWI boosts LearnDetector, an algorithm for learning a single detector.

Boosting. Freund and Shapire's generalized AdaBoost algorithm maintains a distribution $D_t(i)$ over the training examples. Initially, D_0 is uniform. On iteration t, the weak learner is invoked, resulting in hypothesis d_t (what we have called a detector), a weight C_{d_t} is assigned to d_t, and then the distribution is updated as follows:

$$D_{t+1}(i) = D_t(i)\exp(-C_{d_t} d_t(i)(2X(i) - 1))/N_t$$

where $X(i) \in \{1, 0\}$ is the label of i, and N_t is a normalization factor. AdaBoost simply repeats this learn-update cycle T times, and then returns a list of the learned weak hypotheses with their weights.

The LearnDetector Weak Learner. Fig. 2 shows the weak learning algorithm LearnDetector. LearnDetector generates a single detector; BWI invokes LearnDetector (indirectly through AdaBoost) T times to learn the "fore" detectors F, and then T more times to learn the "aft" detectors A. LearnDetector iteratively builds out from the empty detector $\langle[],[]\rangle$. At each step, LearnDetector invokes the functions BestPreExt and BestSufExt, which search for the best extension of length L (the *lookahead* parameter) or less to the prefix and suffix (respectively) of the current detector. These extensions are exhaustively enumerated.

The current detector and the best extensions are then compared to maximize a scoring function. If an extension is found which results in a detector that scores better than the current one, then the first token of the extension (the rightmost of a prefix extension, the leftmost of a suffix extension) is added to the appropriate part of the current detector, and the process repeats. The procedure returns when no extension yields a better score than the current detector.

The function score(d) computes the score of detector $d = \langle p, s\rangle$. Cohen and Singer 1999 describe SLIPPER, a boosting algorithm which infers a single rule at each step. BWI's scoring method is identical to that used by SLIPPER. For a detector d, let M_d^+ be the correctly classified training boundaries (i.e., the boundaries in the training set Y matched by d and labeled 1), and M_d^- be the incorrectly classified examples. Cohen and Singer showed that training error is minimized by using:

$$\text{score}(d) = \sqrt{W_d^+} - \sqrt{W_d^-},$$

and assigning detector d the confidence value:

$$C_d = \frac{1}{2}\ln\left(\frac{W_d^+ + \epsilon}{W_d^- + \epsilon}\right),$$

where $W_d^+ = \sum_{i \in M_d^+} D_t(i)$, is the total weight of the correctly classified boundaries, $D_t(i)$ is the weight of boundary i during boosting iteration t, W_d^- is a similar sum over the set M_d^-, and ϵ is a small smoothing parameter.

Wildcards. As described so far, BWI learns only wrappers that match exact token sequences. We have extended BWI to handle *wildcards*. A wildcard is a special token that matches one of a set of tokens. BWI uses the following wildcards:

- <Alph> matches any token that contains only alphabetic characters
- <ANum>, contains only alphanumeric characters
- <Cap>, begins with an upper-case letter
- <LC>, begins with a lower-case letter
- <SChar>, any one-character token
- <Num>, containing only digits
- <Punc>, a punctuation token
- <*>, any token

Extending BWI to handle wildcards is straightforward: we simply modify BestPreExt and BestSufExt to enumerate all sequences of tokens and wildcards, rather than just tokens.

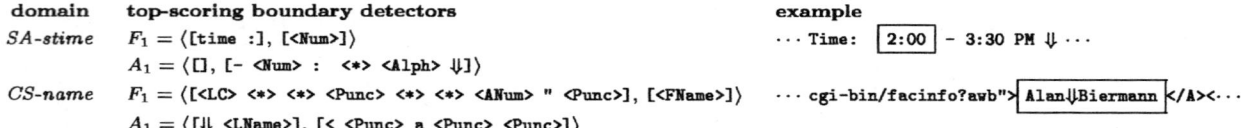

Figure 3: Examples of boundary detectors learned by BWI for the *SA* and *CS* domains. "⇓" is the return character. The wildcards <FName> and <LName> stand for first name and last name; see details below.

Experimental Results

We evaluated BWI on 16 information extraction tasks defined over eight distinct document collections:

- *SA*: A collection of 486 seminar announcements. Fields: *speaker* (speaker's name); *location* (seminar location); *stime* (starting time); and *etime* (ending time).

- *Acq*: A collection of 600 Reuters articles detailing coporate acquisitions. Fields: *acq* (name of purchased company); and *dlramt* (purchase price).

- *Jobs*: A collection of 298 Usenet job announcements. Fields: *id* (message identifier); *company* (company name); *title* (job title).

- *CS*: A collection of Web pages listing the faculty of 30 computer science departments. Field: *name* (faculty member names).

- *Zagats*: A collection of 91 Web pages containing restaurant reviews. Field: *addr* (addresses of restaurants).

- *LATimes*: A collection of 20 Web pages containing restaurant descriptions. Field: *cc* (credit cards accepted by restaurants).

- *IAF*: A collection of 10 pages from an Web email search engine. Fields: *altname* (person's alternate name); and *org* (host organization).

- *QS*: A collection of 10 pages from an Web stock quote service. Fields: *date* (quote date); and *vol* (trading volume).

We chose these collections because they have been widely used in previous research. The first three domains are typical for the traditional IE techniques, while the last five are typical for the wrapper induction techniques. Fig. 3 gives examples of wrappers learned by BWI for two of these tasks.

In our experiments, we adopt the standard *cross validation* methodology: the document collection is partitioned several times into a training set and a testing set. We learn a wrapper using the training set, and then measure its performance using the testing set.

Given a test document, BWI extracts zero or more fields. In order for an extraction to be counted as correct, the exact boundaries of a target fragment must be identified. For the "traditional" domains (*SA*, *Acq* and *Jobs*), we exploit the assumption that each document contains at most one field, and discard all but the highest-confidence prediction. In the "wrapper" domains (*CS*, *Zagats*, *LATimes*, *IAF* and *QS*), documents may contain multiple fields, so we keep all predictions with confidence greater than $\tau = 0$.

We evaluate performance in terms of three metrics: *precision*, the number of correctly extracted fields divided by the total number of extractions; *recall*, the number of correct extractions divided by the total number of fields actually present in the documents, and *F1*, the harmonic mean of precision and recall. We report all values as percentages.

Our experiments were designed to answer four questions:

1. What effect does the number of rounds of boosting T have on performance?
2. What effect does the look-ahead parameter L have on performance?
3. How important are wildcards?
4. How does BWI compare with other learning algorithms on the same tasks?

To address Questions 1–3, we devised a set of experiments using the four *SA* tasks, and we discuss the other domains when the results are significantly different. To answer Question 4, we compare BWI with four alternative learning algorithms.

Question 1: Boosting. To measure sensitivity to the number of rounds of boosting, we fixed look-ahead at $L = 3$, gave BWI the default wildcard set, and varied the number of rounds of boosting from $T = 1$ to 500. As Fig. 4 suggests, the number of rounds required by BWI to reach peak performance depends on the difficulty of the task. On easy tasks, such as *SA-stime*, BWI quickly achieves its peak performance. On more difficult tasks, such as *SA-speaker*, as many as 500 rounds may be required.

On the "wrapper" tasks, many fewer rounds of boosting are required. For example, BWI stops improving after $T = 5$ on *IAF-altname*, and a single round of boosting yields perfect performance on *QS-Date*. These sources are formatted in a highly regular fashion, so just just a handful of boundary detectors are needed.

Question 2: Look-Ahead. Performance improves with increasing look-ahead L, as indicated in Fig. 5. For the *CS* tasks, performance improvements are marginal beyond a look-ahead of 3. This is fortunate, because

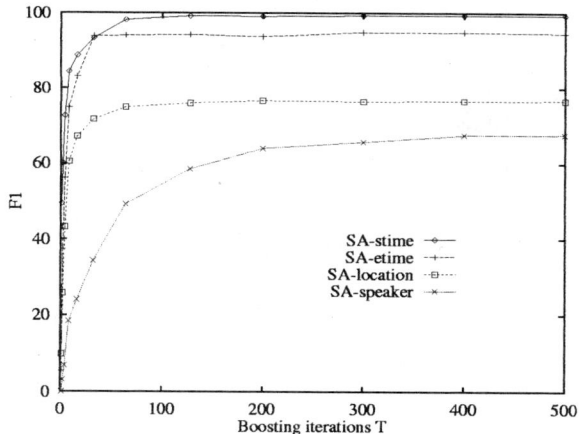

Figure 4: F1 performance on the *SA* tasks as a function of the number of rounds of boosting T.

L	speaker	location	stime	etime
1	7.0	40.1	27.7	7.4
2	51.9	76.6	95.0	84.9
3	67.7	76.7	99.4	94.6
4	69.3	75.5	99.6	93.9

Figure 5: F1 performance on the *SA* tasks as a function of look-ahead L.

training time increases exponentially with look-ahead. With look-ahead set to $L = 3$, BWI took 3,183 sec. to complete 100 rounds of boosting using the default feature set for the speaker task on a 300 MHz. Pentium II; with $L = 4$, it took 13,958 sec.

However, much deeper lookahead is required in some domains. For example, in the *IAF-altname* task, $L = 3$ results in $F1 = 0$, but $L = 8$ yields $F1 = 58.8$. The explanation is that *IAF-altname* requires a 30-token "fore" boundary detector prefix, but shorter prefixes have a very low score, so BWI can find the correct prefix only with very deep lookahead.

Question 3: Wildcards. Wildcards are important to achieve good performance on traditional IE problems. Fig. 6 presents F1 performance on the *SA* task with various wildcard sets. In each case, we performed 500 rounds of boosting with look-ahead set to 3. The "*none*" row lists performance in the absence of wildcards; "*just <*>*" lists performance with only the <*> wildcard; "*default*" lists performance using the full set of eight wildcards listed above.

Finally, we evaluated BWI after adding task-specific lexical resources in the form of three additional wildcards: <FName> matches tokens in a list of common first names released by the U.S. Census Bureau; <LName> matches tokens in a similar list of common last names; and <NEW> matches tokens not found in /usr/dict/words on Unix systems ("NEW" stands for

wildcards	speaker	location	stime	etime
none	15.1	69.2	95.7	83.4
just <*>	49.4	73.5	99.3	95.0
default	67.7	76.7	99.4	94.6
lexical	73.5	—	—	—

Figure 6: F1 performance on the *SA* tasks as a function of various wildcard sets.

"not an English word"). These lexical resources increase F1 from 67.7 to 73.5 on the *SA-speaker* task. It is common in traditional IE to use task-specific lexicons as part of the extraction process. Our results show how such lexicons can be integrated with learning in a way that leads to improved performance.

Question 4: Other Algorithms. Figs. 7–8 compares BWI on the sixteen extraction tasks with four other state-of-the-art learners: two rule learners (SRV (Freitag 1998) and Rapier (Califf 1998)), an algorithm based on hidden Markov models[1], and the Stalker wrapper induction algorithm (Muslea *et al.* 2000).

For the four "traditional" domains, we used $T = 500$ boosting iterations and set the lookahead to $L = 3$, and used the default wildcards. For the five "wrapper" domains we use $T = 50$ and two different settings for L and the wildcards. For *CS-name*, *Zagats-addr*, *LATimes-cc* and *QS-date*, we used $L = 3$ and the lexical wildcards. For *IAF-altname*, *IAF-org* and *QS-vol*, we used $L = 8$ because (as described above) the tasks require very long boundary detectors. Since BWI is exponential in L, the only feasible way to run the BWI with $L = 8$ was to use just the <*> wildcard.

We include precision and recall scores in order to illustrate an interesting aspect of BWI's behavior—its precision bias. The extractors produced by BWI tend to achieve higher precision than the other learners, particularly the HMM, while still managing good recall.

Conclusions

The automatic processing of machine-readable text is becoming increasingly important. Techniques for information extraction—the task of populating a pre-defined database with fragments from free text documents—are central to a broad range of text-management applications.

We have described BWI, a novel approach to building a trainable information extraction system. Like wrapper induction techniques, BWI learns relatively simple contextual patterns identifying the beginning and end of relevant text fields. BWI repeatedly invokes an algorithm for learning such boundaries. By using

---

[1] The HMM in question has four fully connected "target" states, a prefix and suffix, each of length four, and uses shrinkage to mitigate data sparsity. This model has shown state-of-the-art performance on a range of IE tasks; see Freitag and McCallum (1999) for details

	SA-speaker			SA-location			SA-stime			SA-etime					
	Prec	Rec	F1	Prec	Rec	F1	Prec	Rec	F1	Prec	Rec	F1			
HMM	77.9	75.2	76.6	83.0	74.6	78.6	98.5	98.5	98.5	45.7	97.0	62.1			
Rapier	80.9	39.4	53.0	91.0	60.5	72.7	93.9	92.9	93.4	95.8	96.6	96.2			
SRV	54.4	58.4	56.3	74.5	70.1	72.3	98.6	98.4	98.5	67.3	92.6	77.9			
BWI	79.1	59.2	67.7	85.4	69.6	76.7	99.6	99.6	99.6	94.4	94.9	93.9			
	Jobs-id			Jobs-company			Jobs-title			Acq-acq			Acq-dlramt		
HMM	—	—	—	38.6	72.3	50.4	53.2	63.0	57.7	32.8	29.2	30.9	49.3	63.5	55.5
Rapier	98.0	97.0	97.5	76.0	64.8	70.0	67.0	29.0	40.5	57.3	19.2	28.8	63.3	28.5	39.3
SRV	—	—	—	—	—	—	—	—	—	40.7	39.4	40.1	48.1	67.0	56.0
BWI	100	100	100	88.4	70.1	78.2	59.6	43.2	50.1	55.5	24.6	34.1	63.4	42.6	50.9
	LATimes-cc			Zagats-addr			IAF-altname			IAF-org					
HMM	98.5	100	99.3	97.7	99.5	98.6	1.7	90.0	3.4	16.8	89.7	28.4			
Stalker	100	—	—	100	—	—	100	—	—	48.0	—	—			
BWI	99.6	100	99.8	100	93.7	96.7	90.9	43.5	58.8	77.5	45.9	57.7			
	CS-name			QS-date			QS-vol								
HMM	41.3	65.0	50.5	36.3	100	53.3	18.4	96.2	30.9						
Stalker	—	—	—	0	—	—	0	—	—						
BWI	77.1	31.4	44.6	100	100	100	100	61.9	76.5						

Figure 7: BWI compared with four competing algorithms on sixteen tasks.

the AdaBoost algorithm, BWI repeatedly reweights the training examples so that subsequent patterns handle training examples missed by previous rules.

The result is an extraction algorithm with a bias to high precision (because the learned contextual patterns are highly accurate) but with reasonable recall in many domains (due to the fact that dozens or hundreds—but not millions—of such patterns suffice for broad coverage). We have evaluated BWI on a broad range of IE tasks, from traditional free text to machine-generated HTML, and find that BWI is competitive with state-of-the-art algorithms in most domains, and superior in many.

Acknowledgements. This research was funded in part by grant N00014-00-1-0021 from the US Office of Naval Research, and grant ST/1999/071 from Enterprise Ireland.

References

D. Bikel, S. Miller, R. Schwartz, and R. Weischedel. Nymble: a high-performance learning name-finder. In *Proc. ANLP-97*, pages 194–201, 1997.

M.-E. Califf. *Relational Learning Techniques for Natural Language Information Extraction*. PhD thesis, University of Texas at Austin, 1998.

W. Cohen and Y. Singer. A simple, fast, and effective rule learner. In *Proc. Sixteenth National Conference on Artificial Intelligence*, 1999.

Defense Advanced Research Projects Agency. *Proc. Sixth Message Understanding Conference (MUC-6)*. Morgan Kaufmann Publisher, Inc., 1995.

D. Freitag and A. McCallum. Information extraction using HMMs and shrinkage. In *Proc. AAAI-99 Workshop on Machine Learning for Information Extraction*, 1999. AAAI Technical Report WS-99-11.

D. Freitag. Information extraction from HTML: Application of a general machine learning approach. In *Proc. Fifteenth National Conference on Artificial Intelligence*, 1998.

D. Freitag. Machine learning for information extraction in informal domains. *Machine Learning*, 39(2/3), 2000.

C. Hsu and M. Dung. Generating finite-state transducers for semistructured data extraction from the web. *J. Information Systems*, 23(8), 1998.

S. Huffman. Learning information extraction patterns from examples. In *Connectionist, Statistical, and Symbolic Approaches to Learning for Natural Language Processing*, volume 1040 of *Lecture Notes in Artificial Intelligence*, pages 246–260. Springer-Verlag, Berlin, 1996.

J.-T. Kim and D. Moldovan. Acquisition of linguistic patterns for knowledge-based information extraction. *IEEE Trans. on Knowledge and Data Engineering*, 7(5):713–724, 1995.

N. Kushmerick, D. Weld, and R. Doorenbos. Wrapper Induction for Information Extraction. In *Proc. 15th Int. Conf. Artificial Intelligence*, pages 729–35, 1997.

N. Kushmerick. Wrapper induction: Efficiency and expressiveness. *Artificial Intelligence*, 2000. In press.

T. Leek. Information extraction using hidden Markov models. Master's thesis, UC San Diego, 1997.

A. Levy, C. Knoblock, S. Minton, and W. Cohen. Trends and controversies: Information integration. *IEEE Intelligent Systems*, 13(5), 1998.

I. Muslea, S. Minton, and C. Knoblock. Hierachi-

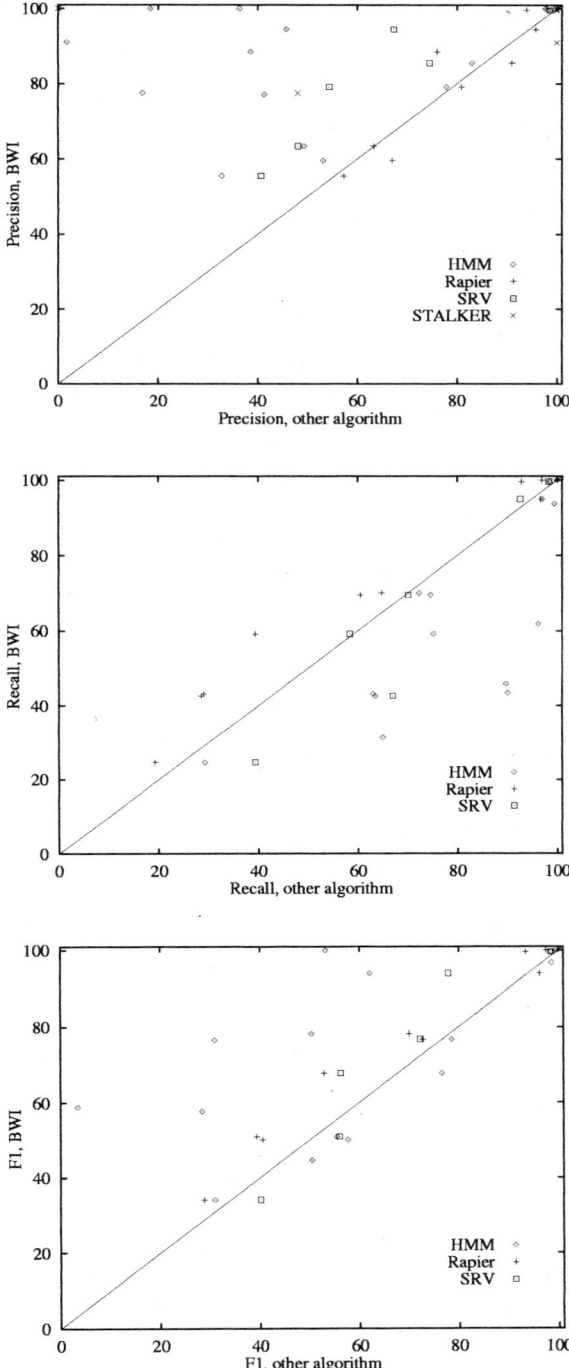

Figure 8: Graphical summaries of the data in Fig. 7. Each point represents a comparison between BWI and one other algorithm; points above the straight lines indicate domains in which BWI performs better.

cal wrapper induction for semistructured information sources. *J. Autonomous Agents and Multi-Agent Systems*, 2000. In press.

R. Schapire and Y. Singer. Improved boosting algorithms using confidence-rated predictions. In *Proc. Eleventh Annual Conference on Computational Learning Theory*, 1998.

S. Soderland. *Learning Text Analysis Rules for Domain-specific Natural Language Processing*. PhD thesis, University of Massachusetts, 1996. CS Tech. Report 96-087.

S. Soderland. Learning information extraction rules for semi-structured and free text. *Machine Learning*, 34(1/3):233–272, 1999.

G. Wiederhold. *Intelligent Information Integration*. Kluwer, 1996.

Information Extraction with HMM Structures Learned by Stochastic Optimization

Dayne Freitag and **Andrew McCallum**

Just Research
4616 Henry Street
Pittsburgh, PA 15213
{dayne,mccallum}@justresearch.com

Abstract

Recent research has demonstrated the strong performance of hidden Markov models applied to *information extraction*—the task of populating database slots with corresponding phrases from text documents. A remaining problem, however, is the selection of state-transition structure for the model. This paper demonstrates that extraction accuracy strongly depends on the selection of structure, and presents an algorithm for automatically finding good structures by stochastic optimization. Our algorithm begins with a simple model and then performs hill-climbing in the space of possible structures by splitting states and gauging performance on a validation set. Experimental results show that this technique finds HMM models that almost always out-perform a fixed model, and have superior average performance across tasks.

Introduction

The Internet makes available a tremendous amount of text that has been generated for human consumption; unfortunately, this information is not easily manipulated or analyzed by computers. *Information extraction* (IE) is the process of filling fields in a database by automatically extracting fragments of human-readable text. Examples include extracting the location of a meeting from an email message, or the name of a corporate takeover target.

Recent research has demonstrated the effectiveness of hidden Markov models (HMMs) for information extraction. HMMs have been applied successfully to many sub-domains of information extraction: the named entity extraction task (Bikel *et al.* 1997); to the task of recovering the sequence of a set of entities occurring in close proximity (*dense extraction*) (Seymore *et al.* 1999); as well as the *sparse extraction* task, in which the object is to extract relevant phrases from documents containing much irrelevant text (Leek 1997; Freitag and McCallum 1999). In many cases, the accuracy of HMMs applied to these tasks is state-of-the-art and often significantly better than alternative learning approaches.

We address the sparse extraction task. We assume that for every document in a corpus there is a corresponding relational record (template), each slot of which is either empty or is filled with a fragment of text from the document. For

Copyright © 2000, American Association for Artificial Intelligence (www.aaai.org). All rights reserved.

example, an electronic seminar announcement might contain the title of the talk, the name of the speaker, the starting time, etc. These typed relevant fragments are called *fields*.

For each field we train a separate HMM. In performing extraction on a particular file, the model must account for all tokens in the document. Special states (called "target states") are trained to emit only those tokens that are part of the phrases to be extracted. Other states ("background states") are designated to emit non-target tokens. By varying the number and connection among states, we can design models that account for a wide range of text patterns, including patterns of language in the neighborhood of target phrases and the structure of the phrases themselves.

A significant problem when applying HMMs to information extraction is the selection of state-transition structure. Certain structures better capture the observed phenomena in the prefix, target and suffix sequences around certain targets. For example, if we know that we want to extract names, we might set aside a single target state for honorifics, one for first names, and one for last names, and connect these states in a way that matches our intuitions. Unfortunately the approach of building structures by hand does not scale to large corpora and is difficult to follow in practice. Furthermore, human intuitions do not always correspond to structures that make the best use of HMM potential.

This paper shows that the selection of state-transition structure effects tremendously the accuracy of the HMM extractor, and presents a stochastic-optimization approach for learning good task-specific structures automatically. Our method begins with a minimal number of states, explores various state splitting operations, selects the operation that gives best performance on a labeled validation set, and recursively explores further splitting operations. The final model is then chosen by cross-validation from those generated.

The idea of automatic structure selection for HMMs is not new (Stolcke and Omohundro 1994; Carrasco and Oncina 1994; Vasko *et al.* 1997; Lockwood and Blanchet 1993), and it has been applied to the problem of dense extraction (Seymore *et al.* 1999). Unlike this and much of the other work—which typically uses goodness of statistical fit to the data—our structure selection process at each step dicriminatively optimizes performance on the task at hand. It also shows much greater improvements due to structure learning. Whether this improvement is possible only in the context of sparse extraction is a question for future research.

We present experimental results on four different data sets. The learned structures give higher accuracy than previously attained using hand-built models, and also outperform SRV and Rapier, two state-of-the-art information extraction systems that employ ILP methods (Freitag 1998; Califf 1998).

HMMs for Information Extraction

Like many tasks involving discrete sequences, good performance on information extraction (IE) tasks relies on powerful modeling of context as well as the current observations. Finite state machines, such as hidden Markov models, offer a good balance between simplicity and expressiveness of context.

Hidden Markov Models

A HMM is a finite state automaton with stochastic state transitions and symbol emissions (Rabiner 1989). The automaton models a probabilistic generative processes whereby a sequence of symbols is produced by starting in some state, transitioning to a new state, emitting a symbol selected by that state, transitioning again, emitting another symbol—and so on until a designated final state is reached. Associated with each of a set of states, $S = \{s_1, \cdots, s_n\}$, is a probability distribution over the symbols in the emission vocabulary $V = \{w_1, w_2, \cdots w_K\}$. The probability that state s_j will emit the vocabulary item w is written $P(w|s_j)$. Similarly, associated with each state is a distribution over its outgoing transitions. The probability of moving from state s_i to state s_j is written $P(s_j|s_i)$. There is also a prior state distribution $P_0(s)$. Training data consists of several sequences of observed emissions, one of which would be written $\{o_1, o_2, \cdots o_m\}$.

Information Extraction with HMMs

Given a model and all its parameters, IE is performed by determining the sequence of states that was most likely to have generated the entire document, and extracting the symbols that were associated with certain designated "target" states. Determining this sequence is efficiently performed by dynamic programming with the *Viterbi* algorithm (Rabiner 1989).

The models we use for IE have the following characteristics:

- Each HMM extracts just one type of field (such as "seminar speaker"). When multiple fields are to be extracted from the same document (such as "seminar speaker" and "seminar location"), a separate HMM is constructed for each field.

- They model the entire document, and thus do not require pre-processing to segment document into sentences or other pieces. The entire text of each training document is used to train transition and emission probabilities.

- They contain two kinds of states, target states and non-target states. Target states are intended to produce the tokens we want to extract.

- They are not fully connected. The restricted transition structure captures context that helps improve extraction accuracy.

For IE, in addition to the traditional HMM parameters and training data, we have labels indicating which are the "target" states and observations. Let $L(s)$ be a binary value indicating whether state s is among the target states. Each training instance is also labeled to indicate which observations are among the target observations for this task, represented by a sequence of binary labels for each observation sequence, written $\{l_1, l_2, \cdots l_m\}$.

Parameter Estimation

Once the state-transition structure is determined, the remaining parameters of the model are the transition and emission probabilities. For IE both are estimated using labeled training data—that is, sequences of words with the target words already identified.

In some HMM structures, the labels determine a unique path through the states. If a unique path does not exist, then we use EM (in the form of Baum-Welch) to iteratively estimate parameters and fill in the missing path. In the E-step we estimate the expected path exactly as in Rabiner 1989, except that we also obey the target label constraints. Hence, for example, the iteration step of the forward procedure becomes:

$$\alpha_{t+1}(s) = \begin{cases} 0 & \text{if } l_{t+1} \neq L(s) \\ \sum_{s'} \alpha_t(s) P(s|s') P(o_{t+1}|s) & \text{otherwise} \end{cases} \quad (1)$$

and the backward procedure is modified analogously.

Transition probabilities are low-degree multinomials, which we estimate by maximum likelihood with ratios of counts, as is traditional. Emission probabilities on the other hand are very high-degree multinomials and require smoothing with a prior because training data is extremely sparse relative to the number of parameters.

Rather than smoothing simply against the uniform distribution, the results in this paper build on work in using shrinkage with HMMs for information extraction (Freitag and McCallum 1999). In many machine learning tasks there is a tension between constructing complex models with many states and constructing simple models with only a few states. The complex model is able to represent intricate structure of the task, but often results in poor (high variance) parameter estimation because the training data is highly fragmented. The simple model results in robust parameter estimates, but performs poorly because it is not sufficiently expressive to model the data (too much bias).

Shrinkage (a general term that includes "hierarchical Bayes" or "empirical Bayes") is a family of statistical techniques that balance these competing concerns. In our HMMs shrinkage is used to "shrink" parameter estimates from data-sparse states of the complex model toward the estimates in related data-rich states of the simpler models. The combination of the estimates is provably optimal under the appropriate conditions. We employ a form of shrinkage that combines the estimates with a weighted average, and

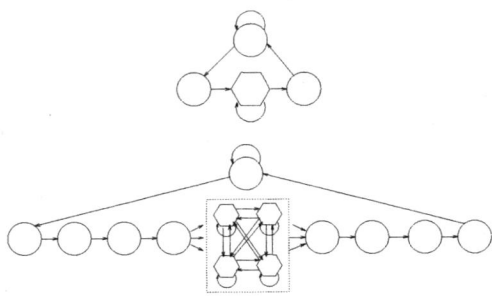

Figure 1: Two example HMM structures. Circle nodes represent non-target states; hexagon nodes represent target states.

learns the weights with Expectation-Maximization. Thus, the smoothed, shrinkage-based emission probability of word w being emitted by state s is

$$\lambda_1 P(w|s) + \lambda_2 P(w|a(s)) + \lambda_3 (1/K) \qquad (2)$$

where the last term represents the uniform distribution, $\lambda_1 + \lambda_2 + \lambda_3 = 1$, and $a(s)$ is the "parent" of state s in the shrinkage hierarchy, (*i.e.* the data-rich abstract state in the simpler model). In our implementation all target states share a parent, and all non-target state share another parent. Space limitations prevent a full description of our shrinkage implementation here; see Freitag and McCallum (Freitag and McCallum 1999) for the details.

Learning State-Transition Structure by Stochastic Optimization

The class of structures we consider for information extraction reflects our intuition that successful extraction requires a learner to model both the typical contents of a field and its context to either side. We distinguish four types of states:

- **Target** States required to model the content of target phrases.
- **Prefix** A prefix is a set of one or more states connected as a string. A prefix state transitions only to the next state in the string or, if it is the last state in the string, to one or more target states. Models are designed in such a way that, if a state sequence (such as that returned by Viterbi) passes through any target state, it must first pass through a prefix.
- **Suffix** A suffix is similar in structure to a prefix. Any state sequence must pass through a suffix upon leaving the set of target states.
- **Background** Background states model any text not modeled by other kinds of states. A background state has outgoing transitions only to itself and to the beginnings of all prefixes, and it has incoming transitions only from itself and the ends of all suffixes.

Figure 1 shows two HMM structures that meet our criteria. The bottom model has a single background state, a prefix and suffix of length four, and four fully interconnected target states. This model performs quite well on a range of information extraction tasks. The top model is the simplest we consider and serves as the starting point for our method's search in structure space.

Beginning with the simple model in Figure 1 we perform hill-climbing in the space of possible structures, at each step applying each of a set of operations to the current model and selecting one of the resulting structures as the next model. For the experiments reported here we define seven operations:

- **Lengthen a prefix** A single state is added to the end of a prefix. The penultimate state now transitions only to the new state; the new state transitions to any target states to which the penultimate state previously transitioned.
- **Split a prefix** A duplicate is made of some prefix. Transitions are duplicated so that the first and last states of the new prefix have the same connectivity to the rest of the network as the old prefix.
- **Lengthen a suffix** The dual of the prefix-lengthening operation.
- **Split a suffix** Identical to the prefix-splitting operation, except applied to a suffix.
- **Lengthen a target string** Similar to the prefix-lengthening operation, except that all target states, in contrast with prefix and suffix states, have self-transitions. The single target state in the simple model in Figure 1 is a target string of length one.
- **Split a target string** Identical to the prefix-splitting operation, except applied to a target string.
- **Add a background state** Add a new background state to the model, with the same connectivity, with respect to the non-background states, as all other background states: the new state has outgoing transitions only to prefix states and incoming transitions only from suffix states.

Note that some of these operations may be applied in several ways, resulting in distinct structures, depending on the model. The result of applying any operation is the set of all topologically distinct models it can generate.

In our experiments, for efficiency, all structures have the same shrinkage configuration, as described in the previous section. Note that the shrinkage configuration can also be determined through optimization, in at least two ways: (1) The two states created in a splitting operation might share a local shrinkage distribution, as well as the distributions created as part of previous splits. The resulting hierarchical configuration would thereby reflect the sequence of operations that led to its construction. (2) We might include an additional set of shrinkage modification operators independently in the stochastic optimization.

Table 1 presents our method for selecting structure. It consists of two loops: one in which a set of structures is generated using one-step look-ahead hill-climbing and F1 performance on a hold-out set;[1] and one in which the models from this set are re-scored using 3-fold cross-validation

---
[1] See the next section for a description of the F1 metric.

```
procedure LearnStructure(LabeledSet, Ops)
    ValidSet ← 1/3 of LabeledSet
    TrainSet ← LabeledSet − ValidSet
    CurModel ← the simple model
    Keepers ← {CurModel}
    I ← 0
    while I < 20 and CurModel has fewer than 25 states
        Candidates ← {M|M ∈ op(CurModel) ∧ op ∈ Ops}
        for M ∈ Candidates
            score(M) ← average of 3 runs trained on
                TrainSet and scored for F1 on ValidSet
        CurModel ← M ∈ Candidates with highest score
        Keepers ← Keepers ∪ {CurModel}
        I ← I + 1
    for M ∈ Keepers
        score(M) ← average F1 from
            3-fold cross-validation on LabeledSet
    return M ∈ Keepers with highest score
```

Table 1: The optimization procedure used to select HMM structure.

on the training set. At any given step in the first loop, **LearnStructure** selects as the next model the single candidate that scores the best average F1 from several training/testing runs. We average several runs in this way, seeding the model in a different way each time, because Baum-Welch settles into different local optima depending on the initial parameter settings. The model returned by **LearnStructure** is the one from the series of generated structures that scores the best F1 in separate runs of three-fold cross-validation on the training set.

Experimental Results

We tested our approach on eight information extraction tasks defined over 4 document collections: **(1)** *SA*: A collection of 485 seminar announcements posted electronically at a large university. Fields include *speaker*, the name of the speaker at the seminar, and *location* the location (e.g., room number) of the seminar. **(2)** *Acq*: A collection of 600 Reuters articles detailing coporate acquisitions. Fields include *acquired*, the name of the company to be purchased, and *dlramt*, the purchase or estimated price of the sale. **(3)** *Jobs*: A collection of 298 Usenet job announcements. Fields include *company*, the name of the company seeking to hire, and *title*, the job title.) **(4)** *CFP*: A collection of 363 Internet "Call for Paper" announcements in ASCII format. Fields include *conf*, the name of the conference, and *deadline*, the full-paper submission deadline. Except for the *CFP* collection, all of these corpora have been used in previously published research.

For each of our experiments we adopt the same basic procedure: The document collection is partitioned several times into a training set and a testing set. We train a learner using the training set and measure its performance using the testing set. In the case of the approach described in this paper, we use the training set both to select a model structure and to set its parameters. With the exception of the *Jobs* partitions, the training and testing sets are of roughly equal size. The *Jobs* partitions—exactly those used in Califf (Califf 1998)—contain 90% training and 10% testing. Results from experiments we ran represent average performance over three training/testing splits. Rapier's scores are those reported in Califf (Califf 1998); they represent average performance over ten training/testing splits.

In the extraction problems we consider here, there is a single correct filler (which may occur several times in a document, with slight variations) for each slot in the answer template. Given a test document, a learner must identify a target fragment or, if none is present, decline to perform an extraction. In order for an extraction to be counted as correct, the precise boundaries of a target fragment must be identified. If a learner issues multiple predictions for a document, we take only the one with highest confidence. Two metrics characterize the performance of a learner: *precision*, the number of correct extractions divided by the number of documents for which the learner issued any prediction; and *recall*, the number of correct extractions divided by the number of documents containing one or more target fragments. We report *F1*, the harmonic mean of precision and recall.

We compare structure learning with four other approaches, two rule-learning approaches previously reported in the literature—SRV (Freitag 1998) and Rapier (Califf 1998)—and two static HMM models. Both SRV and Rapier are relational rule learners that have been shown to perform well on a variety of tasks. SRV induces rules "top down," beginning with a most general rule and specializing. Rapier induces rules bottom up, successively generalizing to cover target phrases. Rows labeled "Simple HMM" and "Complex HMM" show the performance of the two static models shown in Figure 1. Note that the "Simple HMM" is the model with which structure selection begins.

Table 2 shows the F1 performance of the HMM with learned structure on eight tasks and, for each of the four competing approaches, lists the difference in F1 score between the "Grown HMM" and the respective approach. It is clear from these results that, on balance, HMMs are to be preferred over the rule learners mentioned here. They achieve superior performance on almost all tasks, sometimes by substantial margins. Even the "Simple HMM" occasionally out-performs the symbolic methods.

Of course, in order for an HMM to realize its potential, some structure selection is required, as the "vs. Simple HMM" row in Table 2 indicates. The average performance difference with the simple model constitutes an improvement of 24%. A well-designed static model (row "Complex HMM" in Table 2) can achieve good performance, but on average its performance lags behind a dynamically selected model. Note that the complex model was selected based on considerable manual interaction with the *SA* domain, particularly the *speaker* task. It is in some sense optimized for this task, so it comes as no surprise that this is one of the few tasks on which structure learning yields worse results than the static model.

Figure 2 shows parts of the structures of HMMs designed to extract seminar locations and speakers, respectively. Transitions are labeled with the probability assigned to them by Baum-Welch; only transitions with probability greather than 0.1 are shown. Each node in the *location* graph

	speaker	location	acquired	dlramt	title	company	conf	deadline	Average
Grown HMM	76.9	87.5	41.3	54.4	58.3	65.4	27.2	46.5	57.2
vs. SRV	+19.8	+16.0	+1.1	-1.6	—	—	—	—	+8.8
vs. Rapier	+23.9	+14.8	+12.5	+15.1	-11.7	+24.9	—	—	+13.3
vs. Simple HMM	+24.3	+5.6	+14.3	+5.6	+5.7	+11.1	+15.7	+6.7	+11.1
vs. Complex HMM	-2.1	+6.7	+7.5	-0.3	-0.3	+19.1	+0.0	-6.8	+3.0

Table 2: Difference in F1 performance between the HMM using a learned structure and other methods. The + numbers indicate how much better our Grown HMM did than the alternative method.

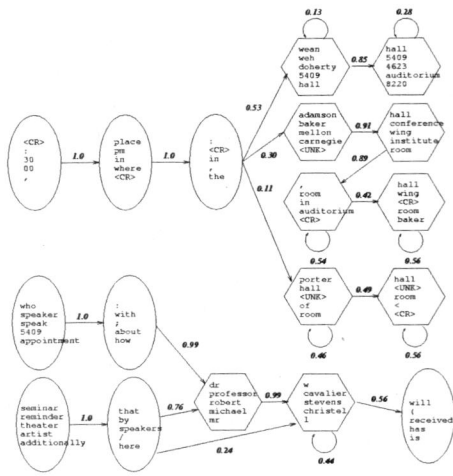

Figure 2: Part of two learned structures designed to extract *locations* (top) and *speakers* (bottom).

displays the top 5 most probable tokens emitted by that state, in order from top to bottom; the nodes in the *speaker* graph show the top 5 tokens according to an odds-ratio metric. The token <CR> stands for a carriage return; the token <UNK> stands for the "unknown" token, in our experiments any token occurring fewer than three times in the training set. Both of these models were the best found in their respective splits. The *location* model was found after 8 states of state splitting, the *speaker* model after 3 steps.

The figure suggests that, in order to extract seminar locations, a single, relatively short prefix context is needed. The fact that the model retains only a single prefix points to the unambiguity and length invariance of the kinds of language leading up to a location. Phrases like "Place:", "Where:", "in the", and "00 pm," are encoded by the prefix. This last phrase is an indication that locations are often preceded by times.

The target states are partitioned into three parallel paths. The top path, accounting for about half of *location* phrases, captures many common *location* phrases consisting of two or three tokens, phrases such as "Weh 5409" and "Wean Hall 5409". Wean and Doherty are buildings on the CMU campus and common meeting places for the talks announced in the SA corpus. The middle path, of length four, appears dedicated to modeling longer *location* phrases, particularly a very popular meeting place which appears in a variety of formats: "Adamson Wing Auditorium in Baker Hall", "Baker Hall, Adamson Wing", "Adamson Wing, Baker Hall". Finally, the bottom path appears to be a "garbage" path, dedicated to modeling locations that are not easily modeled by the other two paths. The high probability of the unknown token in these two states supports this interpretation.

The first target state in the *speaker* model appears dedicated to emitting honorifics and first names, while the other target state emits middle initials and last names. The use of two prefixes suggests that seminar speakers occur in two contexts. The top prefix seems dedicated to accounting for the initial formal presentation, in which phrases like "Who:" and "Speaker:" are common, followed by use of the speaker's full name, including honorific. The bottom prefix seems to be used in the body of the announcement in less formal contexts. It accounts for phrases like "reminder that" and "seminar by". Interestingly, a significant fraction of contexts in which this prefix is used skip to the second target state, apparently because an honorific or first name has been omitted.

Related Work

HMMs have been applied to various versions of the information extraction problem in recent years. The approach described in Freitag and McCallum (Freitag and McCallum 1999) addresses the same problem as in this work—training one HMM per extraction task—but involves manually constructed models. Seymore et al. (Seymore et al. 1999) describe experiments in structure learning, but use HMMs that model all fields simultaneously, and address problems in which an ordering of fields is sought, rather than the location of a single field in a large body of background text. Bikel et al. (Bikel et al. 1997) applies HMMs to the named entity recognition problem, the problem of identifying text fragments that signify particular types of entities, such as people or organizations, without regard to their role in the document. They describe manually designed HMMs with one state per type of entity and use n-gram statistics, rather than HMM structure, to exploit context. The HMMs in Leek (Leek 1997) are carefully designed—both state-transition structure and emission distributions—to model the syntactic constraints of the particular extraction problem.

The problem of learning HMM structure for tasks other than information extraction has seen a fair amount of work. Stolcke and Omohundro (Stolcke and Omohundro 1994) propose a state-merging approach which begins with a large, maximally specific topology and iteratively merges pairs of states. The merging criterion is not performance on any particular task, as in this work, but a Bayesian combination of prior expectations regarding suitable topologies and goodness of fit to the data. Seymore et al. (Seymore et al. 1999) apply the same approach to their extraction problem. Closely related are the state merging algorithms that have been investigated for some years in the field of grammatical inference, particularly those involving stochastic regular grammars (Carrasco and Oncina 1994). State splitting appears better suited than state merging to the sparse extraction problem. Much of the work in state merging presupposes problems that resemble formal language modeling. The problem of dense extraction is much closer in character to formal language identification than is sparse extraction.

Alternatives to state merging/splitting exist. Vasko et al. (Vasko et al. 1997) describe a method which begins with a fully-connected structure and iteratively deletes transitions. Lockwood and Blanchet (Lockwood and Blanchet 1993) propose a method that applies incremental patches to a circuit-free model for speech processing.

Conclusions

Previous work has shown that hidden Markov models are the state-of-the-art method for information extraction. This paper has shown that task-specific state-transition structure of these models is tremendously important to their performance, and has further pushed the state-of-the-art by showing that discriminative stochastic optimization can automatically discover good structures. We hope that these initial investigations will lead to improved methods in the future.

References

Daniel M. Bikel, Scott Miller, Richard Schwartz, and Ralph Weischedel. Nymble: a high-performance learning name-finder. In *Proceedings of ANLP-97*, pages 194–201, 1997.

Mary Elaine Califf. *Relational Learning Techniques for Natural Language Information Extraction*. PhD thesis, University of Texas at Austin, August 1998.

Rafael C. Carrasco and Jose Oncina. Learning stochastic regular grammars by means of a state merging method. In Rafael C. Carrasco and Jose Oncina, editors, *Grammatical Inference and Applications: Second International Colloquium, ICGI-94*. Springer-Verlag, September 1994.

Dayne Freitag and Andrew Kachites McCallum. Information extraction using hmms and shrinkage. In *Papers from the AAAI-99 Workshop on Machine Learning for Information Extration*, pages 31–36, July 1999. AAAI Technical Report WS-99-11.

Dayne Freitag. Information extraction from HTML: Application of a general machine learning approach. In *Proceedings of the Fifteenth National Conference on Artificial Intelligence (AAAI-98)*, 1998.

Timothy R. Leek. Information extraction using hidden Markov models. Master's thesis, UC San Diego, 1997.

Philip Lockwood and Marc Blanchet. An algorithm for the dynamic inference of hidden Markov models (DIHMM). In *1993 IEEE International Conference on Acoustics, Speech, and Signal Processing (ICASSP-93)*, 1993.

L.R. Rabiner. A tutorial on hidden Markov models and selected applications in speech recognition. *Proceedings of the IEEE*, 77(2), February 1989.

Kristie Seymore, Andrew McCallum, and Ronald Rosenfeld. Learning hidden Markov model structure for information extraction. In *Papers from the AAAI-99 Workshop on Machine Learning for Information Extration*, pages 37–42, July 1999. AAAI Technical Report WS-99-11.

Andreas Stolcke and Stephen M. Omohundro. Best-first model merging for hidden Markov induction. Technical Report TR-94-003, International Computer Science Institute, Berkeley, California, January 1994.

Raymond C. Vasko, Jr., Amro El-Jaroudi, J.R. Boston, and Thomas E. Rudy. Hidden Markov model topology estimation to characterize the dynamic structure of repetitive lifting data. In *Proceedings of the 19th Annual International Conference of the IEEE Engineering in Medicine and Biology Society*, 1997.

Localizing Search in Reinforcement Learning

Greg Grudic
Institute for Research in Cognitive Science
University of Pennsylvania
Philadelphia, PA, USA
grudic@linc.cis.upenn.edu

Lyle Ungar
Computer and Information Science
University of Pennsylvania
Philadelphia, PA, USA
ungar@cis.upenn.edu

Abstract

Reinforcement learning (RL) can be impractical for many high dimensional problems because of the computational cost of doing stochastic search in large state spaces. We propose a new RL method, Boundary Localized Reinforcement Learning (BLRL), which maps RL into a mode switching problem where an agent deterministically chooses an action based on its state, and limits stochastic search to small areas around mode boundaries, drastically reducing computational cost. BLRL starts with an initial set of parameterized boundaries that partition the state space into distinct control modes. Reinforcement reward is used to update the boundary parameters using the policy gradient formulation of Sutton et al. (2000). We demonstrate that stochastic search can be limited to regions near mode boundaries, thus greatly reducing search, while still guaranteeing convergence to a locally optimal deterministic mode switching policy. Further, we give conditions under which the policy gradient can be arbitrarily well approximated without the use of any stochastic search. These theoretical results are supported experimentally via simulation.

Introduction

A cornerstone of all Reinforcement Learning (RL) is the concept that an agent uses a trial and error strategy to explore its environment and thus learns to maximize its reward. This trial and error process is usually implemented via stochastic search, which is governed by a probability distribution of actions taken during exploration. Such a stochastic search strategy has proven effective in many RL applications with low dimensional state spaces (Kaelbling, Littman, & Moore 1996).

The difficulty inherent in applying a stochastic search strategy (or any search strategy) to higher dimensional problems is that, in general, the search space grows exponentially with the number of state variables. As a consequence, the computational cost of reinforcement learning quickly becomes impractical as the dimension of the problem increases. The use of function approximation techniques to learn generalizations across large state spaces, and then the use of these generalizations to direct the search process, has been suggested as one possible solution to this curse of dimensionality problem in RL. However, even when function approximation techniques successfully generalize, the dimension of the search remains unchanged, and its computational cost can still be impractical.

We propose to reduce the computational cost of search in high dimensional spaces by searching only limited regions of the state space. The size of the search region bounds the computational cost of RL. Intuitively, the smaller the search region, the lower the computational cost of learning, making it possible to apply RL to very high dimensional problems.

To limit the search, we consider the class of deterministic mode switching controllers, where the action executed by an agent is deterministically defined by its location in state space. (See Figure 1.) Mode switching controllers are commonly used in many control applications in order to allow relatively simple controllers to be used in different operating regimes, such as aircraft climbing steeply vs. cruising at constant elevation (Lainiotis 1976). Mode switching has additional benefit for RL in applications such as robotics, where random actions may result in unsafe outcomes, and therefore actions must be deterministically chosen based on prior knowledge of which actions are both safe and beneficial.

Representing the agent's policy as a deterministic mode switching controller allows us to create a new type of reinforcement learning, Boundary Localized Reinforcement Learning (BLRL), in which the trial and error is limited to regions near mode boundaries. As BLRL is concerned solely with updating the boundary locations between modes, we parameterize these boundaries directly and perform RL on this parameterization using the Policy Gradient formulation of (Sutton *et al.* 2000). In effect, the learning shifts the mode boundaries to increase reward.

This paper presents three new theoretical results. The first result states that any stochastic policy (i.e. stochastic control strategy) can be transformed into a mode switching policy, which localizes search to near mode boundaries. The practical consequence of this result is that an RL problem can be converted to a BLRL problem, thus taking advantage of the convergence properties of BLRL in high dimensional state spaces. The second theoretical result states that convergence to a locally optimal mode switching policy is still obtained when stochastic search is limited to near mode boundaries. This means that most of the agent's state space can be ignored, while still guaranteeing convergence to a locally op-

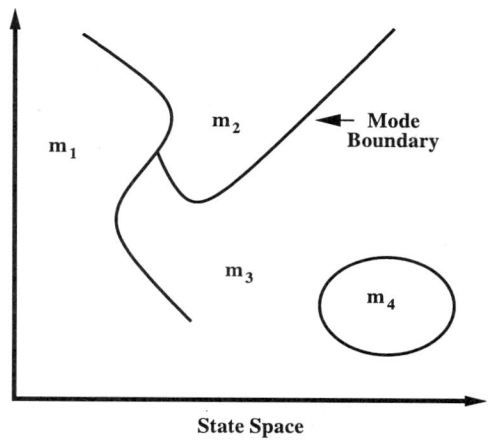

Figure 1: A Mode Switching Controller consists of a finite number of modes $m_1, m_2, ...$ or actions, which are deterministically applied in specific regions of the workspace. The state space is therefore divided into regions specified by Mode Boundaries.

timal solution. The final theoretical result gives a bound on the error in the policy gradient formulation if an agent uses a deterministic search strategy instead of a stochastic one. Surprisingly, convergence to approximately locally optimal deterministic policies does not require the execution of more than one type of action in each region of the state space associated with a single mode. This contrasts with typical RL search where different actions are executed in the same state in order to calculate a gradient in the direction of maximal reward. Avoiding executing multiple modes in each region allows us to limit the use of potentially dangerous or expensive random actions because we search only by making small adjustments in boundary locations. These theoretical results are supported experimentally via simulation.

RL Problem Formulation

Reinforcement Learning as a MDP

The typical formulation of RL is as a Markov Decision Process (MDP) (Kaelbling, Littman, & Moore 1996). The agent has a set of states S (usually discrete), a set of actions A, a reward function $R : S \times A \to \Re$, and a transition function $T : S \times A \to \pi(S)$ where $\pi(S)$ is a probability distribution of actions over the states S. The transition function is written as $T(s, a, s')$ and defines the probability of making a transition from state s to state s' using action a. The goal of reinforcement learning is to find a policy π (i.e. a probability distribution of actions over states), such that the reward obtained is optimized. Optimal policies are typically learned by learning the value of taking a given action in a given state, and then choosing the action which gives the maximum expected reward. The process of finding this optimal policy is formulated as a stochastic search typically dictated by the current policy π.

The basic premise of this standard approach to RL is that a good estimate of the value function can be obtained everywhere in state space. In small state spaces this premise is typically true, however, obtaining such estimates in larger state spaces can require extreme amounts of search.

Policy Gradient RL

The policy gradient formulation of RL which we use differs from the typical RL formulation in that policies are defined by some parameterization vector θ and there is a performance metric ρ that is a function of the policy, and can therefore also be parameterized by θ. Policy Gradient RL is then formulated as a gradient based update of the parameters as follows:

$$\theta_{t+1} = \theta_t + \alpha \frac{\partial \rho}{\partial \theta} \quad (1)$$

where $\partial \rho / \partial \theta$ is the *performance gradient* and α is a positive step size. This formulation relies on the assumption that if the estimate of $\partial \rho / \partial \theta$ is accurate and α is small, then the updated policy parameters θ will give better performance, and the policy will eventually converge to a local optimum.

The policy gradient formulation dates back to Williams' (1987, 1992) REINFORCE algorithm which is known to give an unbiased estimate of the performance gradient $\partial \rho / \partial \theta$. However, REINFORCE suffers from slow convergence resulting from the fact that it requires a good estimate of the actual value of each state (termed the baseline reward parameter) to get a low variance estimate of $\partial \rho / \partial \theta$. This baseline reward parameter is difficult to calculate in practice and therefore REINFORCE has not been widely applied on RL problems.

Recently a number of policy gradient algorithms have been proposed which use function approximation estimates of the state-action value function to give low variance estimates of the performance gradient $\partial \rho / \partial \theta$, and thereby improve rate of convergence (Baird & Moore 1999; Sutton *et al.* 2000; Konda & Tsitsiklis 2000; Baxter & Bartlett 1999). However, there is experimental evidence that direct but *selective* sampling of the value of executing actions in states can give low variance estimates of $\partial \rho / \partial \theta$ without using function approximation (Grudic & Ungar 2000).

In this paper we use the *Action Transition Policy Gradient* (ATPG) algorithm formulation presented in (Grudic & Ungar 2000). The ATPG algorithm selectively samples the state-action value function whenever the agent changes actions, and uses only these samples to obtain estimates of $\partial \rho / \partial \theta$. The performance gradient estimate is based on the relative difference between the values of two different actions which are executed within one time step of each other. This utilization of relative reward gives a low variance estimate of $\partial \rho / \partial \theta$, and allows ATPG to typically converge in many orders of magnitude fewer iterations than other policy gradient algorithms on a variety of RL problems (Grudic & Ungar 2000).

Boundary Localized Policy Gradients (BLPG)

Policy Gradient Formulation

Our formulation of BLRL is based on *Policy Gradient Theorem* of (Sutton *et al.* 2000), which we briefly review below. For each time step $t \in \{0, 1, ...\}$ there is an associated state $s_t \in S$, action $a_t \in A$, and reward $r_t \in \Re$.

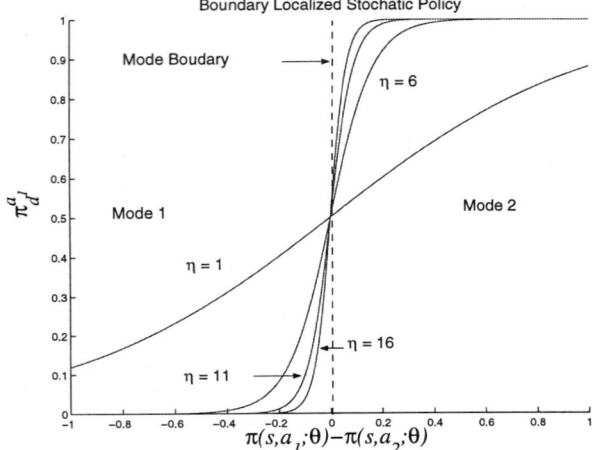

Figure 2: The η-transformation.

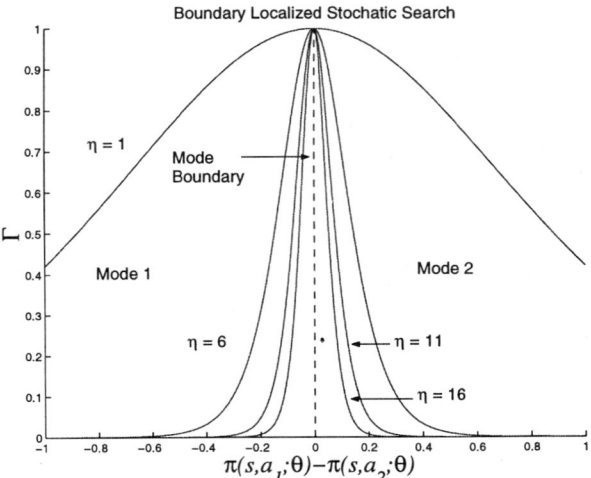

Figure 3: The magnitude of the policy gradient goes to zero everywhere except mode boundaries as $\eta \to \infty$.

Using the usual MDP formulation, the dynamics of the environment are characterized by state transition probabilities $P_{ss'}^a = \Pr\{s_{t+1} = s' | s_t = s, a_t = a\}$, and expected rewards $R_s^a = E\{r_{t+1} | s_t = s, a_t = a\}, \forall s, s' \in S, a \in A$. The agent is assumed to follow a probabilistic policy characterized by $\pi(s, a; \theta) = \Pr\{a_t = a | s_t = s; \theta\}, \forall s \in S, a \in A$ and $\theta \in \Re^l$ is a l dimensional policy parameterization vector. The additional assumption made on the policy is that $\partial \pi / \partial \theta$ exists.

The Policy Gradient Theorem allows for both the average reward and discounted reward formulations for a performance metric. For brevity, we only state the discounted reward formulation here. The discount reward performance metric for an agent that starts at state s_0 is given by:

$$\rho(\pi) = E\left\{\sum_{t=1}^{\infty} \gamma^t r_t \bigg| s_0, \pi\right\} \quad (2)$$

where $\gamma \in [0, 1]$ is a discount reward factor. A *state-action value function* is defined as:

$$Q^\pi(s, a) = E\left\{\sum_{k=1}^{\infty} \gamma^{k-1} r_{t+k} \bigg| s_t = s, a_t = a, \pi\right\} \quad (3)$$

Finally, a discounted weighting of states encountered starting at state s_0 and then following π is defined by $d^\pi = \sum_{t=0}^{\infty} \gamma^t \Pr(s_t = s | s_0, \pi)$.

Given the above definitions, the *Policy Gradient Theorem* states that the exact expression for the policy gradient is:

$$\frac{\partial \rho}{\partial \theta} = \sum_s d^\pi(s) \sum_a \frac{\partial \pi(s, a; \theta)}{\partial \theta} Q^\pi(s, a) \quad (4)$$

Boundary Localization: The η-Transform

The Policy Gradient Theorem assumes that policies are characterized by probability distributions: i.e. $\pi(s, a; \theta) = \Pr\{a_t = a | s_t = s; \theta\}$. In this section we demonstrate that any policies thus formulated can be transformed into approximately deterministic policies, while still preserving the policy gradient convergence results. Consider a policy that consists of only two possible actions: $\pi(s, a_1; \theta)$ and $\pi(s, a_2; \theta)$. These policies can be mapped to boundary-localized stochastic policies, denoted by $\pi_d(s, a_1; \theta)$ and $\pi_d(s, a_2; \theta)$ respectively, using the following transformations:

$$\pi_d(s, a_1; \theta) = \frac{1}{2}[1 + \tanh(\eta(\pi(s, a_1; \theta) - \pi(s, a_2; \theta)))] \quad (5)$$

and

$$\pi_d(s, a_2; \theta) = \frac{1}{2}[1 + \tanh(\eta(\pi(s, a_2; \theta) - \pi(s, a_1; \theta)))] \quad (6)$$

where $\eta \to \infty$. We refer to these transformations as η-transformations. Figure 2 shows the effect of η on the probability distribution of the action a_1 (i.e. $\pi_c^{a_1} \equiv \pi_d(s, a_1; \theta)$). We can see that as $\eta \to \infty$ the probability of executing a_1 in regions of the state space where $(\pi(s, a_1; \theta) - \pi(s, a_2; \theta)) < 0$ becomes arbitrarily small. Similarly, in regions of the state space where $(\pi(s, a_1; \theta) - \pi(s, a_2; \theta)) > 0$ the probability of executing action a_1 is arbitrarily close to 1 as $\eta \to \infty$. Therefore the η-transformation transforms a policy $\pi(s, a_1; \theta)$ which is stochastic everywhere in state space, to a policy $\pi_d(s, a_1; \theta)$ which is stochastic only near the boundaries defined by $(\pi(s, a_1; \theta) - \pi(s, a_2; \theta)) = 0$. We refer to these regions in state space as *mode boundary* regions.

Boundary Localized Policy Gradient

The η-transformation makes the policy gradient become close to zero everywhere except at mode boundaries. To see this, differentiate the BL policy $\pi_d(s, a_1; \theta)$ with respect to the parameters θ as follows:

$$\begin{aligned}\frac{\partial \pi_d^{a_1}}{\partial \theta} &= \frac{\eta}{2}\left(\operatorname{sech}^2(\eta(\pi^{a_1} - \pi^{a_2}))\right)\left(\frac{\partial \pi^{a_1}}{\partial \theta} - \frac{\partial \pi^{a_2}}{\partial \theta}\right) \\ &\stackrel{\Delta}{=} \Gamma(\eta, (\pi^{a_1} - \pi^{a_2}))\left(\frac{\partial \pi^{a_1}}{\partial \theta} - \frac{\partial \pi^{a_2}}{\partial \theta}\right)\end{aligned} \quad (7)$$

where, by definition, $\pi^{a_1} \equiv \pi(s, a_1; \theta)$, $\pi^{a_2} \equiv \pi(s, a_2; \theta)$, $\pi_d^{a_1} \equiv \pi_d(s, a_1; \theta)$ and $\pi_d^{a_2} \equiv \pi_d(s, a_2; \theta)$. Equation (7) indicates that the performance gradient has the following proportionality property:

$$\left|\frac{\partial \rho}{\partial \theta}\right| \propto \Gamma(\eta, (\pi^{a_1} - \pi^{a_2})) \quad (8)$$

This proportionality is plotted in Figure 3, where we see that as $\eta \to \infty$, the policy gradient approaches zero everywhere except near mode boundaries. This means that only regions in state space near mode boundaries need be stochastically searched when BL policies are used. The result is that BL policies have a significantly reduced search space than standard stochastic polices, making them computationally more viable for high dimensional RL problems.

The argument presented above for a policy of two actions can be extended to any finite number of actions. Therefore the η-transformation is valid for any finite set of policies, and one can transform any stochastic policy to a BL policy. Below we state the *Boundary Localized Policy Gradient Theorem*, which is a direct extension of the Policy Gradient theorem.

Theorem: Boundary Localized Policy Gradient *For any MDP, in either the average or discounted start-state formulations,*

$$\frac{\partial \rho}{\partial \theta} = \sum_s d^\pi(s) \sum_a \frac{\partial \pi_d(s, a; \theta)}{\partial \theta} Q^\pi(s, a) \quad (9)$$

Proof Sketch: If $\partial \pi / \partial \theta$ exists then because the η-transformation is continuously differentiable, so does $\partial \pi_d / \partial \theta$. The rest of the proof follows that of (Sutton et al. 2000).

The significance of the BLPG theorem is that locally optimal BL polices can be learned using policy gradients. Therefore, even though search is localized to a very small region of the state space, a policy gradient algorithm (9) will still converge to a locally optimum policy.

Policy Gradients for Deterministic Policies

One of the problems with applying stochastic search-based RL to such applications as robotics is that random actions executed by a robot may result in unsafe or expensive outcomes. For example, if a robot is navigating a hallway and randomly decides to explore the result of the action *go towards a human "obstacle"* rather than try to avoid *"it"*, the result may be an injured human. Therefore, in this section we formulate an error bound on the policy gradient if the agent does not employ a stochastic search policy. Once again, consider a stochastic policy of two actions: $\pi(s, a_1; \theta)$ and $\pi(s, a_2; \theta)$. If an agent executes action a_1 that moves it a distance δ in state space, and thereafter executes action a_2, then the exact policy gradient is given by (4) and can be written as:

$$\begin{aligned}\frac{\partial \rho}{\partial \theta} =\ & d^\pi(s) \left[\frac{\partial \pi(s, a_1; \theta)}{\partial \theta} Q^\pi(s, a_1) + \right.\\ & \left. \frac{\partial \pi(s, a_2; \theta)}{\partial \theta} Q^\pi(s, a_2)\right] + \\ & d^\pi(s+\delta) \left[\frac{\partial \pi(s+\delta, a_1; \theta)}{\partial \theta} Q^\pi(s+\delta, a_1) + \right.\\ & \left. \frac{\partial \pi(s+\delta, a_2; \theta)}{\partial \theta} Q^\pi(s+\delta, a_2)\right]\end{aligned} \quad (10)$$

Note that the exact expression for the policy gradient requires knowledge of the state-action value function for both actions at both locations in state space: i.e. $Q^\pi(s, a_1)$, $Q^\pi(s, a_2)$, $Q^\pi(s+\delta, a_1)$, and $Q^\pi(s+\delta, a_2)$ must all be known. If an agent is executing a deterministic policy, then under the current policy π, action a_2 has never been executed in state s, and action a_1 has never been executed in state $s+\delta$; this means that $Q^\pi(s, a_2)$ and $Q^\pi(s+\delta, a_1)$ are not known. Furthermore, if the agent is performing episodic learning and it is obtaining an estimate of the state-action value-function after each episode, then it also will not have estimates of $Q^\pi(s, a_2)$ and $Q^\pi(s+\delta, a_1)$. However, for both the episodic stochastic and deterministic cases, the agent does have estimates of $Q^\pi(s, a_1)$ and $Q^\pi(s+\delta, a_2)$; i.e. because a_1 is executed in s and a_2 is executed in $s+\delta$. Therefore, we propose the following approximation to the policy gradient approximation, which we term the *Boundary Localized Policy Gradient* (BLPG) Approximation:

$$\begin{aligned}\widehat{\frac{\partial \rho}{\partial \theta}} =\ & d^\pi(s) \left[\frac{\partial \pi(s, a_1; \theta)}{\partial \theta} Q^\pi(s, a_1) + \right.\\ & \left. \frac{\partial \pi(s, a_2; \theta)}{\partial \theta} Q^\pi(s, a_2)\right] + \\ & d^\pi(s+\delta) \left[\frac{\partial \pi(s+\delta, a_1; \theta)}{\partial \theta} Q^\pi(s, a_1) + \right.\\ & \left. \frac{\partial \pi(s+\delta, a_2; \theta)}{\partial \theta} Q^\pi(s+\delta, a_2)\right]\end{aligned} \quad (11)$$

This approximation works if $Q^\pi(\cdot)$ is continuous. Formally, it must satisfy the Lipschitz smoothness condition:

$$\begin{aligned}&\forall s \in S, S \subseteq \Re^N, a \in A, \delta \in \Re^N \\ &\exists k > 0, k \in \Re \text{ s.t.} \\ &|Q^\pi(s, a) - Q^\pi(s+\delta, a)| \leq k \|\delta\|\end{aligned} \quad (12)$$

Note that this smoothness condition is satisfied in both the average and discounted reward formalization of RL. Given this formulation, we state the following lemma.

Lemma: BLPG Approximation *Assume that $Q^\pi(s, a)$ is Lipschitz smooth (12), and that the policy $\pi(s, a; \theta)$ has two actions (a_1 and a_2) and is differentiable with respect to θ. Assume also that the agent takes a step of size δ that takes it from a region where action a_1 is performed to a region where action a_2 is performed. Then if the policy gradient is approximated by (11), the error in the approximation is bounded by:*

$$\left|\frac{\partial \rho}{\partial \theta} - \widehat{\frac{\partial \rho}{\partial \theta}}\right| \leq k \|\delta\| \left(\left|d^\pi(s) \frac{\partial \pi(s, a_2; \theta)}{\partial \theta}\right| + \left|d^\pi(s+\delta) \frac{\partial \pi(s+\delta, a_1; \theta)}{\partial \theta}\right|\right) \quad (13)$$

Proof: Subtracting (11) from (10) and taking the absolute value:

$$\begin{aligned}\left|\frac{\partial \rho}{\partial \theta} - \widehat{\frac{\partial \rho}{\partial \theta}}\right| =\ & \left|d^\pi(s) \frac{\partial \pi(s, a_2; \theta)}{\partial \theta} [Q(s, a_2) - Q(s+\delta, a_2)] + \right.\\ & \left. d^\pi(s+\delta) \frac{\partial \pi(s+\delta, a_1; \theta)}{\partial \theta} [Q(s+\delta, a_1) - Q(s, a_1)]\right| \\ \leq\ & k \|\delta\| \left(\left|d^\pi(s) \frac{\partial \pi(s, a_2; \theta)}{\partial \theta}\right| + \left|d^\pi(s+\delta) \frac{\partial \pi(s+\delta, a_1; \theta)}{\partial \theta}\right|\right)\end{aligned}$$

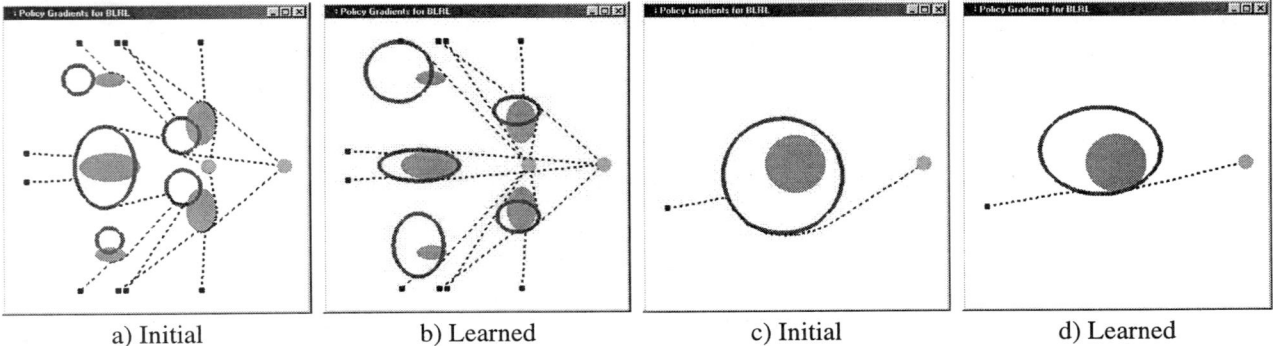

a) Initial b) Learned c) Initial d) Learned

Figure 4: Example of a simulated agent executing episodes in an environment. The agent begins at locations near the top, bottom, and/or left extremes of the environment and goes towards goal positions (small shaded circles) located at the right extreme or near the center. Dashed lines symbolize the agent's path and the obstacles are the larger gray areas. The agent can execute one of two possible actions: if it is executing a deterministic policy and if it is inside one of the regions delineated by a black ellipsoid, it moves away from the ellipsoid's center; otherwise it moves towards a goal position. If the agent is following a stochastic policy, then the ellipsoids indicate regions in state space where the "move away from" action is more probable.

Lemma 1 states that the BLPG approximation error approaches zero as the step size the agent takes approaches zero (i.e. as $\|\delta\| \to 0$).

	Stochastic RL	Stochastic BLRL	Deterministic BLRL
Episodes to converge	6900 (sd 400)	600 (sd 90)	260 (sd 40)

Table 1: 2-D Convergence results with standard deviations.

Simulation Results

We have simulated an agent interacting with its environment using one of two possible actions: the first is *"move towards a goal position"* and the second is *"move away from"* a location in state space. This second action is for obstacle avoidance. If an agent reaches a goal position it gets a reward of +1, if it hits an obstacle it gets a negative reward of -1, and if it is unable to reach its goal within a maximum allotted time, it receives a negative reward of -10.

The agent's state space is *continuously* defined as its Cartesian position, and the policies are parameterized by Gaussians. There are two parameters per dimension per Gaussian - one for position and one for width (i.e. variance). Thus each Guassian adds two parameters per dimension to the policy parameters θ in (4). Typical simulated environments are described in Figure 4. The agent's sensing of position in state space is noisy and is modeled by white noise, which is made proportional to 10% of how far an agent is able to move in one time step. The *Action Transition Policy Gradient* ATPG algorithm (Grudic & Ungar 2000) is used to learn locally optimal policy parameters θ. The ATPG algorithm assumes that the agent interacts with the environment in a series of episodes and the policy parameters θ are updated after each episode. Convergence is therefore measured in number of episodes.

2-D Simulation: Figures 4a and b show a 2-D scenario which has ten possible starting positions, two goal positions, five obstacles, and six Gaussians for defining policies (five for "move away form" which are shown as ellipsoids, and one for "move towards goal", which is most probable everywhere except inside the ellipsoids). Therefore there are a total of 24 policy parameters θ.

Figure 4a shows the initial policy and the resulting paths through the environment. Note that four paths end before a goal is reached and eight paths have collisions with obstacles. Figure 4b shows the paths after the policy parameters have converged to stable values. Note that the location and extent of the Gaussians has converged such that none of the paths now collide with obstacles, and the total distance traveled through state space is shorter.

Table 1 shows the average number of episodes (over ten runs) required for convergence for the three types of polices studied: stochastic, boundary localized stochastic ($\eta = 16$), and deterministic. Note that the purely stochastic polices take the greatest number of episodes to converge, while the deterministic policies take the fewest.

N-D Simulation: We simulated 4, 8, 16, 32, 64, and 128 dimensional environments, with the number of parameters θ ranging from 14 to 512 (i.e. 2 parameters per Gaussian per dimension). The projection of these into the XY plane is shown in Figure 4c and d. Figure 4c shows the starting policies, while Figure 4d shows policies after convergence. In Figure 5, we summarize the convergence results (over ten runs with standard deviation bars) for the three types of policies studied: stochastic, boundary localized stochastic ($\eta = 16$), and deterministic. Note that for both the deterministic and boundary localized policies, convergence is essentially constant with dimension. However, for the stochastic policy, the convergence times explode with dimension. We only report convergence results up to 16 dimensions for stochastic policies - convergence on higher dimensions was still not achieved after 20,000 iterations at which time the simulation was stopped.

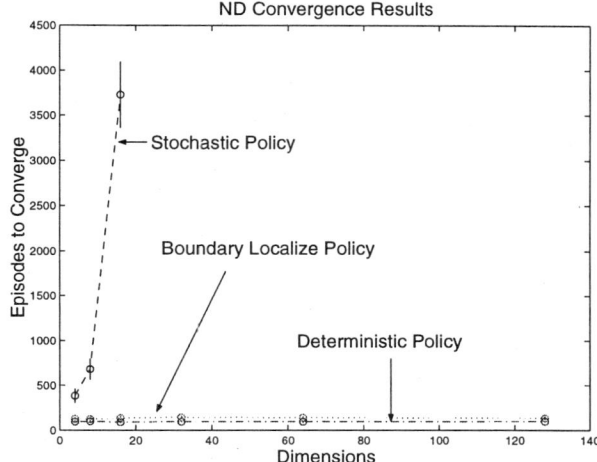

Figure 5: N-D convergence results over ten runs with standard deviation bars.

Discussion and Conclusion

Reinforcement learning (RL) suffers from the combinatorics of search in large state spaces. In this paper we have shown that the stochastic search region in RL can be reduced to mode boundaries by dividing the control policy into a set of state dependent modes. Such controllers are common in complicated control systems, two well-known examples being gain switching controllers (Narendra, Balakrishnan, & Ciliz 1995) and heterogeneous controllers (Kuipers & Åström 1994). The proposed *Boundary Localized Reinforcement Learning* (BLRL) method directly parameterizes the mode boundaries and then uses policy gradients to move the boundaries to give locally optimal policies. Further, we have proven that search can be made deterministic by assuming that the state-action value function is continuous across mode boundaries, a condition that is satisfied in both the average and discounted reward formalization of RL in continuous state spaces.

The policy gradient formulation guarantees that the policies learned are locally, but not necessarily globally, optimal. However, our proposed localization of search means that RL can be applied to high dimensional problems for which global solutions are intractable. Experimental results show that restricting search to boundary regions gives many orders of magnitude reduction in the number of episodes required for convergence. In addition, deterministic policies require slightly fewer episodes to converge than the boundary localized stochastic policies.

The BLRL method is ideally suited for continuous high dimensional RL problems where the agent executes many actions, and each action moves the agent a small distance in state space. One such problem domain is robotics, where actions are executed many times a second (often at 200 Hz or more) and each action moves the robot a small distance through its workspace. In addition, robot controllers can naturally be partitioned into modes, and prior knowledge can be used to define initial boundary parameterizations. Further, domain knowledge can be used to identify which mode transitions are dangerous, and boundaries can be explicitly defined to prohibit such transitions. We are currently applying BLRL to the problem of learning locally optimal policies via reinforcement reward for multiple autonomous robots as they interact with each other and the environment.

Acknowledgements

Thanks to Vijay Kumar and Jane Mulligan for discussing this work with us. This work was funded by the IRCS at the University of Pennsylvania, and by the DARPA ITO MARS grant no. DABT63-99-1-0017.

References

Baird, L., and Moore, A. W. 1999. Gradient descent for general reinforcement learning. In Jordan, M. I.; Kearns, M. J.; and Solla, S. A., eds., *Advances in Neural Information Processing Systems*, volume 11. Cambridge, MA: MIT Press.

Baxter, J., and Bartlett, P. L. 1999. Direct gradient-based reinforcement learning: I. gradient estimation algorithms. Technical report, Computer Sciences Laboratory, Australian National University.

Grudic, G. Z., and Ungar, L. H. 2000. Localizing policy gradient estimates to action transitions. *Forthcoming*.

Kaelbling, L. P.; Littman, M. L.; and Moore, A. W. 1996. Reinforcement learning: A survey. *Journal of Artificial Intelligence Research* 4:237–285.

Konda, V. R., and Tsitsiklis, J. N. 2000. Actor-critic algorithms. In Solla, S. A.; Leen, T. K.; and Mller, K.-R., eds., *Advances in Neural Information Processing Systems*, volume 12. Cambridge, MA: MIT Press.

Kuipers, B., and Åström, K. J. 1994. The composition and validation of heterogeneous control laws. *Automatica* 30(2):233–249.

Lainiotis, D. G. 1976. A unifying framework for adaptive systems, i: Estimation, ii. *Proceedings of the IEEE* 64(8):1126–1134, 1182–1197.

Narendra, K. S.; Balakrishnan, J.; and Ciliz, K. 1995. Adaptation and learning using multiple models, switching and tuning. *IEEE Control Systems Magazine* 15(3):37–51.

Sutton, R. S.; McAllester, D.; Singh, S.; and Mansour, Y. 2000. Policy gradient methods for reinforcement learning with function approximation. In Solla, S. A.; Leen, T. K.; and Mller, K.-R., eds., *Advances in Neural Information Processing Systems*, volume 12. Cambridge, MA: MIT Press.

Williams, R. J. 1987. A class of gradient-estimating algorithms for reinforcement learning in neural networks. In *Proceedings of the IEEE First International Conference on Neural Networks*.

Williams, R. J. 1992. Simple statistical gradient-following algorithms for connectionist reinforcement learning. *Machine Learning* 8(3):229–256.

Recognizing End-User Transactions in Performance Management

Joseph L. Hellerstein, T.S. Jayram, Irina Rish
IBM Thomas J. Watson Research Center
Hawthorne, New York
{hellers, jayram, rish}@us.ibm.com

Abstract

Providing good quality of service (e.g., low response times) in distributed computer systems requires measuring end-user perceptions of performance. Unfortunately, such measures are often expensive or impossible to obtain. Herein, we propose a machine-learning approach to recognizing end-user transactions consisting of sequences of remote procedure calls (RPCs) received at a server. Two problems are addressed. The first problem is labeling an RPC sequence that corresponds to one transaction instance with the correct transaction type. This is akin to text classification. The second problem is transaction recognition, a more comprehensive task that involves segmenting RPC sequences into transaction instances and labeling those instances with transaction types. This problem is similar to segmenting sounds into words as in speech understanding. Using Naive Bayes approach, we tackle the labeling problem with four combinations of feature vectors and probability distributions: RPC occurrences with the Bernoulli distribution and RPC counts with the multinomial, geometric, and shifted geometric distributions. Our approach to transaction recognition uses a dynamic-programming Viterbi algorithm that searches for a most likely segmentation of an RPC sequence into a sequence of transactions, assuming transaction independence and using our classifiers to select a most likely transaction label for a given RPC sequence. For both problems, good accuracies are obtained, although the labeling problem achieves higher accuracies (up to 87%) than does transaction recognition (64%).

Introduction

Providing good quality of service (e.g., low response times) to end-users of distributed computer systems is essential for e-Commerce, among other applications. A first step is to characterize *end-user transactions*. An end-user transaction is a sequence of interactions between the end user and his/her workstation that reflects a logically complete unit of work, such as opening a database, opening a view, reading several records and closing the database. Characterizing end-user transactions (or simply transactions) is needed to (a) better quantify end-user perception of performance, (b) create representative workloads, and (c) provide better resource management. This paper describes a machine-learning approach to recognizing transactions.

Transactions consist of sequences of commands that end-users issue to their workstation. In distributed systems, these commands typically cause *remote procedure calls (RPCs)* to be sent from the user's workstation to one or more tiers of servers that process the RPCs. To illustrate the forgoing, we use the Lotus Notes email system. Common RPCs include OPEN_DB, READ_ENTRIES, and FIND_BY_KEY. Examples of the transactions in Lotus Notes include: replication, search for a note, update notes, and re-sort view.

Because end-user workstations are so numerous and since they are often not the responsibility of the administrative staff, there is often little opportunity to collect measurement data from the workstation itself. Rather, it is at the servers where measurements (e.g., RPCs received) are collected. Unfortunately, little information about end-user transactions is present at the server. In principle, client-server protocols could be instrumented to mark the beginning and end of user interactions. However, this is not sufficient to identify transactions since users often view a sequence of application interactions as a single unit of work. In current practice, this quandary is addressed either by using surrogates for transactions (e.g., synthetic transaction generated by probing stations) or by labeling transactions manually for post-processing. The former often leads to incorrect assessments of service quality. The latter is extremely time consuming. Indeed, it took multiple experts several weeks to segment and label the data we use in this paper.

Our objective is to automatically identify transactions that correspond to a sequence of RPCs from a user. This *transaction recognition* problem involves *segmenting* a sequence of RPCs into transaction instances and *labeling* these instances with the correct transaction types. Labeling alone is a classification problem akin to text classification. The segmentation problem is similar to that faced in speech understanding where an acoustic

Copyright © 2000, American Association for Artificial Intelligence (www.aaai.org). All rights reserved.

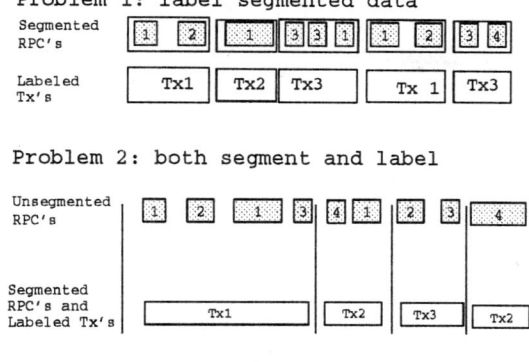

Figure 1: Illustration of labeling and transaction recognition problems.

model is used to partition sounds into words.

Fig. 1 depicts the two problems we address. In problem 1 (labeling), the sequence of RPCs has been separated into sessions (the figure shows one session), which in turn have been segmented into transaction instances. The task here is to label each instance with the correct transaction type based on the RPCs in the instance. For example, in the figure, the third transaction instance, which consists of two RPCs of type 3 and one RPC of type 1, is labeled as Tx3. In problem 2 (transaction recognition), the task is to both segment RPCs into transaction instances and to label these instances. For example, the RPC sequence (1, 2, 1, 3, 4, 1, 2, 3, 4) is segmented into four transaction instances that are labeled Tx1, Tx2, Tx3, and Tx2.

Herein, we propose the use of machine-learning techniques to recognize transactions. For labeling, we use Naive Bayes classifiers specified by the choice of feature vector and by conditional probabilities of each feature given a class (a Naive Bayes model assumes that features are mutually independent given a class). Our approach to transaction recognition uses a dynamic-programming Viterbi algorithm that searches for a most likely segmentation of an RPC sequences into a sequence of transactions, assuming transaction independence and using our classifiers to select a most likely transaction label for a given RPC sequence.

The results herein reported are of three types. First, we provide insight into a new problem domain for machine learning — recognizing end-user transactions to aid in performance management. Second, we demonstrate that Naive Bayes works well for the labeling problem in that it provides an accuracy of approximately 85-87% (with over 30 transaction classes). Third, we describe an approach to the transaction recognition problem that attains an accuracy close to 64%.

The remainder of this paper is organized as follows. Section 2 describes the data characteristics and discusses probabilistic models used later for labeling and for transaction recognition. Section 3 details our results for labeling transaction instances, and Section 4 does the same for labeling with segmentation. Section 5 discusses related work. Our conclusions are contained in Section 6.

Data Characteristics

This section describes the data characteristics and discusses probabilistic models that we use in subsequent sections.

Our data are obtained from a Lotus Notes email server at a large oil company. The data consist of traces of individual RPCs collected during two one-hour measurements of the email interactions of several hundred users. Included in the trace is the type of RPC (e.g., OPEN_COLLECTION), the identity of the server connection (which identifies a single user), and the time (in seconds) at which the request is made. In addition, we have the results of the segmentation and labeling done by Lotus Notes experts, a process that took several weeks.

The data are organized into two data sets, data set 1 and data set 2. Each data set contains approximately 1,500 transaction instances and about 15,000 RPC instances. There are 32 different types of transactions and 92 RPC types. Fig. 2 displays the marginal distributions of transaction and RPC types. Note that the distributions are highly skewed.

The segmentation and labeling done by Lotus Notes experts allows us to structure the data into transaction instances labeled with their types. Instances have a variable number of RPCs. The transaction type is used as the class variable. Our feature vector is a function of the RPC's within a transaction instance.

Our choice of feature vectors is based on what has been employed in related literature (e.g., text classification) and ease of computation. Two feature vectors are considered. Both are represented as a vector of length M (the number of RPC types). The first is the occurrence of each RPC type. Referring to Fig. 1, $M = 4$ and the value of the occurrence feature vector for the third transaction instance is $(1, 0, 1, 0)$. A second feature vector is RPC counts. Again referring to Fig. 1 and the third instance, the value of the count feature vector is $(1, 0, 2, 0)$.

Applying Naive Bayes requires estimating the conditional probability of each feature given a transaction type. For occurrences, the Bernoulli distribution is used. (A Bernoulli random variable takes value 1 with probability p and value 0 with probability $1-p$.) Thus, for each combination of RPC type and transaction type, we estimate $P(o_{ij} = 1|T_i)$, where $o_{ij} = 1$ if RPC of type j occurred in a transaction instance of type i, and 0 otherwise.

For counts, we need to estimate $P(n_{ij}|T_i)$ for each i, j and each value of n_{ij}, where $n_{i,j} = 0, 1, 2, \ldots$ is the number of RPCs of type j in a transaction instance of type i (RPC count). Our approach to these estimation problems is to use several parametric distributions. First,

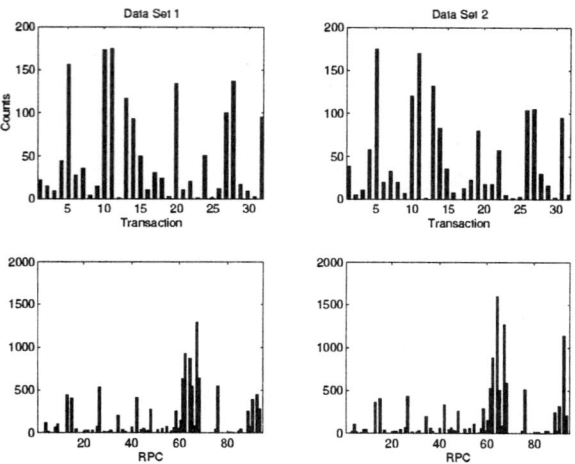

Figure 2: Marginal Distributions of RPC Types and Transaction Types

we consider the multinomial distribution over the RPC counts:

$$P(n_{i1},...,n_{iM}|T_i) = \frac{n!}{\prod_{j=1}^{M} n_{ij}!} \prod_{j=1}^{M} p_{ij}^{n_{ij}},$$

where p_{ij} are the parameters of the distribution satisfying $\sum_{j=1}^{M} p_{ij} = 1$, and n is the total number of RPCs in a transaction, $\sum_{j=1}^{M} n_{ij} = n$. The multinomial distribution has been successfully used for text classification with word counts as features (Nigam et al. 1998; McCallum & Nigam 1998). Note, however, that the multinomial distribution goes beyond the Naive Bayes assumption since it implies a dependency between the RPC counts (they must sum to the total number of RPCs in a transaction instance). Another parametric distribution we consider is the geometric distribution:

$$P(n_{ij}|T_i) = p_{ij}^{n_{ij}}(1 - p_{ij}), n_{ij} = 0, 1, 2, 3, ...$$

This distribution is widely used to describe performance characteristics of queuing systems (Kleinrock 1975), a perspective that is consistent with our application domain.

A closer look at the nature of client-server protocols suggests a third distribution that is a variation on the geometric. Specifically, client-server interactions are broadly of two types. The first are fixed overheads, such as opening a database or accessing a collection of objects. Once this has been done then "payload" operations may take place, such as reads and writes. This suggests that we should mix deterministic distributions with distributions that have substantial variability. It turns out that a variant of the geometric distribution can accommodate these requirements. The variant, which we call the shifted geometric distribution, includes a shift parameter ν_{ij} that specifies the minimum count for RPCs of type j in a transaction

	Data Set 1	Data Set 2
Multinomial	2238	1928
Geometric	490	398
Shifted Geometric	192	178

Figure 3: Chi-Square Statistics for Fits of Parametric Distributions

instance of type i. Namely,

$$P(n_{ij}|T_i) = p_{ij}^{n_{ij}-\nu_{ij}}(1 - p_{ij}),$$

where $P(n_{ij}|T_i) = 0$ if $n_{ij} < \nu_{ij}$. Thus, a shifted geometric distribution with a fixed shift parameter and a probability parameter of 0 is a deterministic distribution. Details of the shifted geometric, including its maximum likelihood estimators, are contained in Appendix A.

Which distribution function best fits the RPC counts in our data? Answering this question is complicated by the fact that we have a mixture of distributions. For the multinomial, there is a distribution for each transaction type. For geometric and shifted geometric, there are 308 distributions—one for each combination of transaction type and RPC type that occurs in our data.

We proceed as follows. For each distribution function, we calculate its parameters for each combination of transaction and RPC type using standard maximum-likelihood estimators. Then, we use Monte Carlo techniques to generate synthetic transaction instances in accordance with the parameters of the distribution function. A large number of synthetic instances is generated in order to achieve a very low variance in the estimation of distribution quantiles. Using a Chi-square goodness of fit test, we compare the empirical distribution of each function's synthetic instances with the empirical distribution of our data. The Chi-square statistics have the interpretation that a lower number indicates that the distribution family better approximates the data. The results are reported in Fig. 3. While no distribution provides a very good fit (primarily due to the frequency of zero counts), it is clear that the shifted geometric provides the best fit and the multinomial has the worst fit.

Labeling

This section describes our approach to assigning transaction types to previously segmented transaction instances. This is a classification task, where $C = \{T_1, ..., T_n\}$ is the set of possible labels (transaction types), $F_k = (f_k^1, ..., f_k^M)$ is the feature vector computed for the kth transaction instance, and f_k^j denotes the feature corresponding to RPC of type j. We consider two feature types: RPC occurrences and RPC counts. More complex features, such as those related to sequencing, are beyond the scope of this paper.

We use Naive Bayes classifiers. Given transaction instance k, we seek T_i that maximizes $P(T_i|F_k)$. Applying

Bayes rule gives $P(T_i|F_k) = \frac{P(F_k|T_i)P(T_i)}{P(F_k)}$. Since Naive Bayes assumes conditional independence between features given class, we get $P(F_k|T_i) = \prod_j P(f_k^j|T_i)$.

We consider several classifiers, each specified by a feature type and a feature distribution: RPC occurrences with the Bernoulli distribution, and RPC counts with the multinomial, geometric, and shifted geometric distributions. These choices are based on previous work in text classification and the data characteristics described in the previous section. We also consider two different parameter estimators for the Bernoulli model: (1) the maximum-likelihood estimator and (2) a non-standard estimator that coincides with the maximum-likelihood estimator of the parameter of the geometric distribution.

Why not use the empirical probability distribution functions (PDFs)? The empirical PDF estimates $P(f = v|c)$ from the frequency of the value v given the feature f and the class c in the training data set. For occurrences, the empirical PDF coincides with the Bernoulli distribution. However, for counts, the situation is more complex. Since the range of count values is potentially unbounded, there may be feature values in the test data for which no probability estimate can be obtained in the training data. This difficult can be addressed by grouping together ranges of values in the test data, but doing so creates a yet another problem–how to form these groups. Because of these complexities, we do not consider the empirical PDF for counts.

The accuracy of the classifiers is gauged in two ways. The first is the fraction of correctly labeled transactions. The second approach is to measure the fraction of correctly labeled RPCs. This approach puts more weight on longer transaction instances. It turns out that the two metrics produce results that are within a few percent of each other. So, we only report results for the first metric.

Our methodology sets aside 10% of the transaction instances for testing, and uses a subset of the remaining data for training the classifier. We varied the size of the training data set from 10% to 90% of the original (input) data set size, to see the effect of the training set size on classification accuracy. We did 30 runs for each subset size, randomly selecting the test set and then randomly selecting the training subset from the remaining data. In each run, the training and the test sets were fixed for all classifiers.

Figure 4 and Table 1 present the results of experiments for data set 1. The x-axis in the figure is training set size, and the y-axis is average labeling accuracy. Table 1 presents both means and standard deviations of the accuracy. The first column, N, is the number of training instances, while the columns 2 to 6 show the classification results for the following distributions: Bernoulli with geometric estimator (**BEG**), Bernoulli with ML estimator (**BE**), multinomial (**MN**), geometric (**GE**), and shifted geometric (**SG**). Note that ac-

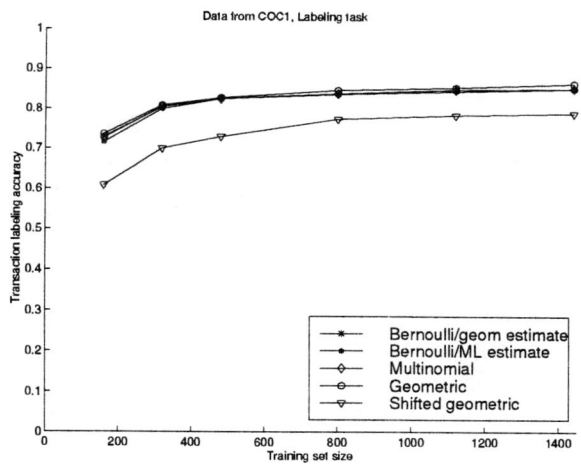

Figure 4: Classification results for the data set 1.

Table 1: Results for the data set 1: mean μ and standard deviation σ of the classification accuracy (in percents).

N	BEG $\mu \pm \sigma$	BE $\mu \pm \sigma$	MN $\mu \pm \sigma$	GE $\mu \pm \sigma$	SG $\mu \pm \sigma$
160	73 ± 6%	72 ± 5%	73 ± 5%	74 ± 6%	61 ± 7%
320	80 ± 5%	80 ± 4%	81 ± 4%	81 ± 5%	70 ± 8%
480	83 ± 3%	83 ± 3%	83 ± 3%	83 ± 3%	73 ± 8%
799	84 ± 4%	84 ± 3%	84 ± 4%	85 ± 3%	78 ± 5%
1119	85 ± 4%	85 ± 3%	85 ± 3%	86 ± 3%	79 ± 5%
1439	86 ± 2%	85 ± 3%	86 ± 2%	87 ± 2%	79 ± 3%

curacy generally improves with the size of the training set. All of the classifiers have an accuracy in excess of 75%. This is quite competitive with the literature on text classification (e.g., (Nigam et al. 1998; McCallum & Nigam 1998)) and is much better than a classifier that always chooses the transaction type that occurs with highest probability in the data (which would provide an accuracy of about 10%). Note that the counts-with-shifted-geometric classifier has accuracies that are consistently lower than the others. This is in contrast to Fig. 3 that shows the shifted geometric provides the best fit to the data. Therefore, the best-fitting distribution may not necessarily provide the best classifier.

Another interesting observation is that occurrences-with-Bernoulli, counts-with-multinomial, and counts-with-geometric yield very similar results. This is usu-

Table 2: Classification results for three data sets using 90% of the data for training and the rest for testing.

Data set	BEG $\mu \pm \sigma$	BE $\mu \pm \sigma$	MN $\mu \pm \sigma$	GE $\mu \pm \sigma$	SG $\mu \pm \sigma$
1	86 ± 2%	85 ± 3%	85 ± 3%	86 ± 2%	79 ± 3%
2	83 ± 2%	84 ± 3%	81 ± 3%	82 ± 3%	78 ± 4%
3	84 ± 1%	85 ± 1%	85 ± 1%	84 ± 1%	77 ± 1%

ally not the case in text classification. For example, others have shown that the counts-with-multinomial classifier is significantly better than occurrences-with-Bernoulli (McCallum & Nigam 1998). That our data do not abide by this principle suggests that its characteristics differ from those of text classification.

Table 2 presents similar results for the data set 2 and for an additional data set 3 obtained from a different customer. Data set 3 contains 73 RPC types, 37 transaction types, and 16210 transaction instances. Here we only report the results for 90% of the data used for training. These data are consistent with the preliminary conclusions stated above. The shifted geometric classifier is significantly less accurate than that for the other distributions. Further, accuracies do not change much between data sets if the same classifier is used.

Transaction Recognition

Here, we consider the more difficult problem of transaction recognition that includes segmentation and labeling. We proceed by assuming that transactions are mutually independent. Then, using the dynamic-programming approach known as Viterbi search (Jelinek 1998; Fu 1982) and the Naive Bayes models described in the previous section, we compute the probability of RPC sequences constituting a transaction.

The transaction recognition algorithm can be derived as follows. Let $R_{1n} = (r_1 r_2 \ldots r_n)$ be the input sequence of RPCs, and let R_{ij} denote the subsequence $(r_i r_{i+1} \ldots r_j)$. Any sequence of integers $V = (i_1, \ldots, i_m)$, where $i_1 = 1$, $i_m \leq n$, and $i_j < i_{j+1}$, is called a *segmentation* of R_{1n}. The interpretation is that each i_j marks the start of j-th transaction instance within R_{1n}. Our objective is to find a most likely segmentation

$$V^* = \arg\max_V P(V|R_{1n}) = \arg\max_V P(V, R_{1n}),$$

where V is a possible segmentation of the sequence R_{1n}. Let $\alpha_k = \max_V P(V, R_{1k})$, where $0 < k \leq n$ and $\alpha_0 = 1$. Using the assumption of transaction independence, we obtain the following dynamic-programming equation:

$$\alpha_k = \max_{0 \leq j < k} \alpha_j \cdot \max_T P(T, R_{j+1,k}),$$

where T is a transaction type. In order to find $P(T, R_{j+1,k})$, we compute the feature vector (using either occurrences or counts) for $R_{j+1,k}$ and apply one of the previously discussed Naive Bayes models. Doing so allows us to compute V^* in $O(n^2)$ time.

Assessing the accuracy of our transaction recognition algorithm is complicated by the fact that the recognizer may not always find the correct transaction boundaries. As a result, our accuracy metric here is the fraction of correctly labeled RPCs. Fig. 5 displays the results of running our algorithm in combination with all four classifiers for data set 1. The x-axis is the fraction of the data set used for training, and the y-axis shows the percent of correctly labeled RPCs. As expected, accuracies are lower for transaction recognition than for

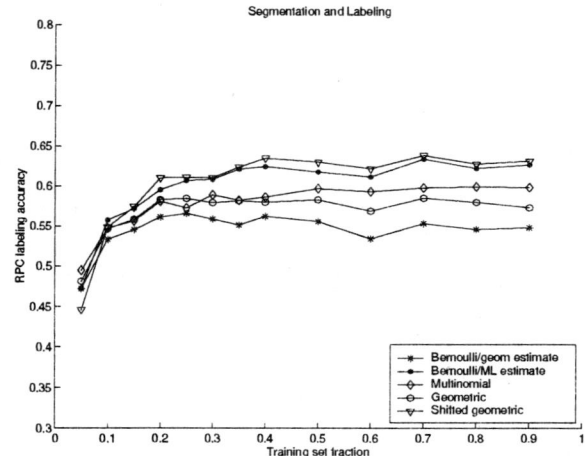

Figure 5: Transaction recognition results for data set 1.

labeling alone – 64% vs. 87% for the best case. Also, in contrast to the labeling problem where 4 of the 5 classifiers performed equivalently, here we see a clear ranking of the classifiers: counts-with-shifted geometric is the best, followed by occurrences-with-Bernoulli. It is interesting that the latter, which uses a more restrictive feature vector, performs better than counts-with-multinomial and geometric. Further, that the ordering of the classifiers in Fig. 5 differs from that in Fig. 4 suggests that the characteristics of a good classier for transaction recognition may differ from that for classification alone.

Related Work and Discussion

To the best of our knowledge, the problem of recognizing end-user transactions has not yet been addressed in the literature. However, the problem of recognizing end-user transactions is closely related to several well-studied machine-learning domains such as text classification, speech recognition, and pattern recognition.

In text classification, a text is represented by a set of features such as word occurrences or word counts, and a classification algorithm, trained on a set of labeled examples, assigns topics (class labels) to previously unseen text instances. Examples include classification of Web pages (Craven et al. 1998; Nigam et al. 1998), sorting electronic mail (Sahami et al. 1998) or news articles (Lewis & Gale 1994; Joachims 1998). A common approach views a text as a "bag of words" (i.e. information about word sequence is ignored), using word occurrences or word counts as features. We employed this approach for assigning a transaction type to a given RPC sequence (labeling problem).

Various learning approaches, such as kNN, Naive Bayes, maximum entropy, neural nets, support-vector machines (SVMs), and many others have been compared on existing benchmarks (Yang 1999; Yang & Pedersen 1997; Joachims 1998; McCallum & Nigam 1998). Surprisingly, the Naive Bayes classifier performs very well in many domains in which its independence assumption is violated. This has been noted elsewhere (e.g., DomingoesPazzani97,McCallum98a). In our domain, RPCs within the same transaction are clearly not independent. However, Naive Bayes achieves quite high accuracy.

Despite similarities with text classification, our domain is inherently more complex because it requires solving the segmentation problem. Related areas include speech recognition (Jelinek 1998) (a stream of sounds must be segmented into words), statistical natural language processing (Manning & Schutze 1999) (segmenting a sequence of words into phrases), and general syntactic pattern recognition (Fu 1982). Commonly used models include Hidden Markov Models (HMMs) and stochastic context-free grammars (SCFGs). A SCFG consist of probabilistic production rules that can be used for constructing a stochastic language with an embedded rich syntactic structure. For example, they have been used as generative models for producing hierarchical workloads in order to evaluate the performance of distributed systems (Raghavan, Joseph, & Haring 1995).

Our approach to segmentation and labeling is closely related to the Viterbi search employed in speech recognition. Further investigation of segmentation techniques that would exploit the structure of our problem is an important direction for future work.

Conclusions

This paper applies machine-learning techniques to a new domain — recognizing end-user transactions. Two problems are addressed. The first is labeling transaction instances with the transaction type. This is similar to problems studied in text classification. The second is transaction recognition, i.e. segmenting RPC sequences into transaction instances and labeling these instances. This more difficult problem is akin to segmenting sounds into words in speech understanding.

We provide three kinds of results. The first characterizes the domain itself. We indicate that there are a substantial number of classes–more than 30 transaction types in the data we obtained from a large oil company. The vocabulary size–the RPC types–is modest, in the range of 50 to 100. There is a highly skewed distributions of both classes and vocabularies (i.e., RPCs). Further, we show that the distribution of RPC counts fits the shifted geometric distribution much better than either the multinomial or the geometric distributions.

Using Naive Bayes, we tackle the labeling problem by employing four combinations of feature vectors and probability distributions: RPC occurrences with the Bernoulli distribution, RPC counts with the multinomial distribution, RPC counts with the geometric distribution, and RPC counts with the shifted geometric distribution. Our experimental results indicate that the classifier using the shifted geometric distribution classifies correctly 78% of transactions. While this is competitive with the literature on text classification, it is considerably lower than the 85-87% achieved by the other classifiers. What is puzzling here is that the shifted geometric provides a much better description of the underlying distribution of RPCs.

Our dynamic-programming approach to transaction recognition uses the Viterbi algorithm, assuming transaction independence and using our classifiers to select most likely transaction label for a given RPC sequence. As an accuracy measure, we use the percent of correctly labeled RPCs rather than transactions, since the transaction recognizer may not always find the correct transaction boundaries. Here, our empirical results indicate that using occurrences with the Bernoulli distribution (assuming ML estimator) and counts with the shifted geometric distribution achieve higher accuracies than the other classifiers (approximately 64%). An interesting observation is that using a better classifier does not always result into a better transaction recognizer (e.g., shifted geometric is the worst classifier, but leads to the best recognizer).

Are our results to date sufficient for the intended applications of recognizing transactions? These applications include: (a) quantifying end-user perceptions of performance (b) creating representative workloads, and (c) anticipating resource management requests. Existing approaches to (a) and (b) attempt to obtain the requisite information through measurement. Item (c) is mostly addressed in an ad hoc manner. Thus, there is little appreciation of the implications of approximate results. This is clearly an area in need of further investigation.

Our results to date provide encouragement that it is possible to recognize end-user transactions using Naive Bayes or other machine-learning techniques. We view this as a starting point. One area of future work is characterizing domain properties that result in a high accuracy for Naive Bayes, especially when the independence assumption does not hold. We also plan to compare Naive Bayes with other state-of-the-art learning techniques, particularly with a general Bayes net classifier and SVMs.

Another direction for further research is the feature selection. By this, we mean both selecting a feature type (e.g., occurrences or counts for single RPCs, or functions on subsets/subsequences of RPCs) and selecting a subset of features of a given type. A commonly used approach to the second problem is selecting a fraction of features having the highest mutual information with the class variable (Yang & Pedersen 1997). This approach is quite effective in text classification where the feature set size is usually large (e.g., when a dictionary contains thousands of words). Since our domain has only about 100 RPCs, there may be little the advantages to employing of feature selection for counts or occurrences. However, if features employing sequence information are considered, then the feature space could grow exponentially and hence feature selection might be essential.

Still other areas of future work include more sophisticated transaction recognition algorithms and an investigation of the properties of a classifier that yield a better transaction recognizer.

Appendix A: Shifted Geometric Distribution

This appendix provides details on the shifted geometric distribution and the estimation of its parameters in our data. This distribution extends the geometric distribution by having a shift parameter, ν_{ij}, that specifies the minimum count for RPCs of type j in a transaction instance of type i. Thus,

$$P(n_{ij}|T_i) = p_{ij}^{n_{ij}-\nu_{ij}}(1-p_{ij})$$

where $P(n_{ij}|T_i) = 0$ if $n_{ij} < \nu_{ij}$.

Let m_i be the number of type i transactions and $q_i = P(T_i)$. Let n_{ilj} be the number of type i RPCs in the l-th segment that is labeled as a transaction of type i. Then the likelihood function is:

$$\begin{aligned} P(\{T_{il}\}, \{n_{ilj}\}) &= \prod_{i=1}^{I}\prod_{l=1}^{m_i}\prod_{j=1}^{J} p_{ij}^{n_{ilj}-\nu_{ij}}(1-p_{ij})q_i \\ &= \prod_i q_i^{m_i} \prod_{j_i} p_{ij}^{n_{ij}-m_i\nu_{ij}}(1-p_{ij})^{m_i} \end{aligned}$$

The maximum likelihood estimators can be found in a straight-forward way. These are: $\hat{p}_{ij} = \frac{n_{ij}-m_i\nu_{ij}}{n_{ij}-m_i\nu_{ij}+m_i}$, $\hat{q}_i = \frac{m_i}{\sum_{i'} m_{i'}}$, and $\hat{\nu}_{ij} = \min_l n_{ilj}$.

References

Craven, M.; DiPasquo, D.; Freitag, D.; McCallum, A. K.; Mitchell, T. M.; Nigam, K.; and Slattery, S. 1998. Learning to extract symbolic knowledge from the World Wide Web. In *Proceedings of AAAI-98, 15th Conference of the American Association for Artificial Intelligence*, 509–516.

Fu, K. S. 1982. *Syntactic Pattern Recognition and Applications*. Engelwood Cliffs, NJ: Prentice Hall.

Jelinek, F. 1998. *Statistical Methods for Speech Recognition*. MIT Press: Cambridge.

Joachims, T. 1998. Text categorization with support vector machines: learning with many relevant features. *European Conf. Mach. Learning, ECML98*.

Kleinrock, L. 1975. *Queueing Systems, Volume 1*. John Wiley and Sons.

Lewis, D. D., and Gale, W. A. 1994. A sequential algorithm for training text classifiers. In *Proceedings of SIGIR-94, 17th ACM International Conference on Research and Development in Information Retrieval*, 3–12.

Manning, C. D., and Schutze, H. 1999. *Foundations of Statistical Natural Language Processing*. MIT Press: Cambridge.

McCallum, A. K., and Nigam, K. 1998. A comparison of event models for naive Bayes text classification. In *Proceedings of the 1st AAAI Workshop on Learning for Text Categorization*, 41–48.

Nigam, K.; McCallum, A. K.; Thrun, S.; and Mitchell, T. M. 1998. Learning to classify text from labeled and unlabeled documents. In *Proceedings of AAAI-98, 15th Conference of the American Association for Artificial Intelligence*, 792–799.

Raghavan, S. V.; Joseph, P. J.; and Haring, G. 1995. Workload models for multiwindow distributed environments. *Lecture Notes in Computer Science* 977:314–326.

Sahami, M.; Dumais, S. T.; Heckerman, D.; and Horvitz, E. 1998. A Bayesian approach to filtering junk E-mail. In *Proceedings of the 1998 Workshop on Learning for Text Categorization*, 55–62.

Yang, Y., and Pedersen, J. O. 1997. A comparative study on feature selection in text categorization. In *Proceedings of ICML-97, 14th International Conference on Machine Learning*, 412–420.

Yang, Y. 1999. An evaluation of statistical approaches to text categorization. *Information Retrieval* 1(1-2):69–90.

ATMOSPHERE - Automatic Track Mining and Objective Satellite Pattern Hunting system using Enhanced RBF and EGDLM

Raymond S. T. Lee and James N. K. Liu

Hong Kong Polytechnic University
Hung Hom, Kowloon, Hong Kong
csstlee@comp.polyu.edu.hk, csnkliu@comp.polyu.edu.hk,

Abstract

Severe weather prediction, such as tropical cyclone (TC) forecast is a typical data mining and forecasting problem that involves high level data manipulation and interpretation of meteorological information such as satellite pictures and other meteorological observation data. In this paper, we present a fully automatic and integrated system known as "ATOMOSPHER" - Automatic Track Mining and Object Satellite Pattern Hunting system using Enhanced RBF and EGDLM - to provide a neural network based TC identification and tracking system. The proposed system consists of two main modules: 1) Object Dvorak technique for TC satellite pattern identification based on an Elastic Graph Dynamic Link Model (EGDLM) and 2) TC tracking system based on an Enhanced Radial Basis Function (RBF) network model.

For system evaluation, 120 TC cases appeared in the period from 1985 to 1998 (provided by National Oceanic and Atmospheric Administration (NOAA)) are adopted. Promising results of over 87% of TC pattern segmentation and 97% of correct classification rate are attained respectively. For TC tracking, an overall of over 86% correct prediction result is achieved.

Keywords: EGDLM, Enhanced RBF, Track mining, TC identification, time series prediction.

1. Introduction

Time series prediction so far is one of the most vital research topics, not only because of its significant practical values, ranging from stock prediction (Liu and Lee 1997; Liu and Tang 1996) to general weather forecast such as rainfall prediction (Li et. al. 1998; Lee and Liu 1999c; Liu and Lee 1999) in meteorology, but also of its academic values.

In a typical weather prediction scenario, factors that affect the coming weather depend not only on local weather elements such as temperatures, relative humidity, air pressure, wind speed and directions, but also regional weather elements such as the effect from global weather pattern, for example El Nino effect (Bao and Xiang, 1991). This constitutes to the handling of a huge amount of information including "extraction", "filtering", "interpretation", "discrimination" and "processing", and also a sophisticate data mining and knowledge discovery process as well. Especially in the case of severe weather prediction such as topical cyclone (TC) forecast, an additional level of complexity with the usage and interpretation of satellite and radar images is being imposed. Unlike those weather elements such as temperature and pressure which can be predicted by classical numerical modeling (Liu 1988) or contemporary neural network models (Liu and Lee 1999), these imagery data are highly variant in the sense that so far only subjective human interpretations by the Dvorak technique is adopted (Dvorak 1973, 1975).

This paper presents an integrated model that provides an effective and fully automatic system for the tropical cyclone (TC) identification and track prediction called ATMOSPHERE (Automatic Track Mining and Satellite Pattern Hunting system using Enhanced RBF and EGDLM). The proposed model consists of two main modules: 1) TC pattern recognition system from satellite pictures known as Elastic Graph Dynamic Link Model (EGDLM), a neural network based model that involves the automatic TC pattern segmentation and elastic pattern matching from the pre-defined TC templates, a process that simulates human TC identification technique called Dvorak analysis (Dvorak 1973, 1975); 2) A time series TC intensity and track mining system using Enhanced Radial Basis Function network, a time series recurrent neural network prediction model that integrates the conventional RBF network with Time Difference and Structural Learning (TDSL) technique.

The paper is organized as follows. Section 2 will present the EGDLM for automatic TC pattern identification. Section 3 will discuss the Enhanced RBF model for TC intensity and track mining. In section 4, an overview of system implementation using 120 TC cases appeared between 1985 to 1998 (information provided by National Oceanic and Atmospheric Administration (NOAA)) will be presented. Comparisons of the proposed system with other contemporary TC tracking system will be conducted as well, together with the conclusion discussed in Section 5.

2. Objective Satellite Pattern Identification of Tropical Cyclone using EGDLM

2.1 Dvorak Technique for TC Identification

In view of the various meteorological phenomena interpreted from satellite images, one of the most valuable contributions is the identification of tropical cyclones - including storms, extra-tropical cyclones, typhoon and hurricanes that threaten numerous human lives and properties.

One of the worldwide accepted methods for TC identification and interpretation was developed by Dvorak (1973; 1975) known as Dvorak technique. From his theory, each TC may go through a life cycle that can be classified into eight categories ranging from TC1 to TC8 (Figure 1). In addition to classifying the tropical cyclones, Dvorak analysis also provides an effective scheme to determine the current strength of the cyclones from the satellite images which are based on the "T-number" (T1-T8) determined from Dvorak technique.

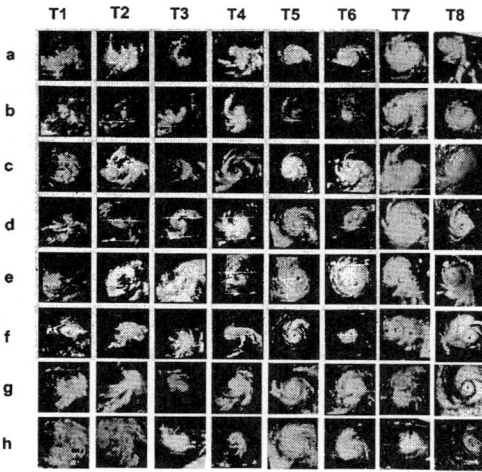

Figure 1 - Dvorak TC templates from T1 to T8 (Each T-number with eight sub-categories corresponds to eight different possible appearance of the TC patterns)

Nowadays, Dvorak technique is still the worldwide agreed official tool for the determination of TC intensity. But due to the highly variation of TC patterns that can appear in satellite pictures, the Dvorak technique is highly subjective which depends on the human justification done by the weather forecasters and meteorologists.

2.2 A Perspective of EGDLM for Invariant TC Pattern Recognition

In this paper, an elastic attribute graph recognition model known as Elastic Graph Dynamic Link Model (EGDLM) is proposed to provide a fully automatic and objective solution for Dvorak technique on TC pattern identification.

In short, object recognition using EGDLM is based on the framework of Dynamic Link Architecture (DLA) (Malsburg 1981) which describes the recognition problem as an elastic graph matching mechanism between the attribute graphs of the image vectors (input layer) with the set of model graphs in the "memory layer". The neural interactions are governed by the onset/offset of the dynamic links between the layers which simulate the functionality of the dynamic memory association in the Short-term memory. Active researches in this area have been done including handwritten character recognition (Liu and Lee 1997, 1998; Lee and Liu 1999e), human face recognition (Lee et. al. 1999, Lee and Liu 1999d) and TC pattern recognition with the integration of Active Snake model for object segmentation based on elastic templates (Lee and Liu 1999a, 2000).

Different from the traditional DLA model, EGDLM makes use of the Composite Neural Oscillatory model to facilitate a fully automatic object segmentation scheme. Recent research of such also involves scene analysis (Lee and Liu 1999b). A schematic diagram of EGDLM for TC pattern matching is shown in Figure 2.

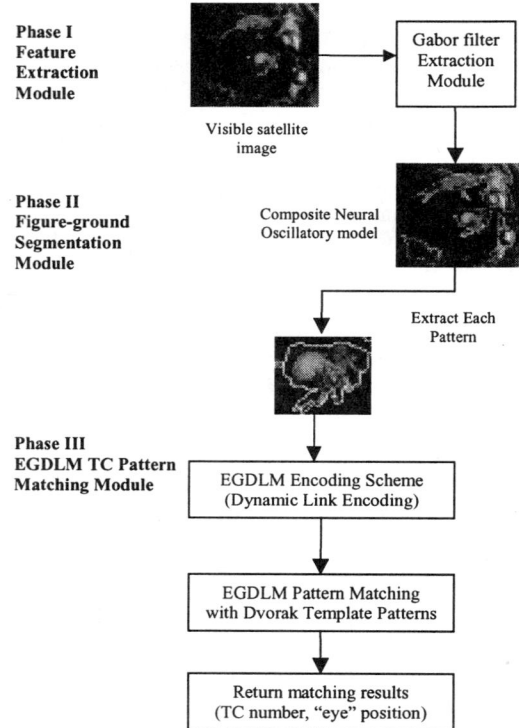

Figure 2 - EGDLM for TC Pattern Identification

2.3 Invariant Properties

One of the most striking features of the EGDLM is the "invariant" property. In the network model, only the topological relations between the composite neural oscillators (ie. dynamic links) are encoded into the network. The pattern matching process is resembled to the "Elastic Graph Matching" which is invariant under various transformations such as translation, rotation, reflection, dilation and occlusion. This occurs commonly in natural scenes (Lee and Liu 1999b).

3. Enhanced Radial Basis Function (RBF) Network for TC Track Mining

3.1 Enhanced RBF Network - System Overview

The proposed Enhanced RBF Network (ERBFN) incorporates with two main technologies into the conventional RBF network for temporal time series prediction problem: 1) Structural learning technique that integrates the "forgetting" factor into the RBF BP algorithm; 2) A Time Difference with Decay (TDD) method is corporated into the network to strengthen the temporal time series relation of the input data sequence for network training. A schematic diagram of the proposed network is shown in Figure 3.

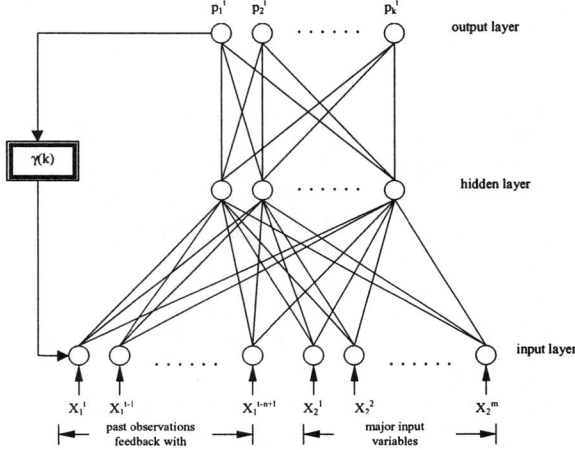

Figure 3 - Schematic diagram of the Enhanced RBF Network

The ERBFN shown in Figure 3 consists of three layers. The first layer is the input layer which consists of two portions: 1) Past network outputs that feedback into the network; 2) Major co-relative variables are concerned with the prediction problem. Past network outputs enter into the network by time-delay unit as the first inputs. These outputs are also affected by a decay factor γ that is governed by the following equation.

$$\gamma = \alpha e^{-\lambda k} \quad (1)$$

where λ is the decay constant, α is the normalization constant and k is the forecast horizon.

In general, the time series prediction of the proposed network is to predict the outcome of the sequence x_1^{t+k} at the time of $t+k$ that is based on the past observation sequence of size n, i.e. $x_1^t, x_1^{t-1}, x_1^{t-2}, x_1^{t-3}, \ldots, x_1^{t-n+1}$ and the major variables that influence the outcome of the time series at time t. For convenience, the following notations are used throughout the following network description: The numbers of input nodes in the first and second portions are set to n and m respectively. The number of hidden nodes is set to p. The predictive steps are set to k, so the number of output nodes is k. At time t, the inputs will be $[x_1^t, x_1^{t-1}, x_1^{t-2}, x_1^{t-3}, \ldots, x_1^{t-n+1}]$ and $[x_2^1, x_2^2, \ldots, x_2^m]$ respectively. The output is given by x^{t+k}, denoted by p_k^t for simplicity, w_{ij}^t denotes the connection weight between the i-th node and the j-th node at time t.

3.2 Enhanced RBF Network - Structural Learning Algorithms

The main idea of RBF learning algorithm with a "forgetting" factor is to introduce a constant decay to connected weights that make the redundancy weight(s) fade out quickly. The cost function of the structural learning algorithm is given by equation (2).

$$E^t = E_1^t + \varepsilon' \sum_{i,j} |w_{ij}^t| \quad (2)$$

where E_1^t denotes the error square in traditional RBF learning, the second term is the penalty criteria.

If delta rule is used, the learning rule of the weights is given by:

$$\Delta w_{ij}^{t+1} = -\eta \frac{\partial E^t}{\partial w_{ij}^t} + \alpha \Delta w_{ij}^t = \Delta w 1_{ij}^t + \alpha \Delta w_{ij}^t - \varepsilon \, \text{sgn}(w_{ij}^t) \quad (3)$$

where the first term in the first line is the weight change obtained by the traditional RBF network, η is the learning rate and α is the momentum. Besides, $\varepsilon = \eta\varepsilon'$ is the "forgetting" factor.

By using this structural learning method, the main "skeleton" of the network can be constructed with weight adapting over a time series of training.

3.3 Enhanced RBF Network – TDD Method

The structural learning algorithm discussed above does provide a "dynamic" structure building of the neural network, but it cannot adapt the temporal time series relations of the input and output feedback data sequences into the model. In order to code with this problem, a temporal difference method with decay feedback is hybridized into the learning algorithm of the proposed model. The basic concepts are presented as follows.

In a typical time series prediction problem, given a series of past observations of time-step n at time t, i.e. $[x_1^t, x_1^{t-1}, x_1^{t-2}, x_1^{t-3}, \ldots, x_1^{t-n+1}]$, with the predictive time-step of k, we not only obtain the predicted output at time t+k, i.e. p_k^t, but more importantly is the sequence of future events starting from time t, i.e. $[p_1^t, p_2^t, p_3^t \ldots, p_k^t]$. In other words, the network can provide an overlapping and inter-related event sequence as an additional "hint" for network learning, which can be implemented by using Temporal Difference technique (Sutton 1983). Besides, by considering a sequence of temporal difference operations from time t+1 to t+k, the prediction from a "nearer" future normally has a higher level of confidence than a "far" future, so a decay operator is integrated into the learning algorithm in order to reflect the situation.

With the integration of TDD methodology, the learning algorithm discussed in equation (3) will be modified into:

$$\Delta w_{ij}^{t+1} = \eta (\sum_{h=2}^{k} \gamma(h) \cdot (p_{h-1}^{t+1} - p_h^t) \sum_{l=1}^{t} \lambda^{t-1} \frac{\partial p_h^l}{\partial w_{ij}^t} + (p_1^t - p_0^t) \cdot \sum_{l=1}^{t} \left[\gamma(l) \cdot \lambda^{t-1} \frac{\partial p_1^l}{\partial w_{ij}^t} \right] + \alpha \Delta w_{ij}^t - \varepsilon'' \text{sgn}(w_{ij}^t) \quad (4)$$

where ε'' is defined as:

$$\varepsilon'' = \begin{cases} \varepsilon & |w_{ij}^t| = < \theta \\ 0 & \text{otherwise} \end{cases} \quad (5)$$

From equation (4), the learning algorithm consists of three basic components, the first two terms refer to the error adjustment based on the temporal differences between the output event sequences between the two consecutive time steps, which is "weighted" by the decay functions $\gamma(l)$, $\gamma(h)$ given by equation (1). The third and fourth terms refer to the structural learning operations, which is explained in equation (4). Also, λ denotes the exponential scale for a connection weight that determines the effective length of the history windows.

4. ATMOSHPERE - System Implementation

4.1 Introduction

In sampling data for simulation, 120 tropical cyclones cases appeared in the period between 1985 and 1998 were identified. All the time series (3-hourly) satellite images and grid point meteorological data are provided by National Oceanic and Atmospheric Administration (NOAA). For the grid point meteorological data being used in the time series prediction, meteorological data including: mean sea level air pressure (MSLP), surface and upper-air (700mb, 500mb, 300mb) wind speed and direction, dry bulb and wet bulb temperature, that is, all the data that will affect the "steering" motion and development of TC are considered.

System implementation tests of ATMOSHPEREE are mainly divided into two phases: 1) TC identification tests based on the TC pattern recognition using EGDLM; 2) TC intensity and track mining tests using Enhanced RBFN Network (ERBFN). Comparisons on system performance with other neural network models and bureau TC tracking system such as OCTM and TKS will be conducted as well. The whole system implementation and performance evaluations were carried out on Sun Sparc 20 workstation.

4.2 TC Pattern Recognition Tests

In the tests, for each of the 120 TC cases, 5 satellite images were randomly chosen for the test, so totally 600 satellite pictures were being used. Two set of tests were conducted for TC pattern recognition using EGDLM:

1) TC patterns segmentation tests

TC patterns segmentation done by EGDLM model using Composite Neural Oscillating technique verse that using Active Contour Model (Lee and Liu 1999a) is shown in Table I. A snapshot of the segmented TC patterns from a satellite image that contains four TCs in 1997 is shown in Figure 4.

TABLE I
TC PATTERNS SEGMENTATION COMPARED WITH ACM MODEL

Segmentation Models	Segmentation Rate			Av. Speed* (sec)
	TC 1-3	TC 4-6	TC 7-8	
EGDLM	92%	96%	99.5%	50 sec
Hybrid ACM	80%	88.2%	97%	195 sec

2) TC patterns recognition tests

In the test, 600 satellite images were undergone TC segmentation and they were matched with the Dvorak templates (Figure 1) using the elastic graph matching technique of EGDLM. Two sets of tests were conducted: They were "TC Pattern Classification Test of the 600 satellite images" and "TC "Eye" Position Identification Test". Results are presented in Tables II and III.

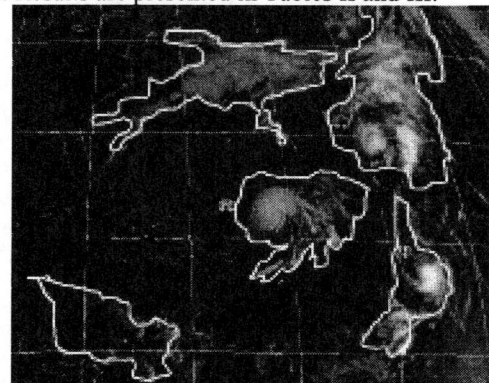

Figure 4 – Segmented TC patterns from satellite image

TABLE II
TC PATTERN CLASSIFICATION RESULTS

	No. of matches for each category			
	TC cat. 1-3 Total no.: 245	TC cat. 4-6 Total no. : 276	TC cat. 7-8 Total no. 231	Overall Total no.:752
EGDLM	229 (93%)	271 (98%)	231 (100%)	731 (97%)
Hybrid ACM	178 (73%)	223 (81%)	211 (91%)	612 (81%)

TABLE III
TC "EYE" POSITION IDENTIFICATION RESULTS

	No. of TC	No. of matches	Recognition rate (%)	"eye" position deviation*
EGDLM	281	278	99%	2.3 km
Hybrid ACM		250	89%	3.0 km

Remark :TC "Eye" position deviation amounts are calculated by the deviation from the TC "eye" location reported by reconnaissance aircraft

4.3 TC Intensity and Track Mining Tests

Using the Enhanced RBF network (ERBFN) for time series TC tracking mining, the 120 TC cases were randomly divided into two sets. The first 60 TC cases were used for network training while the rest used for system testing.

For system evaluation, two types of tests were conducted: 1) Evaluation for the system performance of the Enhanced RBF Network (ERBFN) against two different time series neural network prediction models: conventional RBF network and BBPT (Williams and Zipser, 1995) recurrent network; 2) Comparisons of the TC track mining performance of the proposed ERBFN with the bureau TC tracking systems: OCTM and TKS systems.

In order to provide a systematic performance measure of the proposed model against other neural network prediction tools and the enhancement achieved as compared with the conventional RBF model, the comparison with two other time series prediction models was taken. This included: 1) Conventional RBF network; 2) Backpropagation Time Series Recurrent Network (BBTT). Network training and testing results are shown in Table IV. Storm tracks being successfully mined by all the models for TC Bonnie (1998) against the "Actual" TC track are shown in Figure 5.

TABLE IV
NETWORKS TRAINING AND TESTING RESULTS

Network Models	TC Intensity Prediction		TC Track Prediction	
	MSE training	MSE testing	MSE training	MSE testing
ERBFN	0.014	0.061	0.013	0.079
RBF model	0.412	0.513	0.493	0.581
BPTT model	0.082	0.103	0.093	0.112

Compared with the conventional RBF model, the proposed Enhanced RBF model has achieved a significant enhancement by over 20 and 10 times in mean square error (MSE) in TC intensity and track mining. Even when compared with the BPTT recurrent network, an overall 40% and 30% improvement in these dimensions have been attained respectively.

A quantitative evaluation of the proposed model was performed and tested for its applicability in real time TC track mining as compared with that of the bureau TC Track mining systems: 1) One-way interactive Tropical Cyclone Model (OCTM) used by the JTWC in Guam; 2) Track Forecast System (TKS) – Enhanced numerical prediction forecast used in Central Weather Bureau in Taiwan.

In the experiment, 55 TCs appearing during the period between 1989 to 1992 were used. Track mining accuracy is determined by the great circle distance between the forecast position and the best track position provided by the Central Weather Bureau of Taiwan. Table V shows the comparison results of the Enhanced RBF model with OCTM and TKS models based on the 48-hour TC position forecast during the year 1989-90, detailed TC track mining accuracy figures (in km) for each TC were given for illustration.

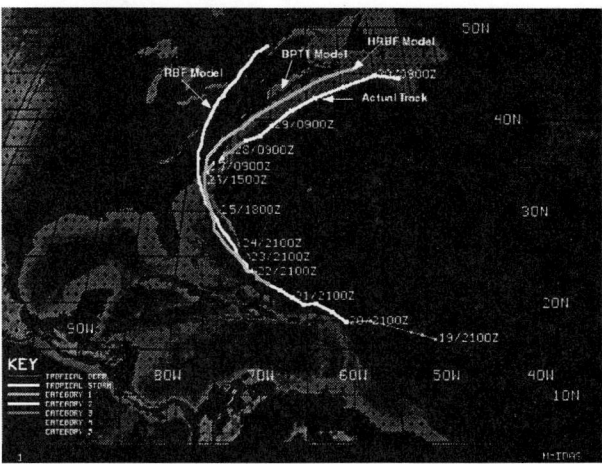

Figure 5 – TC tracks predicted by different models Vs. actual TC track for TC Bonnie (1998)

TABLE V
COMPARISON OF THE HRBF MODEL WITH BUREAU TC TRAC4KING SYSTEMS AT 48-HOUR POSITION FORECAST (1989-1990)

TC/ year	No. of cases	Enhanced RBF	OTCM	TFS
1989	52	296	486	425
1990	41	309	305	322
Overall	93	301	406	379

As shown in Table V, for the 18 TCs appeared in the period between 1989 and 1990, the average 48-hour forecast error reported by Enhanced RBF, OTCM and TFS are 301 km, 406 km and 379 km respectively. The overall improvement comparing with the two models are respectively OTCM (25.8%) and TFS (25.9%), corresponding to less than 3° error. This represents a significant improvement to predict the landfall of TC for warning and precaution measures.

Comparing with the TC track mining results between 1989 and 1990, it can be seen that the errors are somewhat correlated. The track forecasts also depend on the capability in predicting the large scale flow, which is believed to be related to the type of flow regimes. When interpreting Table V, it is worthwhile to realize that 1989 is one of the worst years for OTCM performance. However, the HRBF model still maintains promising track mining capability, giving a good prediction of cyclone movement.

5. Conclusion

This paper proposed a fully integrated and automatic system called ATMOSPHERE (Automatic Track Mining and Objective Satellite Pattern Hunting system using Enhanced RBF and EGDLM) for TC identification and time series intensity and track prediction. Such a task is historically highly dependent on human subjective justification on vast supply of information.

The main contributions of the ATMOSPHERE is two folds: 1) Automate the Dvorak technique for TC identification from satellite images, a process that highly depends on human intervention. With the adoption of EGDLM, the system provides a fully automatic, accurate (over 97% accuracy) solution in a reasonable speed; 2) The adaptability and real time learning track learning technique, which is particularly important for TC Track mining problem due to the rapid development of TC in severe weather conditions. This is also the major weakness of numerical prediction models in forecasting these severe and locally developed weather phenomena.

Acknowledgement

We are grateful to NOAA for the provision of meteorological data and satellite pictures for TC between 1985 to 1998. The authors are also grateful to the partial supports of the Central Research Grants G-S484 of Hong Kong Polytechnic University.

References

Bao C. L. and Xiang Y. Z., 1991. Impact of El Nino Event on the Subtropical High and Meteorological: Oceanic Disaster. In Proceedings of CIES: 25-30, Japan.

Dvorak, V. F., 1973. A Technique for the Analysis and Forecasting of Tropical Cyclone Intensities from Satellite Pictures. NOAA Tech. Memo., NESS 45, U. S. Department of Commerce, Washington, D. C.

Dvorak, V. F., 1975. Tropical Cyclone Intensity Analysis and Forecasting from Satellite Imagery. Mon. Wea. Rev. 103: 420-430.

Lee, R.S.T. and Liu, J.N.K., 1999a. An Automatic Satellite Interpretation of Tropical Cyclone Patterns Using Elastic Graph Dynamic Link Model. To appear in International Journal of Pattern Recognition and Artificial Intelligence.

Lee, R.S.T. and Liu, J.N.K., 1999b. An Oscillatory Elastic Graph Matching Model for Scene Analysis. In Proceedings of International Conference on Imaging Science, Systems, and Technology (CISST'99): 42-45, Las Vegas, Nevada, USA.

Lee, R. and Liu, J., 1999c. Teaching and Learning the A. I. Modeling", Innovative Teaching Tools for Neural Nets, Fuzzy Systems and Genetic Algorithms, eds. L. Jain, CRC Press: 31-86.

Lee, R.S.T. and Liu, J.N.K. 1999d. An Integrated Elastic Contour Fitting and Attribute Graph Matching Model for Automatic Face Coding and Recognition", In Proceedings of the Third International Conference on Knowledge-Based Intelligent Information Engineering Systems (KES'99): 292-295, Australia.

Lee, Raymond S. T. and Liu, James N. K., 1999e. An Oscillatory Elastic Graph Matching Model for Recognition of Offline Handwritten Chinese Characters. In Proceedings of the Third International Conference on Knowledge-Based Intelligent Information Engineering Systems (KES'99): 284-287, Adelaide, Australia.

Lee, Raymond S. T. and Liu, James N. K., 2000. An approach Using Elastic Graph Dynamic Link Model for Automating the Satellite Interpretation of Tropical Cyclone Patterns". To appear in Invariants for Pattern Recognition and Classification: Series in Machine Perception and Artificial Intelligence, World Scientific Publishing.

Lee, R., Liu, J and You, Y., 1999. Face Recognition: Elastic Relation Encoding and Structural Matching. In Proceedings of IEEE International Conference on Systems, Man, and Cybernetics (SMC'99): 172-177, Tokyo, Japan.

Li, B., Liu, J. and Dai, H., 1998. Forecasting from Low Quality Data with Applications in Weather Forecasting. Int. Journal of Computing and Informatics, 22(3): 351-358.

Liu, N. K., 1988. Computational Aspects of a Fine-mesh Sea Breeze Model. M. Phil. Dissertation, Department of Mathematics, Murdoch University, Western Australia.

Liu, N. K. and Lee, K. K., 1997. An Intelligence Business Advisor for Stock Investment. Expert Systems, 14(3): 129-139, Blackwell Publishers, U. K.

Liu, J.N.K. and Lee, R.S.T., 1997. Invariant Character Recognition in Dynamic Link Architecture. In Proceedings of IEEE KDEX97: 188-195, Newport Beach USA.

Liu, J. N. K. and Lee, R. S. T., 1998. Invariant Handwritten Chinese Character Recognition by Dynamic Link Architecture", In Proceedings ICONIP/JNNS'98 (1): 275-278, Kitakyushu, Japan.

Liu, J. N. K. and Lee, R. S. T., 1999. Rainfall Forecasting from Multiple Point Source Using Neural Networks. In Proceedings of IEEE International Conference on Systems, Man, and Cybernetics (SMC'99): 429-434, Tokyo, Japan.

Liu, J. N. K. and Tang, T. I., 1996. An Intelligence System for Financial Market Prediction. In Proceedings of the 2nd South China International Business Symposium: 199-209.

Malsburg, 1981. Nervous Structures with Dynamic Links. Berichte Bunsegesellschaft for Physical Chemistry, 89: 703-710.

Sutton, R. S., 1983. Learning to Predict by the Methods of Temporal Difference. Machine Learning, 3:8-44.

Williams R.J. and Zipser D., 1995. Gradient-based Learning Algorithm for Recurrent Network. Backpropagation: Theory, Architecture and Application, Hillsdale, NJ, Erlbanum.

Learning the Common Structure of Data

Kristina Lerman and Steven Minton

University of Southern California
Information Sciences Institute
4676 Admiralty Way
Marina del Rey, California 90292
{lerman,minton}@isi.edu

Abstract

The proliferation of online information sources has accentuated the need for tools that automatically validate and recognize data. We present an efficient algorithm that learns structural information about data from positive examples alone. We describe two Web wrapper maintenance applications that employ this algorithm. The first application detects when a wrapper is not extracting correct data. The second application automatically identifies data on Web pages so that the wrapper may be re-induced when the source format changes.

Introduction

As the size and diversity of online information grows, many of the common transactions between humans and online information systems are being delegated to software agents (Jennings & Wooldridge 1998). Price comparison and stock monitoring are just two examples of the tasks that can be assigned to an agent. Many protocols and languages have been designed to facilitate information exchange, from primitive EDI protocols to more modern languages like XML and KQML. However, these schemes all require that the agents conform to syntactic and semantic standards that have been carefully worked out in advance. Humans, in contrast, get by with only informal conventions to facilitate communication, and rarely require detailed pre-specified standards for information exchange.

If we examine typical web pages – electronic catalogs, financial sites, *etc.* – we find that information is laid out in a variety of graphical arrangements, often with minimal use of natural language. People are able to understand web pages because they have expectations about the structure of the data appearing on the page and its physical layout. For instance, if we look at online Zagat's restaurant guide, we find a restaurant's name, an address, a review, *etc.* Though none of these are explicitly labeled as such, the page is immediately understandable because we expect this information to be on the page and have expectations about the appearance of these fields (*e.g.*, we know that a U.S. address typically begins with a street address and ends with a zip code).

In this paper we describe a machine learning method for acquiring expectations about the content of data fields. The method learns structural information about data, which we may use to recognize restaurant names, addresses, *etc.* We describe two applications related to wrapper induction that utilize this information. A web page wrapper is a program that extracts data from a web page. Wrappers are used extensively by information integration programs (Knoblock *et al.* 1998). Some types of Web wrappers (Muslea *et al.* 1999, Kushmerick *et al.* 1997) rely primarily on the layout of the Web page to extract data. These wrappers are very efficient at extracting data; moreover, extraction rules can be learned from very few labeled examples. However, sometimes these wrappers stop extracting correctly when the page layout changes. We present a method for verifying that an existing wrapper is correctly extracting data. We also present a method for re-inducing a wrapper when the layout of the Web source changes. Though we focus on web applications, the learning technique is not web-specific, and can be used to learn about text and numeric fields in general. We believe that it is a step towards true agent interoperability, where agents can exchange and aggregate data without needing to know in advance about the detailed syntactic and semantic conventions used by their partners.

The Learning Task

Our objective is to learn the structure of data fields, such as addresses. One example of a street address is "4676 Admiralty Way." In previous work, the structure of information extracted from Web pages was described by a sequence of characters (Goan *et al.* 1996) or a collection of global features, such as the number of words and the density of numeric characters (Kushmerick 1999). We propose an intermediate word-level representation that balances the descriptive power and specificity of the character-level representation with the compactness and computational efficiency of the global representation. Words, or more accurately tokens, are strings generated from an alphabet containing different types of characters: alphabetic, numeric and punctuation. We use the token's character types to assign it to one or more syntactic

Copyright © 2000, American Association for Artificial Intelligence (www.aaai.org). All rights reserved.

categories: alphabetic, numeric, etc. These categories form a hierarchy depicted in Figure 1, where the arrows point from more general to less general categories. A unique token type is created for every string that appears in at least k examples, as determined in a preprocessing step. The hierarchical representation allows for multi-level generalization. Thus, the token "California" belongs to the general token types ALPHANUM (alphanumeric strings), ALPHA (alphabetic strings), CAPS (capitalized words), as well as to the specific type representing the string "California". This representation is flexible and may be expanded to include domain specific information. For example, we may add range to the number category (small, large, 1-, 2-, and 3-digit numbers), or explicitly include knowledge about the type of information being parsed.

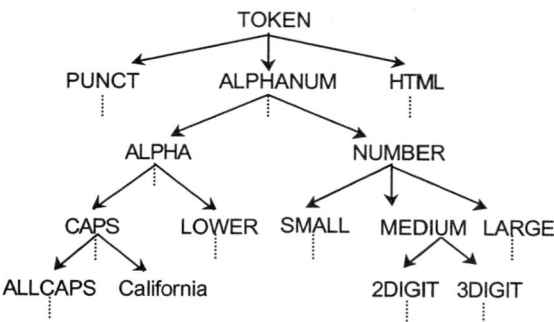

Figure – The token type syntactic hierarchy. Dots indicate the existence of additional types.

We claim that a sequence of specific and general tokens is more useful for describing common data fields than the finite state representations used in previous work (Carrasco & Oncina 1994, Goan et al. 1996). For complex fields, and for purposes of information extraction, it is sufficient to use only the starting and ending sequences as the description of the data field. For example, a set of street addresses – "4676 Admiralty Way", "220 Lincoln Boulevard" and "998 South Robertson Boulevard" – start with a pattern "NUMBER CAPS" and end with "Boulevard" or "CAPS." The starting and ending patterns together define a *data prototype* (*cf.* Datta & Kibler 1995). Note that the patterns in the data prototype are not regular expressions, since they don't allow loops or recursion. We believe that recursive expressions tend to over-generalize and are not useful representations of the types of data we are trying to learn.

The problem of learning the data prototype from a set of examples that are labeled as belonging (or not) to a class, may be stated in one of two related ways: as a classification or as a conservation task. In the classification task, both positive and the negative instances of the class are used to learn a rule that will correctly classify new examples. Classification algorithms, like FOIL (Quinlan 1990), use negative examples to guide the specialization of the rule. They construct discriminating descriptions – those that are satisfied by most of the positive examples and none of the negative examples. The conservation task, on the other hand, attempts to find a characteristic description (Dietterich & Michalski 1981) or conserved patterns (Brazma et al. 1995), in a set of positive examples of a class. Unlike the discriminating description, the characteristic description will often include redundant features. When negative examples are not available to the learning algorithm, redundant features may be necessary to correctly identify new instances of the class. The characteristic description learned from positive examples is the same as the discriminating description learned by the classification algorithm in the presence of negative examples drawn from infinitely many classes. While most of the widely used machine learning algorithms (decision trees and ILP) solve the classification task, fewer algorithms that learn characteristic descriptions are in use (Ditterich & Michalski 1981; Brazma, et al. 1995).

In our applications, an appropriate source of negative examples is problematic; therefore, we chose to frame the learning problem as a conservation task. We introduce DataPro – an algorithm that learns data prototypes from positive examples of the data field alone. DataPro finds statistically significant sequences of tokens, *i.e.*, those that describe many of the positive instances and are highly unlikely to have been generated by chance. DataPro is a statistical algorithm; therefore, it tolerates noisy data. The training examples are encoded in a prefix tree, where each node corresponds to a token type (specific or general category), and a path through the tree corresponds to a sequence of tokens. We present a greedy polynomial time version of the algorithm that relies on significance judgements to grow the tree and prune the nodes.

A sequence of tokens is significant if it occurs more frequently than would be expected if the tokens were generated randomly and independently of one another. We begin by estimating the baseline probability of a token's occurrence from the proportion of all tokens in the examples for the data field that are of that type. Suppose we have already found a significant token sequence – *e.g.*, the pattern consisting of the single token "NUMBER" – in a set of street addresses such as the ones above, and want to determine whether the more specific pattern, "NUMBER CAPS", is also a significant pattern. Knowing the probability of occurrence of type CAPS, we can compute how many times CAPS can be expected to follow NUMBER completely by chance. If we observe a considerably greater number of these sequences, we conclude that the longer pattern is significant.

Formally, we use hypothesis testing (Papoulis 1990) to decide whether a pattern is significant. The null hypothesis is that observed instances of this pattern were generated by chance, via the random, independent generation of the individual tokens. Hypothesis testing decides, at a given confidence level, whether the data supports rejecting the null hypothesis. Suppose n identical sequences have been generated by a random source. The probability that a token T (whose overall probability of occurrence is p) will be the next token in k of these sequences has a binomial distribution. For a large n, the binomial distribution approaches a normal distribution $P(x,\mu,\sigma)$ with $\mu = np$ and $\sigma^2 = np(1-p)$. The cumulative probability is the probability of observing at least n_1 events:

$$P(k \geq n_1) = \int_{n_1}^{\infty} P(x,\mu,\sigma) dx$$

We use approximation formulas (Abramowitz & Stegun 1964) to compute the value of the integral.

The significance level of the test, α, is the probability that the null hypothesis is rejected even though it is true, and it is given by the cumulative probability above. Suppose we set $\alpha = 0.05$. This means that we expect to observe at least n_1 events 5% of the time under the null hypothesis. If the number of observed events[1] is greater, we reject the null hypothesis (at the given significance level), *i.e.*, decide that the observation is significant.

The DataPro Algorithm

We now describe DataPro, the algorithm that finds statistically significant patterns in a set of token sequences. We focus the discussion on the version of the algorithm that learns starting patterns. The algorithm can be easily adapted to learn ending patterns.

During the preprocessing step the text is tokenized, and the tokens are assigned syntactic types (see Figure 1), as described previously. The algorithm builds a prefix tree, in which each node corresponds to a token whose position in the sequence is given by the node's depth in the tree. Every path through the tree starting at the root node is a significant pattern found by the algorithm.

The tree is grown incrementally. Adding a child to a node corresponds to extending the node's pattern by a single token. Thus, each child represents a different way to specialize the pattern. For example, when learning city names, the node corresponding to "New" might have three children, corresponding to the patterns "New Haven", "New York" and "New CAPS".

As explained previously, a child node is judged to be significant with respect to its parent node if the number of occurrences of the child pattern is sufficiently large, given the number of occurrences of the parent pattern and the baseline probability of the token used to extend the parent pattern. A pruning step insures that each child node is also significant given its more specific siblings. For example, if there are 10 occurrence of "New Haven", and 12 occurrences of "New York", and both of these are judged to be significant, then "New CAPS" will be retained only if there are significantly more than 22 examples that match "New CAPS".

Similarly, once the entire tree has been expanded, the algorithm includes a pattern extraction step that traverses the tree, checking whether the pattern "New" is still significant given the more specific patterns "New York", "New Haven" and "New CAPS". In other words, DataPro decides whether the examples described by "New" but not by any of the longer sequences can be explained by the null hypothesis.

We present the pseudocode of the DataPro algorithm below and describe it in greater detail.

DATAPRO MAIN LOOP
Create root node of tree;
For next node Q of tree
   Create children of Q;
   Prune generalizations;
   Determinize children;
Extract patterns from tree;

CREATE CHILDREN OF Q
For each token type T at next position in examples
   Let C = NewNode;
   Let C.token = T;
   Let C.examples = Q.examples that are followed by T;
   Let C.count = |C.examples|;
   Let C.pattern = concat(Q.pattern, T);
   If Significant(C.count, Q.count, T.probability, α)
     AddChildToTree(C, Q)

PRUNE GENERALIZATIONS
For each child C of Q
   Let N = C.count $- \Sigma_i$ (S_i.count | $S_i \in$ {Siblings(C)} &
        S_i.pattern $\subset$ C.pattern);
   If Not(Significant(N, Q.count, C.token.probability, α))
     Delete C;

DETERMINIZE CHILDREN OF Q
For each child C of Q
   For each sibling S of C
     If S.pattern $\subset$ C.pattern
       Delete S.examples from C.examples
     C.count = |C.examples|

EXTRACT PATTERNS FROM TREE
Create empty list;
For every node Q of tree
   For every child C of Q
     Let N = C.count $- \Sigma_i$ (S_i.count | $S_i \in$ {Children(C)}
     If Significant(N, Q.count, C.token.probability, α)
       Add C.pattern to the list;
Return (list of patterns);

DataPro grows the prefix tree greedily by finding specializations of the significant patterns and pruning generalizations. The tree is empty initially, and children are added to the root node. The children represent all tokens that occur in the first position in the training examples more often than expected by chance. The tree is extended incrementally at node Q. A new child is added to Q for

---

[1] Note that the hypothesis we test is derived from observation (data); therefore, we must subtract one from the number of observed events to take into account the reduction in the number of degrees of freedom resulting from an observation. This also prevents the anomalous case when a single occurrence of a rare event is judged to be significant.

every significant specialization of the pattern ending at Q.

In the pruning step, the algorithm checks the children of Q to determine whether the generalizations are significant given the specific patterns. In our notation, $\mathcal{A} \subset \mathcal{B}$ means that $\mathcal{B}$ is a generalization of $\mathcal{A}$. Next, the examples that are explained by any significant patterns are deleted from its sibling generalizations.[2] We refer to this as *determinizing* the tree, because it insures that every sequence of tokens in the training data is used as evidence for at most one pattern in the tree.

The algorithm can in principle be implemented more efficiently than in the pseudocode. The algorithm needs to examine each prefix (a subsequence with which the examples begin) a constant number of times. Given N training examples, the longest one containing L tokens, there are $O(NL)$ prefixes. The size of the tree is, therefore, also $O(NL)$. Pruning and determinization can be folded into node creation, and will not affect the complexity of the algorithm. Note that the algorithm is efficient because we determinize the tree; otherwise, the tree grows exponentially. The complexity of the last step, extracting patterns from tree, is also $O(NL)$.

Application 1: Wrapper Verification

A common problem experienced by information integration applications is wrapper fragility. A Web wrapper is a program that takes a query, retrieves a page from a Web source using the query, and extracts results from it. Many wrappers use layout of HTML pages to extract the data. Therefore, they are vulnerable to changes in the layout, which occur when the site is redesigned. In some cases the wrapper continues to extract, but the data is no longer correct. Wrapper maintenance, *i.e.*, detecting when the wrapper stops working and automatically recovering from failure, is an important problem for information integration research.

Few researchers have addressed the problem of wrapper maintenance. Kushmerick (1999) proposed RAPTURE to verify that a wrapper correctly extracts data from a Web page. Each data field is described by a collection of global numeric features, such as word count, average word length, HTML tag density, etc. Given a set of queries for which the wrapper output is known, RAPTURE checks that the wrapper generates a new result with the expected combination of feature values for each of the queries. Kushmerick found that the HTML tag density feature alone could correctly identify almost all of the changes in the sources he monitored. In Kushmerick's experiment, the addition of other features to the probability calculation about the wrapper's correctness significantly reduced the algorithm's performance.

The prototypes learned by DataPro lend themselves to the data validation task and, specifically, to wrapper verification. A set of queries is used to retrieve HTML pages from which the wrapper extracts N training examples. DataPro learns m patterns that describe the common beginnings and endings of each field of the extracts. In the verification phase, the wrapper generates n test examples from pages retrieved using the same or similar set of queries. Suppose t_i training examples and k_i test examples match the ith pattern. If the two distributions, **k** and **t**, are the same (at some significance level), the wrapper is judged to be extracting correctly; otherwise, it is judged to have failed. Our approach allows us to add other features to the two distributions. In the experiments described below we added the average number of tuples-per-page feature. Goodness of fit method (Papoulis 1990) was used to decide whether the two distributions are the same.

We monitored 27 wrappers (representing 23 distinct Web sources) over a period of several months. For each wrapper, the results of 15-30 queries were stored periodically. All new results were compared with the last correct wrapper output (training examples). The verification algorithm used DataPro to learn the starting and ending patterns for each field of the training examples and made a decision at a high significance level (corresponding to $\alpha = 0.001$) about whether the patterns had the same distribution over the new examples.

Manually checking the results identified 37 wrapper changes[3] out of the total 443 comparisons. Of these 30 were attributed to changes in the source layout and data format, and 7 to changes internal to the wrappers. The verification algorithm correctly discovered 35 of these changes, including the 17 that would have been missed by RAPTURE if it were relying solely on HTML tag density feature. The algorithm incorrectly decided that the wrapper has changed in 40 cases. We are currently working to reduce the high rate of false positives.

Application 2: Wrapper Maintenance

If the wrapper stops extracting correctly, the next challenge is to rebuild it automatically (Cohen 1999). The extraction rules for our Web wrappers (Muslea *et al.* 1999), as well as

---

[2] We have experimented with different procedures and found it useful to not prune the children of the root node, because early pruning may appreciably reduce the number of examples available to the algorithm.

[3] We have found that three effects may change the output of the wrapper. The most important of these is the change in the layout of the pages returned by the Web source. Because our wrappers use positional information to extract data, any alterations in the layout tend to break the wrapper. Changes may also occur in the format of the source data itself: *e.g.*, when street number is dropped from the address field ("Main St" instead of "25 Main St"), or book availability changes from ``Ships immediately" to ``In Stock: ships immediately". It is important to know when these types of changes occur, because information integration applications may be sensitive to data format. Finally, the wrapper code itself may change in a way that affects the wrapper output, *e.g.* to extract "10.00" instead of "$10.00" for the price. The verification algorithm will also pick up these changes.

many others (cf. Kushmerick et al. 1997), are generated by machine learning algorithms, which take as input several pages from the same source and examples of data to extract for each page. Therefore, if we identify examples of data on pages for which the wrapper fails, we can use these examples as input to the induction algorithm to generate new extraction rules.

We propose a method that takes a set of training examples and a set of pages from the same source, and uses a mixture of supervised and unsupervised learning techniques to identify examples of the data field on new pages. Due to paper length limitations, we present an outline of the algorithm, leaving the details to future publication. We assume that the format of data did not change. First, DataPro learns the patterns that describe the start and end of each data field in the training examples. We also calculate the mean and variance of the number-of-tokens distribution. Next, each new page is scanned to identify all text segments that begin with one of the starting patterns and end with one of the ending patterns. These segments, which we call candidates, include examples of the field we want to extract from the new pages. The candidates containing significantly more or fewer tokens than expected based on the number-of-tokens distribution are eliminated from the set, often still leaving hundreds of candidates (we allow up to 300) on each page. The candidates are then clustered to identify subsets that share common features. The features used to describe each candidate are where on the page it occurs, adjacent tokens, and whether it is visible to the user. Each cluster is then given a score based on how similar it is to the training examples. We expect the highest ranked clusters to contain the correct examples of the data field.

We evaluate the algorithm by using it to extract data from Web pages for which correct output is known. The pages were retrieved using the same (or similar) queries that were used to obtain training examples. The output of the extraction algorithm is a ranked list of clusters for every data field being extracted. Each cluster is checked manually, and it is judged to be correct if it contains only the complete instances of the field, which appear in the correct context on the page. For example, if extracting a city of an address, we only want to those city names that are part of an address.

We ran the extraction algorithm for 21 distinct Web sources, attempting to extract 77 data fields from all the sources. In 62 cases the top ranked cluster contained correct complete instances of the data field. In eight cases the correct cluster was ranker lower, while in six cases no candidates were identified on the pages. All except one cluster contained only the correct examples of the field.

The table on the right presents extraction results for six Web sources. The first column lists the source's name and the number of pages provided to the extraction algorithm. The second column lists the data field extracted from the pages. The table also lists the total number of candidates from all pages identified by the data prototypes and the number of the resulting clusters. The last three columns give the rank of the cluster containing correct examples of the field, the number of examples in that cluster and the percent of the examples that are correct and complete. In most cases, the extraction algorithm correctly identifies examples of data fields (rank=1, 100% correct) from several pages. This indicates that our algorithm may be combined with the wrapper induction algorithm to re-induce extraction rules for the correctly identified fields. We note that for three of the sources – *altavista*, *amazon* and *quote* – the existing wrappers failed to produce correct output for the pages used in the extraction task, because the layout of the pages had changed since the extraction rules were created.

source	data field	#candid	#clusters	rank	# in cluster	%correct
altavista	TITLE	896	115	3	5	100
20 pages	LINK	570	32	1	14	100
amazon	AUTHOR	1950	208	2	20	100
20 pages	TITLE	1030	117	2	8	100
	PRICE	49	3	1	15	100
	ISBN	20	2	1	18	100
	AVAILAB.	18	1	1	18	100
arrow	PARTNUM	1447	69	1	6	100
21 pages	MANUFAC	587	25	1	58	100
	PRICE	201	2	1	58	100
	DESCRIP.	718	49	1	58	100
	STATUS	818	45	1	58	100
	PARTURL	0				
bigbook	NAME	192	26	1	14	100
16 pages	STREET	18	2	1	16	100
	CITY	25	4	1	9	100
	STATE	64	7	1	5	100
	PHONE	21	1	1	16	100
quote	PRICECH.	45	5	0	0	0
20 pages	TICKER	29	5	1	11	100
	VOLUME	11	1	1	11	100
	PRICE	0				
showtimes	MOVIE	82	10	1	15	100
15 pages	TIMES	238	13	1	15	100

Table – Results of automatic data extraction for several Web sources.

Related Research

Several researchers have addressed the problem of learning the structure of data. Grammar induction algorithms, for example, learn the common structure of a set of strings. Carrasco and Oncina (1994) propose ALERGIA, a stochastic grammar induction algorithm that learns a regular language given the strings belonging to the language. ALERGIA starts with a finite state automaton (FSA) that is initialized to be a prefix tree that represents all the strings of the language. The FSA is generalized by merging pairs of statistically similar subtrees. We found that ALERGIA tends to merge too many states, even at a high confidence limit, leading to an over-general grammar. The resulting automaton frequently has loops in it, corresponding to regular expressions like a(b*)c. Real data is seldom described by such repeated structures.

Goan et al. (1996) proposed modifications to ALERGIA aimed at reducing the number of bad merges. They also introduced syntactic categories similar to ours. Each symbol can belong to one of these categories. Goan et al. added a new generalization step in which the transitions corresponding to symbols of the same category that are approximately evenly distributed over the range of that category (e.g., 0-9 for numerals) are replaced with a single transition. Though the proposed modifications make the grammar induction algorithm more robust, the final FSA is still sensitive to the merge order. Moreover, it does not allow for multi-level generalization that we have found useful. The algorithm requires dozens, if not hundreds, of examples in order to learn the correct grammar.

A sequence of n tokens can be viewed as a non-recursive n-ary predicate; therefore, we have used FOIL Quinlan 1990) to learn the data prototypes. FOIL learns first order predicate logic clauses defining a class from a set of positive and negative examples of the class. FOIL finds a discriminating description that covers many positive and none of the negative examples.

We have used foil.6 with no-negative-literals option to learn data prototypes for several data fields. In all cases the closed world assumption was used to construct negative examples from the known objects: thus, names and addresses were the negative examples for the phone number class for the *whitepages* source. In most cases there were many similarities between the clauses learned by FOIL and the patterns learned by DataPro; however, FOIL clauses tended to be overly general. Thus, FOIL learned that '(' was a good description of phone numbers for the *whitepages* source. However, '(' will not be sufficient to recognize phone numbers on a random page. We attribute over-generalization to the incompleteness of the set of negative examples presented to FOIL. Another problem was when given examples of a class with little structure, such as names and book titles, FOIL tended to create clauses that covered single examples, or it failed to find any clauses.

Conclusion

In summary, we have presented an efficient algorithm that can be used to learn structural information about a data field from a set of examples. The algorithm promises to be useful in Web wrapper maintenance applications: both for detecting when a wrapper stops extracting correctly and for identifying new examples of the data field in order to rebuild the wrapper.

An important aspect of our work is that we focus on generalizing token sequences according to a type hierarchy. Most previous work in the area has focused on generalizations that capture repeated patterns in a sequence (e.g., learning regular expressions). Though this direction has not yet attracted much attention, we believe that it will prove useful for a wide variety of data validation tasks.

One of the most exciting directions for future work is using the DataPro algorithm for *cross-site* extraction, i.e., learning the author, title and price fields for the Amazon source, and using them to extract the same fields on the Barnes&Noble source. Preliminary results show that this is feasible. A second direction is to use the DataPro approach to learn characteristic patterns within data fields, as opposed to just the starting and ending patterns. The algorithm is efficient enough to be used this way, and there are many applications where this would be useful.

Acknowledgements

This work was supported in part by the Rome Labs and DARPA contract F30602-98-2-0109, by AFOSR contract F49620-98-1-0046, and by the NSF under grant IRI-9610014.

References

Abramowitz, M., and Stegun, I. A. 1964. *Handbook of mathematical functions*. Washington, D.C.: National Bureau of Standards.

Brazma, A.; Jonassen, I.; Eidhammer, I.; and Gilbert, D. 1995. Aproaches to the automatic discovery of patterns in biosequences. Technical report, Dept. of Informatics, University of Bergen.

Carrasco, R. C., and Oncina, J. 1994. Learning stochastic regular grammars by means of a state merging method. *Lecture Notes in Computer Science*, 862.

Cohen, W. W. 1999. Recognizing Structure in Web Pages using Similarity Queries. In *Proc. of AAAI*.

Datta, P.; and Kibler, D. 1995. Learning prototypical concept descriptions. In *Proc. 12th International Conference on Machine Learning*.

Dietterich, T.; and Michalski, R. 1981. Inductive learning of structural descriptions. *Artificial Intelligence*, 16:257-294.

Goan, T.; Benson, N., and Etzioni, O. 1996. A grammar inference algorithm for the world wide web. In *Proc. of AAAI Spring Symposium on Machine Learning in Information Access*.

Jennings, N. R., and Wooldridge, M. eds. 1998. *Agent Technology: Foundations, Applications, and Markets*. Springer-Verlag.

Knoblock, C.; Minton, S.; Ambite, J.L.; Ashish, N.; Modi, P.; Muslea, I.; Philpot, A.; and Tejada, S. 1998. Modeling Web Sources for Information Integration. In *Proc. of AAAI*.

Kushmerick, N.; Weld, D. S., and Doorenbos, R. B. 1997. Wrapper Induction for Information Extraction. In *Proc. of Intl. Joint Conference on Artificial Intelligence (IJCAI)*.

Kushmerick, N. 1999. Regression testing for wrapper mainte-nance. In *Proc. of AAAI*.

Muslea, I.; Minton, S., and Knoblock, C. 1999. A Hierarchical Approach to Wrapper Induction. In *Proc. of the 3rd Conference on Autonomous Agents*.

Papoulis, A. 1990. *Probability and Statistics*. Prentice Hall.

Quinlan, J. R. 1990. Learning logical definitions from relations. *Machine Learning*, 5(3).

Intuitive Representation of Decision Trees Using General Rules and Exceptions

Bing Liu, Minqing Hu and Wynne Hsu

School of Computing
National University of Singapore
Lower Kent Ridge Road, Singapore 119260
(liub, huminqin, whsu)@comp.nus.edu.sg

Abstract

Producing too many rules is a major problem with many data mining techniques. This paper argues that one of the key reasons for the large number of rules is that an inefficient knowledge representation scheme has been used. The current predominant representation of the discovered knowledge is the if-then rules. This representation often severely fragments the knowledge that exists in the data, thereby resulting in a large number of rules. The fragmentation also makes the discovered rules hard to understand and to use. In this paper, we propose a more efficient representation scheme, called *general rules & exceptions*. In this representation, a unit of knowledge consists of a single *general rule* and a set of *exceptions*. This scheme reduces the complexity of the discovered knowledge substantially. It is also intuitive and easy to understand. This paper focuses on using the representation to express the knowledge embedded in a decision tree. An algorithm that converts a decision tree to the new representation is presented. Experiment results show that the new representation dramatically simplifies the decision tree. Real-life applications also confirm that this representation is more intuitive to human users.

Introduction

Much of the existing data mining research has been focused on designing efficient techniques to mine regularities or knowledge from databases. The discovered knowledge is commonly represented as a set of if-then rules. An if-then rule is a basic unit of knowledge.

One of the major problems with many existing mining techniques is that they often produce too many rules, which make manual inspection and analysis very difficult. This problem has been regarded as a major obstacle to practical applications of data mining techniques. It represents a major gap between the results of data mining and the understanding and use of the mining results. This paper aims to bridge this gap by focusing on simplifying the mining results so that they can be easily analyzed and understood by the human user.

In the past few years, a number of techniques have been proposed to deal with the problem of too many rules (e.g., Piatesky-Shapiro & Matheus 1994; Silberschatz & Tuzhilin 1996; Liu & Hsu 1996; Liu, Hsu & Ma 1999). The main idea of these techniques is to use the user's domain knowledge or some statistical measures to filter out those uninteresting rules. This work does not research in this direction. Instead, it identifies an important cause of the problem, and deals with the problem at its root.

We show that one of the key reasons for the large number of rules is that an inefficient scheme is used to represent the discovered knowledge. The simple if-then rules based representation has two major deficiencies:

1. If-then rules *fragment* the knowledge that exists in data, which results in a large number of discovered rules. This large number of rules presents three problems for data mining applications:
   - Manual analysis of the rules is very difficult.
   - Even if some interesting rules can be identified, they may not be actionable because the rules are often too specialized (cover too small a population) due to the fragmentation.
   - The fragmentation obscures the essential relationships in the domain and the special cases (or exceptions). This makes the discovered knowledge hard to understand and to use.

   We will use an example to illustrate the points later.

2. The discovered knowledge is represented only at a single level of detail. This flat representation is not suitable for human consumption because we are more used to hierarchical representation of knowledge. Hierarchical representation allows us to easily manage the complexity of knowledge, to view the knowledge at different levels of details, and to focus our attention on the interesting aspects.

We use a decision tree classification example to illustrate the problems, and to introduce the new representation. Although a decision tree, as its name suggests, is in the form of a tree, it essentially expresses a set of if-then rules. Our example data set has two attributes (A1 and A2), 500 data records and two classes, ▲ and O. The value range of A1 is from 0-100 and A2 from 0-50. The decision tree system C4.5 (Quinlan 1992) is used to build the tree (for classification), which basically partitions the data space into different class regions. The resulting partitioning is expressed as a decision tree. Figure 1 shows the data space and the partitioning produced by C4.5. The resulting tree (not shown here) has 14 leaves, represented

---

Copyright © 2000, American Association for Artificial Intelligence (www.aaai.org). All rights reserved.

by the 14 rectangular regions. The two classes of data are well separated. The 14 regions or the tree can be conveniently represented as a set of if-then rules, with each tree leaf (or a region) forming a single rule:

R1: $A1 \leq 49, A1 > 18 \rightarrow \blacktriangle$
R2: $A1 \leq 10 \rightarrow \blacktriangle$
R3: $A1 > 10, A1 \leq 18, A2 > 18 \rightarrow \blacktriangle$
R4: $A1 > 10, A1 \leq 18, A2 \leq 10 \rightarrow \blacktriangle$
R5: $A1 > 10, A1 \leq 18, A2 > 10, A2 \leq 19 \rightarrow O$
R6: $A1 > 86 \rightarrow O$
R7: $A1 > 49, A1 \leq 60 \rightarrow O$
R8: $A1 > 60, A1 \leq 86, A2 \leq 10 \rightarrow O$
R9: $A1 > 60, A1 \leq 86, A2 > 39 \rightarrow O$
R10: $A1 > 60, A1 \leq 68, A2 > 20, A2 \leq 39 \rightarrow O$
R11: $A1 > 68, A1 \leq 86, A2 \leq 30, A2 > 10 \rightarrow O$
R12: $A1 > 68, A1 \leq 80, A2 \leq 30, A2 \leq 39 \rightarrow O$
R13: $A1 > 60, A1 \leq 68, A2 > 10, A2 \leq 20 \rightarrow \blacktriangle$
R14: $A1 > 80, A1 \leq 86, A2 > 30, A2 \leq 39 \rightarrow \blacktriangle$

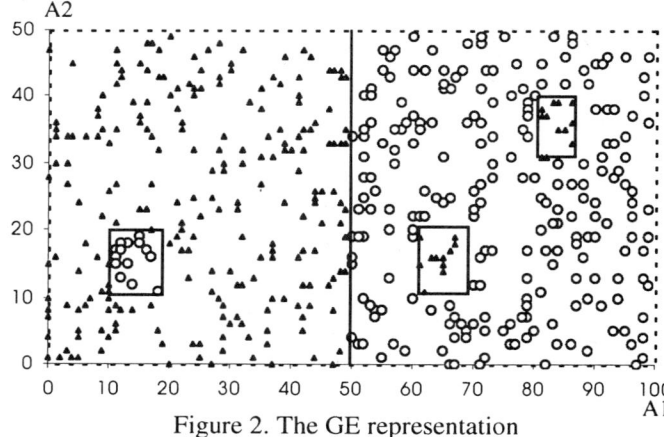

Figure 1. Partitioning produced by C4.5

From Figure 1 and the 14 rules from the decision tree [1], the following observations are made:

- Looking at the 14 rules themselves does not give us a good overall picture of the regularities that exist in data. These rules fragment the knowledge. However, if we change the 14 rules to the following two *general rules & exceptions* (GE) patterns, the picture becomes clear:

  GE-1: $A1 \leq 49 \rightarrow \blacktriangle$ [sup = 47.2%, conf = 94.4%]
     Except R5: $A1 > 10, A1 \leq 18, A2 > 10, A2 \leq 19$
                         $\rightarrow O$ [sup = 2.8%, conf = 100%]

  GE-2: $A1 > 49 \rightarrow O$ [sup = 45.2%, conf = 90.0%]
     Except R13: $A1 > 60, A1 \leq 68, A2 > 10, A2 \leq 20$
                          $\rightarrow \blacktriangle$ [sup = 2.4%, conf = 100%]
           R14: $A1 > 80, A1 \leq 86, A2 > 30, A2 \leq 39$
                          $\rightarrow \blacktriangle$ [sup = 2.4%, conf = 100%]

The first part of a GE pattern is a general rule, and the second part (after "Except") is a set of exceptions to the general rule. From the GE patterns, we see the essential relationships of the domain, the two general rules, and the special cases, the exceptions (R5, R13 and R14). This representation is much simpler than the 14 rules because R1-R4 and R6-R12 are not needed [2]. Figure 2 gives a pictorial representation of the GE patterns. Our real-life application users also confirmed that the new representation is more intuitive, and conforms closely to the representation of knowledge in their daily work.

Note that we have used support (*sup*) and confidence (*conf*) for a rule, which have their usual meanings (Agrawal, Imielinski & Swami 1993). Both support and confidence are useful concepts in practical applications.

- The exception regions are the ones that cause the fragmentation. More exceptions result in more severe fragmentation. For example, in Figure 1, on the left of the $A1 = 49$ line, we have one exception region, and 5 rules were generated. On the right of $A1 = 49$, we have two exception regions, and 9 rules were generated.

Figure 2. The GE representation

The GE patterns simplifies the rules (or decision tree) by:

using general rules and removing those fragmented rules that have the same classes as the general rules.

These fragmented rules are non-essential, and worse still they make the discovered knowledge hard to interpret. This is not to say that the fragmented rules are completely useless. For example, those fragmented rules may have higher confidences (e.g., 100%). They may be useful because of the high confidences. However, the GE patterns have given us a good summary of the knowledge. If the user is interested in the detailed rules, the general rules can direct him/her to them (using a simple user interface).

In the proposed GE representation, each combination of one general rule and a set of exceptions represents a single piece of knowledge. The general rule gives a basic relationship in the domain. The exceptions are unexpected with respect to the general rule. A general rule normally covers a large portion of the data, while an exception covers a relatively small portion of the data. In the next two sections, we will see that the GE representation naturally introduces a knowledge hierarchy, and that it can be expressed in the form of a tree, which we call the *GE tree*.

In the rest of the paper, we develop the idea further in the context of decision trees. An algorithm that converts a

---

[1] C4.5 also has a program to produce a set of classification rules. We do not use them in this paper as these rules can overlap one another, which make them more difficult to comprehend and to process. That program is also very inefficient for large data sets.

[2] The new representation does not affect the classification accuracy.

decision tree to a GE tree is presented. Experiment results and real-life applications show that the proposed method simplifies the decision tree dramatically and also produces a more intuitive representation of knowledge.

General Rules and Exceptions

Since this paper focuses on using the GE representation to express classification knowledge embedded in a decision tree, we define GE patterns in this context. A database D for classification consists of a set of data records, which are pre-classified into q (≥ 2) known classes, $C = \{c_1, ..., c_q\}$. The objective of decision tree building is to find a set of characteristic descriptions of the classes that can be used to predict the classes of future (unseen) cases.

Definition (GE patterns): A GE pattern consists of two parts, a single general rule (which is an if-then rule) and a set of exceptions. It has the following form:
$$X \rightarrow c_i \quad [sup, conf]$$
$$\text{Except} \quad E_1, ..., E_n$$
where:
1. $X \rightarrow c_i$ is the *general rule*. X is a set of *conditions*, and c_i is the *consequent* (a class).
2. $E = \{E_1, ..., E_n\}$ is the set of *exceptions*. E may be empty ($E = \emptyset$). Each E_j is a GE pattern of the form:
$$X, L_j \rightarrow c_k \quad [sup, conf]$$
$$\text{Except} \quad E_{j1}, ..., E_{jm}$$
where ($X, L_j \rightarrow c_k$) is called a *sub-general rule* (if it has no exceptions, we also called it an *exception rule*). L_j is an additional set of conditions, and $c_k \in C$ and $c_k \neq c_i$. E_{jl} are the exceptions of ($X, L_j \rightarrow c_k$).

Notes about the definition:
1. For the sub-general rule, ($X, L_j \rightarrow c_k$), X may not appear explicitly in the conditional part, but needs to be satisfied. For example, if X is A1 > 49, then A1 > 80 can be the only condition of a sub-general rule because data records that satisfy A1 > 80 also satisfy A1 > 49.
2. An exception E_j only covers a subset of the data records covered by its general rule ($X \rightarrow c_i$). The class of E_j's sub-general rule must be different from its general rule.
3. Since each exception is also a GE pattern, this scheme can represent knowledge in a hierarchical fashion.

We now define the (sub-) general rule. We do not need to define exceptions because they are GE patterns.

Definition ((sub-) general rules): A (sub-) general rule is a *significant rule*, and its class is the *majority class* of the data records *covered* by the rule. A rule covers a data record if the data record satisfies the rule's conditions.

It does not make sense that the class of the (sub-) general rule is not the majority class. For example, if our data set has two classes c_1 and c_2, then A1 > 2 $\rightarrow$ c_1 with the confidence of 30% cannot be a general rule. For it to be one, its confidence must be greater than 50%.

Rule significance: The significance of a rule can be measured in many ways. For example, we can measure it using statistical significance tests and/or minimum confidences (*minconf*) from the user. In this work, we use chi-square test/fisher's exact test [3] (Everitt 1977) and minconf. The way that we test the significance of a rule is similar to that in (Liu, Hsu & Ma 1999).

Representing Decision Trees as GE Patterns

Decision tree construction (Quinlan 1992) is a popular method for building classification models. A decision tree has two types of nodes, *decision nodes* and *leaf nodes*. A *decision node* specifies some test to be carried out on an attribute value with one branch for each possible outcome of the test. A *leaf node* indicates a class.

From a geometric point of view, a decision tree represents a partitioning of the data space. A serial of tests (or cuts) from the root node to a leaf represents a hyper-rectangular region. The leaf node gives the class of the region. For example, the five rectangular regions in Figure 3(A) are produced by the decision tree in Figure 3(B). The tree can also be represented as rules. For example, the leaf node 5 in Figure 3(B) can be represented with the rule,

$$A1 > 4, A2 > 2.5 \rightarrow O.$$

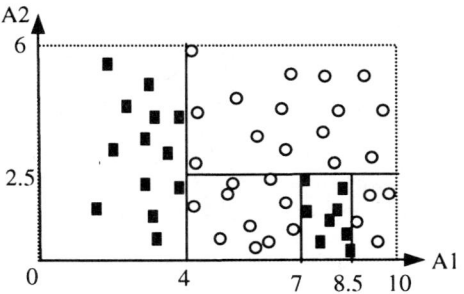

(A). Partitioning produced by the tree in Figure 3(B)

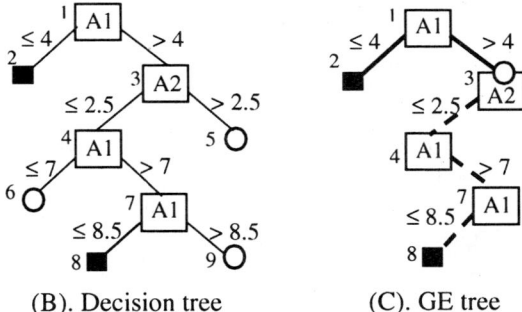

(B). Decision tree   (C). GE tree

Figure 3. An example partitioning of the data space and its corresponding decision tree and GE tree

As mentioned earlier, the GE representation of a decision tree can also be in the form of a tree, which we call the *GE tree*. Below, we present the algorithm that finds general rules and exceptions in the context of a decision tree, or in

---
[3] Chi-square test can be computed very efficiently. However, it is based on the assumption that the expected frequencies should not be small (Everitt 1977). One popular rule of thumb for a 2x2 contingency table is that the chi-square test should not be used when the expected frequency of any cell is smaller than 5. When such a situation occurs, we use fisher's exact test, which is computationally less efficient. However, such cases do not occur often. The computation does not present a problem.

other words, converts a decision tree to a GE tree. The algorithm consists of two steps:
1. Find high-level general rules: The system descends down the tree from the root to find the nearest nodes whose majority classes can form significant rules. We call these rules the *high-level general rules*.
2. Find exceptions: After the high-level general rules are found, the system descends down the tree further to find exceptions. Since an exception is also a GE pattern, with its sub-general rule and exceptions, the question is how to determine whether a tree node should form a sub-general rule or not. We use the following criteria:
   - Significance: A sub-general rule must be significant and has a different class from its general rule.
   - Simplicity: If we use a tree node to form a sub-general rule, it should result in fewer rules in the final GE representation. The complexity of a GE representation is measured by the sum of the number of high-level general rules and the number of sub-general rules (or exception rules). Let the class of the rule R formed by the current node be c_j, and the class of its general rule (before it) be c_i ($i \neq j$). Let the number of leaves below this node in the tree for class c_i be n_i, and for class c_j be n_j. R will be a sub-general rule if the following condition is satisfied:

$$n_j \geq n_i + 1 \quad (1)$$

The formula is intuitive because if the inequality holds it means that using R to form a sub-general rule with class c_j (1 in the formula represents this sub-general rule) cannot result in a more complex final description of the knowledge.

We now use an example to illustrate the idea. In Figure 3(A and B), the following GE patterns can be formed:
GE-1: A1 ≤ 4 → ■
GE-2: A1 > 4 → O
       Except A1 > 7, A1 ≤ 8.5, A2 ≤ 2.5 → ■

A1 ≤ 4 → ■, and A2 > 4 → O are high-level general rules (which are formed by node 2 and 3 in Figure 3(B)). For GE-2, we can have an alternative representation, i.e., forming a sub-general rule at node 7 (Figure 3(B)) with its exception (note that we cannot form a sub-general rule at node 4 because its majority class is the same as that of its general rule at node 3, i.e., O):
GE-2': A1 > 4 → O
        Except A1 > 7, A2 ≤ 2.5 → ■
        Except A1 > 8.5, A2 ≤ 2.5 → O

This representation (GE-2') is, however, more complex than GE-2. If we follow formula (1) above and compare the number of rules, we have
    1 < 1 + 1
This means that we should not use GE-2'. Figure 3(C) gives the GE representation in the tree form. The two thick lines with classes represent the two general rules. The thick dash lines represent the exception of GE-2.

Now let us consider the situation in Figure 4. In this case, a sub-general rule should be formed at node 7 (according to the above formula, 2 ≥ 1 + 1):

GE-2: A1 > 4 → O
       Except A1 > 7, A2 ≤ 2.5 → ■
       Except A1 > 8.5, A2>1.8, A2 ≤ 2.5 → O

If we do not form a sub-general rule here, we will have:
GE-2': A1 > 4 → O
        Except A1 > 7, A1 ≤ 8.5, A2 ≤ 2.5 → ■
        A1 > 8.5, A2 ≤ 1.8 → ■

GE-2 is preferred because it gives us a hierarchy of knowledge and does not increase the knowledge complexity. Intuitively, we can also see that the area within (A1 > 7, A2 ≤ 2.5) is a general area for class ■.

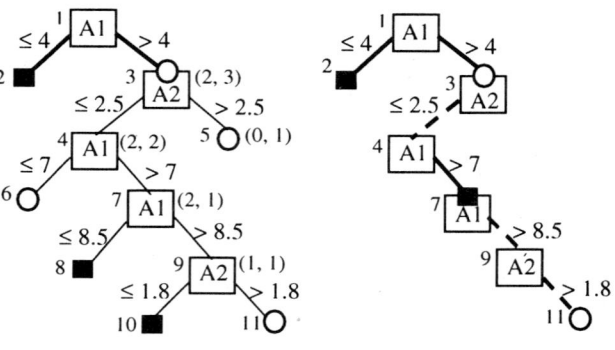

(A). Partitioning produced by the tree in (B)

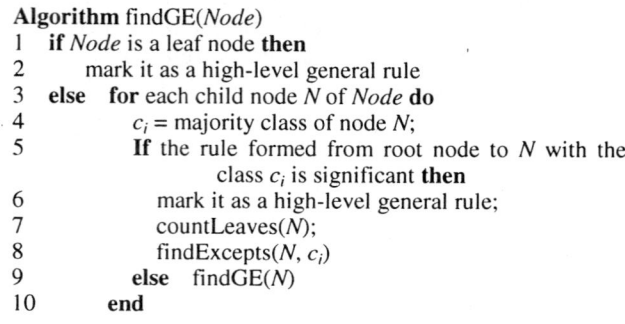

(B). Decision tree   (C). GE tree

Figure 4. A partition of the data space and its corresponding decision tree, and GE tree

The detailed algorithm (findGE) is given in Figure 5. The algorithm first traverses down the tree along each branch recursively to find the high-level general rules (line 2, 5 and 6). In the case of Figure 4(B), it finds two general rules shown in Figure 4(B) and (C), i.e., the two thick lines from the root. The classes (■ or O) are also attached.

Algorithm findGE(*Node*)
1 **if** *Node* is a leaf node **then**
2   mark it as a high-level general rule
3 **else for** each child node *N* of *Node* **do**
4   c_i = majority class of node *N*;
5   **If** the rule formed from root node to *N* with the class c_i is significant **then**
6   mark it as a high-level general rule;
7   countLeaves(*N*);
8   findExcepts(*N*, c_i)
9   **else**   findGE(*N*)
10 **end**

Figure 5: Finding general rules and exceptions

After a high-level general rule is found (line 5), the algorithm goes down the tree further to find its exceptions (line 8). This is carried out by the findExcepts procedure.

As discussed above, to decide whether a node below a general rule should form a sub-general rule or not, we need the numbers of leaves of different classes below the node (formula (1)). The countLeaves procedure (line 7 of Figure 5) performs this task. This procedure is not given here as it is fairly straightforward. In the case of Figure 4(B), the procedure produces the numbers of leaves of different classes below each internal node. These numbers are shown within "()" in Figure 4(B). The first number is the number of ■ class leaves below the node, and the second number is the number of O class leaves.

Finally, the procedure findExcepts is given in Figure 6.

Procedure findExcepts(Node, c_i)
1 **if** Node is a leaf **then**
2   **if** the class of the leaf is different from c_i **then**
3   mark it as an exception
4   **else** delete the node /* it is a fragmented leaf or rule */
5 **else** **for** each child node N of Node **do**
6   c_j = majority class of node N;
7   **if** $c_j \neq c_i$ AND the rule formed from root node to N with the class c_j is significant AND $n_j \geq n_i + 1$ **then**
8   mark it as a sub-general rule
9   findExcepts(N, c_j)
10   **else** findExcepts(N, c_i)
11 **end**
12 **end**

Figure 6: Finding sub-general rules and exceptions

The procedure traverses down the tree from a (sub-)general rule to find its exceptions. c_i is the class of the (sub-)general rule. In lines 1-3, if Node is a leaf and its class is different from the (sub-) general rule's class c_i, it is reported as an exception. Otherwise, the procedure goes down to its children to find exceptions (line 5). If the conditions in line 7 are satisfied, it means that node N can form a sub-general rule. n_i is the number of leaves of class c_i below the node N. The procedure marks this node to form a sub-general rule and recursively goes down (line 8 and 9). For example, in Figure 4(B), node 7 forms a sub-general rule because the conditions in line 7 are met (assume the rule is significant). If the conditions are not met, the procedure goes down further (line 10). For the tree in Figure 4(B), we finally obtain the GE tree in Figure 4(C), which has two high-level general rules, one sub-general rule and one exception rule.

Complexity: Since the algorithm traverses the decision tree at most twice, the complexity of the whole algorithm is $O(m)$, where m is the number of nodes in the decision tree.

Empirical Evaluation

To test the effectiveness and efficiency of the proposed technique, we applied it to the decision trees produced by C4.5 using 20 data sets in the UCI Machine Learning Repository (Merz and Murphy 1996). We also used the technique in a number of real-life applications.

Experiment results on the 20 data sets: Table 1 shows the experiment results. The first column gives the name of each data set. The second column gives the number of leaves in the decision tree produced by C4.5 (after pruning) for each data set. The third column gives the total number of leaves (or rules) in the GE tree (high-level general rules, sub-general rules and/or exception rules).

Table 1: Experiment results

	Data Sets	no. of decision tree leaves	no. of GE tree leaves
1	adult	518	132
2	anneal	53	16
3	austra	31	12
4	auto	49	22
5	breast	18	9
6	chess	28	11
7	cleve	30	16
8	crx	30	11
9	diabetes	22	12
10	german	103	38
11	glass	23	13
12	heart	18	10
13	iono	18	10
14	kdd	330	51
15	mushroom	26	12
16	pima	22	12
17	satimage	216	127
18	splice	157	63
19	tic-tac	95	39
20	waveform	317	146
	Average	105.2	38.1

Comparing column 2 and column 3, we can see that the number of leaves (or rules) in the GE tree is substantially smaller. On average, over the 20 data sets, the number of leaves (or rules) in the GE tree is only 36% of that of the original decision tree. This shows that the GE tree significantly simplifies the decision tree. The execution times are not reported as the algorithm runs so fast that they cannot be logged.

For these experiments, chi-square test at the confidence level of 95% is used to measure the significance of a rule.

Applications: The proposed technique has been used in a number of real-life applications. Due to space limitations, we can only briefly describe one here. In a disease application, the original tree produced by C4.5 from the data has 35 leaves, while the GE tree has only 10 leaves or rules. For instance, a general rule says that if the patient's age is less than 44, the chance of having the disease is very small with 3 exception regions. However, the corresponding sub-decision tree has 14 leaves. Another general rule says that if the patient's age is greater than 62, the chance of having the disease is very high with only one exception. However, C4.5 produces 5 fragmented rules. What is also important is that the users find that the decision tree is hard to understand because it is difficult to obtain a good overall picture of the domain from the fragmented decision tree leaves, which are hard to piece together. The GE tree, on the other hand, is more intuitive.

Related Work

The problem of too many rules has been studied by many researchers in data mining. However, to the best of our knowledge, there is no existing work that tackles the problem from a knowledge representation point of view.

In the *interestingness* research of data mining, a number of techniques (e.g., Piatesky-Shapiro & Matheus 1994; Klemetinen et al 1994; Silberschatz & Tuzhilin 1996; Liu & Hsu 1996; Padmanabhan & Tuzhilin 1998) have been proposed to help the user find interesting rules from a large number of discovered rules. The main approaches are: (1) using some interestingness measures to filter out those uninteresting rules; and (2) using the user's domain knowledge to help him/her identify unexpected rules. However, none of the methods touches the knowledge representation issue.

In (Liu, Hsu & Ma 1999), a method is proposed to summarize the discovered associations (Agrawal, Imielinski, & Swami 1993). The main idea is to find a set of essential rules to summarize the discovered rules. It does not study the knowledge representation issue. Furthermore, the technique cannot be used for decision trees because it requires all possible associations to be discovered. It also does not work with continuous attributes.

(Suzuki 1997; Liu et al 1999) study the mining of exception rules from data given some general rules. (Compton & Jansen 1988) proposes *ripple-down rules* [4], which are rules with exceptions, for knowledge acquisition. (Kivinen, Mannila & Ukkonen 1993) reports a theoretical study of learning ripple-down rules from data. Our work is different. We aim to simplify and summarize the data mining results by using the GE representation. We do not report another technique for mining general rules and/or exceptions from the data. Many existing data mining methods are already able to mine such rules and also the fragmented rules. The mining results are, however, not represented in an intuitive manner. Ripple-down rule mining and exception rule mining do not mine fragmented rules. We believe that such rules should also be discovered because they may be interesting to the user as well (see the Introduction section).

(Vilalta, Blix & Rendell 1997) studies the decision tree fragmentation problem in the context of machine learning. The problem there refers to producing trees that are too large and too deep. The research focus is on reducing the tree size by constructing compound features, by reducing the number of partitions, etc. Our work is different as we do not change the learning process, but only post-process the learning results to produce a more compact and easy-to-understand representation.

(Clark & Matwin 1993; Pazzani, Mani & Shankle 1997) study the problem of producing understandable rules by making use of existing domain knowledge in the learning process. They are different from our work as they are not concerned with different representations.

---

[4] Thanks to an anonymous reviewer for pointing us to the references of ripple-down rules.

Conclusion

In this paper, we have shown that the conventional if-then rules based representation of knowledge is inefficient for many data mining applications because the rules often fragment the knowledge that exists in data. This not only results in a large number of rules, but also makes the discovered knowledge hard to understand. We proposed a more efficient and easy-to-understand representation, which is in the form of general rules and exceptions. This representation is simple and intuitive, and also has a natural way of organizing the knowledge in a hierarchical fashion, which facilitates human analysis and understanding. Experiment results and real-life applications show that the proposed representation is very effective and efficient.

Acknowledgement: We would like to thank Shuik-Ming Lee, Hing-Yan Lee, Shanta C Emmanuel, Paul Goh, Jonathan Phang and King-Hee Ho, for providing us the data and giving us feedbacks. The project is funded by National Science and Technology Board, and National University of Singapore under RP3981678.

References

Agrawal, R., Imielinski, T., Swami, A. 1993. Mining association rules between sets of items in large databases. *SIGMOD-93*.

Clark, P. and Matwin, S. 1993. Using qualitative models to guide induction learning. *ICML-93*.

Compton, P. and Jansen, R. 1988. Knowledge in context: a strategy for expert system maintenance. *Proceedings of 2nd Australian Joint AI Conference (AI-88)*.

Everitt, B. S. 1977. *The analysis of contingency tables*. Chapman and Hall.

Kivinen, J., Mannila, H. and Ukkonen. E. 1993. Learning rules with local exceptions. *EuroCOLT-93*.

Klemetinen, M., Mannila, H., Ronkainen, P., Toivonen, H. and Verkamo, A. 1994. Finding interesting rules from large sets of discovered association rules. *CIKM-94*.

Liu, B. and Hsu, W. 1996. Post-analysis of learned rules. *AAAI-96*.

Liu, B., Hsu, W and Ma, Y. 1999. "Pruning and Summarizing the discovered associations." *KDD-99*.

Liu, H., Lu, H., Feng, R and Hussain, F. 1999. Efficient search of reliable exceptions. *PAKDD-99*.

Merz, C. J. and Murphy, P. 1996. UCI repository of machine learning databases, [http://www.cs.uci.edu/~mlearn].

Padmanabhan, B. and Tuzhilin, A. 1998. A belief-driven method for discovering unexpected patterns. *KDD-98*.

Pazzani, M., Mani, S. and Shankle, W. 1997. Beyond concise and colorful: learning intelligible rules. *KDD-97*.

Piatesky-Shapiro, G. and Matheus, C. 1994. The interestingness of deviations. *KDD-94*.

Quinlan, R. 1992. *C4.5: program for machine learning*. Morgan Kaufmann.

Rivest, R. 1987. Learning Decision Lists. *Machine Learning*, 2.

Silberschatz, A., and Tuzhilin, A. 1996. What makes patterns interesting in knowledge discovery systems. *IEEE Trans. on Know. and Data Eng.* 8(6).

Suzuki, E. 1997. Autonomous discovery of reliable exception rules. *KDD-97*.

Vilalta, R., Blix, G. & Rendell, L. 1997. Global data analysis and fragmentation problem in decision tree induction. *ECML-97*.

Selective Sampling With Redundant Views

Ion Muslea, Steven Minton, and Craig A. Knoblock

Information Sciences Institute and Integrated Media Systems Center
University of Southern California
4676 Admiralty Way
Marina del Rey, CA 90292, USA
{muslea, minton, knoblock}@isi.edu

Abstract

Selective sampling, a form of active learning, reduces the cost of labeling training data by asking only for the labels of the most informative unlabeled examples. We introduce a novel approach to selective sampling which we call *co-testing*. Co-testing can be applied to problems with *redundant views* (i.e., problems with multiple disjoint sets of attributes that can be used for learning). We analyze the most general algorithm in the co-testing family, *naive co-testing*, which can be used with virtually any type of learner. Naive co-testing simply selects at random an example on which the existing views disagree. We applied our algorithm to a variety of domains, including three real-world problems: wrapper induction, Web page classification, and discourse trees parsing. The empirical results show that besides reducing the number of labeled examples, naive co-testing may also boost the classification accuracy.

Introduction

In order to learn a classifier, supervised learning algorithms need labeled training examples. In many applications, labeling the training examples is an expensive process because it requires human expertise and is a tedious, time consuming task. *Selective sampling*, a form of active learning, reduces the number of training examples that need to be labeled by examining unlabeled examples and selecting the most informative ones for the human to label. This paper introduces *co-testing*, which is a novel approach to selective sampling for domains with *redundant views*. A domain has redundant views if there are at least two mutually exclusive sets of features that can be used to learn the target concept. Our work was inspired by Blum and Mitchell (1998), who noted that there are many real world domains with multiple views. One example is Web page classification, where one can identify faculty home pages either based on the words on the page or based on the words in HTML anchors pointing to the page. Another example is perception learning with multiple sensors, where we

can determine a robot's position based on vision, sonar, or laser sensors.

Active learning techniques work by asking the user to label an example that maximizes the information conveyed to the learner (we refer to such selected examples as *queries*). In a standard, single-view learning scenario, this generally translates into finding an example that splits the version space in half, i.e., eliminating half of the hypotheses consistent with the training set. With redundant views, we can do much better. Co-testing simultaneously trains a separate classifier for each redundant view. Each classifier is applied to the pool of unlabeled examples, and the system selects a query based on the degree of disagreement among the learners. Because the target hypotheses in each view must agree, co-testing can reduce the hypothesis space faster than would otherwise be possible. To illustrate this, consider a learning problem where we have two views, **V1** and **V2**. For illustrative purposes, imagine an extreme case where there is an unlabeled example x that is classified as positive by a single hypothesis from the **V1** version space; furthermore, assume that x is classified as positive by all but one of the hypotheses from the **V2** version space. If the system asks for the label of this example, it will immediately converge to a single hypothesis in one of the spaces and no additional examples will be required.

In the real world, where noise and other effects intrude into the learning process, translating this simple intuition into an effective algorithm raises some interesting issues. In this paper we describe co-testing as a family of algorithms, and empirically analyze a simple implementation of the co-testing approach called *naive co-testing*. This paper begins with two in-depth illustrative examples that contrast co-testing with existing sampling approaches. Then we present the naive co-testing algorithm and discuss its application to both wrapper induction and traditional learning problems.

Co-testing and uncertainty sampling

There are two major approaches to selective sampling: uncertainty and committee-based sampling. The former queries the unlabeled examples on which the learned classifier is the least confident; the later gener-

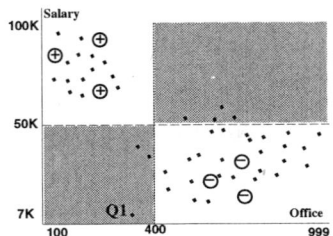 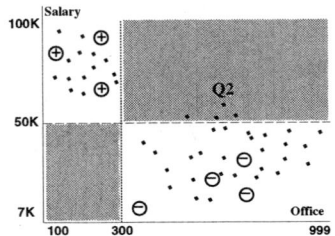 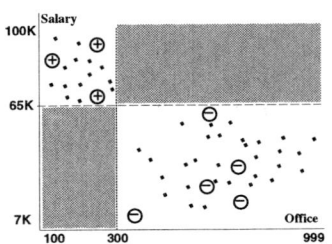

a) Trained on initial training set   b) Re-trained after query **Q1**   c) Re-trained after query **Q2**

Figure 1: **Co-testing at work.**

ates a committee of several classifiers and selects the unlabeled examples on which the committee members disagree the most. In this section, we contrast co-testing with uncertainty sampling, and in the next section we compare our approach with committee-based sampling.

Let us consider the task of classifying the employees of a CS department in two categories: faculty and non-faculty. Let us assume that the classification can be done either by using a person's salary (e.g., only faculty have salaries above $65K) or office number (e.g., only faculty office numbers are below 300). In this case, the domain has two redundant views: one that uses only the salary, and another one that uses only the office number. In both views the target concept is a threshold value: $65K for salary, and 300 for the office number. To learn the target concepts, we use for both views the following learner $\mathcal{L}$: first, $\mathcal{L}$ identifies the pair of labeled examples that belong to different classes and have the closest attribute values; then $\mathcal{L}$ sets the threshold to the mean of these two values.

Co-testing works as follows: initially, the user provides a few labeled examples, and a pool of unlabeled ones. In Figure 1a, the unlabeled examples are denoted by points, while the labeled ones appear as $\oplus$ and $\ominus$ (the former denotes faculty, and the latter represents non-faculty). We use the learner $\mathcal{L}$ to create one classifier for each view (the classifiers are geometrically represented as the dotted and the dashed lines, respectively). Then we apply the classifiers to *all* unlabeled examples and determine the *contention points* – the examples that are labeled differently by the two classifiers. The contention points, which lay in the picture's gray areas, are extremely informative because whenever the two classifiers disagree, at least one of them must be wrong. We select one of the contention points for labeling, add it to the training set, and repeat the whole process.

If the learner can evaluate the confidence of its classification, we can query the contention point on which *both* categorizers are *most confident*, which means that each query *maximally* improves at least one of the hypotheses. In each view from our example, we can measure the confidence level as the distances between the point and the threshold: the larger the distance, the higher the confidence in the classification. In Figure 1a co-testing asks for the label of the example **Q1**, which

is the contention point on which both categorizers are the most confident (i.e., the sum of the distances to the two thresholds is maximal). Once the example is labeled by the user, we re-train, find the new contention points (see Figure 1b), make the query **Q2**, and re-train again. As shown in Figure 1c, the new classifiers agree on all unlabeled examples, and co-testing stops.

As we already mentioned, the traditional approach in uncertainty sampling (Lewis & Gale 1994) consists of learning a single classifier and querying one of the points on which the classifier is the *least confident*. If we use just one of the views in the example above, the lowest confidence points are the ones that are the closest to the threshold. Consequently, uncertainty sampling makes queries that lead to *minimal* improvements of the hypothesis, and it takes more queries to find the correct classifier. In comparison, co-testing has two major advantages. First of all, combining evidence from several views allows us to make queries that lead to maximal improvements. Second, by querying only contention points, we are guaranteed to *always* select an example on which at least one of the classifiers is wrong.

Co-testing & committee-based sampling

Committee-based algorithms (Seung, Opper, & Sompolinski 1972)(Abe & Mamitsuka 1998) take a different approach. First, they generate several classifiers (the *committee*) that are consistent with the training set or sub-samples of it, respectively. Then they make the queries that are the most likely to eliminate half of the hypotheses that are consistent with the training set. More precisely, they apply all committee members to each unlabeled example and query the ones on which the committee vote is the most equally split.

Despite their advantages, committee-based algorithms have difficulties on some types of problems. For example, consider the problem $\mathcal{P}$ of learning *conjunctive concepts* in an instance space with 10,000 binary attributes that can be split into two redundant views: $\mathbf{V1}(a_1, a_2, \ldots, a_{5000})$ and $\mathbf{V2}(a_{5001}, a_{5002}, \ldots, a_{10000})$. Let us assume that the target concept has the following equivalent definitions:

- in **V1**: <t,t,t,?,?,...,?>;
- in **V2**: <f,f,f,?,?,...,?>;
- in **V1**∪**V2**: <t,t,t,?,?,...,?,f,f,f,?,?,...,?>.

Given:
- a problem $\mathcal{P}$ with features $\mathbf{V}=\{a_1, a_2, \ldots, a_N\}$
- a learning algorithm $\mathcal{L}$
- two views $\mathbf{V1}$ and $\mathbf{V2}$ ($\mathbf{V}=\mathbf{V1}\cup\mathbf{V2}$ and $\mathbf{V1}\cap\mathbf{V2}=\emptyset$)
- the sets T and U of labeled and unlabeled examples

LOOP for k iterations
- use $\mathcal{L}$, $\mathbf{V1}(T)$, and $\mathbf{V2}(T)$ to create classifiers h_1 and h_2
- let $ContentionPoints = \{\, x \in U,\ h_1(x) \neq h_2(x)\,\}$
- let $x = \mathbf{SelectQuery}(ContentionPoints)$
- remove x from U, ask for its label, and ad it to T

Figure 2: **The Co-Testing Family of Algorithms.**

The meaning of these concepts is straightforward: for example, in $\mathbf{V1}$, a_1, a_2, and a_3 must be $\mathtt{t}$, and the other attributes do not matter. Finally, let us further assume that the attribute a_4 has the value $\mathtt{t}$ for 99% of the instances (i.e., it rarely has the value $\mathtt{f}$). The scarcity of examples with $a_4=\mathtt{f}$ makes the target concept difficult to learn because it is highly improbable that a random training set includes such an examples. For domains like this one, the challenge consists of identifying these rare and informative examples.[1]

For this problem, we use the FIND-S learner (Mitchell 1997), which generates *the most specific* hypothesis that is consistent with all positive examples. We chose FIND-S because boolean conjunctions are PAC-learnable by FIND-S (i.e., with a high probability, the target concept can be learned in polynomial time based on a polynomial number of *randomly* chosen examples).

Now let us assume that we apply a committee-based approach to the 10,000-attribute instance space. In the initial training set a_4 is unlikely to have the value $\mathtt{f}$, in which case *all* initial committee members will have a_4 set to $\mathtt{t}$; this means that the queries are also unlikely to have $a_4=\mathtt{f}$ because such examples are classified as negative by all committee members (remember that queries are made only on examples on which the committee is split). After several queries, all the committee members become identical (<$\mathtt{t,t,t,t,?,\ldots,?,f,f,f,?,?,\ldots,?}$>) and learning stops. Consequently, even though the target concept is PAC-learnable, with high probability the learned concept will *not* be the correct one.

By contrast, co-testing easily learns the correct concept. First, after several queries, it generates the concepts <$\mathtt{t,t,t,t,?,\ldots,?}$> for $\mathbf{V1}$ and <$\mathtt{f,f,f,?,\ldots,?}$> for $\mathbf{V2}$, which correspond to the concept <$\mathtt{t,t,t,t,?,\ldots,?,f,f,f,?,?,\ldots,?}$> learned above. These two hypotheses disagree on *all* unlabeled examples that have $a_4=\mathtt{f}$ ($\mathbf{V1}$ labels them negative, while $\mathbf{V2}$ labels them positive) *and only on those*. Consequently, co-testing queries such an example and learns the correct hypotheses: <$\mathtt{t,t,t,?,\ldots,?}$> and <$\mathtt{f,f,f,?,\ldots,?}$>, respectively.

---
[1] Later in this paper we will discuss wrapper induction, which is a typical example of problem with rare values.

In order to make the problem more realistic, let us now assume that there are two attributes with rare values. In case they both fall within the same view, the argument above remains valid, and co-testing is guaranteed to find the correct hypothesis. If the two attributes belong to different views, co-testing still finds the perfect hypothesis unless both rare values *always* appear together in all unlabeled examples (which is highly unlikely). A similar argument holds for an arbitrary number of independent attributes with rare values.

The co-testing algorithms

In this section we present a formal description of the co-testing family of algorithms, which was designed for problems with *redundant views*. By definition, a learning problem $\mathcal{P}$ is said to have redundant views if its set of attributes $\mathbf{V} = \{a_1, a_2, \ldots, a_N\}$ can be partitioned in two disjoint views $\mathbf{V1}$ and $\mathbf{V2}$, and either view is sufficient to learn a classifier for $\mathcal{P}$. Ideally, the two views should be able to reach the same classification accuracy, but we will see latter that in practice this is *not* a necessary condition.

Given a learner $\mathcal{L}$, a set T of labeled examples, and a set U of unlabeled ones, co-testing (see Figure 2) works as follows: first, it uses $\mathcal{L}$ to learn two classifiers h_1 and h_2 based on the projections of the examples in T onto the two views, $\mathbf{V1}$ and $\mathbf{V2}$. Then it applies h_1 and h_2 to all unlabeled examples and creates the list $ContentionPoints$ of all unlabeled examples on which they disagree. The difference between the members of the co-testing family comes from the manner in which they select the next query. *Naive co-testing*, on which we will focus in the remaining sections, is the most straightforward member of the family: it *randomly* queries one of the contention points. Naive co-testing is also the most general member of the family because it can be applied to virtually any type of learner (the more sophisticated version discussed in the second section is applicable only to learners that can reliably estimate the confidence of their classification). Despite its simplicity, the empirical results show that naive co-testing is a powerful selective sampling algorithm. We believe that more sophisticated versions of co-testing should lead to faster convergence, but this is a topic that we are still investigating.

Naive co-testing for wrapper induction

A plethora of applications are using data extracted from collections of on-line documents. To avoid hand-writing a large number of extraction rules, researchers focused on learning the rules based on labeled examples. As labeling such examples is an extremely tedious and time consuming task, active learning can play a crucial role in reducing the user's burden. However, relatively little attention has been paid to applying active learning to information extraction. The only approaches that we know about, (Thompson, Califf, & Mooney 1999) and (Soderland 1999), are not general-purpose algorithms because they select the queries based on heuristics specific to their respective learners, RAPIER and WHISK.

Wrapper induction algorithms, like STALKER (Muslea, Minton, & Knoblock 2000), are designed to learn high accuracy extraction rules for semi-structured documents. For instance, let us assume that we want to extract the restaurant names from a collection of documents that look similar to the Web-page fragment shown in Figure 3. To find the beginning of the restaurant name, we can use the *start rule* $\mathbf{R1} = SkipTo(\texttt{Cuisine:})SkipTo(\texttt{<p>})$. $\mathbf{R1}$ starts from the beginning of the page and ignores everything until it finds the string "Cuisine:"; then, again, it ignores everything until it finds "<p>". A similar *end rule* can be used to find the end of the name within the document.

An alternative way to find the start of the name is to use the rule $\mathbf{R2} = SkipTo(\texttt{Phone})SkipTo(Capitalized)$, which is applied *backward*, from the end of the document, and has similar semantics: it ignores everything until it finds "Phone" and then, again, skips to the first capitalized word. In this paper, we call $\mathbf{R1}$ and $\mathbf{R2}$ *forward* and *backward* start rules, respectively. As STALKER can learn both forward and backward rules, we can create the two views in a straightforward manner: $\mathbf{V1}$ and $\mathbf{V2}$ consist of the sequences of characters that *precede* and *follow* the beginning of the item, respectively. More precisely, in $\mathbf{V1}$ we learn forward rules, while in $\mathbf{V2}$ we learn backward rules. Finally, to apply co-testing to wrapper induction, we use STALKER's learning algorithm and the two views described above.

Note that by combining forward/backward start and end rules, one can obtain three types of wrappers: **FB** (**F**orward start and **B**ackward end rules), **FF** (**F**orward start and **F**orward end rules), and **BB** (**B**ackward start and **B**ackward end rules). Out of the 206 extraction tasks described in (Muslea, Minton, & Knoblock 2000), we applied *naive co-testing* on the 10 tasks on which, based on random examples, STALKER failed to generate perfect wrappers of *all three types*. STALKER was successively trained on random training sets of sizes 1, 2, ..., 10; the extraction accuracy was averaged over 20 runs. For co-testing, we started with one random labeled example and made nine queries. We used such small training sets because the learning curves tend to flatten even before reaching 10 examples.

Because of the space constraints, we present here only an overview of the empirical results. Over the 10 tasks, stand-alone STALKER reached the following average accuracies: 82.6% (**FB**), 84.4% (**FF**), and 81.4% (**BB**). By applying co-testing,[2] we obtained significantly higher accuracies for all three classes of wrappers: 90.7% (**FB**), 93.2% (**FF**), and 91.2% (**BB**). These

---

[2]We compared co-testing only with STALKER because there is no other active learning algorithm for wrapper induction. Furthermore, STALKER can not be used in a straightforward manner in conjunction with existing general-purpose selective sampling algorithms (Seung, Opper, & Sompolinski 1972) (Cohn, Atlas, & Ladner 1994) (Abe & Mamitsuka 1998).

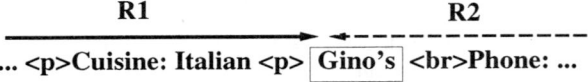

Figure 3: **Extracting the restaurant name.**

results deserve several comments. First, for all three classes of wrappers, co-testing reduced the error rate by 47%, 57%, and 53%, respectively. Second, for four of the 10 tasks, co-testing learned 100% accurate wrappers of *all three types*. Furthermore, these perfect wrappers were learned based on as few as five or six queries. Third, on all 10 tasks co-testing *improved* the accuracy of the *most accurate* of the three types of wrappers. Finally, on eight tasks co-testing also improved the accuracy of the *least accurate* of the wrappers. We can conclude that applying co-testing to STALKER leads to a dramatic improvement in accuracy without having to label more training data.

Beyond wrapper induction

In order to contrast naive co-testing with state-of-the-art sampling algorithms, we applied it to more traditional machine learning domains. In this paper, we compared naive co-testing with query-by-bagging and -boosting (Abe & Mamitsuka 1998) because these are techniques where performance has been reported on several well-studied UCI domains.[3] These two algorithms are also the most general selective sampling approaches in terms of practical applicability (i.e., similarly to co-testing, they can use a large variety of learners). We implemented all three algorithms based on the $\mathcal{MLC}$++ library (Kohavi, Sommerfield, & Dougherty 1997), and we used as learner MC4, which is the $\mathcal{MLC}$++ implementation of C4.5.

First, we applied co-testing on two real world domains for which there is a natural, intuitive way to create the two views: Ad (Kushmerick 1999) and Transfer-Few (Marcu, Carlson, & Watanabe 2000). The former is a Web classification problem with two classes, 1500 attributes, and 3279 examples. It classifies Web images into ads and non-ads and has the following views: **V1** describes the image itself (geometry, words in the image's URL and caption), while **V2** contains all other features (e.g., words from the URL of the page that contains the image, and words from the URL of the page the image points to). The second domain, Transfer-Few, has seven classes, 99 features and 11,193 examples. It uses a shift-reduce parsing paradigm in order to learn to rewrite Japanese discourse trees as English-like discourse trees in the context of a machine translation system. In this case, **V1** describes features specific to a shift-reduce parsing paradigm: the elements in the input list and the partial trees in the stack. **V2** describes features specific to the Japanese tree given as input.

---

[3]http://www.ics.uci.edu/~mlearn/MLRepository.html

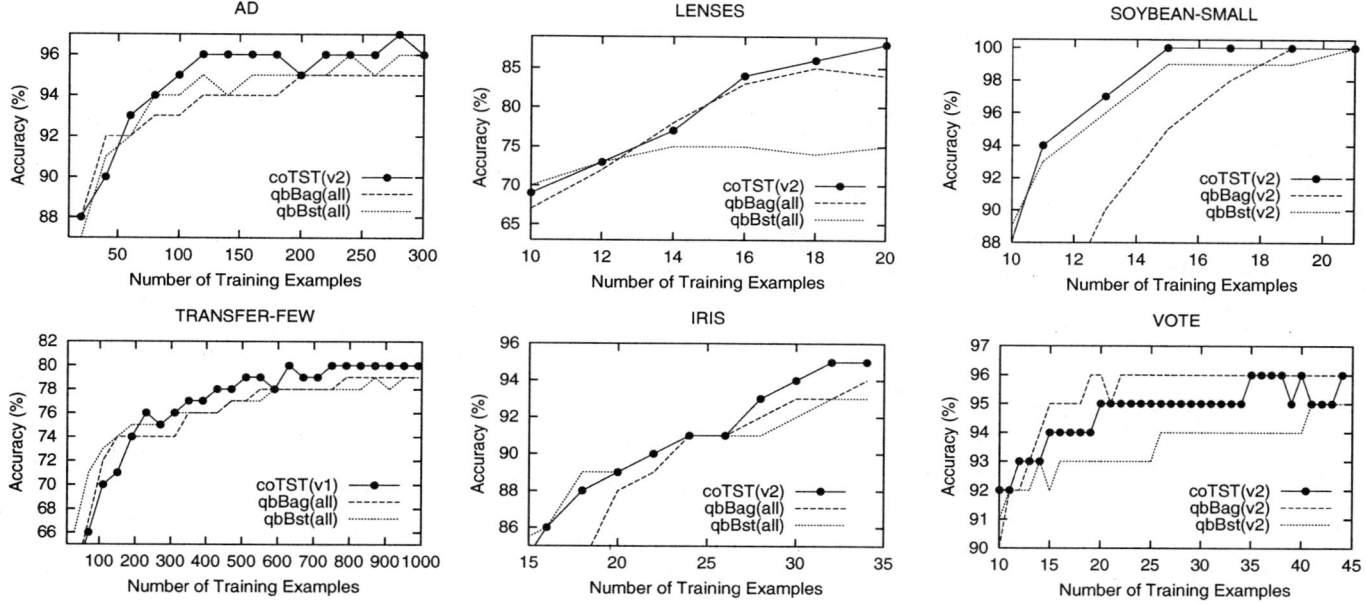

Figure 4: Co-Testing on Traditional Machine Learning Domains.

As the size of these two domains leads to high computational costs, we used 2-fold cross validation and averaged the results over 5 random runs. In both domains we started with a randomly chosen training set of 10 examples, and we made 10 and 20 queries after each learning episode, respectively. As shown in the first column of Figure 4, co-testing clearly outperforms query-by-bagging and -boosting on both domains. We must emphasize that these results were obtained despite the fact that the classifier used by co-testing is less powerful than the other two (i.e., a single decision tree *vs* 20 bagged/boosted decision trees).

To better understand how naive co-testing can outperform such powerful algorithms, we continued our empirical investigation on small size UCI domains. As in most of these domains there is no natural way to create two views, we artificially created the views by splitting the attributes in half[4] (i.e., first and last 50% of them). Finally, in order to have a fair comparison, we selected the domains on which bagging and boosting have accuracies as close as possible to MC4: Lenses, Soybean-Small, Iris, and Vote. For all these domains, we used 10-fold cross validation and averaged the results over 20 random runs. For each domain, we started with a random training set of five examples, and we made one query after each learning episode.

---

[4]The only exception is the iris domain (4 attributes), where there is a large difference in the accuracy of the views $\{a_1, a_2\}$ and $\{a_3, a_4\}$ (72% and 94%, respectively). By using the views $\{a_1, a_2, a_3\}$ and $\{a_4\}$, we obtained closer accuracies: 94% and 95%, respectively. Note that the view $\{a_4\}$ is *not* restricted to single-level decision trees because a_4 has continuous values.

Figure 4 shows the learning curves for both the UCI and the real world domains. For co-testing, we always present the results on the best of the two views. For query-by-bagging and -boosting, we show the best learning curve among **V1**, **V2**, and **V1**$\cup$**V2** (denoted by v1, v2, and all in the legends from Figure 4). Note that on soybean-small and vote, the best accuracy of query-by-bagging and -boosting was obtained on **V2**, not on all features!

The empirical results require a few comments. First of all, co-testing outperforms query-by-boosting on all six domains. Second, co-testing does better than query-by-bagging on five domains; on the sixth one, Vote, both reach the same final accuracies, but query-by-bagging is capable of doing it based on fewer queries. The explanation is quite simple: on this domain, bagging consistently outperforms MC4 by 1%, which means that it reaches the final accuracy based on fewer examples. Third, on all domains except Soybean-Small and Vote, the best accuracy of query-by-bagging and -boosting is obtained on **V1**$\cup$**V2**. This means that co-testing outperforms even more clearly the other two algorithms on the individual views. Last but not least, we found it interesting that the UCI domains contain so much redundancy that our arbitrary views do not lead to any loss of accuracy.

Discussion

In (Blum & Mitchell 1998), the authors showed that redundant views can provide an important source of information for supervised machine learning algorithms. Previously, this topic was largely ignored, though the idea clearly shows up in many unsupervised applications using techniques like EM(Dempster, Laird, & Rubin 1977). However, rather than considering active learning methods, Blum and Mitchell use the two views to learn hypotheses that feed each other with the unlabeled examples on which their classification is the most confident.

Our empirical results show that co-testing is a potentially powerful approach for active learning. In the wrapper induction, `Ad`, and `Transfer-Few` domains, all of which have natural redundant views, naive co-testing clearly improves upon the current state of the art. We believe that co-testing works so well in these domains because it can identify the rarely occurring cases that are relevant, as described in the third section. We note that all these three domains have large number of features, so finding relevant but rare feature-values contributes significantly to performance.

Naive co-testing's good performance on the UCI domains was more surprising, especially since we derived the views by splitting the features arbitrarily. We conjecture that splitting the problem into two views is profitable because it effectively produces committees that are independent, so that the hypotheses produced by one view are quite different than those produced in the other view. Perhaps any committee-based technique that encourages such variation within its committee would do as well.

Whether or not co-testing turns out to do well on traditional single-view domains, we believe that it will have practical value because many large real-world domains do have redundant views. We note that the views are not required to lead to the same accuracy, which makes the constraint easier to fulfill (in fact, none of our domains above had equally accurate views). Clearly, more work needs to be done here, both in exploring the space of co-testing algorithms as well as analyzing the theoretical underpinnings of the approach. Nevertheless, we believe this study presents a step towards an interesting new approach to active learning.

Conclusion

This paper introduced co-testing, a family of selective sampling algorithms. Co-testing queries one of the contention points among multiple, redundant views. We focused on a simple member of the family, *naive co-testing*, which randomly selects one of the contention points. We provided empirical evidence that on domains like wrapper induction, where other sampling methods cannot be naturally applied, *co-testing* leads to significant improvements of the classification accuracy. We also applied *naive co-testing* to traditional machine learning domains, and we showed that its query selection strategy is comparable to the more sophisticated ones used in query-by-bagging and -boosting.

We plan to continue our work on co-testing by following several research directions. First, we will continue studying the various members of the family in order to fully understand both its advantages and its weaknesses. Second, we plan to provide theoretical guarantees for the most interesting members of the family. Third, we will search a formal way to detect the redundant views within a given domain. Last but not least, we will perform a large-scale empirical evaluation by applying co-testing to various real world problems such as Web classification and natural language processing.

Acknowledgments

This work was supported in part by USC's Integrated Media Systems Center (IMSC) - an NSF Engineering Research Center, by the National Science Foundation under grant number IRI-9610014, by the U.S. Air Force under contract number F49620-98-1-0046, by the Defense Logistics Agency, DARPA, and Fort Huachuca under contract number DABT63-96-C-0066, and by research grants from NCR and General Dynamics Information Systems. The views and conclusions contained in this paper are the authors' and should not be interpreted as representing the official opinion or policy of any of the above organizations or any person connected with them.

References

Abe, N., and Mamitsuka, H. 1998. Query learning using boosting and bagging. In *Proc. of ICML*, 1–10.

Blum, A., and Mitchell, T. 1998. Combining labeled and unlabeled data with co-training. In *Proc. of the 1988 Conf. Computational Learning Theory*, 92–100.

Cohn, D.; Atlas, L.; and Ladner, R. 1994. Improving generalization with active learning. *ML* 15:201–221.

Dempster, A.; Laird, N.; and Rubin, D. 1977. Maximum likelihood from incomplete data vie the EM algorithm. *J. of Royal Statistical Society* 39:1–38.

Kohavi, R.; Sommerfield, D.; and Dougherty, J. 1997. Data mining using MLC++, a machine learning library in C++. *Intl. J. of AI Tools* 6(4):537–566.

Kushmerick, N. 1999. Learning to remove internet advetisements. In *Proc. of Auton. Agents-99*, 175–181.

Lewis, D., and Gale, W. 1994. A sequential algorithm for training text classifiers. In *Proc. of Research and Development in Information Retrieval*, 3–12.

Marcu, D.; Carlson, L.; and Watanabe, M. 2000. The automatic translation of discourse structures.

Mitchell, T. 1997. Machine learning. McGraw-Hill.

Muslea, I.; Minton, S.; and Knoblock, C. 2000. Hierarchical wrapper induction for semistructured information sources. *J. Autonom. Agents & Multi-Agent Sys.*

Seung, H.; Opper, M.; and Sompolinski, H. 1972. Query by committee. In *Proc. of COLT-72*, 287–294.

Soderland, S. 1999. Learning extraction rules for semistructured and free text. *ML* 34:233–272.

Thompson, C.; Califf, M.; and Mooney, R. 1999. Active learning for natural language parsing and information extraction. In *Proc. of ICML-99*, 406–414.

A Mutually Beneficial Integration of Data Mining and Information Extraction

Un Yong Nahm and **Raymond J. Mooney**
Department of Computer Sciences,
University of Texas, Austin, TX 78712-1188
{pebronia,mooney}@cs.utexas.edu

Abstract

Text mining concerns applying data mining techniques to unstructured text. *Information extraction* (IE) is a form of shallow text understanding that locates specific pieces of data in natural language documents, transforming unstructured text into a structured database. This paper describes a system called DISCOTEX, that combines IE and data mining methodologies to perform text mining as well as improve the performance of the underlying extraction system. Rules mined from a database extracted from a corpus of texts are used to predict additional information to extract from future documents, thereby improving the recall of IE. Encouraging results are presented on applying these techniques to a corpus of computer job postings from an Internet newsgroup.

Introduction

Data mining, a.k.a. knowledge discovery from databases (KDD), and *information extraction* (IE) are both topics of significant recent interest. KDD considers the application of statistical and machine-learning methods to discover novel relationships in large relational databases. IE concerns locating specific pieces of data in natural-language documents, thereby extracting structured information from unstructured text. However, there has been little if any research exploring the interaction between these two important areas. This paper explores the mutual benefit that the integration of IE and KDD can provide.

KDD assumes that the information to be "mined" is already in the form of a relational database. Unfortunately, for many applications, available electronic information is in the form of unstructured natural-language documents rather than structured databases. Consequently, the problem of *text mining*, i.e. discovering useful knowledge from unstructured text, is beginning to attract attention (Feldman & Dagan 1995; Hearst 1999). Information extraction can play an obvious role in text mining. Natural-language information-extraction methods can transform a corpus of textual documents into a more structured database. Standard

Copyright © 2000, American Association for Artificial Intelligence (www.aaai.org). All rights reserved.

KDD methods can then be applied to the resulting database to discover novel relationships.

In previous research, we have developed a machine-learning system, RAPIER, for inducing rules for extracting information from natural-language texts (Califf & Mooney 1999). Using an IE system constructed by RAPIER, we have extracted a database of over 5,000 computer-related jobs from messages posted to the austin.jobs newsgroup. By applying standard rule induction methods, e.g. C4.5RULES (Quinlan 1993), to the resulting database, we have discovered interesting relationships such as "If a computer-related job requires knowledge of Java and graphics then it also requires knowledge of PhotoShop." This example clearly illustrates the role that IE can play in extending KDD to textual databases.

A less obvious interaction is the benefit that KDD can in turn provide to IE. The predictive relationships between different slot fillers discovered by KDD can provide additional clues about what information should be extracted from a document. For example, if Java∈Programming-Languages and graphics∈areas have been extracted from a job posting, then an IE system might also consider extracting PhotoShop∈Applications as an additional slot filler. Since typically the *recall* (percentage of correct slot fillers extracted) of an IE system is significantly lower than its *precision* (percentage of extracted slot fillers which are correct) (DARPA 1995), such predictive relationships might be productively used to improve recall by suggesting additional information to extract. This paper reports experiments in the job-posting domain demonstrating that predictive rules acquired by applying KDD to an extracted database can be used to improve the recall of information extraction.

The remainder of the paper is organized as follows. Section 2 presents some background information on IE and RAPIER. Section 3 describes a system called DISCOTEX (DISCOvery from Text EXtraction) that improves RAPIER's performance by exploiting prediction rules. Section 4 presents and discusses experimental results obtained on a corpus of job postings from the newsgroup austin.jobs. Section 5 reviews some related work, section 6 discusses directions for future re-

Sample Job Posting
Job Title: Senior DBMS Consultant
Location: Dallas,TX
Responsibilities: DBMS Applications consultant works with project teams to define DBMS based solutions that support the enterprise deployment of Electronic Commerce, Sales Force Automation, and Customer Service applications.
Desired Requirements: 3-5 years exp. developing Oracle or SQL Server apps using Visual Basic, C/C++, Powerbuilder, Progress, or similar. Recent experience related to installing and configuring Oracle or SQL Server in both dev. and deployment environments.
Desired Skills: Understanding of UNIX or NT, scripting language. Know principles of structured software engineering and project management

Filled Job Template
title: Senior DBMS Consultant
state: TX
city: Dallas
language: Powerbuilder, Progress, C, C++, Visual Basic
platform: UNIX, NT
application: SQL Server, Oracle
area: Electronic Commerce, Customer Service
required years of experience: 3
desired years of experience: 5

Figure 1: Sample Text and Filled Template

search, and section 7 presents our conclusions.

Background
Information Extraction

The goal of an IE system is to locate specific data in natural-language text. The data to be extracted is typically given by a template which specifies a list of slots to be filled with substrings taken from the document. IE is useful for a variety of applications, particularly given the recent proliferation of Internet and web documents. Recent applications include apartment rental ads (Soderland 1999), job announcements (Chai, Biermann, & Guinn 1999), and course homepages (Freitag 1998).

In this paper, we consider the task of extracting a database from postings to the USENET newsgroup, austin.jobs. Figure 1 shows a sample message from the newsgroup and the filled computer-science job template where several slots may have multiple fillers. For example, slots such as languages, platforms, applications, and areas usually have more than one filler, while slots related to the job's title or location have only one.

The RAPIER System

RAPIER is a bottom-up relational rule learner for acquiring information extraction rules from a corpus of labeled training examples. It learns patterns describing constraints on slot fillers and their surrounding context using a specific-to-general search. Constraints on patterns can specify the specific words, part-of-speech, or semantic classes of tokens. The hypernym links in WordNet (Fellbaum 1998) provide semantic class information, and documents are annotated with part-of-speech information using the tagger of Brill (1994). In this paper, we use the simpler version of RAPIER that employs only word and part-of-speech constraints since WordNet classes provide no additional advantage in this domain (Califf & Mooney 1999).

The learning algorithm of RAPIER was inspired by several inductive logic programming systems. First, RAPIER creates most-specific patterns for each slot in each example specifying the complete word and tag information for the filler and its full context. New rules are created by generalizing pairs of existing rules using a beam search. When the best rule does not produce incorrect extractions, RAPIER adds it to the rule base and removes existing rules that it subsumes.

By training on a corpus of documents annotated with their filled templates, RAPIER acquires a knowledge base of extraction rules that can then be tested on novel documents. Califf (1998) and Califf & Mooney (1999) provide more information and results demonstrating that RAPIER performs well on realistic applications such as USENET job postings and seminar announcements.

The DISCOTEX System
Text Mining

After constructing an IE system that extracts the desired set of slots for a given application, a database is constructed from a corpus of texts by applying the extractor to each document to create a collection of structured records. Standard KDD techniques can then be applied to the resulting database to discover interesting relationships. Specifically, we induce rules for predicting the information in each database field given the information in all other fields. Standard classification rule-learning methods can be employed for this task.

In order to discover prediction rules, we treat each slot-value pair in the extracted database as a distinct binary feature, such as graphics∈area, and learn rules for predicting each feature from all other features. Similar slot fillers are first collapsed into a pre-determined standard term. For example, "Windows 95" is a popular filler for the platform slot, but it often appears as "Win 95", "Win95", 'MS Win 95", and so on, and "DBA" in the title slot is an abbreviation for "DataBase Administrator". These terms are collapsed to unique slot values before prediction rules are mined from the data. A small domain-dependent synonym dictionary is used to 0 such similar terms. Trivial cases such as "Databases" → "Database" and "Client/Server" → "Client-Server" are handled by manually contrived synonym-checking rules.

Currently, DISCOTEX uses C4.5RULES (Quinlan

- Oracle∈application ∧ QA Partner∈application → SQL∈language
- C++∈language ∧ C∈language ∧ CORBA∈application ∧ Title=Software Engineer → Windows∈platform
- HTML∈language ∧ WindowsNT∈platform ∧ Active Server Pages∈application → Database∈area
- ¬(UNIX∈platform) ∧ ¬(Windows∈platform) ∧ Games∈area → 3D∈area
- Java∈language ∧ ActiveX∈area ∧ Graphics∈area → Web∈area

Figure 2: Sample Mined Prediction Rules for Computer-Science Jobs

Determine T, a threshold value for rule validation
Create a database of labeled examples
   (by applying IE to the document corpus)
For each labeled example D
   S := set of slot fillers of D
   Convert S to binary features
Build a prediction rule base, RB
   (by applying C4.5RULES to the binary data)
For each prediction rule $R \in RB$
   Verify R on training data and validation data
   If the accuracy of R is lower than T
      Delete R from RB

Figure 3: Algorithm Specification: Rule Mining Phase

1993) to induce rules from the resulting binary data by learning decision trees and translating them into pruned rules. We have also applied RIPPER (Cohen 1995) to learn rules, using its ability to handle *set-valued features* to avoid the step of explicitly translating slot fillers into binary features. The two systems produce very similar results and the experiments in this paper employ C4.5rules.

Discovered knowledge describing the relationships between slot values is written in the form of production rules. If there is a tendency for Web to appear in the area slot when ShockWave appears in the applications slot, this is represented by the production rule, ShockWave∈application → Web∈area. Rules can also predict the absence of a filler in a slot; however, here we focus on rules predicting the presence of fillers. Sample rules mined from a database of 5,000 jobs extracted from the USENET newsgroup austin.jobs are shown in Figure 2.

Pseudocode for the text mining phase is shown in Figure 3. A final step shown in the figure is filtering the discovered rules on both the training data and (optionally) a disjoint set of labeled validation data in order to retain only the most accurate of the induced rules. Currently, rules that make *any* incorrect predictions on either the training or validation extracted templates are discarded.

For each example D
   Extract fillers from D using extraction rules
   For each rule R in the prediction rule base RB
      If R fires on the current extracted fillers
         If the predicted filler is a substring of D
            Extract the predicted filler

Figure 4: Algorithm Specification: IE Phase

Using Mined Rules to Improve IE

After mining knowledge from extracted data, DISCOTEX uses the discovered rules to predict missing information during subsequent extraction. Tests of IE systems usually consider two performance measures, *precision* and *recall* defined as:

$$precision = \frac{\#of CorrectFillersExtracted}{\#of FillersExtracted} \quad (1)$$

$$recall = \frac{\#of CorrectFillersExtracted}{\#of FillersInCorrectTemplates} \quad (2)$$

Also, F-measure was introduced to combine precision and recall and is computed as follows (when the same weight is given to precision and recall):

$$F-measure = \frac{2 * Precision * Recall}{Precision + Recall} \quad (3)$$

Since the set of potential slot fillers is very large and not fixed in advance, and since only a small fraction of possible fillers is present in any given document, these performance metrics are generally more informative than the accuracy of predicting the presence/absence across all slot-value pairs.

Many extraction systems provide relatively high precision, but recall is typically much lower. Previous experiments in the job postings domain showed RAPIER's precision (e.g. low 90%'s) is higher than its recall (e.g. mid 60%'s) (Califf 1998). Currently, RAPIER's search focuses on finding high-precision rules and does not include a method for trading-off precision and recall. Although several methods have been developed for allowing a rule learner to trade-off precision and recall (Cohen 1996), this typically leaves the overall F-measure unchanged.

By using additional knowledge in the form of prediction rules mined from a larger set of data automatically extracted from additional unannotated text, it may be possible to improve recall without unduly sacrificing precision. For example, suppose we discover the rule SQL∈language → Database∈area. If the IE system extracted SQL∈language but failed to extract Database∈area, we may want to assume there was an extraction error and add Database to the area slot, potentially improving recall. Therefore, after applying extraction rules to a document, DISCOTEX applies its mined rules to the resulting initial data to predict additional potential extractions. The final decision whether or not to extract a predicted filler is based on whether

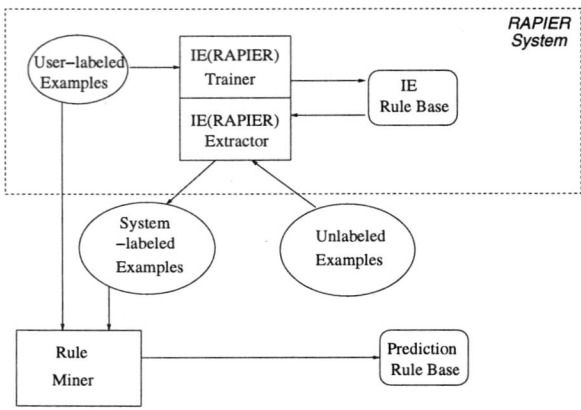

Figure 5: The System Architecture - Training

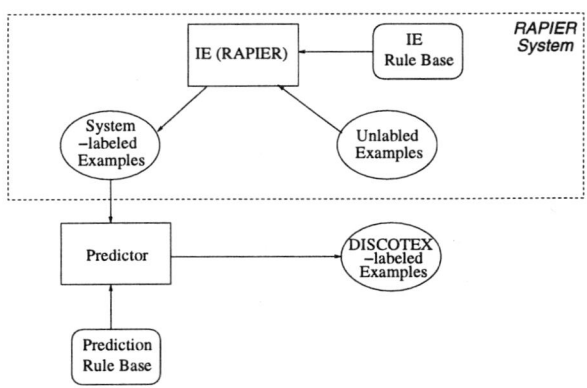

Figure 6: The System Architecture - Test

the filler(or any of its synonyms) occurs in the document as a substring. If the filler is found in the text, the extractor considers its prediction confirmed and extracts the filler. Mined rules that predict the absence of a filler are not used to remove extracted information since there is no analogous confirmation step for improving precision. This overall extraction algorithm is summarized in Figure 4.

One final issue is the order in which prediction rules are applied. When there are interacting rules, such as HTML$\in$languages $\rightarrow$ WWW$\in$area and $\neg$(WWW$\in$area) $\rightarrow$ C++ $\in$languages, different rule-application orderings can produce different results. Without the first rule, a document with HTML$\in$language but without WWW$\in$area in its initial filled template will make the second rule fire and predict C++ $\in$languages. However, if the first rule is executed first and its prediction is confirmed, then WWW will be extracted and the second rule can no longer fire. In DISCOTEX, all rules with negations in their antecedent conditions are applied first. This ordering strategy attempts to maximally increase recall by making as many confirmable predictions as possible.

The overall architecture of the final system is shown in Figures 5 and 6. Documents which the user has annotated with extracted information, as well as unsupervised data which has been processed by the initial IE system (which RAPIER has learned from the supervised data) are all used to create a database. The rule miner then processes this database to construct a knowledge base of rules for predicting slot values. These prediction rules are then used during testing to improve the recall of the existing IE system by proposing additional slot fillers whose presence in the document are confirmed before adding them to final extraction template.

Evaluation
Experimental Methodology

To test the overall system, 600 user-annotated computer-science job postings to the newsgroup austin.jobs were collected. 10-fold cross validation was used to generate training and test sets. In addition, 4,000 unannotated documents were collected as additional optional input to the text miner. Rules were induced for predicting the fillers of the languages, platforms, applications, and areas slots, since these are usually filled with multiple discrete-valued fillers and have obvious potential relationships between their values. The Title slot is also used, but only as a possible antecedent condition of a production rule, not as a consequent. Title has many possible values and is difficult to predict; however, may be useful as a predictor since fillers such as Database Administrator can help determine other values.

Results

Figures 7 and 8 and show the learning curves for recall and and F-measure. Unlabeled examples are not employed in these results. In order to clearly illustrate the impact of the amount of training data for both extraction and prediction rule learning, the same set of annotated data was provided to both RAPIER and the rule miner. Figures 7 and 8 show a comparison between the performance of RAPIER alone, DISCOTEX without filtering rules on independent data, and DISCOTEX with fully filtered rules. As previously stated, there are two ways of filtering rules before they are added to the prediction rule base; simply training and testing induced rules on the entire training set, or holding out part of the original training set as a disjoint validation set. The results were statistically evaluated by a two-tailed, paired t-test. For each training set size, each pair of systems were compared to determine if their differences in recall and F-measure were statistically significant ($p < 0.05$).

DISCOTEX using fully filtered rules performs the best, although DISCOTEX without filtering on disjoint data does almost as well. As hypothesized, DISCOTEX provides higher recall, and although it does decrease precision somewhat, overall F-measure is moderately increased. One interesting aspect is that DISCOTEX retains a fixed recall advantage over RAPIER as the size

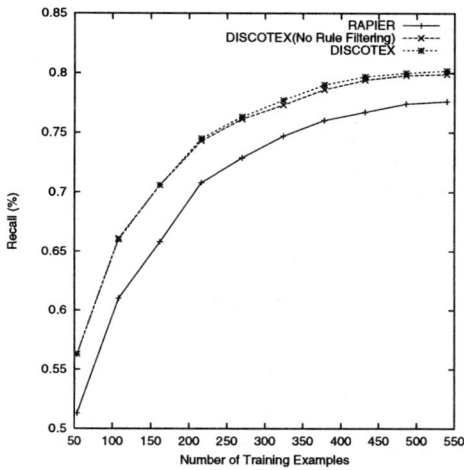

Figure 7: Recall on job postings

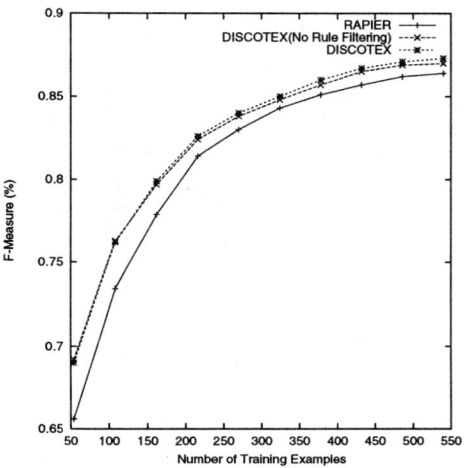

Figure 8: F-measure on job postings

Number of Examples for Rule Mining	Precision	Recall	F-Measure
0	97.4	77.6	86.4
540(Labeled)	95.8	80.2	87.3
540+1000(Unlabeled)	94.8	81.5	87.6
540+2000(Unlabeled)	94.5	81.8	87.7
540+3000(Unlabeled)	94.2	82.4	87.9
540+4000(Unlabeled)	93.5	83.3	88.1
Matching Fillers	59.4	94.9	73.1

Table 1: Performance results of DISCOTEX with unlabeled examples

of the training set increases. This is probably due to the fact that the increased amount of data provided to the text miner also continues to improve the quality of the acquired prediction rules. Overall, these results demonstrate the role of data mining in improving the performance of IE.

Table 1 shows results on precision, recall and F-measure when additional unlabeled documents are used to 0 a larger database prior to mining for prediction rules (which are then filtered on a validation set). The 540 labeled examples used to train the extractor were always provided to the rule miner, while the number of additional unsupervised examples were varied from 0 to 4,000. The results show that the more unsupervised data supplied for building the prediction rule base, the higher the recall and the overall F-measure. Although precision does suffer, the decrease is not as large as the increase in recall. Although adding information extracted from unlabeled documents to the database may result in a larger database and therefore more good prediction rules, it may also result in noise in the database due to extraction errors and consequently cause some inaccurate prediction rules to be discovered as well. The average F-measure without prediction rules is 86.4%, but it goes up to 88.1% when DISCOTEX is provided with 540 labeled examples and 4,000 unlabeled examples. Unlabeled examples do not show as much power as labeled examples in producing good prediction rules, because only 540 labeled examples boost recall rate and F-measure more than 4,000 unlabeled examples. However, unlabeled examples are still helpful since recall and F-measure do slowly increase as more unlabeled examples are provided.

As a benchmark, in the last row of Table 1, we also show the performance of a simple method for increasing recall by always extracting substrings that are known fillers for a particular slot. This version remembers all strings that appear at least once in each slot in the database. Whenever a known filler string, e.g. `Java`, is contained in a test document, it is extracted as a filler for the corresponding slot, e.g. `language`. This is equivalent to replacing the mined rules in DISCOTEX with trivial rules of the form `True → <slot value>` for every known slot value. The reason why this works poorly is that a filler string contained in a job posting is not necessarily the correct filler for the corresponding slot. For instance, `Database` can appear in a newsgroup posting, not in the list of required skills of that particular job announcement, but in the general description for the company. The fact that the precision and F-measure of this strawman are much worse than DISCOTEX's demonstrates the additional value of rule mining for improving extraction performance.

Related Research

There has been relatively little research exploring the integration of IE and KDD. Feldman & Dagan(1995) allude to the use of IE in text mining; however, their KDT system uses texts manually tagged with a limited number of fixed category labels. KDT does not actually use automated text categorization or IE and the paper does not discuss using mined knowledge to improve extraction.

There is a growing interest in the general topic of text mining (Hearst 1999); however, there are few working systems or detailed experimental evaluations. By utilizing existing IE and KDD technology, text-mining systems can be developed relatively rapidly and evaluated on existing IE corpora.

Future Work

Although our preliminary results with job postings are encouraging, a fuller evaluation will apply DiscoTEX to other domains such as business news articles and medical documents.

One step in DiscoTEX that is currently performed manually is collapsing similar slot-fillers in the extracted data into a canonical form, e.g. mapping "NT," "Windows NT," and "Microsoft Windows NT" all to a unique term. In many cases, such collapsing could be automated by clustering slot fillers using a distance metric based on textual similarity, such as character edit distance (Ristad & Yianilos 1998).

Currently, we only consider discrete-valued slots. However, real-valued slots, such as "desired years of experience," could also be provided to the rule miner as additional input features when predicting other slots. Predicting such continuous values using regression methods instead of categorization techniques is another area for future research. The procedure for selecting slots to be used in rule mining also needs to be automated. In the current experiments, we manually chose five slots from the computer-science job template. By identifying and quantifying the correlations between slot values, this decision could be automated.

With regard to using KDD to improve IE, methods for using discovered predictive rules to improve precision as well as recall are needed. Simply eliminating extracted fillers that are not predicted is too course and would likely severely damage recall. Combining confidence measures for both predictive rules and extraction rules during IE could be a productive way to improve both precision and recall.

Conclusions

Information extraction and data mining can be integrated for the mutual benefit of both tasks. IE enables the application of KDD to unstructured text corpora and KDD can discover predictive rules useful for improving IE performance. This paper has presented initial results on integrating IE and KDD that demonstrate both of these advantages.

Text mining is a relatively new research area at the intersection of natural-language processing, machine learning, and information retrieval. By appropriately integrating techniques from each of these disciplines, useful new methods for discovering knowledge from large text corpora can be developed. In particular, the growing interaction between computational linguistics and machine learning (Cardie & Mooney 1999) is critical to the development of effective text-mining systems.

Acknowledgements

This research was supported by the National Science Foundation under grant IRI-9704943.

References

Brill, E. 1994. Some advances in rule-based part of speech tagging. In *Proceedings of the Twelfth National Conference on Artificial Intelligence*, 722–727.

Califf, M. E., and Mooney, R. J. 1999. Relational learning of pattern-match rules for information extraction. In *Proceedings of the Sixteenth National Conference on Artificial Intelligence*, 328–334.

Califf, M. E. 1998. *Relational Learning Techniques for Natural Language Information Extraction*. Ph.D. Dissertation, Department of Computer Sciences, University of Texas, Austin, TX. Also appears as Artificial Intelligence Laboratory Technical Report AI 98-276 (see http://www.cs.utexas.edu/users/ai-lab).

Cardie, C., and Mooney, R. J. 1999. Machine learning and natural language (introduction to special issue on natural language learning). *Machine Learning* 34:5–9.

Chai, J. Y.; Biermann, A. W.; and Guinn, C. I. 1999. Two dimensional generalization in information extraction. In *Proceedings of the Sixteenth National Conference on Artificial Intelligence*, 431–438.

Cohen, W. W. 1995. Fast effective rule induction. In *Proceedings of the Twelfth International Conference on Machine Learning*, 115–123.

Cohen, W. W. 1996. Learning to classify English text with ILP methods. In De Raedt, L., ed., *Advances in Inductive Logic Programming*. Amsterdam: IOS Press. 124–143.

DARPA., ed. 1995. *Proceedings of the 6th Message Understanding Conference*. San Mateo, CA: Morgan Kaufman.

Feldman, R., and Dagan, I. 1995. Knowledge discovery in textual databases (KDT). In *Proceedings of the First International Conference on Knowledge Discovery and Data Mining*.

Fellbaum, C. 1998. *WordNet: An Electronic Lexical Database*. Cambridge, MA: MIT Press.

Freitag, D. 1998. Information extraction from HTML: Application of a general learning approach. In *Proceedings of the Fifteenth National Conference on Artificial Intelligence*, 517–523.

Hearst, M. 1999. Untangling text data mining. In *Proceedings of the 37th Annual Meeting of the Association for Computational Linguistics*, 3–10.

Quinlan, J. R. 1993. *C4.5: Programs for Machine Learning*. San Mateo, CA: Morgan Kaufmann.

Ristad, E. S., and Yianilos, P. N. 1998. Learning string edit distance. *IEEE Transactions on Pattern Analysis and Machine Intelligence* 20(5).

Soderland, S. 1999. Learning information extraction rules for semi-structured and free text. *Machine Learning* 34:233–272.

Multivariate Clustering by Dynamics

Marco Ramoni
Knowledge Media Institute
The Open University
Milton Keynes MK7 6AA, UK
m.ramoni@open.ac.uk

Paola Sebastiani
Department of Mathematics
Imperial College
London SW7 2B, UK
p.sebastiani@ic.ac.uk

Paul Cohen
Department of Computer Science
University of Massachusetts
Amherst MA 01003-4610
cohen@cs.umass.edu

Abstract

We present a Bayesian clustering algorithm for multivariate time series. A clustering is regarded as a probabilistic model in which the unknown auto-correlation structure of a time series is approximated by a first order Markov Chain and the overall joint distribution of the variables is simplified by conditional independence assumptions. The algorithm searches for the most probable set of clusters given the data using a entropy-based heuristic search method. The algorithm is evaluated on a set of multivariate time series of propositions produced by the perceptual system of a mobile robot.

Introduction

Suppose one has a set of time series generated by one or more unknown processes, and the processes have characteristic dynamics. Clustering by dynamics is the problem of grouping time series into clusters so that the elements of each cluster have similar dynamics. Suppose a batch contains a time series of stride length for every episode in which a person moves on foot from one place to another. Clustering by dynamics might find clusters corresponding to "ambling," "striding," "running," and "pushing a shopping cart," because the dynamics of stride length are different in these processes. Similarly, cardiac pathologies can be characterized by the patterns of sistolic and diastolic phases; economic states such as recession can be characterized by the dynamics of economic indicators; syntactic categories can be categorized by the dynamics of word transitions; sensory inputs of a mobile robot can be merged to form prototypical representations of the robot's experiences.

The task of clustering time series can be regarded as the process of finding the partition, i.e. the set of clusters, best fitting the data according to some criteria. Typically, this task involves two steps: (1) model each time series to capture its essential dynamical features; (2) partition the set of time series by clustering. Our approach uses one of the simplest representations of a time series: a first order Markov chain

---

Copyright © 2000, American Association for Artificial Intelligence (www.aaai.org). All rights reserved.

(MC). A MC assumes that the probability distribution of a variable at time t is independent of the variable values observed prior to time $t-1$ (Ross 1996). Furthermore, we regard the task of finding the best partition of the data as a statistical model selection process. Smyth (1999) applied this idea to clustering time series and Sebastiani et al. (1999) devised a Bayesian model-based algorithm to cluster higher-order MCs. The algorithm, called Bayesian Clustering by Dynamics (BCD), has been successfully applied to cognitive robotics (Sebastiani, Ramoni, & Cohen 2000; Cohen et al. 2000), simulated war games (Sebastiani et al. 1999), behavior of stock exchange indices, and unsupervised generation of musical compositions. These applications suggest that even a very simple MC representation of a dynamic process is powerful enough to capture common aspects of different time series. Furthermore, an appealing feature of BCD is an entropy-based heuristic that makes the search over the space of partitions very efficient. In its current formulation, BCD is limited to the univariate case, that is, the algorithm is able to cluster the behaviors of only one variable at a time. But what if the problem at hand is multivariate, that is, it is represented by simultaneous time series of several interacting variables? The assessment of a battlefield situation is done on the basis of several, possibly interacting, factors, like force ratio, number of engaged units, total forces mass, and so on. Similarly, a sensory experience of a mobile robot is given by the simultaneous values of several sensors, and the experience itself can be identified by the correlation among subsets of these variables.

Suppose one wants to cluster a set of multivariate time series of v discrete variables, each taking c values. The straightforward solution is to convert the problem into a univariate one by defining a single variable taking as values all combinations of values of the v variables and then applying the univariate case algorithm (Sebastiani et al. 1999). Unfortunately, this solution is hardly scalable because the number of states of this variable grows exponentially with the number of the original v variables. The solution we present in this paper is a novel clustering technique for multivariate time series, called Multivariate Bayesian Clustering by Dynamics

(MBCD). The clustering algorithm is model-based, as it represents a clustering as a probabilistic model, it is Bayesian, as both the decision of whether grouping MCs and the stopping criterion are based on the clustering posterior probability, and it uses an entropy-based heuristic to reduce the search space over a subset of possible partitions. The clusters of dynamics produced by the algorithm are sets of MCs, which are assumed to be conditional independent given cluster membership. Thus, they capture dynamics involving simultaneously all the variables but the conditional independence assumption makes the algorithm scalable to large data sets. The algorithm is tested on multivariate time series of propositions produced by a mobile robot perceptual system and produces clusters which are significantly different from random clustering and in agreement with human clustering.

Theory

Suppose we have a set $S = \{S_1, \cdots, S_m\}$ of m multivariate time series. Each multivariate time series S_k is a set of v univariate time series $S_{k1}, \cdots, S_{kv}$ recording values of variables $X_1, ..., X_v$. The multivariate clustering algorithm can be outlined as follows. Given the $m \times v$ univariate time series, construct a MC for each series and replace each of the m multivariate time series by a set of v MCs. Rank the m sets of MCs in decreasing order of distance, merge similar sets of MCs into clusters if the merging increases a scoring metric, and repeat the procedure until a stopping criterion is met. The first step is the estimation of a MC from a univariate time series and it is considered next.

Markov Chains

Suppose that, for a variable X, we observe the time series $(x_0, x_1, x_2, ..., x_{i-1}, x_i, ..)$, where each x_i is one of the states $1, ..., s$ of X. The process generating the series is a (first order) MC if the conditional probability that the variable X visits state j at time t, given the sequence $(x_0, x_1, x_2, ..., x_{t-1})$, is only a function of the state visited at time $t-1$. Hence, we write $p(X_t = j|(x_0, x_1, x_2, ..., x_{t-1})) = p(X_t = j|x_{t-1})$, where X_t denotes the variable X at time t, and a MCs is represented by a table $P = (p_{ij})$ of transition probabilities, where $p_{ij} = p(X_t = j|X_{t-1} = i)$ is the probability of visiting state j given the current state i.

Given a time series generated from a MC, we might estimate the probabilities of state transitions $(i \to j) \equiv X_t = j|X_{t-1} = i$ from the data as $p_{ij} = n_{ij}/n_i$, where $n_i = \sum_j n_{ij}$ and n_{ij} is the frequency of the transitions $(i \to j)$ observed in the time series. Instead we prefer a Bayesian estimate in which prior information about transition probabilities can be taken into account. The derivation of this estimate is given in Sebastiani et al. (2000), here we simply give the result: The probability $\hat{p}_{ij}$ is estimated as

$$\hat{p}_{ij} = \frac{\alpha_{ij} + n_{ij}}{\sum_i \alpha_{ij} + n_{ij}} \qquad (1)$$

S	X_1	$\cdots$	X_v
S_1	S_{11}	$\cdots$	S_{1v}
$\vdots$	$\vdots$		
S_m	S_{m1}	$\cdots$	S_{mv}

$\Downarrow$

S	X_1	$\cdots$	X_v
P_1	P_{11}	$\cdots$	P_{1v}
$\vdots$	$\vdots$		
P_m	P_{m1}	$\cdots$	P_{mv}

Figure 1: The first step of the MBCD algorithm replaces time series S_{kh} with transition probability matrices P_{kh}.

where the so called prior hyper-parameter α_{ij} can be thought of as the prior frequency of transition $(i \to j)$, thus encoding prior knowledge about the process. In particular, the ratio α_{ij}/α_i is the prior probability of transition $(i \to j)$ and $\hat{p}_{ij}$ is the posterior probability in the sense of being estimated from prior information α_{ij} and the observed frequency n_{ij} of transition $(i \to j)$.

Clustering

The first step of the algorithm replaces the original time series by MCs represented by transition probability tables, as shown in Figure 1. This conversion process transforms each multivariate time series S_k in S into a set P_k of transition probability matrices P_{kh}, one for each variable X_h. We can now cluster the m sets of transition probability matrices.

As in BCD, the MBCD algorithm is *agglomerative*: it starts by assigning each set of transition matrices P_k to a separate cluster and iteratively merges them until a certain stopping criterion is met. Merging two sets of matrices $P_k = (P_{k1}, \cdots, P_{kv})$ and $P_l = (P_{l1}, \cdots, P_{lv})$ consists of creating a new set C_n of transition probability matrices $(P_{n1}, \cdots, P_{nv})$. The new cluster will be still a set of v transition matrices and each transition probability matrix P_{nh} in C_n is estimated from the cumulative transition frequencies of the variable X_h. The MBCD algorithm does not use a measure of similarity between MCs to decide whether two sets of MCs belong to the same cluster, neither it relies on a separate stopping rule. Both the decision of merging sets and the stopping criterion are based on the posterior probability of the obtained clustering, that is, the probability of the clustering given the data observed: Two sets of MCs are merged if the resulting partition has higher posterior probability than the partition in which these two sets are not merged, and the algorithm stops when no available merging produces a partition with higher posterior probability. MBCD's task is to find a maximum posterior probability partition of sets of MCs. Said in yet another way, MBCD solves a Bayesian model selection problem, where the model M_c it seeks is the most probable partition given the data. Details are given in the next section.

Method

Model selection methods are typically identified by two components: a scoring metrics — in this case, the posterior probability of a partition — and a search strategy to explore the space of possible partitions.

Posterior Probability

The key to the algorithm is the posterior probability of a partition. We regard a partition of the m sets of MCs into c clusters as a statistical model M_c, in which each cluster merges m_k sets of MCs. Components of this statistical model are the sets of MCs, a variable C with states $C_1, ..., C_c$ denoting cluster membership and a structure of dependency among the MCs in each cluster C_k. The variable C is a hidden, discrete variable, as it is not observed in the set S. The number c of states of C is unknown, but the number m of initial sets imposes an upper bound, as the number of clusters will be never higher than the number of initial multivariate time series. For example, if S is given by only two sets of multivariate time series S_1 and S_2, there are only two models describing possible partitions of these data: M_1 in which the two sets are merged into one cluster and M_2 in which the two sets are not merged. In model M_1, variable C takes one value while, in model M_2, C takes two values.

Globally, there are 2^m models describing different partitions. We can compute the posterior probability of these models by Bayes' Theorem:

$$p(M_c|S) = \frac{p(M_c)p(S|M_c)}{p(S)}$$

where $p(M_c)$ is a partition prior probability and $p(S)$ is the marginal probability of the data, and we choose the model with maximum posterior probability. Since we are comparing all models over the same data, $p(S)$ is constant and, for the purpose of maximizing $p(M_c|S)$, it is sufficient to consider $p(M_c)p(S|M_c)$. Furthermore, if all models are *a priori* equally likely, the comparison can be based solely on the *marginal likelihood* $p(S|M_c)$, which is a measure of how likely the data are if the model M_c is true. Reasonable assumptions on the sample space, the adoption of a particular parameterization for the model M_c and the specification of a conjugate prior lead to a simple, closed-form expression for the marginal likelihood $p(S|M_c)$ of which the solution presented in Sebastiani et al. (1999) is a special case for the univariate problem.

Conditional on the model M_c and hence on a specification of c clusters of sets of MCs, we suppose the marginal distribution of the variable C is multinomial, with cell probabilities $p_k = p(C = C_k)$. Furthermore, we suppose that sets of time series assigned to different clusters are mutually independent and that, for each cluster C_k, the v MCs generating the time series assigned to cluster C_k are independent. This last assumption says that, given cluster membership, the MCs are independent: Once we know the cluster we are in, the MC describing the dynamics of each variable X_h is independent of the dynamics describing any other variables. Thus, each cluster captures the overall dynamical features of a set of MCs that can however be treated as independent quantities within clusters. This assumption produces a simple expression for the probability of the data, given a probabilistic specification of model M_c. If we denote by $P_{kh} = (p_{khij})$ the transition probability matrix of the MC for variable X_h in cluster C_k, the probability of observing data S, given the set of probabilities $\theta = (p_k, p_{khij})$ is

$$p(S|\theta) = \prod_{k=1}^{c} p_k^{m_k} \prod_{h=1}^{v} \prod_{ij=1}^{s} p_{khij}^{n_{khij}}$$

where n_{khij} denotes the frequency of transition $(i \to j)$ observed in all the time series generated by the MC with transition probability matrix P_{kh} in cluster C_k, and m_k is the number of sets of time series assigned to cluster C_k. The probability $p(S|\theta)$ is derived as follows. The quantity $\prod_{ij=1}^{s} p_{khij}^{n_{khij}}$ is the probability of observing the transition $(i \to j)$ with frequency n_{khij} in a time series generated from a MC with transition probability matrix P_{kh}. In other words, $\prod_{ij=1}^{s} p_{khij}^{n_{khij}}$ is the probability of observing the time series assigned to the hth component of cluster C_k. Since MCs in a cluster C_k are independent, the probability of the data observed in the whole cluster C_k is computed as the product $\prod_{h=1}^{v} \prod_{ij=1}^{s} p_{khij}^{n_{khij}}$. The joint probability of the data is then computed by simply multiplying these quantity over all clusters defining the partition M_c.

Since quantity $p(S|\theta)$ is a function of the unknown parameter vector θ, in order to maximize the marginal likelihood $p(S|M_c)$, we need to average these unknown parameters out by using prior information. A standard Bayesian solution is to adopt sets of independent Dirichlet prior distributions with hyper-parameters α_{khij}, one Dirichlet for each conditional distribution $(p_{khij})_j$, and one Dirichlet distribution with hyper-parameters β_k for the distribution (p_k) over the clusters. The hyper-parameters α_{khij} and β_k encode prior knowledge about the probabilities p_{khij} and p_k in terms of the ratios $\alpha_{khij}/\sum_j \alpha_{khij}$ and $\beta_k/\sum_k \beta_k$. With this prior specification, the marginal likelihood $p(S|M_c)$ is given by

$$p(S|M_c) = \frac{\Gamma(\sum_k \beta_k)}{\Gamma(\sum_k \beta_k + m)} \prod_{k=1}^{c} \frac{\Gamma(\beta_k + m_k)}{\Gamma(\beta_k)} \times$$

$$\prod_{k=1}^{c} \prod_{h=1}^{v} \prod_{i=1}^{s_h} \frac{\Gamma(\sum_j \alpha_{khij})}{\Gamma(\sum_j [\alpha_{khij} + n_{khij}])} \prod_{j=1}^{s_h} \frac{\Gamma(\alpha_{khij} + n_{khij})}{\Gamma(\alpha_{khij})}$$

where $\Gamma(\cdot)$ is the Gamma function. When $v = 1$, that is, there is only one variable and S is a set of univariate time series, $p(S|M_c)$ equals the expression of the marginal likelihood provided by Sebastiani et al. (2000). Once the *a posteriori* most likely partition has been selected, the set of transition probability matrices P_{kh} associated with the cluster C_k can be estimated as

Similarity Measure

S	X_1	$\cdots$	X_v	D
S_k	P_{k1}	$\cdots$	P_{kv}	
S_l	P_{l1}	$\cdots$	P_{lv}	
	$\downarrow$		$\downarrow$	
	D_{kl1} +	$\cdots$ +	D_{klv}	$\to D_{kl}$

Figure 2: Computation of the similarity measure between two sets of MCs.

$$\hat{p}_{khij} = \frac{\alpha_{khij} + n_{khij}}{\sum_j [\alpha_{khij} + n_{khij}]}$$

and the probability of $C = C_k$ can be estimated as

$$\hat{p}_k = \frac{\beta_k + m_k}{\sum_k \beta_k + m}.$$

The marginal likelihood is a function of the hyper-parameters α_{khij} and β_k. A convenient choice is to set the initial $a = m \times \prod_h s_h^2$ hyper-parameters α_{khij} equal to α/a. In this way, the specification of the prior hyper-parameters requires only the prior precision α, which measures the overall confidence in the prior model. An analogous procedure can be applied to the hyper-parameters β_k associated with the prior estimates of p_k.

Heuristic Search

The number of possible partitions grows exponentially with the number of multivariate time series, and a brute force search in the set of partitions would be infeasible. We introduce here a similarity-based heuristic search. The intuition behind the heuristic is that we have better chances of increasing the marginal likelihood when we merge *similar* clusters. Therefore, if we merge first more similar clusters, we have better chances of reaching the maximum posterior probability partition sooner.

To implement this method, we need to define a measure of similarity able to guide the search process. Our approach is sketched in Figure 2. Recall that each set P_k is a collection of v transition probability matrices P_{kh}, one for each variable X_h. Transition probability matrices P_{kh} and P_{lh} in two sets P_k and P_l are comparable only when they refer to the same variable X_h, and rows with the same index are probability distributions conditional on the same event and they are, therefore, comparable. Thus, a measure of similarity between two sets of MCs can be constructed by evaluating a row-by-row distance between pairs of comparable transition probability tables P_{kh} and P_{lh} and then by summarizing this row-by-row distance for all tables. The measure of similarity currently used by MBCD is an average of the Kullback-Liebler distances between comparable tables so that, by letting p_{khij} and p_{lhij} be the probabilities of transition $(i \to j)$ in P_{kh} and P_{lh}, the Kullback-Liebler distance of the two probability distributions in row i is $D_{klhi} = \sum_j p_{khij} \log(p_{khij}/p_{lhij})$. The average distance between P_{kh} and P_{lh} is then $D_{klh} = \sum_i D_{klhi}/s_h$, with s_h denoting the number of states of variable X_h, and the overall distance between the two sets S_k and S_n is $\sum_h D_{klh}$.

Iteratively, MBCD computes all pairwise distances between sets of transition probability tables, sorts the generated distances, merges the two closest sets and evaluates the result. The evaluation asks whether the new model M_c, in which two sets of MCs are merged, is more probable than the model M_{c+1} in which these sets are separated, given data S. If the probability $p(M_c|S)$ is larger than $p(M_{c+1}|S)$, MBCD replaces the two sets of MCs with the cluster resulting from their merging. Then, MBCD updates the set of ordered distances and repeats the procedure on the reduced set space. If the probability $p(M_c|S)$ is not larger than $p(M_{c+1}|S)$, MBCD tries to merge the second best, the third best, and so on, until no further merging is possible and, in this case, MBCD returns the most probable partition found so far. Note that the similarity measure is just used as a heuristic guide for the search process rather than a grouping criterion.

Evaluation

We evaluated the technique four ways. First, we compared the partitions found by MBCD with those produced by another clustering technique and by a human judge. Second, we developed a measure of the quality of partitions and showed that MBCD partitions score significantly higher than random partitions. Third, we examined MBCD partitions by hand to see whether they make sense. Fourth, we tested MBCD with different values of the prior precision parameter. In previous work, Schmill et al. (1999) constructed a set of 102 trials in which a Pioneer 1 robot interacted with objects in its environment, moving toward or past objects, pushing them, reversing away from them, and so on. Each trial produced two qualitatively different kinds of multivariate time series: a series of a vector of continuous values from roughly 40 sensors, and a series of symbolic states. States are lists of symbolic propositions; for example, ((:STOP :R) (:IS-RED :A) (:IS-OBJECT :A)) is a state in which the robot is stopped and perceives a red object. Schmill et al. clustered the 102 trials in the data set by hand, and also ran a clustering algorithm based on dynamic time warping on the sensor time series, and compared the two sets of clusters S_1 and S_2 as follows: For every pair of trials i and j, record an *agreement* if i and j reside in a single cluster in S_1 and also reside in a single cluster in S_2, or i and j reside in different clusters in S_1 and also reside in a different cluster in S_2. The *concordance* of S_1 and S_2 is just the total number of agreements divided by the total number of pairs of trials. Schmill et al. report concordances greater than 0.9 in a variety of conditions. We apply the same procedure to the same set of 102 trials, computing concordances between MBCD and human clustering, and MBCD and clustering based on dynamic time warping. The results are very good. For the partition MBCD produces with prior precision equal to one, the concordance between MBCD's partition and the human partition is 0.82, and the concordance between MBCD's partition and the dynamic time warping partition is 0.81. To test whether these numbers are significant, we devised a randomization procedure to answer the question, "what is the expected value of the concordance statistic under the null hypothesis that the trials in a partition are distributed in random clusters?" Suppose a partition contains c clusters and each cluster i contains n_i trials. A random partition is generated by randomly selecting (without replacement) trials to construct c clusters of sizes $n_1 \ldots n_c$. The expected value of the concordance between a partition p and a random partition is easily obtained by generating a few hundred random partitions r_i, recording the concordance between p and r_i, and taking the mean of the resulting distribution of r_i. For the partition produced with prior precision equal to one, the expected value of the concordance with a random partition is .73, and the standard deviation of the distribution of r_i is .004. There is essentially no chance that a concordance between two partitions greater than .8 could arise if one of the partitions was random.

Any measure of the quality of a partition must reflect the principle that the similarity of items within clusters is high relative to the similarity of items in different clusters. MBCD clusters episodes, so we need a measure of the similarity of episodes, and ideally it should not be identical to the Kullback-Leibler metric that guides MBCD's search for partitions, because by design MBCD performs well according to that metric. Recall that each state in an episode is a set of propositions (e.g.,((:MOVING-BACKWARD :R) (:IS-RED :A) (:IS-OBJECT :A))). We say a proposition is *frequent* in an episode if the proposition appears in at least $p\%$ of the episode. Let P_1 and P_2 be sets of propositions that are frequent in episodes 1 and 2, respectively. Then a simple measure of similarity, $s = \frac{\|P_1 \cap P_2\|}{\|P_1 \cup P_2\|}$, is the proportion of propositions frequent in either episode that are frequent in both episodes. Let $\bar{s}_i$ be the mean s for all pairs of episodes in cluster i, and let n_i be the number of episodes in that cluster. We want to know whether, for all clusters i, $\bar{s}_i$ is significantly higher that expected under the null hypothesis that MBCD performs no better than an algorithm that builds clusters by grouping randomly-selected episodes. The hypothesis is tested for each cluster by a simple randomization procedure: For cluster i, for c from 1 to k, select n_i episodes at random and calculate $\bar{s}_{i,c}$. The distribution of k values of $\bar{s}_{i,c}$ serves as a sampling distribution of $\bar{s}_i$ under the null hypothesis that clustering is random. The upper 99th percentile of this distribution, $\bar{s}_{i,0.99}$ serves as a critical value; if $\bar{s}_i > \bar{s}_{i,0.99}$, we reject the null hypothesis that cluster i was formed by a random algorithm, with $p \leq .01$. Values of $\bar{s}_i$ and $\bar{s}_{i,0.99}$ for a run of MBCD with prior precision $\alpha = 1$ are shown in Table 1. All of the results are highly significant, MBCD is performing much better than a random algorithm.

Cluster	Mean Similarity	Critical value
1	.5339	.4430
2	.4974	.4008
3	.5780	.4070
4	.7124	.4540
5	.5526	.3741
6	.4696	.3770
7	.6603	.3980

Table 1: Significance values with prior precision $\alpha = 1$.

Qualitatively, the clusters produced by MBCD seem to make sense. Consider the seven clusters produced with prior precision equal to one. The first involves nine trials in which the robot moves toward objects A and C, sometimes bumping A, sometimes C. The second cluster, ten trials, involves the robot moving backwards. In four of these trials, C is the only object in view; in the other six trials, A becomes visible during the trial (by reversing, the robot increases the number of objects visible in its view). The third cluster is a bit of a mess: In all 17 trials, the robot moves forward and object C remains visible throughout. In ten trials, the robot bumps C; in seven trials, object B becomes visible during the trial; and in two trials, object A makes an appearance. In cluster 4, the robot moves forward, all three objects appear, with C in front of B and A appearing late (four trials); or A doesn't appear (two trials). In cluster 5, the robot approaches A in each of 24 trials, and bumps it in 11 trials. Object C enters the picture during 11 trials but disappears before the end of the trial. Cluster 6 incorporates 18 trials in which the robot is either moving forward or moving backward with no object in view, as well as three trials in which either A or C are in view. Cluster 7 also includes forward and backward movement (6 and 9 trials, respectively) in which object A remains in view, appears, or disappears (3, 3, and 9 trials, respectively). Finally, we ran MBCD with several values of the prior precision parameter. Qualitatively, increasing prior precision yields partitions with slightly larger numbers of clusters; the smallest partition contained seven clusters, the largest, sixteen. However, episodes that are grouped together under one value of prior precision are overwhelmingly likely to be grouped together under another: The average concordance of partitions across different values of prior precision is roughly 0.95.

Related and Future Work

Essential features of the MBCD algorithm are the model used to describe univariate time series, the intra-cluster structure of dependency, the model-based Bayesian approach to clustering and the heuristic search. These four features together make the algorithm different from other approaches to clustering multivariate time series.

MBCD uses first order MCs: the simplest model for a time series. More complex models involve the use of

k-order MCs (Saul & Jordan 1999), in which the memory of the time series is extended to a window of k time steps, or Hidden Markov Models (Rabiner 1989), in which hidden variables are introduced to decompose the unknown auto-regressive structure of the time series into smaller components. MBCD can be easily extended to cluster sets of k-order MCs by modifying the expression for the marginal likelihood. Clustering multivariate time series modeled as Hidden Markov Models was considered by Smyth (1997) and future work will compare this approach with MBCD, to point out when one approach is preferable to the other. In another approach known as Dynamic Time Warping (Berndt & Clifford 1996), a series is stretched and compressed within intervals to make it fit the other as well as possible. The intuition behind the method is to cluster time series that have similar shapes. The work has recently been extended by Oates *et al.* (1999) to cluster time series generated from sensory inputs of a mobile robot. Our results, although limited to a single application, showed agreement between the two clustering methods and we are planning a more comprehensive comparison.

Closer to our approach is model-based clustering, originally developed by Banfield & Raftery (1993) to cluster static data and then applied by Smyth (1999) to time series. The probabilistic model used to represent multivariate clustering and its heuristic search sets MBCD apart. The rationale of the heuristic search is that merging sets of similar MCs first should result in better models and increase the posterior probability earlier in the search process. Although the current implementation of MBCD uses the Kullback-Liebler distance to build a similarity measure, other distances could be used and we are currently exploring the effect of replacing the Kullback-Liebler distance with other distance measures.

Conclusions

This paper presented the MBCD algorithm to cluster sets of multivariate time series. The algorithm regards a multivariate time series as a set of univariate time series, models each univariate time series as a MC and clusters sets of MCs using an entropy based heuristic search and a Bayesian scoring metric. An evaluation on a set of multivariate time series showed that the algorithm produces clusters which are significantly different from random clustering and in agreement with human clustering.

Acknowledgments

This research is supported by DARPA/AFOSR under contracts Nos F49620-97-1-0485 and N66001-96-C-8504. The U.S. Government is authorized to reproduce and distribute reprints for governmental purposes notwithstanding any copyright notation hereon. The views and conclusions contained herein are those of the authors and should not be interpreted as necessarily representing the official policies or endorsements either expressed or implied, of DARPA/AFOSR or the U.S. Government.

References

Banfield, J. D., and Raftery, A. E. 1993. Model-based gaussian and non-gaussian clustering. *Biometrics* 49:803–821.

Berndt, D. J., and Clifford, J. 1996. Finding patterns in time series: A Dynamic programming approach. In Fayyad, U. M.; Piatestsky-Shapiro, G.; Smyth, P.; and Uthurusamy, R., eds., *Advances in Knowledge Discovery and Data Mining*. Cambridge, MA: MIT Press. 229–248.

Cohen, P.; Ramoni, M.; Sebastiani, P.; and Warwick, J. 2000. Unsupervised clustering of robot activities: A Bayesian approach. In *Proceedings of the Fourth International Conference on Autonomous Agents (Agents 2000)*. New York, NY: ACM Press.

Oates, T.; Schmill, M. D.; and Cohen, P. R. 1999. Identifying qualitatively different experiences: Experiments with a mobile robot. In *Proceedings of the Sixteenth International Joint Conference on Artificial Intelligence (IJCAI-99)*. San Mateo, CA: Morgan Kaufman.

Rabiner, L. 1989. A tutorial on Hidden Markov Models and selected applications in speech recognition. *Proceedings of the IEEE* 77(2):257–285.

Ross, S. M. 1996. *Stochastic Processes*. New York, NY: Wiley.

Saul, L. K., and Jordan, M. I. 1999. Mixed memory markov models: Decomposing complex stochastic processes as mixture of simpler ones. *Machine Learning* 37:75–87.

Schmill, M. D.; Oates, T.; and Cohen, P. R. 1999. Learned models for continuous planning. In *Proceedings of the Seventh International Workshop on Artificial Intelligence and Statistics (Uncertainty 99)*. San Mateo, CA: Morgan Kaufman. 278–282.

Sebastiani, P.; Ramoni, M.; Cohen, P.; Warwick, J.; and Davis, J. 1999. Discovering dynamics using Bayesian clustering. In *Proceedings of the Third International Symposium on Intelligent Data Analysis (IDA-99)*. New York, NY: Springer. 199–209.

Sebastiani, P.; Ramoni, M.; and Cohen, P. 2000. Bayesian analysis of sensory inputs of a mobile robot. In *Case Studies in Bayesian Statistics*. New York, NY: Springer.

Smyth, P. 1997. Clustering sequences with hidden Markov models. In Mozer, M.; M.I.Jordan; and T.Petsche., eds., *Advances in Neural Information Precessing*. Cambridge, MA: MIT Press. 72–93.

Smyth, P. 1999. Probabilistic model-based clustering of multivariate and sequential data. In *Proceedings of the Seventh International Workshop on Artificial Intelligence and Statistics (Uncertainty 99)*. San Mateo, CA: Morgan Kaufman. 299–304.

Toward a Theory of Learning Coherent Concepts

Dan Roth   Dmitry Zelenko

Department of Computer Science
University of Illinois at Urbana-Champaign
{danr,zelenko}@cs.uiuc.edu

Abstract

We develop a theory for learning scenarios where multiple learners co-exist but there are mutual compatibility constraints on their outcomes. This is natural in cognitive learning situations, where "natural" compatibility constraints are imposed on the outcomes of classifiers so that a valid sentence, image or any other domain representation is produced.

We suggest that work in this direction may help to resolve the contrast between the hardness of learning as predicted by the current theoretical models and the apparent ease at which cognitive systems seem to learn.

A model of concept learning is studied in which the target concept is required to cohere with other concepts of interest. The coherency is expressed via a (Boolean) constraint that the concepts have to satisfy. Under this model, learning a concept is shown to be easier (in terms of sample complexity and mistake bounds) and the concepts learned are shown to be more robust to noise in their input (attribute noise). These properties are established for half spaces and the connection to large margin theory is discussed.

Introduction

The emphasis of the research in learning theory is on the study of learning single concepts from examples. In this framework the learner attempts to learn a single hidden function from a collection of examples (or more expressive modes of interaction) and its performance is measured when classifying future examples. The theoretical research in this direction (Valiant 1984; Vapnik 1995) has already proved useful in that it has contributed to our understanding of some of the main characteristics of the learning phenomenon as well as to applied research on classification tasks (Druker, Schapire, & Simard 1993; Golding & Roth 1999). One puzzling problem from a theoretical and a practical point of view, is the contrast between the hardness of learning problems – even for fairly simple concepts – as predicted by the theoretical models, and the apparent ease at which cognitive systems seem to learn those concepts. Cognitive systems seem to use far less examples and learn more robustly than is predicted by the theoretical models developed so far.

In this paper we begin the study of a new model within which an explanation of this phenomenon may be developed. Key to this study is the observation that cognitive learning problems are do not usually occur in isolation. Rather, the input is observed by multiple learners that may learn different functions on the same input. In our model, the mere existence of the other functions along with the constraints Nature imposes on the relations between these functions – all unknown to the learner – contribute to the effective simplification of each of the learning tasks.

Assume for example that given a collection of sentences where each word is tagged with its part-of-speech (pos) as training instances, one wants to learn a function that, given a sentence as input, predicts the pos tag of the ith word in the sentence. E.g., we would like to predict the pos tag of the word `can` in the sentence `This can will rust`[1]. The function that predicts this pos may be a fairly complicated function of other tokens in the sentence; as a result, it may be hard to learn. Notice, however, that the same sentence is supplied as input to the function that predicts the pos of the word `will` and that, clearly, the predictions of these functions are not completely independent. Namely, the presence of the function for `will` may somewhat constrain the function for `can`. For example, the constraint may be that these functions never produce the same output when evaluated on a given sentence. This exemplifies our notion of coherency: given that these two functions need to produce coherent outputs, the input sentence may not take any possible value in the input space of the functions (that it could have taken when the function's learnability is studied in isolation) but rather may be restricted to a subset of the inputs on which the functions outcomes are coherent.

The learning scenario is that of concept learning from examples, where a learner is trying to identify

---

[1] This may not be the exact way one chooses to model the problem (Brill 1995; Roth & Zelenko 1998). However, this is a reasonable abstraction that helps deliver the intuition behind our point of view.

a concept $f \in \mathcal{F}$ when presented with examples labeled according to f. We study learning in the standard pac (Valiant 1984) and mistake bound (Littlestone 1988) learning models. It is well known that learnability in the pac model depends on the complexity of the hypothesis class. Specifically, it is equivalent to the finiteness of the VC-dimension (Vapnik & Chervonenkis 1971), a combinatorial parameter which measures the richness of the function class (see (Vapnik 1995; Kearns & Vazirani 1994) for details). Moreover, it is known (Blumer et al. 1989; Ehrenfeucht et al. 1989) that the number of examples required for learning is linear in the VC-dimension of the class. Mistake bound learning is studied in an on-line setting (Littlestone 1988); the learner receives an instance, makes a prediction on it, and is then told if the prediction is correct or not. The goal is to minimize the overall number of mistakes made throughout the learning process. The usual way to constrain the learning task is to explicitly restrict the concept class. Instead, here we are mostly concerned with the case in which the restriction is imposed implicitly via interaction between concepts. More precisely, we are interested in a learning scenario that involves several concepts $f_1, f_2, \ldots, f_k$ from the concept class $\mathcal{F}$. Let $g : \{0,1\}^k \to \{0,1\}$ be any Boolean function of k variables. The notion of coherency we study is formalized by assuming that the concepts $f_1, f_2, \ldots, f_k$ are subjected to a constraint g. In all cases, however, we are interested in learning a single function $f_1 \in \mathcal{F}$ under these conditions.

There exists several possible semantics for the coherency conditions and here we present only the one that we find most promising in that we can present results that indicate that the task of learning f becomes easier in these situations. We then study the effect of the coherence assumption on the robustness of the learned concepts. In particular, we study the robustness of learnable concepts to attribute noise. This type of robustness is important in cognitive systems, where multiple concepts are learned and "chained" (Valiant 1999; Khardon, Roth, & Valiant 1999). Namely, the output of one learned predictor may be used as input to another learned predictor. Errors in the output of one predictor therefore translate to attribute noise in the input to another, and predictors have to tolerate it to support chaining well; we show that learning coherent concepts is robust and briefly discuss relations to large margin classification and future work.

Class Coherency

Before getting to the main definition we introduce a condition that turns out to be too strong and leads to a restriction on the function class.

Let $\mathcal{F}$ be a concept class over X. The direct k-product $\mathcal{F}^k$ of the concept class $\mathcal{F}$ is the set $\mathcal{F}^k = \{f : f = (f_1, \ldots, f_k), f_i \in \mathcal{F}, i = 1, \ldots, k\}$. That is, if $f \in \mathcal{F}^k$, $f : X \to \{0,1\}^k$. Thus, learning k functions with a binary range can be reduced to learning a single function with range $\{0, \ldots, 2^k - 1\}$. The following theorem (Ben-David et al. 1995) states that this transformation (and its inverse) preserves PAC learnability[2].

Theorem 1 $\mathcal{F}^k$ is learnable iff $\mathcal{F}$ is learnable.

Definition 1 (Class Coherency) Let $\mathcal{F}$ be a concept class and $g : \{0,1\}^k \to \{0,1\}$ a Boolean constraint. $\mathcal{F}_g^k \subseteq \mathcal{F}^k$ is a coherent collection of functions if $\mathcal{F}_g^k = \{(f_1, \ldots, f_k) \in \mathcal{F}^k : \forall x \in X, (g(f_1(x), \ldots, f_k(x)) = 1)\}$.

Intuitively we can think of g as reducing the range of functions in $\mathcal{F}^k$. That is, if $Y = g^{-1}(1)$, then we do not care about elements $f \in \mathcal{F}^k$ for which $range(f) \not\subseteq Y$.

The observation that a constraint g reduces the range of the functions in $\mathcal{F}^k$ leads to the following sample size bound for pac-learning $\mathcal{F}^k$ (immediate from (Ben-David et al. 1995)).

Theorem 2 Let $m = |g^{-1}(1)|$. Then, the pac learning sample complexity of $\mathcal{F}_g^k$ is $O(\frac{1}{\epsilon}(d(\log m)\log\frac{1}{\epsilon} + \log\frac{1}{\delta}))$ where d is any appropriate capacity measure of $\mathcal{F}_g^k$.

Example 1 Let $\mathcal{F}$ be the class of axis-parallel rectangles inside $[0,1]^2$. Let $g(f_1, f_2) \equiv (f_1 \neq f_2)$. Then $\mathcal{F}_g^2$ is the class of the pairs (f_1, f_2) of axis-parallel rectangles, where f_1 is the complement of f_2 in $[0,1]^2$. Note that in this case $\mathcal{F}_g^2$ is a class of functions with the binary range $\{01, 10\}$. For binary-valued functions, the appropriate capacity measure of Theorem 2 is the VC-dimension of $\mathcal{F}_g^2$. It is not difficult to see that three points can be shattered by the concept class, but no four points can. Therefore, $VCD(\mathcal{F}_g^2) = 3$; however, $VCD(\mathcal{F}) = 4$ and, hence, Theorem 2 implies that the sample complexity of learning the concept class $\mathcal{F}$ alone is greater than the sample complexity of learning it in the presence of other functions when they are all constrained by g. Thus, adding more concepts may make learning easier.

While definition 1 captures the simultaneous nature of the learning scenario, it is too restrictive in that it imposes global constraints on all the k functions. We would like to relax this further and emphasize that the goal here is to study the learnability of a single function, say, f_1, and how it is affected by the presence of the other functions and the requirement that they behave coherently. The next section develops the main definition of this paper.

Distributional Coherency

In the previous section we removed from $\mathcal{F}^k$ any f, such that $g(f(x)) = 0$ for some $x \in X$. Now, we change the semantics of the constraint imposed on the direct product $\mathcal{F}^k$. For each $f \in \mathcal{F}^k$, we simply restrict the domain of f to X', where $\forall x \in X', g(f(x)) = 1$.

Definition 2 (Distributional Coherency) Given a Boolean constraint g and a class $\mathcal{F}$ of functions, we define the class of g-coherent functions $\mathcal{F}_g^\star$ to be the

---

[2] PAC learnability for multi-valued functions is shown to be characterized by the finiteness of a capacity measure of a function class, see (Ben-David et al. 1995) for details.

collection of all functions $f^\star : X \to \{0,1\}^k \cup \{\star\}$ in $\mathcal{F}^k$ defined by

$$f^\star(x) = \begin{cases} f(x) & \text{if } g(f(x)) = 1 \\ \star & \text{otherwise} \end{cases}$$

We interpret the value of "$\star$" as a forbidden value for the function f. In this way we restrict the domain of f to the subset X' of X satisfying the constraint g.

The constraint semantics in Def. 1 is stronger (more restricting) than the one in Def. 2. E.g., let $\mathcal{F}$ be the class of (non-identically false) monotone DNF, and g is $(f_1 \neq f_2)$. Then, $\mathcal{F}_g^2$ is empty, because $f_1(1) = 1 = f_2(1)$, for any $f_1, f_2 \in F$. But, in $\mathcal{F}_g^\star$, we simply restrict the domain of each f_1, f_2 to the non-overlapping areas of f_1, f_2.

In the pac learning model the above constraint can be interpreted as restricting the class of distributions when learning a function $f_1 \in \mathcal{F}$. Only distributions giving zero weight to the region $X \setminus X'$ are allowed.

Definition 3 Let $\mathcal{F}$ be a class of Boolean functions over X. Let $f_1, \ldots, f_k \in \mathcal{F}$ be subjected to a constraint g. Then, a distribution D over X is said to be f_1-compatible w.r.t to $f_2, \ldots, f_k \in \mathcal{F}$ and g, if $D\{x : f^\star(x) = \star\} = 0$, where $f = (f_1, \ldots, f_k)$. We denote by $\mathcal{D}_{f_1}$ the class of all f_1-compatible distributions (w.r.t to $f_2, \ldots, f_k \in \mathcal{F}$ and g).

To motivate investigation into the gain one might expect to have in this learning scenario, consider the following example.

Example 2 Let $\mathcal{F}$ be the class of disjunctions. Consider learning f_1 from examples, in the presence of f_2 and the constraint $g \equiv (f_1 \neq f_2)$. Suppose that both f_1 and f_2 include a literal l. The constraint implies that X' does not contain examples where l is 1 and effectively reduces the size of the target disjunction f_1 since the existence of literals common to f_1 and f_2 in the target disjunction is irrelevant to predictions on X'. Thus, if n_1, n_2 is the number of literals in f_1, f_2, respectively, n_c is the number of common literals, then using a feature efficient algorithm like Winnow (Littlestone 1988) to learn f_1 in the presence of f_2 and the constraint g gives an improved mistake bound of $2(n_1 - n_c)(\log n_1 + 1)$.

The only model we know of that is related to the model studied here is the one studied in (Blum & Mitchell 1998). Our model can be viewed as a generalization of the Blum and Mitchell model. They study learning two functions f_1, f_2 over different domains (X_1 and X_2, respectively), where the learner sees only pairs $(x_1, x_2) \in X = X_1 \times X_2$ that satisfy $f_1(x_1) = f_2(x_2)$. This is a special case of our model, when $x = (x_1, x_2)$ and the functions f_1, f_2 are defined over subdomains X_1, X_2 rather than the whole X. In example 2, if restricted to monotone disjunctions, we get the domain decomposition for free, because the constraint forces the literal sets of the disjunctions to be disjoint. Thus, by applying the results of (Blum & Mitchell 1998)[3], one can quantify the reduction in the number of examples needed for learning constrained monotone disjunctions. Next we analyze a more general case of learning in the coherency model.

Learning Linear Separators

Let $\mathcal{F}$ be the class of half-spaces in R^2 and let g be $(f_1 = f_2)$. f_1 and f_2 are depicted in Figure 1. The arrows point in the direction of the positive half-spaces with respect to the corresponding lines. The constraint g restricts the domains of both f_1 and f_2 to the shaded areas. Therefore, when learning f_1 (and similarly, f_2) we will see examples only from the shaded areas $X' \subseteq X$. For $x \in X'$, $f_1(x) = f_2(x)$. While, in principle, learning f_1 may be hard due to examples nearby the separator, now there are many linear separators consistent with $f_1(x)$. Therefore, at least intuitively, finding a good separator for $f_1(x)$ would be easier. For the case when the linear separator is learned via the Perceptron learning algorithm, we can show the following. (Proof omitted. The theorem is stated for the constraint $(f_1 = f_2)$ but can be phrased to any symmetric constraint.)

Theorem 3 Let f_1 and f_2 be two hyperplanes (w.l.o.g, passing through the origin) with unit normals $w_1, w_2 \in R^n$, respectively. Let $\alpha = \cos(w_1, w_2) = w_1 \cdot w_2$. Let $S = S^+ \cup S^-$ be the sequence of positive and negative examples so that $\forall x \in S, f_1(x) = f_2(x)$. Let S be linearly separable by both f_1 and f_2 with margins $2\delta_1$ and $2\delta_2$, respectively. If $\sup_{x \in S} |x| < R$ then the number of mistakes the Perceptron makes on S is bounded by $\beta \frac{R^2}{\delta^2}$, where $\beta = \frac{1+\alpha}{2}, \delta = \frac{\delta_1 + \delta_2}{2}$.

The general Perceptron mistake bound is $\frac{R^2}{\delta^2}$ (Novikoff 1963), where δ is the margin of the target hyperplane. The presence of f_2 and the constraint g improves the mistake bound by a factor of β. As the shaded regions become smaller, α approaches -1, and, hence, β approaches 0.

While Theorem 3 shows the gain in mistake bound when learning w_1 (as a function of w_2 and the constraint) it is possible to quantify this gain in an algorithmic independent way by characterizing the set $E(w_1, w_2)$ of linear separators consistent with the imposed constraint[4]. Given w_2 and the constraint g, denote by $E(w_1, w_2)$ the set of all linear separators that can be learned without any loss in accuracy when the target concept is w_1. Formally (omitting the dependence on g from the notation), for any two vectors $w_1, w_2 \in R^n$, let $X' = \{x : x \in R^n, sgn(w_1 \cdot x) = sgn(w_2 \cdot x)\}$. That is, X' corresponds to the shaded area in Figure 1. Then:

$$E(w_1, w_2) = \{w : w \in R^n, \forall x \in X', sgn(w \cdot x) = sgn(w_1 \cdot x)\}$$

Theorem 4 uses the well-known Farkas' Lemma (Mangarasian 1969) from linear programming.

---

[3]The results in (Blum & Mitchell 1998) require in addition certain conditional independence assumptions.

[4]The set $E(w_1, w_2)$ depends on the constraint g. The results in this section can be presented for any symmetric constraint on w_1, w_2, but will be presented, for clarity, only for equality.

Lemma 1 For any $m \times n$ matrix A and vector c in R^n, either

$$\{x : Ax \leq 0, c \cdot x > 0\} \text{ is non-empty} \quad (1)$$

or

$$\{y : A^T y = c, y \geq 0\} \text{ is non-empty} \quad (2)$$

but never both.

We now have:

Theorem 4 $E(w_1, w_2) = \{w : w = aw_1 + bw_2; a, b \in R; a, b > 0\}$.

Proof: Denote $W = \{w : w = aw_1 + bw_2; a, b \in R; a, b > 0\}$. Clearly, $W \subseteq E(w_1, w_2)$. In order to prove that $E(w_1, w_2) \subseteq W$, we partition X' in two sets,

$$X'_+ = \{x : x \in R^n, w_1 \cdot x \geq 0, w_2 \cdot x \geq 0\}$$

and

$$X'_- = \{x : x \in R^n, w_1 \cdot x \leq 0, w_2 \cdot x \leq 0\}.$$

Observe that $X'_- = \{-x : x \in X'_+\}$. Fix a $w \in R^n$, so that $w \cdot x \geq 0$ on X'_+. Hence, $w \cdot x \leq 0$ on X'_-, and $w \in E(w_1, w_2)$. Now apply Lemma 1 with $A = \binom{w_1}{w_2}$ (A is an $2 \times n$ matrix whose rows are w_1, w_2), and $c = w$. Since $w \cdot x \leq 0$ on X'_-, (1) is not satisfied; hence, (2) is satisfied, and $w = aw_1 + bw_2$, where a, b are some positive numbers. Thus, $E(w_1, w_2) \subseteq W$. $\square$

Requiring the members of $E(w_1, w_2)$ to be unit vectors, unconstrained learning of f_1 can be viewed geometrically as searching for a point on the unit sphere that is close to the target w_1. In the presence of w_2 and the constraint, we have:

Corollary 1 The intersection of $E(w_1, w_2)$ with the unit sphere is a curve on the unit sphere in R^n connecting w_1 to w_2, with length $cos^{-1}(w_1 \cdot w_2)$.

Thus in the presence of w_2 and the constraint, it is sufficient now for the learning algorithm to find a point on the sphere that is close to any of the curve points; algorithmically, for the Perceptron, this translates to reducing the mistake bound proportionally to the length of this curve.

Robustness

In this section we show that the coherence assumption made in this paper has the effect of making the learned concepts more robust. We start by defining robustness and proving that concepts learned under this model can indeed be evaluated robustly (generalizing previous models of attribute noise); we then show that learning coherent concepts is robust and discuss the relation to large margin theory.

Definition 4 (Attribute Robustness) For $x, y \in \{0, 1\}^n$ let $H(x, y)$ be the Hamming distance between x and y (that is, the number of bits on which x and y differ). Let $S_k(f) = \{x : \forall y, \text{ if } H(x, y) \leq k \text{ then } f(x) = f(y)\}$. We say that the pair (D, f) is (ϵ, k)-robust, if $D(S_k(f)) > 1 - \epsilon$.

Intuitively, the condition means that w.h.p. all the points in a ball of radius k around any point x have the same label. This can be relaxed by requiring $f(y) = f(x)$ to hold only for a $(1 - \gamma)$ portion of the points in the ball $B_k = \{y : H(x, y) \leq k\}$, but we will not discuss this to simplify technical details.

Let f be a concept over $X = \{0, 1\}^n$ and let D be a distribution over X. We denote by D^k_{flip} the distribution that results from choosing k bits uniformly and flipping them. It is easy to see that if (D, f) is (ϵ, k)-robust, and $x \in S_k(f)$, then flipping k bits of x does not change the value of f. Hence, $error_{D^k_{flip}}(f) \leq D(x \notin S_k(f)) \leq \epsilon$ and the robustness condition guarantees a small error when evaluating f on the noisy distribution. It follows that if h is an ϵ-good hypothesis for f under D, and if (D, f) is (ϵ, k)-robust, then h is a 2ϵ-good hypothesis under D^k_{flip}.

We note that the distribution D^k_{flip} is an example of an attribute noise model (Goldman & Sloan 1995; Decatur & Gennaro 1995). These models usually assume the presence of noise in the learning stage and aim at learning a good approximation of the target concept over the original noiseless distribution. However, as can be readily seen (and has been pointed out in (Goldman & Sloan 1995)), in a more realistic setting in which the learned hypothesis is to be evaluated under noisy conditions, this hypothesis may be useless. The robustness condition defined above guarantees that a hypothesis learned in the presence of noise also performs well when being evaluated under these conditions. This holds for a more general attribute noise model, the product attribute noise, defined as follows. Let D be a distribution on the instance space $X = \{0, 1\}^n$. Assume that an attribute i of an example $x \in X$ sampled according to D is flipped independently with probability p_i, $i = 1, \ldots, n$. Denote by $p = \sum_{i=1}^n p_i$ the expected number of bits flipped in an example. We denote the distribution induced this way on X by D^p_{flip}.

Theorem 5 Let (D, f) be (ϵ, k)-robust. If $k \geq p + \sqrt{2n \ln \frac{1}{\epsilon}}$, then $error_{D^p_{flip}}(f) \leq 2\epsilon$.

Proof: Let $(x, f(x))$ be an example sampled according to D. Let x' be the result of flipping the bits of x according to the noise scheme described above. Denote by Pr the product distribution induced by the bit flipping. Then we have:

$$\begin{aligned}
error_{D^p_{flip}}(f) &= D^p_{flip}\{x' : f(x') \neq f(x)\} \\
&= D^p_{flip}\{x' : x \in S_k, f(x') \neq f(x)\} + \\
&\quad D^p_{flip}\{x' : x \notin S_k, f(x') \neq f(x)\} \\
&\leq D^p_{flip}\{x' : x \in S_k, f(x') \neq f(x)\} + \\
&\quad \epsilon \leq Pr\{H(x, x') > k\} + \epsilon
\end{aligned}$$

To bound $Pr\{H(x, x') > k\}$, we let Y be the random variable describing the number of bits flipped in an example. Note that $Y = H(x, x')$ and $E[Y] = p$. Also let

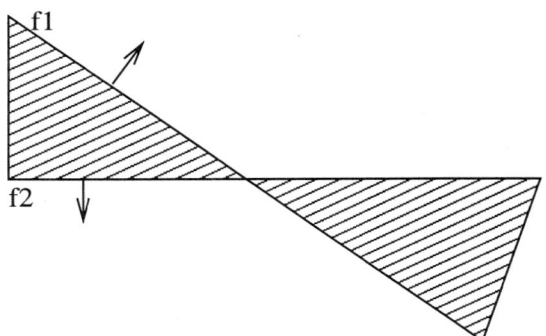

Figure 1: Constrained Half-spaces in R^2.

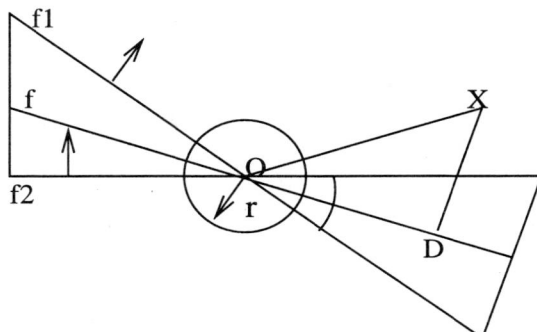

Figure 2: Constrained Robust Half-spaces

$m = \sqrt{2n \ln \frac{1}{\epsilon}}$. Then,

$Pr\{Y > k\} = Pr\{Y > p+m\} = Pr\{Y - E[Y] > m\} \leq e^{\frac{-m^2}{2n}}$,

where the last inequality follows directly from the Chernoff bounds (Hoeffding 1963). Hence, $Pr\{H(x, x') > k\} \leq \epsilon$, and $error_{D^p_{flip}}(f) \leq 2\epsilon$. □

Thus, if we have an ϵ-good hypothesis for noiseless distribution, and the target concept with the underlying distribution satisfy the above (ϵ, k)-robustness condition then the hypothesis will also be 3ϵ-good for the noisy distribution.

Coherency implies Robustness

We now establish the connection between coherency and robust learning. This is done again in the context of learning linear separators. As before, the target function is f_1, and we assume the presence of f_2 (w.l.o.g., both f_1, f_2 pass through the origin), and that they are subjected to the equality constraint g. However, here we restrict the domain of f_1 and f_2 to $X = \{0, 1\}^n$. Let D be a distribution over X. We require the distribution to give small weight to points around the origin. Formally, let $B_r = \{x : x \in X, |x| \leq r\}$ be the origin-centered ball of radius r. Then we require D to satisfy $D(B_r) < \epsilon$.

Notice that in general, when learning a single linear separator f, this property of D does not imply that (D, f) is robust. The following theorem shows that with the equality constraint imposed, the property is sufficient to make (D, f) robust.

Theorem 6 Let f_1 and f_2 be hyperplanes over $\{0, 1\}^n$ (through the origin) with unit normals $w_1, w_2 \in R^n$, respectively. Let $\alpha = \cos(w_1, w_2) = w_1 \cdot w_2$. Let D be a f_1-compatible distribution (w.r.t f_2 and the equality constraint g) that satisfies $D(B_r) < \epsilon$, where $r > k\sqrt{\frac{2}{1-\alpha}}$. Then, there is a linear separator f, so that $D(x : f(x) \neq f_1(x)) = 0$ and f is (ϵ, k)-robust.

Proof: (Sketch) The idea of the proof is to exhibit a linear separator f that is consistent with f_1 on D and, for all points lying outside B_r, has a large "margin" separating positive examples from negative ones. Let f be the hyperplane bisecting the angle between f_1 and f_2. That is, $w = \frac{1}{2}(w_1 + w_2)$, where w is the normal vector of f. By theorem 4, $w \in E(w_1, w_2)$; hence, $D(x : f(x) \neq f_1(x)) = 0$. Now fix a point $x \in R^n$, so that $f_1(x) = f_2(x)$ and $x \notin B_r$. Figure 2. is the projection of f_1, f_2, f to the 2-dimensional plane determined by the origin, the point x and x's projection onto f. (Notice that in Figure 2 X' is the complement of the shaded region in Figure 1.) Then we have that $|XD| = |x|\sin(XOD) \geq r\sqrt{\frac{1-\alpha}{2}}$. If $r > k\sqrt{\frac{2}{1-\alpha}}$, then $|XD| > k$, hence flipping $\leq k$ bits of x will not change the value of f ($|XD|$ is the distance from x to f). Therefore, f is $(0, k)$-robust for any point of the subdomain X' satisfying the constraint and lying outside of the ball B_r (and robustness grows as the size of X' decreases). This implies that (D, f) is (ϵ, k)-robust. □

We note that the assumption $D(B_r) < \epsilon$ in the Theorem 6 is satisfied if there is a margin r separating positive examples of f_1 from its negative examples (Vapnik 1995), so that the weight (with respect D) of examples lying inside the margin is less than ϵ. Also, existence of such a distributional margin implies that a sample of examples from the distribution will be linearly separable with margin at least r with high probability, thus guaranteeing that there is a large margin hyperplane consistent with the sample, that has small error with respect to D (Freund & Schapire 1998). In particular, we construct such a hyperplane f in the proof of Theorem 6.

Conclusions

This paper starts to develop a theory for learning scenarios where multiple learners co-exist but there are mutual compatibility constraints on their outcomes. We believe that these are important situations in cognitive learning, and therefore this study may help to resolve some of the important questions regarding the easiness and robustness of learning that are not addressed adequately by existing models. In addition, we view this model as a preliminary model within which to study learning in a multi-modal environment. Several classifiers feed from the same data, each makes predictions with respect to some facets of the target concept, depending on the modality (identifying images of dogs, identifying barks, etc.). However, these predictions need to satisfy constraints by virtue of representing different aspects of the same concept; this is exactly the situation studied in the coherency model introduced here.

We have shown that within this model the problem of learning a single concept – when it is part of an existing collection of coherent concepts – is easier than in the general situation. Moreover, this gain is due only to the existence of the coherency, even if the learner is unaware of it. Although the results of this paper are restricted mostly to linear separators we do not view this as a severe restriction given their universal nature in theory and applications (Roth 1999; Cortes & Vapnik 1995).

Some of the future directions of this work include the study of coherent concepts under more general families of constraints as well as algorithmic questions that arise from this point of view. These include, in particular, algorithmic questions that aim at exploiting the constraints in order to better learn coherently behaving concepts as in (Munoz et al. 1999).

Acknowledgments

This research is supported by NSF grants IIS-9801638 and IIS-9984168.

References

Ben-David, S.; Cesa-Bianchi, N.; Haussler, D.; and Long, P. M. 1995. Characterizations of learnability of $\{0,\ldots,n\}$-valued functions. Journal of Computer and System Sciences 74–86.

Blum, A., and Mitchell, T. 1998. Combining labeled and unlabeled data with co-training. In Proc. of the Annual ACM Workshop on Computational Learning Theory, 92–100.

Blumer, A.; Ehrenfeucht, A.; Haussler, D.; and Warmuth, M. K. 1989. Learnability and the Vapnik-Chervonenkis dimension. Journal of the ACM 36(4):929–865.

Brill, E. 1995. Transformation-based error-driven learning and natural language processing: A case study in part of speech tagging. Computational Linguistics 21(4):543–565.

Cortes, C., and Vapnik, V. 1995. Support-vector networks. Machine Learning 20:273–297.

Decatur, S. E., and Gennaro, R. 1995. On learning from noisy and incomplete examples. In Proc. of the Annual ACM Workshop on Computational Learning Theory, 353–360.

Druker, H.; Schapire, R.; and Simard, P. 1993. Improving performance in neural networks using a boosting algorithm. In Neural Information Processing Systems 5, 42–49. Morgan Kaufmann.

Ehrenfeucht, A.; Haussler, D.; Kearns, M.; and Valiant, L. 1989. A general lower bound on the number of examples needed for learning. Information and Computation 82(3):247–251.

Freund, Y., and Schapire, R. 1998. Large margin classification using the Perceptron algorithm. In Proc. of the Annual ACM Workshop on Computational Learning Theory, 209–217.

Golding, A. R., and Roth, D. 1999. A Winnow based approach to context-sensitive spelling correction. Machine Learning 34(1-3):107–130. Special Issue on Machine Learning and Natural Language.

Goldman, S. A., and Sloan, R. H. 1995. Can PAC learning algorithms tolerate random attribute noise? Algorithmica 14(1):70–84.

Hoeffding, W. 1963. Probability inequalities for sums of bounded random variables. Journal of the American Statistical Association 58(301):13–30.

Kearns, M., and Vazirani, U. 1994. Introduction to computational Learning Theory. MIT Press.

Khardon, R.; Roth, D.; and Valiant, L. G. 1999. Relational learning for NLP using linear threshold elements. In Proc. of the International Joint Conference of Artificial Intelligence.

Littlestone, N. 1988. Learning quickly when irrelevant attributes abound: A new linear-threshold algorithm. Machine Learning 2:285–318.

Mangarasian, O. L. 1969. Nonlinear Programming. McGraw-Hill.

Munoz, M.; Punyakanok, V.; Roth, D.; and Zimak, D. 1999. A learning approach to shallow parsing. In EMNLP-VLC'99, the Joint SIGDAT Conference on Empirical Methods in Natural Language Processing and Very Large Corpora.

Novikoff, A. 1963. On convergence proofs for perceptrons. In Proceeding of the Symposium on the Mathematical Theory of Automata, volume 12, 615–622.

Roth, D., and Zelenko, D. 1998. Part of speech tagging using a network of linear separators. In COLING-ACL 98, The 17th International Conference on Computational Linguistics, 1136–1142.

Roth, D. 1999. Learning in natural language. In Proc. Int'l Joint Conference on Artificial Intelligence, 898–904.

Valiant, L. G. 1984. A theory of the learnable. Communications of the ACM 27(11):1134–1142.

Valiant, L. G. 1999. Robust logic. In Proceedings of the Annual ACM Symp. on the Theory of Computing.

Vapnik, V. N., and Chervonenkis, A. Y. 1971. On the uniform convergence of relative frequencies of events to their probabilities. Theory of Probability and its applications XVI(2):264–280.

Vapnik, V. N. 1995. The Nature of Statistical Learning Theory. New York: Springer-Verlag.

Empirical Evaluation of a Reinforcement Learning Spoken Dialogue System

Satinder Singh and **Michael Kearns** and **Diane J. Litman** and **Marilyn A. Walker**

AT&T Labs
180 Park Avenue
Florham Park, NJ 07932
{baveja,mkearns,diane,walker}@research.att.com

Abstract

We report on the design, construction and empirical evaluation of a large-scale spoken dialogue system that optimizes its performance via reinforcement learning on human user dialogue data.

Introduction

The formalisms of Markov decision processes (MDPs) and reinforcement learning (RL) have become a standard approach to many AI problems that involve an agent learning to improve performance by interaction with its environment (Sutton, 1991; Kaelbling et al., 1996). While the theory of these formalisms is quite advanced, applications have been limited almost exclusively to problems in control, operations research, or game-playing (e.g., Crites and Barto, 1995; Tesauro, 1995). In this paper, we describe an application of RL to a rather different type of problem, in which the MDP models a system's interaction with a population of human users, and RL is used to optimize the system's performance.

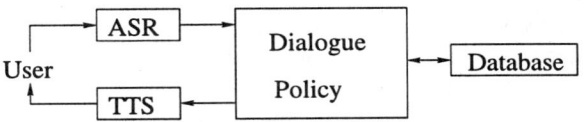

Figure 1: A block diagram representation of a spoken dialogue system.

We have adapted the methods of RL to the problem of automatically learning a good dialogue policy in a *spoken dialogue system* (SDS). The different components of an SDS are shown in block diagram form in Figure 1. In a typical SDS, the user speaks to the system in real time through the telephone, using free-form natural language, in order to retrieve desired information from a back-end database component. The user's speech is interpreted through an automatic speech recognition (ASR) component. The *dialogue policy* decides what the system should say (or in RL terminology, which *action* it should take), again in natural language, through a text-to-speech (TTS) component, at each point in the dialogue.

S1: Welcome to RLDS. How may I help you?
U1: What wineries in Lambertville are open in the morning? [ASR output: *what wineries in Lambertville open in the morning.*]
S2: Did you say you are interested in Lambertville?
U2: Yes.
S3: I found a winery near Lambertville that is open in the morning. It is ... Please give me feedback by saying 'good', 'so-so', or 'bad'.
U3: Good.

Figure 2: A transcription of an example spoken dialogue with our NJFun system. This dialogue happened to go very well, and is relatively short. In general, dialogue length varied between 3 and 20 exchanges between user and system.

Figure 2 shows the transcription of a sample spoken dialogue from the NJFun system we implemented to provide telephone access to a database of activities in New Jersey. In this dialogue, by starting with the open-ended greeting "How may I help you?", the system lets the *user* take the *initiative* in providing information about the activity they are interested in. User responses in such cases may be relatively unconstrained. In contrast, the *system* could take the initiative by saying the more restrictive phrase "Please tell me the location you are interested in", thus constraining the user to provide information about the location of the activity. Which of these contrasting choices of user or system initiative is superior may depend strongly on the properties of the underlying and imperfect ASR, the population of users, as well as the dialogue so far. This choice of initiative occurs repeatedly throughout a dialogue, and is but one example of a class of difficult design decisions.

The traditional, or what we shall call Monte Carlo, approach to learning dialogue policies from data is to pick a set of dialogue policies that experts intuitively feel are good, implement each policy as a separate SDS, collect data from many representative human users for each SDS, and then use standard statistical tests to pick the best dialogue policy and system according to some performance criterion or reward measure (the choice of which we will say more about later).

Copyright © 2000, American Association for Artificial Intelligence (www.aaai.org). All rights reserved.

Only a handful of dialogue policies can be compared this way because of the cost and time of using human subjects. On the other hand, as we will show for our system, many thousands of dialogue policies may still be left after the experts have excluded all policies that are clearly suboptimal.

In this paper we show that the methods of RL are well-suited to the problem of searching the large space of policies that survive after pruning by experts. At a high level, our RL methodology involves the choice of appropriate reward measures and estimates for dialogue state, the deployment of an initial training system that generates deliberately exploratory dialogue data, the construction of an MDP model of user population reactions to different action choices, and the redeployment of the system using the optimal dialogue policy according to this model. This RL method is more data-efficient than the Monte Carlo method, because it evaluates actions as a function of state rather than evaluating entire policies.

While RL has been applied to dialogue system design in previous research (Biermann and Long, 1996; Levin et al., 1997; Walker et al., 1998; Singh et al., 1999), this paper provides a larger scale test of these ideas. We describe our design and implementation of the NJFun system and our controlled experiments with human users verifying our RL-based methodology. The results we describe here provide empirical evidence that, when properly applied, RL can quantitatively and substantially improve dialogue system policy. For example, one of our main results is that the rate of task completion rose from 52% in the training system to 63% in the learned system. In a companion paper (Litman et al., 2000), we describe the same basic system and experiment, but focus on details and analyses more relevant to computational linguistics (such as linguistic analyses of the learned policy, and novice versus expert performance).

Our system and experiments help focus attention on the many challenges spoken dialogue systems present to the prevailing theory and application of RL. These include the fact that the Markov property cannot be guaranteed in an application modeling human users, the difficulty of balancing the need for exploratory data with the need for a functioning training system, and the inherent difficulty of obtaining large amounts of training data in such applications.

Choices in Dialogue Policy

For our purposes, an ASR can be viewed as an imperfect, noisy sensor with an adjustable "parameter" (the *language model* or *grammar*) that can be tuned to influence the types of speech recognition mistakes made. In addition to any perceived matches in the utterance, the ASR also returns a score (typically related to log-likelihood under a hidden Markov model) giving a subjective estimate of confidence in the matches found. This score is important in interpreting the ASR results.

In this work, we concentrate on automating two important types of decisions faced in dialogue policy design, both of which are heavily colored by the ASR facts above. The first type, of which we have already seen an example, is choice of *initiative* — namely, whether the system at any given point should prompt the user in a relatively open-ended manner (often referred to as *user* initiative) or a relatively restrictive manner (*system* initiative).

The second type of choice we investigate is that of *confirmation*. After it has applied the ASR to a user utterance, and obtained a value for some attribute of interest (for instance, town = Lambertville), the system must decide whether to confirm the perceived utterance with the user. In Figure 2, for example, the system chooses to confirm the location but not the activity type (wineries) or the activity time (morning). While we might posit that confirmation is unnecessary for high values of the ASR confidence, and necessary for low values, the proper definitions of "high" and "low" would ideally be determined empirically for the current state (for instance, depending on whether there has been difficulty on previous exchanges), and might depend on our measure of system success.

In the NJFun system, we identified many different dialogue states for which we wanted to *learn* whether to take user or system initiative for the next prompt. Similarly, we identified many different dialogue states in which we wanted to learn whether to confirm the ASR-perceived user utterance, or not to confirm. The actual prompts used in each case were hand-coded; we learn only the choice of initiative and the choice of confirmation, not what natural language utterances to generate. We note that there is genuine and spirited debate over choices of initiative and confirmation among dialogue system designers (Danieli and Gerbino, 1995; Haller and McRoy, 1998, 1999; Smith, 1998; Walker et al., 1998), which is precisely why we wish to automate, in a principled way, the process of making such choices on the basis of empirical data.

RL for Dialogue Policy Design

In this section, we describe the abstract methodology we propose to apply RL to dialogue policy design. In the next section, we will describe in detail the instantiation of this methodology in the NJFun system.

In order to apply RL to the design of dialogue policy, it is necessary to define a *state-based* representation for dialogues. One obvious but impractical choice for this state is a transcript or system log of the entire dialogue so far, which would include the audio so far, the utterances matched by the ASR, the language models used, the confidence scores returned by the ASR, and perhaps many other quantities. In practice, we would like to compress this state as much as possible — representing states by the values of a small set of features — without losing information necessary for making good decisions. We view the design of an appropriate state space as *application-dependent*, and a task for a skilled system designer.

Given choices for the state features, the system designer can think in terms of the state space, and appropriate actions to take in each state. For some states, the proper action to take may be clear (for instance, greeting the user in the start state, or querying the database when all informational attributes are instantiated). For other states, the system designer may debate a choice of actions that may best be determined by *learning* (such as choices of initiative and confirmation). Each mapping from such choice-states to a particular action is a distinct *dialogue policy*.

We also assume that the system designer has chosen a particular *reward function* that can be measured with relative ease on any given dialogue, that takes on scalar values, and whose expectation over the user population is to be maximized. The subject of appropriate measures for dialogue system success is a complex one, and there are many natural choices (Danieli and Gerbino, 1995; Walker et al., 1998), including user satisfaction measures, measures of task completion, and sales figures (in commercial applications). In our empirical results, we commit to a task completion reward measure for the optimization, but also examine several other common reward measures.

Thus, our methodology requires as a starting point that the designer choose a state representation and a reward function, and for perhaps a large number of states, to identify a fixed number of actions to be chosen from. Suppose that the designer implements an initial dialogue policy, and collects a set of dialogues from a sample of the user population. Each dialogue, of course, is a sequence of alternating system and user utterances terminated by a scalar reward:

$$s_1 \to_{a_1, r_1} s_2 \to_{a_2, r_2} s_3 \to_{a_3, r_3} \cdots$$

where the notation $s_i \to_{a_i, r_i} s_{i+1}$ indicates that at the ith exchange, the system was in state s_i, executed action a_i, received reward r_i, and then the state changed to s_{i+1}. From many such sequences, we can estimate *transition probabilities* of the form $P(s'|s, a)$, which denotes the probability of a transition to state s', given that the system was in state s and took action a. Our estimate of this probability is simply the number of times, in all of the dialogues, that the system was in s, took a, *and* arrived in s', divided by the number of times the system was in s and took a (regardless of next state). Similarly, we can estimate a reward function that maps states and actions to rewards. For the reward functions we will examine, the rewards will be nonzero only at terminal states.

The estimated reward function and transition probabilities constitute a *Markov decision process* (MDP) model of the user population's interaction with the system[1]. It (hopefully) captures the stochastic behavior of the users when interacting with the system. Note that in order to have any confidence in this model, the training data must have tried many possible actions from many possible states, and preferably many times. In other words, the training data must be *exploratory* with respect to the chosen states and actions. Perhaps the most straightforward way of ensuring exploratory training data is to take actions randomly. While this is the approach we take, it requires that we be exceptionally careful in designing the actions allowed at each state, in order to guarantee that the random choices made always result in a dialogue sensible to human users. (Keep in mind that there is no exploration in states where the appropriate action is already known and fixed by the system designer.) Other approaches to generating exploratory data are possible.

The final step is to determine the optimal policy in the estimated MDP using a dynamic programming algorithm such as value iteration (e.g., Kaelbling et al., 1996), and then to implement this policy as the learned dialogue policy. To the extent that the estimated MDP is an accurate model of the user population, this final system should maximize the reward obtained from *future* users. Here is a summary of the proposed methodology:

- I. Choose an appropriate reward measure for dialogues, and an appropriate representation for dialogue states.
- II. Build an initial state-based *training* system that creates an *exploratory* data set. Despite being exploratory, this system should provide the desired basic functionality.
- III. Use these training dialogues to build an empirical MDP model on the state space.
- IV. Compute the optimal dialogue policy according to this MDP.
- V. Reimplement the system using the learned dialogue policy.

The NJFun System

In this section, we describe the functionality and construction of the spoken dialogue system on which we tested our methodology. The back-end database for our system contained information on interesting places to visit in New Jersey. The database was indexed by three keys: the activity type (such as historic sites, wineries, museums, etc.); the name of the New Jersey town in which the activity is located (such as Morristown or Lambertville); and the hours in which the place is open. As an example, the Liberty Science Center is indexed under activity type museum, location Jersey City, and hours 10 AM to 6 PM. We binned activities into 9 activity types, and there were 149 distinct database entries[2]. The goal of NJFun is to help the user find all database entries matching a given binding of the desired activity type, location, and period of the day (morning, afternoon, or evening). For any given binding of these three attributes, there may be multiple database matches, which will all be returned to the user.

The system represents the current state of any dialogue by the values of six different state features, whose possible values and meanings are described in Figure 3. At a high level, these state variables tell the system which attribute it is currently working on, whether it has obtained a value for this attribute, what the confidence in that value is, how many attempts have been made to get a value for the attribute, what type of ASR grammar was most recently used, and an indication of whether there have been difficulties in earlier portions of the dialogue. We note that this state representation, in the interests of keeping the state space small, deliberately ignores potentially helpful information about the dialogue so

---

[1]Note that this MDP model is at best an approximation. With a small set of state features, there will be the problem of hidden state or partial observability, for which the richer POMDP model is often more appropriate (e.g., Kaelbling et al., 1996). We leave the use of POMDP models to future work.

[2]To support continuous use, the system's functionality could be extended in a number of ways such as a larger live database and support for followup questions by the users.

Feature	Values	Explanation
Attribute	1,2,3	Which attribute is being worked on
Confidence/ Confirmed	0,1,2, 3,4	0,1,2 for low, medium, and high ASR confidence 3,4 for explicitly confirmed, and disconfirmed
Value	0,1	Whether value has been obtained for current attribute
Tries	0,1,2	How many times current attribute has been asked
Grammar	0,1	Whether open or closed grammar was used
History	0,1	Whether there was trouble on any previous attribute

Figure 3: State features and values.

far. For example, there is no state feature explicitly tracking the average ASR score over all user utterances so far, nor do we keep information about previous attributes [3].

With the state space precisely defined, we can now provide some more detail on the *policy class* we considered[4]. This policy class is obtained by allowing a choice of system or user initiative whenever the system needs to ask or reask for an attribute, and by allowing a choice of confirming or simply moving on to the next attribute whenever the system has just obtained a value for an attribute. For example, in any state in which the *tries* feature has the value 0 and the *attribute* feature has value 1 (which means we are working on activity type, and we have yet to prompt the user for a value for this attribute), the system has a choice of uttering the user initiative prompt "How may I help you", or the system initiative prompt "Please tell me the activity type". In the case of a choice of system initiative, the system has the additional choice of calling the ASR on the user utterance using either a *closed* grammar intended just for that attribute, or an *open* grammar that may correctly recognize information offered on other attributes as well. The open grammar is always used with a user initiative prompt, because the choice of the closed grammar does not make sense in that case.

As another example, choices in confirmation policy are available at states for which the *value* feature is 1 immediately following a prompt to the user for the current attribute. In these states, if the *confidence/confirmed* feature is 0,1 or 2, we allow a choice of whether to confirm the attribute value obtained from the ASR, or to accept the current binding and move on to the next attribute.

We will call the set of all deterministic mappings from the states in which the system has a choice to a particular, fixed choice the *policy class* explored in our experiment. The total number of unique policies in this class was approximately 2^{42}. In keeping with the RL methodology described above, our goal is to compute and implement an approximately optimal policy in this very large class on the basis of RL applied to exploratory training dialogues.

Experimental Methodology

In this section, we describe in some detail the controlled user experiments we conducted. The next section presents the empirical results of these experiments.

Our experimental subjects were 75 fellow employees not involved with the project. The subjects were divided into a training population of 54 people and a test population of 21 people. Although we took the precaution of roughly balancing the male/female, native/non-native and experienced/inexperienced fractions in the training and test sets, subsequent analyses indicated that system performance did not depend significantly on any of these factors. Subjects were not told their training/test classification nor the purpose of our experiments.

As dictated by Step II of the RL methodology above, we first built a *training* version of the system, using the state space and action choices outlined in the preceding section, that used *random exploration*. By this we mean that in any state for which we had specified a choice of system actions, the training system chose randomly among the allowed actions with uniform probability. We again emphasize the fact that the allowed choices were designed in a way that ensured that any dialogue generated by this exploratory training system was intuitively sensible to a human user, and permitted the successful completion of any task the system was intended to perform. Nevertheless, it is important to note that over their multiple calls to the system (see below), training users may have effectively experienced multiple dialogue policies (as induced by the random exploration), while test users experienced a single, fixed, deterministic policy.

We designed a set of six specific tasks each participant was to complete using either the training system or the test system. Each task had an associated web page containing a brief text description of the desired information the participant should obtain, as well as a user survey common to all six tasks[5].

The training participants attempted to complete the six tasks using the exploratory training system. These 54 users generated a total of 311 dialogues[6]. These dialogues were then annotated with an objective *binary task completion* reward function. Since system logs could be matched with which of the six tasks the user was attempting, it was possible to directly compute from the system logs whether or not the user had completed the task. By "completed" we mean binding all three attributes (activity type, location, and time of day) to the exact values specified in the task description given on the associated web page. In this way, each training dialogue was automatically labeled by a +1 in the case of

---

[3]The system of course stores the actual values of previous attributes for the eventual database query, but as these do not influence future dialogue policy in any way, they are not stored as state features.

[4]Greater detail on the policy class can be found in a companion paper (Litman et al., 2000).

[5]Some of these survey questions formed the basis for the subjective reward measures examined in the next section.

[6]The total number of dialogues is less than $54 \times 6 = 324$ because a few users failed to attempt all 6 tasks.

a completed task, or −1 otherwise. We note that this definition of task completion guarantees that the user heard all and only the database entries matching the task specifications. Relaxations of this reward measure, as well as other reward measures, are discussed in the next section.

Finally, the 311 training dialogues, labeled by task completion, were used to build an MDP according the RL methodology, and the optimal policy according to this MDP was computed and implemented as the (now deterministic) dialogue policy in the test system.

The test users carried out the same six experimental tasks using the test system. The primary empirical test of the proposed methodology is, of course, the extent and statistical significance of the improvement in the allegedly optimized measure (task completion) from the training to test populations. The next section is devoted to the analysis of this test, as well as several related tests.

Results

Perhaps our most important results are summarized in the first two rows of Figure 4. In the first row, we summarize performance for the *binary completion* reward measure, discussed in the preceding section. The average value of this reward measure across the 311 dialogues generated using the randomized training system was 0.048 (recall the range is −1 to 1), while the average value of this same measure across the 124 dialogues using the learned test system was 0.274, an improvement that has a p-value of 0.059 in a standard two-sample t-test over subject means.

Reward Measure	Train	Test	Δ	p-value
Binary Completion	0.048	0.274	0.226	0.059
Weak Completion	1.72	2.18	0.46	0.029
Reuse	2.87	2.72	−0.15	0.55
Easy	3.38	3.39	0.01	0.98
NJFun understood	3.42	3.52	0.1	0.58
What to say	3.71	3.64	−0.07	0.71
Web feedback	0.18	0.11	−0.07	0.42

Figure 4: Train versus test performance for various reward measures. The first column presents the different reward measures considered (see text for detail); the second column is the average reward obtained in the training data; the third column is the average reward obtained in the test data; the fourth column shows the difference between the test average and the train average (a positive number is a "win", while a negative number is a "loss"); the fifth column presents the statistical significance value obtained using the standard t-test.

We next examine the performance improvement for a closely related reward measure that we call *weak completion*. In weak completion, if *any* attribute is actually bound to an incorrect value (for instance, if the place was bound to Morristown instead of Lambertville when the latter was specified for the task), a reward of -1 is received. If no attribute is actually bound to an incorrect value, the reward is equal to the number of attributes correctly bound (recall that unbound variables are assigned as don't-care). The motivation for this more refined measure is that reward -1 indicates that the information desired was not contained in the database entries presented to the user, while non-negative reward means that the information desired was present, but perhaps buried in a larger set of irrelevant items for smaller values of the reward.

In the second row of Figure 4, we show the improvement in weak completion from training to test[7]. The training dialogue average of weak completion was 1.72 (recall the range is −1 to 3), while the test dialogue average was 2.18. Thus we have a large improvement, this time significant at the 0.029 level. We note that the policy dictated by optimizing the training MDP for binary completion (which was implemented in the test system), and the policy dictated by optimizing the training MDP for weak completion (which was not implemented) were very similar, with only very minor differences in action choices.

Policy	# Trajs.	Emp. Avg.	MDP Value	p-value
Test	12	0.67	0.534	
SysNoconfirm	11	−0.08	0.085	0.06
SysConfirm	5	−0.6	0.006	0.01
UserNoconfirm	15	−0.2	0.064	0.01
UserConfirm	11	0.2727	0.32	0.30
Mixed	13	−0.077	0.063	0.06

Figure 5: Comparison to standard policies. Here we compare our test policy with several standard policies using the Monte Carlo method. The SysNoconfirm policy always uses system initiative and never confirms; the SysConfirm policy always uses system initiative and confirms; the UserNoconfirm policy always uses user initiative and never confirms; the UserConfirm policy always uses user initiative and confirms; the Mixed policy varies the initiative during the dialogue. For each policy, the second column shows the number of consistent trajectories in the training data, the third column shows the empirical average reward on these consistent trajectories, the fourth column shows the estimated value of the policy according to our learned MDP, and the fifth column shows the statistical significance (p-value) of the policy's loss with respect to the test policy. For all but the UserConfirm policy, the test policy is better with a significance near or below the 0.05 level, and the difference with UserConfirm is not significant.

Although these results indicate an improvement in moving from the randomized training policy to the optimized policy, it is natural to ask how our optimized system compares to systems employing a dialogue policy picked by a human expert. Although implementing a number of hand-picked policies, gathering dialogues from them, and comparing to our learned system would be time-consuming and

---

[7] We emphasize that this is the *improvement* in *weak* completion in the system that was designed to optimize *binary* completion — that is, we only fielded a single test system, but examined performance changes for several different reward measures.

expensive (and in fact, is exactly the methodology we are attempting to replace), our training system provides a convenient and mathematically sound proxy. Since our training dialogues are generated making *random* choices, any dialogue in the training set that is *consistent* with a policy π in our policy class provides an unbiased Monte Carlo trial of π. (This is easily verified formally.) By consistent we mean that all the random choices in the dialogue agree with those dictated by π. We can average the rewards over the consistent training dialogues to obtain an unbiased estimate of the return of π.

Figure 5 compares the performance of our learned test system, on the binary completion reward measure, to 5 fixed policies in our class that are common choices in the dialogue systems literature, or that were suggested to us by dialogue system designers. We see that in 4 cases, our learned policy outperforms these standard policies near or below the 0.05 level of significance, and in one case it is essentially tied. (Not surprisingly, the fixed UserConfirm policy that fared best in this comparison is most similar to the policy we learned.) Thus, in addition to optimizing over a large class of policy choices than is considerably more refined than is typical, the RL approach outperforms a number of natural standard policies.

We next discuss a number of other reward measures that we did not optimize the test system for, but for which we nevertheless examined system improvement or degradation. The two measures considered so far, binary and weak completion, are *objective* reward measures, in the sense that the reward is precisely defined as a function of the system log on a dialogue, and can be computed directly from this log. In contrast, we also examined a number of *subjective* measures that were provided by the human user following each dialogue. Each dialogue task was accompanied by a web survey (see Figure 6), on which we asked the user whether they would use the system again (the *Reuse* reward measure, values 1 (worst) to 5 (best)), whether they found the system easy to use (the *Easy* reward measure, values 1 to 5), whether they thought the system understood what they had said (the *NJFun understood* reward measure, values 1 to 5), whether they knew what they could say at each point in the dialogue (the *What to say* reward measure, values 1 to 5), and finally, whether their experience on this dialogue was good, bad, or neutral (the *Web feedback* reward measure, values −1, 0, and 1 respectively).

Since we did not optimize for any of these subjective measures, we had no *a priori* expectations for improvement or degradation, and indeed Figure 4 shows we did not find statistically significant changes in the mean in either direction for these measures. However, we observed a curious *move to the middle* effect in that a smaller fraction of users had extremely positive or extremely negative things to say about our test system than did about the training system. Although we have no firm explanation for this phenomenon, its consistency (it occurs to varying degree for all 5 subjective measures) is noteworthy.

Let us briefly summarize where we are. Our empirical results have demonstrated improvements in the optimized task completion measures of a complex spoken dialogue system,

Please repeat (or give) your feedback on this conversation. (*good, so-so, bad*)
1. Did you complete the task and get the information you needed? (*yes, no*)
2. In this conversation, it was easy to find the place that I wanted.
3. In this conversation, I knew what I could say at each point in the dialogue.
4. In this conversation, NJFun understood what I said.
5. Based on my current experience with using NJFun, I'd use NJFun regularly to find a place to go when I'm away from my computer.

Figure 6: User survey.

and no statistically significant changes in a number of non-optimized subjective measures, but an interesting move to the middle effect.

# of Trajs.	# of Policies	Corr. Coeff.	p-value	Slope	Inter.
> 0	1000	0.31	0.00	0.953	0.067
> 5	868	0.39	0.00	1.058	0.087
> 10	369	0.5	0.00	1.11	0.11

Figure 7: A test of MDP accuracy. We generated 1000 deterministic policies randomly. For each policy we computed a pair of numbers: its estimated value according to the MDP, and its value based on the trajectories consistent with it in the training data. The number of consistent trajectories varied with policy. The first row is for all 1000 policies, the second row for all policies that had at least 5 consistent trajectories, and the last row for all policies that had at least 10 consistent trajectories. The reliability of the empirical estimate of a policy increases with increasing number of consistent trajectories. The third column presents the correlation coefficient between the empirical and MDP values. The fourth column presents the statistical significance of the correlation coefficient. The main result is that the hypothesis that these two sets of values are uncorrelated can be soundly rejected. Finally, the last two columns present the slope and intercept resulting from the best linear fit between the two sets of values.

The skeptic might wonder if we have simply been fortunate — that is, whether our MDP might have actually been a rather poor predictor of the value of actions, but that we happened to have nevertheless chosen a good policy by chance. As some closing evidence against this view, we offer the results of a simple experiment in which we randomly generated many (deterministic) policies in our policy class. For each such policy π, we used the training dialogues consistent with π to compute an unbiased Monte Carlo estimate $\hat{R}_\pi$ of the expected (binary completion) return of π (exactly as was done for the hand-picked "expert" policies in Figure 5). This estimate was then paired with the value R_π of π (for the start state) in the learned MDP. If the MDP were a perfect model of the user population's responses to system actions, then the Monte Carlo estimate $\hat{R}_\pi$ would simply be a (noisy) estimate of R_π, the correlation between these two quantities would be significant (but of course dependent on the number of samples in the Monte Carlo estimate), and the best-fit linear relationship would be simply $\hat{R}_\pi = R_\pi + Z$ (slope 1 and intercept 0), where Z is a normally distributed noise variable with adjustable mean and variance decreasing as the number of consistent trajectories increases. At the other extreme, if our MDP had no relation to the user population's responses to system actions, then $\hat{R}_\pi$ and R_π would be uncorrelated, and the best we could do in terms of a linear fit would be $\hat{R}_\pi = Z$ (slope and intercept 0) — that is, we ignore R_π and simply model $\hat{R}_\pi$ as noise. The results summarized in Figure 7 indicate that we are much closer to the former case than the latter. Over the 1000 random policies π that we generated, the correlation between $\hat{R}_\pi$ and R_π was positive and rejected the null hypothesis that the variables are uncorrelated well below the 0.01 level of significance; furthermore, the least squares linear fit gave a slope coefficient close to 1.0 and a y-intercept close to 0, as predicted by the idealized case above.

Conclusion

In this paper we presented a detailed methodology for using RL in the design of a spoken dialogue system. We built a large dialogue system using our methodology, and showed that RL is able to effectively search a very large space of dialogue policies (2^{42} in size) using a relatively small amount of training dialogue data (311 dialogues from 54 subjects). Our learned policy outperformed not only our training policy, but also many standard dialogue policies from the literature. We also reported on analyses verifying that the learned MDP is a reasonable model of the user population's interaction with NJFun. As future work, we would like to at least partially automate the choice of the state features used in constructing the MDP, explore the use of richer POMDP models, and do additional empirical evaluation of the RL approach.

Acknowledgements The authors thank Fan Jiang for his substantial effort in implementing our NJFun system, Esther Levin and Roberto Pieraccini for help in using their DMD programming language, Weiland Eckert for maintaining the CTmedia platform, Mazin Rahim for help with Watson, and David McAllester, Richard Sutton, Esther Levin and Roberto Pieraccini for numerous helpful conversations on dialogue system design.

References

A. W. Biermann and Philip M. Long. 1996. The composition of messages in speech-graphics interactive systems. In *Proc. of the 1996 International Symposium on Spoken Dialogue*, pages 97–100.

R. Crites and A. Barto. 1996. Improving elevator performance using reinforcement learning. In *Proc. NIPS 8* pages 1017-1023.

M. Danieli and E. Gerbino. 1995. Metrics for evaluating dialogue strategies in a spoken language system. In *Proc. of the 1995 AAAI Spring Symposium on Empirical Methods in Discourse Interpretation and Generation*, pages 34–39.

S. Haller and S. McRoy, eds. 1998. Special Issue: Computational Models of Mixed-Initiative Interaction (Part I) User Modeling and User-Adapted Interaction: An international journal, Vol. 8, Nos. 3–4.

S. Haller and S. McRoy, eds. 1999. Special Issue: Computational Models of Mixed-Initiative Interaction (Part II) User Modeling and User-Adapted Interaction: An international journal, Vol. 9, Nos. 1–2.

L.P. Kaelbling and M.L. Littman and A.W. Moore 1996. Reinforcement Learning: A survey. In *Journal of Artificial Intelligence Research 4*, pages 237–285.

E. Levin, R. Pieraccini, and W. Eckert. 1997. Learning dialogue strategies within the Markov decision process framework. In *Proc. IEEE Workshop on Automatic Speech Recognition and Understanding*.

D. J. Litman, M. S. Kearns, S. Singh, and M. A. Walker. 2000. Automatic Optimization of Dialogue Management. In *Proc. of COLING 2000*.

S. Singh, M. S. Kearns, D. J. Litman, and M. A. Walker. 1999. Reinforcement learning for spoken dialogue systems. In *Proc. NIPS99*.

R. W. Smith 1998. An Evaluation of Strategies for Selectively Verifying Utterance Meanings in Spoken Natural Language Dialog. In *International Journal of Human-Computer Studies*, 48, pages 627–647.

R. S. Sutton. 1991. Planning by incremental dynamic programming. In *Proc. Ninth Conference on Machine Learning*, pages 353–357. Morgan-Kaufmann.

G.J. Tesauro. 1995. Temporal difference learning and TD-Gammon. In *Comm. ACM 38*, pages 58–68.

M. A. Walker, J. C. Fromer, and S. Narayanan. 1998. Learning optimal dialogue strategies: A case study of a spoken dialogue agent for email. In *Proc. of COLING/ACL 98*, pages 1345–1352.

Unsupervised Learning and Interactive Jazz/Blues Improvisation

Belinda Thom
School of Computer Science
Carnegie Mellon University
Pittsburgh, PA 15207 USA
http://www.cs.cmu.edu/~bthom
bthom@cs.cmu.edu

Abstract

We present a new domain for unsupervised learning: automatically customizing the computer to a *specific* melodic performer by merely listening to them improvise. We also describe BoB, a system that trades customized real-time solos with a specific musician. We develop a probabilistic mixture model, derived from the multinomial distribution, for the clustering and generation of variable sample-sized histograms. With this model, bars of a solo are clustered via the pitch-classes contained therein, adding a new dimension to the problem: the need to learn from sparse histograms. With synthetic data, we quantify the feasibility of handling this issue, and qualitatively demonstrate that our approach discovers powerful musical abstractions when trained on saxaphonist Charlie Parker.

Introduction

This research addresses the problem of the computer interacting with a live, improvising musician in real-time. Although a number of interactive improvisational systems have already been built, (Rowe 1993), (Pennycook & Stammen 1993), (Dannenberg & Bates 1995) and (Walker 1997), these works place the burden of implementing "musically-appropriate" behavior upon the musician/composer/programmer. Rather, we have developed a model of improvisation that automatically customizes itself to its user by first listening to them improvise (warmup), and then probabilistically clustering localized segments (**bars**[1]) of their solos in such a way that the warmup data appears maximally likely.

While the long-term goal is to build an agent that is *fun* to trade solos with, the immediate goal is to develop a method that operationalizes (creates a computer algorithm that does) what the musician does. An an improvisor's insight into what makes their behavior musically-appropriate is necessarily non-technical, vague, and abstract (Thom 2000b); in our approach, notions of musical-appropriateness are inferred (learned) by fitting a probabilistic model to the melodic structure found in the user's warmup bars.

Each bar of a warmup is transformed into a **pitch-class** histogram (PCH), which ignores the temporal ordering of a bar's note-sequence, instead focusing on the musician's preference for certain pitch types. We assume that each

Copyright © 2000, American Association for Artificial Intelligence (www.aaai.org). All rights reserved.

[1] Bold-face terms are musical; see Appendix A.

PCH corresponds to one of the improvisor's C "modes-of-playing," each mode being one of the distinct ways in which the user employs and prefers certain musical **scales**. Under certain assumptions, these histograms can be modeled as a mixture of C multinomials, provided the multinomial components are extended to handle a variable number of sample-sizes.

Existing multinomial mixture model based learners handle at most one count, e.g., *AutoClass* (Hanson, Stutz, & Cheeseman 1991), or one-count-per-bin (Meila & Heckerman 1998). We develop a *variable-sized*-multinomial-mixture model (vMn) in order to handle arbitrary numbers of counts. A new variant of the expectation-maximization algorithm (EM) is derived in order to estimate our model's parameters, using a maximum-a-posteriori (MAP) approach.

This *model-based* approach to clustering is important because it provides essential musical skills: 1) abstract perception (what cluster is a bar in?); 2) abstract generation (sample another bar from some cluster); and 3) an estimation of musical surprise (how likely is a bar?). This approach also gives us a degree of statistical confidence that ad hoc methods — e.g., the melodic clustering methods of (Rolland & Ganascia 1996) or (Hörnel & Ragg 1996), which rely on edit-based distance heuristics — lack (McLachlan & Basford 1988).

While in this paper, learning focuses on a solo's simplest **tonal** features (pitch-class), the same technical learning issues that arise here also apply when learning with a more complete representation. For example, (Thom 1999) also considers intervallic and contour-based musical features; by converting these sequences into per-bar histograms, analogous models are learnable.

By fitting the vMn model to the user's training data, we get abstract, *musician-specific* perception: a bar is perceived via what mode (class, cluster, ...) is most likely to have generated it, which in turn *depends upon the user's warmup data*. It necessarily follows that new PCH samples taken from this vMn model (generation) are musician-specific. As outlined in (Thom 2000b), this model provides the skills needed for real-time musician *and* solo specific response, provided PCH samples can be transformed back into musically-appropriate note-sequences. This transformation is addressed in (Thom 2000c); that appropriate note-sequences can be derived from order-ignorant histograms is due to the fact that in the complete representation scheme, histograms embed more temporal knowledge (intervals depend on successive note pairs; contours upon note strings).

In this paper, we describe our solo trading system and its learning scenario. We introduce the vMn model and an EM-based method for fitting its parameters to the training data. We discuss the unique challenge that arises in this domain. Specifically, training sets are small ($\approx$ 120 histograms), and each histogram is relatively sparse (while there are 12 discrete and nominal pitch-class values, the expected number of counts per histogram is $\approx$ 12.2). This research addresses not only *how* to learn a vMn model, but *what* we can learn from challengingly sparse datasets. The "what" question is investigated by: 1) quantitatively evaluating the performance of synthetic datasets; and 2) qualitatively evaluating the musical-appropriateness of the pitch-class modes that are learned for Bebop saxaphonist Charlie Parker.

In addition to presenting a novel domain and demonstrating that powerful musical abstractions emerge with this vMn approach, our work is significant because it empirically demonstrates that probabilistic clustering of sparse, unlabelled histograms is useful. This success is in part due to the fact that we take advantage of the knowledge that per histogram, *all counts are generated by the same component*, whereas "one count" style approaches treat each as independent of the others. Histograms with larger sample-sizes have more information with which to distinguish themselves — it makes sense to directly incorporate this knowledge into the learning process.

Band-out-of-a-Box (BoB)

We are building Band-OUT-of-a-Box (BoB), an interactive soloist that trades bars of a customized solo with a single musician (Thom 2000b). We now describe how BoB's melodic representation is used to configure itself to the user.

The Domain

BoB is specifically designed for the following scenario. Each time the musician wants to trade solos, they first warmup (for $\approx$ 10 minutes), improvising freely over a desired song at a fixed tempo. During this time, BoB collects training data by recording their note-stream in real-time. Next, BoB goes offline, creating training set $X = < x_1, \ldots, x_i, \ldots, x_n >$ by: 1) segmenting the note-stream into bars; 2) building one PCH per bar. (Note our use of upper- and lower-case letters to distinguish between data points and sets). For PCH x_i, an $m = 12$ dimensional histogram, x_{ij} is the number of times that pitch-class j occurs in bar i. $sz_i = \sum_{j=1}^{m} x_{ij}$ is the total sample-size.

BoB uses a stability/usefulness heuristic to *estimate* how many playing modes, $\hat{C}$, are present in the training data, which in turn, allows a $\hat{C}$-component vMM parameterization, $\hat{\Omega}$, to be estimated so that X appears maximally likely.[2] When BoB goes back online, trading bars of solo with the musician in real-time, $\hat{\Omega}$ is used to abstractly perceive and

---
[2]The hat superscript denotes an estimate.

generate new PCHs with: 1) situation and musician based specificity; and 2) per-bar real-time response.

Representational Issues

Solo segmentation is per bar. While this small, *fixed* time window ($\approx$ 2 [sec]) affords fine-grained responsiveness, it means that PCHs are sparse; it is also the reason that sample-size varies.

Offline learning must occur quickly; small training sets are desirable. Also, musically, local context is crucial (Thom 2000a); one cannot assume that combining multiple warmup sessions necessarily yields better customization.

Unsupervised Learning

We now introduce our probabilistic model, $vMn(\Omega)$, a mixture of C *variable-sized* multinomials. Parametric inference is non-trivial when training data is both observable (histogram bin counts) and unobservable (which component generated what histograms). Learning amounts to segregating the histograms according to those bins that are most heavily used (or vacant).

Example

A subset (21 histograms) of sparse, simulated dataset II (described later) is shown in Figure 1. Each subplot is a different histogram. Bin counts are stacked wire boxes. The gray columns reflect the shape of a histogram's generative probabilities, indicating which bins are highly probable, or *important*.

This dataset, generated by seven components, is displayed so that *each column of subplots has the same generator*. Thus, x_1 is generated by the same component as x_8 and x_{15}. As x_1's first bin has three counts, and this bin is gray, we know these counts make x_1 more likely. "×" marked subplots are less likely, so much so that even when the generative model's parameters are known, if we have to *guess* these histogram generators, we would guess incorrectly.

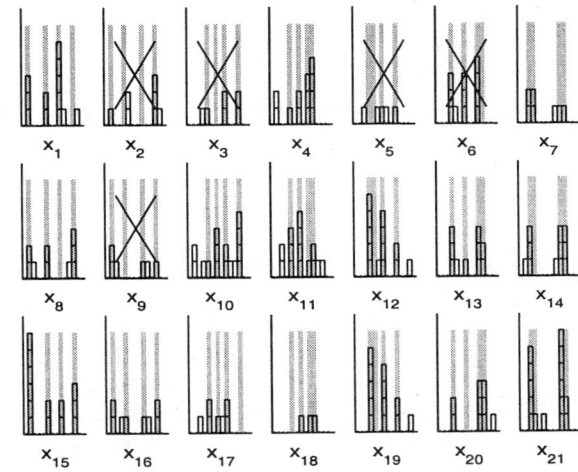

Figure 1: A subset of dataset II

The purpose of this example is to illustrate that learning is *not* trivial. Even knowing the column-arrangement, (which is equivalent to having labels), when the gray columns are hidden, it is not obvious which bins of each component are most important. This figure also illustrates some subtle issues related to sparsity. For example, while smaller than average sample-sizes ($sz_i \leq 8$) coincide with $\frac{4}{5}$ of the ×'s (x_2, x_3, x_5, x_9), the smallest sample-size (x_{18}) is not only correctly classified but also has its counts placed on important bins. On the other hand, while x_{10} has the largest sz, $\frac{1}{3}$ of its counts are misleading (reside on non-important bins). Also, in many cases, counts without gray backgrounds do not hurt classification, although they may hurt learning. On example of this is x_8, where non-important counts happen to reside on bins that do not cause other components to appear more likely.

Larger histogram dimensions mean that more bins *could* be important when estimating generators, which means that sample-size may be distributed amongst more bins, less information regarding a particular bin may be available. On the flip side, more dimensions means less chance for competing components to interfere with one another. Regardless, with sparsity, *specific examples are not likely to contain enough information by themselves,* which also *affords more powerful generalization!* A rigorous probabilistic procedure, one that weighs larger sample-sizes more heavily, especially when they boost other data, is needed.

Music Issues

Modelling PCHs with vMn introduces strong assumptions:

1. For each bar, the musician chooses *at random* from a fixed set of probabilities in order to determine what mode (component) to use. Thus, the musician does not switch modes mid-bar, each bar's mode has nothing to do with its neighboring bar's mode, etc.

2. Per bar, mode and the number of notes played are independent. The number of notes in different bars are also independent.

3. For a given a mode, one pitch-class does not depend upon another (feature independence). Melodically, this means that previously improvised notes do not affect future notes (and vice-versa).

4. Pitch-class bins are nominal/discrete. We do not impose any similarity metric upon pitch-class values.

5. Bars that contain more notes contain more information about what mode the musician is realizing (PCHs are *not* normalized).

The first three items deal with independence, reducing the model's complexity, making it less susceptible to overfitting. As (Nigam *et al.* 1998) notes, the focus on decision boundaries often makes a classifier robust to independence violations. Most serious is Item 1; musical bars certainly affect one another — our datasets are not independently sampled. Fortunately, the quality of our music results empirically validates our approach's usefulness.

Item 4 is crucial. While simpler pitch-class similarity schemes have been used to provide learning feedback — e.g., Euclidean, or the δ-based distance metric used to train melody generation in (Feulner & Hörnel 1994) — other context-dependent aspects (for example, scales) are more perceptible musically (Bartlett 1993). Our *nominal* viewpoint allows another mechanism, and, importantly, a customizable one, to determine pitch-class similarity: how likely is it that certain values are preferred in a given mode?

The Multinomial Distribution

The multinomial family, $Mnom(sz, \theta)$, extends the binomial so as to handle more than two discrete, nominal outcomes. Sample-size sz is *constant*; θ is the r-dimensional probability vector used to weight outcomes $<1, \ldots, 2, \ldots, r>$. When sampling from this distribution, $v \sim Mnom(sz, \theta)$, v is an r-dimensional histogram with sz trials distributed amongst r bins. Histogram likelihood is:

$$\Pr(v|sz, \theta) = \prod_{j=1}^{m} \frac{v_j!}{sz!} (\theta_j)^{v_j}.$$

The vMn Distribution

We now define the variable-sized multinomial mixture model, $vMn(\Omega)$, where $ind(\cdot)$ maps a single-count histogram (vector) into the index of the bin that contains the count (scalar):

$$sz \sim ind(Mnom(1, \eta))$$
$$y = ind(z), \text{ where } z \sim Mnom(1, \pi)$$
$$x|y \sim Mnom(sz, \theta_y).$$

The multinomial components of this model, $\Theta = <\theta_1, \ldots, \theta_c, \ldots, \theta_C>$, control the distribution of counts among bins. Variable sample-size is handled by assuming that a histogram's generator, y, and its sample-size, sz, are independent. Ω refers to parameters Θ, π, and η. $\pi = <\pi_1, \ldots, \pi_c, \ldots, \pi_C>$ controls how often a component is chosen; $\eta = <\eta_{\min(sz)}, \ldots, \eta_{\max(sz)}>$ how often particular sample-sizes occur. The joint likelihood, $<x, y>$, or equivalently $<x, z>$, is:

$$\Pr(x, y|\Omega) = \Pr(sz|\eta)\Pr(y|\pi)\Pr(x|sz, \theta_y).$$

Naive Bayes Classification and vMn

With estimate $\hat{\Omega}$ a Naive-Bayes-Classifier can be built, which maps histograms into one of $\hat{C}$ classes. Bayes-Rule is used to turn the generative model around, so that the *component posteriors,* $\hat{z} = <z_1, \ldots, z_c, \ldots, z_{\hat{C}}>$, can be estimated:

$$z_y = \Pr(y|x, \hat{\Omega}) = \frac{\Pr(y|\hat{\Omega})\Pr(x|y, \hat{\Omega})}{\Pr(x|\hat{\Omega})} = \frac{\hat{\pi}_y \Pr(x|sz, \hat{\theta}_y)}{\sum_{c=1}^{C} \hat{\pi}_c \Pr(x|sz, \hat{\theta}_c)}.$$

Component estimation (abstract perception) is then:

$$\hat{y} = \text{argmax}_c \left(\Pr(c|x, \hat{\Omega}) \right).$$

$\hat{Y}$ and $\hat{Z}$ are the dataset's estimated generators and posteriors respectively. With synthetic data, we also know Y, the true generative components.

With synthetic data, Ω is known, so we can build an Optimal-Bayes-Classifier, whose component estimation (denoted by superscript "*"), is guaranteed to have a minimal expected error rate:

$$err^* = E[y \neq y^*] \approx \frac{|Y \neq Y^*|}{n} = e^*.$$

The "≈" here indicates our estimation of this expectation. err^* quantifies the *hardness* of parameterization Ω, which depends upon the overlap between component distributions, and is a function of the entire input space. Our approximation, e^*, is based on finite dataset X. When the learning algorithm knows C, hardness can also provide a lower bound with which to compute the additional loss of having to infer Ω:[3]

$$\Delta^{err} = E[y \neq \hat{y}] - E[y \neq y^*] \approx \frac{|Y \neq \hat{Y}|}{n} - e^* = \Delta^e.$$

The values of e^* and Δ^e that we report are based on an independent test set.

Unsupervised Learning and vMn

For independent and identically sampled histograms, *average* log-likelihood of *labelled* dataset $<X, Y>$ is:

$$\mathcal{L}_L(X, Y|\hat{\Omega}) = \frac{\log(\Pr(X,Y|\hat{\Omega}))}{n} = \frac{\sum_{i=1}^n \log(\Pr(sz_i|\hat{\eta})) + \log(\hat{\pi}_{y_i}) + \log(\Pr(x_i|sz_i, \hat{\theta}_{y_i}))}{n}. \quad (1)$$

For an *unlabelled* dataset, Y and C are hidden. Average log-likelihood is now the joint marginalized with respect to the posterior:

$$\mathcal{L}_U(X|\hat{\Omega}) = \frac{\log(\Pr(X|\hat{\Omega}))}{n} = \frac{\sum_{i=1}^n \log(\Pr(sz_i|\hat{\eta})) + \log\left(\sum_{c=1}^C z_{ic}\hat{\pi}_c\Pr(x_i|sz_i, \hat{\theta}_c)\right)}{n}. \quad (2)$$

Warmup PCHs are unlabelled; BoB seeks to estimate $\hat{\Omega}$ so that $\mathcal{L}_U$ is maximized. However, $\hat{C}$ must be estimated elsewhere, for to optimize it here is under-constrained.

In vMn, sample-size does *not* affect classification, which is not to say that as sz increases, classification does not become easier. In fact, sz and err^* are inversely related. However, in and of itself, sz provides no information about which component generated a histogram.

With synthetic data, the loss in likelihood associated with having to infer Ω can also be estimated:

$$\Delta^l = l^* - \mathcal{L}_U(X|\hat{\Omega}), \text{ where } l^* = \mathcal{L}_U(X|\Omega)$$

These values are also based on an independent test set.

EM and vMn

Supervised and unsupervised learning both amount to finding an $\hat{\Omega}$ for which their appropriate $\mathcal{L}$ is maximal. It is the log of sums in $\mathcal{L}_U$ that makes its optimization difficult (whereas a closed-form optimum for $\mathcal{L}_L$ exists). $\mathcal{L}_U$'s optimization is non-linear and has multiple roots. We use the EM-algorithm to control the search for local optima (Dempster, Laird, & Rubin 1987). This search is repeated multiple (25) times from different random starting points; the best (most likely) solution is reported.

With each subsequent iteration at time t, EM guarantees that $\mathcal{L}_U(X|\hat{\Omega}^t) \leq \mathcal{L}_U(X|\hat{\Omega}^{t+1})$. In theory, finding a local maximum is equivalent to finding a fixed-point,

---

[3]$\hat{Y}$ must first be permuted to approximate Ω's ordering.

$\mathcal{L}_U(X|\hat{\Omega}^t) = \mathcal{L}_U(X|\hat{\Omega}^{t+1})$. In practice, a computer's precision requires another form of termination (we stop after 8 digits of improvement and/or 1500 iterations).

EM involves two steps per iteration. The E-step calculates $E[\mathcal{L}_L(X, Z|\hat{\Omega}^t)]$. Indicator vector Z is the only random variable, so this expectation amounts to solving $\hat{Z}^t = E[Z|X, \hat{\Omega}^t]$, whose solution is the posteriors, $\hat{z}_i^t = \Pr(y|x_i, \hat{\Omega}^t)$.

In the M-step, $\hat{Z}^t$ is used in place of Z. Ω is re-estimated according to $\hat{\Omega}^{t+1} = \text{argmax}_v(\mathcal{L}_L(X, \hat{Z}^t|v))$. The solution to this equation is

$$\pi_c^{t+1} = \frac{\frac{1}{C} + \sum_{i=1}^n \Pr(z_{ic}|x_i, \hat{\Omega}^t)}{1+n}$$

$$\theta_{cj}^{t+1} = \frac{\frac{1}{m} + \sum_{i=1}^n \Pr(z_{ic}|x_i, \hat{\Omega}^t) x_{ij}}{1 + \sum_{i=1}^n \sum_{j=1}^m \Pr(z_{ic}|x_i, \hat{\Omega}^t) x_{ij}},$$

Both of these estimates are MAP-based: optimal Bayesian parameter estimation, augmented by Laplacean priors on π and θ (Vapnick 1982).

From an improvisational standpoint, the θ priors encode the reasonable musical assumption that no pitch-class is *never* played. The appropriateness of π's priors depends upon the appropriateness of $\hat{C}$; they encode the belief that the musician is never *not* going to use one of their "$\hat{C}$" playing modes.

Estimating C

Estimating C by optimizing $\mathcal{L}_U$ is under-constrained. Rather than adding more constraints, we pick $\hat{C}$ to be the *largest* value that produces a *stable* and *useful* clustering of the training set.

A stable C is defined as one that, when five identical learning experiments are run, produces no disagreements on pair-wise comparisons of solutions. A useful C is defined as one that, on average, is well separated (whose estimated error is below 0.20). Stability quantifies the discrepancies between pairs of solutions' *partitioning* of the training set, shedding light upon how repeatable a learning solution is — how real it is. In BoB, usefulness makes sense: we are most interested in adapting to those playing modes that are markedly different.

Related Work

We know of no other work that empirically validates the feasibility of fully unsupervised vMn learning, or presents learning details for for the fully unsupervised case. While a full-blown vMn style model was used in text-classification (Nigam *et al.* 1998), the focus was on combining labelled and unlabelled data, and sample-size was ignored (histograms were normalized). Fully unsupervised multinomial mixture models usually impose serious restrictions upon the number of samples allowed; in (Hanson, Stutz, & Cheeseman 1991) $sz = 1$. Another common approach, discussed in (Meila & Heckerman 1998), (Hanson, Stutz, & Cheeseman 1991) and (McLachlan & Basford 1988), is to demand that each bin has at most one count. We have developed a new model for this domain because it is important to consider the additional information that larger histograms provide.

Results: Synthetic Data

This domain introduces unique challenges — variable sample-size and sparsity. We now quantify the degree to which learning in such conditions is possible.

In particular, we generate training and test sets with: $C = 7$, $\pi_c = \frac{1}{C}$, $n = 175$ (≈ 25 histograms per cluster), $m = 12$, and $sz \sim Uniform(3, 15)$. On the one hand, we report optimistic results because our learning algorithm knows C. On the other hand, our parameterizations of Ω make learning more difficult than it is likely to be for PCH data. For example, our uniform sz has a larger variance and a smaller mean than Parker's bell-shaped distribution. Also, our components are as "entropic" as possible. Specifically, for each component, four bins are equally *important* (have high probability α of occurring). The other eight bins are equally *non-important* (have low probability β). Each component's important bins are arranged so as to provide maximal interference with the other component's important bins. Thus, discriminating these histograms requires *sets* of features; single features are never sufficient.

We quantified learning performance for three datasets, each harder (having larger e^*) than its predecessors. The values in the right five columns are averaged over 25 experiments. $\Delta^\times$ is the number of misses directly caused by *having* to learn (compare this to $n = 175$ total guesses).

dataset	α	β	l^*	Δ^l	e^*	Δ^e	$\Delta^\times$
I	.248	.001	-9.2	0.18	0.11	0.00	0
II	.21	0.02	-12	0.38	0.22	0.07	12
III	.188	.031	-13	0.40	0.31	0.16	28

While having to learn degrades a classifier's accuracy, and the harder the problem, the worse the degradation, the average cost of having to learn (Δ^e) ranges from negligible to $\frac{1}{2}$ of the optimal (e^*). To add some perspective, consider the worst case, III. We expect to miss 0.47 guesses; an optimal classifier would miss 0.31; a random classifier would miss 0.85. Even with this sparse data (some is shown in Figure 1), learning produces useful results.

Results: Music Data

We now qualitatively argue that our approach produces powerful, customized abstraction when applied to Parker's PCH data. This argument is all the more crucial given that, during solo improvisation, vMn assumptions are likely to be violated.

Our training set was Parker's *Mohawk* improvisations (Goldsen 1978). Figure 2 (left) displays how BoB perceived these solos. Each subsequent row is Parker's next *Mohawk* solo (chorus). The columns are each choruses' bars. The symbol shown in each $< bar, chorus >$ indicates what mode BoB assigned it to. The corresponding mode generator estimates are shown in Figure 2 (right). While $\hat{C} = 4$ and 5 were both stable/useful, solution $\hat{C} = 4$ is presented due to space limitations. Details concerning the **chords**, scales, and melodic styles of the Bebop genre are beyond this paper's scope. The goal here is to merely provide a flavor of the powerful types of musical abstractions that were discussed in (Thom 1999).

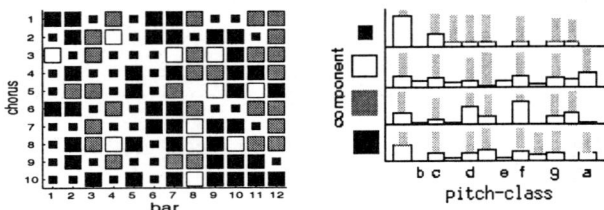

Figure 2: *Mohawk*: Clustering $\hat{Y}$ (left); Parameters $\hat{\theta}_c$ (right)

Several musically appropriate correlations emerge when $\hat{\Omega}$ and $\hat{Y}$ are analyzed. For example, modes ■ and ▪ were most common, accounting for $\frac{80}{119}$ of the bars.[4] The gray backgrounds of these components (right, Figure 2) identify those pitch-classes in the $b^\flat$-Bebop-Major and $e^\flat$-Bebop-Dominant scales respectively. Given the **key** of this song (a 12-bar blues in $b^\flat$), it is appropriate that Parker used these scales, *especially* since they were invented in part to explain his playing style (Baker 1983).

To cite another example, notice the segregation of modes as a function of column (bar), which makes sense given that the chords *change* (and hence the underlying tonal function changes) on bars 1, 5, 7, 9 and 11. A particularly important change occurs in bars 5-6, the only columns in which Parker exclusively uses the Bop-modes. Another case is bars 9-10, the only place were ■ is used more than 50% of the time. Also, bar 12 ends the blues progression. At this point if another chorus is played, it has the musical distinction of being called a "turn-around," whereas if the tune ends, (which is the case in choruses 5 and 10), then a resolution to the tonic ($b^\flat$) is expected. BoB captured Parker's accommodation of these distinctions, using ■ (the $e^\flat$-Major scale) in turn-arounds and restating the tonic via the $b^\flat$-Bop mode.

The component we have not yet discussed, □, exemplifies another powerful aspect of our approach. Notice how all pitch-classes but $e^\flat$ (the bin between d and e) are reasonably probable. While it is musically reasonable to view this component as the $b^\flat$-Major scale (shown in gray), by itself, this viewpoint is limited. For example, with respect to □ we know: 1) how often on average Parker chooses to include non-scalar pitch-classes; 2) that scale-tone $e^\flat$, rather than the non-scalar and musically special "tritone" e, is more surprising; 3) how Parker employs modes in particular contexts (e.g., a choruses' mode-sequence).

In short, a musician's specific improvisational style is *embedded*, or distributed within the learned representation at multiple different and important levels, giving BoB knowledge about what contexts a mode can be used in, what contexts the musician is in, and how to realize a particular mode (i.e., which pitches are most important).

---

[4]No notes were played in $< 5, 8 >$; this bar was omitted.

Conclusion

We have presented a novel domain for unsupervised learning: automatically customizing the computer to its *specific* melodic performer by listening to them improvise. We also described our system BoB, which performs this task in the context of real-time four bar solo trading. We developed a probabilistic mixture model of variable-sized multinomials and a procedure that uses this model to learn how to perceive/generate variable-sized histograms. Because this model was used to cluster per-bar pitch-class histograms, we added a new dimension to the problem: the need to learn from sparse data, and use synthetic data to show that useful results can be learned in this case. We have also shown that when trained on saxophonist Charlie Parker, powerful musical abstractions emerge on many levels. For example, Parker's playing-modes (scales, or sub/supersets of scales) are distributed among a component parameters, which in turn quantifies the relative importance of various pitch-classes, giving us an idea of *how* to realize a particular mode (something rule/scale-based systems must be told how to do). Parker's contextual employment of mode, which allows one to consider generating *new* like-minded contexts, is also embedded within this learned representation, opening up a whole new range of creative possibilities.

Appendix A: Musical Terms

Term	Definition
bar	the grouping caused by the regular recurrence of accented beats, typically 4 taps of a listener's foot (e.g., ≈ 2.5 seconds)
pitch-class (PC)	a pitch's tone, that piano key on the single octave piano that would be played if octave was ignored: $PC \in \{c, d^b, d, ..., b^b, b\}$
octave	two pitches with the same PC and 1:2 frequency ratio
scale	a subset of PC's differing in pitch according to a specific scheme
tonal	the principle of **key** in music conveyed through the family relationship of all its tones and chords, (one affect of this is your being able to sing *doh-re-mi-fa-...* on top of a given harmony/melody)
chord	combination of pitches simultaneously performed, producing more or less perfect harmony

References

Baker, D. 1983. *Jazz improvisation : A Comprehensive Method of Study For All Players*. Frangipani Press.

Bartlett, J. C. 1993. Tonal structure of melodies. In Tighe, T. J., and Dowling, W. J., eds., *Psychology & Music: the Understanding of Melody & Rhythm*. Lawrence Erlbaum Associates, Inc.

Dannenberg, R. B., and Bates, J. 1995. A model for interactive art. In *Proceedings of the Fifth Biennial Symposium for Arts & Technology*, 103–111.

Dempster, A. P.; Laird, N. M.; and Rubin, D. B. 1987. Maximum likelihood from incomplete data via the em algorithm. *Journal of the Royal Statistical Society*.

Feulner, J., and Hörnel, D. 1994. Melonet: Neural networks that learn harmony-based melodic variations. In *Proceedings of the 1994 ICMC*. International Computer Music Association.

Goldsen, M. H., ed. 1978. *Charlie Parker Omnibook: For C Instruments*. Atlantic Music Corp.

Hanson, R.; Stutz, J.; and Cheeseman, P. 1991. Bayesian classification theory. Technical Report FIA-90-12-7-01, NASA Ames Research Center.

Hörnel, D., and Ragg, T. 1996. Learning musical structure and style by recognition, prediction and evoluation. In *Proceedings of the 1996 ICMC*. International Computer Music Association.

McLachlan, G. J., and Basford, K. E. 1988. *Mixture Models: Inference & Applications to Clustering*. Marcel Dekker.

Meila, M., and Heckerman, D. 1998. An experimental comparison of several clustering and initialization methods. Technical Report MSR-TR-98-06, Microsoft Research Center.

Nigam, K.; McCallum, A.; Thrun, S.; and Mitchell, T. 1998. Learning to classify text from labeled & unlabeled documents. In *Proceedings of the 1998 AAAI*. AAAI Press.

Pennycook, B., and Stammen, D. 1993. Real-time recognition of melodic fragments using the dynamic timewarp algorithm. In *Proceedings of the 1993 ICMC*. International Computer Music Association.

Rolland, P., and Ganascia, J. 1996. Automated motive-oriented analysis of musical corpuses: a jazz case study. In *Proceedings of the 1996 ICMC*. International Computer Music Association.

Rowe, R. 1993. *Interactive Music Systems : Machine Listening & Composing*. MIT Press.

Thom, B. 1999. Learning melodic models for interactive melodic improvisation. In *Proceedings of the 1999 ICMC*. International Computer Music Association.

Thom, B. 2000a. Artificial intelligence and real-time interactive improvisation. In *Proceedings from the AAAI-2000 Music and AI Workshop*. AAAI Press.

Thom, B. 2000b. Bob: an interactive improvisational music companion. In *Proceedings of the Fourth International Conference on Autonomous Agents*.

Thom, B. 2000c. Generating musician-specific melodic improvisational response in real-time. Submitted to the International Computer Music Conference.

Titterington, D. M.; Smith, A. F. M.; and Makov, U. E. 1981. *Statistical Analysis of Finite Mixture Distributions*. Wiley & Sons.

Vapnick, V. 1982. *Estimation of Dependences Based on Emperical Data*. Springer-Verlag.

Walker, W. 1997. A computer participant in musical improvisation. In *CHI 97 Electronic Publications*.

Restricted Bayes Optimal Classifiers

Simon Tong
Computer Science Department
Stanford University
simon.tong@cs.stanford.edu

Daphne Koller
Computer Science Department
Stanford University
koller@cs.stanford.edu

Abstract

We introduce the notion of *restricted Bayes optimal classifiers*. These classifiers attempt to combine the flexibility of the generative approach to classification with the high accuracy associated with discriminative learning. They first create a model of the joint distribution over class labels and features. Instead of choosing the decision boundary induced directly from the model, they restrict the allowable types of decision boundaries and learn the one that minimizes the probability of misclassification relative to the estimated joint distribution. In this paper, we investigate two particular instantiations of this approach. The first uses a non-parametric density estimator — Parzen Windows with Gaussian kernels — and hyperplane decision boundaries. We show that the resulting classifier is asymptotically equivalent to a maximal margin hyperplane classifier, a highly successful discriminative classifier. We therefore provide an alternative justification for maximal margin hyperplane classifiers. The second instantiation uses a mixture of Gaussians as the estimated density; in experiments on real-world data, we show that this approach allows data with missing values to be handled in a principled manner, leading to improved performance over regular discriminative approaches.

Introduction

We introduce the notion of *restricted Bayes optimal classifiers*. These classifiers attempt to combine the flexibility of the generative approach to classification with the high accuracy associated with discriminative learning.

Classification methods can generally be separated into two groups: generative and discriminative. Discriminative learning methods such as Support Vector Machines and logistic regression directly optimize a decision boundary and tend to create classifiers possessing higher accuracy than generative methods (Michie, Spiegelhalter, & Taylor 1994; Dumais *et al.* 1998).

In contrast, the generative approach to classification first creates a model of the joint distribution of the class label and features and then classifies a future instance as belonging to the most likely class according to the model. Such a classifier is called a Bayes optimal classifier and is known to minimize the probability of misclassification relative to the estimated density. The presence of a generative model of the joint distribution permits data with missing values, data with missing labels and encoding of prior knowledge to be handled in a principled manner. However, since a model of the full joint distribution has to be constructed, these techniques often tend to have a large number of parameters that need to be estimated. Thus, the learned density is typically quite sensitive to noise in the training data, as is the associated decision boundary. In other words, the Bayes optimal classifier typically has high variance. As a consequence, particularly when doing Bayes optimal classification in high dimensional domains, one commonly uses simple density estimator (e.g., the common use of the Naive Bayes classifier in text classification (Mitchell 1997)).

We propose an alternative approach to dealing with the problem of variance in Bayes optimal classification in a spirit similar to that mentioned in (Duda & Hart 1973; Highleyman 1961). Rather than simplifying the density, we restrict the nature of the decision boundary used by our classifier. In other words, rather than using the classification hypothesis induced by the Bayes optimal classifier, we select a hypothesis from a restricted class. The hypothesis selected is the one that minimizes the probability of error relative to our learned density. We call this error the *estimated Bayes error* of the hypothesis. For example, we can restrict to hypotheses defined by hyperplane decision boundaries. We call the hyperplane that minimizes the estimated Bayes error with respect to a given density a *Bayes optimal hyperplane*.

In this paper, we investigate two particular instantiations of this approach. The first part of the paper discusses using a non-parametric density estimator — Parzen Windows with Gaussian kernels — and hyperplane decision boundaries. We prove that the resulting classifier converges asymptotically to a maximal margin hyperplane classifiers. Maximal margin classifiers are one of the most successful discriminative classifiers, having strong theoretical justifications and empirical successes. By relating them to Bayes optimal classifiers we provide an alternative justification for maximal margin hyperplane classifiers. We also extent our results to a wider class of decision boundaries.

The second part of this paper considers using a semi-parametric density estimator — a mixture of Gaussians — and hyperplane boundaries. We perform experiments on real world data sets. Here, the benefits of having a model of

Copyright © 2000, American Association for Artificial Intelligence (www.aaai.org). All rights reserved.

the joint distribution become apparent, allowing data with missing values to be handled in a principled manner leading to improved performance over regular discriminative approaches.

General Framework

Our focus in this paper is the task of classifying real-valued data cases into two classes. More precisely, suppose we have a feature space $\mathcal{X} = \mathbb{R}^d$ and training data $\mathcal{D} = \{(\mathbf{x}_1, y_1), (\mathbf{x}_2, y_2), \ldots (\mathbf{x}_n, y_n)\}$, where $y_i \in \{C_0, C_1\}$ is called the *class label* for instance $\mathbf{x}_i$. Let n_0 and n_1 be the (non-zero) number of training data in classes C_0 and C_1 respectively. We write $\mathbf{x}_j \in C_i$ when $y_j = C_i$.

Definition 1 *A classifier h is a mapping from $\mathcal{X} - N$ to the set $\{C_0, C_1\}$, where N is a null set. Let $H_0 = \{\mathbf{x} : h(\mathbf{x}) = C_0\}$ and $H_1 = \{\mathbf{x} : h(\mathbf{x}) = C_1\}$.*

In other words, h is a classifier if it maps (almost all) points in $\mathcal{X}$ to one of two class labels.

Let our data instances and their labels be independent and identically distributed according to a joint distribution $P(\mathbf{x}, C)$. We can define the probability that a classifier h makes a classification error:

Definition 2 *Given a joint distributions $P(\mathbf{x}, C)$ and a classifier h we define the* expected misclassification rate *or* Bayes error *of h relative to P, $error(h : P)$, as:*

$$E_P[L(h(\mathbf{x}), C)], \text{ where } L(h(\mathbf{x}), C) = \begin{cases} 1 \text{ if } h(\mathbf{x}) \neq C \\ 0 \text{ otherwise} \end{cases}$$

The *Bayes optimal classifier relative to a distribution P* is given by: $h^*(\mathbf{x}) = C_0$ whenever $P(C_0 \mid \mathbf{x}) > P(C_1 \mid \mathbf{x})$, and $h^*(\mathbf{x}) = C_1$ otherwise. It is well-known that it minimizes the Bayes error.

In order to use the Bayes optimal classifier, we need $P(C_0 \mid \mathbf{x})$ and $P(C_1 \mid \mathbf{x})$. In general, these quantities are not known. The generative approach to classification uses the training data to estimate an approximate joint distribution $\hat{P}(\mathbf{x}, C)$, and then uses the Bayes optimal classifier relative to $\hat{P}$. Let the *estimated Bayes error* denote the Bayes error relative to an estimated distribution $\hat{P}$. The Bayes optimal classifier relative to $\hat{P}$ minimizes the estimated Bayes error.

The Bayes optimal classifier often induces decision boundaries that are fairly complex. Furthermore, the estimate of $\hat{P}$ is often quite sensitive to the noise in the training data, which often implies a similar sensitivity for the decision boundary. In other words, the variance of the Bayes optimal classifier is quite large. A possible approach for reducing this variance is to restrict the class of hypotheses that we allow ourselves to consider. That is, we select the "best" hypothesis within some restricted class $\mathcal{H}$.

Definition 3 *Given a joint distribution $\hat{P}(\mathbf{x}, C)$ and a set of classifiers $\mathcal{H}$, we say that h^* is a* restricted Bayes optimal classifier *with respect to $\mathcal{H}$ and $\hat{P}$ if $h^* \in \mathcal{H}$ and for all $h \in \mathcal{H}$, $error(h^* : \hat{P}) \leq error(h : \hat{P})$.*

One restricted set of classifiers that has received a lot of attention is the set of hyperplane classifiers, where the decision boundary is a hyperplane in feature space.

The above definitions hold in a very general setting. In order to apply them, we need to choose a concrete approach to estimating $\hat{P}$. In most cases, it is easier to estimate $\hat{P}$ using the decomposition $\hat{P}(\mathbf{x}, C) = \hat{P}(C) \cdot \hat{p}(\mathbf{x} \mid C)$ where $\hat{p}(\mathbf{x} \mid C)$ is the *class-conditional density* of the feature vectors $\mathbf{x}$ within the class C. There are many techniques for estimating the class conditional densities (Bishop 1995; Fukanaga 1990; Silverman 1986). We will consider two types of density estimators in this paper: Parzen Windows, and mixtures of k Gaussians.

Parzen Windows and Maximal Margin Hyperplanes

In this section we choose a standard method to estimate the joint density that uses the above decomposition. First, we take the maximum likelihood estimates for $P(C_0)$ and $P(C_1)$. We choose a simple variant of *non-parametric* density estimation: Parzen Windows estimation with Gaussian kernels. To estimate $p(\mathbf{x} \mid C_i)$, we place a Gaussian kernel over each training instance $\mathbf{x}_j$ in class C_i; the estimated density is simply the average of these kernels. We use identical Gaussian kernels for all data cases, each with a diagonal covariance matrix $\sigma^2 I$. More precisely, we define for $i = 0, 1$

$$p_\sigma(\mathbf{x} \mid C_i) = \frac{1}{n_i} \sum_{\mathbf{x}_j \in C_i} \frac{1}{\sigma^d (2\pi)^{\frac{d}{2}}} e^{-\frac{1}{2\sigma^2}(\mathbf{x}-\mathbf{x}_j)^T(\mathbf{x}-\mathbf{x}_j)}$$

where n_i is the number of training instances in class C_i and σ is called the *smoothing parameter*. Together, $\hat{P}(C_0)$, $\hat{P}(C_1)$ and $p_\sigma(\mathbf{x} \mid C_i)$ define a joint density $P_\sigma(\mathbf{x}, C)$ as required. We use $error_\sigma(h)$ to denote $error(h : P_\sigma)$.

Different values for σ correspond to different choices along the bias-variance spectrum: smaller values (sharper peaks for the kernels) correspond to higher variance but lower bias estimates of the density. The choice of σ is often crucial for the accuracy of the Bayes optimal classifier. We can eliminate the bias induced by the smoothing effect of σ by making it arbitrarily close to zero. We prevent the variance of the classifier from growing unboundedly by restricting our hypotheses to the very limited class of hyperplanes. Thus, we choose as our hypothesis the Bayes optimal hyperplane relative to the estimated density induced by the data and σ.

In this section our main result is the following: for linearly separable data, as σ tends to zero, the Bayes optimal hyperplane converges to the maximal margin hyperplane. We further show that a similar result holds for a much wider class of classifiers: for small enough σ, the classifier that maximizes the margin will have a lower estimated error than a classifier with a smaller margin. We also show that for linearly non-separable data, the Bayes optimal hyperplane has a very natural interpretation: it minimizes the training set classification error, and among all the hyperplanes that have the same classification error, it is the one with the largest margin.

Linearly separable data

In this subsection, we assume that the training data are linearly separable. In other words, there exists at least one hyperplane classifier that will correctly classify all of the training data. We will also restrict the hypothesis space $\mathcal{H}$ to be the set of hyperplane classifiers that correctly classify all training data. (These restrictions will be relaxed later on.)

In this case, we can show a tight connection between Bayes optimal hyperplanes and *maximal margin classifiers* (Vapnik 1982).

Definition 4 *The* margin *of a hyperplane h, denoted by* margin(h), *is the smallest Euclidean distance from the hyperplane to a training instance.*

Theorem 5 *Let h^* be some hyperplane in $\mathcal{H}$. The following statements are equivalent:*

- $\forall h \in \mathcal{H}$ s.t. $h \neq h^*$, $\exists S > 0$ s.t. $error_\sigma(h^*) < error_\sigma(h)$ whenever $\sigma < S$.
- h^* has maximal margin.

The intuition behind this result is based on the following alternative expression for the estimated Bayes error, $error_\sigma(h)$:

$$\hat{P}(C_1) \int_{\mathbf{x} \in H_0} p_\sigma(\mathbf{x} \mid C_1) \, d\mathbf{x} + \hat{P}(C_0) \int_{\mathbf{x} \in H_1} p_\sigma(\mathbf{x} \mid C_0) \, d\mathbf{x}.$$

Points that are closer, in Euclidean distance, to one of the Gaussian kernels in $p_\sigma(\mathbf{x} \mid C_1)$ have significantly higher density. Thus, the closer we move the decision boundary to the centers of these kernels, the more mass it will contribute to the estimate Bayes error. As σ shrinks, the kernels that are closest to the decision boundary dominate more and more. A careful analysis shows that the estimated Bayes error of a hyperplane h is dominated by an expression which is exponential in $-margin(h)^2/(2\sigma^2)$. Thus, as σ tends to zero the hyperplane with the larger margin will dominate (have lower error relative to other hyperplanes).

This theorem shows that for any other hyperplane h, once σ is small enough, h^* beats h. However, this does not suffice to show that, as we reduce σ, the Bayes optimal hyperplane h^*_σ for P_σ "converges" to the maximal margin hyperplane h^*. It could, perhaps, be the case that for each $\sigma > 0$, h^*_σ is arbitrarily far away from h^*. In fact, a similar proof to that of Theorem 5 shows that this is not the case.

Corollary 6 *Let $h^* \in \mathcal{H}$ be the maximal margin hyperplane. Let $\delta > 0$ and $\mathcal{H}_\delta$ be the set of hyperplanes in $\mathcal{H}$ with margins less than margin(h^*) $- \delta$. Then there exists $S > 0$ such that, for all $\sigma < S$ and all $h \in \mathcal{H}_\delta$, $error_\sigma(h^*) < error_\sigma(h)$.*

Thus, as $\sigma \to 0$, the margin of h^*_σ tends to the maximal margin. In other words, the Bayes optimal hyperplane converges to the maximal margin hyperplane in terms of margin.

General classifiers

We can generalize the previous framework to more complex classes of classifiers. Instead of letting $\mathcal{H}$ be the set of hyperplanes classifiers we will let $\mathcal{H}$ be any set of classifiers obeying the following condition:

Condition 7 *$\mathcal{H}$ is a set of classifiers such that:*

- *For each $h \in \mathcal{H}$, $H_0 = \{\mathbf{x} : h(\mathbf{x}) = C_0\}$ and $H_1 = \{\mathbf{x} : h(\mathbf{x}) = C_1\}$ are both open sets.*

This condition is fairly mild and allows for a large range of classifiers. For example, any set of classifiers which have hyperplane or polynomial decision boundaries, hinged hyperplanes or decision boundaries induced by neural networks with sigmoidal or linear activation functions satisfy the condition.

We can also generalize the notion of a margin to hold for these more general forms of classifiers. Intuitively the margin is the smallest distance between a training instance and the decision boundary.

Definition 8 *Let h be a classifier. Then margin(h) is:*

$$\min\left(\min_{\mathbf{x}_j \in C_1}(\inf_{\mathbf{x} \in H_0} \|\mathbf{x} - \mathbf{x}_j\|), \min_{\mathbf{x}_j \in C_0}(\inf_{\mathbf{x} \in H_1} \|\mathbf{x} - \mathbf{x}_j\|)\right).$$

In the case of hyperplanes, this definition coincides with the original definition of the margin of a hyperplane classifier. We can now prove the following theorem.

Theorem 9 *Let $\mathcal{H}$ be a set of classifiers that satisfy condition 7. Let h^* be some classifier in $\mathcal{H}$. The following statements are equivalent:*

- $\forall h \in \mathcal{H}$ s.t. margin(h) $\neq$ margin(h^*), $\exists S > 0$ s.t. $error_\sigma(h^*) < error_\sigma(h)$ whenever $\sigma < S$.
- h^* has maximal margin.

This result says that a classifier that has maximal margin will eventually have a lower estimated error than any other particular classifier with a smaller margin. The proof of the theorem (omitted) is rather more involved that that of theorem 5 but the intuition behind it is similar. Suppose we are given two classifiers one of which has a larger margin than the other. It is possible to find a region in $\mathcal{X}$ that is classified one way by the larger margin classifier but the opposite way by the smaller margin classifier and for which the estimated Bayes error incurred by wrongly classifying that area dominates as we reduce the smoothing parameter.

It is interesting to compare this instantiation of restricted Bayes optimal classification with Support Vector Machines (SVMs) (Vapnik 1982; Cortes & Vapnik 1995). An SVM finds the hyperplane that maximizes the margin. The problem of maximizing the margin can be cast as a convex optimization problem then only depends on the training data via inner products between training instances (e.g., $\mathbf{x}_i \cdot \mathbf{x}_j$). One can then apply the "kernel trick" (Cortes & Vapnik 1995), where we replace the inner products with a "kernel function" $K(\mathbf{x}_i, \mathbf{x}_j)$ that satisfies Mercer's condition. (These "kernel functions" are not to be confused with the Gaussian kernels used in Parzen Windows.) Since K satisfies Mercer's condition, we can write $K(\mathbf{x}_i, \mathbf{x}_j) = \Phi(\mathbf{x}_i) \cdot \Phi(\mathbf{x}_j)$ and so by using K we are then implicitly projecting the training data into a different (often higher dimensional) feature space $\mathcal{F}$ and finding the hyperplane that maximizes the margin in that space. By choosing different kernel functions we can implicitly project the training data from $\mathcal{X}$ into spaces $\mathcal{F}$ for which hyperplanes in $\mathcal{F}$ correspond to more complex decision boundaries in the original space $\mathcal{X}$. One commonly

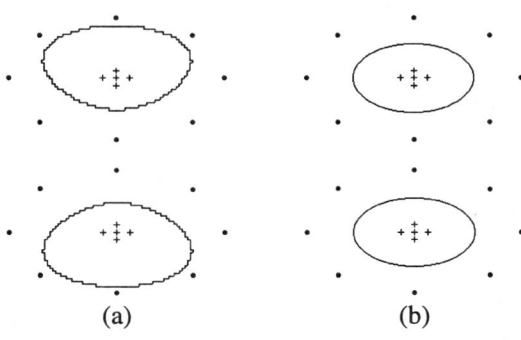 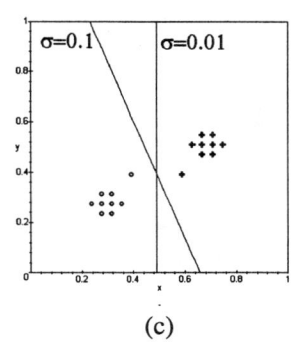 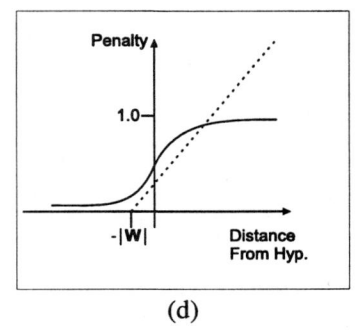

Figure 1: (a) SVM using degree 4 polynomial kernel. (b) Degree 4 polynomial restricted Bayes classifier using Parzen Windows and small σ. (c) Bayes optimal hyperplane for different σ. (d) Parzen Bayes (solid) and Soft Margin (dotted) error functions.

used kernel is $K(\mathbf{x}_i, \mathbf{x}_j) = (\mathbf{x}_i \cdot \mathbf{x}_j + 1)^p$ which induces polynomial decision boundaries of degree p in the original space $\mathcal{X}$.

How does this relate to using restricted Bayes optimal classification with non-parametric density estimation? One fact is that using an SVM that maximizes the margin and that uses a kernel function $K(\mathbf{x}_i, \mathbf{x}_j) = \Phi(\mathbf{x}_i) \cdot \Phi(\mathbf{x}_j)$ corresponds to performing Parzen Window density estimation in the projected space $\mathcal{F}$ and finding the Bayes optimal hyperplane in that projected space for $\sigma \to 0$.

A second fact is that even though the SVM maximizes the margin in the higher dimensional space, the classifier it produces does not necessarily maximize the margin in the original space. So, if we decided to use the kernel $K(\mathbf{x}_i, \mathbf{x}_j) = (\mathbf{x}_i \cdot \mathbf{x}_j + 1)^4$ — which induces degree four polynomial boundaries in the original space — the SVM will not correspond to the degree four polynomial with the largest margin in the original space. However, if we were to use Parzen Windows in our original space and restrict our hypotheses to degree four polynomials then the maximal margin degree four polynomial will have a lower estimated Bayes error than any other polynomial for sufficiently small σ. Figure 1(a) shows the decision boundary produced when using a SVM with a degree four polynomial kernel and figure 1(b) shows the decision boundary produced when using a restricted Bayes optimal classifier where we restrict the set of classifiers to the set of polynomials with degree at most four. The decision boundaries produced by the two approaches do not necessarily coincide.

Data that are not linearly separable

We return to considering the set of hyperplane classifiers and now analyze the behavior of the Parzen Windows Bayes optimal hyperplane for the more general case of data that are not necessarily linearly separable.

Corollary 10 *Given $\sigma > 0$ and hyperplane $h \in \mathcal{H}$ we can write the estimated Bayes error in the following form:*

$$error_\sigma(h) = \frac{1}{n} \left(f_\sigma(\mathcal{D}, h) + \#incorrect \right)$$

where #incorrect is the number of misclassifications on the training data $\mathcal{D}$, and $f_\sigma(\mathcal{D}, h)$ has the following properties:

- $f_\sigma(\mathcal{D}, h) \to 0$ as $\sigma \to 0$
- *if h^* and h both minimize #incorrect and h^* has larger margin than h then there exists $S > 0$ such that $f_\sigma(\mathcal{D}, h^*) < f_\sigma(\mathcal{D}, h)$ whenever $\sigma < S$.*

In other words, as σ tends to zero, the hyperplane with the lowest score will have the lowest classification error on the training data; and, of all such minimum error hyperplanes, it will have the greatest margin with respect to the correctly classified data. Intuitively, this seems a very reasonable hyperplane to pick. This corollary is also consistent with the results we obtained for the linearly separable case; in this case there are hyperplanes in which the number of misclassifications are zero. So, for sufficiently small smoothing parameters the Bayes optimal hyperplane will be a hyperplane which correctly classifies all training data. Hence, for the previous theorems for the linearly separable case we can remove the restriction of the hypothesis space to hyperplanes that correctly classify all training data — we know that for small enough smoothing parameters the Bayes optimal hyperplane will always correctly classify the training data.

The effect of nonzero σ

Until now, we have focused on the behavior of the Bayes optimal hyperplane as σ gets arbitrarily close to zero. As we discussed in the informal justification for Theorem 5, as σ shrinks, the data points closer to the decision boundary have larger and larger impact. At the limit, only the points closest to the boundary, i.e., the ones on the margin, have impact. It is not clear whether focusing only on the margin is necessarily the optimal approach. If we take σ to be non-zero, classifying using the estimated Bayes error will consider the distances of other points from the margin. The larger we make σ, the larger the effect that points further from the margin have on the estimated Bayes error and on the choice of hyperplane. Figure 1(c) illustrates one simple example where a larger value of σ leads to a hyperplane which is arguably more reasonable. In the non-separable case, we also get a similar tradeoff. It is interesting to note that the form of the error function in Corollary 10 resembles the form of the *soft margin* error function often used in SVMs to cope with linearly non-separable data (Cortes & Vapnik 1995): $\|\mathbf{w}\|^2/2 + C(\sum_i \xi_i)$. Briefly, $\mathbf{w}$ is the hyperplane weight vector (including the bias weight b), C is a tunable parameter that influences how much of a penalty to assign errors and the ξ_is are *slack variables* where $(\sum_i \xi_i)$ provides an upper bound on the number of training errors. Thus the soft error function can be decomposed into the sum of a deterministic function of the margin and a "softer" function of the training error whereas our error function can be decomposed into a "soft" function of the margin and the exact training error.

We investigated whether using a non-zero value of σ would achieve a similar effect to that of the soft margin error function.[1] We used the "Pima Indian Diabetes" UC Irvine data set (Blake, Keogh, & Merz 1998) and a synthetic data set. The Pima data set has eight features, with 576 training instances of which 198 are labeled as positive. The synthetic data were generated from two dimensional Gaussian class conditional distributions. In the synthetic case the underlying distribution was known and we could compute the true Bayes error for each of the hypotheses produced, while in the Pima data set classification error on a separate 192 instance test set was measured.

For various values of σ, we searched for the hyperplane that minimizes the estimated Bayes error for P_σ. The error is a differentiable function of the weights of the hyperplane, so we can use gradient descent techniques to find the Bayes optimal hyperplane for any given smoothing parameter. The update rules are easily derived and are omitted.

There are some practical issues to deal with in the implementation of this idea. Unfortunately, the search space is not convex and local minima exist. Furthermore, for small σ, the space consists of numerous very large gently sloping plateaus. Thus, naive gradient descent converges to suboptimal solutions and very slowly. Corollary 6 suggests seeding the search with the maximal margin hyperplane wherever possible and this seemed to improve the speed of convergence and quality of results. We also used *bold driving* (Bishop 1995) to speed up the convergence.

Table 1 lists the errors for various settings of σ and C. For the synthetic data the error is the average true Bayes error over ten data sets, where the optimal parameter was chosen for each data set separately. With the larger data sets we experimented with using cross validation for setting the σ and C parameters and these results are also listed. Many of the synthetic data sets of size nine and fifteen were actually linearly separable and for each of those the maximum margin hyperplane was also computed. These results indicate that the Parzen Windows Bayes optimal hyperplane, optimizing its somewhat different but arguably more natural error function, achieves very similar performance to that of a soft margin hyperplane. This observation is supported by a paired t-test on the cross-validation folds of the Pima data (at 5% significance). Furthermore, the synthetic data support our intuition above that, even for linearly separable data, the Bayes optimal hyperplane can produce a more appropriate classifier than the maximal margin hyperplane, and so reducing the smoothing parameter to zero is not always optimal.

---

[1] We used T. Joachim's SVMlight: www-ai.informatik.uni-dortmund.de/thorsten/svm_light.html

Table 1: Comparison with Soft Margin and Maximal Margin

Parzen σ	Pima Error	Soft Margin C	Pima Error
0.008	28.1	0.1	24.4
0.01	18.8	0.3	21.3
0.02	21.4	0.9	21.9
0.03	22.9	5	22.3
0.04	23.4	10	22.3
0.05	**22.3**	100	22.3
0.1	22.3	**1000**	**22.3**
0.2	27.1	10000	22.3

* Underlined rows indicate settings picked by cross validation.

Synthetic size	9	15	30	5-fold CV 30
Parzen Hyp	8.1 ± 0.35	8.0 ± 0.23	7.6 ± 0.11	8.5 ± 0.62
Soft Margin	8.7 ± 0.73	7.9 ± 0.25	7.6 ± 0.08	8.7 ± 0.55
Max Margin	9.8 ± 0.47	9.4 ± 0.61	—	—

Table 2: Resistance to Outliers. Classification error.

Outlier Percentage	Parzen Hyperplane	Soft Margin Hyperplane	Logistic Regression
0%	16.5 ± 0.2	16.6 ± 0.2	16.8 ± 0.2
1%	16.7 ± 0.2	25.1 ± 0.4	24.7 ± 0.2
2%	16.7 ± 0.4	24.0 ± 0.2	24.0 ± 0.2
3%	17.3 ± 0.8	25.0 ± 0.2	25.1 ± 0.1
4%	18.9 ± 1.5	24.7 ± 0.3	24.4 ± 0.2
5%	17.4 ± 0.9	24.9 ± 0.3	24.7 ± 0.2

With the restricted Bayes hyperplane, the error incurred from a misclassified training instance is eventually saturated the further the instance is from the hyperplane. In contrast, the soft margin error function penalizes a misclassified training instance proportionally to the instance's distance from the margin (see figure 1(d)). This indicates that Parzen Windows Bayes hyperplanes may be more resistant to outliers than Soft Margin SVMs. To test this hypothesis we performed a simple experiment. We sample data from two Gaussians. Each training set consisted of 100 instances and outliers were added to the training sets in various proportions. Outliers were approximately an order of magnitude distance away from the other data points. Again, cross validation was used to select σ and C. Table 2 presents the generalization performance with each row being an average over ten independent runs. The table indicates that Parzen Windows hyperplanes with Gaussian kernels tend to be more resistance to outliers than the other linear methods.

Mixtures of Gaussians

Until now, we have considered using non-parametric density estimation with Gaussian kernels as our density estimator. Clearly we can use other densities with the restricted Bayes optimal classification approach. We now consider using a more parametric density estimator that will allow us to take greater advantage of having a model of the joint distribution. The mixture of k Gaussians density estimator assumes that the class i conditional density $p(\mathbf{x} \mid C_i)$ is a mixture of k Gaussian densities. More precisely, we define for $i = 0, 1$

$$p(\mathbf{x} \mid C_i) = \sum_{j=1}^{k} m_{ij} \left(\frac{1}{\sigma_i^d (2\pi)^{\frac{d}{2}}} e^{-\frac{1}{2\sigma_i^2}(\mathbf{x}-\mu_{ij})^T(\mathbf{x}-\mu_{ij})} \right)$$

Table 3: Average test set error using complete data.

Data Set	Linear SVM	Logistic	MoG Hyp	MoG
Breast	28.74 ± 0.43	**27.38 ± 0.47**	27.42 ± 0.50	29.16 ± 0.53
Diabetes	23.43 ± 0.17	23.37 ± 0.18	**23.23 ± 0.17**	26.50 ± 0.21
German	24.12 ± 0.23	**23.94 ± 0.21**	24.03 ± 0.24	26.35 ± 0.27
Heart	**16.00 ± 0.33**	16.97 ± 0.28	16.33 ± 0.33	17.78 ± 0.37
Hepatitis	32.53 ± 0.59	31.21 ± 0.51	**27.19 ± 0.34**	32.98 ± 0.45
Ionosphere	13.44 ± 0.22	**13.16 ± 0.23**	13.27 ± 0.23	10.55 ± 0.31
Sonar	**25.06 ± 0.42**	25.07 ± 0.41	27.62 ± 0.38	29.95 ± 0.46
Waveform	**12.85 ± 0.05**	13.44 ± 0.07	12.91 ± 0.06	10.65 ± 0.04

Table 4: Average test set error with missing data values.

Data Set	Linear SVM	Logistic	MoG Hyp	MoG
Breast	**29.74 ± 0.49**	30.91 ± 0.50	**29.74 ± 0.47**	32.22 ± 0.58
Diabetes	**26.09 ± 0.23**	26.22 ± 0.27	26.93 ± 0.24	31.50 ± 0.44
German	30.09 ± 0.37	29.46 ± 0.32	**28.38 ± 0.27**	30.91 ± 0.46
Heart	18.21 ± 0.42	18.66 ± 0.43	**17.94 ± 0.40**	20.10 ± 0.46
Hepatitis	28.63 ± 0.40	28.26 ± 0.42	**27.81 ± 0.48**	30.47 ± 0.61
Ionosphere	**13.38 ± 0.21**	13.73 ± 0.22	14.96 ± 0.30	15.46 ± 0.27
Sonar	33.15 ± 0.55	**31.70 ± 0.51**	32.95 ± 0.46	35.42 ± 0.48
Waveform	14.80 ± 0.08	15.89 ± 0.08	**14.59 ± 0.10**	13.88 ± 0.21

Here each m_{ij} is a mixture weight that determines how much the j-th Gaussians contributes towards the overall class i conditional density. Mixtures of Gaussians are semi-parametric density estimators. Notice here that the number of mixture components k is fixed and typically a small value. This is in contrast to the Parzen Windows non-parametric density estimator where the number of kernels grows with the number of training instances.

We can estimate the parameters $m_{ij}, \mu_{ij}, \sigma_i$ for $i \in \{0,1\}, j \in \{1,\ldots k\}$ by using the Expectation Maximization (EM) algorithm (Dempster, Laird, & Rubin 1977). EM finds parameters that locally maximize the likelihood of the observed data. As before, we use the maximum likelihood estimates for the class priors $P(C_0)$ and $P(C_1)$.

We can also handle the presence of missing values in the training data in a principled way. We now use the E-step of EM to not only to compute the mixture components m_{ij}, but also the expected missing values of the data.

Given a density of the above form we can compute the Bayes optimal hyperplane using a similar gradient decent technique as in the Parzen Windows density estimation case.

Experiments

For our experiments we compared three different hyperplane classifier methods: Linear SVMs, logistic regression and Bayes optimal hyperplanes using mixtures of Gaussians (MoG Hyp). We also looked at the Bayes optimal classifier derived from using the mixture of Gaussians density directly (MoG). For the SVM the soft margin parameter, C, needed to be tuned. For the Bayes hyperplane and for the mixture of Gaussians Bayes optimal classifier the number of class mixture components, k, needed to be chosen.

We used data sets from the UC Irvine repository (Blake, Keogh, & Merz 1998).[2] We created 100 randomly generate train/test splits of the data (in a roughly 40/60 split). Each data set contained no missing values. For each realization of the data we learned a SVM, a logistic hyperplane, a Bayes optimal hyperplane using mixtures of Gaussians, and finally the Bayes optimal classifier for a mixture of Gaussians. We used five-fold cross validation on the first five realizations to choose the parameters for each of the methods.

Table 3 contains the test set error rates for the data sets averaged over the one hundred runs. Bold face figures indicate the best *hyperplane* method for each data set. The Bayes optimal hyperplane using mixtures of Gaussians actually outperforms the mixture of Gaussians Bayes optimal classifier on six of the eight data sets. This indicates that restricting the nature of the decision boundary can be better than using the density estimator directly. The Bayes optimal hyperplane is competitive with the two discriminative methods — it is the best hyperplane method on two out of the eight sets, having a lower error rate than the SVM on five sets and outperforming logistic regression on four.

We then looked at how the methods performed with data that contained missing values. For each training instance we randomly removed a feature value with probability 0.75.[3] We used EM to perform density estimation with mixtures of two Gaussians. However, the regular SVM and logistic methods do not handle missing values. For these two discriminative methods we used the common technique (Bishop 1995) of filling in the missing values with their class averages.

Table 4 contains the error rates for the data sets. Here the Bayes hyperplane performs somewhat better, being the first (or equal first) best hyperplane method for five of the eight sets while logistic regression is the best hyperplane method for only one of the data sets and SVMs are the best (or equal best) for three sets. Again, the Bayes hyperplane outperforms the plain mixture of Gaussians Bayes optimal classifier on most of the data sets (seven out of the eight). It is better or equal to the linear SVM on six out of the eight and outperforms logistic regression on five out of eight sets.

As they stand, the gains from the mixture of Gaussian hyperplanes are only suggestive rather than overwhelming. Note that we used a particularly naive form of the Mixture of Gaussian estimator — every Gaussian component within a class had to have an identical and restricted form of covariance matrix. It could well be that allowing more flexible covariance matrices would lead to further improvements in performance.

Conclusions and future work

We have introduced an alternative approach for dealing with the high variance of the Bayes optimal classifier in high dimensional spaces. Our approach is based on finding simple hypotheses that minimize the estimated Bayes error within a certain class, where the Bayes error is estimated relative to the learned distribution.

---

[2]The UC Irvine breast cancer data was obtained from M. Zwitter and M. Soklic at the University Medical Centre, Inst. of Oncology, Ljubljana, Yugoslavia.

[3]The hepatitis data was an exception. We only removed a value with probability 0.4 since otherwise some features consisted entirely of missing values over the whole training set.

We have shown that one very natural instantiation of our approach, where we use Parzen Windows with Gaussian kernels, converges at the limit to the maximal margin hyperplane classifier. We have further analyzed the behavior of the Parzen Windows restricted Bayes method when we consider more general forms of classifiers. While possessing desirable properties, Gaussian kernels tend to cause numerous local minima making a practical system hard to implement well. We are currently investigating choosing different kernels that reduce the jaggedness of the search space while still retaining many of the properties of Gaussian kernels.

The Parzen Windows hyperplane result has several implications. From one perspective, it can be viewed as providing a new probabilistic justification for maximal margin hyperplanes. There have been several other studies exploring probabilistic interpretations, although mainly in the context of Bayesian learning (Cristianini, Shawe-Taylor, & Sykacek 1998; Sollich 1999; Herbrich, Graepel, & Campbell 1998). From another perspective, it provides a strong justification for our intuition that the restricted Bayes optimal classifier avoids the high variance problem of the unrestricted Bayes optimal classifier, even when the representation of the density is very complex. We considered an extremely high variance representation of a density — a non-parametric density with arbitrarily low kernel width. However, the Bayes optimal hyperplane relative to this distribution is (close to) the maximum margin hyperplane, which is known to work well even in high-dimensional spaces. Furthermore, our result suggests that finding a simple classifier optimal relative to a complex density can be better than finding the unrestricted Bayes optimal classifier relative to a simpler density: the maximal margin classifier is better in many domains than most Bayes optimal classifiers.

These observations raise the obvious question as to whether it was the specific choice of non-parametric density estimation and Gaussian kernels that led to the success of restricted Bayes optimal classifier. We addressed this question to some degree by investigating the use of mixture of Gaussians as the density estimator. Our experiments strongly suggest that restricted Bayes optimal classifiers can be used in conjunction with other forms of density estimation to obtain competitive classification performance on complete data. The experiments also suggest that restricted Bayes optimal classifiers can take advantage of having a model of the joint distribution to give an edge over discriminative methods when dealing with data sets with missing values.

This last observation suggests a new perspective on the debate between discriminative learning and the generative approach for classification (Duda & Hart 1973; Rubenstein & Hastie 1997; Jaakola & Haussler 1998; Jaakkola, Meila, & Jebara 1999). In many domains, discriminative learning empirically achieves higher classification accuracy than the Bayes optimal classifier. The usual explanation is that the generative approach spends too much "effort" on minimizing "irrelevant" errors in $P(\mathbf{x}, C)$, and not enough on reducing classification errors. Our approach provides an alternative solution, where the estimated joint density is not used directly in the form of the Bayes optimal decision boundary, but rather to evaluate classifiers in a restricted class.

We intend to investigate the benefits of restricted Bayes optimal classifiers further. Having a model of the joint distribution can provide other advantages. It facilitates the encoding of prior knowledge in a principled way and EM could be used to incorporate unlabeled data. We plan to experiment with this approach for a variety of density estimation approaches. We hope that it will allow us to combine the benefits of the generative approach using realistically expressive representations with the high accuracy classification often associated with discriminative learning.

Acknowledgements

This work was supported by DARPA's *Information Assurance* program under subcontract to SRI International, and by ARO grant DAAH04-96-1-0341 under the MURI program "Integrated Approach to Intelligent Systems".

References

Bishop, C. 1995. *Neural Networks for Pattern Recognition.* Oxford University Press.

Blake, C. Keogh, E. and Merz, C. 1998. UCI repository of machine learning databases.

Cortes, C., and Vapnik, V. 1995. Support vector networks. In *Machine Learning*, volume 20.

Cristianini, N. Shawe-Taylor, J. and Sykacek, P. 1998. Bayesian classifiers are large margin hyperplanes in a Hilbert space. In *Proc. NeuroCOLT2*.

Dempster, A. Laird, N. and Rubin, D. 1977. Maximum likelihood from incomplete data via the EM algorithm. In *Journal of the Royal Statistical Society*.

Duda, R., and Hart, P. 1973. *Pattern Classification and Scene Analysis*. Wiley, New York.

Dumais, S. Platt, J. Heckerman, D. and Sahami, M. 1998. Inductive learning algorithms and representations for text categorization. In *Proc. 7th International Conference on Information and Knowledge Management*.

Fukanaga, K. 1990. *Introduction to Statistical Pattern Recognition*. Boston: Academic Press.

Herbrich, R. Graepel, T. and Campbell, C. 1998. Bayesian learning in reproducing kernel Hilbert spaces. Technical Report TR 99-11, Technical University of Berlin.

Highleyman, W. 1961. Linear decision functions, with application to pattern recognition. In *Proc. IRE*, volume 49, 31–48.

Jaakkola, T. Meila, M. and Jebara, T. 1999. Maximum entropy discrimination. Technical Report AITR-1668, MIT.

Jaakola, T. S., and Haussler, D. 1998. Exploiting generative models in discriminative classifiers. In *Ten Conf. on Advances in Neural Info. Processing Systems (NIPS)*.

Michie, D. Spiegelhalter, D. J. and Taylor, C. 1994. *Machine Learning, Neural and Statistical Classification*. Ellis Horwood.

Mitchell, T. 1997. *Machine Learning*. McGraw-Hill.

Rubenstein, Y., and Hastie, T. 1997. Discriminative vs informative learning. In *Proc. AAAI*.

Silverman, B. 1986. *Density Estimation for Statistics and Data Analysis*. Chapman and Hall, London.

Sollich, P. 1999. Probabilistic interpretation and Bayesian methods for Support Vector Machines. In *Proceedings of ICANN 99*.

Vapnik, V. 1982. *Estimation of Dependences Based on Empirical Data*. Springer Verlag.

A Quantitative Study of Small Disjuncts

Gary M. Weiss* and Haym Hirsh

Department of Computer Science
Rutgers University
New Brunswick, New Jersey 08903
{gweiss, hirsh}@cs.rutgers.edu

Abstract

Systems that learn from examples often express the learned concept in the form of a disjunctive description. Disjuncts that correctly classify few training examples are known as small disjuncts and are interesting to machine learning researchers because they have a much higher error rate than large disjuncts. Previous research has investigated this phenomenon by performing *ad hoc* analyses of a small number of datasets. In this paper we present a quantitative measure for evaluating the effect of small disjuncts on learning and use it to analyze 30 benchmark datasets. We investigate the relationship between small disjuncts and pruning, training set size and noise, and come up with several interesting results.

Introduction

Systems that learn from examples often express the learned concept as a disjunction. The size of a disjunct is defined as the number of training examples that it correctly classifies (Holte, Acker, and Porter 1989). A number of empirical studies have demonstrated that learned concepts include disjuncts that span a large range of disjunct sizes and that the small disjuncts—those disjuncts that correctly classify only a few training examples—collectively cover a significant percentage of the test examples (Holte, Acker, and Porter 1989; Ali and Pazzani 1992; Danyluk and Provost 1993; Ting 1994; Van den Bosch et al. 1997; Weiss and Hirsh 1998). It has also been shown that small disjuncts often correspond to rare cases within the domain under study (Weiss 1995) and cannot be totally eliminated if high predictive accuracy is to be achieved (Holte et al. 1989). Previous studies have shown that small disjuncts have much higher error rates than large disjuncts and contribute a disproportionate number of the total errors. This phenomenon is known as "the problem with small disjuncts".

There are two reasons for studying the problem with small disjuncts. The first is that small disjuncts can help us answer important machine learning questions, such as: how does the amount of available training data affect learning, how does pruning work and when is it most effective, and how does noise affect the ability to learn a concept? Thus, we use small disjuncts as a lens through which to examine important issues in machine learning. The second reason for studying small disjuncts is to learn to build machine learning programs that "address" the problem with small disjuncts. These learners will improve the accuracy of the small disjuncts without significantly decreasing the accuracy of the large disjuncts, so that the overall accuracy of the learned concept is improved. Several researchers have attempted to build such learners. One approach involves employing a maximum specificity bias for learning small disjuncts, while continuing to use the more common maximum generality bias for the large disjuncts (Holte et al. 1989; Ting 1994). Unfortunately, these efforts have produced, at best, only marginal improvements. A better understanding of small disjuncts and their role in learning may be required before further advances are possible.

In this paper we use small disjuncts to gain a better understanding of machine learning. In the process of doing this, we address a major limitation with previous research—that very few datasets were analyzed: Holte et al. (1989) analyzed two datasets, Ali and Pazzani (1992) one dataset, Danyluk and Provost (1993) one dataset, and Weiss and Hirsh (1998) two datasets. Because so few datasets were analyzed, only relatively weak qualitative conclusions were possible. By analyzing thirty datasets, we are able to draw some quantitative conclusions, as well as form more definitive qualitative conclusions than previously possible.[†]

Description of Experiments

The results presented in this paper are based on 30 datasets, of which 19 were collected from the UCI repository (Blake and Merz 1998) and 11 from researchers at AT&T (Cohen 1995; Cohen and Singer 1999). Numerous experiments were run on these datasets to assess the impact of small disjuncts on learning, especially as factors such as training set size, pruning strategy, and noise level are varied. The majority of experiments use C4.5, a program for inducing decision trees (Quinlan 1993). C4.5 was modified by the authors to collect information related to disjunct size. During the training phase the modified software assigns each disjunct/leaf a value based on the number of training examples it correctly classifies. The number of correctly and incorrectly classified examples associated with each disjunct is then tracked during the testing phase, so that at

---

*Also AT&T, 20 Knightsbridge Road, Piscataway, New Jersey
Copyright © 2000, American Association for Artificial Intelligence (www.aaai.org). All rights reserved.

[†] See http://www.cs.rutgers.edu/~gweiss/small_disjuncts.html for a survey of work on small disjuncts.

the end the distribution of correctly/incorrectly classified test examples by disjunct size is known. For example, the software might record the fact that disjuncts of size 3 collectively classify 5 test examples correctly and 3 incorrectly. Some experiments were repeated with RIPPER, a program for inducing rule sets (Cohen 1995), in order to assess the generality of our results.

Since pruning eliminates many small disjuncts, consistent with what has been done previously, pruning is disabled for C4.5 and RIPPER for most experiments (as is seen later, however, the same trends are seen even when pruning is not disabled). C4.5 is also run with the –m1 option, to ensure that nodes continue to be split until they only contain examples of a single class, and RIPPER is configured to produce unordered rules so that it does not produce a single default rule to cover the majority class. All experiments employ 10-fold cross validation and the results are therefore based on averages of the test set calculated over 10 runs. Unless specified otherwise, all results are based on C4.5 without pruning.

An Example: The Vote Dataset

In order to illustrate the problem with small disjuncts and introduce a way of measuring this problem, we examine the concept learned by C4.5 from the Vote dataset. Figure 1 shows how the correctly and incorrectly classified test examples are distributed across the disjuncts in this concept. Each bin in the figure spans 10 sizes of disjuncts. The leftmost bin shows that those disjuncts that classify 0-9 training examples correctly cover 9.5 test examples, of which 7.1 are classified correctly and 2.4 classified incorrectly. The fractional values occur because the results are averaged over 10 cross-validated runs. Disjuncts of size 0 occur because when C4.5 splits a node using a feature f, the split uses all possible feature values, whether or not the value occurs within the training examples at that node.

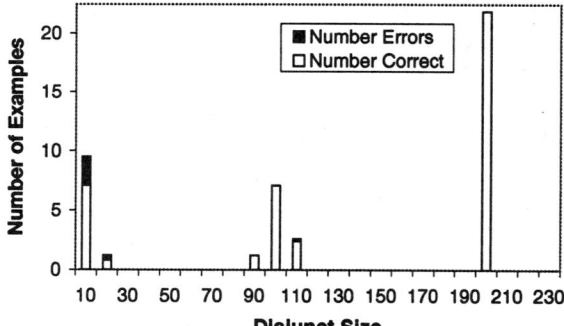

Figure 1: Distribution of Errors

Figure 1 clearly shows that the errors are concentrated toward the smaller disjuncts. Analysis at a finer level of granularity shows that the errors are skewed even more toward the small disjuncts—75% of the errors in the leftmost bin come from disjuncts of size 0 and 1. Space limitations prevent us from showing the distribution of disjuncts, but of the 50 disjuncts in the learned concept, 45 of them are associated with the leftmost bin.

The data may also be described using a new measure, *mean disjunct size*. This measure is computed over a set of examples as follows: each example is assigned a value equal to the size of the disjunct that classifies it, and then the mean of these values is calculated. For the concept shown in Figure 1, the mean disjunct size over all test examples is 124—one can also view this as the center of mass of the bins in the figure. The mean disjunct size for the incorrectly (correctly) classified test examples is 10 (133). Since 10 << 133, the errors are heavily concentrated toward the smaller disjuncts.

In order to better show the extent to which errors are concentrated toward the small disjuncts, we plot, for each disjunct size n, the percentage of test errors versus percentage of correctly classified test examples covered by disjuncts of size n or less. Figure 2 shows this plot for the concept induced from the Vote dataset. It shows, for example, that disjuncts with size 0-4 contribute 5.1% of the correctly classified test examples but 73% of the total test errors. Since the curve in Figure 2 is above the line Y=X, the errors are concentrated toward the smaller disjuncts.

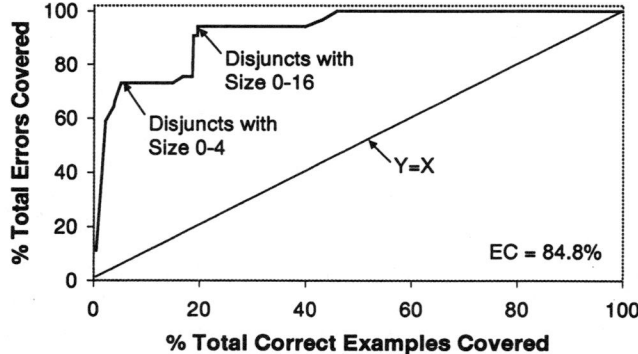

Figure 2: An Error Concentration Curve

To make it easy to compare the degree to which errors are concentrated in the small disjuncts for different concepts, we introduce a measurement called error concentration. *Error Concentration* (EC) is defined as the percentage of the total area above the line Y=X in Figure 2 that falls under the EC curve. EC may take on values between 100 and –100, but is expected to be positive—a negative value indicates that the errors are concentrated more toward the larger disjuncts. The EC value for the concept in Figure 2 is 84.8%, indicating that the errors are highly concentrated toward the small disjuncts.

Results

In this section we present the EC values for 30 datasets and demonstrate that, although they exhibit the problem with small disjuncts to varying degrees, there is some structure to this problem. We then present results that demonstrate how small disjuncts are affected by pruning, training set size, and noise. Due to space limitations, only a few key results are presented in this section. More detailed results are presented elsewhere (Weiss and Hirsh 2000).

Error Concentration for 30 Datasets

C4.5 was applied to 30 datasets and the results, ordered by EC, are summarized in Table 1. We also list the percentage of test errors contributed by the smallest disjuncts that cover 10% of the correctly classified test examples. Note the wide range of EC values and the number of concepts with high EC values.

EC Rank	Dataset	Dataset Size	Error Rate (%)	Largest Disjunct	Number Leaves	% Errors at 10% Correct	Error Conc.
1	kr-vs-kp	3196	0.3	669	47	75.0	87.4
2	hypothyroid	3771	0.5	2697	38	85.2	85.2
3	vote	435	6.9	197	48	73.0	84.8
4	splice-junction	3175	5.8	287	265	76.5	81.8
5	ticket2	556	5.8	319	28	76.1	75.8
6	ticket1	556	2.2	366	18	54.8	75.2
7	ticket3	556	3.6	339	25	60.5	74.4
8	soybean-large	682	9.1	56	175	53.8	74.2
9	breast-wisc	699	5.0	332	31	47.3	66.2
10	ocr	2688	2.2	1186	71	52.1	55.8
11	hepatitis	155	22.1	49	23	30.1	50.8
12	horse-colic	300	16.3	75	40	31.5	50.4
13	crx	690	19.0	58	227	32.4	50.2
14	bridges	101	15.8	33	32	15.0	45.2
15	heart-hungarian	293	24.5	69	38	31.7	45.0
16	market1	3180	23.6	181	718	29.7	44.0
17	adult	21280	16.3	1441	8434	28.7	42.4
18	weather	5597	33.2	151	816	25.6	41.6
19	network2	3826	23.9	618	382	31.2	38.4
20	promoters	106	24.3	20	31	32.8	37.6
21	network1	3577	24.1	528	362	26.1	35.8
22	german	1000	31.7	56	475	17.8	35.6
23	coding	20000	25.5	195	8385	22.5	29.4
24	move	3028	23.5	35	2687	17.0	28.4
25	sonar	208	28.4	50	18	15.9	22.6
26	bands	538	29.0	50	586	65.2	17.8
27	liver	345	34.5	44	35	13.7	12.0
28	blackjack	15000	27.8	1989	45	18.6	10.8
29	labor	57	20.7	19	16	33.7	10.2
30	market2	11000	46.3	264	3335	10.3	4.0

Table 1: Error Concentration for 30 Datasets

While dataset size is not correlated with error concentration, error rate clearly is—concepts with low error rates (<10%) tend to have high EC values. Based on the error rate (ER) and EC values, the entries in Table 1 seem to fit naturally into the following three categories.

1. Low-ER/High-EC: includes datasets 1-10
2. High-ER/Medium-EC: includes datasets 11-22
3. High-ER/Low-EC: includes datasets 23-30

Note that there are no learned concepts with very high EC and high ER, or with low EC and low ER. Of particular interest is that fact that for those datasets in the Low-ER/High-EC group, the largest disjunct in the concept classifies a significant portion of the total training examples, whereas this is not true for the datasets in the High-ER/Low-EC group. Due to space considerations, the results for C4.5 with pruning are not included in Table 1, but the average EC value over the 30 datasets with pruning is 33.5. While this is less than the average without pruning (47.1), it still is well above 0, indicating that even after pruning a substantial proportion of the errors are still concentrated in the smaller disjuncts.

Comparison with Results from RIPPER

Some learning methods, such as neural networks, do not have a notion of a disjunct, while others, such as nearest neighbor methods, do not form disjunctive concepts, but generate something very close, since clusters of examples can be viewed as disjuncts (Van den Bosch et al. 1997). C4.5 is used for most experiments in this paper because it is well known and forms disjunctive concepts. In order to support the generality of any conclusions we draw from the results using C4.5, we compare the EC values for C4.5 with those of RIPPER, a rule learner that also generates disjunctive concepts. The comparison is presented in Figure 3, where each point represents the EC values for a single dataset. Since the results are clustered around the line Y=X, both learners tend to produce concepts with similar EC values, and hence tend to suffer from the problem with small disjuncts to similar degrees. The agreement is especially close for the most interesting cases, where the EC values are large—the same 10 datasets generate the largest 10 EC values for both learners.

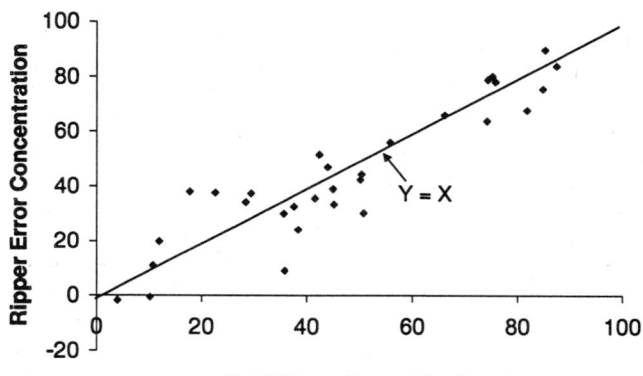

Figure 3: Comparison of C4.5 and RIPPER EC Values

The agreement shown in Figure 3 supports our belief that there is a fundamental property of the underlying datasets that is responsible for the EC values. We believe this property is the relative frequency of rare and general cases in the "true", but unknown, concept to be learned. We recognize, however, that a concept that has many rare cases when expressed as a disjunctive concept may not have them when expressed in a different form. We believe this does not significantly decrease the generality of our results given the number of learners that form disjunction-like concepts.

The Effect of Pruning

Pruning is not used for most of our experiments because it partially obscures the effects of small disjuncts. Nonetheless, small disjuncts provide an opportunity for better understanding how pruning works. Figure 4 displays the same information as Figure 1, except that the results were generated using C4.5 with pruning. Pruning causes the overall error rate to decrease to 5.3% from 6.9%.

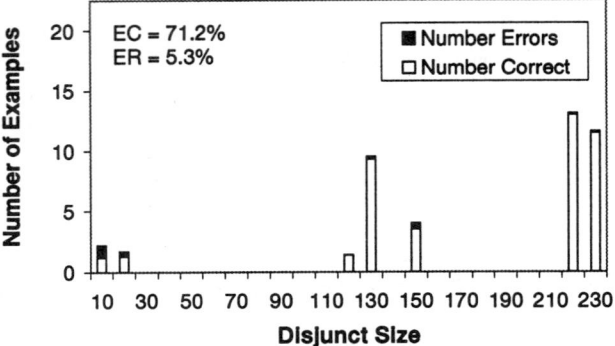

Figure 4: Distribution of Errors with Pruning

Comparing Figure 4 with Figure 1 shows that with pruning the errors are less concentrated toward the small disjuncts (the decrease in EC from 84.8 to 71.2 confirms this). It is also apparent that with pruning far fewer examples are classified by disjuncts with size less than 30. This is because the distribution of disjuncts has changed—whereas before there were 45 disjuncts of size less than 10, after pruning there are only 7. So, pruning eliminates most of the small disjuncts and many of the "emancipated" examples are then classified by the larger disjuncts. Overall, pruning causes the EC to decrease for 23 of the 30 datasets—and the decrease is often large. Looking at this another way, pruning causes the mean disjunct size associated with both the correct and incorrectly classified examples to increase, but the latter increases more than the former. Even after pruning the problem with small disjuncts is still quite evident—after pruning the average EC for the first 10 datasets is 50.6.

Figure 5 plots the absolute improvement in error rate due to pruning against EC rank. The first 10 datasets, which are in the low-ER/high-EC group, show a moderate improvement in error rate. The datasets in the high-ER/medium-EC group, which starts with the Hepatitis dataset, show more improvement, but have more room for improvement due to their higher error rate. The datasets in the high-ER/low-EC group, which start with the Coding dataset, show a net *increase* in error rate. These results suggest that pruning helps when the problem with small disjuncts is quite severe, but may actually increase the error rate in other cases.

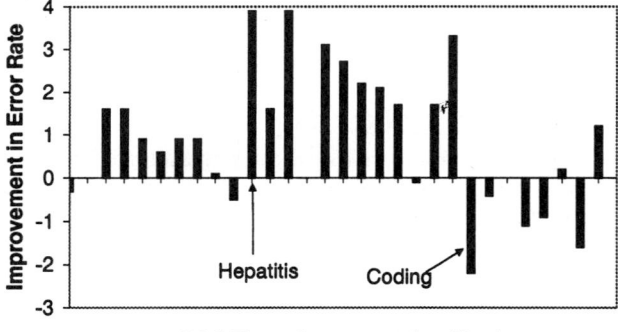

Figure 5: Absolute Improvement in Error Rate vs. EC Rank

The Effect of Training Set Size

Small disjuncts provide an opportunity to better understand how training set size affects learning. We again apply C4.5 to the Vote dataset, except that this time a different 10% (not 90%) of the dataset is used for training for each of the 10 cross-validation runs. Thus, the training set size is 1/9 the size it was previously. As before, each run employs a different 10% of the data for testing. The resulting distribution of examples is shown in Figure 6.

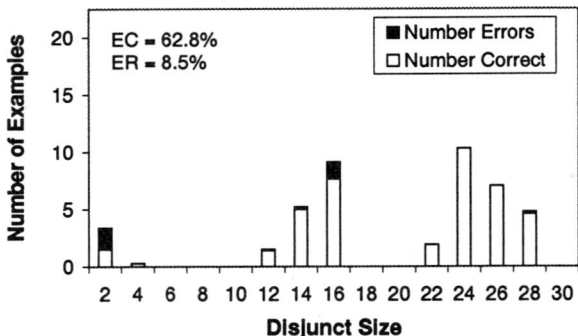

Figure 6: Distribution of Errors (10% Training Data)

Comparing the distribution of errors between Figures 1 and 6 shows that errors are less concentrated toward the smaller disjuncts in Figure 6. This is consistent with the fact that the EC decreases from 84.8 to 62.8 and the mean disjunct size over all examples decreases from 124 to 19, while the mean disjunct size of the errors decreases only slightly from 10.0 to 8.9. Analysis of the results from the 30 datasets shows a similar phenomenon—for 27 of the 30 datasets the EC decreases as the training set size decreases.

These results suggest that the definition of small disjuncts should factor in training set size. To investigate this further, the error rates of disjuncts with specific sizes (0, 1, 2, etc.) were compared as the training set size was varied. Because disjuncts of a specific size for most concepts cover very few examples, statistically valid comparison were possible for only 4 of the 30 datasets. The results for the Coding dataset are shown in Figure 7. Results for the other datasets are available in Weiss and Hirsh (2000).

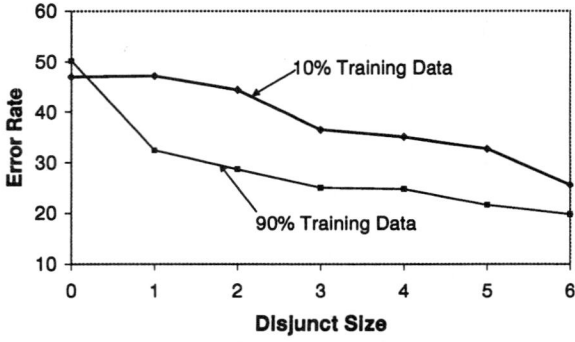

Figure 7: Effect of Training Size on Disjunct Error Rate

Figure 7 shows that the error rates for the smallest disjuncts decrease significantly when the training set size is increased. These results further suggest that the definition of small disjuncts should take training set size into account.

The Effect of Noise

Rare cases cause small disjuncts to be formed in learned concepts. The inability to distinguish between these rare cases (i.e., true exceptions) and noise may be largely responsible for the difficulty in learning in the presence of noise. This conjecture was investigated using synthetic datasets (Weiss 1995) and two real-world datasets (Weiss and Hirsh 1998). We extend this previous work by analyzing 27 datasets (technical difficulties prevented us from handling 3 of the datasets). We restrict the discussion to (random) class noise, since the differing number of attributes in each dataset makes it difficult to fairly compare the impact of attribute noise across datasets.

Although detailed results for class noise are presented elsewhere (Weiss and Hirsh 2000) the results indicate that there is a subtle trend for datasets with higher EC values to experience a greater increase in error rate from class noise. What is much more apparent, however, is that many concepts with low EC values are *extremely* tolerant of noise, whereas none of the concepts with high EC's are. For example, two of the low-EC datasets, blackjack and labor, are so tolerant of noise that when 50% random class noise is added to the training set (i.e., the class value is replaced with a randomly selected valid value 50% of the time), the error rate on the test set increases by less than 1%. The other effect is that as the amount of class noise is increased, the EC tends to decrease. Thus, as noise is added, across almost all of the concepts a greater percentage of the errors come from the larger disjuncts. This helps explain why we find a low-ER/high-EC group of concepts and a high-ER/medium-EC group of concepts: adding noise to concepts in the former increases their error rate and decreases their error concentration, making them look more like concepts in the latter group.

Noise also sometimes causes a radical change in the size of the disjuncts. For low-ER/high-EC group, 10% class noise causes the mean disjunct size of these concepts to shrink, on average, to one-ninth the original size. For the datasets in the high-ER/low-EC group, the same level of noise causes almost no change in the mean disjunct size—the average drops by less than 1%.

Discussion

Many of the results in this paper can be explained by understanding the role of small disjuncts in learning. Learning algorithms tend to form large disjuncts to cover general cases and small disjuncts to cover rare cases. Concepts with many rare cases are harder to learn than those with few, since general cases can be accurately sampled with less training data. This supports the results in Table 1. Concepts in the low-ER/high-EC group contain very general cases—the largest disjunct in these concepts cover, on average, 43% of the correctly classified training examples. The general cases are learned very accurately (the largest disjunct learned in all 10 runs of the Vote dataset never covers *any* test errors). The datasets that are easy to learn and have low error rates have high EC values because so few errors occur in the large disjuncts.

Pruning is the most widespread strategy for addressing the problem with small disjuncts. As was shown earlier, pruning eliminates many small disjuncts. The emancipated examples are then classified using other disjuncts. While this tends to cause the error rate of these other disjuncts to increase, the overall error rate of the concept tends to decrease. Pruning reduces C4.5's average error rate on the 30 datasets from 18.4% to 17.5%, while reducing the EC from 84.8 to 71.2. While this average 0.9% error rate reduction is significant, it is useful to compare this reduction to an "idealized" strategy, where the error rate for the small disjuncts is equal to the error rate of the other (i.e., medium and large) disjuncts. While such a strategy is not achievable, it provides a way of gauging the effectiveness of pruning at addressing the problem of small disjuncts.

Table 2 compares the error rates (averaged over the 30 datasets) resulting from various strategies. The idealized strategy is applied using two scenarios, where the smallest disjuncts covering a total of 10% (20%) of the training examples were assigned an error rate based on the remaining 90% (80%) of the examples.

No Pruning	Default Pruning	Idealized (10%)	Idealized (20%)
18.4%	17.5%	15.2%	13.5%

Table 2: Comparison of Pruning to Idealized Strategy

Table 2 shows that the idealized strategy, even when applied to only 10% of the examples, significantly outperforms C4.5's pruning strategy. These results provide a motivation for finding strategies that better address the problem with small disjuncts.

For many real-world problems, such as identifying those customers likely to buy a product, one is more interested in finding individual classification rules that have high precision than in finding the concept with the best *overall* accuracy. In these situations, pruning seems a questionable strategy, since it tends to decrease the precision of the larger (presumably more precise) disjuncts. To investigate this further, precision/recall curves were generated with and without pruning for each dataset, by starting with the largest disjunct and progressively adding smaller disjuncts. The curves for all 30 datasets were averaged, and the results are shown in Figure 8.

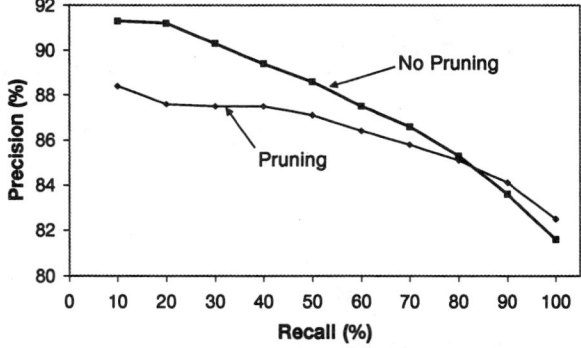

Figure 8: Effect of Pruning on Precision/Recall Curve

The figure shows that while pruning improves predictive accuracy (precision at 100% recall), it reduces the precision of a solution for most values of recall. The break-even point occurs at only 80% recall. This suggests that the use of pruning should be tied to the performance metric most appropriate for a given learning task.

Identifying Error Prone Small Disjuncts

Almost all strategies for addressing the problem with small disjuncts treat small and large disjuncts differently. Consequently, if we hope to address this problem, we need a way to effectively distinguish between the two. The definition that a small disjunct is a disjunct that correctly classifies few training examples (Holte, et al. 1989) is not particularly helpful in this context. What is needed is a method for determining a good threshold t, such that disjuncts with size less than t have a much higher error rate than those with size greater than t. Based on our results we suggest that the threshold t should be based on the relationship between disjunct size and error rate, since error rate is not related to disjunct size in a simple way, and more specifically, using error concentration. Based on the EC curve in Figure 2, for example, it seems reasonable to conclude that the threshold for the Vote dataset should be 4, 16, or a value in between. For datasets such as Market2 or Labor, where the EC is very low, we may choose not to distinguish small disjuncts from large disjuncts at all.

Conclusion

This paper provides insight into the role of small disjuncts in learning. By measuring error concentration on concepts induced from 30 datasets, we demonstrate that the problem with small disjuncts occurs to varying degrees, but is quite severe for many of these concepts. We show that even after pruning the problem is still evident, and, by using RIPPER, showed that our results are not an artifact of C4.5.

Although the focus of the paper was on measuring and understanding the impact of small disjuncts on learning, we feel our results could lead to improved learning algorithms. First, error concentration can help identify the threshold for categorizing a disjunct as small, and hence can be used to improve the effectiveness of variable bias system in addressing the problem with small disjuncts. The EC value could also be used to control the pruning strategy of a learning algorithm, since low EC values seems to indicate that pruning may actually decrease predictive accuracy. A high EC value is also a clear indication that one is likely to be able to trade-off reduced recall for greatly improved precision.

References

Ali, K. M. and Pazzani, M. J. 1992. Reducing the Small Disjuncts Problem by Learning Probabilistic Concept Descriptions, in T. Petsche editor, *Computational Learning Theory and Natural Learning Systems*, Volume 3.

Blake, C. L. and Merz, C. J. 1998. UCI Repository of ML Databases, http://www.ics.uci.edu/~mlearn/MLRepository.html, Irvine, CA: University of California, Department. of Computer Science.

Cohen, W. 1995. Fast Effective Rule Induction. In *Proceedings of the Twelfth International Conference on Machine Learning*, 115-123.

Cohen, W. and Singer, Y. 1999. A Simple, Fast, and Effective Rule Learner. In *Proceedings of the Sixteenth National Conference on Artificial Intelligence*, 335-342. Menlo Park, Calif.: AAAI Press.

Danyluk, A. P. and Provost, F. J. 1993. Small Disjuncts in Action: Learning to Diagnose Errors in the Local Loop of the Telephone Network. In *Proceedings of the Tenth International Conference on Machine Learning*, 81-88.

Holte, R., C., Acker, L. E., and Porter, B. W. 1989. Concept Learning and the problem of small disjuncts. In *Proceedings of the Eleventh International Joint Conference on Artificial Intelligence*, 813-818. San Mateo, CA: Morgan Kaufmann.

Quinlan, J. R. 1993. *C4.5: Programs for Machine Learning*. San Mateo, CA: Morgan Kaufmann.

Ting, K. M. 1994. The Problem of Small Disjuncts: its Remedy in Decision Trees. In *Proceedings of the Tenth Canadian Conference on Artificial Intelligence*, 91-97.

Van den Bosch, A., Weijters, A., Van den Herik, H.J. and Daelemans, W. 1997. When Small Disjuncts Abound, Try Lazy Learning: A Case Study. In *Proceedings of the Seventh Belgian-Dutch Conference on Machine Learning*, 109-118.

Weiss, G. M. 1995. Learning with Rare Cases and Small Disjuncts. In *Proceedings of the Twelfth International Conference on Machine Learning*, 558-565.

Weiss, G. M. and Hirsh, H. 1998. The Problem with Noise and Small Disjuncts. In *Proceedings of the Fifteenth International Conference on Machine Learning*, 574-578.

Weiss, G. M. and Hirsh, H. 2000. A Quantitative Study of Small Disjuncts: Experiments and Results, Technical Report, ML-TR-42, Computer Science Department., Rutgers University. Also available from http://www.cs.rutgers.edu/~gweiss/papers/index.html.

Natural Language Processing and Information Retrieval

Translating with Scarce Resources

Yaser Al-Onaizan, Ulrich Germann, Ulf Hermjakob, Kevin Knight,
Philipp Koehn, Daniel Marcu, and Kenji Yamada

Information Sciences Institute
University of Southern California
4676 Admiralty Way, Suite 1001
Marina del Rey, CA 90292
{yaser,germann,ulf,knight,koehn,marcu,kyamada}@isi.edu

Abstract

Current corpus-based machine translation techniques do not work very well when given scarce linguistic resources. To examine the gap between human and machine translators, we created an experiment in which human beings were asked to translate an unknown language into English on the sole basis of a very small bilingual text. Participants performed quite well, and debriefings revealed a number of valuable strategies. We discuss these strategies and apply some of them to a statistical translation system.

Introduction

Corpus-based approaches to machine translation (MT) have been on the rise recently, partly because of their promise to automate a great deal of dictionary construction and rule writing, partly because they simply represent a new way of attacking a stubborn problem, and partly because they have performed relatively well in MT evaluations (such as those performed by DARPA and the German Verbmobil program). These approaches generally rely on a large bilingual text corpus to provide sample translations. A statistical model is trained on the samples, and it is used to translate new sentences. Most of this research can be classified as either statistical machine translation (SMT) or example-based machine translation (EBMT); it includes work such as (Brown *et al.* 1993; Nagao 1984; Wu 1997; Alshawi, Buchsbaum, & Xia 1997; Melamed 2000; Och, Tillmann, & Ney 1999).

In this area, it is a truism that "there's no data like more data." If a program sees a particular word or phrase one thousand times during training, it is more likely to learn a correct translation pattern than if it sees it ten times, or once, or never. Corpus-based MT approaches have so far been applied to situations where large amounts of bilingual text already exist. For example, (Brown *et al.* 1993) exploit the substantial French-English Canadian parliamentary record. For many language pairs of interest, such a large corpus does not exist, and this severely limits the practicality of statistical approaches for pairs like Polish/Finnish, German/Romanian, etc. This problem is particularly acute for *low-density* languages, which typically have: few native speakers, low levels of computerization, writing not yet standardized, little linguistic work, and/or few linguistic resources online.

Of course, a small amount of bilingual text can be commissioned outright. Current techniques do not work very well on such small data sets, but this does not rule out the possibility of developing new techniques that do. It is also possible that such new techniques would be applicable to improving performance on large data sets.

In this paper, we make an initial investigation into corpus-based translation with severely limited bilingual corpora. For our experiments, we use *Tetun*, one of fifteen distinct languages spoken in East Timor.[1] While carrying out these experiments, we had no background on the Tetun language. This significant blinder forced us to view the linguistic data from an angle similar to that of a knowledge-poor computer program.

Training Corpus

We were able to obtain a small Tetun/English bilingual corpus from Internet sources. These included a United Nations site with a variety of Timor-related legal documents written in up to four languages (English, Tetun, Bahasa Indonesia, and Portuguese). They also included Australian and Japanese sites specializing in East Timorese studies and humanitarian relief. Our bilingual corpus contained:

- 1102 sentence pairs.
- 23652 English word tokens.
- 25576 Tetun word tokens.
- 1993 distinct English word forms.
- 1729 distinct Tetun word forms.

---

[1] Another frequently-used spelling is *Tetum*. East Timorese languages break down into many dialects. We focussed on Tetun-Dili, which is spokenly widely in the East Timorese capital.

Copyright © 2000, American Association for Artificial Intelligence (www.aaai.org). All rights reserved.

1. You can find out where you can go to register in several ways.
   Imi sei hatene oin sa mak atu bele ba hetan fatin tau naran hirak ne'e.
2. UNAMET is responsible for running the popular consultation where you - the people of East Timor - will choose the future of East Timor.
   UNAMET sei responsabiliza atu halao konsulta popular nebe imi - povu Timor Loro Sae - sei hili futuru Timor Loro Sae nian.
3. They will also watch over the whole process to make sure the rules are obeyed and the process is fair.
   Sira mos sei tau matan ba prosesus ne'e tomak atu hatene lolos katak ema lao tuir duni ordem no prosesu ne'e justu duni.

Figure 1: Sample sentence pairs from a small Tetun/English bilingual corpus.

We can contrast this with the 1.6 million sentence pairs available in the French/English Hansard corpus.

Because of the small size of the corpus, it was possible to sentence-align it by hand. We could not be sure that the alignment was correct, of course, but we had many clues: corresponding sentence lengths, sentence pairs containing the same proper nouns, matching paragraph boundaries, matching section markings, etc. The fact that we were able to align the Tetun/English corpus is consistent with positive empirical results reported for knowledge-poor sentence-alignment methods (Church 1993). Figure 1 shows a sample.

Testing Corpus

We held out a short news report from the training corpus and divided it into ten sentences. We circulated the Tetun version (shown in Figure 2), but kept the English translation hidden. One question we wanted to ask was:

> With only a small bilingual training corpus, and no knowledge of the Tetun language (no native speaker, informant, dictionary, grammar book, etc.), can a person translate the material in Figure 2 accurately and fluently?

If the task is impossible for people, then it is probably asking too much to develop new MT techniques for dealing with small training sets. On the other hand, if the task can be accomplished well by people, then post-task debriefings may shed light on potential strategies for MT.

Another way to assess the impact of corpus size is to examine how familiar the test corpus looks after we have seen the training corpus. In this case:

- 18% of the distinct Tetun word forms in the test data are never observed in the bilingual training data.
- 41% of the distinct Tetun word forms in the test data are observed fewer than six times in the bilingual

1. Funsionariu senior UNAMET sira ba Maliana, Suai no Viqueque iha Kuarta-feira hamutuk ho Embaixador Agus Tarmidzi xefe Forsa Serbisu (Forsa Tarefa) Indonezia nian, Brigadeiru Jeneral Satoris, Ofisial Polisia (Polri) iha Timor Lorosa'e nian no Ofisial Senior Indonezia nian sira seluk.
2. Sr Ian Martin, Reprezentante Espesial Sekretariu Jeral nian ba Timor Lorosa'e esplika, "Ami ba fatin tolu ne'e tanba fatin hirak ne'e maka fatin sira be ami iha preokupasaun boot liu."
3. Sr Martin hateten katak, "Maske prosesu tau naran nian la'o di'ak, iha akontesimentu seriu boot ida foin lais ne'e iha Viqueque, tanba nune'e ema barak maka halai husik hela sira nia uma.
4. Ida ne'e maka situasaun ida ne'ebe presiza haree."
5. Iha Suai, UNAMET preokupa loos ho aktividades hosi grupu milisia Laksaur no Mahidi sira.
6. Aktividades hirak ne'e halo numeru ema refujiadu sira barak ba beibeik maka hela iha igreja Suai nian.
7. "Ami nia diskusaun liuliu ko'alia kona ba oinsa atu rezolve aktividade milisia hirak ne'e nian," Sr Martin esplika.
8. Iha Maliana, Sr Martin dehan katak mosu tiha ona hahalok seriu boot sira ne'e molok ninia grupu to'o iha ne'eba.
9. "Problema liuliu ne'e iha Bobonaro maka, hodi uluk kedas, ofisial senior sira lakohi rekonhese sira nia obrigasaun hodi autoriza grupu pro-independensia atu hala'o sira nia servisu.
10. Problema ne'e autoridades Indonezia sira nian hatene kleur ona.

Figure 2: Sentences to be translated in the experiment.

training data.

- 63% of the distinct Tetun word pairs in the test data are never observed.
- 90% of the distinct Tetun word triples in the test data are never observed.

The figures are higher if we consider tokens rather than distinct word forms. This situation is rather difficult in comparison to a similar example in our French/English corpus, where 99.6% of the test words were observed in training, as were 93.5% of the test word-pairs.

Decoding Results

Thirteen people participated in our Tetun/English human translation experiment. They included linguists, computational linguists, computer scientists, and others. Participants were free to organize themselves into teams, and two did so, leaving a total of twelve teams. The instructions, delivered over the web, were to view the Tetun test document as a code for English—and then to decode as best as possible. Participants were given 1102 simple sentence translations in a downloadable file. They were free to work by hand, to implement computer-based tools for assistance, or to completely automate the decoding process. Computer-based tools could be held in private or distributed freely to other teams. The task time was one week; mild incentives were promised to the team with the best decodings.

One very useful keyword-in-context tool was made available. This tool accepts a word or phrase in Tetun or English and displays a list of all sentence pairs containing the word or phrase, highlighting it where it appears.

After all submissions were in, results were evaluated by two non-participant judges. Both judges were native English speakers, and they were asked to score individual sentence decodings on the basis of both accuracy and fluency, on a scale of 1 (bad) to 5 (good). Judgments were made with respect to the reference English translations that were withheld from the participants; the judges were allowed to see the original Tetun sentences, but had no Tetun competence. This kind of monolingual evaluation has its drawbacks. For example, if the reference translator simply gets it wrong, then even a great translation will be scored poorly. Or the reference translator may drop or add minor facts in her quest to produce readable text; two perfectly good translations may then disagree. However, we do not believe such problems hampered our ability to answer our basic question.

Some of the participants were able to produce translations that were strikingly similar to the reference translations, which we therefore assume to be reasonable translations.

We reproduce one participant's decodings in Figure 3. Reference translations are shown in Figure 4. Evaluator judgments appear in Figure 5. See Figure 6 for sample statistical MT results. Each row stands for one participant, and each column stands for one sentence. Each cell in the matrix records the two judges' scores, separated by a colon.

Note that there was a wide range of scores. People differed significantly on how much time they devoted to the task. This is partly a function of patience—when faced with any sort of puzzle or brain-teaser, people sort themselves out according to temperament as well as skill. Also, not all the participants were native English speakers, and this affected fluency. (Note that of the top-scoring three, one was a native English speaker, and two were native German speakers). Finally, one participant entered the (lightly-edited) results of a corpus-based MT system. After the evaluation, judges were asked to identify the best and worst individual sentence translations—the former was produced by a linguist, the latter by the MT system.

We believe that if all decoders had worked as a single team, the resulting translation would have scored better than any individual translation; in our debriefings (described in the next section) we found that even the highest-scoring decoders could have easily been convinced to change their minds on various points.

1. Senior UNAMET Officials ("Functionaries") for Maliana Suai and Viqueque are scheduled for (=planning and expected to go to) Kuarta, along with Ambassador Agus Tarmidzi, President of the Indonesian "Service Force" (Tarriff Force), Brigadier General Satoris, Official of the Police (Polri) in East Timor, and several Indonesian Senior Officials.
2. Mr. Ian Martin, the [UN] Secretary General's Special Envoy (=representative) for East Timor, explained: "We go to the[se] three locations, because these locations are locations that we are very worried about."
3. Mr. Martin said that "Even though the registration process shows signs of improvement, very serious events have taken place since the one in Viqueque, because a number of people have had to give up living in their home.
4. This is a situation that we must watch/look at."
5. In Suai, UNAMET is worried about the activities by the Laksaur and Mahidi militias.
6. These activities, which have left an increasing number of people displaced, occur [mainly?] in the [area around?] Suai.
7. "Our discussion particularly deals with the question how to resolve this militia activity," Mr Martin explained.
8. In Maliana, Mr. Martin said that very serious misconduct had occurred before his group arrived (there).
9. The problems particularly in Bobonaro are, to begin with, that senior officials have refused to recognize their obligation to authorize (permit/allow) pro-independence groups to perform their function/role.
10. The Indonesian authorities have long known about this problem."

Figure 3: Decodings from one participant in the Tetun/English experiment.

1. Senior UNAMET staff went to Maliana, Suai and Viqueque on Wednesday with Ambassador Agus Tarmidzi, Chairman of the Indonesian Task Force, Brigadier General Satoris, Senior Polri Officer in East Timor and other senior Indonesian officials.
2. "We went to those three places because they are places that are of the most concern to us," Mr. Ian Martin, the Special Representative of the Secretary-General for East Timor, explained.
3. "Despite a successful registration, there has recently been serious disorder in Viqueque, and as a result a large number of people have fled from their homes," Mr. Martin said.
4. "That is a situation that urgently needs addressing," he said.
5. In Suai, UNAMET is concerned about the continued activities of the Laksaur and Mahidi militia groups.
6. These activities have led to increases in the numbers of internally displaced people in the church compound in Suai.
7. "Our discussion focussed on the need to take action to reign in the activity of those militia groups," Mr. Martin explained.
8. In Maliana, Mr. Martin said the party arrived soon after several serious incidents.
9. "The fundamental problem in Bobonaro has been, from the beginning, the refusal of senior officials to recognize their obligation to allow pro-independence groups to operate.
10. That problem in Bobonaro has been well known to the Indonesian authorities for some time."

Figure 4: Reference translations.

```
id         scores                              avg
006   3:4 5:5 4:4 5:5 5:5 4:3 5:4 5:5 5:5 5:5  4.55
001   4:5 5:5 3:4 5:5 5:4 5:5 5:5 5:5 4:5 2:3  4.45
003   2:4 5:4 5:4 5:5 5:5 5:5 5:4 5:5 5:2 5:4  4.45
011   4:4 4:4 2:2 4:5 4:3 5:5 4:5 4:4 5:4 5:5  4.10
007   4:4 4:5 4:3 4:2 5:5 5:5 5:5 3:5 4:2 2:2  3.90
010   4:4 3:4 4:3 5:5 5:5 2:4 5:5 3:2 2:2 3:2  3.60
002   4:5 3:4 4:5 3:2 5:4 2:2 4:4 3:2 5:5 2:2  3.50
012   3:3 4:4 2:3 1:4 5:5 3:2 4:4 5:4 5:4 1:2  3.40
008   3:3 2:3 1:2 3:5 4:4 4:4 5:4 2:3 5:3 1:2  3.15
004   2:3 4:3 3:2 5:5 3:5 2:3 3:3 1:1 1:1 2:1  2.65
005   3:3 2:3 1:1 2:3 3:3 2:2 3:4 1:2 2:2 1:2  2.25
009   3:3 2:3 3:3 5:5 3:4 1:1 1:1 1:1 1:1 1:1  2.20
```

Figure 5: Evaluator judgments for all participants. Rows indicate participants, columns indicate sentences, and entries represent the two judges' scores.

6. Aktividades said the new documentation people displaced number journalists serious living igreja Suai.

Figure 6: Sample statistical MT results (IBM model 3).

Decoding Strategies

Here we cover strategies used by human decoders.

Left to Right, Conceptualize

The most common method was to (1) gather potential word translations for each Tetun word, moving left to right over a sentence and using the bilingual corpus, (2) pick word translations that seem to make sense with each other, (3) guess the basic idea of the whole sentence from those translations, and (4) generate a good English sentence expressing that idea. For example, from sentence 4 some decoders could come up with <*situation, need, watch*>, which could then be turned into *it is necessary to watch the situation* or *we must watch the situation*, among many other formulations we observed.

In generating English, we noticed that decoders frequently shifted part of speech. While the bilingual corpus contains many translations for the Tetun word *presiza* (*needed, necessary, need to, required, have to*), decoders felt free to go outside this list (e.g., *must*). This was particularly important for words that were observed only once or twice in the bilingual corpus. Synonym substitution was also frequent. Decoders tapped into extensive English knowledge by supplying articles, copulas, and plurals which they deemed to be missing in Tetun. In expressing the overall idea in English, final word ordering seemed to be a matter of English grammar only, but many decoders reported their discovery that Tetun adjectives often followed nouns and had to be re-ordered.

Intersections and Locality

When consulting the bilingual corpus for instances of a particular Tetun word, decoders would often scroll past long sentence pairs until they found a short one. Short sentence pairs offer a smaller list of potential translations. Given two or three short sentences with the word *ema*, for example, it was easy to look at the intersection of words in the different English translations. This intersection often tolerated inexact matches, e.g., *person/people*. This may be why most decoders preferred to do this operation by hand rather than implement matching algorithms. One decoder implemented IBM Model 1 (Brown *et al.* 1993) but found the resulting probabilistic dictionary to be fairly unhelpful.

Many words do not appear in a large number of sentence pairs. In this case, another strategy was to use locality. Consider trying to determine a translation for *liuliu* in a very long sentence pair. First, decoders easily noticed that the last few phrases often seem to be translations of one another, effectively creating a smaller sentence pair:

...grupu milisia sira liuliu iha loromonu nian iha Timor Lorosa'e.
...militia groups particularly in the west of East Timor.

Next, the phrase *grupu milisia* seems on its face to

translate as *militia groups*, while *Timor Lorosa'e* is clearly *East Timor*. Decoders were then able to hypothesize that *loromonu* translates as *west*. They could then look up this word (which was not in the task-text) and find that it occurred twice, along with the English word *western*. By process of elimination, *liuliu* could then be tentatively linked to the word *particularly*. Another scan of the bilingual corpus showed *liuliu* co-occuring with the phrase *in particular*, effectively confirming this link.

Cognates and Proper Names

To be able to apply locality, decoders needed to know at least some word translations up front. All decoders made heavy use of cognates (Tetun/English word pairs with similar spellings), as shown in the example above. Proper names can be seen as a special case of cognates, undergoing no change in spelling. Punctuation and numerals also provided important anchor points.

Unknown Words

Many words in the translation task did not appear in the bilingual corpus at all, but they still had to be translated. Decoders developed several strategies for handling them. Proper names were easiest, and could be translated without change. However, in the process of "getting the idea" of the sentence, it was important to figure out the type of entity referred to by the proper name. If the rest of the sentence was very clear, the type could be inferred, although this was not foolproof. Some decoders decided to go to web search engines as well. It was not difficult find out from the web that *Viqueque* is a town in East Timor.

Some words were unknown because of the severe lack of spelling standardization in written Tetun. It was difficult for decoders to search for spelling variants, but some were able to compile spelling variation lists while observing sentence pairs retrieved for other purposes. For example, the Tetun translation for *East Timor* appears variously as *Timor Loro sa'e*, *Timor Loro sae*, *Timor Loro-sa'e*, *Timor Lorosa'e*, *Timor Loroasa'e*, and *Timor Lorosae*.

Cognates played a very important role in translating unknown words. It proved easy to decode the phrase *aktividade milisia* even though the first word was never observed in the bilingual corpus. As mentioned above, cognates were also important for anchoring and locality. The bilingual corpus reveals a large number of Tetun/English cognates, such as *grupu/group* and *diskasaun/discussion*. However, there are a much larger number of Tetun/Portuguese cognates. Some decoders could call on friends with Portuguese knowledge to confirm hypotheses. A larger number of decoders knew Spanish, which turned out to be sufficient. For example, the word *igreja* appears in sentence 6, but never in the bilingual corpus. Only half of the decoders were able to translate this word. Several decoders noticed that *igreja* is similar to the Spanish word *iglesia*, which means *church*. One decoder used an online Portuguese/English dictionary to confirm this hypothesis.[2] Other words such as *xefe* (boss), *esplika* (explain), and *preokupasaun* (worry) could be similarly decoded.

Short Tetun Words

Many short Tetun words were easily handled by the decoders. For example, *ho* and *no* both occur frequently translated as *and* in the bilingual corpus. *Iha* seems to translate mostly as *in* or *on*, and decoders easily made this choice when generating fluent English translations.

Other Tetun words were much more difficult because they seemed to have no clear translation, even in the bilingual corpus. These included words like *maka*, *ida*, *sira*, *nian*, *tiha*, and *ona*. The decoders found these frustrating because they were quite frequent in all texts. For example, no decoder could report any theory about the meaning or function of the word *maka*—despite the fact that it occurs forty-two times in the bilingual corpus. The solution adopted by most decoders was to simply ignore these words. This is the reverse of the article/copula/plural situation described above, in which short English words seemed to have no Tetun equivalents.

Some of these puzzles were resolved when we later (subsequent to this experiment) obtained a small handbook for the Tetun language, e.g.:

> A useful word in Tetum is **maka** (often shortened to **mak**) which means 'is what', 'is the one that', 'is the thing that', e.g. **Serveja mak ami hakarak.** = Beer is what we want. (Hull 1999)

Indeed, in Tetun/English translation, it is usually more natural to ignore *maka* than to translate it. We note that *mak* occurred 124 times in our bilingual corpus, but that it did not occur in the test corpus—so decoders had little incentive to figure out that *mak* and *maka* were equivalent.

Phrases

Decoders frequently tried to look up two- and three-word phrases in the bilingual corpus. For example, *prosesu tau naran* occurred several times, translated as *registration process* or simply *registration*. As another example, *tiha ona* was observed many times, but was eventually ignored by decoders, like *maka*. It was convenient that *tiha ona* could be treated as a unit for such reasoning.

Reverse Lookup

Sentence 2 contains the word *ami*, which always co-occurs with the English word *we*, and is therefore easy to translate. Sentence 7, however, begins with the

---

[2]The use of this dictionary, the use of Portuguese-speaking informants, and the use of the web for semantically typing proper names made up the rare use of outside material. The highest-scoring participant used only the bilingual corpus.

phrase *ami nia*. The word *nia* seems to be quite ambiguous, co-occuring with *you*, *your*, *he*, *its*, etc. The phrase *ami nia* never occurs in the bilingual corpus. Almost all decoders were able to work out this puzzle.

The phrase *imi nia* was observed to translate as *your*, while *imi* alone translates as *you*. This was enough for decoders to hypothesize that *nia* is a possessive marker. To confirm this hypothesis, they could look up the English words *they* and *their* and find the Tetun translations *sira* and *sira nia* (note that this type of reasoning reverses the normal Tetun-based lookup process). Some decoders noticed that the English word *he* translates as *nia*; however, there is no such phrase *nia nia*, as the possessive *his* is rendered in short form *ninia*.

In this case, the decoders clearly knew what they were looking for, and could apply reasoning that was more sophisticated than co-occurrence counting.

Negation

Most decoders were able to determine that there is no separate Tetun word indicating negation. Rather, the letters *la-* are frequently prefixed to negate some item. This could be determined again by reverse lookup, i.e., determining which Tetun words co-occur with the English words *not* and *no*. As with reasoning about cognates and spelling variations, it was necessary to look at patterns within words as well as co-occurrences at the word level.

Days of the Week

Sentence 1 contains a puzzle in the phrase *Kuarta-feira*. The bilingual corpus contains the word *Sexta-feira*, translated as *Friday*, but no other instances of either *Kuarta* or *feira*. Most decoders settled on *Wednesday*, while a few picked *Thursday* or nothing at all.

Multi-Sentence Flow

Several decoders reported that it was useful to move back and forth across sentences in the text they were translating. For example, the first sentence mentions *Maliana*, *Suai*, and *Viqueque*, although it is difficult to tell what types of entities these are. However, each is covered in turn by subsequent sentences, where it becomes clear that they are best interpreted as places where things happen. Decoders also reported that the mention of militia problems (in the middle of the text) helped them interpret later passages.

Deliberate Ambiguity

In the phrase *grupu milisia Laksaur no Mahidi sira*, decoders did not agree on the semantic type of *Laksaur*. Some imagined it to be the town where the militia group was, while others imagined it to be the name of the militia group. At least one decoder was unsure, and rather than risk the translation *militia groups in Laksaur and Mahidi*, he translated the phrase ambiguously as *the Laksaur and Mahidi militia groups*.

Non-Strategies

We found that Tetun syntax did not play an important role in any of the decoders' work. No one attempted to draw Tetun parse trees as an intermediate step in decoding. We also found that no decoders drew any conclusions based on the fact that Tetun is in the Austronesian language family, and might therefore behave in certain predictable patterns.

Discussion

Our basic result shows that people can learn to translate a language they do not know if they are given a small bilingual corpus. They do so by employing a number of strategies. Corpus-based MT approaches perform badly on the same task, so there is much room for improvement.

It is interesting to consider which of the decoding strategies are amenable to being formalized in computer algorithms. We consider this to be a good topic for future exploration. Clearly, people can figure out how to translate Tetun without knowing anything about the language. But in this experiment, they knew quite a bit about English, the target language.[3] Moreover, they had some ability to synthesize a number of word translations into a coherent idea of the sentence. These are difficult areas. It would be useful for the machine to locate an appropriate concept for a Tetun word based on its several different translations. For example, the translations for *presiza* (*needed*, *necessary*, *need to*, *required*, *have to*) are enough to identify the general logical concept of necessity. Existing natural language generation programs such as Nitrogen (Langkilde & Knight 1998) can then render this general logical concept in many ways, depending on the other phrases generated in the same sentence. For example, the input:

```
(n / NECESSITY
  :domain (o / OBSERVE
            :patient (s / SITUATION)))
```

is rendered by Nitrogen automatically in over 66,000 ways; relatively highly-ranked ones include:

> The situation must be watched attentively.
> A situation must be watched attentively.
> It must be watched attentively that it is situated.
> It is necessary to watch attentively this situation.

At the very least, a machine should have some basic capability to expand the set of translations beyond those observed in the corpus. In our machine experiments, we frequently observed our program struggling

---

[3] It would be extremely interesting to run such experiment between two unknown languages. Target language considerations such as word order would have to be made on the basis of observed target-language corpora only. (Knight 1997) contains a small artificial corpus along these lines, between imaginary languages Centauri and Arcturan. These languages turn out to be English and Spanish in disguise, allowing human decoders to mentally simulate statistical algorithms without bias.

with a word like *saw* when it needed a word like *sight*. Expanded translation sets can be built from inflectional morphology, derivational morphology, synonym-finding, and other processes.

We carried out some MT experiments using two of the human strategies described above. These were strategies for dealing with cognates and short function words.

We found that standard statistical word-alignments between Tetun and English training sentences were quite inaccurate. Obvious cognate pairs were not connected, as the training algorithm made no use of word-internal features. One easy way to address this problem is to supply a list of cognate pairs as an additional "corpus" appended to the real corpus. This biases the word-alignments search in favor of connecting cognate pairs. We first generate a cognate-pair candidate for each word co-occurrence in the training corpus. For example, from a sentence pair of length n, we will list out n^2 candidates. Most of these candidates are not translations at all, so we restrict candidate pairs to begin with the same letter. We then use an algorithm described by Noah Smith in (Al-Onaizan *et al.* 1999) to find spelling similarities and simultaneously rank the candidate list. We take the top of this list as our cognate corpus, which we append to the regular training corpus. Here are some of the cognates suggested automatically:

```
0.514 problema/problem     0.494 promove/promote
0.496 prova/prove          0.492 proposta/proposal
0.496 imparsial/impartial  0.489 forma/forms
```

Because these word-pairs not only look alike but also co-occur in the corpus, they are fairly reliable. Further down the ranked list, false cognates begin to appear, e.g.,

```
0.302 fila/fear    0.302 pessoal/personnel
```

In inspecting our word alignments, we also found that most of the Tetun function words were connected to various English words. Given a larger corpus, we expect that the training algorithm would learn to generate Tetun function words from the special NULL token, effectively telling the automatic decoder not to hypothesize English translations for them. However, our decoder does not make such hypotheses, loading up English translations with lots of extra words. We do not yet know how to automatically identify such NULL-generated words with a small parallel corpus, but we can make use of our manual analysis. Prior to decoding, we simply remove all "stop-words" (e.g., *maka*) from any Tetun document. We have found that the translations improve when we do this.

For example, before working with cognates and function words, our automatic translation of sentence 4 was:

This is serious situation which was necessary put.

Afterwards, our translation was:

Situation which need to see.

Of course, there is a great deal of the difference between our machine translations and those of human decoders, and we believe it is worth continuing along these lines.

Finally, we note again that our human decoding experiments were run over the web—we provided training and testing corpora, search tools, and evaluation software. This facility is open to the public,[4] and we hope to add other languages. We believe it should be of educational value in computational linguistics, artificial intelligence, and linguistics curricula.

Acknowledgments

We would like to thank Katya Shuldiner for collecting and collating human decodings. Many thanks to David Purdy and Richard Whitney for doing evaluation, and to participants Jonathan Gratch, David Lugo, Franz-Josef Och, Andrew Philpot, Bonnie Glover Stalls, and Marcelo Tallis. This work was supported in part by DARPA-ITO award N66001-00-1-9814.

References

Al-Onaizan, Y.; Curin, J.; Jahr, M.; Knight, K.; Lafferty, J.; Melamed, D.; Och, F.; Purdy, D.; Smith, N. A.; and Yarowsky, D. 1999. Statistical machine translation, final report, JHU Workshop 1999. Technical report, CLSP, Johns Hopkins University.

Alshawi, H.; Buchsbaum, A.; and Xia, F. 1997. A comparison of head transducers and transfer for a limited domain translation applications. In *Proc. ACL*.

Brown, P.; Pietra, S. D.; Pietra, V. D.; and Mercer, R. 1993. The mathematics of statistical machine translation: Parameter estimation. *Computational Linguistics* 19(2).

Church, K. 1993. A program for alinging parallel texts at the character level. In *Proc. ACL*.

Hull, G. 1999. *Tetum: Language Manual for East Timor*. Academy of East Timor Studies.

Knight, K. 1997. Automating knowledge acquisition for machine translation. *AI Magazine* 18(4).

Langkilde, I., and Knight, K. 1998. Generation that exploits corpus-based statistical knowledge. In *Proc. COLING/ACL*.

Melamed, D. 2000. *Empirical Methods for Exploiting Parallel Texts*. MIT Press.

Nagao, M. 1984. A framework of a mechanical translation between Japanese and English by analogy principle. In Elithorn, A., and Bernerji, R., eds., *Artificial and Human Intelligence*. North-Holland.

Och, F.; Tillmann, C.; and Ney, H. 1999. Improved alignment models for statistical machine translation. In *Proc. EMNLP/WVLC*.

Wu, D. 1997. Stochastic inversion transduction grammars and bilingual parsing of parallel corpora. *Computational Linguistics* 23(3).

---

[4] www.isi.edu/natural-language/mt/contest/

The Rules Behind Roles: Identifying Speaker Role in Radio Broadcasts

Regina Barzilay
regina@cs.columbia.edu
CS Dept., Columbia University
New York, NY 10027, USA

Michael Collins   **Julia Hirschberg**   **Steve Whittaker**
{mcollins,julia,stevew}@research.att.com
AT&T Labs — Research
Shannon Laboratory, 180 Park Ave., Florham Park, NJ 07932, USA

Abstract

Previous work has shown that providing information about story structure is critical for browsing audio broadcasts. We investigate the hypothesis that Speaker Role is an important cue to story structure. We implement an algorithm that classifies story segments into three Speaker Roles based on several content and duration features. The algorithm correctly classifies about 80% of segments (compared with a baseline frequency of 35.4%) when applied to ASR derived transcriptions of broadcast data.

Introduction

The amount of browsable online spoken broadcast news data is rapidly increasing. However, due to the serial nature of speech and the costs of hand-indexing, it is very difficult to navigate this data effectively. New technologies use automatic speech recognition (ASR) and information retrieval (IR) techniques to allow audio data to be searched by content. However, in developing such retrieval techniques, it becomes clear that simple term-based retrieval of such large speech "documents", does not enable users to browse audio effectively. Audio is inherently hard to skim, so that accessing a relevant newscast does not guarantee finding the crucial segment within that newscast. Therefore, a critical problem for audio data is to provide information about the internal structure of newscasts. For genres such as broadcast news corpora, we can assist local browsing by exploiting their structural regularities. Regularities include introductory headline teasers, story structuring by correspondents, and predictable program formats. Presenting this information should enable users to navigate to the relevant part of the broadcast. To present such structural information, however, we need to identify structural elements automatically.

We describe a technique for acquiring the structure of broadcast news programs by identifying *participant role*. By identifying role — anchor, journalist, or program guest — we are able to infer a STRUCTURAL SUMMARY of the broadcast. Anchors typically introduce stories and guide the program, appearing throughout. Journalists usually report a specific news story. Program guests are generally interviewed by journalists. Identifying speaker type provides

Copyright © 2000, American Association for Artificial Intelligence (www.aaai.org). All rights reserved.

clues about newscast structure. Both anchors and journalists present explicit structural information. Speaker transitions also yield structural information: when a journalist stops speaking, this is a strong cue that a story has ended. This technique is being developed in the context of an audio browsing project SCAN (Hirschberg *et al.* 1999) on the DARPA Broadcast News corpus.

We present a machine learning algorithm for speaker *role* identification from audio data. The algorithm's input is ASR transcriptions from "All Things Considered" programs, with boundaries between speakers identified, but the identity of speakers unknown. The algorithm's output is a label for each segment, identifying it as either *Anchor*, *Journalist* or *Program Guest*. We use a set of segments with known labels to train a classifier. A separate test corpus evaluates accuracy. The main classifier features relate to the text of each segment. We also include segment duration and textual context features. Our method makes the three-way classification with around 80% accuracy, compared to a baseline result of 35.4% accuracy when every segment is assigned to the most frequent class (Anchor).

We first briefly describe the audio browsing system. We then motivate our use of participant role to define program structure. We describe the Broadcast News Corpus in detail and the task of participant role identification. We then describe the algorithm used for role identification, the features it uses, and how they are computed. We present results of our learning experiments and evaluate their success. Finally, we discuss our future research directions.

The Audio Browsing System

Our system operates on the NIST TREC SDR corpus, a subset of DARPA HUB-4 Broadcast News. The system uses ASR to produce an errorful transcription of each story, after segmenting the speech into audio paragraphs. Stories relevant to a text query are retrieved by a modified version of the SMART IR system. Recognition and retrieval results are then passed to a graphical user interface (GUI). The GUI is designed to support local navigation within speech documents, as well as document retrieval. We employ well-understood text formatting conventions (e.g. headers and paragraphs) to provide useful analogues for speech browsing. The role-based structural information about broadcast programs is intended to augment and extend this interface by providing additional information about where program information is summarized, where individual stories begin and end, and where the most general summarizing portions of these stories are likely to occur.

Motivation

We hypothesized that, in news broadcasts, speaker type should be correlated with program structure. Figure 1 shows a role-based segmentation for the NPR radio program "All Things Considered"[1]. Different parts of the program exhibit different speaker change patterns. Anchor segments, which usually represent headlines or introductions to stories, occur in particular places in broadcasts, and are uninterrupted by guest segments. Anchors also tend to occur more frequently in the program, and to alternate with the journalist they introduce. Individual stories are often characterized by an anchor introduction, a journalist introduction, and then an alternation between journalist and guest segments. A typical journalistic story of this type is marked in figure 1. Given this relationship between speaker role and program structure, roles can be used to categorize program segments according to their type, e.g. headlines or interviews. We hypothesize that this will help users to browse within a broadcast.

(Stolcke et al. 1999) observe that speaker change is a useful feature for story segmentation. However, not all speaker changes correlate with story boundaries. Anchor segments can be used to hypothesize a set of story boundaries, because anchor speech usually separates stories. Guest segments, in contrast, never introduce a story: their contributions always occur within a story.

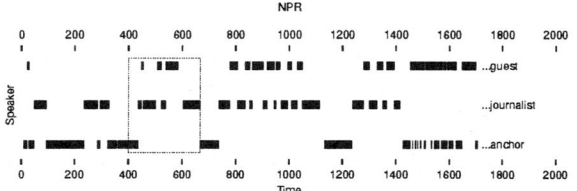

Figure 1: Speaker-type based segmentation.

Information about speaker role may also be beneficial for summarization of news stories. Some segments (for example the anchor segment just before a journalist begins a story, or the first journalist segment within a story) may be particularly important for constructing the summary of a story, and an NLP system for summarization should take this positional information into account.

The Data

The data set used for the development of our speaker type identification consisted of 35 half-hour broadcasts of the radio program "All Things Considered," a subset of the TREC-7 SDR track corpus, which, in turn, represents a subset of the DARPA Broadcast News corpus.

---

[1]For simplicity, figure 1 does not show explicitly all speaker turns. For example, sequence "Anchor, Anchor" appears as one block.

We used both human transcripts provided by NIST and automatically recognized transcripts(ASR) with manually-labeled speaker boundaries from this corpus; segments were tagged for speaker identity and duration. Commercials are excluded from the corpus. We used the ASR transcription of the data provided for the SCAN systems, with an error rate of 31%. We enriched ASR transcripts with manually-labeled speaker boundaries by aligning ASR transcripts with human transcripts using the word time feature, which were provided in both transcripts.

Speaker type was not explicitly provided by the transcripts. Fortunately, it was relatively easy to acquire this information from the hand-labeled speaker names. We compiled a list of the names of anchors and journalists in the corpus[2], and used this to label the segments; any name not appearing in the list was labeled as a program guest. Thus we formed training and test sets of segments labeled with the Anchor/Journalist/Program Guest distinction.

Related Work

Researchers have noted that speaker type change is an important feature for indexing broadcast news (Mani et al. 1997; Huang et al. 1999; Reynar 1999). Huang et al. base their segmentation method on the identification of anchor segments, assuming that two adjacent stories are separated by anchor speech. Detection of anchor segments is implemented using a text-independent speaker recognition technique, based on the acoustic characteristics of speakers. A model for the target speaker, and a background model, are constructed from labeled training data. For the test case, the target speaker is detected according to likelihood ratio values from the constructed models. This method achieved impressive results — a 92% hit rate and a 1.5% false alarm rate, when tested on its ability to detect whether or not one anchor person (Tom Brokaw) was talking. Our method differs from this approach in that we assume no prior knowledge of the acoustic characteristics of the different speakers in the program.

A number of researchers (Chen & Gopalakrishnan 1998; Couvreur & Boite 1999) have considered methods which cluster speaker segments into groups of acoustically similar segments. The goal of this work has usually been the adaptation of speech recognizers to different types of speakers or different channel conditions. Typically, different recognizer models are trained on different clusters. This task is similar but not identical to ours. The output of speech-based systems contains no information about the types of different speakers, although speaker identity would be very useful information in deriving speaker type, if it could be recovered with high accuracy.

Unfortunately, speaker clustering is a difficult task; (Couvreur & Boite 1999) report 70% classification accuracy on broadcast news, even when the number of speakers is given a priori. (Note that this classification accuracy may be quite sufficient for speech recognizer adaptation; in contrast, browsing tasks will usually require a lower error rate.) Fur-

---

[2]We used the list of anchors/journalists on the "All Things Considered" site (http://www.npr.org/programs/atc/).

thermore, this method is sensitive to an increase in the number of speakers and changes in background conditions. This is problematic for broadcast news, where typically there may be thirty speakers, and where channel conditions often vary from microphone speech to telephone speech.

Our algorithm contrasts with the speaker clustering methods in two ways. First, we focus on discovering speaker type, rather than speaker identity. We believe that this is a much more tractable task than full-blown speaker identification, while still providing very useful information for indexing or browsing news programs. Second, our algorithm exploits the lexical information found in ASR transcriptions rather than acoustic information.

Identifying Speaker Type

When we listen to a radio program, we can usually tell whether the speaker is the anchor, a journalist, or a guest speaker in terms of content as well as speaking style.

- An anchor is responsible for reading news, introducing reports from journalists, and announcing upcoming events.
- A journalist is a professional speaker, generally in some remote location where a story is taking place. Journalists often interview guests in the course of presenting their stories.
- A guest speaker is usually a non-professional speaker speaking from a subjective point of view.

Our assumption is that these major functional differences will be reflected in the following features:

Lexical features Intuitively, aspects of what is said should distinguish speaker type. Previously, (Mani et al. 1997) and (Reynar 1999) have observed that "signature phrases", such as "This is CNN's Primenews", are frequently used by anchors and journalists in broadcast news — almost never by guests. These professional speakers also tend to exhibit more 'planned speech' vs. the spontaneous speech of guests. So, we would expect that segments of non-professional speakers would contain more self-repairs and semantically empty words, such as "well".

In previous work, lists of lexical cues have been compiled by hand (see (Mani et al. 1997; Reynar 1999; Teufel & Moens 1998)), with the classifier then using their occurrence as a binary feature. In our approach, we would like to learn these patterns automatically from the training corpus. To do this, we provide as input to the learning algorithm all n-grams from unigrams up to 5-grams from the segment. Thus we generate a large number of lexical features, and allow the machine learning method to find those that are useful.

Note that some lexical patterns are only predictors of speaker type if they are followed by a proper name. For example, the phrase "I'm" is common in broadcast news, but only "I'm ⟨*proper-name*⟩" is a good predictor of an anchor. Because of such observations, we decided to augment the segment text with proper name indicators. In written text, capitalization can be used for identification of proper names, but unfortunately speech transcripts do not provide capitalization. In order to acquire capitalization information, we used a parallel text corpus of written news — the AP corpus from 1996 — which contains 44,171,587 words and 209,426 word types. For each word in the corpus we counted the number of its capitalized vs. un-capitalized occurrences, excluding occurences in initial sentence positions. We consider a word in the speech transcripts to be capitalized, if the ratio of its capitalized appearances is greater than 50%. Of 209,426 word types, 123,649 (59%) were capitalized according to this definition. This method allows us to identify words which are always capitalized, e.g., Clinton, as well as words which have a tendency to be capitalized, e.g., Flowers (in Gennifer Flowers). We substituted all occurrences of words from this list in the broadcast transcripts with a special "capitalized-word" token.

Features from the surrounding context In some cases, the label and the content of adjacent segments may predict the current speaker type. An anchor usually introduces a journalist at the start of a story, and, similarly, a journalist "hands off" the report back to the anchor at the end of a story. In addition, some sequences of labels are more frequent than others (see Figure 1). For example, the sequence "Journalist, Guest, Journalist" occurs sixteen times, while "Journalist, Guest, Anchor" never appears in the graph. We experimented with two types of contextual features: the labels of the n previous segments, and all the features of n previous segments. The first feature type captures the intuition that some label sequences are more frequent than others. The second covers cases in which speakers provide cues about the type of the following speaker.

Duration features Segment duration is another feature which we observe to be correlated with speaker role. Journalist guide books (Mencher 1987) advise controlling the time length of guest speaker segments, and also give suggested lengths for anchor lead-ins and journalist's questions. These features were computed in a straightforward manner, using time labels from the transcripts.

Explicit speaker introductions One of the tasks of professional speakers in radio programs is to introduce themselves and other program participants. Speaker introductions such as "I'm Noah Adams" or "NPR's Claudio Sanchez reports" or "thanks Claudio Sanchez for that report", occur frequently in broadcast news, and can be used for distinguishing anchors and journalists from non-professional speakers. We decided to apply a learning technique to identify speaker introductions in the text (more specifically, proper names in the text where a speaker has introduced herself or a following/preceding speaker), identifying such references in the segments, and tagging, e.g., "Noah Adams" or "Claudio Sanchez" in the above examples.

In the remainder of the section we describe our method for speaker introduction computation. The broadcast news human transcripts include the identity of the speaker of each segment. From this information, we created a training corpus where speaker name were labeled. Out of 133,391 words, 522 (0.4%) fit this definition of speaker name. The identification of speaker introduction was reduced to a binary word-by-word classification problem, which was addressed using the BoosTexter algorithm (described in the following section). The following features were used to represent each word:

- Lexical features aim to discover templates for speaker introduction. For a word in position n, we extracted all trigrams, bigrams and unigrams surrounding the word, including those beginning at position $n-3$ to those ending at position $n+3$. To distinguish all these, we prepend each n-gram with its length and starting position.
- The frequency of the word in the broadcast. Typically, professional speakers are introduced no more than twice during the program, therefore high frequency of the word in the broadcast is an indicator that the word is not a speaker introduction.
- Relative distance from the start and the end of the segment. Self-introduction usually occurs in the start of the segment, while the introduction of other speakers usually happens at the end of the segment.

We approximate capitalization, using the techniques described above. Figure 2 shows an input example for BoosTexter. We evaluated our method on 21,905 words of unseen data. 87 of these words were speaker introductions, our method recovered 70 of them with no false positives (80% recall, 100% precision on this test set). Therefore, it can be used as a reliable feature for our task. This method can also be used for extracting the identity of professional speakers from broadcast transcripts.

```
30_npr's  31_npr's_@  32_npr's_@_@  33_@_@_has
34_@_has_this  35_has_this_report  20_  21_npr's
22_npr's_@  23_@_@  24_@_has  25_has_this  10_  11_
12_npr's  13_@  14_@  15_has, 2, 2, 16.67, 83.33, yes.
```

Figure 2: BoosTexter input for the word "Phillip Davis" in the segment "npr's Phillip Davis has this report". "*xy_www*" stands for a sequence of "_"-delimited words *www* for a window of size *x* in the *y*-th position, "@" stands for capitalized words.

Learning Methods

We applied two algorithms to the classification task. The first, BoosTexter, is a boosting algorithm which was originally applied to text classification (Singer & Shapire 1998). The second technique, maximum entropy modeling, has been previously applied to a variety of natural language tasks, the closest application to ours being part-of-speech tagging as described in (Ratnaparkhi 1996). Both of these methods learn simple weighted rules, each rule using a feature to predict one of the labels with some weight: an example rule would be, *if the segment contains the n-gram "this is NPR news" vote for label Anchor with weight 0.3*. On test data examples, the label with the highest weighted vote is taken as the output of the algorithm. The boosting approach greedily searches for a subset of the features which predict the label with high accuracy; in the maximum entropy method all features occurring above a certain number of times (in our case 12) were used by the model ((Ratnaparkhi 1996) also used a count cut-off to select features).

Results and Evaluation

In this section we first discuss the accuracy of the method on human transcripts, focusing on the contribution of different feature types to the method's performance. We then discuss results on ASR output. We divided our data into a training set containing 27 broadcasts (2336 segments), a development set of 5 broadcasts (339 segments), and a held-out test set containing 5 broadcasts (347 segments). Table 1 shows the numbers of anchors, journalists and guests segments for the training, development and testing sets. On this particular breakdown of the data, a baseline classifier would achieve 35.4% accuracy on the test set by labeling each segment with the most frequent category in the training set — anchor.

	Training	Development	Testing
Anchor	878(37.6%)	123(36.3%)	123(35.4%)
Journalist	630(27%)	83(24.5%)	119(34.3%)
Guest	828(35.4%)	133(39.2%)	105(30.3%)

Table 1: Number of segments per Speaker Type

Using this training/development partition, for each segment we calculated features described in the previous section. Figure 3 shows the classification error on the development set with different types of features included in the model. The following feature types were all found to be useful:

Lexical features We used four textual features: the text of the current segment, the two previous segments and the next segment. Word n-grams of up to length 5 were included. Table 2 shows the textual features with the highest weight found by BoosTexter. The majority of n-grams in the table corresponds to "signature phrases" — these phrases discriminate professional participants from guests, and also help to make the distinction between anchors and journalists. Another group of phrases picked up by BoosTexter, as a predictor of anchors and journalists, corresponds to questions, e.g., "do you, what about". The highest weight predictors of guests, such as "uh, well, you know", are words which are frequent in "everyday" spontaneous speech.

Segment duration The relative segment duration, namely the ratio of current segment duration to previous segment duration, is one of the high-weighted features. When this value is higher than a certain threshold (2.035), it is considered to be journalist predictor. This empirical result can be explained by the fact that a short summary from an anchor often precedes full coverage of the story by a journalist. Absolute segment duration also serves as a predictor of the journalist category: a duration higher than 5.26 minutes corresponds to journalist's segments. On the other hand, very short segments(duration < 0.6 minutes) are indicators that an anchor is speaking.

Speaker introduction The presence of a speaker introduction in the current or previous segment were high-weighted features. A speaker introduction in the previous segment predicts journalist as speaker of the current segment, while a speaker introduction in the current segment predicts anchor as the speaker of the segment.

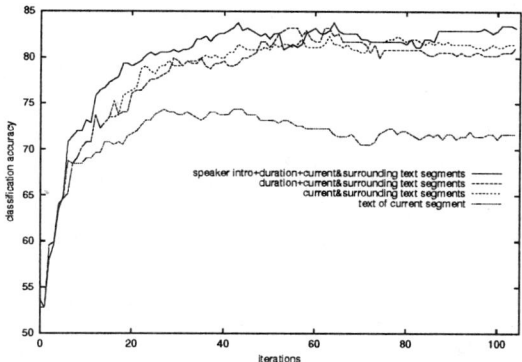

Figure 3: Classification accuracy of BoosTexter on different combinations of features (on development set, human transcripts)

	Human transcripts	ASR transcription
Anchor	npr's, npr, from national, all things considered i'm, and i'm @, us from, good afternoon i'm, reports, do you, what about	nbrs, nbi, things considered an, reports, this is all, commentator @, you, news in
Journ.	but, says, to all things, for national, is @ @ in, his, do you, we've been	reports, @ said, you, explain, @ @ says
Guest	i, we, yeah, well, i think, uh, our	i, i think, that we, it, you know

Table 2: Examples of n-grams with highest weight for human and ASR transcripts found by BoosTexter

Given this set of features, BoosTexter outperforms Maximum Entropy by 4%. BoosTexter has an accuracy of 83.2% on the development set (after 100 rounds), while Maximum Entropy has 79% accuracy. However this picture changes when we add the labels of previously tagged paragraphs to the feature set. In the BoosTexter approach, the labels of the two previous paragraphs as computed by BoosTexter were given as input when tagging the current paragraph. Surprisingly, classification rate decreased significantly — 4.5%. This drop in accuracy occurs because in many cases the categories of previous speakers fully determine the category of current speaker. Therefore, when training BoosTexter weighs these features very highly, "neglecting" other features. In testing, one incorrectly predicted label often causes a "chain reaction" of incorrect labels. This greedy approach could be improved by using the confidence values computed by BoosTexter, and searching for the global sequence with the highest combined confidence. We leave this for future work.

The Maximum Entropy approach provides the conditional probability of label given the segment features and previous labels. Given a broadcast with segments $\{s_1, s_2, \ldots, s_n\}$, a label sequence candidate $\{l_1, l_2, \ldots, l_n\}$ has conditional probability:

$$P(l_1, l_2, \ldots, l_n | s_1, s_2, \ldots, s_n) = \prod_{i=1}^{n} p(l_i | l_{i-1}, l_{i-2}, l_{i-3}, s_i)$$

Beam search aims to find the labeling of the broadcast segments sequence with highest probability. History features included the label of the previous paragraph, the two previous paragraphs and the three previous paragraphs. With a beam-size of $N = 15$, Maximum Entropy outperforms BoosTexter by 1.5% (see Figure 4). Taking into account labels of previous segments improved the accuracy of the Maximum Entropy approach by 5%.

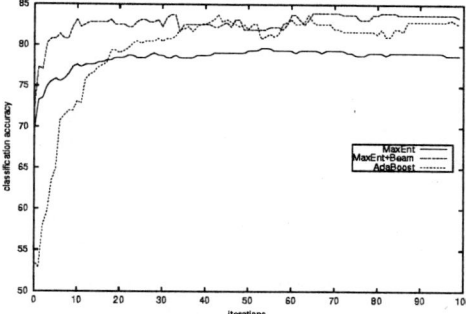

Figure 4: Classification accuracy of different learning algorithms (on development set, human transcripts)

We ran BoosTexter and Maximum Entropy on an unseen test set. The classification accuracy on the test set is 79% for BoosTexter and 80.5% for Maximum Entropy. Table 3 shows prediction accuracy for each of the three speaker types.

	BoosTexter		MaxEnt	
	Recall	Precision	Recall	Precision
Anchor	81.3%	74.6%	91.7%	74.8%
Journalist	70.6%	83.2%	74.0%	90.4%
Guest	82.9%	76.6%	75.2%	78.2%

Table 3: Precision/recall by category on the test set (human transcripts)

After developing the two algorithms on the human transcripts, we examined their performance on ASR transcripts. We formed training, development and test sets of ASR data, and trained BoosTexter and Maximum Entropy classifiers using the same feature types. BoosTexter performance is 75% for development set, and 72.8% for testing set. The accuracy of Maximum Entropy reached 79.9% on the development set and 77% on the test set. It is encouraging that the results were not substantially lower on ASR output, in spite of relatively high speech recognition error rates.

Summary and Future Work

In this paper, we have described how to compute the speaker role in news broadcasts from an automatic transcription of those broadcasts, assuming hand-labeled segmentation of (roughly speaking) speaker turns. We distinguish among three speaker types, Anchor, Journalist (non-Anchor), and Guest Speaker. The main contributions of this paper include identification of features which characterize each category, and an implementation of an algorithm based on those features which identifies speaker roles with high accuracy. A key finding is that content-based features are robust clues to speaker identity, and can be used as a complement to traditional audio-based methods.

Our working hypothesis was that speaker type information is an important cue to story structure. Our immediate future plans therefore involve testing the utility of the speaker type information we can currently identify when it is added to the speech browsing system. We will test the effectiveness of speaker type as an aid for audio browsing of Broadcast News. In addition, the system we have developed gives rise to a number of important issues. First is the question of how to combine our method with methods based on audio features in order to increase the accuracy of our procedure. For example, if the classifier is uncertain about a segment's type based on textual information alone, the acoustic similarity of the segment to other segments classified with high confidence may provide useful information. A related question is whether a combined acoustic-textual method might be extended to a full speaker identification system.

A more ambitious goal is to use speaker roles for parsing broadcast transcripts into structural units, such as headlines, interviews and news summaries. We have observed that each of these broadcast structural units appears to have its own patterns of speaker role changes, so this form of structural identification might indeed be possible. With such additional information, we should be closer to our long-term goal of providing summaries of broadcast news programs.

Acknowledgments

We thank Michiel Bacchiani and Amit Singhal for providing help with the TREC data and ASR transcriptions. Thanks to Aaron Rosenberg, Shimei Pan, Barry Schiffman, Noemie Elhadad, and Carl Sable for useful discussions and comments on earlier versions of this paper.

References

Chen, S., and Gopalakrishnan, P. 1998. Speaker, environment and change change detection and clustering via the bayesian information criterion. In *Proceedings of the DARPA Broadcast News Transcription and Understanding Workshop*.

Couvreur, L., and Boite, J.-M. 1999. Speaker tracking in broadcast audio material in the framework of the thisl project. In *Proceedings of the ESCA ETRW workshop Accessing Information in Spoken Audio*, 84–89.

Hirschberg, J.; Whittaker, S.; Hindle, D.; Pereira, F.; and Singhal, A. 1999. Finding information in audio: A new paradigm for audio browsing and retrieval. In *Proceeding of the ESCA ETRW Workshop*.

Huang, Q.; Liu, Z.; Rosenberg, A.; Gibbon, D.; and Shahraray, B. 1999. Automated generation of news content hierarchy by integrating audio, video, and text information. In *Proceeding of the IEEE International Conference On acoustics, speech, and signal processing*, volume 6, 3025–3028.

Mani, I.; House, M.; Maybury, M.; and Green, M. 1997. Towards content-based browsing of broadcast news video. In Maybury, M., ed., *Intelligent Multimedia Information Retrieval*. AAAI/MIT Press. 241–258.

Mencher, M. 1987. *News Reporting and Writing*. Dubuque, Iowa: William C. Brown, 4 edition.

Ratnaparkhi, A. 1996. A maximum entropy model for part-of-speech tagging. In *Proceeding of the Conference on Empirical Methods in Natural Language Processing*.

Reynar, J. 1999. Statistical models for topic segmentation. In *Proceedings of the 37th Annual Meeting of the ACL*.

Singer, Y., and Shapire, R. 1998. Improved boosting algorithms using confidence-rated predictions. In *Proceeding of 11th Annual Conference on Computational Learning Theory*, 80–91.

Stolcke, A.; Shriberg, E.; Hakkani-Tur, D.; Tur, G.; Rivlin, Z.; and Sonmez, K. 1999. Combining words and speech prosody for automatic topic segmentation. In *Proceedings of the DARPA Broadcast News Workshop*, 61–64.

Teufel, S., and Moens, M. 1998. Sentence extraction and rhetorical classification for flexible abstracts. In *Spring AAAI Symposium on Intelligent Text summarization*.

Cognitive Status and Form of Reference in Multimodal Human-Computer Interaction

Andrew Kehler
Department of Linguistics
University of California, San Diego
9500 Gilman Drive
La Jolla, CA 92093-0108
kehler@ling.ucsd.edu

Abstract

We analyze a corpus of referring expressions collected from user interactions with a multimodal travel guide application. The analysis suggests that, in dramatic contrast to normal modes of human-human interaction, the interpretation of referring expressions can be computed with very high accuracy using a model which pairs an impoverished notion of discourse state with a simple set of rules that are insensitive to the type of referring expression used. We attribute this result to the implicit manner in which the interface conveys the system's beliefs about the operative discourse state, to which users tailor their choice of referring expressions. This result offers new insight into the way computer interfaces can shape a user's language behavior, insights which can be exploited to bring otherwise difficult interpretation problems into the realm of tractability.

Introduction

Despite recent advances in natural language processing (NLP) technology, computers still do not understand natural language interactions very well. Language is rife with complex phenomena that elude our understanding, and thus do not avail themselves of robust methods for interpretation. Solving these difficult problems, of course, is the basis for continuing research in NLP. On the other hand, we might also study the ways in which computer interfaces can shape a user's language behavior, and capitalize on these to reduce the complexity of certain interpretation problems.

In this paper, we consider the problem of resolving reference in human-computer interaction (HCI) with a multimodal interface, to which users can speak and gesture. We show that unlike normal modes of human-human interaction (HHI), reference resolution in an HCI system developed using standard interface design principles admits of a simple algorithm that nonetheless yields very high accuracy. We attribute this unexpected result to the implicit manner in which the interface conveys the system's beliefs about the operative discourse state, to which users tailor their choice of referring expression. This result offers new insight into the way that computer interfaces can shape a user's language behavior,

insights which can be exploited to bring otherwise difficult interpretation problems into the realm of tractability.

Form of Reference, Cognitive Status, and Salience

From a computational linguistic standpoint, it would be nice if speakers always referred to entities using complete and unambiguous referring expressions, thereby rendering reference resolution unproblematic. Of course, this is not what competent speakers do. Instead, natural languages provide speakers with a variety of ways to refer to entities and eventualities when producing an utterance, including pronouns, demonstratives, lexical noun phrases, and proper names. For instance, a particular Four Seasons Hotel might be referred to as *it, this, that, here, there, this hotel, that hotel, the hotel*, or *the Four Seasons*. Importantly, these alternatives are not freely interchangeable, as each encodes different signals about the location of the referent within the hearer's mental model of the discourse – the referent's *cognitive status* – which are necessary for the hearer to identify the intended referent (Chafe 1976; Prince 1981; 1992; Gundel, Hedberg, & Zacharski 1993, inter alia). One reason why accurate algorithms for reference resolution are elusive is the lack of reliably computable methods for determining a potential referent's cognitive status.

To add concreteness to our discussion, we sketch a particular theory of cognitive status, due to Gundel et al. (1993), who propose a *Givenness Hierarchy* containing six cognitive statuses that referents can have and the types of referential expressions that signal them.[1]

in focus	>	activated	>	familiar	>	uniquely identifiable
it		that this this N		that N		the N

Each cognitive status logically implicates those to its right in the hierarchy; for instance, an *in focus* referent is necessarily also *activated*, *familiar*, and *uniquely identifiable*.

---
[1] We will restrict our analysis to definite reference, and thus only the first four statuses in Gundel et al.'s hierarchy.

Thus, a form that normally signals a given cognitive status can be used to refer to an entity with a higher one. However, in a survey of data across several languages, Gundel et al. found that with one exception, each form was found almost exclusively with the status with which it is correlated. The exception in English is the case of definite lexical noun phrases, which were found not only with *uniquely identifiable* referents, but with all higher statuses. Gundel et al. explain these facts using Grice's Maxim of Quantity (Grice 1975), which can be paraphrased as *Make your contribution as informative as required, but not more so*. The first part of the maxim explains why demonstratives are not typically found with referents holding a higher status, as their use conversationally implicates that the higher status does not hold. On the other hand, unlike demonstratives and pronouns, definite lexical noun phrases typically contain the descriptive content necessary to uniquely identify the referent, so an explicit signal of a higher status is unnecessary, per the second half of the maxim.

Theories of information status such as Gundel et al.'s are useful for characterizing the types of referential expression with which a referent is compatible, which helps explain why different referential expressions are used in different contextual circumstances. However, these theories do not contain the degree of specificity required to capture all the constraints required for a computational model for reference resolution: They lack formal, independent conditions for determining the status of a referent in a particular discourse situation, as well as a way to distinguish between several possible referents that hold the same cognitive status. Developers of computational models – who have centered largely on a single cognitive status (in focus) and its correlated referential form (pronominalization) (Sidner 1983; Lappin & Leass 1994; Grosz, Joshi, & Weinstein 1995, inter alia) – have addressed these questions by incorporating a notion of *salience* into their models, along with sets of linguistic factors that are used to compute approximations to degree of salience (e.g., topic continuity, grammatical role, parallelism, and semantic factors). The factors determining salience with respect to other cognitive statuses (e.g., activated), and other types of referring expressions (e.g., demonstrative reference), are even less well understood, and thus have not received as much attention (but cf. Sidner (1983), Passonneau (1989)).

In this paper, we are interested in modeling reference behavior across the spectrum of referential form types for the case of multimodal HCI, which is different from HHI in several respects. First, the discourse state is augmented by the existence of entities in a prominently displayed, shared situational context consisting of icons on a computer screen (compare this, for instance, with the diminished role of situational context in normal HHI settings, and the almost complete lack thereof in a telephone conversation). Second, referring is readily performed using gesture to this shared context, possibly (but not necessarily) augmented with a natural language referring expression. Although these factors might be expected to further complicate the discourse modeling problem, we present an analysis of a corpus of reference data which suggests that, in dramatic contrast to HHI, the interpretation of referring expressions can be computed with very high accuracy with a model consisting of an highly impoverished notion of discourse state and a simple set of rules which are not sensitive to the type of referring expression used. We detail an experiment and its results in the next section, and then explain how these results arise from the implicit manner in which the interface conveys the system's beliefs about the cognitive status of referents to which users tailor their choice of referring expressions.

A Multimodal Map Application and Experiment

The basis for our study is an implemented prototype multimodal travel guide application (Cheyer & Julia 1995; Julia & Cheyer 1997) that was inspired by a multimodal Wizard of Oz simulation (Oviatt 1996). The system provides an interactive interface on which the user may draw, write, or speak. It makes available information about hotels, restaurants, and tourist sites in Toronto that have been retrieved by distributed software agents from commercial Internet World Wide Web sites. The map application is implemented within a multiagent framework called the Open Agent Architecture (OAA) (Martin, Cheyer, & Moran 1999).

```
S:   What do we have here?
     (circles China Town)
     China Town selected
S:   Give me information about this
     (draws arrow to China Town)
     Textual description displayed
S:   Okay so I think I'll visit China Town
     Saturday afternoon
     Calendar displayed and updated
S:   Is there any, uh, good restaurant
     around this area?
     (draws large circle including
     two sites)
     Map scrolled to show restaurant
S:   Well, no, I was looking...that way
     (draws arrow)
     Map scrolled
S:   So what do we have here?
     (circles restaurant)
     Restaurant selected and name displayed
S:   Give me information about this
     Textual description displayed
S:   Okay, I will have dinner there
     Calendar updated
```

Table 1: Example Interaction

Because we were interested in collecting naturally occurring data which may include phenomena not currently handled by the system, we designed a Wizard of Oz (WOZ) experiment. In WOZ experiments, users believe they are interacting directly with an implemented system, but in actuality a human "wizard" intercepts the user's commands and causes the system to produce the appropriate output. Subjects were asked to plan activities during and after a hypothetical business trip to Toronto. They planned places to

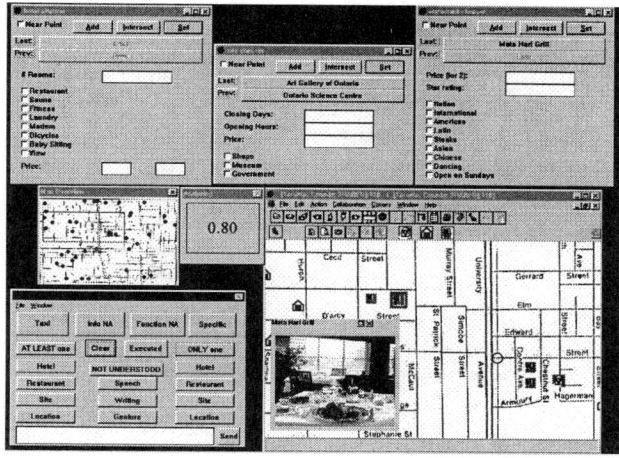 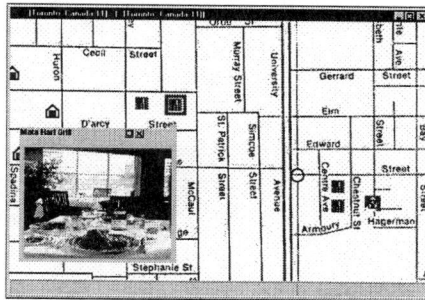

Figure 1: The Wizard Interface (left) and the Subject Interface (right)

stay, sights to see, and places to dine using speech, writing, and pen-based gestures. To first provide experience using each modality in isolation, subjects planned two half days using speech only and pen only respectively. Subjects then planned two half-days using any combination of these modalities they wished. For all tasks, the subjects were given only superficial instruction on the capabilities of the system. The tasks together took an average of approximately 35 minutes. Figure 1 depicts the subject interface and wizard interface, and Table 1 illustrates the type of interaction one finds in the data.

Entities of interest (hotels, restaurants, and tourist sites) were represented as displayed icons. Initially, the screen showed only the map; icons were subsequently displayed in response to questions about or requests to see entities of some type (e.g., "What restaurants are there in this area?"). When a particular entity was referred to (e.g., "Tell me about the museum"), its icon would become *selected* – indicated by highlighting – and previously selected icons would become unselected. Thus, at any given time during the interaction, the screen would usually show some number of icons, with one or more of these possibly highlighted.

We collected data resulting from sessions with 13 subjects. We transcribed 10 of the sessions as a training set, and the final three as a test set. The training and test sets contained 171 and 62 referring expressions respectively.

Results

Table 2 summarizes the distribution of referring expressions within information-seeking commands. (Commands to manipulate the environment, such as to scroll the screen or close a window, were not included.) Training and test data figures are shown without and within parentheses respectively. Listed on the vertical axis are the types of referential form used. The symbol ϕ denotes "empty" referring expressions corresponding to phonetically unrealized arguments to commands (e.g., the command "Information", when information is requested for a particular hotel). Full NPs are noun phrases for which interpretation does not require reference to context (e.g., "The Royal Ontario Museum"), whereas definite NPs (signalled by the determiners "the", "this", "these", or "that", with a head noun and possibly a locative) are reduced noun phrases that do (e.g., "the museum"). The horizontal axis includes two distinctions. First, we distinguish between cases in which an object was gestured to (e.g., by pointing or circling) at the time the command was issued, and cases with no such gesture. Second, we coded the cognitive status of the referents by distinguishing between selected entities, which correspond closely to Gundel et al.'s *in focus*, and unselected but visible entities, which correspond to the status *activated*. As we will see below, further distinctions proved to be unnecessary.[2]

Despite the difficulties in designing accurate reference resolution algorithms for human-human conversational data, it turned out that all of the HCI training data could be captured by a simple decision list procedure:

1. If an object is gestured to, choose that object.

2. Otherwise, if the currently selected object meets all semantic type constraints imposed by the referring expression (i.e., "the museum" requires a museum referent; bare forms such as "it" and "that" are compatible with any object), choose that object.

3. Otherwise, if there is a visible object that is semantically compatible, then choose that object (this happened three times; in each case there was only one suitable object).

4. Otherwise, a full NP (such as a proper name) was used that uniquely identified the referent.

When applied to the blind test data, this algorithm also handled all 62 referring expressions correctly.[3] Strikingly, and

---

[2]The table only includes cases of reference to objects. There was only one case not included, in which the subject used "here" to refer to the area represented by the entire map.

[3]When we began this project, we envisioned our data analysis leading to a more complex set of rules than the intuited rules used in the system at the time. Ironically, the resulting rules are actually *simpler*, yet do in fact exhibit greater coverage.

Form	No Gesture Unselected	No Gesture Selected	Simultaneous Gesture Unselected	Simultaneous Gesture Selected	Total
ϕ		20 (3)	13 (3)	2 (0)	35 (6)
"it"/"they"		7 (4)		2 (0)	9 (4)
"here"			6 (0)	2 (0)	8 (0)
"there"		12 (1)		2 (0)	14 (1)
"this"		3 (2)	8 (1)	6 (1)	17 (4)
"that"		2 (2)	0 (2)		2 (4)
def NP	2 (2)	2 (0)	6 (5)	6 (1)	16 (8)
def NP *locative*	1 (2)				1 (2)
Full NP	21 (17)	35 (13)	9 (3)	4 (0)	69 (33)
TOTAL	24 (21)	81 (25)	42 (14)	24 (2)	171 (62)

Table 2: Distribution of Referring Expressions (Speech and Gesture)

in contrast to what is required for interpreting reference in HHI, this perfect accuracy was achieved despite the fact that the algorithm makes no reference to the *form* of the referring expression – pronouns, demonstratives, and lexical NPs (modulo *semantic* constraints) are all treated identically.

Cognitive Status in Multimodal Systems

Naturally, these results raise the question of why the data can be captured by a small set of rules that are insensitive to referential form. Have we stumbled onto a superior algorithm, or is some other factor at work? The answer lies within the distribution of the data in Table 2 – the central and simplifying aspect of which is that in no case was a referent that was not *in focus* (i.e., unselected) referred to with a pronoun or demonstrative without a disambiguating gesture. Instead, lexical noun phrases were used (21 full NPs and 3 definite NPs in the training data, and 17 full NPs and 4 definite NPs in the test data), and in all cases the content of this noun phrase constrained the choice to one possible referent.

While this is not a property one finds in normal modes of HHI, there is in fact a consistent explanation when one considers the role that the interface plays in these interactions. As we described in Section 2, speakers engaged in HHI must take into account their own beliefs about the hearer's (inaccessible) beliefs concerning the cognitive status of the referent, so that they can choose an appropriate expression to refer to it. The data compiled in the previous section suggests that when conversing with our multimodal interface, speakers inferred their beliefs about the computer's discourse state only from what was explicitly indicated by the (readily accessible) visual display. The display marked two cognitive statuses: selected (in focus) and unselected but visible (activated). As a graphically supplied indication of discourse state, selection is almost certainly a stronger indicator of salience than any linguistic marking afforded by language alone (e.g., placement of a noun phrase in subject or topicalized position), and thus it is unsurprising that reduced expressions are commonly used to refer to selected entities without a disambiguating gesture. Unselected referents, on the other hand, while perhaps carrying different degrees of salience in terms of the properties of the evolving discourse (for instance, some may have been mentioned previously in salient grammatical positions, whereas others appeared in less salient positions or were not previously mentioned at all), remain indistinguishable from each other with respect to their appearance on the screen. Thus, in accommodating the interface's conveyance of cognitive status, speakers could only distinguish between unselected referents by either accompanying their referential expression with a disambiguating gesture, or by choosing a fuller, uniquely-specifying definite description, both of which have the effect of greatly simplifying the interpretation process.

The data also show the effect of Grice's Maxim of Quantity in a speaker's choice of referential expression; in particular, subjects often violated the maxim in a manner which resulted in discourse that human hearers would find to be unnaturally redundant. There were 35 cases in the training data in which the selected (and thus most salient) entity was referred to using a full noun phrase, and 24 cases in which a reference to the selected entity included a gesture; in each case a pronoun unaccompanied by gesture would have sufficed. These two scenarios even overlapped in four cases, in which the selected entity was referred to with a full, unambiguous noun phrase *and* an accompanying disambiguating gesture. An analogous situation in HHI would be one in which a referent is already the topic of discussion (and thus highly salient), where the speaker nonetheless uses a full unambiguous NP *and* simultaneous gesture to refer to it again. Such a referential act would violate conversational principles to the extent that it might confuse listeners or cause them to draw unwanted implicatures. Speakers appear to be far less convinced of a computer's ability to understand natural language, however, and are thus inclined to sacrifice some degree of conversational coherence in an effort to reduce ambiguity. While perhaps not completely natural, one can see this as a fortuitous property upon which computational algorithms can (and do) capitalize in the near term. On the other hand, as users become more confident in the interpretative abilities of HCI systems, one might find an accompanying decline in the amount of redundancy employed.

The Speech-Only Experiment

Recall that in normal modes of HHI, different types of referring expression signal different cognitive statuses so they can, metaphorically speaking, "point" to different places in the hearer's mental model of the discourse. In multimodal

Form	Unselected	Selected	Total
ϕ		20 (13)	20 (13)
"it"/"they"		11 (3)	11 (3)
"there"		6 (0)	6 (0)
"this"		1 (0)	1 (0)
"that"		3 (1)	3 (1)
def NP	14 (0)	12 (3)	26 (3)
def NP *locative*	27 (11)		27 (11)
Full NP	47 (31)	32 (15)	79 (46)
TOTAL	88 (42)	85 (35)	173 (77)

Table 3: Distribution of Referring Expressions (Speech)

HCI, the need to metaphorically point is supplanted by the ability to physically point to objects on the screen, and in our experiments this conversion of modes was total.

This naturally raises the question of what behavior one finds in a speech-only setting, in which gesture is unavailable. One possible outcome is that the reference data becomes more ambiguous, and thus harder to handle, because speakers revert back to a reliance on ambiguous referring expressions to single out referents. The analysis provided in the previous section predicts a different outcome, however: Since the salience of referents within the same cognitive status are undifferentiable with respect to the interface display, speakers will use more descriptive, unambiguous noun phrases in place of reduced, ambiguous ones.

This is in fact what we find upon analyzing the data from the speech-only task, summarized in Table 3. Again, subjects used bare pronominal and demonstrative forms to refer only to selected entities. Without gesture to disambiguate reference to unselected entities, subjects used lexical NPs with uniquely specifying modifiers (such as a locative restricting reference to a single object, e.g., "The hotel on Chestnut Street") much more frequently. (In comparison, a locative modifier was used with a referential expression only three times in the entire corpus of multimodal data.)

Thus, the speech-only setting resulted not in more ambiguous forms of reference, but in less efficient reference than in the multimodal case.[4] This result provides further evidence, therefore, that speakers are accommodating what they perceive to be the system's beliefs concerning the cognitive status of referents from their prominence on the display, and tailoring their referring expressions to those. This fact also provides a potential explanation for why Gundel et al. found that definite NPs co-occurred with all cognitive statuses in their linguistic study, unlike the other forms, as described in Section 2 – such NPs may have been required to distinguish between several referents holding the same cognitive status in a given context, regardless of where on their Givenness Hierarchy the status lies.

---

[4]A similar result was found by Oviatt and Kuhn (1998), who point out that the need to use longer referring expressions can result in a greater number of other types of processing difficulties, such as recognition and parsing errors.

Previous Work

Space precludes a detailed summary of previous work on reference in multimodal systems, but generally speaking, much of this work has proposed methods for reference resolution without focusing on the special properties of multimodal discourse with respect to modeling discourse state and its relation to form of referring expression. A study that nonetheless warrants further discussion is due to Huls et al. (1995), who describe data from interactions with a system using a keyboard to type natural language expressions and a mouse to simulate pointing gestures. To model discourse state, they utilize Alshawi's (1987) framework, in which *context factors* (CFs) are assigned significance weights and a decay function according to which the weights decrease over time. Significance weights and decay functions are represented together via a list of the form $[w_1,...,w_n,0]$, in which w_1 is an initial significance weight which is then decayed in accordance with the remainder of the list. Four "linguistic CFs" and three "perceptual CFs" were encoded. Linguistic CFs include weights for being in a major constituent position ($[3,2,1,0]$), the subject position ($[2,1,0]$, in addition to the major constituent weight), a nested position ($[1,0]$), and expressing a relation ($[3,2,1,0]$). Perceptual CFs include whether the object is visible ($[1,...,1,0]$), selected ($[2,...,2,0]$), and indicated by a simultaneous pointing gesture ($[30,1,0]$).

As in our system, all referring expressions are resolved in the same manner, regardless of the type of referential form: The system simply chooses the most salient entity that meets all semantic constraints imposed by the command and the expression itself (e.g., the referent of "the file" in "close the file" must be an entity that is a file and can be closed). After developing their algorithm using several hundred constructed sentences, Huls et al. tested their framework on a set of user commands containing 125 referring expressions drawn from interactions with 5 subjects, and compared it against two baselines: selecting the most recent compatible referent, and a pencil-and-paper simulation of a focus-based algorithm derived from Grosz and Sidner (1986). They found that all 125 referring expressions were correctly resolved with their approach, 124 were resolved correctly with the Grosz and Sidner simulation, and 119 were resolved correctly with the simple recency-based strategy.

Huls et al. were thus also able to achieve perfect performance using a strategy that does not account for the differences in constraints on cognitive status imposed by different types of referring expressions. They do not, however, use this as a basis to take a deeper look into the nature of multimodal reference, given that this property of the algorithm is obviously untenable for resolving reference in normal HHI. Instead, they promote this simplification as an advantage of their algorithm, and in particular as an improvement over other methods (e.g., the algorithm derived from Grosz and Sidner) which rely on more complex sets of rules.[5] Using

---

[5]It should be noted that this is almost certainly an unfair comparison, as these other methods were originally developed for monomodal (i.e., speech or text only) HHI, which no doubt requires this greater complexity.

this reasoning, we could argue that the greater simplicity of our rule set renders it superior to the Huls et al. method. In actuality, however, the fact that our approach and each of those tested by Huls et al. all obtained very high accuracy supports the thesis of this paper, specifically, that the ability to achieve high accuracy is due to special properties of HCI, and not to the superior adequacy of any particular algorithm.

Nonetheless, this is not to say that these results will extend to any other multimodal HCI system; indeed, the complexity of reference behavior one finds can vary with interface design choices, domain, and task complexity. As a result, the optimal reference resolution strategy will likely also vary on a per-system basis. Other previous systems that use more complex methods for resolving reference include CUBRICON (Neal *et al.* 1988), which uses a focus space model (Sidner 1983), and ALFRESCO (Zancanaro, Stock, & Strapparava 1997), which uses a revision of the centering framework (Grosz, Joshi, & Weinstein 1995). Neither work provides a quantitative evaluation of their algorithm, nor do we have the means to determine the extent to which a simpler method, perhaps coupled with interface choices designed specifically to reduce the complexity of reference, would have provided as good or better results.

Conclusions

We have presented an analysis of a corpus of referring expressions collected from multimodal interactions which suggests that, in dramatic contrast to human-human interaction, the interpretation of referring expressions can be computed with very high accuracy using a model which pairs a highly impoverished notion of discourse state with a simple set of rules that are insensitive to the type of referring expression used. This is contrary to previous research on purely linguistic reference, in which the differences between such forms have been demonstrated to be crucial for understanding. We attributed this result to the implicit manner in which the interface conveys the system's beliefs about the operative discourse state, to which users tailor their choice of referring expression. This result therefore demonstrates one way in which a computer interface can shape the language behavior of users, a fact which can be exploited to turn ordinarily difficult interpretation problems into tractable ones.

Acknowledgements

This work was supported by National Science Foundation STIMULATE Grant IIS-9619126. This work would not have been possible without the contributions of Adam Cheyer, Luc Julia, Jean-Claude Martin, Jerry Hobbs, John Bear, and Wayne Chambliss.

References

Alshawi, H. 1987. *Memory and Context for Language Interpretation*. Cambridge University Press.

Chafe, W. L. 1976. Givenness, contrastiveness, definiteness, subjects, topics, and point of view. In Li, C. N., ed., *Subject and Topic*. New York: Academic Press. 25–55.

Cheyer, A., and Julia, L. 1995. Multimodal maps: An agent-based approach. In *Proceedings of CMC95*, 103–113.

Grice, H. P. 1975. Logic and conversation. In Cole, P., and Morgan, J., eds., *Speech Acts*. New York, New York: Academic Press. 41–58.

Grosz, B., and Sidner, C. 1986. Attention, intentions, and the structure of discourse. *Computational Linguistics* 12(3):175–204.

Grosz, B. J.; Joshi, A. K.; and Weinstein, S. 1995. Centering: A framework for modelling the local coherence of discourse. *Computational Linguistics* 21(2).

Gundel, J. K.; Hedberg, N.; and Zacharski, R. 1993. Cognitive status and the form of referring expressions in discourse. *Language* 69(2):274–307.

Huls, C.; Bos, E.; and Classen, W. 1995. Automatic referent resolution of deictic and anaphoric expressions. *Computational Linguistics* 21(1):59–79.

Julia, L., and Cheyer, A. 1997. Speech: a privileged modality. In *Proceedings of EUROSPEECH'97*, 103–113.

Lappin, S., and Leass, H. 1994. An algorithm for pronominal anaphora resolution. *Computational Linguistics* 20(4):535–561.

Martin, D.; Cheyer, A.; and Moran, D. 1999. The Open Agent Architecture: A framework for building distributed software systems. *Applied Artificial Intelligence* 13(1-2):92–128.

Neal, J. G.; Dobes, Z.; Bettinger, K. E.; and Byoun, J. S. 1988. Multi-modal references in human-computer dialogue. In *Proceedings of the 7th National Conference on Artificial Intelligence (AAAI-88)*, 819–823.

Oviatt, S., and Kuhn, K. 1998. Referential features and linguistic indirection in multimodal language. In *Proceedings of the International Conference on Spoken Language Processing (ICSLP-98)*.

Oviatt, S. 1996. Multimodal interfaces for dynamic interactive maps. In *Proceedings of CHI96*, 95–105.

Passonneau, R. 1989. Getting at discourse referents. In *Proceedings of the 27th Annual Meeting of the Association for Computational Linguistics (ACL-89)*, 51–59.

Prince, E. 1981. Toward a taxonomy of given-new information. In Cole, P., ed., *Radical Pragmatics*. New York, New York: Academic Press. 223–255.

Prince, E. 1992. The ZPG letter: Subjects, definiteness, and information-status. In Thompson, S., and Mann, W., eds., *Discourse Description: Diverse Analyses of a Fundraising Text*. Philadelphia/Amsterdam: John Benjamins B.V. 295–325.

Sidner, C. 1983. Focusing in the comprehension of definite anaphora. In Brady, M., and Berwick, R., eds., *Computational Models of Discourse*. MIT Press. 267–330.

Zancanaro, M.; Stock, O.; and Strapparava, C. 1997. Multimodal interaction for information access: exploiting cohesion. *Computational Intelligence* 13(7):439–464.

Class-Based Construction of a Verb Lexicon

Karin Kipper, Hoa Trang Dang, and Martha Palmer

Department of Computer and Information Sciences
University of Pennsylvania
200 South 33rd Street
Philadelphia, PA 19104, USA
{kipper,htd,mpalmer}@linc.cis.upenn.edu

Abstract

We present an approach to building a verb lexicon compatible with WordNet but with explicitly stated syntactic and semantic information, using Levin verb classes to systematically construct lexical entries. By using verb classes we capture generalizations about verb behavior and reduce the effort needed to construct the lexicon. The syntactic frames for the verb classes are represented by a Lexicalized Tree Adjoining Grammar augmented with semantic predicates, which allows a compositional interpretation.

Introduction

Despite many different approaches to lexicon development (Pustejovsky 1991), (Copestake & Sanfilippo 1993), (Lowe, Baker, & Fillmore 1997), (Dorr 1997), the field of Natural Language Processing (NLP) has yet to develop a clear consensus on guidelines for computational verb lexicons, which has severely limited their utility in NLP applications. Many approaches make no attempt to associate the semantics of a verb with its possible syntactic frames. Others list too many fine-grained sense distinctions due to a lack of a systematic account of verb polysemy. Even WordNet (Miller 1985), one of the most widely used online lexical databases in NLP applications, has elicited much criticism about its representation of verbs.

We address these problems by creating VerbNet, a verb lexicon compatible with WordNet but with explicitly stated syntactic and semantic information, using Levin verb classes (Levin 1993) to systematically construct lexical entries. While previous research on tying semantics to Levin classes (Dorr 1997) has not made explicit the close relation between syntax and semantics hypothesized by Levin, our lexical resource combines traditional lexical semantic information such as thematic roles and semantic predicates, with syntactic frames and selectional restrictions. We have used Lexicalized Tree Adjoining Grammar (LTAG) (Joshi 1985; Schabes 1990) to capture the syntax associated with each verb class. We also show how regular extensions of verb meaning can be achieved through the adjunction of particular syntactic phrases. We base these regular extensions on intersective Levin classes, a fine-grained variation on Levin classes, as a source of semantic components associated with

specific adjuncts (Dang et al. 1998). Unlike work by Saint-Dizier (1999), we do not attempt to automatically construct classes from syntactic criteria. We concentrate on building lexical entries only for the word senses already classified by Levin; future work may add verbs to the classes, as well as construct additional classes for senses not covered by Levin.

Levin Classes and WordNet

Two current approaches to English verb classifications are WordNet and Levin classes. WordNet is an on-line lexical database of English that currently contains approximately 120,000 sets of noun, verb, adjective, and adverb synonyms, each representing a lexicalized concept. A synset (synonym set) contains, besides all the word forms that can refer to a given concept, a definitional gloss and - in most cases - an example sentence. Words and synsets are interrelated by means of lexical and semantic-conceptual links, respectively. Antonymy or semantic opposition links individual words, while the super-/subordinate relation links entire synsets. WordNet was designed principally as a semantic network, and contains little syntactic information. Even as a semantic resource, however, it is missing some of the information that has traditionally been required by NLP applications, including explicit predicate-argument structures. In addition, WordNet senses are often too fine-grained, lacking an underlying notion of semantic components and a systematic extension of basic senses to produce these more fine-grained senses.

On the other hand, the Levin verb classification explicitly states the syntax for each class, but also falls short of assigning semantic components to each class. The classes are based on the ability or inability of a verb to occur in pairs of syntactic frames that are in some sense meaning preserving (diathesis alternations) (Levin 1993). The fundamental assumption is that the syntactic frames are a direct reflection of the underlying semantics. However, Levin classes exhibit inconsistencies that have hampered researchers' ability to reference them directly in applications. Many verbs are listed in multiple classes, some of which have conflicting sets of syntactic frames. Dang et al. (1998) showed that multiple listings could in some cases be interpreted as regular sense extensions, and defined intersective Levin classes, which are a more fine-grained, syntactically and semantically coherent refinement of basic Levin classes. We implement these verb classes and their regular sense extensions in the Lexicalized Tree Adjoining Grammar formalism.

Lexicalized Tree-Adjoining Grammars

Lexicalized Tree-Adjoining Grammars (LTAGs) consist of a finite set of initial and auxiliary elementary trees, and two operations to combine them. The minimal, non-recursive linguistic structures of a language, such as a verb and its complements, are captured by initial trees. Recursive structures of a language, such as prepositional modifiers which result in syntactically embedded verb phrases (VP), are represented by auxiliary trees.

Elementary trees are combined by the operations of substitution and adjunction. Substitution is a simple operation that replaces a leaf of a tree with a new tree. Adjunction is a splicing operation that replaces an internal node of an elementary tree with an auxiliary tree. Every tree is associated with a lexical item of the language, called the *anchor* of the tree. The tree represents the domain over which the lexical item can directly specify syntactic constraints, such as subject-verb number agreement, or semantic constraints, such as selectional restrictions, all of which are implemented as features in Feature-Based LTAG (FB-LTAG) (Vijay-Shanker & Joshi 1991). An example of a simple transitive tree is shown in Figure 1. Alternative syntactic realizations of a lexical item are grouped together into *tree families*. Each family represents a basic argument structure (e.g., intransitive, transitive) and has a set of trees corresponding to transformations (e.g., passive, wh-movement) of the basic structure. The semantic constraints automatically apply to the same arguments in the alternative trees.

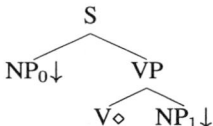

Figure 1: Transitive Tree

Previous work in incorporating semantics into TAG trees has been done. Stone and Doran (1997) described a system used for generation that simultaneously constructs the semantics and syntax of a sentence using LTAGs. Each lexical item is associated with a syntactic tree or family of trees, and each tree has logical forms representing the semantic and pragmatic information selected for that particular lexical item and tree. The meaning of a sentence is the conjunction of the meanings of the elementary trees used to derive it, once the arguments are recovered.

Palmer et al. (1999) and Bleam et al. (1998) defined compositional semantics in FB-LTAG for classes of verbs, representing general semantic components (e.g., motion, manner) as features on the nodes of the trees.

Joshi and Vijay-Shanker (1999), and Kallmeyer and Joshi (1999), describe the semantics of a derivation tree as a set of attachments of trees. The semantics of these attachments is given as a conjunction of formulae in a flat semantic representation. The order of the attachments is not relevant and does not need to be reflected in the semantics. They provide a specific methodology for composing semantic representations much like Candito and Kahane (1998), where the directionality of dominance in the derivation tree should be interpreted according to the operations used to build it.

Description of the Verb Lexicon

VerbNet has two aspects: static and dynamic. The static aspect refers to the verb entries and how they are organized. This aspect provides the characteristic descriptions of a verb sense or a verb class. The dynamic aspect of the lexicon constrains the entries to allow a compositional interpretation in LTAG derivation trees. By incorporating adjuncts we also capture extended verb meanings.

Each verb entry refers to a set of classes, corresponding to the different senses of the verb. For example, the manner of motion sense of "run" is a member of the *Manner of Motion* class, whereas "run" as in "the street runs through the district" is a member of the *Meander* class. For each verb sense there is a verb class as well as specific selectional restrictions (e.g., an instrument of "kick" must be of type $foot$) and semantic characteristics (e.g., a particular manner of directed motion) that may not be captured by the class membership. In order to provide a mapping to other dictionaries, we are also including links to WordNet synsets. Because WordNet has more fine-grained sense distinctions than Levin, each verb sense in VerbNet references the set of WordNet synsets (if any) that captures the meaning appropriate to the class.

Verb classes allow us to capture generalizations about verb behavior. This reduces not only the effort needed to construct the lexicon, but also the likelihood that errors are introduced when adding a new verb entry. Each verb class lists the thematic roles that the predicate-argument structure of its members allows, and provides descriptions of the syntactic frames corresponding to licensed constructions, with selectional restrictions defined for each argument in each frame. Each frame also includes semantic predicates describing the participants during various stages of the event described by the frame.

Verb classes are hierarchically organized, ensuring that each class is coherent enough so that all its members have a common semantics and share a common set of thematic roles and basic syntactic frames. This requires some manual restructuring of the original Levin classes, which is facilitated by using intersective Levin classes. In addition, a particular verb may add more semantic information to the basic semantics of its class.

We decompose each event E into a tripartite structure according to Moens and Steedman (1988). We introduce a time function for each predicate specifying whether the predicate is true in the preparatory ($during(E)$), culmination ($end(E)$), or consequent ($result(E)$) stage of an event. The tripartite event structure allows us to express the semantics of classes of verbs like change of state verbs whose adequate description requires reference to a complex event structure. In the case of a verb such as "break", it is important to make a distinction between the state of the object before the end of the action ($during(E)$), and the new state that results afterwards ($result(E)$).

HIT class

⟨⟨MEMBERS⟩⟩   [⟨hit, 1⟩, ⟨kick, 1⟩, ⟨slap, 1⟩, ⟨tap, 1⟩, ...]
⟨⟨THEMATIC ROLES⟩⟩   Agent(A), Patient(P), Instrument(I)
⟨⟨SELECT RESTRICTIONS⟩⟩   Agent[+animate],
    Patient[+concrete],
    Instrument[+concrete,-animate]

⟨⟨FRAMES and PREDICATES⟩⟩

Basic Transitive	A V P	manner(during(E),directedmotion,A) ∧ manner(end(E),forceful,A) ∧ contact(end(E),A,P)
Transitive with Instrument	A V P with I	manner(during(E),directedmotion,I) ∧ manner(end(E),forceful,I) ∧ contact(end(E),I,P)
Together reciprocal	A V P[+plural] together	manner(during(E),directedmotion,P_i) ∧ manner(during(E),directedmotion,P_j) ∧ manner(end(E),forceful,P_i) ∧ manner(end(E),forceful,P_j) ∧ contact(end(E),P_i,P_j)
Resultative	A V P Adj	manner(during(E),directedmotion,A) ∧ manner(end(E),forceful,A) ∧ contact(end(E),A,P) ∧ Pred(result(E),P)
Resultative	A V P Adj with I	manner(during(E),directedmotion,I) ∧ manner(end(E),forceful,I) ∧ contact(end(E),I,P) ∧ Pred(result(E),P)
Resultative	A V P PP	manner(during(E),directedmotion,A) ∧ manner(end(E),forceful,A) ∧ contact(end(E),A,P) ∧ Pred(result(E),P)
Resultative	A V P PP with I	manner(during(E),directedmotion,I) ∧ manner(end(E),forceful,I) ∧ contact(end(E),I,P) ∧ Pred(result(E),P)
Conative	A V at P	manner(during(E),directedmotion,A)
Conative	A V at P with I	manner(during(E),directedmotion,I)
With/against alternation	A V I against/on P	manner(during(E),directedmotion,I) ∧ manner(end(E),forceful,I) ∧ contact(end(E),I,P)
Body-part object or reflexive object	A V I[+body-part/+refl]	manner(during(E),directedmotion,I) ∧ manner(end(E),forceful,I) ∧ contact(end(E),I,?)
Body-part object or reflexive object	A V I[+body-part/+refl] against/on P	manner(during(E),directedmotion,I) ∧ manner(end(E),forceful,I) ∧ contact(end(E),I,P)
Transitive	I V P	manner(during(E),directedmotion,I) ∧ manner(end(E),forceful,I) ∧ contact(end(E),I,P)
Resultative	I V P Adj	manner(during(E),directedmotion,I) ∧ manner(end(E),forceful,I) ∧ contact(end(E),I,P) ∧ Pred(result(E),P)
Resultative	I V P PP	manner(during(E),directedmotion,I) ∧ manner(end(E),forceful,I) ∧ contact(end(E),I,P) ∧ Pred(result(E),P)

Figure 2: Example entry for the *Hit* class

Transfer of a Message - level 1 class

⟨⟨MEMBERS⟩⟩ [⟨ask, 1⟩, ⟨cite, 1⟩, ⟨demonstrate, 1⟩, ⟨dictate, 1⟩, ...]
⟨⟨THEMATIC ROLES⟩⟩ Agent(A), Recipient(R), Theme(T)
⟨⟨SELECT RESTRICTIONS⟩⟩ Agent[+animate],
Recipient[+animate],
Theme[+message]

⟨⟨FRAMES and PREDICATES⟩⟩

Transitive with Theme	A V T	transfer_info(during(E),A,?,T)
Theme and Recipient	A V T to R	transfer_info(during(E),A,R,T)

Transfer of a Message - level 2 class

⟨⟨PARENT⟩⟩ Transfer of a Message - level 1
⟨⟨MEMBERS⟩⟩ [⟨ask, 1⟩, ⟨dictate, 1⟩, ⟨quote, 1⟩, ⟨read, 1⟩,
⟨show, 1⟩, ⟨teach, 1⟩, ⟨tell, 1⟩, ⟨write, 1⟩]

⟨⟨FRAMES and PREDICATES⟩⟩

Ditransitive	A V R T	transfer_info(during(E),A,R,T)

Figure 3: Example entries for the *Transfer of a Message - levels 1* and *2* classes

Figure 2 shows the entry for the *Hit* class. This class allows for three thematic roles: Agent, Patient and Instrument, with constraints on these roles.[1] The Agent is generally animate; the Patient, concrete; and the Instrument, concrete but inanimate. These selectional restrictions refer to a feature hierarchy where animate subsumes animal and human, concrete subsumes both animate and inanimate, and so forth. The representation does not suffer from some drawbacks of theta role analysis because our roles are not global primitives, but are only meaningful within a class.

The strength of our description comes from the explicit relation between syntax and semantics captured in each entry. The example shows the syntactic frames allowed for the class, with thematic roles as descriptors, which are mapped into predicate-arguments as well as the arguments in a TAG representation. It may be the case that a construction is only possible when a particular lexical item is present; for example, the conative construction[2] needs the lexical item "at", and the *together* reciprocal alternation requires the lexical item "together" to be present. In LTAGs these lexical items would be co-anchors in the initial tree.

Using Levin's description of the allowed frames for the verbs in the *Hit* class, each frame is represented by an ordered sequence of thematic roles. There are two possible simple transitive frames, defined as A V P (Agent Verb Patient) and I V P (Instrument Verb Patient). The *together* reciprocal alternation, as in "John hit the sticks together", requires a plural direct object and the presence of the lexical item "together". The resultative constructions incorporate an adjective(Adj), as in "John kicked the door open", or a prepositional phrase (PP), as in "John kicked the door into an open position". In the *with/against* alternation, in order to have the instrument reading for the direct object, we require a prepositional phrase "against/on Patient", as in "John hit the stick against the fence", where "the stick" is the instrument and "the fence" is the patient.

We use a flat semantic representation in which the semantics of each frame is captured by a conjunction of predicates. Many of the frames allow for a "with Instrument" prepositional phrase, which modifies the arguments of some of the predicates. The basic predicates for the *Hit* class are *manner(during(E),directedmotion,X)*, which specifies that during event E, either the agent or the instrument is in motion, and *manner(end(E),forceful,X)* ∧ *contact(end(E),X,P)*, which captures the idea that at the end of event E the agent or the instrument establishes contact with the patient in a forceful way. The conative construction does not have predicates for contact and manner at the end of the event, since the intended goal of contact is never satisfied. The resultative adds another predicate (*Pred*, instantiated by the particular adjectival or prepositional resultative phrase), which indicates the new resulting state achieved by the patient at the end of the event. Reciprocity for multiple patients selected by a plural direct object is captured by having as many manner predicates as there are patients, since each one is supposedly in motion and forceful. The body-part object and reflexive object alternations are the same as the basic predicates, except that the patient may be unspecified ("John hit his elbow" does not contain any information about what the agent hit his elbow against.)

The hierarchical organization of VerbNet is illustrated in Figure 3. The *Transfer of a Message* verb class is subdivided into three levels. At the top level are thematic roles, syntactic frames and semantic predicates shared by all members of the class. In this particular case, there is a transitive frame with the Theme (message) as the direct object (Agent Verb Theme), as in "John explained trigonometry", and a frame

---
[1] These constraints are more like preferences that generate a preferred reading of a sentence. They may be relaxed depending on the domain of a particular application.

[2] In the conative construction there is an intention of a goal during the event, that is not achieved at the end of the event.

for Theme and Recipient (Agent Verb Theme to Recipient), as in "John taught math to Mary". Both syntactic frames have semantic predicates expressing the transfer of information event, but in the first case the Recipient is underspecified. Some of the verbs in this class are able to participate in other syntactic frames as well. Verbs at the second level can take the ditransitive frame (Agent Verb Recipient Theme) in addition to the frames and predicates inherited from the parent class. A subset of these verbs (*ask, show, teach, tell, write*) can take yet another frame, transitive with Recipient as direct object (Agent Verb Recipient), defining a third level class.

Compositional Semantics

The static description of frames given in the previous section is mapped onto TAG elementary trees, and the semantic predicates are associated with each tree, as was done by Stone and Doran. By using TAGs we get the additional benefit of an existing parser that yields derivations and derived trees from which we can construct the compositional semantics of a given sentence. Kipper et al. (2000), describes the dynamic aspect of VerbNet in greater detail.

Initial trees capture the semantics of the basic senses of verbs in each class. For example, many verbs in the Levin *Run* class can occur in the causative/inchoative alternation, in which the subject of the intransitive sentence has the same thematic role as the direct object in the transitive sentence. Figure 4 shows the initial trees for the causative and inchoative variants for the *Run* class, along with their semantic predicates.

Predicates are associated with not only the verb trees, but also the auxiliary trees. For example, the predicates for a path prepositional phrase headed by "across" specify that an object is in *motion* with a path *via* some other object (the object of the preposition) during the event. The semantics of a sentence is the conjunction of the semantic predicates of the trees used to derive the sentence, in a manner similar to that used by Kallmeyer and Joshi. The ability of verbs to take on extended senses in sentences based on their adjuncts is captured in a natural way by the TAG operation of adjunction and our conjunction of semantic predicates. In cases where the path PP adjoins onto a tree representing a basic motion event, such as for the *Run* class, the *motion* predicate contributed by the PP is redundant but doesn't conflict with existing predicates. However, this *motion* predicate is useful for verb classes such as the *Hit* class, which does not include movement of the direct object as part of the meaning of hit (only sudden contact has to be established); by adjoining a path PP such as "across the room", we get an extended meaning and change in Levin class membership.

The trees are organized into tree families, as is done in the Xtag grammar (XTAG Research Group 1995). Each thematic role is mapped to an indexed node in the basic syntactic tree. For example, $A\ V\ P$ maps to a structure such as the transitive tree shown in Figure 1, with Agent mapped to NP_0 and Patient to NP_1. The selectional restrictions of each role are expressed as semantic features in the nodes. The correspondence between thematic roles and indexing of syntactic arguments in TAG trees is preserved within the tree family, so by specifying the mapping to the basic tree, we also get the mapping to all the transformations applicable to the tree family (e.g., passivization, wh-movement).

Conclusion

We have presented a class-based approach to building a verb lexicon that makes explicit the close association between syntax and semantics, as postulated by Levin. By using verb classes we capture generalizations about verb behavior and reduce not only the effort needed to construct the lexicon, but also the likelihood that errors are introduced when adding new verbs.

Our use of logical forms gives a detailed semantics for each syntactic frame, so that for an event involving motion, it is possible to know not only that the event has a *motion* semantic component, but also which entity is actually in motion. This level of detail is necessary for applications such as animation of natural language instructions (Bindiganavale *et al.* 2000). Another important contribution is that by dividing each event into a tripartite structure, we permit a more precise definition of the associated semantics. Finally, the operation of adjunction in TAGs provides a principled approach to representing the type of regular polysemy that has been a major obstacle in building verb lexicons.

Acknowledgments

This paper is based on research conducted under CAPES grant 0914-95 and NSF grants IIS-9800658 and IIS-9900297.

References

Bindiganavale, R.; Schuler, W.; Allbeck, J. M.; Badler, N. I.; Joshi, A. K.; and Palmer, M. 2000. Dynamically Altering Agent Behaviors Using Natural Language Instructions. *Fourth International Conference on Autonomous Agents*.

Bleam, T.; Palmer, M.; and Vijay-Shanker, K. 1998. Motion Verbs and Semantic Features in TAG. In *Proceedings of the Fourth TAG+ Workshop*.

Candito, M.-H., and Kahane, S. 1998. Can the TAG Derivation Tree Represent a Semantic Graph? An Answer in the Light of Meaning-Text Theory. In *Proceedings of the Fourth TAG+ Workshop*, 21–24.

Copestake, A., and Sanfilippo, A. 1993. Multilingual Lexical Representation. In *Proceedings of the AAAI Spring Symposium: Building Lexicons for Machine Translation*.

Dang, H. T.; Kipper, K.; Palmer, M.; and Rosenzweig, J. 1998. Investigating Regular Sense Extensions Based on Intersective Levin classes. In *Proceedings of COLING-ACL98*.

Dorr, B. J. 1997. Large-Scale Dictionary Construction for Foreign Language Tutoring and Interlingual Machine Translation. *Machine Translation* 12:1–55.

Joshi, A. K., and Vijay-Shanker, K. 1999. Compositional Semantics with Lexicalized Tree-Adjoining Grammar: How Much Under-Specification Is Necessary? . In

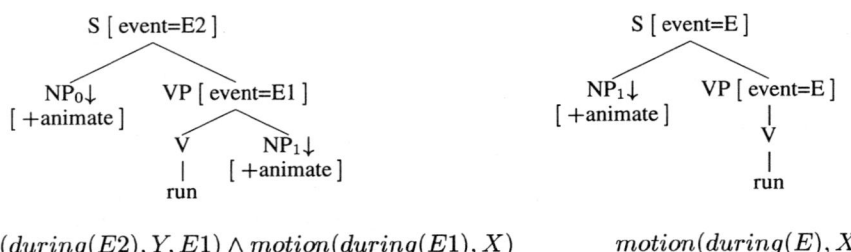

Figure 4: Causative/Inchoative alternation for the *Run* verbs

Proceedings of the Third International Workshop on Computational Semantics (IWCS-3), 131–145.

Joshi, A. K. 1985. How Much Context Sensitivity Is Necessary for Characterizing Structural Descriptions: Tree Adjoining Grammars. In D. Dowty, L. K., and Zwicky, A., eds., *Natural language parsing: Psychological, computational and theoretical perspectives*. Cambridge, U.K.: Cambridge University Press. 206–250.

Kallmeyer, L., and Joshi, A. 1999. Underspecified Semantics with LTAG. In *Proceedings of Amsterdam Colloquium on Semantics*.

Kipper, K.; Dang, H. T.; Schuler, W.; and Palmer, M. 2000. Building a Class-Based Verb Lexicon Using TAGs. In *Proceedings of Fifth TAG+ Workshop*.

Levin, B. 1993. *English Verb Classes and Alternation: A Preliminary Investigation*. The University of Chicago Press.

Lowe, J.; Baker, C.; and Fillmore, C. 1997. A Frame-Semantic Approach to Semantic Annotation. In *Proceedings 1997 Siglex Workshop/ANLP97*.

Miller, G. 1985. WORDNET: A Dictionary Browser. In *Proceedings of the First International Conference on Information in Data*.

Moens, M., and Steedman, M. 1988. Temporal Ontology and Temporal Reference. *Computational Linguistics* 14:15–38.

Palmer, M.; Rosenzweig, J.; and Schuler, W. 1999. Capturing Motion Verb Generalizations in Synchronous Tree-Adjoining Grammar. In Saint-Dizier, P., ed., *Predicative Forms in Natural Language and in Lexical Knowledge Bases*. Kluwer Press.

Pustejovsky, J. 1991. The Generative Lexicon. *Computational Linguistics* 17(4).

Saint-Dizier, P. 1999. Alternations and Verb Semantic Classes for French: Analysis and Class Formation. In Saint-Dizier, P., ed., *Predicative Forms in Natural Language and in Lexical Knowledge Bases*. Kluwer Press.

Schabes, Y. 1990. *Mathematical and Computational Aspects of Lexicalized Grammars*. Ph.D. Dissertation, Computer Science Department, University of Pennsylvania.

Stone, M., and Doran, C. 1997. Sentence Planning as Description Using Tree Adjoining Grammar. In *Proceedings of ACL-EACL '97*.

Vijay-Shanker, K., and Joshi, A. 1991. Unification Based Tree Adjoining Grammars. In Wedekind, J., ed., *Unification-based Grammars*. Cambridge, Massachusetts: MIT Press.

XTAG Research Group. 1995. A Lexicalized Tree Adjoining Grammar for English. Technical report, University of Pennsylvania.

Preserving Ambiguities in Generation via Automata Intersection

Kevin Knight and Irene Langkilde
Information Sciences Institute
University of Southern California
4676 Admiralty Way, Suite 1001
Marina del Rey, CA 90292
{knight,ilangkil}@isi.edu

Abstract

We discuss the problem of generating text that preserves certain ambiguities, a capability that is useful in applications such as machine translation. We show that it is relatively simple to extend a hybrid symbolic/statistical generator to do ambiguity preservation. The paper gives algorithms and examples, and it discusses practical linguistic difficulties that arise in ambiguity preservation.

Introduction

This paper reports on an aspect of a natural language generation system called Nitrogen (Knight and Hatzivassiloglou, 1995; Langkilde and Knight, 1998ab; Langkilde, 2000), which has been used as part of the Gazelle machine translation (MT) system (Knight et al, 1995). In particular, we show how Nitrogen can generate English text that preserves unresolved ambiguities from non-English documents.

One of the first texts translated by Gazelle was a Japanese article with the following noun phrase:

1a. [IC chippu o seizou-suru noni tsukau]
    dorai-echingu soochi ya suteppa
    [*silicon chip construct for use*]
    dry-etching device and stepper motor

In Japanese, relative clauses precede the nouns they modify. In this sentence, it is not clear whether the relative clause [shown bracketed] modifies the whole conjoined noun phrase (dry-etching device and stepper motor) or only the first noun in the conjunction (dry-etching device). Depending on the correct interpretation, reasonable English translations might be:

1b. ((dry-etching devices and stepper motors)
    that are used to construct silicon chips)
1c. ((dry-etching devices that are used to construct
    silicon chips) and stepper motors)

Both of these translations are "unsafe" because they commit to a particular interpretation that may turn out to be wrong. Translators who happen to know about

computer equipment will prefer (1c) over (1b), but even (1c) has its problems—if we remove the parentheses, the sentence is likely to be misparsed by a reader!

The solution is to find a nice English translation that covers both interpretations:

1d. stepper motors and dry-etching devices
    that are used to construct silicon chips

To get this "safe" translation, we simply re-order the nouns in the conjunction. It turns out that this conjunct-flipping technique is often employed by human translators. In this case, the idea is that the reader knows more about stepper motors than the translator does, and can disambiguate more easily. Many structural ambiguities provide opportunities for such ambiguity preservation.

Consider the English sentence:

2a. John saw the man with the telescope.

This sentence has two interpretations, depending on where the prepositional phrase attaches, but both interpretations are covered by the single Spanish translation:

2a. John vió al hombre con el telescopio.

This example shows how word-for-word MT engines frequently perform a simple-minded kind of ambiguity preservation, a fact that explains much of the commercial success of machine translation systems that operate between close language pairs. But even between Spanish and English, syntactic differences suggest careful handling. In the next phrase, the scope of the phrase-initial adjective is unclear:

3a. green eggs and ham

Again, conjunct flipping can help:

3b. (unsafe) huevos verdes y jamón
3c. (unsafe) huevos y jamón verdes
3d. (safe) jamón y huevos verdes

Another usefully vague construction is nominalization. Suppose that I witnessed somebody destroy something, and I only know that Nero was involved. There are safe and unsafe expressions for this situation:

Copyright © 2000, American Association for Artificial Intelligence (www.aaai.org). All rights reserved.

4a. (unsafe) I witnessed Nero being destroyed.
4b. (unsafe) I witnessed the destruction by Nero.
4c. (safe) I witnessed Nero's destruction.

Pronoun reference can also benefit. Consider the English sentence

5. She saw the car in the window and wanted to buy it.

Although we must pick a gender for the German equivalent of "it," we can maintain the ambiguity if we select translations of "car" and "window" that have the same gender:

6a. (unsafe) Sie sah den Wagen$_{masc}$ im
   Schaufenster$_{neut}$ und wollte ihn$_{masc}$ kaufen.
6b. (unsafe) Sie sah den Wagen$_{masc}$ im
   Schaufenster$_{neut}$ und wollte es$_{neut}$ kaufen.
6c. (safe) Sie sah das Auto$_{neut}$ im
   Schaufenster$_{neut}$ und wollte es$_{neut}$ kaufen.

Opportunities for ambiguity preservation occur frequently, but most ambiguities cannot of course be preserved. For example, it is very difficult to preserve lexical part-of-speech ambiguities, as in sentences like "Time flies." Semantic lexical ambiguities are more frequently preservable. In the English sentence "I went to the center," it is not clear whether "center" means "middle" or "an institution devoted to the study of something." When we translate to Spanish, we can simply say "Fui al centro," without resolving the ambiguity.

Sometimes we can preserve an ambiguity only by appealing to awkward and disfluent constructions. Consider the following Japanese phrase:

7a. John no kuruma no kagi
   John genitive-particle car genitive-particle key

There are two possible interpretations: ((John no kuruma) no kagi) and (John no (kuruma no kagi)). A translation like "the keys of John's car" commits to the first interpretation, while "John's car keys" commits to second. In this case, it doesn't really matter too much, but in other cases it will. So we would like to have a general method of preserving this kind of "X no Y no Z" ambiguity. Fortunately, there are two constructions that can do it—unfortunately, neither is very fluent English:

7b. (safe) the keys of the car of John
7c. (safe) John's car's keys

Another pitfall for ambiguity preservation is misdirection. A sentence that supposedly covers two interpretations may employ a syntactic structure that completely obscures one of them. For example, consider:

8. (supposedly safe) The CIA claimed that Jones
              was a spy from 1970 to 1992.

This sentence has a single overwhelmingly strong reading. The author of the sentence can always assert to the reader that it was actually the *claiming* that lasted for 1970 to 1992, not the *spying*, but in that case the reader will feel that he/she has been misdirected.

To sum up, ambiguity preservation is a technique often employed by human translators, among whom it is considered somewhat of an art. There are both opportunities and pitfalls. Ambiguity preservation is particularly interesting for machine translators, because they are not nearly as adept as humans at resolving source-language ambiguities.

Objective

Ideally, we would like to come up with an ambiguity preservation algorithm that is not tied to a specific language pair or even to specific linguistic constructions. Wedekind and Kaplan (1996) consider ambiguity preservation for generators that use LFG-style grammars. They show that the problem is undecidable: an interesting result, but one that is of little use to the practitioner. Emele and Dorna (1998) give an algorithm for preserving ambiguity that relies on packed LFG f-structure representations produced by the transfer component of an MT system. Shemtov (1998) describes the ambiguity preserving version of Kay's (1996) chart generator. Like the above authors, we will discuss ambiguity preservation across semantic inputs, thereby decoupling the problem from translation. For MT applications, we allow source language analysis to generate many possible meanings which are then picked over by an English-only generator. We also imagine non-MT applications for ambiguity preservation, for example, those that generate legal documents. Moreover, a generator that understands how to preserve ambiguity should also be able to steer clear of ambiguities, as again when generating legal documents.

We contribute ambiguity-preservation algorithma different from ones already proposed in (Shemtov, 1998; Emele and Dorna, 1998). Our algorithm uses structures that are somewhat simpler, and we are able to reduce our computations to well-known, generic operations on formal automata. Our goals are that (1) the method we invent is simple, (2) it is efficient, (3) it is a minimal extension to an existing generator, and (4) it is fully implemented and tested. We first describe the generator we use and then describe our method.

Nitrogen

Nitrogen is a broad-coverage sentence realizer that generates English from conceptual expressions that include all concepts of WordNet (Fellbaum, 1998) and a set of sixty semantic relationships drawn from the Gazelle MT interlingua. Because it is difficult to generate on a scale of 100,000 words and concepts without great deal of lexical, conceptual, and grammatical knowledge, Nitrogen supplements its shallow knowledge bases with statistical knowledge gathered from text. The statistical knowledge also helps it build fluent sentences from inputs that are underspecified with respect to number, tense, definiteness, etc.

Nitrogen operates in two stages. First, a meaning representation is transformed into a large network of possible realizations, via an English grammar and lexicon. In the second stage, statistical knowledge is applied to select the most fluent realization.

In the first stage, it is the job of a grammar writer to to produce all possible realizations of input structures, i.e., particular configurations of semantic roles. This is much easier than specifying what are all the correct realizations in a myriad of sub-cases. The first stage of Nitrogen therefore massively overgenerates, producing a lot of ungrammatical and disfluent sentences. Most of these are weeded out by the second-stage statistical component.

Here is an example input to Nitrogen:

```
(p / possible,potential
  :domain (o / obligatory
             :domain (e / eat
                       :agent you
                       :patient chicken-meat)))
```

Nitrogen's grammar produces over ten million realizations, all packed into an efficient data structure. Here are a few randomly selected realizations:

9a. You may be obliged to eat that there was the poulet.
9b. A consumption of poulet by you may be the requirements.
9c. That the eating of chicken by you is obligatory is possible.

It is not trivial to say exactly what is wrong with such sentences, but they are clearly bad. Of the ten million possibilities, however, the statistical component ranks the following reasonable sentences as its top choices for output:

10a. You may have to eat chicken.
10b. You might have to eat chicken.
10c. You may be required to eat chicken.

We designed Nitrogen for scale, robustness, and accuracy, but it turns out that this set-up is good for ambiguity preservation as well.

Ambiguity Preservation with Word Lattices

The original version of Nitrogen packed its alternative realizations into a word-lattice data structure. A small fragment of sample Nitrogen word lattice is shown in Figure 1. The lattice has a start state, an end state, and transitions labeled with words. Each path corresponds to a different sentence, and the whole lattice can be viewed as a set of strings. Typical Nitrogen lattices have hundreds of nodes, thousands of arcs, and billions or more alternative sentences. To extract the most fluent sentence, we use word-pair statistics and n-best search procedures (Knight and Hatzivassiloglou, 1995) similar to those used in speech recognition.

Suppose we have two possible meaning representations (derived, say, from a single Spanish input sentence):

```
1. (s / see
     :agent I
     :patient (m / man
                 :possesses (t / telescope)))

   -> I see the man with the telescope.
   -> I see the man holding the telescope.
      etc.

2. (s / see
     :agent I
     :patient (m / man)
     :instrument (t / telescope))

   -> I see the man with the telescope.
   -> With the telescope, I see the man.
      etc.
```

Nitrogen can compute word lattices for these two meanings independently. Sentences that express both meanings simultaneously (i.e., preserve ambiguity) are exactly the sentences that occur in both lattices. Here, "I see the man with the telescope" appears in both, but "With the telescope, I see the man" does not.

We can compute the desired sentences simply by intersecting the two lattices. There are standard "book" algorithms for doing this. If we convert our lattices into deterministic finite-state acceptors FSA1 and FSA2, then Lewis and Papadimitriou (1981) give a simple algorithm that builds a new acceptor FSA3 which accepts the intersection of the strings accepted by FSA1 and FSA2. However, this algorithm is quadratic in the number of nodes, and is not very practical on large FSAs.

Ambiguity Preservation with Parse Forests

The current version of Nitrogen operates somewhat differently. It packs alternative realizations into a *parse-forest* structure.[1] While a word lattice is best viewed as a set of strings, a parse forest is best viewed as a set of trees. Figure 2 shows three sample forests.

We first designed and implemented an algorithm for intersecting a pair of parse forests, i.e., returning the set of syntactic trees that appear in both forests. While this algorithm preserves certain types of ambiguities, e.g., by conjunct-flipping and nominalization, it fails on others, such as the prepositional-phrase attachment example above. In a case like "I see the man with the

---

[1] Our main motivation is that in observing the behavior of Nitrogen's word-pair-based statistical ranking, we notice many errors due to missed long-distance dependencies. We believe that many of these errors will be corrected if we use a syntax-based ranking, such as that of Collins (1997) or Chelba and Jelinek (1998), operating over trees rather than flat strings. In order to match up with statistically-collected data, our trees are compliant with the labeling and bracketing scheme of the Penn Treebank (Marcus, Santorini, and Marcinkiewicz, 1993). Another advantage of using forests is that they are more compact than lattices, avoiding repetition of substructures.

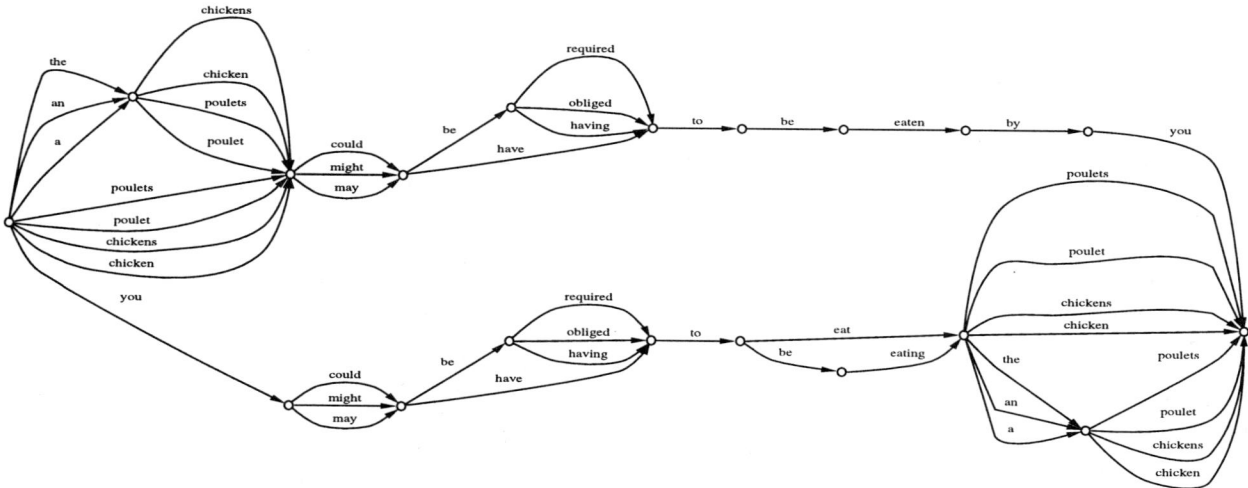

Figure 1: A small fragment of a sample Nitrogen word lattice. One path represents the fluent sentence *you may have to eat chicken*. Other paths correspond to less fluent or appropriate sentences. The full word lattice is many times larger than this fragment.

telescope," there is no single syntactic tree that covers both meanings. However, there *are* strings that cover both meanings.

Suppose we are given parse forests PF1 and PF2. Then we want to build a new parse forest PF3 that includes every tree T such that either (1) T is in PF1 and T's terminal string is in PF2, or (2) T is in PF2 and T's terminal string is in PF1. The following algorithm can do this.

function *preserve-ambiguity*(PF1, PF2):

1. Create a lattice FSA1 that contains the same strings as the forest PF1, using the function shown in Figure 3. (The initial call to this recursive function should be *expand-forest-into-lattice*(PF1, root(PF1)).

2. Create a lattice FSA2 that contains the same strings as the forest PF2.

3. Write down PF1 in the form of a "grammar" composed of a number of context-free rewrite rules, e.g.:

    TOP → S.1   SBAR.6 → NP.9 V.10
    S.1 → NP.2 VP.3   NP.9 → *her*
    NP.2 → *I*   V.10 → *move*
    VP.3 → V.4 SBAR.6   NP.5 → ADJ.7 N.8
    VP.3 → V.4 NP.5   ADJ.7 → *her*
    V.4 → *saw*   N.8 → *move*

    This grammar derives only a finite number of strings.

4. Write down PF2 also using rewrite rules.

5. Compute the intersection of PF1 and FSA2. This results in a new forest that contains all trees in PF1 whose terminal strings are in FSA2. Bar Hillel (1961) describes an exponential-time algorithm for carrying out this intersection. As this is impractical, we instead adopt the efficient polynomial-time formulation described by van Noord (1995):

> It can be shown that the computation of the intersection of a FSA and a CFG requires only a minimal generalization of existing parsing algorithms. We simply replace the usual string positions with the names of the states in the FSA. [p. 160]

Instead of using the PF1 "grammar" to parse a string, we use it to parse the lattice FSA2. We adopt a standard chart parser (Allen, 1989), replacing string positions with lattice states. We process the lattice transitions of FSA2 from left to right (in topological order), adding new constituents to the chart and packing ambiguities in the standard way. This kind of lattice parsing is frequently used in parsing noisy input, as from speech recognition.

6. Compute the intersection of PF2 and FSA1.

7. Compute the union of the resulting forests (results of steps 5 and 6) by merging their root nodes.

To preserve the three-way ambiguity of forests A, B, and C in Figure 2, we apply the above algorithm twice, i.e., *preserve-ambiguity*(*preserve-ambiguity*(A, B), C).

We have implemented this algorithm and integrated it into the Nitrogen generator. When Nitrogen encounters a disjunction in its semantic input, it invokes the ambiguity preservation routine. We have observed this routine employing several different syntactic devices such as those we described in the first section.

* * *

Due to Nitrogen's implementation there is a more efficient algorithm than the one just described for computing ambiguity-preserving trees. This algorithm is based

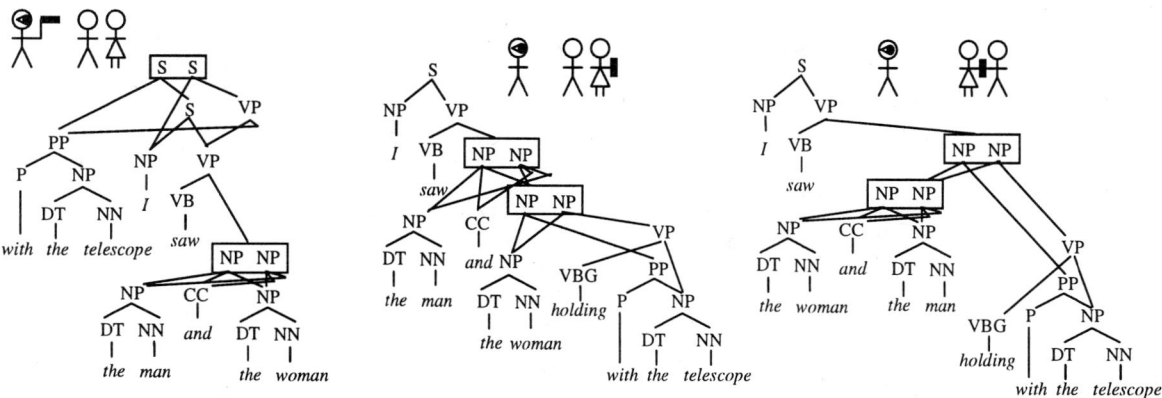

Figure 2: Three parse forests built from three semantic representations. The goal of ambiguity preservation is to identify the trees of just those sentences which cover all meanings.

```
function expand-forest-into-lattice(forest, node)
. lat ← empty-lattice()
. for each rule r in forest with lhs(r) = symbol(node):
. . lat2 ← empty-lattice()
. . for each y in rhs(r):
. . . lat3 ← expand-forest-into-lattice(forest, y)
. . . merge-lattice-states(final-state(lat2), start-state(lat3))
. . merge-lattice-states(start-state(lat), start-state(lat2))
. . merge-lattice-states(final-state(lat), final-state(lat2))
. return(lat)
```

Figure 3: Expanding a forest into a lattice.

on two aspects of Nitrogen's implementation. First, Nitrogen uses a cache to store the results of mapping sub-pieces of the input to sub-forests. The cache avoids duplicate processing during generation because if a particular sub-piece of an input occurs in multiple inputs, the result can retrieved from the cache rather than being regenerated. The effect of the cache is that different forests will share sub-trees if they have sub-units of semantic representation in common. Such shared trees inherently represent an intersection between forests, and automatically preserve ambiguity between different inputs. Unnecessary processing can be avoided by recognizing this in the ambiguity preserving algorithm, rather than continuing to search within the shared sub-tree.

The second aspect of Nitrogen's implementation that facilitates the preservation of ambiguities is the labeling of nodes in the tree. When a sub-forest is generated, it is identified with a unique numeric label. Successive sub-forests are assigned numerically increasing labels. A side effect of this labeling is that a partial order on the nodes in forest is guaranteed, such that a parent node always has a higher-numbered label than any of its children. The ordering on the nodes can be used to guide the search for an intersection between forests. Higher-numbered nodes are always expanded first, ensuring that a shared-subtree will be discovered, if it exists, without doing any unnecessary processing. When a shared sub-tree is found and it is the highest-numbered node among the nodes being examined, the divide-and-conquer method can be used to split the remaining search into two independent sub-problems, thereby significantly reducing the overall search space.

The algorithm in Figure 4 exploits these two aspects of Nitrogen's implementation to achieve more efficient processing. The A and B arguments to the *tree-intersect* function are lists of sequential nodes. Initially, each list contains only the root node of the respective trees being compared. The algorithm is not limited to comparing whole forests, but equally well handles sub-forests and arbitrary sequences of sibling nodes. This gives it another advantage over the previous described algorithm since it can be integrated into the generation process, permitting the preservation of ambiguities within inputs as well as across inputs. The algorithm returns a list of paired trees sharing the same sequence of words, with their differing syntactic structure preserved. This algorithm has been implemented and integrated into the Nitrogen generator.

Discussion

It was very easy to adapt Nitrogen to perform a wide range of ambiguity preservations. Partly, this is because of the simple lattice and forest representations it uses. Nitrogen dispenses with the feature notations that bedevil Wedekind's generator, Shemtov's ambiguity preserving algorithm, and van Noord's lattice parser. In our experience, statistically-gathered knowledge can simulate these features fairly well, while also

```
function tree-intersect (A B)
  if A and B are equal then return the pair (A,B);
  if there are no constituents in A or B then return nil;
  if the highest node of A OR the highest node of B is a leaf node,
  . then return nil;
  if the highest nodes of A and B are the same then
  . high-node := highest node of A;
  . res1 := tree-intersect(left-of-highest(A),left-of-highest(B));
  . res2 := tree-intersect(right-of-highest(A),right-of-highest(B));
  . for every tree pair r1 in res1
  . . for every tree pair r2 in res2
  . . . A1 := append the A tree of res1 to the left of high-node
  . . . . and the A tree of res2 to the right of the high node;
  . . . B1 := append the B tree of res1 to the left of high-node
  . . . . and the B tree of res2 to the right of the high node;
  . . . add the pair (A1,B1) to the tree-pair list;
  . return the tree-pair list.
  if the highest node of A is greater than the highest node of B,
  . for each disjunctive set S of children of A
  . . A1 := substitute S for high-node in A
  . . res := tree-intersect(A1,B);
  . for every tree pair r in res
  . . A2 := replace children in former positions of S
  . . . with new parent node
  . return list of tree-pairs (A2,B);
  otherwise, do the previous seven steps
  . reversing the roles of A and B.
```

Figure 4: Tree-Intersection Algorithm

taking into account the collocational properties of language that are very hard to model with features.

If an ambiguity is not preservable, we union the parse forests instead of doing intersections. This amounts to letting the statistical ranker choose the most fluent sentence regardless of which meaning it expresses. This works better than expected, because strange meanings often make for strange sentences. We do not yet address the problems of disfluent preservations or misdirection (examples 7 and 8), but there are promising avenues in the Nitrogen framework. For example, we might do both intersection and union, but assign higher weights to trees in the intersection. These weights would multiply with those of the statistical ranker, allowing a non-preserving fluent phrase ("John's car keys") to overcome a preserving disfluent one ("John's car's keys"). Misdirection might be attacked by looking at the probabilities assigned to trees by a syntax-based statistical ranker, or by examining the top n statistical parses of proposed generator output.

We would also like to adopt a flat-structure representation for underspecified semantics and massive ambiguity packing (Copestake et al, 1995; Alshawi, 1996; Reyle, 1996, Doerre, 1997), which has been useful to (Shemtov, 1998; Emele and Dorna, 1998). Nitrogen's current meaning representation language, while allowing local disjunctions, is a straightforward but limited feature-based one.

Acknowledgments

We gratefully acknowledge support from NSF Award IIS-9820291.

References

Allen, J. (1989). *Natural Language Understanding*, Benjamin/Cummings.

Alshawi, H. (1996). Underspecified First Order Logics, in Semantic Ambiguity and Underspecification, eds. K. van Deemter and S. Peters.

Bar-Hillel, Y., M. Perles, and E. Shamir (1961). On Formal Properties of Simple for a Structure Grammars, Zeitschrift für Phonetik, SprachWissenschaft und Kommunicationsforschung, 14:143- 172, 1961. Reprinted in *Language and Information - Selected Essays on their Theory and Application*, Addison Wesley series in Logic, 1964, pp. 116-150.

Chelba, C. and F. Jelinek (1998). Exploiting Syntactic Structure for Language Modeling, Proc. COLING/ACL.

Collins, M. (1997). Three Generative, Lexicalised Models for Statistical Parsing, Proc. ACL.

Copestake, A., D. Flickinger, R. Maloufand, S. Riehemann, and I. Sag (1995). Translation using Minimal Recursion Semantics, Proc. Theoretical and Methodological Issues in Machine Translation (TMI).

Doerre, J. (1997). Efficient Construction of Underspecified Semantics under Massive Ambiguity, Proc. ACL/EACL.

Emele, M. and M. Dorna (1998). Ambiguity Preserving Machine Translation using Packed Representations, Proc. COLING/ACL.

Fellbaum, C. (1998). *WordNet*, MIT Press.

Kay, M. (1996). Chart Generation, Proc. ACL.

Knight, K., I. Chander, M. Haines, V. Hatzivassiloglou, E. Hovy, M. Iida, S. Luk, R. Whitney, K. Yamada (1995). Filling Knowledge Gaps in a Broad-Coverage MT System, Proc. IJCAI.

Knight, K. and V. Hatzivassiloglou (1995). Two-Level, Many-Paths Generation, Proc. ACL.

Langkilde, I. Forest-Based Statistical Sentence Generation, Proc. North American ACL.

Langkilde, I. and K. Knight (1998a), The Practical Value of N-Grams in Generation, Proc. of the International Workshop on Natural Language Generation.

Langkilde, I. and K. Knight (1998b), Generation that Exploits Corpus-Based Statistical Knowledge, Proc. COLING/ACL.

Lewis, H. and C. Papadimitriou (1981). *Elements of the Theory of Computation*, Prentice-Hall, Inc.

Marcus, M., B. Santorini, and M. Marcinkiewicz (1993). Building a Large Annotated Corpus of English: The Penn Treebank, *Computational Linguistics*, 19(2).

Reyle, U. (1996). Co-indexing Labelled DRSs to Represent and Reason with Ambiguities, in *Semantic Ambiguity and Underspecification*, eds. K. van Deemter and S. Peters.

Shemtov, H. (1998). *Ambiguity Management in Natural Language Generation*, Ph.D. thesis, Department of Linguistics, Stanford University.

van Noord, G. (1995). The Intersection of Finite State Automata and Definite Clause Grammars, Proc. ACL.

Wedekind, J. and R. Kaplan (1996). Ambiguity-Preserving Generation with LFG- and PATR-style Grammars, *Computational Linguistics*, 22(4).

Statistics-Based Summarization — Step One: Sentence Compression

Kevin Knight and Daniel Marcu
Information Sciences Institute and Department of Computer Science
University of Southern California
4676 Admiralty Way, Suite 1001
Marina del Rey, CA 90292
{knight,marcu}@isi.edu

Abstract

When humans produce summaries of documents, they do not simply extract sentences and concatenate them. Rather, they create new sentences that are grammatical, that cohere with one another, and that capture the most salient pieces of information in the original document. Given that large collections of text/abstract pairs are available online, it is now possible to envision algorithms that are trained to mimic this process. In this paper, we focus on sentence compression, a simpler version of this larger challenge. We aim to achieve two goals simultaneously: our compressions should be grammatical, and they should retain the most important pieces of information. These two goals can conflict. We devise both noisy-channel and decision-tree approaches to the problem, and we evaluate results against manual compressions and a simple baseline.

Introduction

Most of the research in automatic summarization has focused on extraction, i.e., on identifying the most important clauses/sentences/paragraphs in texts (see (Mani & Maybury 1999) for a representative collection of papers). However, determining the most important textual segments is only half of what a summarization system needs to do because, in most cases, the simple catenation of textual segments does not yield coherent outputs. Recently, a number of researchers have started to address the problem of generating coherent summaries: McKeown et al. (1999), Barzilay et al. (1999), and Jing and McKeown (1999) in the context of multidocument summarization; Mani et al. (1999) in the context of revising single document extracts; and Witbrock and Mittal (1999) in the context of headline generation.

The approach proposed by Witbrock and Mittal (1999) is the only one that applies a probabilistic model trained directly on ⟨Headline, Document⟩ pairs. However, this model has yet to scale up to generating multiple-sentence abstracts as well as well-formed, grammatical sentences. All other approaches employ sets of manually written or semi-automatically derived rules for deleting information that is redundant, compressing long sentences into shorter ones, aggregating sentences, repairing reference links, etc.

Our goal is also to generate coherent abstracts. However, in contrast with the above work, we intend to eventually use ⟨Abstract, Text⟩ tuples, which are widely available, in order to automatically learn how to rewrite *Texts* as coherent *Abstracts*. In the spirit of the work in the statistical MT community, which is focused on sentence-to-sentence translations, we also decided to focus first on a simpler problem, that of *sentence compression*. We chose this problem for two reasons:

- First, the problem is complex enough to require the development of sophisticated compression models: Determining what is important in a sentence and determining how to convey the important information grammatically, using only a few words, is just a scaled down version of the text summarization problem. Yet, the problem is simple enough, since we do not have to worry yet about discourse related issues, such as coherence, anaphors, etc.

- Second, an adequate solution to this problem has an immediate impact on several applications. For example, due to time and space constraints, the generation of TV captions often requires only the most important parts of sentences to be shown on a screen (Linke-Ellis 1999; Robert-Ribes et al. 1999). A good sentence compression module would therefore have an impact on the task of automatic caption generation. A sentence compression module can also be used to provide audio scanning services for the blind (Grefenstette 1998). In general, since all systems aimed at producing coherent abstracts implement manually written sets of sentence compression rules (McKeown et al. 1999; Mani, Gates, & Bloedorn 1999; Barzilay, McKeown, & Elhadad 1999), it is likely that a good sentence compression module would impact the overall quality of these systems as well. This becomes particularly important for text genres that use long sentences.

Copyright © 2000, American Association for Artificial Intelligence (www.aaai.org). All rights reserved.

In this paper, we present two approaches to the *sentence compression* problem. Both take as input a sequence of words $W = w_1, w_2, \ldots, w_n$ (one sentence). An algorithm may drop any subset of these words. The words that remain (order unchanged) form a compression. There are 2^n compressions to choose from—some are reasonable, most are not. Our first approach develops a probabilistic noisy-channel model for sentence compression. The second approach develops a decision-based, deterministic model.

A noisy-channel model for sentence compression

This section describes a probabilistic approach to the compression problem. In particular, we adopt the *noisy channel* framework that has been relatively successful in a number of other NLP applications, including speech recognition (Jelinek 1997), machine translation (Brown *et al.* 1993), part-of-speech tagging (Church 1988), transliteration (Knight & Graehl 1998), and information retrieval (Berger & Lafferty 1999).

In this framework, we look at a long string and imagine that (1) it was originally a short string, and then (2) someone added some additional, optional text to it. Compression is a matter of identifying the original short string. It is not critical whether or not the "original" string is real or hypothetical. For example, in statistical machine translation, we look at a French string and say, "This was originally English, but someone added 'noise' to it." The French may or may not have been translated from English originally, but by removing the noise, we can hypothesize an English source—and thereby translate the string. In the case of compression, the noise consists of optional text material that pads out the core signal. For the larger case of text summarization, it may be useful to imagine a scenario in which a news editor composes a short document, hands it to a reporter, and tells the reporter to "flesh it out" ... which results in the article we read in the newspaper. As summarizers, we may not have access to the editor's original version (which may or may not exist), but we can guess at it—which is where probabilities come in.

As in any noisy channel application, we must solve three problems:

- Source model. We must assign to every string s a probability $P(s)$, which gives the chance that s is generated as an "original short string" in the above hypothetical process. For example, we may want $P(s)$ to be very low if s is ungrammatical.
- Channel model. We assign to every pair of strings $\langle s, t \rangle$ a probability $P(t \mid s)$, which gives the chance that when the short string s is expanded, the result is the long string t. For example, if t is the same as s except for the extra word "not," then we may want $P(t \mid s)$ to be very low. The word "not" is not optional, additional material.
- Decoder. When we observe a long string t, we search for the short string s that maximizes $P(s \mid t)$. This is equivalent to searching for the s that maximizes $P(s) \cdot P(t \mid s)$.

It is advantageous to break the problem down this way, as it decouples the somewhat independent goals of creating a short text that (1) looks grammatical, and (2) preserves important information. It is easier to build a channel model that focuses exclusively on the latter, without having to worry about the former. That is, we can specify that a certain substring may represent unimportant information, but we do not need to worry that deleting it will result in an ungrammatical structure. We leave that to the source model, which worries exclusively about well-formedness. In fact, we can make use of extensive prior work in source language modeling for speech recognition, machine translation, and natural language generation. The same goes for actual compression ("decoding" in noisy-channel jargon)—we can re-use generic software packages to solve problems in all these application domains.

Statistical Models

In the experiments we report here, we build very simple source and channel models. In a departure from the above discussion and from previous work on statistical channel models, we assign probabilities $P_{tree}(s)$ and $P_{expand\_tree}(t \mid s)$ to trees rather than strings. In decoding a new string, we first parse it into a large tree t (using Collins' parser (1997)), and we then hypothesize and rank various small trees.

Good source strings are ones that have both (1) a normal-looking parse tree, and (2) normal-looking word pairs. $P_{tree}(s)$ is a combination of a standard probabilistic context-free grammar (PCFG) score, which is computed over the grammar rules that yielded the tree s, and a standard word-bigram score, which is computed over the leaves of the tree. For example, the tree $s =$(S (NP John) (VP (VB saw) (NP Mary))) is assigned a score based on these factors:

$P_{tree}(s) = P(\text{TOP} \to S \mid \text{TOP}) \cdot$
$P(S \to \text{NP VP} \mid S) \cdot P(\text{NP} \to \text{John} \mid \text{NP}) \cdot$
$P(\text{VP} \to \text{VB NP} \mid \text{VP}) \cdot P(\text{VP} \to \text{saw} \mid \text{VB}) \cdot$
$P(\text{NP} \to \text{Mary} \mid \text{NP}) \cdot$
$P(\text{John} \mid \text{EOS}) \cdot P(\text{saw} \mid \text{John}) \cdot$
$P(\text{Mary} \mid \text{saw}) \cdot P(\text{EOS} \mid \text{Mary})$

Our stochastic channel model performs minimal operations on a small tree s to create a larger tree t. For each internal node in s, we probabilistically choose an *expansion template* based on the labels of the node and its children. For example, when processing the S node in the tree above, we may wish to add a prepositional phrase as a third child. We do this with probability $P(S \to \text{NP VP PP} \mid S \to \text{NP VP})$. Or we may choose to leave it alone, with probability $P(S \to \text{NP VP} \mid S \to \text{NP VP})$. After we choose an expansion template, then for each new child node introduced (if any), we grow a new subtree rooted at that node—for example (PP (P in) (NP Pittsburgh)). Any particular subtree is grown

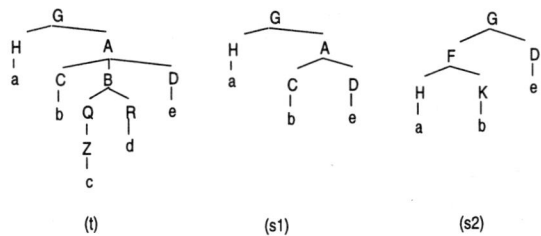

Figure 1: Examples of parse trees.

with probability given by its PCFG factorization, as above (no bigrams).

Example

In this section, we show how to tell whether one potential compression is more likely than another, according to the statistical models described above. Suppose we observe the tree t in Figure 1, which spans the string **abcde**. Consider the compression $s1$, which is shown in the same figure.

We compute the factors $P_{tree}(s1)$ and $P_{expand\_tree}(t \mid s1)$. Breaking this down further, the source PCFG and word-bigram factors, which describe $P_{tree}(s1)$, are:

$P(\text{TOP} \to G \mid \text{TOP})$ $P(H \to a \mid H)$
$P(G \to H A \mid G)$ $P(C \to b \mid C)$
$P(A \to C D \mid A)$ $P(D \to e \mid D)$

$P(a \mid \text{EOS})$ $\boxed{P(e \mid b)}$
$P(b \mid a)$ $\boxed{P(\text{EOS} \mid e)}$

The channel expansion-template factors and the channel PCFG (new tree growth) factors, which describe $P_{expand\_tree}(t \mid s1)$, are:

$P(G \to H A \mid G \to H A)$
$\boxed{P(A \to C B D \mid A \to C D)}$
$P(B \to Q R \mid B)$ $P(Z \to c \mid Z)$
$P(Q \to Z \mid Q)$ $P(R \to d \mid R)$

A different compression will be scored with a different set of factors. For example, consider a compression of t that leaves t completely untouched. In that case, the source costs $P_{tree}(t)$ are:

$P(\text{TOP} \to G \mid \text{TOP})$	$P(H \to a \mid H)$	$P(a \mid \text{EOS})$
$P(G \to H A \mid G)$	$P(C \to b \mid C)$	$\boxed{P(b \mid a)}$
$P(A \to C D \mid A)$	$P(Z \to c \mid Z)$	$\boxed{P(c \mid b)}$
$P(B \to Q R \mid B)$	$P(R \to d \mid R)$	$\boxed{P(d \mid c)}$
$P(Q \to Z \mid Q)$	$P(D \to e \mid D)$	$\boxed{P(e \mid d)}$
		$P(\text{EOS} \mid e)$

The channel costs $P_{expand\_tree}(t \mid t)$ are:

The documentation is typical of Epson quality: excellent.
Documentation is excellent.

All of our design goals were achieved and the delivered performance matches the speed of the underlying device.
All design goals were achieved.

Reach's E-mail product, MailMan, is a message-management system designed initially for VINES LANs that will eventually be operating system-independent.
MailMan will eventually be operating system-independent.

Although the modules themselves may be physically and/or electrically incompatible, the cable-specific jacks on them provide industry-standard connections.
Cable-specific jacks provide industry-standard connections.

Ingres/Star prices start at $2,100.
Ingres/Star prices start at $2,100.

Figure 2: Examples from our parallel corpus.

$P(G \to H A \mid G \to H A)$
$\boxed{P(A \to C B D \mid A \to C B D)}$
$\boxed{P(B \to Q R \mid B \to Q R)}$
$\boxed{P(Q \to Z \mid Q \to Z)}$

Now we can simply compare $P_{expand\_tree}(s1 \mid t) = P_{tree}(s1) \cdot P_{expand\_tree}(t \mid s1))/P_{tree}(t)$ versus $P_{expand\_tree}(t \mid t) = P_{tree}(t) \cdot P_{expand\_tree}(t \mid t))/P_{tree}(t)$ and select the more likely one. Note that $P_{tree}(t)$ and all the PCFG factors can be canceled out, as they appear in any potential compression. Therefore, we need only compare compressions of the basis of the expansion-template probabilities and the word-bigram probabilities. The quantities that differ between the two proposed compressions are boxed above. Therefore, $s1$ will be preferred over t if and only if:

$P(e \mid b) \cdot P(A \to C B D \mid A \to C D) >$
$P(b \mid a) \cdot P(c \mid b) \cdot P(d \mid c) \cdot$
$P(A \to C B D \mid A \to C B D) \cdot$
$P(B \to Q R \mid B \to Q R) \cdot P(Q \to Z \mid Q \to Z)$

Training Corpus

In order to train our system, we used the Ziff-Davis corpus, a collection of newspaper articles announcing computer products. Many of the articles in the corpus are paired with human written abstracts. We automatically extracted from the corpus a set of 1067 sentence pairs. Each pair consisted of a sentence $t = t_1, t_2, \ldots, t_n$ that occurred in the article and a possibly compressed version of it $s = s_1, s_2, \ldots, s_m$, which occurred in the human written abstract. Figure 2 shows a few sentence pairs extracted from the corpus.

We decided to use such a corpus because it is consistent with two desiderata specific to summarization work: (i) the human-written Abstract sentences are grammatical; (ii) the Abstract sentences represent in a compressed form the salient points of the original newspaper Sentences. We decided to keep in the corpus uncompressed sentences as well, since we want to learn not only *how* to compress a sentence, but also *when* to do it.

Learning Model Parameters

We collect expansion-template probabilities from our parallel corpus. We first parse both sides of the parallel corpus, and then we identify corresponding syntactic nodes. For example, the parse tree for one sentence may begin (S (NP ...) (VP ...) (PP ...)) while the parse tree for its compressed version may begin (S (NP ...) (VP ...)). If these two S nodes are deemed to correspond, then we chalk up one joint event (S → NP VP, S → NP VP PP); afterwards we normalize. Not all nodes have corresponding partners; some non-correspondences are due to incorrect parses, while others are due to legitimate reformulations that are beyond the scope of our simple channel model. We use standard methods to estimate word-bigram probabilities.

Decoding

There is a vast number of potential compressions of a large tree t, but we can pack them all efficiently into a shared-forest structure. For each node of t that has n children, we

- generate $2^n - 1$ new nodes, one for each non-empty subset of the children, and
- pack those nodes so that they are referred to as a whole.

For example, consider the large tree t above. All compressions can be represented with the following forest:

```
G → H A      B → R        A → B C      H → a
G → H        Q → Z        A → C        C → b
G → A        A → C B D    A → B        Z → c
B → Q R      A → C B      A → D        R → d
B → Q        A → C D                   D → e
```

We can also assign an expansion-template probability to each node in the forest. For example, to the B → Q node, we can assign P(B → Q R | B → Q). If the observed probability from the parallel corpus is zero, then we assign a small floor value of 10^{-6}. In reality, we produce forests that are much slimmer, as we only consider compressing a node in ways that are locally grammatical according to the Penn Treebank—if a rule of the type A → C B has never been observed, then it will not appear in the forest.

At this point, we want to extract a set of high-scoring trees from the forest, taking into account both expansion-template probabilities and word-bigram probabilities. Fortunately, we have such a generic extractor on hand (Langkilde 2000). This extractor was designed for a hybrid symbolic-statistical natural language generation system called Nitrogen. In that application, a rule-based component converts an abstract semantic representation into a vast number of potential English renderings. These renderings are packed into a forest, from which the most promising sentences are extracted using statistical scoring.

For our purposes, the extractor selects the trees with the best combination of word-bigram and expansion-template scores. It returns a list of such trees, one for each possible compression length. For example, for the sentence *Beyond that basic level, the operations of the three products vary*, we obtain the following "best" compressions, with negative log-probabilities shown in parentheses (smaller = more likely):

Beyond that basic level, the operations of the three products vary widely (1514588)
Beyond that level, the operations of the three products vary widely (1430374)
Beyond that basic level, the operations of the three products vary (1333437)
Beyond that level, the operations of the three products vary (1249223)
Beyond that basic level, the operations of the products vary (1181377)
The operations of the three products vary widely (939912)
The operations of the products vary widely (872066)
The operations of the products vary (748761)
The operations of products vary (690915)
Operations of products vary (809158)
The operations vary (522402)
Operations vary (662642)

Length Selection

It is useful to have multiple answers to choose from, as one user may seek a 20% compression, while another seeks a 60% compression. However, for purposes of evaluation, we want our system to be able to select a single compression. If we rely on the log-probabilities as shown above, we will almost always choose the shortest compression. (Note above, however, how the three-word compression scores better than the two-word compression, as the models are not entirely happy removing the article "the"). To create a more fair competition, we divide the log-probability by the length of the compression, rewarding longer strings. This is commonly done in speech recognition.

If we plot this normalized score against compression length, we usually observe a (bumpy) U-shaped curve, as illustrated in Figure 3. In a typical more difficult case, a 25-word sentence may be optimally compressed by a 17-word version. Of course, if a user requires a shorter compression than that, she may select another region of the curve and look for a local minimum.

A decision-based model for sentence compression

In this section, we describe a decision-based, history model of sentence compression. As in the noisy-channel approach, we again assume that we are given as input

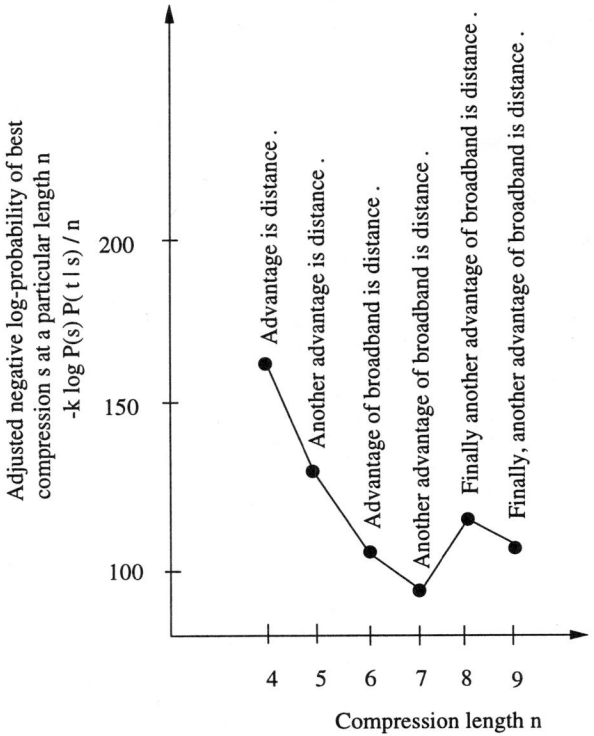

Figure 3: Adjusted log-probabilities for top-scoring compressions at various lengths (lower is better).

a parse tree t. Our goal is to "rewrite" t into a smaller tree s, which corresponds to a compressed version of the original sentence subsumed by t. Suppose we observe in our corpus the trees t and $s2$ in Figure 1. In this model, we ask ourselves how we may go about rewriting t into $s2$. One possible solution is to decompose the rewriting operation into a sequence of shift-reduce-drop actions that are specific to an extended shift-reduce parsing paradigm.

In the model we propose, the rewriting process starts with an empty Stack and an Input List that contains the sequence of words subsumed by the large tree t. Each word in the input list is labeled with the name of all syntactic constituents in t that start with it (see Figure 4). At each step, the rewriting module applies an operation that is aimed at reconstructing the smaller tree $s2$. In the context of our sentence-compression module, we need four types of operations:

- SHIFT operations transfer the first word from the input list into the stack;
- REDUCE operations pop the k syntactic trees located at the top of the stack; combine them into a new tree; and push the new tree on the top of the stack. Reduce operations are used to derive the structure of the syntactic tree of the short sentence.
- DROP operations are used to delete from the input list subsequences of words that correspond to syn-

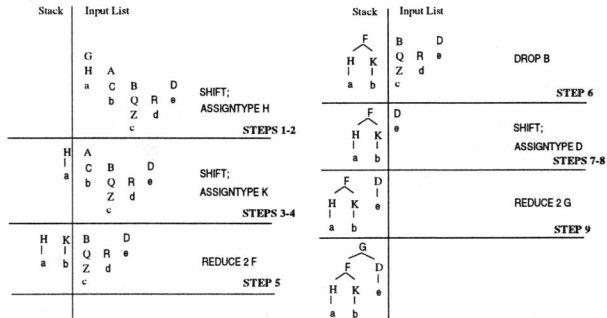

Figure 4: Example of incremental tree compression.

tactic constituents. A DROP X operations deletes from the input list all words that are spanned by constituent X in t.

- ASSIGNTYPE operations are used to change the label of trees at the top of the stack. These actions assign POS tags to the words in the compressed sentence, which may be different from the POS tags in the original sentence.

The decision-based model is more flexible than the channel model because it enables the derivation of trees whose skeleton can differ quite drastically from that of the tree given as input. For example, using the channel model, we are unable to obtain tree $s2$ from t. However, the four operations listed above enable us to rewrite a tree t into *any* tree s, as long as an in-order traversal of the leaves of s produces a sequence of words that occur in the same order as the words in the tree t. For example, the tree $s2$ can be obtained from tree t by following this sequence of actions, whose effects are shown in Figure 4: SHIFT; ASSIGNTYPE H; SHIFT; ASSIGNTYPE K; REDUCE 2 F; DROP B; SHIFT; ASSIGNTYPE D; REDUCE 2 G.

To save space, we show SHIFT and ASSIGNTYPE operations on the same line; however, the reader should understand that they correspond to two distinct actions. As one can see, the ASSIGNTYPE K operation rewrites the POS tag of the word b; the REDUCE operations modify the skeleton of the tree given as input. To increase readability, the input list is shown in a format that resembles as closely as possible the graphical representation of the trees in figure 1.

Learning the parameters of the decision-based model

We associate with each configuration of our shift-reduce-drop, rewriting model a learning case. The cases are generated automatically by a program that derives sequences of actions that map each of the large trees in our corpus into smaller trees. The rewriting procedure simulates a bottom-up reconstruction of the smaller trees.

Overall, the 1067 pairs of long and short sentences yielded 46383 learning cases. Each case was labeled with one action name from a set of 210 possible actions: There are 37 distinct ASSIGNTYPE actions, one for each POS tag. There are 63 distinct DROP actions, one for each type of syntactic constituent that can be deleted during compression. There are 109 distinct REDUCE actions, one for each type of reduce operation that is applied during the reconstruction of the compressed sentence. And there is one SHIFT operation. Given a tree t and an arbitrary configuration of the stack and input list, the purpose of the decision-based classifier is to learn what action to choose from the set of 210 possible actions.

To each learning example, we associated a set of 99 features from the following two classes:

Operational features reflect the number of trees in the stack, the input list, and the types of the last five operations. They also encode information that denote the syntactic category of the root nodes of the partial trees built up to a certain time. Examples of such features are: numberTreesInStack, wasPreviousOperationShift, syntacticLabelOfTreeAtTheTopOfStack, etc.

Original-tree-specific features denote the syntactic constituents that start with the first unit in the input list. Examples of such features are: inputListStartsWithA_CC, inputListStartsWithA_PP, etc.

The decision-based compression module uses the C4.5 program (Quinlan 1993) in order to learn decision trees that specify how large syntactic trees can be compressed into shorter trees. A ten-fold cross-validation evaluation of the classifier yielded an accuracy of 87.16% (± 0.14). A majority baseline classifier that chooses the action SHIFT has an accuracy of 28.72%.

Employing the decision-based model

To compress sentences, we apply the shift-reduce-drop model in a deterministic fashion. We parse the sentence to be compressed (Collins 1997) and we initialize the input list with the words in the sentence and the syntactic constituents that "begin" at each word, as shown in Figure 4. We then incrementally inquire the learned classifier what action to perform, and we simulate the execution of that action. The procedure ends when the input list is empty and when the stack contains only one tree. An inorder traversal of the leaves of this tree produces the compressed version of the sentence given as input.

Since the model is deterministic, it produces only one output. The advantage is that the compression is very fast: it takes only a few milliseconds per sentence. The disadvantage is that it does not produce a range of compressions, from which another system may subsequently choose. It is straightforward though to extend the model within a probabilistic framework by applying, for example, the techniques used by Magerman (1995).

Evaluation

To evaluate our compression algorithms, we randomly selected 32 sentence pairs from our parallel corpus, which we will refer to as the *Test Corpus*. We used the other 1035 sentence pairs for training. Figure 5 shows three sentences from the Test Corpus, together with the compressions produced by humans, our compression algorithms, and a baseline algorithm that produces compressions with highest word-bigram scores. The examples are chosen so as to reflect good, average, and bad performance cases. The first sentence is compressed in the same manner by humans and our algorithms (the baseline algorithm chooses though not to compress this sentence). For the second example, the output of the Decision-based algorithm is grammatical, but the semantics is negatively affected. The noisy-channel algorithm deletes only the word "break", which affects the correctness of the output less. In the last example, the noisy-channel model is again more conservative and decides not to drop any constituents. In constrast, the decision-based algorithm compresses the input substantially, but it fails to produce a grammatical output.

We presented each original sentence in the *Test Corpus* to four judges, together with four compressions of it: the human generated compression, the outputs of the noisy-channel and decision-based algorithms, and the output of the baseline algorithm. The judges were told that all outputs were generated automatically. The order of the outputs was scrambled randomly across test cases.

To avoid confounding, the judges participated in two experiments. In the first experiment, they were asked to determine on a scale from 1 to 5 how well the systems did with respect to selecting the most important words in the original sentence. In the second experiment, they were asked to determine on a scale from 1 to 5 how grammatical the outputs were.

We also investigated how sensitive our algorithms are with respect to the training data by carrying out the same experiments on sentences of a different genre, the scientific one. To this end, we took the first sentence of the first 26 articles made available in 1999 on the *cmplg* archive. We created a second parallel corpus, which we will refer to as the *Cmplg Corpus*, by generating by ourselves compressed grammatical versions of these sentences. Since some of the sentences in this corpus were extremely long, the baseline algorithm could not produce compressed versions in reasonable time.

The results in Table 1 show compression rates, and mean and standard deviation results across all judges, for each algorithm and corpus. The results show that the decision-based algorithm is the most aggressive: on average, it compresses sentences to about half of their original size. The compressed sentences produced by both algorithms are more "grammatical" and contain more important words than the sentences produced by the baseline. T-test experiments showed these differences to be statistically significant at $p < 0.01$ both for individual judges and for average scores across

			Original:	Beyond the basic level, the operations of the three products vary widely.

Original: Beyond the basic level, the operations of the three products vary widely.
Baseline: Beyond the basic level, the operations of the three products vary widely.
Noisy-channel: The operations of the three products vary widely.
Decision-based: The operations of the three products vary widely.
Humans: The operations of the three products vary widely.

Original: Arborscan is reliable and worked accurately in testing, but it produces very large dxf files.
Baseline: Arborscan and worked in, but it very large dxf.
Noisy-channel: Arborscan is reliable and worked accurately in testing, but it produces very large dxf files.
Decision-based: Arborscan is reliable and worked accurately in testing very large dxf files.
Humans: Arborscan produces very large dxf files.

Original: Many debugging features, including user-defined break points and variable-watching and message-watching windows, have been added.
Baseline: Debugging, user-defined and variable-watching and message-watching, have been.
Noisy-channel: Many debugging features, including user-defined points and variable-watching and message-watching windows, have been added.
Decision-based: Many debugging features.
Humans: Many debugging features have been added .

Figure 5: Compression examples

Corpus	Avg. orig. sent. length		Baseline	Noisy-channel	Decision-based	Humans
Test	21 words	Compression	63.70%	70.37%	57.19%	53.33%
		Grammaticality	1.78±1.19	4.34±1.02	4.30±1.33	4.92±0.18
		Importance	2.17±0.89	3.38±0.67	3.54±1.00	4.24±0.52
Cmplg	26 words	Compression	–	65.68%	54.25%	65.68%
		Grammaticality	–	4.22±0.99	3.72±1.53	4.97±0.08
		Importance	–	3.42±0.97	3.24±0.68	4.32±0.54

Table 1: Experimental results

all judges. T-tests showed no significant statistical differences between the two algorithms. As Table 1 shows, the performance of the compression algorithms is much closer to human performance than baseline performance; yet, humans perform statistically better than our algorithms at $p < 0.01$.

When applied to sentences of a different genre, the performance of the noisy-channel compression algorithm degrades smoothly, while the performance of the decision-based algorithm drops sharply. This is due to a few sentences in the *Cmplg Corpus* that the decision-based algorithm over-compressed to only two or three words. We suspect that this problem can be fixed if the decision-based compression module is extended in the style of Magerman (1995), by computing probabilities across the sequences of decisions that correspond to a compressed sentence. Likewise, there are substantial gains to be had in noisy-channel modeling—we see clearly in the data many statistical dependencies and processes that are not captured in our simple initial models. More grammatical output will come from taking account of subcategory and head-modifier statistics (in addition to simple word-bigrams), and an expanded channel model will allow for more tree manipulation possibilities. Work on extending the algorithms presented in this paper to compressing multiple sentences is currently underway.

References

Barzilay, R.; McKeown, K.; and Elhadad, M. 1999. Information fusion in the context of multi-document summarization. In *Proceedings of the 37th Annual Meeting of the Association for Computational Linguistics (ACL-99)*, 550–557.

Berger, A., and Lafferty, J. 1999. Information retrieval as statistical translation. In *Proceedings of the 22nd Conference on Research and Development in Information Retrieval (SIGIR-99)*, 222–229.

Brown, P.; Della Pietra, S.; Della Pietra, V.; and Mercer, R. 1993. The mathematics of statistical machine translation: Parameter estimation. *Computational Linguistics* 19(2):263–311.

Church, K. 1988. A stochastic parts program and noun phrase parser for unrestricted text. In *Proceedings of the Second Conference on Applied Natural Language Processing*, 136–143.

Collins, M. 1997. Three generative, lexicalized models for statistical parsing. In *Proceedings of the 35th Annual Meeting of the Association for Computational Linguistics (ACL-97)*, 16–23.

Grefenstette, G. 1998. Producing intelligent telegraphic text reduction to provide an audio scanning service for the blind. In *Working Notes of the AAAI*

Spring Symposium on Intelligent Text Summarization, 111–118.

Jelinek, F. 1997. *Statistical Methods for Speech Recognition.* The MIT Press.

Jing, H., and McKeown, K. 1999. The decomposition of human-written summary sentences. In *Proceedings of the 22nd Conference on Research and Development in Information Retrieval (SIGIR-99).*

Knight, K., and Graehl, J. 1998. Machine transliteration. *Computational Linguistics* 24(4):599–612.

Langkilde, I. 2000. Forest-based statistical sentence generation. In *Proceedings of the 1st Annual Meeting of the North American Chapter of the Association for Computational Linguistics.*

Linke-Ellis, N. 1999. Closed captioning in America: Looking beyond compliance. In *Proceedings of the TAO Workshop on TV Closed Captions for the hearing impaired people,* 43–59.

Magerman, D. 1995. Statistical decision-tree models for parsing. In *Proceedings of the 33rd Annual Meeting of the Association for Computational Linguistics,* 276–283.

Mani, I., and Maybury, M., eds. 1999. *Advances in Automatic Text Summarization.* The MIT Press.

Mani, I.; Gates, B.; and Bloedorn, E. 1999. Improving summaries by revising them. In *Proceedings of the 37th Annual Meeting of the Association for Computational Linguistics,* 558–565.

McKeown, K.; Klavans, J.; Hatzivassiloglou, V.; Barzilay, R.; and Eskin, E. 1999. Towards multidocument summarization by reformulation: Progress and prospects. In *Proceedings of the Sixteenth National Conference on Artificial Intelligence (AAAI-99).*

Quinlan, J. 1993. *C4.5: Programs for Machine Learning.* San Mateo, CA: Morgan Kaufmann Publishers.

Robert-Ribes, J.; Pfeiffer, S.; Ellison, R.; and Burnham, D. 1999. Semi-automatic captioning of TV programs, an Australian perspective. In *Proceedings of the TAO Workshop on TV Closed Captions for the hearing impaired people,* 87–100.

Witbrock, M., and Mittal, V. 1999. Ultra-summarization: A statistical approach to generating highly condensed non-extractive summaries. In *Proceedings of the 22nd International Conference on Research and Development in Information Retrieval (SIGIR'99), Poster Session,* 315–316.

Estimating Word Translation Probabilities from Unrelated Monolingual Corpora Using the EM Algorithm

Philipp Koehn and Kevin Knight
koehn@isi.edu, knight@isi.edu
Information Science Institute
University of Southern California
4676 Admiralty Way
Marina del Rey, CA 90292

Abstract

Selecting the right word translation among several options in the lexicon is a core problem for machine translation. We present a novel approach to this problem that can be trained using only unrelated monolingual corpora and a lexicon. By estimating word translation probabilities using the EM algorithm, we extend upon target language modeling. We construct a word translation model for 3830 German and 6147 English noun tokens, with very promising results.

1. Introduction

Selecting the right word translation among several options in the lexicon is a core problem for machine translation. The problem is related to word sense disambiguation, which tries to determine the correct sense for a word occurrence (e.g. *river bank* vs. *money bank*).

While the definition of word sense is a tricky issue, the picture is much clearer in translation. If we observe human translators, we can collect up the different ways in which a German word is usually translated into English. In some contexts, certain translations will be more appropriate than others. Determining the sense of a word, as opposed to its translation, is a more subjective enterprise — different experts tend to divide and sub-divide word senses differently. Of course, word sense disambiguation and word-level translation are related. If one cannot determine whether an instance of the word *bank* refers to a river or a financial institution, it is unlikely that one will be able to translate the word accurately into Japanese, and vice versa.

In some ways, word-level translation is easier than word-sense disambiguation. For example, WordNet [Miller et al., 1993] breaks the English word *interest* down into 5 senses. But 3 of these senses all translate to the German word *Interesse* [Resnik and Yarowsky, 1997], so to translate the word correctly in most cases, it may not be necessary to distinguish between these 3 senses. In other ways, word-level translation is harder. Human translators select word translations that accurately describe the source meaning, but they also want

to generate fluent target language output. That means a certain word translation may be preferred if it fits in well with other word translations. Also, the target language may have finer sense distinctions than can be foreseen in the source language. For instance the English word *river* translates as *fleuve* in French when the river flows into the ocean, and otherwise as *rivière* [Ide and Véronis, 1998].

We propose a novel framework for selecting the right translation word in a given sentence context. Using two completely unrelated monolingual corpora and a lexicon, we construct a word translation model for 3830 German and 6147 English noun tokens, with very promising results.

Our method is completely unsupervised: it is not necessary that the two corpora can be aligned in any way. Such monolingual corpora are readily available for most languages, while parallel corpora rarely exist even for common language pairs. Also, no manual sense tagging or definition of senses are required. The corpora we used for the experiments in this paper are the Wall Street Journal (6,892,443 noun tokens) and German newswire (306,982 noun tokens). As lexicon we use the freely available online dictionary LEO[1].

For testing purposes we use parallel corpora (or bitexts), generated from the monthly bulletin of the European Central Bank (ECB[2]) and de-news[3], a daily German news service written by student volunteers. Note that we use the bitexts only for evaluation purposes; they are not required for the construction of the model.

2. Related Research

There has recently been increased interest in empirical word sense disambiguation methods. Most research is reported on supervised methods, which use sense-tagged corpora. A good quantitative comparison of various methods is given by Mooney [1996]. While good results can be achieved, acquiring sufficiently large labeled corpora is prohibitively expensive.

---
[1] http://www.leo.org/cgi-bin/dict-search
[2] http://www.ecb.int/
[3] http://www.isi.edu/ koehn/publications/de-news/

Impressive unsupervised-learning results rivaling supervised methods are also reported by Yarowsky [1995], who trains decision lists for binary sense disambiguation. His bootstrapping method is unsupervised except for the use of a seed definition, which can be obtained manually or from dictionary entries.

Yarowsky deals only with words with very distant senses such as *plant* (*living* vs. *factory*) or palm (*tree* vs. *hand*). It is not clear how well his method will work with words such as the German *Gebiet*, for which our lexicon lists as English translations the following words: *area, zone, district, realm, territory, field, region, department, clime,* and *tract*. Also, seeds for these fine distinctions cannot be easily obtained from dictionaries, and must be created manually.

Schütze [1998] also proposes an unsupervised method, which is in essence a clustering of different usages of a word. The obtained clusters relate to some degree with word senses. It is questionable, however, whether such a method could come up with the proper clusters for the French translations of the word *river*. Also, the mapping of clusters to certain translations requires manual input.

While both Yarowsky and Schütze minimize the amount of supervision, it is still tremendous in the face of thousands of ambiguous lexicon entries. Both report results only on very few examples (less than 20).

The idea of using a second language monolingual corpus for word sense disambiguation is exploited by Dagan and Itai [1994]. They use a target language model to find the correct word-level translation. We expand on this notion and achieve better results, as reported below.

Research in statistical machine translation [Brown et al., 1993] demonstrates that word-level translation models can be learned from large parallel corpora. While there is hope that such corpora are becoming increasingly available, there may never be enough data for each language pair and domain.

Finally, current commercial MT systems seem to rely on always choosing the best word translation, supported by a lexicon of frequent compounds (such as *interest rate*). While this is useful for some instances of the word-level translation problem, it also creates a huge knowledge acquisition bottleneck.

3. Translation Probabilities

We describe an approach that uses a monolingual corpus in the target language to estimate word translation probabilities. These take the form $p_w(f|e)$, the overall probability that the English word e will be translated as f, regardless of context[4]. Brown et al. [1991] show how to estimate $p_w(f|e)$ parameters from a bilingual corpus. Since the translation probabilities cannot be observed directly in non-parallel corpora, one simple idea is to use the frequencies of the translation words in the target language itself.

For instance, if we look at the English noun *question*, our dictionary lists three possible German translations: *Frage, Zweifel,* and *Anfrage*. We can obtain the following counts in our German news wire corpus.

count	translation	sense
241	Frage	*query*
47	Zweifel	*doubt*
44	Anfrage	*request*

So we can estimate that $p_w(Frage|question) = 241/332 = .725$, and so forth. This method often allows us to estimate reasonable translation probabilities. Armed with these translation probabilities, we can decide to always pick the most likely translation word, regardless of context. In testing this approach on the nouns in the evaluation bitexts, we achieve 68.5% word translation accuracy for the ECB and 74.4% for the de-news test set.

However, this simple method frequently fails badly, as for the English noun *interest*, for which we obtain the following counts:

count	translation	sense
187	Anteil	*share, stake*
151	Interesse	*curiosity*
113	Zins	*money paid for money*
66	Bedeutung	*importance*
60	Teilnahme	*participation*
30	Vorteil	*advantage*

Actually, the most common translation *Interesse* ranks only second, behind the very rare translation *Anteil*. This happens because the German word *Anteil* is also the translation of the frequent English words *share, quota, lot, rate, proportion* etc. Most of the occurrences of *Anteil* in the German corpus do not in fact relate to *interest*.

In order to get better translation probabilities estimates, we have to take into account which occurrences of the word translation actually relate to the source word in consideration, and not others. We will address this issue in Section 5.

4. Modeling Context

The simple method described in Section 3 makes no use of context, as it always selects the same translation for a word. One way of deciding among several word translation options is to use a language model of the target language. For example, the machine translation system Gazelle [Knight et al., 1995] uses a word bigram language model to choose among sentence translations. The idea is that the translation of one word will affect the translation of another.

To illustrate this method, consider translating the German compound *Unschuldsvermutung* into English. The ambiguity of *Vermutung* and of the syntactic form of compounds in English yields four different translations. We counted their frequencies in the

---
[4] We follow here the usual notation of translating a foreign word f to an English word e.

World Wide Web using the search engine Altavista (http://www.altavista.com).

count	translation
1	innocence assumption
165	assumption of innocence
24	innocence presumption
6669	presumption of innocence

Clearly, this suggests that the most idiomatic translation is *presumption of innocence*. Also note that the distinction *assumption* vs. *presumption* would not likely be made by a manual German sense tagger for *Vermutung*.

This approach is along the lines of the work by Dagan and Itai [1994], who also use a target language model to disambiguate word translations. They propose the use of syntactic relationships such as subject-verb, verb-object, adjective-noun to disambiguate word translations.

We focus in our experiments on nouns to simplify our experimental setup. This method can be easily extended to include word forms, but for now we strip the corpus of these. Then we collect counts of adjacent words in our reduced English corpus. These counts allow us to estimate language model probabilities $p_{LM}(e_2|e_1)$ that a certain noun e_2 follows a previously observed noun e_1. With the resulting language model we can compute probabilities for sequences of candidate word translations. This is done by

$$p_{LM}(e_1,...,e_n) = p_{LM}(e_1)p_{LM}(e_2|e_1)...p_{LM}(e_n|e_{n-1})$$

Thus, we can pick the word translations that occur in higher scoring candidate sequences (or sentences) than others. For this, we add up all the scores of all sequences that contain the word translation, compare this sum against the sums for the competing translations, and pick the highest.

The advantage of such a model, in addition to being very simple, is that it can be applied to all the nouns we find in a text. Syntactic models, as used by Dagan and Itai [1994], are more restrictive. Still, nothing in the framework that we will describe in the following section prevents us from using their model.

When we apply language probabilities to our evaluation bitexts, we improve on the ECB corpus to 70.6% and on the de-news corpus to 76.6%.

5. Estimation from Unrelated Corpora

We now combine the notion of translation probabilities with the use of context. First, we generate an English noun bigram language model for our English corpus (the target language). Then we use the expectation maximization (EM) algorithm [Dempster et al., 1977] to estimate word-level translation probabilities.

Note that this approach is very similar to research in statistical machine translation [Brown et al., 1993]. There, sentence pairs are given and the word translation model is to be learned without knowing the word alignments. Here, the source sentence is given and the word translation model is to be learned without knowing the target sentence. This is feasible, because we use a lexicon to restrict the space of possible target sentences.

Outline — Consider the following sentence (translation: *Hans visits the bank counter at the end of the day*), annotated with the English noun translations. The correct translations are in bold type.

Hans besucht den Bank	Schalter	am Ende	des Tages
bench	**counter**	bottom	**day**
bank	switch	finish	
		end	
		ending	
		expiration	
		tail	

To compute probabilities for each candidate English noun sequence e_s, we first use Bayes rule:

$$p(e_s|f_s) = p(f_s)^{-1}p(e_s)p(f_s|e_s)$$

So, instead of using direct translation probabilities from German to English, we use a English language model $p_{LM}(e_s)$ and a translation model from English to German $p(f_s|e_s)$. The factor $p(f_s)$ can be discarded for the purpose of comparing different English noun sequences, since it is equal for all possibilities.

We now compute the remaining probabilities $p(e_s)p(f_s|e_s)$ using the language model p_{LM} and word translation probabilities p_w:

$$\begin{aligned} p(e_s)p(f_s|e_s) &= p_{LM}(e_1,...,e_n)p_s(f_1,...,f_n|e_1,..,e_n) \\ &\approx p_{LM}(e_1)p_{LM}(e_2|e_1)...p_{LM}(e_n|e_{n-1}) \cdot \\ & \quad p_w(f_1|e_1)...p_w(f_n|e_n) \end{aligned}$$

Estimation of Translation Probabilities — The translation probabilities p_w are initially set to an uniform distribution. The correct translation will have a higher probability, if it contains more frequent bigrams (*bank counter* vs. *bench switch*).

These noun sequence (or sentence) probabilities are normalized and then used to update the word translation probabilities. Intuitively, after finding the most probable translations of the sentence, we can collect counts for the word translations it contains. Since the English language model provides context information for the disambiguation of the German words, we hope to count only the appropriate occurrences.

In Figure 1 we give a more formal description of our use of the EM algorithm. Given a language model $p_{LM}(e)$ we wish to estimate the translation probabilities $p_w(f|e)$ that best explain the German corpus as a translation from English. The translation probabilities converge after 10 to 20 iterations of the EM algorithm.

This naive algorithm requires integration over c^n possible sentence translations (where c is the average number of translations for any given word). This is too much computation in practice. However, the forward-backward algorithm, which we have implemented, can

```
train language model for English p_LM
initialize word translation probabilities p_w uniformly
iterate
    set score(f|e) to 0 for all dictionary entries (f,e)
    for all German sentences f_s = (f_1, ..., f_n)
        for all possible English sentence translations e_s
            compute sentence transl. probability p_s(e_s|f_s)
                by p_w(f_1|e_1)p_w(f_2|e_2)...p_w(f_n|e_n)·
                   ·p_LM(e_1)p_LM(e_2|e_1)...p_LM(e_n|e_n-1)
        endfor
        normalize p_s(e_s|f_s) so their sum is 1
        for all sentence translations e_s
            for all words e_w in e_s
                add p_s(e_s|f_s) to score(f_w|e_w)
            endfor
        endfor
    endfor
    for all translation pairs (f_w, e_w)
        set p_w(f_w|e_w) to normalized score(f_w|e_w)
    endfor
enditerate
```

Figure 1: The EM Algorithm

accomplish the same in $c^2 n$ steps through the use of dynamic programming [Baum, 1972].

Application — With both language model and translation probabilities in place, we can now find the best word translations for a given German sentence f_s by using the Bayes rule

$$argmax_{e_s} p_s(e_s|f_s) = argmax_{e_s} p_{LM}(e_s) p_w(f_s|e_s)$$

We combine the language model $p_{LM}(e_s)$ with the use of translation probabilities $p_w(f_s|e_s)$ to search for the best translation $p_s(e_s|f_s)$. Again, this is done in $c^2 n$ steps.

6. Results

We now evaluate the generated translation probabilities. First, we look at the translation table for *interest*, as generated by our algorithm:

prob.	translation	sense
33.2%	Interesse	*curiosity*
27.7%	Zins	*money paid for money*
19.8%	Anteil	*share, stake*
12.6%	Teilnahme	*participation*
6.0%	Bedeutung	*importance*
0.5%	Vorteil	*advantage*

These numbers are much closer to a realistic distribution, as the most frequent translations *Interesse* and *Zins* come out on top. The use of the language model clearly helped to discount most instances of *Anteil* that do not translate to *interest*. Our method generated respective translation tables for all 6147 English nouns.

Another way to test the quality of the generated word translation probabilities is to use them to translate German words in context and compare the results against other methods.

For this, we use the ECB and de-news bitexts. After sentence aligning them we can use our lexicon to identify how the nouns in the text were translated. We then measure how accurate the methods match these word-translation pairs. Since sometimes more than one translation of a word may be fully acceptable, we cannot expect 100% accuracy on this task, but it is still a very good metric of the relative performance.

We compare our method (EM) against just using the language model of Section 4 (LM) and just relying of the most frequent translation word in the raw count, as in Section 3 (MF). We also report the performance of a commercial system on this task. Note that there is a slight bias against the commercial system in this evaluation, since we only consider word-translation pairs that are in the dictionary used by our methods.

corpus	commercial	MF	LM	EM
ECB	77.9%	68.5%	70.6%	80.5%
de-news	73.3%	74.4%	76.6%	78.2%

On both texts, our method clearly comes out ahead. The de-news bitext contains 5610 noun word-translation pairs in 2713 sentences, the ECB contains 693 word-translation pairs in 155 sentences. The larger improvement of our EM method over the benchmarks may lie in the fact that it suffices to get a few frequent word translations right.

The results suggest that we can improve substantially upon pure target language modeling, as done by Dagan and Itai [1994]. Although we currently use a different target language model, adding word translation probabilities clearly benefits performance.

7. Discussion

We introduced a completely unsupervised method to estimate translation probabilities. The required monolingual corpora are readily available for most cases. Although a bilingual lexicon is still required and its quality impacts the performance, this should not be a problem for most language pairs in question.

The method works on a large scale: We were able to apply it to a much bigger number of ambiguous words than related research on word sense disambiguation. Our current experimental setup is restricted to nouns, but it will extend to verbs, adjectives, prepositions, etc.

We may improve performance with larger corpora, a larger context window, use of context in the source language, or better language modeling, for instance by exploiting syntactic relations between words. We plan to address these directions in future research.

References

Baum, L. E. (1972). An inequality and associated maximization technique in statistical estimation of probabilistic functions of a Markov process. *Inequalities*, 3:1–8.

Brown, P. F., Della-Pietra, S., Della-Pietra, V., and Mercer, R. (1991). Word-sense disambiguation using statistical methods. In *Proceedings of ACL 29*.

Brown, P. F., Pietra, S. A. D., Pietra, V. J. D., and Mercer, R. L. (1993). The mathematics of statistical machine translation. *Computational Linguistics*, 19(2):263–313.

Dagan, I. and Itai, A. (1994). Word sense disambiguation using a second language monolingual corpus. *Computational Linguistics*, 20(4):563–596.

Dempster, A. P., Laird, N. M., and Rubin, D. B. (1977). Maximum likelyhood from incomplete data via the EM algorithm. *Journal of the Royal Statistical Society*, 39:1–38.

Ide, N. and Véronis, J. (1998). Introduction to the special issue on word sense disambiguation: The state of the art. *Computational Linguistics*, 24(1):1–40.

Knight, K., Chander, I., Haines, M., Hatzivassiloglou, V., Hovy, E., Iida, M., Luk, S. K., Whitney, R., and Yamada, K. (1995). Filling knowledge gaps in a broad-coverage MT system. In *International Joint Conference on Artificial Intelligence*.

Miller, G. A., Beckwith, R., Fellbaum, C., Gross, D., and Miller, K. J. (1993). Introduction to WordNet: An online lexical database. Technical Report CSL 43, Cognitive Science Laboratory Princeton University.

Mooney, R. (1996). Comparative experiments on disambiguation word senses: An illustration of bias in machine learning. In *Proceedings of the Conference on Empirical Methods in Natural Language Processing, EMNLP*.

Resnik, P. and Yarowsky, D. (1997). A perspective on word sense disambiguation methods and their evaluation. In *ACL 35, SIGLEX Workshop at ANLP*.

Schütze, H. (1998). Automatic word sense discrimination. *Computational Lingustics*, 24(1):97–123.

Yarowsky, D. (1995). Unsupervised word sense disambiguation rivaling supervised methods. In *Proceedings of ACL 33*, pages 189–196.

The Automatic Interpretation of Nominalizations

Maria Lapata
Division of Informatics, University of Edinburgh
2 Buccleuch Place, Edinburgh EH8 9LW, UK
mlap@cogsci.ed.ac.uk

Abstract

This paper discusses the interpretation of nominalizations in domain independent wide-coverage text. We present a statistical model which interprets nominalizations based on the co-occurrence of verb-argument tuples in a large balanced corpus. We propose an algorithm which treats the interpretation task as a disambiguation problem and achieves a performance of approximately 80% by combining partial parsing, smoothing techniques and domain independent taxonomic information (e.g., WordNet).

Introduction

The automatic interpretation of compound nouns has been a long-standing unsolved problem within Natural Language Processing (NLP). Compound nouns in English have three basic properties which pose difficulties for their interpretation: (a) the compounding process is extremely productive, (b) the semantic relationship between the compound head and its modifier is implicit (this means that it cannot be easily recovered from syntactic or morphological analysis), and (c) the interpretation can be influenced by a variety of contextual and pragmatic factors.

To arrive at an interpretation of the compound *onion tears* (e.g., onions CAUSE tears) it is necessary to identify that *tears* is a noun (and not the third person singular of the verb *tear*) and to use semantic information about *onions* and *tears* (for example the fact that onions cannot be tears or that tears are not made of onions). Even in the case of a compound like *government promotion* where the head noun is derived from the verb *promote* and the modifier *government* is its argument, it is necessary to determine whether *government* is the subject or the object. One might argue that the preferred analysis for *government promotion* is "government that is promoted by someone". However, this interpretation can be easily overridden in context as shown in example (1) taken from the British National Corpus: here it is the government that is doing the promotion.

(1) By the end of the 1920s, *government promotion* of agricultural development in Niger was limited, consisting mainly of crop trials and model sheep and ostrich farm.

The interpretation of compound nouns is important for several NLP tasks, notably machine translation. Consider the compound *satellite observation* which may mean *observation by satellite* or *observation of satellites*. In order to translate *satellite observation* into Spanish, we have to work out whether *satellite* is the subject or object of the verb *observe*. In the first case *satellite observation* translates as *observación por satelite* (observation by satellite), whereas in the latter it translates as *observación de satelites* (observation of satellites).

A considerable amount of work within NLP focused on the interpretation of two word compounds whose nouns are related via a basic set of semantic relations (e.g., CAUSE relates *onion tears*, FOR relates *pet spray*). With the exceptions of Wu (1993) and Lauer (1995) who have proposed probabilistic models for the interpretation of compounds, the majority of proposals are symbolic: most algorithms rely on hand-crafted knowledge bases or dictionaries containing detailed semantic information for each noun; a sequence of rules exploit this information in order to choose the correct interpretation for a given compound (Leonard 1984; Vanderwende 1994). Most of the proposals contain no qualitative evaluation. The exceptions are Leonard (1984) who reports an accuracy of 76% (although on the training set), Vanderwende (1994) whose algorithm attains an accuracy of 52%, and Lauer (1995) who reports an accuracy of 47%. The low accuracy is indicative of the difficulty of the task given the variety of contextual and pragmatic factors which can influence the interpretation of a compound.

In this paper, we focus solely on the interpretation of nominalizations, i.e., compounds whose head noun is a nominalized verb and whose prenominal modifier is derived from either the underlying subject or direct object of the verb (Levi 1978) (see the examples in (2)–(3)).

(2) a. SUBJ child behaviour ⇒ *child behaves*
    b. OBJ   car lover ⇒ *love cars*
    c. OBJ   soccer competition ⇒ *compete in soccer*
(3) a. SUBJ|OBJ government promotion
    b. SUBJ|OBJ satellite observation

The nominalized verb can either take a subject (cf. (2a)), a direct object (cf. (2b)) or a prepositional object (cf. (2c)). In some cases, the relation of the modifier and the nominalized verb (SUBJ or OBJ) can be predicted either from the subcategorization properties of the verb (cf. (2a) where *child* can only be the subject of the intransitive verb *behave*) or from the semantics of the of the nominalization suffix of the head noun (cf. (2b) where the agentive suffix *-er* of the noun *lover* indicates that the modifier *car* is the object of *love*). In other cases, the relation of the modifier and the head noun is genuinely ambiguous (see (3)).

The interpretation of nominalizations poses a challenge for empirical approaches since the argument relations between a head and its modifier are not readily available in the corpus. We present a probabilistic algorithm which treats the interpretation task as a disambiguation problem, and show how the severe sparse data problem in this task can be overcome by combining partial parsing, smoothing techniques, and domain independent taxonomic information (e.g., WordNet). We report on the results of five experiments which achieve a combined precision of approximately 80% on the British National Corpus (BNC), a 100 million word collection of samples of written and spoken language from a wide range of sources designed to represent a wide cross-section of current British English, both spoken and written (Burnard 1995).

The model

Given a nominalization, our goal is to develop a procedure to infer whether the modifier stands in a subject or object relation to the head noun. In other words, we need to assign probabilities to the two different relations (SUBJ, OBJ). For each relation *rel* we calculate the simple expression $P(rel|n_1,n_2)$ given in (4) below.

(4) $$P(rel|n_1,n_2) = \frac{f(n_1,rel,n_2)}{f(n_1,n_2)}$$

Since we have a choice between two outcomes we will use a likelihood ratio to compare the two relation probabilities (Mosteller & Wallace 1964). In particular we will compute the log of the ratio of the probability $P(\text{OBJ}|n_1,n_2)$ to the probability $P(\text{SUBJ}|n_1,n_2)$. We will call this log-likelihood ratio the argument relation (*RA*) score.

(5) $$RA(rel,n_1,n_2) = \log_2 \frac{P(\text{OBJ}|n_1,n_2)}{P(\text{SUBJ}|n_1,n_2)}$$

Notice, however, that we cannot read off $f(n_1,rel,n_2)$ directly from the corpus. What we can obtain from a corpus (through parsing) is the number of times a noun is the object or the subject of a given verb. By making the simplifying assumption that the relation between the nominalized head and its modifier noun is the same as the relation between the latter and the verb from which the head is derived, (4) can be rewritten as follows:

(6) $$P(rel|n_1,n_2) \approx \frac{f(v_{n_2},rel,n_1)}{\sum_i f(v_{n_2},rel_i,n_1)}$$

where $f(v_{n_2},rel,n_1)$ is the frequency with which the modifier noun n_1 is found in the corpus as the subject or object of v_{n_2}, the verb from which the head noun is derived. The sum $\sum_i f(v_{n_2},rel_i,n_1)$ is a normalization factor.

Parameter estimation

Verb-argument tuples

A part-of-speech tagged and lemmatized version of the BNC (100 million words) was automatically parsed by Cass (Abney 1996). Cass is a robust chunk parser designed for the shallow analysis of noisy text. We used the parser's built-in function to extract verb-subject and verb-object tuples. The tuples obtained from the parser's output are an imperfect source of information about argument relations. For example, the tuples extractor mistakes adjectives for verbs (cf. (7a)) and nouns for verbs (cf. (7b)).

(7)   a.   SUBJ   isolated people
           b.   SUBJ   behalf whose

In order to compile a comprehensive count of verb-argument relations we discarded tuples containing verbs or nouns with a BNC frequency of one. This resulted in 588,333 distinct types of verb-subject pairs and 615,328 distinct types of verb-object pairs.

The data

It is beyond the scope of the present study to develop an algorithm which automatically detects nominalizations in a corpus. In the experiments described in the subsequent sections compounds with deverbal heads were obtained as follows:

1. Two word compound nouns were extracted from the BNC by using a heuristic which looks for consecutive pairs of nouns which are neither preceded nor succeeded by a noun (Lauer 1995).
2. A dictionary of deverbal nouns was created using: (a) Nomlex (Macleod *et al.* 1998), a dictionary of nominalizations containing 827 lexical entries and (b) Celex (Burnage 1990), a general morphological dictionary, which contains 5,111 nominalizations;
3. Candidate nominalizations were obtained from the compounds acquired from the BNC by selecting noun-noun sequences whose head (i.e., rightmost noun) was one of the deverbal nouns contained either in Celex or Nomlex. The procedure resulted in 172,797 potential nominalizations.

From these candidate nominalizations a random sample of 2,000 tokens was selected. The sample was manually inspected and compounds with modifiers whose relation to the head noun was other than subject or object were discarded. Nominalizations whose heads were derived from verbs taking prepositional objects (cf. (2c)) were also discarded. After manual inspection the sample contained 796 nominalizations. From these, 596 tokens were used as training data for the experiments described in the following sections. The remaining 200 nominalizations were used as test data and also to evaluate whether humans can reliably disambiguate the argument relation between the nominalized head and its modifier.

Agreement

Two judges decided whether the modifier is the subject or object of a nominalized head. The nominalizations were disambiguated in context: the judges were given the corpus sentence in which the nominalization occurred together with the preceding and following sentence. The judges were given a page of guidelines but no prior training We measured agreement using the Kappa coefficient (Siegel & Castellan 1988), which is the ratio of the proportion of times, $P(A)$, that k raters agree to the proportion of times, $P(E)$, that we would expect the raters to agree by chance (cf. (8)). If there is a complete agreement among the raters, then $K = 1$, whereas if there is no agreement among the raters (other than the agreement which would be expected to occur by chance), then $K = 0$.

$$(8) \quad K = \frac{P(A) - P(E)}{1 - P(E)}$$

The judges' agreement on the disambiguation task was $K = .78$ ($N = 200$, $k = 2$). The agreement was good given that the judges were given minimal instructions and no prior training. However, note that despite the fact that context was provided to aid the disambiguation task, the annotators were not in complete agreement. This points to the intrinsic difficulty of the task. Argument relations and consequently selectional restrictions are influenced by several pragmatic factors which may not be readily inferred from the immediate context. In the following we propose a method which faces a greater challenge: the interpretation of nominalizations without taking context into account.

Mapping

In order to estimate the frequency $f(v_{n_2}, rel, n_1)$ and consequently the probability $P(rel|n_1, n_2)$, the nominalized heads were mapped to their corresponding verbs. Inspection of the frequencies of the verb-argument tuples contained in the sample (596 tokens) revealed that 372 verb-noun pairs had a verb-object frequency of zero in the corpus. Similarly, 378 verb-noun pairs had a verb-subject frequency of zero. Furthermore, a total of 287 tuples were not attested at all in the BNC either in a verb-object or verb-subject relation. This finding is perhaps not surprising given the productivity of compounds. Considering the ease with which novel compounds are created it is to be expected that some verb-argument configurations will not occur in the training corpus.

We estimated the frequencies of unseen verb-argument pairs by experimenting with three types of smoothing techniques proposed in the literature: back-off smoothing (Katz 1987), class-based smoothing (Resnik 1993) and similarity-based smoothing (Dagan, Lee, & Pereira 1999).

Smoothing

Back-off smoothing

Back-off n-gram models were initially proposed by Katz (1987) for speech recognition but have been also successfully used to disambiguate the attachment site of structurally ambiguous PPs (Collins & Brooks 1995). The main idea behind back-off smoothing is to adjust maximum likelihood estimates like (6) so that the total probability of observed word co-occurrences is less than one, leaving some probability mass to be redistributed among unseen co-occurrences. In general the frequency of observed word sequences is discounted using Good Turing's estimate and the probability of unseen sequences is estimated by using lower level conditional distributions. Assuming that the denominator in (6) $f(v_{n_2}, rel, n_1)$ is zero we can approximate $P(rel|n_1, n_2)$ by backing-off to $P(rel|n_1)$:

$$(9) \quad P(rel|n_1, n_2) = \alpha \frac{f(rel, n_1)}{f(n_1)}$$

where α is a normalization constant which ensures that the probabilities sum to one. If the frequency $f(rel, n_1)$ is also zero backing-off continues by making use of $P(rel)$.

Class-based smoothing

Class-based smoothing recreates co-occurrence frequencies based on information provided by taxonomies such as WordNet or Roget's thesaurus. Taxonomic information can be used to estimate the frequencies $f(v_{n_2}, rel, n_1)$ by substituting the word n_1 occurring in an argument position by the concept with which it is represented in the taxonomy (Resnik 1993). Hence, $f(v_{n_2}, rel, n_1)$ can be estimated by counting the number of times the concept corresponding to n_1 was observed as the argument of the verb v_{n_2} in the corpus.

This would be a straightforward task if each word was always represented in the taxonomy by a single concept or if we had a corpus of verb-argument tuples labeled explicitly with taxonomic information. Lacking such a corpus we need to take into consideration the fact that words in a taxonomy may belong to more than one conceptual classes: counts of verb-argument configurations are reconstructed for each conceptual class by dividing the contribution from the argument by the number of classes it belongs to (Resnik 1993; Lauer 1995):

$$(10) \quad f(v_{n_2}, rel, c) \approx \sum_{n_1' \in c} \frac{count(v_{n_2}, rel, n_1')}{|classes(n_1')|}$$

where $count(v_{n_2}, rel, n_1')$ is the number of times the verb v_{n_2} was observed with noun $n_1' \in c$ bearing the argument relation rel (i.e., subject or object) and $|classes(n_1')|$ is the number of conceptual classes n_1' belongs to. The frequency $f(v_{n_2}, rel, c)$ is reconstructed for all classes c with which the argument n_1 is represented in the taxonomy. Since we do not know which is the actual class of the noun n_1 in the corpus we weigh the contribution of each class by taking the average of the reconstructed frequencies for all classes c:

$$(11) \quad f(v_{n_2}, rel, n_1) = \frac{\sum_{c \in classes(n_1)} \sum_{n_1' \in c} \frac{count(v_{n_2}, rel, n_1')}{|classes(n_1')|}}{|classes(n_1)|}$$

Similarity-based smoothing

Similarity-based smoothing is based on the assumption that if a word w_1' is "similar" to word w_1, then w_1' can provide information about the frequency of unseen word pairs involving w_1 (Dagan, Lee, & Pereira 1999). There are several measures of word similarity which can be derived from lexical co-occurrences, providing an alternative to taxonomies such as WordNet (see Dagan, Lee, & Pereira (1999) for an overview).

We have experimented with two measures of distributional similarity derived from co-occurrence frequencies: the Jensen-Shannon divergence and the confusion probability. The choice of these two measures was motivated by work described in Dagan, Lee, & Pereira (1999) where the

Jensen-Shannon divergence outperforms related similarity measures on a word sense disambiguation task which uses verb-object pairs. The confusion probability has been used by several authors to smooth word co-occurrence probabilities (e.g., Grishman & Sterling 1994). In the following we describe these two similarity measures and show how they can be used to recreate the frequencies for unseen verb-argument tuples (for a more detailed description see Dagan, Lee, & Pereira 1999).

Confusion Probability The confusion probability P_C is an estimate of the probability that word w'_1 can be substituted by word w_1, in the sense of being found in the same contexts.

$$(12) \quad P_C(w_1|w'_1) = \sum_s P(w_1|s)P(s|w'_1)$$

where $P_C(w'_1|w_1)$ is the probability that word w'_1 occurs in the same contexts s as word w_1, averaged over these contexts. Given a tuple of the form w_1, rel, w_2 we chose to treat rel, w_2 as context and smooth over the verb w_1. By taking verb-argument tuples into consideration (12) is rewritten as follows:

$$(13) \quad P_C(w_1|w'_1) = \sum_{rel,w_2} P(w_1|rel,w_2)P(rel,w_2|w'_1)$$
$$= \sum_{rel,w_2} \frac{f(w_1,rel,w_2)}{f(rel,w_2)} \frac{f(w'_1,rel,w_2)}{f(w'_1)}$$

The confusion probability can be computed efficiently as it involves summation only over the common contexts rel, w_2.

Jensen-Shannon divergence The Jensen-Shannon divergence J is a measure of the "distance" between distributions:

$$(14) \quad J(w_1,w'_1) = \frac{1}{2}\left[D\left(w_1 \left\| \frac{w_1 + w'_1}{2}\right.\right) + D\left(w'_1 \left\| \frac{w_1 + w'_1}{2}\right.\right)\right]$$

$$(15) \quad D(w_1\|w'_1) = \sum_{rel,w_2} P(rel,w_2|w_1) \log \frac{P(rel,w_2|w_1)}{P(rel,w_2|w'_1)}$$

where D in (14) is the Kullback-Leibler divergence, a measure of the dissimilarity between two probability distributions (cf. equation (15)) and $(w_1 + w'_1)/2$ is a shorthand for the average distribution:

$$(16) \quad \frac{1}{2}(P(rel,w_2|w_1) + P(rel,w_2|w'_1))$$

Similarly to the confusion probability, the computation of J depends only on the common contexts rel, w_2. Dagan, Lee, & Pereira (1999) provide for the J divergence a weight function $W_J(w, w'_1)$:

$$(17) \quad W_J(w_1,w'_1) = 10^{-\beta J(w_1,w'_1)}$$

The parameter β controls the relative influence of the neighbors (i.e., distributionally similar words) closest to w_1: if β is high, only words extremely close to w_1 contribute to the estimate, whereas if β is low distant words also contribute to the estimate.

We estimate the frequency of an unseen verb-argument tuple by taking into account the similar w_1s and the contexts in which they occur (Grishman & Sterling 1994):

$$(18) \quad f_s(w_1,rel,w_2) = \sum_{w'_1} \text{sim}(w_1,w'_1)f(w'_1,rel,w_2)$$

Given a nominalization n_1 n_2:
1. map the head noun n_2 to the verb v_{n_2} from which it is derived;
2. retrieve $f(verb_{n_2}, \text{OBJ}, n_1)$ and $f(verb_{n_2}, \text{SUBJ}, n_1)$ from the corpus;
3. **if** $f(verb_{n_2}, \text{OBJ}, n_1) < k$ **then**
   recreate $f_s(verb_{n_2}, \text{OBJ}, n_1)$;
4. **if** $f(verb_{n_2}, \text{SUBJ}, n_1) < k$ **then**
   recreate $f_s(verb_{n_2}, \text{SUBJ}, n_1)$;
5. calculate probabilities $P(\text{OBJ}|n_1,n_2)$ and $P(\text{SUBJ}|n_1,n_2)$;
6. compute $RA(rel, n_1, n_2)$;
7. **if** $RA \geq j$ **then**
   n_1 is the subject of n_2;
8. **else**
   n_1 is the object of n_2;

Figure 1: Disambiguation algorithm for nominalizations

where $\text{sim}(w_1,w'_1)$ is a function of the similarity between w_1 and w'_1. In our experiments $\text{sim}(w_1,w'_1)$ was substituted by the confusion probability $P_C(w_1|w'_1)$ and the Jensen-Shannon divergence $W_J(w_1,w'_1)$.

The algorithm

The disambiguation algorithm for nominalizations is summarized in Figure 1. The algorithm uses verb-argument tuples in order to infer the relation holding between the modifier and its nominalized head. When the co-occurrence frequency for the verb-argument relation is zero, verb-argument tuples are smoothed. The sign of the RA score (cf. equation (5) and steps 6–8) indicates the relation between the head n_1 and its modifier n_2: a positive RA score indicates an object relation, whereas a negative score indicates a subject relation. Depending on the task and the data at hand we can require that an object or subject analysis is preferred only if RA exceeds a certain threshold j (see steps 7 and 8 in Figure 1). We can also impose a threshold k on the type of verb-argument tuples we smooth. If for instance we know that the parser's output is noisy, then we might choose to smooth not only unseen verb-argument pairs but also pairs with attested frequencies in the corpus (e.g., $f(verb_{n_2}, rel, n_1) \geq 1$, see steps 3 and 4 in Figure 1).

Experiments

The task

The algorithm was trained on 596 nominalizations and tested on 200. The 596 nominalizations were also used as training data for finding the optimal parameters for the two parameterized similarity-based smoothing approaches. In particular we examined whether the size of the vocabulary (e.g., number of verbs used to find the nearest neighbors) has an impact on disambiguation performance and what the best value for the parameter β is. As far as class-based smoothing is concerned we experimented with two concept hierarchies, Roget's thesaurus and WordNet. Although the class-based and back-off methods are not parameterized, we report their performance both on training and test set for completeness.

The algorithm's output was compared to the manual classification and precision was computed accordingly. For 59%

Method	Accuracy$_{train}$	Accuracy$_{test}$
Default	59.0%	61.8%
Back-off	63.0%	67.0%
Confusion	68.3%	73.7%
Jensen	67.9%	67.0%
WordNet	67.9%	70.6%
Roget	64.6%	66.5%
Ripper	79.7%	78.3%

Table 1: Disambiguation performance

of the nominalizations contained in the train data the modifier was the object of the deverbal head, whereas in the remaining 41% the modifier was the subject. This means that a simple heuristic which defaults to an object relation yields a precision of approximately 59%. Our decision procedure defaults to an object relation when there is no evidence to support either analysis (e.g., when $f(v_{n_2}, \text{OBJ}, n_1) = f(v_{n_2}, \text{SUBJ}, n_1)$).

Results

Before reporting the results of the disambiguation task, we describe our experiments on finding the optimal parameter settings for the two similarity-based smoothing methods.

Figure 2a shows how performance on the disambiguation task varies with respect to the number and frequency of verbs over which the similarity function is calculated. The y-axis in Figure 2a shows how performance on the training set varies (for both P_C and J) when verb-argument pairs are selected from the 1,000 most frequent verbs in the corpus, the 2,000 most frequent verbs in the corpus, etc. (x-axis). The best performance for both similarity functions is achieved using the 2,000 most frequent verbs. Furthermore, performance between J and P_C is comparable (67.9% and 68.3%, respectively). Another important observation is that performance deteriorates less severely for P_C than for J as the number of verbs increases: when all verbs for which verb-argument tuples are extracted from the BNC are used precision for P_C is 66.94%, whereas precision for J is 62.75%. These results are perhaps unsurprising: verb-argument pairs with low-frequency verbs introduce noise due to the errors inherent in the partial parser.

Finally, we analyzed the role of the parameter β. Recall that β appears in the weight function for J and controls the influence of the most similar words. Figure 2b shows how the value of β affects performance on the disambiguation task when the similarity function is computed for the 1,000 and 2,000 most frequent verbs in the corpus. It is clear that performance is low with very high or very low β values (e.g., $\beta \in \{2, 9\}$). We chose to set the parameter β to 5 and the results shown in Figure 2a have been produced for this value for all verb frequency classes.

Table 1 shows how the three types of smoothing, back-off, class-based, and similarity-based, influence performance in predicting the relation between a modifier and its nominalized head. For the similarity-based methods we report the results obtained with the optimal parameter settings ($\beta = 5$; 2,000 most frequent verbs). Let us concentrate on the

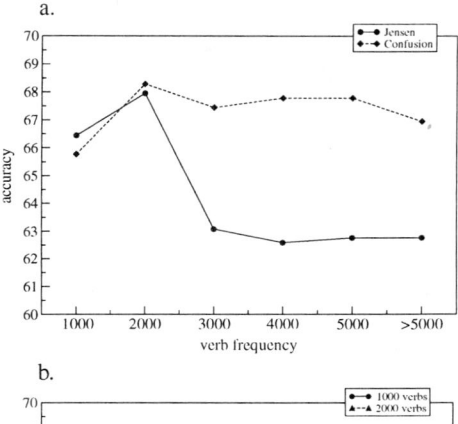

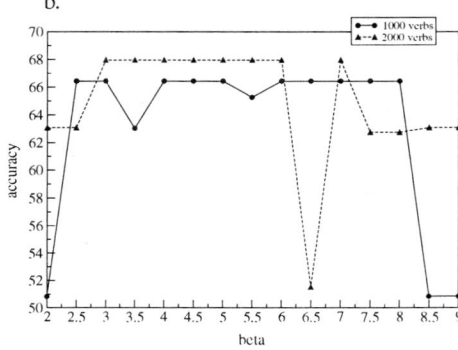

Figure 2: Parameter settings for P_C and J

	Back-off	Jensen	Confusion	WordNet
Jensen	.31			
Confusion	.26	.53		
WordNet	.01	.37	.75	
Roget	.25	.26	.49	0.46

Table 2: Agreement between smoothing methods

training set first. The back-off method is outperformed by all other methods, although its performance is comparable to class-based smoothing using Roget's thesaurus (63% and 64.6%, respectively). Similarity-based methods outperform concept-based methods, although not considerably (accuracy on the training set was 68.3% for P_C and 67.9% for class-based smoothing using WordNet). Furthermore, the particular concept hierarchy used for class-based smoothing seems to have an effect on disambiguation performance: an increase of approximately 2% is obtained by using WordNet instead of Roget's thesaurus. One explanation might be that Roget's thesaurus is too coarse-grained a taxonomy for the task at hand (Roget's taxonomy contains 1,043 concepts, whereas WordNet contains 4,795). We used a χ^2 test to examine whether the the observed performance is better than the simple strategy of always choosing an object relation which yields an accuracy of 59%. The proportion of nominalizations classified correctly was significantly greater than 59% ($p < 0.01$) for all methods but back-off and Roget.

Similar results were observed on the test set. Again P_C outperforms all other methods achieving a precision of 73.7% (see Table 1). The portion of nominalization classified correctly by P_C was significantly greater than 61.8%

Method	SUBJ	OBJ
Back-off	41.6%	78.0%
Jensen	34.7%	91.2%
Confusion	47.3%	82.9%
WordNet	47.8%	80.3%
Roget	50.6%	74.4%

Table 3: Performance on predicting argument relations

($p < 0.05$) which was the percentage of object relations in the test set. The second best method is class-based smoothing using WordNet (see Table 1). The back-off method performs as well as J, reaching an accuracy of 67%.

An interesting question is the extent to which any of the different methods agree in their assignments of subject and object relations. We investigated this by calculating the methods' agreement on the training set using the Kappa coefficient. We calculated the Kappa coefficient for all six pairwise combinations of the five smoothing variants. The results are reported in Table 2. The highest agreement is observed for P_C and the class-based smoothing using the WordNet taxonomy ($K = .75$). This finding suggests that methods inducing similarity relationships from corpus co-occurrence statistics are not necessarily incompatible with methods which quantify similarity using manually crafted taxonomies. Agreement between J and P_C as well as agreement between WordNet and Roget's thesaurus was rather low ($K = .53$ and $K = .46$, respectively). This suggests that different similarity functions or taxonomies may be appropriate for different tasks.

Table 3 shows how the different methods compare for the task of predicting the individual relations for the training set. A general observation is that all methods are fairly good at predicting object relations. Predicting subject relations is considerably harder: no method exceeds an accuracy of approximately 50%. One explanation for this is that selectional constraints imposed on subjects can be more easily overridden by pragmatic and contextual factors than those imposed on objects. J is particularly good at predicting object relations, whereas P_C and class-based smoothing using WordNet seem to yield comparable performances when it comes to predicting subject relations (see Table 3).

An obvious question is whether the precision is increased when combining the five smoothing variants given that they seem to provide complementary information for predicting argument relations. For example, Roget's thesaurus is best for the prediction of subject relations, whereas J is best for the prediction of object relations. We combined the five information sources using a decision tree classifier (Ripper, Cohen 1996). The decision tree was trained on the 596 nominalizations on which the smoothing methods were compared and tested on the 200 unseen nominalizations for which the inter-judge agreement was previously calculated. The average error rate of the decision tree learner was 20.30% ± 1.65% on the training set and 21.65% ± 2.96% on the test set. The latter result translates into a precision of 78.3% (cf. Table 1) which is significantly better ($p < 0.01$) than 61.8%, the percentage of object relations in the test set.

Conclusions

The work reported here is an attempt to provide a statistical model of nominalizations occurring in wide coverage text. We showed that a simple algorithm which combines information about the distributional properties of words and domain independent symbolic knowledge (i.e., WordNet) achieves high performance on unseen data. This is an important result considering the simplifications in the system and the sparse data problems encountered in estimating the probability $P(rel|n_1, n_2)$. Finally, we explored the merits and limitations of various smoothing methods and systematically showed how recreated frequencies can be used in a task other than language modeling to produce interesting results.

References

Abney, S. 1996. Partial parsing via finite-state cascades. In Carroll, J., ed., *Workshop on Robust Parsing*, 8–15. Prague: ESSLLI.

Burnage, G. 1990. Celex – a guide for users. Technical report, Centre for Lexical Information, University of Nijmegen.

Burnard, L. 1995. *Users Guide for the British National Corpus*. British National Corpus Consortium, Oxford University Computing Service.

Cohen, W. W. 1996. Learning trees and rules with set-valued features. In *Proceedings of 13th National Conference on Artificial Intelligence*, 709–716. Portland, Oregon: AAAI Press.

1994. *Proceedings of the 15th International Conference on Computational Linguistics*, Kyoto: COLING.

Collins, M., and Brooks, J. 1995. Prepositional phrase attachment through a backed-off model. In *Proceedings of the 3rd Workshop on Very Large Corpora*, 27–38. Cambridge, MA: ACL.

Dagan, I.; Lee, L.; and Pereira, F. C. N. 1999. Similarity-based models of word cooccurrence probabilities. *Machine Learning* 1–3(34):43–69.

Grishman, R., and Sterling, J. 1994. Generalizing automatically generated selectional patterns. In COLING (1994), 742–747.

Katz, S. M. 1987. Estimation of probabilities from sparse data for the language model component of a speech recognizer. *IEEE Transactions on Acoustics Speech and Signal Processing* 33(3):400–401.

Lauer, M. 1995. *Designing Statistical Language Learners: Experiments on Compound Nouns*. Ph.D. Dissertation, Macquarie University, Sydney.

Leonard, R. 1984. *The Interpretation of English Noun Sequences on the Computer*. Amsterdam: North-Holland.

Levi, J. N. 1978. *The Syntax and Semantics of Complex Nominals*. New York: Academic Press.

Macleod, C.; Grishman, R.; Meyers, A.; Barrett, L.; and Reeves, R. 1998. Nomlex: A lexicon of nominalizations. In *Proceedings of the 8th International Congress of the European Association for Lexicography*, 187–193. Liège, Belgium: EURALEX.

Mosteller, F., and Wallace, D. L. 1964. *Inference and Disputed Authorship: The Federalist*. Addison-Wesley.

Resnik, P. S. 1993. *Selection and Information: A Class-Based Approach to Lexical Relationships*. Ph.D. Dissertation, University of Pennsylvania, Philadelphia, Philadelphia.

Siegel, S., and Castellan, N. J. 1988. *Non Parametric Statistics for the Behavioral Sciences*. New York: McGraw-Hill.

Vanderwende, L. 1994. Algorithm for automatic interpretation of noun sequences. In COLING (1994), 782–788.

Wu, D. 1993. Approximating maximum-entropy ratings for evidential parsing and semantic interpretation. In *Proceedings of 13th International Joint Conference on Artificial Intelligence*, 1290–1296. Chambery, France: Morgan Kaufman.

Predicting and Adapting to Poor Speech Recognition in a Spoken Dialogue System

Diane J. Litman
AT&T Labs - Research
180 Park Avenue
Florham Park, NJ 07932
diane@research.att.com

Shimei Pan
Computer Science Department
Columbia University
New York, NY 10027
pan@cs.columbia.edu

Abstract

Spoken dialogue system performance can vary widely for different users, as well for the same user during different dialogues. This paper presents the design and evaluation of an adaptive version of TOOT, a spoken dialogue system for retrieving online train schedules. Adaptive TOOT predicts whether a user is having speech recognition problems as a particular dialogue progresses, and automatically adapts its dialogue strategies based on its predictions. An empirical evaluation of the system demonstrates the utility of the approach.

Introduction

Most spoken dialogue systems do not try to improve performance by dynamically adapting the system's dialogue behaviors to an individual user during the course of a particular dialogue. But the performance of a spoken dialogue system can vary significantly for different users and even for the same user across dialogues. This paper presents the design and experimental evaluation of a spoken dialogue system that predicts and responds to problematic dialogue situations by automatically adapting its dialogue behaviors.

Figures 1 and 2 show two example dialogues with an adaptive version of TOOT, a spoken dialogue system for retrieving train schedules from the web.[1] In Figure 1, TOOT successfully acquires all of the information that it needs from the user within just one interaction. In Figure 2, however, the *same* system takes much longer to obtain the *same* information from a *different* user, due to repeated automatic speech recognition (ASR) errors (U1, U4, U5, U7).[2] Thus, TOOT's initial configuration of dialogue strategies (*user initiative* and *no confirmation*, as will be detailed below) seems well matched to the user in Figure 1 but poorly matched to the user in Figure 2. In fact, the second dialogue only starts to make real progress after TOOT (twice) adapts its behavior to use more conservative dialogue strategies. After the first adaptation, TOOT starts to preface its utterances with

---

Copyright © 2000, American Association for Artificial Intelligence (www.aaai.org). All rights reserved.

[1]These examples are taken from the experimental corpus described below.

[2]The last column shows ASR confidence, as explained below. Note that the ASR interpretation ("ASR Output") is only shown for misrecognitions.

S1: Hi, this is AT&T Amtrak Schedule System. This is TOOT. How may I help you?
U1: I want a train from Baltimore to New York on Sunday at 8:30 in the evening.
S2: Do you want me to find the trains from Baltimore to New York on Sunday around 8:30 in the evening now?
U2: Yes.
S3: I am going to get the train schedules for you. This may take some time if the internet traffic is heavy. Please wait patiently. [pause] There are 2 trains available approximately at 8:30 in the evening. The first train leaves at 8:38 pm on Sunday, and it takes 2 hours 26 minutes. The second train leaves at 9:08 pm from Sunday to Thursday, and it takes 15 hours 7 minutes. Do you want to continue and find a new set of trains?
U3: No.
S4: Thank you for using AT&T Amtrak train schedule system. See you next time.

Figure 1: A dialogue where the system does not adapt.

"I heard you say" (S5, S8), in order to *implicitly confirm* the most recent ASR hypothesis. When this adaptation still doesn't seem to help the user, the *system* takes the *initiative* by asking the user a series of directed questions (e.g., S9, S11, S13, S15), and asking the user to *explicitly confirm* each ASR hypothesis (e.g., S10, S12, S14, S16). After this second adaptation, the ASR misrecognitions are finally eliminated and the dialogue is successfully completed. Examples such as these suggest that it will be difficult to define a single "best" initial dialogue configuration for all users in all situations, and that a system should also be able to dynamically adapt its initial dialogue strategies.

In previous research, we demonstrated that the use of an *adaptable* spoken dialogue system can indeed increase system performance (Litman & Pan 1999). We developed an adaptable version of TOOT, where *users* were given instructions on how to use voice commands to change TOOT's dialogue strategies at any points in a dialogue. Results from an empirical evaluation showed that an adaptable version of TOOT outperformed a non-adaptable version. Unfortunately, a user-controlled adaptation system is not ideal for many applications, as it requires an initial (although mini-

S1:	Hi, this is AT&T Amtrak Schedule System. This is TOOT. How may I help you?	
U1:	I need to find a train going to New York City. (*ASR Output: DC I don't care on Thursday.*)	-5.293949
S2:	Which city do you want to leave from?	
U2:	Baltimore.	-1.731395
S3:	Do you want me to find the trains from Baltimore to DC on Thursday at anytime now?	
U3:	No.	-2.095545
S4:	How may I help you?	
U4:	I need to leave on Sunday. (*ASR Output: DC between 1 night and 8.*)	-4.916628
*****	**TOOT automatically adapts its behavior to use a more conservative dialogue strategy.** *****	
S5:	I heard you say go to DC between 1 night and 8. Do you want me to find the trains from Baltimore to DC on Thursday between 1 night and 8 now?	
U5:	No. (*ASR Output: Help.*)	-2.801172
S6:	You can say yes or no.	
U6:	No.	-2.509176
S7:	How may I help you?	
U7:	I need to go to New York City from Baltimore on Sunday at 8:30 pm. (*ASR Output: To Chicago Tuesday 8:45 am.*)	-5.948381
S8:	I heard you say go to Chicago on Tuesday around 8:45 am. Do you want me to find the trains from Baltimore to Chicago on Tuesday around 8:45 am now?	
U8:	No.	-3.355405
*****	**TOOT adapts its behavior again, to use an even more conservative dialogue strategy.** *****	
S9:	Which city do you want to go to?	
U9:	New York City.	-1.675092
S10:	Do you want to go to New York City?	
U10:	Yes.	-0.772970
S11:	Which city do you want to leave from?	
U11:	Baltimore.	-1.441275
S12:	Do you want to leave from Baltimore?	
U12:	Yes.	-0.609985
S13:	On which day of the week do you want to leave?	
U13:	Sunday.	-0.548220
S14:	Do you want to leave on Sunday?	
U14:	Yes.	-1.782579
S15:	What time do you want to leave?	
U15:	8:30 pm.	-1.727584
S16:	Do you want to leave around 8:30 pm?	
U16:	Yes.	-0.944121
S17:	Do you want me to find the trains from Baltimore to New York City on Sunday around 8:30 pm now?	
U17:	Yes.	-0.582485
S18:	I am going to get the train schedules for you ...	

Figure 2: A dialogue where the same system infers that things are going poorly, and adapts its behavior twice.

mal) training session for users.

Thus, a natural extension of this approach is to design an *adaptive* spoken dialogue system, where the *system* rather than the user automatically controls the adaptation process. Recently, several machine learning approaches have been developed for detecting problematic dialogue situations that might warrant global dialogue strategy changes (Litman, Walker, & Kearns 1999; Walker *et al.* 2000). To date, however, none of these detection algorithms have actually been used to trigger an automatic adaptation process.

In this paper we show how to combine the above lines of research, by building an adaptive system based on the detection of a problematic dialogue situation, and empirically demonstrating its utility.[3] We first designed adaptive TOOT, which automatically infers and reacts to poor ASR performance in an online manner. We then conducted an experiment comparing the performance of adaptive TOOT to a comparable non-adaptive version. Our results showed that by adapting the dialogue strategies of TOOT in response to inferences regarding repeated ASR misrecognitions, we significantly improved the task success rate.

An Adaptive Spoken Dialogue System

We have developed both adaptive and non-adaptive versions of TOOT, a voice-enabled dialogue system for accessing train schedules from the web via a telephone conversation. TOOT is implemented using a spoken dialogue system platform that combines automatic speech recognition (ASR), text-to-speech synthesis (TTS), a phone interface, and modules for specifying a dialogue manager and application functions (Kamm *et al.* 1997). ASR in our platform is speaker-independent, grammar-based and supports barge-in (which allows users to interrupt the system). The dialogue manager uses a finite state machine to control the interaction, based

---

[3]See (Chu-Carroll & Nickerson 2000) for an evaluation of a spoken dialogue system that automatically adapts initiative based on the current *utterance* and dialogue history.

on the current system state and ASR results.

This section details our methodology for designing an adaptation component for use within the dialogue manager of the adaptive version of TOOT. First, we define the types of dialogue strategy choices that are allowed in TOOT. Second, we illustrate how we instantiate (Litman, Walker, & Kearns 1999) in order to learn a problematic dialogue classifier tailored for TOOT. Third, we describe the adaptation algorithm that we have developed which uses this classifier to predict and react to repeated ASR misrecognitions. Finally, we illustrate how this algorithm generates the dialogue behavior shown in Figure 2.

Dialogue Strategies for Initiative and Confirmation

We allow TOOT to use one of three possible initiative dialogue strategies ("system", "mixed" or "user") and one of three confirmation strategies ("explicit", "implicit", or "no"), at any point in a dialogue. The initiative strategy specifies who has control of the dialogue, while the confirmation strategy specifies how and whether the system lets the user know what it just understood.[4]

Consider the use of *user initiative with no confirmation*, the initial dialogue configuration used in Figures 1 and 2. This approach is the most natural approach in human-human conversation, and is feasible for human-machine conversations when the user knows what can be said at any points of a dialogue, and the system has good recognition performance for the user. By allowing users to specify any number of attributes in a single utterance and by not informing users of every potential misrecognition, this approach can lead to very short and effective dialogues, as in Figure 1.

In contrast, consider the use of *system initiative with explicit confirmation*, our most conservative parameterization of dialogue strategies. Although this configuration is cumbersome and typically increases total dialogue length (Walker, Fromer, & Narayanan 1998; Danieli & Gerbino 1995), it is sometimes effective as in the third portion of Figure 2. Giving the system the initiative about what to ask for next helps to reduce ASR misrecognitions (Walker, Fromer, & Narayanan 1998), by helping to keep the user's utterances within the system's vocabulary and grammar. The use of explicit confirmation also helps increase the user's task success (Danieli & Gerbino 1995), by making it easy for users to correct misrecognitions when they do occur.

A middle setting of dialogue strategies is illustrated in the second portion of Figure 2, where TOOT uses *mixed initiative with implicit confirmation*. In contrast to no confirmation, implicit confirmation makes the user aware of ASR errors; in contrast to explicit confirmation, it is more difficult for users to correct ASR errors after an implicit confirmation (Krahmer *et al.* 1999). In mixed but not system initiative mode, the system can ask both specific questions and open-ended questions (e.g., "How may I help you?"). However, in user but not in mixed initiative mode, the system

---

[4]All other dialogue strategies (e.g., the response strategy for presenting the results of the web query) are fixed in advance, to control the factors in the experimental evaluation described below.

will let the user ignore the specific questions (e.g., after the prompt "On which day of the week do you want to leave?", the user can say "I want a train at 8:00.")

In the non-adaptive version of TOOT, the initiative and confirmation strategies are specified once at the beginning of a dialogue, and cannot be changed until the next dialogue. To allow TOOT to dynamically change its strategies *within* a dialogue, we have augmented the non-adaptive version with a new adaptation component. Whenever the adaptation component predicts that repeated ASR problems have occurred during the course of a dialogue, it changes to a more conservative setting of dialogue strategies.

Learning to Detect Problematic Dialogues

One major functionality of the new adaptation component is that it needs to predict problematic situations during a dialogue, in order to trigger the dialogue strategy adaptations. Previous evaluations of a variety of spoken dialogue systems have suggested that ASR accuracy is one of the most significant predictors of dialogue system performance, e.g., (Walker, Fromer, & Narayanan 1998; Litman & Pan 1999). In our work, we have thus chosen to use poor ASR performance as our adaptation criterion. Following (Litman, Walker, & Kearns 1999), we employ a machine learning approach to automatically derive rules for classifying a dialogue as problematic with respect to ASR.

Our corpus consists of 120 dialogues collected from previous experiments with TOOT (Litman & Pan 1999). The dialogues illustrate many different dialogue strategy configurations, and were collected in interactions with novice users (undergraduate and graduate students). We first classify each dialogue in our corpus as "good" or "bad" with respect to ASR performance, by thresholding on the percentage of user utterances that were previously labeled as semantic misrecognitions.[5] Following (Litman, Walker, & Kearns 1999), our threshold is set to 11%, yielding 45 good dialogues and 75 bad dialogues. For example, the dialogue in Figure 1 would have been classified as "good" because there were no misrecognitions, while the portion of the dialogue in Figure 2 would have been classified as "bad" because 24% (4 out of 17) of the user utterances were misrecognitions.

We also extract a set of prediction features that represent high-level properties of the dialogue history, and that are automatically computable from the system log files generated for each dialogue. Again following (Litman, Walker, & Kearns 1999), we computed a set of 23 features that characterized dialogues along five dimensions: acoustic confidence, dialogue efficiency (e.g. number of system turns), dialogue quality or naturalness (e.g., number of user requests for help), experimental parameters (e.g., initial dialogue strategy configuration), and lexical (e.g. lexical items

---

[5]The labeling of misrecognitions was done prior to the current research, by listening to the recordings and comparing them to the logged ASR results. When ASR did not correctly capture the task-related information, it was labeled as a misrecognition (e.g., U1, U4, U5, and U7 in Figure 2). Since the labeling is semantically based, if U9 had been recognized as "New York" then it still would have been labeled as a correct recognition. Although done manually, the labeling is based on objective criteria.

in ASR output). However, since (as will be seen below) our best learned ruleset uses only a single acoustic feature, only that feature is detailed here.

As shown in the last column of Figure 2, one source of acoustic information directly available in the system log is a per-utterance log-likelihood score from ASR, representing its "confidence" in its interpretation of the user's utterance (Zeljkovic 1996). These confidence measures are typically used to decide whether the system believes it has correctly understood the user's utterance. In our implementation, when the confidence score falls below a predefined threshold for each dialogue state, TOOT generates a rejection utterance such as "Sorry, I can't understand you. Please repeat your answer." The feature *predictedMisrecs%* (predicted percentage of misrecognized utterances) was derived from these utterance confidence scores as follows. First, a threshold of -4 was used to predict whether each non-rejected utterance in the dialogue was a misrecognition; second, the percentage of user utterances in the dialogue that corresponded to these *predicted* misrecognitions was computed. (Recall that our dialogue classifications of "good" and "bad" were determined by thresholding on the percentage of *actual* misrecognitions.) Thus for the excerpt in Figure 2, utterances U1, U4, and U7 would (correctly) be predicted as misrecognitions, and *predictedMisrecs%* would thus be 18% (3 out of 17 utterances). Note that U5 is (incorrectly) predicted to be a correct recognition.

Finally, once each dialogue in our corpus is represented in terms of its features and class value, we employ the machine learning program RIPPER (Cohen 1996) to automatically learn a poor ASR classification model from the training data. The classification model can be used to predict the class of future examples from their features, and is expressed as an ordered set of if-then rules. The best learned dialogue classifier for our data says that if the predicted percentage of misrecognitions is > than 3%, then predict that the dialogue is "bad"; otherwise, predict "good".[6] Based on the results of 10-fold cross validation, this rule successfully classifies almost 80% of the dialogues in our corpus. This performance is better than a majority-class baseline (classify all dialogues as "bad") of 62%. The next section describes how we use this classification model in our adaptation component.

Predicting and Reacting to ASR Problems Online

Intuitively, the automatic adaptation component regularly monitors the conversation with respect to the features in the learned ruleset, and adapts to a more conservative dialogue strategy whenever the rules predict that the dialogue is having repeated ASR problems. The top portion of Figure 3 provides a pseudo-code sketch of the general adaptation algorithm, while the lower portion shows how we instantiate the system-dependent components of the algorithm for our experiments. In particular, the values of AdaptFreq, Ruleset, and CurStrat, as well as the algorithm for

---

[6]While in this experiment RIPPER learned only a single rule and used only a single feature, when the same data was combined with data from two other spoken dialogue systems (Litman, Walker, & Kearns 1999), RIPPER learned 5 rules and used 7 of the 23 features.

Main
  ...
  specify adaptation frequency "AdaptFreq";
  specify classification model "Ruleset";
  specify initial strategy "CurStrat";
  for each user utterance
    if ((turns since CurStrat assignment) $\geq$ AdaptFreq)
      CheckRuleset(Ruleset);
  ...

CheckRuleset(Ruleset)
  for each rule R in Ruleset
    if (CheckPre(R) == "TRUE")
      if (RightHandSide(R) == "bad")
        AdaptStrategy(CurStrat);
  return;

AdaptStrategy(CurStrat)
  CurStrat $\leftarrow$ MakeConservative(CurStrat);

AdaptFreq $\leftarrow$ 4;

Ruleset $\leftarrow$
{if predictedMisrecs% > 3% then "bad";
default "good";}

(Initial) CurStrat:
  CurInit $\leftarrow$ UserInit; CurConf $\leftarrow$ NoConf;

MakeConservative(CurStrat)
  if (CurInit == UserInit) CurInit $\leftarrow$ MixedInit
  elseif (CurInit == MixedInit) CurInit $\leftarrow$ SystemInit;
  if (CurConf == NoConf) CurConf $\leftarrow$ ImpConf
  elseif (CurConf == ImpConf) CurConf $\leftarrow$ ExpConf;

Figure 3: Adaptation algorithm.

MakeConservative(CurStrat), are specified at system initialization and represent parameters that potentially can be tuned to improve the performance of the algorithm.

The system first checks the classification model Ruleset after the number of user utterances specified by AdaptFreq. In our implementation, Ruleset corresponds to the learned classification model described above, and AdaptFreq is set to 4 because humans took approximately 4 utterances on average to initiate adaptation in (Litman & Pan 1999). Note that although our rules were learned by analyzing full dialogues, our adaptation algorithm starts applying the rules after only 4 utterances.[7]

Since in general there is more than one rule in a classification model, CheckRuleset(Ruleset) sequentially checks the precondition of each rule until it finds the first rule that is applicable. (Recall that rules in RIPPER are or-

---

[7]Although we have not investigated the impact this change would have made to the classification accuracy results described above, using the first few utterances rather than the whole dialogue to predict problematic situations did not seriously degrade classification accuracy in the experiments of (Walker *et al.* 2000).

dered. Thus if multiple if-then rules are applicable, the first rule in the ordering determines the class; if no if-then rules are applicable, the default rule is used.) When the first applicable rule is found, if the rule also classifies the dialogue as "bad", dialogue strategy adaptation will be triggered before processing the next user utterance. Otherwise, no adaptation is performed.

More specifically, in order to test the precondition of a rule, `CheckPre(R)` parses the system log file in order to compute the value for each prediction feature presented in the classification rule. Note that each time the features are computed, the system uses only the portion of the log file since the last adaptation (i.e., from the beginning of the dialogue only if there have been no adaptations), because only this part of the dialogue reflects the appropriateness of the current dialogue strategy. If the precondition of the rule is true when it is instantiated with the computed values `CheckPre(R) == ''TRUE''` and the rule gets fired; then, if the fired rule classifies the current dialogue status as ``bad'', `AdaptStrategy(CurStrat)` is activated to change the value of the current dialogue strategy (`CurStrat`) to a more conservative one. Once a rule has been fired and the dialogue classified (and the strategy possibly adapted, depending on the value of the right hand side of the rule), the system continues the monitoring process as the dialogue progresses.

In our specific instantiation of the algorithm, only one feature is employed in the classification model (`predictedMisrecs%`). First, the system parses the log file to extract the ASR confidence score for each user utterance since the last adaptation. Following the definition of `predictedMisrecs%`, the system tests whether each confidence score is less than -4.0, and if so, categorizes the corresponding user utterance as a predicted misrecognition. Then it computes, among all the user utterances considered, the percentage of user utterances just predicted to be misrecognitions. Once `predictedMisrecs%` is calculated, `CheckPre(R)` checks whether this value is greater than 3% (the precondition of the first rule in `Ruleset`). If so, since the portion of the dialogue since the last adaptation is classified as "bad" (`RightHandSide(R) == ''bad''`), `AdaptStrategy(CurStrat)` is called. Note that `AdaptStrategy(CurStrat)` is not called when the if-then rule is not applicable, since the next and last rule will classify the dialogue as "good" by default. `AdaptStrategy(CurStrat)` in turn calls the simple version of `MakeConservative(CurStrat)` shown in Figure 3, which changes user initiative to mixed initiative and mixed initiative to system initiative. Similarly, no confirmation is always changed to implicit confirmation and implicit confirmation to explicit confirmation. Note that when the current dialogue strategy is already the most conservative one (system initiative and explicit confirmation), no further changes are possible.

Example

We now detail how the dialogue strategy adaptations in Figure 2 are automatically generated using the adaptation algorithm in Figure 3. In our experiments, TOOT is always initialized with the dialogue strategy configuration *user initiative with no confirmation*, because these are the most "natural" initiative and confirmation strategies in human-human conversation, and this configuration was shown to benefit most from *user*-controlled adaptation (Litman & Pan 1999).

Because of the user initiative setting, TOOT begins the dialogue in Figure 2 with the open question "How may I help you?" The user's response U1 is then misrecognized by ASR. Because of the no confirmation setting, TOOT does not confirm its interpretation of U1 but instead asks the user for a new piece of information (S2). The user thus doesn't realize the misrecognition until S3, when TOOT asks the user if it should query the web database. (Since this query is an expensive operation, TOOT *always* tells the user the values that will be used for the query – independently of the confirmation strategy.) Since the user now realizes that there was an earlier misrecognition, the user tells TOOT not to query the web (U3). In turn, this causes TOOT to again try to get the information it needs from the user (S4). Since the adaptation frequency is initialized to 4 (`AdaptFreq` in Figure 3), TOOT does nothing with respect to adaptation from U1-U3.

After U4, however, for the first time TOOT checks whether the current dialogue history satisfies the precondition of the adaptation condition, namely the first rule in `Ruleset` in Figure 3. First, TOOT calculates the value of `predictedMisrecs%` for the dialogue segment U1-U4. Because the ASR confidence scores for U1 and U4 are less than the threshold of -4.0, `predictedMisrecs%` is 50%. As a result, the adaptation rule is fired, the dialogue is classified as "bad", and TOOT adapted to a more conservative configuration of dialogue strategies (*mixed initiative with implicit confirmation*, following `MakeConservative(CurStrat)` in Figure 3).

After the first adaptation, the dialogue still doesn't go very well, as TOOT misrecognizes U5 and U7. After U8 (4 turns since the last CurStrat assignment), TOOT checks the classification model for the second time, but only with respect to these last 4 turns. That is because U5-U8 is the only portion of the dialogue obtained using the current strategies. Since the ASR confidence score for U7 is less than -4.0, `predictedMisrecs%` for the new dialogue segment is 25%. This value triggers another adaptation, this time to the most conservative configuration in our implementation (*system initiative with explicit confirmation*).

After this second adaptation, TOOT next checks the adaptation condition after U12 (for the dialogue history U9-U12). This time `predictedMisrecs%` is 0, so the default rule is applicable and no adaptation is triggered. (Given our simple `MakeConservative` algorithm, even if a third adaptation had been triggered, there would have been no more conservative strategies to switch to.) Also, unlike after U4 and U8, the number of turns since the last adaptation does not return to 0. TOOT thus continues to check the adaptation condition with each subsequent utterance (e.g., after U13 the relevant dialogue history is U9-U13), since `predictedMisrecs%` is always 0. Thus, after the second adaptation, the dialogue finally proceeds smoothly and the user's task is successfully completed.

Experimental Evaluation

In order to empirically verify that our automatic adaptation algorithm can actually improve spoken dialogue system performance, we evaluated the adaptive and non-adaptive versions of TOOT discussed in the previous sections. 6 novice users carried out 4 tasks with the adaptive version of TOOT, while 6 different novice users carried out the same 4 tasks with the previous non-adaptive version of TOOT. Our experimental corpus thus consisted of 48 dialogues.

Subjects for both versions of TOOT were undergraduate and graduate students from different universities. Subjects used the web to read a set of experimental instructions, then called TOOT from a phone. The experimental instructions included a brief description of TOOT's functionality, hints for talking to TOOT, and links to 4 task scenarios. The following task scenario was used for the dialogues in Figures 1 and 2: "Try to find a train going *to* **New York City** *from* **Baltimore** on **Sunday** at **8:30 pm**. If you cannot find an exact match, find the one with the **closest** departure time. Please write down the **exact departure time** of the train you found as well as the **total travel time**."

We used the data that we experimentally obtained to compute a number of measures relevant for spoken dialogue evaluation. First, the dialogue manager's log was used to automatically calculate measures representing the efficiency of the dialogue (e.g., total number of **system turns**). As discussed above, we also used each log and the corresponding dialogue recording to hand-label ASR misrecognitions. This allowed us to compute total number of **misrecognized user turns** per dialogue, a measure of dialogue quality. In addition, we manually computed an objective measure representing whether users successfully achieved their task goal or not (**task success**). Task success is 1 if both the **exact departure time** and the **total travel time** (written down by the user at the conclusion of the experiment) are correct, 0.5 if only one value is correct, and 0 if neither is correct. Finally, after each dialogue, users filled out a survey following (Litman & Pan 1999), where 8 questions measured usability factors. For example, "Did you know what you could say at each point of the dialogue?" measured perceived **User Expertise**, and answers from 1 to 5 were possible. A comprehensive **User Satisfaction** measure (ranging from 8 to 40) was then computed by summing each question's score.

We use analysis of variance (ANOVA) to determine whether the adaptive version of TOOT yields significant improvements for any of the evaluation measures used in our experiment.[8] As shown in Table 1, the adaptive version of TOOT outperforms the non-adaptive version.[9] From the

Evaluation Measure	Adaptive (n=24)	Non-Adaptive (n=24)	P
Task Success	.65	.23	.01
User Expertise	4	3.2	.09
User Satisfaction	25.6	21.6	.20
# of Misrecognized Turns	3.9	6.0	.15
# of System Turns	13.7	17.4	.28

Table 1: Dialogue means for different versions of TOOT.

means in column 2 and 3, adaptive TOOT on average has a higher task success rate, higher user satisfaction (particularly due to higher levels of feelings of expertise), less misrecognized user turns and less overall system turns. The *P*-value in column 4 indicates that the improvement in task success rate is significant for the adaptive version of TOOT ($P < 0.01$). In particular, task completion increases from 23% in the non-adaptive version to 65% in the adaptive version. This verifies that adaptation can significantly improve TOOT's performance, in our case by helping users to better achieve their task goals. The improvement for user expertise also shows a trend towards statistical significance ($P < 0.09$). More data is needed to see whether we can obtain significance for the improvements using the other metrics.

It is also interesting to more informally examine how adaptation varies across both dialogues and users. For the 24 dialogues with the adaptive version of TOOT, TOOT didn't adapt at all in 5 dialogues, and adapted at least once in the remaining 19 dialogues. Furthermore, breaking down the .65 overall task success rate (Table 1) by these two conditions shows that the average task success rate was .60 when TOOT chose not to adapt, and .66 when TOOT decided to adapt. Thus, adaptive TOOT does indeed seem to keep the initial dialogue strategy configuration only when appropriate (in contrast to the non-adaptive version of TOOT, where the success rate for the initial configuration is .23), and adapts otherwise. The frequency of adaptation also differs across subjects: for 3 subjects, TOOT adapted in all 4 dialogues; for 1 subject, TOOT adapted in 3 out of 4 dialogues; for the remaining 2 subjects, TOOT adapted for only 2 dialogues. It is particularly interesting to compare the only two subjects who successfully completed all 4 tasks. For one of

---

[8] Our experimental design consisted of 2 factors: the within-in group factor *system adaptability* (with values adaptive or non-adaptive) and the between-groups factor *task* (with values one through four). We use a two-way analysis of variance (ANOVA) to compute whether any main (task-independent) effects of adaptability are statistically significant (probability p<.05) or show a trend (probability p<.1). The ANOVA also tests whether there are any main effects of task, or any interaction effects between adaptability and task, but there are no such significant effects in our data.

[9] Our previous results showed that the utility of user-controlled adaptation was greatest for *user initiative with no confirmation*

TOOT (Litman & Pan 1999). Hence, for our first attempt at automatic adaptation, we focused on adapting only this initial dialogue strategy. However, unpublished results from our previous experiment also showed that in addition to adaptability effects, there were main effects for a factor not considered here: initial dialogue strategy (*user initiative with no confirmation* versus *system initiative with explicit confirmation*). Users had both higher task completion and user satisfaction rates for 1) the adaptable versions of TOOT (independently of strategy), and 2) the *system initiative with explicit confirmation* versions of TOOT (independently of adaptability). In fact, non-adaptable *system initiative with explicit confirmation* TOOT achieved the same task success and the same user satisfaction as *user*-adaptable *user initiative with no confirmation* TOOT (although we speculate that the system initiative version would have done less well with a more expert user population).

these subjects TOOT always adapted twice, while for the other the number of adaptations was either 1 or 0, decreasing as the user gained experience. Observations such as these strengthen our belief that a fixed dialogue strategy will not be ideal for different users, and that even for the same user, different dialogue strategies may be needed in different circumstances.

Summary and Future Work

We have designed and implemented a fully-automated adaptive version of TOOT, and have empirically verified improved levels of system performance compared to a non-adaptive version. Our system incrementally predicts whether a user is having ASR problems as a dialogue progresses, and adapts to a more conservative set of dialogue strategies whenever the predictions classify the dialogue as problematic. Our experimental evaluation demonstrates that the adaptive system outperforms a non-adaptive version of the same system for novice users, by significantly increasing the task success rate from 23% to 65%.

We view our current results as a baseline demonstrating the utility of our approach, and hope to increase system performance by tuning the current implementation. For example, MakeConservative generates only two adaptations (even though many other initiative and confirmation configurations are possible, e.g. *user initiative with implicit confirmation*), and TOOT also can never switch back to a less conservative strategy. These types of sophisticated adaptation behaviors are observed when humans control adaptation (Litman & Pan 1999). We also want to optimize AdaptFreq by examining how our classifier's accuracy depends on the number of utterances used for prediction (Walker *et al.* 2000), and to explore the impact of using a sliding window rather than all the utterances since the last adaptation to compute predictedMisrecs%. Finally, while our current focus is on predicting and adapting to problems at the (sub)dialogue-level, we would like to apply our approach at the utterance level (Levow 1998; Litman, Hirschberg, & Swerts 2000; van Zanten 1999; Smith 1998; Chu-Carroll 2000).

Acknowledgments

We would like to thank Owen Rambow for commenting on an earlier version of this paper, and Sandra Carberry and Janyce Wiebe for their help in recruiting subjects. We especially thank the students at Columbia University, New Mexico State University, and the University of Delaware who participated in our experiment.

References

Chu-Carroll, J., and Nickerson, J. S. 2000. Evaluating automatic dialogue strategy adaptation for a spoken dialogue system. In *Proc. 1st Conference of the North American Chapter of the Association for Computational Linguistics (NAACL)*.

Chu-Carroll, J. 2000. MIMIC: An adaptive mixed initiative spoken dialogue system for information queries. In *Proc. Applied Natural Language Processing (ANLP)*.

Cohen, W. 1996. Learning trees and rules with set-valued features. In *Proc. 13th National Conference on Artificial Intelligence (AAAI)*.

Danieli, M., and Gerbino, E. 1995. Metrics for evaluating dialogue strategies in a spoken language system. In *Proc. AAAI Spring Symposium on Empirical Methods in Discourse Interpretation and Generation*.

Kamm, C.; Narayanan, S.; Dutton, D.; and Ritenour, R. 1997. Evaluating spoken dialog systems for telecommunication services. In *Proc. European Conference on Speech Communication and Technology (EUROSPEECH)*.

Krahmer, E.; Swerts, M.; Theune, M.; and Weegels, M. 1999. Error spotting in human-machine interactions. In *Proc. European Conference on Speech Communication and Technology (EUROSPEECH)*.

Levow, G.-A. 1998. Characterizing and recognizing spoken corrections in human-computer dialogue. In *Proc. 36th Annual Meeting of the Association for Computational Linguistics and the 17th International Conference on Computational Linguistics (COLING-ACL)*.

Litman, D. J., and Pan, S. 1999. Empirically Evaluating an Adaptable Spoken Dialogue System. In *Proc. 7th International Conference on User Modeling (UM)*.

Litman, D.; Hirschberg, J.; and Swerts, M. 2000. Predicting automatic speech recognition performance using prosodic cues. In *Proc. 1st Conference of the North American Chapter of the Association for Computational Linguistics (NAACL)*.

Litman, D. J.; Walker, M. A.; and Kearns, M. J. 1999. Automatic detection of poor speech recognition at the dialogue level. In *Proc. 37th Annual Meeting of the Association for Computational Linguistics (ACL)*.

Smith, R. W. 1998. An evaluation of strategies for selectively verifying utterance meanings in spoken natural language dialog. *International Journal of Human-Computer Studies* 48:627–647.

van Zanten, G. V. 1999. User modelling in adaptive dialogue management. In *Proc. European Conference on Speech Communication and Technology (EUROSPEECH)*.

Walker, M.; Langkilde, I.; Wright, J.; Gorin, A.; and Litman, D. 2000. Learning to predict problematic situations in a spoken dialogue system: Experiments with how may i help you? In *Proc. 1st Conference of the North American Chapter of the Association for Computational Linguistics (NAACL)*.

Walker, M.; Fromer, J.; and Narayanan, S. 1998. Learning optimal dialogue strategies: A case study of a spoken dialogue agent for email. In *Proc. 36th Annual Meeting of the Association for Computational Linguistics and the 17th International Conference on Computational Linguistics (COLING-ACL)*.

Zeljkovic, I. 1996. Decoding optimal state sequences with smooth state likelihoods. In *Proc. International Conference on Acoustics, Speech, and Signal Processing (ICASSP)*.

Social Choice Theory and Recommender Systems:
Analysis of the Axiomatic Foundations of Collaborative Filtering

David M. Pennock

NEC Research Institute
4 Independence Way
Princeton, NJ 08540
dpennock@research.nj.nec.com

Eric Horvitz

Microsoft Research
One Microsoft Way
Redmond, WA 98052-6399
horvitz@microsoft.com

C. Lee Giles

NEC Research Institute
4 Independence Way
Princeton, NJ 08540
giles@research.nj.nec.com

Abstract

The growth of Internet commerce has stimulated the use of collaborative filtering (CF) algorithms as recommender systems. Such systems leverage knowledge about the behavior of multiple users to recommend items of interest to individual users. CF methods have been harnessed to make recommendations about such items as web pages, movies, books, and toys. Researchers have proposed several variations of the technology. We take the perspective of CF as a methodology for combining preferences. The preferences predicted for the end user is some function of all of the known preferences for everyone in a database. Social Choice theorists, concerned with the properties of voting methods, have been investigating preference aggregation for decades. At the heart of this body of work is Arrow's result demonstrating the impossibility of combining preferences in a way that satisfies several desirable and innocuous-looking properties. We show that researchers working on CF algorithms often make similar assumptions. We elucidate these assumptions and extend results from Social Choice theory to CF methods. We show that only very restrictive CF functions are consistent with desirable aggregation properties. Finally, we discuss practical implications of these results.

Introduction

The goal of collaborative filtering (CF) is to predict the preferences of one user, referred to as the *active* user, based on the preferences of a group of users. For example, given the active user's ratings for several movies and a database of other users' ratings, the system predicts how the active user would rate unseen movies. The key idea is that the active user will prefer those items that like-minded people prefer, or even that dissimilar people don't prefer. CF systems have seen growing use in electronic commerce applications on the World Wide Web. For example, the University of Minnesota's GroupLens and MovieLens[1] research projects spawned Net Perceptions,[2] a successful Internet startup offering personalization and recommendation services. Alexa[3] is a web browser plug-in that recommends related links based in part on other people's web surfing habits. Several CF tools originally developed at Microsoft Research are now included with the Commerce Edition of Microsoft's SiteServer,[4] and are currently in use at multiple sites.

The effectiveness of any CF algorithm is ultimately predicated on the underlying assumption that human preferences are correlated—if they were not, then informed prediction would be impossible. There does not seem to be a single, obvious way to predict preferences, nor to evaluate effectiveness, and many different algorithms and evaluation criteria have been proposed and tested. Most comparisons to date have been empirical or qualitative in nature [Billsus and Pazzani, 1998; Breese et al., 1998; Konstan and Herlocker, 1997; Resnick and Varian, 1997; Resnick et al., 1994; Shardanand and Maes, 1995], though some worst-case performance bounds have been derived [Freund et al., 1998; Nakamura and Abe, 1998; Cohen et al., 1999] and some general principles have been advocated [Freund et al., 1998; Cohen et al., 1999]. Initial methods were statistical, though several researchers have recently cast CF as a machine learning problem [Billsus and Pazzani, 1998; Freund et al., 1998; Nakamura and Abe 1998].

We take instead an axiomatic approach, informed by results from Social Choice theory. First, we identify several properties that a CF algorithm might ideally posses, and describe how existing CF implementations obey subsets of these conditions. We show that, under the full set of conditions, only one prediction strategy is possible: The ratings of the active user are derived solely from the ratings of only one other user. This is called the *nearest neighbor* approach [Freund et al., 1998]. The analysis mirrors Arrow's celebrated Impossibility Theorem, which shows that the only voting mechanism that obeys a similar set of properties is a dictatorship [Arrow, 1963]. Under slightly weaker demands, we show that the only possible form for the prediction function is a weighted average of the users' ratings. We also provide a second, separate axiomatization that again admits only the weighted

---

Copyright © 2000, American Association for Artificial Intelligence (www.aaai.org). All rights reserved.

[1] http://movielens.umn.edu
[2] http://www.netperceptions.com

[3] http://www.alexa.com
[4] http://www.microsoft.com/DirectAccess/products/sscommerce

average. The weighted average method is used in practice in many CF applications [Breese *et al.*, 1998; Resnick *et al.*, 1994; Shardanand and Maes, 1995]. One contribution of this paper is to provide a formal justification for it. Stated another way, we identify a set of properties, one of which must be violated by any non-weighted-average CF method. On a broader level, this paper proposes a new connection between theoretical results in Social Choice theory and in CF, providing a new perspective on the task. This angle of attack could lead to other fruitful links between the two areas of study, including a category of CF algorithms based on voting mechanisms. The next section covers background on CF and Social Choice theory. The remaining sections present, in turn, the three axiomatizations, and discuss the practical implications of our analysis.

Background

In this section, we briefly survey previous research in collaborative filtering, describe our formal CF framework, and present relevant background material on utility theory and Social Choice theory.

Collaborative Filtering Approaches

A variety of collaborative filters or recommender systems have been designed and deployed. The Tapestry system relied on each user to identify like-minded users manually [Goldberg *et al.*, 1992]. GroupLens [Resnick *et al.*, 1994] and Ringo [Shardanand and Maes, 1995], developed independently, were the first CF algorithms to automate prediction. Both are examples of a more general class we call *similarity-based* approaches. We define this class loosely as including those methods that first compute a matrix of pairwise similarity measures between users (or between titles). A variety of similarity metrics are possible. Resnick *et al.* [1994] employ the Pearson correlation coefficient for this purpose. Shardanand and Maes [1995] test a few measures, including correlation and mean squared difference. Breese *et al.* [1998] propose a metric called vector similarity, based on the vector cosine measure. All of the similarity-based algorithms cited predict the active user's rating as a weighted sum of the others users' ratings, where weights are similarity scores. Yet there is no *a priori* reason why the weighted average should be the aggregation function of choice. Below, we provide two possible axiomatic justifications.

Breese *et al.* [1998] identify a second general class of CF algorithms called *model-based* algorithms. In this approach, an underlying model of user preferences (for example, a Bayesian network model) is first constructed, from which predictions are inferred.

Formal Description of Task

A CF algorithm recommends items or *titles* to the active user based on the ratings of other users. Let n be the number of users, T the set of all titles, and $m=|T|$ the total number of titles. Denote the $n \times m$ matrix of all users' ratings for all titles as $\mathbf{R}$. More specifically, the rating of user i for title j is R_{ij}, where each $R_{ij} \in \Re \cup \{\bot\}$ is either a real number or $\bot$, the symbol for "no rating". Let $\mathbf{u}_i$ be an n-dimensional row vector with a 1 in the ith position and zeros elsewhere. Thus $\mathbf{u}_i \cdot \mathbf{R}$ is the m-dimensional (row) vector of all of user i's ratings.[1] Similarly, define $\mathbf{t}_j$ to be an m-dimensional column vector with a 1 in the jth position and zeros elsewhere. Then $\mathbf{R} \cdot \mathbf{t}_j$ is the n dimensional (column) vector of all users' ratings for title j. Note that $\mathbf{u}_i \cdot \mathbf{R} \cdot \mathbf{t}_j = R_{ij}$. Distinguish one user $a \in \{1, 2, ..., n\}$ as the active user. Define $NR \subset T$ to be the subset of titles that the active user has not rated, and thus for which we would like to provide predictions. That is, title j is in the set NR if and only if $R_{aj} = \bot$. Then the subset of titles that the active user *has* rated is T-NR.

In general terms, a collaborative filter is a function f that takes as input all ratings for all users, and replaces some or all of the "no rating" symbols with predicted ratings. Call this new matrix P.

$$P_{aj} = \begin{cases} R_{aj} & : \text{if } R_{aj} \neq \bot \\ f_a(\mathbf{R}) & : \text{if } R_{aj} = \bot \end{cases} \quad (1)$$

For the remainder of this paper we drop the subscript on f for brevity; the dependence on the active user is implicit.

Utility Theory and Social Choice Theory

Social choice theorists are also interested in aggregation functions f similar to that in (1), though they are concerned with combining preferences or utilities rather than ratings. Preferences refer to ordinal rankings of outcomes. For example, Alice's preferences might hold that sunny days (*sd*) are better than cloudy days (*cd*), and cloudy days are better than rainy days (*rd*). Utilities, on the other hand, are numeric expressions. Alice's utilities v for the outcomes *sd*, *cd*, and *rd* might be $v_{sd} = 10$, $v_{cd} = 4$, and $v_{rd} = 2$, respectively. If Alice's utilities are such that $v_{sd} > v_{cd}$, then Alice prefers *sd* to *cd*. Axiomatizations by Savage [1954] and von Neumann and Morgenstern [1953] provide persuasive postulates which imply the existence of utilities, and show that maximizing expected utility is the optimal way to make choices. If two utility functions v and v' are positive linear transformations of one another, then they are considered equivalent, since maximizing expected utility would lead to the same choice in both cases.

Now consider the problem of combining many peoples' preferences into a single expression of societal preference. Arrow proved the startling result that this aggregation task is simply impossible, if the combined preferences are to satisfy a few compelling and rather innocuous-looking properties [Arrow, 1963].[2] This influential result forms the

---

[1] We define $0 \cdot \bot = 0$, and $x \cdot \bot = \bot$ for any $x \neq 0$.
[2] Arrow won the Nobel Prize in Economics in part for this result, which is ranked at
http://www.northnet.org/clemens/

core of a vast literature in Social Choice theory. Sen [1986] provides an excellent survey of this body of work. Researchers have since extended Arrow's theorem to the case of combining utilities. In general, economists argue that the absolute magnitude of utilities are not comparable between individuals, since (among other reasons) utilities are invariant under positive affine transformations. In this context, Arrow's theorem on preference aggregation applies to the case of combining utilities as well [Fishburn, 1987; Roberts, 1980; Sen, 1986].

Nearest Neighbor Collaborative Filtering

We now describe four conditions on a CF function, argue why they are desirable, and discuss how existing CF implementations adhere to different subsets of them. We then show that the only CF function that satisfies all four properties is the nearest neighbor strategy, in which recommendations to the active user are simply the preferred titles of one single other user.

Property 1 (UNIV) *Universal domain and minimal functionality.* The function $f(R)$ is defined over all possible inputs R. Moreover, if $R_{ij} \neq \perp$ for some i, then $P_{aj} \neq \perp$.

UNIV simply states that f always provides some prediction for rated titles. To our knowledge, all existing CF functions adhere to this property.

Property 2 (UNAM) *Unanimity.* For all $j,k \in NR$, if $R_{ij} > R_{ik}$ for all $i \neq a$, then $P_{aj} > P_{ak}$.

UNAM is often called the weak Pareto property in the Social Choice and Economics literatures. Under this condition, if all users rate j strictly higher than k, then we predict that the active user will prefer j over k.

This property seems natural: If everyone agrees that title j is better than k, including those most similar to the active user, then it hard to justify a reversed prediction. Nevertheless, correlation methods can violate UNAM if, for example, the active user is negatively correlated with other users. Other similarity-based techniques that use only positive weights, including vector similarity and mean squared difference, do satisfy this property.

Property 3 (IIA) *Independence of Irrelevant Alternatives.* Consider two input ratings matrices, R and R', such that $R \cdot t_j = R' \cdot t_j$ for all $j \in T\text{-}NR$. Furthermore, suppose that $R \cdot t_k = R' \cdot t_k$ and $R \cdot t_l = R' \cdot t_l$ for some $k,l \in NR$. That is, R and R' are identical on all ratings of titles that the active user has seen, and on two of the titles, k and l, that the active user has not seen. Then $P_{ak} > P_{al}$ if and only if $P'_{ak} > P'_{al}$.

---

decor/mathhist.htm as one of seven milestones in mathematical history this century.

The intuition for IIA is as follows. The ratings $\{R \cdot t_j : j \in T\text{-}NR\}$ for those titles that the active user has seen tell us how similar the active user is to each of the other users, and we assume that the ratings $\{R \cdot t_j : j \in NR\}$ do not bear upon this similarity measure. This is the assumption made by most similarity-based CF algorithms. Once a similarity score is calculated, it makes sense that the predicted relative ranking between two titles k and l should only depend on the ratings for k and l. For example, if the active user has not rated the movie "Waterworld", then everyone else's opinion of it should have no bearing on whether the active user prefers "Ishtar" to "The Apartment", or vice versa.

IIA lends stability to the system. To see this, suppose that $NR = \{j, k, l\}$, and f predicts the active user's ratings such that $P_{aj} > P_{ak} > P_{al}$, or title j is most recommended. Now suppose that a new title, m, is added to the database, and that the active user has not rated it. If IIA holds, then the relative ordering among j, k, and l will remain unchanged, and the only task will be to position m somewhere within that order. If, on the other hand, the function does not adhere to IIA, then adding m to the database might upset the previous relative ordering, causing k, or even l, to become the overall most recommended title. Such an effect of presumably irrelevant information seems counterintuitive.

All of the similarity-based CF functions identified here—GroupLens, Ringo, and vector similarity—obey IIA.

Property 4 (SI) *Scale Invariance.* Consider two input ratings matrices, R and R', such that, for all users i, $u_i \cdot R' = \alpha_i (u_i \cdot R) + \beta_i$ for any positive constants α_i and any constants β_i. Then $P_{aj} > P_{ak}$ if and only if $P'_{aj} > P'_{ak}$, for all titles $j,k \in NR$.

This property is motivated by the belief, widely accepted by economists [Arrow, 1963; Sen, 1986], that one user's internal scale is not comparable to another user's scale. Suppose that the database contains ratings from 1 to 10. One user might tend to use ratings in the high end of the scale, while another tends to use the low end. Or, the data might even have been gathered from different sources, each of which elicited ratings on a different scale. For example, in the movie domain, one may want to include data from media critics; however, Mr. Showbiz[1] uses a scale from 0 to 100, TV Guide gives up to five stars, USA Today gives up to four stars, and Roger Ebert reports only thumbs up or down. How should their ratings be compared? We would ideally like to obtain the same results, regardless of how each user reports his or her ratings, as long as his or her mapping from internal utilities to ratings is a positive linear transformation; that is, as long as his or her reported ratings are themselves expressions of utility.

---

[1] http://www.mrshowbiz.com

One way to impose SI is to normalize all of the users' ratings to a common scale before applying f. One natural normalization is:

$$\mathbf{u}_i \mathbf{R}' \leftarrow \frac{\mathbf{u}_i \mathbf{R} - \min(\mathbf{u}_i \mathbf{R})}{\max(\mathbf{u}_i \mathbf{R}) - \min(\mathbf{u}_i \mathbf{R})}$$

This transforms all ratings to the [0,1] range, filtering out any dependence on multiplicative (α_i) or additive (β_i) scale factors.[1]

Another way to ensure SI is to constrain f to depend only on the relative rank among titles (the ordinal preferences of users), and *not* on the magnitude of ratings. Freund *et al.* [1998] strongly advocate this approach.

> One important property of [the collaborative filtering] problem is that the most relevant information to be combined represents *relative preferences* rather than *absolute ratings*. In other words, even if the ranking of [titles] is expressed by assigning each [title] a numeric score, we would like to ignore the absolute values of these scores and concentrate only on their relative order.

By ignoring all but relative rank, Freund *et al.*'s algorithm satisfies SI. On the other hand, the similarity-based methods violate it.

Cohen *et al.* [1999] develop another algorithm for combining ordinal preferences from multiple experts to form a composite ranking of items, applicable for collaborative filtering. Their algorithm proceeds in two stages. The first stage actually satisfies *all four* properties defined in this section: UNIV, UNAM, SI and IIA. As a result, the first-stage preference relation may contain cycles (e.g., title j is preferred to title k, k is preferred to l, and l is preferred to j). The second stage of their algorithm attempts to find the acyclic preference function that most closely approximates the stage one preference relation. The complete two-stage algorithm retains invariance to scale (satisfies SI), but may depend on irrelevant alternatives (violates IIA).

Different researchers favor one or the other of these four properties; the following proposition shows that only one very restrictive CF function obeys them all.

Proposition 1 (Nearest neighbor). Assuming that $|NR| > 2$, then the only function f of the form (1) that satisfies UNIV, UNAM, IIA, and SI is such that:

$$R_{ij} > R_{ik} \quad \Rightarrow \quad P_{aj} > P_{ak} ,$$

for all titles $j,k \in NR$, and for one distinguished user i. The choice of user i can depend on the ratings $\{R \cdot t_j : j \in T\text{-}NR\}$, as long as this dependence is invariant to scale, but once the "best" i is determined, his or her ratings

---
[1] If $\max(\mathbf{u}_i \cdot \mathbf{R}) = \min(\mathbf{u}_i \cdot \mathbf{R})$, then set $\mathbf{u}_i \mathbf{R}' = \mathbf{0}$.

for the titles in *NR* must be fully adopted as the active user's predicted ratings.

Proof (sketch): Let j be a title in *NR*. Rewrite f in equation (1) in the following, equivalent, form:

$$\begin{aligned} P_{aj} &= f(\{R \cdot t_j : j \in T\text{-}NR\}, \{R \cdot t_j : j \in NR\}) \\ &= g(\{R \cdot t_j : j \in NR\}) , \end{aligned}$$

where the choice of function g is itself allowed to depend on $\{R \cdot t_j : j \in T\text{-}NR\}$. With the exception of the "no rating" value $\bot$, the problem has been cast into the same terms as in the Social Choice literature. Doyle and Wellman [1991] point out that Arrow's original proof does *not* require that all users' preference orderings be complete, and the proof insists that the aggregate ordering is complete only for items that some user has expressed a preference over. With the additional assumption of minimal functionality (part of the definition of UNIV), similar to Doyle and Wellman's "conflict resolution" condition, standard social choice proofs become applicable. It follows, from Sen's [1986] or Robert's [1980] extension of Arrow's theorem [1963], that g, and therefore f, must be of the nearest neighbor form specified. •

If the dictatorial user i does not express a rating for some titles, then there exists a secondary dictator h whose preferences are fully adopted among those titles unrated by i and rated by h. This "cascade of dictators" continues until the minimal functionality clause of UNIV is satisfied, as shown in Doyle and Wellman's [1991] axiomatic treatment of default logic.

Weighted Average Collaborative Filtering

We now examine a slight weakening of the set of properties leading to Proposition 1. Under these new conditions, we find that the only possible CF function is a weighted sum: The active user's predicted rating for each title is a weighted average of the other users' ratings for the same title. Our argument is again based on results from Social Choice theory; we largely follow Fishburn's [1987] explication of work originally due to Roberts [1980].

We replace the SI property with a weaker one:

Property 4* (TI) *Translation Invariance.* Consider two input ratings matrices, R and R', such that, for all users i, $\mathbf{u}_i \mathbf{R}' = \alpha (\mathbf{u}_i \mathbf{R}) + \beta_i$ for any positive constant α, and any constants β_i. Then $P_{aj} > P_{ak}$ if and only if $P'_{aj} > P'_{ak}$, for all titles $j,k \in NR$.

This condition requires that recommendations remain unchanged when all ratings are multiplied by the *same* constant, and/or when any of the individual ratings are shifted by additive constants. The TI property, like SI, still honors the belief that the absolute rating of one title by one user is not comparable to the absolute rating of another user. Unlike SI, it assumes that the magnitude of ratings differences, $(R_{ij} - R_{ik})$ and $(R_{hj} - R_{hk})$, *are* comparable between users i and h.

Though they violate SI, the similarity-based methods of GroupLens, Ringo, and vector similarity obey TI.

Proposition 2 (Weighted average). Assuming that $|NR| > 2$, then the only function f of the form (1) that satisfies UNIV, UNAM, IIA, and TI is such that:

$$w \cdot R \cdot t_j > w \cdot R \cdot t_k \implies P_{aj} > P_{ak}$$

for all titles $j,k \in NR$, where $w = <w_1, w_2, \ldots, w_n>$ is a row vector of n nonnegative weights, at least one of which is positive. The specific weights can depend on the ratings $\{R \cdot t_j : j \in T\text{-}NR\}$.

Proof: Follows from Roberts [1980]. •

Proposition 2 does not rule out the nearest neighbor policy, as all but one of the w_i could be zero.

Weighted Average Collaborative Filtering, ... Again

Next, we derive the same conclusion as Proposition 2 working from a different axiomatization. This result is adapted from Harsanyi [1955].

The derivation requires two assumptions.

Property 5 (RRU) *Ratings are utilities*. Each user's rating $u_i \cdot R$ are a positive linear transformation from his or her utilities. That is, the ratings themselves are expressions of utility.

We also assume that users obey the rationality postulates of expected utility theory [Savage, 1954; von Neumann and Morgenstern, 1953]. For example, if user i's ratings for three titles are such that $R_{ij} > R_{ik} > R_{il}$, then there is some probability p for which the user would be indifferent between the following two situations: (1) getting title j with probability p or title l with probability $1 - p$, and (2) getting title k for sure.

Property 2* (UnamE) *Unanimity of Equality*. For all $j,k \in NR$, if $R_{ij} = R_{ik}$ for all $i \neq a$, then $P_{aj} = P_{ak}$.

Proposition 3 (Weighted average, ... again). The only function f of the form (1) that satisfies both RRU and UnamE is such that:

$$P_{aj} = w \cdot R \cdot t_j ,$$

for all titles $j \in NR$, where w is an n-dimensional row vector of real number weights.

Proof: Follows from Harsanyi [1955]. •

Note that this proposition, unlike the previous, admits negative weights.

Implications of the Analysis

What are the implications of the theoretical limitations highlighted in Propositions 1–3? First, we believe that identifying the connection between CF and Social Choice theory allows CF researchers to leverage a great deal of previous work on preference and utility aggregation. A Social Choice perspective on combining default reasoning rules has yielded valuable insights for that task [Doyle and Wellman, 1991], and similar benefits may accrue for CF.

The connection between collaborative filtering and voting has been recognized informally by many authors; indeed, several use the term "vote" to describe users' ratings. Cohen et al. [1999] make the connection more explicit, pointing out the relationship between their rank-merging algorithm and voting methods formulated as early as 1876. In fact, weighted versions of any of the many proposed voting schemes [Fishburn, 1973] are immediate candidates for new CF algorithms. One of the goals of this paper is to extend the analogy beyond terminological and algorithmic similarity to include axiomatic foundations.

Understanding what is theoretically impossible is an important first step in algorithm design. We believe that the results in this paper can help guide CF development in the future. Though our derivations constrain the type of CF function, they do not contain a recommendation as to how exactly to choose the best neighbor, or how to choose the optimal set of weights. Nonetheless, identifying the functional forms themselves can be of value, by constraining the search among algorithms to one of finding the best instantiation of a particular form.

With regards to real-world applications, CF designers for Internet commerce applications might typically be interested more in the predictive performance of a CF algorithm, rather than in the properties of preference coalescence that it does or does not obey. Yet there is no consensus on how best to measure effectiveness, as evidenced by the proliferation of many proposed evaluation scores. As a result, comparisons among the various algorithms are blurred. Even if a standard, accepted evaluation measure is somehow settled upon, empirical performance can be measured only for a limited number of special cases, whereas the theoretical results apply in all circumstances.

Conclusion

We have illustrated a correspondence between collaborative filtering (CF) and Social Choice theory. Both frameworks center on the goal of combining the preferences (expressed as ratings and utilities, respectively) of a group into a single preference relation. Some of the properties that Social Choice theorists have found to be compelling are also arguably desirable in the context of CF. In particular, universal domain (UNIV) is universally accepted. Unanimity (UNAM) is compelling and common. Most of the other properties have been advocated (at least implicitly) elsewhere in the literature. Similarity-based methods with only positive reinforcement obey UNAM, including vector similarity and mean squared difference. Most similarity-based techniques obey independence of irrelevant alternatives (IIA) and translation invariance (TI). Freund *et al.* [1998] and Cohen *et al.* [1999] make the case for scale invariance (SI).

We have identified constraints that a CF designer must live with, if their algorithms are to satisfy sets of these conditions. Along with UNIV and UNAM, IIA and SI imply the nearest neighbor method, while IIA and TI imply the weighted average. A second derivation shows that, if all users' ratings are utilities, and if unanimity of equality holds, then, once again, only the weighted average is available.

Finally, we discussed implications of this analysis, highlighting the fundamental limitations of CF, and identifying a bridge from results and discussion in Social Choice theory to work in CF. This avenue of opportunity includes the implementation of weighted versions of voting mechanisms as potential new CF algorithms.

Acknowledgments

Thanks to Jack Breese and to the anonymous reviewers for ideas, insights, and pointers to relevant work.

References

Kenneth J. Arrow. *Social Choice and Individual Values*. Yale University Press, second edition, 1963.

Daniel Billsus and Michael J. Pazzani. Learning collaborative information filters. In *Proceedings of the Fifteenth International Conference on Machine Learning*, pages 46–54, July 1998.

John S. Breese, David Heckerman and Carl Kadie. Empirical analysis of predictive algorithms for collaborative filtering. In *Proceedings of the Fourteenth Annual Conference on Uncertainty in Artificial Intelligence*, pages 43–52, July 1998.

William W. Cohen, Robert E. Schapire, and Yoram Singer. Learning to order things. *Journal of Artificial Intelligence Research*, 10: 243–270, 1999.

Jon Doyle and Michael P. Wellman. Impediments to universal preference-based default theories. *Artificial Intelligence*, 49: 97–128, 1991.

Peter C. Fishburn. *The Theory of Social Choice*. Princeton University Press, Princeton, New Jersey, 1973.

Peter C. Fishburn. *Interprofile Conditions and Impossibility*. Harwood Academic Publishers, New York, 1987.

Yoav Freund, Raj Iyer, Robert E. Schapire, and Yoram Singer. An Efficient boosting algorithm for combining preferences. In *Proceedings of the Fifteenth International Conference on Machine Learning*, pages 170–178, 1998.

David Goldberg, David Nichols, Brian M. Oki, and Douglas Terry. Using collaborative filtering to weave an information tapestry. *Communications of the ACM*, 35(12): 61–70, December 1992.

John C. Harsanyi. Cardinal welfare, individualistic ethics, and interpersonal comparisons of utility. *Journal of Political Economy*, 63(4): 309–321, August 1955.

Joseph A. Konstan, Bradley N. Miller, David Maltz, Jonathan L. Herlocker, Lee R. Gordon, and John Riedl. GroupLens: Applying collaborative filtering to Usenet news. *Communications of the ACM*, 40(3): 77–87, 1997.

Atsuyoshi Nakamura and Naoki Abe. Collaborative filtering using weighted majority prediction algorithms. In *Proceedings of the Fifteenth International Conference on Machine Learning*, pages 395–403, July 1998.

Paul Resnick and Hal R. Varian. Recommender systems. *Communications of the ACM*, 40(3): 56–58, March 1997.

Paul Resnick, Neophyts Iacovou, Mitesh Suchak, Peter Bergstrom, and John Riedl. GroupLens: An Open architecture for collaborative filtering of netnews. In *Proceedings of the ACM Conference on Computer Supported Cooperative Work*, pages 175–186, 1994.

K. W. S. Roberts. Interpersonal comparability and social choice theory. *Review of Economic Studies*, 47: 421–439, 1980.

Leonard J. Savage. *The Foundations of Statistics*. Dover Publications, New York, 1972.

Amartya Sen. Social Choice theory. In *Handbook of Mathematical Economics*, volume 3, Elsevier Science Publishers, 1986.

Upendra Shardanand and Pattie Maes. Social information filtering: Algorithms for automating "word of mouth." In *Proceedings of Computer Human Interaction*, pages 210–217, May 1995.

John von Neumann and Oskar Morgenstern. *Theory of Games and Economic Behavior*. Princeton University Press, Princeton, New Jersey, 1953 (© 1944).

Learning Subjective Adjectives from Corpora

Janyce M. Wiebe
Department of Computer Science
New Mexico State University, Las Cruces, NM 88003
wiebe@cs.nmsu.edu

Abstract

Subjectivity tagging is distinguishing sentences used to present opinions and evaluations from sentences used to objectively present factual information. There are numerous applications for which subjectivity tagging is relevant, including information extraction and information retrieval. This paper identifies strong clues of subjectivity using the results of a method for clustering words according to distributional similarity (Lin 1998), seeded by a small amount of detailed manual annotation. These features are then further refined with the addition of lexical semantic features of adjectives, specifically *polarity* and *gradability* (Hatzivassiloglou & McKeown 1997), which can be automatically learned from corpora. In 10-fold cross validation experiments, features based on both similarity clusters and the lexical semantic features are shown to have higher precision than features based on each alone.

Introduction

Subjectivity in natural language refers to aspects of language used to express opinions and evaluations (Banfield 1982; Wiebe 1994). *Subjectivity tagging* is distinguishing sentences used to present opinions and other forms of subjectivity (*subjective sentences*) from sentences used to objectively present factual information (*objective sentences*). This task is especially relevant for news reporting and Internet forums, in which opinions of various agents are expressed. There are numerous applications for which subjectivity tagging is relevant. Two examples are information extraction and information retrieval. Assigning subjectivity labels to documents or portions of documents is an example of a non-topical characterization of information. Current information extraction and retrieval technology focuses almost exclusively on the subject matter of the documents. However, additional components of a document influence its relevance to particular users or tasks, including, for example, the evidential status of the material presented, and attitudes adopted in favor of or against a particular person, event, or position.[1] A summarization system would benefit from distinguishing sentences intended to present factual material from those intended to present opinions, since many summaries are meant to include only facts. In the realm of Internet forums, subjectivity

judgements would be useful for recognizing inflammatory messages ("flames") and mining on-line forums for reviews of products and services.

To use subjectivity tagging in applications, good linguistic clues must be found. As with many pragmatic and discourse distinctions, existing lexical resources such as machine readable dictionaries (Procter 1978) and ontologies for natural language processing (NLP) (Mahesh & Nirenburg 1995; Hovy 1998), while useful, are not sufficient for identifying such linguistic clues, because they are not comprehensively coded for subjectivity. This paper addresses learning subjectivity clues from a corpus.

Previous work on subjectivity (Wiebe, Bruce, & O'Hara 1999; Bruce & Wiebe 2000) established a positive and statistically significant correlation with the presence of adjectives. Since the mere presence of one or more adjectives is useful for predicting that a sentence is subjective, this paper uses the performance of the simple adjective feature as a baseline, and identifies higher quality adjective features using the results of a method for clustering words according to distributional similarity (Lin 1998), seeded by a small amount of detailed manual annotation. These features are then further refined with the addition of lexical semantic features of adjectives, specifically *polarity* and *gradability* (Hatzivassiloglou & McKeown 1997), which can be automatically learned from corpora. In 10-fold cross validation experiments, features based on both similarity clusters and the lexical semantic features are shown to have higher precision than features based on each alone. The new adjective features are available on the Web at http://www.cs.nmsu.edu/˜wiebe.

In the remainder of this paper, subjectivity and previous work on automatic subjectivity tagging are first described. The statistical techniques used to create the new adjective features are described next, starting with distributional similarity, followed by learning gradable and polar adjectives. The results are then presented, followed by the conclusions.

Subjectivity

Sentence (1) is an example of a simple subjective sentence, and (2) is an example of a simple objective sentence:[2]

Copyright © 2000, American Association for Artificial Intelligence (www.aaai.org). All rights reserved.

[1] This point is due to Vasileios Hatzivassiloglou.

[2] Due to space limitations, this section glosses over some important distinctions involving subjectivity. The term *subjectivity* is due to Ann Banfield (1982), though I have changed its

(1)
At several different layers, it's a fascinating tale. *Subjective sentence.*

(2)
Bell Industries Inc. increased its quarterly to 10 cents from 7 cents a share. *Objective sentence.*

Sentences (3) and (4) illustrate the fact that sentences about speech events may be subjective or objective:

(3)
Northwest Airlines settled the remaining lawsuits filed on behalf of 156 people killed in a 1987 crash, but claims against the jetliner's maker are being pursued, a federal judge said. *Objective sentence.*

(4)
"The cost of health care is eroding our standard of living and sapping industrial strength," complains Walter Maher, a Chrysler health-and-benefits specialist. *Subjective sentence.*

In (3), the material about lawsuits and claims is presented as factual information, and a federal judge is given as the source of information. In (4), in contrast, a complaint is presented. An NLP system performing information extraction on (4) should not treat the material in the quoted string as factual information, with the complainer as a source of information, whereas a corresponding treatment of sentence (3) would be fine.

Subjective sentences often contain individual expressions of subjectivity. Examples are *fascinating* in (1), and *eroding*, *sapping*, and *complains* in (4). The following paragraphs mention aspects of subjectivity expressions that are relevant for NLP applications.

First, although some expressions, such as *!*, are subjective in all contexts, many, such as *sapping* and *eroding*, may or may not be subjective, depending on the context in which they appear. A *potential subjective element* is a linguistic element that may be used to express subjectivity. A *subjective element* is an instance of a potential subjective element, in a particular context, that is indeed subjective in that context (Wiebe 1994).

Second, there are different types of subjectivity. This work focuses primarily on three: positive evaluation (e.g., *fascinating*), negative evaluation (e.g., *terrible*), and speculation (e.g., *probably*).

Third, a subjective element expresses the subjectivity of a *source*, who may be the writer or someone mentioned in the text. For example, the source of *fascinating* in (1) is the writer, while the source of the subjective elements in (4) is Maher. In addition, a subjective element has a *target*, i.e., what the subjectivity is about or directed toward. In (1), the target is a tale; in (2), the target is the cost of health care. These are examples of *object-centric subjectivity*, which is about an object mentioned in the text (other examples: "I

---

meaning somewhat to adapt it to this work. For references to work on subjectivity, please see (Banfield 1982; Fludernik 1993; Wiebe 1994).

love this project"; "The software is horrible"). Subjectivity may also be *addressee-oriented*, i.e., directed toward the listener or reader (e.g., "You are an idiot").

There may be multiple subjective elements in a sentence, possibly of different types and attributed to different sources and targets. As described below, individual subjective elements were annotated as part of this work, refining previous work on sentence-level annotation.

With colleagues, I am pursuing three applications in related work: recognizing flames, mining Internet forums for product reviews, and clustering messages by ideological point of view (i.e., clustering messages into "camps"). There has been work on these applications: Spertus (1997) developed a flame-recognition system that relies on a small number of complex clues; Terveen et al. (1997) developed a system that mines news groups for Web page recommendations; Sack (1995) developed a knowledge-based system for recognizing ideological points of view; and Kleinberg (1998) discussed using hyperlink connectivity for this problem. Our approach is meant to supplement such approaches: we are developing a repository of potential subjective elements to enable us to exploit subjective language in these applications. This paper takes a significant step in that direction by demonstrating a process for learning potential subjective elements from corpora.

Previous Work on Subjectivity Tagging

In previous work (Wiebe, Bruce, & O'Hara 1999; Bruce & Wiebe 2000), a corpus of 1,001 sentences[3] of the Wall Street Journal Treebank Corpus (Marcus et al. 1993) was manually annotated with subjectivity classifications. Specifically, three humans assigned a subjective or objective label to each sentence. They were instructed to consider a sentence to be subjective if they perceived any significant expression of subjectivity (of any source), and to consider the sentence to be objective, otherwise. The EM learning algorithm was used to produce corrected tags representing the consensus opinions of the judges (Goodman 1974; Dawid & Skene 1979). The total number of subjective sentences in the data is 486 and the total number of objective sentences is 515.

In (Bruce & Wiebe 2000), a statistical analysis of the assigned classifications was performed, showing that adjectives are statistically significantly and positively correlated with subjective sentences in the corpus on the basis of the log-likelihood ratio test statistic G^2. The probability that a sentence is subjective, simply given that there is at least one adjective in the sentence, is 55.8%, even though there are more objective than subjective sentences in the corpus.

An automatic system to perform subjectivity tagging was developed as part of the work reported in (Wiebe, Bruce, & O'Hara 1999). In 10-fold cross validation experiments applied to the corpus described above, a probabilistic classifier obtained an average accuracy on subjectivity tagging of 72.17%, more than 20 percentage points higher than a

---

[3] Compound sentences were manually segmented into their conjuncts, and each conjunct is treated as a separate sentence.

baseline accuracy obtained by always choosing the more frequent class. Five part-of-speech features, two lexical features, and a paragraph feature were used. An analysis of the system showed that the adjective feature was important for realizing the improvements over the baseline accuracy.

Experiments

In this paper, the corpus described above is used, augmented with new manual annotations. Specifically, given the sentences classified as subjective in (Wiebe, Bruce, & O'Hara 1999), the annotators were asked to identify the subjective elements in the sentence, i.e., the expressions they feel are responsible for the subjective classification. They were also asked to rate the strength of the elements (on a scale of 1 to 3, with 3 being the strongest). The subjective element annotations of one judge were used to seed the distributional similarity process described in the next section.

In the experiments below, the precision of a simple prediction method for subjectivity is measured: a sentence is classified as subjective if at least one member of a set of adjectives S occurs in the sentence, and objective otherwise. Precision is measured by the conditional probability that a sentence is subjective, given that one or more instances of members of S appears. This metric assesses feature quality: if instances of S appear, how likely is the sentence to be subjective?

Improving Adjective Features Using Distributional Similarity

Using his broad-coverage parser (Lin 1994), Lin (1998) extracts dependency triples from text consisting of two words and the grammatical relationship between them: $(w1, relation, w2)$. To measure similarity between two words $w1$ and $w1'$, the relation-word pairs correlated with $w1$ are identified and the relation-word pairs correlated with $w1'$ are identified. A similarity metric is defined in terms of these two sets. Correlation is measured using the mutual information metric. Lin processed a 64-million corpus consisting of news articles, creating a thesaurus entry for each word consisting of the 200 words of the same part-of-speech that are most similar to it.

The intuition behind this type of process is that words correlated with many of the same things in text are more similar. It is intriguing to speculate that this process might discover functional and pragmatic similarities. I hypothesized that, seeded with strong potential subjective elements, Lin's process would find others, not all of which would be strict synonyms of the seeds.

A challenging test was performed: in 10-fold cross validation experiments, 1/10 of the data was used for training and 9/10 of the data was used for testing. Specifically, the corpus was partitioned into 10 random sets. For each training set i, all adjectives were extracted from subjective elements of strength 3, and, for each, the top 20 entries in Lin's thesaurus entry were identified. These are the *seed sets* for fold i (each seed set also includes the original seed). The seed sets for fold i were evaluated on the test set for fold i, i.e., the entire corpus minus the 1/10 of the data from which the seeds were selected.

As mentioned above, the precision of a simple adjective feature is used as a baseline in this work, specifically the conditional probability that a sentence is subjective, given that at least one adjective appears. The average precision across folds of the baseline adjective feature is 55.8%. The average precision resulting from the above process is 61.2%, an increase of 5.4 percentage points. To compare this process with using an existing knowledge source, the process was repeated, but with the seed's synonyms in WordNet (i.e., the seed's *synset*) (Miller 1990) in place of words from Lin's thesaurus entry. The performance is slightly better with WordNet (62.0%), but the coverage is lower. When the process below (which gives the best results) is applied using the WordNet synsets, the resulting frequencies are very low. While I believe WordNet is potentially a valuable resource for identifying potential subjective elements, Lin's thesaurus entries appear better suited to the current process, because they include looser synonyms than those in WordNet.

Some adjectives that have frequent non-subjective uses are introduced by the above process. Thus, some simple filtering was performed using the training set. For all seed sets for which the precision is less than or equal to the precision of the baseline adjective feature in the training set, the entire seed set was removed. Then, individual adjectives were removed if they appeared at least twice and their precision is less than or equal to the baseline precision on the training set. This results in an average precision of 66.3% on the test sets, 7.5 percentage points higher than the baseline average. The filtered sets are the ones used in the process below.

Refinements with Polarity and Gradability

Hatzivassiloglou and McKeown (1997) present a method for automatically recognizing the *semantic orientation* or *polarity* of adjectives, which is the direction the word deviates from the norm for its semantic group. Words that encode a desirable state (e.g., *beautiful*, *unbiased*) have a positive orientation, while words that represent undesirable states have a negative orientation.

Most antonymous adjectives can be contrasted on the basis of orientation (e.g., *beautiful–ugly*); similarly, nearly synonymous terms are often distinguished by different orientations (e.g., *simple–simplistic*). While orientation applies to many adjectives, there are also those that have no orientation, typically as members of groups of complementary, qualitative terms (Lyons 1977) (e.g., *domestic*, *medical*, or *red*). Since orientation is inherently connected with evaluative judgements, it is a good feature for predicting subjectivity.

Hatzivassiloglou and McKeown's method automatically assigns a + or − orientation label to adjectives known to have some semantic orientation. Their method is based on information extracted from conjunctions between adjectives in a large corpus—because orientation constrains the use of the words in specific contexts (e.g., compare *corrupt and brutal* with **corrupt but brutal*), observed conjunctions of adjectives can be exploited to infer whether the conjoined words are of the same or different orientation. Using a shallow parser in a 21 million word corpus of Wall Street Journal articles, they developed and trained a log-linear statistical model that predicts whether any two adjectives have the same orientation with 82% accuracy. Combining constraints among many adjectives, a clustering algorithm separates the adjectives into groups of different orientations, and, finally, adjectives are labeled positive or negative. Some manual annotation is required for this process.

Gradability is the semantic property that enables a word to participate in comparative constructs and to accept modifying expressions that act as intensifiers or diminishers. Gradable adjectives express properties in varying degrees of strength, relative to a norm either explicitly mentioned or implicitly supplied by the modified noun (for example, a *small planet* is usually much larger than a *large house*). This relativism in the interpretation of gradable words also makes them good predictors of subjectivity.

A method for classifying adjectives as gradable or nongradable is presented in (Hatzivassiloglou & Wiebe 2000). A shallow parser is used to retrieve all adjectives and their modifiers from a large corpus tagged for part-of-speech with Church's PARTS tagger (Church 1988). Hatzivassiloglou compiled by hand a list of 73 adverbs and noun phrases (such as *a little*, *exceedingly*, *somewhat*, and *very*) that are frequently used as grading modifiers. The number of times each adjective appears modified by a term from this list is a first indicator of gradability. Inflected forms of adjectives in most cases indicate gradability. Thus, a morphological analysis system was implemented to detect inflected forms of adjectives, a second indicator of gradability. A log-linear statistical model was developed to derive a final gradability judgement, based on the two indicators above.

The work reported in this paper uses samples of adjectives identified as having positive polarity, having negative polarity, and being gradable. For each type, we have samples of those assigned manually and samples of those assigned automatically. These samples were determined using a corpus from the Wall Street Journal, but a different corpus from the one used in the current paper. It is important to note that these adjective sets are only samples. Others currently exist, and more could be produced by running the automatic processes on new data.

Results and Discussion

Table 1 presents the results for the seed sets intersected with the gradability and polarity sets (i.e., the lexical sets). Detailed information is given for the features involving the automatically generated lexical sets. Summary information is given in the bottom of the table for the manually classified lexical sets.

The test data for each fold is the entire data set minus the data from which the seeds for that fold were selected. The columns in the table give, in order from the left, the fold number, the number of subjective sentences in the test set (*# Subj*), the number of objective sentences (*# Obj*), and the precision of the baseline adjective feature, i.e., p(subjective sentence | an adjective) (*Adj*). The *Seed-Freq* columns give the number of sentences in the test set that have at least one member of a seed set for that fold and the *Seed-Prec* columns give:

p(subjective sentence | an adjective in the seed set). The *Lex-Freq* columns give the number of sentences that have at least one member of the indicated lexical set, e.g., *Pol+,auto*, and the *Lex-Prec* columns give:

p(subjective sentence | an adjective in that set). For the $S \cap L$ columns, the set is the intersection of the seed sets for that fold and the lexical set. The $S \cap L$-*Freq* and $S \cap L$-*Prec* columns are as above. The *Ave diff* lines give the average difference across folds between the precisions of the indicated sets.

For example, in the test set for Fold 1:

 # Subj: there are 428 subjective sentences.

 # Obj: there are 475 objective sentences.

Adj: the probability that a sentence is subjective, given an adjective, is 55%.

Seed-Freq: 192 sentences contain a member of the seed set.

Seed-Prec: the probability that a sentence is subjective, given an adjective in the seed set, is 58%.

Lex-Freq: 176 sentences contain an automatically identified positive polarity adjective.

Lex-Prec: the probability that a sentence is subjective, given such an adjective, is 59%.

$S \cap L$-*Freq*: 56 sentences contain an adjective that is both in the seed set and in the set of automatically identified positive polarity adjectives.

$S \cap L$-*Prec*: the probability that a sentence is subjective, given such an adjective, is 71%.

The results are very promising. In all cases, the average improvement over the baseline of the $S \cap L$ features is at least 9 percentage points. On average, the gradability/polarity sets and the seed sets are more precise together than they are alone (this information can be found in the *Ave diff* lines). There are many excellent individual results, especially among the *Grad,auto* and *Pol-,auto* sets intersected with the seed sets. Only weak filtering of the original seed sets was done using only the original training data. There are more promising ways in which the various sets could be filtered. For example, some of the data that is currently part of the test set could be used to filter the sets (perhaps 3/10 of the data might be used for training with 1/3 of the training data used for seeding, and 2/3 used for filtering).

Conclusions and Future Work

Learning linguistic knowledge from corpora is currently an active and productive area of NLP (e.g., (Lin 1998; Lee 1999; Rooth *et al.* 1999)). These techniques are often used to learn knowledge for semantic tasks. This paper presents a case study of using such techniques to learn knowledge useful for a pragmatic task, subjectivity tagging.

The results of a clustering method (Lin 1998), seeded by a small amount of detailed manual annotation, were used to develop promising adjective features. These features were then further refined with the addition of lexical semantic

				Pol+,auto						Pol−,auto					
				Seed		Lex		S ∩ L		Seed		Lex		S ∩ L	
Fold	# Subj	# Obj	Adj	Freq	Prec	Freq	Prec	Freq	Prec	Freq	Prec	Freq	Prec	Freq	Prec
1	428	475	55	192	58	176	59	56	71	192	58	75	73	18	61
2	433	469	55	148	64	181	60	53	70	148	64	78	73	14	64
3	444	456	56	86	62	180	60	34	65	86	62	78	74	5	80
4	439	463	56	57	70	178	62	29	69	57	70	77	75	70	71
5	436	465	56	166	63	181	60	52	65	166	63	72	76	10	90
6	443	458	56	133	57	183	60	65	62	133	57	75	75	17	65
7	437	464	56	128	66	181	60	47	70	128	66	76	76	12	75
8	442	459	56	226	60	178	61	58	64	226	60	66	73	18	83
9	439	463	56	147	63	183	61	42	62	147	63	73	73	3	67
10	443	463	56	106	70	179	61	40	68	106	70	68	75	9	89
AVE:			55.8	139	63.3	180	60.4	47.6	66.6	139	63.3	73.8	74.3	11.3	74.5
				Ave diff from Adj to (S ∩ L): 10.8						Ave diff from Adj to (S ∩ L): 18.7					
				Ave diff from Seed to (S ∩ L): 3.3						Ave diff from Seed to (S ∩ L): 11.2					
				Ave diff from Lex to (S ∩ L): 6.2						Ave diff from Lex to (S ∩ L): 0.2					
				Pol−+,auto						Grad,auto					
				Seed		Lex		S ∩ L		Seed		Lex		S ∩ L	
Fold	# Subj	# Obj	Adj	Freq	Prec	Freq	Prec	Freq	Prec	Freq	Prec	Freq	Prec	Freq	Prec
1	428	475	55	192	58	235	63	73	68	192	58	37	68	8	75
2	433	469	55	148	64	243	64	67	69	148	64	37	68	18	78
3	444	456	56	86	62	242	64	39	67	86	62	46	65	10	70
4	439	463	56	57	70	238	66	36	69	57	70	43	67	11	82
5	436	465	56	166	63	238	64	61	69	166	63	43	70	20	85
6	443	458	56	133	57	242	64	79	62	133	57	41	68	12	83
7	437	464	56	128	66	241	65	59	71	128	66	41	68	18	83
8	442	459	56	226	60	233	64	74	68	226	60	39	72	11	82
9	439	463	56	147	63	241	64	45	62	147	63	39	64	23	70
10	443	463	56	106	70	232	65	49	71	106	70	36	72	16	88
AVE:			55.8	139	63.3	238.5	64.3	58.2	67.6	139	63.3	39.6	68.2	14.7	79.6
				Ave diff from Adj to (S ∩ L): 11.8						Ave diff from Adj to (S ∩ L): 23.8					
				Ave diff from Seed to (S ∩ L): 4.3						Ave diff from Seed to (S ∩ L): 16.3					
				Ave diff from Lex to (S ∩ L): 3.3						Ave diff from Lex to (S ∩ L): 11.4					

Pol+,man: Ave diff from Adj to (S ∩ L): 09.1   Ave diff from S to S ∩ L: 01.6   Ave diff from L to (S ∩ L):03.6
Pol−,man: Ave diff from Adj to (S ∩ L): 20.3   Ave diff from S to S ∩ L: 12.8   Ave diff from L to (S ∩ L): 09.1
Grad,man: Ave diff from Adj to (S ∩ L): 13.1   Ave diff from S to S ∩ L: 05.6   Ave diff from L to (S ∩ L): 06.3

Key:
Pol+: positive polarity. **Pol−**: negative polarity. **Grad**: gradable.
Man: manually identified. **Auto**: automatically identified.
 # Subj: number of subjective sentences. **# Obj**: number of objective sentences.
Adj: precision of adjective feature. **Seed**: seed sets. **Lex**: the lexical feature set, e.g., Pol+,auto.
S ∩ L: seed sets ∩ the lexical feature set.

Table 1: Subjectivity Predictability Results

features of adjectives, specifically *polarity* and *gradability* (Hatzivassiloglou & McKeown 1997), which can be automatically learned from corpora. The results are very promising, showing that both processes have the potential to improve the features derived by the other one.

The adjectives learned here are currently being incorporated into a system for recognizing flames in Internet forums. In addition, we plan to apply the methods to a corpus of Internet forums, to customize knowledge acquisition to that genre. This will include deriving a new thesaurus based on distributional similarity, reapplying the processes for identifying gradable and polar adjectives, and annotating subjective elements in the new genre, from which seeds can be selected.

Acknowledgements

This research was supported in part by the Office of Naval Research under grant number N00014-95-1-0776. I am grateful to Vasileios Hatzivassiloglou and Kathy McKeown for sharing the results of their ACL-97 paper; to Dekang Lin for making the results of his COLING-ACL-98 paper available on the Web; to Aravind Joshi for suggesting annotation of subjective elements; to Matthew Bell for performing the subjective element annotations; and to Dan Tappan for performing supporting programming.

References

Banfield, A. 1982. *Unspeakable Sentences*. Boston: Routledge and Kegan Paul.

Bruce, R., and Wiebe, J. 2000. Recognizing subjectivity: A case study of manual tagging. *Natural Language Engineering*.

Church, K. 1988. A stochastic parts porgram and noun phrase parser for unrestricted text. In *Proc. ANLP-88*, 136–143.

Dawid, A. P., and Skene, A. M. 1979. Maximum likelihood estimation of observer error-rates using the EM algorithm. *Applied Statistics* 28:20–28.

Fludernik, M. 1993. *The Fictions of Language and the Languages of Fiction*. London: Routledge.

Goodman, L. 1974. Exploratory latent structure analysis using both identifiable and unidentifiable models. *Biometrika* 61:2:215–231.

Hatzivassiloglou, V., and McKeown, K. 1997. Predicting the semantic orientation of adjectives. In *ACL-EACL 1997*, 174–181.

Hatzivassiloglou, V., and Wiebe, J. 2000. Effects of adjective orientation and gradability on sentence subjectivity. In *18th International Conference on Computational Linguistics (COLING-2000)*.

Hovy, E. 1998. Combining and standardizing large-scale practical ontologies for machine translation and other uses. In *In Proc. 1st International conference on language resources and evaluation (LREC)*.

Kleinberg, J. 1998. Authoritative sources in a hyperlinked environment. In *Proc. ACL=SIAM Symposium on Discrete Algorithms*, 226–233.

Lee, L. 1999. Measures of distributional similarity. In *Proc. ACL '99*, 25–32.

Lin, D. 1994. Principar–an efficient, broad-coverage, principle-based parser. In *Proc. COLING '94*, 482–488.

Lin, D. 1998. Automatic retrieval and clustering of similar words. In *Proc. COLING-ACL '98*, 768–773.

Lyons, J. 1977. *Semantics, Volume 1*. Cambridge, MA: Cambridge University Press.

Mahesh, K., and Nirenburg, S. 1995. A situated ontology for practical nlp. In *Proc. Workshop on Basic Ontological Issues in Knowledge Sharing*. International Joint Conference on Artificial Intelligence (IJCAI-95), Aug. 19-20, 1995. Montreal, Canada.

Marcus, M.; Santorini; B.; and Marcinkiewicz, M. 1993. Building a large annotated corpus of English: The penn treebank. *Computational Linguistics* 19(2):313–330.

Miller, G. 1990. Wordnet: An on-line lexical database. *International Journal of Lexicography* 3(4):??–??

Procter, P. 1978. *Longman Dictionary of Contemporary English*. Addison Wesley Longman.

Rooth, M.; Riezler, S.; Prescher, D.; Carroll, G.; and Beil, F. 1999. Inducing a semantically annotated lexicon via em-based clustering. In *Proc. 37th Annual Meeting of the Association for Computational Linguistics (ACL-99)*, 104–111.

Sack, W. 1995. Representing and recognizing point of view. In *Proc. AAAI Fall Symposium on AI Applications in Knowledge Navigation and Retrieval*.

Spertus, E. 1997. Smokey: Automatic recognition of hostile messages. In *Proc. IAAI*.

Terveen, L.; Hill, W.; Amento, B.; McDonald, D.; and Creter, J. 1997. Building task-specific interfaces to high volume conversational data. In *Proc. CHI '97*, 226–233.

Wiebe, J.; Bruce, R.; and O'Hara, T. 1999. Development and use of a gold standard data set for subjectivity classifications. In *Proc. 37th Annual Meeting of the Assoc. for Computational Linguistics (ACL-99)*, 246–253. University of Maryland: ACL.

Wiebe, J. 1994. Tracking point of view in narrative. *Computational Linguistics* 20(2):233–287.

Planning
and Scheduling

Iterative Flattening: A Scalable Method for Solving Multi-Capacity Scheduling Problems *

Amedeo Cesta
IP-CNR
National Research Council
Viale Marx 15
I-00137 Rome, Italy
cesta@ip.rm.cnr.it

Angelo Oddi
IP-CNR
National Research Council
Viale Marx 15
I-00137 Rome, Italy
oddi@ip.rm.cnr.it

Stephen F. Smith
The Robotics Institute
Carnegie Mellon University
5000 Forbes Avenue
Pittsburgh, PA 15213, USA
sfs@cs.cmu.edu

Abstract

One challenge for research in constraint-based scheduling has been to produce scalable solution procedures under fairly general representational assumptions. Quite often, the computational burden of techniques for reasoning about more complex types of temporal and resource capacity constraints places fairly restrictive limits on the size of problems that can be effectively addressed. In this paper, we focus on developing a scalable heuristic procedure to an extended, multi-capacity resource version of the job shop scheduling problem (MCJSSP). Our starting point is a previously developed procedure for generating feasible solutions to more complex, multi-capacity scheduling problems with maximum time lags. Adapting this procedure to exploit the simpler temporal structure of MCJSSP, we are able to produce a quite efficient solution generator. However, the procedure only indirectly attends to MCJSSP's objective criterion and produces sub-optimal solutions. To provide a scalable, optimizing procedure, we propose a simple, local-search procedure called *iterative flattening*, which utilizes the core solution generator to perform an extended iterative improvement search. Despite its simplicity, experimental analysis shows the iterative improvement search to be quite effective. On a set of reference problems ranging in size from 100 to 900 activities, the iterative flattening procedure efficiently and consistently produces solutions within 10% of computed upper bounds. Overall, the concept of iterative flattening is quite general and provides an interesting new basis for designing more sophisticated local search procedures.

Introduction

Constraint-based search techniques have gained increasing attention in recent years as a basis for scheduling procedures that are capable of accommodating a wide range of constraints. In its most basic form, a constraint based scheduling model operates over some sort of constraint-network encoding of the problem at hand, and problem solving proceeds through the interleaving of three basic actions:

---

* Cesta and Oddi's work has been supported by ASI (Italian Space Agency) under contract ASI-ARS-99-96 and by Italian National Research Council. Smith's work has been sponsored in part by the US Department of Defense Advanced Research Projects Agency under contract F30602-97-20227, and by the CMU Robotics Institute.

Copyright © 2000, American Association for Artificial Intelligence (www.aaai.org). All rights reserved.

constraint propagation: a deduction step where consequences of the current set of scheduling decisions are inferred and inconsistent search states are pruned;

search decision commitment: a choice step where search control heuristics are applied to assign some new value to some decision variable, and move the scheduling search forward;

search decision retraction: a choice step where one or more previously made decisions are retracted, allowing problem solving to back out of and continue from an inconsistent or undesirable state.

Recent research has promoted techniques for each of these basic actions as a means for addressing scheduling problems with increasingly more complex temporal and resource capacity constraints. Work in constraint deduction (Baptiste & Le Pape 1995; Baptiste, Le Pape, & Nuijten 1997; Nuijten 1994) has achieved strong performance through specification of propagation rules that exploit the special structure and character of particular classes of resource constraints. Work in search control heuristics (Smith & Cheng 1993; Cesta, Oddi, & Smith 1998; 1999; Beck & Fox 1999), alternatively, has demonstrated the effectiveness of different forms of constraint analysis in directing the scheduling process toward good solutions. Progress with various local and iterative sampling search frameworks (Zweben *et al.* 1994; Harvey & Ginsberg 1995; Bresina 1996; Crawford 1996; Oddi & Smith 1997; Cesta, Oddi, & Smith 1999), while not directly emphasizing treatment of more complex constraints, has provided several more effective alternatives to simple, backtracking-search retraction schemes.

One challenge in extending constraint-based scheduling models to accommodate more complex constraints is scalability. Quite often, techniques for reasoning about more complex types of temporal and resource capacity constraints come at a computational cost that places fairly restrictive limits on the size of problems that can be effectively addressed. Edge finding techniques, for example, provide a very powerful basis for resource constraint propagation, but are quite computationally heavy and are often impractical in large-scale settings (Baptiste & Le Pape 1995). Likewise, the texture-based heuristics defined in (Beck & Fox 1999) for scheduling with alternative resources are effective on small problems. But they rely on an explicit representation of the entire space of choices, which quickly becomes intractable as larger problems are considered.

In this paper, we focus on developing a scalable heuristic procedure to an extended, multi-capacity resource version of the job shop scheduling problem (MCJSSP) first proposed in (Nuijten 1994). Following from recent successes with non-systematic, local search techniques, we de-emphasize the use of sophisticated constraint propagation and analysis techniques in the generation of any given schedule. Instead, our design approach is to define a simple (and efficient) greedy procedure for generating feasible solutions, and then specify a decision retraction scheme that will allow its repeated use within a larger iterative improvement search framework.

Our starting point is the work of (Cesta, Oddi, & Smith 1998), which developed a procedure for generating feasible solutions to a more complex class of multi-capacity scheduling problem with maximum time lags. By customizing this procedure to exploit the simpler temporal structure of MCJSSP, we are able to produce a quite efficient (though less general) solution generator. To address MCJSSP's objective criteria of minimizing overall schedule makespan and define a scalable, optimizing procedure, we introduce a novel local-search framework called *iterative flattening*. The core solution generation procedure, which is designed to post precedence constraints between activities to reduce (or flatten) resource contention peaks, is first applied to produce an initial feasible solution. New contention peaks are then iteratively created and flattened by (1) retracting some subset of previously posted constraints along the current solution's critical path and (2) restarting the solution generator from this partially developed solution. Any time a lower makespan solution is produced during this iterative process, it becomes the new current solution.

The remainder of the paper is organized as follows. First, we define MCJSSP and a set of reference problems for experimental evaluation. We then describe and evaluate our core greedy search procedure for generating feasible solutions to MCJSSP instances. Next, we introduce our iterative flattening framework for extended local search using the core solution generator previously defined. Experimental results are given that demonstrate the efficacy of the approach across a range of problems of increasing scale. Finally, we briefly discuss opportunities for extending and enhancing the basic iterative flattening search concept.

MCJSSP and its Benchmarks

The Scheduling Problem. The Multi-Capacity Job-Shop Scheduling Problem (MCJSSP) involves synchronizing the use of a set of resources $R = \{r_1 \ldots r_m\}$ to perform a set of jobs $J = \{j_1 \ldots j_n\}$ over time. The processing of a job j_i requires the execution of a sequence of m activities $\{a_{i_1} \ldots a_{i_m}\}$, each a_{ij} has a constant processing time p_{ij} and requires the use of a single unit of resource $r_{a_{ij}}$ for its entire duration. Each resource r_j is required only once in a job and can process at most c_j activities at the same time ($c_j \geq 1$). A *feasible solution* to a MCJSSP is any temporally consistent assignment to the activities' start times which does not violate resource capacity constraints. An *optimal solution* is a feasible solution with minimal overall duration or makespan. Generally speaking, MCJSSP has the same structure as JSSP but involves multi-capacitated resources instead of unit-capacity resources.

Benchmarks. In (Nuijten & Aarts 1996) a method for creating challenging problems is proposed that starts from the JSSP benchmarks of (Lawrence 1984). The idea is to take each original JSSP problem, double (or triple) the capacity of each resource, and then duplicate (or triplicate) the activities of each job. Since all activities continue to require 1 unit of resource capacity, the result is a similarly structured MCJSSP.

We have used this procedure to obtain 80 MCJSSPs from Lawrence's 40 original problems: 40 problems with resources of capacity 2 and 40 with resources of capacity 3. The generated problems range in size from 100 to 900 activities. To organize the presentation of results we subdivide the 80 problems in 4 sets of 20 each:

Set A: LA1-10 x2 x3 (Lawrence's problems numbered 1 to 10, duplicated and triplicated). Using the notation #jobs × #resources (resource capacity), this set consists of 5 problems each of sizes 20x5(2), 30x5(3), 30x5(2), 45x5(3).

Set B: LA11-20 x2 x3. 5 problems each of sizes 40x5(2), 60x5(3), 20x10(2), 30x10(3).

SetC: LA21-30 x2 x3. 5 problems each of sizes 30x10(2), 45x10(3), 40x10(2), 60x10(3).

Set D: LA31-40 x2 x3. 5 problems each of sizes 60x10(2), 90x10(3), 30x15(2), 45x15(3).

Why have we chosen this benchmarks? From one side because in relatively few instances they cover a wide range of problem sizes; from the other because they also provide a direct basis for comparative evaluation. In fact, as noted in (Nuijten & Aarts 1996), one consequence of the problem generation method is that the optimal makespan for the original JSSP is also a tight upper bound for the corresponding MCJSSP. Hence, distance from these upper-bound solutions can provide one useful measure of solution quality.

The problems in set A and the smallest, 20x10 problems in set B have also been solved by (Nuijten & Aarts 1996), providing a further basis for calibrating and evaluating performance on the smaller problems. Nuijten's approach relies on a quite sophisticated set of resource propagation rules including edge-finding, and is well known for its strong performance on this problem subset. The goal of our current investigation is not to perform a competitive comparison with this work per se, but to instead develop a MCJSSP procedure that avoids the computational cost of sophisticated constraint analysis techniques and effectively scales to larger-scale problems such as those in Sets C and D.[1]

---

[1]For example, Nuijten's approach incorporates a family of propagation rules of different computational complexity. The most effective rule of his set is cubic in the number of activities on a resource, which becomes increasingly problematic as the number of activities increases. The decision step of the algorithm we present

A Greedy Algorithm for MCJSSP

As indicated earlier, our approach to designing a scalable heuristic procedure for solving MCJSSPs follows an iterative improvement schema. Our procedure is composed of two basic steps: (a) a greedy search algorithm is first applied to produce an initial feasible solution; (b) a local-search algorithm is then used to iteratively improve the quality of the current solution until a termination condition is met. In this section we first consider the core procedure for generating feasible solutions. In the next, we turn attention to the extended local search process.

Our greedy search algorithm is inspired by prior work on the Earliest Start Time Algorithm (ESTA), proposed originally in (Cesta, Oddi, & Smith 1998) and further refined in (Cesta, Oddi, & Smith 1999). ESTA was designed to address more general, multi-capacity scheduling problems with generalized precedence relations between activities (i.e., corresponding to metric separation constraints with minimum and maximum time lags). We briefly summarize the basic ideas that have been taken from this work, and then describe the modifications made to better address the MCJSSP domain.

Previous Profile-Based Work. ESTA is a variant of a class of profile-based scheduling procedures, characterized by a two-phase, solution generation process:

Construct an infinite capacity solution:
A constraint based representation of the current problem is formulated as an STP (Dechter, Meiri, & Pearl 1991) temporal constraint network.[2] In this initial representation temporal constraints are modeled and satisfied (via constraint propagation) but resource constraints are ignored, yielding a time feasible solution that assumes infinite resource capacity.

Level resource demand by posting precedence:
Resource constraints are super-imposed by projecting "resource demand profiles" over time. Detected resource conflicts are then resolved by iteratively posting simple precedence constraints between pairs of competing activities.

To perform the process of constraint posting ESTA follows a four step cycle:

(a) An ESS (for Earliest Start Solution) consistent with currently imposed temporal constraints is computed. This can be done quickly since the earliest start values of all nodes in any STP network are known to constitute a temporally feasible solution.

(b) Given the ESS, a *contention peak* is recognized on resource r_k at time t if condition $req_k(ESS, t) > c_k$ holds (with req_k being the sum of requirements of resource r_k at time t). Intuitively, a contention peak on resource r_k identifies a set of activities that simultaneously require r_k with a combined capacity requirement $> c_k$.

(c) For each peak, Minimal Critical Sets (MCSs) are computed. A *Minimal Critical Set* (MCS) specifies *a set of activities that simultaneously require a resource r_k with a combined capacity requirement $> c_k$, such that the combined requirement of any subset is $\leq c_k$*. The important advantage of isolating MCSs is that a single precedence relation between any pair of activities in the MCS eliminates the conflict. Since complete enumeration of MCSs is a combinatorial problem, a *sampling strategy* of fixed computational complexity (e.g., linear, quadratic in the number of activities) is proposed in (Cesta, Oddi, & Smith 1999) to collect some subset of MCSs in each peak.

(d) A single MCS is selected and resolved by posting a precedence constraint between two of the constituent activities. MCS selection (variable ordering) is performed according to the K estimator proposed in (Laborie & Ghallab 1995). The specific constraint to be posted (value ordering) is determined so as to preserve maximal temporal slack (in a style similar to that proposed in (Smith & Cheng 1993)).

Previous research has shown ESTA to be effective in overcoming efficiency problems that have plagued other profile-based scheduling procedures, while tending to better minimize the number of precedence constraints posted. As such, it seems a good starting point for building a heuristic approach to MCJSSP.

Adapting ESTA to MCJSSP. Though the basic ESTA procedure just described is directly applicable to MCJSSP, the simpler temporal structure of this problem domain suggests two adaptations in the interest of obtaining a computationally lighter procedure for initial solution generation.

A first change concerns the choice of how to sample MCSs. Previous point (c) performs MCS sampling on each peak detected in the current solution. Simplifying, we not only pay attention to non-redundancy in peak computation but also restrict MCS sampling to only the "maximal peaks", i.e., those peaks that contain the maximum number of activities. This choice is motivated by the observation that in the absence of maximal time lags the criticality of a given resource conflict is more clearly a function of its size.

A second change involves the propagation algorithms used to maintain consistency of the problem's temporal information. The solution of scheduling problems with generalized precedence relations require computation of the transitive closure of the STP representation of the current solution (Dechter, Meiri, & Pearl 1991). Computation of this information is fundamental, for example, for early detection and pruning of temporally infeasible search states. It is well known that such information is computable via all pairs shortest path algorithms, which are quadratic in space and cubic in time with regard to the number of temporal variables in the network. Unfortunately, as problem size increases, this computation tends to increasingly dominate overall solution time.

---

below is also cubic in the worst case. But within the local search framework we propose, this algorithm is executed from scratch only once, as opposed to repeatedly in Nuijten's case.

[2] In a STP (Simple Temporal Problem) network: temporal variables (nodes or time-points) represent beginning and end of activities and beginning and end of temporal horizon; distance constraints (edges) represent duration of activities and separation constraints including simple precedences.

```
ESTA_M(Problem)
1.  TCSP ← CreateCSP(Problem)
2.  loop
3.     Propagate(TCSP)
4.     ConflictSet ← ComputeResourceConflicts(TCSP)
5.     if Empty(ConflictSet)
6.     then return(ExtractSolution(TCSP))
7.     else
8.        if Unsolvable(ConflictSet)
9.        then return(EmptySolution)
10.       else
11.          Conflict ← SelectConflict(ConflictSet)
12.          PrecedenceConstraint
                   ← SelectPrecedence(Conflict)
13.          PostCostraint(TCSP, PrecedenceConstraint)
14.end-loop
15.end
```

Figure 1: Basic $ESTA_M$ Search Procedure

A second observation concerning MCJSSP helps in this case: in any MCJSSP all separation constraints between activities are simple precedence, and the only metric temporal constraints present are activity durations. This being the case, it is possible to detect infeasible orderings between pairs of activities using simpler, single source shortest path algorithms. In fact, temporal consistency can be maintained by a single source shortest path algorithm whose complexity instead depends on the number of edges (or temporal constraints) in the network. Because the STP network representing a scheduling problem is typically sparse (few edges, number of edges of the same order as number of nodes) this leads to a real advantage in terms of lightening the algorithm on problems of significant size.

One side-effect of this shift to a more efficient (but less informative) propagation algorithm is a simplification of the the K estimator computation utilized by the basic search algorithm, In particular, K is instead computed in terms of simple calculations of temporal slack (i.e., given a pair of activities a_i a_j, $slack(a_i, a_j)$ is defined as the difference between a_j's latest start time the and a_i's earliest finish time).

We refer to the procedure resulting from incorporation of the above changes as $ESTA_M$, where the suffix M indicates the modified version. A schematic view of $ESTA_M$ is given in Figure 1. In this formulation we have hidden details of the previous points (a)-(c) in Step 4, where ComputeResourceConflicts performs both peak detection on the ESS, and MCS sampling on the maximal peak.

Experimental Evaluation

In Table 1 we show the performance of $ESTA_M$ on the four benchmark problem sets. The algorithm is implemented in Allegro Common Lisp and the reported results are obtained on a SUN UltraSparc 30 (266MHz). For each algorithm and for each set we report $\Delta_{UB}\%$ (upper row), the average relative deviation from the known upper bound, and CPU_{sec} (lower row), the average CPU time in seconds. The column "All" gives the average values over all 80 problems. We also include the performance results obtained in (Nuijten & Aarts 1996) (the rows labelled CCA), which unfortunately are available only for set A and a few instances of set B.[3] But we note again that the upper-bound reference also provides a very good comparison value.

Observing the Table, two comments are appropriate: (a) it is not surprising that, compared with an algorithm like CCA aimed at finding a solution with an optimal makespan, a single run of $ESTA_M$ is generally not able to find an optimal solution. $ESTA_M$ does not contain any attempt at optimizing, but is designed to simply search for a feasible solution. The fact that it attempts to minimize the number of precedence constraints posted will at best contribute only indirectly to minimizing makespan; (b) Generally, $ESTA_M$ finds a solution quite efficiently, with resulting makespan that varies from 15 to 25% of the upper bound. In fact, the 758 seconds required on average for set D are due mostly to the 5 largest, 900 activity, problems which on average took over 2450 seconds to solve. These problems are characterized by huge peaks that require large numbers of precedence to be leveled. This is the only subset in which the time spent is really relevant.

Table 1: $ESTA_M$ vs. CCA

Algorithm	Set A	Set B	Set C	Set D	All
$ESTA_M$	17.91	16.04	25.27	24.83	21
	45	125	190	758	279
CCA	1.57	*	–	–	–
	369	*	–	–	–

Improving $ESTA_M$ by Local Search

Given an efficient procedure for generating feasible solutions to MCJSSP, the important remaining design issue concerns how to exploit it to perform an extended optimizing search. In both (Nuijten & Aarts 1996; Cesta, Oddi, & Smith 1999), an iterative sampling framework is used to provide a basis for optimization. However, in the interest of scalability we choose instead to emphasize a local search approach. The intuition is simply that computation of neighborhood solutions is likely to be more cost effective than solution regeneration. But this requires an effective approach to generating neighborhood solutions.

To describe our approach, we first introduce a few definitions. Assume that a given solution Sol to a MCJSSP produced by $ESTA_M$ is represented as a directed graph $G_S(A, E)$. A is the set of activities specified in MCJSSP, plus a fictitious a_{source} activity temporally constrained to occur before all others and a fictitious a_{sink} activity temporally constrained to occur after all others. E is the set of precedence constraints imposed between activities in A. E can be partitioned in two subsets, $E = E_{prob} \cup E_{post}$,

---

[3]Only the smallest 5 20x10 problems were solved (not enough for comparison on the whole set). The performance amounts to an average Δ of -0.84% and an average CPU of 591 seconds (i.e., very good solutions but with substantially increasing CPU times).

where E_{prob} is the set of precedence constraints originating in the problem definition, and E_{post} is the set of precedence constraints posted by ESTA$_M$ to resolve various resource conflicts. A *path* in $G_S(A, E)$ is a sequence of activities $a_1 \ldots a_k$, such that, $(a_i, a_{i+1}) \in E$ with $i = 1 \ldots (k - 1)$. The length of a path is the sum of the activities' processing times and a *critical path* is a path from a_{source} to a_{sink} which determines the solution's makespan.

As is well recognized in the scheduling literature, information about *critical paths* can provide a strong heuristic basis for makespan minimization. In the case of solutions generated by ESTA$_M$, any improvement in makespan will necessarily require retraction of some subset of precedence constraints situated on the *critical path*, since these constraints collectively determine the solution's current makespan. Following this observation, we propose a simple, two-step method for generating *moves* in the neighborhood of a given solution:

Shrinking Step: We first randomly retract a subset of precedence constraints $pc_i \in E_{post}$ which fall on the solution's *critical path*. In this way, the Earliest Start Solution is compressed and new peaks appear in the resource profiles.

Flattening Step: We then re-apply the ESTA$_M$ algorithm to level (or flatten) the newly introduced resource conflicts by posting new precedence constraints.

Because of the character of this local search cycle, we call the algorithm *iterative flattening* (i-FLAT).

From a performance standpoint, note that ESTA$_M$ is not applied from scratch (as is done on the initial problem formulation), but in an incremental way to a partially generated solution. In fact, the removal of a subset of precedence constraints generally creates both fewer and smaller peaks than the set of peaks contained in an initial infinite capacity solution. Additional efficiency gains are obtained through use of temporal reasoning techniques that support incremental retraction of precedence constraints $pc_i \in E_{post}$ (Cesta & Oddi 1996).

Figure 2 shows the *iterative flattening* algorithm in more detail. It takes as input three elements: (1) a starting solution Sol; (2) an integer number $P_{rem} \in 1..100$ designating the percentage of precedence constraints $pc_i \in E_{post}$ on the critical path to be removed at each execution of the basic move; and (3) a positive integer $MaxFail$ which specifies the maximum number of moves without an improvement in makespan that the algorithm will tolerate before terminating.

After initialization (Steps 1-2), within the While loop at Step 3, a solution is repeatedly modified by the application of the following subprocedures: SamplingCritical-Path is first applied to randomly select a set of previously posted precedence constraints on the solution critical path; RemovePrecedence then removes this set of constraints through application of incremental temporal reasoning algorithms; ESTA$_M$ is next invoked to find a new earliest start time solution. In the case that a better makespan solution is found (at Step 7), the new solution is stored in S_{best} and the counter is reset to 0 (Steps 9-10). Otherwise, if no improvement is found in $MaxFail$ moves, the algorithm terminates

i-FLAT(Sol,P_{rem},MaxFail)
1. $S_{best} \leftarrow Sol$
2. counter $\leftarrow 0$
3. **while** (counter $\leq$ MaxFail) **do begin**
4.   PrecedenceToRemove
      $\leftarrow$ SamplingCriticalPath(Sol,P_{rem})
5.   RemovePrecedence(Sol,PrecedenceToRemove)
6.   Sol$\leftarrow$ESTA$_M$(Sol)
7.   **if** Mk(Sol) < Mk(S_{best})
8.   **then begin**
9. $S_{best} \leftarrow$ Sol
10.   counter $\leftarrow 0$
11.   **end**
12.   **else** counter $\leftarrow$ counter + 1
13. **end-while**
14. **return**(S_{best})
15. **end**

Figure 2: The *Iterative Flattening* Algorithm

Table 2: i-FLAT Performance

Algorithm	Set A	Set B	Set C	Set D	All
ESTA$_M$	17.91	16.04	25.27	24.83	21
	45	125	190	758	279
i-FLAT(E+1)	8.99	8.29	14.61	12.22	11
	60	161	286	1199	426
i-FLAT(E+5)	7.76	7.10	13.03	11.92	9.95
	124	329	657	1875	746

and returns the best solution found.

Experimental Results

Table 2 shows the performance of i-FLAT on the benchmark problem set. For this set of experiments, P_{rem} was set to 10% and $MaxFail$ to 300. The version of ESTA$_M$ used within i-FLAT is the same as the basic version. We report results for basic ESTA$_M$, for i-FLAT starting from the solution produced by ESTA$_M$ (row labeled i-FLAT(E+1)), and for an extended execution of i-FLAT (row i-FLAT(E+5)) that will be explained below. CPU times reported for the i-FLAT rows include the initial execution of ESTA$_M$, giving the total time taken by the algorithm to produce its best solution.

Two observations are immediate: (a) the time spent by ESTA$_M$ in generating an initial solution dominates the time spent improving it by the iterative i-FLAT process across all problem sets (e.g., 45 seconds versus 15 seconds in the case of Set A); (b) the improvement of ESTA$_M$'s initial solution by i-FLAT is rather significant (lowering an average deviation of 21% to 11%).

It should be noted that i-FLAT currently performs a relatively undirected search (basically a random walk) and there appear several opportunities for further empowering the local search strategy (see concluding discussion below). Here, we consider an alternative approach to improving experimental performance, by simply restarting i-FLAT multiple times from the same ESTA$_M$ solution. This approach is justified by the random step `SamplingCriticalPath`, which guarantees different execution on different restarts. Table 2 shows the results obtained with 5 random restarts of i-FLAT (labeled i-FLAT(E+5)). In this case, performance is improved on all four problem sets and the overall average deviation is lowered below 10%.

Finally, a comment concerning comparison with Nuijten's work. The performance of the two i-FLAT configurations on Set A should be seen as quite positive in relation to the results obtained by the CCA algorithm. If we consider the relatively simple steps that i-FLAT executes in contrast to the rather sophisticated resource propagation rule that is coupled with random restarting in the CCA approach, the difference in deviation of about 6% is quite respectable. If we consider further that i-FLAT's deviation from upper-bound solutions does not worsen substantially with increasing problem scale, and that CCA scalability (particularly with use of the most effective propagation rules) is an open issue, then the results obtained with i-FLAT assume even greater significance.

Conclusions and Future Work

This paper has presented a new iterative improvement technique, called *iterative flattening* for solving large-scale multi-capacity scheduling problems.

Several aspects of this algorithm are worth underscoring. First, the algorithm provides a novel, local search model that integrates naturally with typical constraint-guided schedule generation methods and heuristics. Second, the algorithm is quite general and is applicable not only to the MCJSSP, but also to problems such as resource constrained project scheduling where activities require multiple resources and/or resource capacity of varying amounts. Finally, the algorithm has be shown to scale effectively to large-scale problem instances of the MCJSSP, creating a reference point (being within 10% of computed upper bounds) for other approaches on a rich set of benchmark problems.

The basic concept of iterative flattening presented in this paper is very general, and many possibilities of performance enhancement through incorporation of more sophisticated and better informed local-search procedures appear possible. Among the directions we are considering for future work are the following: examination of different precedence constraint retraction strategies; enrichment of the basic random search with standard concepts such as neighborhood analysis or a taboo-list; and, more generally, the insertion of iterative flattening within a *meta* local search strategy (e.g., (Nowicki & Smutnicki 1996) for the classical JSSP).

References

Baptiste, P., and Le Pape, C. 1995. A Theoretical and Experimental Comparison of Constraint Propagation Techniques for Disjunctive Scheduling. In *Proceedings of the 14th Int. Joint Conference on Artificial Intelligence*.

Baptiste, P.; Le Pape, C.; and Nuijten, W. 1997. Satifiability Tests and Time-Bound Adjustments for Cumulative Scheduling Problems. Technical report, University of Compiégnie. to appear in *Annals of Operations Research*.

Beck, J., and Fox, M. 1999. Scheduling Alternative Activities. In *Proceedings 16th National Conference on AI (AAAI-99)*.

Bresina, J. 1996. Heuristic-biased Stochastic Sampling. In *Proceedings 13th National Conference on AI (AAAI-96)*.

Cesta, A., and Oddi, A. 1996. Gaining Efficiency and Flexibility in the Simple Temporal Problem. In *Proceedings of the Third International Workshop on Temporal Representation and Reasoning (TIME-96)*.

Cesta, A.; Oddi, A.; and Smith, S. 1998. Profile Based Algorithms to Solve Multiple Capacitated Metric Scheduling Problems. In *Proceedings of the 4th Int. Conf. on Artificial Intelligence Planning Systems (AIPS-98)*.

Cesta, A.; Oddi, A.; and Smith, S. 1999. An Iterative Sampling Procedure for Resource Constrained Project Scheduling with Time Windows. In *Proceedings of the 16th Int. Joint Conference on Artificial Intelligence (IJCAI-99)*.

Crawford, J. 1996. An Approach to Resource Constrained Project Scheduling. In *Proceedings of the 1996 Artificial Intelligence and Manufacturing Research Planning Workshop*.

Dechter, R.; Meiri, I.; and Pearl, J. 1991. Temporal Constraint Networks. *Artificial Intelligence* 49:61–95.

Harvey, W., and Ginsberg, M. 1995. Limited Discrepancy Search. In *Proceedings of the 14th Int. Joint Conference on Artificial Intelligence (IJCAI-95)*.

Laborie, P., and Ghallab, M. 1995. Planning with Sharable Resource Constraints. In *Proceedings of the 14th Int. Joint Conference on Artificial Intelligence (IJCAI-95)*.

Lawrence, S. 1984. Resource Constrained Project Scheduling: An Experimental Investigation of Heuristic Scheduling Techniques (Supplement). Technical report, Graduate School of Industrial Administration, Carnegie Mellon University.

Nowicki, E., and Smutnicki, C. 1996. A Fast Taboo Search Algorithm for the Job Shop Problem. *Management Science* 42:797–813.

Nuijten, W., and Aarts, E. 1996. A Computational Study of Constraint Satisfaction for Multiple Capacitated Job Shop Scheduling. *European Journal of Operational Research* 90(2):269–284.

Nuijten, W. 1994. *Time and Resource Constrained Scheduling - A Constraint Satisfaction Approach*. Ph.D. Dissertation, Eindhoven University of Technology, The Netherlands.

Oddi, A., and Smith, S. 1997. Stochastic Procedures for Generating Feasible Schedules. In *Proceedings 14th National Conference on AI (AAAI-97)*.

Smith, S., and Cheng, C. 1993. Slack-Based Heuristics for Constraint Satisfaction Scheduling. In *Proceedings 11th National Conference on AI (AAAI-93)*.

Zweben, M.; Duan, B.; Davis, E.; and Deale, M. 1994. Scheduling and Rescheduling with Iterative Repair. In Zweben, M., and Fox, S. M., eds., *Intelligent Scheduling*. Morgan Kaufmann.

Planning as Satisfiability in Nondeterministic Domains

Paolo Ferraris and Enrico Giunchiglia

DIST — Università di Genova
Viale Causa 13, 16145 Genova, Italy
{otto,enrico}@dist.unige.it

Abstract

We focus on planning as satisfiability in simple nondeterministic domains. By "simple" we mean specified in a simple extension to the STRIPS formalism allowing for specifying actions with nondeterministic effects. This allows us to simplify and extend the theory presented in (Giunchiglia 2000). The result is a planning system which, in simple nondeterministic domains, is competitive with other state-of-the-art planners.

Introduction

Planning as satisfiability (Kautz & Selman 1992) has emerged as one of the most effective approaches to classical planning. Complex problems with 100 actions can be solved in minutes by the latest SAT-based planning system Blackbox (Kautz & Selman 1998). However, the applicability of the SAT-based approach to planning has been confined to classical problems, i.e., to planning domains in which both the effects of actions and the initial state are completely specified. Recently (Giunchiglia 2000), the second author has presented a SAT-based procedure for planning in $\mathcal{C}$ action descriptions (Giunchiglia & Lifschitz 1998) with incompletely specified initial state. The action language $\mathcal{C}$ —among other expressive capabilities— allows to specify domains with concurrent actions, constraints, and nondeterminism.

In this paper we focus on planning as satisfiability in simple nondeterministic domains. By "simple" we mean specified in a simple extension to the STRIPS formalism allowing for specifying actions with nondeterministic effects. This allows us to simplify and extend the encodings and the procedures presented in (Giunchiglia 2000).

About the encodings, we show that various encodings are possible, differing for the action representation ("regular" or "simple-split") and/or planning strategy ("sequential" or "parallel"), see, e.g., (Kautz & Selman 1996; Kautz, McAllester, & Selman 1997; Ernst, Millstein, & Weld 1997) for the corresponding notions in the classical case. These encodings can be automatically generated in polynomial time starting from the initial action description.

Copyright © 2000, American Association for Artificial Intelligence (www.aaai.org). All rights reserved.

About the procedures, we adopt some simple heuristics like the "split on action first" idea from (Giunchiglia, Massarotto, & Sebastiani 1998). We also write down some simple clauses ruling out useless branches from the search space.

The result is a planning system which, in simple nondeterministic domains, is competitive with other state-of-the-art planners.

STRIPS + Nondeterminism

Traditionally, the description of an action in STRIPS consists of the specification of its preconditions and effects as sets of fluent literals. For an action with nondeterministic effects, we specify its possible effects as a set whose elements are sets of fluent literals. Thus, an action A is described using the following notation

$$A \quad \begin{array}{ll} \text{pre}: & P; \\ \text{d-eff}: & E; \\ \text{i-eff}: & N_1, \ldots, N_n; \end{array} \quad (1)$$

($n \geq 1$) in which $\{P\}, \{E\}, N_1, \ldots, N_n$ are finite sets of fluent literals. Intuitively, P represents the preconditions for the action, E lists its determinate effects, while each N_i represent one of the possible indeterminate outcomes for the action. When $\{P\} = \{\}$, or $\{E\} = \{\}$, or $n = 1$ and $N_1 = \{\}$ (corresponding to an action with no preconditions, or no determinate effects or no indeterminate effects) we omit the corresponding field from the specification of A. In the following, we write $pre(A)$, $d\text{-}eff(A)$, and $i\text{-}eff(A)$ to denote respectively the sets $\{P\}$, $\{E\}$, and $\{N_1, \ldots, N_n\}$ respectively. We further assume that for any action A, the sets in $i\text{-}eff(A)$ are consistent with $d\text{-}eff(A)$, i.e., that for any set N in $i\text{-}eff(A)$, it is not the case that the set $N \cup d\text{-}eff(A)$ is inconsistent.

A finite set of actions' specifications is an *action description*. The semantics of an action description can be described in terms of a labeled transition system:

- A *state* is a maximally consistent set of fluent literals, and
- there is a *transition from a state* σ *to a state* σ' *with label* A iff A is an action,

1. $pre(A) \subseteq \sigma$,
2. $\sigma' = (\sigma \cap \sigma') \cup \Gamma$, where Γ is the union of $d\text{-}eff(A)$ with *some* of the sets in $i\text{-}eff(A)$.

The first condition states when A is executable. The second condition says that a fluent keeps its value unless affected either by $d\text{-}eff(A)$ or $i\text{-}eff(A)$.

Action descriptions describe what are the effects of executing actions. Consider for example the following elaboration of the "bomb in the toilet" problem from (Mcdermott 1987). There is a finite set P of packages and a finite set T of toilets. In this section, we assume that there are two packages P_1 and P_2 and one toilet T_1. One of the packages is armed because it contains a bomb. Dunking a package in a toilet disarm the package, but may clog the toilet. Dunking a package in a toilet is possible only if the toilet is not clogged and the package has been not previously dunked. Flushing clears a toilet. This scenario is described by the following action description, in which p and t are metavariables ranging over the sets P and T respectively:

$$\begin{aligned}Dunk(p,t)\quad &\text{pre}: &&\neg Clogged(t), \neg Dunked(p);\\ &\text{d-eff}: &&\neg Armed(p), Dunked(p);\\ &\text{i-eff}: &&\{Clogged(t)\}, \{\};\end{aligned} \quad (2)$$

$$Flush(t)\quad \text{d-eff}: \quad \neg Clogged(t);$$

According to the indeterminate effects of dunking, the toilet will become clogged, or nothing will happen.

In order to specify a planning problem, we need to specify an action description D, but also which are the initial and goal states of D: the task is to determine a "valid plan", i.e., a finite sequence of actions which is "always executable" and such that any of its "possible outcomes" is a goal state.

Formally, a *planning problem* is a triple $\langle I, D, G \rangle$, in which D is an action description while I and G are two fluent formulas. A state σ of D is *initial* [resp. *goal*] if σ satisfies I [resp. G].[1] Thus, for the "bomb in the toilet", the planning problem in which initially one of the packages is armed and the toilet is clear; and with goal to disarm all packages, can be specified by the triple:

$$\langle (Armed(P_1) \equiv \neg Armed(P_2)) \wedge \neg Clogged(T_1),\\ (2), \neg Armed(P_1) \wedge \neg Armed(P_2) \rangle. \quad (3)$$

A *plan* is a finite sequence of actions.
Consider a planning problem $\langle I, D, G \rangle$.
A *history* is a path in the transition diagram of D, that is, a finite sequence

$$\sigma^0, A^1, \sigma^1, \ldots, A^n, \sigma^n \quad (4)$$

($n \geq 0$) such that $\sigma^0, \sigma^1, \ldots, \sigma^n$ are states; $A^1, \ldots, A^n$ are actions; and, for each $i \in \{i, \ldots, n\}$, D has a transition from σ^{i-1} to σ^i with label A^i.

A plan $A^1; \ldots; A^n$ ($n \geq 0$) is *possible* for $\langle I, D, G \rangle$ if there exists a history (4) such that σ^0 is an initial state, and σ^n is a goal state. Notice that —unless the action description is deterministic and there is only one initial state— a possible plan is not ensured to achieve the goal. For example, considering the planning problem (3), the plans $Dunk(P_1, T_1)$ and $Dunk(P_1, T_1); Dunk(P_2, T_1)$ are

---

[1]We say that a state σ satisfies a fluent formula F if $\sigma \cup \{F\}$ is consistent.

both possible. However, intuitively none is valid: the first does not achieve the goal if the bomb is in P_2, while the second is not executable if dunking P_1 clogs the toilet.

An action A is *executable in a state* σ if D has a transition from σ to a state σ' with label A. Let σ^0 be a state. A plan $A^1; \ldots; A^n$ is *always executable in* σ^0 if for any history

$$\sigma^0, A^1, \sigma^1, \ldots, A^k, \sigma^k$$

with $k < n$, A^{k+1} is executable in σ^k. A state σ^n is a *possible result of executing a plan* $A^1; \ldots; A^n$ in σ^0 if there exists a history (4) for D.

A plan $A^1; \ldots; A^n$ is *valid* if for any initial state σ^0,
- $A^1; \ldots; A^n$ is always executable in σ^0, and
- any possible result of executing $A^1; \ldots; A^n$ in σ^0 is a goal state.

Indeed, the plan $Dunk(P_1, T_1); Flush(T_1); Dunk(P_2, T_1)$ is valid for the planning problem (3). Notice that if we assume that flushing is possible only when the toilet is clogged, no valid plan exists for (3).

Encoding possible plans

As in the classical case, various types of encodings are possible. Here we restrict to the generalization of the encodings:

- Explanatory-Regular-Parallel (ERP),
- Explanatory-Regular-Sequential (ERS), and
- Explanatory-simple-Split-Sequential (ESS),

i.e., the ones that experimentally proved to lead to the best computational results in the classical case (see, e.g., (Ernst, Millstein, & Weld 1997; Giunchiglia, Massarotto, & Sebastiani 1998)).

Consider an action description D. In the ERP encodings, for each time point i, we have the following formulas (when we consider the action description (2), p, p' and t, t' are metavariables ranging over P and T respectively):

- an action A executed at time i implies that its preconditions and determinate effects are true at time i and $i+1$ respectively:

$$A_i \supset (\bigwedge_{L \in pre(A)} L_i \wedge \bigwedge_{L \in d\text{-}eff(A)} L_{i+1}).$$

In the case of (2), we have:

$$Dunk_i(p, t) \supset \neg Clogged_i(t) \wedge \neg Dunked_i(p)\\ \wedge \neg Armed_{i+1}(p) \wedge Dunked_{i+1}(p),\\ Flush_i(t) \supset \neg Clogged_{i+1}(t).$$

- An action A executed at time i implies that some of its indeterminate effects are true at time $i+1$:

$$A_i \supset \bigvee_{N \in i\text{-}eff(A)} \bigwedge_{L \in N} L_{i+1}.$$

In the case of (2), the corresponding formulas are tautologies.

- If a fluent literal L becomes true at time $i+1$, then an action A affecting it either through its determinate or indeterminate effects must have been executed at time i:

- If $L \in \textit{d-eff}(A)$ then it is enough to impose that A has been executed at time i,
- If $L \in N \in \textit{i-eff}(A)$ then we have to impose that A has been executed at time i but also that all the literals in N are true at time $i + 1$.

In a formula:
$$L_{i+1} \wedge \neg L_i \supset \bigvee\nolimits_{A: L \in \textit{d-eff}(A)} A_i$$
$$\vee \bigvee\nolimits_A \bigvee\nolimits_{N: N \in \textit{i-eff}(A), L \in N} (A_i \wedge \bigwedge\nolimits_{L': L' \in N} L'_{i+1}).$$

In the case of (2), we get formulas equivalent to:
$$\neg \textit{Armed}_{i+1}(p) \wedge \textit{Armed}_i(p) \supset \bigvee\nolimits_{t \in T} \textit{Dunk}_i(p, t),$$
$$\neg \textit{Armed}_i(p) \supset \neg \textit{Armed}_{i+1}(p),$$
$$\neg \textit{Clogged}_{i+1}(t) \wedge \textit{Clogged}_i(t) \supset \textit{Flush}_i(t),$$
$$\textit{Clogged}_{i+1}(t) \wedge \neg \textit{Clogged}_i(t) \supset \bigvee\nolimits_{p \in P} \textit{Dunk}_i(p, t),$$
$$\textit{Dunked}_{i+1}(p) \wedge \neg \textit{Dunked}_i(p) \supset \bigvee\nolimits_{t \in T} \textit{Dunk}_i(p, t),$$
$$\textit{Dunked}_i(p) \supset \textit{Dunked}_{i+1}(p).$$

- Two distinct actions A and B cannot be executed at time i if they are mutex:
$$\neg(A_i \wedge B_i). \quad (5)$$

For the ERP encodings, A and B are *mutex* if the effects of A contradicts with the possible effects or the preconditions of B; or the other way around. More formally, if there exists two sets $N \in \textit{i-eff}(A)$ and $N' \in \textit{i-eff}(B)$ such that $\textit{d-eff}(A) \cup N \cup \textit{pre}(B) \cup N'$ or $\textit{pre}(A) \cup N \cup \textit{d-eff}(B) \cup N'$ are contradictory. In the case of (2), this imposes
$$\neg(\textit{Dunk}_i(p, t) \wedge \textit{Flush}_i(t)),$$
$$\neg(\textit{Dunk}_i(p, t) \wedge \textit{Dunk}_i(p', t)) \quad p \neq p',$$

and, in the case there is one more than one toilet, also
$$\neg(\textit{Dunk}_i(p, t) \wedge \textit{Dunk}_i(p, t')) \quad t \neq t'.$$

In the ERS and ESS encodings, any two distinct actions A and B are considered to be mutex. As a matter of fact, the ERS encodings are as the ERP, except that we have (5) for any two distinct actions A and B. The ESS encodings are obtained from the ERS encodings by substituting each action
$$\textit{ActionPred}_i(\textit{Arg}_1, \ldots, \textit{Arg}_n)$$
with the conjunction
$$(\textit{ActionPred}_i\_\textit{Arg}_1 \wedge \ldots \wedge \textit{ActionPred}_i\_\textit{Arg}_n)$$
(see, e.g., (Kautz, McAllester, & Selman 1997; Ernst, Millstein, & Weld 1997)). Thus, in our example, we substitute $\textit{Dunk}_i(p, t)$ with $\textit{Dunk\_pkg}_i(p) \wedge \textit{Dunk\_into}_i(t)$. Factorization techniques analogous to those described in (Ernst, Millstein, & Weld 1997) for the classical case, allow to simplify/eliminate some of the clauses. For example, we have the clauses corresponding to, e.g.,
$$\textit{Dunk\_pkg}_i(p) \supset \neg \textit{Dunked}_i(p)$$
instead of those corresponding to
$$\textit{Dunk\_pkg}_i(p) \wedge \textit{Dunk\_into}_i(t) \supset \neg \textit{Dunked}_i(p).$$

It is not difficult to see that, if actions do not have indeterminate effects, each of the above encodings boils down to the corresponding encoding proposed in the classical setting. Let tr_i^D be the conjunction of the above formulas for the particular encoding chosen. Consider a planning problem $\langle I, D, G \rangle$. For each number $n \geq 0$, each assignment[2] μ satisfying
$$I_0 \wedge \bigwedge_{i=0}^{n-1} tr_i^D \wedge G_n \quad (6)$$
corresponds to a possible plan:

- In the case of the ERS encodings, we have that for each $i \in \{0, \ldots, n-1\}$ at most one action variable A_i is assigned to true by μ: this guarantees a totally ordered plan. Analogously for the ESS encodings.
- In the case of the ERP encodings, for each $i \in \{0, \ldots, n-1\}$ more than one action variable A_i may be assigned to true by μ. This results in a partially ordered set of actions. However, any total order consistent with the partial order corresponds to a possible plan. We can choose to lexicographically order any initially unordered pair of actions.

Computing valid plans

Consider a planning problem $\langle I, D, G \rangle$. Let μ be an assignment satisfying (6). Let $act(\mu)$ be the conjunction of the literals in μ corresponding to actions. Let $plan(\mu)$ be the possible plan corresponding to μ.

In order to determine whether $plan(\mu)$ is valid, the fundamental observation is that if each action is executable in any state, $plan(\mu)$ is valid iff
$$act(\mu) \wedge I_0 \wedge \bigwedge_{i=0}^{n-1} tr_i^D \models G_n.$$

On the basis of this observation, our next step is to define a new propositional formula trt_i^D which intuitively represents the transition relation of an automaton Σ

- whose states are doubled (wrt the automaton corresponding to D) by introducing a new fluent symbol Z, and
- whose transitions are labeled with the actions of D and are such that there is a transition from a state σ to a state σ' with label A if and only if
  - σ and σ' satisfy $\neg Z$ and D has a transition from σ_D to σ'_D with label A, or
  - σ satisfies $\neg Z$, σ' satisfies Z and A is not executable in σ_D, or
  - σ and σ' satisfy Z,

where σ_D is the restriction of σ to the fluent signature of D (and similarly for σ'_D).

Thus in Σ any action is "executable" in any state; and (4) is a history of D iff
$$\sigma^0 \cup \{\neg Z\}, A^1, \sigma^1 \cup \{\neg Z\}, \ldots, A^n, \sigma^n \cup \{\neg Z\}$$

---

[2] An *assignment* is a set of literals. An assignment μ *satisfies* a formula P if (i) μ is a maximally consistent set of the literals in P, and (ii) $\mu \cup \{P\}$ is consistent.

is a path of Σ.

Let $Poss_i^D$ be the conjunction of the formulas

$$(A_i \supset \bigwedge_{P \in pre(A)} P_i) \tag{7}$$

over all actions A of D. Intuitively, the formula $Poss_i^D$ says which action is executable in which state at time i. As in (Giunchiglia 2000), we define trt_i^D to be the formula

$$(tr_i^D \wedge \neg Z_i \wedge \neg Z_{i+1}) \vee ((Z_i \vee \neg Poss_i^D) \wedge Z_{i+1}),$$

where Z is a newly introduced fluent symbol. It is not difficult to prove that the above itemized properties hold.

From the above, we have that $plan(\mu)$ is valid iff

$$act(\mu) \wedge I_0 \wedge \neg Z_0 \wedge \bigwedge_{i=0}^{n-1} trt_i^D \models G_n \wedge \neg Z_n. \tag{8}$$

Thus, we can

- *generate* possible plans by finding assignments μ satisfying (6), and
- *test* whether the $plan(\mu)$ is valid by checking whether (8) holds.

This is the idea behind the procedure represented in Figure 1, stated correct and complete in the case of planning problems whose action description is written in $\mathcal{C}$ (Giunchiglia & Lifschitz 1998). Notice that in (Giunchiglia 2000), $Poss_i^D$ is defined as the formula

$$\exists p^1 \ldots \exists p^n tr_i^D [P_{i+1}^1/p^1, \ldots, P_{i+1}^n/p^n] \tag{9}$$

where $P^1, \ldots, P^n$ are all the fluent symbols in D, and $tr_i^D[P_{i+1}^1/p^1, \ldots, P_{i+1}^n/p^n]$ denotes the formula obtained from tr_i^D by substituting each fluent P_{i+1}^k with a distinct propositional variable p^k.

(7) and (9) are not equivalent: (9) entails (7) but not viceversa. However (for the ERP and ERS encodings, and similarly for the ESS), if we add to (7) a conjunct $\neg(A_i \wedge B_i)$ for each pair of actions A and B

- which are mutex, or
- in the case of ERP encodings, such that $d\text{-}eff(A) \cup d\text{-}eff(B)$ is contradictory,

the two formulas become equivalent. These additional conjuncts are not needed for (8) to hold. In fact, in (8), μ is an assignment satisfying (6): as a consequence, $act(\mu)$ entails such additional conjuncts. Notice that, from a computational point of view, computing a propositional formula equivalent to (9) may require an exponential space.

Consider Figure 1. First notice the loop in PLAN_TEST: this takes into account that the assignments generated by PLAN_GEN$_{DP}$ may be partial. Then, notice that the procedure PLAN_GEN$_{DP}$ is essentially the Davis Putnam (DP) procedure (Davis & Putnam 1960; Davis, Longemann, & Loveland 1962) modulo the call to PLAN_TEST whenever it finds an assignment satisfying the input formula. Because of this, we can use any state-of-the-art SAT solvers *almost* as a blackbox. Indeed, we need to modify the source code to

$P := I_0 \wedge \bigwedge_{i=0}^{n-1} tr_i^D \wedge G_n;$
$V := I_0 \wedge \neg Z_0 \wedge \bigwedge_{i=0}^{n-1} trt_i^D \wedge \neg(G_n \wedge \neg Z_n);$
function PLAN() **return** PLAN_GEN$_{DP}$($cnf(P)$, {}).

function PLAN_GEN$_{DP}$(φ, μ)
  if $\varphi = \{\}$ **then return** PLAN_TEST(μ);
  if $\{\} \in \varphi$ **then return** *False*;
  if { a unit clause $\{L\}$ occurs in φ } **then**
    return PLAN_GEN$_{DP}$($assign(L, \varphi), \mu \cup \{L\}$);
  $A := \{$ an atom occurring in φ };
  return PLAN_GEN$_{DP}$($assign(A, \varphi), \mu \cup \{A\}$) **or**
       PLAN_GEN$_{DP}$($assign(\neg A, \varphi), \mu \cup \{\neg A\}$).

function PLAN_TEST(μ)
  foreach {assignment μ' s.t. $\mu \subseteq \mu'$}
    if not SAT($act(\mu') \wedge V$) **then exit with** $plan(\mu')$;
  return *False*.

Figure 1: PLAN and PLAN_GEN$_{DP}$

perform the above mentioned call to PLAN_TEST, and —if implemented— we need to rule out also the pure-literal rule (see, e.g., (Giunchiglia *et al.* 1998) for more details). Such modifications have been carried out on various state-of-the-art SAT solvers, like Bohm's solver (see (Giunchiglia *et al.* 1998)), Zhang's SATO (see (Giunchiglia & Tacchella 2000)), and Bayardo' and Schrag's REL_SAT (see (Wolfman & Weld 1999)).

Heuristics

The procedure PLAN is essentially a "generate and test" procedure. As such, care must be taken in order to avoid the generation of useless cases. To this extent, we have devised the heuristics described in the following paragraphs (here we consider only regular encodings: analogous considerations hold for ESS encodings).[3]

Split on actions first: in PLAN_GEN$_{DP}$, when choosing the atom A, we first give preference to variables corresponding to actions. Splitting on action variables has proven to be a very effective heuristics in the classical case (see (Giunchiglia, Massarotto, & Sebastiani 1998)). In our setting, this imposes that —in PLAN_GEN$_{DP}$ search tree— branching nodes corresponding to fluent variables occur only at the bottom. Given an assignment corresponding to a possible plan which fails the validity test, it is easy to modify PLAN_GEN$_{DP}$ in order to incorporate a simple backjumping schema to the latest assigned action variable. The combined result is that a possible plan will be generated and then tested for validity at most once.

For any two actions A and B such that some of B's preconditions contradict some of the indirect effects of A, we add to (6) the clause

$$\neg A_i \vee \neg B_{i+1},$$

---

[3]We use the term "heuristics" since they are meant to improve the performances "on the average". It is indeed the case that on some problem, better performances can be obtained by turning some heuristic off. However, in our experience, in most cases this does not happen.

for each $i < n$. In fact, any possible plan corresponding to an assignment which violates the above clause, will fail the validity test. In the case of (2), this allows to add the clauses

$$\neg Dunk_i(p,t) \vee \neg Dunk_{i+1}(p',t),$$

for any two packages p and p' and $i < n$.

For each action A such that $pre(A) \cup d\text{-}eff(A)$ is consistent, we can add to (6)

$$\neg A_i \vee \neg A_{i+1},$$

for each $i < n$. In fact, for any such action A, if $A_1, \ldots, A, A, \ldots, A_n$ is a valid plan, then also $A_1, \ldots, A, \ldots, A_n$ is valid. In the case of (2), this implies that

$$\neg Flush_i(t) \vee \neg Flush_{i+1}(t)$$

can be safely added, for any toilet t and $i < n$.

For each time step $i < n-1$, we can assume that if we do not execute any action at i, then we will not execute any action at $i+1$. For (2), if Act is the whole set of actions in the domain, this would imply adding the clauses corresponding to

$$\bigwedge_{A \in Act} \neg A_i \supset \bigwedge_{A \in Act} \neg A_{i+1}.$$

For the bomb-in-the-toilet problem, we will have $|P| \times |T| + |T|$ clauses, each with $|P| \times |T| + |T| + 1$ disjuncts. In order not to have so many long clauses, we introduce the action $NoOp$, and write the clauses

$$\bigvee_{p \in P, t \in T} Dunk_i(p,t) \vee \bigvee_{t \in T} Flush_i(t) \vee NoOp_i,$$

$$NoOp_i \supset NoOp_{i+1},$$

and the $|P| \times |T| + |T|$ binary clauses corresponding to

$$NoOp_i \supset \bigwedge_{p \in P, t \in T} \neg Dunk_i(p,t) \wedge \bigwedge_{t \in T} \neg Flush_i(t).$$

Finally, if we have already checked the non existence of valid plans of length k, when looking for valid plans of length $n > k$, we can restrict our search for possible plans which falsify the goal at step k. In the case of (2), if the goal is to disarm all the packages, we add the clause:

$$\bigvee_{p \in P} Armed_k(p).$$

Even though not necessary (because entailed) we also add the unit clause $\neg NoOp_k$.

Experimental analysis

We have developed $\mathcal{C}$-PLAN, a system implementing the above procedures on top of *SAT (Giunchiglia & Tacchella 2000). For a high-level description of $\mathcal{C}$-PLAN, see (Giunchiglia 2000). Here, it suffices to say that $\mathcal{C}$-PLAN accepts $\mathcal{C}$ action descriptions written in CCALC[4], and that

---

[4]For CCALC, see http://www.cs.utexas.edu/users/tag/cc.

$|P|$-$|T|$	CGP #s	CGP CPU	ERP #s	ERP CPU	ERS #s	ERS CPU	ESS #s	ESS CPU
2-1	3	0.01	3	0.00	3	0.00	3	0.00
3-1	5	0.02	5	0.01	5	0.00	5	0.01
4-1	7	0.07	7	0.01	7	0.01	7	0.02
5-1	9	0.27	9	0.03	9	0.04	9	0.04
6-1	11	1.36	11	0.06	11	0.06	11	0.08
2-2	1	0.01	1	0.00	2	0.01	2	0.00
3-2	3	0.01	3	0.01	4	0.02	4	0.01
4-2	3	0.04	3	0.03	6	0.07	6	0.03
5-2	5	0.52	5	0.06	8	0.16	8	0.13
6-2	5	1.26	5	0.10	10	0.32	10	3.20
2-3	1	0.00	1	0.00	2	0.01	2	0.00
3-3	1	0.01	1	0.01	3	0.05	3	0.04
4-3	3	0.07	3	0.04	5	0.20	5	0.06
5-3	3	0.16	3	0.07	7	0.50	7	0.08
6-3	3	0.35	3	0.17	9	1.11	9	0.14

Table 1: Deterministic actions, multiple initial states

in our tests we have looked for plans of increasing length starting from $n = 1$.

To test $\mathcal{C}$-PLAN effectiveness, we have compared it with CGP (Smith & Weld 1998). CGP has been compiled and run using Allegro Common Lisp Trial Edition 5.0.1. $\mathcal{C}$-PLAN is written in C and has been compiled with gcc -O2. The testing machine has been an Intel PC PII350MHz with 256MbRAM, running SUSE Linux 6.2. Since CGP only deals with nondeterminism in the initial state, we have modified (2) in such a way that dunking a package always clogs the toilet. Initially only one package is armed, the toilets are not clogged, and the goal is to disarm all the packages. As in (Smith & Weld 1998), we (i) have considered problems having from 2 to 6 packages, and from 1 to 3 toilets, and (ii) have assumed that flushing is possible only if the toilet is clogged. For $\mathcal{C}$-PLAN, we have tested its performances using the three encodings ERP, ERS and ESS described previously.

Table 1 shows the results. For CGP, we report the number of levels and the CPU time needed (excluding the time taken by the garbage collector). For each of three encodings used to test $\mathcal{C}$-PLAN, we report the number of steps needed, and the CPU time needed by $\mathcal{C}$-PLAN for the last step. CPU times are in seconds, and repeating the runs produces very similar results.

Consider Table 1. As it can be observed, $\mathcal{C}$-PLAN is competitive with CGP, which experimentally proved to outperform previous planners for nondeterministic domains (like BURIDAN (Kushmerick, Hanks, & Weld 1995) and UDT-POP (Peot 1998)) by orders of magnitude (see (Smith & Weld 1998) for details). Comparing the performances of $\mathcal{C}$-PLAN on the different encodings, we see that ERP leads to the fewest steps and best performances.

In order to evaluate the performances of $\mathcal{C}$-PLAN when using different encodings on nondeterministic domains, we have tested it using the action description (2), in which dunking a package may clog the toilet. The initial and goal states are as before. The results are in Table 2.

Consider Table 2. ERP encodings lead to the best per-

$|P|$-$|T|$	ERP		ERS		ESS	
	#s	last	#s	last	#s	last
2-1	3	0.00	3	0.00	3	0.01
3-1	5	0.01	5	0.01	5	0.01
4-1	7	0.02	7	0.02	7	0.02
5-1	9	0.05	9	0.05	9	0.04
6-1	11	0.09	11	0.08	11	0.08
2-2	1	0.01	2	0.01	2	0.01
3-2	3	0.02	4	0.04	4	0.05
4-2	3	0.07	6	0.12	6	0.75
5-2	5	0.12	8	4.14	8	112.96
6-2	5	6.76	10	538.41	10	5780.81
2-3	1	0.00	2	0.02	2	0.01
3-3	1	0.01	3	0.07	3	0.04
4-3	3	0.07	5	0.55	5	0.72
5-3	3	0.27	7	80.45	8	4.88
6-3	3	0.88	9	7590.51	9	5.85

Table 2: Nondeterministic actions, multiple initial states

formances, sometimes orders of magnitude better than the others. This is not surprising in that it confirms the results obtained in the classical setting. What is more surprising are the performances of C-PLAN when using the ERS or the ESS encodings. Sometime one encoding dominates the other by orders of magnitude, and sometime it is the other way around. Even more, C-PLAN performances do not seem predictable. Introducing an additional package or toilet may cause an unpredictable change in C-PLAN performances. A similar phenomenon has already been observed in propositional satisfiability. As discussed in (Gomes, Selman, & Kautz 1998), the performances of SAT solvers based on the DP procedure can be highly unpredictable: minor changes in the search procedure or in the propositional formula can drastically alter the solution time. As a matter of fact, C-PLAN is heavily based on the DP procedure. Because of this, it may well be the case that by introducing controlled randomization and rapid restart into C-PLAN, we can obtain the speed-ups described in (Gomes, Selman, & Kautz 1998), and, at the same time, make C-PLAN more predictable.

Conclusions

In this paper we have focused on planning as satisfiability in simple nondeterministic domains. We have simplified and extended the theory presented in (Giunchiglia 2000). For example, we have shown that we do not need the (possibly very expensive) computation of a propositional formula equivalent to (9). We have also shown that different encodings are possible, along the lines of what has been done in the classical case: defining "bitwise", or "overloaded simple-split" encodings (see (Ernst, Millstein, & Weld 1997)) seems relatively easy. We have implemented C-PLAN: The experimental analysis shows that C-PLAN is competitive with CGP.

As for CGP, our objective in developing C-PLAN has been to see whether the good performances obtained by SAT-based planners in the classical case, would extend to more complex problems involving concurrency and/or constraints and/or nondeterminism. The experimental analysis shows that, at least in a "simple nondeterministic" setting, the answer is positive.

Acknowledgments

We thank David Smith for having provided CGP code. We thank Norman McCain for the help on CCALC. We thank Armando Tacchella for the help on *SAT. The second author is supported by ASI, CNR and MURST.

References

Davis, M., and Putnam, H. 1960. A computing procedure for quantification theory. *JACM* 7:201–215.

Davis, M.; Longemann, G.; and Loveland, D. 1962. A machine program for theorem proving. *Journal of the ACM* 5(7).

Ernst, M.; Millstein, T.; and Weld, D. Automatic SAT-compilation of planning problems. *Proc. IJCAI-97*.

Giunchiglia, E., and Lifschitz, V. An action language based on causal explanation: Preliminary report. *Proc. AAAI-98*, 623–630.

Giunchiglia, E.; Giunchiglia, F.; Sebastiani, R.; and Tacchella, A. More evaluation of decision procedures for modal logics. *Proc. KR-98*.

Giunchiglia, E.; Massarotto, A.; and Sebastiani, R. Act, and the rest will follow: Exploiting determinism in planning as satisfiability. *Proc. AAAI-98*.

Giunchiglia, E. 2000. Planning as satisfiability with expressive action languages: Concurrency, constraints and nondeterminism. *Proc. KR-00*.

Giunchiglia, E., and Tacchella, A. *SAT: a system for the development of modal decision procedures. In *Proc. CADE-00*.

Gomes, C. P.; Selman, B.; and Kautz, H. Boosting combinatorial search through randomization. *Proc. AAAI-98*, 431–437.

Kautz, H., and Selman, B. Planning as satisfiability. *Proc. ECAI-92*, 359–363.

Kautz, H., and Selman, B. Pushing the envelope: planning, propositional logic and stochastic search. *Proc. AAAI-96*, 1194–1201.

Kautz, H., and Selman, B. BLACKBOX: A new approach to the application of theorem proving to problem solving. *Working notes of the AIPS-98 Workshop on Planning as Combinatorial Search*.

Kautz, H.; McAllester, D.; and Selman, B. Encoding plans in propositional logic. *Proc. KR-96*, 374–384.

Kushmerick, N.; Hanks, S.; and Weld, D. 1995. An algorithm for probabilistic planning. *Artificial Intelligence* 76(1-2):239–286.

Peot, M. 1998. *Decision-Theoretic Planning*. Ph.D. Dissertation, Stanford University. Dept. of Engineering-Economic Systems.

Smith, D., and Weld, D. Conformant graphplan. *Proc. AAAI-98*, 889–896.

Wolfman, S., and Weld, D. The LPSAT-engine & its application to resource planning. *Proc. IJCAI-99*.

Open World Planning in the Situation Calculus

Alberto Finzi and **Fiora Pirri**
Dipartimento di Informatica e Sistemistica
Università degli Studi di Roma "La Sapienza"
Via Salaria 113, 00198 Roma, Italy
{alberto,fiora}@assi.dis.uniroma1.it

Ray Reiter
Department of Computer Science
University of Toronto
Toronto, Canada, M5S 1A4
reiter@cs.toronto.edu

Abstract

We describe a forward reasoning planner for open worlds that uses domain specific information for pruning its search space, as suggested by (Bacchus & Kabanza 1996; 2000). The planner is written in the situation calculus-based programming language GOLOG, and it uses a situation calculus axiomatization of the application domain. Given a sentence σ to prove, the planner regresses it to an equivalent sentence σ_0 about the initial situation, then invokes a theorem prover to determine whether the initial database entails σ_0 and hence σ. We describe two approaches to this theorem proving task, one based on compiling the initial database to prime implicate form, the other based on Relsat, a Davis/Putnam-based procedure. Finally, we report on our experiments with open world planning based on both these approaches to the theorem proving task.

Introduction

Currently, virtually all implemented deterministic planning systems make a closed world assumption that complete information is available about the initial state of the application domain. Conformant Graphplan (Smith & Weld 1998), CMBP (Cimatti & Roveri 1999) and the planner of (Rintanen 1999) are exceptions to this. So also are a few conditional planners incorporating "information gathering" actions, used to fill gaps in the planners' incomplete knowledge base (e.g. (Golden, Etzioni, & Weld 1994; de Giacomo et al. 1997)). Open worlds preclude direct appeal to most planning algorithms in the literature, including the successful SAT (Kautz & Selman 1996) and Graphplan (Blum & Furst 1997) approaches.

In this paper, we describe the theoretical foundations and implementation for an open world planner *without* sensing actions; its job is to find straight line plans using only what is known about the (incomplete) initial state, together with general domain specific facts like state constraints and action preconditions and effects. Ours is a forward reasoning planner, using domain dependent information to prune its search space, as suggested by (Bacchus & Kabanza 1996; 2000); it is axiomatized entirely in the situation calculus.

The Situation Calculus and GOLOG

The situation calculus (McCarthy 1963) is a first order language for axiomatizing dynamic worlds. In recent years, it has been considerably extended beyond the "classical" language to include concurrency, continuous time, processes,

Copyright © 2000, American Association for Artificial Intelligence (www.aaai.org). All rights reserved.

sensing actions, knowledge, etc, but in all cases, its basic ingredients consist of *actions*, *situations* and *fluents*.

Actions Actions are first order terms consisting of an action function symbol and its arguments. In the blocks world, the action of moving block x onto block y might be denoted by the action term $move(x, y)$.

Situations A *situation* is a first order term denoting a sequence of actions. These sequences are represented using a binary function symbol do: $do(\alpha, s)$ denotes the sequence resulting from adding the action α to the sequence s. So $do(\alpha, s)$ is like LISP's $cons(\alpha, s)$, or Prolog's $[\alpha \mid s]$. The special constant S_0 denotes the *initial situation*, namely the empty action sequence, so S_0 is like LISP's ( ) or Prolog's [ ]. Therefore, in a blocks world, the situation term

$$do(move(A, B), do(moveToTable(B), do(move(C, D), S_0)))$$

denotes the sequence of actions

$$[move(C, D), moveToTable(B), move(A, B)].$$

Notice that the action sequence is obtained from a situation term by reading the term from right to left.

Foundational axioms for situations are given in (Pirri & Reiter 1999).

Fluents Relations whose truth values vary from state to state are called *fluents*, and are denoted by predicate symbols with last argument a situation term. For example, in the blocks world, $on(x, y, s)$ might be a relational fluent, meaning that in that state of the world reached by performing the action sequence s, block x will be on block y.

Axiomatizing a Domain Theory

A domain theory is axiomatized in the situation calculus with four classes of axioms (More details in (Pirri & Reiter 1999)):

1. **Action precondition axioms**. There is one for each action function $A(\vec{x})$, with syntactic form

   $$Poss(A(\vec{x}), s) \equiv \Pi_A(\vec{x}, s).$$

   Here, $\Pi_A(\vec{x}, s)$ is a formula with free variables among $\vec{x}, s$. These characterize the preconditions of the action A.

2. **Successor state axioms**. There is one for each fluent $F(\vec{x}, s)$, with syntactic form

   $$F(\vec{x}, do(a, s)) \equiv \Phi_F(\vec{x}, a, s),$$

   where $\Phi_F(\vec{x}, a, s)$ is a formula with free variables among

$a, s, \vec{x}$. These characterize the truth values of the fluent F in the next situation $do(a,s)$ in terms of the current situation s, and they embody a solution to the frame problem for deterministic actions (Reiter 1991).

3. **Unique names axioms for actions.** These state that the actions of the domain are pairwise unequal.
4. **Initial database.** This is a set of first order sentences whose only situation term is S_0 and it specifies the initial state of the domain.

Example 1 The following are successor state and action precondition axioms for a blocks world used in the implementation described below.

Action Precondition Axioms

$Poss(move(x, y), s) \equiv clear(x, s) \land$
$\qquad clear(y, s) \land x \neq y,$
$Poss(moveToTable(x), s) \equiv clear(x, s) \land$
$\qquad \neg onTable(x, s).$

Successor State Axioms

$clear(x, do(a, s)) \equiv$
$\quad (\exists y)\{[(\exists z)a = move(y, z) \lor$
$\quad a = moveToTable(y)] \land on(y, x, s)\} \lor$
$\quad clear(x, s) \land \neg(\exists y)a = move(y, x),$

$on(x, y, do(a, s)) \equiv a = move(x, y) \lor$
$\quad on(x, y, s) \land a \neq moveToTable(x) \land$
$\quad \neg(\exists z)a = move(x, z),$

$onTable(x, do(a, s)) \equiv a = moveToTable(x) \lor$
$\quad onTable(x, s) \land \neg(\exists y)a = move(x, y).$

Planning in the Situation Calculus

The classical definition of planning is (Green 1969).

Definition 1 Plans
Let $\mathcal{D}$ be a background situation calculus axiomatization for some domain, and $G(s)$ a situation calculus formula – the *goal* – with one free situation variable s. A situation term $do(\alpha_n, do(\alpha_{n-1}, \cdots, do(\alpha_1, S_0) \cdots))$ that mentions no free variables is a *plan for* G iff

$\mathcal{D} \models executable(do(\alpha_n, do(\alpha_{n-1}, \cdots, do(\alpha_1, S_0) \cdots)))$
$\quad \land G(do(\alpha_n, do(\alpha_{n-1}, \cdots, do(\alpha_1, S_0) \cdots))).$

Here, the *executable* expression is an abbreviation for $Poss(\alpha_1, S_0) \land Poss(\alpha_2, do(\alpha_1, S_0)) \land \cdots \land Poss(\alpha_n, do(\alpha_{n-1}, \cdots, do(\alpha_1, S_0) \cdots))$. So on this definition, planning is a theorem-proving task: Determine a sequence $\alpha_1, \ldots, \alpha_n$ of variable free action terms such that $G(do(\alpha_n, do(\alpha_{n-1}, \cdots, do(\alpha_1, S_0) \cdots)))$ is provable from the background axioms $\mathcal{D}$, and moreover, this action sequence is executable, meaning that each of its action's preconditions are provable in that situation in which it is to be performed. This is the formal foundation for our open world planner.

GOLOG

Our planner is implemented in the situation calculus-based programming language GOLOG (Levesque *et al.* 1997), a language for defining complex actions in terms of a set of primitive actions axiomatized, as described above, in the situation calculus. It has the standard – and some not so standard – control structures found in most Algol-like languages.

1. *Sequence:* $\alpha\;;\;\beta$. Do action α, followed by action β.
2. *Test actions:* $p?$ Test the truth value of expression p in the current situation.
3. *Nondeterministic action choice:* $\alpha \mid \beta$. Do α or β.
4. *Nondeterministic choice of action arguments:* $(\pi\;x)\alpha$. Nondeterministically pick a value for x, and for that value of x, do the action α.
5. *Procedures, including recursion.*

The semantics of GOLOG programs is defined (see (Levesque *et al.* 1997)) by macro-expansion, using a ternary relation Do. $Do(program, s, s')$ is an *abbreviation* for a situation calculus formula whose intuitive meaning is that s' is one of the situations reached by evaluating the GOLOG *program*, beginning in situation s. Therefore, to execute *program*, one *proves*, using the situation calculus axiomatization of some background domain (e.g. the axioms of Example 1), the situation calculus formula $(\exists s)Do(program, S_0, s)$. Any binding for s obtained by a constructive proof of this sentence is an execution trace, in terms of the primitive actions, of the *program*. A GOLOG interpreter, written in Prolog, is described in (Levesque *et al.* 1997); this is the implementation used for our planner.

A Depth-First Forward Planner

We can now present our planner, written in GOLOG.

proc $wspdf(n)$
$\quad goal?\mid[n > 0?\;;\;(\pi\,a)(primitive\_action(a)?\;;\;a)\;;$
$\quad \neg badSituation?\;;\;wspdf(n-1)]$
endProc

$wspdf(n)$[1] expects the user to provide n, a depth bound, *goal*, a planning goal, *primitive_action*, a predicate characterizing what are the primitive actions of the domain, and finally, an axiomatization of a domain dependent predicate *badSituation*, used to filter out partial plans that are known to be fruitless.

Like any GOLOG program, the planner is executed by proving $(\exists s)Do(wspdf(n), S_0, s)$. Therefore, we start with S_0 as the current situation. In general, if σ is the current situation, $wspdf(n)$ succeeds if $goal(\sigma)$ can be proved, or if $n > 0$ and a primitive action a can be chosen (nondeterministically) such that $Poss(a, \sigma)$ is provable and such that after "performing" a, meaning that $do(a, \sigma)$ becomes the new current situation, $\neg badSituation(do(a, \sigma))$ can be proved, and $wspdf(n-1)$ succeeds with $do(a, \sigma)$ as the current situation. On success, the current situation is a plan for the *goal*. Therefore, the planner works depth-first, generating subplans by increasing length, filtering these with the *badSituation* predicate, and testing the survivors against the *goal*. The *badSituation* filter is our version of Bacchus and Kabanza's use of domain specific information for pruning the search tree of bottom-up planners (Bacchus & Kabanza 2000).

A Regression-Based Theorem Prover

The planner *wspdf* generates potential plans of the form $do(\alpha_n, \ldots, do(\alpha_1, S_0) \cdots)$, where the α_i are action terms; then it tests these potential plans against *goal* and *badSituation*. So the test expressions that must be proved are of the form $W(do(\alpha_n, \ldots, do(\alpha_1, S_0) \cdots))$,

---

[1] *wspdf* stands for the World's Simplest Depth First Planner

for formulas $W(s)$ with a single free situation variable s. These are the kinds of sentences for which regression was designed (Pirri & Reiter 1999). Essentially, regression uses successor state axioms to replace a sentence of the form $W(do(\alpha_n,\ldots,do(\alpha_1,S_0)\cdots))$ by a logically equivalent sentence *about the initial situation only*, and the original sentence is provable iff the regressed sentence is provable *using only the initial database together with the unique names axioms for actions*. So our strategy will be this:

1. Eliminate the quantifiers in the sentence $W(do(\alpha_n,\ldots,do(\alpha_1,S_0)\cdots))$. Here, we insist that all quantifiers be *typed*, and that these types range over finite domains of constants. Formally, a *type* $\tau(x)$ is an abbreviation for a description of a finite domain of constants:

$$\tau(x) \stackrel{def}{=} x = T_1 \vee \cdots \vee x = T_k,$$

where $T_1,\ldots,T_k$ are all constants. Now, introduce *typed quantifiers* $(\forall x : \tau)$ and $(\exists x : \tau)$ according to:

$$(\forall x : \tau)\phi(x) \stackrel{def}{=} (\forall x).\tau(x) \supset \phi(x),$$

$$(\exists x : \tau)\phi(x) \stackrel{def}{=} (\exists x).\tau(x) \wedge \phi(x).$$

Then typed quantification of formulas can be reduced to conjunctions and disjunctions according to the following equivalences

$$(\forall x : \tau).\phi(x) \equiv \phi(T_1) \wedge \cdots \wedge \phi(T_k),$$

$$(\exists x : \tau).\phi(x) \equiv \phi(T_1) \vee \cdots \vee \phi(T_k).$$

Therefore, quantifier elimination for the sentence $W(do(\alpha_n,\ldots,do(\alpha_1,S_0)\cdots))$ amounts to replacing W's quantified subformulas by conjunctions and disjunctions according to these equivalences.

2. Regress the resulting sentence to a sentence about the initial situation only.

3. Convert the regressed sentence to clausal form.

4. Determine whether all clauses of this clausal form are entailed by the initial database. If so, report QED; else report failure.

This is what our implementation does, with one important difference: Rather than regress the entire sentence to the initial situation, it does a depth first regression of the components of the sentence, hoping that the regressed component will simplify in such a way that the remaining components need not be regressed. For example, suppose, in regressing $P \wedge Q$ we first regress P to get R. If R simplifies to $false$, there is no point in next regressing Q, since in any event, the regressed form of $P \wedge Q$ will be $false$. There is a dual principle for regressing formulas of the form $P \vee Q$.

Regression requires successor state axioms, and we allow for these by user-provided Prolog assertions of the form `Atom <=> Expression`. Now we can describe the final details of the regression theorem prover. In regressing an atom A, there are two possibilities:

1. A has a definition of the form `A <=> W`. This means that A has a successor state axiom or is a defined atom, and to regress A, we need to regress W.

2. A has no definition of the form `A <=> W`. Therefore, either A is not a fluent, or it is, but its situation argument is `s0`, so the regression is finished.

The following are the top-level Prolog clauses in our implementation for the regression theorem-prover `prove`, as just described:

A Regression Theorem Prover

```
prove(W) :- eliminateQuantifiers(W,I),
        simplify(I,Simp), regress(Simp,R),
        clausalForm(R,Clauses),
        databaseEntails(Clauses).

regress(P & Q, R) :- regress(P,R1),
        (R1 = false, R = false, ! ;
        regress(Q,R2), simplify(R1 & R2,R)).
regress(P v Q, R) :- regress(P,R1),
        (R1 = true, R = true, ! ;
        regress(Q,R2), simplify(R1 v R2,R)).
regress(-P,R) :- regress(P,R1),
                simplify(-R1,R).
regress(A,R) :- isAtom(A), A <=> W,
    % A is a defined atom.
    % Retrieve and regress its definition.
            eliminateQuantifiers(W,I),
            simplify(I,S), regress(S,R).
regress(A,R) :- isAtom(A), not A <=> W,
    % A is an atom, but it has no definition,
    % so the regression is finished.
        (A = false, R = false, ! ; R = A).
```

Here, `databaseEntails(Clauses)` is a call to a theorem prover for determining whether `Clauses` are a logical consequence of the clauses for the initial database. The precise details of this theorem prover are still open; to complete the implementation, this must be specified, and that is the topic of the next section.

Theorem Proving in the Initial Database

For open world planning, our task is to implement a theorem prover for determining whether `databaseEntails(Clauses)`, as required by the regression-based theorem prover. Here, `Clauses` are the clauses obtained by regressing the expression to be proved. Our overriding concern must be to make this theorem proving task as efficient as possible because the prover will be called each time a test expression must be evaluated, and in the process of searching for a plan, such test expressions (e.g. $on(a,b,do(move(c,d),do(moveToTable(d),S_0)))$) are generated and tested a huge number of times. We have experimented with two approaches, one based on compiling the initial database to prime implicate form, the other using an on-line theorem prover.

Prime Implicates and Compiling an Initial Database

We begin with the initial database, which, being open world, can be any sentences about S_0. Our approach is to transform these sentences into their logically equivalent *prime implicates*.

Definition 2 Prime Implicate

Let $\mathcal{K}$ be a set of clauses. A clause C is a *prime implicate* of $\mathcal{K}$ iff C is not a tautology, $\mathcal{K} \models C$, and there is no clause $C' \neq C$ such that C' subsumes C and $\mathcal{K} \models C'$.[2]

---

[2] A clause is a *tautology* iff it contains A and $\neg A$ for some atom A. Clause C *subsumes* clause C' iff each literal of C occurs in C'.

Theorem 1 (Quine 1959) *Suppose $\mathcal{K}$ is a set of clauses, and $pi(\mathcal{K})$ is the set of all of $\mathcal{K}$'s prime implicates. Then $\mathcal{K}$ and $pi(\mathcal{K})$ are logically equivalent. Moreover, for any non-tautologous clause C, $\mathcal{K} \models C$ iff there is a clause $\Pi \in pi(\mathcal{K})$ such that Π subsumes C.*

This tells us, first, that we can safely replace $\mathcal{K}$ by its prime implicates, and secondly, with these equivalent clauses in hand, we can quickly determine whether a given clause is entailed by $\mathcal{K}$. So it seems that we need only to compute $\mathcal{K}$'s prime implicates, and thereafter we have efficient theorem proving that can be performed in time linear in the number of prime implicates. These prime implicates act like a compiled form of $\mathcal{K}$: All the "hard" reasoning is done at compile time, in computing the prime implicates; after that, reasoning becomes easy. Of course, there is no free lunch, so we have to expect that the compilation phase will have high complexity, and indeed, this is so. In the worst case, the number of prime implicates of a set of clauses is exponential in the number of distinct atoms in those clauses.

The first stage of our implementation converts the initial database to clausal form. In doing so, it first eliminates quantifiers in the sentences of the initial database, making use of various logical simplifications, for example, replacing X = X by true, -true by false, P & true by P, etc. Finally, the implementation computes the prime implicates of these clauses, using a straightforward algorithm based on (Quine 1959).

On-Line Theorem Proving

The alternative to compiling the initial database is on-line theorem proving. This involves a once-only conversion of the initial database to clausal form by quantifier elimination as described in the previous section, but without further processing these clauses into prime implicates. Subsequently, whenever it is required to establish databaseEntails(Clauses) for a regressed set of Clauses, a clausal form theorem prover is invoked. The advantage of this on-line approach is that it avoids the expensive prime implicate computation. The disadvantage is that the theorem proving task becomes much more expensive.

An Open Blocks World

We illustrate an open world axiomatization for the blocks world. Recall that $wspdf(n)$ searches for plans bottom-up, filtering out useless subplans with a user supplied, domain specific *badSituation* predicate. We next describe the predicate we used for our blocks world implementation.

Let $goodTower(x, s)$ be true whenever, in situation s, x is a good tower, meaning that x is the top block of a tower of blocks that is a sub-tower of one of the goal towers. We suppose the planner has available to it a description of all the good towers corresponding to its planning goal. The following are some natural *badSituation*s:

1. The situation resulting from moving a block off a good tower.
2. The situation resulting from moving a block onto a good tower, if the resulting tower is a bad tower.
3. *Opportunistic rule:* The situation resulting from creating a bad tower by moving a block to the table, and some other action could have been performed instead that creates a good tower.

badSituation also imposes certain canonical ordering rules on plans, which we do not describe here. The following Prolog clauses implement rules 1 and 3:

Some Bad Situations for a Blocks World

```
badSituation(do(move(X,Y),S)) :-
      prove(-goodTower(X,do(move(X,Y),S))).
badSituation(do(moveToTable(X),S)) :-
   prove(-goodTower(X,do(moveToTable(X),S))),
   existsActionThatCreatesGoodTower(S).
existsActionThatCreatesGoodTower(S) :-
   (A = move(Y,X) ; A = moveToTable(Y)),
   poss(A,S), prove(goodTower(Y,do(A,S))).
```

Next, we present an example open world blocks problem with 12 blocks, arranged as indicated in the figure.

A Blocks World Problem with Incomplete Initial Situation

```
/* Initial situation: Only the blocks so
   indicated have been specified to be clear.

                        d        m <-- clear;
   clear --> p          a            not on table
   not on--> n         /\
   table              ?/  \?          f <-- not
                     /     \             on table
                    g       b      \
                    h       c       e       k
                   -------------------------
Goal situation          d       k
                        h       g
                        b       m
                        e       f
                        a       c
                      ----------           */

goal(S) :- prove(on(d,h,S) & on(h,b,S) &
   on(b,e,S) & on(e,a,S) & ontable(a,S) &
   on(k,g,S) & on(g,m,S) & on(m,f,S) &
   on(f,c,S) & ontable(c,S) ).

goodTower(X,S) <=> X = a & ontable(a,S) v
   X = e & on(e,a,S) & ontable(a,S) v
   X = b & on(b,e,S) & on(e,a,S) & ontable(a,S) v
   X = h & on(h,b,S) & on(b,e,S) & on(e,a,S) &
        ontable(a,S) v
   X = d & on(d,h,S) & on(h,b,S) & on(b,e,S) &
        on(e,a,S) & ontable(a,S) v
   X = c & ontable(c,S) v
   X = f & on(f,c,S) & ontable(c,S) v
   X = m & on(m,f,S) & on(f,c,S) & ontable(c,S) v
   X = g & on(g,m,S) & on(m,f,S) & on(f,c,S) &
        ontable(c,S) v
   X = k & on(k,g,S) & on(g,m,S) & on(m,f,S) &
        on(f,c,S) & ontable(c,S).

/* Initial database. All references to clear and
   ontable have been eliminated, via their
   definitions, in favor of on.   */

axiom(all([y,block],-on(y,m,s0))).  % m is clear.
axiom(all([y,block],-on(y,p,s0))).  % p is clear.
axiom(all([y,block],-on(k,y,s0))).  % k on the table.
axiom(all([y,block],-on(c,y,s0))).  % c on the table.
axiom(all([y,block],-on(e,y,s0))).  % e on the table.
axiom(all([y,block],-on(h,y,s0))).  % h on the table.
```

```
axiom(on(b,c,s0)).      axiom(on(d,a,s0)).
axiom(on(g,h,s0)).      axiom(on(p,n,s0)).
axiom(on(a,b,s0) v on(a,e,s0)). % a is on b or on e;
axiom(all([x,block],on(x,b,s0) => x = a)). % nothing
axiom(all([x,block],on(x,e,s0) => x = a)). % else
                                           % is on b or e.
axiom(some([x,block],on(f,x,s0))). % f not on table.
axiom(some([x,block],on(m,x,s0))). % m not on table.
axiom(some([x,block],on(n,x,s0))). % n not on table.

% Initial state constraints.

axiom(all([x,block],all([y,block],
                    on(x,y,s0) => -on(y,x,s0)))).
axiom(all([x,block],all([y,block], all([z,block],
          on(y,x,s0) & on(z,x,s0) => y = z)))).
axiom(all([x,block],all([y,block], all([z,block],
          on(x,y,s0) & on(x,z,s0) => y = z)))).

% clear and ontable defined in the initial situation.

clear(X,s0)   <=> all([y,block],-on(y,X,s0)).
ontable(X,s0) <=> all([y,block],-on(X,y,s0)).

% Domain of blocks.

domain(block, [a,b,c,d,e,f,g,h,k,m,n,p]).

% Action preconditions.

poss(move(X,Y),S) :-
        findall(Z,(domain(D), member(Z,D),
               prove(clear(Z,S))),L),
        member(X,L), member(Y,L), not X = Y.
poss(moveToTable(X),S) :- domain(D), member(X,D),
               prove(clear(X,S) & -ontable(X,S)).

% Successor state axioms.

clear(X,do(move(U,V),S)) <=>
                on(U,X,S) v -(X = V) & clear(X,S).
clear(X,do(moveToTable(U),S)) <=>
                on(U,X,S) v clear(X,S).
on(X,Y,do(move(U,V),S)) <=>
                X = U & Y = V v -(X = U) & on(X,Y,S).
on(X,Y,do(moveToTable(U),S)) <=> -(X = U) & on(X,Y,S).
ontable(X,do(move(U,V),S)) <=> -(X = U) & ontable(X,S).
ontable(X,do(moveToTable(U),S)) <=>
                                X = U v ontable(X,S).

primitive_action(move(X,Y)).
primitive_action(moveToTable(X)).
```

There are four things to note about these axioms:

1. The initial database is defined only using the fluent *on*, and not *clear* and *ontable*. In the blocks world, the fluent *on* is primitive, and fluents *clear* and *ontable* can be defined in terms of it:

$$clear(x, s) \equiv (\forall y)\neg on(y, x, s),$$
$$ontable(x, s) \equiv (\forall y)\neg on(x, y, s).$$

Thus, instead of representing the initial fact that h is on the table by $ontable(h, S_0)$, we elected instead to use $(\forall y)\neg on(h, y, S_0)$; similarly for *clear*. With this choice, the initial database does not include facts about *clear* and *ontable*. This considerably reduces the number of clauses for the initial database because these will not include redundant clauses involving *clear* and *ontable*. This, in turn, considerably improves the theorem proving efficiency.

2. The initial database axioms include three *state constraints*, relativized to the initial situation. The *general* state constraints, e.g. $(\forall x, y, s).on(x, y, s) \supset \neg on(y, x, s)$, are not among our axioms because, except for the case $s = S_0$, they are entailed by the successor state and action precondition axioms. See (Lin & Reiter 1994) for a discussion of this issue. In general, for open world planning, the initial database must include all state constraints for the application domain, relativized to the initial situation.

3. The clauses for poss and goal assume responsibility for calling prove on appropriate formulas.

4. The successor state axioms differ from Example 1, which universally quantify over all actions a. In contrast, the open world blocks world axiomatization uses two clauses for clear, one for action move(U,V), the other for action moveToTable(U). There is no deep reason for this choice. It was made only to simplify the implementation of the simplification routine simplify used by the regression theorem prover. To see why, consider the successor state axiom for *clear* in example 1, and consider an instance $move(u, v)$ of a in this sentence:

$$clear(x, do(move(u, v), s)) \equiv$$
$$(\exists y)\{[(\exists z)move(u, v) = move(y, z) \vee$$
$$move(u, v) = moveToTable(y)] \wedge on(y, x, s)\} \vee$$
$$clear(x, s) \wedge \neg(\exists y)move(u, v) = move(y, x).$$

Using the unique names axioms for actions, and some elementary logic, this can be simplified to yield the logical form of the first successor state axiom for clear in the above blocks world axiomatization. Obtaining this logical form from the general successor state axiom was straightforward, but required a lot of simplification based on reasoning about quantifiers, equality and unique names axioms for actions. To avoid having to implement such simplification routines we have opted instead for the user of the system to do this herself, in advance, and to represent the results of these simplifications directly by successor state axioms, particularized to each action, as was done in the above axiomatization.

Experimental Results

We tested our planner on two classes of problems: One class consists of variants of the blocks world problem of the previous section in which we vary the extent to which individual blocks have known information associated with them. The other problem class was drawn from the logistics domain, and again, we varied the amount of known information about the domain's individuals. Moreover, we experimented with two versions of the planner's theorem prover: the prime implicate approach described above, and an on-line theorem prover Relsat 1.0, an implementation of the Davis-Putnam algorithm based on (Bayardo & Schrag 1997).

In designing our experiments, we introduced the concept of an *unknown* for the purposes of measuring a problem's degree of incompleteness. For a given domain individual, an unknown is any property of that individual that is not entailed by the initial database, and whose negation also is not entailed. For the blocks world problem of the previous section, $clear(d)$ is an unknown property of d, because the axioms for the initial database entail neither it, nor $\neg clear(d)$. $(\lambda x)on(m, x)$ is an unknown property of m, and $(\lambda x)(x =$

$b \vee x = e) \wedge on(a, x)$ is an unknown property of a. In total, there are 8 unknown properties for this example.

The Blocks World

Here, we used the axiomatization of the blocks world given in the previous section, but varied the initial situation (so only the first problem in the set of experiments corresponds to the picture associated with those axioms). The remaining four blocks world problem instances used in our experiments were obtained from the problem given in the previous section by adding more blocks to it, and by varying the amount of known information about these additional blocks. The tables given below summarize the comparative performances of Relsat vs the prime implicate implementations of the theorem proving component of our open world planner.[3]

Relsat					
Blocks	12	20	20	22	22
Unknowns	8	8	10	14	10
Plan (sec)	19.7	19.0	31.2	38.7	38.2
Clauses	175	449	502	624	586
Compile (sec)	5.1	44.8	50.1	79.6	82.1
Plan length	14	14	17	17	17

Prime Implicates					
Blocks	12	20	20	22	22
Unknowns	8	8	10	14	10
Plan (sec)	3.9	19.8	-	-	-
Clauses	175	449	502	624	586
Implicates	248	569	-	-	-
Compile (sec)	15.7	119.6	-	-	-
Plan length	14	14	-	-	-

The Logistics Domain

Space limitations prevent us from presenting our situation calculus axiomatization for this domain. They are available, on request, from the authors. To generate open world problems for this domain, we selected a number of the standard closed world benchmarks, and "opened them up" by removing information from their initial state descriptions. As for the blocks world, our measure of the degree of incompleteness of these problems was defined by the number of unknown properties of all domain individuals. In the tables below, the problem numbers are those of the closed world instances of logistics problems used in the First International Planning Competition, described at www.informatik.uni-freiburg.de/~koehler/ipp.html. Our problems were obtained by "opening up" these problem instances.

Relsat: Logistics				
Problem	03	03	04	05
Unknowns	0	1	2	11
Plan (sec)	24.3	31.0	342.8	1405.0
Clauses	776	811	6772	9359
Compile (sec)	9.8	10.5	1146.6	1528.9
Plan length	9	10	11	19

[3] All CPU times here are for a SUN Sparc 10 Ultra, with 333 MHZ processor and 256 MB of RAM.

Prime Implicate: Logistics				
Problem	03	03	04	05
Unknowns	0	1	2	11
Plan (sec)	19.0	24.8	262.5	stack o'flow
Clauses	776	811	6772	9359
Implicates	776	811	6772	9359
Compile (sec)	15.0	16.3	1178.3	2339.2
Plan length	9	10	11	-

Discussion

Our experiments suggest that open world planning is feasible for moderate sized problems (up to 17 step blocks world plans, and 19 step logistics plans). To our surprise, theorem proving with Relsat 1.0 was the clear winner over the prime implicate compilation approach. With larger problems, the latter was overwhelmed by the prime implicate computation, whereas Relsat found plans for all our problem instances. Perhaps a more sophisticated prime implicate algorithm would have helped here, e.g. (de Kleer 1992). We leave such considerations for the future.

Conformant Graphplan (Smith & Weld 1998), CMBP (Cimatti & Roveri 1999) and the planner of (Rintanen 1999) are the only other open world planners that we know. Cimatti and Roveri have extensively tested their planner against those of Smith/Weld and Rintanen, and their data suggests the superiority of their approach over these other planners. The examples on which we tested our planner did not intersect those of Cimatti and Roveri – we did not learn of their work until after we had conducted our experiments. However, we have since done some unsystematic runs with our planner on the bomb and the toilets problem that figured prominently in their experiments. This problem has some straightforward and natural *badSituation*s:

1. Flushing a toilet twice without an intervening package dunking creates a *badSituation*.
2. The problem has a high degree of symmetry, which can be substantially reduced by canonically ordering the packages and toilets:
   (a) Dunking a package creates a *badSituation* if there is an undunked package lower in the package ordering.
   (b) Dunking into a toilet creates a *badSituation* if there is an unclogged toilet lower in the toilet ordering.

We tested our prime implicate-based planner, using these *badSituation*s, on several of the Cimatti and Roveri test problems. None caused it any difficulties. The smallest problem their planner could not solve was BMTC(10,3) – 10 packages, 3 toilets – with high uncertainty, meaning that initially it is unknown whether any of the toilets are clogged; our planner found a 20 step plan in 0.32 seconds. The biggest problem we ran was BMTC(40,6) – 40 packages, 6 toilets – with high uncertainty, producing an 80 step plan in 114 seconds.

In all fairness to CMBP, we must emphasize that it is a domain independent planner, whereas ours relies heavily on its problem specific *badSituation*s. Moreover, CMBP returns all minimal length plans, while ours returns plans one at a time, and these need not be minimal length. Finally, CMBP provides for actions with nondeterministic effects; for us, all actions must be deterministic. On the other hand, we can't think of any reasons for not exploiting domain specific information in planning when it is so obviously useful.

Our planner differs considerably from those of Bacchus/Kabanza in its theoretical foundations and in its implementation. Theoretically, it is based entirely on the situation calculus and Green's Definition 1 for planning, and is arguably more "logically pure" and transparent than the latter, which rely on a combination of STRIPS-like operators and a linear temporal logic. In its implementation, our planner differs in one fundamental respect. The Bacchus/Kabanza planners maintain a current database by *progressing* the previous database in response to the last planned action, whereas our planner does no database progression; instead, it maintains only the initial database, and computes entailments using goal regression together with theorem-proving relative to the initial database. There is a good reason for this: Except for one special case described in (Lin & Reiter 1997), there are no known provably correct and efficient algorithms for progressing an incomplete initial database. Despite these technical differences, our planner is very much in the spirit of the Bacchus/Kabanza approach, and our experiences reinforce their arguments in favor of exploiting domain specific control information in planning systems.

In addition to the open world planner described here, a variety of closed world, forward reasoning, situation calculus planners based on the ideas of Bacchus and Kabanza have also been implemented (Reiter 1999). These include planners for "classical" (totally ordered) problems, as well as for concurrency, and temporally ordered processes, as exemplified by a multi-handed blocks world agent.

(Levesque 1996) has elegantly generalized Green's account of planning in the situation calculus (Definition 1) to *conditional plans*, and we believe that the methods of this paper can be adapted to implement conditional planners based on his foundations.

References

Bacchus, F., and Kabanza, F. 1996. Planning for temporally extended goals. In *Proceedings of the National Conference on Artificial Intelligence (AAAI'96)*, 1215–1222.

Bacchus, F., and Kabanza, F. 2000. Using temporal logics to express search control knowledge for planning. *Artificial Intelligence* 116(1-2):123–191.

Bayardo, R., and Schrag, R. 1997. Using CSP look-back techniques to solve real-world SAT instances. In *Proceedings of the National Conference on Artificial Intelligence (AAAI'97)*, 203–208.

Blum, A., and Furst, M. 1997. Fast planning through planning graph analysis. *Artificial Intelligence* 90(1-2):281–300.

Cimatti, A., and Roveri, M. 1999. Conformant planning via model checking. In Biundo, S., ed., *Proc. ECP99: European Conference on Planning*. Springer-Verlag.

de Giacomo, G.; Iocchi, L.; Nardi, D.; and Rosati, R. 1997. Planning with sensing for a mobile robot. In *Preprints of the Fourth European Conf. on Planning*, 158–170.

de Kleer, J. 1992. An improved incremental algorithm for generating prime implicates. In *Proceedings of the National Conference on Artificial Intelligence (AAAI'92)*, 780–785.

Golden, K.; Etzioni, O.; and Weld, D. 1994. Omnipotence without omniscience: Efficient sensor management for planning. In *Proceedings of the National Conference on Artificial Intelligence (AAAI'94)*, 1048–1054.

Green, C. 1969. Theorem proving by resolution as a basis for question-answering systems. In Meltzer, B., and Michie, D., eds., *Machine Intelligence 4*. New York: American Elsevier. 183–205.

Kautz, H., and Selman, B. 1996. Pushing the envelope: Planning, propositional logic and stochastic search. In *Proceedings of the National Conference on Artificial Intelligence (AAAI'96)*, 1194–1201.

Levesque, H.; Reiter, R.; Lespérance, Y.; Lin, F.; and Scherl, R. 1997. GOLOG: a logic programming language for dynamic domains. *J. of Logic Programming, Special Issue on Actions* 31(1-3):59–83.

Levesque, H. 1996. What is planning in the presence of sensing? In *Proceedings of the National Conference on Artificial Intelligence (AAAI'96)*, 1139–1146.

Lin, F., and Reiter, R. 1994. State constraints revisited. *J. of Logic and Computation, special issue on actions and processes* 4:655–678.

Lin, F., and Reiter, R. 1997. How to progress a database. *Artificial Intelligence* 92:131–167.

McCarthy, J. 1963. Situations, actions and causal laws. Technical report, Stanford University. Reprinted in Semantic Information Processing (M. Minsky ed.), MIT Press, Cambridge, Mass., 1968, pp. 410-417.

Pirri, F., and Reiter, R. 1999. Some contributions to the metatheory of the situation calculus. *Journal of the ACM* 46(3):261–325.

Quine, W. 1959. On cores and prime implicants of truth functions. *American Math. Monthly* 66:755–760.

Reiter, R. 1991. The frame problem in the situation calculus: a simple solution (sometimes) and a completeness result for goal regression. In Lifschitz, V., ed., *Artificial Intelligence and Mathematical Theory of Computation: Papers in Honor of John McCarthy*. San Diego, CA: Academic Press. 359–380.

Reiter, R. 1999. *Knowledge in Action: Logical Foundations for Describing and Implementing Dynamical Systems*. In preparation. Draft available at http://www.cs.toronto.edu/˜cogrobo/.

Rintanen, J. 1999. Constructing conditional plans by a theorem-prover. *Journal of Artificial Intelligence Research* 10:323–352.

Smith, D., and Weld, D. 1998. Conformant graphplan. In *Proceedings of the National Conference on Artificial Intelligence (AAAI'98)*, 889–896. AAAI Press/MIT Press.

Discovering State Constraints in DISCOPLAN: Some New Results

Alfonso Gerevini
Dipartimento di Elettronica per l'Automazione
Università di Brescia
Via Branze 38, 25123 Brescia, Italy
E-mail: gerevini@ing.unibs.it

Lenhart Schubert
Department of Computer Science
University of Rochester
Rochester, NY 14627-0226
E-mail: schubert@cs.rochester.edu

Abstract

DISCOPLAN is an implemented set of efficient preplanning algorithms intended to enable faster domain-independent planning. It includes algorithms for discovering state constraints (invariants) that have been shown to be very useful, for example, for speeding up SAT-based planning. DISCOPLAN originally discovered only certain types of implicative constraints involving up to two fluent literals and any number of static literals, where one of the fluent literals contains all of the variables occurring in the other literals; only planning domains with STRIPS-like operators were handled. We have now extended DISCOPLAN in several directions. We describe new techniques that handle operators with conditional effects, and enable discovery of several new types of constraints. Moreover, discovered constraints can be fed back into the discovery process to obtain additional constraints. Finally, we outline unimplemented (but provably correct) methods for discovering additional types of constraints, including constraints involving arbitrarily many fluent literals.

Introduction

The automated inference of state constraints (invariants) based on a given set of state-transforming operators and initial conditions has emerged as a significant new development in the effort to design effective domain-independent planners (Kelleher & Cohn 1992; Rintanen 1998; Gerevini & Schubert 1996; 1998; Fox & Long 1998). It has been shown that such state constraints, derived in a pre-planning phase, can be used to greatly reduce the planning search space and hence planning time (Gerevini & Schubert 1996; 1998; Rintanen 1998; Kautz & Selman 1998; Fox & Long 1998; 2000; Refanidis & Vlahavas 2000), as well as to aid specification and debugging of planning domains.

In (Gerevini & Schubert 1998) we proposed a collection of techniques for extracting state constraints from a set of operators and an initial state, and we implemented a subset of these techniques in the DISCOPLAN (DIScovering COnstraints for PLANning) package. On the assumption that operators are given in STRIPS-like form, we implemented the derivation of (a) fluent predicate domains (sets of k-tuples that include all possible argument tuples for which a k-ary predicate may hold; these were obtained by a Graphplan-like method); (b) implicative constraints of form

Copyright © 2000, American Association for Artificial Intelligence (www.aaai.org). All rights reserved.

((IMPLIES ϕ ψ) $\sigma_1...\sigma_n$),
where $\phi, \psi, \sigma_1, ..., \sigma_n$ ($n \geq 0$) are literals, the σ_i are static (non-fluent) supplementary conditions such as type and inequality constraints, and the antecedent literal ϕ contains all variables occurring elsewhere; an example is
((IMPLIES (AT ?X ?Y) (AIRPORT ?Y)) (AIRPLANE ?X))
(from the "att-logistics" world, stating that for all ?X, ?Y, if ?X is at ?Y then ?Y is an airport, provided that ?X is an airplane); and (c) simultaneous implicative and single-valuedness (sv-) constraints such as the blocks-world constraint
((IMPLIES (ON ?*X ?Y) (NOT (CLEAR ?Y))) (NEQ ?Y T),
where "starred" variables indicate that there can be at most one value of the argument in the starred position corresponding to any given values for the remaining arguments of the predicate in question, and T stands for the table. In addition, we outlined (but did not implement) algorithms for deriving certain sv-constraints independently of implicative constraints, and for deriving simultaneous implicative and sv-constraints more general than those in (c), allowing both the antecedent and the consequent to contain variables not contained in the other.

Here we describe some major extensions of DISCOPLAN, in both practical and theoretical directions. An across-the-board extension is the allowance for *conditional* effects in operators specifying a planning domain. This is likely to be of considerable practical interest in domain-independent planning, since formalisms permitting operators with conditional effects (e.g., UCPOP and PDDL) facilitate compact encoding of complex operators that would otherwise require unnatural and potentially very large expansions as multiple unconditional operators.

The algorithms and implementation for (b) and (c) above have been generalized accordingly, and the newly implemented and newly proposed techniques similarly allow for conditional effects. These extensions are described in the second section. In the third section, we describe how DISCOPLAN is able to infer additional constraints of the type just mentioned by "expanding" operators so as to include preconditions and effects implied by constraints discovered earlier, and then re-running the discovery algorithms. In the forth section, we describe some further extensions to our methods (mostly unimplemented, but provably correct); this includes methods for inferring strict single-valuedness (and n-valuedness) constraints, and constraints involving arbitrarily many fluent literals. We provide sample results in the fifth section, and then summarize our contribution and its relation to other approaches, and our further plans.

Newly Inferred Constraints

We begin by outlining the generalizations needed to deal with conditional effects in deriving implicative and simultaneous implicative and sv-constraints (a slightly more detailed description is given in (Gerevini & Schubert 2000)). Then we devote a series of subsections to the new capabilities of DISCOPLAN.

Adapting the Hypothesize-and-Test Paradigm to Conditional Effects

We assume operators similar to those handled by UCPOP, except that we do not allow for universal quantification. After (automatic) standardization, each operator consists of a name, a set of parameters, and a set of *when*-clauses. Each *when*-clause contains a set of precondition literals and a set of effect literals, any of which may have constant or parametric arguments and may be positive or negated. The first *when*-clause, called the *primary when*-clause, contains the preconditions that must be verifiable whenever the operator is applied to a state, and the effects whose truth is assured in the resulting state. Each of the remaining, *secondary when*-clauses (if any) specifies additional preconditions and effects, where satisfaction of those preconditions along with the primary ones assures the truth of those effects in the resulting state.

We use several top-level programs to infer different types of constraints from operator structure, but most of them adhere to a hypothesize-and-test paradigm with the following structure. (An exception is the program for finding antisymmetry constraints, in which the first of the following steps is based on single literals rather than pairs). Note that Γ can be logically complex, for instance consisting of both an implicative hypothesis and one or two sv-hypotheses. This is crucial since some hypotheses cannot be verified in isolation, but only by simultaneous induction with other hypotheses.

1. Hypothesize a constraint Γ based on co-occurrences of literals in a *when*-clause w of an operator and in the corresponding primary *when*-clause w_1 (if different). For example, effects ϕ and ψ might lead to an implicative hypothesis (IMPLIES ϕ ψ), and possibly sv-hypotheses about the predicates involved.
2. Add a set of candidate supplementary conditions $\{\sigma_1, ..., \sigma_n\}$, consisting of the static preconditions of w and w_1 and if $w \neq w_1$, the negations of static preconditions of other *when*-clauses (except ones that unify with static preconditions of w or w_1 or their negations).
3. Test hypothesis Γ relative to each *when*-clause of each operator, using the relevant *verification conditions*; for each apparent violation of Γ find the corresponding possible "excuses" for the violation. An excuse is a set of provisos $\{\sigma'_1, ..., \sigma'_m\}$, chosen from the candidate supplementary conditions, that weaken the hypothesis sufficiently to maintain its truth. If a violation has no excuses, abandon the hypothesis Γ, otherwise record the set of possible excuses of the violation on a global list.
4. Find all minimal subsets (up to a given size)[1] of $\{\sigma_1, ..., \sigma_n\}$ that "cover" all apparent violations of Γ; a subset of $\{\sigma_1, ..., \sigma_n\}$ covers an apparent violation of Γ if it contains all elements of at least one "excuse" for that violation;
5. Check hypothesis (Γ $\sigma'_1 ... \sigma'_m$) (i.e., the original hypothesis together with added provisos) for each of the minimal subsets $\{\sigma'_1, ..., \sigma'_m\}$ of $\{\sigma_1, ..., \sigma_n\}$ found in the previous step for truth in the initial conditions of the problem being solved; return the variant hypotheses that pass this test as the verified hypotheses.

Verification Conditions and "Excuses"

Verification conditions are conditions on the precondition-effect structure of operators that are needed to support an inductive proof that the operators maintain a given type of state constraint. (We have such inductive proofs for the constraints found by DISCOPLAN, but space does not allow their inclusion.) The most complex aspect of the above sequence of steps is the collection of possible "excuses" (sets of candidate supplementary conditions) in step 3, when verification conditions for Γ are violated. The details depend on the verification conditions (as determined by the form of Γ), and different verification conditions call for different "excuses" when violated. However, there are commonalities across the various types of hypotheses that are exploited in our code. In particular, there are essentially 4 types of verification conditions: (i) ones that preclude the occurrence of multiple effects of the same type (e.g., in testing (ON ?*X ?Y), we want to guard against multiple effects such as (ON ?U ?W), (ON ?V ?W)); (ii) ones that require the co-occurrence of a certain type of effect with another (e.g, in testing an implicative constraint, whenever an effect instantiates the antecedent, another effect should instantiate the consequent; and similarly for the contrapositive of the implication); (iii) ones that require a *change* (a certain type of precondition and a related effect) whenever a given type of effect is present (e.g., this is needed whenever Γ involves sv-constraints); and (iv) ones that preclude the co-occurrence of certain effects with certain other effects (e.g., this is needed in testing exclusion hypotheses, stating that the truth of one predication implies the falsity of another). Our programs for testing hypotheses and collecting "excuses" are organized around 4 subroutines corresponding to these 4 types of verification condition.[2]

The "excuses" themselves are essentially of two types. One type of "excuse" ensures that a particular *when*-clause of an operator is rendered irrelevant to a hypothesis. In this case the excuse is a singleton $\{\sigma\}$ (chosen from the candidate supplementary conditions) whose falsity is entailed by the preconditions of that *when*-clause (or by the preconditions of the corresponding primary *when*-clause, if differ-

---

[1]For the domains we have tested a size limit of 2 suffices; allowance for up to 5 supplementary conditions yielded no new constraints.

[2]Actually, we have recently added a fifth routine testing for the presence of a "compensating change", which allows us to make stronger use of the induction assumption in testing implicative constraints. We briefly discuss this later.

ent). This type of excuse is considered whenever a *when*-clause generates an effect that should not co-occur with another given effect, or whenever it generates an effect whose co-occurrence requirements are not (provably) met. The second type of "excuse" ensures that the effects of a particular secondary *when*-clause are realized. In this case the "excuse" may contain multiple elements of $\{\sigma_1, ..., \sigma_n\}$, which together entail the preconditions of that *when*-clause. This type of "excuse" is considered whenever a required co-occurring effect is not guaranteed in the *when*-clause under consideration, but can be guaranteed *via* the effects of another *when*-clause, if the preconditions of that other *when*-clause are true. The search for "excuses" for apparent violations of hypothesized constraints has recently been strengthened by the use of subtype/supertype and exclusion relations among static monadic predicates. (These are found in the manner explained in the subsection that follows.)

We now provide some specifics of the discovery process for most types of constraints in the new version of DISCOPLAN, with particular reference to verification conditions (where relevant). We omit discussion of simple implicative constraints (without sv-constraints).

Static Constraints

Static constraints are state invariants involving *type-predicates*, where a type-predicate is a static monadic predicate that occurs positively in the initial state. In general, the result of this analysis gives the following information about types:

- a list of type-predicates, each of which is associated with the set of objects of the domain satisfying the predicate;
- a list of *universal types* (i.e., predicates that are satisfied by every object in the domain), and a list of *empty types* (i.e., predicates that are satisfied by no object);
- a list of supertype/subtype and incompatible relationships between type-predicates.

Type information is computed in polynomial time by processing the initial state in the following way (the algorithm assumes that for each predicate P in the domain it is known whether P is static – this information is computed during the initial standardization of the operators). First we compute the set Θ of the constants appearing in the specification of the initial state, and we associate with each type-predicate the set of the constants appearing in the positive instances of P.[3] This set, indicated with $|P|$, is the *extension* of P. If we have that $|P| = \Theta$, then P is an universal type, while if $|P| = \emptyset$, then P is an empty type; if for some other type-predicate Q, we have that $|P| \subseteq |Q|$, then P is a subtype of Q and Q is a supertype of P, i.e., each object of type P must be of type Q; if $|P| \cap |Q| = \emptyset$, then P and Q are incompatible types, i.e., no object in Θ can be both of type P and of type Q. For example, suppose that the list of static predicates appearing in the initial state is:

((P a) (P b) (Q b) (R a) (S a) (S b)
 (S c) (T a b) (T b c)).

The following information is computed by DISCOPLAN:

- $\Theta = \{a, b, c\}$; Type-predicates: (P Q R S)

[3] Here we assume that all the objects (constant symbols) of the domain appear in the initial state as terms of some positive literal.

- |P| = {a,b}, |Q| = {b}, |R| = {a}, |S| = {a,b,c}
- Universal types: (S ?X); empty types: nil
- Super/sub-type relationships:
  ((IMPLIES (Q ?X) (P ?X)) (IMPLIES (R ?X) (P ?X))
   (IMPLIES (P ?X) (S ?X)) (IMPLIES (Q ?X) (S ?X))
   (IMPLIES (R ?X) (S ?X)))
- Incompatible types:
  ((IMPLIES (Q ?X) (NOT (R ?X)))).

Dedicated Inference of SV-Constraints

An example of an sv-constraint that can be inferred in isolation is the blocks-world constraint ((ON ?X ?*Y)), i.e., any object can be ON at most one other object; or, in unabbreviated FOL,
$\forall x, y, z. (ON(x,y) \land ON(x,z)) \Rightarrow y = z$.
As an example involving a supplementary condition (from the logistics-att world), we have
 ((AT ?X ?*Y) (AIRPLANE ?X)),
i.e., an airplane can be AT no more than one place. Our "dedicated" method of finding sv-constraints of this type starts by forming hypotheses based on the occurrence within a *when*-clause and the corresponding primary *when*-clause of an effect $(P\ t_1...t_n)$ together with a "compensating change", i.e., a P-precondition and corresponding $\neg P$-effect that appears to maintains single-valuedness. The verification conditions ensure (a) that there are no multiple effects that could violate single-valuedness, and (b) that any P-effect is indeed accompanied by a "compensating" change. Violations lead to collection of "excuses" of the sort indicated earlier (if possible), and these provide the basis for deriving minimal sets of supplementary conditions. (a) and (b) suffice for an inductive proof that if a constraint such as ((P ?X ?*Y) (Q ?X)) holds in the initial state, it holds in all reachable states. (Additional starred and unstarred arguments and multiple supplementary conditions are easily dealt with.)

Implicative Constraints + SV-Constraints: The Case of Subsumed Variables

In the introduction, we mentioned the blocks-world constraint
((IMPLIES (ON ?*X ?Y) (NOT (CLEAR ?Y))) (NEQ ?Y T))
as an example of a combined implicative and sv-constraint obtainable by the previous version of DISCOPLAN. In general, the implicative constraints we are considering here have as their antecedent a positive literal that contains at least one "starred" variable not occurring in the consequent, and zero or more "unstarred" variables occurring in the consequent. The stars indicate that for all values of the unstarred variables, the antecedent holds for at most one tuple of values of the starred variables.

The discovery of such constraints in the previous version of DISCOPLAN was limited to domains where operator effects are unconditional. The new algorithm for operators with conditional effects proceeds much as before, though of course with complications due to the fact that multiple *when*-clauses may contribute to the effects of an operator. Potential antecedent-consequent pairs are hypothesized based on co-occurrence of a positive effect literal ϕ with another effect or persistent precondition ψ whose variables are a proper subset of those of ϕ. The complement of the signed predicate of ψ must occur as an effect of some operator (otherwise simultaneous inference of an sv-constraint would be unnecessary), and ϕ and ψ must belong to the pooled effects and persistent preconditions of some *when*-clause w and the corresponding primary *when*-clause w_1. For the special case of an antecedent (P ?X ?*Y) and consequent (Q ?X) the verification conditions are the following (these are easily generalized to allow for multiple shared and starred variables):

(a) There must not be multiple effects matching (P ?X ?*Y) that could directly violate the sv-constraint. The details are as in condition (a) for "dedicated" sv-testing.

(b) If w contains an effect (P x y) for some x and y, there must be a precondition (NOT (Q x')) and an effect (Q x'') in w or the corresponding primary *when*-clause w_1, where $x'' = x' = x$ by symbol identity or EQ-preconditions. (We have recently weakened this condition in a way that makes stronger use of the induction assumption, but leave out details for simplicity.)

(c) If w contains an effect (NOT (Q x)) for some x, there must be a precondition (P x' y) and an effect (NOT (P x'' y')) in w or w_1, where $x'' = x' = x$ and $y = y'$ by symbol identity or EQ-preconditions.

Implicative Constraints + SV-Constraints: The Case of Non-Subsumed Variables

In the implicative constraints considered in the preceding subsection, the antecedent variables were required to subsume the consequent variables. Here we assume instead that both antecedent and consequent contain variables not contained in the other. All such variables are "starred", while the shared variables are unstarred. An example is the following constraint from the Logistics world:
((IMPLIES (AT ?X ?*Y) (NOT (IN ?X ?*Z))) (OBJ ?X)).
This is an *exclusive* state constraint, i.e., it states that no object can simultaneously be AT something and IN something (and in addition an object can be AT no more that one thing, an IN no more than one thing). In (Gerevini & Schubert 1998) we formulated provably correct criteria for deriving such constraints, but once again we did not generalize to operators with conditional effects. The generalized method proceeds much as in the case of implicative constraints with subsumed variables (previous subsection), and we need only point out the main differences. First, hypothesis formation relies on literal co-occurrences as before, except that both the antecedent and consequent are based on effects (with no consideration of persistent preconditions) and the restrictions relevant to exclusive state constraints are placed on signs and variables. There are five verification conditions; for the (easily generalized) special case of an exclusive state constraint with antecedent (P ?X ?*Y) and consequent (NOT (Q ?X ?*Z)), they run as follows. The first two conditions guard against multiple effects matching (P ?X ?*Y) or (Q ?X ?*Z), as in the previous condition (a). The third condition states

(c) If w contains an effect (P x y) for some x, y, there must be a precondition (Q x' z) and an effect (NOT (Q x'' z')) in w or w_1, where $x'' = x' = x$ and $z = z'$ by symbol identity or EQ-preconditions.

The fourth condition is completely analogous to the third, with P and Q and y and z interchanged. The fifth and final condition guards against co-occurrence of an effect (P x y) in one *when*-clause with an effect (Q x' z) in the same or in another *when*-clause, where $x = x'$ by symbol identity or EQ-preconditions. This condition is most easily understood by thinking of an exclusive state constraint as a disjunction of two negative literals, and recognizing that if both literals become false for the same shared argument and some values of the non-shared arguments, then the disjunction cannot remain true for all values of the three variables.

Antisymmetry Constraints

Antisymmetry constraints (as-constraints) are particular implicative constraints of the form
((IMPLIES (P t_1 t_2) (NOT (P t_2 t_1))) σ_1 σ_2...σ_n),
where t_1 and t_2 can be constants or universally quantified variables, and $\sigma_1, ..., \sigma_n$ are supplementary conditions whose variables are a subset of $\{t_1, t_2\}$. An example of an antisymmetry constraint in the blocks-world is
((IMPLIES (ON ?X ?Y) (NOT (ON ?Y ?X)))),
i.e., if one object is on another, then the second is not on the first. Like the previous methods, the method for discovering antisymmetries uses the hypothesize-and-test paradigm described above. In particular, if (P t_1 t_2) is an effect of a *when*-clause in an operator op, then we hypothesize ((IMPLIES (P t_1 t_2) (NOT (P t_2 t_1)))). The hypothesis is then augmented with candidate supplementary conditions in the same manner as for implicative constraints, and tested against the operators to yield variants augmented with minimal sets of supplementary conditions, and finally these variants are tested in the initial state. The verification conditions for an antisymmetry hypothesis Γ, enabling an inductive proof that Γ holds in all reachable states, are the following:

For each when-clause w of each operator o, if w has an effect matching (P t_1 t_2), then assuming that (a) Γ is true in any state s where o is applied and the preconditions of w hold, and (b) Γ becomes false in the state s' resulting by applying o to s, leads to a contradiction (because s or s' would have to be inconsistent).

In order to test this condition, for each *when*-clause w of o, if w has an effect matching (P t_1 t_2) with unifier u, we add $[(P\ t_2\ t_1)]_u$ to the effects of w. Then we test each expanded *when*-clause w_e to see whether the set Ω formed by the effects of w_e, together with the persistent preconditions and effects of the primary *when*-clause w_1 of o (if $w_e \neq w_1$), is *in*consistent. If this is the case, then Γ is confirmed for w. If this is not the case, then we collect sets of supplementary conditions that can excuse the violation of the verification condition.

To strengthen this method, when we test the verification condition against an operator, we use an "expanded" version of the operator, obtained by augmenting the preconditions and effects of each *when*-clause using implicative constraints discovered earlier. (This process is described in the next section). The resulting Ω-sets are inconsistent if Ω contains a pair of contradictory non-static conditions, contradictory EQ/NEQ-conditions, or a pair of static conditions that violate static constraints.

XOR-constraints

XOR-constraints are state-constraints of the form

$((\text{XOR } \phi \; \psi) \; \sigma_1 \; \sigma_2 ... \sigma_n)$,

where ϕ and ψ are positive fluent literals, such that non-shared variables are existentially quantified, while shared variables are universally quantified, and where the variables in $\sigma_1, \sigma_2, ..., \sigma_n$ can only be variables shared by ϕ and ψ. An example of an XOR-constraint in the logistics domain is

((XOR (AT ?X ?Y) (IN ?X ?Z)) (OBJECT ?X)),

stating that in any reachable state, any object is either at some place or in something. The method that we have developed for inferring this type of constraint is based on combining two types of constraints entailing exclusive disjunctions. The first type of constraint consists of those implicative constraints inferred by our previously described methods where ϕ and ψ are fluents, ϕ is positive and ψ is negative. The second type of constraint corresponds to binary "state membership invariants" (Fox & Long 1998). These are binary disjunctions, possibly augmented with supplementary conditions, of the following form $((\text{OR } \phi \; \psi) \; \sigma_1 \; \sigma_2 ... \sigma_k)$, where the non-shared variables of ϕ and ψ are existentially quantified, and the remaining variables are universally quantified. Our method for inferring state membership invariants is a variant of the methods for inferring implicative constraints described in previous sections (for lack of space we omit a detailed description). One of the main differences lies in the way hypotheses are verified in the initial state, and in the way supplementary conditions capable of rescuing the law are collected. When we check a hypothetical membership invariant against the initial state, we consider additional type predicates (not appearing in the operator from which the hypothesis was derived) which restrict the domains of universally quantified variables in ϕ and ψ. For example, in UCPOP's formalization of the *Ferry* domain DISCOPLAN can infer the following membership invariant

((OR (AT ?X ?Y) (ON ?X FERRY)) (AUTO ?X)),

where (AUTO ?X) is a supplementary condition that is required for verifying the law in the initial state, and which does not belong to any operator that suggested the hypothesis. By combining this state membership constraint with the exclusive constraint

((IMPLIES (AT ?X ?Y) (NOT (ON ?X FERRY)))),

DISCOPLAN infers the XOR-constraint

((XOR (AT ?X ?Y) (ON ?X FERRY)) (AUTO ?X)).

Using "Expanded" Operators

As mentioned above DISCOPLAN discovers as-constraints using expanded operators. Moreover, as pointed out in (Gerevini & Schubert 1998), the general hypothesize-and-test process can be enhanced by feeding confirmed constraints back into the process. A straightforward way to do this is to expand each operator by adding extra preconditions and effects that are implied by constraints discovered earlier. In particular, the current version of DISCOPLAN expands the given operators using implicative constraints with subsumed variables.[4]

---

[4]Note that in the current implementation type constraints are not used for expanding the operators. Reasoning about type constraints is incorporated into the various discovery routines.

By re-running all the discovery algorithms using the expanded operators, further constraints can be derived. This process of inferring state-constraints and expanding the operators using discovered constraints can be repeated until no more new constraints are derived.

An operator o is expanded by using each implicative constraint $((\text{IMPLIES } \phi \; \psi) \; \sigma_1, \sigma_2, ..., \sigma_n)$ with subsumed variables in the following way. For each *when*-clause w of o, if a precondition or effect χ of w matches ϕ with unifier u, and $\sigma_1...\sigma_n$ are satisfied under u, then we augment w with $[\psi]_u$. Specifically, we add $[\psi]_u$ to the preconditions of w, if χ is a precondition of w or ψ is a static condition; while we add $[\psi]_u$ to the effects of w if χ is an effect of w and ϕ is non-static. Writing w_1 for the primary *when*-clause of o, if $w = w_1$, then the check for the validity of $\sigma_1...\sigma_n$ is done against the preconditions of w; otherwise (w is a secondary *when*-clause) the supplementary conditions are checked against the preconditions of w extended with the preconditions of w_1. Also, note that if $w = w_1$ and some supplementary preconditions are not satisfied by the preconditions of w_1, then it is still possible that such conditions are satisfied by the preconditions of a secondary *when*-clause w_2. If this is the case, then $[\psi]_u$ is added to the preconditions or effects of w_2 (depending on the conditions indicated above).

Finally, if a *when*-clause is not expanded, and ϕ and ψ involve the same variables, then we try to expand it using the contrapositive implicative constraints

$((\text{IMPLIES } \neg\psi \; \neg\phi) \; \sigma_1 \; \sigma_2 ... \sigma_n)$.

Further Extensions

We previously mentioned our recent weakenening of the verification conditions for combined implicative and sv-constraints, making stronger use of the induction assumptions. The nature of the change is best appreciated from an example. Consider the following simple set of operators describing two ways of getting from one place to another — walking and taking a cab:

```
(define (operator walk)            (define (operator take-cab)
 :parameters (?x ?y)                :parameters (?x ?y)
 :precondition                      :precondition
   (and (at ?x) (neq ?x ?y))          (and (at-cab ?x) (neq ?x ?y))
 :effect (and (at ?y)               :effect (and (at-cab ?y)
              (not (at ?x))))                    (not (at-cab ?x))))

(define (operator get-in)          (define (operator get-out)
 :parameters (?x)                   :parameters (?x)
 :precondition                      :precondition
   (and (at-cab ?x) (at ?x))          (and (at-cab ?x) (in-cab))
 :effect (and (not (at ?x))        :effect (and (at ?x)
              (in-cab)))                        (not (in-cab))))
```

A law that holds in this domain, whenever it holds initially, is (IMPLIES (AT ?*X) (NOT (IN-CAB))). The point of interest is that verification of this law for the walk operator requires the inference, from the induction assumption, that (NOT (IN-CAB)) holds in any state in which the walk-preconditions hold, and since this condition persists, that it also holds after a walk. Our current code does this verification by adding the immediate consequences of the induction assumption to the operator preconditions, and applying the weakened verification conditions (no longer requiring a *change* from (in-cab)) to (NOT (IN-CAB)) in walk). We note that this technique could also be used for simultaneous induction, i.e., we could assume multiple hypotheses in states prior to operator application, add the immediate consequences of these assumptions to the preconditions, and then apply our usual verification conditions for individual hypotheses. If the individual verifications succeed, then all the assumed hypotheses are true (*cf.* (Rintanen 1998)).

Besides the implemented extensions we have outlined so far, we have also formulated a number of extensions theoretically, which we now describe briefly. Their implementation remains as future work.

Strict Single-Valuedness (and n-Valuedness)

The verification conditions we described for "dedicated" inference of sv-constraints essentially ensure that (a) no operator application generates multiple literals that would violate the sv-constraint, and (b) any operator application that generates one instance of the predicate at issue, where there might already be a prior instance with the same "unstarred" arguments, also generates a compensating change from an instance to a negated instance of the predicate. Thus the number of tuples of values of starred variables, for any given values of the unstarred ones, is limited to 1. To establish strict singlevaluedness, we need only add the converse of (b), that any operator that produces a negated instance of the predicate at issue should also produce a "compensating" positive instance. However, both effects must also appear in negated form in the preconditions, since mere affirmation of an effect may just be reaffirmation of something that was already true in the prior state.

In other words, we verify that for any given values of the unstarred arguments, the number of tuples of values of the starred arguments remains fixed. An interesting point is that this enables discovery of "strict n-valuedness" constraints as readily as strict sv-constraints. The only difference lies in what can be confirmed in the initial state.

N-ary Disjunctive Constraints

Our implemented methods in principle allow the inference of constraints involving any number of literals – but only two of these may be fluent literals (the rest are static supplementary conditions). However, our hypothesis generation and verification techniques are rather readily extensible to arbitrary disjunctions of literals, where any number of these may be fluents. We require the hypothesis to be of form $\phi_1 \vee ... \vee \phi_n$, where the ϕ_i are literals, and for each ϕ_i for which some instances can become false (through the effects of some operator), there is another literal ϕ_j whose variables are a subset of those of ϕ_i. All variables are regarded as universally quantified. Then we can verify the law by confirming that whenever one of the literals becomes false (i.e., an instance of its negation is asserted in an operator's effects), a corresponding instance of another literal, with at most the same variables, becomes or remains true (i.e., is asserted as a persistent precondition, or as an effect). We have formulated a method that starts with (potentially) "unnecessarily lengthy" disjunctions, and systematically finds minimal combinations of literals whose disjunction is an invariant.

```
BW-LARGE-B
 ((IMPLIES (CLEAR ?X) (BLOCK ?X)))
 ((IMPLIES (CLEAR ?X) (NOT (FIXED ?X))))
 ((IMPLIES (ON ?X ?Y) (BLOCK ?X)))
 ((IMPLIES (NOT (BLOCK ?X)) (CLEAR ?X)))
 ((IMPLIES (ON ?X ?Y) (BLOCK ?Y)))
 ((IMPLIES (ON ?X ?Y) (NOT (ON ?Y ?X))) )
 ((IMPLIES (ON ?X ?Y) (NEQ ?X ?Y)))
 ((IMPLIES (ON ?X ?Y) (NOT (FIXED ?X))))
 ((IMPLIES (ON ?*X ?Y) (NOT (CLEAR ?Y))) (NOT (FIXED ?Y)))
 ((IMPLIES (FIXED ?X) (BLOCK ?X)) (BLOCK ?X))
 ((ON ?X ?*Y)) ((XOR (ON ?X ?Y) (CLEAR ?Y)) (NOT (FIXED ?Y)))
BW-LARGE-B1
 ((IMPLIES (ON ?X ?Y) (NEQ ?X TABLE)))
 ((IMPLIES (ON ?X ?Y) (NEQ ?X ?Y)))
 ((IMPLIES (ON ?*X ?Y) (NOT (CLEAR ?Y))) (NEQ ?Y TABLE))
 ((IMPLIES (ON ?X ?Y) (NOT (ON ?Y ?X))))
 ((ON ?X ?*Y)) ((XOR (ON ?X ?Y) (CLEAR ?Y)) (NEQ ?Y TABLE))
```

Figure 1: Samples of DISCOPLAN outputs for `bw-large-b` and `bw-large-b1`.

N-ary Disjunctive and SV-Constraints

The second generalization concerns disjunctive laws with simultaneous assumption of sv-constraints. We assume a disjunction of literals $\phi_1 \vee ... \vee \phi_n$, where the ϕ_i literals may contain "starred" occurrences of some variables, subject to the following constraints: (a) only negative literals may contain "starred" variable occurrences; (b) "starred" variables may not occur in more than one literal; and (c) for every ϕ_i that can become false, the set of "unstarred" variables occurring in that literal must include the set of variables (possibly the empty set) of some other literal.

Note that (c) is a generalization of the constraint assumed above for implicative laws without "starred" variables, i.e., without sv-hypotheses. The interpretation of any "stars" occurring in a negative literal is that the predicate of that literal is single-valued in the sense that if we consider all tuples of values of the predicate that satisfy the supplementary conditions on them, then we will find at most one such tuple for any particular choice of values of the unstarred arguments.

For such a generalized disjunctive and sv-hypothesis we have formulated, and proved to be correct, verification conditions enabling an inductive proof that the law holds in all reachable states. These conditions are a generalization of those for n-ary disjunctive constraints, and implicative constraints involving non-subsumed starred variables, that we have described in the previous sections.

Sample Results and Related Work

Figures 1-2 give the outputs of DISCOPLAN for some known problems. For lack of space fluent predicate domains and OR-constraints are not included; moreover, we report only 6 of the 36 static constraints for `T-trains1` and 6 of the 15 static constraints for `att-logistics`. `logistics-a` is from the ATT-logistics domain (Kautz & Selman 1996) for which we used the formalization provided by MEDIC (Ernst, Millstein & Weld 1997); `T-trains1` is from the typed version of the Trains domain (Gerevini & Schubert 1996) containing seven operators, one of which has conditional effects; `bw-large-b` is a problem from SATPLAN formalization of the blocks world (Kautz & Selman 1996) that we translated into four operators with no conditional effects; `bw-large-b1` is the same problems as `bw-large-b`, except that here we used a different domain formalization with just one operator containing conditional effects:

```
T-TRAINS1
((IMPLIES (AT ?X ?Y) (CITY ?Y)))
((IMPLIES (IN ?*X ?Y) (NOT (EMPTY ?Y))))
((IMPLIES (OJ ?X) (NOT (ORANGES ?X))))
((IMPLIES (EMPTY ?X) (CAR ?X)))
((IMPLIES (COUPLED ?X ?Y) (CAR ?Y)))
((IMPLIES (LOOSE ?X) (CAR ?X)))
((IMPLIES (IN ?X ?Y) (OJ ?X)) (TANKER-CAR ?Y))
((IMPLIES (COUPLED ?*X ?Y) (NOT (LOOSE ?Y))))
((IMPLIES (COUPLED ?X ?Y) (ENGINE ?X)))
((AT ?X ?*Y) (ENGINE ?X))
((IMPLIES (AT ?X ?*Y) (NOT (IN ?X ?*Z))) (BANANAS ?X))
((IMPLIES (AT ?X ?*Y) (NOT (IN ?X ?*Z))) (COMM ?X))
((IMPLIES (AT ?X ?Y) (NOT (AT ?Y ?X))))
((IMPLIES (COUPLED ?X ?Y) (NOT (COUPLED ?Y ?X)))))
((XOR (COUPLED ?X ?Y) (LOOSE ?X) (CAR ?X))
((XOR (AT ?X ?Y) (IN ?X ?Z) (BANANAS ?X) (COMM ?X))
((XOR (AT ?X ?Y) (IN ?X ?Z) (BANANAS ?X))
((XOR (IN ?X ?Y) (EMPTY ?Y) (CAR ?Y)))
((IMPLIES (CAR ?X) (NOT (CITY ?X))))
((IMPLIES (CAR ?X) (NOT (TRACK ?X))))
((IMPLIES (CAR ?X) (NOT (ENGINE ?X))))
((IMPLIES (CAR ?X) (NOT (OJ-FAC ?X))))
((IMPLIES (CAR ?X) (NOT (COMM ?X))))
((IMPLIES (BANANAS ?X) (NOT (CAR ?X))))
((IMPLIES (BOXCAR ?X) (CAR ?X)))....

ATT-LOGISTICS-A
((IMPLIES (IN ?X ?Y) (OBJECT ?X)))
((IMPLIES (AT ?X ?Y) (LOCATION ?Y)) (OBJECT ?X))
((IMPLIES (AT ?X ?Y) (AIRPORT ?Y)) (AIRPLANE ?X))
((IMPLIES (AT ?X ?Y) (LOCATION ?Y)) (TRUCK ?X))
((AT ?X ?*Y) (AIRPLANE ?X))  ((AT ?X ?*Y) (TRUCK ?X))
((IMPLIES (AT ?X ?*Y) (NOT (IN ?X ?*Z))) (OBJECT ?X))
((IMPLIES (IN ?X ?Y) (NOT (IN ?Y ?X))))
((IMPLIES (AT ?X ?Y) (NOT (AT ?Y ?X))))
((XOR (AT ?X ?Y) (IN ?X ?Z) (OBJECT ?X))
((IMPLIES (AIRPLANE ?X) (NOT (OBJECT ?X))))
((IMPLIES (AIRPLANE ?X) (NOT (TRUCK ?X))))
((IMPLIES (AIRPLANE ?X) (NOT (LOCATION ?X))))
((IMPLIES (AIRPLANE ?X) (NOT (AIRPORT ?X))))
((IMPLIES (AIRPLANE ?X) (NOT (CITY ?X))))
((IMPLIES (AIRPORT ?X) (LOCATION ?X)))....
```

Figure 2: Samples of DISCOPLAN outputs for att-logistics and T-trains1.

```
(define (operator Put)
  :parameters (?x ?y ?z)
  :precondition (and (on ?x ?) (clear ?x)
                     (neq ?x Table) (neq ?y z) (neq ?x ?y))
  :effect (and (when (eq ?y Table)
                     (and (on ?x ?y) (clear ?z) (not (on ?x ?z))))
               (when (and (neq ?y Table) (clear ?y))
                     (and (on ?x ?y) (clear ?z) (not (on ?x ?z))
                          (not (clear ?y)))) )
```

The tests were conducted on a portable PC 266 MHz with 64 Mbytes, running Allegro Common Lisp 4.3 under Linux.[5] Each type of constraint can be discovered in isolation using a dedicated inference procedure. The total CPU-times that were required for computing all types of constraints for the problems of Figures 1 and 2 were: 0.056 CPU-seconds for logistics-a, 0.098 for T-trains1, 0.026 for bw-large-b and 0.086 for bw-large-b1.

Other approaches for the automatic inference of state invariants have been proposed, including (Kelleher & Cohn 1992; Kelleher 1996), (Fox & Long 1998) and (Rintanen 1998). A major contribution of our work in relation to this prior work and to the original version of DISCOPLAN (1998) is the allowance for conditional effects. Kelleher and Cohn's method is similar to our generation-and-test approach. However, their techniques cannot infer the types of constraints that we have addressed in this paper. The algorithm for computing state invariants proposed in (Rintanen 1998) is limited to propositional operators, and it appears to be computationally more expensive than our techniques.

Fox and Long's TIM system can infer some non-binary

---
[5]DISCOPLAN is written in Lisp and it accepts input domain descriptions specified using either the UCPOP or PDDL formalism.

membership invariants that DISCOPLAN currently cannot infer. On the other hand, TIM does not handle negated preconditions, and cannot infer the following classes of DISCOPLAN constraints: antisymmetry constraints; XOR-constraints; strict n-valuedness; and implicative constraints $\phi \Rightarrow \psi$ where

- ϕ or ψ is a propositional literal, e.g., ((IMPLIES (ON-BOX ?X) (NOT (ON-FLOOR)))) in the Monkey domain;
- both ϕ and ψ are positive literals, e.g., ((IMPLIES (HASBANANAS) (HASKNIFE))) in the Monkey domain; or
- ψ is an EQ/NEQ conditions like the irreflexivity law ((IMPLIES (ON ?X ?Y) (NEQ ?X ?Y))).

Conclusions and Further Work

A significant aspect of the work we have reported here is the allowance for conditional effects in our mechanisms for discovering state constraints in planning domains. Another significant aspect is the greatly expanded range discovery techniques, many of which have been implemented in the new version of DISCOPLAN.

Future work includes the (easy) extension of our methods to use the initial state (in addition to the individual operators) to formulate hypothetical constraints, and the implementation of the techniques that have been developed theoretically but not yet implemented.

Acknowledgments

This research was supported in part by NATO grant CRG951285, and by ARPA/SSTO grant F30602-95-1-0025 DARPA grant F30602-98-2-0133 (second author). We would like to thank Piergiorgio Bertoli for a fruitful discussion that inspired our method of inferring XOR-constraints.

References

Ernst, M.; Millstein, T.; and Weld, D. 1997. Automatic SAT-compilation of planning problems. *Proc. of IJCAI-97*, 1169-1176.

Fox, M. and Long, D. 1998. The Automatic Inference of State Invariants in TIM. *JAIR*, 9, 367–421.

Fox, M. and Long, D. 2000. Utilizing Automatically Inferred Invariants in Graph Construction and Search. *Proc. of AIPS-00*.

Gerevini, A. and Schubert, L.K. 1996. Accelerating partial-order planners: Some techniques for effective search control and pruning, *JAIR*, 5, 95–137.

Gerevini, A. and Schubert, L.K. 1998. Inferring state constraints for domain-independent planning. *Proc. of AAAI-98*, 905–912.

Gerevini, A. and Schubert, L.K. 2000. Extending the Types of State Constraints Discovered by DISCOPLAN. *Proc. of the AIPS-00 Workshop on Analysing and Exploiting Domain Knowledge for Efficient Planning*.

Kautz, H., and Selman, B. 1996. Pushing the envelope: Planning, propositional logic, and stochastic search. In *Proc. of AAAI-96*.

Kautz, H., and Selman, B. 1998. The Role of Domain Specific Knowledge in the Planning as Satisfiability Framework. search. In *Proc. of AIPS-98*.

Kelleher, G. and Cohn, A.G. 1992. Automatically synthesising domain constraints from operator descriptions. *Proc. of ECAI-92.*.

Kelleher, G. 1996. Determining General Consequences of Sets of Actions. TR CMS.14.96. Liverpool Moores Univ.

Refanidis, I. and Vlahavas, I. 2000. Exploiting State Constraints in Heuristic State-Space Planning. *Proc. of AIPS-00*.

Rintanen, J. 1998. A planning algorithm not based on directional search. *Proc. of KR'98*, 617–624.

A logic for planning under partial observability

A. Herzig, J. Lang, D. Longin and T. Polacsek
IRIT-UPS, F-31062 Toulouse Cedex 04, France
{herzig, lang, longin, polacsek}@irit.fr
http://www.irit.fr/~Andreas.Herzig

Abstract

We propose an epistemic dynamic logic EDL able to represent the interactions between action and knowledge that are fundamental to planning under partial observability. EDL enables us to represent incomplete knowledge, nondeterministic actions, observations, sensing actions and conditional plans; it also enables a logical expression of several frequently made assumptions about the nature of the domain, such as determinism, full observability, unobservability, or pure sensing. Plan verification corresponds to checking the validity of a given EDL formula. The allowed plans are conditional, and a key point of our framework is that a plan is meaningful if and only if the branching conditions bear on the knowledge of the agent only, and not on the real world (to which that agent may not have access); this leads us to consider "plans that reason" which may contain branching conditions referring to implicit knowledge to be evaluated at execution time.

Introduction

A large amount of work has been done recently about planning under incomplete information. By incomplete information, we mean (as usual) that the initial state of the world is not fully known and/or the actions are not deterministic. The gap between planning under complete and incomplete information relies on the role of *knowledge* in the latter and especially the *interactions between knowledge and action*. These interactions work in both ways:

- the choice of an action to perform is guided by the knowledge the agent has on the actual state of the world, and especially by the *observations* made after performing previous actions. As soon as performance of an action allows gathering knowledge by a susbsequent observation, the choice of the following action will be generally conditioned by this observation.

- performing an action may bring some more knowledge (and help the agent acting in a better way, as explained just above) by means of consecutive observations; this has led many researchers to focus and formalize *sensing actions*, which do not change the state of the world but only the agent's beliefs.

Copyright © 2000, American Association for Artificial Intelligence (www.aaai.org). All rights reserved.

On the other hand, the planning community has recently paid a lot of attention to the role of logic in representing and solving planning problems. This includes both (1) the SAT-PLAN framework (Kautz & Selman 1996) and its very recent extensions to planning under incomplete knowledge (Rintanen 1999) and (2) the action description languages and their recent application to planning under incomplete knowledge (Lobo, Mendez, & Taylor 1997) (Baral, Kreinovich, & Trejo 1999). The former (1) led to powerful resolution algorithms which benefit from the theoretical and experimental results on satisfiability. The latter (2) gave birth to very expressive languages that enable reasoning with nondeterminism, minimal change, ramifications, concurrent actions, and more recently interactions between action and knowledge. But so far these approaches did not lead yet to the practical development of planning algorithms based on automated proof procedures.

The question now consists of identifying the "simplest" logic containing the notions of incomplete knowledge, nondeterministic actions, observations, conditional plan and sensing actions. Two of these words evoke two well-known families of logics:

- *dynamic logic* aims at reasoning with complex combinations of actions (including sequential and conditional actions). Decidability and complexity results, as well as automated proof procedures for the standard propositional dynamic logic and its variants are a familiar part of the logical landscape. Still, surprisingly, dynamic logic has not been much considered for planning.

- *epistemic logics* aim at reasoning with explicit knowledge of an agent. Some simple epistemic logics are computationally not harder than classical logic.

What is missing to propositional dynamic logic (PDL) so as to render it suitable for planning under incomplete information is (1) the possibility for actions to have epistemic effects and (2) the possibility to branch on epistemic conditions. This second point needs some comments: indeed, PDL enables expressing some kinds of conditional actions, but these conditional actions are not suitable for expressing conditional plans, because while a program can be supposed to know at any instant the value of any variable, this is generally not the case for an agent acting in an incomplete environment, for whom some parts of the world are hidden (see e.g. (Levesque 1996)).

Example 1 *There are d doors. Behind exactly t of the doors, there is a tiger (t < d). Behind one (and only one) of the doors, there is a princess and no tiger. The agent has no prior knowledge about what is behind each of the doors (he only knows the values of d and t). The available actions are listening to what happens behind a given door, which results in hearing the tiger roaring if and only if there is one behind the door, and opening a given door, which may result in marrying the princess or being eaten by the tiger or nothing, depending on what is behind the door. The goal of the agent is to stay alive and marry the princess.*

The propositional variables $p(i)$ and $t(i)$ mean respectively that there is a princess (a tiger) behind door i. Consider the following plan

π_1: if $p(1)$ then $open(1)$
else if $p(2)$ then $open(2)$ (...)

Clearly, π_1 is not executable by the agent, because in general he does not know whether $p(i)$ holds or not, and therefore he is unable to branch on such a condition. The solution is to allow for *epistemic conditions* only. Suppose therefore that our language contains a modal operator **K**. A plan such as

π_2: if $\mathbf{K}p(1)$ then $open(1)$
else if $\mathbf{K}p(2)$ then $open(2)$ else (...)

can then be formulated. However, except when $d = 1$, it misses the goals, because the agent ignores whether $p(i)$ is true or not, therefore he will not open any door.

Thus, agents branch on epistemic conditions only, because they are able to decide whether they *know* a given formula or not, whereas they are not always able to decide whether this formula is *true* in the actual world.

This brings us to the following specificity of our logic: it enables the expression of *plans that explicitly involve a reasoning task*. For Example 1, the shortest succeeding plan (in terms of the average number of actions, given uniform probabilities for princess and tigers locations) can be expressed informally by: repeat (listen to a door and open if there is no tiger) until either the princess is delivered or the two tigers have been found; in this second case, open all remaining doors until the princess is discovered. For $d = 4$ and $t = 2$ this gives

π_3: $listen(1)$;
  if $t(1)$
  then $listen(2)$;
    if $t(2)$
    then $open(3)$; if $\neg p(3)$ then $open(4)$ endif
    else $open(2)$;
      if $\neg p(2)$
      then $listen(3)$; if $t(3)$ then $open(4)$
        else $open(3)$ endif
  else $open(1)$; if $\neg p(1)$ then $listen(2)$; (...)

Such a plan succeeds, but it explicits all branches and it is thus space-consuming: when d and t vary, the size of a valid plan increases exponentially[1]. Now, the branching condi-

---
[1]This is because the evaluation of the condition "the d tigers have been found" after having listened to k doors needs counting the tigers heard so far, which needs explicitly listing the $\binom{k}{t}$ corresponding cases.

tions of such plans are only *conjunctions of elementary observations* (those elementary observations are $t(i)$ or $\neg t(i)$ – one of these is observed after $listen(i)$ is performed), which means that, at any step of the execution, (i) the agent decides in unit time what is the next action to follow and (ii) he is not asked to reason (only to obey, to follow a fully explicited plan).

Let us now consider a plan π_4 where epistemic branching conditions are allowed. We use the following abbreviations: $KnowWherePrincess$ = $\mathbf{K}p(1) \vee \mathbf{K}p(2) \vee \ldots \vee \mathbf{K}p(d)$ and $KnowWhereTigers$ = $(\mathbf{K}t(1) \vee \mathbf{K}\neg t(1)) \wedge \ldots \wedge (\mathbf{K}t(d) \vee \mathbf{K}\neg t(d))$ and we define the procedures:

$OpenIfKnowWherePrincess$:
if $\mathbf{K}p(1)$ then $open(1)$ else if $\mathbf{K}p(2)$ then $open(2)\ldots$

$OpenIfKnowWhereTigers$:
if $\mathbf{K}\neg t(1)$ then $open(1)$;
if $\neg \mathbf{K}married \wedge \mathbf{K}\neg t(2)$ then $open(2)$; ...

π_4: $listen(1)$; $listen(2)$;
  if $\neg KnowWherePrincess \wedge \neg KnowWhereTigers$
  then $listen(3)$;
  if $KnowWherePrincess$
  then $OpenIfKnowWherePrincess$
  else $OpenIfKnowWhereTigers$

It can be checked that π_4 reaches the goals. Interestingly, if d and t vary, there is a plan in the style of π_4 (using epistemic branching conditions) whose size is *linear* in d while any valid plan in the style of π_3 (with no epistemic branching conditions) has an *exponential* size. It is important to notice that this gain in size is counterbalanced by a loss of execution time: indeed, although π_1-like plans have a size in $\mathcal{O}(2^d)$, their execution time (assuming that actions are performed in unit time) takes only $\mathcal{O}(d)$. Contrastedly, for π_4-like plans whose size is in $\mathcal{O}(d)$, their execution requires a linear number of calls to a NP-complete oracle (to compute "KnowWherePrincess" and "KnowWhereTiger"). Therefore, a plan with epistemic branching conditions is all the more interesting as the ratio between cost of space and cost of expensive on-line execution time is high.

An epistemic dynamic logic
Language of EDL

The language of epistemic dynamic logic EDL is constructed from a set of atomic formulas VAR, a set of atomic actions ACT_0, the classical logic operators $\rightarrow, \wedge, \vee, \neg$, the epistemic operator **K**, the dynamic operator $[.]$, and the action operators λ and ;. The formula $[\alpha]q$ is read "after the execution of the action α, q is true". Note that we allow for nested epistemic and dynamic operators. λ is the action "do nothing". The complex action $\alpha;\beta$ is read "execute α and then β". $\langle\alpha\rangle A$ is an abbreviation of $\neg([\alpha]\neg A)$, and $[\texttt{if } A \texttt{ then } \alpha \texttt{ else } \beta]C$ is an abbreviation of $(A \rightarrow [\alpha]C) \wedge (\neg A \rightarrow [\beta]C)$.

An EDL formula is

- *objective* iff it does not contain any modality;
- *static* iff it does not contain any dynamic modality;

- an *epistemic atom* iff it is of the form $\mathbf{K}A$, where A is any EDL formula;
- an *epistemic formula* iff it is formed from epistemic atoms and the connectives of classical logic.

For instance, $a \vee (b \wedge c)$ is objective; $\mathbf{K}(a \vee \neg \mathbf{K}(a \to [\alpha]b))$ is an epistemic atom; $\mathbf{K}(a \vee \neg \mathbf{K}(a \to [\alpha]b)) \vee \neg \mathbf{K}[\beta]c$ is an epistemic formula; $a \vee \neg \mathbf{K}(b \wedge \mathbf{K}c)$ is static but not epistemic; $\mathbf{K}a \vee \neg \mathbf{K}(b \wedge \mathbf{K}c)$ is both static and epistemic.

Semantics of EDL

The semantics of EDL is in terms of possible worlds (states). We interpret the knowledge of the agent at a possible world w by a set of worlds associated to w. Actions are interpreted as transition relations on worlds.

We define a model for EDL as a quadruple $M = \langle W, R_{\mathbf{K}}, \{R_\alpha : \alpha \in ACT_0\}, V \rangle$ where W is a set of possible worlds, $R_{\mathbf{K}} \subseteq W \times W$ and every $R_\alpha \subseteq W \times W$ is an accessibility relation[2], and V associates to each world an interpretation. We require

- $R_{\mathbf{K}}$ to be an equivalence relation on W,
- $R_\lambda\{w\} = \{w\}$,
- $R_{\alpha;\beta} = R_\alpha \circ R_\beta$,
- $R_\alpha \circ R_{\mathbf{K}} \subseteq R_{\mathbf{K}} \circ R_\alpha$.

The truth conditions are defined as usual, in particular:

- $\models_{M,w} \mathbf{K}A$ if $\models_{M,v} A$ for every state $v \in R_{\mathbf{K}}(w)$
- $\models_{M,w} [\alpha]A$ if $\models_{M,w'} A$ for every state $w' \in R_\alpha(w)$

Logical consequence (with global axioms) is noted $\models$.

Axiomatization of EDL

Our axiomatisation of EDL contains that of classical logic together with modal logics S5 for knowledge and K for actions.

N($\mathbf{K}$) $\dfrac{A}{\mathbf{K}A}$

N($[\alpha]$) $\dfrac{A}{[\alpha]A}$

K($\mathbf{K}$) $(\mathbf{K}A \wedge \mathbf{K}(A \to C)) \to \mathbf{K}C$

T($\mathbf{K}$) $\mathbf{K}A \to A$

5($\mathbf{K}$) $\neg \mathbf{K}A \to \mathbf{K}\neg \mathbf{K}A$

Def(λ) $[\lambda]A \leftrightarrow A$

Def($\alpha;\beta$) $[\alpha;\beta]A \leftrightarrow [\alpha][\beta]A$

K($[\alpha]$) $([\alpha]A \wedge [\alpha](A \to C)) \to [\alpha]C$

Acq($[\alpha]$, $\mathbf{K}$) $\mathbf{K}[\alpha]C \to \mathbf{K}[\alpha]\mathbf{K}C$

All the axioms are standard, except Acq($[\alpha]$, $\mathbf{K}$) which means that if the agent knows what will be true after an action then he does not loose this knowledge after the action. Note that Acq($[\alpha]$, $\mathbf{K}$) could be replaced by $\mathbf{K}[\alpha]C \to [\alpha]\mathbf{K}C$ to which it is equivalent given the other axioms.

---

[2] We shall sometimes identify $R_{\mathbf{K}}$ and R_α with mappings $R_{\mathbf{K}} : W \longrightarrow 2^W$ and $R_\alpha : W \longrightarrow 2^W$.

Action and information

Our language is sufficiently expressive to distinguish explicitly between the ontic and the epistemic effects of actions, where ontic (respectively epistemic) effects are meant to be effects on the physical world only (resp. on the epistemic state of the agent only). Two particular classes of actions are *uninformative actions* whose effects are purely ontic and *purely informative actions* whose effects are purely epistemic. Intuitively, uninformative actions cannot bring any new knowledge, which means that everything that is known after the action is performed could be predicted before it was performed. The other way round, purely informative actions do not change the world. In our example, the actions $listen(i)$ are purely informative, while the actions $open(i)$ are not.

A key hypothesis of our logic is that any action α can be decomposed into two actions, namely $\alpha = \alpha^e \circ \alpha^o$, where α^e is purely informative and α^o uninformative. $open(i)$ can be written as $open(i)^e \circ open(i)^o$, where its uninformative component $open(i)^o$ has the effect of making the agent married, eaten, or none of both, *without him being aware*, and its informative component $open(i)^e$ has the effect to make the agent *learn* whether he gets married, eaten or none of both.

Given that $\alpha = \alpha^e \circ \alpha^o$, what is the relation between α^o and α^e? Ideally, all changes brought about by α^o are perceived through α^e. We call actions of this kind (i.e., actions informing the agent about all changes they cause) *fully informant*. Formally, α is fully informant iff for any objective formula A, we have that
$$A \to [\alpha](\neg A \to \mathbf{K}\neg A)$$
holds. Purely informative actions α are fully informant because the ontic part is empty, i.e. $\alpha^o = \lambda$. In our example $open(i)$ is fully informant because it makes the agent aware of the change of truth value of $eaten$ or $married$ when it occurs.

Noticeably, these properties (purely informative, uninformative, fully informant) are about *individual actions*. Nevertheless, global properties of environments (domain descriptions) can be captured from local properties of actions. An *environment* Σ consists of a nonlogical theory T describing the general laws of the world and what is known about the effects of actions, together with the description of what is known about the initial state Σ_{Init}. An environment Σ is *fully observable* iff (i) each $\alpha \in ACT_0$ is fully informant, and (ii) Σ_{Init} is epistemically complete[3]. Σ is *unobservable* iff each $\alpha \in ACT_0$ is uninformative. Σ is *purely informative* iff each $\alpha \in ACT_0$ is purely informative. Σ is *deterministic* iff each $\alpha \in ACT_0$ is deterministic.

Uninformative actions

We characterize uninformative actions by two axioms.

DetEpi($[\alpha]$, $\mathbf{K}$) $\langle\alpha\rangle \mathbf{K}A \to [\alpha]\mathbf{K}A$

Con($[\alpha]$, $\mathbf{K}$) $[\alpha]\mathbf{K}C \to ([\alpha]\bot \vee \mathbf{K}[\alpha]C)$

The first expresses that uninformative actions are epistemically deterministic, in the sense that if *there is* a way of executing α such that A is known afterwards, then A should be

---

[3] i.e. if $\Sigma_{Init} \models \mathbf{K}A \vee \mathbf{K}\neg A$ for all objective A

known after every possible execution of α. This is natural, given that α does not bring any new knowledge (in particular about the way it has been executed). The second says that the epistemic effects of α are known before hand. Semantically, the axioms correspond to the conditions

- If $w', w'' \in R_\alpha(w)$ then $R_\mathbf{K}(w') = R_\mathbf{K}(w'')$
- If $R_\alpha(w) \neq \emptyset$ and $w_1 R_\mathbf{K} \circ R_\alpha w_2$ then $w_1 R_\alpha \circ R_\mathbf{K} w_2$

It can be proved that these two axioms together are equivalent to the more compact criterion of uninformativeness $\neg \mathbf{K}[\alpha]A \rightarrow [\alpha]\neg \mathbf{K}A$. It says that the agent cannot observe anything after α is performed: indeed, for any formula A, if he cannot predict before α is performed that A will hold after α, then he will not know A after α is performed. Acq($[\alpha]$, $\mathbf{K}$) together with Con($[\alpha]$, $\mathbf{K}$) gives us the equivalence $[\alpha]\mathbf{K}C \equiv ([\alpha]\bot \vee \mathbf{K}[\alpha]C)$.

Purely informative actions

Purely informative actions do not change the world but only the knowledge; they are characterized by the axiom

Pres($[\alpha]$) $\quad A \rightarrow [\alpha]A$ if A is an objective formula.

Semantically, this corresponds to the condition

- if $w_1 R_\alpha w_2$ then $V_{w_1} = V_{w_2}$

It follows from Acq($[\alpha]$, $\mathbf{K}$) and standard modal principles that purely informative actions do not diminish the knowledge of an agent.

Proposition 1 *Let A be an objective formula and α a purely informative action. Then*

Pres($[\alpha]$, $\mathbf{K}$) $\mathbf{K}A \rightarrow [\alpha]\mathbf{K}A$

is provable from EDL.

If A is subjective then this does not necessarily hold, in particular if A expresses ignorance. For example $\mathbf{K}\neg \mathbf{K}A \rightarrow [\alpha]\mathbf{K}\neg \mathbf{K}A$ cannot be accepted, given that $\mathbf{K}\neg \mathbf{K}A \leftrightarrow \neg \mathbf{K}A$ is valid in our logic of knowledge S5.

A solution to the Frame Problem

We must solve the Frame Problem in order to put to work our logic. Basically, we could integrate any solution into our framework, given that we have analysed the epistemic effects of an action in terms of its ontic effects on possible worlds. Scherl and Levesque e.g. used Reiter's solution to the Frame Problem, and applied regression as a reasoning method (Scherl & Levesque 1993). We adopt the solution in (Castilho, Gasquet, & Herzig 1999) based on dependence relations, which can be taken over without modifications and which we briefly recall here.

We associate to every atomic action α the set of atomic formulas it influences. Formally, we suppose given a dependency function $DEP : ACT_0 \longrightarrow VAR$. $p \in DEP(\alpha)$ means that α may change the truth value of the atom p. The other way round, if $p \notin DEP(\alpha)$ then α does not change the truth value of p. In other words, DEP represents frame axioms in an economic way. This is expressed by the generic frame axiom

Pres$_{DEP}$($[\alpha]$) if $p \notin DEP(\alpha)$ then $p \rightarrow [\alpha]p$ and $\neg p \rightarrow [\alpha]\neg p$

Semantically, the axiom corresponds to the condition

- For all $w, w' \in W$ and $p \in VAR$, if $w' \in R_\alpha(w)$ and $p \notin DEP(\alpha)$ then $\models_{M,w} p$ iff $\models_{M,w'} p$.

Given a dependence relation DEP, $\models_{DEP}$ is the corresponding extension of the EDL consequence relation.

As a particular case, purely informative actions verify $DEP(\alpha) = \emptyset$. Thus, we have for instance the frame axioms $t(1) \rightarrow [listen(1)]t(1)$ and $p(2) \rightarrow [listen(1)]p(2)$. Combining all these atomic frame axioms by principles of classical logic, we obtain the following.

Proposition 2 *Let A be objective, and let atm(A) be the set of atoms of A. If atm(A) $\cap DEP(\alpha) = \emptyset$ then:*

- $\models_{DEP} A \rightarrow [\alpha]A$;
- $\models_{DEP} \mathbf{K}A \rightarrow [\alpha]\mathbf{K}A$.

Plan verification in EDL

The set of *meaningful plans* is the smallest set such that

- α is a meaningful plan for every $\alpha \in ACT_0 \cup \{\lambda\}$;
- if π and π' are meaningful plans and A is an epistemic formula then $\pi;\pi'$ and if A then π else π' are meaningful plans.

Intuitively, a meaningful plan is a plan whose branching conditions are "epistemically interpretable", which means that the agent can decide whether the branching condition holds or not (which would not necessarily be the case if the formula were not epistemic, cf. example).

A *plan verification problem* $\mathcal{V}$ is defined by a 5-tuple $\langle T, \Sigma_{Init}, DEP, G, \pi \rangle$ where

- $T = \langle S, E, X \rangle$ is an EDL theory composed of a set of state axioms S expressing static laws of the domain, laws about the effects of actions E, and executability laws X. Static laws are static formulas; effect laws are formulas of the form $A \rightarrow [\alpha]C$ with A objective and C an epistemic formula; executability laws are formulas of the form $A \leftrightarrow \langle \alpha \rangle \top$ with A objective.
- Σ_{Init} is an epistemic atom;
- DEP is a dependency function;
- G is a static formula (the goal);
- π is an meaningful plan.

Given a plan verification problem $\mathcal{V}$, π is said to be

- *executable* for $\mathcal{V}$ iff $T \models_{DEP} \Sigma_{Init} \rightarrow \langle \pi \rangle \top$ holds.
- *valid* for $\mathcal{V}$ iff $T \models_{DEP} \Sigma_{Init} \rightarrow [\pi]G$ holds.

The validity problem in EDL is **PSPACE**-hard, and the consequence problem is **EXPTIME**-hard. The reason is that EDL extends modal logic K, where these problems are **PSPACE**- and **EXPTIME**-complete, respectively. Nevertheless, the complexity of the much more specific plan verification problem in EDL is much lower:

Proposition 3 (complexity of plan verification)
PLAN VERIFICATION *in EDL is* Π_2^p-*complete.*

Note that if branching conditions were restricted to elementary conjunctions of observations instead of any epistemic conditions then the problem would be "only" coNP-complete.

It is worth investigating what plan validation becomes when some specific assumptions are made about observability.

Unobservable environments When the environment is unobservable, we can show by induction that uninformativeness extends to any meaningful plan: for any meaningful plan π and any objective formula A,
$$\neg \mathbf{K}[\pi]A \to [\pi]\neg \mathbf{K}A$$
holds, which leads to the following intuitive result: *if there is a meaningful valid plan π for $\mathcal{V} = \langle T, \Sigma_{Init}, DEP, G \rangle$ then there is a nonbranching (i.e., without tests) meaningful valid plan for $\mathcal{V}$.*

Fully observable environments When the environment is fully observable, we can show by induction that for any meaningful plan π and any objective formula A, we have $[\pi](\mathbf{K}A \vee \mathbf{K}\neg A)$ holds, and that the epistemic operator is needless, which is expressed intuitively by the following result: *if there is a meaningful valid plan π for $\mathcal{V}$ then there is an epistemic-free (e.g., without any occurrence of $\mathbf{K}$) meaningful valid plan for $\mathcal{V}$.* Thus, a fragment of PDL is sufficient for capturing plan verification in fully observable environments.

Purely epistemic environments When the environment is fully epistemic, all actions are commutative and knowledge preserving. This leads to the following result: if there is a meaningful valid plan π for $\mathcal{P}$ then $\alpha_1; \alpha_2; ...; \alpha_n$ is a valid plan for $\mathcal{P}$, where $ACT_0 = \{\alpha_1, ..., \alpha_n\}$.

We end up the section with some considerations on plan existence. Informally, the plan existence problem reads: given $\mathcal{P} = \langle T, \Sigma_{Init}, DEP, G \rangle$, is there a plan π for $\mathcal{P}$? Similar to verification problems, we check whether there is a proof of $T, \neg G \models_{DEP} \neg \Sigma_{Init}$. If this is the case, then we can associate a meaningful executable plan π to $\mathcal{P}$. π can then be checked for validity (which will not always be the case, in particular when actions are nondeterministic). π is certainly only a first step towards a plan. We leave this issue to further research.

Example

How we can handle our running example in our logic? For the sake of readability, suppose $d = 2$ and $t = 1$. A meaningful valid plan is

$\pi_{2,1} = listen(1);$ if $\mathbf{K}t(1)$ then $open(2)$ else $open(1)$

Proving the validity of $\pi_{2,1}$ amounts to proving that the formula $T \models_{DEP} \Sigma_{Init} \to [\pi_{2,1}](married \wedge alive)$ is a theorem, where the initial situation Σ_{Init} is

$\Sigma_{Init} = alive \wedge ((t(1) \wedge \neg t(2) \wedge p(2)) \vee (t(2) \wedge \neg t(1) \wedge p(1)))$

and T is the nonlogical theory of the domain, consisting of the following set T of effect axioms:

$T = \{\ t(i) \to [listen(i)]\mathbf{K}t(i),\ \neg t(i) \to [listen(i)]\mathbf{K}\neg t(i),$
$p(i) \to [open(i)]married,\ t(i) \to [open(i)]\neg alive,$
$(\neg p(i) \wedge \neg married) \to [open(i)]\neg married,$
$(\neg t(i) \wedge alive) \to [open(i)]alive,$

$\langle listen(i)\rangle\top\rangle,\ \langle open(i)\top\rangle\}.$

(where we suppose $i \in \{1, 2\}$).

Moreover, let $DEP(listen(i)) = \emptyset$ and $DEP(open(i)) = \{married, alive\}$. (The dependence-based solution to the Frame Problem requires the last two conditional frame axioms of T.) We establish that $T \models_{DEP} \Sigma_{Init} \to [\pi_{2,1}](married \wedge alive)$ by proving $T \models_{DEP} (t(1) \wedge \neg t(2) \wedge p(2) \wedge alive) \to [\pi_{2,1}](married \wedge alive)$ and $T \models_{DEP} (t(2) \wedge \neg t(1) \wedge p(1) \wedge alive) \to [\pi_{2,1}](married \wedge alive)$. Then the disjunction of the respective antecedens is nothing but Σ_{Init}, and since $(\mathbf{K}t(1) \wedge [open(2)](alive \wedge married)) \vee (\mathbf{K}\neg t(1) \wedge [open(1)](alive \wedge married))$ is equivalent to $[listen(1); $ if $\mathbf{K}t(1)$ then $open(2)$ else $open(1)](alive \wedge married)$, putting things together we obtain what we wanted.

Related work and conclusion

There is a significant amount of related work about the interactions between action and knowledge, both in the KR and the planning communities. Combining knowledge and action in a logical framework comes back to the work of (Moore 1985) who provided a theory of action including knowledge-producing actions. Building on this theory, (Scherl & Levesque 1993) represent knowledge-producing actions in the situation calculus by means of an explicit accessibility relation between situations, treated as an ordinary fluent, that corresponds to our epistemic accessibility relation. (Levesque 1996) then uses this knowledge fluents to represent complex plans involving, like ours, nondeterminism, observations and branching (and also loops, that we did not consider). He points out that the executability of a plan requires that the agent *needs to know how to execute it*, which implies that branching conditions must involve knowledge and not objective facts whose truth may not be accessible to the agent. On the one hand, in our logic, consisting of a fragment of propositional PDL extended with epistemic modalities to represent the effects of actions, the interactions between dynamic and epistemic modalities enable a simple representation of various observability assumptions; on the other hand, by using the situation calculus, Levesque handles more easily than us *value tests* returning the value of a variable (for instance, he is able to represent in a simple way a plan such as search Mary's phone number in the phonebook and then dial it whereas we cannot do it unless we write down a finite but unreasonable amount of propositional formulas). This approach was extended in (Lakemeyer & Levesque 1998) so as to introduce the *only knowing* modality. (Bacchus & Petrick 1998) point out the practical impossibility to generate explicit conditional plans, because they get too large, and thus advocate for the need of reasoning about knowledge during plan execution, which is one of the key points of our logic. Their representation model makes use of an epistemic modality. Our approach could be thought of as being complementary to theirs, because we provide a simple way to represent various kinds of interactions between knowledge and action while they focus on the practical computation of the effects of a plan containing sensing actions and knowledge preconditions. (Geffner & Wainer 1998) provide a general language enabling representing nondeterministic actions, sensing actions, observations and conditional plans. Their notion of executable policy is very similar to our notion of meaningful plan, though it is not expressed the same way technically speaking: to avoid generating unreasonably large policies (which happens whenever all accessible belief states are explicitly considered), they express policies on states rather than on belief states; a policy is then said to be executable in a belief state Bel if, roughly speaking, it assigns equivalent actions to all states considered possible in Bel. We choose another way to escape representing explicitly conditional plans, namely by calling for reasoning tasks during execution. (Lobo, Mendez, & Taylor 1997) extend Gelfond and Lifschitz' language $\mathcal{A}$ for reasoning about action so as to represent knowledge effects. An interesting notion in their approach is *knowledge removing actions* that may affect the knowledge the agent has on a fluent. These knowledge removing actions (such as toss) can be easily handled in EDL.

These approaches focus on representing actions and conditional plans involving knowledge preconditions and effects, and checking whether a given plan reaches the goal. Up to know, little has been done in order to generate plans having knowledge preconditions. (Rintanen 1999) extends the planning as satisfiability framework to planning under incomplete knowledge by means of Quantified Boolean Formulae. (Boutilier & Poole 1996) provide a propositional-like representation and resolution framework for POMDPs. None of these works makes use of epistemic nor dynamic modalities.

Lastly, a few authors developed logical systems integrating dynamic and epistemic modalities, but not from a planning perspective. (Del Val, Maynard-Reid II, & Shoham 1997) study from a logical perspective the relations between what the agent perceive and what they believe; this is much related to our logical expressions of observability assumptions in EDL. (Fagin *et al.* 1995) have a language with temporal 'next' and 'always' operators instead of action operators. They have axioms of perfect recall similar to our Acq($[\alpha]$, **K**) (axioms KT1, KT2). They do not integrate a solution to the Frame Problem into their approach. Also slightly related to our work is (Meyer, van der Hoek, & van der Linder 1994) who consider tests as epistemic updates.

Apart from the handling of plan existence, further work includes the study of the complexity of validity for the full logic EDL (so far we only have a complexity result for *plan verification* in EDL) and next, the complexity of plan existence with epistemic preconditions, which would complete the panorama of complexity results for planning under incomplete knowledge (Littman 1997; Baral, Kreinovich, & Trejo 1999).

References

Bacchus, F., and Petrick, R. 1998. Modeling an agent's incomplete knowledge during planning and execution. In *Proc. KR'98*, 423–443.

Baral, C.; Kreinovich, V.; and Trejo, R. 1999. Computational complexity of planning and approximate planning in the presence of incompleteness. In *Proc. of IJCAI'99*, 948–953.

Boutilier, C., and Poole, D. 1996. Computing optimal policies for partially observable decision processes using compact representations. In *Proceedings of AAAI'96*, 1168–1175.

Castilho, M. A.; Gasquet, O.; and Herzig, A. 1999. Formalizing action and change in modal logic I: the frame problem. *J. of Logic and Computation* 9(5).

Del Val, A.; Maynard-Reid II, P.; and Shoham, Y. 1997. Qualitative reasoning about perception and belief. In *Proc. IJCAI'97*, 508–513.

Fagin, R.; Halpern, J.; Moses, Y.; and Vardi, M. 1995. *Reasoning about knowledge*. MIT Press.

Geffner, H., and Wainer, J. 1998. Modeling action, knowledge and control. In *Proc. ECAI'98*, 532–536.

Kautz, H., and Selman, B. 1996. Planning as satisfiability. In *Proc. AAAI'96*, 1139–1146.

Lakemeyer, G., and Levesque, H. 1998. AOL: a logic of acting, sensing, knowing, and only knowing. In *Proc. KR'98*, 316–327.

Levesque, H. J. 1996. What is planning in the presence of sensing? In *Proc. AAAI'96*, 1139–1146.

Littman, M. 1997. Probabilistic planning: representation and complexity. In *Proc. of AAAI'97*, 748–754.

Lobo, J.; Mendez, G.; and Taylor, S. R. 1997. Adding knowledge to the action description language a. In *Proc. AAAI'97*, 454–459.

Meyer, J.-J.; van der Hoek, W.; and van der Linder, B. 1994. Test as epistemic updates. In *Proc. ECAI'94*.

Moore, R. 1985. A formal theory of knowledge and action. In *Formal Theories of the Commensense World*. Norwood. 319–358.

Rintanen, J. 1999. Constructing plans by a theorem prover. *JAIR* 10:323–352.

Scherl, R., and Levesque, H. 1993. The frame problem and knowledge-producing actions. In *Proc. AAAI'93*, 689–695.

Graph Construction and Analysis as a Paradigm for Plan Recognition

Jun Hong
School of Information and Software Engineering
University of Ulster at Jordanstown
Newtownabbey, Co. Antrim BT37 0QB, United Kingdom
j.hong@ulst.ac.uk

Abstract

We present a novel approach to plan recognition in which graph construction and analysis is used as a paradigm. We use a graph structure called a Goal Graph for the plan recognition problem. The Goal Graph is first constructed to represent the observed actions, the state of the world, and the achieved goals at consecutive time steps. It also represents various connections between nodes in the Goal Graph. The Goal Graph can then be analysed at each time step to recognise those achieved goals that are consistent with the actions observed so far. The Goal Graph analysis can also reveal valid plans for the recognised goals or part of the recognised goals. We describe two algorithms, GoalGraphConstructor and GoalGraphAnalyser, based on this paradigm. These algorithms are sound, polynomial-time and polynomial-space. The algorithms have been tested in two domains with up to 245 goal schemata and 100000 possible goals. They perform well in these domains in terms of efficiency, accuracy and scalability.

Introduction

Plan recognition involves inferring the goal of an agent from a set of observed actions and organising the observed actions into a plan structure for the goal. We introduce a novel approach to plan recognition, in which graph construction and analysis is used as a paradigm. Our attempt to do so is in spirit influenced by Blum and Furst's effort on planning with Planning Graphs (Blum & Furst 1995), (Blum & Furst 1997). They introduced a new graph-based approach to planning in STRIPS domains, in which a graph structure called a Planning Graph is first constructed explicitly rather than searching immediately for a plan as in standard planning methods. The Planning Graph is then analysed to generate possible plans.

Since being first introduced, further developments have been made with regard to handling more expressive representation languages (Gazen & Knoblock 1997), (Anderson, Smith, & Weld 1998), (Koehler *et al.* 1997), that allow the use of disjunctive preconditions, conditional effects, and universally quantified preconditions (goal descriptions) and effects in action and goal representation.

Copyright © 2000, American Association for Artificial Intelligence (www.aaai.org). All rights reserved.

We propose to use a different graph structure, called a Goal Graph, for the plan recognition problem. Instead of searching for a plan as in most plan recognition systems, a Goal Graph is first constructed to represent the observed actions, the state of the world as it is changed by these actions, and the fully or partially achieved goals at consecutive time steps. Connections are also made between different kinds of nodes in the Goal Graph. The constructed Goal Graph can then be analysed at each time step to recognise those fully or partially achieved goals that are consistent with the actions observed so far. The Goal Graph analysis also reveals causal links over actions and goals so that valid plans for the recognised goals or part of the recognised goals can be further recognised.

We describe two algorithms based on this paradigm. The GoalGraphConstructor takes a set of partially ordered actions as they are observed and constructs a Goal Graph. The GoalGraphAnalyser analyses the constructed Goal Graph to recognise consistent goals and valid plans. We prove that our algorithms are sound, polynomial-time and polynomial-space. The algorithms have been tested on a 500 MHz Pentium III in two domains. In the extended briefcase domain, we increase the number of locations and objects to create a series of sets of up to over 100000 possible goals for testing the scalability of our algorithms where the approximate linear time performance has been achieved. In the Unix domain, we use a set of data collected in the Unix domain at the University of Washington with over 245 goal schemata and over 10000 possible goals. In this domain, on average it only takes less than a CPU second to update the Goal Graph when an observed action is processed and usually only a very small number of consistent goals remain after a sequence of observed actions has been processed.

The Domain Representation

We use an ADL-like representation (Pednault 1989), including actions with conditional and universally quantified effects, and existentially as well as universally quantified preconditions and goal descriptions. A plan recognition problem consists of

- A set of action schemata specifying primitive actions.
- A finite, dynamic universe of typed objects.
- A set of propositions called the Initial Conditions.

- A set of goal schemata specifying possible goals.
- A set of observed actions that are partially ordered.
- An explicit notion of discrete time.

The solution to a plan recognition problem consists of a set of recognised goals that are consistent with the observed actions together with the valid plans consisting of the observed actions for the recognised goals or part of the recognised goals.

The goal schema consists of a set of goal descriptions. The action schema consists of a set of preconditions and a set of effects. A goal is a ground instance of a goal schema. An action is a ground instance of an action schema. The set of goal descriptions for a goal must be satisfied in the state of the world when the goal is fully achieved. If some but not all goal descriptions are satisfied instead, the goal is partially achieved. The set of preconditions must be satisfied in the state of the world before an action can be executed. The set of effects are taken in the state of the world when an action is executed.

The representation of a simple example domain extended from Pednault's famous example (Pednault 1988) is shown in Figure 1. It involves transportation of two physical objects, a dictionary and a chequebook, between home and office using a briefcase. We assume that only one physical object can be carried in the briefcase at a time. The extended briefcase domain consists of three action schemata and three goal schemata.

In the actual implementation of our plan recognition algorithms, universally quantified preconditions and effects, and conditional effects in an action schema are eliminated and equivalent schemata are created. We use a particular approach we call *dynamic expansion*. Dynamic expansion involves two steps. In the first step, universally quantified preconditions and effects in an action schema are dynamically compiled into the corresponding Herbrand base taking into account the state of the universe at the current time step. In the second step, conditional effects are further eliminated. The universally quantified goal descriptions in a goal schema are treated in the same way as the universally quantified preconditions in an action schema.

Goal Graphs, Valid Plans and Consistent Goals

Goal Graphs

We first describe the structure of the Goal Graph. A Goal Graph is a directed, levelled graph. The levels alternate between proposition levels containing proposition nodes (each labelled with a proposition or negation of a proposition) representing the propositions true or explicitly known to be false in the state of the world at consecutive time steps, goal levels containing goal nodes (each labelled with a goal) representing goals fully or partially achieved at consecutive time steps and action levels containing action nodes (each labelled with an action) representing actions observed at consecutive time steps. The levels in a Goal Graph start with a proposition level at time step 1 that consists of one node for each proposition true in the Initial Conditions. They end

```
(:action mov-b
   :paras (?l ?m - loc)
   :pre (and (neq ?l ?m)(at B ?l))
   :eff (and (at B ?m) (neg (at B ?l))
              (forall (?z - physob)
                 (when (in ?z)
                    (and (at ?z ?m)
                         (neg (at ?z ?l)))))) )
(:action put-in
   :paras (?x - physob ?l loc)
   :pre (and (neq ?x B)(at ?x ?l)(at B ?l))
              (forall (?z - physob)
                    (not (in ?z))) )
   :eff (in ?x) )
(:action take-out
   :paras (?x - physob)
   :pre (in ?x)
   :eff (neg (in ?x)) )
(:goal move-object
   :paras (?x - physob ?l ?m - loc)
   :goal-des (and (neq ?l ?m)
                  (neq ?x B)
                  (imply (neg (at ?x ?l))
                         (at ?x ?m))) )
(:goal keep-object-at
   :paras (?x - physob ?l - loc)
   :goal-des (and (neq ?x B)
                  (imply (at ?x ?l)
                         (not (in ?x)))) )
(:goal keep-object-in
   :paras (?x - physob)
   :goal-des (in ?x) )
```

Figure 1: The representation of the extended briefcase domain

with a goal level at the last time step that consists of a node for each of the goals fully or partially achieved so far.

The goal nodes in goal-level i are connected by description edges to their goal descriptions in proposition-level i. The action node in action-level i is connected by precondition edges to its preconditions in proposition-level i, and by effect edges to its effects in proposition-level $i + 1$. Those proposition nodes in proposition-level i are connected via persistence edges to the corresponding proposition nodes in proposition-level $i + 1$ if their truth values have not been affected by the effects of the action in action-level i. In the Goal Graph shown in Figure 2, three actions have been observed at three consecutive time steps: (mov-b O H), (put-in D H), and (mov-b H O). The Initial Conditions consist of: (at B O), (at D H) and (at C H). Action and goal nodes are on the top and bottom parts of the graph respectively. The proposition nodes are in the middle part of the graph.

Valid Plans

We now define what we mean when we say a set of partially ordered actions forms a valid plan for a goal given the Initial Conditions.

Definition 1 (Causal Link) *Let a_1 and a_2 be two actions. There exists a causal link between a_1 and a_2, written as*

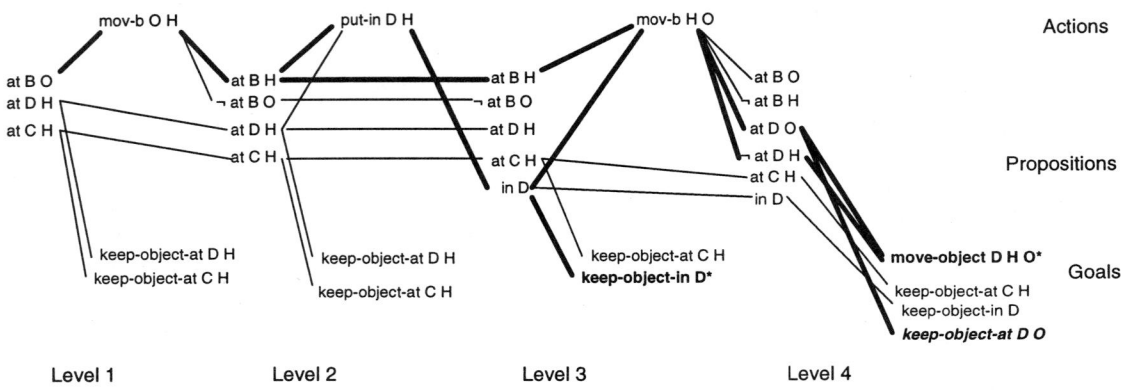

Figure 2: A Goal Graph for an example of the extended briefcase domain

$a_1 \rightarrow a_2$, if and only if one of the effects of a_1 satisfies one of the preconditions of a_2.

A goal can be treated as an action with goal descriptions as its preconditions and an empty set of effects. Therefore causal links can also be established from actions to goals.

Definition 2 (Valid Plan) Let g be a goal, and $P = <A, O, L>$ where A is a set of actions, O is a set of temporal ordering constraints, $\{a_i < a_j\}$, over A, and L is a set of causal links, $\{a_i \rightarrow a_j\}$, over A. Let I be the Initial Conditions. P is a valid plan for g, given I, if and only if

1. the actions in A can be executed in I in any order consistent with O;
2. the goal g is fully achieved after the actions in A are executed in I in that order.

Consistent Goals

We finally define what we mean when we say a goal is consistent with a set of partially ordered actions that have been observed so far.

Definition 3 (Relevant Action) Given a goal g and a set of partially ordered actions, $<A, O>$, where A is a set of actions, O is a set of temporal ordering constraints, $\{a_i < a_j\}$, over A, an action $a \in A$ is said to be relevant to g in the context of $<A, O>$, if and only if

1. there exists a causal link, $a \rightarrow g$; or
2. there exists a causal link, $a \rightarrow b$, where $b \in A$ is a relevant action to g and $a < b$ is consistent with O.

Definition 4 (Consistent Goal) A goal g is consistent with a set of partially ordered actions, $<A, O>$, if and only if every $a \in A$ is relevant to g in the context of $<A, O>$.

Proposition 1 (Valid Plan for Consistent Goal) Let $<A, O>$ be a set of partially ordered actions that have been observed so far, I be the Initial Conditions before $<A, O>$, g be a goal consistent with $<A, O>$. Given I, $P = <A, O, L>$ where L is a set of causal links, $\{a_i \rightarrow a_j\}$, over A, is a valid plan for g when g is fully achieved after $<A, O>$, or otherwise for the achieved part of g when g is partially achieved after $<A, O>$.

Proposition 1 follows Definition 2, 3 and 4. Especially when g is partially achieved, let $g\prime$ be the achieved part of g. So $g\prime$ is fully achieved and $P = <A, O, L>$ is a valid plan for $g\prime$.

Plan Recognition Algorithms

Our plan recognition algorithms run in a two-stage cycle: Goal Graph construction and analysis. This two-stage cycle continues until no action is further observed.

Constructing a Goal Graph

The GoalGraphConstructor starts with a Goal Graph that consists of only proposition-level 1 with nodes representing the Initial Conditions.

Given a Goal Graph ending with proposition-level i, the GoalGraphConstructor first extends the Goal Graph to goal-level i with nodes representing goals fully or partially achieved at time step i. Meanwhile, if a node in proposition-level i satisfies a goal description, a description edge connecting the proposition node to the goal node is added onto the Goal Graph. We call this process *Goal Expansion*.

When an action is observed at time step i, the GoalGraphConstructor then extends the Goal Graph ending with goal-level i, to action-level i with a node representing the observed action. At the same time, the algorithm also extends the Goal Graph to proposition-level $i + 1$ with nodes representing propositions true or explicitly known to be false after the action has been observed. Meanwhile, if a node in proposition-level i satisfies a precondition of the action, a precondition edge connecting the proposition node to the action node is added onto the Goal Graph. For every effect of the action, the GoalGraphConstructor simply adds a proposition node to proposition-level $i + 1$. The effect edge from the action node to the proposition node is also added onto the Goal Graph. Every proposition node at proposition-level i is brought forward to proposition-level $i + 1$ by a maintenance action if its truth value has not been changed by the effect of the action observed at time step i (and it has not been added onto the Goal Graph by the effect of the action). Persistence edges connecting the proposition nodes at two proposition levels are added onto the Goal Graph. We call this process *Action Expansion*.

Theorem 1 (Polynomial Size and Time) *Consider a plan recognition problem with t observed actions in t time steps, a finite number of objects at each time step, p propositions in the Initial Conditions, and m goal schemata each having a constant number of parameters. Let l_1 be the largest number of the effects of any of the action schemata, l_2 be the largest number of the goal descriptions of any of goal schemata. Let n be the largest number of objects at all time steps. Then, the size of the Goal Graph of $t+1$ levels created by the GoalGraphConstructor, and the time needed to create the graph, are polynomial in n, m, p, l_1, l_2 and t.*

The maximum number of nodes in any proposition level is $O(p + l_1 t)$. Let k be the largest number of parameters in any goal schema. Since any goal schema can be instantiated in at most n^k distinct ways, the maximum numbers of nodes and edges in any goal level are $O(mn^k)$ and $O(l_2 mn^k)$ respectively. It is obvious that the time needed to create both nodes and edges in any level is polynomial in the number of nodes and edges in the level.

Theorem 2 *The GoalGraphConstructor is sound: Any goal it adds to the Goal Graph at time step i is one either fully or partially achieved at time step i in the state of the world. The algorithm is complete: If a goal has been either fully or partially achieved by the observed actions up to time step $i-1$, then the algorithm will add it to the Goal Graph at time step i under the assumption that all possible goals are restricted to the categories of goal schemata.*

Proposition-level i of the Goal Graph represents the state of the world at time step i that has been changed from the Initial Conditions after the actions have been observed at time step 1, ..., $i-1$. A fully or partially achieved goal in goal-level i of the Goal Graph is one fully or partially achieved in the state of the world at time step i. On the other hand, goal-level i of the Goal Graph consists of all possible instances of the goal schemata that are fully or partially achieved in the state of the world at time step i.

Recognising Consistent Goals and Valid Plans

We assume that every observed action is relevant to the goal intended by the agent in the context of the agent's actions. Therefore, the goal intended by the agent is consistent with the observed actions and a goal may be the intended goal if it is consistent with the set of the observed actions. Theorem 3 and Theorem 4 state how the recognition of the consistent goals can be achieved by the analysis of a constructed Goal Graph.

Theorem 3 *Given a Goal Graph, there exists a causal link, $a_i \rightarrow g_j$ between an action a_i at time step i and a goal g_j at time step j, where $i < j$, if a_i is connected to g_j via a path of an effect edge, zero or more persistence edges and a description edge. We call such a path a causal link path between a_i and g_j.*

Theorem 4 *Given a Goal Graph, there exists a causal link, $a_i \rightarrow a_j$, and a temporal ordering constraint, $a_i < a_j$,*

between an action a_i at time step i and another action a_j at time step j, where $i < j$, if a_i is connected to a_j via a path of an effect-edge, zero or more persistence-edges and a precondition-edge. We call such a path a causal link path between a_i and a_j.

Based on the structure of the Goal Graph, we can prove the existence of the causal link, $a_i \rightarrow g_j$, in Theorem 3 and $a_i \rightarrow a_j$, in Theorem 4. It is obvious that a causal link path between a_i and a_j guarantees the temporal ordering constraint, $a_i < a_j$.

Given a constructed Goal Graph of t levels, the Goal-GraphAnalyser recognises every consistent goal from the goals in goal-level t by deciding whether every observed action is relevant to it. This is done by first finding those relevant actions from the observed actions, that are connected to the goal by causal link paths. For each of the already-known relevant actions, the algorithm tries to find more relevant actions from the observed actions, that are connected to it by causal link paths. This continues until no more relevant action is found. The algorithm then organises the observed actions as well as temporal ordering constraints and causal links over these actions into a valid plan for the consistent goal.

Proposition 2 *The GoalGraphAnalyser is sound: Any goal g it recognises at time step t is consistent with the observed actions so far, and the plan for g it organises is valid.*

In the example shown in Figure 2, the goal nodes in bold represent three consistent goals among which the goal node in italics represents a partially achieved goal while the other two represent two fully achieved goals. The edges in bold show causal link paths.

Theorem 5 (Polynomial Space and Time) *Consider a t-level Goal Graph. Let l_1 be the number of fully or partially achieved goals at time step t, m_1 be the largest number of goal descriptions in any of these goals, l_2 be the number of the observed actions, and m_2 be the largest number of preconditions in any of these actions. The space size of possible causal link paths that connect the goals to the observed actions and that connect the observed actions to other observed actions, and the time needed to recognise all the consistent goals are polynomial in l_1, l_2, m_1 and m_2.*

Persistence edges do not branch in a Goal Graph. The maximum number of paths that connect a goal to the observed actions is $O(m_1)$. The maximum number of paths that connect an observed action to other observed actions is $O(m_2)$. There are only at maximum l_1 goals in goal-level t and l_2 relevant actions to any of these goals. So the time needed to recognise all the consistent goals is polynomial in $O(l_1(m_1 + l_2 m_2))$.

Experimental Results

Our algorithms have been implemented in Prolog and tested on a 500 MHz Pentium III in two domains in terms of efficiency, accuracy and scalability.

In the extended briefcase domain, we increase the number of locations to 50 and the number of objects up to 40

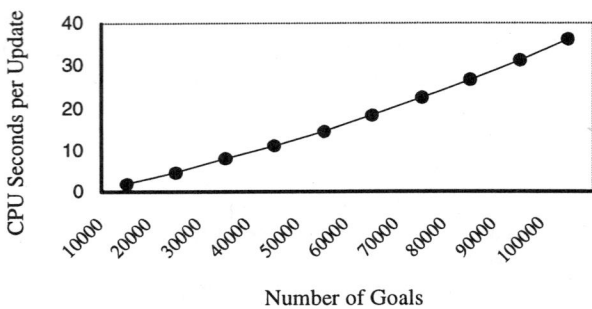

Figure 3: Experimental results of the extended briefcase domain

goal	cpu sec per update	length of observation	fully achieved goals	partially achieved goals	remaining goals
G_1	1.202	2.25	7	12	4
G_2	0.352	16	10	9	1
G_3	0.027	3.0	3	10	1
G_4	1.255	20.5	33	0	1

Table 1: Experimental results of the Unix domain

to create a series of spaces of 10,000, 20,000, up to 100,000 possible goals respectively. The same sequences of observed actions with the same Initial Conditions are used in the experiments in conjunction with these spaces of possible goals. Figure 3 shows that the average CPU time taken to process an observed action is approximately linear in the number of goals.

In the Unix domain, we tested our algorithms on a set of data collected at the University of Washington. To collect the data, the subjects are given goals described in English first and they then try to solve each goal by executing Unix commands. The executed Unix commands are recorded in the data set. We have 29 action schemata for the Unix commands including those executed by the subjects, 245 goal schemata and an estimate of 10000 possible goals. The results show that on average it only takes less than a CPU second to process an observed action and usually only a very small number of consistent goals remain after a sequence of observed actions have been processed.

Table 1 gives a summary of the experimental results. We tested our system on four goals that were originally tested in (Lesh & Etzioni 1995). The CPU second per update is the average time it takes to process an observed action. The length of observation is the average number of observed actions executed by the subjects to achieve the given goal. The fully achieved goals are the goals fully achieved after the last action has been observed. The partially achieved goals are the goals partially achieved. The remaining goals are the goals recognised after the last observed action has been processed. On G_2, G_3 and G_4, our algorithms return single, consistent goals that are the same as the goals given to the subjects. On G_1, four goals are recognised including the goal given to the subjects. Our algorithms recognise that the subjects tried to find one of the four files in the directory but does not know which file it is. This is as good as a human observer can do because you simply can not tell from the observed actions which file the subject was trying to find. These four goals can be generalised into a single, consistent goal 'finding a file in the directory' where variables are allowed in the recognised goals. These results show that our algorithms perform extremely well with regard to efficiency and accuracy. They also demonstrate a significant improvement on the performance of the goal recogniser (Lesh & Etzioni 1995) where 155, 37 and 15 goals remain on G_1, G_2 and G_4 respectively.

Related Work

Most plan recognition systems (e.g., (Allen & Perrault 1980), (Carberry 1986), (Pollack 1986), (Litman & Allen 1987), (Kautz 1987)) search a space of possible plans for candidate plans that account for the observations. To form the search space in a given domain, some kind of plan representation is required. For instance, in Kautz's event hierarchy, plan decompositions are required that describe how low level actions make up complex actions. Even though the use of the plan representation has an obvious advantage of expressive richness, it has a serious limitation in its inability to deal with new plans whose types do not appear in the plan representation. Hand-coding the plan representation in a large and complex domain presents a tedious or impractical task. In some other domains, the knowledge about plans might not be readily available.

Some attempts (e.g., (Lesh & Etzioni 1996), (Bauer 1998)) have recently been made to address this issue in which machine learning techniques have been applied to automate acquisition of plan representation. Even when leaving aside the plan representation consideration, searching the plan space can be expoentially expensive because the number of possible plan hypotheses can be exponential in the number of actions (Kautz 1987). Most plan recognition systems have often been developed in domains in which there are fewer than 100 plans and goals (Lesh & Etzioni 1996).

Our graph construction and analysis approach to plan recognition differs significantly from these plan recognition systems. Instead of immediately searching for candidate plans, our approach explicitly constructs a graph structure in which temporal and causal constraints among the observed actions and the achieved goals are explicitly represented. Our definition of what constitutes a valid plan for a goal eliminates the plan representation in most plan recognition systems. Our plan recognition system only takes the goal schemata and action schemata as input. It recognises consistent goals only from fully or partially achieved goals and organises the observed actions into valid plans for the recognised goals or part of these goals. Under our formulation, the plan recogniser must consider how the observed actions can be composed into plans. Our formation is not limited in its ability to recognise new plans. Our algorithms are sound, polynomial-time and polynomial-space. Our experimental results show that our algorithms can be scaled up and applied to domains in which there are tens of thousands of possible goals and plans. We have therefore accommodated both expressiveness and tractability without the use of plan representation in our system.

Lesh and Etzioni first tried to use a graph representation of actions and goals for the goal recognition problem (Lesh & Etzioni 1995). Their graph representation only consists of action and goal nodes that are fully connected to each other first and then inconsistent goals are repeatedly pruned from this graph representation. This will lead to a set of candidate goals that explain the observed actions. Their graph representation does not explicitly represent temporal constraints and causal links over actions and goals. So their system can only recognise goals rather than plans because it cannot organise the observed actions into plan structures for the recognised goals. Their system is sound and polynomial-time. They have however sacrificed expressiveness of the plan representation for tractability. This is not the case in our system that recognises both goals as well as plans and performs in polynomial time and space. As we indicated in the previous section the number of remaining goals after pruning in their system is usually large.

Our graph-based approach to plan recognition can be seen as a counterpart of planning with Planning Graph in planning (Blum & Furst 1995), (Blum & Furst 1997). Though graph structures are used in both approaches, they consist of different kinds of nodes and edges, take different inputs and aim at producing different outputs.

Conclusions

In this paper, we introduced a new approach to plan recognition in which a graph structure called a Goal Graph is constructed and analysed for plan recognition. We described two algorithms for constructing and analysing a Goal Graph. Our algorithms recognise both goals and plans. They allow redundant and partially ordered actions. They are sound, polynomial-time and polynomial-space. Our empirical experiments show that our algorithms are computationally efficient and they can be scaled up and applied to domains where there are tens of thousands of goals and plans. They recognise goals and plans with great accuracy. Since our new graph-based approach to plan recognition is fundamentally different from the existing methods for plan recognition, it provides an alternative to these methods and shows a new perspective of research into plan recognition.

Our plan recognition system is limited in its ability to recognise every type of erroneous plans. For instance, if an erroneous plan involves an observed action that is completely irrelevant to the intended goal, our system fails to recognise the goal as a consistent one. The GoalGraphAnalyser is not complete: it may not immediately recognise the intended goal as a consistent one when the action currently observed has a causal link with a relevant action that has not yet been observed. So it may temporarily miss the intended goal if it is not yet in the set of consistent goals. This is of course just a delay on updating the set of consistent goals because as soon as the relevant action is observed, the intended goal will be recognised as a consistent one and the set of consistent goals will be updated accordingly. This is natural and inevitable to the human observer: when an observed action is not yet found relevant to a goal in a consistent way, we can either make an unsound guess that it could be relevant to some of the consistent goals we have at moment, or delay the decision for a little while until more actions are observed and this currently observed action is found relevant to a goal in a consistent way. Despite these limitations, our system performs extremely well in our two test domains.

References

Allen, J., and Perrault, C. 1980. Analysing intention in utterances. *Artificial Intelligence* 15:143–178.

Anderson, C.; Smith, D.; and Weld, D. 1998. Conditional effects in graphplan. In *Proc. of 4th Intl. Conf. AI Planning Systems*.

Bauer, M. 1998. Acquisition of abstract plan descriptions for plan recognition. In *Proceedings of AAAI-98*, 936–941.

Blum, A., and Furst, M. 1995. Fast planning through planning graph analysis. In *Proc. of IJCAI-95*, 1636–1642.

Blum, A., and Furst, M. 1997. Fast planning through planning graph analysis. *Artificial Intelligence* 90:281–300.

Carberry, S. 1986. User models: the problem of disparity. In *Proceedings of the 11th International Conference on Computational Linguistics*, 29–34.

Gazen, B., and Knoblock, C. 1997. Combining the expressivity of ucpop with the efficiency of graphplan. In *Proc. 4th Euro. Conf. on Planning*.

Kautz, H. 1987. *A Formal Theory of Plan Recognition*. PhD Thesis, University of Rochester.

Koehler, J.; Nebel, B.; Hoffmann, J.; and Dimopoulos, Y. 1997. Extending planing graphs to an adl subset. In *Proc. of 4th Euro. Conf. on Planning*, 273–285.

Lesh, N., and Etzioni, O. 1995. A sound and fast goal recognizer. In *Proc. 15th Int. Joint Conf. on AI*, 1704–1710.

Lesh, N., and Etzioni, O. 1996. Scaling up goal recognition. In *Proc. of Int. Conf. on Principles of Knowledge Representation and Reasoning*.

Litman, D., and Allen, J. 1987. A plan recognition model for sub-dialogues in conversation. *Cognitive Science* 11:163–200.

Pednault, E. 1988. Synthesizing plans that contain actions with context-dependent effects. *Computational Intelligence* 4(4):356–372.

Pednault, E. 1989. Adl: Exploring the middle ground between strips and the situation calculus. In *Proc. of KR-89*, 324–332. Morgan Kaufman.

Pollack, M. 1986. A model of plan inference that distinguishes between the beliefs of actors and observers. In *Proceedings of the 24th Annual Meeting of the Association for Computational linguistics*, 207–214.

Solving a Supply Chain Optimization Problem Collaboratively

Hoong Chuin Lau and **Andrew Lim**
School of Computing
National University of Singapore
3 Science Drive 2, Singapore 117543

Qi Zhang Liu[*]
Department of Decision Sciences
National University of Singapore
Lower Kent Ridge Road, Singapore 119260

Abstract

We propose a novel algorithmic framework to solve an integrated planning and scheduling problem in supply chain management. This problem involves the integration of an inventory management problem and the vehicle routing problem with time windows, both of which are known to be NP-hard. Under this framework, algorithms that solve the underlying sub-problems collaborate rigorously yet in a computationally efficient manner to arrive at a good solution. We will then present two algorithms to solve the inventory management problem: a complete mathematical model integrating integer programming with constraint programming, and an incomplete algorithm based on tabu search. We present experimental results based on extended Solomon benchmark vehicle routing problems.

Introduction

Supply chain optimization involves the integration of decision-making processes to manage the production and flow of products and services from the source to the customers. An emerging industry trend in supply chain management is the formation of logistics operators that provide a one-stop point-to-point service for the entire distribution operation in the supply chain. Under this system, retailers need not manage their own inventory to ensure timely re-supply while the logistics operator achieves economies of scale by being able to co-ordinate deliveries to multiple retailers. Hence, a system-wide optimization can be achieved through an algorithmic integration of inventory and transportation.

More precisely, consider a distribution system with multiple suppliers, capacitated warehouses, capacitated retailers, identical capacitated vehicles and unit-sized items. The items are to be transported from the suppliers to the warehouses, and subsequently delivered to the retailers by vehicles. Vehicles can combine deliveries to multiple retailers, provided that the items are delivered within stipulated time windows. Given the retailers' time-varying demand forecast over a finite planning horizon, the goal is to find a distribution plan so as to minimize the total operating cost, which comprises the inventory cost (for amounts exceeding demand), backlogging cost (for amounts falling short of demand) and transportation cost.

We call this problem the *Inventory Routing Problem with Time Windows* (IRPTW). Clearly, IRPTW is a complex problem, since it involves the integration of two classical optimization problems: the dynamic capacitated lot-sizing problem and vehicle routing problem with time-windows. Both are proved to be NP-hard even for very simple instances. (See Florian, Lenstra and Rinnooy Kan (1980) and Savelsbergh (1986).)

Many inventory models have been proposed by the OR community in the past. The one-warehouse multi-retailers problem under constant demand has been extensively studied in the past few decades, and the structure of the (near) optimal policies under this system is already well-understood. The reader may refer to Graves, Kan and Zipkin (1993) for a comprehensive review. ¿From the Constraint Programming perspective, an interesting inventory management problem for reusable resources has been recently investigated by Caseau and Kokeny (1998).

As far as integrating inventory and transportation, one of the earliest work in this area is by Federgruen and Zipkin (1984) who considered a *single-period* IRP with stochastic demands at the retailers' end. Their model aims to determine the optimal allocation of inventory to retailers while minimizing routing and inventory costs. This problem in itself already leads to a huge mixed integer programming problem that can only be solved by heuristics. Chan, Federgruen and Simchi-Levi (1998) recently modelled a *single-item, constant demand* distribution system and presented worst case as well as probabilistic bounds for their models. Unfortunately, due to the unrealistic assumption on demand, it is doubtful that any of the asymptotically optimal heuristic proposed will perform well for realistic problems with time-varying demand.

To our knowledge, a supply chain problem as extensive as IRPTW has not been carefully studied in the literature. A notable exception is Carter *et al.* (1996), who proposed a Lagrangean heuristic to solve a single-supplier, single-warehouse IRPTW. Un-

---
[*]Corresponding author
Copyright © 2000, American Association for Artificial Intelligence (www.aaai.org). All rights reserved.

fortunately, their approach cannot guarantee feasibility (even if a solution exists), and the algorithm is sensitive to the values of several parameters where there are no good heuristics for setting them.

In this paper, we present a novel approach based on decomposition into two sub-problems (distribution and routing) plus an interface mechanism to allow the two algorithms to collaborate in a *master-slave* fashion, with the distribution algorithm (A1) driving the routing algorithm (A2). Intuitively, the procedure is as follows. A1 will determine the flow amounts between the suppliers, warehouse and the retailers so as to minimize inventory and backlogging costs subject to warehouse and retailers' capacities. A2, based on the given flow amounts (or customer demands, in Vehicle Routing terminology), sequences the deliveries into routes so as to minimize transportation cost, subject to vehicle capacities and time windows. These routes in turn induce a re-partitioning of the retailers for A1, and the process is repeated. The novelty hinges on the definition of a good interface between A1 and A2 so as to ensure *convergence*, since the objective functions are conflicting when taken separately. (To reduce inventory and backlogging, it is necessary to make more frequent deliveries, but this will increase the transportation cost). To achieve this, we complicate A1 with *vehicle capacity constraints* and impose penalty for flow amounts that have high aggregated transportation cost. This will be explained in greater detail later.

We see several advantages of our approach. First, from the planning and scheduling perspective, it offers an efficient and readily implementable way to tackle the intricacy of integrating two processes along a supply chain. Second, from the computational perspective, our framework is agent-oriented in the sense that the algorithms are agents trying to generate an overall plan collaboratively while guarding their individual interests. Finally, from the software engineering viewpoint, it supports the paradigm of reusability and plug-and-play in the sense that it allows either one of the modules to be replaced without affecting the other. We believe our approach can be adapted to provide decision support for a host of integrated supply chain optimization problems we face today.

Preliminaries

IRPTW is defined as, given the following input:

S: set of suppliers;
R: set of retailers;
J: set of items;
T: consecutive days in the planning period $\{1, 2, \cdots, n\}$;
D_{ijt}: demand of retailer i for item j on day t;
Q_V: vehicle capacity;
Q_W: warehouse storage capacity;
Q_i: storage capacity of retailer i;
W_i: time window of retailer i

C_j: inventory holding cost per unit item j per day at the warehouse;
C_{ij}: inventory holding cost per unit item j per day at retailer i;
B_{ij}: backlogging cost per unit item j per day at retailer i;
T_{ik}: transportation cost incurred by visiting retailer i followed by k on the same route;

output the following:

(1) the distribution plan, which is denoted by:

x_{sjt}: integral flow amount of item j from supplier s to the warehouse on day t; and
x_{ijt}: integral flow amount of item j from the warehouse to retailer i on day t; and

(2) the set of daily transportation routes Φ, which carry the flow amounts in (1) from the warehouse to the retailers such that the sum of the following linear costs is minimized: a) inventory cost at the warehouse (C_j), b) inventory cost at the retailers (C_{ij}), c) backlogging cost (B_{ij}); and d) transportation cost from the warehouse to the retailers (T_{ik}).

We will use indices i, s, j, t for retailers, suppliers, items and days respectively.

The distribution plan must obey the demands and storage capacity constraints. We further assume that items arriving at the warehouse on day t can only be delivered to retailers from day $t+1$ onwards. The transportation routes must obey the standard routing, vehicle capacities and time windows constraints. For notational convenience, we let Φ_t denote the set of routes for day t. Each route is an ordered list of retailers representing the delivery sequence performed by one particular vehicle per day.

Algorithmic Framework

Our algorithmic framework is an iterative approach between 2 sub-problems, namely the distribution problem (DP) and the vehicle routing problem with time-windows (VRPTW).

DP is a *constrained* version of the dynamic lotsizing problem, since it has to iterate with VRPTW in a manner that guarantees convergence. It receives a set of transportation routes Φ as part of the input, and returns a solution that has to be *consistent with* Φ (see definition below). Moreover, its objective function has an additional transportation cost component, which serves as a heuristic in order to generate a distribution plan such that VRPTW will in turn generate low-cost routes subsequently. In this way, the iterative improvement will be sustainable and hence effective.

<u>Definition 3.1.</u> We say that a distribution plan x is *consistent with* a set of transportation routes Φ iff Φ can fulfill the transport needs of x without violating any vehicle capacity constraints. More specially, for all days $t \in T$ and routes $\phi \in \Phi_t$, $\sum_{i \in \phi} \sum_j x_{ijt} \leq Q_V$.

VRPTW is a well-studied NP-hard problem. Several variants of VRPTW have been studied, and many efficient optimal as well as heuristic approaches have been developed to solve them. For a comprehensive review on these algorithms, see Desrosiers *et al.* (1995). Our algorithm framework works for all kinds of VRPTW and any algorithm solving VRPTW. For the convenience of expression, we assume that there is no limit on number of vehicles. However, each vehicle is charged a high penalty so that the number of vehicles used will be minimized. This is to avoid the difficulty of finding feasible solutions for original VRPTW. (Even if there is some limit on number of vehicles, as the iteration between VRPTW and DP progresses, some retailers won't be visited on certain day. Hence the problem instances of VRPTW needed to be solve in the next iteration will decrease. Then the limit may become easy to meet.) With this assumption, we will assume the availability of one such efficient algorithm that returns to us a near-optimal feasible solution when given a VRPTW instance.

Let the algorithms for solving DP and VRPTW be denoted A1 and A2, and let the objective functions be denoted f_1 and f_2, respectively. Let **lowestSoFar** be the objective value of the best DP solution found so far, initialized to ∞. Procedurally, we propose the following:

Algorithm A:
(1) call A2 to generate an initial set of transportation routes Φ
(2) call A1 to generate a distribution plan x that is consistent with Φ
(3) if $f_1(x) =$ **lowestSoFar** return (x, Φ) and stop else set **lowestSoFar** $= f_1(x)$
(4) call A2 to generate a new set of routes Φ' based on x s.t. $f_2(\Phi') < f_2(\Phi)$
(5) if no such Φ' can be found, return (x, Φ) and stop
(6) set $\Phi = \Phi'$; goto Step (2)

It suffices to say now that, by optimality, Step (2) will never return a solution whose objective value is worse than the previous solution. In the next section, we will present details of A1 and A2, and prove that the above algorithm is correct and converges to a solution. More precisely, we will prove that under this framework, the overall objective function of IRPTW decreases monotonically from one iteration to the next.

Integrated IP/CP Model

In this section, we present an exact IP/CP model for solving DP.

Basically, we model DP as a multi-commodity flow problem complicated by side constraints. This model is a time-expanded 3-layer network for suppliers, warehouse and retailers respectively. The warehouse node and each retailer node are replicated n times for the n-day planning period. Arcs between nodes of different layers represent the flow amounts (suppliers to warehouse, warehouse to retailers), while arcs between adjacent replicated nodes represent either inventory carrying over to the next day, or backlogging from the previous day. This model is complicated by the consistency condition and additional transportation component, which can be handled by adding artificial nodes and concave costs on the incident arcs. The resulting model is a fixed-charge (or concave-cost) layered network.

In this section, we present a complete formulation with redundant logic constraints to model interesting relationships between inventory and demands. In the next section, we will present a tabu search strategy with strategic oscillation.

We explain further notations used.

Recall that by A2 (i.e. the VRPTW algorithm) outputs a set of routes Φ to DP. The following variables can be derived directly from Φ:

h_{irt}: 1 if retailer i is served by route $r \in \Phi$ on day t, and 0 otherwise;

c_r: cost of route r, defined as the sum of transportation costs T_{ik} over all adjacent retailers i and k on route r.

The following intermediate variables are used:

z_{ijt}: integral amount of item j held in retailer i on day t;

z_{jt}: integral amount of item j held in the warehouse on day t;

b_{ijt}: integral amount of item j backlog for retailer i on day t;

y_r: $(0,1)$ variable, whether route $r \in \Phi$ is used;

y_{it}: $(0,1)$ variable, whether retailer i is served on day t.

The integer programming formulation of DP is given as follows:
min $\sum_j \sum_t (z_{jt} C_j + \sum_i z_{ijt} C_{ij} + \sum_i b_{ijt} B_{ij}) + \sum_r y_r c_r$
subject to the following linear constraints:

$\sum_j z_{jt} \leq Q_W$, for $t \in T$ \hfill (1)
$\sum_j x_{ijt} + \sum_j z_{ijt} \leq Q_i$, for $i \in R$ and $t \in T$ \hfill (2)
$\sum_i x_{ijt} \leq z_{jt}$, for $j \in J$ and $t \in T$ \hfill (3)
$\sum_s x_{sjt} + z_{jt} - z_{j,t+1} - \sum_i x_{ijt} = 0$,
for $j \in J$ and $t < n$ \hfill (4)
$x_{ijt} + z_{ijt} - z_{ij,t+1} - b_{ijt} + b_{ij,t+1} = D_{ijt}$,
for $i \in R, j \in J$ and $t < n$ \hfill (5)
$x_{ijn} + z_{ijn} - b_{ijn} = D_{ijn}$, for $i \in R, j \in J$ \hfill (6)
$\sum_j x_{ijt} \leq y_{it} Q_i$, for $i \in R$ and $t \in T$ \hfill (7)
$y_{it} \leq y_r$, for $i \in R, r \in \Phi, t \in T$ with $h_{irt} = 1$ \hfill (8)
$\sum_i \sum_j \sum_t x_{ijt} h_{irt} \leq y_r Q_V$, for $r \in \Phi$ \hfill (9)

The objective function comprises 4 components: the warehouse inventory cost, retailers' inventory cost, backlogging cost, and a specially designed function to reflect transportation cost.

Constraint (1) is the warehouse capacity constraint; (2) is the retailers' capacity constraint; (3) means the inventory in the warehouse must exceed daily delivery requirement; (4) is the inventory balance constraint on the warehouse; (5) & (6) are the inventory balance constraints on retailers; (7) defines whether each retailer is served on each day; (8) means a route is used iff at least 1 retailer on this route is served; (9) is the vehicle capacity constraints that enforce the consistency condition on used routes.

The highlight of this model is that, when used cooperatively with the VRPTW algorithm, guarantees convergence. Particularly:

(a) The last component of the objective penalizes usage of *expensive* routes, i.e. it discourages the generation of a distribution plan that will incur a high transportation cost.

(b) Constraint (9) introduces bundle (or knapsack) constraints on the flows to enforce the consistency condition (see Definition 3.1).

Obviously, the above model by itself is much harder to solve than the standard multi-commodity flow problem, due to the following reasons:

(a) The last component of the objective introduces *disjunction* (on y_r) into the problem; and

(b) Typically, a problem with tight bundle constraints takes much longer to solve than one of comparable size without, as shown in Ho and Loute (1983). In fact, it has been shown in Garey and Johnson (1979) that the min-cost network flow problem with bundle constraints is NP-complete, even if all capacities are 1 and all bundles have 2 arcs.

One way to speed up search is to introduce redundant constraints that will trigger constraint propagation. We add the following logical (non-linear) constraints into the IP formulation:

$x_{ijt} > 0 \Rightarrow y_{it} = 1$, for all $i \in R, j \in J$ and $t \in T$ (10)

$(z_{ijt} > 0) + (b_{ijt} > 0) < 2$,
  for all $i \in R, j \in J$ and $t \in T$ (11)

$z_{ijt} > z_{ij,t-1} \Leftrightarrow x_{ijt} > D_{ijt} + b_{ij,t-1}$
  for all $i \in R, j \in J$ and $t \in T$ (12)

$b_{ijt} > b_{ij,t-1} \Leftrightarrow x_{ijt} + z_{ij,t-1} < D_{ijt}$
  for all $i \in R, j \in J$ and $t \in T$ (13)

Constraint (10) says retailer i is served on day t only if there is a positive flow to i that day. (11) is the mutual-exclusivity constraint on inventory holding and backlogging. (12) relates the rise and fall of retailers' inventories between 2 consecutive days with the demand-supply situation. (13) does likewise for retailers' backlogs.

(10) plays the role in forcing early instantiation of the variables y_{it}, which, by Constraint (8), cause an early instantiation of the disjunctive variables y_r. Similarly, (11) to (13) serve to trigger constraint propagation on the variables z_{ijt} and b_{ijt}, by Constraints (2) to (6), cause an early instantiation of the variables x_{ijt}.

The above formulation cannot be solved by traditional MIP solvers which do not support logic constraints, but can be efficiently solved by ILOG Planner (version 3.0) which integrates the ILOG Solver (a constraint propagation search engine) and CPLEX MIP solver.

Having presented enough details, we now proceed to give the convergence proof of algorithm A.

Convergence Proof

Let A1 be an algorithm that solves DP (represented by the above IP/CP model) to optimality, and A2 be any algorithm that returns a feasible solution for a given feasible VRPTW instance. We now prove the convergence of Algorithm A.

Let $f_1(x, \Phi) = \sum_j \sum_t (z_{jt} C_j + \sum_i z_{ijt} C_{ij} + \sum_i b_{ijt} B_{ij}) + \sum_{r \in \Phi} y_r c_r$ denote the objective function of DP and $f_2(\Phi) = \sum_{r \in \Phi} c_r$ denote the objective function of VRPTW. The key argument is that between two consecutive calls to A2, the objective value of f_1 on the same distribution plan must decrease, shown as follows.

Write $f_1(x, \Phi)$ as $f_1(x) + f_1(\Phi)$, where $f_1(x) = \sum_j \sum_t (z_{jt} C_j + \sum_i z_{ijt} C_{ij} + \sum_i b_{ijt} B_{ij})$ and $f_1(\Phi) = \sum_{r \in \Phi} y_r c_r$. Split Φ into $\Phi_1 = \{r \in \Phi | y_r = 1\}$ and $\Phi_2 = \{r \in \Phi | y_r = 0\}$. Then $f_1(\Phi) = f_1(\Phi_1) = f_2(\Phi_1)$. Suppose A2 generates a new set of routes $\Phi' = \Phi'_1 \cup \Phi'_2$, where Φ'_1 (resp. Φ'_2) covers the retailers in Φ_1 (resp. Φ_2). Since $f_2(\Phi') < f_2(\Phi)$, it follows necessarily that $f_2(\Phi'_1) < f_2(\Phi_1)$. Hence, $f_1(\Phi') = f_2(\Phi'_1) < f_2(\Phi_1) = f_1(\Phi)$. This implies, $f_1(x, \Phi') = f_1(x) + f_1(\Phi') < f_1(x) + f_1(\Phi) = f_1(x, \Phi)$. We can therefore easily get the following lemma.

Lemma 1 *Given a feasible instance of IRPTW, Algorithm A converges to a solution.*

Tabu Search

In this section, we present a tabu search (TS) algorithm for solving DP.

TS is a form of local search augmented with adaptive memory. In TS, a *move* operator defines the neighborhood $N(s)$ of the current solution s. Starting with an initial solution, TS proceeds iteratively by replacing current solution s with a *best* neighbor $s' \in N(s)$ among all possible moves. One crucial feature of TS is the notion of a *tabu list*, which is a short-term memory that helps the search avoid cycling as well as escape from local optimality. Another interesting feature is the notion of *strategic oscillation*, which is a long-term memory that achieves an effective interplay between intensification and diversification of search. For a comprehensive description of the tabu search methodology, the reader may refer to the text of Glover and Laguna (1997). In the following, we assume that the reader is familiar with standard TS terminology.

Move Operators

The key move operator is the *transfer move*, which transfer flow amount from one flow variable to another having the same retailer and item (i.e. transfer flow across *different* days). We define two ways to determine the units of amount to be transferred. The first is based on a *variable scaling* strategy where each x_{ijt} is scaled to some discrete units and at each iteration, only 1 unit is transferred. The scaling factor differs over different iterations. We begin with large factors (i.e. coarse-granular flows) and gradually decrease them. When no refinement can be made to obtain better solution, the procedure reverts to a large factor and the process repeats. The second is *greedy feeding* strategy, where we transfer as many units as possible between two flow variables without violating any capacity constraint.

Two other move operators are introduced to speed up the search for better solutions and to escape from local optimality: (1) the *free move*, which frees a retailer on a certain day by transferring all items to other days via the greedy feeding strategy; and (2) the *empty move*, which empties a route by freeing all retailers on the route via free moves.

Note that the moves can result in infeasible solutions (see sub-section on Strategic Oscillation).

Tabu List

The tabu search procedure uses a *tabu list* to store the time (i.e. iteration number) when tabu-active[1] status of each variable ends. Let $\Theta_x = (\tau_{ijt})$, 3D-array of size $|R| \cdot |J| \cdot |T|$, be the tabu list associated with the variables x_{ijt}. We define τ_{ijt} as follows:

$$\tau_{ijt} = start_{ijt} + tenure_{ijt},$$

where $start_{ijt}$ is the iteration number immediately before x_{ijt} was changed, and $tenure_{ijt}$ is the tabu tenure, which is a fraction of the size of Θ_x. Experimentally, TS is effective when the tenure is a random value in the range $[|R||J||T|/5, |R||J||T|/4]$ generated at iteration $start_{ijt}$.

The tabu-active status of other variables, such as retailer coverage y_r and route usage y_{it} are defined likewise.

Candidate List

In general, the neighborhood associated with each move operator can be extremely large. For instance, the transfer move neighborhood has $|R||J||T||T-1|$ elements and hence an exhaustive search of the entire neighborhood at every iteration is too expensive. Instead, we achieve an effective tradeoff between the quality of the best move and the effort expended to find it by determining a much-smaller *candidate list* for each move operator via a greedy strategy.

For the transfer move, we maintain a sorted list of relative inventory costs for each retailer i and item j:

$$w_{ij} = (\sum_t z_{ijt} + \sum_t b_{ijt})/\sum_t D_{ijt}$$

and those variables x_{ijt} whose corresponding costs are within the top $c\%$ (where c is a pre-defined constant) are considered for move.

[1] When a variable is *tabu-active*, its value is not allowed to change during that iteration.

In the same vein, for *free moves* and *empty moves*, we consider retailers and routes (respectively) whose *relative loads* (defined below) are either very high or very low. Low loads can potentially save cost, while high loads may help escape from local optimality. Hence, for free moves, we maintain a sorted list of weights for each retailer i on each day t:

$$w_{it} = max(\sum_j x_{ijt}/\sum_{s,j} D_{ijs}, 1 - \sum_i x_{ijt}/\sum_{s,j} D_{ijs});$$

and for empty moves, we maintain:

$$w_r = max(\sum_{i,t}(h_{irt} \cdot \sum_j x_{ijt})/Q_V, 1 - \sum_{i,t}(h_{irt} \cdot \sum_j x_{ijt})/Q_V);$$

those retailers and routes whose corresponding weights are within the top $c\%$ (where c is a pre-defined constant) are considered for move.

Strategic Oscillation

Strategy oscillation operates in the tabu search procedure by orienting moves in and out of the feasible region. A penalty is imposed on solutions that are infeasible, i.e. those which violate some constraints. For each $i \in R$ and $j \in J$, let $x_{ij,n+1}$ be amount of unfulfilled demand of retailer i for item j, i.e.,

$$x_{ij,n+1} = \sum_t D_{ijt} - \sum_t x_{ijt}.$$

Let $f(x)$ be a function that takes value x if $x > 0$, or 0 otherwise. Denote the amount of items exceeding the capacity of retailer i on day t by

$$v_{it} = f(\sum_j x_{ijt} - Q_i);$$

the amount exceeding the capacity of the warehouse on day t by

$$v_t = f(\sum_j z_{jt} - Q_W);$$

and the amount exceeding the capacity of a vehicle serving route r on day t by

$$v_r = f(\sum_{i,t}(h_{irt} \cdot \sum_j x_{ijt}) - Q_V).$$

We impose an infeasible solution with a penalty cost directly proportional to the degree of constraint violation:

$$P_1 \sum_i \sum_j x_{ij,n+1} + P_2(\sum_i \sum_t v_{it} + \sum_t v_t + \sum_r v_r),$$

where $P_1 < P_2$ are pre-defined parameters. For the intensification phase, they are set high values to reduce the chance of reaching an infeasible solution, while for the diversification phase, they are set lower values. Experimentally, our tabu search scheme is effective when $P_1 = P_2/2$.

Problem	Initial	Final	Iterations	Time(sec)
R101	48929	46022	3	19
R102	47852	44412	3	20
R103	47915	43638	4	40
R104	45692	43184	3	35
R105	46646	43450	3	23
R106	44545	42651	3	35
R107	43050	42193	3	30
R108	41495	40403	2	14
R109	46376	44322	3	24
R110	48283	45283	3	25
R111	47564	44960	3	34
R112	46613	44408	3	38
C101	105608	90667	2	15
C102	146067	104105	3	34
C103	131945	106930	4	44
C104	153228	111894	3	30
C105	120002	106073	2	17
C106	128149	112500	3	34
C107	126839	105747	5	55
C108	128345	102260	5	59
C109	142795	108688	4	38
RC101	110842	106259	4	39
RC102	122789	110580	2	13
RC103	132193	110467	6	70
RC104	119634	102381	4	45
RC105	127889	117552	5	44
RC106	106396	99141	4	32
RC107	117967	109035	2	17
RC108	108388	105446	4	43

Table 1: Experimental Results (Based on Extended Solomon's Benchmarks)

Experimental Results

In this section, we report some preliminary experimental results. To our knowledge, no benchmark test data available in the literature matches our problem exactly. Hence, our experimental results are based on the test data we generated as follows.

Since IRPTW contains VRPTW as a sub-problem, we adopt the well-known Solomon benchmark problems listed in Solomon (1987) to generate the locations and time-windows of the retailers and warehouse (depot). The demands of retailers are randomly generated in the range [0,30]. The capacities of the vehicles, retailers and warehouse are set as 200, 300 and 10000 respectively. In this paper, we consider 3 types of items, 3 suppliers, 1 warehouse and 50 retailers over a 5-day planning horizon. In terms of cost parameters, the inventory cost at the warehouse (C_j), inventory cost of retailer (C_{ij}) and backlogging cost (B_{ij}) are set to be 1, 2 and 4 per unit item per day respectively. The transportation cost of each route is 5 times its total distance plus a fixed vehicle usage cost of 50.

DP is implemented based on the Tabu Search described above, and VRPTW is based on an efficient engine developed inhouse. Note that our concern is not the absolute quality of the solution, but rather, the improvement that can be derived when the two engines collaborate (versus the conventional sequential pipeline approach). Under our proposed collaborative framework, any improvement made to the DP algorithm or VRPTW algorithm will increase the overall solution quality of IRPTW.

We run our program on a Pentium 300 PC and the results are given as follows. In this table, we plot the different test instances against: (1) the initial objective value, (2) final objective value, (3) total number of iterations taken, and (4) CPU run time.

¿From Table 1, we observe that the average number of iterations to convergence is 3.38, and the average percentage improvement in the objective value of the final solution over the initial solution is 10.5%.

References

M. W. Carter, J. M. Farvolden, G. Laporte, J. Xu, Solving an Integrated Logistics Problem Arising in Grocery Distribution, *INFOR*, **34**:4 (1996), 290–306.

L. M. Chan, A. Fedegruen and D. Simchi-Levi, Probabilistic Analysis and Practical Algorithms for Inventory-Routing Models, *Operations Research*, **46**:1 (1998) 96–106.

Y. Caseau and T. Kokeny, An Inventory Management Problem, *Constraints*, 3, (1998), 363–373.

J. Desrosiers, Y. Dumas, M. M. Solomon and F. Soumis, Time Constrainted Routing and Scheduling, in: M. O. Ball *et al*. eds., *Handbooks in Operations Research and Management Science* Vol **8**: Network Routing, (North-Holland, 1995), 35–139.

M. Florian, J. K. Lenstra, and A. H. G. Rinnooy Kan, Deterministic Production Planning: Algorithm and Complexity, *Management Sc.*, **26**:7 (1980), 669–679.

A. Fedegruen and P. Zipkin, An Efficient Algorithm for Computing Optimal (s,S) Policies, *Operations Research*, **22** (1984), 1268–1285.

S. C. Graves, A. H. G. Rinnooy Kan and P. H. Zipkin eds., *Handbook in Operations Research and Management Science* Vol **4**: Logistics of Production and Inventory, (North-Holland, 1993).

M. R. Garey and D. S. Johnson, *Computers and Intractibility*, (Freeman and Company, 1979).

F. Glover and M. Laguna, *Tabu Search*, (Kluwer Academic Publishers, 1997).

J. K. Ho and E. Loute, Computational Experience with Advanced Decomposition of Decomposition Algorithms, *Math Programming*, **27**:3, (1983), 283–290.

M. W. P. Savelsbergh, Local Search for Routing Problems with Time Windows, *Annals of Operations Research*, **4**, (1986), 285–305.

M. M. Solomon, Algorithms for the Vehicle Routing and Scheduling Problem with Time Window Constraints, *Operations Research*, **35**, 1987, 254–265.

From Causal Theories to Successor State Axioms and STRIPS-Like Systems

Fangzhen Lin (flin@cs.ust.hk)
Department of Computer Science
The Hong Kong University of Science and Technology
Clear Water Bay, Kowloon, Hong Kong

Abstract

We describe a system for specifying the effects of actions. Unlike those commonly used in AI planning, our system uses an action description language that allows one to specify the effects of actions using domain rules, which are state constraints that can entail new action effects from old ones. Declaratively, an action domain in our language corresponds to a nonmonotonic causal theory in the situation calculus. Procedurally, such an action domain is compiled into a set of propositional theories, one for each action in the domain, from which fully instantiated successor state-like axioms and STRIPS-like systems are then generated. We expect the system to be a useful tool for knowledge engineers writing action specifications for classical AI planning systems, GOLOG systems, and other systems where formal specifications of actions are needed.

Introduction

We describe a system for generating action effect specifications from a set of domain rules and direct action effect axioms, among other things. We expect the system to be a useful tool for knowledge engineers writing action specifications for classical AI planning systems, GOLOG systems (Levesque et al. 1997), and other systems where formal specifications of actions are needed.

One of our motivations for building such a system is to bridge the gap between formal nonmonotonic action theories on the one hand and STRIPS-like systems on the other. For years, researchers in nonmonotonic reasoning community have been proposing solutions to the frame and ramification problem, aiming for theories of actions that are more expressive than STRIPS-like systems. Until recently, however, these theories were of theoretical interest only because of their high computational complexity. The situation has since changed substantially due to the use of causality in representing domain constraints. For instance, McCain and Turner (McCain and Turner 1998) showed that a competitive planner can be built directly on top of causal action

Copyright © 2000, American Association for Artificial Intelligence (www.aaai.org). All rights reserved.

theories. In this paper, we shall describe a system that takes as input a nonmonotonic action theory and returns as output a full action specification both in STRIPS-like format and as a set of fully instantiated successor state axioms.

The main difference between nonmonotonic action theories and STRIPS-like systems is in the former's use of domain constraints in deriving the indirect effects of actions. Specifying the effects of actions using domain constraints is like "engineering from first principle", and has many advantages. First of all, constraints are action independent, and work on all actions. Secondly, if the effects of actions derived from domain constraints agree with one's expectation, then this will be a good indication that one has axiomatized the domain correctly. Finally, domain constraints can be used for other purposes as well. For instance, they can be used to check the consistency of the initial situation database. In general, when a set of sentences violates a domain constraint, we know that no legal situation can satisfy this set of sentences. This idea can and has been used in planning to prune impossible states. Recently, there are even efforts at "reverse engineering" state constraints from STRIPS-like systems, for instance, (Zhang and Foo 1997) and (Gerevini and Schubert 1998), and use them in planning.

We begin by introducing an action domain description language. A user describes an action domain in this language and submit it as input to the system which will compile it into a complete set of successor state axioms from which a STRIPS-like description similar to Pednault's ADL is then extracted.

An action description language

The best way to look at our action description language is to consider it as a Prolog-user friendly language for writing some simple causal theories in (Lin 1995). Expressions in this language can be thought of as macros for situation calculus formulas in (Lin 1995). Our reasons for not using the situation calculus directly are practical. As far as the specification of action effects is concerned, there is no need for a space of situations, so an action language in the style of (Gelfond and Lifschitz 1999) is more intuitive and easier to use.

Essentially, in this language, one specifies an action domain as a set of domain constraints, and for each action, an action precondition axiom and some direct effect axioms.

The following lines (1) - (12) define a blocks world with three blocks (in the following, variables x, y, and z are assumed to be universally quantified, see the section on formal semantics):

$$domain(block, \{1,2,3\}), \qquad (1)$$
$$Fluent(on(x,y), block(x) \land block(y)), \qquad (2)$$
$$Fluent(ontable(x), block(x)), \qquad (3)$$
$$Complex(clear(x), block(x)), \qquad (4)$$
$$Defined(clear(x), \neg \exists(y, block)on(y,x)), \qquad (5)$$
$$Causes(on(x,y) \land x \neq z, \neg on(z,y)), \qquad (6)$$
$$Causes(on(x,y) \land y \neq z, \neg on(x,z)), \qquad (7)$$
$$Causes(on(x,y), \neg ontable(x)), \qquad (8)$$
$$Causes(ontable(x), \neg on(x,y)), \qquad (9)$$
$$Action(stack(x,y), block(x) \land block(y) \land x \neq y), (10)$$
$$Precond(stack(x,y),$$
$$\qquad ontable(x) \land clear(x) \land clear(y)), \qquad (11)$$
$$Effect(stack(x,y), true, on(x,y)). \qquad (12)$$

where

- Line (1) is an example of *type definitions*. It defines a type called *block* whose domain is the set $\{1,2,3\}$.
- Lines (2) and (3) are examples of *primitive fluent definitions*. For instance, under the type definition (1), (2) yields the following set of fluent constants: $\{on(1,2), on(1,2), on(1,3), on(2,1), on(2,2), on(2,3), on(3,1), on(3,2), on(3,3)\}$.
- Lines (4) and (5) together is an example of *complex fluent definitions*. These are fluents that are defined in terms of primitive fluents. In this case, line (4) defines the syntax of the complex fluent *clear*, and line (5) defines its semantics. In line (5), $\exists(y, block)on(y,x)$ stands for $(\exists y).block(y) \land on(y,x)$. Under line (1), it will be expanded to:

$$Defined(clear(1), \neg(on(1,1) \lor on(2,1) \lor on(3,1))),$$
$$Defined(clear(2), \neg(on(1,2) \lor on(2,2) \lor on(3,2))),$$
$$Defined(clear(3), \neg(on(1,3) \lor on(2,3) \lor on(3,3))).$$

- Lines (6) - (9) are examples of *domain rules*. In general, domain rules are specified by expressions of one of the following forms:

$$Causes(\varphi, f(x_1, ..., x_n)),$$
$$Causes(\varphi, \neg f(x_1, ..., x_n)),$$

where f is a primitive fluent, and φ a fluent formula[1] that has no other unbound variables than those in $x_1, ..., x_n$. The intuitive meaning of a domain rule is that in any situation, if φ holds, then the fluent

[1] A fluent formula is one that is constructed from fluents (both primitive and complex) and equalities.

$f(x_1, ..., x_n)$ will be true as well. A domain rule is stronger than material implication. Its formal semantics is given by mapping it to a causal rule in (Lin 1995), thus the name "causes" in it.

- Line (10) defines a binary action called *stack*, and line (11) defines the precondition of this action: for the action $stack(x,y)$ to be executable in a situation, $clear(x)$, $clear(y)$, and $ontable(x)$ must be true in it. We can similarly define other actions in the blocks world, such as *unstack*.
- Line (12) is an example of *action effect specifications*. In general, action effects are specified by expressions of one of the following forms:

$$Effect(a(x_1, ..., x_n), \varphi, f(y_1, ..., y_k)),$$
$$Effect(a(x_1, ..., x_n), \varphi, \neg f(y_1, ..., y_k)),$$

where f is a primitive fluent, and φ a fluent formula that has no other unbound variables than those in $x_1, ..., x_n, y_1, ..., y_k$. The intuitive meaning of these expressions is that if φ is true in the initial situation, then action $a(x_1, ..., x_n)$ will cause $f(y_1, ..., y_k)$ to be true (false).

Action domain descriptions

While not applicable to the blocks world, in general, an action domain description can also include static proposition definitions and domain axioms. The former are for propositions that are not changed by any actions in the domain, and the latter are constraints about these static propositions. For instance, in the robot navigation domain, we may have a static proposition called $connected(d, r_1, r_2)$ meaning that door d connects rooms r_1 and r_2. The truth value of this proposition cannot be changed by the navigating robot which just rolls from rooms to rooms, but we may have a constraint on it saying that if d connects r_1 and r_2, then it also connects r_2 and r_1.

The following definition sums up our action description language:

Definition 1 *An* action domain description *is a set of type definitions, primitive fluent definitions, complex fluent definitions, static proposition definitions, domain axioms, action definitions, action precondition definitions, action effect specifications, and domain rules.*

A procedural semantics

Given an action domain description $\mathcal{D}$, we use the following procedure called CCP (a Causal Completion Procedure) to generate a complete action effect specification:

1. Use primitive and complex fluent definitions to generate all fluents. In the following let $\mathcal{F}$ be the set of fluents so generated.

2. Use action definitions to generate all actions, and for each action A do the following:

2.1. For each primitive fluent $F \in \mathcal{F}$, collect all A's positive effect about it:[2]

$$Effect(A, \varphi_1, F), \cdots, Effect(A, \varphi_n, F),$$

all A's negative effect about it:

$$Effect(A, \phi_1, \neg F), \cdots, Effect(A, \phi_m, \neg F),$$

all positive domain rules about it:

$$Causes(\varphi'_1, F), \cdots, Causes(\varphi'_k, F),$$

all negative domain rules about it:

$$Causes(\phi'_1, \neg F), \cdots, Causes(\phi'_l, \neg F),$$

and generate the following pseudo successor state axiom for F:

$$succ(F) \equiv init(\varphi_1) \vee \cdots \vee init(\varphi_n) \vee$$
$$succ(\varphi'_1) \vee \cdots \vee succ(\varphi'_l) \vee$$
$$init(F) \wedge \neg[init(\phi_1) \vee \cdots \vee init(\phi_m) \vee$$
$$succ(\phi'_1) \vee \cdots \vee succ(\phi'_k)],$$

where for any fluent formula φ, $init(\varphi)$ is the formula obtained from φ as follows: (1) eliminate first all the quantifiers in φ (this is possible because each type has a finite domain); (2) eliminate all equality literals using unique names assumptions; (3) replace every fluent f in it by $init(f)$. Similarly, $succ(\varphi)$ is the formula obtained from φ by the same procedure except here each fluent f in it is replaced by $succ(f)$. Intuitively, $init(f)$ means that f is true in the initial situation, and $succ(f)$ that f is true in the successor situation of performing the action A in the initial situation.

2.2. Let $Succ$ be the set of pseudo successor state axioms generated from last step, $Succ1$ the following set of axioms:

$$Succ1 = \{succ(F) \equiv succ(\varphi) \mid$$
$$Defined(F, \varphi) \text{ is a complex fluent definition}\}$$

and $Init$ the following set of axioms:

$$Init = \{\varphi \mid Axiom(\varphi) \text{ is a domain axiom}\} \cup$$
$$\{init(\varphi) \supset init(F) \mid Causes(\varphi, F)$$
$$\text{ is a domain rule}\} \cup$$
$$\{init(\varphi) \supset \neg init(F) \mid Causes(\varphi, \neg F)$$
$$\text{ is a domain rule}\} \cup$$
$$\{init(F) \equiv init(\varphi) \mid Defined(F, \varphi)$$
$$\text{ is a complex fluent definition}\} \cup$$
$$\{init(\phi_A) \mid Precond(A, \phi_A)$$
$$\text{ is the precondition definition for } A\}.$$

For each fluent F, if there is a formula Φ_F such that

$$Init \cup Succ \cup Succ1 \models succ(F) \equiv \Phi_F,$$

[2] Notice that when A and F are ground, no variables can occur in formulas φ_i, ϕ_i, φ'_i, and ϕ'_i below.

and Φ_F does not mention propositions of the form $succ(f)$, then output the axiom $succ(F) \equiv \Phi_F$. Otherwise, the action A's effect on F is indeterminate, so output the following two axioms: $succ(F) \supset \alpha_F$, and $\beta_F \supset succ(F)$, where α_F should be as strong as possible, and β_F as weak as possible (see the section on experimental results).

Conceptually, step 2.1 in the above procedure is most significant. Computationally, step 2.2 is most expensive.

Example 1 Consider the blocks world description in Section 2. Steps 1 and 2 use fluent and action definitions to generate all fluent and action constants. Steps 2.1 and 2.2 are then carried out for each action. For instance, for action $stack(1, 2)$, we have:

2.1. For $on(1, 2)$, there is one effect axiom: $Effect(stack(1, 2), true, on(1, 2))$, and seven causal rules:

$$Causes(on(1, 2) \wedge 1 \neq 1, \neg on(1, 2)),$$
$$Causes(on(2, 2) \wedge 2 \neq 1, \neg on(1, 2)),$$
$$Causes(on(3, 2) \wedge 3 \neq 1, \neg on(1, 2)),$$
$$Causes(on(1, 1) \wedge 1 \neq 2, \neg on(1, 2)),$$
$$Causes(on(1, 2) \wedge 2 \neq 2, \neg on(1, 2)),$$
$$Causes(on(1, 3) \wedge 3 \neq 2, \neg on(1, 2)),$$
$$Causes(ontable(1), \neg on(1, 2)).$$

Therefore step 2.1 generates the following pseudo-successor state axiom for $on(1, 2)$:

$$succ(on(1, 2)) \equiv true \vee$$
$$init(on(1, 2)) \wedge \neg[succ(on(2, 2)) \vee succ(on(3, 2)) \vee$$
$$succ(on(1, 1)) \vee succ(on(1, 3)) \vee succ(ontable(1))].$$

Pseudo-successor state axioms for other primitive fluents are generated similarly.

2.2. We then "solve" these pseudo-successor state axioms, and generate fully instantiated successor state axioms such as $succ(on(1, 1)) \equiv false$ and $succ(on(1, 2)) \equiv true$.

Once we have a set of these fully instantiated successor state axioms, we then generate STRIPS-like descriptions like the following:

```
stack(1, 2)           stack(1, 3)           ...
Preconditions:        Preconditions:
  ontable(1)            ontable(1)
  clear(1)              clear(1)
  clear(2)              clear(3)
Add list:             Add list:             ...
  on(1, 2)              on(1,3)
Delete list:          Delete list:
  ontable(1)            ontable(1)
  clear(2)              clear(3)
Cond. effects:        Cond. effects:
Indet. effects:       Indet. effects:       ...
```

We have the following remarks:

- Although we generate the axiom $succ(on(1,3)) \equiv false$ for $stack(1,2)$, we do not put $on(1,3)$ into its delete list. This is because we can deduce $init(on(1,3)) \equiv false$ from $Init$ as well. A fluent is put into the add or the delete list of an action only if this fluent's truth value is definitely changed by the action.
- The STRIPS-like system so generated is best considered to be a shorthand for a set of fully instantiated successor state axioms. This view is consistent with that of (Lifschitz 1986) and (Lin and Reiter 1997).
- As one can see, our CCP procedure crucially depends on the fact that each type has a finite domain so that all reasoning can be done in propositional logic. This is a limitation of our current system, and this limitation is not as bad as one might think. First of all, typical planning problems all assume finite domains, and changing the domain of a type in an action description is easy - all one need to do is to change the corresponding type definition. More significantly, a generic action domain description can often be obtained from one that assumes a finite domain. In our blocks world example, the numbers "1", "2", and "3" are generic names, and can be replaced by parameters. For instance, if we replace "1" by x and "2" by y in the above STRIPS-like description of $stack(1,2)$, we will get a STRIPS-like description for $stack(x,y)$ that works for any x and y. We have found that this is a strategy that often works in planning domains.

Formal semantics

As we mentioned, expressions in our action description language are best considered to be macros for situation calculus formulas in (Lin 1995). Formally, the semantics of an action domain description is defined by a translation into a situation calculus causal theory in (Lin 1995). The translation is quite straightforward. For instance, a domain rule of the form $Causes(\varphi, f(x_1, ..., x_n))$ is translated to

$$(\forall \vec{x}).Fluent(f(x_1, ..., x_n)) \supset$$
$$(\forall s).H(\varphi, s) \supset Caused(f(x_1, ..., x_n), true, s),$$

where $H(\varphi, s)$ is the formula obtained from φ by replacing fluent atom f in it by $H(f, s)$ which stands for that f holds in s, $Caused(f, v, s)$ is another predicate in our version of the situation calculus and stands for that the fluent f is caused (by something unspecified) to have the truth value v in situation s, and $Fluent$ is a predicate constructed from primitive fluent definitions. For instance, corresponding to a primitive fluent definition like $Fluent(ontable(x), block(x))$, we have

$$(\forall x) Fluent(ontable(x)) \equiv block(x),$$

where $block$ is a type predicate. Similarly, an action effect axiom of the form: $Effect(a(x_1, ..., x_n), \varphi, f(y_1, ..., y_k))$ is translated to

$$(\forall \vec{x}, \vec{y}).Action(a(x_1, ..., x_n)) \wedge Fluent(f(y_1, ..., y_k)) \supset$$
$$\{(\forall s).Poss(a(x_1, ..., x_n), s) \wedge H(\varphi, s) \supset$$
$$Caused(f(y_1, ..., y_k), true, do(a(x_1, ..., x_n), s))\},$$

where $Action$ is a predicate constructed from action definitions.

We have shown that under this translation, the procedural semantics given in the previous section is sound, and, under a condition similar to Reiter's consistency condition (Reiter 1991), complete as well. The precise statement of these results and its proof will be given in the full paper[3].

Summary of experimental results

Except for step 2.2, the procedure CCP in section is straightforward to implement. What step 2.2 does is to determine, for each proposition of the form $succ(F)$, whether it can be defined in terms of propositions of the form $init(p)$. If yes, we want an explicit definition, and if not, we want two most general implications: $succ(F) \supset \alpha_F$ and $\beta_F \supset succ(F)$. As it turned out, α_F and β_F are what we have called elsewhere (Lin 2000) the *strongest necessary condition* and *weakest sufficient condition* of $succ(F)$, respectively, and they are also the key in determining whether we can have a successor state axiom for F.

Briefly, given a theory T, a proposition q, and a set of propositions P, a formula φ is a strongest necessary condition (weakest sufficient condition) of q on P if φ is a formula of P, $T \models q \supset \varphi$ ($T \models \varphi \supset q$), and for any such φ', we have that $T \models \varphi \supset \varphi'$ ($T \models \varphi' \supset \varphi$). Although there are some strategies that work particularly well in the action domains (Lin 2000), these two conditions are in general expensive to compute. Thus, our strategy for step 2.2 is to first perform some simple simplification and rewriting, and then use a general procedure for computing these two conditions as a last resort:

1. for each pseudo successor state axiom $succ(f) \equiv \varphi$, do the following: eliminate all $succ(g)$, where g is a complex fluent, in φ using $Succ1$; if under $Init$ the new φ can be simplified into a formula φ' that does not mention any $succ$-propositions, then we have a successor state axiom for f, and we replace each occurrence of $succ(f)$ by φ' in other pseudo-successor state axioms;

2. this step tries to generate frame axioms: for each remaining pseudo-successor state axiom of the form $succ(f) \equiv init(f) \wedge \varphi$ do the following: first replace all $succ$-propositions in φ using their respective pseudo-successor state axioms; if the new φ is entailed by $init(f)$ and $Init$, then we have a frame axiom: $succ(f) \equiv init(f)$, and we replace each occurrence of $succ(f)$ by $init(f)$ in other pseudo-successor state axioms;

3. for each, say f, of the primitive fluents that we do not yet have a successor state axiom: compute first the

---
[3] See http://www.cs.ust.hk/faculty/flin

strongest necessary condition φ of $succ(f)$ on *init*-propositions; if the weakest sufficient condition ϕ of $succ(f)$ under $Init \cup \{\varphi\}$ and the remaining pseudo-successor state axioms is equivalent to *true*, then we have a successor state axiom for f: $succ(f) \equiv \varphi$; otherwise, output $succ(f) \supset \varphi$ and $\phi \wedge \varphi \supset succ(f)$.

4. finally, process complex fluents using their definitions.

By the results in (Lin 2000), this is a sound and complete procedure for step 2.2 of CCP. This is so even when we use a sound but incomplete propositional theorem prover for checking whether a formula can be simplified into one without mentioning any of the *succ*-propositions (step 1 above), or whether a formula is entailed by a propositional theory (step 2 above), as long as a sound and complete procedure is used for step 3 in computing the two conditions. Indeed, in our implemented system,[4] for steps 1 and 2 above, our implemented system uses unit resolution on clauses. Perhaps a bit surprisingly, this turns out to be adequate for many of the context free actions in benchmark planning domains such as the blocks world, logistics domain, and robot navigation domain. For these context free actions, our system finds all successor state axioms even before it reaches step 3, which is the most expensive step in the above procedure. Table 1 shows the performance of our system on action $stack(1,2)$ in the blocks world, and it is representative of the context free actions that we have experimented with. In the table, the "Time" column is the CPU time in seconds on a Sparc Ultra 2 machine running SWI-Prolog, the "Rate" column is the rate of increase of the time over the previous row, and the "Rate of n^6" is the rate of increase of n^6, where n equals to the number of blocks. As one can see, the rate of CPU times conforms well with that of n^6, which is the worst time complexity of our algorithm in the blocks world for a single action: given n blocks, there are $O(n^2)$ of fluents, and for each fluent, computing its successor state axiom needs to do a closure of unit resolution which is $O(m^2)$, where m is the size of clauses, which is in $O(n^2)$. Notice that the STRIPS-like description that our system outputs for the action $stack(1,2)$ is independent of the number of blocks, and is always the one given earlier.

No. of blocks	Time	Rate	Rate of n^6
12	237.57		
13	380.41	1.60	1.62
14	589.98	1.55	1.56
15	893.20	1.51	1.51
16	1314.66	1.47	1.47
17	1886.66	1.44	1.44
18	2655.81	1.41	1.41

Table 1: The blocks world

In addition to the blocks world, we have also successfully applied our system to generate many other benchmark planning domains, including most of the domains in McDermott's collection of action domains in PDDL. The following is a list of some of the common features:

- In many of these domains, it is quite straightforward to decide what effects of an action should be encoded as direct effects (those given by the predicate *Effect*) and what effects as indirect effects (those derived from domain rules).
- The most common domain rules are functional dependency constraints. For instance, in the blocks world, the fluent $on(x,y)$ is functional on both arguments; in the logistics domain, the fluent $at(object, loc)$ is functional on the second argument (each object can be at only one location). It makes sense then that we should have a special shorthand for these domain rules, and perhaps a special procedure for handling them as well. But more significantly, given the prevalent of these functional dependency constraints in action domains, it is worthwhile to investigate the possibility of a general purpose planner making good uses of these constraints.
- Our system is basically propositional. The generated successor state axioms and STRIPS-like systems are all fully instantiated. However, it is often straightforward for the user to generalize these propositional specifications to first-order ones, as we have illustrated it for the blocks world.

Related work

In terms of the action description language, the most closely related work is $\mathcal{A}$-like languages (cf. (Gelfond and Lifschitz 1999)). As we mentioned, action domains described in our language corresponds to special causal theories of (Lin 1995). For these causal theories, a result in (Turner 1997) shows that they are equivalent to some causal theories in (McCain and Turner 1997), and thus equivalent to action domains specified using many $\mathcal{A}$-like languages. As a consequence, our procedural semantics in principle also applies to some action domains specified in these languages.

In planning, the most closely related work is the causal reasoning module in Wilkins's SIPE system (Wilkins 1988). Wilkins remarked (page 85, (Wilkins 1988)): "Deductive causal theories are one of the most important mechanisms used by SIPE to alleviate problems in operator representation caused by the STRIPS assumption." Unfortunately, none of the more recent planning systems have anything like SIPE's causal reasoning module. In SIPE, domain rules have triggers, preconditions, conditions, and effects, and are interpreted procedurally. In comparison, our domain rules are much simpler, and are interpreted declaratively. To a large degree, we can see our system as a rational reconstruction of the causal reasoning module in SIPE.

Concluding remarks

We have described a system for generating the effects of actions from direct action effect axioms and domain

---
[4] Implemented in SWI-Prolog.

rules, among other things.

There are many directions for future work. One of them is on generalizing the propositional STRIPS-like systems generated by our system to first-order case. As we have mentioned, there are some heuristics that seem to work well in many benchmark domains. But a systematic study is clearly needed.

Acknowledgments

This work was supported in part by grants CERG HKUST6091/97E and CERG HKUST6145/98E from the Research Grants Council of Hong Kong.

References

M. Gelfond and V. Lifschitz. Action languages. *Electronic Transactions on Artificial Intelligence, http://www.ep.liu.se/ea/cis*, Vol 3, nr 016, 1999.

A. Gerevini and L. Schubert. Inferring state constraints for domain-independent planning. In *Proc. of AAAI'98*.

H. Levesque, R. Reiter, Y. Lespérance, F. Lin, and R. Scherl. GOLOG: A logic programming language for dynamic domains. *Journal of Logic Programming*, 31:59–84, 1997.

V. Lifschitz. On the semantics of STRIPS. In *Reasoning about Actions and Plans: Proc. of the 1986 Workshop*, pages 1–9. Morgan Kauffmann Publishers, Inc., 1986.

F. Lin. Embracing causality in specifying the indirect effects of actions. In *Proc. of IJCAI'95*, pp 1985-1993.

F. Lin. On strongest necessary and weakest sufficient conditions. In *Proc. of KR2000*.

F. Lin and R. Reiter. How to progress a database. *Artificial Intelligence*, (92)1-2:131–167, 1997.

N. McCain and H. Turner. Causal theories of action and change. In *Proc. of AAAI'97*, pp. 460-465.

N. McCain and H. Turner. Satisfiability planning with causal theories. In *Proc. of KR'98*, pp. 212-221.

R. Reiter. The frame problem in the situation calculus: a simple solution (sometimes) and a completeness result for goal regression. In V. Lifschitz, editor, *Artificial Intelligence and Mathematical Theory of Computation: Papers in Honor of John McCarthy*, pages 418–420. Academic Press, San Diego, CA, 1991.

H. Turner. A logic of universal causation. *Artificial Intelligence*, 1998.

D. Wilkins. *Practical Planning: Extending the Classical AI Planning Paradigm*. Morgan Kaufmann, San Mateo, CA, 1988.

Y. Zhang and N. Foo. Deriving invariants and constraints from action theories. *Fundamenta Informaticae*, 30(1):109–123, 1997.

TCBB Scheme: Applications to Single Machine Job Sequencing Problems

Sakib A. Mondal

Infosys Technologies Limited
27, Bannerghatta Road, JP Nagar 3rd Phase
Bangalore 560 076, INDIA
AbdulSakib@inf.com

Anup K. Sen

School of Management
New Jersey Institute of Technology
University Heights, Newark, NJ 07102, USA
sen@njit.edu

Abstract

Transpose-and-Cache Branch-and-Bound (TCBB) has shown promise in solving large single machine quadratic penalty problems. There exist other classes of single machine job sequencing problems which are of more practical importance and which are also of considerable interest in the area of AI search. In the weighted earliness tardiness problem (WET), the best known heuristic estimate is not consistent; this is contrary to the general belief about relaxation-based heuristic. In the quadratic penalty problem involving setup times (SQP) of jobs, the evaluation function is non-order-preserving In this paper, we present the TCBB scheme to solve these problems as well. Experiments indicate that (i) for the WET problem, the TCBB scheme is highly effective in solving large problem instances and (ii) for the SQP problem, it can solve larger instances than algorithm GREC in a given available memory.

Introduction

Best-first search algorithms like A* require substantial memory to store the generated nodes. On the other hand, depth-first search algorithm uses memory linear in the depth of the search and has very low overhead but runs slower than best-first in search graphs due to generation of duplicate nodes. The trend now is to look for variants of depth-first search which would run in reasonable time to solve problems of larger sizes.

Kaindl et al. (1995) proposed the *Transpose-and-Cache Branch-and-bound* (TCBB) scheme to solve large instances of single machine quadratic penalty job sequencing (QP) problem. The TCBB scheme is a variant of the depth-first branch-and-bound (DFBB) scheme. The DFBB uses a tree search space and it does not utilize the large amount of memory available. The TCBB overcomes this limitation by storing the nodes in the available memory and thus tries to avoid generation of duplicate nodes. This speeds up DFBB considerably. However when memory becomes full, TCBB continues as in DFBB and does not employ any node replacement strategies.

In the weighted earliness-tardiness (WET) problem, jobs with due dates are to be sequenced on a machine such that sum of earliness and tardiness penalty is minimized. A job completing earlier than the due date incurs an earliness penalty (inventory carrying cost) whereas a job completing later incurs a tardiness penalty (imposed by the customer). Currently known best approach for solving this problem is dynamic programming (Ventura and Weng 1995) which runs quickly out of memory. When the penalty coefficients are unity, a branch-and-bound tree search formulation (Hoogeven, Oosterhout, and Van De Velde 1994) has been suggested. Contrary to the general belief (Pearl 1984), the proposed Lagrangian-relaxation based heuristic for the problem is *not consistent*. When the heuristic is not consistent, A* graph search performs poorly since a node may be expanded more than once.

The other problem we consider in this paper is the single machine quadratic penalty problem (SQP) which includes setup times of jobs (Sen and Bagchi 1996). The presence of setup times makes the evaluation function *non-order preserving* (Pearl, 1984) and algorithm A* using graph search space is unsuitable for the problem since no path to a node can be discarded. Algorithm GREC has been suggested by Sen and Bagchi (1996) for finding optimal solutions using graph search space. GREC could solve 20-job problems using a hash queue of 200k nodes and runs faster than tree search, but like A*, it runs out of memory for solving large problems.

In this paper, we employ the TCBB scheme to solve optimally larger instances of the WET and the SQP problems. Instead of using g-values and f-values of nodes (Kaindl et al. 1995), the scheme is rewritten using b-values of nodes to naturally back up values obtained during the search process (Sen and Bagchi 1989). The use of backed-up values can be found in a number of algorithms (Kaindl and Kainz 1997). The use of b-values not only retains the heuristic improvement feature of the algorithm but also makes the approach applicable for the SQP problem. In addition, the scheme is enhanced with a node replacement strategy which would replace the less promising nodes (Reinefeld and Marsland 1994) when memory becomes full. Experimental results encourage the use of the TCBB scheme for the problems considered in the paper.

First, we describe the TCBB scheme and present the code for the algorithm. We then evaluate its performance in the QP problem domain. Next, we describe the WET and the SQP problems respectively, and present our

---

Copyright © 2000, American Association for Artificial Intelligence (www.aaai.org). All rights reserved.

experimental findings. Concluding remarks are given at the end.

The TCBB Scheme

The TCBB scheme is based on the DFBB algorithm. The scheme starts with an upper bound on the cost of the optimal solution and examines all the paths from the start to the goal node in a depth-first manner pruning paths of costs higher than the current upper bound. DFBB never attempts to store the nodes generated except that the nodes on the current path are stored in an implicit stack. On the other hand, TCBB attempts to store the expanded nodes along with their h-values and currently known best g-values if memory is available. Hence when an already stored node is encountered while searching along a different path, TCBB can use the stored g-value and decide whether the node is to be searched again. Thus like A*, it can discard paths to a node if the paths are of higher cost. This approach introduces the graph search feature in the algorithm and the performance of the algorithm becomes comparable to that of A*. The scheme utilizes a transposition table for recognizing transpositions and for caching the best values acquired dynamically (Reinefeld and Marsland 1994).

Unlike A* when memory becomes full, TCBB can still continue as in DFBB and can output optimal solution. Though TCBB cannot store new nodes in such situations, it can still continue to take advantage of already stored nodes. This feature of the scheme may make it more attractive than A*. In the QP problem domain, TCBB was shown to solve 60-job problems within reasonable time.

However, the TCBB scheme can be improved further. For very large problem instances when memory becomes full, use of effective memory management schemes may speed up the search process. Secondly, using g-values of nodes, a graph search algorithm is likely to maintain only the currently known least cost path to a node which in non-order-preserving cases, may lead to nonoptimal solutions. Instead, the scheme can be rewritten using b-values of nodes and arc costs below nodes. The b-value $b(n)$ of a node n stores the cost of the currently known best path below node n. The use of b-values and arc costs not only helps in non-order-preserving cases but also helps in naturally incorporating dynamic heuristic improvements when more accurate estimate is obtained through the search experience (Kaindl and Kainz 1997, pp. 287). The revised TCBB scheme is presented below.

Enhanced TCBB scheme

The enhanced version of the scheme is given in Figure 1. For ready reference, the new scheme is called as *Enhanced TCBB (ETCBB)*. We explain below the working of the scheme in terms of b-values of nodes and arc costs.

The b-value $b(n)$ of a node n store the cost of the currently known best path below node n. When node n is generated for the first time $b(n)$ is set to $h(n)$; $b(n)$ increa-

```
function ETCBBB(n: node; bound: integer): integer;
var  newbound: integer;
     minnode: node;
begin
  if n is a goal node then
  begin   label n SOLVED;
          return 0;
  end;

  newbound := ∞;
  for every successor n_i of n do
  begin
    if n_i is not a stored node then
      b(n_i) := h(n_i);
    if c(n,n_i) + b(n_i) < bound then
      if n_i is NOT SOLVED then
      begin
        b(n_i) := ETCBB(n_i, bound - c(n,n_i));
        if n_i is not a stored node then
          SAVE(n_i); /* Replace non promising node if
                                memory full */
      end;
    if c(n,n_i) + b(n_i) < newbound then
    begin   newbound := c(n,n_i) + b(n_i);
            minnode := n_i;
    end
    else if c(n,n_i) + b(n_i) = newbound and n_i is SOLVED
         then    minnode := n_i;  /*preference to
                                  SOLVED successor */
    bound := min(bound, newbound);
  end;
  if minnode is SOLVED then label n SOLVED;
  return newbound;
end;
```

Figure 1: Algorithm ETCBB

es whenever the cost of the currently known best path below node n (due to exploring the graph below node n) exceeds current value of $b(n)$. As a result, if heuristic is admissible, $h^*(n) >= b(n) >= h(n)$ and hence use of b-value value helps avoiding repetitive search below n.

The algorithm uses the recursive function ETCBB to search the subgraph below the start node s. The current upper bound (we call it *bound*) on the cost of the subgraph below a node is passed as a parameter to the function. Let $c(n,n_i)$ denote the cost of the arc (n,n_i). If for a successor n_i of node n, $c(n,n_i) + b(n_i) < bound$, ETCBB would search the subgraph below node n_i; the value $(bound - c(n,n_i))$ is passed as the current upper bound of the subgraph below the node n_i.

The local variable *newbound* in the function ETCBB stores the minimum of $c(n,n_i) + b(n_i)$, computed amongst all successors of node n. The value of newbound updates the value of $b(n)$ on return from the function. A newbound lower than the current upper bound indicates that a better solution path has been found while a higher newbound indicates that all the paths below node n have been pruned. During execution, newbound also resets the value of bound if it acquires a value lower than that of bound.

When memory becomes full, the simplest alternative is to continue as in DFBB. This strategy was followed in TCBB by Kaindl et al. For large problems, this scheme would run slow since no new nodes get stored and no advantage can be taken out of the stored values of new nodes. A better idea would be to replace the non-promising stored nodes with newly generated promising ones. This decision is critical. Nodes selected for replacement should not be frequently regenerated and reexpanded. In addition, the procedure for selecting nodes for replacement should not significantly increase the overhead of the algorithm. We made special experiments to evaluate a number of node replacement strategies. We found out that TCBB would perform better if, instead of continuing as in DFBB, attempts to replace less recently used nodes when memory becomes full.

ETCBB employs a SOLVE-labelling procedure (Pearl, 1984) if the evaluation function is order preserving. ETCBB labels a node SOLVED if the least cost path below the node has been found. When a SOLVED node is encountered along a different path, ETCBB can use its b-value to update the current bound or may decide to prune the current path. On the other hand, if a non SOLVED node is encountered, ETCBB can use its b-value to prune the current path or may peep below the node to search deeper into the subgraph below the node. We have experimented with or without the SOLVE-labelling procedure. When memory is large, there is hardly any effect of the procedure. But with a lower node limit of 2k nodes for the quadratic penalty (QP)[1] problem (Kaindl et al. 1995), the SOLVE-labelling procedure reduces number of nodes by 69% for 60-job problems, and by 72% for 62-job problems. This result is interesting. However, when the evaluation function is non-order preserving, the SOLVE-labelling procedure may not be in general applicable.

The performance of the ETCBB algorithm was found to be as good as, if not better, than the TCBB scheme for the quadratic penalty (QP) problem. Using reverse[2] search and the same consistent (Pearl 1984) heuristic estimate function, TCBB and ETCBB were run on DEC Alphstation 250 4/266 to solve problems of different sizes. For each problem size, both the algorithms solved the same 100 randomly generated problem instances. Table 1 presents a part of our experimental results when the node limit was fixed at 16k nodes (Kaindl et al 1995). Our experiments indicated the following:

Node limit = 16k nodes				
Job size	TCBB		ETCBB	
	Node Gen.	Time (secs)	Node Gen	Time (secs)
56	139483	12.79	66543	6.94
58	181350	17.72	83723	9.35
60	243602	25.30	108558	13.06
62			131703	16.89

Table 1: TCBB and ETCBB for the QP problem

- ETCBB ran faster than the TCBB scheme generating less number of nodes. For 60-job problems, while the node reduction factor was 2.2, the speedup factor was nearly 2 due the overhead of the algorithm. TCBB could not be run to completion for some instances of 62-job problems since it took long time to execute.
- The node generated per second by both the versions are comparable For 60-job problems, TCBB generated 9626 nodes per second whereas ETCBB generated 8312 nodes per second. Since ETCBB has a higher overhead due to its node replacement strategy, it generated less number of nodes per second than that by TCBB.
- With a node limit of 2k nodes, ETCBB took 77 seconds to solve 62-job problems generating 552790 nodes. As expected, the node generation per second dropped to 7179 as more nodes were replaced due to lower availability of memory. TCBB took long time to complete even for 50-job problem instances.

Thus ETCBB appears to be a refined version of the TCBB scheme. We now investigate its applicability to two important classes of single machine job sequencing problems. We first present the weighted earliness-tardiness problem.

Weighted Earliness-Tardiness (WET) problem

In the weighted earliness-tardiness problem, jobs have due dates. A job completing earlier than the due date incurs an earliness penalty whereas a job completing later incurs a tardiness penalty. The objective is to schedule the jobs in such a way that the weighted sum of earliness and tardiness penalties is minimized. For the class of problem considered in this paper, the earliness and tardiness penalties are measured as the absolute deviation of job completion times around the common due date. The weights, that is, the earliness and tardiness penalty coefficients, depend on whether a job is early or tardy but

---

[1] In the QP problem, a set of jobs J_i with processing times p_i, $1 \leq i \leq N$, are submitted to a machine at time $t = 0$. The jobs are to be processed on the machines one at a time. Let the processing of job J_i be completed at time C_i. The penalty functions are $\Psi_i(C_i) = \beta_i C_i^2$, $1 \leq i \leq N$ where β_i is the given positive penalty coefficient for job J_i. The jobs must be sequenced in such a way that the sum of the penalties for all jobs are minimized.

[2] Kaindl et al (1995) had shown that due to asymmetric distribution of arc costs, searching in the reverse direction from the goal to the start yields much better results in this QP problem.

do not depend on jobs. The problem can be formulated as follows: Given the processing times p_j of N jobs, the common due date d, and the earliness and tardiness penalty coefficients α and β respectively, the objective is to minimize $F = \Sigma_j(\alpha E_j + \beta T_j)$ where $E_j = \max(0, d-C_j)$ and $T_j = \max(0, C_j-d)$ are the earliness and tardiness of job J_j, and C_j denote the completion time of job J_j in a schedule.

The value of the common due date plays an important role in the complexity of the WET problem. When the due date is equal to or larger than a critical value d*, the WET problem becomes unrestricted; otherwise the problem is called restricted. The unrestricted WET problem is polynomially solvable whereas the restricted version is known to be NP-complete (Hall, Kubiak, and Sethi 1991). Other characteristics of the optimal schedule can also be found in (Hall, Kubiak, and Sethi 1991). Dynamic programming (DP) and Depth-first Branch-and-bound have been suggested so far for solving the restricted WET problem. These approaches can hardly be used in practice for solving large problem instances.

Hoogeveen, Oosterhout and Van De Velde (1994) suggested a *Lagrangian-relaxation* based heuristic estimate for the problem which is the best known heuristic estimate available in the literature. Interestingly, this admissible heuristic estimate is not consistent. It relaxes a constraint $W \leq d$ where W is the sum of the processing times of jobs completed before the due date. The heuristic is calculated as $\max_\lambda L(\lambda) = \max_\lambda[\min \{\Sigma_j (\alpha E_j + \beta T_j) + \lambda(W - d)\}]$ where $\lambda \geq 0$. $L(\lambda)$ can be found by Emmon's matching algorithm (Emmon 1987) with positional weights of early jobs increased by λ. Value of $L(\lambda)$ is maximized for that value of λ for which (W-d) changes sign from negative to positive. For a 5-job problem, let $p_1 = 12$, $p_2 = 26$, $p_3 = 32$, $p_4 = 53$ and $p_5 = 56$. Let $\alpha = \beta = 1$ and $d = 122$. Let For the start node s, $h(s) = 161$. Let n be an immediate successor of s where job J_5 is scheduled to complete at time = 179. Then $c(s,n) = 57$ and $h(m) = 82$. Thus the heuristic estimate is not consistent. If heuristic estimates are not consistent, algorithm A* expands a node more than once and performs poorly. Mero (1984) suggested a heuristic modification procedure to improve the performance of A* in such cases. However, this introduces more number of equal f-valued nodes and as a result, tie-resolution becomes an important issue.

We applied algorithm ETCBB to solve the restricted WET problem and achieved significant results. ETCBB could readily solve 2000-job problems using just 16k nodes of memory. Before we present our experimental results, we present salient features of our search formulation.

Search space

A node is represented in the search space as a tuple (U,I) where U represents the number of jobs yet to be scheduled and I is the time when the partial schedule consisting of U unscheduled jobs can start. Thus U can be stored as an index to the above ordered job sequence.

The start node is represented as (N,_) and its successor nodes as (N,0), (N,1), .., (N,d) since the optimal schedule can start at any time between 0 and d. Each of these successor nodes represent a subproblem to be solved. Any subproblem can be decomposed to at most two subproblems since every job may be scheduled either to the left or to the right of the due date. Two different subproblems when decomposed can lead to the same subproblem, thus resulting in a graph search space. For example, the nodes (3,0) and (3,1) may have the same common successor (2,2).

An arc in the search space represents the scheduling of a job and its cost may be taken as the incremental cost of scheduling the job. Therefore, the cost of the two successor arcs below a node would be α times the earliness of the job if the job is scheduled to complete before the due date, and would be β times the tardiness of the job if the job is scheduled to complete after the due date. In this representation, there can be atmost $d+p_N$ nodes at any level. As a result, the total number of nodes in the graph will be $O(N(d+p_N))$.

Successors are ordered in ETCBB following a heuristic rule. At a node n, a job would be scheduled before due date or after due date. Let n.left and n.right denote the unscheduled interval before and after due date at a node n. If $(\alpha + \lambda)$n.left > n.right, the first successor is generated by scheduling before due date else after due date. Heuristic estimates are computed following the Lagrangian-relaxation based heuristic suggested by Hoogeveen, Oosterhout and Van De Velde described above.

Experimental results

In our experiments, we fixed the memory as 16k nodes, and tested ETCBB, DP, DFBB and A* on DEC Alphastation 250 4/266 for problems with different due

Node limit = 16k nodes					
Job size	$\alpha:\beta$	d=0.6d*		d=0.9d*	
		Node Gen.	Time (secs)	Node Gen	Time (secs)
100	5:1	846	0.07	946	0.09
	1:5	682	0.06	740	0.07
500	5:1	1570	0.95	1943	1.22
	1:5	1677	1.04	2197	1.35
1000	5:1	2764	3.47	3319	4.38
	1:5	3301	4.25	4149	5.39
1500	5:1	3082	6.75	5180	10.09
	1:5	4591	9.02	6662	12.87
2000	5:1	5540	14.07	6950	18.22
	1:5	6815	17.38	8663	22.75

Table 2: ETCBB for the WET problem

dates and with different ratios of α and β. Due date was fixed at d=kd*, 0 < k < 1 to solve restricted instances only. The problem criticality increases as d approaches d*, and for a fixed k, it also increases as the ratio of α and β decreases (Bagchi, Sullivan, and Chang 1987). Table 2 reports our findings for ETCBB and Table 3 for other algorithms. Processing times were generated randomly from a uniform distribution in the range 1 to 99. Results were based on the average of 100 randomly problem instances. Our observations are as follows:

- ETCBB could readily solve 2000-job problems; for the most restricted case with d=0.9d* and with $\alpha: \beta$ = 1:5, it took around 23 seconds to solve 2000-job problems.

- DP, A* and DFBB performed poorly in this domain For a node limit of 16k nodes, DP ran out of memory for 20-job problems. A* with heuristic modification (Mero 1984) could solve upto 100-job problems. Other variants of A* with tie resolution in favour of lower or higher g-valued nodes indicated a similar trend. DFBB took 8.28 seconds to solve 100-job problem instances for the most restricted case generating 294463 nodes (Table 3). We could not run DFBB to completion for 200-job problem instances since it took long time to execute.

Job size	Node limit =16k nodes D=0.9d* $\alpha:\beta$=1:5			
	DFBB		A*	
	Node Gen	Time (secs)	Node Gen	Time (secs)
20	300	0.0	251	0.0
40	2968	0.06	877	0.04
60	17258	0.41	3358	0.24
80	20589	0.53	7378	0.80
100	294463	8.28	13023	2.10

Table 3: DFBB and A* for the WET problem

- ETCBB generated 8663 nodes for the most restricted problem which is smaller than the 16k node limit. Hence the node replacement strategy has no role to play. The TCBB version would have performed in a similar way. We have not experimented with the TCBB version because we expect it to perform similarly and secondly, our objective is to show the applicability of the scheme to this domain, not to compare the relative performance of the two versions. Since no nodes were replaced, this remarkable performance of the scheme can thus be attributed to dynamic heuristic improvements incorporated in the algorithm.

We now present the SQP problem and show that ETCBB can optimally solve larger instances than GREC in a given available memory.

Sequence-dependent Quadratic penalty problem (SQP)

The SQP problem is similar in formulation to the QP problem except that jobs may have setup times which are *sequence-dependent*. Setup time s_{ij} for job J_j when it immediately follows job J_i is said to be sequence-dependent if the setup time is dependent on the preceding job J_i. The presence of setup times makes the problem extremely difficult to solve and has been shown to be NP-complete in (Rinooy Kan 1976).

Sen and Bagchi (1996) have shown that due to the presence of sequence-dependent setup times, evaluation function becomes non-order-preserving. As a result, no path can be discarded and A*-based graph search can fail to output optimal solutions. Tree search methods tend to be inefficient because many duplicate nodes get generated. They have suggested a graph search algorithm GREC to optimally solve this problem. GREC has been reported to solve 20-job problems using a hash queue of 200k nodes

We have applied ETCBB to solve this problem optimally. Nodes were represented as pair (V, J_i) where V is the of jobs scheduled and J_i is the last job (Sen and Bagchi 1996). Computation of heuristic estimate and successor ordering are followed as in GREC. Due to the presence of setup times, cost of an arc below a node depends on the incoming path to the node. As a result, cost of a path below a node is also dependent on the incoming path to the node. Hence no node can be labelled SOLVED by the ETCBB algorithm and in our implementation, we have not used the SOLVE labelling procedure.

Job size	Node limit =16k nodes			
	GREC		ETCBB	
	Node Gen	Time (secs)	Node Gen	Time (secs)
10	344	0.01	673	0.01
12	920	0.04	2121	0.06
14	2287	0.12	6089	0.20
16			17369	0.71
18			54180	2.75
20			172110	10.64
22			1298847	98.53

Table 4: GREC and ETCBB for the SQP problem with 16k node limit

The use of b-values of nodes in ETCBB helps in outputting optimal solution in a way similar to that of GREC. Since no g-value of nodes are maintained, no paths need to be discarded. When a node n=(V, J_k) first enters the search graph, the completion time t_k of node n's last job is stored at node n as a parameter T. At a subsequent instant when n is reached along a different path with t'_k being the completion time of job J_k, T is reset to t'_k. The b-value b(n) at the node n depends on the incoming path and thus it depends on T. The value of b(n) along the path of downward movement can be expressed as

$$b(n) = AT^2 + BT + C$$

where A, B and C are parameters dependent on node n but independent of T. Let Q' be the remaining jobs to be processed at n. Then

$A = \Sigma \{ \beta_k \mid J_k \text{ is in } Q' \}$

$B = 2 \Sigma \{ \beta_k t'_k \mid J_k \text{ is in } Q' \}$, and C can be viewed as the b-value at node n with node n as the origin (i.e. with T = 0). The job completion times t'_k in B also take node n as origin. A, B, and C must be stored at each node. Table 4 shows our experimental results and compares the performance of ETCBB with GREC. We can observe the following:

- With 16k node limit, while GREC ran out of space for 16-job problems, ETCBB could solve 22-job problems within 100 seconds. However, GREC ran faster than ETCBB. In (Sen and Bagchi 1996), GREC was shown to solve 20-job problems but using hash queue of size around 200k nodes. We

Job size	Node limit =200k nodes			
	GREC		ETCBB	
	Node Gen	Time (secs)	Node Gen	Time (secs)
20	36646	6.13	151741	8.59
22			460041	32.57

Table 5: GREC and ETCBB for the SQP problem with 200k node limit

ran both ETCBB and GREC with 200k node limit on a faster computer SUN Enterprise 5500. The results are given in Table 5. GREC ran faster than ETCBB for 20-job problems but ran out of "overflow" area for 22-job problems.

- As in the QP problem, the node generation per second is higher in GREC than ETCBB due to higher overhead of node replacement strategy in ETCBB. Since both the algorithms cache nodes, the better performance of ETCBB is due to its memory management scheme.

Conclusion

This paper shows that the Transpose-and-Cache Branch-and-Bound scheme has a future in solving large instances of problems with natural cut-off bound. Specifically, in some single machine job sequencing problems, the scheme has advanced the existing state of solutions. We hope that this paper would encourage future research in the enhancement and application of the scheme.

Many questions remain. The problems with setup times are difficult and needs special attention. Also, how would the TCBB scheme perform in other domains like project scheduling? Future research should address these issues.

Acknowledgments. This research was partly supported by the Indian Institute of Management Calcutta where both the authors were employed. The authors are grateful to Herman Kaindl for invaluable suggestions. The authors also thank Gerhard Kainz for sending us the TCBB code.

References

Bagchi, U.; Sullivan, R.; and Chang, Y. 1987. Minimizing Absolute and Squared Deviation of Completion times About a Common Due date. *Naval Research Logistics* 34: 739—751.

Emmons, H. 1987. Scheduling to a Common Due Date on Parallel Uniform Processors. *Naval Research Logistics* 34:803—810.

Hall, N. G.; Kubiak, W.; and Sethi, S. P. 1991. Earliness Tardiness Scheduling Problems, II: Weighted Deviation of Completion Times About a Restrictive Common Due Date. *Operations Research* 39(5):847—856.

Hoogeven, J. A.; Oosterhout, H.; and Van De Velde, S. L. 1994. New Lower and Upper Bounds for Scheduling around a Small Common Due Date. *Operations Research* 42(1):102--110.

Kaindl, H., and Kainz. G. 1997. Bidirectional Heuristic Search Reconsidered. *Journal of Artificial Intelligence Research* 7:283—317.

Kaindl, H.; Kainz, G.; Leeb, A.; and Smetana, H. 1995. How to Use Limited Memory in Heuristic Search. In *Proc. Fourteenth International Joint Conference on Artficial Intelligence (IJCAI-95).* 236—242. San Francisco, CA: Morgan Kaufman Publishers.

Mero, L. 1984. A Heuristic Search Algorithm with Modifiable Estimate, *Artificial Intelligence* 23(1): 13—27.

Pearl, J. 1984. *Heuristics: Intelligent Search Strategies for Computer Problem Solving.* Addison-Wesley.

Reinefeld, A., and Marsland, T. A. 1994. Enhanced Iterative deepening search. *IEEE Transactions on Pattern Analysis and Machine Intelligence* 16(7):701—710.

Rinooy Kan, A. H. G. 1976. *Machine Complexity Problems: Classification Complexity and Computations.* Nijhoff, The Hague.

Sen, A. K., and Bagchi, A. 1989. Fast Recursive Formulations for Best-first Search that Allow Controlled Use of Memory, In *Proc. Eleventh International Joint Conference on Artificial Intelligence (IJCAI-89).* 297—302. San Francisco, CA: Morgan Kaufman Publishers.

Sen, A. K., and Bagchi, A. 1996. Graph Search Methods for Non-order-preserving Evaluation Functions: Applications to Job Sequencing Problems. *Artificial Intelligence* 86(1):43—73.

Ventura, J., and Weng, M. X. 1995. An Improved Dynamic Programming Algorithm for the Single-Machine Mean Absolute Deviation Problem with a Restrictive Common Due Date. *Operations Research Letters* 17:149--152.

Extracting Effective and Admissible State Space Heuristics from the Planning Graph

XuanLong Nguyen* & Subbarao Kambhampati
Department of Computer Science and Engineering
Arizona State University, Tempe AZ 85287-5406
Email: {xuanlong,rao}@asu.edu

Abstract

Graphplan and heuristic state space planners such as HSP-R and UNPOP are currently two of the most effective approaches for solving classical planning problems. These approaches have hither-to been seen as largely orthogonal. In this paper, we show that the planning graph structure that Graphplan builds in polynomial time, provides a rich substrate for deriving more effective heuristics for state space planners. Specifically, we show that the heuristics used by planners such as HSP-R and UNPOP do badly in several domains due to their failure to consider the interactions between subgoals, and that the mutex information in the planning graph captures exactly this interaction information. We develop several families of heuristics, some aimed at search speed and others at optimality of solutions. Our empirical studies show that our heuristics significantly out-perform the existing state space heuristics.

1 Introduction

The last few years have seen a number of attractive and scaleable approaches for solving deterministic planning problems. Prominent among these are "disjunctive" planners, exemplified the Graphplan algorithm of Blum & Furst [1], and heuristic state space planners, exemplified by McDermott's UNPOP [17] and Bonet & Geffner's HSP-R planners [3; 2]. The Graphplan algorithm can be seen as solving the planning problem using CSP techniques. A compact CSP encoding of the planning problem is generated using a polynomial-time datastructure called "planning graph" [9]. On the other hand, UNPOP, HSP, HSP-R are simple state space planners where the world state is considered explicitly. These planners rely on heuristic estimators to evaluate the goodness of children states. As such, it is not surprising that heuristic state search planners and Graphplan-based planners are generally seen as orthogonal approaches [22].

In UNPOP, HSP and HSP-R, the heuristic can be seen as estimating the number of actions required to reach a state (either from the goal state or the initial state). To make the computation tractable, these heuristic estimators make strong assumptions about the independence of subgoals. Because of these assumptions, state search planners often thrash badly in problems where there are strong interactions between subgoals. Furthermore, these independence assumptions also make the heuristics inadmissible, precluding any guarantees about the optimality of solutions found. In fact, the authors of UNPOP and HSP/HSP-R planners acknowledge that taking the subgoal interactions into account in a tractable fashion to compute more robust and/or admissible heuristics remains a challenging problem [17; 3].

In this paper, we show that the planning graph datastructure computed in polynomial-time as part of the Graphplan algorithm, provides a general and powerful basis for the derivation of state space heuristics that take subgoal interactions into account. In particular, the so-called "mutex" constraints of the planning graph provide a robust way of estimating the cost of achieving a set of propositions from the initial state. The heuristics derived from the planning graph are then used to guide state space search on the problem, in a way similar to HSP-R [2]. Note that this means we no longer use Graphplan's exponential time CSP-style solution extraction phase.

We will describe several families of heuristics that can be derived from the planning graph structure and demonstrate their significant superiority over the existing heuristic estimators. We will provide results of empirical studies establishing that state space planners using our best heuristics easily outperform both HSP-R and Graphplan planners. Our development focuses both on heuristics that speedup search without guaranteeing admissibility (such as those currently used in HSP-R and UNPOP), and on heuristics that retain admissibility and thus guarantee optimality. In the former case, we will show that our best heuristic estimators are more robust and are able to tackle many problem domains that HSP-R does poorly (or fails), such as the grid, travel, and mystery domains used in the AIPS-98 competition [16].

While our empirical results are themselves compelling, we believe that the more important contribution of our work is the explication of the way in which planning graph can serve as a rich basis for derivation of families of heuristic estimators. It is known in the search literature that admissible and effective heuristics are hard to compute unless the interactions between subgoals are considered aggressively [13]. Our work shows that planning graph and its mutex constraints provide a powerful way to take these interactions into account. Since mutex propagation can be seen as a form of directed partial consistency enforcement on the CSP encoding corresponding to the

---

*Copyright ©2000, American Association for Artificial Intelligence (www.aaai.org). All rights reserved.

planning graph, our work also firmly ties up the CSP and state search views of planning.

The rest of the paper is organized as follows. Section 2 reviews the HSP-R planner and highlights the limitations of its "sum" heuristic. These limitations are also shared to a large extent by other heuristic state search planners such as UNPOP. Section 3 discusses how the Graphplan's planning graph can be used to measure the subgoal interactions. Section 4 is the heart of the paper. It develops several families of heuristics, some aimed at search speed and some at solution optimality. Each of these heuristic families are empirically evaluated in comparison to HSP-R heuristic and their relative tradeoffs are explicated. Section 5 discusses the related work, and section 6 summarizes the contributions of our work.

2 Limitation of the HSP-R's sum heuristic

HSP-R [2] is currently one of the fastest heuristic state search planners. It casts planning as search through the *regression space* of world states [19]. In regression state space search, the states can be thought of as sets of *subgoals*. The heuristic value of a state S is the estimated cost (number of actions) needed to achieve S from the initial state. It is important to note that since the cost of a state S is computed from the initial state and we are searching backward from the goal state, the heuristic computation is done only once for each state. Then, HSP-R follows a variation of A* search algorithm, called *Greedy Best First*, which uses the cost function $f(S) = g(S) + w * h(S)$, where g(S) is the accumulated cost (number of actions when regressing from goal state) and $h(S)$ is the heuristic value of state S.

The heuristic is computed under the assumption that the propositions constituting a state are strictly independent. Thus the cost of a state is estimated as the sum of the cost for each individual proposition making up that state.

Heuristic 1 (Sum heuristic) $h(S) := \sum_{p \in S} h(p)$

The heuristic cost $h(p)$ of an individual proposition p is computed using a iterative procedure that is run to fix point as follows. Initially, each proposition p is assigned a cost 0 if it is in the initial state I, and ∞ otherwise. For each instantiated action a, let $Add(a)$, $Del(a)$ and $Prec(a)$ be its Add, Delete and Precondition lists. For each action a that adds some proposition p, $h(p)$ is updated as:

$$h(p) := \min\{h(p), 1 + h(Prec(a))\} \quad (1)$$

Where $h(Prec(a))$ is computed using the sum heuristic (heuristic 1). The updates continue until the h values of all the individual propositions stabilize. This computation can be done before the backward search actually begins, and typically proves to be quite cheap.

Because of the independence assumption, the sum heuristic turns out to be inadmissible (overestimating) when there are positive interactions between subgoals (i.e achieving some subgoal may also help achieving other subgoals), and less informed (significantly underestimating) when there are negative interactions between subgoals (i.e achieving a subgoal deletes other subgoals). Bonet and Geffner [2] provide two separate improvements aimed at handling these problems to a certain extent. Their simple suggestion to make the heuristic admissible is to replace the summation with the "max" function.

Heuristic 2 (Max heuristic) $h(S) := \max_{p \in S} h(p)$

This heuristic, however, is often much less informed than the sum heuristic as it grossly underestimates the cost of achieving a given state.

To improve the informedness of the sum heuristic, HSP-R adopts the notion of mutex relations first originated in Graphplan planning graph. But unlike Graphplan, only *static propositional mutexes* (aka binary invariants) are computed. Two propositions p and q form a static mutex when they cannot both be present in any state reachable from the initial state. Since the cost of any set containing a mutex pair is infinite, we define a variation of the sum heuristic called the "sum mutex" heuristic as follows:

Heuristic 3 (Sum Mutex heuristic)
$h(S) := \infty \ if \ \exists_{p,q \in S} \ s.t. \ mutex(p,q) \ else \ \sum_{p \in S} h(p)$

In practice, the Sum Mutex heuristic turns out to be much more powerful than the sum heuristic and HSP-R implementation uses it as the default.

Before closing this section, we provide a brief summary of the procedure of computing mutexes used in HSP-R[2]. The basic idea is to start with a large set of "potential" mutex pairs and iteratively weed out those pairs that cannot be actually mutex. The set M_0 of potential mutexes is union of set M_A of all pairs of propositions $\langle p, q \rangle$, such that for some action a in A, p in $Add(a)$ and q in $Del(a)$, and set M_B of all pairs $\langle r, q \rangle$, such that for some $\langle p, q \rangle$ in M_A and some action a, r in $Prec(a)$ and p in $Add(a)$. This already precludes from consideration potential mutexes $\langle r, s \rangle$, where r and s are not in the add, precondition and delete lists of any single action. As we shall see below, this turns out to be an important limitation in several domains.

2.1 A pathological example that showcases the limitations of sum mutex heuristic

The *sum mutex heuristic* used by HSP-R, while shown to be powerful in domains where the subgoals are relatively independent such as logistics and gripper domains [2], thrashes badly in problems where there is rich interaction between actions and subgoal sequencing. Specifically, when a subgoal that can be achieved early but that must be deleted much later when other subgoals are achieved, the sum heuristic is unable to recognize this interaction. To illustrate this, consider a simple problem from the grid domain [17] shown in Figure 1: Given a 3x3 grid. The initial state is denoted by two propositions at(0,0) and key(0,1) and the goal state is denoted by 2 subgoals at(0,0) and key(2,2) (See figure 1). Notice the subgoal interaction here: When key(2,2) is first achieved, at(0,0) is no longer true. There are three possible actions: the robot moves from one square to an adjacent square, the robot picks up a key if there is such a key in the square the robot currently resides, and the robot drops the key at the current square. One obvious solution is: The robot goes from (0,0) to (0,1), picks up the key at (0,1), moves to (2,2), drops the key there, and

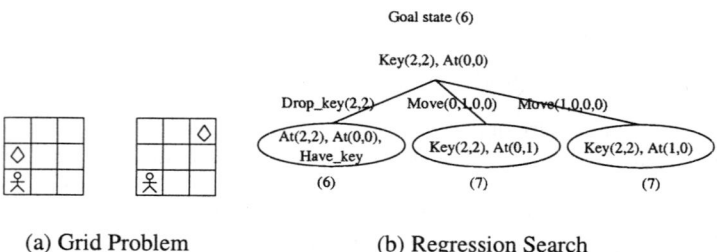

Figure 1: A simple grid problem and the first level of regression search on it.

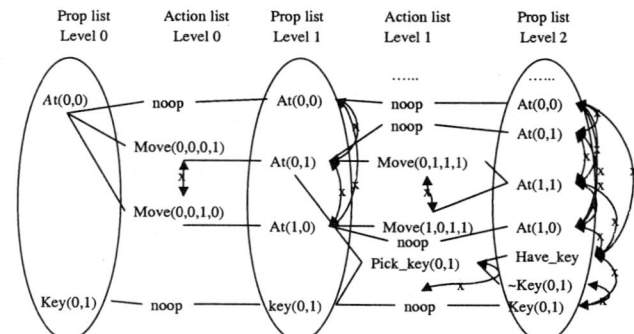

Figure 2: Planning Graph for the 3x3 grid problem

finally moves back to (0,0). This is in fact the optimal 10-action plan. We have run (our Lisp implementation of) HSP-R planner on this problem and no solution was found after 1 hour (generating more than 400,000 nodes, excluding those pruned by the mutex computation). The original HSP-R written in C also runs out of memory (250MB) on this problem.

It is easy to see how HSP-R goes wrong. First of all, according the mutex computation procedure described above, we are able to detect that when the robot is at a square, it cannot be in an adjacent square. But HSP-R's mutex computation cannot detect the type of mutex that says that the robot can also not be in any other square as well (because there is no single action that can place a robot from a square to another square not adjacent to where it currently resides).

Now let's see how this limitation of *sum mutex heuristic* winds up fatally misguiding the search. Given the subgoals (at(0,0), key(2,2)), the search engine has three potential actions over which it can regress the goal state (see Figure 1b). Two of these– move from (0,1) or (1,0) to (0,0)–give the subgoal at(0,0), and the third–dropping key at (2,2), which requires the precondition at(2,2)–gives the subgoal key(2,2). If either of the move actions is selected, then after the regression the robot would be at either (0,1) or (1,0), and that would increase the heuristic value because the cost of at(0,1) or at(1,0) is 1 (greater than the cost of at(0,0)). If we pick the dropping action, then after regression, we have a state that has both at(0,0) (the regressed first subgoal), and at(2,2) (the precondition of drop key at (2,2) action). While we can see that this is an inconsistent state, the mutex computation employed by HSP-R does not detect this (as explained above). Moreover, the heuristic value for this invalid state is actually smaller compared to the other two states corresponding to regression over the move actions. This completely misguides the planner into wrong paths, from which it never recovers.

HSP-R also fails or worsens the performance for similar reasons in the travel, mystery, and grid, blocks world, eight puzzle domains[16].

3 Exploiting the structure of Graphplan's planning graph

In the previous section, we showed the type of problems where ignoring the (negative) interaction between subgoals in the heuristic often lead the search into wrong directions. On the other hand, Graphplan's planning graph, with its wealth of mutex constraints, contains much of such information, and can be used to compute more effective heuristics.

Graphplan algorithm [1] works by converting the planning problem specifications into a planning graph. Figure 2 shows part of the planning graph constructed for the 3x3 grid problem shown in Figure 1. As illustrated here, a planning graph is an ordered graph consisting of two alternating structures, called "proposition lists" and "action lists". We start with the initial state as the zeroth level proposition list. Given a k level planning graph, the extension of the structure to level $k+1$ involves introducing all actions whose preconditions are present in the kth level proposition list. In addition to the actions given in the domain model, we consider a set of dummy "noop" actions, one for each condition in the kth level proposition list (the condition becomes both the single precondition and effect of the noop). Once the actions are introduced, the proposition list at level $k+1$ is constructed as just the union of the effects of all the introduced actions. Planning-graph maintains the dependency links between the actions at level $k+1$ and their preconditions in level k proposition list and their effects in level $k+1$ proposition list.

The critical asset of the planning graph, for our purposes, is the efficient marking and propagation of mutex constraints during the expansion phase. The propagation starts at level 1, with the actions that are statically interfering with each other (i.e., their preconditions and effects are inconsistent) labeled mutex. Mutexes are then propagated from this level forward by using two simple propagation rules: Two propositions at level k are marked mutex if all actions at level k that support one proposition are pair-wise mutex with all actions that support the second proposition. Two actions at level $k+1$ are mutex if they are statically interfering or if one of the propositions (preconditions) supporting the first action is mutually exclusive with one of the propositions supporting the second action. Figure 2 shows a part of the planning graph for the robot problem specified in Figure 1. The curved lines with x-marks denote the mutex relations. The planning graph can be seen as a CSP encoding [11; 22], with the mutex propagation corresponding to a form of directed partial 1- and 2-consistency enforcement [11]. The CSP encoding can be solved using any applicable CSP solving methods (a special case of which is the Graphplan's backward search procedure).

Normally, Graphplan attempts to extract a solution from the planning graph of length l, and will expand it to level $l+1$

only if that solution extraction process fails. Graphplan algorithm can thus guarantee that the solution it finds is *optimal* in terms of number of steps. To make the optimality hold in terms of number of actions (a step can have multiple actions), we need to start with a planning graph that is **serial** [9]. A *serial planning graph* is a planning graph in which every pair of non-noop actions at the same level are marked mutex. These additional action mutexes propagate to give additional propositional mutexes. A planning graph is said to **level off** when there is no change in the action, proposition and mutex lists between two consecutive levels.

Based on the above mutex computation and propagation rules, the following properties can be easily verified:

1. The number of actions required to achieve a pair of propositions is no less than the number of proposition levels to be expanded until the two propositions both appear and are *not mutex* in the planning graph.

2. Proposition pairs that remain mutex at the level where the planning graph levels off can never be achieved starting from initial state.

3. The set of actions present in the level where the planning graph levels off contains all actions that are applicable to states reachable from the initial state.

The three observations above give a rough indication as to how the information in the planning graph after it levels off, can be used to guide state search planners. The first observation shows that the level information in planning graph can be used to estimate the cost of achieving a set of propositions. Furthermore, the set of *level-specific* propositional mutexes help give a finer distance estimate. The second observation shows that once the planning graph levels off, all mutexes in the final level are *static* mutexes. The third observation shows a way to extract a finer (smaller) set of applicable actions to be considered by the regression search, since a new action is introduced into a level only if all of its preconditions appear in the previous level and are non-mutexed, and all actions present in a level are also present in the next level.

4 Extracting heuristics from planning graph

Before we go on to describing a set of effective heuristics extracted from the planning graph, let us briefly describe how these heuristics are used and evaluated. All the heuristics extracted from the planning graph as well as the HSP-R's sum heuristic are plugged into the *same* regression search engine using a variation of A* search's cost function $f(S) = g(S) + w * h(S)$.

We tested the heuristics on a variety of planning domains. These include several well-known benchmark domains such as the blocksworld, rocket, logistics, 8-puzzle, gripper, mystery, grid and travel. Some of these were used in the AIPS-98 competition [16]. These domains are believed to represent different types of planning difficulty. Problems in the rocket, logistics and gripper domains are typical of those where the subgoals are relatively independent. The grid, travel and mystery domains add to logistic domains the hardness of the "topological" combinatorics, while the blocksworld and 8-puzzle domains also have very rich interactions between actions and subgoal sequencing.

Subsection 4.1 is concerned with effective heuristics without consideration of the solution optimality. We set $w = 1$ in all experimental results described in this subsection, except for the parallel domains (e.g rocket, logistics and gripper) where the heuristics work best (in terms of speed) with $w = 5$ [1]. Subsection 4.2 is concerned with improving admissible heuristics for finding optimal solutions. To make the comparisons meaningful, all the planners are implemented in Allegro commonlisp, and share most of the critical data structures. The empirical studies are conducted on a 500 MHz Pentium-III with 512 meg RAM, running Linux. All the times reported include both heuristic computation time and search time, unless specified otherwise.

4.1 Extracting effective heuristics

We are now ready to extract heuristics from the planning graph. Unless stated otherwise, we will assume that we have a serial planning graph that has been expanded until it has leveled off (without doing any solution extraction). In this section, we will concentrate on the effectiveness, without insisting on the admissibility of the heuristics.

Given a set S of propositions, denote $lev(S)$ as the index of the first level in the *leveled serial* planning graph in which all propositions in S appear and are non-mutexed with one another. If no such level exists, then $lev(S) = \infty$. Similarly, denote $lev(p)$ as the index of the first level that a proposition p comes into the planning graph. It takes only a small step from the observations made in the previous section to arrive at our first heuristic:

Heuristic 4 (Set-level heuristic) $h(S) := lev(S)$

Consider the set-level heuristic in the context of the robot example in previous section. In the planning graph, the subgoal key(2,2) first comes into the planning graph at the level 6, however at that level this subgoal is mutexed with another subgoal at(0,0), and the planning graph has to be expanded 4 more levels until both subgoals are present and non-mutex. Thus the cost estimate yielded by this heuristic is 10, which is exactly the true cost achieving both subgoals.

It is easy to see that set-level heuristic is *admissible*. Secondly, it can be significantly more informed than the *max heuristic*, because the max heuristic is only equivalent to the level that a single proposition first comes into the planning graph. Thirdly, a by-product of the set-level heuristic is that it already subsumes much of the static mutex information used by the Sum Mutex heuristic. Moreover, the propagated mutexes in the planning graph wind up being more effective in detecting static mutexes that are missed by HSP-R. In the context of the robot example, HSP-R can only detect that a robot cannot be at squares adjacent to its current square, but using planning graph, we are able to detect that the robot cannot be at any square other than its current square.

Table 1 and 2 show that the set-level heuristic performs reasonably well in domains such as grid, mystery, travel and 8-

---

[1]See [14] for the role of w in BFS.

Problem	sum-mutex	set-lev	adj-sum
bw-large-c	>500000	>500000	8224
rocket-ext-a	769	>500000	658
att-log-a	2978	>500000	2224
gripper	930	>500000	840
8puzzle-2	1399	51561	1540
8puzzle-3	2899	1047	1384
travel-1	4122	25	40
grid3	>200000	49	1151
grid4	>200000	44	1148
aips-grid1	>200000	108	835
mprime-1	>500000	125	96

Table 1: Number of nodes (states) generated by different heuristics, excluding those pruned by mutex computation

puzzle[2] compared to the standard Graphplan [3]. Many of these problems prove intractable for HSP-R's sum-mutex heuristic. We attribute this performance of the set-level heuristic to the way the negative interactions between subgoals are accounted for by the level information.

Interestingly, the set-level heuristic fails in the domains that the *sum heuristic* typically does well, such as rocket world and logistics, where the subgoals are fairly independent of each other. Closely examining the heuristic values reveals that the set-level heuristic remains too conservative and often underestimates the real cost in these domains. A related problem is that the range of numbers that the cost of a set of propositions can take is limited to integers less than or equal to the length of the planning graph. This range limitation leads to a practical problem as these heuristics tend to attach the same numerical cost to many qualitatively distinct states, forcing the search to resort to arbitrary tie breaking.

To overcome these limitations, we pursue two families of heuristics derived by generalizing the set-level heuristic. The first family, called "partition-k" heuristics, attempt to improve the estimate of the cost of a set in terms of costs of its partitions. The second family, called "adjusted sum" heuristics attempt to improve the sum heuristic by considering the interactions among subgoals. These are described in the next two subsections.

4.1.1 Partition-k heuristics

To avoid underestimating and at the same time keep track of the interaction between subgoals, we want to partition the set S of propositions into subsets, each of which has k elements: $S = S_1 \cup S_2 ... \cup S_m$ (if k does not divide $|S|$, one subset will have less than k elements). Ideally, we want a partitioning such that elements within each subset S_i may be interacting with each other, but the subsets are independent of each other. Thus we have the following heuristic:

Heuristic 5 (Partition-k heuristic) $h(S) := \sum_{S_i} lev(S_i)$, where $S_1, ..., S_m$ are k-sized partitions of S.

The question of deciding the partioning parameter k, and how to partition the set S when $1 < k < |S|$, however, is

---
[2] 8puzzle-1, 8puzzle-2 and 8puzzle-3 are two hard and one easy eight puzzle problems of solution length 31, 30 and 20, respectively. Grid3 and grid4 are simplified from the grid problem at AIPS-98 competitions by reducing number of keys and grid's size.
[3] Graphplan implemented in Lisp by M. Peot and D. Smith.

interesting. We find out that this knowledge may be largely domain-dependent. For example, for $k = 1$, the *partition-1* heuristic exhibits similar behavior compared to *sum-mutex* heuristic in domains where the subgoals are fairly independent (e.g gripper, logistics, rocket), and it is clearly better than sum-mutex in all other domains except the blocks world (see table 2).

For $k = |S|$, we have the *set-level* heuristic, which is very good in a complementary set of domains, compared with the sum-mutex heuristic.

For $k = 2$, we implemented a simple pairwise partition scheme as follows: The basic idea is, in order to avoid underestimating, we put propositions of greatest levels into different partitions. Given a set $S = \{p_1, p_2, ..., p_n\}$. Suppose $lev(p_1) \leq lev(p_2) \leq ... \leq lev(p_n)$. We partition
$S = \{p_1, p_n\} \cup \{p_2, p_{n-1}\} \cup ... \cup \{p_{[(n-1)/2]}, p_{[(n+1)/2]}\}$.
As Table 2 shows, the resulting heuristic exhibits interesting behavior: It can solve many problems that are either intractable by the *sum heuristic* or the *set-level heuristic*.

It would be interesting to have a fuller account of behavior of the family of *partition-k heuristics* with respect to different problem domains. Another related idea is to consider "adaptive partition" heuristics that do not insist on equal sized partitions. For example, p and q are put in the same partition if and only if they are mutexes in the planning graph. We intend to pursue these ideas in future work.

4.1.2 Adjusted Sum Heuristics

We now consider improving the sum heuristic by considering both negative and positive interactions among propositions. First of all, it is simple to embed the sum heuristic value into the planning graph. We maintain a cost value for each new proposition. Whenever a new action is introduced into the planning graph, we update the value for that proposition using the same updating rule 1 in Section 2.

We are now interested in estimating the cost $cost(S)$ for achieving a set $S = \{p_1, p_2, ..., p_n\}$. As before, suppose $lev(p_1) \leq lev(p_2) \leq ... \leq lev(p_n)$. Under the assumption that all propositions are independent, we have $cost(S) := cost(S - p_1) + cost(p_1)$. Since $lev(p_1) \leq lev(S - p_1)$, proposition p_1 is possibly achieved before the set $S - p_1$. Now, we assume that there are still no positive interactions, but there are negative interactions between the propositions. Therefore, upon achieving $S - p_1$, subgoal p_1 may have been deleted and needs to be achieved again. This information can be extracted from the planning graph. According to the planning graph, set $S - p_1$ and S are possibly achieved at level $lev(S - p_1)$ and level $lev(S)$, respectively. If $lev(S - p_1) \neq lev(S)$ that means there is some interaction between achieving $S - p_1$ and achieving p_1, because the planning graph has to expand up to $lev(S)$ to achieve both $S - p_1$ and p_1. To take this negative interaction into account, we assign:

$$cost(S) := cost(S-p_1) + cost(p_1) + (lev(S) - lev(S-p_1)) \quad (2)$$

Applying this formula to $S - p_1$, $S - p_1 - p_2$ and so on, we derive:

$$cost(S) := \sum_{p_i \in S} cost(p_i) + lev(S) - lev(p_n)$$

Problem	Graphplan	Sum-mutex	set-lev	partition-1	partition-2	adj-sum	combo	adj-sum2
bw-large-b	18/ 379.25	18/ 132.50	18/ 10735.48	-	18/ 79.18	22/ 65.62	22/ 63.57	18/ 87.11
bw-large-c	-	-	-	-	-	30/ 724.63	30/ 444.79	28/ 738.00
bw-large-d	-	-	-	-	-	-	-	36/ 2350.71
rocket-ext-a	-	36/ 40.08	-	32/ 4.04	32/ 10.24	40/ 6.10	34/ 4.72	40/ 43.63
rocket-ext-b	-	34/ 39.61	-	32/ 4.93	32/ 10.73	36/ 14.13	32/ 7.38	36/ 554.78
att-log-a	-	69/ 42.16	-	65/ 10.13	-	63/ 16.97	65/ 11.96	56/36.71
att-log-b	-	67/ 56.08	-	69/ 20.05	-	67/ 32.73	67/ 19.04	61/53.28
gripper-20	-	59/ 90.68	-	59/ 39.17	-	59/ 20.54	59/ 20.92	59/38.18
8-puzzle1	31/ 2444.22	33/ 196.73	31/ 4658.87	35/ 80.05	47/ 172.87	39/ 78.36	39/ 119.54	31/ 143.559
8-puzzle2	30/ 1545.66	42/224.15	30/ 2411.21	38/ 96.50	38/ 105.40	42/ 103.70	48/ 50.45	30/ 348.27
8-puzzle3	20/ 50.56	20/ 202.54	20/ 68.32	20/ 45.50	20/ 54.10	24/ 77.39	20/ 63.23	20/ 62.56
travel-1	9/ 0.32	9/ 5.24	9/ 0.48	9/ 0.53	9/ 0.62	9/ 0.42	9/ 0.44	9/ 0.53
grid3	16/ 3.74	-	16/ 14.09	16/ 55.40	16/ 46.79	18/ 21.45	19/ 18.82	16/ 15.12
grid4	18/ 21.30	-	18/ 32.26	18/ 86.17	18/ 126.94	18/ 37.01	18/ 37.12	18/ 30.47
aips-grid1	14/ 311.97	-	14/ 659.81	14/ 870.02	14/ 1010.80	14/ 679.36	14/ 640.47	14/ 739.43
mprime-1	4/ 17.48	-	4/ 743.66	4/ 78.730	4/ 622.67	4/ 76.98	4/ 79.55	4/ 722.55

Table 2: Number of actions/ Total CPU Time in seconds. The dash (-) indicates that no solution was found in 3 hours or 250MB.

Since $lev(p_n) = \max_{p_i \in S} lev(p_i)$ as per our setup, we have the following heuristic:

Heuristic 6 (Adjusted-sum heuristic)
$$h(S) := \sum_{p_i \in S} cost(p_i) + lev(S) - \max_{p_i \in S} lev(p_i)$$

Table 1 and 2 show that this heuristic does very well across *all* different types of problems that we have considered. To understand the robustness of the heuristic, notice that the first term in its formula is exactly the *sum* heuristic value, while the second term is the *set-level heuristic*, and the third approximately the *max* heuristic. Therefore, we have

$$h_{adjsum}(S) \approx h_{sum}(S) + h_{lev}(S) - h_{max}(S)$$

It is simple to see that when there is strictly no negative interactions among propositions, $h_{lev}(S) = h_{max}(S)$. Thus, in the formula for $h_{adjsum}(S)$, $h_{sum}(S)$ is the estimated cost of achieving S under the *independence* assumption, while $h_{lev}(S) - h_{max}(S)$ accounts for the additional cost incurred by the *negative* interactions.

Note that the solutions solved by adjusted sum are longer than those provided by other heuristics in many problems. The reason for this is that the first term $h_{sum}(S) = \sum_{p_i \in S} cost(p_i)$ actually overestimates, because in many domains achieving some subgoal typically also helps achieve others. We are interested in improving the *adjusted-sum* heuristic by replacing the first term in its formula by another estimation $cost_p(S)$ that takes into account this type of *positive* interactions while ignoring the negative interactions (which are anyway accounted for by other two terms).

Since there are no negative interactions, once a subgoal is achieved, it will never be deleted again. Furthermore, the order of achievement of the subgoals $p_i \in S$ would be roughly in the order of $lev(p_i)$. Let p_S be the proposition in S such that $lev(p_S) = \max_{p_i \in S} lev(p_i)$. p_S will possibly be the last proposition that is achieved in S. Let a_S be an action in the planning graph that achieves p_S *in the level* $lev(p_S)$, where p_S first appears. (If there are more than one, none of them would be noop actions, and we would select one randomly.)

By regressing S over action a_S, we have state $S + Prec(a_S) - Add(a_S)$. Thus, we have the recurrent relation (assuming unit cost for the selected action a_S)

$$cost_p(S) := 1 + cost_p(S + Prec(a_S) - Add(a_S)) \quad (3)$$

The positive interactions are accounted for by this regression in the sense that by subtracting $Add(a_S)$ from S, any proposition that is co-achieved when p_S is achieved is not counted in the cost computation. Since $lev(Prec(a_S))$ is strictly smaller than $lev(p_S)$, recursively applying equation 3 to its right hand side will eventually reduce to state S_0 where $lev(S_0) = 0$, whose cost $cost_p(S_0)$ is 0.

It is interesting to note that the repeated reductions involved in computing $cost_p(S)$ indirectly extract a sequence of actions (the a_S selected at each reduction), which would have achieved the set S from the initial state if there were no negative interactions. In this sense, $cost_p(S)$ is similar in spirit to (and is inspired by) the "relaxed plan" heuristic recently proposed by Hoffman[8].

Replacing $h_{sum}(S)$ with $cost_p(S)$ in the definition of h_{adjsum}, we get an improved version of adjusted sum heuristic that takes into account both positive and negative interactions among propositions.

Heuristic 7 (Adjusted-sum2 heuristic)
$h(S) := cost_p(S) + (lev(S) - \max_{p_i \in S} lev(p_i))$, where $cost_p(S)$ is computed using equation (3).

Table 2 shows that adjusted-sum2 heuristic can solve all types of problem considered. The heuristic is only slightly worse compared with the adjusted-sum in term of speed, but gives a much better solution quality. In our experiments, with the exception of problems in the rocket domains, the adjusted-sum2 heuristic value is usually admissible and often gives optimal or near optimal solutions.

Finally, another way of viewing the adjusted-sum heuristic is that, it is composed of $h_{sum}(S)$, which is good in domains where subgoals are fairly independent, and $h_{lev}(S)$, which is good in a complement set of domains (see table 2). Thus the summation of them may yield a combination of *differential power* effective in wider range of problems, while discarding the third term $h_{max}(S)$ may sacrifice the solution quality.

Heuristic 8 (Combo heuristic)
$h(S) := h_{sum}(S) + h_{lev}(S)$, where $h_{sum}(S)$ is the sum heuristic value and $h_{lev}(S)$ is the set-level heuristic value.

Problem	Len	max		set-level		w/ memo		GP
		Est	Time	Est	Time	Est	Time	
8puzzle-1	31		-	14	4658	28	1801	2444
8puzzle-2	30	10	-	12	2411	28	891	1545
8puzzle-3	20	8	144	10	68	19	50	50
bw-large-a	12	6	34	8	21	12	16	14
bw-large-b	18	8	-	10	10735	16	1818	433
bw-large-c	28	12	-	14	-	20	-	-
grid3	16	16	13	16	13	16	5	4
grid4	18	10	33	18	30	18	22	22
rocket-ext-a	-	5	-	6	-	11	-	-

Table 3: Column titled "Len" shows the length of the found optimal plan (in number of actions). Column titled "Est" shows the heuristic value the distance from the initial state to the goal state. Column titled "Time" shows CPU time in seconds. "GP" shows the CPU time for **Serial Graphplan**

Surprisingly, as shown in table 2 the Combo heuristic is even slightly faster than adjusted-sum heuristic across all type of problems while the solution quality remains comparable.

4.2 Finding optimal plans with admissible heuristics

We now focus on admissible heuristics that can be used to produce optimal plans. Traditionally, efficient generation of optimal plans has received little attention in the planning community. In [9] Kambhampati et. al. point out that Graphplan algorithm is guaranteed to find optimal plans when the planning graph serial. In contrast, none of the known efficient state space planners [17; 3; 2; 20] can guarantee optimal solutions.

In fact, it is very hard to find an admissible heuristic that is effective enough to be useful across different planning domains. As mentioned earlier, in [3], Bonet et al. introduced the *max heuristic* that is admissible. In the previous section, we introduced the *set-level* heuristic that is admissible and showed that it is significantly better than the max heuristic. We tested the set-level heuristic on a variety of domains using A* search's cost function $f(S) = g(S) + h(S)$. The results are shown in table 3, and clearly establish that set-level heuristic is significantly more effective than max heuristic. Grid, travel, mprime are domains where the set-level heuristic gives very close estimates (see table 2). Optimal search is less effective in domains such as the 8-puzzle and blocks world problem. Domains such as logistics, gripper remain intractable under reasonable limits in time and memory.

The main problem once again is that the set-level heuristic still hugely underestimates the cost of a set of propositions. The reason for this is that there are many n-ary ($n > 2$) *level-specific* mutex constraints present in the planning graph, that are never marked during planning graph construction, and thus cannot be used by set-level heuristic. This suggests that identifying and using higher-level mutexes can improve the effectiveness of the set-level heuristic.

Propagating all higher level mutexes is likely to be an infeasible idea [1; 9] (as it essentially amounts to full consistency enforcement of the underlying CSP). A seemingly zanier idea is to use a limited run of Graphplan's own backward search, armed with EBL [11], to detect higher level mutexes in the form of "memos". We have done this by restricting the backward search to a limited number of backtracks $lim = 1000$. This lim can be increased by a factor $\mu > 1$ as

Problem	Normal PG	Bi-level PG	Speedup
bw-large-b	22/ 63.57	28/ 20.05	3x
bw-large-c	30/ 444.79	38/ 114.88	4x
bw-large-d	-	44/11442.14	100x
rocket-ext-a	34/ 4.72	34/ 1.26	4x
rocket-ext-b	32/ 7.38	34/ 1.65	4x
att-log-a	65/11.96	64/ 2.27	5x
att-log-b	67/ 11.09	70/ 3.58	3x
gripper-20	59/ 20.92	59/ 7.26	3x
8puzzle-1	39/ 119.54	39/ 20.20	6x
8puzzle-2	48/ 50.45	48/ 7.42	7x
8puzzle-3	20/ 63.23	20/ 10.95	6x
travel-1	9/ 0.44	11/ 0.12	4x
grid-3	19/ 18.82	17/ 3.04	6x
grid-4	18/ 37.12	18/ 14.15	3x
aips-grid-1	14/ 640.47	14/ 163.01	4x
mprime-1	4/ 79.55	4/ 67.75	1x

Table 4: Total CPU time improvement from efficient heuristic computation for **Combo** heuristic

we expand the planning graph to next level.

Table 3 shows the performance of the set-level heuristic using a planning graph adorned with learned memos. We note that the heuristic value (of the goal state) as computed by this heuristic is significantly better than the set-level heuristic operating on the vanilla planning graph. For example in 8-puzzle2, the normal set-lev heuristic estimates the cost to achieve the goal as 12, while using memos pushes the cost to 28, which is quite close to the true optimal value of 30. This improved informedness results in a speedup in all problems we considered (up to 3x in the 8-puzzle2, 6x in bw-large-b), even after adding the time for memo computation using limited backward search.

We also compared the performance of the two set-level heuristics with the serial Graphplan, which also produces optimal plans. The set-level heuristic is better in the 8-puzzle problems, but not as good in the blocks world problems (See table 3). Further analysis is needed to explain these results.

5 Discussion on related work

There are a variety of techniques for improving the efficiency of planning graph construction in terms of both time and space, including bi-level representations that exploit the structural redundancy in the planning graph [15], as well as (ir)relevance detection techniques such as RIFO [18] that ignore irrelevant literals and actions while constructing the planning graph. These techniques can be used to improve the cost of our heuristic computation. In fact, in one of our recent experiments, we have used a bi-level planning graph as a basis for our heuristics. Preliminary results show significant speedups (up to 7x) in all problems, and we are also able to solve more problems than before because our planning graph takes less memory (See table 4).

The set of mutex constraints play very important role in improving the informedness of our graph-based heuristics. The *level-specific* mutexes can be used to give finer (longer) distance estimates, while *static* mutexes help prune more invalid and/or unreachable states. Thus, our heuristics can be improved by detecting more mutexes. Indeed, more level-specific mutexes can be discovered through more sophisticated mutex propagation rules [4], while binary and/or higher order static mutexes can be discovered using a variety of different techniques[6; 21; 5].

Several researchers [8; 20] have considered the *positive* interactions while ignoring the negative interactions among subgoals to improve the heuristics in many problem domains. Hoffman [8] uses the length of the first relaxed plan found in a relaxed planning graph (without mutex computation) as the heuristic value. Refanidis [20] essentially extracts the co-achieveness relation among subgoals from the first relaxed plan to account for the positive interactions. These heuristics were reported to provide both significant speedups and improved solution quality.

Concomitant with our work, Haslum & Geffner [7] considered computing admissible state space heuristic based on dynamic programming approach. Interestingly, their most effective *max-pair* heuristic is closely related to our admissible set-level heuristic. Specifically, the heuristic value updating rule in max-pair heuristic has an effect similar to that of the mutex propagation procedure in the planning graph.

Finally, we concentrated on using the heuristics extracted from the planning graph to drive a state search procedure. In contrast, [12] considers the possibility of using such heuristics to drive Graphplan's own backward search. Their results show that some of the same ideas can be used to derive effective variable and value ordering strategies for Graphplan.

6 Conclusion

In this paper, we showed that the planning graph structure used by Graphplan provides a rich source of effective as well as admissible heuristics. We described a variety of heuristic families, that use the planning graph in different ways to estimate the cost of a set of propositions. Our empirical studies show that many of our heuristics have attractive tradeoffs in comparison with existing heuristics. In particular, we provided three heuristics– "adjusted-sum", "adjusted-sum2" and "combo" that are clearly superior to the sum mutex heuristic used by HSP-R across a large range of problems, including those that have hither-to been intractable for HSP-R. State search planners using these heuristics out-perform both HSP-R and Graphplan. We are also one of the first to focus on finding effective *and* admissible heuristics for state search planners. We have shown that the set-level heuristic working on the normal planning graph, or a planning graph adorned with a limited number of higher level mutexes is able to provide quite reasonable speedups while guaranteeing admissibility.

Our approach provides an interesting way of incorporating the strength of two different planning regimes (disjunctive vs. conjunctive search) [10] and views (planning as CSP vs. planning as state search) that have hither-to been considered orthogonal. We use the efficient directed consistency enforcement provided by the Graphplan's planning graph construction to develop heuristics capable of accounting for subgoal interactions. We then use the heuristics to guide a state search engine. In contrast to Graphplan, our approach is able to avoid the costly CSP-style searches in the non-solution bearing levels of the planning graph. In contrast to HSP-R and UNPOP, our approach is able to provide much more informed heuristics that take subgoal interactions into account in a systematic fashion.

Acknowledgements. We thank Minh B. Do, Biplav Srivastava, Romeo S. Nigenda, Hector Geffner and Ioannis Refanidis for helpful discussions and feedbacks. Thanks are also due to Terry Zimmerman for providing with us his fast bi-level planning graph expansion code. This research is supported in part by NSF young investigator award (NYI) IRI-9457634, ARPA/Rome Laboratory planning initiative grant F30602-95-C-0247, Army AASERT grant DAAH04-96-1-0247, AFOSR grant F20602-98-0182 and NSF grant IRI-9801676.

References

[1] A. Blum and M.L. Furst. Fast planning through planning graph analysis. *Artificial Intelligence*. 90(1-2). 1997.

[2] B. Bonet and H. Geffner. Planning as heuristic search: New results. In *Proc. ECP-99*, 1999.

[3] B. Bonet, G. Loerincs, and H. Geffner. A robust and fast action selection mechanism for planning. In *Proc. AAAI-97*, 1997.

[4] M. Do, S. Kambhampati and B. Srivastava. Investigating the effect of relevance and reachability constraints on SAT encodings of planning. To appear in *AIPS-2000*, 2000.

[5] M. Fox and D. Long. Automatic inference of state invariants in TIM. *JAIR*. Vol. 9. 1998.

[6] A. Gerevini and L. Schubert. Inferring state constraints for domain-independent planning. In *Proc. AAAI-98*, 1998.

[7] P. Haslum and H. Geffner. Admissible Heuristics for Optimal Planning. To appear in *AIPS-2000*, 2000.

[8] J. Hoffman. A Heuristic for Domain Independent Planning and its Use in an Enforced Hill-climbing Algorithm. Technical Report No. 133, Albert Ludwigs University.

[9] S. Kambhampati, E. Lambrecht, and E. Parker. Understanding and extending graphplan. In *Proc. ECP-97*, 1997.

[10] S. Kambhampati. Challenges in bridging plan synthesis paradigms. In *Proc. IJCAI-97*, 1997.

[11] S. Kambhampati. EBL & DDB for Graphplan. *Proc. IJCAI-99*. 1999.

[12] S. Kambhampati and R.S Nigenda. Distance based goal ordering heuristics for Graphplan. To appear in *AIPS-2000*, 2000.

[13] R. Korf and L. Taylor. Finding optimal solutions to the twenty-four puzzle. In *Proc. AAAI-96*, 1996.

[14] R. Korf. Linear-space best-first search. *Artificial Intelligence*, 62:41-78, 1993.

[15] D. Long and M. Fox. Efficient implementation of the plan graph in STAN. *JAIR*, 10(1-2) 1999.

[16] D. McDermott. Aips-98 planning competition results. 1998.

[17] D. McDermott. Using regression graphs to control search in planning. *Artificial Intelligence*, 109(1-2):111–160, 1999.

[18] B. Nebel, Y. Dimopoulos and J. Koehler. Ignoring irrelevant facts and operators in plan generation. *Proc. ECP-97*.

[19] N. Nilsson. *Principles of Artificial Intelligence*. Tioga, 1980.

[20] I. Refanidis and I. Vlahavas. GRT: A domain independent heuristic for strips worlds based on greedy regression tables. In *Proc. ECP-99*, 1999.

[21] J. Rintanen. An iterative algorithm for synthesizing invariants. To appear in *AAAI-2000*, 2000.

[22] D. Weld. Recent advances in ai planning. *AI magazine*, 1999.

An Iterative Algorithm for Synthesizing Invariants

Jussi Rintanen
Albert-Ludwigs-Universität Freiburg, Institut für Informatik
Georges-Köhler-Allee, 79110 Freiburg im Breisgau
Germany

Abstract

We present a general algorithm for synthesizing state invariants that speed up automated planners and have other applications in reasoning about change. Invariants are facts that hold in all states that are reachable from an initial state by the application of a number of operators. In contrast to earlier work, we recognize the fact that establishing an invariant may require considering other invariants, and this in turn seems to require viewing synthesis of invariants as fixpoint computation. Also, the algorithm is not inherently restricted to invariants of particular syntactic forms.

Introduction

For a given transition system, for example expressed as an initial state and a set of operators, invariants are facts that hold in all of its reachable states, or more precisely, they are true in the initial state, and their truth is preserved by the application of every operator (which is why they are called invariants.) Invariants can be applied in many kinds of planning algorithms for speeding them up. In algorithms based on backward chaining, like Graphplan (Blum & Furst 1997) and earlier partial-order planners, invariants rule out certain subgoals as unreachable. In algorithms that use neither regression nor progression and represent plan executions explicitly – for example the satisfiability planning approach – invariants extend the incomplete state descriptions and thereby reduce the amount of search needed (Kautz & Selman 1998; Gerevini & Schubert 1998). Invariants are useful also in many other kinds of planning algorithms that operate on partially described states.

Algorithms for computing invariants for automated planning have earlier been given by Kelleher and Cohn (1992), Rintanen (1998), Gerevini and Schubert (1998), and Fox and Long (1998). Kelleher and Cohn as well as Gerevini and Schubert verify that operators preserve the truth of an invariant on the basis of syntactic properties of the operators. Rintanen sketches an algorithm that computes 2-literal invariants from the ground instances of operators. Fox and Long obtain invariants as a byproduct of inferring types for operators.

In this paper we introduce a new algorithm for computing invariants. The algorithm is iterative like mutex computation in Graphplan (Blum & Furst 1997) and the algorithm by Rintanen (1998) (both of which use a ground representation of operators), operates on a schematic representation of operators, and generalizes earlier techniques. The algorithm is motivated by an inductive definition of invariants as formulae that are true in the initial state and are preserved by the application of every operator. Less general (and in restricted cases more efficient) algorithms can be obtained by specializing the general algorithm.

For schemata that represent 2-literal ground invariants we show that the algorithm is efficient. In this case – like with universally quantified invariants in general – the algorithm is strictly stronger than earlier algorithms combined. Invariants with more than two literals are often useful, but the conditions for inferring non-disjunctive facts (literals) from n-literal invariants for high n are very strict because $n - 1$ atomic facts have to be inferred first, so short invariants seem to be the most important ones. Extensions like existential quantification and types can be handled within the algorithm by supplying new subprocedures to the main procedure. No changes in the main procedure are needed.

Operators

An operator $p \Rightarrow e$ consists of a precondition p and a postcondition e that are sets of atomic literals. An operator can be applied if its preconditions are true, and as a result its postconditions become true. Many planning algorithms work with operators as described above but take input in schematic form; that is, a set of operators can be given as a schema from which each individual operator can be obtained by replacing the variables by constants.

In an operator schema $p \Rightarrow e$, the sets p and e consist of literals a or $\neg a$ where a are of the form $P(t_1, \ldots, t_n)$, P is a predicate, and the terms t_i are constants or variables. We sometimes write $P(T)$ where T is a sequence of terms. The ground literals represented by a literal schema are obtained by replacing variables with constants in all possible ways. For simplicity of presentation we assume that all variables have the same type and that different variables are instantiated with different constants. The latter assumption is relevant only in the main procedure of the algorithm.

Copyright © 2000, American Association for Artificial Intelligence (www.aaai.org). All rights reserved.

Form of Invariants

The invariant schemata we consider are of the form $(x_1 \neq x'_1 \land \cdots \land x_n \neq x'_n) \to (L_1 \lor \cdots \lor L_m)$, where L_i are schematic literals $P_i(x_{1,1}, \ldots, x_{1,n_1})$ or $\neg P_i(x_{1,1}, \ldots, x_{1,n_1})$, and x_i and x'_i are variables. All variables and predicate symbols may be different.

Each invariant schema corresponds to a set of ground invariants that are obtained by replacing the variables by constants without violating the inequalities.

Synthesis of Invariants

We present an iterative algorithm for computing invariants from schematic representations of operators. The algorithm produces a sequence $\Sigma_0, \Sigma_1, \ldots, \Sigma_n, \Sigma_{n+1}$ of sets of schemata such that $\Sigma_n = \Sigma_{n+1}$, Σ_0 is satisfied by the initial state, and each Σ_i is obtained from Σ_{i-1} by identifying candidate invariants that may be falsified by operators that are applicable in states that satisfy Σ_{i-1}, and replacing them by weaker candidate invariants. The set Σ_n that is preserved by all operator applications consists of invariants.

Because exact descriptions Σ_i of states reachable with i steps or fewer may be of exponential size and computing invariants is PSPACE-hard (σ is an invariant iff there is no plan that achieves $\neg\sigma$), syntactic restrictions on Σ_i have to be considered. We do not allow constant symbols in the invariants and have an upper bound on clause length. As a consequence, the sets Σ_i are only an upper bound on the reachable states. These restrictions also guarantee a polynomial upper bound on the runtime.

The main procedure of the algorithm is given in Figure 1. The functions $\text{extend}(p, \Sigma)$, $\text{update}(p, e)$, $\text{preserves}(e, u, \sigma)$ and $\text{weaken}(\sigma)$ are described in the following sections. The algorithm first identifies candidate invariants Σ_0, the ground instances of which are true in the initial state. The computation starts from all the atomic schemata with predicates P_i that occur in the problem instance. Here X_i are sequences of distinct variables. Then the algorithm goes through stages $i = 1, 2, \ldots$, considering each operator $o \in O$ at each stage. The ground operator $p \Rightarrow e$ is obtained from o by replacing variables occurring in o by new distinct constant symbols. The function call $\text{extend}(p, \Sigma_{i-1})$ extends the grounded precondition by using the candidate invariants Σ_{i-1} identified at the previous stage. If an inconsistent set is obtained (containing the empty clause), the precondition was not consistent with Σ_{i-1} and the operator is not applicable. For applicable operators a description of the possible successor states is obtained with the function call $\text{update}(p', e)$, and the preservation of each candidate invariant is tested against it. If a candidate invariant cannot be shown to be preserved by an operator, it is replaced by weaker candidate invariants.

In the following sections we describe the auxiliary functions of the algorithm. A familiarity with notions like unification, substitutions and so on is assumed. When we write about unifiers, we mean most general unifiers. Because the algorithm is for efficiency reasons incomplete, there is a certain freedom in implementing the auxiliary functions. We describe the requirements the functions have to satisfy for

INPUT: an initial state I, a set O of operators
OUTPUT: a set of invariants for I, O

$\Sigma_0 := \{P_1(X_1), \neg P_1(X_1), P_2(X_2), \ldots\}$
WHILE there is $\sigma \in \Sigma_0$ that is false in I **DO**
　$\Sigma_0 := (\Sigma_0 \backslash \{\sigma\}) \cup \text{weaken}(\sigma)$;
i := 0;
REPEAT
　$i := i + 1$;
　$\Sigma_i := \Sigma_{i-1}$;
　FOR EACH $o \in O$ **DO**
　　let $p \Rightarrow e$ be a ground instance of o;
　　$p' := \text{extend}(p, \Sigma_{i-1})$;
　　IF p' is consistent
　　THEN
　　　$u := \text{update}(p', e)$;
　　　WHILE not preserves(e, u, σ) for some $\sigma \in \Sigma_i$
　　　DO $\Sigma_i := (\Sigma_i \backslash \{\sigma\}) \cup \text{weaken}(\sigma)$;
UNTIL $\Sigma_i = \Sigma_{i-1}$;
RETURN Σ_i;

Figure 1: The main procedure of the algorithm

the algorithm to be correct, and outline one possible implementation.

The Function $\text{extend}(p, \Sigma)$

To see which facts are true after an operator is applied, we need to know which facts are true before the operator is applied. Obviously, the preconditions p of the operator are true, but assuming that certain facts Σ hold, we can infer the truth of several other facts as well. The function $\text{extend}(p, \Sigma)$ performs these inferences.

For the correctness of the algorithm the function has to satisfy $p \cup \Sigma \models \text{extend}(p, \Sigma)$.

The function extends a set of ground literals p by applying the resolution rule between clauses from Σ and p. Resolving clauses in Σ with each other would produce clauses already in Σ or (for clauses with 3 or more literals) longer clauses that would often violate the upper bound on clause length. Notice that not doing all possible inferences does not sacrifice the correctness of the algorithm.

So for $E \to (A_1 \lor \cdots \lor A_m) \in \Sigma$ choose $n \in \{m-1, m\}$, $\{l_1, \ldots, l_n\} \subseteq p$, and $L_1 = \{A_{i_1}, \ldots, A_{i_n}\} \subseteq L_2 = \{A_1, \ldots, A_m\}$. Then for every $j \in \{1, \ldots, n\}$ unify $\overline{l_j}$ with A_{i_j} to obtain a unifier θ (inequalities E may not be violated.) Now the clause $(E \to L)\theta$ for $L = L_2 \backslash L_1$ can be inferred. If $n = m$ we get the empty clause.

Example 1 Consider an operator that moves a block from the top of a block on top of another block. This operator has a ground instance with the precondition $p = \{on(A, B), clear(A), clear(C)\}$. Let

$$\Sigma = \{x \neq y \to (\neg on(x, z) \lor \neg on(y, z)),$$
$$x \neq y \to (\neg on(z, x) \lor \neg on(z, y)),$$
$$\neg clear(x) \lor \neg on(y, x)\}.$$

Now
$$\text{extend}(p, \Sigma) = \{on(A,B), clear(A), clear(C),\\
x \neq A \rightarrow \neg on(x,B),\\
x \neq B \rightarrow \neg on(A,x),\\
A \neq y \rightarrow \neg on(y,B),\\
B \neq y \rightarrow \neg on(A,y),\\
\neg on(x,A), \neg on(x,C), \neg clear(B)\}.$$

This is because for example the literal $on(y,z)$ in the clause $x \neq y \rightarrow (\neg on(x,z) \vee \neg on(y,z))$ unifies with $on(A,B)$ and hence produces $x \neq A \rightarrow \neg on(x,B)$. ■

The Function update(p, e)

Given an incomplete description p of a state in which a ground operator with the postcondition e is applied, the function update(p, e) computes an incomplete description of the resulting state. This involves modifying members of p according to the ground literals in e that become true. The set p consists of schemata $\sigma = E \rightarrow \phi$ where E is a conjunction of inequalities $x \neq y$ and ϕ is a disjunction of literals. E may be the empty conjunction, which is defined to be true.

For the correctness of the algorithm the function must satisfy the following. If an operator making the atomic literals e true is applied in a state satisfying p, then the successor state satisfies update(p, e).

Updating members of p according to the literals in e can be done one at a time, and separately with respect to every member of e. Positive and negative literals are treated symmetrically, so we consider only positive ground literals $P(c_1, \ldots, c_n) \in e$. We consider every member σ of p in turn, and show how it has to be modified to reflect the update according to $P(c_1, \ldots, c_n)$.

1. If P does not occur in σ, σ is left intact.
2. If ϕ consists of more than one literal, delete σ.[1]
3. If σ is $\neg P(c_1, \ldots, c_n)$, delete σ.
4. If σ is $E \rightarrow \neg P(t_1, \ldots, t_n)$, then unify $P(c_1, \ldots, c_n)$ with $P(t_1, \ldots, t_n)$. If unification succeeds with the unifier θ and the inequalities $E\theta$ are satisfied, the following changes are made. Let $c_{i_1}/x_{i_1}, \ldots, c_{i_m}/x_{i_m}$ be the unifier. Now σ is replaced by m candidate invariants $(c_{i_j} \neq x_{i_j} \wedge E) \rightarrow \neg P(t_1, \ldots, t_n)$ for $j \in \{1, \ldots, m\}$.
   In many cases, like in the example below, at most one variable unifies with a constant and hence $m = 1$.
5. If σ is $E \rightarrow P(t_1, \ldots, t_n)$ and $P(c_1, \ldots, c_n)$ unifies with $P(t_1, \ldots, t_n)$ producing a one-element unifier $\theta = c/x$ and x is the only variable occurring in σ, remove $c \neq x$ from E (if it is in it).[2]

---

[1] The function would be stronger if it retained σ when none of the literals in the ground instances of σ are affected. However, our implementation of *extend* produces clauses with one literal only, and hence the change would not make a difference.

[2] A stronger implementation of this case – or alternatively of the function *preserves* – may sometimes be necessary for obtaining more invariants. Now there is no means for combining schemata that get split in (4). The splitting is essentially a way of handling disjunctive antecedents.

6. If in the resulting set no literal unifies with $P(c_1, \ldots, c_n)$, $P(c_1, \ldots, c_n)$ is added to the set.

Example 2 Let
$$p = \{on(A,B), clear(A), clear(C),\\
x \neq A \rightarrow \neg on(x,B),\\
x \neq B \rightarrow \neg on(A,x),\\
\neg on(x,A), \neg on(x,C), \neg clear(B)\}.$$

We make the following ground literals true in p.
$$e = \{on(A,C), \neg on(A,B), clear(B), \neg clear(C)\}$$

The result is the following.
$$\text{update}(p, e) = \{clear(A), \neg clear(C), \neg on(x,B),\\
x \neq C \rightarrow \neg on(A,x),\\
x \neq A \rightarrow \neg on(x,C),\\
\neg on(x,A), on(A,C), clear(B)\}$$

For example, $x \neq B \rightarrow \neg on(A,x)$ is transformed to $x \neq C \wedge x \neq B \rightarrow \neg on(A,x)$ by $on(A,C)$, and then to $x \neq C \rightarrow \neg on(A,x)$ by $\neg on(A,B)$. ■

The Function preserves(e, u, σ)

When making the ground literals e true in some state so that a state described by u is reached, we check whether the truth of the instances of σ is preserved.

For the correctness of the algorithm the function preserves(e, u, σ) may return true only if $u \models \sigma$ or e does not falsify any literal in any ground instance of σ.

The function first tests whether a literal in a ground instance of σ is falsified when the literals in e become true. If not, the function returns *true*. Otherwise, we unify complements of literals in e with literals in σ in all possible ways. If $\sigma\theta$ is true in u for all unifiers θ we return *true*. Otherwise we return *false*.

The truth of $\sigma\theta$ in u is tested by a function that tests whether all ground instances of the first are entailed by ground instances of the second. Note that the test does not have to be complete for the whole algorithm to be correct, and an incomplete test suffices. We implement it as testing $\sigma' \models \sigma\theta$ for universally quantified first-order clauses (equivalently: refutability of $\sigma' \wedge \neg\sigma\theta$), where $\sigma' \in u$. This is by applications of unit resolution.

Example 3 Let
$$e = \{on(A,C), \neg on(A,B), clear(B), \neg clear(C)\},\\
u = \{clear(A), \neg clear(C),\\
x \neq C \rightarrow \neg on(A,x),\\
x \neq A \rightarrow \neg on(x,C),\\
\neg on(x,A), on(A,C), clear(B)\}, \text{ and}\\
\sigma = y \neq z \rightarrow (\neg on(x,y) \vee \neg on(x,z)).$$

The complement of the disjunct $\neg on(x,y)$ in σ unifies with $on(A,C)$. The unifier θ assigns $x = A$ and $y = C$. To see whether the truth of σ is preserved when e is made true, we have to check whether $(y \neq z \rightarrow \neg on(x,z))\theta = C \neq z \rightarrow \neg on(A,z)$ is included in u. It is, because $x \neq C \rightarrow \neg on(A,x) \in u$ has exactly the same ground instances. ■

The Function weaken(σ)

When it cannot be shown that a candidate invariant is preserved by an operator, it is rejected. There may, however, be closely related invariants that are true in all reachable states and hence preserved by all operators. So when a candidate invariant is rejected, we produce a number of new ones that are weaker in the sense that they hold in more states.

For the termination of the algorithm the schemata $\sigma' \in$ weaken(σ) have to satisfy $\sigma \models \sigma'$ and $\sigma' \not\models \sigma$.

We have three weakening operations: adding a disjunct to the consequent, adding a conjunct $x \neq y$ to the antecedent, and identifying two variables by replacing occurrences of one by the other. As discussed earlier, the computation of arbitrarily complex invariants is not feasible. Hence falsified candidate invariants with a certain number of literals in the consequent or in the antecedent are not weakened, but completely ignored.

Example 4 Consider the schema $\sigma = x \neq y \rightarrow P(x,y) \vee Q(y,z)$. Let P and Q be the only predicates. By adding a new literal we obtain the following four weaker schemata.

$$x \neq y \rightarrow P(x,y) \vee Q(y,z) \vee P(u,v)$$
$$x \neq y \rightarrow P(x,y) \vee Q(y,z) \vee Q(u,v)$$
$$x \neq y \rightarrow P(x,y) \vee Q(y,z) \vee \neg P(u,v)$$
$$x \neq y \rightarrow P(x,y) \vee Q(y,z) \vee \neg Q(u,v)$$

By adding a new inequality we obtain the following.

$$x \neq y \wedge y \neq z \rightarrow P(x,y) \vee Q(y,z)$$
$$x \neq y \wedge x \neq z \rightarrow P(x,y) \vee Q(y,z)$$

By identifying two variables we obtain the following.

$$x \neq y \rightarrow P(x,y) \vee Q(y,x)$$
$$x \neq y \rightarrow P(x,y) \vee Q(y,y)$$

Now weaken(σ) consists of the above schemata. ■

An Example

Consider the blocks world with blocks A, B and C, and the initial state where A and B are on the table, and C is on top of B. The algorithm starts with `on(x,y)`, `ontable(x)`, `clear(x)`, `-on(x,y)`, `-ontable(x)`, and `-clear(x)` and weakens them with the initial state until the following 2-literal schemata Σ_0 are obtained.

```
1. (x!=z)=>(-on(z,u)|-on(x,u))
2. (y!=u)=>(-on(z,u)|-on(z,y))
3. -on(y,y)
4. -on(z,u)|-on(u,y)
5. -on(y,z)|-ontable(y)
6. -clear(z)|-on(x,z)
7. clear(z)|-on(z,y)
8. ontable(z)|-on(x,z)
9. ontable(y)|clear(y)
```

From `-on(z,u)|-on(u,y)` an invariant is later obtained by identifying z and y. Also the last three are not invariants. These schemata essentially say that all stacks of blocks are of height 2.

For producing Σ_i for $i \geq 1$ the operators are considered. If it cannot be shown that a candidate invariant is preserved by the application of an operator, it must be rejected. This happens to schemata 4, 7, 8, 9. The last three do not yield weaker invariants because of the restriction to 2-literal clauses. The first iteration produces the following Σ_1, and at the second iteration we see that Σ_1 is the fixpoint ($\Sigma_1 = \Sigma_2$.)

```
1. (x!=z)=>(-on(z,u)|-on(x,u))
2. (y!=u)=>(-on(z,u)|-on(z,y))
3. -on(y,y)
4. -on(z,u)|-on(u,z)
5. -on(y,z)|-ontable(y)
6. -clear(z)|-on(x,z)
```

Soundness

Proof of soundness of invariant computation is by induction on the number of iterations. States that are reachable from the initial state with i consecutive operations or less satisfy all ground instances of Σ_i.

The base case is directly because the first step of the algorithm ensures that schemata in Σ_0 have only ground instances that are true in the initial state.

For the inductive case we have to show that for a state s reachable with i operations there are no candidate invariants $\sigma \in \Sigma_i$ that are false in s. So assume a candidate invariant σ is false in a state that is reachable from the initial state by i consecutive operations. Hence there is a ground instance $p \Rightarrow e$ of an operator that is applicable after $i - 1$ consecutive operations from the initial state and that makes a ground instance of σ false. By the induction hypothesis Σ_{i-1} does not falsify p. Therefore $p' = $ extend(p, e) is consistent. The schemata in update(p', e) are true in the state that is reached by applying the operator. And preserves$(e, $ update$(p', e), \sigma)$ returns false. The last three facts are directly the correctness criteria the functions satisfy. Therefore $\sigma \notin \Sigma_i$.

The algorithm terminates because the number of states satisfying the candidate invariants increases at each iteration, and as there are finitely many atomic facts, there is an upper bound on the number of states.

Computational Complexity

Given a fixed upper bound on the number of literals in the invariants, the number of candidate invariants is polynomial. All the auxiliary functions run in polynomial time. The number of iterations is bounded by the number of candidate invariants. Hence the algorithm runs in polynomial time.

Interestingly, like shown in the outline of the soundness proof above, the number of iterations is also bounded by the longest of the shortest paths from the initial state to a reachable state. However, like shown by the experiments in the next section, the number of iterations is much lower in practice. This is because the candidate invariants cannot exactly describe all sets of states (assuming that there are no constant symbols and clause length is bounded) and therefore sets Σ_i often represent much larger sets of states than those reachable with i steps. The iteration therefore terminates much faster than what the theoretical upper bounds predict.

domain	ops	2-literal invars	time	3-literal invars	time
bw-large.a/p	3	6	0.43	7	44.19
bw-large.d/p	3	6	1.18	7	105.76
logistics.a	6	4	1.28	4	160.09
logistics.d	6	4	1.68	4	183.92
hanoi.6	1	6	0.45	7	53.41
hanoi.15	1	6	1.15	7	259.82

Table 1: Runtimes of invariant synthesis in seconds. The numbers of iterations when computing 2-literal invariants for bw-large, logistics and hanoi were respectively 2, 6 and 1, and for 3-literal invariants respectively 3, 11 and 3.

Experiments

We have implemented the algorithm, including typed variables, and tried it on a number of benchmarks: the well-known blocks world, logistics and towers of Hanoi.

Data from a number of runs are given in Table 1. The runs were on a 360 MHz Sun Ultra workstation. The program is compiled Standard ML. We give runtimes for the generation of 2-literal invariants (the only important form in many applications) and for comparison also for 3-literal invariants. Only one inequality was allowed in the antecedents. Most of the time is spent in weakening the candidate invariants with the initial state. Main sources of computational overhead are the generation of many candidate invariants by the function *weaken*, almost all of which are later rejected, and the identification of redundancies by testing inclusion between candidate invariants. More sophisticated implementation techniques would reduce these overheads substantially, especially in the 3-literal case.

Not all domains have interesting n-literal invariants for any given n. For the blocks world with n blocks there are m-literal invariants (for $m \leq n$) stating that the *on* relation is acyclic. The only 3-literal invariant for the blocks world (and towers of Hanoi) that is not a consequence of a 2-literal invariant is -on(x,y)|-on(y,z)|-on(z,x). The logistics domain does not have any.

Invariants inferred by our algorithm for common planning benchmarks are given next. The 2-literal invariants for the blocks world were given earlier. For towers of Hanoi we get the following invariants.

1. -on(x:DISK,x:DISK)
2. -on(y:DISK,z:DISK)|-on(z:DISK,y:DISK)
3. -on(x:DISK,y:DISK)|-free(y:DISK)
4. (x!=z)=>(-at(y:DISK,z:PEG)|-at(y:DISK,x:PEG))
5. (x!=z)=>(-on(y:DISK,z:DISK)|-on(y:DISK,x:DISK))
6. (x!=y)=>(-on(y:DISK,z:DISK)|-on(x:DISK,z:DISK))

And for the logistics domain the following.

1. (y!=u)=>(-at(z:{PACKAGE,TRUCK},u:{PORT,AIRPORT})
         |-at(z:{PACKAGE,TRUCK},y:{PORT,AIRPORT}))
2. -at(z:PACKAGE,u:{PORT,AIRPORT})
   |-transport(z:PACKAGE,y:{TRUCK,AIRPLANE})
3. (y!=u)=>(-at(z:{PACKAGE,AIRPLANE},u:AIRPORT)
         |-at(z:{PACKAGE,AIRPLANE},y:AIRPORT))
4. (y!=u)=>(-transport(z:PACKAGE,u:{TRUCK,AIRPLANE})
         |-transport(z:PACKAGE,y:{TRUCK,AIRPLANE}))

Invariants 1 and 3 overlap. This is because airplanes cannot be at a port, and therefore objects at airports and objects at airports or ports get handled separately.

Related Work

Derivation of invariants from first-order formalizations of actions has been investigated by Zhang and Foo (1997). They give a general rule that is based on inferring which fluents are preserved by an action and that corresponds to the computation performed by our function *update*. They also give derivations of many blocks world invariants.

Gerevini and Schubert's (1998) techniques for computing invariants appear to be more general than those by Kelleher and Cohn (1992). Their method for computing implicational invariants is a special case of the computation performed by our functions *update* and *preserves*: a disjunction is an invariant if for every operator, neither disjunct is falsified by the operator, or one disjunct is made true, or one disjunct is a precondition and it is not made false by the operator. For inferring that in the blocks world there can be at most one block on top of a block and that a block with another block on top of it is not clear, Gerevini and Schubert propose techniques that are special cases of our idea of strengthening operator preconditions with candidate invariants. Gerevini and Schubert say that for the blocks world they cannot infer that a block is on top of at most one block or that two blocks cannot simultaneously be on top of each other.

Fox and Long (1998) address the problem of inferring types for objects on the basis of the operators and an initial state. Data obtained in that computation can be used in inferring invariants that state that objects have exactly one of several (positive) properties (or, in some cases, at most n if the initial state had n.) Many invariants are not recognized by Fox and Long, like our blocks world invariants 1, 3, 4 and 6, and the following.

Example 5 Consider the operators $B(x) \Rightarrow \neg A(x)$, $A(x) \Rightarrow \neg B(x)$, $\Rightarrow A(x)$, and $\Rightarrow B(x)$, and an initial state in which for every x at least one of $A(x)$ and $B(x)$ is true. Clearly $A(x) \vee B(x)$ is an invariant. ∎

For example for the logistics domain Fox and Long infer $\forall x \exists y\, at(x, y)$ for vehicles x. Our algorithm as described above does not use existential variables, and hence does not infer this invariant. However, Fox and Long's algorithm is strictly weaker than the obvious extension of our algorithm to existential variables that is pointed out in the conclusions.

Invariants cannot in general be produced separately. Interaction between invariants is often essential in establishing them, and the invariants in the following example cannot be identified with the techniques proposed earlier (Kelleher & Cohn 1992; Gerevini & Schubert 1998; Fox & Long 1998), but our algorithm finds them immediately.

Example 6 Consider the operators $\neg C(x) \Rightarrow \neg A(x)$, $\neg A(x) \Rightarrow \neg C(x)$, and $A(x) \wedge C(x) \Rightarrow \neg B(x)$ and an initial state that satisfies $I = \{A(x) \vee B(x), B(x) \vee C(x)\}$. The formulae I are invariants for the initial state and the operators, but verifying that for example $A(x) \vee B(x)$ is preserved by $\neg C(x) \Rightarrow \neg A(x)$ requires extending the precondition $\neg C(x)$ to $B(x), \neg C(x)$ by the invariant $B(x) \vee C(x)$. ∎

The problem of testing whether given formulae are invariants of a transition system has been extensively investigated in the context of computer-aided verification (Bensalem, Lakhnech, & Saidi 1996).

Conclusions

We have presented an algorithm for computing invariants for automated planning. The main differences to earlier techniques are that the algorithm is not restricted to invariants of particular syntactic forms, it works uniformly for all invariants, and it is formalized as the iterative computation of a fixpoint. Earlier techniques establish each invariant separately and fail to produce invariants that our algorithm produces. Fixpoint computation is needed because interdependencies between invariants may be complex, and it is not in general possible to infer some invariants first and then use them for inferring others. Example 6 shows how two invariants can depend on each other and have to be established in parallel.

We have been able to show that our algorithm can be implemented efficiently for the practically most important case of 2-literal invariants. Improved implementation techniques may make it practical for n-literal invariants for $n \geq 3$.

Our algorithm is not restricted to computing invariants for only one initial state. Given a set S of initial states represented as Σ_0 such that $S \models \Sigma_0$, we start the computation from this Σ_0 instead of the schemata satisfied by I. Similarly, the algorithm can be used for testing whether given (non-automatically identified) schemata Σ_0 are invariants.

This work can be extended to several directions. As an alternative to the formula-based inexact representations of reachable states used in the current paper, standard techniques from symbolic model-checking (Burch et al. 1994) that use binary decision diagrams could be used for performing an exact reachability analysis. Extracting invariants from the resulting binary decision diagrams is straightforward. The main problem in this approach is the size of the binary decision diagrams on bigger problems. Also, only ground invariants could be extracted.

In this paper we only consider schemata with universal variables that represent conjunctions of ground clauses. Schemata with existential variables may represent arbitrarily long disjunctions of ground literals, for example $\forall x(ontable(x) \vee \exists y on(x,y))$ for the blocks world. For handling existential variables one only needs to extend the four auxiliary functions, which is straightforward. Another extension that is not described in the paper is typed variables. Also this extension is an easy exercise.

Acknowledgements

We thank the reviewers for many valuable comments.

References

Bensalem, S.; Lakhnech, Y.; and Saidi, H. 1996. Powerful techniques for the automatic generation of invariants. In Alur, R., and Henzinger, T. A., eds., *Proceedings of the Eighth International Conference on Computer Aided Verification CAV*, volume 1102 of *Lecture Notes in Computer Science*, 323–335. New Brunswick, New Jersey, USA: Springer-Verlag.

Blum, A. L., and Furst, M. L. 1997. Fast planning through planning graph analysis. *Artificial Intelligence* 90(1-2):281–300.

Burch, J. R.; Clarke, E. M.; Long, D. E.; MacMillan, K. L.; and Dill, D. L. 1994. Symbolic model checking for sequential circuit verification. *IEEE Transactions on Computer-Aided Design of Integrated Circuits and Systems* 13(4):401–424.

Fox, M., and Long, D. 1998. The automatic inference of state invariants in TIM. *Journal of Artificial Intelligence Research* 9:367–421.

Gerevini, A., and Schubert, L. 1998. Inferring state constraints for domain-independent planning. In *Proceedings of the Fifteenth National Conference on Artificial Intelligence (AAAI-98) and the Tenth Conference on Innovative Applications of Artificial Intelligence (IAAI-98)*, 905–912. The AAAI Press.

Kautz, H., and Selman, B. 1998. The role of domain-specific knowledge in the planning as satisfiability framework. In Simmons, R.; Veloso, M.; and Smith, S., eds., *Proceedings of the Fourth International Conference on Artificial Intelligence Planning Systems*, 181–189.

Kelleher, G., and Cohn, A. G. 1992. Automatically synthesising domain constraints from operator descriptions. In Neumann, B., ed., *Proceedings of the 10th European Conference on Artificial Intelligence*, 653–655. Wien, Austria: John Wiley & Sons.

Rintanen, J. 1998. A planning algorithm not based on directional search. In Cohn, A. G.; Schubert, L. K.; and Shapiro, S. C., eds., *Principles of Knowledge Representation and Reasoning: Proceedings of the Sixth International Conference (KR '98)*, 617–624. Trento, Italy: Morgan Kaufmann Publishers.

Zhang, Y., and Foo, N. Y. 1997. Deriving invariants and constraints from action theories. *Fundamenta Informaticae* 30(1):109–123.

RealPlan: Decoupling Causal and Resource Reasoning in Planning

Biplav Srivastava
Email: biplav@asu.edu
Department of Computer Science and Engineering
Arizona State University, Tempe, AZ 85287-5406.

Abstract

Recent work has demonstrated that treating resource reasoning separately from causal reasoning can lead to improved planning performance and rational resource management where increase in resources does not degrade planning performance. However, the resources were scheduled procedurally and limited to cases that could be solved backtrack-free. Terming the decoupled framework as RealPlan, in this work, I extend it with a general approach to convert the resource allocation problem as a declaratively specified dynamic constraint satisfaction problem (DCSP), compile it into CSP and solve it with a CSP solver. By doing so, the resource scheduling problem can be handled in its full complexity and can provide a computational characterization of the different scheduling classes. The CSP formulation also facilitates planner-scheduler interaction by helping the scheduler interpret the resource allocation policies proposed by the planner in terms of constraints on values of scheduling variables. Moreover, if the extraction of causal plan is also formulated as a CSP problem, the two CSPs can enable dependency directed backtracking between them. I have implemented declarative scheduling on top of Graphplan and GP-CSP planners (which poses the backward search of Graphplan as a CSP problem), and the resulting planners reiterate the benefits of decoupling planning and scheduling while providing elegant CSP models (RealPlan-MS, RealPlan-PP) for investigating planner-scheduler communication.

Introduction

AI Planning can handle small plans compared to what humans already handle in the real world. In real-world problems, planning and scheduling phases are usually *loosely coupled*. Humans come up with the Work Breakdown Structure (WBS)(Moder & Phillips 1964) to identify the different tasks at some granularity and estimate time and resources for each task. From this information, the critical bottleneck in the project is identified and the sequence of non-critical tasks is re-aligned to optimize on resource usage and meet deadlines. Project management tools like Microsoft Project(Microsoft 1998) help in sequencing the task network using Critical Path Method (CPM) or Program Evaluation and Review Technique (PERT) analysis.

In contrast, most AI planners do not distinguish between causal and resource reasoning and handle them within the same planning algorithm. Experimental results (Srivastava & Kambhampati 1999) show that this strategy severely curtails the scale-up potential of existing planners, including such recent ones as Graphplan(Blum & Furst 1995) and Blackbox (Kautz & Selman 1998). In particular, these planners exhibit the seemingly irrational behavior of worsening in performance with increased resources. The key observation is that the integration of resources explodes the search space of the planner beyond the action sets that are minimal with respect to the logical goals. Actions may be added to achieve the resource goals but may not be necessary for the logical goals. Most planners suffer performance drop due to the expanded flaw resolution.

In our recent work (Srivastava & Kambhampati 1999; Srivastava 2000), we demonstrated that treating resources separately from causal reasoning can lead to improved AI planning performance and rational resource management (for example, planning performance does not worsen with increased resources). However, the resources were scheduled procedurally and only those cases were handled that could be solved backtrack-free. Terming the decoupled framework as RealPlan, in this work, I extend it with a general approach to convert the resource allocation problem into a declaratively specified dynamic constraint satisfaction problem (DCSP(Mittal & Falkenhainer 1990)), compile it into CSP and solve it with a standard CSP solver. By doing so, the full resource scheduling problem can be handled with all its complexity. I provide a computational characterization of the scheduling classes presented in (Srivastava & Kambhampati 1999) in terms of specification of this CSP. The CSP formulation also helps the scheduler to interpret the resource allocation policies proposed by the planner in terms of constraints on values of scheduling variables.

Figures 1 and 2 provide a general overview of the RealPlan approach. The unified framework accepts a domain description along with optional annotations for resources[1], finds a plan modulo the choice of resource abstraction, and then allocates resources to produce a sound final plan (if the plan requires resources). After planning is

---

Copyright © 2000, American Association for Artificial Intelligence (www.aaai.org). All rights reserved.

[1]The primary focus here is on reusable discrete resources which may be sharable or non-sharable.

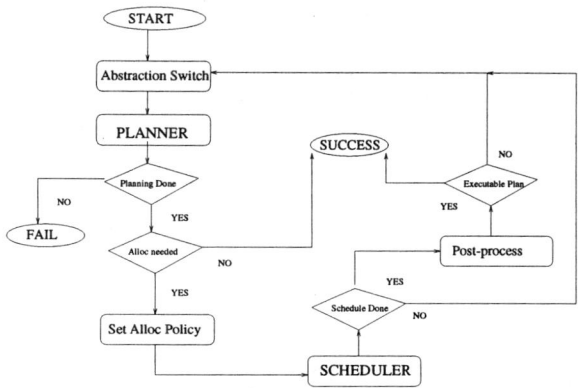

Figure 1: *RealPlan: Unified planning-scheduling framework*

1. Identify resources.
2. If no resource information is available or resources are so low (usually one) that postponing their reasoning is counter-productive, perform conventional planning (i.e. in this case, interactions involving similar resources are addressed during planning).
3. Suppose some of the objects are defined as resources. Planning proceeds as follows:
   (a) Assign dummy values to resource variables in the initial state and goal state such that equivalent resources have the same dummy value.
   (b) Do not compute interference relationships (mutexes) between resource equivalent operators. Operators may still interfere due to other preconditions/effects.
   (c) Complete planning.
4. Once a plan is obtained, allocate resources to the actions in the plan and resolve resource conflicts using any scheduling criteria.
5. Return a valid final plan. As long as the algorithm ensures that all facts achieved during the planning phase are not undone by resource scheduling, the final plan is sound.

Figure 2: *Synopsis of RealPlan approach.*

complete, a scheduler can decide which resources to actually allocate based on resource allocation policies proposed by the planner. The different allocation policies include maintaining the concurrency of the plan, serializing the plan and inserting actions to free and reallocate the resources[2]. If freeing/reallocating actions are allowed, the problem is in fact a dynamic constraint satisfaction problem (DCSP) because these new actions (variables) control the normal action variables.

I have implemented the declarative scheduling (hereafter, referred to as only scheduling) on top of the Graphplan(Blum & Furst 1995) and the GP-CSP(Do & Kambhampati 1999) planners. Planner-scheduler interaction is supported as *master-slave* relationship (called RealPlan-MS, see Figure 3) in Graphplan and GP-CSP. If the declarative scheduling method fails to allocate resources in the context of given resources, time limit and nature of allocation policy, the partial schedule in a failed iteration is not pursued further and destroyed. Further, the responsibility transfers to the planner to change any of the these parameters and try again. If the resource allocation succeeds and new free/reallocation actions were added by the scheduler, the scheduled plan is post-processed for necessary domain translation for

---

[2]The policy of inserting freeing/reallocating actions assumes that actions are reversible in the domain. It could otherwise lead to incompleteness and should be disabled.

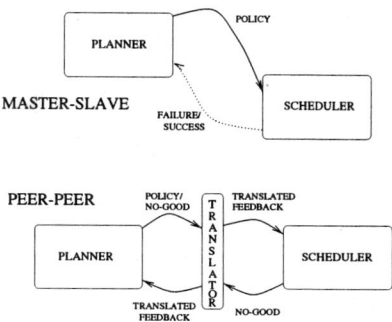

Figure 3: *Communication relationships between the planner and the scheduler. RealPlan-MS is the main focus here whereas RealPlan-PP is currently being developed.*

executability. If all the allocation policies lead to failure or inexecutable plans in a domain, this implies that planning and scheduling were infact, *not loosely coupled* in this instance. In such a case, the framework retains the ability to switch off resource abstraction and resort to traditional planning.

The framework can also support *peer-peer* relationship (called RealPlan-PP) between the planner and the scheduler which is being developed in the GP-CSP context (Srivastava, Kambhampati & Do 2000). In GP-CSP, the plan graph of Graphplan is converted into a CSP problem and solved with a standard solver. Using such a planner, the scheduler can inform the planner about the source of infeasibility in terms of the variables and constraints in the planner's CSP to handle even *tightly coupled* problems. This type of "multi-module dependency directed backtracking" approach is a variation on the hybrid planning methodology developed in (Kambhampati et al 1991), and is also akin to the approach used to link satisfiability and linear programming solvers in (Wolfman & Weld 1999).

Here is the outline of the paper. First, the specification of the constraints for the resource scheduling problem as a dynamic constraint satisfaction problem is described. Next, I discuss planner-scheduler interaction in this context. Through empirical results, we show the effectiveness of the decoupled approach vis-a-vis the nature of resources. The paper concludes with a discussion of related work and comments.

Scheduling as a declarative CSP

For the purpose of illustration, the *"shuffle"* problem, which is the multiple robots version of the 6-block *blocks_facts_shuffle* problem in the Graphplan system, is selected. Here, a stack of blocks has to be systematically shuffled to achieve the goal arrangement. An example of the plan generated for the *shuffle* problem, by disregarding inter-resource conflicts during planning, is shown in Figure 4. The plan consists of 10 time steps (levels) with resource profile of the number of resources left allocated at each level shown in the right column (marked "#Robots"). In our experiments, the problem is generalized to k-block *shuffle* versions so that

Level	Actions by level	# Robots
1	Unstack_R_blkF_blkE	1
2	Unstack_R_blkE_blkD	2
3	Unstack_R_blkD_blkC	3
4	Unstack_R_blkC_blkB	4
5	Putdown_R_blkC	
5	Unstack_R_blkB_blkA	5
6	Stack_R_blkF_blkC	
6	Pickup_R_blkA	5
7	Stack_R_blkB_blkF	4
8	Stack_R_blkE_blkB	3
9	Stack_R_blkA_blkE	2
10	Stack_R_blkD_blkA	1

Figure 4: *A resource-abstracted solution for* shuffle *problem. Curved lines show resource usage spans (see below). The number of resources needed at each level (which equals the number of spans crossing that level) is also shown.*

Action	Vars	Possible Values
A_i	$\langle RA_i, PA_i \rangle$	$\{1..N\}, \{i..L-1\}$
A_j	$\langle RA_j, PA_j \rangle$	$\{1..N\}, \{j..L\}$
F_{ij}	$\langle RF_{ij}, PF_{ij} \rangle$	$\{\bot,1,..N\}, \{\bot,i+1..L-2\}$
U_{ij}	$\langle RU_{ij}, PU_{ij} \rangle$	$\{\bot,1,..N\}, \{\bot,i+2..L-1\}$
N_i	$\langle PN_i \rangle$	$\{i..L\}$

Table 1: *Constraints on action variables and their values while scheduling for resource R. Number of resource of type R are N and the permitted length of the plan is L. $\bot \Rightarrow F_{ij}$, U_{ij} are not needed. N_i is R insensitive.*

Relationship among variables	Comments
$RA_i = RF_{ij} \vee (RF_{ij} = \bot$ $\wedge RA_i = RA_j)$	If freeing action is needed, it uses the same resource as span starting the action
$RA_j = RU_{ij} \vee (RU_{ij} = \bot$ $\wedge RA_i = RA_j)$	If realloc action is needed, it uses the same resource as span ending the action
$RF_{ij} \neq \bot \Leftrightarrow RU_{ij} \neq \bot$	If freeing action occurs, reallocating action also occurs and vice-versa
$PF_{ij} \prec PU_{ij}$ $\vee PF_{ij} = PU_{ij} = \bot$	Position of freeing action is before position of realloc action or both are NULL
$PA_i \prec PF_{ij} \vee PF_{ij} = \bot$	Position of freeing action is after start of span or is NULL
$PA_j \succ PU_{ij} \vee PU_{ij} = \bot$	Position of realloc action is before end of span or is NULL
$RF_{ij} = \bot \Leftrightarrow PF_{ij} = \bot$	If freeing action is not needed, its position is NULL and vice-versa
$RU_{ij} = \bot \Leftrightarrow PU_{ij} = \bot$	If realloc action is not needed, its position is NULL and vice-versa
$PA_i \prec PA_j$	Position of action starting a span is before the action ending it
$PN_i \prec PN_j$, $PN_i \prec PA_j$, $PA_i \prec PN_j$	Relative ordering of actions in the plan is maintained irrespective of resource usage
Non-sharable resource constraints (see Table 3)	If segments of two spans overlap, they cannot share resources over that segment

Table 2: *Relationship among values of action variables.*

the problems can also be scaled independent of the number of resources.

A Constraint Satisfaction Problem (CSP(Beck & Fox 1998)) consists of a set of variables, each with a finite range of values (also called the domain of the variable), and a set of constraints. The aim is to find a satisfying assignment for all the variables which is compatible with the constraint set. In a Dynamic Constraint Satisfaction Problem (DCSP(Mittal & Falkenhainer 1990)), there are two types of variables: activity variables and normal variables. Initially, only a subset of the variables is active, and the objective is to *find assignments for all active variables that is consistent with the constraints among those variables*. In addition, the DCSP specification also contains a set of "activity constraints." An activity constraint is of the form: "if variable x takes on the value v_x, then the variables $y, z, w...$ become active." A DCSP problem can be translated into a normal CSP problem by augmenting the domain of variables with a dummy value $\bot$ (NULL) to signify that those variable may be inactive, and modifying the constraint specification accordingly.

Let us state the resource allocation problem for resource R. The abstract plan has a set of action pairs $\langle A_i, A_j \rangle \mid j \succ i$ where action A_i appears at time step i of the plan (actually written as A_i^m if it is the mth action at level i using resource R but the superscript is omitted for clarity) and they constitute resource spans ($S_{ij} : \langle A_i, A_j, C \rangle$ s) that we have to allocate resources to. The effect C of action A_i is produced at level i and consumed at a later level j for the precondition of action A_j.

Examples of spans in Figure 4 are $S_{1,6}$: $\langle A_1, A_6^1, holding\_R\_blockF \rangle$ and $S_{2,8}$: $\langle A_2, A_8, holding\_R\_blockE \rangle$. We note that the nature of problem is such that every resource allocation choice is a backtrackable point. Moreover, actions can move to lower or upper levels if causal dependencies allow them.

Each action A_i using resource R has two variables associated with it, RA_i for the resource allocated and PA_i for the position or level where the action will appear. Position of an action is also a variable because one way to allocate resources, given a resource limit, is by serializing the parallel plan. Actions that do not participate in manipulation of resources are noted as N_i and their corresponding position variable is PN_i. Given a span S_{ij}:$\langle A_i, A_j, C \rangle$, two additional actions are associated with it, F_{ij} for freeing the resource and U_{ij} to reallocate the resource. The constraints on variables and legal values are listed respectively in Table 1 and Table 2.

As an example, for span $S_{1,6}$, the domain of $RA_1 = RA_6$ = $\{1..7\}$ when 7 is the number of robots in the problem. The domain of position variables are $PA_1 = \{1..12\}$ and $PA_6 = \{6..12\}$ if the allocation policy permits movement of actions in the plan until level 12. If free/ reallocation actions are not allowed, $RF_{1,6} = RU_{1,6} = PF_{1,6} = PU_{1,6} = \bot$. Such an allocation policy in fact allows the scheduler to serialize the planner till level 12 (beyond the abstract plan length of 10 in Figure 4) without adding any new action.

Condition	Constraint on values
$PF^1_{ij} = PU^1_{ij}$ $= PF^2_{ij} = PU^2_{ij} = \bot$	$INTERACT(PA^1_i, PA^1_j, PA^2_i, PA^2_j)$ $\Rightarrow RA^1_i \neq RA^2_i$
$PF^1_{ij} = PU^1_{ij} = \bot;$ $PF^2_{ij}, PU^2_{ij} \neq \bot$	$INTERACT(PA^1_i, PA^1_j, PA^2_i, PF^2_{ij})$ $\Rightarrow RA^1_i \neq RA^2_i$ $INTERACT(PA^1_i, PA^1_j, PU^2_{ij}, PA^2_j)$ $\Rightarrow RA^1_i \neq RA^2_j$
$PF^1_{ij}, PU^1_{ij} \neq \bot;$ $PF^2_{ij} = PU^2_{ij} = \bot$	$INTERACT(PA^2_i, PA^2_j, PA^1_i, PF^1_{ij})$ $\Rightarrow RA^2_i \neq RA^1_i$ $INTERACT(PA^2_i, PA^2_j, PU^1_{ij}, PA^1_j)$ $\Rightarrow RA^2_i \neq RA^1_j$
$PF^1_{ij}, PU^1_{ij},$ $PF^2_{ij}, PU^2_{ij} \neq \bot$	$INTERACT(PA^1_i, PF^1_{ij}, PA^2_i, PF^2_{ij})$ $\Rightarrow RA^1_i \neq RA^2_i$ $INTERACT(PA^1_i, PF^1_{ij}, PU^2_{ij}, PA^2_j)$ $\Rightarrow RA^1_i \neq RA^2_j$ $INTERACT(PU^1_{ij}, PA^1_j, PA^2_i, PF^2_{ij})$ $\Rightarrow RA^1_j \neq RA^2_i$ $INTERACT(PU^1_{ij}, PA^1_j, PU^2_{ij}, PA^2_j)$ $\Rightarrow RA^1_j \neq RA^2_j$

Table 3: *INTERACT(a,b,c,d) = (a ≤ d ∧ c ≤ b). When two sections of resource spans interact, the interacting sections cannot share the same resource. The superscript refers to the spans S_1 or S_2 for which the actions (and variables) are applicable.*

The constraints on resource values enforce that the resource used by A_i is the same as A_j unless the freeing and reallocating actions are present. If they are present, A_i and F_{ij} have the same resource as do U_{ij} and A_j. The constraints on position variables enforce the relative order between the actions. The position of A_i has to be before A_j, while the freeing action, if present, has to be after A_i and the reallocating action, which follows a freeing action, has to be before A_j. The partial ordering of the actions in the abstract plan is also maintained irrespective of resource usage. The exact constraints on the values of variables are summarized in Table 2.

Moreover, if a resource is non-sharable (meaning single capacity), additional constraints have to be specified as summarized in Table 3. The gist of the constraints is that if any segment of a span interacts with that of another, the two spans cannot share a resource. For example, spans $S_{1,6}$ and $S_{2,8}$ interact between levels 2 and 6. Therefore, they cannot share a robot (resource) in this interval unless their allocated robots are freed. Freeing (and reallocating) actions will result in sub-intervals over which a robot cannot be shared.

Finally, in addition to the constraints in Tables 2 and 3, we have the top-level constraints:

- The number of resource allocations at a level must not exceed the available resources.
- To optimize the plan, we can set the objective function as minimizing the total number of actions in the plan and/or amount of resources used. Minimizing resources is usually neglected in AI planning because the number of resources in a problem is part of the initial specification and there is no incentive for saving them.

The resource allocation problem can now be solved by any systematic method. We solve the CSP encodings with GAC-CBJ, a CSP solver in CPLAN(van Beek & Chen 1999)

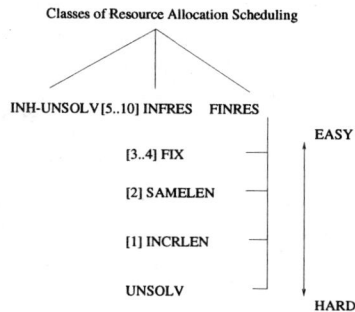

Figure 5: *A classification of resource allocation instances (with resource quantities that put* 6-shuffle *problem in each of the classes). INH-UNSOLV refers to causally infeasible plan for which no scheduling is needed, while UNSOLV refers to an unschedulable plan.*

that performs generalized arc-consistency and conflict directed backjumping.

Policies for Planner-Scheduler Interaction

The communication between planner and scheduler can be seen as policies by the planner about scheduling variables, their domains and constraints. The relationship is *master-slave* as the scheduler responds by flagging success or failure with the suggested parameters. If scheduling method fails to allocate resources in the context of given resources, time limit and nature of allocation policy, the responsibility transfers to the planner to change any of the permissible parameters and try again. The planner also has the option to take up non-abstracted planning at any stage. If resource allocation succeeds, the schedule and the allocation policy are used to derive an executable plan.

In (Srivastava & Kambhampati 1999), the resource allocation problem was classified into a variety of classes (see Figure 5). The complexity of resource scheduling instance increases from left to right and from top to bottom. It was proposed that rather than using one general scheduling method for all classes, one could cycle through the scheduling methods tailored to each of the specific classes. However, the implementation avoided Class INCRLEN and backtracking cases in other classes, and reverted to normal planning.

The CSP formulation allows the different classes to be fully supported in the form of resource allocation policies. The different policies include maintaining the concurrency of the plan, serializing the plan and inserting actions to free and reallocate the resources. Table 4 summarizes the different policies and what they imply in terms of legal values of variables. Maintaining concurrency of the plan corresponds to all actions A_i in the plan being immovable while no freeing/ reallocating actions are permitted. The domain of RA_i is the range of available resources. Serializing the plan implies that the action of the plan can move subject to an upper plan length, L^{MAX}, provided by the planner. Again, no freeing/ reallocating actions are permitted to be inserted. An example of L^{MAX} is the number of actions in the plan, which allows the plan to be completely serialized.

Allocation Policy	Constraint on values
Maintain concurrency (Class INFRES)	$PA_i = i, PA_j = j$, $RA_i = RA_j = \{1,...N\}$ $PF_{ij} = PU_{ij} = \bot$ $RF_{ij} = RU_{ij} = \bot$
Serialize plan	$PA_i = \{i,...L^{MAX}\text{-}1\}$, $PA_j = \{j,...L^{MAX}\}$, $RA_i = RA_j = \{1,...N\}$ $PF_{ij} = PU_{ij} = \bot$ $RF_{ij} = RU_{ij} = \bot$
Introduce Free/ Reallocate action	(Class FINRES)
Class FIX	$PA_i = i, PA_j = j$, $RA_i = RA_j = \{1,...N\}$ $PF_{ij} = \{\bot, i+1\}$, $PU_{ij} = \{\bot, j\text{-}1\}$, $RF_{ij} = RU_{ij} = \{\bot, 1,...N\}$
Class SAMELEN	$PA_i = \{i,...L\text{-}1\}$, $PA_j = \{j,...L\}$, $RA_i = RA_j = \{1,...N\}$ $PF_{ij} = \{\bot, i+1,...L\text{-}2\}$, $PU_{ij} = \{\bot, j\text{-}1,...L\text{-}1\}$, $RF_{ij} = RU_{ij} = \{\bot, 1,...N\}$
Class INCRLEN	$PA_i = \{i,...L^{MAX}\text{-}1\}$, $PA_j = \{j,...L^{MAX}\}$, $RA_i = RA_j = \{1,...N\}$ $PF_{ij} = \{\bot, i+1,...L^{MAX}\text{-}2\}$, $PU_{ij} = \{\bot, j\text{-}1,...L^{MAX}\text{-}1\}$, $RF_{ij} = RU_{ij} = \{\bot, 1,...N\}$

Table 4: *Allocation policy and restrictions on values of variables.* L^{MAX} *is some maximum length ($L^{MAX} \succ L$) upto which the steps of the plan can be increased.*

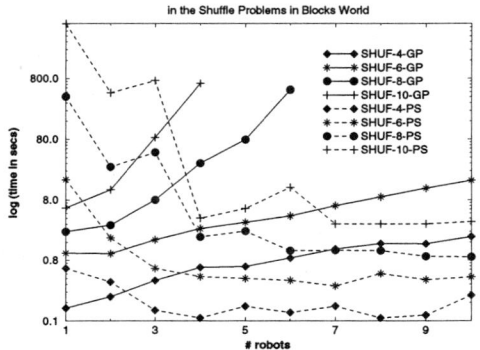

Figure 6: *Comparative performance of my approach of decoupling causal and resource reasoning v/s Graphplan in* shuffle *problem of 4, 6, 8 and 10 blocks. (Total: 80 problems)*

In introducing resource freeing/reallocating actions, three sub-cases are identified. If actions are considered immovable, this corresponds to Class FIX. Here, the freeing action (F_{ij}) can be introduced immediately after A_i while the reallocating action (U_{ij}) can come immediately before A_j. The second sub-case is when the actions are allowed to move upto the length of the abstract plan, and this corresponds to Class SAMELEN. Finally, the actions are allowed to move till any upper limit L^{MAX} ($L^{MAX} \succ L$) in Class INCRLEN.

The advantage of multiple allocation policies is that it helps the planner in communicating the plan preference of the user to the scheduler. For example, the end user may prefer plans with lower number of actions in the plan at the cost of increased plan length. Policies also make sense computationally. The complexity of the CSP problem increases with the domain size of its variables since it is $O(k^n)$ where there are n variables with average domain size of k. The idea of having multiple allocation policies is useful in guiding the scheduler towards easier resource allocation problems first.

Experiments

The aim of the experiments is to show that the declarative scheduling method is not only general but also makes the overall planning efficient vis-a-vis the nature of resources. Implicitly, it also tests if the *master-slave* form of relationship (RealPlan-MS) is effective. We now compare the performance of the approach (as implemented in Graphplan and GP-CSP) to standard Graphplan, when one varies the amount of sharable/ non-sharable resources. I consider the blocks world (robots), the rocket domain (rocket) and the shuttle domain (cranes and shuttles) with varying numbers of resources noted in the parenthesis respectively.

Figure 6 shows the results for the *shuffle* problems with 4, 6, 8 and 10 blocks as the number of robots are varied from 1 to 10. The plots clearly show that planning followed by scheduling (SHUF--PS) is significantly better than original planning in the presence of resources (SHUF--GP). The total time is relatively flat as the number of resources increase in contrast to the performance of Graphplan. Let us consider the 6-block *shuffle* problem in detail.

In RealPlan, the causal reasoning time is constant and the resource reasoning time is dependent on the specific allocation policy (in Table 4) that successfully allocated the resources. For fair comparison, since Graphplan only looks for shorter length of the plan while the serializing allocation policy prefers both shorter length as well as fewer number of actions in the plan, this policy is disabled. The allocation policies are iterated in the following order: class INFRES, class FIX, class SAMELEN and finally class INCRLEN. In the *6-shuffle* case, problems with 5 to 10 robots are solved in class INFRES, problems with 3 and 4 robots are solved in class FIX, and problem with 2 robots is solved in class SAMELEN.

All *k-shuffle* problems with 1 robot can only be solved in class INCRLEN, and are handled straightforwardly, albeit with higher effort (it is reflected by the dip in the plot SHUF--PS after 1 robot case). Note that least commitment on resources makes sense if there are multiple resources so that any resource conflict can be *potentially* overcome during scheduling by assigning different resources to the conflicting actions. In the case of single resource, resource postponement is useless in transferring planning complexity to scheduling and is infact counter-productive, because the planner is banking on concurrency in the plan while resource availability suggests a serial executable plan. This pathological case could have been easily detected and avoided upfront.

Utility of the scheduling classes: The idea of progressively

# Rockets	Normal GP	GP+Sched	GP-CSP+Sched
2	0.13	3.05	0.48
3	0.31	2.97	0.28
4	0.15	2.99	0.31
5	0.23	2.99	0.28
6	0.40	2.96	0.30
7	0.40	2.99	0.29
8	0.55	2.98	0.31

Table 5: Runtime results from experiments in the rocket domain (in cpu sec). GP refers to Graphplan, GP+Sched refers to Graphplan for abstract planning followed by declarative scheduling. In GP-CSP+Sched, the planner is changed to GP-CSP. (Total: 21 problems)

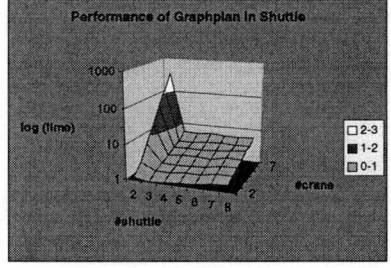

Figure 7: Comparative performance of Graphplan in *shuttle* problems of 2..8 cranes and 2..8 shuttles. (Total: 49 problems)

increasing the domain sizes of variables is very useful in practice. For example, the 10-shuffle problem with 4 robots was solved in 4 sec in class FIX while following the above order, but it took 81 minutes when class INCRLEN was specified upfront.

More results are available in (Srivastava 2000). Let us now investigate the relationship between the nature of resources (sharable v/s non-sharable) and declarative scheduling time. Consider the *rocket* domain where the sharable rocket can be used to transport items between location. Table 5 shows the result of experiments in the *rocket_facts_obj*10 problem in Graphplan distribution where 10 objects have to be moved from one location to another. We see that planning with Graphplan is completed in a fraction of second and it does not change much with the number of sharable resources. On the other hand, the planning time with the new approach is much higher. It turns out that the causal reasoning in the space of abstracted plans takes an average of 2.38 sec (note that causal reasoning is constant for the decoupled approach) while average scheduling time is mere 0.03 sec.

The third column in Table 5 shows the result of using GP-CSP for solving the abstracted planning problem and performing scheduling thereafter. We see that the overall performance is in line with Graphplan confirming that the specific abstracted planning problem is being solved by GP-CSP more efficiently than Graphplan.

The scenario is highlighted if there are non-sharable resources in addition to sharable resources. To study the

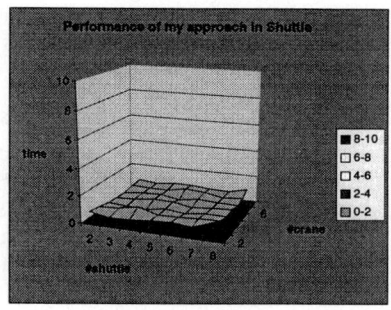

Figure 8: Comparative performance of my approach in *shuttle* problems of 2..8 cranes and 2..8 shuttles (Total: 49 problems).

inter-play between these types of resources, I created a domain called the *shuttle* domain. In this domain, there are sharable shuttles and non-sharable cranes to move boxes between inter-stellar bodies (e.g. Earth and Moon). Problems where the number of both of these resources are varied independently are considered. In Figure 7, we see the performance of Graphplan which degrades sharply with the number of non-sharable cranes and lesser so with the number of sharable shuttles. In Figure 8, the performance of the new approach is shown. We note that run-time is fairly constant and much lesser than Graphplan with varying number of non-sharable cranes and sharable shuttles.

Discussion and related work

Scheduling has been studied widely in Operations Research (OR)(Pinedo 1995) and Artificial Intelligence (AI). In AI, the resource allocation approaches are constraint-based as in systems like OPIS, ISIS and MICRO-BOSS (each summarized in (Zweben & Fox (ed.) 1994)) with very limited action selection choices, if any.

The work on O-Plan (Currie & Tate 1991, pp. 73), has identified the inefficiency of combining resource scheduling with planning (although, to my knowledge, no specific steps were taken to address that inefficiency in the O-Plan work). Among planners that have considered resources, in SIPE(Wilkins 1988), domain-specific operator ordering can be provided by defining what are resource objects in the domain. In IxTeT (Laborie & Ghallab 1995) and HSTS (Muscettola 1994), planning and resource constraints are converted to set of common data-structures and search applied to get a plan. In these systems, planning has been extended to include specification about physical resource usage and this increases expressivity but does not defer flaw resolution. We conjecture that performance degradation with increasing resources will also be seen in these systems.

Work more closer to RealPlan are *parc*Plan (El-Kholy & Richards 1996) and TRP(Cesta & Cristiano 1996) where temporal and resource reasoning is performed after a plan is obtained. In (Liatsos & Richards 1999), planning has been separated into action selection and action sequencing activities, and the latter is expanded to scheduling. In contrast, we consider causal reasoning as planning and resource reasoning as scheduling. Specifically, the causal plan has selected actions along with sequencing information that is independent of resource considerations whereas resource reasoning adds additional sequencing constraints.

Restricted table blocks world from parcPlan[3]: Experiments done in some problems from the restricted table blocks world domain of (Liatsos & Richards 1999) ("arm" is a resource) showed that causal and resource reasoning interact closely here. For smaller problems, e.g. with 4 blocks, 4 table position and 2 arms (b4x4x2), RealPlan-MS performs comparable to Graphplan (in a fraction of seconds). For medium problems, e.g. b6x6x3 and b8x8x4, the performance could suffer if the initial plan is quite parallel because the scheduling cost increases with fewer resources.

These problems are being experimented with RealPlan-PP being studied in (Srivastava, Kambhampati & Do 2000) where the scheduler attempts only cheaper allocation policies and on failure, passes the "failure" explanation back to the planner for re-planning. Initial results show that this approach can solve the medium problems (b6x6x3 and b8x8x4) in drastically less time.

Conclusion

Decoupling of causal and resource reasoning can lead to a big performance edge in planning. To this end, the RealPlan framework allows advances to be made in the two components as well as in planner-scheduler interaction. In this work, I presented a general approach to convert the resource reasoning problem as a declaratively specified DCSP and solved it with a standard CSP solver. The approach is not only more general than previous procedural scheduling methods but also supports intelligent planner-scheduler interaction. In Graphplan and GP-CSP, the *master-slave* relationship (RealPlan-MS) is implemented while in GP-CSP, a truly dependency-directed *peer-peer* relationship (RealPlan-PP) is envisaged. The runtime of RealPlan is much less sensitive to the resource quantity available. Infact, RealPlan-MS admits the paradigm of *plan once and schedule anytime*.

Acknowledgements

I thank Subbarao Kambhampati for his guidance and comments, and BinhMinh Do for discussions on GP-CSP and inter-CSP interactions. I also thank Prof. van Beek for putting the CPLAN planning system and its CSP solvers in public domain, and answering some of my questions. Support for this work comes in part by NSF young investigator award (NYI) IRI-9457634, ARPA/Rome Laboratory planning initiative grant F30602-95-C-0247, Army AASERT grant DAAH04-96-1-0247, AFOSR grant F20602-98-1-0182 and NSF grant IRI-9801676.

References

Beck, J.C., and Fox, M. 1998. A Generic Framework for Constraint-directed Search and Scheduling. *AI Magazine* 19(4).

---

[3] At http://www.icparc.ic.ac.uk/parcPlan/ecp99/index.html.

Blum, A., and Furst, M. 1995. Fast planning through planning graph analysis. *Proc IJCAI-95* 1636–1642.

Cesta, A. and Cristiano, S. 1996. A Time and Resource Problem in Planning Architectures. *Proc. ECP-96*.

Currie, K. and Tate, A. 1991. O-Plan: the open planning architecture. *AI, Vol 52, 49-86*.

Do, B., and Kambhampati, S. 1999. Solving planning graph by compiling it into CSP *To Appear in AIPS 2000*.

El-Kholy, A. and Richards, B. 1996. Temporal and Resource Reasoning in Planning: the *parc*Plan approach. *Proc. ECAI-96*.

S. Kambhampati, M.R. Cutkoksy, J.M. Tenenbaum and S. Lee. Integrating General Purpose Planners and Specialized Reasoners: Case Study of a Hybrid Planning Architecture. *IEEE Trans. on Sys., Man and Cyber., Vol. 23, No. 6, Nov/Dec, 1993*.

Kautz, H., and Selman, B. 1998. BLACKBOX: A New Approach to the Application of Theorem Proving to Problem Solving. *Workshop Planning as Combinatorial Search, AIPS-98, Pittsburgh, PA, 1998*.

Laborie, P., and Ghallab, M. 1995. Planning with sharable resource constraints. *Proc. IJCAI-95*.

Liatsos, V. and Richards, B. 1999. Scaleability in Planning. *Proc. ECP-99*.

Microsoft. 1998. Microsoft Project Version 4.0 User Guide. *Microsoft Press*.

Moder, J. J., and Phillips, C. R. 1964. Project Management with CPM and PERT. *Reinhold Publ., Chapman & Hall Ltd., London*.

Mittal, S., and Falkenhainer, B. 1990. Dynamic Constraint Satisfaction Problems. *Proc. AAAI-90*.

Muscettola, N. 1994. Toward real-world science mission planning. *Proc. AAAI Fall Symposium*.

Pinedo, M. 1995. Scheduling Theory, Algorithms and Systems. *Prentice Hall*.

Srivastava, B. March 2000. Efficient Planning by Effective Resource Reasoning. *Ph.D. Dissertation. Arizona State Univ., USA*.

Srivastava, B., and Kambhampati, S. 1999. Scaling up Planning by teasing out Resource Scheduling *Proc. ECP-99*.

Srivastava, B, Kambhampati, S. and Do, B. 2000. Planning the Project Management Way: Efficient Planning by Effective Integration of Causal and Resource Reasoning. *Technical Report. Arizona State Univ., USA*.

van Beek, P., and Chen, X. 1999 CPlan: A constraint programming approach to planning *Proc. AAAI-99*.

Wolfman, S., and Weld, D. 1999. The LPSAT Engine and its Application to Resource Planning. *Proc. IJCAI-99*.

Wilkins, D. E. 1988. Practical planning: Extending the classical AI planning paradigm. *Morgan Kaufmann Pub., San Mateo, CA*.

Zweben, M., and Fox, M. (ed.). 1994. Intelligent Scheduling. *Morgan Kaufmann Publ., San Mateo, CA*.

Gridworlds as Testbeds for Planning with Incomplete Information

Craig Tovey and **Sven Koenig**
College of Computing, Georgia Institute of Technology
Atlanta, Georgia 30332-0280
{ctovey, skoenig}@cc.gatech.edu

Abstract

Gridworlds are popular testbeds for planning with incomplete information but not much is known about their properties. We study a fundamental planning problem, localization, to investigate whether gridworlds make good testbeds for planning with incomplete information. We find empirically that greedy planning methods that interleave planning and plan execution can localize robots very quickly on random gridworlds or mazes. Thus, they may not provide adequately challenging testbeds. On the other hand, we show that finding localization plans that are within a log factor of optimal is NP-hard. Thus there are instances of gridworlds on which all greedy planning methods perform very poorly, and we show how to construct them. These theoretical results help empirical researchers to select appropriate planning methods for planning with incomplete information as well as testbeds to demonstrate them.

Introduction

Testbeds (prototypical test domains) are planning domains that allow researchers to evaluate their planning methods, communicate performance results of their methods to others, interpret published performance results of others more easily, and compare their methods against these performance results (Hanks, Pollack, & Cohen 1993). Testbeds should be easy to describe, but they should also provide a wide enough variety to mimic real domains. In particular, testbeds must include cases that are not too easy to solve because otherwise planning methods would appear to be more efficient than they actually are in some of the domains of interest. Consequently, planning researchers have studied in detail the properties of their testbeds for planning with complete information, such as blocksworlds and sliding tile puzzles. Examples of such experimental and theoretical studies include (Gupta & Nau 1992; Reinefeld 1993; Slaney & Thiébaux 1996; Koenig & Simmons 1996).

In recent years, planning researchers have become interested in planning with incomplete information. This is an important research direction because, in the real world, complete information is often not available. Gridworlds appear to be by far the most frequently used testbeds for this work. However, not much is known about their properties.

Copyright © 2000, American Association for Artificial Intelligence (www.aaai.org). All rights reserved.

In this paper, we therefore investigate whether gridworlds are good testbeds for planning with incomplete information. We study localization tasks, which are fundamental planning tasks for robots. We find experimentally that greedy planning methods that interleave planning and plan execution can localize robots very quickly on gridworlds with random obstacles or random mazes. Thus, random gridworlds or mazes may not provide adequately challenging cases to push the state of the art. Although the theoretical planning community has shown the complexity of planning tasks with incomplete information to be difficult in general (Littman 1994; Madani, Hanks, & Condon 1999), the reported success of current greedy methods on some gridworlds (Nourbakhsh 1997; Koenig & Simmons 1998a) and our experiments on random gridworlds and mazes reported here suggest that the constrained topology of gridworlds may make them easy to solve. However, we analyze the performance of one greedy planning method in detail, namely the Delayed Planning Architecture (Genesereth & Nourbakhsh 1993), and show that there exist gridworlds on which its performance is poor. Furthermore, we prove that localization even with only suboptimal worst-case performance is NP-hard. Thus there are instances of gridworlds on which *all* greedy planning methods perform very poorly, and we show how they can be constructed. In general, our results improve the understanding of previously used planning methods and testbeds for planning with incomplete information and help empirical researchers to select appropriate planning methods as well as testbeds to demonstrate them.

Gridworlds

We study planning with incomplete information in gridworlds of the kind shown in Figure 1. Gridworlds are finite rectangular areas of square cells. Each cell can be either traversable or untraversable. A robot is always in exactly one cell. It starts in a traversable cell and can then always move north, east, south, or west. Gridworlds have been used as testbeds for different planning methods. Planning tasks with a known start cell and deterministic movement have often been modeled as traditional graph search problems. Planning tasks with nondeterministic movement and automatic sensing that determines the current cell uniquely have been modeled as totally observable Markov decision process models (Dean *et al.* 1993). Planning tasks with

Figure 1: Simple Gridworld

incompletely known start cell or nondeterministic movement, and nondeterministic sensing or sensing on demand have been modeled as partially observable Markov decision process models (McCallum 1995; Hansen 1997). Planning tasks with incompletely known start cell, deterministic movement, and automatic deterministic sensing have been modeled as AND-OR search tasks (Nourbakhsh 1997; Koenig & Simmons 1998a). In this paper, we present a first analysis of the last case.

The Gridworld Planning Tasks

We study localization tasks in gridworlds. Localization is a prototypical planning task with incomplete information. The robot knows a map of the gridworld but does not know its start cell. Evidently, the robot may need to localize prior to performing many other tasks. The sensors on-board the robot tell it in every cell whether the cells immediately adjacent to it in the four compass directions (north, east, south, west) are traversable. (The border of the gridworld is untraversable and observed as such.) The robot can then move one cell to the north, east, south, or west, unless that cell is outside of the gridworld or untraversable (in which case the robot remains in its current cell). We assume that there is no uncertainty in actuation and sensing and that the robot always knows its orientation from the on-board compass. These assumptions are simplifying but sufficiently close to reality to enable one to use the resulting planning methods on real robots (Nourbakhsh 1996).

The robot is localized if it knows its current cell. A deterministic (randomized) localization plan specifies (a probability distribution for) the movement to execute based on all previous movements and observations. A localization plan is valid iff, no matter which cell the robot is started in, it eventually prints out its current cell or correctly determines that localization is impossible. The objective of planning then is to determine a valid deterministic or randomized localization plan that minimizes the expected number of movements for the worst possible start cell (the "worst-case expected performance"), in the following sense: We first calculate the expected number of movements for each possible start cell. The expectation is only important for probabilistic plans and is taken with respect to the randomization of the probabilistic plans. The worst-case expected performance is then the maximum of these values.

Modeling the Planning Tasks

The gridworld planning tasks can be modeled as tree search tasks. The states of the tree search tasks are sets of cells, corresponding to cells that the robot could be in. For example, if the robot has no knowledge of its start cell for the gridworld

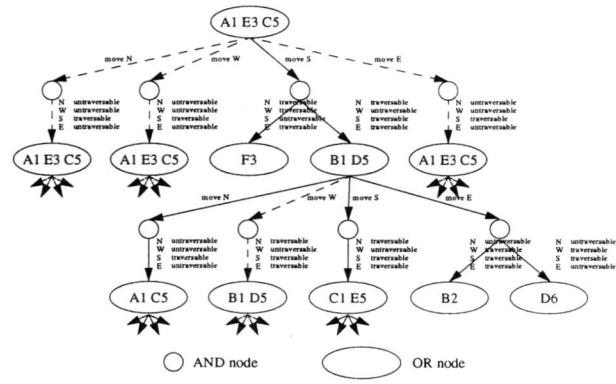

Figure 2: AND-OR Search Tree

planning task from Figure 1 but observes untraversable cells in all compass directions except to its south, then the start state of the robot contains three possible start cells: A1, E3, and C5. In each state, the robot can choose a movement ("OR" nodes of the search tree) and, if it does not stop, then makes a new observation ("AND" nodes of the search tree). For example, Figure 2 shows the beginning of a search tree for the gridworld planning task. (The dashed part of the tree is unnecessary and could be deleted.) A deterministic localization plan assigns each OR node a movement ("deterministic OR node"). Similarly, a randomized localization plan assigns each OR node a probability distribution over the movements ("randomized OR node"). The following theorem shows that valid randomized localization plans cannot perform better than valid deterministic localization plans.

Theorem 1 *No valid randomized localization plan has a better worst-case expected performance than a valid deterministic localization plan with optimal worst-case performance.*

Proof Sketch: Given a valid randomized localization plan, transform it into a valid deterministic localization plan by iteratively pruning all but the best alternative, in the worst-case sense, from the lowest nondeterministic node. ∎

This theorem implies that there is no point in having robots flip coins (that is, move nondeterministically) to localize them in gridworlds with optimal worst-case (expected) performance. In the following, we therefore consider only deterministic localization plans. The tree search tasks in this case are AND-OR search tasks and valid localization plans are decision trees.

Solving the Planning Tasks Greedily

Nourbakhsh and Genesereth noticed experimentally that using a complete AND-OR search to find valid localization plans with optimal worst-case performance for gridworld planning tasks was completely infeasible but that planning methods that interleave planning and plan execution could efficiently find valid localization plans with good worst-case performance for their gridworlds (Genesereth & Nourbakhsh 1993; Nourbakhsh 1997). Their Delayed Planning

Table 1: Random Gridworlds

gridworld size	obstacle density	av. number of subplans	av. number of steps per subplan	av. total number of steps
11 × 11	9.9 %	3.1	1.0	3.2
	29.8 %	1.7	1.0	1.8
	49.6 %	1.2	1.1	1.3
	70.2 %	0.6	1.0	0.7
	90.1 %	0.0	1.0	0.0
31 × 31	10.0 %	5.7	1.1	6.1
	30.0 %	3.0	1.0	3.2
	50.0 %	2.3	1.1	2.5
	70.0 %	1.3	1.1	1.5
	90.0 %	0.3	1.0	0.3
51 × 51	10.0 %	7.2	1.1	7.5
	30.0 %	3.7	1.0	3.9
	50.0 %	2.8	1.1	3.1
	70.0 %	1.6	1.2	1.1
	90.0 %	0.3	1.0	0.3

Table 2: Acyclic Mazes

gridworld size	obstacle density	av. number of subplans	av. number of steps per subplan	av. total number of steps
11 × 11	41.3 %	2.4	1.5	3.6
21 × 21	45.4 %	3.3	1.7	5.4
31 × 31	46.8 %	3.8	1.7	6.6
41 × 41	47.6 %	4.1	1.8	7.5
51 × 51	48.1 %	4.5	1.8	8.0
61 × 61	48.4 %	4.7	1.8	8.6
71 × 71	48.6 %	4.9	1.9	9.1

Architecture with the viable plan heuristic uses breadth-first search (iterative deepening) in the deterministic part of the state space around the current state in conjunction with pruning rules to find a subplan (movement sequence) that reduces the number of possible robot cells with the smallest number of steps (movements). The robot executes the subplan and then repeats the process until it is localized or detects that localization is impossible. Subsequently, Koenig and Simmons developed a generalization of the Delayed Planning Architecture (Koenig & Simmons 1998a). The Delayed Planning Architecture has been applied to a variety of planning problems with incomplete information, including the Bay Area Transit Problem (Hsu 1990) and the Tool Box Problem (Olawsky, Krebsbach, & Gini 1993). In the context of gridworlds, it has been demonstrated experimentally by their authors on real robots and in simulation.

We re-implemented the Delayed Planning Architecture and performed experiments in gridworlds with random obstacles, averaged over 1000 runs with randomly selected start cells. The results in Table 1 show that current planning methods perform very well on random gridworlds. No matter what the size or obstacle density of the gridworld is, the robot can gain information with only slightly more than one move on average, and localizes in a small number of total moves. Table 2 shows that similar results also hold for random acyclic mazes that were generated by depth-first search (using code provided by Joseph Pemberton). Therefore, we need new gridworlds to push the state of the art. Furthermore, the following theorem shows that the worst-case performance of the Delayed Planning Architecture can be extremely suboptimal, much worse than the experimental results in random gridworlds and mazes suggest. All of our example gridworlds are connected and not completely symmetrical (localization is possible). This demonstrates that our lower bounds already hold for these kinds of gridworlds.

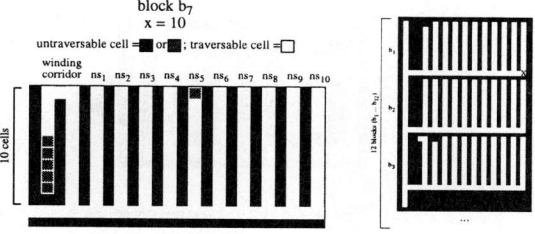

Figure 3: Greedy Performance

Theorem 2 *The worst-case performance of plans generated by the Delayed Planning Architecture can be a factor of $\Omega(\sqrt[3]{s})$ worse than the optimal worst-case performance, where s is the number of cells of the gridworld, even in gridworlds that are connected (every cell can be reached from every other cell).*

Proof Sketch: We construct a gridworld on which the Delayed Planning Architecture has the worst-case performance ratio claimed in the theorem. The gridworld contains many copies of rectangular "blocks" of size $(2x+4) \times (x+2)$. Along the south side of each block is a wall of length $2x+4$ and immediately to the north of the wall is an east-west corridor of length $2x+4$. There are x north-south corridors $ns_1 \ldots ns_x$ of length x each, separated by walls, that branch off of the east-west corridor to the north, starting in the sixth column of the block. To their immediate left is a winding corridor that goes up x cells, goes left two cells, and then goes down $x-2$ cells. Figure 3 (left) shows an example. The gridworld consists of a column of $x+2$ blocks, from block b_1 on top to block b_{x+2} at the bottom. In the extreme west, we add a full length north-south hallway, which makes the gridworld connected. Figure 3 (right) shows an example. We make the last cell of north-south corridor ns_{x-i} of block b_{x+2-i} untraversable, for all $0 \leq i \leq x-1$. We also make the last i cells of the winding corridor of block b_{x+2-i} untraversable, for all $0 \leq i \leq x+1$. This completes the description of how the gridworld is constructed. Clearly, the gridworld is connected and has $s = (2x+5)(x+2)(x+2) = \Theta(x^3)$ cells (which does not include the untraversable border of the gridworld).

The robot can find the beginning of some winding corridor from any starting point with at most $3x+2$ movements and then move at most $2x-1$ into the winding corridor, counting its length, which identifies the block and thus localizes the robot. Thus, the worst-case number of movements in an optimal plan is at most $5x+1 = \Theta(x)$. Now we show that the Delayed Planning Architecture performs many more than $\Theta(x)$ movements if the robot starts at the east end of the east-west corridor of block b_1 (in the figure: marked X). When the robot is started, it knows where it is with the exception of which block it is in. The robot makes $x-1$ movements into north-south corridor ns_x because this is the fastest way of reducing the number of possible robot cells. At this point the robot can eliminate block b_{x+2}. The robot then returns to the east-west corridor and makes $x-1$ movements into north-south corridor ns_{x-1}, at which point it can eliminate block b_{x+1}, and so on. Finally, it makes $x-1$ movements into the winding corridor, at which point it can eliminate block b_2 and has localized. The robot has made a total number of movements equal to $2x^2 + x - 1 = \Theta(x^2)$.

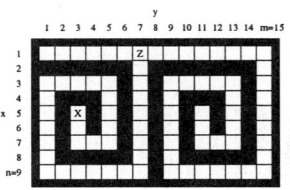

Figure 4: Two Spirals

It follows that the worst-case performance of plans generated by the Delayed Planning Architecture is $\Omega(x^2/x) = \Omega(x) = \Omega(\sqrt[3]{s})$ worse than the worst-case performance of an optimum plan. ∎

Analysis of the Planning Tasks

The Delayed Planning Architecture can be applied to finding homing sequences or adaptive homing sequences for deterministic finite state automata whose states are colored, a concept from theoretical computer science. A homing sequence is a linear plan (movement sequence) with the property that the state colors observed during its execution uniquely determine the resulting state (Kohavi 1978), and it is known that finding a shortest homing sequence is NP-hard in general (Schapire 1992). It could be the case that the constrained topology of gridworlds makes them easy to solve and thus that valid localization plans with optimal worst-case performance for the gridworld planning tasks can be found in polynomial time. We prove, however, that finding valid localization plans even with suboptimal worst-case performance in gridworlds is NP-hard and thus that there are instances of gridworlds on which the Delayed Planning Architecture does not perform well. The following theorem shows that it is easy to find valid localization plans in gridworlds.

Theorem 3 *(Part 1:) For every gridworld of size $m \times n$, there exists a valid localization plan that executes $O(mn)$ movements and that can be found in time $O(mn)$. (Part 2:) This result is the best possible in the sense that there exist gridworlds of size $m \times n$ in which every valid localization plan must execute $\Omega(mn)$ movements and can only be found in time $\Omega(mn)$, even in gridworlds that are connected.*

Proof Sketch: For Part 1, first determine the connected components M_i of the given map of the gridworld. Second, acquire a map M' of the gridworld component where the robot is, by moving the robot in a depth-first search manner. Third, determine which of the M_i are identical to map M', by depth-first search of every map, starting from the west-most cell of the north-most traversable cells. If exactly one M_i matches M', the robot has been localized. If more than one M_i matches M' then the robot cannot localize. This algorithm is correct, needs time $O(mn)$, and executes $O(mn)$ movements. For Part 2, construct a gridworld consisting of two spirals as shown in Figure 4. The gridworld is connected. If the start cell is at the end of one of the spirals (in the figure: X), then any valid localization plan has to execute $\Omega(mn)$ movements (in the figure: move to cell Z) before it can distinguish which spiral it is in. Thus, every valid localization plan must execute $\Omega(mn)$ movements and can only be found in time $\Omega(mn)$. ∎

Theorem 3 leaves open the possibility that optimum localization plans may be so complex that they cannot be encoded in polynomial length. Fortunately, the following theorem shows that finding valid localization plans with optimal worst-case performance is in NP.

Theorem 4 *Determining whether there exists a valid localization plan that executes no more movements than a given value is in NP.*

Proof Sketch: First, use the method from Theorem 3 to find the start cells from which the robot cannot localize. Second, guess a deterministic localization plan (decision tree). Third, simulate a fictitious robot that executes the localization plan on the map of the gridworld from each possible start cell, verifying that the number of movements is smaller than the given value, and that the localization plan yields a correct answer, when it is possible to localize. Therefore, a decision tree can be guessed and verified in polynomial time, *provided that the decision tree has polynomial size*. We now ensure this provision to complete the proof. The algorithm needs to guess only decision trees that have as many leaf nodes as there are possible start cells, that is, no more than mn. This is so because there is at most one branch from the root to a leaf for each start cell. Since there are at most mn leaves, there are at most $mn - 1$ AND nodes with two or more children. The algorithm needs to guess only decision trees that have, on any branch, at most $mn - 1$ AND nodes with only one child between two AND nodes with two or more children. If there were more, then a belief state would repeat on that branch and the part of the branch between two repeating belief states (including one of them) could be cut out. Thus, the decision tree has $O(m^2n^2)$ AND nodes and thus $O(m^2n^2)$ nodes, which is at most quadratic in the size of the problem description. ∎

The following theorem, our main theorem, shows that finding valid localization plans even with suboptimal worst-case performance is NP-hard.

Theorem 5 *It is NP-hard to find a valid localization plan in gridworlds of size $m \times n$ whose worst-case performance is within a factor $O(\log(mn))$ of optimum, even in gridworlds that are connected.*

Proof Sketch: An instance of set cover consists of a base set $S = \{e_1 \ldots e_x\}$ and a collection of sets $S_1, \ldots, S_y \subseteq S$. A set cover is a collection of these sets whose union is S, and the objective is to find a set cover of small cardinality. Finding a set cover whose cardinality is within a factor $O(\log x)$ of minimum is NP-hard (Lund & Yannakakis 1994). Let $y^* \leq x$ denote the cardinality of a minimum set cover for the given instance of the set cover problem. We reduce this problem to finding a valid localization plan in a gridworld of size $m \times n$ with $m = 3x^3y + 1$ and $n = (xy+2)(x+1)$ whose worst-case performance is within a factor $O(\log(mn))$ of optimal. We assume without loss of generality that $\log y = O(\log x)$.

We now explain how the gridworld is constructed from the given instance of the set cover problem. The gridworld contains many copies of rectangular "blocks" of size $(3y) \times (xy + 2)$. Along the south side of each block is a wall of length $3y$ and immediately to the north of the wall is an east-west corridor of length $3y$. There are y north-south corridors $ns_1 \ldots ns_y$ of length xy each, separated by walls, that branch off of the east-west corridor to the north, starting in the second column of the block. Figure 5 shows an example. The gridworld contains an array of $(x^3) \times (x+1)$ blocks. Thus,

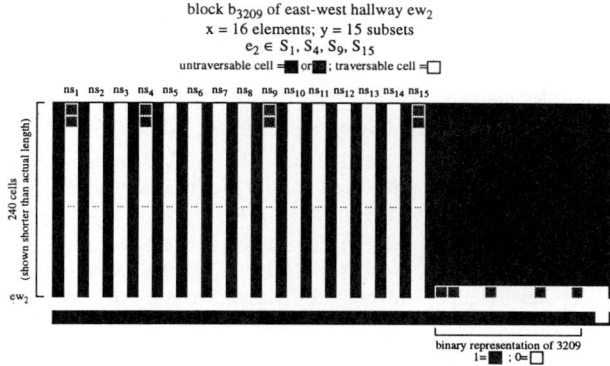

Figure 5: Block for NP-Completeness Proof

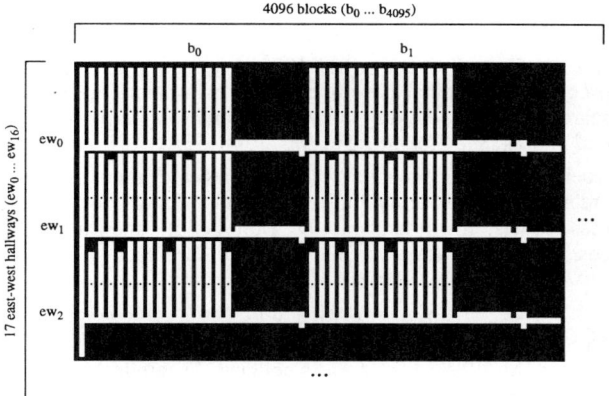

Figure 6: Gridworld for NP-Completeness Proof

Table 3: Gridworlds used to Prove Theorem 2

gridworld size	obstacle density	av. number of subplans		av. number of steps per subplan		av. total number of steps	
11 × 25	50.2 %	4.5	(4)	2.3	(5)	10.2	(20)
13 × 36	50.2 %	5.9	(5)	2.9	(7)	16.9	(35)
15 × 49	50.2 %	7.4	(6)	3.2	(9)	23.7	(54)
17 × 64	50.2 %	8.9	(7)	3.4	(11)	30.6	(77)
19 × 81	50.2 %	10.4	(8)	4.0	(13)	42.0	(104)
21 × 100	50.1 %	11.5	(9)	4.4	(15)	50.0	(135)
23 × 121	50.1 %	13.4	(10)	4.5	(17)	60.4	(170)
25 × 144	50.1 %	14.4	(11)	4.9	(19)	71.1	(209)
27 × 169	50.1 %	16.0	(12)	5.2	(21)	82.5	(252)
29 × 196	50.1 %	18.0	(13)	5.4	(23)	98.0	(299)
31 × 225	50.1 %	19.4	(14)	5.7	(25)	110.5	(350)
33 × 256	50.1 %	20.8	(15)	5.8	(27)	121.5	(405)
35 × 289	50.1 %	22.5	(16)	6.1	(29)	137.7	(464)

there are x^3 blocks $b_0 \ldots b_{x^3-1}$ in the same row. Their east-west corridors form one long east-west hallway. There are $x + 1$ east-west hallways $ew_0 \ldots ew_x$ of length $3x^3y$ each. In the extreme west, we add a full length north-south hallway, which makes the gridworld connected. Figure 6 shows an example. We make the last i cells of north-south corridor ns_j of each block in east-west hallway ew_i untraversable iff $e_i \in S_j$. (Since there is no element e_0, no north-south corridor of any block in east-west hallway ew_0 is shortened.) To be able to distinguish between the blocks in the same east-west hallway, we put a "signature" at the east end of each block. For block b_k, this signature encodes k in binary form, which needs at most $3 \log x$ bits. The signature is in the form of northerly "alcoves," followed by a southerly alcove which marks the beginning of the signature. This completes the description of how the gridworld is constructed in polynomial time.

We now calculate an upper bound z^U on the number of movements of a valid localization plan with optimal worst-case performance. Consider the following localization plan: If only north is unblocked, move north one place (since the robot was in a southerly alcove). Otherwise, move south until the robot sees an opening to the west or east (the robot is now in an east-west hallway), then move east to the end of a signature or until the robot gets blocked (the robot is now directly east of a signature). Move west and read the signature. At this point, the robot knows where it is with the exception of which east-west hallway it is in. The robot then moves west and, every time it encounters one of the y^* north-south corridors in the current block that corresponds to a smallest set cover for the given instance of the set cover problem, it moves to the end of the north-south corridor and back to the east-west hallway. If the robot is in east-west hallway ew_j with $j > 0$ then it will visit at least one north-south corridor that is shorter than xy. Its length uniquely identifies the east-west hallway the robot is in, which localizes the robot. Otherwise the robot must be in east-west hallway ew_0 and is localized as well. Thus, the localization plan is valid. An easy calculation shows that the total number of movements is bounded by $z^U \leq 2y^*xy + 6y \leq 3y^*xy$.

It remains to be shown that a solution to the localization problem implies a solution to the set cover problem. Assume that we have found a valid localization plan whose performance is within a factor $O(\log(mn))$ of optimal. An upper bound on the number of movements of this localization plan is $O(\log(mn))z^U = O(\log((3x^3y+1)(xy+2)(x+1)))3y^*xy = O(\log(x^5y^2))3y^*xy = O(5\log(x) + 2\log(y))3y^*xy = O(7\log(x))3y^*xy = O(\log(x))3y^*xy \leq x3y^*xy \leq 3x^3y$. Thus, the number of movements is no larger than the length of an east-west hallway. Now assume that the robot starts at the east end of east-west hallway ew_0. Thus, it cannot visit a different east-west hallway and, as part of the localization, must determine that no north-south corridor in a block is shorter than xy. If the robot moves into a north-south corridor less than $xy - 1$, it cannot detect whether the corridor is shorter than xy because all north-south corridors are at least $xy - x$ long. Thus, consider all north-south corridors that the robot moves into at least $xy - x - 1$. The collection of subsets that these corridors correspond to must be a set cover, for otherwise the robot could not distinguish between the east-west hallways ew_0 and ew_i for the elements e_i not covered by the collection of subsets. Let y' denote the cardinality of this set cover. To determine how close to minimum the set cover is, we determine a lower bound on the total number of movements of the robot. A straightforward calculation shows that the robot makes at least $(2y'-1)(xy-x-1)$ moves. Combined with the $O(\log(x))3y^*xy$ upper bound shown earlier, this implies that $y' = O(\log(x))y^*$, which implies that the set cover is within a factor $O(\log(x))$ of minimum. ∎

To summarize, Theorem 3 shows that is easy to find valid plans in gridworlds, while Theorems 4 and 5 together show that it is NP-hard to find valid localization plans with optimal or even near-optimal worst-case performance. Combining Theorems 4 and 5 also tells us that the problem stated in Theorem 4 is NP-complete.

Testbeds

As part of the theoretical results in the previous two sections we constructed hard instances of gridworlds on which greedy planning methods, such as the Delayed Planning Architecture, do not perform well. These gridworlds can be used in test suites in addition to random gridworlds or mazes. Table 3 contains the results of the same experiments that Table 1 reported on, except that we now use the Delayed Planning Architecture in conjunction with the gridworlds that we constructed as part of the proof of Theorem 2 instead of random gridworlds. (The numbers in parentheses refer to the particularly bad case used in the proof, where the robot starts at the east end of the east-west corridor of the top-most block.) Clearly, the robot now needs to execute a larger number of movements to reduce the number of possible cells than in random gridworlds or mazes, and the total number of movements is larger than for random gridworlds or mazes of comparable sizes and obstacle densities as well. Similarly, the gridworlds that we constructed as part of the proof of Theorem 5 also provide challenging testbeds.

Conclusions

While testbeds for planning with complete information have been studied extensively, this paper provides a first study of testbeds for planning with incomplete information. We studied localization tasks in gridworlds. Previous experimental work had shown that greedy planning methods, such as the Delayed Planning Architecture (Genesereth & Nourbakhsh 1993; Nourbakhsh 1997), can efficiently find valid localization plans with good performance in random gridworlds and mazes. Our theoretical analysis showed that it is easy to find valid localization plans in arbitrary gridworlds but, perhaps surprisingly, NP-hard to find valid localization plans even with only suboptimal worst-case performance in some gridworlds, even if the gridworlds are connected. This suggests that gridworlds are appropriate testbeds for planning with incomplete information. As part of our proofs, we also showed how to construct hard instances of gridworlds on which the Delayed Planning Architecture and all other greedy planning methods do not perform well at all. These gridworlds can be used in addition to random gridworlds and mazes. In the future, we intend to apply similar ideas to localization tasks where the robots use partially observable Markov decision process models (Koenig & Simmons 1998b).

Acknowledgments

The Intelligent Decision-Making Group is supported by an NSF Career Award under contract IIS-9984827 to Sven Koenig and DARPA's Mobile Autonomous Robot Software (MARS) Program under contract DARPA/SMDC DASG60-99-C-0081.

References

Dean, T.; Kaelbling, L.; Kirman, J.; and Nicholson, A. 1993. Planning with deadlines in stochastic domains. In *Proceedings of the National Conference on Artificial Intelligence*, 574–579.

Genesereth, M., and Nourbakhsh, I. 1993. Time-saving tips for problem solving with incomplete information. In *Proceedings of the National Conference on Artificial Intelligence*, 724–730.

Gupta, N., and Nau, D. 1992. On the complexity of blocks-world planning. *Artificial Intelligence* 56(2–3):223–254.

Hanks, S.; Pollack, M.; and Cohen, P. 1993. Benchmarks, test beds, controlled experimentation, and the design of agent architectures. *AI Magazine* 14(4):17–42.

Hansen, E. 1997. Markov decision processes with observation costs. Technical Report CMPSCI 97-01, Department of Computer Science, University of Massachusetts, Amherst (Massachusetts).

Hsu, J. 1990. Partial planning with incomplete information. In *Proceedings of the AAAI Spring Symposium on Planning in Uncertain, Unpredictable, or Changing Environments*.

Koenig, S., and Simmons, R. 1996. Easy and hard testbeds for real-time search algorithms. In *Proceedings of the National Conference on Artificial Intelligence*, 279–285.

Koenig, S., and Simmons, R. 1998a. Solving robot navigation problems with initial pose uncertainty using real-time heuristic search. In *Proceedings of the International Conference on Artificial Intelligence Planning Systems*, 154–153.

Koenig, S., and Simmons, R. 1998b. Xavier: A robot navigation architecture based on partially observable Markov decision process models. In Kortenkamp, D.; Bonasso, R.; and Murphy, R., eds., *Artificial Intelligence Based Mobile Robotics: Case Studies of Successful Robot Systems*. MIT Press. 91–122.

Kohavi, Z. 1978. *Switching and Finite Automata Theory*. McGraw-Hill, second edition.

Littman, M. 1994. Memoryless policies: Theoretical limitations and practical results. In *From Animals to Animats 3: Proceedings of the Third International Conference on Simulation of Adaptive Behavior*.

Lund, C., and Yannakakis, M. 1994. On the hardness of approximating minimization problems. *Journal of the ACM* 41:960–981.

Madani, O.; Hanks, S.; and Condon, A. 1999. On the undecidability of probabilistic planning and infinite-horizon partially observable Markov decision problems. In *Proceedings of the National Conference on Artificial Intelligence*, 541–548.

McCallum, R. 1995. Instance-based utile distinctions for reinforcement learning with hidden state. In *Proceedings of the International Conference on Machine Learning*, 387–395.

Nourbakhsh, I. 1996. *Robot Information Packet*. Distributed at the AAAI-96 Spring Symposium on Planning with Infomplete Information for Robot Problems.

Nourbakhsh, I. 1997. *Interleaving Planning and Execution for Autonomous Robots*. Kluwer Academic Publishers.

Olawsky, D.; Krebsbach, K.; and Gini, M. 1993. An analysis of sensor-based task planning. Technical Report 93-94, Computer Science Department, University of Minnesota, Minneapolis (Minnesota).

Reinefeld, A. 1993. Complete solution of the eight-puzzle and the benefit of node ordering in IDA*. In *Proceedings of the International Joint Conference on Artificial Intelligence*, 248–253.

Schapire, R. 1992. *The Design and Analysis of Efficient Learning Algorithms*. MIT Press.

Slaney, J., and Thiébaux, S. 1996. Linear-time near-optimal planning in the blocks world. In *Proceedings of the National Conference on Artificial Intelligence Planning*.

Robotics

Performance Comparison of Landmark Recognition Systems for Navigating Mobile Robots

Tom Duckett
Dept. of Technology
University of Örebro
S-70182 Örebro
Sweden
Tom.Duckett@aass.oru.se

Ulrich Nehmzow
Dept. of Computer Science
University of Manchester
Manchester M13 9PL
England
ulrich@cs.man.ac.uk

Abstract

Self-localisation is an essential competence for mobile robot navigation. Due to the fundamental unreliability of dead reckoning, a robot must depend on its perception of external environmental features or landmarks to localise itself. A key question is how to evaluate landmark recognition systems for mobile robots. This paper answers this question by means of quantitative performance measures. An empirical study is presented in which a number of algorithms are compared in four environments. The results of this analysis are then applied to the development of a novel landmark recognition system for a Nomad 200 robot. Subsequent experiments demonstrate that the new system obtains a similar level of performance to the best alternative method, but at a much lower computational cost.

Introduction

The most important requirement for robot navigation — other than staying operational and avoiding collisions — is that of establishing one's own position (*self-localisation*). One possible self-localisation method is by dead reckoning using the robot's odometry. However, major problems with odometry include drift errors caused by wheel slippage and the need for *a priori* knowledge of the robot's position. A solution to both these problems is to use perception of external environmental features (*landmarks*).

The primary motivation for the work presented here was to develop a robust landmark recognition system for a mobile robot navigating over large, real world environments. This goal was achieved by conducting an experimental comparison of existing systems for landmark recognition, based on quantitative performance measures, and then using the results of this analysis to develop a novel landmark recognition system.

The performance criterion applied is *localisation quality versus computational cost*. Experiments are presented in which the self-localisation performance of a Nomad 200 robot equipped with ultrasonic range-finder sensors and a compass (see Fig. 1) is assessed while traversing a series of environments, using each of the different landmark recognition systems under investigation. The new landmark recognition system is shown to obtain a similar level of localisation quality to the best alternative method, but at a significantly reduced computational cost.

Related Work

So far, relatively few attempts have been made to quantify robot-environment interactions or to conduct experimental comparisons of navigating robots. Exceptions include (Schöner & Dose 1992; Smithers 1995), where fundamental sensor-motor behaviors were analysed in terms of dynamical systems theory; (Lee & Reece 1994), where exploration strategies for mapping unfamiliar environments were evaluated; and (Gutmann *et al.* 1998; Thrun 1998), where various algorithms for self-localisation were compared.

Performance Measurement

The experiments were conducted using played-back sensor data recorded by the robot using wall-following. In each environment, the data from the robot's first lap of the environment was used for landmark learning ("map building"), and the data from the subsequent laps was used for testing ("localisation").

Localisation quality was measured using a statistic known as the *uncertainty coefficient*, U, of L given R, which measures the extent to which the robot's response, R (the response of the particular landmark recognition system under investigation to a perceptual stimulus) predicts the robot's true location, L, and is defined by

$$U(L \mid R) = \frac{H(L) - H(L \mid R)}{H(L)},$$
$$H(L) = -\sum_j p_{\bullet j} \ln p_{\bullet j},$$
$$H(L \mid R) = -\sum_{i,j} p_{ij} \ln \frac{p_{ij}}{p_{i\bullet}},$$

where $p_{\bullet j} = \sum_i p_{ij}$, $p_{i\bullet} = \sum_j p_{ij}$, and p_{ij} refers to the probability that the response is i and the true location

Copyright © 2000, American Association for Artificial Intelligence (www.aaai.org). All rights reserved.

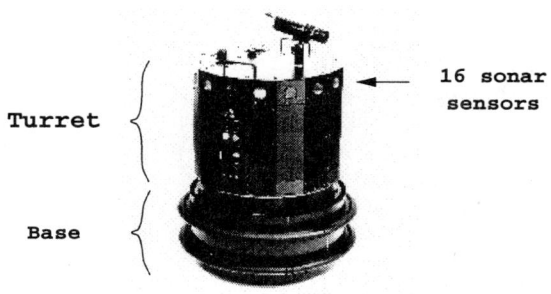

Figure 1: Nomad 200 mobile robot. A flux gate compass was used to keep the turret, and therefore the sensors, at a constant orientation during data collection.

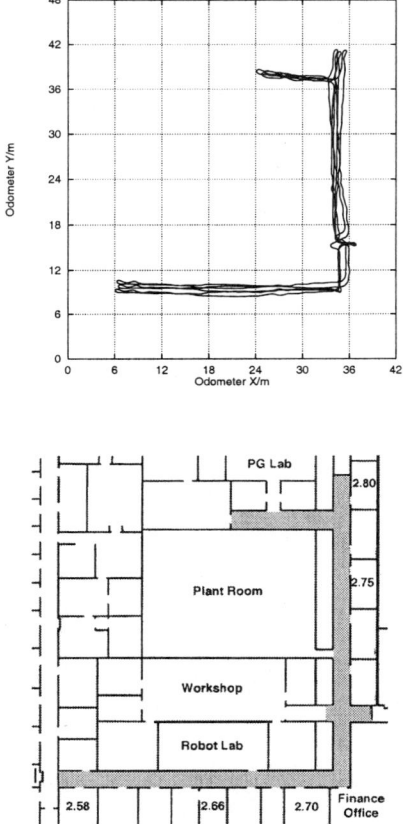

Figure 2: Top: location binning mechanism. Bottom: corresponding floor plan (environment C in Table 1). The dotted grid was used to coarse-code the corrected location data into bins of size 6 m × 6 m — for performance measurement, the current bin was taken as the robot's "true" location L.

is j (Press et al. 1992). A value of $U = 1$ implies that the robot's response always predicts its true location (perfect localisation), while $U = 0$ implies that the response never predicts the true location. The higher the value of U, the better the performance of the system.

To calculate U, some means of tracking the true location L of the robot is required. In initial experiments, the robot's position was measured by hand, but this process was costly and prone to human error. A mechanism for location tracking was therefore developed which is based on retrospectively corrected odometer data. Here, a flux gate compass was used to remove the rotational error affecting the robot's on-line dead reckoning, then the remaining translational drift error was removed by hand (through manual identification of prominent features in the trajectory). The corrected odometer data was coarse-coded into bins, as shown in Fig. 2; see also (Duckett & Nehmzow 1998).

The compass was also used to keep the robot's sensors at a constant orientation, so that the appearance of locations depended only on the robot's position, not the direction of travel.

Landmark Recognition Systems

Robot navigation is possible using artificial landmarks such as beacons, markers or induction loops. However, modifying the robot's environment is costly and inflexible. It is therefore desirable to use "natural" landmarks, i.e., the sensory perceptions a robot obtains in an unmodified environment.

One possible approach is to provide the robot with *a priori* designer-determined landmarks such as doors or ceiling lights. However, this approach can be brittle, due to the different perception of an environment by the designer from that of the robot, and can only be used in environments which contain these features. Instead, we concentrate on landmark recognition systems in which the robot is able to represent its own, *arbitrary* sensor patterns and to exploit whatever features are naturally present in an environment.

RCE Classifier

The first approach considered was the simple classifier mechanism used by (Kurz 1996), in which the robot's sensor patterns are classified according to the nearest neighbour among a set of stored prototypes (see Fig. 3). Each pattern consists of a normalised vector of sonar readings, and the dot product is used to compare vectors. During training, a new pattern is created if the input pattern fails to lie within a fixed sphere of any existing pattern.

ART2 Classifier

Several authors (Racz & Dubrawski 1995; Balkenius & Kopp 1996) have used neural networks based on Adaptive Resonance Theory (Carpenter & Grossberg 1987) for self-localisation. The principal difference between ART and feedforward classifiers such as RCE is the addition of a feedback phase, in which the best matching

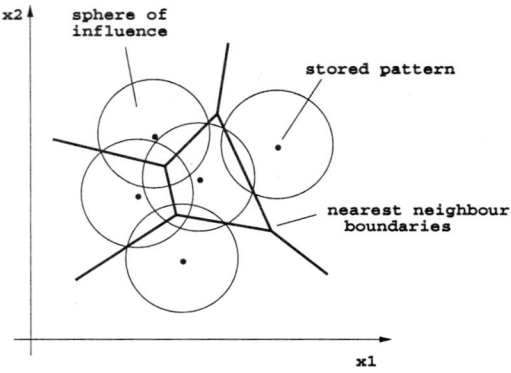

Figure 3: RCE classifier (example in 2 dimensions). The sensory input is classified according to the nearest stored pattern — for performance measurement, the winning pattern was taken as the robot's response R.

unit in the feedforward phase may be rejected and the system searches for another prototype to match the input pattern. This mechanism is used to implement the *self-scaling property*, which prevents any pattern that is a subset of another from being classified in the same category. During training, a new pattern is created if none of the stored patterns is similar enough to the input, otherwise the winning unit is modified to be more similar to the input pattern.

Growing Cell Structures

A number of authors (Nehmzow & Smithers 1991; Kurz 1996; Janet & others 1995) have considered mobile robot localisation using the Self-Organising Map (Kohonen 1993), a neural network which preserves topological relations in its training data. However, both the structure and size of the Kohonen network have to be fixed in advance by the designer, which means that the system cannot be used to map environments whose size is not known *a priori*. To overcome this problem, Fritzke (1994) developed a growing self-organising network which can store an arbitrary number of patterns. Like the Kohonen network, the neighbouring patterns of the best matching unit are adapted during training. In addition, a new pattern is inserted at regular intervals into the most adapted region of the network; see (Fritzke 1994) for full details.

Nearest Neighbour Classifier

This is the landmark recognition mechanism used by (Duckett & Nehmzow 1998). The version used in these experiments was identical to the RCE classifier described above, except that it uses *a priori* position information (from the retrospectively corrected odometry in these experiments, as in Fig. 2) to decide when to add new patterns to the robot's map. In these experiments, new sensor patterns were added to the map at 1.5 m intervals.

Occupancy Grid Matching

Another method for landmark recognition is by matching local occupancy grids (Yamauchi & Langley 1997), where the robot's map consists of a set of stored occupancy grids, one for each place visited by the robot. During localisation, a recognition grid is constructed from the robot's immediate sensor readings and then matched against each of the stored grids. A hill climbing procedure is used to search the space of possible translations[1] between the recognition and stored grids, using an evaluation function to determine the quality of the match. The best matching grid pattern determines the location of the robot. In these experiments, grid patterns were added to the robot's map at 1.5 m intervals, as for the nearest neighbour classifier.

New System: Occupancy Histogram Matching

The main disadvantage of occupancy grid matching its high computational requirements. Here we describe a new landmark recognition system, which introduces a much faster method of matching local occupancy grids.

Again, the robot's map consists of a list of places added at 1.5 m intervals. Landmark information is attached to each of the places as follows. Firstly, the robot takes a detailed sonar scan at its current location and a local occupancy grid consisting of 64×64 cells is constructed, as in (Yamauchi & Langley 1997). However, in the new system, the occupancy grids themselves are not stored or matched. Instead, each grid is reduced to a pair of histograms (one in x direction, and one in y direction), which is then used as a stored signature for that place in the robot's map, as shown in Fig. 4. In the absence of a compass, we would also have to consider angle histograms, as in (Hinkel & Knieriemen 1988).

Each occupancy grid cell represents an area of 15 cm $\times$ 15 cm, and is considered as being in one of three possible states; occupied (O), empty (E) or unknown (U), depending on the corresponding probability of occupancy for that cell, i.e.,

$$State(c_{xy}) = \begin{cases} O & \text{if } p(c_{xy}) > 0.5 \\ U & \text{if } p(c_{xy}) = 0.5 \\ E & \text{if } p(c_{xy}) < 0.5 \end{cases}$$

where $p(c_{xy})$ refers to probability of occupancy for the cell at column x and row y. These probabilities were obtained using the standard method for updating occupancy grids (Moravec & Elfes 1985). One histogram is then derived by adding up the total number of occupied, empty and unknown cells in each of the 64 columns, and the other by adding up the totals for each of the 64 rows.

To begin landmark recognition, the robot takes a new sonar scan. Again, the resulting occupancy grid

---

[1] The self-orientation component of this system was disabled, using the compass instead, in order to make a fair comparison between systems.

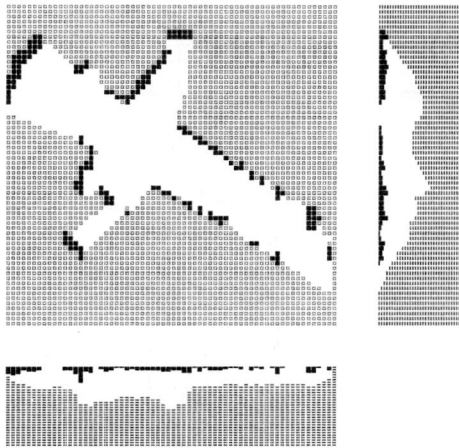

Figure 4: Example occupancy grid and histograms. Occupied cells are shown in black, empty cells in white and unknown cells in grey. A separate pair of histograms is used to represent each individual place in the robot's map.

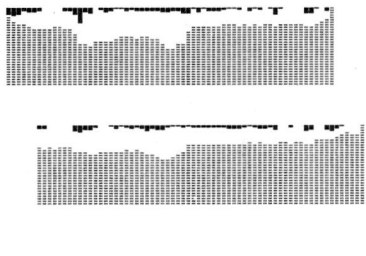

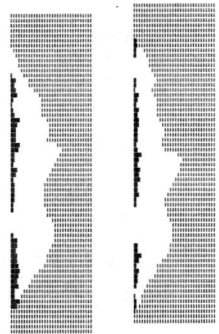

Figure 5: Matching the x and y histograms. The new histograms are convolved with the stored histograms to find the best match.

is processed to produce a pair of histograms. These histograms are then convolved with the corresponding stored histograms for all of the places in the robot's map, as illustrated in Fig. 5. The strength of the match between two histograms T^a and T^b is calculated using the following evaluation function:

$$Match(T^a, T^b) = \sum_j \left[min(O_j^a, O_j^b) + min(E_j^a, E_j^b) + min(U_j^a, U_j^b) \right],$$

where O_j, E_j and U_j refer to the number of occupied, empty and unknown cells contained in the jth element of histogram T. In the convolution, the stored histogram is kept stationary and the recognition histogram is translated against it, using the above function to calculate the best match over the 64 elements of the stored histogram. Any non-overlapping elements in the recognition histogram due to the translation are assumed to consist entirely of unknown cells.

A combined match score M_i for each stored place i is then calculated from best matching alignment for both the x and y histograms, i.e., the translations producing the highest match scores, as

$$M_i = Match(T_x^S, T_x^i) \times Match(T_y^S, T_y^i)$$

where the T^S refer to the x and y histograms for the new sonar scan S, and the T^i to the best matching histograms for place i. During testing, the place with the best match score M_i is taken as the robot's response.

Experiments

Robot sensor data were collected in four real world environments chosen to test the different systems under a variety of conditions, including high levels of perceptual aliasing[2], specular reflection and cross-talk (see Table 1). Environment D is an extreme case, consisting of a very long corridor with few distinctive features. All environments were subject to unpredictable variations in the sensor data, for example, due to people walking past the robot or doors being opened and closed.

The sonar readings were recorded by stopping the wall-following robot every 0.50 m, and rotating its turret to obtain a detailed scan consisting of 144 sonar readings, i.e., nine sets of 16 sonar readings taken at 2.5° intervals.

Performance measurement was carried out for all six landmark recognition mechanisms, in all four environments. The uncertainty coefficient U in each experiment was determined, as was the computational cost of landmark recognition. The latter was determined as the mean processor time required to match a landmark. To enable a fair comparison between systems, the parameters for each of the mechanisms were configured as closely as possible so that each system produced the

---

[2] where several places are perceptually similar enough to be confused by the robot

Environ.	Description	Approx. Size	Route Length	Data Points	N_L	N_R
A	T-shaped hallway	16 m × 13 m	54 m	623	5	16
B	Conference room	16 m × 11 m	49 m	668	6	25
C	L-shaped corridor	34 m × 33 m	147 m	854	12	42
D	Long corridor	53 m × 3 m	111 m	645	9	32

Table 1: Characterisation of environments. N_L denotes the number of location bins, and N_R the average number of responses used in the calculation of the uncertainty coefficient $U(L \mid R)$. The number of data points used for performance evaluation is also indicated.

Environment	RCE	ART2	NstNbr	GCS	OccGrd	OHM
A	0.554	0.573	0.650	0.719	0.732	0.806
B	0.552	0.669	0.715	0.770	0.879	0.850
C	0.462	0.538	0.551	0.502	0.644	0.632
D	0.220	0.265	0.350	0.340	0.487	0.439
$\overline{U}$	0.447	0.509	0.567	0.582	0.686	0.682
T	t	$218\,t$	t	t	$13051\,t$	$31\,t$

Table 2: Localisation quality (uncertainty coefficient) $U(L \mid R)$ and mean uncertainty coefficient $\overline{U}$ for the RCE classifier, ART2 classifier, Nearest Neighbour classifier (NstNbr), Growing Cell Structures (GCS), occupancy grid classifier (OccGrd) and the new landmark recognition system (OHM) in environments A to D. The computational cost T for each algorithm is given in time per landmark match, where $t = 1.8 \times 10^{-5}s$ as measured on a Sparcstation 20.

same number of responses N_R in each environment (see Table 1). Results are given in Table 2 and Fig. 6.

As can be seen from Fig. 6, of the three landmark recognition mechanisms with the lowest computational cost (the RCE, Nearest Neighbour and GCS classifiers), the RCE classifier always comes out worst, with the other two being almost equal in performance.

The remaining classifiers all incur a computational cost increased by one to four orders of magnitude. ART2, despite being two orders of magnitude more computationally expensive, actually performs worse than the Nearest Neighbour and GCS classifiers.

The best landmark recognition mechanism in terms of localisation performance alone is occupancy grid matching ($\overline{U} = 0.686$). Marginally lower in performance ($\overline{U} = 0.682$), but three orders of magnitude cheaper in computation, is the histogram matching classifier. Our conclusion from this data is that for real time, autonomous operation it is optimal to use occupancy histogram matching.

A statistical test was also performed to evaluate the significance of these results. This consisted of a pairwise comparison of the systems, using Student's t-test for paired samples (Press $et\ al.$ 1992) to test the null hypothesis that their performance U over the four environments is really the same. The results in Table 3 indicate significant differences between all of the systems ($p \preceq 0.05$), except in the comparisons between the Nearest Neighbour and GCS classifiers ($p = 0.60$), and the new histogram matching and occupancy grid classifiers ($p = 0.90$). There is a slight anomaly in the com-

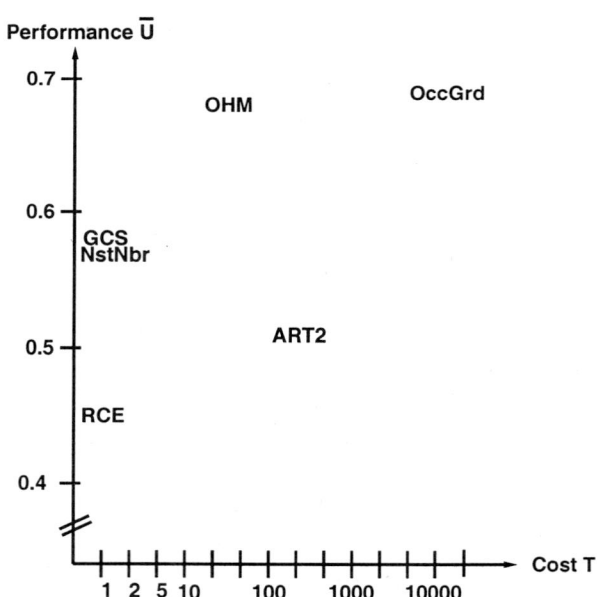

Figure 6: Localisation quality versus computational cost for the systems investigated (see also Table 2). Abbreviations as in Table 2.

p	ART2	NstNbr	GCS	OccGrd	OHM
RCE	0.06	0.01	0.04	0.01	0.01
ART2		0.04	0.16	0.01	0.01
NstNbr			0.60	0.01	0.01
GCS				0.05	0.01
OccGrid					0.90

Table 3: Paired Student's t-test results for the comparative study. Each pair of systems in table 2 was compared in turn, computing the probability p of obtaining these results assuming the null hypothesis that their performance U is really the same.

parison of ART2 and GCS, though we should expect some variations given the size of the samples.

Conclusion

There have been many proposals in the AI literature for navigating mobile robots. However, only recently have there been any attempts to make objective comparisons between different approaches. In this paper, we decided to investigate various methods for performing landmark recognition. The results showed that good localisation can be obtained by matching local occupancy grids, as in (Yamauchi & Langley 1997). Unfortunately, this performance was obtained only at a computational cost four orders of magnitude higher than that of the "cheaper" systems investigated. The new occupancy histogram matching method presented in this paper offers a viable alternative. It has a localisation performance similar to the occupancy grid matching method, at a cost that is only one order of magnitude higher than the "cheaper" methods. Our conclusion is that occupancy histogram matching is a strong candidate for landmark recognition by a navigating mobile robot, especially in situations where computational cost matters. In ongoing work, we have successfully applied this new technique in a complete navigation system which uses previous location information to further improve self-localisation performance (Duckett & Nehmzow 1999).

Acknowledgements

This work was carried out as part of the first named author's PhD thesis at the University of Manchester, who gratefully acknowledges a studentship provided by the Department of Computer Science.

References

Balkenius, C., and Kopp, L. 1996. The XT-1 vision architecture. In *Proc. Symposium on Image Analysis, Lund University, Sweden*.

Carpenter, G., and Grossberg, S. 1987. ART2 : Self-organization of stable category recognition codes for analog input patterns. *Applied Optics* 26(23).

Duckett, T., and Nehmzow, U. 1998. Mobile robot self-localisation and measurement of performance in middle scale environments. *Robotics and Autonomous Systems* 24(1-2). Online at http://www.cs.man.ac.uk/~duckettt.

Duckett, T., and Nehmzow, U. 1999. Knowing your place in real world environments. In *Proc. EUROBOT '99*, 135–142. IEEE Computer Press. Online at http://www.cs.man.ac.uk/~duckettt.

Fritzke, B. 1994. Growing cell structures - a self-organizing network for unsupervised and supervised learning. *Neural Networks* 7(9).

Gutmann, J.-S.; Burgard, W.; Fox, D.; and Konolige, K. 1998. An experimental comparison of localization methods. In *Proc. IROS'98*.

Hinkel, R., and Knieriemen, T. 1988. Environment perception with a laser radar in a fast moving robot. In *Symposium on Robot Control (SYROCO'88)*.

Janet, J., et al. 1995. Global self-localization for autonomous mobile robots using self-organizing Kohonen neural networks. In *Proc. IROS'95*.

Kohonen, T. 1993. *Self-Organization and Associative Memory, 3rd ed.* Springer.

Kurz, A. 1996. Constructing maps for mobile robot navigation based on ultrasonic range data. *IEEE Trans. Systems, Man and Cybernetics B* 26(2).

Lee, D., and Reece, M. 1994. Quantitative evaluation of the exploration strategies of a mobile robot. In *Proc. AAAI'94*.

Moravec, H., and Elfes, A. 1985. High resolution maps from wide angle sonar. In *Proc. ICRA'85*.

Nehmzow, U., and Smithers, T. 1991. Mapbuilding using self-organising networks in really useful robots. In *Proc. SAB'91*.

Press, W.; Teukolsky, S.; Vetterling, W.; and Flannery, B. 1992. *Numerical Recipes in C, 2nd. edition.* Cambridge University Press.

Racz, J., and Dubrawski, A. 1995. Artificial neural network for mobile robot topological localization. *Robotics and Autonomous Systems* 16.

Schöner, G., and Dose, M. 1992. A dynamical systems approach to task-level system integration used to plan and control autonomous vehicle motion. *Robotics and Autonomous Systems* 10:253–267.

Smithers, T. 1995. On quantitative performance measures of robot behaviour. *Robotics and Autonomous Systems* 15(1-2):107–133.

Thrun, S. 1998. Bayesian landmark learning for mobile robot localisation. *Machine Learning* 33(1).

Yamauchi, B., and Langley, P. 1997. Place recognition in dynamic environments. *J. Robotic Systems* 14(2).

Active Audition for Humanoid

Kazuhiro Nakadai[†], Tino Lourens[†], Hiroshi G. Okuno[†*], and Hiroaki Kitano[†‡]

[†]Kitano Symbiotic Systems Project, ERATO, Japan Science and Technology Corp.
Mansion 31 Suite 6A, 6-31-15 Jingumae, Shibuya-ku, Tokyo 150-0001, Japan
Tel: +81-3-5468-1661, Fax: +81-3-5468-1664
* Department of Information Sciences, Science University of Tokyo
‡Sony Computer Science Laboratories, Inc.
{nakadai, tino}@symbio.jst.go.jp, okuno@nue.org, kitano@csl.sony.co.jp

Abstract

In this paper, we present an active audition system for humanoid robot *"SIG the humanoid"*. The audition system of the highly intelligent humanoid requires localization of sound sources and identification of meanings of the sound in the auditory scene. The active audition reported in this paper focuses on improved sound source tracking by integrating audition, vision, and motor movements. Given the multiple sound sources in the auditory scene, *SIG* actively moves its head to improve localization by aligning microphones orthogonal to the sound source and by capturing the possible sound sources by vision. However, such an active head movement inevitably creates motor noise. The system must adaptively cancel motor noise using motor control signals. The experimental result demonstrates that the active audition by integration of audition, vision, and motor control enables sound source tracking in variety of conditions.

Introduction

The goal of the research reported in this paper is to establish a technique of multi-modal integration for improving perception capabilities. We use an upper-torso humanoid robot as a platform of the research, because we believe that multi-modality of perception and high degree-of-freedom is essential to simulate intelligent behavior. Among various perception channels, this paper reports active audition that integrates audition with vision and motor control.

Active perception is an important research topic that signifies coupling of perception and behavior. A lot of research has been carried out in the area of active vision, because it will provide a framework for obtaining necessary additional information by coupling vision with behaviors, such as control of optical parameters or actuating camera mount positions. For example, an observer controls the geometry parameters of the sensory apparatus in order to improve the quality of the perceptual processing (Aloimonos, Weiss, & Bandyopadhyay. 1987). Such activities include moving a camera or cameras (vergence), changing focus, zooming in or out, changing camera resolution, widening or narrowing iris and so on. Therefore, active vision system is always coupled with servo-motor system, which means that active vision system is in general associated with motor noise.

The concept of active perception can be extended to audition, too. Audition is always active, since people hear a mixture of sounds and focus on some parts of input. Usually, people with normal hearing can separate sounds from a mixture of sounds and focus on a particular voice or sound even in a noisy environment. This capability is known as the *cocktail party effect*. While traditionally, auditory research has been focusing on human speech understanding, understanding auditory scene in general is receiving increasing attention. Computational Auditory Scene Analysis (CASA) studies a general framework of sound processing and understanding (Brown 1992; Cooke *et al.* 1993; Nakatani, Okuno, & Kawabata 1994; Rosenthal & Okuno 1998). Its goal is to understand an arbitrary sound mixture including speech, non-speech sounds, and music in various acoustic environment. It requires not only understanding of meaning of specific sound, but also identification of spatial relationship of sound sources, so that sound landscapes of the environment can be understood. This leads to the need of active audition that has capability of dynamically focusing on specific sound in a mixture of sounds, and actively controlling motor systems to obtain further information using audition, vision, and other perceptions.

Audition for Humanoids in Daily Environments

Our ultimate goal is to deploy our robot in daily environments. For audition, this requires the following issues to be resolved:

- Ability to localize sound sources in unknown acoustic environment.
- Ability to actively move its body to obtain further information from audition, vision, and other perceptions.
- Ability to continuously perform auditory scene analysis under noisy environment, where noise comes from both environment and motor noise of robot itself.

First of all, deployment to the real world means that the acoustic features of the environment is not known in advance. In the current computational audition model, the *Head-Related Transfer Function* (*HRTF*) was measured in

---

Copyright ©2000, American Association for Artificial Intelligence (www.aaai.org). All rights reserved.

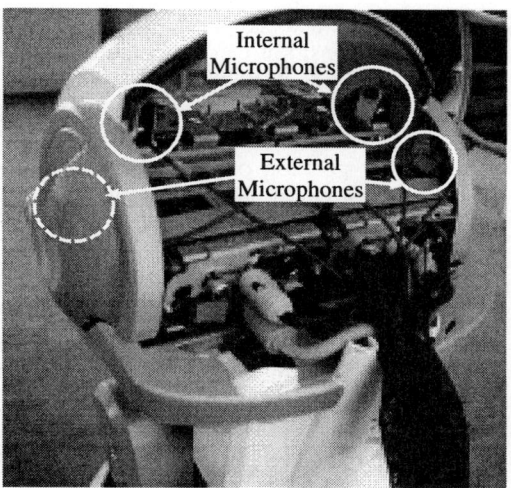

a) Cover   b) Mechanical structure   c) Internal microphones (top) and cameras

Figure 1: *SIG* the Humanoid

the specific room environment, and measurement has to be repeated if the system is installed at different room. It is infeasible for any practical system to require such extensive measurement of the operating space. Thus, audition system without HRTF is an essential requirement for practical systems. The system reported in this paper implements epipolar geometry-based sound source localization that eliminates the need for HRTF. The use of epipolar geometry for audition is advantageous when combined with the vision system because many vision systems uses epipolar geometry for visual object localization.

Second, active audition that couples audition, vision, and motor control system is critical. Active audition can be implemented in various aspects. Take the most visible example, the system should be able to dynamically align microphone positions against sound sources to obtain better resolution. Consider that a humanoid has a pair of microphones. Given the multiple sound sources in the auditory scene, the humanoid should actively move its head to improve localization (getting the direction of a sound source) by aligning microphones orthogonal to the sound source. Aligning a pair of microphones orthogonal to the sound source has several advantages:

- Each channel receives the sound from the sound source at the same time.
- It is rather easy to extract sounds originating from the center by comparing subbands in each channel.
- The problem of front-behind sound from such sound source can be solved by using direction-sensitive microphones.
- The sensitivity of direction in processing sounds is expected to be higher along the center line, because sound is represented by a *sine* function.
- Zooming of audition can be implemented by using nondirectional and direction-sensitive microphones.

Therefore, *gaze stabilization* for microphones is very important to keep the same position relative to a target sound source.

Active audition requires movement of the components that mounts microphone units. In many cases, such a mount is actuated by motors that create considerable noise. In a complex robotic system, such as humanoid, motor noise is complex and often irregular because numbers of motors may be involved in the head and body movement. Removing motor noise from auditory system requires information on what kind of movement the robot is making in real-time. In other words, motor control signals need to be integrated as one of the perception channels. If dynamic noise canceling of motor noise fails, one may end-up using "*stop-perceive-act*" principle reluctantly, so that the audition system can receive sound without motor noise. To avoid using such an implementation, we implemented an adaptive noise canceling scheme that uses motor control signal to anticipate and cancel motor noise.

For humanoid audition, active audition and the CASA approach is essential. In this paper, we investigate a new sound processing algorithm based on epipolar geometry without using HRTF, and internal sound suppression algorithms.

SIG the humanoid

As a testbed of integration of perceptual information to control motor of high degree of freedom (DOF), we designed a humanoid robot (hereafter, referred as *SIG*) with the following components (Kitano *et al.* 2000):

- 4 DOFs of body driven by 4 DC motors — Its mechanical structure is shown in Figure 1b. Each DC motor is controlled by a potentiometer.
- A pair of CCD cameras of Sony EVI-G20 for visual stereo input — Each camera has 3 DOFs, that is, pan, tilt

and zoom. Focus is automatically adjusted. The offset of camera position can be obtained from each camera (Figure 1b).

- Two pairs of nondirectional microphones (Sony ECM-77S) (Figure 1c). One pair of microphones are installed at the ear position of the head to gather sounds from the external world. Each microphone is shielded by the cover to prevent from capturing internal noises. The other pair of microphones are installed very close to the corresponding microphone to gather sounds from the internal world.
- A cover of the body (Figure 1a) reduces sounds to be emitted to external environments, which is expected to reduce the complexity of sound processing.

New Issues of Humanoid Audition

This section describes our motivation of humanoid audition and some related work. We assume that a humanoid or robot will move even while it is listening to some sounds. Most robots equipped with microphones developed so far process sounds without motion (Huang, Ohnishi, & Sugie 1997; Matsusaka *et al.* 1999; Takanishi *et al.* 1995). This *"stop-perceive-act"* strategy, or hearing without movements, should be conquered for real-world applications. For this purpose, hearing with robot movements imposes us various new and interesting aspects of existing problems.

The main problems with humanoid audition during motion includes understanding general sounds, sensor fusion, active audition, and internal sound suppression.

General Sound Understanding

Since computational auditory scene analysis (CASA) research investigates a general model of sound understanding, input sound is a mixture of sounds, not a sound of single source. One of the main research topics of CASA is *sound stream separation*, a process that separates sound streams that have consistent acoustic attributes from a mixture of sounds. Three main issues in sound stream separation are

1. Acoustic features used as clues of separation,
2. Real-time and incremental separation, and
3. Information fusion — discussed separately.

In extracting acoustic attributes, some systems assume the humans auditory model of primary processing and simulate the processing of cocklear mechanism (Brown 1992; Slaney, Naar, & Lyon 1994). Brown and Cooke designed and implemented a system that builds various auditory maps for sound input and integrates them to separate speech from input sounds (Brown 1992).

Nakatani, Okuno, & Kawabata 1994 used harmonic structures as the clue of separation and developed a monaural-based harmonic stream separation system, called HBSS. HBSS is modeled by a multi-agent system and extracts harmonic structures *incrementally*. They extended HBSS to use binaural (stereo microphone embedded in a dummy head) sounds and developed a binaural-based harmonic stream separation system, called Bi-HBSS (Nakatani, Okuno, & Kawabata 1995). Bi-HBSS uses harmonic structures and the direction of sound sources as clues of separation. Okuno, Nakatani, & Kawabata 1999 extended Bi-HBSS to separate speech streams, and uses the resulting system as a front end for automatic speech recognition.

Sensor Fusion for Sound Stream Separation

Separation of sound streams from perceptive input is a nontrivial task due to ambiguities of interpretation on which elements of perceptive input belong to which stream (Nakagawa, Okuno, & Kitano 1999). For example, when two independent sound sources generate two sound streams that are crossing in the frequency region, there may be two possibilities; crossing each other, or approaching and departing. The key idea of Bi-HBSS is to exploit spatial information by using a binaural input.

Staying within a single modality, it is very difficult to attain high performance of sound stream separation. For example, Bi-HBSS finds a pair of harmonic structures extracted by left and right channels similar to stereo matching in vision where camera are aligned on a rig, and calculates the *interaural time/phase difference* (*ITD* or *IPD*), and/or the *interaural intensity/amplitude difference* (*IID* or *IAD*) to obtain the direction of sound source. The mapping from ITD, IPD, IID and IAD to the direction of sound source and vice versa is based on the HRTF associated to binaural microphones. Finally Bi-HBSS separates sound streams by using harmonic structure and sound source direction.

The error in direction determined by Bi-HBSS is about $\pm 10°$, which is similar to that of a human, i.e. $\pm 8°$ (Cavaco 1999). However, this is too coarse to separate sound streams from a mixture of sounds.

Nakagawa, Okuno, & Kitano 1999 improved the accuracy of the sound source direction by using the direction extracted by image processing, because the direction by vision is more accurate. By using an accurate direction, each sound stream is extracted by using a *direction-pass filter*. In fact, by integrating visual and auditory information, they succeeded to separate three sound sources from a mixture of sounds by two microphones. They also reported how the accuracy of sound stream separation measured by automatic speech recognition is improved by **adding more modalities**, from monaural input, binaural input, and binaural input with visual information.

Some critical problems with Bi-HBSS and their work for real-world applications are summarized as follows:

1. **HRTF is needed for identifying the direction**. It is timeconsuming to measure HRTF, and it is usually measured in an aechotic room. Since it depends on auditory environments, re-measurement or adaptation is needed to apply it to other environments.
2. **HRTF is needed for creating a direction-pass filter**. Their direction-pass filter needs HRTF to compose. Since HRTF is usually measured in *discrete* azimuth and elevation, it is difficult to implement sound tracking for continuous movement of sound sources.

Therefore, a new method without using HRTF should be invented for localization (sound source direction) and direction (by using a direction-pass filter). We will propose a new auditory localization based on the epipolar geometry.

Sound Source Localization

Some robots developed so far had a capability of sound source localization. Huang, Ohnishi, & Sugie 1997 developed a robot that had three microphones. Three microphones were installed vertically on the top of the robot, composing a triangle. Comparing the input power of microphones, two microphones that have more power than the other are selected and the sound source direction is calculated. By selecting two microphones from three, they solved the problem that two microphones cannot determine the place of sound source in front or backward. By identifying the direction of sound source from a mixture of an original sound and its echoes, the robot turns the body towards the sound source.

Humanoids of Waseda University can localize a sound source by using two microphones (Matsusaka *et al.* 1999; Takanishi *et al.* 1995). These humanoids localize a sound source by calculating IID or IPD with HRTF. These robot can neither separate even a sound stream nor localize more than one sound source. The Cog humanoid of MIT has a pair of omni-directional microphones embedded in simplified pinnae (Brooks *et al.* 1999a; Irie 1997). In the Cog, auditory localization is trained by visual information. This approach does not use HRTF, but assumes a single sound source. To summarize, both approaches lack for the CASA viewpoints.

Active Audition

A humanoid is active in the sense that it tries to do some activity to improve perceptual processing. Such activity includes to change the position of cameras and microphones by motor control.

When a humanoid hears sound by facing the sound source in the center of the pair of microphones, ITD and IID is almost zero if the pair of microphones are correctly calibrated. In addition, sound intensity of both channels becomes stronger, because the ear cover makes a non-directional microphone directional. Given the multiple sound sources in the auditory scene, a humanoid actively moves its head to improve localization by aligning microphones orthogonal to the sound source and by capturing the possible sound sources by vision.

However, a new problem occurs because gaze stabilization is attained by visual servo or auditory servo. Sounds are generated by motor rotation, gears, belts and ball bearings. Since these internal sound sources are much closer than other external sources, even if the absolute power of sounds is much lower, input sounds are strongly influenced. This is also the case for the SONY AIBO entertainment robot; AIBO is equipped with a microphone, but internal noise mainly caused by a cooling fan is too large to utilize sounds.

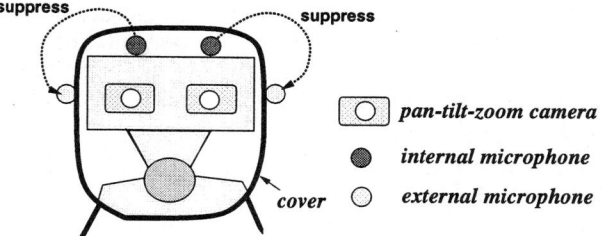

Figure 2: Internal and external microphones for internal sound suppression

Internal Sound Suppression

Since active perception causes sounds by the movement of various movable parts, internal sound suppression is critical to enhance external sounds (see Figure 2). A cover of humanoid body reduces sounds of motors emitted to the external world by separating internal and external world of the robot. Such a cover is, thus expected to reduce the complexity of sound processing caused by motor sounds. Since most robots developed so far do not have a cover, auditory processing cannot become first-class perception of a humanoid.

Internal sound suppression may be attained by one or a combination of the following methodologies:

1. noise cancellation,
2. independent component analysis (ICA),
3. case-based suppression,
4. model-based suppression, and
5. learning and adaptation.

To record sounds for case-based suppression and model-based suppression, each sound should be labeled appropriately. We use data consisting of time and motor control commands as label for sound. In the next section, we will explain how these methods are utilized in our active audition system.

Active Audition System

An active audition system consists of two components; internal sound suppression, and sound stream separation.

Internal Sound Suppression System

Internal sounds of *SIG* are caused mainly by the followings:

- Camera motors — sounds of movement are quiet enough to ignore, but sounds of standby is loud (about 3.7 dB).
- Body motors — sounds of standby and movement are loud (about 5.6 dB and 23 dB, respectively).

Comparison of noise cancellation by adaptive filtering, ICA, case-based suppression and model-based suppression, we concluded that only adaptive filters work well. Four microphones are not enough for ICA to separate internal sounds. Case-based and model-based suppression affect the phase of original inputs, which causes errors of IPD.

Our adaptive filter uses *heuristics with internal microphones*, which specifies the condition to cut off burst noise mainly caused by motors. For example, sounds at stoppers, by friction between cable and body, creaks at joints of cover parts may occur. The heuristics orders that localization by sound or direction-pass filter ignore a subband if the following conditions hold:

1. The power of internal sounds is much stronger than that of external sounds.
2. Twenty adjacent subbands have strong power (30 dB).
3. A motor motion is being processed.

We tried to make as adaptive filter an FIR (Finite Impulse Response) filter of order 100, because this filter is a linear phase filter. This property is essential to localize the sound source by IID (Interaural Intensity Difference) or ITD/IPD (Interaural Time/Phase Difference). The parameters of the FIR filter is calculated by least-mean-square method as adaptive algorithm. Noise cancellation by the FIR filter suppresses internal sounds but some errors occur. These errors make poor localization compared to results of localization without internal sound suppression. Case-based or model-based cancellation is not adopted, because the same movement generates a lot of different sounds and thus it is difficult to construct case or model-based cancellation.

Instead, internal sound suppression system consists of the following subcomponents:

1. **Filtering by threshold** — Since standby sounds of camera motor are stable and limited in frequency range, that is, at frequencies of less than 200 Hz, we confirmed that the filtering of weak sounds less than the threshold is effective.
2. **Adaptive filter** — Since suppression of sounds affects phase information, we design a new adaptive filter that switches through or cut whether the power of internal microphone is stronger than that of an external microphone. If this condition holds, the system assumes that internal sounds are generated.

Sound Stream Separation by Localization

We design a new direction-pass filter with a direction which is calculated by epipolar geometry.

Localization by Vision using Epipolar Geometry Consider a simple stereo camera setting where two cameras have the same focal length, their light axes are in parallel, and their image planes are on the same plane (see Figure 3a). We define the world coordinate (X, Y, Z) and each local coordinate. Suppose that a space point $P(X, Y, Z)$ is projected on each camera's image plane, (x_l, y_l) and (x_r, y_r). The following relations hold (Faugeras 1993):

$$X = \frac{b(x_l + x_r)}{2d}, Y = \frac{b(y_l + y_r)}{2d}, Z = \frac{bf}{d}$$

where f is the focal length of each camera's lens and b is the baseline. Disparity d is defined as $d = x_l - x_r$.

The current implementation of common matching in *SIG* is performed by using corner detection algorithm (Lourens *et al.* 2000). It extracts a set of corners and edges then

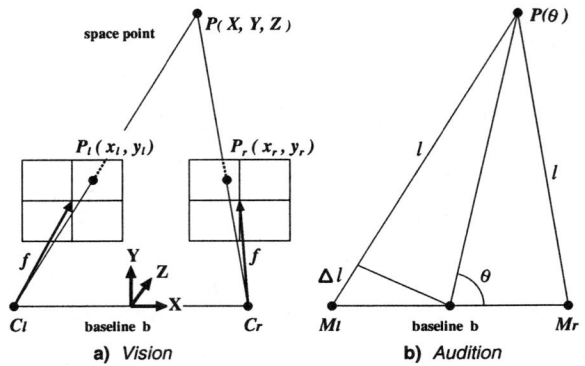

C_l, C_r: camera center, $\quad M_l, M_r$: microphone center

Figure 3: Epipolar geometry for localization

constructs a pair of graphs. A matching algorithm is used to find corresponding left and right image to obtain depth.

Since the relation $y_l = y_r$ also holds under the above setting, a pair of matching points in each image plane can be easily sought. However, for general setting of camera positions, matching is much more difficult and timeconsuming. Usually, a matching point in the other image plane exists on the epipolar line which is a bisecting line made by the epipolar plane and the image plane.

Localization by Audition using Epipolar Geometry
Auditory system extracts the direction by using epipolar geometry. First, it extract peaks by using FFT (Fast Fourier Transformation) for each subband, 47Hz in our implementation, and then calculates the IPD.

Let $Sp^{(r)}$ and $Sp^{(l)}$ be the right and left channel spectrum obtained by FFT at the same time tick. Then, the IPD $\triangle \varphi$ is calculated as follows:

$$\triangle \varphi = \tan^{-1}\left(\frac{\Im[Sp^{(r)}(f_p)]}{\Re[Sp^{(r)}(f_p)]}\right) - \tan^{-1}\left(\frac{\Im[Sp^{(l)}(f_p)]}{\Re[Sp^{(l)}(f_p)]}\right)$$

where f_p is a peak frequency on the spectrum, $\Re[Sp]$ and $\Im[Sp]$ are the real and imaginary part of the spectrum $Sp^{(r)}$. The angle θ is calculated by the following equation:

$$\cos \theta = \frac{v}{2\pi f_p b} \triangle \varphi$$

where v is the velocity of sound. For the moment, the velocity of sound is fixed to 340m/sec and remains the same even if the temperature changes.

This peak extraction method works at 48 KHz sampling rate and calculates FFT for 1,024 points, but runs much faster than Bi-HBSS (12 KHz sampling rate with HRTF) and extracted peaks are more accurate (Nakadai, Okuno, & Kitano 1999).

New Direction-Pass Filter using Epipolar Geometry
As mentioned earlier, HRTF is usually not available in real-world environments, because it changes when a new furniture is installed, a new object comes in the room, or humidity of the room changes. In addition, HRTF should

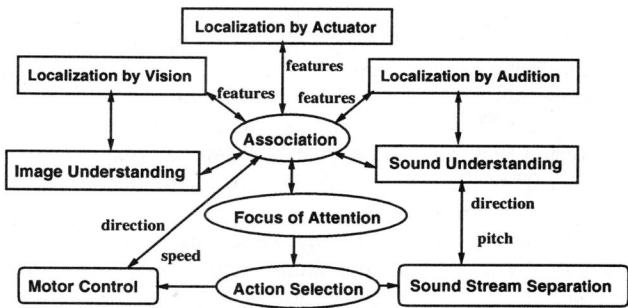

Figure 4: Integrated humanoid perception system

be interpolated for auditory localization of a moving sound source, because HRTF is measured for discrete positions. Therefore, a new method must be invented. Our method is based on the direction-pass filter with epipolar geometry.

As opposed to localization by audition, the direction-pass filter selects subbands that satisfies the IPD of the specified direction. The detailed algorithm is describes as follows:

1. The specified direction θ is converted to $\Delta\varphi$ for each subband (47 Hz).
2. Extract peaks and calculated IPD, $\Delta\varphi'$.
3. If IPD satisfies the specified condition, namely, $\Delta\varphi' = \Delta\varphi$, then collect the subband.
4. Construct a wave consisting of collected subbands.

By using the relative position between camera centers and microphones, it is easy to convert from epipolar plane of vision to that of audition (see Figure 3b). In *SIG*, the baselines for vision and audition are in parallel.

Therefore, whenever a sound source is localized by epipolar geometry in vision, it can be converted easily into the angle θ as described in the following equation:

$$\cos\theta = \frac{\vec{P}\cdot\vec{M_r}}{|\vec{P}||\vec{M_r}|} = \frac{\vec{P}\cdot\vec{C_r}}{|\vec{P}||\vec{C_r}|}.$$

Localization by Servo-Motor System The head direction is obtained from potentiometers in the servo-motor system. Hereafter, it is referred as *the head direction by motor control*. Head direction by potentiometers is quite accurate by the servo-motor control mechanism. If only the horizontal rotation motor is used, horizontal direction of the head is obtained accurately, about $\pm 1°$. By combining visual localization and the head direction, *SIG* can determine the position in world coordinates.

Accuracy of Localization Accuracy of extracted directions by three sensors: vision, audition, and motor control is measured. The results for the current implementation are $\pm 1°$, $\pm 10°$, $\pm 15°$, for vision, motor control, and audition, respectively.

Therefore, the precedence of information fusion on direction is determined as below:

$$\text{vision} > \text{motor control} > \text{audition}$$

Sensor Integrated System The system contains a perception system that integrates sound, vision, and motor control (Figure 4). The association module maintains the consistency between information extracted by image processing, sound processing and motor control subsystems. For the moment, association includes the correspondence between images and sounds for a sound source; loud speakers are the only sound sources, which can generate sound of any frequency. Focus of attention and action selection modules are described in (Lourens *et al.* 2000).

Experiment — Motion Tracking by Three Kinds of Sensors

In this section, we will demonstrate how vision, audition and head direction by potentiometers compensate each missing information to localize sound sources while *SIG* rotates to see an unknown object.

Scenario: There are two sound sources: two B&W Noutilus 805 loud speakers located in a room of 10 square meters. The room where the system is installed is a conventional residential apartment facing a road with busy traffic, and exposed to various daily life noise. The sound environment is not controlled at all for experiments to ensure feasibility of the approach in daily life.

One sound source *A* (Speaker A) plays a monotone sound of 500 Hz. The other sound source *B* (Speaker B) plays a monotone sound of 600 Hz. *A* is located in front of *SIG* (5° left of the initial head direction) and *B* is located 69° to the left. The distance from *SIG* to each sound source is about 210cm. Since the visual field of camera is only 45° in horizontal angle, *SIG* cannot see *B* at the initial head direction, because *B* is located at 70° left to the head direction, thus it is outside of the visual fields of the cameras. Figure 5 shows this situation.

1. *A* plays a sound at 5° left of the initial head direction.
2. *SIG* associates the visual object with the sound, because their extracted directions are the same.
3. Then, *B* plays a sound about 3 seconds later. At this moment, *B* is outside of the visual field of the *SIG*. Since the direction of the sound source can be extracted only by audition, *SIG* cannot associate anything to the sound.
4. *SIG* turns toward the direction of the unseen sound source *B* using the direction obtained by audition.
5. *SIG* finds a new object *B*, and associates the visual object with the sound.

Four kinds of benchmark sounds are examined; fast (68.8 degree/sec) and slow (14.9 degree/sec) movement of *SIG*. Weak signals (similar power to internal standby sounds, which makes signal to noise ratio 0dB) and strong signals (about 50 dB). Spectrogram of each input is shown in Figure 6. Motion tracking by vision and audition, and motion information are evaluated.

Results: Results of the experiment were very promising. First, accurate sound source localization was accomplished without using the HRTF. The use of epipolar geometry for

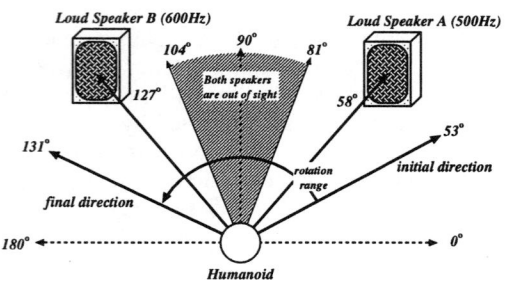

Figure 5: Experiment: Motion tracking by vision and audition while *SIG* moves.

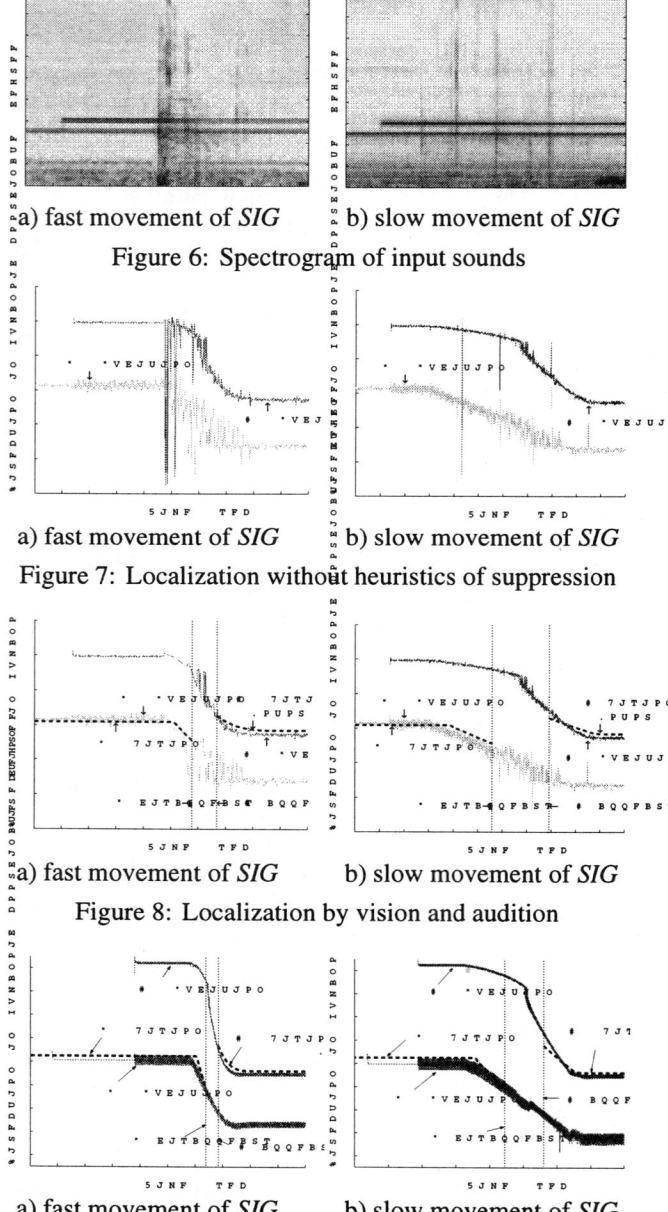

Figure 6: Spectrogram of input sounds
 a) fast movement of *SIG*
 b) slow movement of *SIG*

Figure 7: Localization without heuristics of suppression
 a) fast movement of *SIG*
 b) slow movement of *SIG*

Figure 8: Localization by vision and audition
 a) fast movement of *SIG*
 b) slow movement of *SIG*

Figure 9: Localization for strong signal (50dB)
 a) fast movement of *SIG*
 b) slow movement of *SIG*

audition was proven to be very effective. In both cases of weak and strong sound, epipolar based non-HRTF method locate approximate direction of sound sources (see localization date for initial 5 seconds in Figure 7). In Figure 7, time series data for estimated sound source direction using only audition is plotted with an ego-centric polar coordinate where 0° is the direction dead front of the head, minus is right of the head direction.

The effect of adaptive noise canceling is clearly shown. Figure 7 shows estimated sound source directions without motor noise suppression. Sound direction estimation is seriously hampered when the head is moving (around time 5 - 6 seconds). The spectrogram (Figure 6) clearly indicates extensive motor noise. When the robot is constantly moving to track moving sound sources or to move itself for a certain position, the robot continues to generate such a noise that makes audition almost impossible to use for perception.

The effects of internal sound suppression by heuristics are shown in Figures 8, and 9. The time series of estimated sound source directions for weak and strong signals localized by vision and audition are shown.

Such accurate localization by audition makes association between audition and vision possible. While *SIG* is moving, sound source *B* comes into its visual field. The association module checks the consistency of localization by vision and audition. If the discovered loud speaker does not play sounds, inconsistency occurs and the visual system would resume its search finding an object producing sound. If association succeeds, *B*'s position in world coordinates is calculated by using motor information and the position in humanoid coordinates obtained by vision.

Experimental results indicate that position estimation by audition and vision is accurate enough to create consistent association even under the condition that the robot is constantly moving and generating motor noise. It should be refined that sound source localization by audition in the experiment uses epipolar geometry for audition, and do not use HRTF. Thus, we can simply field the robot in unknown acoustic environment and localize sound sources.

Discussion and Future Work

1. The experiment demonstrates the feasibility of the proposed humanoid audition in real-world environments. Since there are a lot of non-desired sounds, caused by traffic, people outside the test-room, and of course internal sounds, the CASA assumption that input sounds consist of a mixture of sounds is essential in real-world environments. Similar work by Nakagawa, Okuno, & Kitano 1999 was done in a simulated acoustic environment, but it may fail in localization and sound stream separation in real-world environments. Most robots capable of auditory localization developed so far assume a single sound source.

2. Epipolar geometry gives a way to unify visual and auditory processing, in particular localization and sound stream separation. This approach can dispense with HRTF. As far as we know, no other systems can do it. Most robots capable of auditory localization developed

so far use HRTF explicitly or implicitly, and may fail in identifying some spatial directions or tracking moving sound sources.
3. The cover of the humanoid is very important to separate its internal and external worlds. However, we've realized that resonance within a cover is not negligible. Therefore, its inside material design is important.
4. Social interaction realized by utilizing body movements extensively makes auditory processing more difficult. The Cog Project focuses on social interaction, but this influence on auditory processing has not been mentioned (Brooks et al. 1999b). A cover of the humanoid will play an important role in reducing sounds caused by motor movements emitted toward outside the body as well as in giving a friendly outlook to human.

Future Work Active perception needs self recognition. The problem of acquiring the concept of self recognition in robotics has been pointed out by many people. For audition, handling of internal sounds made by itself is a research area of modeling of self. Other future work includes more tests for feasibility and robustness, real-time processing of vision and auditory processing, internal sound suppression by independent component analysis, addition of more sensor information, and applications.

Conclusion

In this paper, we present active audition for humanoid which includes internal sound suppression, a new method for auditory localization, and a new method for separating sound sources from a mixture of sounds. The key idea is to use epipolar geometry to calculate the sound source direction and to integrate vision and audition in localization and sound stream separation. This method does not use HRTF (Head-Related Transfer Function) which is a main obstacle in applying auditory processing to real-world environments. We demonstrate the feasibility of motion tracking by integrating vision, audition and motion information. The important research topic now is to explore possible interaction of multiple sensory inputs which affects quality (accuracy, computational costs, etc) of the process, and to identify fundamental principles for intelligence.

Acknowledgments

We thank our colleagues of Symbiotic Intelligence Group, Kitano Symbiotic Systems Project; Yukiko Nakagawa, Dr. Iris Fermin, and Dr. Theo Sabish for their discussions. We thank Prof. Hiroshi Ishiguruo of Wakayama University for his help in active vision and integration of visual and auditory processing.

References

Aloimonos, Y.; Weiss, I.; and Bandyopadhyay., A. 1987. Active vision. *International Journal of Computer Vision* 1(4):333–356.

Brooks, R.; Breazeal, C.; Marjanovie, M.; Scassellati, B.; and Williamson, M. 1999a. The cog project: Building a humanoid robot. Technical report, MIT.

Brooks, R.; Breazeal, C.; Marjanovie, M.; Scassellati, B.; and Williamson, M. 1999b. The cog project: Building a humanoid robot. In *Lecture Notes in Computer Science*, to appear. Spriver-Verlag.

Brown, G. J. 1992. *Computational auditory scene analysis: A representational approach.* University of Sheffield.

Cavaco, S. ad Hallam, J. 1999. A biologically plausible acoustic azimuth estimation system. In *Proceedings of IJCAI-99 Workshop on Computational Auditory Scene Analysis (CASA'99)*, 78–87. IJCAI.

Cooke, M. P.; Brown, G. J.; Crawford, M.; and Green, P. 1993. Computational auditory scene analysis: Listening to several things at once. *Endeavour* 17(4):186–190.

Faugeras, O. D. 1993. *Three Dimensional Computer Vision: A Geometric Viewpoint.* MA.: The MIT Press.

Huang, J.; Ohnishi, N.; and Sugie, N. 1997. Separation of multiple sound sources by using directional information of sound source. *Artificial Life and Robotics* 1(4):157–163.

Irie, R. E. 1997. Multimodal sensory integration for localization in a humanoid robot. In *Proceedings of the Second IJCAI Workshop on Computational Auditory Scene Analysis (CASA'97)*, 54–58. IJCAI.

Kitano, H.; Okuno, H. G.; Nakadai, K.; Fermin, I.; Sabish, T.; Nakagawa, Y.; and Matsui, T. 2000. Designing a humanoid head for robocup challenge. In *Proceedings of Agent 2000 (Agent 2000)*, to appear.

Lourens, T.; Nakadai, K.; Okuno, H. G.; and Kitano, H. 2000. Selective attention by integration of vision and audition. In *submitted*.

Matsusaka, Y.; Tojo, T.; Kuota, S.; Furukawa, K.; Tamiya, D.; Hayata, K.; Nakano, Y.; and Kobayashi, T. 1999. Multiperson conversation via multi-modal interface — a robot who communicates with multi-user. In *Proceedings of Eurospeech*, 1723–1726. ESCA.

Nakadai, K.; Okuno, H. G.; and Kitano, H. 1999. A method of peak extraction and its evaluation for humanoid. In *SIG-Challenge-99-7*, 53–60. JSAI.

Nakagawa, Y.; Okuno, H. G.; and Kitano, H. 1999. Using vision to improve sound source separation. In *Proceedings of 16th National Conference on Artificial Intelligence (AAAI-99)*, 768–775. AAAI.

Nakatani, T.; Okuno, H. G.; and Kawabata, T. 1994. Auditory stream segregation in auditory scene analysis with a multi-agent system. In *Proceedings of 12th National Conference on Artificial Intelligence (AAAI-94)*, 100–107. AAAI.

Nakatani, T.; Okuno, H. G.; and Kawabata, T. 1995. Residue-driven architecture for computational auditory scene analysis. In *Proceedings of 14th International Joint Conference on Artificial Intelligence (IJCAI-95)*, volume 1, 165–172. AAAI.

Okuno, H. G.; Nakatani, T.; and Kawabata, T. 1999. Listening to two simultaneous speeches. *Speech Communication* 27(3-4):281–298.

Rosenthal, D., and Okuno, H. G., eds. 1998. *Computational Auditory Scene Analysis.* Mahwah, New Jersey: Lawrence Erlbaum Associates.

Slaney, M.; Naar, D.; and Lyon, R. F. 1994. Auditory model inversion for sound separation. In *Proceedings of 1994 International Conference on Acoustics, Speech, and Signal Processing*, volume 2, 77–80.

Takanishi, A.; Masukawa, S.; Mori, Y.; and Ogawa, T. 1995. Development of an anthropomorphic auditory robot that localizes a sound direction (*in japanese*). *Bulletin of the Centre for Informatics* 20:24–32.

Property Mapping: a simple technique for mobile robot programming

Illah R. Nourbakhsh
The Robotics Institute
Carnegie Mellon University
Pittsburgh, PA 15213
illah@ri.cmu.edu

Abstract

In this paper we turn to the mobile robot programming problem, which is a software engineering challenge that is not easily conquered using contemporary software engineering best practices. We propose *robot observability* as a measure of the diagnostic transparency of a situated robot program, then describe *property mapping* as a simple, language-independent approach to implementing reliable robot programs by maximizing robot observability. Examples from real-world, working robots are given in Lisp and Java.

Introduction

The recent availability of inexpensive, reliable robot chassis (e.g. ActivMedia Pioneer, IS-Robotics Magellan, Nomad Scout) has broadened the accessibility of mobile robotics research. Because these robots consist of fixed hardware out-of-the-box, this technology is also shifting the emphasis of mobile robot research from a joint hardware and software design process toward hardware-unaware mobile robot *programming*. Given off-the-shelf robot hardware and a known environment, what software causes the robot to achieve the most desirable behavior?

This is a software design problem, and yet software engineering best practices are not very helpful. Mobile robots suffer from uncertainty in sensing, unreliability in action, real-time environmental interactions and almost non-deterministic world behavior. Mobile robot software engineering combines the hardest aspects of software engineering for the internet and debugging operating systems with a disproportionate measure of environmental and sensing uncertainty.

New programming languages and architectures have been born out of projects to create reliable, real-world robots (Bonasso and Kortenkamp, 1996), (Brooks, 1986), (Firby, 1987), (Horswill, 1999), (Simmons, 1994). Several have demonstrated their efficacy in working mobile robots (Horswill, 1993), (Krotkov et al., 1996).

These existing solutions all effectively constrain the programmer during the process of robot programming, but none provide satisfactory guidance regarding the incremental process of constructing and debugging robot programs. We suggest that one reason the best implementations in these languages succeed is because they facilitate robot debugging. Even more so than with non-robotics systems, diagnosis and subsequent modification of robot software is the chief time sink of robot programming. We believe there is a single key requirement for making robot programming tractable: maximize run-time diagnostic transparency.

In this paper we present *robot observability* as a predictor for diagnostic transparency. Then, we present a language-independent technique called *property mapping* for constructing robot programs that are diagnostically transparent and thereby achieve high degrees of reliability.

The Robot Programming Problem

A mobile robot is a situated automata, or a module that comprises one part of a closed system together with the environment. Fig. 1 shows the standard depiction of a robot, with its outputs labeled as *actions* and the outputs of the environment in turn labeled as *percepts*.

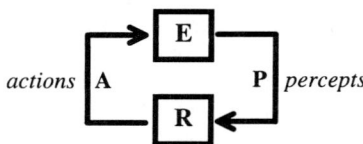

Figure 1: The standard view of an embedded robot

This view can be confusing, as the module R is not meant to depict the physical robot, but rather the automata implemented by the *robot algorithm* (Halperin, Kavraki and Latombe, 1998). The physical robot is a component of the environment, and it is the interface through which the robot automata receives percepts via the physical sensors and acts via physical outputs.

In Fig. 2, we depict the standard view in greater detail. Without loss of generality, we conceptually decompose the automata, or robot program, into a perceptual partitioning module and a control module. *Partition()* is simply a function that may implement perceptual abstraction by mapping various percepts in P to the same abstract percept in Pr. *Control()* is a Moore automata, or a function from the perceptual input (and possibly internal state) to an output (and possibly a new internal state). We use the set Ar, which is a subset of A, to denote the range of *Control()*.

Copyright © 2000 American Association for Artificial Intelligence (www.aaai.org). All rights reserved.

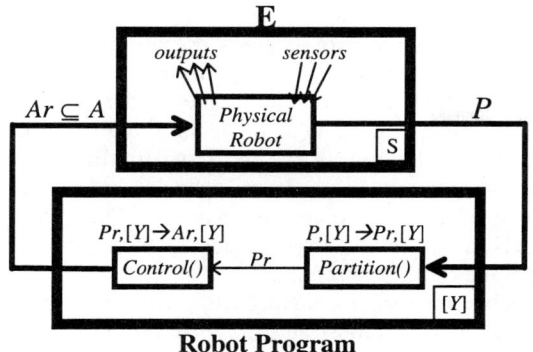

Figure 2: A detailed view of the robot-environment system

The robot programming problem can be posed as follows. The mobile robot software designer is given an environment **E** with state set *S*, including a physical robot with fixed sensors, outputs, a set of possible sensor value-vectors *P* and a set of possible output vectors *A*. The designer creates the Robot Program, and in so doing chooses the effective output range *Ar*, the perceptual partitions *Pr* and the internal state set *Y*, together with the mappings $P, Y \rightarrow Pr, Y$; $Pr, Y \rightarrow Ar, Y$.

Sensor noise is a significant problem in mobile robot programming, and so the separation of the robot program into a perceptual partition followed by state and action update follows the natural course of most robot programming solutions. This is particularly the case in functional programs where state is not used and therefore the robot program simply maps the current perceptual input to an output: $P \rightarrow Pr \rightarrow Ar$.

Fig. 3 shows a working example of a functional program. This program is designed for a differential-drive robot with a sixteen-sonar radial ring. It indefinitely servoes the robot to face the closest object. If one walks around the robot, the robot spins in place, attempting to face the person.

```
Public void turnClosest
  (java.awt.event.MouseEvent event)
{
 int shortestDirection; int speed;
 boolean flag = true;
 RC.turnSonarsOn(); RC.GetState();
 while (flag) {
  RC.GetState();
  shortestDirection=calcShortestDirection() -1;
  if (shortestDirection > 8)
   shortestDirection -= 16;
  if (Math.abs(shortestDirection) > 2)
   RC.setVel(-(shortestDirection*40),
            (shortestDirection*40));
  else RC.setVel(-(shortestDirection*20),
               (shortestDirection*20));
 } } // turnClosest() //

int calcShortestDirection()
{
 int minVal = 255; int minIndex = 0;
 for (int i=1; i<17; i++)
   if (RC.stateArray[i] < minVal) {
     minVal = RC.stateArray[i]; minIndex = i;}
 return minIndex;
} // calcShortestDirection() //
```

Figure 3: Java code for the Turn-Closest program

This code shows the separation of the software into a perceptual reduction, "what direction is the closest object?" in `calcShortestDirection()` followed by action selection, "which way should I turn and how hard?" in the remainder of the `turnClosest()` method.

When students of *Mobile Robot Programming*[1] do the `turnClosest` assignment on their Nomad Scout robots, the two most common reasons for poor behavior correspond to errors in the perceptual partition step and the control step. In the former case, the $P \rightarrow Pr$ mapping fails because students use algorithms that are too complex in determining the location of the closest object (e.g. minimum of adjacent *n* sonar readings). In the latter case, the robot successfully determines the direction to the closest object but the speeds chosen in $Pr \rightarrow Ar$ are too high and so the robot overshoots and oscillates (particularly when the student is unfamiliar with control theory).

The challenge of robot diagnosis is that the same poor robot behavior may be caused by either a bug in *Partition*() or a different bug in *Control*(). Diagnosis would be easier if the robot program were written in a way that enables the history of values for the internal variables of the Robot Program to be observable. In the case of a state-less, functional program, the only internal variable is the abstract percept. We denote the value of the abstract percept over time as *Pr**.

Robot Observability

State observability is defined as the ability of a robot to acquire the value of the state *s* of the Environment E (see Fig. 2). A robot in a fully observable world can acquire the trajectory of environmental state values over time: *S**.

We define the term, *robot observability*, as an analogue to state observability, where the target is not the Environment but its companion, the Robot Program.

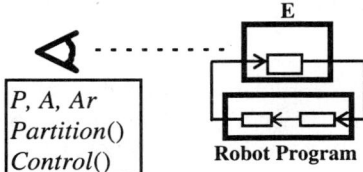

Figure 4: The addition of an observer to the robot system

Suppose that an observer is added to the closed system of Figures 1 and 2. This observer is given a description of the sets *P* and *A* as well as full knowledge of the static robot program, including *Partition*() and *Control*() (See Fig. 4). During run-time, the observer only directly sees the Environment module, but perceives changes in E only to a finite level of acuity.

---

[1] CS2241 at Stanford University; 16x62 at Carnegie Mellon University; CS1699 at University of Pittsburgh.

We define *robot observability* as the degree to which the observer can identify the trajectory of the internal values of the Robot Program, $Pr*$ and $Y*$.

A robot program that is fully observable has transparent internal values. Of course, this depends not only on the structure of the robot program but also on the observability of the Environment. Consider a caterpillar robot with a single forward-facing sonar sensor. The robot program partitions the set of possible sonar values into two possible values that comprise Pr: {*close, far*}. The *Control*() algorithm is functional, simply mapping *close* to zero motion and *far* to positive speed. Lisp code for the robot program is shown in Figure 5.

```
(defun caterpillar-control ()
  (loop
     (r-move (if (close-obstacle) 0
                 *forward-speed*) 0)))
(defun close-obstacle ()
  (< (get-sonar) 6))
```

Figure 5: Code for the caterpillar robot program.

This system has full robot observability for any observer who can reliably discriminate the robot's motion.

It can be shown that for any functional robot program with a bijective mapping from Pr to Ar, the robot is fully observable if the actions in Ar can be discriminated by the observer. This may explain the success of functional and quasi-functional (e.g. reactive) programming in robotics, because viewing the actions of the robot can often provide a direct window into the percept stream arriving at the robot. When the robot misbehaves, the designer can easily determine if the percept violates implicit assumptions made by the designer, or if the functional mapping from percept to action needs to be modified.

Because the composition of Ar is an important design choice for the robot software engineer, we suggest a heuristic that is applicable whether the engineer is designing a functional, reactive or state-based robot program: *prefer robot program solutions with greater robot observability*.

For example, consider a mobile robot that avoids obstacles and must reach a goal location. Fig. 6 shows top-level Lisp code for a synchro-drive robot chassis.

```
(defun swervebot-control ()
  (loop (r-move 10
           (cond ((close-obstacle-right) 30)
                 ((close-obstacle-left) -30)
                 ((goal-way-right) 30)
                 ((goal-way-left) -30)
                 (t 0)))))
```

Figure 6: Code for avoiding an obstacle and achieving a goal

The code in Fig. 6 demonstrates a case-based approach to specifying rotational velocities for the robot. Four most basic cases are identified, and each is assigned a discrete rotational speed and direction. A popular alternative to this case-based approach is a continuous-valued approach, in which the speed is a continuous function of the sensor values (Borenstein and Koren, 1991). For instance, the rotational speed in the case of goal-way-right could be a function of the number of degrees disparity between the heading to the goal and the robot's current heading.

By now it may be apparent to the reader that Fig. 6 contains a simple bug. The signs of the rotation velocities are incorrect in the case of the third and fourth condition; the robot will swerve away from obstacles but also away from the goal when there are no obstacles. This error was not contrived but, rather, it was made by the author on his first try at the robot program.

The behavior that resulted during first testing on a Nomad 150 robot demonstrates the difficulty of debugging mobile robot code. During testing, the robot would, at times, turn away from the goal. Were the sonar sensors seeing phantom obstacles, or was there an error in the rotational encoder? The robot appeared to work correctly at other times, because the designer was standing next to the robot. Unbeknownst to the designer, the robot was executing, not the goal-way-left case (which would have caused a rotation in the "wrong" direction), but the close-obstacle-right (which seemingly turned towards the goal) because its sensors were picking up the designer.

This debugging difficulty stems from a lack of robot observability: when the robot swerves left, it cannot be determined by observation whether it is doing so because of cond case 1 or (in the corrected code) cond case 4. The solution, in keeping with the heuristic to maximize robot observability, is to populate Ar with actions from A that are recognizably different for each of the four different abstract percepts in Pr, as shown in Fig. 7.

```
(defun swervebot-control ()
  (loop (r-move 10
           (cond ((close-obstacle-right) 30)
                 ((close-obstacle-left) -30)
                 ((goal-way-right) -15)
                 ((goal-way-left) 15)
                 (t 0)))))
```

Figure 7: Improved and debugged swervebot code maximizing robot observability

When it is possible to design a robot programming solution with only a handful of cases, this technique may be advantageous relative to the continuous-valued programming approach due to its high robot observability.

This bias toward a small number of cases is just one side effect of the heuristic to maximize robot observability. The general effect of maximizing robot observability is a bias toward reducing the size of Ar maximally, and ideally until the action space is no larger than the robot program's internal feature space: $|Ar| = |Pr \times Y|$. An overly large set of actions in Ar will fail to be discernible by the observer.

In constructing Ar, the designer is performing *action sampling*, in which a subspace of the available action space is being delineated for use by the robot. The perceptual complement is *percept abstraction*, in which the percepts of the robot, P, are partitioned into $|Pr|$ values. If the number of partitions selected is too small, then the robot may fail to recover relevant information from the environment. If |Pr| is too large, then the robot may be discriminating detail that is irrelevant to its task.

In summary, an approach to maximizing robot observability is to minimize the size of Pr and Ar, while including sufficient information in Pr to capture relevant environmental detail and making Ar inclusive enough to maintain the robot's expressiveness. Next, we propose an incremental method for constructing a robot program along these lines.

Property Mapping

A property is a subset of the set of environment states, S. Intuitively, a property captures the value of one feature of the world while allowing other features of the world to range freely. For example, property *p1* may correspond to the robot faced by an obstacle on its left and no obstacle on its right. This property would denote every such state, varying the robot's absolute orientation and the existence of obstacles behind the robot freely, for example.

In the case of robot programming, our intent is to use properties to capture the aspects of environment state that are most relevant to the programming problem. For example, in the case of a mobile robot destined to serve hors d'oeuvres, the designer will care about properties corresponding to the location of obstacles, hungry persons and the status of the tray: {*obstacle near, obstacle far, hungry person near, hungry person far, tray has cookies, tray is empty*}.

When designers think in property space, they can choose to define the set of properties Pr and then the output function g without considering the observability of the properties using the robot's actual sensors. Surprisingly, ignoring the sensory shortcomings of the robot during part of design-time can be beneficial. We propose such a method for robot program design:

1. Suppose that S is fully observable. Select a new property that can map to a single, coherent action.
2. Select a specific action for this property. Avoid choosing the same action for two distinct properties.
3. Implement the property-action pair in code. Test if possible.
4. Unless finished go-to Step 1.

By first ignoring the partial observability problem, the designer avoids simultaneously solving both the action selection problem and the perceptual/state update problems. Instead, the designer creates a set of property-action pairs, where only the most relevant properties are introduced. Since we assume full observability, this approach generates all of the key actions that belong in Ar regardless of the robot's particular perceptual limitations. In Step 3, the designer encodes recognition of the chosen properties into the robot program, thereby addressing the perception/state update problem on a property-by-property basis.

Solving the problem incrementally first minimizes the size of Ar then introduces only as many perceptual partitions into Pr and only as much state Y as is necessary to detect the target properties.

Consider, for example, the robot programming problem for Cheshm, a mobile robot that avoids obstacles using a solitary depth-from-focus sensor. Cheshm's depth-from-focus sensor provides just three levels of range information (i.e *close, medium, far*) in a 3 x 5 grid. The programming challenge is to design a robot program that would actively wander while avoiding both convex and concave (e.g. stairs) obstacles in order to demonstrate the sensor's robustness.

The first property chosen, called danger-closep, recognizes the existence of any convex obstacle dangerously close to the robot. The resulting control program, shown in Fig. 8, made Cheshm a caterpillar robot.

```
(defun cheshm-control ()
  (loop (r-move (if (danger-closep) 0 80) 0)))
```

Figure 8: Preliminary Cheshm control code.

We tested this first version of Cheshm by running the robot in a variety of circumstances, stepping in front of the robot and placing various objects in its way to see if it would react. After debugging the sensing system, additional property-action pairs were added to implement swerving around obstacles based on their positions: {*danger-leftp, danger-rightp, medium-leftp, medium-rightp*}. Fig. 9 shows the complete action control code for Cheshm.

```
(defun cheshm-control ()
  (loop (if (concave-obstaclep) (turn-around)
        (progn
          (setf translation-velocity
            (cond ((danger-closep) 0)
                  ((medium-closep) 40)
                  (t 80)))
          (setf rotation-velocity
            (cond ((danger-leftp) -40)
                  ((danger-rightp) 40)
                  ((medium-leftp) -20)
                  ((medium-rightp) 20)
                  (t 0)))
          (r-move translation-velocity
                  rotation-velocity)))))
```

Figure 9: Cheshm's actual action-selection code

The rotational speeds for medium and close obstacles differ significantly (20 versus 40) so that to the designer/observer can easily recognize the triggering property. An important goal of the Cheshm project was to demonstrate that vision can safely detect concave obstacles. Note that concave-obstaclep uses a different action from those used below it for convex obstacles. This enabled us to observe Cheshm's ability to explicitly recognize concave obstacles, as it turns in place 180 degrees upon encountering stairs and ledges (Nourbakhsh et al., 1997).

A more recent working example is T.A.W. (Texas Alien Woman), a contestant in the 1999 AAAI Hors D'oeuvres competition. In this competition, robots search for humans in the room, offer them appetizers, and return to their refill stations for more appetizers when they run out. T.A.W. was an entry designed to demonstrate the use of inexpensive pyroelectric sensors to detect its human targets. The method, gohome(), was written to control T.A.W. during its return to the refill station once it had run out of cookies. The top-level goal for gohome() is to achieve a specific position, the home base, while avoiding unpredictable, moving obstacles along the way. This code (Fig. 10) was written using the property-mapping technique, starting with the property, closeObstacle.

```
public void gohome() {
  int forwardVel = 0; int goalDist = 0;
  int rotationVel = 0; double rotationGoal;
  int rotIntGoal; int currentRot;
  rc.GetState();
  goalDist = Math.abs(rc.stateArray[rc.XPOS]) +
             Math.abs(rc.stateArray[rc.YPOS]);
  rotationGoal =
    Math.atan2((rc.stateArray[rc.YPOS]),
               (rc.stateArray[rc.XPOS]));
  currentRot = rc.stateArray[rc.THETA];
  rotIntGoal = (int)(3600.0 * rotationGoal /
  if (rotIntGoal < 0) rotIntGoal += 3600;
  if (personp() && (canExcuseMe())) {
    resetExcuseMeTimer();
    System.out.println("I must go get cookies
                        excuse me");
    myTongue.playSound("out.au");
  } // if
  if (goalDist < homeThreshold) {
    move(0,0);
    myState = REFILLING;
    //System.out.println("exitingtoREFILLING");
  } else if (closeObstacle()) {
    //System.out.println("Close obstacle... ");
    forwardVel = 0;
    rotationVel =
      computeRotCloseObstacle(currentRot,
                              rotIntGoal);
  } else {
    //System.out.println("no obstacle...");
    forwardVel = computeForVelTo(goalDist);
    rotationVel = computeRotTo(currentRot,
                               rotIntGoal);
  }
  move(forwardVel, -rotationVel);
} // gohome()

int computeForVelTo(int goalDist) {
  int minF, minS;
  minF = minFront();
  minS = Math.min(minLeft(),minRight());
  int nominal = goalDist / 3; // ILLAH was 2
  if (nominal > 200) nominal = 200;
  if ((minF > 40) && (minS > 20)) {
    return nominal;
  } else if ((minF > 20) && (minS > 10)) {
    return nominal/2;
  } else {
    return nominal/3;
  } }

boolean closeObstacle() {
  return ((minFront() < 17) || (minFLeft() < 8)
       || (minFRight() < 8)); }

int computeRotCloseObstacle(int curRot,
                            int goalRot) {
  if (minLeft() < minRight()) {
    return -50;
  } else {
    return 50;
  }
} // computeRotCloseObstacle() //

// input is between 0 and 3600 and 0 - 3600
// output needs to be -200 to +200 or so...
int computeRotTo(int curRot, int goalRot) {
  int theDiff = goalRot - curRot;
  if (theDiff < -1800) theDiff += 3600;
  if (theDiff > 1800) theDiff -= 3600;
  if ((theDiff > 0) && (minLeft() < 25)) {
    theDiff = 0;
    //System.out.println("left close");
  } else if ((theDiff < 0) &&
             (minRight() < 25)) {
    theDiff = 0;
    //System.out.println("right close");
  }
  return (theDiff / 10);
}

int minLeft() {
  return (Math.min(Math.min(rc.stateArray[11],
    rc.stateArray[12]),rc.stateArray[13])); }
```

Figure 10: T.A.W.'s gohome procedure

When closeObstacle() was first coded, it was given zero rotational speed and the else case directly following it simply set forwardVel at a single speed and set rotationVel at zero. After testing and debugging, the next step was to add rotation to the closeObstacle case and, by inspecting computeRotCloseObstacle() you can see that this was performed using one discrete rotation speed for the sake of robot observability.

Next, the else case was changed from an unintelligent "go straight ahead" command to turn toward the goal. Note in computeRotTo() that the rotational speed was indeed computed as a continuous function of the difference between desired heading and current heading. While this could diminish robot observability, it affords T.A.W. extremely smooth motion and elicited comments to this effect during the competition.

In spite of this continuously-valued function, T.A.W. achieves a high degree of robot observability by depending on *translational* speed to communicate internal state and perceptual state. When the robot is observed during execution of gohome(), it is instantly either moving straight ahead or turning. The observability question is, can an observer tell why the robot is moving the way it is moving?

If T.A.W. is going straight, it is in one of two cases: it believes it is heading in the goal direction, or it cannot turn because it detects an obstacle in computeRotTo(). The forward velocity of T.A.W. is significantly faster in the former case (nominal) than in the latter case (nominal/2), and so this distinction will be obvious.

In the case of turning, T.A.W. turns either toward the goal or away from an obstacle. Turning toward the goal is done at full translational speed (i.e. nominal), as shown by computeForVelTo(), while turning away from an obstacle is done with a forward velocity of *zero* (based on the closeObstacle() case).

The astute reader will note that T.A.W. can speak (myTongue.playSound("out.au")). If so, why not program the robot to communicate internal values verbally, just as a C debugger may sprinkle the code with printf commands. This is acceptable in many situations, but there are two caveats.

First, there remains a bandwidth limitation on the human observer, and this constrains the number of properties and the number of discrete, chosen actions that are feasible. Second, the robot's entire behavior is often relevant to its goals. In the case of T.A.W., the robot speaks to the public, so the audio channel is not freely available.

As shown by the `myState` variable, T.A.W. also makes use of a limited amount of state. The property mapping technique was used for each state's behavior, and furthermore the states were disambiguated by designing intentionally different overall robot motion for each state. The speed achieved by T.A.W. during the GOHOME state is approximately twice the speed used during the SERVEFOOD state.

The control code was designed, implemented and tested over the course of approximately 6 hours of focused work. The result, T.A.W., achieved second place at the 1999 AAAI Competition.

Other, more ambitious mobile robots programmed using this same methodology have demonstrated significant mean time to failure statistics. Chips, in particular, as well as Sweet Lips and Joe, are three full-time tour guide robots that conduct tours in museums. Chips uses a property-mapping, case-based approach to both navigation and obstacle avoidance and has now been running for 22 months autonomously. Its mean time between failure has increased to a stable value of approximately three weeks (Nourbakhsh et al., 1999).

Concluding Remarks

We have used the property mapping technique for more than four years, resulting in several examples of very successful implementations. Our experiences suggest that robot observability is a good predictor of long-term robot reliability. But, is this the most important mechanism by which this technique affects robot reliability?

Property mapping tends to minimize the effective perceptual space via partitioning, and to minimize the effective output range via action sampling. It is conceivable that this form of problem reformulation introduces a real bias toward a space of reliable robot programs, separate from its effect on diagnostic transparency.

The property technique described herein applies to ground percepts and actions. Architectures such at 3T (Bonasso and Kortenkamp, 1996) take advantage of a hierarchical approach in which meta-actions are implemented as primitive behaviors. A next step is to generalize property mapping and robot observability so that they may be applied to such hierarchical systems. This technique also needs to be extended to the multi-threaded case in order to evaluate inherently parallel architectures such as Subsumption (Brooks, 1986).

Finally, we have observed surprising differences in robot reliability when comparing implementations in functional languages (Lisp, ML) and procedural languages (C, Pascal). An examination of whether functional programming languages naturally lead to high degrees of robot observability may be fruitful.

Acknowledgments

Prof. Michael Genesereth teaches CS224 at Stanford University. Profs. Martha Pollack and Don Chiarulli teach CS1699 at University of Pittsburgh. Chris Hardouin created T.A.W. Thanks to Lee Weiss, Iwan Ulrich and the anonymous reviewers for their comments.

References

Bonasso, R. and Kortenkamp, D. 1996. Using a layered control architecture to alleviate planning with inc. info. In *Planning with Incomplete Information*, AAAI Spring Symposium Series.

Borenstein, J. and Koren, Y. 1991. The vector field histogram—fast obstacle avoidance for mobile robots, IEEE J. Robotics and Automation 7 (3) 278-288.

Brooks, R. 1986. A robust layered control system for a mobile robot. *IEEE Journal of Robotics and Automation*, 2:14-23.

Firby, R. 1987. An investigation into reactive planning in complex domains. In *Proc. AAAI-87*.

Halperin, D., Kavraki, L and Latombe J. 1998. Robot algorithms. *CRC Handbook of Algorithms and Theory of Computation*, M. Atallah (ed.), CRC Press.

Horswill, I. 1999. Functional programming of behavior-based systems. In *Proc. IEEE International Symposium on Computational Intelligence in Robotics and Automation*.

Horswill, I. 1993. Polly: A vision-based artificial agent. In *Proc. AAAI-93*, Washington DC, AAAI Press.

Krotkov, E., Simmons, R., Cozman, F. and Koenig, S. 1996. Safeguarded teleoperation for lunar rovers: from human factors to field trials. In *Proc. IEEE Planetary Rover Technology and Systems Workshop*, Minn., MN.

Kunz, C., Willeke, T. and Nourbakhsh, I. 1999. Automatic mapping of dynamic office environments. *Autonomous Robots* 7, 131-142.

Nourbakhsh, I., Bobenage, J., Grange, S., Lutz, R., Meyer, R. and Soto, A. 1999. An affective mobile robot educator with a full-time job. *Artificial Intelligence* 114:95-124.

Nourbakhsh, I., Andre, D., Tomasi, C. and Genesereth, M. 1997. Mobile robot obstacle avoidance via depth from focus. *Robotics and Autonomous Systems* 22, 151-158.

Simmons, R. 1994. Structured control for autonomous robots. *IEEE Transactions on Robotics and Automation*, 10:1.

A Method for Clustering the Experiences of a Mobile Robot that Accords with Human Judgments

Tim Oates, Matthew D. Schmill and Paul R. Cohen

Computer Science Building
University of Massachusetts, Box 34610
Amherst, MA 01003-4610
{oates,schmill,cohen}@cs.umass.edu

Abstract

If robotic agents are to act autonomously they must have the ability to construct and reason about models of their physical environment. For example, planning to achieve goals requires knowledge of how the robot's actions affect the state of the world over time. The traditional approach of hand-coding this knowledge is often quite difficult, especially for robotic agents with rich sensing abilities that exist in dynamic and uncertain environments. Ideally, robots would acquire knowledge of their environment and then use this knowledge to act. We present an unsupervised learning method that allows a robotic agent to identify and represent qualitatively different outcomes of actions. Experiments with a Pioneer-1 mobile robot demonstrate the utility of the approach with respect to capturing the structure and dynamics of a complex, real-world environment, and show that the models acquired by the robot correlate surprisingly well with human models of the environment.

Introduction

If robotic agents are to act autonomously they must have the ability to construct and reason about models of their physical environment. In all but the simplest, static domains, such models must represent the dynamics of environmental change. For example, because the effects of actions are not instantaneous, planning to achieve goals requires knowledge of how the robots actions affect the state of the world over time. The traditional approach of hand-coding this knowledge is often quite difficult, especially for robotic agents with rich sensing abilities that exist in dynamic and uncertain environments. Ideally, agents would acquire knowledge of their environment and then use this knowledge to act.

This paper presents an unsupervised method for learning models of environmental dynamics based on clustering multivariate time series. An unsupervised learning approach to this problem is desirable because, as noted previously, hand-coding models of dynamic,

Copyright © 2000, American Association for Artificial Intelligence (www.aaai.org). All rights reserved.

stochastic environments is a difficult task, and inadequacies of the encoding undermine the agent's autonomy. Experiments with a Pioneer-1 mobile robot demonstrate the utility of the method and show that the models acquired by the robot correlate surprisingly well with human models of the environment.

Individual time series are obtained by recording the output of a subset of an agent's sensors. We call these time series *experiences*. An example of a sensor subset on the Pioneer-1 robot is its array of seven sonars. Each sonar returns the distance to the closest object in the direction that it points. Recording of time series is usually triggered by events, such as the initiation of a particular action. Each time a given event occurs, the time series that was recorded is added to a bucket associated with that event. Once a sufficient number of experiences are recorded, clusters can be formed. Clustering requires a measure of similarity between multivariate time series. One such measure that is particularly appropriate for this problem is Dynamic Time Warping (DTW) (Sankoff & Kruskal 1983). (We discuss DTW in detail in a later section.) Each cluster can then be represented by a prototype, either the cluster centroid or an average of its members. This process is depicted graphically in Figure 1.

Cluster prototypes formed in this manner are useful for a variety of purposes. If the event driving the collection of time series was the initiation of an action, cluster prototypes correspond to qualitatively different outcomes of engaging in that action. As such, they can be used for off-line planning and for on-line prediction by finding the best partial match among the prototypes to current sensor readings.

The remainder of the paper is organized as follows. The next section describes our method for clustering time series in detail, including a discussion of Dynamic Time Warping, the particular clustering algorithm used, and prototype formation. We then present an evaluation of the method as applied to the Pioneer-1 mobile robot. The last two sections review related work, pointing out the connection between Dynamic Time Warping and Hidden Markov Models, and outline future research, respectively.

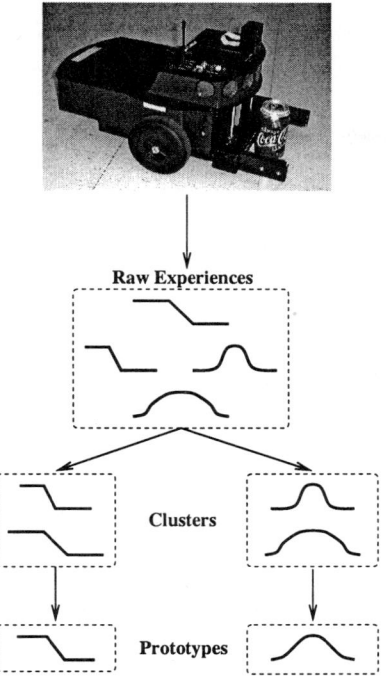

Figure 1: The formation of prototypes of qualitatively difference experiences.

Clustering Experiences

This section presents our method for unsupervised learning of models of environmental dynamics based on clustering of multivariate time series. To ground the discussion, consider the Pioneer-1 mobile robot. Its sensors include, among others, a bump switch on the end of each gripper paddle that indicates when the gripper hits an object, an infrared break beam between the gripper paddles that indicates when an object enters the gripper, and wheel encoders that measure the rate at which the wheels are spinning.

Suppose the robot is moving forward at a fixed velocity. Collectively, the values returned by the sensors mentioned above can discriminate many different situations. For example, if the robot runs into a large immovable object, such as a wall, the bump sensors go high and the wheel velocities abruptly drop to zero. If it bumps into a trash can, which is large but movable, the bump sensors go high and the wheel velocities remain constant. If it comes across an object that can be grasped, the break beam goes high when the object enters the gripper and there is no change in wheel velocity. As observers of the robot's actions, we can label and categorize its experiences. Our goal is to provide mechanisms that will allow the robot to perform that task by itself.

Let E denote an experience, a multivariate time series containing n measurements from a set of sensors such that $E = \{e_t | 1 \leq t \leq n\}$. The e_i are vectors of values containing one element for each sensor. Given a set of m experiences, we want to obtain, in an unsupervised manner, a partition into subsets of experiences such that each subset corresponds to a qualitatively different type of experience. Given such a partition, reasoning with entire sets of experiences is unwieldy, so a simpler representation such as the average experience in a subset is required.

If an appropriate measure of the similarity of two time series is available, clustering followed by prototype extraction is a suitable unsupervised learning method for this problem (see Figure 1). Finding such a measure of similarity is difficult because experiences that are qualitatively the same may be quantitatively different in at least two ways. First, they may be of different lengths, making it difficult or impossible to embed the time series in a metric space and use, for example, Euclidean distance to determine similarity. Second, within a single time series, the rate at which progress is made can vary non-linearly. For example, the robot may move slowly or quickly toward a wall, leading to either a slow or rapid decrease in the distance returned by its forward-pointing sonar. In each case, though, then end result is the same, the robot bumps into the wall. Such differences in rate make similarity measures such as cross-correlation unusable.

The measure of similarity that we use is Dynamic Time Warping (DTW) (Sankoff & Kruskal 1983). It is ideally suited for the time series generated by a robot's sensors. DTW is a generalization of classical algorithms for comparing discrete sequences (e.g. minimum string edit distance (Corman, Leiserson, & Rivest 1990)) to sequences of continuous values. It was used extensively in speech recognition, a domain in which the time series are notoriously complex and noisy, until the advent of Hidden Markov Models which offered a unified probabilistic framework for the entire recognition process (Jelinek 1997).

Given two experiences, E_1 and E_2 (more generally, two continuous multivariate time series), DTW finds the warping of the time dimension in E_1 that minimizes the difference between the two experiences. Consider the two univariate time series shown in Figure 2. Imagine that the time axis of E_1 is an elastic string, and that you can grab that string at any point corresponding to a time at which a value was recorded for the time series. Warping of the time dimension consists of grabbing one of those points and moving it to a new position on the time axis. As the point moves, the elastic string (the time dimension) compresses in the direction of motion and expands in the other direction. Consider the middle column in Figure 2. Moving the point at the third time step from its original location to the seventh time step causes all of the points to its right to compress into the remaining available space, and all of the points to its left to fill the newly created space. Of course, more complicated warpings of the time dimension are possible, as with the third column in Figure 2 in which four points are moved.

Given a warping of the time dimension in E_1, yielding

ROBOTICS 847

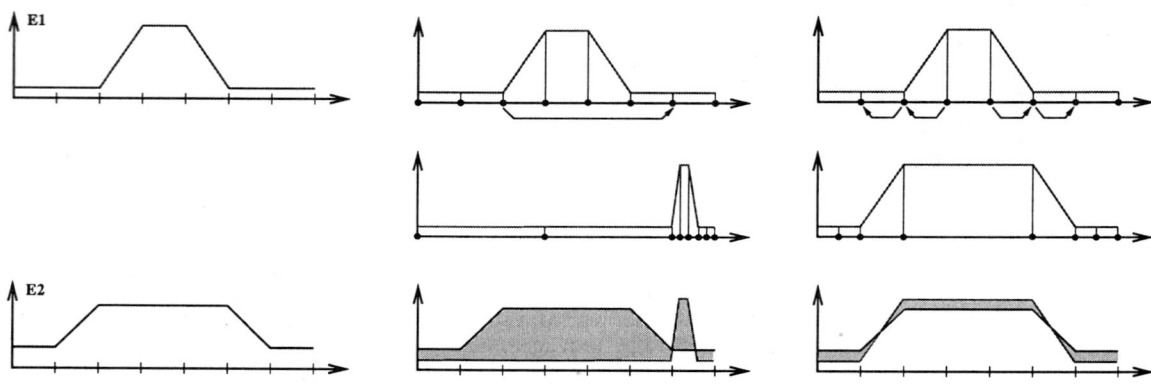

Figure 2: Two time series, E_1 and E_2, (the leftmost column) and two possible warpings of E_1 into E_2 (the middle and rightmost columns).

a time series that we will denote E_1', one can measure the similarity of E_1' and E_2 by determining the area between the two curves. That area is shown in gray in the bottom row of Figure 2. Note that the first warping of E_1 in which a single point was moved results in a poor match, one with a large area between the curves. However, the fit given by the second, more complex warping is quite good. In general, there are exponentially many ways to warp the time dimension of E_1. DTW uses dynamic programming to find the warping that minimizes the area between the curves in time that is a low order polynomial of the lengths of E_1 and E_2, i.e. $O(|E_1||E_2|)$.

DTW returns the optimal warping of E_1, the one that minimizes the area between E_1' and E_2, and the area associated with that warping. The area is used as a measure of similarity between the two time series. Note that this measure of similarity handles nonlinearities in the rates at which experiences progress and is not affected by differences in the lengths of experiences. In general, the area between E_1' and E_2 may not be the same as the area between E_2' into E_1. We use a symmetrized version of DTW that essentially computes the average of those two areas based on a single warping (Kruskall & Liberman 1983). Although a straightforward implementation of DTW is more expensive than computing Euclidean distance or cross-correlation, there are numerous speedups that both improve the properties of DTW as a distance metric and make its computation nearly linear in the length of the time series with a small constant.

Given m experiences, we can construct a complete pairwise distance matrix by invoking DTW $m(m-1)/2$ times (the factor of 2 is due to the use of symmetrized DTW). We then apply a standard hierarchical, agglomerative clustering algorithm that starts with one cluster for each experience and merges the pair of clusters with the minimum average intercluster distance (Everitt 1993). Without a stopping criterion, merging will continue until there is a single cluster containing all m experiences. To avoid that situation, we do not merge clusters for which the mean intercluster distance is significantly different from the mean intracluster distance as measured by a t-test.

Finally, for each cluster we select a prototype. Two methods commonly used are to choose the cluster member that minimizes the distance to all other members of the cluster, or to simply average the members of the cluster. The advantage of the latter method is that it smooths out noise that may be present in any individual data item. Unfortunately, it is only workable when the cluster elements are embedded in a metric space (e.g. Cartesian space). Although we cannot embed experiences in a metric space, DTW allows us to use a combination of the two methods as follows. First, we select the time series that minimizes distance to all other time series in a given cluster. Then we warp all other patterns into that centroid, resulting in a set of patterns that are all on the same time scale. It is then a simple matter to take the average value at each time point over all of the series and use the result as the cluster prototype.

Evaluation

We are interested in the results of our clustering algorithm for two key reasons. First, for the purposes of planning, we would like clusters to map to action outcomes, so that each cluster prototype can serve as the basis for an operator model. Second, we would like agents to be able to acquire a believable ontology of activity. That is, we would like our agents to be able to differentiate actions as a human would so that their representations of outcome are in accordance with our own. As such, our primary means of evaluating cluster quality is to compare the clusters generated by our automated system against clusters generated manually by the experimenter who designed the experiences they comprise.

Data were collected for 4 sets of experiences: 102 experiences with the robot moving in a straight line while collecting data from the velocity encoders, break beams, and gripper bumper (which we will call the *tactile* sensors), 102 move experiences collecting data from

move/tactile	turn/tactile	move/visual	turn/visual
+250 unobstructed	+100 unobstructed	no object	no object
+100 unobstructed	+100 never stops	heavy noise	can't move
-100 unobstructed	+100 bump	approach on right	pass left to right
-250 unobstructed	+100 blocked	approach disappear	pass right to left
+250 temporary bump	+100 temporary bump	discover left reverse	discover right
+100 temporary bump	+100 blocked bump	vanish on right	discover left
+250 push delayed bump	-100 unobstructed	vanish on left	left to right
+250 delayed bump	-100 temporary bump	retreat left	vanish off right
+100 delayed bump	-100 impeded turn	discover right	vanish off left
+250 crash beam1	-100 blocked	approach ahead	
+250 squash		approach, gets big	
+250 push blocked		approach on left	
+250 push		approach, stays small	
+100 push			
+100 push shallow			
+100 blocked			
-100 blocked			

Figure 3: Outcome labels given to the hand built clusters for each of the 4 experience sets.

the Pioneer's vision system, including the X and Y location, area, and distance to a single visible object being tracked (which we will call the *visual* sensors), 50 experiences with the robot turning in place collecting tactile data, and 50 turn experiences collecting visual data. In each experience, the robot attempted to move or turn for a duration between 2 and 8 seconds in the laboratory environment. Visible objects and objects that impeded or obstructed the robot's path were present in many of the trials.

The labels given to the hand-built clusters generated are summarized in table 3. In the visual tracking problems, the clusters correspond to visible objects' relations to the agent during activity; the object may move across the visual field while turning or it may loom while being approached. In the tactile problems, clusters correspond to the Pioneer's velocity and the types of contact made with objects in the environment during the activity; heavy objects halt the Pioneer's progress, and are labeled "crash", while light, small objects merely trigger the break beams and are labeled "push".

We evaluate the clusters generated by DTW and agglomerative clustering with a 2 × 2 contingency table called an *accordance table*. Consider the following table:

	t_e	$\neg t_e$
t_t	n_1	n_2
$\neg t_t$	n_3	n_4

We calculate the cells of this table by considering all pairs of experiences e_j and e_k, and their relationships in the target (hand-built) and evaluation (DTW) clusterings. If e_j and e_k reside in the same cluster in the target clustering (denoted by t_t), and e_j and e_k also reside in the same cluster in the evaluation clustering (denoted by t_e), then cell n_1 is incremented. The other cells of the table are incremented when either the target or evaluation clusterings places the experiences in different clusters ($\neg t_t$ and $\neg t_e$, respectively).

Cells n_1 and n_4 of this table represent the number of experience pairs in which the clustering algorithms are in accordance. We call $n_1 + n_4$ the number of *agreements* and $n_2 + n_3$ the number of *disagreements*. The *accordance ratios* that we are interested in are $\frac{n_1}{n_1+n_2}$, accordance with respect to t_t, and $\frac{n_4}{n_3+n_4}$, accordance with respect to $\neg t_t$.

Table 4 shows the breakdown of accordance for the combination of dynamic time warping and agglomerative clustering versus the ideal clustering built by hand. The column labeled "#" indicates the difference between the number of hand-built and automated clusters. In each problem, the automated algorithm clustered more aggressively, resulting in fewer clusters. The columns that follow present the accordance ratios for experiences grouped together, apart, and the total number of agreements and disagreements.

The table shows very high levels of accordance. Ratios ranged from a minimum of 82.2% for experiences clustered together (t_t) in the move/visual set to 100% for experiences clustered together in the turn problems. For the turn problems, the aggressive clustering may account for the high t_t accuracy, causing slightly lower accuracy in the $\neg t_t$ case.

The disparity in the number of clusters suggests that tuning the parameters of the clustering algorithm to produce more clusters might boost $\neg t_t$ accuracy while preserving the t_t accuracy. The table for this condition is omitted for the sake of brevity, but our findings were that tuning the clustering algorithm in this way leads to a reduction in accuracy in all but the turn/tactile dataset, whose $\neg t_t$ accuracy increased 7 points.

The failure of this strategy to increase $\neg t_t$ accuracy by tuning the clustering algorithm to terminate with more clusters indicates that it is not simply a matter of the number of clusters. Exploration of the t_t disagree-

	#	t_t	$t_t \wedge t_e$	%	$\neg t_t$	$\neg t_t \wedge \neg t_e$	%	Agree	Disagree	%
Move visual	-5	876	720	**82.2**	4275	4125	**96.4**	4845	306	**94.0**
Move tactile	-7	443	378	**85.3**	4708	4468	**95.0**	4846	305	**94.0**
Turn visual	-5	262	262	**100.0**	599	571	**95.3**	833	28	**96.7**
Turn tactile	-6	163	163	**100.0**	698	593	**85.0**	756	105	**87.8**

Figure 4: Accordance statistics for automated clustering against the hand built clustering.

ments in the move/visual data, the problem with the highest error rate, indicates that 132 out of the 156 errors can be traced to two clusters in the automatically generated set that were distributed differently in the target set. The target clusters were "no object" (no visible object being tracked, some minor noise) and "heavy noise" (noise makes it unclear whether anything was being tracked). The automated set had made the split differently; experiences with any noise were grouped together from those that had none. The remaining 24 errors were covered by a handful of six or seven experiences that were also attracted into clusters by experiences the hand builder did not feel were similar.

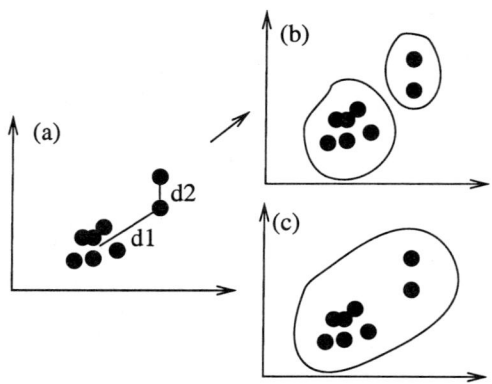

Figure 5: (a) A 2d representation of experiences. (b) The ordering effect of greedily merging based on the shorter distance d2 than the group average distance d1. (c) The most desirable clustering.

The problem is rooted in the tendency of greedy clustering algorithms to suffer from *ordering effects* (Fisher, Xu, & Zard 1992). In clustering schemes based on sorting, the order in which instances are considered biases the clusters that result. In agglomerative clustering algorithms, the clusters that result are biased by the algorithm's greedy choice of always considering merging the lowest distance clusters. Figure 5 illustrates how the ordering effect works on a 2d representation of the move/visual data. Because two of the noisy data are very similar (distance=d_2), they are clustered together early in the clustering process. This early decision creates two cluster centers that individually attract members based on the local greedy policy, where a global view (like our hand-builder's) would cluster them together.

Fortunately, optimization techniques exist that can refine initial clusterings to better reflect a global view (Fisher 1996). We have implemented a simple optimization technique which iteratively reassigns experiences to neighboring clusters if a cluster is found with a smaller group average distance than to the one the experience is in. After applying this optimization technique to the clusters used to generate table 4, many of the errors in the t_t cases disappeared: accordance climbed to 91.9% or better in all cases except the $\neg t_t$ case of turn/tactile, which decreased to below 80%, which reflects the disparity between the number of clusters generated by our algorithm and the hand built clustering.

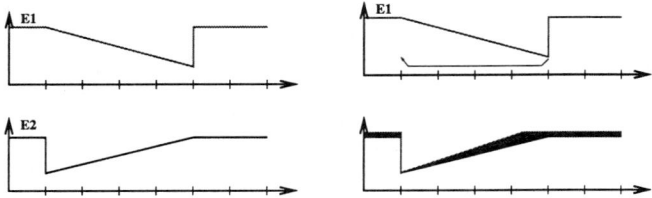

Figure 6: Two time series, E_1 and E_2, and a possible warping of E_1 into E_2 that obscures the salient difference.

The remaining few percent of misses appear to be related to dynamic time warping's ability to manipulate the time dimension. Figure 6 illustrates two time series that correspond to the horizontal location of an object on the Pioneer's visual plane. In experience e_1, the object comes into view from the right, passes across, and disappears off the left side of the visual plane. Experience e_2 represents an object moving in the opposite direction across the visual plane. Clearly, this is a salient distinction for many purposes, including planning, but it is one that DTW is able to obscure by sliding a single point of e_1 backward in time.

Related Work

The use of DTW as a measure of similarity between multivariate time series dates back a number of years to early work in speech recognition (Sakoe & Chiba 1978), although it was ultimately displaced by HMM's (Jelinek 1997). HMM's are actually a powerful generalization of DTW, and recent years have seen renewed interest in DTW for applications where the full power of HMM's may not be required (Berndt & Clifford 1994). That fact notwithstanding, it is unclear how one would apply standard HMM algorithms (such as Baum-Welch and Viterbi) directly to clustering time series. One recent attempt (Smyth 1997) at that problem is much more complex, both computationally and descriptively, than our application of DTW and requires a priori knowledge of the number of clusters (although a method for attempting to determine that number is presented).

Other approaches to measuring similarity between continuous time series have been proposed in the literature (Agrawal et al. 1995; Keogh & Pazzani 1998). However, these approaches are limited to univariate time series and are therefore not applicable to our problem, in which one sensor alone is insufficient to discriminate between experiences.

Conclusion

We have presented an approach to clustering the experiences of an autonomous agent acting in a complex, stochastic environment. Using Dynamic Time Warping as a measure of the similarity between time series sensor data, we produced clusters based on the dynamics of experiences, rather than static features. We evaluated the effectiveness of the unsupervised clustering algorithm by measuring the amount of *accordance* between the clusters it generated and cluster sets generated by hand as an answer key. Using only Dynamic Time Warping and agglomerative clustering on 150 trials of real Pioneer data in a variety of experiences, we measured 82-100% accordance between the automated and hand-built clusterings. By applying a simple iterative optimization algorithm to the initial clusterings, accordance measures increased to 91.9% and better.

Still, pathological cases exist where Dynamic Time Warping was able to find a temporal mapping that glossed over significant differences in time series exist. Though these cases cover only a small percentage of the robot's practical experiences, it is possible to constrain DTW so that these differences will be felt through the distance metric.

Future work will extend the approach described above in three ways. First, we plan on extending the autonomy of our system by utilizing cluster prototypes as bases for planning models, which will allow the Pioneer-1 agent to create basic action sequences to achieve sensorimotor goals. Second, rather than using each experience in its entirety, we will develop methods for identifying subsequences within the experiences that are relevant to the clustering process. Finally, we intend to leverage the relationship between DTW and HMM's to develop a method of clustering time series in which the output is a set of HMM's, one for each cluster.

References

Agrawal, R.; Lin, K.; Sawhney, H. S.; and Shim, K. 1995. Fast similarity search in the presence of noise, scaling and translation in time series databases. In *Proceedings of the 21st International Conference on Very Large Databases*.

Berndt, D. J., and Clifford, J. 1994. Using dynamic time warping to find patterns in time series. In *Working Notes of the Knowledge Discovery in Databases Workshop*, 359–370.

Corman, T. H.; Leiserson, C. E.; and Rivest, R. L. 1990. *Introduction to Algorithms*. MIT Press.

Everitt, B. 1993. *Cluster Analysis*. John Wiley & Sons, Inc.

Fisher, D. H.; Xu, L.; and Zard, N. 1992. Ordering effects in clustering. In *Proceedings of the 9th Annual Conference on Machine Learning*, 163–168.

Fisher, D. 1996. Iterative optimization and simplification of hierarchical clusterings. *Journal of Artificial Intelligence Research* 4:147–179.

Jelinek, F. 1997. *Statistical Methods for Speech Recognition*. MIT Press.

Keogh, E., and Pazzani, M. J. 1998. An enhanced representation of time series which allows fast and accurate classification, clustering and relevance feedback. In *Working Notes of the AAAI-98 workshop on Predicting the Future: AI Approaches to Time-Series Analysis*, 44–51.

Kruskall, J. B., and Liberman, M. 1983. The symmetric time warping problem: From continuous to discrete. In *Time Warps, String Edits and Macromolecules: The Theory and Practice of Sequence Comparison*. Addison-Wesley.

Sakoe, H., and Chiba, S. 1978. Dynamic programming algorithm optimization for spoken word recognition. *IEEE Transaction on Acoustics, Speech and Signal Processing* 26:143–165.

Sankoff, D., and Kruskal, J. B., eds. 1983. *Time Warps, String Edits, and Macromolecules: Theory and Practice of Sequence Comparisons*. Reading, MA: Addison-Wesley Publishing Company.

Smyth, P. 1997. Clustering sequences with hidden markov models. In *Advances in Neural Information Processing 9*.

Coordination for Multi-Robot Exploration and Mapping

Reid Simmons, David Apfelbaum, Wolfram Burgard[1],
Dieter Fox, Mark Moors[2], Sebastian Thrun, Håkan Younes

School of Computer Science, Carnegie Mellon University, Pittsburgh, PA 15213
[1]Department of Computer Science, University of Freiburg, 79110 Freiburg, Germany
[2]Department of Computer Science III, University of Bonn, 53117 Bonn, Germany

Abstract

This paper addresses the problem of exploration and mapping of an unknown environment by multiple robots. The mapping algorithm is an on-line approach to likelihood maximization that uses hill climbing to find maps that are maximally consistent with sensor data and odometry. The exploration algorithm explicitly coordinates the robots. It tries to maximize overall utility by minimizing the potential for overlap in information gain amongst the various robots. For both the exploration and mapping algorithms, most of the computations are distributed. The techniques have been tested extensively in real-world trials and simulations. The results demonstrate the performance improvements and robustness that accrue from our multi-robot approach to exploration.

1 Introduction

Creating maps of the environment is a fundamental challenge in mobile robotics. In general, to do so efficiently requires good exploration strategies. In particular, the robots need to know what areas are worthwhile to explore and how to distribute themselves effectively in order to thoroughly map previously unknown areas.

Most previous work in mapping dealt only with single robots. There are, however, advantages in mapping with multiple robots. The most obvious is that multiple robots can often do the task in less time. This may not always hold, however, due to interference between robots [6, 8]. Thus, it is important for the exploration strategies to keep the robots relatively well separated. Another advantage is that multiple robots may produce more accurate maps, due to merging of overlapping information. This can help compensate for sensor uncertainty and localization error, especially where the robots have different sensor and/or localization capabilities [7].

This paper presents techniques for coordinating multiple, heterogeneous robots in their task of exploring and mapping large, indoor environments. We consider two coordination problems — creating a single global map from the sensor information of the individual robots, and deciding where each robot should go in order to create the map most effectively. While solving the latter problem

Copyright 2000, American Association for Artificial Intelligence (www.aaai.org). All rights reserved.

optimally is intractable, we present a greedy approach that performs quite well, in practice.

Our basic approach to both coordination problems is similar: Distribute most of the computation amongst the individual robots and asynchronously integrate their results by performing some global computations over the data. For instance, each robot processes its own laser data to create a consistent local map. A central mapper module then integrates the local maps to create a consistent global map. The local mappers reduce uncertainty in the data, principally by matching laser scans to decrease localization error. The central mapper further improves the map (minimizing localization error) by iteratively combining data from the robots. This works under the assumption that the robots know their pose relative to one another and have access to high-bandwidth communication.

Similarly, our approach to coordinating exploration combines distributed computation with global decision making. The individual robots construct "bids," which describe their estimates of the expected information gain and costs of traveling to various locations. A central executive receives the bids and assigns tasks in an attempt to maximize overall utility, while trying to minimize overlap in coverage by the robots. In both cases, the majority of the computation is done in a distributed fashion, by the individual robots, and the centralized modules combine and coordinate information in an efficient way.

After presenting related work, Sections 3 and 4 describe our approaches to multi-robot map creation and exploration, respectively. Section 5 presents a case study of three robots combining to map a large indoor area. We also analyze quantitative results from simulations showing the effects of our exploration strategies on task performance. Finally, we discuss future directions that are important to the problems of multi-robot exploration and mapping.

2 Related Work

While there has been work in mapping and exploration for single robot systems [3, 4, 9, 17, 18], there have been relatively few approaches for mapping and exploration with multi-robot systems. Several researchers have studied the problem of using multiple robots to reduce localization error during exploration [10, 13]. For instance, in Rekleitis et. al. [13] the environment is divided into strips. Each strip is explored by a single robot, while the others remain stationary to observe the moving robot and estimate its position. While this has the advantage of improving the overall accuracy of the map, it does nothing to speed the exploration process. On the contrary, the robots are forced to remain near each other in order to stay visible.

Balch and Arkin [1] investigated how communication in multi-robot systems affects different tasks, including the *graze* task where the objective is to completely cover an unknown environment. The robots essentially perform a randomized search of the environment. Their performance results are qualitatively similar to what we observe, but we have not done any direct comparisons of the two methods.

More sophisticated techniques for multi-robot exploration are presented in [15, 21, 22]. Singh and Fujimura [15] present a decentralized on-line approach for heterogeneous robots. When a robot discovers an opening to an unexplored area that it cannot reach because of its size, it selects another robot which can carry out the exploration task. The candidate robot is chosen by trading off the number of areas to be explored, the size of the robot, and the straight-line distance between the robot and the target region.

Yamauchi developed a technique in which the robots build a common map (an occupancy grid) in a distributed fashion [21, 22]. The work introduces the notion of a *frontier*, which is a location near an unexplored part of the environment. The approach groups adjacent cells into frontier regions. Each robot then heads for the centroid of the closest frontier region, but they do so independently — while they share maps, there is no explicit coordination. Thus, the robots may end up covering the same area and may even physically interfere with one another. Our approach, in contrast, tends to keep the robots well separated, which can significantly decrease the time needed to accomplish the mapping task.

The work reported here extends our earlier efforts [2] in several important ways. First, the approach described here distributes the computation, to a large extent. This enables the robots' "bids" to be calculated in parallel, which facilitates scaling to larger numbers of robots and enables the robots to construct bids based on their own capabilities (sensor range, travel costs, etc.). Second, the current method uses a more sophisticated notion of expected information gain that takes current map knowledge and the robots' individual capabilities into account. This allows for more subtle types of coordination, for example, allowing the robots to remain near one another if the map shows that they are separated by a solid wall.

3 Coordinated Mapping

At the core of our approach is a distributed algorithm for concurrent mapping and localization in real-time [19]. The approach makes two major assumptions: First, it assumes the world is reasonably static, and so it cannot handle

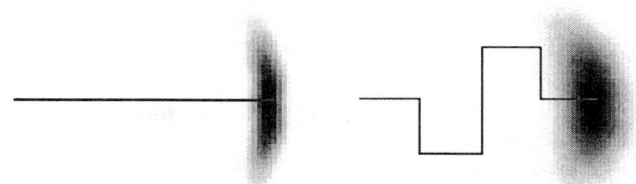

Figure 1: Probabilistic Motion Model
Robot starts at left of each diagram and follows path indicated by solid line. Probability distribution is shown in grey for the robot's posterior location. The darker a location, the more likely it is.

environments that are densely populated or change in major ways (e.g., walls disappearing). Second, it assumes that the robots begin in view of one another, and are told their approximate relative location (within about 1 meter distance and 20 degrees orientation). The first requirement is assumed throughout the literature on concurrent localization and mapping [3, 12, 16, 18]. Fortunately, the second assumption holds for many practical applications, since the problem of team-based mapping in the absence of initial pose information is extremely hard.

Our approach decomposes the mapping problem in a modular, hierarchical fashion: Each robot maintains its own local map, correcting for odometry error as it goes. A central module receives the local maps and combines them into a single, global map. The modules work in real-time and, in fact, adapt their computational requirements to the available resources. The beauty of the approach is that basically the same software runs at both the local and global levels.

To start, each robot receives a sequence of its own odometry and sensor measurements (laser range scans, in our case). From that, it incrementally constructs three things: a maximum likelihood estimate for its own position, a maximum likelihood estimate for the map (location of surrounding objects), and a posterior density characterizing its "true" location, which acknowledges the fact that certain errors cannot be identified when building a map [20].

To illustrate the algorithm, assume that a robot has already developed a partial map. It now wants to augment the map through new sensor and odometry readings. To determine the robot's most likely position, our algorithm maximizes a mixture likelihood function that models (1) the noise in motion (odometry), and (2) the noise in perception. Figure 1 illustrates the motion model. It depicts $P(s \mid s', a)$, the probability of being at pose s, if the robot was previously at s' and executed action a (moving and/or turning). This distribution is obtained by the (obvious) kinematic equations, assuming that robot motion is noisy along its translational and rotational components.

Figure 2 depicts the perceptual model (the likelihood function for sensor readings). The basic idea here is that it is unlikely to receive sensor readings where previous scans saw free-space. The dark region in Figure 2 corresponds to

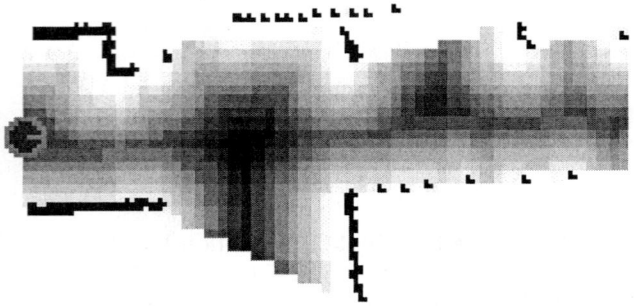

Figure 2: Likelihood Function Generated
Robot is on the left (circle). The scan is depicted by 180 dots in front of the robot. The darker a region, the smaller the likelihood for sensing an object there. Occluded regions are white.

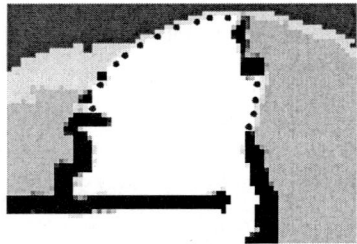

Figure 3: Occupancy Map Used for Exploration
"Obstacle" cells are black, "clear" cells are white, "unknown" cells are grey. Frontier cells are marked by small circles.

the free-space of the scan shown there; the likelihood of detecting something in that region is (inversely) proportional to the grey-level. Thus, scans that nicely align possess much higher likelihood than ones that do not.

A key characteristic of this likelihood function it that it is differentiable. Moreover, search in the relative pose space of the robot can be performed very efficiently using Newton's method (e.g., 1,000 iterations per second). Our approach starts with the odometry measurement reported by the robot as an initial estimate, and uses gradient descent to find the nearest maximum in likelihood space. Since maps are built incrementally and short-term errors are not large, this process converges quickly and, with high reliability, finds the right alignment. The collection of all scans, along with their *corrected scan coordinates*, forms the map. The scan map is then efficiently converted to an occupancy grid map [5], which is required by our motion planner and exploration module.

We now address the problem of building a map using multiple mobile robots. Each robot builds its own local map, using the algorithm described above. Since the robots do not communicate directly, their local coordinate systems are not aligned with each other. Also, due to residual errors in the local maps, the maps typically would not match well even if the coordinate systems were perfectly aligned.

To build a single map, the central mapper module integrates information from the individual robots in real time. Specifically, each robot communicates a subset of its scans (e.g., every 10th) to the central mapper, using the *corrected scan coordinates*. Thus, the maps of the robots are not used directly. Instead, they are used indirectly to produce sequences of scans whose (relative) position errors are already very small to begin with. The central mapper then applies the same gradient descent algorithm described above to minimize the error between the scans of the different robots. Since we assume that the initial positions of the robots are approximately known, our local search approach accurately localizes the robots relative to each other. As additional scans arrive, they are similarly mapped into the global coordinate system, eliminating small deviations. The resulting map integrates every robots' scans into a single, consistent map with relatively little computation. We have tested our procedure for up to 5 robots, and have no doubt that the same architecture easily scales to 10, or more, robots.

4 Coordinated Exploration

The objective in coordinating the exploration of multiple robots is to maximize expected information gain (map knowledge) over time. While the optimal solution is computationally intractable, we have developed a relatively low-cost technique that provides good results, in practice.

To start, each robot constructs a "bid" consisting of the estimated utilities for it to travel to various locations. The bids are sent to a central executive, which assigns tasks to each robot based on all the bids received, taking into account potential overlaps in coverage. Thus, while a robot may prefer to visit one location, the executive might assign it a different location if another robot is expected to gain much the same information. Robots submit new bids when their maps are updated, which can cause them to be retasked. Exploration ends when there is no useful information to be gained.

4.1 Constructing Bids

A robot constructs a new bid each time it receives a map update from the central mapper. It categorizes map cells into three different types (Figure 3) — "obstacle" (probability of occupancy above a given threshold p_o), "clear" (probability below a threshold p_c) and "unknown" (either never been sensed, or probability is between p_o and p_c).

A *bid* is a list of the estimated costs and information gains for visiting various *frontier cells*. We define a *frontier cell* as any "clear" cell adjacent to at least one "unknown" cell (Figure 3). For efficiency, we further stipulate that each frontier cell must be at least some minimum distance from all other frontier cells. For instance, even though our grid has 15 cm resolution, we require frontier cells to be at least 30 cm (approximate radius of the robots) from each other.

To estimate the cost of visiting a frontier cell, we compute the optimal path (shortest distance, assuming deterministic motion) from the robot's current position. All costs are

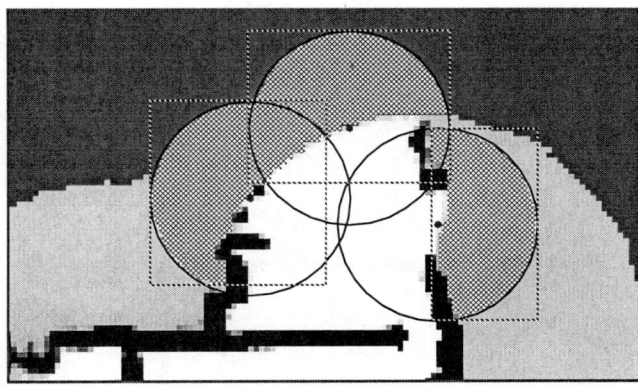

Figure 4: Expected Information Gain
Information gain regions for several representative frontier cells. Circles indicate sensor range. Cross-hatched areas are information gain regions. Dotted lines are the rectangular approximations.

computed simultaneously, using a simple flood-fill algorithm [11] that employs an efficient implementation of a priority queue to propagate minimum path costs through the map. To further decrease computation, we consider only "clear" cells, stopping propagation whenever an "obstacle" or "unknown" cell is reached.

Estimating information gain is more difficult. In fact, the actual information gain is impossible to predict, since it very much depends on the structure of the environment. Our previous work [2] assumed information gain to be constant for each frontier cell, which tended to make the robots spend too much time exploring nearby areas that were nearly known already. Here we use the current map to provide a more informed estimate. Specifically, we assume that the robot has some nominal sensor range and count the number of "unknown" cells that fall within that radius of the frontier cell, subject to the restriction that the resulting *information gain region* forms a connected set (Figure 4). For efficiency, we again use a flood-fill algorithm, this time ending propagation when either a "clear" or "obstacle" cell is encountered, or when the distance to the frontier cell is greater than the sensor range. In addition to counting the number of cells, we record the minimum and maximum extent, forming a rectangle that approximates the information gain region (Figure 4). This enclosing rectangle is used by the executive to estimate potential overlaps in coverage.

While there are definite improvements that can be made in estimating information gain (a simple one would be to bias the count by the occupancy probability of the cells, giving less weight to cells that are already partially known), we have found our metric works quite well in practice. In particular, while the metric usually acts to keep the robots well separated, it still allows them to be spatially near one another if there are known obstacles separating them. Thus, we have seen cases where two robots are tasked to explore adjacent rooms — one goes into the first room and perceives the walls, which get added as obstacles in the map. This separates the room from the adjacent room, information-wise, which allows the executive to send the other robot into the second room. This would not be possible with methods that merely try to maintain a given distance between robots.

4.2 Assigning Tasks

Each robot asynchronously constructs its bids and sends them to a central executive. The executive tries to maximize the total expected utility of the robots by assigning them tasks, based on their bids. A simple greedy algorithm is used to keep the computation real time. The executive first finds the bid location with the highest net utility (information gain minus cost) and assigns that task to the robot that made the bid.[1] It then *discounts* the bids of the remaining robots based on the current assigned tasks (see below) and chooses the highest remaining net utility. This continues until either all robots have been assigned tasks or no task remains whose (discounted) expected information gain is above a minimum threshold.

Key to this algorithm is the discounting. Without it, the robots would act in an uncoordinated manner, being assigned tasks that they, independently, estimate as best. Our previous work discounted the utility of a location as a function of its distance to the other assigned tasks [2]. Here, we explicitly use the estimated information gain for discounting. Specifically, we estimate the percentage of overlap between the information gain regions by how much the approximating rectangles overlap (Figure 4) and decrease the expected information gain by that percentage:

$$d_j = Area\left(IGR_j \cap \left(\bigcup_{i \in R} IGR_i\right)\right) / Area(IGR_j)$$

$$u_j = (1 - d_j) \times i_j - c_j$$

Here, IGR_j is the rectangular approximation of the information gain region for some frontier cell j, the IGR_i are the rectangular information gain regions for the assigned robots R, and i_j and c_j are the expected information gain and path cost of going to cell j. This method is both efficient to compute and a fairly accurate approximation. In one set of experiments, it was within 15% of the true overlap (obtained by counting the actual number of overlapping cells), while being hundreds of times more efficient.

The executive is implemented using the Task Description Language (TDL), an extension of C++ that includes syntactical support for hierarchical task decomposition, task sequencing, execution monitoring, and exception handling [14]. When the executive receives a bid, it waits a short while in case other bids arrive. It then assigns tasks to all robots that are either currently unassigned or have submitted new bids (leaving the currently active ones to continue).

---

1. We found that marginal utility (information gain divided by cost) performed less well, tending to favor areas of small information gain nearby the robot.

Figure 5: Robin, Marian and LittleJohn

Besides assigning tasks, the executive monitors task execution, interfaces with a remote GUI, and interleaves exploration with other tasks. In particular, at any time the user (through the GUI) can request that one of the robots visit a particular location (e.g., to take a closer look). The executive terminates that robot's current task, reassigns other robots to cover for its loss, assigns and monitors the new task, and then integrates the robot back into the exploration pool when it is finished.

One important addition to the task assignment algorithm is the use of *hysteresis*. If a frontier cell for a robot falls within the information gain region of the robot's currently assigned task, then its expected information gain is divided by the *hysteresis ratio* (a constant between 0 and 1, usually 0.85). Lower values for the hysteresis ratio will make the executive less disposed to switching tasks. The basic problem is that, because the robot is continuously sensing the environment, the information gain metric can change drastically after only small motions. For instance, by the time a robot maneuvers to position itself in front of a doorway, it typically has seen a large portion of the room. Without hysteresis, entering and completely exploring the room would not have as much utility as going somewhere else. While not the ultimate solution, hysteresis handles the problem fairly well.

5 Experiments

The multi-robot exploration and mapping system has been tested extensively using a team of three heterogeneous robots — two Pioneer AT robots from RWI and an Urbie robot from IS Robotics (Figure 5). All three robots are equipped with Sick laser scanners that have a 180 degree field of view. The ATs have a 300 MHz on-board laptop running Linux, and all three robots communicate, via Breezecom radio links, with off-board Linux workstations that run the rest of the system, including the mapping, planning, and executive modules.

The most extensive testing was in October, 1999 in an empty hospital building at Fort Sam Houston, San Antonio TX, as part of DARPA's Tactical Mobile Robot (TMR) project. During a five day period, we made repeated runs with the robots, mapping large areas of one floor of the building.

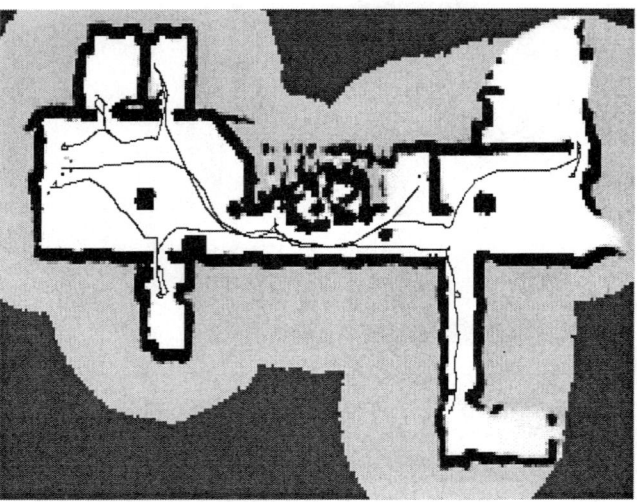

Figure 6: Map Created by Three Robots (62 x 43 m)
Robots start at left. The three solid lines indicate the robots' paths through the environment.

Figure 6 shows one typical run that produced a 62 by 43 meter map in about eight minutes. During these runs, we tended to see similar qualitative behavior — one robot would head down the initial corridor, while the other two would explore rooms on opposite sides of the corridor. When the two finished the initial set of rooms, they would move down the corridor to explore openings that the third robot had discovered, but passed by. We also performed tests where we would teleoperate one of the robots while having the other two autonomously explore the areas not visited by the first.

Some interesting behaviors were observed that are attributable to the coordination algorithm. For one, if three robots start in the middle of a narrow corridor, two tend to head down the corridor in opposite directions, while the third just waits until one of the others spots a doorway. This is because, initially, there are just two distinct frontiers, and assigning one robot to each leaves the third with no expected information gain. Another behavior, noted earlier, is that the robots sometimes explore adjacent offices that, while spatially close, are disconnected in terms of information gain. Finally, in one instance, we noticed a robot having trouble getting near an office it was tasked to explore. A second robot was tasked to explore further down the corridor. However, at some point the executive swapped tasks, since the second robot had fortuitously gotten closer to the office than the first. Such flexibility in dynamically coordinating tasks gives our system the ability to efficiently explore in a wide variety of situations.

To augment the robot tests, we ran experiments in simulation to compare the effects of different numbers of robots in different types of environments. The simulator realistically models the environment and a robot's interaction with it, so that the programs used on real robots can be used with the simulator without modification.

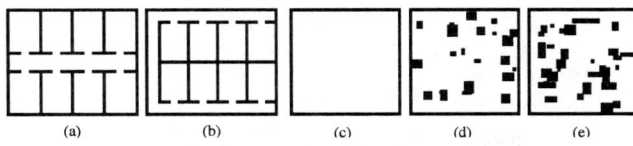

Figure 7: Simulation Environments

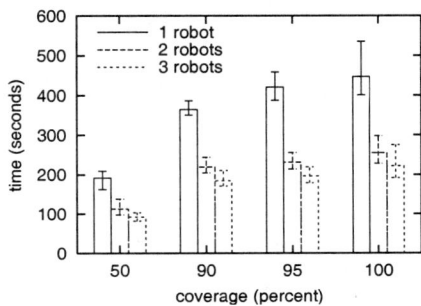

Figure 8: Results from Single-Corridor Environment

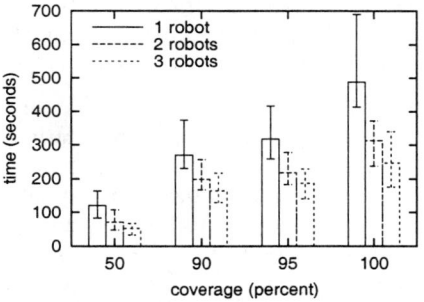

Figure 9: Results from 15% Random Obstacles

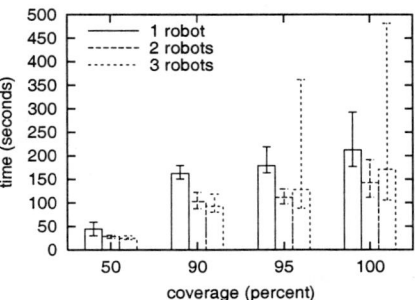

Figure 10: Results from Obstacle-Free Environment

Previously, we demonstrated the performance increase that obtains using coordinated *versus* uncoordinated robots [2]. In the current experiments, we varied the number of robots from one to three, and used five different environments. In the two office-like environments (Figure 7, A and B, 25m x 20m) and the obstacle-free environment (C, 20m x 20m), we ran ten simulations for each number of robots. For the other two environments (D and E, 20m x 20m), we used ten different randomly generated maps, and ran one simulation with each.

While our primary performance metric is the time needed to completely explore the environment, it is also of interest to see how the coverage evolves over time. It might be the case that most of an environment is mapped quickly, while it takes a long time to cover a few last spots at the end. For this reason, we report the time it takes to cover 50, 90, 95 and 100 percent of the environment.

Figure 8 presents the results for the single-corridor office environment (A). It shows that two robots perform significantly better than one, while there is not much gain in having three robots instead of two. The results are similar for two parallel corridors (B). There, two robots can go in separate directions at the beginning, each exploring one part without any overlap. While a third robot can assist initially in the exploration of one of the corridors, once done it must travel a long way in order to help explore the other corridor. In many cases, the other robots do not arrive in time to help out.

In contrast, in the random environments, there is a smaller gain when going from one to two robots and a larger gain when going from two to three robots (Figure 9), compared with the results from the office-like environments. The apparent reason is that the obstacles in the environment help in spreading the robots out.

Surprisingly, in the obstacle-free environment, three robots actually take longer to complete the task, on average, than two (Figure 10). This seems to be because they end up interfering with one another [6, 8]. In contrast, in this environment multiple robots have demonstrable positive effects on map accuracy. With few features, the robots get little help in localizing. This has the greatest impact when there is only one robot exploring — in fact, in 30% of the trials the robot failed to complete the mapping task successfully (i.e., the resultant map was qualitatively wrong). With multiple robots, however, the added sensor information helps significantly: For two robots, only one failure was observed (10%) and with three robots, no failures were observed.

6 Future Work and Conclusions

While we have extensive test results, we still need to quantify the effects of various design decisions, including the effects of hysteresis, the way information overlap is estimated, and the definition of expected information gain itself. We also intend to quantify the performance of the greedy method of task assignment, comparing it to more sophisticated algorithms such as A* or stochastic search.

In both simulation and actual tests, robots are sometimes idle because their discounted utilities are below the minimum threshold. Instead of just staying where they are, they could position themselves strategically so as to minimize the expected distance they would have to travel once they are assigned a task. While for a single robot, a good idle location is one that minimizes the average path cost to all the frontier cells, the problem is much harder if there are several idle robots.

Fundamentally, the approach described in this paper is limited in two respects. First, with respect to mapping, we currently assume that the robots begin in view of one another and are told their initial (approximate) relative location. More sophisticated techniques are needed for mapping and localization when the robots need to merge maps where the coordinate transform is initially unknown and the robots need to find out where they are relative to one another. Second, with respect to exploration, we currently assume it is sufficient to consider the utility of exploring a single point. The approach ignores both the fact that information is gained *en route* and that moving to a given area may facilitate, or possibly hinder, subsequent exploration. We are investigating more sophisticated algorithms that estimate information gain along *paths*, which we believe will improve overall performance significantly.

In conclusion, we have presented an approach to multi-robot exploration and mapping that explicitly coordinates the robots, based on estimates of expected information gain and the cost of exploration. This approach, which builds on our previous work, has demonstrated the types of performance improvements that multiple robots can provide. This includes both reduced exploration time and increased mapping accuracy. While improvements are inevitable in this important area, we now have a benchmark for what is attainable from an effective use of coordination.

Acknowledgments

We thank Greg Armstrong for maintenance of the robots and help with the experiments at CMU. This research is sponsored in part by DARPA via TACOM contract DAAE07-98-C-L032.

References

[1] T. Balch and R.C. Arkin. "Communication in Reactive Multi-agent Robotic Systems." Autonomous Robots 1, pp. 1-25, 1994.

[2] W. Burgard, D. Fox, M. Moors, R. Simmons and S. Thrun. "Collaborative Multi-Robot Exploration." In *Proc. Intl. Conf. on Robotics and Automation*, San Francisco CA, May 2000.

[3] H. Choset. *Sensor Based Motion Planning: The Hierarchical Generalized Voronoi Graph*. Ph.D. Thesis, California Institute of Technology, 1996.

[4] G. Dudek, M. Jenkin, E. Milios and D. Wilkes. "Robotic exploration as graph construction." *IEEE Transactions on Robotics and Automation*, **7:6**, pp. 859-865, 1991.

[5] A. Elfes. *Occupancy Grids: A Probabilistic Framework for Robot Perception and Navigation*. Ph.D. Thesis, Department of Electrical and Computer Engineering, Carnegie Mellon University, 1989.

[6] M. Fontan and M. Mataric. "Territorial Multi-Robot Task Division." *IEEE Transactions on Robotics and Automation*, **14:5**, 1998.

[7] D. Fox, W. Burgard, H. Kruppa and S. Thrun. "Collaborative Multi-Robot Localization." In *Proc. 23rd German Conf. on Artificial Intelligence*. Springer-Verlag, 1999.

[8] D. Goldberg and M.J. Mataric. "Interference as a Tool for Designing and Evaluating Multi-Robot Controllers." In *Proc. AAAI-97*, pp. 637-642, Providence, RI, July, 1997.

[9] B. Kuipers and Y.-T. Byun. "A Robot Exploration and Mapping Strategy Based on a Semantic Hierarchy of Spatial Representations." *Journal of Robotics and Autonomous Systems*, **8**, pp. 47-63, 1991.

[10] R. Kurazume and N. Shigemi. "Cooperative Positioning with Multiple Robots." In *Proc. IEEE/RSJ Intl. Conf. on Intelligent Robots and Systems (IROS)*, 1994.

[11] J.C. Latombe. *Robot Motion Planning*. Kluwer Academic Publishers, 1991.

[12] J. Leonard, H. Durrant-Whyte and I. Cox. "Dynamic Map Building for an Autonomous Mobile Robot." *International Journal of Robotics Research*, **11:4**, pp. 89-96, 1992.

[13] I. Rekleitis, G. Dudek, E. Milios. "Accurate Mapping of an Unknown World and Online Landmark Positioning." In *Proc. of Vision Interface 1998*, pp. 455-461, Nagoya Japan, 1997.

[14] R. Simmons and D. Apfelbaum. "A Task Description Language for Robot Control." In *Proc. Conf. on Intelligent Robotics and Systems (IROS)*, Vancouver Canada, 1998.

[15] K. Singh and K. Fujimura. "Map Making by Cooperating Mobile Robots". In *Proc. Intl. Conf. on Robotics and Automation*, 1993.

[16] R. Smith, M. Self, P. Cheeseman. "Estimating Uncertain Spatial Relationships in Robotics." In *Autonomous Robot Vehicles*, eds. I.J. Cos and G.T. Wilfong, Springer-Verlag, pp. 167-193, 1990.

[17] S. Thrun. "Exploration and Model Building in Mobile Robot Domains." In *Proc. IEEE Intl. Conf. on Neural Networks*, pp. 175-180, 1993.

[18] S. Thrun. "Learning Metric-Topological Maps for Indoor Mobile Robot Navigation." *Artificial Intelligence*, **99:1**, pp. 21-71, 1998.

[19] S. Thrun, W. Burgard and D. Fox. "A Real-Time Algorithm for Mobile Robot Mapping With Applications to Multi-Robot and 3D Mapping". In *Proc. Intl. Conf. on Robotics and Automation*, San Francisco CA, May 2000.

[20] S. Thrun, D. Fox and W. Burgard. "A Probabilistic Approach to Concurrent Mapping and Localization for Mobile Robots." *Machine Learning*, **31**, pp. 29-53, 1998.

[21] B. Yamauchi. "Frontier-Based Exploration using Multiple Robots." In *Proc. Second Intl. Conf. on Autonomous Agents*, Minneapolis MN, 1998.

[22] B. Yamauchi, P. Langley, A.C. Schultz, J. Grefenstette, and W. Adams. "Magellan: An Integrated Adaptive Architecture for Mobile Robots." Tech Report 98-2, Institute for the Study of Learning and Expertise, Palo Alto, CA, May 1998.

Monte Carlo Localization With Mixture Proposal Distribution

Sebastian Thrun   Dieter Fox
School of Computer Science
Carnegie Mellon University
http://www.cs.cmu.edu/~{thrun,dfox}

Wolfram Burgard
Computer Science Department
University of Freiburg, Germany
http://www.informatik.uni-freiburg.de/~burgard

Abstract

Monte Carlo localization (MCL) is a Bayesian algorithm for mobile robot localization based on particle filters, which has enjoyed great practical success. This paper points out a limitation of MCL which is counter-intuitive, namely that *better sensors can yield worse results*. An analysis of this problem leads to the formulation of a new proposal distribution for the Monte Carlo sampling step. Extensive experimental results with physical robots suggest that the new algorithm is significantly more robust and accurate than plain MCL. Obviously, these results transcend beyond mobile robot localization and apply to a range of particle filter applications.

Introduction

Monte Carlo Localization (MCL) is a probabilistic algorithm for mobile robot localization that uses samples (particles) for representing probability densities. MCL is a version of *particle filters* (Dou98; KKR95; LC98; PS99). In computer vision, particle filters are known under the name *condensation algorithm* (IB98). They have been applied with great practical success to visual tracking problems (IB98; DBFT99) and mobile robot localization (DHN99; FBKT00; LV00).

The basic idea of MCL is to approximate probability distributions by sets of samples. When applied to the problem of state estimation in a partially observable dynamical system, MCL successively calculates weighted sets of samples that approximate the posterior probability over the current state. Its practical success stems from the fact that it is nonparametric, hence can represent a wide range of probability distributions. It is also computationally efficient, and it is easily implemented as an *any-time* algorithm, which adapts the computational load by varying the number of samples in the estimation process (FBKT00).

This paper proposes a modified version of MCL, which uses a different sampling mechanism. Our study begins with the characterization of a key limitation of MCL (and particle filters in general). While MCL works well with *noisy* sensors, it actually fails when the sensors are too accurate. This effect is undesirable: Ideally, the accuracy of any sound statistical estimator should *increase* with the accuracy of the sensors.

Copyright © 2000, American Association for Artificial Intelligence (www.aaai.org). All rights reserved.

An analysis of this effect leads to the formulation of a new sampling mechanism (i.e., the proposal distribution), which changes the way samples are generated in MCL. We propose three different ways of computing the importance factors for this new proposal distribution. Our approach, which can be viewed as the natural dual to MCL, works well in cases where conventional MCL fails (and vice versa). To gain the best of both worlds, the conventional and our new proposal distribution are mixed together, leading to a new MCL algorithm with a mixture proposal distribution that is extremely robust.

Empirical results illustrate that the new mixture proposal distribution does not suffer the same limitation as MCL, and yields uniformly superior results. For example, our new approach with 50 samples consistently outperforms standard MCL with 1,000 samples. Additional experiments illustrate that our approach yields much better solutions in challenging variants of the localization problem, such as the *kidnapped robot problem* (EM92). These experiments have been carried out both in simulation and with data collected from physical robots, using both laser range data and camera images for localization.

Our approach generalizes a range of previous extensions of MCL that have been proposed to alleviate these problems. Existing methods include the addition of *random* samples into the posterior (FBKT00), the generation of samples at locations that are consistent with the sensor readings (LV00), or the use of sensor models that assume an artificially high noise level (FBKT00). While these approaches have shown superior performance over strict MCL in certain settings, they all lack mathematical rigor. In particular, neither of them approximates the true posterior, and over time they may diverge arbitrarily. Viewed differently, our approach can be seen as a theory that leads to an algorithm related to the ones above (with important differences), but also establishes a mathematical framework that is guaranteed to work in the limit.

The paper first reviews Bayes filters, the basic mathematical framework, followed by a derivation of MCL. Based on experiments characterizing the problems with plain MCL, we then derive dual MCL. Finally, the mixture proposal distribution is obtained by combining MCL and its dual. Empirical results are provided that illustrate the superior performance of our new extension of MCL.

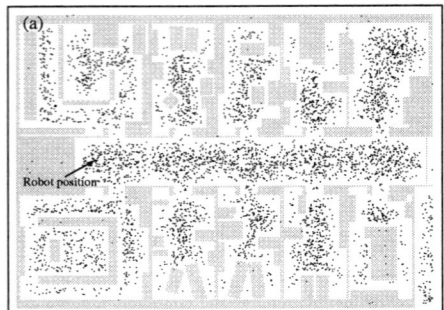 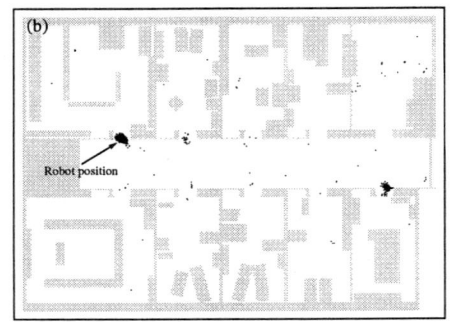 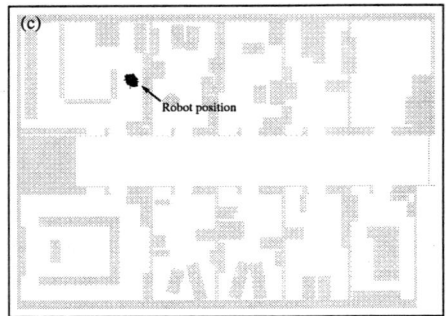

Figure 1: Global localization of a mobile robot using MCL (10,000 samples).

Bayes Filtering

Bayes filters address the problem of estimating the state x of a dynamical system (partially observable Markov chain) from sensor measurements. For example, in mobile robot localization, the dynamical system is a mobile robot and its environment, the state is the robot's pose therein (often specified by a position in a Cartesian x-y space and the robot's heading direction θ). Measurements may include range measurements, camera images, and odometry readings. Bayes filters assume that the environment is *Markov*, that is, past and future data are (conditionally) independent if one knows the current state.

The key idea of Bayes filtering is to estimate a probability density over the state space conditioned on the data. This posterior is typically called the *belief* and is denoted

$$Bel(x^{(t)}) \;=\; p(x^{(t)}|d^{(0\ldots t)})$$

Here x denotes the state, $x^{(t)}$ is the state at time t, and $d^{(0\ldots t)}$ denotes the data starting at time 0 up to time t. For mobile robots, we distinguish two types of data: *perceptual data* such as laser range measurements, and *odometry data* or *controls*, which carries information about robot motion. Denoting the former by o (for *observation*) and the latter by a (for *action*), we have

$$Bel(x^{(t)}) = p(x^{(t)}|o^{(t)}, a^{(t-1)}, o^{(t-1)}, a^{(t-2)} \ldots, o^{(0)}) \quad (1)$$

Without loss of generality, we assume that observations and actions arrive in an alternating sequence.

Bayes filters estimate the belief *recursively*. The *initial belief* characterizes the initial knowledge about the system state. In the absence of such, it is typically initialized by a *uniform distribution* over the state space. In mobile robotics, the state estimation without initial knowledge is called the *global localization problem*—which will be the focus throughout much of this paper.

To derive a recursive update equation, we observe that Expression (1) can be transformed by Bayes rule to

$$\frac{p(o^{(t)}|x^{(t)}, a^{(t-1)}, \ldots, o^{(0)})\, p(x^{(t)}|a^{(t-1)}, \ldots, o^{(0)})}{p(o^{(t)}|a^{(t-1)}, \ldots, o^{(0)})}$$

Under our Markov assumption, $p(o^{(t)}|x^{(t)}, a^{(t-1)}, \ldots, o^{(0)})$ can be simplified to $p(o^{(t)}|x^{(t)})$, hence we have

$$\frac{p(o^{(t)}|x^{(t)})\, p(x^{(t)}|a^{(t-1)}, \ldots, o^{(0)})}{p(o^{(t)}|a^{(t-1)}, \ldots, o^{(0)})}$$

We will now expand the rightmost term in the denominator by integrating over the state at time $t-1$

$$\frac{p(o^{(t)}|x^{(t)})}{p(o^{(t)}|a^{(t-1)}, \ldots, o^{(0)})} \int p(x^{(t)}|x^{(t-1)}, a^{(t-1)}, \ldots, o^{(0)})$$
$$p(x^{(t-1)}|a^{(t-1)}, \ldots, o^{(0)})\, dx^{(t-1)}$$

Again, we can exploit the Markov assumption to simplify $p(x^{(t)}|x^{(t-1)}, a^{(t-1)}, \ldots, o^{(0)})$ to $p(x^{(t)}|x^{(t-1)}, a^{(t-1)})$. Using the definition of the belief Bel, we obtain the important recursive equation

$$Bel(x^{(t)}) \;=\; \frac{p(o^{(t)}|x^{(t)})}{p(o^{(t)}|a^{(t-1)}, \ldots, o^{(0)})} \quad (2)$$
$$\int p(x^{(t)}|x^{(t-1)}, a^{(t-1)})\, Bel(x^{(t-1)})\, dx^{(t-1)}$$
$$= \eta p(o^{(t)}|x^{(t)}) \int p(x^{(t)}|x^{(t-1)}, a^{(t-1)}) Bel(x^{(t-1)}) dx^{(t-1)}$$

where η is a normalization constant. This equation is of central importance, as it is the basis for various MCL algorithms studied here.

We notice that to implement (2), one needs to know three distributions: the initial belief $Bel(x^{(0)})$ (e.g., uniform), the next state probabilities $p(x^{(t)}|x^{(t-1)}, a^{(t-1)})$, and the perceptual likelihood $p(o^{(t)}|x^{(t)})$. MCL employs specific next state probabilities $p(x^{(t)}|x^{(t-1)}, a^{(t-1)})$ and perceptual likelihood models $p(o^{(t)}|x^{(t)})$ that describe robot motion and perception probabilistically. Such models are described in detail elsewhere (FBT99).

Monte Carlo Localization

The idea of MCL (and other particle filter algorithms) is to represent the belief $Bel(x)$ by a set of m weighted samples distributed according to $Bel(x)$:

$$Bel(x) \;=\; \{x_i, w_i\}_{i=1,\ldots,m}$$

Here each x_i is a sample (a state), and w_i is a non-negative numerical factor (weight) called *importance factors*, which sums up to one over all i.

In global mobile robot localization, the *initial* belief is a set of poses drawn according to a uniform distribution over the robot's universe, and annotated by the uniform importance factor $\frac{1}{m}$. The recursive update is realized in three steps.

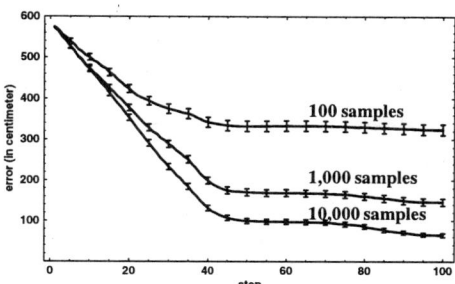
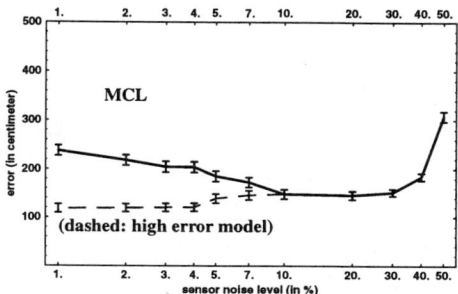

Figure 2: Average error of MCL as a function of the number of robot steps/measurements.

Figure 3: Solid curve: error of MCL after 100 steps, as a function of the sensor noise. 95% confidence intervals are indicated by the bars. Notice that this function is *not* monotonic, as one might expect. Dashed curve: Same experiment with high-error model.

1. Sample $x_i^{(t-1)} \sim Bel(x^{(t-1)})$ using importance sampling from the (weighted) sample set representing $Bel(x^{(t-1)})$.

2. Sample $x_i^{(t)} \sim p(x^{(t)}|x_i^{(t-1)}, a^{(t-1)})$. Obviously, the pair $\langle x_i^{(t)}, x_i^{(t-1)} \rangle$ is distributed according to the product distribution

$$q^{(t)} := p(x^{(t)}|x^{(t-1)}, a^{(t-1)}) \times Bel(x^{(t-1)}) \quad (3)$$

which is commonly called *proposal distribution*.

3. To offset the difference between the proposal distribution and the desired distribution (c.f., Equation (2))

$$\eta \, p(o^{(t)}|x^{(t)})p(x^{(t)}|x^{(t-1)}, a^{(t-1)})Bel(x^{(t-1)}) \quad (4)$$

the sample is weighted by the quotient

$$\frac{\eta \, p(o^{(t)}|x_i^{(t)})p(x_i^{(t)}|x_i^{(t-1)}, a^{(t-1)})Bel(x_i^{(t-1)})}{Bel(x_i^{(t-1)}) \, p(x_i^{(t)}|x_i^{(t-1)}, a^{(t-1)})}$$
$$\propto p(o^{(t)}|x_i^{(t)}) = w_i \quad (5)$$

This is exactly the new (non-normalized) importance factor w_i.

After the generation of m samples, the new importance factors are normalized so that they sum up to 1 (hence define a probability distribution). It is known (Tan93) that under mild assumptions (which hold in our work), the sample set converges to the true posterior $Bel(x^{(t)})$ as m goes to infinity, with a convergence speed in $O(\frac{1}{\sqrt{m}})$. The speed may vary by a constant factor, which depends on the proposal distribution and can be significant.

Examples

Figure 1 shows an example of MCL in the context of localizing a mobile robot globally in an office environment. This robot is equipped with sonar range finders, and it is also given a map of the environment. In Figure 1a, the robot is globally uncertain; hence the samples are spread uniformly trough the free-space (projected into 2D). Figure 1b shows the sample set after approximately 1 meter of robot motion, at which point MCL has disambiguated the robot's position up to a single symmetry. Finally, after another 2 meters of robot motion the ambiguity is resolved, and the robot knows where it is. The majority of samples is now centered tightly around the correct position, as shown in Figure 1c.

Unfortunately, data collected from a physical robot makes it impossible to freely vary the level of noise in sensing. Figure 2 shows results obtained from a robot simulation, modeling a B21 robot localizing an object in 3D with a mono camera while moving around. The noise simulation includes a simulation of measurement noise, false positives (phantoms) and false negatives (failures to detect the target object). MCL is directly applicable; with the added advantage that we can vary the level of noise arbitrarily. Figure 2 shows systematic error curves for MCL in global localization for different sample set sizes m, averaged over 1,000 individual experiments. The bars in this figure are confidence intervals at the 95% level. With 10,000 samples, the computation load on a Pentium III (500 MhZ) is only 14%, indicating that MCL is well-suited for real-time applications. The results also indicate good performance as the number of samples is large. The reader should notice that these results have been obtained for perceptual noise level of 20% (for both false-negative and false-positive) and an additional position noise that is Gaussian-distributed with a variance of 10 degrees. For our existing robot system, the errors are in fact much lower.

A Problem with MCL

As noticed by several authors (Dou98; LV00; LC98; PS99), the basic particle filter performs poorly if the proposal distribution, which is used to generate samples, places too little samples in regions where the desired posterior $Bel(x_t)$ is large.

This problem has indeed great practical importance in the context of MCL, as the following example illustrates. The solid curve in Figure 3 shows the accuracy MCL achieves after 100 steps, using 1,000 samples. These results were obtained in simulation, enabling us to vary the amount of perceptual noise from 50% (on the right) to 1% (on the left); in particular, we simulated a mobile robot localizing an object in 3D space from mono-camera imagery. It appears that MCL works best for 10% to 20% perceptual noise. The degradation of performance towards the right, when there is a lot of noise, barely surprises. The less accurate a sensor, the larger an error one should expect. However, MCL also performs poorly when the noise level is too small. In other words, MCL with accurate sensors may perform *worse* than MCL with inaccurate sensors. This finding is a bit counter-

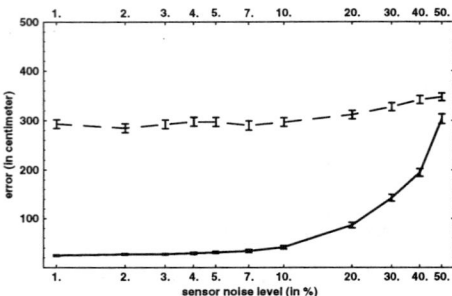

Figure 4: Error of MCL with the dual (dashed line) and the mixture (solid line) proposal distribution—the latter is the distribution advocated here. Compare the solid graph with dashed one, and the curves in Figure 3!

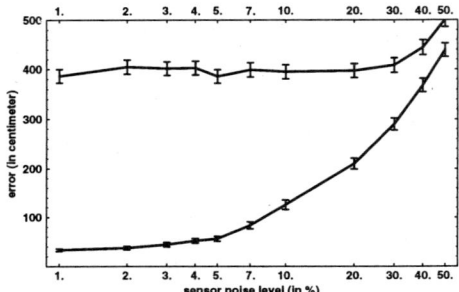

Figure 5: Error of plain MCL (top curve) and MCL with the mixture proposal distribution (bottom curve) with 50 samples (instead of 1,000) for each belief state.

intuitive in that it suggests that MCL only works well in specific situations, namely those where the sensors possess the "right" amount of noise.

At first glance, one might attempt to fix the problem by using a perceptual likelihood $p(o^{(t)}|x^{(t)})$ that overestimates the sensor noise. In fact, such a strategy partially alleviates the problem: The dashed curve in Figure 3b shows the accuracy if the error model assumes a fixed 10% noise (shown there only for smaller "true" error rates). While the performance is better, this is barely a fix. The overly pessimistic sensor model is inaccurate, throwing away precious information in the sensor readings. In fact, the resulting belief is not any longer a posterior, even if infinitely many samples were used. As we will see below, a mathematically sound method exists that produces much better results.

To analyze the problem more thoroughly, we first notice that the true goal of Bayes filtering is to calculate the product distribution specified in Equation (4). Thus, the optimal proposal distribution would be this product distribution. However, sampling from this distribution directly is too difficult. As noticed above, MCL samples instead from the proposal distribution $q^{(t)}$ defined in Equation (3), and uses the importance factors (5) to account for the difference. It is well-known from the statistical literature (Dou98; LC98; PS99; Tan93) that the divergence between (3) and (4) determines the convergence speed. This difference is accounted by the perceptual density $p(o^{(t)}|x^{(t)})$: If the sensors are entirely uninformative, this distribution is flat and (3) is equivalent to (4). For low-noise sensors, however, $p(o^{(t)}|x^{(t)})$ is typically quite narrow, hence MCL converges slowly. Thus, the error in Figure 3 is in fact caused by two different types of errors: one arising from the limitation of the sensor data (=noise), and one that arises from the mismatch of (3) and (4) in MCL. As we will show in this paper, an alternative version of MCL exists that practically eliminates the second error source.

Alternative Proposal Distributions

An alternative proposal distribution, which alleviates this problem, can be obtained by sampling directly from

$$\bar{q}^{(t)} = \frac{p(o^{(t)}|x^{(t)})}{\pi(o^{(t)})} \quad \text{with} \quad \pi(o^{(t)}) = \int p(o^{(t)}|x^{(t)}) \, dx \quad (6)$$

This proposal distribution leads to the *dual* of MCL. It can be viewed as the logical "inverse" of the sampling in regular MCL: Rather than forward-guessing and then using the importance factors to adjust the likelihood of a guess based on an observation, dual MCL guesses "backwards" from the observation and adjusts the importance factor based on the belief $Bel(x^{(t-1)})$. Consequently, the dual proposal distribution possesses complimentary strengths and weaknesses: while it is ideal for highly accurate sensors, its performance is negatively affected by measurement noise. The key advantage of dual MCL is that when the distribution of $p(o|x)$ is narrow—which is the case for low-noise sensors—dual sampling can be much more effective than conventional MCL.

Importance Factors

We will now provide three alternative ways to calculate the importance factors for $\bar{q}^{(t)}$.

Approach 1 (proposed by Arnaud Doucet, personal communication): Draw $x_i^{(t-1)} \sim Bel(x^{(t-1)})$. Hence, the pair $\langle x_i^{(t)}, x_i^{(t-1)} \rangle$ is distributed according to

$$\frac{p(o^{(t)}|x^{(t)})}{\pi(o^{(t)})} \times Bel(x^{(t-1)}) \quad (7)$$

and the importance factor is obtained as follows:

$$\begin{aligned}
w_i &= \left[\frac{p(o^{(t)}|x_i^{(t)})}{\pi(o^{(t)})} \times Bel(x_i^{(t-1)}) \right]^{-1} \\
&\quad \frac{p(o^{(t)}|x_i^{(t)}) \, p(x_i^{(t)}|x_i^{(t-1)}, a^{(t-1)}) \, Bel(x_i^{(t-1)})}{p(o^{(t)}|a^{(t-1)}, \ldots, o^{(0)})} \\
&= \frac{p(x_i^{(t)}|x_i^{(t-1)}, a^{(t-1)}) \, \pi(o^{(t)})}{p(o^{(t)}|a^{(t-1)}, \ldots, o^{(0)})} \\
&\propto p(x_i^{(t)}|x_i^{(t-1)}, a^{(t-1)}) \quad (8)
\end{aligned}$$

This approach is mathematically more elegant than the two alternatives described below, in that it avoids the need to transform sample sets into densities (which will be the case below). We have not yet implemented this approach. However, in the context of global mobile robot localization, we suspect the importance factor $p(x_i^{(t)}|a^{(t-1)}, x_i^{(t-1)})$ will be zero (or very close to zero) for many pose pairs $\langle x_i^{(t)}, x_i^{(t-1)} \rangle$.

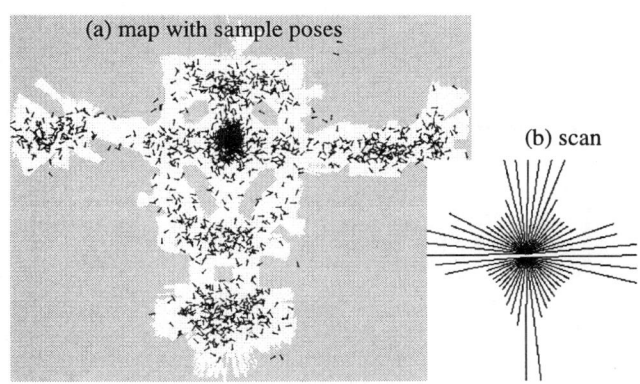

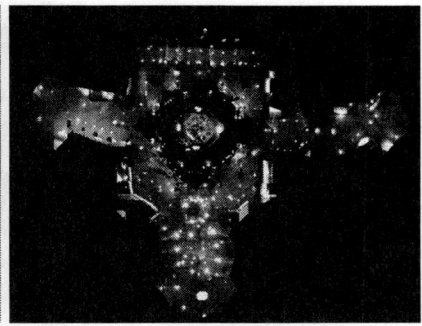

Figure 6: Robot poses sampled according to $\bar{q}$ for the scan shown on the right, using a pre-compiled version of the joint distribution $p(o, x)$ represented by kd-trees.

Figure 7: Left: The interactive tourguide robot Minerva. Right: Ceiling Map of the Smithsonian Museum.

Approach 2 Alternatively, one may in an explicit forward phase sample $x_j^{(t-1)} \sim Bel(x^{(t-1)})$ and then $x_j^{(t)} \sim p(x^{(t)}|x_j^{(t-1)}, a^{(t-1)})$, which represents the robot's belief *before* incorporating the sensor measurement. The "trick" is then to transform the samples $x_j^{(t)}$ into a kd-tree (Ben80; Moo90) that represents the density $p(x^{(t)}|a^{(t-1)}, d^{(0...t)})$, which is again the pose belief just before incorporating the most recent observation $o^{(t)}$.

After this first phase, the importance weights of our samples $x_i^{(t)} \sim \bar{q}^{(t)}$ are then calculated as follows:

$$w_i = \left[\frac{p(o^{(t)}|x_i^{(t)})}{\pi(o^{(t)})}\right]^{-1} \frac{p(o^{(t)}|x_i^{(t)}) \, p(x_i^{(t)}|a^{(t-1)}, d^{(0...t-1)})}{p(o^{(t)}|d^{(0...t-1)}, a^{(t-1)})}$$
$$\propto p(x_i^{(t)}|a^{(t-1)}, d^{(0...t-1)}) \quad (9)$$

This approach avoids the danger of generating pairs of poses $\langle x_i^{(t)}, x_i^{(t-1)} \rangle$ for which $w_i = 0$, but it involves an explicit forward sampling phase.

Approach 3 The third approach combines the best of both worlds, in that it avoids the explicit forward-sampling phase of the second approach, but also tends to generate large importance factors. In particular, it transforms the initial belief $Bel(x^{(t-1)})$ into a kd-tree. For each sample $x_i^{(t)} \sim \bar{q}^{(t)}$, we now draw a sample $x_i^{(t-1)}$ from the distribution

$$\frac{p(x_i^{(t)}|a^{(t-1)}, x^{(t-1)})}{\pi(x_i^{(t)}|a^{(t-1)})} \quad (10)$$

where

$$\pi(x_i^{(t)}|a^{(t-1)}) = \int p(x_i^{(t)}|a^{(t-1)}, x^{(t-1)}) \, dx^{(t-1)} \quad (11)$$

In other words, our approach projects $x_i^{(t)}$ back to a possible successor pose $x_i^{(t-1)}$. Consequently, the pair of poses $\langle x_i^{(t)}, x_i^{(t-1)} \rangle$ is distributed according to

$$\frac{p(o^{(t)}|x_i^{(t)})}{\pi(o^{(t)})} \times \frac{p(x_i^{(t)}|a^{(t-1)}, x_i^{(t-1)})}{\pi(x_i^{(t)}|a^{(t-1)})} \quad (12)$$

which gives rise to the following importance factor:

$$w_i = \left[\frac{p(o^{(t)}|x_i^{(t)})}{\pi(o^{(t)})} \times \frac{p(x_i^{(t)}|a^{(t-1)}, x_i^{(t-1)})}{\pi(x_i^{(t)}|a^{(t-1)})}\right]^{-1}$$
$$\frac{p(o^{(t)}|x_i^{(t)}) p(x_i^{(t)}|x_i^{(t-1)}, a^{(t-1)}) \, Bel(x_i^{(t-1)})}{p(o^{(t)}|d^{(0...t-1)})}$$
$$= \frac{\pi(o^{(t)}) \, \pi(x_i^{(t)}|a^{(t-1)}) \, Bel(x_i^{(t-1)})}{p(o^{(t)}|d^{(0...t-1)})}$$
$$\propto \pi(x_i^{(t)}|a^{(t-1)}) \, Bel(x_i^{(t-1)}) \quad (13)$$

where $Bel(x_i^{(t-1)})$ is calculated using the kd-tree representing this belief density. The only complication arises from the need to calculate $\pi(x_i^{(t)}|a^{(t-1)})$, which depends on both $x_i^{(t)}$ and $a^{(t-1)}$. Luckily, in mobile robot localization, $\pi(x_i^{(t)}|a^{(t-1)})$ can safely be assumed to be a constant, although this assumption may not be valid in general.

The reader should notice that all three approaches require a method for sampling poses from observations according to $\bar{q}^{(t)}$—which can be non-trivial in mobile robot applications. The first approach is the easiest to implement and mathematically most straightforward. However, as noted above, we suspect that it will be inefficient for mobile robot localization. The two other approaches rely on a density estimation method (such as kd-trees). The third also requires a method for sampling poses backwards in time, which further complicates its implementation. However, the superior results given below may well make this additional work worthwhile.

The Mixture Proposal Distribution

Obviously, neither proposal distribution is sufficient, as they both fail in certain cases. To illustrate this, the dashed line in Figure 4 shows the performance for the dual. As in the previous figure, the horizontal axis depicts the amount of noise in perception, and the vertical axis depicts the error in centimeters, averaged over 1,000 independent runs. Two things are remarkable in these experimental results: First, the accuracy if now *monotonic* in perceptual noise: More accurate sensors give better results. Second, however, the overall performance is much poorer than that of conventional MCL. The poor performance of the dual is due to the fact that *erroneous* sensor

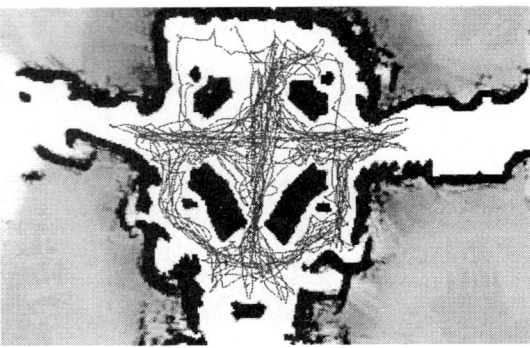

Figure 8: Part of the map of the Smithsonian's Museum of National History and path of the robot.

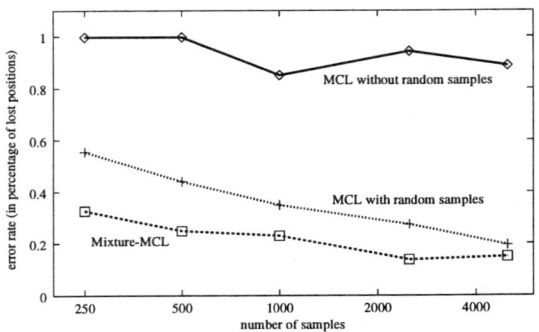

Figure 9: Performance of conventional (top curve), conventional with random samples (middle curve) and our new mixture (bottom curve) MCL for the kidnapped robot problem in the Smithsonian museum. The error rate is measured in percentage of time during which the robot lost track of its position.

measurements have a devastating effect on the estimated belief, since almost all samples are generated at the "wrong" place.

This consideration leads us to the central algorithm proposed in this paper, which uses the following mixture

$$(1 - \phi)q^{(t)} + \phi \bar{q}^{(t)} \qquad (14)$$

with $0 \leq \phi \leq 1$ as the proposal distribution. In our experiments, the mixing rate is set to ϕ throughout. Experiments with an adaptive mixing rate (using pursuit methods) did not improve the performance in a noticeable way.

Sampling Form $\bar{q}$

The remaining principle difficulty in applying our new approach to robotics is that it may not be easy to sample poses x_i based on sensor measurements o. In particular, the previous MCL algorithm "only" requires an algorithm for calculating $p(o|x)$; while there is obvious ways to extend this into a sampling algorithm, sampling *efficiently* from $\bar{q}$ may not a straightforward matter—this is specifically the case for the experiments with laser range finders described below.

Unfortunately, space limitations prohibit a detailed description of our solution. In our implementation, a kd-tree representing the joint distribution $p(o, x)$ is learned in a preprocessing phase, using real robot data (a log-file) as a "sample" of o, and $p(o|x)$ with randomly generated poses x to generate a weighted sample that represents $p(o, x)$. The nice aspect of the tree is that it permits efficient sampling of the desired conditional. Figure 6 shows a set of poses generated for a specific laser range measurement o.

Experimental Results

Our experiments were carried out both in simulation and for data collected with our tour-guide robot Minerva (shown in Figure 7), collected during a two-week period in which it gave tours to thousands of people in the Smithsonian's Museum of National History (TBB+99). The simulation experiments were carried out using the third method for calculating importance factors outlined above. A comparative study showed no noticeable difference between this and the second method. All real-world results were carried out using the second approach, in part because it avoids backwards sampling of poses. As noted above, we did not yet implement the first method.

Simulation Figure 4 shows the performance of MCL with the mixture proposal distribution, under conditions that are otherwise identical to those in Figures 3. As these results suggest, our new MCL algorithm outperforms both MCL and its dual by a large margin. At every single noise level, our new algorithm outperforms its alternatives by a factor that ranges from 1.07 (high noise level) to 9.7 (low noise level). For example, at a noise level of 1%, our new MCL algorithm exhibits an average error of 24.6cm, whereas MCL's error is 238cm and that of dual MCL is 293cm. In comparison, the average error with noise-free sensors and the optimal estimator is approximately 19.5cm (it's not zero since the robot has to face the object to see it).

Our approach also degrades nicely to very small sample sets. Figure 5 plots the error of conventional MCL (top curve) and MCL with mixture proposal distribution (bottom curve) for different error levels, using $m = 50$ samples only. With 50 samples, the computational load is 0.126% on a 500MHz Pentium Computer—meaning that the algorithm is approximately 800 faster than real-time. While plain MCL basically fails under this circumstances to track the robot's position, our new version of MCL performs excellently, and is only slightly inferior to $m = 1,000$ samples.

Real-World Experiments with Lasers Our approach was tested using data recorded during a two-week deployment of the mobile robot Minerva as a museum tour-guide in the Smithsonian's Museum of National History (TBB+99). The data contains logs of odometry measurements and sensor scans taken by Minerva's two laser range-finders. Figure 8 shows part of the map of the museum and the path of the robot used for this experiment.

As reported in (DBFT99; DHN99; FBKT00), conventional MCL reliably succeeds in localizing the robot. To test our new approach under even harder conditions, we repeatedly introduced errors into the odometry information. These errors made the robot lose track of its position with probability of 0.01 when advancing one meter. The resulting localization problem is known as the *kidnapped robot problem* (EM92), which is generally acknowledged as the most challenging localization problem. As argued in (FBT99), this problem tests the ability to recover from extreme failures of

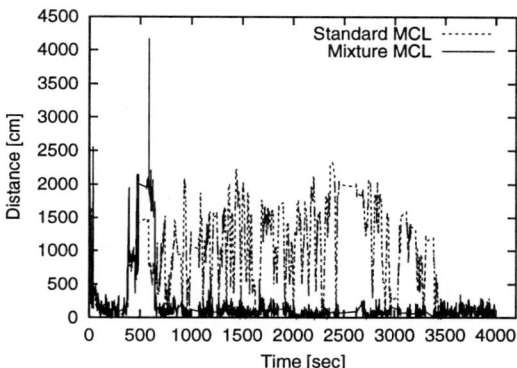

Figure 10: MCL with the standard proposal distribution (dashed curve) compared to MCL with the new mixture distribution (solid line). Shown here is the error for a 4,000-second episode of camera-based localization in the Smithsonian museum.

the localization algorithm.

Figure 9 shows comparative results for three different approaches. The error is measured by the percentage of time, during which the estimated position deviates by more than 2 meters from the reference position. Obviously, the mixture proposal distribution yields significantly better results, even if the basic proposal distribution is mixed with 5% random samples (as suggested in (FBKT00) as a solution to the kidnapped robot problem). The mixture proposal distribution reduces the error rate of localization by as much as 70% more than MCL if the standard proposal distribution is employed; and 32% when compared to the case where the standard proposal distribution is mixed with a uniform distribution. These results are significant at the 95% confidence level, evaluated over actual robot data.

Real-World Experiments with Vision We also compared MCL with different proposal distributions in the context of visual localization, using only camera imagery obtained with the robot Minerva during public museum hours (DBFT99). Figure 7 shows on the right a texture mosaic of the museum's ceiling. Since the ceiling height is unknown, only the center region in the camera image is used for localization.

The image sequence used for evaluation is of extremely poor quality, as people often intentionally covered the camera with their hand and placed dirt on the lens. Figure 10 shows the localization error obtained when using vision only (calculated using the localization results from the laser as ground truth). The data covers a period of approximately 4,000 seconds, during which MCL processes a total of 20,740 images. After approximately 630 seconds, a drastic error in the robot's odometry leads to a loss of the position (which is an instance of the kidnapped robot problem). As the two curves in Figure 10 illustrate, the regular MCL sampler (dashed curve) is unable to recover from this event, whereas MCL with mixture proposal distribution (solid curve) recovers quickly. These result are not statistically significant in that only a single run is considered, but they confirm our findings with laser range finders. Together, our result suggest that the mixture distribution drastically increases the robustness of the statistical estimator for mobile robot localization.

Conclusion

This paper introduced a new proposal distribution for Monte Carlo localization, a randomized Bayesian algorithm for mobile robot localization. Our approach combines two proposal distribution which sample from different factors of the desired posterior. By doing so, our approach overcomes a range of limitations that currently exist for different versions of MCL, such as the inability to estimate posteriors for highly accurate sensors, poor degradation to small sample sets, and the ability to recover from unexpected large state changes (robot kidnapping). Extensive experimental results suggest that our new approach consistently outperforms MCL by a large margin. The resulting algorithm is highly practical, and might improve the performance of particle filters in a range of applications.

Acknowledgments

The authors are indebted to Nando de Freitas and Arnaud Doucet for whose insightful comments on an earlier draft of a related paper. We also thank Frank Dellaert and the members of CMU's Robot Learning Lab for invaluable suggestions and comments.

References

J.L. Bentley. Multidimensional divide and conquer. *Communications of the ACM*, 23(4):214–229, 1980.

F. Dellaert, W. Burgard, D. Fox, and S. Thrun. Using the condensation algorithm for robust, vision-based mobile robot localization. In *CVPR-99*.

J. Denzler, B. Heigl, and H. Niemann. Combining computer graphics and computer vision for probabilistic self-localization. Internal Report, 1999.

A Doucet. On sequential simulation-based methods for bayesian filtering. TR CUED/F-INFENG/TR 310, Cambridge Univ., 1998.

S. Engelson and D. McDermott. Error correction in mobile robot map learning. In *ICRA-92*.

D. Fox, W. Burgard, H. Kruppa, and S. Thrun. Collaborative multi-robot localization. *Autonomous Robots*, 8(3), 2000.

D. Fox, W. Burgard, and S. Thrun. Markov localization for mobile robots in dynamic environments. *JAIR*, 11:391–427, 1999.

R. Fung and B. Del Favero. Backward simulation in bayesian networks. In *UAI94*.

M. Isard and A. Blake. Condensation: conditional density propagation for visual tracking. *IJCV*, 1998.

K. Kanazawa, D. Koller, and S.J. Russell. Stochastic simulation algorithms for dynamic probabilistic networks. In *UAI-95*.

S. Lenser and M. Veloso. Sensor resetting localization for poorly modelled mobile robots. In *ICRA-2000*.

J. Liu and R. Chen. Sequential monte carlo methods for dynamic systems. *Journal of the American Statistical Assoc.*, 93, 1998.

A. W. Moore. *Efficient Memory-based Learning for Robot Control*. PhD thesis, University of Cambridge, 1990.

M. Pitt and N. Shephard. Filtering via simulation: auxiliary particle filter. *Journal of the American Statistical Assoc.*, 1999.

M.A. Tanner. *Tools for Statistical Inference*. Springer, 1993.

S. Thrun et al. MINERVA: A second generation mobile tour-guide robot. In *ICRA-99*.

Appearance-Based Obstacle Detection with Monocular Color Vision

Iwan Ulrich and Illah Nourbakhsh

The Robotics Institute, Carnegie Mellon University
5000 Forbes Avenue, Pittsburgh, PA 15213
iwan@ri.cmu.edu, illah@ri.cmu.edu

Abstract

This paper presents a new vision-based obstacle detection method for mobile robots. Each individual image pixel is classified as belonging either to an obstacle or the ground based on its color appearance. The method uses a single passive color camera, performs in real-time, and provides a binary obstacle image at high resolution. The system is easily trained by simply driving the robot through its environment. In the adaptive mode, the system keeps learning the appearance of the ground during operation. The system has been tested successfully in a variety of environments, indoors as well as outdoors.

1. Introduction

Obstacle detection is an important task for many mobile robot applications. Most mobile robots rely on range data for obstacle detection. Popular sensors for *range-based* obstacle detection systems include ultrasonic sensors, laser rangefinders, radar, stereo vision, optical flow, and depth from focus. Because these sensors measure the distances from obstacles to the robot, they are inherently suited for the tasks of obstacle detection and obstacle avoidance. However, none of these sensors is perfect. Ultrasonic sensors are cheap but suffer from specular reflections and usually from poor angular resolution. Laser rangefinders and radar provide better resolution but are more complex and more expensive. Most depth from X vision systems require a textured environment to perform properly. Moreover, stereo vision and optical flow are computationally expensive.

In addition to their individual shortcomings, all range-based obstacle detection systems have difficulty detecting small or flat objects on the ground. Reliable detection of these objects requires high measurement accuracy and thus precise calibration. Range sensors are also unable to distinguish between different types of ground surfaces. This is a problem especially outdoors, where range sensors are usually unable to differentiate between the sidewalk pavement and adjacent flat grassy areas.

While small objects and different types of ground are difficult to detect with range sensors, they can in many cases be easily detected with color vision. For this reason,

Copyright © 2000, American Association for Artificial Intelligence (www.aaai.org). All rights reserved.

we have developed a new *appearance-based* obstacle detection system that is based on passive monocular color vision. The heart of our algorithm consists of detecting pixels different in appearance than the ground and classifying them as obstacles. The algorithm performs in real-time, provides a high-resolution obstacle image, and operates in a variety of environments. The algorithm is also very easy to train.

The fundamental difference between range-based and appearance-based obstacle detection systems is the obstacle criterion. In range-based systems, obstacles are objects that protrude a minimum distance from the ground. In appearance-based systems, obstacles are objects that differ in appearance from the ground.

2. Related Work

While an extensive body of work exists for range-based obstacle detection, little work has been done in appearance-based obstacle detection (Everett 1995). Interestingly, Shakey, the first autonomous mobile robot, used a simple form of appearance-based obstacle detection (Nilsson 1984). Because Shakey operated on textureless floor tiles, obstacles were easily detected by applying an edge detector to the monochrome input image. However, Shakey's environment was artificial. Obstacles had non-specular surfaces and were uniformly coated with carefully selected colors. In addition, the lighting, walls, and floor were carefully set up to eliminate shadows.

Horswill used a similar method for his mobile robots Polly and Frankie, which operated in a real environment (Horswill 1994). Polly's task was to give simple tours of the 7th floor of the MIT AI lab, which had a textureless carpeted floor. Obstacles could thus also be detected by applying an edge detector to the monochrome input images, which were first subsampled to 64×48 pixels and then smoothed with a 3×3 low-pass filter.

Shakey and Polly's obstacle detection systems perform well as long as the background texture constraint is satisfied, i.e., the floor has no texture and the environment is uniformly illuminated. False positives arise if there are shiny floors, boundaries between carpets, or shadows. False negatives arise if there are weak boundaries between the floor and obstacles.

Turk and Marra developed an algorithm that uses color instead of edges to detect obstacles on roads with minimal texture (Turk and Marra 1986). Similar to a simple motion detector, their algorithm detects obstacles by subtracting two consecutive color images from each other. If the ground has substantial texture, this method suffers from similar problems as systems that are based on edge detection. In addition, this algorithm requires either the robot or the obstacles to be in motion.

While the previously described systems fail if the ground is textured, stereo vision and optical flow systems actually require texture to work properly. A thorough overview of such systems is given by Lourakis and Orphanoudakis (Lourakis and Orphanoudakis 1997). They themselves developed an elegant method that is based on the registration of the ground between consecutive views of the environment, which leaves objects extending from the ground unregistered. Subtracting the reference image from the warped one then determines protruding objects without explicitly recovering the 3D structure of the viewed scene. However, the registration step of this method still requires the ground to be textured.

In her master's thesis, Lorigo extended Horswill's work to domains with texture (Lorigo, Brooks, and Grimson 1997). To accomplish this, her system uses color information in addition to edge information. The key assumption of Lorigo's algorithm is that there are no obstacles right in front of the robot. Thus, the ten bottom rows of the input image are used as a reference area. Obstacles are then detected in the rest of the image by comparing the histograms of small window areas to the reference area. The use of the reference area makes the system very adaptive. However, this approach requires the reference area to always be free of obstacles. To minimize the risk of violating this constraint, the reference area can not be deep. Unfortunately, a shallow reference area is not always sufficiently representative for pixels higher up in the image, which are observed at a different angle. A particular problem are highlights, which usually occur higher up in an image. The method performs in real-time, but uses an image resolution of only 64×64 pixels.

Similar to Lorigo's method, our obstacle detection algorithm also uses color information and can thus be used in a wide variety of environments. Unlike the previously described systems that are all purely reactive, our method permits the use of a deeper reference area by learning the appearance of the ground over several observations. In addition, the learned data can easily be stored and later be reused. Like Lorigo's method, our system also uses histograms and a reference area ahead of the robot, but does not impose the constraint that the reference area is always free of obstacles. In addition, our methods provides binary obstacle images at high resolution in real-time.

3. Appearance-Based Obstacle Detection

Our obstacle detection system is purely based on the appearance of individual pixels. Any pixel that differs in appearance from the ground is classified as an obstacle. The method is based on three assumptions that are reasonable for a variety of indoor and outdoor environments:

1. Obstacles differ in appearance from the ground.
2. The ground is relatively flat.
3. There are no overhanging obstacles.

The first assumption allows us to distinguish obstacles from the ground, while the second and third assumptions allow us to estimate the distances between detected obstacles and the camera.

The classification of a pixel as representing an obstacle or the ground can be based on a number of local visual attributes, such as intensity, color, edges, and texture. It is important that the selected attributes provide information that is rich enough so that the system performs reliably in a variety of environments. The selected attributes should also require little computation time so that real-time performance can be achieved without dedicated hardware. The less computationally expensive the attribute, the higher the obstacle detection update rate, and the faster a mobile robot can travel safely.

To best satisfy these requirements, we decided to use color information as our primary cue. Color has many appealing attributes, although little work has lately been done in color vision for mobile robots. Color provides more information than intensity alone. Compared to texture, color is a more local attribute and can thus be calculated much faster. Systems that solely rely on edge information can only be used in environments with textureless floors, as in the environments of Shaky and Polly. Such systems also have more difficulty differentiating between shadows and obstacles than color-based systems.

For many applications, it is important to estimate the distance from the camera to a pixel that is classified as an obstacle. With monocular vision, a common approach to distance estimation is to assume that the ground is relatively flat and that there are no overhanging obstacles. If these two assumptions are valid, then the distance is a monotonically increasing function of the pixel height in the image. The estimated distance is correct for all obstacles at their base, but the higher an obstacle part is above the ground, the more the distance is overestimated. The simplest approach of dealing with this problem consists of only using the obstacle pixels that are lowest for each column of the image. A more sophisticated approach consists of grouping obstacle pixels and assigning the shortest distance to the entire group.

4. Basic Approach

Our basic approach can best be explained with an example and a *simplified* version of our method. Figure 1 shows a color input image with three reference areas of different depths on the left and the corresponding outputs of the simplified version on the right. The remainder of this section describes the details of the simplified version. Unlike the full version of our method, the simplified version has no memory and uses only one input image. However, all functions of the simplified version are also used by the full version of our method, which will be described in detail in section five.

The simplified version of our appearance-based obstacle detection method consists of the following four steps:

1. Filter color input image.
2. Transformation into HSI color space.
3. Histogramming of reference area.
4. Comparison with reference histograms.

In the first step, the 320×260 color input image is filtered with a 5×5 Gaussian filter to reduce the level of noise.

In the second step, the filtered RGB values are transformed into the HSI (hue, saturation, and intensity) color space. Because color information is very noisy at low intensity, we only assign valid values to hue and saturation if the corresponding intensity is above a minimum value. Similarly, because hue is meaningless at low saturation, hue is only assigned a valid value if the corresponding saturation is above another minimum value. An appealing attribute of the HSI model is that it separates the color information into an intensity and a color component. As a result, the hue and saturation bands are less sensitive to illumination changes than the intensity band.

In the third step, a trapezoidal area in front of the mobile robot is used for reference. The valid hue and intensity values of the pixels inside the trapezoidal reference area are histogrammed into two one-dimensional histograms, one for hue and one for intensity. The two histograms are then low-pass filtered with a simple average filter. Histograms are well suited for this application, as they naturally represent multi-modal distributions. In addition, histograms require very little memory and can be computed in little time.

In the fourth step, all pixels of the filtered input image are compared to the hue and the intensity histograms. A pixel is classified as an obstacle if either of the two following conditions is satisfied:

i) The hue histogram bin value at the pixel's hue value is below the hue threshold.
ii) The intensity histogram bin value at the pixel's intensity value is below the intensity threshold.

If none of these conditions are true, then the pixel is classified as belonging to the ground. In the current implementation, the hue and the intensity thresholds are set

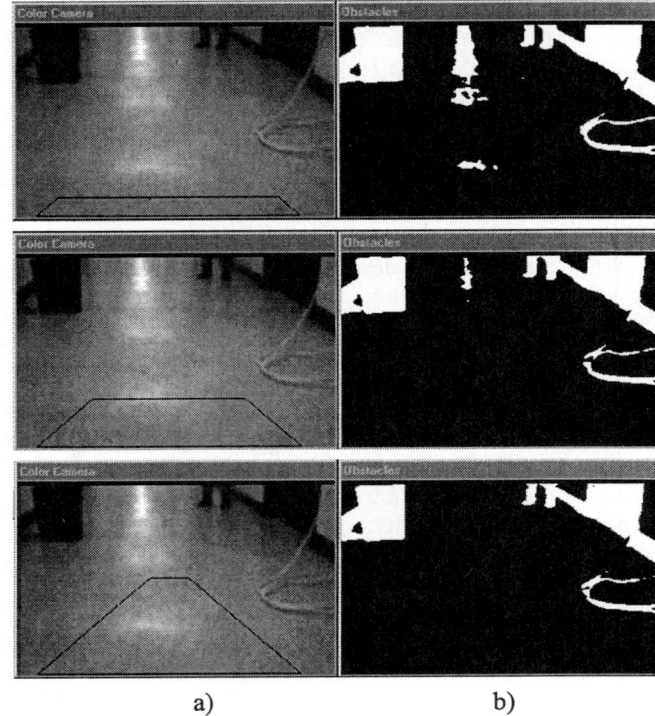

Figure 1: a) Input color image with trapezoidal reference area
b) Binary obstacle output image

to 60 and 80 pixels respectively. The hue threshold is chosen smaller than the intensity threshold because not every pixel is assigned a valid hue value.

As shown in Figure 1, the simplified version of our algorithm performs quite well. Independent of the depths of the reference area, the method detects the lower parts of the right and left corridor walls, the trash can on the left, the door on the right, and the shoes and pants of the person standing a few meters ahead. In particular, the algorithm also detects the cable lying on the floor, which is very difficult to detect with a range-based sensor. The three example images also demonstrate that the deeper the reference area, the more representative the area is for the rest of the image. In the case of the shallow reference area of the top image, the method incorrectly classifies a highlight as an obstacle that is very close to the robot.

5. Implementation

In the previous section, we have shown how the reference area in front of the mobile robot can be used to detect obstacles in the rest of the image. Obviously, this approach only works correctly if no obstacles are present inside the trapezoidal reference area. Lorigo's method, which assumes that the area immediately in front of the robot is free of obstacles, is thus forced to use a reference area with a shallow depth to reduce the risk of violating this constraint. However, as demonstrated in Figure 1, a shallow reference area is not always sufficiently representative.

In order to use a deeper reference area, we avoid the strong assumption that the area immediately ahead of the robot is free of obstacles. Instead, we assume that the ground area over which the mobile robot traveled was free of obstacles. In our current implementation, the reference area is about one meter deep. Therefore, whenever the mobile robot travels relatively straight for more than one meter, we can assume that the reference area that was captured one meter ago was free of obstacles. Conversely, if the robot turns a substantial amount during this short trajectory, it is no longer safe to assume that the captured reference areas were free of obstacles.

The software implementation of the algorithm uses two queues: a *candidate queue* and a *reference queue*. For each acquired image, the hue and intensity histograms of the reference area are computed as described in the first three steps of section four. These histograms together with the current odometry information are then stored in the candidate queue.

At each sample time, the current odometry information is compared with the odometry information of the items in the candidate queue. In the first pass, items whose orientation differs by more than 18° from the current orientation are eliminated from the candidate queue. In the second pass, items whose positions differ by more than 1 m from the current position are moved from the candidate queue into the reference queue.

The histograms of the reference queue are then combined using a simple OR function, resulting in the *combined hue histogram* and the *combined intensity histogram*. The pixels in the current image are then compared to the combined hue and the combined intensity histogram as described in the fourth step of section four.

To train the system, one simply leads the robot through the environment, avoiding obstacles manually. This allows us to easily train the mobile robot in a new environment. The training result consists of the final combined hue and combined intensity histogram, which can easily be stored for later usage as they require very little memory. After training, these histograms are used to detect obstacles as described in the fourth step of section four.

6. Operation Modes

We have currently implemented three operation modes: *regular*, *adaptive*, and *assistive*. In the regular mode, the obstacle detection system relies on the combined histograms learned during training. While this works well in many indoor environments with static illumination, the output contains several false positives if the lighting conditions are different than during training.

In the adaptive mode, the system is capable of adapting to changes in illumination. Unlike the regular version, the adaptive version learns while it operates. The adaptive version uses two sets of combined histograms: a *static* set and a *dynamic* set. The static set simply consists of the combined histograms learned during the regular manual training. The dynamic set is updated during operation as described in section five as if the robot was being manually trained. The two sets are then combined with the OR function. With this approach, we would only add learned items to the reference queue, but never eliminate an item from it. This approach would correspond to the algorithm never forgetting a learned item. For the adaptive set, we actually chose to limit its memory, so that it forgets items that it learned a long distance ago by eliminating these items from the dynamic reference queue. In our current implementation, the dynamic reference queue only retains the ten most recent items.

The assistive mode is well suited for applications of teleoperated and assistive devices. This mode uses only the dynamic set. To start, one simply drives the robot straight ahead for a few meters. During the short training, the reference queue is quickly filled with valid histograms. When the obstacle detection module detects enough ground pixels, the obstacle avoidance module takes control of the robot, freeing the user from the task of obstacle avoidance. If the robot arrives at a different surface, the robot might stop because the second surface is incorrectly classified as an obstacle. The user can then manually override the obstacle avoidance module by driving the robot 1-2 meters forward over the new surface. During this short user intervention, the adaptive obstacle detection system learns the new surface. When it detects enough ground pixels, the obstacle avoidance module takes over again.

7. Experimental Results

For experimental verification, we implemented our algorithm on a computer-controlled electric wheelchair, which is a product of KIPR from Oklahoma. We added quadrature encoders to the wheelchair to obtain odometry information.

The vision software runs on a laptop computer with a Pentium II processor clocked at 333 MHz. The laptop is connected to the wheelchair's 68332 microcontroller with a serial link. Images are acquired from a Hitachi KPD-50 color CCD camera, which is equipped with an auto-iris lens. The camera is connected to the laptop with a PCMCIA framegrabber from MRT. The entire system is shown in Figure 2.

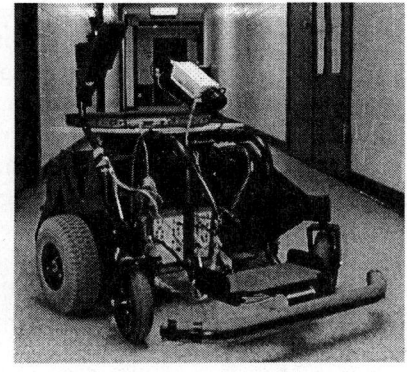

Figure 2: Experimental platform.

Figure 3 shows seven examples of our obstacle detection algorithm. The left images show the original color input images, while the right images show the corresponding binary output images. It is important to note that no additional image processing like blob filtering was applied to the output images. Color versions of the images, as well as additional examples, are available at http://www.cs.cmu.edu/~iwan/abod.html.

The first five images were taken indoors at the Carnegie Museum of Natural History in Pittsburgh. Figure 3a shows one of the best results that we obtained. The ground is almost perfectly segmented from obstacles, even for objects that are more than ten meters ahead. Figure 3b includes a moving person in the input image. Although some parts of the shoes are not classified as obstacles, enough pixels are correctly classified for a reliable obstacle detection. The person leaning onto the left wall is also classified as an obstacle. In Figure 3c, a thin pillar is detected as an obstacle, while its shadow is correctly ignored. However, the system incorrectly classifies a shadow that is cast from an adjacent room on the left as an obstacle. In Figure 3d, the lighting conditions are very difficult, as outdoor light illuminates a large part of the floor through a yellow window. Nevertheless, the algorithm performs well and correctly labels the yellowish pixels as floor. Figure 3e shows an example where our algorithm fails to detect an obstacle. The color of the yellow leg in the center is too similar to the floor. The algorithm also has trouble detecting the lower part of the left wall, which is made of the same material as the floor. However, the darker pixels at the bottom of the wall and the leg are detected correctly due to the high resolution of the image.

The last two images were taken outdoors on a sidewalk. In Figure 3f, both sides of the sidewalk, the bushes and the cars, are detected as obstacles. Moreover, the two large shadows are perfectly ignored. In Figure 3g, the sidewalk's right border is painted yellow. The algorithm reliably detects the grass on the left side and the yellow marking on the right side. Although the yellow marking is not really an obstacle, it does indicate the sidewalk border so that its detection is desirable in most cases. This example is also an argument for the use of color, as the yellow marking would not be recognized as easily with a monochrome camera.

With the current hardware and software implementation, the execution time for the processing of an image of 320 × 260 pixels is about 200 ms. It is important to note that little effort was spent on optimizing execution speed. Beside code optimization, faster execution speeds could also be achieved by subsampling the input image. Another possibility would be to only apply the algorithm to regions of interest, e.g., the lower portion of the image. By only using the bottom half of the image, which still corresponds to a look-ahead of two meters, the current system would achieve an update rate of 10 Hz, which is similar to a fast sonar system. However, our vision system provides information at a much higher resolution than is possible with sonars.

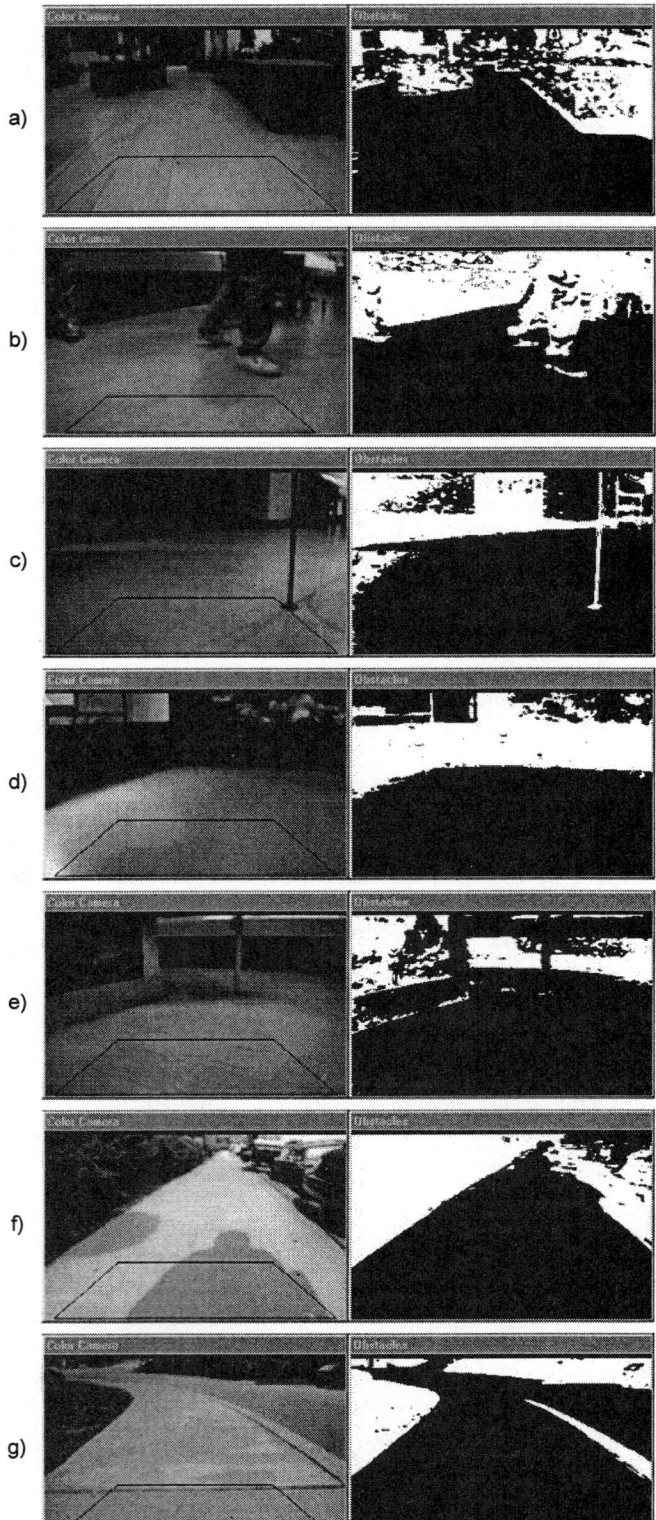

Figure 3: Experimental results.

To further test the performance of our obstacle detection system, we implemented a very simple reflexive obstacle avoidance algorithm on the electric wheelchair. The algorithm is similar to the one used by Horswill's robots (Horswill 1994), but uses five columns instead of three. Not surprisingly, after driving the robot for a few meters in the assistive operation mode, the obstacle detection output allows the wheelchair to easily follow sidewalks and corridors, and avoid obstacles. Another research group at the Robotics Institute has successfully combined our method with stereo vision to provide obstacle detection for an all terrain vehicle (Soto et al. 1999).

8. Evaluation

Our system works well as long as the three assumptions about the environment stated in section three are not violated. We have experienced only a few cases where obstacles violate the first assumption by having an appearance similar to the ground. Figure 3e shows such a case. Including additional visual clues might decrease the rate of false negatives to an even lower number.

We have never experienced a problem with the second assumption that the ground is flat, because our robots are not intended to operate in rough terrain. A small inclination of a sidewalk introduces small errors in the distance estimate. This is not really a problem as the errors are small for obstacles that are close to the robot.

Our system overestimates the distance to overhanging obstacles, which violate the third assumption. This distance estimate error can easily lead to collisions, even when the pixels are correctly classified as obstacles. Although truly overhanging obstacles are rare, tabletops are quite common and have the same effect. However, it is important to note that tabletops also present a problem for many mobile robots that are equipped with range-based sensors, as tabletops are often outside their field of view. The simplest way to detect tabletops is probably to combine our system with a range-based sensor. For example, adding one or two low-cost wide-angle ultrasonic sensors for the detection of tabletops would make our system much more reliable in office environments.

9. Further Improvements

The current algorithm could be improved in many ways. It will be interesting to investigate how color spaces other than HSI perform for this application. Examples of promising color spaces are YUV, normalized RGB, and opponent colors. The final system could easily combine bands from several color spaces using the same approach. Several bands could also be combined by using higher-dimensional histograms, e.g., a two-dimensional histogram for hue and saturation. In addition, several texture measures could be implemented as well.

For large environments with different kinds of surfaces, it would be preferable to have a set of learned histograms for each type of surface. Combining our obstacle detection method with a localization method would allow us to benefit from room-specific histogram sets. In particular, we recently developed a topological localization method that is a promising candidate for combination, because its vision-based place recognition module also relies heavily on the appearance of the ground (Ulrich and Nourbakhsh 2000).

Another possible improvement consists of enlarging the field of view by using a wide-angle lens or a panoramic camera system like the Omnicam. However, it is unclear at this time what the consequences of the resulting reduced resolution will be.

Another promising approach consists of combining the current appearance-based sensor system with a range-based sensor system. Such a combination is particularly appealing due to the complementary nature of the two systems.

10. Conclusion

This paper presented a new method for obstacle detection with a single color camera. The method performs in real-time and provides a binary obstacle image at high resolution. The system can easily be trained and has performed well in a variety of environments, indoors as well as outdoors.

References

Everett, H.R. 1995. *Sensors for Mobile Robots: Theory and Applications*. A K Peters, Wellesley, Massachusetts.

Horswill, I. 1994. Visual Collision Avoidance by Segmentation. In *Proceedings of the IEEE/RSJ International Conference on Intelligent Robots and Systems*, 902-909.

Lorigo, L.M.; Brooks, R.A.; and Grimson, W.E.L. 1997. Visually-Guided Obstacle Avoidance in Unstructured Environments. In *Proceedings of the IEEE/RSJ International Conference on Intelligent Robots and Systems*, 373-379.

Lourakis, M.I.A., and Orphanoudakis, S.C. 1997. Visual Detection of Obstacles Assuming a Locally Planar Ground. Technical Report, FORTH-ICS, TR-207.

Nilsson, N.J. 1984. Shakey the Robot. Technical Note 323, SRI International.

Soto, A.; Saptharishi, M.; Trebi Ollennu, A.; Dolan, J.; and Khosla, P. 1999. Cyber-ATVs: Dynamic and Distributed Reconnaissance and Surveillance Using All Terrain UGVs. In *Proceedings of the International Conference on Field and Service Robotics*, 329-334.

Turk, M.A., and Marra, M. 1986, Color Road Segmentation and Video Obstacle Detection, In *SPIE Proceedings of Mobile Robots*, Vol. 727, Cambridge, MA, 136-142.

Ulrich, I., and Nourbakhsh, I. 2000, Appearance-Based Place Recognition for Topological Localization. In *Proceedings of the IEEE International Conference on Robotics and Automation*, in press.

Multi-Fidelity Robotic Behaviors:
Acting With Variable State Information

Elly Winner and Manuela Veloso

Computer Science Department
Carnegie Mellon University
Pittsburgh, PA 15213
{elly,veloso}@cs.cmu.edu
http://www.cs.cmu.edu/{~elly,~mmv}

Abstract

Our work is driven by one of the core purposes of artificial intelligence: to develop real robotic agents that achieve complex high-level goals in real-time environments. Robotic behaviors select actions as a function of the state of the robot and of the world. Designing robust and appropriate robotic behaviors is a difficult because of noise, uncertainty and the cost of acquiring the necessary state information. We addressed this challenge within the concrete domain of robotic soccer with fully autonomous legged robots provided by Sony. In this paper, we present one of the outcomes of this research: the introduction of *multi-fidelity behaviors* to explicitly adapt to different levels of state information accuracy. The paper motivates and introduces our general approach and then reports on our concrete work with the Sony robots. The multi-fidelity behaviors we developed allow the robots to successfully achieve their goals in a dynamic and adversarial environment. A robot acts according to a set of behaviors that aggressively balance the cost of acquiring state information with the value of that information to the robot's ability to achieve its high-level goals. The paper includes empirical experiments which support our method of balancing the cost and benefit of the incrementally-accurate state information.

Introduction

Intelligent agents operating in dynamic domains rely heavily on real-time information about the world around them to direct and control their behaviors. This information may be raw sensor data, processed sensor data, or sensor data that the agent has to spend effort to acquire.

In most realistic domains, raw sensor data is not refined enough to allow for high-level deliberation or control. The agent must spend effort to process the data it receives from its sensors to support the internal state representation necessary for higher-level control. In addition, sometimes the sensor data the agent needs to select behaviors is not immediately available. The agent must spend time to acquire the raw data in addition to the time spent processing it.

Thus, in many complex and dynamic domains, the quality of the agent's information about the world around it is dependent on the amount of resources the agent is able to devote to acquiring that information. In order for an agent to

Copyright © 2000, American Association for Artificial Intelligence (www.aaai.org). All rights reserved.

act sensibly in such a domain, it must be able to balance its need for information with the benefit this information provides. It must be able to take advantage of all available information and still act sensibly when less is available. Our multi-fidelity behaviors approach provides a framework which allows an agent's performance to respond aggressively to changes in the quality of available information.

The remainder of this paper is organized as follows. We first explain and discuss our multi-fidelity behaviors approach. Then we describe our application of this approach to our RoboCup-99 Sony legged robot team and discuss the strategy we use to balance the costs and benefits of information for the robots.

Multi-Fidelity Behaviors

Dealing with dynamic variations of the cost and availability of resources is a difficult problem that comes up in several areas of computer science. It has been proposed that there is a need in wireless networking for fast algorithms that compute an approximation to the ideal solution. Algorithms that can control the accuracy of their approximations are called *multi-fidelity algorithms* (Satyanarayanan & Narayanan 1999), which inspired our use of the same term for our robotic agent behavior approach.

Such algorithms are also needed to control real-time agent behavior. Our multi-fidelity behaviors approach is a general framework that allows the performance of the system to swiftly upgrade and gracefully downgrade its performance as resource availability varies without disrupting its own activity with potentially frequent behavior changes. We first define general-purpose modes of behavior (Mataric 1992; Brooks 1986). For example, a foraging robot might have three modes of behavior:

1. Search: the robot searches for the desired objects;
2. Acquire: the robot retrieves found objects;
3. Store: the robot returns the foraged objects to some storage location.

We implement modes of behavior at several "fidelity" levels, which correspond to different levels of resource availability. For example, one possible implementation of the store mode of the foraging robot we mentioned above might require that its GPS receiver is working properly. Another implementation would only require that the agent's compass is working. And another might allow the agent to use the stars to navigate. By implementing the same mode, or task, at different fidelity levels, we allow the system to upgrade or downgrade its performance as resource availability changes without changing its behavior drastically. In our example, the robot would never stop trying to store the foraged objects; the efficiency of its method would simply change.

In addition to switching between implementations of individual modes, an agent must also switch between modes. To do this, continuously monitors information about its state, as do Nilsson's teleo-reactive agent programs (Nilsson 1994). In addition to increasing the performance of individual modes, our approach also allows mode-to-mode transitions to depend on the quality of state information. However, care must be taken to avoid a situation that could lead to oscillation between modes as information quality changes with time. The intention of our approach is to allow efficient response to changes in available state information while not allowing the robot to oscillate between states.

RoboCup-99 Legged Robot League

We applied our multi-fidelity behaviors approach to the robotic soccer domain (Kitano *et al.* 1997) in the Sony legged robot league of RoboCup-99.[1] All teams in the RoboCup-99 legged robot league used the same hardware platform: the Sony quadruped legged robots (Fujita, Zrehen, & Kitano 1999), shown in Figure 1.[2] The robots are fully autonomous and have onboard cameras. Our image processing, localization and control algorithms run on the onboard processor. The robots are not remotely controlled in any way, and, as of now, no communication is possible between the robots. The only information available for decision making comes from the robot's onboard camera and from sensors which report on the state of the robot's body.

Figure 1: The Sony quadruped robot dog with a ball.

The soccer game consists of two ten-minute halves, each begun with a kickoff. In the kickoff, the ball begins in the center of the field, and each team may position its robots on its own side of the field. After each goal, play resumes with another kickoff. Each team consists of three robots. Like most of the other 1998 and 1999 teams (Veloso, Pagello, & Kitano 2000), we divided our team into two attackers and one goaltender. In this paper, we will focus on the attackers.

The field is 280 cm in length and 180 cm in width. The goals are centered on either end of the field, and are each 60 cm wide and 30 cm tall. Six unique landmarks are placed around the edges of the field (one at each corner, and one on each side of the halfway line) to help the robots localize themselves on the field.

The robotic soccer domain is a very appropriate one in which to study our approach. Raw data from the robot's camera must be processed to extract the information used to control the robot's behavior. First, the data are sent to the *vision module*, which reports which objects are seen, with what confidence, and at what direction and distance (Bruce, Balch, & Veloso). This information is then sent to the *localization module*, which reports an estimate of the robot's angle, θ, and of its x and y location on the field, along with the standard deviations $\sigma\theta$, σx and σy (Lenser & Veloso 2000).

To estimate the robot's position, the localization system applies Monte Carlo sampling and sensor-based resetting to data about the position of field landmarks relative to the robot. The data provided by the localization system is not accurate when the robot has not recently seen landmarks. Therefore, to get accurate localization information, the robot must look for landmarks.

Because the robot is legged and cannot walk completely smoothly, the camera experiences pitch and roll while it walks. This causes the images it collects to change significantly from one frame to the next. This causes the vision system's identification of objects and the estimate of their distances and angles to degrade. The localization system depends heavily on accurate information about the landmarks, so our approach, like many previous robotic systems, requires that the robot stop moving while looking for landmarks. The process of stopping and scanning for landmarks usually takes the robot between 15 and 20 seconds.

Because of this, it is very costly for the robot to acquire information about its location on the field. Although it is obvious that this information is very useful to a soccer-playing robot, soccer, like other dynamic domains, is time-critical, so every moment spent looking around is lost time. Opponents can also use the robot's inattention to their advantage.

Implementation

To implement our multi-fidelity behaviors approach with the legged robots, we identified the basic modes of behavior and wrote low-fidelity implementations of each of them. We wrote higher-fidelity implementations of some, but not all of the behaviors because some do not benefit from localization information and others are so urgent that we cannot allow them to collect localization information.

We defined four basic modes of behavior for the attackers:

1. Recover: the robot tries to recover a recently lost ball;

2. Search: the robot searches the field for a lost ball;

3. Approach: the robot approaches the ball;

---

[1] Our extensive videos of this event provide invaluable illustrative support to the work presented in this paper.

[2] The Sony AIBO robots were commercially sold in March of 1999. But the robots used for the RoboCup-99 competition are not the same as those commercially available. The robots we used are equipped with slightly different hardware, and, unlike the commercial product, are programmable.

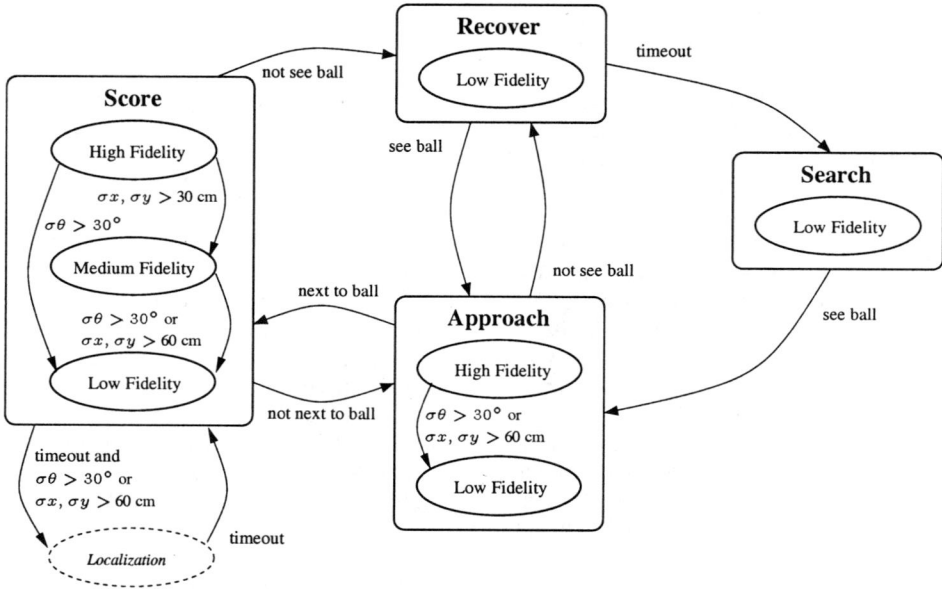

Figure 2: Transitions between the general-purpose modes of behavior and their multi-fidelity implementations. Notice that different behaviors have implementations of different fidelity levels, as appropriate. The transitions are triggered by preset timeouts and processed data sensor, namely visual – see ball, next to ball – and localization information – $\sigma\theta$, σx, σy.

4. Score: the robot pushes the ball towards the goal.

The robot switches between these modes using information about its state. If the robot does not see the ball and did recently, it tries to recover the ball. If this is unsuccessful, it searches for the ball. If the robot sees the ball, it approaches. If it is close to the ball, it pushes the ball towards the goal. Figure 2 shows an illustration of our algorithm. Two modes (approach and score) are implemented using our multi-fidelity behaviors approach.

Low-Fidelity Behavior

Frequently during games, the standard deviations of the robot's localization information are so high that the information should not be used (see the section, "Balancing the Costs of Information"). As explained previously, it is costly for the robot to stop and look every time its localization information is inaccurate. Therefore, we must make sure the robot can choose actions that will help it achieve its goals even when its localization information is not good enough to use. We will describe the algorithms the robot uses to perform these behaviors with no localization information.

- Recover: The robot often loses sight of the ball while it is trying to manipulate it. Its first strategy is to look around only with its head, but if that is not successful, the robot must move around the field to find the ball.

  With no localization information, the robot cannot use a model of the world to try to return to the point at which the ball was last seen. But because, in most cases, the robot has walked past the ball or pushed it to the side, a very efficient way to recover the ball is to walk backwards. If it still does not see the ball, it reverts to the strategy used by last year's team from Carnegie Mellon: it turns in the direction in which the ball was last seen (Veloso & Uther 1999). After this, the robot considers the ball lost and begins a random search for it.

- Search: When the robot does not know where the ball is, it must wander the field to search for it. Without any localization information, the robot cannot do a systematic "oriented" search of the field. Instead, we wrote a random search algorithm that does not rely on localization information at all. Until the robot sees the ball, it alternates between walking forward a random distance and turning a random angle.

- Approach: Although it would be most efficient for the robot to chart an approach to the ball that would allow it to finish "behind" the ball, facing the opponents' goal, this is not possible without localization information. For that reason, when the robot has no localization information, it approaches the ball by running straight towards it.

- Score: Once the robot has possession of the ball, its strategy is simply to push the ball into the goal. This is difficult without localization information because the robot does not know in which direction to push the ball or how far away the goal is. But our behavior allows the robot to score goals without any information from the localization module. The robot walks sideways around the ball until it sees the goal ahead. It then walks forwards into the ball, pushing it towards the goal.

Higher-Fidelity Performance Enhancements

We built higher-fidelity implementations of two of the robot's behavior modes that take advantage of good localization information. Many performance enhancements are possible with perfect localization, but those we developed are robust and reliable even with noisy information.

- Approach: If good localization information is available, the robot is able to use its approach to the ball to get into position behind it. If $\sigma\theta < 30°$, then the robot is able to "skew" its approach to the ball, so that when it reaches the ball, it is closer to its goal position behind the ball.

- Score: Based on knowledge of the robot's position, this implementation decides which direction to circle around the ball, or whether to circle at all. If the robot has $\sigma\theta < 30°$ and $\sigma x, \sigma y < 60$ cm, then the robot can choose the shortest direction to circle around the ball. The robot can also determine that it is facing the right direction and, *even if it does not see the goal*, choose not to circle the ball anymore, but to push the ball forwards, towards the goal. This enables the robot to score goals consistently even when it cannot see the goal at all.

  With $\sigma x, \sigma y < 30$ cm, the robot is able to realize whether this would mean circling into a wall. If the robot is trying to get to the other side of the ball, it will choose to circle in the opposite direction. Otherwise, it will choose not to circle at all, but rather to push the ball forward down the edge of the field.

These enhancements allow the robot to score more consistently than it does with the low-fidelity algorithm. The main reason is that, by making the robot's action more efficient, they reduce the amount of time the robot spends moving around the ball. Because the robot's motion is inaccurate and unpredictable, it often taps the ball away while trying to maneuver around it, forcing the robot to stop and search for the ball. Any reduction in the amount of time the robot spends moving near the ball reduces the chances that the ball will be nudged away.

Unenhanced Behaviors

Although we used localization information to improve the performance of two of the robot's modes, we did not improve the other two. There are two reasons for this. Some behaviors do not benefit from localization information. Other behaviors are so urgent that even if they would benefit from localization information, stopping to acquire it would be too expensive.

Behaviors with No Need for Localization We do not allow the robot to acquire or use localization information at all when it is searching for the ball, whether it has lost the ball recently or is conducting a search of the field for it.

Information about the robot's position on the field does not help it in either of these cases. When the ball has recently been lost, the only important information is that it is probably near the robot. Our unenhanced search already takes advantage of this fact. Even when the ball is completely lost, it is no more likely to be in one area of the field than another, so localization information does not help the robot to determine where to look first.

One way of searching for a lost ball is to build an "oriented" search, in which the robot uses localization information to systematically search each area of the field. This relies on very accurate localization information which takes a lot of time. For comparison, we built an oriented search which uses localization information to walk a circuit of the field. Even on an empty field, in which obstacles do not block the robot's view of landmarks, the random search allows the robot to canvass the field more quickly than the oriented circuit search because the robot never has to stop to look for landmarks.

Urgent Action There are two situations in which we allow the robot to use what localization information it does have, but do not allow it to stop to get more. In these cases, swift action is essential, so there is no time for the robot to stop and look for landmarks.

- Approach: Although we have enhanced the approach mode with a skew feature to allow the robot to position itself behind the ball more efficiently, we do not allow the robot to stop during its approach to scan for landmarks.

  This strategy has negatives, clearly. If the robot does not know where it is on the field, it will not know what to do with the ball when it gets to it. Nevertheless, it is better for a robot to look around when it is in possession of the ball than when it is farther from the ball. When the robot is standing near the ball, it is blocking one side of the ball from visibility and attacks, and is able to respond more quickly to an attack because it is already close by.

- Kickoff: We do not allow the robots to localize during the initial kickoff of the game, because a large advantage is gained by succeeding to push the ball into the opponents' side of the field. When the ball moves to one side of the field, it is very difficult for the robots to move it to the other side of the field.

  Instead of relying on localization information, we take advantage of the information we already have: the robots begin the kickoff behind the ball, facing the opposite goal. When the game begins, the robots charge forward into the ball and try to run with the ball for almost half the length of the field (or almost all the way to the opponents' goal). Stopping to localize would give the opponent a good chance to win the kickoff.

Balancing the Costs of Information

We have already described how we adapt to varying levels of localization information. We will now discuss how we balance the cost and benefits of good localization.

In every domain, system designers must strike a different balance between the costs of acquiring resources and the benefits of using them. Even in the Sony robotic soccer domain, different teams came to different conclusions about how much time should be spent acquiring localization information. This year's team from LRP University in France (Bouchefra *et al.* 1999), for example, chose to localize the robot very infrequently, if at all. However, the benefits of accurate localization are significant.

We use a two-constraint system to balance the cost and benefits of good localization information. One constraint ensures that the robot spend a sufficient amount of time acting. The other ensures that if the robot's localization information quality falls below a preset threshold, the robot will not use it and will stop to look for landmarks as soon as the time constraint allows it to.

We ran two experiments to determine the best values for these two constraints. We tested how long it would take one robot on an open field to score a goal. If the robot took longer than fifteen minutes, we stopped the trial and recorded its time as fifteen minutes.

We positioned the robot at a fixed point, (700, 450) in our coordinate system. This corresponds to 3/4 of the way down the field from the yellow goal, and 1/4 of the way from the right side wall (if facing the yellow goal). We oriented the robot at $-135°$ in our coordinate system, or $45°$ to the left of facing straight towards the yellow goal. We placed the ball directly in front of it, at the midpoint of the width of the field. We timed how many minutes it took the robot to push the ball into the yellow goal.

Figures 3 and 4 show the results of the two experiments we ran. Each trial is represented by a small tick. The mean of each set of trials is indicated as a bold tick. The grey bar around the mean is one standard deviation.

The experiments have, as we expected, a very high variance, which reflects the challenge of the control task inherent in the robots. The results from the robot's sensors have non-neglible variance and the motion of the robot is unreliable. Also, the statistical localization inevitably gives different results even with exactly the same inputs. We believe that most of the variance is due to the high rate of error in the robot's motion. This unreliability is magnified when the ball is involved. Interestingly, when the robot tries to push the ball forward, it often ends up pushing it at an angle or out to the side, or even walking past the ball. When it walks around the ball, it often accidentally taps it, sending the ball off in an unpredictable direction, as described previously.

Constraint 1—Enforcing Action

Our first constraint requires the robot to spend a certain amount of time acting before it stops to look for landmarks. This is crucial for two reasons. The first we mentioned before: soccer is time-critical, so the robot should only localize as much as is necessary. But we must worry about more than the percentage of time the robot spends localizing versus acting. We must also ensure that the robot does not interrupt its action too frequently. Each time the robot stops to look for landmarks, there is some chance that it will have trouble finding the ball when it finishes localizing and looks for it again. This happens because the robot accidentally nudges the ball away, because it fails to stop moving before looking away from the ball or because another robot steals the ball from it. Stopping more frequently increases the chance that this will happen and the robot will have to begin searching for the ball, a time-consuming procedure.

Our scheme uses a counter to require the robot to act for a specified amount of time before looking for landmarks. The amount of time the robot must act before looking could depend on the confidence the robot has in its current localization information or on its current goals. In our scheme, however, it is invariant.

We require that the robot act for the time it takes the image module to proccess 350 frames of data, or about 40 seconds. Recall that stopping to look for landmarks takes the robot between 15 and 20 seconds, not counting the time it takes it to recover the ball afterwards. So we demand that it spend about 2/3 of its time acting.

We chose to count time in image frames processed by the vision module because a full system call is more time consuming than using this information. The number of frames per second is constant (8), and since each processed frame invokes an update in the control module, the cost of updating counters for each processed frame is negligible.

We conducted several tests to discover how long we should force the robot to act before looking for landmarks. Figure 3 shows the results of ten trials of each of three different time intervals that we considered viable.

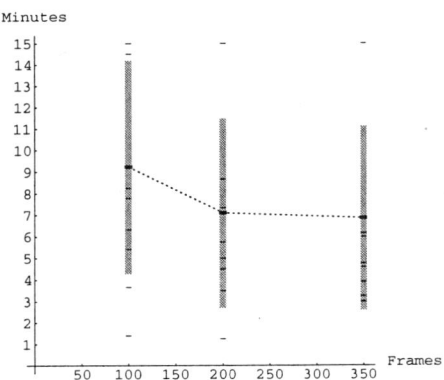

Figure 3: Time taken to score a goal versus how long we require the robot to act before looking for landmarks.

The standard deviations of the trials are, as shown, very high. Nevertheless, there is a clear penalty for localizing too frequently, as shown in the results for the 100-frame (or about 13 second interval). This is because so much stopping to look disrupts the robot's activity. It loses sight of the ball more frequently, and must stop to look for it. Also, scanning for landmarks so often simply takes a lot of time.

Although our results show that 350- and 200-frame intervals (about 40 seconds and 25 seconds, respectively) are roughly equivalent, we chose to use a 350-frame interval. In an actual game, the penalty for stopping more often is much higher than when there is only one robot on the field; when a robot stops to look for landmarks, other robots have a chance to take the ball away.

Constraint 2—Sufficient Localization

The second constraint is how accurate we demand the localization information to be. We measure accuracy with the standard deviations returned by the localization module. If the information is accurate enough, the robot should not stop to look for landmarks when the timing constraint allows it to. But if the localization information is not accurate enough, the robot should not use it.

It is not immediately obvious how good our localization information must be before it is usable. Clearly, if our demands are too high, the robot will rarely be able to use the information it has gathered. And if they are too low, it will use information that is so inaccurate as to be useless at best and damaging at worst.

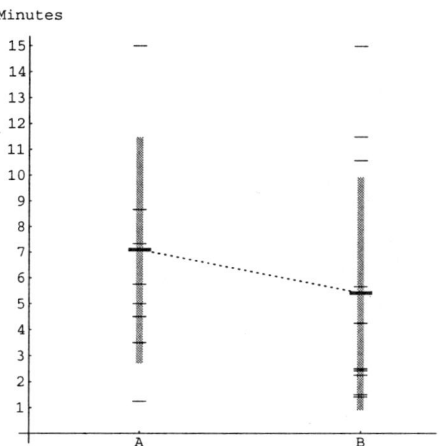

Figure 4: Time taken to score a goal in two setups for transitioning among the multi-fidelity score behavior. Setups A and B correspond to different standard deviation bounds of the localization values for the robot's orientation, θ, and its x, y location on the field.

Figure 4 shows the results of ten trials each of two different sets of standard deviation bounds, labelled A and B. In setup A we set $\sigma\theta < 15°$ and $\sigma x, \sigma y < 30$ cm; in setup B, we set $\sigma\theta < 30°$ and $\sigma x, \sigma y < 60$ cm.

If we demand the localization values be too accurate before allowing the robot to use them, it is often unable to use them and must revert to our low-fidelity strategy, detailed previously. If it is still able to use them sometimes, this just slows it down, as seen in Figure 4, setup A. Other experiments we have run have shown us that if the robot must rely too heavily on the low-fidelity strategy, it is much more likely to tip the ball in the wrong direction and accidentally make an own goal. But, if we demand too little accuracy from the localization values, the robot will rely on them even when they are faulty. We ran other experiments which showed that this too causes the robot to score own goals.

We chose to use the standard deviation values used in setup B from Figure 4 ($\sigma\theta < 30°$, $\sigma x, \sigma y < 60$ cm), because, in our experiments, there was a clear advantage to these settings. These standard deviation bounds mean that the 95% confidence interval for the x and y location of the robot is ± 120 cm, or almost the entire field. These experiments show that, although it is crucial to have a rough estimate of angle, it is not important for the robot to know where it is on the field.

Conclusion

In this paper, we have described our multi-fidelity behaviors approach to designing behaviors for resource-poor realtime environments. We briefly described the approach in general terms. We then elaborated on our implementation of this approach in the RoboCup-99 Sony legged robot league, describing our breakdown of the robot's behavior into modes corresponding to multi-fidelity behaviors. Finally, we presented our two-constraint technique for balancing the cost and benefits of localization information with the Sony robots, along with the results of experiments we ran to determine the best values for those constraints. We are applying the multi-fidelity behaviors approach to several of our other robotic systems.

Acknowledgements

We would like to thank Sony for providing us with wonderful robots and walking movements to work with. We would like to thank Jim Bruce for developing the vision system and Scott Lenser for developing the localization algorithm for our robots. Thanks to Tucker Balch for helpful discussions and suggestions on this work.

This research is sponsored in part by the Defense Advanced Research Projects Agency (DARPA) and the Air Force Research Laboratory (AFRL) under agreement numbers F30602-97-2-0250 and F30602-98-2-0135. The views and conclusions contained in this document are those of the authors and should not be interpreted as necessarily representing official policies or endorsements, either expressed or implied, of the Air Force or the United States Government.

References

Bouchefra, K.; Hugel, V.; Blazevic, P.; Duhaut, D.; and Seghrouchni, A. 1999. Situated agents with reflexive behavior. In *Proceedings of IJCAI-99 Workshop on RoboCup*, 46–51.

Brooks, R. A. 1986. A robust layered control system for a mobile robot. *IEEE Journal of Robotics and Automation* RA-2:14–23.

Bruce, J.; Balch, T.; and Veloso, M. Fast and inexpensive color image segmentation for interactive robots.

Fujita, M.; Zrehen, S.; and Kitano, H. 1999. A quadruped robot for RoboCup legged robot challenge in Paris'98. In Asada, M., and Kitano, H., eds., *RoboCup-98: Robot Soccer World Cup II*. Berlin: Springer Verlag. 125–140.

Kitano, H.; Asada, M.; Kuniyoshi, Y.; Noda, I.; and Osawa, E. 1997. RoboCup: The robot world cup initiative. In *Proceedings of the First International Conference on Autonomous Agents*.

Lenser, S., and Veloso, M. 2000. Sensor resetting localization for poorly modelled mobile robots. In *Proceedings of ICRA-2000, the International Conference on Robotics and Automation*.

Mataric, M. J. 1992. Behavior-based control: Main properties and implications. In *Proceedings of the IEEE International Conference on Robotics and Automation, Workshop on Architectures for Intelligent Control Systems*.

Nilsson, N. J. 1994. Teleo-reactive programs for agent control. *Journal of Artificial Intelligence Research* 1:139–158.

Satyanarayanan, M., and Narayanan, D. 1999. Multi-fidelity algorithms for interactive mobile applications. In *Proceedings of the 3rd International Workshop on Discrete Algorithms and Methods for Mobile Computing and Communications*.

Veloso, M., and Uther, W. 1999. The CMTrio-98 Sony legged robot team. In Asada, M., and Kitano, H., eds., *RoboCup-98: Robot Soccer World Cup II*. Berlin: Springer Verlag. 491–497.

Veloso, M.; Uther, W.; Fujita, M.; Asada, M.; and Kitano, H. 1998. Playing soccer with legged robots. In *Proceedings of IROS-98, Intelligent Robots and Systems Conference*.

Veloso, M.; Pagello, E.; and Kitano, H., eds. 2000. *RoboCup-99: Robot Soccer World Cup III*. Berlin: Springer Verlag. To appear.

Search

Dynamic Representations and Escaping Local Optima: Improving Genetic Algorithms and Local Search

Laura Barbulescu, Jean-Paul Watson, and L. Darrell Whitley
Computer Science Department
Colorado State University
Fort Collins, CO 80523
e-mail: {laura,watsonj,whitley}@cs.colostate.edu

Abstract

Local search algorithms often get trapped in local optima. Algorithms such as tabu search and simulated annealing 'escape' local optima by accepting non-improving moves. Another possibility is to dynamically change between representations; a local optimum under one representation may not be a local optimum under another. *Shifting* is a mechanism which dynamically switches between Gray code representations in order to escape local optima. Gray codes are widely used in conjunction with genetic algorithms and bit-climbing algorithms for parameter optimization problems. We present new theoretical results that substantially improve our understanding of the shifting mechanism, on the number of Gray codes accessible via shifting, and on how neighborhood structure changes during shifting. We show that shifting can significantly improve the performance of a simple hill-climber; it can also help to improve one of the best genetic algorithms currently available.

Introduction

Given a representation and a neighborhood operator, local search methods (Aarts & Lenstra 1997) proceed by gradual manipulation of some initial solution. Because of its myopic nature, local search can become trapped in local optima. Methods such as simulated annealing and tabu search attempt to 'escape' by accepting non-improving or inferior neighbors, with the goal of moving out of the local optimum's basin of attraction. Local optima are induced by the selected representation and neighborhood operator; a local optimum under one representation may not be a local optimum under another representation. Thus, *dynamic representations* are a potentially important, although relatively unexplored, class of escape mechanism.

We focus on parameter optimization. Functions are discretized so that search proceeds in a bit space, with L-bit Gray or Binary encoded function inputs; this is common with Genetic Algorithms (GAs). Empirically, Gray encodings usually perform better than Binary encodings for many real-world functions (Caruana & Schaffer 1988). Gray codes preserve the neighborhood structure of the discretized real-valued search space (Whitley *et al.* 1996). As a result, a

Copyright © 2000, American Association for Artificial Intelligence (www.aaai.org). All rights reserved.

Gray code can induce no more optima than exist in the original function. Further, because there are more neighbors under the Gray code (l bits for each dimension) than in the discretized real-valued function (2 for each dimension), there are usually significantly fewer optima in the Gray code's search space. In contrast, Binary codes often create new optima where none existed in the original function. Finally, many distinct Gray codes exist, each inducing a different neighborhood structure, and potentially different local optima.

These properties motivated (Rana & Whitley 1997) to introduce *shifting* as a mechanism for changing between a restricted set of Gray codes in an effort to escape local optima. A simple hill-climbing algorithm and a state-of-the-art GA were augmented with the shifting mechanism, and evaluated using test functions empirically proven to be both resistant to simple hill-climbing algorithms, and still pose a challenge to GAs.

We establish a new bound on the number of unique Gray codes accessible via shifting. This allows us to focus on a significantly smaller set of representations. We demonstrate that similar Gray codes induce similar search spaces; to escape optima, one must consider dissimilar Gray codes. We use these results to improve the performance of a hill-climbing algorithm, to the point where it is competitive with a state-of-the-art GA.

On Dynamic Representations

For any function, there are multiple representations which make optimization trivial (Liepins & Vose 1990). However, the space of all possible representations is a larger search space than the search space of the function being optimizing. Furthermore, randomly switching between representations is doomed to failure. Suppose we have N unique points in our search space and a neighborhood operator which explores k points before selecting a move. A point is considered a local optimum from a steepest-ascent perspective if its evaluation is better than each of its k neighbors. We can sort the N points in the search space to create a ranking, $R = r_1, r_2, ..., r_N$, in terms of their function evaluation (where r_1 is the best point in the space and r_N is the worst point in the space). Using this ranking, we can compute the probability that a point ranked in the i-th position in R is a local optimum under an arbitrary representation of the search space:

$$P(i) = \frac{\binom{N-i}{k}}{\binom{N-1}{k}} \quad [1 \le i \le (N-k)] \quad (1)$$

Using this result, one can prove that the expected number of local optima under all possible representations for a search space with N points and any neighborhood operator of size k is given by $\sum_{i=1}^{N-k} P(i) = N/(k+1)$ (Whitley, Rana, & Heckendorn 1997).

These equations make it clear that highly ranked points in the search space are local optima under almost all representations. To exploit dynamic representations we cannot randomly change representations. So how do we proceed? First, we assume that most real-world optimization problems have a complexity which is less than that expected from random functions. Two measures of this complexity are: smoothness and number of local optima. We have shown empirically that many test functions and real-world problems tend to be relatively smooth compared to random functions, and that the number of induced local optima are fewer than the expected number of local optima associated with random functions (Rana & Whitley 1997).

It follows that one should use a form of dynamic representation that respects and preserves smoothness and which bounds the number of local optima that can result while changing problem representation. Dynamic Gray codes have these desirable properties.

Gray Codes and Shifting

A Gray code is any integer bit encoding such that adjacent integers are Hamming distance-1 apart. The **standard reflected Gray encoding** of an integer is constructed by applying the exclusive-or operator to a) the standard Binary encoding of the integer and b) the same Binary encoding, shifted one position to the right; the last bit is then truncated. Gray encoding and decoding can be concisely expressed through matrix operations. Let x and y be L-bit Binary-encoded and Gray-encoded integers, respectively, and let G be a transform matrix containing 1's on both the diagonal and upper minor diagonal and 0's elsewhere. The Gray encoding and decoding processes are then simply given by $x^T G$ and $y^T G^{-1}$, respectively.

It can be shown that every permutation of the columns of the G matrix results in another Gray code transform matrix. Note that we can also treat the sequence of integers as a circular chain. Shifting the chain also results in a Gray code. In practice, one can 1) de-Gray a bit string, 2) treat the resulting string as a Binary coded integer and 3) add a constant offset (i.e., a shift) to the integer, mod 2^L (Rana & Whitley 1997).

There are 2^L possible shifting values, and $L!$ permutations over the columns of the Gray transformation matrix. In this paper we prove that all of the $L!$ permutations of the G matrix result in identical Hamming-1 neighborhoods, and only $2^L/4$ of the possible 2^L shifts actually change the Hamming-1 neighborhood.

Given a discretized real-valued function, the number of optima in any Gray encoding under a Hamming-1 neighborhood operator, is less than or equal to the number of optima in the original function. Furthermore, the surface of the original function is a subset of the set of paths induced by the Gray encoding; hence the surface of the original function is preserved and enhanced with greater connectivity by the Gray code (Rana & Whitley 1997). In contrast, the standard Binary coding actually *increases* the number of optima for many test functions (Whitley 1999). This is consistent with the fact that, in practice, search algorithms appear to work better under Gray than Binary encodings.

We now better understand why shifting works. Reflected Gray codes form a circuit. This circuit represents the inputs to a real-valued function. In a Gray coded string of length L, there are L folds, or reflections. As the circuit is shifted, points pass by other points in different reflections. This can be seen in Figure 1 for $L = 4$. The 4 neighbors are North-South-East-West and the graph is a torus. At the order-3 reflection, strings differ only in the 3rd bit; this connects the North-South neighbors in rows 1 and 2, as well as rows 3 and 4. The directional arrows show that these points move in opposite directions when shifting occurs, and hence neighbors flow past each other. The order-4 reflection (where the 4th bit differs) are the North-South connections between rows 2 and 3, as well as the toroidal North-South wrap around between rows 1 and 4. When two local optima "pass" one another in the shifted Gray encoding, one of the two optima must collapse. For example, in Figure 1 positions 4 and 9 are not neighbors in the normal integer mapping induced under standard Gray code. However, when the integer space is shifted by 1, positions 4 and 9 become neighbors. If there are local optima at positions 4 an 9, one of these optima must collapse when the search space is shifted.

We first prove that all permutations of the columns of the Gray transform matrix G yields a transform matrix that induces an identical neighborhood structure.

Theorem 1 *Let G be the L-bit standard reflective Gray transform matrix, and construct G^π by applying a permutation π to the columns of G. Let x be some integer, and let x_G and x_{G^π} be the set of L neighboring integers under G and G^π, respectively. Then $x_G = x_{G^\pi}$.*

Proof: The columns of G and G^π independently produce a single bit of x_G and x_{G^π}, respectively; viewing π as a permutation of the bits of x_G or the columns of G is equivalent. Permuting the bits of each element of x_G does not change the Hamming distance between any element in the set and x, so the Hamming distance-1 neighbors of x under both G and G^π are invariant. □

Next, we show that for any given transform matrix G, only 2^{L-2} shifts result in distinct neighborhood structures. First, note that a reflected Gray code is a symmetric reflection. If we flip the leading bit of each string, the Hamming neighborhood does not change. This is exactly what happens when one shifts by 2^{L-1}. It follows that every shift from $i = 0$ to $2^{L-1} - 1$ is identical to the corresponding shift at $j = 2^{L-1} + i$. As will be shown, shifting by 2^{L-2} also will not change the neighborhood structure, and in general, shifting by 2^{L-k} will result in a change of exactly $k - 2$ neighbors. This can be seen by studying Figure 1: a shift of $2^{4-2} = 4$ (or any multiple of 4) leaves the neighbor-

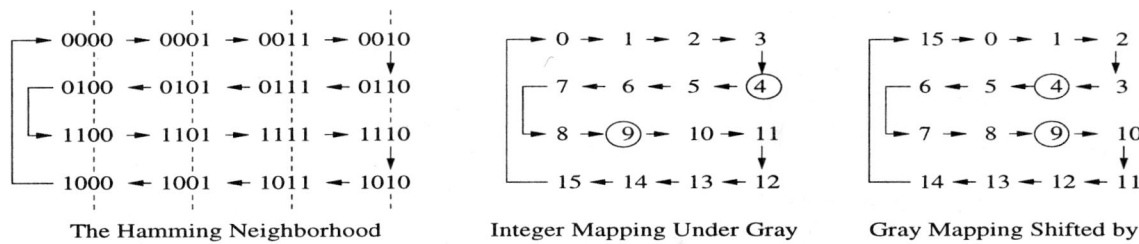

Figure 1: A simple example of shifting. Note that integers are associated with the corresponding positions in the Hamming Neighborhood. Neighbors are N-S-E-W and the arrows map the surface of the real-valued function.

hood structure unchanged. For numbers that are powers of 2, smaller shifts change more neighbors. Note that a shift of 1 implies $1 = 2^0 = 2^{L-L}$, which changes L-2 neighbors. This is the largest number of neighbors which can change in a Gray code. Numbers that are not powers of 2 can be viewed as a combination of large and small shifts.

Theorem 2 *For any Gray encoding, shifting by 2^{L-k} where $k \geq 2$ will result in a change of exactly $k - 2$ neighbors for any point in the search space.*

Proof: Consider an arbitrary Gray coding, and $k \geq 2$. Next, divide the 2^L positions into 2^k continuous blocks of equal size, starting from position 0. Each block contains exactly 2^{L-k} positions (see Figure 2a). Consider an arbitrary block X and arbitrary position P within X. Exactly $L - k$ neighbors of P are contained in X. The periodicity of both Binary and Gray bit encodings ensures that the $L - k$ neighbors of P in X do not change when shifting by 2^{L-k}. Two of the remaining k neighbors are contained in the blocks preceding and following X, respectively. Since the adjacency between blocks does not change under shifting, the two neighbors in the adjacent blocks must stay the same.

The remaining $k-2$ neighbors are contained in blocks that are not adjacent to X. We prove that the rest of these $k-2$ neighbors change. Consider a block Y that contains a neighbor of P. A fundamental property of a Reflected Gray code is that there is a reflection point exactly halfway between any pair of neighbors. For all neighbors outside of block X and which are not contained in the adjacent blocks, the reflection points must be separated by more than 2^{L-k} positions. Shifting X by 2^{L-k} will move it closer to the Reflection point, while Y is moved exactly 2^{L-k} positions farther away from the reflection point (see Figure 2b). Point P in X must now have a new neighbor (also 2^{L-k} closer to the reflection point) in the block Z. If the reflection point between X and Z is at location R, then for the previous neighbor in Y to still be a neighbor of P in X it must have a reflection point at exactly $R + 2^{L-k}$. This is impossible since for all neighbors outside of block X which are not contained in the adjacent blocks, the reflection points must be separated by more than 2^{L-k} positions. A similar argument goes for the case when shifting by 2^{L-k} moves X farther away from the reflection point (while Y is moved closer). Thus, none of the previous $k - 2$ neighbors are neighbors after shifting by 2^{L-k}. □

To better understand how various shifts affect the neigh-

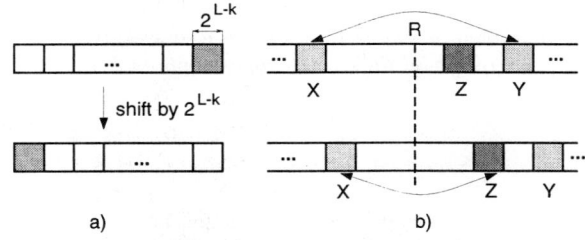

Figure 2: Shifting by 2^{L-k}. **a).** An unwound representation of the Gray codes circuit. **b).** For an arbitrary position in a block X, and an arbitrary neighbor of this position in the block Y, after shifting by 2^{L-k}, the neighbor moves from block Y to block Z.

borhood structure, we consider a 1-dimensional version of Rastrigin's function (described in the experimental section). In Table 1, we list all the function optima under the standard Reflective Gray Code, with $L = 10$. For each optimum, each shift which collapses the optimum is recorded. Clearly, worse optima are collapsible by a larger number of shifts (minimization of $F(X)$ is the objective), simply because a large fraction of the domain (X) has a better evaluation. However, the 'bands' of collapsing shift values were unexpected; similar shifts result in similar neighborhood structures. Next, we formalize this observation by characterizing the difference between neighbors under adjacent shift values; the proof is somewhat lengthy, and is documented in (Barbulescu 2000).

Theorem 3 *For any Gray code, consider two alternative shifts, i and $i + 1$ ($0 \leq i \leq 2^L - 2$). Consider an integer point p in the search space such that its position is not a multiple of 8 after shifting by $i + 1$. Then, $L - 3$ neighbors*

X	$F(X)$	Collapsing Shifts
-2.0	3.9768	22-49, 102-113, 150-177, 201-212, 230-241
-1.0	0.9983	12-18, 76-82, 140-146, 204-210
0.0	0.0	None
-1.0	0.9983	47-53, 111-117, 175-181, 239-245
-2.0	3.9768	16-27, 45-56, 80-107, 144-155, 208-235

Table 1: Enumeration of shifts which collapse the optima of the 1-D Rastrigin's function

of p under the shift $i + 1$ are obtained by subtracting 2 from the neighbors under shift i.

Theorems 1 and 2 might suggest that only small shifts are needed, since small shifts can change a large number of neighbors. Theorem 3 proves that small shifts result in new neighbors that are near to the old neighbors. Empirically, we have found uniform sampling is the best a-priori mechanism for selecting 'good' shifting values. Intensive sampling from the set of shift values can collapse inferior local optima (more sampling increases the probability of collapsing optima). However, not all local optima are collapsible under shifting. The result is formalized in Theorem 4, below.

Theorem 4 *Given an arbitrary Gray code G, let X and Y be two distinct integers with encodings under G given by X_G and Y_G, respectively. Further assume that both X and Y are optima of a function F. If $parity(X_G) = parity(Y_G)$ then no shift exists which allows $hammingDistance(x_G, y_G) = 1$.*

Proof: If $X \neq Y$, and $parity(X_G) = parity(Y_G)$, then $hammingDistance(x_G, y_G)$ is clearly greater than 1. Select an arbitrary shift T to produce a new Gray code G' from G, resulting in X'_G and Y'_G. Application of T produces identical changes in $parity(X'_G)$ and $parity(Y'_G)$. Thus, $parity(X'_G) = parity(Y'_G)$, and $X \neq Y$, implying $hammingDistance(X'_G, Y'_G) \geq 2$. □

Theorem 4 asserts that there may exist optima which cannot be 'collapsed' by shifting. In the next section, we provide an example of such a function.

Experiments

We investigate the utility of incorporating shifting into both a simple hill-climbing algorithm, RBC, and a state-of-the-art genetic algorithm, CHC. Shift values are uniformly sampled from the set of unique shifts. We use the test functions described in (Whitley *et al.* 1996), shown in Table 2 (along with the associated variable domains). These test functions range from simple, separable functions which are easily solved by hill-climbers to more complex non-linear, non-separable functions.

RBC (Random Bit Climber) (Davis 1991) is a next-descent hill-climbing algorithm. Search begins from a random bit string, and proceeds by testing each of the L Hamming-1 neighbors in some randomized order. Both equal and improving moves are accepted. If the search is stuck in a local optimum, it is re-started from a new random bit string. Otherwise, a new random visitation sequence of the L neighbors is generated.

Once a local optimum is detected by RBC, the representation can be shifted to try to escape the local optimum. Search then proceeds from the new bit-string until convergence is re-established. We use two types of restarts: 'soft' and 'hard'. The 'soft' re-start merely changes the representation, without changing the current point in the search space. A 'hard' re-start reinitializes search from a new random point in the search space. Depending on the experiment, we perform either 10 or 50 soft re-starts before each hard re-start.

The Hamming-1 neighborhood at the bit-string level translates into a neighborhood which is capable, in one step, of altering only a single parameter value. This restriction suggests that RBC should perform well on separable test functions, and perform worse on non-separable, non-linear test functions which may require simultaneous manipulation of multiple parameters to yield improvements in the evaluation function. These hypotheses are supported by our experimental results.

The **CHC genetic algorithm** (Eshelman 1991) maintains a parent population of size μ ($= 50$ in our experiments). CHC randomly pairs members of the parent population for reproduction. Once paired, reproduction is only permitted if the Hamming distance between the two parents is greater than some threshold value, resulting in a child population of size λ. The HUX crossover operator is used which ensures that each child is of maximal Hamming distance from the parents. The μ best of the $\mu + \lambda$ individuals form the parent population for the next generation. CHC *guarantees* survival of the best μ individuals encountered during the search.

CHC also uses a re-start mechanism if the parent population remains unchanged for some number of generations. During a re-start, a population containing μ copies of the best individual is formed; all but one copy undergo extensive mutation (35% of the bits). Shifting can be applied each time CHC converges. The best individual is re-encoded using a new, randomly selected shift value.

Methodology

We ran 30 trials of both RBC and CHC on each test function, allowing a maximum of 500K evaluations per run. With the exception of Powell's function (whose dimension was fixed at 4), 10-dimensional versions of each test function were used, with each variable encoded using 10 bits except for Powell's function, which used 20-bit encodings. For the Rana and Whitley functions, 10-dimension versions were constructed using the Weighted-Wrap expansion method, described in (Whitley *et al.* 1996). Two versions of CHC, both with and without shifting, were considered. We tested RBC without shifting, in addition to versions using both 10 and 50 soft re-starts between hard-restarts, denoted RBC-10 and RBC-50 respectively.

Results and Discussion

The results for RBC and CHC are reported in Tables 3 and 4, respectively. The 'Number Solved' column indicates the number of times the algorithm found the optimal solution, out of the 30 total trials. The statistics for both solution quality and number of evaluations are taken over all 30 trials. All statistical comparisons between algorithms are made using two-tailed t-tests (significance level $p < 0.01$).

For RBC (Table 3, RBC-10), shifting yields a statistically significant improvement in both solution quality and number of evaluations for the Rastrigin, Schwefel, and Whitley test functions; for Rana's function, the improvement applies only to solution quality. For both the Powell and Griewangk test functions, no difference in either measure was observed. For CHC (Table 4), shifting fails to yield any significant differences in mean solution quality. However, shifting does sig-

	$x_i \in [-5.12, 5.11]$
Rastrigin	$F(x_i|_{i=1,N}) = (N*10) + [\sum_{i=1}^{N}(x_i^2 - 10\cos(2\pi x_i))]$
	$x_i \in [-512, 511]$
Schwefel	$F(x_i|_{i=1,N}) = \sum_{i=1}^{N} -x_i \sin(\sqrt{|x_i|})$
Griewangk	$F(x_i|_{i=1,N}) = 1 + \sum_{i=1}^{N} \frac{x_i^2}{4000} - \prod_{i=1}^{N}(\cos(\frac{x_i}{\sqrt{i}}))$
Powell	$F(x_1, x_2, x_3, x_4) = (x_1 + 10x_2)^2 + (\sqrt{5}(x_3 - x_4))^2 + ((x_2 - 2x_3)^2)^2 + (\sqrt{10}(x_1 - x_4)^2)^2$
Whitley	$F(x,y) = -x\sin(\sqrt{|x - \frac{y+47}{2}|}) - (y + 47)\sin(\sqrt{|y + 47 + \frac{x}{2}|})$
Rana	$F(x,y) = x\sin(\sqrt{|y + 1 - x|})\cos(\sqrt{|x + y + 1|}) + (y + 1)\cos(\sqrt{|y + 1 - x|})\sin(\sqrt{|x + y + 1|})$

Table 2: The test functions described in (Whitley *et al.* 1996).

Function	Experiment	Mean Sol.	σ	Mean Evals.	σ	Number Solved
Rastrigin	no shift	6.35088	1.34344	500000	0.0	0
	shift-10	0.0	0.0	38368	39201	30
	shift-50	0.0	0.0	4488	1384	30
Schwefel	no shift	-3860.79	116.343	500000	0.0	0
	shift-10	-4189.0	0.0	6888	5481	30
	shift-50	-4189.0	0.0	3588	1058	30
Griewangk	no shift	0.001894	0.007322	160318	150648	28
	shift-10	**0.000818**	0.00448	93488	99037	29
	shift-50	0.009069	0.013182	289021	193251	20
Powell	no shift	0.000258	6.009e-5	500000	0.0	0
	shift-10	**0.000224**	6.53e-5	500000	0.0	0
	shift-50	0.000235	6.95e-5	500000	0.0	0
Whitley	no shift	-770.518	29.7811	500000	0.0	0
	shift-10	-905.879	43.9736	351004	187004	14
	shift-50	**-909.183**	45.014	303511	201526	19
Rana	no shift	-449.115	8.88101	500000	0.0	0
	shift-10	-469.255	7.58475	500000	0.0	0
	shift-50	**-488.151**	5.59812	500000	0.0	0

Table 3: RBC results on six test functions, with 10 and 50 shift attempts before a hard re-start is performed. Results are averaged over 30 independent trials of 500K function evaluations apiece. All functions are being minimized.

nificantly reduce the number of evaluations required for the Rastrigin, Griewangk, and Powell test functions. While substantially improving the performance of both RBC and CHC, significant performance differences between the algorithms still exist. Next, we increase the number of soft re-starts used with RBC (RBC-50), and compare the resulting performance with CHC.

On Rastrigin's and Schwefel's functions, both versions of RBC (RBC-10 and RBC-50) and CHC found the global optimum in all trials. Both of these functions are separable. While there was no statistical difference between RBC-10 and CHC, RBC-50 required significantly fewer evaluations than CHC. Using 50 instead of 10 soft re-starts reduces the variance of the RBC results. The performance improvement can be explained, since all the local optima are collapsible under some shift: Theorem 4 is not applicable. Ten and fifty soft re-starts sample a maximum of 3.9% and 19.6% of the possible (255) unique shifts, respectively. Thus, sampling more shifts increases the chances of collapsing a particular local optimum.

Griewangk's function is the simplest non-separable test function considered: (Whitley *et al.* 1996) show that the function becomes easier (more parabolic) as the dimensionality is increased. Intuitively, a highly parabolic structure should be easily solved by a hill-climbing algorithm. However, CHC significantly outperforms both versions of RBC for the number of evaluations. Furthermore, increasing the number of soft re-starts resulted in poorer RBC performance. To explain this apparent anomaly, we examined the shifting properties of a 1-dimensional version of Griewangk's function. For each local optimum, we enumerated all possible shifts and recorded which shifts were able to collapse the local optimum. We found that Theorem 4 was directly applicable: the two best local optima were not collapsible by any shift - i.e., not collapsible with the global optimum. In addition, these local optima 'flank' the global optimum; to find the global optimum, the initial starting point of RBC must be in its attraction basin to begin with, which is relatively small. Here, shifting is futile - hard re-starts are the only way to find the global optimum.

For both the Powell and Whitley functions, the performance of RBC-10 and RBC-50 is indistinguishable (the increase in the number of trials identifying the global optimum of Whitley's function is a statistical artifact), and both were strongly outperformed by CHC. Although no run of either CHC or RBC ever solved Rana's function to optimal-

Function	Experiment	Mean Sol.	σ	Mean Evals.	σ	Number Solved
Rastrigin	no shift	0.0	0.0	34998	14365	30
	shift	0.0	0.0	**22297**	7299	30
Schwefel	no shift	-4189.0	0.0	9667	31579	30
	shift	-4189.0	0.0	**7148**	2224	30
Griewangk	no shift	0.0	0.0	58723	52101	30
	shift	0.0	0.0	**24354**	12890	30
Powell	no shift	0.0	0.0	200184	80041	30
	shift	0.0	0.0	**96497**	36756	30
Whitley	no shift	-939.88	0.0	**23798**	9038	30
	shift	-939.88	0.0	25331	12881	30
Rana	no shift	-497.10	5.304	500000	0.0	0
	shift	**-494.50**	5.207	500000	0.0	0

Table 4: CHC results on the six test functions, without and with a shifting attempt made each time the algorithm re-starts. Results are averaged over 30 independent trials of 500K function evaluations apiece. All functions are being minimized, with the lowest mean solution or lowest mean number of evaluations in bold.

ity, RBC-50 significantly outperformed RBC-10 in terms of solution quality. While CHC does slightly outperform RBC-50, the difference is minimal (though still statistically significant). This result is particularly interesting, as Rana's function proved to be the most difficult for CHC.

Our results demonstrate that a deeper understanding of shifting can be used to significantly improve the performance of RBC. Looking at both solution quality and number of evaluations, RBC statistically outperforms CHC on Rastrigin's and Schwefel's separable functions, and nearly equals the performance of CHC on non-linear, non-separable problems (Griewangk and Rana's). But on Powell's and Whitley's function, CHC outperforms RBC.

Conclusions

Dynamic representations are an alternative to mechanisms that escape local optima such as re-starts, tabu search, and simulated annealing. Shifting uses multiple Gray code representations to escape local optima. New upper bounds on the number of unique Gray codes under shifting are established. We also characterized neighborhood structures under similar shifted Gray codes. We incorporated the shifting mechanism into both a simple hill-climber and a genetic algorithm. On a test suite containing problems shown to be resistant to hill-climbing strategies, shifting significantly improves the performance of both algorithms. Thus, by augmenting a simple hill-climber with a dynamic representation scheme, we achieve improved performance on test functions which both proved 1) difficult to a simple hill-climbing algorithm and 2) a challenge to a state-of-the-art genetic algorithm.

Acknowledgments

This work was sponsored by the Air Force Office of Scientific Research, Air Force Materiel Command, USAF, under grant number F49620-97-1-0271. The U.S. Government is authorized to reproduce and distribute reprints for Governmental purposes notwithstanding any copyright notation thereon.

References

Aarts, E., and Lenstra, J. K. 1997. *Local Search in Combinatorial Optimization*. John Wiley and Sons.

Barbulescu, L. 2000. Shifting gray codes: The impact on the neighborhood structure. Internal Technical Report, Colorado State University.

Caruana, R., and Schaffer, J. 1988. Representation and Hidden Bias: Gray vs. Binary Coding for Genetic Algorithms. In *Proceedings of the 5th International Conference on Machine Learning*. Morgan Kaufmann.

Davis, L. 1991. Bit-climbing, representation bias, and test suite design. In *Proceedings of the Fourth International Conference on Genetic Algorithms*. Morgan Kaufmann.

Eshelman, L. J. 1991. The chc adaptive search algorithm: How to have safe search when engaging in non-traditional genetic recombination. In Rawlins, G. J., ed., *Foundations of Genetic Algorithms-1*. Morgan Kaufmann.

Liepins, G., and Vose, M. 1990. Representation Issues in Genetic Algorithms. *Journal of Experimental and Theoretical Artificial Intelligence* 2.

Rana, S. B., and Whitley, L. D. 1997. Bit representations with a twist. In *Proceedings of the Seventh International Conference on Genetic Algorithms (ICGA-97)*. Morgan Kaufmann.

Whitley, D.; Mathias, K.; Rana, S.; and Dzubera, J. 1996. Evaluating evolutionary algorithms. *Artificial Intelligence Journal* 85.

Whitley, L. D.; Rana, S.; and Heckendorn, R. 1997. Representation issues in neighborhood search and evolutionary algorithms. In Quagliarelli, D.; Periaux, J.; Poloni, C.; and Winter, G., eds., *Genetic Algorithms in Engineering and Computer Science*. John Wiley.

Whitley, L. D. 1999. A free lunch proof for gray versus binary encodings. In *Proceedings of the Genetic and Evolutionary Computation Conference*. Morgan Kaufmann.

Localizing A^*

Stefan Edelkamp
Institut für Informatik
Am Flughafen 17
D-79110 Freiburg
edelkamp@informatik.uni-freiburg.de

Stefan Schrödl
DaimlerChrysler Research and Technology
1510 Page Mill Road
Palo Alto, CA 94303
schroedl@rtna.daimlerchrysler.com

Abstract

Heuristic search in large problem spaces inherently calls for algorithms capable of running under restricted memory. This question has been investigated in a number of articles. However, in general the efficient usage of two-layered storage systems is not further discussed. Even if hard-disk capacity is sufficient for the problem instance at hand, the limitation of *main memory* may still represent the bottleneck for their practical applications. Since breadth-first and best-first strategies do not exhibit any locality of expansion, standard *virtual memory management* can soon result in thrashing due to excessive page faults.

In this paper we propose a new search algorithm and suitable data structures in order to minimize page faults by a local reordering of the sequence of expansions. We prove its correctness and completeness and evaluate it in a real-world scenario of searching a large road map in a commercial route planning system.

Introduction

Heuristic search algorithms are usually applied to huge problem spaces. Hence, having to cope with memory limitations is an ubiquitous issue in this domain. Since the development of the A^* algorithm (Hart, Nilsson, & Raphael 1968), the main objective has always been to develop methods to regain tractability.

The class of *memory-restricted search algorithms* has been developed under this aim. The framework imposes an absolute upper bound on the total memory the algorithm may use, regardless of the size of the problem space. Most papers do not explicitly distinguish whether this limit refers to disk space or to working memory, but frequently the latter one appears to be implicitly assumed.

IDA^* explores the search space by iterative deepening and uses space linear in the solution length, but may revisit the same node again and again (Korf 1985). It does not use additionally available memory. $MREC$ switches from A^* to IDA^* if the memory limit is reached (Sen & Bagchi 1989). In contrast, SMA^* (Russell 1992) reassigns the space by dynamically deleting a previously expanded node, propagating up computed f-values to the parents in order to save re-computation as far as possible. Eckerle and Schuierer improve the dynamic re-balancing of the search tree (Eckerle & Schuierer 1995). However, it remains to be shown that these algorithms in general outperform A^* or IDA^* since they impose a large administration overhead. A more recent work employs stochastic node caching and is shown to reduce the number of visited nodes compared to $MREC$ (Minura & Ishida 1998).

Even if secondary storage is sufficient, limitation of *working memory* may still represent a bottleneck for practical applications. Modern operating systems provide a general-purpose mechanism for processing data larger than available main memory called *virtual memory*. Transparently to the program, *swapping* moves parts of the data back and forth from disk as needed. Usually, the virtual address space is divided up into units called *pages*; the corresponding equal-sized units in physical memory are called *page frames*. A page table maps the virtual addresses on the page frames and keeps track of their status (loaded/absent). When a *page fault* occurs, i.e., a program tries to use an unmapped page, the CPU is interrupted; the operating system picks a little-used page frame and writes its contents back to the disk. It then fetches the referenced page into the page frame just freed, changes the map, and restarts the trapped instruction. In modern computers memory management is implemented on hardware with a page size commonly fixed at 4096 Byte.

Various *paging strategies* have been explored that aim at minimizing page-faults. Belady has shown that an optimal off-line page exchange strategy deletes the page, which will not be used for the longest time (Belady 1966). Unfortunately, the system, unlike possibly the application program itself, cannot know this in advance. Several different on-line algorithms for the paging problem have been proposed, such as *Last-In-First-Out (LIFO)*, *First-In-First-Out (FIFO)*, *Least-Recently-Used (LRU)*, *Least-Frequently-Used (LFU)*, *Flush-When-Full (FWF)*, etc. (Tanenbaum 1992). Sleator and Tarjan proved that LRU is the best on-line algorithm for the problem achieving an optimal competitive ratio equal to the number of pages that fit into main memory (Sleator & Tarjan 1985).

Programmers can reduce the number of page faults

by designing data structures that exhibit *memory locality*, such that successive operations tend to access nearby memory addresses. However, sometimes it would be desirable to have more explicit control of secondary memory manipulations. For example, fetching data structures larger than the system page size may require multiple disk operations. A file buffer can be regarded as a kind of *"software" paging* that mimics swapping on a coarser level of granularity. Generally, an application can outperform the operating system's memory management because it is well-informed to predict future memory access.

Particularly for search algorithms, system paging can become the major bottleneck. We experienced this problem when applying A^* to the domain of route planning. Node structures become large, compared to hardware pages; moreover, A^* does not respect locality at all; it explores nodes in the strict order of f values, regardless of their neighborhood, and hence jumps back and forth in a spatially unrelated way for only marginal differences in the estimation value.

In the following we present a new heuristic search algorithm to overcome this lack of locality. In connection with software paging strategies, it can lead to a significant speedup. The idea is to organize the graph structure for spatial locality and to expand spatial local data even if it can lead to a possible non-optimal solution. As a consequence, the algorithm cannot stop with the first solution found, but has to do the additional work of exploring all pending paths. However, the increased number of node expansions can be outweighed by the reduction in the number of page faults.

In the next section, we review traditional A^* and extend it so as to allow for node expansions in arbitrary order. We prove its correctness and completeness, and as a byproduct we fix a minor lack of accuracy in the traditional proof for A^*. Then, we describe a data structure called *Heap-Of-Heaps* that is suitable to accommodate locality and is based on a partitioning of the search space. Finally the algorithm is evaluated within a commercial route planning system.

The Algorithm

We start by characterizing the standard A^* algorithm (Hart, Nilsson, & Raphael 1968) in an unusual but concise way on the basis of Dijkstra's algorithm to find shortest paths in (positively) weighted graphs from a *start node* s to a set of *goal nodes* T (Dijkstra 1959). Dijkstra's algorithm uses a priority queue *Open* maintaining the set of currently reached yet unexplored nodes. If $f(u)$ denotes the total weight of the currently best explored path from s to some node u (also called the *merit* of u), the algorithm always selects a node from *Open* with minimum f value for expansion, updates its successors' f-values, and transfers it to the set *Closed* with established minimum cost path.

Traditional A^* = Dijkstra + Re-weighting

Algorithm A^* accommodates the information of a *heuristic $h(u)$*, which estimates the minimum cost of a path from node u to a goal node in T. It can be cast as a search through a re-weighted graph. More precisely, the edge weights w are replaced by new weights $\hat{w}$ by adding the heuristic difference: $\hat{w}(u,v) = w(u,v) - h(u) + h(v)$. At each instant of time in the re-weighted Dijkstra algorithm, the merit f of a node u is the sum of the new weights along the currently cheapest path explored by the algorithm.

By this transformation, negative weights can be introduced. Nodes that have already been expanded might be encountered on a shorter path. Thus, contrary to Dijkstra's algorithm, A^* deals with them by possibly re-inserting nodes from *Closed* into *Open*.

On every path p from s to u the accumulated weights in the two graph structures differ by $h(s)$ and $h(u)$ only, i.e., $w(p) = \hat{w}(p) - h(u) + h(s)$. Consequently, on every cycle c we have $\hat{w}(c) = w(c) \geq 0$, i.e., the re-weighting cannot lead to negatively weighted cycles so that the problem remains solvable.

Let $\delta(u,v)$ and $\hat{\delta}(u,v)$ denote the least-cost path weights between nodes u and v in the initial resp. re-weighted graphs. The heuristic h is called *consistent* if and only if $\hat{w}(u,v) \geq 0$ for all u and v. It is called *optimistic* if $h(u) \leq \min\{\delta(u,t)|t \in T\} = h^*(u)$. This is equivalent to the condition $\min\{\hat{\delta}(u,t)|t \in T\} \geq 0$.

For convenience, since in the following we are dealing only with the transformed weights, we will write w instead of $\hat{w}$.

Invariance Condition

In each iteration of the A^* algorithm, the element u with minimum f value is chosen from the set *Open* and is inserted into *Closed*. Then the set of successors $\Gamma(u)$ is generated. Each node $v \in \Gamma(u)$ is inspected and *Open* and *Closed* are adjusted according to the following procedure *Improve*.

Procedure *Improve* (*Node* u, *Node* v)
    if ($v \in Open$)
        if ($f(u) + w(u,v) < f(v)$)
            Open.DecreaseKey($v, f(u) + w(u,v)$)
        else if ($v \in Closed$)
            if ($f(u) + w(u,v) < f(v)$)
                Closed.Delete(v)
                Open.Insert($v, f(u) + w(u,v)$)
    else
        Open.Insert($v, f(u) + w(u,v)$)

The core of the standard optimality proof of A^* published in AI-literature (Pearl 1985) consists of an invariance stating that while the algorithm is running there is always a node v in the *Open* list on an optimal path with the optimal f-value $f(v) = \delta(s,v)$. In our opinion, this reasoning is true but lacks some formal rigidness: if the child of a node with optimal f-value was already contained in *Closed* (be it with optimal f value), then it wouldn't be reopened and the invariance would be violated. It is part of the proof to show that this situation cannot occur. Thus, we strengthen the invariance condition by requiring the node not to be followed by any *Closed* node on the same optimal solution path.

Invariance I. *Let $p = (s = v_0, \ldots, v_n = t)$ be a least-cost path from the start node s to a a goal node $t \in T$. Application of* Improve *preserves the following invariance: Unless v_n is in* Closed *with $f(v_n) = \delta(s, v_n)$, there is a node v_i in* Open *such that $f(v_i) = \delta(s, v_i)$, and no $j > i$ exists such that v_j is in* Closed *with $f(v_j) = \delta(s, v_j)$.*

Proof: W.l.o.g. let i be maximal among the nodes satisfying (I). We distinguish the following cases:

1. Node u is not on p or $f(u) > \delta(s, u)$. Then node $v_i \neq u$ remains in *Open*. Since no v in *Open* $\cap\, p \cap \Gamma(u)$ with $f(v) = \delta(s, v) \leq f(u) + w(u, v)$ is changed and no other node is added to *Closed*, (I) is preserved.

2. Node u is on p and $f(u) = \delta(s, u)$. If $u = v_n$, there is nothing to show.

   First assume $u = v_i$. Then *Improve* will be called for $v = v_{i+1} \in \Gamma(u)$; for all other nodes in $\Gamma(u) \setminus \{v_{i+1}\}$, the argument of case 1 holds. According to (I), if v is in *Closed*, then $f(v) > \delta(s, v)$, and it will be reinserted into *Open* with $f(v) = \delta(s, u) + w(u, v) = \delta(s, v)$. If v is neither in *Open* or *Closed*, it is inserted into *Open* with this merit. Otherwise, the *DecreaseKey* operation will set it to $\delta(s, v)$. In either case, v guarantees the invariance (I).

   Now suppose $u \neq v_i$. By the maximality assumption of i we have $u = v_k$ with $k < i$. If $v = v_i$, no *DecreaseKey* operation can change it because v_i already has optimal merit $f(v) = \delta(s, u) + w(u, v) = \delta(s, v)$. Otherwise, v_i remains in *Open* with unchanged f-value and no other node besides u is inserted into *Closed*; thus, v_i still preserves (I). □

Note that we have not required f to be optimistic. Under this assumption, the *optimality* of A^* is implied as a corollary, i.e., the fact that a solution returned by the algorithm is indeed a shortest one. To see this, suppose that the algorithm terminates the search process with the first node t' in the set of goal nodes T and $f(t')$ is not optimal. Then $f(t') > \delta(s, u) + \min\{\delta(u, t) | t \in T\} \geq \delta(s, u) = f(u)$, since for an optimistic estimate the value $\min\{\delta(u, t) | t \in T\}$ is not negative. This contradicts the choice of t'. □

General-Node-Ordering A^*

Move ordering is a search optimization technique which has been explored in depth in the domain of two-player games and single-agent applications. It is well-known that substituting the priority queue by a stack or a FIFO-queue results in a depth-first resp. breadth-first traversal of the problem graph. In this case the *DeleteMin* operation is replaced by *Pop* or *Dequeue*, respectively. In the following we will assume a generic operation *DeleteSome* not imposing any restrictions on the selection criteria. The subsequent section will give an implementation that is allowed to select nodes which are "local" to to previously expanded nodes with respect to the application-dependent storage scheme, even though they do not have a minimum f value.

In contrast to A^*, reaching the first goal node will no longer guarantee optimality of the found solution path. Hence, the algorithm has to continue until the *Open* list runs empty. By storing and updating the current best solution path length as a global lower bound value α, we give an anytime extension to A^* that improves the solution quality over time. The concept can be compared to the linear best first algorithm *Depth-First-Branch-and-Bound* (Korf 1993).

Function *General-Node-Ordering* A^*
    Open.Insert$(s, h(s))$
    $\alpha \leftarrow \infty$
    bestSolution $\leftarrow \emptyset$
    while not (*Open.IsEmpty*())
        $u \leftarrow$ *Open.DeleteSome*()
        Closed.Insert(u)
(*)   **if** $(f(u) > \alpha)$ **continue**
        if $(u \in T \wedge f(u) < \alpha)$
            $\alpha \leftarrow f(u)$
            bestSolution $\leftarrow$ retrieved path to u
        else $\Gamma(u) \leftarrow$ *Expand*(u)
            for all v **in** $\Gamma(u)$
                Improve(u, v)
    return *bestSolution*

Theorem 1 *If the heuristic estimate h is optimistic, General-Node-Ordering A^* is optimal.*

Proof: Upon termination, each node inserted into *Open* must have been selected at least once. Suppose that invariance (I) is preserved in each loop, i.e., that there is always a node v in the *Open* list on an optimal path with $f(v) = \delta(s, v)$. Thus the algorithm cannot terminate without eventually selecting the goal node on this path, and since by definition it is not more expensive than any found solution path and *bestSolution* maintains the currently shortest path, an optimal solution will be returned. It remains to show that the invariance (I) holds in each iteration. If the extracted node u is not equal to v there is nothing to show. Otherwise $f(u) = \delta(s, u)$. The bound α denotes the currently best solution length. If $f(u) \leq \alpha$ the condition in (*) is not fulfilled and no pruning takes place. On the other hand $f(u) > \alpha$ leads to a contradiction since $\alpha \geq \delta(s, u) + \min\{\delta(u, t) | t \in T\} \geq \delta(s, u) = f(u)$ (the latter inequality is justified by h being optimistic). □

Theorem 2 *Algorithm General-Node-Ordering A^* is complete, i.e., terminates on finite graphs.*

Proof: For each successor generation, *General-Node-Ordering A^** adds new links to its traversal tree. Moreover, the algorithm only reopens a node in *Closed* when it finds a *strictly* cheaper path to it and, as said above, re-weighting of positively weighted graphs keeps weights of cycles positive. Hence, the algorithm considers at most the number of acyclic path of the underlying finite graph. This number is finite and, therefore, the algorithm terminates. □

The Heap-Of-Heaps Data Structures

Let us briefly review the usual A^* implementation in terms of data structures. The set *Open* is realized as a priority queue (heap) supporting the operations *IsEmpty, Min, Insert, DecreaseKey DeleteMin*. The membership tests $v \in Open$ resp. $v \in Closed$ in procedure *Improve* are implemented using a hash table T. This makes explicit storage of the *Closed* set obsolete, since it is equal to $T \setminus Open$.

For large node structures, it is inefficient to move them physically around; rather, they are maintained in an auxiliary data structure D containing all graph information. D can also contain the links related to the heap and to the hashing chains maximizing *memory locality* with respect to node operations. If the graph is entirely stored, the hash table collapses with D. In some cases there is even no other option than explicit storage, e.g. in the domain of route planning.

Our approach to achieve memory locality is to find a suitable partition of the search space and of all associated data structures into a set of (software) pages $P_1, \ldots, P_k$. We assume a function $\phi : Node \to \{1, \ldots, k\}$ which maps each node to the corresponding page it is contained in.

The data structure *Heap-Of-Heaps* represents the *Open* set. It consists of a collection of k priority queues $H_1, \ldots, H_k$, one for each page. At any instant, one of the heaps, H_{active}, is designated as being *active*. One additional priority queue $\mathcal{H}$ keeps track of the root nodes of all H_i with $i \neq active$; It is used to quickly find the overall minimum across all of these heaps.

The following operations are delegated to the member priority queues H_i in the straightforward way. Whenever necessary, $\mathcal{H}$ is updated accordingly.

Function *IsEmpty*()
 return $\bigwedge_{i=1}^{k} H_i.IsEmpty()$

Procedure *Insert*(*Node u, Merit f(u)*)
 if $(\phi(u) \neq active \ \wedge \ f(u) < f(H_{\phi(u)}.Min()))$
  $\mathcal{H}.DecreaseKey(H_{\phi(u)}, f(u))$
 $H_{\phi(u)}.Insert(u, f(u))$

Procedure *DecreaseKey*(*Node u, Merit f(u)*)
 if $(\phi(u) \neq active \ \wedge \ f(u) < f(H_{\phi(u)}.Min()))$
  $\mathcal{H}.DecreaseKey(H_{\phi(u)}, f(u))$
 $H_{\phi(u)}.DecreaseKey(u, f(u))$

Operation *DeleteSome* performs *DeleteMin* on the active heap.

Function *DeleteSome*()
 CheckActive()
 return $H_{active}.DeleteMin()$

The *Insert* and *DecreaseKey* operations can affect all heaps. However, the hope is that the number of adjacent pages of the active page is small and that they are already in memory or have to be loaded only once; all other pages and priority queues remain unchanged and do not have to reside in main memory.

As the aim is to minimize the number of switches between pages, the algorithm favors the *active* page by continuing to expand its nodes although the minimum f value might already exceed the minimum of all remaining priority queues. There are two control parameters: An *activeness bonus* Δ and an estimate Λ for the cost of an optimum solution.

Procedure *CheckActive*()
 if $(H_{active}.IsEmpty() \ \vee$
   $(f(H_{active}.Min()) - f(\mathcal{H}.Min().Min()) > \Delta$
    $\wedge \ f(H_{active}.Min()) > \Lambda))$
  $\mathcal{H}.Insert(H_{active}, f(H_{active}.Min()))$
  $H_{active} \leftarrow \mathcal{H}.Min()$
  $\mathcal{H}.Remove(H_{active})$

If the minimum f-value of the active heap is larger than that of the remaining heaps plus the *activeness bonus* Δ, the algorithm may switch to the priority queue satisfying the minimum root f value. Thus, Δ discourages page switches by determining the proportion of a page to be explored. As it increases to large values, in the limit each activated page is searched to completion.

However the active page still remains valid, unless Λ is exceeded. The rationale behind this second heuristic is that one can often provide a heuristic for the total least cost path which is, on the average, more accurate than that obtained from h, but which might be overestimating in some cases.

With this implementation, algorithm *General-Node-Ordering* A^* itself remains almost unchanged, i.e., the data structure and page handling is transparent to the algorithm. Traditional A^* arises as a special case for $\Delta = 0$ and $\Lambda < h^*(s)$, where $h^*(s)$ denotes the actual minimum cost between the start node and a goal node.

Optimality is guaranteed, since we leave the heuristic estimates unaffected by the heap prioritization scheme, and since each node inserted into the *Heap-of-Heaps* structure is eventually returned by *DeleteMin*.

Experiments

In our experiments we incorporated our algorithm into a commercially available route planning system running on Windows platforms. The system covers an area of approximately 800 × 400 km at a high level of detail, and comprises approximately 910,000 nodes (road junctions) linked by 2,500,000 edges (road elements). The entire graph structure, together with the members needed for the search algorithm, results in a total memory size of 40 MByte, which already exceeds the advertized minimum main memory hardware requirement of 32 MByte.

For long-distance routes, conventional A^* expands the nodes in a spatially uncorrelated way, jumping to a node as far apart as some 100 km, but possibly returning to the successor of the previous one in the next step. Therefore, the working set gets extremely large, and the virtual memory management of the operating system leads to excessive paging and is the main burden on the computation time.

As a remedy, we achieve memory locality of the search algorithm by exploiting the underlying spatial relation of connected nodes. Nodes are geographically

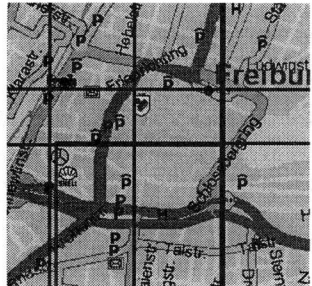

Figure 1: The granularity of the partition (lines indicate bounding rectangles of pages).

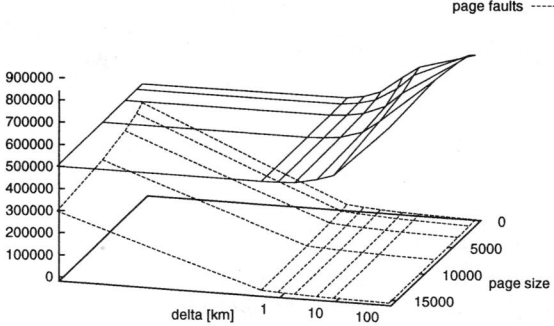

Figure 2: Number of page-faults and node expansions for varying page size and activeness bonus Δ.

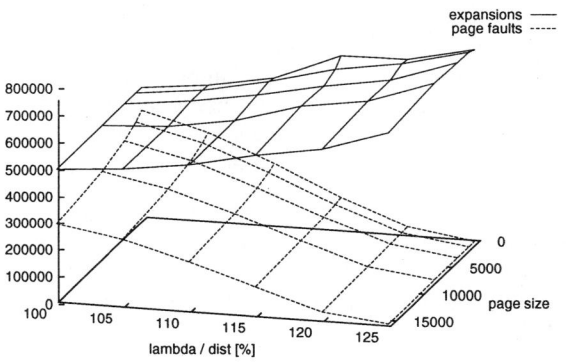

Figure 3: Number of page-faults and node expansions for varying page size and the ratio (in percent) of solution length approximation Λ and the Euclidean distance *dist* between start and goal.

sorted according to their coordinates in such a way that neighboring nodes also tend to appear close to each other. A page consists of a constant number of successive nodes (together with the outgoing edges) according to this order. Thus, pages in densely populated regions tend to cover a smaller area than those representing rural regions. For not too small sizes, the connectivity within a page will be high, and only a comparably low fraction of road elements cross the boundaries to adjacent pages. Fig. 1 shows some bounding rectangles of nodes belonging to the same page.

There are three parameters controlling the behavior of the algorithm with respect to secondary memory, the algorithm parameters Δ and Λ, and the (software) page size. The latter one should be adjusted so that the active page and its adjacent pages together roughly fit into available main memory. The optimum solution estimate Λ is obtained by calculating the Euclidean distance between the start and the goal and adding a fixed percentage.

Fig. 2 opposes the number of page faults to the number of node expansions for varying page size and Δ. We observe that the rapid decrease of page faults compensates the increase of expansions (note the logarithmic scale). Using an activeness bonus of about 2 km suffices to decrease the value by more than one magnitude for all page sizes. At the same time the number of expanded nodes increases by less than ten percent.

Fig. 3 depicts the corresponding influence of Λ. In this case the reduction of page faults by more than a magnitude can be achieved by investing less than 50 percent extra node expansions for Λ equal to 1.25 times the Euclidean distance. The effect is almost independent of the page size.

Unfortunately, the convincing decrease in page faults did not translate proportionally to execution time; the maximum reduction amounted to about 30 percent. We suspect that the reason is that we could not totally control the operating system's hardware paging still working besides and on top of our software paging technique. Hence, more inquiry into the platform-dependent implementation is still required.

We conclude that there is a trade-off between the growth of node expansions and the savings of page faults that has to be resolved by tuning the parameters to improve the overall efficiency for best performance.

Related Work

A couple of dynamic data structures have been proposed which take into account secondary memory structures. Major representatives are tree structured indices, such as B-Trees invented by Bayer and McCreight (Bayer & McCreight 1970) and dynamic hashing variants (Larson 1978), such as extendible hashing (Fagin *et al.* 1970) and virtual hashing (Litwin 1978). External sorting algorithms (Knuth 1973) are special-tailored for handling sequences on disk storage that do not fit into working memory. An extension for the LEDA (Mehlhorn & Näher 1999) C++ library project to secondary storage systems, LEDA-SM for short, is being developed by Crauser and Mehlhorn at

MPI/Saarbrücken.

One currently deeply investigated area in which the advantage of memory locality pays off is the breadth-first synthesis of binary decision diagrams (BDDs) (Bryant 1985). The idea is to construct the diagram structure in a level-wise traversal (Hu & Dill 1993). Since there is a trade-off between low memory overhead and memory access locality, hybrid approaches based on context switches are currently being explored (Yang et al. 1998).

Since each page is explored independently, the algorithms easily lends itself to parallelization by allowing for more than one active page at a time. In fact, a commonly used method for duplicate pruning uses a hash function similar to ϕ defined above to associate with each node of the search space a distinct subspace with a dedicated processor. In (Mahapatra & Dutt 1997), the notion of locality is important to reduce communication between processors and it is implemented as the neighborhood on a hypercube.

There are some related approaches to the re-weighting technique used in our optimality proof. Searching negatively weighted graphs has been intensively studied in literature, cf (Cormen, Leiserson, & Rivest 1990). An $O(|V||E|)$ algorithm for the single-source shortest path problem has been separately proposed by Bellman and Ford. The algorithm has been improved by Yen. The all-pair shortest path problem has been solved by Floyd based on a theorem of Warshall. It has been extended by Johnson for sparse and possibly negatively weighted graphs by re-weighting. All these algorithms do not apply to the scenario of implicitly given graphs with additional heuristic information.

Conclusion

We have presented an approach to relax the order of node expansions in traditional A^*. Its admissibility is shown using a refined invariance condition based on Dijkstra's algorithm and re-weighted graphs. The reordering is used to make the search algorithm take into account memory locality for the price of an increased number of expansions. However, this is offset by the minimization of secondary memory access in a two-layered storage system, which is a major bottleneck for the traditional algorithm. To this end, the data structure *Heap-of-Heaps* has been developed which partitions the underlying graph into pages; two heuristic threshold values discourage page switches and can be tuned for best performance. The count of page switches from an evaluation within a commercially available route planning system supports this view.

References

Bayer, R., and McCreight, E. 1970. Organization and maintenanace of large ordered indexes. *Acta Informatica* 13(7):427–436.

Belady, L. 1966. A study of replacement algorithms for virtual storage computers. *IBM Syst. J* 5:18–101.

Bryant, R. E. 1985. Symbolic manipulation of boolean functions using a graphical representation. In *Design Automation*, 688–694.

Cormen, T. H.; Leiserson, C. E.; and Rivest, R. L. 1990. *Introduction to Algorithms*. The MIT Press.

Dijkstra, E. W. 1959. A note on two problems in connexion with graphs. *Numerische Mathematik* 1:269–271.

Eckerle, J., and Schuierer, S. 1995. Efficient memory-limited graph search. In *KI*, 101–112.

Fagin, R.; Nievergelt, J.; Pippenger, N.; and Strong, H. R. 1970. Extendible hashing - a fast access method for dynamic files. *ACM Trans. Database Syst.* 4(3):315–344.

Hart, P. E.; Nilsson, N. J.; and Raphael, B. 1968. A formal basis for heuristic determination of minimum path cost. *IEEE Trans. on SSC* 4:100.

Hu, A. J., and Dill, D. L. 1993. Reducing BDD size by exploiting functional dependencies. In *Design Automation*, 266–271.

Knuth, D. E. 1973. *The Art of Computer Programming, Vol 3: Sorting and Searching*. Addison-Wesley.

Korf, R. E. 1985. Depth-first iterative-deepening: An optimal admissible tree search. *Artificial Intelligence* 27(1):97–109.

Korf, R. E. 1993. Linear-space best-first search. *Artificial Intelligence* 62(1):41–78.

Larson, P.-A. 1978. Dynamic hashing. *BIT* 18(2):184–201.

Litwin, W. 1978. Virtual hashing: a dynamically changing hashing. In *Very Large Databases*, 517–523.

Mahapatra, N. R., and Dutt, S. 1997. Scalable global and local hashing strategies for duplicate pruning in parallel A* graph search. *IEEE Transactions on Parallel and Distributed Systems* 8(7):738–756.

Mehlhorn, K., and Näher, S. 1999. *The LEDA Platform of Combinatorial and Geometric Computing*. Cambridge University Press.

Minura, T., and Ishida, T. 1998. Stochastic node caching for efficient memory-bounded search. In *AAAI*, 450–459.

Pearl, J. 1985. *Heuristics*. Addison-Wesley.

Russell, S. 1992. Efficient memory-bounded search methods. In *ECAI-92*, 1–5.

Sen, A. K., and Bagchi, A. 1989. Fast recursive formulations for best-first search that allow controlled use of memory. In *IJCAI*, 297–302.

Sleator, D., and Tarjan, R. 1985. Amortized efficiency of list update and paging rules. *Communications of the ACM* 28:202–208.

Tanenbaum, A. S. 1992. *Modern Operating Systems*. New Jersey: Prentice Hall.

Yang, B.; Chen, Y.-A.; Bryang, R. E.; and Hallaron, D. R. 1998. Space- and time-efficient BDD construction via working set control. In *Asia and South Pacific Design Automation*, 423–432.

Speeding up the Convergence of Real-Time Search

David Furcy and **Sven Koenig**
Georgia Institute of Technology
College of Computing
Atlanta, GA 30332-0280
{dfurcy,skoenig}@cc.gatech.edu

Abstract

Learning Real-Time A* (LRTA*) is a real-time search method that makes decisions fast and still converges to a shortest path when it solves the same planning task repeatedly. In this paper, we propose new methods to speed up its convergence. We show that LRTA* often converges significantly faster when it breaks ties towards successors with smallest f-values (*a la* A*) and even faster when it moves to successors with smallest f-values instead of only breaking ties in favor of them. FALCONS, our novel real-time search method, uses a sophisticated implementation of this successor-selection rule and thus selects successors very differently from LRTA*, which always minimizes the estimated cost to go. We first prove that FALCONS terminates and converges to a shortest path, and then present experiments in which FALCONS finds a shortest path up to sixty percent faster than LRTA* in terms of action executions and up to seventy percent faster in terms of trials. This paper opens up new avenues of research for the design of novel successor-selection rules that speed up the convergence of both real-time search methods and reinforcement-learning methods.

Introduction

Real-time (heuristic) search methods interleave planning (via local searches) and plan execution, and allow for fine-grained control over how much planning to perform between plan executions. They have successfully been applied to a variety of planning problems, including traditional search problems (Korf 1990), moving-target search problems (Ishida & Korf 1991), STRIPS-type planning problems (Bonet, Loerincs, & Geffner 1997), robot navigation and localization problems with initial pose uncertainty (Koenig & Simmons 1998), robot exploration problems (Koenig 1999), totally observable Markov decision process problems (Barto, Bradtke, & Singh 1995), and partially observable Markov decision process problems (Geffner & Bonet 1998). Learning-Real Time A* (LRTA*) is probably the most popular real-time search method (Korf 1990). It converges to a shortest path when it solves the same planning task repeatedly. Unlike traditional search methods, such as A* (Nilsson 1971), it can not only act in real time (which is important, for example, for real-time control) but also amortize learning over several planning episodes. This allows it to find a suboptimal path fast and then improve the path until it follows a shortest path. Thus, the sum of planning and plan-execution time is always small, yet LRTA* follows a shortest path in the long run.

Recently, researchers have attempted to speed up the convergence of LRTA* while maintaining its advantages over traditional search methods, that is, without increasing its lookahead. Ishida, for example, achieved a significant speedup by sacrificing the optimality of the resulting path (Ishida & Shimbo 1996; Ishida 1997). We, on the other hand, show how to achieve a significant speedup without sacrificing the optimality of the resulting path. FALCONS (FAst Learning and CONverging Search), our novel real-time search method, looks similar to LRTA* but selects successors very differently. LRTA* always greedily minimizes the estimated cost to go (in A* terminology: the sum of the cost of moving to a successor and its h-value). FALCONS, on the other hand, always greedily minimizes the estimated cost of a shortest path from the start to a goal via the successor it moves to (in A* terminology: the f-value of the successor). This allows FALCONS to focus the search more sharply on the neighborhood of an optimal path. Our experiments on standard search domains from the artificial intelligence literature show that FALCONS indeed converges typically about twenty percent faster and in some cases even sixty percent faster than LRTA* in terms of travel cost. It also converges typically about forty percent faster and in some cases even seventy percent faster than LRTA* in terms of trials, even though it looks at the same states as LRTA* when it selects successors and even though it is not more knowledge-intensive to implement.

This paper, in addition to its relevance to the real-time search community, also sends an important message to reinforcement-learning researchers. Indeed, they are typically interested in fast convergence to an optimal behavior and use methods that, just like LRTA*, interleave planning (via local searches) and plan execution and converge to optimal behaviors when they solve the same planning task repeatedly (Barto, Bradtke, & Singh 1995). Furthermore, during exploitation, all commonly-used reinforcement-learning methods, again just like LRTA*, always greedily move to minimize the expected estimated cost to go (Thrun 1992). The results of this paper therefore suggest that it might be

---

Copyright © 2000, American Association for Artificial Intelligence (www.aaai.org). All rights reserved.

possible to design reinforcement-learning methods that converge substantially faster to optimal behaviors than state-of-the-art reinforcement-learning methods, by using information to guide exploration and exploitation that is more directly related to the learning objective.

Definitions

Throughout this paper, we use the following notation and definitions. S denotes the finite state space; $s_{start} \in S$ denotes the start state; and $s_{goal} \in S$ denotes the goal state.[1] $succ(s) \subseteq S$ denotes the set of successors of state s, and $pred(s) \subseteq S$ denotes the set of its predecessors. $c(s, s') > 0$ denotes the cost of moving from state s to successor $s' \in succ(s)$. The goal distance $gd(s)$ of state s is the cost of a shortest path from state s to the goal, and the start distance $sd(s)$ of state s is the cost of a shortest path from the start to state s. Each state s has a g-value and an h-value associated with it, two concepts known from A* search (Nilsson 1971). We use the notation $g(s)/h(s)$ to denote these values. The h-value of state s denotes an estimate of its true goal distance $h^*(s) := gd(s)$. Similarly, the g-value of state s denotes an estimate of its true start distance $g^*(s) := sd(s)$. Finally, the f-value of state s denotes an estimate of the cost $f^*(s) := g^*(s) + h^*(s)$ of a shortest path from the start to the goal through state s. H-values are called admissible iff $0 \leq h(s) \leq gd(s)$ for all states s, that is, if they do not overestimate the goal distances. They are called consistent iff $h(s_{goal}) = 0$ and $0 \leq h(s) \leq c(s, s') + h(s')$ for all states s with $s \neq s_{goal}$ and $s' \in succ(s)$, that is, if they satisfy the triangle inequality. It is known that zero-initialized h-values are consistent, and that consistent h-values are admissible (Pearl 1985). The definition of admissibility can be extended in a straightforward way to the g- and f-values, and the definition of consistency can be extended to the g-values (Furcy & Koenig 2000).

Assumptions

In this paper, we assume that the given heuristic values are admissible. Almost all commonly-used heuristic values have this property. If $h(s, s')$ denotes $h(s)$ with respect to goal s', then we initialize the g- and h-values as follows: $h(s) := h(s, s_{goal})$ and $g(s) := h(s_{start}, s)$ for all states s. We also assume that the domain is safely explorable, i.e., the goal distances of all states are finite, which guarantees that the task remains solvable by real-time search methods since they cannot accidentally reach a state with infinite goal distance.

Learning Real-Time A*

In this section, we describe Learning Real-Time A* (LRTA*) (Korf 1990), probably the most popular real-time search method. LRTA* (with lookahead one) is shown in Figure 1. Each state s has an h-value associated with it.

[1]We assume that there is only one goal throughout this paper (with the exception of Figure 5) to keep the notation simple. All of our results continue to hold in domains with multiple goals.

---

1. $s := s_{start}$.
2. $s' := \arg\min_{s'' \in succ(s)}(c(s, s'') + h(s''))$.
   Break ties arbitrarily.
3. $h(s) :=$ if $s = s_{goal}$ then $h(s)$[†]
   else $\max(h(s), \min_{s'' \in succ(s)}(c(s, s'') + h(s'')))$.
4. If $s = s_{goal}$, then stop successfully.
5. $s := s'$.
6. Go to 2.

Figure 1: LRTA*

LRTA* first decides which successor to move to (successor-selection rule, Step 2). It looks at the successors of the current state and always greedily minimizes the estimated cost to go, that is, the sum of the cost of moving to a successor and the estimated goal distance of that successor (i.e., its h-value). Then, LRTA* updates the h-value of its current state to better approximate its goal distance (value-update rule, Step 3). Finally, it moves to the selected successor (Step 5) and iterates the procedure (Step 6). LRTA* terminates successfully when it reaches the goal (Step 4). A more comprehensive introduction to LRTA* and other real-time search methods can be found in (Ishida 1997).

The following properties of LRTA* are known: First, its h-values never decrease and remain admissible. Second, LRTA* terminates (Korf 1990). We call a *trial* any execution of LRTA* that begins at the start and ends in the goal. Third, if LRTA* is reset to the start whenever it reaches the goal and maintains its h-values from one trial to the next, then it eventually follows a shortest path from the start to the goal (Korf 1990). We call a *run* any sequence of trials from the first one until convergence is detected. We say that LRTA* breaks ties systematically if it breaks ties for each state according to an arbitrary ordering on its successors that is selected at the beginning of each run. If LRTA* breaks ties systematically, then it must have converged when it did not change any h-value during a trial. We use this property to detect convergence. To represent the state of the art, we use LRTA* that "breaks ties randomly," meaning that ties are broken systematically according to orderings on the successors that are randomized before each run.

Tie-Breaking

LRTA* terminates and eventually follows a shortest path no matter how its successor-selection rule breaks ties among successors. In this section, we demonstrate, for the first time, that the tie-breaking criterion crucially influences the convergence speed of LRTA*. We present an experimental study that shows that LRTA* converges significantly faster to a shortest path when it breaks ties towards successors with smallest f-values rather than, say, randomly or towards successors with largest f-values. Breaking ties towards successors with smallest f-values is inspired by the A* search method, that efficiently finds a shortest path by always ex-

[†]This test could be eliminated by moving Step 4 before Step 2 so that the h-value of s_{goal} is never modified. However, we prefer the current (equivalent) formulation since it makes the value-update rule for the h-values completely symmetrical with the value-update rule for the g-values to be introduced in FALCONS.

1. $s := s_{start}$.
2. $s' := \arg\min_{s'' \in succ(s)}(c(s, s'') + h(s''))$. Break ties in favor of a successor s'' with a smallest f-value, where $f(s'') := g(s'') + h(s'')$. Break remaining ties arbitrarily (but systematically).
3. $g(s) := $ if $s = s_{start}$ then $g(s)$
   else $\max(g(s), \min_{s'' \in pred(s)}(g(s'') + c(s'', s)))$.
   $h(s) := $ if $s = s_{goal}$ then $h(s)$
   else $\max(h(s), \min_{s'' \in succ(s)}(c(s, s'') + h(s'')))$.
4. If $s = s_{goal}$, then stop successfully.
5. $s := s'$.
6. Go to 2.

Figure 2: TB-LRTA*

domain and heuristic values		LRTA* that breaks ties ...		
		towards a largest f-value	randomly	towards a smallest f-value (TB-LRTA*)
8-Puzzle	M	64,746.47	45,979.19	18,332.39
	T	911,934.40	881,315.71	848,814.91
	Z	2,200,071.25	2,167,621.63	2,141,219.97
Gridworld	N	116.50	97.32	82.08
	Z	1,817.57	1,675.87	1,562.46
Permute-7	A	302.58	298.42	288.62
	Z	16,346.56	16,853.69	16,996.51
Arrow	F	1,755.42	1,621.26	1,518.27
	Z	7,136.93	7,161.71	7,024.11
Tower of Hanoi	D	145,246.55	130,113.43	116,257.30
	Z	156,349.86	140,361.39	125,332.52
Words	L	988.15	813.66	652.95
	Z	16,207.19	16,137.67	15,929.81

Table 1: Travel Cost to Convergence

panding a leaf node of the search tree with the smallest f-value, where $f(s) := g^*(s) + h(s)$ for all states s (Pearl 1985). If the g- and h-values are perfectly informed (that is, the g-value of each state is equal to its start distance and its h-value is equal to its goal distance), then the states with smallest f-values are exactly those on shortest paths from the start to the goal. Thus, if LRTA* breaks ties towards successors with smallest f-values, it breaks ties towards a shortest path. If the g- and h-values are not perfectly informed (the more common case), then LRTA* breaks ties towards what currently looks like a shortest path and may thus converge faster. To implement this tie-breaking criterion, LRTA* does not have the g*-values available but can approximate them with g-values. It can update the g-values in a way similar to how it updates the h-values, except that it uses the predecessors instead of the successors. Figure 2 shows TB-LRTA* (Tie-Breaking LRTA*), our real-time search method that maintains g- and h-values and breaks ties towards successors with smallest f-values, where $f(s) := g(s) + h(s)$ for all states s. Remaining ties can be broken arbitrarily (but systematically). We compared TB-LRTA* against versions of LRTA* that break ties randomly or towards successors with largest f-values. We performed experiments in thirteen combinations of standard search domains from the artificial intelligence literature and heuristic values, averaged over at least one thousand runs each. The section on "Experimental Results" contains additional information on the domains, heuristic values, and experimental setup. Table 1 shows that in all cases but one (Permute-7 with the zero (Z) heuristic[2]) breaking ties towards successors with smallest f-values (statistically) significantly sped up the convergence of LRTA* in terms of travel cost (action executions).

FALCONS: A Naive Approach

We just showed that TB-LRTA* converges significantly faster than LRTA* because it breaks ties towards successors with smallest f-values. We thus expect real-time search methods that implement this principle more consequently and always move to successors with smallest f-values to converge even faster. Figure 3 shows Naive FALCONS (FAst Learning and CONverging Search), our real-time search method that maintains g- and h-values, always moves to successors with smallest f-values, and breaks ties to minimize

---

[2]This exception will disappear in our results with FALCONS.

1. $s := s_{start}$.
2. $s' := \arg\min_{s'' \in succ(s)} f(s'')$, where $f(s'') := g(s'') + h(s'')$. Break ties in favor of a successor s'' with the smallest value of $c(s, s'') + h(s'')$. Break remaining ties arbitrarily (but systematically).
3. $g(s) := $ if $s = s_{start}$ then $g(s)$
   else $\max(g(s), \min_{s'' \in pred(s)}(g(s'') + c(s'', s)))$.
   $h(s) := $ if $s = s_{goal}$ then $h(s)$
   else $\max(h(s), \min_{s'' \in succ(s)}(c(s, s'') + h(s'')))$.
4. If $s = s_{goal}$, then stop successfully.
5. $s := s'$.
6. Go to 2.

Figure 3: Naive FALCONS (initial, non-functional version)

the estimated cost to go. Remaining ties can be broken arbitrarily (but systematically). To understand why ties are broken to minimize the estimated cost to go, consider g- and h-values that are perfectly informed. In this case, all states on a shortest path have the same (smallest) f-values and breaking ties to minimize the estimated cost to go ensures that Naive FALCONS moves towards the goal. (All real-time search methods discussed in this paper have the property that they follow a shortest path right away if the g- and h-values are perfectly informed.) To summarize, Naive FALCONS is identical to TB-LRTA* but switches the primary and secondary successor-selection criteria. Unfortunately, we show in the remainder of this section that Naive FALCONS does not necessarily terminate nor converge to a shortest path. In both cases, this is due to Naive FALCONS being unable to increase misleading f-values of states that it visits, because they depend on misleading g- or h-values of states that it does not visit and thus cannot increase.

Naive FALCONS can cycle forever: Figure 4 shows an example of a domain where Naive FALCONS does not terminate for g- and h-values that are admissible but inconsistent. Naive FALCONS follows the cyclic path $s_0, s_1, s_2, s_3, s_2, s_3, \ldots$ without modifying the g- or h-values of any state. For example during the first trial, Naive FALCONS updates $g(s_2)$ to one (based on $g(s_7)$) and $h(s_2)$ to one (based on $h(s_6)$), and thus does not modify them. $g(s_7)$ and $h(s_6)$ are both zero and thus strictly underestimate

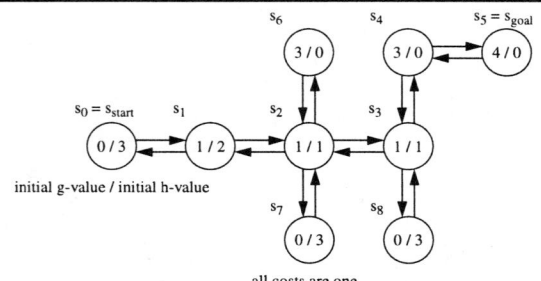

Figure 4: Naive FALCONS Cycles Forever

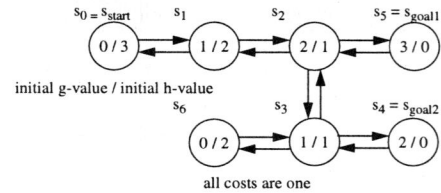

Figure 5: Naive FALCONS Converges to a Suboptimal Path

the true start and goal distances of their respective states. Unfortunately, the successor of state s_2 with the smallest f-value is state s_3. Thus, Naive FALCONS moves to state s_3 and never increases the misleading $g(s_7)$ and $h(s_6)$ values. Similarly, when Naive FALCONS is in state s_3 it moves back to state s_2, and thus cycles forever.

Naive FALCONS can converge to suboptimal paths: Figure 5 shows an example of a domain where Naive FALCONS terminates but converges to a suboptimal path even though the g- and h-values are consistent. Naive FALCONS converges to the suboptimal path $s_0, s_1, s_2, s_3,$ and s_4. The successor of state s_2 with the smallest f-value is state s_3. $f(s_3)$ is two and thus clearly underestimates $f^*(s_3)$. Even though Naive FALCONS moves to state s_3, it never increases its f-value because it updates its g-value to one (based on $g(s_6)$) and $h(s_3)$ to one (based on $h(s_4)$), and thus does not modify them. Naive FALCONS then moves to state s_4. Thus, the trial ends and Naive FALCONS has followed a suboptimal path. Since no g- or h-values changed during the trial, Naive FALCONS has converged to a suboptimal path.

FALCONS: The Final Version

In the previous section, we showed that Naive FALCONS does not necessarily terminate nor converge to a shortest path. Figure 6 shows the final (improved) version of FALCONS that solves both problems. We can prove the following theorems provided that the assumptions described earlier are satisfied.

Theorem 1 *Each trial of FALCONS terminates.*

Theorem 2 *FALCONS eventually converges to a path from the start to the goal if it is reset to the start whenever it reaches the goal and maintains its g- and h-values from one trial to the next one.*

Theorem 3 *The path from the start to the goal that FALCONS eventually converges to is a shortest path.*

1. $s := s_{start}$.
2. $s' := \arg\min_{s'' \in succ(s)} f(s'')$, where $f(s'') := \max(g(s'') + h(s''), h(s_{start}))$. Break ties in favor of a successor s'' with the smallest value of $c(s, s'') + h(s'')$. Break remaining ties arbitrarily (but systematically).
3. $g(s) :=$ if $s = s_{start}$ then $g(s)$
   else $\max(g(s),$
   $\min_{s'' \in pred(s)}(g(s'') + c(s'', s)),$
   $\max_{s'' \in succ(s)}(g(s'') - c(s, s'')))$.
   $h(s) :=$ if $s = s_{goal}$ then $h(s)$
   else $\max(h(s),$
   $\min_{s'' \in succ(s)}(c(s, s'') + h(s'')),$
   $\max_{s'' \in pred(s)}(h(s'') - c(s'', s)))$.
4. If $s = s_{goal}$, then stop successfully.
5. $s := s'$.
6. Go to 2.

Figure 6: FALCONS (final version)

The proofs of these theorems are nontrivial and much more complex than their counterparts for LRTA*. They can be found in (Furcy & Koenig 2000). In the following, we give some intuitions behind the new value-update and successor-selection rules and show that they solve the problems of Naive FALCONS for the examples introduced in the previous section.

FALCONS terminates: The new value-update rules of FALCONS cause it to terminate. We first derive the new value-update rule for the h-values. It provides more informed but still admissible estimates of the h-values than the old value-update rule, by making better use of information in the neighborhood of the current state. The new value-update rule makes the h-values locally consistent and is similar to the path-max equation used in conjunction with A*. If the h-values are consistent, then there is no difference between the old and new value-update rules. To motivate the new value-update rule, assume that the h-values are admissible and FALCONS is currently in some state s with $s \neq s_{goal}$. The old value-update rule used two lower bounds on the goal distance of state s, namely $h(s)$ and $\min_{s'' \in succ(s)}(c(s, s'') + h(s''))$. The new value-update rule adds a third lower bound, namely $\max_{s'' \in pred(s)}(h(s'') - c(s'', s))$. To understand the third lower bound, note that the goal distance of any predecessor s'' of state s is at least $h(s'')$ since the h-values are admissible. This implies that the goal distance of state s is at least $h(s'') - c(s'', s)$. Since this is true for all predecessors of state s, the goal distance of state s is at least $\max_{s'' \in pred(s)}(h(s'') - c(s'', s))$. The maximum of the three lower bounds then is an admissible estimate of the goal distance of state s and thus becomes its new h-value. This explains the new value-update rule for the h-values. The new value-update rule for the g-values can be derived in a similar way.

As an example, we show that Naive FALCONS with the new value-update rules now terminates in the domain from Figure 4. When Naive FALCONS is in state s_2 during the first trial, it increases both $g(s_2)$ and $h(s_2)$ to two and then moves to state s_3. The successor of state s_3 with the smallest f-value is state s_4, and no longer state s_2, because $f(s_2)$

domain and heuristic values		LRTA* that breaks tie randomly	TB-LRTA*	FALCONS
8-Puzzle	M	45,979.19 (100%)	18,332.39	18,332.39 (39.87%)
	T	881,315.71 (100%)	848,814.91	709,416.75 (80.50%)
	Z	2,167,621.63 (100%)	2,141,219.97	1,955,762.18 (90.23%)
Gridworld	N	97.32 (100%)	82.08	57.40 (58.98%)
	Z	1,675.87 (100%)	1,562.46	1,440.02 (85.93%)
Permute-7	A	298.42 (100%)	288.62	284.95 (95.49%)
	Z	16,853.69 (100%)	16,996.51	16,334.67 (96.92%)
Arrow	F	1,621.26 (100%)	1,518.27	1,372.62 (84.66%)
	Z	7,161.71 (100%)	7,024.11	6,763.49 (94.44%)
Tower of Hanoi	D	130,113.43 (100%)	116,257.30	107,058.94 (82.28%)
	Z	140,361.39 (100%)	125,332.52	116,389.79 (82.92%)
Words	L	813.66 (100%)	652.95	569.71 (70.02%)
	Z	16,137.67 (100%)	15,929.81	15,530.42 (96.24%)

Table 2: Travel Cost to Convergence

domain and heuristic values		LRTA* that breaks tie randomly	TB-LRTA*	FALCONS
8-Puzzle	M	214.37 (100%)	58.30	58.30 (27.20%)
	T	1,428.57 (100%)	1,214.63	797.26 (55.81%)
	Z	1,428.59 (100%)	1,227.74	756.47 (52.95%)
Gridworld	N	6.06 (100%)	5.01	2.90 (47.85%)
	Z	32.02 (100%)	26.30	19.77 (61.74%)
Permute-7	A	26.91 (100%)	25.55	22.10 (82.13%)
	Z	117.82 (100%)	92.63	75.22 (63.84%)
Arrow	F	114.94 (100%)	110.60	89.01 (77.44%)
	Z	171.50 (100%)	135.13	105.92 (61.76%)
Tower of Hanoi	D	214.47 (100%)	177.96	109.13 (50.88%)
	Z	216.77 (100%)	166.55	101.44 (46.80%)
Words	L	32.82 (100%)	22.72	18.40 (56.06%)
	Z	71.86 (100%)	55.77	50.10 (69.72%)

Table 3: Trials to Convergence

domain and heuristic values		LRTA* that breaks tie randomly	TB-LRTA*	FALCONS
8-Puzzle	M	311.18 (100%)	452.84	452.84 (145.52%)
	T	1,342.75 (100%)	970.87	1,057.86 (78.78%)
	Z	81,570.22 (100%)	81,585.44	81,526.34 (99.95%)
Gridworld	N	12.15 (100%)	12.70	20.92 (172.18%)
	Z	182.37 (100%)	182.55	183.13 (100.42%)
Permute-7	A	8.14 (100%)	7.75	8.13 (99.88%)
	Z	2,637.86 (100%)	2,639.13	2,639.13 (100.05%)
Arrow	F	15.85 (100%)	16.62	33.61 (212.05%)
	Z	1,016.33 (100%)	1,016.83	1,016.83 (100.05%)
Tower of Hanoi	D	4,457.86 (100%)	3,654.80	3,910.46 (87.72%)
	Z	4,839.49 (100%)	4,803.81	4,801.84 (99.22%)
Words	L	24.27 (100%)	27.79	37.80 (155.75%)
	Z	2,899.73 (100%)	2,900.36	2,900.68 (100.03%)

Table 4: Travel Cost of the First Trial

was increased to four. Thus, Naive FALCONS now moves to state s_4 and breaks the cycle. Unfortunately, the new value-update rules are not sufficient to guarantee that Naive FALCONS converges to a shortest path. The domain from Figure 5 still provides a counterexample.

FALCONS converges to a shortest path: The new successor-selection rule of FALCONS causes it to converge to a shortest path by using more informed but still admissible estimates of the f*-values. In the following, we assume that the g- and h-values are admissible and we present two lower bounds on $f^*(s)$. First, $f^*(s)$ is at least $g(s) + h(s)$, since the g- and h-values are admissible. Second, $f^*(s)$ is at least as large as the cost of a shortest path from the start to the goal, a lower bound of which is $h(s_{start})$, since the h-values are admissible. The maximum of the two lower bounds is an admissible estimate of $f^*(s)$ and thus becomes the new f-value of s. This explains the new calculation of the f-values performed by the successor-selection rule. The other parts of the successor-selection rule remain unchanged. The new f-value of state s, unfortunately, cannot be used to update its g- or h-values, because it is unknown by how much to update the g-value and by how much to update the h-value.

As an example, we show that FALCONS now converges to a shortest path in the domain from Figure 5. When FALCONS reaches state s_2 in the first trial, $f(s_3)$ is now three. All three successors of state s_2 have the same f-value and FALCONS breaks ties in favor of the one with the smallest h-value, namely state s_5. Thus, the trial ends and FALCONS has followed a shortest path. Since no g- or h-values changed, FALCONS has converged to a shortest path.

Experimental Results

In this section, we describe our evaluation of FALCONS, that we tested against LRTA* that breaks ties randomly and TB-LRTA*. We used the following domains from the artificial intelligence literature in conjunction with consistent heuristic values: 8-Puzzle (Korf 1990), Gridworld (Ishida 1997), Permute-7 (Holte et al. 1994), Arrow (Korf 1980), Tower of Hanoi (Holte et al. 1994), and Words (Holte et al. 1996). All of these domains satisfy our assumptions. The domains and heuristic values are described in (Furcy & Koenig 2000). Tables 2, 3, and 4 report the travel cost (action executions) until convergence, the number of trials until convergence, and the travel cost of the first trial, respectively. The data in all three cases were averaged over at least one-thousand runs, each with different start states and ways how the remaining ties were broken in case the successor-selection rule and tie-breaking criterion did not uniquely determine the successor. The remaining ties were broken systematically, that is, for each state according to an ordering on its successors that was selected at the beginning of each run. The orderings were randomized between runs. Convergence was detected when no g- or h-values changed during a trial. Additional details on the experimental setup can be found in (Furcy & Koenig 2000).

Table 2 shows that, in all cases, FALCONS converged to a shortest path with a smaller travel cost (action executions) than LRTA* that breaks ties randomly and, in all cases but one, faster than TB-LRTA*. The percentages in the last column compare the travel cost of FALCONS with that of LRTA*. FALCONS converged 18.57 percent faster over all thirteen cases and in one case even 60.13 percent faster. We tested these results for pairwise significance using the (non-parametric) sign test. All the comparisons stated above are significant at the one-percent confidence level with only one exception: The comparison of FALCONS and TB-LRTA* in the Permute-7 domain with the zero (Z) heuristic is significant only at the five-percent confidence level. The heuristic values for each domain are listed in order of their decreasing informedness (sum of the heuristic values over all states). For example, the (completely uninformed) zero (Z) heuristic is listed last. Table 2 then, shows that the speedup of FALCONS over LRTA* was positively correlated with the informedness of the heuristic values. This suggests that FALCONS makes better use of the given heuristic values. Notice that it cannot be the case that FALCONS converges more quickly than LRTA* because it looks at different (or more) states than LRTA* when selecting successor states. FALCONS looks at both the predecessors and successors of the current state while LRTA* looks only at the successors, but all of our domains are undirected and thus every predecessor is also a successor. This implies that FALCONS and LRTA* look at exactly the same states.

Table 3 shows that, in all cases, FALCONS converged to a shortest path with a smaller number of trials than LRTA* that breaks ties randomly and, in all cases but one, faster than TB-LRTA*. FALCONS converged 41.94 percent faster over all thirteen cases and in some cases even 72.80 percent faster.

To summarize, Table 2 and Table 3 show that FALCONS converges faster than LRTA* and even TB-LRTA*, both in terms of travel cost and trials. The first measure determines the total time during the trials. The second measure determines the total time between the trials, for example, to set up the next trial. This is important in case the set-up time is large.

We originally expected that FALCONS would increase the travel cost during the first trial, since the successor-selection rule of LRTA* (minimize the cost to go) has experimentally been shown to result in a small travel cost during the first trial under various conditions. Table 4 shows that, in four of the thirteen cases, the travel cost of FALCONS during the first trial was larger than that of LRTA*; in seven cases it was approximately the same (99 percent to 101 percent); and in two cases it was lower. The travel cost of FALCONS during the first trial was 19.35 percent larger than that of LRTA* over the thirteen cases. Overall, there is no systematic relationship between the travel cost of FALCONS and LRTA* during the first trial, and the sum of planning and plan-execution times is always small for FALCONS, just like for LRTA*.

Discussion of Results and Future Work

In future theoretical work, we intend to derive analytical upper bounds on the travel cost to convergence of FALCONS, similar to those given in (Koenig & Simmons 1995) for LRTA*.

On the experimental side, all of our domains have uniform costs (i.e., all actions have cost one). Although the theory behind FALCONS guarantees that it will terminate and converge to an optimal path even in domains with non-uniform costs, FALCONS may not converge with smaller travel cost than LRTA* in such domains because the successor-selection rule of FALCONS chooses a successor state with lowest f-value even if the cost of moving to it is very large.

domain and heuristic values		LRTA*	FALCONS	FALCONS without g updates
8-Puzzle	M	45,979.19 (100%)	18,332.39 (39.87%)	19,222.08 (41.81%)
	T	881,315.71 (100%)	709,416.75 (80.50%)	817,078.12 (92.71%)
Gridworld	N	97.32 (100%)	57.40 (58.98%)	58.82 (60.44%)
Permute-7	A	298.42 (100%)	284.95 (95.49%)	263.00 (88.13%)
Arrow	F	1,621.26 (100%)	1,372.62 (84.66%)	1,533.11 (94.56%)
T. Hanoi	D	130,113.43 (100%)	107,058.94 (82.28%)	128,987.97 (99.14%)
Words	L	813.66 (100%)	569.71 (70.02%)	547.35 (67.27%)

Table 5: Travel Cost to Convergence

This property of FALCONS is inherited from A*, which always expands a leaf node of the search tree with the smallest f-value, regardless of the cost of reaching the corresponding state from the current state, since A* only simulates these actions in memory. In future work, we intend to modify the successor-selection rule of FALCONS so that it takes into account the immediate action cost.

So far, one of the main evaluation criteria has been the travel cost to convergence. One may complain that the speedup exhibited by FALCONS over LRTA* comes at an extra computational cost, namely an extra value update per action execution. To decrease the total computational cost (value updates), FALCONS would have to cut the travel cost to convergence at least in half. However, it reduces the travel cost by only 18.57 percent. We also compared FALCONS with a variant of LRTA* that performs two value updates per action execution. This can be done in various ways. Among the ones we tried, our best results were obtained with a variant of LRTA* that first updates $h(s')$ (where s' is the successor of the current state s with the smallest $c(s, s') + h(s')$), then updates $h(s)$, and finally selects the successor s'' of s with the smallest $c(s, s'') + h(s'')$, which may be different from s'. Empirically, this algorithm had a smaller travel cost to convergence than FALCONS. However, we can modify FALCONS so that it never updates the g-values, resulting in one value-update per action execution, just like LRTA*. In (Furcy & Koenig 2000), we prove that our Theorems 1 through 3 can be extended to FALCONS without g updates, provided that the g-values are consistent. Table 5 reports experimental results that clearly show that FALCONS without g updates had a smaller travel cost to convergence than LRTA* (with lookahead one). The speedup was 22.28 percent on average, and up to 58.19 percent. Additional results show that the number of trials to convergence for FALCONS without g updates was 25.97 percent less than for LRTA* on average (and up to 68.71 percent less), and that FALCONS executed an average of 57.51 percent more actions than LRTA* in the first trial.[3] These results are important for two reasons. First, they support the claim that the successor-selection rule of FALCONS speeds up convergence by making better use of the available heuristic knowledge and is able to decrease both the travel cost and computational cost to convergence. Second, they suggest that FALCONS may

---

[3]In domains with uniform costs, with consistent h-values, and with zero-initialized g-values, FALCONS without g updates reduces to LRTA*. Thus, Table 5 does not show results for completely uninformed heuristic values and our averages do not include them.

benefit from an enhanced successor-selection rule that focuses the search even more sharply around an optimal path by speeding up the learning of more accurate g-values, while still making efficient use of the initial heuristic knowledge.

Finally, we intend to apply FALCONS to domains from real-time control. These domains require real-time action-selection and convergence to optimal behaviors but, at the same time, the setup for each trial is expensive and thus it is important to keep the number of trials small. For learning how to balance poles or juggle devil-sticks (Schaal & Atkeson 1994), for example, the pole needs to be picked up and brought into the initial position before every trial. Domains from real-time control are typically directed and sometimes probabilistic, and we have not yet applied FALCONS to domains with these properties. The main difficulty of applying FALCONS to probabilistic domains is to adapt the notion of f-values to probabilistic domains. In contrast, FALCONS can be applied without modification to directed domains since all of our theoretical results continue to hold.

Conclusions

The research presented in this paper is a first step towards real-time search methods that converge to a shortest path faster than existing real-time search methods. We presented FALCONS, a real-time search method that looks similar to LRTA* but selects successors very differently, proved that it terminates and converges to a shortest path, and demonstrated experimentally, using standard search domains from the artificial intelligence literature, that it converges typically about twenty percent faster to a shortest path and in some cases even sixty percent faster than LRTA* in terms of travel cost (action executions). It also converges typically about forty percent faster and in some cases even seventy percent faster than LRTA* in terms of trials. The key idea behind FALCONS is to maintain f-values, that can be used to focus the search more sharply on the neighborhood of optimal paths. First, we demonstrated that breaking ties in favor of successors with smallest f-values speeds up the convergence of LRTA*, resulting in our TB-LRTA*. Then, we demonstrated that selecting successors with smallest f-values (instead of only breaking ties in favor of them) speeds up the convergence of LRTA* even further, resulting in our FALCONS. Our approach differs from that of Ishida who had to sacrifice the optimality of the resulting paths to speed up the convergence of LRTA* (Ishida & Shimbo 1996; Ishida 1997). It opens up new avenues of research for the design of real-time search methods and reinforcement-learning methods that converge substantially faster to a shortest path, by guiding exploration and exploitation with information that is more directly related to the overall learning objective.

Acknowledgments

We thank Eric Hansen, Maxim Likhachev, Yaxin Liu, Bill Murdock, Joseph Pemberton, and Patrawadee Prasangsit for interesting discussions about the convergence behavior of real-time search methods. The Intelligent Decision-Making Group is supported by an NSF Career Award under contract IIS-9984827. The views and conclusions contained in this document are those of the authors and should not be interpreted as representing the official policies, either expressed or implied, of the sponsoring organizations and agencies or the U.S. Government.

References

Barto, A.; Bradtke, S.; and Singh, S. 1995. Learning to act using real-time dynamic programming. *Artificial Intelligence* 73(1):81–138.

Bonet, B.; Loerincs, G.; and Geffner, H. 1997. A robust and fast action selection mechanism. In *Proceedings of the National Conference on Artificial Intelligence*, 714–719.

Furcy, D., and Koenig, S. 2000. Speeding up the convergence of real-time search: Empirical setup and proofs. Technical Report GIT-COGSCI-2000/01, College of Computing, Georgia Institute of Technology, Atlanta (Georgia).

Geffner, H., and Bonet, B. 1998. Solving large POMDPs by real-time dynamic programming. Technical report, Departamento de Computación, Universidad Simón Bolivar, Caracas (Venezuela).

Holte, R.; Drummond, C.; Perez, M.; Zimmer, R.; and MacDonald, A. 1994. Searching with abstractions: A unifying framework and new high-performance algorithm. In *Proceedings of the Canadian Conference on Artificial Intelligence*, 263–270.

Holte, R.; Perez, M.; Zimmer, R.; and MacDonald, A. 1996. Hierarchical A*: Searching abstraction hierarchies efficiently. In *Proceedings of the National Conference on Artificial Intelligence*, 530–535.

Ishida, T., and Korf, R. 1991. Moving target search. In *Proceedings of the International Joint Conference on Artificial Intelligence*, 204–210.

Ishida, T., and Shimbo, M. 1996. Improving the learning efficiencies of real-time search. In *Proceedings of the International Joint Conference on Artificial Intelligence*, 305–310.

Ishida, T. 1997. *Real-Time Search for Learning Autonomous Agents*. Kluwer Academic Publishers.

Koenig, S., and Simmons, R. 1995. Real-time search in non-deterministic domains. In *Proceedings of the International Joint Conference on Artificial Intelligence*, 1660–1667.

Koenig, S., and Simmons, R. 1998. Solving robot navigation problems with initial pose uncertainty using real-time heuristic search. In *Proceedings of the International Conference on Artificial Intelligence Planning Systems*, 154–153.

Koenig, S. 1999. Exploring unknown environments with real-time search or reinforcement learning. In *Proceedings of the Neural Information Processing Systems*, 1003–1009.

Korf, R. 1980. Towards a model of representation changes. *Artificial Intelligence* 14:41–78.

Korf, R. 1990. Real-time heuristic search. *Artificial Intelligence* 42(2-3):189–211.

Nilsson, N. 1971. *Problem-Solving Methods in Artificial Intelligence*. McGraw-Hill.

Pearl, J. 1985. *Heuristics: Intelligent Search Strategies for Computer Problem Solving*. Addison-Wesley.

Schaal, S., and Atkeson, C. 1994. Robot juggling: An implementation of memory-based learning. *Control Systems Magazine* 14.

Thrun, S. 1992. The role of exploration in learning control with neural networks. In White, D., and Sofge, D., eds., *Handbook of Intelligent Control: Neural, Fuzzy and Adaptive Approaches*. Van Nostrand Reinhold. 527–559.

Change Detection in Heuristic Search

Eyke Hüllermeier
IRIT - Université Paul Sabatier
31062 Toulouse Cedex (France)
eyke@irit.fr

Abstract

The order in which nodes are explored in a (depth-first) iterative deepening search strategy is principally determined by the condition under which a path of the search tree is cut off in each search phase. A corresponding criterion, which has a strong influence on the performance of the overall (heuristic) search procedure, is generally realized in the form of an upper cost bound. In this paper, we develop an effective and computationally efficient termination criterion based on statistical methods of change detection. The criterion is local in the sense that it depends on properties of a path itself, rather than on the comparison with other paths. Loosely speaking, the idea is to take a systematic change in the (heuristic) evaluation of nodes along a search path as an indication of suboptimality. An expected utility criterion which also takes the consequence of the suboptimal search decision on the solution quality into account is proposed as a generalization of this idea.

Introduction

Heuristic search strategies (for single-agent path-finding problems) explore more promising paths of a search tree (or, more generally, a search graph) before less promising ones by evaluating search states, thereby putting the successors of an inner node in some order according to their desirability. A frequently used type of (numeric) evaluation function is of the form $f(\eta) = g(\eta) + h(\eta)$, where $g(\eta)$ denotes the cost of the path from the root (initial state) to the node η and $h(\eta)$ is an estimation of the cost, $h^*(\eta)$, of the shortest (= lowest-cost) path from η to some goal state. The value $h(\eta)$ is generally derived from some "features" of the search state associated with η. Considerable attention has been payed to so-called *admissible* heuristics which underestimate the true cost function h^*, i.e., which satisfy $h(\eta) \leq h^*(\eta)$ for all nodes η. Such heuristics are of interest since they allow for realizing search algorithms which are guaranteed to return an optimal (lowest-cost) solution.

One possibility of deriving admissible heuristics in a systematic way is to use simplified (less constrained) models of the original problem (Pearl 1984). Still, the discovery of good admissible heuristics remains a difficult task, let

Copyright © 2000, American Association for Artificial Intelligence (www.aaai.org). All rights reserved.

alone the automatization of this process (Prieditis 1993). Besides, the computation of relaxation-based heuristic functions might be expensive since it calls for solving new, even though simplified, problems. In this paper, we assume heuristic information which does not provide lower bounds but estimations of cost values in a proper (statistical) sense. The (data-oriented) acquisition of this type of heuristic function seems to be less difficult than the (knowledge-oriented) invention of admissible heuristics. For instance, statistical techniques can be used for approximating the cost function h^* from a set of training data (Hüllermeier 1998). Of course, when basing a (best-first) search strategy on inadmissible heuristics, the (first) solution found might not be optimal. Nevertheless, corresponding evaluation functions are often more accurate, and using them in lieu of admissible ones may yield a considerable improvement in (average) time complexity at the cost of an acceptable (perhaps provably bounded (Harris 1974)) deterioration of solution quality.

It is well-known that (depth-first) iterative deepening (ID) search can overcome the main limitations of the basic breadth-first (BFS) and depth-first (DFS) search strategies, namely the exponential space complexity of the former and the non-optimality and non-completeness of the latter (Korf 1985). The criterion used by ID for cutting off search paths is generally given in the form of a global depth-limit or cost-limit. In this paper, we propose alternative termination criteria based on statistical methods of *change detection*. Loosely speaking, the idea is not to use the evaluation of individual (frontier) nodes itself but the *change* in the node evaluation along a search path in order to detect (and cut off) hardly promising paths. The paper is organized as follows: We begin with explaining the problem of change detection in its general form. Then, some basic algorithms for approaching this problem are briefly reviewed. The application of change detection in the context of heuristic search is discussed afterwards. Finally, a generalized approach to search termination based on an expected utility criterion is proposed. The paper concludes with some remarks.

The Problem of Change Detection

The problem of change detection is understood as the detection of *abrupt changes* in some characteristic properties of a system. Generally, such characteristics are not observed directly (e.g., through corresponding sensors) but can only be inferred indirectly from the measurements available. The problem of change detection arises, e.g., in pattern recognition (segmentation of signals), quality control, monitoring in biomedicine, or in connection with the detection of faults in technological processes (Basseville & Nikiforov 1993).

Many problems of this type can be stated as one of detecting a change in the *parameters* of a (static or dynamic) stochastic model. One possibility of approaching change detection is hence from the viewpoint of mathematical statistics. Consider, for instance, a (discrete) sequence $(Y_t)_{1 \leq t \leq T}$ of random variables, where Y_t is characterized by the (parametrized) conditional probability (density) $\phi_\theta(\cdot \mid y_{t-1}, \ldots, y_1)$. We suppose that a change is reflected by the change of the parameter vector θ. Thus, assuming that the random variables are independent of each other and that at most one change has occured, we have

$$\phi(y_t) = \begin{cases} \phi_{\theta_0}(y_t) & \text{if } 1 \leq t < t_0 \\ \phi_{\theta_1}(y_t) & \text{if } t_0 \leq t \leq T \end{cases},$$

where t_0 denotes the change time. The problem of change detection can comprise different tasks: (a) Detecting a change as soon as possible, i.e., deciding at each point of time whether the sequence observed so far contains a change or not. (b) Estimating the change time t_0, if any. (c) Estimating the (possibly unknown) parameters θ_0 and θ_1. These problems can be formalized within the framework of mathematical statistics. The first task, for instance, can be considered as a problem of hypotheses testing: The hypothesis H_0 that $\theta(t) = \theta_0$ for $1 \leq t \leq T$, where $\theta(t)$ denotes the parameter at time t, is tested against the alternative, H_1, that

$$\exists 1 < t_0 \leq T : \theta(1) = \ldots = \theta(t_0 - 1) = \theta_0$$
$$\wedge \; \theta(t_0) = \ldots = \theta(T) = \theta_1.$$

(This test assumes θ_0 and θ_1 to be known.) Likewise, the second task can be approached as a problem of estimating a (discrete) parameter, namely t_0. Note that the second and third task can be considered as auxiliary problems, once the first question has been answered in favor of H_1.

Different performance measures for assessing change detection procedures exist. Even though the importance of a criterion depends on the respective application, the following criteria are relevant in any case: The *expected delay* of a detection is the expected number of time points between t_0 and the time when the change is detected. The *probability of a false detection* is the probability of deciding on H_1 even though H_0 is true. These criteria are irreconcilable, of course: Reducing the probability of a false detection will generally increase the expected delay and vice versa.

Algorithms for Change Detection

In this section, we review one of the basic procedures for change detection, the so-called cumulative sum (CUSUM) algorithm. It is based upon the repeated use of the sequential probability ratio test (SPRT). The CUSUM algorithm was first proposed in (Page 1954).

The Sequential Probability Ratio Test

The SPRT, investigated in depth by WALD (1947), is one of the most important test procedures in sequential statistical analysis, mainly due to its optimality properties (Wald & Wolfowitz 1948) and its computational efficiency. It is a test for deciding between two simple statistical hypotheses

$$H_0 : \theta = \theta_0, \quad H_1 : \theta = \theta_1 \quad (1)$$

about some (constant) parameter θ. Consider a sequence $(Y_t)_{t \geq 1}$ of independent and identically distributed random variables, and let ϕ_{θ_0} and ϕ_{θ_1} denote the probability (density) function of Y_t valid under H_0 and H_1, respectively. Moreover, suppose that this sequence has been observed up to time T. A value of the log-likelihood ratio (the logarithm of the likelihood ratio)

$$\mathcal{L}_T = \sum_{t=1}^{T} \ln(\phi_{\theta_1}(y_t)) - \ln(\phi_{\theta_0}(y_t)) \quad (2)$$

larger (smaller) than 0 can then be interpreted as an indication of the validity of H_1 (H_0). An intuitive decision rule is hence to accept H_0, if $\mathcal{L}_T$ falls below some threshold $\alpha < 0$, and to reject H_0 (i.e., to decide on H_1), if $\mathcal{L}_T$ exceeds a threshold $\beta > 0$. The SPRT realizes this idea by combining a stopping rule and a terminal decision rule:

```
while α < L_T < β
    continue sampling (T = T + 1)
if L_T ≤ α then accept H_0
if β ≤ L_T then reject H_0
```

Observe that the log-likelihood ratio can be written recursively as $\mathcal{L}_T = \mathcal{L}_{T-1} + z_T$, where $z_T = \ln(\phi_{\theta_1}(y_T)) - \ln(\phi_{\theta_0}(y_T))$. Loosely speaking, the SPRT takes observations as long as evidence in favor of either H_0 or H_1 is not convincing enough. The thresholds α and β are directly related to the probabilities of two types of errors, namely of falsely rejecting H_0 and of deciding in favor of H_0 even though H_1 is true. Indeed, α and β can be used for controlling these errors. Of course, a tradeoff between a small probability of an error and the quickness of a decision, i.e., the length of the observed sequence, has to be achieved: The smaller (larger) α (β) is, the smaller is the probability of an error. At the same time, however, the terminal decision will be delayed, i.e., the *exit time*, T_0, will be larger.

The CUSUM Algorithm

The SPRT assumes that the complete data collected during the test is generated by one and the same model. Thus, it has to be modified in the context of change detection, where the data-generating process is assumed to change in-between.

Again, we are interested in testing the hypotheses (1) repeatedly. Now, however, H_0 is definitely true at the beginning, and the sampling is stopped only if a change seems to have occured, i.e., if the test statistic exceeds an upper bound. In order to avoid a detection delay due to the fact that (2) decreases as long as H_0 holds true it is hence reasonable to restrict the accumulated evidence in favor of H_0. This can be achieved by letting α define a lower bound to the test statistic. When choosing $\alpha = 0$ (Lorden 1971), the CUSUM algorithm can be written in its basic form as follows:

```
g₀ = 0, T = 0
repeat until g_T ≥ β
    T = T + 1
    g_T = max{0, g_{T-1} + ln(φ_{θ_1}(y_T)) - ln(φ_{θ_0}(y_T))}
```

If the CUSUM algorithm has terminated at time T_0, the maximum likelihood (ML) estimation of the change time t_0 is given by

$$\hat{t}_0 = \arg \max_{1 < t \leq T_0} \sum_{k=t}^{T_0} \ln(\phi_{\theta_1}(y_k)) - \ln(\phi_{\theta_0}(y_k)).$$

Often, not only the change time t_0 is unknown but also the parameters θ_0 and θ_1. A standard statistical approach, then, is to use the corresponding ML estimations instead. This leads to

$$g_T = \max_{1 < t_0 \leq T} \mathcal{L}_{t_0}(\hat{\theta}_{0,t_0}, \hat{\theta}_{1,t_0}) \qquad (3)$$

$$= \max_{1 < t_0 \leq T} \sum_{t=t_0}^{T} \ln(\phi_{\hat{\theta}_{1,t_0}}(y_t)) - \ln(\phi_{\hat{\theta}_{0,t_0}}(y_t)),$$

where $\hat{\theta}_{0,t_0}$ and $\hat{\theta}_{1,t_0}$ denote, respectively, the ML estimations of θ_0 and θ_1 based on the observations $y_1, \ldots, y_T$ and the assumption that t_0 is a change time. $\mathcal{L}_{t_0}(\theta_0, \theta_1)$ is the log-likelihood ratio associated with the hypotheses

$$H_0 : \forall 1 \leq t \leq T : \theta(t) = \theta_0,$$

$$H_1 : \theta(t) = \begin{cases} \theta_0 & \text{if } 1 \leq t \leq t_0 - 1 \\ \theta_1 & \text{if } t_0 \leq t \leq T \end{cases}.$$

Again, the stopping rule is defined by $g_T \geq \beta$, with β being a predefined threshold. That is, the exit time T_0 is defined as the smallest T such that $g_T \geq \beta$. The (ML) estimation of t_0 is then given by the change time $1 < \hat{t}_0 \leq T_0$ for which the maximum in (3) is attained. Observe that g_T, as defined in (3), can no longer be determined by means of a simple recursive formula.

Changes in Heuristic Search

In this section, we shall apply the idea of change detection to heuristic tree-search algorithms. We assume heuristic information to be available in the form of an estimation h of the cost function h^* which assigns to each node η the cost of the (cost-)optimal path from η to a goal state. A value $h(\eta)$ is considered as the realization of a random variable $H(\eta)$ (Hansson & Mayer 1989). We suppose the random variables associated with different search states to be independent of each other, a simplifying assumption commonly made in the probabilistic analysis of search trees (Zhang & Korf 1995). For the sake of simplicity, we also assume $\mathsf{E}(H(\eta)) = h^*(\eta)$ and $(H(\eta) - h^*(\eta)) \sim \Phi$ for all nodes η, where E denotes the expected value operator.[1] Statistically speaking, $h(\eta)$ is an unbiased estimation of $h^*(\eta)$. Φ is a distribution with associated probability (density) function ϕ, i.e., $\phi(x)$ is the probability (density) that $H(\eta) - h^*(\eta) = x$.

[1] This assumption can easily be relaxed.

The overall cost associated with a node η is given by $f(\eta) = g(\eta) + h(\eta)$, where $g(\eta)$ denotes the cost of the path from the initial state to η. The evaluation function f is used for guiding the search process. According to our assumptions above, $f(\eta)$ can be interpreted as the realization of a random variable $F(\eta)$ such that $(F(\eta) - g(\eta) - h^*(\eta)) \sim \Phi$.

Path Profiles

Consider a search path ρ, i.e., a sequence $(\eta_1, \ldots, \eta_K)$ of nodes with η_1 being the root of the search tree and η_K the (current) frontier node. We associate sequences

$$f(\rho) = (f(\eta_1), \ldots, f(\eta_K)),$$
$$f^*(\rho) = (f^*(\eta_1), \ldots, f^*(\eta_K))$$

with ρ, where $f^*(\eta_k) = g(\eta_k) + h^*(\eta_k)$. $f(\rho)$ is called the *path profile* of ρ. The sequence $f^*(\rho)$ is obviously non-decreasing, i.e.,

$$f^*(\eta_1) \leq f^*(\eta_2) \leq \ldots \leq f^*(\eta_K). \qquad (4)$$

Suppose that we have not made a suboptimal search decision (node generation) so far, i.e., a cost-optimal solution can still be reached from η_K. Then, all inequalities in (4) are in fact equalities. That is, the random variables $F(\eta_k)$ have the same expectation and, hence, the same distribution. Now, suppose all but the kth decision to be optimal. Then,

$$\mu_0 = f^*(\eta_1) = f^*(\eta_2) = \ldots = f^*(\eta_k) \qquad (5)$$
$$< f^*(\eta_{k+1}) = f^*(\eta_{k+2}) = \ldots = f^*(\eta_K) = \mu_1.$$

That is, the expected value of the random variables $F(\eta_1), \ldots, F(\eta_k)$ is μ_0, whereas the expectation of $F(\eta_{k+1}), \ldots, F(\eta_K)$ is μ_1. More generally, we have the case that some (but at least one) of the inequalities in (4) are strict if not all decisions have been optimal. Subsequently, we assume that at most one suboptimal decision has been made.[2]

Change Detection and Search Termination

Iterative deepening search is the method of choice for many applications since it combines the merits of both, BFS (completeness, or even optimality) and DFS (linear space complexity). Taking a repeated (partially informed) depth-first search as a point of departure, the ID algorithm is principally determined by the conditions under which search along a path is broken off. The common approach is to use a depth-limit or, more generally, a cost-limit, for each search phase. For instance, the iterative deepening version of the A* algorithm, IDA*, continues search along a path as long as the frontier node η satisfies $f(\eta) \leq c$, with c being the f-cost-limit valid for the respective search phase.

When being interested in finding good solutions, or even optimal ones, one should obviously avoid the exploration of suboptimal search paths. Indeed, this idea is supported by the gradually increased cost-limit in IDA*. When being also interested in minimizing computational effort, it is

[2] Experimental studies have shown that a generalization of this assumption hardly improves the quality of search decisions.

reasonable, not only to *terminate* search along less promising paths, but also to *continue* search along a path as long as it appears promising, thereby leaving other (perhaps also promising) paths out of account. This idea is actually not supported by the use of an f-cost-limit which brings about a permanent comparison between a (large) set of simultaneously explored paths.[3] In fact, "following a search path as long as it might lead to a (near-)optimal solution" principally requires a *local* termination criterion which makes do with (heuristic) information from nodes of an *individual* path. Here, we shall use statistical methods of change detection in order to realize corresponding termination criteria. As will be seen, these methods allow for estimating the quality of a solution eventually found when following a path without referring to other search paths, or other solutions already encountered.

Consider a path $\rho = (\eta_1, \ldots, \eta_K)$ with path profile $f(\rho) = (f(\eta_1), \ldots, f(\eta_K))$. The parameter of interest, i.e., the change of which has to be detected, is the expected value $E(F(\eta_k))$. Depending on the information available about μ_0 and μ_1, the expected values before and after a change, different algorithms can be applied. Generally, it must be assumed that neither μ_0 nor μ_1 is known. Consequently, the basic CUSUM algorithm cannot be used directly. Rather, we have to proceed from (3). Suppose $1 < k_0 \leq K$ to be a changepoint, i.e., the generation of η_{k_0} was not optimal. The ML estimations $\hat{\mu}_{0,k_0}$ and $\hat{\mu}_{1,k_0}$ of μ_0 and μ_1 are then given by the mean of the values $f(\eta_1), \ldots, f(\eta_{k_0-1})$ and $f(\eta_{k_0}), \ldots, f(\eta_K)$, respectively. The test statistic (3) thus becomes

$$\mathcal{L}(\rho) = \max_{1 < k_0 \leq K} \mathcal{L}_{k_0}(\rho)$$
$$= \max_{1 < k_0 \leq K} \sum_{k=k_0}^{K} \ln(\phi_{\hat{\mu}_{1,k_0}}(f(\eta_k))) - \ln(\phi_{\hat{\mu}_{0,k_0}}(f(\eta_k))),$$

where ϕ_μ denotes the probability (density) function of the random variable $X + \mu$ and $X \sim \Phi$. Observe that we should actually use the *constrained* ML estimations of μ_0 and μ_1, taking into account that $\mu_0 \leq \mu_1$. In fact, the case where $\hat{\mu}_{0,k_0} > \hat{\mu}_{1,k_0}$ indicates an (actually impossible) decrease of the expectation and can hence be ignored. The termination criterion should thus be defined as

$$\mathcal{L}'(\rho) = \max_{1 < k_0 \leq K} \mathcal{L}'_{k_0}(\rho) \geq \beta, \qquad (6)$$

where $\mathcal{L}'_{k_0}(\rho) = \mathcal{L}_{k_0}(\rho)$ if $\hat{\mu}_{0,k_0} \leq \hat{\mu}_{1,k_0}$ and 0 otherwise, and $\beta > 0$ is a predefined threshold. $\mathcal{L}'(\rho)$ can be computed in time $O(K)$ by the algorithm in Figure 1.

An Iterative Deepening Algorithm

When making use of the above termination criterion, a search algorithm cuts of the current path and starts a backtracking whenever (6) is satisfied (or a terminal node has been reached). As already mentioned before, the threshold β can be used for controlling two (conflicting) criteria: The

---

[3]Still, the depth-first component in A* can be strengthened by using a weighted evaluation function (Pohl 1970).

```
function change(f(η_1),...,f(η_K))
  m(1) = f(η_1)
  for k = 2 to K
    m(k) = m(k-1) + f(η_k)
  for k_0 = 2 to K
    μ̂_{0,k_0} = m(k_0 - 1)/(k_0 - 1)
    μ̂_{1,k_0} = (m(K) - m(k_0 - 1))/(K - k_0 + 1)
  L' = 0,  k̂_0 = 0,  s = 0
  for k_0 = K down to 2
    s = s + ln(φ_{μ̂_{1,k_0}}(f(η_k))) - ln(φ_{μ̂_{0,k_0}}(f(η_k)))
    if μ̂_{0,k_0} ≤ μ̂_{1,k_0} and L' < s then
      L' = s,  k̂_0 = k_0
  return L', k̂_0, μ̂_{0,k̂_0}
```

Figure 1: Pseudo-code for computing the termination criterion (6) and the ML estimations $\hat{k}_0$ and $\hat{\mu}_0$.

expected delay of a change detection corresponds to the expected number of nodes explored along a path after a suboptimal search decision has been made. Of course, the smaller the threshold β is, the smaller is the detection delay. The probability of a *false detection* corresponds to the probability of cutting off an optimal search path. Keeping this probability small calls for a large threshold β.

Choosing $\beta = \infty$ leads to a pure depth-first search and, hence, excludes the probability of a false detection completely. In general, however, it may happen that an optimal search path is cut off and the corresponding search process terminates before having found a solution. Suppose, for instance, that a change has occured at $k_0 = 11$. The following table shows the (experimentally determined) probability p of terminating before $k = 11$ and the expected detection delay, d, for different thresholds β if Φ is the standard normal distribution and $\mu_1 = \mu_0 + 2$:

β	p	d	β	p	d
5	0.48	1.51	8	0.28	2.55
6	0.39	1.86	9	0.25	2.85
7	0.33	2.20	10	0.22	3.17

If the search process terminates without a solution, a new search phase with a larger threshold (which might be defined on the basis of the search process so far) has to be started. Based on an increasing sequence $(\beta_i)_{i \geq 0}$ of thresholds we thus obtain an iterative deepening algorithm, IDCD (Iterative Deepening based on Change Detection).

Of course, the first solution found by IDCD is not necessarily an optimal one. In fact, using the kind of heuristic information available does generally not allow for guaranteeing optimality, since the true cost value of a search node might not only be underestimated but also overestimated. It seems hence reasonable to let IDCD return the first solution found. Since the order in which solutions are encountered depends on the order in which (promising) search paths are explored, the successors of inner nodes should be arranged according to their f-evaluations. This way, a partially informed backtracking is realized in each search phase.

An interesting question concerns the completeness of IDCD. It can be shown that IDCD terminates and returns a solution with probability 1 under rather general conditions. This result can be proved by making use of a related termination property of the SPRT (Wald 1947). However, the proof becomes non-trivial due to the fact that one has to consider an infinite number of search paths.

It is worth mentioning that the change detection criterion suggests some kind of (probabilistic) backmarking strategy (Gaschnig 1979): Instead of returning to the closest unexpanded ancestor, one may back up to the parent of the most likely changepoint $\hat{k}_0$ directly, thereby pruning (large) parts of the search tree. Of course, a corresponding algorithm will in general not guarantee completeness.

Utility-Based Search

The principle underlying IDCD is to continue a search path only if it might lead to an optimal solution. Now, suppose that we consider a *comprehensive* value of a computation (Horvitz 1988) including the solution quality as well as the running time, and that we are willing to gain efficiency at the cost of solution quality. In other words, we are interested in finding a "good" solution with reasonable computational effort, rather than finding an optimal one regardless of the running time. In this section, we shall propose a generalization of (6) suitable for supporting search under these assumptions.

Suppose the degree to which a user is satisfied with a solution, x, to depend on some relation between the cost of x and the cost of an optimal solution, say, the difference $\Delta(x)$ between these values. The preferences of the user can then be formalized by means of a (non-increasing) utility function $U : [0, \infty) \to [0, 1]$, where $U(\Delta(x))$ is the utility of a solution x.

Given the preferences of the user thus defined, a reasonable generalization of the termination criterion (6) is to break off search along a path $\rho = (\eta_1, \ldots, \eta_K)$ if the *expected utility* of the best solution reachable from η_K, $x^*(\rho)$, falls below some threshold u_0, i.e., if

$$\mathsf{E}(U(\rho)) = \int_0^\infty U(\Delta) \cdot \pi(\Delta \,|\, f(\rho)) \, d\Delta < u_0. \quad (7)$$

Here $\pi(\Delta \,|\, f(\rho))$ denotes the probability (density) that $\Delta(x^*(\rho)) = \Delta$, given the path profile $f(\rho)$.

Suppose prior knowledge concerning Δ to be available in the form of a (prior) probability (density) function π. The posterior $\pi(\cdot \,|\, f(\rho))$ is then specified by

$$\pi(\cdot \,|\, f(\rho)) \propto \lambda(f(\rho) \,|\, \cdot) \times \pi, \quad (8)$$

where $\lambda(f(\rho) \,|\, \Delta)$ is the probability of observing $f(\rho)$, given the deviation Δ. If we take π as an uninformative prior,[4] then $\pi(\cdot \,|\, f(\rho))$ is proportional to the likelihood function $\lambda(f(\rho) \,|\, \cdot)$, i.e., $\pi(\cdot \,|\, f(\rho)) \propto \lambda(f(\rho) \,|\, \cdot)$, where

$$\lambda(f(\rho) \,|\, \Delta) = \prod_{k=1}^{k_0-1} \phi_{\mu_0}(f(\eta_k)) \prod_{k=k_0}^{K} \phi_{\mu_0+\Delta}(f(\eta_k)). \quad (9)$$

The posterior $\pi(\cdot \,|\, f(\rho))$ cannot be derived from (8) directly if k_0 and μ_0 in (9) are unknown. In Bayesian analysis, such parameters are called *nuisance parameters*. There are different possibilities of deriving a posterior distribution for the parameters of interest in the presence of nuisance parameters (Basu 1977). One might consider, e.g., the marginal distribution of the full posterior distribution which contains both, the parameters of interest as well as the nuisance parameters. This solution may become computationally expensive, however. A further possibility is to replace the nuisance parameters by their ML estimations. This approach seems reasonable in our situation since we can fall back on the results obtained in connection with the detection of changes: Both, the estimation of the change point, $\hat{k}_0$, and of the corresponding expectation, $\hat{\mu}_0$, are computed by the algorithm in Figure 1. A (utility-based) termination criterion can thus be realized as follows:

- Derive $\hat{k}_0$ and $\hat{\mu}_0$ for the current search path ρ.
- Let $\mathsf{E}(U(\rho)) = 1$ if $\hat{k}_0 = 0$. Otherwise, derive $\mathsf{E}(U(\rho))$ according to (7), (8) and (9).
- Break off the search path if $\mathsf{E}(U(\rho)) < u_0$, with $u_0 \leq 1$ being a predefined threshold.

This procedure reveals that the expected utility criterion can be seen as an extension of the change detection approach: Instead of only looking for a jump in the expected value, the decision whether to terminate search or not also depends on the size of this jump. The other way round, (6) corresponds to the special case of (7) in which the utility function is given by $U = 1_{\{1\}}$.

Observe that $\pi(\cdot \,|\, f(\rho))$ is not necessarily 0 on $(-\infty, 0)$ since (9) might be positive (even though small) also for $\Delta < 0$. Instead of incorporating the constraint $\Delta \geq 0$ by means of the usual conditioning (proportional allocation of probability mass) it seems reasonable to take the (actually impossible) event $\Delta < 0$ as evidence for $\Delta = 0$. Formally, this is equivalent to integrating over $(-\infty, \infty)$ in (7) with an extended utility function such that $U(\Delta) = U(0) = 1$ for all $\Delta < 0$.

By making use of (7) in conjunction with a sequence of utility thresholds $(u_i)_{i \geq 0}$ instead of (6) (and the sequence $(\beta_i)_{i \geq 0}$), we obtain an iterative deepening algorithm UBID (Utility-Based Iterative Deepening). Again, the search strategy is not only controlled by (7) but also by $(u_i)_{i \geq 0}$. A threshold $u_i = 0$, for instance, entails a pure depth-first search. The smaller the increments $\Delta u_i = u_i - u_{i-1}$ are defined, the more cautious search paths are explored, i.e., the more UBID resembles an (iterative deepening) best-first search.

Of course, since the expected utility criterion requires the computation of the integral (which is a sum in the case of a discrete distribution Φ) in (7) it is computationally more complex than the change detection criterion. Still, it can be

---
[4] Suppose $\pi(\cdot \,|\, f(\rho))$ to exist under this condition.

realized very efficiently for several special cases. For instance, if Φ is a normal distribution[5] and U corresponds to an (extended) $\{0,1\}$-valued utility function $1_{(-\infty,\Delta_0]}$, the computation of (7) can be realized by simply looking up a value (which depends on $\hat{\mu}_0$, $\hat{\mu}_1$, $\hat{k}_0$) in the table of the (cumulative) standard normal distribution (Hüllermeier & Zimmermann 1998). Let us also mention a further possibility of avoiding integration, namely that of basing the termination rule not on the *expected* but on the *most likely* utility $U(\hat{\mu}_1 - \hat{\mu}_0)$.

Concluding Remarks

We have proposed an iterative deepening strategy in which the decision whether to terminate or continue search along a path is based on properties of the sequence of node evaluations along that path. The basic idea is to "search deep" in the first place, due to reasons of efficiency, but only as long as the expected utility of the solution that will eventually be found is acceptable. This (heuristic) search principle has been formalized based on statistical methods of change detection. The corresponding search algorithm is parametrized by means of a utility function and a sequence of utility thresholds.

Taking the idea of a *local* termination rule for granted, the criteria (6) and (7) appear natural in the sense that they *fully* exploit the information which has become available while following a search path. Observe that admissible (but non-monotone) estimations $f(\eta_k)$ along a path can be aggregated by taking their maximum, which is an obvious way of avoiding a loss of information. As opposed to this, a simple combination (such as, e.g., the average) of all evaluations does hardly make sense in our case since the random variables $F(\eta_k)$ might have different expected values.

Due to reasons of space we could not present experimental results in this paper. Still, a successful implementation providing evidence for the efficiency of our approach as well as a comparison with alternative search methods can be found in (Hüllermeier & Zimmermann 1998), where UBID is applied in the context of knowledge-based configuration. The heuristic function used in this implementation is learned from a set of already solved problems by means of linear regression techniques (Hüllermeier 1998).

The possibility of an efficient parallel implementation served as a main motivation for the development of IDCD and UBID. Indeed, these algorithms are particularly suitable for parallel computation methods since (6) and (7) work with information provided by an individual search path alone and, hence, can lead to a substantial reduction of communication costs. Still, one might think of extending these termination rules by including information from other search paths. This way, it would be possible to base a termination decision on both, the relative change of estimated costs and their absolute values. Particularly, global information can be used for deriving better estimations of the cost of an optimal solution (μ_0 in (5)) and, hence, for improving the test statistic (6). In fact, the methods proposed in this paper can be generalized in further directions as well. Prior information about change points t_0 or deviations Δ, for instance, can be incorporated by means of Bayesian methods or constrained (ML) estimations. Besides, our termination criteria, or variations thereof, might also be useful as stopping rules for selective search in game playing.

Acknowledgements

The author gratefully acknowledges financial support in the form of a TMR research grant funded by the European Commission. Parts of this work have also been supported by the DFG (German Research Association, SFB 376).

References

Basseville, M., and Nikiforov, I. 1993. *Detection of Abrupt Changes*. Prentice Hall.

Basu, D. 1977. On the elimination of nuisance parameters. *J. American Stat. Association* 72:355–366.

Gaschnig, J. 1979. A problem similarity approach to devising heuristics: First results. In *Proc. IJCAI-79*.

Hansson, O., and Mayer, A. 1989. Heuristic search as evidential reasoning. In *Proc. 5th Workshop on Uncertainty in AI*, 152–161. Morgan Kaufmann.

Harris, L. 1974. The heuristic search under conditions of error. *Artificial Intelligence* 5(3):217–234.

Horvitz, E. 1988. Reasoning under varying and uncertain resource constraints. In *Proceeedings AAAI-88*.

Hüllermeier, E., and Zimmermann, C. 1998. A two-phase search method for solving configuration problems. Tech. Rep. tr-rsfb-98-062, Department of Computer Science, University of Paderborn.

Hüllermeier, E. 1998. Approximating cost functions in resource-based configuration. Tech. Rep. tr-rsfb-98-060, Department of Computer Science, University of Paderborn.

Korf, R. 1985. Depth-first iterative deepening: An optimal admissible tree search. *Artif. Intell.* 27(1).

Lorden, G. 1971. Procedures for reacting to a change in distribution. *Annals of Math. Stat.* 42:1897–1908.

Page, E. 1954. Continuous inspection schemes. *Biometrica* 41:100–115.

Pearl, J. 1984. *Heuristics: Intelligent Search Strategies for Computer Problem Solving*. Addison-Wesley.

Pohl, I. 1970. First results on the effect of error in heuristic search. In Meltzer, B., and Michie, D., eds., *Machine Learning* 5. 219–236.

Prieditis, A. 1993. Machine discovery of effective admissible heuristics. *Machine Learning* 12:117–141.

Wald, A., and Wolfowitz, J. 1948. Optimum character of the sequential probability ratio test. *Annals of Mathematical Statistics* 19:326–339.

Wald, A. 1947. *Sequential Analysis*. New York: John Wiley & Sons.

Zhang, W., and Korf, R. 1995. Performance of linear-space search algorithms. *Artif. Intell.* 79:241–292.

---

[5] This distribution often applies at least approximately.

Preference-based Search for Scheduling

Ulrich Junker
ILOG
1681, route des Dolines
06560 Valbonne
France
junker@ilog.fr

Abstract

Preference-based search (PBS) is a new search procedure for solving combinatorial optimization problems. Given a set of preferences between search decisions, PBS searches through a space of preferred solutions, which is tighter than the space of all solutions. The definition of preferred solutions is based on work in non-monotonic reasoning (Brewka 1989; Geffner & Pearl 1992; Grosof 1991) on priorities between defaults. The basic idea of PBS is quite simple: Always pick a locally best decision α. Either make the decision α or make other locally best decisions that allow to deduce $\neg\alpha$ and thus represent a counterargument for α. If there is no possible counterargument then PBS does not explore the subtree of $\neg\alpha$. This pruning of the search space is obtained by non-monotonic inference rules that are inspired by Doyle's TMS and that detect decisions belonging to all or no preferred solution. We show that PBS can optimally solve various important scheduling problems.

Keywords: search, non-monotonic reasoning, scheduling, constraint satisfaction

Introduction

The standard approach for solving combinatorial optimization problems by constraint satisfaction is to apply a Branch-and-Bound method. Each time a solution is found during tree search, an upper bound on the objective is decreased. A lower bound is maintained in intermediate search states, e.g. by encapsulating an OR-algorithm inside a constraint. Furthermore, we can use value-ordering heuristics that select locally better choices first. Unfortunately, if the bounds are far from the optimum, the search space will not be pruned much. If the number of solutions is high, this process will take a long time to converge via the optimum. The problem is that the objective is not sufficiently exploited during search. Since we systematically search through the space of all solutions, locally best choices are more and more abandoned when search is progressing.

Preferred solutions as elaborated in non-monotonic reasoning (Brewka 1989) impose a tighter constraint on the set of all solutions even if the bounds on the objective are not yet tight. The definition of preferred solutions is based on preferences between the possible search decisions. In scheduling, for example, we prefer to assign smaller start times to an activity a. If $t_1 < t_2$ then we prefer the decision $s(a) = t_1$ to $s(a) = t_2$. These preferences define a strict partial order $\prec$ on the set of all possible decisions. A preferred solution is then defined as follows: Firstly, we choose a total order that is a superset of the given partial order. Secondly, we visit the search decisions in this order starting with the best decision. During this process, we will make some of the decisions and abandon the others. When we visit a decision then we check whether it is consistent w.r.t. the initial problem and the already made decisions. If yes then we make the decision. Otherwise, we abandon it. The set of made decisions that is obtained after visiting all possible decisions is a preferred solution. Different preferred solutions can be obtained by choosing different orders.

The same preferred solution can, however, be obtained by several orders. Enumerating all orders therefore is not a good method for computing all preferred solutions. We will elaborate a search procedure which determines each preferred solution exactly once, but which still profits from the preferences between search decisions in order to reduce the search effort. We call this procedure preference-based search (PBS). The basic idea of PBS is quite simple: In each search state, PBS always picks a locally best decision α. PBS branches as follows. It either makes the decision α or it makes other locally best decisions that allow to deduce $\neg\alpha$ and thus represent a counterargument for α. Hence, PBS abandons a locally best decision only if it finds a reason (i.e. a counterargument) for this. If PBS does not find a counterargument for α then it considers $\neg\alpha$ an unjustified choice and does not explore the subtree of $\neg\alpha$ in contrast to standard systematic tree search methods. PBS prunes the search space by applying non-monotonic inference rules that are inspired by Doyle's TMS and that detect decisions belonging to all or no preferred solution. Preference-based search thus does no longer search through the space of all solutions, but only through the space of preferred solutions. It is important to note that PBS is a systematic search procedure for exploring the preferred solutions. It explores all the preferred solutions and does not explore the same preferred solution twice.

PBS itself is a general search procedure that just needs a set of preferences between the possible search decisions.

It can be used as search algorithm for all AI problems that can be treated with Brewka's approach (Brewka 1989). Examples are inheritance of defaults, but also diagnosis and configuration.

In this paper, we show that PBS can also be used to solve optimization problems. Two different definitions for preferred solutions have been proposed in the literature. In (Junker & Brewka 1991), we show that Brewka's definition (Brewka 1989) is stricter than the definition used by Geffner and Grosof (Geffner & Pearl 1992; Grosof 1991). Interestingly, both are useful for solving optimization problems. Brewka's definition can be used for certain scheduling problems, which have a non-linear objective. Grosof/Geffner's definition can be used for integer programming where the objective is linear. The PBS procedure presented in this paper follows Brewka's approach and we consequently apply it to selected scheduling problems.

For each problem, we seek a set of preferences that preserves optimality in the following sense: At least one optimal solution has to be a preferred one w.r.t. the given preferences. If an optimization problem has this property we can use PBS to solve it. For project scheduling problems with precedence constraints and multiple-capacitated resources, we prefer to assign smaller start times to an activity and show that these preferences preserve optimality. The preferred solutions that are obtained by these preferences correspond to the left-shifted schedules.

If optimality is preserved then PBS is a systematic search procedure for the considered optimization problem. That means PBS is able to prove optimality. If PBS does not find a preferred solution that has an objective strictly better than v^* then the optimal value of the objective is not better than v^*. Thus, PBS also reduces the search effort for the optimality proof, which often is very time-consuming.

Compared to existing work in scheduling, we can state that PBS is a generalization and improvement of the schedule-or-postpone method (Le Pape *et al.* 1994; ILOG 1997). This method assigns start times in chronological order, which allows to do efficient constraint propagation in presence of resources with large or time-dependent capacities. PBS gives a clear semantics to the schedule-or-postpone method and shows how to do additional pruning of the search space by analyzing conflicts between start time assignments.

Another method that exploits conflicts between activities is the precedence-constraint-posting approach (PCP) of Cheng and Smith (Smith & Cheng 1993; Laborie & Ghallab 1995; Cesta, Oddi, & Smith 1999). PCP does not assign start times, but posts precedence constraints between pairs of activities that are potentially in conflict. Thus, it also provides an elegant way to search through the space of all left-shifted schedules.

The purpose of this paper is to elaborate the PBS algorithm in a general way and to show that it can be used for scheduling. An empirical comparison between the PBS-scheduler, i.e. the improved schedule-or-postpone method, and the precedence-constraint-posting approach, requires further work and is beyond the scope of this paper.

The paper has five parts: First, we introduce the definition of preferred solutions. Second, we develop the PBS-algorithm. Third, we give preferences for selected scheduling problems. Fourth, we briefly discuss an implementation of PBS for job-shop problems. Finally, we discuss related and future work.

Preferred Solutions

In this section, we give a precise definition of preferred solutions for combinatorial problems that are formulated as constraint satisfaction problems. A constraint satisfaction problem (CSP) consists of a set of variables on which a set of constraints is formulated. Each constraint consists of a relation and a tuple of variables. In this paper, we simply suppose that the set Γ of all constraints of a CSP is given. This set includes domain membership constraints of the form $x \in D$, which are usually introduced separately. We also suppose that a consistency checker is given that checks whether a set of constraints is consistent or not.

We furthermore suppose that a set $\mathcal{A}$ of all possible decisions is given that can be made for solving the problem. A decision can be an arbitrary constraint. For example, we consider constraints of the form $x = v$ which represent an assignment of value v to variable x. We now consider a set of preferences between the decisions in $\mathcal{A}$. In scheduling, for example, we prefer to assign smaller start times to an activity a. If $t_1 < t_2$ then we prefer the decision $s(a) = t_1$ to $s(a) = t_2$. These preferences define a strict partial order $\prec$ on the set $\mathcal{A}$ of all possible decisions.

Definition 1 *Let $<$ be a total order on $\mathcal{A}$ that is a superset of $\prec$. Let $\alpha_1, \ldots, \alpha_n$ be an enumeration of the elements of $\mathcal{A}$ in increasing $<$-order. We then define $A_0 := \emptyset$ and*

$$A_i := \begin{cases} A_{i-1} \cup \{\alpha_i\} & \text{if } \Gamma \cup A_{i-1} \cup \{\alpha_i\} \text{ is consistent} \\ A_{i-1} & \text{otherwise} \end{cases}$$

A_n is a preferred solution.

Thus, we choose a total order $<$ that completes the given partial order. We then visit the decisions of $\mathcal{A}$ in increasing $<$-order and make a decision if it is consistent w.r.t. the decisions made earlier: Thus, a decision can only be retracted if it is inconsistent w.r.t. better decisions. Each suitable total order $<$ defines a preferred solution. The same preferred solution can, however, be obtained by several orders.

Preference-based Search (PBS)

In this section, we introduce two versions of preference-based search. The basic version just exploits preferences, whereas the more sophisticated version also exploits counterarguments and prunes the search space even more.

PBS1: Decide-or-Refute

Since the same preferred solution can be obtained by several orders, enumerating all orders is not a good method for computing all preferred solutions. In order to compute each preferred solution exactly once, we proceed as follows. In each step, we select a best decision α among a set U of unexplored decisions. We also say that α is a $\prec$-best element of U since U does not contain an element β such that $\beta \prec \alpha$.

Algorithm *PBS1*(Γ, $\mathcal{A}$, $\prec$)
1. $A := \emptyset$; $U := \mathcal{A}$; $Q := \emptyset$;
2. **while** $Q \cup U \neq \emptyset$ **do**
3. $B := \{\alpha \in Q \cup U \mid \nexists \beta \in Q \cup U : \beta \prec \alpha\}$;
4.   **if** there is an $\alpha \in B \cap Q$ s.t.
5. $\Gamma \cup A \cup \{\alpha\}$ is inconsistent
6.   **then** $Q := Q - \{\alpha\}$ and continue;
7.   **if** $U = \emptyset$ and $Q \neq \emptyset$ **then** fail;
8.   **if** $B \cap U = \emptyset$ **then** fail;
9.   **if** there is an $\alpha \in B \cap U$ s.t.
10. $\Gamma \cup A \cup \{\alpha\}$ is inconsistent
11.   **then** $U := U - \{\alpha\}$ and continue;
12.   select an $\alpha \in B \cap U$ and set $U := U - \{\alpha\}$;
13.   **choose** $A := A \cup \{\alpha\}$ **or** $Q := Q \cup \{\alpha\}$;
14. **return** A;

Figure 1: Algorithm PBS1

If α is inconsistent w.r.t. a set A of already made decisions then we just drop it. Otherwise, we branch. We either make the decision α by adding it to A or we add it to a set Q of decisions that have to be refuted by subsequent decisions. The set Q thus represents a set of *'refutation queries'*, which impose an additional constraint on the preferred solutions we are computing. We are only interested in preferred solutions that do not contain elements of Q. If, in a subsequent state, an element β of Q is inconsistent w.r.t. an extended set A then we can remove β from Q. The set Q also imposes a constraint on the elements that can be selected in a search state. As long as an element β is in Q, we can't select the decisions that are $\prec$-worse than β. If we can't select any element any more then a dead-end is reached. The non-deterministic algorithm in figure 1 describes this behaviour.

This algorithm can be implemented by a tree search procedure. The following theorem states that PBS1 systematically searches through the space of all preferred solutions:

Theorem 1 *Algorithm PBS1 always terminates. Each successful run returns a preferred solution and each preferred solution is returned by exactly one successful run.*

The algorithm terminates since $2 \cdot |U| + |Q|$ is decreased in each iteration. In each step, the algorithm maintains a state $S := (A, Q, U)$. We say that X is a *preferred solution of the state* S iff X is a superset of A and disjoint to Q and $X - A$ is a preferred solution of the problem $\Gamma \cup A$ with decisions $Q \cup U$ and preferences $\prec \cap (Q \cup U)^2$. Following properties allow to show that PBS1 computes exactly the preferred solutions of state S if PBS1 is in the state S:

P1 if $U = \emptyset$ and $Q = \emptyset$ then A is a preferred solution of (A, Q, U).

P2 if $\alpha \in Q$ and α is a $\prec$-best element of $Q \cup U$ and $\Gamma \cup A \cup \{\alpha\}$ is inconsistent then X is a preferred solution of (A, Q, U) iff X is a preferred solution of $(A, Q-\{\alpha\}, U)$.

P3 if $\alpha \in U$ and α is a $\prec$-best element of $Q \cup U$ and $\Gamma \cup A \cup \{\alpha\}$ is inconsistent then X is a preferred solution of (A, Q, U) iff X is a preferred solution of $(A, Q, U-\{\alpha\})$.

P4 if all $\prec$-best elements α of $Q \cup U$ are in Q and are consistent w.r.t. $\Gamma \cup A$ then (A, Q, U) has no preferred solution.

P5 if $\alpha \in U$ and α is a $\prec$-best element of $Q \cup U$ then X is a preferred solution of (A, Q, U) iff X is a preferred solution of $(A, Q \cup \{\alpha\}, U - \{\alpha\})$ or of $(A \cup \{\alpha\}, Q, U - \{\alpha\})$.

PBS2: Reasoning with Conflicts

As shown in the last section, preference-based search maintains a set Q of refutation queries. For each refutation query α, it has to make a set of decisions that are inconsistent w.r.t. α and that represent a counterargument to α. For this purpose, PBS1 can use any unexplored decision in U except those that are $\prec$-worse than α. Now suppose that there is no such counterargument. In this case, we can make as many additional decisions as possible without being able to refute α. Hence, PBS1 will not find any preferred solution that does not contain α. The problem is that PBS1 detects this only after having explored all elements of U (except those that are worse than α) and this can require a longer search.

In this section, we elaborate a set of non-monotonic inference rules that detect elements that belong to all preferred solutions or to none of them. They help to detect dead-ends earlier and avoid useless branching. In order to do this, the rules exploit the possible conflicts between decisions. A subset C of $\mathcal{A}$ is a *conflict* iff $\Gamma \cup C$ is inconsistent. A conflict C is *minimal* if no proper subset of C is a conflict. If C is a minimal conflict containing α then $C - \{\alpha\}$ is a *counterargument* for α. In order to refute α, we can, for example, make the decisions in $C - \{\alpha\}$. If the set of all possible decisions $\mathcal{A}$ does not contain any conflict then we are not able to refute any element. As a consequence, there is only a single preferred solution, namely $\mathcal{A}$.

Hence, multiple preferred solutions are only obtained if there are conflicts between decisions. Conflicts can therefore help to search for different preferred solution. Different techniques for exploiting conflicts have been proposed.

1. Hitting trees (Reiter 1987) pick a minimal conflict $\{\gamma_1, \ldots, \gamma_k\}$ in each search node and consider all possible ways to resolve it. For each element γ_i, a son node is introduced and γ_i is removed from the set of possible decisions in the son node. The set $\{\gamma_1, \ldots, \gamma_k\} - \{\gamma_i\}$ is a counterargument for γ_i. Elements of this counterargument can, however, be retracted in subsequent steps. If this happens then the retracted element γ_i may be consistent w.r.t. a solution. With other words, we can obtain unjustified retractions in the end.

2. TMS-based provers for default logic (Junker & Konolige 1990) require that all counterarguments for a default are pre-computed. If no counterargument for a default can ever be applied then a TMS-labelling algorithm labels the default with IN, which means that the default belongs to all TMS-labellings (i.e. all solutions).

Whereas the hitting tree approach picks a fixed counterargument in order to refute a decision α, the TMS-based approach just checks whether there exists a potential counterargument. We show how to integrate the TMS-based labelling rules into PBS. The TMS-based approach requires the pre-computation of all possible counterarguments for a decision α. Since there is an exponential number of conflicts in the

Algorithm $PBS2(\Gamma, \mathcal{A}, \prec)$
1. $A := \emptyset; U := \mathcal{A}; Q := \emptyset;$
2. **while** $Q \cup U \neq \emptyset$ **do**
3. $B := \{\alpha \in Q \cup U \mid \not\exists \beta \in Q \cup U : \beta \prec \alpha\};$
4.   **if** there is an $\alpha \in B \cap Q$ s.t.
5. $\Gamma \cup A \cup \{\alpha\}$ is inconsistent
6.   **then** $Q := Q - \{\alpha\}$ and continue;
7.   **if** $U = \emptyset$ and $Q \neq \emptyset$ **then** fail;
8.   **if** $B \cap U = \emptyset$ **then** fail;
9.   **if** there is an $\alpha \in B \cap U$ s.t.
10. $\Gamma \cup A \cup \{\alpha\}$ is inconsistent
11.   **then** $U := U - \{\alpha\}$ and continue;
12.   **if** there is an $\alpha \in Q$ s.t. $A \cup U - succ(\{\alpha\})$
13.   does not contain a counterargument to α
14.   **then** fail;
15.   **if** there is an $\alpha \in B \cap U$ s.t. $A \cup U - succ(\{\alpha\})$
16.   does not contain a counterargument to α
17.   **then** $A := A \cup \{\alpha\}; U := U - \{\alpha\};$ continue;
18.   select an $\alpha \in B \cap U$ and set $U := U - \{\alpha\};$
19.   **choose** $A := A \cup \{\alpha\}$ **or** $Q := Q \cup \{\alpha\};$
20. **return** $A;$

Figure 2: Algorithm PBS2

worst-case, this approach is not feasible. Instead of precomputing all counterarguments, we check for the absence of counterarguments during search. Even the check for the absence of a counterargument can computationally be very hard. We do not need to detect the absence of counterarguments in all cases. Instead, we can check sufficient conditions for the absence of counterarguments if this is computationally cheaper. We thus approximate the subproblem of counterargument checking as follows:

Definition 2 *Let X be a set of possible decisions and α be a decision to be refuted. A counterargument checker is a procedure that satisfies following condition: If applying the checker to X and α returns false then X does not contain a counterargument for α.*

Depending on the problem, we can implement very specific counterargument checkers and choose the sufficient conditions they are checking. We now extend algorithm PBS1 as follows: If an element α of Q has no counterargument in the set $A \cup U - \{\beta \in U \mid \alpha \prec \beta\}$ then we can never refute α and we have reached a dead-end. If we show the same property for an element α of U then we know in advance that we can never refute α. Hence, each preferred solution of the given state contains α and it is not necessary to branch. The resulting algorithm is given in figure 2.

In some cases, the set $A \cup U - \{\beta \in U \mid \alpha \prec \beta\}$ may contain a counterargument for α, but it involves decisions in U that can never be made. Below, we list some more complex properties that allow to limit the set of possible counterarguments even further. In the following, let B be the set of $\prec$-best elements of $Q \cup U$ and $succ(X) := \{\alpha \in U \mid \exists \beta \in X : \beta \prec \alpha\}$ the set of elements of U that are worse than the elements in X:

P6 if $\alpha \in Q$ and $A \cup U - succ(\{\alpha\})$ does not contain a counterargument for α then (A, Q, U) has no preferred solution.

P7 if $\alpha \in U$ and α is a $\prec$-best element of $Q \cup U$ and $A \cup U - succ(\{\alpha\})$ does not contain a counterargument for α then X is a preferred solution of (A, Q, U) iff X is a preferred solution of $(A \cup \{\alpha\}, Q, U - \{\alpha\})$.

P8 if $\alpha \in Q$ and $\beta \in U$ and each counterargument C for α with $C \subseteq A \cup U - succ(\{\alpha\})$ is also a counterargument for β then X is a preferred solution of (A, Q, U) iff X is a preferred solution of $(A, Q \cup \{\beta\}, U - \{\beta\})$.

P9 if there is a $Y \subseteq Q$ s.t. no $\alpha \in Y$ has a counterargument in $A \cup U - succ(Y)$ then (A, Q, U) has no preferred solution.

P10 if there is a $Y \subseteq B \cap U$ s.t. no $\alpha \in Y$ has a counterargument in $A \cup U - succ(Y)$ then X is a preferred solution of (A, Q, U) iff there is an $\alpha \in Y$ s.t. X is a preferred solution of $(A \cup \{\alpha\}, Q, U - \{\alpha\})$.

P11 if there is a $Y \subseteq U$ s.t. for all $\beta \in Y$ there exists an $\alpha \in Q$ s.t. each counterargument C for α with $C \subseteq A \cup U - succ(Y)$ is also a counterargument for β then X is a preferred solution of (A, Q, U) iff X is a preferred solution of $(A, Q \cup Y, U - Y)$.

Properties P6 and P7 are those used in PBS2. P6 allows to detect failures and P7 allows to detect elements that belong to all preferred solutions. P8 allows to detect elements that belong to no preferred solution. P9, P10, and P11 are generalizations of these rules that consider a set Y of decisions instead of a single one. Finding suitable sets Y that allow the application of P9, P10, and P11 is a non-trivial task. Again we can check sufficient conditions for applying P9, P10, and P11. For specific problems such as scheduling there are efficient techniques to identify some sets Y for P9, P10, and P11.

Preferences in Scheduling

We now apply PBS to selected scheduling problems, which are optimization problems. In addition to a set Γ of constraints, these problems have an objective z, which is an integer variable. v^* is the *optimal value* of the optimizations problem iff 1. the objective z is greater than or equal to v^* in all solutions (i.e. Γ implies $z \geq v^*$) and 2. the objective is equal to v^* in some solution (i.e. $\Gamma \cup \{z = v^*\}$ is consistent). A solution with an objective of v^* is called *optimal solution*.

Our purpose is to find a set of preferences that *preserves optimality* in the following sense: At least one optimal solution has to be a preferred one w.r.t. the given preferences. If an optimization problem has this property we can use PBS to solve it. We show that important scheduling problems have this property.

Resource-Constrained Project Scheduling

First we consider project scheduling problems that consist of a set of activities with fixed durations, a set of precedence constraints between the activities, and a set of resources with discrete capacities. For each activity, we introduce a start variable $s(a)$. If $d(a)$ is the fixed duration of the activity then $s(a) + d(a)$ denotes its end time. Activities may have release dates and due dates which leads to constraints of the form $s(a) \geq rd(a)$ and $s(a) + d(a) \leq dd(a)$. If an activity a_1 precedes an activity a_2 then the end time of a_1 is smaller than or equal to the start time of a_2, i.e. $s(a_1) + d(a_1) \leq s(a_2)$. Furthermore, an activity can require a fixed capacity of a given resource. For each time t, the sum of the required capacities of all activities that require a resource r and that are executed during t is smaller than or equal to the capacity of the resource. The objective of the problem is to minimize the makespan, i.e. the latest end time of the activities.

We now introduce preferences between start time assignments of the form $s(a) = t$. Let $\prec_1$ be the smallest strict partial order between those assignments that satisfies:

$$(s(a) = t_1) \prec_1 (s(a) = t_2) \quad \text{if} \quad t_1 < t_2$$
$$(s(a_1) = t_1) \prec_1 (s(a_2) = t_2) \quad \text{if} \quad t_1 + d(a_1) \leq t_2$$

Let $\prec_1$ be the transitive closure of the relation $\leftarrow_1$. The preferred solutions obtained by $\prec_1$ correspond to the left-shifted schedules.

Since PBS constantly does consistency checks it is necessary that those consistency checks are cheap and can be implemented by constraint propagation. Constraints that make the given problem difficult (e.g. due date constraints) are better treated separately.

Theorem 2 *Let Γ be a set of precedence, release date, and resource constraints and Δ be a set of due date constraints for a project scheduling problem. If $\Gamma \cup \Delta$ has a solution then there exists a preferred solution X of Γ and $\prec_1$ that is an optimal solution of $\Gamma \cup \Delta$.*

As usual, we can use an upper bound on the objective to prune the search for an optimal solution. For preferred solutions, we proceed as follows: Suppose we found a preferred solution that satisfies Δ and that has an objective value of v. If PBS explores a state $S := (A, Q, U)$ such that $\Gamma \cup A \cup \Delta \cup \{z < v\}$ is inconsistent then no preferred solution of this state will satisfy Δ and have a better objective than v. In this case, we can prune the subtree of S.

Alternatives Resources

PBS can also be applied to alternative resources. In this case, the resource required by an activity is not given, but belongs to a set of alternative resources. These resources can differ in speed and the duration $d(a, r)$ of an activity a is dependent on the resource r. The chosen resource of a is represented by a constraint variable $r(a)$. The end time of an activity now is $s(a) + d(a, r)$ if $r(a) = r$. A search decision now will assign and schedule an activity and has the form $s(a) = t \wedge r(a) = r$. Of course, we prefer faster resources for an activity a. If the alternative resources have task-independent preferences (i.e. if $d(a_1, r_1) < d(a_1, r_2)$ implies $d(a_2, r_1) < d(a_2, r_2)$ for all a_1, a_2, r_1, r_2) then we can prove that following preferences preserve optimality: Let $\prec_2$ be the smallest strict partial order between those assignments such that:

$$(s(a) = t_1 \wedge r(a) = r_1) \prec_2 (s(a) = t_2 \wedge r(a) = r_2)$$
$$\text{if } t_1 + d(a, r_1) < t_2 + d(a, r_2)$$

$$(s(a_1) = t_1 \wedge r(a_1) = r) \prec_2 (s(a_2) = t_2 \wedge r(a_2) = r)$$
$$\text{if } t_1 + d(a_1, r) \leq t_2$$

Implementation for Job-shop Problems

For first experiments, we implemented a special version of PBS2 for the special case of job-shop scheduling with ILOG SCHEDULER (ILOG 1997). The operations of PBS2 have been expressed in terms of activities and their earliest start times. We also obtain intuitive specializations of properties P6, P7, and P11.

First experimental results are very encouraging. The difficult job-shop problem MT20 has been solved in 56 sec. and with 69344 backtracks (on a Pentium II/300MHz using Linux). This includes the proof of optimality. If additionally the edge-finder of ILOG SCHEDULER is used, MT20 is solved in 6 sec. and with 3542 backtracks. Further improvements might be obtained by variable ordering heuristics and search methods such as LDS.

Related Work

The schedule-or-postpone method (Le Pape et al. 1994; ILOG 1997), which is used in numerous industrial project scheduling applications, can directly be seen as an implementation of the algorithm PBS1 for project scheduling problems and demonstrates its effectiveness. On the other hand, PBS provides a theoretical foundation for this method and PBS2 improves the schedule-or-postpone method significantly.

PBS has some concepts in common with Squeaky-wheel optimization (SWO) (Joslin & Clements 1998). SWO performs a local search through a space of possible prioritizations and uses them to produce greedy solutions. Depending on critical elements (trouble-makers) in the greedy solutions priorities are changed. A greedy solution can be seen as a preferred solution and its prioritization corresponds to the total order that produced the preferred solution. In contrast to SWO, PBS is a systematic search procedure which visits each preferred solution only once, whereas different prioritizations can lead to the same preferred solution.

Similar to PBS, heuristic repair (Minton et al. 1992) only abandons current (best) choices if it finds a reason for this in form of a violated constraint. For example, consider three activities a, b, c of duration 10 that all require the same resource of capacity 1. If the current start times are $s(a) = 0$, $s(b) = 5$, $s(c) = 10$ then a and b are in conflict. We might decide to push a after the end of b by changing $s(a)$ to 15. Next we treat the conflict between b and c and push b after the end of c by setting $s(b)$ to 20. Unfortunately, the reason for delaying a is no longer valid. Since we reproduce the same pattern after each step, we will even run into an infinite repair chain. PBS avoids this problem.

A standard approach for solving project scheduling problems consists in solving conflicts between activities by adding additional precedence constraints (cf. e.g. (Cesta, Oddi, & Smith 1999)). In contrast to this, PBS allows to do start time assignments which results into tighter constraints and more efficient propagation.

Conclusion

We have developed a systematic search procedure for combinatorial optimization problems. PBS uses a set of preferences in order to search through a space of preferred solutions, which is tighter than the space of all solutions. PBS uses non-monotonic inference rules that are inspired by Doyle's TMS and that exploit properties of preferred solution for doing the additional pruning of the search space.

We applied PBS to scheduling. We determined a set of preferences for project scheduling problems which preserve optimality (i.e. guarantee that at least one optimal solution is a preferred one). First experimental results for the job-shop problem MT20 show that PBS is capable to optimally solve difficult optimization problems. Future work is needed to compare PBS with other techniques for solving project scheduling problems (e.g. dominance rules) and to see for which advanced scheduling problems (e.g. with alternative resources) it can provide interesting results.

Future work will be spent to develop a variant of the PBS algorithm that is able to determine the 'G-preferred solutions' as defined by (Geffner & Pearl 1992; Grosof 1991). This will enable us to apply the PBS-idea to other optimization problems such as integer programming, assignment problems, and set covering.

Acknowledgements

I would like to thank the anonymous reviewers for very helpful comments. Without the moral support from my family, this paper would not have been written.

References

Brewka, G. 1989. Preferred subtheories: An extended logical framework for default reasoning. In *IJCAI-89*, 1043–1048. Detroit, MI: Morgan Kaufmann.

Cesta, A.; Oddi, A.; and Smith, S. F. 1999. An iterative sampling procedure for resource constrained project scheduling with time windows. In *IJCAI-99*, 1022–1029.

Geffner, H., and Pearl, J. 1992. Conditional entailment: Bridging two approaches to default reasoning. *Artificial Intelligence* 53:209–244.

Grosof, B. 1991. Generalizing prioritization. In *KR'91*, 289–300. Cambridge, MA: Morgan Kaufmann.

ILOG. 1997. Ilog Scheduler. Reference manual and User manual. V4.0, ILOG.

Joslin, D. E., and Clements, D. P. 1998. "Squeaky Wheel" Optimization. In *AAAI-98*, 340–346.

Junker, U., and Brewka, G. 1991. Handling partially ordered defaults in TMS. In Kruse, R., and Siegel, P., eds., *Symbolic and Quantitative Aspects for Uncertainty. Proceedings of the European Conference ECSQAU*. Berlin: Springer, LNCS 548. 211–218.

Junker, U., and Konolige, K. 1990. Computing the extensions of autoepistemic and default logics with a truth maintenance system. In *AAAI-90*, 278–283. Boston, MA: MIT press.

Laborie, P., and Ghallab, M. 1995. Planning with sharable resource constraints. In *IJCAI-95*.

Le Pape, C.; Couronné, P.; Vergamini, D.; and Gosselin, V. 1994. Time-versus-capacity compromises in project scheduling. In *Proc. of Thirteenth Workshop of the UK Planning Special Interest Group*.

Minton, S.; Johnston, M. D.; Philips, A. B.; and Laird, P. 1992. Minimizing conflicts: a heuristic repair method for constraint satisfaction and scheduling. *Artificial Intelligence* 58:161–205.

Reiter, R. 1987. A theory of diagnosis from first principles. *Artificial Intelligence* 32:57–952.

Smith, S., and Cheng, C. 1993. Slack-based heuristics for constraint satisfaction scheduling. In *AAAI-93*.

Divide-and-Conquer Frontier Search Applied to Optimal Sequence Alignment

Richard E. Korf
Computer Science Department
University of California, Los Angeles
Los Angeles, CA 90095
korf@cs.ucla.edu

Weixiong Zhang
USC Information Sciences Institute
4676 Admiralty Way
Marina del Rey, CA 90292-6695
zhang@isi.edu

Abstract

We present a new algorithm that reduces the space complexity of heuristic search. It is most effective for problem spaces that grow polynomially with problem size, but contain large numbers of short cycles. For example, the problem of finding an optimal global alignment of several DNA or amino-acid sequences can be solved by finding a lowest-cost corner-to-corner path in a d-dimensional grid. A previous algorithm, called divide-and-conquer bidirectional search (Korf 1999), saves memory by storing only the Open lists and not the Closed lists. We show that this idea can be applied in a unidirectional search as well. This extends the technique to problems where bidirectional search is not applicable, and is more efficient in both time and space than the bidirectional version. If n is the length of the strings, and d is the number of strings, this algorithm can reduce the memory requirement from $O(n^d)$ to $O(n^{d-1})$. While our current implementation of DCFS is somewhat slower than existing dynamic programming approaches for optimal alignment of multiple gene sequences, DCFS is a more general algorithm

Introduction: Sequence Alignment

While we present a completely general heuristic search algorithm, it was motivated by a problem in computational biology, known as sequence alignment. Consider the two DNA sequences ACGTACGTACGT and ATGTCGTCACGT. The problem is to align these sequences, by inserting gaps in each one, so that the number of matches between corresponding positions is maximized. For example, if we insert gaps as follows: ACGTACGT_ACGT and ATGT_CGTCACGT, then all the letters in corresponding positions are the same, except for the substitution of T for C in the second position.

The optimal solution to this problem is defined by a cost function. For example, we may charge a penalty of one unit for a mismatch or substitution between characters, and two units for a gap in either string. The cost of an alignment then is the sum of the individual substitution and gap costs. With this cost function, the alignment above has a cost of five, since there is one substitution and two gaps. The optimal alignment of a pair of strings is the alignment with the lowest cost, and the above alignment is optimal. Alignments are important for determining the structural similarity between different genes, and identifying subsequences that are conserved between them.

This problem can be mapped to the problem of finding a lowest-cost path from corner to corner in a two-dimensional grid (Needleman and Wunsch, 1970). One sequence is placed on the horizontal axis from left to right, and the other sequence on the vertical axis, from top to bottom. An alignment is represented by a path from the upper-left corner of the grid to the lower-right corner. Figure 1 shows the path that represents our example alignment. If there is no gap in either string at a given position, the path moves diagonally down and right, since this consumes both characters. The cost of such a move is zero if the corresponding characters match, or the substitution penalty if they differ. A gap in the vertical string is represented by a horizontal move right, since that consumes a character in the horizontal string, but leaves the position in the vertical string unchanged. Similarly, a gap in the horizontal string is represented by a vertical move down. Horizontal and vertical moves are charged the gap penalty. Given this mapping, the problem of finding an optimal sequence alignment corresponds to finding a lowest-cost path from the upper-left corner to the lower-right corner in the grid, where the legal moves at each point are right, down, and diagonally down and right.

This problem readily generalizes to aligning multiple strings simultaneously. For example, to align three strings, we find a lowest-cost path in a cube from one corner to the opposite corner. The cost of a multiple alignment is often computed as the sum-of-pairs cost, or the sum of each of the different pairwise alignments (Setubal and Meidanis, 1997). Equivalently, we can

---

Copyright © 2000, American Association for Artificial Intelligence (www.aaai.org). All rights reserved.

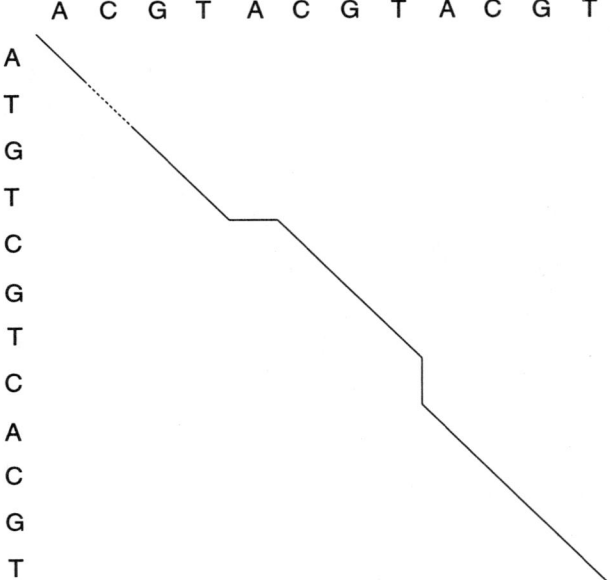

Figure 1: Sequence alignment as path-finding in a grid

score each character position by summing the cost of each of the character pairs. For example, if we have a C, a G, and a gap at one position, the cost at that position is two gap penalties plus a substitution penalty. If we have two gaps and a character at one position, the cost is two gap penalties, since no cost is charged for two gaps in the pair of strings that contain them.

Overview

We first discuss existing techniques for this problem. These include a dynamic programming algorithm (Hirschberg, 1975), a bounded dynamic programming algorithm (Spouge, 1989), and our previous best-first search algorithm, divide-and-conquer bidirectional search (DCBDS) (Korf, 1999). These methods save memory by only storing the frontier nodes of the search, and not the interior nodes. Our new algorithm, divide-and-conquer frontier search (DCFS), is closely related to DCBDS, but uses unidirectional rather than bidirectional search. This is more general, since bidirectional search is not always applicable, more efficient in time and space, and easier to implement. We also discuss the relative efficiencies of unidirectional and bidirectional search. For two-dimensional alignment, Hirschberg's algorithm seems to be the best. For three dimensions, however, an accurate heuristic evaluation function exists, and DCFS outperforms Hirschberg's algorithm and DCBDS, but is slower than bounded dynamic programming. All the algorithms apply to strings of unequal length, but we use strings of equal length in our experiments. Typical size problems that we can readily solve with these techniques are aligning pairs of strings of length 100,000 each, or three strings of length 6,000 each. The sizes of the corresponding grids are 10 billion nodes and 216 billion nodes, respectively.

Previous Work

For simplicity, we describe previous work in the context of aligning two strings, but all the algorithms can be generalized to multiple-string alignment as well. While most of the work in this area finds approximate alignments, we only consider here algorithms that are guaranteed to find optimal alignments.

Problems that Fit in Memory

If the grid is small enough to fit into memory, Dijkstra's single-source shortest path algorithm (Dijkstra, 1959) will solve the problem in $O(n^2)$ time and $O(n^2)$ space, for two strings of length n.

The particular problem of sequence alignment, as opposed to the general shortest-path problem, can also be solved by a much simpler dynamic programming algorithm. We scan the grid from left to right and from top to bottom, storing at each node the cost of a lowest cost path from the start node to that node. For each node, we add the gap cost to the cost of the nodes immediately to the left and immediately above, we add the substitution cost or no cost to the cost of the node diagonally above and to the left, and we store the smallest of these three sums in the current node. This also requires $O(n^2)$ time and $O(n^2)$ space.

Since both algorithms have to store the whole grid in memory, space is the main constraint. For example, if we assume that we can store 100 million nodes in memory, this limits us to aligning two strings of length 10,000 each, or three strings of length 464 each.

Problems that Don't Fit in Memory

The interesting case is when the grid doesn't fit in memory. One approach is to use a heuristic search, such as A* (Hart, Nilsson, and Raphael, 1968), to reduce the size of the search. This requires efficiently computing a lower bound on the cost of a given alignment, and has been applied to sequence alignment by (Ikeda and Imai, 1999). Unfortunately, A* stores every node it generates, and is still memory limited.

The memory limitation of best-first search algorithms like Dijkstra's and A* has been addressed (Korf, 1995). Many algorithms, such as iterative-deepening-A* (IDA*) (Korf, 1985), rely on depth-first search to avoid this memory limitation. The key idea is that a depth-first search only has to store the path of nodes from the start to the current node, and hence only requires space that is linear in the maximum search depth.

While depth-first search is very effective on problem spaces that are trees, or only contain a small number of cycles, it is hopeless on problem spaces with a large number of short cycles, such as a grid. The reason is that a depth-first search must generate every distinct path to a given node. In an $n \times m$ grid, the number of shortest paths from one corner to the opposite corner, ignoring diagonal moves, is $(n+m)!/(n! \cdot m!)$. For example, a 10×10 grid, which contains only 100 nodes, has 184,756 different corner-to-corner paths, and a 25×25 grid, with only 625 nodes, has over 10^{14} such paths. Adding diagonal moves increases these numbers further. As a result, depth-first searches are completely hopeless on this problem.

Other techniques, such as caching some nodes that are generated, have been applied to sequence alignment (Miura and Ishida, 1998). The difficulty with these techniques is that they can only cache a small fraction of the total nodes generated on a large problem, and can only solve relatively easy problems.

Hirschberg's Algorithm

(Hirschberg, 1975) presented an algorithm for computing a maximal common subsequence of two character strings in linear space, based on a two-dimensional grid, with each of the strings placed along one axis. A node of the grid corresponds to a pair of initial substrings of the original stings, and contains the length of a maximal common subsequence of the substrings.

The standard dynamic programming algorithm for this problem requires $O(n^2)$ time and $O(n^2)$ space, for two strings of length n. To compute an element of the grid, however, we only need the value immediately to its left and the value above it. Thus, we can solve the problem by only storing two rows at a time, deleting each row as soon as the next row is completed. In fact, only one row is needed, since we can replace elements of the row as soon as they are used. Unfortunately, this only yields the length of a maximal common subsequence, and not the subsequence itself.

Hirschberg's algorithm computes the first half of this grid from the top down, and the second-half from the bottom up, storing only one row at a time. Then, given the two versions of the middle row, one from each direction, it finds a column for which the sum of the two corresponding elements from each direction is a minimum. This point splits both original strings in two parts, and the algorithm is then called recursively on the initial substrings, and on the final substrings. Hirschberg's algorithm is easily generalized to solve the sequence alignment problem. It can also be generalized to more than two dimensions. These generalizations reduce the space complexity of the d-dimensional alignment problem from $O(n^d)$ to $O(n^{d-1})$, a very significant reduction. The additional cost in time is only a constant factor of two in two dimensions, and even smaller in higher dimensions.

Bounded Dynamic Programming

This algorithm can be improved by using upper and lower bounds on the cost of an optimal solution (Spouge, 1989). For pairwise alignments, a lower bound on the cost to reach the lower right corner of the grid is the gap penalty times the number of gaps needed to reach the corner. For multiple sequence alignments, a much more effective lower bound is available, which will be described in the section on experimental results. An upper bound on the cost of an optimal alignment is the cost of aligning the strings directly, with no gaps in either one. Given an upper bound on the optimal alignment cost, and a lower bound on the cost of aligning any pair of substrings, we can limit the dynamic programming algorithm to that region around the main diagonal in which the cost to reach each node, plus the estimated cost to reach the goal, is no greater that the upper bound on solution cost. For the top-level search, we start with an upper bound equal to the lower bound, and run a series of iterations, incrementally increasing the upper bound until it equals or exceeds the actual optimal alignment cost, and the iteration aligns the entire strings (Ukkonen, 1985). After each recursive search completes, we know the optimal solution costs of the next recursive searches, and use those values for the upper bounds. We refer to this algorithm as iterative-deepening bounded dynamic programming (IDBDP). These ideas are also used in MSA (Gupta, Kececioglu, and Schaffer, 1985), one of the best programs for optimal multiple sequence alignment.

Divide-and-Conquer Bidirectional Search

Divide-and-conquer bidirectional search (DCBDS) (Korf, 1999) generalizes Hirschberg's dynamic programming algorithm to arbitrary path-finding problems. To apply dynamic programming, we have to know in advance which neighbors of a node are its ancestors and which are its descendents, in order to evaluate the ancestors of a node before the node itself. We can do this in the sequence alignment problem because only moves down, right, and diagonally down and right are allowed, making the nodes above, to the left, and diagonally up and left the ancestors. In the general case, where moves to any neighboring nodes are allowed, we can't apply dynamic programming, but rather must apply a best-first search such as Dijkstra's algorithm. DCBDS achieves the same memory savings of Hirschberg's algorithm, but for the general shortest-path problem in any graph.

A best-first search, such as Dijkstra's or A*, stores both a Closed list of nodes that have been expanded, and an Open list of nodes that have been generated, but not yet expanded. The Open list corresponds to the frontier of the search, while the Closed list corresponds to the interior region. In the A* cost function, $f(x) = g(x) + h(x)$, $g(x)$ is the cost from the initial state to node x, and $h(x)$ is a heuristic estimate of the cost from node x to a goal. If h has the property that for all nodes x and their neighbors x', $h(x) \leq c(x, x') + h(x')$, where $c(x, x')$ is the cost from node x to its neighbor x', we say that h is *consistent*. Since consistency is similar to the triangle inequality of all metrics, almost all naturally occurring heuristic functions are consistent. If the heuristic function is consistent, or in the absence of a heuristic function, once an Open node is expanded, an optimal path has been found to it, and it never is expanded again. In that case, we can execute a best-first search without storing the Closed list at all.

In an exponential problem space with a branching factor of two or more, the Open list is larger than the Closed list, and not storing the Closed list doesn't save much. In a polynomial space, however, the dimension of the frontier is one less than that of the interior, resulting in significant memory savings. For example, in a two-dimensional grid, the Closed list is quadratic in size, while the size of the Open list is only linear.

There are two challenges with this approach. The first is that duplicate node expansions are normally eliminated by checking new nodes against the Open and Closed lists. Without the Closed list, to prevent the search from "leaking" back into the closed region, DCBDS stores with each Open node a list of forbidden operators that lead to closed nodes. For each node, this is initially just the operator that leads to its parent. As each node is generated, it is compared against the nodes on the Open list, and if it already appears on Open, only the copy arrived at via a lowest-cost path is saved. When this happens, the new list of forbidden operators for the node becomes the union of the forbidden operators of each copy.

In some problem spaces the operators or edges are directed. For example, in the two-dimensional sequence alignment problem, the only legal operators from a node are to move down, right, or diagonally down and right. After expanding a given node and removing it from Open, if the node immediately above it has not yet been expanded for example, when it is expanded it will regenerate the given node, and place it back on Open. This will cause the search to leak back into the closed region, eliminating the space savings. One solution to this problem is that when a node is expanded, all of its neighboring nodes are generated, including nodes generated by an edge going the wrong way, such as the nodes above, to the left, and diagonally up and left in this case. These latter nodes are also placed on Open, but their cost is set to infinity, indicating that they haven't been arrived at via a legal path yet. By placing all the neighbors of a node on Open when it is expanded, we ensure that a closed node can't be regenerated, and prevent the search from leaking back into the closed region.

Saving only the Open list can be used to speed up the standard Dijkstra's and A* algorithms as well. It is faster not to generate a node at all, than to generate it and then search for it in the Open and Closed lists. On a two-dimensional grid, this technique alone speeds up Dijkstra's algorithm by over 25%.

The main value of this technique, however, is that it executes a best-first search without a Closed list, and never expands a state more than once. When the algorithm completes, it has the cost of an optimal path to a goal, but unfortunately not the path itself. If the path to each node is stored with the node, each node will require space linear in its path length, eliminating all of the space savings. In fact, this approach requires more space than the standard method of storing the paths via pointers through the Closed list, since it doesn't allow the sharing of common subpaths.

One way to construct the path is the following. Perform a bidirectional search from both initial and goal states simultaneously, until the two search frontiers meet, at which point a node on a solution path has been found. Its cost is the sum of the path costs from each direction. Continue the search, saving the middle node on the best path found so far, until the best solution cost is less than or equal to the sum of the lowest-cost nodes on each search frontier. At this point we have a node on a lowest-cost solution path. Save this node in a solution vector. Then, recursively apply the same algorithm to find an optimal path from the initial state to the middle node, and from the middle node to the goal state. Each of these searches adds another node to the final solution path, and generates two more recursive subproblems, etc, until the entire solution is reconstructed.

Divide-and-Conquer Frontier Search

Our new algorithm, divide-and-conquer frontier search (DCFS), also saves memory by storing only the Open list and not the Closed list, but using unidirectional rather than bidirectional search.

Consider our problem of finding an optimal corner-to-corner path in a two-dimensional grid. DCFS begins with a single search from the initial state to the goal state, saving only the Open list, in the same manner as described for DCBDS. When the search encounters a node on a horizontal line that splits the grid in half, each of the children of that node store the coordinates of the node. For every Open node that is past this halfway line, we save the coordinates of the node on the halfway line that is on the current path from the initial state to the given Open node. Once the search reaches the goal state via an optimal path, the corresponding node on the halfway line is an intermediate node roughly halfway along this optimal path. We then recursively solve two subproblems using the same algorithm: find an optimal path from the initial state to this middle node, and find an optimal path from the middle node to the goal node. If the original grid, or one defined by a recursive subproblem, is wider than it is tall, we choose a vertical line to represent the set of possible halfway nodes instead of a horizontal line.

In a grid problem space, we can easily identify a set of nodes that will contain a node roughly halfway along the optimal solution. In a three-dimensional grid, for example, the halfway line becomes a halfway plane, cutting the cube in half either horizontally or vertically. In a general problem-space graph however, identifying such nodes is only slightly more difficult. If we have a heuristic evaluation function, we can choose as a midpoint node one for which $g(x)$, the cost from the initial state to node x, equals $h(x)$, the heuristic estimate from node x to a goal node. If we don't have a heuristic function, but have an estimate of the total solution cost c, we can use as a halfway node any node x for which $g(x)$ is approximately $c/2$.

There are several advantages of unidirectional DCFS over bidirectional DCBDS. One is that unidirectional search is more general, and can be applied to problems that bidirectional search cannot be applied to. For example, if we only have a test for a goal, and don't have an explicit goal state in advance, we may not be able to apply bidirectional search. Secondly, unidirectional search may be more efficient, as we will see below. Finally, unidirectional search is simpler and easier to implement correctly.

Bidirectional vs. Unidirectional Search

Which is more efficient, bidirectional or unidirectional search? The answer is different for brute-force and heuristic searches. A common unidirectional brute-force algorithm is Dijkstra's algorithm or uniform-cost search, a best-first search using the cost function $f(x) = g(x)$. The algorithm terminates when a goal node is chosen for expansion, or the cost of a goal node is less than or equal to the cost of all Open nodes.

To guarantee an optimal solution, bidirectional uniform-cost search terminates when the cost of the best solution found so far is less than or equal to the sum of the minimum $f(x) = g(x)$ costs in the two search frontiers. Thus, the two search frontiers only go half the distance to the goal, instead of one frontier extending all the way to the goal. As a result, bidirectional uniform-cost search usually expands fewer nodes than unidirectional uniform-cost search, with the difference increasing with increasing branching factor of the problem space.

The situation is different for A*, however, which uses $f(x) = g(x) + h(x)$ for its cost function. To guarantee optimal solutions, bidirectional A* terminates when the best solution found so far costs no more than the minimum $f(x) = g(x) + h(x)$ cost in either direction. Since this is the same terminating condition for each of the unidirectional searches, bidirectional A* generates more nodes than unidirectional A*, by virtue of performing two such searches. We could also terminate bidirectional A* when the sum of the minimum $g(x)$ costs in the two directions exceeds the cost of the best solution so far, but with an accurate heuristic function the former terminating condition will occur first.

In addition to the number of nodes generated, we also need to consider the time per node generation. In our experiments, described below, various overheads in bidirectional search made it more expensive per node generation than the unidirectional version.

In terms of memory, unidirectional search only has to maintain a single search horizon, while bidirectional search has to maintain two. This can result in up to a factor of two difference in space complexity. In practice, the difference may be smaller, since the unidirectional search horizon will be larger than an individual bidirectional search horizon.

Finally, unidirectional search is much simpler to implement than bidirectional search. Thus, unidirectional heuristic search is often preferable to bidirectional heuristic search because it generates fewer nodes, takes less time per node generation, requires less memory, and is easier to implement. For a more thorough treatment of bidirectional heuristic search, see (Kaindl and Kainz, 1997).

Experimental Results

We tested our algorithms on random sequence alignment problems. Each triple of DNA base pairs encodes one of 20 different amino acids. For each problem instance we generated random 20-character strings, simulating amino-acid sequences, and computed an opti-

Length	DCBDA*			DCFA*			IDBDP		
	Nodes	Mbytes	Seconds	Nodes	Mbytes	Seconds	Nodes	Mbytes	Seconds
1000	4,385,088	48	4.66	2,428,388	15	1.55	1,478,166	20	2.38
2000	45,956,680	119	50.04	24,147,383	56	17.05	12,419,072	78	15.78
3000	184,459,312	248	212.01	94,778,522	117	77.99	46,080,688	173	55.66
4000	464,723,712	472	665.65	236,315,529	221	192.33	111,106,632	306	136.96
5000	979,234,880	575	1398.18	496,715,891	272	498.53	237,084,672	478	275.41
6000				883,732,606	463	896.78	466,050,656	689	556.162

Table 1: 3-Way Alignment of Random 20-Character Strings

mal alignment between them. We chose random problems to allow generating a large number of problem instances. Our cost function charges nothing for a match, one unit for a substitution, and two units for a gap.

For aligning two strings, the best lower-bound heuristic is the number of gap penalties required to reach the bottom-right corner. This allows us to use the A* cost function, $f(x) = g(x) + h(x)$, with DCBDS and DCFS. We refer to the A* versions of these algorithms as divide-and-conquer bidirectional A* (DCBDA*) and divide-and-conquer frontier A* (DCFA*), respectively. This heuristic is relatively weak, however, and both algorithms examine a large fraction of the nodes in the grid. Since Hirschberg's algorithm has significantly lower overhead per node, it is more efficient in this case. In practice, Hirschberg's algorithm will optimally align two strings of length 100,000 in about 21 minutes, on a 440 megahertz Sun Ultra 10 workstation, the machine used for all our experiments. This requires generating 20 billion nodes.

In three dimensions, corresponding to the simultaneous alignment of three strings, there is a much more effective lower-bound heuristic function available. Recall that the cost function for multiple-string alignment is the sum-of-pairs cost, meaning the sum of the costs of each of the pairwise alignments induced by the three-way alignment. To compute this heuristic function, we optimally align each pair of strings, and then use the sum of the optimal pairwise alignments as a lower bound on the cost of the best three-way alignment. This is a very accurate heuristic function, and greatly reduces the number of nodes that are expanded by the best-first algorithms. The reason this heuristic is not the same as the actual cost is that in the optimal three-way alignment, each of the pairs of strings will not be optimally aligned in general. The reason it is a lower bound is that the cost of the actual alignment of each pair induced by the three-way alignment must be at least as great as the cost of their optimal pairwise alignments. To compute the optimal pairwise alignments, we use the standard dynamic programming algorithm, since it is the most efficient for pairwise alignment.

These values are precomputed and stored, instead of recomputed for each node.

For each problem instance, we generated three random strings, and optimally aligned them. Table 1 shows the average results of 100 problem instances for each case. We ran three different algorithms, all of which return optimal alignments. For each algorithm we give the average number of nodes generated, the amount of memory used in megabytes, and the average running time per problem instance in seconds.

Hirschberg's algorithm is not competitive in more than two dimensions, since it doesn't use a lower bound function, and generates every node in the space at least once. For example, for three strings of length 1000, it generates 1.3 billion nodes, and takes 405 seconds to run, compared to a few seconds for the other algorithms.

The first algorithm in the table is divide-and-conquer bidirectional A* (DCBDA*), and the second is divide-and-conquer frontier A* (DCFA*), both using the same heuristic function. DCFA* generates about half the nodes of DCBDA*, and runs more than twice as fast, due to higher overhead per node. It also uses about half the memory. 640 megabytes was not enough memory to run DCBDA* on strings of length 6000.

The last algorithm in the table is iterative-deepening bounded dynamic programming (IDBDP), described above in the previous work section. IDBDP generates fewer nodes than DCFA*, primarily because DCFA* applies operators in all directions, including the illegal backward directions, to keep the search from leaking into the closed region. IDBDP also runs faster than DCFA* on strings of length 2000 or longer. Our current implementation of IDBDP uses more memory than DCFA*, but this can be reduced.

It should be noted that the absolute performance of these algorithms is sensitive to the cost function, the size of the alphabet, and the correlation of the strings. Thus, these results can only be used for relative comparison of the different algorithms. For example, changing the alphabet to 4 characters to simulate random DNA strings degrades the performance of all three algorithms significantly. On the other hand, since real data is much more highly correlated than random strings, we expect the performance on real data to be significantly better.

Conclusions

We have generalized divide-and-conquer bidirectional search (DCBDS) to unidirectional divide-and-conquer frontier search (DCFS). DCFS is a completely general heuristic search algorithm. Like DCBDS, DCFS reduces the space complexity of finding a lowest-cost path in a d-dimensional grid from $O(n^d)$ to $O(n^{d-1})$. Unlike DCBDS, however, DCFS can be applied to problems that don't allow bidirectional search. In addition, DCFS uses less memory, runs faster, and is easier to implement than DCBDS.

We applied DCFA*, the A* version of DCFS, to find optimal alignments for three random strings of up to 6000 characters each. The performance of DCFA* is compared to that of existing dynamic programming algorithms for optimal sequence alignment of more than three strings. Our current implementation runs faster on problems of length less than 2000 characters, but slower on larger problems.

Acknowledgements

We'd like to thank Matt Ginsberg, Andrew Parks, Louis Steinberg, and Victoria Cortessis for helpful discussions on this research. This research was supported by NSF grants No. IRI-9619447 and IRI-9619554.

References

[1] Dijkstra, E.W., A note on two problems in connexion with graphs, *Numerische Mathematik*, Vol. 1, 1959, pp. 269-71.

[2] Hart, P.E., N.J. Nilsson, and B. Raphael, A formal basis for the heuristic determination of minimum cost paths, *IEEE Transactions on Systems Science and Cybernetics*, Vol. SSC-4, No. 2, July 1968, pp. 100-107.

[3] Hirschberg, D.S., A linear space algorithm for computing maximal common subsequences, *Communications of the ACM*, Vol. 18, No. 6, June, 1975, pp. 341-343.

[4] Gupta, S.K., J.D. Kececioglu, and A.A. Schaffer, Improving the practical space and time efficiency of the shortest-paths approach to sum-of-pairs multiple sequence alignment, *Journal of Computational Biology*, Vol. 3, No. 2, 1995, pp. 459-472.

[5] Ikeda, T., and H. Imai, Enhanced A* algorithms for multiple alignments: optimal alignments for several sequences and k-opt approximate alignments for large cases, *Theoretical Computer Science*, Vol. 210, No. 2, Jan. 1999, pp. 341-374.

[6] Kaindl, H., and G. Kainz, Bidirectional heuristic search reconsidered, *Journal of Artificial Intelligence Research*, Vol. 7, 1997, pp. 283-317.

[7] Korf, R.E., Depth-first iterative-deepening: An optimal admissible tree search, *Artificial Intelligence*, Vol. 27, No. 1, 1985, pp. 97-109.

[8] Korf, R.E., Space-efficient search algorithms, *Computing Surveys*, Vol. 27, No. 3, Sept., 1995, pp. 337-339.

[9] Korf, R.E., Divide-and-conquer bidirectional search: First results, *Proceedings of the Sixteenth International Joint Conference on Artificial Intelligence (IJCAI-99)*, Stockholm, Sweden, August 1999, pp. 1184-1189.

[10] Miura, T., and T. Ishida, Stochastic node caching for memory-bounded search, *Proceedings of the National Conference on Artificial Intelligence (AAAI-98)*, Madison, WI, July, 1998, pp. 450-456.

[11] Needleman, S.B., and C.D. Wunsch, A general method applicable to the search for similarities in the amino acid sequences of two proteins, *Journal of Molecular Biology*, Vol. 48, 1970, pp. 443-453.

[12] Setubal, J., and J. Meidanis, *Introduction to Computational Molecular Biology*, PWS Publishing, Boston, MA, 1997.

[13] Spouge, J.L., Speeding up dynamic programming algorithms for finding optimal lattice paths, *SIAM Journal of Applied Math*, Vol. 49, No. 5, 1989, pp. 1552-1566.

[14] Ukkonen, E., Algorithms for approximate string matching, *Information and Control*, Vol. 64, 1985, pp. 100-118.

Asynchronous Search with Aggregations

Marius Călin Silaghi and **Djamila Sam-Haroud** and **Boi Faltings**
Swiss Federal Institute of Technology, Artificial Intelligence Lab, DI-LIA, CH-1015 Lausanne, Switzerland
{silaghi,haroud,faltings}@lia.di.epfl.ch

Abstract

Many problem-solving tasks can be formalized as *constraint satisfaction problems* (CSPs). In a multi-agent setting, information about constraints and variables may belong to different agents and be kept confidential. Existing algorithms for distributed constraint satisfaction consider mainly the case where access to variables is restricted to certain agents, but constraints may have to be revealed. In this paper, we propose methods where constraints are private but variables can be manipulated by any agent.

We describe a new search technique for distributed CSPs, called *asynchronous aggregation search* (AAS). It differs from existing methods in that it treats sets of partial solutions, exchanges information about aggregated valuations for combinations of variables and uses customized messages to allow distributed solution detection. Three new distributed backtracking algorithms based on AAS are then presented and analyzed. While the approach we propose provides a more general framework for dealing with privacy requirements on constraints, our experiments show that its overall performance is comparable or better than that of existing methods.

Keywords: search, distributed AI, constraint satisfaction

Introduction

Multi-agent systems are often used for solving combinatorial problems such as resource allocation, scheduling, or planning. *Constraint satisfaction* has proven to be a highly successful paradigm for solving such problems in centralized settings. A constraint satisfaction problem (CSP) is given by:

- a set of n *variables* $x_1, ..., x_n$,
- a set of n *domains*, $D_1, ..., D_n$, for the variables,
- a set of k *relations*, $r_1 = (x_i, x_j, ...), ..., r_k$, each of which is a subset of the set of variables, and
- a set of k *constraints*, $C_1, ..., C_k$. C_i gives the allowed value combinations for the corresponding relation r_i.

A *solution* to a CSP is an assignment of values from the corresponding domains to each variable such that for all relations, the combination of assigned values is allowed by the corresponding constraint. Many combinatorial problems, such as resource allocation, scheduling and planning can be modeled as CSPs. A *distributed* CSP (DCSP) arises when information is distributed among several agents. In the common definition of DCSP (Yokoo et al. 92), variables are distributed among agents so that each variable can only be assigned values by a single agent. Several *Asynchronous Search* (AS) algorithms have been developed that allow solving such problems by exchanging messages about variable assignments and conflicts with constraints (called nogoods) (Yokoo et al. 92; Hamadi & Bessière 98).

Asynchronous Search

In this section, we recall the basic background of AS using a small example (Figure 1). Without loosing the fundamental characteristics of AS, we restrict our description to the case with unbounded nogood recording (Yokoo et al. 92) and where each agent has exactly one variable. In this framework, each agent is responsible for maintaining the value of one variable. It has a link toward any agent that owns a constraint involving that variable. Agents are arranged in a priority order. A constraint is enforced by the agent which has the highest priority among those that are responsible for one of the variables in the corresponding relation.

In our example, there are four agents, A^1, A^2, A^3, A^4 who control the variables x_1, x_2, x_3, x_4, with identical domains $D_1=D_2=D_3=D_4=\{0,1,2,3\}$. Agent A^1 wants to ensure that $3x_1 + 1 > x_3$, A^2 wants to have $x_1 > x_2 - 2$, A^3 requires that $x_1 > x_3 - 2$, and A^4 needs $x_2 + x_3 - x_4 > 4$ to hold. In order to solve this problem with conventional AS techniques, we first need to assign a priority to each agent, then move certain constraints to the agent with the higher priority. Let us assume that A^{i+1} has precedence over A^i. In this case, A^1's constraint has to be communicated to A^3 which will be responsible for its enforcement. Each agent will start by randomly assigning to its variable a value from its domain (0 in our example). Upon asynchronous backtracking, the local search space for each agent is determined by its local constraints along with the restrictions imposed by the other agents via **ok?** and **nogood** messages. When an agent assigns a value to its variable, it sends an **ok?**(var=value) message to all the higher-priority agents having a link with it. These agents then evaluate their constraints on that variable. If these constraints are satisfied by the new assignment, given all the known values for the other variables, they do nothing, otherwise they try a new value for

---

Copyright © 2000, American Association for Artificial Intelligence (www.aaai.org). All rights reserved.

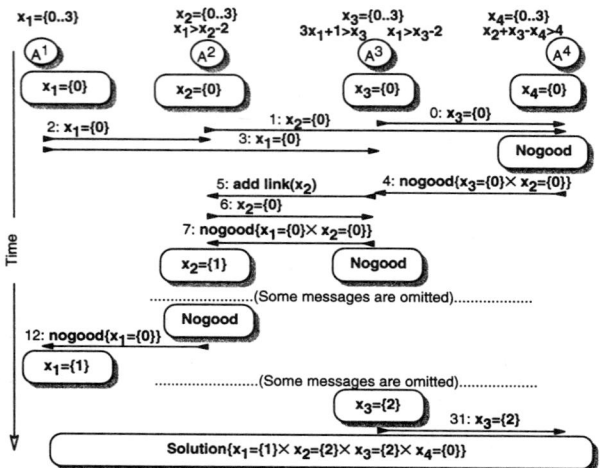
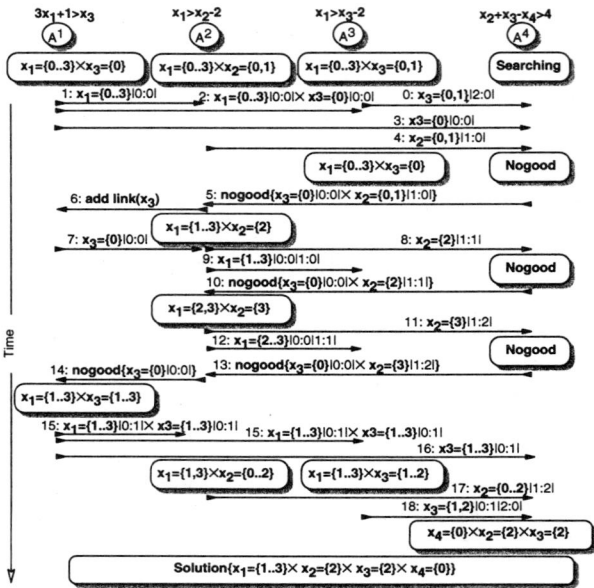

Figure 1: *Simplified trace of an asynchronous search process. Each agent A^i is assorted with a variable x_i, a set of constraints involving this variable and states represented by boxes. A state shows either the assignment chosen for the owned variable or a conflicting situation (nogood). The arrows represent messages. Each message is prefixed by a number.*

Figure 2: *Trace of a search with AAS. The states of the agents can be represented by the current solution to the local CSP defined by their constraints. The pairs $|a, b|$ included in the messages are used for message ordering.*

their variable. If any of them finds no available value, then it generates a **nogood** message. The agent receiving this **nogood** message will then have to incorporate the information in its local search space and change the faulty assignment or generate other nogoods, accordingly. Hence, constraints are always evaluated by higher-priority agents and values always changed by lower priority ones.

Figure 1 shows a simplified trace of message passing obtained for our example using the asynchronous backtracking algorithm described in (Yokoo et al. 92).

Each agent starts by assigning the value 0 to its variable. Agent A^1 then sends an **ok?** message to A^2 and A^3 and agents A^2 and A^3 both send **ok?** messages to A^4. Agents A^2 and A^3 both find the value received from A^1 to be compatible with their constraints. Hence, they do not react. However, A^4's constraint is violated and this agent returns a **nogood** message (4) to A^3.

Private constraints

In the AS formulation, constraints may need to be revealed to any other agent that controls a variable in the corresponding constraint. This corresponds well to certain applications, for example distributed control, but less well to negotiation where variables are public but constraints are private. In this paper, we address this latter case by proposing a technique called *Asynchronous Aggregation Search*. It differs from asynchronous search by the fact that agents exchange messages not about assignments to individual variables, but about tuples of variables. This allows eliminating restrictions on the order in which constraints are treated. Coupled with the fact that AAS allows aggregating ranges of tuples, we obtain efficiency gains over the existing asynchronous backtracking algorithms. The evaluation is done using three different implementations, based respectively on full, partial and no nogood recording.

Asynchronous Search with Aggregations

We now introduce *asynchronous aggregation search* (AAS), a new technique that propagates aggregated tuples of values rather than individual values themselves. In AAS, each agent maintains values for the set of variables in which it is involved. Thus, A^1 maintains value combinations for x_1 and x_3, A^2 for x_1 and x_2, A^3 for x_1 and x_3, and A^4 for all of x_2, x_3 and x_4 (see Figure 2). AAS differs from AS in the fact that message arguments are not just individual assignments, but Cartesian products of assignments (Hubbe & Freuder 92) to different variables. More precisely, in the current implementation of AAS, an assignment is a list of domains, one for each involved variable, which represent all the tuples of their Cartesian product. The assignment $x_1 = \{0..3\}, x_2 = \{0, 1\}$, for example, will represent all the tuples of the Cartesian product $\{0..3\} \times \{0, 1\}$. Similarly, a solution is no longer a list of individual assignments, but a Cartesian product of domains which represents a set of possible valuations. In scheduling and resource allocation problems with large domains, the savings allowed by the Cartesian product representation can be particularly significant.

Figure 2 illustrates the behavior of AAS on our small example. Agent A^1 first selects the Cartesian product $\{x_1 = \{0..3\}\} \times \{x_3 = \{0\}\}$, and sends an **ok?** message with the needed parts of this information to A^2, A^3 and A^4 who manage constraints sharing variables with A^1. The algorithm now works in exactly the same manner as AS, except that messages refer to Cartesian products and agents select different Cartesian products rather than value assignments. More specifically, A^4 finds that no combination in the Cartesian product $\{x_2 = \{0,1\}\} \times \{x_3 = \{0\}\}$ is compatible with its constraint. It therefore generates a **nogood** for this combination which causes A^2 to select the next Cartesian product. Note that since this change selects a subrange of the values allowed by the knowledge of A^2 for x_1, it is not necessary to verify this change with A^1. If it were not possible to find such a subrange, a **nogood** would be generated and sent to A^1 in order to try another Cartesian-product there.

There are several ways in which the agents can build the aggregations. Aggregation algorithms guaranteeing a complete and non-redundant covering of the solution space determined by local constraints are given in (Hubbe & Freuder 92; Haselböck 93; Silaghi, Sam-Haroud, & Faltings 2000).

AAS Algorithms

In this section we will present three distributed backtrack search algorithms based on aggregation. We start by giving the necessary background and definitions. Similarly to the AS algorithm of (Yokoo et al. 92), the agents are assigned priorities. We assume that the agent A^i has priority over another agent A^j if $i > j$. A *link* exists between two agents if they share a variable. The link is directed from the agent with lower priority to the agent with higher priority. Let A^i and A^j be two agents related by a link such that $i > j$. A^i is called the *predecessor* of A^j and conversely, A^j is called the *successor* of A^i. The *end agents* are those without incoming links. The *system agent* is a special agent that receives the subscriptions of the agents for the search. It decides the order of the agents, initializes the links and announces the termination of the search.

Definition 1 (Assignment) *An assignment is a triplet (x_j, set_j, h_j) where x_j is a variable, set_j a set of values for x_j and h_j a history of the pair (x_j, set_j).*

The history provides the information necessary for a correct message ordering. It determines if a given assignment is more recent than another and will be described in more details later. Let $a_1 = (x_j, set_j, h_j)$ and $a_2 = (x_j, set'_j, h'_j)$ be two assignments for the variable x_j. a_1 is *newer* than a_2 if h_j is more recent than h'_j.

Definition 2 *An* aggregate *is a list of assignments.*

An aggregate will be denoted compactly by (V, S, H) where V is the set of variables, and S and H their respective sets of values and histories.

Definition 3 (Explicit nogood) *An explicit nogood has the form $\neg V$, where V is an aggregate.*

The agents communicate using channels without message loss via:

- **ok?** messages which have as parameter an aggregate. They represent proposals of domains for a given set of variables and are sent from agents with lower priorities to agents with higher priorities. An agent sends **ok?** messages containing only domains in which the target agent is interested. He does not send domains for assignments he was proposed and he has never changed. If he has not just

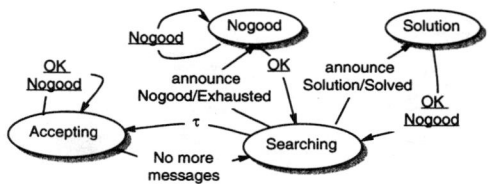

Figure 3: *Backtrack search procedure for each agent*

discarded a recent applicable nogood[1], then he sends only the domains for which he proposes a new modification now. **ok?** messages are also sent as answers to **add-link** messages.

- **nogood** messages which have as parameter an explicit nogood. A **nogood** message is sent from an agent with higher priority to an agent with lower priority, namely to the agent with the highest priority among those that have modified an assignment in the parameter. An empty parameter signals failure.

- **add-link**(vars) messages: sent from agent A^j to agent A^i (with $j > i$). They inform A^i that A^j is interested in the variables $vars$.

Each agent A^i owns a set of local constraints. The variables A^i is *interested in*, are those implied in its local constraints, called the *local variables* and those establishing links with other agents. The *current solution space* of A^i, denoted as C_{A^i}, is described by the local constraints, a list of explicit nogoods and a *view*.

Definition 4 (View) *The view of an agent A^i is an aggregate (V, S, H) such that V contains variables A^i is interested in.*

A view imposes restrictions on the original search space defined by the local constraints of an agent. It contains for each variable, the newest received assignment via **ok?** messages.

Definition 5 (Entailed nogood) *Let V_1 be the view of a given agent, T be the set of tuples disabled from the original solution space by V_1. We say that the nogood $V_1 \rightarrow \neg T$ is entailed by the view V_1.*

A tuple is *contained* in the current solution space of agent A^i if it satisfies the local constraints and is not contained in the explicit or entailed nogoods of C_{A^i}. The *current instantiation* of an agent A^i is a Cartesian product such that all its tuples are contained in C_{A^i}. The list of nogoods, respectively the view, of an agent A^i is updated by the **nogood**, respectively **ok?** messages it receives.

We now propose the following three distributed backtrack search algorithms based on aggregation:

- **AAS-2**: is based on full nogood recording similarly to the AS algorithm of (Yokoo et al. 92).

- **AAS-1**: proceeds similarly to dynamic backtracking (Ginsberg & McAllester 94). It removes the nogoods depending on the instantiation of the modified variables, guaranteeing polynomial space complexity.

---

[1]This refers to nogoods discarded, as described later, since the last instantiation, within the reset CL of AAS0

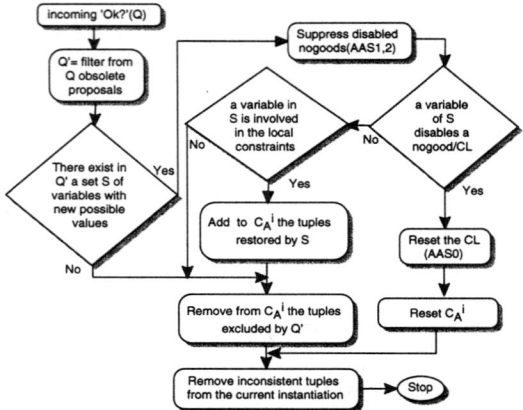

Figure 4: *OK procedure.*

- AAS-0: is a modification of AAS1 with less nogood recording. AAS0 is a novel algorithm which merges all the nogoods maintained by each agent of AAS1 into a single nogood using the relaxation rule:

$$\frac{\begin{array}{c} V_1 \wedge V_2 \rightarrow \neg T^1 \\ V_1 \wedge V_3 \rightarrow \neg T^2 \end{array}}{\Rightarrow \quad V_1 \wedge V_2 \wedge V_3 \rightarrow \neg(T^1 \vee T^2)}, \quad (1)$$

where V_1, V_2 and V_3 are aggregates, obtained by grouping the elements of the nogoods, such that they have no variable in common. Each agent maintains a single explicit nogood which integrates each new incoming explicit nogood using the relaxation rule.

In the case of AAS0, the right part of the nogood description corresponds to the expanded tuples and the left one is referred to as the conflict list (CL).

The core backtrack procedure for each agent is the same for the three algorithms. It is given by the finite state machine of Figure 3. At the beginning, each agent A^i is in the state Searching where it tries to generate a current instantiation from C_{A^i}. At any time in the state Searching, an agent can transit into the state Accepting where it accepts **ok?** or **nogood** messages. These cause the agent to execute the procedures Ok, respectively Nogood which update the local search space (i.e the views, the nogoods lists and the position in the search tree) according to the content of the messages. When, in the state Searching, its C_{A^i} is empty, the agent A^i announces a nogood and transits into the state Nogood. When, on the contrary, a local solution is found (i.e. a set of tuples can be extracted from C_{A^i}), the agent announces the instantiation by sending **ok?** messages to the concerned agents and transits into the state Solution. The current instantiation of the agent is known as long as it remains in the state Solution.

The three algorithms differ by the actions undertaken in the procedures Ok and Nogood, respectively described in Figures 4 and 5.

The procedure Ok treats incoming **ok?** messages. The parameter Q, of such a message is an aggregate. We say that a given assignment (x_j, set_j, h_j) of Q is *obsolete* if the view of the receiving agent contains a newer assignment for x_j. The procedure Ok starts by filtering the obsolete assignments and then proceeds to updating the set C_{A^i} according to the remaining valid assignments. Suppose that one of these assignments offers a new possibility of valuation for an external variable x_j with respect to the current view. In AAS2 or AAS1 all the nogoods which do not take the new possibility into account will be *disabled*. In AAS1 this means that they will be removed. In AAS2 they will be marked and kept for an eventual further usage. In AAS0, if the nogood obtained by the relaxed inference rule contains such a variable but does not take the new value into account, the conflict list will be reset. Resetting C_{A^i} means that all the tuples allowed by the current nogoods and view are introduced in C_{A^i}. In the end, the previous instantiation can be updated and renewed.

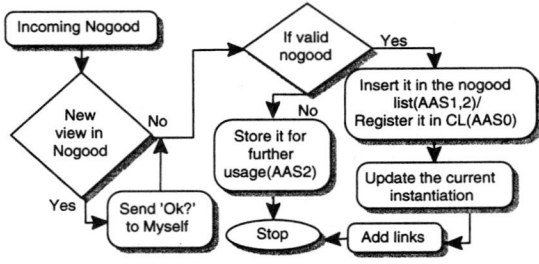

Figure 5: *Nogood procedure.*

The procedure Nogood treats incoming **nogood** messages. The argument, Q, of such a message is an explicit nogood. Let V be the view of the receiving agent. Suppose that there exists in Q, respectively in V, an assignment a_1, respectively a_2 for the variable x_j such that a_1 is newer than a_2. We will say that the nogood gives a *new view* for the variable x_j. In this case, the agent has to update its view by sending an **ok?** message to itself. An explicit nogood is valid if it concerns (i.e. invalidates) the current instantiation of the agent. If the received nogood is valid and if it contains variables that are unknown in the current view of the agent A^i, the procedure *Add links* will establish new links with all the agents $A^j, j < i$, for which these variables are local.

Solution Detection

In the existing asynchronous search algorithms, solutions are only detected upon quiescence[2]. This state is usually recognized using general purpose distributed mechanism (Chandy & Lamport 85). We have noticed that in the particular case of asynchronous search, solutions can be detected before quiescence. This means that termination can be inferred earlier and that the number of messages required for termination detection can be reduced. We have introduced a system message (not considered in the notion of quiescence) called **accepted** which informs the sender of an **ok?** message of the acceptance of its proposal:

- **accepted** messages are sent from an agent to all its predecessors (along all incoming links). If the agent has been an end agent, it also sends an **accepted** to the *system agent*,

---

[2] end of **ok?**, **nogood** and **add-link** messages

- an **accepted** message has as parameter a Cartesian product obtained by intersecting the current instantiation of the sender with the parameters of the last **accepted** messages received from all its outgoing links[3],
- an **accepted** message is sent by an agent only when its parameter is non empty (i.e does not contain empty domains), all the outgoing links have presented an **accepted** message and the agent is in the state Solution,
- the agents checks whether to send **accepted** messages when they reach the state Solution or when they receive **accepted** messages.

accepted messages are FIFO ordered.

Let D_i be the subgraph induced by the agents A^j with $j > i$ such that A^j can be reached from A^i along the directed links initialized by the *system agent*.

Proposition 1 *If a given agent A^i receives an **accepted**(S_k) message from all its outgoing links and if $\forall k, \bigcap S_k \neq \emptyset$, then A^i can infer that $\bigcap S_k$ is a solution for the partial CSP defined by the agents of D_i.*

Proof sketch. D_i is a directed acyclic graph. If a given node A^j of this graph receives an **accepted**(S_k) message from all its k direct successors such that $\bigcap S_k \neq \emptyset$, it is obvious that the k successors have found an agreement on all the elements of $\bigcap S_k$. Following the definition of **accepted** messages, the agent A^j can in turn send an **accepted** through all its incoming links and the process be repeated recursively. The proposition is therefore simply proved by induction on D_i. □

Corollary 1 *A correct solution is detected when the system agent receives an **accepted**(S_i) message from each initial end agent A^i and when $\bigcap_i S_i \neq \emptyset$.*

Message ordering

In asynchronous search (AS), the messages must respect a FIFO channel order of delivery to ensure correct termination (Yokoo *et al.* 92). Our algorithm requires a stronger condition to hold since the channel for each variable is no longer a tree but a graph. This means that several messages can arrive to the same agent, for changing the value of the same variable, through different paths of the graph. For example, in Figure 2 agent A^3 can receive messages concerning variable x_1 from both A^1 and A^2. An order must therefore be established between these kind of messages. In AS it is sufficient to maintain a counter, for the emitter, and include its value within each message sent in order to obtain a FIFO order of delivery. In our algorithm, we include such counters for all the agents that modify a given domain in the message. The history of changes is built by associating a chain of pairs $|a:b|$ to each variable of a message (see Figure 2). Such a pair means that a change of the variable's domain was performed by the agent with index a when its

---
[3]We define the intersection $S_i \cap S_j$ of two Cartesian products S_i and S_j as the Cartesian product of the union of all variables implied in S_i and S_j. The domain of each variable of $S_i \cap S_j$ is given by the intersection of its domains in S_i and S_j.

counter for the corresponding variable had the value b. The local counters are reset each time an incoming **ok?** changes the known history of the corresponding variable. It is incremented each time the agent proposes a change to the domain of that variable. To ensure correct termination, we use the next conventions: The history of changes where the agent with the smaller index or the counter with the larger value occurs first is the most recent. If a history is the prefix of the other, then the longer one is more recent.

Correctness, Completeness, Termination

The detailed proofs are available at (WebProof 2000).

Proposition 2 *AAS0 is correct, complete, terminates.*

Summary of Proof. Correctness is an immediate consequence of Corollary 1.

The proof that quiescence is reached is close to the one given for AS in (Yokoo *et al.* 92), using the additional knowledge that only **ok?** messages could remove nogoods of the agent with the least priority among those implied in the hypothetical infinite loop.

Quiescence can correspond to failure or solution, but it can correspond as well to deadlock. In order to prove that AAS0 cannot lead to deadlock, we have shown that if the system reaches quiescence without having detected solution or failure, a correct solution will be detected in finite time afterwards. Next steps were used:

Step 1 *After receiving the last **ok?** message and performing the subsequent search, either each agent A^i has a final instantiation that is consistent with its view, or failure is detected.*

Step 2 *At quiescence, the view of each agent A^i consists of the intersection of the instantiations of all instantiated agents $A^j, j < i$, for the variables it is interested in. This intersection corresponds, for each variable, to the newest received assignment.*

From the previous steps it results that in a finite time after quiescence, the intersection of the instantiations of all agents $A^j, j \leq i$ is nonempty and consistent with all the constraints in the agents $A^j, j \leq i$, for all i. Consequently, the last **accepted** messages sent by an agent to its predecessors are such that at receiver, $\bigcap S_k \neq \emptyset$. This is true for all the agents, which means that the **accepted** messages needed for solution detection will reach the system agent.

For completeness, we have proved that failure cannot be announced by AAS0 when a solution exists. A nogood, whatever if it is explicit or entailed by a view, is a redundant constraint with respect to the CSP to solve. Since all the additional nogoods are generated by logical inference, an empty nogood cannot be inferred when a solution exists. □

Proposition 3 *AAS1 and AAS2 are correct, complete and terminate.*

Proof. Immediate consequence of the fact that AAS1 and AAS2 only add redundant constraints to AAS0 (under the form of nogoods) and of Proposition 2. □

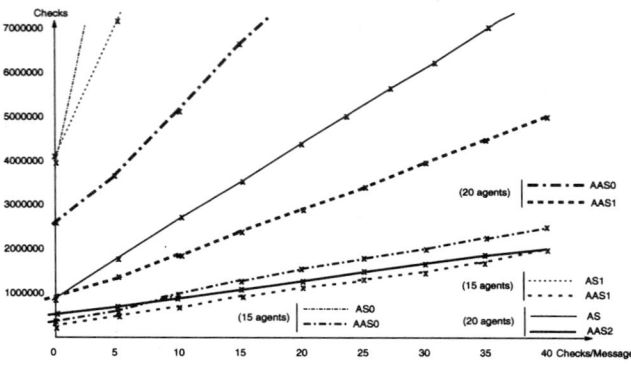

Figure 6: *Comparison of the number of checks on four sets of randomly generated problems near the peak. Abscissae select the relative time needed for sending a message divided by the time for a constraint check.*

Experiments

AAS0, 1 and 2 have been evaluated on randomly generated problems with 15 and 20 agents, situated on distinct computers on a LAN. The constraints have been distributed to the agents in the same way that they would have been in AS so that they can be compared with their variable-oriented counterparts. The size of domains is of 5 values and the problems are generated near the peak of difficulty (Cheesman, Kanefsky, & Taylor 1991) with a density of 30% and a tightness of constraints of 55%. The cost of search is evaluated using the longest sequence of messages and constraint checks. Each test is averaged over 50 instances. The measured parameters used for evaluation are the same as those given in (Yokoo et al. 92). In Figure 6, the slopes of the curves give the number of messages. The intersections with the y-axis give the number of checks when the messages are considered instantaneous. AAS2 performs slightly better than AS. There are specific cases where AS performs better for finding the first solution. However, for discovering that no solution exists AAS2 performs steadily better than AS since the whole search space needs to be expanded. AAS2 also reduces the longest sequence of messages as well as the number of nogoods stored by a factor of 50% on average. AAS1 needs more messages than AAS2, and AAS0 even more. However, they do not present memory problems. We have tested the usefulness of the aggregation by comparing AAS0 and AAS1 against our versions of AS where the equivalent nogood policies are used (AS0 respectively AS1). It spares 95% of the messages. If space is available, it seems useful to store some additional nogoods.

Conclusion

We have presented AAS, a new asynchronous backtrack search technique which requires no artificial redistribution of constraints, allows for aggregating the information transmitted using a Cartesian product representation and includes an enhanced termination detection mechanism. AAS provides a natural support for enforcing privacy requirements on constraints. Its evaluation has been done using three different algorithms called AAS2, AAS1 and AAS0. AAS2 is based on full nogood recording while AAS1 and AAS0 are distributed variants of the centralized dynamic backtracking based on partial nogood recording. In particular, AAS0 is a novel algorithm which only stores a single nogood. The experiments have shown that the overall performance of AAS2 is comparable to that of AS (Yokoo et al. 92). AAS0 and AAS1 have more potential in practice since the space they require is bounded. Their evaluation have shown that aggregation is of interest for reducing the number of messages exchanged in distributed asynchronous search.

In the current implementation, the agents with the lower priority may have to reveal more information about their constraints. If undesirable, such a behavior can be avoided using random or cyclic agent reordering. Moreover, situations where some agents are forced to reveal their whole constraint are not precluded. This can occur, for example, in problems where all the agents but the last accept everything and the last one nothing. Malicious agents can form coalitions and create intentionally such problems in order to determine certain external constraints. In the future we plan to analyze the importance of these issues. We will also investigate how the dynamic change of constraints, which often occurs in human negotiation, can be integrated.

Acknowledgements

This work was performed at the Artificial Intelligence Laboratory of the Swiss Federal Institute of Technology in Lausanne and was sponsored by the Swiss National Science Foundation under project number 21-52462.97.

References

Chandy, K.-M., and Lamport, L. 85. Distributed snapshots: Determining global states of distributed systems. *TOCS'85* 1(3):63–75.

Cheesman, P.; Kanefsky, B.; and Taylor, W. 1991. Where the really hard problems are. In *Proceedings of the 12th International Joint Conference on AI*.

Ginsberg, M., and McAllester, D. 94. Gsat and dynamic backtracking. In J.Doyle., ed., *Proceedings of the 4th IC on PKRR*, 226–237. KR.

Hamadi, Y., and Bessière, C. 98. Backtracking in distributed constraint networks. In *ECAI'98*, 219–223.

Haselböck, A. 93. Exploiting interchangeabilities in constraint satisfaction problems. In *Proceedings of IJCAI'93*, 282–287.

Hubbe, P. D., and Freuder, E. C. 92. An efficient cross product representation of the constraint satisfaction problem search space. In *Proc. of AAAI*, 421–427.

Silaghi, M.-C.; Sam-Haroud, D.; and Faltings, B. 2000. Fractionnement intelligent de domaine pour CSPs avec domaines ordonnés. In *Proc. of RFIA2000*.

WebProof. 2000. Detailed Proof for AAS. http://liawww.epfl.ch/~silaghi/annexes/AAAI2000.

Yokoo, M.; Durfee, E. H.; Ishida, T.; and Kuwabara, K. 92. Distributed constraint satisfaction for formalizing distributed problem solving. In *ICDCS'92*, 614–621.

A* with Partial Expansion for large branching factor problems

Takayuki Yoshizumi, Teruhisa Miura and **Toru Ishida**

Department of Social Informatics, Kyoto University,
Kyoto 606-8501, Japan
{yosizumi, miura, ishida}@kuis.kyoto-u.ac.jp

Abstract

The multiple sequence alignment problem is one of the important problems in Genome Informatics. The notable feature of this problem is that its state-space forms a lattice. Researchers have applied search algorithms such as A* and memory-bounded search algorithms including SNC to this problem. Unfortunately, previous work could align only seven sequences at most. Korf proposed DCBDS, which exploits the features of a grid, and suggested that DCBDS probably solved this problem, effectively. We found, however, that DCBDS was not effective for aligning many sequences. In this paper, we propose a simple and effective search algorithm, A* with Partial Expansion, for state-spaces with large branching factors. The aim of this algorithm is to store only necessary nodes for finding an optimal solution. In node expansion, A* stores all child nodes, while our algorithm stores only promising child nodes. This mechanism enables us to reduce the memory requirements during a search. We apply our algorithm to the multiple sequence alignment problem. It can align seven sequences with only 4.7% of the stored nodes required by A*.

Introduction

The multiple sequence alignment problem is to align several biological sequences and to extract the common pattern. The alignment is used in various ways for biological sequence analysis in Genome Informatics. We can define the multiple sequence alignment problem as the problem of finding the shortest path in a lattice. The state-space is far different from those of typical search problems such as the sliding-tile puzzle and the maze. There are huge numbers of paths through the same node, because the state-space forms a lattice and the branching factor is $O(2^d)$, when d is the number of sequences to be aligned. The multiple sequence alignment problem has notable features that have not been dealt with in the AI search community.

Ikeda and Imai applied the A* algorithm to the multiple sequence alignment problem (Ikeda & Imai 1994). A* must store all child nodes and because of the large branching factors involved, the memory requirements of A* grow rapidly with search progress. Due to memory constraints, A* cannot align more than seven sequences. On the other hand,

Copyright © 2000, American Association for Artificial Intelligence (www.aaai.org). All rights reserved.

linear-space search algorithms such as IDA* (Korf 1985) cannot align more four sequences because of the large number of revisits. We proposed SNC (Miura & Ishida 1998), which can effectively reduce the number of revisits needed by IDA*. SNC, however, cannot align more than seven sequences. Korf was inspired by our research and proposed DCBDS (Korf 1999). This interesting algorithm exploits the features of a grid, stores only the Open list, and performs a series of bi-directional searches. Korf claimed that DCBDS is most effective for a state-space that grows polynomially with problem size, but contains large numbers of short cycles. We applied DCBDS to the multiple sequence alignment problem, which was mentioned as one of the important applications in his paper. We found that not storing the Closed list did not effectively reduce the memory requirements, because the Open list is much larger than the Closed list in the search-space in this case. This weakness is due to the wide distribution of edge costs and a relatively accurate heuristic function. What is worse, DCBDS cannot prevent the search from leaking back into the closed region, when the state-space is a directed graph.

We propose a simple and effective search algorithm, A* with Partial Expansion; it exploits the features of a lattice and effectively reduces the memory requirements. To evaluate the power of our algorithm, we apply it to the multiple sequence alignment problem. We show that it effectively reduces the memory requirements compared to A* and discuss the relation to other search algorithms.

The multiple sequence alignment problem

The alignment of many biological sequences is demanded in various important fields in molecular biology. A biological sequence is composed of alphabetic characters representing its constituents. For example, one protein sequence consists of 20 amino acids. Figure 1 shows a part of the aligned sequences. Hyphens, or gaps, are inserted into the sequences so that the same, or similar, characters occupy the same columns.

In the multiple sequence alignment problem, we want to find the optimal alignment, which is associated with a minimum cost. The cost of the alignment is given by the sum of the costs of pairwise alignments. In a pairwise alignment, the cost of each column is given by the modified PAM-250 matrix in which each sign of score is reversed (Figure 2). The

```
Hal    GASQADNAVLVVAA-D---D-GV-QP-QTQEHVFLARTLGIGELIVAVNKMD-L-VDYGESEYKQVVEEV-KDLLTQVRFDSENAK
Met    GASQADAAVLVVNVDDA--KSGI-QP-QTREHVFLIRTLGVRQLAVAVNKMD-T-VNFSEADYNELKKMIGDQLLKMIGFNPEQIN
Tha    GTSQADAAILVISARDG--E-GV-ME-QTREHAFLARTLGVPQMVVAINKMDATSPPYSEKRYNEVKADA-EKLLRSIGFK-D-IS
Thc    GASQADAAVLVVAV-T---D-GV-MP-QTKEHAFLARTLGINNILVAVNKMD-M-VNYDEKKFKAVAEQV-KKLLMMLGYK-N-FP
Sul    GASQADAAILVVSAKKGEYEAGMSAEGQTREHIILSKTMGINQVIVAINKMDLADTPYDEKRFKEIVDTV-SKFMKSFGFDMNKVK
Ent    GTSQADVAILIVAAGTGEFEAGISKNGQTREHILLSYTLGVKQMIVGVNKMD-A-IQYKQERYEEIKKEI-SAFLKKTGYNPDKIP
Pla    GTSQADVALLVVPADVGGFDGAFSKEGQTKEHVLLAFTLGVKQIVVGVNKMD-T-VKYSEDRYEEIKKEV-KDYLKKVGYQADKVD
Sty    GTSQADAAILIIASGQGEFEAGISKEGQTREHALLAFTMGVKQMIVAVNKMDDKSVNWDQGRFIEIKKEL-SDYLKKIWLQPRQDP
```

Figure 1: A part of the aligned eight sequences

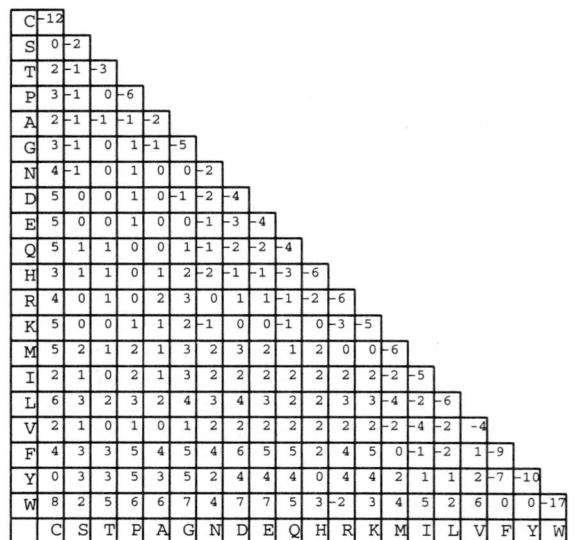

Figure 2: The modified PAM-250 matrix

PAM-250 matrix represents the mutation distance between two amino acids or characters (Dayhoff *et al.* 1978).

Formulation as the shortest path problem

The multiple sequence alignment problem can be formulated as the shortest path problem in the d-dimensional lattice (Carrillo & Lipman 1988). Let d be the number of sequences to be aligned and S_k be the k-th sequence.

$L(S_1, .., S_d)$	State-space which is a d-dimensional lattice. i-th axis corresponds to S_i.
s	The start node.
t	The target node.
γ	Path from s to t in $L(S_1, .., S_d)$.
k	The length of γ.
n_i	The i-th node of γ ($0 \le i \le k$).
$m(\gamma)$	Cost of γ.
u, v	Node in $L(S_1, .., S_d)$.
(u, v)	Edge in $L(S_1, .., S_d)$.
$c(u, v)$	Cost of (u, v).

The notations such as γ_{ij} and u_{ij} represent the projections of γ and u onto the plane determined by S_i and S_j, respectively. The path γ also can be represented as a sequence of nodes $\{n_0, n_1, \ldots, n_k\}$, where $n_0 = s$ and $n_k = t$.

For any given set of d sequences $S_1, \ldots, S_d$, we can define the state-space of the multiple sequence alignment problem. This state-space can be obtained by making the Cartesian product of N sequences (see Figure 3). It forms a d-dimensional lattice. The node that corresponds to the beginning of all the sequences is the start node. The node that corresponds to the end of all the sequences is the target node. The path γ from the start node to the target node in this lattice determines a unique alignment of d sequences. There is a one-to-one relationship between the path and the alignment. The i-th edge of the path corresponds to the i-th column of the alignment. The pairwise alignment of i-th and j-th sequences corresponds to the path γ_{ij}, which is the projection of γ onto the plane determined by the sequences S_i and S_j.

Figure 3 depicts the state-space representation of the multiple sequence alignment problem of three sequences $S_1 =$ ACGH, $S_2 =$ CFG and $S_3 =$ EAC. In this 3-dimensional lattice, the top left-hand corner is the start node and the bottom right-hand corner is the target node. The path drawn with bold line corresponds to the alignment at the lower right of Figure 3. The first edge (n_0, n_1) of this path corresponds to the first column of the alignment, $(-, -, \text{E})$.

In the d-dimensional lattice state-space, the cost of the edge (u, v) is defined as follows.

$$c(u, v) = \sum_{1 \le i < j \le d} c(u_{ij}, v_{ij})$$

The edge (u_{ij}, v_{ij}) is the projection of (u, v) onto the S_i-S_j plane (See Figure 4). In the 2-dimensional lattice, each row and column corresponds to each character in the sequences S_i and S_j, respectively. The diagonal edge associates S_i and S_j, while horizontal and vertical edges represent the insertions of gaps into the pairwise alignment. The cost $c(u_{ij}, v_{ij})$ is given by the value of the modified PAM-250 matrix, which corresponds to their characters. Figure 4 depicts the 2-dimensional path which is the projection of the 3-dimensional path of Figure 3. In this figure, path γ_{12} corresponds to the alignment of two sequences, S_1 and S_2. The second edge $(n_{2_{12}}, n_{3_{12}})$ is the projection of the 3-dimensional edge (n_2, n_3) onto the S_1-S_2 plane. This diagonal edge corresponds two characters, C, C. The cost $c(n_{2_{12}}, n_{3_{12}})$ is given by $p(\text{C}, \text{C})$, which represents the value of the PAM-250 matrix corresponding to characters C and C. On the other hand, the first horizontal edge $(n_{1_{12}}, n_{2_{12}})$ is the projection of (n_1, n_2) and corresponds a character and a gap, A, -. The cost of this edge is given by $p(\text{A}, -)$. The $-$ represents the gap and $p(\text{X}, -)$ or $p(-, \text{X})$ gives the gap

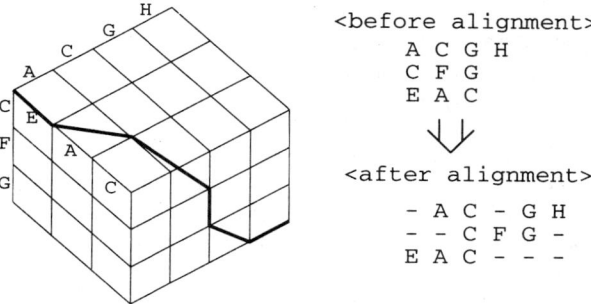

Figure 3: State-space representation

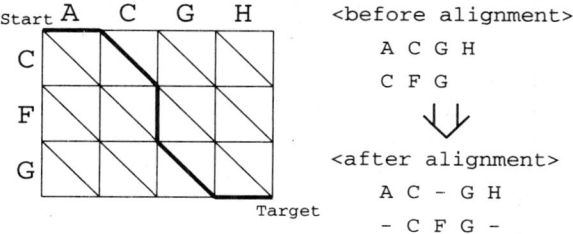

Figure 4: The projection of 3-dimensional path to the S_1-S_2 plane

cost for any character X. There is no corresponding edge for $c(n_0, n_1)$, because the projection of 3-dimensional edge $c(n_0, n_1)$ onto the S_1-S_2 plane is a point. Thus, $p(-,-)$ gives 0 cost, because the pair $(-,-)$ makes no contribution to the pairwise alignment.

Using this definition, we can calculate the cost of the d-dimensional path that corresponds to the alignment of the d sequences. The cost of the path is given by the sum of the edge costs of the path.

$$m(\gamma) = \sum_{i=0}^{k-1} c(n_i, n_{i+1}).$$

Finding the shortest path in d-dimensional lattice is to find the optimal alignment of d-sequences. In Figure 3, $c(n_1, n_2)$ represents the cost of the edge, which corresponds to column $(\mathtt{A}, -, \mathtt{A})$ of the alignment, and equals $p(\mathtt{A}, -) + p(\mathtt{A}, \mathtt{A}) + p(-, \mathtt{A})$.

Using this formulation and the gap cost of 8, Ikeda and Imai (Ikeda & Imai 1994) successfully applied the A* algorithm to the multiple sequence alignment problem. In Ikeda and Imai's experiment, the following heuristic function was used.

$$h(v) = \sum_{1 \leq i < j \leq d} h_{ij}^*(v_{ij})$$

where $h_{ij}^*(v_{ij})$ represents the shortest path length from v_{ij} to t_{ij} in the 2-dimensional lattice for S_i and S_j. h_{ij}^* is computed by the dynamic programming for each pair of S_i and S_j before the search algorithm is applied. In a high dimensional problem such as aligning seven or eight sequences, the time and space needed for the dynamic programming are negligible compared to those taken for solving the problem and do not increase time and space complexity. This heuristic function is admissible and consistent (Ikeda & Imai 1994).

Problem features

The multiple sequence alignment problem has some remarkable features compared to search problems common in the AI search community, such as the sliding-tile puzzle and the maze. Previous work has applied search algorithms to this problem without taking these features into consideration. The features of the multiple sequence alignment problem are as follows.

State-space The state-space forms a lattice. Therefore, there are a large number of distinct paths to the same node.

Branching factor The branching factor is very large. It becomes $O(2^d)$, where d is the number of sequences to be aligned. When $d = 7$ and $d = 8$, for example, the maximum branching factor becomes 127 and 255, respectively.

Distribution of edge cost In the case of a high dimensional lattice, the edge cost $c(u, v)$ can take on a large number of distinct values.

These features are the reasons why IDA* and A* are not effective against the multiple sequence alignment problem. Linear-space search such as IDA* must generate every distinct path to a given node. In the lattice state-space, there are a large number of distinct paths due to the very large branching factor, and the number of revisits becomes very large. What is worse, each iteration relatively expand few nodes, since most paths have different costs due to the wide distribution of edge cost, and the number of iterations becomes very large. Consequently, there is little or no hope of linear-space search algorithms such as IDA* solving this problem in practical time because of the large number of iterations and revisits. On the other hand, best-first search algorithms such as A* cannot solve high dimensional problems given their large memory requirements. Since the branching factor is very large, many child nodes are generated and stored when a node is expanded. The Open list grows rapidly with search progress and consists of those nodes that might be expanded in the future. Among them, there are some nodes that will never be expanded during a search. It is useless and wasteful to store such nodes. Consequently, A* searches often fail because it stores such nodes.

A* with Partial Expansion

It seems logical not to store unpromising nodes; this reduces the space complexity at the cost of solution quality. Recently, this was mentioned as domain-independent pruning rule for beam search (Zhang 1998). Adopting this idea, we present a new admissible algorithm, A* with Partial Expansion, which reduces the memory requirements of A*. In Partial Expansion, if a node has unpromising child nodes after expansion, then the node is put back into the Open list and its priority is lowered.

The algorithm

In addition to $c(n, n_i)$ and $h(n)$ described in the previous section, we use the following notations. $g(n)$ is the shortest path length from the start node s to the node n found so far. $f(n)$ is the static value of node n, which is given by $f(n) = g(n) + h(n)$. $F(n)$ is the stored value of node n. $F(n)$ equals the lowest f-value among all unpromising child nodes of n. C is a predefined and nonnegative cutoff value.

We want to store only those nodes that promise to reach the target nodes. For this purpose, we introduce cutoff value parameter C. The child node is regarded as promising and is stored when the f-value of the child node is less than or equal to C plus the F-value of its parent node. Otherwise, the child node is regarded as unpromising, and is not stored. To guarantee optimality, our algorithm uses an additional stored value $F(n)$. If node n has unpromising child nodes after expansion, then n is put back into the Open list with $F(n)$. Initially, the F-value of a node equals its f-value. After expansion of node n, our algorithm sets the $F(n)$ to the lowest f-value among its unpromising child nodes. A* expands nodes in incremental order of f-value, while our algorithm expands nodes in incremental order of F-value. If there are no promising child nodes, then it does not store child nodes at all and only revises the parent's F-value to the lowest f-value among unpromising child nodes. In this case, in other words, it only lowers the priority of its parent node for expansion.

The pseudo-code of our algorithm is as follows. In this code, T represents the set of target nodes, and $succ(n)$ represents the set of child nodes of a node n. The cutoff value C is given in advance.

Algorithm A* with Partial Expansion

```
1   g(s) := 0
2   F(s) := g(s) + h(s)
3   OPEN ← {s}
4   CLOSED ← ∅
5   while OPEN ≠ ∅ do
6       n := arg min F(n_i), n_i ∈ OPEN
7       OPEN ← OPEN − {n}
8       if n ∈ T then return
9       SUCC_≤C ← {n_j | n_j ∈ succ(n), f(n_j) ≤ F(n)+C}
10      SUCC_>C ← {n_k | n_k ∈ succ(n), f(n_k) > F(n)+C}
11      for each n_l ∈ SUCC_≤C do
12          if n_l ∉ OPEN ∪ CLOSED then
13              g(n_l) := g(n) + c(n, n_l)
14              F(n_l) := g(n_l) + h(n_l)
15              OPEN ← OPEN ∪ {n_l}
16          else if n_l ∈ OPEN and
                     g(n) + c(n, n_l) < g(n_l) then
17              g(n_l) := g(n) + c(n, n_l)
18              F(n_l) := g(n_l) + h(n_l)
19          else if n_l ∈ CLOSED and
                     g(n) + c(n, n_l) < g(n_l) then
20              g(n_l) := g(n) + c(n, n_l)
21              F(n_l) := g(n_l) + h(n_l)
22              CLOSED ← CLOSED − {n_l}
23              OPEN ← OPEN ∪ {n_l}
24          end if
25      end for each
26      if SUCC_>C = ∅ then
27          CLOSED ← CLOSED ∪ {n}
28      else
29          F(n) := min f(n_m), n_m ∈ SUCC_>C
30          OPEN ← OPEN ∪ {n}
31      end if
32  end while
```

In this code, there are some additional operations beyond those of A*. In order to selectively store child nodes, we need the operations shown on line 9 and 10 in the pseudocode. Lines 2, 14, 18, 21 and 29 are needed to manage F-value. The operation on line 30 puts an expanded node back into the Open list.

In extreme cases, when $C = \infty$, our algorithm is identical to A*. On the other hand, when $C = 0$, it stores nodes in best-first order, so those nodes whose f-value exceed the optimal cost will never be stored. This means that we can perform a search with the same size of memory as the Closed list used by A*.

Thus, our algorithm is very effective for those problems wherein the ratio of the Open list to the Closed list is large. Suppose that we apply A* to the problems where the state-space forms a tree and the branching factor is b. Then the ratio of the Open list to the Closed list becomes $b - 1$ to 1. We can reduce the memory requirements by a factor of the branching factor b, since our algorithm only needs the same size of memory as the Closed list by A*. The branching factor of the multiple sequence alignment problem is very large as described in the previous section. In this case, we can effectively reduce the memory requirements by a factor of a few hundred in the best case. Thus, the effect of our algorithm is non trivial for this application.

Search behavior of A* with Partial Expansion

Figure 5 shows the search behavior of our algorithm when $C = 0$. The solid circles represent stored nodes and the dotted circles represent unstored nodes. The digits in the circles represent the F-value, i.e. expansion priority. The digits on the right side of the arrow represent revised F-value after expansion. The digits on the top left of the circles represent the order of expansion.

Figure 5(a) shows the first expansion. The F-value of node A is initialized to its f-value, 6. Only one child node B is stored at this expansion, because the f-value of node B equals the F-value of node A. We revise F-value of node A to the lowest f-value, 7, among all unpromising child nodes and put node A back into the Open list. Figure 5(b) shows the second expansion. Node B with the lowest F-value is expanded. There are no child nodes with the same f-value as the F-value of B, so no child nodes are stored in this expansion. We put node B back into the Open list after revising its F-value to the lowest f-value, 8, among all child nodes. Figure 5(c) shows the third expansion. Node A with the lowest F-value is expanded again and child node C is stored. We set F-value of node A to 9 and puts node A back into the Open list.

In the same search space, it is necessary for A* to store the nodes represented by the dotted circles in addition to those stored by our algorithm. That is to say, we can find the optimal solution with fewer stored nodes than A*.

Evaluation

Experiment

In our experiments, we used the same conditions as in Ikeda and Imai's experiments, as mentioned before. We use 21 se-

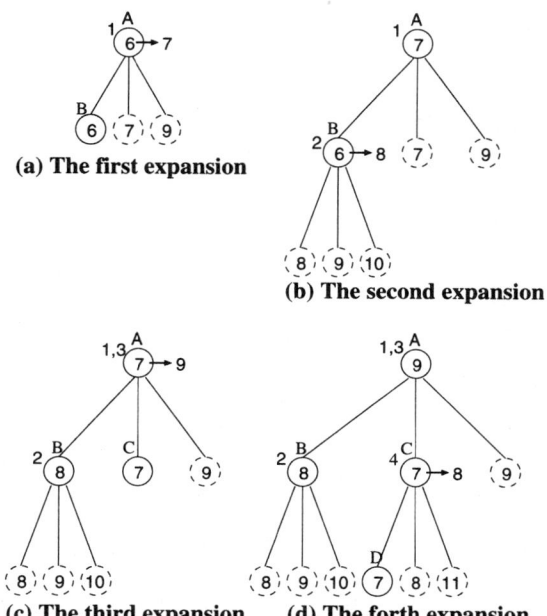

(a) The first expansion
(b) The second expansion
(c) The third expansion
(d) The forth expansion

Figure 5: Search behavior of A* with Partial Expansion(C=0)

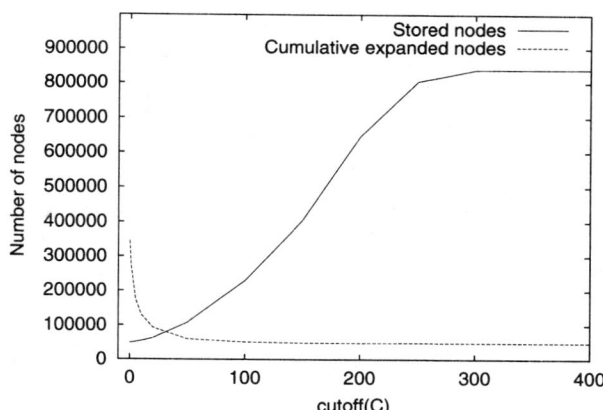

Figure 6: Number of stored and cumulative expanded nodes for each cutoff value(the seven sequence alignment)

quences from various species[1], which code for the elongation factor (EF-TU, EF-1α). The average length of these sequences is 448. The first seven of the 21 sequences are the same as those in their experiments. We applied our algorithm and A* to ten instances of seven and eight sequence alignment problems, respectively. It is natural for the maximum number of sequences, which are aligned by each search algorithm, to depend on sequence length, cost function, heuristic function and so on. We, however, can use their setting as benchmark test, because previous work also uses this setting to evaluate search algorithms. Each instance consists of seven or eight sequences that were randomly selected from 21 sequences. The maximum number of nodes stored by both algorithms is 2,000,000. This corresponds to about 160 megabytes of memory. For each instance, we assess performance from the cumulative number of expanded nodes and the maximum number of stored nodes with the cutoff values (C) of $0, 10, 50$ and ∞. When $C = \infty$, our algorithm is identical to A*. The cumulative number of expanded nodes corresponds to computational complexity and the number of

---

[1]These species are as follows. (0) haloacula marismortui, (1) methanococcus vannielii, (2) thermoplasma acidophilum, (3) thermococcus celer, (4) sulfolobus acidocaldarius, (5) entamoeba histolytica, (6) plasmodium falciparum, (7) stylonychia lemnae, (8) euglena gracilis,(9) dictyostelium dscoideum, (10) lycoperscon esculentum, (11) arabidopsis thaliana, (12) absidia glauca, (13) rhizomucor racemosus, (14) candida albicans, (15) saccharomyces cerevisiae, (16) onchocerca volvulus, (17) artemia salina, (18) drosophila melanogaster, (19) xenopus laevis, (20) homo sapiens. The figure in a parenthesis corresponds to sequence number in this paper. These sequences are available in Genome database on the WWW.

stored nodes corresponds to space complexity.

Table 1 and 2 show the experimental results for the seven and the eight sequence alignment problems. The results are very similar. Due to space limitations, we show only the results of five instances. In the case of A*, the cumulative number of expanded nodes equals the number of nodes included in the Closed list, because the heuristic function we used is consistent. This value is approximately equal to the number of stored nodes in the case of $C = 0$. This shows that our algorithm can perform a search with just the same size of memory as the Closed list used by A*. Averaging the five instances, the cumulative number of nodes expanded by our algorithm is about 5 times larger than that by A*, due to re-expansion of the same node. On the other hand, we can reduce the number of stored nodes to 4.7% of what A* requires. In addition, our algorithm can align the eight sequences, while A* cannot because it demands excessive memory. This result shows the effectiveness of our algorithm against the multiple sequence alignment problem.

Figure 6 shows the cumulative number of expanded nodes and the number of stored nodes for various cutoff values in the case of a first instance of the seven sequence alignment problem. In this instance, the maximum difference in f-values between a node and its child is 396. When $C \geq 396$, our algorithm is virtually identical to A* because it stores all child nodes for each expansion. Figure 6 shows that we can effectively reduce the number of stored nodes, while the cumulative number of expanded nodes increases only a little if the cutoff value is appropriate. In the case of $C = 50$, for example, our algorithm reduces the memory requirements by 87%, while the computational complexity increases by only 20% compared to A*.

In Figure 6, it seems that the number of stored nodes is proportional to the cutoff value, while the cumulative number of expanded nodes is inversely proportional to the cutoff value. The intuitive explanation is as follows. As to the cumulative number of expanded nodes, every node n, whose f-value is lower than the cost of an optimal solution path,

Table 1: Experimental results for the seven sequence alignment problem

instance	sequence number	cutoff	0	10	50	∞(A*)
1	0,1,2,3, 4,5,6	Cumulative Expansion	344,640	129,986	59,592	48,575
		Stored Nodes	48,882	53,948	107,157	839,150
2	0,1,2,8, 10,14,17	Cumulative Expansion	234,582	101,211	53,504	44,405
		Stored nodes	45,144	49,956	87,987	911,218
3	0,2,4,7, 8,14,15	Cumulative Expansion	169,618	82,499	45,859	38,639
		Stored Nodes	38,810	42,851	75,045	859,307
4	5,7,8,9, 10,12,18	Cumulative Expansion	30,702	19,249	12,644	11,650
		Stored Nodes	11,877	13,031	22,801	451,033
5	0,3,6,9, 11,12,19	Cumulative Expansion	463,446	210,544	107,432	85,437
		Stored Nodes	86,611	94,853	164,879	1,576,920

Table 2: Experimental results for the eight sequence alignment problem

instance	sequence number	cutoff	0	10	50	∞(A*)
1	0,1,2,3, 4,5,6,7	Cumulative Expansion	6,945,069	1,956,430	804,602	unsolvable
		Stored Nodes	545,114	596,782	931,689	
2	0,3,4,10, 14,16,17,18	Cumulative Expansion	6,090,700	2,123,360	935,680	unsolvable
		Stored Nodes	648,240	702,099	1,133,568	
3	0,2,5,9, 11,12,16,19	Cumulative Expansion	1,162,528	525,715	265,425	unsolvable
		Stored Nodes	213,999	238,323	461,453	
4	1,4,9,10, 12,15,16,20	Cumulative Expansion	6,321,726	2,095,884	899,443	unsolvable
		Stored Nodes	635,294	697,740	1,165,797	
5	0,1,3,4, 6,11,14,17	Cumulative Expansion	13,938,989	3,953,400	1,580,348	unsolvable
		Stored Nodes	1,016,453	1,098,194	1,639,663	

has to be stored by our algorithm. If the cutoff value is large, the cumulative number of expanded nodes is relatively small, because the expansion of a node stores many child nodes. On the other hand, with a low cutoff value, the cumulative number of expanded nodes is relatively large because the expansion stores few child nodes. As to the number of stored nodes, it is proportional to the cutoff value. This is because the number of stored node, whose f-value is more than the cost of an optimal solution path, increases as the cutoff value increases.

The number of stored nodes for eight sequences is about ten times larger than that for seven sequences in the case of $C = 0$ in our experiments. This implies that the memory requirements for the nine sequence alignment problem may be ten times larger than that for the eight sequence alignment problem. Accordingly, we cannot currently align more than eight sequences by algorithms based on A*, including our algorithm, under the common memory capacity.

Related work

SMA* (Russel 1992) and RBFS (Korf 1993) were proposed to avoid the memory problems of A*. In this section, we compare our algorithm to these algorithms. All explore nodes in best-first order, however, there are some differences between them.

A* Our algorithm is identical to A*, when the cutoff value $C = \infty$. Thus, it includes A* as the special case. Our algorithm stores nodes in best-first order and never stores nodes whose evaluated costs are larger than the cost of an optimal solution path when $C = 0$. It reduces the space complexity at the cost of node re-expansion overhead. As the experimental results show, however, we can effectively reduce the space complexity while only slightly increasing the computational complexity by selecting the appropriate cutoff value.

RBFS (Korf 1993) RBFS is a linear-space best-first search algorithm. For each recursive call, RBFS uses a local cost threshold, which enables it to explore nodes in best-first order. The threshold value equals to the cost of its lowest-cost brother. On the other hand, our algorithm memorizes the cost of its lowest-cost unpromising child for each node and reduces the space complexity without losing admissibility. Unfortunately, RBFS cannot avoid revisits because it stores only nodes along the current search path. Our algorithm has advantages over RBFS when the state-space forms a lattice, because there are no revisits in our algorithm.

SMA* (Russel 1992) SMA* behaves like A* until SMA* stores the maximum number of nodes. When the number of stored nodes reaches the limit, SMA* prunes the node with highest cost in the Open list and continues to search. On the other hand, our algorithm stores only promising nodes and never prunes them. Here is an essential difference between the algorithms. The algorithm of SMA* is much more complicated than that of A*. In addition, we have to use more complicated version of SMA* (Kaindl & Khorsand 1994), when we apply SMA* to problems whose state-space is a graph. Our algorithm is very simple with little modification of the A* algorithm and is applicable to graph problems without any modification.

Conclusion

We have proposed a simple and effective search algorithm, A* with Partial Expansion, to reduce the memory requirements of A* for problems wherein the branching factor is large. It reduces the space complexity of A*, without losing the merits of A*. It is admissible if a heuristic function is admissible. Consequently, we can solve problems wherein the branching factor is large, while A* cannot due to its excessive memory requirements.

We applied our algorithm and A* to the multiple sequence alignment problem. Experimental results show our algorithm can, on average, align seven sequences with only 4.7% of the amount of memory required by A*. We also applied it to the eight sequence alignment problem, which has not been solved up to now, and successfully aligned eight sequences.

In typical search problems such as the sliding-tile puzzle, the branching factor is much smaller than it is in the multiple sequence alignment problem. For such problems, our algorithm may be less effective in reducing the amount of memory, compared to the case of the multiple sequence alignment problem. However, there are several important applications for which our algorithm will be effective. One such application is the route finding problem in cities with massive and complicated road networks. Usually, the data of a road network occupies a huge volume. It cannot be fitted into main memory and is stored in a geographical database in secondary memory or in distributed databases over the Internet. Suppose that we want to find the shortest route from our house to the nearest bookstore. In a complicated city, there are countless routes because of the many intersections and transportation methods; the branching factor of this problem is very large. Most routes, such as a route to Paris by airplane or to a station by taxi, are useless for finding the shortest route. Thus, it is difficult to directly apply A* to this application. In order to reduce the memory requirements, such useless choices are eliminated when an application is formalized by the search problem. However, it is desirable for the search algorithm to be capable of coping with such useless choices instead of manually eliminating them from the model. The importance of our algorithm lies in its applicability to real world applications.

References

Carrillo, H., and Lipman, D. 1988. The multiple sequence alignment problem in biology. *SIAM Journal Applied Mathematics* 48: 1073-1082.

Dayhoff, M. O.; Schwartz, R. M.; and Orcutt, B. C. 1978. *Atlas of protein sequence and structure*, volume 5, 345-352. National Biomedical Research Foundation.

Ikeda, T., and Imai, T. 1994. Fast A* algorithms for multiple sequence alignment. *Genome Informatics Workshop 94*, 90-99.

Kaindl, H., and Khorsand, A. 1994. Memory-bounded bidirectional search. *AAAI-94*, 1359-1364.

Korf, R. E. 1985. Depth-first iterative-deepening: An optimal admissible tree search, *Artificial Intelligence* 27, 97-109.

Korf, R. E., 1993. Linear-space best-first search, *Artificial Intelligence* 27, 97-109.

Korf, R. E. 1999. Divide-and-conquer bidirectional search: first results. *Proc IJCAI-99*, 1184-1189.

Miura, T., and Ishida, T. 1998. Stochastic node caching for memory-bounded search. *AAAI-98*, 450-456.

Russel, S., 1992. Efficient memory-bounded search methods. *ECAI-92*, 1-5.

Zhang, W., 1998. Complete anytime beam search. *AAAI-98*, 425-430.

Depth-First Branch-and-Bound versus Local Search: A Case Study

Weixiong Zhang

Information Sciences Institute and Computer Science Department
University of Southern California
4676 Admiralty Way, Marina del Rey, CA 90292
Email: zhang@isi.edu

Abstract

Depth-first branch-and-bound (DFBnB) is a complete algorithm that is typically used to find optimal solutions of difficult combinatorial optimization problems. It can also be adapted to an approximation algorithm and run as an anytime algorithm, which are the subjects of this paper. We compare DFBnB against the Kanellakis-Papadimitriou local search algorithm, the best known approximation algorithm, on the asymmetric Traveling Salesman Problem (ATSP), an important NP-hard problem. Our experimental results show that DFBnB significantly outperforms the local search on large ATSP and various ATSP structures, finding better solutions faster than the local search; and the quality of approximate solutions from a prematurely terminated DFBnB, called truncated DFBnB, is several times better than that from the local search.

1 Introduction and Overview

Depth-first branch-and-bound (DFBnB) [2; 22] and local search [17; 12; 10; 11] are the two most applied search methods for solving combinatorial optimization problems, such as planning and scheduling. DFBnB is usually the algorithm for finding optimal solutions of large problems, due to the virtue of its linear-space requirement. Local search, on the other hand, is a method for high-quality approximate solutions, and has been shown to be effective and efficient on many combinatorial optimization problems, such as the symmetric Traveling Salesman Problem (TSP) [17; 10; 11].

Besides that DFBnB is an efficient complete algorithm for optimal solutions, it can be used as an approximation algorithm[1], as suggested in [9]. DFBnB explores a state space in a depth-first order, and finds many suboptimal solutions with increasingly better qualities. These solutions are approximations to the optimal solution if DFBnB is terminated prematurely. Furthermore, DFBnB is also an anytime algorithm. An anytime algorithm [4] can provide a solution at any time during its execution, and is able to improve the quality of the current best solution with more computation. DFBnB finds better suboptimal solutions with more computation and eventually reaches the optimal solution. In contrast to the importance of anytime problem solving and the effort of developing new anytime algorithms [7; 8], DFBnB has not been studied as an approximation or anytime algorithm so far.

We study DFBnB as an approximation and anytime algorithm in this paper. We compare it against the Kanellakis-Papadimitriou local search algorithm on the asymmetric Traveling Salesman Problem (ATSP) [12]. This local search algorithm is an adaptation and extension of the well-known Lin-Kernighan local search algorithm [17], and the only local search algorithm for the ATSP which we found in the literature. We choose the ATSP due to the following two reasons. First, the ATSP is an important problem in the NP-hard class [22] and has many practical applications. Many difficult combinatorial optimization problems, such as vehicle routing, workshop scheduling and computer wiring, can be formulated and solved as the ATSP [16]. Second, despite its importance, little work has been done on the ATSP, which is disproportional to that on the symmetric TSP (see [11] for an excellent survey and references cited). It will be very helpful if information regarding which algorithm should be used for a particular type of ATSP is available to guide algorithm selection in practice.

The paper is structured as follows. We discuss the ATSP, DFBnB, truncated DFBnB and the Kanellakis-Papadimitriou local search algorithm in Section 2. In Section 3, we describe various ATSP structures used in our experiments. In Section 4, we investigate initial tour-construction heuristics. In Section 5, we compare DFBnB with the local search algorithm. We discuss the features of DFBnB and the weakness of the local search

---

Copyright ©2000, American Association for Artificial Intelligence (www.aaai.org). All rights reserved.

[1]We use the term *approximation algorithm* loosely to refer to an algorithm that is able to find a suboptimal solution. Such an algorithm does not provide a quality guarantee under the definition of ϵ-approximation algorithm [20].

algorithm on the ATSP in Section 6. Finally, we conclude and discuss future work in Section 7.

2 The Problem and the algorithms

Given n cities, $\{1, 2, \cdots, n\}$, and a matrix $(c_{i,j})$ that defines the costs of pairs of cities, the Traveling Salesman Problem (TSP) is to find a minimum-cost tour that visits each city once and returns to the starting city. When the cost matrix is asymmetric, i.e., the cost from city i to city j is not necessarily equal to the cost from j to i, the problem is the asymmetric TSP (ATSP).

2.1 DFBnB and truncated DFBnB

Branch-and-bound (BnB) [2; 22] solves an ATSP as a state-space search and uses the assignment problem as a lower-bound cost function. The *assignment problem* (AP) [18; 22] is to assign to each city i another city j, with $c_{i,j}$ as the cost of the assignment, such that the total cost of all assignments is minimized. The AP is a relaxation of the ATSP, since the assignments need not form a complete tour. Therefore, the AP cost is a lower bound on the ATSP tour cost. If the AP solution happens to be a complete tour, it is also the solution to the ATSP. The BnB search takes the original ATSP as the root of the state space and repeats the following two steps. First, solve the AP of the current problem. If the AP solution is not a complete tour, decompose it into subproblems by subtour elimination. Specifically, select a subtour from the AP solution, and generate subproblems by excluding some edges from the assignments, so as to eliminate the subtour. There are many subtour-elimination heuristics [2], and we use the Carpaneto-Toth scheme in our experiments [3], which generates no duplicate subproblem. Next, select as the current problem a new subproblem that has been generated but not yet expanded. This process continues until there is no unexpanded problem, or until all unexpanded problems have costs greater than or equal to the cost of the best complete tour found so far. Note that a subproblem is more constrained than its parent problem, therefore the AP cost to the subproblem must be as much as that to the parent. This means that the AP cost function is monotonically nondecreasing with search depth. The AP to the root node can be computed in $O(n^3)$ time; and the APs to non-root nodes can be computed in $O(n^2)$ time [18].

Depth-first branch-and-bound (DFBnB) is a special BnB that explores nodes or subproblems in a depth-first order. DFBnB uses an upper bound α on the optimal cost, whose initial value can be infinity or the cost of a tour generated by a polynomial-time heuristic (cf. Section 4). Starting at the root node, DFBnB always selects a recently generated node n to examine next. If the AP solution of n is a complete tour, meaning that n is a leaf node in the search tree, and its cost is less than the current upper bound α, α is revised to the cost of n. If n's AP solution is not a complete tour and its cost is greater than or equal to α, n is pruned, because node costs are non-decreasing along a path from the root so that no descendent of n will have a cost smaller than n's cost. Otherwise, n is expanded, generating all its child nodes. To find an optimal goal node quickly, the children n should be searched in an increasing order of their costs. This is called *node ordering*. We use node ordering in this study.

DFBnB can be used as an anytime algorithm. During the depth-first exploration of a state space, DFBnB may encounter many leaf nodes and improve the best solution at hand continuously. Furthermore, DFBnB can be stopped at any time during its execution. This is an extension to the M-Cut strategy suggested in [9], which terminates BnB with a fixed amount of computation. We call DFBnB with an early termination *truncated DFBnB*. Among all possible stopping points, of particular interest is where the first leaf node is reached. When no initial tour is used, this simple, special truncated DFBnB is a greedy search in a search space, which always chooses to explore next the minimum-cost child node of the current state until it reaches a leaf node. When a high-quality initial tour is employed, DFBnB may not necessarily encounter a leaf node before the total allocated computation is exhausted. Without confusion, we call DFBnB that terminates when it reaches a leaf node or consumes all allowed computation *truncated DFBnB* in the rest of this paper.

2.2 Kanellakis-Papadimitriou local search

Local search is based on a fundamental concept called *neighborhood structure*. If two TSP tours differ by λ edges, and one can be changed to the other by swapping the different edges, one tour is a λ-change neighbor of the other. A neighborhood structure is established by defining the legitimate changes. Within a neighborhood, a tour is a local optimum if it is the best among its neighbors. Given a neighborhood structure, a local search moves from a tour to a neighboring tour that has a smaller cost until a local optimum is reached.

The Kanellakis-Papadimitriou local search algorithm for the ATSP [12] follows the Lin-Kernighan local search algorithm for the symmetric TSP [17], and uses *primary changes*, which change an odd number of edges in a tour. Figure 1 shows a primary 3-change. Primary changes are found by the following *sequential* process. To construct a primary change of a tour π, we first remove an arc x_1 of π, resulting in a directed path (Figure 2(a)). We then add a new arc y_1, which determines an arc x_2 that needs to be deleted and creates a cycle C_1 (Figure 2(b)). We can immediately break the cycle C_1 by adding a new arc y_2 as shown in Figure 2(c). We end up with a directed path, as we started with in Figure 2(a). In general, we call two subsequent pairs of deleted and added arcs, $< x_i, y_i >$ and $< x_{i+1}, y_{i+1} >$ for $i = 1, 3, 5, \cdots$, a *pair of steps*, if y_{i+1} subsequently breaks the cycle produced by y_i. The sequential process proceeds in pairs of steps, searching for a primary change by a sequence of cycle creations, each immediately followed by a breaking of the cycle. Obviously, a path can be closed by linking its two end cities, resulting in a complete tour, e.g. Figure

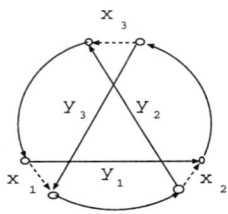
Fig. 1: Primary 3-chage.

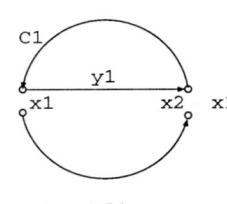
Fig. 2: Sequential search of primary changes.

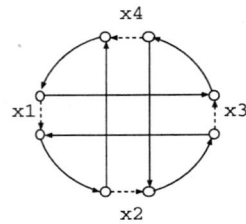
Fig. 3: Quad change.

2(c). Another useful change is the *quad* change, shown in Figure 3. It is not primary, but seems to substantially enrich the neighborhood structure [12].

The Kanellakis-Papadimitriou algorithm uses all the primary changes, obtained sequentially, and quad changes. Starting at an initial tour, it first searches for improving primary $2k+1$ changes, making k as large as possible. To reduce computation, the algorithm requires that it has a favorable change at every pair of steps, i.e., in searching for a better $2k+1$ primary change, it must have already retained a $2k-1$ primary change that improves the starting tour. The algorithm also presorts the intercity distances to facilitate the search of favorite primary changes. The algorithm repeatedly searches for primary changes, until none exists. It then repeatedly improves the tour by quad changes, until no improvement is possible. It then starts to search for primary changes again, and the process repeats. If the tour cannot be improved by a primary or a quad change, it is a local optimum. The process can be restarted on different initial tours, until no computation is available.

3 Problem structures

In our experiments, we considered the ATSP of various sizes, ranging from a few dozen to 1,000 cities, and used the following five problem structures. (1) Random matrices with $c_{i,j}$ uniformly chosen from $\{0, 1, 2, \cdots, r\}$, where $r = 2^{24} - 1$. We used a large intercity cost range r to generate difficult problem instances, because there exists an average-case complexity transition for BnB, i.e., the ATSP is relatively easy to solve when r is small, with respect to the number of cities n; while relatively difficult when r is large [24; 25]. (2) Matrices with the triangle inequality, $c_{i,j} \leq c_{i,k} + c_{k,j}$, for all possible i, j, k. We first generated random matrices as in (1), and then used a closure procedure to enforce the triangle inequality. (3) Matrices satisfying the constraint $c_{i,j} \leq i \times j$, which are believed to be difficult for a method using the AP cost function [19]. We chose $c_{i,j}$ independently and uniformly from $\{0, 1, \cdots, i \times j\}$. (4) Matrices converted from no-wait flowshop scheduling problems for four machines, which are NP-complete [21]. We first generated random scheduling problems, by setting the required processing time of a job on a machine to be an integer independently and uniformly chosen from $\{0, 1, 2, \cdots, 2^{16} - 1\}$, and then converted the problems into ATSPs using the method suggested in [23]. (5) Matrices of individual problems from the TSP library [1].

4 Initial Tour Construction Heuristics

Local search requires an initial tour to start, and its performance depends on the quality of the initial tour. A high-quality initial tour can also improve the performance of DFBnB. The known polynomial-time tour construction heuristics for the ATSP include nearest neighbor [6; 10], nearest insertion [6; 10], greedy algorithm [6; 10], repeated assignment [6], and Karp's patching algorithm [13]. Due to space limit, the interested reader is referred to [6; 10; 13] for the details of the methods.

To find the best tour construction heuristic, we experimentally compared these heuristics using the first four cost matrices described in Section 3. Due to space limit, detailed experimental results are not included here. Our experimental results show that Karp's patching algorithm has the best tour quality, followed by repeated assignment, greedy, nearest neighbor, and nearest insertion. The quality of the tours from the patching algorithm is more than an order of magnitude smaller than those from the other methods on all problem structures that we considered. Therefore, Karp's patching algorithm was used in our experimental comparison of DFBnB and local search.

5 Experimental Results

We implemented the Kanellakis-Papadimitriou local search algorithm and DFBnB in C and compared them on a Sun Ultra Sparc 10 workstation. The algorithms used an initial tour from Karp's patching algorithm.

5.1 Truncated DFBnB versus local search

We first compared truncated DFBnB and the local search algorithm for finding approximate solutions. Table 1 summarizes the results on the ATSP with the first four cost matrices, i.e., random matrices, matrices with triangle inequality, matrices with $c_{i,j} \leq i \times j$, and matrices converted from no-wait flowshop scheduling problems. In this set of experiments, truncated DFBnB did not use a limit on the total amount of computation, but terminated when it reached a leaf node, a node whose AP solution is a complete tour. Table 1 shows the tour qualities and CPU times of these two algorithms, averaged over 500 instances for 100- to 500-city ATSPs, and 100 instances for 600- to 1,000-city ATSPs. The tour

# of cities			100	200	300	400	500	600	700	800	900	1,000
random matrices	error (%)	LS	6.352	5.228	4.312	3.898	3.675	3.323	3.157	2.760	2.841	2.628
		TDFBnB	1.798	0.930	0.650	0.491	0.375	0.291	0.266	0.251	0.209	0.189
	time (sec.)	LS	0.022	0.108	0.296	0.604	1.036	1.658	2.495	3.164	4.190	5.798
		TDFBnB	0.013	0.072	0.195	0.426	0.756	1.178	1.805	2.434	3.450	4.621
	win (%)	LS	2.60	0.60	0.20	0.80	0.20	0.00	0.00	1.00	0.00	0.00
		TDFBnB	95.40	98.20	99.40	98.60	99.60	99.60	99.80	99.00	100.00	100.00
matrices with triangle inequality	error (%)	LS	1.066	0.629	0.506	0.426	0.343	0.305	0.275	0.264	0.238	0.200
		TDFBnB	0.660	0.334	0.235	0.172	0.138	0.113	0.105	0.100	0.088	0.087
	time (sec.)	LS	0.024	0.118	0.322	0.659	1.097	1.870	2.595	3.560	4.846	6.267
		TDFBnB	0.014	0.068	0.191	0.392	0.705	1.144	1.603	2.389	3.327	5.552
	win (%)	LS	10.20	4.80	5.80	4.00	3.60	3.00	2.00	1.00	1.00	1.00
		TDFBnB	59.00	60.60	61.00	57.80	63.20	60.60	63.00	68.00	62.00	60.00
matrices with $c_{i,j} \leq i \times j$	error (%)	LS	3.445	2.558	2.113	1.898	1.605	1.543	1.522	1.336	1.311	1.250
		TDFBnB	1.649	0.863	0.587	0.466	0.357	0.298	0.255	0.215	0.206	0.194
	time (sec.)	LS	0.036	0.206	0.613	1.295	2.294	4.043	5.840	8.103	11.100	15.096
		TDFBnB	0.023	0.127	0.365	0.740	1.267	2.141	3.148	4.606	5.981	7.901
	win (%)	LS	10.60	4.20	2.20	1.20	1.75	1.40	1.00	0.00	2.00	1.00
		TDFBnB	83.00	94.20	95.80	97.40	97.00	98.20	99.00	100.00	98.00	99.00
no-wait flowshop scheduling	error (%)	LS	0.035	0.013	0.008	0.006	0.004	0.003	0.003	0.003	0.002	0.002
		TDFBnB	0.030	0.011	0.007	0.005	0.003	0.003	0.002	0.002	0.002	0.001
	time (sec.)	LS	0.063	0.468	1.797	4.812	9.881	19.631	33.353	49.026	70.553	98.802
		TDFBnB	0.029	0.177	0.543	1.213	2.222	3.891	5.748	8.552	2.249	5.781
	win (%)	LS	11.80	9.60	7.60	7.20	8.20	7.40	6.00	7.00	6.00	7.00
		TDFBnB	34.80	40.40	45.80	50.20	47.00	52.60	48.00	51.00	49.00	55.00

Table 1: Truncated DFBnB vs. local search.

quality is expressed as the error of tour costs relative to the AP lower bounds. The relative error of truncated DFBnB is less than 1.8% for 100-city instances, and decreases to less than 0.20% for 1,000-city instances on all four types of cost matrices. Across all problem structures and sizes we examined, the average tour quality of truncated DFBnB is better than that of the local search, and the average execution time of truncated DFBnB is less than that of the local search. Table 1 also shows the percentage of the instances on which truncated DFBnB finds better tours than the local search, as well as the percentage of the instances on which the local search is better than truncated DFBnB (labeled as win). The results show that on most problem instances, truncated DFBnB outperforms the local search.

We also compared truncated DFBnB with the local search on all ATSP instances in the TSP library [1]. In the first set of experiments, the termination condition of truncated DFBnB is when it reaches a leaf node. The experimental results are shown in Table 2, where AP is the cost of the assignment problem, patch the tour cost from the patching algorithm, LS the tour cost from the local search, LS(millisec.) the CPU time of the local search in milliseconds, TDFBnB1 the tour cost from truncated DFBnB, TDFBnB1(millisec.) the CPU time of truncated DFBnB, TDFBnB1 win the indicator if truncated DFBnB finds better tours, and LS win the indicator if the local search finds better tours. As the results show, truncated DFBnB is not very effective on some of these problems. We observed that these problems are the ones on which the difference between the tour cost from the patching algorithm and the AP cost is relatively large. This may be due to some semisymmetric structures embedded in the problems, which defeat the effectiveness of the assignment problem.

Truncated DFBnB can be enhanced by Karp's patching algorithm. The patching algorithm can be applied to a node that needs to be expanded by DFBnB, i.e. a node whose AP cost is less than the current upper bound. The application of the patching algorithm has a great impact on the total running time of truncated DFBnB as well as the quality of the best tour that can be found. By applying the patching algorithm, a tour better than the best solution at hand may be found, which reduces the value of the current upper bound. Consequently, a smaller upper bound prevents truncated DFBnB from reaching a leaf node soon, which means that truncated DFBnB needs to explore more nodes. The results of the experiment are shown in the last four columns of Table 2, where the enhanced truncated DFBnB is labeled as TDFBnB2. The results show that the enhanced truncated DFBnB is very effective, increasing the number of problems on which truncated DFBnB finds better tours than the local search from six to 11.

5.2 Anytime DFBnB versus local search

To better understand DFBnB and the local search algorithm, we compared the quality of the tours that they find over the time of their executions on randomly generated ATSPs. That is, we considered the anytime performance of these algorithms. Figure 4 shows the result on the 300-city ATSP with random cost matrices, averaged over 100 instances. The horizontal axis of Figure 4 is the CPU time, in a logarithmic scale, and the vertical axis is the average error of tour costs relative to the optimal tour costs. Both algorithms start with a complete tour generated by Karp's patching algorithm. Since the local search typically finishes earlier than DFBnB, which finds an optimal tour at the end, we restart the local search on initial tours generated by the other tour construction heuristics of Section 4 – in the order

problem	AP	patch	LS	LS (millisec.)	TDF-BnB1	TDF-BnB1 (millisec.)	TDF-BnB1 win	LS win	TDF-BnB2	TDF-BnB2 (millisec.)	TDF-BnB2 win	LS win
xbr17	0	40	39	0	39	1			39	1		
ft53	5931	7932	7364	0	7917	8		x	7372	9		x
ft70	37978	39401	38947	2	38855	2	x		38855	2	x	
ftv170	2631	2793	2783	5	2776	14	x		2767	153	x	
ftv33	1185	1455	1390	0	1443	0		x	1329	3	x	
ftv35	1381	1493	1493	1	1490	2	x		1487	3	x	
ftv38	1438	1550	1550	0	1547	2	x		1546	5	x	
ftv44	1521	1737	1699	0	1663	1	x		1613	4	x	
ftv47	1652	1787	1784	0	1787	8		x	1787	8		x
ftv55	1435	1680	1649	0	1675	1		x	1624	8	x	
ftv64	1721	1970	1851	1	1853	0		x	1839	20	x	
ftv70	1766	2016	1990	1	1999	2		x	1954	21	x	
kro124p	33978	40183	36787	5	40180	18		x	37241	43		x
p43	43	5629	5625	1	5623	1	x		5623	1	x	
rbg323	1326	1326	1326	71	1326	32			1326	32		
rbg358	1163	1163	1163	79	1163	33			1163	33		
rbg403	2465	2465	2465	302	2465	164			2465	164		
rbg443	2720	2720	2720	382	2720	183			2720	183		
ry48p	12517	15430	14792	1	15285	3		x	14735	5	x	
SUM							6	8			11	3

Table 2: Truncated DFBnB vs. local search on problems from TSP library.

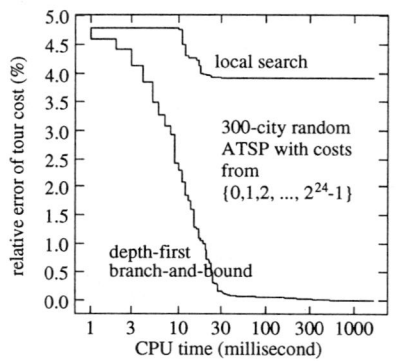

Fig. 4: DFBnB vs. local search on 300-city random ATSP.

of repeated assignment, greedy algorithm, nearest neighbor and nearest insertion – until the local search uses the same amount of time as used by DFBnB. However, the local search generally fails to improve the best tour found based on the patching algorithm, since these tour construction heuristics are not very effective.

Figure 4 shows that DFBnB significantly outperforms the local search on the ATSP with random cost matrices. Similar results have also been observed on other problem sizes and structures. DFBnB typically finds better tours earlier than the local search. This is partially because the AP can be computed in $O(n^2)$ time on a non-root node of the search tree [18], rather than in $O(n^3)$ time on the root node. Based on our experiments, the AP on a non-root node can be computed in roughly one tenth, one twentieth, and one seventeenth of the CPU time required for the AP of the initial ATSP with random cost matrices, matrices with triangle inequality, and matrices with $c_{i,j} \le i \times j$, respectively. Thanks to the superior performance of truncated DFBnB, DFBnB can obtain a high-quality tour very early in its execution, which can further help to restrict the search to the areas where better solutions can be found.

6 Discussions

The superior performance of DFBnB and truncated DFBnB on the ATSP is primarily due to two factors. The first is the assignment problem (AP) lower-bound cost function. As observed in previous research [2] and in our own experiments, this cost function gives a superb estimation on the actual ATSP tour cost, approaching the ATSP cost from below as problem size increasing. In our experiments on the random ATSP with the elements of cost matrices independently and uniformly chosen from $\{0, 1, 2, \cdots, 2^{24} - 1\}$, the cost of the AP is 99.090% of the ATSP cost on average for 100-city instances, 99.816% for 500-city instances, and 99.916% for 1,000-city instances. A good lower-bound cost function can usually give rise to a strong branch-and-bound algorithm by providing a good node ordering. This has also been observed on number partitioning using branch-and-bound with Karmarkar-Karp heuristics [15].

The second factor that leads to the superb performance of DFBnB is that the state space under BnB subtour elimination with the decomposition rules of [3] is a shallow but bushy tree without duplicate nodes. Our experiments revealed that with random cost matrices, the depth of an ATSP state-space tree is typically less than $n/20$, and its average branching factor of the nodes is around $n/5$. For a random 500-city ATSP for instance, the tree depth is less than 25 and the branching factor is around 100. Since leaf nodes are shallow, they can be reached easily, so as to give rise to solutions quickly.

The poor performance of the Kanellakis-Papadimitriou algorithm for the ATSP indicates that its local-search neighborhood structure may be restricted. Comparing to the symmetric TSP, there is no primary change with an even number of edges in the ATSP. Thus, finding a better primary change of large steps is difficult. Furthermore, the local search searches for increasingly better primary changes, which may substantially curtail the effectiveness of the algorithm. In addition, to find favorable pairs of steps, edges need to be sorted, further preventing the local search to quickly improve the initial tour, as shown in Figure 4.

7 Conclusions and Future Work

Depth-first branch-and-bound (DFBnB) is not only a general technique for *optimally* solving difficult NP-complete combinatorial optimization problems, but can also be adapted to efficient anytime and approximation algorithms. In this paper, we studied DFBnB and truncated DFBnB, a DFBnB with an early termination, on the asymmetric Traveling Salesman Problem (ATSP) of various structures and sizes. Specifically, we experimentally compared DFBnB and truncated DFBnB against the Kanellakis-Papadimitriou local search algorithm, the best known approximation algorithm for the ATSP. Our experimental results showed that DFBnB outperforms the local search algorithm, finding better ATSP tours significantly earlier than the local search, on large ATSP and various problem structures.

The contribution of this work is twofold. First, to the specific problem of the ATSP, it provides a thorough comparison of DFBnB and the local search, showing that DFBnB and truncated DFBnB are the choices of algorithms for the problem in practice. Second, beyond the specific problem of the ATSP, this work shows that DFBnB, a systematic approach, is also well suited for approximate and anytime problem solving. The results of this paper demonstrated that DFBnB can compete with and outperform a local search algorithm for finding both approximation and anytime solutions.

The poor performance of the Kanellakis-Papadimitriou algorithm suggests two possible future research for the ATSP. One is to define more effective local-search neighborhood structures, and the other is to develop strategies for escaping local minima, such as random walk, to strengthen a local search algorithm.

We would like to conclude the paper by pointing out that one of the major results of the paper, i.e., a systematic search may significantly outperform a nonsystematic search, is not an isolated observation on a particular problem. Similar observations have been made on number partitioning [15] and random coding networks [5; 14], on which DFBnB significantly outperforms the best known stochastic search. Our future research will concentrate on characterizing the common features of these different application domains and identifying the conditions under which a systematic search is able to outperform a nonsystematic search.

Acknowledgments

This work was funded by NSF Grant #IRI-9619554.

References

[1] ftp://ftp.zib.de/pub/packages/mp-testdata/tsp/tsplib/tsplib.html.

[2] E. Balas and P. Toth. Branch and bound methods. In *The Traveling Salesman Problem*, pages 361–401. John Wiley & Sons, Essex, England, 1985.

[3] G. Carpaneto and P. Toth. Some new branching and bounding criteria for the asymmetric traveling salesman problem. *Management Science*, 26:736–743, 1980.

[4] T. Dean and M. Boddy. An analysis of time-dependent planning. In *Procceedings of the 7th National Conference on Artificial Intelligence (AAAI-88)*, pages 49–54, St. Paul, MN, August 1988.

[5] R. Dechter and K. Kask. Personal communications. 1999-2000.

[6] A. Frieze, G. Galbiati, and F. Maffioli. On the worst-case performance of some algorithms for the asymmetric traveling salesman problem. *Network*, 12:23–39, 1982.

[7] L. Hoebel and S. Zilberstein, editors. *Proceedings of the AAAI Workshop on Building Resource-Bounded Reasoning Systems*, Providence, RI, July 1997. AAAI.

[8] E. Horvitz and S. Zilberstein, editors. *Proceedings of the AAAI Fall Symposium on Flexible Computation in Intelligent Systems: Results, Issues and Opportunities*, Cambridge, MA, 1996. AAAI.

[9] T. Ibaraki, S. Muro, T. Murakami, and T. Hasegawa. Using branch-and-bound algorithms to obtain suboptimal solutions. *Zeitchrift für Operations Research*, 27:177–202, 1983.

[10] D. S. Johnson. Local optimization and the traveling salesman problem. In *Proc. of the 17th Intern. Colloquium on Automata, Languages and Programming*, pages 446–461, England, July 1990.

[11] D. S. Johnson and L. A. McGeoch. The Traveling Salesman Problem: A case study. In *Local Search in Combinatorial Optimization*, pages 215–310. John Wiley & Sons, 1997.

[12] P. C. Kanellakis and C. H. Papadimitriou. Local search for the asymmetric traveling salesman problem. *Operations Research*, 28:1086–1099, 1980.

[13] R. M. Karp. A patching algorithm for the nonsymmetric Traveling-Salesman Problem. *SIAM Journal on Computing*, 8:561–573, 1979.

[14] K. Kask and R. Dechter. Stochastic local search for bayesian networks. In *Proc. Intern. Workshop on AI and Statistics*, 1999.

[15] R. E. Korf. A complete anytime algorithm for number partitioning. *Artificial Intelligence*, 105:133–155, 1998.

[16] E. L. Lawler, J. K. Lenstra, A. H. G. Rinnooy Kan, and D. B. Shmoys. *The Traveling Salesman Problem*. John Wiley & Sons, Essex, England, 1985.

[17] S. Lin and B. W. Kernighan. An effective heuristic algorithm for the traveling salesman problem. *Operations Research*, 21:498–516, 1973.

[18] S. Martello and P. Toth. Linear assignment problems. *Annals of Discrete Math.*, 31:259–282, 1987.

[19] D. L. Miller and J. F. Pekny. Exact solution of large asymmetric traveling salesman problems. *Science*, 251:754–761, 1991.

[20] C. H. Papadimitriou. *Computational Complexity*. Addison-Wesley, Reading, MA, 1994.

[21] C. H. Papadimitriou and P. C. Kanellakis. Flowshop scheduling with limited temporary storage. *Journal of ACM*, 27:533–549, 1980.

[22] C. H. Papadimitriou and K. Steiglitz. *Combinatorial Optimization: Algorithms and Complexity*. Prentice-Hall, Englewood Cliffs, NJ, 1982.

[23] S. S. Reddi and C. V. Ramamoorthy. On the flowshop sequencing problem with no wait in process. *Operational Research Quarterly*, 23:323–331, 1972.

[24] W. Zhang and R. E. Korf. Performance of linear-space search algorithms. *Artificial Intelligence*, 79:241–292, 1995.

[25] W. Zhang and R. E. Korf. A study of complexity transitions on the asymmetric Traveling Salesman Problem. *Artificial Intelligence*, 81:223–239, 1996.

Innovative Applications:
Deployed Applications

SciFinance: A Program Synthesis Tool for Financial Modeling

Robert L. Akers, Ion Bica, Elaine Kant, Curt Randall, Robert L. Young

SciComp Inc.
5806 Mesa Drive, Suite 250
Austin, TX 78731
phone: 512-451-1050, fax: 512-451-1622
email: info@scicomp.com or <lastname>@scicomp.com
www.scicomp.com

Abstract

The SciFinance^{TM} software synthesis system automates the programming task for financial risk management activities ranging from algorithms research to production pricing to risk control. Introduced commercially in late 1998, the system is currently licensed to a number of major investment banks. SciFinance's high-level, extensible specification language, ASPEN, enables quantitative analysts to generate code from concise model descriptions that are written in application-specific and mathematical terminology. From these specifications, typically one page or less, the system will produce a C program thousands of lines long. The specification language's abstractions help analysts focus on their primary tasks—model description, validation, and analysis—rather than on programming details. Compared with manual programming, automating the programming process produces codes that are more sophisticated, accurate, and consistent. Analysts can develop modeling codes within a day that previously took weeks or were not even attempted. SciFinance is an extension to a system that generates scientific computing codes in a variety of target languages including Fortran and C. The implementation integrates an object-oriented knowledge base, refinement and optimization rules, computer algebra, and a planning system. The same knowledge base is used by the specification checking, synthesis, and information portal subsystems.

Problem Description

Financial risk management increasingly demands new and customized simulation codes to implement its sophisticated computational models. These codes, typically designed by the quantitative analysts at investment banks, help determine prices for investment products, make trading decisions, and assess and control financial risk. The rate of growth in this area is striking. For example, the volume of the parent industry, custom ("over-the-counter") derivative securities trading, has increased twelve-fold since 1990 to eighty trillion dollars. Spending for modeling software is close to a billion dollars per year with an expected growth rate of about 10 percent. One way quantitative analysts can keep on top of this growth is with a tool like SciFinance^{TM}, which automates code generation.

Copyright © 2000, American Association for Artificial Intelligence (www.aaai.org). All rights reserved.

A derivative security is one whose value depends on that of some other underlying security. Derivatives allow firms to hedge risk. For example, a multi-national firm may use foreign exchange options to limit its exposure to volatile exchange rates. In 1973, Myron Scholes and Fischer Black derived a partial differential equation, the Black-Scholes equation (for which a Nobel Prize was later awarded), that estimates the fair value of a derivative security as a function of the characteristics of the underlying security and time. Since then, the mathematical theory of derivative pricing has been greatly refined, supporting the explosive growth in the volume and variety of derivatives sold in the marketplace.

Analysts need codes that accurately value and hedge derivative portfolios because as the global derivatives market grows in size, complexity, and competitiveness, clients increasingly demand products tailored to their specific investment requirements. As a bank's suite of investment products grows, corresponding simulation codes must be rapidly and accurately produced.

Large investment banks, brokerage firms, insurance companies, and hedge funds employ quantitative analysts to develop pricing models for these complex derivative structures. Analysts must create a new pricing model whenever a customer needs a price quote on a custom derivative instrument; thus new models must be produced rapidly and frequently. This demand is straining the ability of derivatives houses to model and price these instruments in a timely manner. The complexity of the deals may require a team of analysts, financial engineers, and programmers to work days or even weeks to develop the pricing model. Because a small programming or design error can cost the holding institution millions of dollars, accuracy and consistency of pricing strategies are critical. Quick turnaround is also essential, or the institution may lose the deal to a competitor.

The simulation codes involve the solution of a set of partial differential equations, each of which is an equation like the Black-Scholes equation described in Figure 1. The solution is subject to appropriate boundary conditions, initial conditions, constraints, and possible discrete events such as dividend payments. Especially important are the sensitivities of the solution to the various input parameters. Closed-form solutions are not available for any but the most trivial examples of these problems, and thus numerical approximation codes must be written.

The value V of a derivative security whose underlying stock has current price S, dividend yield D_0, volatility σ, and risk-free interest rate r satisfies the equation:

$$\frac{\partial V}{\partial t} + \frac{1}{2}\sigma^2 S^2 \frac{\partial^2 V}{\partial S^2} + (r - D_0) S \frac{\partial V}{\partial S} - rV = 0$$

Figure 1: The Black-Scholes equation.

Analysts ensure the accuracy and efficiency of models, but because they are highly trained and compensated, they make very expensive programmers. Consequently the objective is to greatly reduce programming time while maintaining or improving the accuracy and consistency of the pricing models. In addition, new tools must be both easy to use and familiar enough to inspire confidence in their function.

The problems of financial modeling, although similar to those in other areas of engineering and scientific computing, are especially acute because the field of finance evolves much more rapidly and new models are needed much more quickly. Conventional approaches to producing modeling codes involve combinations of library packages, object libraries, and manual programming. However, these approaches are unsatisfactory for many users (one of our customers evaluated more than 10 products before choosing SciFinance). The reason for the dissatisfaction is that such approaches obscure the model and force the problem solver to think at too low a level of abstraction (reasons are described in more detail in (Akers et al. 1998)). Thinking in terms of the tools or components, rather than in terms of the problem, application, and mathematical solution techniques, can potentially lead the analyst to make compromises that cause inaccurate or incomplete solutions. Large-grained library packages, for example, do not address how to produce new codes when the specifications do not exactly match an existing library routine. Finer-grained libraries shift the emphasis to problems of matching interfaces and connecting components and fail to provide component-spanning optimizations. Manual programming is time consuming and error prone.

To address some of these shortcomings, both object-oriented libraries (including in financial applications) and expert systems (in other application areas) have been developed. Object-oriented libraries can provide more generality by abstracting data structure representations, but they are usually not independent of the specific equations being solved or of properties such as spatial dimensionality and order of accuracy of the algorithm. Even with object-oriented libraries, however, assembly and bottom-up optimization of individual modules is the analyst's focus rather than top-down decision making and global optimization.

Conventional expert systems can select and combine library modules, relieving the user of some of the programming burden. However, expert systems alone do not address issues such as an appropriate specification level, generation of arbitrary higher-order methods, global and problem-specific optimization, and platform re-targeting.

Software synthesis can solve these problems by integrating the best aspects of object libraries and expert systems and augmenting them with the power of computer algebra, program transformation, and planning. Program synthesis accepts specifications in financial and mathematical terms, provides intelligent assistance in making choices, validates specifications and generates error checking code, and optimizes globally with problem-specific knowledge.

Application Description

SciFinance transforms specifications written in a high-level language called ASPEN (Algorithm SPEcification Notation) into executable C code. The synthesis process allows mixed user/system decision making and provides feedback to users in the form of summaries of its work at a sequence of levels of problem refinement.

SciFinance is a customized version of an underlying technology called SciNapse (Kant 1993), (Akers et al. 1997) and part of a general tradition of software synthesis (e.g., (Lowry and McCartney 1991), (Johnson)). Related techniques include the use of planning, theorem proving, or expert systems to compose library modules or to construct scripts. Although these techniques have proved fruitful in other domains, for example using planning to reconfigure software libraries for image analysis (Chien et al. 1999), they typically do not generate the complex control structures and customized data representations that are required in financial applications.

The SciFinance implementation is an object-oriented knowledge base containing application, mathematical, and programming constructs. Integrated with the objects are program transformations (for program elaboration, numerical approximation, data-structure selection and program optimization) and a scheduling mechanism. SciFinance successively refines ASPEN specifications through increasingly detailed levels of representation paralleling a best-practice version of human scientific computing. The levels-of-refinement approach, consistent with state-of-the-art literature (Gallopoulos and Sameh 1997) helps give the user a sense of familiarity and confidence. It also allows mixed user/system decision making. Design choices include questions about the desired results (which only the user can answer) and selection of numerical techniques. SciFinance will make selections in the absence of user specification. SciFinance is implemented in Mathematica^R (Wolfram 1999).

High-Level Specification Language. The ASPEN specification language represents problems in a way that is both clear to the user and suitable for manipulation by the system. Because ASPEN is concise, expressive, and flexible, users can easily write both simple and sophisticated specifications. Many numerical algorithms, equations, and other mathematical entities can be specified with keywords, and it is easy to specify equations algebraically or to define new, parameterized equation families.

Specification Checking. A front-end specification parser processes specifications and sets up the object instances representing the user's problem statement. Its extensive diagnostics trap and report specification errors early in the synthesis process. The parser is partially dynamically generated; it constructs its semantic actions based upon the current content of the knowledge base and automatically incorporates the relevant knowledge base content from the user's problem specification. Thus, the knowledge base itself defines what the front end will process and many of the actions it will take. In this sense, the front end is merely a machine presenting and processing a language defined in the knowledge base, which means that new concepts can be introduced with no impact on the front-end processor.

Knowledge Representation. SciFinance mixes rules and objects to represent knowledge about mathematics and programming and to present design choices in appropriate terms and in a logical order. Objects represent entities such as equation sets, individual equations, variables, and solvers. Attributes on object instances not only store object relationships between equations and variables, but also store the design choices that must be made for specific problems. For example, a representation attribute on an array variable can be filled by alternatives such as full, diagonal, time-independent, and stencil. Associated design choice rules encapsulate the details of the knowledge about how to make choices. Representation choice rules, for example, examine the equations in which a variable participates to determine the best data structure for a variable. Choices are not always from a fixed set but may be algebraically constructed based on equation discretizations.

We developed an object-oriented programming system, built on top of Mathematica, that supports dynamically created classes as well as instances. Tools use the dynamic classes to translate declarative, human-oriented descriptions of discrete events, algorithm templates, and discretization rules into the internal object and rule representations. The goals and agendas mechanism, which manages the synthesis and user interactions by ordering the resolution of object attribute values according to their dependencies, is tightly integrated with the object system. It allows attribute values to be computed with methods, constraints, heuristics, and both user-defined and system-defined defaults. Thus, the object system is used not only to organize the knowledge base, but also to encode the synthesis process itself.

Design Choice Rules. Associated with each choice (object attribute) are a result type, constraint and heuristic rules (which both can use previous choices), and defaults. Constraints filter the legal values of the alternatives type. Heuristics (with a simple voting scheme) and defaults are applied next if the ASPEN specification or constraints do not indicate a unique design choice. The specification may contain general default choices, such as an input file for variables not otherwise initialized.

Algorithm Templates. After most design decisions are made, SciFinance constructs a program by instantiating algorithm templates. Templates are special objects that represent mathematical algorithms such as time-evolution loops, equation-system solvers, and interpolations. Template objects are generic algorithm descriptions, free of specific equations and data-structure representations, which provide links to other synthesis entities, including other templates. SciFinance fills out the network of templates, and expands the template objects into pseudocode, inserting assignment statements based on the specific equations and representation selections.

Templates are introduced to the system declaratively. A template translator processes these declarations and incorporates them into the knowledge base in such a way that they are smoothly integrated with the synthesis process.

Elaboration Rules and Global Optimization. Unlike a library-combining process, SciFinance optimizes throughout synthesis, not just as a final code-transformation pass. For example, it eliminates unnecessary problem variables as soon as possible, maximizes parallelism based on equation dependencies, and makes space-time tradeoffs via algorithm choices and problem-specific representation selections. SciFinance also applies conventional optimizations such as the introduction of temporary variables, loop merging, and loop unrolling.

Computer Algebra. SciFinance would be much less powerful without its extensive use of computer algebra to make coordinate system transformations, numerical approximations, error estimates, and data structure and operator optimizations. Various rule-based simplifiers and transformation engines perform the algebraic manipulations of problem entities. Examples include a pseudocode optimizer integrated with a pseudocode elaboration transformer, an inequality simplifier, and translators to convert the system's low-level pseudocode to various target languages, including Fortran and dialects of C.

Platforms. The synthesis engine, SciFinance, runs on a wide variety of platforms (anything that Mathematica runs on), including UNIX, WindowsNT, and Windows9x. SciFinance-generated codes adhere to the standards of the target languages (ANSI C, Microsoft C, and Fortran-77) and may be compiled and run on any platform supporting those languages.

The Mathematica system has two separate parts. The first part is an evaluator/interpreter called the kernel, in which SciFinance objects and rules are implemented. The other part is the Mathematica Notebook, which provides window-based communication between a user and the kernel. The notebooks provide access to a built-in set of WYSIWYG document writing capabilities that can mix text and kernel instructions. We have added new menus for interacting with SciFinance to those already present on notebooks.

Information Portal.

SciFinance's information portal (Young, Kant, and Akers 2000) provides easy access to a suite of Mathematica notebooks presenting information about the system's capabilities and the synthesis in process. The notebooks all utilize a semantic network of information nodes. The semantic network uses the same knowledge representation tools as the rest of SciFinance and can refer to classes in the synthesis knowledge base corresponding to domain entities. The notebooks include reference documents, example catalogs, summaries describing the state of the problem (program) after each level of refinement, and human-authored documents automatically processed to convert selected references to hyperlinks.

```
(* Continuous knockout put, barrier X2,
   leveraged by # samples below X1 *)
Region[SMin<=S<=X2 && 0<=L<=LMax &&
       0<=t<=TMax, Cartesian[{S,L},t]];
When[Interior, BlackScholes1D[]];
When[Boundary,AutomaticBC];
When[max[S], V==0];
When[max[t], V==L*Max[0,K-S]/nsamp];
DiscreteEvents[
 Path[direction[L],
      function[L==SumOf[if[S<=X1,1,0]]],
      ReadFile[tsample, "tsamp.dat"],
      nsample==nsamp]];
Default[TaggedInputFile["DayCount.dat"]];
Output[V, "atSpot.out", spottable,
       L==LSpot, Labelled, NoInitialOutput];
ReadTable[spottable, nspot,
          "spottable.dat"];
CrankNicholson;
```

Figure 2: APSEN Specification - daycount problem

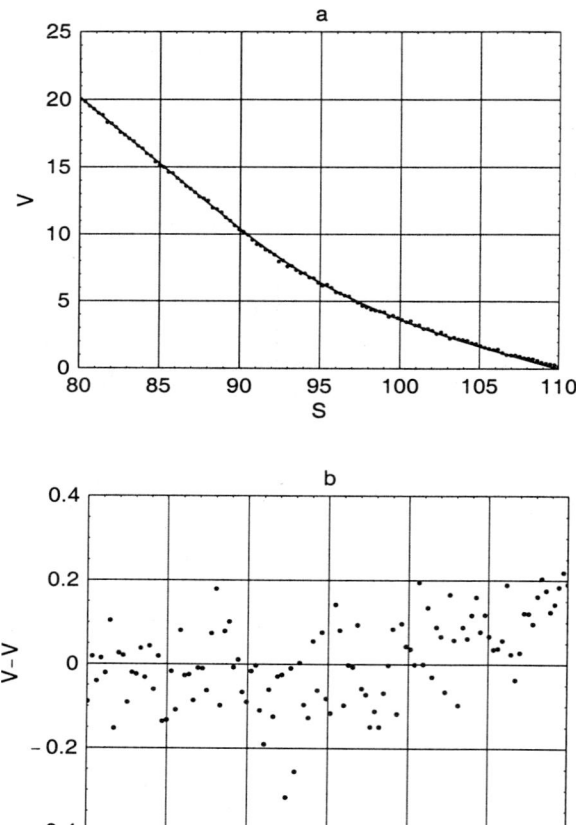

Figure 3: (a) The present value of a daycount-knockin/continuous knockout put option as a function of present stock price: the smooth curve shows results from the finite difference code generated by SciFinance and the dots show the results of the Monte Carlo (random number simulation) code. (b) The difference between the methods: the Monte Carlo code has a slight over-pricing bias near the barrier at 110, is noisy, and is about a factor of 50 slower than the finite difference code.

Examples of System Use. Quantitative analysts at risk-management institutions, university professors, and industry consultants use SciFinance to price custom equity-based derivative securities instruments (such as convertible bonds) and foreign exchange instruments. Some of these pricing codes are embedded in production systems for securities valuations, and some are used in research or for validating other approximations. Numerous examples have been published (Gatheral et al. 1999), (Brown and Randall 1999), (Randall, Kant, and Chhabra 1997). SciFinance is also used in university classes in computational finance.

A typical SciFinance application is modeling a derivative security. The model is specified in mathematical and numerical terms familiar to a financial analyst. Many common notions, such as equations, discretization methods, special problem conditions, and numerical algorithms are denoted by name, with variants specifiable via parameterization.

An Example Specification. The example in Figure 2 specifies a simple but non-trivial code that prices a "daycount knockin, continuous knockout put option." The generated code will solve the one-dimensional Black-Scholes equation in a two-dimensional region defined by the underlying stock price S and the knockin path variable L, which counts the number of days. `AutomaticBC` is an ASPEN specification statement that defines linearity boundary conditions. A specific boundary condition overrides this default at `max[S]` to define the continuously monitored knockout boundary condition (at X2). The "put" is described by the payoff condition `When[max[t], V==L*Max[0,K-S]/nsamp];` The knockin condition—the fraction of samples (L/nsamp) for which the spot price is below a second barrier (X1)—is given by the `DiscreteEvents[Path[...]];` specification. The `tsample` in the `Path` descriptor defines the set of sampling dates, and the `ReadFile` specifies their input source. By default, all other inputs are read from the file `DayCount.dat`. The output is the option value V interpolated to a specific series of spot prices (read into the array `spottable` from `spottable.dat`) and on a specific value of L, namely `L == LSpot`. The specification of numerical methods is optional. For example, The discretization scheme `CrankNicholson` is given, but since no solver is given, SciFinance will make the choice. Given this simple ASPEN specification, SciFinance generates about 1000 lines of C code. Figure 3 shows that the result produced by the SciFinance code is a significant improvement over traditional methods.

Uses of AI Technology

We attribute the success of SciFinance to the naturalness of its high-level specification language and the extensibility of the specification language and of the implementation. As noted previously, the implementation relies heavily on the integration of object-oriented design with transformation rules, symbolic algebra, and plan-based scheduling. All of these features are extremely useful for a system that is easy to build and extend, has sufficient mathematical flexibility, and is fully automated. For example, rather than plan-based scheduling, the original prototype had a more straightforward concept expansion and rule application procedure. But after attacking some very complex examples, it became obvious the system had difficulty understanding and controlling the rule interactions and rule firings when generating varied and sophisticated codes. Other approaches to software synthesis such as automated deduction do not seem appropriate here for a number of reasons. For example, the numerical methods are only approximations, and the error is not always known, so proving the methods or deriving them automatically would be extremely difficult and time consuming. Given the high degree of accuracy needed, automated learning of methods from examples also seems impractical, although learning how to make some default settings of numerical parameters based on experimentation could be a useful new tool.

We selected Mathematica as the commercial implementation platform that provided the most of the capabilities we need—a multi-platform, unified system including a symbolic programming language with sophisticated pattern matching, a computer algebra system, and a notebook interface with a rich set of capabilities for displaying or entering traditional-looking mathematical notation. Many of our potential customers are already Mathematica users. We built the missing object representation and user interface capabilities as additional layers over Mathematica.

A declarative knowledge representation and good model of the domain were key aspects in developing SciFinance. The domain model includes problem structures, simulation code structures, and the human code-construction process. The synthesis process can thus be derived directly from the domain model. The combination of a good model with easy access to the declarative knowledge and meta-knowledge unifies and simplifies many tasks.

SciFinance classes representing mathematical and programming constructs have attributes corresponding to their properties and various design choices, along with methods for elaborating these attributes. The methods are elaboration and transformation rules that sometimes include substantial algebraic manipulations. The two technologies are appropriately mixed; knowledge representation provides meaningful locations for the methods, and robust, high-quality algebraic transformations produce the needed results.

The planner exploits the knowledge and meta-knowledge to set goals to decompose tasks or to instantiate objects and then refine them by filling in attributes. Its agenda mechanism schedules refinements and design decisions for algorithms, numerical approximations, and data structures. The planning system uses method descriptions to automatically determine refinement orderings that ensure that all data to make choices are in place before decisions are considered. Currently, SciFinance customers provide the specification in a file, but the knowledge representation and planner are formulated such that it would be easy to develop specifications interactively if that became desirable.

SciFinance's reflective implementation does trade ease and speed of development for performance. Fortunately, because the synthesis speed is roughly proportional to CPU speed, given reasonable amounts of memory, we can take advantage of the hardware improvement curve to increase the practical problem size that SciFinance can handle without major tuning.

Application Use and Payoff

SciFinance was first announced in October 1998, after some beta testing, and the first commercial sale came in January 1999 when Merrill Lynch licensed the product for use by quantitative analysts in its Global Equity-Linked Product and Technology Unit. Some other customers we are permitted to list are Bear Stearns, MeesPierson, and KBC Financial Products. All report that specifying problems in a high-level language and automating the code generation has many advantages, primarily the ability to quickly develop complex models, focus precious human resources on the most critical analytic tasks, and reap accurate, high-quality, and consistent code. We have no way to obtain an exact count, but we know that hundreds of codes have been generated.

Customers' descriptions of benefits

Promoting a focus on the modeling tasks. Analysts at Merrill Lynch have been using SciFinance for a year. In a detailed case study co-authored with SciComp (Gatheral et al. 1999), they write that software synthesis makes it much easier to handle complex problems and allows them to focus on the problem and modeling choices, rather than on programming and debugging. In doing research, they can now solve within a day or two problems that appeared too complex to solve in a reasonable time using conventional techniques. In addition, quick turnaround gives their busy analysts the time to experiment with alternative techniques and fine-tune production codes. The analysts have also found that automatically generating codes ensures a consistent set of assumptions about the valuation of a portfolio and a consistent style across all models, even when those models are generated by different people over an extended period of time.

Reducing labor in a risk-control environment. Dr. Raymond Hawkins, Associate Director of Risk Control at Bear, Stearns Securities Corporation, uses SciFinance in a risk-control rather than trading environment. The risk-control department performs risk analysis for clearance of client portfolios on a daily basis, re-pricing every single security within a portfolio and doing a variety of stress tests to determine the portfolio risk. For each security, the department first develops an ASPEN specification that incorporates the terms and conditions of the security, then develops a pricing tool from the code that SciFinance generates. Bear, Stearns Securities previously depended on proprietary models for the pricing tools, but moved to SciFinance because they felt it would be an extremely cost-effective approach. For Dr. Hawkins, an important feature of software synthesis is its ability to reduce labor while producing consistent, highly accurate programs. With program synthesis, highly trained analysts can focus their energy on the analysis and risk control, not on programming.

Increasing code accuracy and development speed. Dr. Anastasios Politis, currently a quantitative analyst at KBC Financial Products, has been using SciFinance for a year and a half to generate codes for pricing new options (both for research and production) and to determine whether closed-form solutions are precise enough. Dr. Politis says that SciFinance makes code development faster and easier for him, and that his bank benefits from more accurate models and fewer deals lost because of slow pricing. SciFinance allows Dr. Politis to develop many models within a single day rather than over the course of a week. Using conventional manual programming methods to develop finite difference codes of the variety SciFinance produces, he says, is immensely time consuming (exactly how time-consuming depends on the resemblance to existing codes). By putting the correct numerical elements, such as solvers, at his disposal, SciFinance enables Dr. Politis to develop some new models in just a few hours. For generating certain types of models (those for American-style options and barrier options) SciFinance has become Dr. Politis' preferred method. He finds codes generated by SciFinance to be superior to the more traditional lattice-based codes. In addition, because certain features can be expressed with a single ASPEN specification statement, SciFinance greatly facilitates his pricing of the varied complex features of options such as convertible bonds.

Gaining confidence in models. MeesPierson analysts use SciFinance primarily to gain confidence in their existing models and to test new modeling approaches. They expect to generate production pricing models in the future. With SciFinance, analysts have been able to rapidly generate a variety of accurate, PDE-based codes to validate existing pricing products. Also, they can more quickly and confidently test new pricing models, which helps bring new exotic-option products to market faster. MeesPierson analysts also use SciFinance to research new pricing approaches and conduct experiments that give them a better feel for more sophisticated models.

Changes to business processes

For many financial institutions, using SciFinance would require changing the way they integrate codes into their production environment. To minimize these changes, ASPEN provides several integration constructs, both producing top-level codes that are callable from spreadsheets or C++ methods and providing stub functions to call customer routines. Customization of these interfaces is also relatively straightforward because ASPEN can be easily extended.

Merrill Lynch analysts, in addition to writing new codes with SciFinance, expect to rewrite much of their existing codes using the ASPEN specifications as documentation for what the codes do. They consider the business process changes to be positive, indicating an evolution from having traders responsible for everything from designing models to executing transactions into a mature industry characterized by a cooperative division of labor. This division pairs the customer's regular uncovering of new mathematical problems in their derivatives structuring activity with SciComp's experience with numerical PDE solution techniques, thus benefiting both parties.

Future benefits

As synthesis from high-level languages becomes more widely used, we can expect continued extensions in the varieties of financial and numerical methods made available and continued improvements in the efficiency of the generated codes. We also expect analysts to increasingly delegate the responsibility for design choices about numerical methods and parameters to automated systems with expertise in these areas. And as more knowledge is incorporated into the systems, specifications will be couched in even more natural "deal-sheet" terms.

The ASPEN language itself can become a useful communication tool within a large company or even industry-wide. It provides a clear conceptual framework for computational models that separates the problem from numerical algorithms and is free from unimportant implementation details. ASPEN could become a concise vehicle for auditors, risk managers, and regulators to assess portfolio risk at a high level of abstraction. Yet because it is tied to a code generating tool, the exchange and refinement of ASPEN specifications can lead directly into producing high quality executable models. We also see a possibility for ASPEN to evolve into the next-generation language for more general mathematical modeling.

Application Development and Deployment
A Brief History

SciFinance and its underlying SciNapse technology evolved over about eight years with an average of two or three computer scientists as implementors and one or two mathematicians and physicists as advisors, testers, and users. The precursor project, called Sinapse, began at Schlumberger in late 1990 with the application of modeling seismic and acoustic logging tools and with a target language of Connection Machine Fortran. Several generated codes (after some hand tuning) were used in internal logging tool design projects. In 1995, Elaine Kant, the head of the Schlumberger Sinapse project, acquired the rights to the code and founded SciComp to further develop the system. A three-year NIST Advanced Technology Program award funded additional research to advance software synthesis technology for scientific computing on multiple architectures. After about two years, the focus began to narrow to financial applications and the generation of C code. After some venture funding from the Verticality Investment Group and about a year of additional development and beta testing, full-fledged commercial sales of SciFinance began in October 1998.

The development process, though not formal, is close in spirit to a spiral model. After initial prototyping, system evolution was essentially incremental, adding new mathematical constructs and new programming or optimization knowledge based on project plans and customer demand. Major replacement of the specification language and parser, the planning system, and the code generator occurred without interruption to system availability. After every major change, a growing set of regression tests (based on examples generated in-house and examples that customers chose to share) is run. Subsets of the tests are run after smaller changes.

Development Issues

Building a rapidly extensible underlying technology has always been a goal and has occupied much of the first years of SciNapse development. Success has been based on the object-oriented design with an emphasis on making the system interface, specification language, and documentation self-generative from the knowledge base (it took three tries to develop the most workable specification language). Also, the template representation of algorithms brings regularity and discipline to the definition of new algorithms and their availability in specifications. And Mathematica, despite its shortcomings in execution speed, programming environment, and user interface modifiability, has served as a flexible programming language that integrates programming, computer algebra and notebook interface in a single system.

Focusing on the application area and involving users in the process began early, though even earlier would have been better. After we published some textbook-level financial modeling examples in August 1996, potential customers started sending us challenge problems. We generated some increasingly sophisticated financial modeling codes, and eventually committed ourselves to finance as our initial application area. At that time, we stopped new work on parallel computing and Fortran, both useful for numerical modeling but not necessary for SciFinance. We tried, but to date have failed, to set up any formal development partnerships.

Deployment Issues

Customers typically evaluate SciFinance for several months before deciding to buy. During this period, quantitative analysts learn how to write ASPEN specifications and determine how easy it is to produce the codes they need. Usually they generate the equivalent of some of their own codes and compare them for accuracy and efficiency. When convinced that automatically generated codes are of at least comparable quality, they move on to a current problem of substantially greater difficulty to ensure that it too can be specified and correctly generated. The last step is usually to determine whether they can easily adapt the generated codes to the bank's production environment. In some cases this involves a customization of the ASPEN interface specification features to the particular information technology needs of the bank.

Convincing analysts that they can spare the time to try a new paradigm is a continuing hurdle. Enormous consequence falls on the appropriateness and accuracy of their models, and they are accustomed to working with familiar methods in a tightly controlled way. Some analysts do not regularly use PDE methods. Although time is still a major issue, the initial skepticism about whether SciFinance could generate sophisticated and accurate codes is rapidly diminishing as our customer list and technical publication list grow. We must, however, continually increase the scope of the system's applications and mathematical sophistication in order to keep existing customers and attract the new customers that already have substantial bases of existing codes.

Rapidly developing interfaces to customers' proprietary environments is an important part of making the system useful to a broad range of institutions. Unfortunately, there are no industry standards for trading system interfaces or error handling. There are too many different commercial and in-house developed back-office systems to develop in advance for all possibilities. Instead we provided some basic solutions and developed tools to simplify customization. ASPEN has many constructs for reading and otherwise initializing data, specifying external calls to user functions, and making the generated codes callable. It also has ways to specify dynamic memory management (in C) and an error-handling scheme that propagates error codes. Based on customer requests, we have created half a dozen parameterizations for the structure of the top-level generated routine, and we have modified the original error-handling scheme to make it thread-safe.

Maintenance

SciFinance serves a competitive market with rapidly evolving needs. As a commercial product, it will grow and be maintained for a long time. Evolution includes not only bug fixes, but also the addition of new algorithms, performance enhancements, better design choice heuristics, new design choice options, and interface extensions. As previously discussed, SciFinance was designed with continuous update in mind, and many system features are derived directly from the knowledge base, which also has many internal consistency checks. We update the internal development version continually, with commercial releases about once every two months. A release typically includes about a half dozen new or extended features as well as several bug fixes.

Users can make some extensions through specification macros, and eventually we will make an algorithm description language available. More extensive additions to the knowledge base must be made by the developers based on suggestions from customer or staff mathematicians and financial analysts. Typically, staff mathematicians and computer scientists must work together to devise the most appropriate generalizations of the financial-construct and mathematical-optimization suggestions before they are implemented. In addition to keeping up with new financial constructs and improvements in numerical methods, we plan the more intensive addition of a new class of methods, Monte Carlo simulations. Over the long term, we may expand into additional areas of financial modeling, produce generic PDE packages for students and professional engineers, extend the system to specific applications, and provide interfaces for less technically oriented users.

It is crucial that SciFinance generate correct code, which

is especially challenging because the system is most attractive to people who push the limits with complex, marginally tractable problems (professional practitioners already have solutions to the easy problems). We attack the correctness problem with the specification parsing previously described and with automated development-time tests and regression tests. During development, the template translator employs extensive semantic checking, providing diagnostic assistance like that of a helpful compiler. The object methods are checked for circularity and type conformance. Synthesis-time appropriateness checks encoded in our object methods help guarantee that the process is running as expected. An object examiner and various process-monitoring tools assist in unit testing and debugging. Much of the documentation is re-generated from the system's semantic network of information whenever it changes, minimizing maintenance effort and eliminating the possibility of making certain kinds of errors. A mechanical validity check of the information network verifies that every alleged node reference is to a node that actually exists and checks that every node in the network can be reached. We always subject proposed system updates to extensive regression testing, which compares the regenerated codes with previous versions, runs them through Purify^R, tests the numerical results, and monitors execution times. We test widely over the cross product of new features, including incorrect specifications, to ensure graceful error recovery and cogent diagnostics.

Summary

SciFinance brings an integrated set of AI, knowledge-based, and computer-algebra techniques to bear on the real-world problems of numerical modeling, providing a commercial software synthesis system for solving PDEs in computational finance. Customers testify that the system increases productivity, reduces development time, and yields consistently high-quality codes that can conform to institutional environments. The system's mathematical knowledge can lower the entry barrier for non-mathematicians, and the extensive data structure and programming knowledge completely relieve the user of coding burdens. The system's common knowledge base minimizes maintenance efforts. The evolution of the target application from sonic and seismic modeling to computational finance demonstrates the adaptability of the system's fundamental design. This flexibility also allows developers to respond rapidly to user needs, a necessity in the fast-moving world of securities option pricing.

Acknowledgments

SciFinance would not exist as a product without contributions from our consultants and other SciComp team members; thanks to Stanly Steinberg, David Johansen, Larry Schumann, Miriam Boral, and Monica Garcia. We also are grateful to Elaine Rich and the IAAI reviewers for critical readings of this paper, and to our customer/colleagues who have graciously shared their experiences.

This work was supported in part by the National Institute of Standards and Technology under Advanced Technology Program Cooperative Agreement Number 70NANB5H1017.

References

Akers, R.; Kant, E.; Randall, C.; Steinberg, S.; and Young, R. 1997. SciNapse: A Problem-Solving Environment for Partial Differential Equations. *IEEE Computational Science and Engineering*. 4(3):32-42.

Akers, R.; Baffes, P.; Kant, E.; Randall,C.; Steinberg, S.; and Young, R. 1998. Automatic Synthesis of Numerical Codes for Solving Partial Differential Equations. Special Issue *Non-Standard Applications of Computer Algebra* of *Mathematics and Computers in Simulation* 45(1-2):3-22.

Brown, G. and Randall, C. 1999. If the Skew Fits. *Risk Magazine* 12(4):62-65.

Chien, S.; Fisher, F.; Lo, E.; Mortensen, H.; and Greeley, R. 1999. Using Artificial Intelligence Planning to Automate Science Data Analysis for Large Image Databases. *Intelligent Data Analysis* 3:159-176.

Gallopoulos, E., and Sameh, A. 1997. *CSE: Content and Product. IEEE Computational Science and Engineering* 4(2):39-43.

Gatheral, J.; Epelbaum, Y.; Han, J.; Laud, K.; Lubovitsky, O.; Kant, E.; and Randall, C. 1999. Implementing Option-Pricing Models Using Software Synthesis. *Computing in Science and Engineering* 1(6):54-64.

Johnson, W. L., and Nuseibeh, B., eds. *Automated Software Engineering: An International Journal*.

Kant, E. 1993. Synthesis of Mathematical Modeling Software. *IEEE Software* 10(3):30-41.

Lowry, M. R., and McCartney, R. D., eds. 1991. *Automating Software Design*. Menlo Park, CA:AAAI Press/The MIT Press.

Randall, C.; Kant, E.; and Chhabra, A. 1998. Using program synthesis to price derivatives. *Journal of Computational Finance* 1(2):97-129.

Wolfram, S. 1999. *The Mathematica Book*. Wolfram Media/Cambridge University Press.

Young, R. L; Kant, E.; and Akers, L. A. 2000. A Knowledge-Based Electronic Information and Documentation System. In *Proceedings of the 2000 International Conference on Intelligent User Interfaces*, 280-285. New Orleans, LA:ACM Press.

Assentor®: an NLP-based Solution to E-mail Monitoring

Chinatsu Aone, Mila Ramos-Santacruz, William J. Niehaus

SRA International, Inc.
4300 Fair Lakes Court
Fairfax, VA 22033
{aonec, mila, niehaus}@verdi.sra.com

Abstract

This paper describes the Natural Language Processing (NLP) component of an e-mail monitoring product called Assentor®. Assentor monitors electronic correspondence for brokerage firms. It uses pattern-matching-based information extraction technology to find and quarantine e-mail messages that indicate, among others, customer complaints, insider trading, stock hyping, hard-pressure sales tactics, and firm preservation issues such as jokes and obscenities. This paper presents a quantitative evaluation of applying pattern matching vs. keyword-based searching to e-mail monitoring. Our evaluation shows that pattern matching performs significantly better than keyword-based searching both in terms of recall (false negatives) and precision (false positives).

Introduction

As e-mail replaces more traditional means of communication in the business arena, firms and institutions need ways to guarantee that their e-mail correspondence is in full compliance with laws and regulations. This is especially true of tightly regulated industries such as the securities industry, where traditionally *compliance officers* review hardcopy correspondence. The securities industry's regulatory bodies (the Securities and Exchange Commission, the National Association of Securities Dealers, and the New York Stock Exchange) have regulations that require a reasonable review of broker e-mail communications (i.e., SEC Rules 17a-3 and 17a-4, NASD Rule 3010 and NYSE Rule 342). The monitoring is designed to prevent violations such as stock hyping, insider trading, and hard-pressure sales tactics, as well as to properly handle customer complaints. Because of the difficulty of monitoring large amounts of e-mail messages, many securities firms have not fully implemented e-mail; others go through tedious manual review procedures to guard against illegal communications. However, manual review of e-mail messages is costly, time-consuming, inconsistent, and simply not feasible for firms with large volumes of e-mail correspondence. Most importantly, manual (pre-)review of e-mail messages defeats the purpose of e-mail, which is immediate delivery.

Copyright © 2000, American Association for Artificial Intelligence (www.aaai.org). All rights reserved.

The problem of e-mail monitoring, therefore, calls for an automated solution. In this paper we describe an e-mail message screening system called Assentor®, which relies on Natural Language Processing (NLP) technology, in particular pattern-matching-based information extraction. The system has been tailored for securities and investment firms. It flags potentially improper communications, such as illegal stock hyping, high-pressure sales tactics, insider trading, and other potentially litigious issues, for human review. In this paper, we describe Assentor's screening capability and present a quantitative evaluation of the NLP-based vs. keyword-based approaches. This evaluation shows that Assentor's NLP-based approach performs significantly better than keyword searching both in terms of precision and recall.

Application Description

Assentor is an e-mail monitoring system tailored for brokerage and investment firms. Assentor sits inside the firm's firewall. As illustrated in Figure 1, the system monitors e-mail messages to and from brokers. The system administrator provides the list of users to monitor and sets the level of monitoring (threshold) for individual users. The system can be configured to apply different levels of monitoring based on seniority and past performance of individual brokers. For instance, senior or highly trusted brokers may be subject to less scrutiny than junior brokers. When Assentor flags a message, it quarantines it for human review. The system can be configured to either let a copy of the message go to its intended recipient or hold the message until a human reviewer approves or rejects it. A compliance officer reviews the message quarantined and can reject it, approve it, or send a warning to the sender.

Assentor integrates a number of Original Equipment Manufacturer (OEM) products. As outlined in the architecture diagram in Figure 2, messages are first decomposed (e.g., attachments are separated) using Integralis MAILsweeper™. Then, messages are checked for viruses using Command Software™ and converted to ASCII text (e.g., Microsoft Word to ASCII text) using INSO Outside In™.

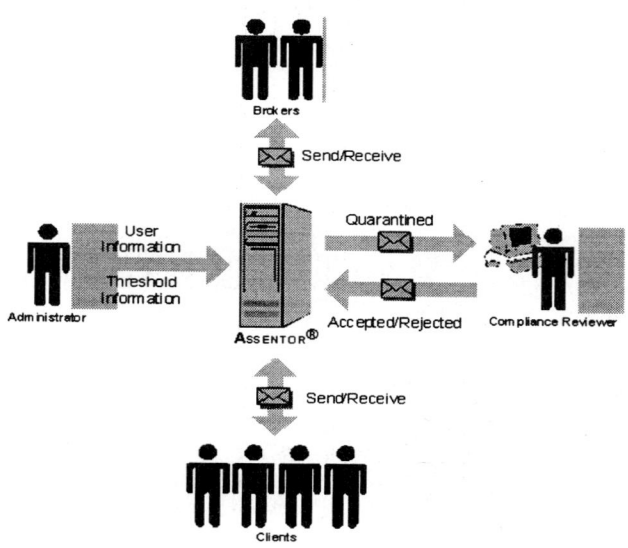

Figure 1: Assentor's Concept of Operation

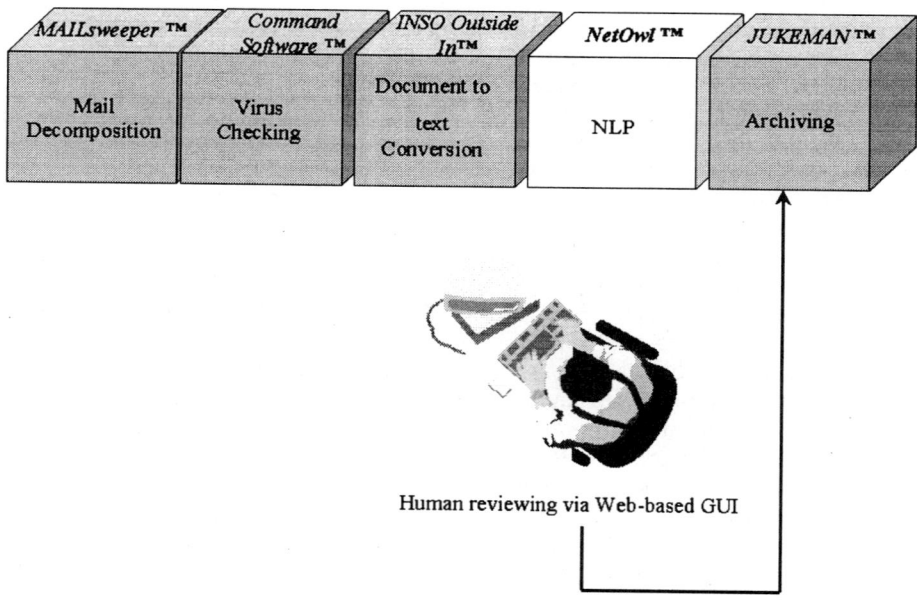

Figure 2: Assentor's Architecture Diagram

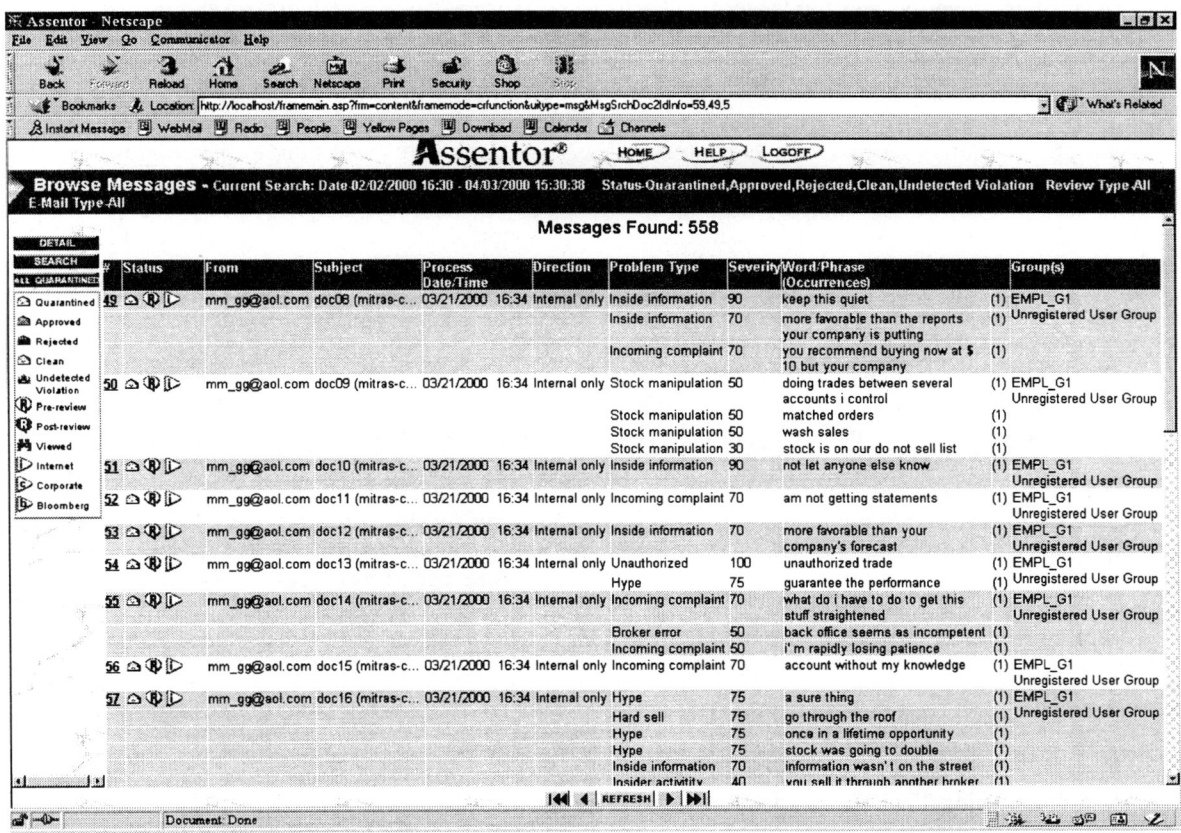

Figure 3: Assentor's "Browse Messages" Screen

At the heart of Assentor is SRA's information extraction engine NetOwl™, which flags potentially improper messages to be quarantined. A compliance reviewer reviews quarantined messages through Assentor's Web-based Graphical User Interface (GUI). Figure 3 shows a list of sample quarantined messages on Assentor's "Browse Messages" screen. Finally, Assentor archives all messages using JUKEMAN™ and generates e-mail management reports. Assentor runs on NT.

In this paper we will concentrate on Assentor's NLP component. Table 1 lists the problem categories tracked by Assentor and the e-mail direction (i.e., inbound or outbound) to which they apply. When Assentor finds an e-mail message containing one of these potential violations, the system quarantines the message.

Category	Direction
Incoming Complaint	In
Legal	In
Money Laundering	In
Stock Manipulation	In
Unauthorized	In
Hard Sell	Out
IPO	Out
Puffery	Out
Reply to Complaint	Out
Restricted Issue	Out
Broker Error	In/Out
Encryption Key	In/Out
Encryption Signature	In/Out
Encryption Message	In/Out
Hype	In/Out
Inappropriate	In/Out
Insider Activity	In/Out
Inside Information	In/Out
Profanity	In/Out
Rumor	In/Out
Terms to Monitor	In/Out

Table 1: Issues Monitored by Assentor

Each problem category (e.g., complaints, rumors, insider trading, etc.) is divided into three sublevels (i.e., high severity, medium severity, and low severity). Each sublevel contains a set of concepts to be monitored. The concepts are organized into these sublevels according to the severity of the content they convey and the ambiguity they may carry. For instance, the high level of the complaint category contains concepts such as complaints about big money losses or broker's recommendations, and requests that an account be terminated. The medium severity includes complaints about unexpected commissions and unsuitable investments. The low severity level is for concepts such as trouble contacting the broker, mild blaming for stock performance, and ambiguous indications of unhappiness by the customer (e.g., "*I'm disappointed*", which could occur in the context of a personal message). The Assentor system administrator at the firm can set up broker groups and turn sublevels on and off depending on the firm's policy for each group. The application can thus be configured to apply different levels of monitoring based on seniority and past performance of individual brokers.

Uses of AI Technology

Assentor relies on NLP technology, in particular information extraction. Information extraction (IE) is emerging as a new technology in commercial solutions. Commercial IE tools include SRA's NetOwl™, IBM's Intelligent Miner™ for Text (Dorre, Gerstl, and Seiffert 1999), and Inxight's Thing Finder™ (www.inxight.com/products/developer/ad_tf.html). To the best of our knowledge, Assentor is the first industry-wide solution that applies pattern-matching-based IE technology to e-mail monitoring and categorization.

Assentor integrates NetOwl and applies generic and domain-specific patterns for the securities industry compliance domain. The generic patterns recognize names of people, companies, locations, e-mail and http addresses, telephone numbers, monetary figures, dates, and time expressions. The domain-specific patterns that we developed specifically for Assentor recognize phrases and sentences relevant to the securities industry compliance domain. Domain knowledge is thus represented in patterns. We worked closely with compliance officers to knowledge engineer the patterns for NetOwl. NetOwl is written in C++ and runs on Windows NT and Sun Solaris.

Various approaches can be adopted for e-mail monitoring from simple keyword-based searching to machine-learning-based techniques. In order to find the most suitable AI technology for e-mail monitoring, we have also evaluated a supervised learning-based approach (nearest neighbor). Our experiments showed than the learning-based categorization approach does not perform well when there is not a large amount of training data available. In our experience only 2% of all messages merit flagging in this e-mail monitoring application for the securities industry. Thus, it is very difficult to collect enough training examples for categories that are rare, such as Stock Manipulation and Insider Trading.

By contrast, since humans can easily generalize a comparatively small set of examples, pattern matching is especially suitable for e-mail monitoring. Moreover, pattern matching has rendered the best results in information extraction, as shown in the series of Message Understanding Conferences (cf. Aone *et al.* 1998).

Some firms use keyword-based searching for e-mail monitoring. A common perception is that keywords flag as many *bad* messages as patterns (or even more), but produce more incorrect hits (*false positives*). To compare the performance of Assentor's NLP-based solution and keyword-based searching, we ran both Assentor and a list of keywords on two sets of unseen messages, or *blind sets*. The first set contains 2000 incoming messages, 163 of which are *bad* messages. The second set contains 1800 outgoing messages, 129 of which are *bad* messages. All our training and blind sets are real-world messages provided by brokerage firms. Our list of keywords was the combination of 3 keyword lists we obtained from 3 brokerage firms (a total of 300 unique keywords).

Our evaluation showed that Assentor's NLP-based approach performs significantly better than keyword searching both in terms of *recall* and *precision*. Recall is the percentage of *bad* messages that were correctly identified as such. Assentor identified 30% more *bad* messages than keyword-based searching. *Precision* is the percentage of flagged messages that were correctly identified as *bad* messages. Assentor's precision was four times better than keyword-based searching. Low precision translates into a higher number of messages that need human review. In other words, the more incorrect hits (*false positives*) a system outputs, the more expensive it is to review the messages.

It is easy to see why pattern matching produces better precision than keyword-based searching. Keywords are typically single words or short phrases. If a document or message contains a keyword, the document is automatically flagged regardless of the keyword's actual meaning. Because of this, keywords generate a high number of false positives. For instance, a keyword like "tip" will not distinguish between a relevant phrase (e.g., "*I'll give you a tip for your investments*") and an irrelevant one (e.g., "*they never tip the waiter*"). Similarly, the keyword "sue" will not distinguish between a relevant phrase (e.g., "*I'm going to sue your company*") and an irrelevant one (e.g., "*Sue called*").

By contrast, Assentor's pattern-matching-based technology incorporates linguistic context, which helps to remove ambiguity. For instance, "safest" and other superlatives are stock-hyping keywords, but only when they are predicated of things like "accounts" or "stocks". Assentor recognizes when superlative terms describe stock phrases. Thus, it flags "*this stock is the best investment*" but not "*an education is the best investment.*"

It is very important to note that our NLP-based approach also produces better recall than keyword-based searching. There are a number of reasons for this. First, Assentor's patterns benefit from its dynamic name recognition capability. It dynamically identifies names of companies, people, and locations based on the linguistic properties of these phrases, instead of relying on static lists of names. It also identifies dates and monetary expressions which cannot be listed. Assentor's patterns take advantage of these semantic classes. For instance, a hard-pressure sales tactic pattern for phrases like "you must buy <COMPANY>" will match both known companies as in "*You must buy IBM*" as well as new companies as in "*You must buy XYZ Corp.*" Keyword lists, by contrast, are not likely to include a complete list of all companies and are usually not capable of recognizing new company names.

Second, Assentor's NLP-based technology includes the capability to recognize morphological variants, i.e., the different shapes that a single word can take (e.g., "mismanage, mismanagement", "look, looks, looked, looking"). This morphological capability makes its patterns more flexible and robust than a keyword-based system. In a keyword-based system, compliance officers have to think of all possible word variants and combinations of variants. It is easy to forget to list some of these variants or combinations. By contrast, Assentor's morphological analysis capability enables the system to avoid such omissions. For instance, a single pattern for the concept of "mishandling or mismanaging accounts" can match the following phrases:

"You have mishandled my account"
"Mishandling our accounts"
"You mismanaged the account I opened with you"
"Your broker has mishandled my account"
"I see mismanagement of my accounts"
"Mishandling of my account"

Third, relevant concepts are often expressed with sentences consisting only of *common* words such as "*want*," "*told*," "*consented*," "*buy*," "*fee*," etc. Keyword lists do not usually include common words because they flag too many messages. Assentor's patterns can recognize expressions involving common words without generating many false positives. For instance, Assentor's patterns can recognize the following types of expressions, which are difficult for the keyword-based approach to recognize without generating many false positives.

Broker Errors:
"I did not want to do this in the first place"
"I thought you were going to buy that Japan Fund"
Unauthorized Activities:
"We never told you to use our margin"
"We had never actually consented to make that purchase"
Complaints:
"We don't think it's fair to be charged these fees"
"This trust has been returning less than I expected"

IPO:
"The firm is looking to do a deal"
"Major systems integration company will be coming to market"
Hard-pressure Sales Tactics:
"You owe it to yourself"
"You know that you deserve it"
Stock Hyping:
"Buy it while you still can"
"Stock is priced like it's going out of business"

In summary, contrary to the common perception that keywords can catch as many relevant messages as more sophisticated techniques, the keyword-based approach not only produces more false positives but also catches fewer relevant messages than Assentor's NLP approach.

Application Development and Deployment

The first step in the development of Assentor was to gather domain knowledge about the securities industry's special needs for e-mail monitoring. During this early stage, securities industry consultants and a group of early adopters and pilot firms provided their insight as well as hardcopy and electronic copy of their correspondence under a strict confidentiality agreement.

As the second step, this correspondence data was split into training and blind sets. With the help of a GUI-based annotation tool, human annotators highlighted questionable messages, and marked and categorized relevant phrases in them.

Computational linguists then performed a data analysis of the training data and wrote patterns. Patterns are generalizations of the examples found in the training corpus. For instance, the example "*I did not receive a confirmation for my IBM trade*" is a complaint about not receiving something. Computational linguists generalize examples using synonyms, domain knowledge, and linguistic constructs. By adding synonyms in the patterns, variations such as "*I did not get a confirmation for my IBM trade*" are also captured. Using domain knowledge, other relevant objects are added to the pattern to cover variations such as: "*I did not receive stocks/certificates/information/dividends,*" etc. Through linguistic variations (e.g., passivization, contractions, reordering, etc.) of the original example, further variations are captured: "*you did not send me/I didn't get/we never got/we haven't got*" etc.

An automated scoring tool provided feedback about the effectiveness of the rule set on both training and blind sets in terms of standard information extraction metrics: recall, precision, and f-measure. The false positives and false negatives found in the development sets were used to further refine the pattern set.

Most errors in the blind sets are false positives. Assentor's patterns are tailored to brokers' business correspondence, but brokers' correspondence includes a fair amount of non-business related messages. The latter often contain language that is very similar to the problems that Assentor is searching for. For instance, complaints such as "I'm very unhappy and disappointed" may well occur in the context of a personal message.

Application Use and Payoff

At present, Assentor has been deployed at 77 brokerage and investment firms, with a total of 89,195 seats. Some firms have been using it for as long as two years. Firms' compliance officers use the system on a daily basis. It is estimated that for a firm with 1000 brokers, the complete manual human review solution (randomly selecting 15% of all messages) costs about 5 times as much as the Assentor solution, and that the keyword-based solution costs more than twice as much. As an additional benefit of using Assentor, firms report that it reduces non-business e-mail correspondence. Moreover, the amount of e-mail messages containing inappropriate language (e.g., obscenities and jokes) tends to decrease considerably after the first two weeks of deployment.

Maintenance

Pattern refinement continues on a regular basis as we receive feedback and new sets of sample e-mail messages from firms. As actual examples of violations are scarce, client feedback is an essential part of improving the NLP performance. So far, we have analyzed over 60,000 messages. Pattern updates are provided to the firms quarterly as part of maintenance. Releases are distributed by CD. Patches can be downloaded from the Assentor customer website.

Summary and Future Directions

We have described an e-mail monitoring tool that uses pattern-matching-based information extraction. We presented an evaluation of its performance vs. keyword-based searching. Our evaluation shows that pattern matching performs significantly better than keyword-based searching both in terms of precision and recall.

We are planning to apply Assentor technology to other areas. One area is website monitoring i) to ensure that sensitive or proprietary information of organizations is not publicly disclosed on their webpages, and ii) to allow companies to monitor negative news about themselves. Another exciting application is to use this technology in e-mail response management systems (ERMS) to dramatically improve e-mail-based customer service in e-Business. The NLP technology that underlies Assentor will enable automated or semi-automated response to customer's e-mail messages.

Acknowledgments

Assentor would have not been possible without the contributions of the entire Assentor team and the feedback provided by Assentor's early adopters, pilot firms, and customers. Our thanks to all of them.

References

Aone, Chinatsu, Lauren Halverson, Tom Hampton, and Mila Ramos-Santacruz. 1998. "SRA: Description of the IE^2 System Used for MUC-7." In Proceedings of the 7th Message Understanding Conference (MUC-7). www.muc.saic.com.

Dorre, Jochen, Peter Gerstl, and Roland Seiffert. 1999. "Text Mining: Finding Nuggets in Mountains of Textual Data." In Proceedings of the Knowledge Discovery and Data Mining Conference (KDD-99).

Nurse Rostering at the Hospital Authority of Hong Kong

Andy Hon Wai Chun

City University of Hong Kong
Department of Electronic Engineering
Tat Chee Avenue, Kowloon
Hong Kong
eehwchun@cityu.edu.hk

Steve Ho Chuen Chan, Garbbie Pui Shan Lam, Francis Ming Fai Tsang, Jean Wong and Dennis Wai Ming Yeung

Advanced Object Technologies Limited
Unit 602A, HK Industrial Technology Center
72 Tat Chee Avenue, Kowloon
Hong Kong
{steve, garbbie, francis, jean, dennis}@aotl.com

Abstract

This paper describes the Rostering Engine (RE) that we have developed for the Hospital Authority (HA), Hong Kong as part of their Staff Rostering System (SRS) using AI constraint-programming techniques. The Hospital Authority manages over 40 public hospitals in Hong Kong. With close to 1500 wards total, the amount of resources needed to produce weekly staff rosters for each ward is tremendous and extremely time consuming. Previously, most staff rosters were generated manually. Without computer records, it was difficult for HA to produce workforce statistics or to improve resource efficiency. In early 1997, the Hospital Authority embarked on a strategic Staff Rostering System project to provide automation support in managing their large workforce of over 48,000 full-time hospital staff. The Staff Rostering System performs ward-level rostering based on ward-specific constraints, staff requests, and work patterns. Version 1 of the system was completed early 1998 and Version 2 was released early 1999. The system is gradually being deployed in different public hospitals across Hong Kong.

Task Description

The Hong Kong Hospital Authority (http://www.ha.org.hk) was established in 1990 as an independent body to manage all public hospitals in Hong Kong. It is accountable to the Hong Kong Government through the Secretary for Health and Welfare. It provides medical treatment and rehabilitation services to patients through hospitals, specialist clinics and outreaching services. At the end of 1997, the Authority managed over 26,400 hospital beds; representing roughly 4.06 public hospital beds per 1,000 population. To fulfil its roles, the Authority employs over 48,000 full-time staff. In 1997, the Authority managed over 44 public hospitals/institutions and 49 specialist outpatient-centers.

Copyright © 2000, American Association for Artificial Intelligence (www.aaai.org). All rights reserved.

The wards within each HA hospital schedules and manages its own nurses and clinical supporting staffs. Some staff members work across wards and need to be scheduled at the departmental level. This is obviously a very time-consuming task but needs to be performed regularly. In 1997, the Hospital Authority started to work with the City University of Hong Kong to design and develop the core rostering engine of their Staff Rostering System.

Ward managers use the Staff Rostering System (SRS) to schedule, reschedule and manage different types of staff such as nurses, student nurses and clinical supporting staff. Since the SRS will be used by a wide variety of different wards and hospitals which have their own specific needs and requirements, in additional to the standard Hospital Authority rules and constraints, the SRS was designed to be flexible enough to capture different types of operational needs. The way rostering is performed may also be different from ward to ward. For instance, rostering may be performed in stages for different ranks and shifts – a night roster may be prepared before the day duties are planned, or nursing officer's night shifts might be rostered first. For course, different groups of staff and different shifts will have different sets of rules and constraints. Rostering may also be performed in different intervals. For example, night shift rostering might be performed once every 4 weeks while other shifts may be rostered on a weekly or bi-weekly manner.

SRS will be used to roster many different types of staff and by many different types of wards and hospitals. Designing a sufficiently comprehensive set of rules and constraints and a rostering algorithm that is sufficiently flexible to handle all the different types of rostering needs were the main challenges in this project.

System Goals

Although many of the constraints used in SRS are unique to the Hospital Authority, the main goals and objectives of the SRS are similar to those of many other rostering systems. For example, the SRS should ensure that there is an adequate number and mixture of skilled staff present to maintain committed level of service quality. At the same time, each staff member should be assigned an appropriate number of working hours in accordance with their terms of appointment, i.e., should not be over-worked or under-utilized.

For course the roster should also be as fair as possible to all staff members. For example, each staff should be equally given the same number of days off on weekends and public holidays or the same number of night duties. Understanding that each person has their individual needs, staff requests and preferences should also be considered during rostering and accepted as long as they do not impact the overall roster.

Another key objective is to make the roster as "friendly" as possible. For example, it should maximize the interval between performing two night duties. It should prevent or avoid shift patterns that are not desirable. For example, having to work two night duties on consecutive Sundays or having to work an afternoon shift just before a night shift.

The fundamental requirement that any rostering system must follow is of course to ensure that all Government labor regulations are followed and that all appointment terms are met. The system should also produce rosters within a reasonably short period of time.

Application Description

The Staff Rostering System (SRS) is a computer system developed by HA's Information Technology Division to improve the delivery of health care services. It provides assistance to HA hospitals at the ward level in assigning shifts for nursing staff and supporting staff. Through process re-engineering, the system supports the streamlining of the rostering process and hence increases productivity. The functions of SRS include:

- Generating rosters using constraint programming
- Printing rosters for distribution to staff
- Storing roster records into a database
- Generating management reports

SRS adopts a two-tiered client-server architecture. Database operations such as retrieval, display, and modification of rosters, personnel information, and constraints are performed using Microsoft Visual Basic as the front-end to the back-end Microsoft SQL Server database. The Rostering Engine is a component of the front-end and is invoked when rosters need to be generated.

Typically, when a ward manager uses the Staff Rostering System, he/she would first update the system with any changes. These can be changes in ward information, such as special duty days, or staff information, such as promotions or resignations, etc. The ward manager would also adjust any constraints or parameters that might have changed. Normally, rules and constraints, once set are fairly stable. The ward manager then enters any staff requests, such as day off, leave encashment, etc., and any pre-assigned duties, such as training. Once all the pre-assignments, requests and changes have been made, the ward manager then invokes the Rostering Engine to produce a roster for a particular set of staff, shifts, and rostering period.

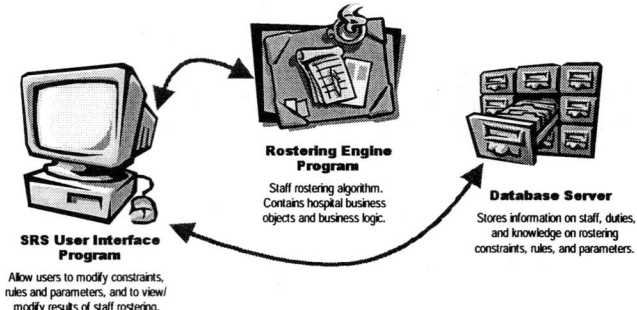

Figure 1. Overall system architecture.

The Rostering Engine creates business objects for the ward being rostered using the following four main types of information:

- **Static information about the ward.** This includes the department this ward belongs to, the shifts within a ward, the special duty days, and how rosters should be generated.

- **Staff information.** This includes information on rank, seniority, assigned wards, leave balances, and personal requests.

- **Constraints and parameters.** These are the constraints and parameters used during rostering. Constraints are described in further detail in Sections below.

- **Historical information.** This includes a set of roster-related statistics, such as number of accumulated leave, etc. and the previous roster history.

Figure 2. Typical operation of the Staff Rostering System.

Guided by the constraints of a ward, the past roster, and staff requests, the Rostering Engine produces the desired roster for the selected set of staff, shifts, and rostering period using AI constraint programming techniques (Chun 1999, Puget 1994).

Uses of AI Technology

The nurse rostering problem is modeled as a constraint satisfaction problem (CSP) (Cohen 1990, Kumar 1992, Steele 1980, Van Hentenryck 1989). The key components to any CSP algorithm are, of course, the variables, their domains, and the constraints that restrict how these variables may be assigned values from their domains. In our Rostering Engine, each variable represents the unknown shift that a nurse should work in, on a particular day. The domain consists of all the shifts defined for the group of staff that the roster is being generated for.

Our rostering constraints are classified as either hard or soft. Hard constraints must be followed strictly, such as enforcing labor regulations. Soft constraints represent preferences. Users are allowed to define different levels of preferences for each soft constraint. To further control how rostering constraints are used, two "scoping" mechanisms are provided – a "when-to-apply" scope and a "who-to-apply" scope. The "when-to-apply" scope defines when a constraint should be applicable, such as only during weekends or on Mondays as examples. The "who-to-apply" scope defines those staffs that are affected by a constraint, such as a particular individual, a group of staff, or staffs belonging to a particular rank.

The following highlights the key constraints considered by our Rostering Engine:

- **Manpower Demand Constraint**

This type of constraint defines manpower requirement for a specific rank, staff group, gender or their combination in a particular shift, as well as the alternative manpower demand patterns in case the original demand cannot be satisfied. For example:

- *Exactly 4 registered nurses on Monday morning can be replaced by 3 registered nurses and 1 enrolled nurse or by 2 registered nurses and 1 student nurse.*
- *At least 1 male registered nurse in night shift.*

- **Working Hours Constraint**

This type of constraint defines the total number of working hours for a staff within the specified time period. For example:

- *An enrolled nurse should work exactly 88 hours per fortnight.*
- *A registered nurse should work at least 40 hours per week.*

- **Shift Distribution Constraint**

This type of constraint defines the frequency that a staff may be assigned a particular shift during the specified time period. For example:

- *At most 1 night shift on Sunday per fortnight.*
- *At least 1 day off on Sunday every 4 weeks.*

- **Days Between Same Shift Constraint**

This type of constraint defines the number of days that should elapse before a staff member takes another shift of the same type. For example:

- *Minimum 4 days between night shifts.*
- *Exactly 3 days between afternoon shifts.*
- *A night shift on Thursday must be followed by a night shift on Sunday.*

- **Consecutive Day-Of-Week Constraint**

This type of constraint defines the total number of consecutive occurrences of a particular shift assigned to a staff on a certain day. For example:

- *Cannot assign night shifts on two consecutive Sundays.*
- *Morning shifts must be assigned in two consecutive Saturdays each time.*
- *Cannot assign day off on two consecutive public holidays.*

- **Shift Sequence Pattern Constraint**

This type of constraint defines a pattern of shifts to be assigned on consecutive days.

- *Afternoon shift is not preferred if before a night shift.*

- *Prefer a day off right after a night shift.*
- *Prefer a morning shift to be followed by a day off and then an afternoon shift.*
- *Should avoid assigning three morning shifts in a row.*
- *Should not assign three night shifts in a row.*

The Rostering Algorithm

The problem of nurse rostering or rostering in general have been subjects for decades of scheduling research (Abdennadher and Schlenker 1999, Martello and Toth 1886, Miller, Pierskalla, and Rath 1990, Randhawa 1983, Rosenbloom and Goertzen 1987). The combinatorial problems of shift assignment are well documented. It is only in recent years that researchers have begun to look into constraint programming as an alternative approach. Several researchers have documented successful applications of constraint programming to nurse and staff rostering (Dresse 1995, Kusumoto 1996, Lau and Lau 1997, Lazaro and Aristondo 1995).

The scheduling algorithm we have created for the Hospital Authority combines the power of constraint propagation with intelligent heuristics to avoid combinatorics associated with rostering. Constraint propagation reduces the search space early on while our heuristics guide the search through the remaining search space. The technique we use is a combination of look-ahead and intelligent scoring to determine which nurse to roster next and which shift would satisfy most of the soft constraints. Through half a year of pilot run, we have refined our heuristics so that the scheduling algorithm yields fairly good results within a short reasonable time.

Application Use and Payoff

Hospital Authority's SRS has been in daily use in wards of the Prince of Wales Hospital, Alice Ho Miu Ling Nethersole Hospital, and Shatin Hospital for over a year. Since then, Kwai Chung Hospital, Kwong Wah Hospital, Bradbury Hospice, and the United Christian Hospital have also gone live. Altogether, over 250 seats of SRS have been installed. Over three hundred people have been trained to use the system. Further deployment at other HA hospitals are being scheduled.

There are numerous benefits in using AI techniques for staff rostering. Some of the key application payoffs are outlined below:

- **Increased Productivity**

Just the process of sitting down and drafting a weekly roster for a single ward is already quite time consuming, not to mention trying to make the roster more efficient and "friendly." Unfortunately, this mundane task of staff rostering must be performed by a highly experienced and skilled staff - the ward manager. In a large hospital, there may be twenty to thirty such ward managers each performing staff rostering for their respective wards. The availability of an automated system, such as the SRS, greatly improves productivity by relieving ward managers of the more mundane aspects of staff scheduling and lets them focus on the actual management of staffs and problem solving. SRS, by using intelligent AI techniques, also produces rosters that assigns staff more efficiently and hence improves the overall productivity of the hospital.

- **Increased Morale**

Because the rules, constraints and parameters used by our Rostering Engine for each ward are clearly specified and well publicized, suspicions of favoritism are eliminated. Having a set of open criteria, by itself, has already greatly improved staff morale in general. In addition, our Rostering Engine ensures that all staffs are treated fairly by using different types of historical statistics to generate the roster. The statistics indicate how "well" each staff has been treated so far, in terms of the number of more desirable or less desirable shifts assigned in the past. Based on the statistics, the Rostering Engine tries to evenly assign "good" shifts to balance out the statistics. Using fairness measures is another way of improving staff morale. Furthermore, the Rostering Engine also tries to satisfy as many staff preferences and requests as possible without violating the fairness criteria, which provides a better sense of belonging. Due to complexity of all the computations involved, the time needed to produce rosters of this quality manually will be overly time consuming.

- **Facilitate Quality Management**

Previously, many wards used only manual approaches to staff scheduling with only paper records of staff work assignments and leave schedules. Trying to produce any management statistics or reports from the paper records was difficult and prone to errors. SRS, with its connected databases, allows the Hospital Authority to quickly and accurate produce any type of management reports at a click of a button. This allows senior management instant access to statistics on workforce productivity and utilization for planning and review.

- **Improved Quality of Service**

The most important objective of any workforce scheduling system is, of course, to improve the quality of service provided by the organization. This quality of service can be ensured by scheduling an adequate number of staff with a well-balanced set of skills and experiences to handle any potential work that might be needed in the ward. The most important criterion considered by the Rostering Engine is to ensure that all workload requirements are satisfied first.

Application Development and Deployment

The SRS project began in early 1997 and was considered as one of the key strategic IT projects of the Hospital Authority.

The project began with an extensive user requirement study. Several larger hospitals within Hong Kong were selected for requirement analysis. The objective was to be able to obtain a board set of requirements that balanced the needs of a wide variety of wards across Hong Kong.

Based on the results of the requirement study, a set of generalized rules and constraints was extracted that encapsulated a majority of the rostering knowledge used by different wards in Hong Kong. Although the Hospital Authority has a fixed set of rules and guideline governing the scheduling of staff, each ward operates slightly differently and has additional constraints and parameters that must also be considered.

Software and database design of the Staff Rostering System began mid-1997. A set of Booch Diagrams (Booch 1994) was used to document the design of the Rostering Engine. Actual software development began soon after that and lasted roughly nine months. Development was performed in parallel; the Hospital Authority designed and implemented the backend database and the front-end Visual Basic graphic user interfaces, while we focused on the C++ Rostering Engine. Total project team size was roughly fifteen people.

The Rostering Engine was developed using the MS Visual Studio development environment. C++ class libraries from RogueWave (http://www.roguewave.com) were used to create the foundation classes and hospital business objects. Class libraries from ILOG (http://www.ilog.com) were used to implement the CSP algorithm and to provide constraint-programming capabilities.

The Hospital Authority began to field test the Staff Rostering System early 1998 in a few selected sites including Prince of Wales Hospital and Alice Ho Miu Ling Nethersole Hospital. During this period, comments and feedback from end users were used to refine the user interfaces, reporting facilities and the backend rostering component. The Rostering Engine was extended, in terms of its scheduling algorithm and heuristics, to better match the needs for individual test wards but without loosing generality. After half a year of field-testing and refinement, Version 1 of the system was officially deployed in mid-1998.

By end of 1998, SRS was deployed in all the general wards of Alice Ho Miu Ling Nethersole Hospital and all the wards of the Shatin Hospital. The Prince of Wales Hospital also began to roll out SRS in all its wards starting early 1999. Also within 1999, over a hundred seats of SRS were installed at Kwai Chung Hospital and Kwong Wah Hospital. In early 2000, SRS began roll out at Bradbury Hospice and the United Christian Hospital. The Staff Rostering System is now in daily use at seven of the larger hospitals in Hong Kong, with a total application installation base of roughly 250 wards total. The implementation of SRS at other public hospitals are still underway.

The Staff Rostering System is an ongoing HA strategic project. New enhancements and software features were added in 1999 and also planed for 2000. One potential enhancement is departmental-level rostering that further enhances staff utilization by sharing staff across wards depending on workload requirements of the wards and the skill sets of the available staff. There are numerous other areas, within the hospital environment, that can also benefit from AI constraint programming technology. For instance, scheduling and managing operation theatres, radiology rooms and operators, hospital beds, ambulance dispatching, etc. The Hospital Authority is now looking into some of these potential areas as well.

Maintenance

The rules and constraints used by the Rostering Engine were designed to be fully maintainable by the hospital end-user, which are mainly the ward managers. A set of simple-to-use MS Visual Basic screens and menus allow HA staff to quickly and conveniently display and update the knowledge base. All ward-specific knowledge, constraints, parameters and data are stored in the local MS SQL Server database. Changes in the knowledge base to reflect changes in operational needs can be routinely performed without any Rostering Engine source code modification. HA's IT Department provides front-line technical and end-user support while we provide additional assistance whenever needed. The City University of Hong Kong (http://www.cityu.edu.hk) and its subsidiary Advanced Object Technologies Limited (http://www.aotl.com) provides development and consulting services on enhancements to the Rostering Engine.

Conclusion

This paper provided a brief overview of the Rostering Engine, which is part of the Hong Kong Hospital Authority's Staff Rostering System. The Rostering

Engine is the scheduling program that generates a roster using constraint-programming techniques given a set of rostering parameters and constraints. The paper described the general architecture of the SRS and the key constraints considered by the RE. Given that there are over a thousand public hospital wards in Hong Kong, our Rostering Engine might eventually become one of the largest installation of any AI system in the Asia Pacific region.

Acknowledgements

The authors would like to thank the Hospital Authority, Hong Kong for providing us with an opportunity to participate in this crucial project. We would also like to thank HA for allowing us to include information on the Rostering Engine in this paper. In particular, we would like to thank Barbara Kwan and her team members Deirdre Chiu and Derek Tang for suggestions made to an earlier version of this paper.

Research performed was funded in part by a Hong Kong RGC Earmarked Grant and a Strategic Research Grant provided by the City University of Hong Kong.

References

Abdennadher, S. and Schlenker, H. 1999. Nurse Scheduling using Constraint Logic Programming. In *Proceedings of the Eleventh Conference on Innovative Applications of Artificial Intelligence*, 838-843. Menlo Park, Calif.: AAAI Press.

Chun, H.W. 1999. Constraint Programming in Java with JSolver. In *Proceedings of the First International Conference and Exhibition on the Practical Application of Constraint Technologies and Logic Programming*. London.

Cohen, J. 1990. Constraint Logic Programming. *Communications of the ACM* 33(7):52-68.

Booch, G. 1994. *Object-Oriented Analysis and Design with Applications*, 2nd ed. Benjamin/Cummings Publishing Company Inc.

Dresse, A. 1995. A Constraint Programming Library Dedicated to Timetabling. In *Proceedings of the First ILOG Solver and Scheduler Users Conference*. Paris: ILOG.

Kumar, V. 1992. Algorithms for Constraint Satisfaction Problems: A Survey. *AI Magazine* 13(1):32-44.

Kusumoto, S. 1996. Nurse Scheduling System Using ILOG Solver. In *Proceedings of the Second ILOG Solver and Scheduler Users Conference*. Paris: ILOG.

Lau, H.C. and Lau, S.C. 1997. Efficient Multi-Skill Crew Rostering via Constrained Sets. In *Proceedings of the Second ILOG Solver and Scheduler Users Conference*. Paris: ILOG.

Lazaro, J.M. and Aristondo, P. 1995. Using Solver for Nurse Scheduling. In *Proceedings of the First ILOG Solver and Scheduler Users Conference*. Paris: ILOG.

Martello, S. and Toth, P. 1986. A Heuristic Approach to the Bus Driver Scheduling Problem. *European Journal of Operations Research* 24 (1):106-117.

Miller, H.E., Pierskalla, W.P. and Rath, G.J. 1990. Nurse Scheduling Using Mathematical Programming. *Naval Research Logistics* 37:559-577.

Puget, J.-F. 1994. A C++ Implementation of CLP. In *ILOG Solver Collected Papers*. ILOG SA, France.

Randhawa, S.U. and Sitompul, D. 1983. A Heuristic Based Computerized Nurse Scheduling System. *Computers and Operations Research* 20(8):837-844.

E.S. Rosenbloom, E.S. and Goertzen, N.F. 1987. Cyclic Nurse Scheduling. *European Journal of Operations Research* 31:19-23.

Steele, G.L. Jr. 1980. The Definition and Implementation of a Computer Programming Language Based on Constraints, Ph.D. Thesis, MIT.

Van Hentenryck, P. 1989. *Constraint Satisfaction in Logic Programming*, MIT Press.

PTV: Intelligent Personalised TV Guides

Paul Cotter & Barry Smyth

Smart Media Institute
Department of Computer Science, University College Dublin
Belfield, Dublin 4, Ireland
{Paul.Cotter, Barry.Smyth}@ucd.ie

Abstract

Although today's world offers us unprecedented access to greater and greater amounts of electronic information, we are faced with significant problems when it comes to finding the right information at the right time – this is the essence of the *information overload problem*. One of the proposed solutions to this problem is to develop technologies for automatically learning about the implicit and explicit preferences of individual users in order to customise and personalise the search for relevant information. In this paper we describe the development of the PTV system (Personalised Television Listings – http://www.ptv.ie) which tackles the information overload problem associated with modern TV listings data, by providing an Internet-based personalised TV listings service so that each registered user receives a daily TV guide that has been specially compiled to suit their particular viewing preferences.

Introduction

The term *information overload* has become almost synonymous with the Internet and the World Wide Web, and today the Internet's 200+ million users are finding it increasingly difficult to efficiently locate precisely relevant information content among its growing repository of 500+ million pages. For example, modern search engines provide only a first cut through the information space, leaving the user with a significant search task in order to locate individual information items. This is beginning to cause problems on the Internet and is seen as a serious barrier to its future success.

This problem takes on even more significance when one considers the new generation of mobile phones, which offer users an alternative Internet access route through the Wireless Application Protocol (WAP). Web content (including text, graphics, forms, hyperlinks etc.) is displayed as WML encoded pages; WML is the equivalent of HTML on WAP devices. At the present time, these devices suffer from greatly reduced display sizes, limited bandwidth, and restricted on-board memory (see Figure 1). Under these conditions it becomes even more important to

Copyright © 2000, American Association for Artificial Intelligence (www.aaai.org). All rights reserved.

be able to offer WAP users personalised information content, since current WAP devices do not facilitate a trawl through even moderate quantities of information in conventional Web terms.

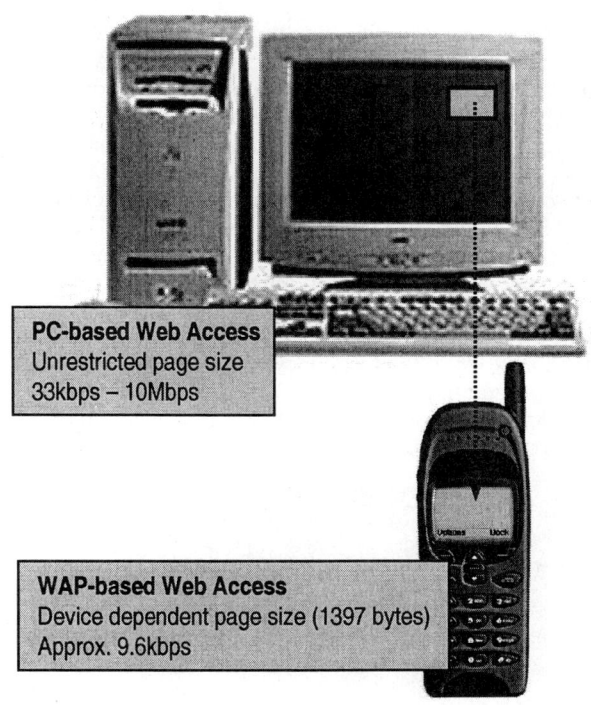

Figure 1. Compared to the traditional mode of Web access (that is, the PC), WAP-based access devices, such as mobile phones, can suffer from greatly reduced screen real-estate, bandwidth, and page sizes.

Content personalisation is one potential solution to the information overload problem. It promises the precise delivery of user-targeted information by automatically learning about the preferences of individual users over time, and by using this information to guide the search for, and presentation of, relevant information.

In this paper we focus on an emerging information overload problem that is associated with the new generation of digital TV systems. We suggest that it will become almost impossible for people to cope with the promise of hundreds of TV channels and thousands of TV programmes daily, and that traditional TV guides will fail to provide any practical assistance. We present PTV (http://www.ptv.ie) as a real solution to this problem. In short, PTV is an innovative Internet service that uses content personalisation techniques to automatically learn about the TV viewing preferences of individual users to provide them with highly customised and personalised daily TV guides. In particular, we focus on two versions of PTV, a fully deployed Web-based system and a newly developed version for WAP-based mobile phones (making PTV one of the world's first fully personalised WAP information services for the mobile phone market).

Problem Description

With the arrival of new cable and satellite television services, and the next generation of digital TV systems, we will soon be faced with an unprecedented level of programme choice. Tens of TV channels today will become hundreds of channels tomorrow, and thousands soon after that. Even today, in Europe and the US, many subscribers have access to upwards of one hundred channels, broadcasting over 2500 programmes per day. The service providers tell us that this new level of channel choice will revolutionise the way we use and view TV, but they rarely tell us of the pit-falls that lie just around the corner. These developments will introduce a whole new set of information overload issues since we have not yet developed the tools that are necessary to deal with this new level of choice. It will become increasingly difficult to find out what programmes are on in a given week, never mind locating a small set of relevant programmes for a quiet evening's viewing.

Figure 2. Compared to the traditional mode of Web access (that is, the PC), WAP-based access devices, such as mobile phones, can suffer from greatly reduced screen real-estate, bandwidth, and page sizes.

Consider the traditional TV guide, which lists programming information for perhaps a week in advance. The days of a slim, easy to digest 30-page volume are numbered. Instead we are faced with TV guides of telephone book proportions, running into hundreds of pages of indigestible schedule charts. Moreover, the way that we interact with our TV sets will also have to change. For better or for worse, "channel surfing" will become a thing of the past as a means for finding out what's on now – while a rapid surf through 20 or 30 channels takes an acceptable few minutes, surfing through 200 or 300 channels could take a number of hours.

Of course the digital TV vendors are aware of such issues, and do recognise the beginnings of a serious information overload problem. They are now offering electronic programme guides (EPGs) to help users to navigate through the TV listings maze. These guides provide an on-screen menu system for searching online TV listings information. Figure 2 shows an example of Sky Digital's EPG, listing programmes on 10 channels for a 1 hour time-slot. However, Sky's full 60 channel line-up requires up to 6 screens of information for each viewing hour (that is, over 140 screens per viewing day). Clearly the burden of search remains with the user and these EPGs face the same problems of scale as existing TV guides.

Some EPG's attempt to help the user further by providing a genre-based view of the listings data. For example, a user might request a list of all comedies, or drams, or films that are on a given day, and this will help to focus the search further. However, these static genre-based approaches are still relatively crude, and at best provide only short-term relief from the information overload problem, after all, there may still be hundreds of comedies showing on a given night, and many of these may be of no interest to a given user.

Application Description

The PTV project is motivated by the belief that the TV listings domain can benefit greatly from an EPG that incorporates content personalisation techniques as a means of filtering and customising TV listings information for individual users (Kay 1995; Perkowitz and Etzioni 1997). In this section we describe the PTV system, focusing in particular on how it produces personalised TV guides by integrating user profiling, case-based reasoning, and collaborative profiling techniques.

Hardware & Software

PTV is a Java-based client-server system and includes a specially designed optimised, multi-threaded server and dynamic HTML/WML page generator, plus all of the artificial intelligence and user profiling components necessary for personalisation. It currently runs on WindowsNT on an Intel 450MHz processor with 64MB of RAM and has been stress-tested beyond 7 million hits per month without any substantial performance degradation.

System Architecture

PTV users can register, login, and view their personalised TV guides as specially customised HTML pages (for conventional PC-based access) or as WML pages (for mobile phone access). The architecture of PTV (Figure 3) does not depend on the mode of access (PC vs. WAP-based device) and all user interaction is handled via HTTP. The heart of the system lies with its server-side components, which handle all the main information processing functions such as user registration and authentication, user profiling, guide compilation, and the all-important programme recommendation and grading.

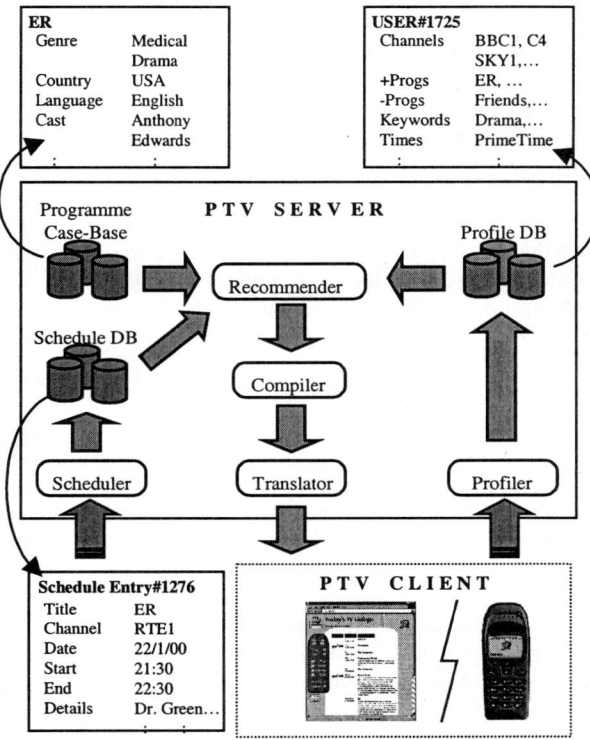

Figure 3. An overview of the PTV system architecture.

Profile Database & Profiler: The key to PTV's personalisation facility is an accurate database of user profiles. Each profile encodes the TV preferences of a given user, listing channel information, preferred viewing times, programme and genre preferences, guide preferences etc. (see Figure 3). Preliminary profile information is collected from the user at registration time in order to bootstrap the personalisation process. However, the majority of information is learned from grading feedback provided by the user; each recommended programme is accompanied with grading icons or links that allow the user to explicitly evaluate the proposed recommendation (see also Section 4.1).

Programme Case-Base: This database contains the programme content descriptions (programme cases). Each entry describes a particular programme using features such as the programme title, genre information, the creator and director, cast or presenters, the country of origin, and the language; an example programme case for the comedy 'Friends' is shown in Figure 3. This information repository is crucial for the content-based (case-based) recommendation component of PTV (see Section 4.2).

Schedule Database: This database contains TV listings for all supported channels. Each listing entry includes details such as the programme name, the viewing channel, the start and end time, and typically some text describing the programme in question (see the schedule entry example in Figure 3). The schedule database is constructed automatically from electronic schedule resources.

Recommender: The recommender component is the intelligent core of PTV. Its job is to take user profile information and to select new programmes for recommendation to a user. In the next section we will explain how PTV uses a hybrid recommendation approach that combines content-based and collaborative recommendation strategies (see Sections 4.2 and 4.3).

Guide Compiler: To compile a personalised guide for a user, PTV uses two programme lists: (1) programmes listed as positive in the user's profile, along with those programmes selected for recommendation (that do not occur in the profile); (2) a list of programmes to be aired on the specified date by channels listed in the user's profile. The intersection of these lists is the set of programmes that will finally appear in the personalised guide.

Guide Translator: The guide compiler produces a generic guide format, which is automatically converted into a HTML or WML page by the guide translator as appropriate. While individual guides are converted into single HTML pages for the Web, they are converted into multiple WML pages (or cards) for mobile phone usage; this is necessary to solve the problems of limited presentation space (and memory space) that exist on current WAP phones

Problem Description

Artificial Intelligence techniques are central to the success of the PTV system. Specifically, the ability to accurately personalise the television guide of an individual user relies on the availability of an accurate model of this user (user profiling), and an ability to relate this profile to relevant programme content (programme recommendation). In this section we outline PTV's user profiling component and its content recommendation strategies

Acquiring User Profiles

The success of PTV depends ultimately on the quality of its personalised guides, and this depends largely on the quality of the user profiles and their ability to represent the viewing preferences of users (Jennings and Higuchi 1993; Kay 1995; Perkowitz and Etzioni 1997)). In PTV each user profile contains two types of information: *domain preferences* and *programme preferences*. The former describe general user preferences such as a list of available TV channels, preferred viewing times, subject keywords and genre preferences, and guide format preferences. Programme preferences are represented as two lists of programme titles, a positive list containing programmes that the user has liked in the past, and a negative list containing programmes that the user has disliked.

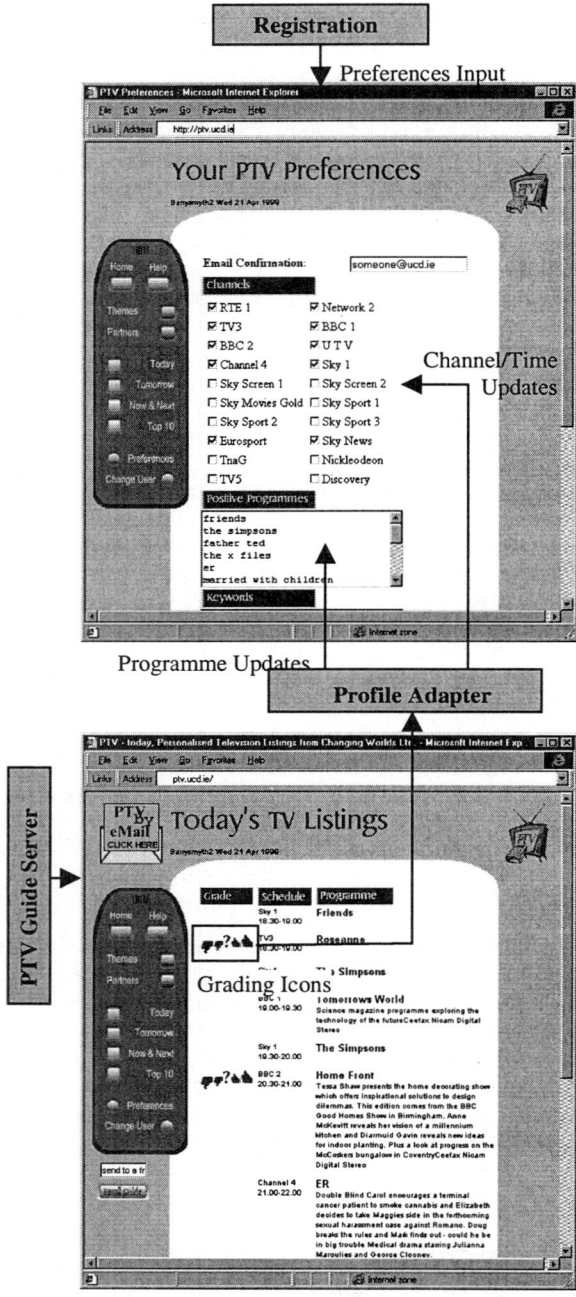

Figure 4. User profiles and feedback in PTV (Web-based).

Profile information is gathered in two ways. Users are encouraged to manually update their profiles directly by specifying viewing preferences. However, while manual profile editing has its advantages (usually in terms of profile accuracy) it is a burden for the users. In particular, we have found that users are happy to provide fairly complete domain preferences but tend to provide only limited programme preferences. For this reason, PTV includes a profile update facility that is driven by direct user feedback through a set of grading icons listed beside guide programmes. PTV's profiler uses this information to automatically alter a user's profile in a number of ways. The simplest modification is to update the programme preference lists by adding positively or negatively graded programmes to the appropriate list. However, the domain preferences can also be altered. For example, viewing time preferences can be adjusted if a user frequently prefers prime-time programmes to morning shows. In general, this long-term feedback connection between user and system is vital if PTV is to maintain an accurate picture of each user over time.

Figure 4 outlines how user profiles are updated in the Web-based PTV system. A similar scenario operates in the WAP-based version of PTV except that preference and grading options require a number of individual pages, rather that having a single preferences page or integrating the grading icons with the main guide pages as in the Web-based version (see Section 5 for further details and example screen shots).

A Content-Based Recommendation Approach

Ultimately in PTV, personalising a given user's TV guide boils down to recommending the right programmes for that user given their various viewing constraints. PTV harnesses two complementary recommendation strategies to base its recommendations on the programmes that a given user has liked in the past (case-based or content-based) and on the programmes that similar users like (collaborative). In this section we look at the more traditional content-based (or case-based) approach (Watson 1997) and in the following section we will look at the complementary collaborative recommendation strategy.

The basic philosophy in content-based recommendation is to recommend items that are similar to those items that the user has liked in the past; see also (Balabanovic and Shoham 1997; Hammond et al. 1996; Smyth and Cotter 1999). For PTV, this means recommending programmes that are similar to the programmes in the positive programme list and dissimilar to those in the negative programme list. Three components are needed for content-based recommendation: (1) content descriptions for all TV programmes (see the programme case-base in Section 2 and Figure 3); (2) a compatible content description of each user's profile; (3) a procedure for measuring the similarity between a programme and a user.

PTV's programme case-base has already been outlined (Section 3.2) and an example case is shown in Figure 3. Each case is described as a set of features and the similarity between two cases can be defined as the weight sum of the similarity between corresponding case features. However, there is no direct means of computing the similarity between a case and a user profile, as user profiles are not described as a set of case features. Instead each raw user profile is converted into a feature-based representation called a *profile schema*. Basically, the profile schema corresponds to a content summary of the programme preferences contained in a user profile, encoded in the same features as the programme cases. The similarity between a profile and a given programme case can then be computed using the standard weighted-sum similarity metric as shown in equation 1; Where $f_i^{Schema(u)}$ and f_i^p are the ith features of the schema and the programme case respectively.

1. $$\Pr gSim(Schema(u),p) = \sum w_i \bullet sim\left(f_i^{Schema(u)}, f_i^p\right)$$

A problem with content-based methods is the knowledge-engineering effort required to develop case representations and similarity models. Furthermore, because content-based methods make recommendations based on item similarity, the newly recommended items tend to be similar to the past items leading to reduced diversity. In the TV domain this can result in narrow recommendation lists, for example, a lot of comedies if the majority of profile programmes are comedies.

A Collaborative Recommendation Approach

Collaborative recommendation methods such as automated collaborated filtering are an alternative to content-based techniques. Instead of recommending new items that are similar to the ones that the user has liked in the past, they recommend items that other *similar users* have liked (Balabanovic and Shoham 1997; Billsus and Pazzani 1998; Goldberg et al. 1992; Konstan et al. 1997; Maltz and Ehrlich 1995; Shardanand and Maes 1995). And instead of computing the similarity between items, we compute the similarity between users, or more precisely the similarity between user profiles. In PTV the recommendations for a target user are based on the viewing preferences of the k most similar users.

PTV computes user similarity by using a simple graded difference metric shown in equation 2; where p(u) and p(u') are the ranked programmes in each user's profile, and $r(p_i^u)$ is the rank of programme p_i in profile u. The possible grades range from –2 to +2 and missing programmes are given a default grade of 0. Of course this is just one possible similarity technique that has proved useful in PTV, and any number of techniques could have been used, for example statistical correlation techniques such as Pearson's correlation coefficient (see eg., Billsus and Pazzani 1998).

2. $$PrfSim(u,u') = \frac{\sum_{p(u) \cup p(u')} \left| r\left(p_i^u\right) - r\left(p_i^{u'}\right) \right|}{4 \bullet \left| p(u) \cup p(u') \right|}$$

3. $$PrgRank(p,u) = \sum_{u \in U} PrfSim(u,u')$$

Once PTV has selected k similar profiles for a given target user, a recommendation list is formed from the programmes in these similar profiles that are absent from the target profile. This list is then ranked and the top r programmes are selected for recommendation. The ranking metric is shown in equation 3; U is the subset of k nearest profiles to the target that contain a programme p. This metric biases programmes according to their frequency in the similar profiles and the similarity of their recommending user. In this way popular programmes suggested by very similar users tend to be recommended.

Collaborative filtering is a powerful technique that solves many of the problems associated with content-based methods. For example, there is no need for content descriptions or sophisticated case similarity metrics. In fact, high quality recommendations, that would ordinarily demand a rich content representation, are possible. Moreover, recommendation diversity is maintained as relevant items that are dissimilar to the items in a user profile can be suggested.

Collaborative filtering does suffer from some shortcomings. There is a startup cost associated with gathering enough profile information to make accurate user similarity measurements. There is also a latency problem in that new items will not be recommended until these items have found their way into sufficiently many user profiles. This is particularly problematic in the TV domain because new and one-off programmes occur regularly and do need to be considered for recommendation even though these programmes will not have made it into any user profiles.

The key to PTV's success is the use of a combined recommendation approach. For a given guide, a selection of programmes is suggested, some are content-based recommendations (including new or one-off programmes) while others are collaborative recommendations. In particular, recommendation diversity is ensured through the use of collaborative filtering and the latency problem can be solved by using content-based methods to recommend new or one-off programmes.

System Demonstration

In this section we look at the use of the PTV system by a new user, stepping through each of the basic stages, from initial registration through to guide viewing. To avail of PTV's personalisation facilities, each new user must register an account with PTV. In addition to submitting the usual username and password details the user is also asked to provide initial profile information (as discussed in Section 4.2) and this is shown by the screen shots in Figure 5. Figure 5(a) shows the preferences screen for the web-based version of PTV, whereas Figure 5(b) shows the equivalent screens in the WAP-based version.

The presentation restrictions introduced by the current generation of WAP enabled mobile phone should now be clear. As a result the single-screen preferences of the Web-based version is replaced by multiple screens in the WAP-based version.

Incidentally, access to the preferences information shown in Figure 5 is not restricted to registration time. Users can access and edit their profiles at any time as a means of supplementing any updates made by the programme grading process.

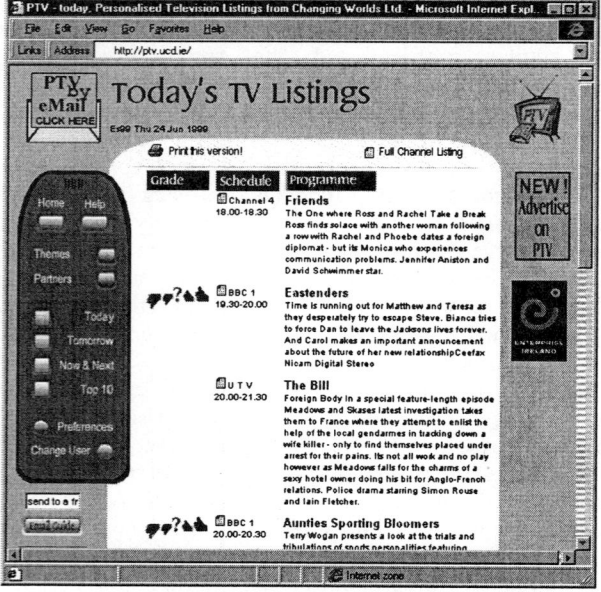

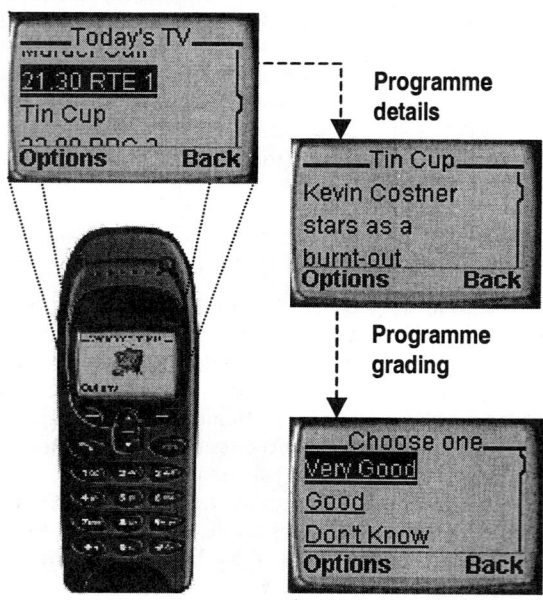

Figure 5. The initial profile screen during user registration.

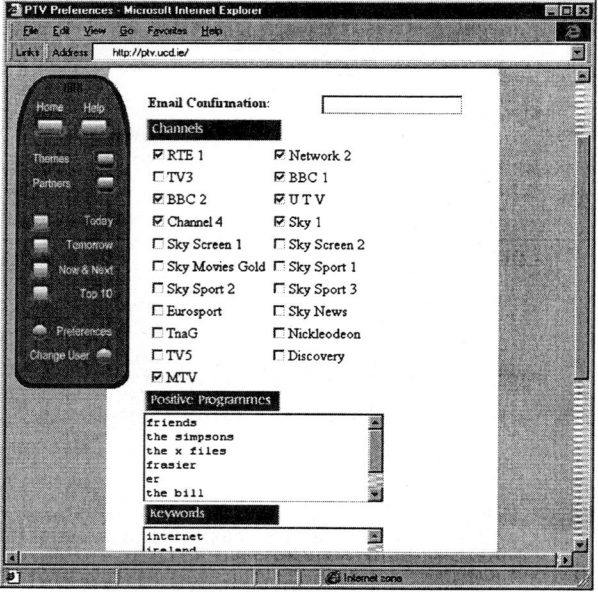

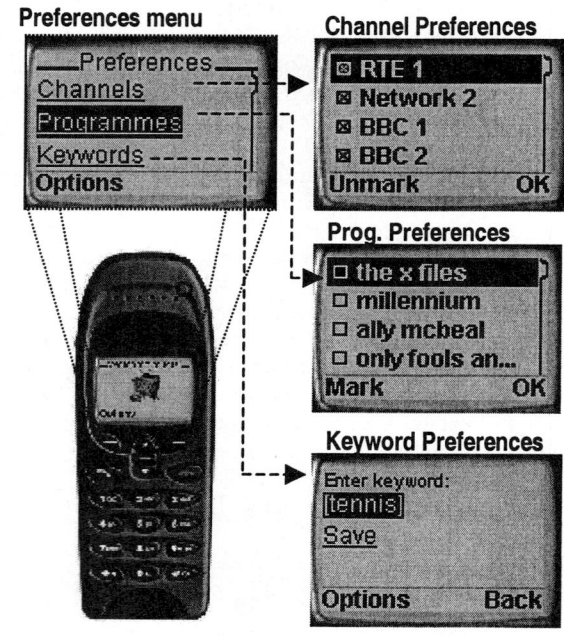

Figure 6. A personalised guide for today's TV.

Once a user has registered they can access their personalised guides. The main interface has been kept simple and all of the site features and guide options are available from a simple menu on both the Web and WAP versions. The user can receive personalised guides for programmes on today or tomorrow, as well as what's on now and next, a list of the top 10 programmes (as compiled from the user profiles currently in the system), a wide range of subject-specific guides (eg, comedy, drama, film, etc), plus of course full TV listings.

Figure 6(a&b) shows examples of a personalised daily guide from the Web and WAP versions of PTV. On the Web-based version, Figure 6(a), we can see four programmes from BBC, Channel 4 and UTV; the full guide contains about 10 programmes. Two of the visible programmes have been selected for this guide because the user is known to enjoy them (Friends and The Bill are both listed in the user's profile). Two of the programmes (Eastenders and Auntie's Sporting Bloomers) are *recommendations* based on this user's profile, and as such they are annotated with grading icons so that the user can provide feedback on the quality of these recommendations. Similar information is carried by the WAP version but because of presentation and memory restrictions it is not possible to display complete guide information (programme name, details, channel, time, and grading options) on a single screen. Instead, the main guide screen contains only programme title, channel, and time information as shown. A user is free to request more information on any particular programme by a simple selection, and at this point can continue on to grade that programme as desired; see Figure 6(b).

PTV's personalisation facility is also used to compile a variety of so-called *themed guides* which are analogous to the genre-based guides used by modern EPGs (see Section 2). These guides are not compiled with respect to a particular user but rather with respect to a particular theme. For example, PTV provides themed guides for comedy, sport, news, drama, soap operas, chat shows etc, and the programmes for these guides are automatically selected using PTV existing recommendation engine by creating profiles to represent 'virtual' users with specialized interests in a particular theme.

Deployment, Evaluation, and Maintenance

PTV was originally developed as part of a three-year basic research project in the Department of Computer Science at University College Dublin, Ireland. The resulting personalisation technology was re-implemented as a commercially viable personalisation engine during 1999 (approximately 9 person months). A well developed set of tools and systems now exist for rapidly developing new commercial versions of PTV to suit a wide range of client needs. For example, the latest development of the WAP-based version of PTV required only 8 person-weeks of development time.

Application Use and Payoff

PTV went live in January 1999 and the number of registered users has grown to nearly 20,000 with about 50,000 personalised guides generated per month. Furthermore, as yet PTV has not been publicised, so its current popularity is based largely on word of mouth and unsolicited press coverage. In fact, since the launch the site has received a Yahoo! Site of the Month award plus many favourable press reviews from Irish and UK magazines and newspapers including ComputerActive, Dot.ie, PC Live, Business & Finance, the Sunday Business Post, and the Irish Times. PTV was a finalist in the Irish Golden Spider Internet Awards under the best use of technology category.

PTV has been so successful that a campus company called Changing Worlds (http://www.changingworlds.com) has been established in University College Dublin to market the PTV system and its underlying personalisation technology. For example, a re-branded version of PTV has already been licensed and launched on the Ireland.com portal site (http://www.ireland.com) run by the Irish Times newspaper group. This re-branded version is called MyTV and since its launch in August 1999 has attracted approximately 8,000 new users to produce approximately 40,000 personalised guides per month. MyTV adds a valuable 'sticky' content service to the ireland.com site and helps to secure user loyalty and increase traffic levels.

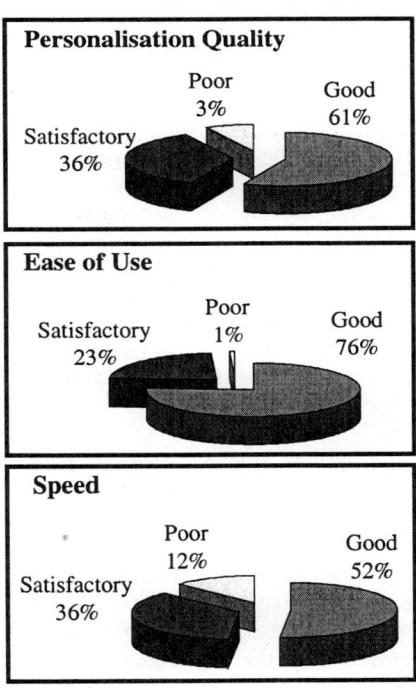

Figure 7. User survey summary results.

End-User Evaluation

Of course, from a scientific viewpoint, the big question concerns the accuracy of PTV's personalisation facility.

From January to June, 1999, real users carried out an extensive and detailed study on PTV. In total 310 users completed a comprehensive questionnaire regarding all aspects of PTV including its personalisation quality, speed, and ease of use, the results of which are summarised in the pie charts shown in Figure 7; see Smyth & Cotter (1999) for further experimental results.

Clearly, the results are extremely positive. Critically, only 3% of users found the personalised guides to be of poor quality and 99% of users found the site to be easy to use as a source of TV listings. Moreover, 88% of users found the response time to be acceptable, which we view very positively, especially considering the fact that PTV's pages are created dynamically and the limited speed of today's Internet.

Maintenance

The PTV systems are designed to have minimal ongoing maintenance requirements. For example the maintenance of the user profiles and the programme schedules is fully automatic. In fact, in our experience, the only manual maintenance that is required involves the addition of new programme cases and the addition of new channels and cable-regions. Even a relatively inexperienced user can manage both of these maintenance options by using PTV's in-built tools.

Conclusions

We believe that PTV represents a convergence of technologies that provides an effective solution to the very real problem of providing people with relevant TV listings information as digital TV becomes a reality. PTV personalises TV information to meet the viewing preferences of individual users by integrating two different information-filtering strategies, case-based reasoning and collaborative filtering, with user profiling techniques. The resulting hybrid personalisation technique allows programme recommendations to be made according to the type of programmes a target user has enjoyed in the past as well as the programmes that other similar users have enjoyed.

To date this technology has been deployed on the Internet as the PTV (www.ptv.ie) and MyTV (www.ireland.com) web sites. These applications have proven to be successful with widespread adoption across Irish Internet market. In the near future, a WAP version of PTV will be formally launched and we believe a similar success story will unfold as mobile phone users recognise the real benefits of high-quality content personalisation on their restricted mobile handsets. In fact, we argue that traditional TV listings services are not appropriate given the screen and bandwidth limitations of the current generation of WAP devices – a personalised service such as PTV is the best available solution.

Of course PTV's personalisation technology is not restricted to personalising TV listings content. The PTV systems are built around a content personalisation engine that can be readily adapted to practically any source of information content and Changing Worlds is currently using this technology to develop the next generation of intelligent, personalised information services.

References

Balabanovic M., Shoham Y. 1997. FAB: Content-Based Collaborative Recommender. *Communications of the ACM*, 40(3): 66-72.

Billsus, D. & Pazzani, M. J. 1998. Learning collaborative Information Filters. In *Proceedings of the International Conference on Machine Learning*, Wisconsin, USA.

Goldberg D., Nichols D., Oki B. M., Terry D. 1992. Using Collaborative Filtering to Weave an Information Tapestry. *Communications of the AC* 35(12) 61-70.

Hammond, K. J., Burke, R., and Schmitt, K. 1996. A Case-Based Approach to Knowledge Navigation. In *Case-Based Reasoning Experiences Lessons and Future Directions*. MIT Press, 125-136

Jennings, A. & Higuchi, H. 1993. A user model neural network for a personal news service. *User Modeling and User-Adapted Information*: 3(1).1-25

Kay J. 1995. Vive la Difference! Individualised Interaction with Users. In *Proceedings of the 14th International Joint Conference on Artificial Intelligence*, 978-984. Menlo Park, Calif.: International Joint Conferences on Artificial Intelligence Inc.

Konstan J. A., Miller B. N., Maltz D., Herlocker J. L., Gordan L. R., Riedl J. 1997. Grouplens: Applying Collaborative Filtering to Usenet News. *Communications of the ACM*. 40(3) 77-87.

Maltz D., Ehrlich K. 1995. Pointing the Way: Active Collaborative Filtering. In *Proceedings of the ACM Conference on Human Factors in Computing Systems (CHI '95)*. ACM Press, New York, N.Y., 202-209.

Perkowitz, M. & Etzioni, O. 1997. Adaptive Web Sites: An AI Challenge. In *Proceedings of the 15th International Joint Conference on Artificial Intelligence*. Menlo Park, Calif.: International Joint Conferences on Artificial Intelligence Inc.

Shardanand, U. & Maes, 1995. P. Social Information Filtering: Algorithms for Automating 'Word of Mouth'. In *Proceedings of the Conference on Human Factors in Computing Systems (CHI95)*. ACM Press, New York, N.Y. 210-217

Smyth, B. & Cotter, P. 1999. Surfing the Digital Wave: Generating Personalised TV Listings using Collaborative, Case-Based Recommendation. In *Proceedings of the International Conference on Case-Based Reasoning*, 561-571. Springer-Verlag, Germany.

Watson, I. (1997) *Applying Case-Based Reasoning: Techniques for Enterprise Systems*. Morgan-Kaufmann.

LifeCode™ - A Natural Language Processing System for Medical Coding and Data Mining

Daniel T. Heinze Ph.D., Mark L. Morsch, Ronald E. Sheffer, Jr., Michelle A. Jimmink, Mark A. Jennings, Willam C. Morris Ph.D., Amy E. W. Morsch Ph.D.

A-Life Medical, Inc.
9555 Chesapeake Drive – Suite 101
San Diego, California 92123
dheinze, mmorsch, rsheffer, mjimmink, mjennings, bmorris, amorsch@alifemedical.com

Abstract

LifeCode™ (patent pending) is a Natural Language Processing and Expert System that extracts demographic and clinical information from free-text clinical records. The initial application of LifeCode is for the Emergency Medicine clinical specialty. An application for Diagnostic Radiology is now in beta-test. A pilot program for performing data mining on acute care clinical records has been completed. The LifeCode NLP engine uses a large number of specialist readers whose particular outputs are combined at various levels to form an integrated picture of the patient's medical condition(s), course of treatment and disposition. The LifeCode Expert System performs the tasks of combining complementary information, deleting redundant information, assessing the level of medical risk and level of service represented in the clinical record and producing an output that is appropriate for input to an Electronic Medical Record (EMR) system or a billing system. Because of the critical nature of the tasks, LifeCode has a unique "self-awareness" feature that enables it to recognize the limits of its competence and thus ask for assistance from a human expert when faced with information that is beyond the bounds of its competence. The LifeCode NLP and Expert Systems are wrapped as DCOM servers and reside in various delivery packages including On-Line Transaction Processing (OLTP), a web-browser interface and an Automated Speech Recognition (ASR) interface.

Problem and Task Description

LifeCode™ (patent pending) is a Natural Language Processing (NLP) system that extracts clinical information from free-text medical records. In the United States alone, medicine is a trillion dollar per year business and generates in excess of seven hundred million clinical documents in transcribed free-text form. Viewing medicine as a business, the clinical information in the free-text records has a necessary application in producing a bill for services and facility utilization. This is the realm of medical coding and billing. Another desirable business application of the information is tracking physician performance and resource utilization. From the clinical perspective, the information in the clinical notes can be used to improve communications between multiple providers for the same patient, to monitor the efficacy of alternate courses of treatment and to provide feedback and alerts relative to the course of care for a particular patient.

Although the Electronic Medical Record (EMR) has been a major goal in Health Information Management (HIM) for more than two decades, the success of such systems has been seriously limited due to the relative inaccessibility of the information in free-text clinical documentation. Attempts to change the documentation habits of physicians have not had significant success largely due to the increased time and inconvenience associated with using computer interfaces that require formatted input. Further, numerous consultations with practicing physicians have taught us that there is a basic inability of fully structured systems to represent many of the nuances that make each case unique.

Other programs for NLP of medical free-text differ substantially from LifeCode. Medical document retrieval and classification systems determine only if a particular subject is discussed within a document (Aronow and Shmueli, 1996; Aronow, Cooley and Sonderland, 1995; Aronow, et.al., 1995; Aronow and Feng, 1997; Croft, Callan and Aronow, 1995; Hirsch and Aronow, 1995; Lenhert, et. al., 1994; Sonderland, et.al., 1995). Such approaches do not distinguish typical roles such as agent (who performed the surgery) or patient (who had the illness). They do not discern temporal information such as duration (how long has the patient been ill) or timing (how frequent are the bouts of pain). They do not discern negation (the patient was diagnosed not to have the illness under discussion). The list goes on, but these examples should be sufficient. Medical word and phrase tagging systems operate at a much more granular level to apply tags that disambiguate semantic senses (Sager, et.al., 1994a; Sager, et.al, 1996). They would discern, for example, between the verbal use of "burning" (e.g. the

---

Copyright © 2000, American Association for Artificial Intelligence (www.aaai.org). All rights reserved.

flame was burning the patients finger) and the adjectival use (e.g. the patient had a burning substernal chest pain). Tagging does not in itself solve issues such as roles, negation and temporality. Attempts to do medical coding (assignment of predefined medical codes that identify diseases, injuries, medical procedures, etc.) typically have not dealt with the issues of role, negation, timing, etc. (Larkey and Croft, 1995; Lenert and Tovar, 1993; Yang and Chute, 1992). Some, however, use very complex linguistic processing and achieve very high accuracy (Sager, et.al. 1994b), but such systems require many years of development and have not been able to move easily into the commercial marketplace. Systems that use a less rigorous linguistic approach either in specific medical specialties such as radiology (Ranum, 1988; Zingmond and Lenert, 1993) or in general medical texts (Sneiderman, et. al., 1995; Sneiderman, Rindflesch and Aronson, 1996) typically lack both the specificity (in terms of roles, temporality, etc.) and the accuracy (in terms of precision and recall) to be used in critical tasks such as medical billing or populating an EMR from free-text. None of the systems and projects discussed thus far incorporate the inference and logic capabilities necessary to refine medical diagnosis and procedure codes per the extensive medical and legal guidelines, nor do they have the knowledge required to use coded information for reporting purposes.

Further, by way of comparison, commercial products that advertise medical NLP (e.g. HBOC's Autocoder, or Medicode's Encoder Pro) are essentially keyword recognition systems for searching online versions of paper reference manuals. They lack NLP competence but do have some level of knowledge regarding the proper use and reporting of user selected codes.

Aside from the issues already discussed, a major drawback of all these systems is that they are unable to discern the presence of information that is beyond the scope of their competency. To be useful in a real-world application, a medical NLP system must be able to discern when it is able to operate unassisted and when it needs to seek human intervention in order to maintain the appropriate quality level. We refer to this ability as "self-awareness".

LifeCode provides both linguistic competence and medical knowledge and logic to:
- Use NLP to extract from a free-text clinical note...
  - the patient demographics (name, age, gender, etc),
  - the patient's chief complaint,
  - the history of the present illness (duration, severity, time of onset, circumstances of medical relevance, related signs and symptoms, location of the injury/illness, context of onset, etc.),
  - the medical history of the patient and (as applicable) the patient's family,
  - relevant social history (use of tobacco, alcohol and drugs, living arrangements, etc.)
  - the nature and extent of the physical examination performed by the physician,
  - the nature and extent of old records consulted, professional consultations and medical tests performed by the physician,
  - the final diagnoses, potentially also including possible and ruled-out diagnoses,
  - the course of treatment including surgical procedures, drug therapy and monitoring levels, and
  - the disposition of the patient at the end of the clinical encounter with the physician.
- Use an Expert System to determine from the extracted information...
  - the most specific version of each diagnosis and procedure,
  - the level of documentation of the history and physical examination,
  - the risk to the patient presented by the medical condition and treatment,
  - the complexity of the medical decision making for the physician,
  - the level of service provided by the physician, and
  - the appropriate manner to report the event for billing purposes based on the type of medical provider, the place of medical care and the particular requirements of the insurance carrier.

Application Description

The LifeCode system is organized into two layers, as seen in Figure 1. The top layer is the executable portion, implemented largely in C++ together with several finite-state and context sensitive processors. This top layer contains two modules, the NLP extraction engine and the Expert System. As shown in Figure 1, documents flow into the NLP extraction engine and are transformed into a collection of discrete data elements. These data elements are represented in Figure 1 as a poorly aligned group of shaded and unshaded blocks, signifying the unfinished nature of the information at this stage. The Expert System module takes this collection as input and applies rules that filter, combine, and restructure the data elements into the data records that are then saved in an SQL database. The bottom layer represents the system knowledge base. In an effort to abstract the domain knowledge away from the source code, the knowledge bases contains the medical vocabulary; definitions covering anatomy, microbiology, medications, signs, symptoms, diagnoses, and procedures; and rules for medical coding. This data (and more) comprises the

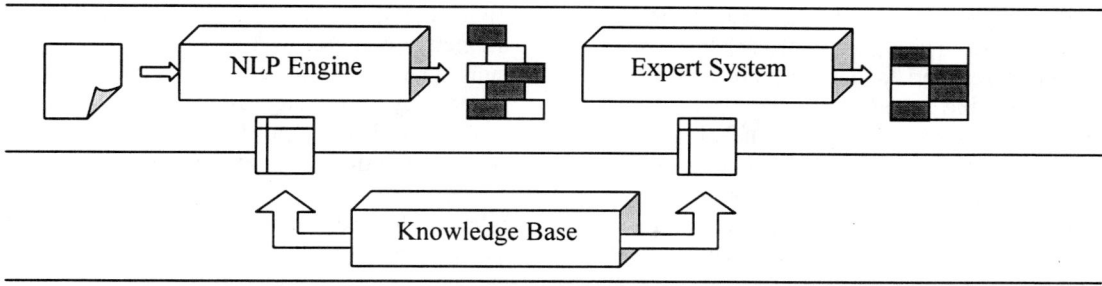

Figure 1. LifeCode Architecture

knowledge base and is written using proprietary specification languages that are compiled using custom utility programs into C++ data objects. These data objects are read in at initialization of the top layer executable modules. In Figure 1 these data objects are illustrated by the icons that are shown flowing from the knowledge base to the NLP engine and Expert System modules. This design allows system upgrades through modification of the knowledge bases, without requiring recompilation of the C++ source code for the NLP engine or Expert System.

Looking more closely at the executable layer, the NLP module blends multiple types of text processing techniques - including morphological reduction, pattern matching, bottom-up parsing, synonym substitution, and vector analysis - to recognize, extract, and categorize the key information in a clinical note. There are four components that make up the NLP module: document segmenter, lexical analyzer, phrase parser, and concept matcher. These components execute in sequence, accepting the note as ASCII text and producing a list of discrete data elements that are organized by type with each assigned a semantic label. The types broadly categorize the extracted information according to the main themes of the note. These include procedures, diagnoses, symptoms, current history, past history, physical examination, and medications. The semantic labels assign a meaning to each element that corresponds to a definition in the system's external knowledge base.

Clinical notes are typically composed of multiple paragraphs, divided into blocks of text by headings. The document segmenter identifies and categorizes the text based on the meaning of the heading that precedes each block. The meanings of the headings are determined by comparing, using a flexible pattern-matching scheme, against a set of possible heading definitions specified in the knowledge base. This process places each portion of a note in a broad context as defined by the meaning of an associated section heading. Examples of section headings are History of Present Illness, Review of Systems, Physical Examination, Medical Decision Making, and Final Diagnosis. As the text is processed by subsequent modules, this context is preserved and is used later on to compute the type of each extracted data element. The output of the document segmenter is a linked list of text sections, stored in the order they appear in the original note. As we will discuss later on, knowing the context of each data element is required in order to reach the level of precision required of medical coding.

The lexical analyzer module is a series of processors designed to transform the text into a string of symbols that are consistent with the vocabulary of the knowledge base specifications. This functionality includes acronym expansion and morphological reduction. In the acronym expansion, each unambiguous acronym in the text is converted into its full definition. Acronyms considered ambiguous, having more than one potential meaning, are either left unchanged, allowing the concept matcher to resolve conflicts, or an appropriate default definition is selected. Morphological reduction transforms multiple morphological variants of a word into a base form. This is done for words where morphological variation does not affect the underlying concept being expressed. In addition to text transformation, scalar values representing temporal information, vital signs and laboratory test results such as body temperature and oxygen saturation are extracted and stored. Cardinal and ordinal numbers are replaced by tokens that uniquely encode their values.

After all of the tokens have been generated by the lexical analyzer, the phrase parser performs a bottom-up syntactic analysis. The parser is highly resilient and tolerant of the incorrect grammar that characterizes clinical documents and unknown words. The information needed for medical coding is expressed primarily in the noun phrases of a text. The boundaries of a noun phrase are typically defined by prepositions, verbs or some type of punctuation. The phrase parser uses these delimiters to form chunks of text of a size, from two or three words up to a complete sentence, that roughly corresponds to the granularity of the definitions within the knowledge base. Although nouns and noun phrases are the focus, verbs are not ignored in this process. Verbs can be key terms in the definitions of medical procedures. Therefore, the phrase parser preserves verbs and most other modifying words as it forms chunks of text.

The concept matcher uses vector analysis to assign meanings to each phrase. These meanings are represented as labels and can correspond to one or more chunks of texts, depending upon the scope of the definition in the knowledge base. In vector analysis, meanings are assigned by modeling the knowledge base as a vector space. Each word is a separate dimension. Every definition in the knowledge base is represented by a vector in this vector space. To find the meaning of a phrase, the concept matcher plots a vector representing the phrase into the knowledge base vector space to determine the closest meaning.

The following example illustrates the vector analysis performed by the concept matcher for a simple ICD-9 dictionary. Consider a dictionary with four ICD-9 codes:

786.50 Chest pain unspecified
786.51 Substernal chest pain
786.52 Chest wall pain
786.59 Musculoskeletal chest pain

These four codes cover the chest pain category within the ICD-9 coding guidelines. Codes 786.53 through 786.58 are not defined but are available for future expansion of the guidelines. In these four definitions, there are six unique words (ignoring case): chest, pain, unspecified, substernal, wall, and musculoskeletal. For the purposes of vector analysis, these six unique words can be treated as six dimensions. Thus, the four definitions in the example dictionary can be represented as four unit vectors within a six dimensional space. The concept matcher assigns meaning to a phrase by identifying the vector from the dictionary, and thereby the definition, that most closely matches the vector formed from the words in the phrase. The closest match is determined by computing the angular difference between the vector from the phrase and each vector from the dictionary. The angular difference is computed using a simple inverse cosine formula. The vector from the dictionary with the smallest angular difference, as long as that difference is below a defined threshold, is the best match. A threshold is required to ensure that the best match from the dictionary has significant similarity with the words in the phrase. Typically this threshold is set between 0° and 45°. To obtain a perfect match, an angular difference of 0°, a phrase must contain every word in a definition, but no more. For the simple ICD-9 dictionary defined above, the phrase 'chest wall pain' is a perfect match for the definition of the ICD-9 code 786.52.

A second evaluation phase after the initial vector difference computation is used to refine the matches. This includes using anatomy, medication, and microbiology concept hierarchies and synonym lists to improve chances of a match. Also, syntactic heuristics may be applied. These heuristics join and redistribute words from two or more consecutive phrases that were divided by the phrase parser and compute the meaning for the newly combined phrase. With meanings assigned to individual chunks of text, the extracted data elements are formed by collecting all of the semantic labels and forming a list. The labels are grouped on this list according to their context in the note.

The Expert System module applies specialty-specific rules of medical coding, assigning a final set of diagnosis and procedure codes. The codes are derived from the semantic labels. In fact in many cases the actual ICD-9 (diagnosis) (Medicode, 1999) or CPT (medical procedure) (AMA, 1999) codes are used as labels. This module consists of specialized algorithms and business rules that have been developed through analysis of published guidelines and consultation with medical coding experts. The context is important at this stage because elements with similar definitions may have different roles in different contexts. For example, in emergency medicine the review of systems (a subjective inventory of symptoms from the patient) and the physical examination (an objective report of findings made by the physician) may have similar language and therefore similar concepts. However, they serve different roles in assigning an overall level of service code to the encounter. Data elements from these two contexts cannot be intermingled. In addition to computing the final codes, the expert system assesses the quality of the coding, flagging notes that should be reviewed by a human expert. The criteria for this assessment are the consistency of the data extracted, the complexity of the diagnoses and procedures, and incomplete information.

The entire LifeCode system runs at the core of a continuously operating (24/7) data center. Our business operates as a service bureau, receiving electronic notes via ftp or dial-up connections. The notes are held for a period of time until payor demographics and addenda have been received. From there, LifeCode runs on the documents with the results stored in an SQL database. The document, medical codes, and payor demographics are returned to the client electronically, and their staff reviews the results using a coding review workstation. The data center operates within a Windows NT environment on high-end Intel Pentium platforms.

Uses of AI Technology

In the sense that LifeCode is the brain-child of its inventors and developers, it is in the lineage of cognitive linguistics. We cannot, however, claim that LifeCode is a truly cognitive system. "Cognitive linguistics and cognitive grammar are 'cognitive' in the sense that, insofar as possible, language is seen as drawing on other, more basic systems of abilities (e.g. perception, attention, categorization) from which it cannot be dissociated." (Langacker, 1999) LifeCode, of course, does not have "more basic systems of abilities" as listed by Langacker.

It is, however, designed to operate as if it did possess these basic systems and, more importantly, the corresponding mental capacities, e.g. the assessment of duration, ability to shift attention to different narrators and events, a sense of urgency, etc. In terms of the core AI components, there is little in LifeCode that has not been available in NLP work for some time. This includes such basic functions as lexical, syntactic and semantic analysis. What makes LifeCode unique is the organization of basic components in a manner that reduces each of the functions into a myriad of agents that work either independently or cooperatively. At this level of reduction, the lines between lexical, syntactic and semantic analysis begin to blur. However, for the sake of illustration, there are nearly three dozen agents that operate primarily at the lexical and syntactic level. It is, then, not so much the advances in AI techniques that have made LifeCode possible, rather it is the particular reduction that we have applied to the top-level functions and the system-level organization that has been imposed to synthesize a domain specific level of natural language understanding.

At the algorithm or technique level, there are two noteworthy advances in LifeCode. LifeCode represents an advance in the sheer amount of knowledge that it is able to apply to NLP within a reasonable amount of time. The computationally intensive nature of NLP is well known. In dealing with a single sentence, LifeCode's core engine will reference the linguistic and medical knowledge bases from several thousand to several million times. The average number of references is about fifty thousand per sentence. In addition to techniques such as caching, LifeCode employs a novel dynamic programming technique that is, to the best of our knowledge, on the order of ten times faster than other algorithms. Typical of dynamic programming techniques (Bentley, 1996), this algorithm utilizes a large table to store partial results during the vector analysis. As a result of this technique, LifeCode (on a 500MHz Pentium PC running Windows NT) is able to run a knowledge base with well more than three million entries against a four hundred word document in ten to twenty seconds.

The second noteworthy technique is LifeCode's "self-awareness". For the medical applications against which LifeCode is applied, it is unrealistic to think that a computer could at this time reach a level of understanding that would enable it to work unsupervised and unaided. In fact, human professionals frequently find themselves resorting to reference materials or consulting experts. In this respect, humans are largely aware of the limits of their mental abilities and are able to determine when consultation is required. For our applications, a computer would not be particularly useful if it did not know when it was at the limits of its knowledge or abilities. This would require that a human expert review all of the computer's output, thus negating the computer's usefulness. In one sense, the ability to know when to ask for help can be construed as the ability to recognize the difference between those unknowns that matter and those that do not matter. To achieve this ability in LifeCode, we have developed a technique that we call semi-knowledge. That is, LifeCode has, beyond it's core knowledge, a very broad but shallow knowledge of application relevant aspects of medicine. This semi-knowledge enables LifeCode to distinguish between relevant and irrelevant information, and further between medical information that is within its expertise versus that which is outside its expertise.

The core LifeCode engine is wrapped in an industrial strength data center that controls local and remote I/O, document reformatting, database storage and archival, version control, QA review, user interfaces and accounting. Within the medical applications that we have approached, LifeCode is patent pending as a top-level business process method. At the NLP system level, it is patent pending in terms of its organization and approach to NLP. And, at the algorithm level, the high-speed dynamic programming and the semi-knowledge algorithms are patent pending.

Application Use and Payoff

A-Life has over 400 hospitals under contract of which 26 hospitals have been implemented as of the date of writing (January 2000). A-Life completed a successful testing program of the first application for the coding of emergency medicine at two billing company sites in early 1998. Full commercial operations started in July 1998. A-Life's solutions for Emergency Medicine and Radiology are used by billing companies and providers (hospitals and health centers) to completely automate daily coding operations for the vast majority of medical charts. LifeCode codes approximately 70% of documents with no human intervention. The remaining documents are coded as completely as possible and categorized as either requiring additional QA review or as incomplete charts due to documentation deficiencies. Of the charts sent for additional QA review, about half are already coded correctly and completely and require no further changes. From a statistical standpoint, this seemingly high review level is needed in order to keep LifeCode's false-positive rate below 1% for billable procedures (observed false-positive rates for human coders in production settings is 2% to 4%).

The payoffs and benefits for using LifeCode can be summarized as:
- significant overall reduction in medical coding costs via enhanced productivity;
- far more accurate, consistent and complete assignment of codes than is humanly possible;
- more efficient operations by reducing a large labor force that is difficult to recruit and retain;

- greatly increased uniformity and validity of codes assigned and data produced;
- elimination of coding inconsistency typically found with manual processes;
- a major asset in developing in-house compliance programs;
- reduction of accounts receivable cycle due to faster turnaround, decreased error rate and fewer payer rejections;
- an audit trail showing coding logic matched with coding results, stored for use during a payer audit;
- compliance guaranteed – HCFA-compliant coding reduces risk of fines for fraud and abuse; and
- a competitive advantage for customers allowing them to expand their sales.

Other benefits that will accrue in time from the use of LifeCode are:
- Electronic data availability/retrieval allows for utilization review, clinical protocol analysis and process enhancement for billing and claims submission.
- Instant feedback to physicians on the quality of documentation thus improving patient care and optimization of accurate, allowable reimbursement.

Positive operational effects for the users of LifeCode include:
- By automating the medical coding task, human coders are able to focus on tasks that require human expertise such as quality control, review of difficult documents, and physician education.
- Optimization of existing staff, overall reduction of staff and reduced costs for hiring and training.
- Reduction of paper flow and reduced storage costs.
- Operational, statistical and clinical reports assist customers in better managing operations.

Application Development and Deployment

The development of LifeCode began with the founding of A-Life Medical, Inc. in February 1996. The R&D department started with two part-time and has grown to now be seven full-time individuals. The group is composed of three AI software experts, three linguists (all computationally oriented), and one knowledge engineer. Additionally, the company has grown to include medical specialty experts both as employees and as regular consultants. The R&D group has also been aided greatly by our beta-customers. The application infrastructure was developed by our Information Systems department that currently consists of six software engineers, two systems administrators and two installation engineers. Finally, our marketing staff has contributed in terms of market driven requirements and expectations. The development time, to date, from the R&D department has been close to twenty person-years. The time contributed by other departments within A-Life and by our beta-customers would easily exceed that number. The development methodology for R&D has been iterative thus leading to an organic growth of the core product. The application infrastructure was developed with a standard design-build-test approach with version control. We are now at the point where mature portions of the core technology are being transferred from R&D to IS where they will be reimplemented based on lessons learned in the initial development phase.

During the initial development phase, the two greatest difficulties were the rapidly changing regulations governing clinical documentation and the widespread uncertainty within the medical community as to how to respond to these changes. Both the changes and the growing complexity of the regulations (driven primarily by the Health Care Financing Administration (HCFA) and secondarily by private insurers) have been both a bane and a blessing: a bane in that they have made it far more difficult to produce a product that can deal with the complexity, and a blessing in that it is increasingly difficult for humans to deal with the regulations and so automation has become very appealing in the market place. It can be expected that this duality, with the attendant banes and blessings, will exist in any highly regulated market. The lesson is to be prepared for the unavoidable drain on capital and time as well as the risk of being regulated out of business.

A further deployment issue has been market acceptance. LifeCode is significantly different from anything else that has been in use in the medical coding marketplace, and users are predictably skeptical. A quality product that meets a real need and staying power are both necessary to penetrate such a market. As of the time of writing, LifeCode is beginning to enjoy the rewards of widespread market acceptance. The pathway to acceptance led through small, enterprising billing companies such as Applied Medical Systems of Durham, North Carolina to large, prestigious clients such as Louisiana State University Health Sciences Center in Shreveport, Louisiana and MedAmerica in Oakland, California. But direct sales alone do not make up the whole story. In the long run, industry partners will make up the largest part of the business for a specialty product such as LifeCode. As with the direct sales, these partnerships began with joint selling agreements with small medical records companies such as ER Records in Irving, Texas and range to full OEM relationships with health information systems and services giants such as Dictaphone and MedQuist. Even larger partnerships are in the negotiation stage. It is this diversity of both direct customers and OEMs that will ensure the acceptance and success of LifeCode.

Maintenance

After the initial deployment of the LifeCode NLP engine in a production environment, the maintenance and subsequent development of the core knowledge bases is "real world" data driven. A cycle of feedback and maintenance is an integral part of the system. The first source of this data is analysis of the free-text, physician-dictated medical record. The second, and equally important, source of data is QA and customer use of the system. LifeCode's "self-awareness" feature routes certain medical records to human experts who "fix" the coding of the record. Targeted comparison analyses allow linguists and software engineers to iteratively improve the accuracy of the system. Knowledge bases and software algorithms are continually refined to better match the language used by the physician and the domain knowledge elicited from professional medical coders.

As medical specialties are added, knowledge bases are created and a cycle of maintenance and "natural language adaptation" is used to adjust to phrasings employed by physicians in these specialties. Within specialties, coding knowledge is currently very much in a state of flux and LifeCode must be regularly updated to reflect the dynamic nature of this. This includes changes in the practice of medicine and the effects this has on medical coding, yearly updates of codes, and major, but less frequent, changes in coding guidelines. LifeCode's unique design permits independent editing of source code, knowledge bases, and the expert coding system. Linguists, knowledge engineers, and software engineers with differing areas of expertise may contribute to improving the system without being limited by their individually varying knowledge of programming, linguistics, or the intricacies of coding.

Currently LifeCode does not use learning techniques because changes in medical codes and policies must be imparted to the system prior to the existence of any real world data by which learning could be driven. Also, for purposes of compliance, it is necessary to have a system that can be precisely audited in terms of why and how a particular decision was made. We believe, however, that in the future, automated learning techniques could be applied as an aid to dealing with variations in language use between physicians.

Conclusion

LifeCode advances the state-of-the-art in NLP along several boundaries. Its architecture brings together a number of NLP and Expert Systems technologies in a coherent commercial product. At the algorithm level, it represents a step forward in terms of high processing speed with very large linguistic knowledge bases. Also, its "self-awareness" capability is a necessity for system output to be used without human intervention on every decision and is, to our knowledge, unique among NLP applications. Finally, as a method for doing business, LifeCode has the potential to significantly influence the future course of medical records management. Given the current growth in direct sales and partnerships, the future for LifeCode is bright. Automation of medical coding and data mining will soon move from nicety to necessity.

References

AMA. 1999. *Current Procedural Terminology: CPT 2000.* American Medical Association.

Aronow, D. B., James R. Cooley, J. R., Sonderland, S. 1995. Automated Identification of Episodes of Asthma Exacerbation for Quality Measurement in a Computer-Based Medical Record. Technical Report IR-61, University of Massachusetts at Amherst – Center for Intelligent Information Retrieval.

Aronow, D. B., Sonderland, S., Ponte, J. M., Feng, F., Croft, W. B., Lehnert, W. G. 1995. Automated Classification of Encounter Notes in a Computer Based Medical Record. Technical Report IR-67, University of Massachusetts at Amherst – Center for Intelligent Information Retrieval.

Aronow, D. B., Shmueli, A. 1996. A PC Classifier of Clinical Text Documents: Advanced Information Retrieval Technology Transfer. *Proceedings – American Medical Informatics Association Fall Symposium.* 932ff.

Aronow, D. B., Feng, F. 1997. Ad-Hoc Classification of Electronic Clinical Documents. *D-Lib Magazine*, January.

Aronow, D. B., Feng, F., Croft, W. B. 1999. Ad Hoc Classification of Radiology Reports. *Journal of the American Medical Informatics Association.* 6(5): 393-411.

Bentley, J. 1996. The Impossible Takes a Little Longer. *Unix Review*, December, 75-79.

Croft, W. B., Callan, J. P., Aronow, D. B. 1995. Effective Access to Distributed Heterogeneous Medical Text Databases. *Proceedings – MEDINFO 95.* 1719ff.

Hirsch, M., Aronow, D. B. 1995. Suggesting Terms for Query Expansion in a Medical Information Retrieval System. Technical Report IR-63, University of Massachusetts at Amherst – Center for Intelligent Information Retrieval.

Langacker, R. W. 1999. Explanation in Cognitive Linguistics and Cognitive Grammar – Seminar hand-out

UCSD Department of Linguistics Conference on The Nature of Explanation in Linguistic Theory. University of California at San Diego. December 3-5, 1999.

Larkey, L. S., Croft, W. B. 1995. Automatic Assignment of ICD9 Codes to Discharge Summaries. Technical Report IR-64, University of Massachusetts at Amherst – Center for Intelligent Information Retrieval.

Lenert, L. A., Tovar, M. 1993. Automated Linkage of Free-text Descriptions of Patients with Practice Guidelines. *Proceedings – Symposium on Computer Applications in Medical Care.* 274-278. New York: Institute of Electrical and Electronics Engineers.

Lehnert, W., Sonderland, S., Aronow, D. B., Feng, F., Smith, A. 1994. Inductive Text Classification for Medical Applications. Technical Report TC-32, University of Massachusetts at Amherst – Center for Intelligent Information Retrieval.

Medicode. 1999. *Physician ICD-9-CM: International Classification of Diseases, 9th Revision, Clinical Modification.* Fifth Edition.

Ranum, D. L. 1988. Knowledge Based Understanding of Radiology Text. *Proceedings – Symposium on Computer Applications in Medical Care.* 141-145. New York: Institute of Electrical and Electronics Engineers.

Sager, N., Lyman, M., Nhan, N. T., Tick, L. J. 1994. Automatic Encoding into SNOMED III: A Preliminary Investigation. *Proceedings – Symposium on Computer Applications in Medical Care.* 230-234. New York: Institute of Electrical and Electronics Engineers.

Sager, N., Lyman, M., Bucknall, C. 1994. Natural Language Processing and the Representation of Clinical Data. *Journal of the American Medical Informatics Association.* 1(2):142-160.

Sager, N., Nhan, N.T., Lyman, M.S., Tick, L.J. 1996. Medical Language Processing with SGML Display. *Proceedings of the 1996 AMIA Annual Fall Symposium.* 547-551. Hanley & Belfus.

Sneiderman, C. A., Rindflesch, T. C., Aronson, A. R., Browne, A. C. 1995. Extracting Physical Findings from Free-Text Patient Records. *Proceedings – American Medical Informatics Association Spring Congress.*

Sneiderman, C. A., Rindflesch, T. C., Aronson, A. R. 1996. Finding the Findings: Identification of Findings in Medical Literature Using Restricted Natural Language Processing. *Proceedings – American Medical Informatics Association Fall Symposium.* 239-243.

Sonderland, S., Aronow, D. B., Fisher, D., Aseltine, J., Lehnert, W. 1995. Machine Learning of Text Analysis Rules for Clinical Records. Technical Report TC-39, University of Massachusetts at Amherst – Center for Intelligent Information Retrieval.

Yang, Y., Chute, C.G. 1992. An Application of Least Squares Fit Mapping To Clinical Classification. *Proceedings – Symposium on Computer Applications in Medical Care.* 460-464. New York: Institute of Electrical and Electronics Engineers.

Zingmond, D., Lenert, L. A. 1993. Monitoring Free-Text Data Using Medical Language Processing. *Computers and Biomedical Research.* 26:467-481.

The Emergence Engine:
A Behavior Based Agent Development Environment for Artists

Eitan Mendelowitz

AI Lab - 4532 Boelter Hall
Computer Science Department, University of California, Los Angeles
Los Angeles, California 90095
eitan@cs.ucla.edu

Abstract

Many artists are intrigued by the creative possibilities presented to them by virtual worlds populated with autonomous agents. Artists wishing to explore these possibilities face many obstacles including the need to learn artificial intelligence programming techniques. The Emergence Engine allows artists with no programming experience to create complex virtual worlds. Using behavior based action selection, the Emergence Engine allows artists to populate their worlds with autonomous situated agents. Artists can then direct the agents' behaviors using Emergence's high level scripting language. Artists have used the Emergence Engine successfully since 1998 to create numerous art installations exhibited both in the US and abroad.

Introduction

Computers are becoming increasingly important in the art world. Not only are computers being used as tools for creating traditional art (e.g. drawing, animation, and video) but they are being used as an artistic medium in their own right. Of particular interest is the growing field of interactive computer art. The best of these art pieces often use artificial intelligence technologies to create a meaningful and aesthetically engaging experience for the user.

David Rokeby's piece, *Very Nervous System,* uses vision systems and neural networks to turn a person's movements into music. *A-Volve,* by Christa Sommerer & Laurent Mignonneau, allows users to evolve virtual "creatures" using genetic algorithms. Steve Wilson's *Is Anyone There,* uses digitized speech and voice recognition to call pay phones and engage those who answer in conversation. Each of these installations received critical acclaim in the art world.

While many artists and designers are interested in creating interactive pieces, only a small number have the technical ability to do so. The Emergence Engine addresses the needs of artists who wish to explore the artistic and aesthetic issues of user interaction with autonomous situated agents in real-time 3D virtual environments. The agents created with the Emergence Engine are "believable" as defined by Loyall and Bates (Bates & Loyall 1997). Users are able to suspend belief and accept the agent as genuine. The Emergence Engine allows the artist to create inhabited virtual worlds without first requiring them to master the complexities of programming and artificial intelligence technologies.

The key component in the success of the Emergence Engine is the use of behavior based artificial intelligence for agent control. The Emergence Engine's control system allows artists to create and direct the behaviors of situated agents. The artist's direction of agent behavior can be done interactively in real-time through a graphical front-end or through the Emergence scripting language. Artists have exhibited pieces using the Emergence Engine in numerous art shows including Ars Electronica, and SIGGraph.

Related Applications and Research

A number of research groups have worked on the task of creating and directing autonomous agent interaction in real-time virtual environments. While not geared towards digital artists, their work was helpful in giving Emergence a point from which to start.

The Oz project (Bates, Loyall, & Reilly 1992), allows designers to give agents sets of goals. Each goal contains of sets of behaviors and sub-goals. An agent chooses from the set in order to best satisfy its goals. Behaviors are essentially action scripts heavily influenced by Dyer's work in story understanding (Dyer 1983). Most of the interaction in Oz worlds is linguistic.

Motivate is a commercial product whose main target is game creation. Motivate is a hierarchical finite state machine. Its strength for game companies is that it supports animation blending. For example the "walk" animation can be combined with the "chew gum" animation and the result would be an agent that is both walking and chewing gum. Motivate's "behaviors" are on the level of actions, for example sit and walk. Game designers wanting complex interaction are forced to build their own artificial intelligence libraries.

Copyright © 2000, American Association for Artificial Intelligence (www.aaai.org). All rights reserved.

Bruce Blumberg and the ALIVE project (Blumberg & Galyean 1995) use a goal oriented behavior system for situated agents. Behaviors represent both high level goals like "find food" and low level goals such as "move to." Behaviors can execute motor actions, change internal variables, and inhibit other goals. Action is taken on a winner take all basis. Once an action is taken it is performed by the motor system and often involves a sequence of animations. Unlike the Emergence Engine, behaviors are created specifically for an individual agent and require c++ programming. The system runs on an Onyx Reality Engine.

Improv (Perlin & Goldberg 1996) is the system most similar to the Emergence Engine. Like Emergence, Improv also has a behavior based scripting language. In Improv a script is a sequence of actions. Scripts are grouped. When a script in a group is chosen for execution all other scripts in that group are suppressed. Scripts are chosen probibalistically based on decision rules. While the Improv scripting approach seems very different from the Emergence scripting language, Emergence can simulate the Improv approach through probabilistic transition rules. Each character in the Improv system requires a dedicated computer for its behavior system.

Like Motivate and ALIVE (and unlike Emergence) Improv's animation is procedural. Actions taken determine the state of limbs and joints. The Emergence Engine supports key frame animation rather than procedural animation. Digital artists are often skilled animators and desire a high level of control over how their creations move. It was because of Emergence's focus on the artist that the decision was make to use interpolated key frame animation.

Improv was created with virtual theater in mind. As a result, Improv's scripts are performance oriented consisting of behaviors like "turn to camera" and "walk offstage." In contrast, the Emergence Engine was created for virtual environments. There is no on and off stage. More significantly, Emergence agents are situated in the world. Emergence agents sense and react to their environment.

Task Description

The Emergence Engine was created to allow artists and designers to create complex aesthetically pleasing worlds. To that end it was decided that: (1) The Emergence engine must be immersive. (2) The Emergence engine must support the creation of complex agent interactions with relative ease. (3) The Emergence Engine must be usable by artists. And (4), The Emergence Engine must be accessible.

In order to be immersive, the virtual world must engage the users' senses. It was decided that the Emergence Engine must be able to render geometrically complex texture mapped 3D worlds at high resolutions and high frame-rates. Because hearing is an important part of an immersive experience, the Emergence Engine was required to support multiple voices, stereo panning, and distance attenuation. Finally, there was a strong desire on the part of artists to explore other interface modalities such as voice and touch. The design of the Emergence Engine should take these desires into account.

The primary design goal of the Emergence Engine was to support artist creation of intra-agent (i.e. agent/user) and inter-agent (i.e. agent/agent) interactions. Emergence should enable artists to create societies of agents that exhibit such social behaviors as flocking, collective foraging, and construction. Artists should be able to exert as much control over the agents as they please. Emergence should support the continuum of artist direction of agent behavior, ranging from completely autonomous agents to completely scripted agents.

The Emergence design philosophy was to allow artists to use tools with which they were already familiar. To better aid visual artists Emergence would need a graphical interface for behavior control. Finally, most artists are not programmers. The Emergence scripting language would have to be compact and easy to learn.

The last requirement for the Emergence Engine is that it be accessible to artists. Most artists work on tight budgets. While most interactive virtual environments run on high-end computer graphics machines (e.g. SGIs and Onyx reality engines) the Emergence Engine would be designed to run on high-end personal computers. The requirement of running a real-time system on a PC platform affected many choices in the implementation of the Emergence Engine's artificial intelligence components.

Application Description

To appreciate the Emergence Engine, it is important to understand for what Emergence is used. To that end, this paper describes an example Emergence Engine installation. It then describes the design process used by artists to create such an installation. After describing how the system is used, this paper will describe the software architecture of the Emergence Engine. Special attention will be given to artificial intelligence techniques used in its execution.

An example installation

The Emergence Engine has been installed in many art shows all over the world. Its first installation was Rebecca Allen's work entitled "The Bush Soul (2)" in SIGGraph 1998's "Touchware" art show. The installation used three networked personal computers to render a three screen first person panoramic view of the virtual environment. Because the system is interactive, no two user experiences were the same. What follows is a brief narrative description of a typical user experience.

The installation begins with a view of the avatar, the user's embodiment in the virtual world, perched on a hilltop. Below the avatar is a "village" teeming with life-like but abstract creatures.

Figure 1: Photograph of the Emergence Engine's three-screen installation at SIGGraph 1998

Through the use of a gamepad, the user is free to explore the world by controlling the avatar's movements. As the Avatar moves down the hill into the Village the user encounters three tall creatures made out of whirling 5 pointed stars. The Whirlers by pass the user uninterested, mumbling among themselves. A small childlike Whirler follows them. Upon seeing the avatar the child playfully follows the user around bouncing happily and giggling. The small Whirler is conflicted; it wants to stay playing with the avatar but also wants to stay with the adult Whirlers. The Whirler plays with the avatar for a time then decides to rejoin its group.

Also inhabiting the Village are two large lumbering three legged creatures, Tripods. Occasionally the Tripods get tired and curl up into a protective rocklike ball. The Tripods feel threatened by strangers; when the avatar approaches, they try to scare off the user by rearing-up on a single leg. If the user continues to approch, the Tripods try to push away the user's avatar with their two free legs.

Overhead soars a flock of birds. Scattered about the Village, swaying in the breeze, are colorful flowers resembling oversized tulips.

Tribal music starts to play and, upon hearing the music, one flower manages to wiggle its way out of the ground. The flower glides across the village to coax a second flower out of the ground. Once together, the flowers begin a coordinated dance.

The above narration only describes a fraction of the interactions and behaviors present in the Village. The village is a small part of the entire virtual world. The world has four other regions of equal complexity. Artists were able to create such complicated intra-agent and inter-agent relations by using the artificial intelligence components built in to the Emergence Engine.

The Design Process

Using behavior based situated agents and a high level behavior scripting language, the Emergence Engine allows artists to create populated worlds without worrying about technical details. Using the Emergence Engine, the virtual world design process does not begin with software design. Rather, artists begin the design process as they usually do with concept drawings, descriptions of scenarios, and character sketches.

Once done with the concept, the artists create "bodies" for their agents. Emergence allows artists to create animated models using the standard animation packages with which they are already familiar (e.g. SoftImage, 3DMax and Maya). These models are imported into Emergence for use as agent bodies. The Emergence Engine uses a simple gray scale image as a topographical map to create world terrain.

Once the bodies of the agents are complete, artists concentrate on agent behavior and interaction. Typically, designers will have a character sketch of an agent (or a set of agents). The sketch may be something like "this character is wary of strangers." Artists can choose from a palette of behaviors which behaviors each agent should exhibit. Using a graphical interface, artists can modify behaviors in real-time allowing them to work visually, as they are accustomed. Once an artist is satisfied with an agent's behavior he/she can export the behavior settings directly into a script.

The final step of the design process is script creation. Scripts support higher level interaction. Using scripts artists can simulate changes in emotional state or goals. In addition, artists can use scripts to directly instruct agents to take a particular action.

The Emergence Architecture

The Emergence Engine has five components: the graphics module, physics module, the networking module, the behavior module, and the scripting module. Each component works independently and communicates with each of the other components through well defined interfaces. All five components will be described below with special attention given to those of interest to this conference: the behavior module and the scripting module.

The Graphics Module

The graphics module was designed to support real-time 3D environments. The Emergence graphics engine makes the most of available consumer-level OpenGL acceleration to provide performance that rivals high-end graphics workstations. The graphics engine renders an average of 6000 texture mapped or vertex colored polygons. The Emergence Engine supports interpolated key frame model animation, dynamic lighting with multiple light sources, and particle systems.

The graphics module receives model locations from the physics module. The scripting module provides the graphics module with key frame information for animating agent models.

The Physics Module

The Emergence Engine supports reasonably realistic real-world physics. To that end the physics module has two tasks, collision detection and force application.

Every object in the world has a collision model. For computational efficiency, the collision model is usually a simplified version of the agent model. When an agent moves between frames, its collision model sweeps out a collision volume. A frame is the smallest unit of time in the Emergence Engine. If the collision volumes of two objects are interpenetrating they are said to be colliding. Collisions are computed using hierarchical bounding boxes allowing for quick and efficient collision detection. This approach is similar to that used by I-Collide (Cohen, Lin, Manocha, &. Ponamgi 1995)

All agents in the world may be subjected to physical forces. The artists can choose what forces should be applied to a given object in the world. The artists are given a standard set of forces from which to choose (e.g. friction, gravity, and drag). In addition to choosing the forces to which an agent is subjected, artists can set the physical qualities of an agent (e.g. mass, coefficient of friction, elasticity).

The physics engine runs on a separate thread than the graphics engine. Given a fast enough computer or multiple processors, threading allows the physics engine to run at a higher frame rate than the graphics engine. The result is better physical realism through super sampling.

The physics module provides the graphics module with the location and orientation of objects in the world. It also provides the situated agents with many of their senses by sending events to the behavior and scripting modules.

When the physics engine detects a collision is sends the agent a collision event. The collision event tells the agent with what it collided, where the collision took place and with how much force the collision occurred. The collision events constitute the agents' sense of touch.

In addition to having a collision model every agent has a vision model. The vision model represents the agent's field of vision. When the physics engine detects an object within an agent's vision model it sends a vision event to the agent. Agents are given knowledge of visible objects and their position through the vision events.

Finally, the physics module keeps track of sound attenuation. When an agent make a sound, all agents within hearing distance are sent a hearing event along with the sound that was made (in the form of the sound's filename).

The Networking module

The Emergence Engine supports networking between computers over TCIP. While each machine on the Emergence network has a local copy of agents, only one computer on the network, the server, has "ownership" of that agent. The server broadcasts changes in that agent's state over the network to other participating machines. The network is tolerant to lost packets, if information about an agent's position is lost the local machine interpolates the agent's current position until accurate information is received. Any machine on the network can act as a display and render the world.

At SIGGraph '98, the Emergence system displayed a three screen panoramic first person view of the Emergence world using three networking computers.

Another feature of the networking module is that it allows arbitrary string messages to be sent over the network. The network messaging was included to allow for the integration of sensors and other devices with the emergence system.

For example, at SIGGraph '99, a separate PC with a touch sensor was used as a networked input device. The sensor informed agents in the virtual world when a user approached the installation. The networking module allows artists flexibility in examining interface modalities.

The last two modules of the Emergence Engine, the behavior module and the scripting module constitute Emergence's use of artificial intelligence technology.

Uses of Artificial Intelligence Technology

The Behavior Module

Agents are situated in the virtual environment and thus respond to external stimuli or lack thereof. In addition to the senses sight, touch, and hearing, agents can sense string "messages" and can sense the passing of time. At every frame, the agents must arbitrate between different and possibly competing behaviors to arrive at a single action.

The Emergence Engine behavior module resembles Craig Reynolds' steering behaviors (Reynolds 1999). The Emergence Engine uses a system of relative weights to choose between competing behaviors for action selection. This approach is not so different from the inhibition/excitations approach often used by other behavior systems. Raising the weight of one behavior will increase its influence while simultaneously decreasing the influence of all other behaviors. In effect, excitation of one behavior inhibits all other competing behaviors.

Low-level behaviors do not depend on sensory input. Such behaviors are of the type: move to a specific point, face a particular direction, move around at random, slow down, etc.

Other behaviors are higher level and require vision or other senses. Such behaviors include: agent following, collision avoidance, path following, agent watching, move in formation with other agents (e.g. to an agent's left), etc.

Every active behavior, those with non-zero weights and the required stimuli, chooses a goal point. A single unified goal point is decided upon by computing the weighted average of all the behaviors' goal points. While more complex arbitration schemes exist including decision-theoretic approaches (Pirjanian & Mataric 1999) and constraint-based approach (Bares, Grigoire, & Lester 1998) they are often computationally expensive.

The Emergence Engine is required to arbitrate between dozens of behaviors for scores of agents on a single personal computer. Weighted averaging was chosen for its computational frugality. The choice of a simple arbitration method does not require a sacrifice in behavioral complexity. Many of the benefits gained from more complex arbitration schemes can be achieved using weighted averages if behaviors are allowed to modify their own weights. For example, if a collision is imminent the collision avoidance behavior can temporarily double (or quadruple) its own weight in order to suppress the influence of other competing behaviors.

Once a single goal point is selected, it is passed on to the agent's motor system. Not all agents have the same motor abilities. Some agents can fly while others are restricted to movement on the ground. Some agents can move sideways while others must move in the direction they are facing. Agents move by telling the physics module to apply a force and/or a torque to their bodies.

In addition to its computational efficiency, behavior based control has a representational advantage for the artist. The approach allows artists to be presented with a palette of behaviors. Each behavior has a concrete meaning and the system of relative weights is intuitive. Using the Emergence Engine's graphical front-end artists can change behavior weightings while the system is active. Such interactivity greatly shortens the amount of time required by the artist to arrive at desired agent behaviors.

The Scripting Module

The Emergence scripting language was designed to be small and easy for artists to learn. The scripting module is used for high level control over agent behavior.

Similar to Brooks' subsumption architecture (Brooks 1986), the Emergence scripting module implements multiple augmented finite state machines running in parallel. Communication between different finite state machines is done by passing string messages. Unlike the subsumption architecture there is no hierarchy. All finite state machines have equal influence over an agent.

The scripting module is tightly coupled with the Emergence Engine's behavior module. Any behavior value an artist can set interactively, through Emergence's graphical front end, can be scripted. Usually, this feature is used to simulate changes in an agent's emotional state or mood by changing the relative weights of different steering behaviors.

In addition to changing behavior variables, the Emergence scripting language allows for the creation and destruction of agents, the playing of sound files, the playing of key framed animations, and the sending of messages. Scripts can also call other scripts (and wait for them to terminate), or spawn other scripts (and run them in parallel).

Like a standard finite state machine, every script has a special start state which is entered when an script is executed. Upon entering a state, a list of statements is executed sequentially. Executed statements perform the aforementioned actions.

Every state has a list of transitions. Each transition has a condition and a state. When a transition's condition is satisfied the script enters the transition's state.

Emergence transitions are associated with sensory events. These events correspond to an agent's senses and include vision, collision, hearing, message, timer, immediate, and animation-end. The physics module generates the vision, collision, and hearing events. The timer event is generated at a set time interval specified in the state. The immediate event is generated once, immediately after the last statement in the state executed. The animation-end event is called when the graphics module displays the last key-frame of an animation sequence.

Transition conditions are only checked when their associated event is sent.

Another departure from traditional finite state machines is the use of local variables. Every state can have a list of parameters. Upon entering a state, values are bound to the members of the parameter list. The use of parameters allows scripts to be compact and reusable.

The following is an example of a script. It instructs an agent to follow creatureA. If creatureA bumps into the agent the agent is instructed to avoid creatureA and the script terminates. CreatureA is a parameter and is bound to a value when the script is called.

```
State FollowTheCreature(string CreatureA) {
   Follow.Weight[CreatureA] = 10;
   // follow CreatureA with a weight of 10
   Follow.Distance[CreatureA] = 2;
   // follow A from a distance of 2 meters
} transitions {
   OnCollision {
     if that T== CreatureA then
       AviodTheCreature(CreatureA);
     // if that with which you collided
     // is creatureA then go to state
     // AviodTheCreature
```

```
    }
}
state AviodTheCreature(string CreatureA) {
  Follow.Weight[CreatureA] = 0;
  //stop following creatureA
  Aviod.Weight[CreatureA] = 10;
  //avoid creatureA with a weight of 10
}
//since there are no transition statements
 //the script terminates in state
 //AviodTheCreature
```

Application Use and Payoff

Since the spring of 1998, the Emergence Engine has been used by dozens of artists to create interactive virtual environments. Artists typically require less than two weeks of learning before becoming comfortable with the Emergence Engine. Installed in art shows and conferences including SIGGraph 1998, SIGGraph 1999, and Ars Electronica 1999, Emergence has been experienced by thousands of users. The Emergence Engine has allowed artists to examine issues of human-computer interaction, artificial intelligence, and virtual interactive environment without requiring them to learn how to program.

Application Development and Deployment

The Emergence Engine began in 1997, when Professor Rebecca Allen of UCLA's Department of Design | Media Arts assembled a team of artists and computer scientists to explore issues of human–agent interaction. This original team created a prototype Emergence Engine that supported agents with a few hand-coded behaviors. This prototype system was exhibited at Art Futura in Madrid, Spain in 1997.

Using lessons learned from the prototype, Loren McQuade and I collaborated to create the Emergence Engine architecture. The development process began with months of discussions with Professor Allen and other artists. After determining the needs of said artists we spent a month planning the Emergence software architecture. The Emergence Engine itself was written in C++ and some assembly over the course of seven months. Flex and Bison were used in the creation of the Emergence scripting language.

The Emergence Engine runs on any Intel platform machines using Windows NT as an operating system. The Emergence Engine requires a graphics card that supports OpenGL.

Current efforts involve making the scripting language even easier to use. A script editor was created in the spring of 1999. In the future we hope to develop a graphical interface for the scripting language completely freeing the artist from having to write code.

Conclusion

The Emergence Engine provides a unique development environment for designers and artists to explore virtual world creation. Using behavior based techniques and a high level scripting language, the Emergence Engine allow designers with little or no programming experience to create situated agents that interact with the user in intelligent and meaningful ways. The Emergence Engine has been used to create a number of successful interactive computer art installations enjoyed by thousands of users all over the world.

Acknowledgments. I would like to thank Professor Rebecca Allen, Director of the Emergence Lab, and the other artists who used the Emergence Engine to create works of art I could not have imagined. I would also like to thank Intel for their support of the Emergence Lab.

References

Dyer, M. 1983. *In-Depth Understanding.* , Cambridge, Mass.: The MIT Press.

Loyall, A. and Bates, J. 1997. Personality-Rich Believable Agents That Use Language. *Proceedings of the First International Conference on Autonomous Agents,* 106-113. New York, N.Y.: The Association for Computing Machinery.

Bates, J., Loyall, B., and Reilly, W. 1991. Broad Agents, *Proceedinge of the AAAI Spring Symposium on Intergrated Intelligent Architectures.* Stanford University, Calf.: AAAI Press.

Blumberg, B., and Galyean, T. 1995. Multi-Level Direction of Autonomous Creatures for Real-Timer Virtual Enviroments. *Proceedings of SIGGRAPH95.* New York, N.Y.: The Association for Computing Machinery.

Perlin, K., and Goldberg, A., 1996. Improv: A system for Scripting Interactive Actors in Virtual Worlds. *Proceedings of SIGGRAPH96.* New York, N.Y.: The Association for Computing Machinery.

Brooks, R. 1986a. A Robust Layered Control System for a Mobile Robot. *IEEE Journal of Robotics and Automation.* RA-2:14-23.

Bares, W., Grigoire, J., and Lester, J. 1998. Realtime Constraint-Based Cinematography for Complex Interactive 3D Worlds. *Proceedings of the Tenth Conference on IAAI.* Menlo Park, Calf.: AAAI Press.

Pirjanian, P. and Mataric, M. 1999. A decision-theoretic approach to fuzzy behavior coordination. *Proceedings of the IEEE Conference on Computational Intelligence in Robotics and Automation,* Monterey, Calif:, IEEE.

Reynolds, C. 1999. Steering Behaviors For Autonomous Characters. Computer Game Developers Confernece. San Francisco, Calf: Computer Game Developers Confernece.

Cohen, J., Lin, M., Manocha, D., and Ponamgi. K. 1995. I-COLLIDE: An Interactive and Exact Collision Detection System for Large-Scaled Environments. Proceedings of Association for Computing Machinery International 3D Graphics Conference. New York, N.Y.: The Association for Computing Machinery.

Innovative Applications:
Emerging Applications

The TheaterLoc Virtual Application

Greg Barish, Craig A. Knoblock, Yi-Shin Chen, Steven Minton, Andrew Philpot, Cyrus Shahabi

Information Sciences Institute, Integrated Media Systems Center, and Department of Computer Science
University of Southern California
4676 Admiralty Way, Marina del Rey, CA, 90292
{barish, knoblock, minton, philpot}@isi.edu {yishinc, shahabi}@pollux.usc.edu

Abstract

Although much has been written about various information integration technologies, little has been said regarding how to combine these technologies together to build an entire "virtual" application. In this paper, we describe the design and implementation of TheaterLoc, an information integration application that allows users to retrieve information about theaters and restaurants for a variety of cities in the United States, including an interactive map depicting their relative locations and video trailers of the movies playing at the selected theaters. The data retrieved by TheaterLoc comes from five distinct heterogeneous and distributed sources. The enabling technology used to achieve the integration includes the Ariadne information mediator and wrappers for each of the web-based data sources. We focus in detail on the mediator technologies, such as data modeling, source axiom compilation, and query planning. We also describe how the wrappers present an interface for querying data on web sites, aiding in information retrieval used during data integration. Finally, we discuss some of the major integration challenges we encountered and our plans to address them.

Introduction

There is a wealth of interesting data sources and applications available on the World Wide Web, but it is difficult to do much with the information except look at it or build a specific application to process the data available. Writing separate applications each time is a time-consuming and redundant task. We have developed a system called Ariadne (Knoblock et al. 1998) that makes it possible to rapidly construct an information agent that can integrate data sources that were not originally designed to work together. The resulting virtual application dynamically performs the integration in order to minimize the problems associated with storing and maintaining data. Ariadne includes tools for constructing wrappers that make it possible to query web sources as if they were databases and the mediator technology required to dynamically and efficiently answer queries using these sources.

Copyright © 2000, American Association for Artificial Intelligence (www.aaai.org). All rights reserved.

We claim that Ariadne makes it possible to rapidly build virtual applications and in this paper we describe exactly what is involved. Specifically, we provide a detailed, behind-the-scenes look at one of the recent applications we have built. This application, called TheaterLoc (Barish et. al. 1999a), integrates data related to movie theaters and restaurants, allowing users to view their locations on a map, look up restaurant reviews and movie showtimes, and watch trailers of films.

There has already been substantial work on information integration (Weiderhold 1996) and projects that focus on applying this technology to the World Wide Web, including Information Manifold (Levy et. al. 1996), Occam (Kwok and Weld 1996), Infomaster (Genesereth et. al. 1997), and InfoSleuth (Bayardo et. al. 1997), as well as related work specifically on information extraction (Hammer et. al. 1997; Doorenbos et. al. 1997; Kushmerick 1997). But what is noticeably absent from the literature is a study on what it takes to put together an entire application using the various integration technologies. To that end, we describe the details of how TheaterLoc works and how it was developed.

The next section describes what the application does from the user's point of view. Then, we describe how it works, including the domain modeling, the query planning, and the wrappers for extracting the data from web pages. Next, we enumerate TheaterLoc development tasks and their costs. Lastly, we identify some remaining challenges and how we are currently addressing them.

The TheaterLoc Application

TheaterLoc (http://www.isi.edu/ariadne/demo/theaterloc) is a web site that allows users to retrieve information about restaurants and movie theaters for various cities in the United States. Users first choose the city in which to query. The system then returns information about the theaters and restaurants in that city, as well as a custom, interactive map identifying their relative locations within that city, illustrated in Figure 1.

Users can then click on any of the plotted points to be taken to a web page containing further details about that particular place. For example, when a restaurant is chosen, users are taken to its corresponding CuisineNet web page (as shown in Figure 2), which contains reviews,

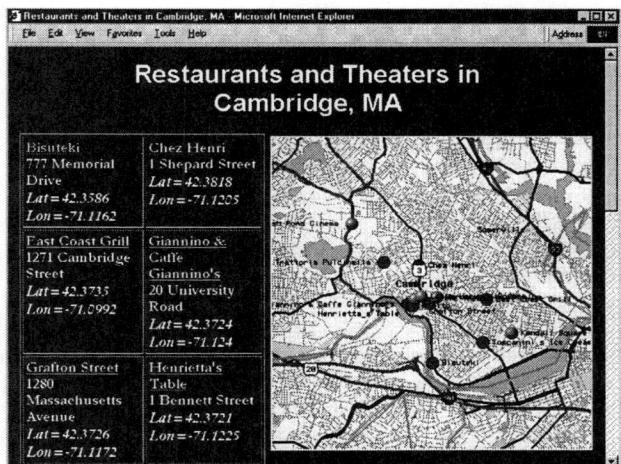

Figure 1: Theaters and restaurants in Cambridge, MA

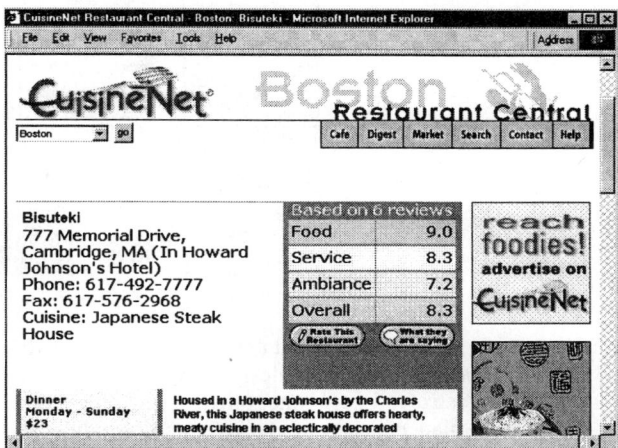

Figure 2: Restaurant detail page

Figure 3: Theater detail page

pricing information, and ratings. Alternatively, choosing a theater returns a listing of the current movies playing there, along with their showtimes, and links to video trailers, as shown in Figure 3.

The information integrated by TheaterLoc comes from five distinct online sources. Restaurant information is gathered from CuisineNet, theater and movie showtime information from Yahoo Movies, and the trailers come from Film.com. Construction of the interactive map is facilitated by two sources: the E-TAK geocoder (to geocode all addresses for plotting) and the US Census Tiger Map Service. The TheaterLoc application is effective because it saves the user from having to go to these sites separately, navigate through different user interfaces, and integrate the data manually. Instead, what is presented is a single, cohesive application that seamlessly integrates the useful data from these sources and automatically correlates them as necessary.

System Architecture

TheaterLoc is a client/server application, where the server side is composed of three major pieces: a web server, an information mediator, and a set of wrappers to access data sources. For the purposes of this paper, we will focus on the details of the mediator and wrappers, since they are the centerpiece of the integration effort.

The system architecture is shown in Figure 4. When a user issues a query though the web interface, the HTTP request is processed by the web server, and a corresponding query is sent to Ariadne for resolution. The mediator, in turn, constructs a plan indicating which sources should be queried and how the data retrieved should be integrated. This plan also contains information about how to order the steps of information retrieval (since there may be dependencies), which steps can be executed in parallel, and what other data manipulation functions (such as relational joins or projections) need to be done to answer the query.

Many of the data sources comprising Ariadne applications are web sites. Access to their data is accomplished through communication with data source *wrappers*, which provide a standard, flexible query interface to a set of logically related web pages. Web pages are considered semi-structured sources, in that they contain useful information, organized in a predictable manner, which can be extracted automatically.

Wrappers are used to parse the data from these web pages, essentially providing a database-like interface to the data contained on those pages. They allow the mediator to interrogate web sites for information in a standard and structured manner, specifically, a subset of the SQL language. The TheaterLoc wrappers and their underlying web site sources are listed in Table 1.

Example Query

To illustrate the details of integration within the system, consider the following example. Suppose a user wants to map restaurants and theaters in Cambridge, Massachusetts.

As described earlier, this HTTP request is translated by the web server into an query sent to Ariadne, which then plans a solution. The resulting plan consists of several

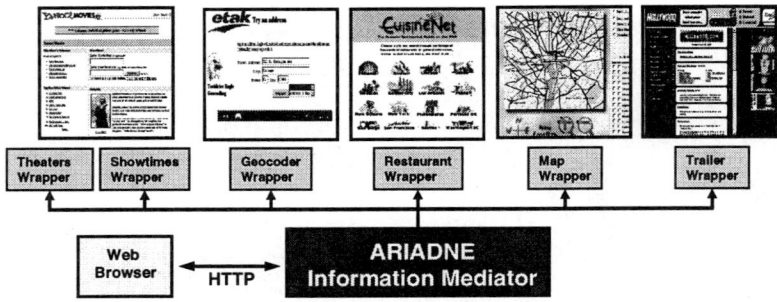

Figure 4: TheaterLoc System Architecture

subqueries to the various data sources that the mediator knows about, so that the desired information can be efficiently retrieved and integrated. For the example query, this plan consists of retrieving information about the various restaurants and theaters in Cambridge, and retrieving a map showing their relative locations.

The detailed plan needed to accomplish these two tasks includes a few additional steps, based on the information sources available. Recall that it is not possible to simply get all of this information from a single source. The mediator must reason about what data the various sources can offer and then construct a plan which retrieves the desired information based on the features, limitations, and dependencies between the sources. These detailed steps are described below.

Retrieving Theaters and Restaurants. For our example query, since the user has chosen to get information on all theaters and restaurants in Cambridge, the mediator will initially determine that it needs to query the Restaurant and Theater wrappers to get demographic information (names, addresses, and URLs) for both types of establishments. In contrast, if the application interface had allowed the user to search only for information about theaters in Cambridge, the mediator would realize that there would be no need to query the Restaurant wrapper, as CuisineNet only provides data about restaurants.

Retrieving the Interactive Map. The next step in the plan for our Cambridge query involves using the Geocoder source to convert theater and restaurant street addresses into latitudes and longitudes. This is necessary in order to construct a query to the Map wrapper, which retrieves a dynamic, interactive map indicating the locations of these places.

The map returned is an HTML "image map", where each plotted point is associated with a hyperlink to a page containing more details about that location. Thus, users can click on a particular point to explore more detail about either a restaurant or theater. If they choose a restaurant they are taken to the CuisineNet page for that restaurant. If, on the other hand, they choose the URL attribute for a theater, another Ariadne query is invoked to collect movie showtime and video trailers for those movies. Again, the web server translates an HTTP-based request into a domain-level query.

Retrieving Movie Information. The query to Ariadne for theater details contains the name of the theater chosen. The corresponding plan that the mediator constructs to solve this query consists of two steps: (a) interrogating the Yahoo Movies site via the Showtimes wrapper for information about movie showtimes and (b) for each movie, querying the Trailer wrapper to locate the URL for the video trailer, if any, associated with that movie. The combined information is joined into a single relation and subsequently returned to the user as an HTML table. Users can then view the trailer by clicking on the link provided in this table.

How TheaterLoc Works

We now take a detailed look at the inner workings of TheaterLoc, focusing primarily on the Ariadne mediator and wrapper technologies.

Data Modeling

In Ariadne, relationships between data are expressed in the application *domain model*. This model contains information about classes, their attributes, and their relationship to other classes. The domain model provides a unifying ontology for describing the contents of the sources.

The model supports both *functional sources* and *data sources*. The former essentially has a set of input and output attributes: when given the required input attributes, functional sources perform some computation and produce the output attributes. Data sources, on the other hand, simply contain a relation to be returned. There are often instances when data sources require some input in order to return a relation (for web sites, this is the case when executing an HTTP POST request), so they can be very similar to functional sources. However, in Ariadne,

Wrapper	Source	URL
Restaurant	*CuisineNet*	www.cuisinenet.com
Theater	*Yahoo*	movies.yahoo.com
Showtimes	*Yahoo*	movies.yahoo.com
Geocoder	*E-TAK*	www.geocode.com
Tiger	*USGS*	tiger.census.gov
Trailer	*Film.com*	www.film.com

Table 1: TheaterLoc wrappers and underlying sources

functional sources are typically local and they always involve computation performed locally. Data sources are either local or remote and, if they do involve computation, that computation is performed remotely.

The TheaterLoc domain model is shown in Figure 5. The model shows the domain level classes of Map, Place, Movie, Restaurant, and Theater. Restaurant, for example, is a class that has several attributes (such as cuisine) and is related to other classes (such as Theater). Classes in the domain model are mapped to zero or more actual information sources. For example, in TheaterLoc, the Restaurant class is mapped to the CuisineNet source.

The directed arc edge from Restaurant to Theater indicates a *covering*, referring to the fact that the only types of Place in TheaterLoc are either restaurants or theaters. Since the Restaurant and Theater classes are sub-classes of Place, they naturally inherit attributes of their parent class, namely: street, city, state, city-state, latitude, and longitude. The sources associated with each class are shown as gray cylinders or cubes, near the class. The cylinders indicate data sources, the cubes indicate functional sources. Also shown for each source is a list of the attributes it provides along with any binding constraints (Kwok and Weld, 1996), the latter prepended with a "$" character. Binding constraints are simply input requirements that a source has before it can provide data.

The Geocoder is an example of a data source that has a binding constraint. It requires street, city, and state attributes in order to provide latitude and longitude information about an address. Intuitively, this type of constraint makes sense: one cannot geocode an address without knowing the address first.

Functional sources can also have binding constraints. The Article-Fn source, for example, takes as input an attribute called raw-movie-nm and returns an attribute called movie-name. This purpose of this source is to normalize the ordering of the words of a movie title, so that semantic equivalence can be detected with another source. Specifically, this source is used to move any grammatical article which might appear at the end of a movie title to the front of the title. For example, the raw-movie-nm might be "Bug's Life, A" and the movie-name returned would be "A Bug's Life".

Although data sources with binding constraints appear similar to functional sources at the modeling level, they are usually different at the implementation level. Functional sources typically perform local computation based on input and derive original data based on that input. In contrast, data sources with binding constraints

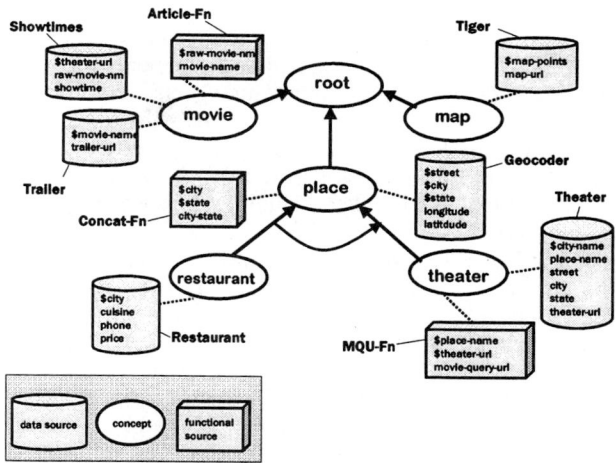

Figure 5: TheaterLoc domain model

typically use the input information as a means to either perform remote computation or as a means to filter out a logical subset of data from a much larger set.

Query Planning

Planning in Ariadne consists of two major steps: an initial axiom compilation phase and then a run-time planning phase. The first step is executed once, when the application is first initialized. The second step is executed each time the mediator receives a query.

Axiom Compilation. The reasoning done by the mediator about the domain model leverages the results of an initial domain axiom compilation step (Ambite et. al. 1998) that generates rules about what source combinations can be used to solve various domain queries. Specifically, axiom compilation is based on applying a set of inference rules to construct a lattice describing how various combinations of data modeled at the domain level can be retrieved given the available functional and data sources.

For example, consider the axioms for the TheaterLoc Restaurant domain class, shown in Figure 6. Notice the second axiom, which has a *head* declaring that various attributes of restaurant (such as cuisine and latitude) can be retrieved by combining the CuisineNet and Geocoder sources, as shown in the *body* of the axiom. Essentially, axioms represent how to map domain level terms onto one or more source level terms.

The initial axiom compilation step significantly reduces the run-time execution of the system. Instead of performing a costly search to locate those sources

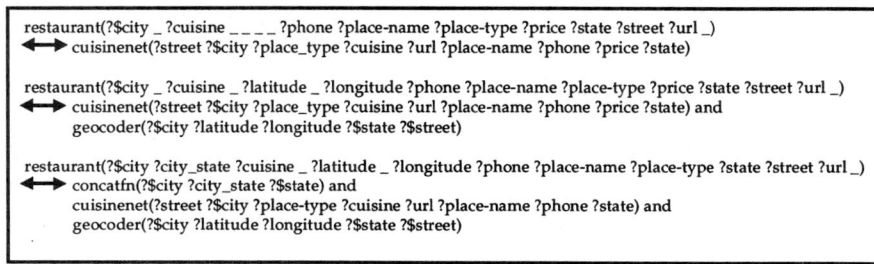

Figure 6: Partial list of TheaterLoc axioms

required to answer a given query, the planner can instead quickly consult the pre-compiled axiom lattice.

Planning By Rewriting. When queries are posed to the system, Ariadne reasons about the domain model and source descriptions in order to develop an efficient plan for retrieving and integrating the data. The method used to accomplish this is called Planning-by-Rewriting (PBR) (Ambite and Knoblock 1997). Under PBR, an initial, sub-optimal plan is quickly generated and then iteratively improved by applying a series of rewriting rules. Rewriting relies on local search algorithms that can alter both the sources used to resolve portions of a query as well as the ordering of operations performed by the mediator during information integration.

The resulting plans produced by PBR can significantly optimize and simplify the linear portions of the plan, as well as exploiting opportunities for parallelism between tasks, where possible. For example, the planning for the query about restaurants and theaters in Cambridge would discover that the collection of demographic information and the geocoding of that information was a necessarily serial sequence, whereas the collection of the demographic data from the Theater wrapper and the collection of data from the Restaurant Wrapper were independent plan steps that could be parallelized.

An example plan to locate the theaters in Cambridge, which represents a sub-plan of the original example presented earlier, is shown in Figure 5. Generally, what is illustrated here is that a list of theaters is being retrieved from the Theaters wrapper, geocoded and the relevant attributes returned as output. In addition, for each theater, a *movie-query-URL* (which is the basis for the movie-showtimes query) is derived. In looking at the figure, we can identify a series of plan operators associated with these general tasks. For example, notice that there is a retrieval done for Theaters, the result used as the basis for geocoding (Geocoder retrieve step), and the subsequent results are joined along the *street*, *city*, and *state* attributes. Later, there is a join done between this information and the *movie-query-URL* information, based on *place-name*. Finally, the output contains the attributes of the class, provided by the integrated sources.

Wrapper-based Information Extraction

Wrappers, as described previously, provide a generic mechanism by which a web site can be queried as a traditional database, in a subset of the SQL syntax. In TheaterLoc, for example, when querying the list of restaurants from CuisineNet for Cambridge, the SQL query:

```
select name, address, url from CuisineNet
where city='Cambridge'
```

is issued to the Restaurant wrapper by the mediator. The wrappers work by using a *page model* to describe the location and type of web page(s), an *embedded catalog* to define the hierarchical relationship between data on a page, and a set of *extraction rules* describing how to parse data from that page (Muslea et. al.. 1999).

The page model describes how the pages should be contacted in order to prepare for data extraction. For example, the E-TAK Geocoding site consists of an HTML form that requires address information as input to return the geographic coordinates for that address. Thus, the extraction of those coordinates is contingent on submitting the form (an HTTP POST request). The automatic entering of data onto the form and subsequent POST request are described in the page model.

An embedded catalog is used to model the hierarchical relationships between the attributes on a page. For example, the Showtimes wrapper contains a two-level embedded catalog which describes the fact that each theater page contains a list of one or more movies. The embedded catalog is used as a basis for how to parse a given web page. Multiple levels in the catalog typically indicate list-like structures on pages, so that nested lists of information can be extracted in a structured manner.

Finally, the extraction rules describe how a page should be split into a hierarchy of regions, and where the data is located within each of these regions. Whereas the embedded catalog describes the general tree-like structure of a page, the extraction rules define how to locate the nodes and leaves of that tree, the latter being the actual data to be extracted. Rules are expressed in a regular-expression like syntax, and are based on identifying

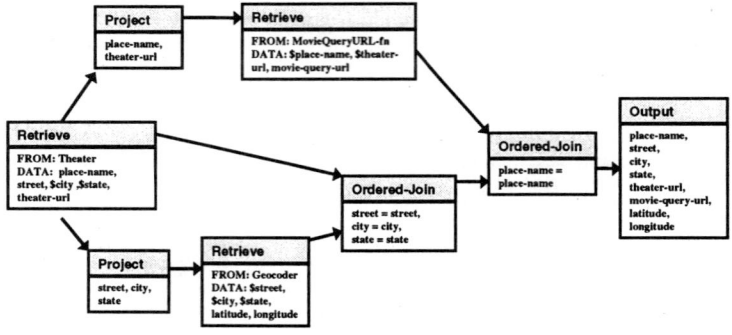

Figure 7: Part of the TheaterLoc query plan

landmarks near where the matching expression will appear.

Generation of the page model, embedded catalog, and extraction rules is accomplished through training the system via a graphical user interface (GUI). Application developers use the wrapper GUI to choose web pages they want to extract data from, as well as where the various parts of data on that page are located – they actually point and click to indicate this information. Using inductive learning, a system called STALKER (Muslea et. al. 1998) generates the rules associated with the user-defined catalog and model.

As an example of how wrappers extract data from a web page, consider the TheaterLoc Showtimes wrapper. As shown in Figure 8, the Yahoo Movies web page for a theater shows a list of movies and their showtimes. Obviously, there are some natural structures and patterns associated with the data for that page. Wrappers take advantage of this semi-structure to perform information extraction. For example, the figure shows that on each page there is a notion of a *movielist*, which is composed of a list of *movies*.

Figure 9a shows the actual page model file for the Showtimes wrapper. Notice that a binding pattern relationship (indicated by the "?" symbol) exists: a URL for a theater must be supplied in order to receive information about movies and showtimes. Figure 9b shows the hierarchical embedded catalog for the same wrapper. The movielist/movie relationship, as described above, is captured here. Finally, Figure 9c presents the extraction rules. These rules describe how to locate relevant data on a web page. Notice that they are somewhat related to the embedded catalog, in the sense that hierarchical relationships must have special rules which show how to locate multiple child instances. For example, the notion that *movielist* contains one or more *movies* requires that the extraction rules specify not only where the *movielist* can be found on the page, but also how to iterate through it, so that multiple instances of its children can be identified.

It is also interesting to note the two-level embedded catalog which mirrors the list-like structure of the actual web page (Figure 8), where each theater contains a list of movies, and each movie has a set of showtimes. Notice that we also could have extended the catalog to a third-level, to capture the *list* of showtimes, instead of just the showtimes as one large string. But, that sort of

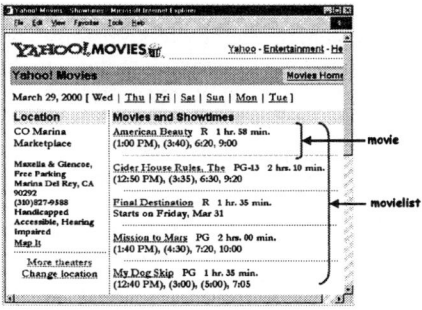

Figure 8: Web page for Yahoo! Movies

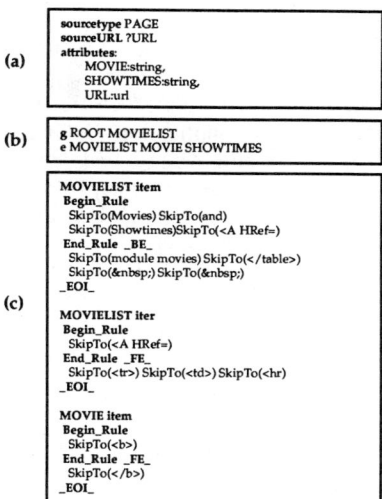

Figure 9 (a) page model, (b) emedded catalog, (c) extraction rules

enumeration would not be useful at the application level (we do not need to extract the individual showtimes), so we used just two levels.

The Development Process

We constructed TheaterLoc in a very short amount of time. Table 2 enumerates the time spent on each part of the development process. In total, building TheaterLoc required 3-4 days. One of the more important things to note from this table is that, with the exception of the Tiger Map wrapper, using our wrapper GUI tool to automate the construction of all TheaterLoc wrappers cost about 3 hours of total project time. The Tiger wrapper required special integration (coordinate translation) and ended up taking us an entire day to complete.

Task	Time Required
Application design	3-4 hours
Domain modeling	2-3 hours
Wrapping web sources (w/GUI)	2-3 hours
Tiger Map wrapper	1 day
Building functional sources	1-2 hours
Interface/HTML	2-3 hours
Web server integration	3-4 hours
Application testing	2-3 hours
Total	3-4 days

Table 2: Project development Time

The tools and approach that we used to build TheaterLoc also make it an application that is easy to maintain and extend. For example, adding a new source into the application is simply a matter adding this source to the domain model and using the wrapper GUI tool to automate its construction. Similarly, dealing with changes to the sources is also a straightforward process that does not require re-engineering the entire system.

It is worthwhile to note the amount of reusability inherent in virtual applications like TheaterLoc. The wrappers, in particular, could be integrated into another virtual application without any modifications. For example, if some future application required plotting hospitals and schools on an interactive map based on their street addresses, the geocoder and map wrappers from TheaterLoc could simply be reused for this purpose.

Challenges and Extensions

Using the Ariadne technologies we have described allows us to rapidly build information integration applications. However, there are still some challenges that remain. In this section, we list two of these challenges and briefly describe our ongoing research at addressing them.

Resolving Data Inconsistencies

One problem frequently encountered when integrating data from multiple sources involves semantically equivalent objects that exist in inconsistent text formats across these sources. With TheaterLoc, for example, although the movie "A Bug's Life" was listed by Film.Com as such, Yahoo Movies listed it as "Bug's Life, A". This made it difficult for us to correlate the two objects, something we needed to do when associating a movie and its showtimes with a video trailer. As described earlier, we solved this problem for TheaterLoc specifically by building a functional source that normalized the textual format of this data. However, it is clear that a more general solution is necessary.

Towards that end, we have been designing an approach that identifies semantic equivalence by matching all of an objects' shared attributes (Tejada et. al. 1998). With our technique, certain attributes have more importance (weight) in deciding a match than others. For example, in TheaterLoc, we could resolve the similarity between "A Bug's Life" and "Bug's Life, A" by computing a similarity metric between all of the shared attributes (such as movie title, director, and actors) and then judge equivalence based on this metric. Since the manual encoding of attribute weighting is time consuming and error-prone, we are also developing an active learning approach for tailoring attribute weighting rules, through limited user input, for specific application domains.

Improving Performance and Scalability

Data Materialization. At their core, information integration applications are only as fast as their most latent sources. One slow website can substantially affect overall application performance. For TheaterLoc, a major bottleneck was the Tiger map source, which occasionally took several seconds to render a map. In addition, web-based data sources are not always reliable. For example, there were times when CuisineNet was temporarily unavailable or simply overloaded with requests.

As a remedy for these issues, we are investigating the optimization of data access by selective pre-fetching and caching of source data (Ashish et. al. 1998). Since information integration applications are frequently associated with very large databases, we must be careful to cache only the subset of data that returns the greatest improvement to overall application performance. Our selective approach is based on the frequency of queries, as well as other source-specific metadata, such as source responsiveness. We are also exploring a solution for highly fragmented classes, where a single class may be associated with many sources. In this case, we would like to collapse the cache into a minimal set of classes.

Dataflow Execution. Web-based information integration usually involves retrieving data from multiple web sites at once and applying a series of relational algebra operations (i.e., Select, Join) to achieve a final result. Complicating this are instances where retrieving a logical set of data (a logical relation) involves extracting data from a series of linked web pages. In general, execution could be optimized by (a) parallelizing as much of the data retrieval as possible and (b) streaming retrieved data back to the plan so that it can be processed as soon as possible.

To accomplish this, we are developing the Theseus plan execution system (Barish et. al. 1999b). Based on a hybrid dataflow architecture, Theseus naturally supports the high degree of parallelism and data pipelining that web-based information integration demands. Eventually, we intend to combine both Ariadne and Theseus, such that former is responsible for plan generation and latter is responsible for execution.

Discussion

In this paper, we have described TheaterLoc, an example of a virtual application that integrates data from a set of independent online data sources. We have also described the details of the information integration technology that was used to build TheaterLoc. In particular, we have focused on how state-of-the-art artificial intelligence techniques (planning, knowledge representation, information extraction, and machine learning) were combined to produce the final result. In addition, we have shown that using Ariadne technology makes virtual application development both simple and quick.

It is important to note that TheaterLoc is merely one example of the type of virtual application that can be built using Ariadne. The enabling technologies described in this paper are generic enough to be readily applied to any information domain. In addition, future applications can easily reuse parts of existing ones, further expediting the development process.

New applications are being deployed on the Internet at a rapid rate. While many all offer some measure of independent usefulness, they lack integration with each other. The technology of information integration, such as that embodied by Ariadne, promises a future in which developers can have the power to mix-and-match useful data from any number of these sources to create endless types of novel virtual applications.

Acknowledgements. This work was supported in part by the Integrated Media Systems Center, a NSF Engineering Research Center, in part by research grants from NCR and General Dynamics Information Systems, in part by NASA/JPL under contract number 961518, in part by the Rome Laboratory of the Air Force Systems Command and the Defense Advanced Research Projects Agency under contract number F30602-98-2-0109, and in part by the United States Air Force under contract number F49620-98-1-0046. Views and conclusions contained in this article are the authors' and should not be interpreted as representing the official opinion or policy of the above organizations or any person connected with them.

We would like to also thank the rest of the Ariadne team: José Luis Ambite, Yigal Arens, Naveen Ashish, Dan DiPasquo, Kristina Lerman, Ion Muslea, Maria Muslea, Jean Oh, and Sheila Tejada. We are also grateful for the help of Chris Stuber, at the USGS Tiger Mapping Service, for his coordinate system translation assistance.

References

Ambite, J.L. and Knoblock, C.A. 1997. Planning by Rewriting: Efficiently Generating High-Quality Plans. *AAAI-97*, Providence, RI.

Ambite, J.L. and Knoblock, C.A. 1998. Flexible and Scalable Query Planning in Distributed and Heterogeneous Environments. *Proc of 4th Intl Conf on Artificial Intelligence Planning Systems*, Pittsburgh, PA.

Ambite, J.L.; Knoblock, C.A.; Muslea, I.; and Philpot, A. 1998. Compiling Source Descriptions for Efficient and Flexible Information Integration. USC/ISI Technical Report.

Ashish, N.; Knoblock, C.A.; and Shahabi, C. 1999 Selective materializing data in mediators by analyzing user queries. *Fourth IFCIS Conference on Cooperative Information Systems*.

Barish, G.; Knoblock, C.A.; Chen, Y-S.; Minton, S.; Philpot, A; Shahabi, C. 1999a. TheaterLoc: A Case Study in Information Integration. *IJCAI-99 Information Integration Wkshp*.

Barish, G.; DiPasquo, D.; Knoblock, C.A.; Minton, S. Efficient Execution for Information Management Agents. 1999b. *ACM CIKM Workshop on Web Information and Data Management*. Kansas City, MO, USA.

Bayardo Jr., R.J.; Bohrer, W.; Brice, R.; Cichocki, A.; Fowler, J.; Helal, A.; Kashyap, V.; Ksiezyk, T.; Martin, G.; Nodine, M.; Rashid, M.; Rusinkiewicz, M.; Shea, R.; Unnikrishnan, C.; Unruh, A.; and Woelk, D. 1997. InfoSleuth: Agent-based semantic integration in open and dynamic environments. *Proceedings of ACM SIGMOD-97*.

Doorenbos, R.B.; Etzioni, O.; and Weld, D.S. 1997. A scalable comparison shopping agent for the world-wide-web. *Agents-97*.

Genesereth, M.R.; Keller, A.M.; and Duschka, O.M. 1997. Infomaster: An information integration system. *Proceedings of ACM SIGMOD-97*.

Hammer, J.; Garcia-Molina, H.; Nestorov, S.; Yerneni, R.; Breunig, M.; and Vassalos, V. 1997. Template-based wrappers in the TSIMMIS system. *Proceedings of ACM SIGMOD-97*.

Knoblock, C.A.; Minton, S; Ambite, J.L.; Ashish, N.; Modi, J.; Muslea, I.; Philpot, A. and Tejada, S. 1998 Modeling Web Sources for Information Integration. *AAAI-98*, Madison, WI.

Kushmerick, N. 1997. *Wrapper Induction for Information Extraction*. PhD Thesis, Computer Science Dept. University of Washington.

Kwok, C.T and Weld, D.S. 1996. Planning to gather information. In *Proceedings of AAAI-96*.

Levy, A.Y; Rajaraman, A.; and Ordille, J.J. 1996. Query-answering algorithms for information agents. *Proceedings of AAAI-96*.

Muslea, I.; Minton, S.; and Knoblock, C.A. 1998. STALKER: Learning Extraction Rules for Semistructured, Web-based Information Sources. *AAAI-98 Workshop on "AI & Information Integration"*, Madison, WI.

Muslea, I.; Minton, S.; and Knoblock, C.A. 1999. A Hierarchical Approach to Wrapper Induction. *Agents-99*, Seattle, WA.

Tejada, S.; Knoblock, C.A.; and Minton, S. 1998. Handling inconsistency for multi-source integration. Technical Report, *AAAI-98 Workshop on "AI & Information Integration"*, Madison, WI.

Weiderhold, G. 1996. *Intelligent Integration of Information*. Kluwer.

Exploiting a Thesaurus-Based Semantic Net for Knowledge-Based Search

Peter Clark, John Thompson, Heather Holmback, Lisbeth Duncan
Mathematics and Computing Technology
The Boeing Company, PO Box 3707, Seattle, WA 98124
{peter.e.clark,john.a.thompson,heather.h.holmback,lisbeth.e.duncan}@boeing.com

Abstract

With the growth of on-line information, the need for better resource location services is growing rapidly. A popular goal is to conduct search in terms of concepts, rather than words; however, this approach is frequently thwarted by the high up-front cost of building an adequate ontology (conceptual vocabulary) in the first place. In this paper we describe a knowledge-based Expert Locator application (for identifying human experts relevant to a particular problem or interest), which addresses this issue by using a large, pre-built, technical thesaurus as an initial ontology, combined with simple AI techniques of search, subsumption computation, and language processing. The application has been deployed and in use in our local organization since June, 1999, and a second, larger application was deployed in March 2000. We present the Expert Locator and the AI techniques it uses, and then we evaluate and discuss the application. The significance of this work is that it demonstrates how years of work by library science in thesaurus-building can be leveraged using AI methods, to construct a practical resource location service in a short period of time.

Introduction

With the rapid growth of on-line information, it is becoming increasingly hard for users to find the information they need. The phenomenon of posing a query to a Web search engine and receiving many thousands of "hits", few of which are really relevant, is a familiar one. A well-known contributor to this problem is that search is organized around *words* (contained in the target documents) rather than the *concepts* which those words denote. As a word can denote many concepts (polysemy) and a concept can be denoted by many words (synonymy), a user's query may both miss relevant documents and hit irrelevant ones. In addition, without an unambiguous representation of what the user is interested in, it is impossible to apply domain knowledge to reason about the user's information request.

In this paper, we describe our recent work in conducting search in terms of *concepts* (unambiguous denotations of the entities of interest) rather than words, to reduce the ambiguity problem and also exploit domain knowledge for

---

Copyright © 2000, American Association for Artificial Intelligence (www.aaai.org). All rights reserved.

search. In particular, we have exploited an extensive technical thesaurus to provide both a conceptual vocabulary ("ontology") and a source of domain knowledge, avoiding the high up-front cost of ontology-building from scratch. We have combined this with simple AI techniques of search, subsumption computation, and language processing. We have used this for building an "Expert Locator" search tool for identifying human experts within our 200 person organization relevant to a user's problem or interest. This application has been deployed and in use within our organization since June 1999, and a similar, larger application was recently deployed in March, 2000, indexing a larger group of technical experts within Boeing. We describe the initial version of the thesaurus-based Expert Locator and the AI techniques that have been used to enhance it in various ways, and then we discuss and evaluate the application. Our conclusion is that, when the thesaurus and application domain are well matched, the many years of work by library science in thesaurus-building can be leveraged using AI methods to construct a practical resource location service.

Approach

A Thesaurus as a Conceptual Vocabulary

One challenge for working in concept space is the construction of an appropriate ontology ("conceptual vocabulary") appropriate to the domain of interest. To address this, we have used a technical thesaurus as the initial ontology, seeking to exploit the many years of effort already spent by librarians in constructing a conceptual vocabulary for a domain. Other alternative (but more costly) approaches would be to hand-build the ontology from scratch, e.g., CoalSORT (Monarch & Carbonell 1987), or learn it automatically from analysis of text corpora, e.g., PhraseFinder (Jing & Croft 1994).

It is important to note that a library thesaurus is distinct from a synonym dictionary (a common misconception) in two important ways. First, each term (concept) in the thesaurus has a unique name, precisely to remove word ambiguity. Sometimes concept names will include a parenthetical qualification if a single word would be ambiguous, e.g., "planes (geometry)", "beams (radiation)". Second, a thesaurus encodes not only the conceptual vocabulary but also semantic relationships (of a rather informal kind) between

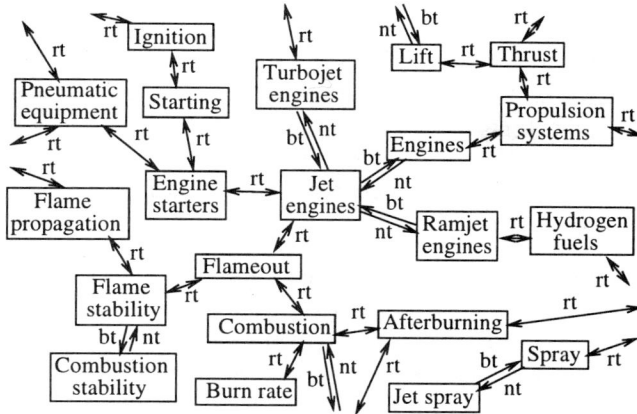

Figure 1: Sketch of a tiny fragment of Boeing's Thesaurus. The full Thesaurus contains approximately 37,000 concepts and 100,000 relationships between them.

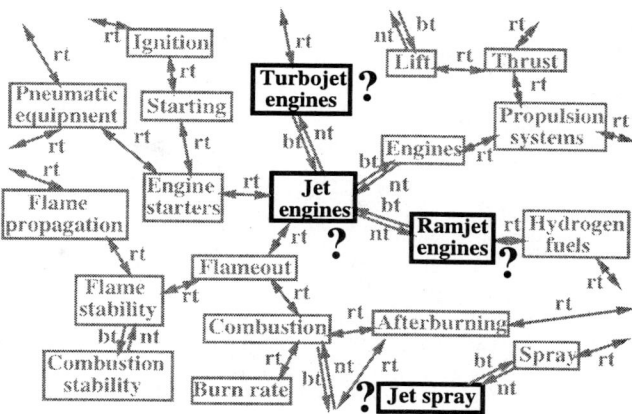

Figure 2: From the user's initial query word(s) (here the word "jet"), the system identifies possible concepts he/she may be referring to by simple stemming then substring matching.

concepts, the three most important types being named 'bt' (broader term), 'nt' (narrower term), and 'rt' (related to). A broader term denotes a subject area which encompasses the original term, usually[1] corresponding to a generalization (superclass) link in an inheritance hierarchy (e.g., "jet engines" −bt→ "engines"), while a narrower term is the inverse of this. The rt relation expresses that some (unspecified) close conceptual relationship exists between the two concepts. Although the semantics of these links are rather informal, they nevertheless provide (by design) knowledge about conceptual relationships in the domain, specifically for the task of information retrieval.

The particular thesaurus we have used is Boeing's Technical Thesaurus, built by Boeing Technical Libraries. This Thesaurus is a vast network of approximately 37,000 concepts (plus another 19,000 synonym concept names), with approximately 100,000 links between them (of the three types mentioned above), plus additional relationships ('subject note', 'used for', etc.) for other purposes. It is well suited to our purposes as it is highly customized to our target domain (aerospace) and organization (Boeing), and is rich in aerospace and "Boeing-speak" concepts, and also in concepts from the related areas in which Boeing is involved (e.g., computing, finance, sales, personnel management). A tiny fragment (0.05%) of this Thesaurus, sketched as a graph, is shown in Figure 1, where boxes denote Thesaurus concepts and arcs denote relationships.

Performing Concept-Based Search using a Thesaurus

For typical word-based search tools, an indexing engine (e.g., a Web crawler) builds ahead of time a word index of resources (e.g., Web pages) to be searched. At search time, a user enters a set of query words, and a matching algorithm then compares these with the word index to identify

---

[1]but not always, for example "France" may be declared as a narrower term of "Europe", expressing a meronymic (part-of) rather than hypernymic (subclass) relation.

the "best" resources that match the user's query. Our goal is to do an analogous thing in concept space, requiring three main tasks to be performed:

1. A concept index needs to be built, in which target resources are indexed in terms of the concepts (not words) characterizing them.

2. A user's query needs to be (re-)formulated in terms of concepts.

3. A "concept-based search" algorithm is needed to match the user's concept query with the concept index of resources.

In our application, the Expert Locator, the "resources" we are interested in searching for are, in fact, not documents but human experts. We adopted straightforward approaches to the three tasks listed above:

1. The concept index was built manually, by asking each expert to characterize his/her area(s) of expertise by a list of concepts drawn from the Thesaurus.

2. After the user enters a set of search words, the system finds possible concepts he/she might be referring to (by stemming the user's words and then substring matching on concept names in the Thesaurus), and then asks the user to select his/her intended concept(s). This is illustrated in Figure 2, where the user has entered the word "jet", to which the system will ask: "By 'jet' did you mean: (i) jet engine (ii) ramjet engine (iii) jet spray (iv) ...?" If none of these are appropriate, the user can browse the Thesaurus by iteratively clicking on a concept to see its neighbors in the Thesaurus graph, to help locate his/her concept(s) of interest.

3. Thus having a set of concept(s) the user is interested in, the system searches for experts who either know about one of those concepts or know about concepts "closely related to" the user's concepts of interest, where "closely related to" corresponds to the distance between the user's

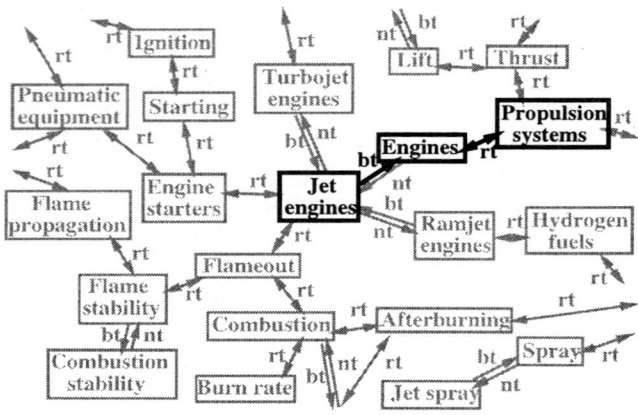

Figure 3: The distance between concepts in the Thesaurus graph is used to assess relevance between an expert's area of expertise (here "propulsion systems") and a user's concept of interest (here "jet engines").

and expert's concepts in the Thesaurus graph[2]. This is illustrated in Figure 3, where an expert in "propulsion systems" is considered moderately relevant to a query for information about "jet engines", as the concepts "propulsion systems" and "jet engines" are relatively close in the graph.

An example of the Expert Locator application itself is shown in Figure 4. The user asks for someone who knows about "graphics", to which the system asks (via a menu): "By 'graphics' did you mean: (i) graphic arts (ii) raster graphics (iii) graphic methods ...?" The user ticks the box(es) to identify his/her intended concept(s) (here "computer graphics"), then the system retrieves experts who either tagged themselves as having expertise in that concept(s) or in concepts closely related to it. In Figure 4, the system reports both the expert's technical area (e.g., "digital video") and the semantic path of associations from that concept to the user's original concept of interest (e.g., "via computer graphics → digital video").

Initial Results and Development

Initial, informal trials with the Expert Locator were encouraging, and in particular illustrated how even the semi-formal semantic relationships in the Thesaurus could help search. At the same time, these trials highlighted several issues which needed to be addressed:

1. The length of the shortest path between two concepts in the thesaurus graph is a crude measure of "semantic distance" or "relevance" between two concepts, and further tight controls on the graph search are needed.

2. Despite the 100,000 relationships in the Thesaurus, we frequently found cases where (at least for our purposes) desirable links were missing. In fact, of the 37,000 concepts in the Thesaurus, approximately 15,000 are "orphans" (i.e., not connected with any other concept), mean-

[2]This is an oversimplification; we elaborate shortly.

ing that knowledge of concept associations could not be applied in those cases[3].

3. Even with 37,000 concepts, experts occasionally found that their area of expertise was missing, i.e., not properly characterized by any of the original Thesaurus concepts.

We now describe how these issues were (and continue to be) addressed.

Semantic Distance and Relevance

Evaluating semantic relatedness using network representations has a long history in artificial intelligence and psychology, e.g., (Resnik 1995; Brooks 1998; Tudhope & Taylor 1997), and we are exploiting this basic idea for our application. Intuitively, a short path (measured by counting links) between concepts in the Thesaurus graph might be expected to correspond to some loose notion of "relevance" between those concepts. For example, "artificial intelligence" and "semantics" are two links apart ("artificial intelligence" −rt→ "inference" −rt→ "semantics") and also intuitively appear to be related. Unfortunately, this is not always the case, as relevance is not always transitive. For example, "flood control" and "artificial intelligence" appear 'close' as they are just three links apart ("artificial intelligence" −rt→ "cybernetics" −rt→ "control" −nt→ "flood control"); similarly, "battle management" is within three links of "library science" ("battle management" −bt→ "management" −nt→ "information management" −rt→ "library science"). Table 1 gives a coarse quantification of this phenomenon using data from the evaluation (described later), showing the average relevance of concepts at distance D to an initial concept C. Due to this rapid degradation of relevance with distance, we severely constrain the search for relevant concepts to those at distance two or less from an initial concept. Work by other researchers suggests that this degradation might be partially reduced by weighting links using statistical methods, e.g., (Resnik 1998; Manning & Schutze 1999; Chen et al. 1993), an avenue which we are considering exploring.

One simple refinement we made to this "link counting" approach was to disallow paths which include a generalization (bt) link followed (either immediately or otherwise) by a specialization (nt) link. This avoids paths such as "battle management" −bt→ "management" −nt→ "information management", where the path first moves to a general concept and then specializes to a concept disjoint with the original. An informal evaluation of this approach suggests that this improves the credibility of the paths as explaining relevance (as these questionable paths are removed), but often alternative (more plausible) paths can be found and the list of relevant concepts is not significantly altered (e.g., blocking the path "battle management" −bt→ "management" −nt→ "information management" −rt→ "library science" causes

[3]One factor contributing to this relatively high proportion of orphans was that a separate database of "identifiers" (additional, non-Thesaurus keywords) was merged into the Thesaurus several years ago, with connections to Thesaurus terms still being added. As described later, our graph enhancement algorithm can assist with this linking process.

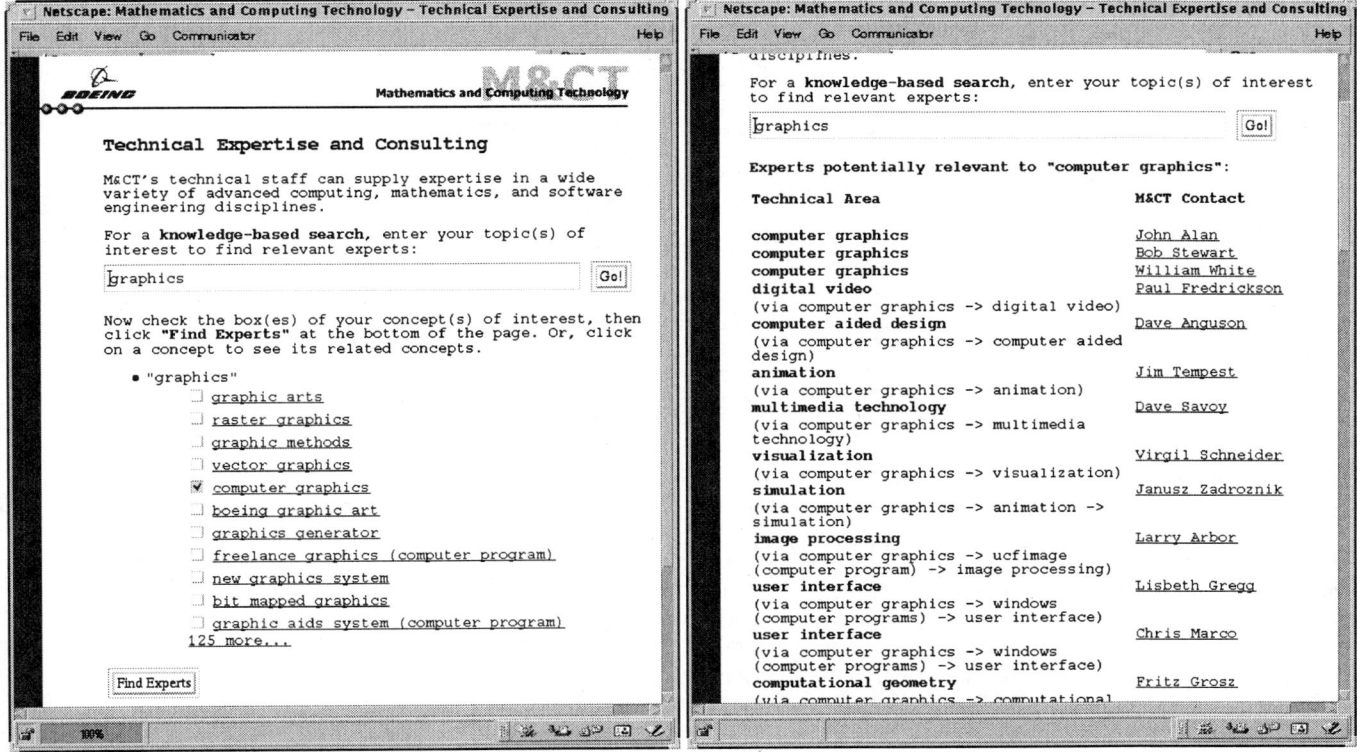

Figure 4: Two consecutive screen shots of the Expert Locator in use. First the user identifies the concept(s) he/she is interested in (by browsing and checking boxes), then experts are retrieved based on the proximity of their areas of expertise to those concept(s) in the semantic graph.

	Distance D from C			
	0	1	2	3
Number of concepts at D from C (mean)	1	2.69	46	356
(median)	1	1	10	96
Mean relevance of concepts at D to C	10.0 ±0	7.8 ±0.3	4.3 ±0.3	3.2 ±0.4

Table 1: Relevance degrades rapidly with distance, as judged by a human expert on a 0 (irrelevant) to 10 (relevant) scale. ± denotes standard error. The table also shows the rapid increase in concept accessibility with distance.

a different path "battle management" −rt→ "command control" −nt→ "information systems" −rt→ "library science" to be found instead).

Enhancing the Thesaurus Connectivity: Computing Extra Subsumption and Association Relationships

Although the Boeing Thesaurus is highly connected (100,000 links), it is often the case that desirable links, at least for our purposes, were missing, including 40% (15,000) of the 37,000 concepts being orphans and thus inaccessible to search.

However, an important characteristic of technical thesauri is that many concept names are compound (multi-word) terms. In Boeing's Thesaurus, 32,000 (85%) of the concept names are compound nouns or phrases. This allows some automated analysis of the concepts to be performed, based on the constituent words in these terms, using subsumption computation techniques (Woods 1991). For example, the concept "space shuttle main engine" is an orphan in the Thesaurus, but by comparing its constituents with other concept names, an algorithm can infer that it is related to the concept "space shuttle" (as "space shuttle" is a concept in the Thesaurus) and generalizes to "engines". Similarly, "metal pipe welding" can be inferred as a specialization of "tube joining", as "pipe" is a specialization of "tube" and "welding" is a specialization of "joining" in the Thesaurus.

We implemented a graph enhancement algorithm for this task, that automatically inferred these missing links using using word-spotting/natural language processing technology. This algorithm computes subsumption relationships between terms in a similar style to (Woods et al. 1999), and can be viewed as a simple classification engine using the limited semantics that a thesaurus affords. The algorithm

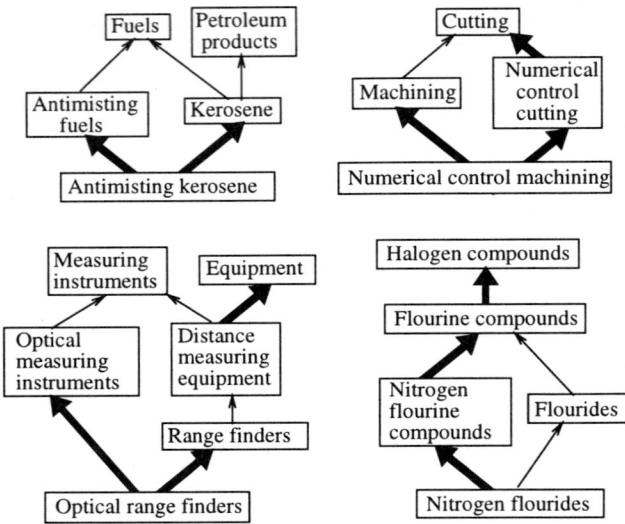

Figure 5: Four subgraphs of the enhanced Thesaurus, showing generalization (bt) links. The thin arcs were part of the original Thesaurus, the thick arcs were inferred automatically by the graph enhancement algorithm and added to the Thesaurus. "related-to" (rt) links (not shown) are inferred in a similar way. Approximately 58,000 links were inferred in total.

behaves as follows. First, individual words in a compound term are stemmed, and then the compound is generalized (in all possible ways) by repeatedly either removing the first word (e.g., "turbojet engine" becomes "engine") or generalizing one of its words/sub-phrases using the taxonomic links in the Thesaurus (e.g., "turbojet engine" becomes "jet engine"). If the generalization thus created exists in the Thesaurus as a concept in its own right, then taxonomic (bt/nt) links are added. This is repeated for all concepts, and then a final sweep of the resulting graph is performed to remove redundant taxonomic links (e.g., A−bt→C is considered redundant if A−bt→B and B−bt→C). This algorithm is extended to also add "related to" links by also allowing the last word in the compounds to be removed in the the 'generalization' step (e.g., "space shuttle engine" is related to "space shuttle"). Compounds created in this way (if they are also Thesaurus concepts), and any new ones derived from them, are then linked to the original concept using "related-to" (rt) links, rather than taxonomic (bt/nt) links.

Applying this algorithm, approximately 21,000 generalization/specialization links and 37,000 related-to links were automatically added, and the number of orphans was reduced from approximately 15,000 ($\approx$40%) to 4,600 ($\approx$13%). This approach relies heavily on the choice of name the Thesaurus authors decided to use for a concept. The algorithm will sometimes make mistakes due to changing word sense (e.g., "mean value analysis" becomes mistakenly related to the concept "values", in the sense of ethics), or finding unintended sub-phrases (mis-bracketing). However, interestingly, such mistakes were unusual, mainly attributable to the Boeing Thesaurus being a domain-specific rather than general thesaurus, where words in concept names tend to be used in a single sense (namely the aerospace sense). As a result, almost all of the (many) mis-generalizations hypothesized by the algorithm are non-Thesaurus concepts, and thus do not contribute links to the enhanced Thesaurus. We qualitatively evaluate the effect of the graph enhancement algorithm later in this paper.

Natural Language Processing of Compound Nouns

As a generalization of this approach, we have started work applying more sophisticated natural language processing technology to analyze compound nouns in the Thesaurus. This offers several advantages:

1. It provides better regularization of word variations (e.g., recognizing that "antisubmarine", "anti-submarine", and "anti submarine" are all variants of the same concept).

2. It can help disambiguate the appropriate word sense, based on the other words in the compound (e.g., "manual" in "transmission manual" refers to the concept of "manuals (documentation)", not "hand-operated").

3. It can help identify appropriate word grouping (bracketing), e.g., "advanced knowledge engineering" = "advanced (knowledge engineering)", not "(advanced knowledge) engineering".

4. It can refine the all-encompassing "related to" link into finer semantic categories, e.g., identifying that "coal" is the result of "coal mining", while "strip" is the manner of "strip mining".

An interactive prototype system called NCAS (Noun Compound Analysis System) was developed to perform this task. Word regularization, part of speech information, and identification of possible bracketings are performed by a standard parsing component. For word sense disambiguation, preferred bracketing, and identification of the head-modifier relation, we follow a knowledge-based linguistic approach of using a set of noun-noun (and also adjective-noun) interpretation rules. Similar approaches to noun compound interpretation have been performed by others, for example (Barker & Szpakowicz 1998; Vanderwende 1993; Finin 1986). An example of an interpretation rule is:

For compound "*modifier head*" (e.g., "metal tube"):
    IF   *modifier* is a Material
    AND *head* is a Physical-Object
    THEN *head* is-made-of *modifier*.

A set of 27 noun-noun relation types were chosen (e.g., agent, causes, contains, location) by merging relations from our previous NLP work (Holmback, Duncan, & Harrison 2000) with Barker's list (Barker & Szpakowicz 1998), and then these were augmented to fit the Thesaurus data. This latter step was based on manual analysis of the 450 most common noun compounds that were either a Thesaurus concept name or a subphrase of a concept name. As well as identifying the relation type, the rules constrain which word senses can co-occur. For example, the above rule constrains "tube" in "metal tube" to be a physical object (e.g., a pipe), thus ruling out "tube" in the senses of an abstract geometric shape or a subway.

Our work in this area is still preliminary, and the rule base, word sense classification hierarchy, and association of word senses with Thesaurus concepts are still incomplete. However, processing of noun compounds in this way, or more generally dictionary definitions, e.g., similar to MindNet (Dolan, Vanderwende, & Richardson 1993), may prove to be a useful additional way to augment the semantic knowledge base.

Handling non-Thesaurus Concepts

In addition to processing the concepts within the Thesaurus, the natural language processing of compound nouns offers a way of dealing with concepts that are missing in the Thesaurus, but are of interest to the user (either to express his/her area of expertise, or to perform a search). Currently, if an expert cannot find a suitable concept to characterize his/her expertise, a common strategy is to use a set of concepts, each representing an element of his/her desired concept name. For example, an expert in "document releasing" (missing in the Thesaurus) may tag him/herself with the concepts "documents" and "releasing". This is problematic because his/her expertise is not about releasing in general, but about a particular *type* of releasing (namely of documents). However, by tagging him/herself with the general "releasing" concept, he/she will be considered highly relevant to concepts neighboring "releasing" in the Thesaurus, such as "venting", "emission", etc., a clearly undesirable consequence.

Instead, we would like the system to accept this compound noun as a new concept represented as a structure denoting the relationship between its constituents, rather than as a set of independent concepts, which we can informally sketch as:

"Document Releasing" $\neq$ [Documents] + [Releasing]
= [Releasing, object: Documents]

The noun-noun processing technology we have implemented can be used for exactly this task, by interactively (or automatically) linking the user's new concept to existing concepts, both for classifying resources and posing a search query. This would mark a significant shift in cataloging/classification from a task of concept *selection* to one of concept *construction* from primitives.

Evaluation

Finding good evaluation metrics for this style of application is challenging. The ultimate success of the Expert Locator application relies on several factors: the quality of the underlying knowledge-base (the enhanced thesaurus), the search algorithm, the ability of experts to label themselves appropriately with thesaurus concepts in the first place, the ability of users to identify their concepts of interest to perform a search, and other issues such as speed and the friendliness of the interface. Thus it is important to consider which aspect(s) of the system are being evaluated (the original Thesaurus? the enhancements? the experts' ability to describe themselves?). In addition, it is difficult to select what to compare the the Locator against (i.e., what constitutes "success"?).

There are several weak indicators of the system's utility that we can point to. The system is deployed and has achieved limited but sustained use (averaging approximately 1.2 searches per workday since June 1999), with 163 experts in our organization currently self-registered using 314 subject areas (concepts), mainly in the fields of computer science and mathematics (our organization's main technologies). Feedback has been very positive, and has spawned the construction of a second, larger application, indexing a separate, larger community of experts. This second application was deployed in March 2000, and has been used for 596 searches during its first three weeks of use (i.e., to time of writing), even though its availability has not been widely advertised yet. The most significant requirement people have pointed to is not with the concept-based search itself, but to restrict this search to a subset of the database constrained by simple attribute filters, e.g., years at Boeing, job type. This is a straightforward extension which we are planning to incorporate.

In a trivial way, the Expert Locator improves on simple word-based searches of an expertise database simply because, by definition, it does not require the user to enter exactly (or indeed any) of the subjects the experts classified themselves under, but will instead find "relevant" experts even if there is not an exact match with a user's query. Two specific questions are how the size of the search (i.e., the distance bound on the search from the initial concept(s), in number of links) affects precision and recall, and what effect the automatic enhancement of the original Thesaurus with subsumption and related-to links has had.

As a rough evaluation of this phenomenon, we performed an analysis in which a human expert selected a concept he knew about, and then scored a random sample of the concepts at distances 1, 2, and 3 away according to a subjective measure of "relevance", similar to semantic distance experiments in psychology, e.g., (Brooks 1998), on a score of 0 (completely irrelevant) to 10 (completely relevant). The assumption here is that to the extent a concept is relevant, an expert on that concept would be able to answer a question about the original selected concept. This assessment was performed using both the original Thesaurus alone and with the additional links automatically added.

We can use these measures to assess the Expert Locator's search as follows: for each concept C_i in the Thesaurus, let $r_{ij} = 0$ if concept C_j is deemed completely irrelevant to it, or 1 if it is deemed completely relevant. Thus, if a search for concepts relevant to a concept C_i retrieves concepts $C_1, \ldots, C_N$, then (using standard definitions) **precision** = $\sum_{j=1}^{N} r_{ij}/N$ (the proportion of hit concepts which are relevant), and **recall** = $\sum_{j=1}^{N} r_{ij} / \sum_{j=1}^{M} r_{ij}$ (the proportion of relevant concepts which are hit), where M is the total number of concepts in the Thesaurus. In our case, where we have 'degrees of relevance', we allow r_{ij} to also take fractional values between 0 and 1 (= (the manually judged relevance on the 0 to 10 scale)/10). As assessing $\sum_{j=1}^{M} r_{ij}$ (the total number of concepts relevant to C_i in the Thesaurus,

Radius D	Original Thesaurus Graph		Enhanced Graph	
of search	Precision (%)	Relative Recall (%)	Precision (%)	Relative Recall (%)
0	100 ±0	6 ±2	100 ±0	6 ±2
1	84 ±3	26 ±6	80 ±3	39 ±1
2	58 ±6	48 ±7	57 ±5	75 ±9
3	50 ±6	65 ±10	42 ±7	100 *

Table 2: Variation of precision and recall (relative to recall within distance 3 in the enhanced graph, *) in locating concepts relevant to some initial starting concept. ± denotes standard error. The results show that the Thesaurus enhancements significantly improve recall, with only a minimal negative effect on precision.

weighted by relevance) is impractical (M = 37,000), we instead assume all relevant concepts are within a distance three in the enhanced Thesaurus, and thus the recall scores are only relative to concepts in this set (hence "relative recall"). This assumption only affects the factor by which the recall scores are normalized, not their relative sizes, which is our main interest for this comparative study. The results, averaged over five different trials, i.e., for five different concepts C_i, are shown in Table 2.

These results suggest that enhancing the Thesaurus has had only a minimal negative effect on precision, while significantly increasing recall. In other words, the automatically added links are apparently of comparable quality, in denoting relevance, as the original manually added links, and allow a significantly larger number of relevant concepts (thus experts) to be identified during search. The occasional errors in the linking algorithm (e.g., due to not recognizing word sense change) is probably one contributing factor to the fractional difference in these figures.

Discussion, Critique, and Conclusion

Perhaps the most significant result of this work is to highlight the potential value of combining a technical thesaurus with simple AI techniques of search, subsumption computation, and language processing, allowing us to construct and deploy a practical expert location system in a very short time. Library science has spent many years building conceptual taxonomies in the form of thesauri, and the resources available there are sometimes overlooked in AI research. We have demonstrated how we can exploit this work for a practical task in combination with AI techniques, and have also speculated on more sophisticated AI methods which could be applied to further enhance the application.

In some ways, the utility of the Expert Locator is somewhat surprising, given the well-known difficulties in equating "number of links" with "relevance", e.g., (Resnik 1995). In fact, our experience largely confirms previous findings that, in general, link distance is a weak measure of relevance, and only in the restricted case of very short paths (lengths 1 or 2) was this a meaningful measure to use (Table 1), contrary to our initial expectations. A second point of note is that we are using a technical (rather than general) thesaurus, highly customized to our particular application domain and company's activities. This provides an important filter, as only aerospace/Boeing-specific concepts and relationships are present, thus automatically "biasing" the knowledge to just that required for the domain at hand. In fact our initial work started with WordNet (Miller et al. 1993) (a general-purpose lexical reference system of linked concepts), but was quickly abandoned precisely because many of the links it contained were irrelevant and detrimental to aerospace-specific queries. The domain-specificity of the Boeing Thesaurus not only constrains search by encoding just a domain-specific notion of relevance, but also constrains the Thesaurus enhancement algorithm to add only aerospace-relevant links (e.g., "giant hangar" will not be related to the concept "giants" precisely because the concept "giants" is not in the Thesaurus). In addition, mistakes from word ambiguity in concept names are significantly reduced, as words tend to be used in the same (aerospace) sense.

It is also clear that there are further developments which can be made. In particular, a list of concepts is a rather crude characterization of an expert's ability or a user's information need, and using structured representations would help considerably in this respect, as discussed earlier. Similarly, migrating the Thesaurus to a knowledge-base with more rigorous semantics would enable inferencing and question-answering services to be added, and provide a basis for computing relevance using more principled domain knowledge rather than concept associations. However, the simplicity of the presented approach is also a considerable strength – it has allowed a practical system to be built and deployed, and in a way which is easily reproducible by others. It also provides a springboard from which these refinements can now be explored.

Specific to the expert location task, we have assumed that expert relevance is equated with concept relevance. While there is obviously an important relationship, it is also clear there are other important factors which we have not taken into account, e.g., an expert's years of experience, location, and position in the company, which should be added for selecting the portion of the database to search. We have also not attempted to quantify the "quality" of an expert, e.g., through recommendations from others or "social filtering", as performed by so-called recommender systems (Kautz 1998) such as ReferralWeb (Kautz, Selman, & Shah 1997). This would be another possible dimension for expert location to explore.

Although we have focussed on expert location, there is essentially nothing in the presented approach which is specific to this task, and the same approach could be applied or integrated with search for other resource types, e.g., projects, documents, and work groups. Again, a concept-based index of the resource entities would be needed, which could be constructed either manually or (in the case of text) automatically using statistical methods (Manning & Schutze 1999). This points to the exciting possibility of using a thesaurus-derived knowledge-base for organizing and indexing a wide variety of information resources, again coupling many years work in library science with AI techniques to provide potentially valuable information management services, an avenue which we are currently exploring.

Acknowledgements:

We are greatly indebted to Boeing Technical Libraries, in particular Gail Shurgot, Mary Whittaker, and Corinne Campbell, for their work on the Boeing Thesaurus and their encouragement and support for this work. Thanks also to Don Retallack, Steve Woods, Mike Uschold, and Rob Jasper for ideas and feedback on this work and its application.

References

Barker, K., and Szpakowicz, S. 1998. Semi-automatic recognition of noun modifier relationships. In *Proc. COLING-ACL'98*, 96–102.

Brooks, T. 1998. The semantic distance model of relevance assessment. In *Information Access in the Global Information Economy (Vol 35): Proceedings of the 61st Annual Meeting of ASIS*, 33–44.

Chen, H.; Lynch, K. J.; Basu, K.; and Ng, T. D. 1993. Generating, integrating, and activating thesauri for concept-based document retrieval. *IEEE Expert* 25–34.

Dolan, W. B.; Vanderwende, L.; and Richardson, S. 1993. Automatically deriving structured knowledge-bases from a machine-readable dictionary. In *Proc. of the Pacific Assoc. for Computational Linguistics*.

Finin, T. W. 1986. Constraining the interpretation of nominal compounds in a limited context. In Grishman, R., and Kittredge, R., eds., *Analyzing Language in Restricted Domains*. NJ: Erlbaum. 163–173.

Holmback, H.; Duncan, L.; and Harrison, P. 2000. A word sense checking application for simplified english. In *Third International Workshop on Controlled Language Applications*.

Jing, Y., and Croft, W. B. 1994. An association thesaurus for information retrieval. Technical Report UM-CS-1994-017, Dept CS, Univ Massachusetts at Amherst.

Kautz, H.; Selman, B.; and Shah, M. 1997. ReferralWeb: Combining social networks and collaborative filtering. *Communications of the ACM* 40(3).

Kautz, H., ed. 1998. *Proc. AAAI Workshop on Recommender Systems*. AAAI Tech Report WS-98-08.

Manning, C. D., and Schutze, H. 1999. *Foundations of Statistical Natural Language Processing*. MA: MIT Press.

Miller, G. A.; Beckwith, R.; Fellbaum, C.; Gross, D.; and Miller, K. 1993. *Five Papers on WordNet*. NJ: Prinston Univ. (http://www.cogsci.princeton.edu/~wn/).

Monarch, I., and Carbonell, J. 1987. CoalSORT: A knowledge-based interface. *IEEE Expert* 39–53.

Resnik, P. 1995. Using information content to evaluate semantic similarity in a taxonomy. In Mellish, C. S., ed., *IJCAI-95*, 448–453. Kaufmann.

Resnik, P. 1998. Semantic similarity in a taxonomy: An information-based measure and its application to problems of ambiguity in natural language. *Journal of AI Research* 11:95–130.

Tudhope, D., and Taylor, C. 1997. Navigation via similarity: Automatic linking based on semantic closeness. *Information Processing and Management* 33(2):233–242.

Vanderwende, L. 1993. SENS: The system for evaluating noun sequences. In Jensen, K.; Heidorn, G. E.; and Richardson, S. D., eds., *Natural Language Processing: The PLNLP Approach*. Boston, MA: Kluwer.

Woods, W. A.; Bookman, L. A.; Houston, A.; Kuhns, R. J.; Martin, P.; and Green, S. 1999. Linguistic knowledge can improve information retrieval. Tech Report TR-99-81, Sun Labs. (http://www.sun.com/research).

Woods, W. A. 1991. Understanding subsumption and taxonomy: A framework for progress. In Sowa, J. F., ed., *Principles of Semantic Networks*. CA: Kaufmann. 45–94.

ICARUS: Intelligent Content-Based Retrieval of 3D Scene

Raffaella Colaci and Marco Schaerf

Dipartimento di Informatica e Sistemistica, Università di Roma "La Sapienza"
Via Salaria 113, I-00198
Roma, Italy
{colaci, schaerf}@dis.uniroma1.it

Abstract

We present a tool for the analysis, classification and content-based retrieval of 3D scene. The system ICARUS analyzes files in VRML format, searching for the presence of complex 3D-objects and relative geometrical relationships between them. Descriptions of the virtual scenes are classified in a Terminological System, and reasoning mechanisms are used for querying.

Keywords: virtual reality, description logics, information retrieval, geometric reasoning, knowledge representation, multimedia.

Introduction

Multimedia information systems, such as those supporting image and video databases, are more and more widespread and widely used. The particular nature of data types involved in multimedia databases might require special facilities for optimal storage, access and retrieval. An intelligent data management should provide the capability of querying multimedia object content, rather than being simply a file repository that does not understand the stored data. Multimedia data must be interpreted before it can be queried and this process demands data-specific analysis algorithms to generate content descriptions. The richness of the data model used to represent content information plays a key role in its usability. Many papers [1,6] focus on the importance of having appropriate description and querying mechanisms to describe and retrieve multimedia information. While traditional approaches use keyword indexing, we aim to show that rich object description languages can provide several advantages.

In this paper we present a prototype system, called ICARUS (Intelligent Classification And Retrieval Of Unlabelled Scene), for intelligent management of virtual scenes collections. In particular, we focus our attention on three-dimensional scenes modeled using the Virtual Reality Modeling Language (VRML). Interesting scenes represent situation on a specific domain, and knowledge of the modeled domain is used to classify and retrieve properties of the scenes.

Copyright © 2000, American Association for Artificial Intelligence (www.aaai.org). All rights reserved.

The system purpose is to analyze VRML files, extract information on their content, and use a concept description language (CLASSIC) to describe the characteristics of the virtual scenes. Such descriptions are then classified in a conceptual structure, representing the knowledge of the domain, and reasoning mechanisms are used for information retrieving and querying.

The analysis aims to discover the presence in a virtual scene of complex 3D-objects, calculate their absolute positions in the 3D-space, and verify geometrical relationships between objects. The analyzer produces simple descriptions, while the inference engine deducts all other interesting properties about the scenes. The user does not need to specify any information. This is the reason why we call our scenes "unlabelled".

At the current status of development, ICARUS only focuses on a simple domain: a set of characters, a number of relations among them, and a set of furniture elements and accessories. Each object corresponds with a particular VRML model (prototype) that represents it in virtual scenes. The system provides the users with a rich collection of prototypes in order to model a scene. ICARUS is able to identify all the instances of the prototypes present in a file, and uses the geometrical and semantic knowledge of the models during the analysis process. In this way the system can deal with complex structured-objects, rather than only with geometric primitives.

The access to the system facilities is allowed via the World Wide Web. Users can upload their VRML files, verify the analysis results and decide whether classifying their scenes. The system provides a suitable graphical user interface for querying and data presentation.

ICARUS has been developed using the object-oriented programming languages Java. This language is well suited for network programming, in particular as it provides applets for client-side and servlets, which can replace CGI scripts, for server-side. LISP language is used for the interface to the CLASSIC KBMS, whose implementation is in LISP.

Description Logics as Data Model

At the heart of ICARUS lays its knowledge base (KB). It is defined using CLASSIC [2], a concept language in the family of Description Logics (DLs), or Terminological Logics. DLs are a fragment of first-order logic particularly well suited for specifying data classes (called *concepts*) and relationships among classes. Moreover DLs are equipped with both a formal semantics and efficient inference mechanisms.

A distinguishing feature of DLs is that classes can be defined *intensionally*, in terms of descriptions that specify the properties that objects must satisfy to belong to the concept. In DLs-systems the KB is made up of two components: the Terminological Box (TBox) is the general schema concerning the classes, their properties and mutual relationship, and the AssertionalBox (ABox) is a instantiation of this schema, containing assertions relating individuals to classes, or individuals to each other. Formally, concepts are interpreted as sets of individuals, and *roles* are binary relations used to specify their properties. E.g., a role "father-of" can relate a father to his child. Functional relations are called *attributes*. A role-hierarchy is used to state that a role is a *subrole* of another one, meaning that the binary relations interpreting them are contained one in the other. E.g., one may state that "father-of" is a subrole of "parent-of".

A concept language allows the construction of composite *descriptions*, built up recursively as term from subterms, using different constructors, as boolean operators on concepts - conjunction (AND), union (OR) and negation (NOT). E.g., the concept MAN can be defined as (AND PERSON MALE). Also restrictions on roles are possible: universal role quantification (ALL), unqualified existential role quantification, and restrictions on the number of role fillers (AT-LEAST, AT-MOST). E.g. the concept FATHER can be defined as (AND MAN AND (AT-LEAST (1, father-of) ALL (father-of, PERSON))).

A significant feature of descriptions is that they can be reasoned with, as they form a logical theory. The fundamental logical relationship between descriptions is *subsumption* (containment): C is subsumed by B iff every possible individual instance of C would also be an instance of B. Through subsumption, concepts are put into a taxonomy (*classification*). Individuals are classified determining all concepts they satisfy.

DL-systems provide numerous other deductive services, as *consistency checking* on individuals, *incoherent concept detection*, information *propagation* and *rule application*.

DLs are particularly useful as query languages for structured data [3]. Both intensional and extensional knowledge can be retrieved. One can detect whether a query is incoherent, i.e. that cannot possibly return any individuals because of the semantics of the KB, or a query is coherent but it returns an empty set as answer because there is no known individual that satisfies all the given constraints.

CLASSIC language uses only a subset of the above possible language constructors - it does not use OR and NOT constructors - even if it offers others useful ones, such as SAME-AS and TEST. As a matter of fact CLASSIC project philosophy prefers more restricted expressiveness, but more efficient reasoning. When efficient systems, based on much more powerful DLs, will be available, ICARUS would adopt them in place of CLASSIC.

ICARUS

Architecture of ICARUS

ICARUS has a client-server architecture, as shown in figure 1. It allows using system capabilities on a remote host connected via the Internet.

We can recognize the following different components:
- An HTML Browser Java-compatible, with a plug-in capable to display VRML files;
- A Java Applet, that implements the graphical interface for querying and that allows the connection to servers;
- A Web Server, providing system access;

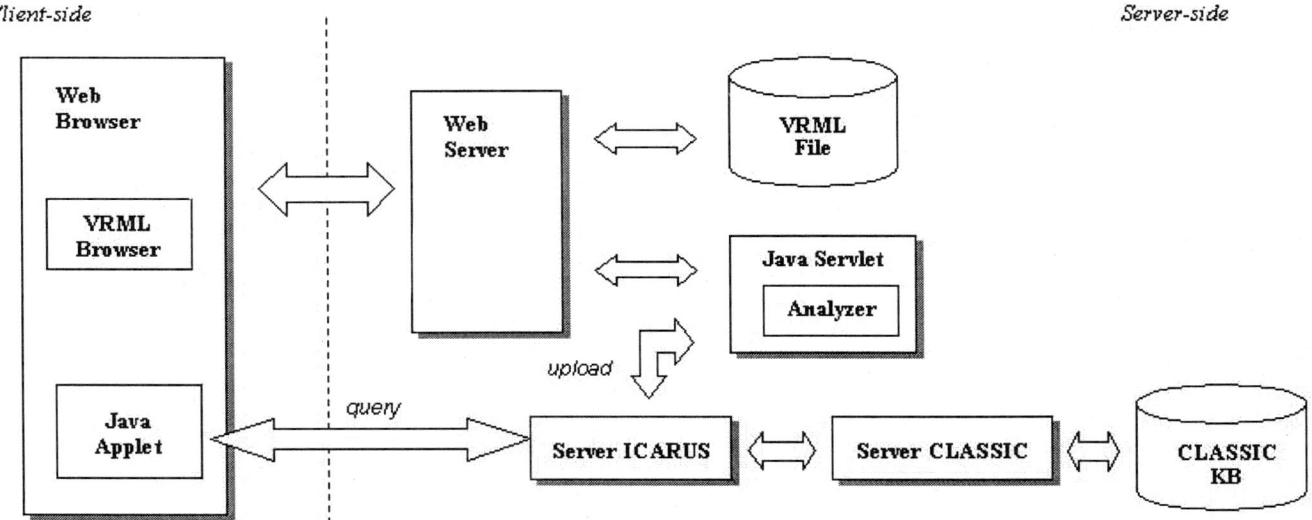

Figure 1. Architecture of ICARUS

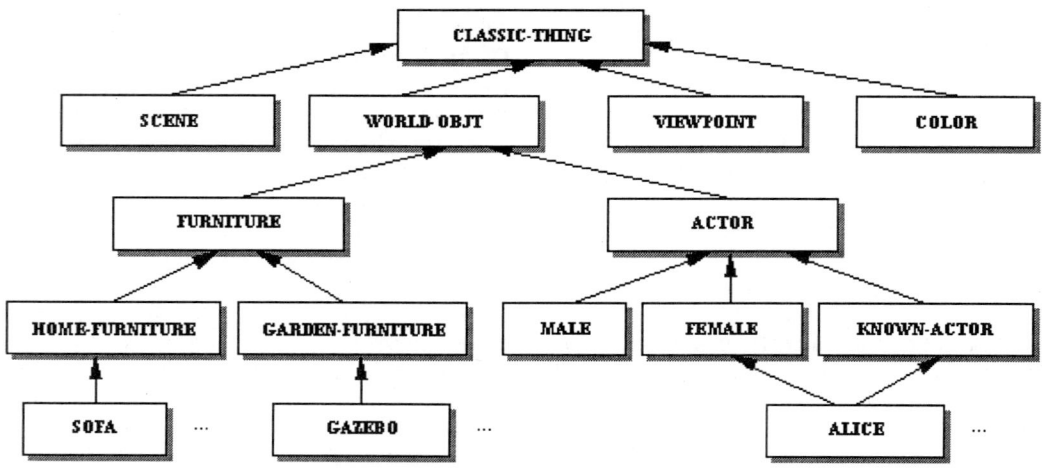

Figure 2. General conceptual structure

- A Java Servlet that the Web Server loads to manage user requests. In particular, the servlet is able to complete the upload session running the Analyzer, which parses files and produces scene descriptions for the KB.
- A Java Server, called Server ICARUS, is connected with the servlet for upload process and with the clients for querying the KB. It translates queries in CLASSIC format and synchronizes accesses to the KB.
- A LISP Server, called Server CLASSIC, is the interface between the CLASSIC KB and the other components;
- The CLASSIC KBMS that defines the structured concepts and stores the descriptions of the analyzed scenes.

ICARUS does not need special hardware features, even if users hosts should have a graphic engine support for an optimal visualization of 3D scenes. Internet connection should be as fast as possible to gain efficiency.

Software compatibility is needed. In particular the Java servlet and the LISP server should be run on the same host, in order to share files information. This should not be a problem because of the Java language is architecture-neutral and Java software platforms are ported onto various hardware-based platforms. Java 2 Platform, Standard Edition, version 1.2.2, is used. Moreover Java3D and Java Servlet packages are necessary.

For client-side, notice that HTML browser must be able to accept cookies, its JVM must be update at least at version 1.7, and it must have installed a VRML plug-in.

The Knowledge Base

Currently, the application domain of ICARUS is quite simple. The system focuses on scenes, which involve furnished environments (houses or gardens) and a set of characters, male and female (Alice, Bob, Charlie, etc.), whose physical features (skin, hair, beard colors) and clothes (shirt, skirt, trousers, shoes colors) are known. Also relations among actors are defined. E.g. Alice is a relative of Bob, friend of Diana, colleague of Charlie and loves Frank, and so on. The ICARUS KB models this knowledge of the domain. In particular every piece of furniture and character matches a specific concept. Individuals identified during file analysis process, and whose properties and geometrical information are maintained, populate the KB. The domain is described through a concept hierarchy, whose simplified view is shown in figure 2.

Relations between individuals are represented as roles. E.g. the roles furnishing and characters relate a scene, respectively, with its furniture and actors. Geometrical information, such as dimension, position and orientation are stored for every object in a scene. Roles representing geometrical relation between WORLD-OBJECT (in-front-of, behind, over, beside, and so forth) are also defined.

Roles have a hierarchical structure too. As we suppose love implies friendship, role "lover-of" is defined as subrole of "friend-of". A particular use of role hierarchy allows relating specific information within a role. For example, one can join a scene to a male actor through the role character-male, instead of using its parent role character. With this structure of roles, it is possible to define a special form of qualified existential role quantification. So the concept SCENE-AT-LEAST-1-MALE can be expressed as (AND SCENE (AT-LEAST 1 character-male)). Using simply not-structured roles, we can specify only universal role quantification, such as SCENE-ALL-MALE = (AND SCENE (AT-LEAST 1 characters)(ALL characters MALE)).

Inverse roles are possible: for symmetric relation one can define a role and its inverse as the same (near-near), otherwise a different inverse name is allowed (inside-outside).

Some relations among concepts, such as friendship between ALICE and ELIZABETH, can be expressed using roles. In this case, since a role cannot relate two concepts, a role joins one of the concepts to an individual representing the other concept (meta-individual). Using the *rules* mechanism, relations among concepts and concept meta-individuals are inferred to individuals.

Rules are also used to deduce that a generic character, when it possesses specific physical features, is a KNOWN-ACTOR, thus retrieving the other relationships.

In the KB some pairs of concepts are defined as disjoint primitive concepts (FURNITURE and ACTOR, or MALE and FEMALE), in order to show that no individual can satisfy both of them.

As the system aims to classify scenes, the concept SCENE has a particular meaning. This concept is described as a primitive concept, while a number of *defined-concept* is based on it. A defined-concept is a concept expressing both necessary and sufficient conditions for an individual to be an instance of it. This type of concept is essentially as views in databases. A considerable advantage gained with defined-concepts is that the system itself can be charged with organizing these views into a hierarchy. Notice that the relations expressed are more complex than just the class-subclass relation. In ICARUS the taxonomy of defined-concepts provides a mechanism to describe scene properties to final users. For this reason defined-concepts are used to describe special properties of the scenes or particular situation. For example, we have defined concepts representing:

- The presence/absence of known actors (SCENE-PRESENT-ALICE, SCENE-NOT-PRESENT-BOB), or pieces of furniture (SCENE-WITH-TABLE);
- The number of characters present (SCENE-NO-CHARACTERS, SCENE-AT-LEAST-3-CHARACTERS, etc.);
- The presence of particular kind of actors (SCENE-NO-FEMALE, SCENE-ALL-FEMALE, SCENE-AT-LEAST-1-FEMALE);
- The kind of environment, based on the presence of particular furniture. For example we can recognize a ROOM, if walls, floor and door are present, or a GARDEN, if there are grass and garden furniture. Also particular kind of rooms is defined: SITTING-ROOM, KITCHEN, LIBRARY, BEDROOM, OFFICE.
- Special relations among actors (SCENE-ALL-FRIENDS, SCENE-AT-LEAST-2-COLLEAGUES) or among generic objects (SCENE-ALL-OBJECTS-NEAR);
- Particular situation (job-meeting, Christmas-party, romantic scene).

A number of described concepts cannot be expressed in CLASSIC without the use of the TEST constructor, which allows LISP procedures to be used in specifying concepts. Passing a test restriction represents a sufficient condition to satisfy a concept. Tests are used to retrieve information in querying. E.g. if we want to retrieve "a scene where is present a man in front of a table", we define the restriction (TEST-C retrieve-geometric-rel-test MALE TABLE in-front-of).

It's worth noticing that ICARUS can adapt to different application domains by defining domain-specific knowledge bases, without modifying other system components, but only providing a suitable user interface.

Parsing and Geometrical Analysis

The main purpose of ICARUS is the analysis of three-dimensional scenes modeled using the Virtual Reality Modeling Language (VRML). The VRML file format integrates 3D graphics and multimedia and is widely used in a distributed environment such as the Web.

An important characteristic of VRML files is the ability to compose files together through inclusion and to relate files together through hyperlinking. Hierarchical file inclusion enables the creation of arbitrarily large worlds that can be dynamically modified through a variety of mechanisms that encourage composition, encapsulation, and extension.

Each VRML file:
- Implicitly establishes a world coordinate space for all objects defined in the file, as well as all objects included by the file;
- Explicitly defines and composes a set of 3D and multimedia objects;
- Can specify hyperlinks to other files and applications;
- Can define object behaviors.

In a VRML file it is implicitly defined a scene graph, which contains hierarchically grouped nodes describing objects and their properties, as well as nodes that participate in the event generation and routing mechanism.

Prototypes allow the set of VRML node types to be extended by the user. Prototype definitions can be included in the file in which they are used or defined externally. ICARUS provides its users with a rich collection of prototypes, i.e. 3D-object models defined in terms of other VRML nodes, which can be used to model a virtual scene.

The system has specific information about its prototype library, such as their possible use (furniture or characters), the concept that represents them and their appearance (original dimension, orientation and position). This information is used during the analysis process in order to obtain a CLASSIC description of a scene. VRML offers different mechanisms in order to include instances of prototypes in a scene:

- Direct use of EXTERNPROTO nodes, i.e. prototypes defined externally;
- Definition and reuse of PROTO nodes, i.e. prototypes node defined completely in the file, including others prototypes;
- Use of INLINE node, in order to include directly another VRML file;
- Definition and reuse of grouping nodes that include others prototypes.

Parsing a VRML file, the ICARUS Analyzer is able to identify all the instances of the system prototype library that are present in a virtual scene. At the same time absolute position in the world coordinate space is calculated for each identified instance. For this purpose, the analyzer uses both local geometric transformations (scaling, translation, and rotation) extracted from the scene graph and initial geometric knowledge of prototypes.

The parsing phase is followed by a geometrical analysis, whose purpose is to retrieve special geometric relationships

between recognized prototype instances. In particular the relations that can be determined between two objects are:
- *Symmetrical relations*, which join a pair of objects.
  - Near: both dimensions and relative distances between objects are used. A special use of this relation involves determining objects that are near to viewpoints in the scene;
  - Opposite: involving objects position, dimension and orientation. Objects must have inverse orientations.
  - Behind: as for opposite, but the same orientation is required.
  - Inside (Outside): used to describe if an object is completely contained in another one.
- *Asymmetrical relations*, which relate an object to another one, but the inverse relation is not necessarily true. Each relation involves dimensions and positions of both objects, while orientation is implicitly assumed choosing a specific face of the object.
  - In front of;
  - Back;
  - Beside;
  - Over;
  - Under.

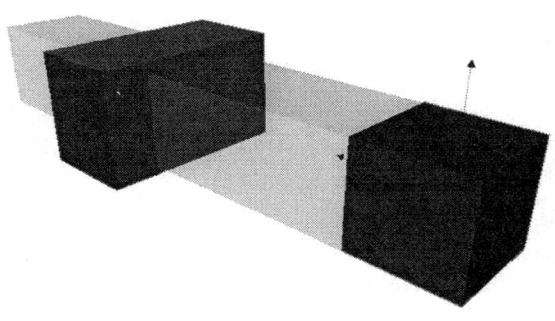

Figure 3. Relation between bounding-

Geometrical analysis is carried out taking into consideration not objects themselves but their bounding-boxes, i.e. rectangular parallelepipeds surrounding objects. For example, the relation "in front of" between the object bounding-boxes is shown in figure 3. Note that before starting the analysis of the relations the bounding-boxes of the objects are scaled (in function of their average dimension) and their projection planes inclined. Using this technique we can get better results in computing the relationships, because we can take into consideration both the dimensions and the distances between objects.

The last part of the analysis process aims at constructing a description of the analyzed scene in the format of CLASSIC. In particular, the analyzer creates individuals with specific properties:
- An individual for each prototype instance;
- An individual for the scene.

Each individual is defined indicating the most significant concept it satisfies, such as TABLE, BED, for furniture prototypes and MAN or WOMAN for character prototypes. Positions and orientation information are stored and others individuals are indicated as geometric role fillers, according to geometrical relationships retrieved. Colors can be related to ACTOR individuals through specific color roles. The individual related to the scene is defined indicating that it satisfies directly only the concept SCENE. All others interesting concepts are deduced during classification. A scene is described by listing all the objects that are contained in it. Moreover information about defined viewpoints is also stored. An important phase in defining a description is *role-closure*. In fact CLASSIC adopts the *Open World Assumption* and only if roles are explicitly closed each individual can be well classified taking into account all its properties.

Querying the KB

ICARUS provides its users with the capability of submitting their VRML files for analysis. If no error is reported during parsing phase, the system creates new individuals and classifies scene description in the KB.

The other main service provided by ICARUS is querying the KB and retrieving information about scenes. For this purpose a suitable graphic interface is available.

The user can obtain a scene description, in the form of a list of all defined-concepts the scene satisfies. Selected scenes can be visualized and the user can navigate through the virtual worlds. Using a query panel one can specify compound queries, in order to retrieve all scenes:
- Whose environment is a particular room (kitchen, sitting room, library, bedroom) or a garden;
- Where specific characters (Alice, Bob, ...) are necessarily present (or not present);
- Where there is at least, at most or exactly a certain number of elements. An element can be a specific kind of object (Chair) or a particular actor (Frank), but generic categories of element (Furniture or Characters) are also allowed.
- Where a specific geometric relation between elements (objects or actors) is satisfied. E.g. Bob near a bed.
- Where all (or at least two) characters are in a particular relationship. E.g. a scene with all friend or at least 2 lovers.
- Where there is at least a character with specific clothes or physical features (blue trousers or white beard).
- That can be classified as particular situation, such as a job meeting, a romantic scene, a Christmas party, etc.

An important feature is incoherent queries detection. Then error messages are shown in dialog frames. Inconsistent queries cause only warning messages.

Examples

We propose some examples to show how ICARUS can be used. Notice that we used only prototypes present in the system library to model these scenes.

Example 1. This scene is visualized in figure 4. The analysis of this scene recognizes the presence of three

characters and several pieces of furniture. An interesting defined-concept the environment satisfies is KITCKEN. In fact the scene is a ROOM because the prototype of a room was used, and all the furniture that are indicated in the KITCKEN concept definition (a cooker, a sink, a fridge, a table, two chairs, a cabinet) appear. This scene can be retrieved by a query that requires, for example:
- Exactly three characters;
- At least two female characters;
- A female actor near a table;
- A generic character in front of a chair;
- A male character opposite a sink;
- A fridge beside a cooker.

Example 2. A view of the scene in this example is shown in figure 5. Note that this is a SCENE-IN-GARDEN. However the scene is classified as a much more specific concept: a ROMANTIC-SCENE. To understand why it can happen you must know that the two actors represent the characters ALICE and FRANK, who are known as lovers. Hence, all conditions that describe our idea of romantic scene are satisfied: there are exactly two lover characters

and they stand near and opposite.

Conclusions

In this paper we have presented a prototype systems that provides domain specific content-based classification and retrieval of VRML scenes. In our system the emphasis is on the representation of the logical and geometrical properties of scenes and their use for classification and retrieval. Many other systems aim at classifying complex data (e.g. images) by the use of logical relations. For example in [4] Corridoni et al. extract from an image a set of relations based on the color and these relations are then used for retrieval. While we are not aware of any other system that use a concept description language, such as CLASSIC, for the classification of 3D scenes, it is worth mentioning the system ALFRESCO [5] that uses YAK (a concept description language) for accessing information on 14th century Italian frescoes and monuments.

An important research issue that needs to be addressed in the near future is extending ICARUS analysis mechanisms to other 3D file format (CAD format). Another fundamental aspect to investigate is description and classification of dynamic scenes. Since this behavior is expressed via an event model, we are currently working on a logical language that can express the dynamic relation between objects.

References

1. Adjeroh, D. A.; and Nwosu, K. C. 1997. Multimedia database management: Requirements and issues. *IEEE Multimedia* 4(3): 24-33.
2. Brachman, R. J.; McGuinness, D.L.; Patel-Schneider, P. F.; Alperin Resnick, L.; and Borgida, A. 1991. Living with CLASSIC: when and how to use a KL-ONE-like language. In Sowa, J. F., editor, *Principles of Semantic Networks*, 401-456. Morgan Kaufmann, Los Altos.
3. Calvanese, D.; De Giacomo, G.; and Lenzerini, M. 1996. Structured objects: Modeling and reasoning. In *Proceedings of DOOD-95*, 229-246. LNCS 1013.
4. Corridoni, J. M.; Del Bimbo, A.; De Magistris, S.; and Vicario, E. 1996. A visual language for color-based painting retrieval. In *Proceeding of IEEE Symposium of Visual Languages*, 68-75.
5. Stock, O. et al. 1993. Alfresco: enjoying the combination of natural language processing and hypermedia for information exploration. In Maybury, M. T., editor, *Intelligent Multimedia Interfaces*, 197-224.
6. Subrahmanian, V. S. 1998. *Principles of Multimedia Database Systems.* Morgan Kaufmann, Los Altos.

Acknowledgments

We thank Francesco M. Donini and Emilio Domenicucci for their work on a previous version of ICARUS. Work partially supported by ASI (Italian Space Agency) and MURST.

Integrating a Spoken Language System with Agents for Operational Information Access

Jody Daniels

Lockheed Martin Advanced Technology Laboratories
1 Federal Street
Camden, NJ 08102 USA
jdaniels@atl.lmco.com

Abstract

Changing the way users interact with their data is the principal objective of the Listen, Communicate, Show (LCS) paradigm. LCS is a new paradigm being applied to Marine Corps tactical logistics. Using a spoken language understanding system a Marine converses with the system to place a supply or information request, which is passed to a mobile, intelligent agent to execute at the proper database. Upon successful return, the agent notifies the spoken language system of its results, and the Marine is given a verbal and/or visual response.

Introduction

Marines work in a dynamic, fluid environment where requirements and priorities are constantly subject to change. It currently takes 72 hours before a Marine in a Combat Service Support Operations Center (CSSOC) can confirm with a requesting unit that their order is in the logistics system. This is unacceptable for most requests, particularly if the request is for mission-critical supplies. CSSOC personnel spend a great deal of their time placing and then tracking requests, trying to keep the requesting units appraised of the status of their supplies. When it takes so long to place and check on a request, all involved become frustrated and operational plans may have to be altered to accommodate the slowness of the supply system.

The focus of the LCS - Marine project is to provide Marines in the field with the logistical support that they need, when they need it, where they need it. In an LCS system, the computer *listens* for information requests, *communicates* both with the user and networked information resources to compute user-centered solutions, and *shows* tailored visualizations to individual warfighters.

This is done by integrating a spoken language understanding system (SLS) (for assisting the user in placing a request) with mobile, intelligent agents (for information access). The SLS converses with the user to gather information for placing a new request, or to check status, amend, or cancel an existing request. Once sufficient information is obtained from the user, the SLS launches an agent to accomplish the requested task. The agent accesses a snapshot of the Marine databases by traveling over existing tactical communications networks. Once the agent's itinerary is complete, it returns to the SLS, which generates an appropriate response to the user. This may be visual in addition to verbal, depending on the available media. By integrating these AI technologies, we hope to reduce the 72-hour response time to less than 7.2 minutes.

Through a quick conversation between the user and the LCS system, many potential pitfalls can be reduced or eliminated in the processing of a request. For example, the system can observe that the user has requested an amount that exceeds the capacity of the requesting unit and can attempt to resolve this problem directly with the user. Additionally, the user can establish monitor agents that will track the request and send notification agents back to the user to report either status updates or observations that the request isn't being given the attention the user needs.

Achieving near real-time access to logistics databases via spoken language and agents greatly increases the confidence that the proper supplies will arrive and in a more timely fashion. Thus, commanders are able to more accurately generate operations plans that are less likely to be subject to supply shortfalls.

We next describe the LCS - Marine task. Then we discuss the system and its components. Finally we give an overview of the operational testing and results of using the LCS - Marine system.

Task Description

To submit requests through the logistics system, units pass their requests to the CSSOC, which prepares a Rapid Request form. LCS - Marine supports both ordinance (Class V) and subsistence (Class I) supply requests through the use of the Rapid Request form. LCS – Marine users provide their input to the CSSOC via radio and use radio protocols when communicating. This requires the system to understand call signs, military times, etc.

To support the flow of information using the Rapid Request form, the initial set of LCS - Marine activities are to submit a request, check on its status, change a request, and cancel a request. Figure 1 shows a partially completed Rapid Request form when placing a new request.

Copyright © 2000, American Association for Artificial Intelligence (www.aaai.org). All rights reserved.

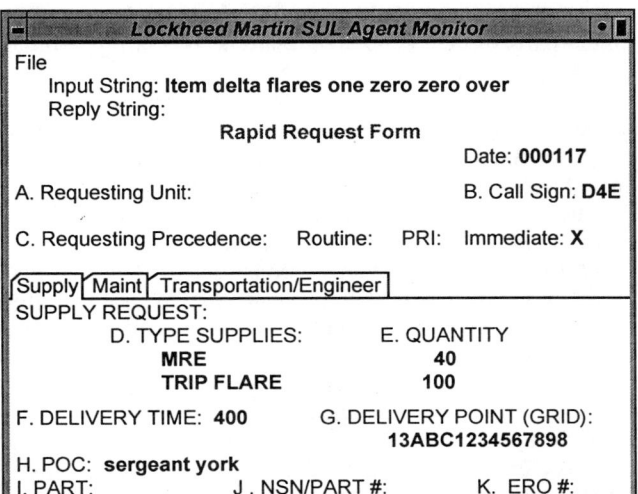

Figure 1. Partially Completed Marine Corps Rapid Request Form

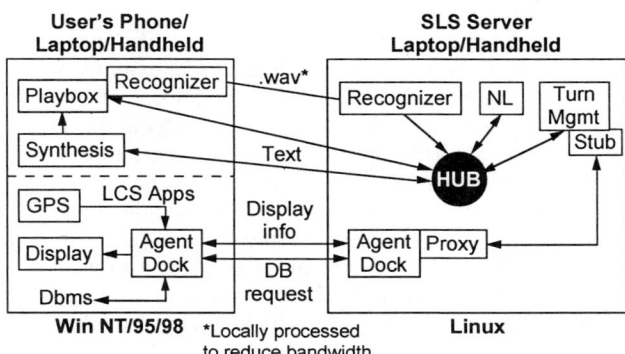

Figure 2. LCS - Marine Architecture

Overview of the LCS – Marine System

The LCS - Marine system consists of four major components: an SLS, a collection of agents for information access, real-world operational databases, and communications networks to connect the user to the SLS and the agents to the databases. Operationally, the Marine speaks into a microphone attached to a hand-held device. The recognition process begins on the hand-held and sends a compressed version of the speech over a wireless communications link to the main portion of the SLS, which resides a short distance away.

The other SLS components complete the recognition process, parse the *n*-best possibilities, create a semantic representation, add historical context from the on-going human-machine interchange, and decide what step to take next. Possible next steps include prompting the user for additional information, requesting a clarification, or sending an agent to an information source to process a completed user request.

When the dialogue is sufficiently progressed, the SLS will send a mobile agent over another communications link (either SINCGARS or Wavelan) to the remote database management system (dbms). After processing the request at the dbms, the agent returns to the SLS to confirm placing the request (or the modification or deletion). The SLS then generates a response for the user, which may be both verbal and visual. The SLS transforms the verbal response from a semantic frame into text, which is then synthesized into speech on the hand-held device. Visual updates are handled by agents, which manage a custom display server. Figure 2 provides an overview of the current LCS – Marine architecture.

We next describe each of the components of the system, starting with the SLS, then the extendible mobile agent architecture system, the dbms, and finally the communications system.

Spoken Language Understanding System (SLS)

The SLS uses the MIT Galaxy II architecture customized with the domain application and specialized servers (Seneff, Lau, and Polifroni 1999). The architecture is designed to be "plug and play."

Galaxy II is a DARPA-developed, GOTS, distributed, component-based middleware product maintained by the MITRE Corporation. Specialized servers handle specific tasks, such as translating audio data to text. All Galaxy II-compliant servers communicate with each other through a central server known as the Hub. The Hub manages flow control, handles traffic among distributed servers, and provides state maintenance.

Using the Hub architecture, information is passed in the form of a frame. Specific frames are built throughout the processing to handle and store such items as the input utterance, prior context, and the response to the user.

In terms of overall processing, speech is moved from the Playbox to the Recognizer. Speech is translated, prior context added, and processed using the Natural Language (NL) and Turn Manager servers to verify the new input's validity. The Turn Manager generates a response, NL converts it to text, and the Synthesis server generates the verbal response. The Playbox then speaks the waveform file to the user.

Audio. The Audio Input/Output server, known as the Playbox, uses the COTS Microsoft SAPI Speech Development Kit (Beta). Using SAPI audio objects enables LCS - Marine to capture and play back speech. The server captures speech and sends it as an audio waveform file to the Recognizer.

To support low-bandwidth communications, such as tactical and cellular, the initial steps of the Recognizer (spectral compression) were added to the audio capture modules to reduce the amount of bandwidth needed to move the waveform file.

At the other end of a processing cycle (sometimes called a turn) the Synthesis server converts text to speech, creating an audio waveform file. Synthesis also uses Microsoft SAPI audio objects. This waveform file is then passed directly to the Playbox for audio generation, completing the user-machine dialogue loop.

Recognizer. The Recognizer is the server responsible for speaker-independent speech recognition. Audio waveform data is analyzed for component sounds and examined with respect to models of known combinations of sounds. Candidate results are selected using an *n*-best algorithm.

The *n*-best algorithm produces a list of the *n* most likely possible utterances produced that map to the waveforms being examined. The list is merged into a single network, a word graph. Three conceptual models are used in this process. The acoustic model maps sounds to phones, the base unit of pronunciation. The pronunciation model maps groups of phones to words, and the language model groups words into sequences.

The LCS - Marine acoustic model is derived from data collected by the Spoken Language Systems Group at MIT for another speech application (Glass and Hazen 1998). The data is from narrow-band telephone speech and contains 24,000 samples. LCS - Marine has adapted and expanded upon this model as the vocabulary and the operational environment evolves.

The Recognizer combines the pronunciation and language models into one process, a class bigram model. This combined model is constructed and trained using a pronunciation lexicon of vocabulary words, a collection of word classifications, and a training set of common sentences and phrases.

Classification rules assist the language model by identifying groups of words that could appear in similar locations within an utterance. These could be "numbers," "city names," "colors" or any other group of related terms.

A large set of textual sentences, phrases, and other types of user inputs exist to train the class bigram model. These range in length from "Third platoon needs four thousand m sixteen rounds at checkpoint bravo before sixteen hundred hours zulu" to "no." The text samples provide order information to the Recognizer and are used to generate the relative probabilities found in the language model.

The Recognizer merges the *n*-best sequences into a single directed word graph. The nodes in the graph correspond to particular pinpoints in time. The edges connecting the nodes are labeled with a word and score. NL will use these scores when matching against the parse rules.

Natural Language (NL). The NL component handles text parsing and generation. A semantic frame is built to represent knowledge and the user's meaning. This knowledge representation is initially built by NL and is passed to the other components. NL parses text, both syntactically and semantically, to create a semantic representation (the semantic frame) to pass to the Turn Manager. NL also takes semantic frames representing replies from the system back to the user and transforms the frame into text to be synthesized into speech.

NL first syntactically parses the possible sequences in the word graph provided by Recognizer. NL uses a grammar specific to the application domain. The most likely parsable word sequence from the word graph is converted into a syntax tree for further manipulation.

A second domain-specific grammar maps the resulting syntax tree into a semantic tree. The semantic tree is an intermediate step in which meanings are mapped onto salient parts of the syntax tree, ready to be rearranged into a semantic frame.

Using another set of rules, NL constructs a semantic frame from the semantic tree. While both the semantic tree and the semantic frame represent the meaning of an utterance, the structure of the semantic tree reflects the form of the utterance, while the semantic frame reflects the form of the ideas expressed within that utterance.

Information from previously constructed frames (which represent the history of the discourse) may be used to augment the current frame through a collection of rules. The final semantic frame incorporates this historical context and represents the current semantic state of the dialogue. It is passed to the Turn Manager.

When the Turn Manager has completed its processing and has created a reply to speak to the user, NL again takes action. NL translates turn management output, also a semantic frame, into natural language text. This is accomplished by selecting the appropriate text templates from a catalog of templates and filling in the blanks with information from fields within the semantic frame. The text generated by NL is then passed to the Synthesis server.

Turn Manager. The Turn Manager manages dialogue with the user and interfaces with the agent system. The logic contained in the Turn Manager governs the order of clarifying questions from the system back to the user and triggers agent creation and tasking. This turn management stage reflects the system's end of the dialogue with the user.

The Turn Manager examines the current semantic state of the dialogue, represented by the semantic frame created by NL. The Turn Manager checks the information contained in the semantic frame to determine which data elements of a request are present, which are missing, and whether the information is consistent with domain knowledge. If the semantic frame contains insufficient or inconsistent information, a request for clarifying information is generated and sent back to the NL server in the form of a semantic frame.

One of the Turn Manager's greatest strengths is its support of mixed-initiative dialogue. That is, while the Turn Manager requests information in a predictable order, it is able to accept information from the user that it has not yet requested. For example, if the system asks the user, "Where should the shipment be delivered?" and the user replies "Deliver by noon to Checkpoint Charlie," the Turn Manager recognizes that both a location and a time have been given. It will, therefore, not ask for a time, which might otherwise have been requested later.

When the request by the user is sufficiently complete, the second responsibility of the Turn Manager comes into play. The Turn Manager distributes tasks to agents to gather and/or disseminate information to and from data sources. For example, this might mean making an SQL query to a database. When an agent returns information, the Turn Manager accepts it and translates it into a semantic frame. This semantic frame is passed back to the NL server and will be used to generate a response.

Extendible Mobile Agent Architecture System

LCS - Marine's information discovery and dissemination is accomplished using the Extendible Mobile Agent Architecture (EMAA) (Lentini, et. al. 1998) (Hofmann, McGovern, and Whitebread 1998). This agent architecture is used to integrate the LCS - Marine system with logistical databases, whether Lotus Notes, Oracle, or another dbms.

The agent architecture is a framework on which to build autonomous, intelligent, mobile agent systems. It defines an object-oriented interface for programming agent systems. It follows the principles of component-oriented and reusable object-oriented software. The agent architecture provides a mobile agent platform that gives an application the ability to dynamically create asynchronous mobile software agents. These agents can migrate among computing nodes in a network and can exploit resources at those nodes.

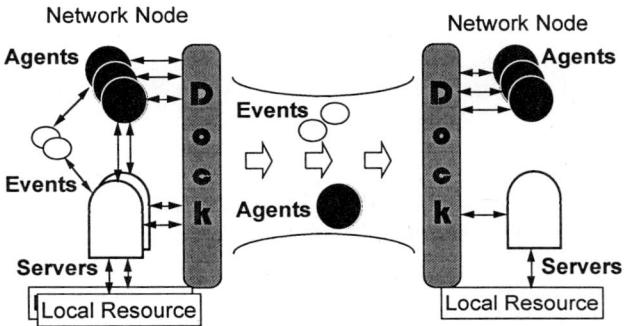

Figure 3. Extendible Mobile Agent Architecture

The agent architecture has three major components: the agents, servers, and the dock. At the most basic level, the agents perform the specialized, user-defined work (i.e., tasks). Agents travel through the system of computing nodes via the docks. The dock serves as a daemon to send and receive agents between docks at other nodes. Nodes that offer specialized services to agents do so via servers that provide packaged components. The relationship of the agents, servers, and docks is shown in Figure 3.

Agents. Mobile agents carry and execute tasks at different nodes. The goal of the agent is to complete all of its tasks. Since the agent is mobile, one must consider both the task and where that task is performed when creating the agent itinerary. EMAA supports mapping tasks to nodes; the set of these task/node pairs is defined as the itinerary of the agent.

EMAA Agent itineraries are Finite State Machines. Agents constructed using this model can exhibit complex behavior while maintaining the ability to execute itinerary subgoals.

Mobile agents can be tasked with database actions (i.e., query, submit, monitor, modify). They migrate to the dbms machine and execute the database actions and return with the results. The mobile agents gain access to the database using the Java Database Connection Standard (JDBC). A server component is run at the node that provides the functionality to make the JDBC connection. The agent accesses the server when it arrives at the node to obtain the functionality to establish the database connection. Once a connection is established, interaction to the database is done using standard SQL commands.

Servers. The agents rely on servers at each node to provide the underlying mechanism to interface with resources; they do not carry programs, merely well defined tasks. It is beneficial to package the code needed to access resources into separate components known as servers. Servers provide a repository of common functionality and processes that an agent may access at a given node. The agent architecture provides the following features with its resource servers. First, they are code repositories: migrating agents carry as little code as possible, thus conserving bandwidth. Second, the servers provide common APIs for the code or logic needed to exploit the resources at a node that keeps the agent machine-independent. Third, because of the component design of servers, the implementation of node-specific resources is separate from the implementation of the agent application.

Dock. The dock is the operating environment for agents and servers. The dock consists of four components: communication server, agent manager, server manager, and event manager.

A communications server is the daemon process itself and it handles all connections to any other computing nodes. It manages the transmission of agents to and from the local node.

An agent manager registers the agent and initializes it for execution. It is used in agent collaboration and agent validation for security reasons.

A server manager handles the server components at a node and provides a control mechanism to start and stop a service.

An event manager "listens" for component events. An event is an announcement that some component in the system has reached an important state, which may be of interest to other components. Often it is unknown if and when a component will generate an event. For this reason, agents and servers dependent on events must have an event manager "listen" for an event.

How Agents Are Used in LCS - Marine. The LCS - Marine system uses the agent architecture to interact with the Marines' logistical dbms. Mobile agents make ordinance (Class V) and subsistence (Class I) requests such as for water, 5.56 rounds, or flares. When making a request, agents are created with request criteria, (e.g., the amount of a particular type of supply to order, delivery location, etc.). If necessary, an agent will first make sure that the request criteria satisfy all dynamic request constraints. Values for these constraints are stored external to the agent system and need to be accessed for validity checking.

When a unit places a request for the water, the agent retrieves the allowable limit from the unit information and checks to see if the requested amount is allowable. If so, then the agent migrates to the logistical database, connects with the database, and executes the request.

Logistical Database (dbms)

LCS - Marine's focus has been on simplifying the logistics process by gathering and disseminating information in a more effective and timely manner. If data can be inserted into and obtained from a database quickly and efficiently, it can effectively provide the information needed to make knowledgeable decisions for appropriate actions.

LCS - Marine uses an Oracle-based logistical database provided by the 1st Marine Expeditionary Force (MEF) for research, development, testing, and prototyping potential spoken user interactions with logistical data sources. The database supports logging, processing, and monitoring logistics requests. It incorporates a number of logistical systems including the Rapid Request Tracking System, Command Information System, and various administrative tools. The front end to these systems is a web-based interface using Cold Fusion to dynamically update the web pages. These systems support both the tactical community ordering supplies through the logistical database, and the watch officers in the rear monitoring the incoming requests and outgoing shipments of supplies.

By using a subset of the 1st MEF's database, which contains "real" logistic data gathered during one of their training exercises (data is spread across 121 tables), LCS - Marine can approximate the interaction that users have with the system.

Communications System

To benefit Marines in the field, the LCS system has been made more portable. The system's basic architecture was reduced to lightweight equipment (PC laptops) without a loss in functionality. Hand-held computing devices have been added and the microphone replaced with an ear/microphone headset. Increased mobility and accessibility were added via wireless access.

Testing

To measure the effectiveness of the LCS paradigm under operational conditions—real users placing real requests, accessing a live dbms, and using existing communications links—we slated four Integrated Feasibility Demonstrations (IFDs) over a twelve-month period. The first was held in September of 1999, the second in December, and the third is projected for April 2000, with the final one to be in July 2000. The IFDs range from scripted dialogue, replicated databases, and testing in the lab with prior military personnel, to active duty Marines using the system operationally over a series of days as their sole means of interaction with the logistics system for rapid requests.

The first IFD used five former military personnel as test subjects, although none were a Marine and none had used the Rapid Request form. All were familiar with radio operations and the military alphabet. All were native English speakers. Four were male and one was female. Each person attempted to accomplish three tasks: input a simple request, check on the status of the request, and make a modification to an existing request.

The second IFD took place concurrent with the Marine exercise Desert Knight. In this IFD, ten active-duty Marines attempted five tasks: the prior three plus a more complex request and canceling of an order. Nine of the subjects had used radio communications before, but only one had used the Rapid Request form before.

In a strenuous test of the speaker independence portion of the system, the users represented a diverse set of demographics: three of the subjects came from the Western US, two from the Southern US, one from the Mid-Atlantic Coast, one from the Midwestern US, one from Algeria, one from Mexico, and one from Burma. Seven subjects were male; three were female.

The third IFD is to take place in April 2000 concurrent with a Marine combined arms exercise and the fourth IFD will follow in July. The third IFD will allow greater flexibility in the dialogue and will integrate the LCS - Marine system into the existing logistics system: agents will be accessing the live dbms, rather than a replica. For the fourth IFD the system will be operational for a longer period of time and from a variety of locations.

At the conclusion of the IFDs we will review progress and evaluate the system's robustness. Depending on the outcome, LCS - Marine could be either directly integrated into CSSOC operations or development could continue with further testing in preparation for a future integration.

Results

There are a variety of metrics that can be used to measure an SLS. Among these are measures for task completion, accuracy, and user satisfaction. For the IFDs we prepared and revised a user satisfaction survey and instrumented the system to collect a variety of pieces of data. We also made manual annotations within the conversation log files to collect additional metrics.

We reported task complexity, task completion rate, system understanding, and user satisfaction across the set of three or five tasks. We also attempted to pinpoint errors down to a specific component(s) of the system, although we do not discuss specific results here.

We computed task complexity as the number of information items that the system needed to understand before it could task an agent. For example, stating: "Item delta M R E three hundred," represents three information items, specifying the line in the form, the type of supply, and the quantity. Table 1 gives a breakdown by task.

In IFD-1 an overall task completion rate for all tasks was 60%, which improved to 89% in IFD-2 for these same three tasks. For the set of five tasks in IFD-2, the average task completion rate was 82%. (The data from one subject was not included in the final results because of the difficulty of other humans in understanding this person.)

Task	Items	Turns	Time (Min)	Completion Rate
Simple request	11	21.0	7.0	78%
Complex request	22	27.0	16.6	44%
Status check	4	6.0	2.8	100%
Change request	6	11.5	4.1	89%
Cancel request	4	8.0	3.3	100%

Table 1. IFD-2 results.

For system understanding, we measured the number of "turns" to complete each task. We considered a turn to be a complete cycle, including both a user input and a system response.

For both completed IFDs, we measured user satisfaction after the completion of the entire test session. In the future, we may measure user satisfaction after the testing of each task, rather than at the end of the session. Because there is currently no standard for measuring user satisfaction of dialogue systems, we are still adapting our survey to attempt to glean the most information. Unfortunately, in retrospect, the changes we made to the survey between IFD-1 and IFD-2 were likely to have hurt our results. (For example, there were several questions where a negative response would have been the best response, and, if these questions were not closely read, the user could easily misinterpret the question.) For IFD-1, overall user satisfaction was at 1.85 on a 1 to 5 scale where 1 was best. For IFD-2, overall user satisfaction was at 6.4 on a 1 to 10 scale where 10 was best.

It is important to note that the amount of time spent training personnel to use the LCS - Marine system is generally less than 10 minutes. After a short introduction, the user is shown a sample dialogue for familiarization. The user is also given information about meta-instructions, such as how to start over or clear their previous statement, before they begin the tasks.

Conclusion

We have built a system that integrates an SLS with a mobile, intelligent agent system that allows users to place and access data requests via a conversational interface. The system is speaker independent and requires little training. The time to accomplish a task is significantly lower than the old, manual input method, but can still be improved. Being able to rapidly access, insert, modify, and delete data gives the users greater confidence in the supply system and allows commanders to generate operations plans that are less likely to be subject to supply shortfalls.

Acknowledgements

Thanks to members of the LCS - Marine team: Josh Brody, Phil Crawford, Jerry Franke, Michael Frew, Steve Knott, Lizz McCormick, Jose Rivera, and Kathy Stibler.

This research was supported by DARPA contract N66001-98-D-8507 and Naval contract N47406-99-C-7033.

References

Glass, J., and Hazen, T.J. 1998. Telephone-Based Conversational Speech Recognition in the Jupiter Domain. In *Proceedings of ICSLP '98*. Sydney, Australia.

Hofmann, M.O., McGovern, A., and Whitebread, K.R. 1998. Mobile Agents on the Digital Battlefield, in *Proceedings of the 2nd International Conference on Autonomous Agents (Agents '98)*. Minneapolis/St. Paul.

Lentini, R., Rao, G., Thies, J., and Kay, J. 1998. EMAA: An Extendable Mobile Agent Architecture. In *Proceedings for the Software Tools for Developing Agents Workshop at the 15th National Conference on Artificial Intelligence (AAAI '98)*. Madison, Wisconsin.

Seneff, S., Lau, R., and Polifroni, J. 1999. Organization, Communication, and Control in the GALAXY-II Conversational System. In *Proceedings for Eurospeech '98*. Budapest, Hungary.

DMML: An XML Language for Interacting with Multi-modal Dialog Systems

Nanda Kambhatla, Malgorzata Budzikowska, Sylvie Levesque, Nicolas Nicolov, Wlodek Zadrozny, Charles Wiecha and Julie MacNaught

IBM T.J. Watson Research Center
30 Saw Mill River Road, Hawthorne, NY 10532
{nanda,sm1,nicolas,wlodz,wiecha,jmacna}@us.ibm.com, slevesqu@ca.ibm.com

Abstract

We present Dialog Moves Markup Language (DMML): an extensible markup language (XML) representation of modality independent communicative acts of automated conversational agents. In our architecture, DMML is the interface to and from conversational dialog managers for user interactions through any channel or modality. The use of a common XML interface language across different channels promotes high cost efficiency for the business. DMML itself has no application or domain specific elements; DMML elements embed elements representing application business logic. DMML captures the abstractions necessary to represent arbitrary multi-agent dialogs and to build cost-efficient, sophisticated natural language dialog systems for business applications.

Introduction

Our goal is to create a framework for building conversational dialog agents for business applications, where users can converse with the agents using any channel of interaction (e.g. web, telephone, PDA, cellular phone, etc.) or modality (speech, text, graphics, etc). Conversational dialog agents are automated software agents that can participate fully in natural dialog (Allen 1995) and whose internal state may include beliefs, desires, and intentions (BDI models; e.g. see (Bratman et al. 1988; Cohen et al. 1990) and references therein). Examples of conversational agents include natural language dialog based telephony banking and stock trading systems (Zadrozny et al. 1998) and planning systems for disaster handling (Ferguson and Allen 1998).

We are building several multi-modal conversational agents for different business applications. In our architecture (see Figure 1), there are several presentation managers (PMs), one for each channel of interaction. A channel can encompass several modalities. For example, users may interact with web sites using speech, text, or graphics (the

Copyright © 2000, American Association for Artificial Intelligence (www.aaai.org). All rights reserved.

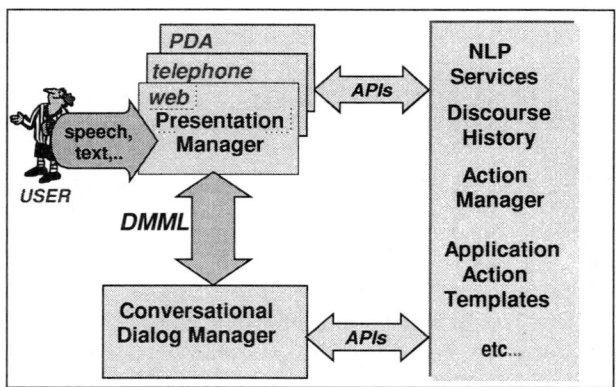

Figure 1: Architecture for multi-modal, multi-channel conversational agents for business applications.

web presentation manager will handle all these interactions).

Each presentation manager (PM) is responsible for interacting with the user through its specific channel, sending any user input to a conversational dialog manager (CDM) in a common dialog interaction format (which we call dialog moves markup language or DMML). The PM calls APIs to access natural language understanding and generation modules specific to the modalities in use and to generate or parse DMML messages. For example, a telephony PM might call APIs for accessing a speech recognition module. The PM receives DMML messages (if any) from the CDM and communicates to the user the relevant information though appropriate modalities over the same channel of interaction.

The CDM is responsible for managing the dialog with the user. The CDM interacts with the PMs using a modality- and channel-independent language called DMML. The CDM uses a suite of APIs to interact with specialized services and managers to execute business transactions (through an action manager), to fetch or update the discourse history, to fetch application templates, etc.

The Dialog Moves Markup Language (DMML) is a language designed for representing the communicative acts of conversational agents for communication between such agents. For successful multi-agent communication, the communicative intent of one agent must be recognized by the other agent. DMML attempts to capture such intentions. DMML can be used for messaging between a human (one kind of conversational agent) and a conversational dialog manager (another conversational agent). Notice how this view associates the PM with the human user to result in a software agent communicating with other software agents through DMML (cf. Figure 1). DMML can also be used for communication between any two (or more) agents that have a notion of intentions to communicate, actions they want to achieve through the communication, and a shared view of their environment. DMML can represent a synchronous turn taking dialog between two agents. We believe it is also general enough to represent arbitrary asynchronous multi-party dialogs.

DMML is an application of eXtensible Markup Language (XML; (Bray et al. 1998)), a standard for document and message markup. DMML has been designed to be an open markup language with no domain- or application-specific markup tags. It is open to enable developers to use further refinements of the basic speech acts in use. All application- and domain-specific markup is encoded using application-specific tags, which reside *underneath* (i.e. are embedded in) the DMML markup. This concept is explained in greater detail in section 3.

The use of DMML as a standard common interface between conversational agents facilitates tremendous cost-efficiency in developing dialog applications. DMML also enables relatively easy portability to new channels of interaction, since only presentation managers need to be developed for such channels. This is because there is only one conversational dialog manager managing conversations with users across different channels with different modalities. The use of well recognized and emerging standards like XML and XSL is crucial, since the DMML messages can be transformed using XSL (eXtensible Stylesheet Language; (Clark and Deach 1998)) with relative ease to channel or modality dependent languages like VoiceXML (VoiceXML 2000), HTML, or Wireless Markup Language.

In this paper, we present the DMML language (Section 2) and show an example (Section 3) illustrating its components with a dialog between a human and an automated conversational agent for stock trading. We contrast DMML with some related work in section 4, such as the work in philosophy of language, the Elephant 2000 programming language, KQML and agent markup languages. We explain our work in progress with DMML in section 5 and present some conclusions in section 6.

Dialog Moves Markup Language (DMML)

The basic elements of DMML are dialog profiles and dialog moves. Dialog profile elements enable agents to send to each other the constraints on their respective environments or the constraints on the communication itself. For instance, an agent may be unwilling (as a result of its internal decision making process) or unable (due to its environmental constraints) to process requests of a certain kind. Dialog profiles enable agents to communicate such constraints to each other.

A dialog move by agent1 to agent2 represents a set of communicative acts by agent1 directed towards agent2, with the intention of changing agent2's model of the state of the world and/or convince agent2 to take actions based on agent2's revised model of the state of the world.

Dialog profiles

Dialog profiles enable dialog agents to communicate to each other the constraints of their respective environments and constraints on the communication itself. The basic elements of profiles are templates (e.g. XML Schemas (Thompson et al. 2000)) describing these constraints. DMML supports four basic types of templates—assertion templates, command templates, request templates and response templates—corresponding to the four basic types of dialog moves. These templates may contain "schemas" (Thompson et al. 2000) expressing constraints on the corresponding dialog moves. For instance, a response template contains a schema defining the syntax of a valid response. By exchanging such templates, dialog agents can negotiate the parameters of communication before or during a dialog.

Shown below is a profile that defines a template for valid XML elements for representing stock transactions to a stock trading CDM (cf. Figure 1). Due to space constraints, we have only shown the schema for buy transactions. The notion is similar to that of defining valid types for communication. This template specifies that a valid BUY element must contain zero or one instances of a COMPANY element, a QUANTITY element, an ACCOUNT element, and a PRICE element. Each COMPANY element has a text string representing the name of the COMPANY, and so on. The CDM sends profiles like the one below to PMs that are requesting stock trading services. After receiving this profile, each receiving agent (PM) knows the syntax of the XML messages for buying shares, for selling shares, for inquiring about the price of certain shares, etc. Note that profiles are not required to be sent before dialog moves are communicated. DMML allows profiles to be sent at any point in a dialog session. This enables agents to dynamically communicate to each other any changes in their environments or any changes to the constraints of their communication.

```xml
<profile>
 <template type="document">
  <schema id="stock_transactions">
   <ElementType name="COMPANY" model="closed" content="textOnly"
         dt:type="string">
   </ElementType>
   <ElementType name="QUANTITY" model="closed" content="textOnly"
         dt:type="number">
   </ElementType>
   <ElementType name="ACCOUNT" model="closed" content="textOnly"
         dt:type="string">
   </ElementType>
   <ElementType name="PRICE" model="closed" content="textOnly"
         dt:type="amount">
   </ElementType>
   <ElementType name="BUY" model="closed" content="eltOnly">
    <element type="COMPANY" minoccurs="0" maxoccurs="1"/>
    <element type="QUANTITY" minoccurs="0" maxoccurs="1"/>
    <element type="ACCOUNT" minoccurs="0" maxoccurs="1"/>
    <element type="PRICE" minoccurs="0" maxoccurs="1"/>
   </ElementType>
   ...
  </schema>
 </template>
</profile>
```

Dialog moves

Currently, DMML includes four basic types of dialog_moves: assertions, commands, requests and responses.

- *Assertions* represent unsolicited information by an agent that does not necessarily require a response: greetings, warnings, reminders, thanks and welcome messages, offers, etc. Assertions also include statements of fact by agents.
- *Commands* represent speech acts where the commanding agent's expectation is of unconditional action execution: e.g. help, exit, cancel and operator commands.
- *Requests* represent requests for information, confirmation, clarification, identification, action execution, notification, etc. Note that most request elements will have business/application elements as their descendents describing the specific things being requested for the given application. Request elements may also contain response template elements describing valid responses to the request and validation scripts (in a standard language like ECMAScript) that can verify the validity of responses with respect to some other (semantic) constraints.
- *Responses* represent responses to request moves. Thus, a response element always contains an attribute referring to the id of the request move to which it is the response. DMML does not mandate response elements to immediately follow request elements; i.e. the responses can be asynchronous and out of turn. Responses may include notifications, clarifications, confirmations (confirmed or rejected), action_results, information, answer_lists and descriptions. Answer_lists include a list of answers. A description may include a summary, identity of responder, a rationale, and a list of suggestions. Suggestions are lists of alternative answers. Note that most response elements will have business/application elements as their descendants describing the specific things being sent as a response to the request for the given application.

Currently DMML represents mostly directive and assertive communicative acts, due to the limitations of the conversational agents for which it is an interface language. However, in future we plan to also support commisive (e.g. *promise*), permissive (e.g. *permit*), prohibitive (e.g. *forbid*), declarative (e.g. *declare*), and expressive (e.g. *wish*) communicative acts (cf. Singh 1998).

DMML is an open markup language. Thus, a user query "Can you tell me the price of IBM" could be represented as

```
<REQUEST>
  Can you tell me the price of IBM?
</REQUEST>
```

Or as

```
<REQUEST>
  <TELL>
    the price of IBM?
  </TELL>
</REQUEST>
```

Or as

```
<REQUEST REQUEST_TYPE="INFORMATION">
  <PRICE_INFO>
    <COMPANY>IBM</COMPANY>
  </PRICE_INFO>
</REQUEST>.
```

All the above fragments are valid DMML fragments. Allowing open markup enables developers to extend the pre-specified dialog moves by specifying their own sub-categories of requests, commands, assertions, responses, notifications, etc.

In DMML, all the application specific markup is embedded within the DMML markup to support heterogeneous agents and to ensure that DMML is not domain or application dependent. DMML can encapsulate any content as long as it is provided in XML compliant format. For example, in the last excerpt above, all the business application markup (within the request element) is shown in bold and is not part of DMML. This enables separate XSL transformations that can transform the 'conversational style' independent of the specific application or even the domain of the application. Thus, the same DMML message can be used for completely different applications or for different implementations of the same application.

An example: use of DMML for a stock trading application

In this section, we present an example of a dialog between a user and a conversational agent for stock trading. We show a sequence of user utterances, the corresponding DMML messages sent by the PM (presentation manager) to the CDM (conversational dialog manager; see Figure 1), the DMML messages sent by the CDM to the PM, and the corresponding content of the user screen. While this example does not illustrate all the elements of DMML, it gives a flavor of the use of DMML elements and elements representing the embedded business logic. All application specific business logic encoding is shown in bold type and is not part of DMML. Note that the references to the schema "stock_transactions" in response-templates are to the example schema shown in the previous section that defines the syntax of valid XML messages for communication for this domain.

USER: Hi! I want to buy one hundred shares of IBM

```
<dmml version="1.0">
  <move from="PM1" to="CDM "
        channel="web" id="m1">
    <assertion type="greet" id="a1">
      <xml schema="assert_schema">
        <MESSAGE>Hi</MESSAGE>
      </xml>
    </assertion>
    <assertion type="info" id="a2">
      <xml schema="logon_schema" >
        <NAME>Steve</NAME>
        <PASSWORD>adroit</PASSWORD>
        <ACCOUNT>12345</ACCOUNT>
      </xml>
    </assertion>
    <request type="action" id="r1">
      <xml schema="stock_transactions">
        <BUY>
          <COMPANY>IBM</COMPANY>
          <QUANTIY>100</QUANTITY>
        </BUY>
      </xml>
    </request>
  </move>
</dmml>
```

SYSTEM: Hello, Steve!
  You said you wanted to buy 100 shares of IBM.
  Do you want to use your checking account?
  At what price do you want to buy these shares?

```
<dmml version="1.0">
  <move from="CDM" to="PM1"
        channel="web" id="i2">
    <assertion type="greet" id="a3"
               previousmoveid="a2">
      <xml schema="assert_schema">
        <MESSAGE>
          Hi Steve!!!
        </MESSAGE>
      </xml>
    </assertion>
    <request type="info" id="r2" previousmoveid="r1">
      <xml schema="stock_transactions">
        <BUY>
          <COMPANY origin="user_specified">
          IBM</COMPANY>
          <QUANTIY origin="user_specified">
          100</QUANTITY>
          <ACCOUNT origin="system_inferred">
          12345</ACCOUNT>
        </BUY>
      </xml>
      <responsetemplate>
        <schema id="stock_transactions/>
      </responsetemplate>
    </request>
  </move>
</dmml>
```

USER: What is the current price of IBM?
```
<dmml version="1.0">
  <move from="PM1" to="CDM" channel="web" id="i3">
    <request type="info" id="r3">
      <xml schema="stock_transactions">
        <PRICE_INFO>
          <COMPANY>IBM</COMPANY>
        </PRICE_INFO>
      </xml>
      <responsetemplate>
        <schema id="stock_transactions"/>
      </responsetemplate>
    </request>
  </move>
</dmml>
```

SYSTEM: The current price of IBM is 110 1/2.
  Do you want to buy 100 shares at this price from your checking account?

```
<dmml version="1.0">
  <move from="CDM" to="PM1" channel="web" id="i4">
    <response type="info" id="rp1" previousmoveid="r3">
      <xml schema="stock_transactions" > >
        <PRICE_INFO>
          <COMPANY origin="user_specified">
          IBM</COMPANY>
          <PRICE origin="system_specified">
          110 ½</PRICE>
        </PRICE_INFO>
      </xml>
    </response>
    <request type="confirmation" id="r4" previousmoveid="r1">
      <xml schema="stock_transactions">
        <BUY >
          <COMPANY origin="user_specified">
          IBM</COMPANY>
          <QUANTITY origin="user_specified">
          100</QUANTITY>
          <ACCOUNT origin="system_inferred">
```

```
                12345</ACCOUNT>
               <PRICE origin="system_inferred">
                110 ½</PRICE
              </BUY >
            </xml>
          </responsetemplate>
             <schema id="stock_transactions"/>
          </responsetemplate>
        </request>
      </move>
</dmml>
```

USER: Make that 75 shares.

```
<dmml version="1.0">
    <move from="PM1" to="CDM" channel="web" id="i5">
       <request type="correction" id="r5" previousmoveid="r4">
         <xml schema="stock_transactions">
            <BUY >
               <QUANTITY origin="user_specification">
                75</QUANTITY>
             </BUY>
         </xml>
       </responsetemplate>
             <schema id="stock_transactions"/>
       </responsetemplate>
       </request>
    </move>
</dmml>
```

SYSTEM: Do you want me to execute a buy order of 75 shares of IBM at 110 1/2 from your checking account?
...

As suggested by the example above, the use of DMML for messaging between PM and CDM enables tremendous cost-efficiency for the development of multi-modal and multi-channel stock trading systems. The development costs are greatly reduced since we need to build one dialog manager instead of one for each channel. Also, enabling conversational access through new channels is relatively easy, since it entails only the building of another PM (e.g. using XSL) and not another dialog engine. Moreover, DMML gives us a mechanism to specify business specific syntactic and/or some semantic constraints using XML Schemas and ECMAScript.

Related Work

The act of uttering a sentence (through speech, typed in text, etc.) is called a speech act. When a speech act occurs, the following acts are preformed (Austin 1962):
- locutionary act: the act of the utterance being produced,
- illocutionary act: the act the speaker performs in uttering the words, and
- perlocutionary act: the act that actually occurs as a result of the utterance.

In DMML, we attempt to capture the illocutionary acts of human users when they interact with a conversational agent and the illocutionary acts of conversational agents when interacting with other conversational agents or a human user.

The Elephant 2000 programming language (McCarthy 1998) is a language sharing some of the design goals of DMML. However, while Elephant is intended to be a declarative programming language (based on speech act theory) for building intelligent agents, DMML is intended to be an interface language between such agents.

DMML can also be used for representing human-to-human dialogs. When used for this purpose, DMML is similar in spirit to the SGML annotation scheme (Isard et al. 98) used in the new version of the Edinburgh Map Task corpus[1] for providing abstract annotations for sophisticated human-to-human task-oriented dialogs. The annotations include dialog moves, dialogue games, dialog transactions, POS tagging etc. DMML offers additional constructs (like profiles) that facilitate the annotation of environmental (and other) constraints that the above work lacks.

DMML can also be used as a general agent communication markup language (e.g. KQML (Finin et al 1994)). DMML provides a standard (e.g. XML, XSL, XML Schemas, etc.) interface for interacting with dialog agents with certain characteristics. DMML satisfies Singh's (Singh 1998) criteria for a flexible and powerful agent markup language. DMML is an open language since its syntax can be extended (e.g. by defining different kinds of *requests*) and it allows open application markup embedded within the speech acts. DMML also satisfies the heterogeneity criterion since it allows agents of different design to talk to each other by exchanging their respective constraints. However, DMML does not satisfy the requirement that it's semantics be based on social agency, because (currently) DMML does not allow for the specification of norms of interpretation. For DMML-based languages, such norms have to be developed independently of specifying communication protocols (cf. Singh 1998). The DMML design assumes that the automated agents using DMML for communication are working together--without necessarily having knowledge of each other's environment--to achieve common business goals. Thus, (currently) there is an implicit assumption that the agents are benign, honest, cooperative, and share the semantics of the business transactions. These assumptions alleviate the need for a more rigorous semantic specification.

Work in progress

We are planning to use DMML in our architecture for building multi-modal multi-channel software applications. The goal is to build an architectural framework and tools that empower an application developer to author a business

---

[1] Currently the annotation scheme is being converted to XML.

application that can scale to multiple channels of interaction and modalities with relative ease. We intend to use this broad architecture as a platform to developing a series of conversational systems that can be accessed by multiple channels and modalities, e.g. web, telephone, etc.

In our architecture, DMML provides a modality- and channel-independent mechanism for describing communicative intent and environmental constraints of agents. The use of XML and related standards like XSL, ECMAScript, XML Schemas promotes inter-operability across heterogeneous platforms and software vendors.

We are currently finalizing a specification of version 1 of DMML, and implementing a series of APIs and accessory modules—as suggested in Figure 1—for use in the architecture described above. We plan to have a prototype system ready by fall 2000.

Conclusions

In this paper, we have presented Dialog Moves Markup Language (DMML), an XML language for interaction between conversational dialog agents. The elements of DMML are dialog moves representing communicative acts like requests, responses, assertions and commands, and dialog profiles representing constraints on dialog moves. DMML is designed to be an open markup language that allows agents to define and use their own sub-categorizations of the basic dialog moves. Hence DMML supports multiple levels of granularity/abstractions in representing natural language and multi-modal dialogs. Moreover, DMML supports communication between heterogeneous agents, because of the use of shared, common speech acts for communicating intentions and goals, rather than procedures for achieving these goals. All application specific markup is embedded within DMML elements and is in itself not part of DMML.

DMML supports multi-party, multi-modal, multi-channel interactions with a single dialog engine. The constructs of DMML are modality- and channel- independent by design and represent the abstract intentions of communicating agents. The use of XML enables relatively easy transformation to modality specific presentation languages such as VoiceXML and HTML. Thus, DMML enables tremendous cost efficiency in building conversational systems.

We believe DMML can be the basis for developing a standard XML based language for representing the communicative acts of arbitrary multi-modal multi-agent dialogs. However, currently DMML represents mainly assertive and directive communicative acts. In future work, we plan to evolve DMML to include other categories of communicative acts and representations of the social context shared by all communicating agents in the environment.

Acknowledgments

We thank all of our colleagues in the conversational machines group and in the DMML project team for many valuable insights and for their constant help.

References

Allen J. 1995. *Natural Language Understanding.* The Benjamin/Cummings Publishing Company, Inc., Redwood City, CA, USA. Second Edition.

Austin, J. L. (1962). *How to do things with words.* Oxford: Clarendon Press.

Bratman, M. E.; Israel, D.; and Pollack, M. E. 1988. Plans and resource-bounded practical reasoning. *Computational Intelligence*, 4:349—355.

Bray, T.; Paoli, J.; and Sperberg-McQueen, C., M. 1998. *Extensible Markup Language (XML) 1.0. Technical Report* http://www.w3.org/TR/REC-xml, World Wide Web Consortium Recommendation.

Clark, J. and Deach, S. 1998. *Extensible Stylesheet Language (XSL) 1.0. Technical Report*, http://www.w3.org/TR/WD-xsl-19980818.html, World Wide Web Consortium Working Draft.

Cohen, P. R.; Morgan, J.; and Pollack., M. E. eds., 1990. *Intentions in Communication*, The MIT Press, Cambridge, Massachusetts, USA.

Ferguson, G.; and Allen, J. 1998. TRIPS: An Integrated Intelligent Problem-Solving Assistant, Proceedings of AAAI-98 and IAAI-98, AAAI Press/ MIT Press, pp 567-572.

Finin, T.; Fritzson, R.; McKay, D.; and McEntire, R. 1994. KQML – A Language and Protocol for Knowledge and Information Exchange. Technical Report CS-94-02, Computer Science Department, University of Maryland and Valley Forge Engineering Center, Unisys Corporation.

Isard, A.; McKelvie, D.; and Thompson, H. 1998. Towards a minimal standard for dialogue transcripts: A new SGML architecture for the HCRC Map Task Corpus. Proceedings of ICSLP'98. Sydney.

McCarthy, J. 1998. Elephant 2000: A Programming Language Based on Speech Acts, Stanford University, http://www.formal.stanford.edu/jmc/elephant/elephant.html.

Singh, M.P., (1998). Agent Communication Languages: Re-thinking the principles. IEEE Computer, 31(12), pp 40-47.

Thompson, H. S.; Beech, D.; Maloney, M.; and Mendelsohn, N. (2000). XML Schema Part 1: Structures, http://www.w3.org/TR/xmlschema-1/.

VoiceXML (2000). Web site: www.voicexml.org, v1.0 specification: http://www.voicexml.org/specs/VoiceXML-100.pdf

Zadrozny, W.; Wolf, C.; Kambhatla, N.; and Ye, Y. (1998), Conversation Machines for Transaction Processing, Proceedings of IAAI'98, AAAI Press/MIT Press, pp 1160-1166.

Applying Learnable Evolution Model to Heat Exchanger Design

Kenneth A. Kaufman and Ryszard S. Michalski*

Machine Learning and Inference Laboratory
George Mason University
Fairfax, Virginia 22030-4444
{kaufman, michalski}@gmu.edu

* Also with the Institute of Computer Science, Polish Academy of Sciences, Warsaw, Poland

Abstract

A new approach to evolutionary computation, called *Learnable Evolution Model* (LEM), has been applied to the problem of optimizing tube structures of heat exchangers. In contrast to conventional Darwinian-type evolutionary computation algorithms that use various forms of mutation and/or recombination operators, LEM employs machine learning to guide the process of generating new individuals. A system, ISHED1, based on LEM, automatically searches for the highest capacity heat exchangers under given technical and environmental constraints. The results of experiments have been highly promising, often producing solutions exceeding the best human designs.

Introduction

This paper describes an application of a new approach to evolutionary computation, called *Learnable Evolution Model* (LEM), which employs machine learning to guide the process of generating new populations (Michalski 1998; 2000). LEM integrates two modes of operation, a Darwinian Evolution mode, which is based on traditional evolutionary computation methods (e.g., Holland 1975; Michalewicz 1996), and Machine Learning mode, which generates new individuals through a process of theory formation and instantiation. Specifically, Machine Learning mode generates hypotheses that characterize differences between groups of high performing and low performing individuals, and then instantiates these hypotheses to generate new individuals.

LEM has been applied to a range of function optimization problems (Michalski and Zhang 1999; Cervone 1999), and to the design of nonlinear filters (Coletti et al. 1999). In both applications, LEM significantly outperformed the evolutionary computation algorithms used in the experiments, sometimes speeding up the evolution process by two or more orders of magnitude in terms of the number of births (or generations).

This paper describes the application of LEM to the very complex practical problem of optimizing heat exchangers. The implemented program, ISHED1 (Intelligent System for Heat Exchanger Design) searches for the best arrangement of the evaporator tubes in the heat exchanger of an air conditioner. This is a very difficult problem because the search space is poorly structured and extremely large (there are about 10^{80} possible tube arrangements in a medium-sized heat exchanger). In order to avoid the cost of solving this problem for different operating conditions, manufacturers of air conditioning systems currently assume in their models average operating conditions (regarding the temperature, humidity, airflow, etc.). Since real conditions are often different from the assumed averages, such air conditioning systems tend to perform sub-optimally.

ISHED1 does not make such assumptions. It evolves toward structures that are best suited for any given technical constraints and environmental conditions. In the process of evolutionary design, it employs a heat exchanger simulator that serves as an evaluator of the proposed designs under the assumed conditions (Domanski 1989).

Problem Description

The problem of heat exchanger design is to seek a structure of tubes that provides the maximum heat transfer given technical and environmental constraints. These constraints include the size of the exchanger (the number of rows of tubes and the number of tubes per row), the refrigerant used, the outside air temperature and humidity, the flow of air through the heat exchanger, and others.

In an air conditioner, refrigerant flows through a loop. It is superheated and placed in contact with cooler outside air (within the condenser unit), where it transfers heat out and liquefies. Coming back to the evaporator, it comes into contact with the warmer interior air that is being pushed through the heat exchanger, thus cooling the air, and heating and evaporating the refrigerant.

The heat exchanger itself consists of an array of parallel tubes through which the refrigerant flows back and forth. A typical model is shown in Figure 1. In this figure, there

---

Copyright © 2000, American Association for Artificial Intelligence (www.aaai.org). All rights reserved.

are three rows of 16 tubes, with one inlet tube and two outlet tubes. The path from the inlet tube to the outlet tubes splits along the way. In general, there can be multiple inlet tubes, and the paths from each of them to the outlet tubes may or may not split. Individual tubes may be connected to each other in many different ways. The efficiency of the heat exchanger strongly depends on the

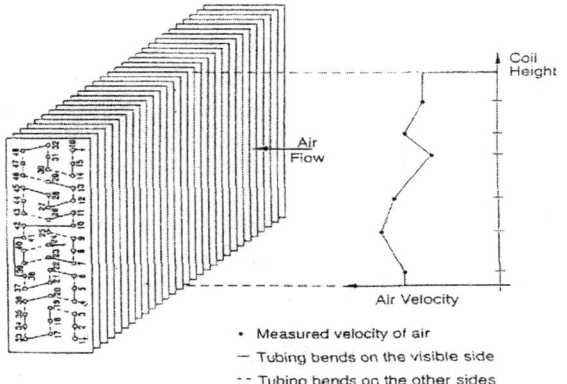

order in which the tubes are connected.

Figure 1: An Architecture of Evaporator Circuitry: A sample 16 x 3 configuration.

While the refrigerant flows through the tubes, air is forced through the unit, whose velocity/volume profile may be as illustrated in the figure. The air first comes into contact with and is cooled by the refrigerant in the first depth row, then in the subsequent rows.

The amount of cooling the air conditioner provides is the aggregate of the heat transfer provided by each of its tubes. Each tube's transfer is a function of the temperature and volume per unit time of both the air and the refrigerant coming into contact at that tube. Different orderings of the tubes affect the temperature and pressure of the refrigerant passing through each tube. The results of prior air/refrigerant interactions affect their temperatures at later interactions. Additionally, the refrigerant loses pressure (and velocity) while passing through the bends between tubes; it thus helps in maximizing heat transfer if adjoining tubes are physically close to each other.

In short, the goal of ISHED1 is to determine how to order the flow through the tubes such that heat transfer is maximized for the given constraints. Note that the number of depth rows and the number of tubes per row are mutable, and ISHED1 can handle different heat exchanger sizes so long as there are equal numbers of tubes in each row, the number of depth rows does not exceed 5, and the total number of tubes does not exceed 130.

ISHED1 is able to apply background knowledge reflecting the nature of the problem in order to constrain the search to plausible architectures. A user-defined parameter (or its default value) imposes limitations on the lengths of most tube bends. ISHED1 also enforces six real-world constraints on architectures, ranked from suggested to essential. The program rejects structures that violate a required constraint, and only under special circumstances (namely when designing a more compliant architecture is very difficult) generates structures that violate the most lenient constraints.

Two of the six constraints state that inlet tubes should not, and that tubes from which exit tubes receive their refrigerant should, be located next to exit tubes. These constraints allude to the fact that while through most of its travels through the heat exchanger the refrigerant is a mixture of liquid and gaseous coolant, and thus at a temperature close to its evaporation point at its current pressure, the refrigerant in the exit tube is all gas, and as such is warmed rapidly to a higher temperature by the exchange of heat (as opposed to the heat being used in a phase shift). There is some noticeable conduction of heat between the exit tubes and their immediate neighbors; this is minimized when the refrigerant in those neighboring tubes is also close to leaving the heat exchanger system. Similarly another constraint, the constraint that exit tubes should be in the first depth row, is based on the fact that the overall cooling will be most effective when this warmest refrigerant encounters some of the warmest air, and the coolest refrigerant meets already cooled air.

A constraint limiting splits in refrigerant paths is based on the unacceptable drops in refrigerant pressure that will occur if a single path undergoes multiple splits. Another constraint requiring inlets and outlets to be on the same side of the heat exchanger manifold is based on the structural requirements of the air conditioning unit, as is one that forbids looping in the refrigerant path.

Overview of ISHED1

The goal of ISHED1 is to apply the recently developed Learnable Evolution Model (Michalski 2000) to assist an expert in designing optimal heat exchanger architectures under given operating conditions. ISHED1 works in conjunction with two other major systems, a simulator, EVAP5, that evaluates the performance of given heat exchanger architectures (Domanski 1989) and a general purpose AQ-type inductive learning system (Michalski 1983, 2000; Kaufman and Michalski, 1998) that is employed in the Symbolic Learning Module of ISHED1.

Following the LEM methodology, ISHED1 integrates two evolutionary strategies: *Darwinian evolutionary learning* and *Symbolic evolutionary learning*. Figure 2 presents a general diagram of the implemented ISHED1 system. Darwinian evolutionary learning is performed by the Evolutionary Learning Module, and Symbolic evolutionary learning is performed by the Symbolic

Learning Module, which implements AQ-type inductive learning and a hypothesis instantiation module.

The Control Module takes the current population of candidate heat exchanger designs and determines which evolutionary strategy to apply. The selected strategy operates on the population, generates the subsequent population, and passes it to the simulator for evaluation of the individual structures. These structures and their evaluations are returned to the Control Module for the next generation (iteration).

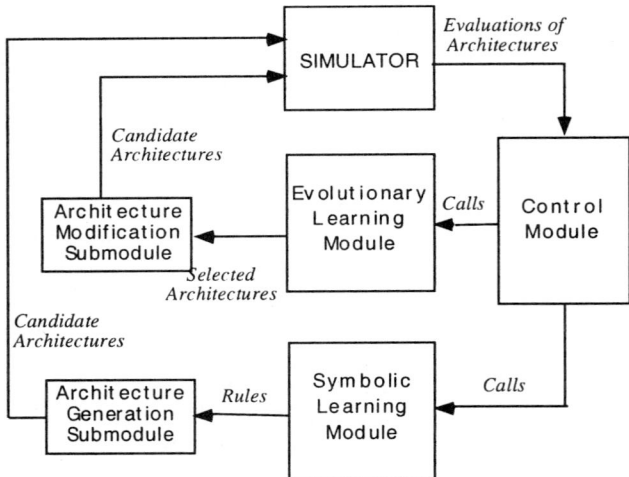

Figure 2: A general functional architecture of ISHED1.

Two related parameters guide the Control Module in determining which strategy to apply. Basically, ISHED1 applies Darwinian evolution until the population is no longer improving. It then switches to symbolic learning until similarly the performance (both in terms of the best individual and the population overall) has plateaued, continuing to alternate modes based on performance. Experiments have indicated that the application of a new strategy is often sufficient to remove the evolutionary process from the point where it has stalled.

Because of the nature of the problem and the feasible ways of internally representing heat exchanger structures, both evolutionary modules required problem-specific customization from previous LEM applications (e.g., Coletti et al. 1999; Michalski and Zhang 1999; Cervone and Michalski 2000). Traditional genetic operators would be, for the most part, unworkable in this domain, so eight analogous domain-specific *structure modifying* (SM) operators were implemented, such as swapping the positions of two adjacent tubes in the flow, or moving the source of a tube's refrigerant further upstream, in the process creating a split path. The SM operators change the characteristics of the candidate exchangers in ways that will most likely lead to *admissible* new structures, that is, structures satisfying the given physical and environmental constraints, as described above. A selected operator is tried repeatedly with different operands in order to generate a feasible structure, until it either succeeds or "times out" (based on limits specified in the user's control parameters), in which case another operator, hopefully more applicable, will be tried.

The second strategy, based on symbolic learning, examines the characteristics of both well- and poorly-performing designs, and automatically creates hypotheses (in the form of attributional rules) that characterize the better-performing architectures. These hypotheses are then applied to generate a new population of designs.

Due to the complexity of the domain, the learning program uses an abstract, rather than precise, specification of the different structures. Consequently, the learned rules also refer to abstract designs. These abstract rules allow the system to instantiate them in many different ways to produce specific designs. The rule instantiation process must, however, follow the previously mentioned constraints on designs. Generating heat exchanger architectures satisfying these constraints from a specification of inlet, outlet and split tubes is a computationally complex problem. To simplify it, ISHED1 usually generates only one architecture from a given specification of the key tubes.

To summarize, given instructions characterizing the environment for the sought heat exchanger design, an initial population of designs (either specified by the user, randomly generated, or a combination of the two), and parameters for the evolutionary process, ISHED1 evolves populations of designs using the above two strategies for a specified number of generations. At the end, it produces a report stating the best designs (architectures) found and their estimated capacity, as determined by the simulator. The ISHED1 control module determines when to apply each of the two evolutionary strategies (see Figure 2).

System Operation

Control Parameters

The first step of the ISHED1 operation is to read a file that defines the control parameters for the program and the characteristics of the desired architecture. These parameters, which override defaults when read, allow users latitude in controlling the system run. They can be grouped into the following clusters (some individual parameters are alluded to in multiple clusters):

- Parameters defining the characteristics of a heat exchanger: its size and its shape

- Parameters defining the characteristics of the initial population: its size, any user-specified first generation individuals, and the nature of the individuals randomly specified by the system

- Parameters defining the length of the evolutionary process
- Parameters describing the airflow through the heat exchanger, defined by a list of locations in the cross-section of the exchanger, and the velocities of the air at these locations. The velocities in other locations are linearly interpolated.
- Run control parameters, including the persistence of the Darwinian and symbolic learning modes, parameters for guiding Darwinian mode operation and symbolic mode architecture generation, and the level of detail to be presented in the output file.

Defining the Initial Set of Structures

ISHED1 allows a user to define an initial set of heat exchanger architectures. If the user does not define them, the system generates the initial set randomly. The user may define one or more initial architectures, and specify the number of copies of each architecture to be generated to fill the initial population. User-specified architectures may be based either on previous ISHED1 runs, or draw upon the user's knowledge of the problem, so as to test hypotheses or to try to improve upon industry models.

It is also possible that the user may define only a portion of the initial population, in which case the system randomly generates the remaining designs. The random generation process creates different types of architectures in proportions defined a priori in the program. These proportions are determined through estimations of the form promising architectures are likely to take, based on the number of tubes in the target heat exchanger.

System Control

The control module starts in Darwinian evolution mode using an elitist strategy (i.e., the best performing architecture so far *always* gets passed to the next generation as the first element of the new population). Elitism also is used in Symbolic learning mode; there the best architecture explored by the program so far *and* all architectures that were in the "good" class for rule learning propagate directly to the next generation. Elitism has proven to be an important feature of evolutionary computation processes and is used in many algorithms.

In Darwinian mode, the structure modifying operator selected for application to a given structure is chosen probabilistically, based on the topology of the heat exchanger structure (the number of inlets, outlets and splits). The probabilities are based on an estimate of how likely an application of this operator is likely to result in a favorable change. Typically, the less catastrophic operators and those that will maintain architectures with three inlets or fewer are favored.

Darwinian Evolution Module

A generation in the Darwinian Evolution Module follows the same three-step pattern that is followed by traditional genetic algorithms: a step in which individuals are probabilistically selected to be the basis for the next generation, with selection probability proportional to their evaluated fitness; a step in which the selected individuals are modified by various operators; and finally a step in which the members of this new population are evaluated.

To guide the modification of structures in the evolutionary design process in harmony with the heat exchanger design constraints, we developed and implemented eight Structure Modifying (SM) Operators for ISHED1, each of which makes a change in the heat exchanger design on which it is operating.

The system probabilistically selects an operator to apply, based on the topology of the heat exchanger design being operated on (the data representation maps out the architecture precisely by encoding a vector of each tube's refrigerant source). It will search for a feasible application of the operator, trying it with several different sets of operands if necessary. If it seems that the operator will not lead to a feasible change in the structure, another operator is tried; if the system is unable to admissibly apply an SM operator after a large number of iterations, the program has an escape clause, so as not to get stuck in an exit-less loop. In such a rare case, ISHED1 will apply a null operator to the structure.

Symbolic Learning Module

When the Symbolic Learning module is applied, members of the current population are divided into three classes based on their cooling capacity. If all individuals have identical performance, evolution in this mode is not possible, and Darwinian evolution will take place instead.

The range from best performance level in the population to the worst is examined. Individuals with performance in the top HFT% of this range are placed in the "good" class. Similarly, individuals in the bottom LFT% are placed in the "bad" class, where HFT and LFT (high and low fitness thresholds) are program parameters (in ISHED1 HFT=LFT=25%). Other individuals are placed in the "indifferent" class.

The AQ18 rule learning program (Kaufman and Michalski, 2000) generates a set of rules that distinguish "good" architectures from "bad", based on abstractions of the specific architectures. These rules are then instantiated in a different ways to generate new architectures. During consecutive generations, rules are used in the context of their predecessors, so as to further focus the concept of design optimality.

Each new generation consists of the best architecture discovered so far, architectures of the "good" class, and new architectures generated by instantiating the learned rules. If there are enough open slots in the population, each rule is applied at least twice, by rotating among them, ordered by the number of training examples satisfying each rule (called t-weights, which are indicators of the rule's strength). Finally, any other individuals are generated based on rules chosen probabilistically, with rules' probabilities proportional to their t-weights.

Experiments

During the course of ISHED1 development, many experiments with the system were conducted. The initial experiments concentrated on a well-known problem, using a common heat exchanger size and a fairly uniform airflow pattern. In these experiments, ISHED1 designs were comparable to the industry standard. One concern in some of these designs was that after many generations of Darwinian evolution, the designs would become chaotic in terms of their inter-tube connections. Nonetheless, using available tools, an engineer can smooth the connections, hopefully at little cost to the capacity of the exchanger.

In later experiments, the refrigerant was changed, and the airflow pattern was defined as highly non-uniform. Under such conditions, industry-standard heat exchangers do not perform well. The best ISHED1-produced architectures conformed intuitively to expectations of what a successful architecture in a non-uniform airflow should look like, and indeed performed far better than the currently used expert-designed structures.

Subsequent experiments varied the size and shape of the heat exchanger -- between 2 and 4 depth rows, with between 40 and 90 total tubes. Similar results were observed. During the final stage of development, we began experimenting with pre-specified members of initial populations. These results were to some degree mixed. When a very large portion of the initial population was pre-specified with known good architectures, further improvement could often be found. To some degree, the pre-specification is analogous to an initial symbolic learning step using the prior background knowledge; as a result, ISHED1 begins with a solid population.

But when fewer individuals were used to seed the initial population, improvement was hard to come by. While further experimentation is needed to determine if this is a regular occurrence, and if so its cause, it is possible that a level of imbalance is reached in the population that hinders both the establishment of large numbers of seeded examples and their kin for improvement, and the blossoming of promising, but relatively weak, randomly generated individuals. It is also possible that system parameters then need to be adjusted from default values.

While it is not possible to include an entire run log from even a single experiment due to the space limitation, a small sample of the ISHED1 output may be useful to provide a flavor of the program's operation. Such an excerpt, with some annotations added for readability (in italics), is shown in Figure 3. Parameters t, u and q associated with a rule characterize the rule's quality (Kaufman and Michalski, 2000).

In general, these experiments served to confirm the ability of ISHED1 to generate improved designs, and to adapt to different environmental situations. Thus, it has proven its potential to be a powerful tool for automating the heat exchanger design processes.

```
Exchanger Size: 16 x 3
Population Size: 15     Generations: 40
Operator Persistence: 5
Mode Persistence: GA-probe=2 SL-probe=1
Initial population:
Structure #0.3:  17  1  2  3  4  5  6  7  8  9 12 13 29 15
         31  I 18 33 20 36 22 38 24 40 26 42 11  2  7
         45 14 47 16 34 35 19 37 21 39 23 41 25 43
         44 28 46 30 48 32:  5.5376
Structure #0.8:  17  1 20  3  4 22  6 24  8 26 10 28
         27 15 16 32 33  2 18 19  5 38  7 40  9 42 11
         44 13 46 30 48 34 35 36  I 21 37 23 39 25
         41 27 43 29 45 31 47:  Capacity = 5.2099
and 13 others

Selected Members:  3, 2, 3, 7, 9, 3, 9, ...
Operations: NS(23, 39), SWAP(8), SWAP(28), ...,
            SWAP(29), SWAP(25), SWAP(1)
```

Below is one of the structures created by the application of a SM operator in Darwinian mode (by swapping the two tubes following tube 29 in Structure #0.8)

Generation 1:

```
Structure #1.13:  17  1 20  3  4 22  6 24  8 26 10 28
         27 15 16 32 33  2 18 19  5 38  7 40  9 42 11  4
         13 45 30 48 34 35 36  I 21 37 23 39 25 41
         27 43 46 29 31 47:  Capacity=5.2093
and 14 others.

Selected Members:  6, 15, 11, 3, 13, 1, ...
```

The program soon shifts into Symbolic Learning Mode:
Generation 5: Learning mode
```
Learned rule:
  [x1.x2.x3.x4.x5.x6.x7.x8.x9.x11.x12.x13.x14.x
  15.x17.x18.x19.x20.x21.x22.x23.x24.x25.x26.x2
  7.x28.x29.x30.x31.x32.x33.x34.x35.x36.x37.x38
  .x39.x40.x41.x42.x43.x44.x45.x46.x47.x48=regu
  lar] & [x10=outlet]&[x16=inlet]  (t:7,u:7,q:1)

An example of a generated structure:
Structure #5.1:  17  1  2  3  4  5  6  7  8  9 12 29 45 30
         31  I 18 33 20 36 22 38 24 40 26 42 11 27
         13 15 47 48 34 35 19 37 21 39 23 41 25 43
         44 28 46 14 32 16:  Capacity=5.5377
```

Below is a structure from the 21st generation:
Generation 21: Learning mode
```
Structure #21.15 2 18  4  1  6  3  5  7  8  9 12 13 45 15
         31  I 33 17 35 36 22 39 24 40 42 25 11 44
         30 46 32 47 34 19 20 37 21 23 38 41 26 43
         28 27 29 14 48 16:  5.5387
and 14 others

Selected Members:  11, 4, 4, 13, 15, 10, 12, 13,
15, 15, 12, 2, 3, 5, 10.
```

Finally, ISHED1 achieves:

```
Generation 40:
Structure #40.15:  33 17  2 41  4  5  6  9  7  8 12
                   29 46 45 47  I  1 34 20 36 22 38 24  3
                   42 43 44 27 13 15 32 16 18 11 19 37
                   21 32 23 25 40 26 28 35 30 14 48 31:
                   Capacity=6.3686
```

Figure 3: An excerpt from the log of an ISHED1 run.

Conclusion

A method and system ISHED1 was described that assists engineers in optimizing heat exchanger designs. The method is based on the Learnable Evolution Model, which uses machine learning to guide evolutionary computation.

Among the areas for potential improvement of ISHED1 are several aspects of the Symbolic Learning module. One of them concerns the rule instantiation process, which is currently fixed and may constrict the diversity of the population generated. It is also not clear how well the representation space we chose reflects the realities of the design task. An interesting topic for future development is the integration of constructive induction into the symbolic learning engine in order to find the best fit between the representation space and the problem at hand.

Experiments with ISHED1 have demonstrated that it is capable of generating designs equal or superior to the best human designs, particularly in cases of non-uniform airflow. It thus provides a powerful new tool for assisting engineers in designing heat exchangers based on the synergistic application of Darwinian evolution and symbolic learning from examples. It is believed that the described methodology can also be applied to other problems in engineering design.

ISHED1 was developed in collaboration with the National Institute of Standards and Technology (NIST), which is currently conducting extensive experiments with ISHED1 and introducing it to the air-conditioning manufacturing industry (Domanski 2000) for use in their design processes.

Acknowledgments

The authors express their deep gratitude to Dr. Piotr Domanski from the National Institute of Standards and Technology for introducing to them the problem of designing optimal heat exchangers, for his excellent collaboration on the project, and for providing the heat exchanger simulator used in ISHED1. They also thank the National Institute of Standards and Technology and International Intelligent Systems, Inc. for their support of this project. The LEM methodology and the basic machine learning algorithms used were developed in the Machine Learning and Inference Laboratory at George Mason University, which is supported by the National Science Foundation under grants IIS-9904078 and IRI-9510644.

References

Cervone, G. 1999. An Experimental Application of the Learnable Evolution Model to Selected Optimization Problems. Master's Thesis. *Reports of the Machine Learning and Inference Laboratory*, MLI 99-8, George Mason University, Fairfax, VA.

Cervone, G. and Michalski, R.S. 2000. Design and Experiments: LEM2 Implementation of the Learnable Evolution Model. *Reports of the Machine Learning and Inference Laboratory*, MLI 00-2, George Mason University, Fairfax, VA.

Coletti, M., Lash, T., Mandsager, C., Michalski, R.S., and Moustafa, R. 1999. Comparing Performance of the Learnable Evolution Model and Genetic Algorithms on Problems in Digital Signal Filter Design. *Proceedings of the 1999 Genetic and Evolutionary Computation Conference (GECCO)*.

Domanski, P.A. 1989. EVSIM - An Evaporator Simulation Model Accounting for Refrigerant and One Dimensional Air Distribution. NISTIR 89-4133.

Domanski, P.A. 2000. Evaporator Model with A Visual Interface. Presentation at *Winter Meeting of the American Society of Heating, Refrigeration and Air-conditioning Engineers (ASHRAE)*, Dallas, TX.

Holland, J. 1975. *Adaptation in Artificial and Natural Systems*. Ann Arbor: The University of Michigan Press.

Kaufman, K.A. and Michalski, R.S. 2000. The AQ18 System for Machine Learning: User's Guide. *Reports of the Machine Learning and Inference Laboratory*, MLI 00-3, George Mason University, Fairfax, VA.

Michalewicz, Z. 1996. *Genetic Algorithms+Data Structures = Evolutionary Programs*. Springer Verlag, 3rd edition.

Michalski, R.S. 1983. A Theory and Methodology of Inductive Learning. In Michalski, R.S. Carbonell, J. and Mitchell,T., eds., *Machine Learning: An Artificial Intelligence Approach*. Palo Alto: TIOGA Publishing Co., 83-134.

Michalski, R.S. 1998. Learnable Evolution: Combining Symbolic and Evolutionary Learning. *Proceedings of the Fourth International Workshop on Multistrategy Learning (MSL'98)*, 14-20.

Michalski, R.S. 2000. LEARNABLE EVOLUTION MODEL: Evolutionary Processes Guided by Machine Learning. *Machine Learning* 38, 9-40.

Michalski. R.S. and Zhang, Q. 1999. Initial Experiments with the LEM1 Learnable Evolution Model: An Application to Function Optimization and Evolvable Hardware. *Reports of the Machine Learning and Inference Laboratory*, MLI 99-4, George Mason University, Fairfax, VA.

A Campus-wide University Examination Timetabling Application

Andrew Lim, Ang Juay Chin, Ho Wee Kit, Oon Wee Chong

School of Computing,
National University of Singapore, Singapore
{alim, angjc, howeekit, oonwc}@comp.nus.edu.sg

Abstract

The authors of this paper were tasked to create an automated campus-wide timetabling system, for both course and examination timetable scheduling, for the National University of Singapore. This paper explains the development and design of the exam-scheduling portion of the University Timetable Scheduler (UTTS) software. The preliminary results of the application of the AC3 algorithm on this problem are also shown, and indicate the tremendous potential benefits of such a system.

Introduction

Beginning in the 1993/1994 academic year, the National University of Singapore (NUS) introduced a modular academic course structure to give students greater control over the content of their course of study. This new structure has overall been a welcome change, but the students have largely been restricted to choosing courses within their own faculty. NUS is now following up by introducing cross-faculty modules, which are subjects that can be taken by students from various faculties. It is the intention of NUS to eventually offer program comprising of up to 30% cross-faculty modules. More information on the National University of Singapore and its course structure can be found at the NUS Website[1].

The introduction of cross-faculty modules greatly increases the difficulty in scheduling both the course and examination timetables. In particular, examination timetable scheduling (handled by the administration department for the entire university) is made much more difficult as cross-faculty modules must be placed in an available timeslot for students from several faculties. In view of this, NUS has tasked the authors of this paper to create an automated course and examination timetable scheduler, with the working title of University Timetable Scheduler (UTTS).

---

[1] http://www.nus.edu.sg

Copyright © 2000, American Association for Artificial Intelligence (www.aaai.org). All rights reserved.

Aspects of the course-scheduling portion of UTTS are described in a separate paper (Lim et al. 2000a). This paper describes the development of the exam-scheduling portion. We will first give an account the way examination timetabling is done currently in NUS. We then describe the system design of UTTS, bearing in mind the possible conversion to a Client/Server application in the future. Finally, we will describe the current status of our program, with the results and statistics of our preliminary testing.

The Current System

At present, the University's policy is to schedule all examinations before student enrolment. Hence, it is the duty of all students to make sure that they choose courses with examinations that do not clash. Obviously, this is undesirable as it unnecessarily restricts the students' choices. It is therefore an aim of any timetable to have as few such potential clashes as possible.

The University's examination timetable scheduling is currently handled by the Administration department, which must organize and schedule all the examinations in a particular semester for each and every faculty. We interviewed the timetabling officer from the Administration department to find out their current timetabling process.

At the moment, this difficult process is still being done by hand. The process of creating the resultant timetable is as follows:

1. Each faculty puts forward a request for a certain number of days, timeslots and seats to the Administration Department.

2. The timetabling officer assigns each faculty a certain number of days, timeslots and seats. The number for each faculty is based on a combination of the requested number, enrolment figures, availability of resources and previous experience. History has shown that there are never enough resources to accommodate the wishes of all the faculties. The timetabling officer also reserves a number of "spare" slots for emergencies.

3. Each faculty then attempts to create a feasible examination timetable using the resources they have been assigned. Some faculties further break down these resources to departmental level, and produce a collated timetable of all the departments.

4. Inevitably, some faculties will find that the resources allocated to them are insufficient to create a feasible timetable. They then contact the Administration department to request for more resources. Depending on need and availability, the timetabling officer would then allocate more resources to the requesting faculty from the pool of "spare" slots.

5. This cycle of request/allocation continues until all the examinations have been scheduled satisfactorily.

In practice, this procedure has many disadvantages:

1. The initial allocation of days and slots is likely to be sub-optimal. This is because it is difficult to judge the effect of changes in student enrolment and registration.

2. Human nature and expediency dictates that the initial request for resources would be a value somewhat greater than what is strictly required. This is understandable, as the individual faculties would like some room to maneuver in case of unforeseen emergencies.

3. Due to the above points, the process is extremely time-consuming. The cycles of request and allocation (coupled with episodes of negotiation an compromise) can take several weeks to resolve.

4. The process is also error-prone, due to the large amount of data to consider. The act of verification is difficult, and there has been a case of a conflict that was overlooked until a very late stage, and its correction was awkward and troublesome.

The automated examination timetable scheduler aims to eliminate these problems. In particular, the UTTS Exam Scheduler would take as its most important inputs the set of examinations and candidates, and the set of constraints from each faculty. Hence the adequacy of resources could be more accurately determined, along with the task of their allocation. Furthermore, if the system proves successful, we can then experiment with scheduling the examinations only after student registration.

Functions of the Automated System

When we started work on the UTTS Examination Scheduler, we strove to achieve the following aims:

- To create an examination timetable that schedules all examinations, invigilators, registrar staff and required equipment. The most important criterion is that two examinations taken by the same student should not be scheduled at the same time. The preferences of invigilators and registrar staff are relatively less important than the ability of a candidate to sit for his registered examination. Equipment required for an examination can be treated simply as an attribute for the examination, and should have little or no effect on the actual timetable scheduling.

- To drastically reduce the time taken to schedule the examination timetable, while at the same time satisfying (as much as possible) the constraints imposed by the user. Aside from the obvious benefits of saved time, an automated timetable scheduler that can produce a timetable in minutes rather than days or weeks opens up possibilities of simulating policy changes.

- To minimize the total number of days taken for the entire examination period. The total number of days occupied is used to judge the "goodness" of a timetable solution.

- To reduce the number of examinations held at the IMM Building, which would result in a definite monetary saving (see the Problem Domain section below).

- To produce a candidates' seating plan. This is the least important aim, as it is just a tool of convenience for the users. To the scheduling engine, where a particular student sits within an examination venue is irrelevant.

Problem Domain

In order to test our eventual system, we obtained student registration data from the NUS Computer Center for both semesters of the academic years 1997/1998 and 1998/1999, as well as for the first semester of academic year 1999/2000. The data that was obtained from the Computer Center consisted of a set of text files, each containing the list of student-examination tuples. We converted the text files into *Microsoft Access*™ files, which enabled us to make use of SQL queries for the data.

As an example of our problem domain, we present the

statistics for Semester I of the 1998/1999 academic year. This consists of 21607 students, each taking one or more of 1561 papers. Some relevant facts include:

- The number of candidates sitting for an examination ranges from as few as 1 (152 papers) and as many as 1283 (Mathematics A, EG1401).

- Each examination requires a number of invigilators to be present, of which at least one must be a Chief Invigilator.

- Most examinations also require one or more members of the Registrar's Office to be present.

- Some of the examinations are labeled "open-book" examinations, meaning that the candidates are allowed to bring reference materials into the examination venue. The remaining are considered "closed-book", where no reference materials are allowed.

These examinations are scheduled to the following venues:

Alias	Venue	Capacity
IMM	IMM Exhibition Hall	1600
GYM	Gymnasium	312
MPH1	Multi-Purpose Sports Hall 1	750
MPH2	Multi-Purpose Sports Hall 2	850
CH	Competition Hall	396

Table 1: List of Examination Venues

The IMM Building is a commercial building that is not owned by NUS. The venues in the IMM Building must be rented by the University for the purpose of holding the examinations.

Using the current manual system, the timetable that was produced started from 27 October 1998 to 28 November 1999, comprising 47 sessions.

System Design

The UTTS system design is based on the 3-Tier architecture that is commonly used when building Client/Server applications. It keeps distinct the GUI, object oriented and data storage portions of our program. By separating the system into 3 tiers, they can be worked on independently (Reese, 1997).

UTTS is divided into the following 3 tiers. The *View* tier involves the graphical user interface. The *Application* tier is composed of the modules in an object-oriented paradigm that manipulate the objects in the system. This includes the scheduling engine, the printing modules and the report generator. Finally, the *Persistence* layer consists of the actual database access. Figure 1 shows the UTTS system design.

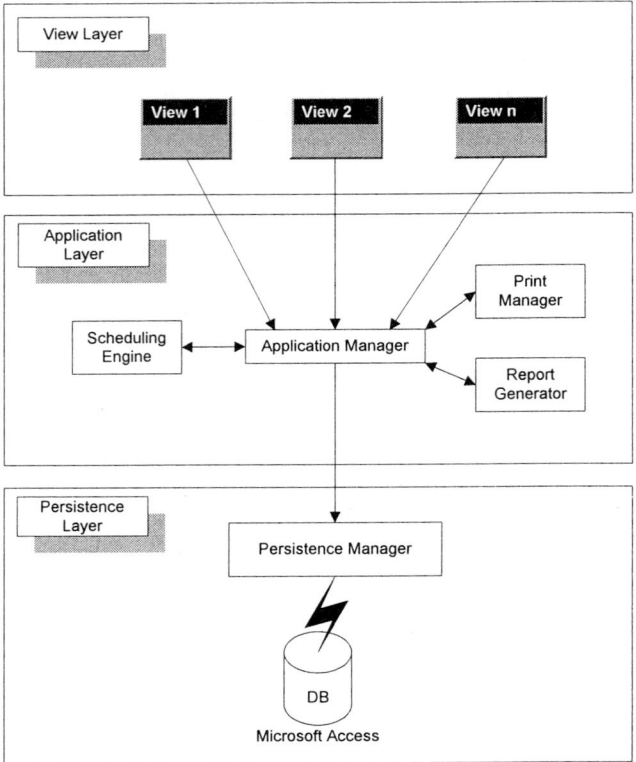

Figure 1: UTTS System Architecture

When deciding on our system design, we had to balance the factors of program speed and memory use. One naïve implementation would be to load all data into the main memory during program load time. However, this would take up an unnecessary amount of memory, since it is unlikely that all the information stored in the databases would be required. The starting load time would also increase. In our design, we read information into memory on an "as-needed" basis. We keep a `MasterList` in the *persistent* layer that retains the list of objects read from the database, and the actions performed on them. This `MasterList` is also useful for undoing actions. For example, when the user requests for information on a particular student, the information flow is as follows:

1. The GUI requests for the student information from the *application server* layer by calling `server.getStudent(studentIndex)`.
2. The *application server* layer uses the *persistence manager* class to retrieve this information, calling `persistent.get(studentIndex)`.

3. The *persistence manager* class first checks if the wanted student can be found in the `MasterList`. If it can, the correct student object is returned straight from the `MasterList`. If not, it asks the *student* class to load the required student object.
4. The *student* class delegates its *studentPeer* class to retrieve the appropriate information from the database. The student object is then returned to the GUI, and that student object is updated to the `MasterList`.

In this way, both database access and memory usage are minimized.

Scheduling Engine

The Examination Timetabling Problem is both a constraint satisfaction problem (CSP) as well as an optimization problem. In the exam-timetabling problem, we are typically given a set of both hard and soft constraints. Two *hard* constraints that must be satisfied are:

- No student is required to be present for two or more examinations in the same time slot.
- There number of seats at a venue is sufficient to accommodate all the students scheduled to take an examination there.

In addition, we would also like to handle the following constraints if possible (*soft* constraints):

- *Staff S* is required to invigilate at least x sessions and at most y sessions.
- Separate all open and closed-book examinations.
- Separate all examinations with different duration.
- Spread all examinations of a student over the examination period as much as possible.
- Any 2 papers of a student should be placed minimally x sessions or y days apart.
- *Paper A* be placed x days away from *Paper B*
- *Paper A* to be held before *Paper B*
- *Paper A* and *Paper B* to be held simultaneously
- *Paper A* and *Paper B* are not to be held simultaneously
- *Paper A* to be held as early/late as possible in the examination period
- *Paper A* is to be held in session s
- *Paper A* is to be held on/before/after date d
- *Paper A* is to be held within period $(d1, d2)$
- *Paper A* must not be held during period $(d1, d2)$
- *Paper A* is to be held in week n.
- *Paper A* is to be held at venue v.
- *Paper A* is to be held at a venue belonging to venue group g.

The user can assert any or all of the above soft constraints. Our objective in any case is to generate a conflict-free timetable, which minimizes the number of time slots used. In consideration of the nature of our problem and the variety of constraints that we have to handle, we have combined our main scheduling algorithm together with a consistency algorithm.

For our first attempt, the main scheduling algorithm used is based on a weighted sum of three measures. Each paper has a weight computed as follows:

- Measure 1 is based on the number of candidates taking this paper
- Measure 2 is based on the constraint degree of this paper (i.e., the number of other papers affected by the scheduling of this paper)
- Measure 3 is based on the number of slots that cannot be used for scheduling this paper, due to one or more constraint conflicts

PaperWeight = α*Measure1* + β*Measure2* + γ*Measure3* where $\alpha + \beta + \gamma = 1$

With this weighted scheme, the main algorithm can be described as follows:

1. Let Q be a Priority Queue of papers sorted by *PaperWeight*
2. While Q is not empty
   Dequeue paper p in Q
   Find the first available time slot for paper p
   If the time slot is found then
       Assign paper p to the found time slot
   Else
       Return Failure
3. Return Success

We model our problem as a CSP and derive a constraint graph. Each paper corresponds to a vertex of the constraint graph with its associated domain. Each constraint relation P(X, Y) corresponds to the two arcs (X, Y) and (Y, X) in the graph.

We apply the arc consistency algorithm, AC-3 (Mackworth 1977), to perform domain reduction at the start of the scheduling algorithm, as well as during each assignment of a paper to a time slot. The AC-3 algorithm basically makes the entire graph arc-consistent by considering a set of potentially inconsistent arcs. While the queue is not empty, an arc is removed from the queue and considered. If it is not consistent, its domain is revised and made consistent. As a result, all other consistent arcs that could have become inconsistent are inserted back into the queue.

Exam Data Information	1998/99 semester 1			1998/99 semester 2		
No. of Candidates	21607			21591		
No. of Candidates_Paper	101197			93693		
No. of Time Conflicts	23751			24424		
Max Degree of Time Conflicts	277			285		
Connectivity of Constraint Graph	1.95%			2.05%		
Comparison	Papers	# Slots	Time(s)	Papers	# Slots	Time(s)
Manual System	1282	47	-	1248	48	-
UTTS (M1=0.1, M2=0.8, M3=0.1)	1561	30	381	1545	29	368

Table 2: UTTS test results

One advantage of performing domain reduction using AC-3 is that we can handle the various constraints easily. In addition, with the use of AC-3, our main scheduling algorithm requires a minimum effort in finding the first available slot for each paper. We could also determine the number of slots that are being eliminated for a given paper (as used in Measure 3) easily.

When using AC-3, we need to perform an arc-consistency check whenever a paper is assigned a slot. However, this overhead is relatively cheap compared to naïve implementation of computing the availability of the all time slots for every unscheduled paper. Thus, making use of AC-3 helps to improve the efficiency of our scheduling algorithm.

Test Results

The data we acquired from the computer center contained some anomalies of students taking an illogical number of examinations. In particular, there were instances of students taking more than 20 papers in the semester. We suspect that this is due to the inclusion of non-examinable and/or exempted papers in the database. As there was no convenient way to remove these cases, they remained in our test data.

Another discrepancy between our test data is the number of examinations to be scheduled. Our test data includes non-examinable subjects, which as previously stated cannot be conveniently extracted. Furthermore, some examinations in the manual timetable were scheduled in small classrooms and laboratories, and these alternative sites are not used in our simulation. Hence, our results are based on more papers, to be scheduled in fewer venues, and may be worse than in an actual implementation.

Table 2 shows the results of running the UTTS program on our sets of test data, and also compares the actual timetables that were created by the manual process and the timetables generated by our program. In these results, we have only taken into account the 2 hard constraints.

As can be seen, despite having to schedule more papers in a smaller capacity, our heuristic produced much better results than the actual manual system. For Semester I of the 1998/1999 academic year, UTTS produced a timetable that makes use of a mere 30 slots, compared to 47 for the manual system. Similarly, 29 slots were used compared to 48 for Semester II of the same academic year. These results were obtained in around 6 minutes per test case.

Since our tests only take into account the 2 hard constraints, we cannot view these results as ironclad. Nonetheless, it is obvious that our automated system can potentially result in a timetable with a shorter duration than the traditional manual system.

Our tests were performed on a Pentium-500 PC with 128MB RAM. The system was coded in JDK 1.1 and JFC 1.03 using *IBM VisualAge™ for Java*.

Future Directions

The development of an automated examination-timetabling program is a large project, and there will be several cycles of development, testing, user feedback and implementation to be done before the final product is deployed. The major aspects include the handling of more constraints, the advancement to the Client/Server architecture, and better scheduling algorithms. Efforts have already been made in the direction of improved scheduling algorithms by the UTTS team (Lim and Fu, 2000).

UTTS is an ongoing project, with improvements and refinements to be made as the program undergoes actual use.

Conclusion

This paper details the development process and techniques of an automated examination-timetabling program. We show our system design based on the 3-tier architecture, which is appropriate for our purposes. We also show the results of implementing the AC-3 algorithm on our constraint-propagation scheduling engine, and note that the results are at least comparable to those achieved by the current manual system, and in a much shorter time, when implemented on the basic hard constraint set.

We believe that our system shows the great potential benefits of automating the examination-timetabling task in a large university like NUS.

References

The National University of Singapore Website, http://www.nus.edu.sg

A. Lim, W. C. Oon, J. C. Ang, W. K Ho, *Development of a Campus-wide University Course Timetabling Application: Input Issues*, forthcoming.

A. Lim, Z. Fu, *The Examination Scheduling Problem*, forthcoming.

A. K. Mackworth, Consistency in Networks of Relations, *Artificial Intelligence* 8 (1977): 88-119

G. Reese, *Database Programming with JDBC and Java*, O'Reilly 1997.

An Expert System for Recognition of Facial Actions and Their Intensity

M. Pantic and L.J.M. Rothkrantz

Delft University of Technology
Faculty of ITS - Department of Knowledge Based Systems
P.O. Box 356, 2600 AJ Delft, the Netherlands
{M.Pantic,L.J.M.Rothkrantz}@cs.tudelft.nl

Abstract

The Facial Action Coding System (FACS) is an objective method for quantifying facial movement in terms of 44 component actions, i.e. Action Units (AUs). This system is widely used in behavioral investigations of emotion, cognitive process and social interaction. Highly trained human experts (FACS coders) presently perform the coding. This paper presents a system that can automatically recognize 30 AUs, their combinations and their intensity. The system employs a framework for hybrid facial feature detection and an expert system for facial action coding in static dual-view facial images. Per facial feature, multiple feature detection techniques are applied and the resulting redundant data is reduced so that an unequivocal facial expression geometry ensues. Reasoning with uncertainty is used to encode and quantify the encountered facial actions based on the determined expression geometry and the certainty of that data. Eight certified FACS coders tested the system. The recognition results demonstrated rather high concurrent validity with human coding.

Introduction

Facial expressions play the main role in the non-verbal aspect of human communication [11]. Besides, facial movements that comprise facial expressions provide information about affective state, personality, cognitive activity and psycho-pathology. The Facial Action Coding System (FACS) [4] is the leading method for measuring facial movement in behavioural science. FACS is currently executed manually by highly trained human experts (i.e. FACS coders). Recent advances in computer technology open up the possibility for automatic measurement of facial signals. An automated system would make classification and quantification of facial expressions widely accessible as a tool for research and assessment in behavioural science and medicine. Such a system could also form the front-end of an advanced human-computer interface that performs interpreting (e.g. [10]) communicative facial expressions.

This paper presents a system that performs facial expression recognition as applied to automated FACS encoding. From 44 facial actions defined by FACS, our system automatically recognizes 30 facial actions, their combinations and their intensity by applying different AI techniques and non-AI techniques integrated into a single system. We use a hybrid approach, i.e. a combination of different image processing techniques, to extract facial expression information from a static dual-view image. Then we employ a rule-based expert system to encode and quantify the encountered facial actions from the extracted facial expression information and the certainty of that data. Finally another expert system is applied to adjust this result (if necessary), based on an emotional classification of the encountered facial expression. Validation studies on the prototype demonstrated that the recognition results achieved are in 90% consistent with those of eight FACS coders. In addition it has been shown that the quantification of the facial action codes achieved by the system deviates in average for 8% from that done by the FACS coders.

Facial Action Coding System

The Facial Action Coding System (FACS) [4] has been developed to facilitate objective measurement of facial activity for behavioural science investigations of the face. It is a system designed for human observers to visually detect independent subtle changes in facial appearance caused by contractions of the facial muscles. In a form of rules, FACS provides a linguistic description of all possible visually detectable facial changes in terms of 44 so-called Action Units (AUs). Using these rules, a trained human FACS coder decomposes an observed expression into the specific AUs that produced the expression.

Although FACS is the most prominent method for measuring facial expressions in behavioral science, a major impediment to its widespread use is that its manual application is time consuming in addition to the time required to train human experts. Each minute of videotape takes approximately one hour to score and it takes 100 hours of training to achieve minimal competency on FACS. Automating FACS would not only make it widely accessible as a research tool, it would also increase the speed of coding and improve the precision and reliability of facial measurement.

In addition to providing a tool for behavioral science research, a system that outputs facial action codes would provide an important basis for man-machine interaction systems. In natural interaction only 7% of the meaning of a communicative message is transferred vocally while 55% is transferred by facial expressions [11]. FACS provides a description of the basic elements of any facial expression. Integration of automated systems for facial action coding, speech recognition and interpretation of those communicative signals would make human-computer interaction more natural, more efficient and more effective.

Automatic Recognition of Facial Actions

Recent advances in computer vision and pattern analysis facilitated automatic analysis of facial expressions from images. Different approaches have been taken in tackling the problem: analysis of facial motion [6], [1], [12], grey-level pattern analysis [20], analysis of facial features and their spatial arrangements [2], [8], [13], [10], holistic spatial pattern analysis [7], [17]. The image analysis techniques in these systems are relevant to the goal of automatic facial expression data extraction, but the systems themselves are of limited use for behavioural science investigations of the face. In many of these systems the discrimination of expressions remained at the level of few emotion categories, such as happy, sad or surprised, rather than on a finer level of facial actions. Yet, for investigations of facial behaviour itself, such as studying of the difference between genuine and simulated affective state, an objective and detailed measure of facial activity such as FACS is needed.

Explicit attempts to automate facial action coding in images are few [3]. Black et al. [1] use local parameterised models of image motion and few mid-level predicates that are derived from the estimated motion parameters and describe the encountered facial change. Here the specificity of optical flow to action unit discrimination has not been described. Essa et al. [6] use spatio-temporal templates to recognise two facial actions and four prototypic emotional expressions. Cohn et al. [2] achieved some success in automating facial action coding by feature point tracking of a set of points manually located in the first frame of an examined facial image sequence. Their method can identify 8 individual AUs and 7 AUs combinations. Here, each image sequence should start with a neutral facial expression and may not contain more than one face action in a row.

In fact, it is not known whether any of the methods reported up-to-date is sufficient for describing the full range of facial behaviour. None of the systems presented in the literature deals with both, facial action coding and quantification of the codes.

A New Approach

This paper presents a system capable of interpreting static dual-view facial images in terms of facial actions and their intensities involved in the shown facial expression. The system was developed to achieve both:
1. person independent, robust, fully automatic extraction of facial expression information from a dual-view
2. robust, fully automatic quantified facial action coding.

The study of feasibility demonstrated that a rule-based expert system, combined with image analysis techniques for facial expression information extraction, is appropriate paradigm for expression recognition as applied to automated FACS encoding. Here, the rule-based character of FACS and the overall characteristics of the task (i.e. it is a cognitive task that involves reasoning rather than numerical computation on a stable and narrow knowledge domain defined by FACS) decided the issue.

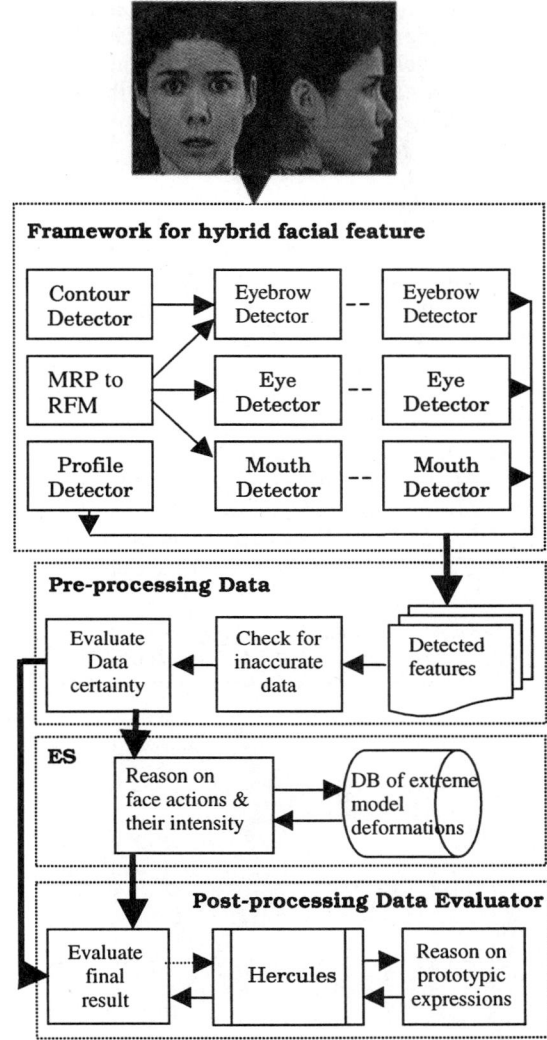

Figure 1. System architecture

Our system consists of four integral parts (Figure 1): data generator, data evaluator, data analyzer and post-processor. The Facial Data Generator is a framework for "hybrid" facial expression information extraction from a dual-view facial image where for each prominent facial feature (eyes, eyebrows, nose and mouth) multiple feature detectors are applied. This part of the system is presented first. Then the Data Evaluator is explained. The Facial Data Evaluator selects per facial feature the best from the results of the applied detectors, substitutes missing data by setting and checking hypotheses about the overall facial appearance and assigns certainty measures (i.e. our confidence in data) to the evaluated data. The Facial Data Analyzer, presented next in this paper, has been implemented as a rule-based expert system that converts the evaluated facial expression data into quantified facial action codes. Finally the Post-Processor is presented. It is a CLIPS implemented rule-based expert system, which classifies the current expression into one of the six basic emotions [5] and based on the result adjusts (if necessary) the result obtained in the previous processing stages. The paper provides technical data on system development, software environment, testing procedures and results. A discussion about the strengths and limitations of the system concludes the paper.

Facial Data Generator

FACS was primarily developed for human observers to perform facial action encoding from full-face photographs of an observed person. Efforts have recently turned to measuring facial actions by image processing of video sequences [2], [6], [1]. This became a trend since there is a growing psychological research that argues that facial expression dynamics are critical in expression analysis. Nevertheless, our work is more in line with the original purpose of FACS – measuring of static facial actions. In our system only the end-state of the facial movement is measured in comparison to an expressionless face of the same subject. The movement itself is not measured.

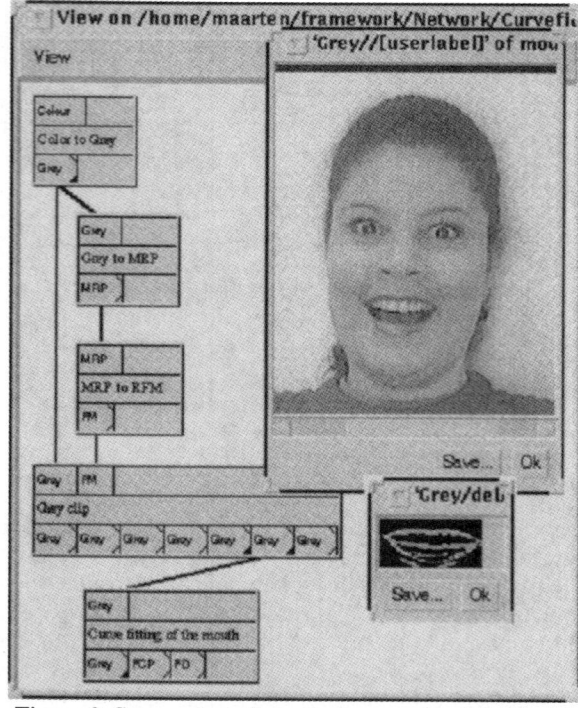

Figure 2. Screen shot of stand-alone mode of the Facial Data Generator

The system deals with static dual-view facial images. Two digitized cameras mounted on the head of the user acquire the images. The cameras are fastened to two holders attached to a headphone-like device. One camera holder is placed in front of the face at approximately 15 centimeters from the tip of the nose (obtains the frontal view). The other camera is placed on the right side of the face at approximately 15 centimeters from the center of the right cheek (obtains the side view). The camera setting ensures the presence of the face in the scene and some out-of-plane head motions cannot be encountered together with the non-rigid facial motion (i.e. the images are scale and orientation invariant).

The existing systems for facial image analysis usually utilize a single kind of feature detectors [3]. In contrast, we are proposing a hybrid approach to facial expression data extraction. To localize the contours of the prominent facial feature (eyebrows, eyes, nose and mouth), for each feature the Facial Data Generator concurrently applies multiple detectors of different kinds. For instance, a neural network-based approach originally proposed by Vincent et al. [16] that finds the micro-features of the eyes and an active contour method proposed by Kass et al. [9] with a greedy algorithm for minimizing the snake's energy function [19] perform currently automatic detection of the eyes. But, any other detector picked up "off the shelves" that achieves localization of the eye contour can be used instead. For profile detection, a spatial approach to sampling the profile contour from a thresholded side-view image is applied [18]. Instead of fine-tuning the existing feature detectors or inventing new ones, known techniques are combined.

The motivation for integrating multiple detectors is the increase in quality of a "hybrid detector". Each typical feature detector has circumstances under which it performs better than another detector. Hence, the chances for successful detection of a given feature increase with the number of integrated detectors. Therefore, by integrating different detectors per facial feature into a single framework, the percentage of missing data is reduced.

The requirement posed on the development of the Facial Data Generator was the integration of the existing detectors in an easy-to-enlarge interactive user-friendly platform that can operate stand-alone as well as a part of a larger system. The stand-alone mode, illustrated in Figure 2, is used for testing of different detectors. Availability of JDK and JNI made Java perfectly suitable for the development of such a software platform. More details about the design of the Facial Data Generator and the integrated feature detectors can be found in [14].

After invoking all integrated detectors, each localized facial feature contour is stored in a separate file. The files form the input to the Facial Data Evaluator (Figure 1).

Facial Data Evaluator

The Facial Data Evaluator operates in two stages. First it delimits the geometry of the encountered expression by choosing the "best" of the redundantly detected facial features stored in the files, which form the output of the Facial Data Generator. In the second stage, the defined facial expression geometry is represented in terms of our face model. The set of the face-model points, together with the assigned *certainty factors* (CFs), forms the input to the Facial Data Analyzer.

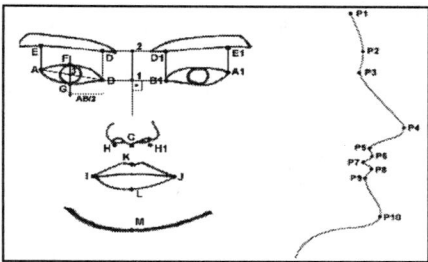

Figure 3. Face model

Selection among the Detected Facial Features

The reasoning of the first stage applies the knowledge about the facial anatomy (e.g. the inner corners of the eyes are immovable points) to check the correctness of the results achieved by the facial feature detectors. Based on this check, each file forming the output of the Facial Data Generator is flagged with one of the labels: *good*, *missing*, *missing one*, *highly inaccurate* and *highly inaccurate one*. If a single point represents the localized contour of a facial feature, the file containing that result is labeled as *missing*. In the case of the pair features (eyes and brows), the file may be labeled as *missing one*. A file is labeled as *highly inaccurate* if there is a lack of consistency in the extracted facial expression geometry. For example, a file containing the result of an eye detector is labeled as *highly inaccurate one* if the localized inner corner of an eye deviates for more than 5 pixels from the inner corner of the pertinent eye localized in the expressionless face of the same subject. The files that pass this check are labeled as *good*. Finally an inter-file consistency check is performed. If the contour stored in the tested file deviates for more than 10 pixels in any direction from relevant contours stored in the other files, the tested file is discarded.

When all of the files are evaluated in terms of missing and highly inaccurate data, the files labeled as *missing* or *highly inaccurate* are discarded and the facial expression geometry is determined by the results stored in the left over files. To make the best choice between the results of different detectors, which detect the same feature, the priorities $n \in \mathbb{N}$ are used. These have been off-line manually assigned to the integrated detectors based on their overall evaluation results. Each facial feature is delimited by the content of a not discarded file that comprises that feature detected by the detector of the highest priority. The priority of the selected detector n (where $n = N$ is the highest priority a detector can have) determines the CF assigned to the feature as given in formula (1).

In the case of the eyes and eyebrows it may happen that the remained files are labeled as *missing one* or *highly inaccurate one*. The eye/eyebrow that has been successfully localized by a detector with the highest priority is used to substitute its pair feature that has been badly localized. The CF of the successfully detected feature is set according to formula (1), while the CF of the feature being replaced is calculated as given in formula (2).

$$CF = (1 / N) * n \quad (1)$$
$$CF = (1 / (N + 1)) * n \quad (2)$$

If detection of a certain feature fails (i.e. all of the relative files are discarded), the pertinent feature detected in the expressionless face of the same subject is used to substitute the missing feature. The CF assigned to the feature being substituted in this way is set to *1/2N*.

Representation by the Face Model

We utilize a point-based face model composed of two 2D facial views, namely the frontal and the side view (Figure 3). There are two main motivations for this choice. First, the rules of FACS can be converted straightforwardly into the rules for deforming a point-based face model. Second, the validity of the model can be inspected visually by comparing the changes in the model and the changes in the modeled expression.

The frontal-view face model is composed of 19 facial points. The utilized side-view face model consists of 10 profile points, which correspond with the peaks and valleys of the curvature of the profile contour function [18].

Since all of the detectors integrated into the Facial Data Generator extract contours of the facial features and since the images are scale- and orientation invariant, localizing the model points from the extracted contours of the facial features is straightforward. For instance, point A and point B are localized as the outermost left, respectively, the outermost right point of the contour of the left eye. Point F and point G are localized as the upper, respectively, the lower intersection point of the eye contour with a line going parallel to the vertical face axis through the middle of the line AB (as illustrated in Figure 3).

To each of the model points a CF is assigned that is equal to the CF assigned to the facial feature to which the point belongs. For example, the CF assigned to the points of the side-view model is equal to the CF that has been assigned to the sampled profile contour.

Facial Data Analyzer

The Facial Data Analyzer is the kernel of our system. It performs reasoning with uncertainty about facial actions and their intensity. Table 1 provides the mapping between 30 FACS rules and 30 rules of our expert system.

Each rule of the knowledge base given in Table 1 recognizes activation of a single AU based on the facial change caused by that AU. This means that each rule encodes a certain facial action based on discrepancy of the spatial arrangement of the model points between the current and the neutral expression of the same person.

Table 1. User-oriented pseudo-code of the rules for facial action coding from the face model deformation (Figure 3)

AU	FACS rule	ES rule	AU	FACS rule	ES rule	AU	FACS rule	ES rule
1	Raised inner brows	increased ∠BAD and ∠B1A1D1	13	Mouth corners pulled sharply up	decreased IB, decreased JB1, decreased CI, decreased CJ	25	Lips parted	increased P6P8, P4P10<t2
2	Raised outer brow	increased ∠BAD or ∠B1A1D1				26	Jaw dropped	t2<P4P10<t3
			15	Mouth corner downwards	increased IB or increased JB1	27	Mouth stretched	P4P10>t3
4	Lowered / frowned brows	P2 downwards, not increased curvature P2-P3	16	Depressed lower lip	P8 downwards, P8 outwards, decreased P8P10	28	Lips sucked in	Points P6 and P8 are absent
5	Raised upper lid	increased 3F or increased 4F1	17	Raised chin	P10 inwards	28b	Bottom lip sucked in	Point P8 is absent
6	Raised cheek	activated AU12	18	Lips puckered	decreased IJ>t1	28t	Top lip sucked in	Point P6 is absent
7	Raised lower lid	no AU12 & AU9 FG>0 F1G1>0, 3F>0, 4F1>0, decreased 3G or decreased 4G1	19	Tongue showed	curvature P6-P8 contains 2 valleys and a peak	36t	Bulge above the upper lip caused by tongue	increased curvature P5-P6
			20	Mouth stretched	increased f16, not increased f12 not increased f13	36b	Bulge under the lower lip	Point P9 is absent
8	Lips towards each other (teeth visible, lips tensed & less visible)	increased P5P6, P6 outwards, P8 outwards, curvature P6-P8 [increased P8P10	23	Lips tightened but not pressed	no AU28b, no AU28t, no AU8, decreased KL, KL>0, not decreased IJ, not increased IB, not increased JB1	38	Nostrils widened	absent AUs: 8, 9, 10, 12, 13, 14, 15, 18, 20, 24, 28 increased HH1
9	Wrinkled nose	increased curvature P2-P3				39	nostrils compressed	decreased HH1
10	Raised upper lip	P6 upwards, P6 outwards, decreased P5P6, not increased curvature P2-P3	24	Lips pressed together	no AU28b, no AU28t, no AU8, decreased KL, KL>0, decreased IJ<t1	41	Lid dropped	not decreased 3G decreased FG, decreased 3F or decreased F1G1, decreased 4F1, not decreased 4G1
12	Mouth corners pulled up	decreased IB, decreased JB1, increased CI, increased CJ						

The rules have been uniquely defined. In other words, each model deformation corresponds to unique set of AU-codes.

We utilized a *relational list* (R-list) to represent the relations between the rules of the knowledge base. The used R-list is a four-tuple list where the first two columns identify the conclusion clause of a certain rule that forms the premise clause of another rule, identified in the next two columns of the R-list. Each premise clause of each rule given in Table 1 is associated with an S-function, as defined in (3), which influences a so-called cumulative *membership grade* (MG) of the premise of the rule.

$$S(x; \alpha, \beta, \gamma) = 0 \quad \text{for } x \leq \alpha$$
$$S(x; \alpha, \beta, \gamma) = 2[(x-\alpha)/(\gamma-\alpha)]^2 \quad \text{for } \alpha < x < \beta$$
$$S(x; \alpha, \beta, \gamma) = 1 - 2[(x-\gamma)/(\gamma-\alpha)]^2 \quad \text{for } \beta < x < \gamma \quad (3)$$
$$S(x; \alpha, \beta, \gamma) = 1 \quad \text{for } x \geq \gamma$$

where α and γ are function's end points and $\beta=(\alpha+\gamma)/2$ is so-called crossover point

The parameters of S-function are on-line defined by the contents of the database (DB) containing the maximal encountered deformations of the face model. For instance, the S-functions associated with the premises of the rule for recognition of AU5 are defined as $S5\_1(x; 0, \frac{1}{2}max\_3F, max\_3F)$ and $S5\_2(x; 0, \frac{1}{2}max\_4F1, max\_4F1)$ where x is the actual deformation of the distance 3F, respectively 4F1, and the *max_3F* and *max_4F1* are retrieved from the DB.

The database of extreme model deformations is on-line altered. For each facial-distance/ profile-contour (defined in Table 1), the difference is calculated between that feature detected in the expressionless face and the pertinent feature detected in the current expression. If the determined difference is higher than the related value stored in the DB, the content of the DB is adjusted. The initial values of the extreme model deformations are set off-line, prior the system execution, based on a representative set of facial expressions of the currently observed person. This representative set of facial expressions, i.e. observed persons' *individual extreme-displays (IED)* set, consists of the 6 basic emotional expressions, neutral expression and 4 maximal displays of AU8, AU18, AU39 and AU41. This set of 11 expressions has been experimentally proved to be sufficient for initialisation of the values stored in the DB of extreme model deformations (see rules for facial expression emotional classification in [13]).

Fast direct chaining as defined by Schneider et al. [15] has been applied as the inference procedure. It is a breadth-first search algorithm that starts with the first rule of the knowledge base and then searches the R-list to find if the conclusion of the fired rule forms a premise of another rule that will be fired in the next loop. Otherwise, the process will try to fire the rule that in the knowledge base comes after the rule last fired.

The model points delimited by the Facial Data Evaluator (Figure 3) determine the facial-distances/ profile-contours employed by the rules (Table 1). The CFs associated with the model points define the CF of the related distance/ contour as given in formula (4).

$$CF\_feature = min\ (CF\_point1,...,CF\_pointN)\ (4)$$

The overall certainty of the premise of a fired rule is calculated as defined by Schneider et al. [15]:
1. For the portion of the premise that contains clauses $c1$ and $c2$ related as $c1\ AND\ c2$, $CF = min\ (CF\_c1,\ CF\_c2)$.
2. For the portion of the clause that contains clauses $c1$ and $c2$ related as $c1\ OR\ c2$, $CF = max\ (CF\_c1,\ CF\_c2)$.
3. If the premise contains only clause c, $CF = CF\_c$.

Further, the cumulative membership grade MG_p of the premise of a rule is calculated and multiplied by 100% to obtain the quantification of the AU code encrypted by that rule. MG_p of a rule's premise p is calculated from the membership grades MG_c associated with the clauses c of the premise p.
1. For a clause c of a kind "certain AU (not) activated", $MG\_c = 1$. For the portion of the premise that contains c AND $c1$ or c OR $c1$, where the clause $c1$ is of another kind, $MG\_p = MG\_c1$.
2. For a clause c of a kind "certain point absent /present", $MG\_c = 1$. For the portion of the premise that contains c AND $c1$ or c OR $c1$, where the clause $c1$ is of another kind, $MG\_p = MG\_c1$.
3. For a clause c where two values are compared, $MG\_c = S(x;\ \alpha,\ \beta,\ \gamma)$, where S is the S-function associated with c. For a portion of the premise that contains c AND $c1$, where c and $c1$ are of the same kind, $MG\_p = avg\ (MG\_c,\ MG\_c1)$. For a portion of the premise that contains c OR $c1$, $MG\_p = max\ (MG\_c,\ MG\_c1)$.
4. If the premise contains only clause c, $MG\_p = MG\_c$.

A processing loop of the inference engine ends with updating the DB of the extreme model deformations, updating a *list of fired rules* (LFR) and searching the R-list for a rule that the process will try to fire in the next loop. LFR prevents the inference engine from firing a rule twice. If a rule has fired, its number is added to this list.

Post Processor

In the case a certain facial feature fails to be detected by the Facial Data Generator, the Facial Data Evaluator utilises the pertinent feature detected in the expressionless face to substitute missing data. Hence, exact information about the examined expression is lost. To diminish this loss, we exploit a higher level "emotional grammar" of facial expressions defined by Ekman [5]. The main idea is that there is a higher possibility that a smile is coupled with "smiling" eyes than with expressionless eyes.

The system's post-processor utilizes an existing CLIPS-implemented expert system, HERCULES, to classify the observed facial expression into the six basic emotion categories. Since HERCULES has been presented elsewhere [13], just a short description of its processing is provided here. The attention is paid on integration and actual employment of HERCULES within the system for automated facial action encoding.

HERCULES accepts an AU-coded description of the encountered expression and converts this into a set of emotion labels. The rules for emotional classification of the facial actions are straightforwardly acquired from the linguistic descriptions of the prototypic facial expressions given by Ekman [5]. Five certified FACS coders have validated these rules using a set of 129 dual view images representing the relevant combinations of AUs. In 85% of the cases, the human observer and the system evenly labeled the observed expression [13].

HERCULES returns a set of quantified emotion labels. An emotion label is quantified according to the assumption that each AU, forming a part of a certain basic expression, has an equal influence on that expression's intensity.

Input to the Post-Processor consists of the expression geometry delimited by the Facial Data Evaluator and the quantified AU-codes determined by the Facial Data Analyzer. The geometry of the current expression is checked for presence of an expressionless facial feature. A simple control of the assigned CFs performs this check. A CF equal to *1/2N* is assigned to a facial feature only if the pertinent feature detected in the expressionless face has substituted the feature. If there is a feature having CF equal to *1/2N*, HERCULES is invoked. Otherwise, the system's processing terminates and displays the result – the quantified AU-codes and the certainty of these conclusions.

If HERCULES is invoked, this result is adjusted upon the acquired emotional classification of the analyzed expression. The returned list of emotion labels is searched and a kind of backward reasoning of HERCULES' inference engine is performed for the emotion label with the highest weight and the facial feature marked as expressionless. The rules given in Table 2 are used to reason about the possible deformation of the marked facial feature whereupon the system's final result is then adjusted.

Table 2. The rules for determining the appearance of the missing facial feature (i.e. the appropriate AU code) based on emotional classification of the encountered expression

	Eyes	Eyebrows	Mouth
Sadness	7 if 1	1	15
Fear	5+7	1 if 5	20
Happiness	6	-	12
Surprise	5	1+2	26
Disgust	9	9	9
Anger	7	4	24

In order to quantify appropriately the newly added AU, the AU-codes comprising the analyzed expression are compared to the AU-codes comprising the prototypic expression, which characterizes the emotion category to which the analyzed expression has been classified. The AU-codes that belong to both are marked and their average intensity is assigned to the newly added AU. The CF assigned to this AU is obtained as given in formula (5).

$$CF = \frac{1}{2} * min\{CFs\_marked\_AU\text{-}codes\} \quad (5)$$

System Development and Evaluation

The system is developed according to the Incremental Development model. This model is characterized by integrated prototyping where the design phases - coding, integration and implementation - are split in successive increments of functionality. The successive increments, covering the full breadth of the system in an easy-to-integrate way, were selected according to the main parts of the system: Facial Data Generator, Data Evaluator, Data Analyzer and Post-Processor. Each part has been developed independently and then integrated into the operational and tested prototype presented in this paper. Chronologically, the Facial Data Generator and the Post-Processor have been developed in parallel and before the other parts of the system.

Since the system is to be used on different software platforms for purposes of behavioral science research as well as a part of human-computer interface, robustness, user-friendliness and portability were the requirements posed on the development. Integrating multiple detectors into a single workbench for facial expression information extraction and applying the reasoning with uncertainty on the extracted data insure robustness and precision of the system. JDK and JNI made Java a proper tool for fulfilling all other constraints posed on the development.

The operational prototype presented here has not been deployed in a real-world environment. The aim is to develop a robust, fully operational, intelligent multi-modal/media human-computer interface which will perform encoding and interpreting of all human communicative signals, namely, speech, facial expressions, body movements, vocal and physiological reactions. Still, if regarded merely in the scope of human-behavior-interpretation application domain, the prototype has been evaluated by the end-users since eight certified FACS coders have performed the validation studies on the prototype. Validation studies addressed the question whether the interpretations acquired by the system are acceptable to human experts judging the same images.

Testing Images and Testing Subjects

The overall performance of the system's prototype has been evaluated on a database containing 1040 dual views (see Figure 1 for a testing image example). Eight certified FACS coders participated in building of this database. Subjects were of both sexes and ranged in age (22-34) and ethnicity (European, South American and Asian).

The database of testing images contains the dual views of each subject displaying 2x30 expressions of separate AU activation, 4 maximal displays of AU8, AU18, AU39 and AU41, 2x6 basic emotional expressions, a neutral expression and 53 expressions representing combinations of AU activation. The images have been recorded under constant illumination using fixed light sources attached next to the mounted cameras and none of the subjects had a moustache, a beard or wear glasses.

Facial Action Encoding Performance

Two certified FACS coders validated the rules for AU coding by evaluating 90 expressions of separate AU activation displayed by other three coders. In 100% of the cases the image representing the activation of a certain AU, produced according to our rules (Table 1), has been labeled with the same AU-code by the coders. This result has been expected, however, since all of the rules have been acquired from FACS in a straightforward manner.

The facial action coding achieved by the system was 89.6% (i.e. 90% for the upper face AUs, 85% for the lower face AUs and 94% for the AUs combinations) when compared to human coding of all images in the database.

Facial Action Codes Quantification Performance

In order to compare quantification of the AU-codes done by our system with that done by humans, we collected the data from a questionnaire. For each image from the database shown by a certain subject, we asked the other seven subjects to assign an *individual index of intensity impression* to each of the activated AU(s) displayed in the image. While determining the indexes for the images of an observed subject, the coders used that persons' individual extreme-displays (IED) set. Finally, for each image in the database, an average index of intensity impression has been calculated.

For each of the eight subjects, his/her IED-set was also used to set the initial values in the database of extreme model deformations. The rest of his/her dual views have been used to evaluate the performance of the system by comparing the system's result and the average index of intensity impression related with a relevant image. Then the results for a total of 952 testing images have been averaged. The average disagreement between the AU intensity assigned by the system and the relevant average index of intensity impression was 0.08 (i.e. 8%), respectively 0.16 (i.e. 16%), in the case of the correctly recognized AU with a CF >= 0.3, respectively CF < 0.3. Disagreements were mostly caused by "inaccuracy" of the human eye when comparing the currently observed facial deviation with a relevant deviation shown in the images of the observed subject's IED-set.

Conclusion

The system presented in this paper brings together three fundamentally diverse technologies: psychologically and anatomically founded FACS [4], image analysis and AI. The system encodes and quantifies 30 different facial actions from static dual-view facial images.

By a large number of experiments, a confident system performance measurement is obtained that indicates rather robust and accurate facial action coding that the system accomplishes. When tested on 1040 dual-view images, facial action correct recognition rate achieved by the system was 89.6%. Average disagreement between the facial action intensity calculated by the system and that assigned by human experts was 0.08 (i.e. 8%), respectively 0.16 (i.e. 16%), in the case of the correctly recognized facial action with a CF $>=$ 0.3, respectively CF $<$ 0.3.

In comparison to the existing explicit attempts to automate facial action coding [2], [1], [6], the system presented in this paper is new and fundamentally different by the use of AI technology. Also it deals with automatic facial action coding in a more effective way. The best of the existing similar systems [2] performs recognition of 15 different facial actions. None of the existing similar systems quantifies the facial action codes. Our system performs accurate fully automatic coding and quantification of 30 different facial actions in static facial dual-views.

There are a number of ways in which the presented system could be improved. First of all, the system cannot encode the full range of facial behavior. From a total of 44 AUs defined in FACS, the presented prototype can encode 30 AUs from a dual-view image of encountered facial expression. The facial feature detectors integrated into the system are far from perfect and have not been proved capable of detecting all facial changes underlying a full range of facial behavior. The facial motions should be modeled and real-time spatio-temporal detectors of facial movement should be integrated into the system to allow tracking of fast facial actions such as wink, blink and wiping of the lips. Modeling the facial motion will also allow analysis of facial expression dynamics, which seems to be crucial in expression analysis.

Another limitation of the presented prototype is evident in a time-consuming performance. While the execution of the reasoning process takes some 3-4 seconds, complete processing of a single image takes 3 minutes in average due to the time-consuming image processing. Real-time image analysis would need to be achieved if the system is to be used as a part of a realistic man-machine interface.

We are not aware of any system, including our own, which perfects automatic facial action coding either in photographs or in video sequences. We still seek and investigate the possibilities.

References

[1] Black, M.J.; Yacoob, Y. 1998. Recognizing facial expressions in image sequences using local parameterized models of image motion. *International Journal on Computer Vision* 25(1): 23-48.

[2] Cohn, J.F.; Zlochower, A.J; Lien, J.J.; Kanade, T. 1998. Feature-point tracking by optical flow discriminates subtle differences in facial expression. *Proc. IEEE FG*, 396-401.

[3] Donato, G.; Bartlett, M.S.; Hager, J.C.; Ekman, P.; Sejnowski, T.J. 1999. Classifying Facial Actions. *TPAMI* 21(10): 974-989.

[4] Ekman, P.; Friesen, W.V. 1978. *Facial Action Coding System (FACS)*. Palo Alto: Consulting Psychologists Press.

[5] Ekman, P. 1982. *Emotion in the Human Face*. Cambridge: Cambridge University Press.

[6] Essa, I.; Pentland, A. 1997. Coding, analysis, interpretation and recognition of facial expressions. *TPAMI* 19(7): 757-763.

[7] Hong, H.; Neven, H.; von der Malsburg, C. 1998. Online facial expression recognition based on personalized galleries. *Proc. IEEE FG*, 354-359.

[8] Huang, C.L.; Huang, Y.M. 1997. Facial expression recognition using model-based feature extraction and action parameters classification. *Journal of Visual Communication and Image Representation* 8(3): 278-290.

[9] Kass, M.; Witkin A.; Terzopoulos, D. 1987. Snake: Active Contour Model. *Proc. IEEE ICCV*, 259-269.

[10] Kearney G.D.; McKenzie, S. 1993. Machine interpretation of emotion: design of JANUS. *Cognitive Science* 17(4): 589-622.

[11] Mehrabian, A. 1968. Communication without words. *Psychology Today* 2(4):53-56.

[12] Otsuka, T.; Ohya, J. 1998. Spotting segments displaying facial expression from image sequences using HMM. *Proc. IEEE FG*, 442-447.

[13] Pantic, M.; Rothkrantz, L.J.M. 1999. An expert system for multiple emotional classification of facial expressions. *Proc. IEEE ICTAI*, 113-120.

[14] Rothkrantz, L.J.M.; van Schouwen, M.R.; Ververs, F.; Vollering, J.C.M. 1998. A multimedia workbench for facial expression analysis. *Proc. Euromedia*, 94-101. Ghent: SCS Press.

[15] Schneider, M.; Kandel, A.; Langholz, G.; Chew, G. 1996. *Fuzzy Expert System Tools*. Chichester: John Wiley & Sons Ltd.

[16] Vincent, J.M.; Myers, D.J.; Hutchinson, R.A. 1992. Image feature location in multi-resolution images. *Neural Networks for Speech, Vision and Natural Language*, 13-29. Chapman & Hall.

[17] Wang, M.; Iwai, Y.; Yachida, M. 1998. Expression recognition from time-sequential facial images by use of expression change model. *Proc. IEEE FG*, 324-329.

[18] Wojdel, J.C.; Wojdel, A.; Rothkrantz, L.J.M. 1999. Analysis of facial expressions based on silhouettes. *Proc. of ASCI*, 199-206. Delft, NL: ASCI Press.

[19] Williams, D.J.; Shah, M. 1992. A fast algorithm for active contours and curvature estimation. *Computer Vision and Image Processing* 55 (1): 14-26.

[20] Zhang, Z.; Lyons, M.; Schuster, M.; Akamatsu, S. 1998. Comparison between geometry-based and Gabor wavelets-based facial expression recognition using multi-layer perceptron. *Proc. IEEE FG*, 454-459.

AI for the Web — Ontology-based Community Web Portals

Steffen Staab[a,b], Jürgen Angele[b], Stefan Decker[a,b], Michael Erdmann[a], Andreas Hotho[a], Alexander Maedche[a], Hans-Peter Schnurr[a,b], Rudi Studer[a,b], York Sure[a]

email: {staab, angele, decker, erdmann, hotho, maedche, schnurr, studer, sure}@aifb.uni-karlsruhe.de
[a]Institute AIFB, University of Karlsruhe, 76128 Karlsruhe, Germany
http://www.aifb.uni-karlsruhe.de/WBS
[b]ontoprise GmbH, Hermann-Löns-Weg 19, 76275 Ettlingen, Germany
http://www.ontoprise.com

Abstract

Community web portals serve as portals for the information needs of particular communities on the web. We here discuss how a comprehensive, ontology-based approach for building and maintaining a high-value community web portal has been conceived and implemented. The ontology serves as a semantic backbone for accessing knowledge on the portal, for contributing information, as well as for developing and maintaining the portal. In particular, the ontology allows for flexible querying and inferencing of knowledge. Actual usage of our technology is facilitated through a set of tools that are about to turn our research system into a portal for wide-spread usage right now. The development of these tools has greatly benefited from some first experiences we had with actual users of the community web portal of the knowledge acquisition community.

1 Introduction

One of the major strengths of the World Wide Web is that virtually everyone who owns a computer may contribute high-value information — the real challenge is to make valuable information be found. Search machines help with this task, but ultimately they fail to provide appropriatly structured views onto the web.

From the very beginning of the web, communities of interest have formed that covered what they deemed to be of interest to their members in — what we here call — community web portals. Community web portals are similar to Yahoo!™ and its likes by their goal of presenting a structured view onto the web, however they are dissimilar by the way knowledge is provided in a collaborative process with only few resources (manpower, money) for maintaining and editing the portal. Thus, their is a need for automation of management of community web portals.

Community web portals try to weave loose pieces of information into a coherent presentation adequate for sharing knowledge with the user. Support through ontologies appears as an appropriate means in order to facilitate the tool-supported structuring of knowledge. The ontology formally represents common knowledge and interests that people share within their community. It is used to support the major tasks of a portal, viz. accessing the portal through manifold, dynamic, conceptually plausible views onto the information

Copyright © 2000, American Association for Artificial Intelligence (www.aaai.org). All rights reserved.

of interest in a particular community (Section 2), and providing information in a number of ways that reflect different types of information resources held by the individuals (Section 3). The subsequent Section 4 shows how an ontology-based web portal may be developed and maintained using our set of methods and tools and how the overall architecture of the portal looks like. Before we conclude, we compare our work with related approaches (Section 5).

The Example. The example that we draw from in the rest of this paper is the portal for the *"Knowledge Annotation Initiative of the Knowledge Acquisition community"* (KA2; *cf.* (Benjamins, Fensel, & Decker 1999)). The KA2 initiative has been conceived for semantic knowledge retrieval from the web building on knowledge created in the KA community. To structure knowledge, an ontology has been built in an international collaboration of researchers. The ontology constitutes the basis to annotate WWW documents of the knowledge acquisition community in order to enable intelligent access to these documents and to infer implicit knowledge from explicitly stated facts and rules from the ontology.

Given this basic scenario, which may be easily transferred towards other settings for community web portals, we have investigated the techniques and built the tools that we describe in the rest of this paper. Nevertheless the reader may note that we have not yet achieved a complete integration of all tools and neither have we exploited all our technical capabilities in our up and running demonstration KA2 community web portal (http://ka2portal.aifb.uni-karlsruhe.de).

2 Accessing the Community Web Portal

Navigating through a, maybe unknown, portal is a rather difficult task in general. Information retrieval may of course help, but it may also be more of a hindrance, because the user may not know the conceptualization that underlies the portal. Hence, we provide query and navigating capabilities and make the conceptual background transparent to the user.

Our description of access capabilities in this section starts with the query capabilities of our representation framework. The framework builds on the very same F-Logic (Kifer, Lausen, & Wu 1995) mechanism for querying as it does for ontology representation and, thus, it may also exploit and explicate the ontological background knowledge. In addition to these facilities for explanation and exploration, the ontology also acts as a mediator between proprietary information sources that provide additional background knowledge to the portal (cf. (Wiederhold & Geneserth 1997) on mediators). Nevertheless, F-Logic is as poorly suited for presentation to naive users as any other query language. Hence, its use is mostly disguised in various easy-to-use mechanisms that more properly serve the needs of the common user (*cf.* Section 2.2), while it still gives the editor all the power of the principal F-Logic representation and query capabilities. Finally in this section, we touch upon some very mission-critical issues of the actual inference engine that answers queries and derives new facts by combining facts with structures and rules from the ontology.

2.1 Query Capabilities

Though information may be provided in a number of different formats our underlying language for representation and querying is F-Logic. For instance, using a concrete example from our showcase the following query asks for all publications of the researcher "Steffen Staab".

(1) FORALL $Pub \leftarrow$
    EXISTS ResID ResID:*Researcher* [NAME $\twoheadrightarrow$
    "Steffen Staab"; PUBLICATION $\twoheadrightarrow$ Pub].

The substitutions for the variable *Pub* are the desired publications. The expressiveness and usability of such queries is strongly increased by the possibility to use a simple form of information retrieval using regular expressions whithin queries.

In addition, the query capabilities enable using the background knowledge expressed in the KA2 ontology using rules. For example, one rule states that, two researchers cooperate, if a *Researcher* X works at a *Project Proj* and if a *Researcher* Y works at the same *Project Proj* and X is another person than Y. The rule is formulated in F-Logic as follows:

(2) FORALL $X, Y, Proj$
    $X : Researcher$ [COOPERATESWITH $\twoheadrightarrow Y : Researcher$]
    $\leftarrow$
    $X : Researcher$ [WORKSATPROJECT $\twoheadrightarrow Proj : Project$]
    AND
    $Y : Researcher$ [WORKSATPROJECT $\twoheadrightarrow Proj : Project$]
    AND NOT equal(X, Y).

If we take a look at web pages about research projects, typically information about the researchers (*e.g.* their names, their affiliation, ...) involved in the projects is explicitly stated in HTML. However, the fact that researchers who are working together in projects are cooperating is not explicitly stated on the web pages. A question might be: "Which researchers are cooperating with other researchers?" Querying for cooperating researchers the implicit information about project cooperation of researchers is retrieved. The query may be formulated using F-Logic:

(3) FORALL ResID1, ResID2 $\leftarrow$
    ResID1: *Researcher* [COOPERATESWITH $\twoheadrightarrow$ ResID2].

The result set includes explicit information about a researchers cooperation relationships, which are stored in the knowledge warehouse, and also implicit information about project cooperation between researchers derived using the project-cooperation rule modeled in (2)..

2.2 Navigating and Querying the Portal

Usually it is too inconvenient for users to query the portal using F-Logic. Therefore, we offer a range of techniques that allow for navigating and querying the community web:

- A *hypertext link* may contain a query which is dynamically evaluated when one clicks on the link. Browsing is realized by defining views on the top-level concepts of the KA2 ontology, such as *Persons*, *Projects*, *Organizations*, *Publications*, *Research Topics* and *Events*. For example clicking on the *Projects* hyperlink results in a query for all projects known to the portal. The query is evaluated and the results are presented to the user in a table.

- A choice of concepts, instances, or combinations of both may be issued to the user in *HTML forms*. Choice options may be selected through check boxes or radio buttons. For instance, clicking on the *Projects* link (*cf.* upper part of Figure 1) an F-Logic query is evaluated and all projects contained in the portal are retrieved. The results can be restricted using topic-specific attributes contained in the KA2 ontology for projects, such as topics of a project, people involved etc. The selection list (*e.g.* for all people involved in projects) is generated dynamically from the information contained in the knowledge warehouse (*cf.* Section 3.4).

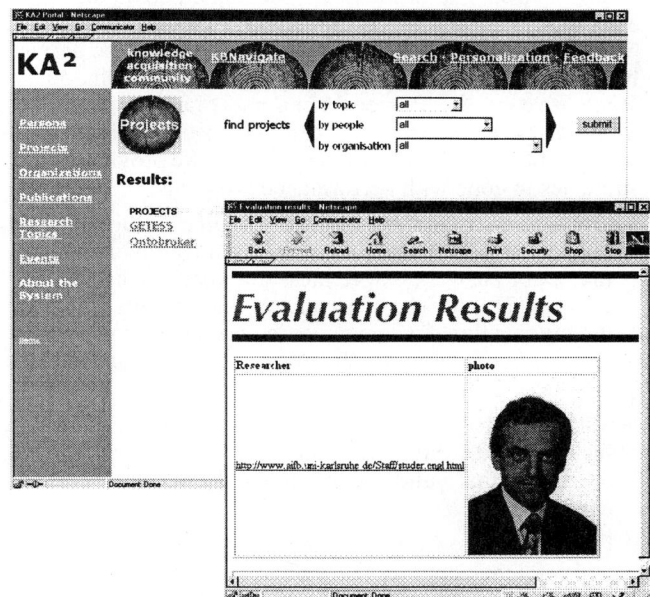

Figure 1: Accessing the Community Web Portal

- A query may also be generated by using the *hyperbolic view interface*. The hyperbolic view visualizes the ontology as a hierarchy of concepts. The presentation is based on hyperbolic geometry (*cf.* (Lamping, Rao, & Pirolli 1995)). When a user selects a node from the hyperbolic concept hierarchy, a form is presented which allows the user to select attributes or to insert values for the attributes. A result of the user request searching for the community member "Rudi Studer" and his photo is shown in the left part of Figure 1. Based on the selected node and the corresponding attributes, a query is compiled.

- Furthermore, queries created by the hyperbolic view interface may be stored using the personalization feature. Queries are personalized for the different users and are available for the user in a selection list. The stored queries can be considered as *semantic bookmarks*. By selecting a previously created bookmark, the underlying query is evaluated and the updated results are presented to the user. By this way, every user may create a personalized view on the portal.
- Finally, we offer an expert mode. The most technical (but also most powerful and flexible) way for querying the portal requires that F-Logic is typed in by the user. This way is only appropriate for users who are very familiar with F-Logic and the KA2 ontology.

2.3 The Inference Engine

The inference engine answers queries and it performs derivations of new knowledge by an combination of facts and the ontology. While the expressiveness of F-Logic and its Java powered realization in our inference engine is one of the major arguments for using it in a semantic community web portal, wide acceptance of a service like this also depends on *prima facie* unexciting features like speed of service. The principal problem we encounter here is that there exist worst case situations (not always recognizable as such by the user) where a very large set of facts must be derived by the inference engine in order to solve a particular query. While we cannot guarantee for extremely fast response times in all cases, unless we drastically cut back on the expressiveness of our representation formalism, we provide several strategies to cope with performance problems:

- The inference engine may be configured to subsequently deliver answers to the query instead of waiting for the entire set of answers before these answers are presented to the user. This has the consequence that answers which are directly available as facts may be presented immediately while other anwers which have to be derived using rules are presented later.
- The inference engine caches all facts and intermediate facts derived from earlier queries. Thus, similar queries or queries that build on previously derived facts may be answered fast.
- Finally, we allow the inference engine to be split into several inference engines that execute in parallel. Every engine may run on a different processor or even a different computer. Every inference engine administers a subset of the rules and facts. A master engine coordinates user queries and distributes subqueries to the slave engines. These slave engines either answer these subqueries directly or distribute incoming subqueries to other inference engines.

3 Providing Information

An essential feature of a community web portal is the contribution of information from all (or at least many) members of the community. Though they share some common understanding, the pieces of information they may contribute may come in many different (legacy) formats. Hence, one needs a set of methods and tools that may account for the diversity of information sources of potential interest to the community portal. These methods and tools must be able to cope with different syntactic mechanisms and they must be able to integrate different semantic formats based on the common ontology.

Considering the syntactic and/or interface side, we support three major, different, modes of information provisioning: First, we handle *metadata-based information sources* that explicitly describe contents of documents on a semantic basis. Second, we align regularities found in documents or data structures with the corresponding semantic background knowledge in *wrapper-based* approaches. Third, we allow the direct provisioning of facts through our *fact editor*. All the information is brought together in the knowledge warehouse. Thus, it mediates between the original heterogeneous information sources.

3.1 Metadata-based Information

Metadata-based information enriches documents with semantic information by explicitly adding metadata to the information sources. Over the last years several metadata languages have been proposed which can be used to annotate information sources. Current web standards can be handled within our semantic web portal approach. On the one hand, RDF (W3C 1999) facts serve as direct input for the knowledge warehouse, on the other hand, RDF facts can be generated from information contained in the portal knowledge warehouse. We developed *SiLRI* (Simple Logic-based RDF Interpreter), a logic-based inference engine implemented in Java that can draw inferences based on the RDF data model (Decker *et al.* 1998). XML provides the chance to get metadata for free, *i.e.* as a side product of defining the document structure. For this reason, we have developed a method and a tool called *DTDMaker* for generating DTDs out of ontologies (Erdmann & Studer 1999). DTDMaker derives an XML document type definition from a given ontology in F-Logic, so that XML instances can be linked to an ontology. The linkage has the advantage that the document structure is grounded on a true semantic basis and, thus, facts from XML documents may be directly integrated into the knowledge warehouse.

HTML-A, our HTML extension, adds annotations to HTML documents using an ontology as a metadata schema. HTML-A has the advantage to smoothly integrate semantic annotations into HTML and prevents the duplication of information. To facilitate the annotation of HTML, we have developed an HTML-A annotation tool called *OntoPad*.

3.2 Wrapper-based Information

In general, annotating information sources by hand is a time consuming task. Often, however, annotation may be automated when one findes regularities in a larger number of documents. The principle idea behind wrapper-based information is that there are large information collections that have a similar structure. We here distinguish between semi-structured information sources (*e.g.* HTML) and structured information sources (*e.g.* relational databases).

Semi-structured Sources. In recent years several approaches have been proposed for wrapping semi-structured documents, such as HTML documents. Wrapper factories (*cf.* (Sahuguet & Azavant 1999)) have considerably facilitated the task of wrapper construction. In order to wrap directly into our knowledge warehouse we have developed our own wrapper approach OntoWrapper that directly aligns regularities in semi-structured documents with their corresponding ontological meaning.

Structured Sources. Though, in the KA2 community web there are no existing information systems, we would like to emphasize that existing databases and other legacy-systems may contain valuable information for building a community web portal.

3.3 Fact Editor

The process of providing new facts into the knowledge warehouse should be as easy as possible. For this reason we offer the *Fact Editor*, which is another mode in which the hyperbolic interface tool may be used. At this time the forms are not used to ask for values, but to introduce values for attributes of instances of a corresponding concept from the ontology. The Fact Editor is also used for maintaining the portal to add, modify, or delete facts.

3.4 Knowledge Warehouse

The different methods and tools we have just described feed directly into the knowledge warehouse or indirectly when they are triggered by a web crawl. The warehouse itself hosts the ontology, *i.e.* the metadata level, as well as the data proper. The knowledge warehouse is indirectly accessed, through a user query or a query by an inference engine such as described in Section 2. Hence, one may take full advantage of the distribution capabilities of the inference engine and, likewise, separate the knowledge warehouse into several knowledge bases or knowledge marts. Facts and concepts are stored in a relational database, however, they are stored in a *reified* format that treats relations and concepts as first-order objects and that is therefore very flexible with regard to changes and amendments of the ontology.

4 Development of Web Portals

4.1 The Development and Maintenance Process

Even with the methodological and tool support we have described so far, developing a web portal for a community of non-trivial size remains a complex task. Strictly ad-hoc rapid prototyping approaches easily doom the construction to fail or they easily lead up to unsatisfactory results. Hence, we have thought about a more principled approach towards the development process that serves as means for documenting development, as well as for communicating principal structures to co-developers and editors of the web portal. We distinguish different phases in the development process that are illustrated in Figure 2. For the main part this model is a sequential one. Nevertheless, at each stage there is an evaluation as to whether and as to how easily further development may proceed with the design decisions that have been accomplished before. The results feed back into the results of earlier stages of development.

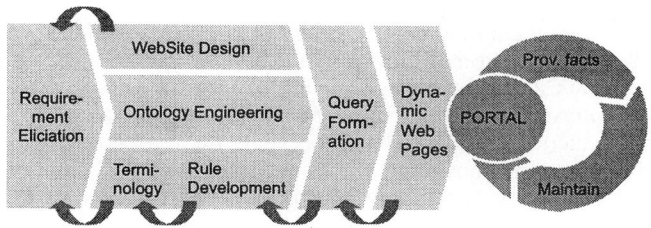

Figure 2: The Development Process of the Community Web Portal

The main stages of the development process and their key characteristics are given in the following:

- The process starts with the *elicitation* of user requirements in the requirements elicitation phase. In this phase, requirements about important and interesting topics in the domain are collected, the information goals of potential users of the portal are elicited, and preferences or expectations concerning the structure and layout of presented information is documented. Results of this very first phase constitute the input for the design of the web site and for preliminary HTML pages and affect the formal domain model embodied in the ontology.

- The requirements determine, *e.g.*, which views and queries are useful for users of the portal, which navigation paths they expect, how different web pages are linked, or which functionality is provided in different areas of the portal. Requirements like these are realized in the *web site design*. This design phase may be performed independently to a very large extent from the underlying formal structuring, *i.e.* the ontology.

- In parallel to the development of the structure and layout of the web site an *ontology engineering* process is started. The first phase elicits relevant *domain terms* that need to be refined and amended in the ontology engineering phase. First, the static ontology parts, *i.e.* the concept hierarchy, the attributes, and relations between concepts are formally defined. Thereafter, *rules* and constraints are developed. Rule development may incur a major revision of the concept hierarchy as consequence.

- In the *query development* step the views and queries described in one of the earlier phases are formalized. At first, their functionality is tested independently from the web site design. To express the information needs formally, the developer has to access the ontology, whereby additional rules or relations that define new views or ease the definition of queries may become necessary.

- Finally, web pages are populated, *i.e.* the queries and views developed during website design, and formalized and tested during query formalization are integrated into the operational portal. Information may be accessed via the portal as soon as a sufficient amount has been made available as outlined in Section 3.

During operation of the community portal it must be fed and maintained:

- The user community provides facts via numerous input channels (*cf.* Section 3).

- These facts may contain errors or undesired contents, or the integration of different sources may lead to inconsistencies. To counter problems like these a person is responsible to detect these cases and act appropriately. The detection of inconsistencies is supported by the inference engine via constraints formulated in F-Logic. The editor then has to decide how to proceed. He may contact responsible authors of conflicting information, he may simply ignore it, or he may manually edit the information.
- Changing requirements of the community must be reflected in the portal, *e.g.* popularity increasing in new fields of interests or technologies or viewpoints that shift may incur changes to the ontology, new queries, or even a new web site structure. In order to meet such new requirements, the above mentioned development process may have to be partially restarted.

4.2 Tools for Development and Maintenance

The previous subsection has described the principal steps for developing a community web portal. For efficient development of a community web portal, however, the process must be supported by tools. In the following, we describe the most important tools that allow us to facilitate and speed up the development and maintenance process. The tools cover the whole range from ontology engineering (OntoEdit), query formulation (Query Builder), up to the creation of dynamic web pages with the help of HTML/JavaScript templates. An overview of the tool suit is given in Table 1.

Table 1: Tool Suit for Community Portals

Tool	Description
OntoEdit	Ontology Engineering Environment
OntoPad	HTML Annotation Tool
Inference Engine	Reasoning service for query answering
OntoWrapper	Extracting information from semi-structured documents
Query Builder	Visual creation of queries
Fact Editor	Manual provision and maintenance of facts
Knowledge Warehouse	Fact base of the community web portal
HTML and JavaScript templates	Support the development of virtual HTML pages
Hyperbolic View	Visual querying the community web portal

OntoEdit. OntoEdit is a Ontology Engineering Environment delivering a wide range of functionalities for the engineering of ontologies including the modeling of concepts, relations, rules, and general ontology metadata (cf. (Maedche *et al.* 2000)). It includes several views on the modeling primitives that enable the user to state common legalities (*e.g.* the symmetry of the cooperation relationship between two persons).

Query Builder. While queries with low complexity can be expressed in F-Logic using the rule debugger alone, in other cases it is more convenient to create queries using our Query Builder tool. Such queries may then be integrated as links in a web page within a web editor by copying and pasting it into the web editors form. The Query Builder also contains a rule debugger, providing different views on different levels of detail to the proof tree that visualize relevant rules and rule parts for tracing the derivation process. In addition, generated queries by the Query Builder can be directly embedded into HTML/JavaScript Templates.

HTML/JavaScript Templates. Another time consuming activity is the development of the web pages that assemble queries from parts and that display the query results. For that purpose we have developed a library of template pages:

- Templates with check boxes, radio boxes, and selection lists are available. These HTML forms produce data which are used in Javascript functions to generate queries.
- The results of a query are fed into a template page as Javascript arrays. From these data different presentation forms may be generated:
  - A general purpose template contains a table that presents answer tuples returned by the inference engine in a HTML table. The template provides functions to sort the table in ascending or descending order on different columns. Substitutions of certain variables may be used as URLs for other entries in the table. Different data formats are recognized and processed according to their suffixes, *i.e.* a ".gif" or ".jpg" suffix is interpreted as a picture and rendered as such (*cf.* Figure 1 for an example).
  - Results may also be fed into selection lists, radio boxes, or check lists. Thus, query results can provide the initial setting of further HTML form fields.
- As a personalization feature of our web portal users store queries by assigning a personal label. All stored queries can be accessed through a selection list, to restart the query and retrieve the most up to date answers. This list of stored queries provides individual short cuts to often needed information.

5 Related Work

Our work combines approaches from different areas and extends these concepts in many directions. We here just give a short survey of this related work — a more detailed comparison may be found in (Staab *et al.* 2000).

Portals: Typically, portals like Yahoo!™ are indices of web pages that are maintained by editors that manually classify web documents into a tree-like taxonomy of topics. In contrast to our approach those portals only utilize a very lightweight ontology that solely consists of categories arranged in a hierarchical manner. Due to its weak ontology Yahoo! cannot extend given information with facts derived by ontological axioms.

A community focused and ontology-based portal is RiboWeb (Altmann *et al.* 1999) that offers ribosome data and computational models for their processing. RiboWeb specifies ontologies in OKBC (Chaudri *et al.* 1998). The primary source of data is given by scientific literature which is manually linked to the different ontologies. Both systems, RiboWeb and our community portal, rely on ontologies for offering a semantic-based access to the stored data. However, the OKBC component of RiboWeb does not support the kind of automatic deduction that is offered by the inference engine of Ontobroker. Furthermore, RiboWeb does not include wrappers for automatically extracting information from the given published articles. On the other hand, the computational modules of RiboWeb offer processing functionalities that are not part of (but also not intended for) our community web portal.

Database approaches: STRUDEL (Fernandez et al. 1998) and Hyperwave (Maurer 1996) apply concepts from database management systems to the process of building Web sites. They use database queries to generate web pages from database contents — allowing for multiple views onto the same content. When compared to our approach, these systems lack the semantic level that is provided in our approach by the domain ontology and the associated inference engine.

Knowledge representation for the web: The Ontobroker project (Decker et al. 1999) lays the technological foundations for the KA2 portal. Similar to Ontobroker are SHOE (Luke et al. 1997) and WebKB (Martin & Eklund 1999). All three systems aim at providing intelligent access to Web documents (though, with different means). However, they all lack an environment of methods and tools that are needed to build a community portal on their top and, thus, to make an application out of a core technology.

From our point of view, our community portal system is a rather unique AI application with respect to the collection of methods used and the functionality provided. Our approach for accessing information, providing information and maintaining the portal are more comprehensive than those found in other portals. We are able to offer this functionality since our backbone system Ontobroker and its add-ons provide more powerful techniques for e.g. inferencing or extracting information from various sources than those offered by comparable systems.

6 Conclusion

We have demonstrated in this paper how a community may build a community web portal. The portal is centered around an ontology that structures information for the purpose of presenting and provisoning information, as well as for the development and maintenance of the portal. We have described a particular application, the KA2 community web portal, that illustrates some of our techniques and methods.In particular, we have developed a set of ontology-based tools that allow to present multiple views onto the same information appropriate for browsing, querying, and personalizing web pages. Queries are responded to by an inference engine for F(rame)-Logic that integrates knowledge from many different sources.

For the future we are planning to integrate several semi-automatic information extraction-based approaches supporting the information provisioning part of our portal framework. Ontology revision and maintenance and the impact on the facts stored in the knowledge warehouse are currently not well understood and have to be researched further.

References

Altmann, R.; Bada, M.; Chai, X.; Carillo, M. W.; Chen, R.; and Abernethy, N. 1999. RiboWeb: An Ontology-based System for Collaborative Molecular Biology. *IEEE Intelligent Systems* 14(5):68–76.

Benjamins, R.; Fensel, D.; and Decker, S. 1999. KA2: Building Ontologies for the Internet: A Midterm Report. *International Journal of Human Computer Studies* 51(3):687.

Chaudri, V.; Farquhar, A.; Fikes, R.; Karp, P.; and Rice, J. 1998. OKBC: A Programmatic Foundation for Knowledge Base Interoperability. In *Proceedings 15th National Conference on Artificial Intelligence (AAAI-98)*, 600–607.

Decker, S.; Brickley, D.; Saarela, J.; and Angele, J. 1998. A Query and Inference Service for RDF. In *Proceedings of the W3C Query Language Workshop (QL-98), December 3-4*.

Decker, S.; Erdmann, M.; Fensel, D.; and Studer, R. 1999. Ontobroker: Ontology Based Access to Distributed and Semi-Structured Information. In Meersman, R., et al., eds., *Database Semantics: Semantic Issues in Multimedia Systems*. Kluwer Academic Publisher. 351–369.

Erdmann, M., and Studer, R. 1999. Ontologies as Conceptual Models for XML Documents. In *Proceedings of the 12th International Workshop on Knowledge Acquisition, Modelling and Mangement (KAW'99), Banff, Canada, October*.

Fernandez, M.; Florescu, D.; Kang, J.; and Levy, A. 1998. Catching the Boat with Strudel: Experiences with a Web-Site Management System. In *Proceedings of the 1998 ACM Int. Conf. on Management of Data (SIGMOD'98), Seattle, WA*.

Kifer, M.; Lausen, G.; and Wu, J. 1995. Logical Foundations of Object-Oriented and Frame-Based Languages. *Journal of the ACM* 42.

Lamping, L.; Rao, R.; and Pirolli, P. 1995. A Focus+Context Technique Based on Hyperbolic Geometry for Visualizing Large Hierarchies. In *Proceedings of the ACM SIGCHI Conference on Human Factors in Computing Systems*.

Luke, S.; Spector, L.; Rager, D.; and Hendler, J. 1997. Ontology-based Web Agents. In *Proceedings of First International Conference on Autonomous Agents*.

Maedche, A.; Schnurr, H.-P.; Staab, S.; and Studer, R. 2000. Representation language-neutral modeling of ontologies. In *Modellierung-2000: Proceedings of the German Workshop on Modeling. Koblenz, April, 2000*. Fölbach-Verlag.

Martin, P., and Eklund, P. 1999. Embedding Knowledge in Web Documents. In *Proceedings of the 8th Int. World Wide Web Conf. (WWW'8), Toronto, May 1999*. Elsevier Science B.V.

Maurer, H. 1996. *Hyperwave. The Next Generation Web Solution*. Addison Wesley.

Sahuguet, A., and Azavant, F. 1999. WysiWyg Web Wrapper Factory (W4F). Technical Report. http://db.cis.upenn.edu/DL/WWW8/index.html.

Staab, S.; Angele, J.; Decker, S.; Erdmann, M.; Hotho, A.; Maedche, A.; Studer, R.; and Sure, Y. 2000. Semantic Community Web Portals. In *Proceedings of the 9th World Wide Web Conference (WWW-9), Amsterdam, Netherlands*.

W3C. 1999. RDF Schema Specification. http://www.w3.org/TR/PR-rdf-schema/.

Wiederhold, G., and Genesereth, M. 1997. The Conceptual Basis for Mediation Services. *IEEE Expert / Intelligent Systems* 12(5):38–47.

Defining and Using Ideal Teammate and Opponent Agent Models

Peter Stone
AT&T Labs — Research
180 Park Ave., room A273
Florham Park, NJ 07932
pstone@research.att.com
http://www.research.att.com/~pstone

Patrick Riley and **Manuela Veloso**
Computer Science Department
Carnegie Mellon University
Pittsburgh, PA 15213
{pfr,veloso}@cs.cmu.edu
http://www.cs.cmu.edu/{~pfr,~mmv}

Abstract

A common challenge for agents in multiagent systems is trying to predict what other agents are going to do in the future. Such knowledge can help an agent determine which of its current action options is most likely to achieve its goals. There is a long history in adversarial game playing of using a model of an opponent which assumes that it always acts optimally. Our research extends this strategy to adversarial domains in which the agents have incomplete information, noisy sensors and actuators, and a continuous action space. We introduce "ideal-model-based behavior outcome prediction" (IMBBOP) which models the results of other agents' future actions in relation to their optimal actions based on an ideal world model. Our technique also includes a method for relaxing this optimality assumption. IMBBOP was a key component of our successful CMUNITED-99 simulated robotic soccer application. We define IMBBOP and illustrate its use within the simulated robotic soccer domain. We include empirical results demonstrating the effectiveness of IMBBOP.

Introduction

A common challenge for agents in multiagent systems is trying to predict what other agents are going to do in the future. Such knowledge can help an agent determine which of its current action options are most likely to help it achieve its goals.

Ideally, an agent could learn a model of other agents' behavior patterns via direct observation of their past actions. However, that is only possible when agents have many repeated interactions with one another.

We explore the use of agent models in an application where extensive interactions with a particular agent are not possible, namely robotic soccer. In robotic soccer tournaments, such as RoboCup (Kitano *et al.* 1997), a team of agents plays against another team for a single, short (typically 10-minute) period. The opponents' behaviors are usually not observable prior to this game and there are not enough interactions during the game to build a useful model.

In this paper, we introduce "ideal-model-based behavior outcome prediction" (IMBBOP). This technique predicts an agent's future actions in relation to the optimal behavior in its given situation. This optimal behavior is agent-independent and can therefore be computed based solely on

Copyright © 2000, American Association for Artificial Intelligence (www.aaai.org). All rights reserved.

a model of the world dynamics. IMBBOP does not assume that the other agent *will* act according to the theoretical optimum, but rather characterizes its expected behavior in terms of deviation from this optimum.

The Application: Goal-Scoring in Soccer

Our IMBBOP implementation is carried out in the simulated robotic soccer domain using the RoboCup soccer server (Corten *et al.* 1999; Noda *et al.* 1998). In this domain, there are 22 agents, each acting up to 10 times per second. Each agent gets local, incomplete perceptory information, making it impossible to determine another agent's impression of the world state based only upon the actual world state. Sensors, actuators, and world dynamics are all noisy. However, both the ball and players have maximum speeds enforced by the simulation.

Over the past several years, we have created teams of soccer-playing agents for use in the RoboCup simulator. The teams are all called "CMUnited-XX," where "XX" indicates the year in which they first participated in the RoboCup international simulator tournament. For example, the most recent incarnation, "CMUNITED-99," was introduced at the RoboCup-99 tournament in Stockholm, Sweden which was held in August of 1999.

Although CMUNITED-98 (Stone, Veloso, & Riley 1999), the champion of RoboCup-98, out-scored its opponents by a combined score of 66–0, it failed to score on many opportunities in which it had the ball close to the opponent's goal, especially against the better opponents. Similarly, when playing against itself, there are many shots on goal, but few goals (roughly one by each team every 3 games). Since CMUNITED-98 became publicly available after the 1998 competition, we expected there to be several teams at RoboCup-99 that could beat CMUNITED-98, and indeed there were. In order to improve its performance, we introduced IMBBOP into the CMUNITED-99 team, specifically to improve its goal-scoring ability.

IMBBOP is used in several ways in CMUNITED-99. Most significantly in terms of performance, it is used to decide when to shoot and when to pass when an agent has the ball very near to the opponent's goal. It is also used by agents to determine when the opponents are likely to be able to steal the ball from them. The remainder of this section motivates the specific robotic soccer tasks to which IMB-BOP has been applied.

When to Shoot

One of the most important offensive decisions in robotic soccer is the decision of when to shoot the ball towards the goal. In CMUNITED-98, decisions about when to shoot were made in one of three ways:

- Based on the distance to the goal
- Based on the number of opponents between the ball and the goal
- Based on a decision tree.

All of these methods have significant problems in this domain. Distance to goal completely ignores how the opponents are positioned. The number of opponents between the ball and the goal does not accurately reflect in how *good* of a position the defenders are. Lastly, the decision tree was trained for passing(Stone 2000), so its performance on the related but different behavior of shooting is questionable.

Empirically, these methods were not effective when playing against good opponents, as indicated by the low number of goals scored by CMUNITED-98 both against itself and against the closest two competitors at the RoboCup-98 competition.

When to Pass Near the Goal

When near the opponent's goal, an agent may often be faced with the decision of whether to shoot the ball or to pass to a teammate. CMUNITED-98 agents never passed the ball when near the opponent's goal under the assumption that an agent should always shoot when given the opportunity.

However, we observed several situations in which an agent shot the ball from a bad angle and missed, even though there was a nearby teammate with a much better angle at which to shoot. In order to remedy this situation, it is necessary to equip the agents with a method for evaluating whether passing the ball would lead to a higher chance of scoring than would shooting.

Breakaways

An important idea in many team ball sports like soccer is the idea of a *breakaway*. Intuitively, this is when some number of offensive players get the ball and themselves past the defenders, leaving only perhaps a goalie preventing them from scoring. Shooting and passing at the proper time is particularly important on breakaways. If the agent shoots too early, the goalie will have plenty of time to stop the ball. If the agent shoots too late, then the goalie may have time to get the ball before the kick is complete.

When on a breakaway, an agent must decide when to shoot the ball. Therefore, by improving upon the solution to the shooting problem described above, the resulting breakaway performance can also be improved. The empirical results in this paper are based on performance statistics when using different shooting strategies on breakaways.

Cycles to Steal

CMUNITED-99 makes use of teammate and opponent models most prominently in the situations described above. However, it also makes use of opponent models to determine whether or not an agent can keep control of the ball without an opponent stealing it. Such an ability is a prerequisite for an agent being able to safely *dribble* (interleave short kicks and dashes in a given direction so that the agent in effect moves with the ball). As such, it also impacts on the agent's ability to execute breakaways and score goals.

IMBBOP

IMBBOP is designed for situations in which an agent X has a goal G to be achieved by time T. X must determine whether agent Y can prevent (if an "opponent") or achieve (if a "teammate")[1] G after X takes action A. In particular, X must determine which of its possible actions $A_1, \ldots, A_n$ is most likely to achieve G by time T.

IMBBOP makes the following assumptions:

- X must select an action from among $A_1, \ldots, A_n$ to be executed immediately. It then ceases to affect the achievement of G.

- Whether or not Y can achieve or prevent X's goal depends on T. That is, $\exists t$ s.t. Y could achieve G by, or prevent G from being achieved by, time t.

- X has a model of the world dynamics.

- X has incomplete information regarding Y's current state.

- X has an incomplete model of Y's capabilities (how it can affect the world). That is, X knows (through the world model) what actions Y can take, but has no model of how Y chooses its action. However, based on the world model, X can deduce an upper bound on Y's capabilities in terms of the minimum time necessary to execute tasks. For example, the world model could specify a maximum possible agent speed.

Given these assumptions, IMBBOP works as follows.

1. Using the model of world dynamics and the resultant upper bounds on agent capabilities, determine analytically the minimum t such that Y could prevent or achieve G by time t after X takes action A.

2. Use a threshold on $T - t$ to predict whether or not action A will succeed: the greater $T - t$, the more likely Y is to be able to prevent or achieve G by time T. Thus, $T - t$ is an indication of the likelihood that action A will result in goal G being achieved by time T.

In step 1, such an analysis is made possible under the simplifying assumption that the world dynamics and a time-based bound on the action capabilities of Y are known. In addition, X fills in missing information about Y with best-case values from Y's perspective (i.e., if Y could be in one of n states, X assumes that Y is in the state from which it

---

[1] Here we consider an agent to be a teammate if it also has the goal G and to be an opponent if it has the goal of preventing G. We assume that X knows which agents are teammates and which are opponents.

could most quickly achieve or prevent G). Note that there is no guarantee that Y could *actually* achieve G by time t.

For example, if Y is currently located at location (x_1, y_1) and must get to location (x_2, y_2) in order to prevent G, then, using a theoretical maximum speed of s, X could compute analytically that Y cannot get to location (x_2, y_2) in time less than $\frac{\sqrt{(x_2-x_1)^2+(y_2-y_1)^2}}{s}$. In actual fact, it may be unlikely that Y could actually arrive at (x_2, y_2) so quickly given the time necessary for it to figure out that it needs to get there and possibly accelerate to the maximum speed.

In practice, X will execute action A based on whether or not $T - t$ exceeds some threshold.

IMBBOP in CMUNITED-99

This section details the application of IMBBOP to the specific robotic soccer tasks laid out above. The CMUNITED-99 simulated robotic soccer team includes all of these applications.

While IMBBOP is principally concerned with predicting the outcomes of other agents' behaviors, it also makes use of a model of the agent's own action outcomes. In general, it is possible to predict an agent's own action outcomes via empirical testing. For example, we determined empirically that an agent can generally position the ball and kick it with high power in a chosen direction in 4 or fewer simulator cycles. While 4 is not a hard upper bound on the number of cycles due to the noise in the simulator, it is an empirically reliable estimate and is used in our estimate of the number cycles it will take an opponent to steal the ball.

When to Shoot

As mentioned above, CMUNITED-98's methods for deciding when to shoot were ineffective against good opponents. CMUNITED-99 makes this decision in a more principled way by using a model of an "optimal" opponent goalie. That is, we use a model of a goalie that reacts instantaneously to a kick, moves to exactly the right position to stop the ball, and catches with perfect accuracy.

When deciding whether to shoot, the agent first identifies its best shot target. It generally considers two spots, just inside each of the two sides of the goal. The agent then considers the lines from the ball to each of these possible shot targets. *shot-target* is the position whose line is further from the goalie's current position.

The agent then predicts, given a shot at *shot-target*, the ball's position and goalie's reaction using the optimal goalie model. We use the following predicates:

blocking-point The point on the ball's path for which an optimal goalie heads.

ball-to-goalie-cycles The number of cycles for the ball to get to the *blocking-point*

goalie-to-ball-cycles The number of cycles for the goalie to get to the *blocking-point*

shot-margin =*ball-to-goalie-cycles*−*goalie-to-ball-cycles*

better-shot(k) Whether teammate k has a better shot than the agent with the ball, as judged by *shot-margin*

The value of *ball-to-goalie-cycles* corresponds to T in our definition of IMBBOP, while *goalie-to-ball-cycles* corresponds to t. The value *shot-margin* is a measure of the quality of the shot. The smaller the value of *shot-margin*, the more difficult it will be for the goalie to stop the shot. For example, for a long shot, the ball may reach the *blocking-point* in 20 cycles (*ball-to-goalie-cycles*= 20), while the goalie can get there in 5 cycles (*goalie-to-ball-cycles*= 5). This gives a *shot-margin* of 15. In terms of IMBBOP, $T = 20$, $t = 5$, and $T - t = 15$. This is a much worse shot than if it takes the ball only 12 cycles (*ball-to-goalie-cycles*= 12) and the goalie 10 cycles to reach the *blocking-point* (*goalie-to-ball-cycles*= 10). The latter shot has a *shot-margin* of only 2 ($T = 12, t = 10, T - t = 2$). Further, if *shot-margin*$ < 0$ ($T - t < 0$), then the "optimal" goalie could not reach the ball in time, and the shot should succeed.

When to Pass Near the Goal

Using a model of opponent behavior gives us a more reliable and adaptive way of making the shooting decision. We can also use it to make better passing decisions via a model of teammate behavior outcomes. As mentioned above, CMUNITED-98 never passed the ball when near the opponent's goal. In CMUNITED-99, the agent with the ball simulates the situation in which its teammate is controlling the ball, using the goalie model to determine how good a shot the teammate has. If the teammate has a much better shot, then the predicate *better-shot*(k) will be true, indicating that the agent should pass rather than shooting itself.

In this case, the agent is using an optimal model of both the teammate *and* the opponent goalie. The *shot-target* is computed from the teammate's perspective, and the speed at which the teammate will be able to propel the ball towards the goal is assumed to be as high as possible according to the world model. The *blocking-point*, *ball-to-goalie-cycles*, and *goalie-to-ball-cycles* are all computed from the teammate's and goalie's current positions. Now, since we are primarily predicting the teammate's performance, T is the *goalie-to-ball-cycles* and t is the *ball-to-goalie-cycles*. The greater the value of $T - t$, the more likely the teammate is to succeed in getting the ball past the goalie.

There is one complication here; it takes time to pass the ball. In the time that elapses during a pass, the world changes, and the receiving agent may then decide the original agent has a better shot. This could lead to passing loops where neither agent shoots. CMUNITED-99 does two things to avoid this loop. First, the agent only passes to a teammate with a better shot if, given the current state, the goalie cannot stop the shot ($T - t > 0$). Secondly, the extra time difference between the passing and receiving agents must be greater than some threshold (5 in CMUNITED-99).

Note that this analysis of shooting ignores the presence of defenders. Just because the goalie can not stop the shot (as judged by the optimal goalie model) does not mean that a nearby defender can not run in to kick the ball away.

Breakaways

The above technique for using a model of teammates and opponent goalies can be incorporated into a special-purpose breakaway behavior. We precisely define a breakaway using several predicates:

controlling-teammate Which teammate (if any) is currently controlling the ball. "Control" is judged by whether the ball is in the area defined by the simulator within which the player can physically kick the ball.

controlling-opponent Which opponent (if any) is currently controlling the ball

opponents-in-breakaway-cone The breakaway cone is shown in Figure 1. The cone has its vertex at the player with the ball and extends to the opponents goal posts.

teammates-in-breakaway-cone The same as the previous definition, but for the other side of the field. This is used when judging whether the opponents currently have a breakaway.

our-breakaway = (*controlling-teammate*≠ None) ∧ (*controlling-opponent*=None) ∧ (*opponents-in-breakaway-cone*≤1)

their-breakaway = (*controlling-opponent*≠ None) ∧ (*controlling-teammate*=None) ∧ (*teammates-in-breakaway-cone*≤1)

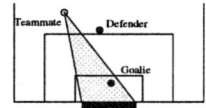

Figure 1: The Breakaway Cone

Once the agent determines that it is on a breakaway (*our-breakaway* is true), it starts dribbling the ball towards the opponent's goal (actually slightly across the front of the goal). It continues to do so until deciding to shoot, at which point it kicks the ball as hard as possible towards a corner of the goal (*shot-target*). The decision of when to stop dribbling in order to shoot is the key decision when on a breakaway.

We use the optimal model described above to help make this decision. During a breakaway, the agent shoots when either one of the following is true:

1. *shot-margin* (or $T - t$) gets below a certain threshold (1 cycle in CMUNITED-99)

2. The time that it would take for the goalie to proceed directly to the ball and steal it gets below a certain threshold (6 cycles in CMUNITED-99). This time is again determined analytically using an optimal model of the goalie's movement capabilities (See the description of "cycles to steal" that follows).

This skill was extremely effective in the competition, with the vast majority of our goals being scored using the specialized breakaway code.

Cycles to Steal

CMUNITED-99 also makes use of opponent models to determine whether or not an agent can keep control of the ball without an opponent stealing it. In this case, it is necessary to determine whether the nearest opponent could get to the ball in less time than it would take to safely kick the ball away. Thus, T is the time it would take to kick the ball away. In CMUNITED-99, we use the constant $T = 3$ since an agent can generally position the ball and kick it with high power in a chosen direction in 3 simulator cycles.

The time (t) it would take the opponent to get to the ball's current position is computed based on the opponent's current position, the maximum speed of the opponent in the simulator, and an estimate of how long it would take the opponent to move around the agent to get to the ball (only if the agent is between the ball and the opponent).

The agent bases its decision of whether or not to dribble based on a threshold of on $T-t$. In CMUNITED-99, players only dribble when $T - t < 1$. That is, they need to be fairly certain that the opponent will not be able to steal the ball before they are willing to dribble.

Results

In this section we present empirical results demonstrating the effectiveness of IMBBOP in the robotic soccer domain. First we evaluate the performance of an individual agent on a breakaway when using IMBBOP. Second, we present evidence of IMBBOP's usefulness to the team as a whole.

Isolated Testing

In order to test the effectiveness of IMBBOP in simulated robotic soccer, we ran simulations involving only 2 players: a goalie and a striker. The striker and ball were repeatedly placed 30m away from the goal. The goalie was placed next to the goal. The task of the striker is to attempt to shoot the ball past the goalie into the goal, while the goalie aims to thwart the striker. This setup creates a breakaway situation.

In all cases, the striker dribbles the ball roughly towards the goal until deciding to shoot.Meanwhile, the goalie must decide when to start moving towards the ball in an attempt to block it. At one extreme, it could wait until the player shoots, thereby ensuring that it will no longer be able to change the ball's direction. At the other extreme, it could immediately move towards the striker in an attempt to "cut down the angle," or reduce the amount of open goal from the striker's perspective.

The strategies we use for the goalie during testing are:

1. Wait for the striker to shoot the ball before trying to get it.

2. Once the striker gets to within 24m of the goal, run out to try and catch the ball.

3. Once the striker gets to within 35m of the goal (effectively immediately), run out to try and catch the ball.

Meanwhile, we tested several striker strategies with IMBBOP and without against each of the possible goalie strategies. As described in the previous section, the CMUNITED-99 strikers use two different types of opponent models when executing breakaways: one based on *shot-margin* (Condition 1 above) and one based on the predicted number of cycles it would take the goalie to steal the ball (Condition 2). Thus, the striker can use neither, either, or both models when deciding when to shoot. When using neither model, it shoots purely based on its distance to the goal.

Thus, the strategies for the striker are:

1. Use both models to determine when to shoot (conditions 1 and 2).
2. Use only the stealing ball model (condition 2).
3. Use only the *shot-margin* model (condition 1).
4. Shoot as soon as within 17m of the goal.
5. Shoot as soon as within 25m of the goal.

Each striker strategy was tested against each goalie strategy for 10,000 simulator cycles, which allows between 95 and 215 separate breakaway attempts. The percentage of breakaways that result in goals for each of these combinations of strategies is shown in Figure 2. The numbered goalie strategy indicated on the x-axis corresponds the goalie strategy as numbered above.

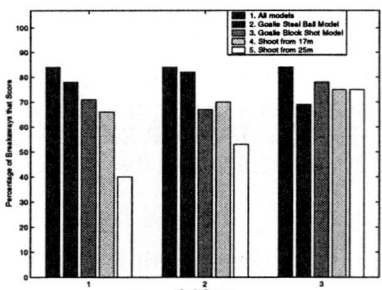

Figure 2: The effectiveness of different types of models. The percentage of breakaways which result in a goal is shown for various goalie strategies and uses of models. The numbered goalie strategy indicated on the x-axis corresponds the strategy as numbered in the text.

When using both models, the striker performs consistently better than in all other cases regardless of the goalie's strategy. But when using only one of the models, the results are sometimes *worse* than shooting based just on distance. A goalie has two basic ways to stop a shot (as reflected in the two models): by getting in the way once the ball is kicked, or by stealing the ball before the shot can be taken. Using only one of the models only reflects one of these possibilities. On the other hand, a distance threshold takes into account both of these abilities *for a particular goalie strategy*.

For any particular breakaway, there is some distance from the goal at which the striker should shoot. This distance depends mostly on the strategy which the goalie is using. Therefore, for any particular goalie strategy, *some* distance threshold for shooting will probably perform quite well. The importance of using the goalie models is that with the models, the agent can perform well no matter what strategy the goalie uses. The players do not need to know the goalie strategy *a priori*, and if the goalie changes its strategy, the agents will adapt effectively.

Full Games

IMBBOP has proven to be very useful to us in creating the CMUNITED-99 team of soccer-playing agents (Stone, Riley, & Veloso 2000). While CMUNITED-98 could rarely score when playing against itself (roughly 1 goal every 3 games), CMUNITED-99 scores about 9 goals per game when playing against CMUNITED-98.

Since there were several improvements over CMUNITED-98 incorporated into CMUNITED-99, it is usually difficult to isolate a single change as being responsible for the team's overall improvement. However, in this case, there is clear evidence that incorporating IMBBOP into the agents' breakaway strategy is itself enough to lead to a significant improvement in the team's performance.

In order to demonstrate this claim, we played five versions of CMUNITED-99 against the CMUNITED-98 team. The only difference among these 5 versions was that their agents used the 5 different breakaway strategies listed above. Each version played 9 10-minute games against CMUNITED-98. Table 1 displays the mean goals per game scored by each of these versions, as well as the standard deviation. CMUNITED-98 never scored a goal.

Goals/Game	Breakaway Strategy				
	1	2	3	4	5
Mean	8.9	10.6	8.6	3.6	3.6
Std. Dev.	± 1.5	± 1.3	± 2.6	± 1.4	± 1.0

Table 1: Goals scored by CMUNITED-99 against CMUNITED-98 when using the different breakaway strategies. Each trial represents 9 10-minute games. CMUNITED-98 never scored.

The three strategies (1–3) using some form of IMBBOP all performed significantly better than the two (4–5) which do not. Note that the the CMUNITED-98 team used breakaway strategy 4 (always shooting from 17m). Although breakaway strategy 2, which only uses one of the two types of opponent models, outperforms strategy 1, which uses both, the result is only borderline significant. In addition, as noted above, each strategy will work against *some* specific goalie. When testing against different goalie types as in the previous subsection, we found that breakaway strategy 1 was most effective overall.

Since the RoboCup tournaments do not provide controlled testing environments, we cannot make any definite conclusions based on the competitions. However, when watching the games during RoboCup-99, we noticed many goals scored as a result of well-timed shots and passes near the opponent's goal. In the end, CMUNITED-99 went on to win the RoboCup-99 championship, outscoring its opponents, many of which were ale to beat CMUNITED-98, by a combined score of 110–0.

Related Work

There is a long history in adversarial game playing of using a model of an opponent which assumes that it always acts optimally. For example, in the minimax search algorithm, one enumerates all the possible actions that the other agent may take and then always assumes that the other agent takes the action that is the ideal action from its own viewpoint, which would be the worst action for us. This means that minimax acts safely, but not opportunistically: it maximizes worst-case performance. If the other agent does not perform its ideal action, then minimax's choice yields an outcome better than predicted.

Minimax is designed for turn-taking adversarial domains with complete information and discrete actions (such as chess). In contrast, our research focuses on adversarial domains in which the agents have incomplete information, noisy sensors and actuators, and a continuous action space (such as adversarial robotic control). Nonetheless, we are able to build on one key feature of minimax—the use of a model of the other agent's future actions in relation to its theoretical optimal actions—in our model-based technique, IMBBOP. Our technique also includes a method for relaxing this optimality assumption.

An alternative to minimax, in which other agents aren't necessarily assumed to act optimally, is the recursive modeling method (RMM) (Gmytrasiewicz, Durfee, & Wehe 1991). Using RMM, an agent models the internal state and action selection strategy of another agent in order to predict its actions. This method is recursive because the other agent might similarly be modeling the original agent, leading to an arbitrary depth of reasoning (techniques for limiting this depth have been studied (Durfee 1995; Vidal & Durfee 1995)).

A limitation of both minimax and RMM is that they rely on knowing the state of other agents and their action capabilities in order to construct payoff matrices. In contrast, our research is concerned with situations in which the agent's state and action capabilities may not be known (we do assume a known upper bound on their capabilities).

Past approaches have examined methods for deducing agents' action capabilities through observation (Wang 1996); deducing agent's plans given their actions (Huber & Durfee 1995); and deducing agents' actions given incomplete observations of their states (Tambe 1995). All of these approaches address situations in which an agent does not have the information necessary to determine the optimal actions of other agents in the environment. IMBBOP addresses similar situations, but differs from all of these approaches in that it does not directly deduce an agent's actions, plans, or capabilities. Rather, it uses an idealized world model and observable agent state information to estimate the agent's optimal action. It characterizes the *actual* capabilities of the agent in relation to this estimated optimal action.

Conclusion and Future Work

Ideal-model-based behavior outcome prediction is potentially applicable and useful in any domain in which an agent does not know the states and action capabilities of other agents in the environment. By using a model of the world dynamics to determine an upper-bound on agent performance (the ideal), an agent's actual performance can be characterized in relation to this ideal.

The presentation of IMBBOP and its first application as reported in this paper include engineered aspects that may be specific to the robotic soccer domain. For example, the time-based threshold and the particular parameter values and predicates used to define the agent behaviors are tailored to this domain. However, we hope to extend this technique to additional domains in the future.

When evaluating whether a potential action is likely to achieve an agent's goal, an agent using IMBBOP uses a time-based threshold $(T-t)$ to represent the predicted maximum or minimum difference between another agent's actual performance and its ideal performance. Our work reported in this paper uses hard-wired thresholds. However, the opportunity exists for on-line learning of these threshold values. Learning models, or adaptively modeling other agents, is a part of our on-going and future research.

Meanwhile, our IMBBOP implementation has played a significant role in our successful development of a team of simulated robotic soccer-playing agents.

References

Corten, E.; Dorer, K.; Heintz, F.; Kostiadis, K.; Kummeneje, J.; Myritz, H.; Noda, I.; Riley, P.; Stone, P.; and Yeap, T. 1999. Soccer server manual, version 5.0. Technical Report RoboCup-1999-001, RoboCup. At URL http://ci.etl.go.jp/˜noda/soccer/server/Documents.html.

Durfee, E. H. 1995. Blissful ignorance: Knowing just enough to coordinate well. In *Proceedings of the First International Conference on Multi-Agent Systems (ICMAS-95)*, 406–413. Menlo Park, California: AAAI Press.

Gmytrasiewicz, P. J.; Durfee, E. H.; and Wehe, D. K. 1991. A decision-theoretic approach to coordinating multiagent interactions. In *Proceedings of the Twelfth International Joint Conference on Artificial Intelligence*, 62–68.

Huber, M. J., and Durfee, E. H. 1995. Deciding when to commit to action during observation-based coordination. In *Proceedings of the First International Conference on Multi-Agent Systems (ICMAS-95)*, 163–170. Menlo Park, California: AAAI Press.

Kitano, H.; Tambe, M.; Stone, P.; Veloso, M.; Coradeschi, S.; Osawa, E.; Matsubara, H.; Noda, I.; and Asada, M. 1997. The RoboCup synthetic agent challenge 97. In *Proceedings of the Fifteenth International Joint Conference on Artificial Intelligence*, 24–29. San Francisco, CA: Morgan Kaufmann.

Noda, I.; Matsubara, H.; Hiraki, K.; and Frank, I. 1998. Soccer server: A tool for research on multiagent systems. *Applied Artificial Intelligence* 12:233–250.

Stone, P.; Riley, P.; and Veloso, M. 2000. The CMUnited-99 champion simulator team. In Veloso, M.; Pagello, E.; and Kitano, H., eds., *RoboCup-99: Robot Soccer World Cup III*. Berlin: Springer Verlag.

Stone, P.; Veloso, M.; and Riley, P. 1999. The CMUnited-98 champion simulator team. In Asada, M., and Kitano, H., eds., *RoboCup-98: Robot Soccer World Cup II*. Berlin: Springer Verlag.

Stone, P. 2000. *Layered Learning in Multiagent Systems: A Winning Approach to Robotic Soccer*. Intelligent Robotics and Autonomous Agents. MIT Press.

Tambe, M. 1995. Recursive agent and agent-group tracking in a real-time, dynamic environment. In *Proceedings of the First International Conference on Multi-Agent Systems (ICMAS-95)*, 368–375. Menlo Park, California: AAAI Press.

Vidal, J. M., and Durfee, E. H. 1995. Recursive agent modeling using limited rationality. In *Proceedings of the First International Conference on Multi-Agent Systems (ICMAS-95)*, 376–383. Menlo Park, California: AAAI Press.

Wang, X. 1996. Planning while learning operators. In *Proceedings of the Third International Conference on AI Planning Systems*.

Rapid Development of a High Performance Knowledge Base for Course of Action Critiquing

Gheorghe Tecuci, Mihai Boicu, Dorin Marcu, Michael Bowman, Florin Ciucu, and Cristian Levcovici

Learning Agents Laboratory, Department of Computer Science, MS 4A5
George Mason University, 4400 University Drive, Fairfax, VA 22030-4444
{tecuci, mboicu, dmarcu, mbowman3, fciucu, clevcovi}@gmu.edu, http://lalab.gmu.edu

Abstract

This paper presents a practical learning-based methodology and agent shell for building knowledge bases and knowledge-based agents, and their innovative application to the development of a critiquing agent for military courses of action, a challenge problem set by DARPA's High Performance Knowledge Bases program. The agent shell consists of an integrated set of knowledge acquisition, learning and problem solving modules for a generic knowledge base structured into two main components: an ontology that defines the concepts from a specific application domain, and a set of task reduction rules expressed with these concepts. The rapid development of the COA critiquing agent was done by importing an initial ontology from CYC and by teaching the agent to perform its tasks in a way that resembles how an expert would teach a human apprentice when solving problems in cooperation. The methodology, the agent shell, and the developed critiquer were evaluated in several intensive studies, and demonstrated very good results.

1 Introduction

The purpose of this paper is twofold: 1) to present a maturing learning-based methodology and tool for developing knowledge-based agents, and 2) to present an innovative application of this methodology and tool.

This work was performed as part of the High Performance Knowledge Bases (HPKB) program which ran from 1997 to 1999, with support from DARPA and AFOSR (Cohen et al. 1998). The goal of HPKB was to produce the technology needed to rapidly construct large knowledge-bases that provide comprehensive coverage of topics of interest, are reusable by multiple applications with diverse problem-solving strategies, and are maintainable in rapidly changing environments. The organizations participating in HPKB were given the challenge of solving a selection of knowledge-based problems in a particular domain, and then modifying their systems quickly to solve further problems in the same domain. The aim of the exercise was to test the claim that, with the latest AI technology, large knowledge bases can be built quickly and efficiently.

Our approach to HPKB is based on the Disciple apprenticeship multistrategy learning theory, methodology and shell for rapid development of knowledge bases and knowledge-based agents (Tecuci 1998). The challenge problem for the first year of HPKB was to build a knowledge-based workaround agent that is able to plan how a convoy of military vehicles can "work around" (i.e. circumvent or overcome) obstacles in their path, such as damaged bridges or minefields (Tecuci et al. 1999). The challenge problem for the second year of HPKB was to build a critiquing agent that can evaluate military Courses of Action (COA) that were developed as hasty candidate plans for ground combat operations. The developed Disciple agents and the Disciple shell were evaluated during intense DARPA annual evaluations, together with the other systems developed in the HPKB program by the other participating teams. In both cases the Disciple agents were developed very rapidly and demonstrated performance superior to the other developed systems.

In this paper we will present the successful application of the Disciple approach to the COA challenge problem. We will first describe this challenge problem which in itself represents an innovative application of Artificial Intelligence. Then we will present the Disciple tool and methodology used to build the COA critiquing agent. After that we will present the results of DARPA's evaluation of the developed tools and COA critiquers. We will also briefly present the results of a separate knowledge acquisition experiment with Disciple. We will conclude the paper with a discussion of these results and the future direction of our work.

2 The Course of Action Challenge Problem

A military COA is a preliminary outline of a plan for how a military unit might attempt to accomplish a mission. A COA is not a complete plan in that it leaves out many details of the operation such as exact initial locations of friendly and enemy forces. After receiving orders to plan for a mission, a commander and staff complete a detailed and practiced process of analyzing the mission, conceiving and evaluating potential COAs, selection of a COA, and the preparation of detailed plans to accomplish the mission based on the selected COA. The general practice is for the staff to generate several COAs for a mission, and then to

---

Copyright © 2000, American Association for Artificial Intelligence (www.aaai.org). All rights reserved.

make a comparison of those COAs based on many factors including the situation, the commander's guidance, the principles of war, and the tenets of army operations. The commander makes the final decision on which COA will be used to generate his or her plan based on the recommendations of the staff and his or her own experience with the same factors considered by the staff (Jones, 1999).

The COA challenge problem consisted of rapidly developing a knowledge-based critiquing agent that can automatically critique COAs for ground force operations, can systematically assess selected aspects of a COA, and can suggest repairs to it. The role of this agent is to act as an assistant to the military commander, helping the commander to choose between several COAs under consideration for a certain mission. The agent could also help students to learn to develop courses of action.

The input to the COA critiquing agent consists of the description of a COA that includes the following aspects:

a) The COA sketch, such as the one in the top part of Figure 1, is a graphical depiction of the preliminary plan being considered. It includes enough of the high level structure and maneuver aspects of the plan to show how the actions of each unit fit together to accomplish the overall purpose, while omitting much of the execution detail that will be included in the eventual operational plan. The three primary elements included in a COA sketch are: control measures which limit and control interactions between units; unit graphics that depict known, initial locations and make up of friendly and enemy units; and mission graphics that depict actions and tasks assigned to friendly units. The COA sketch is drawn using a palette-based sketching utility.

b) The COA statement, such as the partial one shown in the bottom part of Figure 1, clearly explains what the units in a course of action will do to accomplish the assigned mission. This text includes a description of the mission and the desired end state, as well as standard elements that describe purposes, operations,

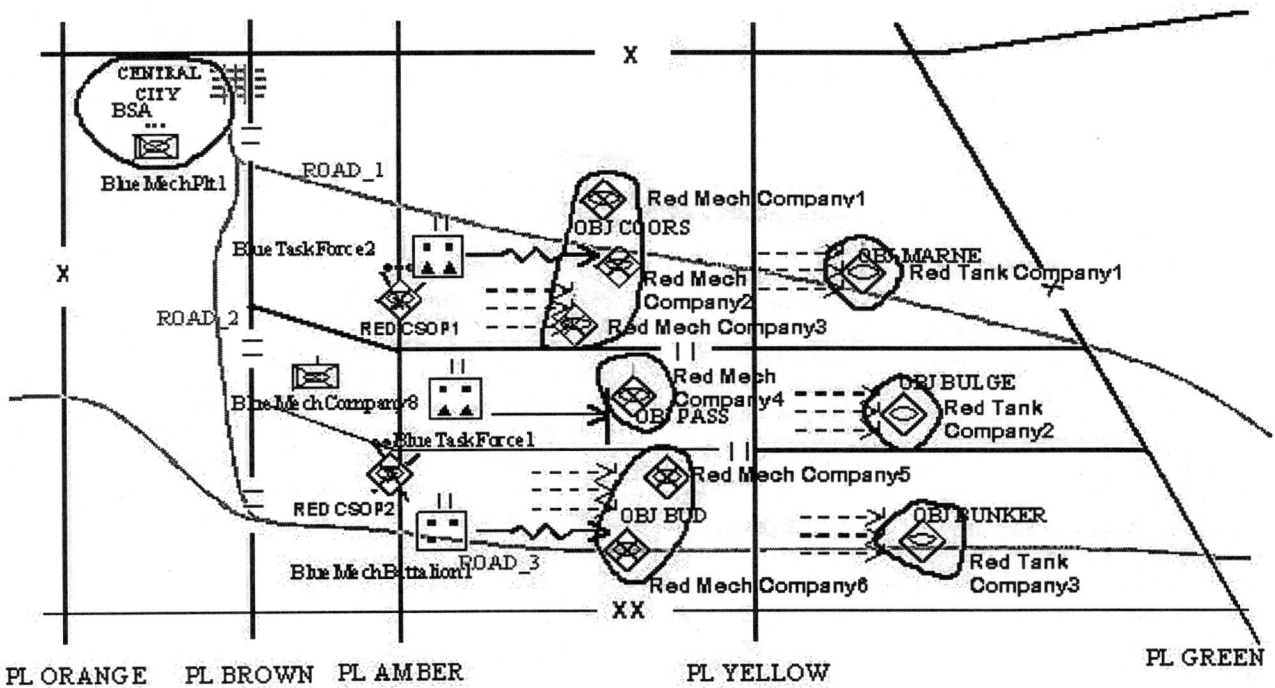

Mission: BLUE-BRIGADE2 attacks to penetrate RED-MECH-REGIMENT2 at 130600 Aug in order to enable the completion of seize OBJ-SLAM by BLUE-ARMOR-BRIGADE1.

Close: BLUE-TASK-FORCE1, a balanced task force (MAIN-EFFORT) attacks to penetrate RED-MECH-COMPANY4, then clears RED-TANK-COMPANY2 in order to enable the completion of seize OBJ-SLAM by BLUE-ARMOR-BRIGADE1.

BLUE-TASK-FORCE2, a balanced task force (SUPPORTING-EFFORT1) attacks to fix RED-MECH-COMPANY1 and RED-MECH-COMPANY2 and RED-MECH-COMPANY3 in order to prevent RED-MECH-COMPANY1 and RED-MECH-COMPANY2 and RED-MECH-COMPANY3 from interfering with conducts of the MAIN-EFFORT1, then clears RED-MECH-COMPANY1 and RED-MECH-COMPANY2 and RED-MECH-COMPANY3 and RED-TANK-COMPANY1.

...

Figure 1: A sample of a COA sketch and a fragment of a COA statement.

tasks, forms of maneuver, units, and resources to be used in the COA. The COA statement is expressed in a restricted but expressive subset of English.

c) Selected products of mission analysis, such as the areas of operations of the units, avenues of approach, key terrain, unit combat power, and enemy COAs.

Based on this input, the critiquing agent has to assess various aspects of the COA, such as its viability (suitability, feasibility, acceptability and completeness), its correctness (array of forces, scheme of maneuver, command and control), and its strengths and weaknesses with respect to the Principles of War and the Tenets of Army Operations, to justify the assessments made and to propose improvements to the COA.

In the HPKB program, the COA challenge problem was solved by developing an integrated system composed of several critiquers, each built by a different team, to solve a part of the overall problem. The teams were Teknowledge-Cycorp, ISI/Expect, ISI/Loom, and GMU. All these teams shared an input ontology and used the same internal representation of the input generated by Teknowledge, AIAI, and Northwestern Univ., from COA descriptions provided by Alphatech.

We developed a COA critiquer, called Disciple-COA, that identifies the strengths and the weaknesses of a course of action with respect to the principles of war and the tenets of army operations (FM-105, 1993). There are nine principles of war: objective, offensive, mass, economy of force, maneuver, unity of command, security, surprise, and simplicity. They provide general guidance for the conduct of war at the strategic, operational and tactical levels. The tenets of army operations describe the characteristics of successful operations. They are: initiative, agility, depth, synchronization and versatility. Figure 2, for instance, shows some of the strengths of the COA from Figure 1 with respect to the Principle of Mass, identified by Disciple-COA.

In addition to generating answers in natural language, Disciple also provides the reference material based on which the answers are generated, as shown in the bottom of Figure 2. Also, the Disciple-COA agent can provide justifications for the generated answers at three levels of detail, from a very abstract one that shows the general line of reasoning followed, to a very detailed one that indicates each of the knowledge pieces used in generating the answer.

In the next section we will present the general methodology used to build Disciple-COA and the architecture of Disciple-COA.

3 General Presentation of Disciple-COA

Disciple is the name of an evolving theory, methodology and shell for rapid development of knowledge bases and knowledge-based agents, by subject matter experts, with limited assistance from knowledge engineers (Tecuci, 1998). The current Disciple shell consists of an integrated set of knowledge acquisition, learning and problem solving modules for a generic knowledge base (KB) structured into two main components: an ontology that defines the concepts from a specific application domain, and a set of problem solving rules expressed with these concepts. The problem solving approach of an agent built with Disciple is task reduction, where a task to be accomplished by the agent is successively reduced to simpler tasks until the initial task is reduced to a set of elementary tasks that can be immediately performed. Therefore, the rules from the KB are task reduction rules. The ontology consists of hierarchical descriptions of objects, features and tasks, represented as frames, according to the knowledge model of the Open Knowledge Base Connectivity (OKBC) protocol (Chaudhri et al. 1998).

The development of a specific Disciple agent includes the following processes: 1) the customization of the problem solver and the interfaces of the Disciple shell for that particular domain; 2) the building of the domain ontology by importing knowledge from external repositories of knowledge and by manually defining the other components of the ontology, and 3) teaching the agent to perform its tasks, teaching that resembles how an expert would teach a human apprentice when solving problems in cooperation. Following this process we have developed Disciple-COA which is presented in Figure 3.

Assess COA411 with respect to the Principle of Mass

There is a major strength in COA411 with respect to mass because BLUE-TASK-FORCE1 is the MAIN-EFFORT1 and it acts on the decisive point of the COA (RED-MECH-COMPANY4) with a force ratio of 10.6, which exceeds a recommended force ratio of 3.0. Additionally, the main effort is assisted by supporting action SUPPRESS-MILITARY-TASK1 which also acts on the decisive point. This is good evidence of the allocation of significantly more than minimum combat power required at the decisive point and is indicative of the proper application of the principle of mass.

There is a strength in COA411 with respect to mass because BLUE-TASK-FORCE1 is the main effort of the COA and it has been allocated 33% of available combat power but this is considered just a medium level weighting of the main effort.

There is a strength in COA411 with respect to mass because BLUE-MECH-COMPANY8 is a COMPANY-UNIT-DESIGNATION level maneuver unit assigned to be the reserve. This is considered a strong reserve for a BRIGADE-UNIT-DESIGNATION level COA and would be available to continue the operation or exploit success.

Reference: FM 100-5 pg 2-4, KF 113.1, KF 113.2, KF 113.3, KF 113.4, KF 113.5 - To mass is to synchronize the effects of all elements of combat power at the proper point and time to achieve decisive results Observance of the Principle of Mass may be evidenced by allocation to the main effort of significantly greater combat power than the minimum required throughout its mission, accounting for expected losses. Mass is evidenced by the allocation of significantly more than minimum combat power required at the decisive point.

Figure 2: Solutions generated by Disciple-COA.

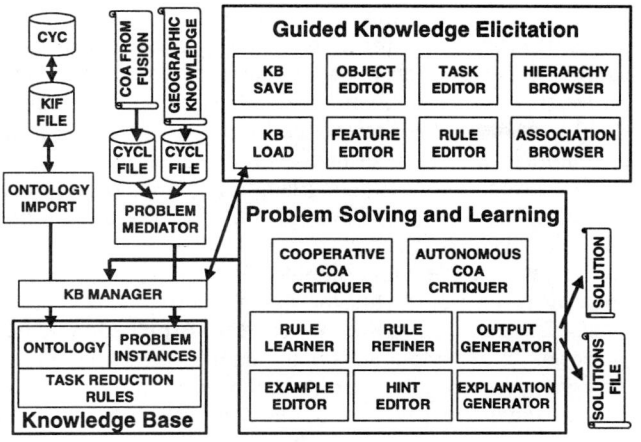

Figure 3: The architecture of Disciple-COA.

For Disciple-COA, an initial ontology was defined by importing the input ontology built by Teknowledge and Cycorp for the COA challenge problem. The input ontology contains the terms needed to represent the COAs to be critiqued, and was shared by all the developed critiquers. The top level of this ontology is represented in Figure 4. It includes concepts for representing geographical information, military organizations and equipment, descriptions of specific COAs, military tasks, operations and purposes. As shown in the top left of Figure 3, this ontology was first translated from CYC's language into KIF (Genesereth and Fikes, 1992) and from there it was translated into the representation language of Disciple and the other critiquers.

The imported ontology was further developed by using the ontology building tools of Disciple shown in the top right side of Figure 3 (the object, feature, task and rule editors and browsers).

As presented in the previous section, the COA to be critiqued is represented as a sketch and a textual description. A statement translator (developed by AIAI), a COA sketcher (developed by Teknowledge), and a geographic reasoner (developed by Northwestern Univ.) transform and fuse these external representations into a description in the CYC language, according to the input ontology. This description is imported into Disciple's ontology by the problem mediator module of Disciple.

Figure 4: Top level of the ontology imported from CYC.

The next step in the development of the Disciple-COA critiquer was to teach Disciple to critique COAs with respect to the principles of war and the tenets of army operations. The expert loads the description of a specific COA, such as COA411 represented in Figure 1, and then invokes the Cooperative Problem Solver with an initial task of critiquing the COA with respect to a certain principle or tenet. Disciple uses its task reduction rules to reduce the current task to simpler tasks, showing the expert the reductions found. The expert may accept a reduction proposed by the agent, may reject it or may decide to define a new reduction. From each such interaction Disciple will either learn a new task reduction rule or will refine a previously learned rule, as explained in the following. After a new rule is learned or an existing rule is refined, the Cooperative Problem Solver resumes the task reduction process until a solution of the initial problem is found.

Initially Disciple does not contain any rules. Therefore all the problem solving steps (i.e. task reductions) must be provided by the expert, as illustrated in Figure 5, and explained in the following.

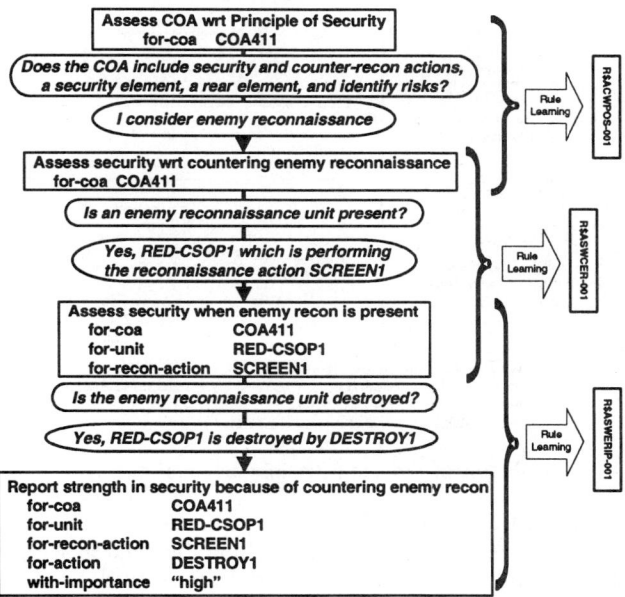

Figure 5: Task reductions and the rules learned from them.

To assess COA411 with respect to the Principle of Security the expert (and Disciple) needs a certain amount of information which is obtained by asking a series of questions (see Figure 5). The answer to each question allows one to reduce the current assessment task to a more detailed one. This process continues until the expert (and Disciple) has enough information about COA411 to make the assessment. As shown in Figure 5, the initial task is reduced to that of assessing the security of COA411 with respect to the countering of enemy reconnaissance. Then one asks whether there is any enemy reconnaissance unit

INNOVATIVE APPLICATIONS 1049

present in COA411. The answer identifies RED-CSOP1 as being such a unit because it is performing the task SCREEN1. Therefore, the task of assessing security for COA411 with respect to countering enemy reconnaissance is now reduced to the better defined task of assessing security when enemy reconnaissance is present. The next question to ask is whether the enemy reconnaissance unit is destroyed or not. In the case of COA411, RED-CSOP1 is destroyed by the task DESTROY1. Therefore one can conclude that there is a strength in COA411 with respect to the Principle of Security because the enemy reconnaissance unit is countered.

To define a reduction of the current task the expert uses the Example Editor. This, in turn, may invoke the Object Editor, the Feature Editor or the Task Editor, if the specification of the example involves new knowledge elements that are not present in the current ontology. Once the reduction has been defined by the expert the Rule Learner is invoked to learn a general rule from each specific task reduction. Figure 6 shows some details of the process of teaching Disciple.

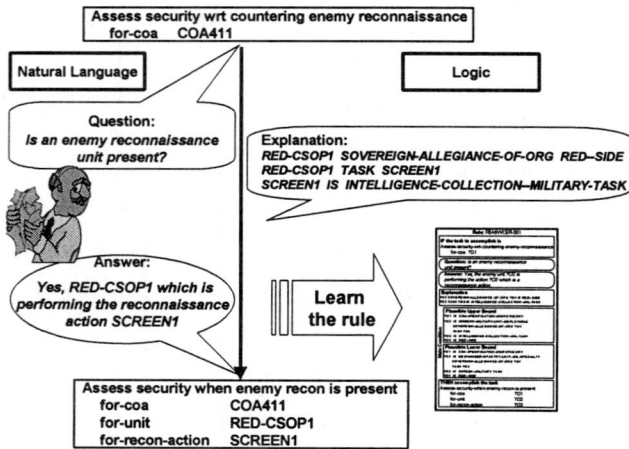

Figure 6: Teaching Disciple to reduce a task.

The left hand side of Figure 6 represents the reasoning process of the expert, the question and the answer being in free natural language format. To learn a rule from this example of task reduction, Disciple needs to find an explanation of why the task from the top of Figure 6 is reduced to the task from the bottom of Figure 6. The explanation to be found, expressed in Disciple's language, is shown in the right hand side of Figure 6. Formally, this explanation consists of a set of paths in Disciple's ontology, each path being a sequence of objects and features. The information from the explanation is included in the question and the answer from the left hand side of Figure 6. However, the current version of Disciple does not have the ability to understand natural language. The main role of the question and the answer is to focus the reasoning process of the expert. Also, the domain expert is not a knowledge engineer and therefore cannot be assumed to be able to provide Disciple with the explanation. This would be very difficult for the expert for at least two reasons. First of all there are many hundreds of object names and feature names and the domain expert should not be required to learn them. Secondly, the domain expert should not be required to use the formal syntax of Disciple, to be able to correctly define formal explanations.

The current approach to explanation generation relies on the complementary abilities of the domain expert and Disciple. The expert cannot formulate correct explanations, but he can provide some hints to Disciple, for instance by pointing to an object that the explanation should contain. Also, he can recognize a correct explanation piece proposed by Disciple. Disciple, on the other hand, can generate syntactically correct explanation pieces. It can also use analogical reasoning and the hints received from the expert to focus its search and to identify a limited number of plausible explanations from which the expert will have to select the correct ones.

The explanation generation strategy is based on an ordered set of heuristics for analogical reasoning. They exploit the hierarchies of objects, features and tasks to identify the rules that are similar to the current reduction, and to use their explanations as a guide to search for similar explanations for the current example. This cooperative explanation-generation process proved to be very effective, as demonstrated by the successful knowledge acquisition experiment described in section 4.

From the example reduction and its explanation in Figure 6, Disciple automatically generated the plausible version space rule in Figure 7. This is an IF-THEN rule, the components of which are generalizations of the elements of the example in Figure 6. In addition, the rule contains two conditions for its applicability, a plausible lower bound condition and a plausible upper bound condition. These conditions approximate an exact applicability condition that Disciple attempts to learn. The plausible lower bound condition covers only the example in Figure 6, restricting the variables from the rule to take only the values from this example. It also includes the relations between these variables that have been identified as relevant in the explanation of the example. The plausible upper bound condition is the most general generalization of the plausible lower bound condition. It is obtained by taking into account the domains and the ranges of the features from the plausible lower bound conditions and the tasks, in order to determine the possible values of the variables. The domain of a feature is the set of objects that may have that feature. The range is the set of possible values of that feature. For instance, ?O2 is the value of the task feature "FOR-UNIT", and has as features "SOVEREIGN-ALLEGENCE-OF-ORG" and "TASK". Therefore, any value of ?O2 has to be in the intersection of the range of "FOR-UNIT", the domain of "SOVEREIGN-ALLEGENCE-OF-ORG", and the domain of "TASK". This intersection is "MODERN-MILITARY-UNIT-DEPLOYABLE".

The learned PVS rules, such as the one in Figure 7, are used in problem solving to generate task reductions with

```
Rule: R$ASWCER-001
IF the task to accomplish is
Assess-security-wrt-countering-enemy-reconnaissance
    for-coa  ?O1

Question: Is an enemy reconnaissance
unit present?

Answer: Yes, ?O2 which is performing the
reconnaissance action?O3.

Explanation
?O2 SOVEREIGN-ALLEGIANCE-OF-ORG ?O4 IS RED--SIDE
?O2 TASK ?O3 IS INTELLIGENCE-COLLECTION--MILITARY-TASK

Main Condition
  Plausible Upper Bound Condition
  ?O1 IS COA-SPECIFICATION-MICROTHEORY
  ?O2 IS MODERN-MILITARY-UNIT--DEPLOYABLE
       SOVEREIGN-ALLEGIANCE-OF-ORG ?O4
       TASK ?O3
  ?O3 IS INTELLIGENCE-COLLECTION--MILITARY-TASK
  ?O4 IS RED--SIDE

  Plausible Lower Bound Condition
  ?O1 IS COA411
  ?O2 IS RED-CSOP1
       SOVEREIGN-ALLEGIANCE-OF-ORG ?O4
       TASK ?O3
  ?O3 IS SCREEN1
  ?O4 IS RED--SIDE

THEN accomplish the task
Assess-security-when-enemy-recon-is-present
    for-coa           ?O1
    for-unit          ?O2
    for-recon-action  ?O3
```

Figure 7: Plausible version space rule learned
from the example and explanation in Figure 6.

different degrees of plausibility, depending on which of its conditions are satisfied. If the Plausible Lower Bound Condition is satisfied, then the reduction is very likely to be correct. If the Plausible Lower Bound Condition is not satisfied, but the Plausible Upper Bound Condition is satisfied, then the solution is considered only plausible. Any application of a PVS rule however, either successful or not, provides an additional (positive or negative) example, and possibly an additional explanation, that are used by the agent to further improve the rule through the generalization and/or specialization of its conditions.

Let us consider again the task reductions from Figure 5. At least for the elementary tasks, such as the one from the bottom of the figure, the expert needs also to express them in natural language:

"There is a strength with respect to surprise in COA411 because it contains aggressive security/counter-reconnaissance plans, destroying enemy intelligence collection units and activities. Intelligence collection by RED-CSOP1 will be disrupted by its destruction by DESTROY1".

Similarly, the expert would need to indicate the source material for the concluded assessment. The learned rules will contain generalizations of these phrases that are used to generate answers in natural language, as illustrated in Figure 2. Similarly, the generalizations of the questions and answers from the rules applied to generate a solution are used to produce an abstract justification of the reasoning process.

Comparing the left hand side of Figure 6 (which is defined by the domain expert) with the rule from Figure 7 (which is learned by Disciple) suggests the usefulness of Disciple for knowledge acquisition. In the traditional knowledge engineering approach, a knowledge engineer would need to manually define and debug a rule like the one in Figure 7. With Disciple, the domain expert (possibly assisted by a knowledge engineer) needs only to define an example reduction, because Disciple will learn and refine the corresponding rule. That this approach works very well is demonstrated by the intense experimental studies conducted with Disciple and reported in the next section.

4 Evaluation of the COA Critiquers and of the Knowledge Acquisition Tools

In addition to GMU, other three research groups have developed COA critiquers as part of the HPKB program. Teknowledge and CYC have developed a critiquer based on the CYC system (Lenat, 1995). The other two critiquers have been developed at ISI, one based on the Expect system (Kim and Gil, 1999), and the other based on the Loom system (MacGregor, 1999). All the critiquers were evaluated as part of the HPKB's annual evaluation that took place during the period July 6-16, 1999, and included five evaluation items of increasing difficulty. Each item consisted of descriptions of various COAs and a set of questions to be answered about each of them. Item1 consisted of COAs and questions that were previously provided by DARPA to guide the development of the COA critiquing agents. Item2 included new test questions about the same COAs. Items 3, 4, and 5 consisted of new COAs that were increasingly more complex and required further development of the COA agents in order to properly answer the asked questions. Each of the Items 3, 4 and 5 consisted of two phases. In the first phase each team had to provide initial system responses. Then the evaluator issued the model answers and each team had a limited amount of time to repair its system, to perform further knowledge acquisition, and to generate revised system responses.

The responses of each system were scored by a team of domain experts along the following dimensions and associated weights: Correctness-50% (matches model answer or is otherwise judged to be correct), Justification-30% (scored on presence, soundness, and level of detail), Lay Intelligibility-10% (degree to which a lay observer can understand the answer and the justification), Sources-10% (degree to which appropriate sources are noted), and Proactivity-10% extra credit (appropriate corrective actions or other information suggested to address the critique). Based on these scores several classes of metrics have been computed, including Recall and Precision. Recall is obtained by dividing the score for all answers provided by a critiquer to the total number of model answers for the asked questions. This was over 100% in the case of our critiquer, primarily because of the extra credit received for generating additional critiques that were not among the model answers provided by the evaluator. "Precision" is obtained by dividing the same score by the total number of answers provided by that system (both the model answers provided by the evaluator and the new answers provided by the critiquer). The results obtained by the four evaluated critiquers are presented in Figure 8 and show that Disciple-COA has obtained the best results.

Figure 9 compares the recall and the coverage of the developed critiquers for the last three most complex items of the evaluation. For each item, the beginning of each arrow shows the coverage and recall for the initial testing phase, and the end of the arrow shows the same data for the modification phase. This graph shows that all the systems increased their coverage during the evaluation. In particular, the KB of Disciple increased by 46% (from the equivalent of 6229 simple axioms to 9092 simple axioms), which represents a very high rate of knowledge acquisition of 286 simple axioms/day.

During August 1999 we conducted a one week knowledge acquisition experiment with Disciple-COA, at the US Army Battle Command Battle Lab, in Fort Leavenworth, Kansas. In this experiment, four military experts that did not have any prior knowledge engineering experience received around 16 hours of training in Artificial Intelligence and the use of Disciple-COA. They then succeeded in training Disciple to critique COAs with respect to the Principle of Offensive and the Principle of Security, starting with a KB containing the complete ontology of objects and features but no rules. During the training process that lasted around three hours, and without receiving any significant assistance from knowledge engineers, each expert succeeded in extending the KB of Disciple-COA with 28 tasks and 26 rules, following a modeling of the critiquing process (such as the one in Figure 5) that was provided to them at the beginning of the experiment. At the end of the experiment they completed a detailed questionnaire that revealed high scores for the perceived usefulness and usability of Disciple.

5 Conclusions

We have presented an approach to the development of knowledge based agents and its rapid and successful use for the development of a critiquing agent that acts as an assistant to a military commander. This approach and the developed agent have been evaluated in two intensive studies. The first study concentrated on the quality of the developed critiquer and the ability to rapidly extend it by its developers and subject matter experts. The second study

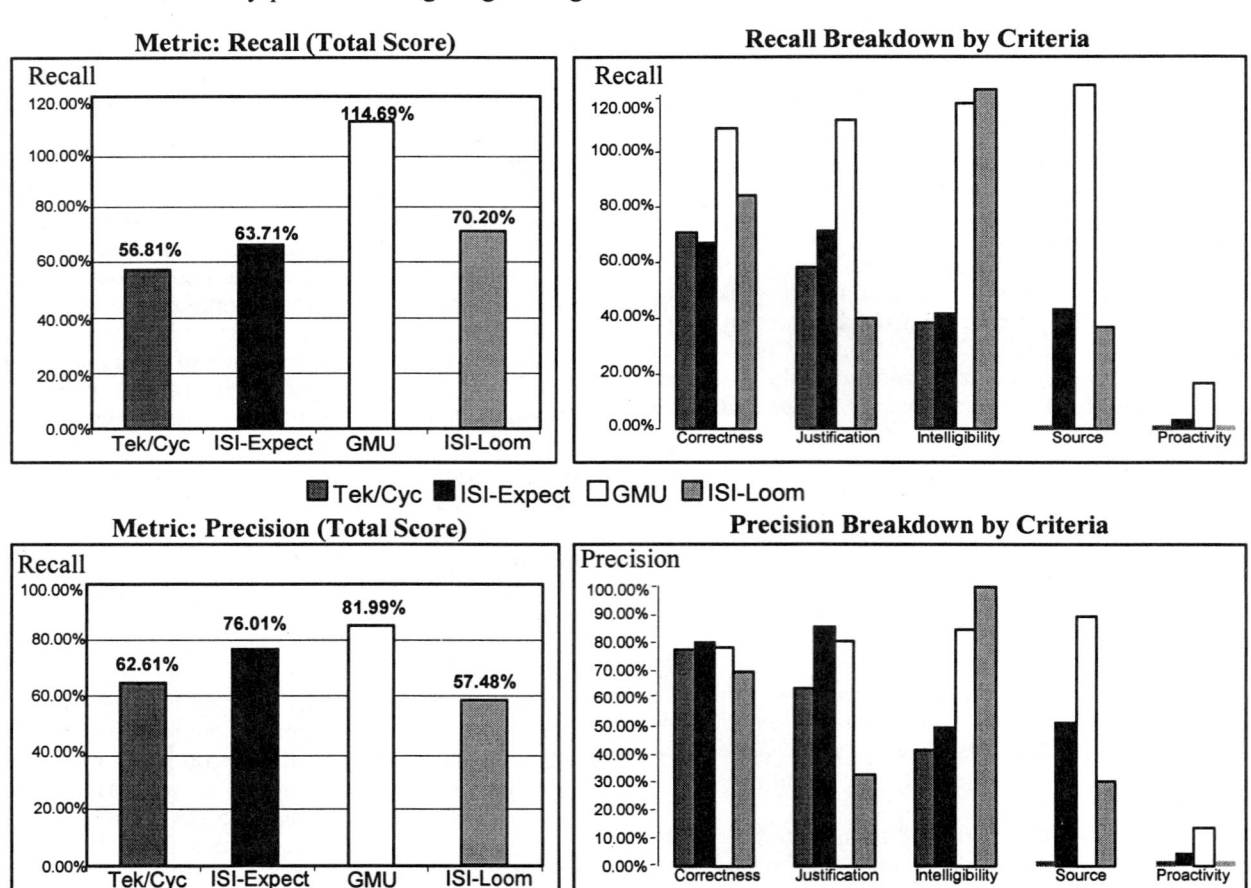

Figure 8: Comparison of the performance of the developed COA critiquers.

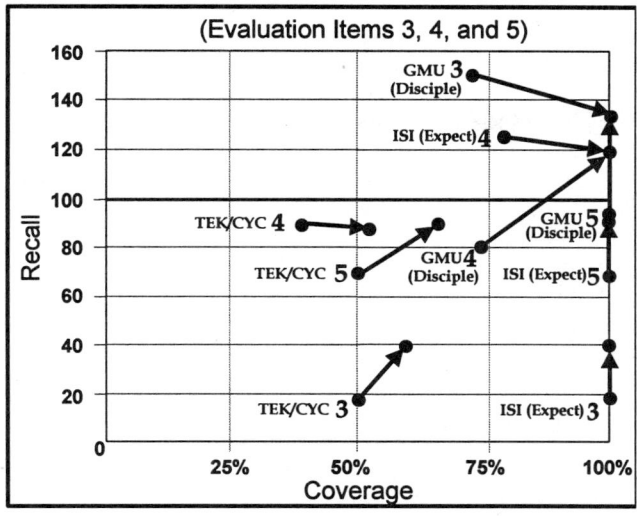

Figure 9: Coverage vs Recall, Pre- and Post-Repair.

concentrated on the ability of domain experts to extend the knowledge base of the critiquer with very limited assistance from knowledge engineers. Both studies have shown that Disciple has reached a significant level of maturity, being usable to rapidly develop complex knowledge based agents. The Disciple approach facilitates the process of knowledge base development because it reduces the complex operations that are necessary in order to build a knowledge base to simpler operations. Rather than creating an ontology from scratch, one can import it from a repository of knowledge and update it accordingly. Rather than defining general problem solving rules the expert needs only to provide specific examples because Disciple can generalize them into rules. Rather than creating sentences in an unfamiliar formal language, the domain expert needs only to understand sentences generated by Disciple and select the relevant ones. Finally, rather then providing explanations to the system the expert may only need to provide hints and let the agent find the explanations. As the knowledge acquisition experiment has demonstrated, even the current version of Disciple allows a domain expert to perform several such operations without being assisted by a knowledge engineer. This shows that by further developing this approach it will become possible for domain experts to directly build knowledge bases. Our long term vision for Disciple, that guides our future work, is to evolve it to a point where it will allow normal computer users to build and maintain knowledge bases and knowledge based agents, as easily as they use personal computers for text processing or email.

Acknowledgments.

This research was supported by AFOSR and DARPA through the grants F49620-97-1-0188 and F49620-00-1-0072. The evaluation of the COA critiquers was conducted by Alphatech. The experts that participated in the knowledge acquisition experiment were LTC John N. Duquette, LTC Jay E. Farwell, MAJ Michael P. Bowman, and MAJ Dwayne E. Ptaschek. Ping Shyr, Bogdan Stanescu, Liviu Panait, Marinel Alangiu and Cristina Cascaval are contributing to the new version of Disciple. The anonymous reviewers of this paper provided insightful comments on our research.

References

Boicu, M., Wright, K., Marcu, D., Lee, S. W., Bowman, M. and Tecuci, G. 1999. The Disciple Integrated Shell and Methodology for Rapid Development of Knowledge-Based Agents. In *Proceedings of the Sixteenth National Conference on Artificial Intelligence*, 900-901, Menlo Park, California: AAAI Press.

Chaudhri, V. K., Farquhar, A., Fikes, R., Park, P. D., and Rice, J. P. 1998. OKBC: A Programmatic Foundation for Knowledge Base Interoperability. In *Proceedings of the Fifteenth National Conference on Artificial Intelligence*, 600–607, Menlo Park, California: AAAI Press.

Cohen, P., Schrag, R., Jones, E., Pease, A., Lin, A., Starr, B., Gunning, D., and Burke, M. 1998. The DARPA High-Performance Knowledge Bases Project. *AI Magazine* 19(4): 25-49.

FM-105. 1993. US Army Field Manual 100-5, Operations, Headquarters, Department of the Army.

Genesereth, M. R., and Fikes, R. 1992. Knowledge Interchange Format, Version 3.0 Reference Manual. Logic-92-1, Computer Science Department, Stanford University.

Jones, E., 1999. HPKB Course of Action Challenge Problem Specification, Alphatech, Inc., Burlington, MA.

Kim, J., and Gil, Y. 1999. Deriving Expectations to Guide Knowledge Base Creation. In *Proceedings of the Sixteenth National Conference on Artificial Intelligence*, 235-241, Menlo Park, California: AAAI Press.

Lenat, D. B. 1995. CYC: A Large-scale Investment in Knowledge Infrastructure. *Communications of the ACM* 38(11): 33-38.

MacGregor, R. 1999. Retrospective on LOOM. Available online at: http://www.isi.edu/isd/LOOM/papers/macgregor/Loom_Retrospective.html.

Tecuci, G. 1998. *Building Intelligent Agents: An Apprenticeship Multistrategy Learning Theory, Methodology, Tool and Case Studies*. London, England: Academic Press.

Tecuci, G., Boicu, M., Wright, K., Lee, S. W., Marcu, D. and Bowman, M. 1999. An Integrated Shell and Methodology for Rapid Development of Knowledge-Based Agents. In *Proceedings of the Sixteenth National Conference on Artificial Intelligence*, 250-257, Menlo Park, California: AAAI Press.

A Case-Based Reasoning Application for Engineering Sales Support using Introspective Reasoning

Ian Watson

AI-CBR
Dept. of Computer Science
University of Auckland
New Zealand
ian@ai-cbr.org

Abstract

This paper describes the implementation of a case-based reasoning application that supports engineering sales staff. The application is distributed and operates on the world wide web using the XML standard as a communications protocol between client and server side Java applets. The paper describes the distributed architecture of the operational prototype, the two case retrieval techniques used, its implementation, trial, and subsequent improvements to its architecture and retrieval techniques using introspective reasoning to improve retrieval efficiency.

Introduction

Western Air is a distributor of HVAC (heating, ventilation and air conditioning systems in Australia with a turnover in 1997 of $25 million (US dollars). Based in Fremantle the company operates mainly in Western Australia, a geographic area of nearly two million square miles. The systems supported range from simple residential HVAC systems to complex installations in new build and existing factories and office buildings.

Western Air has a distributed sales force numbering about 100. The majority of staff do not operate from head office but are independent, working from home or a mobile base (typically their car). Until recently, sales staff in the field would gather the prospective customer's requirements using standard forms and proprietary software, take measurements of the property and fax the information to Western Air in Fremantle. A qualified engineer would then specify the HVAC system. Typically the engineer would have to phone the sales staff and ask for additional information and the sales staff would have to make several visits to the customer's building and pass additional information back to the head office engineer.

Western Air felt that basing a quote on the price of a previous similar installation gave a more accurate estimation than using prices based on proprietary

Copyright © 2000, American Association for Artificial Intelligence (www.aaai.org). All rights reserved.

software, catalogue equipment prices and standard labor rates. To try to help engineers make use of all the past installations a database was created to let engineers search for past installations. The database contained approximately 10,000 records, each with 60 fields describing the key features of each installation and then a list of file names for the full specification. Initially the engineers liked the database and it increased the number of past installations they used as references. However, after the honeymoon ended, they started to complain that it was too hard to query across more than two or three fields at once. And that querying across ten or more fields was virtually impossible. In fact most of them admitted to using the database to laboriously browse through past installations until they found one that looked similar to their requirements.

Prototype Development

Western Air decided that merely improving the efficiency of the engineers in Fremantle would not solve the whole problem. Ideally they would like the sales staff to be able to give fast accurate estimates to prospective customers on the spot. However, they were aware that there was a danger that the less knowledgeable sales staff might give technically incorrect quotes.

The solution they envisaged was to set up a web site that sales staff could access from anywhere in the country. Through a forms interface the prospect's requirements could be input and would be passed to a CBR system that would search the library of past installations and retrieve similar installations. Details of the similar installations along with the FTP addresses of associated files would then be available to the sales staff by FTP. The sales staff could then download the files and use these to prepare an initial quote. All this information would then be automatically passed back to an engineer to authorize or change if necessary. Once an installation was completed its details would be added to the library and its associated files placed on the FTP server.

The development team comprised:
- a senior engineer from Western Air (one of the firms owners) as project champion,
- an engineer from Western Air to act as project manager and domain expert,
- a consultant Java/HTML programmer,
- a consultant from AI-CBR to advise on CBR issues (resident in the UK), and
- a part-time data entry clerk.

Because the project had the direct involvement of one of the firms owners management commitment was not a problem. It was decided that creating a partially functional prototype was sensible and that a carefully controlled and monitored trial was essential for two reasons:
1. It was still not certain that sales staff could create technically sound first estimates and therefore a small carefully monitored trial was essential to avoid losing the firm money.
2. There were resource implications since although all sales staff had portable PCs, some were old 486 Windows 3.1 machines and few had modems or Internet accounts.

A fixed (non-negotiable) budget was given to the project of $32,000 (US) and it was decided that six months would be given for development and trial of the system. The project started in October of 1997 and the trial was planned for March of 1998.

It was decided initially to deal with moderately complex residential HVAC systems because it was felt that this would provide a reasonable test of the system without undue risk. Western Air felt that it was commercially unwise to risk experimentation on high value commercial contracts. Western Air realised they wanted a system that could find similar installations without making the query too complex for the engineers. Web-based CBR applications have been demonstrated for a few years now such as the FAQFinder and FindME systems [Hammond et al., 1996] and those at Broderbund and Lucas Arts [Watson, 1997].

The solution they envisaged was to set up a web site that sales staff could access from anywhere in the country. Through a forms interface the prospect's requirements could be input and would be passed to a CBR system that would search the library of past installations and retrieve similar installations. Details of the similar installations along with the FTP addresses of associated files would then be available to the sales staff by FTP. The sales staff could then download the files and use these to prepare an initial quote. All this information would then be automatically passed back to an engineer to authorise or change if necessary. Once an installation was completed its details would be added to the library and its associated files placed on the FTP server.

Since a simple nearest neighbour retrieval algorithm would suffice implementing our own system was a viable option. Java (Visual Café) was chosen as the implementation language for both the client and server side elements of the CBR system. XML (eXtensible Markup Language) [WWW Consortium, 1997] was used as the communication language between client and server-side applets. The World-Wide Web Consortium (W3C) finalised XML 1.0 in December 1997 as a potential successor to HTML.

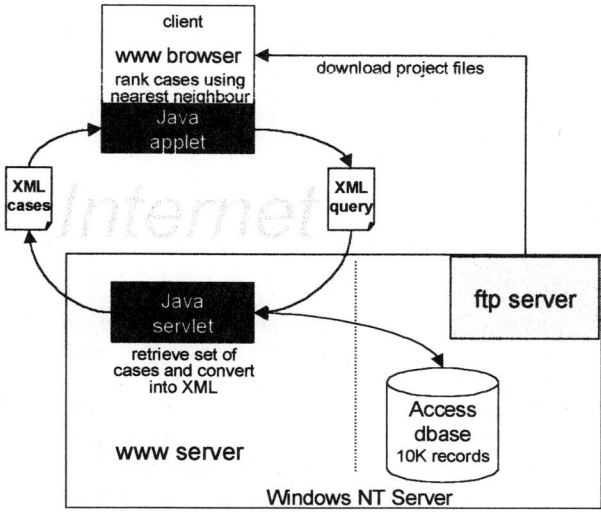

Figure 1. System Architecture

System Architecture

On the sales staff (client) side a Java applet is used to gather the customer's requirements and send them as XML to the server. On the server side another Java applet (a *servlet*) uses this information to query the database to retrieve a set of relevant records. The Java servlet then converts these into XML and sends them to the client side applet that uses a nearest neighbour algorithm to rank the set of cases.

Case Representation

Cases are stored within a database. Each record (case) comprises 60 fields used for retrieval and many more used to describe the HVAC installations. In addition, links to other files on the FTP server are included to provide more detailed descriptions. Once retrieved from the database the records are ranked by a nearest neighbour algorithm and dynamically converted into XML for presentation to the client browser. An XML case representation is used by our system [Shimazu, 1998]. XML pages can contain any number of user defined tags defined in a document type definition (DTD) file. Tags are nested hierarchically from a single root tag that can contain any number of child tags. Any child tag in turn can contain any number of child tags. Each tag contains a begin statement (e.g. <Case>) and an end statement (e.g. </Case>).

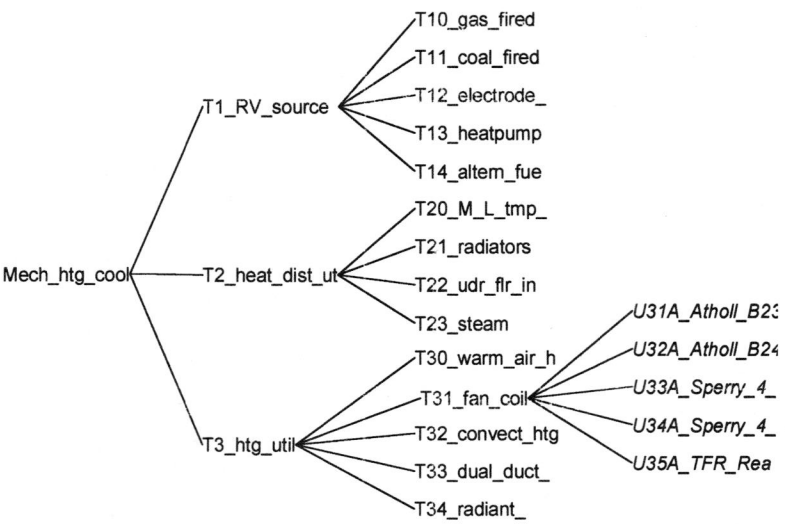

Figure 2. A Portion of the Symbol Hierarchy for Mechanical Heating & Cooling Systems

Case Retrieval

Case retrieval is a two stage process. In stage one the customer's requirements are relaxed through a process of *query relaxation*. This process takes the original query and relaxes terms in it to ensure that a useful number of records are retrieved from the database. This is similar to the technique used by Kitano & Shimazu [1996] in the SQUAD system at NEC, although as is discussed later, we have improved it efficiency using an introspective learning heuristic.

For example, assume we are trying to retrieve details of installations using Athol B25 equipment. An SQL query that just used "Athol_B25" as a search term might be too restrictive. Using an ordered symbol hierarchy (as in Figure 2) our system knows that "Athol B25" is a type of "Fan Coil" system so the query is relaxed to "Where (((EquipmentReference) = "T31_fan_coil"")..)). This query will include equipment from Athol, Sperry and TFR. An ordering of each set of symbols in the hierarchy is obtained through the reference number suffixes to each symbol (e.g. T10, T11, T12, T13, T14 as shown in Figure 2). The symbol hierarchies are stored in tables in the database.

Other specific criteria, elevations or temperatures that are numbers (integers or reals) can be relaxed by using simple ranges (e.g. a temperature of 65° F. could be relaxed to "Between 60 and 70"). Knowledge engineering was required to determine by what amounts numeric features should be relaxed. The relaxation is expressed as a term ± a percentage (e.g., "Relax_Temp = ± 10%"). These relaxation terms are stored in tables in the database.

In the second stage the small set of retrieved records are compared by the client-side applet with the original query and similarity is calculated using the simple nearest neighbour algorithm shown in Figure 3. The resulting similarity measure is normalized to give a percentage range of 0% (i.e. completely dissimilar) to 100% (i.e. completely similar). The weighting on the features by default is set to 1 (i.e., all features are by default considered of equal importance) However, the sales engineers can change the feature weightings to reflect client priorities or their own preferences.

$$Similarity(T,S) = \sum_{i=1}^{n} f(T_i, S_i) \times w_i$$

where:
T is the target case
S is the source case
n is the number of features in each case
i is an individual feature from 1 to n
f is a similarity function for feature i in cases T and S
and
w is the importance weighting of feature I

Figure 3 The Nearest Neighbour Algorithm

Once an HVAC installation is completed its details are added to the database and its associated files placed on the FTP server. Having a database management system for the case repository has proved essential since it makes it easier to generate management reports and ensure data integrity. It would be almost impossible to maintain a collection of 10,000 cases without a DBMS.

Interface Design

The interface to the system is a standard Java enabled web browser (Netscape or Internet Explorer). The forms within the Java applet were designed to look as similar to the original forms, HVAC specification tools and reports that the sales staff were already familiar with. Microsoft FrontPage 98 and Macromedia's DreamWeaver were the primary tools used to create the web site.

Testing

Two weeks before trial five test scenarios were created that were representative of the range of more complex residential installations the system would be expected to handle in use. These were given to the five sales staff who would initially use the system and they were asked to test the system. Out of the 25 tests (5x5) 22 were correct. Although the remaining three were not specified as expected they were felt to be technically acceptable solutions.

The prototype was rolled out for trial to the five sales staff in March of 1998. Acceptance of the system from the five sales staff was very good once they understood what it was doing. During the month's trial the system dealt with 63 installations all of which were felt to be technically sound. The sales staff had not had to use the expertise of the HVAC engineers at all for this work although the engineers checked the final specifications.

During the trial month the five sales staff were able to handle 63 installation projects without having an HVAC engineer create the specification. This resulted in a considerable saving in engineers time allowing them more time to deal with complex high value commercial HVAC contracts.

Prototype Enhancements

Since its test the original prototype of the system has experienced increasing load performance problems. The Java servlet approach suffered from poor performance because the web server loads, executes and terminates a new servlet program for each user access. Large data sets and complex queries especially burden the system because data querying takes place via the Java servlet program rather than directly via the database. This coupled with the fact that MS Access is not a particularly fast database caused time out problems as the server load increased. To rectify this problem the database was ported to mySQL (http://www.mysql.org) a freeware database with much better performance. In addition Netscape's LiveWire database integration tool was used. This product has excellent database query functions, and importantly, because the LiveWire engine runs within the Netscape Web Server process it can share database connections across all Web accesses.

Introspective Learning

The initial query relaxation method of first performing a precise query and then relaxing the query through successive iterations until a sufficiently large set of cases was retrieved also compounded the performance problems. A suggestion was made to turn this process around – namely, why not relax the initial query far enough to ensure that a large set of cases would be retrieved (e.g. several hundred cases) and then refine the query to reduce the sub-set to around twenty cases). The obvious speed advantage in this approach is that only a small sub-set of the whole case-base is used in any subsequent iterations as opposed to the entire case-base in the original query relaxation approach.

However, deciding how much to relax the query was not straightforward so an introspective learning approach was taken. This is an approach in CBR where the reasoning system itself learns over time to modify its internal representation to improve its performance [Markovitch & Scott, 1993]. For example, CBR systems may learn to modify feature weights, adaptation rules [Leake, et al., 1995; Hanney & Keane, 1996], or even learn to forget redundant cases [Smyth & Cunningham, 1996].

A decision was made to log each time a feature was relaxed during the query relaxation process. When the same query term is encountered again the query is automatically relaxed by one of three methods:

1) by the precise amount it was relaxed the previous time,
2) by the average amount it was relaxed the previous N times it had been relaxed (where n is the total number of times it has been relaxed), and
3) by the mean amount it was relaxed the previous N times it had been relaxed.

Experiments were then conducted to see which, if any, of these simple heuristics most improved retrieval efficiency. This of course required that we decided what we meant by efficiency, was it:

- Time efficiency, i.e. purely a measure of retrieval speed, or
- Accuracy, i.e., a measure of the quality of the final suggested set of cases.

It was felt by us that both metrics were important so both were considered. Because of problems due to network and server loads and the way command stacks were executed it was difficult to directly measure retrieval speed accurately so the concept of precision was used as an analogue. That is, how many cases were returned in the set of retrieved cases. The fewer the number the more precise. A smaller number of cases would always be processed faster by the system, hence retrieval time would be quicker (unless network traffic beyond our control slowed down the exchange of information).

Therefore, if the query relaxation algorithm returned a single case that was a 100% match to the target case we would have an accuracy rating of a perfect 100% with a precision of 100%. It is worth remembering that this only tests the first stage of retrieval. In the second stage a nearest neighbour algorithm selects the most similar case from the retrieved set.

Testing

Tests were conducted by partitioning the case-base. Approximately one fifth of the cases (2000) were removed at random from the case-base. These were then used in a random sequence as probes to query the case-base. Our hypothesis therefore was that if the introspective learning algorithm worked either the precision or accuracy or both of the system should improve over time.

Results

Three methods were used by the introspective learning algorithm to learn how to relax the query:
1) *precise relaxation* – i.e., relax query features by the precise amount they were relaxed the previous time.
2) *average relaxation* – i.e., relax query features by the average amount they were relaxed the previous N times they had been relaxed (where N is the total number of times it has been relaxed), and
3) *mean relaxation* – i.e., relax query features by the mean amount they had been relaxed the previous N times they had been relaxed.

The results for percentage accuracy were entirely inconclusive. Percentage accuracy did not improve using either of the three introspective learning algorithms. This is not surprising since the objective of the query relaxation method is not to retrieve the "best" matching case but rather to retrieve a set of good candidate cases upon which the nearest neighbour algorithm can work. However, conversely there was no evidence that introspective learning reduced the accuracy of the set of retrieved cases.

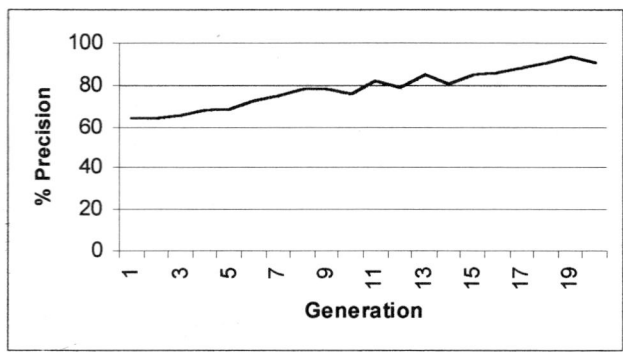

Figure 4 % Precision for Mean Relaxation
(Generation is in 100s)

The results for precision were more encouraging, except for when the precise retrieval learning algorithm was used. It's results unsurprisingly showed wild fluctuations as each query relaxation was based purely on the previous query relaxation. Sometimes this worked and sometimes it didn't; in effect the learning algorithm had no long term memory. However, the average and mean relaxation results showed improvement with time. Precision for average relaxation improved from about 64% to 84%, whilst with mean relaxation percentage precision improved from about 64% to 94%. In addition, mean relaxation showed smaller fluctuations because this method is less perturbed by outliers. This shows that the system has been able to improve its precision (i.e., retrieve a smaller set of candidate cases) without harming its accuracy. This would improve the system's overall retrieval time.

Conclusions

This implementation has shown how a distributed CBR system can be created on the web in a relatively short space of time (six months). Implementing the system for web delivery will make the system much more viable. Just a few years ago we would have had to install the entire system (including the database of 10,000 records) on each of the sales staffs PCs. We would then have had to regularly send them updates to the database. This would significantly increase the operational costs of the system. Thus the web is an ideal medium for delivering intelligent support of all types.

The project was most certainly helped by having a ready made case library. Although knowledge engineering work was still required in determining valid ways of relaxing the SQL queries and creating similarity metrics. This was not surprising as the similarity measure is one of the most important *knowledge containers* of any CBR system [Richter, 1998].

XML is a useful communications protocol enabling large packets of formatted information to be exchanged thereby reducing network traffic. As a possible replacement to HTML it should help the web support intelligent applications [Hayes, et al., 1998; Doyle, et al., 1998]. However, we have demonstrated that implementing a simple CBR system is not difficult and is a viable alternative to purchasing a commercial tool. We will see CBR systems playing an increasingly important role in product selection and specification on-line, since similarity-based retrieval is very useful for Internet e-commerce systems [Wilke, et al., 1998].

However, under increasing use the prototype's performance started to become an issue that would reduce its effectiveness. Several measures were taken to improve performance including using a faster database to store the cases, improving the way database access was managed on the server side and improving the way the query relaxation algorithm worked. This later improvement was significant because it involved the use of an introspective learning a accuracy of the algorithm that learns by how much to relax case features during the relaxation process. Our experimental findings show that although the learning algorithm does not improve the accuracy of the system it does improve its precision. For the future we would like to find a way to make the learning algorithm consider the interaction of case features. Currently features are considered in isolation which is obviously a weakness since there are certainly both strong and weak dependencies between case features.

Acknowledgements

I would like to acknowledge the cooperation of Western Air in the development of this system and in particular their permission to publish. Hideo Shimazu provided valuable information on the use of XML and David McSherry had the idea to improve the efficiency of the query relaxation algorithm.

References

Doyle, M., Ferrario, M.A, Hayes, C., Cunningham, P., Smyth, B. (1998). CBR Net: Smart Technology Over a Network, Internal Report Trinity College Dublin, TCD-CS-1998-07.
http://www.cs.tcd.ie/Padraig.Cunningham/publications.html

Hammond, K.J., Burke, R., & Schmitt, K. (1996). A Case-Based Approach to Knowledge Navigation. In, Case-Based Reasoning: Experiences, Lessons, & Future Directions. Leake, D.B. (Ed.) pp.125-136. AAAI Press/The MIT Press Menlo Park, Calif., US.

Hanney, K. & Keane, M. (1996). Learning Adaptation Rules From a Case-Base. Advances in Case-Based Reasoning, Smith, I. & Faltings, B. (Eds.) Lecture Notes in AI # 1168 pp.179-192. Springer-Verlag, Berlin.

Hayes, C., Doyle, M., Cunningham, P., (1998). Distributed CBR Using XML, Internal Report Trinity College Dublin, TCD--CS-1998-06.
http://www.cs.tcd.ie/Padraig.Cunningham/publications.html

Kamp, G. Lange, S. & Globig, C. (1998). Case-Based Reasoning Technology: Related Areas. In, Case-Based Reasoning Technology: From Foundations to Application. Lenz, M. et al (Eds.) LNAI # 1400 pp.325-351. Springer-Verlag, Berlin.

Kitano, H., & Shimazu, H. (1996). The Experience Sharing Architecture: A Case Study in Corporate-Wide Case-Based Software Quality Control. In, Case-Based Reasoning: Experiences, Lessons, & Future Directions. Leake, D.B. (Ed.) pp.235-268. AAAI Press/The MIT Press Menlo Park,Calif., US.

Leake, D.B., Kinley, A. & Wilson, D. (1995). Learning to Improve Case Adaptation by Introspective Reasoning and CBR. In, Case-Based Reasoning Research & Development, Veloso, M. & Aamodt, A. (Eds.), Lecture Notes in AI # 1010, pp.229-240. Springer-Verlag, Berlin.

Markovitch, S. & Scott, P.D. (1993). Information Filtering. Selection mechanisms in Learning Systems. Machine Learning, 10, pp.113-151.

Richter, M. (1998). Introduction - the basic concepts of CBR. In, Case-Based Reasoning Technology: from foundations to applications. Lenz, M., Bartsch-Sporl, B., Burkhard. H-D. & Wess, S. (Eds.). Lecture Notes In AI # 1400 Springer-Verlag, Berlin.

Shimazu, H. (1998). Textual Case-Based Reasoning System using XML on the World-Wide Web. To appear in the Proc. Of the 4th European Workshop on CBR (EWCBR98), Springer Verlag LNAI.

Smyth, B., & Cunningham,). (1996). The Utility Problem Analysed: A Case-Based Reasoning Perspective. Advances in Case-Based Reasoning, Smith, I. & Faltings, B. (Eds.) Lecture Notes in AI # 1168 pp.392-399. Springer-Verlag, Berlin.

Watson, I. (1997). Applying Case-Based Reasoning: techniques for enterprise systems. Morgan Kaufmann Publishers Inc. San Francisco, CA.

Watson, I. (1998). Case-Based Reasoning is a Methodology not a Technology. Research & Development in Expert Systems XV, Mile, R., Moulton, M. & Bramer, M. (Eds.), pp.213-223. Springer-Verlag, London.

Wilke, W. Lenz, M. Wess, S. (1998). Intelligent Sales Support with CBR. In, Case-Based Reasoning Technology: from foundations to applications. Lenz, M., Bartsch-Sporl, B., Burkhard. H-D. & Wess, S. (Eds.). Lecture Notes In AI # 1400 91-113. Springer-Verlag, Berlin.

World Wide Web Consortium, (1997). Extensible Markup Language 1.0, recommendation by W3C:
www.w3.org/TR/PR-xml-971208

Student Abstracts

Identifying words to explain to a reader: A preliminary study

Greg Aist

Language Technologies Institute, Carnegie Mellon University
5000 Forbes Ave.
Pittsburgh, Pennsylvania 15213
Phone: (412) 268-5726   Email: aist@cs.cmu.edu   Web: http://www.cs.cmu.edu/~aist/cv.html

Explain words to help kids learn vocabulary: Elicit, capture, and utilize expert explanations

The core idea of this paper is familiar to teachers: While a child is reading, explain unfamiliar words. Project LISTEN's Reading Tutor (http://www.cs.cmu.edu/~listen) listens to children read aloud and helps them learn to read. We want the Reading Tutor to explain unfamiliar words.
To *elicit* explanations from an expert, the computer should suggest -- or let the expert select -- words to annotate.
To *capture* explanations, the expert will type in and then narrate an explanation. Text and narration will be saved for later use (Mostow & Aist 1999).
To *utilize* explanations during assisted reading, we will display the explanations as extra sentences to be read aloud with the computer's help. Explanations will be provided on student request or computer tutor initiative.
We focus here on how to select words for annotation. How? Annotating all words may be too expensive in preparation time or storage space. Kids may not know which words they need help on. Grade-level wordlists may not include all the hard words in a story. Perhaps adult readers can identify words to explain.

Preliminary experiment: *Paul Revere's Ride*

Three people (male, native speakers of North American English, (at least) college graduates) annotated the 989-word poem *Paul Revere's Ride* (Henry Wadsworth Longfellow, 19th century American). The instructions were to insert one explanation for each word or phrase that the rater thinks should be explained to the reader. With annotations in bold:

> Listen, my children, and you shall hear
> Of the midnight ride of Paul Revere, …
> He said to his friend, "If the British march
> **British** → **from England**
> By land or sea from the town to-night,
> Hang a lantern aloft in the belfry arch
> **aloft** → **up**
> **belfry** → **church bell tower**
> **arch** → **[picture of arch]**

Copyright © 2000, American Association for Artificial Intelligence (www.aaai.org). All rights reserved.

> Of the North Church tower as a signal light,--
> **North Church** → **an old church in Boston**
> **signal** → **like a sign**
> One, if by land, and two, if by sea; …

For analysis, each word token was coded **1** if contained in an annotation and **0** otherwise. We summarize below:

Rater	Words coded **1** out of all words	Words coded **1** out of words w/out *the, a*
J	16% (160/989)	19% (159/840)
A	3% (26/989)	3% (26/840)
G	6% (59/989)	7% (59/840)
At least one rater	18% (175/989)	21% (174/840)

Pairwise interrater reliabilities using kappa (Carletta 1996):

	J	A	G
J	-	0.178 all words 0.172 w/out *the, a*	0.405 all words 0.397 w/out *the, a*
A	-	-	0.426 all words 0.422 w/out *the, a*
G	-	-	-

All values of kappa were significantly greater than zero. Kappa of zero is chance, less than 0.40 shows poor agreement, between 0.40 and 0.75 shows fair agreement, and above 0.75 shows excellent agreement (SPSS 1999).
Why did J-G and A-G agree well, but not J and A? J explained more words than A. A remarked that the instructions did not say who was the intended reader of the story. Finally, none of the raters were reading experts.
Nonetheless, even annotating all the words that any rater annotated (174/840) would require less effort than annotating all the non-article words. Also, more specific instructions and better-trained raters may improve results.

References

Carletta, Jean. 1996. Assessing agreement on classification tasks: The kappa statistic. *Computational Linguistics*, 22(2), 249-254. http://www.iccs.informatics.ed.ac.uk/~jeanc/squib.ps

USPTO99 Mostow, J. and Aist, G. Reading and Pronunciation Tutor. United States Patent No. 5,920,838. Filed June 2, 1997; issued July 6, 1999. US Patent and Trademark Office.

SPSS. 1999. SPSS® Base 9.0 Applications Guide. Chicago IL: SPSS. See also company web site at http://www.spss.com

Speculative Execution for Information Agents

Greg Barish, Craig A. Knoblock, Steven Minton

Information Sciences Institute and Department of Computer Science
University of Southern California
4676 Admiralty Way, Marina del Rey, CA 90292
{barish, knoblock, minton}@isi.edu

Practical deployments of information agents can suffer from sub-optimal performance and scalability for a number of reasons. In the case of web-based information integration, for example, data sources are remote and their latency can have a substantial effect on overall execution performance. Scalability can also be poor, since concurrent queries can cause multiple, simultaneous remote data retrievals (often of the same information), quickly consuming available bandwidth. The frequency of remote retrievals also makes such agents inherently I/O-bound, wasting CPU cycles.

One way of optimizing execution in such scenarios is to engage in speculative execution. Tasks likely to be executed in the future can be performed in advance, such as when an agent is I/O-bound. Correctly guessing can be profitable – the overall end-to-end application could perform faster, bandwidth could be conserved, and the CPU could be scheduled more optimally. Still, designing a technique for speculative information agent execution is not simple. For one, there are competing justifications. For example, an agent could speculate based on the profile of a current user or on the activity of past clients, or on resource availability. Secondly, speculation itself incurs additional overhead: it should not interfere with normal execution and there must be some method of coordinating speculative execution between multiple agents. Third, speculative execution itself needs to be scalable - hinting done on a per-user basis could lead to a prohibitive number of hints in popular agents.

Consider an "information portal" application, where users can view news headlines and stock quotes and charts. Suppose that 90% of the users currently logged into the system have portfolios that contain Cisco Systems stock. In this case, we could speculate that at least one will request detailed information about this stock and thus we could pre-fetch this data, or just the costly part (for example, the chart graphic).

Note that the idea of speculative execution is not limited to pre-fetching data. Other costly operators (i.e., relational joins) could be pre-executed based on branch and data value predictions. The only requirement of speculatively executing an operator is that there exist a way to "undo" the speculated action, should a guess be wrong.

Our research deals with specifying an approach for the scalable speculative execution of information agents. In particular, we are exploring how different *speculative contexts* can be integrated to reduce the risk of speculation. Contexts are different paradigms under which speculative hints can be generated. Example contexts include: the availability of system resources, past user agent requests, and the list of most recently requested agents. Each context can establish its own speculative hints. Hints can then be merged to determine optimal speculation. We are also interested in recovery when making bad guesses as well as making speculative execution itself scalable. In terms of the latter, we are exploring *decentralized speculation* and *speculative bundling*. Decentralized speculation is a technique allowing individual operators (or agents) autonomy in speculation - avoiding the need to have global entity to deal with all of the speculative choices in the system. Speculative bundling suggests that, under heavy load, many speculative hints will be generated, and that it can be more efficient to periodically merge groups of hints, rather than to react to each one.

Speculative execution has historically been associated with computer architecture and compilers. Recently, it has been successfully applied to workflow (Hull et. al. 2000) and operating systems (Chang et. al. 1999). Based on these results and the opportunities for execution in I/O-bound agents, we believe speculative execution is an exciting direction for future research.

Chang. F.; Gibson, G.A. 1999. Automatic I/O hint generation through speculative execution. *Proc 3rd Symposium on OS Design & Implementation*

Hull, R; Lirbat, F; Kumar, B; Zhou, G; Dong, G; Su, J. 2000. Optimization Techniques for Data-intensive Decision Flows. *ICDE-00*

Copyright © 2000, American Association for Artificial Intelligence (www.aaai.org). All rights reserved.

Heterogeneous Neuron Models based on Similarity

Lluís A. Belanche Muñoz

Dept. de Llenguatges i Sistemes Informàtics
Universitat Politècnica de Catalunya
c/Jordi Girona Salgado, 1-3
08034 Barcelona, Spain.

belanche@lsi.upc.es

In this research, artificial neural models are extended to handle missing and non-real data and weights, and made to compute an explicit similarity relation. Artificial Neural Networks (ANN) constitute a class of models amenable to learn non-trivial tasks from representative samples. When exposed to a supervised training process, they build an internal representation of the underlying target function by combining a number of parameterized base functions (PBF). The network relies in the representation capacity of the PBF (that is, of the neuron model) as the cornerstone for a good approximation. This is true at least for the most widespread PBF: that used in the MultiLayer Perceptron –basically a scalar product between the input and weight vectors plus an offset, followed by a squashing function– and that used in Radial Basis Function networks –a distance metric followed by a localized response function. The task of the hidden layer(s) is to find a new, more convenient representation for the problem *given* the data representation chosen, a crucial factor for a successful learning process that can have a great impact on generalization ability (Bishop 1995, p. 296).

Additionally, in theory ANN design should follow the principle: *Similar patterns should yield similar outputs* (Rumelhart et al 1993). However, what "similar patterns" means is problem-dependent, and only in counted occasions will coincide with the fixed interpretation of similarity that a network is going to perform. In this respect, a marked shortcoming of the neuron models existent in the literature is the difficulty of adding prior knowledge to the model, either of the data or of the problem to be solved. Furthermore, in classical neuron models, inputs are continuous real-valued quantities. However, in many important domains from the real world, objects are described by a mixture of continuous and discrete variables, where some values may be lacking, and usually characterized by some source of uncertainty.

This work deals with the development of general classes of neuron models, accepting heterogeneous inputs by aggregation of continuous (crisp or fuzzy) numbers, linguistic information, and discrete (either ordinal or nominal) quantities, with provision also for missing information. The internal stimulation of these neural models is based on an explicit *similarity relation* between the input and the weight tuples (which are also heterogeneous). The framework is very comprehensive and several particular models can be derived as instances thereof –in particular, the two mentioned standard models are shown to compute a specific similarity function provided all inputs are real-valued and complete. A family of models defined as a composition of a Gower-based similarity function (Gower 1971) with a sigmoid squashing function is shown to be a useful brick for constructing layered architectures (Heterogeneous Neural Networks or HNN) (Belanche 2000), trained by means of Evolutionary Algorithms.

These networks –limited thus far to feed-forward structures– are capable to learn from non-trivial data sets with an effectiveness comparable, and often better, than that of classical networks, specially exhibiting a remarkable robustness when information degrades due to the growing presence of missing data. There is also an increase in flexibility by accepting training processes using imprecise or vague data, both in the input *and* the weights. The rationale behind the approach is that, by respecting the nature of the data, and endowing the neuron models with the properties of an explicit and *ad hoc* similarity measure, it is expected that the resulting neural structures are able to learn from datasets in a satisfactory way, both from the point of view of generalization performance and readability of results.

This hypothesis has been validated by experimentation in classification and regression problem domains, coming either from standard benchmarks or from real-world problems (e.g. Valdés, Belanche and Alquézar 2000) with encouraging results. Work is in progress towards proving the universal approximation property of these networks.

References

Belanche, Ll. 2000. A Theory for Heterogeneous Neuron Models based on Similarity. Technical Report LSI-00-06-R. Dept. of Llenguatges i Sistemes Informàtics. Univ. Politècnica de Catalunya.

Bishop, C. 1995. *Neural Networks for Pattern Recognition*. Oxford: Clarendon Press.

Gower, J.C. 1971. A General Coefficient of Similarity and some of its Properties. *Biometrics* 27: 857-871.

Rumelhart, D.E., Durbin, R., Golden, R., Chauvin, Y. 1993. Backpropagation: The Basic Theory. In *Mathematical Perspectives of Neural Networks*. Smolensky, Mozer, Rumelhart (eds.): Erlbaum.

Valdés, J.J., Belanche, Ll., Alquézar, R. 2000. Fuzzy Heterogeneous Neurons for Imprecise Classification Problems. *International Journal of Intelligent Systems*, 15(3): 265-276.

Mixed-Initiative Reasoning for Integrated Domain Modeling, Learning and Problem Solving

Mihai Boicu and Gheorghe Tecuci

Learning Agents Laboratory, Department of Computer Science, MS 4A5
George Mason University, 4400 University Drive, Fairfax, VA 22030-4444
(703) 993-4669, URL: lalab.gmu.edu, Email: mboicu@gmu.edu

The main challenge addressed by this research is the knowledge acquisition bottleneck defined as the difficulty of creating and maintaining a knowledge base that represents a model of the expertise domain that exists in the mind of a domain expert. The mixed-initiative approach we are investigating, called Disciple (Tecuci et al. 1999; Boicu et al., 2000), relies on developing a very capable agent that can collaborate with the domain expert to develop its knowledge base. In this approach both the agent and the expert are accorded responsibility for those elements of knowledge engineering for which they have the most aptitude, and together they form a complete team for knowledge base development. The domain modeling and problem solving approach is based on task reduction paradigm. The knowledge base to be developed consisting of an OKBC-type ontology that defines the terms from the application domain, and a set of plausible task reduction rules expressed with these terms.

The main focus of our research is the development of a powerful and flexible mixed-initiative plausible reasoner that allows the expert to train the agent in a variety of ways, and in as natural a manner as possible, similar to the way the expert would train a human apprentice. This reasoner exploits the structure of the ontology and of the plausible task reduction rules to integrate the domain modeling, learning and problem solving processes involved in developing the knowledge base of the agent. The goal is to develop a knowledge base that will allow the agent to exhibit a problem solving competence that is similar with that of the domain expert. We call the set of all correct solutions generated with this "final" knowledge base the Target Solution Space. However, the current knowledge base of the agent is incomplete and may be partially incorrect. Therefore, part of the Target Solution Space is not even included in the Current Representation Space of the agent which will have to be extended by introducing new terms in the ontology.

The plausible reasoner allows the agent to distinguish between four types of increasingly complex problem solving situations: routine, innovative, inventive and creative. This capability guides the interaction with the domain expert, leading to a cooperative problem solving process where the agent solves the more routine parts of the problem and the expert solves the more creative ones. In this process the agent will learn from the expert improving its knowledge base.

A very important feature of the mixed-initiative reasoner is that it fulfils multiple roles, supporting domain modeling, learning and problem solving, depending of the agent's knowledge. Initially, when the agent does not have much knowledge, the emphasis is on domain modeling where most of the problems require "creative" or "inventive" solutions. During this phase, the plausible reasoner supports the definition of the inventive solutions and the explanation-based learning of the rules. As the agent learns from the expert, it is increasingly able to propose routine and innovative solutions. During this phase the plausible reasoner supports solution generation and explanation-based rule refinement.

In summary, this mixed-initiative reasoner allows the achievement of several levels of synergism between the expert that has the knowledge to be formalized and the agent that is able to formalize it: synergism in cooperative problem solving, synergism between teaching and learning, and synergism between different learning strategies.

Acknowledgments

This work was supported by AFOSR and DARPA through the grants F49620-97-1-0188 and F49620-00-1-0072.

References

Boicu, M., Tecuci, G., Marcu, D., Bowman, M., Ciucu F., and Levcovici C. 2000. Disciple-COA: From agent Programming to Agent Teaching. In *Machine Learning: Proceedings of the Seventeenth International Conference*, San Francisco, Calif.: Morgan Kaufmann Pub.

Tecuci, G., Boicu, M., Wright, K., Lee, S.W., Marcu, D. and Bowman, M. 1999. An Integrated Shell and Methodology for Rapid Development of Knowledge-Based Agents. In *Proc. of the Sixteenth National Conference on Artificial Intelligence*, 250-257, Menlo Park, Calif.: AAAI Press.

A Methodology for Modeling and Representing Expert Knowledge that Supports Teaching-Based Intelligent Agent Development

Michael Bowman, Gheorghe Tecuci and Mihai Boicu

Learning Agents Laboratory, Department of Computer Science, MS 4A5
George Mason University, 4400 University Drive, Fairfax, VA 22030-4444
{mbowman3, tecuci, mboicu}gmu.edu, http://lalab.gmu.edu

The long term research goal of our research group is to change the way a knowledge-based agent is built, from being programmed by a knowledge engineer (based on what he or she has learned from a domain expert) to being directly taught by a domain expert that receives limited or no support from a knowledge engineer. The investigated approach, called Disciple (Tecuci, 1998), relies on developing a very capable learning and reasoning agent that can collaborate with a domain expert to develop its knowledge base consisting of an ontology that defines the terms from the application domain, and a set of general task reduction rules expressed with these terms.

An important component of this research is the development of a general methodology for modeling and representing expert knowledge that supports teaching-based intelligent agent development. With respect to this methodology we formulate the following claims: 1) it is natural for the expert, 2) it is applicable to a wide variety of domains; 3) it identifies the tasks to be represented in the agent's knowledge base, 4) it identifies the necessary concepts and features to be represented in the ontology, 5) it guides the rule learning process 6) it supports natural language generation of solutions by the agent and their abstract justifications.

We will briefly illustrate this methodology with the Course Of Action (COA) challenge problem that consists of rapidly developing a knowledge-based critiquer that receives as input the description of a military course of action and assesses various aspects of the COA, such as its strengths and weaknesses with respect to the Principles of War and the Tenets of Army Operations. The domain expert is given a specific problem to solve (such as, to "Assess COA411 with respect to the Principle of Objective") and solves it through task reduction. To perform this assessment, the expert needs a certain amount of information about COA411. This information is obtained through a series of questions and answers that help reduce the initial assessment task to simpler and better defined ones, until the expert has enough information to perform the assessment. Thus, to "Assess COA411 with respect to the Principle of Objective", one has to consider the features that characterize the objective, and these are specified by the expert as being "identification", "attainability", and "decisiveness". Therefore, the current task is reduced to three simpler assessment tasks. Assessing the attainability of the objective is applicable for the main effort and an offensive mission. Therefore, the ontology has to contain a classification of COA missions into offensive missions and defensive missions. To effectively assess the attainability of the objective one would have to determine whether there is a suitable path between the main effort and the objective. This reveals other necessary concepts, such as different types of paths (avenues of approach, mobility corridors, and infiltration lanes), and different types of units. Moreover, each path would need to be characterized by its capacity, and each unit would need to be described in terms of its path requirements.

This methodology was used to build the knowledge base of Disciple-COA that demonstrated the highest knowledge acquisition rate and the best performance results out of four systems evaluated in the DARPA's HPKB program. Also, in August 1999, we conducted a knowledge acquisition experiment with Disciple-COA at the US Army Battle Command Battle Lab where domain experts that did not have any prior knowledge engineering experience found this methodology very natural and easy to use.

In conclusion, we are developing a domain modeling methodology that is tightly integrated with an apprenticeship multistrategy learning approach to knowledge acquisition that allows domain experts to naturally express their expertise in a form that supports many aspects of KB development, including ontology formation, rule learning, and natural language generation.

Acknowledgments

This work was supported by AFOSR and DARPA through the grants F49620-97-1-0188 and F49620-00-1-0072.

References

Tecuci, G. 1998. *Building Intelligent Agents: An Apprenticeship Multistrategy Learning Theory, Methodology, Tool and Case Studies.* London, England: AP.

Tecuci, G., Boicu, M., Marcu, D., Bowman, M., Ciucu F., and Levcovici C. 2000. Rapid Development of a High Performance Knowledge Base for Course of Action Critiquing. In *AAAI-2000/IAAI-2000 Proceedings,* Menlo Park, CA: AAAI Press.

Automated Learning of Pricing and Bundling Strategies in Information Economies

Christopher H. Brooks and **Edmund H. Durfee**
Artificial Intelligence Laboratory
University of Michigan
Ann Arbor, MI 48109
{chbrooks,durfee}@umich.edu
http://www.eecs.umich.edu/~chbrooks

The advent of automated commerce and the ability to electronically distribute information goods, or articles, have created a new set of problems for producers of information content. Since information goods have negligible marginal cost, producers are presented with a huge space of potential bundling and pricing strategies to choose from. Producers potentially have two separate decision problems to solve: what to offer and how to price it. For example, in deciding what to offer, producers may choose to offer articles from a wide variety of categories, or just offer in-depth content in a few selected categories. In deciding what to charge for their goods, a producer might choose from a number of schedules such as a flat fee, a per-article price, or a schedule which changes nonlinearly based on the number of articles purchased. The choice of schedule and goods offered will impact both the producer's per-iteration profit and also what it is able to learn about consumer preferences. In an online environment with a large number of goods and rapid transaction times, it will be advantageous for a producer to automate this decision-making. In (Brooks et al. 1999), we describe this problem and show how a monopolist producer can acquire higher aggregate profit by learning a simpler pricing schedule. Our current work considers two other factors that complicate the producer's learning and decision-making problems: the presence of other producers and differences in article content.

In a world in which a producer is competing with other producers for a market of consumers, the producer must consider both the strategy of other producers and the preferences of the consumers. Typically, neither of these are known, but instead must be learned over time. What makes this difficult is that the other producers are also trying to learn about consumer preferences, so producer strategies are not necessarily stationary. One question we are concerned with is the extent to which reasoning about opponent strategies is actually useful; there will be a tradeoff between an increase in the degree of modeling detail and the marginal gain in the value of the information acquired.

One factor that makes this problem different from a traditional game theory problem is that we are explicitly interested in the nonequilibrium rewards that a producer receives. That is, it's not enough for a producer to eventually learn an optimal pricing schedule; the producer also wants to maximize its interim profits while learning this price schedule. This leads to a tradeoff between the quality of the solution that is learned and the time needed to perform this learning. The reason for this is that, in real-world e-commerce problems, the consumer population is typically changing, either due to entry and exit of consumers or shifting consumer tastes. Therefore, a producer may not have enough time to find an optimal strategy.

The decision as to how to price a set of articles is only half of the problem. A producer must also decide which articles to offer. Typically, consumers will have heterogeneous preferences over articles. The producer's decision problem is then to find a set of articles which can be priced so as to maximize its profits.

One advantage of information goods is that it is their content which is valued by consumers. This content can often be categorized and placed within a taxonomy. Under some assumptions, similarity within a taxonomy can be used as a predictor of consumer utility for an article. For example, if a producer sees that consumers highly value an article on Michael Jordan, it might conclude that consumers would also value articles on Magic Johnson, since both men are former NBA players. Of course, this is only a bias; it may be that consumers use a different taxonomy than the producer assumes. Determining the taxonomy used by the consumer then becomes a learning problem in itself.

Again, we would like for the producer to not only find a good set of articles to offer, but also to perform well during learning, since the consumer population is likely to be changing.

All of this work takes place under a decision-theoretic framework, in which a producer estimates the value of its actions with respect to a possibly unknown problem horizon and takes a series of actions which will maximize its profits. By viewing the choice of articles to sell and the selection of prices as a set of decisions which yield both information and profit and then estimating the value of each decision, we will gain a greater understanding of how to explore complex decision spaces.

References

Brooks, C. H.; Fay, S.; Das, R.; MacKie-Mason, J. K.; Kephart, J. O.; and Durfee, E. H. 1999. Automated strategy searches in an electronic goods market: Learning and complex price schedules. In *Proceedings of ACM EC-99*.

---

*This work was supported in part by an IBM University Partnership Grant and by the National Science Foundation under grant IIS-9872057
Copyright © 2000, American Association for Artificial Intelligence (www.aaai.org). All rights reserved.

Incremental and Distributed Learning with Support Vector Machines

Doina Caragea, Adrian Silvescu, and Vasant Honavar

Artificial Intelligence Research Laboratory
Department of Computer Science
Iowa State University, Ames, IA 50011
{dcaragea|silvescu|honavar}@cs.iastate.edu

Due to the increase in the amount of data gathered every day in the real world problems (e.g., bioinformatics), there is a need for inductive learning algorithms that can incrementally process large amounts of data that is being accumulated over time in physically distributed, autonomous data repositories. In the incremental setting, the learner gradually refines a hypothesis (or a set of hypotheses) as new data become available. Because of the large volume of data involved, it may not be practical to store and access the entire dataset during learning. Thus, the learner does not have access to data that has been encountered at a previous time. Learning in the distributed setting can be defined in a similar fashion. An incremental or distributed learning algorithm is said to be exact if it gives the same results as those obtained by batch learning (i.e., when the entire dataset is accessible to the learning algorithm during learning). We explore exact distributed and incremental learning algorithms that are variants and extensions of the support vector machine (SVM) family of learning algorithms.

For the sake of simplicity, suppose that we have two data sets D_1 and D_2, and we want to learn from them in an incremental setting using SVM. A naive approach (Syed, Liu & Sung, 1999) works as follows:

1. Apply the SVM algorithm to D_1 and generate a set of support vectors SV_1
2. Add SV_1 to D_2 to get a data set D_2'
3. Apply the SVM algorithm to D_2' and generate a set of support vectors SV_2

One can envision a similar approach in the distributed setting. The naive approach works reasonably well in practice if the two data sets D_1 and D_2 each individually are representative of the entire training set $D_1 \cup D_2$, so that the *maximal margin* separating hyperplane determined by the support vectors derived from either one of them doesn't differ very much from that derived from the entire data set. In general, however, we can prove that the hyperplane obtained using such a naive approach can have arbitrarily high error with respect to the hyperplane obtained by applying the SVM algorithm directly to $D_1 \cup D_2$.

We have explored a more sophisticated approach to distributed and incremental learning of SVM (Caragea, Silvescu & Honavar, 2000). Let L be an inductive learning algorithm for pattern classification, which outputs hypotheses that are encoded directly in terms of training examples. SVM has this property because the maximal margin hyperplane is completely specified by a linear combination of a subset of training examples (the so-called support vectors). Given such a learning algorithm L and data sets $D_1, D_2, \cdots, D_N$, a sufficient condition for exact learning, i.e. $(L...L(L(D_1) \cup D_2)... \cup D_N) = L(D_1 \cup ... \cup D_N)$ (incremental case), is the following (*u-closure*) property: $L(L(D) \cup D') = L(D \cup D')$, for any arbitrary sets D and D'. We can state a similar property for distributed learning.

It is easy to show that the naive approach to incremental learning using SVM violate the *u-closure* property. However, the subset of the the positive (and negative) examples that form the vertices of the convex hulls of the positive (and negative) examples in the respective data sets do satisfy the *u-closure* property. So exact incremental and distributed learning algorithms can be obtained by combining the vertices of the respective two convex hulls (one for the positive examples, and another for the negative examples) and then applying SVM to generate a hyperplane that maximizes the margin of separation between the two classes. Our experiments using carefully constructed artificial data sets verify the soundness of this approach. However, since complexity of convex hull computation has a linear dependence on the number of facets of the convex hull (and the number of facets can be exponential in dimension of the space), this approach is likely to be practical only when the convex hulls are simple (i.e., have relatively few facets). We have a characterization of the necessary and sufficient subset of each of the two convex hulls that guarantee exact incremental and distributed learning. Work in progress seeks to precisely characterize hypotheses classes that lend themselves to efficient learning in exact or approximate incremental and distributed settings.

References

Caragea, D., Silvescu, A., Honavar, V. (2000). *Distributed and Incremental Learning with Support Vector Machines*, Tech. Rep.ISU-CS-TR 2000-04.

Syed, N.A., Liu, H., Sung, K.K. (1999). *Incremental Learning with Support Vector Machines*, In: KDD'99, San Diego, CA.

System that Identifies Writers

Sung-Hyuk Cha and Sargur N. Srihari
Center of Excellence for Document Analysis and Recognition
State University of New York at Buffalo
{scha,srihari}@cedar.buffalo.edu

Since the writer identification plays an important investigative and forensic role in many types of crime, various automatic techniques, feature extraction, comparison and performance evaluation methods have been studied (see [1] for the extensive survey). It has been practiced based on the hypothesis that people's handwritings are as distinctly different from one another as their individual natures, as their own finger prints [2,3]. However, relatively little study has been carried out to demonstrate its scientific and statistical validity and reliability as forensic evidence [4] or to answer the question whether one can build a machine that can identify writers. For this reason, we present a simple model to establish the individuality of handwriting based on Hilton's model. Hilton calculated the *odds* by taking the likelihood ratio statistic that is the ratio of the probability calculated on the basis of the similarities, under the assumption of identity, to the probability calculated on the basis of dissimilarities, under the assumption of non-identity [3,5].

There exist various parametric and non-parametric techniques to solve the multiple category classification problem or simply called *polychotomizer* where the number of classes is finite and small [6]. As the number of classes is too large to observe all (U.S. population), these techniques are of no use and the problem is seemingly insurmountable. For this reason, we suggest to transform a large and intractable polychotomizer to a simple *dichotomizer*, a classifier that places a pattern in one of only two categories: distance data between two writings of the same author and those of two different authors. In this model, one need not observe all classes and still allows the inferential classification. We state the problem as follows; given two randomly selected handwritten documents, the *writer identification* problem is to determine whether the two documents were written by the same person with two types of confusion error probabilities. To illustrate, suppose there are three writers, $\{W_1, W_2, W_3\}$. Each writer provides three documents and two scalar value features extracted per document. Fig. 1 (a) shows the plot of two features from documents for every writer and Fig. 1 (b) represents the transformed plot in the two dimensional feature distance domain.

Using eleven feature distance values, we trained an *artificial neural network* and obtained 97% overall correctness.

Copyright © 2000, American Association for Artificial Intelligence (www.aaai.org). All rights reserved.

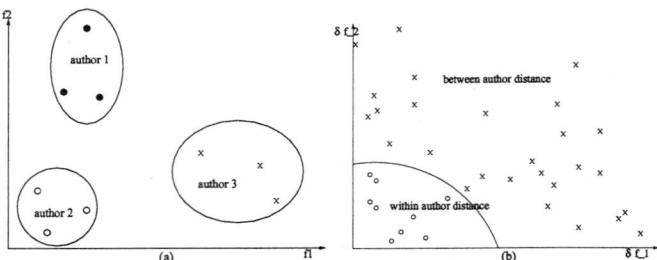

Figure 1: *Transformation from Feature domain to Feature distance domain*

In this experiment, 571 people provided three sample handwritings resulting in 1,713 within and 1,464,615 between author distance data. The type I and II error rates are 2.1% and 3.5%, respectively. Type I error occurs when two documents are determined to be written by two different authors even though they were written by one author and type II error is vice versa.

Acknowledgments This research is funded by National Institute of Justice (NIJ): Award Number 1999-IJ-CX-K010.

References

[1] R. Plamondon and G. Lorette, "Automatic signature verification and writer identification - the state of the art," *Pattern Recognition*, vol. 22, no. 2, pp. 107–131, 1989.

[2] R. R. Bradford and R. B. Bradford, *Introduction to Handwriting Examination and Identification*. Nelson-Hall Publishers: Chicago, 1992.

[3] R. A. Huber and A. M. Headrick, *Handwriting Identification: Facts and Fundamentals*. CRC Press LLC, 1999.

[4] J. Travis, "Forensic document examination validation studies." Solicitation: http://ncjrs.org/pdffiles/sl297.pdf, October 1998.

[5] O. Hilton, "The relationship of mathematical probability to the handwriting identification problem," in *Proceedings of Seminar No. 5*, pp. 121–130, 1958.

[6] R. O. Duda, D. G. Stork, and P. E. Hart, *Pattern Classification and Scene Analysis*. John Wiley & Sons, Inc., 2nd ed., 2000.

Using Anytime Planning for Centralized Coordination of Multiple Robots in Real-time Dynamic Environments

Gabriel J. Ferrer, Glenn S. Wasson, James P. Gunderson and **Worthy N. Martin**

Computer Science Department, Thornton Hall
University of Virginia, Charlottesville, VA 22903
{ferrer, wasson, gunders, martin}@virginia.edu

We are investigating the use of planning in multi-robot, real-time, dynamic environments. Each individual robot is considered to be an effector of a centralized planning system. In a real-time environment, it is important to be careful to ensure that the time required to find a good plan does not itself reduce the system's ability to complete its tasks in a timely manner. Our physically situated system coordinates a group of security robots that guard an area against intruders. Our approach uses a variation of the three-level paradigm for robot architectures (e.g. (Bonasso *et al.* 1997) (Brill *et al.* 1998)) in conjunction with an anytime approach to planning (Dean *et al.* 1995) (Zilberstein & Russell 1993). In this domain, the system must ensure that the total amount of time spent planning and then executing the plan is short enough that the security robots can still capture the intruders. Too much time spent planning prevents the security robots from achieving this objective. Our system uses anytime planning to ensure that plans are found in a timely manner. Anytime algorithms return results with a quality proportional to the amount of time the algorithm had available for execution.

Our planner initially assigns patrol routes to the security robots that ensure sensor coverage of the area. As intruders enter the area, our planner assigns some of the robots sequences of intruders to pursue, and plans patrols for the remaining robots to maintain sensor coverage. Once tasks are assigned, the security robots carry out their tasks reactively (Brooks 1986) (Brill *et al.* 1998). Once reactive execution begins, the security robots act independently of the planner until they are assigned new tasks. Each robot reports the current locations of any intruders sensed to the sequencer. The sequencer determines if reassignments are necessary, and if so, reinvokes the planner. Task reassignments are made when new intruders are detected or a security robot is out of range to capture an assigned target.

An anytime approach is used by our planner for robot task replanning. For an anytime algorithm to be effective, it is important to specify a progression of results that the algorithm will return. Our progression is based on the concept of *plan locality*. That is, when a plan fails and needs to be replanned, much of the plan may still be valid and useful as is, and repairing the failure may be sufficient. On the other hand, local failures in a plan can have non-local implications. Our approach initially limits replanning to the part of the plan that failed, while leaving the rest of the plan alone. This constrains the amount of search that the planner must conduct. Once that is done, the amount of the plan to be replanned is enlarged. This allows the planner to search a larger space. This process of iteratively enlarging the part of the plan to be replanned continues until either the planner is interrupted or the scope of replanning has grown to the point that it encompasses the entire plan. The smaller search space of the early phase of the replanning algorithm ensures that there is a new plan available quickly, while the larger spaces searched in the later phases enable plans of higher potential quality to be considered.

Our system currently uses a geometric measure of locality when replanning. That is, it replans for security robots that are within a progressively increasing radius of the plan failure point. Some of the research questions we are investigating include: How can we generalize the concept of locality for replanning in other domains? If the intermediate data structures (e.g. partial plans and world states) of the planning algorithm are preserved, can we use locality as an indexing device to enable us to find partial plans quickly that we can use as starting points for replanning? How should we progress locality when two or more plan failures occur?

References

Bonasso, R. P.; Firby, R. J.; Gat, E.; Kortenkamp, D.; Miller, D. P.; and Slack, M. G. 1997. Experiences with an architecture for intelligent, reactive agents. *Journal of Experimental and Theoretical Artificial Intelligence* 9(2).

Brill, F. Z.; Wasson, G. S.; Ferrer, G. J.; and Martin, W. N. 1998. The effective field of view paradigm: Adding representation to a reactive system. *Engineering Applications of Artificial Intelligence* 11:189–201.

Brooks, R. A. 1986. A robust layered control system for a mobile robot. *IEEE Journal of Robotics and Automation* RA-2(1):14–23.

Dean, T.; Kaelbling, L. P.; Kirman, J.; and Nicholson, A. 1995. Planning under time constraints in stochastic domains. *Artificial Intelligence* 76(1-2):35–74.

Zilberstein, S., and Russell, S. J. 1993. Anytime sensing, planning and action: A practical model for robot control. In *Proceedings of IJCAI-1993*, 1402–1407.

MURDOCH: Publish/Subscribe Task Allocation for Heterogeneous Agents

Brian P. Gerkey and **Maja J Matarić**
Computer Science Department
University of Southern California
941 West 37th Place, Mailcode 0781
Los Angeles, CA 90089-0781
bgerkey|mataric@cs.usc.edu, http://www-robotics.usc.edu/~agents/projects/pub-sub.html

Introduction In this paper, we describe a novel approach to the problem of dynamic task allocation among groups of heterogeneous agents. Specifically, we advocate the use of *publish/subscribe* messaging, a well-researched ((S$^+$98)) and commercially proven ((TIB97)) message brokering paradigm that is readily applicable to distributed control. We present MURDOCH, an implemented publish-subscribe system, and explain how it can facilitate multi-robot coordination.

Publish/Subscribe Messaging At the heart of MURDOCH is an implementation of publish/subscribe messaging, which in turn depends on subject-based addressing. *Subject-based addressing* is an addressing scheme in which individual messages are addressed by content rather than destination. *Publish/subscribe messaging* is a messaging paradigm that uses *subject-based addressing* to divide a network into a loosely-coupled association of anonymous data producers and consumers. A data producer simply tags a message with a subject (or set of subjects) and "publishes" it onto the network; any data consumers who have "subscribed" to that subject (or set of subjects) will automatically receive the message. The goal of publish/subscribe messaging is to enable a loosely-coupled distributed system in which the data producers have no knowledge of the data consumers and vice versa.

Subject Namespace In our system, each robot subscribes to a set of subjects which represent its "capabilities". A mobile robot might subscribe to subjects such as `sonar`, `speech`, `camera`, `compass`, and `mobile`; a desktop PC, on the other hand, might subscribe to subjects such as `compute-server` and `mass-storage`. Thus, to reach all robots who have sonar sensors and cameras, one can publish a message to the subject (`sonar camera`); only those machines with the specified capabilities will receive the message. In addition to those subjects which represent concrete robot capabilities, subjects can be more abstract representations of state information. For example, when a team of robots is engaged a cooperative box-pushing task, a robot's current perception of the box is extremely useful; thus domain-specific subjects such as `see-box` and `contacting-box` will be introduced and used to coordinate the robots' behavior throughout the progression of the task. These subscriptions can and do change over time. For example, with regard to our box-pushing task, which is a truly dynamic domain, individual sub-tasks will be periodically generated and published to subjects such as `contacting-box`; an agent's state with respect to this subscription will be constantly changing throughout the task, and sub-task assignments will reflect this.

Negotiation In MURDOCH, task allocation is performed by matching the set of resources needed to perform the task with agents who are capable of achieving it. An agent's capabilities at any point in time are described by the subjects to which it subscribes. So, in order to match a given task to capable agents, messages regarding the task should be tagged with a subject that describes the necessary resources. Resource requirements specified in this way (i.e. in the subject of a message) are "hard", in that they are not negotiable. Of course, more than one agent may be capable of performing a task and so there must be a method for selecting among a group of willing participants. We introduce metric functions, or simply *metrics* for this purpose. Along with a task description, a message concerning a task to be performed will also include a set of metrics which will be evaluated on each respondent, assigning it a "score", so that the system may (in a distributed fashion) select the agent best suited. In order to actually allocate the various pieces of a task, MURDOCH employs a simple, efficient, and decentralized negotiation protocol. The user phrases the task to be performed in terms of task components, each one described in terms of behavioral primitives, resource requirements, and eligibility metrics. MURDOCH then iterates through the components, and each agent claims those for which it most capable.

References

Ronald C. Arkin. *Behavior-Based Robotics*. MIT Press, Cambridge, MA, 1998.

Maja J. Matarić. Behavior-based control: Examples from navigation, learning, and group behavior. *Journal of Experimental and Theoretical Artificial Intelligence*, 9(2–3):323–336, 1997.

Robert Strom et al. Gryphon: An information flow based approach to message brokering. In *Proceedings of the International Symposium on Software Reliability Engineering*, Paderborn, Germany, November 1998.

TIBCO Software, Inc. *TIB®/Rendezvous™ Concepts*, August 1997. http://www.rv.tibco.com.

Domain-Specific Knowledge Acquisition Using WordNet

Roxana Girju
Department of Computer Science and Engineering
Southern Methodist University
Dallas, Texas, 75275-0122
roxana@seas.smu.edu

This paper presents a method that acquires new concepts and connections associated with user-selected *seed* concepts, and adds them to the WordNet linguistic knowledge structure. New domain knowledge can be acquired around some seed concepts that a user considers important. The knowledge we seek to acquire relates to one or more of these concepts, and consists of new concepts not defined in WordNet and new relations that link the concepts with other concepts.

The approach consists of forming a corpus with sentences containing seed concepts and then identifying on this corpus lexico-syntactic patterns that reflect semantic relations.

The algorithm has four procedures outlined below.
`Procedure 1`: Concept extraction.
`Input`: Noun phrases that contain a seed concept.
`Output`: New concepts constructed around the seed concept.

After the sentences in the corpus are parsed, new concepts are sought in the noun phrases where seed concepts reside. This procedure searches in WordNet and other electronic dictionaries for possible concepts in the noun phrases. The final acceptance of the concepts rests with the user.

The next step is to create a taxonomy for the newly acquired concepts that is consistent with WordNet.
`Procedure 2`: Classification by subsumption
`Input`: A list of NPs containing the seed as head noun
`Output`: An ontology of concepts under the seed

The classification algorithm is based on the simple idea that a compound concept [word, seed] is ontologically subsumed by concept [seed]. Similarly, for a relative classification of any two concepts [word1, seed] and [word2, seed], the ontological relation between word1 and word2, if it exists, is extended to the two concepts. In the case that word1 subsumes word2, then a relation is formed between the two concepts.

Texts are a rich source of information from which in addition to concepts we can also learn relations between concepts. We are interested here on finding out semantic relations that may link the concepts extracted above with other concepts. The approach is to search for lexico-syntactic patterns comprising the concepts of interest. These new re-

Copyright © 2000, American Association for Artificial Intelligence (www.aaai.org). All rights reserved.

lations can be learned automatically from clauses and sentences in which the seeds occur.
`Procedure 3`: Learn lexico-syntactic patterns.
`Input`: A training corpus and semantic relation types.
`Output`: Basic lexico-syntactic patterns in which semantic relations can be expressed.
A pair of words is selected, not necessarily seeds, among which a semantic relation of interest holds. Let's consider the INFLUENCE relation. An example is:
interest rate INFLUENCES *earnings*
The corpus is searched for all instances when the pairs of two concepts selected above occur in the same sentence. Extract the lexico-syntactic patterns that link the two concepts in a pair. For example:
The economic policy will have an immediate impact on inflation this year. From this sentence extract the generally applicable pattern: [*impact on NP2 from NP1*] $\implies$ INFLUENCE(NP1, NP2).
`Procedure 4`: Learn new relationships between concepts.
`Input`: (1) The seed concepts list, (2) concepts learned with `Procedure 1`, (3) the 5000 sentences corpus and (4)the patterns acquired with `Procedure 3`.
`Output`: New relationships between concepts.

Using the new lexico-syntactic patterns found with `Procedure 3`, search the corpus and find other concepts that are connected with a seed via the same patterns. Repeat this for all the patterns found above.

The method was tested with five seeds from the financial domain and the system working in a semi-automated mode found 362 new concepts and 62 relationships.

The knowledge acquisition technology described in this paper is applicable to any domain, by simply selecting appropriate seed concepts. Most importantly, the new concepts can be integrated with an existing ontology, and the type of the new relations is small which is helpful for reasoning activities.

References

Christiane Fellbaum. WordNet - *An Electronic Lexical Database*, MIT Press, Cambridge, MA, 1998.

Marti Hearst. Automated Discovery of WordNet Relations. In *WordNet: An Electronic Lexical Database and Some of its Applications*, editor Fellbaum, MIT Press, Cambridge, MA, 1998.

Graph Based Concept Learning

Jesus A. Gonzalez, Lawrence B. Holder, Diane J. Cook

University of Texas at Arlington, Department of Computer Science and Engineering
Box 19015, Arlington, TX 76019-0015
{gonzalez,holder,cook}@cse.uta.edu
URL: http://cygnus.uta.edu/subdue/ConceptLearning

Concept Learning is a Machine Learning technique in which the learning process is driven by providing positive and negative examples to the learner. From those examples, the learner builds a hypothesis (concept) that describes the positive examples and excludes the negative examples. Inductive Logic Programming (ILP) systems have successfully been used as concept learners. Examples of those are Foil (Quinlan and Cameron 1993) and Progol (Muggleton 1995). The main engine of these systems is based in first order logic. In this research we introduce a graph based relational concept learning system called SubdueCL, which through the experiments has shown that it is competitive with ILP systems in different types of domains. SubdueCL is an extension made to the Subdue (Cook and Holder 1994) system, which is an unsupervised graph based learner.

The Subdue system takes as input a labeled graph and discovers substructures (sub-graphs) that compress the input graph, according to the minimum description length principle and represent structural concepts in the data. The main discovery algorithm is a computationally constrained beam search. The algorithm begins with the substructure matching a single vertex in the graph. Each iteration the algorithm selects the best substructure and incrementally expands the instances of the substructure. The algorithm searches for the best substructure until all possible substructures have been considered or the total amount of computation exceeds a given limit. Evaluation of each substructure is determined by how well the substructure compresses the description length of the input graph. The best substructure found by Subdue can be used to compress the input graph, which can then be input to another iteration of Subdue. After several iterations, Subdue builds a hierarchical description of the input data where later substructures are defined in terms of substructures discovered on previous iterations. Subdue has been applied to several domains including image analysis, CAD circuit analysis, chemical reaction chains, and artificially-generated databases (Cook and Holder 1994).

The SubdueCL system is an extension to Subdue. It uses Subdue's core functions to perform graph operations, but the learning process is different because it works as a supervised learner by differentiating positive and negative examples using a set-covering approach. The hypothesis found by SubdueCL is a disjunction of conjunctions. SubdueCL forms one of these conjunctions (rules) in each iteration. Positive example graphs covered in a previous iteration are removed from the graph for subsequent iterations. SubdueCL evaluates the generated substructures (or rules) according to how well they describe the positive examples without describing the negative examples. For this evaluation, the positive examples that are not covered and the negative examples covered by the substructure are considered errors because the ideal substructure would be one covering all the positive examples without covering any negative example. SubdueCL allows hypotheses where some of the rules may cover negative examples. We are working on a version of SubdueCL that produces only consistent hypotheses, and the application of the PAC learning framework to SubdueCL.

A comparison of SubdueCL with the two ILP systems Foil and Progol using attribute-value databases showed that SubdueCL performs better for non-numeric domains and Progol for numeric domains. The goal now is to show how SubdueCL performs with relational domains where ILP systems have produced very good results. Some preliminary results using this type of domains show that SubdueCL is able to learn the tic-tac-toe domain and produce a perfect output just as Foil and Progol do. The figure shows a rule learned in the tic-tac-toe domain that describes a winning board with X's in the top line (tls=top-left-side, tms=top-medium-side and trs=top-right-side).

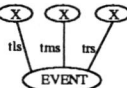

References

Cook, D. J. and Holder, L. B. 1994. Substructure discovery using minimum description length and background knowledge. *Journal of Artificial Intelligence Research* 1:231-255.

Muggleton, S. 1995. Inverse entailment and Progol. *New Generation Computing* 13:245-286.

Quinlan, J. R. and Cameron-Jones, R. M. 1993. FOIL: A Midterm Report. *In Proceedings of the European Conference on Machine Learning.* Vienna, Austria 3-20.

Copyright © 2000, American Association for Artificial Intelligence (www.aaai.org). All rights reserved.

An Adaptive Planner Based on Learning of Planning Performance

Kreshna Gopal   Thomas R. Ioerger

Department of Computer Science, Texas A&M University, College Station, TX 77843-3112
Email: {kgopal/ioerger}@cs.tamu.edu

Saving and reusing previously constructed plans is largely regarded as a promising approach to deal with the intractability of domain-independent planning (Hammond 1989; Kambhampati and Hendler 1992). But it has been shown that syntactically matching a new problem with a candidate case is NP-hard, and modifying a plan to suit a new problem can be strictly more difficult than generating a plan from scratch (Nebel and Koehler 1995). We present a case-based planning system that does not involve any plan modification and performs case matching very efficiently.

The system involves essentially a default planner, a plan library and learning from a set of training examples (cases solved by the default planner). To solve a new problem (with initial state I_{NEW} and goal state G_{NEW}), a case (with initial state I_R, goal state G_R and solved plan P_R) is retrieved from the library, such that the original task of finding a plan is reduced to that of finding two potentially simpler sub-plans. The first sub-plan P_I transforms I_{NEW} into I_R. The second sub-plan P_G transforms G_R into G_{NEW}. If an appropriate case is retrieved, P_I and P_G can be constructed by the default planner with less computational effort, and a concatenation of P_I, P_R and P_G constitutes a solution plan, as shown in the figure below. The most appropriate case is one where the predicted combined cost of developing P_I and P_G is the least, and significantly smaller than planning from scratch.

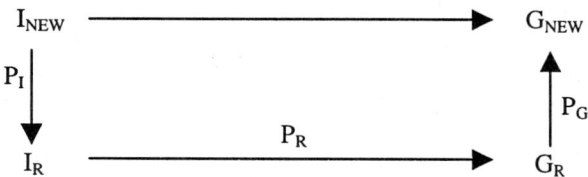

We used a neural network to learn how to predict the time the default planner would take to transform I_{NEW} into G_{NEW}, I_{NEW} into I_R and G_R into G_{NEW}. The predicted time taken is represented as a weighted combination of features of the problem. In our experiments, features were manually constructed, and both domain-dependent as well as domain-independent features were tested on.

Let $Distance(I,G)$ be the time the default planner is predicted to take to transform state I into state G. Then the retrieved case $<I_R, G_R, P_R>$ is the one with the highest $Gain$, defined by the following:

$$Gain = \frac{Distance(I_{NEW}, G_{NEW})}{Distance(I_{NEW}, I_R) + Distance(G_R, G_{NEW})}$$

$Gain$ can be computed very efficiently. Other target functions can also be learned (e.g. the quality of plan produced) and the $Gain$ metric can be accordingly defined in alternative ways.

A prototype of the system was implemented, with a STRIPS-based planning system developed by N. Short and L. Dickens as the default planner. A single-layer network was used for training and the system was tested in the blocks-world domain. A 25-35% improvement in planning performance was observed on the average for problems with 3-7 blocks. It is hypothesized that this method can be used to improve the average-case performance of other planners as well. The effectiveness of the system was found to depend heavily on how successful learning is, which relies primarily on the extraction of relevant problem features. Another determining factor is the library size. The overhead of searching a large library may exceed the gain obtained by reuse. This is the *utility* problem, which can be addressed in a number of ways (Minton 1985). The presented case-based framework has considerable potential to improve efficiency of planning in real-world domains, especially because it avoids plan modification and enables matching a problem with stored cases in a highly efficient way.

References

Fikes, R. E., Hart, P. E., and Nilsson, N. J. 1972. Learning and executing generalized robot plans. *Artificial Intelligence* 3:251-288.

Hammond, K. J. 1989. *Case-based planning: viewing planning as a memory task*. San Diego, Calif.: Academic Press.

S. Kambhampati, S., and Hendler, H. A. 1992. A validation-structure-based theory of plan modification and reuse. *Artificial Intelligence* 55:193-258.

Minton, S. 1985. Selectively generalizing plans for problem-solving. In *Proceedings IJCAI-85*, 596-599. San Mateo, Calif.: Morgan Kaufmann.

Nebel, B., and Koehler, J. 1995. Plan reuse versus plan generation: a theoretical and empirical analysis. *Artificial Intelligence* 76:427-454.

Knowledge Representation on the Internet:
Achieving Interoperability in a Dynamic, Distributed Environment

Jeff Heflin

Department of Computer Science
University of Maryland
College Park, MD 20742, USA
heflin@cs.umd.edu

The Internet's explosive growth is making it harder and harder to harness its potential. There is so much information available that users are frequently overwhelmed by information overload. Due to limitations in modern natural language processing, an important part of search involves keyword-based techniques, which tend to have poor precision and recall. Some systems use the format of a web page to extract information, but due to the changing nature of these pages, such systems are very fragile. It has been claimed that the Extensible Markup Language (XML) will solve these problems by replacing the presentation-oriented tags of HTML with content-specific tags. While it is true that XML will be useful for data exchange and separating content from format, once XML is in widespread usage there will be significant interoperability problems. Unless all content providers agree on the same set of tags and the meanings of these tags it will be impossible to automatically integrate their information.

The field of knowledge representation has studied techniques for storing, modifying and reasoning with complex information. A growing subfield of KR is the study of ontologies, which are reusable knowledge components. Recent research has shown that semantically marking up web pages using terms from an explicit ontology can greatly improve retrieval, integrate the data of many pages, and enable intelligent internet-based agents as well. However two characteristics of the Internet provide significant challenges for an ontology approach: it is ever changing and it is decentralized. Thus, it must be possible to adapt ontologies to meet existing needs in a timely fashion, but such changes must not have an adverse impact on the objects that depend on the ontology (i.e., those ontologies and web pages that use the ontology to define their terms).

My work with SHOE, which stands for Simple HTML Ontology Extensions, has given me a lot of experience with the design and application of semantic markup languages for the Web. SHOE distinguishes between two types of web pages: ontologies and instances. A SHOE ontology describes a domain by defining categories, relations, inference rules, and other elements. Each ontology may extend other ontologies, thus refining their definitions for use in another context. A SHOE instance consists of a number of assertions that describe one or more entities, and commits to an ontology that provides definitions for these descriptions. This approach enables interoperability by allowing content providers to share ontologies when appropriate and by allowing new ontologies to be created that reuse existing definitions when possible. However, although these capabilities are important, they are insufficient for a dynamic, distributed environment. To ensure that a change to an ontology does not adversely affect existing instances, each version of a SHOE ontology is given its own web page and assigned a unique version number, while each instance references a particular version of an ontology.

I have a developed a formal model for reasoning with ontologies in dynamic, distributed environments. This model separates the notion of ontologies from that of data, and provides for multiple versions of each ontology. In this model I introduce the concept of perspectives, which allows us to use different ontologies to provide different semantics over a data source. I will continue to refine this model as my research progresses.

In the SHOE approach, interoperability is dependent on authors reusing concepts from existing ontologies whenever possible. However, when there is concurrent development of ontologies in a large distributed environment such as the Web, this can not be guaranteed, and it is likely that over time ontologies will diverge and become less interoperable. I have begun to look at means for reintegrating these ontologies without breaking the dependencies that other objects have on them.

In order to demonstrate the SHOE approach, I have built a set of tools and ontologies, and have applied the techniques to various domains. The SHOE specification, tutorials, papers, and demos can be found at http://www.cs.umd.edu/projects/plus/SHOE/.

Acknowledgements

I thank my advisor, James Hendler, for his direction and support. I also thank Sean Luke who originally conceived of SHOE.

Copyright © 2000, American Association for Artificial Intelligence (www.aaai.org). All rights reserved.

Using Pattern Databases to Find Macro Operators

István T. Hernádvölgyi
University of Ottawa
School of Information Technology & Engineering
Ottawa, Ontario, K1N 6N5, Canada
Email: istvan@site.uottawa.ca

In this work we employ heuristic search to obtain *macro operators* for spaces defined in our production system. A macro operator is a sequence of original operators which reaches a subgoal from a state without search. A *macro table* has operators for each subgoal. Korf (Korf 1985) used macro operators to find suboptimal solutions for the Rubik's Cube and the 15-Puzzle. While the paths found by the macro method are not guaranteed to be optimal, once the macro table is calculated the search effort is negligible. Traditionally macro operators were found by uninformed search methods, because there were no obvious heuristics. We have devised a simple notation, PSVN (Hernádvölgyi & Holte 1999), to represent state spaces. In PSVN, states are vectors of labels and the operators are simple rewriting rules. For this notation we invented a technique to automatically generate admissible and monotonic heuristics to guide the A* family of algorithms. We apply a simple transformation – *domain abstraction* – on the description of the original space to obtain the abstract space where the distance between two states in the original space is never shorter than the distance between their images in the abstract space. The heuristic values are the lengths of shortest paths in the abstract space. We calculate the distance between the image of the goal state and the rest of the abstract states and store them in a look-up table indexed by the abstract states. This look-up table is also called a pattern database and the method was first used by Culberson and Schaeffer to solve the 15-Puzzle (Culberson & Schaeffer 1994). Korf used pattern databases to solve random instances of the Rubik's Cube for the first time. So far pattern databases have only been used to obtain shortest paths. In this work we use them to find macro operators.

A macro operator reaches a subgoal state without search. To solve for a goal state, each macro brings one (*or a few*) of the labels in the vector representing the state to the index where they occur in the goal state. Subsequent application of the macros in the order of the subgoals fixes all labels and the goal state is reached. The subgoals are patterns where labels at specific indices are identical to the labels of the goal state at those indices. The first subgoal is to fix the label at index i_1, the next subgoal is to fix the label at index i_2 such that the label at index i_1 remains intact and the last subgoal is to fix the last label leaving already fixed labels undisturbed. It is very simple to describe subgoals in PSVN. We introduce a special label which represents "don't care". If our current subgoal is to move the label from index i_x to index i_y while leaving the labels at indices i_1 to i_k intact, then the labels at the other indices can be relabeled to the "don't care" label and the macro operator is a (shortest) path from the relabeled states where i_x and i_y are out of order to the one where they are in order. The labels i_1 to i_k mentioned above are the ones to be left intact. The abstract space is derived by a domain map which renders some of these labels identical. By applying this method we were able to build optimal macro-tables for the Rubik's Cube, where the longest optimal macros are composed of 13 moves. The average branching factor of our IDA* search tree was 14.35.

Establishing the order of subgoals for permutation groups can be done automatically, but for a general PSVN search space it may require the user's intervention. It may also take some experimentation to find a pattern database which is not too large but provides good heuristic values. The size of the pattern database is determined by the domain abstraction, which is simple to encode in our notation. Korf's partial-match with bi-directional search (Korf 1985) is expected to expand $b^{d/2}$ states, where b is the branching factor and d is the optimal macro's length, but it must store the entire frontier of the search trees. Our pattern databases with modest size (1M entries) provide average heuristic values which are greater or equal to $d/2$ for the macros of the Rubik's Cube resulting in less than $b^{d/2}$ states expanded. We use IDA*, hence no memory additional to the database is needed.

I would like to thank Dr. Jonathan Schaeffer and Dr. Robert Holte for their encouragement and guidance to complete this work.

References

Culberson, J. C., and Schaeffer, J. 1994. Efficiently searching the 15-puzzle. Technical report, Department of Computer Science, University of Alberta.

Hernádvölgyi, I. T., and Holte, R. C. 1999. PSVN: A vector representation for production systems. Technical Report TR-99-04, School of Information Technology and Engineering, University of Ottawa.

Korf, R. E. 1985. Macro operators: A weak method for learning. *Artificial Intelligence* 26:35–77.

Autonomous Multi-Agent Docking using Color Segmentation

Jeffrey Hyams
University of South Florida
4202 East Fowler Avenue, ENB 118
Tampa, FL 33620-5399
813-974-1347
hyams@csee.usf.edu
http://www.csee.usf.edu/~hyams/docking

This poster will look at the work in progress of an autonomous multi-agent scheme for ego-centric docking, meaning that the agent docking has no communication or help from the agent to which it is docking. Docking has become a major issue in marsupial robots, and has applications in space exploration, urban search and rescue, and reconnaissance. This work attempts to make use of color segmentation of a fiducial and affordances in reactive behaviors to autonomously dock a mobile robot agent, specifically a marsupial type of heterogeneous team. To this end, a real-time solution was also needed, and thus limited the algorithm to the lowest order complexity that could be managed while still being robust.

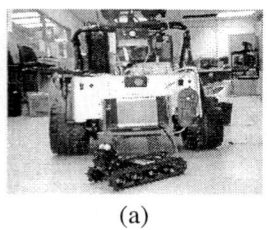 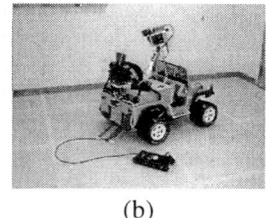

(a) (b)

Figure 1: In (a), Bujold is shown next to the docking bay, with the gate and fiducial in view. In (b), the USF Perceptual Robotics Labs's Marsupial team, Silverbullet and Bujold.

In any real-world docking situation, there are different lighting conditions, and most current vision applications do not work well in in these conditions. This work uses a specific color segmentation which is better in unstructured lighting(Hyams, Powell, & Murphy 1999). Future work will use other techniques such as adaptation and imprinting to adapt to different lighting conditions. Having two heterogeneous mobile robot agents coordinate is difficult, and the current work implies no communication between them. Future work will also include mother-centric docking, as well as a cooperative docking.

For the color segmentation task, a two-color fiducial of dimensions seven inches long by four and a half inches high was used. The left half is painted magenta, while the right half is painted cyan. The image is transformed into the Spherical Coordinate color space, which has been shown to be very good at distinguishing the color from the type and intensity of the lighting conditions.(Hyams, Powell, & Murphy 1999) The magenta and cyan are segmented on the color triangle, then then a connected components algorithm is run on these images to remove noise and to provide a more exact segmentation. This gives statistics for the segmentation of the fiducial, the most important of which is the size of each color region in the image.

With the size and position in the image derived from the color segmentation, a daughter robot then uses a reactive behavior to dock to the mother. There are two main ideas in this docking algorithm, perspective and looming. These provide the information necessary to get to the dock from anywhere behind the mother robot within about two meters from the dock.

Current work in progress includes implementing an adaptive method which will change the segmentation parameters over time (Murphy & Arkin 1990) and imprinting the colors by taking a quick check when Bujold first leaves Silverbullet. This will hopefully eliminate many of the problems with unknown or unstructured lighting conditions. It has been demonstrated that the current autonomous docking system works 17% faster than 22 human operators who teleoperated the robot, and has a 96% success rate while teleoperation had 95%. Further, the segmentation algorithm runs with a low order of complexity, with a worst case of $O(m \times n^2)$ and an average case of $O(m \times n)$. Also, the color segmentation works well in unstructured lighting conditions(Hyams, Powell, & Murphy 1999) and can be run on an off-the-shelf platform. This work could be used for numerous situations where multi-agents are in use, such as space exploration, urban search and rescue, or surveillance.

References

Hyams, J.; Powell, M.; and Murphy, R. 1999. Cooperative navigation of micro-rovers using color segmentation. In *IEEE International Symposium on Computational Intelligence in Robotics and Automation*, 195–201.

Murphy, R., and Arkin, R. 1990. Adaptive tracking for a mobile robot. In *IEEE International Symposium on Intelligent Control*, 1044–1049.

Ontology Integration in XML

Euna Jeong
Department of Computer Science and Information Engineering
National Taiwan University
eajeong@agents.csie.ntu.edu.tw

Chun-Nan Hsu
Institute of Informationi Science, Academia Sinica
chunnan@iis.sinica.edu.tw

Abstract

We study the problem of automatically generating an integrated schema for XML DTDs. Introducing a novel *view inference* approach, we shows that the set of views and source descriptions can be automatically derived.

Introduction The problem of information integration has become significant as the growing number of information sources on the Internet. Information integration systems provide users with an integrated schema of underlying sources. The integrated schema is designed by hand and a mapping between the integrated schema and the source schemas is needed for the system to answer queries. As XML (Bray, Paoli, & Sperberg-McQueen 1998) as become a new standard for representation and exchange of data on the Internet, in this article, we consider the problem of automatically generating an integrated schema for different XML DTDs with similar document types.

Architecture XML with a DTD is self-descriptive and provides a semistructured data model. These properties render that DTDs defining similar document type have structural and naming similarities. Given a collection of source DTDs, we propose a view inference approach which automatically derives the set of integrated views and source descriptions.

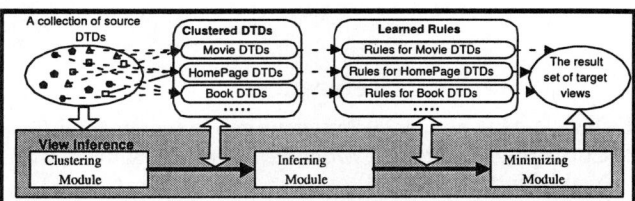

Step 1: Clustering DTDs takes a collection of source DTDs as an input. A DTD is modeled as an edge-labeled graph. The type of an object is defined by adjacent objects and the relation between them. Our strategy is to merge types by *top-down merge*. If two types have the same parent type, they will be merged into a new type. Based on merged types, DTDs are re-defined with them and clustered into one of DTD classes. Generic matching methods (Sanfeliu 1990) are used to know how similar two DTDs are.

Step 2: Learning Rules learns the general rules describing source DTDs in the same class. Our approach is based on tree grammar inference(Miclet 1990). The technique of the generalization of k-tails' concept is applied to learning tree grammars(Levine 1982). At first, the automaton contains one state for each subtree of the sample set T, if they have the same set of k-tails, then their states are made identical. This gives an automaton that recognizes a tree language containing T.

Step 3: Minimization of Tree Automata optimizes the learned rules. The learned rules are a set of states in a tree grammar and need to be transformed to an integrated view. The integrated views allow the user to formulate queries to XML documents. In this step, we use *bottom-up merge*. If two states have the same subtree, but different root labeling, then they will be merged. As a result, the minimized tree automaton will be more flexible than before.

Conclusions We have presented how to automatically generate integrated views for XML from source DTDs. Our approach allows for fully automatic generation of integrated views from a collection of DTDs.

References

Bray, T.; Paoli, J.; and Sperberg-McQueen, C. M. 1998. Extensible Markup Language(XML) 1.0. Technical report, W3C.

Levine, B. 1982. The use of tree derivatives and a sample support parameter for inferring tree systems. In *IEEE Transactions on Pattern Analysis and machine Intelligence*, 25–34.

Miclet, L. 1990. *Syntactic and structural pattern recognition*. World Scientific. chapter 9.

Sanfeliu, A. 1990. *Syntactic and structural pattern recognition*. World Scientific. chapter 6.

Graph-Based Hierarchical Conceptual Clustering in Structural Databases

Istvan Jonyer, Lawrence B. Holder and Diane J. Cook
University of Texas at Arlington
Department of Computer Science and Engineering
Box 19015, Arlington, TX 76019-0015
{jonyer|holder|cook}@cse.uta.edu
URL: http://cygnus.uta.edu/subdue/clustering

Introduction

Cluster analysis has been studied and developed in many areas for a wide variety of applications. The purpose of applying clustering to a database is to gain better understanding of the data, in many cases through revealing hierarchical topologies. We are working on extending the Subdue structural knowledge discovery system with clustering functionalities. Past works related to ours are an incremental approach called Cobweb [Fisher 1987], and its extension, Labyrinth [Thompson & Langley 1991], that can represent structured objects using a probabilistic model.

Conceptual Clustering Using Subdue

Subdue [Holder and Cook 1993] is a knowledge discovery system that can deal with structured data by working on their graph representation. This includes vertex and edge labels, as well as directed and undirected edges, where objects and data usually map to vertices, and relationships and attributes map to edges.

Subdue's discovery algorithm discovers interesting, repetitive substructures in the input graph, which is used by our new Graph-Based Hierarchical Conceptual Clustering (GBHCC) algorithm. This algorithm builds a *classification lattice*, versus a tree suggested by other work. We have found that in structured domains the strict tree representation is inadequate. GBHCC begins with an empty lattice and calls Subdue to find a substructure S that maximally compresses the input graph G according to our Minimum Description Length heuristic. If S achieves some compression of G, then S is added to the lattice and used to compress the graph G. S becomes the definition of a cluster. The compressed graph is passed again to Subdue to find another substructure. This iterative approach on successively more compressed graphs allows Subdue to find new substructures defined in terms of previously discovered substructures. Therefore, when substructures are added to the lattice, their parents may include other, non-root nodes in the lattice. This approach allows the discovery of conceptual clustering hierarchies of the database.

To illustrate Subdue's strength–the ability to work with structured data–we present a task that involves describing a DNA sequence by clustering. To represent the DNA as a graph, atoms and small molecules are mapped to vertices, and bonds are represented by undirected edges. The edges are labeled according to the type of bond, single or double. A portion of the lattice generated is shown in the figure.

The lattice closely resembles a tree, with the exception that two nodes (bottom-left) have two parents. The lattice describes 71% of the DNA sequence. As the figure shows, smaller, more commonly occurring compounds are found first that compose the first level of the lattice. These account for more than 61% of the DNA. Subsequently identified clusters are based on these smaller clusters that are either combined with each other, or with other atoms or molecules to form a new cluster. The second level of the lattice extends the conceptual clustering description such that an additional 7% of the DNA is covered. Future work on Subdue will continue discovery of hierarchical clusterings in real-world domains, and both objective and expert-based comparisons to other clustering systems.

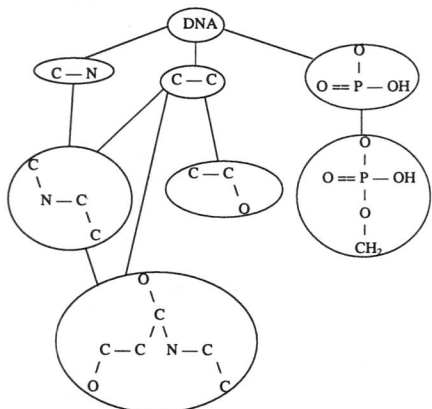

References

Fisher, D. H. Knowledge Acquisition Via Incremental Conceptual Clustering, *Machine Learning*. Kluwer, The Netherlands, 1987.

Holder, L. B. and D. J. Cook. Discovery of Inexact Concepts from Structural Data. In *IEEE Transactions on Knowledge and Data Engineering*, Volume 5, Number 6, 1993, pages 992-994.

Thompson, K. and P. Langley. Concept formation in structured domains. In Fisher, D.H., & Pazzani, M. (Eds.), *Concept Formation: Knowledge and Experience in Unsupervised Learning*, chap. 5. Morgan Kaufmann Publishers, Inc., 1991.

Situation Awareness with The Limited Visual Attention

Youngjun Kim, Randall W. Hill, Jr., Jonathan Gratch

Information Science Institute
University of Southern California
4676 Admiralty Way, Suite 1001
Marina del Rey, California 90292
{yjkim,hill,gratch}@isi.edu

Situation awareness (SA) is the perception of the elements in the environment within a volume of time and space, the comprehension of their meaning, and the projection of their status in the near future (Endsley M. 1988). A critical aspect of the situation awareness (SA) problem is that agents must construct an overall view of a dynamically changing world using limited sensor channels. For instance, a (virtual) pilot, who visually tracks the location and direction of several vehicles that he cannot see simultaneously, must shift its visual field of view to scan the environment and to sense the situation involved. We developed the perceptual coordination that helps a virtual pilot efficiently track one or more objects.

Simulation worlds usually offered all information to virtual humans. However, providing all information to the virtual humans not only is unrealistic but can also cause perceptual overload since extracting the pertinent information from the available sensors is challenging and results in unpredictable consequences. In order to reduce perceptual overload, we reduced the amount of input to the perceptual system by limiting a virtual human's visual field. By restricting the visual field, the virtual human needs a way of coordinating the tracking of multiple objects when one or more of the objects are outside the visual field. This calls for a focus of attention and a way of controlling it. For instance, if a virtual human with a limited field of view (e.g., 15 degrees) is tracking two objects, one of which is not currently in view, the agent has to shift its visual attention between the objects, and it has to do it frequently enough to remain sufficiently aware of the situation to avoid disasters (like collisions). A central issue that emerges from shifting visual attention is how long the virtual human can look away from the primary target without losing track of it since there has to be a reasonable prediction of where the object will be located to ease the reacquisition when it is time to shift visual attention back to a target. We have developed a method for predicting a target's future position, and the amount of time the prediction is valid, given the observed motion of the object (e.g. speed, velocity, heading) and the key elements of an environment, which are strategically important terrain features (e.g., hill, mountain, road, river, and lake), surrounding the target.

In our approach, we have focused on learning how to mentally track entities whose behavior will be influenced by key elements of the environment (i.e. maintaining a representation of an object's position when outside the visual field). We implemented the approach on a virtual pilot in a distributed, interactive simulation system called ModSAF. The virtual pilot flies a synthetic helicopter and performs tactical operations with a team of other team pilots. To predict the amount of time the pilot looks away, a neural network is applied since the expected output is how many degrees the object will turn based on the key environment elements surrounding the object and the degree of turning (-35 to 35) of the object is discrete. Given a number of training examples, a neural net learns how the formation of key elements of an environment surrounding a specific target (e.g. tank) affected the movements. In the process of predicting the future positions (e.g. each arrow), the trust factor, which is similar to uncertainty threshold in (Sonu Chopra, 1999), was applied to decrease the degree of trusting the output of the neural network and its value is varied by the task (e.g. battle, reconnaissance).

We found that the method for perceptual coordination we proposed is a way to create more realistic agents since it provides a reasonable time constraint on shifting the visual field. We will extend our approaches by integrating perceptual coordination with organizational and spatial structures (Weixiong Zhang, 1999) that can give a deliberate method of describing spatial relationships between a target and key elements of an environment.

References

Endsley M. 1988. Design and evaluation of situation awareness enhancement. In Proc of the Human Factors Society 32nd Annual Meeting, Santa Monica, CA.

Sonu Chopra and N.Badler. "Where to Look? Automating Visual Attending Behaviors of Virtual Human Characters," Proceedings of the Third International Conference on Autonomous Agents. May 1-5, 1999. Seattle,WA.

Weixiong Zhang, Randall W. Hill, Jr. 1999. A Template-based and pattern-driven approach to situation awareness and assessment in virtual humans. To appear in the Fourth International Conference on Autonomous Agents, Agents-2000.

Copyright ©2000, American Association for Artificial Intelligence (www.aaai.org). All rights reserved.

Language Learning in Large Parameter Spaces

Karen T. Kohl
MIT Artificial Intelligence Laboratory
545 Technology Square, Room 809
Cambridge, MA 02143
ktkohl@ai.mit.edu

Introduction

Various theories of linguistics have proposed that the differences among natural languages can be parameterized. Certainly syntactic theories such as Principles and Parameters (Chomsky, 1981) assume the existence of such parameters. Along with the problem of defining parameters, we need to address the problem of a child's acquisition of the settings of these parameters.

Several algorithms for parameter setting have been proposed and examined on small spaces. Unless we have a realistic space to study, we cannot fully understand the predictions of these algorithms. Having an implemented computational model of these algorithms is important for studying them at greater depths. This study examines one such parameter-setting algorithm in realistic spaces.

The TLA

Gibson and Wexler (Gibson and Wexler, 1994) propose the Triggering Learning Algorithm, or TLA, for binary-valued parameters. If the learner hears a trigger, or a sentence which she cannot analyze under the current parameter settings, she randomly selects one parameter and changes its value if the new value allows her to analyze the sentence. Niyogi and Berwick (Niyogi and Berwick, 1996) have characterized the TLA as a local hill-climbing search algorithm with memoryless learning.

Gibson and Wexler's proposal studied a space with only three parameters. They found that certain target languages were not learnable if the learner started in certain states, called local maxima. One proposed solution was to start with a default value for one parameter. Another proposal was that the local maxima would disappear with a larger, more realistic parameter space.

A 12-Parameter Space

To examine potential solutions to the local maxima problem, we used Stefano Bertolo's implementation of the TLA. His system added nine syntactic parameters to Gibson and Wexler's original three parameters. The twelve parameters involved position and. We added several enhancements allowing users to select and to add parameters.

We found that the likelihood of finding local maxima in a space increased with the size of the space. As the spaces grew more realistic, more parameter interaction resulted in more local maxima. Therefore, the problem of local maxima is not specific to Gibson and Wexler's three-parameter space and does not disappear as the space becomes more realistic.

Since we found that local maxima were common in this large twelve-parameter space, we considered several solutions. When looking at default settings of parameters, we found no initial setting of all parameters that would guarantee the learnability of all target languages.

Next we tried to find default settings of a few parameters that would make most target languages learnable. If we could find parameter settings that patterned together in the unlearnable languages, then we could predict and try to verify that these kinds of languages are unattested in natural language. However, we found that the best default settings still predicted several known natural languages to be unlearnable.

Conclusion

The problem of local maxima is very real for the TLA. More parameters means that there will be more interaction. The solutions of using default settings of parameters made the wrong predictions.

Although we did not find a solution to the problem of local maxima in the TLA, we did show how to study the algorithm in depth. Without this implementation, we could not have been sure of the extent of the problem of local maxima. Any theory of the acquisition of parameter setting should be studied closely with large parameter spaces.

References

Broihier, K. 1997. *Case Studies in Language Learnability*. Ph.D. diss., Dept. of Brain and Cognitive Science, MIT.

Chomsky, N. 1981. *Lectures on Government and Binding*. Dordrecht: Foris.

Gibson, E., and K. Wexler. 1994. Triggers. *Linguistic Inquiry* 25:407-454.

Niyogi, P., and R. Berwick. 1994. Learning from Triggers. *Linguistic Inquiry* 27:605-622.

Niyogi, P., and R. Berwick. 1996. A Language Learning Model for Finite Parameter Spaces. *Cognition* 61:162-193.

Reinforcement Learning for Algorithm Selection

Michail G. Lagoudakis
Department of Computer Science
Duke University
Durham, NC 27708
mgl@cs.duke.edu

Michael L. Littman
AT&T Labs – Research and Duke University
Florham Park, NJ 07932
mlittman@research.att.com

Many computational problems can be solved by multiple algorithms, with different algorithms fastest for different problem sizes, input distributions, and hardware characteristics. We consider the problem of *algorithm selection*: dynamically choose an algorithm to attack an instance or subinstances (due to recursive calls) of a problem with the goal of minimizing the overall execution time. We formulate the problem as a kind of Markov Decision Process (MDP), and use ideas from reinforcement learning (RL) to solve it.

The process' state consists of a set of instance features, such as problem size. Actions are the different algorithms we can choose from. Non-recursive algorithms are terminal in that they solve the problem completely (terminal state). Recursive algorithms create subproblems and therefore cause transitions to other states, making the task a sequential decision task. The immediate cost of a decision is the real time taken for executing the selected algorithm on the current instance, excluding time taken in recursive calls. Thus, the total (undiscounted) cost during an episode is the time taken to solve the problem. The goal is a policy that minimizes the total cost/time. This process differs from a standard MDP as it allows one-to-many state transitions (multiple recursive calls at one level).

Our initial experiments focus on the problem of *order statistic selection*: given an array of n (unordered) numbers and some index i, select the number that would rank i-th if the array were sorted. We picked two algorithms such that neither is best in all cases, otherwise learning would not help. DETERMINISTIC SELECT (D) is an $O(n)$ recursive algorithm and HEAP SELECT (H) is an $O(n \log n)$ algorithm that performs best for indices close to 1 or n. The process' state consists of the size n and the distance d of the index i from the closest end of the array (assuming symmetry). The value of choosing H at some state $s = [n, d]$ is simply the time it takes to solve the corresponding instance, since this is a terminal algorithm. The optimal value of choosing D can be expressed in terms of other state-action values:

$$Q\left([n,d], D\right) = \min_{a=\{H,D\}} \{Q\left([n/5, n/10], a\right)\} + \min_{a=\{H,D\}} \{Q\left([n', d'], a\right)\} + R([n,d], D),$$

where $R(s, a)$ is the immediate cost of choosing action a in state s, and $n' \leq 7n/10 + 6$. The states $[n/5, n/10]$

Copyright © 2000, American Association for Artificial Intelligence (www.aaai.org). All rights reserved.

and $[n', d']$ correspond to the two recursive calls of D. This Bellman equation resembles the recurrence equation for the running time of DETERMINISTIC SELECT (Cormen, Leiserson, and Rivest 1990):

$$T(n) \leq T(\lceil n/5 \rceil) + T(7n/10 + 6) + O(n).$$

Our learning rule is a variation of Q-learning that combines Monte-Carlo (MC) and Temporal Difference (TD) learning:

$$\begin{aligned}Q(s,a) &= (1-\alpha)Q(s,a) + \\ &\quad \alpha \left[\left(R(s,a) + \Re_\pi(s_{n/5})\right) + \min_{a'}\{Q(s',a')\}\right],\end{aligned}$$

where $\Re_\pi(s)$ is the total cost of solving the subproblem s using the current greedy policy (no exploration). Thus, the smaller subproblem is effectively pushed into the immediate cost (MC) and the bigger one is used for bootstrapping (TD).

We trained the system on thousands of randomly generated inputs of size 10000 and various indices, using an $1 - \epsilon$ policy and decreasing learning rate. Results are shown below. The "cut-off point algorithm" uses H when the index is within the first 13% or the last 7% of the input (as suggested by the plot), and D otherwise. The learned algorithm performs better with one exception due to the lack of the assumed symmetry. Additional results and extensions are available (Lagoudakis and Littman 2000).

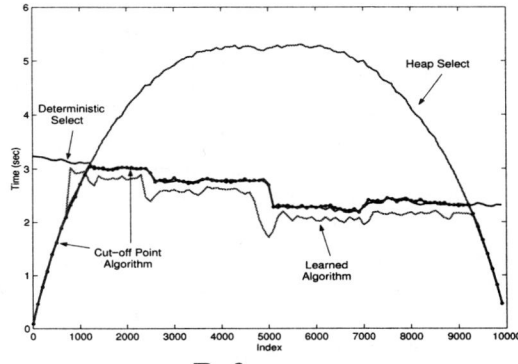

References

Cormen, T.H.; Leiserson, C.E.; and Rivest R.L. 1990. *Introduction to Algorithms*. Cambridge, Mass: MIT Press.

Lagoudakis, M.G., and Littman, M.L. 2000. Algorithm Selection using Reinforcement Learning. In *Proceedings of the Sixteenth International Conference on Machine Learning*. AAAI Press. To appear.

Tracing Dependencies of Strategy Selections in Agent Design

Dung N. Lam, K. S. Barber

The Laboratory for Intelligent Processes and Systems
Department of Electrical and Computer Engineering, ENS 240
University of Texas at Austin, Austin, TX 78712-1084
{dnlam, barber}@lips.utexas.edu

Given the diverse multi-agent system (MAS) implementations developed for various domains, there has been a lack of a comprehensive method for analyzing and evaluating the assortment of MAS architectures and technologies resident in those architectures. With a formal method to investigate agent architectures, MAS designers can answer 1) how performance criteria affect design decisions, 2) how design decisions affect MAS behavior, and 3) which combinations of design decisions are best suited for the application. This research proposes that the first step in answering these questions is to decompose an agent into its *core competencies* (CC), which define the major functionalities of an agent. Some example core competencies include agent organization (AO), plan generation (PG), task allocation (TA), plan integration (PI), plan execution (PE), world modeling, communication, actuation, and perception (Barber, Liu, and Han 1999). CCs affect the behavior of the agent and of the system.

For each CC, the designer chooses to implement a *core competency strategy* from a library of existing strategies. With each design decision, the number of possible strategy combinations decreases due to the dependencies among strategies across CCs. In solving a given problem, an agent coordinates itself with other agents in the system to organize and to create a plan and/or reactively generate actions that leads to a solution. The agent uses its chosen agent organization, which defines how agents interact with each other, to manage the agents during the planning process. First, the agent works alone or cooperates with other agents in PG. Next, in TA, those plans and subtasks are distributed to the appropriate agents. Finally, in PI, the agents' schedules are combined according to the chosen strategy, which results in task-coordinated agents. After planning, the agents must monitor the execution of the subtasks and make any necessary adjustments.

Each CC strategy has dependencies based on its *demands* on the functionality of other CCs (e.g., a market AO demands that TA be composed of proposals, bids, and agreements). Additionally, the selection of a CC strategy is dictated by dependencies among *variables* (factors and properties that affect the choice of strategy used), such as available resources and the number and type of agents involved. CCs are instantiated as CC strategies and are illustrated in Figure 1 as a sequence of adaptors that links the problem to a solution. Each CC strategy adaptor is built upon the previous adaptor and thus is constrained by the dependencies of the previous CC strategy. The male pin connectors represent the variables and demands of that CC strategy that can be passed on to the next CC strategy. The female pin connectors suggest the demands that are passed on from the previous CC strategy. The pin connectors must match, or the demands must be satisfied, for CC strategies to be compatible. It is possible to have an adaptor that encompasses more than a single CC, such as Partial Global Planning.

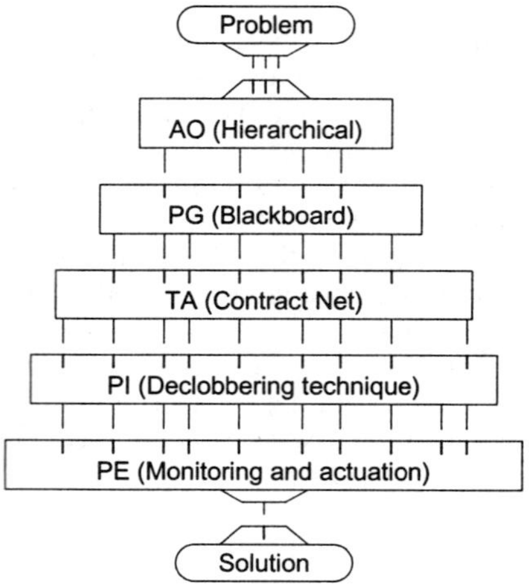

Figure 1: CC strategies are shown as adaptors that build upon previous adaptors.

With the resulting method to analyze agents at an abstract level, MAS designers can investigate the system-level implications of selecting strategies that have dependencies spanning across multiple CCs and across agents. Design decisions can be traced from the domain performance criteria that motivated the decisions to the resulting MAS behavior. Continuing research will develop a fundamental understanding of how and why certain combinations of strategies produce specific agent-level and system-level behaviors.

References

Barber, K. S., Liu, T. H., and Han, D. C. 1999. Agent-Oriented Design. Multi-Agent System Engineering. In *Proceedings of the Ninth European Workshop on MAAMAW*, 28-40. Berlin, Germany: Springer.

Copyright © 2000, American Association for Artificial Intelligence (www.aaai.org). All rights reserved.
This research was supported in part by the Texas Higher Education Board (#3658-0188-1999).

Programming Robot Behavior Primitives Through Human Demonstration

Amy Larson and Richard Voyles
Department of Computer Science and Engineering, University of Minnesota
4-192 EE/CS Bldg, 200 Union Street SE
Minneapolis, MN 55455
{larson,voyles}@cs.umn.edu

Robotic systems are capable of complex behavior by sequencing simpler skills called *primitives* (Voyles, Morrow, & Khosla 1997). A primitive is a sensor/actuator mapping robust enough to perform appropriately in various situations. Programming one primitive can be tedious and requires an accurate translation of human knowledge to machine code. Once a sufficient set of primitives *is* coded, the user must write code to sequence the primitives – also tedious and difficult. Programming by human demonstration addresses these problems of acquiring and combining primitives.

To create primitives, programming by demonstration can be implemented with a supervised learning technique such as artificial neural networks (ANN) to learn a sensor/actuator mapping. Problems exist with such techniques, however, including creating a training set which is comprehensive (for robustness) and concise (for efficient training). Here, we present a method for nonexpert users to collect "good" training data from an intuitive understanding of task behavior, not from knowledge of the underlying learning mechanism.

Good training data includes anomalous situations and corrective behavior. For example, when road-following, data should include examples of how to return to the road if the robot inadvertently strays from the lane. However, if the demonstrator veers off the road to show the robot how to correct itself, the system also learns to veer off the road. Pomerleau's solution (1992) is to simulate corrective behavior, but this requires task domain knowledge. Our solution, applied to wall-following for indoor mobile robots, is to filter real data, automatically separating good data from bad.

Data from a demonstration consists of sensor and actuator vectors. A sensor vector contains all sensor readings and an actuator vector contains all actuator values at a given timestep. Together, these vectors comprise training data from which the learning method extracts the inherent sensor/actuator mapping. Our filtering process determines which of these vector pairs qualify as good.

We first calculate standard deviation of each sensor across time, providing a measure of consistency. Each sensor whose standard deviation falls below a threshold is labelled a key sensor. For each, the most frequent reading is determined and used as its characteristic reading. The result is

the *characteristic vector*, depicting the desired behavior.

We filter data by taking the vector difference of the characteristic vector and the key sensor readings at each timestep, then we analyze the slope of the smoothed differences across time. A positive slope at a data point indicates the robot is moving away from the desired behavior. This data point is assumed bad and is removed.

Other possible uses for a characteristic vector include: a guide for selecting a subset of sensors for more efficient ANN training; a guide to include or exclude additional data keeping the training set from becoming prohibitively large for on-line learning (similar to that proposed in Pomerleau but without task domain knowledge); and most importantly, as behavior models for Hidden Markov Models (HMMs). The ultimate goal of this work is to create a robotic system capable of learning sequential tasks from human demonstration. HMMs have been used successfully for this purpose in robotics (Pook & Ballard 1993) and are good candidates for success here.

Preliminary experiments on RWI's ATRV Jr. and Nomadic's SuperScout resulted in a comprehensive training set with a single, continuous demonstration. Note this method relies on the assumption that key sensors are those with relatively constant readings. This holds for many tasks; nonetheless, we may be able to relax it by using correlation coefficients of sensors and actuators.

Acknowledgements

This work sponsored by Air Force Research Lab under contract F30602-96-2-0240.

References

Pomerleau, D. 1992. *Neural Network Perception for Mobile Robot Guidance*. Ph.D. Dissertation, Carnegie Mellon University, Pittsburgh, PA.

Pook, P., and Ballard, D. 1993. Recognizing teleoperated manipulations. In *Proc. IEEE Int'l Conf. on Robotics and Automation*, volume 2, 578–585.

Voyles, R.; Morrow, J.; and Khosla, P. 1997. Towards gesture-based programming: Shape from motion primordial learning of sensorimotor primitives. *Journal of Robotics and Autonomous Systems* 22(3-4):361–375.

An Implementation of the Combinatorial Auction Problem in ECL^{i}PS^e

Robert Menke and Rina Dechter

University of California, Irvine
Irvine, California 92717-3425
http://www.ics.uci.edu/~rmenke/
{rmenke, dechter}@ics.uci.edu

In a traditional auction, items are placed "up for bids" in an arbitrary sequence. For many bidders, this model is inadequate because the individual items increase in value when held in conjunction with other items. *Combinatorial auctions* allow bidders to bid upon multiple items simultaneously. While this resolves the problems for the bidders, it increases the problem of the auctioneer: determining the optimal selection of bids to maximize revenue is NP-complete.

(Sandholm 1999) suggests an algorithm that reduces the search space considerably. His algorithm, a DFS of the problem space using an ancillary data structure called a *Bidtree*, takes advantage of two properties of "real-life" auctions: that the bids submitted would be sparse and that the order in which bids are selected is irrelevant. The Bidtree helps select the next bid to be considered.

The goal of this project is to evaluate the general principles and algorithms developed for constraint processing in recent years, as well as the tools and languages facilitating the use of constraints for problem solving using the auction problem as a benchmark. By comparing general constraint-processing algorithms against methods tailored for this task, the power of such general algorithms can be demonstrated. This project was initiated during a class in the department of Information and Computer Science at the University of California, Irvine. Specifically, the constraint processing language ECL^{i}PS^e (ECLiPSe 1995) was used, which has as its basic algorithm backtracking with forward-checking and uses branch-and-bound for optimization tasks. There were three subgoals of this project: first, implement the combinatorial auction problem in ECL^{i}PS^e; second, implement Sandholm's solution using ECL^{i}PS^e; and third, investigate the possibility of improving the search using other heuristics.

It is important to realize that the Bidtree algorithm does not take into account the values the bidders have associated with each bid, nor does it consider (in this form of the algorithm) whether a mechanism for forward checking has been incorporated into the implementation language. Since ECL^{i}PS^e *does* support forward checking, the Bidtree algorithm simply becomes a static ordering of the variables.

The alternative bid selection rules used dynamic variable ordering to improve performance. The first approach was *most constrained bid* (MCB), which selected the bid whose set of items had the most non-empty intersections with all of the bids, thus elimintating more feasible future bids.

The second algorithm used the *most valuable bid* (MVB) rule. MVB selected the bid that had the largest amortized value (the value divided by the size of the set). It was hoped that the MVB selection rule would produce a higher revenue in its initial solution. This is desirable because the auctioneer may wish to stop the search before the algorithm completes. Additionally, a higher revenue discovered earlier would produce a better bound and would result in faster convergence to the optimal solution.

The data sets in the full report were generated by the same methods as in the Sandholm paper, but with scaled parameters because of resource limitations. Two results using unscaled parameters are summarized in Table 1. In most cases the MVB algorithm showed significant improvement over Bidtree in time to completion and the number of refinements to the bound. More experimental results may be seen at http://www.ics.uci.edu/~rmenke/runs/.

References

1995. *ECLiPSe User Manual, v. 3.5*. Available at http://www.ecrc.de/eclipse/eclipse.html.

Sandholm, T. W. 1999. An algorithm for optimal winner determination in combinatorial auctions. In *International Joint Conference on Artificial Intelligence (IJCAI)*, 542–547.

Experiment	Method	Total search time	Best revenue found at
150 bids,	MCB	20627.70 s	13517.25 s
25 items,	Bidtree	18739.12 s	7847.97 s
3 items/bid	MVB	2960.42 s	326.79 s
50 bids,	MCB	315.57 s	238.05 s
75 items,	Bidtree	208.47 s	1.85 s
value by size	MVB	78.66 s	11.69 s
50 bids,	MCB	624.75 s	457.21 s
75 items,	Bidtree	4220.93 s	2811.56 s
3 items/bid	MVB	231.41 s	55.74 s

Table 1: Comparison of performance of the three algorithms

A Semi-Complete Disambiguation Algorithm for Open Text

Rada Mihalcea
Department of Computer Science and Engineering
Southern Methodist University
Dallas, Texas, 75275-0122
rada@seas.smu.edu

Word Sense Disambiguation (WSD) is one of the most difficult areas of Natural Language Processing (NLP); the semantic comprehension of a text, and the possibility to expand a text with semantically related information, drastically depends on the availability of a highly accurate WSD algorithm. Solutions considered so far by researchers for the WSD problem, are making use of machine readable dictionaries (Leacock, Chodorow and Miller 1998), or the information gathered from raw or semantically disambiguated corpora (Yarowsky 1995). These methods are designed either to work with a few pre-selected words, in which case a high accuracy is obtained, or they are general methods which disambiguate, with lower precision, all the words in a text.

With the present work, we are trying to achieve a compromise between these two different directions. There are fields in NLP, like Information Retrieval and others, which could benefit from a method which performs a semi-complete disambiguation (i.e. it disambiguates only a certain percentage of the words in a text), but which is highly accurate.

The method described in this abstract uses information gathered from a MRD, namely WordNet (Fellbaum 1998), and from SemCor - a corpus in which all words are sense tagged based on WordNet definitions. It differs from previous approaches in that it uses an iterative approach: the algorithm has as input the set of nouns and verbs extracted from the input text, and incrementally builds a set of disambiguated words. This approach allows us to identify, with high precision, the semantic senses for a subset of the input words. About 55% of the nouns and verbs are disambiguated with a precision of 91%.

Below, we are going to briefly describe the various procedures used to identify the correct sense of a word. These procedures are iteratively invoked within the main algorithm.

PROCEDURE 1. This procedure uses a Named Entity (NE) component to recognize and identify person names, locations, company names and others. We add TPER (person), TORG(group) and TLOC(location) tags. The words or word collocations marked with such tags are replaced by their role (i.e. person, group, location) and marked as having sense #1.

PROCEDURE 2. Identify the words having only one sense in WordNet (*monosemous* words). Mark them with sense #1.

PROCEDURE 3. For a given word W_i, at position i in the text, form two pairs, with the word before W_i (pair W_{i-1}-W_i) and the word after W_i (pair W_i-W_{i+1}). Then, we extract all the occurrences of these pairs found within the semantic tagged corpus formed with the 179 texts from SemCor. If, in all the occurrences, the word W_i has only one sense #k, and the number of occurrences of this sense is larger than 3, then mark the word W_i as having sense #k.

Copyright © 2000, American Association for Artificial Intelligence (www.aaai.org). All rights reserved.

PROCEDURE 4. Find words which are semantically connected to the already disambiguated words, and for which the connection distance is 0. The distance is computed based on the WordNet hierarchy; two words are semantically connected at a distance of 0 if they belong to the same synset.

PROCEDURE 5. Find words which are semantically connected with each other, and for which the connection distance is 0.

PROCEDURE 6. Find words which are semantically connected to the already disambiguated words, and for which the connection distance is maximum 1; two words are semantically connected at a maximum distance of 1 if they are *synonyms* or they belong to a *hypernymy/hyponymy* relation.

PROCEDURE 7. Find words which are semantically connected with each other, and for which the connection distance is maximum 1.

The text to be disambiguated is first tokenized and part of speech tagged using Brill's tagger. We also identify the concepts based on WordNet definitions. Two sets of words are maintained, a set of ambiguous words SAW and the set of disambiguated words SDW. The procedures presented above are applied iteratively, until no more words can be disambiguated. Initially, all the words from the text are included in the SAW set and SDW is initialized with the empty set. As words are disambiguated by one of the procedures, they are removed from SAW and added to SDW. This allows us to identify a set of nouns and verbs which can be disambiguated with high precision.

We performed several tests using 6 randomly selected files from SemCor. Each of these files has been divided into sets of 15 sentences; these sets are used as input to the algorithm. The results have shown that about 55% of the nouns and verbs are disambiguated with 91% accuracy.

The method described here is a continuation of our previous work in the WSD field (Mihalcea and Moldovan 1999), and it is part of the work we are currently doing in the field of semantic indexing.

References

Fellbaum, C. *WordNet, An Electronic Lexical Database*. The MIT Press, 1998.

Leacock, C.; Chodorow, M. and Miller, G.A. Using Corpus Statistics and WordNet Relations for Sense Identification, *Computational Linguistics vol.24 no.1*, pages 147-165, 1998.

Mihalcea, R. and Moldovan D. A method for Word Sense Disambiguation of unrestricted text *Proceedings of the 37th Annual Meeting of the Association for Computational Linguistics (ACL-99)*, pages 152-158, College Park, MD, 1999.

Yarowsky, D. Unsupervised word sense disambiguation rivaling supervised methods. *Proceedings of the 33rd Annual Meeting of the Association of Computational Linguistics (ACL-95)*, pages 189-196, Cambridge, MA, 1995.

Combining Classification and Temporal Learning

Matthew Winston Mitchell
School of Computer Science and Software Engineering,
Faculty of Information Technology, Monash University
P.O Box 197 Caulfield East, 3145 Australia
matt@insect.sd.monash.edu.au

Background

This introduces TRACA (Temporal Reinforcement-learning and Classification Architecture), a connectionist learning system for solving problems in large state spaces. These types of problems, such as robot control, commonly include the presence of irrelevant attributes and hidden-state.

TRACA is capable of dealing with both irrelevant information and hidden-state while addressing two common shortcomings of other learning systems. The first shortcoming is requiring a large number of training examples which is unrealistic for learning in the real world. The second is having to pre-determine or constrain network structure and size.

System Overview

TRACA dynamically develops a model of its environment while learning. This model consists of *combination* groups, which are used to construct general rules, and *temporal* groups, which implement a memory mechanism.

Groups represent one or more situations and are connected to detector inputs and/or other groups by arcs which are used to pass a variety of messages. Based on the situations they represent, groups contain nodes which store estimates of action-values (Sutton 1998) - and maintain transition probabilities to other situations.

New groups are created incrementally while learning by combining existing nodes as selected by a localized probabilistic mechanism. Each new combination of nodes is given a small number of trials to determine its usefulness and is then retained only while it demonstrates an improved value estimate over those of its lower level component nodes.

Relationship to Other Work

TRACA has several distinguishing features. It is able to reduce the complexity of structures by representing NOT and XOR using only logical AND combinations in conjunction with the organisation of nodes into groups

and a suppression mechanism. When compared to Neural Networks (Lin 1993), nodes in TRACA store value estimates independently, allowing it to exploit learning from only a few training examples. Finally, TRACA will not continue to solve hidden-state problems if the solution provides no useful improvement in achieving reinforcement. This avoids the problem of choosing to either have a fixed-size history window or to artificially restrict the number of temporal nodes (McCallum 1996; Ring 1994).

TRACA's creation of new groups through combinations has strong parallels to both Holland's Learning Classifier Systems (Holland 1975) and Drescher's Schema Mechanism (Drescher 1991).

Results

Experimental results have demonstrated that TRACA is capable of representing a number of problems - including those with hidden-state - without having to pre-determine network size or structure. The performance of TRACA in experiments indicate that it can match the accuracy of a number of other systems with a relatively small number of training examples.

References

Drescher, G. 1991. *Made-Up Minds*. The MIT Press.

Holland, J. 1975. *Adaption in natural and artificial systems*. University of Michigan Press.

Lin, L. 1993. *Reinforcement Learning for Robots Using Neural Networks*. Ph.D. Dissertation, School of Computer Science, Carnegie Mellon University, Pittsburgh USA.

McCallum, A. 1996. *Reinforcement Learning With Selective Perception and Hidden State*. Ph.D. Dissertation, Department of Computer Science, University of Rochester, NY.

Ring, M. 1994. *Continual Learning in Reinforcement Environments*. Ph.D. Dissertation, The University of Texas at Austin.

Sutton, R. 1998. *Reinforcement Learning: An Introduction*. The MIT Press.

Copyright © 2000, American Association for Artificial Intelligence (www.aaai.org). All rights reserved.

Deriving and Using Abstract Representation in Behavior-Based Systems

Monica N. Nicolescu and **Maja J. Matarić**

Computer Science Department
University of Southern California
941 West 37th Place, Mailcode 0781
Los Angeles, CA 90089-0781
monica|mataric@cs.usc.edu, http://www-robotics.usc.edu/~agents/projects/abn.html

We present a representation that addresses two current limitations of the behavior-based systems (BBS) (Matarić 1992), (Arkin 1998): the lack of abstract representation within behaviors (which makes them hard to use in complex, sequential problems) and the need for behavior redesign even for tasks that use subsets of the same behavior set. We introduce the concept of behavior networks, based on the abstract behaviors representation described below.

We distinguish the following two types of behavior preconditions: *world preconditions* (activate the behaviors based on the state of the environment) and *sequential preconditions* (task-dependent conditions, often postconditions of other existing behaviors). In standard BBS behaviors, both types of preconditions are tested together, thus hard-coding a particular solution. The key step in adapting specialized behaviors to more general use is in the separation of the execution conditions from the outputs or actions, which allows for a more general set of activation conditions. The pairing of a behavior's conditions and its effects, without the specification of its inner workings, constitutes an *abstract behavior*. Intuitively, this is simply an explicit specification of the behavior's execution conditions (i.e., preconditions) and its effects (i.e., postconditions). The result is an abstract and general operator much like those used in classical deliberative systems (Fikes & Nilsson 1971). The behaviors that do the work that achieves the specified effects under the given conditions are called *primitive behaviors*, and may involve one or an entire collection of sequential or concurrently executing behaviors, as is typical for BBS. Behavior networks are a means of specifying strategies or general "plans" in a way that merges the advantages of both abstract representations and behavior-based systems. The nodes in the networks are abstract behaviors, and the links between them represent precondition and postcondition dependencies. The task plan or strategy is represented as a network of such behaviors.

We have implemented the proposed concepts on a physical mobile robot (Pioneer 2-DX) given an object delivery task in an enclosed, 2-section environment. The robot successfully finds a box, which may be in either section, goes with it through the door and pushes it to the delivery point. The solution makes use of two behavior networks and captures the important aspects of the proposed concepts: abstract representation, behavior reuse, behavior networks and the importance of relying on real embedded behaviors.

As a next goal, we seek to automate the behavior network generation and to use the representation to address human-robot interaction. The abstract representation should allow us to employ simple communication mechanisms which would enable the robots to benefit from the human and also learn from and share their acquired knowledge and experiences.

The abstract behavior representation we are proposing combines the advantages of deliberative, STRIPS-like architectures (Fikes & Nilsson 1971), and those of BBS' capability to operate in dynamically changing environments. However, it is important to note that we are not describing a *hybrid architecture*. Our work is related to the approaches of Kaelbling & Rosenschein (1990) (the *situated automata* model) and of Lyons & Arbib (1989) who developed a *robot schema* model of computation for sensory-based robot programming. However, their implementations do not allow generalization and reuse of the compiled high level circuitry and respectively the *robot schemas* to multiple tasks. Maes (1990) describes an action selection mechanism for a situated agent, based on spreading activation within a network created dynamically from a given behavior repertoire. A key difference is that the network nodes, at least in the demonstrated examples, consist of STRIPS-like high-level operators much more abstract than those we employ.

References

Arkin, R. C. (1998), *Behavior-Based Robotics*, MIT Press, CA.

Fikes, R. E. & Nilsson, N. J. (1971), 'STRIPS: A new approach to the application of theorem proving to problem solving', *Artificial Intelligence* **2**, 189–208.

Kaelbling, L. P. & Rosenschein, S. J. (1990), 'Action and planning in embedded agents', *Robotics and Autonomous Systems(1&2), June 1990* **6**, 35–48.

Lyons, D. M. & Arbib, M. A. (1989), 'A formal model of computation for sensory-based robotics', *IEEE Transactions on Robotics and Automation* **5**(3), 280–293.

Maes, P. (1990), 'Situated Agents Can Have Goals', *Journal for Robotics and Autonomous Systems* **6**(3), 49–70.

Matarić, M. J. (1992), 'Integration of Representation Into Goal-Driven Behavior-Based Robots', *IEEE Transactions on Robotics and Automation* **8**(3), 304–312.

Model-Based-Diagnosis for Fault Management in telecommunications Networks

Aomar Osmani

LIPN, Avenue J.-B. Clément F-93430 Villetaneuse
ao@lipn.univ-paris13.fr, http://www-lipn.univ-paris13.fr/~osmani

Abstract

Fault management is a crucial problem for telecommunication networks. The network complexity requires artificial intelligence techniques to assist the operators in supervision tasks. Initially expert systems techniques were proposed, presently various techniques are used: neural networks, constraint satisfaction problems, Petri networks. These methods are based on the analysis of the breakdown situations observed in the real system, consequently, they have the same problem as expert systems: they are enable to reason about new faults and the level of explanation of fault is poor.

The continual change of the telecommunication networks reduces the effectiveness of these methods. The model based techniques propose a framework based on the adaptive modeling of the system and the prediction of the behavior of the system from the simulation model.

Model-based-techniques are recognized more adapted to the evolutive systems, and give a good explanation of the faults. Model-based techniques typically compare observations of the behavior of a system being diagnosed to expectations based upon a model of the system in order to diagnosis faults. These approaches take a detailed view of the network. A generally accepted model for detailed system representation is that of a discrete-event system.

We have proposed in the GASPAR project a model-based approach to diagnose fault situations in greatest French telecommunication networks: TRANSPAC (BCD^+). This approach is based on two steps (see figure 1): (1) *Off-line step:* The first step to studying faults management is to build a model (Osm99c). This construction is done using two abstraction levels: structural abstraction where components of the network are modeled by temporal graph and behavioral model where each component is modeled by temporal and communicating finite state machines.

When the model is built, single and multiple faults are simulated in the model. The model is completed by a new kind of components "fault component". These components simulate faults (Osm00). Corresponding to the two level abstraction I have proposed two kind of algorithm: propagating algorithm associated to the structural level and deducting algorithm associated to the behavioral level (ORC^+99; Osm99b; OL00). The simulation process generates for each simulated situation a set of possible sequences of alarms could by received by the supervisor center. At the end of simulation a learning database of fault situations is built. This database is used by discrimination module to classify given fault in the space of sequences of alarms (Osm99a); (2) On-line step: the expert system generated by the off-line step is used to recognize on-fly fault situations from the stream of alarms arriving at the supervisor.

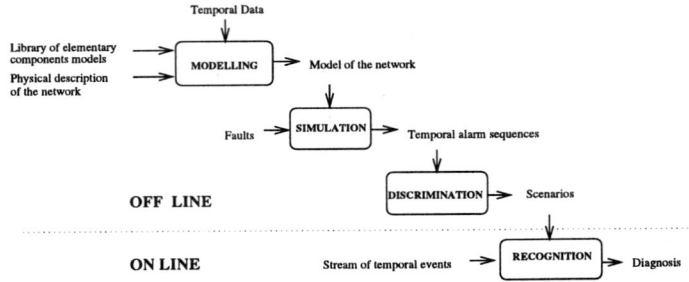

Figure 1: *Different steps of our approach*

References

S. Bibas, M.O. Cordier, P. Dague, F. Lévy, E. Mayer, A. Osmani, and L. Rozé. Supervision des réseaux de télécommunications : une approche à base de modèles dossier. In *Dossier : IA et Télécom (AFIA-Avril98)*.

A. Osmani and F. Lévy. Generation d'une base d'apprentissage pour l'apprentissage de pannes dans un reseau de télécommunications. In *(RFIA'2000)*.

A. Osmani, L. Rozé, M.O. Cordier, P. Dague, F. Lévy, and E. Mayer. Supervision of telecommunication networks. In *(ECC-99)*, 1999.

A. Osmani. Generalized intervals to learn and to recognize faults in telecommunication networks. In *(ACAI-99)*, 1999.

A. Osmani. Introduction to reasoning about cyclic intervals. In *(IEA/AIE-99)*, 1999.

A. Osmani. Modeling and simulating breakdown situations in telecommunication networks. In *(IEA/AIE-99)*, 1999.

A. Osmani. Simulating faults in telecommunication networks: reasoning about uncertain propagation of events. In *(CATA-2000)*, 2000.

Copyright © 2000, American Association for Artificial Intelligence (www.aaai.org). All rights reserved.

Representation and Evolution of Lego-based Assemblies

Maxim Peysakhov, Vlada Galinskaya, William C. Regli

Geometric and Intelligent Computing Lab
Department of Mathematics and Computer Science
Korman Computing Center
Drexel University
Philadelphia, PA 19104
{umpeysak, uvgalins, regli}@mcs.drexel.edu

Abstract

This research presents an approach to the automatic generation of engineering designs. Our approach is to apply Messy Genetic Algorithm optimization techniques to the evolution of assemblies composed of Lego elements. Design evaluations are based on a set of behavior and structural equations. Initial populations are generated at random, and the system evaluates and assigns numeric fitness values to each member in the population. The design candidates for subsequent generations are produced by a user-specified selection technique. Single point crossovers are applied by using cut and splice operators at random points of the messy chromosomes; random mutations are applied with a certain low probability to modify individual nodes of the graph. This cycle continues until a suitable design is found or until the time limit has expired. We have selected the domain of Lego assemblies because it represents a sufficiently complex, multi-disciplinary design domain and includes a wide variety of realistic engineering constraints. Further, the domain is sufficiently discrete as to be tractable.

The main contribution of this research is not in the genetic algorithm itself, but rather in its application to the practical task of Lego design generation. Representing Lego designs as a mechanical assembly graph has a number of potential advantages over the assembly tree approach, which was mentioned as a limiting factor in earlier research. A labeled assembly graph is more expressive and can represent a greater variety of Lego assemblies, including kinematic mechanisms as well as static structures. The nodes of the graph represent different Lego elements, and the edges of the graph represent connections between elements. We have developed a graph grammar to define valid combinations of nodes and edges precisely and unambiguously. This language aids in classifying the Lego blocks and connections. For now we have used this notation only to formally define the requirements documentation. In the future, we plan to introduce another level of abstraction and represent Lego mechanisms as sentences in a language of Lego assemblies, rather than graphs, which will make it easier to validate the assembly against grammar rules.

Although the current system can handle only static structures composed of block-type elements, the general approach can be applied to much more elaborate kinematic mechanisms. We have developed specifications on the representation of wheels, gears, and axles, and their connections. Each structure has a number of attributes, such as weight, number of nodes, and size in each dimension. These parameters are used by the evaluation function to calculate the fitness of the structure. Our eventual goal is to introduce simulation of electro-mechanical devices into our evaluation functions.

Figure 1 shows the result of evolution of static Lego structures with predefined geometric parameters. In these experiments, mutation and crossover rates were 0.01 and 0.7, respectively, and we used a *rank selection strategy* and *elitism* on a population of 100 members. In the first experiment the goal was to evolve a structure with a size of 10 Lego units in each *x-y-z* dimension with minimal weight. The resulting structure is shown on the left; it was discovered at generation 3367 and exactly matches the desired size. Also, it is one of the lightest possible structures that can be created from the set of elements that we have. In the other experiment, we evolved a pillar-like structure, with 2 by 4 base and length equal to 20, 40 or 60 Lego units and having maximal density. The output of the system is shown on the right. The resulting structures exactly match desired sizes and have very few defects.

We believe that this research creates a foundation for future work, and that we will be able to apply GA techniques to the evolution of more complex and realistic electro-mechanical structures.

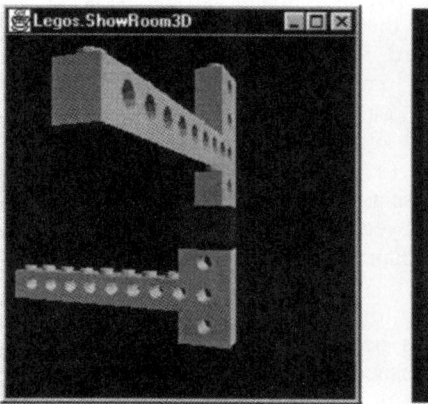

Figure 1: Experimental Results.

Acknowledgments

Support provided by the NSF Knowledge and Distributed Intelligence in the Information Age (KDI) Initiative Grant CISE/IIS-9873005 and CAREER Award CISE/IIS-973354 to William C Regli.

Copyright © 2000, American Association for Artificial Intelligence (www.aaai.org). All rights reserved.

Intelligent Monitoring in a Robotic Assistant for the Elderly

Sailesh Ramakrishnan

Intelligent Systems Program
University of Pittsburgh
sai+@pitt.edu

Martha E. Pollack

Department of Computer Science and
Intelligent Systems Program
University of Pittsburgh
pollack@cs.pitt.edu

The NurseBot project is developing a mobile robot that is intended to assist elderly people suffering from mild cognitive disorders in their everyday life (see http://www.cs.cmu.edu/~nursebot). One of the main components of the project is intelligent reminding, which is useful when an elderly person has mild memory problems. The robot possesses information about the elder's daily activities, and monitors their performance, providing reminders when needed. The reminders may address activities that are critical to the elder's health and safety (taking their medications), as well as activities that support the elder's general happiness (their favorite TV program). An intelligent reminder system must be able to analyze its user's plans and compute a monitoring plan of its own.

One of the main aspects of intelligent monitoring is to identify which activities should be monitored. It is infeasible to monitor *everything*, for several reasons. First, the robot may not be able, or might choose not to follow its user around all the time, for example, it might not enter the user's bathroom. Second, the kinds of and the accuracy of the sensors may limit the ability of the robot to monitor certain activities. Third, too much monitoring may annoy the elderly user, who may be attentive to and punctual about certain activities, only requiring monitoring for other activities. Prior work on selecting activities to monitor during plan execution (e.g. Pollack and McCarthy 1999) has not focused on these aspects of the problem, but instead has distinguished between environmental changes that influence an existing plan in some way, and those that do not.

The intelligent monitoring system we are developing learns which activities need to be monitored, and when reminders need to be issued. It is initially provided with a detailed representation of the user's plans, which may be modified, via additions, deletions, or changes, as time passes. These modifications are handled by PMA, the Plan Management Agent (Pollack, Tsamardinos and Horty 1999). The representation may identify certain activities as *critical*: these must be monitored all the time (e.g. medicine-taking). Non-critical activities fall into two classes: those that should be monitored, with reminders presented as needed; and those that only need to be periodically monitored.

Our approach makes use of a Bayesian belief network that represents our belief about the likely time of the user's performance of each planned activity, contingent on his or her performance of certain earlier activities. (For instance, the time at which the user eats breakfast may depend on the time at which s/he got up.) We then run simulations on the model of the user's activities to identify which ones are likely to be late and hence should be monitored. More specifically, our algorithm involves four steps: (1) Convert the elderly person's plan from PMA's temporal network representation to a Bayesian belief network. (2) Perform numerous simulations. In each, a time interval for each activity is randomly chosen, subject to the conditional probabilities in the network. (We make use of a discretized notion of time.). (3) Use the results of the simulations to compute the probability distribution of each activity's execution over time. The probability of an activity's occurrence during time interval I is the fraction of simulations in which that interval was chosen for that activity. (4) This probability is combined with a weighting factor for that activity and is then compared to a threshold. The weighting factor for critical activities is infinitely large. An activity is flagged if the probability it will be late exceeds the threshold. Currently, we are using thresholds as a simplified mechanism for identifying activities to monitor; we plan to incorporate a more decision theoretic mechanism in a future version. Monitoring actions for the flagged activities are incorporated into the robot's plan and are executed. Each time the robot observes an activity or has information about a change, this process is repeated with the new information incorporated into the network, and if necessary the monitoring plan is modified.

References

Pollack M. E. and McCarthy, C., Towards Focused Plan Monitoring: A Technique and an Application to Mobile Robots, *IEEE International Symposium on Computational Intelligence in Robotics and Automation (CIRA)*, 1999.

Pollack, M. E., Tsamardinos, I. and Horty, J. F. Adjustable Autonomy for a Plan Management Agent, *AAAI Spring Symposium on Adjustable Autonomy*, Stanford, CA, March, 1999.

Towards Efficient Negotiation Mechanisms for Collaboration*

Timothy Rauenbusch
Division of Engineering and Applied Sciences
Harvard University
Cambridge MA 02138 USA
tim@eecs.harvard.edu

Autonomous agents can achieve more by working together in a team than if each agent acted alone, but disagreements about exactly how to accomplish a group task will arise (e.g., over subtask assignment). The goal of this work is to develop a negotiation mechanism that is suitable for agents involved in a collaboration.

A significant problem in multi-agent systems is that there is no central authority to settle disagreements. Even though a resolution may be globally optimal from the group perspective, an individual agent will not agree to a deal unless that deal is in its own self-interest. For this reason, search techniques that find some globally optimal resolution, such as one that seeks to maximize the sum of the utility of agents in the group (Sandholm 1998) are not directly applicable. For example, even though an outcome that gives $5 to each robot may maximize a group's gain, a self-interested robot would prefer an outcome of $6, even if that left another robot with $1.

Much work in AI on negotiation has adopted methods from the economic field of game theory(Kraus, Wilkenfeld, & Zlotkin 1995; Ephrati & Rosenschein 1991) and has focused on the design of negotiation mechanisms (or protocols) that guarantee *stability*, that is, the incentive for agents to adhere to the strategies prescribed by the mechanism designer.

There is a mismatch between these approaches and the needs of agents negotiating in the context of a collaboration. Game theoretic approaches assume that the evaluation of an agent's preferences is cost-free. Additionally, work based on bargaining assumes common knowledge of agents' preferences. Voting can be applied to more general settings but at the cost of wasting resources (i.e., by an externally imposed tax).

Similarly, familiar auction mechanisms where agents can bid for tasks do not meet the needs of collaborative agents. Arguments for efficiency and stability in auctions assume that there will be a large number of agents bidding on a given item.

We argue that negotiation among collaborators requires a new approach and use the SharedPlans formalism for collaboration (Grosz & Kraus 1999) to identify several important properties of such negotiations which conflict with the assumptions of game-theoretic mechanisms. Specifically, negotiations among collaborators are integrative instead of zero-sum; they are frequent, so resources squandered can quickly accumulate; the evaluation of collaborators' preferences involves costs; and frequently only one agent in a group is capable of performing a given task. Thus, in the setting of collaborative activity, the properties of outcome efficiency, minimization of preference computation, and simplicity are more important than stability.

We describe a new mechanism called Blind Mediation (BM) that can be applied in a collaborative setting. BM implements an anytime search algorithm through the space of possible agreements a group could make. It has the desirable properties of outcome efficiency, minimization of preference computation and simplicity. Simulations have shown that the performance of BM (in terms of long term efficiency and decreased computation cost) is significantly superior to full revelation of preferences and negotiations among people.

References

Ephrati, E., and Rosenschein, J. S. 1991. The Clarke tax as a consensus mechanism among automated agents. In *Proceedings of the Ninth National Conference on Artificial Intelligence*, 173–178.

Grosz, B., and Kraus, S. 1999. The evolution of SharedPlans. In Wooldridge, M., and Rao, A., eds., *Foundations and Theories of Rational Agency*, number 14 in Applied Logic Series. The Netherlands: Kluwer Academic Publishers. 227–262.

Kraus, S.; Wilkenfeld, J.; and Zlotkin, G. 1995. Multiagent negotiation under time constraints. *Artificial Intelligence* 75:297–345.

Sandholm, T. 1998. Contract types for satisficing task allocation: I theoretical results. In *AAAI 1998 Spring Symposium: Satisficing Models*.

---

*The research reported in this paper was partially supported by National Science Foundation grants IIS-9978343 and CDA-94-01024, and the DARPA Autonomous Negotiating Teams Program, Contract F30602-99-C-0169.
Copyright © 2000, American Association for Artificial Intelligence (www.aaai.org). All rights reserved.

Behavior Acquisition and Classification: A Case Study in Robotic Soccer

Patrick Riley and **Manuela Veloso**

Computer Science Department, Carnegie Mellon University, Pittsburgh, PA 15213

Increasingly in domains with multiple intelligent agents, each agent must be able to identify what the other agents are doing. This is especially important when there are adversarial agents inferring with the accomplishment of goals. Once identified, the agents can then respond to recent strategies and adapt to improve performance.

This research works under the hypothesis that fast and useful adaptation can be done by analogy to previous observations. We introduce methods to extract similarities in temporal observations of the world. First, past observations are organized into a set of behavior classes. By analyzing similarities, the current adversary can be classified into this set of behavior classes. The agents can then employ the most effective strategy against that behavior group.

The test domain for this research is the Soccer Server System (Noda *et al.* 1998) as used in the Robot World Cup Initiative (Kitano *et al.* 1997). The server provides a realistic *simulation* of a soccer game. Distributed software agents interact in a complex, noisy, inaccessible environment. The software was developed based on the champion CMUnited99 agent team (Stone, Riley, & Veloso 2000).

The raw data of the simulation consists of locations of players and the ball over time. The data is first broken into windows of fixed size. For each window, several features are extracted. Each feature extractor watches for a particular type of event (such as an opponent's pass or an opponent's shot). Upon observing an event of the right type, the feature extractor records where on the field, but not when in the window the event occurred.

The recordings of all the games at RoboCup-98 and RoboCup-99 were used as the data sets. A behavior class is created for each team in the competitions. The teams are first observed on a fraction of the games they played. Then, for each type of feature, the data from each window is averaged together to create a "target configuration" for that feature type. In other words, a behavior class consists of a set of examples for what each feature extractor should return if the current opponent is in that class.

After creating these behavior classes, the goal is to correctly identify which teams were playing based on these observations. In order to perform any classification, there must be a notion of similarity between the target configuration and what was actually observed. A novel similarity metric was developed that takes in account spatial localities of topological differences.

Classification was performed in two ways. First with a standard nearest-neighbor approach and then by training a decision tree with the similarities to all of the target configurations as the feature set.

Copyright © 2000, American Association for Artificial Intelligence (www.aaai.org). All rights reserved.

The number of teams in the two competitions was 34 and 37 respectively, making the accuracy of random guessing about 3%. The nearest-neighbor approach performed very poorly on both data sets, with both a 500 cycle window and a 1000 cycle window, doing better than random guessing in only one case. The decision tree approach performed much better (Figure 1). The results also point out an interesting tradeoff in the window length. A long window gives a more accurate sample of the opponent, but a short window gives more data for better learning as well as faster adaptation.

Future work could include smarter creation of behavior classes. Rather than the *a priori* distinction of team name, a clustering approach could be used, such as (Sebastiani, Ramoni, & Cohen 1999). Also, Hidden Markov Models may be useful in capturing more complex events for the features (Han & Veloso 1999). Also, automatically determining the correct window length, perhaps on a per-feature basis, could be very useful.

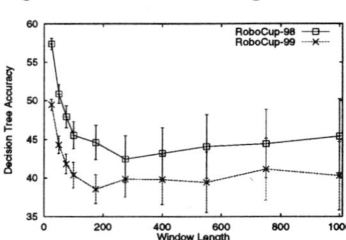

Figure 1: Decision Tree Accuracy

The main contributions of this research are: a windowing approach to abstracting features in complex domains; a novel discrete spatial similarity metric; and a demonstration that the windowing approach can capture important strategic features in a particular complex, dynamic domain.

References

Han, K., and Veloso, M. 1999. Automated robot behavior recognition applied to robotic soccer. In *Proceedings of IJCAI-99 Workshop on Team Behaviors and Plan Recognition*.

Kitano, H.; Tambe, M.; Stone, P.; Veloso, M.; Coradeschi, S.; Osawa, E.; Matsubara, H.; Noda, I.; and Asada, M. 1997. The robocup synthetic agent challenge. In *Proceedings of IJCAI-95*, 24–49.

Noda, I.; Matsubara, H.; Hiraki, K.; and Frank, I. 1998. Soccer server: A tool for research on multiagent systems. *Applied Artificial Intelligence* 12:233–250.

Sebastiani, P.; Ramoni, M.; and Cohen, P. 1999. Unsupervised classification of sensory inputs in a mobile robot. In *Proceedings of the IJCAI Workshop on Neural, Symbolic, and Reinforcement Methods for Sequence Learning*.

Stone, P.; Riley, P.; and Veloso, M. 2000. The CMUnited-99 champion simulator team. In Veloso; Pagello; and Kitano., eds., *RoboCup-99: Robot Soccer World Cup III*. Berlin: Springer.

Tambe, M., and Rosenbloom, P. 1995. Resc: An approach for dynamic, real-time agent tracking. In *Proceedings of IJCAI-95*.

"Small-World" Networks of Mobile Robots

Stergios I. Roumeliotis and Maja J. Mataric

$stergios|maja@robotics.usc.edu\ http://www-robotics.usc.edu/\sim stergios/aaai2000.html$

Department of Computer Science
University of Southern California
Los Angeles, CA 90089-0781

In order for a group of robots to coordinate collaboration during multi-robot tasks (Fontan & Mataric 1998), they need to communicate in an intelligent, purposeful way (Gerkey & Mataric 2000). If small groups of robots are involved, global communication (broadcasting, or one-to-all) is usually sufficient. The main advantage is that all the acquired information is available to all the members of the group. However when the number of robots increases so does the amount of data to handle. Information overflow can affect the performance of the separate teams working on different sub-tasks while limitations of the communication channel can cause interference and reduce the overall performance. A potential alternative to this would be to support local (one-to-a few) communication amongst the robots. The connectivity of such networks (communication topology) is usually assumed to be either completely regular (each robot communicates with its immediate neighbors forming a communication lattice), or completely random (each member of the group communicates with some random other members). However many biological, technological, and social networks lie somewhere between these two extremes (regular lattices vs. random graphs). Recently, a new form of coupled systems called "small-world" networks (Watts & Strogatz 1998), (Collins & Chow 1998), have been used to successfully describe the interactions of systems that can be highly clustered, like regular lattices, yet have small characteristic path lengths like random graphs.

Regular networks are also known as "large-world" networks. They are highly clustered while the characteristic path length is large, scaling with the typical dimension n of the network. High clustering is appropriate for certain types of robotic tasks when information produced by individual robots is more likely to be used by neighboring robots. For example, a large number of robots distributed amongst a few teams each performing a different task that requires only local collaboration (e.g. one team is drilling and analyzing soil samples from a certain area while another team is assembling a solar panel) would benefit from such an arrangement of the communication sub-networks between the robots. On the other end, if these teams perform tasks that call for global collaboration (e.g. each team maps neighboring areas) then the size of the characteristic path length results in increased delays for the information to flow from one robot to all the others in the colony. This type of communication topology would reduce the efficiency of the collaboration amongst the sub-groups. In this latter case a random-graph type of connectivity would be ideal. Small characteristic path lengths would ensure that the information gathered by each individual team member would be diffused during a few only communication cycles (re-broadcasting of the data to robots connected on the same Ethernets) to all the robots in the colony. In many cases the members of a robot colony are required to switch from tasks that require primarily local collaboration to tasks that depend on global communication. Instead of redesigning the communication topology each time there is a new task from a regular to a random graph and vice-versa, "small-world" networks can be used. Starting from a ring lattice and rewiring a few edges at random with some probability p we can "tune" the graph between regularity ($p = 0$) and disorder ($p = 1$). Graphs belonging in this intermediate region $0 < p < 1$, shift gradually from regular network to a random network. Both the characteristic path length $L(p)$ and the clustering $C(p)$ of the network can be described as functions of the amount of randomness p.

The implementation of a "small-world" network topology when designing the communication graph of a large colony of mobile robots has the following advantages: 1. The communication overload that each of the robots would experience if all of them were connected on the same network (1 Ethernet, one-to-all communication) is obviated, 2. The amount of clustering for local teams of robots remains almost the same and thus relevant information produced within this team is quickly shared amongst its members, and 3. The characteristic path length is significantly reduced compared to the case of a regular (lattice-like) network, therefore facilitating the fast diffusion of information across the colony when this is necessary for a global task. The critical parameters of such a network are the total number of robots in the colony n, the connectivity dimension k and the degree of randomness p. In most cases n is pre-specified while k and p are the design parameters to be determined in order to bring an initially regular network to its "small-world" form.

References

Collins, J., and Chow, C. 1998. It's a small world. *Nature* 393(6684):409–410.

Fontan, M., and Mataric, M. 1998. Territorial multi-robot task division. *IEEE Transactions on Robotics and Automation* 14(5):815–822.

Gerkey, B., and Mataric, M. 2000. Murdoch: Publish/subscribe task allocation for heterogeneous agents. In *Fourth International Conference on Autonomous Agents*. (to appear).

Watts, D., and Strogatz, S. 1998. Collective dynamics of 'small-world' networks. *Nature* 393(6684):440–442.

Copyright © 2000, American Association for Artificial Intelligence (www.aaai.org). All rights reserved.

Towards Approximately Optimal Poker

Jiefu Shi and Michael Littman
Department of Computer Science, Duke University
Durham, NC 27705
{jshi | mlittman}@cs.duke.edu

Creating strategies for different games forces us to grapple with different types of decision-making challenges. Poker is a stochastic game of imperfect information; unlike games of complete information, game-theoretic optimal strategies for poker can be randomized. Koller and Pfeffer [1] argue that two-player poker can be solved efficiently in the size of the game tree using a clever mapping to linear programming.

Texas Hold'em is the variant of poker used in championship tournaments. We are working on methods for generating approximately optimal strategies for Texas Hold'em. To give the flavor of our approach, we describe initial experiments in using abstraction.

For games with a single betting round, we use a grouping method to reduce the number of distinct hands considered. We enumerate all possible hands by their hand strength to obtain a raking of each hand (a hand with higher value always beats the hand with a lower value). Next, we group hands into *bins*. Each bin contains hands with similar rankings, so, a hand belonging in a bin with a rank of three beats all hands in bins one and two. The game is then solved at the level of bins: we imagine that players are randomly assigned to bins, with the highest ranking bin the winner; betting strategies are computed for the resulting game. The number of bins used in the approximation controls the degree of abstraction and can be adjusted to accommodate space and time requirements.

For our test-bed, we used a game with 200 possible hands. We first generated the optimal strategy for the first player (dealer). We then ran experiments dividing hands into from 4 to 200 bins and produced strategies for the second player (gambler) based on each of these groupings. Figure 1 shows how well the gambler fared against the optimal strategy of the dealer based on 100,000 games (the gambler has an advantage in this and most poker games). The results are quite encouraging; using as few bins as 10% of the number of hands, the resulting play is almost as good as that of the optimal strategy.

In games with multiple betting rounds, the principle concern is "hand potential". The player is forced make decisions based on partial hands. The same ranking trick would not work as in the one round case. A hand with high potential of developing into a strong hand may not have high hand value currently (for example, four-card flush). For these games, we rank the hands based on the average value of all possible complete hands that a partial hand can develop into. We then group them into bins and play each bin against another to get the expected payoff; this is used in defining the payoffs for the "abstracted" game. And, for cards yet to come, we also use the notion of abstraction. Instead of performing our calculation based on each possible card to come, we also group those cards yet to come into bins (for example, only knowing a low diamond is coming rather than knowing that the three of diamonds is coming).

We introduced a reduced version of Texas Hold'em that consists of a 52 card deck but with 3 cards in play. Figure 2 shows the result of the gambler versus the dealer (the dealer is using the optimal strategy). Just as in the game with the single betting round, we can do quite well just using a very small number of bins.

Figure 1. No Hand Potential

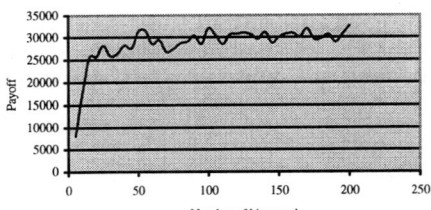

Figure 2. Hand Potential

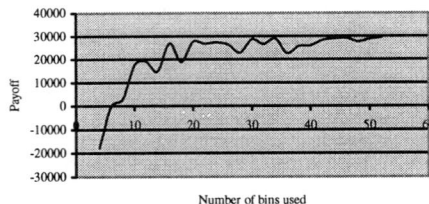

References

[1] D. Koller and A. Pfeffer, 1997. "Representations and Solutions for Game-Theoretic Problems," *Artificial Intelligence,* vol. 94, no. 1-2, pp. 167-215

Team-aware Multirobot Strategy for Cooperative Path Clearing

Gita Sukthankar
Robotics Institute, CMU
Pittsburgh, PA 15213
gitars@cs.cmu.edu
http://www.cs.cmu.edu/~gitars/AAAI-2000

In this paper, we present a simulated version of a potential demining problem in which robotic minesweepers clear a battle area of anti-tank mines to enable troops to breach the field. The demining problem is modeled as a distributed optimization problem in which the robots strive to minimize an abstract cost function. Robots were simulated using the Java based simulator, *TeamBots* (www.teambots.org).

The demining robots are responsible for clearing a direct vertical path between the top and bottom edges of the minefield. At each time step, robots must select one of three possible actions: *move*, *scan*, or *defuse*. Each action has a time cost associated with it that represents the relative difficulty of the task for the robot; deactivating mines is not explicitly modeled in the simulation as an actuation task. This problem has characteristics of the *consume* and *graze* tasks described in (Balch & Arkin 1995); robots explore unknown areas until they isolate a path that has few mines before converging to "consume" the mines. By varying the costs associated with each action, we can model the characteristics of different robotic deminers.

Previous work suggests that a homogeneous strategy should perform well in this domain, given its similarity to other foraging-type tasks. However we show that robots using a simple homogeneous approach have difficulty completing the task due to high inter-robot interference. We suggest that the proper way to approach the problem of interference is to make the the robots more "team-aware"; each robot plans its strategy based on assumptions about what its teammates are doing and current sensor data. This approach works well and substantially outperforms the simple homogeneous approach in which each robot individually optimizes. Although this type of global optimization can become intractable for large numbers of robots, we present an efficient algorithm that only considers local interactions.

For the "team-aware" optimization strategy, each robot models the decision-making process of its nearest peers. Since robots outside this neighborhood are less likely to interfere the robot's goal, their impact on the choice of next action is not considered. For each teammate within this neighborhood the robot determines whether the teammate is also heading for its chosen column. This calculation can be performed in $O(K)$ time for K neighbors and creates a list of potential interference points. The obvious algorithm for finding an optimal arrangement of peers to cells in the chosen column requires an exhaustive enumeration. Fortunately the same result can be calculated far more efficiently. A robot need only consider its K best choices rather than all N cells, because it can never be assigned to a worse option. This enables us to determine the optimal solution while only considering K^K potential assignments. Preliminary results indicate that the "team-aware" strategy performs favorably compared to the individual optimization strategy; in scenarios with larger number of robots (> 3), the team robots clear a path faster and are less likely to get trapped by other robots.

Unfortunately, a multirobot system cannot always be created by cloning a group of single robots programmed for the same task. There has to be some awareness, either on the part of the robots or the system designer, of the role that other team members will play in completing the task. Unless the global task is somehow partitioned among the robots, they will either interfere with each other or converge on a sub-optimal division of labor.

Heterogeneity, either behavioral or functional, can serve as prior agreement on labor division. *Functional* heterogeneity usually means that not all the robots are capable of performing all the tasks, whereas *behavioral* heterogeneity occurs when not all the robots are interested in performing the same section of the task, at least not at the same time. This inhibits SPST (same place, same time) interference, as described in (Fontan & Mataric 1998).

Homogeneous systems are well suited for using teamwork since it is relatively trivial for a a homogeneous system to "model" its fellow teammates. This approach shares some similarities with the central planner method, although it is often computationally faster since each robot only has to infer the actions of fellow robots within sensor range, rather than the actions of the entire team.

References

Balch, T., and Arkin, R. 1995. Communication in reactive multiagent robotic systems. *Autonomous Robots* 1(1).

Fontan, M., and Mataric, M. 1998. Territorial multi-robot task division. *IEEE Transactions on Robotics and Automation* 15(5).

Interfacing Issues for Information Extraction

Peter Vanderheyden and **Robin Cohen**
Department of Computer Science, University of Waterloo
Waterloo, Ontario, Canada N2L 3G1
{*pbvander, rcohen*}@*uwaterloo.ca*

Traditional approaches to information extraction implicitly assume that many elements of the task are static — the user's query, and the description of domain and corpus, for example. We believe that in many real situations, however, this assumption does not hold and it is important to consider how the system could best support interaction with the user when the assumption breaks down. Current goals in the information extraction community are for the system to produce accurate results while being easy to retrain and port to a new domain. We seek to extend current approaches to handle dynamic elements of the problem.

"Evolving queries", discussed in the information retrieval (IR) literature, need to be supported by information extraction (IE) systems; IR and IE are both, after all, tools for gathering information from documents in response to a user query. When a casual user — neither an expert in the use of the system, nor in the domain — engages in any information gathering task, there will be an initial phase of investigation and discovery during which the user becomes familiar with the system, the domain, and the documents in the corpus and the user's query may change over time or evolve. For example, a user may have a query about terrorist activities, asking for the names of perpetrators and the locations of targets; an interim system output prompts the user to refine the query, redefining terrorist activities as involving only a subset of weapons while generalizing to allow for additional (*e.g.*, government) perpetrators.

The query is not the only element that may change over time; certainly the domain evolves as additional documents are processed. As well, when the corpus is very large or dynamic (*e.g.*, the Internet), the corpus itself may be seen as evolving — rules for mapping text patterns to query items that apply at one time or for one portion of the corpus no longer apply for another.

To provide more robust support for information extraction in a dynamic environment, we consider such issues as:

- appropriate "modalities" for an interface to large amounts of natural language text — the user and system need shared access to all information in order to interact about the current problem state. In existing systems, these include document text, that text annotated with system-specific markups (Bird & Liberman 1999), and possibly a syntax of markup rules; we add additional modalities (*e.g.*, heuristics in the user model; tripartite model of the query, domain, and corpus).

- appropriate opportunities when the system or user should take initiative to interact with one another or to modify the current state — we have proposed a "mixed-initiative" approach (Vanderheyden & Cohen 1999), expanding the opportunities for interaction and shared control of modalities; the system continuously evaluates the need and cost-benefits of its actions. Regularities in the document text not yet identified by the user, or interim results produced by the system (*e.g.*, a partial answer to the user's query recognized in a document) may prompt the system to initiate interaction with the user.

- features for knowledge representation — we allow the user multiple views of the data, and direct manipulation of the domain and query representations. Modifying or navigating through one modality will update others.

- features for machine learning — while the rule of thumb has been that larger increments (batch learning) give better accuracy, smaller increments (online learning) allow better adaptivity; and active learning (Engelson & Dagan 1996) lets the system control its own training examples.

We intend to investigate how choices made on these and related issues affect performance. Specifically, our initial focus will be on how best to support evolving information models (query and domain) interactively.

References

Bird, S., and Liberman, M. 1999. Annotation graphs as a framework for multidimensional linguistic data analysis. In *Towards Standards and Tools for Discourse Tagging, Proc. of the Workshop*, 1–10. ACL.

Engelson, S. P., and Dagan, I. 1996. Sample selection in natural language learning. In Wermter, S.; Riloff, E.; and Scheler, G., eds., *Connectionist, Statistical, and Symbolic Approaches to Learning for Natural Language Processing*, Lecture Notes in AI. Springer, Berlin. 230–245.

Vanderheyden, P., and Cohen, R. 1999. Designing a mixed-initiative information extraction system. In *Working Notes of the AAAI'99 Workshop on Mixed-Initiative Intelligence*, 142–146.

Clustering with Instance-level Constraints

Kiri Wagstaff and Claire Cardie
Department of Computer Science
Cornell University
Ithaca, NY 14850
(607) 255-5033
{wkiri,cardie}@cs.cornell.edu
http://www.cs.cornell.edu/home/wkiri/research/constraints.html

Clustering algorithms seek to discover underlying patterns in a data set automatically. To this end, they conduct a search through the space of possible organizations of the data, preferring those which group similar instances together and keep dissimilar instances apart. We claim that this search can be aided by the addition of constraints, which serve to restrict the search space and to guide the search through it.

Although clustering remains a popular area of research, to our knowledge no previous attempt has been made to incorporate hard constraints into a clustering algorithm. However, constraints have been used successfully in other unsupervised domains (e.g. interactive knowledge base construction (De Raedt, Bruynooghe, & Martens 1991)). Additionally, work has been done on incorporating general background knowledge (e.g. as a starting point in the search space (Thompson & Langley 1992) or as declarative knowledge in the form of rules on cluster membership (Talavera & Béjar 1999)).

In this work, we focus on two kind of constraints: *must-link* and *cannot-link* constraints. Both are considered hard constraints that must be satisfied (we defer an exploration of other kinds of constraints, including soft constraints, to future work). Must-link constraints specify that two instances have to be in the same cluster, while cannot-link constraints prevent two instances from being in the same cluster. We experimented with constraints using a modified version of COBWEB (Fisher 1987) that constructs a partition of the data (rather than a hierarchy). For any real-world application of this technique, constraints would be derived from problem-specific background knowledge. However, we here used randomly generated sets of constraints based on the (known but not visible to the clustering algorithm) class labels. Evaluation was done using 10-fold cross-validation with 50 random trials per fold.

We found that the incorporation of constraints can improve clustering accuracy, i.e. how close the resulting partition is to the correct partition. In experiments on four data sets (three from UCI (Blake & Merz 1998) and a part-of-speech tagging data set; $n = 50$), we saw improvements of up to 11% after incorporating 50 constraints, and up to 17% with 100 constraints. We also discovered that the type of constraint that is most effective can vary between data sets; greater increases can be obtained, for example, by using only must-link constraints with the mushroom data set. In addition, because constraints restrict the search space, we observed a corresponding decrease in runtime as more constraints were added.

We intend to apply this technique to other clustering algorithms so that they can likewise take advantage of constraint information. In addition, we plan to experiment with a variety of other data sets. In particular, some real-world domains appear likely to benefit from the inclusion of constraints, such as noun phrase coreference. In this task, background linguistic knowledge offers useful hints as to which noun phrases should be grouped together and which should not. In conclusion, we have reported on work which shows that incorporating constraints in a clustering algorithm can lead to an increase in accuracy for class discovery.

This work was supported in part by a National Science Foundation Graduate fellowship and by NSF Grant IRI-9624639. We would like to thank Westley Weimer for his suggestions as the work progressed and Peter Cheeseman, Doug Fisher, and John Stutz for email discussions.

References

Blake, C. L., and Merz, C. J. 1998. UCI Repository of Machine Learning Databases. http://www.ics.uci.edu/~mlearn/MLRepository.html.

De Raedt, L.; Bruynooghe, M.; and Martens, B. 1991. Integrity Constraints and Interactive Concept-Learning. In *Proceedings of the Eighth International Workshop on Machine Learning*, 394–398. Northwestern University, Chicago, IL: Morgan Kaufmann.

Fisher, D. 1987. Knowledge Acquisition Via Incremental Conceptual Clustering. *Machine Learning* 2:139–172.

Talavera, L., and Béjar, J. 1999. Integrating Declarative Knowledge in Hierarchical Clustering Tasks. In *International Symposium on Intelligent Data Analysis*, 211–222. Amsterdam, The Netherlands: Springer-Verlag.

Thompson, K., and Langley, P. 1992. Case Studies in the Use of Background Knowledge: Incremental Concept Formation. In *AAAI-92 Workshop on Constraining Learning with Prior Knowledge*, 60–68. San Mateo, CA: The AAAI Press.

An ILP Method Based on Instance Graph

Runqi Zhang

Department of Computer Science and Engineering
State University of New York at Buffalo
rzhang@cse.buffalo.edu

A necessary function of ILP systems is to test whether rulesets intensionally cover examples. In general, when R contains recursive clauses, the above test may not terminate. In order that ILP techniques can serve end users directly in applications such as knowledge discovery in databases, general methods must be provided to ensure that the learned rulesets are executable and, in particular, that they do not lead to infinite recursion. To the best of our knowledge, all current methods are based on some kind of "Literal Order" or analog. Among them, the method "Ordering a Set of Constants and then Ordering Recursive Literals" that FOIL used (Cameron-Jones & Quinlan 1993) is one of the most advanced. However, this method suffers in at least three ways. ❶It can not be extended to Multiple Predicate Learning (MPL) (Raedt et cl. 1993) that involves more than one relation, e.g. when relation R invokes S and S invokes R. ❷It may not order constants correctly so as to have to rely on users to define constant orders for many recursive learning tasks. Sometimes this is necessary but not easy for users. ❸It needs to define theory constants that are strong hints of ground clauses.

In our opinion, in order to overcome the above shortcomings, FOIL should memory more of previous learning to help further search in rule space. If we can efficiently record and update the effects that are made to the instance space every time when a new (recursive) clause is added to the rule, we can design more powerful heuristics to help search the rule space. Based on this idea, we invented **instance graph** $H_{(R,E)}$, where R is a ruleset and E is an instance space.

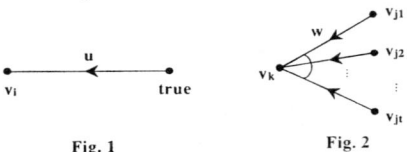

Fig. 1   Fig. 2

Instance graph is a type of directed hypergraph. In instance graph, every vertex denotes an example of the target predicate. Every hyperarc in instance graph $H_{(R,E)}$ denotes an instance of a clause in R that contains no negative background examples in its body. There are two types of hyperarcs. The first type illustrated in Fig. 1 denotes an instance of a non-recursive clause. v_i denotes the head of the instance, and "true" is a special vertex we defined. The second type illustrated in Fig. 2 denotes an instance of a recursive clause. v_k denotes the head of the instance and $v_{j1},...,v_{jt}$ denote all target examples appearing in the body of the instance. Clearly, instance graph $H_{(R,E)}$ can detail the relationship between ruleset R and target example space E. An example is **intensionally covered** by R if and only if there is a hyper-path from "true" to the vertex that denotes the example in $H_{(R,E)}$.

Because of the powerful description of instance graph, we can take account of **hung** examples rather than just covered and abandoned examples (a hung example is an example that is extensionally covered by current ruleset and may be intensionally covered after some new clause(s) added into the ruleset).

We designed a data structure to maintain instance graph efficiently. Then we designed a new ILP algorithm FOILBIG (First-Order Inductive Learner Based on Instance Graph). FOILBIG guarantees that **if FOILBIG believes a ruleset R covers an example e, then there certainly is a hyper-path from "true" to the vertex that denotes e in the instance graph, i.e. R intensionally covers e**. FOILBIG guarantees executability of learned rulesets, and does not substantially raise computational complexity compared to FOIL. FOILBIG has no restriction of ordering, and hence makes it possible to complete more learning tasks in ILP context. The method based on instance graph could also be used by any learning system that grows elements from ground facts by repeated specialization. FOILBIG has been implemented superficially and preliminary experiment shows that it can solve problems beyond the scope of FOIL.

In addition, unlike the method used by FOIL, our method can be extended to MPL with the extension of instance graph. We believe this is truly significant because MPL is much more complex than SPL (Single Predicate Learning) (detailed in Raedt et cl. 1993).

Part of our research has been published (Zhang et cl. 1999). See http://www.cse.buffalo.edu/~rzhang/research for more details.

Acknowledgments Thanks to my advisors Prof. Xiaoping Chen and Prof. Xin He, and colleague Guiquan Liu. Special thanks to Prof. Robert L Givan for his comments and suggestions, and to my English Tutor Perry Caldwell for his constant help.

References

Cameron-Jones, R.M. and Quinlan, J.R. 1993. Avoiding pitfalls when learning recursive theories. In *Proceedings of the Thirteenth International Joint Conference on Artificial Intelligence.* 1050-1055.

Raedt, L.De; Lavrac, N. and Dzeroski, S. 1993. Multiple predicate learning. In *Proceedings of the Thirteenth International Joint Conference on Artificial Intelligence.* 1037-1042.

Zhang, R., Chen, X. and Liu, G. 1999. An ILP algorithm without restriction of constant ordering. *The Chinese Journal of Software* (10)8: 868-876.

Doctoral Consortium

Helping children learn vocabulary during computer assisted oral reading

Greg Aist

Language Technologies Institute, Carnegie Mellon University
5000 Forbes Ave.
Pittsburgh, Pennsylvania 15213
Phone: (412) 268-5726   Email: aist@cs.cmu.edu   Web: http://www.cs.cmu.edu/~aist/cv.html

Help children learn vocabulary by reading

Vocabulary is fundamental to reading. As elementary students cross over from learning to read into reading to learn, vocabulary knowledge becomes increasingly important. The massive amount of vocabulary a student must learn precludes large amounts of time spent on any single word (Carver 1994, Schwanenflugel et al. 1997), except perhaps for some words that the student will read and write many times over the course of a lifetime. Therefore students must learn vocabulary from text.

Help children learn vocabulary during computer assisted oral reading

Project LISTEN's Reading Tutor listens to children read aloud, and helps them learn to read (Mostow & Aist CALICO 1999). The Reading Tutor shows the child a story one sentence at a time, listens to the child read all or part of the sentence out loud, and responds with help in recorded human voices. When the Reading Tutor has heard the student read every content word, the Reading Tutor shows the next sentence. Besides reading, the student may click *Go* to see the next sentence, *Back* to move back, on a word or on *Help* to hear the word read by the Tutor or get other help, or *Goodbye* to log out.
To learn new words from interacting with the Reading Tutor, a student must:
• spend time reading,
• read new material hard enough to have new words, and
• learn the meaning of new words when encountered.
We excluded the first factor -- time on task -- as outside the scope of this thesis. We addressed the second factor by modifying the Reading Tutor to take turns picking stories with students, to expose students to more new material than they would have read if they picked all the stories themselves. We addressed the third factor by designing, implementing, and evaluating ways to augment stories with extra help -- such as synonyms or glossary definitions -- to make the most of encounters with novel words.

Copyright © 2000, American Association for Artificial Intelligence (www.aaai.org). All rights reserved.

How to get kids to read more new material? Take turns picking stories

Prior to the 1999-2000 version, the Reading Tutor let the child choose any story he or she wanted, although it did try to guide the student to a story of appropriate difficulty.
In a four-month study in Spring 1998, children were reading new material as little as 40% of the time. Reports from teachers and other observations indicated that some kids tended to just re-read familiar stories rather than choose new material. We wanted to revise the story choice policy to not ensure that every student read new material.
We made the Reading Tutor take turns picking stories:
1. Every day, decide randomly whether the student or the Reading Tutor will pick the first story.
2. After the first story of the day, take turns picking stories.
Informal usability and acceptance testing at an urban elementary school and at CHIkids 1999 confirmed that kids would tolerate taking turns with the Reading Tutor. We included the new turn-taking story choice policy in the Fall 1999 Reading Tutor, deployed at two elementary schools. We measured new material read as percent of novel sentences encountered out of all sentences encountered. Analysis of variance and post-hoc testing (SPSS 1999; used here and throughout this paper) revealed that the Fall 1999 kids with the mixed-choice Reading Tutor read about 7% more new material than the Spring 1998 kids with the student-choice Reading Tutor (rate of new material normally distributed; $F=4.67$, $p=.033$; 65.7% vs. 58.5% new material by estimated marginal means).

How to help kids learn new words? Augment stories with extra vocabulary help

Next we present an experiment to test if augmenting text with information about words would help children learn the meanings of those words better than they would have from the text alone. We modified the Reading Tutor to augment some words in stories the child was reading with synonyms (X means Y), antonyms (X is the opposite of Y) or hypernyms (X is a kind of Y). For a given child, some of the words were augmented and others were left augmented to serve as a control group. The next time the child logged in (typically the next day) the computer presented multiple-choice vocabulary probes. Sometimes, the expected answer in the multiple-choice question was the same as the comparison word shown the previous day, and sometimes the expected answer was a different word.

We analyzed the results for three groups of words encountered during fall 1999: all of the words, the subset of words with only one sense in WordNet (Fellbaum 1998), and a set of words which would allow detection of a non-lexical effect (giving the help "X means Y" and then asking a multiple-choice question with expected answer Z). We built a loglinear model for each subset, using FACTOID (whether a word received help or not), ID (student), ANSWER (right or wrong), and FACTOID*ANSWER (to test for effect of factoid on answer). No significant effects of FACTOID on ANSWER were found. Why?

Help not helpful. Perhaps the factoids were not informative enough.

Questions too hard. Some of the automatically constructed questions were hard even for adults to answer.

Questions confusing. The questions contained answers that were taken from different senses of the target word, archaic vocabulary, and rare meanings.

Kids may have ignored the help or the question. The existence of some poor help or poor questions may have led some students to ignore ALL of the vocabulary assistance.

Target words were too easy. Perhaps students already knew the words that the Reading Tutor was giving them help on. We identified a set of words that were rare and thus more likely to be unknown to the students before the experiment began. We chose as the "rare" criterion any word that occurred 15 times or less in the Brown corpus (Kucera and Francis 1967), using the MRC psycholinguistic database available at http://www.psy.uwa.edu.au/MRCDataBase/uwa_mrc.htm. For these rare words:

1. All words: N=1753, FACTOID*ANSWER=0.19 +/- 0.10 (significant at 90%)
2. Single-sense words: N=319, FACTOID*ANSWER=0.30 +/- 0.23 (not significant)
3. Non-lexical effect: N=894, FACTOID*ANSWER=-0.04 +/- 0.15 (not significant)

These results should of course be considered suggestive, due to the relatively low (90%) level of confidence. However, an overall picture is emerging for when automatically generated factoids may help kids learn vocabulary: Give help on words with a single sense that are rare enough that they are likely to be new to the student.

Conclusion

We have described progress towards increasing children's encounters with novel words, and also towards increasing children's learning from encounters with new words. What remains?

During 1999-2000, a separate study is comparing children's learning with human tutors to children's learning with the Reading Tutor. We expect the human-tutored children to do better than the computer-tutored children. Since the human tutors and the computer tutor are using the same stories, we can analyze the human tutors' story choice patterns for ways to improve the Reading Tutor's story choices.

Besides synonyms, what else may help kids learn words from context? Having kids write definitions for words may encourage them to think deeply about the meaning of words, at a large additional cost in time for younger students. Human-written glossary definitions may also help, for both single-sense words and for words with more than one sense. We can test whether human-written and narrated glossary definitions help kids learn words better than just reading a story alone.

Acknowledgements

First we thank our thesis committee: Jack Mostow (advisor), Albert Corbett, Chuck Perfetti (University of Pittsburgh), and Alex Rudnicky. Brian Junker provided statistical advice. This material is based upon work supported in part by the National Science Foundation under Grant Nos. IRI-9505156, CDA-9616546, REC-9720348, and REC-9979894, and by the author's NSF Graduate Fellowship and Harvey Fellowship. Any opinions, findings, conclusions, or recommendations expressed in this publication are those of the author(s) and do not necessarily reflect the views of the National Science Foundation or the official policies, either expressed or implied, of the sponsors or of the United States Government.

References

Carver, R. P. 1994. Percentage of unknown vocabulary words in text as a function of the relative difficulty of the text: Implications for instruction. Journal of Reading Behavior 26(4) pp. 413-437.

Fellbaum, C. 1998. WordNet: An electronic lexical database. Cambridge MA: MIT Press. Searchable index for WordNet 1.6 at http://www.cogsci.princeton.edu/cgi-bin/webwn

Kucera, H and Francis, W. N. 1967. Computational Analysis of Present-Day American English, Brown University Press, Providence, Rhode Island, 1967.

Mostow, J. & Aist, G. 1999. Giving help and praise in a reading tutor with imperfect listening -- because automated speech recognition means never being able to say you're certain. CALICO Journal 16(3), 407-424. Special issue (M. Holland, Ed.), Tutors that Listen: Speech recognition for Language Learning, 1999.

Schwanenflugel, P. J., S. A. Stahl, and E. L. McFalls. 1997. Partial word knowledge and vocabulary growth during reading comprehension. Journal of Literacy Research 29(4): 531-553.

SPSS. 1999. SPSS® Base 9.0 Applications Guide. Chicago IL: SPSS. See also company web site at http://www.spss.com

Adaptive Learning Systems: A model for business entrepreneurs to implement IT

Dessa David

Zicklin School of Business -Baruch College; Graduate Center,
City University of New York, 17 Lexington Avenue, Room 435, New York, New York, 10010
Dessa_David@baruch.cuny.edu

Adaptive Learning Systems [ALS] have garnered tremendous attention in recent years from academia, practitioners and trade press [Jennings et al. 1998; Nwana 1996]. The numerous agent conferences and World Wide Web agent sites developed lately evidence this prevailing trend [Murch 1999; http://www.agentlink.com]. ALS are part of the agent paradigm 'invading' the research world that provides new ways of analyzing, designing and implementing complex software systems [Jennings et al. 1998]. Although varied in description, these systems are characterized by behaviors that are adaptable (by self-automation of actions) and flexible (by learning the user's preferences, styles, and cognitive levels thereby offering proactive forms of interaction/support). ALS are user-centered, and have the potential to revolutionize the way users interact with computers, overcoming many of the limitations of current systems. A review of the literature indicates that researchers have been complaining about the lack of these systems' use as practical tools for real world problems [Bradshaw 1997; Hook 1996; Jennings et al. 1998; Maes 1994; Nwana 1996]. This dissertation agrees with these researchers and identifies a domain that can significantly benefit from this technology.

The author posits that ALS hold the potential to facilitate the decision-making process regarding Information Technology (IT) implementation. The potential benefits that IT promises business entrepreneurs will compel them to make IT implementation decisions. The decision-making process poses many challenges. Failure to adopt IT or incorrect decisions regarding IT implementation can be detrimental to a business. In short, the decision to adopt IT is weighted, complex, challenging and risky. Technology acceptance has been the heart of research for many years. The Technology Acceptance Model [TAM] and other technology acceptance research postulate and empirically validate that perceptions are key determinants to one's decision regarding IT [Agarwal et al. 1998; Davis et al. 1991; Gefan et al. 1998; Harrison et al. 1998; Moore et al. 1991]. However, simply acquiring the technology is not sufficient in realizing the returns on investments. It has been hypothesized that one of the reasons for the productivity paradox is that systems acquired are never used [Agarwal et al. 1998]. To date, several researchers have studied technology acceptance [Agarwal et al. 1998; Gefan et al. 1998, Iacovou et al. 1995, Igbaria et al. 1997, Karahanna et al. 1999], but there is a lack of research on mediating influences to augment the decision-maker's perceptions [Agarwal et al. 1998, Gefan et al. 1998, Iacovou 1995, Igbaria et al 1997, and Karahanna et al 1999]. This study postulates that ALS can be effective tools that mediate the decision-maker's perceptions during IT implementation. Prior research indicates that any decision support tool should be adaptable to the user's preferences and habits [Agarwal 1994, Chaung 1998, El-Najdawi et al. 1993, and Shaw 1993]. ALS have the characteristics needed to develop tools to support the business entrepreneur during the IT implementation decision-making process. ALS are flexible, self-adapting systems capable of accomplishing task on behalf of the user. Consequently, ALS can be used as tools for business entrepreneur's IT implementation decision-making.

More specifically, this research will attempt to answer the following questions:
Will an adaptive learning system [ALS] assist the business entrepreneur in making more effective IT implementation decisions?
What is the framework for a support system to be utilized by business entrepreneurs in making IT decisions?

This research adopts a two-phase approach. (1) Based on a review of the literature a conceptual model of the ALS was developed. (2) An ALS based on the conceptual model will be developed, evaluated and validated. In this study, the researchers will test the effectiveness of an Adaptive Learning System Technology Advisor (henceforth referred to as ALSTA) during the IT implementation decision-making process. The results will be empirically tested by laboratory experiment. Validation will follow steps outlined by Straub [1989] to ensure ALSTA is reliable and robust tool. The constructs for measurement to be used during the experiment will be developed from prior empirically validated research.

This research hopes to contribute to the following areas of research: theories and applications of software agents; and IT implementation.

Copyright © 2000, American Association for Artificial Intelligence (www.aaai.org). All rights reserved.

Automatic Generation of Memory Based Search Heuristics

István T. Hernádvölgyi
University of Ottawa
School of Information Technology & Engineering
Ottawa, Ontario, K1N 6N5, Canada
Email: istvan@site.uottawa.ca

Our goal is to automatically generate heuristics to guide state space search. The heuristic values are distances computed in an abstract space which is automatically derived from the original space. The search space is described in a production system. Simple syntactic transformations of this description give rise to another search space. The distances of abstract states from the abstract goal state are stored in a look-up table and provide admissible and monotonic heuristics for search algorithms such as IDA*. The size of the abstract space is the size of the look-up table and different transformations on the description of the space give rise to abstract spaces of different size. We are interested in the relationship between the memory required to store the heuristic and the speed of search. We are also interested in ranking abstractions which generate abstract spaces of the same cardinality with respect to their predicted performance without actually performing searches in the original space. We also plan to use our technique to search for macro operators to find suboptimal paths very quickly. A macro operator is a sequence of operators which immediately reaches a subgoal state applied to a state without performing search.

Culberson and Schaeffer (Culberson & Schaeffer 1996) developed a technique (*pattern database*) to represent heuristic look-up tables and effectively used it on the 15-Puzzle. Korf used pattern databases to find optimal paths for random instances of the Rubik's Cube for the first time. In his paper he conjectured that the size of the pattern database and the speed of search can be linearly traded for each other. We verified his conjecture in a large scale experiment and reported it in (Holte & Hernádvölgyi 1999). Korf and Reid in (Korf & Reid 1998) gave a more formal derivation of the expected number of states generated by the search algorithm based on the distribution of heuristic values. We used their ideas to select the best heuristics in a large pool of heuristics with equal memory requirements. We devised a simple vector notation for representing state spaces and a method for automatically creating abstractions based on this notation. Our technique based on mapping labels (*domain abstraction*) is guaranteed to create abstract spaces where the distances provide admissible and monotonic heuristic values. Some abstractions are non-surjective; there are states in the abstract space which have no pre-image in the original

space. These states take up space in the pattern database and they often shorten the optimal path in the abstract space resulting in small heuristic values. Non-surjective abstractions arise frequently in our experience.

We have identified some structural properties which may be used to avoid non-surjective abstractions, but to date we have no automatic way of avoiding them in general. We are working on efficiently computable methods which can quickly determine if the state has a pre-image. These involve invoking suboptimal but very fast search techniques – such as refinement and macro search – to test membership. Traditionally macro operators were found by blind search techniques (Korf 1985) and by macro composition due to the lack of heuristics for searching for the macros. Domain abstraction can provide heuristics to search for macro operators and we plan to use it to find shorter macro operators and to build macro tables for very large spaces. Domain abstraction proved very successful in many problem spaces but it has no use in binary domains. We are investigating other techniques which also give rise to abstract spaces by reducing the dimension of the state representation rather than map labels. We are also working on extending our current production system to encode more complex spaces. Our preliminary data suggests that combining more than one smaller abstractions with total size m results in faster searches than a single one with size m. We plan to study how to select those abstractions from a pool of abstractions whose combined performance is the best.

References

Culberson, J. C., and Schaeffer, J. 1996. Searching with pattern databases. *Advances in Artificial Intelligence (Lecture Notes in Artificial Intelligence 1081)* 402–416.

Holte, R. C., and Hernádvölgyi, I. T. 1999. A space-time tradeoff for memory-based heuristics. *Proceedings of the Sixteenth National Conference on Artificial Intelligence (AAAI-99)* 704–709.

Korf, R. E., and Reid, M. 1998. Complexity analysis of admissible heuristic search. *Proceedings of the Fifteenth National Conference on Artificial Intelligence (AAAI-98)* 305–310.

Korf, R. E. 1985. Macro operators: A weak method for learning. *Artificial Intelligence* 26:35–77.

Copyright © 2000, American Association for Artificial Intelligence (www.aaai.org). All rights reserved.

Reasoning and Acting in Time

Haythem O. Ismail
Department of Computer Science and Engineering
and Center for Cognitive Science
State University of New York at Buffalo
226 Bell Hall
Buffalo, NY 14260-2000
hismail@cse.buffalo.edu

Cognitive robotics is that branch of artificial intelligence concerned with "the study of the knowledge representation and reasoning problems faced by an autonomous robot (or agent) in a dynamic and incompletely known world" (Levesque & Reiter 1998, p. 106). My work is not aimed at solving *all* the problems of cognitive robotics; rather, it is about studying, fleshing out, and investigating solutions to a subset of them. In particular, a subset of those problems that face an agent *reasoning and acting in time*. To understand what this exactly means, a number of general assumptions about what is reasonably to be expected from an embodied cognitive agent should first be pointed out.

First, to appropriately behave in a changing world, an agent must be aware of its environment and the outcome of its acts, and ready to recover from errors, interrupts, and failure. Second, while acting, it should be capable of carrying out on-line natural language conversations with human operators. An operator may direct the agent on how to act, provide it with general knowledge about its environment (including knowledge about past events), or inquire on what it has done, is doing, and intends to do. Third, reasoning and acting are not two unrelated activities that the agent may perform; they are both temporally and causally interleaved. The agent does reasoning in the service of acting and acting in the service of reasoning. (Kumar & Shapiro 1994). It needs to reason about what to do, when to do it, and how to do it. This is particularly crucial for interrupt handling. In addition, the agent may act in order to add a missing link to a chain of reasoning (perform a sensory act, for instance).

For the above requirements to be met, the agent should have a personal sense of time— a NOW pointer that moves whenever the agent perceives a change in the environment (Shapiro 1998). Not only does the agent reason *about* the moving time, it reasons *in* that time. More precisely, since the agent may act in the service of reasoning, reasoning takes time. That is, the value of the NOW pointer at the beginning of a reasoning process may be different from its value at the end. Thus, the agent may be reasoning about NOW, when the very process of reasoning results in NOW moving. This gives rise to what has been dubbed *the problem of the fleeting now* (Ismail & Shapiro 2000).

It is my goal to develop a theory of time that includes a multi-granular representation of NOW, so that changes at some level of temporal granularity do not result in NOW moving at coarser levels. In addition, a theory of conscious sequential acting and interrupt handling is being developed to allow the agent to reason, from very general knowledge of context-sensitive priorities of acts, about what to do next. The research is done within the framework of the SNePS knowledge representation and reasoning system (Shapiro & Rapaport 1992) and the GLAIR agent architecture (Hexmoor & Shapiro 1997).

References

Hexmoor, H., and Shapiro, S. C. 1997. Integrating skill and knowledge in expert agents. In Feltovich, P. J.; Ford, K. M.; and Hoffman, R. R., eds., *Expertise in Context*. Menlo Park, CA / Cambridge, MA: AAAI Press/MIT Press. 383–404.

Ismail, H., and Shapiro, S. 2000. Two problems with reasoning and acting in time. In Cohn, A. G.; F.Giunchiglia; and Selman, B., eds., *Principles of Knowledge Representation and Reasoning: Proceedings of the Seventh International Conference (KR 2000)*. San Francisco: Morgan Kaufmann. In press.

Kumar, D., and Shapiro, S. C. 1994. Acting in service of inference (and vice versa). In Dankel, II, D. D., ed., *Proceedings of the Seventh Florida Artificial Intelligence Research Symposium*, 207–211. St. Petersburg, FL: The Florida AI Research Society.

Levesque, H., and Reiter, R. 1998. High-level robotics: Beyond planning. In *Cognitive Robotics: Papers from the 1998 AAAI Fall Symposium*, 106–108. Menlo Park, CA: AAAI Press. Technical report FS-98-02.

Shapiro, S., and Rapaport, W. 1992. The SNePS family. *Computers and mathematics with applications* 23(2–5):243–275. Reprinted in F. Lehman, ed. *Semantic Networks in Artificial Intelligence*, pages 243–275. Pergamon Press, Oxford, 1992.

Shapiro, S. 1998. Embodied Cassie. In *Cognitive Robotics: Papers from the 1998 AAAI Fall Symposium*, 136–143. Menlo Park, CA: AAAI Press. Technical report FS-98-02.

Copyright © 2000, American Association for Artificial Intelligence (www.aaai.org). All rights reserved.

Ontology Integration in XML

Euna Jeong
Department of Computer Science and Information Engineering
National Taiwan University
eajeong@agents.csie.ntu.edu.tw

Chun-Nan Hsu
Institute of Informationi Science, Academia Sinica
chunnan@iis.sinica.edu.tw

Abstract

We study the problem of automatically generating an integrated schema for XML DTDs. Introducing a novel *view inference* approach, we shows that the set of views and source descriptions can be automatically derived.

Introduction The problem of information integration has become significant as the growing number of information sources on the Internet. Information integration systems provide users with an integrated schema of underlying sources. The integrated schema is designed by hand and a mapping between the integrated schema and the source schemas is needed for the system to answer queries. As XML (Bray, Paoli, & Sperberg-McQueen 1998) as become a new standard for representation and exchange of data on the Internet, in this article, we consider the problem of automatically generating an integrated schema for different XML DTDs with similar document types.

Architecture XML with a DTD is self-descriptive and provides a semistructured data model. These properties render that DTDs defining similar document type have structural and naming similarities. Given a collection of source DTDs, we propose a view inference approach which automatically derives the set of integrated views and source descriptions.

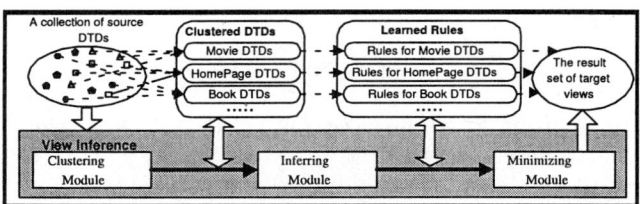

Step 1: Clustering DTDs takes a collection of source DTDs as an input. A DTD is modeled as an edge-labeled graph. The type of an object is defined by adjacent objects and the relation between them. Our strategy is to merge types by *top-down merge*. If two types have the same parent type, they will be merged into a new type. Based on merged types, DTDs are re-defined with them and clustered into one of DTD classes. Generic matching methods (Sanfeliu 1990) are used to know how similar two DTDs are.

Step 2: Learning Rules learns the general rules describing source DTDs in the same class. Our approach is based on tree grammar inference(Miclet 1990). The technique of the generalization of k-tails' concept is applied to learning tree grammars(Levine 1982). At first, the automaton contains one state for each subtree of the sample set T, if they have the same set of k-tails, then their states are made identical. This gives an automaton that recognizes a tree language containing T.

Step 3: Minimization of Tree Automata optimizes the learned rules. The learned rules are a set of states in a tree grammar and need to be transformed to an integrated view. The integrated views allow the user to formulate queries to XML documents. In this step, we use *bottom-up merge*. If two states have the same subtree, but different root labeling, then they will be merged. As a result, the minimized tree automaton will be more flexible than before.

Conclusions We have presented how to automatically generate integrated views for XML from source DTDs. Our approach allows for fully automatic generation of integrated views from a collection of DTDs.

References

Bray, T.; Paoli, J.; and Sperberg-McQueen, C. M. 1998. Extensible Markup Language(XML) 1.0. Technical report, W3C.

Levine, B. 1982. The use of tree derivatives and a sample support parameter for inferring tree systems. In *IEEE Transactions on Pattern Analysis and machine Intelligence*, 25–34.

Miclet, L. 1990. *Syntactic and structural pattern recognition*. World Scientific. chapter 9.

Sanfeliu, A. 1990. *Syntactic and structural pattern recognition*. World Scientific. chapter 6.

Belief Revision in a Deductively Open Belief Space

Frances L. Johnson

Department of Computer Science and Engineering, Center for Multisource Information Fusion, and
Center for Cognitive Science
State University of New York at Buffalo
226 Bell Hall, Buffalo, NY 14260-2000
flj@cse.buffalo.edu

I am researching the traditional belief revision integrity constraints and postulates, which are designed for deductively closed belief spaces, and revising them so that they are applicable to implemented knowledge representation and reasoning systems with deductively open belief spaces (DOBS).

A knowledge representation and reasoning system must be able to deal with contradictions and revise beliefs. This is especially important to data fusion, where information is combined from multiple sources, which might contradict each other. Most theoretical postulates for belief revision and belief contraction assume a deductively closed belief space (DCBS), where all beliefs derivable *from* a belief space are *in* that belief space. This is hard (or impossible) to produce in an implemented belief revision system, which has real-world limitations on computation time and database size. This makes it difficult to evaluate such a system using the theoretical postulates; yet evaluating system adherence to these postulates is a pressing issue for those doing belief revision research in computer science.

Unlike a DCBS, a DOBS uses a base set of assertions (hypotheses), but only deduces beliefs from that base gradually over time – i.e. some implicit beliefs may not yet be explicit (or part of the belief space). Thus, it can grow even if the base remains static, and it can never be referred to as consistent – only either inconsistent or "not known to be inconsistent." My research begins with a formalism that describes a DOBS and its integrity constraints (ICs) and postulates, which will guide belief revision techniques for implemented systems. This formalism can then be used to better enable system/postulate comparisons.

I plan to offer a DOBS version of the AGM postulates (Alchourron, Gärdenfors, and Makinson 1985), Hansson's base contraction postulates (Hansson 1993), and postulates proposed for ranked beliefs, and to provide brief comments regarding postulate adherence for paraconsistent logics and incomplete systems. Using these postulates, I hope to develop a theory for comparing systems, so that implementers will be able to (a) evaluate how well their systems meet the standards of the postulates and (b) compare their systems to other systems.

Of the four ICs listed by (Gärdenfors & Rott 1995), there remains an open discussion on how to properly weight and combine constraints IC3 (minimizing damage to the belief space) and IC4 (removing the least important or entrenched beliefs over those more entrenched) during contraction or revision. For example: How do you choose between retracting many weak beliefs vs. one strong belief?

As I develop my theories, I will continue revising my enhancement of our implemented belief revision system, SNeBR (Martins and Shapiro 1988), to adhere to the DOBS postulates and to improve its method of weighting and combining IC3 and IC4. Also, although many systems require quantitative measures of entrenchment (or belief strength), our system will use qualitative, partial orderings – thus allowing the inclusion of information whose credibility is only known relative to that of another belief. This ordering information is stored as beliefs and can also be reasoned about and revised.

Acknowledgements: I would like to thank my advisor Stuart Shapiro and the SNePS Research Group, specifically Haythem Ismail and Bill Rapaport. This work has been supported in part by the US Army Communications and Electronics Command (CECOM), Ft. Monmouth, NJ through a contract with CACI Technologies.

References

Alchourron, C. E.; Gärdenfors, P.; and Makinson, D. 1985. On the Logic of Theory Change: Partial Meet Contraction and Revision Functions. *The Journal of Symbolic Logic*, Vol 20, Num. 2, 510-530.

Gärdenfors, P.; and Rott, H. 1995. Belief Revision. In: Gabbay, Hogger and Robinson (Eds.), *Handbook of Logic in Artificial Intelligence and Logic Programming*, Vol 4, Epistemic and Temporal Reasoning. Clarendon Press, Oxford. 35-131.

Hansson, S.O. 1993. Reversing the Levi Identity. *Journal of Philosophical Logic* 22:637-669

Martins, J.P. and Shapiro, S.C. (1988), A Model for Belief Revision, *Artificial Intelligence* 35 25-79.

Selective Sampling With Co-Testing: Preliminary Results

Ion Muslea, Steven Minton, and Craig A. Knoblock
Information Sciences Institute and Integrated Media Systems Center
University of Southern California
4676 Admiralty Way
Marina del Rey, CA 90292, USA
{muslea, minton, knoblock}@isi.edu

Abstract

We present a novel approach to selective sampling, *co-testing*, which can be applied to problems with *redundant views* (i.e., problems with multiple disjoint sets of attributes that can be used for learning). The main idea behind co-testing consists of selecting the queries among the unlabeled examples on which the existing views disagree.

Selective sampling, a form of active learning, reduces the number of training examples that need to be labeled by examining unlabeled examples and selecting the most informative ones for the human to label. We introduce *co-testing*, which is a novel approach to selective sampling for domains with *redundant views*. A domain has redundant views if there are at least two mutually exclusive sets of features that can be used to learn the target concept. Our work was inspired by (Blum & Mitchell 1998), who noted that there are many real world domains with multiple views. For example, in Web page classification, one can identify faculty home pages either based on the words on the page or based on the words in HTML anchors pointing to the page.

Active learning algorithms ask the user to label an example that maximizes the information conveyed to the learner (we refer to such selected examples as *queries*). In a standard, single-view learning scenario, this generally translates into finding an example that splits the version space in half, i.e., eliminating half of the hypotheses consistent with the training set. With redundant views, we can do much better. Co-testing simultaneously trains a separate classifier for each redundant view. Each classifier is applied to a pool of unlabeled examples, and the system selects a query based on the degree of disagreement among the learners. As the target hypotheses in each view must agree, co-testing can reduce the hypothesis space faster than would otherwise be possible. To illustrate this, consider a learning problem where we have two views, **A** and **B**. For illustrative purposes, imagine an extreme case where there is an unlabeled example x that is classified as positive by a single hypothesis from the **A** version space; furthermore, assume that x is classified as positive by all but one of the hypotheses from the **B** version space. If the system asks for the label of x, it will immediately converge to a single hypothesis in one of the spaces and no additional examples will be required.

Co-testing works as follows: initially, the user provides a few labeled examples, and a pool of unlabeled ones. We use a learner $\mathcal{L}$ to create one classifier for each view, apply the classifiers to *all* unlabeled examples, and determine the *contention points* – the examples that are labeled differently by the two classifiers. The contention points are extremely informative because whenever the two classifiers disagree, at least one of them must be wrong. We select one of the contention points for labeling, add it to the training set, and repeat the whole process.

In fact, co-testing is a *family of algorithms* that differ from each other only with respect to the manner in which they select the next query among the contention points. The simplest member of the family, *naive co-testing*, selects at random one of the contention points. More sophisticated approaches to query selection may lead to faster convergence. For instance, if the learner can evaluate the confidence of its classification, we can query the contention point on which *both* categorizers are *most confident*, which means that each query *maximally* improves at least one of the hypotheses.

We applied naive co-testing to three real-world problems that have natural ways to create redundant views: wrapper induction, Web page classification, and natural language discourse-tree parsing. On 10 wrapper induction problems, naive co-testing reduced the average error rate by 47%, from 82.6% to 90.7%. On the other two domains, our algorithm clearly outperformed two powerful selective sampling algorithms: query-by-bagging and -boosting (Abe & Mamitsuka 1998).

References

Abe, N., and Mamitsuka, H. 1998. Query learning using boosting and bagging. In *Proc. of ICML*, 1–10.

Blum, A., and Mitchell, T. 1998. Combining labeled and unlabeled data with co-training. In *Proc. of the 1988 Conf. Computational Learning Theory*, 92–100.

Grounding State Representations in Sensory Experience for Reasoning and Planning by Mobile Robots

Daniel Nikovski
The Robotics Institute, Carnegie Mellon University
5000 Forbes Ave., Pittsburgh, PA 15213
nikovski@cs.cmu.edu

Abstract

We are addressing the problem of learning probabilistic models of the interaction between a mobile robot and its environment and using these models for task planning. This requires modifying the state-of-the-art reinforcement learning algorithms to deal with hidden state and high-dimensional observation spaces of continuous variables. Our approach is to identify hidden states by means of the trajectories leading into and out of them, and perform clustering in this embedding trajectory space in order to compile a partially observable Markov decision process (POMDP) model, which can be used for approximate decision-theoretic planning. The ultimate objective of our work is to develop algorithms that learn POMDP models with discrete hidden states defined (grounded) directly into continuous sensory variables such as sonar and infrared readings.

Mobile robots often have to reason and plan their course of action in unknown, non-deterministic, and partially observable environments. Acquiring a model of the environment that reflects the effect of the robot's actions is essential in such cases. The framework of partially observable Markov decision processes (POMDPs) is especially suitable for representing stochastic models of dynamic systems.

Reasoning, planning, and learning in fully-observable state spaces is relatively well understood, and finding optimal policies for problems with huge numbers of states is now feasible. On the contrary, planning and learning in problems with partially-observable state spaces have proven to be very difficult. Finding optimal policies for POMDPs has been shown to be PSPACE-hard and currently solvable problems rarely have more than a hundred states. Learning POMDPs is harder still – even for problems with discrete state spaces and discrete observations, the number of states for the largest problems solved are in the dozens.

The usual approach to learning POMDPs has been to unfold the model in time and employ a general method for learning probabilistic networks such as Baum-Welch (BW), which tunes the parameters of the model so as to increase the likelihood of the training data given these model parameters. Such algorithms often get trapped in shallow local maxima of the optimization surface and can rarely recover the true POMDP that has generated the data. In an attempt to find a learning method that can overcome this problem, we have adapted the best-first model merging (BFMM) algorithm, originally proposed by Stolcke and Omohundro for learning hidden Markov models. An extensive experimental study over 14 synthetic worlds showed that this algorithm has advantages over the BW for learning POMDPs (Nikovski and Nourbakhsh 1999).

In spite of its advantages, the BFMM algorithm also leads to local maxima in likelihood, because it selects mergers greedily and never reconsiders suboptimal ones. We have developed a new algorithm for learning POMDPs based on merging states by performing clustering in the space of trajectories of percepts and actions leading into and out of hidden states. The advantage of this algorithm is that it considers all possible mergers at once and chooses only the best ones, based on similarities between trajectories. We have compared experimentally this algorithm with BW and BFMM in a simulated environment resembling a typical office space with moderate perceptual aliasing (Nikovski and Nourbakhsh 2000). Seven similarity measures have been tested and one of them yielded results far exceeding those of the other algorithms.

We are presently working on reducing the computational complexity of the learning algorithm from $O(N^3)$ to $O(N \log N)$, where N is the length of the observation/action sequence. We are also working on modifying the algorithm to handle continuous observations by designing similarity measures between pairs of trajectories consisting of continuous sensor readings, using several techniques from the fields of system identification and optimal control.

References

D. Nikovski and I. Nourbakhsh. Learning discrete Bayesian models for autonomous agent navigation. In *Proceedings of the 1999 IEEE International Symposium on Computational Intelligence in Robotics and Automation.*, 137–143. IEEE, Monterey, CA, 1999.

D. Nikovski and I. Nourbakhsh. Learning probabilistic models for decision-theoretic navigation of mobile robots. To be published in *Proceedings of the Seventeenth International Conference in Machine Learning*. Stanford, CA, 2000.

Online Ensemble Learning

Nikunj C. Oza
Computer Science Division
University of California
Berkeley, California 94720–1776
oza@cs.berkeley.edu

Ensemble learning methods train combinations of base models, which may be decision trees, neural networks, or others traditionally used in supervised learning. Ensemble methods have gained popularity because many researchers have demonstrated their superior prediction performance relative to single models on a variety of problems especially when the correlations of the errors made by the base models are low (e.g., (Freund & Schapire 1996; Tumer & Oza 1999)). However, these learning methods have largely operated in batch mode—that is, they repeatedly process the entire set of training examples as a whole. These methods typically require at least one pass through the data for each base model in the ensemble. We would instead prefer to learn the *entire* ensemble in an *online* fashion, i.e., using only one pass through the entire dataset. This would make ensemble methods practical when data is being generated continuously so that storing data for batch learning is impractical, or in data mining tasks where the datasets are large enough that multiple passes would require a prohibitively large training time.

We have so far developed online versions of the popular bagging (Breiman 1994) and boosting (Freund & Schapire 1996) algorithms. We have shown empirically that both online algorithms converge to the same prediction performance as the batch versions and proved this convergence for online bagging (Oza 2000). However, significant empirical and theoretical work remains to be done. There are several traditional ensemble learning issues that remain in our online ensemble learning framework such as the number and types of base models to use, the combining method to use, and how to maintain diversity among the base models.

When learning large datasets, we may hope to avoid using all of the training examples and/or input features. We have developed input decimation (Tumer & Oza 1999), a technique that uses different subsets of the input features in different base models. We have shown that this method performs better than combinations of base models that use all the input features because of two characteristics of our base models: they overfit less by using only a small number of highly-relevant input features, and they have lower correlations in their errors because they use different input feature subsets. However, our method of selecting input features currently examines the entire training set at once, which makes it unsuitable for our online ensemble framework. We are working on extending input decimation to select appropriate feature subsets online. We may also be able to select a small subset of the training examples without a significant degradation in generalization performance. There are many possible reasons for this, such as: the available data may be very dense in the space of possible points, the user may explicitly choose to learn using a subset of the examples (e.g., examples with a particular attribute value), or the user may only need a relatively low-quality solution. For example, the last possibility is often true when learning ensemble models—we often do not need high-performing base models because, if the correlations of their errors are low, then the ensemble will still perform well. We would also like to devise confidence measures for the base models or entire ensemble to help us determine when we have reached a suitable accuracy and; therefore, reduce the number of data points that we have to learn.

We need to formally characterize the performance of our online ensembles relative to batch ensembles and the best base models. We would also like to extend our work to learn time-series data which may have changing underlying statistical properties (e.g., in a factory, there may be 24-hour cycles in the data). This requires that our learning algorithms detect the different regimes in the data and devise base models for each of these regimes online.

References

Breiman, L. 1994. Bagging predictors. Technical Report 421, Department of Statistics, University of California, Berkeley.

Freund, Y., and Schapire, R. 1996. Experiments with a new boosting algorithm. In *Proceedings of the Thirteenth International Conference on Machine Learning*, 148–156. Bari, Italy: Morgan Kaufmann.

Oza, N. C. 2000. Learning bagged and boosted ensembles online. Submitted for Publication.

Tumer, K., and Oza, N. C. 1999. Decimated input ensembles for improved generalization. In *Proceedings of the International Joint Conference on Neural Networks (IJCNN-99)*.

Copyright © 2000, American Association for Artificial Intelligence (www.aaai.org). All rights reserved.

Learning Landmarks for Robot Localization

Robert Sim and Gregory Dudek

Centre for Intelligent Machines,
McGill University
3480 University St, Room 409
Montréal, QC
H2W 2B6
{simra,dudek}@cim.mcgill.ca

Abstract

Our work addresses the problem of *learning* a set of visual landmarks for mobile robot localization. The learning framework is designed to be applicable to a wide range of environments, and allows for different approaches to computing a pose estimate. Initially, each landmark is detected using a model of visual attention and is matched to observations from other poses using principal components analysis. Attributes of the observed landmarks can be parameterized using a generic parameterization method and then evaluated in terms of their utility for pose estimation. We discuss the status of the work to date, and future directions.

Problem Statement

Our goal is to develop a framework for a robotic system which can automatically acquire knowledge of its environment that is useful for the task of navigation. An important aspect of this system is the ability to localize. It is well known that odometry alone is not sufficient for a robot to maintain an accurate estimate of its position or pose. As a result, a robot requires other external cues in order to localize accurately. In previous work (Sim & Dudek 1999), we have developed a framework for the localization problem which employs supervised learning to infer the correlation between attributes of the observed landmarks and the pose of the robot. The landmarks themselves are initially extracted as the maximal responses of an attention operator.

Our prior work serves as a proof-of-concept of the approach. There remain several unanswered questions. First, what attention operators are best suited to the task of localization? Second, how should the correlation between landmark attributes and pose be calculated? Finally, what is the best approach to collecting training data? We intend to address these issues in our future work.

Previous Work

Prior work on the localization problem includes the Markov localization framework (Fox *et al.* 1998), which computes a probability density function over the pose space and updates this funtion over time by exploiting the Markov assumption and a prior map. There are two disadvantages to that approach – first, computational conciderations require that the pose space be discretized; and second, in the basic framework pose estimates are derived from the global sensor output – outliers in the field of view can pose problems for the estimator. Furthermore, the goal of the Markov localization framework is to minimize the positional uncertainty over the *trajectory* of the robot, and hence assumes a prior probability density estimate of the pose at each stage, requiring the robot to move in order to refine its pose estimate.

Our prior work addressed these issues in the context of computing a precise pose estimate without any *a priori* knowledge or motion on the part of the robot (Sim 1998). The mechanism operates by first *exploring* the environment, collecting images from a set of sample positions. From this training data a set of *tracked landmarks* are computed by first selecting a set of candidates on the basis of the output of an attention operator, and then tracking the candidates over the input images. Figure 1 depicts a set of candidates extracted from an image taken in our lab. A supervised learning scheme is employed to compute a set of parameterizations from the variations of visual attributes of the tracked landmarks with respect to changes in robot pose. For example, we consider the variation in appearance and position of a landmark as a function of the robot's position. The uncertainty of these parameterizations can then be estimated from the training data using a cross-validation scheme.

Once training is complete, the robot is equipped to generate a pose estimate from anywhere in its pose space. When an estimate is required, it acquires an input image and extracts a set of candidate landmarks. These candidates are matched to the learned tracked landmarks, and a separate pose estimate is generated for each match. The resulting estimates are then combined in a robust manner, taking into account the *a priori* uncertainty of the tracked landmark parameterizations. Figure 2 demonstrates the accuracy of the method. Each 'x'–'o' pair represents a generated pose estimate and the actual pose of the robot, over a 2m by 2m pose space in a laboratory environment.

Future Work

Currently, we are evaluating the suitability of different attention operators for the task of extracting candidate landmarks. The generic nature of our framework allows for a straight-

---

Copyright © 2000, American Association for Artificial Intelligence (www.aaai.org). All rights reserved.

Figure 1: A scene with extracted landmark candidates.

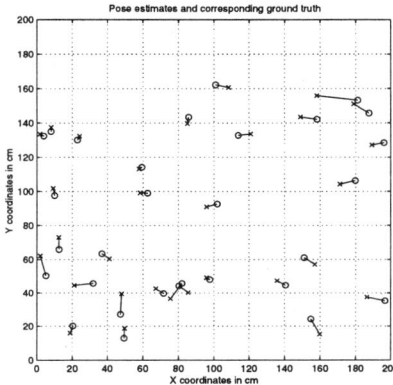

Figure 2: A set of pose estimates obtained from a 2m by 2m laboratory environment.

forward substitution of a new attention operator. The quality of the results will be measured in terms of the raw accuracy of the resulting pose estimation system, as well as its ability to measure the uncertainty of the pose estimates.

In order to address the problem of selecting an appropriate attention operator, we will consider the prior work of Shi and Tomasi (Shi & Tomasi 1994), which selects features which are well disposed to tracking, Reisfeld et al. (Reisfeld, Wolfson, & Yeshurun 1995), which selects features on the basis of symmetry, and Itti and Koch (Itti, Koch, & Niebur 1998), which employs a variety of criterion in order to select regions of high saliency.

Second, we are investigating alternative parameterization paradigms. Our initial parameterization method linearizes the joint data-pose space, and the results are very good compared to the standard linear least-squares estimation approaches which treat the pose and data spaces as duals. We are also considering non-linear parameterization approaches such as neural networks and regularization.

Finally, we are considering the important problem of deciding what are the best poses from which to collect training observations. In formulating a solution to such a problem, one must consider seriously the issue of what constitutes a good model of a landmark, as well as the costs associated with physically moving the robot to new vantage points.

Our consideration of these issues will rely heavily on the theoretical framework for inverse problem theory developed by Tarantola (Tarantola 1986), Whaite's approach to model parameter estimation using active vision (Whaite & Ferrie 1990) and the approach to map-building developed by Kuipers and Byun (Kuipers & Byun 1991), which constructs local regions of reliability in the pose space.

We expect that a theoretically rigorous approach to the problem of learning to estimate pose from visual landmarks will lead to an implementation that is successful both experimentally and in practical settings.

Acknowledgements

This work is funded by a PGS-B scholarship from the Canadian Natural Sciences and Engineering Research Council.

References

Fox, D.; Burgard, W.; Thrun, S.; and Cremers, A. B. 1998. Position estimation for mobile robots in dynamic environments. In *Proceedings of the 15th National Conference on Artificial Intelligence (AAAI-98) and of the 10th Conference on Innovative Applications of Artificial Intelligence (IAAI-98)*, 983–988. Menlo Park: AAAI Press.

Itti, L.; Koch, C.; and Niebur, E. 1998. A model of saliency-based visual attention for rapid scene analysis. *IEEE Transactions on Pattern Analysis and Machine Intelligence* 14:1254–1259.

Kuipers, B., and Byun, Y.-T. 1991. A robot exploration and mapping strategy based on a semantic hierarchy of spatial representations. *Robotics and Autonomous Systems* 8:47–63.

Reisfeld, D.; Wolfson, H.; and Yeshurun, Y. 1995. Context free attentional operators: the generalized symmetry transform. *International Journal Of Computer Vision* 14:119–130.

Shi, J., and Tomasi, C. 1994. Good features to track. In *Proceedings of the Conference on Computer Vision and Pattern Recognition*, 593–600. Los Alamitos, CA, USA: IEEE Computer Society Press.

Sim, R., and Dudek, G. 1999. Learning and evaluating visual features for pose estimation. In *Proceedings of the IEEE International Conference on Computer Vision(ICCV)*. Kerkyra, Greece: IEEE Press.

Sim, R. 1998. Mobile robot localization from learned landmarks. Master's thesis, McGill University, Montreal, Canada.

Tarantola, A. 1986. *Inverse Problem Theory*. Amsterdam, The Netherlands: Elsevier Science Publishers B. V.

Whaite, P., and Ferrie, F. P. 1990. From uncertainty to visual exploration. In *Proceedings of the 3rd International Conference on Computer Vision*.

Refining Inductive Bias in Unsupervised Learning via Constraints

Kiri Wagstaff
Department of Computer Science
Cornell University
Ithaca, NY 14853
wkiri@cs.cornell.edu

Algorithmic bias is necessary for learning because it allows a learner to generalize rationally. A bias is composed of all assumptions the learner makes outside of the given data set. There exist some approaches to automatically selecting the best algorithm (and therefore bias) for a problem or automatically shifting bias as learning proceeds. In general, these methods are concerned with supervised learning tasks. However, reducing reliance on supervisory tags or annotations enables the application of learning techniques to many real-world data sets for which no such information exists. We therefore propose the investigation of methods for refining the bias in unsupervised learning algorithms, with the goal of increasing accuracy and improving efficiency. In particular, we will investigate the incorporation of background knowledge in the form of constraints that allow an unsupervised algorithm to automatically avoid unpromising areas of the hypothesis space.

Background Knowledge as Constraints. There is a natural connection between the bias in an algorithm and background knowledge. Often, the bias hardcoded into an algorithm was chosen due to background knowledge about the class of tasks to be targeted. This bias encodes certain assumptions about what sort of hypotheses are valid solutions for *any* problem it is applied to. However, for a specific task it is often the case that more precise information is available that can be used to augment the bias in useful ways. In such cases, it is desirable to leverage this background knowledge to refine the algorithmic bias in the proper direction.

In particular, we are interested in improvements that can be obtained with the addition of problem-specific constraints. Constraints are derived from background knowledge and specify relationships between instances that may not be expressible in the traditional feature-value representation used for machine learning data sets.

Current and Proposed Work. To date, we have investigated the incorporation of instance-level hard constraints into one clustering algorithm (a partitioning variation of COBWEB (Fisher 1987)). We found that incorporating constraints results in improved clustering accuracy (Wagstaff & Cardie in press). The types of constraints investigated were specific to algorithms that create flat partitions of the input data. We plan to investigate the relative merits of different kinds of constraints (e.g. hard vs. soft, feature-level vs. instance-level, probabilistic vs. deterministic) as applied to a variety of algorithms (partitioning vs. hierarchical, those that use a distance measure vs. those that do not, etc.).

In addition, a number of interesting questions were raised in the course of our previous work. First, does the distribution of instances (how many are from each class) affect the efficacy of constraints? Second, in our experiments, we observed that the category utility (CU) of the "correct" (fully-constrained) partition was *lower* than that obtained without using constraints. Does this indicate that CU is a poor choice of objective function in clustering? What does this signify about the correlation of the class label and other attributes, and ultimately about the relative "difficulty" of the data set? Lastly, how can we generate constraints to be used by these techniques?

Evaluation of Constraint Techniques. In order to assess the techniques developed, we plan to evaluate them on a variety of real-world and artificial data sets. Of particular importance is a determination of the relationship between the amount of information contained in the constraints and the magnitude of any accuracy improvements observed.

For some domains, constraints on which instances can or cannot reside in the same cluster are known or are automatically computable from background knowledge. In the problem of noun phrase coreference, for example, instance-level constraints can be computed from background linguistic knowledge. Other good candidates for evaluating constraint techniques are domains where class labels are known for a small subset, but not all, of the instances. Artificial data sets will be useful for exploring what effect the class distribution of instances has on clustering accuracy. In addition, we expect to use them to investigate the observed effect on category utility when constraints are used.

Acknowledgements: We would like to thank Claire Cardie for research advice and Westley Weimer for proofreading and suggestions. This work is supported by an NSF Graduate Fellowship.

References

Fisher, D. 1987. Knowledge Acquisition Via Incremental Conceptual Clustering. *Machine Learning* 2:139–172.

Wagstaff, K., and Cardie, C. in press. Clustering with Instance-Level Constraints.

Artificial Intelligence-Based Computer Modeling Tools for Controlling Slag Foaming in Electric Furnaces

Eric Wilson

Aerospace Engineering and Mechanics Dept.
University of Alabama
Tuscaloosa, AL 35487
elwilson@earthlink.net

Abstract

Due to increased competition in a world economy, steel companies are currently interested in developing techniques that will allow for the improvement of the steelmaking process, either by increasing output efficiency or by improving the quality of their product, or both. Slag foaming is one practice that has been shown to contribute to both these goals. This paper describes an effort in progress to both model and control the slag foaming process using neural networks in tandem with genetic algorithms and fuzzy logic.

Introduction

Slag foaming is a common process used within the steel industry to improve steel production. It involves the injection of oxygen and carbon into a molten steel bath. Carbon monoxide bubbles are formed, which rise and begin to foam the surface of the steel bath. This process results in less energy consumption, less refractory wear, and improved quality of the steel produced.

Overall, slag foaming has greatly improved the efficiency of steel production in electric arc furnaces. However, slag foaming is a highly dynamic process, which makes it difficult to model and control. Several different artificial intelligence-based tools exist for creating models of such complex systems. Two approaches have been found to be particularly effective in developing data-driven computer models: (1) neural networks and (2) fuzzy mathematics with genetic algorithms.

The project discussed in this paper proposes a dual approach to modeling the slag foaming process. Two computer models of the slag foaming process will be developed: (1) a neural network model and (2) a geno-fuzzy model. Both computer models will be data-driven; they will use data obtained from an industrial electric arc furnace operation. The data will consist of input/output pairs. Once developed, these models will be connected with genetic algorithm / fuzzy logic controllers that will be trained to maximize the quality of the foamy slag being modeled. These controllers would then be installed into steel plants, where final adjustments would occur.

Results

Progress has already been made towards developing a slag foaming model. Specifically, two different models have been developed. One of these models (developed in conjunction with Martin Marietta) predicts slag composition at various times during a steel heat. Results show that the neural network model makes accurate predictions (within five percent error) on eighty-five percent of the slag composition data. The second model (developed in conjunction with Georgetown Steel and Albany Research Center) takes data given on the amount of raw material and energy coming into the refractory, and predicts slag height in the refractory at every two to three seconds. Figure 1 shows how closely the neural network models the actual slag height over time.

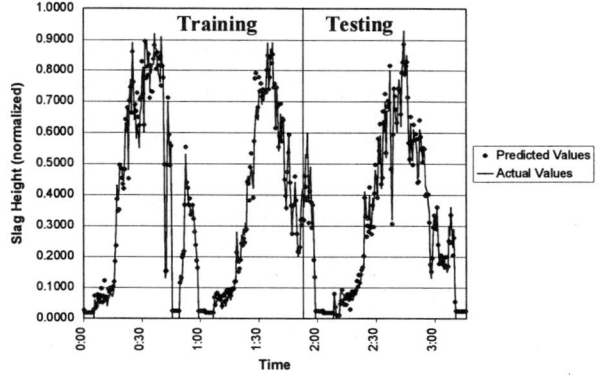

Figure 1 — Neural Network Prediction of Slag Height

Future work will include the development of a slag foaming controller using genetic algorithms and fuzzy logic in conjunction with the neural network slag foaming models already developed. This controller will then be installed, tested, and refined at Georgetown Steel. Completion of this project should occur in May 2001.

Copyright © 2000, American Association for Artificial Intelligence (www.aaai.org). All rights reserved.

Intelligent Systems Demonstrations

Sensible Agents: Demonstration of Dynamic Adaptive Autonomy

K. S. Barber, A. Goel, D. C. Han, J. Kim, D. N. Lam, T. H. Liu, C. E. Martin, R. McKay

The Laboratory for Intelligent Processes and Systems
Electrical and Computer Engineering
The University of Texas
Austin, TX 78712
barber@mail.utexas.edu

Research Overview

Multi-agent Systems (MAS) meld the research fields of Distributed Computing and Artificial Intelligence into a field called Distributed Artificial Intelligence (DAI). MAS fit nicely into domains that are naturally distributed and require automated reasoning to solve problems. Sensible Agents are one MAS designed for domains with a high level of dynamism and uncertainty. A central problem in MAS is finding the correct organizational structure for the agents (e.g. hierarchical, peer group, etc.) in which responsibilities to plan for and execute goals are allocated. In dynamic situations, it is unreasonable to expect a single organizational structure to be appropriate at all times. For proof of this, one needs only look at human management theory and practice. Human corporations often reorganize to face new environmental conditions. Sensible Agents attack this problem with Dynamic Adaptive Autonomy (DAA), which allows them to reorganize themselves during runtime to solve different problems in the face of a changing environment.

Some specific research that has contributed to flexible, adaptive multi-agent coordination includes partial global planning (Durfee and Lesser, 1987), organizational self-design (Ishida et al., 1992), STEAM flexible teamwork (Tambe, 1997), and RETSINA matchmaking (Sycara and Pannu, 1998). However, these techniques do not specifically adapt agent planning-interaction styles.

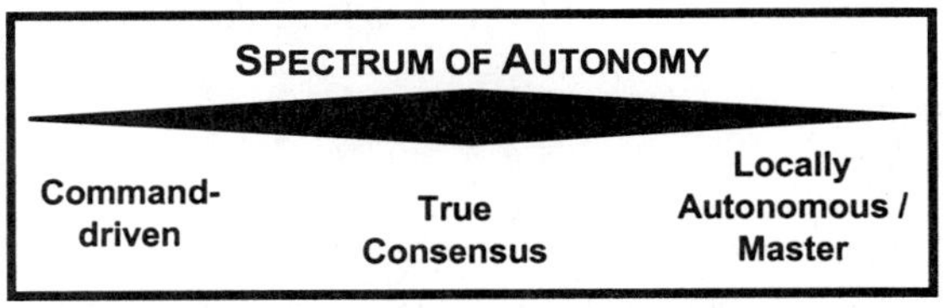

Figure 1: Spectrum of Autonomy

DAA allows agents to dynamically form, modify, and dissolve goal-oriented problem-solving agreements with other agents in a robust and flexible manner. As a member of a problem-solving organization, Sensible Agents establish their role in interacting with others by selecting an autonomy level for each goal they intend to pursue: (1) **Command driven**—agent does not plan but obeys orders given by another agent, (2) **Consensus**—agent works as a team member to devise plans, (3) **Locally Autonomous / Master**—the agent plans alone, unconstrained by other agents, and may or may not give orders to command-driven followers.

Each Sensible Agent (Barber et al., 2000) is composed of the following components: (1) the *Action Planner*; (2) the *Perspective Modeler*; (3) the *Conflict Resolution Advisor*; and (4) the *Autonomy Reasoner*. Domain-specific information, processing rules, and state are restricted to the Action Planner module, while remaining modules are domain-independent.

Sensible Agents are capable of performing: (1) trade-off assessment regarding the impact of local decision-making and goal satisfaction on system objectives, (2) their own behaviors by planning for a goal (local or system) and/or executing actions to achieve the goal, (3) group behaviors by forming binding autonomy agreements (e.g. consensus groups, master agent planning for group of command-driven agents) (4) self-organization by determining the best problem-solving organization, autonomy level, to optimally satisfy a goal, and (5) preferential learning for associating autonomy levels to situations.

Demonstration

The Sensible Agent Testbed provides an infrastructure of well-defined, publicly available interfaces where distributed agents operate and communicate. The end-user can interact with the testbed from the viewpoint of (1) the environment, by defining scenarios and injecting contingencies, or (2) the decision maker, by participating in planning and execution and receiving assistance from other Sensible Agents.

Sensible Agent capabilities will be demonstrated in the naval radar frequency management (NRFM) domain. This domain requires maintaining a set of position and frequency relationships among geographically distributed radars such that radar interference is minimized. Radar interference occurs primarily when two or more radars are operating in close proximity at similar frequencies. For a typical group of naval ships, it may take hours or days for a human assisted by a rule-based system to determine an optimal position and frequency. Unfortunately, the environment typically changes much faster than the human can respond. Local decisions impact the entire system,

---

Copyright © 2000, American Association for Artificial Intelligence (www.aaai.org) All right reserved.

requiring tradeoffs between local goal (e.g. keep my radars interference free) and system goals (e.g. keep radars in my group of ships interference free).

The NRFM Sensible Agent demonstration is used to determine the performance of Sensible Agents under different problem solving organizations. Agents monitor a naval radar for interference from external sources, and, if interference is detected, attempt to eliminate it by working alone or with others (Goel et al., 1998). Several different operating scenarios are demonstrated. Each Sensible Agent has the following capabilities:

Communication: the ability to send messages to another agent and to asynchronously respond to sent messages. Communication takes the form of (1) requesting/supplying information, (2) forming Autonomy Level Agreements, (3) reporting a conflict, (4) reporting a solution to a conflict.

Sensing: the ability to sense the position of other ships. Agents can also sense their level of interference, but cannot sense the source. If an agent detects interference it initiates problem solving to minimize the interference.

Environmental modeling: the ability to maintain an internal, local, model of the agent's world, separate from the simulation model of the world. Each agent is aware of the initial state of the system (ship positions and frequencies), however as the simulation progresses, an agent's local model may deviate from the world model. The agents use communication and sensing to update their local models.

Planning: the ability to plan at each of the autonomy levels described above. Successful planning for this problem hinges on an agent's ability to determine interference-free frequency assignments. Agents do this by modeling the spectrum of available frequencies and the necessary frequency differences (delta frequencies) for each known pair of radars. Agents then attempt to make assignments that meet all delta-frequency constraints within the restricted frequency space. Three algorithms are available to each agent's planner and are associated with the appropriate autonomy level classification.

An agent attempting to resolve interference in a locally autonomous fashion will plan alone. The agent will use its internal world model to find a frequency that is likely to be interference-free. The frequencies of other radars in the system are modeled as constraints on the search process. If no frequencies are found, searching continues at regular time intervals until one is found or a random "deadlock" time limit is reached. If the agent determines that the system is in deadlock (with respect to its interference state), it will choose a random frequency to pull the system out of deadlock.

Only the master plans in a master/command-driven relationship. If the master or its command-driven agents are experiencing interference, the master attempts to eliminate the interference through iterative assignments. First, it chooses its own frequency in the manner described above, but without considering the frequencies of its command-driven agents as constraints. It then determines an interference-free frequency for each command-driven agent, adding these frequencies as constraints, until all assignments have been made. If no set of satisfying assignments is found, the planning process is restarted. Once a solution has been found, the assignments are passed to the command-driven agents. Command-driven agents may report back to the master if they are still experiencing interference after the assignment. This may occur when the master's internal model does not match the world state.

Each agent involved in consensus interaction plays an equal part in determining frequency assignments. First, each agent independently carries out the master/command-driven planning algorithm with the other members of the consensus group treated as command-driven agents. At the conclusion of this phase, each agent proposes its solution to the rest of the consensus group during a synchronization phase. Each agent includes an estimate (based on its internal model) of the expected interference for each radar. Each consensus member deterministically selects the proposal with the least amount of estimated interference, and the agents assign frequencies accordingly.

Acknowledgements

The research was funded in part by The Texas Higher Education Coordinating Board Advanced Technology Program (003658-0188-1999), The National Science Foundation and The Naval Surface Warfare Center.

References

Barber, K. S., Goel, A., Han, D., Kim, J., Liu, T. H., Martin, C. E., and McKay, R. M. 2000. Simulation Testbed for Sensible Agent-based Systems in Dynamic and Uncertain Environments. Accepted to *TRANSACTIONS: Quarterly Journal of the Society for Computer Simulation International, Special Issue on Modeling and Simulation of Manufacturing Systems*.

Durfee, E. H. and Lesser, V. R. 1987. Using Partial Global Plans to Coordinate Distributed Problem Solvers. In *Proceedings of the Tenth International Joint Conference on Artificial Intelligence*, 875-883. : International Joint Conferences on Artificial Intelligence, Inc.

Ishida, T., Gasser, L., and Yokoo, M. 1992. Organization Self-Design of Distributed Production Systems. *IEEE Transactions on Knowledge and Data Engineering* 4(2): 123-134.

Sycara, K. P. and Pannu, A. S. 1998. The RETSINA Multiagent System: Towards Integrating Planning, Execution and Information Gathering. In *Proceedings of the Second International Conference on Autonomous Agents*, 350-351. Minneapolis/St. Paul, MN: ACM Press.

Tambe, M. 1997. Towards Flexible Teamwork. *Journal of Artificial Intelligence Research* 7: 83-124.

The Systems Engineering Process Activities (SEPA) Methodology and Tool Suite

K. Suzanne Barber, Thomas Graser, Paul Grisham, Stephen Jernigan, Sutirtha Bhattacharya

The Laboratory for Intelligent Processes and Systems
Electrical and Computer Engineering, The University of Texas, Austin, TX 78712
barber@mail.utexas.edu

Research Objective and Motivation

The Systems Engineering Process Activities (SEPA) Program delivers a documented formal methodology and tool suite supporting traceable system analysis and design activities for development of modular, reusable software systems. The SEPA tool suite demands efficient knowledge representations as well as efficient search techniques to manage and interrogate the large, complex associations of artifacts generated in the software engineering process.

The analysis and design of large, complex software systems mandates a formal methodology and supporting tools to assist system development teams throughout the software system lifecycle. The magnitude of personnel, the diversity of personnel backgrounds and agendas, and the transient nature of personnel and technology in relation of the software system lifecycle places a number of requirements on the process by which 1) application domain requirements are acquired, analyzed and model, 2) a system architecture is derived from those requirements, 3) technology decisions are made and implementation progresses, and 4) the system is tested and maintained. A formal methodology provides a *gameplan* for the entire lifecycle keeping team members "on the same page" and offering a mechanism by which to gauge progress. Large software projects with large numbers of personnel making large numbers of decisions require not only a formal process but tools to assist team members in executing their jobs and documenting their decisions. Traceability of decisions and documentation of decision rationale is key to understanding resulting decisions as well as understanding the impact of changes to decisions (e.g. decisions related to modeling, design, implementation, test and maintenance). Current object-oriented design approaches provide minimal guidance to software engineers working to derive an object-oriented design from a functionally specified domain model. Both a formal process methodology and tools are required to assist the engineer in answering the question, *what are the objects (software modules)?* and the required specification of those modules for maximum reuse and ease of integration.

Copyright © 2000, American Association for Artificial Intelligence (www.aaai.org) All right reserved.

Research Approach

The SEPA effort proposes both a methodology and supporting tool suite to facilitate capture of evolving requirements and object-oriented design for the graceful realization and evolution of systems targeting particular applications. SEPA creates traceable, comprehensible, and extensible system design specifications based on requirements from system clients and domain experts. The funnel, or cone, abstraction is chosen to represent a spectrum of user inputs/requirements that are narrowed, refined, and structured into a system design. User inputs require refinement for a number of reasons, including the need to: (1) merge inputs from multiple sources, and (2) distinguish between inputs relating to system requirements and those relating to general domain knowledge.

Three tenets are key to the SEPA methodology:

♦ Traceability between artifacts generated at each SEPA phase is critical to assuring 1) accurate modeling and subsequent understanding of the domain and system requirements, 2) derived architecture satisfies and captures requirements, and 3) justifiable and documented rationale for the architecture and design. Artifacts are shown in above boxes at the end of arrows.

♦ Separation of systems requirements for a particular implementation from those requirements inherent to the general domain

♦ Reuse of requirements, architecture specifications and designs are all three necessary to evaluate the similarities of requirements across development efforts and subsequently assess the appropriateness of architecture components and designs.

During **Knowledge Model Creation and Synthesis**, Knowledge Engineers employ *knowledge models* (e.g., message sequence charts, task descriptions) to graphically depict and document knowledge acquired from Domain Experts and promote verification and validation feedback cycles. Each Knowledge Model (KM) is the result of a single KA session. However, a single KA session may result in several new KMs. The KM synthesis effort seeks to detect conflicts and similarities among KMs across a particular user perspective or across the entire domain.

Knowledge Models reflecting user requirements often describe service and data requirements inherent to the domain and system implementation constraints/ requirements for a targeted application (**Application Requirements**) as well as example **Current Technologies**

Solutions. Separation of requirements and technology specifications promote a separation of concerns for developers as well as a reusable Domain Model which can "live" beyond technology choices to be used for multiple application system implementations where different technology choices are appropriate.

A **Reference Architecture (RA)** is described as a repository of domain components (known as Domain Reference Architecture Classes) which can be reused in a family of applications in a domain. DRACs are special domain classes that are defined at a business entity level of abstraction. A single DRAC may be realized by one or more actual objects during implementation. DRACs are represented by the set of: (1) attributes and services that characterize them, (2) the behavior of the DRAC, (3) the constraints and dependencies between the DRAC being described and (4) other DRACs. These DRACs are defined from model elements in the Domain Model. The resulting RA is completely domain-specific and highly flexible for building similar systems in the future. The translation process from the DM to the RA involves the methodical querying and analyzing of various views in the domain model (concepts, tasks, etc.) to arrive at DRACs with assigned responsibilities such that all responsibilities/requirements identified in the DM have been satisfied. DRACs are technology independent, focusing on what domain requirements exist rather than how technology solutions satisfy those domain requirements. System constraints specifying how available or potential technology solutions must fulfil domain requirements are captured in the **Application Infrastructure Requirements Model** (AIRM). Following the object oriented decomposition of Reference Architecture, the AIRM is likewise represented in a OO representation (Infrastructure Reference Architecture Classes, IRACs) with links from the IRACs to the applicable DRACs.

KAM manages and monitors artifacts from Knowledge Acquisition (KA) to establish a baseline for traceability. KAM also provide project management facilities to assist in the coordination of personnel (knowledge engineers, developers, domain experts) as well as the documents produced or obtained during the KA process. **HyDRA** aids in creating Knowledge Models (KMs), detecting conflicts between KMs and synthesizing the KMs into a single, functional Unified Knowledge Model. The synthesis process merges domain information from multiple experts while preserving traceability to KA. **SEPArator** distinguishes the information present in the SEPA Unified Knowledge Model into a Domain Model containing domain-based requirements, a Technology Solutions Repository capturing legacy systems, and an Application Requirements Model containing requirements for specific system implementations. **RARE** guides the developer in transitioning from a functional Domain Model produced by HyDRA to an object-oriented Reference Architecture of domain-based components (DRACs). Primarily, RARE assists in the decision process regarding what entities in the domain model should be represented as DRACs in the reference architecture. **MeTER** complements RARE by modeling application requirements gathered from KA and represented in the Unified Knowledge Model to represent IRACs and respective instances. ASERT is used to specify application technology. These technology specification models are linked to DRACs and IRACs for subsequent use in generating a system design specification satisfying domain and application requirements.

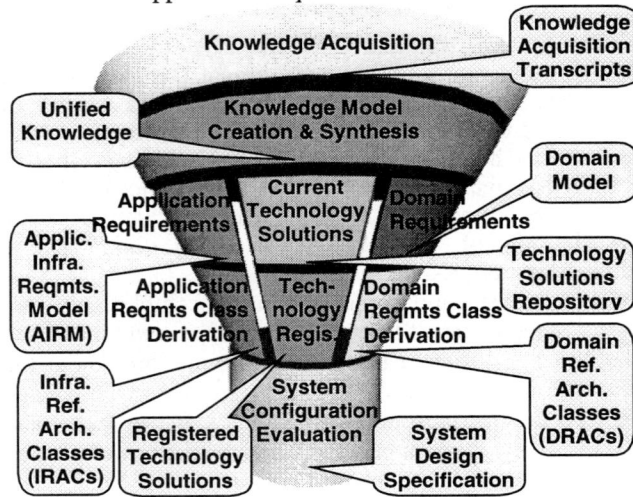

RIVT provides a design configuration and trade-off analysis environment to 1) select intended portions of the RA (domain services and data requirements) to be included in the targeted system, 2) select technologies satisfying/delivering requirements posed by selected DRACs and corresponding constraints in the CARM, and 3) evaluate feasibility of integrating selection technologies. As components are integrated, relevant integration rules describing application performance requirements and DRAC interaction (data and service dependencies between DRACs) will trigger. The resulting transcript of rules triggered as well as actions taken by the user to satisfy any detected integration violation (e.g. selection of another technology or relaxation of constraints) provides a validation of system integrity and a trace-ability to user requirements. Allowing the specification of notional technology specifications, users can specify "what if" designs.

Demonstration of the SEPA tool suite will show the need and utilization of rich knowledge representations as well as efficient search techniques to support artifact capture, artifact associations and traceability, progression and evolution of artifacts, and interrogation to support analysis and design decisions. SEPA has been applied to a number of domains. The SEPA tool demonstrations show how the SEPA tools were used in a DARPA initiative to develop information systems support first responders in emergency situations (e.g. fire, natural disaster, ChemBio).

Qualitative Spatial Interpretation of Course-of-Action Diagrams

Ronald W. Ferguson*
ferguson@cs.nwu.edu

Robert A. Rasch, Jr.[‡]
raschr@leavenworth.army.mil

William Turmel*
turmel@ils.nwu.edu

Kenneth D. Forbus*
forbus@ils.nwu.edu

*Qualitative Reasoning Group
Computer Science Department, Northwestern University
Evanston, IL 60201, USA

[‡]Battle Command Battle Lab (BCBL)
415 Sherman
Ft. Leavenworth, Kansas 66027

This paper describes two reasoners built for a real-world diagrammatic reasoning task: Course-of-Action (COA) diagrams. COA diagrams are a useful test bed for diagrammatic reasoning due to their inherently spatial domain and extensible visual symbology. Using a qualitative spatial reasoning engine, GeoRep, we built two COA diagram interpreters. We first describe COA diagrams, then the GeoRep engine, and then the resulting COA interpreters.

COA diagrams are used by the military to depict a region's military units and their assigned tasks (Figure 1). COA diagrams also depict topographical features, movement types (via various arrow types and polyline symbols), available routes, and tasks such as blocking enemy movement. A written plan accompanies the diagram (note: "COA diagram" refers solely to the diagram). COA diagrams are often hand-sketched, and redrawn as needed during planning.

COA diagram interpretation requires two kinds of qualitative spatial reasoning. Locally, symbol shapes indicate object types and characteristics. Globally, relative symbol placement indicates geographically-based relations.

Locally, COAs communicate meaning via their simply-drawn and broadly composable symbology. Symbols are easily classified via their visual structure. Figure 2 shows standard symbols for boundaries, task forces, minefields, friendly and enemy armor battalions, and attacks on objectives. All these symbols use composable subparts. For an armor battalion (Figure 2-d), the rectangle indicates a friendly unit, the contained ellipse indicates armor, and the two "antennae" indicate a battalion. Many parts, such as echelon markers, apply across many symbol classes.

More globally, COA diagrams also communicate meaning via symbol placement. For example, Figure 1 depicts (in the dashed rectangle) three task forces attacking objective SLAM. Units are assigned to the attack by placement along an attack arrow. Here, the attack paths cross an enemy minefield, and indicate an enemy regiment "behind" that minefield. The diagram boundaries divide the map into "areas of operation" to which units are assigned.

We built our COA interpreters using a qualitative spatial representation engine, GeoRep (Ferguson & Forbus, 2000). As input, GeoRep takes a drawing in a vector graphics format. From this, it creates a qualitative spatial representation of the drawing in a domain-specific spatial vocabulary.

GeoRep's architecture contains two stages: the low-level relational describer (LLRD) and the high-level relational describer (HLRD). The LLRD handles the domain-independent representation of the drawing, representing primitive visual relations such as proximity, parallel line segments, polygons, and connection and containment relations. These relations are salient in early vision. The HLRD in turn uses domain-specific rules to extend the LLRD's representation to detect domain-specific spatial relations and symbols types, which are given as output.

The COA diagram describer

Our first reasoner is the *COA diagram describer* (COADD). COADD uses GeoRep to describe COA diagrams containing a simplified symbology. Its symbol set includes assembly, engagement, and objective areas, basic unit and attack types, and borders.

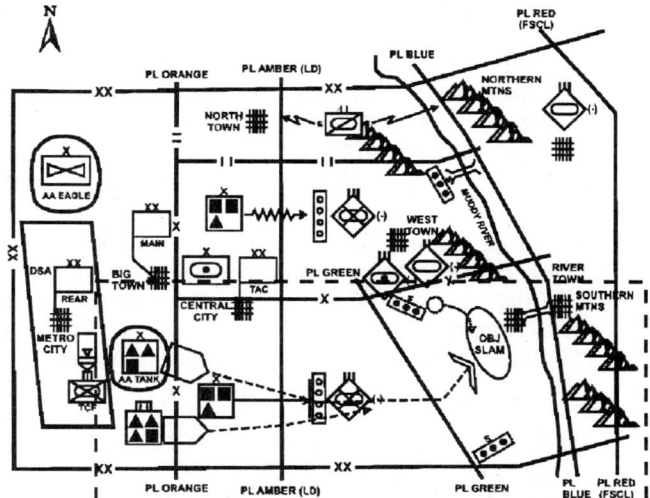

Figure 1: A COA diagram (Dept of the Army, 1997), Figure 5-5). For brevity, we focus on the dashed rectangle area, depicting the main attack (and two supporting attacks) on Objective SLAM.

Copyright © 2000, American Association for Artificial Intelligence (www.aaai.org). All rights reserved.

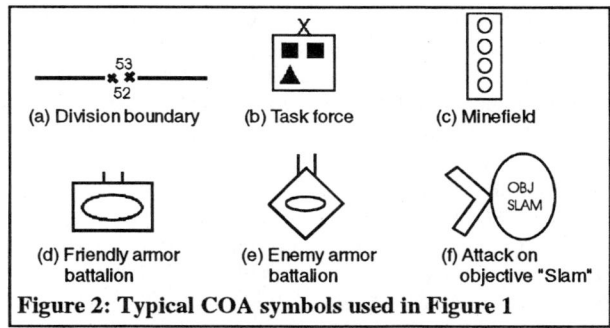

Figure 2: Typical COA symbols used in Figure 1

HLRD rules are used to recognize COA symbols using low-level relations. For example, friendly armor units are recognized as rectangles containing horizontally-oriented ellipses. These rules reflect the compositionality of COA symbols. For example, echelon markers are detected and then linked to specific units and boundaries, reflecting how echelon markers apply across different symbol types. Other rules infer unit intent by proximity to attack arrows and assembly areas. The rule set is small but expressive, with 37 HLRD rules covering 18 object types and relations.

To test COADD, we built a COA retriever. We used MAC/FAC (Forbus, Gentner, & Law, 1995), a retriever based on the Structure-Mapping Theory of similarity (Gentner, 1983), as the retrieval engine. Given a target diagram, COADD built a description and MAC/FAC retrieved the most similar COA diagram, using a casebase of previously-built descriptions.

Preliminary testing with a casebase of 10 cases showed that performance was adequate, but not exceptional: similar cases were often retrieved (e.g., for simple attack plans), and the aligned parts were often useful, but the depth of COADD's simplified domain did not provide enough variability for proper testing. Useful test results required a broader subset of the COA symbology.

The COA Geographic Reasoner

In our second prototype (which was designed for the DARPA HPKB initiative), attempts to expand the COADD prototype soon made clear that a deeper revision was needed. A broader symbology and larger diagrams made COADD's recognition difficult and slow.

First, GeoRep's input was changed to use *knowledge-enriched vector graphics*. This format contains primitive visual elements as before, but also links visual elements to specific COA objects—in effect pre-classifying them. Identified symbols are handled by a *glyph* visual element, which contains component shapes that have display characteristics, extent, and location, but are not analyzed by GeoRep's low-level vision routines. For example, while GeoRep previously had to recognize armor battalions, the input now specifies which visual elements are armor battalions. This leaves the more tractable task of representing geographic relations between glyphs.

In collaboration with other HPKB research teams, we determined a set of 15 geographic queries. These queries emphasize relative distance and direction, areas of operation, paths, and metric distance measures.

The resulting geographic reasoner answers a broad set of queries, and was used successfully by other research teams to build a knowledge-based COA critiquer. In our testing, the reasoner handled 190 geographic queries over four different COA diagrams and answered all but 8 correctly. While the system is powerful, the visual domain theory is small, containing 51 axiomatic rules and 23 base statements (categories and category relations) for 15 query types.

The geographic reasoner combines spatial and semantic knowledge to determine critical relationships. Figure 3 shows several of its queries and answers. Its answers show

---

Units A, B, and C are friendly units in the dotted region of Figure 1. Unit Z is the enemy unit to their right.

What is a path between friendly unit B and enemy unit Z? How far apart are they along that path? **Path-880** *(a path between the units)*. **2.96 km**.

What obstacles are between unit B and enemy unit Z? How far from unit B to the obstacle along that previous path? What is the ordinal direction from unit B to the obstacle? **Minefield-84. 2.12 kilometers. East—directly.**

What is the area of operations for unit A? *Answer returns an area, bounded by brigade-level borders, around unit A.*

What is the area of operations for unit B? *Same area, located east of the unit. Unit B is outside this area, but Unit B's task is inside, meaning that it is unit B's responsibility.*

Figure 3: Questions and answers to the Geographic Reasoner for Figure 1, re-written in English.

---

a clean interaction between knowledge about the glyphs ("Which glyphs are minefields?"), semantic categories ("Are minefields an obstacle?") and qualitative spatial relations ("Is there an obstacle between this unit and its goal?"). Often "spatial" relationships turn on conceptual knowledge ("Is this unit a part of the area of operations it is inside? Only if its task's goal is not elsewhere.").

Conclusion

COA diagrams constitute a useful test bed for research into diagrammatic reasoning. Using a two-level qualitative spatial reasoner like GeoRep, one can quickly build powerful diagrammatic reasoners.

There are many limitations in the current prototypes. The difficulty with scaling COADD is telling, and highlights the difficult task of distinguishing between many similar glyph types. While the Geographic Reasoner works well, its query set is limited. In addition, performance is sometimes slow due to inefficiencies in proximity-detection.

Development continues. We hope to extend the low-level visual vocabulary to clarify COADD's scaling difficulties. We also plan to extend the Geographic Reasoner, adding query types and increasing reasoner efficiency. This system is currently being evaluated for integration into a prototype COA decision support system.

Acknowledgments. This research was supported by the DARPA High Performance Knowledge Bases initiative, by the Office of Naval Research's Cognitive and Computer Science programs, and by the National Science Foundation under the Learning and Intelligent Systems program.

References

Department of the Army. (1997). *Staff Organizations and Operations* (Field Manual 101-5). Washington, DC.

Ferguson, R. W., & Forbus, K. D. (2000). GeoRep: A flexible tool for spatial representation of line drawings. AAAI-2000. Austin, TX.

Forbus, K. D., Gentner, D., & Law, K. (1995). MAC/FAC: A model of similarity-based retrieval. *Cognitive Science, 19*(2), 144-206.

Gentner, D. (1983). Structure-Mapping: A theoretical framework for analogy. *Cognitive Science, 7*, 155-170.

TV Content Recommender System

Srinivas Gutta, Kaushal Kurapati, KP Lee, Jacquelyn Martino, John Milanski, J. David Schaffer, John Zimmerman

Philips Research
345 Scarborough Rd.
Briarcliff Manor, NY 10510
{srinivas.gutta, kaushal.kurapati, kp.lee, jacquelyn.martino, john.milanski, dave.schaffer, john.zimmerman}@philips.com

Abstract

The plethora of content available to the consumer has become overwhelming. Increasing amounts of information are being disseminated through terrestrial broadcast, satellite, and cable leading to an information overload. Common modes of searching for TV programs currently in existence include: TV-guide, PreVue channel and rudimentary search tools available through satellite dish TV programming service. These tools are general-purpose in nature and are not specifically tailored to the individual viewer's taste. Towards that end we advance in this paper a recommender system that searches for TV programs based on their likes/dislikes through implicit personalization techniques.

Introduction

Today, most consumers face an exhausting task of having to find something to watch on TV that fits their interests. Currently, the main modes for searching and identification of relevant TV content are the following: (a) browsing through pages of the 2D grid-format paper TV guide, (b) waiting on the PreVue channel, which is an automated scrolling version of the paper TV-guide grid and (c) using the rudimentary search tools that are available with a satellite dish TV programming service. The specific problems associated with them include the inability of the viewers to weed out irrelevant content, non-interactivity and difficulty in navigation. An alternative way is to provide viewers with a personalized means to provide intuitive user interfaces and the ability to filter program information. We propose a combination of the following two approaches to assist the users:

Search Engines & Information Visualization - Provide them with easy-to-use tools for search and present the abstract information in a way that is intuitive and easy to comprehend.

Recommender Systems - Provide them with a system that tracks and recognizes their preferences and organizes the TV program content accordingly.

Copyright © 2000, American Association for Artificial Intelligence (www.aaai.org). All rights reserved.

Background

Researchers in information visualization have taken several approaches to visualize multidimensional data in various application contexts [Card et al., 1999]: finding movies and homes, news articles in a database, and web pages on the Internet. The specific problems associated with them include the use of scatter plots which are not particularly helpful in visualizing text-based TV program data, due to occlusion problems and the use of immersive visualization techniques leading to slower response time of the system, and loss of user orientation. The literature is rich with descriptions of other visualization systems for scientific and data mining applications; however, researchers have not focussed their attention on the consumer domain, which is what our work addresses.

The research in adaptive systems aims to build recommender systems that help the user in filtering information based on the user's profile. Several such systems have been built in recent years to help users deal with various sources of information [Etzioni, 1999]. However, these systems have a major source of information missing, the TV. The TV Advisor by Das and Horst [Das and Horst, 1998] is one example of a recommender system for TV found in the literature. They make use of explicit techniques to generate recommendations for a TV viewer. Such techniques require the user to take the initiative and explicitly specify their interests, in order to get high quality recommendations. Implicit techniques, on the other hand, provide a non-intrusive approach to lessen the burden on the user by inferring the user's preferences from the use of a TV set.

Application Prototype

Our application prototype aims to be a 'smart electronic program guide (smart EPG)' that enables a user to search and browse through a TV programs database. It is 'smart' because it maintains an adaptive user profile and makes recommendations of TV programs, computed according to the profile. The application can be divided into 3 parts as described below.

The search environment provides the tools for the user to formulate a search for retrieval from a TV-programs database. We organize the valid search criteria along 'strings' or 'bracelets', which represent individual dimensions of the multi-dimensional TV programs database. Each 'bracelet' is a grouping of complementary 'beads' where each 'bead' is a visual representation of information contained in the database. In our prototype, we have 7 bracelet categories: day of the week, time of the day, program genres, channels, keywords, user profile names and saved searches. This notion of beads evolves from ancient prayer beads or the abacus, where the beads served as information holding units and were useful for counting. The navigation and selection of search criteria takes place through a standard remote control.

The overview environment is concerned with the visual representation of the search results. The results are TV shows matching the search criteria, retrieved from the database. Our approach to visualization was to map this abstract information in a manner that parallels the human tendency to put physical objects closer when they are important and to let them fade into the background as their importance decreases. We use depth as a cue to achieve this notion. A tunnel model was used for displaying the results comprising of rings, each of which serves as a placeholder for the recommended TV shows. The TV-shows that are highly recommended for a user will be displayed closer to the user, on the first few rings, than those that are not.

In the current version of our prototype, user profiles can be used as search criteria to generate system recommendations of TV content. The search results are visualized, in the overview environment, in the order of high to low relevancy based on a desirability score that is computed according to the person's profile. The scores are the output of either of two recommender engines that we have built as part of our research. Both of our approaches to generating TV program recommendations are based on implicit profiles of TV viewers. At the current time, we pursued approaches that could deal with incremental updates of the viewing history, and inconsistencies in the indexing of shows in the TV show data. An implicit profile is built from the viewing history of a TV viewer. The viewing history is a list of shows that a viewer has watched (positive examples) and not watched (negative examples). The implicit nature of our profiling method stems from the fact that the process does not involve any explicit interaction with TV viewers, regarding their likes and dislikes, other than collecting information about what shows have been watched.

The first of our TV program recommender systems uses the Bayesian classifier [Billsus and Pazzani, 1996] approach to compute the likelihood that the viewer will like or dislike a particular TV program. We approach the problem with a 2-class Bayesian decision model, where a show belongs to either the class, watched, or the class, not watched. The user profile, in the Bayesian context, is a collection of attributes (or features) together with a count of how many times an attribute occurs in positive and negative examples. From this profile, we first compute the prior probability that a show belongs to a particular class and then the conditional probability that a given feature will be present if a show is in either of the two classes. Using these probabilities we finally compute the a posteriori probability for a new show, given its feature set, that it belongs to a particular class.

The second approach construct rules for classifying shows given a *training set* of positive and negative shows that are part of the TV viewing history. We begin by deriving a decision tree (DT) which is then decomposed into rules for classifying the shows. The decision tree employed is Quinlan's C4.5 [Quinlan, 1993] that uses an information-theoretic approach based on entropy. C4.5 builds the decision tree using a top-down, divide-and-conquer approach: it first selects an attribute, then divides the training set into subsets characterized by the possible values of the attribute, and follows the same procedure recursively with each subset until no subset contains objects from more than one class. The single-class subsets correspond to the leaves of the decision tree, while a node indicates that a further test needs to be performed on that show to determine which class the show belongs to. When a new show, which is not part of the training set, is encountered, the DT is parsed to obtain a probabilistic class distribution for the show and the class with the highest probability is the predicted class.

Future Work

We have tested our application with potential users in order to get an appraisal of our visualization and personalization techniques. We got very encouraging endorsements of our concepts. Users also gave helpful suggestions for improvement, which are under consideration.

References

[Billsus and Pazzani, 1996] D. Billsus and M. Pazzani. Revising User Profiles: The Search for Interesting Web Sites. *Proceedings of 3rd International Workshop on Multistrategy Learning*. AAAI Press, 1996.

[Card et al., 1999] Stuart Card, Jock Mackinlay, and Ben Shneiderman. *Readings in Information Visualization*. Morgan Kaufmann Publishers Inc., San Francisco, California, 1999.

[Das and Horst, 1998] Duco Das and Herman ter Horst. Recommender Systems for TV. *Proceedings of 15th AAAI Conference*, Madison, Wisconsin, July 1998.

[Etzioni, 1999] Oren Etzioni, Jorg Muller, Jeffrey Bradshaw. Proceedings of the 3rd Annual Conference on Autonomous Agents, ACM Press, 1999.

[Quinlan, 1993] Ross J. Quinlan. C4.5: *Programs for Machine Learning*. Morgan kaufmann Publishers Inc., San Francisco, California, 1993.

The Chimaera Ontology Environment

Deborah L. McGuinness, Richard Fikes, James Rice, and Steve Wilder

Knowledge Systems Laboratory
Stanford University, Stanford, CA
{dlm, fikes, wilder}@ksl.stanford.edu

CommerceOne
Mountain View, CA
rice@jrice.com

Ontologies have become central components in many applications including search, e-commerce, configuration and, arguably, every large web site (at least for organization and navigation). As ontologies become larger, more distributed, and longer-lived, the need for ontology creation and maintenance environments grows. In our work with ontologies and tool environments over the last few years, we have observed growing needs for automated support of two tasks: (1) merging multiple ontologies and (2) diagnosing (and evolving) ontologies. Chimaera is aimed at supporting these two tasks.

We believe these areas will become more critical over time. Merging becomes imperative when multiple terminologies must be used and viewed as one ontology (e.g., when an e-commerce company needs to merge the terminologies of UNSPSC and RosettaNet into one consistent ontology). Merging is also critical when distributed team members need to assimilate two or more ontologies that should work together in an integrated fashion. Similarly, diagnosis of ontologies becomes more critical as ontologies are obtained from more varied sources. One may need to use a number of "standard" vocabularies that make differing assumptions about design, representation, or reasoning. For example, some vocabularies may allow cycles while others do not and some may support disjoint partitions while others may not be able to express the notion (and thus not expect any associated reasoning). Additionally outside vocabularies may not follow required internal naming conventions. Diagnosis along many dimensions may be required to focus a human's attention in areas that are likely to need modification before use in a particular environment. Finally, diagnostic log generation is useful, but even more useful is an environment that supports interaction with the log and assistance in fixing identified problems.

Chimaera is a merging and diagnostic web-based browser ontology environment. Its design and implementation is based on our experience developing other user interfaces for knowledge applications such as the Ontolingua ontology development environment [Farquhar, et al, 1997], the Stanford CML editor [Iwasaki, et al, 1997], the Stanford JAVA Ontology Tool (JOT), the Intraspect knowledge server [Intraspect 1999], two web interfaces [McGuinness, et. al., 1995; Welty, 1996] for the CLASSIC knowledge representation system [Borgida, et. al, 1989], and a collaborative environment for building ontologies for FindUR [McGuinness, 1998]. Its goal is to work with many ontologies, thus we chose to build on a platform that handles any OKBC-compliant [Chaudhri, et. al, 1998] representation system. Chimaera accepts over 15 designated input format choices (such as ANSI KIF, Ontolingua, Protégé, CLASSIC, iXOL, etc.) as well as any other OKBC-compliant form. It will soon be compliant with other emerging standards such as RDF and DAML.

Chimaera contains a simple editing environment in the tool and also allows the user to use the full Ontolingua editor/browser environment for more extensive editing. Ontolingua is not a requirement however; other editors could be used in its place. It facilitates merging by allowing users to upload existing ontologies into a new workspace (or into an existing ontology). Figure 1 shows the result of someone loading in two ontologies (Test1 and Test2) and then choosing the name resolution mode for the ontologies. Chimaera will suggest potential merging candidates based on a number of properties. It generates a name resolution list that may be used as a guide through the merging task. The displayed option in the name resolution list in the figure below shows a suggestion to merge Mammal and Mammalia (since they had similar names). The user sees a display of the places where the two terms appear in the hierarchy (with only the connected portions of the hierarchy displayed). The user may browse the hierarchy in more detail by doing things like expanding subclasses (both Mammal and Mammalia are closed as represented by the closed triangle in the figure). The user may also view the definitions of the terms and, within Ontolingua, the user may also obtain the results of similarly and difference structural comparisons of the definitions as well. The user may then choose to merge the terms with a simple menu choice from the class menu.

Chimaera allows the user to choose the level of vigor with which it suggests merging candidates. Higher settings, for example will look for things like possible acronym expansion (which was extremely valuable in our use of Chimaera on some government knowledge bases).

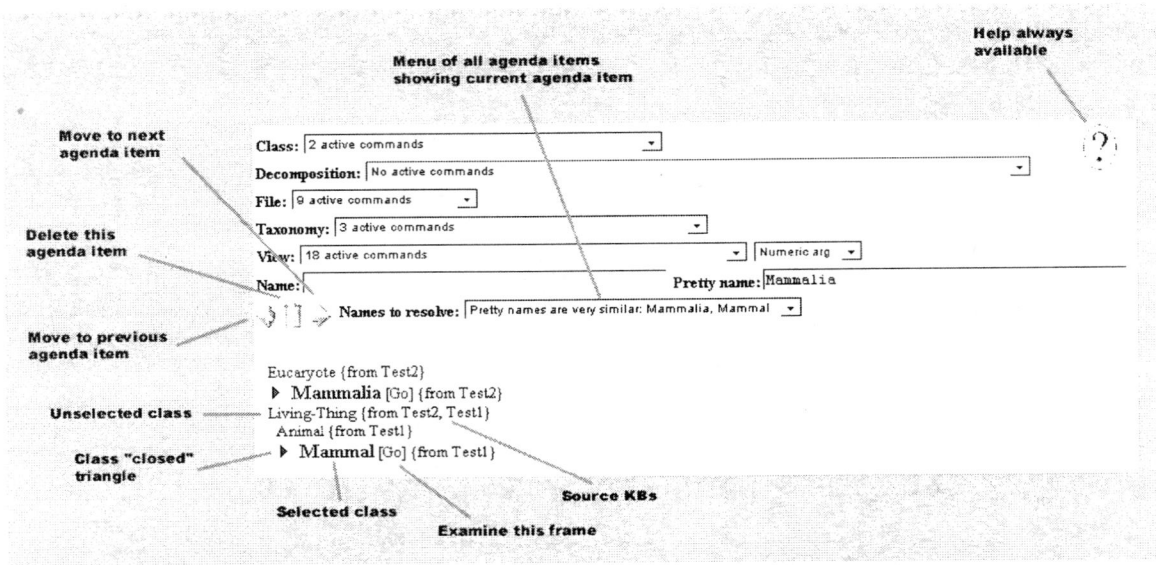

Figure 1: Chimæra in name resolution mode suggesting a merge of Mammal and Mammalia

Chimaera also supports a taxonomy resolution mode. It looks for a number of syntactic term relationships (such as <X-Y> and <Y> since the two are usually subclass related). When attached to a classifier, it can look for semantic subsumption relationships as well

Chimaera includes an analysis capability that allows users to run a diagnostic suite of tests selectively or in their entirety. The output is displayed as an interactive log that allows users to see the results of the tests and also to explore the results. The tests include incompleteness tests, syntactic checks, taxonomic analysis, and semantic checks. We built this system to provide collaborators with varying training essentially a "todo" list containing updates that would likely need to be done before the ontologies would be of the most use to us. The list contains things such as terms that are used but that are not defined, to terms that have contradictory ranges, to cycles detected in the ontology definitions. We are extending the system to include a rule language that allows users to specify additional tests that our environment should include in its diagnostic tool suite so that users may customize the diagnostics to their particular environment.

Chimaera was used in the High Performance Knowledge Base project to analyze incoming ontologies. It is also being used and/or evaluated by companies including VerticalNet and Cisco. More information is available from [McGuinness, et. al, 2000], or from the web site http://www.ksl.Stanford.EDU/software/chimaera/ which also includes links to a tutorial and a movie demonstration. It is licensable for use.

Acknowledgments. The authors wish to thank DARPA for its support of this work under contract N66001-97-C-8554, *Large-Scale Repositories of Highly Expressive Knowledge.*

References.
A. Borgida, R.J. Brachman, D.L. McGuinness, and L.A. Resnick; *CLASSIC: A Structural Data Model for Objects*, SIGMOD, Oregon, 1989
V. Chaudhri, A. Farquhar, R. Fikes, P. Karp, and J. Rice; *OKBC: A Programmatic Foundation for Knowledge Base Interoperability*; AAAI-98.
A. Farquhar, R. Fikes, and J. Rice; *The Ontolingua Server: a Tool for Collaborative Ontology Construction*; Intl. Journal of Human-Computer Studies **46**, 1997.
Intraspect Knowledge Server, Intraspect Corp., 1999. (http://www.intraspect.com/product_info_solution.htm)
Y. Iwasaki, A. Farquhar, R. Fikes, & J. Rice; *A Web-based Compositional Modeling System for Sharing of Physical Knowledge.* Morgan Kaufmann, Nagoya, Japan, 1997.
D.L. McGuinness; *Ontological Issues for Knowledge-Enhanced Search*; Proceedings of Formal Ontology in Information Systems, June 1998. Also in Frontiers in Artificial Intelligence and Applications, IOS-Press, Washington, DC, 1998.
D.L. McGuinness, R. Fikes, J. Rice, and S. Wilder. *An Environment for Merging and Testing Large Ontologies.* Proceedings of Knowledge Representation 2000.
D.L. McGuinness, L.A. Resnick, and C. Isbell; *Description Logic in Practice: A CLASSIC: Application*; IJCAI, 1995.
United Nations Standard Product and Services Classification (UNSPSC) Code organization. http://www.unspsc.org/home.htm
C. Welty; *An HTML Interface for CLASSIC*; Proceedings of the 1996 International Workshop on Description Logics; AAAI Press; November, 1996.

Matchmaking to Support Intelligent Agents for Portfolio Management

Massimo Paolucci
Zhendong Niu
Katia Sycara
Constantine Domashnev
Sean Owens
Martin Van Velsen

The Robotics Institute, Carnegie Mellon University, Pittsburgh, PA
{paolucci,niu,katia,dconst,owens,vvelsen}@cs.cmu.edu

Abstract

A-Match is a matchmaking system that allows agents to enter and exit the system dynamically. It employs a Matchmaker to support agents in the system in their exchange of services. A-Match lets human users interact with the Matchmaker. Through the A-Match users find agents that can provide needed services or advertise new agents. The functionality of the A-Match is displayed in the context of the Warren System, a system that supports the user to manage its own stock portfolio.

Research Overview

The Internet is both a powerful resource and a powerful challenge for AI applications. While it provides a great deal of information, it is also a dynamic source of information in which sites might disappear while new and better sites are added. The A-Match System and the Warren System (Sycara, Decker, & Zeng 1999) demonstrate how Multi Agent Systems (MAS) naturally deals with the dynamism of the Internet. A-Match is a web based matchmaking service that records which agents are available and the services that they provide. Through the A-Match, agents and human users with specific needs find agents that satisfy those needs. Warren is a portfolio management application based on the RETSINA Open MAS (Sycara et al. 1996). Agents in the Warren System find each other through A-Match's matchmaking capabilities in such a way that the system can automatically reconfigure itself when new services are provided or old service providers disappear.

As pages dynamically appear and disappear on the Web, agents dynamically enter and exit Open MAS, such as Warren. This dynamism makes impossible to maintain hard-wired relations between agents. Agents in the system should be able to reconfigure automatically and gather up to date information from the agents that are functional. A-Match supports this automatic reconfiguration process by providing a special agent, called Matchmaker, that maintains an updated mapping between the agents that are currently in the system and the services that they provide. The Matchmaker function as the yellow pages: it collects advertisements of the services provided by the agents that enter the system and it matches these advertisements against the requests that come from agents that request services. The result of the request to the Matchmaker is contact information of agents that provide the needed service. The Matchmaker does not get involved in the transaction between the requester agent and the provider agent, it is the responsibility of the requesting agent to contact the provider directly.

In addition to the Matchmaker, the A-Match System provides to human users a way to access the Matchmaker. This functionality is of great value for users since they gain direct access to the services provided by all agents in the system. A-Match consists of an interface between humans and the Matchmaker, through this interface users can query the matchmaker to find which agents provide a specific service, retrieve a list of agents advertised and query the agents retrieved directly. In addition, the A-Match provides a mean to advertise agents when the agent does not advertise itself automatically. A-Match is a deployed system that is publicly available on the web (A-Match is on-line at the following address http://www.cs.cmu.edu/ softagents/a-match/).

The Warren System shows how multiagent systems can take advantage of A-Match's matchmaking to manage heterogeneous information and to use redundant functionalities to increase the reliability of the system. Warren provides the user with information that comes from different sources: it provides stock quotes directly from the web, it monitors news casts to find news about stocks of interest to the user, and it advises the user when the portfolio does not match the user's risk profile. Agents in the Warren system use the Matchmaker in the A-Match to find the agents that provide the services and to recover when service providers fail.

A-Match

A-Match is a web based interface to the Matchmaker that allows human users to find agents that can provide needed services. Agents in the Matchmaker are represented on the bases of the inputs that they take and the outputs that they return. For instance, an agent that reports the stock value of a specific ticker is expressed as a transformation from the ticker to the value of the stock. Through the A-Match the user can compile a query to the Matchmaker requesting a specific service: queries are expressed through the output that user expects from the agent and the inputs that she is ready to provide. The Matchmaker matches the require-

Copyright ©1999, American Association for Artificial Intelligence (www.aaai.org). All rights reserved.

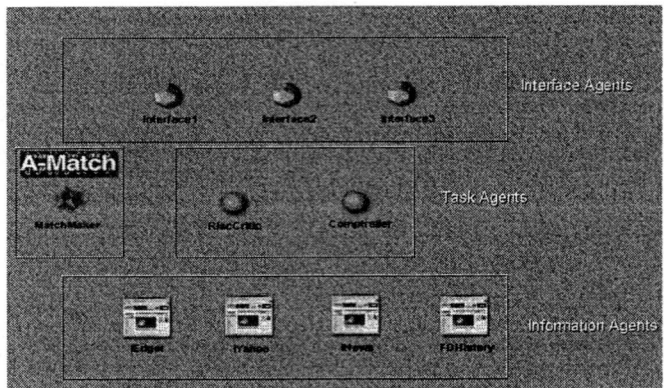

Figure 1: The Warren Architecture.

ments of the user against the advertisements stored and it reports the list of agents whose advertisement matches the request of the user. The match performed by the Matchmaker is based on a taxonomy of terms. For example, an agent A might advertise that, given a ticker name, it reports the value of the corresponding stock, while the user might look for an agent that given a stock name returns the price of the stock. The Matchmaker would recognize a similarity between ticker and stock name, and a similarity between value and price and report to the user the agent A provides the service requested. Once an agent is found, the user can use the A-Match to query the agent directly and display the answer from the agent. Users can also use the A-Match to browse the ontology used during the matching process. The browser allows them to find the definition of terms, and to estimate the similarity between terms in the ontology. In addition, the A-Match provides functionalities that allow the user to browse advertisements, advertise new agents, unadvertise agents and update the advertisement of agents. The browse functionality displays the list of all agents that already advertised with the Matchmaker; humans can advertise functionalities of agents that cannot advertise on their own; unadvertise is used to remove references of agents from the matchmaker; while update is an editing facility that allows the user to modify advertisements to correct mistakes.

A-Match can store different types of advertisements coming from different applications. Purposely, the Matchmaker does not pose any boundary between applications: any agent that matches the request can be suggested as provider of a service. Ultimately, the same agent can provide a service in two different systems provided that it responds to the needs of those systems. This blurring of boundaries between systems is a very important feature for multiagent systems since it allows automatic reusability of functionalities.

Warren

Warren shows how a multiagent system can take advantage of the A-Match and the Matchmaker. As shown in figure 1, Warren is composed of three types of agents: interface agents that display the portfolios to the users, task agents that assist the user in the management of its portfolio, and information agents that are used to gather information about stocks in the portfolio. Through the interface agent the user can buy stocks, sell stocks, monitor the value of its own portfolio and monitor news about the stocks in the portfolio. In addition the user can monitor the value of prospective stocks that she does not own yet. Two task agents assist the user, the Comptroller records the portfolio and could interact with brokers (At the moment though, Warren does not allow real stock trading) to actually acquire stocks. The Risk Critic acts as a financial advisor and signals to the user when the acquisition of new stocks in the portfolio or the sale of some stocks modifies the risk associated with the portfolio. Information agents monitor the web to report the value of stocks and their current risk profile, so that the risk critic can suggest to the user whether to buy or sell. Furthermore, some information agents monitor news casts to find news that can be of interest for the user.

The interaction between agents is a key aspect of MAS, but this interaction is very difficult to appreciate because it is always hidden in the computation of the agents. The Retsina MAS offers a tool, called Demo Display, that monitors and graphically displays the agents and their exchange of messages.

Acknowledgments

The authors wish to acknowledge the contribution of many people that through the years worked on different versions of Warren. This research has been sponsored in part by ONR grant N-00014-96-16-1-1222 by DARPA grant F-30602-98-2-0138.

References

Sycara, K.; Decker, K.; Pannu, A.; Williamson, M.; and Zeng, D. 1996. Distributed intelligent agents. *IEEE Expert, Intelligent Systems and their Applications* 11(6):36–45.

Sycara, K.; Decker, K.; and Zeng, D. 1999. Intelligent agents in portfolio management. In Agent Technology: Foundations, Applications, and Markets., eds., *N. Jennings and M. Woolridge*. Springer.

Adaptive User Interfaces through Dynamic Design Automation

Robin R. Penner
University of Minnesota
College of Mechanical Engineering
111 Church Street SE
Minneapolis, MN 55455
rpenner@me.umn.edu

Erik S. Steinmetz
University of Minnesota
Dept. of Computer Science and Engineering
200 Union Street SE
Minneapolis, MN 55455
steinmet@cs.umn.edu

Christopher L. Johnson
Honeywell Technology Center
Human Centered Systems
3660 Technology Drive
Minneapolis, MN 55418
chris.l.johnson@honeywell.com

Abstract

The inherent difficulty in supporting human usability in large control systems—such as building environmental and security systems—derives from the large diversity of components and users within each domain. Each system is different, with different types and organizations of devices; each user is different, and takes different roles; each task a user performs varies with the situation. As a result, applying traditional methods of interface design to these systems is insufficient. Designers end up handcrafting each diagram required by each type of user, the effort needed to add new functionality quickly bloats, and users end up juggling multiple disparate applications. We have begun to deploy a tool called DIG (Dynamic Interaction Generation) that addresses this difficulty. DIG uses models of domain, task, and presentation knowledge to automatically design and present interfaces specialized to a user's current role and task, the current situation, and the capabilities of the current display hardware. In this demonstration, DIG will convert a real-life building management configuration into a dynamic interface that building managers can operate using either a standard PC or a Palm Pilot.

Introduction

Designing a user interface is difficult, time-consuming, and expensive. Designing a *good* user interface is even harder. Even though industry support of the practice of UI design has improved in recent years—although still often inadequate—complex, distributed systems pose a particular usability problem. Because of the variability and expandability of these systems, the potential situations and tasks that arise during the life of a user interface become unpredictable. And if traditional, static design is the only available method for delivering these interfaces, responding to non-determinate situations becomes impossible. At the very least, adapting the interface in response to changes in task requirements, system configuration, user roles, or evolving technology or culture becomes difficult and costly.

For instance, consider the domain of building management. Even though the basics of day-to-day management are the same, individual installations are very different from each other, with different users, tasks, equipment, and requirements. Small buildings differ from large buildings, forced air systems differ from boiler systems, automated security installations differ from buildings staffed with human security guards. Large installations may employ large numbers of users, each assigned a well-specified role limited to one or two tasks required by the system; small installations may employ one user who is manager/operator/technician all in one.

This variability among systems in terms of configuration, criticality, tasks, roles, and security levels drives up the cost of traditional user interface methods considerably. In current systems, each visualization display that each user requires must be individually handcrafted, at a cost of up to 5% of the entire system.

We have been conducting large-scale research programs to address these issues, and believe that an appropriate and effective response is to develop systems that automatically design interfaces, responsive to the specific situation that holds at the particular time the interface is needed.

Dynamic Interaction Generation

Dynamic Interaction Generation (DIG) is a solution in which an automated reasoning system designs a user interface for a control system on demand and presents it on whatever display device is in use (Penner 1998). As a result, the interface is consistent, well-designed, and adapted to users' privileges, roles, and tasks; the objects of interest; the value and type of data displayed; and the hardware devices displaying the interface. As a user's interaction progresses, DIG continues to dynamically adapt the interface to these factors.

We have implemented a working DIG system in DIGBE (DIG for Building Environments), which converts a building management configuration database into a dynamic, adaptive interface for building managers. DIGBE currently uses the Honeywell Excel Building Supervisor (XBS) as the source of real-time operational data, as well as information about the domain objects present in the system. However, DIGBE's architecture (Figure 1) is modular, so that the system is neutral about its data sources. Efforts are currently underway to provide conduits to other real-time data sources and to automatically create configurations through discovery.

Copyright © 2000, American Association for Artificial Intelligence (www.aaai.org). All rights reserved.

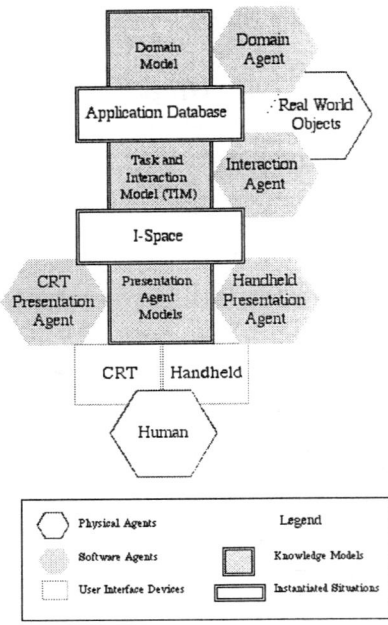

Figure 1: DIGBE Architecture

Architecture

The DIGBE architecture contains three basic knowledge structures, each manipulated by different types of software agents. A *domain agent* manages understanding of the relevant data in the real world. An *interaction design agent* performs automatic compositional interaction design. And a *presentation agent* determines how to present these interactions on the user's selected interaction device.

Each DIGBE agent maintains multiple models of the kinds of objects and actions it is interested in. DIGBE's knowledge models are:

- the *Domain Model*, used by the domain agent, which defines an ontology of the objects, relationships, actions, user roles, data roles, and data types in the domain
- the *Task and Interaction Model* (TIM), used by the interaction agent, which contains a multi-layer description of a compositional process for designing interactions to support applications and their tasks
- the *Presentation Agent Models*, used by presentation agents, which contain platform-specific widget libraries and platform-generic tables of heuristics and equivalencies, allowing conversions of the above interaction designs into working user interfaces.

DIGBE also contains two shared situation representations; the Application Database—which represents the current situation in the system—is shared by the domain agent and the interaction agent, and the I-Space—which represents the current interaction—is shared by the interaction and presentation agents.

Design Process

The basis of DIGBE's adaptive design capabilities is the TIM, which has five levels:

- *Applications*, like Building Management, which are composed of tasks
- *Tasks*, like Monitoring or Specifying, which are composed of sub-tasks
- *Sub-tasks*, like Plotting or Selection, which are composed of elements
- *Element*s, like Discrete Set or Value Over Time, which are composed of primitives
- *Primitives*, like Selector and Labeler, which are the basic units of interaction

The TIM is a *self-composing productive system*. When an instance of a TIM object is created in the I-Space, that instance is responsible for adapting to the current situation and producing its own parts. Each object fine-tunes its sub-components for the specific context, based on appropriateness to the situation and the user. Using this process of self-composition, an entire interface—or only parts that have changed—can be created in real-time as needed. After an I-Space is fully composed, the interaction agent passes the interaction design to the appropriate presentation agent, which expresses the interaction using device-specific resources.

Benefits of Interaction Generation

When graphical user interfaces became practical in the 1980's, an emphasis on user interface management systems (UIMS) resulted in attempts to automate interface generation. Industry and university researchers generally concluded that user interface generation was too difficult (Szekely 1996), because it depends on human knowledge of task structures and domain requirements. In contrast, we hypothesize that the unpredictability of tasks and information available within emerging systems will only become more important, outweighing the difficulty and expense of defining and applying dynamic design knowledge. DIGBE demonstrates that dynamic interaction adaptation through separation of interface and application function is not only feasible, but possible as an automated real-time process, with minimal demand on domain semantics.

References

Penner, R. 1998. Automating User Interface Design. In Proceedings of Systems, Man, and Cybernetics 1998, San Diego.

Szekely, P. 1996. Retrospective and Challenges for Model-Based Interface Development. In Proceedings of CADUI '96, ed. J. Vanderdonckt. Namur, Belgium: Namur University Press.

User interface softbots

Robert St. Amant and Luke S. Zettlemoyer
Department of Computer Science
North Carolina State University
EGRC-CSC Box 7534
Raleigh, NC 27695-7534
stamant@csc.ncsu.edu

Softbots in the interface

Human-computer interaction (HCI) and artificial intelligence (AI) share a long history of research. Concepts such as problem spaces, goals and operators, rationality, and computational models of cognition have significantly influenced research directions in both fields. Recently the concept of *agents* has sparked a common interest among AI and HCI researchers. Our demonstration focuses on interface agents, those that assist the user in the rich, often complex environment of the graphical user interface (Maes 1994; Lieberman 1995).

Our general interest lies in the interaction between agents and their environments. Conventional interface agents interact with other applications through an application programming interface (API) or access to source code. We have developed a novel class of agents we call interface softbots, or *ibots*, that control interactive applications through the graphical user interface, as human users do (Zettlemoyer & St. Amant 1999; Zettlemoyer, St. Amant, & Dulberg 1999). Our ibots are based on a programmable substrate that provides sensors and effectors for this purpose. Sensor modules take pixel-level input from the display, run the data through image processing algorithms, and build a structured representation of visible interface objects. Effector modules generate mouse and keyboard gestures to manipulate these objects. These sensors and effectors act as the eyes and hands of an artificial user, controlled by an external cognitive system. Together the sensors, effectors, and controller provide a general-purpose means of managing interactive applications, through the same medium as a real user.

System components

Conceptually, we can break down ibot functionality into three components, as we might do with any physically realized robot: perception, action, and control.

Perception

Ibot perception relies on conventional image processing techniques. Object identification follows a three-stage process of segmentation, feature computation, and interpretation. The process starts by examining the contents of the screen buffer, at the pixel level, as shown in Figure 1. Segmentation breaks the image into pixel groups of different colors. Bottom-up feature computation follows, to associate properties such as color, bounding box points, area, and perimeter with each group. Finally, interpretation rules combine these features to identify interface objects in top-down fashion.

The process recognizes all familiar user interface controls in Microsoft Windows, including buttons, scroll bars (including the scroll box, scroll arrows, and background regions), list boxes, menu items, check boxes, radio buttons and application windows. It can even parse text, doing a simple form of optical character recognition, for the standard system typeface.

Action

Ibot effectors insert events into the operating system's event queue, resulting in actions indistinguishable from user-generated events. Primitive events include `move-mouse`, `mouse-down`, `mouse-up`, `key-down`, and `key-up`. This allows ibots to select icons, click buttons, pull down menus, turn on radio buttons, and carry out other standard, familiar operations that human users are capable of.

Control

Control of ibot sensors and effectors is through standard AI planning techniques. We find that the assumptions made by theoretically motivated planning systems (e.g., Graphplan and its relatives (Blum & Furst 1997; Weld 1999)) are

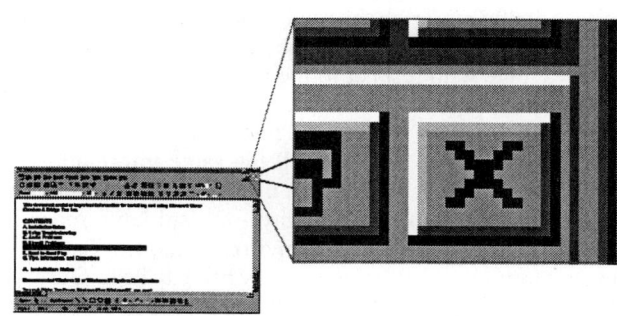

Figure 1: Source data for visual processing

closely matched by design features built into graphical user interfaces. Planners often abstract away the continuous, uncertain, dynamic, and unobservable properties of an environment, such that it becomes discrete, deterministic, static, and accessible—properties associated with broad classes of modern graphical user interfaces (St. Amant 1999). In our most recent work (St. Amant & Zettlemoyer 2000) we have developed a very simple hierarchical planner to control the perception and action components of an ibot.

The planner can direct an ibot to take a wide variety of action sequences, ranging from selecting objects to choosing pulldown menu items to more complex, domain-specific activities in the interface.

Discussion

We have built ibots for a number of interactive applications, including a word processor (St. Amant 2000), an illustration package (St. Amant & Zettlemoyer 2000), the Windows OS interface (Dulberg, St. Amant, & Zettlemoyer 1999), and even Microsoft Solitaire (Zettlemoyer & St. Amant 1999). A generic ibot architecture is shown in Figure 2. The implementation is in C++ and Common Lisp; it bears some similarity at the most basic level to the Java Robot class. The work has significant limitations, but progress has been surprisingly rapid.

Our long-term goal, as stated, is the development of ibots that can solve real-world problems of significant complexity, those that a user might be interested in to turn over to an automated system. We have only taken a few initial steps in this direction. Nevertheless, we have found ibots to be a flexible, powerful vehicle for agents research. Our preliminary work has given us insights in areas such as intelligent interaction mechanisms (Dulberg, St. Amant, & Zettlemoyer 1999), programming by demonstration (St. Amant *et al.* 2000), user interface evaluation (Zettlemoyer, St. Amant, & Dulberg 1999), programmable user models (St. Amant, Riedl, & Zettlemoyer 2000), and most importantly the relationship between AI planning and the user interface (St. Amant 1999; St. Amant & Zettlemoyer 2000; Zettlemoyer & St. Amant 1999).

We believe that our work on ibots sets the stage, in the longer term, for agents that can use interactive applications with all the facility of human users. Consider the human-oriented environments that agents can act in today: robots in offices, hallways, or on the road, or softbots moving through file systems and over the Internet. Agents are often at some disadvantage with respect to their sensing and effecting capabilities in these environments, in comparison with human agents. In contrast, ibots in the restrictive environment of a user interface have access to all the same information and all the same actions that human users have, with little or no degradation in quantity or quality—the only difference between users and agents in this environment is the knowledge and cognitive processing power they bring to bear. Our work will level the playing field for humans and agents solving real-world problems in an extremely powerful and flexible environment.

References

Blum, A., and Furst, M. 1997. Fast planning through planning graph analysis. *Artificial Intelligence* 90:281–300.

Dulberg, M. S.; St. Amant, R.; and Zettlemoyer, L. 1999. An imprecise mouse gesture for the fast activation of controls. In Proceedings of INTERACT '99, 375–382.

Lieberman, H. 1995. Letizia : An agent that assists web browsing. In Proceedings of the International Joint Conference on Artificial Intelligence, 924–929.

Maes, P. 1994. Agents that reduce work and information overload. *Communications of the ACM* 37(7):31–40.

St. Amant, R., and Zettlemoyer, L. S. 2000. The user interface as an agent environment. Forthcoming.

St. Amant, R.; Lieberman, H.; Potter, R.; and Zettlemoyer, L. S. 2000. Visual generalization in programming by example. *Communications of the ACM* 43(3):107–114.

St. Amant, R.; Riedl, M. O.; and Zettlemoyer, L. S. 2000. A practical perception substrate for cognitive modeling in HCI. Forthcoming.

St. Amant, R. 1999. User interface affordances in a planning representation. *Human Computer Interaction* 14(3):317–354.

St. Amant, R. 2000. Interface agents as surrogate users. Forthcoming.

Weld, D. S. 1999. Recent advances in AI planning. *AI Magazine* 20(2):93–123.

Zettlemoyer, L., and St. Amant, R. 1999. A visual medium for programmatic control of interactive applications. In CHI '99 (ACM Conference on Human Factors in Computing), 199–206.

Zettlemoyer, L.; St. Amant, R.; and Dulberg, M. S. 1999. Ibots: Agent control through the user interface. In Proceedings of the Fifth International Conference on Intelligent User Interfaces, 31–37.

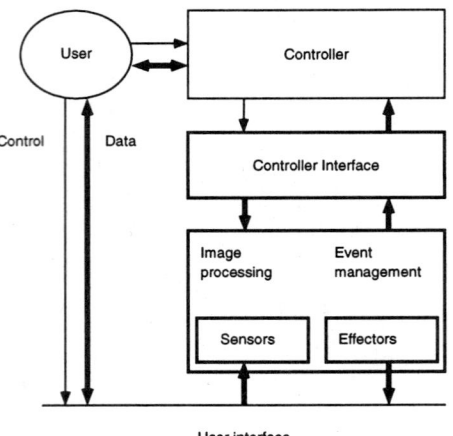

Figure 2: A generic ibot architecture

O-Plan: a Web-based AI Planning Agent

Austin Tate, Jeff Dalton and John Levine

Artificial Intelligence Applications Institute
Division of Informatics, The University of Edinburgh,
80 South Bridge, Edinburgh, EH1 1HN, UK.
{a.tate, j.dalton, j.levine}@ed.ac.uk
http://www.aiai.ed.ac.uk/~oplan/

Abstract

In these demonstrations we show O-Plan, an AI planning agent working over the WWW. There are a number of demonstrations ranging from a simple "single shot" generation of Unix systems administration scripts through to comprehensive use of AI technologies across the whole planning lifecycle in military and civilian crisis situations The applications are derived from actual user requirements and domain knowledge. The AI planning technologies demonstrated include:
- Domain knowledge elicitation
- Rich plan representation and use
- Hierarchical Task Network Planning
- Detailed constraint management
- Goal structure-based plan monitoring
- Dynamic issue handling
- Plan repair in low and high tempo situations
- Interfaces for users with different roles
- Management of planning and execution workflow

The featured demonstrations, and others, are available at http://www.aiai.ed.ac.uk/~oplan/isd/

Introduction

O-Plan (Currie and Tate, 1991; Tate et. al., 1998; Tate et.al, 2000) is shown running as a planning agent on the world wide web. Other AI planning technologies used include a planning domain editor and knowledge acquisition methodology (Polyak, 1998; Tate et.al. 1998), execution monitoring support (Reece and Tate, 1994), plan repair methods (Drabble et. al, 1996), planning workflow and process management panels (Tate et.al., 1999). These are used in a range of progressively more challenging situations in the featured demonstrations. The O-Plan system employs an underlying representation of plans termed <I-N-OVA> which expresses plans as a set of constraints on behaviour (Tate, 1996a).

In the later demonstrations, the work provides a rare example of a comprehensive use of AI technologies across the whole planning lifecycle, set in a realistic application in which the actual user community set the requirements and provided the domain knowledge employed.

Copyright© 2000, American Association for Artificial Intelligence (www.aaai.org). All rights reserved.

The demonstrations are available on-line at http://www.aiai.ed.ac.uk/~oplan/isd/ where full details, sample scenarios, maps, demonstration scripts, and access to a copy of the code of the system itself are available for educational and further research purposes. A password is required to run some of the longer demonstrations. This is available on request to oplan@ed.ac.uk

Unix Systems Administration Scripts

We recommend you start with a simple demonstration such as the Unix Systems Administrators Script writing aid (a very simple packaged use of planning technology accessible over the web). Fill in the form for your requirements on mapping physical to logical Unix disk volumes, and it writes the script for you. The maintenance of such scripts in Unix was proving problematic for a Unix system vendor to maintain. The demonstration shows how AI planning can be used in such cases where the basic ingredients used are not very numerous, but the way they can be combined varies.

Pacifica Non-combatant Evacuation Operations (NEO)

After that, try a simple prepackaged disaster relief planning aid. You select the number of people to be evacuated from various places around the island of Pacifica and the local circumstances (for example stormy weather will prevent helicopters from being used). O-Plan will then generate one plan that may be suitable. This example introduces one of the domains that we use in our later more comprehensive demonstrations, but in a very simple form.

Pacifica Disaster Relief using COA/Evaluation Matrix Interface

In the next demonstration we provide a Course of Action (COA)/Evaluation Matrix interface to enable the user to develop a number of options or alternatives using different initial conditions or differing objectives and guidance. We recommend that you start with a simple matrix interface demonstration for Pacifica Disaster Relief. It does not need a password. This demonstration introduces the type of COA/Evaluation Matrix interface we use in most of our work (ate et.al., 1999), but in a simple single user role form. You just list the types of problem to be addressed, give some information about the local circumstances and time available, then generate a plan in a one shot exercise (without interacting with the planner in a mixed initiative mode) and view the results. You can move on and generate other options with different initial conditions and different objectives if you wish.

Pacifica Disaster Relief using Multi-user Role COA/Evaluation Matrix Interface

If you feel comfortable with the earlier demonstrations and have a little more time available (15 minutes is suggested), then move on to one of the demonstrations needing a password. The COA/Evaluation matrix interface in this more comprehensive Pacifica Island Disaster Recovery demonstration allows for multiple users with different roles to work together with automated planning agent in a mixed initiative fashion. User roles can be as commander/task assigner or planner. The Planning Process Panel (Tate et.al. 1999) interface supports the coordination of the planning process between users and the automated planning agent in the development of multiple options at various stages of generation and evaluation.

You do not need to type in a session name unless several users want to engage in collaborative development of the options (in which case they should select different user roles from those available in the pull down menu, and type in a session name which they have agreed).

US Army Small Unit Operations using Multi-user Role COA/Evaluation Matrix Interface

In this final demonstration, we have identified the stages in the overall Small Unit Operations SUO) command, planning and execution process at US Army company level from receipt of mission through to a successful outcome and after-action activities (US Army, 1999). Within this process there are opportunities for a range of planning and decision aids, all facilitated by a common approach to representing the objectives and plans involved.

The demonstration (Tate et. al., 2000) addresses all the phases of the operation. It uses O-Plan and its associated planning technology to address the whole lifecycle of the generation and use of plans:
- Domain and initial plan representation
- Deliberative initial planning and generation of multiple options
- Plan execution monitoring and dynamic repair of plans
- Tailored interfaces for various user roles including planning process workflow support

Further information of the technology employed in these demonstrations is available in the references below or at the O-Plan Home Page (http://www.aiai.ed.ac.uk/~oplan/).

Acknowledgements

The O-Plan project is sponsored by the Defense Advanced Research Projects Agency (DARPA) and the U.S. Air Force Research Laboratory (AFRL) via the Planning Initiative (Tate, 1996b) under grant number F30602-99-1-0024. The U.S. Government and the University of Edinburgh are authorized to reproduce and distribute reprints for their purposes notwithstanding any copyright annotation hereon.

References

Currie, K. and Tate, A., 1991, O-Plan: the Open Planning Architecture, Artificial Intelligence, Vol. 52, pp.49-86, Elsevier, 1991.

Polyak, S., 1998, A Common Process Methodology for Engineering Process Domains, *Proceedings of the Systems Engineering for Business Process Change (SEBPC) workshop*, University of Ulster, March 1999.

Reece, G., and Tate, A., 1994, Synthesizing Protection Monitors from Causal Structure, *Proceedings of the Second International Conference on Planning System*, Chicago, June, AAAI Press.

Tate, A., 1996a, Representing Plans as a Set of Constraints – the <I-N-OVA> Model, *in Proceedings of the Third International Conference on Artificial Intelligence Planning Systems*, Edinburgh, UK.

Tate, A. (ed.), 1996b, *Advanced Planning Technology: Technological Achievements of the ARPA/Rome Laboratory Planning Initiative*, AAAI Press.

Tate, A., Dalton, J., and Levine, J., 1998, Generation of multiple qualitatively different plans, *Proceedings of the 4th International Conference on AI Planning System*, Pittsburgh, USA.

Tate, A., Levine, J., Dalton, J., and Aitken, S., 1999, O-P3: Supporting the Planning Process using Open Planning Process Panels, *Proceedings of the AAAI Workshop on Agent Based Systems in the Business Context*, AAAI-Press WS-99-02.

Tate, A., Levine, J., Jarvis, P., and Dalton, J., 2000, Using AI Planning Technology for Army Small Unit Operations, Proceedings of the Fifth International Conference on Artificial Intelligence Planning Systems (AIPS_2000), May 2000.

Tate, A., Polyak, S., Jarvis, P., 1998, TF Method: An Initial Framework for Modeling and Analyzing Planning Domains, *Proceedings of the AIPS-98 workshop on Knowledge Engineering and Acquisition for Planning: Bridging Theory and Practice*, AAAI Technical Report WS-98-03.

US Army, 1999, Center for Army Lessons Learned, Virtual Research Library, http://call.army.mil

Customer Coalitions in the Electronic Marketplace

M. Tsvetovat, K. Sycara, Y. Chen and J. Ying

The Robotics Institute
Carnegie Mellon University
Pittsburgh, USA.

Abstract

In the last few years, the electronic marketplace has witnessed an exponential growth in worth and size, and projections are for this trend to intensify in coming years. While the Internet offers great possiblities for creation of spontaneous communities, this potential has not been explored as a means for creating economies of scale among similar-minded customers.

This demonstration (TSCY00) [1] will illustrate the economic incentives behind formation of buying clubs and achivement of effect of economies of scale within temporary agent coalitions. The demonstration will also focus on coalition formation mechanisms for creation of such buying clubs.

Introduction

A coalition is a set of self-interested agents that agree to cooperate to execute a task or achieve a goal. Such coalitios were thoroughly investigated within game theory (Pel84; RZ94; SS97; SLA+99). There, issues of solution stability, fairness and payoff disbursements were discussed and analyzed. The formal analysis provided there can be used to compute multi-agent coalitions, however only in a centralized manner and with exponential complexity. DAI researchers (SLA+99; SS97) have adopted some of the game-theoretical concepts and upon them developed coalition formation algorithms, to be used by agents within a multi-agent system. These algorithms concentrate on distribution of computations, complexity reduction, efficient task allocation and communication issues. Nevertheless, some of the underlying assumptions of the coalition formation algorithms, which are essential for their implementation, do not hold in real-world multi-agent systems.

This demonstration will illustrate the economic incentives behind formation of buying clubs and achivement of effect of economies of scale within temporary agent coalitions. The demonstration will also focus on coalition formation mechanisms for creation of such buying clubs.

The demonstration will start by illustrating the protocol and scenarios in coalition formation, and presenting the economic models that show how both suppliers and customers can benefit from advent of such buying clubs (i.e. *incentives* to create buying clubs), which are critical in any real-world system. We will proceed by demonstrating a multi-agent system that implements formation of buying clubs based on abovementioned mechanisms. Coference attendees would be able to interact with the system using a web-based interface, and form buying clubs for procurement of technical books. This system would be used to collect empirical data on user's reactions to different coalition formation scenarios in a real-world setting, as well as data on economic incentives in a situation that maximally approaches real world deployment of such a system.

Issues in Design of Coalition Systems

It is possible to construct a number of coalition models and protocols, all of which would have different properties and requirements. In general, all coalition models include several stages:

- **Negotiation:** The coalition leader or representative negotiates with one or more suppliers to provide the good or service, addressing the choice of suppliers, and evaluation of competetive bids.

- **Coalition Formation:** The coalition leader solicits new members to join his coalition, based on a set of admission constraints.

- **Leader Election/Voting:** The members elect a coalition leader or cast direct votes for or against certain bids.

- **Payment Collection:** The coalition leader or third party collects the payments from coalition members and is responsible for conveying the full amount to the supplier

- **Execution/Distribution stage:** As a transaction is executed and the purchased goods arrive, they must be distributed to the members of the coalition.

As one designs a coalition protocol, he must take into account issues such as coalition stability, distribution of costs and risks among coalition memebers, allocation of utility after the transaction is completed, and need for trust in members of coalition, suppliers or third parties.

Most coalition protocols can be divided into two classes (*pre-negotiation and post-negotiation*), based on the order in which negotiation and coalition formation happen. In pre-negotiated coalitions, the coalition leader negotiates a deal with one or more suppliers using an estimated coalition size or order volume, and then advertises the creation of the coalition and waits for other members to join. In pre-negotiation protocols, the coalition leader must estimate the group size and thus carries the risk of not being able to form a suitable coalition. Other pre-negotiation protocols may shift some of the risk onto coalition members (by introducing a small price uncertainty) or onto the supplier.

In post-negotiation scenario, the group is formed first, based on some admission criteria. Then, a group leader negotiates with suppliers, and offers the resulting deal to the group. Here, the group must be able to trust its leader to negotiate on its behalf. Unless the group is formed by a number of people who know each other through other channels (i.e. a group of students in a class), there would have to be an explicit leader selection/verification mechanism, or a mechanism for collective negotiation.

Demonstration System

In order to verify the abovementioned hypotheses, we have designed a flexible test-bed that can be used to evaluate different coalition creation protocols, as well as determine the real-world feasibility of automated agent-based coalition formation and negotiation protocols.

As an initial problem domain, we chose collective book purchasing. Often, in the university setting, one sees large number of students that are enrolled in the same class purchasing the same books reqiored for a class. Such groups are natural coalitions, given the ease of collection of payments and distribution of goods, and a large number of potential users of the system.

The testbed system (see figure 1) consists of a coalition server, an auctioneer agent, set of supplier agents, and a web-based interface for end users. The system is based on a simple pre-negotiation protocol.

Users use the WWW interface to conduct reverse auctions with supplier agents. The supplier agents, in turn, are given a step function volume discount schedule and make their bids accordingly to projected sizes of coalitions. After the reverse auction is complete, the coalition server opens the coalition to new members, which can join the group if they meet the entrance requirements. After the group is formed, the coalition server proceeds to execute the transaction.

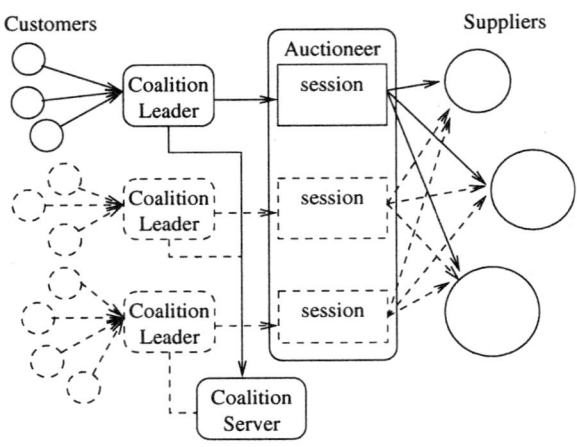

Figure 1: System Architecture

Conclusion

The demonstration system will illustrate issues in formation of spontaneous buying clubs and offer conference attendees a chance to have a hands-on experience with coalition formation in a virtual market environment.

References

B Peleg. *Game Theoretic Analysis of Voting in Commities.* Cambridge University Press, 1984.

Jeffrey Rosenschein and Gilad Zlotkin. *Rules of Encounter.* MIT Press, Cambridge, MA, 1994.

T. Sandholm, K. Larson, M. Andersson, O. Shehory, and F. Tohme. Coalition structure generation with worst case guarantees. *Artificial Intelligence Journal*, 1999.

O. Shehory and K. Sycara. Multi-agent coordination through coalition formation. In *Proceedings of the Agent Theories, Languages and Methodologies (ATAL97)*, 1997.

M. Tsvetovat, K. Sycara, Y. Chen, and J. Ying. Customer coalitions in the electronic marketplace. In *Proceedings of Fourth International Conference on Autonomous Agents, to appear*, June 2000.

Non-Axiomatic Reasoning System (Version 4.1)

Pei Wang
Research Division, Intelligenesis Corporation
and
Center for Research on Concepts and Cognition, Indiana University
http://www.cogsci.indiana.edu/farg/pwang.html

Introduction

NARS (Non-Axiomatic Reasoning System) is an intelligent reasoning system. It answers questions according to the knowledge originally provided by its user. What makes it different from conventional reasoning systems is its ability to learn from its experience and to work with insufficient knowledge and resources.

The NARS 4.1 demo is a Java applet. It comes with help information and simple examples to show how the system does deduction, induction, abduction, analogy, belief revision, membership evaluation, relational inference, backward inference, new concept formation, and so on, in a unified manner.

The demo also allows its user to create new examples to test the system, as well as to see the internal structure and process when the system is running. The on-line help document contains links to relevant publications.

A previous version of the system, NARS 3.0, is described in detail in (Wang, 1995), which, and other related publications, are available at the author's web page.

The System

NARS is based on the conjecture that what we call "intelligence" can be built into a computer system by making it to adapt to its experience, that is, to answer questions according to available knowledge and resources.

Concretely, it means that the system should open to new knowledge and questions in real time, and answer questions according to its available knowledge when the knowledge and resources are insufficient to provide a perfect answer.

Knowledge Representation

NARS does not use first-order predicate logic. Instead, each piece of knowledge in NARS has the form "$SrP < f, c >$". Here S is the subject term, and P is the predicate term. In the simplest situation, both of them are words. r is an inheritance relation. In this demo, three types of inheritance relations can be used:

- "$S \subset P$" means that "S is a special type of P";
- "$S \in P$" means that "S is an instance of P";
- "$S = P$" means that "S and P are similar to each other".

"$< f, c >$" is the truth value of the sentence, where f is the "frequency", a real number in [0, 1], indicating the ratio of positive evidence among all evidence of the relation, and c is the "confidence", a real number in (0, 1), indicating the amount of evidence the system has on the relation.

Each question that can be asked to the system has the form SrP. A question looks just like a piece of knowledge, except that there is no truth value, and that S or P (but not both) can be a special symbol "?". A question without "?" is like a "yes/no" question — the system is asked to evaluate the truth value of the given relation. A question with "?" is like a "what" question — the system is asked to find a term that have more positive evidence and less negative evidence for the given relation.

Since the confidence of a piece of knowledge cannot reach 1.0, no answer is absolutely sure. Instead, the system needs to compare the available candidates to choose a "best answer", which may be overturned by new knowledge or further consideration.

Inference Rules

The following basic rules are involved in this demo. Each of them in NARS takes two pieces of existing knowledge as premises, and derive a piece of new knowledge as conclusion. The premises must share at least one common term.

$$
\begin{array}{cc}
\textbf{Revision} & \textbf{Deduction} \\
S \subset P < f_1, c_1 > & S \subset M < f_1, c_1 > \\
S \subset P < f_2, c_2 > & M \subset P < f_2, c_2 > \\
\hline
S \subset P < f, c > & S \subset P < f, c >
\end{array}
$$

$$
\begin{array}{cc}
\textbf{Abduction} & \textbf{Induction} \\
S \subset M < f_1, c_1 > & M \subset S < f_1, c_1 > \\
P \subset M < f_2, c_2 > & M \subset P < f_2, c_2 > \\
\hline
S \subset P < f, c > & S \subset P < f, c >
\end{array}
$$

$$
\begin{array}{cc}
\textbf{Analogy} & \textbf{Comparison} \\
S \subset M < f_1, c_1 > & S \subset M < f_1, c_1 > \\
M = P < f_2, c_2 > & P \subset M < f_2, c_2 > \\
\hline
S \subset P < f, c > & S = P < f, c >
\end{array}
$$

Since by definition $S \in P$ is identical to $\{S\} \subset P$, rules on the "$\in$" relation can be derived from those on the "$\subset$" relation.

In each rule, there is a truth value function that calculate the strength and confidence of the conclusion ($<f, c>$) from those of the premises ($<f_1, c_1>$ and $<f_2, c_2>$). Different rule use different function.

According to how the confidence c is calculated, the above rules can be put into three categories:

1. In Deduction and Analogy, the confidence of the conclusion can be very close to the confidence of a premise, so these types of inference can produce relatively sure answers.

2. In Abduction, Induction, and Comparison, the confidence of the conclusion is always much lower than that of the premises, so these types of inference are more tentative.

3. Revision is the only rule where the confidence of the conclusion is higher than that of the promises, because this rule merges the evidence of the premises into that of the conclusion.

Besides these basic rules, NARS 4.1 also has compound-term composition and decomposition rules, such as "$S \subset (P1 \cap P2)$ if and only if $S \subset P1$ and $S \subset P2$". Another type of rule is backward inference rule that derive question from question and knowledge, such as from available knowledge "$S \subset M$" and question "$? \in M$" to derive a new question "$? \in S$", whose answer and the knowledge can derive an answer to the original question. This kind of rule allows the system to work in a goal-directed manner.

Control Mechanism

Because of the assumption of real time input, NARS cannot work on a task at a time, but must allow multiple tasks to be under processing at the same time. Because of the assumption of insufficient knowledge and resources, it cannot assume that all tasks will be processed to their "logical end", or to be solved by considering all relevant knowledge in the system.

Instead, the system processes multiple inference tasks by time-sharing. Each task is given a priority value, which indicates the frequency for it to be processed for a time slice. After a task is selected for processing, a piece of knowledge is also selected according to a priority distribution, then the derived task and knowledge are put back into the task pool and knowledge base, and the priority of the involved task and knowledge is adjusted according to the feedback obtained in this inference step.

When an answer is found for a user question, it is reported, then the system continue to look for a better one, if the task still have a high enough priority.

The Demonstration

NARS has been implemented several times. The current version, 4.1, is a Java applet which is available at the author's web page. There is also a file for download, which contains both the code and the documentation.

User Interface

The user interface of NARS 4.1 allows the user to provide knowledge and questions to the system in a text field. The system will return answers to the questions in another window. Since the timing of input influences the system's processing, the user can also specify the number of inference steps allowed between input events.

The user can let the system to work step by step, or to run continuously. The user can open several display windows to watch the internal inference process, as well as the content and priority distribution of the task pool and knowledge base.

There are several system parameters the user can adjust to change the system's behavior, such as the forgetting rate of the knowledge base, and so on.

There is an on-line User's Guide that explains how the demo can be used.

Examples

The NARS 4.1 demo has a set of examples attached, and each of which shows a basic function or property of the system. By observing how the examples are processed in the system, the user can get direct experience on how the system works.

The examples include: input and output, context sensitivity, deduction, induction, abduction, mixed inference, confidence processing, backward inference, contradiction handling, similarity evaluation, compound term formation, Hempel's paradox, relation operators, and fuzzy concept formation.

In the on-line documentation, each example comes with a simple explanation about the system's processing and the result, as well as links to related publications.

All of these examples can be given to the system by copy/paste. When a user becomes familiar enough to the system, he or she can create new examples to test the system, as long as they can be expressed in the formal language of NARS.

These examples show that NARS is different from other reasoning systems in terms of the knowledge representation language, the semantics of the language, the inference rules, the knowledge base structure, the control mechanism, and the relation with users. NARS provides a unified solution to many problems that are traditionally handled in isolation to one another.

References

Wang, P. 1995. Non-Axiomatic Reasoning System: Exploring the essence of intelligence. Ph.D. diss., Dept. of Computer Science and Program of Cognitive Science, Indiana Univ.

Untangle: A new ontology for card catalog systems

Christopher Welty and Jessica Jenkins

Vassar College Computer Science Dept.
Poughkeepsie, NY 12604-0462
weltyc@cs.vassar.edu
http://untangle.cs.vassar.edu/

Abstract

The ontology used by most card catalog and bibliographic systems is based on a now outdated assumption that users of the systems would be looking for *books on shelves,* and therefore only books were first-class objects, with people, organizations, etc. as simple attributes. This limited the ability of a user to browse. A new ontology for card catalog systems is proposed that suggests that persons, organizations, conferences, etc., should be first-class objects with attributes and relations of their own, creating a rich space of background information that helps users find what they are looking for. This new ontology has been implemented in a knowledge-based system called Untangle, which demonstrates two key advantages of this rich information space: it enables automatic augmentation of the data through reasoning, and it enables a new paradigm for search that combines querying and browsing.

Introduction

Library card-catalog systems are quite old, with evidence of recorded indexes dating back at least as far as the 12th century. Through the centuries the underlying assumption of these systems – implicit or explicit – was simple: the only object of any search is a book. This assumption led to an *ontology* that still exists today: the only type of object in a card-catalog system is a book, which has attributes such as author, title, publisher, date, etc. While we understand that these attributes correspond to people, organizations, etc., in implemented systems they are nothing more than strings.

As the size of, and access to, libraries increase dramatically with modern communication, this ontology no longer serves, and a new ontology, that supports a new paradigm in library search, is called for. The new ontology supports the notion that persons, places, events, organizations, etc., are first-class objects, and that a user *browsing* through the information may submit individual queries whose results may be these objects, *not books*. For the web, the consequence of this is the same, the result of an individual query does not always have to be a web page. A search may be for information about a person, place, organization, etc.

This implies that search must be, in this age of information, an iterative process that alternates between *browsing* the information space, and *querying* it. The results of queries will be new starting places for browsing, and information discovered during browsing may suggest new queries, since clearly users may not have perfect knowledge of what they are looking for.

We present here the ontology of the Untangle system, and then describe the system itself, which is available on the web.

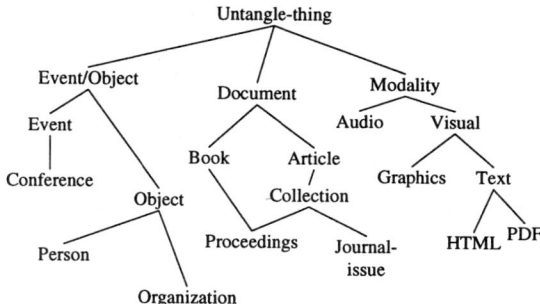

Figure 1: Taxonomy of Untangle concepts.

The Ontology

The Untangle Ontology contains two types of objects: things related to topics (TOPICAL-THING) and things related to entities in the real world (UNTANGLE-THING). A more complete description of topic related issues can be found in (Welty and Jenkins, 1999), and will not be discussed here.

Basic Types

The domain of real entities for Untangle is split into three main types: Modalities, Documents, and Event/Objects (Welty, 1996). Some of the taxonomy is shown in Figure 1, and in the demo you can select "list the main objects in the ontology" to get a textual view of the ontology taxonomy.

Documents are the central objects in the system. The background information is there mainly to support finding these objects. Although the result of any particular query may be any type of object, it is assumed that the result of any sustained interaction will be a document. The document hierarchy is fairly straightforward, and was derived from Bibtex with a few extras added for web support.

Modalities are an object type which are used to represent the physical manifestations of a document in the real world (Welty, 1998). A single document, e.g. a book, may have a published hard-copy version, an on-line PDF version, an on-line HTML version, and an audio-cassette version. Each of these real things are *the same book*, they share the author, title, subject, they contain the same information. They each also have attributes of their own; on-line versions have a URL and format, hardcopy books have a shelving code, etc. In addition to making more sense, breaking these attributes out of the document object makes it possible to represent the fact that several web pages may be the same thing, and therefore returning a single "hit" for a query instead of one per web page helps prune and narrow search results.

Event/Objects are the background information that enhances the catalog and makes browsing possible. Events are things like conferences, workshops, etc., that often result in people getting together exchanging information and publishing papers. It is not unusual, for example, for a person to search for a paper they remember *hearing* at a conference, without remembering the author or title. Objects are things like people and organizations.

Relationships

Each type of object has a set of attributes and relationships that help define it. To explore the ontology and see the relationships defined for each type of entity, in the demo you may click on "list the main objects in the ontology" and then click on any concept. Another good starting place is "explore the Untangle topic space" select some topics, and then look at the entities classified under that topic. Each entity has links for all the entities it is related to.

The complete set of relationships for each object can be accessed through the demo, we provide here the basic set of relationships for navigating through the space.

Articles have an *author*, and are *published-in* some kind of *COLLECTION*, such as a *JOURNAL-ISSUE* or a proceedings. Collections may have editors, and are published-by an organization. A journal-issues may be an issue-of a journal, and a proceedings is the proceedings-of a conference. A conference has participants, a location, and is sponsored by an organization. A person may have an affiliation, and may be a student-of some school. We also support former-employee-of and former-student-of.

Reasoning

In addition to supporting combined querying and browsing, the new ontology supports reasoning to enrich the information space. The main point of using a KR system instead of a database is that reasoning can be used to enhance the data that can be automatically mined from existing bibliographic databases. The bulk of the reasoning is used to support the spatial representation of topics used in the system, and to support data consistency. We describe here a few examples of the reasoning over the types described above that are used to augment the data:

- A publisher is any organization that publishes something.
- Two people are collaborators if they are authors of the same document.
- A person participates in a conference if they author a paper published in the conference proceedings.
- A person is interested in a topic if they write a paper on that subject.
- If a person is an employee-of a department, they are an employee-of the organization the department is a part of.

Demo Tour

Click on the small blue "home" icon at the bottom of the screen to get to the untangle home page, or go to the URL: http://untangle.cs.vassar.edu/. The first three links in the list you see are the main links for exploring the demo.

Let's say you're looking for articles on ontologies for information systems. You remember hearing a talk about this at a conference in Florida some years ago.

1. Hit the "query" link on the Untangle home page.
2. Select conference from the taxonomy (under event).
3. Type "Florida" into the text box labelled "location", and click "do it." The result is a list of conferences in Florida.
4. Click on "FLAIRS-96" (you can select it with the radio button, but in this case clicking on it is a shortcut). The result is a dynamically generated page that describes all the information the system has about the conference. At this point you may recognize someone in the list of participants. Let's say you don't.
5. Click on the proceedings. This results in a list of articles published in the proceedings (and in the knowledge base). You notice one, "Intelligent Assistance for Navigating the Web." which sounds familiar.
6. Click on it. You get information on this article. Aha! That's the one. Now you see in the list of topics "formal ontologies in information systems."
7. Click on that topic, and you get a list of people, events, publications, and organizations that have been classified under this topic.

Continue to explore. The icons on the bottom of every page go to the home page, to the query page, and to the FAQ page.

References

Welty, Chris and Jenkins, Jessica. An Ontology for Subject. *J. Data and Knowledge Engineering.* **31**(2):155-182. September, 1999. Elsevier.

Welty, Chris and Ide, Nancy. Using the Right Tools: Enhancing Retrieval of Marked-Up Documents. *J. Computers in the Humanities.* Summer, 1999. 33(10):59-84. Kluwer.

Welty, Chris. Towards an Ontology for Library Modalities. In S. Ali, ed. *Proceedings of the AAAI-98 Workshop on Representations for Multi-Modal Human-Computer Interaction.* AAAI Press. July, 1998.

Welty, Chris. Intelligent Assistance for Web Navigation. *Proceedings of the 1996 Florida AI Research Symposium.* May, 1996.

Welty, Chris. A Knowledge-Based Email Distribution System. *Proceedings of the 1994 Florida AI Research Symposium.* Journal of AI Press. May, 1994.

Robot Competition and Exhibition

Symbol Recognition and Artificial Emotion for Making an Autonomous Robot Attend the AAAI Conference

François Michaud, Dominic Létourneau, Jonathan Audet and François Bélanger

LABORIUS - Research Laboratory on Mobile Robotics and Intelligent Systems
Department of Electrical and Computer Engineering
Université de Sherbrooke, Sherbrooke (Québec Canada) J1K 2R1
{michaudf,letd01,audj01,belf02}@gel.usherb.ca
http://www.gel.usherb.ca/laborius

Introduction

LABORIUS is a young research laboratory interested in designing autonomous systems that can assist human in real life tasks. To do so, robots require some sort of "social intelligence", giving them the ability to interact with various types of agents (humans, animals, robots and other physical agents). Our team of robots is made of six Pioneer 2 robots, three indoor and three outdoor models, with each robot equipped with 16 sonars, a compass, a gripper, a camera with a frame grabber and a Fast Track Vision System, a RF Ethernet-modem connection and a Pentium 233 MHz PC-104 onboard computer. The programming environment used is Ayllu (Werger 2000), a tool for development of behavior-based control systems for intelligent mobile robots.

Figure 1: Hercules, the Pioneer 2 robot that will attempt to attend AAAI'2000.

According to Dautenhahn (Dautenhahn 1999), three important characteristics of social robotics are that 1) agents can recognize and interact with each other and engage in social interactions as a prerequisite to developing social relationships, 2) agents can explicitly communicate with each other, and 3) agents have 'histories' and they perceive and interpret the world in terms of their own experiences. The first two characteristics have been accomplished mostly by using explicit radio communication of the position of the robots, obtained by a positioning system (GPS or radio triangulation), and by using other electronic media communication method (like infrared) (Cao, Fukunaga, & Kahng 1997). Vision is also put to contribution, for instance by using color recognition (e.g., RoboCup and (Michaud & Vu 1999)). Using vision for agent recognition and communication does not limit interaction to specific environments, and it is an ability that humans and animals have. One mechanism that we are currently developing it to make a robot capable of recognizing symbols used to identify other agents or to give indications to the robot.

Another project that we are working on is concerned with the concept of artificial emotion (Michaud *et al.* 2000), which is increasingly used in designing autonomous robotic agents. Artificial emotion has up to now been principally used in making robots respond emotionally to situations experienced in the world or to interactions with humans (Velásquez 1998; Breazeal 1998). However, they can also play an important role in solving what is called the **universal problems of adaptation** (Plutchik 1980): hierarchy, territoriality, identity and temporality. Artificial emotion can help a robot manage its own limitations in interacting with the world, interact socially with others and establish a shared meaning for interpersonal communication.

We plan to use our symbol recognition mechanism and the concept of artificial emotion to take part to the *Robot Challenge* and make a Pioneer 2 AT robot attend the AAAI Conference. The goal is to use signs to guide the robot to the registration desk, to let the robot move around in the crowd, recognize dignitaries and recharge itself whenever necessary, go to a conference room and give a short presentation, in HTML using a Web interface, about the whole experience.

Symbol Recognition

Social interaction in a heterogeneous group of robots and humans can be done in various ways: gesture, signs, speech, sounds, touch, etc. Making a robot recognize printed signs

---

Copyright © 2000, American Association for Artificial Intelligence (www.aaai.org). All rights reserved.

is an interesting idea because it can be a very general method for robots to communicate information to and identify each other.

Our symbol recognition technique is done in four steps: 1) image segmentation using colors, 2) robot positioning, 3) features extraction of color segments and 4) symbol identification using an artificial neural network. Image segmentation is achieved using 32 colors and commodity hardware (Bruce, Balch, & Veloso 2000). Each recognizable symbol are assumed to be contained in one segment, i.e., all the pixels of the same color representing the symbol must be connected (8 neighbors) together to avoid recombination of boundary boxes. The robot positioning phase consists of orienting the robot using the Sony Pan-Tilt-Zoom camera, and to extract black on white printed symbols in the robot's environment. Special symbols like arrows and letters are used to guide the robot to specific locations. Features extraction are rotation and scaling independent, using a centroid based method. Finally, character identification is implemented with a standard back-propagation network. The network is trained with designated symbols of different rotations, scales and noise ratios.

Software Architecture with Artificial Emotion

The fundamental objective of the robot's software architecture is to combine various properties associated with 'intelligence', like reactivity, emergence, situatedness, planning, deliberation and motivation, while still preserving their underlying principles (Michaud & Vu 1999). To summarize the approach, the architecture is based on behavior-producing modules (or behaviors) that are dynamically selected using modules that monitor specific conditions (which can be sensed or derived from internal mechanisms). The goals of the robot (e.g., going to the registration desk, schmooze, recharge, etc.) are managed using internal activation variables called motives (Michaud & Vu 1999). A behavior-producing module that is selected may or may not be used to control the robot, according to the sensory conditions it monitors and the arbitration mechanism used to coordinate the robot's behaviors. By observing how behavior-producing modules are used over time, the architecture can infer important information about the overall behavior of the robot in the environment. We believe this to be essential for the implementation of artificial emotions. The emotional capability is incorporated in the control architecture like a global background state, allowing emotions to influence and to be influenced by all of the architecture's modules.

The artificial emotions used for the task are related to temporality, i.e., they allow to take into consideration the limited duration of an individual's life. Sadness, distress and joy contributes in solving this adaptation problem. In our implementation, distress is used to detect external conflicts (like being trapped somewhere, stalling, not being able to grasp something, etc.) or internal conflicts (like the simultaneous activation of too many goals at once). Sadness and joy are used to prioritize the goals of the robots according to what is experienced in the world. These three emotions will be used to express the robot's state. The evolution of these states over time will be memorized for the robot's presentation. We also plan to use a simple interface to communicate these states, other information and requests with the outside world.

Current Status

As of the end of March, our symbol recognition approach has been validated off-line, and we still have to implement it on the robot. The architectural methodology with artificial emotion is functional, as for the charging station, and new behavior-producing modules and mechanisms (like for the Internet HTML presentation) specific to our participation to the AAAI *Robot Challenge* are under development. We do not plan to address the map navigation and elevator use skills of the challenge.

Acknowledgments

Research conducted by LABORIUS is supported financially by the Natural Sciences and Engineering Research Council of Canada (NSERC), the Canadian Foundation for Innovation (CFI) and the Fonds pour la Formation de Chercheurs et l'Aide à la Recherche (FCAR) of Québec.

References

Breazeal, C. 1998. Infant-like social interactions between a robot and a human caretaker. *Adaptive Behavior, special issue on Simulation Models of Social Agents*.

Bruce, J.; Balch, T.; and Veloso, M. 2000. Fast color image segmentation using commodity hardware. In *Workshop on Interactive Robotics and Entertainment*.

Cao, Y. U.; Fukunaga, A. S.; and Kahng, A. B. 1997. Cooperative mobile robotics: antecedents and directions. *Autonomous Robots* 4:1–23.

Dautenhahn, K. 1999. Embodiment and interaction in socially intelligent life-like agents. In *Computation for Metaphors, Analogy and Agent. Lecture Notes in Artificial Intelligence*, volume 1562. Springer-Verlag. 102–142.

Michaud, F., and Vu, M. T. 1999. Managing robot autonomy and interactivity using motives and visual communication. In *Proc. Conf. Autonomous Agents*, 160–167.

Michaud, F.; Prijanian, P.; Audet, J.; and Létourneau, D. 2000. Artificial emotion and social robotics. Submitted to *Fifth International Symposium on Distributed Autonomous Robotic Systems (DARS)*.

Plutchik, R. 1980. A general psychoevolutionary theory of emotion. In *Emotion: Theory, Research, and Experience*, volume 1. Academic Press. chapter 1, 3–33.

Velásquez, J. D. 1998. A computational framework for emotion-based control. In *Workshop on Grounding Emotions in Adaptive Systems, Conference on Simulation of Adaptive Behavior*.

Werger, B. B. 2000. Ayllu: Distributed port-arbitrated behavior-based control. Submitted to *Fifth International Symposium on Distributed Autonomous Robotic Systems (DARS)*.

The Blue Swarm

Dan Stormont

Utah State University
9590 Old Main Hill
Logan UT 84322-9590
stormont@hass.usu.edu

Why a swarm?

There are a number of robotics applications that require covering a large area thoroughly and in a minimum amount of time. Some examples of these types of applications are: exploring planetary bodies for items of interest, such as trace water, Helium 3, or magnetic flux lines; clearing mine fields; and the urban search and rescue (USAR) problem that will be simulated as part of the AAAI 2000 Robotics Competition. The usefulness of "swarms" of cooperating mobile robots for solving these kinds of problems is nothing new – as is evidenced by the encouragement to use multiple robots in the rules for this year's contest.

About the Blue Swarm

The Blue Swarm is named after the Utah State University mascot "Big Blue". It was started as part of the engineering project required for the EE (industry-oriented PhD) degree at Utah State. This project will take approximately two years to complete, so the swarm brought to this year's competition will demonstrate an interim capability. In fact, the USAR competition is being used as a testing ground for the first iteration of the swarm. The primary Blue Swarm will be made up of modified toy cars. The cars are "Red Fox" remote-controlled cars purchased from Kay-Bee Toys. These cars were selected because they are cheap (less than $10 each), easy to modify (the cable to the remote control can be cut, providing access to the power wires to the motors), and they have two motors for differential steering. The navigation method to be used this year is still being simulated. The three methods being compared are a random walk, preprogrammed path, and reinforcement learning without communications. The random walk method is illustrated in figure 1. As the name implies, it is just a random path through the competition area. If this method is selected, it will probably be implemented using analog circuitry. The preprogrammed path is illustrated in figure 2. This method follows a fixed path, but reacts if

Copyright © 2000, American Association for Artificial Intelligence (www.aaai.org). All rights reserved.

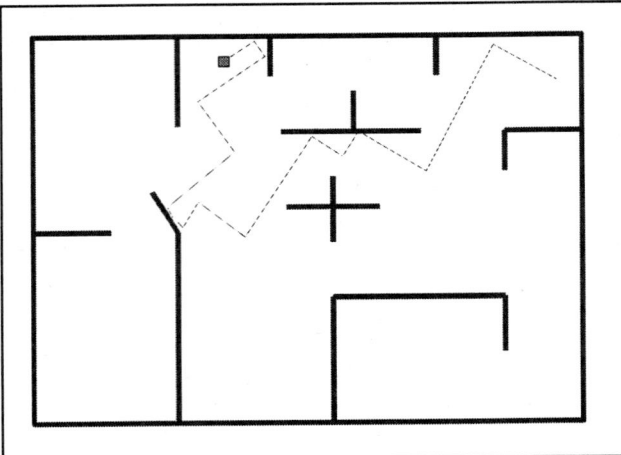

Figure 1. An example of the random walk method.

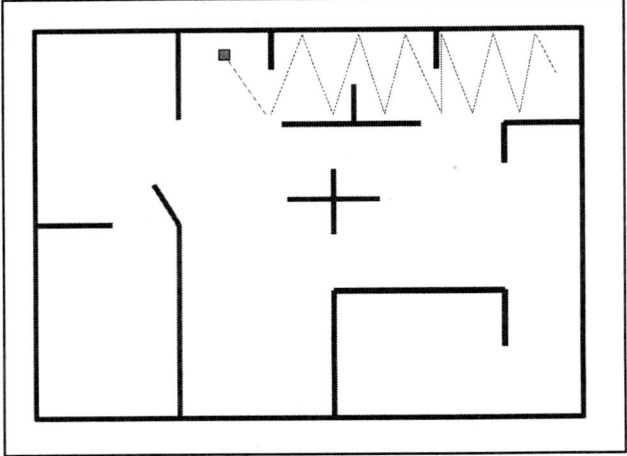

Figure 2. An example of the preprogrammed path method.

an obstacle is encountered by trying to go around the obstacle. If this method is selected as a result of simulation, it will most likely be implemented using a microcontroller like a PIC 17X or a BASIC Stamp. The reinforcement learning method will use $TD(\lambda)$ learning with a backpropagation neural network. How this will be implemented for the swarm hasn't been decided yet, if it is selected. For this first phase, none of the robots will be using inter-robot communications. The sensor to be used for the competition will be an infrared detector, so the swarm will only be able to find the infrared heat source (simulated survivor) for this year's competition. Depending on funding, there may be two more Blue Swarms at the competition: one based on the Parallax Board of Education (BOEbot) and one based on the Scorpio muscle wire legged robot.

Future Research

As mentioned above, the Blue Swarm brought to the AAAI 2000 Robot Competition is just an interim step toward a swarm that could be made suitable for planetary exploration. Between the 2000 and 2001 competitions, the swarm will be improved with the addition of inter-robot communications to enable coordination, the possible addition of other sensors, and the potential incorporation of more advanced learning algorithms. The decision about adding these capabilities will be based on the results of this year's competition and additional simulation work. More information about this project can be found at http://www.usu.edu/afrotc/cadre/stormont/swarm.html.

Invited Talks

Decision Making under Uncertainty: Operations Research meets AI (Again)

Craig Boutilier
Department of Computer Science
University of Toronto
Toronto, ON M5S 3H5
cebly@cs.toronto.edu

Abstract

Models for sequential decision making under uncertainty (e.g., Markov decision processes, or MDPs) have been studied in operations research for decades. The recent incorporation of ideas from many areas of AI, including planning, probabilistic modeling, machine learning, and knowledge representation) have made these models much more widely applicable. I briefly survey recent advances within AI in the use of fully- and partially-observable MDPs as a modeling tool, and the development of computationally-manageable solution methods. I will place special emphasis on factored problem representations such as Bayesian networks and algorithms that exploit the structure inherent in these representations.

1 AI Meets OR

When one is reminded of the crossroads where artificial intelligence (AI) meets operations research (OR), the vital and active area of combinatorial optimization immediately springs to mind. The interaction between researchers in the two disciplines has been lively and fruitful. Linear and integer programming, constraint-based optimization, stochastic local search, all have broken from their "home communities" and spurred interdisciplinary advances to the extent that it is impossible to classify much of this research as strictly AI or strictly OR (except by the affiliations of the researchers). As a result, optimization problems of incredible scale are being solved on a daily basis, and our understanding of the relative strengths of various methods and how they can be combined has advanced considerably.

AI and OR meet at another, less-traveled, less-visible crossroads, passing through the area of sequential decision making under uncertainty. Sequential decision making—that is, *planning*—has been at the core of AI since its inception. Yet only in the last half-dozen years has the planning community started to seriously investigate stochastic models. *Decision-theoretic planning* (DTP) has allowed us to move beyond the classical (deterministic, goal-based) model to tackle problems with uncertainty in action effects, uncertainty in knowledge of the system state, and multiple, conflicting objectives. In this short time, *Markov decision processes* (MDPs) have become the *de facto* conceptual model for DTP.

MDPs were introduced in the OR community in the 1950s [2] and have studied and applied in OR and stochastic optimal control for decades. Both the fully-observable and partially-observable variants (FOMDPs and POMDPs, respectively) have proven to be very effective for capturing stochastic decision problems; in fact, one might view POMDPs as offering a general model in which most sequential decision problems can be cast.[1] A number of algorithms have been developed for constructing optimal policies, for both FOMDPs [2, 27] and POMDPs [45], generally based on Bellman's dynamic programming principle.

The generality of these models and algorithms comes at a price: the modeling of any specific problem as an MDP can be tedious, and the computational cost of applying a general-purpose solution algorithm is typically very high, often too high to be practical. Thus, special problem structure must generally be exploited in order to render the models practically solvable. Examples of models with special structure include linear-quadratic control problems (using Kalman filters) for POMDPs, or queuing models for FOMDPs.

AI planning problems also exhibit considerable structure. System states are composed of a number of different features (or variables or propositions). In classical planning, this fact has been exploited to great effect in the representation of deterministic actions using STRIPS [21], the situation calculus [35, 42], and a host of other formalisms. Furthermore, classical planning techniques such as regression [47] and partial-order planning [33] have exploited the structure inherent in such representations to construct plans much more effectively (in many cases) than one can through explicit, state-based methods. Other techniques such as hierarchical abstraction, decomposition, and so on, have rendered certain types of planning problems tractable as well.

The use of MDPs for DTP requires than analogous insights be applied to the decision-theoretic generalizations of classical planning problems. Two crucial tasks are therefore:

---

[1] For example, the exploration/exploitation tradeoff in reinforcement learning and bandit problems is best formulated as a POMDPs [3]. General models of sequential games are often formulated as (multiagent extensions of) POMDPs [37]. Models from control theory such as Kalman filters [29] are also forms of POMDPs.

(1) the development of natural and concise representations for stochastic, dynamic systems and utility functions, so that MDPs can be specified in a convenient form that exploits regularity in the domain and problem structure; and (2) the development of algorithms for policy construction that exploit this structure computationally. Fortunately, some good progress has been made in both of these directions. This is a key area where AI has much to offer in making MDPs more easily solved and, therefore, more widely applicable as a model for DTP.

In this talk I will survey a few of the techniques that have been developed recently for solving both FOMDPs and POMDPs. I will focus on a specific primarily on techniques that exploit concise system representations, much as regression or partial-order planning use (say) STRIPS action representations and propositional goal descriptions to discover structure in the set of plans they construct. There are, of course, many more concepts from various areas of AI (planning, learning, etc.) that can be—and have been—brought to bear on the effective solution of MDPs. Many techniques developed in the reinforcement learning community, for example, discover various forms of problem structure without being provided with a concise system representation: essentially structure in the representation of the *solution* is discovered without explicitly requiring that the problem be represented this way. The use of function approximation to represent value functions in reinforcement learning is a prime example of this [4]. Other techniques involve using search [1, 23], sampling [30, 46], and region-based problem decomposition [18, 25, 41, 38].

2 Action Representation

To represent stochastic actions and systems, a number of researchers have adapted a tool used for the representation of probability distributions, namely *Bayesian networks* [39], to the problem of action representation. Bayesian networks provide a formal, graphical way of decomposing a probability distribution by exploiting probabilistic independence relationships. Bayesian networks can also be augmented to represent *actions*, for instance, using the methods of *influence diagrams* [43, 39], or representations such as *two-stage* or *dynamic* Bayesian networks (DBNs) [17]. The use of DBNs has not only provided a natural and concise means of representing stochastic dynamic systems, but has also given rise to a number of computationally effective techniques for inference tasks such as monitoring, prediction and decision making.

In the talk I will briefly review DBNs and discuss why they are suitable representations for MDPs as applied to DTP. Roughly, DBNs exploit the fact that the (stochastic) effect of an action on different system variables often exhibits great probabilistic independence; furthermore, the effect on one variable may depend on the state of only a subset of system variables. For instance, the action of moving five meters in a certain direction may stochastically influence the state of a robot's battery, as well as its location; but the probabilities of various changes in these variables may be independent. Furthermore, the robot's ending location may depend on its starting location, but not on the variable denoting the load it is carrying. These facts imply that the transition probabilities for this action—the probabilities of moving from state to state when the action is executed—exhibit a certain regularity. This regularity is exploited in the DBN representation, and we can often specify and represent system dynamics in time and space polynomial in the number of system variables (in contrast to the exponential space required by transition matrices used in the "standard" treatment of discrete-space MDPs). DBNs can be augmented with the structured representation of conditional probability tables for individual variables (e.g., using decision trees [11], algebraic decision diagrams [26], or Horn rules [40]), giving additional space savings and allowing even more natural specification. Similar remarks can be made for other components of MDPs such as reward function and observation probabilities. For a survey of these issues, see [9].

3 Abstraction

When solving an FOMDP, our aim is to produce a policy, or a mapping that associates an action to be executed with each state of the system. An optimal policy is one that has greatest expected value, where value is generally measured using some simple function of the rewards associated with the states the agent passes through as it executes the policy. For POMDPs, the goal is similar, except that we do not assume that the agent knows the true state of the system: it only obtains noisy observations of the system state. Instead, we consider a mapping from *belief states*—or probability distributions over system states—into actions. An agent's belief state reflects its uncertainty about the true state of the system when it is forced to act. For both FOMDPs and POMDPs, we generally produce optimal policies indirectly by first constructing a *value function* that measures the expected value of acting optimally at any state (or belief state), and then choosing actions "greedily" with respect to this optimal value function. Value functions are typically produced using dynamic programming algorithms.

Once again, the "standard" MDP model is intractable when we consider feature-based problems, as the number of states grows exponentially with the number of variables needed to describe the problem. Value functions and policies, which map system states (or belief states) into values or actions, cannot be represented or computed in an explicit fashion.[2] However, given that such problems generally exhibit regularity in their transition probabilities and reward functions, we might hope that value functions and policies would exhibit regularity as well. If so, then these mappings may be represented compactly.

For instance, it might be that the robot should always move to the mailroom when mail is ready to be picked up unless it's battery is low. This component of the policy mapping can be represented very concisely using a rule such as $MailReady \wedge$

---

[2] In fact, the space of belief states is continuous; however, value functions and policies have a nice structure that allows them to be represented finitely [45] using a set of system state-based mappings, as we discuss below.

¬LowBattery → Do(MoveMailRoom). This rule represents the policy mapping for *all* states where MailReady ∧ ¬LowBattery holds. We can view this as a form of *abstraction*: details involving *other* variables are irrelevant to the choice of action when MailReady ∧ ¬LowBattery is known.

To make use of this structure, we require techniques that discover these regularities without enumerating states. Decision-theoretic generalizations of goal regression for FOMDPs have been developed recently that do just this [11, 6, 20]. These methods exploit the structure in the MDP representation to determine which variables are relevant to prediction of expected value and action choice, and which can be ignored. Furthermore, these determinations are conditional (e.g., MailReady may be relevant when ¬LowBattery holds, but may be irrelevant when LowBattery is true). These methods essentially organize and "cluster" the classic dynamic programming computations using the structure laid bare by the MDP representation. For instance, in [11] we use decision trees to represent policies and value functions, and exploit DBN and decision tree MDP representations to discover the appropriate decision tree structure. These methods often render large MDPs tractable because they obviate the need for state space enumeration.

These techniques have been extended to other representations such as algebraic decision diagrams [26] (which have proved to offer very large impact on computational savings). A general view of this approach in terms of automaton minimization is proposed in [14]. Furthermore, these representations provide tremendous leverage for approximation [19, 10, 16]. I will briefly review some of these developments in the talk.

Similar ideas have been applied to POMDPs. Though value functions for POMDPs map belief states to expected value, rather than system states, Sondik [45] has shown that these continuous functions are piecewise linear and convex: as a result they can be represented using a finite collection of *state-based* value functions. These state-based value functions can be computed by dynamic programming. In [12], we apply abstraction algorithms similar to those described above to discover suitable decision-tree structure for the state-based value functions that make up the POMDP belief state-based value function. Hansen and Feng [24] extend these ideas to more sophisticated POMDP algorithms and use an ADD representation, providing some encouraging results.

POMDPs offer an additional complication: for the approaches described above, an agent must maintain a belief state as the system evolves. After each action and observation of the system, this distribution over system states is updated and the optimal action for the new belief state is determined. This is, of course, a computationally intractable process in general since the number of system states is itself unmanageable. Furthermore, the process is online rather than offline, so computational intractability is a much more pressing concern. DBN representations are designed for precisely this reason, exploiting independencies among variables in order to more compactly maintain distributions as they evolve over time. Unfortunately, as shown convincingly by Boyen and Koller [13], exact belief state monitoring is intractable even given very concise DBN representations. However, they have shown how partially-observable processes can be monitored approximately. The choice of approximation method can be informed by the DBN representation of the system and error bounds on the difference between the true and approximate belief state can be constructed quite easily. In fact, we can view their approximation scheme as a form of abstraction.

Though the Boyen and Koller scheme was not designed for POMDPs, it can certainly be applied to POMDP belief state monitoring. The method for generating error bounds is not directly applicable unfortunately: it does not account for error in decision quality induced by error in belief state. Recent work by McAllester and Singh [34] has related belief state error to decision quality error in POMDPs. In the talk, I briefly describe work done jointly with Pascal Poupart on using DBN representations to make construct such bounds and to select an appropriate "abstraction" for the belief state monitoring process.

4 Decomposition

Another important way in which DBN problem representations can be exploited computationally is through problem decomposition. In many instances, MDPs have reward function devised of several additive, independent components (in the sense of multi-attribute utility theory [31]). Often the individual components of the reward function can be influenced only by certain actions or certain system variables. For each individual objective, we can often use the DBN representation of an MDP to (often rather easily) construct a smaller MDP comprised of only those variables relevant to the achievement of that objective [7]. In other cases, the decomposition may be given to us directly. These sub-MDPs will be considerably smaller than the original MDP (exponentially smaller in the number of irrelevant variables), and can be solved using standard techniques to produce a policy (and value function) that dictates how best to achieve that individual objective. Given the policies and value functions for these sub-MDPs, the question remains: how does one produce a globally-optimal (or near-optimal) policy using the component value functions for guidance?

The question of merging policies has been addressed in [7, 36, 44]. Essentially, the component value functions can be used as heuristics to guide the search for a global policy.

A related viewpoint is adopted in [32], where an additive structure is *imposed* on a value function. Given a set of basis functions (generally defined over some subset of the system variables), value determination for a given policy can be constrained to have the form of a weighted sum of the basis functions. The factored nature of the state space can be thus exploited in constructing basis functions. It seems clear that DBN representations of MDPs could be used to construct reasonable basis functions automatically, though this idea hasn't been pursued.

5 The Future

The use of structured representation to bring about the effective solution of both FOMDPs and POMDPs shows great promise. With FOMDPs, very large problems involving up to one billion states have been solved exactly using structured representations and solution techniques such as those described above. While POMDPs have proven to be more difficult to handle efficiently, structured approaches are beginning to offer some encouragement. There is of course much that remains to be done.

An important set of tasks involves the integration of structured representations and solution methods with other methods for solving MDPs. For example, while sampling has proven to be an effective means of belief state monitoring [28] and shows hope for solving POMDPs [46], DBN representations of dynamics and structured representation of value functions can be used to make sampling far more effective by focusing attention on (or diverting attention from) those areas of state space where variance in estimates can have a greater (or lesser) impact on decision quality. Many of these techniques (e.g., decomposition and abstraction) can be integrated with one another rather easily, since they tend to focus on complementary forms of structure.

Many other types of MDP structure can be captured or discovered more easily using AI-style problem representations as well. Reachability analysis can be made much more effective using DBN problem representations [8], and can aid in the solution of MDPs (much like the reachability analysis implemented by GraphPlan [5] accelerates goal regression). Large action spaces can sometimes be represented compactly using such representations [15], as well.

One of the most glaring deficiencies of these representations is the inability to deal with relational concepts and quantification, things taken for granted in classical AI knowledge representation. This isn't to say that logical representations of probabilistic concepts are unknown. Poole's independent choice logic [40] (to take one example) offers a means of representing stochastic action using relations and variables. Extensions of Bayesian networks offer similar possibilities [22]. An extension of the abstraction and decomposition ideas discussed in the talk to first-order representations of MDPs will provide a major step toward making MDPs a standard, practical tool for AI applications. Similarly, the extension of these ideas to continuous or hybrid domains will expand the range of practical applicability of MDPs considerably.

The activity at the MDP crossroads, where AI and OR meet yet again, is increasing. AI style representational methods and computational techniques are leading the way in taking FOMDPs and POMDPs from being simply a nice, conceptual, mathematical model of sequential decision making to becoming a practical technology for stochastic decision problems. This is indeed fortunate since the conceptual model is the right one for so many problems within AI, and outside.

References

[1] A. G. Barto, S. J. Bradtke, and S. P. Singh. Learning to act using real-time dynamic programming. *Artificial Intelligence*, 72(1–2):81–138, 1995.

[2] Richard E. Bellman. *Dynamic Programming*. Princeton University Press, Princeton, 1957.

[3] Donald A. Berry and Bert Fristedt. *Bandit Problems: Sequential Allocation of Experiments*. Chapman and Hall, London, 1985.

[4] Dimitri P. Bertsekas and John. N. Tsitsiklis. *Neurodynamic Programming*. Athena, Belmont, MA, 1996.

[5] Avrim L. Blum and Merrick L. Furst. Fast planning through graph analysis. In *Proceedings of the Fourteenth International Joint Conference on Artificial Intelligence*, pages 1636–1642, Montreal, 1995.

[6] Craig Boutilier. Correlated action effects in decision theoretic regression. In *Proceedings of the Thirteenth Conference on Uncertainty in Artificial Intelligence*, pages 30–37, Providence, RI, 1997.

[7] Craig Boutilier, Ronen I. Brafman, and Christopher Geib. Prioritized goal decomposition of Markov decision processes: Toward a synthesis of classical and decision theoretic planning. In *Proceedings of the Fifteenth International Joint Conference on Artificial Intelligence*, pages 1156–1162, Nagoya, 1997.

[8] Craig Boutilier, Ronen I. Brafman, and Christopher Geib. Structured reachability analysis for Markov decision processes. In *Proceedings of the Fourteenth Conference on Uncertainty in Artificial Intelligence*, pages 24–32, Madison, WI, 1998.

[9] Craig Boutilier, Thomas Dean, and Steve Hanks. Decision theoretic planning: Structural assumptions and computational leverage. *Journal of Artificial Intelligence Research*, 11:1–94, 1999.

[10] Craig Boutilier and Richard Dearden. Approximating value trees in structured dynamic programming. In *Proceedings of the Thirteenth International Conference on Machine Learning*, pages 54–62, Bari, Italy, 1996.

[11] Craig Boutilier, Richard Dearden, and Moisés Goldszmidt. Exploiting structure in policy construction. In *Proceedings of the Fourteenth International Joint Conference on Artificial Intelligence*, pages 1104–1111, Montreal, 1995.

[12] Craig Boutilier and David Poole. Computing optimal policies for partially observable decision processes using compact representations. In *Proceedings of the Thirteenth National Conference on Artificial Intelligence*, pages 1168–1175, Portland, OR, 1996.

[13] Xavier Boyen and Daphne Koller. Tractable inference for complex stochastic processes. In *Proceedings of the Fourteenth Conference on Uncertainty in Artificial Intelligence*, pages 33–42, Madison, WI, 1998.

[14] Thomas Dean and Robert Givan. Model minimization in Markov decision processes. In *Proceedings of the Fourteenth National Conference on Artificial Intelligence*, pages 106–111, Providence, 1997.

[15] Thomas Dean, Robert Givan, and Kee-Eung Kim. Solving planning problems with large state and action spaces. In *Fourth International Conference on Artificial Intelligence Planning Systems*, pages 102–110, Pittsburgh, PA, 1998.

[16] Thomas Dean, Robert Givan, and Sonia Leach. Model reduction techniques for computing approximately optimal solutions for Markov decision processes. In *Proceedings of the Thirteenth Conference on Uncertainty in Artificial Intelligence*, pages 124–131, Providence, RI, 1997.

[17] Thomas Dean and Keiji Kanazawa. A model for reasoning about persistence and causation. *Computational Intelligence*, 5(3):142–150, 1989.

[18] Thomas Dean and Shieu-Hong Lin. Decomposition techniques for planning in stochastic domains. In *Proceedings of the Fourteenth International Joint Conference on Artificial Intelligence*, pages 1121–1127, Montreal, 1995.

[19] Richard Dearden and Craig Boutilier. Abstraction and approximate decision theoretic planning. *Artificial Intelligence*, 89:219–283, 1997.

[20] Thomas G. Dietterich and Nicholas S. Flann. Explanation-based learning and reinforcement learning: A unified approach. In *Proceedings of the Twelfth International Conference on Machine Learning*, pages 176–184, Lake Tahoe, 1995.

[21] Richard E. Fikes and Nils J. Nilsson. STRIPS: A new approach to the application of theorem proving to problem solving. *Artificial Intelligence*, 2:189–208, 1971.

[22] Nir Freidman, Daphne Koller, and Avi Pfeffer. Structured representation of complex stochastic systems. In *Proceedings of the Fifteenth National Conference on Artificial Intelligence*, pages 157–164, Madison, 1998.

[23] Hector Geffner and Blai Bonet. High-level planning and control with incomplete information using POMDPs. In *Proceedings Fall AAAI Symposium on Cognitive Robotics*, Orlando, FL, 1998.

[24] Eric A. Hansen and Zhengzhu Feng. Dynamic programming for pomdps using a factored state representation. In *Proceedings of the Fifth International Conference on AI Planning Systems*, Breckenridge, CO, 2000. to appear.

[25] Milos Hauskrecht, Nicolas Meuleau, Leslie Pack Kaelbling, Thomas Dean, and Craig Boutilier. Hierarchical solution of Markov decision processes using macroactions. In *Proceedings of the Fourteenth Conference on Uncertainty in Artificial Intelligence*, pages 220–229, Madison, WI, 1998.

[26] Jesse Hoey, Robert St-Aubin, Alan Hu, and Craig Boutilier. SPUDD: Stochastic planning using decision diagrams. In *Proceedings of the Fifteenth Conference on Uncertainty in Artificial Intelligence*, pages 279–288, Stockholm, 1999.

[27] Ronald A. Howard. *Dynamic Programming and Markov Processes*. MIT Press, Cambridge, 1960.

[28] Michael Isard and Andrew Blake. CONDENSATION—conditional density propagation for visual tracking. *International Journal of Computer Vision*, 29(1):5–18, 1998.

[29] R. E. Kalman. A new approach to linear filtering and prediction problems. *Journal of Basic Engineering*, 82:35–45, 1960.

[30] Michael Kearns, Yishay Mansour, and Andrew Y. Ng. A sparse sampling algorithm for near-optimal planning in large Markov decision processes. In *Proceedings of the Sixteenth International Joint Conference on Artificial Intelligence*, pages 1324–1331, Stockholm, 1999.

[31] R. L. Keeney and H. Raiffa. *Decisions with Multiple Objectives: Preferences and Value Trade-offs*. Wiley, New York, 1976.

[32] Daphne Koller and Ronald Parr. Computing factored value functions for policies in structured mdps. In *Proceedings of the Sixteenth International Joint Conference on Artificial Intelligence*, pages 1332–1339, Stockholm, 1999.

[33] David McAllester and David Rosenblitt. Systematic nonlinear planning. In *Proceedings of the Ninth National Conference on Artificial Intelligence*, pages 634–639, Anaheim, 1991.

[34] David McAllester and Satinder Singh. Approximate planning for factored POMDPs using belief state simplification. In *Proceedings of the Fifteenth Conference on Uncertainty in Artificial Intelligence*, pages 409–416, Stockholm, 1999.

[35] John McCarthy and P.J. Hayes. Some philosophical problems from the standpoint of artificial intelligence. *Machine Intelligence*, 4:463–502, 1969.

[36] Nicolas Meuleau, Milos Hauskrecht, Kee-Eung Kim, Leonid Peshkin, Leslie Pack Kaelbling, Thomas Dean, and Craig Boutilier. Solving very large weakly coupled Markov decision processes. In *Proceedings of the Fifteenth National Conference on Artificial Intelligence*, pages 165–172, Madison, WI, 1998.

[37] Roger B. Myerson. *Game Theory: Analysis of Conflict*. Harvard University Press, Cambridge, 1991.

[38] Ronald Parr. Flexible decomposition algorithms for weakly coupled Markov decision processes. In *Proceedings of the Fourteenth Conference on Uncertainty in Artificial Intelligence*, pages 422–430, Madison, WI, 1998.

[39] Judea Pearl. *Probabilistic Reasoning in Intelligent Systems: Networks of Plausible Inference*. Morgan Kaufmann, San Mateo, 1988.

[40] David Poole. The independent choice logic for modelling multiple agents under uncertainty. *Artificial Intelligence*, 94(1–2):7–56, 1997.

[41] Doina Precup, Richard S. Sutton, and Satinder Singh. Theoretical results on reinforcement learning with temporally abstract behaviors. In *Proceedings of the Tenth European Conference on Machine Learning*, pages 382–393, Chemnitz, Germany, 1998.

[42] Raymond Reiter. The frame problem in the situation calculus: A simple solution (sometimes) and a completeness result for goal regression. In V. Lifschitz, editor, *Artificial Intelligence and Mathematical Theory of Computation (Papers in Honor of John McCarthy)*, pages 359–380. Academic Press, San Diego, 1991.

[43] Ross D. Shachter. Evaluating influence diagrams. *Operations Research*, 33(6):871–882, 1986.

[44] Satinder P. Singh and David Cohn. How to dynamically merge Markov decision processes. In *Advances in Neural Information Processing Systems 10*, pages 1057–1063. MIT Press, Cambridge, 1998.

[45] Richard D. Smallwood and Edward J. Sondik. The optimal control of partially observable Markov processes over a finite horizon. *Operations Research*, 21:1071–1088, 1973.

[46] Sebastian Thrun. Monte Carlo POMDPs. In *Proceedings of Conference on Neural Information Processing Systems*, 1999. to appear.

[47] Richard Waldinger. Achieving several goals simultaneously. In E. Elcock and D. Mitchie, editors, *Machine Intelligence 8: Machine Representations of Knowledge*, pages 94–136. Ellis Horwood, Chichester, England, 1977.

Why do we Need a Body Anyway?

Justine Cassell

MIT Media Lab
E15-315
20 Ames Street
Cambridge MA 02139
justine@media.mit.edu
http://www.media.mit.edu/~justine/

Embodiment is all the rage: humanoid agents, robots with eyelashes. It brings back those glory days of AI when "human-like" was a goal in and of itself.

And yet, the trend is towards smart environments, disappearing computers, intelligent rooms. These systems are said to allow people to interact with the room "as they interact with another person".

In this talk I will agree with Harry Potter that one should "never trust anything that can think for itself, if you can't see where it keeps its brain". I'll argue that humans need to *locate* intelligence, and that this issue poses problems for the disappearing computer. Bodies are the best possible example of located intelligence, of course, and interacting with another person is best done when there is another person to interact with. On this basis of this discussion, I will support the use of embodiment in certain AI domains and demonstrate with a series of implemented systems, including some new work on "shared reality" -- a paradigm in which both human and computer share a real physical space within which to make hand gestures, facial displays, body movements, and real physical objects that can be passed back and forth between the real and virtual world.

But I will claim that unless we understand the "affordances" of the body -- for face-to-face conversation, for situating intelligence, for establishing trust and other kinds of interactional glue -- then neither embodied systems nor invisible computers will ever be more than just another Cheshire Cat face.

Cassell, J., Sullivan, J., Prevost, S., and Churchill, E. (eds.), (2000). *Embodied Conversational Agents.* Cambridge, MA: MIT Press.

Cassell, J. (2000). "More than Just Another Pretty Face: Embodied Conversational Interface Agents." *Communications of the ACM*

Cassell, J., Ananny, M., Basu, A., Bickmore, T., Chong, P., Mellis, D., Ryokai, K., Vilhjálmsson, H., Smith, J., Yan, H. (2000) "Shared Reality: Physical Collaboration with a Virtual Peer". *Proceedings of ACM SIGCHI Conference on Human Factors in Computing Systems (CHI).* April 4-9, Amsterdam, NL.

Cassell, J. and Vilhjálmsson, H. (1999). "Autonomy vs. Direct Control: Communicative Behaviors in Avatars." *Autonomous Agents and Multi-Agent Systems*, 2(1): 45-64.

Cassell, J., and Thórisson, K. (1999). "The Power of a Nod and a Glance: Envelope vs. Emotional Feedback in Animated Conversational Agents." *Journal of Applied Artificial Intelligence* 13 (3): 519-538.

Copyright © 2000, American Association for Artificial Intelligence (www.aaai.org). All rights reserved.

Structure, Duality, and Randomization: Common Themes in AI and OR

Carla P. Gomes
Computer Science Department
Cornell University
Ithaca, NY 14853
gomes@cs.cornell.edu

Abstract

Both the Artificial Intelligence (AI) community and the Operations Research (OR) community are interested in developing techniques for solving hard combinatorial problems. OR has relied heavily on mathematical programming formulations such as integer and linear programming, while AI has developed constrained-based search and inference methods. Recently, we have seen a convergence of ideas, drawing on the individual strengths of these paradigms. Furthermore, there is a great deal of overlap in research on local search and meta-heuristics by both communities. Problem structure, duality, and randomization are overarching themes in the study of AI/OR approaches. I will compare and contrast the different views from AI and OR on these topics, highlighting potential synergistic benefits.[1]

Introduction

In recent years we have seen an increasing dialog between the Artificial Intelligence (AI) and Operations Research (OR) communities, in particular in the area of combinatorial problems. These problems are ubiquitous and occur in areas as diverse as planning, scheduling, automated reasoning, and protein folding. AI approaches encompass a rich collection of knowledge representation formalisms for dealing with a wide variety of real-world problems. Some examples are constraint programming representations, logical formalisms, declarative and functional programming languages such as Prolog and Lisp, Bayesian models, rule-based formalism, etc. The downside of such rich representations is that in general they lead to intractable problems, and we therefore often cannot use such formalisms for handling realistic size problems. OR, on the other hand, has focused on more tractable representations, such as linear programming formulations. OR based techniques have demonstrated the ability to identify optimal and locally optimal solutions for well-defined problem spaces. In general, however, OR solutions are restricted to rigid models with limited expressive power. AI techniques, on the other hand, provide richer and more flexible representations of real-world problems, supporting efficient constraint-based reasoning mechanisms as well as mixed initiative frameworks, which allow the human expertise to be in the loop. The challenge lies in providing representations that are expressive enough to describe real-world problems and at the same time guaranteeing good and fast solutions.

Problem structure, *duality*, and *randomization* are overarching themes in the study of AI/OR approaches. In this paper I compare and contrast the different views from AI and OR on these topics, highlighting potential synergistic benefits.

Problem Structure

The ability to capture and exploit problem structure is of central importance, a way of taming computational complexity. In general structured models are easier to understand and compute with.

The OR community has identified several classes of problems with very interesting, *tractable*, structure. Linear Programming (LP) is a notable example of such a class. Linear Programming plays a major role in OR methods. Work done by Leonid Kantorovich in 1939 is considered the main precursor to Linear Programming (LP). In 1947, George Dantzig developed LP and the simplex method, initially conceived to speed up the process of providing a time-staged deployment, training and logistical program in military applications.[2] Interestingly, the word "programming" in Linear Programming has nothing to do with computer programming, but rather with the notion of "program" as used by the military to refer to plans of military operations. The simplex method made it possible to consider larger problems in areas as diverse as transportation, production, resource allocation, and scheduling problems.

The complexity of LP was not known for a long time. In the 70's, Klee and Minty (1972) created an example that showed that the simplex method can require exponential time. However, despite its worst-case exponential complexity, the simplex method generally performs very well

---

Copyright © 2000, American Association for Artificial Intelligence (www.aaai.org). All rights reserved.
[1]This paper is based on Gomes (2000).

[2]Ironically, Dantzig was not considered for the Nobel Prize in Economics for work related to the discovery and application of LP. The prize was given to Koopmans and Kantorovich for their work applying LP to problems in economics.

in practice. In the late 70's, Khachian (1979) developed a polynomial-time algorithm for linear programming. On practical problems, however, this method was much less efficient than the simplex method. In 1984, Karmarkar devised an interior point method that is more efficient and can outperform the simplex method on certain large problems instances. Still, the simplex method is often the method of choice. ILOG-CPLEX simplex based method, one of the leading LP commercial software, was shown to be very competitive or even outperforming interior point based methods on several benchmarks (Bixby 1999).

The main extensions of LP are Integer Programming (IP) and Mixed Integer Programming (MIP). IP and MIP extend LP to deal with integrality constraints and are the "bread and butter" of OR.

The standard OR approach for solving MIP problems is to use a branch-and-bound search. Branch-and-bound entails solving several LP's, which are relaxations of the original IP or MIP that provide guidance and tighten bounds for branch and bound techniques. First, an LP relaxation of the problem instance is considered. In such a relaxation, all variables of the problem are treated as continuous variables. If the solution to the LP relaxation problem has non-integer values for some of the integer variables, we have to branch on one of those variables. This way we create two new subproblems (nodes of the search tree), one with the floor of the fractional value and one with the ceiling. (For the case of binary (0/1) variables, we create an instance with the variable set to 0 and another with the variable set to 1.) Following the strategy of repeatedly fixing integer variables to integer values will lead at some point to a subproblem with an overall integer solution (provided we are dealing with a feasible problem instance). (Note we call any solution where all the integer variables have integer values an "integer solution".) In practice, it often happens that the solution of the LP relaxation of a subproblem already is an integer solution, in which case we do not have to branch further from that node. Once we have found an integer solution, its objective function value can be used to prune other nodes in the tree, whose relaxations have worse values. This is because the LP relaxation bounds the optimal solution of the problem. For example, for a minimization problem, the LP relaxation of a node provides a lower-bound on the best possible integer solution. Interestingly, branch-and-bound is a particular case of A*: the admissible heuristic is the LP relaxation.

Successful solutions of large-scale MIPs require formulations whose LP relaxations give a good approximation to feasible solutions. For instance, it is known that the Knapsack problem is relatively easy to solve if using the "right" LP formulations whose relaxations are very insightful for a branch and bound algorithm. However, some formulations of the Knapsack problem lead to poor relaxations of the corresponding LP, in the sense that they do not provide much information for a branch and bound algorithm.

Another very successful way of exploiting structure is the work of Dantzig and Wolfe on solving LP by means of *Decomposition*. It has had a major impact on solving large-scale problems. In fact, even though the simplex method can handle sparse problems with several thousands of rows quite comfortably, it does not scale up when it comes to truly huge problems. For such problems the simplex method is out of the question and the Dantzig-Wolfe decomposition is needed. An example of the application of such decomposition methods is column generation techniques. They have been successfully applied, *e.g.*, in Airline Crew Scheduling (see *e.g.*, Barnhart *et al.* 1994). Branch-and-price is an example of a column generation technique.

The crew scheduling problem is the problem of assigning crews to a given set of flights, in general all the flights of a specific fleet type. In this problem, sequences of flights (pairings) are assigned to crews so that each flight is assigned to exactly one crew. Since pairings are subject to complicated rules (safety and contractual rules) it would be difficult to express constraints and costs if a direct encoding were used.[3] Instead, valid pairings are enumerated and the problem is formulated as a set partitioning problem (SPP). In this formulation each column or variable corresponds to a pairing and the objective is to partition all of the flights into a set of minimum cost pairings.

The main drawback is that the number of pairings grows exponentially with the number of flights. For example, Vance (1993) found more than 5 million valid pairings in a daily problem with 253 flights. Problems with 1000 flights, a typical size for a U.S. domestic carrier, are likely to have billions of pairings.

The approach used to solve this formidable problem uses Dantzig-Wolfe column generation. The LP relaxation of the SPP is solved, but only a subset of columns are initially considered. This problem is called the *restricted master problem*. New columns are generated only as needed, and if needed, and based on the information provided by the solution to the *restricted master problem*, *i.e.*, the *dual prices*. These *dual prices* allow one to determine which flights should be included in "good" columns for the master problem. The problem of generating new columns is called the *subproblem* or *pricing problem*.

Trans-Shipment Problems or *Network Flow Problems* are also notable examples of the importance of exploiting structure. Even though these problems are MIPs, which in general are NP-hard, the special structure of Network Flow Problems allows for very efficient (polynomial) algorithms. An interesting aspect of Network Flow Problems is that the optimal solution of instances involving only integral constraints are guaranteed to be also integer-valued. Many combinatorial problems, well beyond cases that deal with physical shipments of some commodity, such as scheduling problems, can be efficiently formulated as Network Flow Problems.[4]

Typically, when using OR methods, one starts by categorizing the problem into a class of problems for which efficient solution methods have been developed such as LP or

---

[3] By direct encoding we mean a formulation with variables x_{ij}, where $x_{ij} = 1$ if crew i is assigned to flight j.

[4] Unfortunately, Network Flow Algorithms cannot be used when there are global constraints on the nodes of the network. An example of a global constraint would state that the amount of goods shipped through certain nodes corresponds to 30 % of the total amount of goods shipped.

Network Flow. If the problem does not fit into such a class, one uses a more general formulation such as IP or MIP. At a second level, in general using an automated process, structure is detected using inference methods. For example, when solving IP's or MIP's, the derivation of "cutting planes" is very important to eliminate parts of the search space that are guaranteed not to contain the optimal solution. Cutting planes are linear inequalities that can be added to the original formulation of an IP with the guarantee that no integer solution will be eliminated, but with the advantage of eliminating fractional solutions generated by the linear relaxation of the problem. The addition of cutting planes leads to tighter relaxations, and therefore their solutions are better approximations of the IP's solution. Gomory (1958, 1963) pioneered this approach, showing how to systematically generate "cuts" that lead to an integer solution. "Cuts" or "cutting planes" are *redundant* constraints, in the sense that they do not eliminate feasible solutions. However, although these constraints are redundant in terms of the solution, they can play a major role during the search process. A classical example of the importance of cutting planes involves the pigeonhole problem: by adding the appropriate redundant constraints to a linear programming formulation, its relaxation immediately returns infeasibility. Without such redundant constraints, the results of the LP relaxation are useless. The OR community has developed several techniques for the generation of cuts, but, in general, it is not clear how to construct such cuts. A direction of research is the study of techniques that will lead to the generation of better cuts as well as efficient domain reduction techniques, and the combination of cuts with domain reduction techniques. Relevant work in this area is that of Lovasz and Schrijver (1991) and Balas, Ceria, and Cornuejols (1993). They have developed the *lift-and-project* technique. Hooker (1992) has developed cutting plane algorithms for IP and resolution methods in propositional logic. Work on the automated generation of cutting planes for problems such as the pigeonhole problem has been done by Barth (1996).

The OR community has identified several classes of problems with very a interesting, *tractable*, structure. LP, and Network Flow problems are good examples of such problems. OR also exploits the structure of problems during inference by generating "cutting planes", which allow for tighter relaxations that are therefore closer to the optimal integer solution. The AI community, on the other hand, has also identified interesting tractable problem classes: The most successful case, involving logical formalisms, is probably the Horn clausal form, which led to the development of expert systems.

The CSP community, on the other hand, has identified the special structure of several global constraints that are ubiquitous in several problems, which allow for the development of efficient constraint propagation techniques for the reduction of the variable domains. The CSP community mainly relies on domain reduction techniques for inference during search. A very successful strategy is to exploit the structure of special constraints and treat them as a global constraint (Beldiceanu and Contejean 1994, Caseau and Laburthe 1997; Regin 1994 and 1996). Some examples of such propagation methods are the constraint that guarantees that all elements of a vector are different (all-different constraint) and the constraint that enforces that certain values occur a given number of times in a given vector of variables (cardinality constraint). The implementation of such constraints is an interesting use of Network Flow algorithms (Regin 1994, 1996). The work done at Kestrel Institute using a transformational approach to scheduling encompasses the generation of very efficient constraint propagation techniques (Smith and Parra 1993). Dixon and Ginsberg (2000) combine satisfiability techniques from AI and OR, more specifically pseudo-Boolean representations and the cutting plane proof system with restricted learning methods such as relevance-bounded learning. They propose a new cutting plane proof for the pigeonhole principle of size n^2, and show how to implement intelligent backtracking techniques using pseudo-Boolean representation.

In general, however, the notion of structure is very hard to define, even though "we recognize structure when we see it." For example, there is not a methodology that shows how to construct good cutting planes. Therefore, formalizing the notion of structure and understanding its impact in terms of search is a key challenge for both AI and OR.

AI has made some progress in this area, namely in the study of phase transition phenomena, correlating structural features of problems with computational complexity. This is a new emerging area of research that is changing the way we characterize the computational complexity of NP-Hard problems, beyond the worst-case complexity notion: Using tools from statistical physics we are now able to provide a fine characterization of the spectrum of computational complexity of instances of NP-Complete problems, identifying typical *easy-hard-easy* patterns (Hogg et al. 1996). For example, in the Satisfiability problem it is known that the difficulty of problems depends on the ratio between number of clauses and number of variables (Kirkpatrick and Selman 1994).

We have studied phase transition phenomena in a more structured domain, the so-called Quasigroup Completion Problem (Gomes and Selman 1997). We introduced this domain to bridge the gap between purely random instances, such as Satisfiability, and highly structured problems, such as those from finite algebra (Fujita et al. 1993; Lam et al. 1989). The best way to view the quasigroup completion problem is in terms of the completion of a Latin square (which technically defines the multiplication table of the quasigroup). Given N colors, a Latin square is defined by an N by N table, where each entry has a color and where there are no repeated colors in any row or column. N is called the *order* of the square. The quasigroup completion problem (QCP) is the problem of whether a partially colored Latin square can be completed into a full Latin square by assigning colors to the open entries of the table. QCP is NP-complete (Colbourn 1984) and it has been used to study the effectiveness of a variety of local consistency measures for constraint satisfaction procedures (Stergiou and Walsh (1999a, 1999b), Walsh 1999, Regin 1994). (See www.cs.cornell.edu/gomes/ for a java applet demonstrating the quasigroup completion problem.)

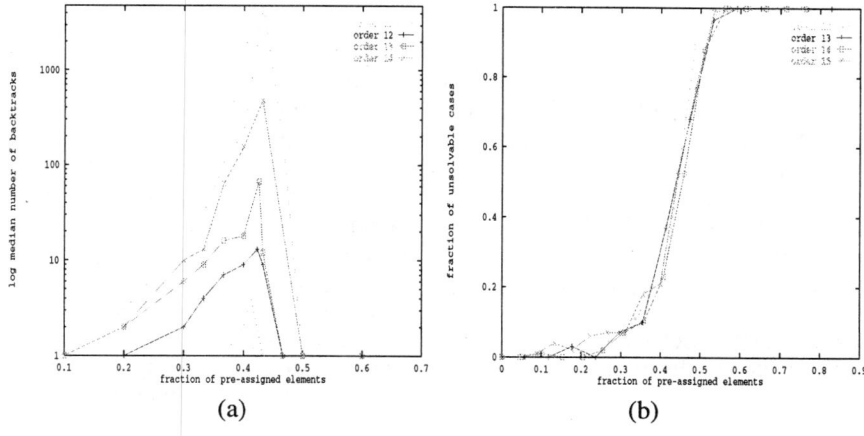

Figure 1: (a) Cost profile, and (b) phase transition for the quasigroup completion problem (up to order 15).

In our work we identified a phase transition phenomenon for QCP (Gomes and Selman 1997). At the phase transition, problem instances switch from being almost all solvable ("under-constrained") to being almost all unsolvable ("over-constrained"). The computationally hardest instances lie at the phase transition boundary. Figure 1 shows the median computational cost and phase transition. Along the horizontal axis we vary the ratio of pre-assigned colors. We note that even though all the instances are from an NP-complete problem, we clearly distinguish various regions of problem difficulty. In particular, both at low ratios and high ratios of preassigned colors the median solution cost is relatively small. However, in between these two regimes, the complexity peaks and, in fact, exhibits strong exponential growth. Somewhat surprisingly, the computational cost curves (curves for quasigroups of order 11, 12, 13, 14, 15) all peak at approximately at the same ratio, which is approximately 42% of the total number of cells of the matrix. [5]

The underlying phenomenon is explained by the left panel of figure 1 which shows the phase transition curve. The figure shows the probability of an instance being satisfiable as a function of the ratio of pre-assigned colors. At low ratios, almost all formulas are satisfiable; at high ratios, almost all formulas are unsatisfiable; whereas at the phase transition (around a ratio of 42%) 50% of the instances are satisfiable and 50% are unsatisfiable. This phase transition point directly corresponds to the peak in the computational complexity: This is a much finer characterization of the computational complexity of NP-complete problems than the standard worst-case exponential results (Cheeseman et al. 1991, Mitchell et al. 1992; Kirkpatrick and Selman 1994). (See Hogg et al. (1996) for a collection of papers on the topic.)

Another structural feature that has been recently formalized is the concept of *backbone*. The backbone of an instance corresponds to the shared structure of all the solutions of a problem instance. In other words, the set of variables and corresponding assignments that are common in all the solutions of a problem instance is the backbone (Monasson et al. 1999). We can link the computational hardness area to a phase transition which corresponds to a clear threshold phenomenon in the size of the backbone of the problem instances. The size of the backbone is measured in terms of the percentage of variables that have the same value in all possible solutions. We have observed a transition from a phase where the size of the backbone is almost 100% to a phase with a backbone of size close to 0%, for our quasigroup domain. The transition is sudden and it coincides with the hardest problem instances both for incomplete and complete search methods. Fig. 2 shows the backbone fraction as a function of the fraction of unassigned colors in satisfiable quasigroups (see also Achlioptas et al. 2000). The figure also includes the normalized cost of local search. The figure shows a sharp phase transition phenomenon in the backbone fraction, which coincide with the hardness peak in local search.[6]

The correlation between problem hardness and the appearance of the backbone suggests that search methods have the worst performance when a non-negligible fraction of the variables must appear in the backbone. When the backbone fraction nears 1, however, the problems are so constrained that incorrect choices near the root are quickly detected and corrected. For local search procedures, an explanation might be developed by considering the relationship between the backbone and set of solutions to the instances. When the backbone is small, there are many solutions widely distributed in the search space, and so local search may quickly

---

[5] The exact location of the phase transition appears to be characterized in terms of *Number-of-preassigned-colors*$/N^p$, where $p \neq 2$. However, and given that for low orders of quasigroups $p = 2$ is a good approximation, for simplification we talk about proportion of preassigned colors in terms of the total number of cells of the matrix, i.e., N^2. See also Achlioptas et al. (2000).

[6] The figure gives data for $N = 36$. The hardness peak for our complete search method also lies in the phase transition region but is shifted slightly to the right. We are currently investigating whether that shift is real or part of the uncertainty in our data.

find one. When the backbone is near 1, the solutions are tightly clustered, so that that all clauses "vote" to push the search in the same direction. A partial backbone, however, may indicate that solutions are in different clusters that are widely distributed, with different clauses pushing the search in different directions. The role that backbone variables play in search is still not fully understood and requires further research. Nevertheless, we believe that the notion of backbone is critical when solving real-world problems. A good strategy for building real systems may encompass the use of powerful pre-processing techniques identifying backbone variables[7]. In practice, humans tend to implicitly use the notion of backbone variables ("critical resources") when dealing, for example, with tasks such as scheduling and planning.

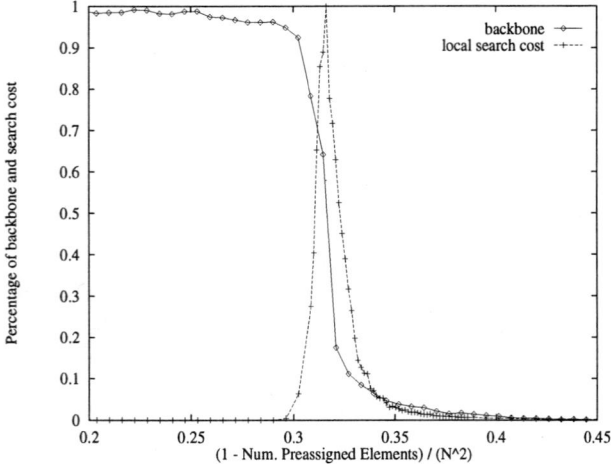

Figure 2: Backbone phase transition with cost profile.

Another interesting structural concept involves the identification of the tractable components of a problem. Monasson et al. (1999) introduced the 2+p SAT formulation to study the behavior of problems that are a mixture of 2-SAT and 3-SAT clauses. The proportion of 3-SAT clauses is defined by the parameter p. Note that this hybrid problem is NP-complete, for $p > 0$. However, and somewhat surprisingly, Monasson et al. showed that the problem scales linearly as long as the fraction of 3-SAT clauses is below 0.4. This is a promising result, suggesting that several problems that are NP-complete in the worst case may behave in a tractable way as long as a "good-size" well structured component is identified. Such a result makes it even more compelling for us to try to identify the well structured components of problems for which good efficient algorithms exist.

Duality

Duality plays an important role in OR. The basic idea is that, in general, problems can be considered both from a primal and dual perspective — maximizing the profit is equivalent to minimizing costs. Every maximization LP problem gives rise to a minimization LP problem, its *dual*. Interestingly, every feasible solution of one problem provides a bound on the optimal value of the other problem, and if one of them has an optimal solution, so does the other and their optimal values are the same. This is what the famous Duality Theorem states, formally proved by Gale et al. (1951). Its notions originated in conversations between Dantzig and von Neumann in the fall of 1947. The theory of duality is also used to perform sensitivity analysis and parametric analysis, *i.e.*, the study of the impact on the objective function when the level of resources (the right hand sides of the linear constraints) vary or when the coefficients of the objective function vary. The technique of *penalties* uses sensitivity analysis to tighten bounds during branch-and-bound search.

Duality is a powerful concept that has been extensively exploited by the OR community, a very elegant theory in the context of LP. There are dual theories for IP (Schrijver 1991), but, in general, as the problem grows they become very complex and are rarely used in practice. Furthermore, in general, duality is not yet well understood for problems involving constraints other than inequality constraints. Hooker et al. (2000) propose an interesting general approach to duality and sensitivity analysis that applies to both continuous and discrete problems. They generalize the classical idea of a dual to that of "inference dual", which can be defined for any optimization problem. To solve the inference dual corresponds to obtaining a proof of the optimal value of the problem. Sensitivity analysis can be interpreted as an analysis of the role of each constraint in this proof. Traditional sensitivity analysis for LP is a special case of such an approach. Recently there have also been several promising results in the CSP community using dual formulation approaches (*e.g.*, to solve hard timetabling problems: McAloon et al. 1997 and Gomes et al. 1998b). Such approaches, by considering simultaneously two perspectives — the primal and dual view of the problem, allow for stronger inferences in terms of variable domain reductions. Research in this area, coupled with the study of the design of global constraints and good relaxation schemes for primal and dual formulations, is very promising. The study of new ways for performing sensitivity analysis based on duality is also a promising research area.

Randomization

Randomization and stochastic strategies have been very successful in local search methods. Local search methods or meta-heuristics are often used to solve challenging combinatorial problems. Such methods start with an initial solution, not necessarily feasible, and improve upon it by performing small "local" changes. One of the earliest applications of local search was to find good solutions for the Traveling Salesman Problem (TSP) (Lin (1965) and Lin and Kernighan (1973)). Lin and Kernighan showed that by performing successive swaps of cities to an arbitrary initial tour of cities, until no such swaps are possible, one can generate solutions that are surprisingly close to the shortest possible tour. There are several ways of implementing local search methods, depending on the choice of the initial so-

---

[7]Of course, the identification of all the backbone variables may be as difficult as solving the initial problem.

lution, types of "local" changes allowed, and feasibility and cost of (intermediate) solutions.

There is a great deal of overlap in research on local search by the AI and OR communities, namely in simulated annealing (Kirkpatrick *et al.* 1983), tabu search (Glover 1989), and genetic algorithms (Holland 1975). A recent new area of application for local search methods is in solving NP-complete *decision problems*, such as the Boolean satisfiability (SAT) problem. In 1992, Selman *et al.* showed that a greedy local search method, called GSAT, could solve instances with up to 700 hundred variables. Currently GSAT and variants (*e.g.,* WALKSAT) are among the best methods for SAT, enabling us to solve instances with up to 3000 variables (Selman *et al.* 1994). Closely related work in the area of scheduling is the technique of "MinConflicts" proposed by Minton *et al.* (1992).

Stochastic strategies have been very successful in the area of local search. However, local search procedures are inherently incomplete methods. An emerging area of research is the study of Las Vegas algorithms, *i.e.*, randomized algorithms that always return a model satisfying the constraints of the search problem or prove that no such model exists (Motwani and Raghavan 1995). The running time of a Las Vegas style algorithm can vary dramatically on the same problem instance. The extreme variance or "unpredictability" in the running time of complete search procedures can often be explained by the phenomenon of "heavy-tailed cost distributions" (Gomes *et al.* 2000). The understanding of these characteristics explains why "rapid restarts" and portfolio strategies are very effective. Such strategies eliminate the heavy-tailed behavior and exploit *any significant probability mass early on in the distribution.* Restarts and portfolio strategies in fact reduce the variance in runtime and the probability of failure of the search procedures, resulting in more robust overall search methods (Frost *et al.* 1997; Gomes and Selman 1999; Gomes *et al.* 1998a; Gomes *et al.* 2000; and Hoos 1999). So, somewhat counterintuitively, randomization actually provides a way for making solution methods more robust.

Conclusions

I have discussed the rich set of connections between artificial intelligence and operations research, focusing on approaches for dealing with hard combinatorial problems. We have seen how these connections can be grouped around three themes: *problem structure, duality,* and *randomization.* The overarching goal of these different themes in AI and OR is to uncover hidden tractable problem structure combined with a need for increased robustness and predictability of solution methods.

Acknowledgments

This work is funded by the Air Force Research Laboratory, Information Directorate and the Air Force Office of Scientific Research, under the New World Vistas Initiative (F30602-99-1-0005, F30602-99-1-0006, and AFOSR NWV project 2304, LIRL 97RL005N25).

References

Achlioptas, D., Gomes, C., Kautz, H. and Selman B. (2000) Generating satisfiable instances. *Proceedings of the Seventeenth National Conference on Artificial Intelligence (AAAI-00)*, 2000.

Anderson, L. (1985). Completing partial Latin Squares. *Mathematisk Fysiske Meddelelser*, 41, 1985, 23–69.

Balas, E., Ceria, S., and Cornuejols, G. (1993) A lift and project cutting plane algorithm for mixed 0-1 programs. *Mathematical Programming* 58 (1993), 295-324.

Barnhart, C., Johnson, E., Nemhauser, G., Savelsbergh, M., and Vance, P. (1994) Branch-and-Price: column generation for solving huge Integer Programs. *Mathematical Programming. State of the Art* Birge, J., and Murty, K. (eds.), 1994, 186-207.

Barth,P. (1996) Logic based 0-1 Constraint Programming. Kluwer, 1996.

Beldiceanu N. and Contejean, E. (1994) Introducing global constraints in CHIP. *Mathl. Comput. Modelling*, 20 (12), 1994, 97–123.

Bixby R., (1999) MIP: Closing the gap between theory and practice. *19th IFIP TC7 Conference on System Modelling and Optimization* (Plenary Lecture), Cambridge, England, 1999.

Caseau, Y. and Laburthe, F. (1997) Solving various weighted matching problems with constraints. *Principles and Practice of Constraint Programming*, vol. 1330 of *Lecture Notes in Computer Science*, 1997, 17–31.

Caseau, Y., Laburthe, F., Le Pape, C., and Rottembourg B. (2000) Combining local and global search in a constraint programming environment. *Knowledge Engineering Review*, Vol. 15 (1), 2000.

Cheeseman, P., Kanefsky, B., and Taylor W. (1991) Where the really hard problems are. *Proc. IJCAI*, 1991.

Clements D., Crawford J., Joslin D., Nemhauser G., Puttlitz, M, and Savelsbergh, M. (1997) Heuristic optimization: a hybrid AI/OR approach. *Workshop of Constraint Programming*, Austria, 1997.

Colbourn, C. (1984). The complexity of completing Latin Squares. *Discrete Appl. Math.*, 8, (1984), 25-30.

Dantzig, G.B. (1991) Linear Programming. *History of Mathematical Programming, A collection of Reminiscences* Lenstra, J., Kan, R., Schrijver, A. (eds.), CWI, Amsterdam, 1991, 19-31.

Dantzig, G.B. and Wolfe, P. (1960) Decomposition principle for linear programs. *Operations Research*, 8, 1960, 101-111.

Denes, J. and Keedwell, A. (1974) Latin Squares and their applications. *Akademiai Kiado, Budapest, and English Universities Press*, London, 1974.

Dixon, H. and Ginsberg, M. (2000) Combining satisfiability techniques from AI and OR. *Knowledge Engineering Review*, Vol. 15 (1), 2000.

Frost, D., Rish, I., and Vila, L. (1997) Summarizing CSP hardness with continuous probability distributions. *Proceedings of the Fourteenth National Conference on Artificial Intelligence (AAAI-97)*, 1997.

Fujita, M., Slaney, J., and Bennett, F. (1993). Automatic generation of some results in Finite Algebra. *Proc. IJCAI*, 1993.

Gale, D., Kuhn H, and Tucker A. (1951) Linear programming and the theory of games. *Activity Analysis of Production and Allocation,*, Wiley, New York, (1951) 317–329.

Glover, F. (1989) Tabu search — part I. *ORSA Journal on Computing*, 1(3) (1989) 190–206.

Gomes, C. (2000) Artificial Intelligence and Operations Research: challenges and opportunities in planning and scheduling. *Knowledge Engineering Review*, Vol. 15 (1), 2000.

Gomes, C.P., Kautz, H., and Selman, B. (1998a) Boosting combinatorial search through randomization. *Proceedings of the Fifteenth National Conference on Artificial Intelligence (AAAI-98)*, 1998.

Gomes, C.P. and Selman, B. (1997) Problem structure in the presence of perturbations. *Proceedings of the Fourteenth National Conference on Artificial Intelligence (AAAI-97)*, New Providence, RI, 1997, 221–226.

Gomes, C.P. and Selman, B. (1999) Search strategies for hybrid search spaces. *Proceedings of the Eleventh International Conference on Tools with Artificial Intelligence (ICTAI-99)*, 1999.

Gomes, C.P., Selman, B., Crato, N, and Kautz, H. (2000) Heavy-Tailed phenomena in Satisfiability and Constraint Satisfaction Problems. *Journal of Automated Reasoning*, Vol. 24 (1/2) 2000, 67–100.

Gomes, C.P. and Selman, B., McAloon, K., and Tretkoff C. (1998b). Randomization in backtrack search: Exploiting Heavy-Tailed Profiles for Solving Hard Scheduling Problems. *Proc. AIPS-98*.

Gomory, R. (1958) An outline of algorithm for integer solutions to linear programs. *Bulletin of the American mathematical Society*, 1958, 64, 275–278.

Gomory, R. (1963) An algorithm for integer solutions to linear programs. *Recent Advances in Mathematical Programming* McGraw-Hill, Graves, R. and Wolfe, P. (eds.) 1963, 64, 260–302.

Holland, J.H (1992) *Adaptation in natural and artificial systems*. University of Michigan Pres, 1992.

Hooker, J. (1992) Generalized resolution for 0-1 linear inequalities. *Annals of Mathematics and Artificial Intelligence*, 6, 1992, 271–286.

Hooker, J., Ottosson, G., Thorsteinsson, E. and Kim, H. (2000) A scheme for unifying optimization and constraint satisfaction methods. *Knowledge Engineering Review*, Vol. 15 (1), 2000.

Hoos, H. (1999) On the run-time behaviour of stochastic local search algorithms for SAT. *Proceedings of the Fifteenth National Conference on Artificial Intelligence (AAAI-99)*, 1999, 661-666.

Jeroslow, R. (1980) A cutting plane game for facial disjunctive programs. *SIAM J. Control and Optimization*, 18, 1980, 264–280.

Kantorovich, V. (1939) Mathematical Methods in the organization of planning of production. *Management Science*, 6, 1960, 366–422 [English translation.]

Karmarkar, N. (1984) A new polynomial time algorithm for linear programming. *Combinatorica*, 4, 1984, 373–395.

Khachian, V. (1979) A polynomial time algorithm for linear programming. *Math. Doklady*, 20, 1979, 191–194. [English translation.]

Kirkpatrick, S., Gelatt, C.D., and Vecchi, M.P. (1983) Optimization by simulated annealing. *Science*, 220 (1983) 671–680.

Kirkpatrick, S. and Selman, B. (1994) Critical behavior in the satisfiability of random boolean expressions. *Science*, 264 (May 1994) 1297–1301.

Klee, V. and Minty, G. (1972) How good is the simplex algorithm? *Inequalities-III* Shisha, O. (ed.) New York: Academic Press, 1972, 159–175.

Lam, C., Thiel, L., and Swiercz, S. (1989) The non-existence of finite projective planes of order 10. *Can. J. Math.*, Vol. XLI, 6, 1989, 1117–1123.

Lin, S. (1965) Computer solutions of the traveling salesman problem. *BSTJ*, 44, no 10 (1965), 2245–69.

Lin, S. and Kernighan, B.W. (1973) An effective heuristic for the traveling-salesman problem. *Oper. Res.* 21 (1973) 498–516.

Lovasz, L. and Schrijver A. (1991) Cones of matrices and set functions and 0-1 optimizations. *SIAM J. Control and Optimization*, 1991, 166–190.

Luby, M., Sinclair A., and Zuckerman, D. (1993). Optimal speedup of Las Vegas algorithms. *Information Process. Lett.*, 17, 1993, 173–180.

McAloon, K., Tretkoff C. and Wetzel G. (1997). Sports League Scheduling. *Proceedings of Third Ilog International Users Meeting*, 1997.

McAloon, K., Tretkoff C. and Wetzel G. (1998). Disjunctive programming and and cooperating solvers. *Advances in Computational and Stochastic Optimization, Logic Programming, and Heuristic Search*, 1998. Kluwer, Woodruff, D. (ed.), 75–96.

Mitchell, D., Selman, B., and Levesque, H.J. (1992) Hard and easy distributions of SAT problems. *Proc. AAAI-92*, San Jose, CA (1992) 459–465.

Minton, S., Johnston, M., Philips, A.B., and Laird, P. (1992) Minimizing conflicts: a heuristic repair method for constraint satisfaction and scheduling problems. *Artificial Intelligence*, 58 (1992) 161–205,

Monasson, R., Zecchina, R., Kirkpatrick, S., Selman, B., and Troyansky, L. (1996). Determining computational complexity from characteristic 'phase transitions'. *Nature*, Vol. 400(8), 1999.

Motwani, R. and Raghavan P. (1995) Randomized algorithms. Cambridge University Press, 1995.

Nemhauser, G., and Wolsey L. (1988) Integer and Combinatorial Optimization. John Wiley, New York, 1988.

Nemhauser, G., and Trick, M. (1997) Scheduling a major college basketball conference. Georgia Tech., Technical Report, 1997.

Oddi A. and Smith, S. (1997) Stochastic procedures for generating feasible schedules. *Proceedings of the Fourteenth National Conference on Artificial Intelligence (AAAI-97)*, New Providence, RI, 1997.

Puget, J-F., and Leconte, M. (1995). Beyond the black box: constraints as objects. *Proceedings of ILPS'95*, MIT Press, 513–527.

Regin J.C. (1994). A filtering algorithm for constraints of difference in CSPs. *Proceedings of the Eleventh National Conference on Artificial Intelligence (AAAI-94)*, Seattle, 1994.

Regin J.C. (1996). Generalized arc consistency for global cardinality constraint. *Proceedings of the Thirteenth National Conference on Artificial Intelligence (AAAI-96)*, Oregon, 1996.

Rodosek, R., and Wallace, Mark (1998). One model and different solvers for hoist scheduling problems. Manuscript in preparation.

Schrijver A. (1991) Theory of linear and integer programming. Wiley, 1986.

Selman, B., Kautz, H., and Cohen, B. (1994) Noise strategies for improving local search. *Proc. AAAI-94,* Seattle, WA (1994) 337–343.

Selman, B., Levesque, H.J., and Mitchell, D. (1992) A new method for solving hard satisfiability problems. *Proc. AAAI-92*, San Jose, CA (1992) 440–446.

Smith D., and Parra E. (1993). Transformational approach to transportation scheduling. *Proceedings of the Eigth Knowledge-Based Software Engineering Conference*, 1993, Chicago,

Stergiou, K. and Walsh, T. (1999a) The Difference All-Difference Makes Proc. of *IJCAI-99*, Stockholm, Sweden.

Stergiou, K. and Walsh, T. (1999b) Encodings of non-binary constraint satisfaction problems. *Proc. AAAI-99*, Orlando, FL. 1999.

Vance, P., (1993) Crew scheduling, cutting stock, and column Generation: solving huge integer programs. Georgia Tech., PhD Thesis, 1993.

Walsh, T. (1999) Search in a Small World. Proc. of *IJCAI-99*, Stockholm, Sweden, 1999.

Modelling High-Dimensional Data by Combining Simple Experts

Geoffrey E. Hinton
Gatsby Computational Neuroscience Unit
University College London
17 Queen Square, London WC1N 3AR, U.K.
http://www.gatsby.ucl.ac.uk/

Abstract

It is possible to combine multiple non-linear probabilistic models of the same data by multiplying the probability distributions together and then renormalizing. A "product of experts" is a very efficient way to model data that simultaneously satisfies many different constraints. It is difficult to fit a product of experts to data using maximum likelihood because the gradient of the log likelihood is intractable, but there is an efficient way of optimizing a different objective function and this produces good models of high-dimensional data.

Introduction

One way of modeling a complicated, high-dimensional data distribution is to use a large number of relatively simple probabilistic models and to somehow combine the distributions specified by each model. A well-known example of this approach is a mixture of Gaussians in which each simple model is a Gaussian and the combination rule consists of taking a weighted arithmetic mean of the individual distributions. This is equivalent to assuming an overall generative model in which each data vector is generated by first choosing one of the individual generative models and then allowing that individual model to generate the data vector. Combining models by forming a mixture is attractive because it is easy to fit mixtures of tractable models to data using EM or gradient ascent and, if sufficiently many models are included in the mixture, it is possible to approximate complicated smooth distributions arbitrarily accurately.

Unfortunately, mixture models are very inefficient in high-dimensional spaces. Consider, for example, the manifold of face images. It takes about 35 real numbers to specify the shape, pose, expression and illumination of a face and, under good viewing conditions, our perceptual systems produce a sharp posterior distribution on this 35-dimensional manifold. This cannot be done using a mixture of simple models each of which is tuned in the 35-dimensional manifold because the posterior distribution cannot be sharper than the individual models in the mixture and the individual models must be broadly tuned to allow them to cover the 35-dimensional manifold.

Copyright © 2000, American Association for Artificial Intelligence (www.aaai.org). All rights reserved.

A very different way of combining distributions is to multiply them together and renormalize. If the individual distributions are uni- or multivariate Gaussians, their product will also be a multivariate Gaussian so, unlike mixtures of Gaussians, products of Gaussians cannot approximate arbitrary smooth distributions. If, however, the individual models are a bit more complicated and each contain one or more latent (*i.e.* hidden) variables, multiplying their distributions together (and renormalizing) can be very powerful. Individual models of this kind will be called "experts".

Products of Experts (PoE) have the advantage that they can produce much sharper distributions than the individual expert models. For example, each expert model can constrain a different subset of the dimensions in a high-dimensional space and their product will then constrain all of the dimensions. For modeling handwritten digits, one low-resolution model can generate images that have the approximate overall shape of the digit and other more local models can ensure that small image patches contain segments of stroke with the correct fine structure. For modeling sentences, each expert can enforce a nugget of linguistic knowledge. For example, one expert could ensure that the tenses agree, one could ensure that there is number agreement between the subject and verb and one could ensure that strings in which colour adjectives follow size adjectives are more probable than the the reverse.

The idea of combining the opinions of multiple different expert models by using a weighted average in the log probability domain (i.e. a product) is far from new (Genest and Zidek, 1986; Heskes 1998), but research has focussed on how to find the best weights for combining experts that have already been learned separately rather than training the experts cooperatively. This may be because fitting a PoE to data appears very difficult. It appears to be necessary to compute the derivatives, with repect to the parameters, of the partition function that is used in the renormalization. As we shall see, however, these derivatives can be finessed by optimizing a less obvious objective function than the log likelihood of the data.

Learning PoE's by maximizing likelihood

We consider individual expert models for which it is tractable to compute the derivative of the log probability of a data vector with respect to the parameters of the expert. We combine n individual expert models as follows:

$$p(\mathbf{d}|\theta_1...\theta_n) = \frac{\Pi_m p_m(\mathbf{d}|\theta_m)}{\sum_\mathbf{c} \Pi_m p_m(\mathbf{c}|\theta_m)} \quad (1)$$

where $\mathbf{d}$ is a data vector in a discrete space, θ_m is all the parameters of individual model m, $p_m(\mathbf{d}|\theta_m)$ is the probability of $\mathbf{d}$ under model m, and $\mathbf{c}$ indexes all possible vectors in the data space [1]. For continuous data spaces the sum is replaced by the appropriate integral.

For an individual expert to fit the data well it must give high probability to the observed data and it must waste as little probability as possible on the rest of the data space. A PoE, however, can fit the data well even if each expert wastes a lot of its probability on inappropriate regions of the data space provided different experts waste probability in different regions.

The obvious way to fit a PoE to a set of observed *iid* data vectors is to compute the derivative of the log likelihood of each observed vector, $\mathbf{d}$, under the PoE. This is given by:

$$\frac{\partial \log p(\mathbf{d}|\theta_1...\theta_n)}{\partial \theta_m} = \frac{\partial \log p_m(\mathbf{d}|\theta_m)}{\partial \theta_m}$$
$$- \sum_\mathbf{c} p(\mathbf{c}|\theta_1...\theta_n) \frac{\partial \log p_m(\mathbf{c}|\theta_m)}{\partial \theta_m} \quad (2)$$

The second term on the RHS of Eq. 2 is just the expected derivative of the log probability of an expert on fantasy data, $\mathbf{c}$, that is generated from the PoE. So, assuming that each of the individual experts has a tractable derivative, the obvious difficulty in estimating the derivative of the log probability of the data under the PoE is generating correctly distributed fantasy data. This can be done in various ways. For discrete data it is possible to use rejection sampling: Each expert generates a data vector independently and this process is repeated until all the experts happen to agree. Rejection sampling is a good way of understanding how a PoE specifies an overall probability distribution and how different it is from a causal model, but it is typically *very* inefficient. A Markov chain Monte Carlo method that uses Gibbs sampling is typically much more efficient. In Gibbs sampling, each variable draws a sample from its posterior distribution given the current states of the other variables. Given the data, the hidden states of all the experts can always be updated in parallel because they are conditionally independent. This is a very important consequence of the product formulation. If the individual experts also have the property that the components of the data vector are conditionally independent given the hidden state of the expert, the hidden and visible variables form a bipartite graph and it is possible to update all of the components of the data vector in parallel given the hidden states of all the experts. So Gibbs sampling can alternate between parallel updates of the hidden and visible variables. To get an unbiased estimate of the gradient for the PoE it is

---

[1] The symbol p_m has no simple relationship to the symbol p used on the LHS of Eq. 1. Indeed, so long as $p_m(\mathbf{d}|\theta_m)$ is positive it does not need to be a probability at all, though it will generally be a probability in this paper.

necessary for the Markov chain to converge to the equilibrium distribution.

Unfortunately, even if it is computationally feasible to approach equilibrium before taking samples, there is a second serious difficulty. Samples from the equilibrium distribution generally have very high variance since they come from all over the model's distribution. This high variance swamps the derivative. Worse still, the variance in the samples depends on the parameters of the model. This variation in the variance causes the parameters to be strongly repelled from regions of high variance even if the gradient is zero. To understand this subtle but powerful effect, consider a horizontal sheet of tin which is resonating in such a way that some parts have strong vertical oscillations and other parts are motionless. Sand scattered on the tin will accumulate in the motionless areas even though the time-averaged gradient is zero everywhere.

Learning by maximizing contrastive likelihood

There is a simple and very effective alternative to maximum likelihood learning which eliminates almost all of the computation required to get samples from the equilibrium distribution and also eliminates almost all of the variance that masks the gradient signal. Instead of maximizing the log likelihood of the data, we maximize the *difference* between the log likelihood of the data vectors and the log likelihood of "one-step" reconstructions of the data vectors. This objective function will be called the "contrastive log likelihood". The reconstructions are generated by one full step of Gibbs sampling, which involves the following four stages:

1. Compute, for each expert separately, the posterior probability distribution over its hidden variables given the data vector, $\mathbf{d}$.

2. Pick a value for each latent variable from its posterior distribution.

3. Given the chosen values of all the latent variables, compute the conditional distribution over each visible variable by multiplying together the conditional distributions specified by each expert.

4. Pick a value for each visible variable from its conditional distribution. These values constitute the reconstructed data vector, $\hat{\mathbf{d}}$.

Each expert is chosen to be tractable, so it is possible to compute the exact value of the first term on the RHS of Eq. 2 for both $\mathbf{d}$ and $\hat{\mathbf{d}}$. The second term on the RHS is the same for $\mathbf{d}$ and $\hat{\mathbf{d}}$. So if we ignore the fact that, unlike the data, the distribution of the reconstructions depends on the parameters of the experts, we get a simple rule for approximately following the gradient of the contrastive log likelihood:

$$\Delta \theta_m \propto \frac{\partial \log p_m(\mathbf{d}|\theta_m)}{\partial \theta_m} - \frac{\partial <\log p_m(\hat{\mathbf{d}}|\theta_m)>_{\hat{\mathbf{d}}}}{\partial \theta_m} \quad (3)$$

where the angle brackets denote expectations over the distribution of the one-step reconstructions of $\mathbf{d}$. This works very well in practice even when a single reconstruction of each data vector is used in place of the full probability distribution over reconstructions. Changing θ_m changes the distribution of $\hat{\mathbf{d}}$ but this effect only makes a small contribution to the derivative of the contrastive log likelihood so the expected vector of changes in the parameters given by Eq. 3 almost always has a positive cosine with the true gradient of the contrastive log likelihood (see Hinton (1999) for details).

The difference in the derivatives of the data vectors and their reconstructions has some variance because the reconstruction procedure is stochastic. But when the PoE is modelling the data moderately well, the one-step reconstructions will be very similar to the data so the variance will be very small. The close match between a data vector and its reconstruction reduces sampling variance in much the same way as the use of matched pairs for experimental and control conditions in a clincal trial. The low variance makes it feasible to perform online learning after each data vector is presented, though the simulations described in this paper use batch learning in which the parameter updates are based on the summed gradients measured on all of the training set or on relatively large mini-batches.

The idea of simultaneously maximizing the log likelihood of the data and minimizing the log likelihood of the one-step reconstructions is central to this paper. Its main justification is that it is computationally easy and it works well in practice, but it also has a number of intuitive justifications.

In high-dimensional datasets, the data nearly always lies on, or close to, a much lower-dimensional, smoothly curved manifold. The PoE needs to find parameters that make a sharp ridge of log probability along the low-dimensional manifold. By starting with a point on the manifold and ensuring that this point has higher log probability than the typical reconstructions from the latent variables of all the experts, the PoE ensures that the probability distribution has the right local curvature (provided the reconstructions are close to the data). It is possible that the PoE will accidentally assign high probability to other distant and unvisited parts of the data space, but this is unlikely if the log probabilty surface is smooth and if both its height and its local curvature are constrained at the data points. It is also possible to find and eliminate such points by performing prolonged Gibbs sampling without any data, but this is just a way of improving the learning and not, as in Boltzmann machine learning, an essential part of it.

Perhaps the best intuitive justification comes from considering the convergence of the Gibbs sampling procedure towards the equilibrium distribution. To maximize the log likelihood of the observed data we need to minimize the Kullback-Liebler divergence between the data distribution and the marginal over the visible variables of the equilibrium distribution. If we already have a perfect model and we use the data distribution to initialize the Gibbs sampling, we will already be at equilibrium. So maybe we can find a good model by initializing the Gibbs sampling with the data, observing how one step of convergence to equilibrium causes us to diverge from the initial distribution, and adjusting the parameters to cancel out this divergence. The obvious way to reduce the tendency to wander away from the data distribution is to increase the log likelihood of the data vectors we start with and to decrease the log likelihood of the reconstructed data vectors. Because Gibbs sampling moves towards the equilibrium distribution of the model, the reconstructed vectors cannot, on average, be less likely under the model than the data vectors and they can only have the same average likelihood when the model is perfect (assuming that the Markov chain mixes).

Although these intuitive justifications are each somewhat vague, their product is sharper.

PoE's and Boltzmann machines

The Boltzmann machine learning algorithm (Hinton and Sejnowski, 1986) is easy to implement in hardware, but it is very slow in networks with interconnected hidden units. Smolensky (1986) introduced a restricted type of Boltzmann machine with one visible layer, one hidden layer, and no intralayer connections. Freund and Haussler (1992) realised that in this restricted Boltzmann machine (RBM), the probability of generating a visible vector is proportional to the product of the probabilities that the visible vector would be generated by each of the hidden units acting alone. An RBM is therefore a PoE with one expert per hidden unit[2]. When the hidden unit of an expert is off it specifies a factorial probability distribution in which each visible unit is equally likely to be on or off. When the hidden unit is on, it specifies a different factorial distribution by using the weight on its connection to each visible unit to specify the log odds that the visible unit is on. Multiplying together the distributions over the visible states specified by different experts is achieved by simply adding the log odds. Exact inference is tractable in an RBM because the states of the hidden units are conditionally independent given the data.

The learning algorithm given by Eq. 2 is exactly equivalent to the standard Boltzmann learning algorithm for an RBM. Consider the derivative of the log probability of the data with respect to the weight w_{ij} between a visible unit i and a hidden unit j. The first term on the RHS of Eq. 2 is:

$$\frac{\partial \log p_j(\mathbf{d}|\mathbf{w}_j)}{\partial w_{ij}} = <s_i s_j>^0 - <s_i s_j>^{j\infty} \quad (4)$$

where $\mathbf{w}_j$ is the vector of weights connecting hidden unit j to the visible units, $<s_i s_j>^0$ is the expected value of $s_i s_j$ when $\mathbf{d}$ is clamped on the visible units and s_j is sampled from its posterior distribution given $\mathbf{d}$, and $<s_i s_j>^{j\infty}$ is the expected value of $s_i s_j$ when alternating Gibbs sampling of the single hidden unit and the visible units is iterated to get samples from the equilibrium distribution in a network whose only hidden unit is j.

The second term on the RHS of Eq. 2 is:

$$\sum_{\mathbf{c}} p(\mathbf{c}|\mathbf{w}) \frac{\partial \log p_j(\mathbf{c}|\mathbf{w}_j)}{\partial w_{ij}} = <s_i s_j>^\infty - <s_i s_j>^{j\infty} \quad (5)$$

---

[2]Boltzmann machines and Products of Experts are very different classes of probabilistic generative model and the intersection of the two classes is RBM's

where **w** is all of the weights in the RBM and $<s_i s_j>^\infty$ is the expected value of $s_i s_j$ when alternating Gibbs sampling of all the hidden and all the visible units is iterated to get samples from the equilibrium distribution of the RBM.

Subtracting Eq. 5 from Eq. 4 gives the gradient of the log likelihood of d:

$$\frac{\partial \log p(\mathbf{d}|\mathbf{w})}{\partial w_{ij}} = <s_i s_j>^0 - <s_i s_j>^\infty \qquad (6)$$

The high sampling variance in $<s_i s_j>^\infty$ makes learning difficult. It is much more effective to follow the approximate gradient of the contrastive log likelihood. For an RBM this approximate gradient is particularly easy to compute:

$$\frac{\partial \log p(\mathbf{d}|\mathbf{w})}{\partial w_{ij}} - \frac{\partial <\log p(\hat{\mathbf{d}}|\mathbf{w})>_{\hat{\mathbf{d}}}}{\partial w_{ij}} \approx <s_i s_j>^0 - <s_i s_j>^1 \qquad (7)$$

where $<s_i s_j>^1$ is the expected value of $s_i s_j$ when a one-step reconstruction of **d** is clamped on the visible units and s_j is sampled from its posterior given the reconstruction.

Learning the features of handwritten digits

When presented with real, high-dimensional data, a restricted Boltzmann machine trained to maximize the contrastive log likelihood using Eq. 7 should learn a set of probabilistic binary features that model the data well. To test this conjecture, an RBM with 500 hidden units and 256 visible units was trained on 8000 16 × 16 real-valued images of handwritten digits from all 10 classes. The images, from the training set on the USPS Cedar ROM, were normalized but highly variable in style. The pixel intensities were normalized to lie between 0 and 1 so that they could be treated as probabilities and Eq. 7 was modified to use probabilities in place of stochastic binary values for both the data and the hidden units. The binary values of the hidden units were still used for generating the one-step reconstructions.

It took two days in matlab on a second millenium workstation to perform 658 epochs of learning. In each epoch, the weights were updated 80 times using the approximate gradient of the contrastive log likelihood computed on mini-batches of size 100 that contained 10 exemplars of each digit class. To improve the learning speed a momentum method was used. Except for the first 10 epochs, the parameter updates were supplemented by adding 0.9 times the previous update.

The PoE learned localised features whose binary states yielded almost perfect reconstructions. For each image about one third of the features were turned on. Some of the learned features had on-center off-surround receptive fields or vice versa, some looked like pieces of stroke, and some looked like Gabor filters or wavelets. The weights of 100 of the hidden units, selected at random, are shown in figure 1.

Learning to discriminate handwritten digits

An attractive aspect of PoE's is that it is easy to compute the numerator in Eq. 1 so it is easy to compute the log probability of a data vector up to an additive constant, $\log Z$, which

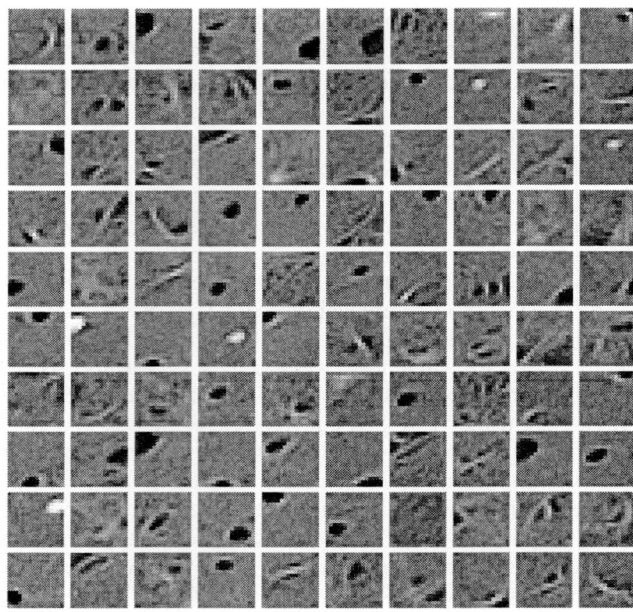

Figure 1: The receptive fields of a randomly selected subset of the 500 hidden units in a PoE trained on 8000 images of digits with equal numbers from each class. Each block shows the 256 learned weights connecting a hidden unit to the pixels. The scale goes from +2 (white) to −2 (black).

is the log of the denominator in Eq. 1. Unfortunately, it is hard to compute this additive constant. This does not matter if we only want to compare the probabilities of two different data vectors under the PoE, but it makes it difficult to evaluate the model learned by a PoE by summing the log probabilities that the PoE assigns to test data vectors.

An alternative way to evaluate the learning procedure is to learn two different PoE's on different datasets such as images of the digit 2 and images of the digit 3. After learning, a test image, **t**, is presented to PoE_2 and PoE_3 and they compute $\log p(\mathbf{t}|\theta_2) + \log Z_2$ and $\log p(\mathbf{t}|\theta_3) + \log Z_3$ respectively. If the difference between $\log Z_2$ and $\log Z_3$ is known it is easy to pick the most likely class of the test image, and since this difference is only a single number it is quite easy to estimate it discriminatively using a set of validation images whose labels are known.

Figure 2 shows features learned by a PoE that contains a layer of 100 hidden units and is trained on 800 images of the digit 2. Figure 3 shows some previously unseen test images of 2's and their one-step reconstructions from the binary activities of the PoE trained on 2's and from an identical PoE trained on 3's.

Figure 4 shows the unnormalized log probability scores of some test images under a model trained on 825 images of the digit 7 and a model trained on 825 images of the digit 9. These two classes were chosen because they are the most difficult to discriminate. Discrimination is not perfect on the test images, but it is encouraging that all of the errors are close to the decision boundary, so there are no confident mis-

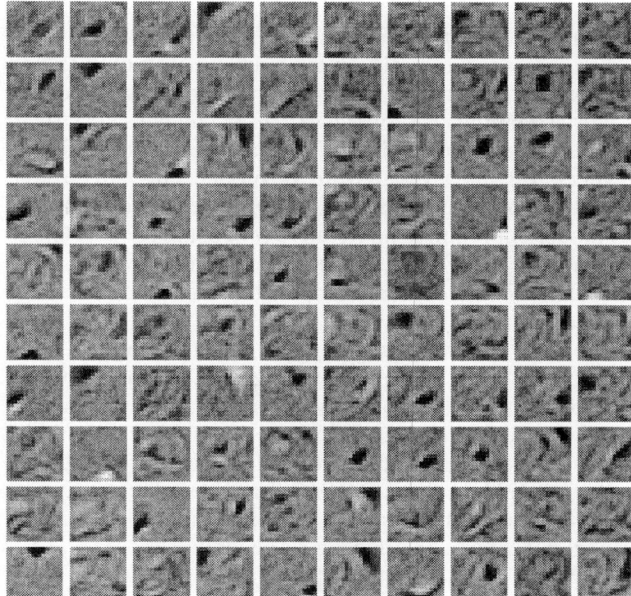

Figure 2: The weights learned by 100 hidden units trained on 16 x 16 images of the digit 2. The scale goes from +3 (white) to −3 (black). Note that the fields are mostly quite local. A local feature like the one in column 1 row 7 looks like an edge detector, but it is best understood as a local deformation of a template. Suppose that all the other active features create an image of a 2 that differs from the data in having a large loop whose top falls on the black part of the receptive field. By turning on this feature, the top of the loop can be removed and replaced by a line segment that is a little lower in the image.

classifications. To achieve this excellent separation, it was necessary to use models with two hidden layers and to average the scores from two separately trained models of each digit class. For each digit class, one model had 200 units in its first hidden layer and 100 in its second hidden layer. The other model had 100 in the first hidden layer and 50 in the second. The units in the first hidden layer were trained without regard to the second hidden layer. After training the first hidden layer, the second hidden layer was then trained using the probabilities of feature activation in the first hidden layer as the data.

If there are 10 different PoE's for the 10 digit classes it is slightly less obvious how to use the 10 unnormalized scores of a test image for discrimination. One possibility is to use a validation set to train a logistic regression network that takes the unnormalized log probabilities given by the PoE's and converts them into a probability distribution across the 10 labels (see Hinton (1999) for details). This gives an error rate of 1.1% which compares very favorably with the 5.1% error rate of a simple nearest neighbor classifier on the same training and test sets and is about the same as the very best classifier based on elastic models of the digits (Revow, Williams and Hinton, 1996). If 7% rejects are allowed (by

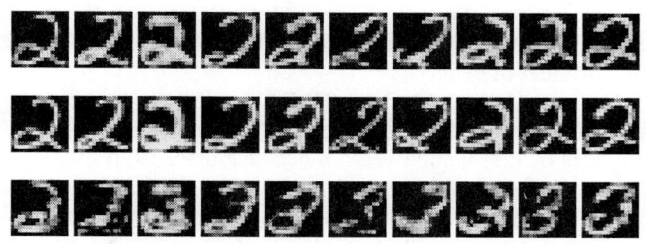

Figure 3: The center row is previously unseen images of 2's. The top row shows the pixel probabilities when the image is reconstructed from the binary activities of 100 feature detectors that have been trained on 2's. The bottom row shows the reconstruction probabilities using 100 feature detectors trained on 3's.

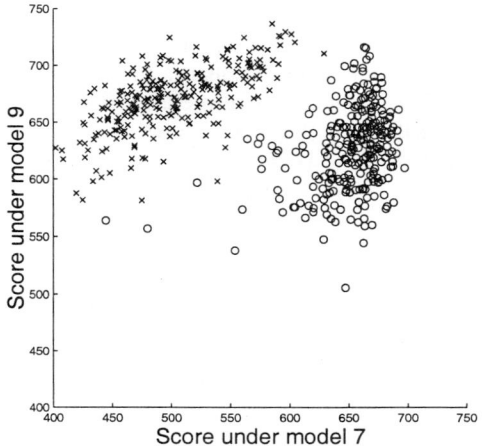

Figure 4: The unnormalised log probability scores of the previously unseen test images of 7's and 9's. Although the classes are not linearly separable, all the errors are close to the best separating line.

choosing an appropriate threshold for the probability level of the most probable class), there are no errors on the 2750 test images.

Other types of expert

Binary stochastic pixels are not unreasonable for modeling preprocessed images of handwritten digits in which ink and background are represented as 1 and 0. In real images, however, there is typically very high mutual information between the real-valued intensity of one pixel and the real-valued intensities of its neighbors. This cannot be captured by models that use binary stochastic pixels because a binary pixel can never have more than 1 bit of mutual information with anything. An interesting approach is to use experts that each consist of a mixture of a uniform distribution and a factor analyser with just one factor. Each expert has a binary latent variable that specifies whether to use the uniform or the factor analyser and a real-valued latent variable that specifies the value of the factor. Experts of this type have been explored in the context of directed acyclic graphs (Hinton, Sallans and Ghahramani, 1998) but they should work better in a product of experts.

Hidden Markov Models (HMM's) are of great practical value in modeling sequences of discrete symbols or sequences of real-valued vectors because there is an efficient algorithm for updating the parameters of the HMM to improve the log likelihood of a set of observed sequences. HMM's are, however, quite limited in their generative power because the only way that the portion of a string generated up to time t can constrain the portion of the string generated after time t is via the discrete hidden state of the generator at time t. So if the first part of a string has, on average, n bits of mutual information with the rest of the string the HMM must have 2^n hidden states to convey this mutual information by its choice of hidden state. This exponential inefficiency can be overcome by using a product of HMM's as a generator. During generation, each HMM gets to pick a hidden state at each time so the mutual information between the past and the future can be linear in the number of HMM's. It is therefore exponentially more efficient to have many small HMM's than one big one. However, to apply the standard forward-backward algorithm to a product of HMM's it is necessary to take the cross-product of their state spaces which throws away the exponential win.

For products of HMM's to be of practical significance it is necessary to find an efficient way to train them. Andrew Brown (Brown and Hinton, *in preparation*) has shown that for a toy example involving a product of four HMM's, the learning algorithm in Eq. 3 works well. The forward-backward algorithm is used to get the gradient of the log likelihood of an observed or reconstructed sequence *w.r.t.* the parameters of an individual expert. The one-step reconstruction of a sequence is generated by using the forward-backward algorithm in each expert separately to calculate the posterior probability distribution over paths through the hidden states, then stochastically selecting a hidden path in each expert from the posterior. At each time step in the reconstructed sequence, an output symbol or output vector is then chosen from the product of the output distributions specified by the hidden state selected for that time step in each HMM. If more realistic products of HMM's can be trained successfully by maximizing the contrastive likelihood, they should be far better than single HMM's for many different kinds of sequential data.

Comparison with directed acyclic graphical models

Inference in a PoE is trivial because the experts are individually tractable and the product formulation ensures that the hidden states of different experts are conditionally independent given the data. This makes them relevant as models of biological perceptual systems, which must be able to do inference very rapidly. Alternative approaches based on directed acyclic graphical models suffer from the "explaining away" phenomenon. When such graphical models are densely connected exact inference is intractable, so it is necessary to resort to clever but implausibly slow iterative techniques for approximate inference (Saul and Jordan, 1998) or to use crude approximations that ignore explaining away during inference and rely on the learning algorithm to find representations for which the shoddy inference technique is not too damaging (Hinton, Dayan, Frey and Neal, 1995).

The ease of inference in PoE's is balanced by the difficulty of generating fantasy data from the model. This can be done trivially in one ancestral pass in a directed acyclic graphical model but requires an iterative procedure such as Gibbs sampling in a PoE. If, however, Eq. 3 is used for learning, the difficulty of generating samples from the model does not impede learning.

The most attractive property of a set of orthogonal basis functions is that it is possible to compute the coefficient on each basis function separately without worrying about the coefficients on other basis functions. If the generative model is causal, this attractive property can only be achieved by using basis functions that are orthogonal. A product of experts, however, retains this attractive property whilst allowing non-orthogonal experts and non-linear generative models.

Acknowledgements

This research was funded by the Gatsby Charitable Foundation. Thanks to Peter Dayan, Zoubin Ghahramani, David MacKay, David Lowe, Yee-Whye Teh, Guy Mayraz, Andy Brown, and other members of the Gatsby unit for helpful discussions.

References

Freund, Y. and Haussler, D. (1992) Unsupervised learning of distributions on binary vectors using two layer networks. *Advances in Neural Information Processing Systems 4*. J. E. Moody, S. J. Hanson and R. P. Lippmann (Eds.), Morgan Kaufmann: San Mateo, CA.

Genest, C. & Zidek, J. V. (1986) Combining probability distributions: A critique and an annotated bibliography. *Statistical Science* **1**, 114-148.

Heskes, T. (1998) Bias/Variance decompositions for likelihood-based estimators. *Neural Computation* **10**, 1425-1433.

Hinton, G. E. (1999) Training Products of Experts by Maximizing Contrastive Likelihood. Technical Report: GCNU TR1999-001. Gatsby Computational Neuroscience Unit, University College London (www.gatsby.ucl.ac.uk).

Hinton, G., Dayan, P., Frey, B. & Neal, R. (1995) The wake-sleep algorithm for self-organizing neural networks. *Science*, **268**, 1158-1161.

Hinton, G. E. Sallans, B. and Ghahramani, Z. (1998) Hierarchical Communities of Experts. In M. I. Jordan (Ed.) *Learning in Graphical Models*. Kluwer Academic Press.

Hinton, G. E. & Sejnowski, T. J. (1986) Learning and relearning in Boltzmann machines. In Rumelhart, D. E. and McClelland, J. L., editors, *Parallel Distributed Processing: Explorations in the Microstructure of Cognition. Volume 1: Foundations*, MIT Press.

Revow, M., Williams, C. K. I. and Hinton, G. E. (1996) Using Generative Models for Handwritten Digit Recognition. *IEEE Transactions on Pattern Analysis and Machine Intelligence*, **18**, 592-606.

Saul, L. K., Jaakkola, T. & Jordan, M. I. (1996) Mean field theory for sigmoid belief networks. *Journal of Artificial Intelligence Research*, **4** 61-76.

Smolensky, P. (1986) Information processing in dynamical systems: Foundations of harmony theory. In Rumelhart, D. E. and McClelland, J. L., editors, *Parallel Distributed Processing: Explorations in the Microstructure of Cognition. Volume 1: Foundations*, MIT Press.

Recent Progress in the Design and Analysis of Admissible Heuristic Functions

Richard E. Korf
Computer Science Department
University of California, Los Angeles
Los Angeles, CA 90095
korf@cs.ucla.edu

Abstract

In the past several years, significant progress has been made in finding optimal solutions to combinatorial problems. In particular, random instances of both Rubik's Cube, with over 10^{19} states, and the 5×5 sliding-tile puzzle, with almost 10^{25} states, have been solved optimally. This progress is not the result of better search algorithms, but more effective heuristic evaluation functions. In addition, we have learned how to accurately predict the running time of admissible heuristic search algorithms, as a function of the solution depth and the heuristic evaluation function. One corollary of this analysis is that an admissible heuristic function reduces the effective depth of search, rather than the effective branching factor.

Introduction

The Fifteen Puzzle consists of fifteen numbered square tiles in a 4×4 square grid, with one position empty or blank. Any tile horizontally or vertically adjacent to the blank can be moved into the blank position. The task is to rearrange the tiles from some random initial configuration into a desired goal configuration, ideally or optimally using the fewest moves possible.

The Fifteen Puzzle was invented by Sam Loyd in the 1870s (Loyd, 1959), and appeared in the scientific literature shortly thereafter (Johnson and Story, 1879). The editor of the journal added the following comment to the paper: "The '15' puzzle for the last few weeks has been prominently before the American public, and may safely be said to have engaged the attention of nine out of ten persons of both sexes and of all ages and conditions of the community."

One reason for the world-wide Fifteen Puzzle craze was that Loyd offered a $1000 cash prize to transform a particular initial state to a particular goal state. Johnson and Story proved that it wasn't possible, that the entire state space was divided into even and odd permutations, and that there is no way to transform one into the other by legal moves.

Rubik's Cube was invented in 1974 by Erno Rubik of Hungary, and like the Fifteen Puzzle a hundred years earlier, became a world-wide sensation. More than 100 million Rubik's Cubes have been sold, and it is the best-known combinatorial puzzle of all time.

In the remainder of this paper, we'll use these example problems to illustrate recent progress in heuristic search. In particular, the design of more accurate heuristic evaluation functions has allowed us to find optimal solutions to random instances of both the 5×5 Twenty-Four puzzle, and Rubik's Cube for the first time. In addition, we'll present a theory that allows us to accurately predict the running time of admissible heuristic search algorithms from the solution depth and the heuristic evaluation function. One consequence of this theory is that an admissible heuristic function decreases the effective depth of search, relative to a brute-force search, rather than the effective branching factor.

Search Algorithms

The 3×3 Eight puzzle contains only 181,440 reachable states, and hence can be solved optimally by a brute-force breadth-first search in a fraction of a second.

To solve the 4×4 Fifteen Puzzle however, with about 10^{13} states, we need a heuristic search algorithm, such as A* (Hart, Nilsson, and Raphael 1968). A* is a best-first search in which the cost of a node n is computed as $f(n) = g(n) + h(n)$, where $g(n)$ is the length of the current path from the start to node n, and $h(n)$ is a heuristic estimate of the length of a shortest path from node n to a goal. If $h(n)$ is *admissible*, meaning it never overestimates the distance to a goal, A* is guaranteed to find a shortest solution, if one exists.

The classic heuristic function for the sliding-tile puzzles is Manhattan distance. It is computed by taking each tile, counting the number of grid units between its current location and its goal location, and summing these values for all tiles. Manhattan distance is a lower bound on actual solution length, because every tile must move at least its Manhattan distance, and each move only moves one tile.

Unfortunately, A* can't solve the Fifteen Puzzle, because it stores every node it generates, and exhausts the available memory on most problems before finding a solution. Iterative-Deepening-A* (IDA*) (Korf, 1985) is a linear-space version of A*. It performs a series of depth-first searches, pruning a path and backtracking when the cost $f(n) = g(n) + h(n)$ of a node n on the path exceeds a cutoff threshold for that iteration. The initial threshold is set to the heuristic estimate of the initial state, and increases in each iteration to the lowest cost all the nodes pruned on the last iteration, until a goal node is expanded. Like A*, IDA* guarantees an optimal solution if the heuristic function is admissible. Unlike A*, however, IDA* only requires memory that is linear in the maximum search depth. IDA*, using the Manhattan distance heuristic, was the first algorithm to find optimal solutions to random instances of the Fifteen Puzzle (Korf, 1985). An average of about 400 million nodes are generated per problem instance, requiring about 6 hours of running time in 1985.

Design of Heuristic Functions
Classical Explanation

The standard explanation for the origin of heuristic functions is that they compute the cost of exact solutions to a simplified version of the original problem (Pearl, 1984). For example, in the sliding-tile puzzles, if we ignore the constraint that we can only move a tile into the empty position, we get a new problem where any tile can be moved to any adjacent position, and multiple tiles can occupy the same position. In this simplified problem, we can solve any instance by taking each tile one at a time, and moving it along a shortest path to its goal position, counting the number of moves made. The cost of an optimal solution to this simplified problem is just the Manhattan distance of the original problem. Since we simplified the problem by removing a constraint on the moves, any solution to the original problem is also a solution to the simplified problem, and hence the cost of an optimal solution to the simplified problem is a lower bound on the cost of an optimal solution to the original problem. Thus, any heuristic derived in this way is admissible.

What makes it possible to efficiently compute the Manhattan distance is that in the simplified problem, the individual tiles can move independently of each another. The reason the original problem is difficult, and why the Manhattan distance is only a lower bound on actual cost, is that the tiles interact. By taking into account some of these interactions, we can compute more accurate admissible heuristic functions.

Pattern Databases

Pattern databases (Culberson and Schaeffer, 1998) are one way to do this. Consider any subset of tiles, such as the seven tiles in the right column and bottom row of the Fifteen Puzzle, which they called the *fringe pattern*. The minimum number of moves required to get the fringe tiles from their initial positions to their goal positions, including any required moves of other tiles as well, is obviously a lower bound on the minimum number of moves needed to solve the entire problem.

It would be too expensive to calculate the moves needed to solve the fringe tiles for each state in the search. This number, however, depends only on the positions of the fringe tiles and the blank position, but not on the positions of the other tiles. Since there are only a limited number of such configurations, we can precompute all of these values, store them in memory in a table, and look them up as needed during the search. Since there are seven fringe tiles and one blank, and sixteen different locations, the total number of possible configurations of these tiles is $16!/(16-8)! = 518,918,400$. For each table entry, we can store the number of moves needed to solve the fringe tiles from their corresponding locations, which takes only a byte of storage. Thus, we can store the whole table in less than 500 megabytes of memory.

We can compute this table by a single breadth-first search backward from the goal state. In this search, the non-pattern tiles are all considered equivalent, and a state is uniquely determined by the positions of the pattern tiles and the blank. As each configuration of these tiles is encountered for the first time, the number of moves made to reach it is stored in the corresponding entry of the pattern database. The search continues until all entries of the table are filled. Note that this table is only computed once for a given goal state, and its cost can be amortized over the solution of multiple problem instances with the same goal state.

Once the table is built, we use IDA* to search for an optimal solution to a problem instance. As each state is generated, the positions of the pattern tiles and the blank are used to compute an index into the pattern database, and the corresponding entry, which is the number of moves needed to solve the pattern tiles, is used as the heuristic value for that state.

Using the fringe pattern database, (Culberson and Schaeffer, 1998) reduced the number of nodes generated to solve the Fifteen Puzzle by a factor of 346, and reduced the running time by a factor of 6. Combining this with another pattern database, and taking the maximum of the two database values as the heuristic value, reduced the nodes generated by about a thousand, and the running time by a factor of 12, compared to Manhattan distance.

Rubik's Cube Pattern databases have also been used to find optimal solutions to Rubik's Cube (Korf, 1997). The standard $3 \times 3 \times 3$ Rubik's Cube contains about 4.3252×10^{19} different reachable states. Of the 27 subcubes, or *cubies*, 20 of them move. These can be divided into eight *corner cubies*, with three faces each, and twelve *edge cubies*, with two faces each. There are only $88,179,840$ different configurations of the corner cubies, and the number of moves to solve just the corner cubies ranges from zero to eleven moves. At four bits per entry, a pattern database for the corner cubies requires about 42 megabytes of memory. Six of the twelve edge cubies generate $42,577,920$ different possibilities, and a corresponding pattern database requires about 20 megabytes of memory. Similarly, the remaining six edge cubies generate another pattern database of the same size.

Given multiple pattern databases, the best way to combine them without overestimating the actual solution cost, is to take the maximum of their values, even if the cubies in the different databases don't overlap. The reason for this is that every twist of the cube moves eight different cubies, and hence moves that contribute to the solution of the cubies in one pattern may also contribute to the solution of the others. Taking the maximum of the values in all three pattern databases described allowed IDA* to find the first optimal solutions to random instances of Rubik's Cube (Korf, 1997). The median optimal solution length is 18 moves. At least one problem instance generated a trillion nodes, and required a couple weeks to run. With further improvements by Michael Reid, Herbert Kociemba, and others, most states can now be solved optimally in a day.

Disjoint Pattern Databases

The main limitation of Culberson and Schaeffer's pattern databases is that the only way to combine the values from different databases without overestimating actual cost is to take their maximum value. Returning to the Fifteen Puzzle, even if we compute a separate pattern database for the remaining eight tiles not in the fringe pattern, the best admissible combination of these two heuristic values is their maximum. The reason is that Culberson and Schaeffer counted all moves required to solve the pattern tiles, including moves of tiles not in the pattern. As a result, moves used to solve tiles in one pattern may also be used to solve tiles in another pattern.

One way to improve on this is when computing the heuristic value for a pattern of tiles, only count the moves of the tiles in the pattern. Then, given two or more patterns that have no tiles in common, we can add together the heuristic values from the different databases, and still get an admissible heuristic. This is because in the sliding-tile puzzle, each operator only moves a single tile. We call such a set of databases a *disjoint pattern database*, or a disjoint database for short. Summing the values of different heuristics results in a much larger value than taking their maximum, and thus greatly reduces the amount of search that is necessary.

A trivial example of a disjoint pattern database is Manhattan distance. Manhattan distance can be viewed as the sum of a set of individual pattern database values, each representing only a single tile. It could be "discovered" by running a pattern search for each tile, recording the number of moves required to get that tile to each location from its goal location.

A non-trivial example of a disjoint database divides the Fifteen Puzzle in half horizontally, into a group of seven tiles on top, and eight tiles on the bottom, assuming the goal position of the blank is the upper-left corner. We precompute the number of moves required to solve the tiles in each of these two patterns, from all possible combinations of positions, but only counting moves of the tiles in the given pattern. Instead of explicitly representing the blank position in the database, we store the minimum value for all possible positions of the blank. The eight-tile pattern contains $16!/(16-8)! = 518,918,400$ entries, each of which requires a byte, or 495 megabytes of memory. The 7-tile pattern contains only $16!/(16-7)! = 57,657,600$ entries, or 55 megabytes of storage.

The memory requirement can be reduced by only storing in the database the number of moves needed in addition to the sum of the Manhattan distances of the pattern tiles, which only takes four bits. Then, during the search, we compute the Manhattan distances of the pattern tiles, and add the database value to the Manhattan distance to get the overall heuristic.

Once these pattern databases are computed and stored, we get another set of heuristic values by reflecting all the tiles and their positions about the main diagonal of the puzzle. This gives us a 7-tile database on the left side of the puzzle, and an 8-tile pattern database on the right. The values from these two different sets of databases can only be combined by taking their maximum, since their individual tiles overlap.

This heuristic can be used to optimally solve random Fifteen Puzzle instances, generating an average of about 37,700 nodes, and taking about 43 milliseconds per problem instance on a 440 Megahertz Sun Ultra 10 workstation with 640 megabytes of memory. This is in comparison to 400 million nodes and about 75 seconds per problem on the same machine for simple Manhattan distance. This is a factor of over 10,000 in nodes generated, and over 1700 in actual running time.

Pairwise Distances

The original pattern database idea allows the most general combination rule, since the maximum of any set of admissible heuristics is always an admissible heuristic. Conversely, disjoint pattern databases admit the most powerful combination rule, by allowing the values from different heuristics to be added together, but are not very general, since they require each operator to effect only subgoals within a given pattern. Disjoint databases cannot be used on Rubik's Cube, for example, since each twist moves eight different cubies. Between these two extremes lies a technique that combines the two ideas.

Consider a database that contains the number of moves required to correctly position every pair of tiles, from every possible pair of positions they could be in. In most cases, this will be the sum of their Manhattan distances. In some cases, however, this *pairwise distance* will exceed the sum of the Manhattan distances. For example, if two tiles are in the same row, which is also their goal row, but they are reversed with respect to each other, one tile will have to move vertically out of the row, to allow the other to pass by, and then move back into the row. This adds two moves to the sum of their Manhattan distances, which only reflects the moves within their goal row. This is the idea behind the "linear conflict" heuristic function (Hansson, Mayer, and Yung, 1992), the first significant improvement to Manhattan distance. There are also other situations where the pairwise distance of two tiles from their goal location exceeds the sum of their Manhattan distances (Korf and Taylor, 1996).

The difficulty with the pairwise distance heuristic comes in applying it to a given state. We can't simply sum the pairwise distances of all pairs of tiles, because moves of the same tile will be counted repeatedly. Rather, we must partition the tiles into non-overlapping groups of two, and then sum the pairwise distances of each of the disjoint groups. Ideally, we want to choose a grouping for each state that maximizes the heuristic value. This is known as a maximal matching problem, and must be solved for each state in the search. Thus, heuristics based on pairwise distances are relatively expensive to compute. The idea of pairwise distances can obviously be generalized to distances of triples or quadruples of tiles as well.

Twenty-Four Puzzle An admissible heuristic based on linear conflicts and other pairwise distances lead to the first optimal solutions to random instance of the 5×5 Twenty-Four Puzzle (Korf and Taylor, 1996), containing almost 10^{25} states. Some of these problems generated trillions of nodes, and required weeks to run. Currently, we are applying disjoint databases to this problem, using patterns of six tiles, with significant reductions in nodes generated and running times.

Time Complexity of Heuristic Search

We now turn our attention to the time complexity of heuristic search algorithms. The central difficulty is that the running time depends on the quality of the heuristic function, which has to be characterized in some way. We begin with computing the brute-force branching factor, and then consider heuristic search.

Brute-Force Branching Factor

The running time of a brute-force search is $O(b^d)$, where b is the branching factor of the search space, and d is the solution depth of the problem instance. In the sliding-tile puzzles, the branching factor of a node depends on the position of the blank. If the blank is in a corner, there are two places it can go, if it's on a side it can go to three places, and from a center position it can to to four places. If we assume that all possible positions of the blank are equally likely, we get a branching factor of $4 \cdot 2 + 8 \cdot 3 + 4 \cdot 4/16 = 3$ for the Fifteen Puzzle. Subtracting one to eliminate the move back to the parent node yields a branching factor of 2.

Unfortunately, the blank is not equally likely to be in any position in a deep search. In particular, the more central location of the middle positions causes those positions to be over-represented in the search space. To compute the asymptotic branching factor, we need to compute the equilibrium fraction of nodes with the blank in the different types of positions at a given depth of the search tree, in the limit of large depth. When this is done correctly (Edelkamp and Korf, 1998), we get an asymptotic branching factor of about 2.13 for the Fifteen Puzzle.

A similar situation occurs in Rubik's Cube, even though all operators are always applicable. In this case, we restrict the operators applied to avoid redundant states. For example, if we allow any twist of a single face as a primitive operator, we don't want to twist the same face twice in a row, since the same effect can be achieved by a single twist. Furthermore, since twists of opposite faces are independent, these operators commute, and we only allow two consecutive twists of opposite faces to occur in one particular order. These considerations result in a branching factor of about 13.34847 for Rubik's Cube, compared to $6 \cdot 3 = 18$ for the naive problem space.

Conditions for Node Expansion

We now turn our attention to heuristic search. The running time of a heuristic search is proportional to the number of nodes expanded. Both A* and IDA* expand all nodes n whose total cost is less than the optimal solution cost, i.e. $f(n) = g(n) + h(n) < c*$, where $c*$ is the optimal solution cost (Pearl, 1984). An easy way to understand this node expansion condition is that any admissible search algorithm must continue to expand every partial solution path, until its cost equals or exceeds the cost of an optimal solution, lest it lead to a better solution.

Characterization of the Heuristic

As mentioned above, the central difficulty in analyzing the time complexity of heuristic search lies in characterizing the heuristic. Previous work on this problem (Pearl, 1984) characterized the heuristic by its accuracy as an estimator of optimal solution cost, and relied on an abstract analytic model of the search space. There are several problems with this approach. The first is that to determine the accuracy of a heuristic function on even a single problem instance, we have to determine the optimal solution cost, which is computationally very expensive on large problems. Secondly, most real problems don't fit the restrictive assumptions of the abstract model, namely that the problem space contain only a single solution path to the goal. Finally, the results obtained are only asymptotic results in the limit of large depth. As a result, this previous work cannot predict the actual performance of heuristic search on real problems such as the sliding-tile puzzles or Rubik's cube.

In our analysis (Korf and Reid, 1998), we characterize the heuristic function by the distribution of heuristic values over the problem space. In other words, we only need to know the fraction of states with each different heuristic value. Equivalently, let $P(x)$ be the fraction of total states in the problem space with heuristic value less than or equal to x. In other words, $P(x)$ is the probability that a randomly chosen state in the problem space has heuristic value less than or equal to x. More precisely, we need the distribution of heuristic values at a given depth of the brute-force search tree, in the limit of large depth, but we ignore this detail here. Note that the heuristic distribution says nothing directly about the accuracy of the heuristic function, except that distributions shifted toward larger values are more accurate, since we assume that our heuristics are admissible.

For heuristics based on a pattern database, we can compute the heuristic distribution exactly, simply by scanning the database. If the heuristic is based on several different pattern databases, we assume that the different heuristic values are independent. For heuristics based on functions, such as Manhattan distance, we can randomly sample states from the problem space, and use the heuristic values of the samples to approximate the heuristic distribution. Note that in either case, we don't have to solve any problem instances to get the heuristic distribution.

Main Theoretical Result

Here's the main result of our analysis (Korf and Reid, 1998). Let N_i be the number of nodes at depth i in the brute-force search tree. For example, N_i might be b^i, where b is the brute-force branching factor. In a heuristic search to depth d, the number of nodes expanded by A* or IDA* at depth i is simply $N_i \cdot P(d-i)$. At one level, the argument for this is simple. The nodes n at depth i have $g(n) = i$, and $P(d-i)$ is the fraction of nodes n for which $h(n) \leq d-i$. Thus, for these nodes, $f(n) = g(n) + h(n) \leq i + d - i = d$, which is the condition for node expansion in a search to depth d.

The key property that makes this work is consistency of the heuristic function. We say that h is consistent if for all nodes n and their neighbors n', $h(n) \leq c(n, n') + h(n')$, where $c(n, n')$ is the cost from node n to its neighbor n'. This is akin to the triangle inequality of metrics, and almost all admissible heuristics are consistent. If our heuristic is consistent, then the pruning that occurs in the tree doesn't effect the heuristic distribution of the nodes that are expanded. Given the number of nodes expanded at a given depth, we sum these values for all depths up to the optimal solution depth to determine the total number of nodes expanded, and hence the running time of the algorithm.

Experimental Results

We have experimentally verified this analysis on Rubik's Cube, the Eight Puzzle, and the Fifteen Puzzle. In each case, for N_i we used the actual numbers of nodes in the brute-force tree at each depth. For Rubik's cube, we determined the heuristic distribution from the pattern databases, assuming the values from different databases are independent. For the Eight Puzzle, we computed the heuristic distribution of Manhattan distance exactly by exhaustively generating the space, and for the Fifteen Puzzle, we approximated the Manhattan distance distribution by a random sample of ten billion states. We then compared the number of node expansions predicted by our theory to the average number of nodes expanded by IDA* on different random initial states. For Rubik's cube, we got agreement to within one percent, and for Fifteen puzzle we got agreement to within 2.5 percent at typical solution depths. For the Eight Puzzle, our theoretical predictions agreed exactly with our experimental results, since we could average the experimental results over all states in the problem space. This indicates that our theory accounts for all the relevant factors of the problem.

The "Heuristic Branching Factor"

From previous analyses, it was thought that the effect of an admissible heuristic function is to reduce the effective branching factor of a heuristic search relative to a brute-force search. The effective branching factor of a search is the limit at large depth of the ratio of the number of nodes generated at one level to the number generated at the next shallower level. One immediate consequence of our analysis, however, is that the effective branching factor of a heuristic search is the same as the brute-force branching factor of the problem space. The effect of the heuristic is merely to decrease the effective depth of search, by a constant based on the heuristic function. This prediction is also verified by our experimental results.

Conclusions

Pattern databases (Culberson and Schaeffer, 1998) automate the design of more effective lower-bound heuristics. We have used them to find optimal solutions to Rubik's cube. We have also extended the original idea to disjoint databases, which allow the values from different pattern databases to be added together, rather than just taking their maximum. Disjoint databases reduce the time to find optimal solutions to the Fifteen Puzzle by over three orders of magnitude, relative to the Manhattan distance heuristic. In addition, pairwise and higher order distances can also be used to compute more effective heuristics, but at greater cost per node evaluation. We have used both disjoint databases and pairwise distances to find optimal solutions to the 5 × 5 Twenty-Four puzzle.

We have also developed a new theory that allows us to predict the running time of heuristic search algorithms. The heuristic is characterized simply by the distribution of heuristic values over the problem space. Our theory accurately predicts our experimental results on the sliding-tile puzzles and Rubik's Cube. One consequence of our theory is that the effect of a heuristic is to reduce the effective depth of search, rather than the effective branching factor.

Acknowledgements

I would like to thank my collaborators in this work, including Stefan Edelkamp, Ariel Felner, Michael Reid, and Larry Taylor. This research was sponsored by NSF grant No. IRI-9619447.

References

[1] Culberson, J., and J. Schaeffer. Pattern Databases, *Computational Intelligence*, Vol. 14, No. 4, 1998, pp. 318-334.

[2] Edelkamp, S. and R.E. Korf, The branching factor of regular search spaces, *Proceedings of AAAI-98*, Madison, WI, July, 1998, pp. 299-304.

[3] Hansson, O., A. Mayer, and M. Yung, Criticizing solutions to relaxed models yields powerful admissible heuristics, *Information Sciences*, Vol. 63, No. 3, 1992, pp. 207-227.

[4] Hart, P.E., N.J. Nilsson, and B. Raphael, A formal basis for the heuristic determination of minimum cost paths, *IEEE Transactions on Systems Science and Cybernetics*, Vol. SSC-4, No. 2, July 1968, pp. 100-107.

[5] Johnson, W.W. and W.E. Storey, Notes on the 15 puzzle, *American Journal of Mathematics*, Vol. 2, 1879, pp. 397-404.

[6] Korf, R.E., Depth-first iterative-deepening: An optimal admissible tree search, *Artificial Intelligence*, Vol. 27, No. 1, 1985, pp. 97-109.

[7] Korf, R.E., and L.A. Taylor, Finding optimal solutions to the twenty-four puzzle, *Proceedings of AAAI-96*, Portland, OR, Aug. 1996, pp. 1202-1207.

[8] Korf, R.E., Finding optimal solutions to Rubik's Cube using pattern databases, *Proceedings of AAAI-97*, Providence, RI, July, 1997, pp. 700-705.

[9] Korf, R.E., and M. Reid, Complexity analysis of admissible heuristic search, *Proceedings AAAI-98*, Madison, WI, July, 1998, pp. 305-310.

[10] Loyd, S., *Mathematical Puzzles of Sam Loyd*, Selected and Edited by Martin Gardner, Dover, New York, 1959.

[11] Pearl, J. *Heuristics*, Addison-Wesley, Reading, MA, 1984.

Human-level AI's Killer Application: Interactive Computer Games

John E. Laird and Michael van Lent

University of Michigan
1101 Beal Ave.
Ann Arbor, Michigan 48109-2110
laird@umich.edu, vanlent@umich.edu

Abstract

Although one of the fundamental goals of AI is to understand and develop intelligent systems that have all of the capabilities of humans, there is little active research directly pursuing that goal. We propose that AI for interactive computer games is an emerging application area in which this goal of human-level AI can successfully be pursued. Interactive computer games have increasingly complex and realistic worlds and increasingly complex and intelligent computer-controlled characters. In this paper, we further motivate our proposal of using interactive computer games, review previous research on AI and games, and present the different game genres and the roles that human-level AI could play within these genres. We then describe the research issues and AI techniques that are relevant to each of these roles. Our conclusion is that interactive computer games provide a rich environment for incremental research on human-level AI.

Introduction

Over the last thirty years, research in AI has fragmented into more and more specialized fields, working on more and more specialized problems using more and more specialized algorithms. This approach has led to a long string of successes with important theoretical and practical advancements. However, these successes have made it easy for us to ignore our failure to make significant progress in building human-level AI systems. Human-level AI systems are the ones that you dreamed about when you first heard of AI: HAL from "2001, a Space Odyssey"; Data from "Star Trek"; or CP30 and R2D2 from "Star Wars". They are smart enough to be both triumphant heroes and devious villains. They seamlessly integrate all the human-level capabilities: real-time response, robust, autonomous intelligent interaction with their environment, planning, communication with natural language, common sense reasoning, creativity, and learning.

If this is our dream, why isn't any progress being made? Ironically, one of the major reasons that nobody (well almost nobody - see Brooks et al. 2000 for one high-profile

exception) is working on this grand goal of AI to achieve human-level intelligence is that current applications of AI do not need full-blown human-level AI. For almost all applications, the generality and adaptability of human thought isn't needed - specialized, although more rigid and fragile, solutions are cheaper and easier to develop. Unfortunately, it is unclear whether the approaches that have been developed to solve specific problems are the right building blocks for creating human-level intelligence. The thesis of this paper is that interactive computer games are the killer application for human-level AI. They are the application that will soon need human-level AI, and they can provide the environments for research on the right kinds of problems that lead to the type of the incremental and integrative research needed to achieve human-level AI.

Computer Generated Forces

Given that our personal goal is to build human-level AI systems, we have struggled to find the right application for our research that requires the breadth and depth of human-level intelligence. In 1991, we found a start in computer generated forces for large-scale distributed simulations. Effective military training requires a complete battle space with tens if not hundreds or thousands of participants. The real world is too expensive and dangerous to use for continual training, and even simulation is prohibitively expensive and cumbersome when fully manned with humans. The training of four pilots to fly an attack mission can require over twenty planes plus air controllers. The military doesn't even have a facility with twenty manned simulators, and if it did, the cost in personnel time for the other pilots and support personnel to train those four pilots would be astronomical. To bypass those costs, computer generated forces are being developed to populate these simulations. These forces must integrate many of the capabilities we associate with human behavior - after all they are simulating human pilots. For example, they must use realistic models of multiple sensing modalities, encode and use large bodies of knowledge (military doctrine and tactics), perform their missions autonomously, coordinate their behavior, react quickly to changes in the environment, and dynamically replan missions. Together with researchers at the Information Sciences Institute/University Southern California and Carnegie Mellon University, we set off to build human-level AIs for military air missions (Tambe, et al. 1995). In 1997, we successfully demonstrated fully autonomous simulated aircraft (Jones, et al. 1999), and research and development continues on these systems. Although computer generated forces are a good starting application for developing human-level AI, there are extremely high costs for AI researchers to participate in this work. It requires a substantial investment in time and money to work with the simulation environments and to learn the extensive background knowledge, doctrine, tactics, and missions. Furthermore, much of the current funding is for building and fielding systems and not for research.

Computer Games

In late 1997, we started to look for another application area, one where we could use what we learned from computer generated forces and pursue further research on human-level intelligence. We think we have found it in interactive computer games. The games we are talking about are not Chess, Checkers, Bridge, Othello, or Go, which emphasize only a few human capabilities such as search and decision making. The types of games we are talking about use the computer to create virtual worlds and characters for people to dynamically interact with - games such as Doom, Quake, Tomb Raider, Starcraft, Myth, Madden Football, Diablo, Everquest, and Asheron's Call.

Human-level AI can have an impact on these games by creating enemies, partners, and support characters that act just like humans. The AI characters can be part of the continual evolution in the game industry to more realistic gaming environments. Increasing realism in the graphical presentation of the virtual worlds has fueled this evolution. Human-level AI can expand the types of experiences people have playing computer games by introducing synthetic intelligent characters with their own goals, knowledge, and capabilities. Human-level AI can also recreate the experience of playing with and against humans without a network connection. Current players of computer games are driven to networked games because of the failings of the computer characters. In massively multiplayer online games, human-level AIs can populate the worlds with persistent characters that can play the game alongside humans, providing opportunities for interesting interactions that guide players in the game and enhance the social dynamics between players. Our hypothesis is that populating these games with realistic, human-level characters will lead to fun, challenging games with great game play.

From the AI researcher perspective, the increasing realism in computer games makes them an attractive alternative to both robotics in the real world and home-grown simulations. By working in simulation, researchers interested in human-level AI can concentrate on cognitive capabilities and finesse many of the pesky issues of using real sensor and real motor systems - they must still include some sensor modeling to get realistic behavior, but they don't have to have a team of vision researchers on their staff. They can do this in worlds that are becoming increasingly realistic simulations of physical and social interactions, without having to create these worlds themselves. Computer games are cheap ($49.95), reliable, and sometimes surprisingly accessible, with built-in AI interfaces. Moreover, computer games avoid many of the criticisms often leveled against simulations. They are real products and real environments on their own that millions of humans vigorously interact with and become immersed in. Finally, unlike military simulations, we do not need to hunt out experts on these games; they surround us.

Another reason for AI researchers to work in computer games is that if we don't start working in this area, the computer game industry will push ahead without us (Woodcock 1999). Already there are at least five AI Ph.D's working in the industry (Takahashi, 2000). This is a chance for AI researchers to team with an aggressive, talented, and caffeine-charged industry in the pursuit of human-level AI. Below is a list of reasons for AI researchers to take the computer game industry seriously.

1. Computer game developers are starting to recognize the need for human-level AI. Synthetic human-level characters are playing an increasingly important role in many genres of computer games and have the potential to lead to completely new genres.
2. The computer game industry is highly competitive and a strong component of that competition is technology. AI is often mentioned as the next technology that will improve games and determine which games are hits. Thousands of new computer games are written every year with overall development time averaging nine months to two year, so technological advances sweep through the industry quickly. Already, many computer games are marketed based on the quality of their AI. This is a field in which AI will have a significant impact.
3. Game developers are technologically savvy and they work hard to stay current with technology. AI programmer is already a common job title on game development teams.
4. The game industry is big. More money is spent on computer games than on movies.
5. Computer game hardware is going to provide cheap, high-end computation power for AI in computer games in the next five years. The newest PC 3D video boards and the next generation consoles, such as Sony's Playstation 2 and Micosoft's X-box, move the entire graphics pipeline off of the increasingly powerful CPU, freeing it for AI. It is not at all unthinkable that in five

years there will be dedicated AI processors in game consoles - we just have to tell them what we need.
6. Computer games need help from academic AI. The current emphasis in computer game AI is on the *illusion* of human-like behavior for very limited situations. Thus, most, if not all, of the current techniques that are used for controlling game AIs (such as big C functions or finite-state machines) will not scale up. However, just as computer game graphics and physics have moved to more and more realistic modeling of the physical world, we expect that game developers will be forced into more and more realistic modeling of human characters. Moreover, as researchers we can get a step ahead of the game designers by using their environments for research on human-level AI

One thing that is missing in the computer game field is significant research funding. Some of the military funding to support computer generated forces is spilling over to computer games research and some of the biggest computer game companies have started research centers that include research in AI. More funding could become available as more game developers discover they need help with the AI in their products to push for a competitive advantage. Much of the research could get done in non-traditional ways, with the involvement of undergraduates, game developers, and game players. This is a way to move AI research out of the labs and into the hands of millions.

Related Research on Computer Games

Other researchers have argued that great game play comes from "believable" agents. These agents don't necessarily have to be human-level in their intelligence, as long as they have a façade of intelligence supported by great personality. Joe Bates' OZ research group at Carnegie Mellon University (Bates 1992) and Barbara Hayes-Roth's group at Stanford University (Hayes-Roth and Doyle 1998) have worked on developing believable agents for interactive fiction and related computer games. Their research emphasized personality, AI agent to human interaction, and shallow but broad agents. We think these are important aspects, but want to emphasize that computer games provide an arena for attempting to also build knowledge-rich, complete, integrated AI that incorporate many "deep" capabilities.

John McCarthy (1998) has also argued that interactive computer games should be considered as a topic of study for AI, where we can study how an AI system could play a game (his example is Lemmings, Jr. - a real-time scheduling and resource allocation game) and solve problems that a human attempts. Other researchers have used other computer games such as Pengi (Agre and Chapman 1987), and Simcity (Fasciano 1996). Our extension is to propose research on the AI characters that are part of the game. Clearly, these efforts are related because human-level AI characters often require the skills of human players. One advantage of creating game characters is that we can influence how games are made and played.

RoboCup (Asada et al., 2000) is another related project where competitors develop AI systems to defeat other AI systems in both real robotic and simulated soccer games. In RoboCup the goal is to build the best soccer-playing robots, not to create the best game play or human-like behavior. RoboCup is stimulating the development of integrated systems, but none with the variety of capabilities we expect to see in interactive computer games.

Computer Game Genres

In this section we review the major genres of computer games to which human-level AI is relevant. There are other game genres, like hunting games, fishing games and life-like creatures games (Stern 1999), where deer-level, fish-level, or dog-level AI is necessary. For each of the genres in this section, we discuss the different roles that human-level AI can play: enemies, partners, support characters, strategic opponents, low-level units and commentators. Other roles are possible, but these are the most common. In the following sections, we go through these roles and discuss how AI could improve the games and how these games provide research problems for human-level AI. Finally, we review the areas of AI that are applicable to these problems. This information is collected together in Figure 1 on the next page.

Action Games

"Shortly after landing on an alien surface you learn that hundreds of your men have been reduced to just a few. Now you must fight your way through heavily fortified military installations, lower the city's defenses and shut down the enemy's war machine." – Quake II

Action games involve the human player controlling a character in a virtual environment, usually running around and using deadly force to save the world from the forces of evil. These games vary in the perspective that the human has of their character, be it first-person where the human sees what the character would see, or third-person, where the player looks over the shoulder of the character. Popular examples include Doom, Quake, Descent, Half-Life, and Tomb Raider. In pure action games, AI is used to control the enemies, which are invariably alien monsters or mythical creatures. Realism in graphics has been the point of competition for these games; however, the graphics race seems to have run its course, with better AI becoming the point of comparison. Recent games have extended the genre so that the human player may be part of a team, which includes either human or AI partners.

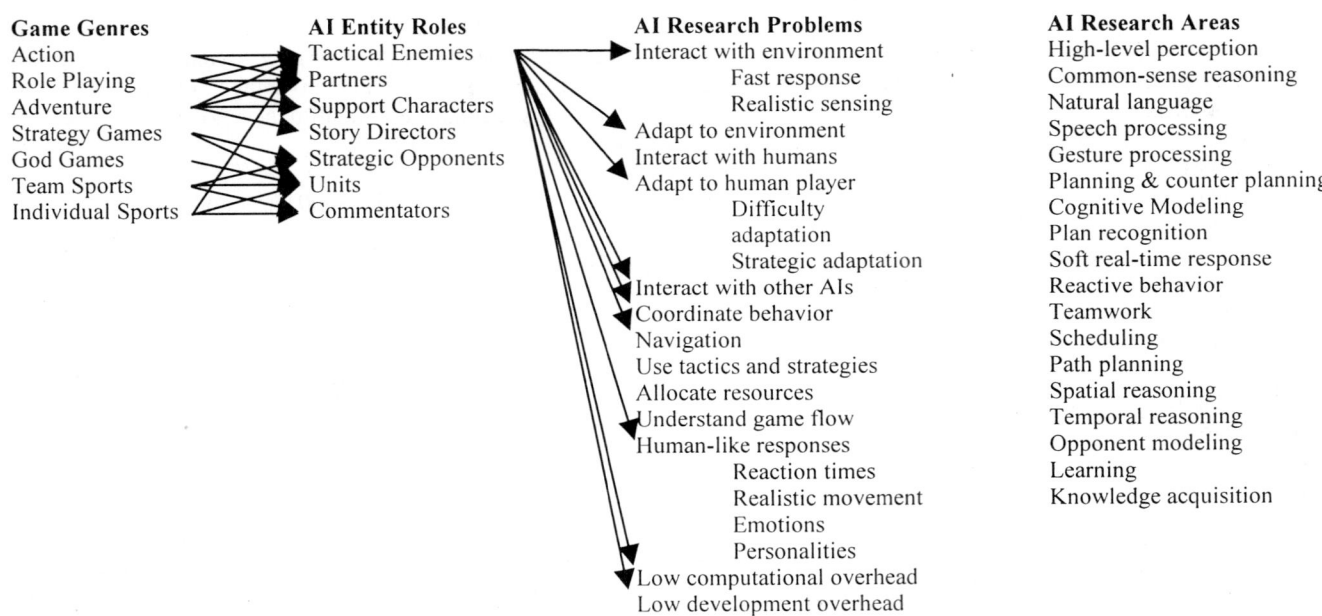

Figure 1: AI roles in game genres with illustrative links to their associated research problems and relevant AI research areas.

Role-Playing Games

"Immerse yourself in a...world, where nations hang in the balance of your actions, dark prophecies test your resolve, and heroic dreams can be fulfilled at last." – Baldur's Gate

In role-playing games, a human can play different types of characters, such as a warrior, a magician, or a thief. The player goes on quests, collects and sells items, fights monsters, and expands the capabilities of their character (such as strength, magic, quickness, etc.), all in an extended virtual world. Example games include Baldur's Gate, Diablo, and Ultima. Recently, massively multiplayer role-playing games have been created where thousands of people play and interact in the same game world: Ultima Online, Everquest, and Asheron's Call. In both types of role-playing games AI is used to control enemies, like in action games, partners who travel and adventure with the players and also supporting characters, such as shopkeepers. The massively multiplayer games provide an additional opportunity to use AI to expand and enhance the player to player social interactions, perhaps with AI controlled kings who war by sending player controlled knights to battle each other.

Adventure Games

"Aye, 'tis a rollicking piratey adventure that's sure to challenge the mind and shiver a few timbers!" – The Curse of Monkey Island

Adventure games, and the related genre of interactive fiction, move further from action games, as they de-emphasize armed combat and emphasize story, plot and puzzle solving. In these games, players must solve puzzles and interact with other characters, as they progress through an unfolding adventure that is determined in part by their actions. Early adventure games, such as Adventure, and Zork were totally text based, but more recent games sport 3D graphics (sometimes using the graphics engines developed for action games). Example games include the Infocom series, King's Quest, and many games from Lucas Arts, such as Full Throttle, Monkey Island, and Grim Fandango. AI can be used to create realistic supporting goal-driven characters that the player must interact with appropriately to further their progress in the game. One of the Holy Grails of interactive fiction is to have a computer director who can dynamically adjust the story and plot based on the actions of the human. The majority of games have fixed scripts and use many tricks to force the human player through essentially linear stories. However, a few games, such as Blade Runner, have incorporated some autonomy and dynamic scripting into their characters and story line (Castle 1998).

Strategy Games

"Players must successfully construct and rule their medieval empire while engaging in real-time tactical warfare over land, sea, and air." – Warcraft

In strategy games, the human controls many units (usually military units, like tanks, or the ever present alien war machines) to do battle from a god's eye view against one or more opponents. Strategy games include reenactments of different types of battles: historical (Close Combat), alternative realities (Command and Conquer), fictional future (Starcraft), and mythical (Warcraft, Myth). The human is often faced with problems of resource allocation, scheduling production, and organizing defenses and attacks (Davis 1999). AI is used in two roles: to control the detailed behavior of individual units that the human commands, and as a strategic opponent that must play the same type of game against the human. The AI needs of the individual units differs from the enemies and partners of action and role-playing games because they are not meant to be autonomous but are meant to be good soldiers who "follow orders."

God Games

"You're in charge of creating an entire city from the ground up – and the sky's the limit." – SimCity 3000

God games give the player god-like control over a simulated world. The human can modify the environment and to some extent its inhabitants. The entertainment comes by observing the effects of his or her actions on individuals, society, and the world. SimCity is the classic example of a god game where the human acts as mayor and the AI controls individual units or citizens of the simulated city. The Sims is probably the most intriguing example. The player creates individual characters (units) that have significant autonomy, with their own drives, goals, and strategies for satisfying those goals, but where God (the human player) can come in and stir things up both by managing the individual characters and their environment.

Team Sports

"Welcome to Madden NFL 97, the game that captures the excitement of a 30 yard touchdown pass, the strategy of a well executed scoring drive, and the atmosphere of a crisp autumn afternoon in the stadium." – Madden NFL 97

Team sports games have the human play a combination of coach and player in popular sports, such as football (Whatley 1999), basketball, soccer, baseball, and hockey. AI is used in two roles that are similar to the roles in strategy games, the first being unit level control of all the individual players. Usually the human controls one key player, like the quarterback, while the computer controls all the other members of the team. A second role is as the strategic opponent, which in this case is the opposing coach. One unique aspect of team sport games is that they also have a role for a commentator, who gives the play by play, and color commentary of the game (Frank 1999).

Individual Sports

"Rip up the course on inline skates, speed on the street luge, pull serious air on the skateboard, and shred courses on the mountain bike." – ESPN Extreme Games

For individual competitive sports, such as driving, flying, skiing, and snowboarding, the computer provides a simulation of the sport from a first or third person perspective. The human player controls a participant in the game who competes against other human or computer players. The computer player is more like an enemy in an action game than a strategic opponent or unit from a strategy game because the game is usually a tactical, real-time competition. Individual sports can also require commentators.

Although we listed specific genres, the genres are fuzzy concepts, with many games being hybrids, incorporating components of multiple genres. For example, there are strategy games (Dungeon Keeper) that allows the human to "jump in the body" of one of their units and play as if it is an action game for a while. Also, there are actions games where you must also manage resources and multiple units (such as Battlezone). Although there will be a continual blurring of the genres, the basic roles for AI stay the same: enemies, partners, support characters, strategic opponents, units and commentators.

Roles

Tactical Enemies

In early games, the tactics of the computer-controlled enemies were generally limited to running directly at the player. Later enemies were scripted or controlled by simple finite-state machines. In these early games, the enemies were made more challenging, not with improved intelligence, but with bigger guns, tougher hides, and superior numbers. They also usually "cheated" by being able to see through walls or out of the back of their heads. More recently, games such as Half Life (Birdwell 1999), Descent 3, Quake III (Keighley 1999), and Unreal Tournament have incorporated path-planning and many tactics that make these enemies more human-like. Our own research (Laird and van Lent 1999; Laird 2000) has concentrated on building enemies for Quake II that have the same strengths and weaknesses as human players. To beat them, you have to out-think them as much as you have to outshoot them. Our Soar Quakebot is essentially a real-time expert system that has multiple goals and extensive tactics and knowledge of the game. It is built within the Soar architecture and has over 800 rules. While exploring a level, it creates an internal model of its world and it uses that model in its tactics, to collect nearby weapons and health, to track down an enemy, and to set ambushes. It also tries to anticipate the actions of human players by putting itself in their shoes (creating an internal model of their situation garnered from its perception of the player) and projecting what it would do if it were the human player.

Building human-level enemies for these games requires solving many general AI problems and integrating the solutions into coherent systems. The enemies must be autonomous. They must interact with complex dynamic environments, which requires reactive behavior, integrated planning, and common sense reasoning. As they advance, they will also need models of high-level vision that have the same strengths and weaknesses as humans. One common complaint among game players is that the enemy AI is cheating, which destroys the game playing experience. For example, if the human is in a dark room, the AI would be cheating if it could easily sense, identify, and locate the human. However, if the human is back-lit by a bright hall, the AI enemy should be able to easily sense and locate the human, but possibly not identify him. This is important for game play so that the same tactics and behaviors that work well with humans work well with AI enemies.

There are many other applications of AI to building intelligent enemies. Because of the extended geography of the environment, they must navigate, use path planning, spatial reasoning, and temporal reasoning. As the games become more complex, the enemies will need to plan, counter-plan, and adapt to the strategies and tactics of their enemies, using plan recognition and opponent modeling techniques, and learning. Their responses need to be within the range of humans in terms of reaction times and realistic movement. One can even imagine adding basic models of emotions, where the enemies get "mad" or "frustrated" and change their behavior as a result.

Partners

Creating AI controlled partners involves many of the same research issues as tactical enemies. However, while enemy AI systems emphasize autonomy, partners emphasize effortless cooperation and coordination between the human player and the AI partner. Current games restrict the human to using specific commands to interact with partners, such as defend, attack, follow me - commands much more limited than used in human-to-human interactions. In the extreme, this brings in speech recognition and natural language processing and even gesture recognition. The partner AI must coordinate its behavior, understand teamwork, model the goals of the human, and adapt to his style. Building such partners can build on previous research in AI in these areas, but within the context of all of the other cognitive activities involved in playing the game.

Support Characters

Support characters are usually some of the least sophisticated AI characters in computer games, but they have the most promise to improve games and are the most interesting in terms of developing human-level AI. They currently have sets of canned responses that they spit back to the user based either on menu-selected questions or keywords. The most complex ones, such as in Blade Runner (Castle 1998) have some autonomy and some simple goals, but they are extremely narrow goals with limited sets of behaviors for achieving those goals.

Adding other AI controlled support characters could help populate the games with interesting opportunities for interaction that guide the player along various plot lines. Since these characters need to exist in a virtual world and generally play a human role in this world, they provide a useful first step towards human-level AI. In this role, support characters must interact with and adapt to the environment, interact with and adapt to human players and other support characters and provide human-like responses, possibly including natural language understanding and generation. In order to do all this, and because these support characters are most directly playing the role of embodied virtual humans, they require a wide range of integrated AI capabilities including everything from natural language to path planning to teamwork to realistic movement.

Strategic Opponents

When creating strategic opponents for strategy games and team sports games, most game developers have had to resort to "cheating" to make the opponent challenging. Often strategic opponents are given extra units or resources, additional information about the map or the human player's position, or they play the game by a different set of rules. Even with these advantages, most strategic opponents are predictable and easily beaten once their weaknesses are found. Strategic opponents for team sports games face an additional difficulty in that their style of play must match a real world team about which the human players are likely to be very knowledgeable.

The tasks a strategic opponent must perform can be divided into two categories: allocating resources and issuing unit control commands. Involved in both of these tasks is the development of a high level strategy. Creating this strategy, which is where current strategic opponents are weakest, involves integrated planning, common sense reasoning, spatial reasoning, and usually plan recognition and counter-planning to react to the human's attack. One of the most important aspects of strategy creation is the coordination of multiple types of units into a cohesive strategy. Once the plan is decided, the strategic opponent must determine how to best use limited resources (mined minerals or substitute players on a team) to compose an attack force appropriate to implement the battle plan. This resource allocation involves scheduling production and temporal reasoning about when the resulting units will be available. The strategic opponent must also issue commands to the newly created individual units, causing them to carry out the battle plan. Controlling a large force of units with only a single mouse is a significant part of the challenge for human players. Because of this, the strategic opponent must enforce human-like limitations, such as reaction times and realistic movements, when issuing commands to make the battle fair.

Units

In strategy games, god games, and team sports games, AI is used to control individual units. Generally these units are given high level commands from either the human player or the strategic opponent and need to carry out these commands. Units are usually controlled via finite-state machines (or large C functions) that are augmented with special routines for path planning and path following. In addition to following orders, units often need some ability to act autonomously. For example, a platoon of marines moving from one position to another should not ignore an enemy tank. Instead they should autonomously choose to attack if appropriate or else find a new path. This semi-autonomous behavior involves common sense reasoning and perhaps coordination with other units. Since there can be hundreds of units active in a game at one time, the issues of computational and memory overhead are particularly important for unit AI (Atkin et al. 1999).

Commentators

The role of the commentator is to observe the actions of the AI and the human and generate natural language comments suitable to describe the action (Frank 1999). In the Robocup competition, there is a separate competition for commentator agents (Binsted 1998). Although sports games, both team and individual, are the most obvious genres for commentators, they can also be found in some action games, such as Unreal Tournament. The obvious challenge for a commentator is to create a natural language description of the on-going action in the game. The description may include both the moment to moment action as well as key tactical and strategy events that can require complex plan recognition and a deep understanding of the game.

Resource and Development Issues

A constant issue for game developers is the need to meet the limited computational power, in both memory and processing power, available in the average home computer. These resource issues can be finessed within the academic research community when the goal is just to do research on human-level AI independent of the commercial applications. However, we encourage researchers to take resource issues seriously because the more accessible our research is, the more likely it is that game developers and other industries will understand the need for research on human-level AI and AI techniques in general. Our experience with the Soar Quakebot has driven us to research on comparisons of Soar with other architectures (Wallace and Laird 1999, Bhattacharyya and Laird 1999) and the overall efficiency of Soar. The Soar Quakebot requires 3 Mbytes and 10% of the processing power of a 400Mhz Windows NT Pentium II.

An additional constraint is that these AI systems must be developed at moderate cost. A game company will not be able to spend more than one man-year on development of the AI for a game. We need to develop techniques for quickly building and customizing human-level AI systems. Research on software engineering, knowledge acquisition, and machine learning will definitely play a role.

Conclusion

From a researcher's perspective, even if you are not interested in human-level AI, computer games offer interesting and challenging environments for many, more isolated, research problems in AI. We are most interested in human-level AI, and wish to leverage computer games to rally support for research in human-level AI. One attractive aspect of working in computer games is that there is no need to attempt a "Manhattan Project" approach with a monolithic project that attempts to create human-level intelligence all at once. Computer games provide an environment for continual, steady advancement and a series of increasingly difficult challenges. Just as computers have inexorably gotten faster, computer game environments are becoming more and more realistic worlds, requiring more and more complex behavior from their characters. Now is the time for AI researchers to jump in and ride the wave of computer games.

Acknowledgments

The authors are indebted to the many students and staff who have worked on the Soar/Games project, most notably Steve Houchard, Karen Coulter, Mazin Assanie, Josh Buchman, Joe Hartford, Ben Houchard, Damion Neff, Kurt Steinkraus, Russ Tedrake, and Amy Unger.

References

Agre, P. E. and Chapman, D. 1987. Pengi: An implementation of a theory of activity, In *Proceedings of AAAI-87*, 268-272, AAAI Press.

Asada, M., Veloso, M., Tambe, M., Noda, I., Kitano, H., and Kraetzschmar, G. K., 2000. Overview of RoboCup-98, *AI Magazine,* 21(1):9-19.

Atkin, M. S., Westbrook, D. L., and Cohen, P. R., 1999. Capture the Flag: Military Simulation Meets Computer Games. In *Papers from the AAAI 1999 Spring Symposium on Artificial Intelligence and Computer Games*, Technical Report SS-99-02, AAAI Press, 1-5.

Bates, J. 1992. Virtual Reality, Art, and Entertainment. *Presence: The Journal of Teleoperators and Virtual Environments* 1(1):133-138.

Bhattacharyya, S. and Laird, J. E., 1999. Lessons for Empirical AI in Plan Execution. The IJCAI-99 workshop on Empirical AI.

Binsted, K. 1998. Character Design for Soccer Commentary, In Proceedings of the Robo-Cup Workshop, 23-35.

Birdwell, K. 1999. The CABAL: Valve's Design Processing for Creating Half-Life. *Game Developer.* 6(12):40-50.

Brooks, R. A., Breazeal. C., Marjanovic, M., Scassellati, B., and Williamson, M. 2000. *The Cog Project: Building a Humanoid Robot.* Forthcoming.

Castle, L. 1998. The Making of Blade Runner, Soup to Nuts! In *Proceedings of the Computer Game Developers' Conference*, Long Beach, CA, 87-97.

Cavazza, M., Bandi, S., and Palmer, I. 1999. "Situated AI" in Video Games: Integrating NLP, Path Planning and 3D Animation. In *Papers from the AAAI 1999 Spring Symposium on Artificial Intelligence and Computer Games*, Technical Report SS-99-02, 6-12. AAAI Press.

Davis, I. 1999. Strategies for Strategy Game AI. In *Papers from the AAAI 1999 Spring Symposium on Artificial Intelligence and Computer Games*, Technical Report SS-99-02, 24-27. AAAI Press.

Fasciano, M. J. 1996. Real-time Case-based Reasoning in a Complex World. Technical Report TR-96-05, Computer Science Department, University of Chicago, 1996

Frank, I. 1999. Explanations Count. In *Papers from the AAAI 1999 Spring Symposium on Artificial Intelligence and Computer Games*, Technical Report SS-99-02, 77-80. AAAI Press.

Hayes-Roth, B. and Doyle, P. 1998. Animate Characters. *Autonomous Agents and Multi-Agent Systems*, 1(1):195-230.

Jones, R.M., Laird, J. E., Nielsen, P. E., Coulter, K.J., Kenny, P.G., and Koss, F.V. 1999. Automated Intelligent Pilots for Combat Flight Simulation, *AI Magazine*, 20(1):27-42.

Keighley, G. 1999. The Final Hours of Quake III Arena: Behind Closed Doors at id Software, GameSpot, http://www.gamespot.com/features/btg-q3/index.html.

Laird, J. E. and van Lent, M. 1999. Developing an Artificial Intelligence Engine. In *Proceedings of the Game Developers' Conference*, San Jose, CA, 577-588.

Laird, J. E. 2000. It Knows What You're Going To Do: Adding Anticipation to a Quakebot. In *Papers from the AAAI 2000 Spring Symposium on Artificial Intelligence and Interactive Entertainment*, Technical Report SS-00-02, 41-50. AAAI Press.

McCarthy, J. 1998. Partial Formalizations and the Lemmings Game, http://www-formal.stanford.edu/jmc/lemmings.html

Stern, A. 1999. AI Beyond Computer Games. In *Papers from the AAAI 1999 Spring Symposium on Artificial Intelligence and Computer Games*, Technical Report SS-99-02, 77-80. AAAI Press.

Takahashi, D. 2000. Artificial Intelligence Gurus Win Tech-Game Jobs. *The Wall Street Journal*, March 30, 2000, B14.

Tambe, M., Johnson, W. L., Jones, R. M., Koss, F., Laird, J. E., Rosenbloom, P. S., and Schwamb, K. 1995. Intelligent Agents for Interactive Simulation Environments, *AI Magazine*, 16 (1):15-39.

Wallace, S. and Laird, J. E., 1999. Toward a Methodology for AI Architecture Evaluate: Comparing Soar and CLIPS. ATAL-99, July.

Whatley, D. 1999. Designing Around Pitfalls of Game AI. In *Proceedings of the Game Developers' Conference*, San Jose, CA, 991-999.

Woodcook, S. 1999. Game AI: The State of the Industry. Game Developer, 6(8).

The Games Computers (and People) Play

Jonathan Schaeffer
Computing Science Dept.
University of Alberta
Edmonton, Alberta
Canada T6G 2H1
jonathan@cs.ualberta.ca

Abstract

The development of high-performance game-playing programs has been one of the major successes of artificial intelligence research. The results have been outstanding but, with one notable exception (Deep Blue), they have not been widely disseminated. This talk will discuss the past, present, and future of the development of games-playing programs. Case studies for backgammon, bridge, checkers, chess, go, hex, Othello, poker, and Scrabble will be used.

The research emphasis of the past has been on high performance (synonymous with brute-force search) for two-player perfect-information games. The research emphasis of the present encompasses multi-player imperfect/non-deterministic information games. And what of the future? There are some surprising changes of direction occurring that will result in games being more of an experimental testbed for mainstream AI research, with less emphasis on building world-championship-caliber programs.

One of the most profound contributions to mankind's knowledge has been made by the artificial intelligence (AI) research community: the realization that intelligence is not uniquely human.[1] Using computers, it is possible to achieve human-like behavior in nonhumans. In other words, the illusion of human intelligence can be created in a computer.

This idea has been vividly illustrated throughout the history of computer games research. Unlike most of the early work in AI, game researchers were interested in developing high-performance, real-time solutions to challenging problems. This led to an ends-justify-the-means attitude: the result—a strong chess program—was all that mattered, not the means by which it was achieved. In contrast, much of the mainstream AI work used simplified domains, while eschewing real-time performance objectives. This research typically used human intelligence as a model: one only had to emulate the human example to achieve intelligent behavior. The battle (and philosophical) lines were drawn.

The difference in philosophy can be easily illustrated. The human brain and the computer are different machines, each with its own sets of strengths and weaknesses. Humans are good at, for example, learning, reasoning by analogy, and image processing. Computers are good at numeric calculations, repetitious computations, and memorizing large sets of data. These machine architectures are largely complimentary: the human's processing strengths are the computer's weaknesses and the computer's strengths are human weaknesses. Given a problem to be solved and a specified architecture (human brain or silicon computer), a good solution should cater to the strengths of the machine being used, not the weaknesses. When viewed in this light, it is not surprising that the unhuman-like approaches have won out.

Building high-performance game-playing programs has been one of AI's major triumphs. This is due, in part, to the success achieved in games such as backgammon, chess, checkers, Othello, and Scrabble, where computers are playing as well as or better than the best human players. However, it is also due to the examples it set to the research community. These include tackling challenging problems (rather than trivial subsets, as is still often seen in AI research) and the emphasis on the results of the system without regard for the methods used to achieve those results (the ends justify the means). More details can be found in (Schaeffer 1999).

The success of *Deep Blue* at chess was an enormous publicity win for the AI community. With the 50-year challenge of building a world-class chess program finally out of the way, no other games-related grand challenge problem has emerged that fires the imagination of AI researchers like chess did. A new generation of games are being actively researched (e.g. bridge, go, poker, shogi) which promise to produce research results that will likely have a wider impact on the AI community. The games cannot benefit significantly from the silver bullet of chess—deep search—and it will take a a plethora of new ideas to achieve success. Research into building game programs continues, but the work will be less visible and more academic.

Acknowledgments

This work was funded by the Natural Sciences and Engineering Research Council of Canada. Thanks to Haym Hirsh for prompting me to put these ideas into words.

References

Schaeffer, J. 1999. The role of games in understanding computational intelligence. *IEEE Intelligent Systems* (November/December):10–11.

Copyright © 2000, American Association for Artificial Intelligence (www.aaai.org). All rights reserved.

[1] Many of the comments in this note originally appeared in (Schaeffer 1999).

Conceptual Indexing: Practical Large-Scale AI for Efficient Information Access

William A. Woods
Sun Microsystems Laboratories
One Network Drive
Burlington, MA 01803
william.woods@east.sun.com

Abstract

Finding information is a problem shared by people and intelligent systems. This paper describes an experiment combining both human and machine aspects in a knowledge-based system to help people find information in text. Unlike many previous attempts, this system demonstrates a substantial improvement in search effectiveness by using linguistic and world knowledge and exploiting sophisticated knowledge representation techniques. It is also an example of practical subsumption technology on a large scale and with domain-independent knowledge. Results from this experiment are relevant to general problems of knowledge-based reasoning with large-scale knowledge bases.

Introduction

Long-term solutions to many problems in AI require efficient access to large amounts of knowledge. To be effectively scalable, such applications need to be able to find specific items of relevant information in an amount of time that is sublinear with respect to the size of the body of knowledge employed. This paper will describe the use of KL-One-style subsumption technology (Woods & Schmolze 1992) to address this problem in the context of a system to help people find specific information in online text. It will also discuss the extrapolation of these techniques to other large-scale knowledge-based applications.

The system in question uses a combination of linguistic content processing and intensional subsumption logic (Woods 1991) to automatically construct a conceptual index (Woods 1997) of all the words and phrases that occur in a body of text, organized by a relationship of generality (subsumption). The system uses intensional subsumption technology to classify each word and phrase into a conceptual taxonomy in which each concept is linked to the most specific concepts that subsume it (i.e., that are more general). This taxonomy, together with records of where each concept occurs in the indexed material, constitutes the conceptual index. Subsumption paths through the taxonomy can be used to connect terms in an information request to related terms in indexed material, and the positional information in the index can be used to identify small, focused passages in the material where the requested information is likely to be.

Copyright © 2000, American Association for Artificial Intelligence (www.aaai.org). All rights reserved.

This ability to locate specific answers to specific questions in unrestricted text is a useful intermediate capability between true question answering and traditional document retrieval. Experiments have shown that using this system results in a substantial improvement in human search productivity (Woods *et al.* 2000).

Background

I began this study by looking at what goes wrong when people fail to find what they want online. By catching people in what I came to call an information-seeking state, I was occasionally able to capture a spontaneous statement of the information need and watch the process by which people searched for information. In some cases I was able to compare what they eventually found to what they said they wanted. As a result of this study, I identified two principal problems that stand in the way of effective search. The first is that the terms used in the request are often different from the terms that are used by the author of the needed material (the paraphrase problem). The second is that it is usually difficult to find the relevant information in the documents that are retrieved (the information location problem).

I conjectured that an intensional subsumption methodology that I had been working on in the context of knowledge-based reasoning (Woods 1991) could be applied to both problems by locating specific places in the source material where particular things were said, and by dealing with the generality relationships that hold between the terms used in a query and those used in the indexed material. An experimental conceptual indexing and retrieval system was designed and constructed to test this hypothesis (Ambroziak & Woods 1998). Before describing it, I will first introduce the problems that the system needs to solve.

The problems

There are four sources of difficulty inherent in natural language that stand as potential obstacles to effective search. These problems are:

- Morphological variation – e.g., acid glass vs. acidic glass
- Differing terminology – e.g., moon rocks vs. lunar rocks
- Word relationships that alter meaning – e.g., man bites dog vs. dog bites man

- Word sense – e.g., dolphins as marine mammals vs. the Miami Dolphins

In the first case, morphological differences in inflection or in derivation give rise to different forms of a word. In the second, semantic relationships between different words with related meanings constitute the link between what was asked for and what was needed. In the third case, the mere presence of the requested elements is not sufficient to guarantee that they are being used in the desired relationships. In the fourth case, only some senses of ambiguous words are of interest.

To address these problems, we need to consider the following questions:

- What information is required to connect the concepts in a query to concepts in a relevant passage?
- How can this information be organized and used efficiently?
- To what extent can conceptual descriptions of the content of a document be automatically extracted and organized from the document itself?

Subsumption and paraphrase

In dealing with terminological variation, I chose to use an approach based on subsumption of less general terms by more general terms and subsumption of derived and inflected forms of words by their roots and base forms. This was chosen over the more traditional approach of using a synonym thesaurus and a stemming algorithm because it preserves information and gives control of the granularity of searching to the user. There are actually very few true synonyms in natural language, and if one puts terms that are not truly synonymous into a synonym thesaurus mechanism, the result is a lack of precision in being able to specify what is desired. In contrast, subsumption technology enables the searcher to specify a request at the level of generality of interest, and only those terms that are subsumed by the requested term are automatically searched for. Subsumption technology handles all of the phenomena of synonyms and more. In fact, synonymy is just the special case of mutual subsumption. Thus, in a technical sense, one can say that "subsumption subsumes synonymy."

With this approach, we answer the above questions in the following way:

- We use semantic relationships between concepts, morphological relationships between words, and syntactic relationships between words and phrases to connect terms of a request with relevant material.
- We use intensional subsumption algorithms to organize words and phrases into a conceptual taxonomy in order to use this information efficiently.
- We use a robust syntactic phrase extractor to extract words and phrases from the indexed material and parse them into conceptual structures which are then automatically organized into the conceptual taxonomy by taxonomic subsumption algorithms.

Conceptual Indexing

In conceptual indexing, the indexing system performs a significant, but limited amount of linguistic content processing at indexing time in order to support later retrieval operations. Every word that is encountered is looked up in a lexicon to determine its syntactic part of speech, any morphological structure that it exhibits, what specific word senses it may have, and any semantic relationships that it has to other words or word senses. Words that are not already in the lexicon are subjected to a knowledge-based morphological analysis (Woods 2000) in order to construct a new lexical entry that will be used for any subsequent occurrences of the same word. This system deals with prefixes, suffixes, and lexical compounds (e.g., *bitmap*). The system is capable of making plausible analyses of completely unknown words and is integrated with the conceptual taxonomy so that rules can make use of subsumption facts about words as well as syntactic and spelling information. Many rules also infer semantic subsumption relationships as a result of their analyses.

After lexical analysis, sequences of words that can form basic phrases (simple noun phrases and some simple verb phrases) are identified and parsed into conceptual structures. These structures are then automatically classified into the conceptual taxonomy by a taxonomic subsumption algorithm that can efficiently locate the place in the evolving taxonomy where the new concept should be placed. This algorithm, known as an MSS algorithm (for "most specific subsumer"), finds the most specific concepts in the taxonomy that subsume the new concept, and links the new concept directly under those concepts. A related algorithm, known as the MGS algorithm (for "most general subsumee"), finds the most general concepts that are subsumed by the new concept and links them directly under the new one.

When a single word is added to the taxonomy, any subsuming words or word senses that are listed in the lexical entry for that word are also added to the taxonomy and subsumption links are created to link these words and word senses to their most specific subsumers. When a phrase is added, the MSS algorithms searches the conceptual taxonomy to find its most specific subsumers, using the conceptual structures of the phrases to align corresponding constituent elements and using semantic subsumption relationships already in the taxonomy to relate constituents to each other. For example, in one taxonomy, the phrase *automobile cleaning* subsumes *car washing* because of the way corresponding elements of these phrases are aligned and the facts (derived from semantic subsumption information in lexical entries) that a car is a kind of automobile and washing is a kind of cleaning.

Because of the conceptual subsumption algorithms, it is possible to look up a phrase that doesn't occur in the taxonomy and still find useful concepts in the "neighborhood." This is because the algorithm automatically locates the places in the taxonomy where the query concept would belong, using the same MSS and MGS algorithms that are used to construct the taxonomy. For example, one can look up *automobile cleaning* in a taxonomy and find *car washing*. One can think of the subsumption logic that governs the taxonomy as providing a conceptual space in which to search that is an "oriented topology." The orienting principle is the up/down relationship of generality and the topological neighborhoods are determined (and linguistically labeled) by the subsuming concepts and their descendants. This conceptual space provides a naturally intuitive structure for browsing and navigating, and allows subsumption algorithms to be used to get quickly to the right neighborhood (without having to navigate all the way down from the top). This is a more effective structure to navigate than a strictly hierarchical classification tree, and it provides more informative browsing capabilities than approaches based on linking concepts according to measures of term-term distance.

The utility of a conceptual index can be illustrated by an example (shown in Figure 1) from the conceptual index of a collection of encyclopedia articles about animals. An initial request for *brown fur* retrieved the phrase (BROWN FUR) and the subsumed phrases (GRAY BROWN FUR), (RICH BROWN FUR), and (WHITE-SPOTTED BROWN FUR). However, a display of more general concepts showed that the query was subsumed by the phrase (BROWN COAT), revealing that the request was inadvertently more specific than intended. Generalizing the request to (BROWN COAT) produced the substantially more useful collection of concepts shown in Figure 1. By displaying the more general concepts in the taxonomy that subsumed the stated request, the system unobtrusively suggested an exceedingly useful generalization of the request.

Note that morphological relationships are incorporated into the subsumption framework by treating derived and inflected forms of words as subsumed by their base forms. For example, *brownish* is subsumed by *brown*. Morphological variations and terminology variations are thus automatically related in the conceptual taxonomy, and syntactic relationships are incorporated into the structures of the parsed phrases. Different senses of words can be represented by distinct concepts that have different places in the taxonomy but are subsumed by an abstract concept corresponding to the undisambiguated word.

Specific Passage Retrieval

The conceptual index supports direct access to places in the indexed material where concepts subsumed by a query occur. However, there are often situations in which elements of a query occur in a text without being explicitly related in ways that would enable a strict subsumption. For example, in the Encyclopedia example illustrated above, subsumption fails to pick up a passage of text that says, *The coat is reddish brown,* because there is no explicit phrase subsumed by *brown coat*. To handle such cases, we use a technique called "relaxation ranking" (Woods 1997; Ambroziak & Woods 1998; Woods *et al.* 2000) to find specific passages where as many as possible of the elements of a query occur near each other, preferably in the same form and word order and preferably closer together. These passages are given a penalty score based on the amount of deviation from an exact copy of the query (same words, same forms, same order, and nothing else in between). Penalties are assigned in proportion to the amount of intervening material occurring between the desired terms. When the elements occur in a different order for reasons that are not accounted for, an extra penalty is assigned proportional to the amount of reordering of terms. In addition, small penalties can be assigned for subsumed terms and different inflected forms of the requested terms, and substantial penalties are assigned for elements that are missing from passages that contain some, but not all, of the elements of a request.

```
(BROWN COAT)
  |-k- (BRIGHT REDDISH BROWN COAT)
  |-k- (BROWN BLACK COAT)
  |-k- (BROWN COATS)
  |    |-k- (FAWN COATS)
  |    |    |-v- ((FAWN) COATS)
  |    |
  |    |-k- (REDDISH BROWN UPPER COATS)
  |
  |-k- (BROWN FUR)
  |    |-k- (GRAY BROWN FUR)
  |    |-k- (RICH BROWN FUR)
  |    |-k- (WHITE-SPOTTED BROWN FUR)
  |
  |-k- (BROWN HAIR)
  |    |-k- (BROWN HAIRS)
  |    |    |-k- (REDDISH BROWN GUARD HAIRS)
  |    |
  |    |-k- (BROWN WOOL)
  |    |    |-k- (REDDISH BROWN WOOL)
  |    |
  |    |-k- (BROWNISH HAIR)
  |    |-k- (REDDISH BROWN HAIR)
  |         |-k- (REDDISH BROWN GUARD HAIRS)
  |         |-k- (REDDISH BROWN WOOL)
  |
  |-k- (BROWN-GRAY COAT)
  |-k- (BROWNISH COAT)
  |    |-k- (BROWNISH HAIR)
  |    |-k- (BROWNISH SUMMER COAT)
  |    |-k- (COARSER BROWNISH COAT)
  |    |-k- (DARK BROWNISH COAT)
  |
  |-k- (COAT OF BROWN)
  |    |-k- (WOOLLY COAT OF REDDISH BROWN)
  |-k- (TAWNY COAT)
```

Figure 1: A fragment of a conceptual taxonomy, illustrating the utility of navigating in conceptual space.

Retrieved passages are constructed dynamically in response to a query, using information from the conceptual index about where concepts occur in the text. The hit passages from a single query may range in size from a single word or phrase to several sentences or a paragraph, with penalty scores generally increasing as passages get longer. This is in contrast with passage retrieval methods in which the indexed material is presegmented into paragraphs or sentences at indexing time. Because of the way scores are assigned, the penalty scores are highly correlated with the likelihood that the terms in the passage are related in the way that is requested, so the best passages tend to occur at the top of the ranking. This is because the likelihood that the terms are related in the desired way and are being used in the desired senses tends to decrease as the terms in the passage get further apart and their order departs from that of the input request.

For example, the following is a passage retrieved by this system, when applied to the UNIX® operating system on-line documentation (man pages):

Query: print a message from the mail tool
6. -2.84 *print mail mail mailtool*
Print sends copies of all the selected mail items to your default printer. If there are no selected items, mailtool sends copies of those items you are currently...

The indicated passage is ranked 6th in a returned list of found passages, indicated by the 6 in the above display. The number -2.84 is the penalty score assigned to the passage, and the subsequent words *print*, *mail*, *mail*, and *mailtool* indicate the words in the text that are matched to the corresponding words in the input query. In this case, *print* is matched to *print*, *message* to *mail*, *mail* to *mail*, and *tool* to *mailtool*. This is followed by the content of the actual passage located. The information provided in these hit displays gives the information seeker a clear idea of why the passage was retrieved and enables the searcher to quickly skip down the hit list with little time spent looking at irrelevant passages. In this case, it was easy to identify that the 6th ranked hit was the best one and contained the relevant information.

The retrieval of this passage involved use of a semantic subsumption relationship to match *message* to *mail*, because the lexical entry for *mail* recorded that it was a kind of *message*. It used a morphological root subsumption to match *tool* to *mailtool* because the morphological analyzer analyzed the unknown word *mailtool* as a compound of *mail* and *tool* and recorded that its root was *tool* and that it was a kind of *tool* modified by *mail*. Taking away the ability to morphologically analyze unknown words would have blocked the retrieval of this passage, as would eliminating the lexical subsumption entry that recorded *mail* as a kind of *message*.

Precision Search Benefits

Precision Content Retrieval offers users three key benefits. The first is specific passage retrieval–that is, finding specific passages of information that are responsive to specific requests. The second is an effective ranking and scoring of the found passages, so that the best passages are listed first. The third is "conceptual navigation," the ability to move around in the structured conceptual taxonomy, a "conceptual space" that is intuitively organized for efficient browsing and navigation and includes all of the concepts found in the indexed material.

In quantitative evaluations of these benefits (Woods *et al.* 2000), one experiment showed that without any of its knowledge sources, the relaxation ranking algorithm is roughly as good as a state-of-the art commercial search engine at finding documents, and it becomes substantially better (41% better) when semantic and morphological knowledge is used. This is in contrast to most previous attempts to use linguistic knowledge to improve information retrieval (Fagan 1989; Lewis & Sparck Jones 1996; Mauldin 1991; Sparck Jones 1998; Varile & Zampolli 1997; Voorhees 1993; Mandala, Tokunaga, & Tanaka 1999) (but see the latter for some successes as well). This experiment doesn't measure the benefit of being able to locate the specific passages where the information occurs.

In another experiment, informally measuring the time it took to find specific information on a web site or to conclude that it is not in the indexed material, using a commercial search engine versus our conceptual indexing technology, showed a five-fold improvement in search productivity from using the conceptual indexing technology (55 minutes versus 11 minutes to work through a suite of 15 typical queries).

Large-Scale Knowledge Representation

The system that I have just described is an example of a large-scale application of subsumption technology. When we began this project, it was not clear that it would be possible to build large conceptual taxonomies in a reasonable amount of time. In fact, most of the theoretical work on KL-One-style techniques had produced unattractive complexity results at that time (Woods & Schmolze 1992). However, (Woods 1991) described an approach, called "intensional subsumption," that appeared likely to resolve some of the complexity issues and would at the same time increase the expressive power of the representational system. The system I have just described is the first large-scale test of this approach, and so far, the predictions of (Woods 1991) seem to have held up.

To date, the largest conceptual index that we have built contained over three million concepts. It was derived from a 3.1-million-word corpus of technical material. The core lexicon that we used contains approximately 80,000 words (150,000 word forms) and contains semantic subsumption facts for more than 15,000 words. More than 18,000 words were encountered in the 3.1-million-word corpus that were not in this lexicon (not counting numbers and hyphenated words), illustrating the importance of morphological analysis. The morphological analysis system that we used to analyze these words (and the hyphenated words as well) contains approximately 1,200 morphological rules. In addition to patterns of spelling of the analyzed words, these rules test syntactic and sometimes semantic information about hypothesized root words, in order to form hypotheses about the structure and meanings of the unknown words and to construct lexical entries for them.

When I began the exploration of subsumption technology for conceptually indexing text, one of the things I was interested in understanding was the behavior of taxonomic classification algorithms on large collections of naturally occurring concepts. The automatic extraction of words and phrases from unrestricted text provides an almost unlimited supply of naturally occurring concepts. This provides a more realistic testing environment than would an algorithmic study on synthesized examples. While we are still in the process of studying the behavior of large-scale classification algorithms, we have at least demonstrated that large scale conceptual taxonomies can be constructed and used and that they provide real benefit for the information location problem.

Other Applications of Large-Scale Subsumption

The intensional subsumption technology described here was originally motivated by the problem of organizing the rules of a large-scale knowledge-based reasoning system that would be able to deal with millions of rules and handle the kinds of fluent shifts in levels of generality that people exhibit when reasoning (Woods 1986). The idea was that the pattern parts of rules could be organized into a subsumption taxonomy so that the most specific rules that match a given subgoal could be found efficiently using the MSS algorithm. Although there are likely to be some differences between classifying the pattern parts of rules and the classification of natural English phrases, our experiences with the latter nevertheless give some idea of the feasibility and complexity of such classifications in large taxonomies. Moreover, there are reasons to suspect that the behavior for rule patterns might not be too different. For example, predicates used in logical rules are usually amenable to translation into ordinary English.

Our experiences with classifying English phrases show that it is at least possible to construct and use large conceptual taxonomies and to deal with the subsumption relationships between different levels of generality. It would be interesting to try to extend this approach to handling large-scale rule-based systems. Woods (1991) presents a number of advantages of such an approach, such as the ability to quickly determine the most specific subsuming rule patterns from very large collections of rules. In addition to the benefit of finding matching rules efficiently from a large collection, this approach has the added benefit of automatically organizing the pattern parts of the rules by generality, so that the most specific matching patterns are found, and any information from more general rules can be found by inheritance or overridden by the more specific rules.

Woods (1991) also presents an analysis of the structure of concepts in representations such as frames, semantic networks, object-oriented class systems, and conventional data base records, that makes it possible to correctly apply subsumption logic to such representations. One of the key insights is the observation that slots in frames, fields in data records, and class and instance variables in object-oriented systems, all have a quantificational import that determines how those elements participate in inheritance and subsumption reasoning. By making this quantificational import explicit, in the form of a system of quantificational tags, it is possible to develop a clean separation between the logical structure of concepts, which can be interpreted by subsumption and inheritance algorithms, and the domain-specific content of those concepts, which is then reasoned about by the subsumption logic and reasoning system. For example, different quantificational tags are used to express the different relationships implied by the superficially similar statements:

- birds have wings
- people need vitamins

In the first case, for every bird, there are some wings that it has, while in the second, for every person and every vitamin, that person needs that vitamin.

Quantificational tags can also be used to distinguish relationships that are governed by statistical probabilities, as opposed to strict logical implications, and those that are definitional versus those that are assertional. Using these distinctions, a subsumption taxonomy can integrate probabilistic with strictly logical information, as well as absolute and defeasible inheritance.

Furthermore, a classification process based on intensional subsumption can be used to efficiently resolve conflicts between competing rules in multiple inheritance situations. For example, in the famous "Nixon diamond" scenario, in which Richard Nixon, who was both a Republican and a Quaker, would be expected to inherit hawkishness from the REPUBLICAN concept and non-hawkishness from the QUAKER concept, a conceptual subsumption approach can identify the locus of the problem at the level of the greatest-lower-bound concept, REPUBLICAN QUAKER. This then suggests that an experiment needs to be conducted to determine the likelihoods of hawkishness for Republican Quakers. (This is an empirical fact that needs to be determined, not something that can be resolved by any principle of inheritance.) Once such likelihoods have been determined and associated with the REPUBLICAN QUAKER concept, individual instances like Richard Nixon, that would be classified under both REPUBLICAN and QUAKER, will automatically be classified under this combined concept by the MSS algorithm. Thus, they will inherit the resolved result from the immediate parent concept, REPUBLICAN QUAKER, without needing to even notice the conflicting sources of information above it.

The detection of such potential conflicts can be done either as a consequence of finding an individual case which inherits conflicting information (in which case a combined concept is then created from the parents that participate in the conflict), or it can be done as a background process, searching for greatest-lower-bound concepts whose parent concepts would provide conflicting information. In the latter case, one need not wait to encounter conflicting instances in order to ask the necessary questions to resolve the conflicts.

In summary, the organizing principles of intensional subsumption hold a lot of promise for organizing very large collections of rules for efficient use. The experiments in conceptual indexing of text suggest that such an approach might be tractable. However, it is difficult to test this hypothesis without a problem that provides a source of millions of rules. One wonders what a naturally occurring population of such rule patterns might be like and how a taxonomic classification approach would behave on such a population.

Conclusion

I have described a system that constructs and uses large-scale conceptual taxonomies of English concepts that are automatically extracted from unrestricted text. These taxonomies of meaningful words and phrases are used to help people find specific information in online text by efficiently finding connections between terms used in a request and related terms used by authors of the text material. It provides an example of practical subsumption technology on a large scale and with domain-independent knowledge.

This system has demonstrated a substantial improvement in search effectiveness from using linguistic and world knowledge and exploiting intensional subsumption technology in conjunction with a relaxation-ranking passage retrieval algorithm. Conceptual taxonomies in excess of three million concepts have been automatically constructed, indexing previously unseen bodies of text material and using a pre-existing body of general-purpose linguistic and semantic rules and knowledge.

Results from this experiment are relevant to general problems of knowledge-based reasoning with large-scale knowledge bases and with domain-independent knowledge. An important issue is the problem of scale – how to find a small amount of information relevant to a given problem out of a truly encyclopedic body of knowledge. Intensional subsumption technology (Woods 1991) is used to find the most specific subsumers of a concept in an amount of time that is sublinear in the size of the taxonomy. Such taxonomies can be used to organize the pattern parts of rules, as well as facts, and thus find matching rules from very large rule sets in a reasonable amount of time. Subsumption technology can also efficiently resolve conflicting inheritance paths.

The conceptual indexing system described is an example of practical AI using large-scale and domain-independent knowledge bases that provides a significant improvement in human information access.

Acknowledgments

Many people have been involved in creating and testing the conceptual indexing and retrieval system described here. These include: Gary Adams, Jacek Ambroziak, Cookie Callahan, Chris Colby, Jim Flowers, Stephen Green, Ellen Hays, Ann Houston, Robert Kuhns, Patrick Martin, Paul Martin, Peter Norvig, Tony Passera, Philip Resnik, Scott Sanner, Robert Sproull, and Mark Torrance.

Sun and Sun Microsystems are trademarks or registered trademarks of Sun Microsystems, Inc. in the U.S. and other countries.

UNIX is a registered trademark in the United States and other countries, exclusively licensed through X/Open Company, Ltd. UNIX est une marque enregistree aux Etats-Unis et dans d'autres pays et licenciée exclusivement par X/Open Company Ltd.

References

Ambroziak, J., and Woods, W. A. 1998. Natural language technology in precision content retrieval. In *International Conference on Natural Language Processing and Industrial Applications*. Moncton, New Brunswick, Canada: Université de Moncton. www.sun.com/research/techrep/1998/abstract-69.html.

Fagan, J. L. 1989. The effectiveness of a nonsyntactic approach to automatic phrase indexing for document retrieval. *Journal of the American Society for Information Science* 40(2):115–132.

Lehmann, F., ed. 1992. *Semantic Networks in Artificial Intelligence*. Pergamon Press.

Lewis, D. D., and Sparck Jones, K. 1996. Natural language processing for information retrieval. *CACM* 39(1):92–101.

Mandala, R.; Tokunaga, T.; and Tanaka, H. 1999. Combining multiple evidence from different types of thesaurus for query expansion. In *Proceedings of the 22nd Annual International ACM SIGIR Conference on Research and Development in Information Retrieval*. ACM-SIGIR.

Mauldin, M. L. 1991. Retrieval performance in FERRET a conceptual information retrieval system. In *14th Annual International ACM/SIGIR Conference on Research and Development in Information Retrieval*, 347–355.

Sparck Jones, K. 1998. A look back and a look forward. *SIGIR* 13–29.

Varile, G., and Zampolli, A., eds. 1997. *Survey of the State of the Art in Human Language Technology*. Cambridge Univ. Press.

Voorhees, E. M. 1993. Using wordnet to disambiguate word senses for text retrieval. In *Proceedings of 16th ACM SIGIR Conference*. ACM-SIGIR.

Woods, W. A., and Schmolze, J. G. 1992. The kl-one family. *Computers & Mathematics with Applications* 23(2–5):133–177. Reprinted in (Lehmann, 1992).

Woods, W. A.; Bookman, L. A.; Houston, A. C.; Kuhns, R. J.; Martin, P. A.; and Green, S. 2000. Linguistic knowledge can improve information retrieval. In *Proceedings of ANLP-2000*. Seattle WA: ACL ANLP.

Woods, W. A. 1986. Important issues in knowledge representation. *Proceedings of the IEEE* 74(10):1322–1334. Reprinted in (Woods, 1990).

Woods, W. A. 1990. Important issues in knowledge representation. In Raeth, P. G., ed., *Expert Systems: A Software Methodology for Modern Applications*. IEEE Computer Society Press. 180–204.

Woods, W. A. 1991. Understanding subsumption and taxonomy: A framework for progress. In Sowa, J., ed., *Principles of Semantic Networks: Explorations in the Representation of Knowledge*. San Mateo, CA: Morgan Kaufmann. 45–94.

Woods, W. A. 1997. Conceptual indexing: A better way to organize knowledge. Technical Report SMLI TR-97-61, Sun Microsystems Laboratories, Mountain View, CA. www.sun.com/research/techrep/1997/abstract-61.html.

Woods, W. A. 2000. Aggressive morphology for robust lexical coverage. In *Proceedings of ANLP-2000*. Seattle WA: ACL ANLP.

Index

A* with Partial Expansion for Large Branching Factor Problems, 923
Achlioptas, Dimitris, 256
Acquiring Problem-Solving Knowledge from End Users: Putting Interdependency Models to the Test, 223
Active Audition for Humanoid, 832
Adaptive Learning Systems: A Model for Business Entrepreneurs to Implement IT, 1102
Adaptive Planner Based on Learning of Planning Performance, An, 1073
Adaptive User Interfaces through Dynamic Design Automation, 1127
ADVISOR: A Machine Learning Architecture for Intelligent Tutor Construction, 552
Agent Capabilities: Extending BDI Theory, 68
AI for the Web - Ontology-Based Community Web Portals, 1034
Aist, Greg, 1061, 1100
Akers, Robert L., 937
Al-Onaizan, Yaser, 672
Algorithm for Multi-Unit Combinatorial Auctions, An, 56
Amir, Eyal, 456
Anchoring Symbols to Sensor Data: Preliminary Report, 129
Anderson, David, 209
Anderson, Emily, 209
Angele, Jürgen, 1034
Anshelevich, Vadim V., 189
Answering Queries Using Views over Description Logics Knowledge Bases, 386
Antoniou, G., 405
Aone, Chinatsu, 945
Apfelbaum, David, 852
Appearance-Based Obstacle Detection with Monocular Color Vision, 866
Applying Learnable Evolution Model to Heat Exchanger Design, 1014
Arseneau, Shawn, 3
Artificial Intelligence-Based Computer Modeling Tools for Controlling Slag Foaming in Electric Furnaces, 1113
Ashley, Kevin D., 316
Assentor®: An NLP-Based Solution to E-mail Monitoring, 945
Assessing Relevance with Extensionally Defined Principles and Cases, 316
Asynchronous Search with Aggregations, 917
ATMOSPHERE - Automatic Track Mining and Objective Satellite Pattern Hunting System Using Enhanced RBF and EGDLM, 603
Audet, Jonathan, 1140
Automated Learning of Pricing and Bundling Strategies in Information Economies, 1066

Automatic Generation of Memory Based Search Heuristics, 1103
Automatic Interpretation of Nominalizations, The, 716
Automatic Invention of Integer Sequences, 558
Autonomous Multi-Agent Docking Using Color Segmentation, 1076

Back to the Future for Consistency-Based Trajectory Tracking, 370
Baral, Chitta, 62, 545
Barber, K. Suzanne, 1082, 1115, 1117
Barbulescu, Laura, 879
Barish, Greg, 980, 1062
Barzilay, Regina, 679
Basin, David, 195
Bayardo, Roberto J. Jr., 157
Bayesian Fault Detection and Diagnosis in Dynamic Systems, 531
Beal, Carole R., 552
Beck, Joseph E., 552
Bednar, James A., 117
Behavior Acquisition and Classification: A Case Study in Robotic Soccer, 1092
Béjar, Ramón, 262
Belanche Muñoz, Lluís A., 1063
Bélanger, François, 1140
Belief Revision in a Deductively Open Belief Space, 1106
Bell, A. M., 9
Ben-Eliyahu-Zohary, Rachel, 267
Bennett, Brandon, 503
Besnard, Philippe, 411
Bhattacharya, Sutirtha, 1117
Bica, Ion, 937
Billington, D., 405
Biswas, Gautam, 531
Bjäreland, Marcus, 62
Blue Swarm, The, 1142
Blumberg, Bruce M., 249
Boicu, Michael, 1065
Boicu, Mihai, 1046, 1064
Boosted Wrapper Induction, 577
Boufkhad, Yacine, 273
Boutilier, Craig, 22, 355, 1145
Bowman, Michael, 1046, 1065
Brooks, Christopher H., 1066
Broxvall, Mathias, 464
Bucklew, J. A., 9
Budzikowska, Malgorzata, 1008
Bui, Hung H., 524
Bundy, Alan, 195, 558
Burgard, Wolfram, 852, 859
Burke, Robert C., 249

Calvanese, Diego, 386
Campus-Wide University Examination Timetabling Application, A, 1020
Caragea, Doina, 1067
Cardie, Claire, 1097

Case-Based Reasoning Application for Engineering Sales Support Using Introspective Reasoning, A, 1054
Cassell, Justine, 1151
cc-Golog: Towards More Realistic Logic-Based Robot Controllers, 476
Cesta, Amedeo, 742
Cha, Sung-Hyuk, 1068
Chajewska, Urszula, 363
Chan, Steve Ho Chuen, 951
Change Detection in Heuristic Search, 898
Chaudhri, Vinay K., 436
Chen, Yi-Shin, 980, 1133
Chimaera Ontology Environment, The, 1123
Chin, Ang Juay, 1020
Choe, Yoonsuck, 123
Chong, Oon Wee, 1020
Chun, Andy Hon Wai, 951
Ciucu, Florin, 1046
Clark, Peter, 988
Class-Based Construction of a Verb Lexicon, 691
Clustering with Instance-Level Constraints, 1097
Cobot in LambdaMOO: A Social Statistics Agent, 36
Coen, Michael H., 15
Cognitive Status and Form of Reference in Multimodal Human-Computer Interaction, 685
Cohen, Paul R., 633, 846
Cohen, Philip R., 42
Cohen, Robin, 1096
Cohn, Anthony G., 503
Colaci, Raffaella, 996
Collective Intelligence and Braess' Paradox, 104
Collins, Michael, 679
Colton, Simon, 558
Combining Classification and Temporal Learning, 1086
Combining Knowledge and Search to Solve Single-Suit Bridge, 195
Compilability of Abduction, 349
Complexity of Restricted Consequence Findings and Abduction, The, 337
Computing Circumscriptive Databases by Integer Programming: Revisited, 429
Conceptual Indexing: Practical Large-Scale AI for Efficient Information Access, 1180
Conjunctive Query Language for Description Logic Aboxes, A, 399
Consistency-Based Model for Belief Change: Preliminary Report, A, 392
Cook, Diane J., 1072, 1078
Cooperstock, Jeremy R., 3
Coordination Failure and Congestion in Information Networks, 9
Coordination for Multi-Robot Exploration and Mapping, 852
Coradeschi, Silvia, 129

Cotter, Paul, 957
Counting Models Using Connected Components, 157
Cowley, Wes, 470
Customer Coalitions in the Electronic Marketplace, 1133

Dalton, Jeff, 1131
Dang, Hoa Trang, 691
Daniels, Jody, 1002
DATALOG with Constraints — An Answer-Set Programming System, 163
David, Dessa, 1102
Dechter, Rina, 1084
Decision Making under Uncertainty: Operations Research Meets AI (Again), 1145
Decision-Theoretic, High-Level Agent Programming in the Situation Calculus, 355
Decker, Stefan, 1034
(De)Composition of Situation Calculus Theories, 456
Defining and Using Ideal Teammate and Opponent Agent Models, 1040
de Giacomo, Giuseppe 386
del Val, Alvaro, 279, 337, 343
Delgrande, James P., 392
Deliberation in Equilibrium: Bargaining in Computationally Complex Problems, 48
Demand-Driven Algorithm for Generating Minimal Models, A, 267
Depth-First Branch-and-Bound versus Local Search: A Case Study, 930
Deriving and Using Abstract Representation in Behavior-Based Systems, 1087
Describing Rigid Body Motions in a Qualitative Theory of Spatial Regions, 503
Discovering State Constraints in DISCOPLAN: Some New Results, 761
Disjunctive Temporal Reasoning in Partially Ordered Models of Time, 464
Distributed Algorithm to Evaluate Quantified Boolean Formulae, A, 285
Divide-and-Conquer Frontier Search Applied to Optimal Sequence Alignment, 910
DMML: An XML Language for Interacting with Multi-Modal Dialog Systems, 1008
Domain-Specific Knowledge Acquisition Using WordNet, 1071
Domashnev, Constantine, 1125
Domike, Steffi, 236
Domingos, Pedro, 564
Duckett, Tom, 826
Dudek, Gregory, 1110
Duncan, Lisbeth, 988
Durfee, Edmund H., 1066
Dynamic Case Creation and Expansion for Analogical Reasoning, 323
Dynamic Ontologies on the Web, 443
Dynamic Representations and Escaping Local Optima: Improving Genetic Algorithms and Local Search, 879

East, Deborah, 163
Edelkamp, Stefan, 885
Efficient Global-Search Strategy in Discrete Lagrangian Methods for Solving Hard Satisfiability Problems, An, 310
Egly, Uwe, 417
Eiter, Thomas, 417
Elomaa, Tapio, 570
Emergence Engine: A Behavior Based Agent Development Environment for Artists, The, 973
Empirical Evaluation of a Reinforcement Learning Spoken Dialogue System, 645
Erdmann, Michael, 1034
Estimating Word Translation Probabilities from Unrelated Monolingual Corpora Using the EM Algorithm, 711
Execution of Temporal Plans with Uncertainty, 491
Expert System for Recognition of Facial Actions and their Intensity, An, 1026
Exploiting a Thesaurus-Based Semantic Net for Knowledge-Based Search, 988
Extracting Effective and Admissible State Space Heuristics from the Planning Graph, 798

Faltings, Boi, 917
Feldmann, Rainer, 285
Ferguson, Ronald W., 510, 1119
Ferraris, Paolo, 748
Ferrer, Gabriel J., 1069
Fikes, Richard, 1123
Finzi, Alberto, 754
Flexible Framework for Defeasible Logics, A, 405
Forbus, Kenneth D., 323, 510, 1119
Fox, Dieter, 852, 859
Frank, Ian, 195
Freitag, Dayne, 577, 584
From Causal Theories to Successor State Axioms and STRIPS-Like Systems, 786
Furcy, David, 891

Galinskaya, Vlada, 1089
Game of Hex: An Automatic Theorem Proving Approach to Game Programming, The, 189
Game-Theoretic Approach to Constraint Satisfaction, A, 175
Games Computers (and People) Play, The, 1179
Generalizing Boundary Points, 570
Generating Satisfiable Problem Instances, 256
Generation of Ideologically-Biased Historical Documentaries, 236
GeoRep: A Flexible Tool for Spatial Representation of Line Drawings, 510
Gerevini, Alfonso, 761
Gerkey, Brian P., 1070
Germann, Ulrich, 672
Gil, Yolanda, 223
Giles, C. Lee, 729
Girju, Roxana, 1071
Giunchiglia, Enrico, 748
Goel, A., 1115
Gomes, Carla P., 256, 1152
Gonzalez, Jesus A., 1072
Gopal, Kreshna, 1073
Gorniak, Peter, 217
Governatori, G., 405
Graph Based Concept Learning, 1072
Graph Construction and Analysis as a Paradigm for Plan Recognition, 774

Graph-Based Hierarchical Conceptual Clustering in Structural Databases, 1078
Graser, Thomas, 1117
Gratch, Jonathan, 1079
Greiner, Russell, 230
Gridworlds as Testbeds for Planning with Incomplete Information, 819
Grisham, Paul, 1117
Grosskreutz, Henrik, 476
Grounding State Representations in Sensory Experience for Reasoning and Planning by Mobile Robots, 1108
Grudic, Greg, 590
Gunderson, James P., 1069
Gutta, Srinivas, 1121

Han, D. C., 1115
Hazarika, Shyamanta, 503
Heflin, Jeff, 443, 1074
Heinze, Daniel T., 965
Hellerstein, Joseph L., 596
Helping Children Learn Vocabulary during Computer Assisted Oral Reading, 1100
Hendler, James, 443
Hermjakob, Ulf, 672
Hernádvölgyi, István T., 1075, 1103
Herzig, A., 768
Heterogeneous Neuron Models Based on Similarity, 1063
Hill, Randall W. Jr., 1079
Hinton, Geoffrey E., 1159
Hirschberg, Julia, 679
Hirsh, Haym, 665
Holder, Lawrence B., 1072, 1078
Holmback, Heather, 988
Honavar, Vasant, 1067
Hong, Jun, 774
Hoos, Holger H., 22
Horikoshi, Tsutomu, 330
Horrocks, Ian, 399
Horvitz, Eric, 729
Hotho, Andreas, 1034
Hsu, Chun-Nan, 1077, 1105
Hsu, Wynne, 615
Hu, Minqing, 615
Huang, Thomas S., 243
Huber, Marcus J., 42
Hüllermeier, Eyke, 898
Human-Guided Simple Search, 209
Human-Level AI's Killer Application: Interactive Computer Games, 1171
Hunsberger, Luke, 30
Hunter, Anthony, 411
Hyams, Jeffrey, 1076

ICARUS: Intelligent Content-Based Retrieval of 3D Scene, 996
Identifying Words to Explain to a Reader: A Preliminary Study, 1061
ILP Method Based on Instance Graph, An, 1098
Imai, Michita, 142
Implementation of the Combinatorial Auction Problem in ECLiPSe, An, 1084
Improved Algorithms for Optimal Winner Determination in Combinatorial Auctions and Generalizations, 90
Incremental and Distributed Learning with Support Vector Machines, 1067
Information Extraction with HMM Structures Learned by Stochastic Optimization, 584

Integrating a Spoken Language System with Agents for Operational Information Access, 1002
Integrating Equivalency Reasoning into Davis-Putnam Procedure, 291
Intelligent Monitoring in a Robotic Assistant for the Elderly, 1090
Inter-Layer Learning Towards Emergent Cooperative Behavior, 3
Interactive Training for Synthetic Characters, 249
Interfacing Issues for Information Extraction, 1096
Interval Algebra for Indeterminate Time, An, 470
Intuitive Representation of Decision Trees Using General Rules and Exceptions, 615
Ioerger, Thomas R., 1073
Isbell, Charles Lee Jr., 36
Ishida, Toru, 923
Ismail, Haythem O., 1104
Iterative Algorithm for Synthesizing Invariants, An, 806
Iterative Combinatorial Auctions: Theory and Practice, 74
Iterative Flattening: A Scalable Method for Solving Multi-Capacity Scheduling Problems, 742

Jayram, T. S., 596
Jenkins, Jessica, 1137
Jennings, Mark A., 965
Jeong, Euna, 1077, 1105
Jernigan, Stephen, 1117
Jimmink, Michelle A., 965
Johnson, Christopher L., 1127
Johnson, Frances L., 1106
Jonsson, Peter, 464
Jonyer, Istvan, 1078
Junker, Ulrich, 904
Jussien, Narendra, 169

Kaelbling, Leslie Pack, 378
Kambhampati, Subbarao, 798
Kambhatla, Nanda, 1008
Kant, Elaine, 937
Kaufman, Kenneth A., 1014
Kautz, Henry, 256
Kearns, Michael, 36, 645
Kehler, Andrew, 685
Kim, Jihie, 223, 1115
Kim, Youngjun, 1079
Kipper, Karin, 691
Kit, Ho Wee, 1020
Kitano, Hiroaki, 832
Knight, Kevin, 672, 697, 703, 711
Knoblock, Craig A., 621, 980, 1062, 1107
Knowledge Representation on the Internet: Achieving Interoperability in a Dynamic, Distributed Environment, 1074
Koehn, Philipp, 672, 711
Koenig, Sven, 819, 891
Kohl, Karen T., 1080
Kojima, Haruhiko, 330
Kolaitis, Phokion G., 175
Koller, Daphne, 363, 531, 538, 658
Korf, Richard E., 201, 910, 1165
Kormann, Dave, 36
Korvemaker, Benjamin, 230
Kreinovich, Vladik, 545

Kumar, Sanjeev, 42
Kurapati, Kaushal, 1121
Kurien, James, 370
Kushmerick, Nicholas, 577

Lagoudakis, Michail G., 1081
Laird, John E., 1171
Lakemeyer, Gerhard, 476
Lam, Dung N., 1082, 1115
Lam, Garbbie Puishan, 951
Lambrix, Patrick, 68
Lang, J., 768
Langkilde, Irene, 697
Language Learning in Large Parameter Spaces, 1080
Lapata, Maria, 716
Larson, Amy, 1083
Larson, Kate, 48
Lau, Hoong Chuin, 780
Learning Landmarks for Robot Localization, 1110
Learning Subjective Adjectives from Corpora, 735
Learning the Common Structure of Data, 609
Lee, K. P., 1121
Lee, Raymond S., 603
Lenzerini, Maurizio, 386
Lerman, Kristina, 609
Lerner, Uri, 531
Lesh, Neal, 209
Létourneau, Dominic, 1140
Levcovici, Cristian, 1046
Levesque, Hector J., 42
Levesque, Sylvie, 1008
Levine, John, 1131
Leyton-Brown, Kevin, 56
Lhomme, Olivier, 169
Li, Chu Min, 291
Liberatore, Paolo, 349
LifeCode™ – A Natural Language Processing System for Medical Coding and Data Mining, 965
Lim, Andrew, 780, 1020
Lin, Fangzhen, 786
Litman, Diane J., 645, 722
Littman, Michael L., 1081, 1094
Liu, Bing, 615
Liu, James N., 603
Liu, Qi Zhang, 780
Liu, T. H., 1115
Local Search Characteristics of Incomplete SAT Procedures, 297
Local Search with Constraint Propagation and Conflict-Based Heuristics, 169
Localizing A*, 885
Localizing Search in Reinforcement Learning, 590
Logic for Planning under Partial Observability, A, 768
Longin, D., 768
Lourens, Tino, 832
Love, Bradley C., 136

MacNaught, Julie, 1008
Maedche, Alexander, 1034
Maher, M. J., 405
Maintainability: A Weaker Stabilizability Like Notion for High Level Control, 62
Making Rational Decisions Using Adaptive Utility Elicitation, 363
Manyà, Felip, 262

Marcu, Daniel, 672, 703
Marcu, Dorin, 1046
MarketSAT: An Extremely Decentralized (but Really Slow) Algorithm for Propositional Satisfiability, 303
Markman, Arthur B., 136
Marks, Joe, 209
Martin, C. E., 1115
Martin, Worthy N., 1069
Martino, Jacquelyn, 1121
Mataric, Maja J., 1070, 1087, 1093
Matchmaking to Support Intelligent Agents for Portfolio Management, 1125
Mateas, Michael, 236
Matsubara, Shigeo, 110
McCallum, Andrew, 584
McGee, David R., 42
McGuinness, Deborah L., 1123
McIlraith, Sheila A., 483
McKay, R., 1115
McLaren, Bruce M., 316
Mechanism for Group Decision Making in Collaborative Activity, A, 30
Memory-Based Forecasting for Weather Image Patterns, 330
Mendelowitz, Eitan, 973
Menke, Robert, 1084
Method for Clustering the Experiences of a Mobile Robot that Accords with Human Judgments, A, 846
Methodology for Modeling and Respresenting Expert Knowledge that Supports Teaching-Based Intelligent Agent Development, A, 1065
Meverden, Cara, 323
Michalski, Ryszard S., 1014
Michaud, François, 1140
Mihalcea, Rada, 1085
Miikkulainen, Risto, 117, 123
Milanski, John, 1121
Minton, Steven, 609, 621, 980, 1062, 1107
Mirtich, Brian, 209
Mitchell, Matthew Winston, 1086
Miura, Teruhisa, 923
Mixed-Initiative Reasoning for Integrated Domain Modeling, Learning and Problem Solving, 1064
Model-Based-Diagnosis for Fault Management in Telecommunications Networks, 1088
Modeling Actions with Ramifications in Nondeterministic, Concurrent, and Continuous Domains — and a Case Study, 497
Modeling Classification and Inference Learning, 136
Modeling High-Dimensional Data by Combining Simple Experts, 1159
Mondal, Sakib A., 792
Monien, Burkhard, 285
Monte Carlo Localization with Mixture Proposal Distribution, 859
Mooney, Raymond J., 627
Moors, Mark, 852
Morris, Paul, 491
Morris, William C., 965
Morsch, Amy E. W., 965
Morsch, Mark L., 965
Mostek, Thomas, 323
Multi-Fidelity Robotic Behaviors: Acting with Variable State Information, 872
Multivariate Clustering by Dynamics, 633

MURDOCH: Publish/Subscribe Task Allocation for Heterogeneous Agents, 1070
Muscettola, Nicola, 491
Musen, Mark, 450
Muslea, Ion, 621, 1107
Mutually Beneficial Integration of Data Mining and Information Extraction, A, 627

Nahm, Un Yong, 627
Nakadai, Kazuhiro, 832
Nakamura, Mutsumi, 62
Nayak, P. Pandurang, 370
Nehmzow, Ulrich, 826
Nguyen, XuanLong, 798
Nicolescu, Monica N., 1087
Nicolov, Nicolas, 1008
Niehaus, William J., 945
Nikovski, Daniel, 1108
Niu, Zhendong, 1125
Non-Axiomatic Reasoning System (Version 4.1), 1135
Non-Deterministic Social Laws, 15
Nourbakhsh, Illah R., 840, 866
Noy, Natalya Fridman, 450
Nurse Rostering at the Hospital Authority of Hong Kong, 951

O-Plan: A Web-Based AI Planning Agent, 1131
Oates, Tim, 846
Oddi, Angelo, 742
Okamoto, Hidenori, 429
Okuno, Hiroshi G., 832
On 2-SAT and Renamable Horn, 279
On Pruning Techniques for Multi-Player Games, 201
On the Recognition of Abstract Markov Policies, 524
Online Ensemble Learning, 1109
Ono, Tetsuo, 142
Ontology Integration in XML, 1077, 1105
Open World Planning in the Situation Calculus, 754
Ordóñez, Iván, 517
Ortiz, Luis E., 378
Osmani, Aomar, 1088
Otsuka, Kazuhiro, 330
Owens, Sean, 1125
Oza, Nikunj C., 1109

Padgham, Lin, 68
Palmer, Martha, 691
Pan, Shimei, 722
Pantic, M., 1026
Paolucci, Massimo, 1125
Parkes, David C., 74, 82
Parr, Ronald, 363, 531
Pehoushek, J. D., 157
Penner, Robin R., 1127
Pennock, David M., 729
Performance Comparison of Landmark Recognition Systems for Navigating Mobile Robots, 826
Peysakhov, Maxim, 1089
Pfeffer, Avi, 538
Philpot, Andrew, 980
Pirri, Fiora, 754
Planning as Satisfiability in Nondeterministic Domains, 748
Plexousakis, Dimitris, 470

Polacsek, T., 768
Pollack, Martha E., 1090
Poole, David, 217
Pratt-Hartmann, Ian, 423
Predicting and Adapting to Poor Speech Recognition in a Spoken Dialogue System, 722
Predicting Future User Actions by Observing Unmodified Applications, 217
Predicting UNIX Command Lines: Adjusting to User Patterns, 230
Preference-Based Search for Scheduling, 904
Preserving Ambiguities in Generation via Automata Intersection, 697
Preventing Strategic Manipulation in Iterative Auctions: ProxyAgents and Price-Adjustment, 82
Programming Robot Behavior Primitives through Human Demonstration, 1083
PROMPT: Algorithm and Tool for Automated Ontology Merging and Alignment, 450
Property Mapping: A Simple Technique for Mobile Robot Programming, 840
PTV: Intelligent Personalised TV Guides, 957

Qualitative Spatial Interpretation of Course-of-Action Diagrams, 1119
Quantitative Study of Small Disjuncts, A, 665

Ramakrishnan, Sailesh, 1090
Ramoni, Marco, 633
Ramos-Santacruz, Mila, 945
Randall, Curt, 937
Rapid Development of a High Performance Knowledge Base for Course of Action Critiquing, 1046
Rasch, Robert A. Jr., 1119
Ratajczak, David, 209
Rauenbusch, Timothy, 1091
Reading a Robot's Mind: A Model of Utterance Understanding Based on the Theory of Mind Mechanism, 142
RealPlan: Decoupling Causal and Resource Reasoning in Planning, 812
Reasoning and Acting in Time, 1104
Recent Progress in the Design and Analysis of Admissible Heuristic Functions, 1165
Recognizing End-User Transactions in Performance Management, 596
Redundancy in Random SAT Formulas, 273
Refining Inductive Bias in Unsupervised Learning via Constraints, 1112
Regli, William C., 1089
Reinforcement Learning for Algorithm Selection, 1081
Reiter, Ray, 355, 754
Representation and Evolution of Lego-Based Assemblies, 1089
Restricted Bayes Optimal Classifiers, 658
Rice, James, 1123
Riley, Patrick, 1040, 1092
Rintanen, Jussi, 806
Rish, Irina, 596
Robust Combinatorial Auction Protocol against False-Name Bids, 110

Roth, Dan, 639
Rothkrantz, L. J., 1026
Roumeliotis, Stergios I., 1093
Roussel, Olivier, 273
Rousu, Juho, 570
Rules behind Roles: Identifying Speaker Role in Radio Broadcasts, The, 679
Ryall, Kathy, 209

Saffiotti, Alessandro, 129
St. Amant, Robert, 1129
Sakurai, Yuko, 110
Sam-Haroud, Djamila, 917
Sampling Methods for Action Selection in Influence Diagrams, 378
Sandholm, Tuomas, 48, 90
Satoh, Ken, 429
Schaeffer, Jonathan, 1179
Schaerf, Marco, 349, 996
Schaffer, J. David, 1121
Schamberger, Stefan, 285
Schaub, Torsten, 392
Scherl, Richard, 483
Schmill, Matthew D., 846
Schneider, Gerald E., 249
Schnurr, Hans-Peter, 1034
Schrödl, Stefan, 885
Schubert, Lenhart, 761
Schuurmans, Dale, 297
SciFinance: A Program Synthesis Tool for Financial Modeling, 937
Sebastiani, Paola, 633
Selective Sampling with Co-Testing: Preliminary Results, 1107
Selective Sampling with Redundant Views, 621
Self-Organization of Innate Face Preferences: Could Genetics Be Expressed through Learning?, 117
Self-Organizing Neural Network for Contour Integration through Synchronized Firing, A, 123
Self-Supervised Learning for Visual Tracking and Recognition of Human Hand, 243
Selman, Bart, 256
Semantics and Inference for Recursive Probability Models, 538
Semantics of Agent Communication Languages for Group Interaction, 42
Semi-Complete Disambiguation Algorithm for Open Text, A, 1085
Sen, Anup K., 792
Sensible Agents: Demonstration of Dynamic Adaptive Autonomy, 1115
Sethares, W. A., 9
Shahabi, Cyrus, 980
Sheffer, Ronald E. Jr., 965
Shi, Jiefu, 1094
Shoham, Yoav, 56
Silaghi, Marius Calin, 917
Silvescu, Adrian, 1067
Sim, Robert, 1110
Simmons, Reid, 852
Singh, Satinder, 36, 645
Siskind, Jeffrey Mark, 149
Situation Awareness with the Limited Visual Attention, 1079
Small-World Networks of Mobile Robots, 1093
Smith, Barbara, 182
Smith, Stephen F., 742

Smyth, Barry, 957
Social Choice Theory and Recommender Systems: Analysis of the Axiomatic Foundations of Collaborative Filtering, 729
Solving a Supply Chain Optimization Problem Collaboratively, 780
Solving Advanced Reasoning Tasks Using Quantified Boolean Formulas, 417
Solving Combinatorial Auctions Using Stochastic Local Search, 22
Solving the Round Robin Problem Using Propositional Logic, 262
Some Tractable Combinatorial Auctions, 98
Soutchanski, Mikhail, 355
Southey, Finnegan, 297
Speculative Execution for Information Agents, 1062
Speeding up the Convergence of Real-Time Search, 891
Srihari, Sargur N., 1068
Srivastava, Biplav, 812
STA: Spatio-Temporal Aggregation with Applications to Analysis of Diffusion-Reaction Phenomena, 517
Staab, Steffen, 1034
Statistics-Based Summarization — Step One: Sentence Compression, 703
Steinmetz, Erik S., 1127
Stergiou, Kostas, 182
Stickel, Mark E., 436
Stone, Peter, 36, 1040
Stormont, Dan, 1142
Structure, Duality, and Randomization: Common Themes in AI and OR, 1152
Studer, Rudi, 1034
Sturtevant, Nathan R., 201
Sukthankar, Gita, 1095
Sun, Wei, 3
Sure, York, 1034
Suri, Subhash, 90
Suzuki, Satoshi, 330
Sycara, Katia, 1125, 1133
Symbol Recognition and Artificial Emotion for Making an Autonomoius Robot Attend the AAAI Conference, 1140
System that Identifies Writers, 1068
Systems Engineering Process Activities (SEPA) Methodology and Tool Suite, The, 1117

Tate, Austin, 1131
TCBB Scheme: Applications to Single Machine Job Sequencing Problems, 792
Team-Aware Multirobot Strategy for Cooperative Path Clearing, 1095
Tecuci, Gheorghe, 1046, 1064, 1065
Tennenholtz, Moshe, 56, 98
Tessaris, Sergio, 399
TheaterLoc Virtual Application, The, 980
Thielscher, Michael, 497
Thom, Belinda, 652
Thomere, Jerome F., 436
Thompson, John, 988
Thrun, Sebastian, 355, 852, 859
Tompits, Hans, 417
Tong, Simon, 658
Torrini, Paolo, 503
Total Knowledge, 423
Tovey, Craig, 819

Toward a Theory of Learning Coherent Concepts, 639
Towards a Logic-Based Theory of Argumentation, 411
Towards Approximately Optimal Poker, 1094
Towards Efficient Negotiation Mechanisms for Collaboration, 1091
Towards Feasible Approach to Plan Checking under Probabilistic Uncertainty: Interval Methods, 545
Tracing Dependencies of Strategy Selections in Agent Design, 1082
Tractable Classes for Directional Resolution, 343
Translating with Scarce Resources, 672
Trejo, Raúl, 545
Truszczynski, Miroslaw, 163
Tsang, Francis Ming Fai, 951
Tsvetovat, M., 1133
Tumer, Kagan, 104
Turmel, William, 1119
TV Content Recommender System, 1121

Ulrich, Iwan, 866
Ungar, Lyle H., 74, 82, 590
Unified Bias-Variance Decomposition for Zero-One and Squared Loss, A, 564
Unsupervised Learning and Interactive Jazz/Blues Improvisation, 652
Untangle: A New Ontology for Card Catalog Systems, 1137
User Interface Softbots, 1129
Using Anytime Planning for Centralized Coordination of Multiple Robots in Real-Time Dynamic Environments, 1069
Using Auxiliary Variables and Implied Constraints to Model Non-Binary Problems, 182
Using Pattern Databases to Find Macro Operators, 1075
Using Prior Knowledge: Problems and Solutions, 436

Vanderheyden, Peter, 1096
van Lent, Michael, 1171
van Velsen, Martin, 1125
Vanouse, Paul, 236
Vardi, Moshe Y., 175
Veloso, Manuela, 872, 1040, 1092
Venkatesh, Svetha, 524
Visual Event Classification via Force Dynamics, 149
Voyles, Richard, 1083

Wagstaff, Kiri, 1097, 1112
Wah, Benjamin W., 310
Waldinger, Richard J., 436
Walker, Marilyn A., 645
Walsh, Toby, 182, 558
Walsh, William E., 303
Wang, Pei, 1135
Wasson, Glenn S., 1069
Watson, Ian, 1054
Watson, Jean-Paul, 879
Wiecha, Charles, 1008
Weiss, Gary M., 665
Wellman, Michael P., 303
Welty, Christopher, 1137
West, Geoff, 524

What Sensing Tells Us: Towards a Formal Theory of Testing for Dynamical Systems, 483
Whitley, L. Darrell, 879
Why Do We Need a Body Anyway?, 1151
Wiebe, Janyce M., 735
Wilder, Steve, 1123
Wilson, Eric, 1113
Winner, Elly, 872
Wittaker, Steve, 679
Wolpert, David, 104
Woltran, Stefan, 417
Wong, Jean, 951
Woods, William A., 1180
Woolf, Beverly Park, 552
Wu, Ying, 243
Wu, Zhe, 310

Yamada, Kenji, 672
Yamauchi, Takashi, 136
Yeung, Dennis Wai Ming, 951
Ying, J., 1133
Yokoo, Makoto, 110
Yoon, Song-Yee, 249
Yoshizumi, Takayuki, 923
Younes, Hakan, 852
Young, Robert L., 937

Zadrozny, Wlodek, 1008
Zancanaro, Massimo, 30
Zelenko, Dmitry, 639
Zettlemoyer, Luke S., 1129
Zhang, Runqi, 1098
Zhang, Weixiong, 910, 930
Zhao, Changpeng, 3
Zhao, Feng, 517
Zimmerman, John, 1121